The Good Pub Guide 2002

The Good Pub Guide 2002

Edited by Alisdair Aird

Deputy Editor: Fiona Stapley

Managing Editor: Karen Fick
Research Officer: Elizabeth Adlington
Associate Editor: Robert Unsworth
Editorial Assistance: Fiona Wright

EBURY PRESS
LONDON

Please send reports on pubs to

The Good Pub Guide
FREEPOST TN1569
WADHURST
East Sussex
TN5 7BR

or contact our website:
www.goodguides.com

This edition first published in 2001 by Ebury Press,
Random House, 20 Vauxhall Bridge Road,
London SW1V 2SA

The Random House Group Limited Reg. No. 954009

www.randomhouse.co.uk

1 3 5 7 9 10 8 6 4 2

A CIP catalogue record for this book is available from the British Library.

ISBN 0 09 18679794 0

Typeset from author's disks by Clive Dorman & Co.
Edited by Pat Taylor Chalmers
Printed and bound in Great Britain by Cox and Wyman Ltd, Reading, Berkshire

Contents

Introduction 6
What is a Good Pub? 15
Using the *Guide* 16
Author's Acknowledgements 22

ENGLAND
Bedfordshire 24
Berkshire 32
Buckinghamshire 50
Cambridgeshire 69
Cheshire 90
Cornwall 111
Cumbria 141
Derbyshire 171
Devon 197
Dorset 255
Durham *see* Northumbria
Essex 279
Gloucestershire 299
Hampshire 337
Herefordshire 371
Hertfordshire 385
Isle of Wight 399
Kent 407
Lancashire *with* Greater Manchester *and* Merseyside 435
Leicestershire *and* Rutland 462
Lincolnshire 484
Norfolk 499
Northamptonshire 523
Northumberland *see* Northumbria
Northumbria (County Durham, Northumberland
    and Tyneside) 537
Nottinghamshire 560
Oxfordshire 573
Rutland *see* Leicestershire
Shropshire 607
Somerset 624
Staffordshire 659
Suffolk 669
Surrey 693
Sussex 712
Warwickshire *with* Birmingham *and* West Midlands 754
Wiltshire 775
Worcestershire 805
Yorkshire 819

LONDON 884
SCOTLAND 927
WALES 968
CHANNEL ISLANDS 1005

Overseas Lucky Dip 1010
Special Interest Lists 1018
Report Forms 1035
Maps . . . . .at back of book

Introduction

This *Guide* is now 20 years old. As it has been under the same editorship throughout that time, we are particularly conscious of the changes that have taken place. One of the most striking is in the choice of drinks available. The so-called nitrokegs (the Smooths, Creamflows and so on) hadn't even been invented when we started, and the designer lagers such as Grolsch had only just begun their assault on the market-place. Much more importantly for most of our readers, there is now an altogether richer choice of cask-conditioned real ales than there was then. And whereas in that first edition only nine of the pubs brewed their own beers, in this one nearly 50 of the main entries do, with dozens more among the small-print entries.

There's been an even more fundamental transformation on the wine side. Back in our first edition wine deserved only the barest mention, and then in scarcely more than a dozen pubs. Things have changed dramatically since. In this edition, over 300 pubs have qualified for our Wine Award.

In our first edition, pub food was typically pretty dull. What were called 'basket meals' were quite common; a little wicker basket, with some chips and scampi or chicken nuggets, say, nesting in a paper napkin. Back in those days, we categorised as 'good' a choice of baked potatoes, salads, lasagne, moussaka, scampi, a couple of casseroles and steak. Together with lasagne and moussaka, the mainstays of pub food were chilli con carne, curry and steak pie, and it was very rare to find pubs cooking anything more interesting. A glance through a few pages of this edition shows how enormous the change has been, with most pubs now aiming altogether higher than that.

Changes on the food side have not all been good, however. Twenty years ago, almost all pubs would do a sandwich or a filled roll. For a great many of our readers, that's quite enough for a pub lunch. However, now nearly one in five pubs that do food won't do a sandwich or filled roll at all. And most that do now produce not an honest-to-goodness sandwich, but instead either a hefty baguette with all sorts of trappings, or a sandwich accompanied by salad or chips or both. Putting stuff that people don't want on their plates not only drives up the price unnecessarily, but also makes customers feel uneasy at the waste. And it can be an excuse for serving sandwiches – which should be the ideal quick snack – no more promptly than a full-scale hot meal. This is now becoming quite a common cause of reader complaints.

A closely related problem is the over-generous helping. Although many of our readers like to see a heaped plate, many more do not. People watching their weight, many older folk, any luncher expecting a big evening meal – all these find overfilled plates a waste of money as well as of food. We hope far more pubs will follow the example of those which now offer smaller helpings at a reduced price.

Pub attitudes to children have changed out of all recognition in these 20 years. Of the pubs featured in our first edition, 58% excluded children from all parts of the pub. Today, only 8% do. Back in those days, the most common provision for children was an unprepossessing 'family room' tucked somewhere out of sight. Today, children are allowed pretty freely throughout in over one in three of the pubs that allow them at all, and in the others are normally allowed throughout the dining areas.

Twenty years ago, hardly any pubs tried to segregate smokers (even then there were pioneers: the New Inn at Appletreewick in Yorkshire was the first pub to ban smoking). Today, recognising that smokers are now in the minority, nearly two-thirds restrict smokers to certain parts of the pub – even if in most cases that's the main part.

During these 20 years, we have watched the decline and fall of the juke box. When we started the *Guide*, nearly one in five pubs had one. Now, the proportion has fallen to one in 17. The reason, no doubt, is that people now have access to such a wide range of music at home, or via their personal stereos, that they are less prepared to pay per play in a pub. However, over the same period a different auditory invader has taken over all too many pubs. Twenty years ago, about one in five pubs had piped music. Now, more than half do. A few pubs do win real praise for carefully selected and well reproduced real music. But our postbag shows clearly that many customers generally find piped music intensely irritating, and that very few actively enjoy it, at least in its normal form – a mindless wash of pop music, or 'middle of the road', or the jolly bits from Vivaldi's *Four Seasons*.

When the *Guide* first came out, Scottish pubs and inns had for a few years been allowed to open all day, and at that time about one in three did so. That proportion has steadily increased, until now over 80% do. English and Welsh pubs were not allowed to open all day until 1988. Just as in Scotland, all-day opening has increased year by year since then. Getting off to a later start, England and Wales still have some way to go before reaching Scottish levels of all-day opening, but 46% of English and Welsh pubs do now open all day, at least for part of the week or part of the year.

Who owns what

There have been tremendous changes in pub ownership since the *Guide* started. Twenty years ago a high proportion was owned by five big national brewing combines: Allied, Bass, Courage, Scottish & Newcastle (S&N) and Whitbreads.

Today, only S&N still owns pubs (a slimmed-down estate of around 1,500), and also brews beer. Its real ale brands are Theakstons, McEwans, Youngers and Home, and the former Courage brands – Courage itself, John Smiths and Websters. Pubs formerly owned by Courage (many of them rebranded as Inntrepreneur) are now owned by a Japanese bank, Nomura, which has swiftly come from nowhere to become Britain's biggest pub landlord, with around 5,500 pubs; Unique is its main pub company.

The former Allied beer brands (Tetleys, Ansells, Friary Meux and Benskins) now belong to Carlsberg-Tetleys, owned by the Danish firm Carlsberg. Carlsberg also owns the Ind Coope Burton brand, but has contracted out the brewing of that beer to a smaller brewing group, Wolverhampton & Dudley (W&D – see below). Carlsberg owns no pubs. Most pubs formerly owned by Allied are now owned by another new pub group, Punch, which was set up in 1998 with American financial backing, and now owns some 5,000 pubs.

Both Bass and Whitbreads have recently sold their breweries to the Belgian firm Interbrew, which has a string of international lager brands. So Interbrew took on Bass, Worthington, M&B, Hancocks, Stones, Boddingtons, Flowers and Whitbreads. However, the British competition authorities are making Interbrew sell on a part of their Bass/Whitbreads interests (as we went to press it seems probable that the buyer would be another foreign-based brewer).

Bass sold its tenanted pubs to Punch in 1998, and has now sold its managed pubs to Nomura. Nomura is converting these managed pubs into tenancies, like all its other pubs. Bass has kept its flagship Vintage Inns and new Ember Inns chain of a few dozen pubs, but the terms of its breweries sale to Interbrew means that it is having to change its name from Bass to Six Continents.

Whitbreads has also virtually entirely dropped out of the pub business. It has now sold its main estate of 3,000 pubs to a subsidiary of Deutsche Bank, keeping just 270 Brewers Fayre pubs and 258 Beefeaters, with the intention of increasing the number of Brewers Fayres and (sharply) reducing the number of Beefeaters. It thinks of both these chains as restaurants rather than as pubs.

So the former Big Five brewing/pub groups have now been whittled down to just one, alongside two foreign-owned brewing combines (one of which the competition authorities aim to split).

The next tier down of brewing/pub combines has also seen a lot of change. Greenalls, a major player in the *Guide*'s early years, has dropped out of the pub scene altogether, and its 1,200 or so pubs are now owned by Nomura (under the Inn Partnership name), while its beers are now brewed by Carlsberg-Tetleys. W&D has expanded from its original West Midlands base (with the Banks's and Hansons brands) to acquire the Camerons, Marstons and Mansfield breweries, and owns about 1,100 pubs. But it has itself now become a takeover target, with those interested in buying it wanting the pubs but likely to sell on the breweries (W&D have their own plans to dispose of the Camerons brewery and close the Mansfield one).

The other main semi-national brewing/pub group is Greene King, based firmly in East Anglia when the *Guide* started but now expanding far beyond. It now also owns the Morlands and Ruddles brands, has nearly 1,600 pubs, and looks likely to make further acquisitions: Badger, the Dorset brewer with pubs across much of southern England, might make an apt target.

Many other new pub companies have sprung up since the *Guide* started, on broadly similar lines to Nomura and Punch, in that they have taken on wholesale chunks of pub estates disposed of by national or regional brewers. The next biggest is Enterprise, which has some 3,400 pubs and has been growing fast. A close rival is Pubmaster, the former Brent Walker pub property company, owned since by a financial syndicate including the Prudential and a former subsidiary of NatWest. This has 2,000 or more pubs, and is also looking to expand.

A major point about these and other new non-brewing pub companies is that they are primarily financial institutions owning pubs as properties, rather than direct operators of pub chains. This means that a great many pubs which used to have managers, reporting directly to a brewery or other central office, are being converted to tenancies. In this way, the pub company can rely on a steady income stream through the fixed rent from each pub, instead of the less certain direct income gained from its sales. This steady income from tenanted pubs can be traded or 'securitised' by the pub company; money which the company makes through controlling the supply of beer and so forth to its tenants is the gravy on top of that solid income.

Another major new influence is pushing pub-owning chains, including the brewers, towards converting managed pubs into tenancies. The EU working hours directive which has just come into effect in the UK, limiting employees' hours, means that pub managers should now work for no more than 48 hours a week. In practice, many pub managers have been working for 60 hours a week. For a pub company to restructure its pubs' administrative systems to cope with this problem would be very costly. However, letting a previously managed pub to a tenant eliminates the problem, as there is nothing to stop the tenant (self-employed, not an employee) from working for as long as there are hours in the day.

We have some doubts about whether the conversion of so many previously managed pubs to let pubs will prove trouble-free. Our main worry is simply about whether the pool of available tenant talent is big enough to supply all the newly vacant tenancies and leases. A good pub tenant is rather a special breed. Besides all the skills needed to manage the staffing, drink and food sides of a pub well, the tenant must also have the extra aptitudes needed to make a success of being self-employed and running his or her own business. And of course this includes the inclination and ability to provide and manage the financial cushion that's needed to cope with fluctuations in trade – not just the usual seasonal ones, but the potential disaster such as foot and mouth.

The proliferation of tenancies and leases tempts many existing successful tenants to expand. This can work very well indeed. Someone who runs a single pub well, as its very full-time tenant/manager, may make a great success of taking on the tenancy of say three or four nearby pubs, putting managers in all, and working part-time in each of them. However, this sort of doubling up can also be a catastrophe: the single good pub can all too easily expand into a small group of bad ones.

A further problem is that whereas tenants of the former big brewing combines had the legal right to buy a guest beer more cheaply from a different brewer, tenants of the big non-brewing pub companies do not have that right. So the company can control entirely the sale of beer to its tenants, without the moderating influence on price and on choice of the right to a guest beer. Punch is typical of pub companies which do exercise this close control. We compared the price of the cheapest bitter in the 19 Punch pubs in this edition with the average price in other pubs in the same county. Four Punch pubs were cheaper than the local average; one cost the same; 14 were more expensive. Taking all these Punch pubs together, their customers were on average paying 11p a pint more than the local average for their beer.

When we started the *Guide* 20 years ago, we, like everyone else, worried about the monopoly stranglehold which the five big pub-owning brewers had over pubs and pub prices. That worry has gone. But the huge non-brewing pub companies which have replaced them now bring new worries. Basically, they are financial institutions dealing in pubs as commercial property. If they left it at that, then fine. But as instead they normally also control the supply of drinks to their tenants, they should surely be subject to the same consumer safeguards as the big brewers were. It seems to us essential that their tenants should be given the right to choose and buy a guest beer, and wines, spirits and soft drinks, from a different supplier. We are less convinced that there should be the same limit on the number of pubs owned by a pub company as there was with the brewers (the brewers were limited to 2,000 tied pubs). But that case should at least be explored formally by the competition authorities.

Beer prices

Often, the best way of getting value for money on the beer front is to choose a beer from one of the smaller brewers. The Table which follows shows how smaller brewers compare with the national average price of £1.92 a pint, and with the big brewing combines, which averaged between £1.86 and £1.91 a pint (that is, fractionally below the national norm). We have included only those brewers whose beers we found offered as the cheapest by at least two pubs, and we have excluded Channel Islands brewers, which work under a more lenient tax regime. The number in brackets after each name shows the number of pubs we found offering their beer as its cheapest – obviously, the more pubs, the more reliable our price.

Table: How beer prices compare
£/pint

£/pint	
£1.46	Sam Smiths (8)
£1.51	Barnsley (2)
£1.56	Burton Bridge (2)
£1.60	Hydes (2)
£1.62	Hanby (2)
£1.63	Castle Rock (2)
£1.64	Thwaites (4)
£1.65	Tomos Watkins (2)
£1.68	**Own brew** (43)
£1.70	Highgate (2), Lees (2)
£1.71	Robinsons (7)
£1.73	Daleside (2), York (3)
£1.74	Greenalls (brewed for Nomura by Carlsberg-Tetleys; 7)
£1.77	Donnington (3)
£1.78	Hardys & Hansons (2), Oakham (2)
£1.79	Jennings (19)
£1.80	Burtonwood (3), Teignworthy (3)
£1.82	Hobsons (9), Batemans (8)
£1.83	St Austell (9), Wye Valley (5), Yates (3), Branoc (2)
£1.84	Archers (7)
£1.85	Summerskills (3), Skinners (2), Weltons (2)
£1.86	Sharps (18), Cotleigh (11)
£1.87	Banks's (14), Hambleton (3), Branscombe Vale (2)
£1.88	Camerons (2), Moles (2)
£1.89	Black Sheep (26), Princetown (4)
£1.90	Mansfield (6), Broughton (4), Goachers (3), Moorhouses (2), Ridleys (3)
£1.91	Butcombe (19), Everards (7)
£1.92	Hook Norton (55), Otter (9)
£1.93	Buffys (2)
£1.94	Brains/Buckley (9), Grainstore (4), Goffs (2)
£1.95	Belhaven (14), Cheriton (6), Blackawton (2), Butts (2)
£1.96	Exmoor (9), Palmers (9)
£1.97	Tolly (5)
£1.98	Marstons (13), Wickwar (2)
£1.99	Ushers (brewed by Hardy; 4)
£2.00	Ringwood (18), Shepherd Neame (14), Gales (8), Cains (2), fff (2)

£2.01	Wadworths (32), Dartmoor Best (brewed for Carlsberg-Tetleys by St Austell; 7)
£2.02	Charles Wells (7), West Berkshire (5)
£2.03	Greene King (103), Adnams (80), Badger (33), Timothy Taylors (3), Hop Back (2), Ventnor (2)
£2.05	Fullers (24), Youngs (18), St Peters (3), Ballards (2)
£2.06	Woodfordes (6)
£2.08	Hardy (5), Goddards (2)
£2.09	Harveys (21)
£2.10	Larkins (5)
£2.11	Brakspears (31), Caledonian (8)
£2.13	Brewery on Sea (2)
£2.15	Morrells (brewed by Hardy; 4)
£2.23	Harviestoun (2)
£2.30	Nethergate (2)

Other beers we found at extremely low prices, but just in single pubs, were Holts, Wyre Piddle, Bathams, Passageway, Clarks, Orkney, Falstaff and Woolhampton. All these were £1.70 a pint or less (very much less in the case of Holts and Wyre Piddle).

The cheapest area for drinks is unquestionably Lancashire. In a survey of prices in 1,314 pubs nationwide, we found beer there was typically 24p a pint less than the national average. There is no reason why prices for beer in other areas should be any higher than they are in Lancashire. In effect, pub-goers everywhere else are having their money creamed off, like the froth on the top of a pint. The Table below shows how much extra people in other areas now have to pay for their beer:

Table: How much extra you pay per pint

5p	Cheshire
10p	Cumbria, Yorkshire
12p	Staffordshire, Nottinghamshire, Worcestershire
13p	Derbyshire, Herefordshire
14p	Shropshire
16p	Wales
17p	Cornwall, Northumbria
21p	Warwickshire/West Midlands)
22p	Lincolnshire
23p	Devon, Gloucestershire, Leicestershire/Rutland
24p	Somerset
26p	Wiltshire
27p	Hertfordshire, Northamptonshire
28p	Dorset, Essex
29p	Bedfordshire
30p	Norfolk
31p	Scotland, Suffolk
32p	Isle of Wight
33p	Hampshire, Sussex
35p	Cambridgeshire
36p	Kent
38p	Oxfordshire
42p	Buckinghamshire
46p	Berkshire
50p	London, Surrey

Awards

Many pubs which do serious cooking now put so much thought into their fish dishes that these account for nearly half their menu. This is a tremendous change since even a few years ago, let alone when the *Guide* first came out back in those days of breaded defrosted scampi and very battered cod. There are far too many of these pubs to list here. Instead, we are concentrating on those which specialise in fish above all else. Places that stand out are the Trinity Foot at Swavesey in Cambridgeshire; the

Victory in St Mawes, Cornwall; the Drewe Arms at Broadhembury, Anchor at Cockwood, Devon (its concentration on such a wide range of fish and seafood has proved so popular that it has spawned a similar menu in a small group of sister pubs), Passage House in Topsham, and Start Bay at Torcross, Devon; the New Inn at Shalfleet, Isle of Wight; the Dering Arms at Pluckley, Kent; the Applecross Inn at Applecross, Old Inn at Gairloch, Seafood Restaurant & Bar, St Monance, Tayvallich Inn at Tayvallich, and Morefield Motel at Ullapool, Scotland; the Penhelig Arms in Aberdovey, Wales; and the Rozel Bay Hotel at Rozel, Jersey. From this impressive group, Philip and Bridget Savage's Victory in St Mawes emerges as our **Fish Pub of the Year**.

In the bigger towns and cities, it's fairly easy to find pubs that do cheap meals, but really interesting cheap pub food is much harder to come by. Prime examples are the Sweeney & Todd in Reading, Berkshire; the Cambridge Blue in Cambridge and Brewery Tap in Peterborough, Cambridgeshire; the Derby Tup in Whittington Moor on the edge of Chesterfield, Derbyshire; the Adam & Eve in Norwich; the Dukes 92 in Manchester; and the Fat Cat in Sheffield. In smaller places, the Black Horse in Croston, Lancashire, and Pendre at Cilgerran, Wales, stand out. In fact the Pendre does more than stand out. We've decided that Jeff and Debra Warren there must be closet philanthropists, subsidising their remarkably good interesting food out of their own pockets. If they can put as much imagination and care as this into their dishes at these prices, why can't many more pubs follow suit? So for the second year running, the Pendre at Cilgerran is **Bargain Food Pub of the Year**.

The individual county chapter introductions show how wide the choice of excellent dining pubs has become. Most areas now have several pubs that are quite special for meals out. All of these now go to great lengths to satisfy themselves about the quality of their raw ingredients. Usually, this now means using local producers, and increasingly suppliers with organic certification. Here, we list places which are worth travelling quite a long way to, for their exceptional food. The Winterbourne Arms at Winterbourne, Berkshire; the Five Arrows in Waddesdon, Buckinghamshire; the Punch Bowl at Crosthwaite, Cumbria; the Three Crowns at Ullingswick, Herefordshire; the Albion in Faversham, Kent; the Burlton Inn at Burlton, Shropshire; the Queens Head at Bramfield, Suffolk; the Horse Guards at Tillington, Sussex; the Fox & Goose at Armscote, Warwickshire; the Crab & Lobster at Asenby, Blue Lion at East Witton, Star at Harome, Angel at Hetton, Yorke Arms at Ramsgill, Three Acres in Shelley, General Tarleton at Ferrensby and Sportsmans Arms at Wath in Nidderdale (all Yorkshire – why is this richly provided county so far from the *Guide* staff's homes?); the Wheatsheaf at Swinton, Scotland; the Nantyffin Cider Mill near Crickhowell, Walnut Tree at Llandewi Skirrid (under its new owners) and Nags Head in Usk, Wales. The top dog in the dining pub world this year is undoubtedly Paul Klein's Blue Lion at East Witton – our **Dining Pub of the Year**.

Nearly 50 pubs among the main entries brew their own beer. Ones where the taste stands out include the Brewery Tap in Peterborough, Cambridgeshire; the Black Bull in Coniston and Sun in Dent, Cumbria; the Fountain Head at Branscombe, Devon; the Brunswick in Derby; the Flower Pot at Cheriton, Hampshire; the Grainstore in Oakham, Rutland and Exeter Arms at Barrowden (Leicestershire); the Swan in West Peckham, Kent; the Marble Arch in Manchester (all organic now), in the Lancashire chapter; the Dipton Mill at Diptonmill near Hexham, Northumbria; the Six Bells in Bishop's Castle, Shropshire; the Burton Bridge Inn in Burton upon Trent, Staffordshire; the Victoria at Earl Soham, Suffolk; the Beacon in Segley, West Midlands (with the Warwickshire chapter); and the New Inn at Cropton and Fat Cat in Sheffield, Yorkshire. Sandra Lee's New Inn at Cropton has a fine distinctive range, usually five at a time, from a potential choice of eight: it is **Own Brew Pub of the Year**.

We have never excluded a pub from this book on the grounds that it doesn't keep cask conditioned beers – real ale. We are proud of the fact that we are a good pub guide, rather than merely a good beer guide. However, virtually all the pubs in the *Guide* do keep real ale, in good condition. It seems that being prepared to go to the trouble of keeping real ale (no easy task) is almost the mark of a good publican. Many licensees go beyond this, enjoying tracking down a range of interesting beers, even a quickly changing choice from all around the country. Champion pubs for the beer lover are the Brown Bear in Biggleswade, Bedfordshire; the Bhurtpore at Aston, Cheshire; the Watermill at Ings, Cumbria; the Brunswick and Alexandra in Derby; the Double Locks just outside Exeter and Bridge in Topsham, Devon; the Wine Vaults in Southsea, Hampshire; the White Horse in Hertford (remarkable for a brewery-owned pub to have such an interesting choice); the Marble Arch in Manchester and Station Buffet in Stalybridge, Lancashire; the Fat Cat in Norwich, Norfolk; the Victoria in Beeston and Lincolnshire Poacher in Nottingham (both are in the same small chain as the Alexandra in Derby); and the Fat Cat and New Barrack in Sheffield and Maltings in York. Trevor Harris's Brunswick in Derby carries off the top title of **Beer Pub of the Year**.

Sam Smiths of Tadcaster in Yorkshire is notable for supplying its Old Brewery real ale throughout the country at relatively very low prices – on average, nearly 50p a pint lower than the norm, and bringing a particular touch of price sanity to its London pubs. Because of its customer-friendly pricing, Sam Smiths is our **Brewer of the Year**.

Even in the grim days when pub wine was usually an undrinkable joke, quite a few independent licensees went out of their way to keep decent wines. Now, even big chains are making a point of giving their customers a good choice of wines by the glass (Vintage Inns is an example), and some beer suppliers and pub owners such as Adnams and Hardy/Eldridge Pope distribute very good pub wines. The vast majority of pubs in the *Guide* now have decent house wines, and in quite a few the choice and/or quality is excellent. Favourite wine pubs are the Bell at Boxford, Berkshire; the Trengilly Wartha near Constantine, Cornwall; the Bull & Butcher at Turville, Buckinghamshire; the Nobody Inn at Doddiscombsleigh and Maltsters Arms at Tuckenhay, Devon; the New Inn at North Nibley, Gloucestershire; the Red Lion at Boldre and Wykeham Arms in Winchester, Hampshire; the Gate at Boyden Gate, Kent; the Olive Branch at Clipsham, Leicestershire; the George of Stamford, Lincolnshire; the Old Ram at Tivetshall St Mary, Norfolk; the Crown in Southwold, Suffolk; the Pear Tree at Whitley, Wiltshire; the Fox & Hounds at Carthorpe and Angel at Hetton, Yorkshire. The Nobody Inn at Doddiscombsleigh has had more enthusiastic reports about its wines from readers this year than any other pub – scarcely a surprise, with its rich and rewarding choice of 800 by the bottle, 20 by the glass kept oxidation-free, and tutored tastings. Nick Borst-Smith's Nobody Inn is our **Wine Pub of the Year**.

Is Scotland losing its edge as the best place in the world for whiskies? There are pubs and inns in Scotland with a great range of malts to try: the Cawdor Inn at Cawdor, Bow Bar in Edinburgh and Eilean Chraggan at Weem each has over 100. But these are now being rivalled by many pubs south of the Border, some of which have an even more impressive choice of Scotland's own drink. Pubs with a fine collection include the Bhurtpore at Aston, Cheshire; the Nobody Inn at Doddiscombsleigh, Devon (240); the Gumstool near Tetbury and Anchor at Oldbury-on-Severn (Gloucestershire); the Clarendon (Wight Mouse) at Chale, Isle of Wight (365); the Britons Protection in Manchester (175); the Bulls Head at Clipston, Northamptonshire (over 500); the Victoria in Beeston and Lincolnshire Poacher in Nottingham; the Armoury in Shrewsbury, Shropshire; the Fox & Hounds at Great Wolford, Warwickshire (200); the Quarrymans Arms near Box, Cross Guns near Bradford-on-Avon and Haunch of Venison in Salisbury (Wiltshire); the New Barrack in Sheffield, Fox & Hounds at Starbotton and Pack Horse at Widdop, Yorkshire (130); and Richard and Paula David's Old House at Llangynwyd in Wales, which with its fine collection of over 350 whiskies including real rarities is our **Whisky Pub of the Year**.

Though it is hard enough to run one pub well, it is clearly a lot more difficult to run a chain of them well. One small chain based in the East Midlands is Tynemill, started by Chris Holmes in 1977 with a single pub in Newark, which then featured in the first edition of the *Guide*. There are 17 now, typically unpretentious places, plainly furnished, with simple, enjoyable and often interesting food, a good range of real ales (now including ones from their own Castle Rock brewery), and low prices. Seven Tynemill pubs now feature as main entries in the *Guide*; this very high proportion shows the quality of the chain. Tynemill is our **Pub Group of the Year**.

This year's edition has around 120 new main entries (or pubs which have not been in the *Guide* for some while, making a reappearance usually after one or more changes of management). Some of our finds this year have been particularly memorable. We'd pick out the Five Bells at Stanbridge (Bedfordshire), the Sun in the Wood at Ashmore Green (Berkshire), the Carpenters Arms at Slapton (Buckinghamshire), the Fitzwilliam Arms in Castor (Cambridgeshire), the Napoleon in Boscastle and Driftwood Spars at Trevaunance Cove (Cornwall), the Farmers Arms in Ulverston (Cumbria), the Ship in Noss Mayo and Kings Arms at Winkleigh (Devon), the Museum Hotel at Farnham (Dorset), the Whalebone at Fingringhoe and Mole Trap near Stapleford Tawney (Essex), the Bell at Sapperton (Gloucestershire), the Fox & Hounds at Crawley (Hampshire), the Derby Arms near Longridge and Red Lion in Mawdesley (Lancashire), the Olive Branch at Clipsham (Leicestershire), the Rat at Anick and County in Aycliffe (Northumbria), the Blewbury Inn at Blewbury (Oxfordshire), the Cookhouse at Bromfield (Shropshire), the Duke of Cumberland Arms at Henley (Sussex), the Durham Ox at Crayke, White Swan in Pickering and Bay Horse at Terrington (Yorkshire), and the Glasfryn in Mold (Wales). Of these, the Museum Hotel at Farnham in Dorset, newly reopened under Vicky Elliot and Mark Stephenson, looks set to become a real star, and is our **Newcomer of the Year**.

People have always worried that the True Pub is disappearing – probably, ever since pubs began. It was certainly a common theme among writers in the late 19th and early 20th centuries. Many people have an idealised vision of a down-to-earth tavern with an open fire, chatty regulars and landlord or landlady, plain old-fashioned furnishings and simple honest food – if any. It has to be agreed that most of the pubs in this *Guide* are a far cry from that, with a good deal of comfort, and food that's definitely more sophisticated. However, there's no shortage of truly unspoilt pubs in this edition – certainly well over 100 among the main entries, not to mention hundreds more in the Lucky Dip sections at the end of each chapter. What's more, our impression is that there are more of these than there were in the first edition, 20 years ago. Here, we give our pick of the bunch: places with a truly timeless feel, and an absolute absence of pretention: the Cock at Broom, Bedfordshire; the Bell at Aldworth, Berkshire; the Crown at Little Missenden, Buckinghamshire; the Queens Head at Newton, Cambridgeshire; the White Lion at Barthomley, Cheshire; the Quiet Woman at Earl Sterndale, Barley Mow at Kirk Ireton and Three Stags Heads at Wardlow, Derbyshire; the Square & Compass at Worth Matravers, Dorset; the Drewe Arms at Drewsteignton, Duke of York at Iddesleigh, Warren House near Postbridge, Stag at Rackenford, Bridge in Topsham, Rugglestone near Widecombe and Northmore Arms at Wonson, all in Devon; the Red Lion at Ampney St Peter and Boat at Ashleworth Quay, Gloucestershire; the Flower Pots at Cheriton and Harrow at Steep, Hampshire; the Carpenters Arms at Walterstone, Herefordshire; the Gate at Boyden Gate and Red Lion at Snargate, Kent; the Church Inn at Uppermill, Lancashire; the Cap & Stocking in Kegworth and New Inn at Peggs Green, Leicestershire; the Star in Bath, Tuckers Grave at Faulkland, Halfway House at Pitney and Rose & Crown at Huish Episcopi, Somerset; the Kings Head at Laxfield, Suffolk; the Blue Ship near Billingshurst, Sussex; the Vine in Brierley Hill, Case is Altered at Five Ways and Beacon in Sedgley, Warwickshire/West Midlands; the Haunch of Venison in Salisbury, Wiltshire; the Fleece at Bretforton and Monkey House at Defford, Worcestershire; the Birch Hall at Beck Hole, White Horse in Beverley and Whitelocks in Leeds, Yorkshire; the Nags Head in Central London, Compton Arms in North London and George in South London; the Cresselly Arms at Cresswell Quay, Plough & Harrow at Monknash and Old House at Llangynwyd, Wales; and the original public bar in Les Fontaines in St John, Jersey. The Bell at Aldworth, in the Macaulay family for over 200 years, is our **Unspoilt Pub of the Year**.

Over 500 of the main entries this year have bedrooms. Of these, about half now have our Place to Stay Award, showing that we know they can be recommended firmly for this. Some are really outstanding: the Five Arrows in Waddesdon, Buckinghamshire; the Trengilly Wartha near Constantine, Halzephron near Helston and Driftwood Spars at Trevaunance Cove, Cornwall; the Museum Hotel at Farnham, Dorset; the Horns at Goosnargh, Lancashire; the White Horse at Brancaster Staithe and Hoste Arms in Burnham Market, Norfolk; the Lamb in

Burford, Oxfordshire; the Burlton Inn and Wenlock Edge Inn, Shropshire; the George at Norton St Philip and Royal Oak at Luxborough, Somerset; the Abbey Inn at Byland Abbey, Crab & Lobster at Asenby, Blue Lion at East Witton, White Swan in Pickering, Yorke Arms at Ramsgill and Sportsmans Arms at Wath in Nidderdale, Yorkshire; the Eilean Iarmain at Isle Ornsay, Plockton Hotel in Plockton, Tigh an Eilean Hotel at Shieldaig and Wheatsheaf at Swinton, Scotland; and the Bear in Crickhowell, Wales. Cecil Barrow's Royal Oak at Luxborough is our **Inn of the Year**.

All sorts of different things can make a pub rewarding, and sometimes these wrap together to create somewhere particularly memorable. This top flight of exceptional pubs, all on peak form these days, includes the Five Arrows in Waddesdon, Buckinghamshire; the Trengilly Wartha near Constantine, Cornwall; the Five Bells at Clyst Hydon, Nobody Inn at Doddiscombsleigh and Double Locks near Exeter, Devon; the Wykeham Arms in Winchester, Hampshire; the Rose & Crown near Selling, Kent; the Hoste Arms in Burnham Market, Norfolk; the Lamb in Burford, Oxfordshire; the Burlton Inn at Burlton and Wenlock Edge Inn in Shropshire; the Strode Arms at Cranmore and Royal Oak at Luxborough, Somerset; the Blue Lion at East Witton, Angel at Hetton and Chequers at Ledsham, Yorkshire; and the Bear in Crickhowell, Wales. The welcome at the Wenlock Edge Inn is so warmly embracing, with everything just right, that everyone comes away really enthusiastic about the place, and looking forward to their next chance of a visit; Stephen and Di Waring's Wenlock Edge Inn at Wenlock Edge is **Pub of the Year**.

The heart of a good pub is its landlord or landlady. Star licensees this year are H E Macaulay of the Bell at Aldworth, Berkshire; Duncan Rowney and Lisa Chapman of the White Hart at Preston Bissett, Buckinghamshire; Robin Bean and Charles Hume Smith of the Five Bells at Clyst Hydon, and Nick Borst-Smith of the Nobody Inn at Doddiscombsleigh, Devon; John Barnard of the Red Lion at Ampney St Peter, and Michael Dowdeswell and Alex de la Torre of the Anchor at Oldbury-on-Severn, Gloucestershire; Anthony Goodrich of the Rose & Crown at Snettisham, and Iain Salmon of the Three Horseshoes at Warham, Norfolk; Gerald Bean of the Burlton Inn, and Stephen and Di Waring of the Wenlock Edge Inn, in Shropshire; Alistair and Sarah Cade of the Notley Arms at Monksilver, Somerset; Alan East of the Yew Tree at Cauldon, Staffordshire; and Chris Wraith of the Chequers at Ledsham, Yorkshire. The welcoming warmth and great professional skill of Robin Bean and Charles Hume Smith of the Five Bells at Clyst Hydon earn them the title of **Landlords of the Year**.

A couple of dozen licensees and their families have the distinction of having steered their pubs and inns into every single edition of the *Guide* since it was first published 20 years ago. These **long service champions** are the Macaulay family of the Bell at Aldworth, Berkshire; Peter and Janet Hodges of the Peacock at Bolter End, Buckinghamshire; Norman and Pauline Rushton of the Chequers at Fowlmere, and David and Juliet Short of the Queens Head at Newton, Cambridgeshire; William Morris of the Turks Head in Penzance, and Marjorie Ross of the Port Gaverne Inn near Port Isaac, Cornwall; Judith Fry of the Britannia at Elterwater, and Steph Barton of the Drunken Duck near Hawkshead, Cumbria; John Thompson of the John Thompson Inn at Ingleby, near Melbourne, Derbyshire; Neil Girling of the Sloop at Bantham; Nick Borst-Smith of the Nobody Inn at Doddiscombsleigh, Roger Newton of the Blue Ball at Sidford, James Henry of the Oxenham Arms at South Zeal, and Sally Pratt of the Diggers Rest at Woodbury Salterton, Devon; Penny Doe and the Ferguson family at the Bell in Castle Hedingham, Essex; the McCutcheon family in the Harrow at Steep, Hampshire; Toby Wingfield Digby of the Brocket Arms at Ayot St Lawrence, Hertfordshire; Richard Bowman of the Inn at Whitewell, Lancashire; Valerie Hope at the Wig & Mitre in Lincoln, and Ivo Vannocci at the George of Stamford, Lincolnshire; Alan and Jean Glen at the Olde Ship in Seahouses, Northumbria; Julie Griffiths of the Sir Charles Chinnor above Chinnor, and the Howard family of the White Hart at Fyfield, Oxfordshire; Alan East of the Yew Tree at Cauldon, Staffordshire; Antony and Victoria Leroy at the Haunch of Venison in Salisbury, Wiltshire; and Nicolas Ryan of the Crinan Hotel at Crinan, and Graham and Anne Henderson at Burts Hotel in Melrose, Scotland. Each of these has given great pleasure to hundreds of *Guide* readers over the years – a real achievement.

What is a Good Pub?

The main entries in this book have been through a two-stage sifting process. First of all, some 2,000 regular correspondents keep in touch with us about the pubs they visit, and nearly double that number report occasionally. We are now also getting quite a flow of reports through our **www.goodguides.com** web site. This keeps us up-to-date about pubs included in previous editions – it's their alarm signals that warn us when a pub's standards have dropped (after a change of management, say), and it's their continuing approval that reassures us about keeping a pub as a main entry for another year. Very important, though, are the reports they send us on pubs we don't know at all. It's from these new discoveries that we make up a shortlist, to be considered for possible inclusion as new main entries. The more people that report favourably on a new pub, the more likely it is to win a place on this shortlist – especially if some of the reporters belong to our hard core of about 500 trusted correspondents whose judgement we have learned to rely on. These are people who have each given us detailed comments on dozens of pubs, and shown that (when we ourselves know some of those pubs too) their judgement is closely in line with our own.

This brings us to the acid test. Each pub, before inclusion as a main entry, is inspected anonymously by the Editor, the Deputy Editor, or both. They have to find some special quality that would make strangers enjoy visiting it. What often marks the pub out for special attention is good value food (and that might mean anything from a well made sandwich, with good fresh ingredients at a low price, to imaginative cooking outclassing most restaurants in the area). Maybe the drinks are out of the ordinary (pubs with several hundred whiskies, with remarkable wine lists, with home-made country wines or good beer or cider made on the premises, with a wide range of well kept real ales or bottled beers from all over the world). Perhaps there's a special appeal about it as a place to stay, with good bedrooms and obliging service. Maybe it's the building itself (from centuries-old parts of monasteries to extravagant Victorian gin-palaces), or its surroundings (lovely countryside, attractive waterside, extensive well kept garden), or what's in it (charming furnishings, extraordinary collections of bric-a-brac).

Above all, though, what makes the good pub is its atmosphere – you should be able to feel at home there, and feel not just that *you're* glad you've come but that *they're* glad you've come.

It follows from this that a great many ordinary locals, perfectly good in their own right, don't earn a place in the book. What makes them attractive to their regular customers (an almost clubby chumminess) may even make strangers feel rather out-of-place.

Another important point is that there's not necessarily any link between charm and luxury – though we like our creature comforts as much as anyone. A basic unspoilt village tavern, with hard seats and a flagstone floor, may be worth travelling miles to find, while a deluxe pub-restaurant may not be worth crossing the street for. Landlords can't buy the Good Pub accolade by spending thousands on thickly padded banquettes, soft music and menus boasting about signature dishes nesting on beds of trendy vegetables drizzled by a jus of this and that – they can only win it, by having a genuinely personal concern for both their customers and their pub.

Using the *Guide*

THE COUNTIES

England has been split alphabetically into counties, mainly to make it easier for people scanning through the book to find pubs near them. Each chapter starts by picking out the pubs that are currently doing best in the area, or are specially attractive for one reason or another. Metropolitan areas have been included in the counties around them – for example, Merseyside in Lancashire. And occasionally we have grouped counties together – for example, Rutland with Leicestershire, and Durham with Northumberland to make Northumbria. If in doubt, check the Contents.

Scotland and Wales have each been covered in single chapters, and London appears immediately before them at the end of England. Except in London (which is split into Central, East, North, South and West), pubs are listed alphabetically under the name of the town or village where they are. If the village is so small that you probably wouldn't find it on a road map, we've listed it under the name of the nearest sizeable village or town instead. The maps use the same town and village names, and additionally include a few big cities that don't have any listed pubs – for orientation.

We always list pubs in their true locations – so if a village is actually in Buckinghamshire that's where we list it, even if its postal address is via some town in Oxfordshire. Just once or twice, while the village itself is in one county the pub is just over the border in the next-door county. We then use the village county, not the pub one.

STARS ★

Specially good pubs are picked out with a star after their name. In a few cases, pubs have two stars: these are the aristocrats among pubs, really worth going out of your way to find. The stars do NOT signify extra luxury or specially good food – in fact some of the pubs which appeal most distinctively and strongly of all are decidedly basic in terms of food and surroundings. The detailed description of each pub shows what its special appeal is, and this is what the stars refer to.

FOOD AND STAY AWARDS ⊕ ⇌

The knife-and-fork rosette shows those pubs where food is quite outstanding. The bed symbol shows pubs which we know to be good as places to stay in – bearing in mind the price of the rooms (obviously you can't expect the same level of luxury at £40 a head as you'd get for £100 a head). Pubs with bedrooms are marked on the maps as a square.

♀

This wine glass symbol marks out those pubs where wines are a cut above the usual run, and/or offer a good choice of wines by the glass.

◗

The beer tankard symbol shows pubs where the quality of the beer is quite exceptional, or pubs which keep a particularly interesting range of beers in good condition.

£

This symbol picks out pubs where we have found decent snacks at £2.10 or less, or worthwhile main dishes at £5.25 or less.

RECOMMENDERS

At the end of each main entry we include the names of readers who have recently recommended that pub (unless they've asked us not to).

Important note: the description of the pub and the comments on it are our own and not the recommenders'; they are based on our own personal inspections and on later verification of facts with each pub. As some recommenders' names appear quite often, you can get an extra idea of what a pub is like by seeing which other pubs those recommenders have approved.

LUCKY DIPS

The Lucky Dip section at the end of each county chapter includes brief descriptions of pubs that have been recommended by readers, with the readers' names in brackets. As the flood of reports from readers has given so much solid information about so many pubs, we have been able to include only those which seem really worth trying. Where only one single reader's name is shown, in most cases that pub has been given a favourable review by other readers in previous years, so its inclusion does not depend on a single individual's judgement. In all cases, we have now not included a pub in the list unless the reader's description makes the nature of the pub quite clear, and gives us good grounds for trusting that other readers would be glad to know of the pub. So the descriptions normally reflect the balanced judgement of a number of different readers, increasingly backed up by similar reports on the same pubs from other readers in previous years. Many have been inspected by us. In these cases, LYM means the pub was in a previous edition of the *Guide*. The usual reason that it's no longer a main entry is that, although we've heard nothing really condemnatory about it, we've not had enough favourable reports to be sure that it's still ahead of the local competition. BB means that, although the pub has never been a main entry, we have inspected it, and found nothing against it. In both these cases, the description is our own; in others, it's based on the readers' reports. This year, we have deleted many previously highly rated pubs from the book simply because we have no very recent reports on them. This may well mean that we have left out some favourites – please tell us if we have!

Lucky Dip pubs marked with a ☆ are ones where the information we have (either from our own inspections or from trusted reader/reporters) suggests a firm recommendation. Roughly speaking, we'd say that these pubs are as much worth considering, at least for the virtues described for them, as many of the main entries themselves. Note that in the Dips we always commend food if we have information supporting a positive recommendation. So a bare mention that food is served shouldn't be taken to imply a recommendation of the food. The same is true of accommodation and so forth.

The Lucky Dips (particularly, of course, the starred ones) are under consideration for inspection for a future edition – so please let us have any comments you can make on them. You can use the report forms at the end of the book, the report card which should be included in it, or just write direct (no stamp needed if posted in the UK). Our address is The Good Pub Guide, FREEPOST TN1569, WADHURST, East Sussex TN5 7BR. Alternatively, you can get reports to us immediately, through our web site (**www.goodguides.com** – see below).

MAP REFERENCES

All pubs outside the big cities are given four-figure map references. On the main entries, it looks like this: SX5678 Map 1. Map 1 means that it's on the first map at the end of the book. SX means it's in the square labelled SX on that map. The first figure, 5, tells you to look along the grid at the top and bottom of the SX square for the figure 5. The third figure, 7, tells you to look down the grid at the side of the square to find the figure 7. Imaginary lines drawn down and across the square from these figures should intersect near the pub itself.

The second and fourth figures, the 6 and the 8, are for more precise pin-pointing, and are really for use with larger-scale maps such as road atlases or the Ordnance Survey 1:50,000 maps, which use exactly the same map reference system. On the relevant Ordnance Survey map, instead of finding the 5 marker on the top grid you'd find the 56 one; instead of the 7 on the side grid you'd look for the 78 marker. This makes it very easy to locate even the smallest village.

Where a pub is exceptionally difficult to find, we include a six-figure reference in the directions, such as OS Sheet 102 map reference 654783. This refers to Sheet 102 of the Ordnance Survey 1:50,000 maps, which explain how to use the six-figure references to pin-point a pub to the nearest 100 metres.

MOTORWAY PUBS

If a pub is within four or five miles of a motorway junction, and reaching it doesn't involve much slow traffic, we give special directions for finding it from the motorway. And the Special Interest Lists at the end of the book include a list of these pubs, motorway by motorway.

PRICES AND OTHER FACTUAL DETAILS

The *Guide* went to press during the summer of 2001. As late as possible, each pub was sent a checking sheet to get up-to-date food, drink and bedroom prices and other factual information. By the summer of 2002 prices are bound to have increased a little – to be prudent, you should probably allow around 5% extra by then. But if you find a significantly different price please let us know.

Breweries or independent chains to which pubs are 'tied' are named at the beginning of the italic-print rubric after each main entry. That means the pub has to get most if not all of its drinks from that brewery or chain. If the brewery is not an independent one but just part of a combine, we name the combine in brackets. When the pub is tied, we have spelled out whether the landlord is a tenant, has the pub on a lease, or is a manager; tenants and leaseholders of breweries generally have considerably greater freedom to do things their own way, and in particular are allowed to buy drinks including a beer from sources other than their tied brewery.

Free houses are pubs not tied to a brewery, so in theory they can shop around to get the drinks their customers want, at the best prices they can find. But in practice many free houses have loans from the big brewers, on terms that bind them to sell those breweries' beers. So don't be too surprised to find that so-called free houses may be stocking a range of beers restricted to those from a single brewery.

Real ale is used by us to mean beer that has been maturing naturally in its cask. We do not count as real ale beer which has been pasteurised or filtered to remove its natural yeasts. If it is kept under a blanket of carbon dioxide to preserve it, we still generally mention it – as long as the pressure is too light for you to notice any extra fizz, it's hard to tell the difference. (For brevity, we use the expression 'under light blanket pressure' to cover such pubs; we do not include among them pubs where the blanket pressure is high enough to force the beer up from the cellar, as this does make it unnaturally fizzy.) If we say a pub has, for example, 'Whitbreads-related real ales', these may include not just beers brewed by the national company and its subsidiaries but also beers produced by independent breweries which the national company buys in bulk and distributes alongside its own.

Other drinks: we've also looked out particularly for pubs doing enterprising non-alcoholic drinks (including good tea or coffee), interesting spirits (especially malt whiskies), country wines (elderflower and the like), freshly squeezed juices, and good farm ciders. So many pubs now stock one of the main brands of draught cider that we normally mention cider only if the pub keeps quite a range, or one of the less common farm-made ciders.

Bar food refers to what is sold in the bar, not in any separate restaurant. It means a place serves anything from sandwiches and ploughman's to full meals, rather than pork scratchings or packets of crisps. We always mention sandwiches in the text if we know that a pub does them – if you don't see them mentioned, assume you can't get them.

The *food listed* in the description of each pub is an example of the sort of thing you'd find served in the bar on a normal day, and generally includes the dishes which are currently finding most favour with readers. We try to indicate any difference we know of between lunchtime and evening, and between summer and winter (on the whole stressing summer food more). In winter, many pubs tend to have a more restricted range, particularly of salads, and tend then to do more in the way of filled baked potatoes, casseroles and hot pies. We always mention barbecues if we know a pub does them. Food quality and variety may be affected by holidays – particularly in a small pub, where the licensees do the cooking themselves (May and early June seems to be a popular time for licensees to take their holidays).

Any separate *restaurant* is mentioned. But in general all comments on the type of food served, and in particular all the other details about bar food at the end of each entry, relate to the pub food and not to the restaurant food.

Children's Certificates exist, but in practice *children* are allowed into at least some part of almost all the pubs included in this *Guide* (there is no legal restriction on the movement of children over 14 in any pub, though only people over 18 may get alcohol). As we went to press, we asked the main-entry pubs a series of detailed questions about their rules. *Children welcome* means the pub has told us that it simply lets them come in, with no special restrictions. In other cases we report exactly what arrangements pubs say they make for children. However, we have to note that in readers' experience some pubs make restrictions which they haven't told us about (children only if eating, for example), and very occasionally pubs which have previously allowed children change their policy altogether, virtually excluding them. If you come across this, please let us know, so that we can clarify the information for the pub concerned in the next edition. Beware that if children are confined to the restaurant, they may occasionally be expected to have a full restaurant meal. Also, please note that a welcome for children does not necessarily mean a welcome for breast-feeding in public. If we don't mention children at all, assume that they are not welcome. All but one or two pubs (we mention these in the text) allow children in their garden or on their terrace, if they have one. In the Lucky Dip entries we mention children only if readers have found either that they are allowed or that they are not allowed – the absence of any reference to children in a Dip entry means we don't know either way.

Dogs, cats and other animals are mentioned in the text if we know either that they are likely to be present or that they are specifically excluded – we depend chiefly on readers and partly on our own inspections for this information.

Parking is not mentioned if you should normally be able to park outside the pub, or in a private car park, without difficulty. But if we know that parking space is limited or metered, we say so.

We now say if a pub does **not** accept *credit cards*; some which do may put a surcharge on credit card bills, as the card companies take quite a big cut.

Telephone numbers are given for all pubs that are not ex-directory.

Opening hours are for summer; we say if we know of differences in winter, or on particular days of the week. In the country, many pubs may open rather later and close earlier than their details show unless there are plenty of customers around (if you come across this, please let us know – with details). Pubs are allowed to stay open all day Mondays to Saturdays from 11am (earlier, if the area's licensing magistrates have permitted) till 11pm. However, outside cities most English and Welsh pubs close during the afternoon. Scottish pubs are allowed to stay open until later at night, and the Government has announced plans to allow later opening in England and Wales too, though again it's unlikely that the law will be changed during the currency of this edition. We'd be very grateful to hear of any differences from the hours we quote. You are allowed 20 minutes' drinking-up time after the quoted hours – half an hour if you've been having a meal in the pub.

Bedroom prices normally include full English breakfasts (if these are available, which they usually are), VAT and any automatic service charge that we know about. If we give just one price, it is the total price for two people sharing a double or twin-bedded room for one night. Otherwise, prices before the / are for single occupancy, prices after it for double. A capital B against the price means that it includes a private bathroom, a capital S a private shower. As all this coding packs in quite a lot of information, some examples may help to explain it:

£65	on its own means that's the total bill for two people sharing a twin or double room without private bath; the pub has no rooms with private bath, and a single person might have to pay that full price.
£65B	means exactly the same – but all the rooms have private bath.
£50(£65B)	means rooms with private baths cost £15 extra
£35/£50(£65B)	means the same as the last example, but also shows that there are single rooms for £35, none of which have private bathrooms

If there's a choice of rooms at different prices, we normally give the cheapest. If there are seasonal price variations, we give the summer price (the highest). During the winter, many inns, particularly in the country, will have special cheaper rates. And at other times, especially in holiday areas, you will often find prices cheaper if you stay for several nights. On weekends, inns that aren't in obvious weekending areas often have bargain rates for two- or three-night stays.

MEAL TIMES

Bar food is commonly served from 12-2 and 7-9, at least from Monday to Saturday (food service often stops a bit earlier on Sundays). If we don't give a time against the *Bar food* note at the bottom of a main entry, that means that you should be able to get bar food at those times. However, we do spell out the times if we know that bar food service starts after 12.15 or after 7.15; if it stops before 2 or before 8.45; or if food is served for significantly longer than usual (say, till 2.30 or 9.45).

Though we note days when pubs have told us they don't do food, experience suggests that you should play safe on Sundays and check first with any pub before planning an expedition that depends on getting a meal there. Also, out-of-the-way pubs often cut down on cooking during the week, especially the early part of the week, if they're quiet – as they tend to be, except at holiday times. Please let us know if you find anything different from what we say!

NO SMOKING

We say in the text of each entry what, if any, provision a pub makes for non-smokers. Pubs setting aside at least some sort of no-smoking area are also listed county by county in the Special Interest Lists at the back of the book.

DISABLED ACCESS

Deliberately, we do not ask pubs questions about this, as their answers would not give a reliable picture of how easy access is. Instead, we depend on readers' direct experience. If you are able to give us help about this, we would be particularly grateful for your reports.

PLANNING ROUTES WITH THE GOOD PUB GUIDE

Computer users may like to know of a route-finding programme, Microsoft® AutoRoute™ Great Britain 2002 Edition, which shows the location of *Good Pub Guide* pubs on detailed maps, works out the quickest routes for journeys, adds diversions to nearby pubs – and shows our text entries for those pubs on screen.

OUR WEB SITE (www.goodguides.com)

Our Internet web site combines material from *The Good Pub Guide* and its sister publication *The Good Britain Guide* in a way that gives people who do not yet know the books at least a taste of them. We also hope that we can use it to give readers of the books extra information (and allow them to report quickly to us). As part of an ongoing improvement program we have significantly increased the amount of information on the site this year. You can use the site to send us reports – this way they get virtually immediate attention.

CHANGES DURING THE YEAR – PLEASE TELL US

Changes are inevitable, during the course of the year. Landlords change, and so do their policies. And, as we've said, not all returned our fact-checking sheets. We very much hope that you will find everything just as we say. But if you find anything different, please let us know, using the tear-out card in the middle of the book (which doesn't need an envelope), the report forms here, or just a letter. You don't need a stamp: the address is The Good Pub Guide, FREEPOST TN1569, WADHURST, East Sussex TN5 7BR. As we have said, you can also send us reports by using our web site: **www.goodguides.com.**

Author's Acknowledgements

In this the *Guide*'s 20th year, I'd like to record my particular thanks to David Perrott, who has drawn the maps since it started; to Pat Taylor Chalmers, who has punctiliously edited the text each year; to John Holliday of Trade Wind Technology, who has built our state-of-the-art database; to Michael Sissons my agent and his colleagues at PFD, who assisted at the *Guide*'s birth and have been vital to its health ever since; and to Amelia Thorpe and her colleagues at Ebury Press, who have been the publishers from Heaven. I'm deeply grateful too to the many people who have worked alongside me on the *Guide*, and especially to Fiona Stapley, who has been with it almost since it started. Above all, warm thanks to Helena, who for 20 years has put up with the way that my annual total immersion in the editorial process has stopped me functioning as anything remotely resembling a normal human being between May and October.

The *Guide* could never have started, let alone grown as it has, without the unstinting help we have had from the many thousands of readers who report to us on the pubs they visit. For the tremendous amount of help they've given us this year, I am deeply grateful to Richard Lewis, Ian Phillips, George Atkinson, Susan and John Douglas, Kevin Thorpe, Michael and Jenny Back, CMW, JJW, Steve Whalley, Martin and Karen Wake, Michael Doswell, LM, Dennis Jenkin, Phil and Jane Hodson, Peter and Audrey Dowsett, Phyl and Jack Street, Roger Huggins, Dave Irving, Ewan McCall, Tom McLean, John Beeken, Lynn Sharpless, Bob Eardley, Eric Larkham, the Didler, Rona Murdoch, Tom Evans, Ann and Colin Hunt, Joan and Michel Hooper-Immins, Ian and Nita Cooper, Margaret Dickinson, Catherine Pitt, Jonathan Smith, Ted George, Derek and Sylvia Stephenson, MDN, Darly Graton, Graeme Gulibert, Pete Baker, Pat and Tony Martin, Tracey and Stephen Groves, Esther and John Sprinkle, Val and Alan Green, Mr and Mrs C Roberts, Andy and Jill Kassube, Paul and Ursula Randall, Charles and Pauline Stride, Brian and Anna Marsden, Guy Vowles, P and M Rudlin, Joyce and Maurice Cottrell, Dr M E Wilson, Tony and Wendy Hobden, E G Parish, Simon Collett-Jones, Martin Jennings, Tina and David Woods-Taylor, Mike Gorton, Comus and Sarah Elliott, Kevin Blake, Jenny and Brian Seller, W W Burke, J F M and M West, Jim Bush, G Coates, Alan and Paula McCully, B, M and P Kendall, John Wooll, Basil Minson, Anthony Longden, Dick and Madeleine Brown, Bruce Bird, John Foord, Paul and Penny Rampton, Mayur Shah, JP, PP, Andy Sinden, Louise Harrington, John Evans, Eric Locker, John and Vivienne Rice, R T and J C Moggridge, Richard and Margaret Peers, KC, John Kane, Mike Ridgway, Sarah Miles, Marjorie and David Lamb, Mary Kirman and Tim Jefferson, Howard Dell, DWAJ, Michael Buchanan, David Peakall, David J Miles, Bob and Maggie Atherton, Peter Meister, Nigel Woolliscroft, Peter F Marshall, Dr and Mrs A K Clarke, Jenny and Dave Hughes, Keith and Chris O'Neill, P Abbott, Richard Fendick, Bernie Adams, Pamela and Merlyn Horswell, Ian Jones, Joan Thorpe, Mike and Mary Carter, Gill Waller, Tony Morriss, Dave Braisted, Rob Fowell, Jayne and Peter Capp, Edward Jago and Stephen, Julie and Hayley Brown.

Thanks too to the thousands of devoted publicans, who have given me and our readers 20 years of delighted pub-hunting.

Alisdair Aird

England

Bedfordshire

Three new entries here this year: the Brown Bear in Biggleswade, a cheerful place that specialises in a changing choice of interesting real ales; the Five Bells at Stanbridge, an attractively redesigned pub with interesting food; and the Three Fyshes at Turvey, a well run traditional riverside pub. The friendly Fox & Hounds at Riseley is a great place for steak lovers, but our clear choice as Bedfordshire Dining Pub of the Year is the Knife & Cleaver at Houghton Conquest, an excellent place for a special meal out. Our favourite traditional country pub in this county is the Cock at Broom, doing very well these days; and the Three Tuns at Biddenham deserves a special mention as the only Bedfordshire pub to have kept its place in all 20 editions of the Guide so far. Some pubs to pick out particularly from the Lucky Dip at the end of the chapter are the Black Horse at Ireland, Lynmore at Sharpenhoe, Bedford Arms at Souldrop and White Horse at Southill. On the whole this is not an expensive county: drinks prices are around the national average, with the Brown Bear giving the best beer value.

BIDDENHAM TL0249 Map 5
Three Tuns £

57 Main Road; village signposted from A428 just W of Bedford

Bustling and friendly, this thatched village pub is especially popular at lunchtime for its reasonably priced, enjoyable food. This might include sandwiches (from £2; soup and sandwich £3.50), ploughman's (£3.50), ham and egg (£4), home-made dishes such as curry (£6), steak and kidney pie and meaty or vegetarian lasagne (£6.50), steaks (from £8.50), and children's menu (£2.50); the dining room is no smoking. The bustling lounge has low beams and country paintings, and well kept Greene King IPA, Abbot and Ruddles County on handpump. A simpler public bar has darts, table skittles, dominoes and a fruit machine. There are seats in the attractively sheltered, spacious garden, and a big terrace has lots of picnic-sets. The very good children's play area has swings for all ages. *(Recommended by BKA, Ian Phillips, Terry Mizen, Steve Chambers, Michael Tack, Bob and Maggie Atherton)*

Greene King ~ Tenant Alan Wilkins ~ Real ale ~ Bar food (not Sun evening) ~ No credit cards ~ (01234) 354847 ~ Children in dining room ~ Open 11.30-2.30, 6-11; 12-3, 7-10.30 Sun

BIGGLESWADE TL1944 Map 5
Brown Bear ◧

29 Hitchin Street; from A6001 follow sign for Hitchin Street shops

Definitely one for the beer buffs, this cheery local specialises in unusual real ales from microbreweries and regional brewers. Over the last three years the warmly welcoming licensees have served nearly two and a half thousand different brews, with usually nine on at any one time. They say it's their aim to try out every beer in Britain, and given the effort they put into tracking them down seem quite likely to succeed. On our visit the choice included Ballards Best, Hanby Cascade, Humpty Dumpty Lemon and Ginger, Mighty Oak Obeer, and Wye Valley Dorothy Goodbodys and Old Skippers. They offer tastings of beers you might not have come across and also keep four Belgian beers on draught (and dozens more by the bottle).

During their lively May and November beer festivals they can have up to 70 different beers. Bigger than you'd expect from outside, the partly bare-boards bar has patterned wallpaper and carpets, and masses of beer mats and pump clips across the ceiling; it stretches back into no smoking areas, and there are a few outdoor tables at the side. Generously served home-made bar food such as lasagne (£3.65), chilli (£3.90), and cumberland sausage (£3.95); fruit machine, piped music. *(Recommended by Richard Lewis, Pete Baker, Nev)*

Free house ~ Licensees Mary and Alan ~ Real ale ~ Bar food (not Sun evening) ~ No credit cards ~ (01767) 316161 ~ Live music most Fridays ~ Open 12-3, 5-11 (11-11 Fri, Sat); 12-10.30 Sun

BROOM TL1743 Map 5
Cock ★

23 High Street; from A1 opposite northernmost Biggleswade turnoff follow Old Warden 3, Aerodrome 2 signpost, and take first left signposted Broom

Praise for this unspoilt, friendly 17th-c pub is as consistent as ever. Its four cosy rooms have remained almost untouched over the years with simple latch doors, low ochre ceilings, stripped panelling and farmhouse-style tables and chairs on their antique tiles; winter log fires. There's no counter, and the very well kept Greene King IPA, Abbot and Ruddles County are tapped straight from the cask, by the cellar steps off a central corridor running down the middle of the building; piped music, darts, table skittles, cribbage and dominoes. Readers enjoy the good straightforward bar food which includes sandwiches (from £2.55), home-made soup (£2.95), ploughman's (from £4.55), vegetarian lasagne (£5.95), scampi or filled yorkshire puddings (£5.95), breaded plaice filled with prawns and mushrooms or large cod (£6.95), cajun chicken (£7.25), 8oz sirloin steak (£7.95), and Sunday roast (£6.95). There are picnic-sets on the terrace by the back lawn, and a fenced-off play area; caravanning and camping facilities are available. *(Recommended by Pete Baker, JP, PP, Dez and Jen Clarke, Phil and Sally Gorton, the Didler, Stephen, Julie and Hayley Brown, Ian Phillips, Mark Blackburn, David R Crafts, B, M and P Kendall)*

Greene King ~ Tenants Gerry and Jean Lant ~ Real ale ~ Bar food (not Sun evening) ~ Restaurant ~ (01767) 314411 ~ Children in restaurant and family room ~ Open 12-3(4 Sat), 6-11; 12-5, 7-10.30 Sun

HOUGHTON CONQUEST TL0441 Map 5
Knife & Cleaver 🍽 ♀ 🛏

Between B530 (old A418) and A6, S of Bedford

Bedfordshire Dining Pub of the Year

This attractive 17th-c brick-built dining pub is great for stylishly presented, imaginative and fully flavoured food; service is really welcoming and efficient. The bar menu (there is a separate restaurant one, particularly strong on daily fresh fish) includes sandwiches (from £3), soup of the day such as honey parsnip and ginger (£3), mozzarella, tomato and pesto on toasted baguette (£4.75), sautéed mushrooms and black pudding on baked walnut bread (£5.25), baked oysters (£6.50 for six), moules marinières (£7.25), Welsh lamb shank on pesto mash (£7.95) and a dish of the day such as guinea fowl in red wine with woodland mushrooms (£6.25). Puddings (£3.25) might include strawberry and rhubarb salad with home-made crumble ice cream or chocolate sponge with black cherry sauce, and there's a proper cheeseboard (£4). The relaxed and comfortable bar has maps, drawings and old documents on the walls, panelling which is reputed to have come from nearby ruined Houghton House, and a blazing fire in winter; the airy no smoking conservatory restaurant has rugs on the tiled floor, swagged curtains, cane furniture and lots of hanging plants, and there's also a no smoking family room. Well kept Bass and Batemans XB on handpump, Stowford Press farm cider, over two dozen good wines by the glass, and a fine choice of up to 20 well aged malt whiskies; unobtrusive piped music. Beware that it does get very busy, and on Saturday evening if the restaurant is fully booked they may not serve bar meals. There's no denying that this is a very restaurantry place, but given the scarcity of good dining pubs in this part of the country we'd be doing readers a disservice if we decided that its thorough-going emphasis on food disqualified it as a pub. There are new tables on the terrace in the neatly kept garden, and the church opposite is worth a look. *(Recommended by David and Ruth Shillitoe, Simon Cottrell, Bob and Maggie Atherton, JCW, Enid and Henry Stephens, Simon King, Maysie Thompson, Anthony Barnes)*

Free house ~ Licensees David and Pauline Loom ~ Real ale ~ Bar food (not Sun evening; not Sat evening if restaurant is busy) ~ Restaurant ~ (01234) 740387 ~ Children away from main bar ~ Open 12-2.30, 7-10.30(11 Sat); 12-3(closed evening) Sun; closed 27-30 Dec ~ Bedrooms: £49B/£64B

KEYSOE TL0762 Map 5
Chequers
Pertenhall Road, Brook End (B660)

The friendly licensees at this pleasant village local go out of their way to make customers feel at home. Comfortable seats in one of the two neat and simple beamed rooms (which are divided by an unusual stone-pillared fireplace) lend an air of the 1960s; this room is no smoking; darts, shove-ha'penny, bar billiards, dominoes; piped local radio or music. Bar food is very popular, with sandwiches (from £2), which you can have toasted, home-made soup (£2.50), garlic mushrooms on toast (£3.50), ploughman's (£4), chilli con carne (£5.50), home-made steak and ale pie (£6.00), chicken breast stuffed with stilton in a chive sauce (£8), steaks (from £9.25) and puddings such as Kahlua-flamed bananas or banana ice cream with home-made butterscotch sauce (from £2.25); children's menu (£3.25). Well kept Fullers London Pride and Hook Norton Best on handpump from the stone bar counter; some malt whiskies, and mulled wine in winter. Tables and chairs on the back terrace look over the garden, which has a wendy house, play tree, swings and a sand-pit. *(Recommended by Michael and Jenny Back, Stephen, Julie and Hayley Brown)*

Free house ~ Licensee Jeffrey Kearns ~ Real ale ~ Bar food (not Tues) ~ (01234) 708678 ~ Children in eating area of bar and in separate family room ~ Open 11.30-2.30, 6.30-11; 12-2.30, 7-10.30 Sun; closed Tues

LINSLADE SP9225 Map 4
Globe
Globe Lane, off Stoke Rd (A4146) nr bridge; outside Linslade proper, just before you get to the town sign

Nicely set below the embankment of the Grand Union Canal, this whitewashed 19th-c pub is a perfect spot to while away an afternoon watching life on the water. Understandably busy in summer when there's a jolly bustling atmosphere, there are enough tables outside to cope, most of them along the towpath with others in a very well equipped fenced-off play area with climbing forts and equipment, and also some in the garden under the trees alongside the car park. Inside, a series of cosy beamed and flagstoned rooms with intriguing quotations on the walls, and an open fire, afford the same fine views from a warmer environment. Well kept beers are Adnams, Courage Best, Marstons Pedigree, Theakstons Best and a guest; piped music. Bar food includes a soup of the day such as carrot and orange (£2.75), doorstep sandwiches (from £3.25), ploughman's (£4.50), grilled salmon (£8.50), steak (from £9.55) and puddings such as sticky toffee or chocolate and whisky mousse (£3.50); efficient service. To get there you come down a little private road that seems to take you further into the countryside than you really are, and the Cross Bucks Way leads off from just along the canal. *(Recommended by Ian Phillips, Susan and John Douglas)*

Old English Inns ~ Manager Peter Morris ~ Real ale ~ Bar food (not winter Sun evenings) ~ Restaurant ~ (01525) 373338 ~ Children in eating area of bar and restaurant ~ Open 11-11; 11-10.30 Sun; 11.30-3, 6.30-11(10.30 Sun) winter

MILTON BRYAN SP9730 Map 4

Red Lion 🍽

Toddington Road, off B528 S of Woburn

This comfortably relaxing pub, handy for Woburn Abbey and Safari Park, is changing hands as the *Guide* comes out, so we cannot guarantee that it will continue to be run along the same lines. Up to now it's been one of the county's best pubs, with a good range of food at sensible prices from chunky sandwiches to typical pub dishes, fresh fish specials and a good value pensioners' lunch. The beamed bar area has white-painted walls, some exposed brickwork, big fading rugs on the part wood and part flagstoned floors, a case of sporting cups, and fresh flowers on the round wooden tables; piped music. Well kept Greene King IPA and Old Speckled Hen and a fortnightly changing guest on handpump. There are plenty of tables, chairs and picnic-sets out on the terrace and lawn, which looks across to a delightfully thatched black and white timbered house; there's a climbing frame out here too. Times and other details were those in force as we went to press. *(Recommended by Ron and Val Broom, Ian Phillips, David and Ruth Shillitoe, Joy and Peter Heatherley, Keith Barker, Maysie Thompson, Steve Chambers, Karen and Graham Oddey)*

Greene King ~ Real ale ~ Bar food (12-2.30, 6.30-10) ~ Restaurant ~ (01525) 210044 ~ Children welcome ~ Open 11-3(4 Sat), 6-11; 12-4, 6-10.30 Sun

ODELL SP9658 Map 4

Bell £

High Street/Horsefair Lane; off A6 S of Rushden, via Sharnbrook

The five small homely low-ceilinged rooms in this pretty stone and thatched village pub – some with shiny black beams – loop around a central servery and are furnished with handsome old oak settles, bentwood chairs and neat modern furniture; there's a log fire in one big stone fireplace, and two coal fires elsewhere, with well kept Greene King IPA, Abbot, Triumph and seasonal ales on handpump. Reasonably priced bar food includes sandwiches (from £2.20), ploughman's (from £4.40), omelettes (£4.10), ham, egg and chips (£4.65), vegetable pie (£4.50), liver and bacon (£5.50), and daily specials from the board such as asparagus and mushroom pasta (£5.20), smoked bacon steak with cumberland sauce (£7.25), vegetable lasagne (£5.60), braised lamb shank (£8.95) or lamb or chicken curry (£7.50); usual children's dishes (from £2.30) and puddings such as crunchy Dime bar gateau and cheesecake (from £2.20)). Picnic-sets on the flower-filled terrace overlook a wooded garden, and from here there's an attractive walk down through a wild area to a bridge over the Great Ouse. Children will enjoy watching the garden roamings of Lucy the ten-year-old goose, and golden pheasants, cockatiels and canaries. Further along the road is a very pretty church, and the pub is handy for the local country park. *(Recommended by Ian Phillips, Anthony Barnes, Maysie Thompson)*

Greene King ~ Tenants Derek and Doreen Scott ~ Real ale ~ Bar food (not Sun evening) ~ (01234) 720254 ~ Children in eating area of the bar and in separate family room ~ Open 11-3, 6-11; 12-3, 7-10.30 Sun

RIDGMONT SP9736 Map 4

Rose & Crown

2 miles from M1 junction 13: follow Ampthill signposts, and the pub is on A507, on Ridgmont High Street

Run by the same landlord for 23 years, this attractive 17th-c brick house was once part of the Duke of Bedford's estate. Inside there's a charming collection of Rupert Bear memorabilia and old english sheepdog china. Its neat lounge is pleasantly arranged with a sofa and other comfortable chairs, brasses, prints of white geese and an open fire in its sizeable brick fireplace. If you just want a drink, there's plenty of standing room in the low-ceilinged traditional public bar (with fruit machine, shove-ha'penny, cribbage and dominoes). There's more Rupert memorabilia up a couple of steps in the no smoking dining area. Home-made pub food includes sandwiches (from £2), sausage and mash (£4.95), macaroni cheese (£5.25), pies (from £5.85), and curries (from £5.95). Besides well kept Charles Wells Eagle and Bombardier on handpump, they usually have two guests such as Greene King Abbot and Adnams Broadside, and up to 50 whiskies; friendly service and piped music. In summer the long and attractive suntrap tree-lined garden behind, full of flowers and shrubs, is a big plus; there are also some picnic-sets out in front, below the pretty hanging baskets. There's easy parking and good wheelchair access, and it's handy for Woburn Abbey. The pub grounds offer plenty of room for reasonably priced camping and caravanning. *(Recommended by Ian Phillips, Dez and Jen Clarke, R T and J C Moggridge, Bob and Val Collman)*

Charles Wells ~ Tenant Neil McGregor ~ Real ale ~ Bar food (7-9.30, 6-9.30 Fri and Sat) ~ Restaurant ~ (01525) 280245 ~ Children in restaurant ~ Open 10.30-2.30, 6-11; 12-3, 7-10.30 Sun

RISELEY TL0362 Map 5
Fox & Hounds

High St; village signposted off A6 and B660 N of Bedford

If you like steaks, you should be really happy here: you can choose the piece of meat you want and how you want it cooked, and you're then charged by the weight – say, £10.60 for 8oz rump, £11.60 for 8oz of sirloin and £12.80 for fillet (not Saturday lunchtime). Blackboards show other dishes, using local supplies, such as stilton and broccoli soup (£2.75), salmon rolls marinated in a juniper and dill sauce (£3.50), mushrooms in white wine, double cream, ham and mustard sauce (£3.75), steak and kidney pie (£7.95), chicken cordon bleu (£7.95), poached plaice in parsley and dill, and puddings such as spotted dick or steamed ginger (£3.25). Even if you don't see anything you fancy, it's worth asking: they're very obliging here, and will try and cope with particular food requests. It's a cheerfully bustling place, and does get busy. As they don't take bookings on Saturday night be prepared for a long wait for your table, and your food; and this year, you'll find the dining tables are bigger. A relaxing lounge area with leather chesterfields, lower tables and wing chairs contrasts with the more traditional pub furniture spread among timber uprights under the heavy low beams; unobtrusive classical or big band piped music. Charles Wells Eagle and Bombardier with maybe a changing guest such as Adnams are kept well on handpump, alongside a decent collection of other drinks including bin-end wines and a range of malts and cognacs. An attractively decked terrace with wooden tables and chairs has outside heating, and the pleasant garden has shrubs and a pergola. *(Recommended by Colin and Janet Roe, Michael Sargent, Sarah Markham, Ian Phillips, Nigel and Olga Wikeley)*

Charles Wells ~ Managers Jan and Lynne Zielinski ~ Real ale ~ Bar food (12-1.45, 6.30-9.30; 12-2, 7-9 Sun) ~ Restaurant ~ (01234) 708240 ~ Children welcome ~ Open 11.30-2.30, 6.30-11; 12-3, 7-10.30 Sun

STANBRIDGE SP9623 Map 4
Five Bells

Station Road; pub signposted off A5 N of Dunstable

Transformed by the current owners, this attractive old pub has been shortlisted for various pub design awards in recent months, and deservedly so; it's been very stylishly refurbished and redecorated, keeping the feel of a smartly relaxed country pub, but adding a fresh, contemporary zip. There are rugs, armchairs and sofas, candles on the neatly polished tables, exposed beams and wooden floors, and careful spotlighting that creates quite different moods around the various areas (of which perhaps the cosiest is the small corner by the fireplace). The big, brighter restaurant leads into a large garden with plenty of good wooden tables and chairs, and perfectly mown lawns; more outside tables nestle under a big tree at the front. There's quite an emphasis on the good imaginative food, which might include big well presented sandwiches (£4.95), tatin of marinated tomatoes with mozzarella and honey-roast figs (£10.95), fried bass on buttered linguini with raspberry and ginger sauce

(£11.95), and roast poussin on a cassoulet of spring vegetables (£13); the menu highlights which wines will best suit most dishes. They have occasional themed evenings – on St George's Day for example, or during Wimbledon; the chefs trained at hotels such as the Lanesborough in London, and see the gourmet nights as the perfect opportunity to show off what they can do. Well kept Bass and two changing guests such as Badger Best and Marstons Pedigree on handpump; piped music. *(Recommended by MP, Stephen Archer)*

Free house ~ Licensees Carl May and Corinne Bell ~ Real ale ~ Bar food ~ No credit cards ~ (01525) 210224 ~ Children welcome ~ Open 12-3, 5-11; 11-11 Sat; 12-10.30 Sun

TURVEY SP9452 Map 4
Three Cranes
Just off A428 W of Bedford

The prices at this stone-built 17th-c coaching inn have hardly changed since last year. The airy two-level carpeted bar has a solid-fuel stove, a quiet décor including old photographs and Victorian-style prints, and an array of stuffed owls and other birds in the main dining area; there are plenty of sensible tables with upright seats. Well kept Adnams, Courage Best and Directors, Fullers London Pride and Hook Norton Best on handpump. The specials board might include lunchtime sandwiches (from £2.25), soup (£2.50), ploughman's (£4.75), curried vegetable pancake (£6.50), steak and ale pie or lasagne (£6.95), medallions of pork with prune and armagnac sauce or fresh salmon with prawn and dill butter (£8.75), chicken medallions with brandy and peppercorn sauce (£8.85), tuna steak topped with cucumber butter (£9.50), steaks (from £10.25) and puddings such as treacle tart or fruit pie (£3.25); the good sausages (£6.50) come from the butcher next door. The staff are friendly; there are picnic-sets in a neatly kept garden with a climbing frame, and in summer, the pub front is filled with colourful hanging baskets and window boxes. *(Recommended by I C Millar, Maysie Thompson, Anthony Barnes, Colin and Janet Roe, Steve and Sue Griffiths)*

Old English Inns ~ Managers Paul and Sheila Linehan ~ Real ale ~ Bar food (12-2, 6.30-9.30) ~ Restaurant ~ (01234) 881305 ~ Children in eating area of bar and restaurant ~ Open 11-2.30, 6-11; 12-10.30 Sun ~ Bedrooms: £39.50S/£55S

Three Fyshes
A428 NW of Bedford; Bridge Street, W end of village

Next to the River Ouse, this friendly traditional pub shows the marks of past floods on the honey-coloured outside walls. A charming squint-walled stone corridor links the cosy flagstoned public bar (which has a big inglenook) with the main room: heavy beams, a carpet and flagstone floor, dark wood close-set tables and chairs, a large box window seat and another stone inglenook fireplace flanked by comfortable sofas (lovely roaring fires in winter). The good choice of mostly traditional bar food might include soup (from £2.50), baguettes (from £4.25), venison pie (£6.50) and steaks (from £5.75) as well as specials (with an emphasis on fresh fish). Pleasant efficient service; real ales on handpump such as Adnams Extra and Best, Marstons Pedigree and guests such as Greene King Ruddles County or Old Speckled Hen. There are good views of a mill and the river from the garden at the back, which has picnic-sets and room for children to run around. Hanging baskets in summer; piped music. The car park is 100 yards away. *(Recommended by Michael Tack, George Atkinson, Mike Ridgway, Sarah Miles, Colin and Janet Roe, Ian Phillips)*

Old English Inns ~ Managers Alan and Joanne Wainwright ~ Real ale ~ Bar food (12-2.30, 6-10) ~ Restaurant ~ (01234) 881264 ~ Children welcome ~ Open 11-3, 5.30-11; 11-11 Sat; 12-10.30 Sun

Lucky Dip

Besides the fully inspected pubs, you might like to try these Lucky Dips recommended to us and described by readers (if you do, please send us reports: www.goodguides.com).

Ampthill [TL0338]
Queens Head [Woburn St]: Friendly local with cosy lounge, rather bigger bar, simple cheap home-made food, well kept Charles Wells Bombardier, character landlord *(MP)*
Barton-le-Clay [TL0831]
Coach & Horses [Bedford Rd]: Big helpings of good low-priced wkdy food inc Mon roast and Fri fresh fish, very obliging licensees *(David and Michelle Bailey)*
Bedford [TL0549]
Crossed Keys [High St]: Refurbished as Greene King café/bar, their ales, cheap plentiful lunchtime food *(Tony and Wendy Hobden)*
Foxy Fish [Barns Hotel, Cardington Rd]: Smartly refurbished hotel bar in converted 17th-c manor house just outside town; lots of tables on polished flagstones, decent food; keg beers, piped music; charming relaxing terrace by calm stretch of River Ouse, attractive bedrooms *(Ian Phillips, BB)*
Wellington Arms [Wellington St]: Traditional corner local with Adnams, B&T Shefford Bitter and Mild and up to eight guest beers, also draught Hoegaarden and Czech Budweiser, bottled Belgian beers; cheap lunchtime rolls, darts, dominoes, food skittles, no juke box; open all day *(Peter Lamswood)*
Biggleswade [TL1944]
Wheatsheaf [Lawrence Rd]: Unpretentious local, as they used to be a few decades ago; one small very friendly room, well kept Greene King ales inc Mild, darts, dominoes and cards, TV for horseracing, no food or music *(Pete Baker)*
Bromham [TL0050]
Swan [Bridge End; nr A428, 2 miles W of Bedford]: Friendly and comfortable beamed family dining pub, good choice of food from sandwiches to seafood specials, quick service, lots of pictures, well kept Greene King IPA and Abbot, decent coffee, evening log fire; quiet piped music; public bar with darts and fruit machine, provision for children, garden *(Ian Phillips, Colin and Janet Roe, Michael Tack)*
Cardington [TL0847]
Kings Arms [The Green; off A603 E of Bedford]: Recently extended Brewers Fayre, usual food not too expensive, real ales such as Flowers Original and Wadworths 6X, airship photographs; sheltered picnic-sets under weeping willows *(Ian Phillips)*
Colmworth [TL1058]
☆ *Wheatsheaf* [Wilden Rd]: Early 17th-c pub, now largely a restaurant with interesting stylish food, but does have well kept Bass and Adnams; big log fire and low armchairs in small low-beamed bar, helpful young waitresses; front picnic-sets, small garden, comfortable and stylish new bedroom extension *(Michael Sargent)*
Eggington [SP9525]
Horseshoes [High St]: Cosy, comfortable and unpretentious country pub with three individually decorated rooms, friendly efficient service, three well kept interesting ales, good imaginative evening meals (not Mon) and lunchtime snacks, solid wooden tables; pub games; roomy garden with pretty hanging baskets, hens, chicks and friendly dog, country views; cl Mon lunchtime *(Margaret and Roy Randle, MP)*
Ireland [TL1341]
☆ *Black Horse* [off A600 Shefford—Bedford]: Busy and attractive dining pub with wide choice of good value plentiful piping hot food, good fresh ingredients, very good puddings, sizeable lounge or family dining area, well kept Bass and Worthington, good range of wines and good coffee, lots of very helpful friendly staff, plenty of tables in lovely front garden with play area – peaceful rural setting *(Mike and Marian Bister, Michael Sargent, BB, Maysie Thompson)*
Kensworth [TL0218]
Farmers Boy [B4540, Whipsnade end]: Village pub with good value food from sandwiches to good Sun roasts, generous and freshly made (so may be a wait), well kept Fullers, cheerful staff, roaring fire, pleasant beamed lounge bar split into three areas, nooks and crannies, good old-fashioned dining room (more restauranty evenings and Sun); children very welcome, and dogs, piped pop music, separate bar with pool, fruit machine and SkyTV; play area, maybe bouncy castle and rabbit hutches in big fenced-off back garden by fields with horses *(George Atkinson, MP)*
Northill [TL1546]
Crown [Ickwell Rd; village signed from B658 W of Biggleswade]: Black and white thatched pub with expanded food side under new regime, former public bar now a dining room, low-beamed main bar, huge open fire, well kept Bass and Greene King ales, wines by the glass; front seats by village pond, play area in huge back garden, tranquil village not far from the Shuttleworth Collection *(Pete Baker, Michael Dandy)*
Radwell [TL0057]
☆ *Swan* [Felmersham Rd]: Charming beamed and thatched pub, two spacious rooms joined by narrow passage, woodburner, lots of prints, wide choice of good food, service friendly even when very busy, well kept Charles Wells IPA and Eagle with a guest such as Camerons 80/-, decent coffee, popular evening restaurant (must book Fri/Sat); unobtrusive piped music; pleasant garden, attractive quiet village *(Maysie Thompson, Stephen, Julie and Hayley Brown)*
Sharpenhoe [TL0630]
☆ *Lynmore*: Woodburner and lots of old local photographs, prints and bric-a-brac in long low-beamed rambling family lounge and back no smoking dining area (good views), plentiful quick consistently good value food inc fresh veg and children's, well kept Bass, Fullers London Pride and Hancocks HB, good service; good garden for children, big wendy house; popular

with walkers *(Phil and Heidi Cook)*
Shillington [TL1234]
Musgrave Arms [Apsley End Rd, towards
Pegsdon and Hexton]: Friendly and civilised
lounge with settles and tables, comfortable
public bar, small dining room, wide choice of
generous home-made food inc good Sun roast,
Greene King IPA and Abbot tapped from the
cask, cheerful service; big back garden with
picnic-sets *(Len Banister)*
Souldrop [SP9861]
☆ *Bedford Arms* [High St; off A6 Rushden—
Bedford]: Bright, jolly and spacious, with good
range of interesting food esp fish in dining
section and other areas off; well kept Greene
King ales, big stone fireplace, brasses, settles
and prints; piped music; very peaceful village
(Bernie Adams, Sarah Markham)
Southill [TL1542]
☆ *White Horse* [off B658 SW of Biggleswade]:
Country pub with comfortable lounge, dining
room with spotlit well, small public bar with
prints, harness and big woodburner; enjoyable
food, Flowers, Fullers London Pride, and
Greene King IPA, children in eating areas;
delightful big garden maybe with children's
rides on diesel-engine miniature train, separate
sheltered lawn with bird feeders, garden shop
and good play area *(LYM, Michael Dandy)*
Steppingley [TL0135]
Chaneys [Flitwick Rd]: Good interesting food
esp seafood, large conservatory dining area
with rattan and chrome furniture, rattan and
matt black steel in bar with Adnams Broadside,
extensive wine list; well spaced picnic-sets out
behind, marquee *(Ian Phillips)*
Stotfold [TL2136]
Coach & Horses [The Green]: Revived and
flourishing under enthusiastic new tenant,
welcoming comfortable feel, well kept Greene
King IPA and a guest such as Courage
Directors, Marstons Pedigree or Morlands Old
Speckled Hen, darts, dominoes and cribbage
(Mike Rowley)
Studham [TL0215]
Bell [Dunstable Rd]: Friendly two-bar village
pub dating from 16th c, very pretty outside;
masses of brasses in beamed and timbered
lounge (partly no smoking), plentiful good
value freshly cooked food inc big baguettes,
Adnams and Greene King Abbot, pool and
SkyTV in public bar; booking advised Sat, Sun
lunch very popular; tables and views in big
garden, handy for Whipsnade and the Tree
Cathedral *(John Brightley, BB)*
Thurleigh [TL0558]
Jackal [High St]: Friendly and welcoming, with
skilful cooking by landlord/chef, roaring winter
fires in both bars, interesting wines, summer
Sun barbecues in nice garden; dogs allowed in
public bar *(Karen and Steve Brine)*
Toddington [TL0028]
Angel [Luton Rd]: Tucked away by green, part

16th-c but largely Victorian, lots of rooms and
now has a thai restaurant (where children
allowed), real ales such as Banks's, Courage
and Marstons, tea and coffee all day; has had
jazz Sun lunchtime, SkyTV; tables in garden,
attractive large village *(Maggie and Peter
Shapland)*
Bell [Market Sq]: Comfortable, with pleasant
atmosphere, decent food inc well cooked veg,
well kept Flowers *(Maggie and Peter Shapland)*
Sow & Pigs [Church Sq; handy for M1
junction 12]: Quaint 19th-c pub named after
carving on church opp, bare-boards front bar
with old wall bench, carpeted saloon, mixed
bag of furnishings inc pews, two armchairs and
a retired chesterfield, lots of pig decorations,
also old books and knick-knacks inc armless
mannequin, friendly landlord, particularly well
kept Greene King ales, good coffee, basic food
(not Sun; back Victorian-style dining room can
be booked for parties), two real fires, children
allowed; picnic-sets in small garden, attractive
village *(Kevin Thorpe, Maggie and Peter
Shapland)*
Totternhoe [SP9821]
☆ *Cross Keys* [Castle Hill Rd; off A505 W of M1
junction 11]: Neat low-beamed thatched and
timbered local below remains of a mott and
bailey fort, very popular, with friendly
accommodating hard-working licensees, small
public bar and slightly larger lounge bar,
enjoyable honest home-made food inc
interesting snacks and good choice of puddings;
big attractive garden, play equipment in
orchard below *(BB, Len Banister, Helen
Whitmore)*
Woburn [SP9433]
Bell [Bedford St]: Long narrow bar/dining area,
pleasantly furnished and cosy, with warm
woodburner, settles and hunting prints; friendly
helpful staff, generous reasonably priced bar
food, well kept Greene King ales, reasonable
wine choice, good coffee, roomy restaurant;
children welcome at lunchtime; tables outside,
hotel part across road, handy for Woburn Park
(Mike Ridgway, Sarah Miles, June Shamash)
☆ *Black Horse* [Bedford St]: Spacious open-plan
19th-c food pub, wide choice from sandwiches
and baked potatoes to steaks and fish cut to
order and grilled in the bar, also children's and
special orders, separate back restaurant; well
kept Adnams, Courage Directors, Fullers
London Pride and Theakstons; open all day
summer Sat and bank hols, summer barbecues
in pleasant sheltered garden; children in eating
areas *(LYM, Michael Dandy)*
Flying Fox [A5 Bletchley—Hockcliffe, away
from village]: Renamed and reworked as
Vintage Inn dining pub, with hop-hung beams,
pictures and artefacts, pleasant atmosphere,
decent food from open sandwiches up, Bass and
Worthingtons, attentive service; piped music;
tables out on grass *(George Atkinson)*

Berkshire

A marked split is developing in Berkshire's pubs, between places putting the emphasis very firmly on food, and pubs proudly keeping up the traditional virtues of an unassuming tavern with a welcome for all. In the foody camp, front-runners this year are the Bell at Boxford (a remarkable choice of wines by the glass), the ancient Bel & the Dragon in Cookham (smart, imaginative and seriously pricy), the Italian-leaning White Hart at Hamstead Marshall, the Hare & Hounds near Lambourn (new licensees making their mark), the George & Dragon in Swallowfield, and the Royal Oak so prettily set at Yattendon (it's been in all 20 issues of the Guide). All these can offer really good food, and quite a sense of occasion. By contrast, the more traditional camp includes two great favourites: the unchanging, marvellously simple Bell up on the downs at Aldworth, the only other Berkshire pub to have featured in every edition of the Guide so far – always in the same hands (it's been in the same family for many generations); and the secluded Pot Kiln at Frilsham, brewing its own beer, and also doing very well indeed these days. These two had the cheapest drinks we found in the county, which is in general very expensive for drinks, with beer jumping in price by 10p a pint this year, and now costing over 15p a pint more than the national average. Relatively few Berkshire pubs successfully have a foot in both camps, doing really good food yet keeping a truly pubby style. A new entry this year, the Sun in the Wood at Ashmore Green near Newbury, is a fine example of these. Others showing they can do this balancing act particularly well are the individualistic Horns at Crazies Hill, the cheerful Queen Victoria at Hare Hatch, the Rose & Crown at Woodside, and the Winterbourne Arms at Winterbourne. The Winterbourne Arms, with imaginative restaurany food from the new chef, but friendly new managers keeping a good pubby atmosphere, combines these two sides so enjoyably that it is our Berkshire Dining Pub of the Year. Current front-runners in the Lucky Dip section at the end of the chapter are the Hinds Head in Bray, Blade Bone at Bucklebury, Thatched Tavern at Cheapside, Jolly Farmer at Cookham Dean, Bunk at Curridge, Swan at East Ilsley, Pheasant at Great Shefford, Dew Drop near Hurley, Dundas Arms at Kintbury, Fishermans Cottage and Hobgoblin in Reading, Bull in Wargrave, Five Bells at Wickham and Two Brewers in Windsor; we have inspected and so can firmly vouch for the great majority of these.

ALDWORTH SU5579 Map 2

Bell ★ ♀ ▣ £

A329 Reading—Wallingford; left on to B4009 at Streatley

A favourite with many readers, this unchanging 14th-c country pub has been run by the same family for over 200 years. It is simply furnished with benches around the panelled walls, an ancient one-handed clock, a glass-panelled hatch rather than a bar counter for service, beams in the shiny ochre ceiling, and a woodburning stove. The timeless, welcoming atmosphere is helped by the ban on games machines, mobile phones and piped music. Apart from winter home-made soup (£2.50), appetising bar food is confined to exceptionally good value filled hot crusty rolls such as cheddar (£1.30), stilton, ham or pâté (£1.50), turkey (£1.60), smoked salmon, prawn or salt beef (£1.95), and delicious crab in season (£2), plus filled french bread (£2.50), and ploughman's (from £3); very good service. Particularly well kept and very cheap Arkells BBB and Kingsdown, Crouch Vale Bitter, and from the local West Berkshire Brewery, Old Tyler and Dark Mild on handpump (they won't stock draught lager); good quality house wines. Darts, shove-ha'penny, dominoes, and cribbage. The quiet, old-fashioned garden by the village cricket ground is lovely in summer, and the pub is handy for the Ridgeway. At Christmas, local mummers perform in the road by the ancient well-head (the shaft is sunk 400 feet through the chalk), and steaming jugs of hot punch and mince pies are handed round afterwards; occasional morris dancing in summer; Christmas mummers. It can get busy at weekends. *(Recommended by Jonathan Smith, Derek and Sylvia Stephenson, Dick and Madeleine Brown, Guy Vowles, JP, PP, Kevin Thorpe, Paul Vickers, Mark and Diane Grist, the Didler, CMW, JJW, Ian Phillips, Pat and Tony Martin, Susan and John Douglas)*

Free house ~ Licensee H E Macaulay ~ Real ale ~ Bar food (11-2.45, 6-10.45; 12-2.45, 7-10.15 Sun) ~ No credit cards ~ (01635) 578272 ~ Children must be well behaved ~ Open 11-3, 6-11; 12-3, 7-10.30 Sun; closed Mon exc bank holidays, 25 Dec

ASHMORE GREEN SU5069 Map 2
Sun in the Wood

NE of Newbury, or off A4 at Thatcham; off A34/A4 roundabout NW of Newbury, via B4009 Shaw Hill, then right into Kiln Road, then left into Stoney Lane after nearly 0.5 miles; or get to Stoney Lane sharp left off Ashmore Green Road, N of A4 at W end of Thatcham via Northfield Road and Bowling Green Road

Well named, this country pub is surrounded by tall trees, seeming many miles and not just a few minutes away from the heart of Newbury. It's very popular locally for consistently good food, with lunchtime freshly baked baguettes (from £3.25; steak and onions £4.95), starters such as home-made soup (£3.25), hotpot of mushrooms in a creamy stilton and port sauce (£4.20), hot chicken and bacon salad (£4.50), and main dishes such as lamb and mint sausages braised in red wine on lentils, savoy cabbage and bacon, with onion mash (£8.50), monkfish on a saffron and spring onion risotto with a mild thai red curry sauce (£10.95), and roast duck breast with a kumquat, port and marmalade sauce (£12.50); the puddings show some enjoyable variations on old favourites, such as chocolate bread and butter pudding with white chocolate ice cream (£3.95). Part of the bar and the restaurant are no smoking. The high-beamed front bar has bare boards on the left, carpet on the right, with a mix of old bucket chairs, padded dining chairs and stripped pews around sturdy tables, and opens into a big back dining area with the same informal feel, candles on tables, and some interesting touches like the big stripped bank of apothecary's drawers. It looks out over the big woodside garden, which has plenty of picnic-sets, and a play area with slide and climber. Well kept Badger Best and Wadworths IPA and 6X on handpump, decent house wines, well organised friendly attentive service. There is a small conservatory sitting area by the side entrance. *(Recommended by Charlie Woods, A and G Rae, Mr and Mrs A Chandler, Edward Mason)*

Wadworths ~ Tenant Philip Davison ~ Real ale ~ Bar food (12-2, 6.30-9.30; not Sun evening or Mon) ~ Restaurant ~ (01635) 42377 ~ Children in eating area of bar and restaurant ~ Open 12-2.30(3 Sat), 6(5.30 Sat)-11; 12-4, 7-10.30 Sun; closed Mon (exc Dec)

BOXFORD SU4271 Map 2
Bell ♀

Back road Newbury—Lambourn; village also signposted off B4000 between Speen and M4 junction 14

Although this civilised mock-Tudor inn is notable for its popular food and impressive range of wines (over 60) and champagnes by the glass, it manages to retain the relaxed atmosphere of a country local as well. The bar is quite long but snug, with a nice mix of racing pictures, old Mercier advertisements, red plush cushions for the mate's chairs, some interesting bric-a-brac, and a coal-effect fire at one end. Changing regularly, enjoyable meals might include good sandwiches, half a dozen oysters (£6), steak in ale pie (£8.95), thai fish curry (£12.95), shank of lamb or roast salmon (£13), and fillet steak (£17); the summer lobster dishes (£25) are great favourites. Most people eat in the rather smart, partly no smoking restaurant area on the left, but you can also dine on the covered and heated terrace. Well kept changing beers might include Badger Tanglefoot, Courage Best, Morrells Oxford Blue and Wadworths 6X on handpump, kept under light blanket pressure, and they stock a wide range of whiskies. Pool, shove-ha'penny, cribbage and dominoes, plus a fruit machine, TV, juke box, and piped music. A side courtyard has white cast-iron garden furniture. *(Recommended by James Morrell, P Bennett, A H and J A Morris, J M M Hill)*

Free house ~ Licensee Paul Lavis ~ Real ale ~ Bar food (12-2, 7-9.45) ~ Restaurant (till 10) ~ (01488) 608721 ~ Children welcome ~ Open 11-11; 12-10.30 Sun ~ Bedrooms: £65S/£75S

BRAY SU9079 Map 2

Crown

1½ miles from M4 junction 9; A308 towards Windsor, then left at Bray signpost on to B3028; High Street

This is a welcoming, friendly pub dating back to the 14th c. There are lots of beams (some so low you have to watch your head), and plenty of old timbers conveniently left at elbow height where walls have been knocked through. The partly panelled main bar has a good mix of customers, oak tables, leather backed armchairs, and a good open fire. One dining area has photographs of WWII aeroplanes. Reliable bar food is cooked to order and includes soup (£3.60), tagliatelle with olive oil, basil and parmesan (£7.50), wild boar sausages and mash (£7.95), home-made beef and Guinness pie (£9.95), oriental chicken salad (£10.95), a huge bowl of moules marinières (£11.75), a fillet of Scottish salmon on a roast mixed pepper salad with a sweet dill vinaigrette (£12.95), with puddings such as apple pie and treacle tart (£3.50). Well kept Brakspears Special, Courage Best and Directors on handpump and a fair choice of wines; helpful service. There are tables and benches in an attractive and sheltered flagstoned front courtyard with a flourishing grape vine, with more under cocktail parasols in a large back garden. *(Recommended by Lesley Bass, Mike and Jennifer Marsh, J Hale, Jayne and Peter Capp, Susan and John Douglas, Chris Glasson)*

Scottish Courage ~ Lease John and Carol Noble ~ Real ale ~ Bar food (12-2.30, 7-9; not Sun or Mon evenings) ~ Restaurant ~ (01628) 621936 ~ Open 11-3, 6-11; 12-3, 7-10.30 Sun; closed 25 Dec

BURCHETTS GREEN SU8381 Map 2

Crown

Side rd from A4 after Knowl Green on left, linking to A404

It might be best to book a table at weekends if you want to enjoy the popular food here. At lunchtime, there might be soup (£3.95), sandwiches (from £3.95), smooth chicken liver parfait with home-made chutney (£4.75), baked avocado and prawn thermidor (£5.25), cumberland sausage and onion gravy (£7.25), and steak and kidney pudding (£8.25); evening dishes include thai-style curried mushrooms with garlic bread (£4.75), poached fillet of salmon with a prawn and herb cream (£9.55), calves liver with bubble and squeak, bacon and caramelised onion jus (£11.75), and roast rack of lamb with rosemary jus and dauphinoise potatoes (£12.25). The civilised main bar is clean and comfortable, with a restauranty layout and unobtrusive piped music; the very small plain bar has one or two tables for casual customers. Well kept Bass and Greene King IPA on handpump, kept under light blanket pressure, and a good range of wines by the glass. There are tables out in a pleasant quiet garden. *(Recommended by Gordon Prince, Ian Phillips)*

Greene King ~ Lease Ian Price ~ Real ale ~ Bar food (till 9.30) ~ Restaurant ~ (01628) 822844 ~ Children in restaurant ~ Open 12-2.30, 6-11

CHIEVELEY SU4774 Map 2
Blue Boar

2 miles from M4 junction 13: A34 N towards Oxford, 200 yds left into Chieveley, then about 100 yds after Red Lion left into School Rd; at T-junction with B4494 turn right towards Wantage and pub is 500 yds on right; heading S on A34, don't take first sign to Chieveley

A handy escape from the M4, this thatched inn is set in a lovely but lonesome spot on a country road, with views over rolling fields. Three rambling rooms are furnished with high-backed settles, windsor chairs and polished tables, and decked out with a variety of heavy harness (including a massive collar); the left-hand room has a log fire and a seat built into the sunny bow window. Bar food includes sandwiches (from £3.50), soup (£2.45), thai crab cakes (£4.75), ploughman's (£5.10), local sausages (£5.95), breaded mediterranean kiev or chilli con carne (£6.50), poached salmon with hollandaise sauce (£7.70), and puddings (from £2.95); there's also a civilised oak-panelled restaurant. Well kept Boddingtons, Fullers London Pride and Wadworths 6X on handpump; several malt whiskies; soft piped music. Tables are set among the tubs and flowerbeds on the rough front cobbles outside. *(Recommended by John Robertson, Roger and Jenny Huggins, Christopher and Jo Barton, D B, John H Smith)*

Free house ~ Licensees Ann and Peter Ebsworth ~ Real ale ~ Bar food (12-1.45, 7(8.30 Sun)-9.30) ~ Restaurant ~ (01635) 248236 ~ Open 11-3, 6-11; 12-3, 7-10.30 Sun; closed 25 and 26 Dec ~ Bedrooms: £57B/£69B

COOKHAM SU8884 Map 2
Bel & the Dragon
High Street; B4447 N of Maidenhead

The three carefully furnished rooms in this fine old pub have comfortable seats, heavy Tudor beams and open fires contrasting with the pastel walls and up-to-date low voltage lighting. It's the imaginative food that many customers come to enjoy, and as well as specials at lunchtime which include battered haddock or avocado filled with smoked chicken and orange segments with a lime mayonnaise (£8.95), with evening choices such as rack of lamb (£17.95), halibut (£18.95), and fillet steak (£21.95), the menu offers chargrilled chicken and prawn tikka kebabs with a cucumber and mint yoghurt dip (£6.95), warm salad of pancetta, black pudding, chorizo and marinated field mushrooms topped with a poached egg (£7.25), trio of sausages on grain mustard mash with onion gravy (£9.95), fresh asparagus, mushroom and roast garlic gnocchi topped with sage frite and parmesan, served with a rocket and cherry tomato salad (£12.25), slow roasted lamb shoulder on garlic and rosemary infused butterbean cassoulet, with an orange and rosemary jus (£13.50), and thai marinated duck breast sliced on a nest of stir-fried vegetables and egg noodles with plum and ginger sauce (£15.95). Well kept Brakspears Bitter, Courage Best, and Marstons Pedigree are served from the low zinc-topped bar counter, and there's a good choice of wines, whiskies, liqueurs and fruit juices; good service. Three carefully furnished rooms have comfortable seats, heavy Tudor beams and open fires contrasting with the pastel walls and up-to-date low voltage lighting. Street parking can be very difficult. The town's rewarding Stanley Spencer Gallery is almost opposite. *(Recommended by B and M A Langrish, A F P Barnes, Iain Robertson, Guy Charrison, Ian Phillips)*

Free house ~ Licensee Michael Mortimer ~ Real ale ~ Bar food (12-2.30, 7-10; not evening 25 Dec) ~ Restaurant ~ (01628) 521263 ~ Well behaved children welcome ~ Open 11-11; 12-10.30 Sun

---

Pubs brewing their own beers are listed at the back of the book.

COOKHAM DEAN SU8785 Map 2
Uncle Toms Cabin

Hills Lane, Harding Green; village signposted off A308 Maidenhead—Marlow – keep on
down past Post Office and village hall towards Cookham Rise and Cookham

One reader was delighted, on his visit, to find a carthorse with all its harness
standing by the front door. The pretty cream-washed cottage remains friendly and
unpretentious, and the mainly carpeted little rooms are filled with chatting
customers. At the front are low beams and joists and lots of shiny dark brown
woodwork, whilst furnishings such as old-fashioned plush-cushioned wall seats, beer
advertisements and old brass kitchen scales lend a nostalgic 1930s feeling. There's
also quite a lot of breweryana, and some interesting gold discs. Bar food (with prices
unchanged since last year) includes thick-cut sandwiches with salad and crisps (from
£2.95), soup (£3.25), filled baked potatoes (from £3.95), rice, tomato and courgette
gratin (£5.75), steak and ale pie or chicken wrapped in bacon with blue cheese sauce
(£6.95), chargrilled halibut with tomato sauce (£7.75), steaks (£9.75), and puddings
such as home-made treacle tart and apple flan (£2.75). Well kept Benskins Best,
Fullers London Pride, and a regularly changing guest beer like Adnams Broadside or
Wells Bombardier on handpump; darts, shove-ha'penny, cribbage, and dominoes.
Piped music, if on, is well chosen and well reproduced. The attractive, sheltered
sloping back garden has picnic-sets, and there are a couple of old teak seats under a
chestnut tree at the front. The two cats Jess (black and white) and Wilma (black)
enjoy the winter coal fire, and Oggie the busy black and white dog welcomes other
dogs (who get a dog biscuit on arrival). *(Recommended by Simon Chell, Mrs A Pantin,
Ian Phillips)*

*Vanguard ~ Lease Nick and Karen Ashman ~ Real ale ~ Bar food (12(12.30 wknds)-
2(2.30 wknds), 7.30-10) ~ Restaurant ~ (01628) 483339 ~ Children in eating area of
bar ~ Open 11-3, 5.30-11; 12-3, 7-10.30 Sun*

CRAZIES HILL SU7980 Map 2
Horns 🍺

From A4, take Warren Row Road at Cockpole Green signpost just E of Knowl Hill, then
past Warren Row follow Crazies Hill signposts

The gentrified country atmosphere and friendly welcome in this tiled whitewashed
cottage are much enjoyed by its many customers – plus the fact that there is no juke
box, fruit machine or piped music. The comfortable welcoming bars have rugby
mementoes on the walls, exposed beams, open fires and stripped wooden tables and
chairs. The no smoking barn room is opened up to the roof like a medieval hall, and
terracotta walls give it a cosy feel. Popular bar food includes lunchtime baguettes,
soup (£4.25), thai crabcakes or breaded butterfly prawns with chilli and garlic
mayonnaise (£5.95), tagliatelle with a creamy feta cheese, smoked salmon and
coriander sauce (£7.75), beef, mushroom and Guinness pie (£7.95), roast chicken
supreme with a sherry and tarragon sauce on a bed of roasted courgettes (£9.95),
and daily specials like green shell mussels in white wine, coriander and chilli butter
(£5.25), spinach and mushrooms lasagne (£6.95), and cod fillet with English
mustard and breadcrumbs with lemon butter (£12.95). Fish comes daily from
Billingsgate, and it is essential to book a table at weekends (it does get particularly
busy on Sunday lunchtimes). Well kept Brakspears Bitter, Special, and seasonal ales
on handpump, a thoughtful wine list, several malt whiskies – and they make a good
bloody mary. There's plenty of space in the very large garden. *(Recommended by
M Borthwick, Simon Collett-Jones, T R and B C Jenkins, J Hale, Mr and Mrs T A Bryan,
Marion Turner, Burton Brown, Keith and Margaret Kettell, Adrian and Felicity Smith)*

*Brakspears ~ Tenant A J Hearn ~ Real ale ~ Bar food (not Sun evening) ~ Restaurant
~ (0118) 940 1416 ~ Children in restaurant lunchtimes only ~ Open 11.30-2.30(3
Sat), 6-11; 12-10.30 Sun*

If we know a pub has an outdoor play area for children, we mention it.

FRILSHAM SU5573 Map 2

Pot Kiln ★ ◖

From Yattendon take turning S, opposite church, follow first Frilsham signpost, but just after crossing motorway go straight on towards Bucklebury ignoring Frilsham signposted right; pub on right after about half a mile

'Well worth getting lost for' is how one reader describes this hard-to-find, unassuming brick pub. It's in a lovely rural spot, approached via single track roads which give it quite an isolated feel – but once inside, there's a lively, chatty atmosphere and plenty of customers. Three basic yet comfortable bar areas have wooden floorboards, bare benches and pews, and a good winter log fire, too. Well kept Brick Kiln Bitter and Goldstar Honey (from the pub's own microbrewery behind) is served from a hatch in the panelled entrance lobby – which has room for just one bar stool – along with well kept Arkells BBB, and Morlands Original on handpump. Decent straightforward food includes tasty filled hot rolls (from £1.65), home-made soup (£2.95), ploughman's (from £4), vegetable chilli (£6.85), salmon and broccoli fishcake (£7.25), and evening specials such as chicken lasagne with brandy and cream sauce (£7.50), fresh salmon fillet (£8.95), and venison casserole (£10.60); no chips, and vegetables are fresh. Rolls only on Sundays. The public bar has darts, dominoes, shove-ha'penny, table skittles, and cribbage. The pink candlelit back room/dining room is no smoking. There are picnic-sets in the big suntrap garden, with good views of the nearby forests and meadows. The pub is surrounded by plenty of walks, and dogs are allowed in the public bar on a lead. *(Recommended by JP, PP, the Didler, Kevin Thorpe, Simon Chell, Susan and John Douglas, Mark and Diane Grist, Sheila Keene, Adrian and Felicity Smith, J Hale)*

Own brew ~ Licensee Philip Gent ~ Real ale ~ Bar food (not Tues evening) ~ (01635) 201366 ~ Children in back room ~ Irish music first Sun evening of month ~ Open 12-2.30(3 Sat), 6.30-11; 12-3, 7-10.30 Sun; closed Tues lunchtimes; 25 Dec

GREAT SHEFFORD SU3875 Map 2

Swan

2 miles from M4 junction 14 – A338 towards Wantage

In summer, the tables on the quiet lawn and terrace are a fine place to enjoy a drink or meal while watching the ducks on the River Lambourn; the restaurant enjoys the same view. Inside, the low-ceilinged, spacious bar has bow windows and is comfortably furnished, with racing-related and other sporting memorabilia on the walls (as well as old photographs and other bric-a-brac), reminding you that this is deepest horse-training country; newspapers and magazines to read. The Village Bar has a large open fire, a good mix of both locals and visitors, and a friendly welcome. A reasonable choice of food includes baguettes, home-made soup (£2.95), chicken liver pâté (£4.25), broccoli and cream cheese bake (£6.50), pork cooked in cider, apples and cream (£7.25), sweet beef curry (£7.50), pie of the day (£7.75), chicken balti (£8.95), salmon steak cooked in honey and ginger (£9.25), and steaks (from £10.95). Well kept Bass, and Courage Best and Directors on handpump; friendly attentive service. TV and piped music. *(Recommended by Joy and Peter Heatherley, H W Clayton, Susan and John Douglas, Simon Pyle)*

Eldridge Pope (Hardy) ~ Manager Terry Cook ~ Real ale ~ Bar food ~ Restaurant ~ (01488) 648271 ~ Children in eating area of bar and restaurant ~ Open 11-3, 6-11; 12-3, 7-10.30 Sun

HAMSTEAD MARSHALL SU4165 Map 2

White Hart ⇌

Village signposted from A4 W of Newbury

The highly enjoyable Italian food continues to draw lots of customers to this popular dining pub. The much liked daily specials might include sogliole (fillet of lemon sole with olive oil, lemon juice and herbs, £12.50) or rognoni (lambs kidneys fried with wine, mustard, cream and mushrooms, £11.50), plus dishes from the menu such as home-made soup (£4.50), mozzarella, tomato, basil and olive oil salad (£4.50), Italian salami with olives (£5.50), fritatta omelette (£7.50), spaghetti Napolitana (£7.50), lasagne (£8.50), steaks (from £16.50), and puddings (£4.50) like torta di mele or crespelle dolce (warm pancakes with poached plums and vanilla ice cream); the food boards are attractively illustrated with Mrs Aromando's drawings, many of the herbs and vegetables are home-grown, the bread is home-made, and their beef is from a local organic farm; no smoking restaurant. Hardy Country and Wadworths 6X are served on handpump alongside decent Italian wines in the L-shaped bar with red plush seats built into the bow windows, cushioned chairs around oak and other tables, a copper-topped bar counter, and a log fire open on both sides; piped music. The flower-bordered walled garden is lovely in summer, and there are quiet and comfortable beamed bedrooms in a converted barn across the courtyard. The pony in the paddock with jumps behind the garden is called Solo. *(Recommended by James A Waller, J M M Hill, Lynn Sharpless, Bob Eardley, Keith Allen, John Evans, Mrs M Horgan)*

Free house ~ Licensees Nicola and Dorothy Aromando ~ Real ale ~ Bar food (not Sun) ~ Restaurant (not Sun) ~ (01488) 658201 ~ Children in eating area of bar ~ Open 12-2.30, 6-11; closed Sunday, 25, 26 Dec, 1 Jan, and two wks in summer ~ Bedrooms: £60B/£80B

HARE HATCH SU8077 Map 2
Queen Victoria
Blakes Lane; just N of A4 Reading—Maidenhead

As well as being a friendly local where you can enjoy the consistently well kept real ales, this is also a pub with good, interesting food and a welcome for visitors. The two chatty, low-beamed bars are nicely furnished with flowers on tables, strong spindleback chairs, wall benches and window seats, and decorations such as a stuffed sparrowhawk and a delft shelf lined with beaujolais bottles; the tables on the right are no smoking. Changing daily, popular bar food might include sandwiches (from £2.20), olive and stilton pâté (£2.95), sautéed chicken livers with brandy and cream (£3.95), steak and oyster pie (£5.80), sizzling thai pork, Chinese chicken, pepper and onion kebab, smoked fish medley, and cheese and chilli beef tortillas (all £5.95), and barbary duck breast in rosemary and garlic (£9.95); vegetables are fresh. Well kept Brakspears Bitter, Special, Old and a seasonal beer on handpump, a fair choice of wines by the glass, and obliging service. Dominoes, cribbage, fruit machine, and three-dimensional noughts and crosses. There's a flower-filled no smoking conservatory, and a robust table or two in front by the car park. *(Recommended by Simon Collett-Jones, Colin and Sandra Tann, D J and P M Taylor, Brian Root, J Hale, R Huggins, D Irving, E McCall, T McLean)*

Brakspears ~ Tenant Ron Rossington ~ Real ale ~ Bar food (12-2.30, 6.30-10.30; 12-10 Sun) ~ Restaurant ~ (0118) 940 2477 ~ Children welcome ~ Open 11-3, 5.30-11; 12-10.30 Sun

HOLYPORT SU8977 Map 2
Belgian Arms
1½ miles from M4 junction 8/9 via A308(M), A330; in village turn left on to big green, then left again at war memorial (which is more like a bus shelter)

Although this popular pub places quite an emphasis on the varied choice of good food, drinkers feel comfortable here, and the staff offer a friendly welcome. The L-shaped, low-ceilinged bar has interesting framed postcards of Belgian military uniform and other good military prints, and some cricketing memorabilia on the walls, a china cupboard in one corner, a variety of chairs around a few small tables, and a roaring log fire. Well kept Brakspears Bitter and Special on handpump, or the few good malt whiskies they stock. The daily specials are especially popular, and at lunchtime might include fresh smoked haddock with poached eggs, vegetarian shepherd's pie, steak in ale or fish pie, and chilli con carne or lasagne (all £5.95), with evening examples like fresh salmon fillet in red onion sauce (£8.95) and breast of duck in orange sauce (£9.95). Other bar food includes sandwiches (the toasted 'special' is well recommended, £3), a good ploughman's (£4), pizzas with different toppings (£5), steaks (from £9.95), and Sunday roast beef (£7.95). In summer, sitting in the charming garden looking over the duck pond towards the village green, it is hard to believe that you are so close to the M4. *(Recommended by Chris Glasson, Simon Collett-Jones, MP, R Huggins, D Irving, E McCall, T McLean)*

Brakspears ~ Tenant Alfred Morgan ~ Real ale ~ Bar food (12-2, 6.30-9.30; not Sun evening) ~ (01628) 634468 ~ Children in eating area of bar ~ Open 11-3, 5.30-11; 12-3, 7-10.30 Sun

INKPEN SU3564 Map 2
Swan

Lower Inkpen; coming from A338 in Hungerford, take Park Street (first left after railway bridge, coming from A4)

As well as running this beamed country pub, the licensees also have an organic beef farm, and their farm shop next door sells a plethora of gifts, books, vegetables and other organic foods. Naturally, you can expect to find plenty of home-grown ingredients among the decent bar meals, which include sandwiches, broccoli, mushroom and pasta bake or beef curry (£6.95), home-made salmon, cod and smoked haddock fishcakes or steak in ale pie (£7.25), steaks (from £8.50), and puddings such as bread and butter pudding, fresh fruit salad and pear tart (£3.50); they do cream teas in summer. The eating areas are no smoking. Well kept Butts Bitter, Hook Norton Bitter and Mild, and a guest such as Butts Blackguard on handpump; local Lambourn Valley cider and home-made sloe gin. The rambling bar rooms have cosy corners, fresh flowers, polished furniture, and three open fires (there's a big old fireplace with an oak mantelbeam in the restaurant area). The games room has old paving slabs, bench seating and darts, shove-ha'penny, cribbage, and dominoes; piped music. Out in front there are flowers by the picnic-sets raised above the quiet village road on old brick terraces, and also a small quiet garden. *(Recommended by Mark Percy, Lesley Mayoh, Peter and Jean Hoare, Mrs A Pantin, John Robertson, John Parker)*

Free house ~ Licensees Mary and Bernard Harris ~ Real ale ~ Bar food (12-2.30, 7-9.30) ~ Restaurant ~ (01488) 668326 ~ Well behaved children in eating area of bar and restaurant ~ Open 11-2.30, 7-11; 11-11 Sat; 12-2.30, 7-10.30 Sun; closed 25 and 26 Dec ~ Bedrooms: £40S/£70S

LAMBOURN SU3175 Map 2
Hare & Hounds

Lambourn Woodlands, 3½ miles from M4 junction 14: A336 N, then first left on to B4000; pub is 2½ miles S of Lambourn itself

New licensees have taken over this smart dining pub and have refurbished throughout – though readers have been quick to point out that the friendly, relaxing character is essentially the same. Several rooms lead off the narrow bar but perhaps the nicest area is the mustard coloured room with attractive pine chairs and wooden tables and a lovely fireplace off to the left as you head along the central passageway; equine prints and pictures on the walls. The room next to that has a mix of simple wooden and marble-effect tables, a church-style pew, and neatly patterned curtains. Good, enjoyable bar food now includes home-made soup (£3.95), plum tomato tart with an onion compote and pesto dressing (£5.95), chicken liver parfait flavoured with a port caramel or salmon fishcakes (£6.50), scallops and mussels in a light saffron sauce, served with fresh linguini (£7.95), grilled goats cheese served with chives, artichoke and a marinated tomato risotto (£11.50), brill fillet with chargrilled potatoes, rocket salad and a lime and coriander dressing (£12.50), rack of lamb roasted with garlic and thyme, fennel confit and gratin dauphinois (£14.50), and sirloin steak with a shallot confit and basil butter (£15); they add a 10% service charge in the evenings. Well kept Wadworths IPA and 6X on handpump, and good wines and a choice of malt whiskies; pleasant service, piped music, TV. Outside, there are new benches in the garden behind, and a decent children's play area.

(Recommended by M and J Cottrell, J Hale, Michael Sargent, J M M Hill)

Free house ~ Licensee Andy Vine ~ Real ale ~ Bar food (12-2.30, 7-9.30) ~ Restaurant ~ (01488) 71386 ~ Children in eating area of bar ~ Open 11-3, 6-11; 12-3 Sun; closed Sun evening

MARSH BENHAM SU4267 Map 2
Red House ⓦ ♀

Village signposted from A4 W of Newbury

This smartly renovated, thatched dining pub is not the place to drop into for a casual pint, as much of the emphasis is on the imaginative food. The comfortable bar has a light stripped wood floor and magenta walls, and a mix of Victorian and older settles. The library-style front restaurant (which is no smoking) is lined with bookcases and hung with paintings. The wide choice of interesting (if not cheap) food might include crab spring roll (£5.50), good caesar salad with poached egg (£5.95), salmon fishcakes with a sweet and sour sauce (£8.50), lamb shank with a red wine sauce (£12.50), and puddings such as iced praline mousse and baked marshmallow filled with apple and blackberry compote (£4.50); there's also a two-course bar lunch (£11.95). Well kept Fullers London Pride and Ruddles County on handpump, good wines, lots of malt whiskies, and quite a few brandies and ports. A terrace with teak tables and chairs overlooks the long lawns that slope down to water meadows and the River Kennet. *(Recommended by Jane and Graham Rooth, David Peakall, John Voos, A J Smith)*

Free house ~ Licensee Xavier Le-Bellego ~ Real ale ~ Bar food (lunchtime only) ~ Restaurant ~ (01635) 582017 ~ Children over 6 in restaurant ~ Open 12-11; 12-3 Sun; closed Sun evening and all day Mon

PEASEMORE SU4577 Map 2
Fox & Hounds

Village signposted from B4494 Newbury—Wantage

The picnic-sets outside this cheerful local give views across rolling fields, and on a clear day you can look right over to the high hills of the Berkshire/Hampshire border about 20 miles southward. Inside, the two bars have brocaded stripped wall settles, chairs and stools around shiny wooden tables, a log-effect gas fire (open to both rooms), and piped music. One wall inside has a full set of Somerville's entertaining *Slipper's ABC of Fox-Hunting* prints, and another sports a row of flat-capped fox masks, reflecting the customs of the surrounding horse-training country. Bar food includes baguettes, home-made soup (£2.50), hot garlic mushrooms (£3.95), roasted red pepper and mushroom lasagne, speciality sausages with onion gravy or home-made pie (£5.50), spiced lamb with apricots (£6.95), and steaks (from £8.95); there's also a board dedicated to fish dishes. The restaurant is no smoking. Well kept Fullers London Pride, Greene King IPA and a guest beer on handpump, decent wines, and a good few malt whiskies. Darts, pool, dominoes, cribbage, fruit machine, discreet juke box, and TV. More reports please. *(Recommended by Richard Gibbs)*

Free house ~ Licensees David and Loretta Smith ~ Real ale ~ Bar food (not Mon; 12-2, 5.30(6.30 Sat, 7 Sun)-9.45(10 Sat, 9.30 Sun)) ~ Restaurant ~ (01635) 248252 ~ Children welcome ~ Singer/guitarist monthly ~ Open 5.30-11; 12-3, 6.30-11 Sat; 12-3, 7-10.30 Sun; closed Mon and Tues-Fri lunchtimes

READING SU7272 Map 2
Sweeney & Todd £

10 Castle Street; next to Post Office

Though you'd never guess it from the street, a lively bar is hidden behind the baker's shop in this unique patisserie-cum-pub, selling pies, soft drinks and even fresh eggs. Behind the counter and down some stairs, a surprising number of tiny tables are squeezed into one long thin room, most of them in rather conspiratorial railway-carriage-style booths separated by curtains, and each with a leather-bound menu to match the leather-cushioned pews. Old prints line the walls, and the colonial-style fans and bare-boards floor enhance the period feel. Among the impressive choice of pies might be chicken, honey and mustard, hare and cherry, duck and apricot, goose and gooseberry, partridge and pear, or the rugby-influenced five nations – a medley of beef, Guinness, garlic, mustard and leeks (all £3.60), with other bar food such as soup (£2.50), sandwiches (from £2.50), casseroles (£5.10), and roasts (£6). Helpings are huge, and excellent value. Well kept Adnams Best, Badger Tanglefoot, Wadworths 6X and a changing guest are served on handpump from the small bar, with various wines and a range of liqueurs and cigars. You can buy the pies in the shop to take away. *(Recommended by Paul Vickers, Colin and Sandra Tann, David Symons, Mark and Diane Grist, Jonathan Smith, Andy and Jill Kassube, Richard Lewis, Adrian and Felicity Smith)*

Free house ~ Licensee Mrs C Hayward ~ Real ale ~ Bar food ~ Restaurant ~ (0118) 958 6466 ~ Children welcome away from bar ~ Open 11-11; closed Sun, 25 and 26 Dec, and bank holidays

SONNING SU7575 Map 2
Bull

Village signposted on A4 E of Reading; off B478, in village by church

When the wisteria is out, this unpretentious black and white timbered inn looks especially pretty, and the courtyard is bright with tubs of flowers. Inside, the two old-fashioned bar rooms have low ceilings and heavy beams, cosy alcoves, cushioned antique settles and low wooden chairs, and inglenook fireplaces; the back dining area is no smoking. You need to find a table before you can order the good bar food, which might include home-made soup, filled french bread (from £4.50), ploughman's, lasagne or chilli (£9.50), lamb tagine with pine nut, coriander and raisin couscous (£11.50), thai green chicken curry (£11.95), lamb shank in a red wine and redcurrant jus (£12.50), and roast pheasant with a blackberry and raisin sauce (£13.95); popular puddings. Well kept Gales Best, HSB and Butser, with a guest such as Fullers London Pride on handpump, and lots of country wines; darts, fruit machine, and TV. If you bear left through the ivy-clad churchyard opposite, then turn left along the bank of the River Thames, you come to a very pretty lock. *(Recommended by Val Stevenson, Rob Holmes, Mark and Diane Grist, Paul Vickers, Karen and Graham Oddey, Catherine Pitt)*

Gales ~ Manager Dennis Mason ~ Real ale ~ Bar food (12-2, 6-9.30; all day summer wknds) ~ (0118) 969 3901 ~ Children in eating area of bar ~ Open 11-3, 5.30-11; 11-11(11-3, 5.30-11 winter) Sat; 12-10.30(12-3, 7-10.30 winter) Sun ~ Bedrooms: £85B/£85B

STANFORD DINGLEY SU5771 Map 2
Bull

From M4 junction 12, W on A4, then right at roundabout on to A340 towards Pangbourne; first left to Bradfield, and at crossroads on far edge of Bradfield (not in centre) turn left signposted Stanford Dingley; turn left in Stanford Dingley

New licensees have taken over this attractive 15th-c brick pub and have added bedrooms, opened up a no smoking dining room, and built a new kitchen to cope with demand. The beamed tap room, with its new soft furnishings, is firmly divided into two parts by standing timbers hung with horsebrasses, and Brakspears Bitter, and Gold Star, Good Old Boy and Skiff from the West Berkshire brewery are all well kept and cheap for the area. The main part has an old brick fireplace, red-cushioned seats carved out of barrels, a window settle, wheelback chairs on the red quarry tiles, and an old station clock. The half-panelled lounge bar has been redecorated to reflect the motorsport and classic car interests of the owners, and there are refectory-type tables. Bar food now includes home-made soup (£3.25), sandwiches or baguettes (from £3.50), ploughman's (from £4.50), crispy baked potatoes (from £4.55), vegetarian stir fry (£6.75), liver and bacon with lyonnaise sauce (£7.95), daily specials such as seafood chowder (£4.25), traditional Irish stew (£7.95), and lemon sole stuffed with salmon and tarragon (£10.95), and puddings such as sticky toffee sponge with custard (£3). Ring the bull and piped music. In front of the building are some big rustic tables and benches, and to the side is a small garden with a few more seats. The Kennet Morris Men visit on August Bank Holiday and New Year's Day, and on summer Saturdays, owners of classic cars and bikes gather in the grounds. *(Recommended by Lynn Sharpless, Bob Eardley, Klaus and Elizabeth Leist)*

Free house ~ Licensees Robert and Kate Archard and Robin Walker ~ Real ale ~ Bar food (12-2.30(2 Sun), 6.30-9.30; no food winter Sun evenings) ~ Restaurant ~ (0118) 974 4409 ~ Children in eating area of bar and restaurant ~ Open 12-3, 6-11; 11(12 in winter)-3, 6-11 Sat; 12-3, 7-10.30 Sun ~ Bedrooms: £45S/£70S(£75B)

Old Boot

Off A340 via Bradfield, coming from A4 just W of M4 junction 12

The neatly kept and friendly beamed bar in this stylish 18th-c beamed pub has fine old pews, settles, old country chairs, and tables smelling nicely of furniture polish, attractive fabrics for the old-fashioned wooden-ring curtains, some striking pictures and hunting prints, two welcoming fires (one in an inglenook), and bunches of fresh flowers. Well kept Brakspears, West Berkshire Good Old Boy, and Youngs Special on handpump, and generously poured good wine. Enjoyable bar food might include home-made soup (£3.50), garlic mushroom tart (£3.95), duck liver pâté (£4.25), baguettes or grilled goats cheese with sesame seeds and red onion marmalade (£4.95), prawn stir fry (£6.75), home-made steak and kidney pie (£7.95), beef stroganoff (£8.50), chicken supreme on sweet potato with braised celery and mushroom sauce (£11.95), cajun tuna (£13.95), and puddings (£3.95); no smoking dining conservatory. In summer the peaceful sloping back garden and terrace – with their pleasant rural views – are popular places to sit, with more tables outside the front. *(Recommended by J Hale, Alan and Ros Furley)*

Free house ~ Licensees John and Jeannie Haley ~ Real ale ~ Bar food ~ Restaurant ~ (0118) 974 4292 ~ Children welcome ~ Open 11-3, 6-11; 12-3, 7-10.30 Sun

SWALLOWFIELD SU7364 Map 2

George & Dragon ♀

Church Road, towards Farley Hill

The imaginative – if not cheap – food in this attractive and cottagey dining pub continues to drawn lots of customers, so it might be best to book a table beforehand. Using fresh seasonal produce, the menu might include lunchtime ciabatta sandwiches or moules marinières (£5.50), smoked haddock risotto topped with a poached egg (£8.50), whole bass marinated in chillies, garlic, lime leaves and coriander (£10.90), confit of duck, rabbit and chicken with a mixed bean cassoulet and a tomato and harissa sauce (£13.25), seared tuna loin with a mango, ginger, coriander and chilli salsa (£14.50), grilled ostrich steak served with herbed bulgar wheat and thyme jus (£14.95), and puddings such as chocolate indulgence, raspberry and strawberry pavlova and crunchy praline cheesecake (£4.95); the dining conservatory can be no smoking. The atmosphere is cosily old-fashioned and relaxed, with rather a smart décor of stripped beams, red walls, rugs on flagstones and good solid wooden furnishings; there's a large log fire. Well kept Adnams, Fullers London Pride and Wadworths 6X on handpump, and good wines. Service is friendly and prompt, and the staff bring drinks to your table. Piped music. *(Recommended by R Lake, Mrs L Hanson, Catherine Pitt)*

Free house ~ Licensee Paul Dailey ~ Real ale ~ Bar food (12-2, 6.30-9.30(10 Sat)) ~ Restaurant ~ (0118) 988 4432 ~ Well behaved children welcome ~ Open 11.30-11; 11.30-3, 6-11 Sat; 12-4, 7-10.30 Sun; closed evenings 25 and 26 Dec and 1 Jan

---

Pubs in outstandingly attractive surroundings are listed at the back of the book.

WALTHAM ST LAWRENCE SU8276 Map 2
Bell

In village centre

The licensees here were on the point of leaving as we went to press, but such is the charm of this timbered black and white pub in its pretty village setting, that we are keeping our fingers crossed that things will not change too much. The lounge bar has finely carved oak panelling and a log fire, and the public bar has heavy beams, an attractive seat in the deep window recess, and well kept Bass, and Brakspears Bitter and one of their seasonal ales on handpump; the small front room is no smoking. Bar food has included a fair choice of vegetarian meals, plus daily specials, evening extras, and home-made puddings; we'd be grateful for any feedback on the new menu. In summer, pretty flower baskets add colour to the front of the building, and there are seats in the garden and terrace behind. *(Recommended by Nick Holmes, Susan and John Douglas)*

Free house ~ Real ale ~ Bar food (not Sun or Mon evenings) ~ Restaurant ~ (0118) 934 1788 ~ Children in restaurant and family room ~ Open 11-3, 6-11; 12-3, 7-10.30 Sun; closed pm 25-26 Dec

WEST ILSLEY SU4782 Map 2
Harrow ♀

Signposted at East Ilsley slip road off A34 Newbury—Abingdon

On fine days, you can enjoy a drink or a meal at the picnic-sets in the big garden of this white-painted village pub, and there are other tables under cocktail parasols looking out over the duck pond and cricket green. Inside, the open-plan bar has yellow walls, mainly hung with Victorian prints, and a mix of antique oak tables, unpretentious old chairs, and a couple of more stately long settles; there's also an unusual stripped twin-seated high-backed settle between the log fire and the bow window. Enjoyable home-made bar food might include interestingly filled baguettes (from £4.25), mussels with white wine, cream and garlic (£4.95), ploughman's (£5.50; the pickle is home-made), grilled goats cheese on chargrilled vegetables (£5.50), salmon and skate terrine (£6.50), pork chop with home-made pork sausage on red cabbage (£9.95), and puddings such as fresh lemon tart with raspberry sauce and cream or hot chocolate fondant with pistachio sauce and cookie ice cream (from £4.50). The dining room is no smoking. Greene King Abbot, Morlands Original and Old Speckled Hen on handpump, and a good wine list with around ten by the glass. *(Recommended by D J and P M Taylor, Charlie Woods, Adrian and Felicity Smith, Mr and Mrs T A Bryan, Dr D Taub, J Hale, Nick Holmes)*

Greene King ~ Tenants Emily Hawes and Scott Hunter ~ Real ale ~ Bar food (not winter Sun or Mon evenings) ~ Restaurant ~ (01635) 281260 ~ Well behaved children welcome; not Fri/Sat evenings ~ Open 11-3, 6-11; 12-3, 7-10.30 Sun

WINTERBOURNE SU4572 Map 2
Winterbourne Arms 🍴

3½ miles from M4 junction 13; A34 N, first left through Chieveley and on to B4494, then left and right

Berkshire Dining Pub of the Year

With new licensees and a new chef, this country pub remains popular for its wide choice of interesting food – but also manages to keep its friendly pubby atmosphere. From the lunchtime snack menu, there might be soup (£4.50), oven-baked potatoes or ciabatta with fillings such as stilton, onion confit and crispy parma ham, mozzarella, mediterranean vegetables and pesto sauce or turkey, brie and bacon (from £4.50), duck salad with orange segments and balsamic dressing (£7.25), and stir-fried vegetables in sesame oil with a selection of seafood (£7.50); weekly changing specials such as wild mushrooms in a sherry cream sauce with puff pastry topping (£5.25), terrine of foie gras and duck with home-made piccalilli (£7.25), breast of quail with potato pancake, mushroom duxelle and beetroot jus (£13.50), and ravioli of crab garnished with langoustines and shellfish sauce (£16.50), with home-made puddings like zesty lemon tart or chocolate marquise with white chocolate sauce. Well kept Bass with two guests such as Fullers London Pride and West Berkshire Good Old Boy on handpump, and a decent wine list with 12 wines by the glass. The bars have been gently refurbished but have kept the collection of old irons around the fireplace, early prints and old photographs of the village, and a log fire; you can see the original bakers' ovens in the restaurant area, which was once a bakery. The peaceful view over the rolling fields from the big bar windows cunningly avoids the quiet road, which is sunken between the pub's two lawns; flowering tubs and hanging baskets brighten up picnic-sets, and the garden boasts a big weeping willow. There are nearby walks to Snelsmore and Donnington. *(Recommended by Lyn and Geoff Hallchurch, Dr and Mrs A K Clarke, Chris Glasson, David and Nina Pugsley)*

Free house ~ Licensees Don Gregor and Carole Gent ~ Real ale ~ Bar food (12-2.30(2 Sun), 7-9.30) ~ Restaurant ~ (01635) 248200 ~ Children in restaurant, over 7 in evenings ~ Open 11.30-3(4 Sat), 6-11; 12-4 Sun; closed Sun pm, all day Mon – exc bank holidays

WOODSIDE SU9270 Map 2

Rose & Crown

Woodside Road, Winkfield, just off A332 Ascot—Windsor

Very handy for Ascot (and on a big race day, there may be a lively group in a corner around the TV), this attractive low white building is run by warmly friendly, helpful licensees. Quite a bit of emphasis is placed on the food, but there is a thriving atmosphere, with plenty of regulars dropping in for a drink. The long narrow bar has neatly painted low beams, tall chairs by its brick bar counter, comfortably cushioned wall seats, and plenty of space for eating, with most of the dark wooden tables set for diners. It's best to get there early for lunch, with the numbers building up not long after noon, and it might be wise to book at weekends. The food is good and reasonably priced, and includes sandwiches (from £2.95), lots of baked potatoes (£4.95), omelettes, honey-roast ham and eggs and home-made lasagne (£5.95), home-made pie of the day or chicken curry (£6.95), and poached salmon in white wine and cream (£7.95). The choice is widest (and most expensive) in the evenings. Well kept Greene King Abbot, Morlands Original and Ruddles County on handpump; piped music and fruit machine. Service is good. The side garden has tables and a swing, and the setting backed by woodland is peaceful and pretty. *(Recommended by J Hale, Mr and Mrs T A Bryan, Nigel Williamson)*

Greene King ~ Lease A Morris ~ Real ale ~ Bar food (12-2.30, 7-9.30; not Sun or Mon evenings) ~ Restaurant (evening) ~ (01344) 882051 ~ Children in eating area of bar and in restaurant, but must be over 12 in evening ~ Open 11-11; 12-7 Sun; closed Sun evening ~ Bedrooms: /£40

YATTENDON SU5574 Map 2

Royal Oak ♀ ⇌

The Square; B4009 NE from Newbury; turn right at Hampstead Norreys, village signposted on left

Most people come to this elegantly handsome and rather upmarket inn to enjoy the imaginative food. You can eat in the panelled and prettily decorated brasserie/bar with its marvellous log fire, fresh flowers and relaxed atmosphere or in the no smoking (and more expensive) restaurant. From a changing menu, there might be roasted red pepper and tomato soup with a goats cheese dumpling (£4.25), tournedos of fresh poached salmon on a salad of marinated vegetables (£6.75), smoked haddock kedgeree with a poached egg and curry cream (£13.75), roast loin of pork with pomme fondant, carrot purée and a morrel mushroom jus and chervil oil (£14.50), and corn-fed breast of chicken on a rösti with fennel, roasted onions and anchovy mayonnaise and red wine jus (£14.95), with puddings like warm chocolate brownie with white chocolate ice cream and pistachio tuile or vanilla crème brûlée with compote of rhubarb and shortcake biscuit (from £4.75); vegetables are extra. Well kept Wadworths 6X, and a good wine list. The restaurant is no smoking; best to book. In summer, you can eat at tables in the pleasant walled garden – and there are more in front on the village square. Some of the attractive, well appointed bedrooms (not cheap) overlook the garden. The poet Robert Bridges once lived in the attractive village – one of the few still privately owned. *(Recommended by JP, PP, Simon Chell, D B, Susan and John Douglas, Peter and Giff Bennett, Adrian and Felicity Smith, John Davis, Peter B Brown, Derek Thomas)*

Regal-Corus ~ Manager Corinne Macrae ~ Real ale ~ Bar food (12-2.30, 7-10) ~ Restaurant ~ (01635) 201325 ~ Children in eating area of bar and restaurant ~ Open 11-11; 11-10.30 Sun ~ Bedrooms: £116B/£136B

Lucky Dip

Besides the fully inspected pubs, you might like to try these Lucky Dips recommended to us and described by readers (if you do, please send us reports: www.goodguides.com).

Ascot [SU9268]
Wells [London Rd]: Neatly refurbished, light and airy, with calm welcoming lunchtime atmosphere, long blackboard list of good sensibly priced food inc fresh seafood (crisp linen napkins), well kept beers, good wine list; extended family room, big garden with terrace and play equipment *(MJVK, John Sibley)*
Aston [SU7884]
Flower Pot [signed off A4130 Henley—Maidenhead at Crazies Hill]: Friendly old place with nice orchard garden looking over meadows to cottages and far side of Thames – busy with walkers and families wknds, when service can slow; well kept Brakspears inc Mild, good unusual reasonably priced food inc lots of fish, bare-boards public bar, lively and brightly lit, with lots of stuffed fish in glass cases, darts; unobtrusive piped music, friendly siamese cats and elderly dog *(Susan and John Douglas, Mr and Mrs E W Howells)*
Beech Hill [SU6964]
Old Elm Tree: Friendly new licensees doing well in two-bar pub, redecorated inside and out; tempting choice of good generous food in tastefully set out conservatory restaurant and barn-style eating area (may be a wait for a table even midweek evenings), alluring puddings, well kept real ales such as Brakspears and Ruddles, decent house wines, attentive cheerful service *(Lucie Robson, Tony Beaulah)*
Binfield [SU8571]
Stag & Hounds [Forest Road (B3034)]: Comfortable 14th-c pub with interesting array of low-beamed bars, open fires, antiques, brass, wide changing food choice, well kept ales such as Courage Best and Directors, Theakstons XB and Wadworths 6X, decent wines, daily papers; piped music; children allowed in partly no smoking eating area, tables out on front terrace and in back garden *(David H T Dimock, Mr and Mrs Capp, LYM)*
Bray [SU9079]
☆ *Fish* [1¾ miles from M4 junction 8, via A308 and B3028; Old Mill Lane]: Restaurant not pub despite its pubby layout, with close-set tables, really good fresh fish, fine range of New World wines, attractive pictures, rugs, candles at night, no smoking conservatory (with plenty of

blinds); children allowed lunchtime, service can be slow, cl Sun evening, Mon *(Karen and Graham Oddey, C L Kauffmann, LYM, J Hale, Marion Turner, B J Harding)*
☆ *Hinds Head* [High St]: Handsome Tudor pub, panelling and beams, sturdy oak furniture, leather porter's chairs and other comfortable seating, two blazing log fires, nice pictures, soft lighting, interesting food range (not cheap) from substantial sandwiches to upstairs restaurant, well kept ales such as Brakspears SB, Courage Best and Fullers London Pride, good wines, friendly locals, helpful attentive staff; piped music; plans for tables on front terrace *(Susan and John Douglas, George Atkinson, Ian Phillips, LYM, J F M and M West, David and Nina Pugsley)*
Bucklebury [SU5769]
☆ *Blade Bone* [Chapel Row]: Large pub doing well under new licensees; warm, friendly and clean, with plush seats and dark tables, tasteful pictures and plates on pastel walls, matching carpets, small dining room with no smoking conservatory, wide choice of good well presented food inc good puddings and cheeseboard (and they do children's helpings), well kept ales such as Fullers London Pride and ESB and West Berkshire Mr Chubleys; tables in big neat garden with play area *(Mark and Liz Wallace, Colin and Sandra Tann)*
Cheapside [SU9469]
☆ *Thatched Tavern* [off B383 at Village Hall sign; village signed off A332/A329]: Civilised dining pub (not cheap) keeping a cottagey feel despite extension and upgrading, little bar with polished flagstones, very low gnarled beams, old cast-iron range in big inglenook and comfortably padded seats and cushions, three smart dining rooms off with deep carpet, crisp linen and big church candles, cheerful service, well kept Brakspears Bitter, Fullers London Pride and Greene King Abbot, lots of wines, daily papers, no games or piped music; attractive small garden, handy for Virginia Water walks; children in restaurant, open all day wknds *(J S M Sheldon, Susan and John Douglas, Marion Turner, Stephen A'Court, LYM, Simon and Laura Habbishow)*
Cookham Dean [SU8785]

☆ *Jolly Farmer* [Church Rd, off Hills Lane]:
Friendly, cosy and deliberately kept traditional
by the village consortium which owns it, with
small rooms, open fires, well kept ales such as
Brakspears and Courage Best, attractive dining
room, pub games, no music or machines, good
quiet garden with play area; well behaved
children welcome away from bar *(Chris
Glasson, LYM, Simon Chell)*
Curridge [SU4871]

☆ *Bunk* [3 miles from M4 junction 13: A34
towards Newbury, then first left to Curridge,
Hermitage, and left into Curridge at Village
Only sign]: Stylish recently extended and
refurbished dining pub with wide choice of
good interesting food (not cheap, not Sun
evening), smart stripped-wood tiled-floor bar
on left, wooded-meadow views and
conservatory; four well kept ales inc Fullers
London Pride, good choice of wines, buoyant
atmosphere, welcoming efficient service, tables
in neat garden, fine woodland walks nearby
*(Angus and Rosemary Campbell, Lord
Sandhurst, J Hale, BB)*
Datchet [SU9876]

Royal Stag [not far from M4 junction 5; The
Green]: Above-average food and well kept
Tetleys-related and guest beers in friendly and
picturesque traditional local; beautiful beams,
ecclesiastical windows overlooking churchyard,
attractively carved armchairs (and bar), one
wall panelled in claret case lids, log fire, daily
papers, welcoming old retriever; separate bar
with TV and football posters, occasional juke
box; open all day *(Simon Collett-Jones, Chris
Glasson)*
East Ilsley [SU4981]

☆ *Swan* [High St]: Spacious, neat and well
decorated, with a slightly formal look but
pleasantly informal dining-pub feel; wide range
of good bar food (busy with families Sun – best
to book), friendly landlord, well kept Morlands
Original and Charles Wells Bombardier, daily
papers; no smoking restaurant, tables in
courtyard and walled garden with play area;
excellent bedrooms, some in house down road
*(Mr and Mrs T A Bryan, LYM, Paul S
McPherson)*
Fifield [SU9076]

Fifield Inn [A424 Burford—Stow, away from
village]: Neatly kept and attractive old stone-
built pub with eclectic décor, generous good
food esp Sun roasts (restaurant-type meals only
that day, best to book wknds), well kept
Greene King, lots of wines by the glass; live jazz
Sun evening; children welcome, tidy garden
(Chris and Karen Dixon, A K and J J Dixon)
Great Shefford [SU3875]

☆ *Pheasant* [less than ½ mile N of M4 junction 14
– B4000, just off A338]: Rather isolated pub
under new ownership (a National Hunt
jockey), with four neat rooms, bistro
atmosphere, lots of horse-racing pictures and
cartoons and horsey customers; end dining area
with emphasis on good tapas alongside other
interesting dishes, well kept Butts Jester, log
fires, no music; public bar with games inc ring
the bull; attractive views from pleasant garden

(George Atkinson, LYM)
Halfway [SU4068]

Halfway Inn [A4 Hungerford—Newbury]:
Wide choice of imaginative food, great
attention to detail and colour, fresh veg, good
children's dishes (and children's helpings of
most main ones); good range of wines and
beers, friendly helpful staff, partitions dividing
dining room into cosy areas *(John Davis)*
Holyport [SU8977]

☆ *George* [1½ miles from M4 junction 8/9, via
A308(M)/A330; The Green]: Low-ceilinged
open-plan bar with new landlord cooking
enjoyable generous food inc several fish dishes,
cheerful landlady and friendly bustle, nice old
fireplace, pictures and warming pans, small
dining area (usually booked Sun), well kept
beer; picnic-sets outside, lovely village green
(Mr and Mrs T A Bryan)
Hungerford [SU3368]

Plume of Feathers [High St]: Big open-plan pub
with slight brasserie feel, good food from soup
and well made sandwiches up, well kept Greene
King, cosy fire towards the back; bedrooms
(Margaret Ross)
Hurley [SU8283]

Black Boy [A404]: Old-fashioned cottagey pub
concentrating on wide-ranging food (freshly
cooked, so may be a wait), but a few tables for
drinkers, with very well kept Brakspears PA,
Mild and SB, decent house wines, friendly
service, open fire, attractive garden by paddock,
picnic-sets looking over countryside rolling
down to Thames *(R J Cox)*

☆ *Dew Drop* [pub signed off A423 via Honey
Lane]: Isolated country pub reopened after
refurbishment and extension, fine inglenook log
fire, old pews and informal mix of furniture,
prints on dusky pink walls, popular food from
sandwiches (not Sun) to enjoyable meals,
relaxed friendly staff (ditto the couple of cats),
well kept Brakspears Bitter, Special and
seasonal ales, quite a few malt whiskies, darts,
shove-ha'penny, backgammon and dominoes;
children in eating area, french windows to
courtyard and attractive sloping garden with
barbecue, good walks *(Susan and John
Douglas, J C Upshall, J Hale, Mark and Diane
Grist, LYM)*

Red Lion [Henley Rd]: Old-fashioned
comfortable Vintage Inn, two log fires, amiable
service, decent food; picnic-sets in garden *(Bob
and Laura Brock)*

Rising Sun [High St]: Cottagey three-room pub,
low beams and flagstones, assorted chairs
around scrubbed pine tables, pleasant
atmosphere, good well priced food, well kept
Boddingtons, Brakspears and Fullers London
Pride, friendly staff cope efficiently with
summer wknd popularity; pretty Shaker-style
dining room, attractive spot nr Thames *(Susan
and John Douglas, Bill Sykes, John Herbert)*
Inkpen [SU3864]

☆ *Crown & Garter* [Great Common]: Three areas
around central bar, oak settle by open fire,
attractive décor and relaxed atmosphere, good
choice of good reasonably priced home-made
food, imaginative without being too way-out,

well kept Archers, Boddingtons and West Berkshire, friendly helpful service and a real welcome for families; children's play area in pleasant small garden; bedrooms; cl lunchtime Mon/Tues *(Mark Foden, J V Dadswell, K and C Tindal)*

Kintbury [SU3866]

☆ *Dundas Arms* [Station Rd]: Clean and tidy, with well priced fresh home-made food (not Mon evening or Sun) from sandwiches up, well kept real ales from smaller breweries, good coffee and wines by the glass, no piped music, fine range of clarets and burgundies in evening restaurant; tables out on deck above Kennet & Avon Canal, children welcome, pleasant walks; comfortable bedrooms with own secluded waterside terrace *(Keith Allen, J M M Hill, Charles and Pauline Stride, LYM, Roger and Pauline Pearce, Mrs J H S Lang)*

Lambourn [SU3278]

George [Market Pl]: Very good value food, well kept Arkells, friendly efficient service without frills *(anon)*

Littlewick Green [SU8379]

☆ *Cricketers* [not far from M4 junction 9; A404(M) then left on to A4, from which village signed on left; Coronation Rd]: Charming spot opp cricket green, well kept Brakspears and Fullers London Pride, freshly squeezed orange juice, decent low-priced food inc good free Sun bar nibbles, neat housekeeping, lots of cricketing pictures, cosy local atmosphere; big-screen TV *(Tom Evans, Chris Glasson, LYM)*

Maidenhead [SU8582]

Stag & Hounds [Lee Lane, just off A308 N]: Refurbished pub with reasonably priced food in carpeted dining lounge, good choice of well kept guest ales, friendly newish landlord, small side bar; pictures for sale, skittle alley *(Chris Glasson)*

Vine [Market St]: Well kept Brakspears PA, SB and Old, basic food *(Chris Glasson)*

Midgham [SU5566]

Coach & Horses [Bath road (N side)]: Main-road pub with friendly helpful licensees, New Zealand décor, wide choice of food; garden behind *(Angus and Rosemary Campbell, BB)*

Newbury [SU4666]

☆ *Lock Stock & Barrel* [Northbrook St]: Popular modern pub standing out for canalside setting, with suntrap balcony and terrace looking over a series of locks towards handsome church; clean and spacious wood-floored bar with antique-effect lights and fittings, and quite a sunny feel – lots of windows; good choice of reasonably priced food all day, well kept Fullers beers, even an organic beer, plenty of newspapers, lots of tables and chairs; no smoking back bar; busy with young crowds at wknds, upstairs lavatories; canal walks *(T G Thomas, BB, Peter and Audrey Dowsett, W W Burke)*

Old Windsor [SU9874]

☆ *Union* [Crimp Hill Rd, off B3021 – itself off A308/A328]: Friendly old pub with interesting collection of nostalgic show-business photographs, good bar food from sandwiches up, well kept ales such as Brakspears and

Courage Directors, consistently good service, log fire in big fireplace, fruit machine; good value attractive copper-decorated restaurant, white plastic tables under cocktail parasols on sunny front terrace (heated in cooler weather), country views; comfortable bedrooms *(BB, Gordon Prince, R A Watson, Ian Phillips)*

Pangbourne [SU6376]

Cross Keys [opp church]: Well kept Greene King and a guest beer, decent bar food from sandwiches to steaks, simple wooden interior with relaxed lounge, two connecting family rooms, open fires; good largely covered back terrace, with decorative Japanese bridge over little stream and popular Sun lunchtime barbecues *(Catherine Pitt, Jonathan Smith)*

Swan [Shooters Hill]: Attractive 17th-c Thames-side pub with good range of bar food all day, modern interior, dining balcony and conservatory, Greene King ales inc Old Speckled Hen, decent wines, friendly cat; piped music, sports TV; picnic-sets overlooking the weir and moorings *(Jonathan Smith, Catherine Pitt)*

Reading [SU7273]

3Bs Bar [Town Hall, Blagrave St]: Light and airy café-bar in town hall expansively redeveloped as arts/museum/concert centre, four well kept changing ales from microbreweries, all-day side food servery with pastries and cakes as well as bar lunches, friendly staff, magazines and daily papers, plenty of posters about Reading's three Bs – beer, biscuits and bulbs; lots of tables out in pedestrian zone, open all day; young pubby atmosphere evenings, esp Tues blues night, also open mike Weds, indie Thurs *(Richard Lewis, Jonathan Smith, Catherine Pitt)*

Back of Beyond [Kings Rd]: Large Wetherspoons by Kennet & Avon Canal, comfortable and airy, with usual food and wide choice of well kept beers, good prices, plenty of seating indoors and out *(Jonathan Smith)*

Butler [Chatham St]: Bare-boards Fullers pub, their beers kept well, reasonably priced usual food lunchtime and early evening *(Jonathan Smith)*

☆ *Cock-a-Snook* [Queens Walk]: Friendly new split-level pub behind shopping mall, nothing special in décor or furnishings but notable for its range of well kept ales tapped from the cask such as Arkells 2B, 3B and Kingsdown, Ringwood and guests such as Hydes and Moorhouses at low prices (enthusiastic landlord open to suggestions and wants lists), farm ciders, cosy atmosphere, filled rolls; Sun quiz nights, darts teams *(Jonathan Smith, Catherine Pitt, Richard Houghton)*

Corn Exchange [Forbury Rd]: Imaginative split-level conversion, lots of stone and wood, chandler's equipment, Fullers full range excellently kept (inc their bottled beers), friendly staff and locals, food in larger upstairs bar with bare boards, photographs and ornaments; SkyTV, piped music; wheelchair access, open all day wkdys, cl Sun, no food Fri/Sat evening *(Catherine Pitt, Jonathan Smith)*

☆ *Fishermans Cottage* [Kennet Side – easiest to

walk from Orts Rd, off Kings Rd]: Good friendly backwater respite from Reading's bustle, by canal lock and towpath (gasometer view), with waterside tables, lovely big back garden and light and airy conservatory; modern furnishings of character, pleasant stone snug behind woodburning range, good value lunches inc lots of hot or cold sandwiches (very busy then but service quick), full Fullers beer range with perhaps a guest such as Brakspears, small choice of wines, small darts room, SkyTV; dogs allowed (not in garden) *(Andy and Jill Kassube, Jonathan Smith, Catherine Pitt, Mark Percy, Lesley Mayoh)*

Griffin [Church Rd]: Roomy food pub with good varied blackboard choice inc vegetarian, Courage, Theakstons and a guest beer, efficient young staff, several separate areas; tables in courtyard, beautiful spot on Thames overlooking swan sanctuary *(Tony Hobden)*

☆ *Hobgoblin* [Broad St]: Popular, friendly and individual basic drinkers' pub, with up to nine daily-changing well kept interesting guest beers (several hundred a year) and one or two farm ciders as well as their well kept Wychwood ales and bottled beers, country wines, filled rolls, lively landlord, friendly staff and locals, daily papers, bare boards, raised side area, alcovey panelled back rooms, hundreds of pumpclips on walls and ceiling; no mobile phones, but games machine, TV, piped music; open all day *(Catherine Pitt, Richard Lewis, Jonathan Smith, Andy and Jill Kassube, Paul Vickers, Mark and Diane Grist)*

Hook & Tackle [Katesgrove Lane, off A4 next to flyover inner ring rd]: Pretty little pub with pastiche but comfortable traditional décor, usual lunchtime food (may be a wait, Tannoy food announcements), plenty of long tables at the back, good range of well kept ales from Fullers to Tisbury, outstanding twice-yearly beer festivals, warm-hearted old-fashioned landlady, quick caring service, two coal-effect gas fires, bar billiards; evenings can fill with young people and loud music; picnic-sets on side lawn by flyover *(Ian Phillips, T G Thomas, Jonathan Smith, Catherine Pitt)*

☆ *Hop Leaf* [Southampton St]: Recently refurbished friendly bustling local tied to Hop Back of Wiltshire with their full beer range kept well, also occasional Reading Lion beers brewed on the premises, fine farm cider, nice family atmosphere, simple bar snacks, no smoking area, family room, darts, bar billiards; one-way system making parking close by difficult *(Jonathan Smith, Catherine Pitt, Mark and Diane Grist, JP, PP)*

Hope [Friar St]: Large comfortable open-plan Wetherspoons pub handy for shops, with good mix of customers, lots of books and old Reading prints, some no smoking areas, good menu inc specials, good choice of well kept ales, friendly efficient service; open all day, good disabled facilities, pleasant back terrace *(T G Thomas, Richard Lewis)*

Retreat [St Johns St]: Basic 1960ish backstreet local just as friendly under new landlord, particularly well kept ales such as Brakspears,

Hook Norton and Theakstons, good simple food, back bar with darts and bar billiards *(Catherine Pitt, Richard Houghton, Jonathan Smith)*

Three Guineas [Platform 4, Station]: Large friendly railway-theme pub in former booking office building, central bare-boards bar with pleasant furnishings, wide choice of food inc lots of specials, Adnams and three other well kept ales, friendly staff; piped music may be loud evenings, games machines; tables on terrace, open from 7.30am *(Catherine Pitt)*

Remenham [SU7683]

Little Angel [A4130, just over bridge E of Henley]: Good atmosphere in low-beamed dining pub popular with business people, attractive restaurant area with panelling and darkly bistroish décor (bar itself small and pretty basic), friendly helpful unhurried service, splendid range of wines by the glass, well kept Brakspears, big conservatory, floodlit terrace *(Sheila Keene, LYM, Mike and Jennifer Marsh)*

Stratfield Mortimer [SU6664]

☆ *Fox & Horn* [The Street; 4 miles W of A33]: Roadside pub done up for dining by Californian licensees, largely dark green and buff décor, open-plan big-windowed front bar with log fire, well kept Fullers London Pride, Hook Norton Best and Wadworths 6X, good choice of wines in big glasses, espresso machine; some emphasis on comfortable two-room no smoking restaurant with good unusual changing food from light lunches up, inc some inspired puddings; may be piped Richard Clayderman; tables outside *(Steve Clifton, BB, Dr and Mrs R E S Tanner)*

Streatley [SU5980]

Bull [A417/B4009]: Efficient staff in large friendly pub with emphasis on good generous food; Hardy beers, friendly dog, tables outside – lovely setting; good walks *(anon)*

Wargrave [SU7878]

☆ *Bull* [off A321 Henley—Twyford; High St]: Good friendly atmosphere in cottagey low-beamed pub popular for interesting and enjoyable food esp good value lunchtime filled baguettes and hot dishes, well kept Brakspears, good log fires; tables on pretty partly covered terrace, bedrooms *(Michael Porter, M Borthwick, LYM)*

Wickham [SU3971]

☆ *Five Bells* [3 miles from M4 junction 14, via A338, B4000; Baydon Rd]: Neatly kept local in racehorse-training country, big log fire, tables tucked into low eaves, inviting choice of good value food, well kept ales inc Greene King Old Speckled Hen and Ringwood, friendly landlord, good lunchtime mix from regulars to family groups, garden with good play area; children in eating area, good value bedrooms *(Dick and Madeleine Brown, K H Frostick, LYM)*

Windsor [SU9676]

Highlander [Castle Hill]: Opp castle, with friendly service, decent food, very Scottish theme; children welcome *(Don and Leanne Palmer, Chris Glasson)*

Royal Oak [Datchet Rd, opp Riverside Stn]: Big and busy, looking up to castle, with quick friendly service, red plush and panelling, some fine stained glass, good choice of good value food from big servery in airy bistro family eating area (children welcome here), Marstons Pedigree and Wadworths 6X; white furniture on L-shaped terrace *(BB, Carol and Dono Leaman)*

Swan [Mill Lane, Clewer]: Traditional local, no music or machines, well kept Fullers IPA and London Pride; bedrooms *(Alistair Forsyth)*

Three Tuns [Market St]: Big bar with Courage ales from central servery, food inc good sandwiches (same baker as the Queen), quick service; piped music, can be busy with tourists *(R Huggins, D Irving, E McCall, T McLean)*

☆ *Two Brewers* [Park St, off High St next to Mews]: Quaint snug three-roomed pub with relaxed atmosphere, good interesting home-made food (not Sat evening) inc unusual hot sandwiches, well kept beers such as Courage Directors, Wadworths 6X and Charles Wells Bombardier, good choice of wines by the glass and bottle (and of Havana cigars), fair prices, pleasant service, daily papers, bare boards and beams (covered with sayings and quotes), walls lined with corks; tables out on pavement of pretty Georgian street next to Windsor Park's Long Walk; has been open all day summer *(Chris Glasson, Sue Demont, Tim Barrow, Dr Stuart Reed)*

Winkfield [SU9072]

☆ *White Hart* [between Windsor and Bracknell; Church Rd (A330)]: Smartly traditional Tudor dining pub, quietly comfortable if a bit over-furnished, with ex-bakery bar and ex-courthouse restaurant, good varied food esp Sun lunch, candlelit tables, real ales such as Brakspears and Fullers London Pride, good wine choice, friendly attentive young staff; sizeable attractive garden *(LYM, Chris Glasson, Simon Collett-Jones)*

Wokingham [SU8068]

Broad Street Tavern [Broad St]: Old building smartly but not over-trendily done up with stripped wood, good range of filling lunchtime food, well kept Wadworths IPA, 6X and guest beers tapped from the cask, low prices, very friendly service, nice local atmosphere, quarterly beer festivals *(R T and J C Moggridge, Jonathan Smith)*

Crooked Billet [Honey Hill]: Busy country pub with pews, tiles, brick serving counter, crooked black joists, generous plain lunchtime food, well kept Brakspears, small no smoking restaurant area where children allowed; nice outside in summer, very busy wknds *(LYM, Colin and Sandra Tann)*

Woolhampton [SU5767]

☆ *Rowbarge* [Station Rd]: Big canalside family dining place with beamed bar, panelled side room, small snug, bric-a-brac, candlelit tables, wide choice of good freshly made food inc Sun lunch, decent choice of well kept ales inc Fullers London Pride, helpful staff; large no smoking back conservatory, tables by water and in big garden with fishpond, moorings not far *(Colin McKerrow, LYM, Roger and Pauline Pearce, Mrs P Shakespeare, Charles and Pauline Stride)*

Post Office address codings confusingly give the impression that some pubs are in Berkshire, when they're really in Oxfordshire or Hampshire (which is where we list them).

Buckinghamshire

Quite a change-around here this year, with several former main entries moving to the Lucky Dip section at the end of the chapter, making room for half a dozen newcomers: the unspoilt Three Horseshoes in a lovely peaceful spot at Bennett End, the Dinton Hermit at Ford (reopened as a nicely relaxed dining pub), the Hampden Arms at Great Hampden (enjoyable food and friendly atmosphere; back in the Guide after a break), the Crooked Billet at Newton Longville (good food, fine range of wines), the Carpenters Arms at Slapton (a unique and engaging combination of second-hand bookshop with good pub) and the Chequers at Wheeler End (a nice old pub restored to its traditional roots by old Guide stalwarts from the Prince Albert at Frieth). Other pubs doing particularly well here these days are the Red Lion at Chenies (good food in relaxed pubby atmosphere), the Seven Stars at Dinton (good all round, good value food), the Stag & Huntsman at Hambleden (another good all-rounder), the Rising Sun at Little Hampden (a good secluded dining pub), the Crown at Little Missenden (a spotless classic chatty country pub), the affable White Hart at Preston Bissett (nice balance between food, drink and conversation), the friendly and bustling Polecat at Prestwood (imaginative food), the Five Arrows in Waddesdon (first-class pub/hotel, gaining a star this year for its all-round quality), and the Chequers at Wooburn Common with its thriving hotel and restaurant side. More restauranty than any of these, and by no means cheap, is the Angel at Long Crendon: its good imaginative food, and popularity with readers, earn it our accolade of Buckinghamshire Dining Pub of the Year. We should emphasise that this county does very well for food in pubs. Even the most unpretentious places among our main entries here, from cheerful walkers' taverns in the lovely countryside to unspoilt locals, are now serving enjoyable honest food without much recourse to the freezer pack. Peter and Janet Hodges deserve a special mention: they have won an entry for their Peacock at Bolter End in all 20 editions of the Guide. The handsome and interesting old Royal Standard of England at Forty Green, and the Bull & Butcher at Turville, have the same consistent record of achievement, though under different managements. Lucky Dip pubs to note particularly this year (and almost all already inspected and vouched for by us) are the Old Thatched Inn at Adstock, Bottle & Glass near Aylesbury, Pheasant at Brill, Chequers at Fingest, Crooked Billet at Flackwell Heath, Red Lion at Great Kingshill, White Horse at Hedgerley, Blackwood Arms on Littleworth Common, Stag at Mentmore, Carrington Arms at Moulsoe, Swan in Olney, Crown at Penn, Lone Tree at Thornborough, Red Lion in Wendover and George & Dragon in West Wycombe. Drinks prices in the county are rather higher than the national average.

Planning a day in the country? We list pubs in really attractive scenery at the back of the book.

BENNETT END SU7897 Map 4
Three Horseshoes

Horseshoe Rd; from Radnage follow unclassified road towards Princes Risborough and turn left into Bennett End Road, then right into Horseshoe Road

Simple yet civilised, this hard-to-find old country inn is in a lovely tranquil setting, the surroundings made particularly distinctive by a red phone box rising inexplicably from the fenced-off duck pond. There are plenty of tables behind to take in the view. Inside, the more appealing room is the snug front bar, with flagstone floors, high wooden settles, and a few seats tucked around an antique range – though the friendly labrador seems to prefer the sofas in the comfortable, sitting-roomish lounge. Well kept Brakspears, Flowers and Fullers London Pride on handpump; maybe quiet piped music. Appetising bar food – all home-made – ranges from lunchtime sandwiches and simple things like macaroni cheese (£4) to evening dishes such as chicken with cashew nuts (£10). They do a roast on Sundays, when the pub can get busy; at other times you might have it almost to yourself. One of the bedrooms has a large water bed. *(Recommended by Catherine and Richard Preston)*

Free house ~ Licensees Tim and René Ashby ~ Real ale ~ Bar food ~ No credit cards ~ (01494) 483273 ~ Open 12-3, 7-11(10.30 Sun); closed Mon ~ Bedrooms: £45B/£55B

BOLTER END SU7992 Map 4
Peacock

Just over 4 miles from M40 junction 5, via A40 then B482

The brightly modernised bar in this bustling little pub has a rambling series of alcoves, and a good log fire, and the Old Darts bar is no smoking. Well kept Brakspears Bitter and Fullers London Pride on handpump, decent wines (ten by the glass), and freshly squeezed orange juice; no piped music. Enjoyable bar food includes local sausages (£6), spicy beef and bean chilli or cheesy mushroom pancakes (£6.50), home-made steak and kidney pie (£8), marinated grilled salmon fillet (£8.90), steaks (from £10) and gammon hock cooked in herbs (£11/half £8); every day, there are up to three main course and three pudding specials such as spicy Moroccan vegetable pie (£6.90), rabbit gently cooked with wine and herbs (£7.50) or Whitby cod (£7.90), and citron tart, sticky toffee pudding or home-made syllabub. Cribbage and dominoes. In summer there are seats around a low stone table and picnic-sets in the neatly kept garden. The 'no children' is strictly enforced here. *(Recommended by Comus and Sarah Elliott)*

Punch ~ Lease Peter and Janet Hodges ~ Real ale ~ Bar food (12-2, 6.30-9.15; not Sun evening) ~ (01494) 881417 ~ Open 11.45-2.30, 6-11; 12-3 Sun; closed Sun evening

CADMORE END SU7892 Map 4
Old Ship ◀

B482 Stokenchurch—Marlow

Carefully restored, this 17th-c tiled cottage, huddled just below a country road, has kept its unpretentious character and charm. The tiny low-beamed two-room bar (now separated by standing timbers rather than a wall) is simply furnished with new brocaded banquettes and stools in the carpeted room on the right, and scrubbed country tables, bench and church chair seating (one still has a hole for a game called five-farthings), and bare boards on the left. Shove-ha'penny, cribbage, and dominoes. Bar food includes sandwiches and baguettes (from £2.75), home-made soup (£2.50), garlic prawns (£5.95), home-made chilli (£6.25), home-made steak in ale pie (£8.25), barnsley chop or seared salmon (£8.75), and chicken in parma ham with a sun-dried tomato and basil sauce (£8.95); 2-course curry evening meal £10.00). Well kept Brakspears Bitter, Old, Special, seasonal and Mild, and a guest like Fullers London Pride or Hook Norton Old Hooky tapped from the cask. There are seats on the terrace, and more in the sheltered garden with a large pergola. Parking is on the other side of the road. *(Recommended by Pete Baker, Barbara Wilder, Andy Meaton,*

Susan and John Douglas, the Didler, Paul Vickers)

Free house ~ Licensee Ian Wingfield ~ Real ale ~ Bar food (12-2, 6.30-9.30; not Sun) ~ Restaurant ~ (01494) 883496 ~ Children at licensee's discretion ~ Open 11-3, 5.30-11; 12-3, 7-10.30 Sun

CHEARSLEY SP7110 Map 4
Bell

The Green; minor rd NE of Long Crendon and N of Thame

Built with bricks from a clay unique to the surrounding area called Witchert, this bustling pub has a welcoming traditional feel. The cosy bar has mugs and tankards hanging from the beams, a collection of plates at one end of the room, an enormous fireplace, and handsome counter; there may be batches of local eggs for sale. Well kept Fullers Chiswick, London Pride and seasonal brews, and a small but well chosen selection of wines by the glass. Much of the simple good bar food is made from local ingredients and might include lunchtime sandwiches (from £3.45), leek and mushroom crumble (£5.95), generously served ham, egg and chips (£6.25), lamb casserole and minty dumpling (£7.25), tuna steak with coriander, lemon and white wine (£7.95), and puddings such as apricot and mango oaty crumble (£3.25). They sell ice pops and various drinks for children. You can't book tables, so there's ample space for drinkers, but it's best to get there early if you intend to eat. On Friday evenings you might find the licensees or one of the locals coming round the bar with sausages. Prompt friendly service; cribbage, dominoes. Play equipment such as slides, a rope bridge, wendy house, climbing frames and the like fill the spacious back garden, which has rabbits and chickens in one corner. There are plenty of tables out here, with more on a paved terrace, where there may be barbecues in summer. A couple of tables in front overlook the very grassy village green. More reports please. *(Recommended by Richard Gibbs)*

Fullers ~ Tenants Peter and Sue Grimsdell ~ Real ale ~ Bar food (12-1.45, 7-9; not Sun evening or Mon (exc bank holidays)) ~ No credit cards ~ (01844) 208077 ~ Children in eating area of bar ~ Open 12-2.30(3 Sat), 6-11; 12-3, 7-10.30 Sun; closed Mon lunchtime (exc bank holidays)

CHENIES TQ0198 Map 3
Red Lion ★

2 miles from M25 junction 18; A404 towards Amersham, then village signposted on right; Chesham Road

The landlord is keen that this bustling place should be thought of as a pub that sells good food, rather than a restaurant selling real ales – and the relaxed, unstuffy atmosphere reflects this. The unpretentious L-shaped bar has original photographs of the village and traction engines, comfortable built-in wall benches by the front windows, and other traditional seats and tables; there's also a small back snug and a dining room. Good enjoyable food includes soup (£3.25), interestingly filled hot and cold baps (from £3.25), filled baked potatoes (with interesting fillings, from £3.85), a trio of dips (hummous, tapenade and salsa with corn chips £3.95), fresh tuna on mixed leaves with tomatoes, olives and caraway seeds or pasta with aubergine and tomato sauce (£4.95), ploughman's (from £5.25), baked avocado and chicken in a rich neapolitan sauce topped with mozzarella (£5.75), sweet and sour vegetable balti (£6.50), home-made pies such as steak, stout and orange or vegetable and bean (from £6.50), pork, chilli and lentil casserole (£7.50), fishcakes with a lemon and parsley sauce (£9.95), steaks (from £10.95), daily specials like pasta, olive oil, pepperoni and parsley with tomatoes and parmesan (£6.25), pork and leek sausages with mustard gravy (£7.95), and crispy duck legs with stir-fried vegetables and black bean sauce (£8.50), and puddings (from £2.50); vegetables and salad are extra. Well kept Benskins Best, Marlow Rebellion Lion Pride (brewed for the pub), Vale Notley and Wadworths 6X on handpump. The hanging baskets and window boxes are pretty in summer. No children, games machines or piped music; handy for the M25. *(Recommended by Mike and Jennifer Marsh, Pat and Tony Martin, Evelyn and*

Derek Walter, Tracey and Stephen Groves, Marjorie and Bernard Parkin, Ian Phillips, Mike and Heather Watson, Dick and Penny Vardy, Joan and Andrew Life, Angela Cerfontyn, Mark Percy, Lesley Mayoh)

Free house ~ Licensee Mike Norris ~ Real ale ~ Bar food (12-2, 7-(9.30 Sun)10) ~ (01923) 282722 ~ Open 11-2.30, 5.30-11; 12-3, 6.30-10.30 Sun; closed 25 Dec

DINTON SP7611 Map 4
Seven Stars £

Stars Lane; follow Dinton signpost into New Road off A418 Aylesbury—Thame, near Gibraltar turn-off

A firm favourite with its many customers, this pretty white-rendered tiled house, tucked away in a quiet village, is popular for its good value food and genuinely friendly welcome. The public bar (or Snug) is lent character by two highly varnished ancient built-in settles which face each other across a table in front of a vast stone inglenook fireplace, while the spotless lounge bar – comfortably and simply modernised – has beams, joists and a burgeoning collection of old tools on the walls. Although these rooms are not large, the restaurant area is spacious and comfortable. Good, straightforward bar food includes sandwiches (from £1.75; toasties 25p extra), soup (£2.75), filled baked potatoes (from £3.50), ploughman's or vegetable pasta bake (£4.50), home-made lasagne (£5), battered haddock (£5.50), gammon and egg (£6.25), steaks (from £9.50), daily specials, and puddings (from £2.75). Well kept Fullers London Pride and Vale Edgar's Golden Ale on handpump. The affable landlord has a penchant for flamboyant ties.There are tables under cocktail parasols on the terrace, with more on the lawn of the pleasant sheltered garden. The pub is handy for the Quainton Steam Centre, and Dinton itself and nearby Westlington are pleasant villages. *(Recommended by Marjorie and David Lamb, Ian Phillips, SLC, Colin Parker, R F Ballinger, J Hale)*

Free house ~ Licensee Rainer Eccard ~ Real ale ~ Bar food (not Sun or Tues evenings) ~ Restaurant ~ (01296) 748241 ~ Children in eating area of bar ~ Open 12-3, 6-11; 12-4, 7-10.30 Sun; closed Tues evening

EASINGTON SP6810 Map 4
Mole & Chicken 🍴 ♀

From B4011 in Long Crendon follow Chearsley, Waddesdon signpost into Carters Lane opposite the Chandos Arms, then turn left into Chilton Road

To be sure of getting a table in this friendly dining pub – set in rolling open countryside – it's best to book beforehand. This is very much the place for a special meal out (they don't offer bar snacks), and from the changing restauranty menu you might find enjoyable starters such as home-made soup (£3.50), grilled crostini of smoked fish and cream cheese or roasted large field mushrooms with spinach and cheese (£5.95), and sautéed king prawns with garlic and chilli (£6.95), with main courses like pasta tossed with roasted vegetables and parmesan or much liked duck and bacon salad with a warm plum sauce (£8.95), chargrilled salmon fillet with a lemon and parsley butter (£9.95), roasted guinea fowl thighs stuffed with pork and garlic and served with wild rice and a red wine and mushroom sauce (£11.50), and Gressingham duck with orange sauce or chargrilled English steak (£12.95); several daily changing fish choices, too. Decent French house wines (and a good choice by the bottle), over 40 malt whiskies, and well kept Greene King IPA and Morlands Old Speckled Hen on handpump. The open-plan layout is very well done, so that all the different parts seem quite snug and self-contained without being cut off from what's going on, and the atmosphere is chatty and relaxed. The beamed bar curves around the serving counter in a sort of S-shape, and there are pink walls with lots of big antique prints, and (even at lunchtime) lit candles on the medley of tables to go with the nice mix of old chairs; good winter log fires.The garden, where they sometimes hold summer barbecues and pig and lamb roasts, has quite a few tables and chairs. *(Recommended by Lesley Bass, J Hale, Karen and Graham Oddey, Mrs L Lyons, Ian Dawson, Maysie Thompson, Marion Turner, David and Michelle Bailey, John Robertson, Brian Root)*

Free house ~ Licensees A Heather and S Ellis ~ Real ale ~ Restaurant (12-2, 7-10; 12-9.30 Sun) ~ (01844) 208387 ~ Children welcome ~ Open 12-3, 6-11; 12-10.30 Sun

FORD SP7709 Map 4
Dinton Hermit
Village signposted between A418 and B4009, SW of Aylesbury

Recently taken over by Johnny Chick, who's made something of a speciality of turning quiet country pubs into popular food places, this 16th-c stone cottage has kept its attractively old-fashioned layout. Beside the huge inglenook fireplace hangs a very old print of John Bigg, the supposed executioner of Charles I and the man later known as the Dinton Hermit. The bar has scrubbed tables on the original black and red tiled floor and well kept Adnams, Morrells Oxford Blue, and Wadworths 6X tapped from the cask, and decent wines are served from the thick solid oak counter. The cosy restaurant has church candles burning on each table, and it's best to book in advance to be sure of a seat. The menu was changing as we went to press, but there will be sandwiches (from £3), ploughman's (£6.50; the hot chicken one is liked, £6.95), and dishes such as vegetable lasagne and good steak pie with a proper suet crust (£7.95) at lunchtime, with evening choices like bayonne ham with poached eggs and muffins (£7.95), home-made blinis with sour cream and gravadlax (£8.95), baked halibut (£12.95), big dover soles (£18.50), and good home-made puddings (from £4); Sunday roast beef (£10.95). Seats in the attractive courtyard, where they hold barbecues and live jazz events in summer, and there's an acre of garden. *(Recommended by J Osborn-Clarke, Tim and Ann Newell, Torrens Lyster, Karen and Graham Oddey)*

Free house ~ Licensee Johnny Chick ~ Real ale ~ Bar food ~ Restaurant ~ (01296) 747473 ~ Children at landlord's discretion ~ Open 11-3, 6-11; 12-4, 7-11 Sun

FORTY GREEN SU9292 Map 2
Royal Standard of England
3½ miles from M40 junction 2, via A40 to Beaconsfield, then follow sign to Forty Green, off B474 ¾ mile N of New Beaconsfield

This ancient pub has enormous appeal, both in the layout of the building itself and in the fascinating collection of antiques which fills it. There are rifles, powder-flasks and bugles, ancient pewter and pottery tankards, lots of brass and copper, needlework samplers and stained glass. The rambling rooms also have lots to look at – huge black ship's timbers, finely carved old oak panelling, roaring winter fires with handsomely decorated iron firebacks, and a massive settle apparently built to fit the curved transom of an Elizabethan ship. Charles II is believed to have hidden, during the Battle of Worcester in 1651, in the high rafters of what is now the food bar. Two areas are no smoking. Enjoyable bar food includes home-made soup (£3.75), thai fishcakes with tomato and pepper salsa (£4.25), sandwiches (from £4.25), chicken, bacon and onion terrine with apricot chutney or ploughman's (£5.25), liver and bacon with onion gravy (£5.95), home-made pies like game with rabbit, pheasant and venison or sweet potato, haricot bean and mushroom (from £7.95), fillet of salmon with a tapenade crust on wilted greens with basil dressing (£8.75), daily specials such as wild mushroom risotto (£7.95) or seared tuna steak with niçoise salad (£10.95), and home-made puddings such as rhubarb and orange cinnamon crumble or chocolate cheesecake (£3.95). Well kept Brakspears Bitter, Fullers London Pride, Marstons Pedigree, Greene King Old Speckled Hen, and a guest beer on handpump, and country wines and mead. There are seats outside in a neatly hedged front rose garden, or in the shade of a tree. *(Recommended by Simon Collett-Jones, Anthony Longden, Ian Phillips, Roger and Pauline Pearce, Lesley Bass, Peter and Elizabeth May, the Didler, JP, PP, Ian Dawson)*

Free house ~ Licensees Cyril and Carol Cain ~ Real ale ~ Bar food (12-2,30, 6.30-9.30) ~ Restaurant ~ (01494) 673382 ~ Children in eating area of bar and in family room until 9.30 ~ Open 11-3, 5.30-11; 12-3.30, 7-10.30 Sun; closed evening 25 Dec

FRIETH SU7990 Map 2
Prince Albert ◗

Village signposted off B482 in Lane End; turn right towards Fingest just before village

Cheerful new licensees had just taken over this old-fashioned cottagey pub as we went to press and planned some minor refurbishments, as well as opening up a dining room. On the left, there are low black beams and joists, brocaded cushions on high-backed settles (one with its back panelled in neat squares), a big black stove in a brick inglenook, and a leaded-light built-in wall cabinet of miniature bottles. The slightly larger area on the right has more of a medley of chairs and a big log fire. The menu was in the planning stage, but they hoped to include sandwiches (from £2.50), ploughman's (from £3.95), vegetarian dishes (from £4), roast rib of beef or chicken with stilton mash and tomato concasse (£6.95), and puddings (from £2.50). Well kept Brakspears Best and Special on handpump. A nicely planted informal side garden has views of woods and fields, and there are plenty of nearby walks. *(Recommended by the Didler, Pete Baker, Ron and Val Broom, Dr D E Granger, Ian Phillips, Martin and Karen Wake)*

Brakspears ~ Tenant Steve Anderson ~ Real ale ~ Bar food ~ (01494) 881683 ~ Open 11-(2.30 Mon)3, 5.30-11; 12-4, 7-10.30 Sun

GREAT HAMPDEN SP8401 Map 4
Hampden Arms ❨❢❩

Village signposted off A4010 N and S of Princes Risborough

In a lovely quiet spot opposite the village cricket pitch, this friendly pub is popular for its good, interesting food. There might be home-made soup (£3.50), good value light lunches such as cottage pie, chicken and ham bake or cannelloni (all £4.95), vegetarian lasagne (£5.95), steak and mushroom pie, ham and egg, butterfly prawns, various omelettes or coquilles St Jacques (all £6.95), giant cod or rib-eye steak (£8.95), orange pork (£10.95), chicken maryland (£11.95), and puddings such as sticky toffee pudding or banana pancake (£3.50). A small corner bar has well kept Adnams, Brakspears, and Fullers London Pride on handpump, and winter mulled wine; service is quietly obliging. The green-walled front room has broad dark tables, with a few aeroplane pictures and country prints; the back room has a slightly more rustic feel, with its cushioned wall benches and big woodburning stove; one room is no smoking. There are tables out in the tree-sheltered garden; on the edge of Hampden Common, the pub has good walks nearby. *(Recommended by J Hale, Jack Clarfelt, John Branston, Maysie Thompson, Francis and Deirdre Gevers-McClure, P Price, Lynne Adler)*

Free house ~ Licensees Terry and Barbara Matthews ~ Real ale ~ Bar food (12-2, 6.30-9.30) ~ (01494) 488255 ~ Children welcome ~ Open 12-3, 6.30-11; 12-3, 6.30-10.30 Sun; may close some Sun or Mon evenings

HADDENHAM SP7408 Map 4
Green Dragon ★ ❨❢❩ ♀

Village signposted off A418 and A4129, E/NE of Thame; then follow Church End signs

The interesting choice of food still remains the main reason for coming to this popular dining pub. As well as sandwiches (from £3.25), there might be home-made soup (£3.50), baked courgette and goats cheese cake served with roast vegetables (£4.95), crab and salmon fishcakes with mango salsa (£5), special steak sandwich on garlic bread with home-made chips (£6.95), a trio of pork sausages on mash with onion gravy and crisp fried onions (£7.50), home-made pie of the day (£8.50), Cornish fillets of bass on braised fennel with juniper berries (£11), sautéed Gressingham duck breast with wild mushroom and thyme jus or fillet steak encased in cashel blue cheese with a port sauce (£11.50), and puddings like lemon tart with raspberry sorbet or sticky toffee pudding with toffee sauce (£3.95); they offer a set price menu on Tuesday and Thursday evenings which they call Simply a Tenner, which is very popular and best to book in advance. Well kept Fullers London Pride and Vale Wychert on handpump, and sensibly priced well chosen wines including a few by the glass. The main area is divided into two high-ceilinged communicating rooms, decorated with attractive still lifes and country pictures; piped music. For those just wanting a drink, there is still a respectable corner set aside. A big sheltered gravel terrace behind the pub has white tables and picnic-sets under cocktail parasols, with more on the grass, and a good variety of plants. This part of the village is very pretty, with a duckpond unusually close to the church. *(Recommended by John Branston, Karen and Graham Oddey, Brian Root, Tracey and Stephen Groves, Ian Phillips, Barbara Wilder, Andy Meaton, Maysie Thompson, J Hale, Matthew Last, Patricia Purbrick)*

Whitbreads ~ Lease Peter Moffat ~ Real ale ~ Bar food (not Sun evening) ~ Restaurant ~ (01844) 291403 ~ Well behaved children in restaurant (must be over 7 in the evenings) ~ Open 11.30-2.30, 6.30-11; 12-2 Sun; closed Sun evening

HAMBLEDEN SU7886 Map 2
Stag & Huntsman ⬤

Turn off A4155 (Henley—Marlow Rd) at Mill End, signposted to Hambleden; in a mile turn right into village centre

Even on a cold miserable winter lunchtime, this attractive brick and flint pub is usually still packed with walkers, here to enjoy the hearty home-made food. And in summer, the seats in the spacious and neatly kept country garden are quickly snapped up. The half-panelled, L-shaped lounge bar has a cheerful, lively atmosphere, low ceilings, a large fireplace, and upholstered seating and wooden chairs on the carpet. Enjoyable bar food includes soup (£3.75), a bowl of chilli (£5.95), marinated chicken (£7.95), lambs liver and bacon (£8.25), beef in Guinness pie (£8.95), steaks (from £11.25), and puddings such as treacle tart pecan pie (£3.75). Well kept Brakspears Bitter, Wadworths 6X and a guest beer on handpump, farm ciders, and good wines are served by friendly staff in the attractively simple public bar; darts, dominoes, shove-ha'penny, and piped music. There's a dining room, and a cosy snug at the front. Set opposite the church on the far edge of one of the prettiest Chilterns villages, it's just a field's walk from the river. *(Recommended by Susan and John Douglas, Gwen and Peter Andrews, Catherine and Richard Preston, T R and B C Jenkins, J Hale, Lesley Bass, Bob and Laura Brock, Klaus and Elizabeth Leist, Cyril S Brown, Mike and Heather Watson)*

Free house ~ Licensees Hon. Henry Smith and Andrew Stokes ~ Real ale ~ Bar food (not Sun evenings) ~ (01491) 571227 ~ Children in eating area of bar and restaurant ~ Open 11-2.30(3 Sat), 6-11; 12-3, 7-10.30 Sun; closed 25 Dec ~ Bedrooms: £58B/£68B

LITTLE HAMPDEN SP8503 Map 4
Rising Sun ⬤

Village signposted from back road (ie W of A413) Great Missenden—Stoke Mandeville; pub at end of village lane; OS Sheet 165 map reference 856040

After a stroll along one of the surrounding woodland tracks, many walkers head for this secluded and comfortable dining pub to enjoy the imaginative food. Dining tables dominate the opened-up bar, and there's a woodburning stove and log fire to add to the cosiness in winter. Changing blackboards display popular food such as grilled black pudding on a sweetcorn fritter with apple sauce (£4.50), grilled goats cheese on garlic bread with cranberries (£4.75), warm duck and bacon salad with pine nuts and croutons with a basil vinaigrette (£4.95), breadcrumbed breast of chicken filled with cream cheese and prawns, served with lemon and tarragon sauce (£8.95), fried strips of veal on a bed of spaghetti with a creamy wild mushroom sauce or deep-fried whole tail scampi (£9.95), and puddings like hot walnut cake with date and butterscotch sauce and vanilla ice cream, chocolate toffee mousse with sultanas soaked in brandy or baked rice pudding flavoured with cardamom and served with stewed plums and cream (£3.75). Well kept Adnams, Brakspears Bitter and Marstons Pedigree on handpump, with home-made mulled wine and spiced cider in winter, and a short but decent wine list. There are some tables on the terrace by the sloping front grass. Muddy boots must be left outside. *(Recommended by Peter and Jan Humphreys, Gordon Neighbour, Tim Brierly, Maysie Thompson, David and Michelle Bailey, Matthew Last, J Hale, Kenneth and Sybil Court, Brian Root, Ian Dawson, Karen and Graham Oddey, Dr M Owton)*

Free house ~ Licensee Rory Dawson ~ Real ale ~ Bar food (not Sun evening, not Mon) ~ Restaurant ~ (01494) 488360 ~ Children must be well behaved ~ Open 11.30-3, 6.30-10(11 Sat); 12-3 Sun; closed Sun evening and all Mon (exc bank hol Mon lunchtimes) ~ Bedrooms: £30B/£58B

LITTLE MISSENDEN SU9298 Map 4
Crown ★ ◀

Crown Lane, SE end of village, which is signposted off A413 W of Amersham

'Everything a pub should be' commented one reader about this unspoilt country brick cottage. It has been run by the same family now for over 90 years, and the present licensees (third generation) offer a traditional welcome, and keep the pub spotlessly clean. The bustling bars are more spacious than they might first appear, with old red flooring tiles on the left, oak parquet on the right, built-in wall seats, studded red leatherette chairs, a few small tables, and a complete absence of music and machines; a good mix of customers adds to the chatty relaxed atmosphere. Very well kept real ales include Adnams Broadside, Brakspears, Marstons Pedigree, and a guest such as Black Sheep or Marlow Rebellion IPA on handpump, and they also have farm ciders, decent malt whiskies, and winter mulled wine. Popular straightforward home-made bar food includes a decent choice of generous very good value sandwiches (from £2.50), as well as ploughman's and pasties (from £4), buck's bite (a special home-made pizza-like dish £4), and steak and kidney pie (£4.75); darts, shove-ha'penny, cribbage, dominoes, and table skittles. The attractive sheltered garden behind has picnic-sets and other tables, and may occasionally give a view of Fighter Command pilots practising startling aerobatics in small propeller aeroplanes overhead. The pretty village has an interesting church. No children. *(Recommended by D B, Simon Collett-Jones, Tracey and Stephen Groves, Doug Sawyer, Susan and John Douglas, Ian Phillips)*

Free house ~ Licensees Trevor and Carolyn How ~ Real ale ~ Bar food (lunchtime only) ~ (01494) 862571 ~ Open 11-2.30(3 Sat), 6-11; 12-3, 7-10.30 Sun

LONG CRENDON SP6808 Map 4
Angel ★ ⑪

Bicester Rd (B4011)

Buckinghamshire Dining Pub of the Year

Smartly expensive, this partly 17th-c dining pub is the place to come for a special treat. The comfortable and pleasantly decorated lounge has a mix of ample sofas, and there are sturdy tables and chairs in another area; two dining areas are no smoking. A no smoking conservatory dining room at the back looks out on the garden, and the terrace is a popular spot in summer. At lunchtime, the imaginative food includes open sandwiches and baguettes (from £5.25; chargrilled vegetables and mozzarella cheese £5.25, Scottish smoked salmon and avocado salsa £6.95), fried Highland black pudding on crispy bacon and potato rösti with deep-fried haggis fritter and English mustard jus (£6.25), wild mushrooms and asparagus millefeuille in a roast garlic and tarragon cream sauce (£6.50), chargrilled sausages with onion gravy (£7.25), and seafood and saffron risotto flavoured with basil and parmesan cheese (£12.50); also, smoked goose and rocket salad topped with seared duck foie gras (£8.50), Culham Wood partridge on a confit of wild mushrooms and roasted root vegetables in a port and redcurrant sauce (£14.95), and daily specials like roast Spanish sardines in garlic butter (£4.50), poached fillet of natural smoked haddock on leek and mustard mash with cheese sabayon (£10.25), and fried fillet of bream on black noodles with a lobster cream sauce (£11.75). Puddings such as hot fig tart tatin with home-made caramel ice cream or rhubarb crème brûlée (£4.50);

vegetables are extra. Well kept Hook Norton and Ridleys on handpump, quite a few malt whiskies and an extensive wine list. Obliging friendly service; piped music. *(Recommended by J Hale, Richard Fendick, Patricia Purbrick, Mrs Jackie Williams, Iain and Joan Baillie, Keith Barker, Roger Braithwaite, Tim Brierly)*

Free house ~ Licensees Trevor Bosch and Angela Good ~ Real ale ~ Bar food (not Sun evening) ~ Restaurant ~ (01844) 208268 ~ Children welcome ~ Open 12-3, 7-10; 12-3 Sun; closed Sun evening ~ Bedrooms: £55B/£65B

NEWTON LONGVILLE SP8430 Map 4
Crooked Billet ♀

Off A421 S of Milton Keynes; Westbrook End

Busily efficient, this brightly modernised thatched pub wins praise for its carefully prepared and often imaginative food, as well as its thoughtfully chosen wines – all 260 of which are available by the glass in the restaurant, or in the bar if you're eating. The changing menu might include crispy duck with spring onion and cucumber salad (£4.50), sausages and mash (£7.50), loin of lamb with lamb kidney sausage and deep-fried leeks (£11.50), and roast bass with pea purée and wilted curly kale (£13); they have some interesting cheeses. The menu warns of a 25-minute wait for main courses at busy times. They don't take bookings at lunchtimes (except on Sundays), but for the evening restaurant tables need to be reserved well in advance – up to a month some weekends. The restaurant is no smoking. Though the focus is very much on the food, it still feels like a proper pub; the extended bar has beam and plank ceilings, some partly green-painted walls, sporting trophies on the shelves, and usually a few chatting locals. There are a few tables out on the lawn. Greene King IPA, Abbot and seasonal beers on handpump, along with maybe a guest such as Brakspears or Morrells; piped music, fruit machine. They don't allow mobile phones. On bank holiday weekends there may be pig roasts or other special events. *(Recommended by Simon Fisher, June and Malcolm Farmer, Karen and Graham Oddey)*

Greene King ~ Licensee John Gilchrist and Emma Sexton ~ Real ale ~ Bar food (not Sun evening or Mon) ~ (01908) 373936 ~ Children in restaurant ~ Open 11.30-3, 5.30-11; closed Mon lunchtime

PRESTON BISSETT SP6529 Map 4
White Hart

Pound Lane; village can be reached off A421 Buckingham bypass via Gawcott, or from A4421 via Chetwode or Barton Hartshorn

The friendly licensees of this charming little 18th-c thatched and timbered white-painted pub have a very sensible evening policy which keeps all their customers happy. While they offer bar snacks at lunchtime, evening food is only served in the (usually fully booked) dining room, and the main bar is kept for those just wanting a chat and a drink. The three cosy little rooms are genuinely traditional, and have old lamps hanging from the low beams, captain's chairs, red banquettes and stools nestling around the tables, local prints and memorabilia from the local Tetleys-owned Aylesbury Brewing Company around the walls, and a log fire with perhaps their friendly golden retriever slumbering beside it. The quality of the food matches the warmth of the welcome, and the nicest place to enjoy it is the largest room (no smoking) with a well polished wooden floor and high-backed wooden settle. As well as nibbles such as moroccan spiced bread, olives, and spiced pickled herrings (from £1.50), lunchtime choices include hot baguettes (from £2.50), various soups (£3.25), filled Aga-baked potatoes (from £4.50), and large flat mushrooms sautéed in garlic and fresh herb butter, au gratin with goats cheese (£4.95); in the dining room, there might be bresaola, parmesan, virgin oil and lemon juice (£4.95), prawn moneybags with two dips (£4.75), cod and chips served in the *Financial Times* (£5.95/£7.95), fresh linguini with roasted vine tomatoes and pesto (£8.25), lamb, apricot and rosemary pie (£8.50), and chicken breast filled with mozzarella and pesto wrapped in prosciutto and baked (£9.50); service is chatty and helpful. Adnams Best and a guest such as Batemans XB or Jennings Cumberland on handpump, extensive wine list with 13 by the glass, a dozen malt whiskies, country wines, and home-made elderflower cordial and lemonade in summer, with mulled wine in winter. There are tables behind on a terrace and in a walled garden, and they hold occasional barbecues or wine tastings. So many dogs accompany their owners that they sell dog biscuits at the tiny central bar counter. No children. *(Recommended by J Hale, Peter and Jean Hoare, Bob and Maggie Atherton, Karen and Graham Oddey, Trevor Ives, Iain and Joan Baillie, Mr and Mrs D S Price, Lynn Sharpless, Bob Eardley, R R Thompson, Brian Root)*

County Estates ~ Tenants Duncan Rowney and Lisa Chapman ~ Real ale ~ Bar food (12-1.45, 7-9; not Mon or Tues) ~ Restaurant ~ (01280) 847969 ~ Open 12-2.30, 6.30-11; 12-3, 7-10.30 Sun; closed Mon and Tues lunchtimes

PRESTWOOD SP8700 Map 4
Polecat

170 Wycombe Rd (A4128 N of High Wycombe)

Very well run by cheerful, friendly people, this much enjoyed pub offers particularly good food and a decent choice of well kept beers and wines. Several smallish rooms open off the low-ceilinged bar, with a medley of tables and chairs, all sorts of stuffed birds as well as the stuffed white polecats in one big cabinet, small country pictures, rugs on bare boards or red tiles, and a couple of antique housekeeper's chairs by a good open fire; the Gallery room is no smoking. At lunchtime there tend to be chatty crowds of middle-aged diners, with a broader mix of ages in the evening. Lunchtime snacks include sandwiches (from £3), filled baked potatoes (from £4.40), and ploughman's (£4.95), while other dishes include home-made soup (£3.40), leek and potato soufflé baked in filo with chive sour cream (£4.50), curried vegetable rissoles with mint dip (£7.20), home-made pies or salmon fishcakes with tomato and herb sauce (£7.90), supreme of chicken filled with smoked cheese, wrapped in bacon and served with red wine sauce (£8.90), lamb shank with button onions and pearl barley (£9.40), daily specials such as medallions of pork in a walnut crumb with apple, sage and spring onion salsa (£7.40), grilled trout fillets on root vegetable rösti with coriander cream sauce (£8.90), and magret of duck with pear and claret sauce (£10.80), and puddings like coconut meringues with mango syllabub, sherry trifle or chocolate sables (£3.75). Well kept Marstons Pedigree, Greene King Old Speckled Hen, Ruddles County, Theakstons Best, and Wadworths 6X on handpump at the flint bar counter, nine wines by the glass, and a good few malt whiskies. As well as pretty hanging baskets and tubs, the attractive garden has hundreds of herbaceous plants, and there are picnic-sets on neat grass out in front beneath a big fairy-lit pear tree, with more on a big well kept back lawn. *(Recommended by P Price, Simon Collett-Jones, Matthew Last, Desmond Hall, D and M T Ayres-Regan, Lesley Bass, Klaus and Elizabeth Leist, Marion Turner, Ken Richards, Kevin Thomas, Nina Randall, Gordon Tong)*

Free house ~ Licensee John Gamble ~ Real ale ~ Bar food (12-2, 6.30-9; not Sun evening) ~ Restaurant ~ No credit cards ~ (01494) 862253 ~ Children in eating area of bar ~ Open 11.30-2.30, 6-11; 12-3 Sun; closed Sun evening, 25-26 Dec, evening 31 Dec, 1 Jan

SKIRMETT SU7790 Map 2
Frog 🛏

From A4155 NE of Henley take Hambleden turn and keep on; or from B482 Stokenchurch—Marlow take Turville turn and keep on

As this bustling country inn is set in the heart of the Chiltern hills with lots of surrounding hiking routes, it's not surprising that walkers find their way here to enjoy the well kept beer and generously served food. Although brightly modernised, it still has something of a local feel with leaflets and posters near the door advertising raffles and so forth. The neatly kept beamed bar area has a mix of comfortable furnishings, a striking hooded fireplace with a bench around the edge (and a pile of logs sitting beside it), big rugs on the wooden floors, and sporting and local prints around the salmon painted walls. The function room leading off, with a fine-looking dresser, is sometimes used as a dining overflow. To be sure of a table, you must book in advance: sandwiches, home-made soup (£2.95), baked goats cheese with roast beetroot (£5.50), warm potato rösti, black pudding, smoked salmon and poached egg salad (£5.95), lasagne of wild mushrooms and asparagus with chervil butter sauce (£8.95), fried turkey escalope in a tarragon cream sauce (£9.50), roast fillet of salmon with onion marmalade and sautéed potatoes (£10.50), braised and glazed shank of lamb in a port and redcurrant jus (£12.50), and puddings such as banoffi pie, orange and Grand Marnier pancakes stuffed with ice cream and an orange sauce or chocolate nut brownies (from £3.50); they also offer a two-course (£13.95) and three-course meal (£17.50). The restaurant is no smoking; piped music. Well kept Brakspears, Fullers London Pride and a weekly changing guest on handpump such as Adnams Best or Black Sheep Bitter, a good range of wines, and various coffees. A side gate leads to a lovely garden, with a large tree in the middle, and unusual five-sided tables well placed for attractive valley views. The bedrooms are engaging, and it's a nice base for the area; Henley is close by, and just down the road is the delightful Ibstone windmill. *(Recommended by P G Plumridge, Phil and Sarah Kane, Matthew Last, Ian Phillips, Gill and Keith Croxton)*

Free house ~ Licensees Jim Crowe and Noelle Greene ~ Real ale ~ Bar food ~ Restaurant ~ (01491) 638996 ~ Children in restaurant and family room ~ Open 11.30-3, 6.30(6 Fri and Sat)-11; 12-4, 6.30-10.30 Sun; closed Sun evening Oct-Easter Sun ~ Bedrooms: £53.50S(£53.50B)/£65S(£65B)

SLAPTON SP9320 Map 4

Carpenters Arms

Village signposted off B488 S of Linslade, just N of Horton; or can be reached off A4146 S of Leighton Buzzard, via Billington

A delightfully quirky oddity, this old thatched house doubles as a second-hand bookshop. Shelves and tables around the four small and cottagey connecting rooms were filled on our last visit with everything from a coffee-table guide to the Peak District to biographies of Churchill and the weighty *Famous Trials of History* (they also had an equally daunting sequel), and there's plenty more in an adjacent barn. Worth a visit simply to wade through the thousands of titles, the pub has other pleasures to merit a detour: the food and drink for a start, and a nicely unpretentious atmosphere. The changing menu includes sandwiches and baguettes (not Sun), usually a couple of soups such as ham, lentil and vegetable (£3.50), and promptly served meals such as cottage pie (£6.75), wild rabbit in a creamy white wine and coriander sauce (£8.50), or a good vegetarian dish. Even in summer you may find Christmas pudding on the menu; they enjoy making them so much they usually end up with too many. Booking is recommended on Saturday evenings – the cottagey bar has only around 10 tables. Two well kept changing beers such as Buckleys IPA, and Side Pocket from the Tring Brewery; half a dozen or so well chosen wines by the glass; friendly attentive service. One of the rooms has a brick fireplace, and elsewhere are beams, the odd timber, mismatched old chairs and cushioned settles, and tiled or carpeted floors; they sell local honey. A sleeping cat clearly enjoys the unspoilt restful feel of the place. There are a few plastic tables under trees on a terrace, with nice tulips in spring. *(Recommended by Kate Colgrave, Susan and John Douglas, Andrew Scarr, Helen Whitmore)*

Free house ~ Licensee Jim Vogler ~ Real ale ~ Bar food (not Sun) ~ No credit cards ~ (01525) 220563 ~ Open 12-3.30, 7-11; closed Dec 25/26

TURVILLE SU7690 Map 2

Bull & Butcher

Valley road off A4155 Henley—Marlow at Mill End, past Hambleden and Skirmett

The emphasis in this civilised black and white timbered dining pub is firmly placed on its imaginative restauranty food. There might be soup (£3.95), hot home-smoked beef pastrami on rye or thai fishcakes with sweet chilli sauce (£5.95), terrine of confit duck leg and smoked duck breast with piccalilli (£6.95), spaghetti with pepperonata sauce or pork and leek sausages, mash, roast shallots and gravy

(£8.95), breast of chicken, roquefort leeks, rösti potato and pea velouté (£10.95), Tamworth pork medallions, bubble and squeak and mustard sauce (£11.95), and grilled king prawns and marinated monkfish, beef tomato and onion salad, warm chorizo and caper vinaigrette or chargrilled sirloin steak (£12.95). Well kept Brakspears Bitter, Mild, Special and Old, and a couple of guest beers on handpump, Weston's cider, and 37 wines by the glass. There are two low-ceilinged, beamed rooms (one has a well), with cushioned wall settles and an inglenook fireplace. Once a month (Tuesday evenings) the MG car club meets here. It does get crowded at weekends. The pub is set among ancient cottages in a lovely Chilterns valley crowned by a white windmill, and after a walk, the seats on the lawn by fruit trees in the attractive garden are a fine place to end up. *(Recommended by Simon Collett-Jones, Joel Dobris, D B, the Didler, JP, PP, Peter Walters, Lesley Bass, Torrens Lyster, Martin and Karen Wake)*

Brakspears ~ Tenant Nicholas Abbott ~ Real ale ~ Restaurant ~ (01491) 638283 ~ Open 11-3, 6(6.30 Sat)-11; 12-5, 7-10.30 Sun

WADDESDON SP7417 Map 4
Five Arrows ★ ⑪ ♀ ◨ ⟳

A41 NW of Aylesbury

This is a lovely civilised place – part of the Rothschild Esate – with consistently friendly service, exceptionally good food, and a fine choice of drinks. A series of light and airy high-ceilinged rooms makes up the unstuffy open-plan pubby bar, with family portrait engravings, lots of old estate-worker photographs, heavy dark green velvet curtains on wooden rails, mainly sturdy cushioned settles and good solid tables on parquet flooring (though one room has comfortably worn-in armchairs and settees). Newspapers and copies of *Country Life* are kept in an antique magazine rack. From the interesting menu, there might be soups such as broad bean minestrone or tomato and orange (£4.95), thai marinated fillet of red mullet on a bed of soy noodles (£4.95; main course £8.95), spring vegetable risotto with lemon and parmesan (£5.25), crayfish tail salad with dill mayonnaise (£5.95; main course £11.95), chargrilled breast of chicken with mango vinaigrette (£8.95), roasted darne of salmon wrapped in parma ham with a citrus jus (£11.25), confit of duck with raspberry and red wine jus (£12.95), pigeon breasts with black pudding on potato rösti with a port and redcurrant jus (£13.50), and puddings such as bourbon mousse with a duo of mango and rapsberry coulis, banoffi pie, and warm chocolate fudge cake with traditional custard (£4.15). No sandwiches or snacks on Sundays. The country-house-style restaurant is no smoking; must book at busy times. The formidable wine list runs to Rothschild first-growth clarets as well as lesser-known Rothschild estate wines. Well kept Fullers London Pride on handpump, many malt whiskies, champagne by the glass, proper cocktails, and freshly squeezed orange juice; efficient service, unobtrusive piped music. The sheltered back garden has attractively grouped wood and metal furnishings. This is an ideal base for visiting Waddesdon Manor. *(Recommended by Lesley Bass, Gerard McCaffrey, Ian Phillips, M A and C R Starling, Paul and Ursula Randall, Mrs Jackie Williams, Patricia Beebe, Karen and Graham Oddey, Dick and Penny Vardy, Maysie Thompson, J Osborn-Clarke, Bob and Maggie Atherton)*

Free house ~ Licensees J A Worster and F Bromovsky ~ Real ale ~ Bar food (12-2.30, 7-9.30; 12-2, 7.30-9 Sun) ~ Restaurant ~ (01296) 651727 ~ Children welcome ~ Open 11-11; 11-3, 6-11 Sat; 12-3, 7-10.30 Sun ~ Bedrooms: £60S/£85S(£85B)

WESTON UNDERWOOD SP8650 Map 4
Cowpers Oak ◨

High Street; village signposted off A509 in Olney

Children are welcomed in this wisteria-covered old pub in its charming setting among pretty thatched cottages. There's a large and attractive garden, with tame rabbits, a pig, goats, sheep, ponies and chickens – as well as a play area; also, seats on a small suntrap terrace by the lane in front. Inside are beams and stripped stone, with a pleasant medley of furnishings on the left-hand bar's bare boards, including old settles, a rocking chair, and even a long school desk. Lots of photographs, prints, and dark panelling, and newspapers and magazines to read. They keep five real ales in fine condition on handpump including Adnams, Fullers London Pride, Greene King IPA and Marstons Pedigree, with guests such as Shepherd Neame Spitfire or Wadworths 6X, also farm cider and several malt whiskies. Simple good value food includes soup (£2.95), hearty sandwiches (£2.50), baguettes (£3.50), crispy coated vegetables (£3.95), home-made lasagne (£6.50), chicken fillet with stilton and mushrooms (£6.95), salmon with tarragon sauce (£7.95), and chargrilled steaks (from £10.50); there's a no smoking back restaurant. Service is friendly and attentive. The right-hand games room has darts, bar billiards, hood skittles, table football, shove-ha'penny, cribbage, dominoes and TV; piped music. Dogs may be allowed in the bar (but not the main garden). *(Recommended by George Atkinson, Eric Locker, Mike Ridgway, Sarah Miles, Sue Demont, Tim Barrow)*

Unique Pub Co ~ Lease Paul Burchill and Zoe Cushnie ~ Real ale ~ Bar food (12-2.30, 7-9.30; not Sun or Mon evenings) ~ Restaurant ~ (01234) 711382 ~ Children welcome ~ Open 12-3, 5.30-11; 12-11(10.30 Sun) Sat; 12-3, 6(Sun)-11(10.30) winter wknds

WHEELER END SU8093 Map 4
Chequers ⬛

Off B482 in Lane End NW of Marlow, then first left also signposted Wheeler End

The new tenants in this small white-painted tiled house have thrown out the fruit machines, big-screen TV and piped music, gently redecorated, and ended up with a warm relaxed local with well kept beers and a roaring log fire in the grate. Under the low ceiling, the bar has what might be called an inherently friendly layout: it's so small, and shaped in such a way, that you can't help but feel part of the general conversation. It angles back past the inglenook (where Jazz the black cat likes to sit), and a little roomlet, to a bigger back room with a couple of dart boards. Furniture is mainly scrubbed country-kitchen with a few board-backed wall benches, and the walls are hung with small hunting prints, cartoons and so forth; darts, shove-ha'penny, cribbage, and dominoes. Well kept Brakspears and Fullers London Pride and ESB on handpump. Bar food at lunchtime includes home-cooked ham and eggs (£4.95), ciabatta sandwiches or granary rolls filled with things like sausage and fried onions, avocado and prawns, BLT or stilton and bacon (from £4.95), and steak and kidney pie (£5.95), with evening dishes such as thai fishcakes (£6.95), chicken in two mustards and cream (£7.25), steak (£8.95), and home-made puddings from bread and butter pudding to tiramisu (£3.45). There are a few tables outside; no car park to speak of, but plenty of parking nearby. No children. *(Recommended by Anthony Longden, Ron and Val Broom)*

Fullers ~ Tenants Joss and Frank Reynolds ~ Real ale ~ Bar food ~ (01494) 883070 ~ Open 11-2.30, 5.30-11; 12-3, 7-10.30 Sun

WOOBURN COMMON SU9187 Map 2
Chequers 🍴 🛏

From A4094 N of Maidenhead at junction with A4155 Marlow road keep on A4094 for another ¾ mile, then at roundabout turn off right towards Wooburn Common, and into Kiln Lane; if you find yourself in Honey Hill, Hedsor, turn left into Kiln Lane at the top of the hill; OS Sheet 175 map reference 910870

Even when really busy, the enthusiastic young staff here remain friendly and efficient. It's a welcoming place with a good mix of customers – many drawn from its thriving hotel and restaurant side. The low-beamed, partly stripped-brick bar has standing timbers and alcoves to break it up, comfortably lived-in sofas on its bare boards, a bright log-effect gas fire, and various pictures, plates, a two-man saw, and tankards; one room is no smoking. Changing daily, enjoyable food includes sandwiches (from £3.75), soup (£3.95), ploughman's (£5.25), popular vegetarian dishes such as chilled melon with grapes, mint and muscat wine (£6.95) and glazed swiss cheese soufflé with garlic cream sauce (£7.95), deep-fried calamari with sweet chilli dressing (£7.95), seared black bream with spinach and newburg sauce (£9.95), a nage of fish and shellfish with saffron and dill sauce (£10.95), fried calves liver with potato purée and onion jus (£11.95), and puddings (from £3.75); there's a more formal restaurant. Well kept Greene King IPA, Original, and Ruddles County on handpump, a sizeable wine list (champagne and good wine by the glass), and a fair range of malt whiskies and brandies. The spacious garden set away from the road, has cast-iron tables. Attractive stripped-pine bedrooms are in a 20th-c mock-Tudor wing; breakfasts are good. *(Recommended by Kevin Thomas, Nina Randall, Chris Glasson, T R and B C Jenkins, Ian Phillips, Colin Campbell, Simon Chell, Desmond Hall, Simon Collett-Jones, Peter and Giff Bennett, Dick and Penny Vardy, Mr and Mrs Gordon Turner)*

Free house ~ Licensee Peter Roehrig ~ Real ale ~ Bar food (12-2.30, 7-9.30 (10 Fri and Sat) ~ Restaurant ~ (01628) 529575 ~ Children welcome ~ Open 11-11; 11-10.30 Sun ~ Bedrooms: £97.50B/£102.50B

Lucky Dip

Besides the fully inspected pubs, you might like to try these Lucky Dips recommended to us and described by readers (if you do, please send us reports: www.goodguides.com).

Adstock [SP7330]
☆ *Old Thatched Inn* [Main St, off A413]: Attractive and spacious beamed and flagstoned pub/restaurant doing well under new regime, friendly and comfortable, with cosy corners and open fires, generous good food from sandwiches to game and theme nights, well kept Bass and Hook Norton Best, decent wines, welcoming attentive staff; may be piped music; seats out in sheltered back garden, children in restaurant and eating area *(George Atkinson, LYM, Arthur Baker, Karen and Graham Oddey)*
☆ *Verney Arms* [Verney Junction, Addington]: Cheery and cottagey, more bistro than pub, with Shaker-style furniture, imaginative décor, colourful walls and chairs, plates on bright red dado, fresh flowers; very good interesting (if not cheap) food, also small bar area around tiny brick counter; well kept Greene King ales, smartly relaxed atmosphere, open fire, good friendly service, soft piped jazz; tables in garden *(BB, George Atkinson, Mr and Mrs B J P Edwards)*
Amersham [SU9597]
Crown [Market Sq]: Small peaceful modernised bar in old hotel, beams and polished wood floors, neat tables all set for dining, interesting 16th-c features in comfortable lounge, good value food from baguettes up, afternoon teas, good restaurant, quick friendly service, Bass and Hancocks HB; attractive split-level outside seating area with cobbled courtyard and plant-filled garden, comfortable bedrooms *(BB, Jenny and Brian Seller, Norman Fox)*
Eagle [High St]: Low-beamed rambling pub with good helpings of usual food lunchtime and Sat evening, well kept ales such as Adnams, Fullers London Pride, Tetleys and Youngs Special, quick service even when busy, log fire, simple décor with a few old prints; maybe soft piped music, fruit machine; pleasant streamside back garden *(Simon Collett-Jones, Ian Phillips, Iain and Joan Baillie)*
☆ *Kings Arms* [High St]: Picture-postcard timbered building in charming street, lots of heavy beams and snug alcoves, big inglenook, high-backed antique settles and other quaint

old furnishings among more standard seating; good value bar food, restaurant, pleasant service, well kept Tetleys-related and other ales, children in eating area; open all day, rather a young person's pub evening; nice garden *(Charles Gysin, LYM)*
☆ *Saracens Head* [Whielden St (A404)]: Friendly unspoilt 17th-c local, neat, clean and largely no smoking, with beams, gentle lighting, massive inglenook with roaring fire in ancient decorative fire-basket, interesting décor, simple inexpensive generous fresh food from baguettes up, well kept Greene King IPA, Abbot, Old Speckled Hen and Ruddles Best, cheery chatty landlord; soft piped music; little back terrace *(LYM, Jenny and Brian Seller, Susan and John Douglas, Simon Collett-Jones)*
Aston Clinton [SP8712]
☆ *Oak* [Green End St]: Cosy and attractively refurbished beamed Fullers pub, good bar and plenty of dining room, friendly efficient service, generous home-made food (not Sun pm) cooked to order with good veg, decent wines, real fire, no music or machines *(B Brewer)*
Astwood [SP9547]
☆ *Old Swan* [Main Rd]: Doing well under new ownership, attractive, clean, airy and spacious, beams and flagstones, furnishings traditional yet modern, inglenook with woodburner, pictures, brasses and bric-a-brac, darts and pews in side area; well kept Adnams, Fullers London Pride and Greene King Old Speckled Hen, good value bar food from hot filled baps up, warm cosy atmosphere, friendly quick service, restaurant; large garden, side garden bar *(George Atkinson, LYM)*
Aylesbury [SP7510]
☆ *Bottle & Glass* [A418 some miles towards Thame, beyond Stone]: Friendly low-beamed thatched pub, tiled floor, attractive rambling layout, wide choice of good imaginative (if not cheap) food inc good fresh fish and seafood range (best to book, two sittings wknds), lively atmosphere, attentive friendly service, well kept ales, good choice of wines, neat garden *(LYM, Iain and Joan Baillie, Tim and Ann Newell)*

Kings Head [Kings Head Passage]: Famously well preserved 15th-c inn owned by NT, recently reopened, with wonderful early Tudor window lighting lofty bar, well kept real ale, good choice of food in bar and restaurant, more seats in side room; tables out in original courtyard with small corner arts and crafts shop (cl Mon) *(Tim and Ann Newell)*

Beaconsfield [SU9490]

☆ *Greyhound* [a mile from M40 junction 2, via A40; Windsor End, Old Town]: Welcoming and cosily rambling coaching inn with wide choice of home-made food (not Sún evening) from baps through bubble and squeak in variety to unusual fish dishes, two bars and partly no smoking back bistro area, well kept Courage Best, Fullers London Pride, Wadworths 6X and two guest beers, daily papers, professional young staff, no music or machines, no children *(David and Ruth Shillitoe, Joy and Peter Heatherley, Simon Collett-Jones, LYM, Geoffrey Kemp)*

Bierton [SP8415]

Bell [Aylesbury Rd]: Good wide choice of food esp fresh fish, good service, well kept Fullers London Pride; traditional two-bar layout; arrive early to get a seat *(MP)*

Brill [SP6513]

☆ *Pheasant* [off B4011 Bicester—Long Crendon; Windmill St]: Unpretentious simply furnished beamed pub in marvellous spot looking over to ancient working windmill, nearby view over nine counties, bar food running up to steaks and good salads, well kept Marstons Pedigree and Tetleys, good value house wines, prompt friendly service, attractive dining room up a step; piped music, no dogs (they have two golden retrievers); children welcome, tables in verandah and garden, bedrooms, open all day wknds *(Iain and Joan Baillie, R J Walden, Howard and Margaret Buchanan, LYM, C and G Fraser)*

Butlers Cross [SP8406]

Russell Arms [off A4010 S of Aylesbury, at Nash Lee roundabout; or off A413 in Wendover, passing stn; Chalkshire Rd]: Straightforward roadside pub with well kept real ales, good speedy service, short choice of enjoyable food; small sheltered garden, well placed for Chilterns walks *(B Brewer, LYM)*

Cheddington [SP9217]

Old Swan [off B488 N of Tring; High St]: Pretty thatched pub under newish landlord, open-plan but pleasantly laid out, well kept Bass, Brakspears, Fullers London Pride and Tetleys, usual food (not Sun evening) from sandwiches and baked potatoes to steaks, partly no smoking restaurant; children welcome, good family garden with enclosed play area, furnished wendy house and child-size wooden bench and tables *(LYM, Karen and Graham Oddey)*

Chicheley [SP9045]

☆ *Chester Arms* [quite handy for M1 junction 14]: Cosy and pretty beamed Charles Wells pub with rooms off semicircular bar, log fire, comfortable settles and chairs, wide choice of chef-served food from sandwiches to daily fresh fish and Aberdeen Angus beef, children's helpings, friendly service, Greene King IPA, Abbot and Ruddles, sizeable back dining room down steps; darts, fruit machine, quiet piped music; picnic-sets in small back garden *(Ian Phillips, George Atkinson)*

Clifton Reynes [SP9051]

Robin Hood [off back rd Emberton—Newton Blossomville; no through road]: Friendly new landlord widening range of decent food (inc Sun roasts) in pleasant stone-built pub, small and unpretentious, with inglenook, dark beams, good service, well kept Greene King IPA and Abbot, lots of Robin Hood film stills, nice grapevine conservatory; table skittles and juke box in plain public bar; very big garden with plenty of tables, horses in neighbouring field, riverside walks to Olney. *(BB, George Atkinson)*

Cuddington [SP7311]

Crown [village signed off A418 Thame—Aylesbury; Spurt St]: Small cosy village pub, olde-worlde with candles and open fire, friendly service, unusual choice of good food, Fullers Chiswick, London Pride and ESB, curry night Thurs, summer mediterranean nights *(Neil Dury)*

Dagnall [SP9916]

Golden Rule [Main Rd S]: Comfortable, friendly and bustling small pub, good home-cooked food, changing range of real ales, occasional beer festivals *(MP)*

Denham [TQ0486]

Falcon [Village Rd]: Open-plan but cosy and traditional with inglenook fireside seats below ancient cupboards, well kept ales inc Brakspears, lunchtime food inc good value sandwiches, welcoming staff; steps up to entrance *(Helen Hazzard, LM)*

Green Man: Warm and lively 18th-c pub, beams and flagstones in original part, dining area in raised extension, well kept beers, pleasant staff *(Francis and Deirdre Gevers-McClure)*

☆ *Swan* [¼ mile from M40 junction 1; follow Denham Village signs]: Pretty pub in lovely village, friendly atmosphere, comfortable mix of easy chairs and old drop-leaf tables, open fires, lots of plates, old bottles and prints on timbered walls, picture windows overlooking splendid floodlit back garden with picnic-sets and play area; well kept Courage Best and Directors and Marstons Pedigree, enjoyable straightforward food from sandwiches up; games machine, maybe piped pop music *(Simon Collett-Jones, Helen Hazzard, Ian Phillips, LYM, LM, Dave Hess)*

Emberton [SP8849]

Bell & Bear [off A509 Olney—Newport Pagnell; High St]: Wide choice of well priced food inc interesting dishes, Charles Wells Eagle and a guest such as Youngs AAA, farm cider, convivial homely atmosphere, friendly efficient staff, comfortable lounge with two fireplace features, dining area and attractive flower displays, bar with darts, juke box and machines; big garden with swings and large rabbit hutch, open all day Sat, attractive village *(Mike Ridgway, Sarah Miles)*

Fawley [SU7586]

☆ *Walnut Tree* [signed off A4155 or B480, N of Henley]: Relaxed and roomy Chilterns dining pub, wide choice from sandwiches up inc good fish in both bars, restaurant and no smoking conservatory, well kept Brakspears PA and SB, good range of wines; may be a delay at busy times; well spaced tables on big lawn, more in covered terrace extension; children welcome, open all day wknds, simple bedrooms *(Brian Root, LYM, Keith and Margaret Kettell, Tracey and Stephen Groves, Chris Glasson)*

Fingest [SU7791]

☆ *Chequers* [signed off B482 Marlow—Stokenchurch]: Several rooms around old-fashioned Tudor core, roaring fire in vast fireplace, sunny lounge by good-sized charming country garden with lots of picnic-sets, small no smoking room, interesting furniture, well kept Brakspears PA, SB and Old, dominoes and cribbage, enjoyable traditional food, quick friendly service, attractive restaurant; children in eating area; interesting church opp, good walks – can get crowded wknds *(Simon Collett-Jones, Klaus and Elizabeth Leist, Piotr Chodzko-Zajko, the Didler, P G Plumridge, LYM, Martin and Karen Wake, JP, PP)*

Flackwell Heath [SU8889]

☆ *Crooked Billet* [off A404; Sheepridge Lane]: Cosily well worn and comfortable old-fashioned 16th-c pub with lovely views (beyond road) from flower-filled suntrap front garden, low beams, good choice of reasonably priced tasty lunchtime food (not Sun), eating area spread pleasantly through alcoves, charming landlord, prompt service, well kept Brakspears and Whitbreads-related ales, good open fire; juke box *(Mayur Shah, BB, Susan and John Douglas)*

Frieth [SU7990]

☆ *Yew Tree* [signed off B482 N of Marlow]: Concentration on the food side (with quite a Greek flavour), but locals still dropping in for a drink, and walkers with dogs welcome; enjoyable peaceful atmosphere, exemplary service, well kept ales such as Brakspears PA, Fullers London Pride and Gibbs Mew Bishops Tipple, pleasant dining conservatory; may be unobtrusive piped music *(LYM, David and Michelle Bailey, J Hale)*

Great Horwood [SP7731]

Crown [off A4033 N of Winslow; The Green]: Smartly attractive and comfortable two-room Georgian pub with good value fresh home-made food from popular hot lamb sandwiches to Sun lunches, well kept Flowers IPA, Greene King Old Speckled Hen and a guest such as Youngs, farm ciders; fresh flowers in striking inglenook fireplace in summer, old-fashioned gramophone, parlour-like dining room with big wooden tables, board games; maybe soft piped music; quiz and theme nights inc jazz, friendly spaniel called Toby; tables on neat front lawn, very handy for Winslow Hall *(BB, Karen and Graham Oddey)*

Swan [B4033 N of Winslow]: Friendly and roomy front lounge with inglenook fire and dining area, small back bar with pool and darts, well kept Greene King IPA and Hook

Norton Best, very wide choice of straightforward food; open all day wknds, nice side garden *(Karen and Graham Oddey)*

Great Kimble [SP8206]

☆ *Bernard Arms* [Risborough Rd (A4010)]: Plush but friendly, with some nice prints (and photographs of recent Prime Ministers dropping in for a drink, even Yeltsin with the Majors), daily papers, good imaginative food in bar and restaurant, four changing real ales, decent wines, good range of malt whiskies and bottled beer, games room; no dogs, attractive fairy-lit gardens, well equipped bedrooms *(Chris Glasson)*

Swan & Brewer [Grove Lane (B4009, nr A4010)]: Beamed and tiled tap room, pleasantly furnished dining area with good reasonably priced food, real ales such as Adnams, Fullers London Pride and Hook Norton Best, friendly staff; well behaved children allowed, tables out on village green *(J V Dadswell)*

Great Kingshill [SU8798]

☆ *Red Lion* [A4128 N of High Wycombe]: Really a fish restaurant rather than the roadside local that it looks like, but there is a bar where you can get just a drink; friendly staff, wide choice of enjoyable very fresh fish and shellfish simply prepared, lots of home-baked melba toast to nibble, good puddings, good value wine, recent extension giving a no smoking area; quiet lunchtime but busy evenings, cl Sun evening, Mon *(David and Michelle Bailey, Marion Turner, Matthew Last, LYM)*

Grendon Underwood [SP6820]

Swan [Main St]: Divided open-plan pub with good value home-made food, good welcoming service, back games area with darts and pool *(Karen and Graham Oddey)*

Hawridge [SP9505]

☆ *Rose & Crown* [signed from A416 N of Chesham; The Vale]: Roomy and recently refurbished open-plan pub with wide choice of enjoyable food, well kept Brakspears and good range of wines, warmly welcoming attentive service, big log fire, peaceful country views from restaurant area; children allowed, broad terrace with lawn dropping down beyond, play area *(Marion Turner, LYM, B Brewer)*

Hedgerley [SU9686]

☆ *White Horse* [Village Lane, towards Gerrards X]: Friendly old country local with enjoyable lunchtime food inc good pies, sandwiches, bangers and mash, home-made fishcakes, particularly well kept Greene King IPA, Charles Wells Eagle and several unusual changing ales tapped from the cask, welcoming service; relaxed atmosphere in charming flagstoned public bar, jugs, ball cocks and other bric-a-brac, coal or log fires, larger lounge with cold food display cabinet, occasional beer festivals; no dogs, can be very busy; open all day wknds, occasional barbecues in big pleasant back garden, lovely window boxes, attractive village, good walks nearby *(J M Pitts, Paul Vickers, the Didler)*

High Wycombe [SU8792]

Beech Tree [Amersham Rd]: Cosy little red brick local, roomy back conservatory eating area, well kept Courage Best and Directors, friendly staff, decent food all day; quiet piped music; excellent big children's play area, lots of picnic-sets on grassy area, pleasant semi-rural setting *(Tony W Dickinson)*

Terriers [Amersham Rd]: Former Black Boy, friendly and helpful new management and staff, Greene King ales inc Old Speckled Hen, good value food esp Sun lunch, warm local feel; piped music; tables out on raised deck, swings in big garden *(Tony W Dickinson)*

Iver [TQ0381]
Red Lion [Langley Park Rd]: Formerly the Gurkha, refurbished and extended under new name, popular ambitious food, good service *(Nick Holmes)*

Ivinghoe [SP9416]
Rose & Crown [Vicarage Lane, off B489 opp church]: Cosy and spotless low-ceilinged L-shaped bar with back lounge up a few steps, generous popular freshly made food, well kept Adnams Best and Greene King IPA, friendly service, separate dining area, children welcome; quiet piped music, no muddy boots – nr one end of Ridgeway long-distance path; small secluded suntrap walled garden, pleasant village *(John Brightley, MP)*

Kingswood [SP6918]
☆ *Crooked Billet* [A41]: Rambling white weatherboarded dining pub divided into several cosy and attractively reworked rooms, stripped tables and mixed seats, log fire in big fireplace, no smoking dining area up a step or two, wide range of interesting food from baguettes up, well kept Adnams, Fullers London Pride and Hook Norton, pleasant efficient service, piped classical music; can be busy, esp wknds; tables out on terrace and in back garden – attractive surroundings, handy for Waddesdon Manor *(Arthur Baker, BB)*

Lacey Green [SP8201]
☆ *Pink & Lily* [from A4010 High Wycombe–Princes Risboro follow Loosley sign, then Gt Hampden, Gt Missenden one]: Charming little old-fashioned taproom (apostrophised sillily by Rupert Brooke – poem framed here) in much-extended Chilterns pub with warm welcome, airy and plush main dining bar (tables may all be reserved for diners), well presented good food; well kept ales such as Boddingtons, Brakspears PA, Courage Best and Glenny Hobgoblin, good well priced wines, friendly efficient service, open fire, dominoes, cribbage, ring the bull; piped music, children over 5 if eating; conservatory, big garden *(the Didler, Mr and Mrs R A Buckler, JP, PP, LYM, B Brewer)*

Whip [Pink Rd]: Cheery pubby local welcoming walkers, layout recently improved by repositioning of bar, mix of simple traditional furnishings, reliable food from good lunchtime soup and sandwiches to Sun lunches, well kept ales inc Brakspears and Courage Best, copious coffee, friendly service; fruit machine, TV; tables in sheltered garden, just below windmill *(Ian Phillips, David and Michelle Bailey, BB)*

Lavendon [SP9153]
Green Man [A428 Bedford—Northampton]: Roomy and attractive thatched and beamed

17th-c pub in pretty village, enjoyable food from baguettes and interesting soups up, snacks all afternoon, friendly attentive staff, restful atmosphere, woodburner and hops around bar, Courage Directors, Ruddles, Theakstons Best and XB, big restaurant with no smoking area; children welcome, maybe unobtrusive piped music; open all day, some seats out behind *(Mike Ridgway, Sarah Miles)*

Horseshoe [A428 Bedford—Northampton; High St]: Big spotlessly kept beamed village pub doing well under friendly new licensees, good home cooking in bar and restaurant, well kept Charles Wells real ales, small but interesting wine list, plush furnishings; appealing good-sized garden with play area. *(BB, Chris Matthews)*

Little Horwood [SP7930]
Shoulder of Mutton [Church St; back road 1 mile S of A421 Buckingham—Bletchley]: Partly thatched timbered pub with rambling bar, extensively refurbished under new licensees; woodburner in huge inglenook, french windows to pleasant back garden with plenty of tables *(LYM)*

Little Missenden [SU9298]
Red Lion: Small 15th-c pub, locals crowded around two coal fires, well kept Tetleys-related and other ales, decent wines, generous good value food from lots of sandwiches up, preserves for sale; piped music; tables (some under awning) and busy aviary in sunny side garden by river with ducks, swans and fat trout *(Mr and Mrs T A Bryan, LM)*

Little Tingewick [SP6432]
☆ *Red Lion* [off A421SW of Buckingham]: Welcoming 16th-c thatched Fullers pub, now bypassed, with roomy divided bar, low beams, pictures, well kept Chiswick and London Pride, good home-made food inc interesting dishes, good service, big log fire, small cosy no smoking dining room; family garden *(George Atkinson)*

Littleworth Common [SP9386]
☆ *Blackwood Arms* [3 miles S of M40 junction 2; Common Lane, OS Sheet 165 map ref 937864]: Doing well after recent takeover by a former landlord, pleasantly redecorated, with wide changing range of well kept ales on handpump or tapped from the cask, friendly atmosphere, good value simple food, roaring log fire; dogs welcome, tables outside, lovely spot on edge of beech woods – good walks *(Bob and Laura Brock, LYM, Anthony Longden)*

Long Crendon [SP6808]
Churchill Arms [B4011 NW of Thame]: Neatly refurbished village local, long and low, with terracotta walls, end public bar, well kept Brakspears, Fullers London Pride, Greene King Abbot and maybe a guest such as Youngs Special, friendly service, good log fire in big fireplace, generous usual lunchtime bar food, evening restaurant; piped music; children welcome, pleasant garden overlooking cricket field *(LYM, Tim and Ann Newell)*

Marlow [SU8486]
Claytons [Quoiting Sq, Oxford Rd]: Former Clayton Arms reworked as trendy tapas bar,

good food, several beer taps (inc Brakspears – not on handpump), pleasant atmosphere, good mix of customers, friendly staff, smooth piped jazz; busy Fri/Sat night, heated terrace *(the Didler, Ian Hall)*

Crown & Anchor [Oxford Rd]: Reopened as tap for Sam Trumans brewery with their changing ales and even a lager, maybe a guest beer, smallish take-us-as-you-find-us bar with part set aside Fri/Sat for live music, friendly service, some tables set for the enjoyable food, more out behind; piped music, quiz night Weds; comfortable bedrooms, pleasant back garden *(Richard Houghton, D and M T Ayres-Regan, BB)*

Marsh Gibbon [SP6423]

☆ *Greyhound* [West Edge]: Traditional furnishings, stripped beams and stonework, and surprisingly good fresh interesting thai food, half-price for children (no under-6s), in bar and two-room restaurant with oriental statuary; well kept Fullers London Pride, Greene King Abbot and IPA, decent house wines, handsome woodburner, dominoes, cribbage, and classical piped music; tables outside with play area *(Karen and Graham Oddey, LYM)*

Plough [opp church]: Old stone-built beamed village pub with comfortable banquettes in bays, soft lighting, good bar food from baguettes to lots of blackboard dishes, parlour dining room, Morrells Oxford Blue and Varsity and John Smiths, decent house wine, helpful staff, games room off public bar *(Michael and Jenny Back)*

Marsworth [SP9114]

☆ *Red Lion* [village signed off B489 Dunstable—Aylesbury; Vicarage Rd]: Low-beamed partly thatched village pub with cheerful service, well kept ales such as Bass, Fullers London Pride, Greene King Old Speckled Hen and Hancocks HB, decent wines, good value food inc good vegetarian dishes, quiet lounge with two open fires, steps up to snug parlour and lively games area (children allowed there with an adult); sheltered garden, not far from impressive flight of canal locks *(LYM, Sue Demont, Tim Barrow)*

Mentmore [SP9119]

☆ *Stag* [The Green]: Enthusiastic chef doing small choice of good value well presented bar food with wider evening choice, friendly chatty landlord, well kept Charles Wells Eagle and Bombardier, relaxed atmosphere in small civilised lounge bar with low oak tables, attractive fresh flower arrangements, open fire, restaurant and public bar leading off; charming sloping garden, dogs welcome *(Marjorie and David Lamb, Sally Hill, Katherine Guiton, BB)*

Milton Keynes [SP8335]

☆ *Old Beams* [Osier Lane, Shenley Lodge; off Childs Way via Livesey Hill and Paxton Cres, or Fulmer St via Faraday Dr]: Lots of brick and wood in sizeable comfortably extended former farmhouse, old photographs, paintings and brass, candles on dining tables, flagstoned bar, well kept McMullens ales with a guest such as Courage Directors, good choice of enjoyable food, keen young staff, speciality coffees, good pubby atmosphere; business faxes sent and

received free, very popular with local office staff; piped music; big garden with two ponds, swans and ducks *(George Atkinson, E J and M W Corrin)*

Moulsoe [SP9041]

☆ *Carrington Arms* [1¼ miles from M1, junction 14: A509 N, first right signed Moulsoe; Cranfield Rd]: Interesting pub featuring meats and fresh fish sold by weight from refrigerated display then cooked on indoor barbecue, with wide range of other food, even a lobster tank and separate oyster and caviar bar (no, not a cheap place); well kept Bass, Caledonian Deuchars IPA and Theakstons Best, champagnes by the glass, comfortable mix of wooden chairs and cushioned banquettes; open all day Sun, children allowed, long pretty garden behind, separate bedroom block *(Dr A Sutton, Roger and Pauline Pearce, Karen and Graham Oddey, Alan Sutton, Tim Lawrence, Mike and Wendy Proctor, Bob and Maggie Atherton, Martin and Karen Wake, Charles and Pauline Stride, Prof M J Kelly, LYM, Mike and Mary Carter, Charlie Harris)*

Naphill [SU8497]

Black Lion [Woodlands Dr]: Good choice of reasonably priced food from generous baguettes and baked potatoes up, real ales and friendly efficient staff in comfortable open-plan bar with aircraft pictures (Strike Command HQ nearby), and conservatory dining extension; maybe piped music; picnic-sets in good-sized garden with swings and slides, nearby Chilterns walks; has been open all day *(David and Michelle Bailey, LYM)*

Olney [SP8851]

☆ *Swan* [High St S]: Cosy and civilised, calls itself a bistro but much pubbier than you'd expect, especially the beamed and timbered bar with well kept real ales such as Fullers London Pride, Hook Norton, Jennings and Morrells; very busy and popular at lunchtime, good atmosphere, candles on pine tables, log fires, good choice of excellent value food inc a bargain daily special, superior wines, cheery service; tables in courtyard, one under cover *(Michael Jones, Sue Parsons, Keith Campbell, Michael Sargent, BB)*

Penn [SU9193]

☆ *Crown* [B474 Beaconsfield—High Wycombe]: Friendly and very carefully extended Chef & Brewer family dining pub, very welcoming to children, with good generous food in three attractively furnished low-ceilinged bars, one with medieval flooring tiles, interesting varied décor, well kept Courage Directors, decent short wine list, good prompt service; air conditioning, unobtrusive piped music, fruit machine, trivia; perched opp 14th-c church on high ridge with distant views, lots of tables in attractive gardens with good play area, wknd barbecues, open all day *(LYM, David and Michelle Bailey, Matthew Last, Simon Collett-Jones, Ian Dawson, Jill Bickerton, D J Mann, Peter and Elizabeth May, Ian Phillips, B Brewer)*

Penn Street [SU9295]

☆ *Hit or Miss* [off A404 SW of Amersham, then keep on towards Winchmore Hill]: Well laid out low-beamed three-room pub with own cricket ground, pleasant atmosphere, welcoming bustle and helpful service, well kept if not cheap Badger ales, decent wines, log fire, Trivial Pursuit cards, some cricket and chair-making memorabilia, well behaved children over 5 allowed, separate largely no smoking restaurant; may be soft piped music; picnic-sets out in front, pleasant setting *(LYM, Howard Dell, J Hale, Simon Collett-Jones, Graham Johnson, Mike Tucker, Mark and Diane Grist, Cyril S Brown, S Roberts)*

Stewkley [SP8526]

☆ *Carpenters Arms* [junction of Wing and Dunton rds]: Welcoming low-ceilinged village pub with generous reasonably priced fresh home-made food from sandwiches to imaginative main dishes inc speciality pies, well kept ales inc Fullers London Pride and Marstons Pedigree, sociable alsatian called Boon; bookcases in extended dining lounge, darts in jolly little public bar, subdued piped music; garden with play area *(LYM, Marjorie and David Lamb)*

Stoke Goldington [SP8348]

☆ *White Hart* [High St (B526 NW of Newport Pagnell)]: Friendly thatched and beamed stone-built pub with two smartly modernised bars and restaurant, cheerful attentive landlord, good value well presented usual food from sandwiches and baked potatoes up, quick service, Charles Wells beers with a guest such as Greene King Old Speckled Hen, decent coffee; piped music; picnic-sets on sheltered back lawn with play area, footpath network starts just across rd *(George Atkinson, LYM, CMW, JJW)*

Stoke Green [SU9882]

☆ *Red Lion* [off B416 signed Wexham and George Green]: Rambling and roomy refurbished Vintage Inn, lots of little separate areas, pleasant atmosphere, well presented good value food, Bass and another changing ale, good choice of decent wines, log fires, no smoking room, children welcome; tables outside, may be summer barbecues, open all day Fri/Sat *(LYM, Bob and Laura Brock)*

Stony Stratford [SP7840]

☆ *Bull* [High St]: Famous old coaching inn, smartened up but keeping panelling and beams, comfortable lounge bar, nice little area used for (good) coffee with coal-effect fire, small dining room, separate more rustic flagstoned bar with country hardware; decent food, well kept Bass, Benskins, Fullers London Pride and Youngs, friendly service; may be piped pop music; bedrooms *(Ian Phillips, LYM, Karen and Graham Oddey)*

☆ *Cock* [High St]: Comfortable old-fashioned hotel, quiet at lunchtime but lively in the evenings, with leather settles and library chairs on bare boards, good bar food from filled baps to chargrills, very friendly service, well kept Courage Directors, Theakstons and a guest beer; tables out in attractive back courtyard, barbecues; bedrooms *(Ian Phillips, Karen and Graham Oddey, LYM)*

Fox & Hounds [High St]: Friendly 17th-c two-bar pub with pictures and photographs, fresh

flowers, well kept Greene King and Yates, decent cheap lunchtime food from sandwiches and burgers to bargain specials; piped radio, games area with hood skittles, darts, folk, blues or jazz Thurs, Sat and first Tues; tables in walled garden *(Pete Baker, CMW, JJW)*

Taplow [SU9082]

Feathers [opp Cliveden entrance]: Much modernised family dining pub, wide range of reasonably priced enjoyable food, efficient service even when busy, Greenalls ales, decent wines, farm cider; tables in courtyard, play area, dogs allowed only by front picnic-sets *(Brian and Carole Polhill)*

Thornborough [SP7433]

☆ *Lone Tree* [A421 4 miles E of Buckingham; pub named on OS Sheet 165]: Nicely converted old roadside house, open-plan with two side areas and unspoilt feel, friendly service, vast range of home-made traditional food inc unusual sandwiches, local cheeses and good Sun roasts, well kept ales such as Batemans, Black Sheep, Shepherd Neame Spitfire and Youngs Special, big log fire; may be piped classical music *(George Atkinson, Karen and Graham Oddey, Colin Parker, R M Corlett, LYM, Neil Dury)*

Wendover [SP8607]

☆ *Red Lion* [High St]: Bustling and friendly 17th-c inn with wide choice of good value changing food, generous and imaginative, inc fish specialities, Sun lunch and children's dishes in refurbished oak-beamed flagstoned bar and adjacent good value restaurant; four well kept ales such as Henley Ted & Bens Organic Bitter, Youngs Special and one brewed for the pub, good wines, many by the glass, efficient service; can get smoky, dogs allowed till 7; walker-friendly (on Ridgeway Long Distance Path), tables and heaters out behind, with colourful flowering tubs; comfortable bedrooms *(Catherine and Richard Preston, Eric Locker, BB)*

West Wycombe [SU8394]

☆ *George & Dragon* [High St; A40 W of High Wycombe]: Handsome and popular Tudor inn with comfortable colourfully decorated rambling bar, massive beams, sloping walls, big log fire, well kept Courage Best and Directors and guests such as Fullers London Pride and Charles Wells Bombardier, food inc upmarket and good vegetarian dishes, small no smoking family dining room (wknd children's menu); spacious peaceful garden with fenced play area, bedrooms (magnificent oak staircase), handy for West Wycombe Park *(Barbara Wilder, Andy Meaton, Desmond Hall, Piotr Chodzko-Zajko, Chris Glasson, LYM, Susan and John Douglas)*

Whitchurch [SP8020]

☆ *White Swan* [High St]: Homely and pubby thatched two-bar local with well kept Fullers ales, well prepared food, picnic-sets in rambling garden behind *(LYM)*

Wycombe Marsh [SU8992]

Disraeli Arms [Ford St]: Cosy two-room pub with emphasis on food esp cajun, Brakspears, Flowers and Fullers London Pride, good choice of wines, good friendly service, restaurant *(anon)*

Cambridgeshire

Four pubs here have been in all 20 editions of the Guide *so far, two with the same licensees throughout that time: Norman and Pauline Rushton's smart Chequers at Fowlmere, a fine dining pub; and the Queens Head at Newton, kept wonderfully unspoilt by David and Juliet Short. Both seem to get better and better each year. The other two old faithfuls here are the Three Horseshoes at Madingley (a dining pub with elaborate food) and the Haycock at Wansford, which has grown and grown over the years we've known it. To offset these are four pubs making their very first appearance in the main entries this year: the Fitzwilliam Arms at Castor (an interestingly different style of food pub), the relaxing Ancient Shepherds in Fen Ditton, the bustling Navigator at Little Shelford (good authentic thai food) and the Red House at Longstowe (a nice find on the Old North Road). Other pubs doing particularly well here these days are the cheerful White Hart at Bythorn (emphasis on its bistro food), the no smoking Cambridge Blue in Cambridge, the friendly King William IV at Heydon (packed with curios, doing notable vegetarian dishes), the charming Old Bridge Hotel in Huntingdon (stylish if pricy food, good wines, nice place to stay), the Brewery Tap in Peterborough (interesting modern pub brewing its own good beers), and the Anchor at Sutton Gault (well worth tracking down, for its food and atmosphere). With no fewer than seven pubs in the county now qualifying for our cherished Food Award, there's no shortage of places for a special meal out; from among them we select the Chequers at Fowlmere as Cambridgeshire Dining Pub of the Year, for its carefully thought out imaginative food. Drinks prices in the county are slightly higher than the national average – it's now broken through the £2 a pint barrier; we found the cheapest beer in our two Peterborough entries. In the Lucky Dip at the end of the chapter, places to note particularly this year (almost all already inspected and vouched for by us) are the Lion in Buckden, Free Press in Cambridge, John Barleycorn in Duxford, Three Tuns at Fen Drayton, Oliver Twist at Guyhirn, Blue Lion at Hardwick, Plough & Fleece at Horningsea, Plough at Shepreth, Red Lion in Wisbech and Three Blackbirds at Woodditton.*

BARNACK TF0704 Map 5
Millstone ◧

Millstone Lane; off B1443 SE Stamford; turn off School Lane near the Fox

Steady and reliable, this well liked old stone-built village local is run by a particularly friendly and accommodating landlord. It's especially popular for its enjoyable food, so much so that you may need to get there early for a seat, even during the week. As well as their famous home-made pies such as steak in ale, chicken and bacon, minted lamb or pork with apple and cider (all £6.95), there might be home-made soup like good carrot and coriander or broccoli and stilton (£2), sandwiches (from £2.95), freshly baked filled baguettes (£3.25), generous pâté (£3.45), ploughman's, stilton and vegetable crumble or liver and bacon hotpot (£6.95), mixed grill (£8.95), and home-made puddings such as white chocolate and rum torte or home-made blackberry crumble (£2.95); on Thursday and Friday, there's fresh fish from Grimsby (battered haddock or plaice, £6.25). Smaller helpings for OAPs, a straightforward children's menu, and maybe marmalades, jams, pickles and fruit cakes for sale with the funds going to a charity. You may find Stone the ancient pub dog sitting motionless on one of the cushioned wall benches in the traditional timbered bar which is split into comfortably intimate areas, and also has a patterned carpet and high beams weighed down with lots of heavy harness. A little snug displays the memorabilia (including medals from both World Wars) of a former regular. The snug and dining room are no smoking. Beers include consistently well kept Adnams, Everards Old Original and Tiger and an interesting guest on handpump. They also keep a good choice of Gales country wines. In summer the window baskets and window boxes are attractive. *(Recommended by Mr and Mrs J Glover, Michael and Jenny Back, Norma and Keith Bloomfield, Eric Locker, M J Morgan, Anthony Barnes, Roger and Pauline Pearce, Conus and Sarah Elliott, Ted and Jan Whitfield)*

Everards ~ Tenant Aubrey Sinclair Ball ~ Real ale ~ Bar food (not Sun evening) ~ Restaurant ~ (01780) 740296 ~ Children in eating area of bar and restaurant ~ Open 11.30-2.30, 5.30(6 Sat)-11; 12-4, 7-10.30 Sun

BYTHORN TL0575 Map 5
White Hart 🍴 ♀
Village signposted just off A14 Kettering—Cambridge

The main emphasis here is very much on Bennett's Bistro (taking its name from the chatty ebullient landlord Bill), although there remains a good, informal pubby atmosphere. You are welcome to enjoy just a drink – they keep Everards Tiger, Greene King IPA and Abbot, and maybe a guest such as Morlands Old Speckled Hen in good condition on handpump, and there's a well chosen affordable wine list. The popular and interesting food might include home-made soup (£3.50), spicy thai chicken, braised lamb shank, game and Guinness casserole, steak and mushroom pie, tomato, onion and garlic pasta, wild boar sausages, and minted lamb kebabs (all £8.50), and steaks (from £8.95). The restaurant menu (it's no smoking in here) is more elaborate. Much better on the inside than it looks from the exterior, the homely main bar and several linked smallish rooms have a pleasant mix of furnishings, such as a big leather chesterfield, lots of silver teapots and so forth on a carved dresser and in a built-in cabinet, and wing armchairs and attractive tables. One area with rugs on stripped boards has soft pale studded leather chairs and stools, and a cosy log fire in a huge brick fireplace. There are cookery books and plenty of magazines for reading, staff are courteous and friendly, and there's a good mix of customers. *(Recommended by G S B G Dudley, David and Mary Webb, Gordon Tong, Pat and Roger Fereday, Moira and John Cole, A J Bowen, Anthony Barnes, Ian Phillips, R C Wiles, Bob and Maggie Atherton)*

Free house ~ Licensee Bill Bennett ~ Real ale ~ Bar food (not Sun pm, not Mon) ~ Restaurant ~ No credit cards ~ (01832) 710226 ~ Children welcome ~ Open 11-3, 6-11; 12-4 Sun; closed Sun evening, all day Mon

CAMBRIDGE TL4658 Map 5
Anchor 🍺 £
Silver St (where there are punts for hire – with a boatman if needed)

Perhaps this pub sums up what Cambridge is all about. It's in a lazy setting on the bank of the River Cam with punts drifting past its suntrap terrace, but is also the first pub we've come across with internet access – and one of the last with video games. However, we're more likely to be heading there for the eight real ales on handpump which include Boddingtons, Flowers Original, Marstons Pedigree, Whitbread Castle Eden and guests such as Fullers London Pride, Greene King Old Speckled Hen and Youngs Special. Unsurprisingly, it's at its liveliest in term time with plenty of students spreading around the four levels. The entrance area has some nooks and crannies with lots of bric-a-brac, church pews, and a brick fireplace at either end. Upstairs, the pubby bar (no smoking during food service times), has pews and wooden chairs and fine river and Mill Pond views, while the downstairs café-bar has enamel signs on the walls and a mix of interesting tables, settles, farmhouse chairs, and hefty stools on the bare boards. More steps take you down again, to a simpler flagstoned room with french windows leading out to the terrace (which is heated in the evenings). Simple but very good value bar food includes home-made soup (£1.95), filled baked potatoes (£2.95), ploughman's (£4.20), salads (from £4.50), battered cod (£4.70), and usually four daily specials such as steak and ale pie, cauliflower cheese and chicken curry (all £4.75), with puddings such as sticky toffee pudding and apple and blackberry crumble (£2.25); juke box, fruit machine, TV. *(Recommended by Giles and Liz Ridout, John Wooll, Keith Jacob, Mark Stoffan, Michael Buchanan, Paul S McPherson, Rob Fowell, Patricia Beebe, Laura and Stuart Ballantyne)*

Whitbreads ~ Managers Alastair and Sandra Langton ~ Real ale ~ Bar food (12-7 Mon-Thurs; 12-3.45 Fri, Sat; 12-2.30 Sun) ~ (01223) 353554 ~ Children welcome in eating area of bar during food service hours ~ Open 11-11; 11-10.30 Sun

Cambridge Blue ◖ £

85 Gwydir Street

Totally no smoking and completely free of piped music, this quiet backstreet pub is run in the attractively distinctive and friendly style of the couple who made a runaway success of the Free Press in Cambridge a couple of years ago. Its two simple uncluttered rooms have simple, old-fashioned bare-boards-style furnishings with candles on the tables, a big collection of oars and so many rowing photographs that you feel you're browsing through someone's private family album. Beers are picked from interesting, mostly East Anglian but sometimes distantly located small breweries such as Iceni, Hobsons, Milton and Potton with a few from more usual brewers such as Adnams, Nethergate, Woodfordes. There's a decent choice of wines and malt whiskies. Good value, generous home-made food is served in the attractive little conservatory dining area, and might include filled ciabattas (from £2.50), two home-made soups (£2.95), a cold table with game or picnic pies, nut roast, various quiches, and so forth (from £4.25), chilli (£4.75), chicken or vegetable burritos (£5), daily specials such as navarin of lamb or cod and lime leaf pie (£4.75), and puddings such as treacle tart or apricot crumble (£1.95). The surprisingly large back garden is home to a couple of rabbits and a boules pitch. *(Recommended by John Wooll, Hazel and Michael Duncombe, Patricia Beebe, Sue Demont, Tim Barrow, Mike and Mary Carter, Peter J Holmes, the Didler)*

Free house ~ Licensees Chris and Debbie Lloyd ~ Real ale ~ Bar food (12-2.30, 6-9.30) ~ (01223) 361382 ~ Children welcome in conservatory till 9pm ~ Open 12-2.30(3 Sat), 6-11; 12-3, 6-10.30 Sun; closed evening 25 Dec

Eagle ♀ £

Bene't Street

This bustling old stone-fronted town centre coaching inn is worth visiting just for the building. The five rambling rooms (one is no smoking) retain many charming original architectural features. There are lovely worn wooden floors and plenty of original pine panelling, two fireplaces dating back to around 1600, two medieval mullioned windows, and the remains of two possibly medieval wall paintings. The high dark red ceiling has been left unpainted since the war to preserve the signatures of British and American airmen worked in with Zippo lighters, candle smoke and lipstick. The creaky old furniture is nicely in keeping. An attractive cobbled and galleried courtyard is atmospherically screened from the street by sturdy wooden gates and has heavy wooden seats and tables and pretty hanging baskets. The straightforward food is served from a counter in a small back room, and includes filled baguettes (from £4.95), vegetable tikka (£5.45), gammon and egg (£5.85), sausage and mash (£5.95), tagliatelle with chicken and bacon (£6.45), barbecued spare ribs (£7.45), salmon steak with hollandaise (£8.50) and two or three daily specials, too. Well kept Greene King IPA, Abbot and Old Speckled Hen and a guest such as Shepherd Neame Spitfire on handpump; friendly service from well dressed staff. At Christmas, choristers from King's College Choir sing here – perfectly complemented by mulled wine. No children inside. *(Recommended by Terry Mizen, Joel Dobris, John Wooll, Keith and Janet Morris, Martin and Lois Sheldrick, the Didler, Simon Chell, Patricia A Bruce, Patricia Beebe, Rob Fowell, Sue Demont, Tim Barrow)*

Greene King ~ Manager Alastair Morrison ~ Real ale ~ Bar food (12-8.45(8 Fri-Sun)) ~ (01223) 505020 ~ Open 11-11; 12-10.30 Sun

Live & Let Live 🍺 £

40 Mawson Road; off Mill Road SE of centre

You'll find a good mix of customers at this friendly and unpretentious little backstreet local which still has a lively buoyant atmosphere under its new licensees. The heavily timbered brickwork rooms have sturdy varnished pine tables with pale wood chairs on bare boards, real gas lighting, lots of interesting old country bric-a-brac and posters about local forthcoming events; piped music. Part of the bar is no smoking until 9pm, and basic but generous bar food includes home-made soup (£2.25), filled baguettes (from £2.95, hot beef £3.20), vegetable lasagne (£5.25) and one or two daily specials such as liver and bacon or stuffed peppers (£4.25); Saturday morning big breakfast (£4.30) and Sunday roast (£4.95). Well kept Adnams, Everards Tiger and Nethergate Umbel and three or four guests from independent brewers such as Milton, Oakham and Tring and 20 or so malts; friendly service. On Sunday evenings they serve free snacks with the live music. Well behaved dogs are welcome. *(Recommended by Colin and Janet Roe, Patricia Beebe, Giles Francis, Dr David Cockburn, John Brightley)*

Burlison Inns Ltd ~ Lease Alan Kilker ~ Real ale ~ Bar food ~ (01223) 460261 ~ Children welcome in eating area of bar till 8pm ~ Folk most Sun evenings ~ Open 11.30-2.30, 5.30(6 Sat)-11; 12-2, 7-10.30 Sun

CASTOR TL1298 Map 5
Fitzwilliam Arms ♀

Village signposted off A47 just W of Peterborough

Recently taken over by the Cheesemans, who made their previous pub, the Carrington Arms at Moulsoe in Bedfordshire, a popular *Guide* main entry, this thatched stone building has been very attractively reworked as a rather unusual dining pub. The most striking feature is towards the far end, where the foody heart of the pub consists of a smart free-standing green-enamelled cooker, a cabinet of choice meats and fish waiting for the chef-manager's deft chopping and griddling, a shellfish bar with several types of Iranian caviar as well as oysters and so forth, and even a lobster tank. Beyond here, a no smoking room has a striking combination of finely detailed and interesting Mogul-style Indian pictures with elegant spindly black metal furniture, and this somewhat esoteric note echoes elsewhere in the pub's long pleasantly divided bar: Indonesian-style heavy metal and hardwood tables among more orthodox pub ones, some silvery alloy café tables and chairs alongside conventional seats. Well kept Adnams, Brewsters Marquis and Marstons Pedigree on handpump, and a good choice of wines – with shelves of sparkling wine glasses. It's a very well run place, with good quick service, but maybe piped music. The village, now peacefully bypassed, is a pretty one. *(Recommended by anon)*

Free house ~ Licensees Edwin and Trudy Cheeseman ~ Real ale ~ Bar food (12-2, 6.30-10(7-9.30 Sun)) ~ Restaurant ~ (01733) 380251 ~ Children welcome if eating ~ Open 11-3, 6-11; 12-3, 7-10.30 Sun

ELSWORTH TL3163 Map 5
George & Dragon

Off A604 NW of Cambridge, via Boxworth

It's best to book a table at this brick-built dining pub, particularly if you want to enjoy the good value three-course lunch (£10). Very polite smartly uniformed staff will show you to your table and hand you a menu which includes light snacks such as sandwiches (from £3), soup (£3.20), ploughman's (£5), as well as trout fillet (£9), turkey schnitzel with asparagus or chicken in sesame batter with leek and mustard sauce (£9.50), lemon sole or roast duckling (£11) and steaks (from £12) and home-made puddings (£3.25). A pleasant panelled main bar with lots of shiny brassware opens on the left to a slightly elevated no smoking dining area with flowers on comfortable tables, and a good woodburning stove. From here, steps lead down to another quiet no smoking garden room behind, with tables overlooking attractive garden terraces. On the right is a more formal restaurant; soft piped music. Well kept Greene King IPA, Morlands Old Speckled Hen, and Ruddles County on handpump, and decent wines. *(Recommended by Michael and Jenny Back, Martin and Lois Sheldrick, Rob Fowell, O K Smyth, Eric George, Maysie Thompson, Keith and Janet Morris, Penny Miles)*

Free house ~ Licensees Barrie and Marion Ashworth ~ Real ale ~ Bar food (not Sun evening) ~ Restaurant ~ (01954) 267236 ~ Children in eating area of bar, restaurant and family room ~ Open 11-3, 6-11; 12-2.30 Sun; closed Sun evening

ELTON TL0893 Map 5
Black Horse
B671 off A605 W of Peterborough and A1(M); Overend

There's a cheery atmosphere here, with little to suggest that this nice old place was once the village morgue – it's also said to have its own dungeon. It has a homely and comfortable mix of furniture, with no two tables and chairs seeming the same, roaring fires, hop-strung beams, antique prints, and lots of ornaments and bric-a-brac including an intriguing ancient radio set. Dining areas at each end of the bar have parquet flooring and tiles, and the stripped-stone back lounge towards the restaurant has an interesting fireplace. The main emphasis here is on an interesting choice of food which might include home-made soup (£3.75), sandwiches (from £3.65), filled baguettes such as emmenthal and red pepper (from £4.95), goats cheese salad or seafood medley (£5.95), mussels cassoulet (£6.95/£10.95), ploughman's (from £7.25), steak and kidney or vegetable pies (£9.95), roast chicken breast stuffed with black cherry and pork and served with an orange butter sauce (£12.50), three or four fish dishes such as baked cod with crispy noodles and a sage and onion sauce (£12.95), rack of lamb with kidneys and a mustard sauce (£14.95), and home-made puddings such as lemon tart with citrus sorbet, banoffi pie or summer fruit pudding with mascarpone (all £4.95). Well kept Bass, Caledonian Deuchars IPA and a guest such as Nethergate Suffolk County on handpump, good value wines, and good service from friendly staff; the family area is no smoking. There are tables, some shaded by horse chestnut trees in a garden that's prettily divided into separate areas. Behind the low-built pub is Elton Hall, and this attractive bypassed village has a lovely Saxon church (and an oak which is said to have the widest spread in Europe). *(Recommended by Sally Anne and Peter Goodale, Richard Lewis, George Atkinson)*

Free house ~ Licensee John Clennell ~ Real ale ~ Bar food (12-2.30, 6-9.30) ~ Restaurant ~ (01832) 280240 ~ Children welcome ~ Open 12-3, 6-11; 12-4, 6-11.30 Sat; 12-6 Sun; closed Sun evening

ELY TL5380 Map 5
Fountain ◖
Corner of Barton Square and Silver Street

This basic but genteel town corner pub takes a very simple traditional approach: well kept beers, no food, and a pleasant atmosphere that attracts a real mix of age groups. Though very close to the cathedral it escapes the tourists, and is the kind of place to come for a chat rather than to shout over music or fruit machines. Old cartoons, local photographs, regional maps and mementoes of the neighbouring King's School punctuate the elegant dark pink walls, and neatly tied-back curtains hang from golden rails above the big windows. Above one fireplace is a stuffed pike in a case, and there are a few antlers dotted about – not to mention a duck at one end of the bar. Adnams Southwold and Broadside, Fullers London Pride, and a changing guest such as Charles Wells Bombardier or Everards Tiger on handpump; very efficient service. A couple of tables are squeezed on to a tiny back terrace. Note the limited opening times, and a couple of readers have found it closed even then so it might be best to ring first. *(Recommended by Lynn Sharpless, Bob Eardley, the Didler)*

Free house ~ Licensees John and Judith Borland ~ Real ale ~ No credit cards ~ (01353) 663122 ~ Children welcome away from bar and until 8pm ~ Open 5-11; 12-2, 6-11 Sat; 12-2, 7-10.30 Sun

FEN DITTON TL4860 Map 5
Ancient Shepherds
Off B1047 at Green End, The River signpost, just NE of Cambridge

The nicest room at this solidly beamed old place is the central one, with lots of fat dark red button-back leather settees and armchairs, low solid Indonesian tables, heavy drapes around a window seat with big scatter cushions, and a warm coal fire. Above a black dado the walls (and ceiling) are dark pink, and decorated with little steeplechasing and riding (or comic fox and policeman) prints, and the lighting is soothing: evidently just the place for Cambridge researchers to restore their equilibrium. On the right is a smallish convivial bar with Adnams and Flowers IPA on handpump, and another coal fire; on the left a pleasant restaurant. Bar food includes sandwiches (from £3), ploughman's (from £5.95) and steak baguettes (£6.25), as well as a menu that changes every six weeks or so but might include Newmarket sausages and gravy (£7.25), liver and bacon (£8), steak and ale pie (£8.50), wild mushroom lasagne (£8.95) and fish such as smoked haddock or cajun-style bass (up to £14). The friendly pub dog is called Hugo. *(Recommended by Roy and Margaret Jones, Roy Bromell, John Shields)*

Pubmaster ~ Lease J M Harrington ~ Real ale ~ Bar food (not Sun evening) ~ Restaurant ~ (01223) 293280 ~ Children in restaurant ~ Open 12-3, 6-11; 12-5 Sun; closed Sun evening

FORDHAM TL6270 Map 5
White Pheasant ♀
Market Street; B1085, off A142 and A11 N of Newmarket

This fresh-feeling simply decorated dining pub is under the same management as the very successful Red Lion at Icklingham over in Suffolk, and the Crown & Punchbowl at Horningsea in this county, and like them specialises in good imaginative food: soup of the day (£3.55), chicken liver pâté (£3.75), prawn cocktail (£4.95), Newmarket sausage and mash (£6.10), lambs liver, bacon and onion gravy (£7.75), pork chops with apple sauce (£9.57), chicken breast with sherry and mushroom sauce (£10.95), daily specials such as salmon and cod fishcakes with tomato and chive sauce (£6.10), and roast beef with bourguignon sauce (£7.85), and puddings like apple crumble and lemon and ginger crunch tart (£3.95). The smallish but airy bar has a mix of big farmhouse tables and chairs, a couple of turkey rugs on the bare boards, folded white napkins and flowers in bottles on the tables, prints and simple black iron candle lamps on white walls, some stripped brickwork and a cheery log fire at one end. One or two steps lead down to a small similarly furnished green-carpeted room. Service is friendly and helpful (they try to help out people with food allergies), and they have well kept Adnams and Tolly Cobbold Original on handpump from the horseshoe bar that faces the entrance, and good house wines; maybe piped light jazz or classical music *(Recommended by Ian and Nita Cooper, J H Ling)*

Excalibur ~ Licensees Ian Hubbert and Jonathan Gates ~ Real ale ~ Bar food (12-2.30, 6-10(7-9 Sun)) ~ Restaurant ~ (01638) 720414 ~ Children welcome ~ Open 12-3, 6-11(7-10.30 Sun)

If we know a pub has a no smoking area, we say so.

FOWLMERE TL4245 Map 5

Chequers 🏮 ♟

B1368

Cambridgeshire Dining Pub of the Year

The thoughtfully creative menu at this civilised and professionally run 16th-c dining pub will be very appealing if you're looking for a change from the usual pub fare. Vegetable and salad accompaniments are well chosen to complement each imaginative dish. The menu changes from time to time but you might expect white Normandy onion and chicken soup with gruyère croutons (£3.20), smoked haddock with chopped chives and sliced tomatoes and baked with cream and lancashire cheese (£5.40), brochette of king prawns with aïoli and thai dipping sauce (£7.80), sautéed pigeon breasts on raw spinach and truffle oil salad or duck and port pâté (£5.20), creamy aubergine crumble with falafel, fried okra, tomatoes and fennel and orange salad (£7.60), navarin of lamb with baked winter vegetables and dumplings (£8.60), grilled wild venison fillet on blackberry and veal jus with onion confit, potato and celeriac rösti and baby spinach and truffle oil salad (£13.80), and puddings such as treacle, orange and coconut tart or hot date sponge with sticky toffee sauce (£3.90) and English cheeses (£4); Sunday roast beef (£11.20). The attractively priced fine wines by the glass (including vintage and late-bottled ports) are particularly well chosen. There's also a good list of malt whiskies, well kept Adnams with a guest such as Gales HSB or Timothy Taylors Landlord on handpump, freshly squeezed orange juice, and several brandies. Two warm and cosy comfortably furnished communicating rooms downstairs have an open log fire – look out for the priest's hole above the bar. Upstairs there are beams, wall timbering and some interesting moulded plasterwork above the fireplace. The airy no smoking conservatory overlooks white tables under cocktail parasols among flowers and shrub roses in a charming well tended floodlit garden. *(Recommended by Michael and Jenny Back, Alan Jones, Mrs Jackie Williams, Dr David Cockburn, Tony Beaulah, JMC, Kay Vowles, Ian Phillips, K Carr-Brion, R C Wiles, Martin and Lois Sheldrick, Hilary Edwards, Peter Mueller)*

Free house ~ Licensees Norman and Pauline Rushton ~ Real ale ~ Bar food ~ Restaurant ~ (01763) 208369 ~ Children welcome lunchtimes ~ Open 11.30-2.30, 6-11; 12-2.30, 7-10.30 Sun; closed 25 Dec

GOREFIELD TF4111 Map 8

Woodmans Cottage

Main St; off B1169 W of Wisbech

The spacious modernised bar at this friendly village local rambles back around the bar counter, with leatherette stools and brocaded banquettes around the tables on its carpet. There's a big collection of china plates in a comfortable side eating area, as well as 1920s prints on its stripped brick walls; the Cellar is no smoking, and beyond is an attractive pitched-ceiling restaurant – best to book early. At the other end of the pub, a games area has darts, pool, fruit machine, TV, cribbage, dominoes and a juke box. One of the main draws here is the popular pubby food that includes toasties (from £1.50), burgers (from £2), omelettes or ploughman's (from £4), half a dozen vegetarian meals including vegetable curry (£6.50), steak and kidney pie (£6.75), steaks (from £8.50), a huge array of counter-displayed home-made puddings (£3), and quite a few daily specials such as lamb shank with mint gravy and turkey ham stilton (£6.50). Well kept Greene King IPA and Abbot and a couple of guests such as Everards Tiger or Morlands Old Speckled Hen on handpump; piped music. There's a children's play area, and tables out in a sheltered back terrace, with a few more on a front verandah. *(Recommended by Michael and Jenny Back, R C Wiles, Ian Phillips)*

Free house ~ Licensees R and J Martin, M and R Tuck ~ Real ale ~ Bar food (till 10) ~ Restaurant ~ (01945) 870669 ~ Children in eating area of bar and restaurant ~ Live entertainment Fri evenings monthly ~ Open 11-3, 7-11; 12-3, 7-10.30 Sun

HEYDON TL4340 Map 5
King William IV 🍷
Off A505 W of M11 junction 10

For years the licensee here, Elizabeth Nicholls, has led the way forward in vegetarian cooking in pubs, showing others what can easily be done with a little extra thought and effort. Last year this immaculately run place won our National Vegetarian Pub of the Year award. It isn't just that they offer around a dozen vegetarian dishes, it's the fact that they are genuinely interesting, too: asparagus, broccoli and roquefort lattice puff with a cheese fondue, cashew and pine kernel stir fry with noodles and crackers, baked field mushrooms with mediterranean fruits and emmenthal crust, ricotta, leek and sweet chestnut crumble, nutty and date curry, and nutmeg, spinach and cream cheese crispy pancakes with a tomato and chive sauce (from £7.95). Meat lovers are by no means left out though, with other enjoyable bar food including lunchtime sandwiches (from £3.15), filled baguettes (from £4), bangers and mash (£6.95), steak and kidney shortcrust pie (£7.95), confit of duck or beef and mushrooms in stout with herb dumplings (£9.25), braised lamb shank with redcurrant jus or grilled swordfish steak with avocado and mango salsa (£10.95), with puddings like bread and butter pudding and fresh cream mousse or dark chocolate torte with raspberry coulis (from £4.95). Part of the restaurant is no smoking. The nooks and crannies of the beamed rambling rooms, warmed in winter by a log fire, are crowded with a delightful jumble of rustic implements like ploughshares, yokes and iron tools as well as cowbells, beer steins, samovars, cut-glass, brass or black wrought-iron lamps, copper-bound casks and milk ewers, harness, horsebrasses, smith's bellows, and decorative plates and china ornaments. Half a dozen well kept real ales include Adnams, Fullers London Pride, Greene King IPA and Abbot and Ruddles County and a guest such as Morrells Graduate on handpump. They'll also do you a cocktail here; friendly, efficient staff. Fruit machine and piped music. A new wooden deck has teak furniture and outdoor heaters, and there are more seats in the pretty garden. *(Recommended by Jack Clarfelt, Philip and Julia Evans, Keith and Janet Morris, Martin and Lois Sheldrick, S Horsley)*

Free house ~ Licensee Elizabeth Nicholls ~ Real ale ~ Bar food (till 10 (9.30 Sun)) ~ Restaurant ~ (01763) 838773 ~ Children welcome in snug ~ Open 12-2.30, 6(6.30 winter)-11; 12-3, 7-10.30 Sun; closed 25 Dec

HINXTON TL4945 Map 5
Red Lion
Between junctions 9 and 10, M11; just off A1301 S of Gt Shefford

There's a cheery atmosphere at this pretty pink-washed twin-gabled old pub which is especially popular for its very well prepared food. The interesting and regularly changing menu might include lunchtime sandwiches (from £1.95), home-made soup (£3.75), home-made pâté with onion marmalade (£4.25), grilled goats cheese with red onion and apricot chutney (£4.75), cheese basket with garlic mushrooms and mozzarella (£4.95), roast mediterranean vegetables and pasta with parmesan shavings and garlic ciabatta (£7.50), lamb souvlakia with tabouleh and a pie of the week such as steak and ale (£8.75), Malaysian chicken curry (£8.95), fried tiger prawns with mango, avocado and chilli salsa and toasted ciabatta (£13.95), and home-made puddings such as crème caramel, apricot bread and butter pudding and sticky toffee with mascarpone and poached pear (£3.25). The dusky mainly open-plan bustling bar has leather chesterfields on wooden floors and a chatty amazon parrot called George is occasionally around; trivia and cribbage. The smart no smoking restaurant is filled with mirrors, pictures, grandfather and assorted clocks. Real ales include well kept Adnams, Greene King IPA and a couple of guests such as Everards Tiger and Woodfordes Wherry on handpump, and Adnams wines too. There are picnic-sets and a pleasant terrace in the tidy and attractive garden (the magnolia's nice in spring). The pub is not far from Duxford Aeroplane Museum. *(Recommended by Mrs V Brown, Jenny and Dave Hughes, Patricia Beebe, David and Mary Webb, J and D Boutwood, F M Craven, Eric Locker, Ian Phillips)*

Free house ~ Licensees Jim and Lynda Crawford ~ Real ale ~ Bar food ~ Restaurant ~ (01799) 530601 ~ Children over 10 in eating area of bar ~ Open 11-2.30, 6-11; 12-2.30, 7-10.30 Sun; closed evenings 25 and 26 Dec

HORNINGSEA TL4962 Map 5
Crown & Punchbowl

Just NE of Cambridge; first slip-road off A14 heading E after A10, then left at T; or via B1047 Fen Ditton road off A1303

Moving steadily in a more restauranty direction, this friendly and rather civilised, spacious low-beamed pub has four or five open-plan rooms which work their way round the central counter. It's fairly simply but atmospherically decorated with good solid stripped pine tables which are well spaced on the mainly bare boards and some striking dark blue paintwork picking out the woodwork. The little bar area has a nice pulpit at one end and some stained glass and a big blue and white flag. There are a few big prints and mirrors dotted around and simple black iron candle lamps, and big stag's head on the cream walls; piped classical music. There are two intimate and slightly separate feeling little conservatory areas, one of which has recently been refurbished. They aim to have over a dozen fresh fish dishes a day such as scallops with hazelnut and basil butter (£8.95), ling with tomato sauce and cheese (£10.95) and bass with chilli butter or barracuda with black peppercorn sauce (£15.95), and seasonal game dishes such as partridge breast fillets with honey and mango sauce (£12.95) and game grill (£15.95). Other interesting and well prepared bar food might include soup (£4.25), warm bacon and mushroom salad (£5.25), sausages and mash (£6.25), leek, potato and mushroom layer in cream sauce (£7.95), Mexican chicken and bacon salad (£8.95), sardines in garlic butter (£9.95) and rabbit with plum sauce (£11.55). The two or three well kept real ales on handpump might be from Adnams, Morlands or Tolly, also country wines and elderflower pressé. There are seats in the simple back garden, and you can just catch a glimpse of the River Cam from the end of the car park. We haven't heard from readers yet about the newly refurbished bedrooms. The Red Lion in Icklingham and the White Pheasant at Fordham are in the same small group. *(Recommended by Ian Phillips, John Wooll, Kevin Thorpe, Brian Kneale, Charles and Pauline Stride)*

Excalibur ~ Licensees Jonathan Gates and Ian Hubbert ~ Real ale ~ Bar food (till 10(9 Sun)) ~ Restaurant ~ (01223) 860643 ~ Children welcome ~ Open 12-3, 6-11(7-10.30 Sun); closed 25 Dec and 26 Dec, 1 Jan evenings ~ Bedrooms: £50B/£85B

HUNTINGDON TL2371 Map 5
Old Bridge Hotel ★ ⑭ ♀ ⇌

1 High St; just off B1043 entering town from the easternmost A604 sliproad

A first view of the handsomely elegant exterior of this 18th-c building – once a private bank – is a lovely introduction to the elegantly civilised time you'll enjoy here. It's tucked away in a good spot by the River Great Ouse with its own landing stage, and tables on the well kept garden's waterside terraces (unfortunately there may be some traffic noise out here). The bar, with its fine polished floorboards, good log fire, and quietly chatty atmosphere, serves three well kept real ales including Adnams Bitter and a couple of guests such as City of Cambridge Hobsons Choice and Potton Shambles on handpump. An excellent wine list includes a really fine choice by the glass, there's also freshly squeezed orange juice and smoothies, and good coffee, too. The main emphasis is on the excellent, imaginative food (though not cheap) which is served in the big no smoking airy Terrace with its lovely verdant murals, or in the slightly more formal, panelled, no smoking restaurant. The seasonally styled menu changes once a month but might include spinach soup with nutmeg cream (£4.50), braised leek, smoked quail eggs and hazelnuts (£5), marinated raw tuna with chilli, hot Asian spices and mooli (£7), braised shoulder of lamb with rosemary, tomato, garlic, mashed potato and roasted root vegetables (£12), bass fillet with rösti potato, kale, fennel and cardamom sauce (£18), braised pork with ginger and hot spicy green vegetables salad (£13), beef fillet with potato truffle gratin, buttered cabbage and black pudding (£18); you may want to order additional vegetables (from £2). They will do smaller helpings of some of the dishes for children. Generally quite continental puddings might include lemon or chocolate tart, pears roasted in calvados with cinnamon ice cream, sticky toffee pudding with caramel sauce or pistachio soufflé with chocolate ice cream (£4.50-£7) and a very good cheese platter (£6). Very good waitress service. *(Recommended by David R Crafts, R C Wiles, Martin and Lois Sheldrick, J F M and M West, Andy Sinden, Louise Harrington, Peter Mueller, Ian Phillips, Mrs Thomas, Gordon Tong, Michael Sargent; also in* The Good Hotel Guide*)*

Huntsbridge ~ Licensee Martin Lee ~ Real ale ~ Bar food (12-2.15, 6.30-9.30) ~ Restaurant ~ (01480) 424300 ~ Children welcome ~ Open 11-3, 6-11; 12-3, 7-10.30 Sun ~ Bedrooms: £80B/£100B

KEYSTON TL0475 Map 5

Pheasant ⑪ ♀

Village loop road; from A604 SE of Thrapston, right on to B663

This civilised place is well known for its imaginative menu and high standard of cooking. Changing dishes might include pea soup with crumbled goats cheese and minted olive oil (£4.95), marinated fresh tuna on raw fennel and lemon salad with sorrel (£6.50), fishcakes on buttered spinach or potato gnocchi with broad beans, pea shoots, lemon and fresh parmesan (£7.95), linguini pasta with moules marinières (£8.50), sausage and mash with caramelised onion chutney (£9), smoked and roast chicken breast with truffled spring cabbage (£12.95), skirt of Aberdeenshire beef with watercress purée, celeriac gratin and mushrooms (£14.50) and puddings such as soft almond meringue with compote of summer berries and basil ice cream or orange tart with bitter chocolate sorbet (£5.50), hot raspberry souffle with hazelnut ice cream (£6.95), and cheese platter (£5.95); two course set lunch (£9.90 Mon-Sat). An exceptionally good wine list includes an interesting choice of reasonably priced bottles and around 20 wines by the glass (plus two champagnes). There's also fine port and sherry, freshly squeezed juices, and well kept Adnams Bitter with changing guests such as Potton Village Bike and Nethergate Old Growler. The oak beamed spreading bar has open fires, simple wooden tables and chairs, guns on the pink walls, country paintings and a restful atmosphere. The more formal little restaurant is no smoking. Service is courteous and efficient. Wooden tables are set in front of the pub. *(Recommended by Ian Phillips, Dr B and Mrs P B Baker, Mandy and Simon King, J F M and M West, Mike and Heather Watson, R C Wiles, Brian Kneale, Martin and Lois Sheldrick, Stephen, Julie and Hayley Brown, Michael Sargent, Gwen and Peter Andrews, O K Smyth, Gordon Tong, Howard and Margaret Buchanan, Di and Mike Gillam)*

Huntsbridge ~ Licensee Clive Dixon ~ Real ale ~ Bar food ~ Restaurant ~ (01832) 710241 ~ Children welcome ~ Open 12-2, 6.30(6 Sat)-10.30; 12-2, 7-9.30 Sun; closed 25/26 Dec, 1 Jan evenings

LITTLE SHELFORD TL4451 Map 5

Navigator

2½ miles from M11 junction 11: A10 towards Royston, then left at Hauxton, The Shelfords signpost

The lively bustle here, at lunchtime and in the evenings, combines the conviviality of a good local with the expectant relish of a place where the food really counts for something. There's an easy mix of drinkers and diners, with the best place for eating being up a step on the right: candles on tables set close together on the tiled floor, a mix of pews, wheelback chairs and spindleback elbow chairs, and a hot coal fire in the cast-iron fireplace. In the rest of the pub, which is carpeted and has pine-panelled walls, the furnishings are much the same, with plenty of brown beams. There's a clue to the food in the oriental embroidered black wall decorations: the Thai lady chef produces good thai dishes in varying strengths such as tum yum soups from (£6.80, seafood £10.40), green vegetarian curry (£6.80), panang beef (£7.60), prawn curry (£9.40), an interesting mixed seafood curry (£9.50) and roast duck curry (£10.40). Well kept Greene King IPA, Abbot and Old Speckled Hen on handpump or tapped from the cask; maybe piped pop music. There are a few picnic-sets on some grass under an ash tree out beyond the small car park. *(Recommended by M A C Rutherford, Catherine and Richard Preston)*

Greene King ~ Tenant Chris Adomite ~ Real ale ~ Bar food (not Mon/Sat lunchtime, Sun evening) ~ (01223) 843901 ~ Children welcome ~ Open 11-2.30, 6-11; 12-2, 7-10.30 Sun; closed Mon/Sat lunchtime

LONGSTOWE TL3154 Map 5
Red House 🚩

Old North Road; A1198 Royston—Huntingdon, S of village

A roadside pub of the sort that you might all too easily whizz past without a second glance, this well repays a stop. The atmosphere has that relaxed and easy-going feel that so often seems to envelop people who spend much time with horses – and there's ample evidence of where the licensees' interest lies, from the fox mask and horse tack through quite a few good hunting prints to the rosettes mounted proudly behind the bar. From the bar counter with its red-tiled floor go round to the right, past the big log fire with its fat back kettle and a couple of tables beside it, and step down into another dark-tiled area with chintzy easy chairs and settees; a very comfortable haunt, looking out into a sheltered and attractive little garden with picnic-sets. On the left is an attractive restaurant area. On our inspection visit, the changing well kept beers on handpump were Greene King IPA, Fenland Hell & High Water (yes, we were there early last winter) and Potton Shambles; daily papers, maybe piped music. Bar food includes sandwiches (from £2.95), soup (£3.45), sausages and mash with mushy peas (£7.25), kidney bean and red pepper goulash (£7.50), poached salmon with asparagus and hollandaise (£11.50), mixed grill (£13.95), and daily specials such as chicken tikka masala or pasta carbonara (£7.95) and home-made puddings (£3.25). *(Recommended by Nick Marshall)*

Free house ~ Licensees Gillian and Martin Willis ~ Real ale ~ Bar food (12-2, 6-9.30; 12-2.30, 7.30-9.30 Sun) ~ (01954) 718480 ~ Children welcome in restaurant if eating ~ Open 12-3, 5.30-11(7.30-10.30 Sun); closed Mon am

MADINGLEY TL3960 Map 5
Three Horseshoes 🍴 ♀

Off A1303 W of Cambridge

These days this attractive and civilised thatched dining pub will please the adventurous diner who's willing to follow the chef on his culinary explorations, daringly mixing ingredients from all corners of the world in surprising combinations. It is very popular here so you may struggle just to get a reservation. There is a slightly simpler bar menu – toasted brioche with peach, onion and mustard chutney, rocket and parma ham (£4.50), penne with saffron butter and pecorino (£6.50) or pizzetta with piquillo peppers, tapenade, ricotta and thyme (£7.50), but most people are here for the very innovative à la carte menu which is served in the bar or conservatory-restaurant, and changes monthly. You might find spring vegetable soup with pecorino crostini (£4.50), steamed crab custard with sweetcorn purée and a crab, fennel, dill and sweet potato salad (£6), peppered carpaccio with celeriac and horseradish pannacotta, olive and marjoram relish and hot mustard oil (£7.50), tea-smoked duck with soba noodles, thai grass, enoki mushrooms, green tea, miso broth and white truffle oil (£6.50), salmon fillet with green herb risoni, tempura green beans, spinach salad and red wine and mustard sauce (£13.50), fried venison loin with star anise spätzle, fried bok choi, shi-itake mushrooms and oyster sauce and chilli sambal (£14.95), roast halibut with wild mushroom crust, truffle and bacon mash, parsley and garlic purée, asparagus saltimbocca and truffle aïoli (£14.75), steamed bass with prawn-stuffed aubergine, szechuan pickled cucumber and kombu salad with shallot and ginger oil (£16.95); creatively prepared vegetables (£3). Puddings might include caramelised lemon tart or tahini and honey spice cake with honey and saffron figs and crème fraîche or coconut pannacotta with mango and chilli sorbet and coconut mango salad (from £4.75). The pleasantly relaxed little no smoking airy bar has an open fire, simple wooden tables and chairs on the bare floorboards, stools at the bar and pictures on the Wedgwood green walls. An outstanding wine list includes around 20 by the glass, plus sweet wines and ports, and there are two or three real ales on handpump which might be Adnams Southwold, Batemans XXXB or Everards Tiger. *(Recommended by Michael Sargent, Martin and Lois Sheldrick, Keith and Janet Morris, Mr and Mrs J Glover, David and Mary Webb, J Hale, Brian Root, John Shields, Maysie Thompson, Patricia Beebe, B N F and M Parkin, Richard Siebert, Terry Mizen, R C Wiles, Penny Miles)*

Huntsbridge ~ Licensee Richard Stokes ~ Real ale ~ Bar food ~ Restaurant ~ (01954) 210221 ~ Children welcome ~ Open 11.30-2.30, 6-11; 12-2.30, 7-10.30 Sun

NEWTON TL4349 Map 5
Queens Head ★ ◖ £

2½ miles from M11 junction 11; A10 towards Royston, then left on to B1368

Splendid in its genuine simplicity, this unspoilt friendly country pub has been traditionally run by the same licensee for more than quarter of a century. Each year we're all relieved to know that once again there's been absolutely no change since the year before, and the year before that and so on (we're not counting the fact that the price of a baked potato or mug of soup went up by 10p). There's always a good crowd of locals – even on a Monday lunchtime, and visitors love it too. The well worn main bar has a low ceiling and crooked beams, bare wooden benches and seats built into the walls, paintings on the cream walls, and bow windows. A curved high-backed settle stands on the yellow tiled floor, a loudly ticking clock marks the unchanging time here while a lovely big log fire heartily warms the place. The little carpeted saloon is similar but cosier. Adnams Bitter and Broadside are tapped straight from the barrel, with Regatta in summer, Old Ale in winter and Tally Ho at Christmas, Crone's and Cassell's ciders, and fresh orange and organic apple juice. Darts in a no smoking side room, with shove-ha'penny, table skittles, dominoes, cribbage, and nine men's morris. Basic, hearty food is limited to a range of very good value lunchtime sandwiches (from £2) including enjoyable roast beef ones, and mugs of lovely home-made brown soup and filled baked potatoes (both £2.40); in the evening and on Sunday lunchtime they serve plates of excellent cold meat, smoked salmon, cheeses and pâté (from £3.50). There are seats in front of the pub, with its vine trellis. *(Recommended by John Shields, Ian Phillips, Duncan Slater, Pat and Tony Martin, Pam and David Bailey, Martin and Lois Sheldrick, Keith and Janet Morris, R C Wiles, M A C Rutherford, Klaus and Elizabeth Leist, Rob Fowell, Michael Buchanan, Christine and Neil Townend, Susan and Nigel Wilson, Jonathan Tong, Tony Beaulah, R E Davidson)*

Free house ~ Licensees David and Juliet Short ~ Real ale ~ Bar food (not 25 Dec) ~ (01223) 870436 ~ Very well behaved children in eating area of bar ~ Open 11.30-2.30, 6-11; 12-2.30, 7-10.30 Sun; closed 25 Dec

PETERBOROUGH TL1999 Map 5
Brewery Tap ◖ £

Opposite Queensgate car park

A good modern feeling entry for the *Guide*, this American-style place is a striking conversion of an old labour exchange, and is said to be one of the largest microbreweries in Europe. Contemporary industrial décor continues throughout its vast open-plan areas, with blue-painted iron pillars holding up a steel-corded mezzanine level, light wood and stone floors, and hugely enlarged and framed newspaper cuttings on its light orange walls. It's stylishly lit by a giant suspended steel ring with bulbs running around the rim, and steel-meshed wall lights. A band of chequered floor tiles traces the path of the long sculpted light wood bar counter which is boldly backed by an impressive display of uniform wine bottles in a ceiling-high wall of wooden cubes. A huge glass wall on one side gives a view of the massive copper-banded stainless brewing vessels that produce the award-winning Oakham beers. Up to a dozen real ales on handpump might include Bishops Farewell, Harlequin, Helterskelter, JHB, Old Tosspot and White Dwarf, all from the brewery here, with guests from other independent brewers like Elgoods, Newby Wyke and Payn. The staff are young and friendly, and there's a surprisingly mixed clientele, though the piped music may be a bit loud for some. We're told it gets very busy at night, and there might be an entry fee on Friday and Saturday nights. Thai bar food includes tempura vegetables (£2.75), spring rolls or won ton (£2.90), chicken satay or dim sum (£3.50), green, red or yellow curries or beef with oyster sauce, peppers, mushrooms and spring onions (£4.50), noodles stir fried with sweet radish, spring onions, peanuts, egg and either tiger prawns or vegetables (£4.95), aromatic duck stir fried in tamarind sauce with cashew nuts (£5.50), and good value set menus. It's owned by the same people as Charters. *(Recommended by Peter H Stallard, Richard Lewis, Ian Phillips, the Didler, JP, PP, Stephen, Julie and Hayley Brown, Ted and Jan Whitfield, M J Morgan)*

Own brew ~ Licensee Neil Poulter ~ Real ale ~ Bar food (all day Fri/Sat) ~ (01733) 358500 ~ No children ~ DJ Fri/Sat evenings, live bands wkdays ~ Open 12-11(till 1.30 am Fri/Sat); 12-10.30 Sun

Charters 🍺 £

Town Bridge, S side

Worth a visit for its novelty value alone, but actually a worthy entry in its own right, this unusual pub is housed in a remarkable conversion of a sturdy 1907 commercial Dutch grain barge afloat on the River Nene. There's plenty of seating in the well timbered sizeable nautically themed bar which is below decks in the cargo holds; above deck a glazed restaurant replaces the tarpaulins that used to cover the hold. It's a popular place with a bustling lively atmosphere, piped music and friendly staff. Up to a dozen handpumps serve quickly changing ales such as well kept Bass, Everards Tiger, Fullers London Pride, beers from the owner's own nearby microbrewery (see the Brewery Tap entry above) like Oakham JHB (very cheap), Bishops Farewell and Old Tosspot, and guests from brewers such as Black Sheep, Cottage, Iceni and Fenland. Simple but good value bar food includes soup (£1.75), filled baguettes (from £2), steak and ale, chilli or mushroom stroganoff over fries (£2.35), filled baked potatoes (from £2.75), burger (from £3.95), lasagne or fish and chips (£4.95), roast chicken breast (£5.25); maybe barbecues in summer. Landlubbers can opt for tables in one of the biggest pub gardens in the city, often overrun with rabbits. *(Recommended by Richard Lewis, the Didler, Ted and Jan Whitfield, JP, PP, Stephen, Julie and Hayley Brown)*

Free house ~ Licensee Paul Hook ~ Real ale ~ Bar food (12-2.30, 6-9.30) ~ Restaurant (evening) ~ (01733) 315700 ~ Children in eating area of bar and restaurant ~ Open 12-11(10.30 Sun)

SPALDWICK TL1372 Map 5

George

Just off A14 W of Huntingdon

Recently bought from Charles Wells by the licensee here, this very well liked black beamed pub has otherwise remained largely unchanged. Even when busy – which it usually is – the staff here are friendly and helpful. There's a chatty local atmosphere in the red-carpeted bar which also has pewter mugs hanging from the black beams, a mix of understated comfortable seats grouped cosily around little tables, each with a posy of flowers in a vase on a lace doyley, and a candle as well as nice little prints on the walls and some house plants; piped music, pool and fruit machine. To be sure of a table it's best to book if you're coming to enjoy the popular food: red thai chicken curry (£6.50), fresh battered Grimsby cod, grilled sardines, and breaded pork with pepper sauce (all £6.95), breast of chicken stuffed with salmon and watercress (£8.95), roast duck with apple sauce or rump steak (£8.95), fresh grilled lemon sole (£9.95) and baked bass (£11.95); the restaurant is no smoking. Their three well kept real ales are Charles Wells Bombardier and Eagle IPA and Adnams Broadside on handpump. *(Recommended by Dr Brian and Mrs Anne Hamilton, Stephen, Julie and Hayley Brown, David and Mary Webb, Eric Locker, Margaret and Roy Randle, George Atkinson, Geoffrey and Brenda Wilson, Michael Sargent)*

Free house ~ Licensee Mr Watson ~ Real ale ~ Bar food (12-2, 7-10) ~ Restaurant ~ (01480) 890293 ~ Children in restaurant ~ Open 12-3, 6-11(7-10.30 Sun)

STILTON TL1689 Map 5
Bell ♀ 🛏

High Street; village signposted from A1 S of Peterborough

Dick Turpin is alleged to have hidden from the law for nine weeks at this elegant 16th-c old stone coaching inn and once inside it's not hard to imagine the pub as it was in those days. The two neatly kept bars have bow windows, sturdy upright wooden seats on flagstone floors, a large warm log fire in a handsome stone fireplace and a giant pair of blacksmith's bellows hanging in the middle of the front bar. There are also big prints of sailing and winter coaching scenes on the partly stripped walls and plush-cushioned button-back built-in banquettes; backgammon, dominoes, cribbage and piped music. Well kept Greene King Abbot, Marstons Pedigree, Oakham JHB and a guest such as Burton Bridge on handpump, and a good choice of wines by the glass. Reliably enjoyable bar food is served in generous helpings, and might include broccoli and stilton soup (£3.50), chicken liver and garlic pâté with red onion marmalade (£4.50), chorizo, oyster mushroom and artichoke salad (£5.25), thai fishcakes with sweet and sour cucumber sauce or tempura tiger prawns with chilli relish (£5.50), stilton and spinach quiche (£8.25), braised beef and ale with stilton dumplings (£8.95), game pie (£9.50), lamb tagine with apricots and buttered couscous (£9.95) and rib eye steak (£11.95). The eating area of the bar and lower part of the restaurant are no smoking; friendly service. Through the fine coach arch there's a lovely sheltered courtyard with tables, and a well which supposedly dates back to Roman times; attractive chintzy bedrooms. *(Recommended by Ian and Jane Irving, Geoffrey Kemp, Brian and Janet Ainscough, David Peakall, B N F and M Parkin, Ted and Jan Whitfield, Charles and Pauline Stride, Mrs Margaret Leale, Kevin Thorpe, Bob and Maggie Atherton, Peter H Stallard, Anthony Barnes, Darly Graton, Graeme Gulibert)*

Free house ~ Licensee Liam McGivern ~ Real ale ~ Bar food ~ Restaurant ~ (01733) 241066 ~ Well behaved children in eating area of bar at lunchtime ~ Irish band last Sun in month ~ Open 12-2.30(3 Sat), 6-11; 12-3, 7-10.30 Sun; closed 25 Dec ~ Bedrooms: £69.50B/£89.50B

SUTTON GAULT TL4279 Map 5
Anchor ★ 🍴 ♀ 🛏

Village signed off B1381 in Sutton

Although this very special old place is mainly popular for dining, the licensees are determined to keep a relaxed and informal pubby atmosphere. The four heavily timbered stylishly simple rooms have three log fires, antique settles and well spaced scrubbed pine tables on the gently undulating old floors, good lithographs and big prints on the walls, and lighting by gas and candles. As well as a thoughtful wine list (including a wine of the month and eight by the glass), winter mulled wine and freshly squeezed fruit juice, they have a real ale tapped from the cask which could be from a fairly local brewer like City of Cambridge, Nethergate or Humpty Dumpty. The new head chef here was formerly head chef at the Old Bridge Hotel in Huntingdon, and we're already detecting signs of even warmer than usual approval for the good imaginative food. It currently includes thai chicken and coconut soup (£3.95), chicken liver and brandy pâté with red onion marmalade (£4.95), fried quail with fresh rhubarb chutney (£5.50), venison carpaccio with pesto dressing and parmesan shavings (£6.95), crisp risotto cake with baby sweetcorn and oyster mushrooms (£10.75), steak, kidney and Guinness pie (£11.95), roast fillet of salmon, vermouth sauce and fennel purée (£12.50), roast loin of wild rabbit with sherry sauce (£12.95), barbary duck breast with braised red cabbage (£14.95), and calfs liver with potato rösti (£13.95); home-made puddings such as hot sticky toffee pudding, home-made bakewell tart, and chocolate and brandy terrine with raspberry coulis (£4.45), and a particularly good changing British cheeseboard (£5.50). From

Monday to Friday lunchtimes (not bank holidays), there's a very good value two-course menu (£7.95), and children can have most of their dishes in smaller helpings; three-course Sunday lunch (£16.50); booking advised. In summer you can sit outside and there are good walks and birdwatching near here as the pub is well set by the high embankment of the New Bedford river; no dogs. *(Recommended by Derek Thomas, Gwen and Peter Andrews, Michael Sargent, Gordon Neighbour, Maysie Thompson, Martin and Lois Sheldrick, DF, NF, Alan Clark, John Shields, Bruce Bird, K W West, R C Wiles, Pat and Tony Hinkins, MDN, Bill and Pat Pemberton, Tina and David Woods-Taylor, Patricia Beebe)*

Free house ~ Licensee Robin Moore ~ Real ale ~ Bar food (12-2, 7-9(6.30-9.30 Sat); not 26 Dec) ~ Restaurant ~ (01353) 778537 ~ Children welcome ~ Open 12-3, 7-11(10.30 Sun) ~ Bedrooms: £50S(£65B)/£66.50S(£95B)

SWAVESEY TL3668 Map 5
Trinity Foot
A14 eastbound, NW of Cambridge; from westbound carriageway take Swavesey, Fen Drayton turn

Head to this busy pub for their incredible range of very fairly priced fresh and well prepared fish which is delivered daily from the east coast ports. Depending on the day's catch, there might be soft herring roes on toast (£4.25), king scallops wrapped in bacon (£5.50), grilled mackerel with Portuguese dressing or rock eel with garlic butter (£7.75), grilled cod or haddock (£8), grilled or baked black bream (£9), crayfish salad (£10) or monkfish medallions cooked in white wine and cream (£11). If you don't feel like fish there are plenty of other options such as pâté (£4.25), ploughman's (£4.50), and sirloin steak (£12). They have quite a few other daily specials such as cream of white onion soup (£2.75), avocado pear and prawns (£4.75), vegetable and stilton quiche (£6.50), beef goulash (£7.75) and chicken breast in madeira and mushroom sauce (£8). As well as decent wines, and freshly squeezed fruit juice, they may have Boddingtons, Elgoods Pageant Ale and Whitbread, kept under light blanket pressure. There are well spaced tables, fresh flowers, a light and airy flower-filled conservatory, and a no smoking dining room. The big enclosed garden has shrubs and trees, though you may find the nearby A14 is too noisy to enjoy it. The pub owns a fresh fish shop next door (open Tues-Fri 11-2.30, 6-7.30, Sat 11-2.30). *(Recommended by Mr and Mrs K J Morris, Rob Fowell, Pat and Tony Martin, DF, NF, Gordon Theaker, Martin and Lois Sheldrick)*

Whitbreads ~ Lease H J Mole ~ Real ale ~ Bar food (till 10 Fri/Sat, 12-1.30 Sun) ~ Restaurant ~ (01954) 230315 ~ Children in restaurant ~ Open 11-2.30, 6-11; 12-3 Sun; closed Sun evenings

THRIPLOW TL4346 Map 5
Green Man ◀
3 miles from M11 junction 10; A505 towards Royston, then first right; Lower Street

The chatty landlord – an ex-classical conductor – is the collector of all the nice old bric-a-brac at this welcoming Victorian pub. But your first impression will probably be of the striking green on the vertical planked panelling and the darker green Anaglypta wallpaper, all nicely topped with an ochre ceiling, and countrified with dried flowers, hop bines and copper kettles. There's a good mix of furniture, mostly sturdy stripped tables and attractive high-backed dining chairs and pews on a flowery red carpet, and an enjoyable collection of teddy bears jostling on shelves with pewter mugs, decorated china, old scales, and illustrated boy's annuals. The Memorial Lounge is a sweet and cosy little room round to the right of the bar with unusual old Broads posters and comfortable sofas and armchairs. Two arches lead through to a no smoking dining area on the left, with red walls, a couple of old brocaded seats, lots more bric-a-brac and a mix of candlesticks on the tables; piped classical music, darts. Big helpings of lunchtime bar food might include filled baked potatoes or filled baguettes (from £3.90), ham and egg (£4.25), ploughman's (£4.50), good sausages with egg and chips (£4.95), chicken and broccoli in white wine and green peppercorn sauce (£7.35), and steak, Guinness and mushroom pie

(£7.95). In the evening, slightly more elaborate dishes might include steamed giant mussels in parsley white wine (£4.90), chicken rogan josh (£7.25), timbale of wild mushrooms topped with braised fennel with a yeni raki and turmeric sauce (£8.40) and rib eye steak (£10.90), with puddings such as chocolate truffle torte or carrot cake (£3.50). The landlord is very keen on supporting the smaller breweries so alongside well kept Timothy Taylors Landlord two or three interesting changing guests on handpump might be from Badger, Milton or Woodfordes. There are picnic-sets on the terrace, and globe lights throughout the landscaped garden. Very handy for Duxford. *(Recommended by Ian Phillips, Stephen, Julie and Hayley Brown, Catherine and Richard Preston, Pam and David Bailey, P and D Carpenter)*

Free house ~ Licensee Roger Ward ~ Real ale ~ Bar food (not Tues) ~ (01763) 208855 ~ Children over 5 welcome in eating area of bar ~ Open 12-2.30, 6-11(7-10.30 Sun); closed Tues

WANSFORD TL0799 Map 5
Haycock ★ ♀ ⇔

Village clearly signposted from A1 W of Peterborough

The main entrance hall at this handsome old coaching inn (which is very handy for the A1) has a fine flagstoned floor with antique hunting prints, seats and a longcase clock. This leads into a smart panelled main bar with dark terracotta walls, sturdy rail above a mulberry dado, and old settles. Through two comely stone arches is another attractive area, while the comfortable front sitting room has some squared oak panelling by the bar counter, a nice wall clock, and a big log fire. The airy stripped brick Orchard room by the garden has dark blue and light blue basketweave chairs, pretty flowery curtains and nice modern prints; doors open on to a big sheltered courtyard with lots of tables and cream Italian umbrellas; piped music. They serve only sandwiches (from £4.95), filled ciabattas (from £5.85), ploughman's (£6.25) and cream teas (£5.50) in the bar, but you can have a full (but not cheap) meal in the Orchard room: soup (£3.50), goats cheese and tomato tart (£6.25), fish and chips (£9.50), papardelle carbonara (£9.95), seared calves liver with crispy bacon, mash and red wine jus or chicken supreme with wild mushroom risotto (£10.25) and roast salmon fillet with haggis crust and ginger broth (£12.50). The restaurant is no smoking. Well kept Adnams and Bass on handpump and a good wine list. *(Recommended by Derek Thomas, Mr and Mrs J Glover, Francis Johnston, Mr and Mrs T B Staples, Gordon Neighbour, M H Fallside, M J Morgan, Barbara Wensworth, R C Wiles)*

Free house ~ Licensee Shelby Neale ~ Real ale ~ Restaurant ~ (01780) 782223 ~ Children in eating area of bar and restaurant ~ Open 11-11; 12-10.30 Sun ~ Bedrooms: £80B/£90B

Lucky Dip

Besides the fully inspected pubs, you might like to try these Lucky Dips recommended to us and described by readers (if you do, please send us reports: www.goodguides.com).

Alconbury [TL1776]
White Hart [Vinegar Hill, Alconbury Weston; handy for A1, nr A14/M11 turnoffs]: Friendly and comfortable respite from trunk roads, spotlessly and extensively refurbished with plush dining room, good value home cooking inc good vegetarian choice and OAP bargains, well kept Ruddles County and John Smiths, lively local back bar with darts; piped radio; charming village, ducks on stream *(Rev John Hibberd)*
Arrington [TL3250]
Hardwicke Arms: Handsome and substantial coaching inn with beamed and panelled lounge, decent bar food with good vegetarian choice, well kept Greene King IPA with a guest such as

Coniston Bluebird, good friendly service; bedrooms with own bathrooms, handy for Wimpole Hall *(LYM, Norman Fox, A G Morris)*
Babraham [TL5150]
George [High St; just off A1307]: Beams and timbers, old pictures and artefacts, good imaginative food in bar and restaurant inc pudding club, well kept Greene King and unusual guest beers, no smoking area, friendly efficient staff; very quiet piped music; tables on front grass, attractive setting on quiet road *(Keith and Janet Morris)*
Barrington [ST3818]
☆ *Royal Oak* [from M11 junction 11 take A10 to Newton, turn right; West Green]: Rambling

thatched Tudor pub with tables out overlooking classic village green, heavy low beams and timbers, lots of character, well kept Courage Best and Directors and Greene King IPA and Old Speckled Hen, prompt service, decent bar food and full restaurant menu in pleasant no smoking dining conservatory; maybe piped music, children in one area *(LYM, Michael Dandy, Jim Bush)*

Brampton [TL2170]

Grange [High St]: Pleasant elegant refurbished bar used by locals, enterprising newish chef/landlord doing good interesting food from sandwiches and more substantial bar meals (not Sun evening) to fine restaurant meals (not Sun evening or Mon), good service; comfortable bedrooms *(Gordon Theaker)*

Buckden [TL1967]

☆ *Lion* [High St]: Lovely partly 15th-c coaching inn, oak beams and carvings in small comfortable bar, good well presented food inc lots of fresh veg, appealing summer cold table, generous helpings, friendly attentive staff, roaring log fire, good choice of wines, John Smiths and Ruddles on electric pump, no music or machines; bedrooms *(Michael Sargent, David and Ruth Shillitoe, Mr and Mrs J Glover)*

Cambridge [TL4658]

☆ *Boathouse* [Chesterton Rd]: Well kept Boddingtons, Castle Eden and Wadworths 6X, good choice of ciders, decent coffee and generous usual food from sandwiches and baked potatoes up in easy-going pub with verandah overlooking river and punt station (wonderful playground on opp bank), L-shaped main room with varnished wood tables, framed prints and rowing memorabilia; juke box; children welcome, no dogs, pretty garden with hungry ducks, even a car park, open all day *(Ian Phillips, LYM)*

Bun Shop [King St]: Atmospheric studenty pub with new chef doing enterprising reasonably priced food, Boddingtons and Marstons Pedigree; piped music *(Dr David Cockburn, Patricia Beebe)*

☆ *Castle* [Castle St]: Large, airy and well appointed, with full Adnams range kept well and guests such as Wadworths Farmers Glory, generous quickly served food inc burgers, no smoking area with easy chairs upstairs, friendly staff; may be piped pop music, picnic-sets in good garden *(Brian and Anna Marsden, the Didler, Abi Benson, Keith and Janet Morris)*

Champion of the Thames [King St]: Small and cosy local with plenty of character, wonderfully decorated windows, padded walls and seats, painted Anaglypta ceiling, lots of woodwork, no music, welcoming atmosphere, simple lunchtime sandwiches, particularly well kept Greene King IPA and Abbot *(the Didler, Dr David Cockburn, Keith and Janet Morris)*

Clarendon Arms [Clarendon St]: Quaint partly flagstoned pub with well kept Greene King IPA and Abbot, friendly staff, wide choice of good value food; may be piped music; open all day, bedrooms simple but clean and comfortable *(Keith and Janet Morris)*

☆ *Fort St George* [Midsummer Common]: Picturesque, and very popular for its charming waterside position on Midsummer Common, overlooking ducks, swans, punts and boathouses; extended around old-fashioned Tudor core, interesting bar and traditional Sun lunches, well kept Greene King ales, decent wines, oars on beams, historic boating photographs, stuffed fish and bric-a-brac; lots of tables outside *(LYM, Kevin Blake)*

☆ *Free Press* [Prospect Row]: Friendly bare-boards pub kept deliberately simple, no smoking throughout, no piped music, machines or mobile phones; plain wooden tables and benches, open fires, well kept Greene King IPA, Abbot and Mild, good value honest food inc good soup and ploughman's and plenty of vegetarian dishes, cribbage and dominoes; sheltered paved back garden *(Patricia Beebe, Terry Mizen, Sue Demont, Tim Barrow, LYM, the Didler, Geoffrey Plow, Michael Buchanan)*

Granta [Newnham Terr]: Quiet balcony and terrace take full advantage of view over mill pond, ducks and attractive adjoining open area; good value usual food from sandwiches to steaks, Greene King ales, efficient service; punt hire *(Abi Benson)*

Green Dragon [Water St]: Attractive late medieval timber-framed building, friendly and comfortable with beams, huge inglenook fireplace and so forth, good value substantial food lunchtime and late evening (not Sat), well kept Greene King IPA, Abbot and Mild; waterside tables across quiet street, easy parking *(Keith and Janet Morris)*

Maypole [Portugal Pl/Park St]: Welcoming Italian-run pub with tasty filling food, well kept ales such as Adnams, Wadworths 6X and Charles Wells Bombardier, notable cocktails, prompt service; fruit machines, darts and TV in public bar; ice-cream hatch for tables outside *(Anthony Barnes, Dr David Cockburn)*

Mitre [Bridge St, opp St Johns Coll]: Dark and dim back-to-basics alehouse décor, good range of real ales, farm cider, good wines, no smoking area, log-effect fire *(Jonathan Smith, Keith and Janet Morris)*

Old Spring [Ferry Path; car park on Chesterton Rd]: Well worn in old-fashioned furnishings and décor, bare boards, gas lighting, lots of old pictures, decent straightforward food inc Sun roasts, well kept Greene King IPA and Abbot, two log fires, long back conservatory, summer barbecues; children till 8, has been open all day Sat *(LYM, Abi Benson, John Shields)*

Pickerel [Magdelene St]: Spacious pub with low beams and cosy corners, friendly staff, real ales such as Flying Scotsman and Theakstons XB, good food inc imaginative dishes; juke box, machines *(John Brightley)*

Six Bells [Covent Garden]: Small slightly modernised two-roomed local with vibrant atmosphere, friendly service, bargain food, well kept Greene King ales *(Chris Glasson)*

Chatteris [TL3986]

Cross Keys [Market Hill]: Attractive 16th-c coaching inn opp church in sleepy fenland town, relaxing open fire in long bar is part public and part comfortable armchairs, pleasant back courtyard, very good reasonably priced food in bar and restaurant inc good Sun lunches, warm friendly service, Greene King beers, inexpensive wine, tea and coffee; comfortable bedrooms *(R L Turnham)*

Chittering [TL4970]
Travellers Rest [Ely Rd (A10)]: Roomy open-plan roadside pub done up in comfortable chain-pub style, all very neat and clean, partly no smoking bar and no smoking dining room, polite pleasant service, wide choice of good generous freshly prepared food (real chips and home-made puddings), well kept ales such as Greene King IPA and Old Speckled Hen, properly served coffee, easy wheelchair access at back, spotless lavatories; may be soft piped music; children in family area, picnic-sets among fruit trees behind, camp site *(Michael and Jenny Back, BB)*

Conington [TL3266]
White Swan [signed off A14 (was A604) Cambridge—Huntingdon; Elsworth Rd]: Friendly and attractive quietly placed country local with children welcome in several eating areas on right of cheerful traditional bar, no smoking restaurant, games inc bar billiards and juke box on left, good range of reasonably priced popular food from sandwiches and children's dishes to decent steaks, quick friendly service, well kept Greene King IPA and Abbot tapped from the cask, snuffs; good big front garden with play area and play house *(Peter J Holmes, Keith and Janet Morris)*

Croydon [TL3149]
☆ *Queen Adelaide* [off A1198; High St]: Comfortably roomy beamed dining bar with standing timbers dividing off separate eating area, sofas, banquettes and stools, good value enjoyable home-made food esp fish, well kept ales such as Boddingtons and Greene King, impressive array of spirits, efficient friendly service; unobtrusive piped music; garden, play area *(P and D Carpenter, Keith and Janet Morris)*

Dry Drayton [TL3862]
☆ *Black Horse* [signed off A428 (was A45) W of Cambridge; Park St, opp church]: Olde-worlde village local under new management, clean and spacious, with very generous food inc wide vegetarian choice and good Sun lunch, well kept Greene King and other ales inc weekly changing guests, friendly prompt service, welcoming fire in central fireplace, games area, tables on pretty back terrace and neat lawn *(Keith and Janet Morris, David and Mary Webb, BB)*

Duxford [TL4745]
☆ *John Barleycorn* [off A1301; Moorfield Rd, pub at far end]: Useful food pub in thatched and shuttered early 17th-c cottage, good plain food all day (cooked to order, so may be a wait), Greene King IPA and Abbot and a guest such as Black Sheep, decent wines, good friendly service, softly lit spotless but relaxed bar with old prints, decorative plates and so forth; may be piped music, could do with a no smoking area; tables out among flowers, open

all day *(Don and Marilou Brooks, Charles Gysin, David Twitchett, Rob Fowell, Mr and Mrs T B Staples, Stephen, Julie and Hayley Brown, Uta and John Owlett, LYM, Christopher Turner)*

Eltisley [TL2659]
☆ *Leeds Arms* [signed off A428; The Green]: Knocked-through beamed bar overlooking peaceful village green, huge log fire, very friendly staff, close-set tables for substantial food from nicely presented sandwiches to good home-made hot dishes, well kept Adnams Broadside and Greene King IPA, Stowford Press cider, pleasant no smoking restaurant; children in eating area, pleasant garden with play area; simple comfortable bedrooms in separate block *(Simon Mighall, P and D Carpenter, LYM)*

Elton [TL0893]
☆ *Crown* [Duck St]: Carefully rebuilt stone pub with above-average varied food from chunky sandwiches (wknd baguettes instead) to enjoyable hot dishes, well kept Adnams and Greene King IPA and Abbot, cheerful helpful uniformed staff, banknotes on low beams, big log fire, large dining conservatory (cl Sun pm and Mon); steps up to no smoking restaurant and lavatories; opp green in beautiful small village *(Michael and Jenny Back, Michael Sargent)*

Ely [TL5380]
Cutter [Annesdale, off Station Rd just towards centre from A142 roundabout; or walk S along Riverside Walk from Maltings car park]: Lovely riverside setting, with plenty of tables outside and a genuine welcome for children, friendly series of unpretentious bars, Courage Directors, Greene King IPA and Old Speckled Hen and John Smiths, good house wines; piped music can be obtrusive *(Michael Buchanan, LYM)*
Lamb [Brook St (Lynn rd)]: Good lunchtime bar food in impressively panelled hotel lounge bar, friendly staff, well kept Tetleys; bedrooms *(Nigel Williamson, Roger and Pauline Pearce)*
Prince Albert [Silver St]: Spotless traditional two-bar local with Greene King IPA, Abbot, XX Mild and Triumph kept well, good value straightforward food (or you can bring your own food if you buy a drink), friendly long-serving landlord, books for sale, no juke box; trim and attractive garden with two aviaries *(Keith and Janet Morris, the Didler, MDN)*
West End House [West End, off Cambridge Rd]: Vibrant atmosphere; good choice of well kept beer, friendly landlord and customers; can be smoky *(Dr Roger Turner)*

Etton [TF1406]
☆ *Golden Pheasant* [just off B1443 N of Peterborough, signed from nr N end of A15 bypass]: Looks like the 19th-c private house it once was, notable for consistently well kept ales usually inc Adnams Broadside, Batemans XXXB, Cottage Goldrush, Greene King IPA, Kelham Island Pale Rider, Timothy Taylors Landlord and six weekly guests; homely plush bar, airy glass-walled no smoking side room (children allowed here), tasty food in bar and restaurant, quick friendly service, pub games;

well reproduced piped music, friendly dogs; good-sized garden with soccer pitch, floodlit boules pitch, interesting aviary, adventure playground and marquee; bedrooms, open all day at least in summer *(Ted and Jan Whitfield, M J Morgan, Peter Burton, BB)*

Fen Drayton [TL3368]
☆ *Three Tuns* [signed off A14 NW of Cambridge at Fenstanton; High St]: Well preserved ancient thatched building, relaxed and friendly bar with two inglenook fireplaces, interesting heavy-set moulded Tudor beams and timbers, wide choice of enjoyable food from warm baguettes to unusual dishes in partly no smoking restaurant, well kept Greene King IPA, Abbot, Old Speckled Hen and Ruddles Best, helpful well trained staff; seats on neat back lawn, good play area *(David and Ruth Hollands, LYM, Peter J Holmes, Eric Locker)*

Fulbourn [TL5156]
Bakers Arms [Hinton Rd]: Picturesque pub in pleasant village, popular lunchtime with local business people for good choice of generous if not cheap food; Greene King ales *(R C Vincent)*

Godmanchester [TL2470]
Black Bull [signed off A14 (was A604) just E of Huntingdon; Post St]: Interesting heavily beamed old pub by church, big inglenook log fire, settles forming booths by leaded-light windows, glinting brassware, side room with lots of black rustic ironwork, well kept Black Bull (brewed for the pub locally), Boddingtons, Flowers Original and Wadworths 6X under light blanket pressure, no smoking dining room, big courtyard, pretty garden *(Michael Buchanan, D P Brown, LYM, Iain Robertson)*
Exhibition [London Rd]: Doing well under current welcoming management, interesting choice of well priced good food, good service, flagstones, plain furniture, flowers on tables, mural of village shops *(Robbie Dobson)*

Grantchester [TL4455]
Red Lion [High St]: Busy family food pub, comfortable and spacious, with helpful service, generous soft drinks, Greene King IPA and Abbot; paid-entry toddlers' ball room, sheltered terrace and good-sized lawn with animals to entertain the many children *(Brian and Anna Marsden, John Shields, Chris Glasson, LYM)*

Guyhirn [TF3903]
☆ *Oliver Twist* [follow signs from A47/A141 junction S of Wisbech]: Comfortable open-plan lounge with big welcome from cheerful Geordie landlord, well kept sturdy furnishings, good range of home-made generous food from huge crusty warm rolls to steaks, well kept Everards Beacon and Tiger with a weekly guest beer, big open fires; may be piped music; restaurant, very popular as lunchtime business meeting place *(M J Morgan, BB, Bernie Adams, Phil and Jane Hodson)*

Hail Weston [TL1662]
Royal Oak [High St; just off A45, handy for A1 St Neots bypass]: Picturesque 17th-c thatched and beamed pub in quiet and pretty village nr Grafham Water, with unpretentious neatly kept low-beamed bar, cosy log fire, simple food, well kept Charles Wells ales and maybe a guest beer,

pleasant service, family room; darts, piped music and fruit machine in room off; open all day, big neat attractive garden with good play area *(Michael Sargent)*

Hardwick [TL1968]
☆ *Blue Lion* [signed off A428 (was A45) W of Cambridge; Main St]: Enjoyably friendly and photogenic old local with lots of beams, open fire and woodburner, fairly priced food from lunchtime sandwiches and baguettes to fresh Whitby fish (good value fish and chips Mon night), very extensive restaurant area (evening booking recommended), well kept Greene King IPA and Abbot tapped from the cask, old farm tools, two cats, conservatory; piped music; pretty roadside front garden, car park; handy for Wimpole Way walkers *(Keith and Janet Morris, Michael Sargent, John Brightley, BB, Penny Miles)*

Hildersham [TL5448]
Pear Tree [off A1307 N of Linton]: Thriving atmosphere in straightforward village local with odd crazy-paved floor, generous home cooking inc home-baked bread, children's helpings, cheerful service, well kept Greene King IPA and Abbot, daily papers, board games; children welcome, tables outside *(BB, Alan Jones)*

Holme [TL1987]
Admiral Wells [Station Rd]: Picturesque and well refurbished, with three seating areas, cheerful unfussy atmosphere, well kept Greene King and several guest ales such as Oldershaws Old Boy, good friendly service and cheerful obliging landlord, good bar menu inc sandwiches, ploughman's and other more substantial snacks, conservatory, games area on left; lively summer beer festival, tables out on gravel and in pleasant side garden (Inter-City trains hurtling by); open all day Fri-Sun *(O K Smyth, A G Morris, Michael and Jenny Back, Richard Lewis)*

Horningsea [TL4962]
☆ *Plough & Fleece* [just NE of Cambridge: first slip-road off A14 heading E after A10, then left; or B1047 Fen Ditton road off A1303; High St]: Rambling country pub, low black beams, comfortably worn high-backed settles and other sturdily old-fashioned wooden furnishings, dark cool recesses in summer, log fires in winter, more modern no smoking back dining room and comfortable conservatory, enjoyable food inc interesting light dishes, good service, well kept Greene King IPA and Abbot; dominoes and cribbage; garden with nice mix of wild and cultivated flowers; can be busy lunchtime, handy for Cambridge Science Park; cl Mon evening *(Bob and Maggie Atherton, J F M and M West, B and K Hypher, Pam and David Bailey, LYM)*

Houghton [TL2772]
Three Jolly Butchers [Huntingdon Rd, Wyton]: Welcoming family atmosphere, wide choice of imaginative food inc lots of fish specials, friendly accommodating staff, well kept Bass, Greene King IPA and Abbot and Hancocks HB, beams and brasses, restaurant; huge back garden, play area and occasional barbecues *(Ian Phillips, Roger and Pauline Pearce, Mrs A Chesher)*

Leverington [TF4410]

Rising Sun [just NW of Wisbech; Dowgate Rd]: Decent food, very helpful and efficient chef/landlord *(Michael and Jenny Back)*

Little Thetford [TL5374]

Fish & Duck [Holt Fen; track off A1123 Wicken—Stretham]: Neatly kept rambling family pub by remote fenland marina where rivers Cam, Old West and Great Ouse join, good food all day inc Sun carvery, friendly service, interesting memorabilia, lovely Ely cathedral view from conservatory; dogs on leads allowed, tables outside, good play area *(C Norman, Patricia Beebe)*

Marholm [TF1402]

Fitzwilliam Arms [Stamford Rd]: Handsome thatched stone-built inn, its rambling three-room bar comfortably opened up and modernised, good value food, efficient service, well kept Tetleys-related real ales; fruit machine; good big garden *(Tom Evans)*

Milton [TL4763]

Waggon & Horses [off A10 N of Cambridge; High St]: Welcoming mock-Tudor local with L-shaped lounge, good value food, faultlessly kept Elgoods ales, cheerful efficient service, games corner with darts and bar billiards, friendly dalmatian, lots of hats; attractive garden with slide and swing, apple trees, barbecues, picnic-sets and boules *(Pete Baker)*

Newborough [TF1805]

Decoy [Werrington Bridge Rd, Milking Nook (B1443 E of Peakirk)]: Smartly updated old-fashioned pub, friendly and comfortable, two spacious bars, eating area off, Adnams, Bass, Marstons and Theakstons, interesting food, log fire; pool, quiet piped music; sheltered garden, real fen country *(Peter H Stallard)*

Perry [TL1467]

Wheatsheaf [nr Grafham Water sailing club]: Clean and pleasant, with good food choice, quick welcoming service, good value coffee, plenty of tables in pleasant garden; bedrooms *(David and Mary Webb)*

Peterborough [TL1798]

Boathouse [Thorpe Meadows, off Thorpe Rd]: Big busy boathouse-theme Greene King pub by River Nene and famous boating lake, lots of bare brick, wood and nautical bric-a-brac; open all day, food all day too, reasonable prices, well kept real ales, friendly staff; family room with satellite TV, tables outside, summer barbecues; good disabled facilities *(Richard Lewis)*

Bogarts [North St]: Half a dozen well kept ales mainly from small breweries in friendly open-plan Victorian pub with central bar, good simple lunchtime food, daily papers, fine mix of customers, lots of Humphrey Bogart pictures; TV, games machine; handy for Westgate shopping centre, tables outside, open all day *(JP, PP, Richard Lewis)*

Bull [Westgate]: Rambling elegance, numerous bar rooms, attractive nooks and crannies with plush armchairs, low tables and attentive liveried staff – civilised yet comfortably pubby feel; Adnams and Tetleys-related ales, decent house wine, limited bar menu inc good sandwiches, smart restaurant; bedrooms

(John Wooll, Kevin Blake)

College Arms [Broadway]: Large open-plan Wetherspoons conversion with well kept ales such as Courage Directors, Fullers London Pride, Marstons Pedigree and Nethergate Priory Mild, good value varied food inc bargains, friendly helpful staff, comfortable seating inc upstairs, side alcoves and no smoking areas, bookshelves and paintings; open all day *(Richard Lewis, Ted and Jan Whitfield, M J Morgan, Beryl and Bill Farmer)*

Glass Onion [Burghley Rd]: Friendly straightforward open-plan local with well kept Courage Directors, Everards Beacon, Tiger and Original, and Payns (from landlord's Ramsey microbrewery), low prices, pool; no children inside; open all day, picnic-sets and climber in back garden *(Richard Lewis)*

Great Northern [Station Rd]: Well kept ales such as Fullers London Pride, Grainstore Ten Fifty and Greene King Abbot in pleasant station hotel bar, friendly staff, good facilities; bedrooms, open all day *(Richard Lewis)*

Palmerston Arms [Oundle Rd]: 16th-c stone-built pub with old tables, chairs, benches and a sofa in carpeted lounge, tiled-floor public bar, lots of well kept real ales tapped from the cask behind hop-hung counter, even organic lager, good pork pies, friendly landlord, no music or machines; step down into pub, steps to lavatory; small garden, open all day, but at busy times, esp wknds, they lock doors and restrict access to locals only *(Richard Lewis, the Didler, JP, PP, G Coates)*

Purls Bridge [TL4787]

☆ *Ship*: Overlooking Old Bedford River and RSPB reserve at end of long fenland road; warm and welcoming, with friendly courteous licensees and laid-back staff, well kept Flowers and Wadworths, generous good value varied food inc good Sun lunch; cl wkdy lunchtimes and Mon evening *(Judy Wayman, Bob Arnett)*

Shepreth [TL3947]

☆ *Plough* [signed just off A10 S of Cambridge; High St]: Neatly kept bright and airy local (would have been a main entry this year, but for its unco-operative landlord), popular generous home-made food from good sandwiches, baguettes and home-made soup up, quick service, welcoming and helpful to customers, changing well kept ales such as Adnams, Greene King IPA, Tetleys and Wadworths 6X, decent wines, modern furnishings, family room, popular side dining room; maybe evening piped music; well tended back garden with fairy-lit arbour and pond, summer barbecues and play area *(Joy and Colin Rorke, Keith and Janet Morris, Catherine and Richard Preston, BB)*

Stapleford [TL4651]

Rose [London Rd]: Wide range of good plain well presented food in family-friendly dining pub with tap room to left, small bar and big lounge with beams, inglenook and open fire; prompt service, particularly well kept beers inc Fullers London Pride; picnic-sets out on grass *(Keith and Janet Morris, John Shields)*

Stow cum Quy [TL5260]
☆ *White Swan* [just off B1102 – follow Bottisham sign]: Comfortable and cosy village local popular for growing choice of good value generous food from hot or cold sandwiches to piping hot main dishes (may stop early lunchtime), no smoking dining room with fresh flowers, well kept ales such as Adnams, Greene King IPA, Milton Pegasus, Wolf and a house beer, friendly service; picnic-sets in garden, cl Mon *(BB, Michael Buchanan, P and D Carpenter, Pam and David Bailey, Bill and Marian de Bass)*

Swaffham Prior [TL5764]
Red Lion [B1102 NE of Cambridge; High St]: Attractive and interesting local in pleasant village, well kept Greene King ales, wide range of generous fresh food from sandwiches, baked potatoes and exemplary ploughman's to steaks, comfortably divided dining area, prompt service *(Ian Wilson, Michael Buchanan, Jack Clarfelt)*

Trumpington [TL4454]
Coach & Horses [High St (A1309)]: Roomy and tastefully restored, decent fairly priced food from sandwiches to good value meals, well kept beers, dining area, open fire; may be quiet piped music *(P and D Carpenter, Catherine and Richard Preston)*

Ufford [TF0904]
☆ *Olde White Hart* [back rd Peterborough—Stamford, just S of B1443]: Old-fashioned 17th-c village pub with interesting features and nice snug (not always open), well kept ales such as Theakstons Old Peculier and Wadworths 6X, wide choice of bottled beers, farm cider, good coffee, decent food, kind service, traditional games; big garden with terrace and play area, camping; children welcome, folk music Sun evening, cl Mon lunchtime *(Tom Evans, LYM)*

Willingham [TL4070]
Three Tuns [Church St]: Old village pub with new management doing food from bar snacks to full meals, well kept Greene King and guest ales, darts and dominoes *(Peter J Holmes)*

Wisbech [TF4609]
☆ *Red Lion* [North Brink]: Hospitable and civilised long front bar in lovely Georgian terrace on River Nene, closest Elgoods pub to the brewery with their beer kept well (also a German lager on tap), decent wines, good value food from interesting baguettes to wide range of home-made dishes inc fish, Fri bargain salad bar, particularly friendly landlord and welcoming staff, good river views; nr NT Peckover House, very popular lunchtime *(John Brightley, Tony and Wendy Hobden, Carl and Jackie Cranmer, M J Morgan)*

Woodditton [TL6659]
☆ *Three Blackbirds* [signed off B1063 at Cheveley]: Pretty thatched pub with attractively old-fashioned flagstoned bar on left, second bar opening into large dining area with more tables upstairs, some interesting food inc enterprising vegetarian dishes (as well as lunchtime sandwiches), friendly service, well kept Greene King IPA and Old Speckled Hen, quite a few malt whiskies, racing photographs and cartoons; children welcome, pretty garden; cl first Tues of month *(M Lickert, LYM)*

Post Office address codings confusingly give the impression that some pubs are in Cambridgeshire, when they're really in the Leicestershire or Midlands groups of counties (which is where we list them).

Cheshire

Though we carried out a lot of inspections here this year on pubs we'd not visited before, we found only one that definitely merited promotion to the main entries: the Egerton Arms at Astbury, a thriving old village inn in a very pretty spot. Other pubs on top form here this year are the Grosvenor Arms at Aldford (an excellent dining pub), the Bhurtpore at Aston (great beers and other drinks, enjoyable food, plenty of atmosphere), the charming old thatched White Lion at Barthomley (one of the very few pubs so consistently good that they have been in all 20 editions of this Guide), the Cholmondeley Arms near Bickley Moss and the Dysart Arms at Bunbury (two more first-rate dining pubs), the Calveley Arms at Handley (imaginative food, especially fish), the charmingly set Bells of Peover at Lower Peover (another of our 'long service' pubs, in every edition so far – a fine all-rounder), and the Sutton Hall Hotel near Macclesfield (stylish, even rather grand, yet unfailingly welcoming to all). Of these, the Grosvenor Arms earns our title of Cheshire Dining Pub of the Year, for its imaginative food in relaxed and interesting surroundings. Some other interesting pubs to note here are the Blue Bell at Bell o' th' Hill (very ancient, very friendly), the Albion in Chester (fine World War I memorabilia, good all round), the cosy old Hanging Gate up on the moors near Langley (the third of the county's pubs to have won a place in the Guide *every year since it started), the chatty Leathers Smithy near Langley (another traditional moorland pub), and the Smoker at Plumley (a reliable off-motorway standby). Drinks prices here are well below the national average; the Sam Smiths at the Olde Park Gate, Over Peover, was particularly cheap. In the Lucky Dip section at the end of the chapter several pubs stand out as particularly worth checking out, almost all of them inspected and vouched for by us: the White Lion at Alvanley, Boot in Chester, Copper Mine at Fullers Moor, Harrington Arms at Gawsworth, George & Dragon at Great Budworth, Foxcote at Little Barrow, Swan With Two Nicks at Little Bollington, Dun Cow at Ollerton, Highwayman at Rainow, Ryles Arms at Sutton, Setter Dog at Walker Barn and Boot and Slipper at Wettenhall.*

ALDFORD SJ4259 Map 7

Grosvenor Arms ★ ⊕ ♀ ◖

B5130 Chester—Wrexham

Cheshire Dining Pub of the Year

A real favourite with readers, this lively pub is popular for its enjoyable food and an impressive choice of beers, wines and spirits. There's a traditional feel throughout the spacious open-plan layout, and a chatty atmosphere in the huge panelled library with tall book shelves along one wall and long wooden floor boards with lots of well spaced substantial tables. Several quieter areas are well furnished with good individual pieces including a very comfortable parliamentary-type leather settle. Throughout there are plenty of interesting pictures, and the lighting's exemplary; cribbage, dominoes, Trivial Pursuit and Scrabble. Huge helpings of well presented imaginative bar food might include home-made soup (£3.50), sandwiches (from £3.75), roast duck leg with a red onion marmalade (£5.95), fresh salmon and horseradish pâté with a vinaigrette dressing (£5.45), spicy lamb kebabs with coriander yoghurt in pitta bread with mixed salad (£7.45), grilled cod with crab risotto and shellfish butter sauce (£10.95), and medallions of beef cooked in a mustard, brandy, cream and wild mushroom sauce (£14.95). Unusual vegetarian dishes might be baby corn fritters on stir-fried vegetables and noodles with a chilli and sesame sauce (£7.45) or ricotta, spinach and pine kernel strudel with a tomato and red pepper sauce (£7.25), and there are puddings such as coffee and whisky cheesecake and sticky date pudding with butterscotch sauce (£3.95). Up to five well kept real ales on handpump include Batemans XB, Flowers IPA and guests such as Shepherd Neame Best, Hanby Drawwell and Weetwood Eastgate, all 20 wines (largely New World) are served by the glass, and an awesome choice of whiskies includes 75 malts, 25 bourbons, and 25 from Ireland. There are canapés on the bar at Sunday lunchtime, and it's best to book on weekend evenings. The airy terracotta-floored conservatory has lots of huge low hanging flowering baskets and chunky pale wood garden furniture, and opens on to a large elegant suntrap terrace and neat lawn with picnic-sets, young trees and a tractor. *(Recommended by Denis and Dorothy Evans, Tom Hargreaves, Pat and Tony Hinkins, Mike and Wena Stevenson, Rob Fowell, MLR, Lorna and Howard Lambert, W K Wood, Paul Boot, Joan and Michel Hooper-Immins, Mrs P J Carroll, Mr and Mrs M Cooper, Graham and Lynn Mason)*

Brunning & Price ~ Licensees Gary Kidd and Jeremy Brunning ~ Real ale ~ Bar food (12-10(9 Sun); not 25 Dec) ~ (01244) 620228 ~ No children under 14 inside after 6pm ~ Open 11.30-11; 12-10.30 Sun

ASTBURY SJ8461 Map 7
Egerton Arms
Village signposted off A34 S of Congleton

In a pretty spot overlooking an attractive old church, this busy village inn is well liked by locals and passing visitors for its reliable, promptly served food; though the car park is huge, you may have to move fast to bag a spot on a Sunday lunchtime. Originally a farmhouse, it has a cheerily pubby feel in the brightly yellow-painted rooms that ramble around the bar; some parts date back to the 14th c. Around the walls are the odd piece of armour, shelves of books, and mementoes of the Sandow Brothers, who performed as 'the World's Strongest Youths' (one of them was the landlady's father). In summer dried flowers fill the big fireplace. Served in either bar or restaurant, the wide range of food includes sandwiches (from £2.60), hot baguettes (£3.50), ploughman's (£4.25), chicken, cheese and corn pie (£5.25), parsnip and leek bake (£5.75), salmon grilled with ginger and coriander butter (£6.75), crispy roast half duckling (£9.50) and daily specials such as chicken stroganoff; children's menu. Parts of the bar and restaurant are no smoking. Robinsons Best and Frederics on handpump; TV. There are a few well placed tables in front, and a play area with wooden fort. Though she's not been spotted for a while, the ghost of a murdered neighbour is said to haunt the pub. We look forward to hearing from readers who have tried the bedrooms here. *(Recommended by Andy Gosling, Mrs P A King)*

Robinsons ~ Licensees Alan and Grace Smith ~ Real ale ~ Bar food (12-2, 6.30-9; 12-2, 7-8.30 Sun) ~ Restaurant ~ (01260) 273946 ~ Children welcome ~ Open 11.30-11; 11.30-3, 7-10.30 Sun ~ Bedrooms: £25B/£50B

ASTON SJ6147 Map 7
Bhurtpore ★ ♀ ◖
Off A530 SW of Nantwich; in village follow Wrenbury signpost

There are up to a thousand beers a year at this deservedly popular roadside inn, which takes its name from a town in India where local landowner Lord Combermere won a battle. Though frequently dubbed a real ale enthusiasts' dream, there's a lot more to it: this year they've added a selection of fine wines to their already decent wine list, there's a choice of 90 different whiskies, and their menu contines to expand. The cheerful, willing staff remain cool under pressure and are not averse to a chat with customers. Nine handpumps serve a rotating choice of really unusual and very well kept beers which might include Abbeydale Absolution, Durham Sanctuary, Hydes Dark Mild, Marston Moors Mongrel, Salopian Heaven Sent and Wye Valley Wholesome Stout, as well as European beers such as Bitburger Pils or Timmermans Peach Beer. They also have dozens of good bottled beers, fruit beers (and fruit-flavoured gins) and a changing farm cider or perry. The carpeted lounge bar bears some Indian influences, with an expanding collection of exotic artefacts (one turbaned statue behind the bar proudly sports a pair of Ray-Bans), as well as good local period photographs, and some attractive furniture. Enjoyable reasonably priced bar food includes sandwiches (from £2.25, hot filled baguettes £3.50), filled baked potatoes (from £2.95), locally produced sausages, egg and chips (£4.25), lemon sole fillets with parma ham in a cream and herb sauce (£8.95), steak, kidney and ale pie (£6.95), and very good home-made Indian dishes such as chicken tikka kebabs (£4.25), and a choice of about six curries and baltis (from £6.95). The licensees are constantly adapting the specials board which might include fillet of bass and spinach in filo pastry with citrus sauce (£10.25), venison casserole (£8.95), a decent vegetarian choice such as leek and cheese cakes in a cheesy mustard sauce (£6.95) or ratatouille (£6.95), and puddings such as rhubarb crumble and local ice cream (from £2.95). At weekends it can get extremely busy, but at lunchtime or earlyish on a weekday evening the atmosphere is cosy and civilised. Tables in the comfortable public bar are reserved for people not eating, and the snug area and dining room are no smoking. Strictly no children. Darts, dominoes, cribbage, pool, TV, fruit machine; readers highly recommend their occasional beer festivals. By the time this book goes to press they will have two new bedrooms. *(Recommended by Mike and Wendy Proctor, Andy Chetwood, Andy Lace, E G Parish, Rob Fowell, Nigel Woolliscroft, the Didler, Sue and Bob Ward, Alan and Paula McCully, JP, PP, Giles and Liz Ridout, Derek and Sylvia Stephenson, Richard Lewis, Edward Leetham, Sue Holland, Dave Webster)*

Free house ~ Licensee Simon George ~ Bar food (not 26 Dec) ~ Restaurant ~ (01270) 780917 ~ No children ~ Folk third Tues of month ~ Open 12-(3 Sat)2.30, 6.30-11; 12-3, 7-10.30 Sun; closed 25 Dec and 1 Jan

BARTHOMLEY SJ7752 Map 7
White Lion ★ £

A mile from M6 junction 16; take B5078 Alsager road, then Barthomley signposted on left

The seats and picnic-sets on the cobbles outside this unspoilt black and white thatched pub have a charming view of the attractive village. A good place to bring overseas visitors, the main bar of this listed building feels timeless, with an inviting open fire, heavy oak beams dating back to Stuart times, attractively moulded black panelling, Cheshire watercolours and prints on the walls, latticed windows, and wobbly old tables. As we went to press they'd just finished repainting. Up some steps, a second room has another open fire, more oak panelling, a high-backed winged settle, a paraffin lamp hinged to the wall, and shove-ha'penny, cribbage and dominoes; a third room is much used by local societies. The generous lunchtime bar food, which is very good value, fits in well with the overall style of the place, and includes cheese and onion oatcakes with beans and tomatoes or pie, peas and gravy (£2), stilton and local roast ham ploughman's (£4.50), local pork sausages with onion gravy (£3.50) and specials such as chilli con carne or Sunday roast (£4.50); to be sure of a table at weekends, it's best to arrive early. Very well kept Burtonwood Bitter and Top Hat, and a monthly guest on handpump; friendly efficient service; no noisy games machines or music. The early 15th-c red sandstone church of St Bertiline across the road is worth a visit. *(Recommended by JP, PP, John Robertson, Pat and Tony Martin, the Didler, A C Stone, John and Anne McIver, V N Stevenson, Edward Leetham, Rob Fowell, Tony Middis, Barbara Wilder, Andy Meaton, Dr and Mrs J Hills, Nigel Woolliscroft, Sue Holland, Dave Webster, Angus Lyon, Jenny and Brian Seller, Jim Bush)*

Burtonwood ~ Tenant Terence Cartwright ~ Real ale ~ Bar food (lunchtime) ~ (01270) 882242 ~ Children welcome away from public bar ~ Open 11.30-11(5-11 only Thurs); 12-10.30 Sun

BELL O' TH' HILL SJ5245 Map 7

Blue Bell ◖

Signposted just off A41 N of Whitchurch

The friendly Californian landlord and his Russian wife have a real welcome for both walkers and their dogs in this cosily attractive partly 14th-c country local. The entrance to the heavily beamed building – with its massive central chimney – is through a great oak door by a mounting-block; you then find yourself in a small quarry-tiled hallway, with stairs up, and another formidable oak door on your right. This leads into three communicating rooms, two served by hatch; the main bar is in an inglenook with an attractively moulded black oak mantelbeam. Comfortably plush wall seats among the cheerful mix of furnishings, lots of brass ornaments and newspapers to read on Sundays; several trophies reflect the regulars' passion for dominoes. As well as soup and sandwiches (£1.75), reasonably priced home-cooked bar food (which may sometimes be served outside their usual hours) includes pâté (£2.50), cumberland sausage or gammon (£4.95), trout (£6.50), steaks (from £6.50), and daily specials including (with notice) vegetarian meals (mostly under £6); puddings (from £1.75). Well kept Hanby Drawwell and an unusual guest such as Plassey Bitter from a small local brewer. Children will enjoy getting to know the sociable pub dogs. Picnic-sets among flowers on the front grass, and maybe cows and a donkey or two in the adjoining field where you can camp. *(Recommended by Sue and Bob Ward, Graham and Lynn Mason, Nigel Woolliscroft, G Coates)*

Free house ~ Licensees Pat and Lydia Gage ~ Real ale ~ Bar food (12-2, 7-9) ~ Restaurant ~ (01948) 662172 ~ Children welcome ~ Open 12-3, 7-11(10.30 Sun)

BICKLEY MOSS SJ5650 Map 7

Cholmondeley Arms ★ ⑪ ♍ 🛏

Cholmondeley; A49 5½ miles N of Whitchurch; the owners would like us to list them under Cholmondeley Village, but as this is rarely located on maps we have mentioned the nearest village which appears more often

Very popular with readers for its enjoyable food, this imaginatively converted Victorian building, with a steeply pitched roof, gothic windows and huge old radiators, was the local school until 1982. There's a relaxing informal atmosphere in the cross-shaped high-ceilinged bar, which is filled with eye-catching objects such as old school desks above the bar on a gantry, masses of Victorian pictures (especially portraits and military subjects), and a great stag's head over one of the side arches. There's a mix of seats from cane and bentwood to pews and carved oak settles, and the patterned paper on the shutters matches the curtains. You'll have to book at weekends for the bar food; the menu changes daily but might include home-made courgette soup (£3.25), sandwiches (from £3.95), green mussels grilled with a lobster butter or duck and brandy pâté with cumberland jelly(£4.75), game pie with a puff pastry crust or leek and cheddar soufflé grilled with cheese (£7.95), bass fillets on buttered samphire with a light velouté sauce, rack of lamb with a garlic and thyme sauce or pheasant in an apple and calvados sauce (£9.95), chicken breast with mushroom, dijon mustard and cream (£9.25), and puddings such as syrup tart and cream or spotted dick and custard (£4.25). Well kept Adnams Bitter, Banks's Mild, Marstons Pedigree, Weetwood Old Dog and a guest such as Timothy Taylors Landlord on handpump. An old blackboard lists 10 or so interesting and often uncommon wines by the glass; big (4-cup) pot of cafetière coffee, teas, and hot chocolate. Comfortable and clean bedrooms are across the old playground in the headmaster's house; there are seats out on a sizeable lawn. Cholmondeley Castle and gardens are close by. *(Recommended by Mike and Wena Stevenson, Mike and Mary Carter, Mike and Wendy Proctor, John McDonald, Ann Bond, Kevin Blake, Mrs P J Carroll, Mr and Mrs M Cross, Ray and Winifred Halliday, Sarah Holden, Pat and Dick Warwick, Rob Fowell, Nigel Woolliscroft)*

Free house ~ Licensees Guy and Carolyn Ross-Lowe ~ Real ale ~ Bar food (12-2.30, 6.30-9.30) ~ Restaurant ~ (01829) 720300 ~ Children in eating area of bar and restaurant ~ Open 11-3, 6.30-11; 12-3, 6.30-10.30 Sun ~ Bedrooms: £45B/£60B

BUNBURY SJ5758 Map 7

Dysart Arms ★ ⑪ ♀

Bowes Gate Road; village signposted off A51 NW of Nantwich; and from A49 S of Tarporley
– coming this way, coming in on northernmost village access road, bear left in village centre

Although this friendly, cheerful pub is popular for its good food, it's a nice place to
come just for a drink. The tables on the terrace and in the immaculately kept slightly
elevated garden are very pleasant in summer, with views of the splendid church at
the end of the picturesque village, and the distant Peckforton Hills beyond. Inside,
nicely laid out airy spaces ramble around a pleasantly lit central bar. Under deep
venetian red ceilings, the knocked-through cream-walled rooms have red and black
tiles, some stripped boards and some carpet, a comfortable variety of well spaced big
sturdy wooden tables and chairs, a couple of tall bookcases, some carefully chosen
bric-a-brac, properly lit pictures and warming fires in winter. One area is no
smoking, and they have dominoes. They've lowered the ceiling in the more
restauranty end room (with its book-lined back wall), and there are lots of plants on
the window sills. Interesting food from a changing menu might include home-made
soup (£3.25), sandwiches (from £3.75), grilled bruschetta of goats cheese topped
with walnut crumble on a beetroot and chive salad (£4.95), sautéed tiger prawns
with tomato salsa and ciabatta bread (£5.95), local sausages with mash and onion
gravy (£7.95), salmon fillet teriyaki on roasted asparagus (£10.95), turkey escalope
dusted with paprika on linguini with creamy mustard sauce, shoulder of lamb with a
red wine and rosemary sauce (£10.95) and well liked puddings such as baked vanilla
cheesecake, apple pie or raspberry crème brûlée with shortbread biscuits (£3.75) as
well as a good, changing selection of cheeses. Well kept Boddingtons and Timothy
Taylors Landlord, and a couple of guests such as Weetwood Eastgate and Yorks
Yorkshire Terrier on handpump, good interesting wines by the glass. The staff are
friendly and efficient; it's part of the small pub group which includes the Grosvenor
Arms at Aldford. *(Recommended by Joy and Peter Heatherley, Revd D Glover, Lynette and
Stuart Shore, Rob Fowell, SLC, Denis and Dorothy Evans, Gill and Keith Croxton,
Mrs P J Carroll, Paul Boot, Mr and Mrs M Cooper, D Bryan, Nigel Woolliscroft, J C Temple,
Mr and Mrs G Owens, Sue Holland, Dave Webster, Paul and Margaret Baker, Graham and
Lynn Mason, Jim Bush)*

*Brunning & Price ~ Managers Darren and Elizabeth Snell ~ Real ale ~ Bar food (12-
2.15, 6-9.30; 12-9.30(9 Sun)Sat) ~ (01829) 260183 ~ Under 10s in eating area of bar,
and only until 6pm ~ Open 11-11; 12-10.30 Sun*

CHESTER SJ4166 Map 7

Albion ★ ◀

Park Street

The landlord of this old-fashioned corner pub is devoted to his striking collection of
World War I memorabilia: throughout, you'll find big engravings of men leaving for
war, similarly moving prints of wounded veterans, and other more expected aspects
– flags, advertisements and so on. Free from piped music, noisy machines and
children, its separate rooms are an oasis of calm, tucked away in a quiet part of
town just below the Roman Wall. The attractively muted post-Edwardian décor
includes floral wallpaper, appropriate lamps, leatherette and hoop-backed chairs, a
period piano, and cast-iron-framed tables, with an attractive side dining room.
Appealing to a good mix of ages, it's friendly and chatty; it can get quite smoky.
Well kept Cains, Greenalls, Timothy Taylors Landlord and maybe a couple of
weekly guests such as Batemans XXXB and Caledonian Deuchars IPA on
handpump, up to 30 malt whiskies and fresh orange juice; the wines are non-French.
Service is very friendly (though they don't like people rushing in just before closing
time – and won't serve crisps or nuts). Home-cooked food in huge helpings includes
Staffordshire oatcakes filled with black pudding, honey-roast gammon with
cumberland sauce, roast turkey, vegetarian haggis, and lincolnshire sausages in red
wine and shallot sauce (all £5.95); they are used to being asked for one dish with
two sets of cutlery. Puddings might include cold melted chocolate pudding, home-

made brandy and apricot ice cream and fresh lemon and lime cheesecake (£2.95); they also do great doorstep sandwiches. The landlord still has plans for a couple of bedrooms with bathrooms, maybe by early 2002. *(Recommended by John Brightley, Joy and Peter Heatherley, the Didler, Rob Fowell, P G Plumridge, Alan and Paula McCully, JP, PP, Joe Green, Darly Graton, Graeme Gulibert, Sue Holland, Dave Webster, John and Jackie Chalcraft, Stephen, Julie and Hayley Brown, M Joyner)*

Inn Partnership (Nomura) ~ Lease Michael Edward Mercer ~ Real ale ~ Bar food (12-2, 5.30(7 Sun)-8, 6-8.30 Sat) ~ (01244) 340345 ~ Open 11.30-3, 5(6 Sat)-11; 12-3, 7-10.30 Sun

Old Harkers Arms ♀ ◖

1 Russell Street, down steps off City Road where it crosses canal – under Mike Melody antiques

From inside this well converted Victorian canalside warehouse you can watch the canal boats drift past. The lofty ceiling and tall windows give a feeling of space and light, yet the tables are carefully arranged to create a sense of privacy. The nicely decorated bar has attractive lamps, interesting old prints on the walls, and newspapers and books to read from a well stocked library at one end. The menu changes frequently, and popular tasty bar food might include sandwiches (from £3.25), toasted ciabattas and baguettes (£3.95), soup (£3.25), ploughman's (£5.25), grilled salmon marinated in sherry and soya sauce with mange tout and crispy ginger (£7.50), baked avocado filled with stilton and mixed nuts or penne pasta with gammon, apricots, mushrooms, chicory and cream sauce (£6.95), and rib-eye steak (£12.95), with puddings such as belgian chocolate, biscuit and nut slice or passion fruit sorbet (£3.25); Sunday roast; on Monday evening two courses and half a bottle of wine are £12.95. The bar counter, apparently constructed from salvaged doors, serves well kept real ales on handpump including Boddingtons, Lees and Weetwood Best and up to five guests such as Caledonian 80/-, Fullers London Pride, Greene King Old Speckled Hen and Roosters Yankee; around 50 malt whiskies, and decent well described wines. Popular with a young crowd on Saturday evening. The pub is part of the same small group that owns the Grosvenor Arms at Aldford and the Dysart Arms at Bunbury. *(Recommended by Darly Graton, Graeme Gulibert, Keith Fairbrother, Kerry Law, Angela Westwood, Sue Holland, Dave Webster, John McDonald, Ann Bond, Rob Fowell, Paul Boot, Pat and Tony Martin, Kevin Blake)*

Brunning & Price ~ Lease Barbie Hill and Catryn Devaney ~ Real ale ~ Bar food (12-(2 Fri)2.30, 5.30-9.30; 12-9.30 Sat(9 Sun); not Fri evening) ~ Restaurant ~ (01244) 344525 ~ Children welcome till 7pm ~ Open 11.30-11; 12-10.30 Sun

COTEBROOK SJ5865 Map 7
Fox & Barrel

A49 NE of Tarporley

This well run bar and restaurant does well in suiting both drinkers and diners. The snug distinct areas are interestingly furnished, with a good mix of tables and chairs including two seats like Victorian thrones, an oriental rug in front of a very big log fireplace, a comfortable banquette corner, and a part with shelves of rather nice ornaments and china jugs; silenced fruit machine, unobtrusive piped music. Beyond the bar, there's a huge uncluttered candlelit dining area (no smoking) with varying-sized tables, comfortable dining chairs, attractive rugs on bare boards, rustic pictures above the panelled dado, and one more extensively panelled section. The choice of tasty, nicely presented food, which changes every ten to twelve weeks, might typically include home-made soup (£2.75), sandwiches (readers recommend the toasted triple decker) and baguettes (from £3.50), tandoori chicken salad (£5.75), ploughman's (£5.50), home-made pie of the day (£7.95), mixed cheese ravioli with white wine cream sauce and black grapes (£8.95), fish stew (£11.75), roast rump of veal on horseradish, potato and parsnip mash (£11.75) and steaks (from £11.95), with puddings such as profiteroles and crème brûlée (£3.75); three-course Sunday lunch (£11.50). Well kept Boddingtons, Marstons Pedigree and a couple of guests such as Flowers Original and Greene King Old Speckled Hen are served (through a sparkler) by handpump, and there's a decent choice of wines. Friendly attentive service from the uniformed staff. A traditional jazz band plays every Monday evening. *(Recommended by Olive and Ray Hebson, D Gaston, Mr and Mrs M Cooper, Ray and Winifred Halliday, Angela Gibson, Pat and Tony Hinkins)*

Inn Partnership (Nomura) ~ Tenant Martin Cocking ~ Real ale ~ Bar food (12-2.30, 6.30-9, 6-9.30 Fri and Sat, 12-3, 6-9 Sun) ~ Restaurant ~ (01829) 760529 ~ Children in restaurant ~ Trad jazz band Mon evening ~ Open 12-3, 5.30-11; 12-(11 Sat)10.30 Sun; closed 25 Dec

DARESBURY SJ5983 Map 7
Ring o' Bells ♀ ◼

1½ miles from M56 junction 11; A56 N, then turn right on to B5356

From the front of this roomy pub you can see the church where Lewis Carroll's father was vicar – it has a window showing all the characters in *Alice in Wonderland*. Successfully combining a spacious and airy atmosphere (the dining rooms are no smoking) with a cosy, homely feel, there is a good variety of places to sit. On the right is a comfortable, down-to-earth part where walkers from the nearby canal can relax, while the left has more of a library style, and some reflection of its 19th-c use as a magistrates' court; all rooms have wheelchair access. Service is friendly and efficient. The long bar counter has well kept Boddingtons, Cains, Greenalls Bitter and Mild and two weekly guest beers such as Batemans Miss Whiplash or Exmoor Beast on handpump, half a dozen each of red and white wines by the glass, and a dozen malts. Readers recommend the lunchtime bar food which might include soup (£2.95), sandwiches (from £2.85), ploughman's (£4.20), steak and ale pie (£6.95) and curry of the day (£7.25). Blackboards show a wide choice of more sophisticated food, with some interesting dishes such as duck breast in fruits of the forest sauce (£10.95) or sizzling sweet and sour chicken with oriental vegetables (£8.95), and they do fresh fish every day; puddings include chocolate orange sponge and sticky toffee pudding (from £2.95), and in winter there's a roaring fire. There are plenty of tables out in a long partly terraced garden which can get busy in the summer; the village is an attractive place to stroll through. *(Recommended by Marianne and Peter Stevens, Edward Leetham, Bernie Adams, Roy and Lindsey Fentiman, Graham and Lynn Mason)*

Scottish Courage ~ Manager Martin Moylon ~ Real ale ~ Bar food (12-2.30, 6-9.30 Mon-Sat; 12-8.45 Sun) ~ Restaurant ~ (01925) 740256 ~ Children in restaurant ~ Open 11-11; 12-10.30 Sun

HANDLEY SJ4758 Map 7
Calveley Arms

Whitchurch Road, just off A41 S of Chester

In summer you can play boules in the secluded garden of this cosy black and white country pub. Most people, however, come for the well prepared imaginative food. Especially good for fresh fish, they have at least four fish specials every day, such as plaice fillet with prawn and lobster sauce (£7.75), baked bass on fennel or seared scallops with mange tout and ginger (£9.95). Other dishes from the changing menus (bound in the covers of old children's annuals) range from whole roast spring chicken in tarragon sauce (£8.25) to more standard bar food such as soup (£2.25), sandwiches (from £2.50), home-made steak and kidney pie (£5.50), roasted seasonal vegetables with couscous and minted yoghurt (£5.85), and rump steak (£8.50); service is courteous and welcoming. Well kept Boddingtons and Theakstons Black Bull and occasional guests such as Black Sheep Best and Timothy Taylors Landlord on handpump, and an interesting selection of soft drinks. The attractively furnished roomy beamed lounge has leaded windows, an open fire at one end and some cosy alcove seating; shove-ha'penny, dominoes, cribbage, table skittles and piped music. In summer if the weather is nice they hold a Thursday evening barbecue. *(Recommended by Kevin Blake, MH, BD, Olive and Ray Hebson, Paul and Margaret Baker)*

Enterprise ~ Lease Grant Wilson ~ Real ale ~ Bar food (12-2.15, 6-9.30; 12-2.30, 7-9 Sun) ~ (01829) 770619 ~ Children in eating area of bar ~ Open 12-3, 6-11; 12-4, 7-10.30 Sun

HIGHER BURWARDSLEY SJ5256 Map 7
Pheasant 🍺

Burwardsley signposted from Tattenhall (which itself is signposted off A41 S of Chester) and from Harthill (reached by turning off A534 Nantwich—Holt at the Copper Mine); follow pub's signpost on up hill from Post Office; OS Sheet 117 map reference 523566

This superbly placed half-timbered and sandstone 17th-c pub is best on a clear day, when the telescope on the terrace lets you make out even the pier head and cathedrals in Liverpool, while from inside there's a fine view over the Cheshire plain. After a recent refurbishment the bar has a bright modern feel, with wooden floors and light-coloured furniture; the see-through fireplace is said to house the largest log fire in the county. There's a pleasant no smoking conservatory and a new restaurant. The atmosphere is relaxed and walkers are welcome. Interesting bar food includes soup (£3.75), pressed gammon terrine and fried quail egg with pineapple chutney and onion dressing (£4.95), slow roast lamb shank with bubble and squeak potato cake and butterbean red wine sauce (£8.50), twice baked cheese soufflé with asparagus and grape walnut sauce (£6.50), seafood and red pepper pesto risotto (£7.25), sirloin steak (£13.50) and puddings such as sticky toffee, date and chocolate pudding with butterscotch sauce or local ice creams (£3.95). The three changing well kept ales on handpump might include Timothy Taylors Landlord and Weetwood Eastgate with a guest such as Greene King Old Speckled Hen, and they stock over 30 malts; friendly staff. The big side lawn has picnic-sets, and is host to barbecues on some summer weekends. The bedrooms in the attractively converted sandstone barn have been refurbished. The pub is well placed for the Sandstone Trail on the Peckforton Hills, and the nearby Candle Workshops are quite a draw in summer. *(Recommended by Sue Holland, Dave Webster, Alan and Paula McCully, Rob Fowell, Steve Whalley, Brian and Anna Marsden, Mr and Mrs M Cooper, Graham and Lynn Mason)*

Free house ~ Licensees Bridget and Lee McKone ~ Real ale ~ Bar food (12-2.30, 6.30-9.30) ~ Restaurant ~ (01829) 770434 – fax (01829) 771097 ~ Children in eating area of bar till 8pm ~ Open 11-11; 12-10.30 Sun ~ Bedrooms: /£80S(£80B)

LANGLEY SJ9569 Map 7
Hanging Gate

Meg Lane, Higher Sutton; follow Langley signpost from A54 beside Fourways Motel, and that road passes the pub; from Macclesfield, heading S from centre on A523 turn left into Byrons Lane at Langley, Wincle signpost; in Sutton (½ mile after going under canal bridge, ie before Langley) fork right at Church House Inn, following Wildboarclough signpost, then 2 miles later turning sharp right at steep hairpin bend; OS Sheet 118 map reference 952696

The three low-beamed rambling rooms in this cosy old drovers' pub are simply and traditionally furnished, and have big coal fires, and some attractive old prints of Cheshire towns. Perched high on a Peak District ridge, it is thought to have been built long before it was first licensed, nearly 300 years ago. Good straightforward bar food includes soup (£2.25), fresh fried cod (£6.95), steaks (from £8.95) and (a readers' favourite here) lamb cutlets (£8.95), and there are puddings such as bread and butter pudding (£2.75). Well kept Hydes Bitter, Jekylls Gold and a guest from the brewery on handpump, and there are quite a few malt whiskies; piped music. The blue room is no smoking. There's an airy garden room down some stone steps and from seats outside on a crazy-paved terrace, there are spectacular views over a patchwork of valley pastures to distant moors, and the tall Sutton Common transmitter above them. *(Recommended by the Didler, Rob Fowell, JP, PP, Dr W J M Gissane, Nigel Woolliscroft, Mike and Wendy Proctor)*

Free house ~ Licensees Peter and Paul McGrath ~ Real ale ~ Bar food (not Sun evening) ~ Restaurant ~ (01260) 252238 ~ Children in family area ~ Open 12-3, 7-11; 12-11 Sat; 12-10.30 Sun

Leathers Smithy ◼

From Macclesfield, heading S from centre on A523 turn left into Byrons Lane at Langley,
Wincle signpost; in Langley follow main road forking left at church into Clarke Lane – keep
on towards the moors; OS Sheet 118 map reference 952715

Popular with walkers, the bustling, partly flagstoned right-hand bar of this cheerful
place has lots of traditional pubby character, with its bow-window seats, wheelback
chairs, and roughcast cream walls hung with motoring memorabilia. On the left,
there are more wheelback chairs around cast-iron-framed tables on a turkey carpet,
and open fires give the place a cosy feel in winter. Popular good value bar food
includes sandwiches (from £2.30), smoked salmon and prawns (£4.50), wild
mushroom lasagne or thai red chicken curry (£5.50), home-made steak pie (£5.25),
halibut in prawn and dill sauce, duck in orange sauce or gammon and egg (£6.95)
and good steaks (from £9.75), with puddings such as bilberry or apple pie (£2.50).
Alongside a good collection of spirits including well over 80 whiskies, they have
farm cider, gluhwein in winter from a copper salamander, and very well kept real
ales such as Greene King Abbot, Jennings Snecklifter and Timothy Taylors Landord.
Chatty landlord and wife; no piped music. Good views of Ridgegate Reservoir; close
to Macclesfield Forest and Teggs Nose country park. *(Recommended by Dr W J M
Gissane, Mr and Mrs C Roberts, Mike and Wena Stevenson, Derek Stafford, Lynette and Stuart
Shore)*

*Free house ~ Licensee Paul Hadfield ~ Real ale ~ Bar food (12-2, 7-9.30(8.30 Tues-
Thurs); 12-8.30 Sun; not Mon evening) ~ (01260) 252313 ~ Open 12-3 (exc winter
Mon), 7-11; 12-10.30 Sun*

LOWER PEOVER SJ7474 Map 7

Bells of Peover ★

The Cobbles; from B5081 take short cobbled lane signposted to church

This charming wisteria-covered pub, parts of which date back some 750 years, is
nicely tucked away in a peaceful hamlet. The seats on the crazy-paved terrace in front
overlook a fine black and white 14th-c church, and a spacious lawn beyond the old
coachyard at the side spreads down through trees and under rose pergolas to a little
stream. The cosy tiled bar has side hatches for its serving counter, toby jugs and comic
Victorian prints, and the original lounge has antique settles, high-backed windsor
armchairs and a spacious window seat, antique china in the dresser, pictures above
the panelling, and two small coal fires. There's a second similar lounge. Friendly,
efficient staff serve generous bar food which includes home-made soup (£2.25),
sandwiches and baguettes (from £3.90), filled baked potatoes (from £3.85),
ploughman's (from £4.20), chicken breast with white wine and pepper sauce (£7.50),
lambs liver with port and stilton sauce, (£7.85), broccoli and salmon bake (£6.75),
sirloin steak (£11.95), and daily specials with an emphasis on fish such as grilled brill
with parsley butter (£8.55) or grilled gilthead bream in a prawn and chive sauce
(£9.55) and puddings such as pecan pie and chocolate fudge brownie with white
chocolate sauce (from £2.95). Most people wear a jacket and tie in the restaurant.
Well kept Marstons Pedigree and Theakstons on handpump; dominoes, cribbage and
piped music. Children are not allowed in the pub. *(Recommended by Roger and Pauline
Pearce, Revd D Glover, Simon and Laura Habbishow, Leo and Barbara Lionet, Mrs P J Carroll,
Keith and Janet Eaton, Mr and Mrs P Smith, R F Grieve, Dr A J Williams, the Didler, W K Wood,
Darly Graton, Graeme Gulibert, P R and S A White, R Davies, Denis and Dorothy Evans, Mr and
Mrs Johnson, Eric Locker, Lesley Bass, JP, PP, Sue Holland, Dave Webster)*

*Scottish Courage ~ Manager Richard Casson ~ Real ale ~ Bar food (12(3 Sat)-2.30, 6-
9.30, 12-9 Sun) ~ Restaurant ~ (01565) 722269 ~ Open 11.30-3, 5.30-11; 11.30-11
Sat; 12-10.30 Sun*

People named as recommenders after the main entries have told us that the pub
should be included. But they have not written the report – we have, after
anonymous on-the-spot inspection.

MACCLESFIELD SJ9271 Map 7
Sutton Hall Hotel ★ 🛏

Leaving Macclesfield southwards on A523, turn left into Byrons Lane signposted Langley, Wincle, then just before canal viaduct fork right into Bullocks Lane; OS Sheet 118 map reference 925715

Peacocks strut among the tables on the tree-sheltered lawn, and ducks and moorhens swim in the pond in front of this elegant but unstuffy 16th-c baronial hall. Inside, the bar is divided into separate areas by tall black oak timbers, with some antique squared oak panelling, lightly patterned art nouveau stained-glass windows, broad flagstones around the bar counter (carpet elsewhere), and a raised open fire. It is mostly furnished with straightforward ladderback chairs around sturdy thick-topped cast-iron-framed tables, and there are a few unusual touches such as a suit of armour by a big stone fireplace, a longcase clock, a huge bronze bell for calling time and a brass cigar-lighting gas taper on the bar counter itself. Reasonably priced home-made bar food includes soup (£1.95), sandwiches (from £3.50), moules marinières (£4.75), broccoli and cheese bake (£5.75), tasty steak, kidney and oyster pie (£6.95), daily specials such as roast turkey with tarragon cream sauce (£6.45), grilled halibut in teriyaki marinade (£7.95), venison steak with cream, brandy and peppercorn sauce (£8.50), and puddings such as blueberry crème brûlée and chocolate, hazelnut and rum flan (£3). Well kept Bass, Greene King IPA, Marstons and a guest beer on handpump, 40 malt whiskies, decent wines, freshly squeezed fruit juice, and a proper pimms. They can arrange clay shooting, golf or local fishing for residents, and there's access to canal moorings at Gurnett Aqueduct on the Macclesfield Canal 200 yards away. *(Recommended by JP, PP, Mike and Wendy Proctor, Stephen, Julie and Hayley Brown, Bill Sykes, Adrian and Gwynneth Littleton, the Didler, Mrs P J Carroll, Dr W J M Gissane)*

Free house ~ Licensee Robert Bradshaw ~ Real ale ~ Bar food (12-2.30(2 Sun), 7-10) ~ Restaurant ~ (01260) 253211 ~ Children in restaurant and family room wknd and bank hol lunchtimes only ~ Open 11-11(10.30 Sun) ~ Bedrooms: £75S(£75B) /£90S(£90B)

NANTWICH SJ6552 Map 7
Crown

High Street; in pedestrian-only centre, close to church; free public parking behind the inn

The overhanging upper galleries and uncertain black and white perpendiculars and horizontals of this strikingly quaint three-storey timbered hotel have dominated the High Street since 1583. The cosy rambling beamed bar is simply furnished with various antique tables and chairs on its sloping creaky floors. Lunchtime bar food includes soup (£2.25), sandwiches (from £2.55), filled baked potatoes (from £3.75), ploughman's (£4.45), plaice (£4.60), steak (£9.75), daily specials such as grilled lamb cutlets or steak and kidney pie (£5.35); children's menu (£2.85); the evening restaurant specialises in Italian food. Boddingtons and Flowers IPA on handpump; very busy weekend evenings; piped music, fruit machine and TV. *(Recommended by M Joyner)*

Free house ~ Licensees Phillip and Susan Martin ~ Real ale ~ Bar food (lunchtime) ~ Restaurant (evening, all day Sat) ~ (01270) 625283 ~ Children welcome ~ Open 11-11; 12-10.30 Sun ~ Bedrooms: £69.95B/£87.90B

OVER PEOVER SJ7674 Map 7
Olde Park Gate

Stocks Lane; off A50 N of Holmes Chapel at the Whipping Stock

Inside this traditional pub, each small room has a character of its own: flowery wallpaper and an oriental rug on parquet floor in one place, carpeting, coach horns, horse tack and guns in another, small hunting and other country prints in yet another. Most are quiet and civilised, with black beams and joists, and a good mix of various-sized Macclesfield oak seats and more workaday chairs. The back room with its darts and basic wall seats is a real locals' haunt; no smoking area. Like the well kept Sam Smiths OB on handpump, the bar food (virtually all home-made) is good value, and includes soup (£2.50), sandwiches (from £3.45), hot rolls such as sausage and fried onions (£4.25), proper pies such as lamb and apricot or beef, ale and mushroom (£7.95-£9.95), ploughman's (£6.95), roast of the day or curry (£7.15), and puddings such as blueberry bakewell or blackcurrant and apple pie (£2.95). The pub has teams for darts and dominoes; piped music, juke box, fruit machine and TV. *(Recommended by Rob Fowell, Steve Whalley, Peter F Marshall)*

Sam Smiths ~ Manager Gillian Carter ~ Real ale ~ Bar food (12-2, 6.30-9, not Sun or Mon evening) ~ (01625) 861455 ~ Children in separate family room ~ Open 11.30-11; 12-3.30, 7-10.30 Sun

OVERTON SJ5277 Map 7
Ring o' Bells ◗ £

Just over 2 miles from M56 junction 12; 2 Bellemonte Road – from A56 in Frodsham take B5152 and turn right (uphill) at Parish Church signpost

The charm of this friendly pub is that things never seem to change here, and in summer the outside is festooned with a mass of colourful hanging baskets. Dating from the early 17th c, a couple of the little rambling rooms have pleasant views over a stone-built church and the Mersey far below. It's very much the sort of place where drinkers stand around the bar chatting. The room at the back has some antique settles, brass-and-leather fender seats by the log fire, and old hunting prints on its butter-coloured walls; a beamed room with antique dark oak panelling and stained glass leads through to a darts room (there's also a TV, dominoes, cribbage, and other board games). An old-fashioned hatch-like central servery dispenses Flowers IPA, Greenalls and Timothy Taylors Landlord along with four or five guest ales a week on handpump, and they also stock over 80 different malt whiskies. Very reasonably priced lunchtime bar food includes sandwiches and toasties (from £2), filled baked potatoes (£2.75), home-made steak and mushroom pie, chicken tikka masala or cumberland sausage and mash, (£3.95), and puddings such as spotted dick; friendly waitress service. There's one no smoking room, and a secluded garden at the back has tables and chairs, a pond, and lots of trees. Look out for the friendly pub cats. *(Recommended by Stephen, Julie and Hayley Brown, MH, BD, Bernie Adams, Joy and Peter Heatherley)*

Greenalls ~ Tenant Shirley Wroughton-Craig ~ Real ale ~ Bar food (lunchtime) ~ Restaurant ~ No credit cards ~ (01928) 732068 ~ Children welcome away from bar ~ Open 11.30-3(4 Sat), 5.30(6 Sat)-11; 12-4, 7-10.30 Sun

PEOVER HEATH SJ7973 Map 7
Dog 🛏

Off A50 N of Holmes Chapel at the Whipping Stocks, keep on past Parkgate into Wellbank Lane; OS Sheet 118 map reference 794735; note that this village is called Peover Heath on the OS map and shown under that name on many road maps, but the pub is often listed under Over Peover instead

There are usually lots of drinkers among the diners at this civilised, friendly place, and readers praise the fact that children are welcome in the games area. Service is relaxed but efficient. As well as home-made soup (£2.50), a very good range of sandwiches (from £2.95), and ploughman's (from £4.95), the large helpings of straightforward bar food might include starters such as smoked scottish salmon, prawn and avocado salad or deep-fried brie with cranberry sauce (£4.50), with main courses such as roast local leg of lamb, mushroom stroganoff, roast duck in black cherry sauce, ham shank with parsley sauce or spinach and mushroom lasagne (£9.95), steaks (from £10.95) and puddings such as cheesecakes, fruit pies and pavlovas (£3.50). It's best to book at weekends; the dining room is no smoking. Well kept Hydes, Moorhouses Black Cat and Weetwood Best and Old Dog are served on handpump, along with Addlestone's cider, over 50 malt whiskies, freshly squeezed orange juice, and a decent expanding wine list; darts, pool, dominoes, TV, juke box and piped music. The main bar has comfortable easy chairs and wall seats (including one built into a snug alcove around an oak table), and two wood-backed built-in seats either side of a coal fire, opposite which logs burn in an old-fashioned black grate. There are picnic-sets out on the quiet lane, underneath the pub's pretty hanging baskets, and the attractive garden is nicely lit on summer evenings. Well equipped bedrooms. One reader tells us that there's a good walk from here along cross-country paths and quiet country lanes to the Jodrell Bank Centre and Arboretum. *(Recommended by Dr Paull Khan, Steve Whalley, Mr and Mrs Gordon Turner, Charles and Pauline Stride, Pat and Dick Warwick, E G Parish, Graham and Lynn Mason, Denis and Dorothy Evans)*

Free house ~ Licensee Steven Wrigley ~ Real ale ~ Bar food (12-2.30, 7-9.30, not evening 25 Dec) ~ Restaurant ~ (01625) 861421 ~ Children in eating area of bar and restaurant ~ Theme night 2nd Fri in month ~ Open 11.30-3, 5(5.30 Sat)-11; 12-10.30 Sun ~ Bedrooms: £55B/£75B

PLUMLEY SJ7175 Map 7
Smoker

2½ miles from M6 junction 19: A556 towards Northwich and Chester

Taking its name from a favourite racehorse of the Prince Regent, this partly thatched, popular old pub is a good haven from the M6. Its three well decorated connecting rooms have dark panelling, open fires in impressive period fireplaces, military prints, a collection of copper kettles, and an Edwardian print of a hunt meeting outside which shows how little the appearance of the pub has changed over the centuries. It's comfortably furnished throughout with deep sofas, cushioned settles, windsor chairs, and some rush-seat dining chairs. The same menu covers both the bar and brasserie (though they will reserve tables and give full waitress service in the brasserie); this has created a relaxed atmosphere, with the brasserie becoming even more part of the pub. Reasonably priced bar food, which changes every three months to reflect the season, includes home-made soup (£2.35), sandwiches and baguettes (from £2.95), haggis (£4.55), smoked duck breast with orange (£7.35), beef, pork and chicken fillet stir fry (£9.75), beef stroganoff (£7.95), steaks (from £10.95), a vegetarian daily special and a selection of fish and seafood such as lemon sole goujons or seafood tagliatelle (£7.35); puddings such as lemon torte with raspberry coulis and jam roly-poly with custard (£2.95); two-course Sunday set menu (£10.95). Well kept Robinsons Best and Old Stockport on handpump, 30 malt whiskies and a good choice of wines; friendly efficient service. There are no smoking areas in the bar, and they plan to make the brasserie no smoking as well; piped music. The sizeable side lawn has roses and flowerbeds, and there's a children's play area in the extended garden. *(Recommended by Mr and Mrs C M Pearson, Ian Phillips, Simon J Barber, Lynette and Stuart Shore, John and Elspeth Howell, Revd D Glover, Joy and Peter Heatherley, Rob Fowell, E G Parish, Nigel and Sue Foster, Stan and Hazel Allen, D S Jackson, R Mathews, Colin Parker)*

Robinsons ~ Tenants John and Diana Bailey ~ Real ale ~ Bar food (12-2.15, 6.30-9.30; 12-9.15 Sun) ~ Restaurant ~ (01565) 722338 ~ Children in eating area of bar and restaurant ~ Open 1.30-3, 6-11; 12-10.30 Sun

TARPORLEY SJ5563 Map 7
Rising Sun

High Street; village signposted off A51 Nantwich—Chester

This bustling village pub, prettiest in summer with its mass of hanging baskets and flowering tubs, is popular with locals and visitors alike. The cosy rooms contain well chosen tables surrounded by eye-catching old seats including creaky 19th-c mahogany and oak settles; there's also an attractively blacked iron kitchen range (and three open fires), sporting and other old-fashioned prints on the walls, and a big oriental rug in the back room. Good hearty bar food includes sandwiches (from £2.50), toasties from (£2.95), filled baked potatoes (from £2.95), stuffed mushrooms (£3.45), home-made turkey and ham pie (£6.75), lasagne (£6.95), gammon steak (£7.95), and a good vegetarian choice such as quorn and butter bean goulash or black bean sizzler (£8.10), mixed grill (£11.20), and 16oz rump steak (£11.95). Well kept Robinsons Best and Mild on handpump. The surrounding village is attractive. *(Recommended by E G Parish, Brian Wainwright, Sue Holland, Dave Webster, the Didler, Mike and Mary Carter, Rob Fowell)*

Robinsons ~ Tenant Alec Robertson ~ Real ale ~ Bar food (12-2, 5.30-9; 12-10.30 Sun) ~ Restaurant (evening) ~ (01829) 732423 ~ Children in lounge and eating area of bar, over 12s in restaurant only in evening ~ Open 11.30-3.30, 5.30-11; 11.30-11 bank holidays and Sat; 12-10.30 Sun

WESTON SJ7352 Map 7
White Lion 🛏

3½ miles from M6 junction 16; A500 towards Crewe, then village signposted on right

Originally a Tudor farmhouse, this pretty black and white timbered inn has a bustling low-beamed main room divided into smaller areas by very gnarled black oak standing timbers. There's a varied mix of seats from cushioned modern settles to ancient oak ones, with plenty of smaller chairs. In a smaller room on the left are three fine settles, carved in 18th-c style; the atmosphere is relaxed and friendly. Straightforward bar food includes home-made soup (£1.95), sandwiches (from £2.50), filled baguettes (from £3.75), vegetable lasagne (£5.25), good value daily specials such as haddock mornay, chicken and ham or steak and mushroom pie, and mixed grill (£5.25), poached local Dee salmon (£7.95) and steak (£11.25); as well as home-made puddings (£3.25), they do a range of ice cream sundaes. Attentive service from the pleasant young staff. You may need to book at the weekend, and it's worth noting that they stop serving lunch at 1.45 on Sunday. Well kept Bass and Boddingtons on handpump, and a sizeable wine list; dominoes, TV and piped music. The two side rooms are no smoking. It has its own bowling green by a sheltered lawn with picnic-sets behind. *(Recommended by Klaus and Elizabeth Leist, Sue Holland, Dave Webster)*

Free house ~ Licensee Alison Davies ~ Real ale ~ Bar food (not 25 Dec) ~ Restaurant ~ (01270) 500303 ~ Children in restaurant and family room ~ Open 11-3, 5(6.30 Sat)-11; 12-3, 7-10.30 Sun ~ Bedrooms: £58B/£68B

WHITEGATE SJ6268 Map 7
Plough

Foxwist Green; along Beauty Bank, opp Methodist chapel – OS Sheet 118 map reference 624684; from A556 at W end roundabout of Northwich bypass take Whitegate road, bear right in village and then take Foxwist Green turn left; or from A54 W of Winsford turn off at Salterswell roundabout, then first left

They now serve more than 10 different types of coffee at this cheerful old pub. The two pleasant rooms inside have simple but comfortable furnishings (the intimate little dining room has just half a dozen tables), and a fire lends a cosy feel to the lounge. Especially popular with locals, the wide choice of enjoyable home-made food often uses fresh local produce, and might range from soup (£2.25), sandwiches (from £2.95), and filled baked potatoes (from £4.95), to steak pie, grilled breaded haddock or chicken curry (£6.25), half lamb shoulder in port and rosemary sauce (£7.95), 8oz sirloin steak (£8.75), a decent choice of vegetarian dishes such as moussaka or mushroom and sweetcorn stroganoff (£6.50); daily specials could be pork with stilton and port cream sauce (£7.75) and diced lamb with mint and mango (£7.25), and they do puddings such as chocolate and Baileys pie and home-made meringues with butterscotch sauce (from £2.95); two sittings for Sunday lunch. In summer, children's meals are served in the garden only, which has a new play area (children are not allowed inside). Well kept Robinsons Best Hatters Mild and Old Stockport; Monday quiz night; piped music, TV and dominoes. The Whitegate Way – a rehabilitated former railway track – is one of several popular walks nearby. *(Recommended by Jeff and Miriam Hancock, Carol and Dono Leaman, Pat and Dick Warwick)*

Robinsons ~ Tenant David Hughes ~ Real ale ~ Bar food (12-2, 6.30-9, all day Sun in summer) ~ Restaurant ~ (01606) 889455 ~ Children under 14 in garden only ~ quiz night on Mon ~ Open 12-(10.30 Sun)11; 12-3.30, 7-10.30 Sun winter

WHITELEY GREEN SJ9278 Map 7
Windmill

Hole House Lane; village signposted off A523 a mile N of B5091 Bollington turn-off

The interior of this large, well restored slate-roofed white house has been refitted in the style of a country farmhouse, with attractive wood-floored open-plan extensions leading off from the original heavily beamed 16th-c core. Nothing much has changed since the new landlord took over, with much space still given over to dining – well spaced tables and a good-sized no smoking area. But there's room too to sit over the daily papers with a pint of well kept Greene King Old Speckled Hen, Tetleys or their guest beer (maybe Adnams Broadside or Bass) from handpump. Using local produce when possible, the weekly changing bar food might include soup (£1.95), sandwiches (from £2.45), ploughman's (£4.95), broccoli bake (£5.95), chicken with stilton and pepper sauce (£9.95) and sirloin steak (from £8.95), with puddings such as treacle sponge (£2.75); three-course Sunday lunch (£11.95). Look out for the pegged wall draughts; fruit machine, TV, and piped music. The attractive four-acre garden has pretty shrub borders around the lawn, plenty of picnic-sets, and a bar and barbecue in summer; there are smart wooden benches and green parasols at the front. Tucked away up a quiet country lane, the pub is close to the Middlewood Way, a sort of linear country park along a former rail track, and there are nearby canal and other walks. *(Recommended by Roger and Pauline Pearce)*

Bass ~ Manager Neil Gaffin ~ Real ale ~ Bar food (12-3 Sun, 6.30-9) ~ Restaurant ~ (01625) 574222 ~ Well behaved children away from bar ~ Open 12-3, 5-11; 12-11 Sat; 12-10.30 Sun

WILLINGTON SJ5367 Map 7
Boot

Boothsdale, off A54 at Kelsall

Well placed for walks, this relaxed dining pub is attractively set on a wooded hillside looking out over the lush farmland and hedgerows of the Cheshire plain towards the Welsh hills. Converted from sandstone cottages, it has a new extension with french windows overlooking the garden. Inside has been carefully opened up, leaving small unpretentiously furnished room areas around the central bar with its woodburning stove. The restaurant has wheelback chairs around plenty of tables on its flagstones, and a good log fire. As well as simpler dishes such as soup (£2.40), sandwiches and baguettes (from £3.50), ploughman's (£5.90), asparagus and brie bake (£8.25), fried chicken and bacon (£8.50) and steaks (from £10.95), there are interesting daily specials such as grilled black pudding with smoked bacon, shallot and tarragon cream sauce (£4.95), or deep-fried fillets of bass coated in sesame batter with chilli, ginger and lemon salsa (£10.50); puddings (£3.95). Well kept Cains, Flowers Original, Greenalls and a guest from the local Weetwood brewery on handpump, 30 malt whiskies, and a decent wine list. Outside, the raised stone terrace with picnic-sets is a summer suntrap, and children enjoy meeting the three donkeys, pot-bellied pig, golden retriever H, and Monty the cat. There's a good fruit farm nearby. *(Recommended by Joy and Peter Heatherley, E G Parish, MH, BD)*

Inn Partnership (Nomura) ~ Lease Mike Gollings and Liz Edwards ~ Real ale ~ Bar food (11-2.30, 6-9.30, all day wknds and bank holidays) ~ Restaurant ~ (01829) 751375 ~ Children in restaurant lunchtime and early evening ~ Open 11-3, 6-11; 11-11 bank holidays and Sat; 11-10.30 Sun; closed 25 Dec

WINCLE SJ9666 Map 7
Ship ◖

Village signposted off A54 Congleton—Buxton

An ideal stop for walkers, this cosy 16th-c pub is reputedly one of Cheshire's oldest. Two old-fashioned and simple little tap rooms (no piped music or games machines) have thick stone walls, a coal fire, and Boddingtons, Wye Valley, and a constantly changing guest ale on handpump. From a changing blackboard, enjoyable bar food might include home-made soup (£2.95), smoked salmon and dill pâté (£3.95), local trout with almonds sautéed in garlic butter, brie and leek parcels with mustard cream sauce or pasta tossed with roasted vegetables, pesto, pine nuts and goats cheese (£7.95), chicken breast stuffed with mozzarella and sun-dried tomato with provençal sauce (£8.95), steaks (from £10.95), and home-made puddings such as rhubarb crumble or crêpes (£2.95). It can get busy Saturday evenings and Sunday lunchtimes (when you might have to park on the steep, narrow road outside), so it's a good idea to book. There's a small garden with wooden tables and swings. Friendly staff can give you advice on the best local walks through the picturesque surrounding countryside, and they may stay open all day on summer weekends. *(Recommended by the Didler, Nigel Woolliscroft, Rob Fowell, DC, Hugh A MacLean, Dr D J and Mrs S C Walker, Mike and Wendy Proctor, E G Parish, A Maclean)*

Free house ~ Licensee Steven Mark Simpson ~ Real ale ~ Bar food (not Mon exc bank holidays) ~ Restaurant ~ (01260) 227217 ~ Children in family room ~ Open 12-3, 7-(10.30 Sun)11; closed Mon (exc bank holidays)

WRENBURY SJ5948 Map 7
Dusty Miller
Village signposted from A530 Nantwich—Whitchurch

This handsomely converted 19th-c mill is perfectly positioned in a tranquil spot by the Shropshire Union Canal. The comfortable modern main area has long low-hung hunting prints on terracotta walls, and the variety of seats includes tapestried banquettes, an ornate church pew and wheelback chairs flanking rustic tables. If you go further in there's a quarry-tiled standing-only part by the bar counter (dogs are welcome here), which has well kept Robinsons Best and Hatters Mild and (in winter) Old Tom on handpump. Good service; piped music, dominoes. Made largely from fresh local ingredients, good hearty bar food might include home-made soup (£2.95), filled rolls (from £3.50), coarse goose pâté with rhubarb and ginger jam (£3.95), deep-fried hot and spicy creel prawns with yoghurt dip (£5.55), oatcakes filled with spinach, mushrooms and garlic and glazed with cheese (£7.50), vegetable gratin (£5.75), smoked haddock with prawns baked in mustard and cider sauce (£8.25), chargrilled chicken fillet in creamy stilton sauce with buttery peppered cabbage (£8.95), and local steaks (from £10.75); vegetables (£1.75); the upstairs dining area and three tables in the bar are no smoking. From a series of tall glazed arches inside, you can see the striking counter-weighted drawbridge going up and down, and in summer you can look on from the picnic-sets on the gravel terrace among rose bushes by the canal (reached either by the towpath or by a high wooden catwalk over the River Weaver which, unusually, passes beneath the canal). *(Recommended by Mike and Wendy Proctor, Mr and Mrs J Underwood, P J Holt, E G Parish)*

Robinsons ~ Tenant Mark Sumner ~ Real ale ~ Bar food (not Mon in winter) ~ Restaurant ~ (01270) 780537 ~ Children in eating area of bar and restaurant ~ Open 11-3, 6-11; 12-3, 7-10.30 Sun; closed Mon lunchtime in winter

---

Post Office address codings confusingly give the impression that some pubs are in Cheshire, when they're really in Derbyshire (and therefore included in this book under that chapter) or in Greater Manchester (see the Lancashire chapter).

Lucky Dip

Besides the fully inspected pubs, you might like to try these Lucky Dips recommended to us and described by readers (if you do, please send us reports: www.goodguides.com).

Acton Bridge [SJ5975]
☆ *Maypole* [Hill Top Rd; B5153 off A49 in Weaverham, then right towards Acton Cliff]: Civilised and warmly welcoming beamed dining pub very popular for wide choice of good varied generous food (booking advised wknds), close-set tables in big dining area with lots of brass, copper and china, some antique settles as well as more modern furnishings, two coal fires, well kept Greenalls, gentle piped music; attractive outside with hanging baskets and tubs, seats in well kept garden with orchard behind *(Mr and Mrs B Hobden, LYM)*

Alderley Edge [SJ8478]
Royal Oak [Heyes Lane]: Large comfortably revamped pub with cosy book-lined corners, good range of reasonably priced hot dishes, sandwiches too, well kept beers, good value house wines; back terrace with grassy play area *(Mrs E E Sanders)*

Allgreave [SU9767]
Rose & Crown [A54 Congleton—Buxton]: Small, very friendly, in remote spot in great walking country, good Dane valley views; small choice of interesting food (may be best to book wknds), good choice of well kept ales and of wines, excellent service; three refurbished bedrooms *(Guy Vowles)*

Allostock [SJ7572]
Drovers Arms [A50 Knutsford—Holmes Chapel]: Well spaced tables in roomy bar with wide choice of popular food from well filled sandwiches and baguettes up; some music nights *(E G Parish)*

Alpraham [SJ5959]
Travellers Rest [A51 Nantwich—Chester]: Particularly well kept Tetleys Bitter and Mild in unchanging four-room country local in same family for three generations, chatty involving atmosphere presided over by veteran landlady, leatherette, wicker and Formica, some flock wallpaper, fine old brewery mirrors, darts, back bowling green; no games machines, no piped music and no food (apart from crisps and nuts), cl wkdy lunchtimes *(the Didler, Pete Baker, JP, PP, E G Parish)*

Alsager [SJ8054]
Manor House [Audley Rd]: Part of hotel complex, cosy and charming oak-beamed lounge bar, relaxing atmosphere, good choice of food inc lunchtime salad bar, comfortable restaurant, friendly staff, Flowers Original; good bedrooms *(E G Parish)*

Alvanley [SJ4974]
☆ *White Lion* [Manley Rd; handy for M56 junction 14]: Comfortable and civilised 16th-c dining pub with good slightly upscale food inc good fish and children's dishes, friendly service, plush low-beamed lounge, busy restaurant extension (booking recommended), games in smaller public bar, Greenalls Mild, Bitter and Original; tables on terrace, play area, farm animals and duck pond *(Myke and Nicky Crombleholme, E G Parish, LYM, MH, BD,*

Graham and Lynn Mason)

Audlem [SJ6543]
☆ *Shroppie Fly* [Shropshire St]: Beautifully placed by Locks 12/13 of Shropshire Union Canal, one bar shaped like a barge, good canal photographs, brightly painted bargees' china and bric-a-brac, usual food inc children's, well kept Boddingtons and Flowers IPA and Original, friendly staff, mainly modern furnishings, children in room off bar and restaurant; piped music; seats on waterside terrace, open almost all day summer, cl winter lunchtimes *(LYM, E G Parish, L Davenport)*

Barbridge [SJ6156]
☆ *Barbridge Inn* [just off A51 N of Nantwich]: Well run and lively open-plan family dining pub done out in olde-worlde style with tiled floors, faded woodwork, hessian curtains, country prints and artefacts; pretty setting by lively marina at junction of Shropshire Union and Middlewich canals, with play area in busy riverside garden, flagstoned conservatory with washtub tables, no smoking area, friendly helpful staff, simple well cooked food, well kept Boddingtons, Cains and Greenalls, games room, quiet piped music; good disabled facilities, open all day, quiz Tues, jazz Thurs, barbecue *(LYM, Mike and Wendy Proctor, Richard Lewis)*

Beeston [SJ5459]
☆ *Beeston Castle Hotel* [A49 S of Tarporley]: Clean and comfortable, in good walking country below the castle, polite cheerful staff, good choice of attractively presented food, small wing chairs and sensible tables in spacious bar, well kept Bass and Worthington, short but well chosen wine list, restaurant; children until 8, comfortable bedrooms, open all day Sun *(E G Parish)*

Bradfield Green [SJ6859]
Coach & Horses [A530 NW of Crewe]: Attractive and comfortably cottagey, good value properly cooked food inc children's, well kept ales inc Greenalls, decent wines, good friendly staff, horse pictures; discreet piped music *(E G Parish)*

Brereton Green [SJ7864]
Bears Head [handy for M6 junction 17; set back off A50 S of Holmes Chapel]: Handsome old heavily timbered inn, its warren of old rooms pleasantly refurbished as a comfortable brasserie-style Vintage Inn, with old-fashioned furniture, good choice of well prepared fresh straightforward food, well kept Bass, Worthington BB and a guest such as Fullers London Pride, cheerful log fire, welcoming service; open all day, good value bedrooms in modern block *(LYM, Margaret Ross, A C Sullivan, E G Parish, Dorsan Baker)*

Broxton [SJ4858]
☆ *Egerton Arms* [A41/A534 S of Chester]: Neatly kept welcoming family pub, well polished old furniture, antique plates and prints in roomy dark-panelled bar, warmly decorated no

smoking dining area off; wide choice of good food (all day wknds) from sandwiches up inc lots for children, helpful efficient staff, maybe well kept Burtonwood Top Hat and a guest such as local Beartown Bearskinful, decent wines, children very welcome, colouring materials; discreet piped music; picnic-sets out under cocktail parasols, play area, balcony terrace with lovely views, open all day, recently refurbished bedrooms *(LYM, MH, BD, MLR)*

Chelford [SJ8175]

Egerton Arms [A537 Macclesfield—Knutsford]: Good Chef & Brewer, candles on oak tables, bottles on shelves, bric-a-brac, enjoyable blackboard food inc thai curries, Theakstons; tables outside *(Kevin Blake)*

Chester [SJ4066]

Boathouse [The Groves, off Grosvenor Park Rd; on Dee 5 mins from centre]: Modern pub on site of 17th-c boat house by River Dee next to rowing clubs, super views, large airy family room, good range of lunchtime food inc children's promptly served to numbered tables, ales such as Greene King Old Speckled Hen and Ruddles County and Theakstons XB (more in Ale Taster back bar, which specialises in them), fruit machines; good disabled facilities; picnic-sets on small terrace *(E G Parish)*

☆ *Boot* [Eastgate Row N]: Down-to-earth unpretentious pub atmosphere in lovely 17th-c Rows building, heavy beams, lots of woodwork, oak flooring and flagstones, even some exposed Tudor wattle and daub, black-leaded kitchen range in lounge beyond good value food servery, no smoking oak-panelled upper area popular with families (despite hard settles), good service, cheap well kept Sam Smiths, relaxed feel; piped music, children allowed *(Sue Holland, Dave Webster, the Didler, Rona Murdoch, LYM)*

Falcon [Lower Bridge St]: Striking building with good bustling atmosphere, handsome beams and brickwork, well kept Sam Smiths, decent basic bar meals (not Sun), fruit machine, piped music; children allowed lunchtime (not Sat) in airy upstairs room; jazz Sat lunchtime, open all day Sat, interesting tours of the vaults; can get packed *(LYM, Sue Holland, Dave Webster)*

Mill [Milton St]: Pleasantly relaxed real ale bar in ex-mill hotel, up to ten changing well kept ales from smaller breweries inc a Mild, friendly efficient staff, enjoyable bar food till late evening, good value Sun lunch, restaurant overlooking canal; piped music, jazz Mon; good with children, waterside tables, boat trips; bedrooms *(the Didler, Sue Holland, Dave Webster)*

Union Vaults [Francis St/Egerton St]: Classic corner alehouse with enthusiastic staff, three quiet and friendly split-level rooms, well kept and reasonably priced Greenalls, Plassey and unusual changing beers and stouts (guest beer suggestions book), bar billiards and bagatelle, back room with pool; maybe sandwiches (nothing else), piped music; open all day *(the Didler, Sue Holland, Dave Webster, Joe Green)*

Watergates [Watergate Sq]: Rambling candlelit medieval crypt, good wines by the glass, quickly served food; late evenings fills with young people and loud well reproduced music *(BB, Andy, Julie and Stuart Hawkins)*

Clotton [SJ5364]

Bulls Head [A51 Chester—Nantwich]: Attractive building, spaciously refurbished, with civilised but friendly atmosphere, well presented food inc interesting dishes, good service, John Smiths, pool room; country views *(E G Parish)*

Congleton [SJ8663]

Beartown Tap [Willow St]: Reworked as light and airy tap for local Beartown small brewery, their beers from six handpumps, several rooms off bar *(Edward Leetham)*

Heath Farm [Padgbury Lane]: Popular open-plan country-theme Big Steak family dining pub in converted farmhouse with animal pictures, no smoking and family areas inc attached indoor play area for younger children (but also a child-free dining area), usual food all day inc bargains for two and Sun carvery, well kept Marstons Pedigree and Tetleys, maybe a guest such as Greene King Triumph, smart friendly staff; karaoke and disco nights; good disabled facilities, open all day *(Rob Fowell, Richard Lewis)*

Cotebrook [SJ5765]

Alvanley Arms [A49/B5152 N of Tarporley]: Handsome Georgian-fronted sandstone inn dating partly from 16th c, two comfortable rooms (one no smoking) off chintzy hall, new landlady providing wide choice of good reasonably priced food from sandwiches up, well kept Hartleys XB, decent house wines, a good few malt whiskies, big open fire, neat high beams, interesting sporting and other prints; attractive fairy-lit pond-side garden; children in restaurant, comfortable good value bedrooms *(LYM, Phyl Karsenbarg, Jill and Peter Small)*

Crewe [SJ7053]

Albion [Pedley St]: Backstreet local refurbished and brightened up under new landlord, well kept Tetleys Bitter and Dark Mild, friendly staff, railway-theme lounge, lively bar with darts, dominoes, TV and pool room; piped music, quiz night Weds *(JP, PP, E G Parish)*

Borough Arms [Earle St]: Recently reopened and regaining its original name, new landlord keeping nine or ten interesting changing ales in top condition, four Belgian beers on draught and dozens in bottle, two real lagers; railway theme, green décor, plans for basement restaurant, tables outside and even a microbrewery; initially has been cl lunchtime *(E G Parish, Edward Leetham, the Didler)*

Brocklebank [Weston Road]: Roomy open-plan Brewers Fayre family dining pub, bric-a-brac, railway prints, comfortable seating, big conservatory, Lego play room, lots of high chairs, baby-changing room, adventure playground; wide food choice, Greene King Old Speckled Hen, friendly efficient staff; open all day *(Richard Lewis)*

Cross Keys [Remer St]: Large, comfortable and expertly run, current chef/landlord doing good generous food (all day Sat) inc popular Sun lunches, real ales *(E G Parish)*

Crown [Earle St]: Sociable and popular local

comfortably refurbished and opened up, but keeping its high ceilings, old-fashioned furnishings and wallpaper, 1940s snug with service bell pushes, back games area with pool and juke box, welcoming landlady, well kept Robinsons; handy for Railway Heritage Centre *(Pete Baker, E G Parish, Sue Holland, Dave Webster)*

Express [Mill St]: Comfortable local with well kept ale, sports TV *(E G Parish)*

Rising Sun [Middlewich Rd (A530), Wolstanwood]: After refurbishment settling down well under current management, good food range from ploughman's and distinctive open sandwiches up, well kept Greenalls, Tetleys and an interesting guest beer, panelling, prints and comfortable seating in lots of separate areas, raised eating area, children's facilities; tables and play area outside, open all day, good disabled access (inc lift), bedrooms, quiet countryside *(E G Parish)*

Delamere [SJ5669]

☆ *Fishpool* [A54/B5152]: Bright china and brasses on green walls of four small rooms, good relaxed atmosphere, well kept ales such as Greenalls Bitter, Mild and Original, Marstons Pedigree, John Smiths, Tetleys and Weetwood Old Dog, no games or music, well behaved children allowed; lunchtime sandwiches and snacks, wider evening choice, open all day, picnic-sets on peaceful lawn, good spot nr pike-haunted lake and Delamere Forest *(Stephen, Julie and Hayley Brown, MH, BD, Revd D Glover, LYM, Olive and Ray Hebson)*

Faddiley [SJ5753]

☆ *Thatch* [A534 Wrexham—Nantwich]: Attractive cottagey thatched, low-beamed and timbered dining pub with carefully done new barn-style restaurant extension and charming country garden, well kept Courage Directors, Theakstons Best and Mild, Websters Yorkshire and a local guest such as Plassey Best, food (all day Sun) from imaginatively filled baguettes to some interesting main dishes, children in restaurant, no smoking area; dominoes, fruit machine, piped music; open all day Sun *(LYM, Sue Holland, Dave Webster, Rob Fowell, E G Parish, MH, BD)*

Frodsham [SJ5278]

Helter Skelter [Church St]: Wide range of good food inc speciality Welsh rarebit and vegetarian choice, good choice of well kept beers (inc guests) and ciders from long counter on right, nice atmosphere with tall stools, leaning-post seating, window tables and raised deck, real fire, upstairs restaurant Thurs-Sat; poor disabled access *(Owen Campbell, G Coates)*

Fullers Moor [SJ4954]

☆ *Copper Mine* [A534]: Busy and comfortable dining pub, fresh, light and airy in summer, cosy coal fire in winter; wide choice of well presented tasty food from big lunchtime sandwiches to good Sun lunches, well kept Bass, friendly staff, pine furnishings, interesting copper-mining memorabilia and lots of copper kettles and warming pans, pretty nooks and crannies; children welcome, spacious garden with barbecues and lovely views; handy for

Sandstone Trail *(MDN, E G Parish, MLR, LYM, John Brightley)*

Gawsworth [SJ8969]

☆ *Harrington Arms* [Church Lane]: Ancient farm pub's two traditional small panelled rooms (children allowed in one) with bare boards, fine carved oak bar counter, well kept Robinsons Best and Hatters Mild served in big old enamelled jugs, friendly service, pickled eggs, sandwiches and pies freshly made; benches on small front cobbled terrace *(the Didler, JP, PP, E G Parish, LYM)*

Grappenhall [SJ6386]

Parr Arms [nr M6 junction 20; A50 towards Warrington, left after 1½ miles; Church Lane]: Pleasant pub with good genuine home cooking, Greenalls and two guest ales; tables out by church, picture-postcard setting *(Edward Jago)*

Great Budworth [SJ6778]

☆ *George & Dragon* [signed off A559 NE of Northwich; High St]: Attractive and unusual 17th-c building in delightful village, rambling panelled lounge, beams hung with copper jugs, interesting things to look at, red plush button-back banquettes and older settles, helpful service, sensibly priced bar food inc good Sun lunch, well kept Tetleys and two quickly changing guest beers (over 100 a year), farm cider, decent coffee, no smoking area, games in public bar, recently redone upstairs restaurant and (Weds-Sun – worth booking) family dining area; open all day Sat/Sun *(E G Parish, LYM, Bernie Adams, R F Grieve)*

Guilden Sutton [SJ4468]

☆ *Bird in Hand* [Church Lane]: Good well presented food in quiet civilised dining pub, friendly service, good selection of well kept beer; children welcome *(Philip Hastain, Dawn Baddeley)*

Gurnett [SJ9271]

☆ *Old Kings Head* [just S of Macclesfield]: Beamed former coaching house and smithy, now a welcoming split-level local by Macclesfield Canal aqueduct (moorings), old-fashioned unlit kitchen range, well kept Banks's, very generous reasonably priced good food, restaurant, attentive service; quiet piped music *(Bill Sykes)*

Haughton Moss [SJ5856]

Nags Head [Long Lane, off A49 S of Tarporley]: Very friendly black and white pub with low beams, pristine furnishings, fresh food cooked to order, also well filled sandwiches; excellent welcoming service, real ales, big garden with unobtrusive play area, bowling green for hire; children welcome, no dogs *(Mrs P J Carrol, Sue Holland, Dave Webster)*

Heatley [SJ7088]

Railway [Mill Lane (B5159)]: Friendly traditional local with four distinct rooms, good value soup and hot lunches, fresh filled barm cakes other times, particularly well kept Boddingtons and Timothy Taylors Landlord; alongside disused railway, now part of Trans-Pennine Trail *(R Davies)*

Huxley [SJ5162]

Farmers Arms [off A51 SE of Chester]: Friendly local with two fires, bric-a-brac and real ales, smallish separately run restaurant popular for good food esp steaks, well priced sensibly chosen wines, attractive personal feel *(Michele Burrow)*

Little Barrow [SJ4769]

☆ *Foxcote* [Station Lane]: Attractive and neatly kept isolated country pub, old-world beamed lounge with pine bar and log fire, notable food inc seafood specialities and good value well presented Sun lunch, well kept beers inc guests, good range of wines, good service; largely no smoking *(Lynette and Stuart Shore, David Owens)*

Little Bollington [SJ7286]

☆ *Swan With Two Nicks* [the one nr Altrincham, 2 miles from M56 junction 7 – A56 towards Lymm, then first right at Stamford Arms into Park Lane; use A556 to get back on to M56 westbound]: Welcoming bustle in refurbished beamed village pub full of brass, copper and bric-a-brac, snug alcoves, some antique settles, log fire, good choice of popular freshly made generous food from good value filling baguettes up, well kept ales inc Boddingtons, Greene King Old Speckled Hen and Timothy Taylors Landlord, decent wines, cheerful quick staff; tables outside, open all day, attractive hamlet by Dunham Hall deer park, walks by Bridgewater Canal *(Mr and Mrs C Roberts, LYM, Alun Howells, E G Parish, Adrian and Gwynneth Littleton, Lawrence Mitchell)*

Lymm [SJ6787]

☆ *Spread Eagle* [not far from M6 junction 20; Eagle Brow]: Beamed local with traditional décor, central bar serving big comfortable lounge with dining tables, cosy snug with coal fire, cheery atmosphere, reasonably priced food from sandwiches to good value home-made lunches, particularly well kept Lees, proper public bar with darts, dominoes, TV and juke box; bedrooms, attractive village *(R Davies, Pete Baker)*

Macclesfield [SJ9273]

☆ *Castle* [Church St]: Deceptively big unchanging local popular with older people, with two lounges, small public bar, lots of nooks and crannies inc end glass-roofed area up steps, well kept Courage Directors and Theakstons Bitter and Mild, simple lunchtime food inc proper chips *(the Didler, Sue Holland, Dave Webster, BB)*

Sun [Mill Lane/London Rd]: Beams and bare boards in two basic rooms off central servery, one with games, well kept Burtonwood, Cains and three changing guest beers, coal fires, friendly landlord may knock up a sandwich for you; open all day Sat *(Pete Baker, Dave Irving)*

Middlewich [SJ7066]

Kings Arms [Queen St]: Well kept games-oriented pub, exceptionally friendly service *(L Davenport)*

Mobberley [SJ8079]

☆ *Bird in Hand* [Knolls Green; B5085 towards Alderley]: Cosy low-beamed rooms with comfortably cushioned heavy wooden seats, warm coal fires, small pictures on Victorian wallpaper, little panelled snug, good no smoking top dining area, good choice of

promptly served reasonably priced food from enjoyable hot baguettes up, summer afternoon teas, helpful quietly friendly service, well kept Sam Smiths, lots of malt whiskies, decent house wines, pub games; occasional piped music; children allowed, open all day *(E G Parish, LYM, Mrs P J Carroll, Mr and Mrs C Roberts, Mrs E E Sanders)*

Chapel House [Pepper St; Ashley rd out towards Altrincham]: Small, clean and homely, nicely carpeted, darkish woodwork, upholstered stools and wall settles, good value simple food (not Mon) from generous filled barm cakes, club sandwiches and baked potatoes to chilli and curries etc, good friendly service, well kept Boddingtons and Marstons Pedigree, two open fires, small games room; courtyard seats *(Mr and Mrs C Roberts)*

Church Inn [opp church]: Current chef doing enjoyable food inc good sandwich menu, well kept Greenalls inc Mild, big log fire, cheerful service (can slow at busy times), friendly atmosphere; children welcome, tables outside, play area, own bowling green *(Mrs P J Carroll)*

Moulton [SJ6569]

Travellers Rest [Whitlow Lane]: Popular and convivial three-room village inn with lots of bric-a-brac, good choice of well kept Whitbreads-related real ales, welcoming atmosphere, pool, darts etc, separate restaurant; very reasonably priced bedrooms *(E G Parish)*

Nantwich [SJ6552]

Black Lion [Welsh Row]: Three atmospheric little rooms alongside main bar, old-fashioned nooks and crannies, beams and bare floors, big grandfather clock, maybe chess set laid out on tables; four changing real ales inc well kept local Weetwood brews, farm cider, cheap sandwiches, very friendly cat; outside seats on narrow side terrace; occasional live music, open all day *(Pete Baker, Sue Holland, Dave Webster, BB)*

Globe [Audlem Rd]: Quality home cooking (all day wknds) with fresh veg and unusual vegetarian dishes, friendly relaxed atmosphere, Greenalls and Worthington; pretty floral displays *(E G Parish)*

Shakespeare [Beam St]: Roomy town pub with lots of special drinks offers, large dining room with very reasonably priced food inc authentic dishes from Indian chef *(E G Parish)*

☆ *Vine* [Hospital St]: Popular town pub, dates from 17th c though sympathetically modernised inside, stretching far back with dimly lit quiet corners (seem to get better the deeper you penetrate), good value food from hearty sandwiches up inc good proper puddings, well kept Hydes beers, friendly staff, dog and locals, pub games; piped music; children welcome, open all day Sat, cl Mon lunchtime *(MH, BD, Sue Holland, Dave Webster, Andy Chetwood, Andy Lace, BB, Edward Leetham)*

Ness [SJ3076]

Wheatsheaf [Neston Rd]: Thwaites pub by Ness Gardens, overlooking Dee Estuary, sturdy comfortable furnishings, spacious alcoves, 1940s stained glass, good value lunchtime home cooking inc children's meals, charming young managers; picnic-sets on lawn, play area, open all day *(E G Parish)*

Ollerton [SJ7776]

☆ *Dun Cow* [Chelford Rd; outskirts of Knutsford towards Macclesfield]: Attractive country pub, comfortable and very hospitable, good solid furnishings in small snug rooms, good choice of generous honest food (booking advised for restaurant), particularly pleasant service, well kept Greenalls, John Smiths and a guest beer, decent wines, two fine log fires; open all day in summer *(LYM, E G Parish, A Preston)*

Over Peover [SJ7674]

☆ *Whipping Stocks* [Stocks Lane]: Several neatly kept rooms, good oak panelling and fittings, solid furnishings, well kept cheap Sam Smiths, wide choice of low-priced popular straightforward food all day from good sandwiches up, friendly smartly dressed staff; children in eating area, picnic-sets in good-sized garden with safe play area, easy parkland walks *(LYM, Graham and Lynn Mason, Steve Whalley)*

Parkgate [SJ2878]

Boathouse [village signed off A540]: Black and white timbered Greenalls dining pub with several interesting connecting rooms and big conservatory (booking needed wknds), spectacular views to Wales over silted grassy estuary behind, generous if not cheap food inc children's, busy young staff, well kept Greenalls, Tetleys and guest beers, maybe art exhibitions; nearby marshes good for birdwatchers *(Sue and Bob Ward, E G Parish)*

Poynton [SJ9483]

☆ *Boars Head* [Shrigley Rd, Higher Poynton, off A523]: Welcoming Victorian country pub next to Middlewood Way (ex-railway walk and cycle route) and Macclesfield Canal, well refurbished with button-back leather seats (and darts) in bar, lounge with enjoyable home-made food (all day wknds) inc speciality pies, well kept reasonably priced Boddingtons with a guest such as Bass, coffee etc, big open fire; handy for Lyme Park *(Adam Wainwright, Brian and Anna Marsden)*

Prestbury [SJ9077]

☆ *Legh Arms*: Striking long heavy-beamed 16th-c building with newish licensees, friendly, cheerful and willing staff, lots of woodwork, gallery, smart atmosphere, tables laid with cloths and cutlery in comfortably opened-up and enlarged dining bar, good choice of enjoyable food inc decent sandwiches, vegetarian and good value three-course lunch with interesting choices, well kept Robinsons Best and maybe Frederics, good coffee; open all day, children welcome *(Mr and Mrs C Roberts)*

Rainow [SJ9576]

☆ *Highwayman* [A5002 Whaley Bridge—Macclesfield, NE of village]: Timeless unchanging moorside pub with small rooms, low 17th-c beams, well kept Thwaites ales, bar food inc good sandwiches, good winter fires (electric other times), plenty of atmosphere, lovely views *(LYM, the Didler)*

Rushton Spencer [SJ9161]

Fox [Beat Lane, off A523 towards Bridgestones

and Timbersbrook]: Has had enthusiastic reports on newish licensees for their good interesting food inc fresh fish, friendly helpful staff, well kept beer, decent wines, but found unexpectedly closed early summer 2001; bedrooms in hotel extension behind; tables and play area out behind; delightful hill setting *(Mrs P J Carroll)*

Sandbach [SJ7661]

Limes [Sweettooth Lane]: Elegant and imposing, formerly a Victorian country house, pleasant bar area, distinctive comfortably padded seating around attractively set tables in dining part, good friendly service, well kept Boddingtons, Marstons and Tetleys; small conservatory, seats out around bowling green, in cottagey estate *(E G Parish)*

Smallwood [SJ8260]

Blue Bell [Spen Green]: Smallbeamed country pub carefully refurbished to keep its comfortable lived-in feel, welcoming new licensees, good service, well kept interesting real ales, winter mulled wine; home-cooked Sun lunches planned, open all day Sun *(E G Parish)*

Stoak [SJ4273]

Bunbury Arms [Little Stanney Lane; 1 mile from M53 junction 10, A5117 W then first left]: Small snug and big but cosy beamed lounge with interesting antique furniture, lots of pictures and books, friendly staff and locals, enjoyable food (all day Sun) with unusual starters making good light lunches (very popular wkdys with local business people), well kept Cains; tables on grass by car park (M-way noise), short walk for canal users from bridge 136 or 138 *(Edward Leetham, Barbara Smith)*

Sutton [SJ9271]

☆ *Ryles Arms* [Hollin Lane, Higher Sutton]: Large popular dining pub in fine countryside, thriving atmosphere, consistently good generous food from sandwiches to game and interesting dishes, well kept ales such as Coach House Best, Marstons Pedigree and Ruddles County, good choice of whiskies, no smoking dining area and family room, some attractively individual furnishings, french windows to terrace, no music or games *(Annette and John Derbyshire, Hugh A MacLean, C L Kauffmann, LYM)*

Swettenham [SJ8067]

☆ *Swettenham Arms* [off A54 Congleton—Holmes Chapel or A535 Chelford—Holmes Chapel]: Attractive and prettily placed old country pub very popular for wide choice of good if not cheap food efficiently served in charming series of individually furnished rooms from sofas and easy chairs to no smoking dining area (must book Sun), well spaced tables, well kept ales such as Beartown Bearskinful and Bearton, Hydes, Jennings and Tetleys, farm cider, picnic-sets on quiet side lawn; children welcome, live music Weds *(Mrs P J Carroll, LYM, Revd D Glover, Peter F Marshall, E G Parish, Brian and Anna Marsden, Mike and Wendy Proctor, Graham and Lynn Mason)*

Tarporley [SJ5563]

☆ *Swan* [High St, off A49]: Tastefully modernised

Georgian inn with cosy little spaces, well kept Ruddles and three guests such as Adnams, Charles Wells Bombardier and Jennings, bottled Belgian beers, dozens of malt whiskies, civilised informal brasserie with rather smart food from lunchtime sandwiches and snacks up, separate restaurant, polite service; tables outside, provision for children; comfortable well equipped bedrooms *(LYM, Sue Holland, Dave Webster, E G Parish, Mike and Wendy Proctor)*

Walker Barn [SJ9573]

☆ *Setter Dog* [A537 Macclesfield—Buxton]: Warm, clean and civilised stone-built pub with windswept Pennine views, real ales such as Bass, local Storm or Timothy Taylors Landlord in small low-beamed pubby bar, good friendly service, high-backed settles, roaring fire, small separate restaurant with appetising sensibly priced food inc good value Sun lunch; tables in car park across road (watch for fast moving traffic), fantastic setting, handy for Teggs Nose Country Park, open all day *(BB, Derek and Sylvia Stephenson, Dr W J M Gissane, JP, PP)*

Warmingham [SJ7161]

☆ *Bears Paw* [School Lane]: Luxurious pub doing well under current manager, well prepared food from enormous filled baguettes to substantial main courses, plush seating around marble-top tables in raised areas, well kept Bass, Boddingtons and Worthington BB, relaxed atmosphere, friendly helpful staff, charming restaurant, pool room, children very welcome; good spot by river and ancient church in picturesque village, seats in front garden, bedrooms *(E G Parish)*

Warrington [SJ5686]

☆ *Ferry Inn* [leave A562 in Penketh – park in Station rd off Tannery Lane]: Pretty building in lovely isolated spot between St Helens Canal and Mersey, four well kept real ales inc very quickly changing guest beers, over 100 whiskies, good home-cooked food (not Sun evening) inc huge fresh cod with proper chips and mushy peas, nice upstairs dining room, friendly service, cosy low-beamed bar, log fires, provision for children; tables outside with play area, pets corner, pony paddock *(LYM, Lyn and Geoff Hallchurch)*

Stag [Chester Rd, Walton]: Modern pub with friendly efficient service, good food and beer, nice atmosphere *(John Shepherd)*

Wettenhall [SJ6261]

☆ *Boot & Slipper* [off B5074 just S of Winsford; Long Lane – OS Sheet 118 map ref 625613]: Only a shortage of recent readers' reports keeps this engaging old country pub out of the main entries this year; attractive layout and décor,

hard-working cheerful landlady, good generous food from sandwiches to inventive main dishes, well kept Marstons Pedigree and Tetleys, good choice of malt whiskies, decent wine list, children welcome in eating areas; picnic-sets on front cobbles, play area, comfortable bedrooms, open all day wknds *(Mr and Mrs A Craig, LYM, Dave and Margaret Bush, Dr C D and Mrs S M Burbridge)*

Wheelock [SJ7559]

Commercial [off new A534 bypass; Game St]: Old-fashioned unspoilt local, two smaller rooms (one no smoking) off high-ceilinged main bar, unaltered décor, Boddingtons, Marstons Pedigree, Thwaites and an occasional guest beer, real fire, firmly efficient service, no food; pool in games room, maybe Thurs folk night, open from 8 evenings only, and Sun lunchtime *(Pete Baker, the Didler)*

Willington [SJ5367]

Willington Hall [just off A51]: Good informal atmosphere in country hotel's public and lounge bars, good reasonably priced bar meals, helpful staff, choice of beers; ten comfortable bedrooms *(E G Parish)*

Wilmslow [SJ8481]

George & Dragon [Church St]: Good meals at extraordinarily low price in comfortably worn local by parish church, well kept Bass or Worthington, quick friendly helpful service *(Mr and Mrs C Roberts)*

Victoria [Green Lane]: Banks's conversion of high-ceilinged former police station, first called the Blue Lamp and now renamed; bare boards, two cosy snugs, 19th-c fireplaces, panelled dados and interesting interior windows, well kept Best, Original and Marstons Pedigree, very cheap food from separate counter, friendly staff, tables outside; games machine, piped music *(Doug Christian)*

Wrenbury [SJ5948]

Cotton Arms [Cholmondeley Rd]: Beamed and timbered pub in popular spot by canal locks and boatyard, with good value food in two large dining areas, friendly staff, Greenalls and a guest beer, lots of brass, open fire, side games room *(E G Parish, Mike and Wendy Proctor)*

Wybunbury [SJ6950]

☆ *Swan* [B5071]: Spotless family-friendly bow-windowed pub with nooks and crannies in homely rambling lounge, snug dining areas inc no smoking one, pleasant public bar, well kept ales inc Jennings, good house wines, good home-made food, reasonable prices, efficient helpful service, plenty of bric-a-brac; tables in garden by beautiful churchyard; bedrooms *(Sue Holland, Dave Webster, Lynette and Stuart Shore, Edward Leetham, LYM)*

If a service charge is mentioned prominently on a menu or accommodation terms, you must pay it if service was satisfactory. If service is really bad you are legally entitled to refuse to pay some or all of the service charge as compensation for not getting the service you might reasonably have expected.

Cornwall

New entries here this year are the pleasantly individual and relaxed old Napoleon up at the top of the hill in Boscastle (doing well under its ex-musician landlord), the Plume of Feathers at Mitchell (attractively reworked inside, and doing very imaginative specials), the Who'd Have Thought It at St Dominick (charming layout, nice country views – good all round) and the Driftwood Spars in a great spot at Trevaunance Cove near St Agnes (lively interesting bars, brewing its own beer – a pleasant place to stay in). Other pubs currently on top form here are the Trengilly Wartha near Constantine (nice for families or for a quiet midweek pint, good food and bedrooms), the well run Olde Plough House at Duloe, the Earl of St Vincent at Egloshayle (try to be there on the hour, for the clocks striking), the ancient Blue Anchor in Helston (brewing unusual beers), the Halzephron on the coast just south of there (great all-rounder), the friendly and relaxed Crown at Lanlivery, the Royal Oak in Lostwithiel (another good all-rounder), the Pandora set beautifully by the water near Mylor Bridge, the cheerful Turks Head in Penzance, the ever-popular Roseland at Philleigh, the Ship superbly placed in Porthleven, the Turks Head in its idyllic spot on the island of St Agnes, the Sloop, a famous focal point in St Ives, the St Kew Inn (particularly welcoming atmosphere, good all round), and the Victory tucked away in St Mawes (its food, specialising in local fish, is getting really rather exciting). The Maltsters Arms at Chapel Amble earns our award of Cornwall Dining Pub of the Year, for imaginative food (and a great choice of wines by the glass) in nice surroundings. William Morris of the Turks Head in Penzance and Marjorie Ross of the Port Gaverne Inn near Port Isaac both deserve high praise, as they have won a main entry for their establishments in all 20 annual editions of the Guide. Other Cornish pubs with this fine record of consistency (even under changing licensees) are the Shipwrights Arms at Helford, Blue Anchor in Helston, Miners Arms at Mithian, Pandora near Mylor Bridge, Roseland at Philleigh and Ship in Porthleven. In the Lucky Dip section at the end of the chapter, pubs to note particularly this year are the Cadgwith Cove Inn at Cadgwith, Old Shire in Camborne, Seven Stars in Falmouth, Galleon and King of Prussia both in Fowey, Watermill at Lelant, Bush at Morwenstow, Old Coastguard in Mousehole, Notter Bridge Inn at Notter, Golden Lion and London both in Padstow, Victoria at Perranuthnoe, Blue Peter in Polperro, Lugger at Polruan, Railway Inn in St Agnes, Rising Sun in St Mawes, White Hart at St Teath, New Inn at Veryan, Tinners Arms at Zennor, and on St Marys in the Isles of Scilly the Atlantic Inn and the Bishop & Wolf. We have inspected and can vouch for the great majority of these. Drinks prices here, hardly changed over the year and certainly held steadier than in most other areas, are rather lower than the national average.

Pubs staying open all afternoon at least one day a week are listed at the back of the book.

BODINNICK SX1352 Map 1

Old Ferry ★

Across the water from Fowey

On the banks of the pretty Fowey river and next to the steep lane in front of the ferry slipway (make sure your brakes work well if you park here), this 400-year-old inn is a friendly, relaxed place. The three simply furnished little rooms have quite a few bits of nautical memorabilia, a couple of half model ships mounted on the wall, and several old photographs, as well as wheelback chairs, built-in plush pink wall seats, and an old high-backed settle. The family room at the back is actually hewn into the rock; piped music and TV. Decent bar food includes home-made soup (£2.95), sandwiches (from £2.25; toasties 30p extra), ploughman's (from £5.25), quite a few dishes with chips (from £3.95; home-cooked ham and egg £4.50), home-made cream cheese and broccoli pasta bake (£5.95), curry of the day or home-made steak and kidney pie (£6.50), fresh smoked haddock with scrambled egg (£7.95), puddings (£2.95), good daily specials like stir-fried chicken (£9.50) or bass (£13.95), and children's meals (from £2.75); the attractive restaurant is no smoking (try and bag a window seat). Sharps Own on handpump, kept under light blanket pressure. Most of the bedrooms look out over the river. *(Recommended by Mayur Shah, Dr M W A Haward, Sue Demont, Tim Barrow, Mrs P G Newton, Peter Salmon, Dennis Jenkin, Charlie Harris, M Joyner, B, M and P Kendall)*

Free house ~ Licensees Royce and Patricia Smith ~ Real ale ~ Bar food (12-2.30, 6-9 (12-2, 6.30-8.30 in winter)) ~ Restaurant ~ (01726) 870237 ~ Children in eating area of bar and in family room ~ Open 11-11; 12-10.30 Sun; 11.30-2.30, 6.30-10.30 Mon-Fri and Sun in winter ~ Bedrooms: /£45(£55S)(£65B)

BOSCASTLE SX0990 Map 1

Napoleon

High Street; up at the top of the village

Built in 1549, this cosy thick-walled white cottage is up at the top of its steep, quaint village, and there are splendid views on the way. Several little flagstoned rooms ramble around up and down, with oak beams, slate floors, log fires, an exposed oven, an interesting and unusual collection of Napoleon prints and memorabilia, pottery boots, walking sticks and lots of other knick-knacks. The friendly, relaxed landlord dispenses well kept Bass and St Austell Tinners, HSD and seasonal ales from casks behind the bar; decent wines. Good bar food includes home-made soup with herb scones (£2.50), garlic mushrooms (£3), grilled mackerel (£6.50), chick pea and vegetable korma (£5.95), thai red chicken curry or steak in ale pie (£6.75), rump steak (£7.75), puddings such as Cointreau, orange and treacle tart or toffee apple pancake with toffee sauce (£2.75), and Sunday roast (£5.50); it's best to book for the restaurant. Bar billiards, table skittles, darts, shove-ha'penny, cribbage, dominoes, and toad-in-the-hole. There are seats (and boules) out on a small sheltered terrace. *(Recommended by Jonathan Gibbs, Chris and Elaine Lyon, the Didler, George Atkinson, G K Smale)*

St Austell ~ Tenant Mike Mills ~ Real ale ~ Bar food (12-2, 6.30-9(9.30 in summer) ~ Restaurant ~ (01840) 250204 ~ Children in eating area of bar ~ Live acts Tues evening and jazz Fri evening ~ Open 11-2.30, 5.30-11; 11-11 Sat; 12-10.30 Sun; 11-3, 5.30-11 Sat winter

CALLINGTON SX3669 Map 1

Coachmakers Arms

Newport Square (A388 towards Launceston)

This imposing 18th-c pub is a warmly friendly place with an irregularly shaped, comfortable beamed and timbered bar, and a growing collection of antique clocks, prints of coach making and transport on the walls, and lots of fresh flowers; little winged settles and stools made from polished brass-bound casks, and well kept Bass, with St Austells HSD and Dartmoor Best on handpump, kept under light blanket pressure. Good home-made food in the bar and open-plan restaurant area includes soup (£2.50), garlic egg mayonnaise (£2.95), open sandwiches (from £4.25), a pie of the day (£5.50), stilton and prawn flan (£5.95), fisherman's crunch (£6.25), salmon steak poached in cream, with prawns (£8.95), steaks (from £8.95), and puddings (£2.95). Quiz night on Wednesdays, fruit machine; dogs welcome. *(Recommended by Bryan Robinson, David Z West, Mr and Mrs N Smith)*

Free house ~ Licensees John Cook and Les Elliott ~ Real ale ~ Bar food (not 25 Dec) ~ Restaurant ~ (01579) 382567 ~ Children in eating area of bar and restaurant ~ Open 11-3, 6-11; 12-3, 7-10.30 Sun ~ Bedrooms: /£40B

CHAPEL AMBLE SW9975 Map 1
Maltsters Arms ★ ⑨ ♀

Village signposted from A39 NE of Wadebridge, and from B3314

Cornwall Dining Pub of the Year

Especially warm and welcoming, this bustling pub is well worth the drive down the little high-hedged roads. The attractively knocked-together rooms have black oak joists in the white ceiling, partly panelled stripped stone walls, heavy wooden tables on the partly carpeted big flagstones, a large stone fireplace, and a pleasant, relaxed atmosphere; the bar extension is hung with ship pictures, a large collection of keyrings, and a growing collection of seafaring memorabilia. There's also a side room and upstairs family room, and the eating areas are all no smoking. Popular bar food at lunchtime includes open sandwiches and ploughman's, home-made soup (£3.15), curry of the day or pork stroganoff (£5.50), chicken liver parfait with orange and red onion marmalade or steak and kidney pie (£5.95), langoustines with whisky and horseradish cream sauce (£6.25), and Cornish sirloin steak (£9.95); in the evening, it is more elaborate with dishes such as chargrilled vegetable salad (£5.25), oven baked sardines (£5.50), asparagus tart with chargrilled baby fennel and carrots with a béarnaise sauce (£9.95), roasted duck breast on braised red cabbage with chilli, spring onion, ginger and sesame, served with a chinese-style sherry, orange and vanilla jus (£13.25), whole megrim sole baked with local crab, white wine and cream, topped with gingered breadcrumbs (£13.95), and puddings like lemon brûlée or chocolate cheesecake. Well kept Bass, Greene King Abbot, Sharps Coaster, Maltsters Special (brewed specially for the pub by Sharps), and maybe a couple of guests like Fullers London Pride or Sharps Will's Resolve on handpump kept under light blanket pressure; 22 wines by the glass, a growing collection of malt whiskies, a good range of brandies and armagnacs, and even milk shakes. Cribbage, dominoes, backgammon, and piped music. Benches outside in a sheltered sunny corner, and pretty hanging baskets and tubs. *(Recommended by R L Turnham, J Davidson, R J Walden, Mrs J Reeves, B A Dale, Mr and Mrs Ian Matthews, G U Briggs, Kevin Thorpe, Michael and Ann Cole, Betsy Brown, Nigel Flook, the Didler, Tracey and Stephen Groves, R and S Bentley, Steve Dark, Joy and Peter Heatherley, Rita Horridge)*

Free house ~ Licensees David & Marie Gray and David Coles ~ Real ale ~ Bar food (12-2(1.45 in winter), 6.15-9.30) ~ Restaurant ~ (01208) 812473 ~ No children in the bar and must be over 8 in restaurant ~ Open 11-2.30, 6-11; 12-2.30, 7-10.30 Sun; closed evening 25 Dec

CONSTANTINE SW7229 Map 1
Trengilly Wartha ★ ⑨ ♀ ◧ ⮕

Constantine signposted from Penryn—Gweek rd (former B3291); in village turn right just before Minimarket (towards Gweek); in nearly a mile pub signposted left; at Nancenoy, OS sheet 204 map reference 731282

Cleverly, the licensees have managed to make this tucked-away inn appeal to a wide range of customers – not an easy thing to do. Families are made welcome, but for those in search of a good pint, a proper pub meal and a glance at a newspaper, this is also a smashing place to visit (quieter during the week). Food in both the bar and restaurant has had consistent praise this year, the wine list is especially good and thoughtful, and it's a super place to stay, with tasty breakfasts. The long low-beamed main bar has a woodburning stove and attractive built-in high-backed settles boxing in polished heavy wooden tables, and at one end, shelves of interesting wines with drink-in and take-out price labels (they run their own retail wine business, Cochonnet Wines). There's a bright no smoking family conservatory with an area leading off that houses pool, darts, shove-ha'penny, dominoes, cribbage, and shut the box; they run their own cricket team. Popular bar food includes soup (£2.40), local feta cheese, bean and tomato salad (£3.90), Cornish meaty or vegetarian pasties (£4), devon blue cheese and walnut pâté (£4.80), sausages with mustard mash and onion gravy (£5.20), ploughman's and salads (from £5.30), leek and cheese soufflé (£7.80), thai pork (£8.20), crab cakes (£10.50), specials like half a dozen Helford oysters (£8), duck tagine with preserved lemon, tomato and spiced couscous (£10.40) or monkfish and king prawns in a green thai curry sauce (£10.50), and proper food for children (from £3.50). Well kept Skinner's Knocker, Sharps Cornish, and maybe a local guest on handpump or tapped from the cask. Over 50 malt whiskies (including several extinct ones), 20 wines by the glass (from a fine list of 250), and around 10 armagnacs. The pretty landscaped garden has some tables under large parasols, an international sized piste for boules, and a lake; lots of surrounding walks. *(Recommended by Sue Demont, Tim Barrow, Martin and Karen Wake, Mike Gorton, Mike and Mona Clifford, Mrs G Breare, Bruce Bird, Joyce and Maurice Cottrell, Mike and Sue Loseby, the Didler, Joy and Peter Heatherley, Charlie Harris, Mr and Mrs M Cooper, JP, PP, M A Borthwick, Lorna and Howard Lambert, Dr Paull Khan, David Rule, R J Walden, T A Smith, Martin and Lois Sheldrick, Marion Turner, Mike and Alison Stevens, Mr and Mrs M A Cook, JCW, Nigel Long, Patricia A Bruce, Bernard Stradling, Simon and Laura Habbishow, Ian)*

Free house ~ Licensees Nigel Logan and Michael Maguire ~ Real ale ~ Bar food (12-2.15(2 Sun), 6.30(7 Sun)-9.30) ~ Restaurant ~ (01326) 340332 ~ Children welcome ~ Open 11-3, 6.30-11; 12-3, 7-10.30 Sun ~ Bedrooms: £40(£48B)/£60(£72B)

CREMYLL SX4553 Map 1
Edgcumbe Arms
End of B3247, off A374 at Crafthole (coming from A38) or Antony (from Torpoint car ferry)

From this bustling pub there are splendid walks in the nearby waterfront parkland or a more energetic one through Mount Edgcumbe to the seaside villages of Kingsand and Cawsand – though for the less hearty, there's a foot ferry from Plymouth. The several old-fashioned small rooms (some with fine Tamar views from bow-window seats) have panelling, beam-and-plank ceilings, slate flagstones and bare boards, and furnishings to match – big stripped high-backed settles, pews, fireside sofa, housekeeper's chairs, pretty cushions and the like, with candles on tables and plenty of decorative china, copper, brass and old pictures; there's a no smoking area. Bar food includes sandwiches from £2.95; baguettes from £3.95), filled baked potatoes (from £3.95), vegetable lasagne or grilled cod (£5.95), rump steak (£7.95), puddings (£3.25), and daily specials like home-made steak and kidney pie (£5.95), skate wings with lemon butter (£11.95) or local fresh scallops with garlic and smoked bacon (£12.95). Well kept St Austell HSD, Tinners, and Tribute on handpump, and friendly, helpful service; darts, pool, fruit machine, juke box, and piped music. There are tables outside close to the water. *(Recommended by Ralph and Gloria Maybourn, Angela, Shirley Mackenzie, Pete and Rosie Flower, Ian Phillips, Carole and John Smith)*

St Austell ~ Managers David and Amanda Rowe ~ Real ale ~ Bar food ~ (01752) 822294 ~ Children in eating area of bar and in family room ~ Open 11-11; 12-10.30 Sun ~ Bedrooms: £35S/£60S(£50B)

DULOE SX2358 Map 1
Olde Plough House
B3254 N of Looe

This is a pub that readers like to come back to – which is always a good sign. The two communicating rooms have a lovely dark polished Delabole slate floor, some turkey rugs, a mix of pews, modern high-backed settles and smaller chairs, foreign banknotes on the beams, three woodburning stoves, and a restrained décor – some prints of waterfowl and country scenes, a few copper jugs and a fat china pig perched on window sills. The public side (just as comfortable) has darts; piped music. Popular, reasonably priced food at lunchtime includes home-made soup (£2.10), filled baguettes (from £2.75; smoked salmon and cream cheese £4.25), ploughman's (from £3.95), a roast of the day (£4.95), home-cooked ham and egg (£5.25), leek and mushroom crumble (£5.95), and fish pie (£6.95), with evening dishes such as smoked duck pâté with red onion chutney (£4.55), scallops and salmon (£4.75), gammon topped with honey, pineapple and cheese (£7.55), medallions of pork in a creamy peppercorn and brandy sauce (£9.25), and steaks cooked on hot stones (£8.95), and daily specials like grilled cod fillet with prawn, cucumber and dill butter (£9.45) and fried venison steak with fried vegetables and red wine (£9.95). Sunday roasts. Bass and Sharps Doom Bar on handpump, sensibly priced wines, and good attentive service. There is a small more modern carpeted dining room, and a few picnic-sets out by the road. The two friendly jack russells are called Jack and Spot, and the cat, Willow. *(Recommended by Peter and Jenny Quine, R L Turnham, Sue and David Arnott, Nick Lawless, D S Jackson, Peter and Anne-Marie O'Malley, Mrs P G Newton, Mrs June Wilmers, M Joyner, Glenys and John Roberts)*

Free house ~ Licensees Gary and Alison Toms ~ Real ale ~ Bar food ~ Restaurant ~ (01503) 262050 ~ Children in eating area of bar ~ Open 12-2.30, 6.30-11; 12-2.30, 7-10.30 Sun; closed evenings 25-26 Dec

EDMONTON SW9672 Map 1

Quarryman

Village signposted off A39 just W of Wadebridge bypass

Run by especially friendly people, this interesting pub is built around a carefully reconstructed slate-built courtyard of former quarrymen's quarters. The three beamed rooms (one is no smoking) have simple pleasant furnishings, a set of interesting old brass spirit optics above the fireplace nestling among some fine old whisky advertising figurines, fresh flowers on tables, a woodburner, and a couple of bow windows (one with a charming stained-glass quarryman panel) looking out to a distant wind farm; there's some interesting sporting memorabilia – particularly the Roy Ullyett menu cartoons for British Sportsman's Club Savoy lunches for visiting cricket and rugby international teams. Good bar food includes sandwiches, home-made soup (£2.90), warm goats cheese salad with pears and walnut (£4.90), tiger prawns in tempura batter with a sweet chilli dip (£5.50), vegetarian cannelloni (£6.50), Aberdeen Angus steaks (from £10.50), and specials such as toad-in-the-hole with shallot and red wine jus (£7.50), chargrilled loin of pork topped with red onion and chilli marmalade and welsh rarebit with cider sauce (£9.50), and roast cod wrapped in parma ham on a bed of bubble and squeak with a light parsley sauce (£9.90). They have four well kept beers on handpump such as Sharps Doom Bar and Skinners Betty Stogs, with guests from Kitchen and Greene King, decent house wines and some interesting good value bottles, and 20 malt whiskies; pool and piped music. The dog is called Floyd. There's a cosy no smoking bistro on the other side of the courtyard. The pub forms part of an attractively understated small health and holiday complex. *(Recommended by Rita Horridge, Bruce Bird, Joy and Peter Heatherley, B J Harding, Geoff Calcott, Geoff Edwards, Sheila and Phil Stubbs, Mike and Sue Loseby, Sandy Thomson, Kevin Thorpe)*

Free house ~ Licensees Terry and Wendy De Villiers Kuun ~ Real ale ~ Bar food (12-2.30, 6-9; not 25 Dec) ~ Restaurant ~ (01208) 816444 ~ Well behaved children in eating area of bar ~ Open 12-11; 12-10.30 Sun

EGLOSHAYLE SX0172 Map 1

Earl of St Vincent

Off A389, just outside Wadebridge

Full of interest, this pretty pub is well worth spending some time in – especially on the hour when the fascinating collection of antique clocks (all in working order) start chiming; there's also golfing memorabilia and art deco ornaments, and all sorts of rich furnishings. Well kept St Austell Tinners and HSD, and a guest on handpump; piped music. Enjoyable, good value food such as sandwiches (from £2), home-made soup £2.25), and daily specials like smashing liver and bacon or cod and chips (£4), steak pie (£4.50), and gammon and egg (£5); the evening menu is more elaborate. The snug is no smoking. In summer, there are picnic-sets in the lovely garden and marvellous flowering baskets and tubs. The pub is tucked away in a narrow quiet back street behind the church. *(Recommended by the Didler, Mr and Mrs Capp, M A Borthwick, Kevin Thorpe, David Eberlin, James Nunns, Dr M W A Haward, G U Briggs, George Atkinson, Joy and Peter Heatherley, Brian and Bett Cox, Terry Mizen, John and Sarah Perry, P and M Rudlin)*

St Austell ~ Tenants Edward and Anne Connolly ~ Real ale ~ Bar food (not Sun evening) ~ Restaurant ~ (01208) 814807 ~ Children in eating area of bar ~ Open 11-3, 6.30-11; 12-3, 7-10.30 Sun

HELFORD SW7526 Map 1
Shipwrights Arms
Off B3293 SE of Helston, via Mawgan

Seats on the terrace here are set above a lovely wooded creek, and there are plenty of surrounding walks (a long distance coastal path goes right past the door), so in good weather, this thatched pub does get very busy. There's quite a nautical theme inside, with navigation lamps, models of ships, sea pictures, drawings of lifeboat coxswains and shark fishing photographs – as well as a collection of foreign banknotes behind the bar counter. A dining area has oak settles and tables; winter open fire. Well kept Castle Eden and Greene King IPA on handpump, and bar food such as home-made soup (£2.50), crab cocktail (£4.25), ploughman's (from £4.90; the crab is well liked £6.95), smoked fish platter (£6.25), steak and mushroom or fresh fish pies (£7.95), and home-made puddings (£4.25); piped music. The pub is quite a walk from the nearest car park. *(Recommended by Miss J E Winsor, Brian Skelcher, Mr and Mrs M Cooper, Peter Salmon, Mrs B Rogers, Simon and Laura Habbishow, JP, PP, the Didler, Betsy Brown, Nigel Flook, Ruth and Paul Lawrence, Tina and David Woods-Taylor, Anthony and Elizabeth Barker)*

Greenalls ~ Lease Charles Herbert ~ Real ale ~ Bar food (not Sun or Mon evenings in winter) ~ (01326) 231235 ~ Children welcome ~ Open 11-2.30, 6-11; 12-3, 7-10.30 Sun; closed Sun evenings in winter

HELSTON SW6527 Map 1
Blue Anchor ◀ £
50 Coinagehall Street

This old thatched pub, once a monks' hospice, remains, happily, a basic drinkers' tavern and the own brew beers – Middle, Spingo Special, and Easter and Christmas Special – come from what is probably the oldest brewing house in the country; they also sell farm cider. A series of small, low-ceilinged rooms opening off the central corridor has simple old-fashioned furniture on the flagstones, interesting old prints, some bared stone walls, and in one room a fine inglenook fireplace. A family room has darts; dominoes. Bar food includes rolls and sandwiches (from £1.50), home-made soup (£1.80), ham and egg (£3.95), ploughman's (from £4.25), liver and bacon hotpot (£4.75), steak and kidney pie (£5.50), and daily specials (£2.95). Past an old stone bench in the sheltered little terrace area is a skittle alley which you can hire. At lunchtimes you can usually go and look round the brewery and the cellar. *(Recommended by P J Holdsworth, the Didler, Kevin Thorpe, Trish and Ian Avis, Giles Francis, Miss J E Winsor, Sue Holland, Dave Webster, JP, PP)*

Own brew ~ Licensee Simon Stone ~ Real ale ~ Bar food (12-3) ~ (01326) 562821 ~ Children in own room ~ Jazz Mon, folk Thurs ~ Open 10.30-11; 12-10.30 Sun ~ Bedrooms: £27S/£40S

Halzephron 🍴 ♟ 🍺

Gunwalloe, village about 4 miles S but not marked on many road maps; look for brown sign on A3083 alongside perimeter fence of RNAS Culdrose

Even at their busiest, the hard-working licensee and her staff at this fomer smugglers' haunt are unfailingly welcoming and helpful – and the imaginative food continues to delight readers. The bustling and pleasant bar is spotlessly clean with comfortable seating, copper on the walls and mantelpiece, and a warm winter fire in the big hearth; there's also quite a small no smoking family room. At lunchtime, bar snacks include sandwiches (from £2.90; super crab £7.50), home-made soup (£3.80), freshly made pâté or mushrooms sautéed with herbs in a cream sauce with garlic bread (£5), ploughman's (from £5), and platters such as crab, prawn or smoked salmon (from £10.50), with evening choices like breast of chicken marinated in herbs and dijon mustard, breadcrumbed and deep fried (£9.50), and chargrilled sirloin steak (£11.90); evening specials might include smoked salmon pâté (£5), duck leg confit on oriental cabbage with sweet and sour sauce (£6.10), pasta with mediterranean vegetables, artichokes, olives and sun-dried tomatoes with olive oil and basil, topped with parmesan (£8.30), sweet and sour pork with egg fried rice (£9.90), roast saddle of lamb with an apricot and rosemary stuffing on garlic pomme purée, with a date compote and red wine sauce (£10.90), wild boar, juniper and borlotti bean casserole (£11.80), caramelised Gressingham duck on butternut squash purée with redcurrant juniper jus (£13), and home-made puddings like lemon mousse, hot chocolate fudge cake or caramel cream pots (from £3.20); all the eating areas are no smoking. Well kept Sharps Cornish Coaster, Own and Doom Bar, and St Austell Daylight Robbery on handpump, a good wine list, 40 malt whiskies, and around 25 liqueurs; dominoes and cribbage. There are lots of lovely surrounding unspoilt walks with fine views of Mount's Bay, Gunwalloe fishing cove is just 300 yards away, and there's a sandy beach one mile away at Church Cove. *(Recommended by Mike and Mona Clifford, Dr D J and Mrs S C Walker, D and H Broodbank, Nick Lawless, Mr and Mrs M Cooper, John and Sarah Perry, Brian Skelcher, Cliff Blakemore, Miss J E Winsor, Sue Demont, Tim Barrow, Joyce and Maurice Cottrell, James Nunns, Betsy Brown, Nigel Flook, Jacquie and Jim Jones, Dr P Brown, Mrs Romey Heaton, Trish and Ian Avis, Sue Holland, Dave Webster)*

Free house ~ Licensee Angela Thomas ~ Real ale ~ Bar food (not 25 Dec) ~ Restaurant ~ (01326) 240406 ~ Children in family room ~ Open 11-2.30, 6(6.30 winter)-11; 12-2.30, 6.30-10.30 Sun; closed 25 Dec ~ Bedrooms: £38B/£68B

KINGSAND SX4350 Map 1
Halfway House 🍺

Fore St, towards Cawsand

To reach this attractive old inn, it might be most enjoyable to park and walk through the narrow hilly streets down towards the sea and harbour. The simply furnished but quite smart bar is mildly Victorian in style, and rambles around a huge central fireplace, with low ceilings, soft lighting, and plenty of locals – though there's a warm welcome for the many summer visitors. Bar food (with prices little changed since last year) is good and enjoyable and includes daily specials such as home-made soup (£2.75; fish soup with rouille and croutons £3.50), crab cocktail (£4.95), medallions of pork with a creamy mushroom sauce or poached salmon with tomato salsa (£9.95), grilled duck breast with parsnip crumble and cranberry sauce (£9.95), and puddings such as squidgy chocolate roulade, orange and rhubarb pie or sticky ginger pudding (£3.45); also, baguettes (from £2.25), baked potatoes (from £3.50), ploughman's (from £5), home-cooked ham and egg (£5.75), cashew nut paella (£7.65), daily curry (£7), steaks (from £9.45), and children's meals. There are often attractive fresh flowers on the tables. Well kept Courage Best, Sharps Doom Bar, and a guest beer on handpump kept under light blanket pressure, and decent wines. Service is quick and friendly, and the bar staff add a lot to the enjoyable atmosphere. The piped music is generally unobtrusive; cribbage, dominoes, backgammon, and fruit machine. The village is well placed for visiting Mount Edgcumbe House and Country Park, and there are marvellous surrounding walks, especially on the cliffs at

Rame Head. *(Recommended by S J and C C Davidson, M Joyner, R L Turnham, Steve Whalley)*

Free house ~ Licensees Sarah and David Riggs ~ Real ale ~ Bar food ~ Restaurant ~ (01752) 822279 ~ Children welcome ~ Choir Weds evenings ~ Open 12-3(3.30 Sat), 6.30-11; 12-4, 6.30-10.30 Sun; 7pm opening in winter ~ Bedrooms: £27.50S/£55S

LAMORNA SW4424 Map 1
Lamorna Wink
Off B3315 SW of Penzance

One of the best collections of warship mementoes, sea photographs and nautical brassware in the county can be found in this neat little local. There are simple furnishings, a little coal fire in cold weather, and Sharps Own and Doom Bar, and Skinners Cornish Knocker on handpump. Bar food includes sandwiches (from £1.60; fresh local crab £4.50), filled baked potatoes (from £2.75), ploughman's (£4), and fresh local crab salad (in season, £10). Pool and fruit machine. There are front benches outside where you can just hear the sound of the sea and the burble of the stream behind. The attractive little cove is worth a look, and there are bracing walks along the coastal path in either direction. *(Recommended by Mike and Sue Loseby, Paul and Penny Rampton, Alan and Hillie Johnson)*

Free house ~ Licensee Robert Drennan ~ Real ale ~ Bar food ~ No credit cards ~ (01736) 731566 ~ Children in eating area of bar ~ Open 11-11; 12-10.30 Sun; 11-4, 6-11 in winter

LANLIVERY SX0759 Map 1
Crown ◖
Signposted off A390 Lostwithiel—St Austell (tricky to find from other directions)

This is one of Cornwall's oldest inns, and the rambling rooms have no noisy games machines, music or pool tables – just a good chatty and relaxed atmosphere and friendly licensees. The small, dimly lit public bar has heavy beams, a slate floor, and built-in wall settles and attractive alcove of seats in the dark former chimney; darts. A much lighter room leads off here with beams in the white boarded ceiling, some new settees in one corner, cushioned black settles, a small cabinet with wood turnings for sale, owl and badger pictures, and a little fireplace with an old-fashioned fire; there's another similar small room. Enjoyable bar food includes sandwiches (from £1.65), good meaty or vegetarian pasties (from £1.75), home-made soup (£3), ploughman's (from £3.75), daily specials such as smoked fish pâté wrapped in smoked salmon (£3.50), fresh mackerel or plaice (when available, from £5.75), steak and stout pie with herb pastry or fish pie (£8.15), and puddings like fruit crumbles (£3.50). Well kept Sharps Own, Doom Bar, and Eden Ale on handpump; darts, dominoes, cribbage, table skittles, and shove-ha'penny. The slate-floored porch room has lots of succulents and a few cacti, and wood-and-stone seats, and at the far end of the restaurant is a no smoking sun room, full of more plants, with tables and benches. There's a sheltered garden with granite faced seats and white cast-iron furniture. *(Recommended by Tina and David Woods-Taylor, R M Corlett, Dennis Jenkin, J Davidson, Terry Mizen, George Atkinson, Dr M W A Haward, BKA, Sue and David Arnott, Mrs June Wilmers, Ian Phillips, Joy and Peter Heatherley, David Edwards, R J Herd, Paul R White, Roger and Jenny Huggins, Tracey and Stephen Groves)*

Free house ~ Licensees Ros and Dave Williams ~ Real ale ~ Bar food (12-2.15, 7-9.15(9.30 Sat)) ~ Restaurant ~ (01208) 872707 ~ Children in eating area of bar and restaurant ~ Trad jazz every 2nd Sun evening ~ Open 11-3, 6-11; 12-3, 6-10.30 Sun ~ Bedrooms: £27.50S/£45S

The ◖ symbol shows pubs which keep their beer unusually well or have a particularly good range.

LOSTWITHIEL SX1059 Map 1

Royal Oak ◖

Duke Street; pub just visible from A390 in centre – best to look out for Royal Talbot Hotel

A consistently popular long-standing entry in our *Guide*, this well run pub has friendly, welcoming staff, a good range of real ales, and enjoyable food. Good, popular bar food includes lunchtime snacks such as sandwiches (from £1.45; toasties 25p extra), ploughman's (from £3.75), fried chicken (£4.95), and scallops in cheese and white wine sauce (£5.25), as well as soup (£2.40), stuffed mushrooms (£3.85), vegetarian crêpes (£6.75), fresh local trout (£8.50), steaks (from £9.25), daily specials such as a curry or steak and kidney in ale pie (£7.50), fresh salmon in a cucumber and cream sauce (£8.95), and garlic king prawns (£9.75), and puddings like home-made treacle tart or cherry pie (£2.30). Well kept Bass, Fullers London Pride, Marstons Pedigree, Sharps Own, and a couple of changing guests on handpump – as well as lots of bottled beers from around the world. The neat lounge is spacious and comfortable, with captain's chairs and high-backed wall benches on its patterned carpet, and a couple of wooden armchairs by the log-effect gas fire; there's also a delft shelf, with a small dresser in one inner alcove. The flagstoned and beamed back public bar has darts, dominoes, cribbage, fruit machine, TV, and juke box, and is popular with younger customers; piped music. On a raised terrace by the car park are some picnic-sets. *(Recommended by George Atkinson, John and Pat Horne, Dr M E Wilson, Mayur Shah)*

Free house ~ Licensees Malcolm and Eileen Hine ~ Real ale ~ Bar food (not 25 Dec) ~ Restaurant ~ (01208) 872552 ~ Children in restaurant and family room ~ Open 11-11; 12-10.30 Sun ~ Bedrooms: £37.50B/£63B

LUDGVAN SW5033 Map 1

White Hart

Churchtown; off A30 Penzance—Hayle at Crowlas; OS Sheet 203 map reference 505330

Unspoilt and friendly, this bustling old pub is enjoyed by both locals and visitors. The cosy beamed rooms are full of interest: a fascinating mix of interesting old seats and tables, masses of mugs and jugs glinting in cottagey corners, bric-a-brac, pictures and photographs (including some good ones of Exmoor), soft oil-lamp-style lighting, and stripped boards with attractive rugs on them; the two big woodburning stoves run radiators too. One little area is no smoking. As well as daily specials such as fresh cod (£4.95), smoked bacon, chicken and broccoli bake, toad-in-the-hole or stilton, red pepper and sweetcorn quiche (£5.25), and roast beef or cider braised pork chop (£5.50), simple bar food includes sandwiches (from £1.50), home-made souup (£1.75), locally-made pasties (£1.80), ploughman's (from £3.25), omelettes (£4.25), and ham and egg (£4.40). Well kept Bass, Flowers IPA, and Marstons Pedigree tapped from the cask, and quite a few whiskies; cribbage, dominoes. *(Recommended by Joy and Peter Heatherley, Joyce and Maurice Cottrell, the Didler, P and M Rudlin, Dennis Jenkin, P J Holdsworth, Mrs Romey Heaton, Paul R White)*

Inn Partnership (Nomura) ~ Tenant Denis Churchill ~ Real ale ~ Bar food (not Mon evenings Oct-Whitsun) ~ No credit cards ~ (01736) 740574 ~ Children in restaurant ~ Open 11-2.30(3 Sat), 6-11; 12-3, 7-10.30 Sun

MITCHELL SW8654 Map 1

Plume of Feathers

Just off A30 Bodmin—Redruth, by A3076 junction; take the southwards road then turn first right

Since the licensees took over a year ago, they have worked hard at refurbishing and redecorating this friendly roadside pub. A new kitchen has been added, extra garden space incorporated, a new cellar installed, and they are in the process of transforming barns at the back of the building into letting bedrooms and a self-catering cottage. There are stripped old beams and an enormous open fire, the walls are fresh pastel colours, and a natural spring well has been made into a glass-topped table. There's a no smoking restaurant, and an eating area near the main bar for the minority who want to smoke. As well as a straightforward menu which includes things like home-made soup (£2.30), sandwiches (from £2.40; ciabatta from £3.70), baked potatoes (from £2.65), and steak (£9.25), there are lunchtime specials such as deep-fried brie (£4.25), steak and kidney pie (£5.50), and salmon on roasted vegetables with tomato tapenade (£7.50), with evening specials such as fried scallops on a spinach and parmesan salad (£4.25), grilled john dory fillets with tomatoes, olives, lemon and rosemary (£10.95), grilled bass with rocket and spring onion and parmesan mash (£11.95), and beef fillet with seared scallops (£12); puddings include crunchy apple tart with clotted cream or baked chocolate cheesecake (from £3.25). Well kept Courage, Sharps Doom Bar and Skinners on handpump, a comprehensive wine list, freshly squeezed orange juice and good fresh Italian coffees. Piped music, juke box, darts, and fruit machine. The raised lawn at the back has an adventure playground for children. *(Recommended by Mr and Mrs Capp, Jack and Rosalin Forrester, Karen Hands)*

Free house ~ Licensees M F Warner and J Trotter ~ Real ale ~ Bar food (12-10) ~ Restaurant ~ (01872) 510387 ~ Children welcome ~ Occasional jazz ~ Open 1-11; 12-10.30 Sun

MITHIAN SW7450 Map 1
Miners Arms
Just off B3285 E of St Agnes

Today this is a friendly old pub, but it has been used as many things in its 400 years. One upstairs room was a court and still has the original barrel ceiling, there's a passage behind the fireplace in the sitting room that once led to a tunnel connecting it to the manor house, and it has even served as a chapel. The small back bar has an irregular beam and plank ceiling, a wood block floor, and bulging squint walls (one with a fine old wall painting of Elizabeth I); another small room has a decorative low ceiling, lots of books and quite a few interesting ornaments, and there are warm winter fires. The Croust Room is no smoking. Bar food includes sandwiches, home-made soup (from £3), ploughman's (from £4.75), steak, kidney and oyster pie or wild boar and apple sausages (£6.75), sweet hickory chicken salad or butternut squash and barley bake (£7.25), local dover sole (£12.50), puddings (from £2.75), and children's dishes (from £2.75). Bass, Courage Best and Sharps Doom Bar on handpump, and quite a few wines by the glass. Shove-ha'penny, bar billiards, cribbage, and dominoes. There are seats on the back terrace, with more on the sheltered front cobbled forecourt. *(Recommended by Peter Salmon, Ted George, JP, PP, R L Turnham)*

Inn Partnership (Nomura) ~ Lease Andrew Bown ~ Real ale ~ Bar food ~ (01872) 552375 ~ Children welcome away from bar ~ Open 12-2.30, 6-11(10.30 Sun)

MOUSEHOLE SW4726 Map 1
Ship
Follow Newlyn coast road out of Penzance; also signposted off B3315

As we went to press this bustling harbourside local set in a lovely village was about to have new licensees. It's been such an enjoyable local that we are keeping our fingers crossed that things won't change too much. The opened-up main bar has black beams and panelling, built-in wooden wall benches and stools around the low tables, photographs of local events, sailors' fancy ropework, granite flagstones, and a cosy open fire. Bar food has included filled baked potatoes or sandwiches, ploughman's, ham and egg, steak and kidney pie, spinach and mushroom lasagne, and local fish. On 23 December they bake Starry Gazy pie to celebrate Tom Bawcock's Eve, a tradition that recalls Tom's brave expedition out to sea in a fierce storm 200 years ago. He caught seven types of fish, which were then cooked in a pie with their heads and tails sticking out. Well kept St Austell BB, Tinners, HSD and Daylight Robbery on handpump, and several malt whiskies. The elaborate harbour lights at Christmas are worth a visit; best to park at the top of the village and walk down. *(Recommended by Kevin Flack, Alan and Hillie Johnson, Stuart Turner, Mr and Mrs P Eastwood)*

St Austell ~ Manager D W Adams ~ Real ale ~ Bar food ~ Restaurant ~ (01736) 731234 ~ Children welcome away from bar ~ Open 10.30-11; 12-10.30 Sun ~ Bedrooms: £35S/£50S

MYLOR BRIDGE SW8137 Map 1

Pandora ★★ ♀

Restronguet Passage: from A39 in Penryn, take turning signposted Mylor Church, Mylor Bridge, Flushing and go straight through Mylor Bridge following Restronguet Passage signs; or from A39 further N, at or near Perranarworthal, take turning signposted Mylor, Restronguet, then follow Restronguet Weir signs, but turn left down hill at Restronguet Passage sign

In fine weather you can sit with your drink on the long floating pontoon in front of this delightful medieval thatched pub, and watch the visiting dinghies pottering about in the sheltered waterfront; it's at its best at high tide out of season; showers for yachtsmen. Inside, the several rambling, interconnecting rooms have low wooden ceilings (mind your head on some of the beams), beautifully polished big flagstones, cosy alcoves with leatherette benches built into the walls, a kitchen range, and a log fire in a high hearth (to protect it against tidal floods); half the bar area is no smoking – as is the restaurant. Bar food (with prices unchanged since last year) includes home-made soup (£3.20), sandwiches (from £3.50, good local crab £6.50), sausages with onion marmalade (£5.50), mediterranean fish stew (£6.75), smoked haddock, salmon and prawn bake (£7.25), crab cakes (£7.95), puddings, and children's menu (from £3). Bass, St Austell Tinners, HSD, and IPA on handpump from a temperature controlled cellar, lots of good wines by the glass, and local cider. It does get very crowded in summer, and parking is difficult at peak times. Good surrounding walks. *(Recommended by JP, PP, Dr M E Wilson, B A Dale, Brian Skelcher, J Davidson, Tina and David Woods-Taylor, Simon and Laura Habbishow, the Didler, Martin and Karen Wake, Kevin Macey, Stephen and Jean Curtis, M Borthwick, Charlie Harris, Nigel and Olga Wikeley, Tracey and Stephen Groves, Joyce and Maurice Cottrell, Betsy Brown, Nigel Flook, Val Stevenson, Rob Holmes, Ian Phillips, Joy and Peter Heatherley, Ian Arthur, Paul R White, J Forbes)*

St Austell ~ Tenant John Milan ~ Real ale ~ Bar food ~ Restaurant ~ (01326) 372678 ~ Children welcome ~ Open 11-11; 12-10.30 Sun; 12-2.30, 7-11 in winter

PENZANCE SW4730 Map 1

Turks Head

At top of main street, by big domed building (Lloyds TSB), turn left down Chapel Street

Both visitors and locals are welcomed just as warmly in this reliably friendly, unchanging pub. The bustling bar has old flat irons, jugs and so forth hanging from the beams, pottery above the wood-effect panelling, wall seats and tables, and a couple of elbow rests around central pillars; piped music. A good choice of popular bar food includes soup (£2.60), lunchtime open sandwiches (from £2.95, white crabmeat £5.75), filled baked potatoes (from £3.95), ham and egg (£4.50), ratatouille topped with cheese (£4.95), steak and kidney pie (£6.75), steaks (from £7.50), and daily specials such as a lunchtime vegetable cottage pie (£5.50) or daily roast l(£5.95), local cod in beer batter (£6.95), chargrilled cajun chicken breast (£8.25), sizzling tandoori monkfish (£9.55), and duck breast with brandy and orange sauce (£10.95). Well kept Boddingtons, Green King Old Speckled Hen, Sharps Cornish Coaster, and a guest like Fullers London Pride on handpump; helpful service. The suntrap back garden has big urns of flowers. There has been a Turks Head here for over 700 years – though most of the original building was destroyed by a Spanish raiding party in the 16th c. *(Recommended by Jonathan Smith, Ken Flawn, David Clifton, Val Stevenson, Rob Holmes, Alan and Hillie Johnson, Paul R White)*

Inn Partnership (Nomura) ~ Tenant William Morris ~ Real ale ~ Bar food (11(12 Sun)-2.30, 6-10) ~ Restaurant ~ (01736) 363093 ~ Children in family room ~ Open 11-3, 5.30-11; 12-3, 5.30-10.30 Sun; closed 25 Dec

PHILLEIGH SW8639 Map 1

Roseland ★ ♀

Between A3078 and B3289, just E of King Harry ferry

Handy for Trelissick Gardens and the King Harry ferry, this charming little place remains as consistently friendly and as popular as ever. The two bar rooms (one with flagstones and the other carpeted) have wheelback chairs and built-in red-cushioned seats, open fires, old photographs and some giant beetles and butterflies in glasses, and a relaxed chatty atmosphere; the little back bar is used by locals. Enjoyably good bar food includes home-baked pasty (£2.60), sandwiches (from £3.50; bocatta bread with chargrilled chicken, hummous, mint and tzatziki £6.50), ploughman's or filled baked potatoes (from £4.50), crevettes sautéed in lime and chilli butter (small £5.95, large £7.95), beef and stilton pie (£8.25), braised shank of lamb (£8.95), crab cakes with a tomato and basil dressing (£9.95), daily specials like pork and stilton pâté (£5.95), scallops with brandy and coriander with a herb crust (£9.95), and Aberdeen Angus steak (£12.50), puddings (£3.95), and children's menu; you must book to be sure of a table. The restaurant is no smoking. Well kept Bass, Ringwood Best, Marstons Pedigree, and Sharps Own and Doom Bar on handpump, local cider, quite a few wines by the glass, and several malt whiskies; dominoes and cribbage. The pretty paved front courtyard is a lovely place to sit in the lunchtime sunshine beneath the cherry blossom, and the back garden has a small outdoor children's play area. *(Recommended by Nick Lawless, Christopher Wright, the Didler, Kevin Macey, Mrs S Cripps, D A Boylett, Miss E Murphy, JP, PP, Sheila and Phil Stubbs, Sharon Doe, Mrs Cole, Mike Gorton, Mr and Mrs E Borthwick, Joy and Peter Heatherley)*

Greenalls ~ Tenant Colin Phillips ~ Real ale ~ Bar food ~ Restaurant ~ (01872) 580254 ~ Children welcome ~ Open 11-3, 5.30-11; 12-3, 6-10.30 Sun

POLKERRIS SX0952 Map 1

Rashleigh

Signposted off A3082 Fowey—St Austell

In wet, miserable weather this little pub is a popular spot – though there is little doubt that it comes into its own in the summer. You can sit on the stone terrace and enjoy the views towards the far side of St Austell and Mevagissey Bays, and the isolated beach with its restored jetty is just a few steps away. The bar is snug and cosy, and the front part has comfortably cushioned seats and well kept St Austell HSD, Sharps Doom Bar and up to four changing guest beers on handpump, a decent wine list and over 40 whiskies; the more simply furnished back area has local photographs on the brown panelling, a winter log fire and maybe piped classical music. Bar food includes sandwiches (from £2; open ones from £4.25), ploughman's (from £4.50), home-cooked ham with pineapple or cottage pie (£5.50), hazelnut and vegetable crumble (£6), a lunchtime cold buffet (£6.50), fish pie (£6.95), daily specials such as chargrilled rump steak (£10.50), john dory (£11.50), and whole bass (£15), puddings (from £2.80), and children's menu (from £1.95). Though parking space next to the pub is limited, there's a large village car park, and there are safe moorings for small yachts in the cove. This whole section of the Cornish Coast Path is renowned for its striking scenery. *(Recommended by Charlotte Latham, Joy and Peter Heatherley, Nigel and Olga Wikeley, Mayur Shah, JP, PP, the Didler, R L Turnham, Pete and Rosie Flower, Meg and Colin Hamilton)*

Free house ~ Licensee Bernard Smith ~ Real ale ~ Bar food (11-2.15, 6-10) ~ Restaurant ~ (01726) 813991 ~ Children allowed if well behaved ~ Pianist Sat evening ~ Open 11-3, 6-11; 12-3, 6-10.30 Sun; 11.30-2.30, 6.30-11 winter

POLPERRO SX2051 Map 1

Old Mill House

Mill Hill; bear right approaching harbour

On a narrow lane close to the harbour, this pretty white cottage is a friendly, pleasant place to stay. There are polished boards, solid stripped pine furniture, dado and stall dividers, a couple of housekeeper's chairs and some hefty rustic implements by the big log fireplace, fishing-boat pictures, and netting and some nautical hardware overhead. Flagstones by the serving counter, and well kept Sharps Cornish Coaster and Eden Ale on handpump. Bar food (they tell us prices have not changed since last year) includes home-made soup (£2.25), sandwiches (from £2.20), locally made pasties (£2.95), ploughman's (£4.95), home-made steak and kidney pie (£5.95), home-made lasagne or fresh grilled cod (£6.95), daily specials like home-made chilli (£5.95), grilled prawns (£6.95), and scallops with bacon (£7.95), and puddings such as sticky toffee cheesecake or apple pie with clotted cream (from £2.75). Round the corner is an area with darts and pool, shove-ha'penny, cribbage, dominoes, and shut the box. A little room opens off on the left; piped music. There is a picnic-set in front, with more under parasols in a streamside garden with a terrace behind. *(Recommended by Mayur Shah, Roger and Jenny Huggins, Mike and Sue Loseby, Richard Butler, Marie Kroon, Ted George, R J Walden, Stuart Turner, Mrs P G Newton, Dave Irving, Marion Turner, Rona Murdoch, E M and H P N Steinitz, E G Parish)*

Free house ~ Licensee Suzanne Doughty ~ Real ale ~ Bar food ~ (01503) 272362 ~ Children in eating area of bar, restaurant, and family room ~ Open 11(12 in winter)-11; 12-10.30 Sun ~ Bedrooms: /£55B

PORT ISAAC SX0080 Map 1
Golden Lion
Fore Street

The views over the harbour of the lovely steep village here can be enjoyed from seats on the terrace or from window seats in the cosy rooms of this friendly local. There's a bustling, chatty atmosphere, a bar with a fine antique settle among other comfortable seats, and decorative ceiling plasterwork. Bar food includes sandwiches (lunchtime only, from £2.30), filled baked potatoes (from £3.25), proper fish and chips or home-made vegetable korma (£6.95), home-made fish pie (£7.95), home-made steak in ale pie (£8.25), chargrilled sirloin steak (£11.95), and daily specials like fresh crab sandwich (£4.95) or warm goats cheese and bacon salad (£7.95); during the summer, evening meals are served in the no smoking bistro. Well kept St Austell Tinners, HSD and a changing guest on handpump and several malt whiskies. Darts, shove-ha'penny, dominoes, a fruit machine in the public bar, and piped music. You can park at the top of the village unless you are lucky enough to park on the beach at low tide. *(Recommended by Linda Norsworthy, Nigel Pittman, George Atkinson, Joy and Peter Heatherley, the Didler, R J Walden, Kevin Macey, Karen and Graham Oddey, Betsy Brown, Nigel Flook, Sue Demont, Tim Barrow)*

St Austell ~ Tenants Mike and Nikki Edkins ~ Real ale ~ Bar food (not winter Sun evenings) ~ Restaurant (evening) ~ (01208) 880336 ~ Children in eating area of bar and restaurant ~ Open 11.30-11; 12-10.30 Sun; closed evening 25 Dec

Port Gaverne Inn ♀ ⇌
Port Gaverne signposted from Port Isaac, and from B3314 E of Pendoggett

As we went to press, we heard that this 17th-c inn was up for sale. It's been somewhere our readers have enjoyed very much over the years, so we will keep our fingers crossed that things won't change too much. The bar has big log fires and low beams, flagstones as well as carpeting, some exposed stone, and lots of chatty locals. In spring, the lounge is filled with pictures from the local art society's annual exhibition, and at other times there are interesting antique local photographs. Bar food includes sandwiches, ham and egg, bangers and mash or vegetarian lasagne (£4.25), ploughman's or home-made cottage pie (£4.95), deep-fried local plaice (£6.25), and daily specials such as seafood pancakes (£4.95), chicken, bacon and leek pie (£6.95), and moules normandes (£8.95); you can eat in the bar, the Captain's Cabin – a little room where everything is shrunk to scale (old oak chest, model sailing ship, even the prints on the white stone walls) or on a balcony overlooking the sea; the restaurant is no smoking. On Sunday lunchtime, there's a choice of two roasts and a vegetarian dish (two courses £6.95). Well kept Bass,

Greene King Abbot, and Sharps Doom Bar and Cornish Coaster on handpump, a good bin-end wine list with 60 wines, a very good choice of whiskies and other spirits. There are seats in the garden close to the sea. Some bedrooms have their own balcony with views out over the cove and up to the cliffs, and there are splendid surrounding clifftop walks, and plenty of bird life. *(Recommended by John and Jackie Chalcraft, P Price, Kevin Macey, G U Briggs, Peter Salmon, Tony and Valerie Marshall, Charles Gysin, Joy and Peter Heatherley, Betsy Brown, Nigel Flook, Sue Demont, Tim Barrow, P Fisk)*

Free house ~ Licensee Marjorie Ross ~ Real ale ~ Bar food ~ Restaurant ~ (01208) 880244 ~ Children in Captain's Cabin or snug; must be over 7 in restaurant ~ Open 11-11; 12-10.30 Sun; 11-2.30, 6-11 winter; closed early Jan-mid Feb ~ Bedrooms: £45S/£90B

PORTHALLOW SW7923 Map 1
Five Pilchards

SE of Helston; B3293 to St Keverne, then village signposted

A new conservatory with a waterfall has been added to this friendly and sturdy stone-built pub. The walls and ceilings of the bars are hung with an abundance of salvaged nautical gear, lamps made from puffer fish, and interesting photographs and clippings about local shipwrecks. Good bar food includes sandwiches (from £2.50; good crab £4.50), home-made seafood chowder (£3.95), fish pie (£6.95), breast of duck in redcurrant and port sauce (£11.95), and scallops in saffron and wine (£12.95). Well kept Greene King Abbot and Sharps Doom Bar, Coaster, and Eden Ale on handpump, good wines. Seats out on the terrace. Tides and winds allowing, you can park on the foreshore. *(Recommended by Ian Wilson, Miss J E Winsor, Trish and Ian Avis, P and M Rudlin, Stuart Turner, Canon Michael Bourdeaux)*

Free house ~ Licensee Brandon Flynn ~ Real ale ~ Bar food ~ Restaurant ~ (01326) 280256 ~ Children in eating area of bar and restaurant ~ Open 12-2.30, 6-11; 12-3, 7-10.30 Sun; closed Sun evening in winter, cl all day Mon

PORTHLEVEN SW6225 Map 1
Ship

Village on B3304 SW of Helston; pub perched on edge of harbour

Whether you are cosily tucked away inside this old fisherman's pub on a cold winter's day or enjoying sunshine out in the terraced garden, the cheerful, hard-working landlord will make you feel welcome. To reach it, you have to climb a flight of rough stone steps – it's actually built into the steep cliffs, and there are marvellous views over the pretty working harbour and out to sea; at night, the harbour is interestingly floodlit. The knocked-through bar has log fires in big stone fireplaces and some genuine character, and the family room is a conversion of an old smithy and has logs burning in the huge open fireplace. Popular bar food includes sandwiches (from £3.95; fine toasties from £4.50; excellent crusties from £4.95), filled baked potatoes (from £3.50), grilled goats cheese on a pesto crouton or smoked fish platter (£4.95), ploughman's (from £5.95), home-made chilli (£7.90), a vegetarian dish (£8.50), steaks (from £10.50), local crab claws (£11.95), daily specials like home-made crab soup (£4.50), cumberland sausage with spicy red cabbage (£9.95), crab and prawn mornay (£10.95) or duck with oriental stir-fried vegetables (£14.95), puddings such as home-made apple torte or chocolate sponge (from £3.25), and children's meals (£2.95); the candlelit dining room also enjoys the good view. Well kept Courage Best and Directors, Greene King Abbot, and Sharps Doom Bar on handpump, and several malt whiskies; dominoes, cribbage, fruit machine and piped music. *(Recommended by John and Helene Hammond, James Nunns, Mr and Mrs P Eastwood, the Didler, Bruce Bird, Joyce and Maurice Cottrell, P and M Rudlin, Mike Gorton, Mike and Sue Loseby, Paul R White, Miss J E Winsor, Marion Turner)*

Free house ~ Licensee Colin Oakden ~ Real ale ~ Bar food ~ (01326) 564204 ~ Children in family room ~ Open 11.30-3, 6.30-11; all day in summer; 12-3.30, 6.30-10.30 Sun

RUAN LANIHORNE SW8942 Map 1

Kings Head

Village signposted off A3078 St Mawes road

Careful refurbishments have taken place recently in this attractive, neatly kept pub, set opposite a fine old church in a pleasant out-of-the-way village. The beamed bar has a welcoming local atmosphere, and is decorated with hanging china and framed cigarette cards, and there's an attractive family room with lots of mirrors next door. Good bar food inludes ciabatta rolls (from £3.95), ploughman's (£4.75), roast tomato and dolcelatte tart (£4.50), thai chicken salad with mango salsa (£4.95), a selection of local fish (from £8.95), rump of lamb with polenta and pesto rosso or scallopine of veal with white wine, sage and lemon (£10.95), steaks (from £10.95), and puddings such as Belgian chocolate truffle, lemon tart and sticky toffee pudding (£3.15). The dining room is no smoking. Well kept Fullers London Pride, Skinners Cornish Knocker and a beer brewed for the pub by Skinners, and guest beers on handpump, local cider, and a decent wine list; cribbage, dominoes, cards and draughts. There are seats in the suntrap, sunken garden and views down over the pretty convolutions of the River Fal's tidal estuary. *(Recommended by Dr P Brown, Bernard Stradling, S Horsley, John and Joan Calvert, John and Sarah Perry, Mrs J Anderton, David Wallington, Mr and Mrs F Farnham-Flower, Joy and Peter Heatherley)*

Free house ~ Licensee Russell Weightman ~ Real ale ~ Bar food (12-1.45, 6-8.45; not winter Mon) ~ Restaurant ~ (01872) 501263 ~ Children in family room ~ Open 12-2.30, 6-11; 12-2.30, 7-10.30 Sun; closed Mon from Sept to Easter

ST AGNES SV8807 Map 1

Turks Head 🍺

The Quay

From the few tables on a patch of lawn across the sleepy lane from this little slate-roofed white cottage are wonderful views, and there are steps to the slipway so you can walk down with your drinks and food and sit right on the shore. Inside, the simply furnished but cosy and very friendly pine-panelled bar has quite a collection of flags, helmets and headwear and banknotes, as well as maritime photographs and model ships. The real ale arrives in St Agnes via a beer supplier in St Austell and two boat trips: Dartmoor Best and a beer named for the pub, well kept on handpump, besides decent house wines, a good range of malt whiskies, and hot chocolate with brandy. At lunchtime, the decent bar food includes legendary huge locally made pasties (though they do sell out; £3.65), open rolls (from £2.75; local crab £4.75), ploughman's (from £4.65), salads (from £5.65; local crab £7.75), cold roast beef with chips (£5.40), vegetable pasta bake (£5.95), and puddings like sticky toffee pudding (£2.85), with evening gammon in port wine sauce (£6.50), fresh fish of the day, and sirloin steak (£9.95); children's meals (from £2.70). Ice cream and cakes are sold through the afternoon, and in good weather they may do evening barbecues. The dining extension is no smoking, and the cats are called Taggart and Lacey, and the collie, Tess. Darts, cribbage, dominoes and piped music. In spring and autumn hours may be shorter, and winter opening is sporadic, given that only some 70 people live on the island; see below. *(Recommended by Jonathan Smith, Dr M E Wilson, Trish and Ian Avis, P and M Rudlin, Canon Michael Bourdeaux)*

Free house ~ Licensees John and Pauline Dart ~ Real ale ~ Bar food (12-2.30, 6.30-9) ~ (01720) 422434 ~ Children in eating area of bar ~ Open 11-11; 12-10.30 Sun; closed Nov-Mar (but open Weds and Sat evenings, and Sun lunchtime) ~ Bedrooms: /£53B

ST BREWARD SX0977 Map 1

Old Inn

Old Town; village signposted off B3266 S of Camelford, also signed off A30 Bolventor—Bodmin

Sharing its hilltop with a church whose tower is a landmark for miles around, this country pub is a friendly, welcoming place. The spacious middle bar has plenty of seating on the fine broad slate flagstones, banknotes and horsebrasses hanging from the low oak joists that support the ochre upstairs floorboards, and plates on the stripped stonework; two massive granite fireplaces date back to the 11th c. Generous helpings of bar food include home-made soup (£2.50), filled baps or sandwiches (from £2.75), filled baked potatoes (from £3.95), ploughman's (from £4.50), ham and eggs (£5.25), all-day breakfast (£5.75), pie of the day (£5.95), mixed grill (£10.50), daily specials like vegetable masala (£5.95), large battered cod (£5.95), and hot smoked salmon fillet with dill sauce (£7.95), puddings such as blackberry and apple crumble (£2.95), and children's meals (from £3.25). The restaurant is no smoking. Well kept Bass, Sharps Doom Bar and Special Ale, and John Smiths Bitter on handpump, decent wines, and a huge range of malt whiskies; sensibly placed darts, piped music, SkyTV, and fruit machine. Picnic-sets outside are protected by low stone walls. There's plenty of open moorland behind, and cattle and sheep wander freely into the village. In front of the building is a very worn carved stone; no one knows exactly what it is but it may be part of a Saxon cross. *(Recommended by Sheila and Phil Stubbs, Joy and Peter Heatherley, Mr and Mrs Capp, the Didler)*

Free house ~ Licensee Darren Wills ~ Real ale ~ Bar food (11-2.30, 6-9.30) ~ Restaurant ~ (01208) 850711 ~ Children in eating area of bar, restaurant, and family room ~ Monthly live entertainment in winter ~ Open 11-11; 12-10.30 Sun; 11-3, 6-11 Mon-Thurs in winter

ST DOMINICK SX3967 Map 1
Who'd Have Thought It
Village signposted a mile E of A388, S of Callington

The peaceful country views can best be appreciated from the spacious no smoking conservatory of this friendly country pub, which has a great deal of individuality. The comfortable lounge bars have plush stools and solid antique furniture on the turkey carpet, high shelves of Staffordshire pottery, gleaming copper jugs and lamps, and a winter open fire. The Silage Bar has darts, juke box and TV. Good reasonably priced food includes soup (£1.90), sandwiches (from £2.80), pasty (£3.15), filled baked potatoes (from £3.50), basket meals (from £4.25), ploughman's (from £4.35), fruity curry (£5.75), platters (from £5.95; salmon and dill tart £6.95; roasted smoked salmon £7.35), steak and kidney pie or chicken and broccoli crumble (£6.95), fish pie (£7.25), sirloin steak (£10.25), and puddings such as spotted dick or fruit crumble with clotted cream (£2.60); children's menu. Well kept Bass, St Austell HSD, Skinners Betty Stogs and Worthington Best on handpump, and decent wines. There are seats in the garden; Cotehele House (NT) is nearby. *(Recommended by Ted George, Jacquie and Jim Jones, R L Turnham, Joy and Peter Heatherley)*

Free house ~ Licensee J D Potter ~ Real ale ~ Bar food (12-1.45, 7-9.45) ~ (01579) 350214 ~ Children in conservatory ~ Open 11.30-2.30, 6.30-11; 12-3, 7-10.30 Sun

ST IVES SW5441 Map 1
Sloop ⬛
The Wharf

Even in mid-winter, this quaint old waterside inn is busy – so in summer, it's best to get here early, especially for one of the very few seats out on the little cobbled area in front of the pub, looking over the road to the harbour. The front bar has kept quite a bit of character – and there are bright St Ives School paintings on the walls. To the right of the door is a tiny, simple public bar with two very long tables, which is connected to the front part of the low-beamed lounge: cushioned, built-in wall seats, cast-iron-framed pub tables on the flagstones, and in both rooms, quite a few portrait drawings by Hyman Segal. At the back is the beamed Cellar Bar (which isn't actually downstairs) with plenty of booth seating against the brown vertical panelled walls, a slate floor, and a bustling atmosphere. Well kept Bass, John Smiths, Greene King Old Speckled Hen and Sharps Doom Bar on handpump, and good fresh coffee (you keep the mug); juke box, fruit machine, TV, and piped music. Well liked bar food includes home-made soup (£2.95), sandwiches (from £2.75; good crab £4.50;

baguettes from £4.75), popular locally caught fresh fish such as mackerel simply cooked in seasoned flour (£5.95), home-made smoked salmon and crab fishcakes (£6.50) or a trio of monkfish, haddock and lemon sole in a prawn, cream and white wine sauce (£7.95), home-made chicken and bacon lasagne or ham and eggs (£5.95), their speciality seafood chowder (£6.95), crab, prawn and mussel salad (£8.95), and sirloin steak (£9.95); staff are friendly and cope efficiently with the crowds. *(Recommended by the Didler, Alan and Hillie Johnson, Kevin Macey, Stuart Turner, Joyce and Maurice Cottrell, N H E Lewis, Liz and John Soden, Ted George, Paul R White, Peter and Gwyneth Eastwood, Edward Jago)*

Unique Pub Co ~ Lease Maurice and Sue Symons ~ Real ale ~ Bar food (12-3, 6-8.45) ~ (01736) 796584 ~ Children in eating area of bar until 9pm ~ Open 10.30-11; 12-10.30 Sun ~ Bedrooms: /£60B

ST KEW SX0276 Map 1
St Kew Inn

Village signposted from A39 NE of Wadebridge

'A thoroughly enjoyable place' is how several readers describe this rather grand-looking old stone building. The neatly kept bar has winged high-backed settles and varnished rustic tables on the lovely dark Delabole flagstones, black wrought-iron rings for lamps or hams hanging from the high ceiling, a handsome window seat, and an open kitchen range under a high mantelpiece decorated with earthenware flagons. At lunchtime, the good, popular bar food includes sandwiches, soup (£2.50), filled baked potatoes or good ploughman's (£4.25), leeks and bacon in a cheese sauce or plaice and chips (£5.95), and sirloin steak (£11.95), with evening dishes like home-made chicken liver pâté (£3.50), vegetarian curry (£5.95), beef in Guinness with herb dumplings or lambs liver in a crème fraîche, mushroom and sherry sauce (£7.50), and honey roast duck with a red wine and orange sauce (£11.95); daily specials such as gruyère and onion tart, several fresh fish dishes, seasonal game or steak and kidney pie, and children's menu (from £3.50). Well kept St Austell Tinners, HSD, and Summer Ale tapped from wooden casks behind the counter (lots of tankards hang from the beams above it), a couple of farm ciders, a good wine list, and several malt whiskies; darts, cribbage, and dominoes. The big garden has seats on the grass and picnic-sets on the front cobbles. Parking is in what must have been a really imposing stable yard. The church next door is lovely. *(Recommended by Dennis Jenkin, the Didler, Tony Mott, R J Walden, Michael and Ann Cole, Steve Dark, M A Borthwick, Karen and Graham Oddey, Brian Skelcher, Kevin Thorpe, George Atkinson)*

St Austell ~ Tenant Desmond Weston ~ Real ale ~ Bar food ~ Restaurant ~ (01208) 841259 ~ Children in restaurant ~ Open 11-11; 12-10.30 Sun; 11-2.30, 6-11 winter wkdys; 12-3, 7-10.30 Sun in winter

ST MAWES SW8533 Map 1
Victory 🍽 ♀

Victory Hill

How things have changed at this former fisherman's local. The bar has been refurbished and a restaurant opened upstairs (where there had been letting bedrooms) with sisal carpeting, pale grey and pastel blue colours, and original seascapes by a local artist on the walls. They now specialise in fish which comes from local fishermen and producers, and have a curer from Penryn who provides smoked fish exclusively for them. They bake their own bread, make their own pickles, relishes, flavoured oils and other preserves, gather marsh samphire and seaweed from the local coast, and sell home-produced and local specialities in the pub which you can take home. In the bar, the menu might include fish soup with a crouton and rouille (£4.95), crostini of soft herring roes with lemon and caper dressing (£7.95), thai fishcakes with a sweet and sour salad and dipping sauce or deep-fried local cod in beer batter with home-made tartare sauce (£8.25), grilled whole mackerel with herb salad and salsa verde (£8.50), treacle-glazed ham, bubble and squeak and home-made tomato chutney (£8.95), and

Falmouth Bay whole crab salad (£9.95); they offer two-course (£24.95) and three-course (£29.95) meals in the restaurant. Good local cheeses, and puddings such as caramelised rice pudding with armagnac prunes, lemon and lime tart with crème fraîche or apple crumble with clotted cream (£3.95). Well kept Flowers IPA, Marstons Pedigree, and Sharps Doom Bar on handpump, a dozen wines by the glass, and malt whiskies. The flowering baskets and tubs outside are very pretty in summer, and in warm weather you can sit at the benches outside on the cobbles which give a glimpse of the harbour just down the road. *(Recommended by Kevin Macey, Mike Gorton, Peter and Jenny Quine, Mrs B Rogers, R and S Bentley, Geoff Calcott, L W T Mercer, Dr David Skeggs, Dr M W A Haward, Dr M E Wilson)*

Inn Partnership (Nomura) ~ Lease Philip and Bridget Savage ~ Real ale ~ Bar food ~ Restaurant ~ (01326) 270324 ~ Children welcome ~ Open 10.30-11; 12-10.30 Sun

ST MAWGAN SW8766 Map 1
Falcon 🍺
NE of Newquay, off B3276 or A3059

In a pretty village with a handsome church, this friendly and comfortable pub is a popular place for a meal. The big bar has a log fire, small modern settles and large antique coaching prints on the walls, and plenty of space to enjoy the good bar food, which might include lunchtime sandwiches, home-made soups such as cheese and ale or parsnip and apple (£2.75), pheasant breast in raspberry and port sauce (£8.25), whole lemon sole (£8.50), trio of fresh fish fillets with lime butter (£8.75), and langoustines in garlic butter (£9.95); hearty breakfasts, served promptly. The restaurant is no smoking and has paintings and pottery by local artists for sale. Well kept St Austell Tinners, HSD and Tribute on handpump, and a decent wine list; efficient service even when busy; piped music, darts, dominoes, and euchre. Particularly when the fine wisteria is flowering, the cobbled courtyard in front with its stone tables is a lovely spot to relax. The peaceful, attractive garden has plenty of seats, a wishing well, and play equipment for children. *(Recommended by Jane O'Mahoney, Helen Hazzard, Sheila and Phil Stubbs, Carol and Dono Leaman, Canon Michael Bourdeaux, Theo, Anne and Jane Gaskin, John Crafts, Peter and Jenny Quine, Deborah and Ian Carrington, P J Holdsworth, Mike and Sue Loseby)*

St Austell ~ Tenant Andy Banks ~ Real ale ~ Bar food (not 25 Dec) ~ Restaurant ~ (01637) 860225 ~ Children in restaurant and family room ~ Open 11-3, 6-11; 12-3, 7-10.30 Sun ~ Bedrooms: £20/£60S

TREBURLEY SX3477 Map 1
Springer Spaniel 🍽 🍷
A388 Callington—Launceston

Now run by the same energetic licensee as the very popular Roseland at Philleigh, this bustling pub remains well liked for its food. The relaxed bar has a lovely, very high-backed settle by the woodburning stove in the big fireplace, high-backed farmhouse chairs and other seats, and pictures of olde-worlde stage-coach arrivals at inns; this leads into room with chintzy-cushioned armchairs and sofa in one corner, and a big solid teak table. Up some steps from the main bar is the beamed, attractively furnished, no smoking restaurant. From the menu, there might be sandwiches, mushroom pots (with bacon in a cream and brandy sauce £4.50), mediterranean tart (£5.60), steak and kidney pie or scallops sautéed with bacon and shallots (£6.50), fresh vegetable risotto (£6.95), chicken breast with a glaze of caramelised red onions and balsamic vinegar (£8.95), cod steak baked with a cheesy herb crust on a provençale sauce (£9.50), shank of lamb with fresh orange, red wine, garlic and rosemary or local crab salad (£9.95), duck breast with a whisky and stem ginger sauce (£11.95), and puddings like minted white chocolate cheesecake on a bitter chocolate sauce, treacle and lemon tart with clotted cream or espresso crème brûlée (from £4.25); children's dishes (from £3.75). Well kept Sharps Doom Bar, Eden Ale, and a beer named for the pub on handpump, a good wine list, and 20 malt whiskies. *(Recommended by Jacquie and Jim Jones, Mrs Cole, Dr M W A Haward,*

John Kirk, Basil Minson, Richard and Margaret Peers, John and Sarah Perry, Joy and Peter Heatherley, Martin and Karen Wake, John and Elizabeth Thomason)

Free house ~ Licensee Colin Phillips ~ Real ale ~ Bar food ~ Restaurant ~ (01579) 370424 ~ Children welcome ~ Open 11-3, 5.45-11; 12-3.30, 6.30-10.30 Sun; closed 4 days over Christmas

TREGADILLETT SX2984 Map 1

Eliot Arms

Village signposted off A30 at junction with A395, W end of Launceston bypass

New licensees again for this creeper-covered house, but many of the interesting collections have remained. The charming series of little softly lit rooms is filled with 72 antique clocks (including 7 grandfathers), 400 snuffs, hundreds of horsebrasses, old prints, old postcards or cigarette cards grouped in frames on the walls, quite a few barometers, and shelves of books and china. Also, a fine old mix of furniture on the Delabole slate floors, from high-backed built-in curved settles, through plush Victorian dining chairs, armed seats, chaise longues and mahogany housekeeper's chairs, to more modern seats, and open fires; piped music. The licensee had only just moved into the pub as we went to press and had not organised his menu, but they will offer doorstep sandwiches (from £3.05), home-made soup (£3.50), and main dishes such as steak, kidney and mushroom pie, chicken curry, gammon and egg, puddings, and Sunday lunch. Well kept Courage Best and Directors, and Sharps Doom Bar and Eden Ale on handpump; darts, fruit machine. There are seats in front of the pub and at the back of the car park; more reports please. *(Recommended by Mike and Sue Losebey, JP, PP, the Didler, Joy and Peter Heatherley, Helen Hazzard, Peter and Audrey Dowsett, Joan and Michel Hooper-Immins, Kevin Blake, Sue Demont, Tim Barrow, Joyce and Maurice Cottrell, G K Smale, Andy Smith, Paul R White)*

J P Leisure ~ Managers Jamie Player and Debbie Cooper ~ Real ale ~ Bar food ~ (01566) 772051 ~ Children welcome ~ Open 11-3, 6-11; 12-3, 7-10.30 Sun ~ Bedrooms: /£40(£50S)

TRESCO SV8915 Map 1

New Inn 🍷 🛏

New Grimsby; Isles of Scilly

While locals tend to sit by the bar counter on one of the high bar chairs and chat amiably to each other or the friendly bar staff, visitors enjoy the main bar room or the light, airy dining extension. There are some comfortable old sofas, banquettes, planked partition seating, and farmhouse chairs and tables, a few standing timbers, boat pictures, a large model sailing boat, a collection of old telescopes, and plates on the delft shelf. The Pavilion (as they call the new extension) has plenty of seats and tables on the blue wooden floors and cheerful yellow walls, and looks over the terrace with its new teak furniture. Well liked bar food at lunchtime includes sandwiches (from £3.90; soup and a sandwich from £5.90), pasties (from £4.20), chargrilled burgers or ploughman's (from £4.95), and daily specials; evening dishes such as stone-baked pizzas (£3.95), oak smoked Scottish salmon slices (£5.95), chicken breast marinated in lemon and cracked pepper, tarragon and lemon sauce or tuna steak flavoured with Chinese five spice served with oriental dressing (£9.50), and steaks (from £9.90); children's menu (£3.95). The five well kept real ales are all Cornish: Sharps Eden Ale, Skinners Betty Stogs Bitter and Summer Blonde, a beer named for the pub, and St Austell Daylight Robbery on handpump; interesting wines (by the large glass), 25 malt whiskies, and 10 vodkas; real espresso and cappuccino coffee. Darts, pool, juke box, cribbage, dominoes, and euchre. Note that the price below is for dinner, bed and breakfast. They open earlier for coffee in the morning, and serve afternoon tea. *(Recommended by BKA, Jonathan Smith, Dr M E Wilson, P and M Rudlin, R J Herd)*

Free house ~ Licensee Robin Lawson ~ Real ale ~ Bar food ~ Restaurant ~ (01720) 423006 ~ Children in eating area of bar ~ Live entertainment Fri, Sat or Tues evening every 2 or 3 wks ~ Open 11-11; 12-10.30 Sun; 12-2.30, 7-11 in winter ~ Bedrooms: £80B/£160B

TREVAUNANCE COVE SW7251 Map 1

Driftwood Spars ◖ ◄

Quay Road, off B3285 in St Agnes

In a lovely spot just up the road from the beach and dramatic cove, this 17th-c building (originally a marine warehouse and fish cellar) was constructed from local slate and granite, and timbered with massive ships' spars – the masts of great sailing ships, many of which were wrecked along this coast. There's said to be an old smugglers' tunnel leading from behind the bar, up through the cliff. The two lower bars are bustling and popular, with a variety of wooden tables and chairs, old ship prints and lots of nautical and wreck memorabilia, a winter log fire, and a good mix of customers; one bar has a juke box, pool, fruit machine and TV. Upstairs, the comfortable dining areas offer plenty of space (and residents have the use of a similarly comfy gallery bar). Decent bar food includes sandwiches (from £1.90), filled baked potatoes (from £3), ploughman's (from £3.85), chilli crab cakes (£5.20), ham and eggs (£5.40), steaks (from £7.50), and daily specials like local boar burgers (£4.50), honey mustard chicken, or lamb and mint casserole (£6.25), fish pie (£6.30), steak in ale pie (£6.50), a carvery on summer evenings and winter Sundays, and puddings such as banoffi pie, bread and butter pudding or sherry trifle (£2.50). They have their own microbrewery where they produce Cuckoo Ale, and keep five guests from Bass, Sharps, Skinners and St Austell on handpump; over 100 malt whiskies, and friendly helpful staff. There are seats in the garden, and the summer hanging baskets are pretty. Readers have enjoyed staying here; plenty of surrounding coastal walks. *(Recommended by Richard Butler, Marie Kroon, P and M Rudlin, Val Stevenson, Rob Holmes, Brian Websdale)*

Own brew ~ Licensees Gordon and Jill Treleaven ~ Real ale ~ Bar food (12-2.30, 6.30-9.30) ~ (01872) 552428 ~ Children welcome ~ Live music Fri/Sat evenings ~ Open 10.30-11; 12-10.30 Sun; 11 opening in winter ~ Bedrooms: £32S/£64B

TRURO SW8244 Map 1

Old Ale House ◖ £

Quay Street

They keep up to 14 real ales on handpump or tapped from the cask in this bustling, chatty pub, and changing regularly, there might be beers from Bass, Courage, Exmoor, Fullers, Sharps, Skinners, John Smiths, and Theakstons; 21 country wines. Enjoyable bar food is freshly prepared in a spotless kitchen in full view of the bar: doorstep sandwiches (from £2.65; delicious hot baked garlic bread with melted cheese from £2.70), filled oven-baked potatoes (from £2.95), ploughman's (from £3.65), good hot meals served in a skillet pan like five spice chicken, sizzling beef or vegetable stir fry (small helpings from £4.25, big helpings from £5.25), daily specials such as sausage or vegetable hotpots or munster bake (£2.50), and puddings (£2.30). The dimly lit bar has a good mix of customers, an engaging diversity of furnishings, some interesting 1920s bric-a-brac, beer mats pinned everywhere, matchbox collections, and newspapers and magazines to read. Cribbage, dominoes, giant Jenga, giant Connect Four, and piped music. *(Recommended by R J Walden, Brian Skelcher, Joyce and Maurice Cottrell, Jonathan Smith, JP, PP, Pat and Robert Watt, Mrs S Cripps, P and M Rudlin, Jacquie and Jim Jones, Mr and Mrs Capp, Ted George, the Didler, Chris and Sandra Taylor, Jeff Davies, Tracey and Stephen Groves, Martin Edwards, Jonathan Gibbs, S Horsley)*

Scottish Courage ~ Manager Mark Jones ~ Real ale ~ Bar food (12-3(5 Sat), 7-9; no food Sat or Sun evenings) ~ (01872) 271122 ~ Children in eating area of bar until 9 ~ Live music Mon, Thurs, Sat ~ Open 11-11; 12-10.30 Sun

---

Bedroom prices normally include full English breakfast, VAT and any inclusive service charge that we know of. Prices before the '/' are for single rooms, after for two people in double or twin (B includes a private bath, S a private shower).

Lucky Dip

Besides the fully inspected pubs, you might like to try these Lucky Dips recommended to us and described by readers (if you do, please send us reports: www.goodguides.com).

Altarnun [SX2182]
Rising Sun [NW, towards St Clether]: Basic 16th-c local in attractive spot, with two small traditional flagstoned or tiled-floor rooms, coal fire, six well kept changing ales, good value simple food, friendly staff and locals, restaurant; open all day wknds and summer, tables outside, bedrooms *(the Didler, P J Holdsworth)*
Blisland [SX0973]
Blisland Inn [signed off A30 and B3266 NE of Bodmin]: Five well kept changing ales (hundreds each year, and one at a bargain price) in very friendly genuine two-bar pub, sensibly priced fresh food (much of it local) inc small helpings for children or a spare plate to share; efficient service, family room, a real welcome for dogs, pool room, no music or machines; tables outside *(P and M Rudlin, the Didler)*
Bodmin [SX0767]
Weavers [Honey St]: Welcoming refurbished local, wide choice of usual food, good service, busy but relaxing atmosphere, full St Austell beer range kept well; SkyTV sports *(Sue and Mike Todd)*
Boscastle [SX0990]
☆ *Cobweb* [B3263, just E of harbour]: Bustling old pub, hundreds of old bottles hanging from heavy beams, two or three high-backed settles, dark stone walls, cosy log fire, maybe real ales such as Dartmoor or St Austell, reasonably priced bar food from sandwiches and filled baked potatoes to steaks, another fire in big family room, darts, dominoes, cribbage, pool, fruit machine and juke box; more machines in good-sized children's room, no smoking area; live music Sat, open all day *(Mike and Sue Loseby, the Didler, JP, PP, Deborah and Ian Carrington, LYM)*
Breage [SW6128]
Queens Arms [3 miles W of Helston]: Long thriving bar with log fire each end, beams festooned with plates, six well kept changing ales, wide range of food inc children's dishes, no smoking dining room, welcoming landlord, daily papers, games area; tables and children's games room outside, another play area and garden over the lane; quiz night Weds, jazz Thurs; bedrooms, medieval wall paintings in church opp *(P and M Rudlin)*
Bude [SS2006]
Falcon [Falcon Terrace]: 19th-c hotel overlooking canal, old-fashioned furnishings and atmosphere, lots of quick good value food in bar and restaurant inc crunchy veg, daily roast, local fish and good puddings, well kept Bass and St Austell Tinners and HSD, good coffee and herbal teas; big family room with two pool tables, dogs welcome; bedrooms comfortable and well equipped, good breakfast *(Rita Horridge, Derek Allpass, KJWM)*
Cadgwith [SW7214]
☆ *Cadgwith Cove Inn*: Friendly new licensees

doing good food from simple bar snacks to interesting main dishes inc local crab and fresh fish in unpretentious pub with big front terrace overlooking fish sheds and bay; roomy and clean, local seascapes and nautical memorabilia, four or five well kept ales such as Marstons Pedigree, Sharps Own and Wadworths 6X, choice of wines by the glass, separate restaurant; dogs welcome, and children away from main bar, folk and jazz evenings; on Coast Path and open all day at least in summer *(Colin Parker, Mike and Alison Stevens, Nigel Hopkins, Martin and Karen Wake, Sue Holland, Dave Webster)*
Calstock [SX4368]
Tamar [Quay]: Spotless pub yards from the river, new licensees doing good reasonably priced food, well kept Courage Best and Directors and Greene King Ruddles County, neatly kept terrace making the most of this year's riverside rejuvenation; hilly walk or ferry to Cotehele (NT) *(Carole and John Smith, Brian, Dill, Jenni and Kate Hughes)*
Camborne [SW6438]
☆ *Old Shire* [Pendarves; B3303 towards Helston]: Largely extended family dining pub with popular carvery, generous good food, Bass, decent wines, friendly ever-present landlady, attentive young staff, modern back part with lots of easy chairs and sofas, pictures for sale and great coal fire, conservatory; picnic-sets on terrace, summer barbecues *(Renee and Dennis Ball, P and M Rudlin, Mr and Mrs P Eastwood)*
Camelford [SX1083]
Darlington [Market Pl]: Friendly pub on busy main street, food nearly all day, helpful staff, St Austell Tinners; open all day, seats on cobbled front terrace, bedrooms *(George Atkinson)*
Cargreen [SX4362]
☆ *Crooked Spaniard* [off A388 Callington—Saltash]: Much-altered pub in grand spot by Tamar, with smart river-view dining extension and waterside terrace – always some river activity, esp at high tide; cosy and comfortable panelled bar, huge fireplace in another room, good generous food inc Sun carvery, well kept ales; under same management as Crooked Inn at Trematon *(Ted George, R L Turnham)*
Charlestown [SX0351]
Harbour Inn [by Pier House Hotel]: Small well managed somewhat hotelish bar, good value traditional food, well kept Bass and Flowers Original, good wine choice, welcoming attentive service; first-class location alongside and looking over the classic little harbour, interesting film-set conservation village with shipwreck museum *(Anthony and Elizabeth Barker, Betty Laker, Brian Skelcher, Myke and Nicky Crombleholme)*
Chilsworthy [SX4172]
White Hart: Friendly new licensees for well restored village pub, enterprising choice of good food, well kept beer, lots of local activities (and

cats); nice (steep) garden, great views *(Brian, Dill, Jenni and Kate Hughes)*

Coverack [SW7818]

Paris [The Cove]: Friendly old-fashioned pub above harbour in beautiful fishing village, spectacular bay views, well kept ale, enjoyable generous food esp local fish and seafood, also children's, good Sun lunch and maybe teas, well kept Ushers, nautical items inc large model of namesake ship, interesting wooden moulds from Falmouth churchyard; garden, bedrooms *(Eamonn and Natasha Skyrme, Miss J E Winsor, Tina and David Woods-Taylor)*

Crackington Haven [SX1396]

☆ *Coombe Barton*: Beautifully placed open-plan pub in tiny village, good for families with young children; spectacular sea view from roomy and spotless lounge/dining area, no smoking area, family room, good value food inc local fish, well kept Sharps Doom Bar and another local guest ale, good coffee, tables on big terrace, games room with pool tables; bedrooms, on Coast Path *(G K Smale, P and M Rudlin, Brian, Dill, Jenni and Kate Hughes, Bruce Bird)*

Crafthole [SX3654]

☆ *Finnygook*: Clean and comfortable much-modernised lounge bar, light and airy dining room, good range of cheap bar food inc wholesome baguettes, well kept St Austell beers, reasonably priced wines, hospitable staff; discreet piped music, one car park is steep, and beware of the high pressure taps in the lavatories; good sea views from residents' lounge, low-priced bedrooms *(Dennis Jenkin, BB)*

Liscawn Inn: Converted farmhouse in lovely valley looking over Tamar to Plymouth, wide choice of good value food, reasonably priced drinks, friendly staff; play area, bedrooms *(Ian and Deborah Carrington)*

Crantock [SW7960]

☆ *Old Albion* [Langurroc Rd]: Pleasantly placed photogenic thatched village pub, low beams and flagstones, old-fashioned tastefully decorated small bar with brasses and open fires, larger more open room with local pictures, friendly relaxed atmosphere keeping informal local feel despite all the summer visitors (and the souvenirs sold here), good range of generous basic home-made food inc giant ploughman's, Courage ales with a guest from Sharps or Skinners; open all day, tables on small terrace *(Colin Gooch, Brian Skelcher, S Horsley, David and Carole Chapman, LYM, Paul R White, JP, PP)*

Crows Nest [SX2669]

☆ *Crows Nest* [signed off B3264 N of Liskeard; OS Sheet 201 map ref 263692]: Old-fashioned 17th-c pub with gleaming horsey bits hanging from bowed dark oak beams, mining pictures and some interesting and unusual furnishings, big log fire, no smoking area (children welcome here), friendly atmosphere, well kept St Austell Tinners and HSD and a guest beer, decent wines, food from pasties and ploughman's to usual hot dishes; piped music; picnic-sets on terrace by quiet lane, handy for Bodmin Moor

walks *(Dr M E Wilson, LYM, B, M and P Kendall, R L Turnham, JP, PP)*

Cubert [SW7858]

☆ *Smugglers Den* [Trebellan, off A3075 S of Newquay]: Welcoming bustle in 16th-c thatched stone pub, long bar with small barrel seats and tables, dining side with enormous inglenook woodburner and steps down to big family room, other side with armchairs, settees and pool; helpful friendly staff, fresh generous quickly served good food inc local seafood, good choice of well kept ales inc one or two guest beers tapped from the cask, farm cider, no machines or juke box; tables in sheltered courtyard, cl winter Mon–Weds lunchtime *(P and M Rudlin, A Wheeler, Anna Jenkins, JP, PP, Comus and Sarah Elliott, Paul R White)*

Falmouth [SW8033]

Boathouse [Trevethan Hill/Webber Hill]: Friendly and interesting two-level pub with lots of woodwork, nautical theme, log fire, well kept beer; jam nights, deck overlooking estuary *(Dr M E Wilson)*

Masons Arms [Killigrew St]: Small friendly town pub, warm atmosphere, good beer *(Dr M E Wilson)*

☆ *Quayside Inn & Old Ale House* [ArwenackSt/Fore St]: Bustling bare-boards dark-panelled bar with fine range of real ales and lots of pub signs (also piped music, fruit machine, TV), upstairs harbour-view lounge with armchairs and sofas one end, doorstep sandwiches, hot bloomers, baked potatoes and unpretentious main dishes (served all day in summer), children welcome; live music Fri/Sat, open all day, picnic-sets out by Custom House Dock *(Mayur Shah, Chris and Sandra Taylor, Nigel and Olga Wikeley, E G Parish, LYM, Ted George, Dr M E Wilson)*

Seaview [Wodehouse Terr]: Convivial maritime local above 111-step Jacob's Ladder, lots of appropriate bric-a-brac, stunning harbour view from picture windows and a couple of tables outside, good range of well kept ales inc Bass; bedrooms *(Dr M E Wilson)*

☆ *Seven Stars* [The Moor (centre)]: Classic unchanging 17th-c local with wonderfully entertaining vicar-landlord, no gimmicks, warm welcome, well kept Bass, Sharps Own and changing beers such as Skinners Who Put The Lights Out tapped from the cask, home-made rolls, garrulous regulars, big key collection, quiet back snug, tables on roadside courtyard *(the Didler, Ian Phillips, Kevin Thorpe, BB)*

Flushing [SW8033]

Royal Standard [off A393 at Penryn (or foot ferry from Falmouth); St Peters Hill]: Trim and traditional waterfront local, great views from front terrace, neat bar with pink plush and copper, alcove with pool and darts, simple well done food inc good baked potatoes and home-made pasties, well kept Bass, Flowers IPA and Sharps Doom Bar, very long-serving welcoming landlord, plenty of genuine characters; outside gents' *(the Didler)*

Fowey [SX1252]

☆ *Galleon* [Fore St; from centre follow Car Ferry signs]: Superb spot overlooking harbour and estuary, well refurbished with solid pine and modern nautical décor, dining areas off, generous good value food inc fine fresh local fish, well kept and priced Bass, Flowers IPA, Sharps Coaster and changing guest beers, fast friendly service; jazz Sun lunchtime; tables out on attractive extended waterside terrace, good estuary-view bedrooms *(D and M T Ayres-Regan, Pete and Rosie Flower, JDM, KM, Peter and Audrey Dowsett, Keith and Katy Stevens, BB)*

☆ King of Prussia [Town Quay]: Upstairs bar in handsome quayside building, large, clean and neatly refurbished, with bay windows looking over harbour to Polruan, St Austell ales, sensibly priced wines, good friendly service, side family food bar with good value food inc fish and seafood; maybe piped music; seats outside, open all day at least in summer, bedrooms *(Will Evans, LYM, Nick Lawless, Val Stevenson, Rob Holmes, David Edwards, Sue Holland, Dave Webster)*

Golant [SX1155]

☆ Fishermans Arms [Fore St (B3269)]: Plain but charming waterside local, nice garden, lovely views from terrace and window; warm welcome, good generous straightforward home-made food all day in summer (cl Sun afternoon), well kept Ushers Bitter, Founders and seasonal ales, log fire, interesting pictures, tropical fish *(Rob Thorley, Julia Turner, the Didler)*

Goldsithney [SW5430]

Crown [B3280]: Tidy pub with roomy and comfortable L-shaped bar and small dining room, wide range of enjoyable food inc bargain Thurs lunches, local fresh fish and Sun roasts, St Austell ales, decent house wines, friendly service; pretty suntrap glass-roofed front loggia and pavement tables, masses of hanging baskets *(P and M Rudlin)*

Gorran Haven [SX0141]

Llawnroc [Chute Lane]: Comfortable family-friendly granite pub overlooking harbour and fishing village, good value home-made food inc local fish in bar and no smoking restaurant, Scottish Courage and local ales, prompt smart and friendly service, family/games room; sunny tables out in front, barbecues; good value bedroom block *(Nick Lawless, John Brightley, Christopher Wright, Peter Salmon, B A Dale)*

Grampound [SW9348]

☆ Dolphin [A390 St Austell—Truro]: Unpretentious village pub with good value generous home-made food, local veg, Weds OAP lunch, well kept St Austell ales, decent house wines, two-level bar with comfortable chintzy settees and easy chairs, interesting prints, log fire; children allowed, pool, fruit machine, piped music; handy for Trewithen Gardens; bedrooms *(D S Price, Catriona and Fiona Picken, Dr and Mrs R Booth)*

Gulval [SW4831]

☆ Coldstreamer: Busy but very clean and civilised local, caring landlady and polite young staff, comfortable dining atmosphere, attractive and popular hop-girt restaurant with military prints, very enjoyable generous food inc local fish and

popular good value Sun carvery, well kept Bass, Flowers IPA and Greene King Old Speckled Hen, decent wines, unusual high ceilings; quiet pleasant village very handy for Trengwainton Gardens, and for Scillies heliport – turn right opp entrance *(Dr Phil Putwain, Peter Salmon)*

Gurnards Head [SW4338]

☆ Gurnards Head Hotel [B3306 Zennor—St Just]: Hotel in a great spot, with good pub atmosphere in flagstoned bar, log fires each end, imaginative good value food (not Mon evening) esp fish soup, seafood and vegetarian, well kept ales such as Bass, Flowers Original, Fullers London Pride and Skinners, good wine list, friendly licensees and staff; plain family room, piped music, folk nights Weds and Fri; well equipped comfortable bedrooms with own bathrooms, glorious walks in outstanding NT scenery, inland and along the cliffy coast *(Annette Morley, David Whittaker)*

Gweek [SW7027]

Gweek Inn [back roads E of Helston]: Happy and comfortable family chain pub, large low-ceilinged bar with open fire, quick good-humoured service, well kept Greene King Old Speckled Hen and Wadworths 6X, reasonably priced standard food, decent wines, lots of motoring trophies (enthusiast licensees); pleasant restaurant Tues-Sat (summer); live music Fri, children welcome, tables on grass (safe for children), summer kiosk with all-day snacks, short walk from seal sanctuary *(P and M Rudlin, Cliff Blakemore)*

Halsetown [TL5038]

Halsetown Inn [B3311 SW of St Ives]: Old-fashioned pub in nice country setting, old Cornish range, friendly staff, good value home-made food inc local fish and game, well kept beers; bedrooms *(N Hughes)*

Helford Passage [SW7627]

☆ Ferry Boat [signed from B3291]: Extensive modern bar in great – and popular – summer spot by sandy beach with swimming, small boat hire, fishing trips and summer ferry to Helford, full St Austell range kept well, very good range of wines by the glass, wide choice of good generous food from separate servery inc fresh fish and afternoon teas, comfortable no smoking restaurant, prompt cheerful helpful service; maybe piped music, games area with juke box and SkyTV; suntrap waterside terrace, barbecues, usually open all day summer (with cream teas and frequent live entertainment); about a mile's walk from gate at bottom of Glendurgan Garden (NT); steep walk down from the overflow car park; we haven't yet had reports on the bedroom side – some emphasis on this now *(Geoff Calcott, P and M Rudlin, LYM, Martin and Karen Wake)*

Langdon [SX3091]

Countryman [Boyton, B3254 N of Launceston]: Good choice of well kept beers, reasonably priced food inc good snacks, quick friendly service, simple bar, dining area, restaurant and family room; very busy Sun lunchtime and school hols; tables and swings outside, handy for Tamar Otter Sanctuary *(Dennis Jenkin)*

Lanner [SW7240]

☆ *Fox & Hounds* [Comford; A393/B3298]:
Relaxed rambling bar with very friendly helpful
staff, black beams, stripped stone, dark
panelling, high-backed settles and cottagey
chairs, warm fires, good choice of generous
reasonably priced food from sandwiches to
duck or guineafowl, well kept Bass and St
Austell Tinners and HSD tapped from the cask,
partly no smoking restaurant, children in dining
area; pub games, piped music; great floral
displays in front, neat back garden with pond
and play area; open all day wknds
(Paul R White, LYM)

Lanreath [SX1757]

☆ *Punch Bowl* [signed off B3359]: Rambling
17th-c inn under new landlord, traditional
flagstoned public bar and comfortable black-
panelled lounge, usual lunchtime bar food, well
kept Courage, Greene King Old Speckled Hen
and Skinners Betty Stogs or Cornish Knocker,
striking panelled medieval restaurant with
chandeliers, gargoyles and mead feasts; children
welcome, cl Mon lunchtime in winter,
bedrooms, pleasant tucked-away village
*(LYM, Dr Paull Khan, Pete and Rosie Flower,
Mrs P G Newton, Nick Lawless)*

Lelant [SW5437]

☆ *Badger* [Fore St]: Dining pub with good range
of food from sandwiches to fresh fish and
lavish home-made puddings, OAP carvery
bargain, attractively softly lit modern L-shaped
interior, partly no smoking, with panelled
recesses, airy back conservatory, St Austell
Tinners and other beers, friendly efficient
service; bedrooms good value, prettily
decorated; wonderful breakfast *(Mr and Mrs M
Cooper, Alan and Hillie Johnson)*

☆ *Watermill* [Lelant Downs, just off A3074]:
Neatly kept interesting former mill, working
waterwheel behind with gearing inside, some
emphasis on upstairs restaurant, thriving newly
extended black-beamed downstairs bar with
well kept Sharps Eden and Skinners Betty Stogs,
decent wines, good coffee, good interesting
reasonably priced food inc thoughtful children's
choices, good fire, cheerful young managers
(same owners as Trengilly Wartha nr
Constantine), attentive service; nice grounds,
tables out among trees *(P and M Rudlin, R J
Howdle, Joyce and Maurice Cottrell, C Jones)*

Lerryn [SX1457]

☆ *Ship* [signed off A390 in Lostwithiel; Fore St]:
Partly no smoking, real ales such as Bass,
Courage Best, Greene King Old Speckled Hen
and Sharps Doom Bar, local farm cider, fruit
wines and malt whiskies, friendly regulars, wide
food choice inc proper pasties, good
sandwiches and popular Sun carvery, efficient
service even when busy, huge woodburner;
games room with pool, dogs on leads and
children welcome; pretty spot esp when tide's
in, with picnic-sets outside, play area; famous
stepping-stones and three well signed waterside
walks nearby, nice bedrooms in adjoining
building, wonderful breakfast *(R L Turnham,
Dennis Jenkin, Peter and Audrey Dowsett,
Graham Brooks, LYM)*

Liskeard [SX1665]

Halfway House [Two Waters Foot, off A38 E
towards Bodmin]: Rebuilt after fire in 2000,
shuttered brick building in lovely wooded valley
with plenty of tables on lawn by river (trout
and salmon); two restaurants (one no smoking),
good range of generous food using carefully
chosen produce (local ostrich, wild boar, fish
from boats at Looe and hormone-free beef),
well kept Sharps ales, Tetleys and Wadworths
6X, good friendly atmosphere; children and
dogs welcome *(M Joyner)*

Lizard [SW7012]

☆ *Top House* [A3083]: Spotless well run pub
particularly popular with older people, in same
friendly family for 40 years; lots of interesting
local sea pictures, fine shipwreck relics and
serpentine craftwork (note the handpumps) in
neat bar with generous good value bar food
from sandwiches to local fish and seafood
specials, ales such as Sharps Doom Bar and
Special and Wadworths 6X, reasonably priced
wines, roaring log fire, big no smoking area, no
piped music (occasional live); tucked-away fruit
machine, darts, pool; tables on terrace,
interesting nearby serpentine shop *(Eric
George, Nigel Hopkins, P and M Rudlin, BB,
Miss J E Winsor, Sue Holland, Dave Webster,
Edward Jago)*

Looe [SX2553]

Olde Salutation [Fore St, E Looe]: Big
squareish beamed and tiled room with red
leatherette seats and neat tables, some old-
fashioned fireplace, lots of local fishing
photographs, side snug with olde-worlde
harbour mural and fruit machine, step down to
simple family room; decent usual food from
notable crab sandwiches to Sun roasts, fast
friendly service, well kept Ushers Best; piped
music may be obtrusive, forget about parking;
popular locally as The Sal – open all day,
handy for coast path *(BB, E G Parish, Dr and
Mrs B D Smith)*

Lostwithiel [SX1059]

Globe [North St]: Large rambling traditional
pub with lots of small rooms, friendly landlady
and staff, nice pubby atmosphere, open fire,
pleasant plain décor, good food choice, well
kept Cotleigh Tawny; tables in attractive
garden *(Dr and Mrs B D Smith)*

Luxulyan [SX0458]

Kings Arms [Bridges]: Recently refurbished
open-plan village pub by bridge, pleasant
atmosphere, friendly helpful staff, enjoyable
reasonably priced home-made food, well kept
St Austell PA, Tinners and HSD, country bric-
a-brac, back games area with pool; small front
terrace, new back garden, handy for Eden
Project *(J F M and M West, Ian and Nita
Cooper)*

Madron [SW4532]

King William IV: Attractive and unusual local
with friendly helpful licensees, plenty of
horsebrasses and other country knick-knacks
(but not too much), enjoyable simple food from
good sandwiches to locally popular Sun lunch,
good choice of beers inc Ushers, warm fire;
handy for Trengwainton (NT) *(Dennis Jenkin)*

Malpas [SW8442]

☆ *Heron* [Trenhaile Terr, off A39 S of Truro]: Extended and airily refurbished, blonde modern furniture and sky-blue material and paintwork, good food choice, well kept St Austell Tinners and HSD, friendly staff, log fire, lots of local photographs, children welcome; pool, machines, piped music, can be very busy; stunning setting above wooded creek, suntrap slate-paved terrace; *(David Wallington, Ian Wilson, S Horsley, LYM)*

Manaccan [SW7625]

New Inn [down hill signed to Gillan and St Keverne]: Attractive old thatched local, friendly helpful landlady, well kept ales such as Flowers IPA and Wadworths 6X, wide choice of bar meals from lots of good sandwiches served with chips to local seafood and wonderful Sun lunch, traditional games – but modern tables and chairs; children welcome, sweet little terrier, winter darts and euchre nights, pleasant back garden with swing, pretty waterside village *(LYM, the Didler, P and M Rudlin, Valerie Pitts)*

Marazion [SW5231]

Godolphin Arms [West End]: Very extensive redeveloped pub with great views across beach and Mounts Bay towards St Michael's Mount, popular food, real ales inc local beers, good service, comfortable and civilised upper lounge bar and no smoking dining room, family room with play area, informal lower bar, roomy terrace; carefully decorated bedrooms, most with sea view *(P and M Rudlin)*

Metherell [SX4069]

☆ *Carpenters Arms* [follow Honicombe sign from St Anns Chapel just W of Gunnislake A390; Lower Metherell]: Heavily black-beamed local with huge polished flagstones and massive stone walls in cosy bar and brightly lit lounge, good choice of reasonably priced honest food and well kept ales, friendly considerate landlord, helpful efficient service; darts, may be piped radio; children welcome in the two modern carpeted eating areas (one no smoking), bedrooms, handy for Cotehele *(Tim Whiteley, Joy and Peter Heatherley, LYM)*

Mevagissey [SX0145]

☆ *Fountain* [Cliff St, down alley by Post Office]: Welcoming unpretentious beamed and slate-floored harbourside local with good value tasty simple food inc fresh fish, well kept St Austell ales, lovely fire, obliging service, plenty of atmosphere, lots of old local prints and photographs, cosy back bar with glass-topped cellar; local artist does piano sing-song Fri, good fish in popular upstairs restaurant; SkyTV sports; open all day, bedrooms, pretty frontage *(Christopher Wright, the Didler, Nick Lawless, John and Marian Greenwood)*

Sharks Fin [The Quay]: Right on the pretty working harbour (which has £2 parking charge), with snug bar reminiscent of smugglers' cave with part-painted stone walls, ship's timbers and packing cases, reasonable choice of bar food, seafood restaurant; open all day in summer for food (also has large tea room), good value bedrooms *(Edward Jago)*

Morwenstow [SS2015]

☆ *Bush* [signed off A39 N of Kilkhampton; Crosstown]: One of Britain's oldest pubs, quiet, individual and unchanging; part Saxon, with serpentine Celtic piscina in one wall, ancient built-in settles, beams and flagstones, and big stone fireplace, upper bar with interesting bric-a-brac, well kept St Austell HSD and Worthington BB tapped from the cask, Inch's cider, friendly service, lunchtime food (not Sun) mainly sandwiches and pasties, maybe a stew, darts; no piped music, children or dogs, seats out in yard; lovely setting, interesting village church with good nearby teashop, great cliff walks; cl Mon in winter *(the Didler, Basil Minson, Martin and Karen Wake, Miss J F Reay, LYM, Debbie and Neil Hayter)*

Mousehole [SW4726]

☆ *Old Coastguard* [The Parade]: Spacious yet cosy and relaxed, with light décor, board floor, pine and cane furniture, interesting prints and superb Mounts Bay views, esp from conservatory; friendly attentive staff, good enterprising food from snacks inc delicious fish soup to substantial fresh main dishes esp seafood and rich puddings, ales such as Bass, Sharps Doom Bar, St Austell Trelawnys Pride; children welcome, piped music, lots of musical events; pleasant terrace and sizeable gardens leading down to rocky beach; comfortable bedrooms, good breakfast *(Angela Thomas, Janet Edwards, Tamsyn Bond)*

Newquay [SW8061]

☆ *Fort* [Fore St]: Former master mariner's house extensively refurbished after recent takeover by St Austell, good food all day from sandwiches, hot baguettes and baked potatoes up in big family dining area, roomy front bar with sofas, back conservatory, friendly service, real ales, games area; sizeable garden with sea-view terrace, good bedrooms, fine setting high above beach and small harbour *(David and Carole Chapman, Alan M Pring)*

Skinners Ale House [East St]: Open-plan bar well refurbished in bare boards and sawdust style, steps up to back part, good choice of Skinners ales with some guests tapped from the cask, good value food; live music wknds inc trad jazz Sun night, open all day *(JP, PP, the Didler)*

Notter [SX3861]

☆ *Notter Bridge Inn* [signed just off A38 Saltash—Liskeard]: Lovely spot just off trunk road, tables in conservatory and fairy-lit garden looking down on sheltered stream, neatly kept open-plan dining lounge, wide choice of food esp particularly good home-made curries, good value children's meals and puddings inc delicious local farm ice creams, welcoming bustling atmosphere, well kept Bass, Courage Best and Greene King Abbot, friendly helpful service, darts in public bar; children very welcome, friendly fat tortoiseshell cat, maybe unobtrusive piped music; open all day wknds, must book Fri/Sat, very handy for nearby holiday parks *(Mayur Shah, Wendy Hollas, BB)*

Padstow [SW9175]

☆ *Golden Lion* [Lanadwell St]: Friendly and cosy

backstreet pub with pleasant black-beamed front bar, high-raftered back lounge with plush banquettes against ancient white stone walls; cheerful local bustle, reasonably priced simple lunches inc very promptly served good sandwiches, evening steaks and fresh seafood, well kept real ales, good staff, coal fire; pool in family area, piped music or juke box, fruit machines; bedrooms *(the Didler, P J Holdsworth, Joyce and Maurice Cottrell, BB)*

☆ London [Llanadwell St]: Kindly down-to-earth fishermen's local a bit off the beaten track, lots of pictures and nautical memorabilia, pretty flowers out in front, good buzzing atmosphere (get there early for a table), well kept St Austell beers, decent choice of malt whiskies, good choice of wknd lunchtime bar food inc good value crab sandwiches and fresh local fish, more elaborate evening choice (small back dining area), great real fire; can be smoky, games machines but no piped music; open all day, bedrooms good value *(G U Briggs, Brian Skelcher, LYM, Ted George, M Joyner, Charles Eaton, Val Stevenson, Rob Holmes, Sue Demont, Tim Barrow, Joyce and Maurice Cottrell)*
Shipwrights [North Quay; aka the Blue Lobster]: Stripped brick, lots of wood, flagstones, lobster pots and nets in big popular low-ceilinged quayside bar with well kept St Austell ales, good friendly service, bar food and upstairs restaurant; popular with young people evenings; a few tables out by water *(BB, David and Carole Chapman, Geoff Calcott, Edward Jago)*

Pelynt [SX2055]
☆ Jubilee [B3359 NW of Looe]: Neatly kept 16th-c inn with interesting Queen Victoria mementoes and some handsome antique furnishings in relaxed beamed lounge bar and Victoria Bar, enjoyable bar food from sandwiches and baked potatoes to steaks inc children's dishes (they like to get two sittings in at busy times), well kept Bass, Skinners Betty Stogs and St Austell Daylight Robbery, children welcome in eating areas; separate public bar with sensibly placed darts, pool, fruit machine, and piped music; picnic-sets under cocktail parasols in inner courtyard with pretty flower tubs, good play area, comfortable bedrooms, open all day wknds *(Dennis Jenkin, LYM, Dr and Mrs B D Smith, Peter and Jenny Quine)*

Pendeen [SW3834]
Radjel [Boscaswell Terr]: Friendly two-bar local with lots of wreck and other photographs on stripped stone walls, St Austell Tinners and other ales, good value food inc popular take-away pizzas, TV one end of lounge, separate games room with pool; bedrooms, popular with walkers, nr Cape Cornwall *(LYM, Jeanne and Paul Silvestri)*

Pendoggett [SX0279]
Cornish Arms: Big locals' bar with games, TV and piped music, attractive more sedate front part with traditional oak settles on fine polished slate floor, real ales inc Bass and Sharps Doom Bar, welcoming service, separate restaurant; provision for children, open all day, terrace

with distant sea view; bedrooms *(Roger and Jenny Huggins, LYM)*

Penelewey [SW8240]
☆ Punch Bowl & Ladle [B3289]: Much extended thatched pub in picturesque setting, cosy rooms, big settees and rustic artefacts, strong emphasis on plush and spreading dining side, wide choice of good fresh generous food inc good help-yourself salads and fish; Bass, Courage Directors, Fullers London Pride and Sharps Own, unobtrusive piped music, children and dogs on leads welcome; handy for Trelissick Gardens, small back sun terrace, open all day summer *(R and S Bentley, Ian Phillips, LYM, B J Harding)*

Penryn [SW7834]
Famous Barrel [St Thomas St, between A394 and B3291]: Huge half-barrel door opens into old low-ceilinged local, barrel theme, red plush seats, woodburner, Flowers and Sharps Doom Bar *(Dr M E Wilson)*

Penzance [SW4730]
☆ Admiral Benbow [Chapel St]: Well run pub with elaborately nautical décor in interesting maze of areas, friendly staff, decent food inc good curries, four well kept ales, downstairs restaurant, pleasant view from top back room; children allowed, open all day summer *(LYM, Anthony and Elizabeth Barker, P and M Rudlin)*
☆ Dolphin [The Barbican; Newlyn road, opp harbour after swing-bridge]: Busy welcoming local with attractive nautical décor, good harbour views, quick bar food inc good pasties, well kept St Austell ales, great fireplace, big pool room with juke box etc; children in room off main bar; no obvious nearby parking *(LYM, the Didler)*
☆ Globe & Ale House [Queen St]: Small low-ceilinged tavern, lots of old pictures and artefacts, bare boards and dim lighting, well kept Bass, Sharps Own and Skinners Betty Stogs and Bettys Mild with guest beers, some tapped from the cask, such as Ash Vine, RCH, Ridleys and Teignworthy, enthusiastic helpful landlord *(Jonathan Smith, the Didler)*

Perranuthnoe [SW5329]
☆ Victoria [signed off A394 Penzance—Helston]: Comfortable and relaxed L-shaped local refurbished by friendly and efficient new management, cosy low-beamed bar, some stripped stonework, coastal and wreck photographs, freshly baked lunchtime baguettes and doorstep sandwiches, interesting evening specials inc seafood and home-made gravadlax, well kept beers such as Courage, Gibbs Mew Bishops Tipple and Ushers, unusual choice of good wines, neat coal fire, no smoking and family areas; quiet piped music; good bedrooms, handy for Mounts Bay *(Kevin McEleny, Jeanne and Paul Silvestri, LYM, Clare McLaughlin, Sally McEleny, Simon Carter)*

Phillack [SW5638]
Bucket of Blood [Churchtown Rd]: Welcoming bustle in traditional low-ceilinged village pub, thick whitewashed stone walls, stripped pine, generous attractive food, well kept St Austell

Tinners and HSD, jolly gruesome ghost stories; tables outside *(LYM, Edward Jago)*

Pillaton [SX3664]

☆ *Weary Friar* [off Callington—Landrake back road]: Pretty tucked-away 12th-c pub with four spotless and civilised knocked-together rooms (one no smoking), comfortable seats around sturdy tables, easy chairs one end, log fire, well kept Bass, Greene King Old Speckled Hen and Sharps, farm cider, nicely presented bar food inc lunchtime sandwiches, children's helpings and good puddings, quick cheerful helpful service; big back restaurant (not Mon), children in eating area; maybe piped radio; tables outside, Tues bell-ringing in church next door; comfortable bedrooms *(LYM, Mrs June Wilmers, Ted George, Joy and Peter Heatherley, Jacquie and Jim Jones)*

Polperro [SX2051]

☆ *Blue Peter* [Quay Rd]: Dark and cosy, in great setting up narrow steps above harbour; unpretentious little low-beamed wood-floored friendly local with nautical memorabilia, well kept St Austell and guest beers such as Sharps Doom Bar, farm cider, quick service, log fire, traditional games, some seats outside, family area upstairs with video game; open all day, can get crowded, and piped music – often jazz or nostalgic pop – can be loudish; often live music Sat, no food (you can bring in pasties) *(the Didler, Richard Butler, Marie Kroon, Pete and Rosie Flower, LYM, E M and H P N Steinitz, Roger and Jenny Huggins, Dave Irving, Mayur Shah)*

Noughts & Crosses [Lansallos St; bear right approaching harbour]: Steps down to cosy and cheerful beamed terraced pub with flagstoned woody servery, small food bar, more steps to bigger tiled-floor stripped stone streamside bar, upstairs family room; Ushers seasonal ale, decent food inc local crab sandwiches, good specials and cheap children's food, friendly young staff; children welcome, open all day wknds *(Helen Hazzard, Mrs P G Newton, BB)*

☆ *Three Pilchards* [Quay Rd]: Welcoming low-beamed fishermen's local high over harbour, lots of black woodwork, dim lighting, simple furnishings, enjoyable food from good crab sandwiches and pasties to lots of local seafood, open fire in big stone fireplace, well kept Ushers Best and Founders, tables on upper terrace up steep steps; piped music, can get very busy; open all day *(John and Vivienne Rice, Val Stevenson, Rob Holmes, BB)*

Polruan [SX1251]

☆ *Lugger* [back roads off A390 in Lostwithiel, or passenger/bicycle ferry from Fowey]: Beamed waterside local with high-backed wall settles, big model boats etc, fine views from upstairs partly no smoking family room, good straightforward bar food inc children's and local fish, wider evening choice, restaurant, St Austell ales, pub games; piped music (occasional live), games machine, children and well behaved dogs welcome; good walks, open all day *(Mrs P G Newton, Nick Lawless, the Didler, Graham Brooks)*

Porthleven [SW6225]

Harbour Inn [Commercial Rd]: Large well looked-after pub/hotel worth knowing for outstanding setting with tables out on big harbourside terrace, good value simple food in dining area off expansive lounge and bar, quick friendly service, well kept St Austell ales, comprehensive wine list, restaurant; decent bedrooms, some with harbour view *(Paul R White, Sue Demont, Tim Barrow, Alan and Hillie Johnson, Charlie Harris)*

Portreath [SW6545]

Basset Arms [Tregea Terr]: Welcoming village pub with enjoyable food in comfortable bar, no smoking dining room and big bright conservatory, friendly caring service, well kept beers inc a local one; unobtrusive piped music; tables on grass with play area, short stroll from beach, open all day Sun and summer *(P and M Rudlin)*

☆ *Portreath Arms* [by B3300/B3301 N of Redruth]: Smartly refurbished, with quiet comfortable lounge, steps down to no smoking dining room, friendly atmosphere, well kept real ales inc a local one, decent house wine, good choice of home-made bar food from open sandwiches to steaks, local fish and good value Sun roast, friendly helpful staff; separate large public bar with pool, darts etc; bedrooms, well placed for coastal walks *(P and M Rudlin)*

Portscatho [SW8735]

Plume of Feathers [The Square]: Comfortable pub in pretty fishing village, side locals' bar, well kept St Austell and other ales, good value usual food, restaurant; very popular with summer visitors but perhaps most welcoming out of season *(Kevin Macey, LYM)*

Praze An Beeble [SW6336]

☆ *St Aubyn Arms* [The Square]: Quietly welcoming two-bar country pub, traditional furnishings, good choice of well kept ales inc Sharps and Skinners, wide choice of enjoyable food inc children's (two restaurants, one upstairs); fruit machines; large garden *(Colin Gooch, P and M Rudlin)*

Redruth [SW6843]

Cornish Arms [Sparnon Gate, off B3300 NW; OS Sheet 203 map ref 686436]: Honest 17th-c local with Sharps Own and Doom Bar and big fire in small bar on right, another fire in bigger lounge on left, central family dining room, good value generous food from sandwiches to steaks, friendly owners; a couple of tables outside *(P and M Rudlin)*

☆ *Tricky Dickys* [Tolgus Mount; OS Sheet 203 map ref 686427]: Spotless and well run conversion of isolated former tin-mine smithy, dark inside, with forge bellows, painting of how it might have looked; buoyant atmosphere, well kept beers, decent wines, good value food, exemplary service; children welcome, partly covered terrace with barbecues, aviary, jazz Tues, other entertainment Thurs; bedroom block, squash and fitness centre *(P and M Rudlin)*

St Agnes [SW7250]

☆ *Railway Inn* [Vicarage Rd, via B3277]: Village local with fascinating shoe collection, also splendid original horsebrasses, interesting naval memorabilia and photographs; decent bar food from lunchtime sandwiches to steaks and OAP specials, well kept Bass, Boddingtons and Flowers IPA, friendly cat, no smoking restaurant; juke box; children in eating area, open all day summer, tables on terrace *(Trevor Swindells, Terry Mizen, Val Stevenson, Rob Holmes, Mr and Mrs Capp, Paul R White, LYM)*

St Erth [SW5535]
Star [Church St]: Low-beamed 17th-c pub, well worn in and deceptively spacious, with lots of bric-a-brac, wide blackboard food choice using local produce and fresh local fish, Bass, Banks's Mild and guest beers, good wine list, friendly service; dogs welcome, comfortable bedrooms, open all day *(Alan and Hillie Johnson, Ken Flawn)*

St Ewe [SW9746]
☆ *Crown* [signed from B3287]: Attractive cottage pub, modestly posh but pleasantly simple; 16th-c flagstones, spick and span traditional furnishings inc church pews and fine settle, lovely log fire, homely plump cat, toby jug collection, well kept St Austell HSD, Daylight and Tinners, well drilled staff, wide food choice from good pasties, lots of baked potatoes and baguettes to steaks, also OAP specials, large back dining room up steps; several picnic-sets on raised back lawn, handy for the Lost Gardens of Heligan *(LYM, Nick Lawless, J M and P M Carver, Dr M W A Haward, Sue Holland, Dave Webster, Christopher Wright, Kevin Thorpe, Mayur Shah)*

St Issey [SW9271]
☆ *Ring o' Bells* [Churchtown; A389 Wadebridge—Padstow]: Neatly modernised cheerful village local with consistently good home-made food in bustling bar or quieter restaurant inc children's helpings, well kept Bass and Courage Directors, welcoming service, open fire; darts, pool, some tables in flowery courtyard; can get packed in summer; bedrooms *(Theo, Anne and Jane Gaskin, Sheila and Phil Stubbs, LYM)*

St Ives [SW5441]
Castle [Fore St]: Cosy and spotless local, low ceilings and lots of dark panelling in one long room, stained-glass windows, old local photographs, maritime memorabilia, well priced wholesome bar food, well kept ales such as Bass and Wadworths 6X tapped from the cask, good value coffee, friendly staff; unobtrusive piped music; bustling in summer, relaxing out of season *(Ted George)*
Lifeboat [Wharf Rd]: Busy harbourside pub, good atmosphere, cosy corners, nautical theme, friendly staff, bar food, good views, bar billiards; open all day *(David and Carole Chapman)*
Pedn Olva [The Warren]: Tastefully reworked in modern style by St Austell (who took it over recently), great spot with large bar overlooking sea and handsome restaurant overlooking Porthminster beach, new chef doing good modern food; comfortable bedrooms *(Ken Flawn)*
Three Ferrets [Chapel St]: Small and simple,

with well kept real ale, friendly feel, pool, darts and dominoes; piped music *(N Hughes)*
Union [Fore St]: Spotless friendly pub under same management as the Sloop, roomy but cosy dark interior, low beams, small fire, masses of old local photographs, neatly ordered tables, food from filled baguettes to local fish, Bass and John Smiths, decent wines, coffee; piped music, can get very crowded *(Liz and John Soden, Alan and Hillie Johnson, Ted George)*

St Just in Penwith [SW3631]
Kings Arms [Market Sq]: Friendly local, comfortable and clean, with plenty of character, good bar meals, St Austell ales, some tapped from the cask; popular live music nights; reasonably priced bedrooms with own bathrooms, prodigious breakfast *(the Didler, Mrs P G Newton)*
☆ *Star* [Fore St]: Harking back to the 60s in customers, style and relaxed atmosphere; interesting and informal dimly lit low-beamed local with old-fashioned furnishings, good value home-made food from sandwiches and pasties up, well kept St Austell ales, farm cider in summer, mulled wine in winter, and old-fashioned drinks like rum shrub; traditional games inc bar billiards, nostalgic juke box, tables in attractive back yard; simple bedrooms, good breakfast *(the Didler, LYM, Chris and Sandra Taylor)*

St Mabyn [SX0473]
St Mabyn Inn: Cheerful bustling country pub, good choice of appetising restaurant food inc lots of good fish, pleasant service, attractive décor, good choice of real ales inc Sharps and Skinners, farm cider, interesting wines; darts *(the Didler, Karen and Graham Oddey, J M and P M Carver)*

St Mawes [SW8433]
Idle Rocks [Tredenham Rd (harbour edge)]: Hotel with good bar lunches, attentive welcoming service, evening restaurant (must book), superb sea view; tables on terrace, bedrooms *(Dennis Jenkin)*
☆ *Rising Sun* [The Square]: Carefully and comfortably refurbished open-plan hotel bar used by boaters and local fishermen, dozens of old Cornwall prints, reasonably priced good food in bar and restaurant esp popular bargain Fri fish supper, well kept St Austell ales, decent wines, good coffee, genial landlord and helpful staff; attractive conservatory, slate-topped tables on sunny terrace just across lane from harbour wall of this pretty seaside village; open all day summer, good value attractive bedrooms *(Dennis Jenkin, Mike Gorton, Andy Sinden, Louise Harrington, Dr David Skeggs, E G Parish, Sue Holland, Dave Webster, LYM)*

St Neot [SX1867]
☆ *London* [N of A38 Liskeard—Bodmin]: Spotless 16th-c beamed country pub on Bodmin Moor, comfortable and airy, with cheerful efficient staff, good home-made food from sandwiches (normal or doorstep) up, well kept Sharps Own and Doom Bar tapped from the cask, decent house wines (choice of glass sizes), two log fires, dining area behind trellis;

unobtrusive piped music; attractive village in wooded valley, 15th-c church with outstanding stained glass *(Dennis Jenkin, Andy Smith)*

St Teath [SX0680]

☆ *White Hart* [B3267; signed off A39 SW of Camelford]: Friendly and unpretentious flagstoned village pub with sailor hat-ribands and ship's pennants from all over the world, swords and a cutlass, coins embedded in ceiling, coal fire, neat dining room off, straightforward popular food from sandwiches to fresh fish, good steaks and all-day Sun roasts, well kept Bass, Greene King Ruddles and Sharps Doom Bar, decent wines, friendly efficient service; games bar with darts, pool, sports TV etc, live music most Sats; children very welcome, open all day wknds, comfortably refurbished bedrooms, good breakfast *(Sue and Dave Harris, Mr and Mrs Capp, Dr Paull Khan, LYM, David Eberlin, Roger and Jenny Huggins, Steve Dark, Karen and Graham Oddey)*

Stithians [SW7037]

Golden Lion [Stithians Lake, Menherion]: Friendly pub with lakeside terrace, good food esp Sun lunch with good vegetarian choices, particularly well kept St Austell ales *(Dr D J and Mrs S C Walker)*

Stratton [SS2406]

Kings Arms [Howells Rd (A3072)]: Lively and friendly three-room 17th-c local with well kept Exmoor, Sharps and several guest beers, reasonably priced food, good service, children welcome; piped music and TVs may obtrude *(James Flory, P and M Rudlin)*

Tintagel [SX0588]

Old Malthouse [Fore St]: Useful stop, good range of bar meals, cream teas too, welcoming staff; roadside terrace with ice-cream servery *(George Atkinson)*

Wharncliffe Arms [Fore St]: Comfortable lounge with fine doll display, lots of local photographs and memorabilia, Redruth Cornish Rebellion, usual food, pleasant attentive staff *(George Atkinson)*

Trebarwith [SX0585]

Port William [Trebarwith Strand]: Lovely seaside setting with glorious views, waterside picnic-sets across road and on covered terrace, fishing nets and maritime memorabilia inside, no smoking room with interesting fish tanks, gallery with local artwork, food from nice pasties and filled rolls to fresh fish, Bass, Flowers Original and St Austell Tinners and HSD, piped music, Fri folk music, limited nearby parking; children in eating area, well equipped comfortable bedrooms (but if you book by credit card they may debit your account right away, keeping the money if you have to cancel), open all day *(LYM, George Atkinson, Ray and Jacki Davenport)*

Treen [SW3824]

Logan Rock [just off B3315 Penzance—Lands End]: Cheerful relaxed local nr fine coast walks, fine low-beamed traditional bar with high-backed modern oak settles, wall seats, inglenook seat by hot coal fire, well kept St Austell ales, lots of games in family room,

friendly dogs (others allowed on leads); food (all day in summer) from sandwiches and pasties up inc children's, local fish and cream teas, may be juke box or piped music; tables in small sheltered garden *(Nigel Hopkins, the Didler, LYM)*

Tregony [SW9245]

☆ *Kings Arms* [Fore St (B3287)]: Unpretentious old pub, two chatty comfortable bars, dining area with no smoking room, good value quickly served food inc some interesting new dishes and good Sun lunch, well kept Sharps Doom Bar and Wadworths 6X, decent wine, friendly staff; tables in pleasant garden, charming village *(M Borthwick, Christopher Wright, Mrs Joan Knight)*

Trematon [SX3959]

☆ *Crooked Inn* [off A38 just W of Saltash]: A tucked-away surprise, relaxed and friendly, down a long bumpy drive: lots of animal drawings and photographs, a good mix of furnishings in the big stepped bar, new conservatory, generous enjoyable bar food using local produce, well kept Bass, Sharps Own and Doom Bar, Skinners Cornish Knocker and St Austell HSD, decent wines, friendly service; children welcome, open all day wknds, courtyard tables, more in back garden with a good play area and far views, new bedroom block *(Joy and Peter Heatherley, David and Sarah Gilmore, George Little, Peter Salmon, LYM)*

Truro [SW8244]

Barley Sheaf [Old Bridge St, behind cathedral]: Refurbished, keeping its beams and adding a conservatory; Boddingtons, Sharps Doom Bar and Skinners Cornish Knocker, decent food, good service; piped music, TVs; pleasant terrace *(Alan M Pring, James Nunns)*

☆ *City* [Pydar St]: Rambling bar refurbished under new licensees with excellent track record, enjoyable with lighter dishes lunchtime and main menu evenings, well kept Courage Best, Skinners Betty Stogs, Sharps Doom Bar and a guest beer, genuine character, cosy atmosphere, attractive bric-a-brac, cheerful helpful service, pool in room off; sheltered back courtyard *(P and M Rudlin)*

William IV [Kenwyn St]: Clean and fresh panelled split-level bar with well kept St Austell beers, decent wine, wide range of enjoyable food, elegantly tiled airy two-level conservatory dining room opening into small flowery garden; evening piped music *(Minda and Stanley Alexander)*

Tywardreath [SX0854]

New Inn [off A3082; Fore St]: Friendly, informal and busy conversion of private house in nice village setting, well kept Bass tapped from the cask and St Austell ales on handpump, food (till 8 evening), games and children's room; secluded garden, bedrooms *(the Didler, BB)*

Veryan [SW9139]

☆ *New Inn* [village signed off A3078]: Good value nourishing food inc home-made pizzas, fresh veg and popular Sun lunch in neat and homely one-bar beamed local, no smoking dining area, leisurely atmosphere, genial landlord, well kept St Austell Tinners and HSD tapped from the cask, good value house wines, good coffee, two stone fireplaces; friendly alsatian and burmese cat; quiet garden behind the pretty house, bedrooms, interesting partly thatched village – nearby parking unlikely in summer *(the Didler, Christopher Wright, Nick Lawless, Paul R White, BB, Bernard Stradling, Sue Holland, Dave Webster)*

Widemouth [SS2002]

Bay View [Marine Dr]: Open-plan, with fine views over beach, good value food, Sharps Doom Bar and Own, Skinners Betty Stogs and a beer brewed for the pub; open all day in summer *(the Didler)*

Zelah [SW8151]

Hawkins Arms [A30]: Cosy, warm and comfortable, with open fires, good choice of generous well priced food, good range of beers inc Skinners *(P and M Rudlin, Dr M E Wilson)*

Zennor [SW4538]

☆ *Tinners Arms* [B3306 W of St Ives]: Unaffected country local in lovely windswept setting by church nr coast path, limited food (all day in summer), usually ales such as Sharps and Wadworths 6X kept well in casks behind bar, Lane's farm cider, decent coffee, rather spartan feel with flagstones, lots of granite and stripped pine, real fires each end, back pool room (where children may be allowed), no music; cats and friendly dogs, tables and maybe chickens in small suntrap courtyard, fine long walk from St Ives; parking space has been increased *(Brian Skelcher, Guy Consterdine, S Horsley, the Didler, LYM, Kevin Flack)*

ISLES OF SCILLY

St Martins [SV9215]

Seven Stones [Lower Town]: New licensees now keeping a couple of St Austell real ales and doing enjoyable freshly made food inc pasties and pizzas; doubles as village hall and looks it, but has decent interior and superb view, with tables outside; limited winter opening *(P and M Rudlin, Jonathan Smith)*

St Marys [SV9010]

☆ *Atlantic Inn* [The Strand; next to but independent from Atlantic Hotel]: Spreading rather dark bar with nice little room at one end, boat hanging from ceiling and lots of nautical bits and pieces, flowery-patterned seats, usual bar food (local fish is good), reasonably priced St Austell ales inc XXXX Mild, friendly landlord, efficient service, mix of locals and tourists, sizeable brighter dining area overlooking harbour; darts, pool, fruit machines; little terrace with green cast-iron furniture and wide views, good bedrooms *(P and M Rudlin, John Knighton, BB, Jonathan Smith)*

☆ *Bishop & Wolf* [Hugh St/Silver St (A3110)]: Lively and friendly local atmosphere, interesting sea/boating décor with secluded corners and gallery above road, nets, lots of woodwork and maritime bric-a-brac, lifeboat photographs, helpful staff, well kept St Austell Tinners and HSD, very wide choice of good generous food from locally caught megrim to exotica (should book, attractive upstairs restaurant); piped music, popular summer live music *(Steve and Carolyn Harvey, Edward Jago)*

Cumbria

Many of even the best pubs and inns here faced an almost impossibly lean time in the first half of 2001, with foot and mouth disease severely limiting visitor numbers and making even the locals wary of getting out and about. It says a great deal for Lakeland attitudes that landlords and landladies (and their local regulars) have stayed so cheerful and friendly. It is a great area for pub lovers, with many surrounded by glorious scenery, some simple places ideal for walkers, others with inventive food, and quite a few now brewing their own beer. Pubs scoring particularly highly in readers' affections here are the Royal Oak in Appleby (good food, plenty of character), the Dukes Head at Armathwaite (good food here too, and a nice place to stay), the prettily placed Punch Bowl at Askham, the Pheasant at Bassenthwaite Lake (a rather smart country hotel with an engagingly pubby bar), the Wheatsheaf at Beetham (new licensee doing imaginative food), the unspoilt Blacksmiths Arms at Broughton Mills, the Oddfellows Arms at Caldbeck (a thriving country local), the Masons Arms up on Cartmel Fell (seems on particularly good form since the landlady's recent marriage; it's been in all 20 Good Pub Guide editions so far), the Pheasant at Casterton (very good food and a nice place to stay, yet very much a pub still), the Sun at Crook (very good food here too, in a pubby atmosphere), the very foody Punch Bowl at Crosthwaite, the unspoilt Britannia at Elterwater (a great favourite ever since our first edition, and still in the same family), the well run Travellers Rest just outside Grasmere, the civilised Drunken Duck near Hawkshead (elaborate and imaginative evening food, simpler at lunchtime), the friendly Watermill at Ings (a great place for beer enthusiasts), the well run Shepherds at Melmerby (enjoyable food), the bustling Tower Bank Arms at Near Sawrey (straight out of Beatrix Potter, yet another pub that's been in all our editions so far), the expanding Queens Head at Troutbeck (great atmosphere, another special favourite), the Wasdale Head Inn (great for walkers and climbers), the friendly and simple Bay Horse at Winton (good all round) and the Gate Inn at Yanwath (imaginative food in nicely unpretentious surroundings). To these we'd add a clutch of new entries: the Bitter End in Cockermouth, brewing its own ales; the Sun in Coniston, attractively 'defurbished' by its friendly newish owner; the cheerful and welcoming Black Dog near Dalton-in-Furness; the Kings Arms in Hawkshead (convivial bar, pleasant hotel); and the Farmers Arms in Ulverston (a focal point for the town, good all round). For a special meal out, the Pheasant at Casterton, Sun at Crook, Punch Bowl at Crosthwaite, Drunken Duck near Hawkshead and Queens Head at Troutbeck would all do you proud; our choice as Cumbria Dining Pub of the Year is the Punch Bowl at Crosthwaite. One further pub has been in all 20 Guide editions so far: the Old Dungeon Ghyll in Langdale. In the Lucky Dip section at the end of the chapter, pubs to note particularly are the Kirkstone Pass Inn above Ambleside, Hole in t' Wall in Bowness, Wheatsheaf at Brigsteer, Dutton Arms at Burton-in-Kendal (very foody), Kings Arms in Cartmel, Royal at Dockray, General Burgoyne at Great Urswick, Queens Head in Hawkshead, Swinside near Keswick, Mill Inn at Mungrisdale, Herdwick at Penruddock, Yew Tree at Seatoller, Eagle & Child at Staveley, Blacksmiths Arms at Talkin and Kings Head at Thirlspot (we have already inspected and approved the great majority of these). Drinks prices have held almost unchanged in the area this year, with a pint of beer typically costing nearly 20p less than the national average – and very much less than that in the Blue Bell at Heversham with its bargain Sam Smiths.

AMBLESIDE NY3804 Map 9
Golden Rule

Smithy Brow; follow Kirkstone Pass signpost from A591 on N side of town

Happily, nothing changes in this honest Lakeland local – it is still a place where there are plenty of friendly regulars to chat to, and where the landlord welcomes walkers and their dogs. The bar has lots of local country pictures and a few fox masks decorating the butter-coloured walls, horsebrasses on the black beams, built-in leatherette wall seats, and cast-iron-framed tables; dominoes and cribbage. The room on the left has darts and a fruit machine, and the one down a few steps on the right is a quieter sitting room. Well kept Hartleys XB and Robinsons Best, Old Stockport, and Hatters Mild on handpump; pork pies (50p), and filled rolls (£1.50). There's a back yard with tables, and especially colourful window boxes. The golden rule referred to in its name is a brass measuring yard mounted over the bar counter. *(Recommended by P Price, Andy and Jill Kassube, P Abbott, H K Dyson, Margaret and Roy Randle, Ian Dawson, Jim Gardiner, Sarah and Peter Gooderham)*

Robinsons ~ Tenant John Lockley ~ Real ale ~ Bar food ~ No credit cards ~ (015394) 32257 ~ Children welcome until 9pm ~ Open 11-11; 12-10.30 Sun

APPLEBY NY6921 Map 10
Royal Oak

Bongate; B6542 on S edge of town

A good mix of customers fills the bars at this old-fashioned coaching inn, creating a relaxed, chatty atmosphere. The oak-panelled public bar has a good open fire, and the beamed lounge has old pictures on the timbered walls, some armchairs and a carved settle, and a panelling-and-glass snug enclosing the bar counter; dominoes. Enjoyable bar food includes home-made soup (£1.95), sandwiches (from £3.25), tortilla wraps filled with chicken and sour cream or steak with green pepper and guacamole (£4.95), lasagne or beef in ale (£6.95), gammon and peach (£7.95), and a skillet of sweet potato with cheese and fresh thyme (£8.95), with daily specials such as wild boar pâté or mussels steamed in beer (£3.95), haddock fillet with nut brown butter or rabbit casserole (£8.95), peppered pork fillet (£9.95), salmon with thai spices (£10.95), and puddings such as lemon tart or raspberry crème brûlée (£3.25); Sunday roast lunch (£7.95). Part of the restaurant is no smoking. Well kept Black Sheep, John Smiths, Yates Bitter, and a changing guest on handpump, and a good range of wines and malt whiskies; dominoes, cribbage, and TV. There are seats on the front terrace, and masses of flowering tubs, troughs and hanging baskets. You can get here on the scenic Leeds/Settle/Carlisle railway (best to check times and any possible delays to avoid missing lunch). *(Recommended by Susan and John Douglas, Paul Boot, Anthony Barnes, Guy Vowles, Christine and Malcolm Ingram, Steve Whalley, Barbara Wilder, Andy Meaton, Ian S Morley, Richard J Holloway, Mr and Mrs R Peacock, Vicky and David Sarti, C A Hall, Walter and Susan Rinaldi-Butcher, Tony Middis, Mr and Mrs T B Staples, Edward Watson)*

Mortal Man Inns ~ Manager Hugo Broadbent ~ Real ale ~ Bar food (12-2.30, 6-9) ~ Restaurant ~ (01768) 351463 ~ Children in eating area of bar and restaurant ~ Open 11-11; 12-10.30 Sun ~ Bedrooms: £37B/£76B

If you report on a pub that's not a main entry, please tell us any lunchtimes or evenings when it doesn't serve bar food.

ARMATHWAITE NY5146 Map 10
Dukes Head ★ 🛏

Off A6 a few miles S of Carlisle

A very pleasant place to stay (and the breakfasts are good), this is an unpretentious village pub with a warm welcome for all. The civilised lounge bar has oak settles and little armchairs among more upright seats, oak and mahogany tables, antique hunting and other prints, and some brass and copper powder-flasks above its coal fire. Consistently good bar food includes home-made soup (£2.50), sandwiches (from £2.50), pork and venison terrine (£3.95), omelettes (from £5.95), platters (from £6.85), lentil, carrot and cashew nut loaf (£6.90), grilled trout with chervil and lemon stuffing or fillet of pork with creamy cider and apple sauce (£7.95), roast duckling with apple sauce (£10.95), daily specials such as butterbean and red pepper casserole with couscous (£6.45), braised chicken with chorizo (£6.95), game casserole (£7.20), and whole bass (£10.95). The restaurant is no smoking. Well kept Tetleys, and a guest such as Castle Eden, Greene King Old Speckled Hen or Wadworths 6X on handpump; dominoes and cribbage; separate public bar with darts, table skittles, and fruit machine. There are tables out on the lawn behind; boules. You can hire bicycles. *(Recommended by Richard J Holloway, Helen Flaherty, R and M Wallace, Mr and Mrs J McRobert, E R Thirkell, Dave Braisted, R Davies, John and Christine Lowe, Christopher Ross, Michael Sargent, Joan Thorpe)*

Pubmaster ~ Tenant Henry Lynch ~ Real ale ~ Bar food (12-2, 6.15-9) ~ Restaurant ~ (016974) 72226 ~ Children welcome ~ Open 12-3, 5.45-11; 12-3, 5.45-10.30 Sun ~ Bedrooms: £28.50B/£48.50B

ASKHAM NY5123 Map 9
Punch Bowl

Village signposted on right from A6 4 miles S of Penrith

Quietly set facing the lower village green, this is an attractive inn, well run by its friendly licensees. The rambling bar has coins stuck into the cracks of the dark wooden beams (periodically taken out and sent to charity), and local photographs and prints of Askham – as well as an antique settle by a log fire, interesting furnishings such as Chippendale dining chairs and rushwork ladder-back seats around sturdy wooden tables, and well cushioned window seats in the white-painted thick stone walls. Between the lounge and the games room is an open log fire. Bar food (prices have stayed the same for two years now) includes lunchtime sandwiches (£2.70), home-made soup (£2.85), deep-fried mushrooms with herb and garlic butter (£2.95), cumberland sausage (£6.10), vegetarian lasagne (£6.50), beef in ale (£6.60), grilled salmon with a tangy lemon dressing (£6.80), stir-fry duck with plum sauce (£8.80), steaks (from £9.80), daily specials, and children's dishes (£3). Well kept Barngates Cracker Ale, Castle Eden, and Greene King IPA on handpump; dominoes, cribbage, fruit machine, and piped pop music, and in the separate public bar darts and pool. There are tables out on a flower-filled terrace. *(Recommended by Malcolm Taylor, Mr and Mrs Maurice Thompson, Angus Lyon, Dr Paull Khan, Brian and Lynn Young, Karen and Graham Oddey, Ian Jones, Justin Hulford, Jim Abbott)*

Whitbreads ~ Lease David and Frances Riley ~ Real ale ~ Bar food (12-2, 6-9) ~ Restaurant ~ (01931) 712443 ~ Children welcome until 9pm ~ Open 11-3, 5.30-11; 11-11 Sat; 12-10.30 Sun ~ Bedrooms: £40B/£59B

BARBON SD6282 Map 10
Barbon Inn 🛏

Village signposted off A683 Kirkby Lonsdale—Sedbergh; OS Sheet 97 map reference 628826

Readers enjoy staying in this 17th-c coaching inn. The licensees and locals are friendly and welcoming, there are marvellous surrounding walks, and excellent breakfasts. Several small rooms lead off the simple bar with its blackened range, each individually and comfortably furnished: carved 18th-c oak settles, comfortable sofas and armchairs, a Victorian fireplace. Reasonably priced bar food includes sandwiches, home-made soup (£2.50), home-made pâté (£2.95), home-made cottage pie (£4.95), cod and chips (£5.50), local cumberland sausage (£5.95), home-made lasagne (£6.25), and rump steak (£7.95); the restaurant is no smoking. Well kept Theakstons Best and a guest such as Greene King Old Speckled Hen on handpump; dominoes and piped music. The lovely sheltered garden here is prettily planted and neatly kept. *(Recommended by Ben and Chris Francis, Jayne and Peter Capp, Dr J D Bassett)*

Free house ~ Licensee Lindsey MacDiarmid ~ Real ale ~ Bar food ~ Restaurant ~ (015242) 76233 ~ Children welcome ~ Open 11.30-3, 6.30-11 ~ Bedrooms: £30(£35B)/£60B

BASSENTHWAITE LAKE NY1930 Map 9
Pheasant ★ ⇌

Follow Pheasant Inn sign at N end of dual carriageway stretch of A66 by Bassenthwaite Lake

Although this is a rather smart and civilised hotel, its little bar is pleasantly old-fashioned and pubby, with mellow polished walls, cushioned oak settles, rush-seat chairs and library seats, hunting prints and photographs, and well kept Bass, Jennings Cumberland, and Theakstons Best on handpump; a dozen good wines by the glass. Several comfortable lounges have log fires, fine parquet flooring, antiques, and plants; one is no smoking – as is the restaurant. Enjoyable lunchtime bar food includes soup with home-made bread (£2.95), salmon mousse (£5.25), open sandwiches (from £5.25), potted Silloth shrimps (£5.35), ploughman's (£5.95), spaghetti napolitana (£6.25), lambs liver and black pudding with red onion gravy (£7.25), fillets of smoked haddock on a bed of spinach with a light cheese sauce and topped with a poached egg (£7.55), and puddings (from £3.25). From the garden, you can stroll into the very attractive surrounding woodlands, and there are plenty of walks in all directions. *(Recommended by Vicky and David Sarti, Nigel Woolliscroft, Tracey and Stephen Groves, Tina and David Woods-Taylor, Nick Lawless, Ben and Sheila Walker, Michael Butler, Karen and Graham Oddey; also in* The Good Hotel Guide*)*

Free house ~ Licensee Matthew Wylie ~ Real ale ~ Bar food (not in evening – restaurant only) ~ Restaurant ~ (017687) 76234 ~ Children in eating area of bar and in restaurant if over 8 ~ Open 11.30-2.30, 5-10.30(11 Sat); 12-2, 6-10.30 Sun; closed 25 Dec ~ Bedrooms: £65B/£106B

BEETHAM SD5079 Map 7
Wheatsheaf 🍴 ♀ ⇌

Village (and inn) signposted just off A6 S of Milnthorpe

A new licensee has taken over this 16th-c coaching inn, but it remains a friendly place for an enjoyable meal. The opened-up front lounge bar has lots of exposed beams and joists and is decorated in warm ochre shades and gingham fabrics; the main bar is behind on the right, with well kept Jennings Bitter and Cumberland and a changing guest beer on handpump, and a fine choice of New World wines by the glass; there's also a cosy and relaxing smaller room for drinkers, and a roaring log fire. Imaginative, popular food includes good soups such as mushroom and tarragon (£2.95), interesting lunchtime sandwiches (from £3.95), deep-fried herb-crusted camembert on a toasted citrus salad (£4.85), warm salad of confit of duck with a blackcurrant relish (£5.50), crispy filo basket filled with a stir-fry of mushrooms, sweet potatoes and feta cheese (£8.25), chargrilled barnsley lamb chop with garlic and thyme mash and redcurrant and tomato gravy or caribbean chicken with lime and coconut (£9.95), and puddings such as sticky fudge and walnut pudding with butterscotch sauce (£4.75); they also offer a two-course lunch (£7.95). Daily newspapers and magazines to read. The upstairs no smoking dining room is candlelit at night. *(Recommended by Steve Whalley, Karen Eliot, David Atkinson, Gordon Neighbour, Malcolm Taylor, Tony Middis, Alan and Judith Gifford, MLR, DC, G P McGovern, David Cooke, Margaret Dickinson)*

Free house ~ Licensee Emma Lamb ~ Real ale ~ Bar food ~ Restaurant ~ (015395) 62123 ~ Children in eating area of bar ~ Open 11-3, 6-11; 12-3, 7-10.30 Sun ~ Bedrooms: £45S/£60B

BOOT NY1701 Map 9
Burnmoor ♀

Village signposted just off the Wrynose/Hardknott Pass road, OS Sheet 89 map reference 175010

A perfect haven for walkers, this partly 16th-c inn is in a pretty and incredibly peaceful hamlet. The beamed and carpeted white-painted bar has an open fire (burning all day), comfortable seats, well kept Black Sheep, Jennings Bitter and Cumberland, and a guest such as Barngates Cracker on handpump from the new slate-topped bar counter, a thoughtful wine list (one of the licensees is in the wine trade), quite a few malt whiskies (specialising in Islay malts), and good mulled wine (served all year); pool, cribbage, dominoes, darts, cards, TV, and juke box. Good lunchtime bar food – using home-grown vegetables, beef and venison from Scotland, and fish from local lakes – includes sandwiches (from £2.25; sandwich and soup from £4.25), home-made soup (£2.50), filled baked potaotes (from £3.25), home-made pâté (£3.50; large £5.50), thin and crispy pizza (from £3.75; large from £6.25), home-roasted ham and egg (£5; large £8.50), vegetable chilli with home-made chutney (£6; large £9.50), and game pie (£7; large £11.50), with evening dishes such as apple and stilton melt (£4), home-made quiche (£6; large £9.50), lamb, black pudding and potato hotpot with pickled red cabbage (£6.75; large £9.50), and rump steak with herb butter (£7); they usefully serve morning coffee, and all day breakfast. The restaurant is no smoking. There are seats outside on the sheltered front lawn with a children's play area – slide, swings, and rope assault course. The inn is handy for the Ravenglass and Eskdale steam railway and for a restored watermill, said to be the oldest working example in the country. *(Recommended by Tony and Wendy Hobden, Roger Braithwaite, Nicholas Paint, H K Dyson, David and Julie Glover)*

Free house ~ Licensees Harry and Paddington Berger ~ Real ale ~ Bar food (11-5, 6-9; not 25 Dec) ~ Restaurant ~ (019467) 23224 ~ Children welcome ~ Open 11-11; 11-10.30 Sun ~ Bedrooms: £30B/£60B

BOUTH SD3386 Map 9
White Hart

Village signposted off A590 near Haverthwaite

There's a good friendly, bustling atmosphere in this small inn, and although many customers know each other, visitors are made very welcome. The sloping ceilings and floors show the building's age, and there are lots of old local photographs and bric-a-brac – farm tools, stuffed animals, a collection of long-stemmed clay pipes – and two log fires, one in a woodburning stove. The games room has darts, pool, pinball, dominoes, fruit machine, TV, and juke box; piped music. A fair choice of home-made food – using locally supplied, naturally produced meat from rare breed animals – includes sandwiches, good soups (£2.20), garlic mushrooms (£3.95), home-made steak in ale pie or cumberland sausage (£6.95), chicken or vegetable balti or pasta with a rich tomato, olive and basil sauce (£7.25), halibut steak with garlic and parsley butter (£9.25), sirloin steak (£8.95), daily specials, puddings (£2.75), and children's meals (from £2.75); the restaurant is no smoking. Well kept Black Sheep, Boddingtons, Jennings Cumberland, and Tetleys, with guests such as Barnsley Bitter, Coniston Bluebird or Yates Bitter on handpump, and 40 malt whiskies. There are plenty of surrounding walks, and tables out in the attractively planted garden. *(Recommended by Mrs Romey Heaton)*

Free house ~ Licensees Nigel and Peter Barton ~ Real ale ~ Bar food (12-2, 6-8.45; not Mon or Tues lunchtime) ~ No credit cards ~ (01229) 861229 ~ Children welcome until 8.30 ~ Open 12-2, 6-11; 12-11 Sat; 12-10.30 Sun; closed Mon and Tues lunchtimes ~ Bedrooms: £26B/£46B

It is illegal for bar staff to smoke while handling your drink.

BROUGHTON MILLS SD2190 Map 9
Blacksmiths Arms
Off A593 N of Broughton-in-Furness

Unspoilt and charming, this bustling, friendly pub is tucked away in a little hamlet in peaceful countryside. The four simply but attractively decorated small rooms have open fires in three of them, ancient slate floors, and well kept Barngates Tag Lag, Dent Aviator, and Jennings Cumberland on handpump, farm cider, and interesting bottled beers. Enjoyable food (not served in the bar) is cooked by the licensee and includes lunchtime sandwiches and baked potatoes as well as home-made soup (£1.95), home-made pâté (£3.65), steak in ale pie (£6.50), mushroom stroganoff (£6.45), cumberland sausage (£5.95), marinated lamb shoulder in minted gravy (£7.25), tuna steak in a mediterranean sauce (£7.45), steaks (from £10.20), and daily specials such as cod fillet baked in tomato sauce, topped with mozzarella cheese (£6.95), cajun pork (£7.15), and Aberdeen Angus steak in stilton sauce (£8.95). There are three smallish dining rooms (the back one is no smoking). Darts, cards, dominoes, and children's books and games. The hanging baskets and tubs of flowers in front of the pub are very pretty in summer. *(Recommended by Dr and Mrs Anthony Smith, BKA, Derek Harvey-Piper, JP, PP, Margaret Dickinson, Kevin Thorpe, Ian and Liz Rispin)*

Free house ~ Licensee Philip Blackburn ~ Real ale ~ Bar food (not winter Mon lunchtime) ~ Restaurant ~ (01229) 716824 ~ Children welcome ~ Open 12-11; 12-10.30 Sun; 5-11 Mon (cl winter Mon), 12-2.30, 5-11 Tues-Fri in winter; closed 25 Dec

BUTTERMERE NY1817 Map 9
Bridge Hotel 🛏
Just off B5289 SW of Keswick

This chatty, friendly inn is a fine place to stop for lunch while enjoying some of the lovely surrounding walks. The flagstoned area in the beamed bar is good for walking boots, and has built-in wooden settles and farmhouse chairs around traditional tables, a panelled bar counter and a few horsebrasses, and there's a dining bar with brocaded armchairs around copper-topped tables, and brass ornaments hanging from the beams; the restaurant and guest lounge are no smoking. Good bar food includes soup with home-made bread (£2.70), interesting sandwiches such as brie and sun-dried tomato or barbecue spiced chicken and mayonnaise (£2.75; toasties £3.50), home-made smoked salmon pâté (£3.10), ploughman's or warm bacon, onion, chopped egg, and seasonal salad with parmesan cheese croutons (£4.30), butterbean casserole (£6.30), tasty cumberland hotpot, home-made steak and kidney pie or crispy duck stir fried with vegetables and soy sauce (£6.75), poached Borrowdale trout (£7.50), steaks (from £10.50), and children's menu (£2.50). Well kept Black Sheep, Flowers IPA, and Theakstons Old Peculier on handpump, quite a few malt whiskies, and a decent wine list. Outside, a flagstoned terrace has white tables by a rose-covered sheltering stone wall. The views from the bedrooms are marvellous; please note, the bedroom prices are for dinner, bed and breakfast; self-catering, too. *(Recommended by Jim Abbott, David Field, Michael and Ann Cole, Dick and Madeleine Brown, Meg and Colin Hamilton, H K Dyson, Tracey and Stephen Groves, Risha Stapleton, GD, KW, J Greenwood)*

Free house ~ Licensee Peter McGuire ~ Real ale ~ Bar food (all day at peak times) ~ Restaurant ~ (017687) 70252 ~ Children in eating area of bar and, if over 7, in restaurant ~ Open 10.30-11; 10.30-10.30 Sun ~ Bedrooms: £65B/£130B

CALDBECK NY3239 Map 9
Oddfellows Arms
B5299 SE of Wigton

With particularly well kept beer and enjoyable food, this comfortably extended pub is popular with its many customers – locals, walkers, and those touring the area. The bar and attractive no smoking dining room have a good thriving atmosphere,

Jennings Bitter and Cumberland and seasonal guests on handpump, and bar food such as soup (£2), filled baked potatoes or lunchtime sandwiches (from £2.95), cumberland sausage (£5.25), chicken curry or steak in ale pie (£5.75), vegetarian dishes (£5.95), braised shoulder of lamb with redcurrant and mint gravy (£8.25), and poached swordfish with lemon butter (£8.45). Darts, pool, fruit machine, juke box, TV, dominoes, and piped music. John Peel is buried in the village. *(Recommended by Mike and Penny Sutton, Mr and Mrs W D Borthwick, Canon David Baxter, Dr Paull Khan, Steve and Liz Tilley)*

Jennings ~ Manager Allan Bowe ~ Real ale ~ Bar food (12-2, 6.15-8.30) ~ Restaurant ~ (016974) 78227 ~ Children welcome until 9.30 ~ Open 12-11; 12-10.30 Sun; 12-3, 6-11 weekdays in winter ~ Bedrooms: £28S/£48S

CARTMEL FELL SD4288 Map 9
Masons Arms ◖

Strawberry Bank, a few miles S of Windermere between A592 and A5074; perhaps the simplest way of finding the pub is to go uphill W from Bowland Bridge (which is signposted off A5074) towards Newby Bridge and keep right then left at the staggered crossroads – it's then on your right, below Gummer's How; OS Sheet 97 map reference 413895

In a lovely spot, this very popular pub has a main bar with plenty of character: low black beams in the bowed ceiling, country chairs and plain wooden tables on polished flagstones, and a grandly Gothick seat with snarling dogs as its arms. A small lounge has oak tables and settles to match its fine Jacobean panelling, and a plain little room beyond the serving counter has pictures and a fire in an open range; the family room has an old-parlourish atmosphere, and there's also an upstairs room which helps at peak times. Well kept Boddingtons, Jennings Cumberland, Yates Bitter, Wadworths 6X, and Wells Eagle IPA on handpump, their own bottled Damson Ale, a huge range of bottled beers, quite a few Belgian fruit beers, and – in summer – Normandy cider; carefully chosen wines, too. Good, wholesome food includes home-made soup (£2.95), sandwiches (from £3.55), spare ribs (£4.95), lentil and hazelnut pâté (£5.25), cajun sausage and black pudding (£5.95), ploughman's (£6.95), and steak pie (£7.95), with specials such as leek and butter bean pie or garlic roasted vegetable quiche (£7.25), caramelised onion and chicken bake (£7.50), lamb and apricot casserole or braised steak in ale (£7.95), and puddings like good orange crème brûlée, sticky toffee pudding or apple and blackcurrant pie with almond pastry (£3.25). On the front terrace, there are rustic benches and tables with an unrivalled view overlooking the Winster Valley to the woods below Whitbarrow Scar, and they sell leaflets outlining local walks of varying lengths and difficulty. *(Recommended by Ewan and Moira McCall, Mike and Wendy Proctor, Nigel Woolliscroft, Jean Tremlett, David Field, Pat and Clive Sherriff, Mrs Romey Heaton, Nick Lawless, Peter Burton, Mr and Mrs Richard Osborne, Bob and Val Collman, John Barrow, SLC, Jane Taylor, David Dutton)*

Own brew ~ Licensee Helen Walsh ~ Real ale ~ Bar food (12-2, 6-8.45) ~ (015395) 68486 ~ Children in eating area of bar ~ Open 11.30-11; 12-10.30 Sun; 11.30-3, 6-11 winter; closed 25 Dec and evening 26 Dec

CASTERTON SD6279 Map 10
Pheasant ⑪ ♀ ⇐

A683 about a mile N of junction with A65, by Kirkby Lonsdale; OS sheet 97 map reference 633796

The licensees of this civilised inn work very hard to ensure that – despite the fact that it is a pleasant place to stay overnight and the food is good and imaginative – they remain a proper pub with a relaxed, chatty atmosphere and a warm welcome for both the friendly crowd of locals and for the many visitors. The neatly kept and attractively modernised beamed rooms of the main bar have padded wheelback chairs, plush wall settles, newspapers and magazines to read, a woodburning stove surrounded by brass ornaments in a nicely arched bare stone fireplace with polished brass hood, and well kept Theakstons Bitter and Old Peculier and guests such as

Black Sheep Bitter, Dent Bitter or Wye Valley Bitter on handpump; over 30 malt whiskies, and a good wine list offering 12 by the glass. There's a further room (which is no smoking) across the passage with a piano. Good bar food includes home-made soup (£2.50), lunchtime sandwiches (from £2.75) and smoked salmon and scrambled eggs or ploughman's (£5.95), home-made Chinese vegetable spring rolls with a mild chilli dip (£4.95), local cumberland sausage with apple and sultana chutney (£6.75), beef in ale pie or spinach, feta cheese and mushroom strudel with salsa sauce (£6.95), Aberdeen Angus steaks (from £12.95), and daily specials such as creamed mushrooms with chives topped with herbed crumbs and oven baked (£4.25), dressed crab with mango mayonnaise (£4.95), roast leg of lamb with minted gravy and roasted vegetables (£7.95), guinea fowl with a rich red wine and mushroom sauce (£8.95), and seafood mixed grill (salmon, tuna, halibut, swordfish and crevettes £13.95); hearty breakfasts. The restaurant is no smoking. Darts, dominoes, chess, cards, draughts, piped music, and weekly winter quiz evenings. There are some tables with cocktail parasols outside by the road, with more in the pleasant garden. The nearby church (built for the girls' school of Brontë fame here) has some attractive pre-Raphaelite stained glass and paintings. Dogs welcome. *(Recommended by Christine and Malcolm Ingram, Jayne and Peter Capp, Ken Richards, Mr and Mrs R Barclay, Deborah Altringham, Mrs V Goldie, John Watson, Pierre and Pat Richterich, Mrs Pat Crabb, Mr and Mrs C J Frodsham)*

Free house ~ Licensees Melvin and May Mackie ~ Real ale ~ Bar food ~ Restaurant ~ (015242) 71230 ~ Children welcome ~ Open 11-3, 6-11(10.30 Sun) ~ Bedrooms: £40B/£72B

CHAPEL STILE NY3205 Map 9
Wainwrights
B5343

From the picnic-sets on the terrace in front of this white-rendered Lakeland house, there are good views; lots of surrounding walks. Inside, the characterful slate-floored bar has plenty of room, and it is here that walkers and their dogs are welcomed. There's a relaxed and friendly atmosphere, an old kitchen range, cushioned settles, and well kept Jennings Bitter, Cumberland Ale, and Sneck Lifter, with a guest beer such as Black Sheep or Barngates Tag Lag on handpump. Bar food includes sandwiches (from £3.25), filled baked potatoes (from £3.95), home-made steak in ale pie or cumberland sausage (£6.95), tasty lamb shoulder with honey and mint (£7.95), children's dishes (from £3.75), and daily specials; they don't take bookings, so best to get there early. The dining area is no smoking; darts, dominoes, fruit machine, and piped music. *(Recommended by Ewan and Moira McCall, W W Burke, Paul Roughley, Julia Fox, Dave Braisted)*

Free house ~ Licensees M Darbyshire and D Banks ~ Real ale ~ Bar food (12-2, 6-9) ~ (015394) 38088 ~ Children in eating area of bar and in restaurant until 9.30 ~ Quiz night Tues evening ~ Open 11.30-11; 12-10.30 Sun; 11.30-3, 6-11 weekdays in winter

COCKERMOUTH NY1231 Map 9
Bitter End ◧ £
Kirkgate, by cinema

As well as a good mix of customers which creates a bustling, friendly atmosphere, this interestingly refurbished place keeps eight real ales – including its own-brewed ones. From a tiny Victorian-style shop window, there's a view of the little brewery where the landlord brews Cockersnoot and Cuddy Luggs, and he also keeps Coniston Bluebird, Jennings Bitter and Sneck Lifter, and three weekly changing guest beers on handpump, in good condition; quite a few bottled beers from around the world. The three main rooms have a different atmosphere in each – from quietly chatty to sporty, with the décor reflecting this, such as unusual pictures of a Cockermouth that even Wordsworth might have recognised, to more up-to-date sporting memorabilia, and framed beer mats. Some tables in the front bar are no smoking. At lunchtime, simple snacks include home-made soup (£1.75), filled rolls (from £1.65), and filled baked potatoes (from £1.95), with a larger evening choice such as five-bean casserole (£5.15), home-made chicken tikka (£5.50), home-made steak and mushroom in ale pie (£5.50), puddings like home-made sticky toffee pudding (£2.10), children's meals (from £2), and roast Sunday lunch (£4.95). Service is very welcoming; piped music; the public car park round the back is free after 6. *(Recommended by G Coates, Tom McLean, Richard Lewis, Rona Murdoch, David Field, Mr and Mrs Richard Osborne)*

Own brew ~ Licensee Susan Askey ~ Real ale ~ Bar food ~ No credit cards ~ (01900) 828993 ~ Children in eating area of bar ~ Open 12(11.30 Sat)-2.30(3 Sat), 6-11; may open all day summer Sat; 12-3, 7-10.30 Sun

CONISTON SD3098 Map 9

Black Bull 🍺 🛏️

Yewdale Rd (A593)

One of the beers brewed on site here is named after Donald Campbell's Bluebird, and there's quite a lot of memorabilia devoted to the attempting of the water speed records. Other own-brewed beers include Coniston Old Man, and Opium on handpump, plus a guest such as Theakstons Old Peculier. The cheerful back area has slate flagstones and is liked by walkers and their dogs, while the beamed and carpeted front part has cast-iron-framed tables, comfortable banquettes and stools, an open fire, and a relaxed, comfortable feel; part of the bar and all of the restaurant are no smoking. You can buy their T-shirts, bottles, and clocks in the little 'shop'. Bar food includes home-made soup (£2.35), sandwiches (from £2.95; toasties £3.45), filled baked potatoes (from £3.95), ploughman's (£5.95), 10oz cumberland sausage (£6.25), spicy chilli (£7.45), leek and vegetable crumble (£7.95), local Esthwaite smoked trout (£8.45), gammon and eggs (£9.95), sirloin steak (£11.95), and daily specials such as strips of pork with shallots and mushroom in cream and wholegrain mustard sauce, steak in ale pie or braised knuckle of local lamb with root vegetables (from around £7.25); puddings (£2.90), and children's menu (£3.95). Farm ciders, and quite a few bottled beers and malt whiskies. There are tables out in the former coachyard; parking may not be easy at peak times. *(Recommended by Jayne and Peter Capp, MP, Karen and Graham Oddey, Dr D J and Mrs S C Walker, Richard Lewis, Kevin Thorpe)*

Own brew ~ Licensee Ronald Edward Bradley ~ Real ale ~ Bar food (all day) ~ Restaurant ~ (015394) 41335/41668 ~ Children in eating area of bar and restaurant ~ Open 11-11; 12-11 Sun; closed 25 Dec ~ Bedrooms: £50S(£35B)/£65S(£75B)

Sun 🍺

Pub signposted from centre

This is a friendly and comfortable 16th-c inn with an informal Edwardian hotel attached. The pub part has been completely 'unmodernised' to reveal an old-fashioned classic Lakeland bar. The walls have been stripped back to the stonework (finding two pre-Victorian windows in the process), the ceiling beams have been exposed, the flagstoned floor has been extended (using old flagstones), and a 19th-c range fitted to replace the previous 1960s fireplace. There are cask seats (including two heavy ones), cast-iron-framed tables, some built-in blue seating and old Victorian settles, and Donald Campbell photographs (this was his HQ during his final attempt on the world water speed record). As well as lunchtime snacks such as rolls or sandwiches or filled baked potatoes (from £3.50), macaroni cheese (£4.50), omelettes (£5.95), and ploughman's (£6), the good food might include home-made soup (£2.75), home-made pork and apricot pâté (£4.25), cauliflower and three cheese or bacon and mushroom pasta (£5.95), vegetable lasagne (£7.75), cumberland sausage (£7.95), steak, kidney and ale pie (£8.30), sirloin steak (£11.95), and braised whole pheasant in red wine sauce (£12.50); some dishes can also be ordered in small helpings for those with small appetites or for children. The dining room is no smoking as is the children's area in the bar. Well kept Black Sheep, Coniston Bluebird, and Moorhouses Black Cat, with a couple of guest beers like

Barngates Tag Lag, Jennings Bitter or Timothy Taylors Landlord on handpump, a decent wine list, several malt whiskies, and friendly staff. Darts, table skittles, cribbage, dominoes, and occasional piped music. There are seats and tables in front of the building and in the big tree-sheltered garden, which make the most of the lovely views; there's also a new conservatory and terrace in front of the hotel. Fishing, riding and shooting can all be arranged for residents (we haven't yet had reports from readers who have stayed here). *(Recommended by Tina and David Woods-Taylor, Ewan and Moira McCall, Kevin Flack, David Whitehead)*

Free house ~ Licensee Alan Piper ~ Real ale ~ Bar food (12-2, 6-9; all day high season) ~ Restaurant ~ (015394) 41248 ~ Children in eating area of bar and in restaurant until 9.30 ~ Open 11-11; 12-10.30 Sun ~ Bedrooms: £35S/£70B

CROOK SD4795 Map 7
Sun 🍴

B5284 Kendal—Bowness

Although much emphasis is placed on the consistently good, interesting food here, there's still something of the atmosphere of a village local, and the staff are very friendly. The two rooms are opened together so that the dining area now dominates, and one area is no smoking. The food is highly enjoyable and includes lunchtime sandwiches and baked potatoes, and moules marinières or garlic mushrooms and smoked bacon salad (£4.50), honey and orange roasted duck breast with a citrus crème fraîche dressing or smoked shell-on prawns with aïoli (£4.95), Italian seafood salad (£5.50), home-made steak in ale pie (£7.50), garlic and herb tagliatelle or seared tuna with fresh fruit (£9.50), venison and red wine casserole (£9.95), warm smoked salmon steak with hollandaise and dauphinoise potatoes or fried lemon sole fillets with shallots, lemon, thyme and capers (£9.95), roast guinea fowl with grapes in a white wine and tarragon sauce or roast duck with fresh ginger and Grand Marnier (£10.50), and proper puddings such as spotted dick, damson fool or chocolate and hazelnut roulade (£3.85). Well kept Boddingtons, Courage Directors, Greene King Old Speckled Hen, and Theakstons on handpump, an interesting choice of good value wines, and a welcoming fire; darts and dominoes. The pub is set away from the Windermere bustle and looks over rolling hills. *(Recommended by Michael Doswell, Tina and David Woods-Taylor, Hugh Roberts, Joan Yen, Sarah and Peter Gooderham, Ray and Winifred Halliday, John and Sarah Perry)*

Free house ~ Licensee Adrian Parr ~ Real ale ~ Bar food ~ Restaurant ~ (01539) 821351 ~ Children in eating area of bar and restaurant ~ Open 11-3, 5-11; 11-11 Sat; 12-10.30 Sun

CROSTHWAITE SD4491 Map 9
Punch Bowl 🍴 ♀

Village signposted off A5074 SE of Windermere

Cumbria Dining Pub of the Year

While people do just drop into this idyllically placed 16th-c inn for a drink, it would seem a shame to miss out on the excellent, imaginative food. Readers very much enjoy staying here as well. There are several separate areas carefully reworked to give a lot of space, and a high-raftered central part by the serving counter with an upper minstrel's gallery on either side; the bar and snug area are no smoking. Steps lead down into a couple of small dimly lit rooms on the right, and there's a doorway through into two more airy rooms on the left. It's all spick and span, with lots of tables and chairs, beams, pictures by local artist Derek Farman, and an open fire. As well as a set-price lunch (two courses £8, three courses £10.95), the imaginative food might include sandwiches, home-made tomato and basil soup with pesto (£2.70), crispy duck leg confit salad with provençale mixed leaf salad (£5.25), baked goats cheese salad on oven-baked beetroot with button onions, watercress and a walnut oil dressing (£5.50), layered white crab meat salad with a sweet chilli, red pepper and lime sauce (£6.25), grilled aubergine, courgette and polenta topped with melted lancashire cheese and a tomato sauce (£8.25), chargrilled tuna steak on crushed potatoes with braised ginger, leeks and five spice sauce or grilled chicken with a spicy tomato, red and green pepper sauce (£10.95), chargrilled fillet of lamb with a creamy thai curry sauce (£11.25), escalope of calves liver with sage leaves (£12.25), and puddings such as honey and Drambuie crème brûlée, sticky tunisian-style orange and lemon cake, and chocolate brownie with home-made chocolate chip ice cream and a chocolate sauce (from £3.75); popular Sunday lunch. Well kept Barngates Tag Lag, Black Sheep, and Wells Bombardier on handpump, a carefully chosen wine list, and several malt whiskies. There are some tables on a terrace stepped into the hillside. *(Recommended by Peter and Anne-Marie O'Malley, Ian and Jane Irving, P Fisk, Joan Yen, A Preston, Revd D Glover, Paul Boot, Hugh Roberts, D J Hulse, Karen Eliot)*

Free house ~ Licensee Steven Doherty ~ Real ale ~ Restaurant ~ (015395) 68237 ~ Children welcome ~ Open 11-11; 12-3 Sun; closed Sun evening, all day Mon (open bank hols and all through Easter) ~ Bedrooms: £37.50B/£55B

DALTON-IN-FURNESS SD2376 Map 7
Black Dog 🍺 £

Holmes Green, Broughton Road; a mile N of town, beyond A590

Morris dancers were entertaining the locals outside this friendly country inn as we arrived late one Friday in early summer. The evening ended with leading neighbouring farmers joining the landlord in a session of traditional folk songs – something we're told happens fairly regularly (and often quite spontaneously). A former farmhouse, the pub itself is a simple, comfortable local, but it's lifted out of the ordinary by the cheery couple who run it – and by the very good choice of six real ales. On our visit these included Brakspears, Coniston Opium, Cropton Honey Gold and York Up 'n' Under, but the choice can change every couple of days; they also have farm cider. The unpretentious bar has beer mats and brasses around the beams, two log fires, partly tiled and flagstoned floor, and plain wooden table and chairs; there may be several dried hams hanging above the bar counter. A side terrace has a few plastic tables and chairs. Good value hearty bar food – all home-made – includes sandwiches, several vegetarian dishes such as chilli or an Italian fennel bake (£3.95), and scallops and bacon in a creamy sauce or beef in red wine (£4.95); children's menu. They didn't accept credit cards when we visited, but were planning to in the future. The pub is handy for the South Lakes Wild Animal Park. *(Recommended by Dr B and Mrs P B Baker)*

Free house ~ Licensees Jack Walker and Julia Taylor ~ Real ale ~ Bar food ~ No credit cards ~ (01229) 462561 ~ Children welcome ~ Open 12-3 Weds-Fri and some school hols; 5-11; 12-11(10.30 Sun) Sat; closed Mon-Tues am ~ Bedrooms: £25/£35B

DENT SD7187 Map 10
Sun 🍺

Village signposted from Sedbergh; and from Barbon, off A683

The Dent Brewery which supplies this bustling own-brew pub is actually a few miles up in the dale; well kept on handpump, there's Bitter, T'Owd Tup, Kamikazee, and Aviator Ale, and monthly guests. The bar has a pleasant traditional atmosphere, simple furniture, a coal fire, some timbers and beams, and several local snapshots; one room to the left of the bar is no smoking. Straightforward bar food (with prices unchanged since last year) includes tasty home-made soup (£1.95), sandwiches (£2.25; toasties £2.75), ploughman's (£4.75), home-made steak and kidney pie (£4.95), cumberland sausage or brie and courgette crumble (£5.25), steaks (from £6.95), daily specials such as vegetable hotpot (£5.25), pork and garlic crumble or chicken in white wine (£5.95), and children's helpings (£2.95). Darts, pool, dominoes, fruit machine, and juke box (in the pool room). There are rustic seats and tables outside. *(Recommended by Ewan and Moira McCall, Rona Murdoch, David Dutton, Jane Taylor, JP, PP, A C and E Johnson)*

Own brew ~ Licensee Martin Stafford ~ Real ale ~ Bar food (12-2, 7-8.30) ~ (015396) 25208 ~ Children welcome ~ Open 11-11; 12-10.30 Sun; 11-2.30, 7-11 weekdays in winter ~ Bedrooms: £22S/£49B

ELTERWATER NY3305 Map 9

Britannia ★ ◧ ⇌

Off B5343

Being at the heart of the Lake District – and being such a smashing pub – does mean crowds at peak times, but there's a very relaxed, informal atmosphere, and the staff remain friendly and helpful. There's a small and traditionally furnished back bar, plus a front one with a couple of window seats looking across to Elterwater itself through the trees on the far side: cosy coal fires, oak benches, settles, windsor chairs, a big old rocking chair, and well kept Coniston Bluebird, Dent Aviator, Jennings Bitter, and two guest beers such as Hop Back Summer Lightning or Moorhouses Pendle Witches Brew on handpump, 24 malt whiskies, a few country wines, and winter mulled wine; the lounge is comfortable. Good, popular bar food includes lunchtime filled rolls (from £2.50; beef with onion gravy £3), filled baked potatoes (£3.75), home-made quiche (£4.95) or home-made cumberland pie (£6.50), with evening dishes such as home-made pâté with cumberland sauce or deep-fried brie wedges with fruit coulis (£3.25), home-made lamb rogan josh or steak and mushroom pie (£7.95), poached fresh salmon steak with lemon and dill butter (£8.25), and puddings like hot banana with butterscotch pancakes or bread and butter pudding (£3.25); super breakfasts and home-baked fruit scones for afternoon cream teas. The restaurant is no smoking; dominoes and cribbage. In summer, people flock to watch the morris and step and garland dancers. *(Recommended by Tina and David Woods-Taylor, Dr Bob Bland, MP, Mr and Mrs Richard Osborne, Mr and Mrs W D Borthwick, Brian and Anna Marsden, Tracey and Stephen Groves, Keith and Janet Eaton, Richard Lewis, SLC, W W Burke, David Cooke, P Price, JDM, KM, Jayne and Peter Capp, Ewan and Moira McCall, Doug Christian, Tom McLean, Mrs S E Griffiths, Geoffrey and Carol Thorp, Ian Dawson, H K Dyson)*

Free house ~ Licensees Judith Fry and Christopher Jones ~ Real ale ~ Bar food (all day) ~ Restaurant ~ (015394) 37210 ~ Children welcome until 9 ~ Quiz Sun evenings ~ Open 11-11; 12-10.30 Sun; closed 25 Dec and evening 26 Dec ~ Bedrooms: £30/£60(£78S)(£70B)

GARRIGILL NY7441 Map 9

George & Dragon ◧

Village signposted off B6277 S of Alston

Originally a posting inn, this simple stone-built place looks across a small tree-shaded village green, and is popular with walkers. On the right, the bar has solid traditional furnishings on the very broad polished flagstones, a lovely stone fireplace with a really good log fire, and a friendly, relaxed atmosphere; there's a separate tartan-carpeted games room with sensibly placed darts, pool and dominoes. Good value, straightforward bar food includes sandwiches (from £1.70), filled yorkshire pudding (from £2.20), soup (£2.25), cumberland sausage (£5.50), broccoli and cream cheese bake (£5.60), and steak pie (£6.25). The dining room is no smoking; piped music. Well kept Black Sheep, Flowers IPA, Fullers London Pride and Marstons Pedigree on handpump. *(Recommended by Edward Watson, Sue and Geoff Price, Dr Paull Khan, Ted Tomiak)*

Free house ~ Licensees Brian and Jean Holmes ~ Real ale ~ Bar food ~ Restaurant ~ (01434) 381293 ~ Children welcome ~ Open 12-4, 6.30-11; 11.30-11 Sat; 12-4, 7-10.30 Sun; 12-3, 7-11 in winter ~ Bedrooms: £18/£36(£40B)

GRASMERE NY3406 Map 9

Travellers Rest

Just N of Grasmere on A591 Ambleside—Keswick; OS sheet 90 map reference 335089

The hard-working, friendly owners have now been running this bustling inn for 10 years – and are looking forward to the next decade. This year, they have refurbished the bar and games room using local stone for the floors and oak boards for the walls, and have created a lounge area with settles and upholstered armchairs and sofa benches; newspapers and magazines to read, a warming log fire, local watercolours and suggested walks and coast-to-coast information on the walls, and a relaxed atmosphere; piped classical music. Good bar food includes home-made soup (£2.95), sandwiches (from £3.25; open ones £6.25), cumberland sausage, bacon and mushroom skillet (£4.25), steak and kidney in ale pie (£7.25), thai vegetable curry (£7.95), steaks (from £11.95), daily specials such as chicken liver and chestnut pâté (£3.95), wild mushroom risotto and fresh asparagus spears (£6.25), honey-roasted gammon with peaches and plums or crispy skinned grey mullet with mange tout and orange sauce (£6.95), and roasted leg of Herdwick lamb with minted onions (£7.95), and home-made puddings such as sticky date and caramel pudding or a trio of chocolate puddings (£3.45). Well kept Greene King IPA, Jennings Bitter, Cumberland, and Sneck Lifter, and a guest such as Coniston Bluebird on handpump, and up to 20 malt whiskies. The games room is popular with families: darts, pool, fruit machine, TV, and dominoes. The restaurant is no smoking. This is a lovely spot with wonderful surrounding scenery and good walks, and there are picnic-sets in the side garden from which you can admire the marvellous views. As well as the telephone number listed below, they have a reservations number – 0870 0112152. *(Recommended by A S and P E Marriott, Richard Lewis, Dr Paull Khan, Roy and Margaret Jones, Jim Abbott, Peter and Anne-Marie O'Malley, Michael Doswell, Karen Eliot, W W Burke, Tina and David Woods-Taylor, Ian and Jane Irving, Mrs Romey Heaton, P Price, G J French)*

Free house ~ Licensees Lynne, Derek and Graham Sweeney ~ Real ale ~ Bar food (12-9.30; 12-3, 6-9.30 in winter) ~ (015394) 35604 ~ Children in eating area of bar and restaurant ~ Open 11-11; 12-10.30 Sun ~ Bedrooms: £32B/£64B

HAWKSHEAD NY3501 Map 9
Drunken Duck ★ 🍴 ♀ 🍺 🛏

Barngates; the hamlet is signposted from B5286 Hawkshead—Ambleside, opposite the Outgate Inn; or it may be quicker to take the first right from B5286, after the wooded caravan site; OS Sheet 90 map reference 350013

Civilised and friendly, this attractive 17th-c inn remains very popular with a large number of our readers. It is at its pubbiest at lunchtime when the food is simpler and there's a more informal, chatty atmosphere. Emphasis in the evening is on the restaurant-style meals enjoyed by residents relaxing after a day's touring or walking or by those out for a special occasion. The bar and snug are traditional beamed rooms with good winter fires, cushioned old settles and a mix of chairs on the fitted turkey carpet, pictures, cartoons, cards, fox masks, and cases of fishing flies and lures, and maybe the multi-coloured cat. All of the pub is no smoking except the bar. Good lunchtime food includes sandwiches on ciabatta such as hummous and grated carrot, smoked salmon, bacon and sour cream or hot fried chicken breast with caesar dressing (from £3.95), port and stilton pâté (£4.20), fish pie (£6.95), cumberland sausage with caramelised red onion and rosemary jus (£8.50), steak and red wine pie (£8.95), slowly roasted duck leg with basil and parmesan mash, whole roast red onion, and madeira gravy (£9.50), and puddings like baked white chocolate cheesecake with griottine cherries or lemon brûlée with citrus scented shortbread (from £3.95). Evening dishes such as mussels grilled with pesto, tomato concasse and parmesan shavings (£5.25), smoked haddock and chive risotto with extra virgin truffle oil (£5.50), stir-fried tiger prawns marinated in coriander, lime and chilli (£8), chargrilled red peppers and asparagus with sun-dried tomato polenta and grilled goats cheese (£8.95), herb-crusted lamb noisettes on leek purée and roast sweet potatoes, served with rosemary and redcurrant jus or fillet of cod served on fondant red peppers, sautéed potatoes and spring onions with a crab and saffron sauce (£11.95), and local Fellbred beef fillet on tomato and herb potatoes, watercress mousse, shallots and red wine jus (£15.95), with puddings such as nutty treacle torte with vermouth apples and clotted cream or poached pear set in blackberry jelly with lemon curd ice cream and poppy seed tuile (from £4.25). As well as Chesters Strong & Ugly, Cracker, and Tag Lag brewed in their cellar, they have Jennings Bitter and Yates Bitter on handpump; 25 malt whiskies, a dozen wines by the glass, and foreign bottled beers. Dominoes and cribbage. There are seats on the front verandah with stunning views and quite a few rustic wooden chairs and tables at the side, sheltered by a stone wall with alpine plants along its top; the pub has fishing in a private tarn behind. This is a super place to stay. *(Recommended by Ian Dawson, John and Joan Calvert, Mrs Romey Heaton, Nick Lawless, Tom McLean, Philip and Wendy McDonald, Les Brown, Richard Lewis, Giles and Liz Ridout, Margaret Dickinson, Walter and Susan Rinaldi-Butcher, J H Bell, Olive and Ray Hebson, David Field, Ewan and Moira McCall, Anne and Paul Horscraft, JDM, KM, John Knighton, G J French, Brian and Anna Marsden, Phil and Heidi Cook, Tracey and Stephen Groves)*

Own brew ~ Licensee Steph Barton ~ Real ale ~ Bar food (12-2.30, 6-9; not 25 Dec) ~ Restaurant ~ (015394) 36347 ~ Children welcome ~ Open 11.30-11; 12-10.30 Sun; closed evening 25 Dec ~ Bedrooms: £60B/£100B

Kings Arms ◗ 🛏

The Square

Set on the glorious main square, this inn has been welcoming travellers since Elizabethan times, and the present licensees have been here for over 21 years. The relaxed and informal bar is a friendly meeting place for both locals and visitors, with traditional pubby furnishings, low ceilings, and well kept Black Sheep, Coniston Bluebird, Theakstons, and Tetleys on handpump; lots of malt whiskies. Good bar food at lunchtime includes home-made soup (£2.35), sandwiches (from £2.75), mushrooms in a creamy garlic and tarragon sauce (£3.50), filled baked potatoes (£3.95), ploughman's (£5.25), mixed bean chilli (£5.50), and home-made steak in ale pie or fish and chips (£6.25); in the evening, there might be deep-fried prawns in filo pastry with hoisin dipping sauce (£3.50), game casserole in rich red wine and herb sauce (£6.50), grilled lamb chops with mint peso and ratatouille or baked organic Esthwaite trout with bacon and tomato salad (£7.95), steaks (from £9.25), and roast duck breast with parsnip purée and a damson jus (£9.50). As well as comfortable bedrooms, they offer self-catering cottages. *(Recommended by R C Vincent, Nick Lawless, Richard Butler, Marie Kroon, Mr and Mrs S Mason)*

Free house ~ Licensee Rosalie Johnson ~ Real ale ~ Bar food (12-2.30, 6-9.30; not evening 25 Dec) ~ Restaurant ~ (0153 94) 36372 ~ Children in eating area of bar and restaurant ~ Occasional one-man band or folk group ~ Open 11-11; 12-10.30 Sun ~ Bedrooms: £34(£39S)/£29(£34S)

HESKET NEWMARKET NY3438 Map 10
Old Crown ◗

Village signposted off B5299 in Caldbeck

One of the main draws to this relaxed and unfussy local is the particularly good, own-brewed real ales on handpump: Hesket Newmarket Great Cockup Porter, Skiddaw Special Bitter, Blencathra Bitter, Old Carrock Strong Ale, and Catbells Pale Ale. You can arrange to see the brewery on Wednesdays; also, traditional cider, and quite a few wines. Another speciality is the very popular evening curries (meaty ones £6.75 and vegetarian £6) – though they also offer sandwiches, mushroom, parsley and garlic soup with home-made bread (£2), ham and egg (£4.25), chicken, pheasant and apricot pie (£4.25), lamb casserole (£6), and roast Sunday lunch (£4.50). The dining room is no smoking. The little bar has a few tables, a coal fire, and shelves of well thumbed books, and a friendly atmosphere; juke box, darts, pool, shove-ha'penny, cribbage and dominoes. They have a self-catering cottage. The pub is in a pretty setting in a remote, attractive village. *(Recommended by David Cooke, Tracey and Stephen Groves)*

Own brew ~ Licensee Kim Mathews ~ Real ale ~ Bar food (12-3, 6.30-8.30; not Sun, Mon or Tues) ~ Restaurant ~ No credit cards ~ (016974) 78288 ~ Children welcome ~ Live entertainment 1st Sun of month ~ Open 12-3, 5.30-11; 12-3, 7-10.30 Sun; closed Mon and Tues lunchtimes

Pubs with attractive or unusually big gardens are listed at the back of the book.

HEVERSHAM SD4983 Map 9
Blue Bell
A6 (now a relatively very quiet road here)

Dating back to 1460, this partly timbered country hotel is civilised and comfortable and was originally a vicarage. The lounge bar has warm winter fires, pewter platters hanging from the beams, an antique carved settle, cushioned windsor armchairs and upholstered stools, and small antique sporting prints and a display cabinet with two stuffed fighting cocks on the partly panelled walls. One big bay-windowed area is divided off as a children's room, and the long, tiled-floor public bar has darts, pool, cribbage, dominoes, fruit machine, TV, and piped music. Decent bar food includes soup (£2.95), sandwiches (£2.95; open ones from £3.95), filled baked potatoes (from £3.95), lovely Morecambe Bay potted shrimps (£4.95), grilled fresh salmon with a tomato cream sauce (£6.95), roast guinea fowl with a raspberry sauce (£7.45), sizzling sirloin steak (£11.95), puddings (£2.95), daily specials, and children's menu (£4.95); they also do morning coffee and afternoon tea. The restaurant is no smoking. Well kept Sam Smiths OB on handpump kept under light blanket pressure, quite a few malt whiskies, and a fair wine list; helpful staff. Crossing over the A6 into the village itself, you come to a picturesque church with a rambling little graveyard; if you walk through this and on to the hills beyond, there's a fine view across to the estuary of the River Kent. The estuary itself is a short walk from the pub down the country road that runs by its side. *(Recommended by D Bryan, David Carr, W W Burke, Stephen Denbigh, Dr Paull Khan, SLC)*

Sam Smiths ~ Managers Susan and Richard Cowie ~ Real ale ~ Bar food (12-9.30) ~ Restaurant ~ (015395) 62018 ~ Children in eating area of bar and restaurant ~ Open 11-11; 12-11 Sun ~ Bedrooms: £49.50S/£66S

INGS SD4599 Map 9
Watermill ◀
Just off A591 E of Windermere

With story telling sessions on Tuesday evenings, a marvellous range of real ales, no piped music or noisy games machines, and a friendly welcome, it's not surprising that there's always a good mix of customers in this well run ivy-covered stone inn. Perfectly kept on handpump, there are up to 16 real ales: Black Sheep Special and Best, Coniston Bluebird, Jennings Cumberland, Lees Moonraker, and Theakstons Best and Old Peculier, with changing guests like Adnams Regatta, Batemans XXXB, Dent Ramsbottom, Fullers London Pride, Hop Back Summer Lightning, Hughes Dark Ruby Mild, Isle of Skye Young Pretender, Moorhouses Pendle Witches Brew, and Tomintoul Caillie; also, Hoegaarden wheat beer and Old Rosie scrumpy on draught, bottled beers, and up to 50 malt whiskies; thirsty dogs are kindly catered for, too, with a biscuit and bowl of water. The bars have a very friendly, bustling atmosphere, and a happy mix of chairs, padded benches and solid oak tables, bar counters made from old church wood, open fires, and on the wall amusing cartoons by a local artist. The spacious lounge bar, in much the same traditional style as the other rooms, has rocking chairs and a big open fire; two areas are no smoking. Enjoyable bar food includes lunchtime sandwiches, splendid home-made soup (£2.30), deep-fried crispy vegetables with a garlic dip (£3.85), home-made pâté (£3.95), Whitby haddock (£6.50), beef in ale pie (£6.95), cajun chicken (£7.80), lamb cutlets roasted in honey and coarse grain mustard (£9.95), steaks (from £11.25), and home-made daily specials such as thai fishcakes or spinach filled pancakes with a wild mushroom sauce glazed with mozzarella (£4), moroccan-style lamb and apricot tagine (£6.60), chicken, leek and smoked bacon pie (£6.80), sweet and sour pork (£6.95), and braised venison and chestnut casserole (£7). Darts, cribbage, and dominoes. There are seats in the front garden. Lots of climbing, fell-walking, fishing, boating of all kinds, swimming and pony-trekking within easy reach. Note that even residents cannot book a table for supper. *(Recommended by MLR, P Abbott, Hugh Roberts, Paul Boot, David and Barbara Knott, JDM, KM, Richard Lewis, Nick Lawless, Mr and Mrs D W Mitchell, Mrs S Miller, Jayne and Peter Capp, Paul Roughley, Julia Fox, Paul Fairbrother, Helen Morris, GD, KW)*

Free house ~ Licensees Alan and Brian Coulthwaite ~ Real ale ~ Bar food (12-2, 6.15-9) ~ (01539) 821309 ~ Children in eating area of bar ~ 1st Tues of month story telling club ~ Open 12-2.30, 6-11; 12-3, 6-10.30 Sun; closed 25 Dec ~ Bedrooms: £27S/£48B

KESWICK NY2623 Map 9
Dog & Gun
Lake Road; off top end of Market Square

Lively and unpretentious, this bustling pub remains a friendly place with a good, relaxed atmosphere. There are low beams, a partly slate floor (the rest are carpeted or bare boards), some high settles, a fine collection of striking mountain photographs by the local firm G P Abrahams, brass and brewery artefacts, coins in beams and timbers by the fireplace, and log fires. Well kept Theakstons Best, Old Peculier, and XB on handpump, and well liked bar food (with unchanged prices) such as home-made soup (£1.95), sandwiches (from £2.20), five bean chilli with garlic bread (£5.25), lamb curry or goulash (£5.75), baked Borrowdale trout (£6.25), and puddings (from £2.25). 25 malt whiskies, piped music. *(Recommended by Karen and Graham Oddey, Jim Abbott, SLC, Eric Locker, K Chard, Dick and Madeleine Brown, Richard Lewis, Vicky East)*

Scottish Courage ~ Manager Peter Ede ~ Real ale ~ Bar food (12-9) ~ (017687) 73463 ~ Children welcome until 9 ~ Open 11-11; 12-10.30 Sun

George ◖ 🛏
3 St Johns Street, off top end of Market Street

The bedrooms in this fine old inn have been refurbished this year and now all have their own bathrooms. There's an attractive traditional black-panelled side room with an interesting Wordsworth connection and good log fire, an open-plan main bar with old-fashioned settles and modern banquettes under Elizabethan beams, pleasant efficient staff, and daily papers. Well kept Jennings Bitter, Cumberland, Cocker Hoop, and Sneck Lifter on handpump, and enjoyable bar food such as sandwiches, home-made soup (£2.25), mussels cooked in white wine topped with pesto (small £3.95; large £7.25), fish and chips (£5.95), home-made chilli (£6.50), local cumberland sausage on minted mash with pickled red cabbage or mushroom strudel (£6.95), and daily specials like baked aubergine and sun-dried tomato tartlet (£7.95), fried chicken stuffed with goats cheese and parma ham served with a chunky tomato and roast garlic sauce (£9.95), and duckling with a spicy pear, ginger chutney, and a honey and calvados orange sauce (£11.95). The restaurant is no smoking; piped music, fruit machine, and dominoes. *(Recommended by Vicky and David Sarti, Mike and Bridget Cummins, H K Dyson, P and M Rudlin, Lesley Bass, Jim Abbott)*

Jennings ~ Managers Angela Fletcher and Peter Clarke ~ Real ale ~ Bar food (12-2.30, 6-9.30(10 Fri/Sat)) ~ Restaurant ~ (017687) 72076 ~ Children welcome away from bar ~ Open 11-11; 12-10.30 Sun ~ Bedrooms: £30B/£60B

KIRKBY LONSDALE SD6278 Map 7
Snooty Fox
Main Street (B6254)

Although a new licensee has taken over this rambling pub, we are happy to note that the interesting items on the walls in the various rooms, still remain: eye-catching coloured engravings, stuffed wildfowl and falcons, mounted badger and fox masks, guns and a powder-flask, stage gladiator costumes, and horse-collars and stirrups. The bar counters are made from English oak, as is some panelling, and there are also country kitchen chairs, pews, one or two high-backed settles and marble-topped sewing-trestle tables on the flagstones, mugs hanging from the beams, and two coal fires. Bar food now includes sandwiches, pork chops with apple compote (£5.95), steak and kidney pudding with red wine sauce (£6.95), cumberland sausage with mustard mash (£7.45), chicken stir fry (£7.50), a plate of seafood with herb cream (£7.95), breast of chicken stuffed with wild mushrooms (£8.95), and rib-eye steak (£10.95). The dining annexe is partly no smoking. Well kept Black Sheep, Theakstons Best, Timothy Taylors Landlord, and a guest such as Batemans XB, Greene King IPA or Oakham JHB on handpump, and several country wines; piped music and fruit machine. There are tables out in the pretty garden. *(Recommended by Malcolm Taylor, Paul S McPherson, Christine and Neil Townend, Clive Flower, David Carr, J F M and M West, Angus Lyon, Andrew and Ruth Triggs, Julian Heath, Mrs Pam Mattinson)*

Mortal Man Inns ~ Manager Stuart Rickard ~ Real ale ~ Bar food (12-2.30, 6.30-10; 12-9.30 Sun) ~ Restaurant ~ (01524) 271308 ~ Children in eating area of bar and restaurant ~ Open 11-11; 12-10.30 Sun ~ Bedrooms: £33S/£56S

LANGDALE NY2906 Map 9
Old Dungeon Ghyll 🍺

B5343

Full of character and atmosphere, this boisterous place is a real fell-walkers' and climbers' haven, and in the evening, the down-to-earth bar is full of heroic feats and the smell of drying clothes. There's no need to remove boots or muddy trousers, and you can sit on the seats in old cattle stalls by the big warming fire, and enjoy the well kept Black Sheep, Jennings Cumberland, Theakstons XB and Yates Bitter with guests such as Coniston Bluebird or Marstons Pedigree on handpump. The pub is in a marvellous position at the heart of the Great Langdale Valley and surrounded by fells including the Langdale Pikes flanking the Dungeon Ghyll Force waterfall; there are grand views of the Pike of Blisco rising behind Kettle Crag from the window seats cut into the thick stone walls; part of the bar is no smoking. Straightforward food includes lunchtime sandwiches (from £2.25), and dishes such as home-made soup (£2.25), game pie, lasagne, curry and chilli (all around £6.50); if you are not a resident and want to eat in the restaurant you must book ahead; friendly, helpful staff, darts and dominoes. It can get really lively on a Saturday night (there's a popular National Trust campsite opposite). They usefully open at 9am for breakfast. *(Recommended by SLC, Ewan and Moira McCall, MP, H K Dyson, Fred and Lorraine Gill, Mrs Romey Heaton, David Hoult, Dr Bob Bland, Michael Buchanan, Mrs S Miller, Nigel Woolliscroft)*

Free house ~ Licensee Neil Walmsley ~ Real ale ~ Bar food (12-2, 6-9) ~ Restaurant ~ (015394) 37272 ~ Children in eating area of bar ~ Open 11-11; 12-10.30 Sun; closed 22-26 Dec ~ Bedrooms: /£66S

LITTLE LANGDALE NY3204 Map 9
Three Shires 🍺

From A593 3 miles W of Ambleside take small road signposted The Langdales, Wrynose Pass; then bear left at first fork

The 'three shires' are Cumberland, Westmorland and Lancashire, which used to meet at the top of the nearby Wrynose Pass. From seats on the terrace there are lovely views over the valley to the partly wooded hills below Tilberthwaite Fells, with more seats on a well kept lawn behind the car park, backed by a small oak wood. The summer flowers regularly win competitions. The comfortably extended back bar has stripped timbers and a beam-and-joist stripped ceiling, antique oak carved settles, country kitchen chairs and stools on its big dark slate flagstones, Lakeland photographs lining the walls, and a warm winter fire in the modern stone fireplace with a couple of recesses for ornaments; an arch leads through to a small, additional area. Good bar food at lunchtime includes soup (£2.50), sandwiches (£3; baguettes £4.50), filled baked potatoes (£4.50), ploughman's (£5), cumberland sausage (£7.25), and beef in ale or fresh vegetable pies (from £7.50); in the evening, there might be rich game terrine with an apple and sultana compote (£4.95), grilled fillet of fresh salmon on a bed of spinach with rich Pernod and butter sauce (£8.50), chargrilled breast of chicken with sage and stilton sauce (£8.95), and daily specials like pasta with a wild mushroom cream, topped with toasted almonds (£7.95), roast loin of pork with a sage and fennel crust finished with honey and mustard sauce

(£8.25), and grilled fillet of sea bream on a bed of mediterranean-style vegetables with a light tomato sauce (£8.95); children's meals (£3.50). The restaurant and snug are no smoking. Well kept Coniston Old Man, Jennings Bitter, and a guest such as Black Sheep or Coniston Bluebird on handpump, quite a few malt whiskies, and a decent wine list; darts and dominoes. *(Recommended by Linda Montague, Ewan and Moira McCall, JDM, KM, Brian and Anna Marsden, Dr and Mrs J Hills, Tina and David Woods-Taylor)*

Free house ~ Licensee Ian Stephenson ~ Real ale ~ Bar food (12-2, 6-8.45; no evening meals Dec or Jan) ~ Restaurant ~ (015394) 37215 ~ Children welcome until 9 ~ Open 11-11; 12-10.30 Sun; 11-3, 8-10.30 midweek in winter; closed 25 and 26 Dec ~ Bedrooms: £33B/£72B

LOWESWATER NY1222 Map 9
Kirkstile Inn

From B5289 follow signs to Loweswater Lake; OS Sheet 89 map reference 140210

Between Loweswater and Crummock Water, this popular little country inn is surrounded by arresting peaks and fells; you can enjoy the view from picnic-sets on the lawn, from the very attractive covered verandah in front of the building, and from the bow windows in one of the rooms off the bar. The bar is low-beamed and carpeted, with a roaring log fire, comfortably cushioned small settles and pews, and partly stripped stone walls. New licensees again this year, and bar food now includes home-made soup (£2.50), baguettes (£3.50), filled baked potatoes (£3.95), ploughman's (£4.75), vegetarian lasagne (£5.95), home-made braised beef in ale or local cumberland sausage with apple purée (£6.25), gammon and egg (£6.50), lamb cobble with a warm herb scone (£6.95), and home-made puddings such as sticky toffee pudding or fruit crumble (£3); children's dishes (£3.25). Well kept Coniston Bluebird and Jennings Bitter and Cumberland on handpump; darts, cribbage, dominoes, and a slate shove-ha'penny board; a side games room called the Little Barn has pool. *(Recommended by John and Christine Lowe, H K Dyson, K Chard, R Huggins, D Irving, E McCall, T McLean, Stephen McNees, Dr Paull Khan)*

Free house ~ Licensees Roger and Helen Humphreys ~ Real ale ~ Bar food ~ Restaurant ~ (01900) 85219 ~ Children welcome ~ Occasional jazz ~ Open 11-11; 11-10.30 Sun ~ Bedrooms: £35B/£56B

MELMERBY NY6237 Map 10
Shepherds ★ ♀

About half way along A686 Penrith—Alston

There's a good bustling atmosphere in this very well run pub and a happy mix of locals and visitors – all welcomed by the friendly licensees. The bar is divided up into several areas; the heavy beamed no smoking room to the left of the door is carpeted and comfortable with bottles on the mantelbeam over the warm open fire, sunny window seats, and sensible tables and chairs, and to the right is a stone-floored drinking part with a few plush bar stools and chairs. At the end is a spacious room with a high-raftered ceiling and pine tables and farmhouse chairs, a woodburning stove, and big wrought-iron candelabra, and steps up to a games area with pool; darts, dominoes, fruit machine and juke box. Enjoyable food at lunchtime includes a vegetarian or meat based soup (£3), hot filled ciabatta bread (from £4.80), quiche of the day (£5.60), shepherd's pie (£5.20), various ploughman's with home-made rolls and their prize winning cheeses (£5.95), and shepherd's pie (£5.20), with weekly specials such as garlic mushrooms (£4.80), grilled sardines with caper and lemon butter (£5.20), chicken korma (£6.90), steak and kidney pie (£7.20), apricot stuffed chicken breast (£7.60), and cider braised halibut fillet (£9.20); daily roasts (£5.95), and puddings like lemon cheesecake or chocolate torrone (from £2.95); half helpings for children, and traditional Sunday roast. Much of the main eating area is no smoking. Well kept Jennings Cumberland and Dent T'Owd Tup and a couple of guests such as Black Sheep Bitter or Youngs Special on handpump, as well as over 50 malt whiskies, draught cider, a good wine list, country wines, and quite a few bottled continental beers. Hartside Nursery Garden, a noted alpine and primula plant specialist, is just over the Hartside Pass, and there are fine views across the green to the Pennines. *(Recommended by Malcolm Taylor, Tony and Wendy Hobden, John and Sylvia Harrop, Paul Fairbrother, Helen Morris, David Cooke, Mrs Pat Crabb, Richard J Holloway, Edward Watson, Mr and Mrs P Smith, MLR, R Davies, Andy and Jill Kassube)*

Free house ~ Licensee Martin Baucutt ~ Real ale ~ Bar food (10.30-2.30, 6-9.45; 12-2.30, 7-9.45 Sun; not 25 Dec) ~ Restaurant ~ 0870 745 3383 ~ Children in eating area of bar and restaurant ~ Occasional live entertainment Fri evening in winter ~ Open 10.30-3, 6-11; 12-3, 7-10.30 Sun; closed 25 Dec

NEAR SAWREY SD3796 Map 9
Tower Bank Arms ◖

B5285 towards the Windermere ferry

This was known as the small country inn in *The Tales of Jemima Puddleduck* and Beatrix Potter's Hill Top Farm (owned by the National Trust) backs on to the pub – so at peak times, unsurprisingly, it does get very busy. The low-beamed main bar has a fine log fire in the big cooking range, high-backed settles on the rough slate floor, local hunting photographs and signed photographs of celebrities on the walls, a grandfather clock, and good traditional atmosphere. Good bar food includes home-made soup (£2.25), lunchtime filled rolls (from £2.75) or ploughman's (from £4.35), Morecambe Bay potted shrimps (£4.50), cumberland sausage, home-made flan or a vegetarian dish of the day (£5.50), Whitby scampi (£6.75), wild boar and pheasant or game pies (£7.50), and duckling à l'orange (£7.75). Well kept Theakstons Best and Old Peculier, and weekly changing guest beers on handpump, as well as lots of malt whiskies, and Belgian fruit beers and other foreign beers; darts, shove-ha'penny, and dominoes. Seats outside have pleasant views of the wooded Claife Heights. This is a good area for golf, sailing, birdwatching, fishing (they have a licence for two rods a day on selected waters in the area), and walking, but if you want to stay at the pub, you'll have to book well in advance. *(Recommended by Giles and Liz Ridout, Nick Lawless, David Carr, Mrs Romey Heaton, Rona Murdoch, P Abbott, Tina and David Woods-Taylor)*

Free house ~ Licensee Philip Broadley ~ Real ale ~ Bar food (not 25 Dec) ~ Restaurant ~ (015394) 36334 ~ Children in eating area of bar lunchtime but in restaurant only in evenings ~ Open 11-3, 6-11; 12-3, 6-10.30 Sun; closed evening 25 Dec ~ Bedrooms: £37S/£52S

PENRITH NY5130 Map 10
Agricultural ◖

Castlegate; ¾ mile from M6 junction 40 – A592 into town, just off entrance roundabout

This is an excellent alternative to the M6 service areas – both as somewhere simple but comfortable to stay or for a good meal. The pub is carefully refurbished to retain much of its original charm and Victorian elegance, and has a bustling market town atmosphere. The comfortable L-shaped beamed lounge has partly glazed panelling, plenty of seating, a lovely log fire, curved sash windows over the bar, and a good down-to-earth local atmosphere with a thorough mix of customers. Jennings Bitter, Dark Mild, Cumberland, Cocker Hoop and Sneck Lifter on handpump are particularly well kept, and service from the chatty landlord is prompt and helpful; over 25 malt whiskies, and darts, dominoes, and piped music. At lunchtime, good bar food includes sandwiches (from £2.20; toasties from £2.60; baguettes from £3.05), baked potatoes (from £2.75), home-made soup with a sandwich (£3.10), as well as grilled black pudding on a bed of herb and onion mashed potato with mustard sauce (£2.95), cumberland sausage (£5.35), Whitby scampi (£5.90), home-made steak and kidney pie (£5.95), lamb marinated in honey, garlic and mint (£8.55), steaks (from £8.75), and daily specials like chicken and mushroom pie (£5.45), beef stroganoff (£6.95), and grilled fresh haddock with a mustard glaze (£7.45). The restaurant is no smoking. There are good views from the picnic-sets out at the side. *(Recommended by Andy Rudge, Peter Salmon, Mrs Roxanne Chamberlain, Andy and Jill Kassube)*

Jennings ~ Tenants Jim and Margaret Hodge ~ Real ale ~ Bar food (12-2, 6-8.30(9 Sat) ~ Restaurant ~ (01768) 862622 ~ Children in eating area of bar and restaurant ~ Open 11-11; 12-10.30 Sun ~ Bedrooms: £25/£40

SEATHWAITE SD2396 Map 9
Newfield Inn

Duddon Valley, nr Ulpha (ie not Seathwaite in Borrowdale)

The slate-floored bar here has a genuinely local and informal atmosphere, with wooden tables and chairs, and some interesting pictures, and well kept real ales such as Coniston Bluebird, Jennings Bitter, J W Lees Bitter, and Wells Bombardier on handpump. There's a comfortable side room and a games room with shove-ha'penny, cribbage, dominoes, and piped music. Good value bar food includes filled granary baguettes or proper home-made soup (£2.95), vegetarian dishes (£5.95), big cumberland sausages or home-made steak pie (£6.45), huge gammon steaks with free range eggs (£7.95), and daily specials such as mushroom pasta bake (£5.95), Chinese spare ribs (£6.95), and local Herdwick lamb (£8.95); one area is no smoking. Tables out in the nice garden have good hill views. The pub owns and lets the next-door self-catering flats. It is popular at weekends with climbers and walkers, and there are lovely views. *(Recommended by M Tempest, Karen and Graham Oddey, Rona Murdoch, A Preston)*

Free house ~ Licensee Paul Batten ~ Real ale ~ Bar food (12-9) ~ No credit cards ~ (01229) 716208 ~ Children in eating area of bar and restaurant ~ Open 11-11; 11-10.30 Sun

SEDBERGH SD6692 Map 10
Dalesman 🍺

Main St

The Dales Way and Cumbrian Cycle Way pass the door of this nicely modernised pub, and there are lots of walks of varying difficulty all around. Inside, the various rooms (one of which is no smoking) have quite a mix of decorations and styles – lots of stripped stone and beams, cushioned farmhouse chairs and stools around dimpled copper tables, and a raised stone hearth with a log-effect gas fire; also, horsebrasses and spigots, Vernon Stokes gundog pictures, various stuffed animals, tropical fish, and a blunderbuss. Through stone arches on the right a no smoking buttery area serves tasty food (with prices unchanged since last year) such as home-made soup (£2), filled rolls (from £2.50; toasties from £2.70), lots of baked potatoes with fillings like grilled bacon and tomatoes or chargrilled chicken with tangy barbecue sauce (£5), big breakfast (£6.90), home-made cumberland sausages, steak and kidney pie or 12oz gammon and egg (£7), spinach and ricotta chestnut parcel (£8.50), Aberdeen Angus steaks (from £11), daily specials, and Sunday roast (£6). Well kept Tetleys Bitter and Theakstons Best on handpump, and around 30 malt whiskies; dominoes and piped music. Some picnic-sets out in front, and a small car park. *(Recommended by Stan and Hazel Allen, Carol and Dono Leaman, Rita and Keith Pollard, Brian and Pat Wardrobe, Mike and Wendy Proctor)*

Free house ~ Licensees Michael Garnett and Graham Smith ~ Real ale ~ Bar food (12-2.30, 6-9.30) ~ Restaurant ~ (015396) 21183 ~ Children in eating area of bar and restaurant ~ Open 11-11; 12-10.30 Sun ~ Bedrooms: £30B/£60B

STAINTON NY4928 Map 10
Kings Arms

1¾ miles from M6 junction 40: village signposted from A66 towards Keswick, though quickest to fork left at A592 roundabout then turn first right

Handy for the M6, this pleasantly modernised, friendly pub has a neatly kept open-plan bar with a rather cosy feel. Also, leatherette wall banquettes, stools and armchairs around wood-effect tables, brasses on the black beams, and prints and paintings of the Lake District on the swirly cream walls; one room is no smoking during mealtimes. Enjoyable traditional bar food includes lunchtime snacks such as sandwiches (from £2.25; toasties from £2.65; open ones from £3.55), filled baked potatoes (from £3.75), and ploughman's (£4.35); also, home-made soup (£1.95), crispy mushrooms with garlic dip (£3.05), cumberland sausage with egg (£4.95), steak and kidney pie (£5.75), vegetarian lasagne (£6.25), sirloin steak (£9.95), daily specials, roast Sunday lunch, and puddings (£2.75). Well kept Castle Eden and summer guests like Theakstons Old Peculier and Wadworths 6X on handpump, and 20 malt whiskies; welcoming staff. Sensibly placed darts, dominoes, cribbage, scrabble, fruit machine (summer only), and piped music. There are tables on the side terrace, with more on a small lawn. *(Recommended by R W Slawson, Mrs P Gregory, Jack and Heather Coyle, Christine and Neil Townend, Brian and Lynn Young)*

Pubmaster ~ Tenants James and Anne Downie ~ Real ale ~ Bar food (not winter Mon exc bank hols) ~ No credit cards ~ (01768) 862778 ~ Children in eating area of bar if dining until 9 ~ Open 11.30-3, 6.30-11; 12-4, 7-10.30 Sun; closed Mon Oct-May exc bank hols

THRELKELD NY3325 Map 9

Salutation

Old main rd, bypassed by A66 W of Penrith

Walkers are fond of this down-to-earth, old-fashioned local, handsomely set below the fells and challenging brow of Blencathra. The low-beamed connecting rooms have simple furnishings, a roaring log fire, and Courage Directors, Ruddles Best, Theakstons Old Peculier, Best and Mild, and Youngers Scotch on handpump, and quite a few malt whiskies; the tiled floor is used to muddy boots. Bar food includes sandwiches (from £2.20), soup (£2.65; the leek is good), basket meals (from £4.15), large ploughman's (from £4.95), meaty or vegetarian lasagne, steak and mushroom pie or hungarian goulash (all £5.95), steaks (from £10.95), daily specials, and puddings like sticky toffee pudding (£2.95). The spacious upstairs children's room has a pool table and juke box (oldies); also, darts, cribbage, dominoes, fruit machine, TV, and piped music. They hope to have bedrooms next year. *(Recommended by Tina and David Woods-Taylor, James Nunns, Mrs S Miller, Olive and Ray Hebson, Michael Butler, Mel Swales, Neil Spink)*

Scottish Courage ~ Tenants Ian Leonard, Marian Burnip ~ Real ale ~ Bar food (12-2, 6-9) ~ Restaurant ~ (017687) 79614 ~ Children welcome ~ Open 11-3, 5.30-11; 11-11 Sat; 12-10.30 Sun; 12-2, 6.30-11 winter

TIRRIL NY5126 Map 10

Queens Head ★ ⦿ ⛉

3½ miles from M6 junction 40; take A66 towards Brough, A6 towards Shap, then B5320 towards Ullswater

Although this pub has many attributes, it's the genuinely warm and friendly welcome from the helpful staff that our readers comment on so often. Their beer also draws favour, and from their own little brewery in one of the old outhouses behind the pub, they brew Bewshers Best (after the landlord in the early 1800s who bought the inn from the Wordsworths and changed its name to the Queens Head in time for Victoria's coronation), Academy Ale, and Old Faithful, and keep guest beers such as Dent Aviator, and Jennings Cumberland on handpump; they also hold a popular Cumbrian Beer & Sausage Festival during August. Over 40 malt whiskies, a good choice of brandies and other spirits, a carefully chosen wine list. The oldest parts of the bar have original flagstones and floorboards, low bare beams, black panelling, high-backed settles, and a roomy inglenook fireplace (once a cupboard for smoking hams); the little back bar has a lot of character; piped music. At lunchtime, good bar snacks include baguettes (from £3.25; hot sirloin steak and fried onions £4.25), filled baked potatoes (from £3.95), pasta dishes (£3.75 or £7.50), stuffed pitta breads (from £4.25; peppered beef strips and cooling cucumber dip £4.95), ploughman's (from £5.50), chilli (£7.25), home-made pie of the day (£7.50),

chargrilled gammon and eggs (£7.75), OAP specials (from £4.75), and puddings
such as banoffi pie, chocolate crush or summer pudding (from £2.75). Also, home-
made soup (£2.50), steak in ale pudding or mediterranean carrot roll (£7.95),
Lakeland lamb shoulder in redcurrant gravy (£9.50), and daily specials such as
grilled black pudding on coarse grain mustard sauce (£2.95), thai fishcakes on
hollandaise sauce (£8.75), crab, spinach and cream cheese strudel (£8.95), and tuna
steak in lime and ginger butter (£9.25); the restaurant is no smoking. Pool, juke box,
and dominoes in the back bar. The pub is very close to a number of interesting
places, such as Dalemain House at Dacre. *(Recommended by Christine and Neil Townend,
Roger and Jenny Huggins, Tony Middis, Peter and Anne-Marie O'Malley, Dr Paull Khan,
Margaret and Roy Randle, Gwyneth and Salvo Spadaro-Dutturi, Dr and Mrs L Wade, Karen and
Graham Oddey, D Stephenson, Peter F Beever, Guy Vowles, Trish Carter, Charles Gysin, David
Cooke, Dr B and Mrs P B Baker, Richard Lewis, Tracey and Stephen Groves, J Roy Smylie,
D S Jackson)*

*Own brew ~ Licensee Colin Tomlinson ~ Real ale ~ Bar food (12-2, 6-9.30) ~
Restaurant ~ (01768) 863219 ~ Children in eating area of bar and in restaurant; for
accommodation, under 3, over 13 ~ Open 12-3, 6-11; 12-11 Sat; 12-10.30 Sun; closed
evening 25 Dec ~ Bedrooms: £35B/£50B*

TROUTBECK NY4103 Map 9
Queens Head ★ ⑪ ♀ ◖ ⇦
A592 N of Windermere

By the time this book is published, there will be two new dining areas here, built on
the site of the former kitchen (which will be rebuilt in the back car park), and six
new bedrooms. The dining rooms will also be somewhere you can drop into for a
casual drink, and will have oak beams and stone walls, an open fire, settles along big
tables, and similar décor to the existing bars. The big rambling original U-shaped bar
has a little no smoking room at each end, beams and flagstones, a very nice mix of
old cushioned settles and mate's chairs around some sizeable tables (especially the
one to the left of the door), and a log fire in the raised stone fireplace with horse
harness and so forth on either side of it in the main part, with a woodburning stove
in the other; some trumpets, cornets and saxophones on one wall, country pictures
on others, stuffed pheasants in a big glass case, and a stag's head with a tie around
his neck, and a stuffed fox with a ribbon around his. A massive Elizabethan four-
poster bed is the basis of the finely carved counter where they serve Boddingtons,
Coniston Bluebird, and Jennings Bitter, with guests such as Barngates Cracker, Dent
Ramsbottom and Timothy Taylors Landlord on handpump. Very good, imaginative
bar food includes light lunches such as a bowl of fresh mussels steamed with garlic
and herbs and finished with cream (£4.95), confit of chicken leg on braised cabbage
with roasted shallots or mixed bean and wild mushroom cassoulet served on pasta in
a rich butter sauce (£5.95), and peppered venison and redcurrant casserole with a
timbale of braised rice (£6.25), as well as soup with home-made bread (£2.75), wild
mushroom, stilton and black olive terrine served on sun-dried tomato dressed leaves
(£5.25), steak, ale and mushroom cobbler (£7.25), asparagus, courgette and spinach
mousse set on sautéed mange tout and cherry tomatoes with a smoked garlic cream
(£9.50), pieces of smoked haddock wrapped in filo pastry filled with a garlic cream
and baked on to a tomato compote (£13.25), and calves liver seared on to creamed
celeriac with a raspberry vinegar spiked jus (£14.25); puddings like sticky toffee
pudding with crème anglaise, chocolate truffle cheesecake with a Baileys cream or
mixed fruit parfait with fruit coulis (£3.75), and a thoughtful children's menu (from
£3); they also have a three-course menu £15.50); piped music. Seats outside have a
fine view over the Trout valley to Applethwaite moors. This is a very nice place to
stay, with excellent breakfasts – but check beforehand if you want an early start.
*(Recommended by John and Christine Lowe, Ian and Jane Irving, Philip and Wendy McDonald,
Karen and Graham Oddey, John McEver, R J Ruffell, Tim and Beryl Dawson, Richard Lewis,
Tracey and Stephen Groves, Derek Thomas, Phil and Heidi Cook, Tina and David Woods-Taylor,
Sarah and Peter Gooderham, RJH, A Piasecki, Dick and Madeleine Brown, Margaret and Roy
Randle, Ian Dawson, Simon J Barber, R N and M I Bailey, Paul Boot, Bob and Marg Griffiths,
Comus and Sarah Elliott, Revd D Glover, Peter and Anne-Marie O'Malley, Pierre)*

Free house ~ Licensees Mark Stewardson and Joanne Sherratt ~ Real ale ~ Bar food ~ Restaurant ~ (015394) 32174 ~ Children welcome ~ Open 11-11; 12-10.30 Sun; closed 25 Dec ~ Bedrooms: £51.50B/£75B

ULVERSTON SD2978 Map 7

Bay Horse 🍴 ♀

Canal Foot signposted off A590 and then you wend your way past the huge Glaxo factory

Standing on the water's edge of the Leven Estuary with views of both the Lancashire and Cumbrian fells, this civilised hotel was once a staging post for coaches that crossed the sands of Morecambe Bay to Lancaster in the 18th c. It's at its most informal at lunchtime when the good, imaginative bar food might include sandwiches (from £3.70; smoked chicken with curry mayonnaise and toasted coconut £3.95), home-made soup (£3.25), cheese platter with home-made biscuits and soda bread (£5.95), home-made herb and cheese pâté, savoury terrine or button mushrooms in a tomato, cream and brandy sauce on a peanut butter crouton (£6.25), smoked haddock and sweetcorn chowder served with hot garlic and paprika bread (£6.75), strips of chicken, leeks and button mushrooms on savoury rice with a sweet and sour sauce or braised lamb, apricot and ginger puff pastry pie (£8.50), flakes of smoked haddock and brandied sultanas cooked in a rich cheddar cheese sauce and served in a puff pastry case, venison burger with onion marmalade, and sage and apple sauce or smoked salmon, leek and waterchestnut quiche (£9), and home-made puddings (£4.50); it's essential to book for the restaurant. Well kept Jennings and Thwaites and a guest such as Greene King Old Speckled Hen on handpump, a decent choice of spirits, and a carefully chosen and interesting wine list with quite a few from South Africa. The bar has a relaxed atmosphere and a huge stone horse's head, as well as attractive wooden armchairs, some pale green plush built-in wall banquettes, glossy hardwood traditional tables, blue plates on a delft shelf, and black beams and props with lots of horsebrasses. Magazines are dotted about, there's a handsomely marbled green granite fireplace, and decently reproduced piped music; darts, bar billiards, shove-ha'penny, cribbage, and dominoes. The no smoking conservatory restaurant has fine views over Morecambe Bay (as do the bedrooms) and there are some seats out on the terrace. Please note, the bedroom price includes dinner as well. (Recommended by Jenny and Chris Wilson, A D Ryder, Ray and Winifred Halliday, John and Christine Lowe, Revd D Glover)

Free house ~ Licensee Robert Lyons ~ Real ale ~ Bar food (bar food lunchtime only; not Mon) ~ Restaurant ~ (01229) 583972 ~ Children in eating area of bar and in restaurant if over 12 ~ Open 11-11; 12-10.30 Sun ~ Bedrooms: /£170B

Farmers Arms 🍴 ♀ 🍺

Market Place

Right in the heart of Ulverston, and very much a focal part of town, this busy place has a wonderfully welcoming atmosphere – and an excellent choice of well above average food and drink. The building dates back to the 16th c, and is pretty much unchanged from the outside, but has been appealingly modernised and extended inside. The original fireplace and timbers blend in well with the more contemporary furnishings in the front bar – mostly wicker chairs on one side, comfortable sofas on the other; the overall effect is rather unusual, but somehow it still feels like the most traditional village pub. A table by the fire has newspapers, glossy magazines and local information, then a second smaller bar counter leads into a big raftered eating area, part of which is no smoking. Six swiftly changing well kept real ales on handpump, some chosen because they're local brews, others simply because they have amusing names; on our visit the choice included Coniston Ambleside, Eccleshall Slaters, Moorhouses Pendle Witches Brew and Theakstons Best. They specialise in carefully chosen New World wines, with around a dozen by the glass. The very good food includes excellent sandwiches or hot baguettes (usually available all day and made with their own bread) such as salami with mozzarella, olives and tomatoes, goats cheese and sweet pepper or chicken, brie and cranberry (£3.95), and main courses such as mushroom and sweet pepper stroganoff or peppered pork steak with a cajun and wild mushroom sauce and sweet paprika glaze (£6.95), and seared tuna fillet with spicy couscous and lemon and honey (£8.95); children's menu. They open early for a good choice of breakfasts and coffees. It's worth booking at busy times. In front is a very attractive terrace with plenty of good wooden tables looking on to the market cross, big heaters, and lots of colourful plants in tubs and hanging baskets (the landlord is a keen gardener). If something's happening in town the pub is usually a part of it: events range from weekly quiz nights to the world's largest gathering of pantomime ponies. They can be busy on Thursday market day. *(Recommended by Lee Potter, Mrs M Granville-Edge)*

Free house ~ Licensee Roger Chattaway ~ Real ale ~ Bar food ~ (01229) 584469 ~ Children welcome ~ Open 11(10 for breakfast)-11(10.30 Sun)

WASDALE HEAD NY1808 Map 9
Wasdale Head Inn 🏠

To NE of lake; long detour off A595 from Gosforth or Holmrook

Well away from the main tourist areas and surrounded by steep fells, this three-gabled mountain hotel makes an excellent base for walking and climbing. The high-ceilinged, spacious no smoking main bar has an old-fashioned country-house feel with its shiny panelling, cushioned settles on the polished slate floor, great George Abraham early mountaineering photographs on the walls, and a log fire. It's named for the first landlord, Will Ritson, who by his death in 1890 had earned the reputation of being the World's Biggest Liar for his zany tall stories. There's a comfortably old-fashioned residents' bar and lounge (the oak-panelled walls covered with photographs of ground-breaking climbs), snug and restaurant. Popular bar food includes sandwiches, soup (£2.20), cumberland sausage and black pudding, local Herdwick lamb, and steak in ale pie (£6.75). Lively, helpful staff, and up to nine well kept real ales on handpump such as Dent, Derwent Bitter, Hesket Newmarket Blencathra Bitter, Jennings Cumberland and Sneck Lifter, Yates Bitter, and others from local microbreweries; a decent choice of malt whiskies, and good wine list; dominoes, cribbage, chess and quoits. The drive below the plunging majestic screes by the lake is quite awesome. Besides the comfortable bedrooms, they offer well equipped self-catering accommodation; nice breakfasts. *(Recommended by Linda Montague, H K Dyson, Nigel Woolliscroft, Paul Thompson, Anna Blackburn, Peter Brueton, Dr Bob Bland, Mrs Jane Wyles; also in* The Good Hotel Guide*)*

Free house ~ Licensee Howard Christie ~ Real ale ~ Bar food (12-9(8 in winter)) ~ Restaurant ~ (019467) 26229 ~ Children allowed if well behaved ~ Open 11-11(10 in winter); 12-10.30 Sun ~ Bedrooms: £45B/£90B

WINTON NY7810 Map 10
Bay Horse £ 🏠

Just off A685, N of Kirkby Stephen

In a fine setting, this low white building has two simple, low-ceilinged rooms with Pennine photographs and local fly-tying, and well kept Black Sheep and beers from local breweries such as Border, Coniston, Dent, and Hambleton on handpump. Served by quick, friendly staff, the good, very reasonably priced bar food includes sandwiches (from £1), home-made soup (£1.65), steak and kidney pie or cumberland sausage (£3.75), vegetable and stilton bake or hot spiced breast of chicken (£6.50), sirloin steak (£9.50), daily specials such as pork fillet in orange sauce or tortellini with a tomato and basil sauce (£6.50), and puddings like rum and raisin pudding or sticky toffee pudding (£2.75); three-course Sunday lunch (£5.95). The dining room is no smoking; pool, darts, and dominoes. From the garden behind the inn (which is surrounded by farms and faces the village green), there are tables looking up to Winton and Hartley fells. *(Recommended by P T Sewell, Dr Paull Khan, Geoffrey and Brenda Wilson)*

Free house ~ Licensee Derek G Parvin ~ Real ale ~ Bar food (not Tues lunchtime) ~ (017683) 71451 ~ Children in eating area of bar ~ Open 12-2.30, 6.30-11; 12-4,

6.30-10.30 Sun; closed Tues lunchtimes; best to check wkdy lunchtimes in winter ~ Bedrooms: /£35B

YANWATH NY5128 Map 9

Gate Inn 🍽

2¼ miles from M6 junction 40; A66 towards Brough, then right on A6, right on B5320, then follow village signpost

An engaging combination of really good inventive food with the welcoming environment of an unpretentious village local, this remains a very popular and friendly entry in our *Guide*. The simple turkey-carpeted bar, full of chatting regulars, has a log fire in an attractive stone inglenook and one or two nice pieces of furniture and middle-eastern brassware among more orthodox seats; or you can go through to eat in a two-level no smoking restaurant. Carefully prepared, imaginative food might include home-made soup (£2.50), good 'black devils' (sliced black pudding with cream and peppercorn sauce £3.30), seafood pancake (£3.95), pies such as sweet potato or chicken and leek (£6.25), good fish pie (£6.75), much enjoyed steak baguette (£6.95), salmon and monkfish wrapped in parma ham with a creamy prawn sauce (£9.95), steaks (from £9.95), daily specials such as venison steak with mushroom and red wine sauce (£9.75) and breast of barbary duck with cranberry and orange sauce (£10.95), and puddings like sticky ginger pudding or rich chocolate pudding with hot chocolate fudge sauce (£3); friendly, helpful service. Well kept Hesket Newmarket Skiddaw Special Bitter and Theakstons Best on handpump, and a decent wine list; darts, dominoes, cribbage, and shove-ha'penny; the friendly border collie is called Domino and is good with children. There are seats on the terrace and in the garden. *(Recommended by Ian and Jane Irving, Richard J Holloway, Roger and Jenny Huggins, B, M and P Kendall, James Oliver, IHR, Christine and Neil Townend, Michael Doswell, Carol and Dono Leaman, Mrs S Miller, Malcolm Taylor)*

Free house ~ Licensees Ian and Sue Rhind ~ Real ale ~ Bar food ~ Restaurant ~ (01768) 862386 ~ Children welcome ~ Open 12-3, 6.30(6 Sat and Sun)-11(10.30 Sun); 12-2.30, 6.30-11 in winter

---

Lucky Dip

Besides the fully inspected pubs, you might like to try these Lucky Dips recommended to us and described by readers (if you do, please send us reports: www.goodguides.com).

Ambleside [NY4007]
☆ *Kirkstone Pass Inn* [A592 N of Troutbeck]: Splendid position and surrounding scenery – Lakeland's quaint highest inn; hard-working and very friendly licensees, lots of old photographs and bric-a-brac, two log fires, hearty food lunchtime and evening, well kept Jennings, good coffee, hot chocolate, mulled wine, daily papers; tables outside, three refurbished bedrooms *(LYM, Mrs S Miller, Tina and David Woods-Taylor)*
Arnside [SD4578]
Albion [Promenade]: Popular Thwaites corner local included for its great views over estuary to Lakeland mountains from bar and tables outside; pleasant atmosphere, good simple food *(Pat and Clive Sherriff)*
Bardsea [SD3074]
Bradylls Arms: Particularly welcoming landlady, plush refurbishment, some stripped stone, wide choice of good home-made food from sandwiches to fresh seafood, children's menu, popular richly decorated back conservatory restaurant with lovely Morecambe

Bay views, well kept Flowers IPA; garden with play area, very attractive village nr sea; open all day Sun *(David Carr, Jenny and Brian Seller, BB)*
Bassenthwaite [NY2228]
Sun [off A591 N of Keswick]: Opened-up rambling bar with low 17th-c beams, two big log fires, good choice of well kept Jennings ales, usual food, interesting local photographs, friendly service, pool; provision for children, tables in pretty front yard looking up to the fells *(David Cooke, LYM, Michael Butler)*
Blencogo [NY1948]
☆ *New Inn* [signed off B5302 Wigton—Silloth]: Must book for fine choice of very good food – real serious cooking, yet at sensible prices – in bright and simply modernised former village local, log fire, real ale, decent wines and whiskies, a few big Cumbrian landscapes, pleasant service; cl Mon *(Mrs Jane Wyles, BB)*
Boot [NY1700]
Brook House: Converted small Victorian hotel with wide choice of good generous home-cooked food on solid timber tables, small plush

bar, comfortable hunting-theme lounge, log fires, well kept Black Sheep and Theakstons, friendly service, good views; handy for Ravenglass railway and great walks, good bedrooms *(S C Cowell)*

Borrowdale [NY2515]
Borrowdale Hotel [B5289, S end of Derwentwater]: A hotel, but very good choice of reasonably priced 'pub lunch' food from sandwiches up, roomy bar, pleasant staff, tables in garden; bedrooms *(Lord Sandhurst)*

Bowness-on-Windermere [SD4097]
☆ *Hole in t' Wall* [Lowside]: Ancient beams, stripped stone, lots of country bric-a-brac and old pictures, splendid log fire under vast slate mantelpiece, upper room with attractive plasterwork (and dominoes and juke box), reasonably priced bar food from sandwiches to steak, well kept Robinsons Frederics, Best and Hatters Mild, may be home-made lemonade or good winter mulled wine; very busy in tourist season; sheltered seats in tiny flagstoned front courtyard *(Richard Lewis, Jayne and Peter Capp, Alan Thomas, Giles and Liz Ridout, Mike and Wendy Proctor, LYM, P Abbott)*

Braithwaite [NY2324]
☆ *Coledale Hotel* [signed off A66 W of Keswick, pub then signed left off B5292]: Bustling inn perfectly placed at the foot of Whinlatter Pass, fine views of Skiddaw, winter coal fire, little 19th-c Lakeland engravings, plush banquettes and studded tables, well kept Jennings, Theakstons XB, Yates and Youngers; darts, dominoes, piped music, hearty food, no smoking dining room; garden with slate terrace and sheltered lawn, pretty bedrooms, open all day *(Karen and Graham Oddey, Stephen McNees, Betsy and Peter Little, LYM, Michael Butler, Tracey and Stephen Groves, DC)*

Brigsteer [SD4889]
☆ *Wheatsheaf*: Cosy traditional pub in quiet village, comfortable atmosphere, well presented food from good if not cheap sandwiches to plenty of fish, local ostrich and good value Sun lunch, mid-week lunchtime bargains, welcoming efficient staff, well kept Boddingtons, Theakstons and guests such as Coach House Coachmans and Ridleys IPA, good wines; country views *(Michael Doswell, Mrs B Cadman, Malcolm Taylor, Margaret Dickinson)*

Brough Sowerby [NY7913]
Black Bull: Spacious beamed bar, clean and comfortable, with friendly licensees, Jennings beer, wide choice of beautifully presented food from good sandwiches up, warm fire, small separate dining room *(R L Gorick)*

Broughton-in-Furness [SD2187]
☆ *Manor Arms* [The Square]: 18th-c inn with six well kept changing ales mixing interesting microbrews with the nationals; good sandwiches, comfortable relaxed atmosphere even when busy, friendly owners and locals, pool table; well appointed good value bedrooms, big breakfast *(H K Dyson, Dr B and Mrs P B Baker)*

Burton-in-Kendal [SD5376]
☆ *Dutton Arms* [4 miles from M6 junction 35;

just off A6070 N of Carnforth (and can be reached – unofficially – from M6 northbound service area between junctions 35 and 36)]: Stylishly refurbished popular pub/restaurant with two well kept real ales in very small smartly comfortable pre-meal bar, roomy two level restaurant, partly no smoking, dark tables, hop bines, grand piano, wide choice of good food from baguettes (not cheap) to imaginative hot dishes (the vegetarian ones tempt even meat eaters), well chosen wines, good young staff, log fire, toys for children; smallish back garden with play area and view of Virgin trains; new bedrooms, open all day Sun and summer wkdys *(Michael Doswell, Margaret Dickinson, BB)*

Buttermere [NY1817]
☆ *Fish*: Spacious, fresh and airily refurbished former coaching inn on NT property between Buttermere and Crummock Water, wide range of good value generous food from fresh sandwiches to delicious fish, well kept Jennings, Theakstons XB and guest beers, friendly service, fine views, tables out on terrace; can get crowded; bedrooms *(BB, Dick and Madeleine Brown)*

Cartmel [SD3879]
Cavendish Arms [Cavendish St, off main sq]: Scottish & Newcastle pub with open fire, well kept ales, no smoking restaurant, children welcome; tables out in front and behind by stream, comfortable bedrooms, good walks, open all day *(Mike Tucker, MLR, John and Christine Lowe, Margaret Dickinson, LYM, Paul Boot, Lord Sandhurst)*
☆ *Kings Arms* [The Square]: Picturesque and inviting, nicely placed at the head of the attractive town square – rambling and neatly kept heavy-beamed bar, mix of furnishings from traditional settles to banquettes, usual generous bar food and no smoking restaurant all day, reasonable prices, good friendly service and attentive landlord, two well kept real ales, children welcome (get lollipops), seats out on square and in attractive back part by beck; teashop, craft and gift shop upstairs *(Mary Belshaw, Margaret Dickinson, LYM, John Foord)*
Pig & Whistle: Friendly well run local with adjoining bistro, well kept beers, good well priced food *(David Field)*
Royal Oak [The Square]: Tastefully refurbished, with low ceilings, cosy nooks, generous good value food from baguettes up, well kept real ales such as Wadworths 6X, friendly helpful service; nice big garden, bedrooms *(Margaret Dickinson, BB)*

Cockermouth [NY1231]
☆ *Trout* [Crown St]: Solid old fishing hotel with pink plush sofas, captain's chairs and open fire in comfortable and friendly bar reached through other public rooms, good bar food from good sandwiches up (large or small helpings), well kept Jennings Cumberland, Marstons Pedigree and Theakstons Best, over 50 malt whiskies, decent wines, freshly squeezed juices, friendly helpful staff; coffee lounge and comfortable restaurant (best to book Sun lunch) both no smoking; shame

about the piped music; nice gardens down to river, children welcome, good bedrooms, fishing courses in season *(Peter and Pat Frogley, LYM, David Field, Dr W V Anderson)*

Crooklands [SD5384]

Crooklands Hotel [A65/B6385, nr M6 junction 36]: Big Best Western hotel dating from 16th c, pleasant pubby bar with good atmosphere, exposed brick and stonework, comfortable chairs and settles, log fires, Theakstons Best, pleasant staff, snug brick-floored second bar, good value straightforward food at sensible prices in intimate stable-theme carvery and romantic upstairs bistro, afternoon teas, games area with pool; good new shop doing local produce and crafts (normal shop hours only), comfortable bedrooms *(Margaret Dickinson, BB)*

Dacre [NY4626]

Horse & Farrier [between A66 and A592 SW of Penrith]: Pleasant 18th-c village pub with jovial landlord, friendly helpful staff, generous good value straightforward food in dining extension, particularly well kept Bass and a guest beer, quiz night; integral post office *(D R and A J Linnell, Peter F Beever, David Cooke)*

Dockray [NY3921]

☆ *Royal* [A5091, off A66 W of Penrith]: Bright open-plan bar in great spot, wide choice of good food from lunchtime rolls and baked potatoes up, children's helpings, friendly helpful service, well kept Black Sheep, Boddingtons, Castle Eden, Jennings Cumberland, Theakstons and Timothy Taylors Landlord, decent wines by the glass, two dining areas (one no smoking), walkers' part with stripped settles on flagstones; darts, cribbage and dominoes; piped music; picnic-sets in garden; open all day, comfortable bedrooms, good breakfast *(Ken Richards, Richard J Holloway, Brian Wall, Peter and Anne-Marie O'Malley, LYM, Peter F Beever)*

Durdar [NY4051]

☆ *Black Lion* [from M6 junction 42 follow Dalston sign]: Generous well presented home-made food, well kept Theakstons Best, pleasant staff, no smoking room, all extremely clean; handy for Carlisle racecourse *(Mike and Penny Sutton)*

Ennerdale Bridge [NY0716]

Shepherds Arms: Friendly village inn with good substantial food inc children's in spacious dining bar with polished wood floor, cheerful service, well kept Courage Directors, Jennings, Theakstons Best and XB, decent coffee; bedrooms – on coast-to-coast path, by car-free dale great for walkers, with weather forecast blackboard *(Tina and David Woods-Taylor, Lord Sandhurst)*

Eskdale Green [NY1300]

Bower House [½ mile W]: Civilised old-fashioned stone-built inn popular with older people, good log fire (when they light it) in main lounge bar extended around beamed and alcoved core, well kept Coniston Bluebird, Hartleys XB, Hesket Newmarket Cat Bells, Jennings and Theakstons XB, bar food, no noisy machines (but may be piped music), no

smoking restaurant; nicely tended sheltered garden by cricket field, charming spot, bedrooms, open all day *(LYM, Rona Murdoch, Bob and Val Collman, Pat and Clive Sherriff, Tina and David Woods-Taylor)*

Foxfield [SD2185]

Prince of Wales [opp stn]: Friendly and homely, with wide choice of well kept ales inc beers brewed in the former stables here and at the Tigertops brewery down in Wakefield (same owners), enthusiastic licensees, enjoyable home-made food wknds, open fire, pub games, papers and beer-related reading matter; children very welcome, games for them; cl Mon, bedrooms planned *(Gill and David Weild, Richard Lewis, Dr B and Mrs P B Baker)*

Gosforth [NY0703]

Horse & Groom [towards Santon]: Well kept Jennings and Tetleys, good food from Swiss chef/landlord *(H K Dyson)*

Lion & Lamb: Thriving local with well kept John Smiths, Theakstons Best and guest beers, enjoyable food; tables outside, open all day *(H K Dyson)*

Grasmere [NY3406]

☆ *Swan* [A591]: Upmarket hotel but individual and relaxed even when busy, with friendly service, lively little public bar, quieter old-fashioned lounge popular with older people (children allowed here), oak beams, armchairs, velvet curtains, prints and swords, inglenook log fires; varied reasonably priced well prepared food in bar and restaurant, keg beers but good malt whiskies and coffee; terrace tables in garden, picturesque surroundings, drying room for walkers; easy parking, open all day, comfortable bedrooms *(Richard Lewis, LYM, Canon David Baxter)*

Wordsworth Hotel [in village]: Well kept and stylish hotel with huge choice at good buffet lunch in very comfortable surroundings, also cheerful separate Dove & Olive Branch bar with log fire and well kept ales inc Tetleys; conservatory, nice garden, comfortable bedrooms *(LYM, T D Surgenor)*

Great Salkeld [NY5536]

Highland Drove: Neatly kept old inn doing well under friendly and helpful father-and-son licensees, large dining area, innovative food based on local produce, fish and game, Black Sheep, Theakstons and a monthly guest beer *(David Cooke, Kevin Tea)*

Great Urswick [SD2674]

☆ *General Burgoyne* [Church Rd]: Flagstoned early 18th-c village pub overlooking small tarn; four small cosy rambling rooms with log fires, bustling cheerful country atmosphere, lots of mugs and glasses hanging from beams, friendly efficient service, good generous food, Hartleys beers; board games, piped music *(Margaret and Roy Randle, BB)*

Hawkshead [SD3598]

☆ *Queens Head* [Main St]: Bustling dining pub, bow-tied barmen in red plush low-beamed and panelled bar, open fire, shiny brasses, no smoking snug, decent bar food and restaurant meals, well kept Hartleys XB and Robinsons Bitter, Frederics and Mild, dominoes, cribbage;

piped music, children in eating areas and snug,
open all day; good bedrooms *(Angus Lyon,
John and Sarah Perry, Mrs J Walker, Margaret
Dickinson, LYM, Bernard Stradling)*

Hayton [NY5157]

Lane End [A69 Carlisle—Brampton]: Well run
rather foody stone-built pub with pleasant
softly lit low-beamed bar, rugs on flagstones,
banquettes and settles, roaring log fire, good
bustling atmosphere, welcoming service, wide
choice of good value food from sandwiches up,
well kept Jennings, good coffee, dining room
and attractive conservatory restaurant; pool
room, piped music; open all day, play area
(Audrey and Derek Lambert, Michael Doswell)

Kendal [SD5192]

Globe [Market Pl]: Compact town pub, lively
but civilised, with carpeted beamed split-level
bar, pleasant décor, good popular
straightforward bar food and more ambitious
evening menu, well kept Thwaites ales, friendly
attentive service, short list of well chosen wines
at keen prices, separate dining room upstairs
(where children welcome) *(Michael Doswell,
Janet and Peter Race)*

Keswick [NY2623]

Lake Road Inn [Lake Rd]: Straightforward
two-room Victorian town pub with well kept
Jennings Bitter, Cumberland and Sneck Lifter,
usual food, informal service; tables in small
sheltered courtyard with converted stables,
open all day wknds and summer wkdys *(Peter
and Pat Frogley)*

☆ *Pheasant* [Crosthwaite Rd (A66, a mile out)]:
Small friendly beamed local with lots of
customer cartoons, good value generous food
(esp ham and eggs) lunchtime and early
evening, fast service, consistently well kept
Jennings beers, no smoking dining room;
children if eating; bedrooms, nr ancient church
of St Kentigern *(P and M Rudlin, Ian Dawson,
Olive and Ray Hebson)*

☆ *Swinside* [only pub in Newlands Valley, just
SW; OS Sheet 90 map ref 242217]: Attractive
neatly modernised but rustic and rambling pub
very popular for good reasonably priced freshly
made food from sandwiches, baguettes or soup
and warm rolls up in bar and restaurant, well
kept Jennings beers, decent wines, good log
fires, welcoming service, family room; dogs
allowed, plenty of tables outside with play area,
open all day Sat and summer; bedrooms,
peaceful valley setting, stunning views of crags
and fells *(Michael Butler, Dick and Madeleine
Brown, Jim Abbott, LYM, H K Dyson, David
Cooke, DC, Tina and David Woods-Taylor)*

Kirkby Lonsdale [SD6278]

☆ *Sun* [Market St (B6254)]: Bustling rambling
low-beamed and partly stripped-stone bar, one
room no smoking, cosy pews, good winter fires,
well kept Black Sheep, Boddingtons, Dent and a
guest beer, lots of malt whiskies, bar food;
piped music; bedrooms *(Darly Graton, Graeme
Gulibert, Andrew and Ruth Triggs, Julian
Heath, David Carr, Shaun Pinchbeck, LYM)*

Kirkoswald [NY5641]

Crown: Friendly recently renovated 16th-c
coaching inn, beams covered with plates,

brasses around fireplace, teapots over bar, good
generous home-cooked usual food using local
produce and fish, pleasant service, well kept
Jennings ales *(Neil and Anita Christopher,
Kevin Tea)*

Langdale [NY2906]

Stickle Barn [by car park for Stickle Ghyll]:
Lovely views from café-style walkers' and
climbers' bar, good choice of food inc packed
lunches, well kept Scottish Courage beers, small
no smoking area, mountaineering photographs;
fruit machines, TV, piped music; big pleasant
terrace, open all day; bunkhouse
accommodation, live music in loft *(Brian and
Lynn Young)*

Metal Bridge [NY3564]

Metal Bridge Hotel [off A74 Carlisle—Gretna,
nr Rockcliffe]: Friendly staff, decent bar food,
good choice of Scottish Courage beers, nice
river view from sun lounge *(Mike and Lynn
Robinson)*

Mungrisdale [NY3630]

☆ *Mill Inn* [off A66 Penrith—Keswick, a bit over
a mile W of A5091 Ullswater turn-off]:
Delightfully placed pub neatly cleaned up by
experienced new licensees (also run the
Agricultural in Penrith), enjoyable food in bar
and separate no smoking restaurant, well kept
Jennings Bitter and Cumberland, good choice
of wines by the glass and malt whiskies, helpful
service, games room; children and walkers
welcome, open all day, tables on gravel
forecourt and neat lawn sloping to little river,
warm pleasant bedrooms (note that there's a
quite separate Mill Hotel here) *(Mike and
Penny Sutton, LYM, Nick Lawless, Alan
Sutton)*

Nenthead [NY7843]

Crown [Overwater]: Cosy relaxing bar, well
kept Jennings and a guest ale, friendly landlord,
wife cooks interesting food from imaginative
vegetarian dishes to great steaks, lots of fresh
veg, elegant no smoking dining room, good
wines; no children or dogs, cl Tues *(Mrs Laurie
Humble, Mr and Mrs D Logan, Anthony and
Elizabeth Hartnett)*

Miners Arms: Friendly and unpretentious
family-run pub, good genuine home cooking,
reasonable prices, Jennings Cumberland and
guest beers from afar such as Tisbury
Stonehenge and Woodfordes Wherry, no piped
music; homely family bedrooms, filling
breakfasts, also bunkhouse *(Anthony Barnes)*

Newby Bridge [SD3786]

Swan: Fine setting below fells next to river with
waterside picnic-sets under cocktail parasols by
old stone bridge, good atmosphere in large
hotelish bar (can get very busy) with all sorts of
nooks and crannies, decent food from
sandwiches (not cheap) to Sun roasts, well kept
Boddingtons, efficient staff; bedrooms *(Chloe
and Robert Gartery, Meg and Colin Hamilton,
Eddie Edwards)*

Outgate [SD3599]

☆ *Outgate Inn* [B5286 Hawkshead—Ambleside]:
Attractively placed and very hospitable country
pub with three pleasantly modernised rooms,
well kept Robinsons Bitters, Frederics and

Hartleys XB, usual food inc sandwiches; trad jazz Fri, open all day wknds, comfortable bedrooms *(SLC, BB)*

Patterdale [NY3916]

White Lion: Cheerful bar with a captive market of walkers and climbers (can be crowded wknds), well kept ales inc Castle Eden, food inc speciality flaming steaks in long narrow room on left; bedrooms *(Dick and Madeleine Brown, Mr and Mrs Maurice Thompson)*

Penruddock [NY4327]

☆ *Herdwick* [off A66 Penrith—Keswick]: Recently refurbished cottagey 18th-c inn, neat and well cared for, with emphasis on consistently good well priced food esp Sun roast and good fresh veg, good atmosphere, welcoming fast service, well kept Tetleys from unusual curved bar, cosy atmosphere, stripped stone, attractive restaurant with upper gallery (worth booking evenings), pool room; five bedrooms *(Mike and Penny Sutton, Mr and Mrs P Smith, Charles Gysin, BB)*

Port Carlisle [NY2462]

Hope & Anchor: Bright, cheerful and lively, popular with locals and holiday-makers, attractively priced straightforward food, Jennings ales *(John and Kathleen Potter)*

Ravenglass [SD0894]

Ratty Arms: Ex-railway bar in main line station (a bit of a trek from the narrow-gauge steam railway) with well kept real ales, interesting food, good value restaurant, service friendly and efficient even when busy; pool table in busy public bar; open all day wknds and summer *(LYM, Gordon Neighbour)*

Ravenstonedale [NY7204]

☆ *Black Swan* [just off A685 Kirkby Stephen to M6]: Hotel bar with open fire and some stripped stone, for sale early 2001; has had real ales such as Black Sheep, Jennings and Timothy Taylors Landlord, country wines, good set food inc some interesting dishes, friendly staff; dogs welcome, tables in charming tree-sheltered streamside garden over road; comfortable bedrooms inc some for disabled, good serious walking country *(Margaret Dickinson, Mike Tucker, BB)*

Fat Lamb [Crossbank; A683 Sedbergh—Kirkby Stephen]: Remote inn with pews in cheerfully modernised bar, log fire in traditional black kitchen range, good local photographs and bird plates, friendly staff, well kept Tetleys, food from filled baguettes to restaurant meals; facilities for disabled, children really welcome; comfortable bedrooms with own bathrooms, tables out by sheep pastures, good walks *(Abi Benson, BB, Margaret Dickinson)*

Rosthwaite [NY2615]

☆ *Scafell* [B5289 S of Keswick]: Good base for area, in beautiful tranquil spot, plain slate-floored fairly modern-feeling bar in back extension, with separate entrance and a few tables out overlooking beck, well kept Theakstons Best and XB, log fire, good value usual food, children's helpings of most dishes; friendly helpful service even when packed with walkers (weather forecasts up on a board); afternoon teas, piped music, pool; hotel has

appealing cocktail bar/sun-lounge and dining room; bedrooms not big but good *(David Heath, H K Dyson, BB)*

Sandford [NY7316]

Sandford Arms [just off A66 W of Brough]: Immaculate 18th-c former farmhouse in peaceful village, beams and stripped stone, well kept Black Sheep and Theakstons, decent wines, friendly new owners, good food freshly made using local ingredients, pretty dining room; well equipped bedrooms, fishing on River Eden *(Michael Doswell)*

Scales [NY3427]

☆ *White Horse* [A66 W of Penrith]: Cheerful new Irish landlord in light and airy beamed pub-restaurant with cosy corners, interesting farmhouse-kitchen memorabilia and good open fires, well kept Jennings ales, wide choice of good food inc some local specialities; a couple of no smoking tables, well behaved children welcome (over 5 evening), lovely setting below Blencathra *(Mike and Penny Sutton, LYM)*

Seatoller [NY2414]

☆ *Yew Tree:* Restaurant rather than pub, with well presented imaginative food inc local specialities in attractive low-ceilinged restaurant at foot of Honister Pass, good choice of whiskies and wines in cosy beamed and slate-floored back bar with open range and wonderful collections from old police hats through cameras to antique scales, garden behind; can get crowded, but efficient friendly staff *(Miss D V Tindale)*

Sedbergh [SD6692]

Red Lion [Finkle St (A683)]: Cheerful beamed Jennings local, comfortable and friendly, with their full beer range kept well, good value generous tasty food, helpful service, coal fire *(BB, Margaret Dickinson)*

Shap [NY5615]

Greyhound [A6, S end]: Doing well under current management (ex-lecturers from local college), friendly, bustling and unpretentious, with good unfussy food in bar or restaurant, real ales inc Wadworths 6X, really quick attentive service; bedrooms, popular with coast-to-coast walkers *(David Cooke)*

Southwaite [NY4046]

Crown [away from village, towards Gaitsgill]: Very welcoming, with good cheap food from sandwiches and home-made soup up, Theakstons and guest beers, open fire, recent dining room extension; handy for Carlisle races *(David Cooke)*

Spark Bridge [SD3185]

☆ *Royal Oak* [off A5092 N of Ulverston]: Large popular riverside food pub with good food (all day Sun, with well-priced two-course lunch) inc wonderful steaks and interesting specials, good children's menu, relaxed informal atmosphere in beamed and carpeted bar, friendly service, well kept Marstons Pedigree and Tetleys, decent house wines, open fire; large pool room, small garden *(Chris Macandrew, Doug Christian, BB)*

Staveley [SD4798]

☆ *Eagle & Child* [off A591 Windermere—Kendal]: Sensitively refurbished two-bar pub with good home-made food inc fresh fish and veg, imaginative dishes, thoughtful provision for children and generous Sun lunch, well kept Jennings Cumberland and guests such as Barngates Chesters and Black Sheep, farm cider, attentive friendly service; small neat riverside garden, comfortably renovated bedrooms, good breakfast *(BB, Jim Gardiner, Jackie Moffat, MLR)*

Stonethwaite [NY2613]

☆ *Langstrath* [Borrowdale]: Welcoming, neat and clean rather upmarket pub with decent bar food, well kept Black Sheep, Jennings and Theakstons, lots of malt whiskies, enthusiastic landlord, good service, open fires; quite separate restaurant; delightful peaceful village, pleasant good value bedrooms, great views *(H K Dyson, Alan Thomas)*

Talkin [NY5557]

☆ *Blacksmiths Arms*: Welcoming bustle, good generous food in bar or informal dining room inc fresh fish and popular cheap Sun lunch (booking advisable), attentive service, well kept Black Sheep and Theakstons, open fire, local pictures; unobtrusive piped music, fruit machine; five comfortably refurnished bedrooms, prettily set village nr good walks *(Ken Richards, Alan Clark, Alun Llewellyn, LYM)*

Tebay [NY6204]

Cross Keys [very handy for M6 junction 38]: Comfortable roadside pub with plentiful tasty food in separate eating area, prompt polite service, well kept beer, decent wine, coal fire, darts, pool, cribbage; bedrooms *(Mrs C Gray, Abi Benson)*

Thirlspot [NY3217]

☆ *Kings Head* [A591 Grasmere—Keswick]: Well refurbished beamed bar, long and low, with inglenook fires, wide choice of food inc fresh fish and good puddings in no smoking eating area (they look after special dietary needs), well kept Jennings, Theakstons Best, XB and Mild, Yates and a guest ale, fast service, tables in garden, games room with pool; piped music; children welcome, with toy box; good spot, good value bedrooms (the hotel part and restaurant are separate) *(LYM, P and J Shapley, Mr and Mrs M Cross, Alina Bibby)*

Threlkeld [NY3325]

☆ *Horse & Farrier*: Comfortably enlarged 17th-c dining pub, roomy, warm and pleasant, with hunt cartoons, imaginative rather restauranty food, three well kept Jennings ales, good house

wines, good welcoming service, plenty of space for drinkers; open all day, dogs allowed when restaurant is closed *(James Nunns, Gerald and Valerie Popper, Mel Swales, Mike Cowley, Helen Coster, IHR, J M Hill)*

Torver [SD2894]

☆ *Church House* [A593/A5084 S of Coniston]: Cheerfully civilised low-beamed bar, keen staff, splendid hill views (if weather allows), good log fire, particularly well kept Castle Eden, reasonably priced food inc good baguettes, big garden; children welcome, attractive evening restaurant; open all day at least in summer; bedrooms *(Lord Sandhurst)*

Troutbeck [NY4103]

Mortal Man [A592 N of Windermere; Upper Rd]: Neatly kept partly panelled beamed hotel bar with big log fire, mix of seats inc a cushioned settle, copper-topped tables, cosy eating room, no smoking picture-window restaurant, food from sandwiches to steaks with some tempting specials, well kept ales such as Jennings, John Smiths and Theakstons Best, courteous young staff, darts, dominoes; piped music may obtrude, TV room, Sun folk/blues night; children welcome, open all day, bedrooms – lovely village, great scenery *(Dr M E Wilson, Kevin Thorpe, Revd D Glover, Mrs S Miller, Ian Dawson, IHR, LYM, GD, KW, Tim and Beryl Dawson, JDM, KM)*

Uldale [NY2436]

Snooty Fox: Unpretentious but comfortable two-bar local in tiny village, friendly helpful landlord, well kept Theakstons and a beer brewed for them in Hesket Newmarket, good generous food; reasonably priced bedrooms *(anon)*

Watermillock [NY4523]

☆ *Brackenrigg* [A592, Ullswater]: Opened-up rustic 19th-c inn in lovely spot overlooking Ullswater, good imaginative food, cheery helpful staff, particularly well kept Black Sheep Special, Theakstons and Jennings Cumberland, friendly mix of holiday-makers and locals; bedrooms and self-catering *(David Cooke, Derek Cash)*

Whitehaven [NY0017]

Sal Madges [Duke St]: Unpretentious town pub with well kept Jennings and good low-priced food inc children's bargains and home-made cakes; pool room *(Mrs M Granville-Edge)*

Windermere [SD4198]

Elleray Hotel [Cross St]: Good value pub meals, also restaurant; bedrooms *(Abi Benson)*

People don't usually tip bar staff (different in a really smart hotel, say). If you want to thank a barman – dealing with a really large party say, or special friendliness – offer him a drink. Common expressions are: 'And what's yours?' or 'And won't you have something for yourself?'

Derbyshire

A couple of good new entries here, both attractively placed: the Chequers on Froggatt Edge, storming back into these pages after a bit of a break; and the Plough, a charming dining pub just outside Hathersage. Other pubs doing particularly well this year are the hospitable Devonshire Arms at Beeley (Friday night is fish night), the Waltzing Weasel at Birch Vale (nice atmosphere, good cooking reflecting the licensees' passion for Italy and peasant casseroles), the Olde Gate at Brassington (this classic country pub gains a Star Award this year), the Old Sun in Buxton (thoroughly traditional virtues), the Brunswick in Derby (great collection of real ales, including ones brewed here, and always cheerful), and the cosy and very welcoming old Red Lion on the green at Litton. Of the three pubs here to have gained our Food Award, all of them good for special meals out, the Waltzing Weasel gains our award as Derbyshire Dining Pub of the Year. The Monsal Head Hotel gains both a Beer Award and a Place to Stay Award this year; and John Thompson, landlord of the Trent-side pub named for him near Melbourne, deserves special praise for having steered his establishment into all 20 editions of the Guide so far – a unique record for the county; and he brews his own good value beers. Drinks prices elsewhere in the county are also generally on the attractive side of the national average; the Olde Dolphin in Derby had especially cheap beer. In the Lucky Dip at the end of the chapter, we'd recommend particularly the Queen Anne at Great Hucklow, Royal at Hayfield, Black Swan at Idridgehay, Dewdrop in Ilkeston, Malt Shovel in Shardlow and Bell at Smalley.

ASHBOURNE SK1846 Map 7
Smiths Tavern

St Johns St; bottom of market place

There's an enjoyably pubby atmosphere at this neatly kept traditional pub, which is just at the foot of the town's market place. The attractive chatty bar stretches back a lot further than you might think from the relatively narrow shop-front entrance, with horsebrasses and tankards hanging from heavy black beams, a delft shelf of antique blue and white china, old cigarette and drinks advertisements, a plush wall seat facing the bar counter, and a good choice of newspapers to read. Steps lead up to a middle room with more plush seating around solid tables, a piano and log-effect gas fire, and beyond that a light and airy no smoking dining room. Good hearty food includes soup (£2.25), steak and kidney pie, pasta bake or lasagne (£5.25) and about a dozen daily specials such as recommended Derbyshire oak cake with cheese and onion (£4.50), curry (£5.25) and leek and mushroom crumble or trout with lemon and almond butter (£6.50); three-course Sunday lunch (£6.95). Well kept Banks's, Marstons Pedigree and a guest such as Morrells Varsity on handpump, over 30 whiskies, and a range of vodkas; very friendly obliging service. Darts, dominoes and cribbage. *(Recommended by JP, PP, David Carr, Adrian and Felicity Smith, Sue Holland, Dave Webster, John Foord)*

Union Pub Company ~ Tenant Paul Mellor ~ Real ale ~ Bar food (12-3, 6-9.30) ~ Restaurant ~ (01335) 342264 ~ Children welcome ~ Quiz night every second Sun ~ Open 11-11; 12-10.30 Sun; 11-3, 5-11 Mon-Fri winter

BARLOW SK3375 Map 7
Trout

Valley Road, Common Side; B6051 NW of Chesterfield

You'll probably need to book to be sure of a table at this good dining pub. Enjoyable bar food from a sound menu includes soup (£3.10), pasta with tomato sauce and parmesan (£3.50), smoked salmon terrine on a light lime and lemon mayonnaise (£4.25), sandwiches (from £4.50), filled baguettes (£5.50), steak and kidney pudding (£7.50), battered cod, chips and mushy peas (£7.95), seared salmon with dill lemon and whole grain mustard mayonnaise (£8.95), 8oz sirloin (£10.50). The carpeted interior is surprisingly more inviting than you might have guessed from the road, with neat good-sized tables (candlelit at night), comfortable brocaded banquettes, old-world prints and beams; a second smaller dining room opens off. There's a good pubby atmosphere on the other side of the bar, with big stripped and scrubbed tables on bare boards, more banquettes and cushioned stools, a big brick fireplace and Bass, Boddingtons and a guest such as Greene King Abbot on handpump or tapped from the cask. They also offer a couple of weekly guest wines alongside a decent wine list. The bottom part of the pub is no smoking; unobtrusive piped music. There are tables out on the terrace. *(Recommended by Darly Graton, Graeme Gulibert, Keith and Chris O'Neill, Steven and Sally Knight)*

Free house ~ Licensees Brian Tookey and Katie Whitton ~ Real ale ~ Bar food (12-2.30, 6.30-9.30) ~ Restaurant ~ (0114) 2890893 ~ Children in restaurant ~ Open 12-3, 6-11(7-10.30 Sun); closed 25 Dec evening

BEELEY SK2667 Map 7
Devonshire Arms

B6012, off A6 Matlock—Bakewell

This handsome old stone pub is beautifully set in a pretty Peak District estate village and is handy for Chatsworth House and for gourmands visiting the Duchess of Devonshire's produce shop at Pilsley. The building was successfully converted from three early 18th-c cottages to a prosperous coaching inn in the mid 18th c (when Dickens is said to have been a regular). These days big log fires cheerfully warm its charmingly atmospheric black-beamed rooms which are furnished with comfortably cushioned stone seats along stripped walls, and antique settles and simpler wooden chairs on flagstoned floors. The restaurant and cocktail bar are no smoking. Very good, sensibly imaginative bar food is served all day and might include home-made soup (£2.75), filled baguettes (from £3.95), grilled goats cheese (£5.50), avocado and prawn cocktail (£5.75), a good value ploughman's (£5.95), haggis and neaps (£6.25), salmon hollandaise or black pudding and bacon salad (£7.95), gammon hock with white bean sauce (£8.50), venison in plum sauce (£11.50), and mixed grill (£12.95); puddings (from £2.95). They do around a dozen fish dishes for their Friday fish night, and on Sundays they do a special Victorian breakfast with a glass of bucks fizz and the Sunday newspapers (£10.95). You will need to book for both, and it's also best to book at weekends; service remains friendly and efficient, even when busy. Well kept Black Sheep Best and Special, Theakstons XB and Old Peculier, and a guest such as Jennings on handpump, decent good value house wine, and about three dozen malt whiskies. *(Recommended by Prof John and Mrs Patricia White, Arthur Williams, Dr D J and Mrs S C Walker, Dr and Mrs J Hills, Paul and Margaret Baker, Darly Graton, Graeme Gulibert, Steven and Sally Knight, Mike and Sue Loseby, JP, PP, W W Burke, the Didler, Andy and Ali, Albert and Margaret Horton, Peter F Marshall, Keith and Chris O'Neill, Annette and John Derbyshire, Kevin Thorpe, Christopher Turner, Mr and Mrs J McRobert, O K Smyth, Tony Middis)*

Free house ~ Licensee John A Grosvenor ~ Real ale ~ Bar food (12-9) ~ (01629) 733259 ~ Children welcome ~ Open 11-11; 12-10.30 Sun; closed 25 Dec

---

By law pubs must show a price list of their drinks. Let us know if you are inconvenienced by any breach of this law: www.goodguides.com

BIRCH VALE SK0286 Map 7

Waltzing Weasel 🍴 ♀ 🛏

A6015 E of New Mills

Derbyshire Dining Pub of the Year

A new chef at this friendly place has broadened the scope of the menu which includes dishes that reflect the landlord's passion for Italy, and there's something of a peasant stew crusade going on here too. The home-made food is consistently very enjoyable and might include soup (£3.50), sandwiches (from £3.50), sardine tapenade or ploughman's or pepper tart (£5.75), pizzas (£5.75/£7.75), crayfish tails (£6.75), steak baguette (£8.75), seafood tart or the casserole of the day such as Italian beef or tagine (£9.75), lamb shank marinated in anchovies, garlic, rosemary and wine (£11.50), Italian platter (£11.75) and puddings such as cold lemon soufflé, bread and butter pudding or brandy snap baskets with fruit and ice cream (£3.75); Sunday roast (£10.50). The evening menu is slightly different. The building is high on a hill with fine views of Kinder Scout and the Peak District from its charming back restaurant, pretty garden and terrace. The comfortable bar – pubbier than ever, feel some readers, in contrast to so many places that are getting all too restauranty – has a cheerful fire, plenty of houseplants on corner tables, daily papers on sticks, and a greeting from Bess, the friendly dog. Some of the furnishings reflect the licensees' interest in antiques (they're former dealers), with handsome oak settles and tables among more usual furniture, lots of nicely framed mainly sporting Victorian prints, and a good longcase clock. Well kept Marstons Best and Timothy Taylors with maybe a guest beer on handpump, and a good choice of decent wines and malt whiskies. The spacious bedrooms are comfortably furnished, and lovely breakfasts include home-made marmalade. (*Recommended by Dr J H and Mrs J M Hills, David Heath, Mike and Wendy Proctor, Mike and Lynn Robinson, Revd D Glover, Darly Graton, Graeme Gulibert, Glenys and John Roberts, Helen Whitmore, Annette and John Derbyshire, Mike and Mary Carter, Mr A Wright, M N Carey, Mrs P J Carroll*)

Free house ~ Licensee Michael Atkinson ~ Real ale ~ Bar food ~ Restaurant ~ (01663) 743402 ~ Children over 5 in restaurant ~ Open 12-3, 5.30-(10.30 Sun)11 ~ Bedrooms: £45S/£75B

BIRCHOVER SK2462 Map 7

Druid 🍴

Village signposted off B5056

The emphasis at this popular creeper-clad dining pub is quite firmly on the food, and it's best to book for evening and weekend meals. As well as blackboards displaying a remarkably large choice of daily specials, an extensive menu includes port and stilton pâté (£4.20), deep-fried breaded blue cheese with apricot dip (£4.90), crispy prawns with garlic and soy dip (£5.30), moussaka (£6.90), half aubergine filled with rice, peppers, mushrooms, cheese and peanut and garlic sauce, or lentil, carrot and nut rissoles with piquant salsa (£7.40), steak and kidney pudding or thai chicken (£8.90), halibut baked with orange, ginger and garlic with black olives and water chestnuts (£10.90), marinated rack of lamb with redcurrant and gooseberry sauce (£13.20) and lots of puddings like sherry and fruit trifle or dime bar crunch pie (£3.20). The spacious and airy two-storey dining extension, candlelit at night, is really the heart of the place, with pink plush seats on olive-green carpet. The small plain bar has plush-upholstered wooden wall benches around straightforward tables, a big coal fire and three or four well kept real ales including Druid (brewed for the pub by nearby Leatherbritches) and a couple of guests such as Boddingtons and Mansfield Bitter; good collection of malt whiskies. The Garden Room, tap room and part of the bar are no smoking. There are picnic-sets in front, and good walks in the area. (*Recommended by Mike and Wendy Proctor, John and Christine Lowe, Mrs P J Carroll, A Preston, Andy and Ali, Wendy Dye, Annette and John Derbyshire, JP, PP, Richard Cole, JDM, KM, Geoff and Kath Nicholson, Keith and Chris O'Neill, Keith and Di Newsome, Colin Parker*)

Free house ~ Licensee Brian Bunce ~ Real ale ~ Bar food (7-8.30 winter Sun-Fri; till

9.30 in summer) ~ Restaurant ~ (01629) 650302 ~ Children welcome till 8 ~ Open 12-3, 7-11; closed 25 Dec, evening 26 Dec

BRASSINGTON SK2354 Map 7
Olde Gate ★
Village signposted off B5056 and B5035 NE of Ashbourne

There's an agreeably old-fashioned atmosphere at this village pub, which is said to be haunted by a Spanish ghost. Although the date etched outside is 1874, it was originally built in 1616 of magnesian limestone and timbers salvaged from Armada wrecks and exchanged for locally mined lead. Furnishings in the relaxing public bar are appealingly traditional. There's a lovely ancient wall clock, rush-seated old chairs, antique settles, including an ancient partly reframed one of black solid oak, and log fires. Gleaming copper pots sit on a lovely 17th-c kitchen range, pewter mugs hang from a beam, and a side shelf boasts a collection of embossed Doulton stoneware flagons. On the left of a small hatch-served lobby, another cosy beamed room has stripped panelled settles, scrubbed-top tables, and a roaring fire under a huge mantelbeam. Good (if not cheap) changing bar food might include open sandwiches (from £4.95), pies (£7.50), cajun chicken or aubergine and courgette crumble (£8.95), marinated lamb steak (£12.95) and balti king prawns (£13.95) and puddings like chocolate fudge cake or strawberry pavlova (£3.15). The dining room is no smoking. Well kept Marstons Pedigree and a guest on handpump, and a good selection of malt whiskies; cribbage and dominoes. Stone-mullioned windows look across lots of tables in a pleasant garden to small silvery-walled pastures. In summer, the small front yard with a couple of benches is a nice spot to listen to the village bell-ringers practising on Friday evenings. Carsington reservoir, ideal for water sports and activities, is a five-minute drive away. *(Recommended by Mr and Mrs S Oxenbury, Pat and Roger Fereday, Peter F Marshall, Anthony Barnes, Rob Fowell, Keith and Di Newsome, Kevin Thorpe, Darly Graton, Graeme Gulibert, JP, PP, John and Christine Lowe, Dr W J M Gissane, JDM, KM, the Didler, Kevin Blake, Mike and Wendy Proctor)*

Marstons (W & D) ~ Tenant Paul Burlinson ~ Real ale ~ Bar food (not Mon evening) ~ No credit cards ~ (01629) 540448 ~ Children over 10 in bar ~ Open 12-2.30(3 Sat), 6-11(7-10.30 Sun); cl Mon am autumn-spring

BUXTON SK1266 Map 7
Bull i' th' Thorn
Ashbourne Road (A515) 6 miles S of Buxton, nr Hurdlow

Deriving its name from a hybrid of its 15th-c and 17th-c titles, the Bull and Hurdlow House of Hurdlow Thorn, this place is a curious cross between a medieval hall with a fairly straightforward roadside pub atmosphere. Among the lively old carvings that greet you as you enter, is one of the eponymous bull caught in a thornbush, and there are also images of an eagle with a freshly caught hare, and some spaniels chasing a rabbit. In the hall which dates from 1471 a massive central beam runs parallel with a forest of smaller ones, there are panelled window seats in the embrasures of the thick stone walls, handsome panelling, and old flagstones stepping gently down to a big open fire. It's furnished with fine long settles, an ornately carved hunting chair, a longcase clock, a powder-horn, and armour that includes 17th-c German helmets, swords, and blunderbusses and so forth. Stuffed animals' heads line the corridor that leads to a candlelit hall, used for medieval themed evening banquets. Served all day, the enormous choice of bar food is popular with families and includes soup (£2), filled baguettes (from £2.75), stir fry vegetables (£6), a huge lamb shank (£8.25), duck (£8.25), wild boar steak (£10.95); Sunday lunch (£5). An adjoining room has darts, pool, dominoes and a juke box; piped music. Robinsons Best on handpump. The three bedrooms have four-poster and rococo beds. A simple no smoking family room opens on to a terrace and big lawn with swings, and there are more tables in a sheltered angle in front. The pub is handy for the High Peak Trail. *(Recommended by Mike and Wendy Proctor, Adrian and Felicity Smith, the Didler, Dr Paull Khan, Kevin Blake, Mike and Lynn Robinson, JP, PP)*

Robinsons ~ Tenant Mrs Annette Maltby-Baker ~ Real ale ~ Bar food (9.30am-9pm) ~ (01298) 83348 ~ Children welcome ~ Open 9.30-11(10.30 Sun) ~ Bedrooms: /£60B

Old Sun ♀ ◖

33 High St

There's a genuinely relaxing atmosphere in the cosy little rooms of this rambling traditional pub. Several small well furnished and softly lit areas lead off the central bar, with open fires, low beams, bare boards or terracotta tiles, comfortable leather armchairs and chesterfields, fresh flowers, terracotta tiles, stripped wood screens, old local photographs, and some carefully chosen bric-a-brac (such as the 19th-c Guinness bottles found during refurbishment of the cellar). As well as Marstons Best and Pedigree served in lined oversized glasses, there may be a guest such as Camerons Strongarm. They also stock an impressive range of bottled beers and malt whiskies, farm cider, and a good choice of wines, with about a dozen by the (huge!) glass. Bar food includes home-made soup (£2.25), sandwiches (from £3), hot king prawns with limes and chilli mayonnaise (£3.75), a daily pasta dish (£4.75), chicken fajitas (£6.85), 10oz rump steak (£11), and a couple of daily specials such as sausages and mash (£5.95) and baked salmon on parsley mash (£7.50); puddings (from £2). Friendly staff; piped music, TV. *(Recommended by Joan and Michel Hooper-Immins, David Carr, David and Heather Stephenson, Simon and Laura Habbishow, Brian and Anna Marsden, Rob Fowell, the Didler, Margaret and Roy Randle, Peter F Marshall, Mike and Wendy Proctor, David Hoult, JP, PP)*

Marstons (W & D) ~ Manager Mr A Johnson ~ Real ale ~ Bar food (12-2, 5.30-9, 12-9 Sat and Sun) ~ (01298) 23452 ~ Children in back bar till 8pm ~ Open 11.30(11 Sat)-11; 12-10.30 Sun

BUXWORTH SK0282 Map 7

Navigation

Silkhill, off B6062, which itself leads off the A6 just NW of Whaley Bridge roundabout

Barges chugging along the newly restored canal add to the atmosphere at this extended early 18th-c free house. It's arguably at its best in summer when you can sit outside on a sunken flagstoned terrace and enjoy the attractive surroundings. Inside, a clutter of brassware and china brightens up the cosy linked low-ceilinged rooms, which have plenty of snug corners, good coal and log fires, and flagstone floors. Interesting prints and other canalia recall the days when the old Peak Forest Tramway ran from what is now the car park, connecting the canal with limestone quarries in nearby Dove Holes. Bar food includes soup (£2.25), prawn cocktail (£3.95), steak and kidney pie or broccoli and cheese bake (£6.50), fish of the day (£6.95), grilled salmon with lemon, caper and parsley butter (£7.50), thai chicken curry (£7.75), 8oz rump steak (£8.95), and puddings such as apple pie and hot chocolate fudge cake (£2.75); children's dishes. Well kept good value Marstons Pedigree, Timothy Taylors Landlord, Websters Yorkshire and a guest such as Abbeydale Moonshine on handpump, farm ciders in summer and mulled wine in winter. A games room has pool, darts, shove-ha'penny, dominoes, and TV; quiet piped music. We haven't yet had feedback about the refurbished bedrooms; play area and pets corner outside. *(Recommended by Bernie Adams, Annette and John Derbyshire, Kevin Blake, David Carr, Bob and Lisa Cantrell, Rob Fowell, Dr Paull Khan, Mike and Lynn Robinson)*

Free house ~ Licensees Alan and Lynda Hall ~ Real ale ~ Bar food (12-9.30(9 winter)) ~ Restaurant ~ (01663) 732072 ~ Children welcome ~ Open 11-11; 12-10.30 Sun ~ Bedrooms: £29.50B/£48B

Anyone claiming to arrange or prevent inclusion of a pub in the *Guide* is a fraud. Pubs are included only if recommended by genuine readers and if our own anonymous inspection confirms that they are suitable.

CASTLETON SK1583 Map 7

Castle Hotel 🛏

High Street at junction with Castle Street

The welcoming bar at this neatly kept hotel has stripped stone walls with built-in cabinets, a nice open fire, finely carved early 17th-c beams and, in one room, ancient flagstones. If you're in the area, the colourful Garland Ceremony procession, commemorating the escape of Charles II, passes by on 29th May and is worth seeing, or there are more ghoulish stories associated with the pub to distract you at other times, including one about the ghost of a bride who, instead of enjoying her planned wedding breakfast here, died broken-hearted when she was left at the altar. Seasonally changing bar food includes soup (£2.35), lunchtime sandwiches (from £3.60), sausages and mash (£4.95), braised marinated lamb (£5.45) lemon chicken or baked macaroni and spinach (£5.95), good cod and chips (£6.35), seafood salad (£6.95), baked trout with parsley butter (£7.70) and puddings such as fruit brûlée or toffee bread and butter pudding (£2.95). They keep Bass and Tetleys on handpump, service is pleasant and efficient, a good part of the pub is no smoking, and there's a fruit machine and piped music. You can sit in the pretty garden. *(Recommended by Rev John Hibberd, Duncan Cloud, Albert and Margaret Horton, JP, PP, Dr W J M Gissane, Mike and Wendy Proctor, John and Christine Lowe, P Holland, Ruth and Paul Lawrence, James A Waller, Emma Napper)*

Vintage Inns ~ Manager Glen Mills ~ Real ale ~ Bar food (12-10) ~ (01433) 620578 ~ Children welcome ~ Open 11.30-11; 12-10.30 Sun ~ Bedrooms: £40B/£50B

DERBY SK3435 Map 7

Alexandra 🍺 £

Siddals Rd, just up from station

Like the other pubs in this successful little independent chain, they keep an interesting ever-changing range of real ales at this two-roomed Victorian town pub. The friendly beer-loving landlord knows how to keep a decent pint too, and alongside Bass, Batemans XB, Hook Norton Best and Timothy Taylors Landlord, you'll find around half a dozen or so unusual guests from all sorts of microbreweries such as Beowulf, Leadmill, Moles and Oldershaw. They also have up to five continental draft beers, country wines, cider tapped from the cask and around two dozen malt whiskies. There's a cheerfully chatty atmosphere in the simple bustling bar which has good heavy traditional furnishings on dark-stained floorboards, shelves of bottles, and lots of railway prints and memorabilia – signalling the fact that it's just two minutes away from Derby station; the lounge is no smoking. Straightforward good value bar food includes filled hot or cold rolls (from £1.60), gammon and egg (£4.25), beef in ale with dumplings or chicken in cream and asparagus sauce (£4.95), and Sunday lunch (£3.25, two for £6); darts, cribbage, dominoes and piped music. *(Recommended by the Didler, David Carr, JP, PP, C J Fletcher, Richard Lewis, Rob Fowell)*

Tynemill ~ Manager Mark Robins ~ Real ale ~ Bar food (12-2; also 7-8.30 Sun) ~ No credit cards ~ (01332) 293993 ~ Open 11-11; 12-3, 7-10.30 Sun ~ Bedrooms: £25S/£35S

Brunswick 🍺 £

1 Railway Terrace; close to Derby Midland railway station

The changing range of very good own brew beers here is produced in the purpose-built brewery tower which is visible from a viewing area at the back of this traditional old railwaymen's pub. Said to be the first railwaymen's hostelry in the world, it's situated at the apex of a row of preserved railway cottages. Of the incredible range of up to 17 beers on handpump or tapped straight from the cask by the hands-on chatty landlord, around four – including Second Brew, the highly-praised Railway Porter, Triple Hop and Old Accidental – are from the Brunswick Brewery. Others beers are sourced from far and wide and might include Bass, Hook Norton Old Hooky,

Marstons Pedigree, Sarah Hughes Dark Ruby and Timothy Taylors Landlord and Golden Best; farm cider is tapped from the cask. The very welcoming high-ceilinged serving bar has heavy, well padded leather seats, whisky-water jugs above the dado, and a dark blue ceiling and upper wall, with squared dark panelling below. The no smoking room is decorated with little old-fashioned prints and swan's neck lamps, and has a high-backed wall settle and a coal fire; behind a curved glazed partition wall is a quietly chatty family parlour narrowing to the apex of the triangular building. Darts, dominoes, fruit machine and TV. Reasonably priced home-made lunchtime bar food includes filled beef, ham, cheese or tuna and sweetcorn rolls (£1.65), soup (£1.95), hot beef, cheese and bacon or sausage cobs (£2), home-made pies (£3.35), ploughman's or chilli (£3.50), and there's always a vegetarian dish such as vegetable lasagne (£3.75); they only do rolls on Sunday. There are seats in the terrace area behind. A beer festival in the first week of October commemorates the pub's anniversary, and they hold another popular one in February. *(Recommended by Richard Lewis, Kevin Flack, JDM, KM, JP, PP, C J Fletcher, Mike Pugh, Keith and Chris O'Neill, Sue Holland, Dave Webster, the Didler, David Carr, Kevin Blake)*

Own brew ~ Licensee Trevor Harris ~ Real ale ~ Bar food (11.30-2.30 Mon-Sat) ~ No credit cards ~ (01332) 290677 ~ Children in family room ~ Jazz Thurs evenings ~ Open 11-11; 12-10.30 Sun

Olde Dolphin £

Queen St; nearest car park King St/St Michaels Lane

The new beer garden at this friendly well-run little place provides a welcome refuge from the bustle of the city centre. Dating from 1530, this claims to be Derby's oldest pub and judging by its big bowed black beams it's not hard to believe they're right. Its four snug old-fashioned feeling rooms – two with their own separate street doors – have shiny panelling, opaque leaded windows and coal fires. They're traditionally decorated, with varnished wall benches in the tiled-floor public bar, and a brocaded seat in the little carpeted snug, as well as cast-iron-framed tables and lantern lights. There's no piped music here, just daily papers, board games and chat. Ten handpumps dispense well kept real ales which might include Bass, Black Sheep, Dolphin Ale (brewed locally for them), Deuchars IPA, Greene King Abbot, Marstons Pedigree and Ruddles County; there's a beer festival in the last week in July. Hearty good value bar food includes soup (£2.25), sandwiches (from £1.90), hot filled baguettes (£2.95), spinach and mushroom pancakes (£3.25), fish and chips (£3.75), lasagne (£4.75) and 8oz rump steak (£5.95); three-course Sunday lunch (£3.50). A no smoking upstairs restaurant serves good value steaks. Good service from helpful uniformed staff. *(Recommended by JDM, KM, David Carr, the Didler, JP, PP, Richard Lewis, Richard Houghton)*

Bass ~ Tenant Janina Holmes ~ Real ale ~ Bar food (9-11) ~ Restaurant (6-11pm) ~ (01332) 267711 ~ Children welcome ~ Open 10.30-11; 12-11 Sun

EARL STERNDALE SK0967 Map 7
Quiet Woman 🛏 £

Village signposted off B4053 S of Buxton

Apart from a new pub sign outside nothing really changes at this unspoilt stone cottage. It's a treasure for those who like their pubs really basic and old-fashioned. The whole place is suffused with an honest and unfussy atmosphere, and you can buy free-range bantam and goose eggs, local cheese, local poetry books or even silage as easily as a pint of beer. It's very simple inside, with hard seats, plain tables (including a sunken one for dominoes or cards), low beams, quarry tiles, lots of china ornaments and a roaring winter coal fire; pool table in the family room. As well as well kept Marstons Best and Pedigree and Mansfield there are three guests from brewers such as Adnams, Everards and Whim on handpump. When not pulling pints, the landlord has been keeping himself busy on what has turned out to be quite a long-term project, which is renovating the kitchen. At the moment they serve sandwiches (£1.50), home-made pork pies 80p (using their own pork), and occasional winter hotpots. There are picnic-sets out in front, and budgies, hens, turkeys, ducks, donkeys and pigs to keep children amused; the small campsite next door can be hired through the pub, and they have a caravan (for hire) in the garden. *(Recommended by Ann and Colin Hunt, David Edwards, David Hoult, Adrian and Felicity Smith, Paul Roughley, Julia Fox, the Didler, L Davenport, JP, PP)*

Free house ~ Licensee Kenneth Mellor ~ Real ale ~ No credit cards ~ (01298) 83211 ~ Children in family room ~ Jamming sessions most Sun lunchtimes ~ Open 12-3(4.30 Sat), 7-11; 12-5, 7-10.30 Sun

EYAM SK2276 Map 7
Miners Arms 🍽

Signposted off A263 Chesterfield—Chapel-en-le-Frith

The great plague, drunken vicars and the ghosts of two young girls who perished in a fire all feature in the history of this very welcoming popular village pub. The three little plush beamed rooms each have their own stone fireplace, and a pleasantly relaxed atmosphere becomes more lively in the evening, when locals drop in for the well kept Stones and a couple of guests such as Bass and Fullers London Pride on handpump. Good home-cooked bar food includes soup (£1.95), sandwiches (from £2.35), cumberland sausages with onion gravy (£4.95), ploughman's (£4.55), poached salmon in white wine sauce, chicken breast in cream and prawn sauce, decent vegetarian meals such as vegetable pasta bake or nut and vegetable stir fry (all £6.95), and crispy duck (£7.95); puddings (£3); cheerful attentive service. The village is a good base for exploring the Peak District, and there are decent walks nearby, especially below Froggatt Edge. *(Recommended by IHR, Ann and Colin Hunt, JP, PP, Dr and Mrs J Hills, DC, the Didler)*

New Century Inns ~ Tenants Neil and Sal Hunt ~ Real ale ~ Bar food (12-9(6 Sun); not Sun evening) ~ Restaurant ~ (01433) 630853 ~ Children welcome ~ Open 12-11(10.30 Sun) ~ Bedrooms: £30S/£60B

FENNY BENTLEY SK1750 Map 7
Coach & Horses

A515 N of Ashbourne

The comfortable front bar at this steadily reliable 17th-c rendered stone house has flowery-cushioned wall settles and library chairs around the dark tables on its stone flagged floor, waggonwheels hanging from the black beams, horsebrasses, pewter mugs, and prints on the walls. There are more prints on the stained pine panelling in the little back room, with country cottage furnishings, and a lovely old fireplace (one of three) which was hidden away until last year's renovations. There's a very pleasant atmosphere, and the quietly friendly licensees are always warmly welcoming. Enjoyable reasonably priced bar food from a changing blackboard might include soup (£2.50), lunchtime sandwiches (from £3.25), hot sandwiches such as black pudding and onion (£3.50), potato shells filled with brandied mushrooms (£3.75), ploughman's (£4.95), steak and kidney shortcrust pie (£5.95), chilli bean and vegetable tortilla (£6.50), lamb and rosemary sausages (£6.25), salmon fillet with white wine, cream and asparagus sauce or honey-roast duck breast with mango and ginger sauce (£8.50), traditional home-made puddings (£2.50). The dining room and back bar are no smoking. Very well kept Marstons Pedigree, and two or three guests such as Abbeydale Moonshinie, Timothy Taylors Landlord and Titanic Best on handpump, and several malt whiskies; cribbage, dominoes and piped music. There are views across fields from picnic-sets in the back garden by an elder tree, and wood tables and chairs under cocktail parasols on the front terrace. *(Recommended by Sue Holland, Dave Webster, Derek and Sylvia Stephenson, A Preston, Mr and Mrs S Oxenbury, Dr W J M Gissane, JP, PP, Kevin Blake, John and Christine Lowe, Brian and Anna Marsden, John Foord, Bernie Adams, the Didler, Ben and Sheila Walker)*

Free house ~ Licensees John and Matthew Dawson ~ Real ale ~ Bar food (12-2.30, 6.30-9; all day Sat/Sun) ~ Restaurant ~ (01335) 350246 ~ Children in restaurant and family room ~ Open 11-3, 5-11; 11-11 Sat; 12-11 Sun

FOOLOW SK2077 Map 7
Barrel

Bretton; signposted from Foolow, which itself is signposted from A623 just E of junction with B6465 to Bakewell; can also be reached from either the B6049 at Great Hucklow, or the B6001 via Abney, from Leadmill just S of Hathersage

There are splendid views over five surrounding counties from this unspoilt old stone turnpike inn, which is perched on the edge of an isolated ridge and claims to be the highest pub in Derbyshire. Stubs of massive knocked-through stone walls divide it into several areas. The cosy and peaceful oak-beamed bar, its old-fashioned charm still very much intact, has flagstones, studded doors in low doorways, lots of pictures, antiques and a collection of bottles. The snuggest area is at the far end with an open wood fire, a leather-cushioned settle, and a built-in corner wall-bench by an antique oak table. As well as soup (£1.95) and sandwiches (from £2.45), whitebait (£3.95), ploughman's (from £4.80), steak and ale pie or daily roast (£6.25), fish and chips (£6.75), daily specials might include chicken with apricot and tarragon sauce (£8.50), game hotpot with herb dumplings (£8.95), halibut baked with spinach, mussels and garlic (£9.95); puddings (£3.40); friendly service. Well kept Tetleys with a couple of guests such as Adnams Broadside, Greene King Abbot and Marstons Pedigree and on handpump, and over 20 malts. The same Irish ceilidh band has been playing at the pub for 24 years. There are seats out on the breezy front terrace. The pub is in excellent walking country, and is handy for Chatsworth. Maybe open all day in summer school holidays – phone to check. *(Recommended by Annette and John Derbyshire, Nigel Woolliscroft, IHR, John Brightley, Peter F Marshall, Jack Morley, JP, PP, DC, the Didler, Carol and Steve Spence, R A Watson, Rev John Hibberd, Mr and Mrs D Moir)*

Free house ~ Licensee Paul Rowlinson ~ Real ale ~ Bar food (12-2.30, 6.30-9.30) ~ Restaurant ~ (01433) 630856 ~ Children in eating area of bar and restaurant ~ Irish ceilidh band Weds evening ~ Open 11-3, 6-11; 11-11 wknds; closed 25 Dec ~ Bedrooms: £45B/£60B

FROGGATT EDGE SK2477 Map 7
Chequers 🍴 🛏

B6054, off A623 N of Bakewell; OS Sheet 119 map reference 247761

Froggatt Edge is just up through the woods behind this beautifully situated busy country inn, flourishing under its new licensees. The fairly smart bar has library chairs or small high-backed winged settles on the well waxed floorboards, an attractive richly varnished beam-and-board ceiling, antique prints on the white walls, partly stripped back to big dark stone blocks, and a big solid-fuel stove; one corner has a nicely carved oak cupboard. One of the main draws here is the tasty unusual bar food in the partly no smoking dining area. The menu changes all the time but there might be soup (£2.25), very enjoyable hearty sandwiches (from £3.25, smoked salmon £5.50), smoked duck with kumquat chutney or bresaola with truffle oil and parmesan (£3.95), walnut and seared sweet pepper penne (£5.50), sausage of the day, mushroom and red pepper stroganoff (£5.95), chicken on pasta with ratatouille (£7.25), baked salmon and leeks (£7.95), minted lamb chops with sweet pepper cracked wheat (£8.95), whole baked grey mullet with vegetable pilau rice (£9.95), pork fillet with poached pear and mustard sauce (£10.20), 8oz sirloin (£10.95) and puddings such as chocolate and chestnut mousse and rhubarb puff pastry tart with greek yoghurt (£2.50-£4.95); pleasant efficient service. Well kept Marstons Pedigree, Theakstons and a guest such as Black Sheep on handpump, a good range of malt whiskies and a changing wine board; piped music. There are seats in the peaceful back garden; six nicely furnished comfortable bedrooms. *(Recommended by Christopher Turner, Darly Graton, Graeme Gulibert, David Carr, John and Sheila Lister, JDM, KM, B C Hammond, Chris and Elaine Lyon, Mrs G M Roberts, John Evans, Mr and Mrs Hugh Wood, Steven and Sally Knight, Paul and Margaret Baker, James A Waller, Mike and Wendy Proctor, P J and Avril Hanson, Emma Napper)*

Pubmaster ~ Tenant Stephen Burgess ~ Real ale ~ Bar food (12-3, 5.30-9.30) ~

(01433) 630231 ~ Children in no smoking section ~ Jazz last Weds of month ~ Open 12-3, 5.30-11; 12-11 Sat; 12-10.30 Sun ~ Bedrooms: £48B/£64B.

HARDWICK HALL SK4663 Map 7
Hardwick Inn

2¾ miles from M1 junction 29: at roundabout A6175 towards Clay Cross; after ½ mile turn left signed Stainsby and Hardwick Hall (ignore any further sign for Hardwick Hall); at sign to Stainsby follow road to left; after 2½ miles staggered road junction, turn left

Owned by the National Trust and originally built around 1600 as a lodge for the nearby Elizabethan Hall, this 17th-c golden stone house draws a lot of its trade from the tourists visiting the house and its surrounding grounds. It's also handy for the M1 so can get crowded (at which times it might get smoky), especially at weekends. Its cosy rooms – one has an attractive 18th-c carved settle – have stone-mullioned latticed windows. The carpeted lounge is the most comfortable with its upholstered wall settles, tub chairs and stools around varnished wooden tables. Good value bar food is served all day and includes soup (£1.70), sandwiches (from £2.80), ploughman's (from £4.45), roast of the day (£6.50), as well as daily specials such as game and ale casserole (£6.50), grilled trout with orange and black pepper (£6.75) and bream with thai coating (£6.95); puddings such as damson crumble (£2.65). The carvery restaurant is no smoking. Well kept Courage Directors, Greene King Old Speckled Hen, Ruddles County and Theakstons XB and Old Peculier on handpump, and a growing collection of over 150 malt whiskies; friendly efficient service. There's a nice view from the tables in the garden. *(Recommended by the Didler, June and Ken Brooks, Walter and Susan Rinaldi-Butcher, Ian and Nita Cooper, D B, Jayne and Peter Capp, IHR, M Borthwick, Darly Graton, Graeme Gulibert, Keith and Chris O'Neill, Jenny and Brian Seller, Simon and Laura Habbishow, JP, PP, Mike and Mary Carter, GD, KW, Mr and Mrs J E C Tasker, John and Christine Lowe)*

Free house ~ Licensees Peter and Pauline Batty ~ Real ale ~ Bar food (11.30-9.30, 12-9 Sun) ~ Restaurant ~ (01246) 850245 ~ Children welcome in family room and restaurant ~ Open 11.30-11; 12-10.30 Sun

HASSOP SK2272 Map 7
Eyre Arms

B6001 N of Bakewell

The Eyre coat of arms, painted above a stone fireplace (which has a coal fire in winter), dominates the beamed no smoking lounge bar at this 17th-c stone-built inn. There's also a longcase clock, cushioned settles around the walls, comfortable plush chairs and lots of brass and copper. A smaller public bar has dominoes and another fire; the snug is no smoking too, and there's a small separate dining area; maybe quiet piped classical music. Good seasonal food might include soup (£2.65), lunchtime sandwiches (from £2.75), sliced duck and mango (£4.25), aubergine and mushroom lasagne (£5.95), ham and mushroom tagliatelle (£6.55), steak and kidney pie (£7.25), salmon with orange and basil sauce (£7.45), chicken stuffed with leeks and stilton in a creamy sauce (£8.95), puddings such as bread and butter pudding or brandy snap basket filled with coffee ice cream (£2.65), and daily specials such as chicken breast stuffed with avocado and mozzarella with tomato and basil sauce (£8.45) and rabbit, cider and bacon pie topped with suet crust pastry (£8.95); efficient and cheerfully helpful service. Black Sheep Special, John Smiths and Marstons Pedigree on handpump. Colourful hanging baskets, and in autumn the virginia creeper, brighten up the exterior, and a new fountain plays in the small garden, which has tables looking out over beautiful Peak District countryside. There are good walks near here. *(Recommended by DC, JP, PP, Sir Richard FitzHerbert, the Didler)*

Free house ~ Licensee Lynne Smith ~ Real ale ~ Bar food ~ (01629) 640390 ~ Well behaved children in dining area if eating ~ Open 11.30-3, 6.30-11; 12-2.30, 7-10.30 Sun; closed 25 Dec

HATHERSAGE SK2380 Map 7
Plough ♀

Leadmill; A622 (ex B6001) towards Bakewell, OS Sheet 110 map reference 235805

Based on a former farmhouse, this is beautifully placed just south of the village, by the River Derwent, with tables in a pleasant garden running down to the water. Inside, the emphasis is on the food side. There's a very wide choice: not always a good sign, but in this case the landlord, who used to be a butcher, is proud of his sources, and the food is fresh, imaginatively prepared and full of taste. It might include sandwiches (from £2.95), soup (£3.25), aubergine pâtés with lemon relish (£3.95), roulette of duck with sweet and sour marmalade and brioche (£4.95), steak and kidney pie (£7.95), gammon and pineapple (£8.50), vegetarian platter (£9.95), blackened chicken with sweetcorn fritters, chilli jam and sweet pepper sauce (£10.95), baked monkfish and prawns with pepper and tomato sauce (£13.95) and puddings such as chocolate cherry torte or steamed syrup pudding (from £2.95). The attractive cosy-feeling bar, furnished with solid comfort, is on two levels, with a big log fire at one end and a woodburning stove at the other. Everything is spotless, and service is both cheerful and hospitable and so well organised that things go smoothly even at very busy times (it's worth booking for Sunday lunch); piped music and no smoking restaurant. Well kept Theakstons and a couple of guests such as Exmoor Gold, Fullers London Pride and Theakstons Old Peculier on handpump, cafetière coffee, around nine good value wines by the glass (on hot summer days people like the well chilled whites). We have not yet had reports from people staying here, but would expect it to be a nice place to stay. *(Recommended by E E Atkins, W W Burke, John Evans, IHR, GD, KW, M C and S Jeanes, Kathy and Chris Armes, Tom and Ruth Rees, Darly Graton, Graeme Gulibert, B and M A Langrish)*

Free house ~ Licensee Bob Emery ~ Real ale ~ Bar food (11.30-2.30, 6.30-9.30; 11.30-9.30 Sat; 12-9 Sun) ~ Restaurant ~ (01433) 650319 ~ Children welcome if eating ~ Open 11.30-11; 12-10.30 Sun ~ Bedrooms: £45B/£65B

HOGNASTON SK2350 Map 7
Red Lion ⊕

Village signposted off B5035 Ashbourne—Wirksworth

Although there is an emphasis on the enjoyable food at this friendly welcoming place, it's still very much a pub where locals drop in for a drink. The open-plan oak-beamed bar has a good relaxed atmosphere, with almost a bistro feel around the attractive mix of old tables (candlelit at night) on ancient flagstones, and copies of *Country Life* to read. There are old-fashioned settles among other seats, three open fires, and a growing collection of teddy bears among other bric-a-brac. Well cooked popular bar meals include home-made soup (£3.95), devilled kidneys (£4.25), warm goats cheese tart (£5.25), thai green chicken curry (£10.50), seafood marinara (£10.95), asparagus, sun-dried tomato and black olive risotto (£12.50), braised shank of lamb on olive mash (£14.95), fried beef fillet on puy lentils and béarnaise sauce (£16.95), puddings (from £3.95); booking is recommended for weekends. Well kept Marstons Pedigree, Greene King Abbot, Greene King Old Speckled Hen and a guest such as Timothy Taylor Landlord on handpump; country wines. Service is friendly and attentive; piped music. Handy for Carsington Reservoir. *(Recommended by Mr and Mrs G Owens, Mr and Mrs S Oxenbury, David Atkinson, Bernard Stradling, John Kane, June and Malcolm Farmer, JP, PP)*

Free house ~ Licensee Pip Price ~ Real ale ~ Bar food (not Sun evening, not Mon) ~ (01335) 370396 ~ Open 12-3, 6-11(7-10.30 Sun); closed Mon lunchtime ~ Bedrooms: £45S/£75S

'Children welcome' means the pub says it lets children inside without any special restriction; readers have found that some may impose an evening time limit – please tell us if you find this: www.goodguides.com

HOPE SK1783 Map 7
Cheshire Cheese ⌂

Edale Road – off A625 at W end of village

Each of the three very snug oak-beamed rooms at this friendly 16th-c village pub has its own coal fire, making the pub particularly cosy during the winter months. It's close to the Pennine Way and is well situated for a walk in the lovely Edale Valley. Originally built on the salt-carrying route from Cheshire across the Pennines to Yorkshire, the pub takes its name from the payments that were made in the form of cheese for an overnight stop, and you can still see the original cheese hooks in the lower room. Tasty bar food includes soup (£2.50), sandwiches (from £3.50), gammon and mixed grill (£8.95), with daily specials such as cheese and broccoli bake (£5.25), steak pie (£6.95), chicken in leek and stilton sauce (£7.75) and puddings such as ginger pudding with lemon sauce (£3.50); the lower dining room is no smoking. Well kept Barnsley Best, Whim Hartington and a couple of guests such as Black Sheep and Timothy Taylors Landlord on handpump, a good choice of house wines and malt whiskies; attractively furnished bedrooms. Parking can be a problem when busy. *(Recommended by David Edwards, Ken and Joan Bemrose, Steven and Sally Knight, Derek and Sylvia Stephenson, Kevin Thorpe, A C and E Johnson, Michael Buchanan, DC, Brian and Anna Marsden, JP, PP, John Brightley, Ruth and Paul Lawrence, Mike and Lynn Robinson, David and Heather Stephenson)*

Free house ~ Licensee David Helliwell ~ Real ale ~ Bar food ~ Restaurant ~ (01433) 620381 ~ Children in eating area and restaurant till 9pm ~ Open 12-3, 6.30-11; 12-11 Sat; 12-4, 6.30-10.30 Sun ~ Bedrooms: /£60S

KIRK IRETON SK2650 Map 7
Barley Mow ⬛ ⌂

Village signed off B5023 S of Wirksworth

There's a charmingly timeless atmosphere, traditional furnishings and civilised old-fashioned service at this tall gabled Jacobean brown sandstone inn. There are no games machines or other gadgets, just the occasional game of cards or dominoes. Dimly lit passageways and narrow stairwells open into a small main bar, which has a pubby feel, with antique settles on the tiled floor or built into the panelling, a roaring coal fire, four slate-topped tables, and shuttered mullioned windows. Another room has built in cushioned pews on oak parquet flooring and a small woodburner, and a third has more pews, tiled floor, beams and joists, and big landscape prints. One room is no smoking. Well kept and good value Hook Norton Best and Old Hooky, Leatherbritches, Marstons Pedigree, Whim Hartington and possibly a guest from a little brewer like Black Sheep or Cottage are kept in their casks behind a modest wooden counter; farm ciders. Food consists of lunchtime filled rolls (75p) and good home-cooked imaginative evening meals, which are for residents only. The pub is home to a couple of friendly pugs and a good-natured newfoundland. There's a decent-sized garden, and a couple of benches out in front. The pretty village is in good walking country and is handy for Carstington Water. *(Recommended by Willie Bell, JP, PP, the Didler, Dr W J M Gissane, Pete Baker, Bernard Stradling, Joan and Tony Walker, Kevin Thorpe, Tim Lawrence)*

Free house ~ Licensee Mary Short ~ Real ale ~ No credit cards ~ (01335) 370306 ~ Children welcome out of the bar ~ Open 12-2, 7-11(10.30 Sun); closed 25 Dec, 1 Jan ~ Bedrooms: £25S/£45B

LADYBOWER RESERVOIR SK1986 Map 7
Yorkshire Bridge ⌂

A6013 N of Bamford

This bustling roadside hotel is attractively situated near lots of pleasant countryside walks, including the Ladybower, Derwent and Howden reservoirs which were immortalised by the World War II Dambusters. This is a popular part of the world so you'll probably need to get here early for a table in summer to enjoy the generous bar food which includes soup (£2.50), lunchtime sandwiches (from £2.80), filled baked potatoes (from £3.10), lunchtime ploughman's (£5.95), chicken breast stuffed with herbs, topped with tomatoes and mozzarella (£6.95), lamb pot roast (£9.40), and steaks (from £9.95), with specials such as parma ham and black pepper tortelloni (£6.40), battered haddock (£6.95) and venison steak with tarragon butter (£9.95), and puddings such as bread and butter pudding and rum truffle (from £2.95). All three dining rooms are no smoking. One area has a country cottage atmosphere, with floral wallpaper, sturdy cushioned wall settles, Staffordshire dogs and toby jugs on a big stone fireplace with a warm coal-effect gas fire, china on delft shelves, a panelled dado and so forth. Another extensive area, with a fire, is lighter and more airy with pale wooden furniture, good big black and white photographs and lots of plates on the walls. The Bridge Room has a coal-effect fire and oak tables and chairs and there are pleasant views across a valley to steep larch woods from the small no smoking conservatory. Bass, Stones and Theakstons Best and Old Peculier are well kept on handpump, and there's good coffee with real cream; darts, dominoes, fruit machine, and piped music; disabled lavatories. The comfortable bedrooms are prettily decorated. *(Recommended by A Preston, Keith and Chris O'Neill, Kevin Blake, Mike and Wena Stevenson, Revd D Glover, Mike and Mary Carter, Annette and John Derbyshire, John and Christine Lowe)*

Free house ~ Licensee Trevelyan Illingworth ~ Real ale ~ Bar food (12-2, 6-9(9.30 Fri/Sat); 12-8.30 Sun) ~ Restaurant ~ (01433) 651361 ~ Children welcome ~ Open 11-11; 12-10.30 Sun ~ Bedrooms: £43B/£64B

LITTLE HUCKLOW SK1678 Map 7
Old Bulls Head

Pub signposted from B6049

A little low door here takes you into two neatly kept, oak-beamed rooms at this friendly old country pub. One room is served from a hatch, the other over a polished bar counter. The low ceilings and walls are packed with brasses, tankards and mining equipment, local photographs, thickly cushioned built-in settles, and a coal fire in a neatly restored stone hearth; darts, dominoes. For years a shaft in the cellar led down to a mine, until an explosion in the shaft blew off a piece of the cellar roof to create the unusual little 'cave' room at the back – at this point one assumes the mining innkeeper of the day probably stopped going to work that way. The neatly tended garden boasts lovely views over to the Peak District, and an unusual collection of well restored and attractively painted old farm machinery. Enjoyable hearty home-made bar food includes garlic mushrooms (£3.95), lasagne or stilton and vegetable bake (£6.75), battered cod (£7.50), gammon steak (£9.95) and puddings such as spotted dick or fruit crumble (from £2.95). Well kept John Smiths and Tetleys are served from carved handpumps, and they keep several malt whiskies. *(Recommended by Ann and Colin Hunt, Mike and Lynn Robinson, John and Beryl Brown, JP, PP, John and Christine Lowe)*

Free house ~ Licensee Julie Denton ~ Real ale ~ Bar food ~ (01298) 871097 ~ Children in eating area of bar ~ Open 12-3, 6-11(6.30-10.30 Sun) ~ Bedrooms: £35B/£56B

LITTON SK1675 Map 7
Red Lion

Village signposted off A623, between B6465 and B6049 junctions; also signposted off B6049

Very much at the heart of the community, this 17th-c pub is lovely at Christmas when a brass band plays carols, and bustling during the annual village well-dressing carnival, when villagers create a picture from flower petals, moss and other natural materials on a clay backing (usually the last weekend in June). Its two homely linked front rooms are very welcoming, with low beams, some panelling and blazing log fires. There's a bigger no smoking back room with good-sized tables and large antique prints on its stripped stone walls. The small bar counter has well kept Barnsley Bitter, Jennings Cumberland, Tetleys and a guest such as Shepherd Neame

Spitfire on handpump, with decent wines and 30 malt whiskies. Good food includes excellent hot and cold sandwiches (from £2), soup (£2.40), breaded garlic mushrooms (£2.85), steak and ale pie, gammon or battered cod (£5.80), 8oz sirloin (£7.35) and daily specials such as thai chicken curry (£5.85) or garlic lamb knuckle or salmon in white wine sauce or salmon in dill hollandaise (£6.95); puddings (£2.30). Service is friendly and helpful, and well behaved dogs are allowed; darts, shove-ha'penny, cribbage and dominoes. The quiet tree-studded village green in front is attractive, and there are good walks nearby. *(Recommended by Mike and Wendy Proctor, the Didler, JP, PP, Lynette and Stuart Shore, Eric Locker, David Atkinson, J Boggon, Andrew Pashley, Roy and Margaret Jones, Mrs P J Carroll, Neil and Anita Christopher)*

Free house ~ Licensees Terry and Michele Vernon ~ Real ale ~ Bar food (12-2, 6-8(8.30 Thurs-Sat); not Sun evenings) ~ (01298) 871458 ~ Well behaved children over 6 welcome ~ Open 11.30-3, 6-11; 11-11 Sat; 12-10.30 Sun

MELBOURNE SK3427 Map 7
John Thompson ◖ £

Ingleby, which is NW of Melbourne; turn off A514 at Swarkestone Bridge or in Stanton by Bridge; can also be reached from Ticknall (or from Repton on B5008)

The Thompson family have lived in this part of the world for generations. In 1969 John Thompson (look out for his citation for bravery on the wall for trying to save a drowning man) converted his 15th-c farmhouse into the present public house. He's been enthusiastically brewing his own real ales here since 1977. Very attractively priced, they include JT Bitter, Summer Gold and winter Porter. They make fine accompaniments to the good straightforward lunchtime carvery, which includes sandwiches or rolls (from £1.40, nothing else on Sundays), home-made soup (£1.50), salads with cold ham or beef (£4), excellent roast beef with yorkshire puddings (£5, not Mondays) and well liked puddings such as bread and butter pudding or fruit crumble (£2). This is a fairly simple place with a big, pleasantly modernised lounge with ceiling joists, some old oak settles, button-back leather seats, sturdy oak tables, antique prints and paintings, and a log-effect gas fire; a couple of smaller cosier rooms open off, with a piano, pool, fruit machine and a juke box in the children's room. There's a no smoking area in the lounge; piped music. There are lots of tables by flowerbeds on the well kept lawns, and on a partly covered outside terrace with its own serving bar. *(Recommended by Bernie Adams, Rosemary Kennell, the Didler)*

Own brew ~ Licensee John Thompson ~ Real ale ~ Bar food (lunchtime) ~ No credit cards ~ (01332) 862469 ~ Children in eating area of bar if eating, and family room ~ Open 10.30-2.30, 7-11; 12-2.30, 7-10.30 Sun

MILLTOWN SK3561 Map 7
Miners Arms

Off B6036 SE of Ashover; Oakstedge Lane

Set in former lead-mining country (hence the pub's name), with vestiges of the old workings adding interest to attractive country walks right from the pub's door, this impeccably kept, comfortable stone-built dining pub is virtually on the edge of Ashover. It's won firm friends for its particularly good value very tasty home-made food. Dishes are listed on a changing board and although they're not that unusual the quality is high. Things come with particularly good vegetables – say, three different sorts of potato, and half a dozen different vegetables including less common ones such as squash. There might be home-made soup (£1.85), chicken liver pâté (£3.25), spinach pasta bake (£6.25), steak and mushroom pie (£6.35), roasted chicken with lemon and tarragon (£6.95), braised beef in Murphy's or grilled cod (£7.95) and puddings such as mixed fruit bake or bread and butter pudding (£2.50). You may have to book a day or two ahead for lunch and do take note of their opening times. The layout is basically L-shaped, with a local feel up nearer the door; the dining room is no smoking. Two constantly rotating real ales are usually from smaller brewers such as Grainstore and Hampshire (it's a delight to see such glisteningly polished glasses), good value wines, very friendly efficient service, maybe quiet piped classical music. *(Recommended by Mr and Mrs R Willimott, John and Christine Lowe, Mr and Mrs Hugh Wood, JDM, KM, the Didler)*

Free house ~ Licensees Andrew and Yvonne Guest ~ Real ale ~ Bar food (not Mon/Tues, Sun evening, Weds evening in winter) ~ No credit cards ~ (01246) 590218 ~ Children welcome ~ Open 12-3, 7-11.30 Weds-Sun; closed Weds evening winter; closed Mon/Tues, Sun evening

MONSAL HEAD SK1871 Map 7
Monsal Head Hotel 🍺 🛏️

B6465

The best place to admire the magnificent view from this busy extended hotel which is perched high above Monsal Dale is from the conservatory, from the balconies and big windows in the lounge, and from four of the eight comfortable bedrooms. The cosy side stable bar once housed the horses that used to to pull guests and their luggage up from the station at the other end of the steep valley. There's reference to its past role in the stripped timber horse-stalls, harness and brassware and lamps from the local disused railway station. There's a big warming woodburning stove in an inglenook, flagstones, cushioned oak pews around tables, farm tools, and piped music. Eight well kept real ales include Courage Directors, Marstons Pedigree, Monsal Best Bitter (brewed for them by Lloyds), Theakstons Old Peculier and Best, Timothy Taylors Landlord, Whim Hartington and a couple of guests such as Kelham Island Pale Rider and Abbeydale Matins on handpump – friendly helpful staff may allow a little taster before you commit yourself to a pint. There's also a very good choice of bottled German beers, and sensibly priced wines. Decent reasonably priced bar food is served all day and might include soup (£2.50), smoked haddock fishcakes with ginger and lime sauce (£3.50), burgers (£4.50), baked aubergine filled with sweet and sour vegetables and topped with brie (£5.95), stilton stuffed chicken breast wrapped in bacon (£6.95), lamb in honey and mint (£7.10), seafood tagliatelle (£7.50), game pie (£8.50) and a couple of daily specials such as fried king scallops on caramelised orange (£4.95), pork fillet and asparagus on whole grain mustard and thyme sauce (£9.95), bass on watercress crushed potatoes with balsamic dressing (£11.95); no smoking restaurant. The boundary of the parishes of Little Longstone and Ashford runs through the hotel, and the spacious restaurant and smaller lounge are named according to which side of the line they sit; beer garden. *(Recommended by Mike and Wendy Proctor, Ian S Morley, Keith and Chris O'Neill, JP, PP, Nigel Woolliscroft, P and M Rudlin, the Didler, Mike and Lynn Robinson, Phil and Heidi Cook, Sue Demont, Tim Barrow, M G Hart, A C and E Johnson)*

Free house ~ Licensees Christine O'Connell and Philip Smith ~ Real ale ~ Bar food (12-9.30) ~ Restaurant ~ (01629) 640250 ~ Children welcome ~ Open 11-11; closed 25 Dec ~ Bedrooms: £38.50B/£46.60B

OVER HADDON SK2066 Map 7
Lathkil

Village and inn signposted from B5055 just SW of Bakewell

Nice outside for its marvellous views in summer and inside by the warming fire in winter, this unpretentious hotel is next to Lathkil Dale, one of the quieter dales, which lies steeply down below, with paths from the village leading straight into the tempting harmonious landscape of pastures and copses. Unsurprisingly, it's very popular with walkers, who can leave their muddy boots in the pub's lobby. The airy room on the right as you go in has a nice fire in the attractively carved fireplace, old-fashioned settles with upholstered cushions or plain wooden chairs, black beams, a delft shelf of blue and white plates, original prints and photographs, and big windows. On the left, the spacious and sunny family dining area – partly no smoking – doubles as a restaurant in the evenings; it's not quite as pubby as the bar, but there isn't a problem with shorts or walking gear. Bar food includes home-made soup (£2.25), filled rolls (from £2.25), smoked mackerel (£5.25), a vegetarian dish (£5.50), steak and kidney pie (£6.10), chicken breast and smoked salmon in stilton sauce (£6.40), cold topside of beef (£6.75), venison casserole (£7.50) and puddings (£2.75). Four well kept real ales include Charles Wells Bombardier, Whim Hartington and a couple of guests such as Marstons Pedigree and Timothy Taylors Landlord on handpump (samples are offered in sherry glasses); select malt whiskies and a good range of new world wines. Darts, bar billiards, shove-ha'penny, backgammon, dominoes, cribbage, and piped music. It does get very busy so it's best to get here early in good weather. *(Recommended by Mike and Wendy Proctor, the Didler, Richard Cole, Ben and Sheila Walker, Prof John and Mrs Patricia White, JP, PP, Rob Fowell, Anthony Barnes, Dr and Mrs M Locker, Carol and Steve Spence, JDM, KM, James A Waller, Eric Locker, Albert and Margaret Horton, Catherine and Richard Preston, Sue Holland, Dave Webster, Mike and Heather Watson, Nigel Woolliscroft, Paul and Margaret Baker)*

Free house ~ Licensee Robert Grigor-Taylor ~ Real ale ~ Bar food (not 25 Dec) ~ Restaurant ~ (01629) 812501 ~ Children welcome in restaurant and family room ~ Open 11.30-3, 6.30(7 winter)-11; 11.30-11(11.30-4, 7-11 winter) Sat; 12-10.30(12-4, 7-10.30 winter) Sun ~ Bedrooms: £37.50B/£70B

SHARDLOW SK4330 Map 7
Old Crown 🍺

Cavendish Bridge, off old A6 at Trent Bridge, actually just over Leics boundary

This friendly 17th-c coaching inn was once a deportation point for convicts bound for the colonies. These days the warmly welcoming bar is packed with hundreds of jugs and mugs hanging from the beamed ceiling, brewery and railway memorabilia and other bric-a-brac, with pictures and old brewery adverts covering the walls (even in the lavatories). Tasty bar food includes soup (£1.50), sandwiches (including a good range of baguettes, from £2), filled baked potatoes (from £2.50), liver and bacon casserole or beef and stilton pie (£6.30), game pudding (£6.50), lamb chops with rich port and orange sauce (£6.95), roast shank of lamb (£8.25), and puddings like treacle sponge and cherry pancake (from £1.95). The cellar restaurant has a patio overlooking the garden. About half a dozen well kept real ales include Black Sheep, Fullers London Pride, Greene King Old Speckled Hen and Timothy Taylors Landlord with a guest such as Everard Beacon on handpump; there's also a nice choice of malt whiskies. Shove-ha'penny, cribbage, fruit machine and piped music. Handy for the A6 and M1. *(Recommended by Christopher Turner, the Didler, Mr and Mrs J E C Tasker, Mike and Heather Watson, Sue Holland, Dave Webster, Dr and Mrs J Hills, Mrs C Monk, A C and E Johnson, Kevin Blake, JP, PP)*

Free house ~ Licensees Peter and Gillian Morton-Harrison ~ Real ale ~ Bar food (lunchtime) ~ (01332) 792392 ~ Children in eating area of bar at lunchtime only ~ Open 11.30-3.30, 5-11 (11-11 Fri); 12-5, 7-10.30 Sun ~ Bedrooms: £25S/£35S

WARDLOW SK1875 Map 7
Three Stags Heads 🍺

Wardlow Mires; A623 by junction with B6465

The robust character of this simple unchanging white-painted cottage will appeal to anyone who likes their pubs to be full-bloodedly traditional. While it certainly doesn't aim to attract a smart dining crowd, beer lovers happy to swap stories with the friendly locals and landlord over a hearty home-cooked meal won't want to leave. The tiny flagstoned parlour bar, warmed right through the winter by a cast-iron kitchen range, has old leathercloth seats, a couple of antique settles with flowery cushions, two high-backed windsor armchairs and simple oak tables – one curiosity is the petrified cat in a glass case. The well kept beer here is pretty no-nonsense too, with Abbeydale Absolution, Black Lurcher (brewed for the pub) at ABV 8% and Matins and Broadstone on handpump, as well as lots of bottled continental and English beers (the stronger beers can be quite pricey). They try to vary the seasonal menu to suit the weather, so dishes served on their hardy home-made plates (the barn is a pottery workshop) might include saag aloo or mushroom and spinach pie (£6.50), lamb and spinach curry or fish pie (£7.50), rabbit and pigeon pie (£8.50) and hare stew or pigeon breasts (£9.50). They also do a roaring trade in mugs of tea, and in winter there might be free hot chestnuts on the bar. You can book the tables in the small no smoking dining parlour with open fire. Cribbage and dominoes, nine men's morris and backgammon. It's situated in a natural sink, so don't be surprised to find the floors muddied by boots in wet weather (and the dogs muddy). The front terrace looks across the main road to the distant hills. The pub opens only on weekday evenings in high summer or when there's sufficient demand, so it's best to phone before visiting. *(Recommended by JP, PP, Kevin Thorpe, Rob Fowell, Mike and Wendy Proctor, C J Fletcher, the Didler, Nigel Woolliscroft, Pete Baker, Mike and Lynn Robinson, A C and E Johnson, L Davenport)*

Free house ~ Licensees Geoff and Pat Fuller ~ Real ale ~ Bar food ~ No credit cards ~ (01298) 872268 ~ Folk music most Sat evenings ~ Open 7-11 Fri; 12-11 Sat; 12-10.30 Sun; closed wkdys exc Fri evenings and bank hol Mons

WHITTINGTON MOOR SK3873 Map 7
Derby Tup ☜ £
387 Sheffield Rd; B6057 just S of A61 roundabout

The main draw at this simple unpretentious corner house is the impressive range of drinks they keep: just under a dozen well kept real ales, a good stock of continental and bottle-conditioned beers, fruit beers, farm ciders, perry and decent malt whiskies. Alongside five rotating guest beers such as Archers Golden, Caledonian Deuchars, Fullers London Pride and Woodfordes Wherry, you'll find Black Sheep Bitter, Greene King Abbot, Theakstons Old Peculier, Timothy Taylors Landlord and Whim Hartington. The plain but sizeable rectangular bar, with frosted street windows and old dark brown linoleum, has simple furniture arranged around the walls (there's a tremendously long green plastic banquette), leaving lots of standing room. There are two more small no smoking rooms; daily papers, possibly piped rock and blues, darts, dominoes and cribbage. Changing daily, a wide choice of good value food might include enjoyable sandwiches made with fresh bread from the neighbouring bakery (from £1.65), home-made soup (£2), corned beef hash (£3.75), Mexican vegetable quiche (£4), thai peanut chicken or moroccan lamb, and a range of home-made pies (all £4.50). Despite the remote-sounding name, Whittington Moor is on the northern edge of Chesterfield. It can get very busy on weekend evenings. *(Recommended by the Didler, CMW, JJW, JP, PP, Darly Graton, Graeme Gulibert, Keith and Chris O'Neill)*

Tynemill ~ Tenant Peter Hayes ~ Real ale ~ Bar food (12-2.30; 6-8 Thurs-Sat) ~ (01246) 454316 ~ Children in two side rooms ~ Open 11.30-11.00; 12-4, 7-10.30 Sun

WOOLLEY MOOR SK3661 Map 7
White Horse ⑪
Badger Lane, off B6014 Matlock—Clay Cross

There are lovely views over the Ogston reservoir and the Amber Valley from this delightfully situated, attractive old pub. A sign outside shows how horses and carts carried measures of salt along the toll road in front – the toll bar still stands at the entrance of the road. The chatty tap room, still very much in its original state, serves well kept Bass and Ruddles and a couple of guests such as Greene King Abbot and Old Speckled Hen. They also do home-made lemonade and decent wines. There is piped classical music in the lounge, and the views are from the no smoking conservatory. It's best to book for the restaurant. Using fresh local produce, very enjoyable bar food includes good soup (£2.95), toasted paninis (from £3.25), mezze plate (£3.75), sandwiches (from £3.95), steak sandwich (£4.95), steak and kidney pie (£5.75), creole sweetcorn fritter with jambalaya rice and salsa (£6.25), fish and chips (£6.75), roast pork leg with apricot and almond stuffing or roast red pepper and goats cheese strudel (£7.25), beef and prune tagine (£7.75), fried entrecote on mushroom ragoût with watercress butter (£8.25), fried tuna with niçoise salad (£8.95), duck breast with blackberry and apple sauce (£9.95); good children's meals come with a puzzle sheet and crayons. Picnic-sets in the garden have lovely views too, and there's a very good children's play area with wooden play train, climbing frame and swings, and boules. *(Recommended by Don and Shirley Parrish, DAV, Simon and Carol Hadwick, Richard Cole, A Preston, Peter and Audrey Dowsett, Norma and Keith Bloomfield, Rob Fowell, the Didler, Peter F Marshall, Rita and Keith Pollard, Keith and Chris O'Neill, JDM, KM, Steven and Sally Knight, DC, Bernie Adams)*

Free house ~ Licensees Graeme Jones and Keith Hurst ~ Real ale ~ Bar food (12-2, 6-9 Mon-Sat, 12-8 Sat) ~ No credit cards ~ (01246) 590319 ~ Children in eating area of bar and restaurant ~ Open 12-3, 6-11; 12-11 Sat; 12-10.30 Sun

Lucky Dip

Besides the fully inspected pubs, you might like to try these Lucky Dips recommended to us and described by readers (if you do, please send us reports: www.goodguides.com).

Alderwasley [SK3153]
Bear [½ mile SW, on Ambergate—Wirksworth high back road]: Unspoilt and not smart, small-roomed softly lit bar, good blackboard choice of imaginative food, also carvery, good wines, enthusiastic friendly staff, two smallish warm and comfortable dining rooms, log fires *(Mrs J Hinsliff, A Preston)*
Apperknowle [SK3878]
☆ *Yellow Lion* [High St]: 19th-c stone-built village local with very welcoming long-serving licensees, comfortable banquettes in L-shaped lounge with TV, old organ, brass lamps, fruit machine, no smoking dining room, wide choice of good value food from sandwiches and toasties up inc vegetarian, five well kept ales inc Timothy Taylors Landlord, reasonable prices, good choice of wines by glass, garden with play area; Mon and Weds quiz nights; children welcome, cheap bedrooms *(Keith and Chris O'Neill, C R Tyler, Peter F Marshall, JP, PP, the Didler)*
Ashford in the Water [SK1969]
☆ *Bulls Head* [Church St]: Cosy and homely comfortable lounge, busy bar, well kept Robinsons Best, Old Stockport and Hartleys XB, well prepared adventurous food, prompt friendly service, no piped music; children in public bar, tables out behind and by front car park *(Darly Graton, Graeme Gulibert, Annette and John Derbyshire, Brian and Anna Marsden, June and Malcolm Farmer, Albert and Margaret Horton)*
Ashover [SK3463]
Crispin [Church St]: Pleasant and friendly, with good value food from sandwiches up, real ales, real fires in comfortable beamed lounge (which with dining room is oldest part), and in split-level bar with games and sporting mementoes, family room, back conservatory *(Paul Bridgett)*
Bakewell [SK2168]
☆ *Castle Inn* [Bridge St]: Friendly Georgian pub with three candlelit rooms, smart wine-bar feel mixing flagstones with comfortable furnishings and lots of pictures, well kept ales such as Boddingtons, Flowers and a guest such as Barnsley, cafetière coffee, good value home-made food inc unusual dishes, friendly staff, two real fires, daily papers; jazz and blues wknds, tables outside *(Carol and Steve Spence, David Carr, Kevin Blake)*

Manners [Haddon Rd]: Well kept Robinsons, friendly and interesting licensees, convivial atmosphere (esp Mon market days) *(D G Chapman)*
Peacock [Bridge St]: Clean, bright and cheerful, well kept Theakstons and guest such as Adnams Bitter and Broadside, popular food (not Mon-Weds evenings), good prices and service *(Darly Graton, Graeme Gulibert, Ian and Nita Cooper)*
Baslow [SK2672]
Robin Hood [A619/B6050]: Fairly modern, well decorated and comfortable, with tidy banquettes, well kept Banks's and Mansfield ales, good reasonably priced food from sandwiches up, brisk friendly service, soft piped music; big back uncarpeted bar for walkers and climbers (boots and dogs on leads welcome); bedrooms, good walking country nr Baslow Edge *(M G Hart, Dr D J and Mrs S C Walker, Ian and Nita Cooper)*
Belper [SK3549]
Fishermans Rest [Broadholme Lane]: Good generous reasonably priced food inc monster grill, well kept Marstons Pedigree, friendly atmosphere, great view, no machines, well reproduced piped music such as blues; play area *(James Edge)*
Talbot [Bridge Foot]: Italian-owned coaching inn with Mediterranean-theme décor, good changing lunchtime bar food from sandwiches and baguettes to short choice of reasonably priced main dishes, evening more steak-bar style, Marstons Pedigree and bottled Italian beers, welcoming staff, open fire *(Geoff and Tricia Alderman, Martin Lucas)*
Biggin [SK1559]
☆ *Waterloo* [W of A515]: Reasonably priced generous food inc help-yourself salads and children's dishes, Bass, welcoming service; pleasant farmland views from picnic-sets out in front, camping in field behind, handy for Tissington Trail *(Richard Fendick)*
Birch Vale [SK0287]
☆ *Sycamore* [Sycamore Rd; from A6015 take Station Rd towards Thornsett]: Good reasonably priced food inc children's dishes and rich puddings in thriving four-roomed dining pub; well kept ales, friendly helpful service, piped music, fountain in downstairs drinking bar; spacious streamside gardens with good

play area, pets corner and summer bar; restaurant open all day Sun, children welcome, handy for Sett Valley trail; bedrooms comfortable, good breakfast *(Mrs M A Cameron, LYM)*

Bonsall [SK2858]

Barley Mow [off A6012 Cromford—Hartington; The Dale]: Friendly tucked-away pub with particularly well kept Whim Hartington and two or three guest beers, fresh sandwiches and other food, character furnishings; live music wknds inc landlord playing accordion, organises local walks; cl wkdy lunchtimes (may open Fri by arrangement, open all day Sat) *(the Didler, JP, PP)*

Brackenfield [SK3658]

Plough [A615 Matlock—Alfreton, about a mile NW of Wessington]: Much modernised oak-beamed stone-built 18th-c former farmhouse in lovely setting, cosy and welcoming three-level bar, cheerful log-effect gas fire, several well kept ales inc Adnams and Greene King Old Speckled Hen, sensibly priced freshly made food inc children's, OAP bargain lunch and splendid puddings range; big beautifully kept gardens with play area *(Ian and Nita Cooper)*

Bradwell [SK1781]

☆ *Bowling Green* [Smalldale, off B6049 at Gore Lane/Townend]: Good views from tables on terrace and garden outside attractive 16th-c stone-built local, much modernised inside, with wide choice of good food from sandwiches to duck, well kept Bass, John Smiths Magnet, Stones, and Boothys brewed for the pub, lots of malt whiskies; games room, fruit machine, unobtrusive piped music; decent bedrooms in separate building *(LYM, P and M Wakely, Jim Bush)*

Buxton [SK0572]

Bakers Arms [West Rd]: Homely family-run terraced local with well kept Greene King Abbot, Tetleys and several guest beers such as Kelham Island Pale Rider, welcoming comfortable atmosphere, good mix of customers *(anon)*

Old Hall [The Square, almost opp Opera House]: Large hotel worth knowing for its wine bar, open most of the day, with good value food from generous sandwiches to main dishes; bedrooms *(M G Hart)*

Calver [SK2474]

Bridge Inn [Calver Bridge, off A623 N of Baslow]: Unpretentious welcoming village local, quick good value food (not Mon evening or winter Sun evening), particularly well kept Hardys & Hansons ales, good friendly service, lots of areas and cosy corners, coal fires, old brass and local prints; tables in nice big garden by River Derwent *(R A Watson, Gill Waller, Tony Morriss)*

Derwentwater Arms [Low Side]: Neat and simple décor, plenty of room, courteous efficient attentive staff, good freshly cooked food esp fish and fresh veg, bargain OAP lunches; raised garden (but disabled access) *(IHR, Frank Gorman)*

Eyre Arms [Chesterfield Rd, Calver Sough]: Large Mansfield family dining pub, helpful friendly staff, food all day wknds, wide drinks choice inc three real ales and good coffee, smart beamed lounge with blazing fire, shelves of bottles and plates, lots of copper and brass, family room, fish tank and piano; piped music, fruit machines; tables outside, open all day *(CMW, JJW, Kevin Blake)*

Carsington [SK2553]

Miners Arms [just N of B5035 Wirksworth—Ashbourne]: Popular for reasonably priced usual food, efficient service, tables and climbing frame in garden behind; pleasant village in good walking and cycling country nr Carsington reservoir *(Richard Fendick)*

Castleton [SK1583]

☆ *George* [Castle St]: Good friendly relaxed atmosphere, good food from nourishing sandwiches to interesting and individual main dishes, two roomy bars, one mainly for eating, with beams and stripped stone, helpful efficient staff, well kept Bass ales; tables on wide forecourt, lots of flower tubs; popular with young people – nr YHA; dogs welcome *(JP, PP, Steven and Sally Knight, Ruth and Paul Lawrence)*

Olde Cheshire Cheese [How Lane]: Two communicating beamed areas, cosy and spotless, lots of photographs, cheery landlord, well kept Stones and Worthington tapped from the cask, back lounge set for wide choice of usual reasonably priced food, open fire, toby jugs and local paintings; sensibly placed darts, quiet piped music; bedrooms *(BB, David Edwards, Rona Murdoch)*

☆ *Olde Nags Head* [Cross St (A625)]: Small but solid hotel dating from 17th c, interesting antique furnishings in civilised main bar, coal fire, well kept Marstons Pedigree, good coffee, impressive bar food from sandwiches up, cosy Victorian restaurant; open all day, comfortable bedrooms *(LYM, JP, PP)*

Chapel-en-le-Frith [SK0581]

Cross Keys [Chapel Milton]: Pleasant atmosphere and good generous fresh food (all day Sun) in popular old local with smartly decorated small restaurant, well kept beers, very friendly service; children welcome *(Dr and Mrs R E S Tanner)*

Chelmorton [SK1170]

Church [between A6 and A515 SW of Buxton]: Comfortable split bar, ample space for diners, good range of reasonably priced generous food inc fresh veg, friendly landlord and golden labrador, well kept Marstons Bitter, Pedigree, seasonal ale and a guest such as Adnams, tables out on terrace, well tended flower boxes; piped music, outside lavatories; superb walking country *(Dr W J M Gissane, JP, PP)*

Chesterfield [SK3871]

Market Hotel [New Sq]: Festival Ale House, bare boards and panelling, several well kept changing real ales, generous straightforward food; open all day, cl Sun lunchtime *(Keith Jacob)*

☆ *Royal Oak* [Chatsworth Rd]: Friendly pub, always a good atmosphere, fine choice of well kept beers, enthusiastic young landlord *(Keith and Chris O'Neill)*

Rutland [Stephenson Pl]: Very old L-shaped pub next to crooked spire church, now a Hogshead, with rugs and assorted wooden furniture on bare boards, a dozen well kept ales and a farm cider, good value food, darts, pinball machine, old photographs; children welcome, open all day *(Keith and Chris O'Neill, W W Burke)*

Chinley [SK0482]

☆ *Lamb* [just off A624 S of Hayfield]: Profusely decorated three-room stone-built pub tucked below road, good range of food (all day wknds and bank hols) inc notable specials and large or small helpings of Sun roast, well kept Bass and other ales, friendly licensees; children welcome, lots of tables out in front with good views *(Greta and Christopher Wells, BB, Jack Morley)*

Codnor [SK4249]

Red Admiral [Alfreton Rd]: Pleasant atmosphere, friendly staff, good home-cooked food and well kept range of beers *(R P Webb)*

Combs [SK0478]

Beehive: Roomy and comfortable, with good generous home cooking (bargain suppers Mon, Weds/Thurs steak nights) evenings and all day wknd, well kept ales such as Black Sheep and Hydes Jekyll Gold, pleasant piped jazz, quiet piped jazz, quiz night Tues; bedrooms, tables outside, by lovely valley tucked away from main road *(Bob and Lisa Cantrell)*

Coxbench [SK3743]

Fox & Hounds [off B6179 N of Derby; Alfreton Rd]: Friendly village local with long partly flagstoned bar, raised restaurant area, wide choice of good interesting fresh food, well kept Fullers London Pride, Marstons Pedigree and Tetleys, good service; may be piped music *(John Beeken)*

Crich [SK3554]

Cliff [Cromford Rd, Town End]: Cosy and unpretentious two-room pub with real fire, well kept Hardys & Hansons ales, good value generous standard bar food; great views, handy for National Tramway Museum *(Gill Waller, Tony Morriss, the Didler, JP, PP, C J Fletcher)*

Cromford [SK2956]

Boat [Scarthin, off Mkt Pl]: Spotless 18th-c traditional local in quaint village, long narrow low-beamed bar with stripped stone, bric-a-brac and books, friendly relaxed atmosphere, log fire, well kept ales such as Adnams and Marstons Pedigree, darts; TV may be on for sports; children welcome, garden *(JP, PP, Dr and Mrs J Hills, the Didler)*

Cutthorpe [SK3273]

☆ *Gate* [Overgreen; B6050 W of village]: Picture-window views over eastern Peak District (good peaceful walks) from chatty area around bar, neat and comfortable no smoking dining lounge down steps, good value food (not Sun-Tues evenings) inc bargain lunches popular with older people, well kept ales such as Bass, Boddingtons, Flowers Original and Mansfield Riding, friendly efficient staff, coal fire, lots of biggish pictures; children welcome if eating, no dogs *(L Davenport)*

Peacock [School Hill (B6050 NW of Chesterfield)]: Neatly kept and comfortable, good straightforward food, good service, well kept real ales *(Keith and Chris O'Neill)*

Derby [SK3438]

☆ *Abbey Inn* [Darley St, Darley Abbey]: Notable for massive stonework remnants of 11th-c abbey; brick floor, studded oak doors, big stone inglenook, stone spiral stair to upper bar with handsome oak rafters; well kept cheap Sam Smiths, decent lunchtime bar food, children allowed; opp Derwent-side park, pleasant riverside walk out from centre *(JP, PP, David Carr, the Didler, Anthony Barnes, LYM)*

Exeter Arms [Exeter Pl]: Several comfortable and friendly areas inside, inc super little snug with black-leaded and polished brass range, black and white tiled floor, two built-in curved settles, lots of wood and bare brick, HMS *Exeter* and regimental memorabilia and breweriana; friendly staff, well kept Banks's and Camerons Strongarm, fresh rolls and pork pies, daily papers, well reproduced piped music; open all day *(Kevin Blake, the Didler, JP, PP, Richard Lewis, Richard Houghton)*

Falstaff [Silver Hill Rd, off Normanton Rd]: Lively and friendly three-room former coaching inn, basic and unsmart, with changing well kept ales such as Greene King Abbot and Marstons Pedigree; right-hand bar with coal fire usually quieter; open all day *(the Didler)*

☆ *Flower Pot* [King St]: Extended real ale pub with excellent changing choice of well kept beers, some tapped from the cask – a dozen or more at a time, glassed panels show cellarage, regular beer festivals; friendly staff, several rooms inc comfortable back bar with lots of books and old Derby photographs, brewery memorabilia, good value food till early evening, daily papers, pub games, some good live bands; open all day, tables on terrace; same small group runs the Smithfield *(Richard Lewis)*

Friargate [Friar Gate]: Good choice of interesting well kept ales (some tapped from the cask) in comfortable and relaxing pub, part carpeted, padded banquettes, high ceilings and light green décor, hatch service from heavily panelled central bar, bar food inc all-day rolls, daily papers, friendly landlady, disabled facilities; open all day, popular with students *(the Didler, David Carr, G Coates)*

Old Silk Mill [Full St]: Attractively decorated and welcoming two-room 1920s pub with old prints and full-scale mural of 1833 Derby turnout, good range of beers under light carbon dioxide blanket such as Bathams Best, Boddingtons, Brewsters Bellydance, Fullers London Pride, Marstons Pedigree, Springhead Leveller and Youngs Special, lots of country wines, good value cheap food from sandwiches to steaks all day (back dining area, breakfasts from 9am), daily papers, real fires; open all day, handy for cathedral and Industrial Museum *(Richard Houghton, the Didler, Richard Lewis, G Coates, JP, PP)*

Rowditch [Uttoxeter New Rd (A516)]: Popular good value roadside pub, friendly atmosphere, well kept Mansfield Riding and Old Baily, Marstons Pedigree and guest beers, country wines, attractive small snug on right, coal fire, quiz and food nights *(the Didler)*

Smithfield [Meadow Rd]: Friendly and comfortable bow-fronted pub with big bar, snug, back lounge full of old prints, curios and breweriana, well kept Bass, Oakham JHB, Whim Hartington and other Oakham, Whim and guest ales such as Fullers London Pride, filled rolls and hearty lunchtime meals, real fires, daily papers; juke box, pub games inc table skittles, board games, TV and games machines, quiz nights, live music; open all day, children welcome, riverside garden *(the Didler, Richard Lewis, JP, PP, David Carr)*

☆ *Standing Order* [Irongate]: Vast Wetherspoons conversion of imposing bank, central bar, booths down each side, elaborately painted plasterwork, pseudo-classical torsos, high portraits of mainly local notables; usual popular food all day, good range of well kept ales, reasonable prices, daily papers, neat efficient young staff, no smoking area; rather daunting acoustics; disabled facilities *(the Didler, JP, PP, BB)*

Station Inn [Midland Rd]: Friendly and bustling basic local with good food lunchtime and early evening in large back lounge, particularly well kept Bass in jugs from cellar, M&B Mild and Marstons Pedigree on handpump, tiled floor bar, side room with darts, pool and TV, ornate façade; piped music, open all day Fri *(Richard Lewis, the Didler)*

Draycott in the Clay [SK1630]

Boars Head [Aston Bridge; A515, about 1½ miles N]: Rambling pub/hotel handy for Sudbury Hall, lunchtime carvery and well presented bar food, very reasonable prices, well kept Bass and Greene King Ruddles County, cheerful efficient service despite the bustle; restaurant; motel-type bedrooms *(John and Christine Lowe)*

Dronfield [SK3378]

Old Sidings [B6057]: Railway-theme pub by main line, upstairs lounge with lots of local railway memorabilia, no smoking part up a couple of steps, plush seating, velvet curtains, well kept Stones Bitter and Mild and Tetleys, reasonably priced usual food inc children's and bargains for early suppers or students, games inc revolving pool table past narrow bar, separate restaurant; open all day *(Kevin Blake)*

Duffield [SK3543]

Pattern Makers Arms [Crown St, off King St]: Tall Victorian backstreet local with growing choice of interesting guest beers under enthusiastic new landlord, piano wknds *(the Didler)*

Edale [SK1285]

☆ *Old Nags Head* [off A625 E of Chapel-en-le-Frith; Grindsbrook Booth]: Popular neatly refurbished pub at start of Pennine Way, flagstoned area for booted walkers, food from basic hearty sustenance to more interesting dishes, well kept Scottish Courage and other ales, open fire; children in airy back family room, tables on front terrace and in garden – short path down to pretty streamside cottages; open all day *(JP, PP, LYM, P and M Rudlin)*

Ednaston [SK2442]

Yew Tree: Unusual and attractive village pub with four rooms served from central bar, best one with lots of copper and brass, dark beams hung with whisky-water jugs, bay window overlooking garden, wall seats, large round table and open fire; good range of well cooked food, friendly efficient service, Bass beers with a guest such as Charles Wells Bombardier, separate games room out by car park *(Kevin Blake, O Richardson)*

Elton [SK2261]

☆ *Duke of York* [Main St]: Unspoilt old-fashioned local, like stepping back in time, lovely little quarry-tiled back tap room with coal fire in massive fireplace, glazed bar and hatch to corridor, two front rooms – one like private parlour with dining table (no food, just crisps); Mansfield and occasional guest beer such as Adnams; lavatories out behind by the pig sty; open 8.30-11, and Sun lunchtime *(John Brightley, C J Fletcher, the Didler, JP, PP)*

Fenny Bentley [SK1750]

Bentley Brook [A515 N of Ashbourne]: Big open-plan bare-boards bar/dining room, log fire, communicating restaurant, one or two changing own-brewed Leatherbritches ales and well kept guest beers such as Mansfield Riding and Marstons Pedigree, food inc some unusual dishes (maybe free meals for children eating with adults early evening), well reproduced piped music; picnic-sets on terrace with barbecue area, skittles, kitchen shop; marquee for spring bank hol beer festival, open all day, handy for Dovedale; bedrooms *(BB, the Didler, MLR, JP, PP, Dr B and Mrs P B Baker, Alun Howells)*

Foolow [SK1976]

☆ *Bulls Head*: Attractive moorland village pub with friendly flagstoned bar, prompt cheerful service, well kept changing ales such as Black Sheep, enjoyable food from generous sandwiches up in bar and pleasant no smoking restaurant area, interesting photographs inc good collection of Edwardian naughties; bedrooms, fine views, cl Sun evening *(LYM, B and M A Langrish, A Preston)*

Froggatt Edge [SK2577]

Grouse [B6054 NE of Froggatt]: Plush front bar, open fire and wooden benches in back bar, big dining room, good home cooking, Adnams and Banks's beers, friendly service, handsome views; verandah and terrace, clean bedrooms, good gritstone moorland walking country *(DC)*

Great Hucklow [SK1878]

☆ *Queen Anne*: Good family atmosphere, friendly new landlord, beams and gleaming copper, well kept Mansfield and guest beers such as Adnams, open fire, unpretentious blackboard food, french windows to small back terrace and charming garden with lovely views, walkers' bar; unobtrusive piped music; two quiet bedrooms, good walks *(CMW, JJW, the Didler, Peter F Marshall, Rona Murdoch, Mrs P A King, Trevor Swindells)*

Grindleford [SK2478]

☆ *Maynard Arms* [Main Rd]: Spacious high-ceilinged hotel bar, civilised and comfortable, with dark panelling, local and autographed cricketing photographs, wide choice of food from sandwiches to steaks, well kept Boddingtons and Castle Eden, well chilled white wines, friendly staff; no smoking restaurant overlooking neat gardens with water feature; piped music; children in eating areas, open all day Sun, comfortable bedrooms, nice setting *(D J and P M Taylor, Dr W J M Gissane, Kathy and Chris Armes, David Carr)*

Sir William [B6001]: Comfortable and friendly, with wide choice of good value food, well kept ales, good coffee, pool table in spacious room; splendid view esp from terrace, walking nearby *(IHR)*

Hartington [SK1360]

Devonshire Arms [Market Pl]: Newish chef doing good choice of tasty food in attractive old pub, three well kept real ales, friendly staff; comfortable bedrooms, tables out in front facing village duck pond, more in small garden behind, good walks *(Richard Fendick, Dr W J M Gissane)*

Hathersage [SK3187]

Fox House [A625 about 6 miles SW of Sheffield]: Handsome 18th-c stone-built pub with well kept Bass ales, good value well presented food, good service; nice moorland location *(BB, Keith and Chris O'Neill, Susan and Nigel Wilson)*

☆ *George* [Main Rd (A625 W of Sheffield)]: Substantial old hotel, comfortable and restful, with old-fashioned attentive service, good value well presented food from sandwiches with home-baked bread to good hot dishes such as scallops or lamb, well kept Boddingtons, decent wine, attentive service, neat flagstoned back terrace by rose garden; a nice place to stay (the back bedrooms are the quiet ones) *(John and Christine Lowe, Tom and Ruth Rees, LYM)*

Little John [Station Rd]: Comfortable and friendly, with good value generous food, real ales such as Boddingtons, games room; disabled access, bedrooms *(Mary Morris)*

☆ *Scotsmans Pack* [School Lane, off A625]: Big clean welcoming open-plan local very popular with walkers, huge choice of generous nicely presented imaginative food (best to book Sun lunch), reasonable prices, Burtonwood beers with a guest such as Ridleys ESX, decent wines, good service; some seats on pleasant side terrace by trout stream; good bedrooms, huge breakfast *(David Carr, Rev John Hibberd, Darly Graton, Graeme Gulibert, Steven and Sally Knight, Vicky and Matt Wharton)*

Hayfield [SK0388]

☆ *Lantern Pike* [Glossop Rd (A624 N)]: Cosily unpretentious and welcoming, with plush seats, lots of brass, china and toby jugs, well kept Boddingtons, Flowers IPA and Timothy Taylors Landlord, good choice of malt whiskies, decent fresh bar food from sandwiches up inc children's and OAP wkdy lunches; no smoking back dining room, darts, dominoes, maybe piped nostalgic music; back terrace looking up to Lantern Pike, great spot for walkers; children welcome, open all day wknds, good value bedrooms (quieter at back) *(Kevin Blake, LYM, MP)*

Pack Horse [off A624 Glossop—Chapel-en-le-Frith; Market St]: Busy dining pub open all day, good proper food cooked to order from baguettes to steaks at close-set tables; great decorations for Christmas and other festivals *(Mike and Wendy Proctor, John and Christine Lowe)*

☆ *Royal* [Market St]: Spacious and well run 18th-c former vicarage, oak panelling, six well kept ales (civilised beer festival early Oct), Weston's farm cider, relaxed cheerful atmosphere, friendly efficient service, local papers, good sensibly priced food from hot beef or pork rolls up; jazz Sun afternoon, pleasantly decorated bedrooms, open all day wknds *(Mike and Wendy Proctor, Bob and Lisa Cantrell)*

Heage [SK3650]

White Hart [Church St]: Friendly, with Bass, Courage Directors and Marstons Pedigree, good value food from sandwiches to big mixed grill, no smoking restaurant; secluded garden with play area *(Geoff and Tricia Alderman)*

Heanor [SK4345]

Mundy Arms [Ilkeston Rd]: Recently reworked as smart character dining pub, good reasonably priced choice, well kept Hardys & Hansons, country dressers with china and ornaments, beams and alcoves *(Kevin Blake)*

Holbrook [SK3644]

☆ *Dead Poets* [Chapel St; off A6 S of Belper]: Connected to the Brunswick in Derby, with well kept ales from there, three guest beers on handpump and Marstons Pedigree served by the jug from the cellar; beams, settles, candles on scrubbed tables, flagstones, big open fire; folk music every other Sun, bring your own instrument and join in; open all day Fri-Sun *(Bernie Adams, JP, PP, the Didler)*

Spotted Cow [Town St]: Traditional pub extended behind, Jennings, good value food inc vegetarian and generous help-yourself veg, comfortable no smoking eating area *(Bernie Adams, Richard and Jean Green)*

☆ *Wheel* [Chapel St]: Friendly beamed country local with well kept ales such as Courage Directors, Marstons Pedigree, Theakstons Best and Old Peculier, Whim Hartington and a guest beer, some in jugs from the cellar, good value home-made food (not Sun evening or Mon) from sandwiches and baguettes up, good log fire, cheerful attentive staff, snug, family room, attractive separate restaurant; tables on terrace and in pleasant secluded garden with hawk in aviary, open all day Sat, cl Mon lunchtime *(Geoff and Tricia Alderman, the Didler, Bernie Adams, JP, PP)*

Holmesfield [SK3277]

☆ *Robin Hood* [B6054 towards Hathersage]: Neatly extended moorland pub with wide choice of popular food (all day wknd) from sandwiches to steaks, half helpings for OAPs and children, well kept real ale, smart pleasant staff, good open fires, beams, partly carpeted flagstones, plush banquettes, high-raftered restaurant with big pictures; children in eating areas, piped music, stone tables out on cobbled front courtyard *(LYM, Keith and Chris O'Neill)*

Holymoorside [SK3469]

Lamb [Loads Rd, just off Holymoor Rd]: Small, cosy and spotless two-room village pub in leafy spot, Bass, Home, Theakstons XB and up to six guest beers inc one from Adnams, pub games, tables outside; cl lunchtime Mon-Thurs *(Martin Wyss, the Didler, Mike and Bridget Cummins)*

Hope [SK1783]

Woodroffe Arms [Castleton Rd]: Several friendly rooms inc conservatory, good choice of generous good value food inc children's and Sun lunch, well kept Boddingtons and Wadworths 6X, real fire, cheerful service; Sun quiz night, garden with swings; bedrooms *(Rev John Hibberd, Ann and Colin Hunt)*

Hulland [SK2647]

Black Horse [Hulland Ward; A517 Ashbourne—Belper]: 17th-c pub with décor to match, good freshly made food, not over-priced and inc interesting dishes, in bar or dining room, well kept Bass and Marstons Pedigree with a guest such as Timothy Taylors Landlord or Wychwood, friendly licensees; children welcome, tables in garden, comfortable bedrooms, nr Carsington Water *(Derek and Sylvia Stephenson, Gill Waller, Tony Morriss, J V Dadswell)*

Idridgehay [SK2848]

☆ *Black Swan* [B5023 S of Wirksworth]: Attractive bistro-style pub with conservatory extension, nice unhurried atmosphere, good food with plentiful fresh veg (not cheap, but some winter bargains), friendly efficient staff, guest beers; occasional jazz and other events, pleasant garden views across valley *(A Preston, R P and L E Booth, John and Christine Lowe)*

Ilkeston [SK4643]

Bridge Inn [Bridge St, Cotmanhay; off A609/A6007]: Two-room local by Erewash Canal, popular with fishermen and boaters for early breakfast and sandwich lunches; extremely well priced well kept Hardys & Hansons Best and Best Mild; well behaved children allowed, nice back garden with play area, open all day *(the Didler)*

☆ *Dewdrop* [Station St, Ilkeston Junction, off A6096]: Large welcoming three-room Victorian pub in old industrial area, two blazing coal fires, pictures and plates, friendly staff and locals, good value bar snacks inc huge cheap sandwiches, Ind Coope Burton, Hook Norton Old Hooky and half a dozen interesting guest beers from countrywide microbreweries (Feb and Dec beer festivals), good choice of whiskies, darts and TV in small public bar and impromptu piano sessions in lounge; sheltered outside seating, barbecue; cl Sat lunchtime, good value bedrooms *(JP, PP, Kevin Blake, James and Laura Newton, the Didler)*

King's Newton [SK3826]

Hardinge Arms [not far from M1 junction 23A, via A453 to Isley, then off Melbourne/Wilson rd; Main St]: Cosily plush rambling front bar with open fires, beams and fine panelled and carved bar counter, food from sandwiches and baked potatoes to popular carvery, Bass beers with a guest such as Marstons Pedigree, stately and spacious back lounge; piped music; children in eating area, open all day Sun, motel bedrooms *(John and Christine Lowe, LYM, JDM, KM)*

Kniveton [SK2050]

Red Lion [Main St]: Small village pub, friendly and helpful licensees (he gives good walking advice), three well kept changing ales often from small local breweries, enjoyable food inc good vegetarian choice; children very welcome *(Dr Chris Hammond)*

Little Eaton [SK3642]

Fox & Hounds [Alfreton Rd]: Dining pub with good food and welcoming staff *(David and Helen Wilkins)*

Little Longstone [SK1971]

☆ *Packhorse* [off A6 NW of Bakewell via Monsal Dale]: Snug unchanging 16th-c cottage, a pub since 1787, with old wooden chairs and benches in two homely well worn in beamed rooms, well kept Marstons Best and Pedigree, simple food lunchtime and evening, informal service, pub games, terrace in steep little back garden, hikers welcome; Weds folk night, opens 5 wkdys *(Kevin Thorpe, LYM, JP, PP, the Didler, Peter F Marshall)*

Makeney [SK3544]

☆ *Holly Bush* [A6 N, cross river Derwent, before Milford turn right, then left]: Unspoilt two-bar village pub, cosy and friendly, with five well kept ales brought from cellar in jugs, besides Ruddles County and one named for the pub – also annual beer festival; three roaring open fires (one by curved settle in snug's old-fashioned range), flagstones, beams, tiled floors; lunchtime rolls, basic evening food inc Thurs steak night, dining area; games machines in lobby; children allowed in back conservatory, dogs welcome, aviary on small terrace *(the Didler, JP, PP, Bernie Adams)*

Matlock [SK2959]

☆ *Boat House* [Dale Rd, Matlock Bridge – A6 S edge of town]: Friendly old-fashioned three-room Hardys & Hansons pub by River Derwent, between road and cliff of old limestone quarry; their ales kept well and priced reasonably, seafood specialities inc great seafood platter for two served with moules marinières, family room; pool, traditional games, old juke box; open all day – tea at teatime; some seats outside, interesting walks, bedrooms *(Derek and Sylvia Stephenson, JP, PP, Hugh A MacLean)*

Matlock Bath [SK2958]

Princess Victoria [South Parade]: Small pub with comfortable long beamed bar, Mansfield, Marstons Pedigree and guests such as Black Sheep and Charles Wells Bombardier, bar food, coal fire, upstairs restaurant *(Kevin Blake)*

Millers Dale [SK1473]

Anglers Rest [just down Litton Lane; pub is PH on OS Sheet 119 map ref 142734]: Friendly and comfortable creeper-clad pub with wonderful gorge views, good value food in cosy lounge, ramblers' bar and candlelit no smoking dining room, well kept Marstons Pedigree, Tetleys and changing guest beers such as Coach House Posthorn and Ruddles County, lots of toby jugs, plates and teapots, pool room; attractive village, good riverside walks *(Peter F Marshall, JP, PP)*

Milltown [SK3562]

Nettle [Fallgate, Littlemoor]: Extensively improved, now with small good value carvery restaurant, Hardys & Hansons real ales *(Paul Bridgett)*

Mugginton [SK2843]

☆ *Cock* [back road N of Weston Underwood]: Clean, comfortable and relaxing, with tables and settles in rambling panelled L-shaped bar, big dining area, wide choice of good value food from lunchtime sandwiches and snacks to more adventurous specials, interesting fresh veg, well kept Bass, Marstons Pedigree and Wadworths 6X, sensibly priced wines, friendly staff; tables outside, nice surroundings, good walks *(Richard and Jean Green, JDM, KM)*

New Mills [SK0085]

Beehive [Albion Rd, not far from A6]: Friendly bar with marble-top cast-iron tables on flagstones, woodburner, old local photographs, well kept Boddingtons and interesting guest beers, good value generous Indian food in separately run upstairs restaurant, cheap wines, good range of hot drinks, daily papers, air conditioning; children and dogs welcome, disabled facilities *(Bob and Lisa Cantrell)*

Fox [Brookbottom; OS Sheet 109 map ref 985864]: Friendly and unchanging old country pub cared for well by long-serving landlord, open fire, well kept Robinsons, plain good value food inc sandwiches, darts, pool; children welcome, handy for walkers (can get crowded wknds); splendid tucked-away hamlet down single-track lane *(the Didler, David Hoult)*

Newbold [SK3772]

Nags Head: Stone-built pub next to historic chapel and observatory, Mansfield and related ales, food lunchtime and evening, no smoking dining room, attentive licensees *(Faith Gorman)*

Newton Solney [SK2825]

Unicorn [Repton Rd]: Friendly pub with good value food in bar and small restaurant; good bedrooms, huge breakfast *(Theo, Anne and Jane Gaskin, the Didler)*

Oakerthorpe [SK3856]

Peacock [B6013 Belper—Clay Cross]: Spacious and attractive dining pub, nooks and crannies, plenty of character, lots of pictures and plates, shelves of tasteful bric-a-brac, smart separate restaurant, enjoyable food, well kept beers such as Mansfield and Marstons Pedigree; play area, open all day *(Kevin Blake)*

Ockbrook [SK4236]

Royal Oak [Green Lane]: Quiet 18th-c village local run by same family for 47 years, small unspoilt rooms (one no smoking), well kept Bass and guest beers such as Black Sheep, open fire, limited but enjoyable lunches, evening rolls, traditional games inc popular darts in lively tap room, house plants, flowers, clocks and homely local photographs, no music or machines; tables in charming cottage garden with play area, lovely hanging baskets; still has former (unused) brewhouse *(Pete Baker, Mike and Bridget Cummins, the Didler, JP, PP)*

Old Brampton [SK3171]

Fox & Goose [off A619 Chesterfield—Baslow at Wadshelf]: Friendly refurbished hilltop pub looking over Chesterfield and towards Sheffield, roomy pleasant low-ceilinged main bar with big stone fireplace, two smaller side rooms, interesting sandwiches, good range of beers *(Keith and Chris O'Neill)*

Parwich [SK1854]

Sycamore: Fine old welcoming unspoilt pub, jovial landlady, lively chat and roaring log fire in simply furnished but comfortable main bar, lots of old local photographs, hatch-served tap room with games and younger customers; plain wholesome fresh food lunchtimes and Weds-Sat evenings, big helpings, well kept Robinsons inc seasonal Old Tom, and Theakstons; tables out in front and on grass by car park, quiet village not far from Tissington *(John Foord, Paul Bridgett, A C and E Johnson, JP, PP, Pete Baker)*

Pilsley [SK2471]

☆ *Devonshire Arms* [off A619 Bakewell—Baslow; High St]: Delightfully tastefully refurbished real with good value home-made fresh food, carvery Thurs evening (may need to book), well kept Mansfield Riding and Old Baily and a guest such as Batemans, public bar area for walkers and children; quiz and music nights; very handy for Chatsworth farm and craft shops, lovely village *(B and M A Langrish, Kevin Thorpe)*

Renishaw [SK4578]

Sitwell Arms [A616, 2 miles from M1 junction 30]: Food from good value sandwiches up and well kept changing ales in civilised high-ceilinged bar, restaurant; bedrooms in comfortable back extension, handy for Renishaw Hall (gardens and Sitwell family memorabilia) *(A Preston, LYM)*

Ripley [SK4050]

Moss Cottage [Nottingham Rd]: Welcoming, with choice of joints from good carvery, well kept Bass and Highgate Mild *(Arthur Baker)*

Rowsley [SK2566]

☆ *Grouse & Claret* [A6 Bakewell—Matlock]: Spacious and comfortable chain family dining pub in well refurbished old stone building, good reasonably priced food (all day wknd) from carvery counter with appetising salad bar, friendly helpful service, no smoking area, decent wines, open fires; tap room popular with walkers, tables outside; good value bedrooms, small camp site behind nr river *(Robert and Patricia Battarbee)*

Saltergate [SK3871]

Barley Mow [Saltergate]: Usual lunchtime food from sandwiches to main dishes inc two for the price of one Sat and Mon, Marstons Pedigree and Theakstons Best, L-shaped room with no smoking in snug at lunchtime, original coloured Wards Brewery windows *(Keith and Chris O'Neill)*

Sawley [SK4931]

Steamboat [off B6540; not far from M1 junction 25 via Long Eaton slip road]: Great setting by Trent lock, tables out on terrace overlooking colourful narrowboats, nautical theme, ship's lanterns, well kept Theakstons and a guest beer, coal fire, pool and games in second bar, separate restaurant *(Kevin Blake)*

Shardlow [SK4330]

☆ *Malt Shovel* [3½ miles from M1 junction 24, via A6 towards Derby; The Wharf]: Old beamed pub in 18th-c former maltings attractively set by canal, pretty hanging baskets etc, interesting odd-angled layout, good cheap lunchtime food from baguettes and baked potatoes to enterprising specials, well kept Banks's Best and Marstons Pedigree, welcoming quick service (but meal orders stop 2 sharp), good central open fire, farm tools and bric-a-brac; no small children, lots of tables out on waterside terrace *(JP, PP, John Beeken, the Didler, LYM, Kevin Blake, Kevin Flack)*

Sheldon [SK1768]

Cock & Pullet: New conversion of old cottage, small and cosy, with cheerful helpful staff, plenty of atmosphere, good value tasty food inc Sun roasts and home-made puddings, well kept beer, morning coffee, open fire and scrubbed oak tables, pool in adjacent room; welcomes ramblers; tables outside *(DC, Keith and Di Newsome, Eric Locker)*

Shottlegate [SK3247]

☆ *Hanging Gate* [A517 W of Belper]: Charming Bass dining pub, above-average sensibly priced food all day, Bass and a guest ale, decent choice of sensibly priced wines esp New World, friendly helpful staff, pleasant rooms with attractive settles; garden *(Stephen, Julie and Hayley Brown, JDM, KM)*

Smalley [SK4044]

☆ *Bell* [A608 Heanor—Derby]: Two-room village pub with atmosphere all the better for being both small and popular, dining area with good reasonably priced changing food, well kept cheap real ales such as Adnams Broadside, Bass, Batemans Valiant, Glentworth Early Bird, Mallard Duckling, Marstons Pedigree, Whim IPA and Hartington, good choice of wines, smart efficient friendly staff; post office annexe, tables out in front and on big relaxing lawn with play area, beautiful hanging baskets, attractive bedrooms behind *(JP, PP, Bernie Adams, the Didler, A Preston, Derek and Sylvia Stephenson)*

South Normanton [SK4457]

Castlewood [just off M1 junction 28, via A38; Carter Lane E]: Brewers Fayre with large friendly collection of rooms and dining nooks, good choice of beers and wines, good value food inc children's, quick service, huge indoor play area; piped music; attached Travel Lodge *(Peter and Audrey Dowsett, Keith and Chris O'Neill)*

South Wingfield [SK3755]

Old Yew Tree [B5035 W of Alfreton; Manor Rd]: Cosy and convivial local with lots of character, log fire, panelling, kettles and pans hanging from beams, good food, well kept Marstons Pedigree and guests such as Greene King Abbot, Jennings Cumberland or Shepherd Neame Spitfire, separate restaurant area *(Kevin Blake)*

Sparrowpit [SK0980]

Wanted Inn [junction A623/B6061]: Attractive

easy-going 16th-c stone-built inn, all beams, copper and brasses one end, tidy plainer end with local photographs (dogs allowed here), friendly service, well kept Robinsons Bitter and Mild, sensibly priced home-made food inc good Sun lunch; piped music; picnic-sets by car park, beautiful countryside *(CMW, JJW, Mike and Lynn Robinson)*

Spitewinter [SK3366]

☆ *Three Horse Shoes* [Matlock Rd, Spitewinter; A632 SW of Chesterfield]: Good value food inc good curries and fresh fish sold in three sizes, Bass and Worthington, pleasant service, no smoking restaurant; panoramic views of Chesterfield *(Keith and Chris O'Neill, Derek and Sylvia Stephenson)*

Spondon [SK3935]

Malt Shovel [Potter St]: Unspoilt village pub, cosy panelled and quarry-tiled rooms off corridor, also lounge and large games room, decent choice of inexpensive food, well kept Bass and guest beers; lovely hanging baskets, tables in back garden *(the Didler, L Davenport, JP, PP, Brian and Halina Howes)*

Stanton in Peak [SK2464]

Flying Childers [off B5056 Bakewell—Ashbourne; Main Rd]: Cool in summer, warm in winter with coal fire in cosy and unspoilt right-hand room, well kept Bass or Marstons Pedigree and a guest beer such as Batemans, very welcoming old-fashioned landlord, chatty locals, dominoes and cribbage, good value filled rolls; in delightful steep stone village overlooking rich green valley; cl Mon-Thurs lunchtime *(the Didler, Peter F Marshall, JP, PP, C J Fletcher)*

Staveley [SK4374]

☆ *Speedwell* [Lowgates]: Former typical industrial local attractively reworked in late 1990s, brewing its own Townes beers, all good with distinctive flavours and served cheaply in top condition, friendly staff, no smoking area, no juke box or machines (nor food); cl wkdy lunchtimes, open all day wknds *(Derek and Sylvia Stephenson, G W Town)*

Ticknall [SK3423]

☆ *Chequers* [High St (B5006 towards Ashby)]: Small, friendly and full of atmosphere, with vast 16th-c inglenook fireplace, bright brass, old prints, no food, well kept Marstons Pedigree and seasonal beers; nice garden, good walking area *(LYM, Brian and Genie Smart, the Didler, JP, PP)*

Staff of Life [High St (Ashby Rd)]: Neat and attractive old local, small rooms off large bar, well kept beers such as Timothy Taylors Landlord (some tapped from the cask), good generous straightforward food at attractive prices, very wide choice, meat cooked wonderfully, pleasant staff; open fire, restaurant *(M Borthwick)*

Tideswell [SK1575]

☆ *George* [Commercial Rd (B6049, between A623 and A6 E of Buxton)]: Well worn in traditional L-shaped bar/lounge (partly no smoking), good value generous food inc children's, three well kept Hardys & Hansons ales, open fires, friendly licensees and staff, soft piped music; popular with young people evenings, games room with darts, pool, juke box and machines; children and dogs welcome, 60s music Fri; by remarkable church, tables in front overlooking pretty village, sheltered back garden; good value simple bedrooms (church clock strikes the quarters), pleasant walks *(C J Fletcher, BB, CMW, JJW, Mike and Penny Sutton, Ann and Colin Hunt, Steven and Sally Knight, JP, PP, Dr D J and Mrs S C Walker)*

Wensley [SK2661]

Red Lion [B5057 NW of Matlock]: Virtually a pub with no beer (may not even have bottles now), but worth a visit for its unspoilt appeal; friendly two-room no smoking farmhouse with chatty brother and sister owners, an assortment of 1950s-ish furniture, piano in main bar (landlord likes sing-songs), unusual tapestry in second room (usually locked, so ask landlady), no games or piped music, just tea, coffee, soft drinks and filled sandwiches or home-baked rolls maybe using fillings from the garden; outside lavatories; open all day *(John Brightley, the Didler, JP, PP, Pete Baker, Kevin Thorpe)*

Whittington [SK3875]

Cock & Magpie [Church Street N, behind museum]: Tap room, snug, lounge and no smoking conservatory dining room, Banks's or Mansfield Riding and Marstons Pedigree, good choice of good food inc sandwiches and early evening bargains for two (booking suggested for Sun), friendly service; handy for museum *(Keith and Chris O'Neill)*

Whittington Moor [SK3873]

Red Lion [Sheffield Rd (B6057)]: Small 19th-c stone-built pub tied to Old Mill with their Bitter, Bullion and a seasonal beer kept well,

thriving atmosphere, old local photographs in two rooms, very friendly landlady *(Keith and Chris O'Neill)*

Winster [SK2460]

Bowling Green [East Bank, by NT Market House]: Refurbished but bar still pleasantly traditional and local-feeling, with friendly staff, well kept beers such as Whim Hartington, wide choice of generous reliable home cooking inc good Sun lunch, log fire, dining area and conservatory *(Darly Graton, Graeme Gulibert, Anthony Barnes, JP, PP, Carol and Steve Spence)*

Miners Standard [Bank Top (B5056 above village)]: Welcoming 17th-c local, friendly family service, well kept Boddingtons and Marstons Pedigree, attractively priced generous food inc huge pies, big open fires, lead-mining photographs and minerals, ancient well; children allowed away from bar; restaurant, attractive view from garden, interesting stone-built village below; open all day (at least Sun) *(Anthony Barnes, JP, PP, Darly Graton, Graeme Gulibert, L Davenport)*

Youlgreave [SK2164]

☆ *George* [Alport Lane/Church St]: Handsome yet unpretentious stone-built 17th-c inn opp church, quick friendly service, welcoming locals, good straightforward home cooking inc game, comfortable banquettes, well kept John Smiths, Theakstons Mild and a guest such as Hartington or Ruddles; flagstoned locals' and walkers' side room, dogs welcome, games room, juke box; attractive village handy for Lathkill Dale and Haddon Hall, roadside tables, open all day *(Darly Graton, Graeme Gulibert, JP, PP)*

Stars after the name of a pub show exceptional quality. One star means most people (after reading the report to see just why the star has been won) would think a special trip worth while. Two stars mean that the pub is really outstanding – many that for their particular qualities cannot be bettered.

Devon

Five licensees here have the proud record of steering their pubs into every annual edition of the Guide, throughout its 20 years: Neil Girling of the Sloop at Bantham; Nick Borst-Smith of the Nobody Inn at Doddiscombsleigh; Roger Newton of the Blue Ball at Sidford; James Henry of the Oxenham Arms at South Zeal; and Sally Pratt of the Diggers Rest at Woodbury Salterton. All these places are on fine form – particularly the Nobody Inn, a great favourite with readers. Other pubs with a similar record of long and distinguished service in the Guide, though under changing licensees, are the Anchor at Cockwood (hugely popular for its fish and seafood), the Cott at Dartington, the unspoilt and unchanging Drewe Arms at Drewsteignton (surprisingly good food), the White Hart in Exeter (we await reports on the new regime here), the Elephants Nest up on Dartmoor at Horndon (another favourite), and the tiny Millbrook at South Pool. By contrast, we welcome as new entries (or pubs returning to the Guide after a break) the Castle Inn at Lydford, the Two Mile Oak south of Newton Abbot (interesting bars, good beer and home cooking), the civilised Ship above the water at Noss Mayo, the Passage House in Topsham (good fresh fish), the cheerful Kingsbridge Inn in Totnes (good all round) and the attractive Kings Arms at Winkleigh (enterprising food, good drink). Other pubs on particularly good form are the Masons Arms at Branscombe (an all-round success), the Drewe Arms at Broadhembury (excellent fish-cooking in a nice pubby atmosphere), the Old Thatch Inn at Cheriton Bishop (a very popular break from the A30), the nicely run Five Bells at Clyst Hydon and Hunters Lodge at Cornworthy, the Cherub in Dartmouth (warm and friendly, full of history), the chatty Union at Dolton (good food), the Freebooter at East Prawle (a warmly welcoming all-rounder), the Turf Hotel at Exminster (getting there is half the fun), the ancient Church House at Harberton, the friendly and individual Duke of York at Iddesleigh (gaining a Star Award this year), the Masons Arms at Knowstone (newish licensees settling in very successfully), the Tower at Slapton (the new chef is a find – and gains a Food Award), the busy Sea Trout at Staverton (good all round), and the Tradesmans Arms at Stokenham (relaxed and civilised, also gaining a Food Award this year). With so much good food on offer here, you're spoilt for choice: the Masons Arms at Branscombe wins the overall accolade of Devon Dining Pub of the Year. Drinks prices in the county are approaching the national average, with bargains to be had among the many pubs stocking beers from small local breweries, or the several which brew their own. The cheapest beer we found was in the Imperial, a grand Wetherspoons in Exeter. In the Lucky Dip section at the end of the chapter, we'd particularly pick out the Ship at Axmouth, Claycutters Arms at Chudleigh Knighton, Church House at Churchstow, Skylark at Clearbrook, Linny at Coffinswell, Union at Denbury, Well House in Exeter, Old Inn at Halwell, Church House at Holne, Barn Owl at Kingskerswell, Flintlock at Marsh, Fox & Goose at Parracombe, Harris Arms at Portgate, Jack in the Green at Rockbeare, Globe in Topsham and Old Church House at Torbryan; we have inspected and approved most of these already.

ASHPRINGTON SX8156 Map 1
Durant Arms
Village signposted off A381 S of Totnes; OS Sheet 202 map reference 819571

Set in a pretty village opposite the church, this is a spotlessly kept, popular inn. The beamed open-plan bar has several open fires, lamps and horsebrasses, fresh flowers, and a mix of seats and tables on the red patterned carpet; there's a lower carpeted lounge too, with another open fire. Good, enjoyable bar food includes sandwiches, soup (£2.35), ham and eggs (£5.95), chicken in brandy lasagne, good liver and onions, tasty spinach and mushroom risotto or cottage pie (all £6.45), steak and kidney pie (£7.25), fish dishes such as grilled salmon steak with a tomato and cucumber salsa (£8.95) or scallops and monkfish in a bacon and cream sauce (£9.50), medallions of Barbary duck breast with gooseberry sauce (£10.95), and puddings such as blackberry and apple pie or home-made brûlée (£3.50); best to book if you want to be sure of a table. The no smoking dining room has lots of oil paintings and watercolours by local artists on the walls. Good, attentive service. Well kept Flowers Original and Wadworths 6X on handpump, and local Pigsqueal cider; no games machines but they do have piped music. There is some wooden garden furniture on the terrace with more seats on the sheltered back garden. *(Recommended by Richard and Margaret Peers, Andy and Elaine Grant, Mrs Thomas, Bob and Ann Westbrook, Lyn and Geoff Hallchurch)*

Free house ~ Licensees Graham and Eileen Ellis ~ Real ale ~ Bar food ~ Restaurant ~ (01803) 732240 ~ Children welcome ~ Open 11.30-2.30, 6-11; 12-2.30, 7-10.30 Sun; closed evenings 25 and 26 Dec ~ Bedrooms: £35B/£55B

AVONWICK SX7157 Map 1
Avon
Off A38 at W end of South Brent bypass; village signposted from exit

Mr Velotti's enjoyable Italian cooking continues to draw customers to this busy pub; best to book to be sure of a table. Listed on boards in the small back bar, there might be filled baguettes, soup (£2.50), chargrilled vegetable salad £4.75), fritto misto (£5.50), penne barese (£6.45), risotto pescatore or seafood spaghetti (£7.25), chicken stuffed with artichokes and parma ham in a mascarpone sauce (£9.50), veal escalopes in a mushroom, cream and masala sauce (£10.50), fresh tuna fish with a tomato, anchovy and olive sauce (£11.50), and fillet of beef au poivre (£13); espresso coffee. Some decent Italian wines alongside the well kept Badger Best and Bass on handpump; fruit machine and piped music. Décor and furnishings are comfortable and pleasant in a fairly modern style. There are tables out in a pleasant garden by the River Avon. *(Recommended by John Evans, Paul Boot)*

Free house ~ Licensees Mario and Marilyn Velotti ~ Real ale ~ Bar food (not Sun) ~ Restaurant (closed Sun) ~ (01364) 73475 ~ Children in restaurant ~ Open 11.30-2.30, 6-11; 7-10.30 Sun; closed Sun lunchtime

AXMOUTH SY2591 Map 1
Harbour Inn
B3172 Seaton—Axminster

Even on a winter weekday, this prettily set and friendly thatched pub fills up quickly, so it's best to get there early to be sure of a seat. The Harbour Bar has black oak beams and joists, fat pots hanging from pot-irons in the huge inglenook fireplace, brass-bound cask seats, a high-backed oak settle, and an antique wall clock. A central lounge has more cask seats and settles, and over on the left another room is divided from the no smoking dining room by a two-way log fireplace. At the back, a big flagstoned lobby with sturdy seats leads on to a very spacious and simply furnished family bar. Well kept Flowers IPA and Original, Otter Ale, and Wadworths 6X on handpump; pool, and winter skittle alley. Good bar food includes sandwiches (from £1.75), soup (£2.50), home-made pâté (£3.25), ploughman's (from £4), half a roast chicken (£5.50), lamb cutlets in mint and honey gravy (£7.25; the lamb is from their own flock), popular fresh local fish (the lemon sole is well liked, £7.75), steaks (from £8), puddings (from £2.75), and children's menu (£2.75); cheerful service even when busy, and friendly cat. They have a lavatory for disabled people, and general access is good. There are some tables in the neat back flower garden. The handsome church opposite has fine stone gargoyles. *(Recommended by Alan and Paula McCully, Basil Minson, Mike and Mona Clifford, Lyn and Geoff Hallchurch, Peter Burton, John and Vivienne Rice, Chris Reeve)*

Free house ~ Licensees Dave and Pat Squire ~ Real ale ~ Bar food (not winter Sun evenings) ~ Restaurant ~ (01297) 20371 ~ Children in eating area of bar and in summer family room ~ Live entertainment weekly summer, every 2 wks winter ~ Open 11-3, 6-11; 12-3, 7-10.30 Sun; closed Sun evenings end Oct-Easter

BANTHAM SX6643 Map 1
Sloop ♀ ⇔

Off A379/B3197 NW of Kingsbridge

One of the best surfing beaches on the south coast is only a five minute walk over the dunes from this popular 16th-c pub – lots of rock pools and fine sandcastle sand, too. The black-beamed bar has a good bustling atmosphere, country chairs around wooden tables, stripped stone walls and flagstones, a woodburning stove, and easy chairs in a quieter side area with a nautical theme. Enjoyable bar food includes sandwiches, tasty home-made soups (from £2.60), sausage and chips (£2.95), lava bread, ham and cockles or hot potted shrimps (£4.45), liver with caramelised onion mash and sage gravy (£5.85), citrus cured salmon or vegetable and lentil pie (£5.65), steamed fillet of smoked haddock with a cream and spinach sauce (£7.90), breast of chicken stuffed with apricot mousse (£8.45), grilled Devon lamb with fresh rosemary sauce (£8.85), deep-fried squat lobster with a lemon and tarragon mayonnaise (£9.25), fillet of bass with spring onions, lemon grass and ginger (£12.45), and home-made puddings like lemon crunch, treacle tart or summer pudding (£3.10); hearty breakfasts. Part of the dining room is no smoking. Well kept Bass, Dartmoor IPA, and Palmers IPA on handpump, Luscombe farm cider, 25 malt whiskies, 12 wines by the glass from a carefully chosen wine list (including some local ones), and a good choice of liqueurs and west country drinks like rum and shrub or brandy and lovage. Darts, dominoes, cribbage, and table skittles. There are some seats at the back. The bedrooms in the pub itself have the most character; they also have self-catering cottages. Plenty of surrounding walks. *(Recommended by Tracey and Stephen Groves, Roger Wain-Heapy, Hugh Roberts, R and D Gray, Lorna and Howard Lambert, Mrs J Ekins-Daukes, MP, Geoff and Tricia Alderman, Ian Jones, Trevor and Lynda Smith)*

Free house ~ Licensee Neil Girling ~ Real ale ~ Bar food (12-2, 7-10; not 25-26 Dec) ~ Restaurant ~ No credit cards ~ (01548) 560489/560215 ~ Children in restaurant ~ Open 11-2.30, 6-11; 12-2.30, 6.30(7 in winter)-10.30 Sun ~ Bedrooms: £34B/£68B

BEER SY2389 Map 1
Dolphin ◖

Fore Street, off B3174 W of Seaton

Set in an attractive village, this seaside local is one of the oldest buildings. The good-sized friendly open-plan bar is lively and bustling (especially in summer), its décor old-fashioned, with oak panelling and interesting nooks. You soon find yourself looking past the other customers, and spotting all sorts of bric-a-brac and memorabilia, not just nautical hardware (though there's plenty of that, too); piped music, darts, dominoes, cribbage, fruit machines, and TV. Particular favourites are the giggly old fairground distorting mirrors, and the antique prize-fighting prints on the way through to the back (where there are sometimes antique stalls). Particularly well kept Bass and Cotleigh Tawny on handpump, and decent wine. As well as good local fish such as skate, plaice or lemon sole, and crab (from £8.25), enjoyable bar food includes sandwiches (from £1.95; fresh crab £5.25), soup (£2.25), such as sandwiches (from £1.95), ploughman's (£3.75), roast beef or lamb (£5.75), home-made steak and kidney pie (£6), with daily specials such as fried squid (£4.50), curries (£8.50), and scallops thermidor or rib-eye steak with pepper sauce (£10.25), and puddings like home-made spotted dick with custard or fruit pie (£3.25). There's a dining room, and one or two tables out by the pavement keeping an eye on the high street action. The village street, with a little stream bubbling along one side, leads steeply down to a beach with fishing huts (and motor boat hire). *(Recommended by Paul Hathaway, Lyn and Geoff Hallchurch, Richard Fendick, Graham and Rose Ive, AL and Gill, Basil Minson)*

Free house ~ Licensee Mrs Lee Gibbs ~ Real ale ~ Bar food ~ Restaurant ~ No credit cards ~ (01297) 20068 ~ Children welcome ~ Open 11-3, 6-11; 12-3, 7-11 Sun; closed 5 wks Jan/Feb ~ Bedrooms: £25S/£40(£50B)

BERRYNARBOR SS5646 Map 1
Olde Globe ★ £
Village signposted from A399 E of Ilfracombe

Full of character, the series of dimly lit homely rooms in this rambling 13th-c pub has low ceilings, curved deep-ochre walls, and floors of flagstones or of ancient lime-ash (with silver coins embedded in them). There are old high-backed oak settles (some carved) and plush cushioned cask seats around antique tables, and lots of cutlasses, swords, shields and fine powder-flasks, a profusion of genuinely old pictures, priests (fish-coshes), thatcher's knives, sheep shears, gin-traps, pitchforks, antlers, and copper warming pans; the family room has a ball pool and other play equipment. Well kept Courage Directors, Ushers Best and a guest beer on handpump, and several country wines; sensibly placed darts, pool, skittle alley, dominoes, cribbage, fruit machine, and piped music. Bar food includes sandwiches (from £1.60), home-made soup (£1.75), ploughman's (from £2.95), home-made vegetable lasagne (£4.75), steak and kidney pie (£5.30), steaks (from £8.20), puddings (from £2.20), and children's dishes (£2.20); quick, friendly service. The gaslit restaurant is no smoking. The crazy-paved front terrace has some old-fashioned garden seats, and there is a children's activity house. *(Recommended by Pat and Tony Martin, Maysie Thompson, Linda Norsworthy, Mr and Mrs I Bennett)*

Unique Pub Co ~ Lease Phil Bridle ~ Real ale ~ Bar food ~ Restaurant ~ (01271) 882465 ~ Children in own room ~ Open 11.30-2.30, 6(7 in winter)-11; 12-2.30, 7-11 Sun

BLACKAWTON SX8050 Map 1
George ◀
Main Street; village signposted off A3122 W of Dartmouth, and off A381 S of Halwell

This is a traditional and friendly local with courteous staff and convivial locals. The main bar has some timbering, a mix of cushioned wooden chairs, cushioned wall benches, and wheelbacks on the bare boards, mounted butterflies and a collection of beer mats and pump clips, and hop bines above the bar; another bar has old pictures of the village and has been redecorated this year. On one wall is a quaint old bow-windowed panel with little drawings of customers scratched on the black paint. There's also a cosy end lounge with an open fire and big bow window with a pleasant view. Bar food is almost totally home-made and includes lunchtime sandwiches, jumbo mussels (£3.35), walnut and stilton tagliatelle (£4.50), freshly made pizzas (from £4.50), liver, bacon and onions (£5.25), thai pork with coconut or steak and kidney pie (£5.95), chicken korma (£6.75), beef stroganoff (£7.50), daily specials such as rabbit and tarragon casserole (£6.50), skate wing in creamy caper sauce (£7.95), and whole grilled gilt head bream (£10.50), and puddings like chocolate fudge brownie or a crumble of the day (£2.70); they also have a take-away menu. Well kept Princetown Dartmoor IPA, Teignworthy Spring Tide, and a couple of interesting changing guests on handpump, dozens of Belgian bottled beers, and quite a few whiskies; they hold a beer festival around the late May bank holiday with live bands. Cribbage, dominoes and euchre. The garden, set below the pub, has several picnic-sets and nice views. *(Recommended by Tracey and Stephen Groves)*

Free house ~ Licensee Stuart O'Dell ~ Real ale ~ Bar food (till 10) ~ No credit cards ~ (01803) 712342 ~ Children welcome away from public bar ~ Live entertainment during beer festivals ~ Open 12-2.30, 6(7 in winter)-11; 12-3, 7-10.30 Sun; closed Mon lunchtime ~ Bedrooms: £20S/£40S

Normandy Arms 🛏

Signposted off A3122 W of Dartmouth; OS Sheet 202 map reference 807509

This pub's name refers to the time the whole village was commandeered as a training ground to prepare for the Normandy landings – you may still be able to see some of the bullet scars. The main bar has an interesting display of World War II battle gear, a good log fire, and well kept Branscombe Vale Branoc and Summa That plus two guest beers on handpump. Enjoyable bar food includes home-made soup (£2.10), sandwiches (from £2.10; the crab is good, £3.35), devilled mushrooms (£3.65), ploughman's (£3.95), prawns flamed in brandy (£4.65), steak and kidney pie (£4.95), pork in cider and cream (£8.95), steaks with quite a choice of sauces (from £8.95), whole lemon sole (£9.25), and home-made puddings like tipsy cake or apple pie (from £2.95). The restaurant is no smoking. Sensibly placed darts, pool, shove-ha'penny, cribbage, dominoes, and piped music. Some tables out in the garden. *(Recommended by Alan Cowell, Richard and Margaret Peers, G R Taylor, Mr and Mrs J French)*

Free house ~ Licensees Jonathan and Mark Gibson ~ Real ale ~ Bar food ~ Restaurant ~ (01803) 712316 ~ Children in restaurant ~ Open 12-2.30, 7-11; 12-11 Sat; 12-2.30, 7-10.30 Sun; closed 25 Dec, 1 Jan ~ Bedrooms: £35B/£52B

BRANSCOMBE SY1988 Map 1
Fountain Head 🍺

Upper village, above the robust old church; village signposted off A3052 Sidmouth—Seaton, then from Branscombe Square follow road up hill towards Sidmouth, and after about a mile turn left after the church

If you arrive much after opening time, the car park here will be full – even in mid-winter. It's a much enjoyed and very friendly old-fashioned place with a lot of real character, and has the added attraction of brewing its own beers in the Branscombe Vale Brewery: Branoc, Jolly Geff (named after Mrs Luxton's father, the ex-licensee), summer Summa That, winter Hells Belles, Christmas Yo Ho Ho, and summer guest beers; they also hold a midsummer weekend beer festival which comprises three days of spitroasts, barbecues, live music, morris men, and over 30 real ales; farm cider, too. The room on the left – formerly a smithy – has forge tools and horseshoes on the high oak beams, a log fire in the original raised firebed with its tall central chimney, and cushioned pews and mate's chairs. On the right, an irregularly shaped, more orthodox snug room has another log fire, white-painted plank ceiling with an unusual carved ceiling-rose, brown-varnished panelled walls, and rugs on its flagstone-and-lime-ash floor; the children's room is no smoking, the airedale is called Max, and the black and white cat, Casey Jones. Bar food such as home-made soup (£2.75), sandwiches (from £2.50; fresh crab £3.75), filled baked potatoes or ploughman's (£4.50), home-made meaty or vegetarian lasagne or cottage pie (£5.25), home-made steak and kidney pie (£5.70), evening grills (from £6.95), daily specials like breaded mushrooms with garlic dip (£4.50), fresh battered cod (£5.75), and pork steak in mustard sauce (£6.95), and children's meals (from £1.75). Darts, shove-ha'penny, cribbage, and dominoes. There are seats out on the front loggia and terrace, and a little stream rustling under the flagstoned path. They offer self-catering. *(Recommended by David Carr, Ron Shelton, Phil and Sally Gorton, the Didler, A C and E Johnson, Joan and Michel Hooper-Immins, JP, PP, Brian and Bett Cox, Basil Minson, L Flannigan, R T and J C Moggridge, Frank Smith)*

Own brew ~ Licensee Mrs Catherine Luxton ~ Real ale ~ Bar food ~ (01297) 680359 ~ Children in own room; must be over 10 in evening restaurant ~

Folk/Irish/folk summer Thurs ~ Open 11.30-3, 6-11; 12-3, 6-10.30 Sun; 11.30-
2.30, 6.30-11 in winter

Masons Arms ⑪ ♀ 🛏

Main St; signed off A3052 Sidmouth—Seaton

Devon Dining Pub of the Year

As well as comfortable bedrooms in this very popular inn, they now have three
cottages across the road which can be let with full hotel facilities or as self-
catering units. There's a hundred-year-old photograph up on the wall featuring
the inn and these cottages and one proudly bears a sign 'Devon Constabulary' –
so no after hours drinking in those days. The rambling low-beamed main bar has
a massive central hearth in front of the roaring log fire (spit roasts on Tuesday
and Sunday lunch and Friday evenings), windsor chairs and settles, and a good
bustling atmosphere. The no smoking Old Worthies bar has a slate floor, a
fireplace with a two-sided woodburning stove, and woodwork that has been
stripped back to the original pine. The no smoking restaurant (warmed by one
side of the woodburning stove) is stripped back to dressed stone in parts, and is
used as bar space on busy lunchtimes. Under the new head chef, they now bake
much of their bread and make their own jams, chutneys, and pickles. Good bar
food includes soups such as roasted tomato and fennel (£2.95), a terrine of pasta
and spinach wrapped in prosciutto ham (£4.25), moules marinières (£5.25), their
own oak smoked salmon with horseradish cream (£6.50), deep-fried cod in beer
batter (£7.95), grilled cumberland sausage with spring onion mash and a
redcurrant reduction (£8.75), well liked steak and kidney pudding (£9.25),
sautéed local crab cakes with lemon mayonnaise (£9.50), crispy roasted duckling
on a potato and celeriac rösti and caramelised parsnips with an orange sauce and
spiced plum chutney (£13.75), and daily specials such as smoked haddock terrine
(£4.75), grilled herrings (£7.25), fillet of pork with oriental-style vegetables
(£10.50), and whole grilled bass stuffed with baby spinach and garlic (£12.95);
puddings like sherry trifle, crème brûlée or apple crumble. Well kept Bass, Otter
Ale and Bitter, and two guest beers on handpump; they hold a beer festival in July
and keep 30 malt whiskies, 12 wines by the glass, and farm cider; polite, attentive
staff. Darts, shove-ha'penny, dominoes, and skittle alley. Outside, the quiet
flower-filled front terrace has tables with little thatched roofs, extending into a
side garden. *(Recommended by Mr and Mrs R Woodman, Pat and Dick Warwick, Basil
Minson, R J Walden, David Carr, David Peakall, Shaun Pinchbeck, L Flannigan, Alan Cowell,
Mike and Mona Clifford, Mike and Wendy Proctor, Steve Whalley, Michael Buchanan, Charlie
Harris, Gethin Lewis, Peter Meister, Andy Sinden, Louise Harrington, A C and E Johnson,
Paul R White, Mrs Thomas, Ewan and Sue Hewitt, Alan and Paula McCully)*

*Free house ~ Licensees Murray Inglis and Andrew Painter ~ Real ale ~ Bar food ~
Restaurant ~ (01297) 680300 ~ Children welcome but must be well behaved ~
Open 11-11; 12-10.30 Sun; 11-3, 6-11 in winter ~ Bedrooms: £22/£44
(£72S)(£60B)*

BROADHEMBURY ST1004 Map 1
Drewe Arms ★ ⑪ ♀

Signposted off A373 Cullompton—Honiton

One of the things that makes this marvellous place so special – apart from the
delicious fish dishes – is the way the hard-working licensees have managed to
create a friendly, chatty atmosphere in which anyone walking in for just a drink
would not feel remotely awkward. The bar has a proper pubby feel, neatly carved
beams in its high ceiling, and handsome stone-mullioned windows (one with a
small carved roundabout horse), and on the left, a high-backed stripped settle
separates off a little room with flowers on the three sturdy country tables, plank-
panelled walls painted brown below and yellow above with attractive engravings
and prints, and a big black-painted fireplace with bric-a-brac on a high
mantelpiece; some wood carvings, walking sticks, and framed watercolours for

sale. The flagstoned entry has a narrow corridor of a room by the servery with a couple of tables, and the cellar bar has simple pews on the stone floor; the dining room is no smoking. Most people do come to enjoy the unfailingly good food: open sandwiches (from £5.25); gravadlax £5.75; sirloin steak and melted stilton £6.95), daily specials such as spicy tomato soup (£5), griddled sardines (£7 small helping, £9 large helping), smoked haddock and stilton rarebit (£7 small helping, £10.50 large helping), wing of skate with black butter and capers (£11), fillet of brill with horseradish hollandaise (£11.50), sea bream with orange and chilli (£12.50), fillet of beef with pesto (£16), whole lobster (£18.50), and puddings such as spiced pears with stem ginger ice cream or rhubarb compote with vanilla ice cream (£4.50); they also offer a three-course meal (£25.25) with choices such as marinated herring with a glass of aquavit, fillet of turbot, and St Emilion chocolate pudding. Best to book to be sure of a table. Well kept Otter Bitter, Ale, Bright and Head tapped from the cask, and a very good wine list laid out extremely helpfully – including 12 by the glass; shove-ha'penny, dominoes and cribbage. There are picnic-sets in the lovely garden which has a lawn stretching back under the shadow of chestnut trees towards a church with its singularly melodious hour-bell. Thatched and very pretty, the 15th-c pub is in a charming village of similar cream-coloured cottages. *(Recommended by the Didler, Kevin Blake, Anthony Longden, Basil Minson, Ian Phillips, Howard and Margaret Buchanan, Charlie Harris, Roger Braithwaite, E H and R F Warner, David and Elizabeth Briggs, JP, PP, James Flory, Peter Craske)*

Free house ~ Licensees Kerstin and Nigel Burge ~ Real ale ~ Bar food (not Sun evening) ~ Restaurant ~ (01404) 841267 ~ Well behaved children in eating area of bar and in restaurant ~ Open 11-3, 6-11; 12-3 Sun; closed Sun evening, 31 Dec

BUCKLAND BREWER SS4220 Map 1
Coach & Horses ★

You can be sure of a genuine welcome from the friendly staff in this carefully preserved, 13th-c thatched house – and there's a good mix of customers, too. The attractively furnished and heavily beamed bar has comfortable seats (including a handsome antique settle), a woodburning stove in the inglenook, and maybe Harding the friendly cat; a good log fire also burns in the big stone inglenook of the cosy lounge. A small back room has darts and pool. Good bar food includes sandwiches (from £2.75), home-made pasty (£3.25), filled baked potatoes (from £3.50), ploughman's (£4.25), ham and egg (£5.95), five home-made curries (£7.25), daily specials such as mushroom and cheddar cheese puff pastry pie (£6.25), steak, mushroom and ale pie or pork in apples and cider (£6.50), lamb in orange and redcurrant (£7.25), fillets of bream in spicy tomato sauce (£8.95), and beef fillets in wholegrain mustard and mushroom sauce (£11.95); home-made puddings (£2.95), and Sunday lunch (£5.50). The restaurant is no smoking. Well kept Flowers Original or Fullers London Pride on handpump; dominoes, fruit machine, skittle alley, and piped music. There are tables on a terrace in front, and in the side garden. The bedrooms have been refurbished this year. *(Recommended by Jill Thomas, Neil Dury, Steve and Liz Tilley, Dr Paull Khan, Richard Fendick, Mrs L M Hardwick, R M Corlett, Steve Chambers)*

Free house ~ Licensees Oliver Wolfe and Nicola Barrass ~ Real ale ~ Bar food (not evening 25 Dec) ~ Restaurant ~ (01237) 451395 ~ Children in eating area of bar and restaurant until 9.30 ~ Open 12-3, 6-11; 12-3, 7-10.30 Sun; closed evening 25 Dec ~ Bedrooms: £25B/£50B

BUCKLAND MONACHORUM SX4868 Map 1
Drake Manor
Off A386 via Crapstone, just S of Yelverton roundabout

This is a smashing little pub with well kept beer, good food, and a friendly, relaxed atmosphere. The heavily beamed public bar on the left has brocade-cushioned wall seats, prints of the village from 1905 onwards, some horse tack and a few ship badges on the wall, and a really big stone fireplace with a woodburning stove; a small door leads to a low-beamed cubby hole where children are allowed. The snug Drakes Bar has beams hung with tiny cups and big brass keys, a woodburning stove in an old stone fireplace hung with horsebrasses and stirrups, a fine stripped pine high-backed settle with a partly covered hood, and a mix of other seats around just four tables (the oval one is rather nice). On the right is a small, beamed, recently refurbished dining room with settles and tables on the flagstoned floor. Shove-ha'penny, darts, euchre, cribbage, and dominoes. Enjoyable bar food includes soup (£2.25), lunchtime baguettes and ploughman's (from £3.25), sausage, ham and chips (£4.20), hot, spicy prawns (£3.75), home-made lasagne or garlic mushrooms with chilli and prawns (£5.50), steak and kidney pie (£5.95), gammon and pineapple (£6.25), steaks (from £8.95), and daily specials like barbecued spare ribs (£3.50), fresh halibut with a sweet pepper sauce (£8.95), and roast rack of lamb with fruit and port sauce (£9.50). Particularly warmly friendly staff serve the well kept Courage Best, Ushers Founders, and a guest such as Bass or Greene King Abbot on handpump, and they keep nearly 100 malt whiskies, a decent wine list, and country wines. The prettily planted and sheltered back garden has some new picnic-sets. The pub (originally built to house the masons constructing the church in the 12th c; it was rebuilt in the 16th c) is handy for Garden House; more reports please. *(Recommended by Ian Phillips, Joy and Peter Heatherley, Gordon Stevenson)*

InnSpired Inns ~ Lease Mandy Robinson ~ Real ale ~ Bar food (12-2, 7-10(9.30 Sun)) ~ Restaurant ~ (01822) 853892 ~ Children in restaurant and family room ~ Open 11.30-2.30(3 Sat), 6.30-11; 12-3, 7-10.30 Sun

BUTTERLEIGH SS9708 Map 1
Butterleigh Inn

Village signposted off A396 in Bickleigh; or in Cullompton take turning by Manor House Hotel – it's the old Tiverton road, with the village eventually signposted off on the left

As unspoilt as ever, this bustling village pub has plenty to look at in its little rooms: pictures of birds and dogs, topographical prints and watercolours, a fine embroidery of the Devonshire Regiment's coat of arms, and plates hanging by one big fireplace. One room has pine dining chairs around country kitchen tables, another has an attractive elm trestle table and sensibly placed darts, and there are prettily upholstered settles around the three tables that just fit into the cosy back snug. Tasty bar food includes filled lunchtime rolls or home-made soup (£2.50), ploughman's (£3.95), home-made burger or vegetarian dish (£4.95), tuna with a hot tomato salsa (£6.95), bacon chops with a red wine and berry sauce (£7.95), steaks (from £8.95), and daily specials. Well kept Cotleigh Tawny and Barn Owl, and a guest such as RCH East Street Cream or Scattor Rock Devonian on handpump; darts, shove-ha'penny, cribbage, dominoes, and piped music; jars of snuff on the bar. Outside are tables on a sheltered terrace and neat small lawn, with a log cabin for children. *(Recommended by Mrs Sylvia Elcoate, Jacquie and Jim Jones, James Flory, Ian Phillips, Jane and Adrian Tierney-Jones, Richard and Margaret Peers, Bryan Robinson)*

Free house ~ Licensee Jenny Hill ~ Real ale ~ Bar food ~ (01884) 855407 ~ Children in eating area of bar lunchtime only ~ Open 12-2.30, 6(5 Fri)-11; 12-3, 7-10.30 Sun

CHAGFORD SX7087 Map 1
Ring o' Bells

Off A382 Moretonhampstead—Whiddon Down

Run by warmly friendly licensees, this big, old black and white pub is popular with both locals and visitors. The oak-panelled bar has black and white photographs of the village and local characters past and present on the walls, comfortable seats, a choice of newspapers, a big fireplace full of copper and brass, and a log-effect gas fire; newspapers to read and no noisy games machines or piped music. There's a small no smoking candlelit dining room. Generous helpings of good food include two home-made soups (£3; soup and a pudding £5.95), sandwiches (from £3), filled baked potatoes (from £5), cod in batter (£5.95), mixed fruit and vegetable pilaf (£7), daily specials using local produce, such as home-made liver pâté (£4.95), warm bacon and diced avocado salad with croutons (£5), red onion and courgette tart (£7.25), whiting with citrus herb butter (£7.50), pork curry (£7.95), and brace of duck legs with cumberland sauce (£9.25), and puddings such as treacle tart, chocolate and lime cream roulade or steamed sponge pudding (£3.50); Sunday roasts (from £7.25). Well kept Butcombe Bitter and Gold, and Exmoor Ale on handpump, Addlestone's cider, and quite a few malt whiskies. Shove-ha'penny, dominoes, and darts (if the pub is not busy). The sunny walled garden behind the pub has seats on the lawn; dogs are welcome and there are dog biscuits on the corner of the bar; the pub cat Coriander keeps visiting dogs in control. There are walks on the nearby moorland. *(Recommended by Robert Gomme, Ann and Colin Hunt, Gartlen and Wally Rogers, John and Sarah Perry, Mr and Mrs C Roberts)*

Free house ~ Licensee Mrs Judith Pool ~ Real ale ~ Bar food (they serve breakfast and snacks from 8.30am) ~ Restaurant ~ (01647) 432466 ~ Children in eating area of bar and restaurant ~ Open 11-3, 5-11; 12-3, 6-10.30 Sun; may close early on quiet evenings in winter ~ Bedrooms: £20/£40(£45S)

CHERITON BISHOP SX7793 Map 1
Old Thatch Inn
Village signposted from A30

A handy break from the A30, this pleasant, friendly pub is popular for its good food. The rambling beamed bar is separated from the lounge by a large open stone fireplace (lit in the cooler months), and has well kept Branscombe Vale Branoc, and a couple of guests such as Otter Ale or Skinners Figgys Brew on handpump. Over the May spring bank holiday, they hold a weekend beer festival featuring only west country ales from small independent breweries. Enjoyable bar food includes sandwiches, home-made soup (£2.95), grilled sardines with provençale sauce (£3.95), warm smoked mozzarella with sun-dried tomato salad in a puff pastry case (£4.25), braised lamb shank with cheese and onion mash and red wine jus (£7.95), braised venison with redcurrant sauce (£8.75), veal escalope with mushrooms and white wine and cream sauce (£9.50), and whole black bream baked with mediterranean vegetables (£10.25). During the winter they hold themed food evenings. The family room is no smoking; piped music. *(Recommended by Esther and John Sprinkle, Mr and Mrs D S Price, Peter and Audrey Dowsett, R J Walden, Dr and Mrs J Lakic, Deborah and Ian Carrington, Peter Meister, Ann and Colin Hunt, M H Lendrum, Laura Wilson, Cath Donne, Ruth and Paul Lawrence)*

Free house ~ Licensee Stephen James Horn ~ Real ale ~ Bar food ~ Restaurant ~ (01647) 24204 ~ Children in eating area of bar and in family room ~ Open 11.30-3, 6-11; 12-3, 7-10.30 Sun; closed 25 Dec ~ Bedrooms: £35B/£49B

CHITTLEHAMHOLT SS6521 Map 1
Exeter Inn 🛏
Off A377 Barnstaple—Crediton, and B3226 SW of South Molton

This friendly old inn in a quiet village makes a good base for Exmoor National Park with all its outdoor facilities. The bars are full of matchboxes, bottles and foreign banknotes, and there's an open stove in the huge stone fireplace, and cushioned mate's chairs, settles and a couple of big cushioned cask armchairs. A side area has seats set out as booths around the tables under the sloping ceiling. Good bar food includes sandwiches (from £2.25; baguettes from £2.50), soup (£2.25), filled baked potatoes (from £3.20), home-made chicken liver pâté (£3.50), ploughman's and salads (from £4.50), a vegetarian dish (£5.20), local trout (£7.20), good local steaks (£11), daily specials, and home-made puddings (£2.60); Sunday roast (£6). The restaurant is no smoking. Well kept Dartmoor

Best, Greene King Abbot, and a guest such as Adnams Best, Brains or Marstons Pedigree on handpump or tapped from the cask, and farm ciders; darts, shove-ha'penny, dominoes, cribbage, fruit machine, and piped music. The pub's cricket team play on Sundays. *(Recommended by Mrs P G Newton, Shaun Pinchbeck, David and Michelle Bailey)*

Free house ~ Licensees David and Deborah Glenister ~ Real ale ~ Bar food ~ Restaurant ~ (01769) 540281 ~ Children in eating area of bar and restaurant ~ Open 11.30-2.30, 6(7 Jan-Mar)-11; 12-3, 7-10.30 Sun ~ Bedrooms: £25S/£50S

CLYST HYDON ST0301 Map 1

Five Bells 🍴

West of the village and just off B3176 not far from M5 junction 28

'What a nice pub' is a comment many readers make about this most attractive, thatched place, and the licensees are extremely friendly and welcoming. The bar is spotlessly kept and divided at one end into different seating areas by brick and timber pillars; china jugs hang from big horsebrass-studded beams, there are many plates lining the shelves, lots of sparkling copper and brass, and a nice mix of dining chairs around small tables (fresh flowers and evening candles in bottles), with some comfortable pink plush banquettes on a little raised area; the pretty no smoking restaurant is up some steps to the left and has been redecorated this year in blue and gold. Past the inglenook fireplace is another big (but narrower) room they call the Long Barn with a pine dresser at one end and similar furnishings. Good, popular home-made daily specials might include garlic mushrooms (£3.95), crispy bacon and stilton salad (£4.25), avocado baked with Somerset brie and pepperoni (£4.25), mussels in cider and cream or kiln-roasted hickory-smoked salmon fillet (£4.95), home-made steak and kidney pudding (£8.25), lamb shank roasted with honey and rosemary (£10.25), smoked fish platter (£10.95), pink sea bream (£11.50), and T-bone steaks (£14.45); also, sandwiches (from £3), home-made soup (£2.95), courgettes provençale (£5.25), platters (from £5.50), cold home-cooked ham (£7.25), steaks (from £10.45), and children's menu (£2.25). Well kept Cotleigh Tawny, O'Hanlon's Blakeley's Best, and Otter Bitter on handpump, a thoughtful wine list, and several malt whiskies. The cottagey front garden is a fine sight with its thousands of spring and summer flowers, big window boxes and pretty hanging baskets; up some steps is a sizeable flat lawn with picnic-sets, a play frame, and pleasant country views. *(Recommended by R J Herd, Jacquie and Jim Jones, Brian and Genie Smart, Basil Minson, Dr P F A Watkins, Nigel and Sue Foster, John and Sarah Perry, Joan E Hilditch, James Flory, R J Walden, Hugh Roberts, Joy and Peter Heatherley, Haydn Jones, L G Owen, Brian and Bett Cox)*

Free house ~ Licensees Robin Bean and Charles Hume Smith ~ Real ale ~ Bar food ~ Restaurant ~ (01884) 277288 ~ Well behaved children in eating area of bar ~ Open 11.30-2.30, 6.30-11(10.30 Sun); evening opening 7 (6.30 Sat) in winter

COCKWOOD SX9780 Map 1

Anchor 🍴

Off, but visible from, A379 Exeter—Torbay

Immensely popular, this is a very well run place with obliging, speedy service, and particularly good fish dishes. From a large menu, there are 30 different ways of serving mussels (£5.95 normal size helping, £9.95 for a large one), 12 ways of serving scallops (from £5.25 for a starter, from £12.95 for a main course), 10 ways of serving oysters (from £6.95 for starter, from £13.95 for main course), and 5 'cakes' such as crab cakes or mussel cakes (£5.95 for starter, £9.95 for main course), as well as tuna steak in tomato and garlic (£5.95), locally caught cod (£6.25), whole grilled plaice (£6.50), and a shellfish selection (£14.95), and lots of daily specials. Non-fishy dishes feature as well, such as home-made soup (£2.50), sandwiches (from £2.65), home-made chicken liver pâté (£3.85), cheese and potato pie (£4.50), home-made steak and kidney pudding (£5.50), rump steak (£8.95), and children's dishes (£2.50). But despite the emphasis on food, there's still a pubby atmosphere, and they keep six real ales on handpump or tapped from the cask: Bass, Flowers Original, Fullers London Pride, Greene King Old Speckled Hen, Otter Ale and Wadworths 6X. Also, a rather a good wine list (10 by the glass – they do monthly wine tasting evenings September-June), 25 brandies, 70 malt whiskies, and west country cider. The small, low-ceilinged, rambling rooms have black panelling, good-sized tables in various alcoves, and a cheerful winter coal fire in the snug; the cosy restaurant is no smoking. Darts, dominoes, cribbage, table skittles, fruit machine, and piped music. From the tables on the sheltered verandah you can look across the road to the bobbing yachts and crabbing boats in the harbour. Nearby parking is difficult when the pub is busy – which it usually is. *(Recommended by Basil Minson, John and Vivienne Rice, Bob and Ann Westbrook, David Carr, Alan and Paula McCully, Canon Michael Bourdeaux, Darly Graton, Graeme Gulibert, Mike Gorton, Susan and Nigel Wilson, Jayne and Peter Capp, John Beeken, Mr and Mrs Capp, Tracey and Stephen Groves)*

Heavitree ~ Tenants Mr Morgan and Miss Sanders ~ Real ale ~ Bar food (12-3(2.30 Sun), 6.30-10(9.30 Sun)) ~ Restaurant ~ (01626) 890203 ~ Children in eating area of bar and in restaurant ~ Open 11-11; 12-10.30 Sun; closed evening 25 Dec

COLEFORD SS7701 Map 1
New Inn 🍴 🍷 🛏

Just off A377 Crediton—Barnstaple

The garden of this 600-year-old inn has been landscaped, and new chairs, tables and umbrellas placed on the new decking under the willow tree along the stream; there are more seats on the terrace. Inside, there are several interestingly furnished areas that spiral around the central servery, with ancient and modern settles, spindleback chairs, plush-cushioned stone wall seats, some character tables – a pheasant worked into the grain of one – and carved dressers and chests; also, paraffin lamps, antique prints and old guns on the white walls, and landscape plates on one of the beams, with pewter tankards on another; the resident parrot Captain is chatty and entertaining. The servery itself has settles forming stalls around tables on the russet carpet, and there's a winter log fire. Using good local produce, the highly enjoyable bar food might include soup (£3.50), filled baguettes (from £3.95), omelettes or smoked fish platter (£4.95), ploughman's or mediterranean vegetables and pasta bake (£5.95), creamy fish pie, chicken and mushroom stroganoff or liver and bacon (all £6.95), steaks (from £6.95), Italian beef (£7.95), confit of duck with caramelised onions (£8.95), fillet of beef with green peppercorn sauce and roasted cherry tomatoes (£15.95), and puddings such as treacle and lemon tart with clotted cream, fruit crumble or sticky date pudding (from £3.50); the restaurant is no smoking. Well kept Badger Best, Everards Beacon Ale, Exmoor Gold, and Otter Ale on handpump, and quite a range of malt whiskies, ports and cognacs. Fruit machine (out of the way up by the door), darts, and piped music. This is one of the oldest 'new' inns in the country. *(Recommended by John and Sarah Perry, Jed and Virginia Brown, Ian Phillips, John and Vivienne Rice, Mrs Sylvia Elcoate, Lynn Sharpless, Bob Eardley, G C Buckle, Sarah and Simon House, Sandy Thomson, Pat and Tony Martin, L Flannigan, Dr Brian and Mrs Anne Hamilton, Cathy Robinson)*

Free house ~ Licensees Paul and Irene Butt ~ Real ale ~ Bar food (till 10(9.30 Sun)) ~ Restaurant ~ (01363) 84242 ~ Children in eating area of bar and in restaurant ~ Open 12-2.30, 6-11; 12-2.30, 7-10.30 Sun; closed 25 and 26 Dec ~ Bedrooms: £55B/£65B

COMBEINTEIGNHEAD SX9071 Map 1
Wild Goose

Just off unclassified coast road Newton Abbot—Shaldon, up hill in village

New licensees have taken over this 17th-c pub, and as well as continuing to keep six real ales, have placed more emphasis on the bar food. The spacious back beamed lounge has a mix of wheelbacks, red plush dining chairs, a decent mix of tables, and french windows to the garden; the front bar has some red Rexine seats in the window embrasures of the thick walls, flagstones in a small area by the door, some beams and standing timbers, and a step down on the right at the end, with dining chairs around the tables and a big old fireplace with an open log fire. In the main part are standard lamps in corners, a small carved oak dresser with a big white goose, and a fruit machine; darts, pool, cribbage, dominoes, shove-ha'penny, and a general knowledge quiz every second Sunday evening; there's also a cosy section on the left with an old settee and comfortably well used chairs. Well kept ales from Bath, Exe Valley, Otter Ale, Princetown, Scattor Rock, Skinners, and Teignworthy on handpump, over 30 malt whiskies, and local Luscombe cider. Good bar food now includes lunchtime snacks like jumbo sausage and onions in a baguette (£2.50), filled granary rolls (from £2.50), omelettes (from £4.50), and ploughman's (from £4.95), as well as home-made soup (£2.75), home-made pâté such as smoked mackerel or duck with port, or king prawns in filo pastry with a dip (£4.50), Mexican chilli (£5.50), vegetable crumble (£5.75), their very popular, huge whole rack of ribs with barbecue or sweet and sour sauce (£7.50), chicken breast in stilton sauce (£8.50), fresh fish dishes like cod in dill batter (£8.50) or whole lemon sole (£10.95), and puddings such as home-made bread and butter pudding, cheesecakes or banoffi pie (£2.95); curry night in on Thursday (£6.50 which includes a pint of beer or large glass of wine). Some picnic-sets in the garden. *(Recommended by the Didler, Mrs Sylvia Elcoate, David and Elizabeth Briggs, Bob and Ann Westbrook, Peter Winter-Hart, JP, PP, Ian and Nita Cooper)*

Free house ~ Licensees Jerry and Kate English ~ Real ale ~ Bar food (till 10(9.30 Sun)) ~ (01626) 872241 ~ Well behaved children in eating area of bar and in restaurant ~ Open 11.30-2.30, 6.30-11; 12-2.30, 7-10.30 Sun

CORNWORTHY SX8255 Map 1
Hunters Lodge

Off A381 Totnes—Kingsbridge ½ mile S of Harbertonford, turning left at Washbourne; can also be reached direct from Totnes, on the Ashprington—Dittisham road

This is a smashing little pub, spotlessly kept by its warmly friendly licensees, and newly redecorated outside. The two rooms of the small low-ceilinged bar have only around half a dozen red plush wall seats and captain's chairs around heavy elm tables, and there's also a small and pretty no smoking cottagey dining room with a good log fire in its big 17th-c stone fireplace. Good, well presented food at lunchtime includes sandwiches, tomato and fresh basil soup (£2.50), port, pear and stilton pâté (£3.75), cumberland sausage and mash (£4.50), chicken curry (£5.95), steak and kidney pie with suet crust (£6.95), fried plaice fillets (£7), and baked skate with peppered butter (£7.75), with evening dishes such as smoked haddock and cheese fishcake (£3), spinach pancake filled with crab (£4.50), grilled fillet of cod with sun-dried tomato dressing, topped with gruyère cheese (£8.95), fillet of pork tenderloin with apricot stuffing (£9.50), roast rack of English lamb with plum and fresh mint sauce (£11.75), and puddings like chocolate and brandy mousse, blackberry and apple crumble or tarte au citron (£3.25). Well kept Badger Best and Fullers London Pride on handpump, a few malt whiskies, and a decent wine list. Dominoes, cribbage, Jenga, shut the box, and piped music. In summer, there is plenty of room to sit outside – either at the picnic-sets on a big lawn stretching up behind the car park or on the flower-filled terrace closer to the pub. They have a lovely black labrador, Henry (who is happy to take a spare seat at your table), and they welcome other dogs (and their walking masters). *(Recommended by David and Elizabeth Briggs, John Evans, Mark Sheard, Mr and Mrs R Reece, Brian Lynch)*

Free house ~ Licensees John and Jill Diprose ~ Real ale ~ Bar food ~ Restaurant ~ (01803) 732204 ~ Children welcome ~ Open 11.30-2.30, 6.30-11; 11-3, 6-11 Sat; 12-3, 6.30-10.30 Sun

DALWOOD ST2400 Map 1
Tuckers Arms
Village signposted off A35 Axminster—Honiton

Parts of this pretty cream-washed thatched longhouse date back to the 13th c, and after the church, it is the oldest building in the parish. The fine flagstoned bar has lots of beams, a random mixture of dining chairs, window seats, and wall settles (including a high-backed winged black one), and a log fire in the inglenook fireplace. The back bar has an enormous collection of miniature bottles. From the elaborate menu, you can choose a main course (£10.95), two courses (£14.50 and £17.50), and three courses (£17.95 and £20.95), with starters such as sharp and sweet chicken livers, game terrine, warm salad of mushrooms with garlic prawns or smoked salmon platter, and a main course like finnan haddock with prawns in a sauce of fresh rosemary, cream and vermouth, escalope of pork with green ginger wine, lime and garlic, steak, kidney and oyster pie, wild mushroom and roasted vegetables provençale style, fillets of john dory and king prawns with bananas, and tournedos of venison and stilton on a port gravy; half the restaurant is no smoking. Well kept Courage Directors, and Otter Ale and Bitter on handpump kept under light blanket pressure; skittle alley and piped music. The flowering tubs, window boxes and hanging baskets are lovely in summer. *(Recommended by Basil Minson, Laura Wilson, Esther and John Sprinkle)*

Free house ~ Licensees David and Kate Beck ~ Real ale ~ Bar food (not 26 Dec) ~ Restaurant ~ (01404) 881342 ~ Children in eating area of bar, restaurant and family room until 9.30 ~ Open 12-3, 6.30-11; 12-3, 7-10.30 Sun ~ Bedrooms: £32.50S/£55S

DARTINGTON SX7762 Map 1
Cott
In hamlet with the same name, signposted off A385 W of Totnes opposite A384 turn-off

Yet more new licensees for this lovely thatched 14th-c place – and this time, the long-serving chef has gone too; we're keeping our fingers crossed for a period of stability now. The traditional, heavy-beamed bar has several communicating rooms with big open fires, flagstones, and polished brass and horse-harness on the white washed walls; one area is no smoking – as are a few tables in the restaurant. Bar food at lunchtime now includes sandwiches (from £3.25), soup (£3.50), filled baked potatoes (from £3.75), ploughman's (£5.75), a hot buffet (£6.95), a cold buffet (from £6.95), and puddings (£3.50), with evening dishes such as venison and game pâté with pear and rosemary jelly (£5.50), sautéed king prawns with garlic, lemon and herb butter (£5.95), beef casserole with mushrooms or oriental stir-fried vegetables (£7.95), calves liver flamed in brandy (£9.95), fillet of wild bass on a sweet pepper coulis (£13.95), and puddings like spotted dick or Swiss chocolate torte (£3.50). Well kept Courage Directors, Theakstons Best, and a guest such as Wadworths 6X on handpump. There are picnic-sets in the garden, with more on the terrace amid attractive tubs of flowers. Good walks through the grounds of nearby Dartington Hall, and it's pleasant touring country – particularly for the popular Dartington craft centre, the Totnes—Buckfastleigh steam railway, and one of the prettiest towns in the West Country, Totnes. *(Recommended by Malcolm Taylor, Mr and Mrs Capp, Mr and Mrs M Cooper, R T and J C Moggridge, Dave Braisted, Carol Ackroyd, Peter McNamara, John and Vivienne Rice, MP, Andrew Hodges, Revd A Nunnerley, P Rome, Mike and Mary Carter, David and Elizabeth Briggs, Richard and Margaret Peers, Paul R White, Bob and Ann Westbrook, Brian Skelcher, Tony Baldwin, Tony and Jill Cawley, Lyn and Geoff Hallchurch)*

Old English Inns ~ Managers Adrian and Jan Skinner ~ Real ale ~ Bar food (12-2.30, 6.30-9) ~ Restaurant ~ (01803) 863777 ~ Children welcome ~ Open 11-11; 12-10.30 Sun; maybe 11-2.30, 6-11 in winter ~ Bedrooms: £55B/£70B

DARTMOUTH SX8751 Map 1

Cherub

Higher St

Although new licensees have taken over this Grade II* listed, 14th-c pub, readers tell us it's as warm and friendly as ever. The bustling bar has tapestried seats under creaky heavy beams, leaded-light windows, and a big stone fireplace; upstairs is the low-ceilinged no smoking restaurant. Well kept Brakspears, Everards, Exmoor, and a beer named for the pub on handpump, 20 malt whiskies, and 10 wines by the glass; piped music. Good bar food includes soup (£2.50), sandwiches (from £2.75), filled baked potatoes (£4.50), deep-fried stilton mushrooms (£5), smoked haddock in white wine sauce (£5.75), steak, mushroom and Guinness pie (£6.75), fish pie (£7.25), curry of the day (£7.50), and steak and chips (£8.50). In summer particularly, the building is a striking sight with each of the two heavily timbered upper floors jutting further out than the one below, and the hanging baskets are at their best. *(Recommended by Gordon Stevenson, Charles Eaton, Dr B and Mrs P B Baker, Alan Thomas, R T and J C Moggridge, Betsy and Peter Little, Ken Flawn, JP, PP, John Knighton, David Carr, Tracey and Stephen Groves)*

Free house ~ Licensees Charles Veals and Laurie Scott ~ Real ale ~ Bar food ~ Restaurant ~ (01803) 832571 ~ Children in restaurant only and must be over 10 ~ Open 11-11; 12-10.30 Sun; 11-2.30, 5-11 Mon-Thurs in winter

Royal Castle Hotel 🛏

11 The Quay

Originally two Tudor merchant houses but with a Regency façade, this friendly place overlooks the inner harbour and the river beyond. There are two ground floor bars, each with their own atmosphere. On the left of the flagstoned entrance hall is the Harbour bar, with an assortment of pine and mahogany furniture on wooden floors, lots of chatty locals, and dominoes, cribbage, TV, and piped music; live music is held here. On the right is the Galleon bar which is more lounge-like, and has some fine antiques, a Tudor fireplace, and a no smoking area. Well kept Courage Directors, Exe Valley Dob's Best Bitter, Flowers IPA, and Wadworths 6X on handpump. Bar food includes home-made soup (£2.50), sandwiches (from £2.85; smoked chicken and avocado £3.65; crab £3.95), baked potatoes (from £3.95), deep-fried brie with a port and orange sauce (£4.45), broccoli, mushroom and tomato bake with a stilton and garlic crumble (£4.95), ploughman's (from £4.95), home-baked ham with eggs (£5.25), local venison sausages with cumberland sauce or home-made steak and kidney in ale pie (£6.25), braised lamb shank in a rich mint and rosemary sauce (£7.95), fresh crab (£9.95), steaks (from £11.75), and puddings (£2.95); on winter lunchtimes, they serve spit-roasts from their 300-year-old Lidstone range – pork, lamb and beef, all from local suppliers. The restaurant is no smoking. *(Recommended by Rona Murdoch, JP, PP, Mr and Mrs R Head, David Carr, D S Price, George Atkinson)*

Free house ~ Licensees Nigel and Anne Way ~ Real ale ~ Bar food (all day) ~ Restaurant ~ (01803) 833033 ~ Children welcome ~ Live music Weds, Thurs, and Sun ~ Open 11-11; 12-10.30 Sun ~ Bedrooms: £68.95B/£107.90B

DODDISCOMBSLEIGH SX8586 Map 1

Nobody Inn ★★ 🍽 ♀ 🍷 🛏

Village signposted off B3193, opposite northernmost Christow turn-off

For many readers, a visit to this immensely popular inn is a yearly pilgrimage. Mr Borst-Smith is very much a hands-on licensee, working hard with his staff to ensure that whether you are coming in for a light lunch and a pint, an evening meal, or an overnight stay, you will be warmly welcomed. The two rooms of the lounge bar have handsomely carved antique settles, windsor and wheelback chairs, benches, carriage lanterns hanging from the beams, and guns and hunting prints in a snug area by one of the big inglenook fireplaces. They keep perhaps the best pub wine cellar in the country – 800 well cellared wines by the bottle and 20 by the glass kept oxidation-free; there's also properly mulled wine and twice-monthly tutored tastings (they also sell wine retail, and the good tasting-notes in their detailed list are worth the £3.50 it costs – anyway refunded if you buy more than £30-worth); also, a choice of 240 whiskies, local farm ciders, and well kept Bass, Nobody's (brewed by Branscombe), Otter Ale, and a guest such as RCH East Street Cream on handpump. Good bar food includes good home-made soups (£3.50) and daily specials such guinea fowl and chestnut terrine with tomato and apple chutney, wild mushroom risotto with garlic and cream dressing, and thai prawn fishcakes with salsa (£3.90), sausage and mash with onion gravy (£5.50), hot lentil and walnut cakes with red onion marmalade and yoghurt or creamy salmon, green peppercorn, and white wine tagliatelle (£5.80), beef in ale, lamb casseroled with honey, mint, pine nuts and apricots, and breast of chicken in an apple, celery and calvados sauce (£7.90), and herb-crumbed butterfish on sweet potato mash with coriander sauce (£8.50); puddings like treacle and house malt whisky tart, raspberry and passion fruit mousse with a hazelnut biscotti or plum pudding with toffee sauce (all £3.90). They keep an incredible choice of around 50 west country cheeses (half a dozen £5; you can buy them to take away as well). The restaurant is no smoking. There are picnic-sets on the terrace with views of the surrounding wooded hill pastures. The medieval stained glass in the local church is some of the best in the west country. No children are allowed inside the pub. *(Recommended by David Peakall, Basil Minson, Pat and Sam Roberts, Betsy Brown, Nigel Flook, Sarah and Simon House, Mr and Mrs Thomas, Matt Britton, Alison Cameron, Lynn Sharpless, Bob Eardley, Shaun Pinchbeck, A Moore, V N Stevenson, Paul Thompson, Anna Blackburn, Jenny and Chris Wilson, Richard and Margaret Peers, Tracey and Stephen Groves, LM, N and S Alcock, Mr and Mrs S Oxenbury, P and J Shapley, Charlie Harris, P R and S A White, John Beeken, Anne and Barry Coulton, Steve Whalley, Hugh Roberts, the Didler, C M; also in* The Good Hotel Guide)

Free house ~ Licensee Nick Borst-Smith ~ Real ale ~ Bar food (till 10) ~ Restaurant ~ (01647) 252394 ~ Open 12-2.30, 6-11; 12-3, 7-10.30 Sun; closed 25 and 26 Dec ~ Bedrooms: £23(£38B)/£66(£70B)

DOLTON SS5712 Map 1
Union 🛏

B3217

There's a warm welcome for all at this enjoyable and comfortable village inn. The little lounge bar has a comfortably cushioned window seat, a pink plush chesterfield, a nicely carved priest's table and some dark pine country chairs with brocaded cushions, and dagging shears, tack, country prints, and brass shell cases. On the right and served by the same stone bar counter is another bar with a chatty atmosphere and liked by locals: heavy black beams hung with brasses, an elegant panelled oak settle and antique housekeeper's chairs, a small settle snugged into the wall, and various dining chairs on the squared patterned carpet; the big stone fireplace has some brass around it, and on the walls are old guns, two land-felling saws, antlers, some engravings, and a whip. As well as lunchtime snacks like baguettes filled with bacon and mushrooms or locally made sausages (£3.95), ploughman's (from £4.95), ham and egg (£5), local cod in beer batter (£5.50), the good food might include sardines freshly grilled with olive oil and sea salt (£3.95), fresh mussels in wine, shallots and cream (£4.95), stilton and pasta bake (£5.50), home-made lasagne (£5.50), steak, Guinness and oyster pie (£6.50), and puddings such as home-made chocolate truffle torte and tarte au citron (£3.25). The restaurant is no smoking. Well kept St Austell HSD and a guest such as Clearwater Beggars Tipple, Exmoor Ale or Sharps Doom Bar, and decent wines. Outside on a small patch of grass in front of the building are some rustic tables and chairs. *(Recommended by Mr and Mrs P A A Stocker, R J Walden, Mrs M Bagnall, Dr M W A Haward, P and J Shapley, Mrs V M Hodgson, Graham Sumner, Jed and Virginia Brown, David Hoult, Anthony Longden)*

Free house ~ Licensees Ian and Irene Fisher ~ Real ale ~ Bar food (not Weds) ~

Restaurant ~ (01805) 804633 ~ Children in eating area of bar (until 9) and in restaurant ~ Open 12-2.30, 6-11; 12-2.30, 7-10.30 Sun; closed Wednesdays ~ Bedrooms: /£55S(£65B)

DREWSTEIGNTON SX7390 Map 1
Drewe Arms

Signposted off A30 NW of Moretonhampstead

It's well worth leaving the A30 to have a good lunch in this unpretentious and friendly old thatched pub. The small room on the left has hardly changed at all, thankfully, since the outstandingly long tenure of the former landlady, the late Mabel Mudge, and still has its serving hatch and basic seats; the room on the right with its assorted tables and chairs has a log fire, and is not much bigger. Well kept Bass, Flowers IPA, Gales HSB, and Greene King Old Speckled Hen kept on racks in the tap room behind, and local cider. At the back is a sizeable eating area, with good food such as a huge bowl of soup with a loaf of bread (£3.50), sandwiches (£3.95 with chips or salad), a proper ploughman's (£4.95), pork and sage sausage with bubble and squeak or crispy belly of pork on tatties and leeks with apple sauce (£5.95), jumbo cod fillet in beer batter or vegetarian dishes like crispy potato wedges with a leek sauce topped with stilton (£6.95), and shank of lamb with an orange and red wine sauce £12). The restaurant is no smoking. Dominoes, darts, shove-ha'penny, and skittle alley. Castle Drogo nearby (open for visits) looks medieval, though it was actually built earlier last century. *(Recommended by Robert Gomme, Peter Meister, Mrs J Reeves, Richard and Margaret Peers, JP, PP, Kevin Thorpe, David Biggins, G and A Wall, Mr and Mrs McKay, Veronica Brown, the Didler, David and June Harwood, John and Vivienne Rice, Mike and Mona Clifford, Malcolm and Faith Thomas, Dr P F A Watkins, Jason Caulkin)*

Whitbreads ~ Lease Janice and Colin Sparks ~ Real ale ~ Bar food (not 25 Dec) ~ Restaurant ~ (01647) 281224 ~ Children in eating area of bar and in restaurant ~ Open 11-3, 6-11; 12-3, 7-10.30 Sun ~ Bedrooms: /£55B

EAST PRAWLE SX7836 Map 1
Freebooter

Village signposted off A379 E of Kingsbridge, at Frogmore and Chillington

The warmth of the welcome alone makes a visit to this unspoilt local special, but the beers and food are also particularly good. To the right of the door are wheelback chairs and brocaded wall seats on the parquet floor and a stone fireplace with its surround supposedly taken from a Spanish ship captain's cabin door; on the left, there's another stone fireplace (which has holes in the huge granite block over it that were packed with explosives for blasting rock out of a nearby quarry), a couple of armchairs and a curved high-backed settle, flowers on chunky elm tables, and more wheelback chairs; plenty of books on the area, shipping memorabilia, and a friendly, relaxed atmosphere; some tables are no smoking. Good, enjoyable food (using organic or additive free meat and poultry) includes sandwiches (from £2), home-made soups like parsnip and ginger (£2.75), home-made burgers or free-range three-egg omelettes (from £3), garlic mushrooms in cream and white wine (£3.50), grilled goats cheese on walnut bread (£3.50), scallops in ginger or creamy leek croustade (£5.50), sweet potato and chick pea curry (£7), seafood au gratin (£8.50), beef in ale (£8.50), organic steaks (from £10.50), and puddings such as gooseberry or plum pies or treacle sponge (£3). Well kept Dartmoor Best, Greene King Abbot, and a guest such as Princetown Jail Ale on handpump, kept under light blanket pressure, Heron Valley cider, and good wines by the glass; darts, shove-ha'penny, cribbage, dominoes, board games, and piped music. From the walled garden and picnic-sets behind the pub, are views of the sea, and the coastal path between Salcombe and Start Point is nearby. The name Freebooter means pirate's ship. *(Recommended by Simon C Tallett, Mr and Mrs C R Little, Mr and Mrs M Dalby, Philip and Julia Evans, Caroline Raphael, Eric Locker)*

Free house ~ Licensees John and Delphine Swaddle ~ Real ale ~ Bar food (not winter Mon) ~ Restaurant ~ No credit cards ~ (01548) 511208 ~ Children welcome ~ Open 12-3, 6.30-11; 12-3, 7-10.30 Sun; closed winter Mon lunchtime

EXETER SX9190 Map 1
Double Locks ✦

Canal Banks, Alphington; from A30 take main Exeter turn-off (A377/396) then next right into Marsh Barton Industrial Estate and follow Refuse Incinerator signs; when road bends round in front of the factory-like incinerator, take narrow dead end track over humpy railway bridge, cross narrow canal swing bridge, then turn sharp right and follow track along canal; much quicker than it sounds, and a very worthwhile diversion from the final M5 junction

Although not easy to find, this converted lock-keeper's cottage at the end of an isolated canalside road is well worth the trek. It's consistently friendly and has a very relaxed, laid-back atmosphere; students (and an enormous number of our readers of all ages) love it. They keep up to a dozen real ales on handpump or tapped from the cask: Adnams Broadside, Badger Tanglefoot, Batemans XB, Branscombe Branoc, Everards Original, Green King Abbot, Hop Back Summer Lightning, Mauldons Black Adder, Shepherd Neame Spitfire, and Youngs Bitter and Special; farm cider. Good, tasty bar food includes sandwiches (£2.95; garlic bread with goats cheese £3.70), filled baked potatoes (from £4.70), ham and eggs or feta cheese and spinach pie (£5.45), ploughman's (£5.50), Wednesday evening curries (from £6.25), breakfast special (plus a pint of beer, £6.25), chicken satay (£6.75), and puddings like treacle tart. There's quite a nautical theme in the bar – with ship's lamps and model ships, and darts, shove-ha'penny, cribbage, and piped music. The decking by the canal is a fine place to sit on a warm evening, and there's a large children's play area with rope walk, swings, slides and climbing area; cycle paths along the ship canal. *(Recommended by Joan and Michel Hooper-Immins, Matt Britton, Alison Cameron, John and Vivienne Rice, John Beeken, Esther and John Sprinkle, JP, PP, Geoff and Linda Dibble, the Didler, John Wilson, R T and J C Moggridge, Dave Irving, Mike Gorton)*

Youngs ~ Managers Tony Stearman and M Loades ~ Real ale ~ Bar food (11-10.30; 12-10 Sun) ~ Restaurant ~ (01392) 256947 ~ Children in restaurant ~ Trad jazz Thurs evening, soft rock/folk weekends ~ Open 11-11; 12-10.30 Sun

Imperial ✦ £

Crediton/Tiverton road near St Davids Station

In 1801, this splendid building was built as a private mansion, and to get to it, you have to go along a sweeping drive; it stands in a 6-acre hillside park with plenty of picnic-sets in the grounds and elegant metal garden furniture in an attractive cobbled courtyard. Inside, there are all sorts of areas such as a couple of little clubby side bars and a newly located bar on the left-hand side looking into a light and airy former orangery – the huge glassy fan of its end wall is lightly mirrored – and a glorious ex-ballroom filled with elaborate plasterwork and gilding brought here in the 1920s from Haldon House (a Robert Adam stately home that was falling on hard times). One area is no smoking. The furnishings give Wetherspoons' usual solid well spaced comfort, and there are plenty of interesting pictures and other things to look at. Well kept and very cheap Courage Directors, Exmoor Gold, Greene King Abbot, Shepherd Neame Spitfire, Theakstons Best, and a couple of guest beers tapped from the cask. Decent bar food includes soup (£2.10), filled baps (from £2.55), filled baked potatoes (from £2.95), ham and eggs (£3.99), quite a few burgers (from £4.59), Aberdeen Angus pie (£4.99), vegetable lasagne or spaghetti with mushrooms, sun-dried tomatoes, basil and rocket, served with garlic bread (£4.79), rump steak (after 2pm, £5.99 with a choice of sauces), and puddings like treacle sponge (from £1.99); on Monday-Thursday, they offer two meals for £5.99 (2-10pm; 2-8pm Friday and Saturday). Silenced fruit machines and video game. No under-

18s. *(Recommended by Dr and Mrs A K Clarke, JP, PP, Dr B and Mrs P B Baker, Mike Gorton, P A Legon, Ian Phillips, Tony and Wendy Hobden, David Carr)*

Wetherspoons ~ Manager Jonathan Randall ~ Real ale ~ Bar food (11-10; 12-9.30 Sun) ~ (01392) 434050 ~ Open 11-11; 12-10.30 Sun

White Hart

4 rather slow miles from M5 junction 30; follow City Centre signs via A379, B3182; straight towards centre if you're coming from A377 Topsham Road

The rambling bar in this pleasantly old-fashioned 14th-c inn has heavy bowed beams in the dark ochre terracotta ceiling hung with small copper jugs, windsor armchairs and built-in winged settles with latticed glass tops to their high backs, oak tables on the bare oak floorboards (carpet in the quieter lower area, and a log fire in one great fireplace with long-barrelled rifles above it. In one of the bay windows is a set of fine old brass beer engines, the walls are decorated with pictorial plates, old copper and brass platters, and a wall cabinet holds some silver and copper. From the latticed windows, with their stained-glass coats of arms, one can look out on the cobbled courtyard – lovely when the wisteria is flowering in May. Bottlescreu Bill's (closed Sunday evening) is a dimly candlelit bar with bare stone walls, and offers straightforward bar food and summer barbecued dishes. The bars, lounge area and part of the restaurant are no smoking. Bass, Courage Directors, and John Smiths on handpump, and a respectable range of fine wines. Bedrooms are in a modern extension. More reports please. *(Recommended by P A Legon, JP, PP, David Carr, Ian Phillips, Andrew Hodges)*

Eldridge Pope (Hardy) ~ Manager G F Stone ~ Real ale ~ Bar food (till 10) ~ Restaurant ~ (01392) 279897 ~ Children in eating area of bar and restaurant ~ Open 11.30-3, 5.30-11; 11-11 Sat; 12-3, 7-10.30 Sun; closed evening 25 Dec, 26 Dec ~ Bedrooms: £49B/£64B

EXMINSTER SX9487 Map 1
Turf Hotel ★

Follow the signs to the Swan's Nest, signposted from A739 S of village, then continue to end of track, by gates; park, and walk right along canal towpath – nearly a mile; there's a fine seaview out to the mudflats at low tide.

Getting to this isolated, friendly pub is part of the enjoyment of the whole visit. You can either walk (which takes about 20 minutes along the ship canal) or cycle, or take a 40-minute ride from Countess Wear in their own boat, the *Water Mongoose* (bar on board; £5 adult, £2 child return, charter for up to 56 people £200). They also operate a 30-seater boat which brings people down the Exe estuary from Topsham quay (15 minute trip, adults £3, child £2). For those arriving in their own boat there is a large pontoon as well as several moorings. From the bay windows of the pleasantly airy bar there are views out to the mudflats – which are full of gulls and waders at low tide – and mahogany decking and caulking tables on the polished bare floorboards, church pews, wooden chairs and alcove seats, and pictures and old photographs of the pub and its characters over the years on the walls; woodburning stove and antique gas fire. Good bar food includes sandwiches (from £2.50; toasties from £3), home-made soup (£2.95), warm chicken salad with a sweet chilli sauce (£3.95 starter, £6.95 main course), hummous in pitta bread with roasted vegetables (£5.25), ploughman's using local cheeses (£5.95), fresh and smoked salmon pasta (£6.50), thai prawn and noodle curry or fish pie (£7.95), and puddings like sticky toffee pudding or apple crumble (from £2.95); hugely enjoyable, popular self-cook barbecues in summer. The dining room is no smoking. Well kept Dartmoor Best, and Otter Bright and Otter Ale on handpump, Green Valley farm cider, wines from the Loire Valley that they import themselves, and several gins; cribbage, dominoes, and piped music. The garden has a children's play area built using a lifeboat from a liner that sank off the Scilly Isles around 100 years ago; there's also a deck area by the water. *(Recommended by Graham and Rose Ive, John and Vivienne Rice, Esther and John Sprinkle, Chris and Sandra Taylor, James Flory, David Carr, Mike Gorton, Chris Parsons, John Beeken, the Didler, Canon Michael Bourdeaux, Alan and Paula McCully)*

Free house ~ Licensees Clive and Ginny Redfern ~ Real ale ~ Bar food ~ (01392) 833128 ~ Children in eating area of bar ~ Open 11.30-11; 11.30-10.30 Sun; 11.30-5 winter weekends; closed weekdays Oct, Nov, Mar; closed Jan/Feb ~ Bedrooms: £30/£60

HARBERTON SX7758 Map 1
Church House
Village signposted from A381 just S of Totnes

You can be sure of a friendly welcome in this ancient pub, part of which may actually be Norman, as it was probably used as a chantry-house for monks connected with the church. The open-plan bar has some magnificent medieval oak panelling, and the latticed glass on the back wall is almost 700 years old and one of the earliest examples of non-ecclesiastical glass in the country. Furnishings include attractive 17th- and 18th-c pews and settles, candles, and a large inglenook fireplace with a woodburning stove; one half of the room is set out for eating. The family room is no smoking. Bar food is most enjoyable and people tend to choose from the daily specials board: mussel and prawn chowder (£3.75), stilton, brandy and walnut pâté (£3.95), fresh battered scallops (£4.95), mixed mushroom and spinach lasagne or fresh salmon and smoked salmon fishcakes (£6.95), chicken breasts wrapped in bacon and filled with blue brie, almonds and apricots (£8.95), and kleftico (leg of lamb for two people, £17.90). From the standard menu, there's home-made soup (£2.95), sandwiches (from £2.95), prawns in garlic butter (£3.95), three locally made sausages (£4.75), ploughman's (from £4.50), fry-up (£6.50), rainbow trout (£7.95), steaks (from £8.50), and puddings like treacle tart with clotted cream or sticky toffee pudding (from £2.95). Well kept Bass and Wells Bombardier and guest beers like Greene King Abbot, Exmoor Ale or St Austell XXX Mild on handpump, farm cider, a dozen wines by the glass, and several malt whiskies; darts, cribbage, and dominoes. Tabitha the cat is very friendly. *(Recommended by J H Bell, Bob and Ann Westbrook, Basil Minson, John and Sarah Perry, Richard and Margaret Peers, Brian and Bett Cox, Dr Phil Putwain)*

Free house ~ Licensees David and Jennifer Wright ~ Real ale ~ Bar food (12-1.45, 7-9.30; not 25, 26 Dec, 1 Jan) ~ (01803) 863707 ~ Children in family room ~ Open 12-3, 6-11; 11.30-3.30, 6-11 Sat; 12-3.30, 6(7 in winter)-10.30 Sun; closed evenings 25 and 26 Dec and 1 Jan ~ Bedrooms: £25/£40

HATHERLEIGH SS5404 Map 1
George ♀
A386 N of Okehampton

A little bar that had been shut in this black and white timbered old pub for some years has been re-opened and extended to create the Mad Monk bar; there are amusing murals of monks on the light gold walls, and a mix of country tables and chairs. They are also revamping another bar as a dining area. The little front bar in the original part has huge oak beams, stone walls two or three feet thick, an enormous fireplace, and easy chairs, sofas and antique cushioned settles. The spacious L-shaped bar was built from the wreck of the inn's old brewhouse and coachmen's loft, and has more beams, a woodburning stove, and antique settles around sewing-machine treadle tables; piped music. Well kept Bass, St Austell Dartmoor Best and HSD, a beer named for the pub and Whitbreads on handpump, lots of malt whiskies, and farm cider. Under the new licensees, bar food includes sandwiches (from £2.20), home-made soup (£2.95), filled baked potatoes (from £3.95), ploughman's (£4.95), daily specials (around £4.25; delicious roast chicken), beef and vegetable pie (£5.95), salmon in a creamy dill and tarragon sauce (£7.50), steaks (from £8.95), and seafood medley £9.50). The courtyard has very pretty summer window boxes and hanging baskets, and there are rustic wooden seats and tables on the cobblestones; there's also a walled cobbled garden. Some of the bedrooms have four-poster beds. *(Recommended by the Didler, David and Ruth Hollands, Rita Horridge, Geoff and Linda Dibble, JP, PP, R J Walden)*

Free house ~ Licensees Janice Anderson and J Pozzetto ~ Real ale ~ Bar food (12-3, 6.30-9.30) ~ Restaurant ~ (01837) 810454 ~ Children in eating area of bar and restaurant ~ Jazz and Irish music ~ Open 11-11.30; 12-10.30 Sun ~ Bedrooms: /£69.50B

Tally Ho 🍺

Market St (A386)

They continue to brew their own ales at this friendly pub: Tarka Tipple, Midnight Madness, and Nutters, and a guest such as Clearwater Cavalier. The opened-together rooms of the bar have heavy beams, sturdy old oak and elm tables on the partly carpeted wooden floor, decorative plates between the wall timbers, shelves of old bottles and pottery, and a woodburning stove, and huge open fire. Bar food includes lunchtime sandwiches, soup (£3.20), home-made pâté (£3.85), sausages (£4.95), half a rack of ribs in barbecue sauce (£5.50), a vegetarian dish (£6.60), and gammon and pineapple (£7.95). The restaurant is no smoking. Darts, shove-ha'penny, dominoes, cribbage, and piped music. There are tables in the sheltered garden. *(Recommended by the Didler, R J Walden, Ron and Sheila Corbett, Tony and Wendy Hobden, JP, PP)*

Own brew ~ Licensee D Hemsley ~ Real ale ~ Bar food ~ Restaurant ~ (01837) 810306 ~ Children in eating area of bar ~ Open 11-3, 6-11; 12-3, 7-10.30 Sun ~ Bedrooms: £25B/£50B

HAYTOR VALE SX7677 Map 1

Rock ★ 🛏

Haytor signposted off B3387 just W of Bovey Tracey, on good moorland road to Widecombe

Very neatly kept and civilised, this peaceful place is handy for Dartmoor National Park. The two communicating, partly panelled bar rooms have easy chairs, oak windsor armchairs and high-backed settles, polished antique tables with candles and fresh flowers, old-fashioned prints and decorative plates on the walls, and good winter log fires (the main fireplace has a fine Stuart fireback); the restaurant, lounge and children's area are no smoking. Served by friendly staff, the impressive choice of very good bar food might include home-made soup (£2.95), English brie with onion, pepper and orange chutney (£4.25), Teign River mussels in a three-mustard sauce or wild boar and apple sausages (£5.95), ploughman's with west country cheeses, pickles and chutneys (£6.25), pasta with an artichoke, courgette and red onion chilli oil (£7.95), fish and chips (£8.50), and tossed salmon with dill dressing or steak and kidney pudding (£8.95), with puddings such as fresh passion fruit cheesecake with a vanilla and passion fruit sauce, treacle and walnut tart or chocolate pot with clotted cream and chocolate curls (£3.75). Well kept Bass, Dartmoor Best and Hardy Royal Oak on handpump, and several malt whiskies. In summer, the pretty, large garden opposite the inn is a popular place to sit and there are some tables and chairs on a small terrace next to the pub itself. Plenty of walks, golf, horse riding and fishing are nearby. *(Recommended by Mr and Mrs S Oxenbury, Mr and Mrs J McRobert, J H Bell, Pat and Robert Watt, Basil Minson, Mr and Mrs R Head, Ann and Colin Hunt, Sue Demont, Tim Barrow, Mike Gorton, Ken and Jenny Simmonds, Jane and Adrian Tierney-Jones, Richard and Margaret Peers)*

Free house ~ Licensee Christopher Graves ~ Real ale ~ Bar food (not 25 Dec) ~ Restaurant ~ (01364) 661305 ~ Children welcome ~ Open 11-11(10.30 in winter); 12-10.30 Sun; closed 25 Dec ~ Bedrooms: £50.50S(£60.50B)/£71S(£81B)

HOLBETON SX6150 Map 1
Mildmay Colours ◀

Signposted off A379 W of A3121 junction

In a quiet, off-the-beaten-track village, this friendly pub has a neat bar with various horse and racing pictures, and the framed racing colours of Lord Mildmay-White on the partly stripped stone and partly white walls, plenty of bar stools as well as cushioned wall seats and wheelback chairs on the turkey carpet, and a tile-sided woodburning stove; an arch leads to a smaller, similarly decorated family area. Though the brewery has moved away, they still offer Mildmay SP and Colours, and a guest beer on handpump; local farm cider. There's a decent, carpeted family area with pool, TV, pinball, juke box, and fruit machine. Bar food includes sandwiches (from £2.95; baguettes from £3.95), home-made soup (£2.99), home-made chicken liver pâté (£3.10), ham and egg (£3.95), ploughman's (from £4.95), mushroom stroganoff (£5.50), Mexican chicken enchilada (£6.35), pork chops with apple sauce (£7.15), steaks (from £9.95), daily specials such as steak and kidney pie (£5.60), liver and bacon (£5.95), and rack of lamb (£8.95), home-made puddings (£2.99), and children's meals (£2.40). The well kept back garden has picnic-sets, a swing, and an aviary, and there's a small front terrace. *(Recommended by Dr Paull Khan, Martin Jennings, G R Taylor, R J Walden, Geoff and Tricia Alderman, Norman and Sarah Keeping, Carol Ackroyd, Peter McNamara)*

Free house ~ Licensee Louise Price ~ Real ale ~ Bar food ~ Restaurant ~ (01752) 830248 ~ Children in family room ~ Monthly live entertainment ~ Open 11-3(2.30 in winter), 6-11; 12-3, 7-10.30 Sun ~ Bedrooms: £30S/£50S

HORNDON SX5280 Map 1
Elephants Nest ◀

If coming from Okehampton on A386 turn left at Mary Tavy Inn, then left after about ½ mile; pub signposted beside Mary Tavy Inn, then Horndon signposted; on the OS Outdoor Leisure Map it's named as the New Inn

'As good as ever' is a phrase used to describe this popular pub by several of our readers, and customers do seem to return, again and again. There's a good log fire, large rugs and flagstones, a beams-and-board ceiling, and cushioned stone seats built into the windows, with captain's chairs around the tables; the name of the pub is written up on the beams in 80 languages; what was an old beer cellar is another bar with views over the garden and beyond to the moors. Enjoyable home-made bar food includes soup (£2), filled rolls (from £2), west country mushrooms or home-made crab or chive and cashew nut pâté (£3.70), half a dozen burgers (from £3.90), ploughman's (from £4), ratatouille (£5.70), sweet and sour pork or beef curry (£6.50), local game pie (£7.30), and steaks (from £10). Well kept Boddingtons, Palmers IPA, St Austell HSD, and two changing guest beers on handpump. Sensibly placed darts, cribbage, dominoes, shut the box, and piped music. They have three dogs, cats, ducks, chickens, rabbits, and horses; customers' dogs are allowed in on a lead. Benches on the spacious lawn in front of this 400-year-old place look over dry-stone walls to the pastures of Dartmoor's lower slopes, and the rougher moorland above; plenty of walks. *(Recommended by Esther and John Sprinkle, Ann and Colin Hunt, JP, PP, Dr and Mrs Nigel Holmes, Bruce Bird, John and Vivienne Rice)*

Free house ~ Licensee Nick Hamer ~ Real ale ~ Bar food (11.30-2, 6.30-10(9.30 Sun)) ~ Restaurant ~ (01822) 810273 ~ Children in family room ~ Open 11.30-2.30, 6.30-11(10.30 Sun)

Most pubs in the *Guide* sell draught cider. We mention it specifically only if they have unusual farm-produced 'scrumpy' or specialise in it. Do please let us know about any uncommon draught cider you find in a pub: www.goodguides.com

HORNS CROSS SS3823 Map 1
Hoops
A39 Clovelly—Bideford

This friendly 13th-c inn has an oak-beamed bar with an ancient well set into the floor, paintings and old photographs of the pub on the walls, cushioned window seats, oak settles, and logs burning in big inglenook fireplaces; leading off here is a small similarly furnished room with another fireplace. Generous helpings of enjoyable bar food, quickly served by cheerful staff, include home-made soup, sandwiches (from £3.50), ploughman's (from £4.50), roasted comice pear wrapped in parma ham (£4.80), fresh courgette flowers filled with local goats cheese (£5.50), popular beer-battered fish and chips (£6.50), lambs liver and bacon (£7.90), steaks (from £8.75), fresh spinach pancake filled with leeks and brie or grilled natural smoked haddock with creamed sweetcorn and poached egg (£8.95), local skate wing with black butter or venison casserole (£9.50), steak and kidney pudding (£9.75), crackly pork (£10.90), whole grilled lemon sole with beurre blanc (£11.50), and puddings such as banoffi pie, fresh lemon tart or spotted dick (£3.50); they grow much of their salad produce. There are several no smoking areas. Well kept Bass, Barum, Cotleigh Barn Owl, Jollyboat Buccaneers, Mainbrace Bitter, and Plunders tapped from the cask, farm cider, 40 malt whiskies, and 20 wines by the glass (including champagne); piped music, darts, shove-ha'penny, dominoes, table skittles, and TV. Outside, it is particularly pretty in summer with lots of flowering tubs and baskets and picnic-sets in a sheltered central courtyard. *(Recommended by Alan and Paula McCully, Rita Horridge, the Didler, George Atkinson, Derek Thomas, Steve and Liz Tilley, D and S Ainsworth, Steve Chambers)*

Free house ~ Licensee Gay Marriott ~ Real ale ~ Bar food (12-3, 6-9.30) ~ Restaurant ~ (01237) 451222 ~ Well behaved children welcome but not in evening restaurant ~ Open 11-11; 12-10.30 Sun; closed 25 Dec ~ Bedrooms: £50B/£60B

IDDESLEIGH SS5708 Map 1
Duke of York ★
B3217 Exbourne—Dolton

Particularly friendly, helpful licensees run this old thatched pub, tucked down narrow winding lanes in a quiet hamlet, and readers have enjoyed their visits so much in the last year or so that we have decided to award them a star. The bar has a lot of character, rocking chairs by the roaring log fire, cushioned wall benches built into the wall's black-painted wooden dado, stripped tables, and other homely country furnishings, and well kept Adnams Broadside, Cotleigh Tawny, and a guest such as Exe Valley Dobs or Sharps Doom Bar tapped from the cask; farm cider and freshly squeezed orange and pink grapefruit juice. Good bar food includes sandwiches, two or three home-made soups (£2.75 small, £3.25 large), chicken liver and brandy or port and liver pâté (£4.50), crab mayonnaise (£4.50 small, £7.50 large), liver, bacon and mash, two salmon fishcakes or spinach, mushroom and brie filo parcel (all £6.50), duck parcel (£7), leg of lamb steak (£7.50), steak and kidney pudding (£8), and steak (£11); hearty breakfasts. Cribbage, dominoes, shove-ha'penny, cards, chess and draughts. Through a small coach arch is a little back garden with some picnic-sets. Fishing nearby. *(Recommended by Dr P F A Watkins, JP, PP, Mike Gorton, Theo, Anne and Jane Gaskin, the Didler, Anthony Longden, Sharon Doe, Jed and Virginia Brown, Miss E Murphy, G K Smale, Guy Consterdine, George Atkinson, R J Walden, Sarah Meyer, Alan and Paula McCully, Jane and Adrian Tierney-Jones)*

Free house ~ Licensees Jamie Stuart and Pippa Hutchinson ~ Real ale ~ Bar food (all day except 25 Dec) ~ Restaurant ~ (01837) 810253 ~ Children welcome ~ Open 11-11; 12-10.30 Sun ~ Bedrooms: £25B/£50B

KINGSTEIGNTON SX8773 Map 1
Old Rydon

Rydon Rd; from A381/A380 junction follow signs to Kingsteignton (B3193), taking first right turn (Longford Lane), go straight on to the bottom of the hill, then next right turn into Rydon Rd following Council Office signpost; pub is just past the school, OS Sheet 192 map reference 872739

Although a new licensee has taken over here and it is now brewery-owned, reports seem as positive as ever. The small, cosy bar has a big winter log fire in a raised fireplace, cask seats and upholstered seats built against the white-painted stone walls, and lots of beer mugs hanging from the heavy beam-and-plank ceiling. There are a few more seats in an upper former cider loft facing the antlers and antelope horns on one high white wall; piped music. Well liked bar food includes home-made soup (£2.95), filled baked potatoes or toasted muffins with various toppings (from £3.95), ploughman's (from £4.85), warm salads (from £4.95; charcoal grilled escalope of lemon and marjoram chicken £6.95), warm Spanish potato, fresh vegetable and egg tortilla (£5.95), chargrilled chicken satay (£6.95), daily specials, and children's meals (£3.50). The restaurant is no smoking (though you may smoke in the restaurant lounge). Well kept Bass, Fullers London Pride and a guest beer such as Greene King Abbot or Otter on handpump, and helpful, friendly service. The nice biggish sheltered garden has seats under parasols, with more on the terrace, and a popular conservatory with prolific shrubbery. This is not the easiest pub to find, and in a rather surprising location when you do – in the middle of a residential area. *(Recommended by Peter and Jenny Quine, Betsy and Peter Little, Bob and Ann Westbrook, John and Sarah Perry, Dr P F A Watkins, Mr and Mrs M Cross, Lyn and Geoff Hallchurch, June and Ken Brooks)*

Heavitree ~ Manager Martin Webb ~ Real ale ~ Bar food ~ Restaurant ~ (01626) 354626 ~ Children in eating area of bar and restaurant ~ Open 11-3, 6-11; 12-3, 7-10.30 Sun

KINGSTON SX6347 Map 1
Dolphin 🛏

Off B3392 S of Modbury (can also be reached from A379 W of Modbury)

Half a dozen tracks lead down to the sea from this charming, shuttered 16th-c inn, and there are plenty of surrounding walks. Several knocked-through beamed rooms have a good mix of customers, a relaxed, welcoming atmosphere (no noisy games machines or piped music), amusing drawings and photographs on the walls, and rustic tables and cushioned seats and settles around their bared stone walls; one small area is no smoking. Good honest seasonally changing bar food includes sandwiches (from £2.50; crab £4.75), home-made soup (£2.75), ploughman's (£4.50), ham and chips (£4.95), lasagne (£5.25), spinach, brie and yellow pepper tart (£5.95), steak in ale casserole or fish pie (£6.50), chicken breast in tarragon and cream sauce (£9.95), steaks (from £9.95), home-made puddings like treacle tart or banana and walnut pudding with caramel sauce (£2.75), and children's meals (from £1.50); nice breakfasts. Well kept Courage Best and Ushers Founders and a guest such as Bass or Wadworths 6X on handpump. Outside, there are tables and swings. *(Recommended by R and D Gray, Eric Locker, David and Helen Wilkins, Peter and Susan Turner, John Wilson, Ian Jones, James and Penny Abell, G R Taylor, P and J Shapley)*

InnSpired ~ Lease Neil and Annie Williams ~ Real ale ~ Bar food ~ (01548) 810314 ~ Children welcome ~ Open 11-3, 6-11; 12-3, 6-10.30 Sun ~ Bedrooms: £39.50B/£55B

We checked prices with the pubs as we went to press in summer 2001. They should hold until around spring 2002 – when our experience suggests that you can expect an increase of around 10p in the £.

KNOWSTONE SS8223 Map 1

Masons Arms ★ ♀

Signposted from A361 Tiverton to South Molton road and B3227 Bampton to South Molton

The new dining room, kitchen, lavatories and garden area are all up and running now at this 13th-c thatched inn, and although they don't offer bedrooms in the pub itself, they have a very popular cottage a walk from the pub, with an ensuite bedroom and downstairs sitting room with an inglenook fireplace and woodburning stove, and breakfast supplied from the pub. The simple little main bar has heavy medieval black beams, farm tools on the walls, pine furniture on the stone floor, and a fine open fireplace with a big log fire and side bread oven – the warmly friendly licensee tell us that there is always a fire lit, whatever the weather. Good bar food includes soups such as cream of parsnip, lemon and ginger soup (£2.95), light lunches such as filled ciabatta loaves (£4.50) or ploughman's or oven-baked ham and eggs (£5.50), breaded thai prawns with ginger mayonnaise (£4), chargrilled cajun chicken with pesto butter, steak, kidney and Guinness pie or popular spare ribs (all £6.50), lamb shank casserole (£7.50), baked salmon escalope with garlic mayonnaise (£8.50), duck breast with Grand Marnier sauce (£10.50), and daily specials such as Greek spinach, feta cheese and filo pie (£6.50), seafood pancakes (£7.50), and lovely puddings such as chocolate roulade with chocolate mousse and cream, banana and caramel crème brûlée or sticky toffee pudding with butterscotch sauce. Well kept Cotleigh Tawny tapped from the cask, and a decent wine list; piped music. *(Recommended by Bruce and Jody Davie, Mrs M S Porter, Shaun Pinchbeck, Mrs S Matthews, Sarah Holden, Jed and Virginia Brown, JP, PP, J C Brittain-Long, Debbie and Neil Hayter, Hazel Boundy, Anne Westcott, the Didler)*

Free house ~ Licensees Paul and Jo Stretton-Downes ~ Real ale ~ Bar food (not evening 24 Dec, not 25 Dec) ~ (01398) 341231 ~ Children in family room if over 8 and until 9pm ~ Open 12-3, 6-11.30; 12-3, 7-10.30 Sun; closed 25 Dec ~ Bedrooms: £35S/£50S

LITTLEHEMPSTON SX8162 Map 1

Tally Ho!

Signposted off A381 NE of Totnes

There's lots to look at in the neatly kept and cosy rooms of this friendly little pub and the bare stone walls are covered with porcelain, brass, copperware, mounted butterflies, stuffed wildlife, old swords, and shields and hunting horns and so forth; there's also an interesting mix of chairs and settles (many antique and with comfortable cushions), two coal fires, low beams and panelling, and fresh flowers and candles on the tables. Well liked bar food (with prices unchanged since last year) includes sandwiches (from £2.95), home-made soup (£3.50), home-made chicken liver pâté (£3.95), lasagne (£6.95), steak and kidney pie (£7.95), pork fillet with cider, almond, apple and cream sauce (£9.25), steaks (from £10.95), whole local plaice with dill and lemon butter (£8.95), duck with black cherry and kirsch sauce (£11.95), and home-made puddings. Well kept Bass and a guest such as Robinsons or Wadworths 6X on handpump; they hold charity quiz evenings. The three friendly cats are called Monica, Thomas and Ellwood. The terrace is full of flowers in summer. *(Recommended by Mrs J Ekins-Daukes, Basil Minson, P G Wooler, John Bowling)*

Free house ~ Licensees P Saint, A Greenwood, G Waterfield ~ Real ale ~ Bar food (not 25 Dec) ~ Restaurant ~ (01803) 862316 ~ Children in eating area of bar ~ Open 12-3, 6(7 Sun)-11; closed evening 25 Dec ~ Bedrooms: £50S/£60S

LOWER ASHTON SX8484 Map 1

Manor Inn ◖

Ashton signposted off B3193 N of Chudleigh

Very well run by friendly, professional licensees, this creeper-covered pub is set in a charming valley, and has pretty summer hanging baskets. There's a good mix of customers, although the left-hand room with its beer mats and brewery advertisements on the walls is more for locals enjoying the well kept Princetown Jail Ale, RCH Pitchfork, Teignworthy Reel Ale, and a constantly changing guest on handpump; local cider and decent wines by the glass. On the right, two rather more discreet rooms have a wider appeal, bolstered by the good, popular home-made food which might include soup (£2.10), sandwiches (from £2.10), lots of filled baked potatoes (from £2.75), home-made burgers with various toppings (from £3.50), ploughman's (from £4.75), vegetable bake (£5.25), home-cooked ham and egg (£5.95), steak, mushroom and ale pie (£6.25) and steaks (from £8.95), with a good choice of changing specials such as vegetable and nut curry (£5.25), beef casserole or venison sausages (£6.25), chicken, smoked bacon and mushroom pasta in a creamy cheese sauce (£6.95), pork steak with an apple and cider sauce (£7.25), salmon and prawns au gratin (£7.95), and duck breast with a morello cherry sauce (£9.50). Shove-ha'penny, spoof. The garden has lots of picnic-sets under cocktail parasols (and a fine tall Scots pine). No children inside. *(Recommended by Phil and Sally Gorton, JP, PP, the Didler, LM, John and Vivienne Rice, Mike Gorton, Jeanne and Paul Silvestri, G and A Wall, Alan and Paula McCully, Richard and Margaret Peers)*

Free house ~ Licensees Geoff and Clare Mann ~ Real ale ~ Bar food (12-1.30, 7-9.30; not Mon) ~ (01647) 252304 ~ Open 12-2.30, 6.30(7 Sat)-11; 12-2.30, 7-10.30 Sun; closed Mon (except bank hols)

LUSTLEIGH SX7881 Map 1
Cleave
Village signposted off A382 Bovey Tracey—Moretonhampstead

Before or after a walk, this old thatched pub is an enjoyable place for lunch. The low-ceilinged lounge bar has granite walls, attractive antique high-backed settles, cushioned wall seats, and wheelback chairs around the tables on its patterned carpet, and a roaring log fire. A second bar has similar furnishings, a large dresser, harmonium, an HMV gramophone, and prints, and the no smoking family room has crayons, books and toys for children. Decent bar food includes home-made soup (£3.50), good lunchtime sandwiches (from £3.95; hot sardines £4.95), home-made chicken liver and brandy pâté (£4.95), home-made cheese and onion flan or local butcher's sausages with mash and onion gravy (£6.50), roast beef and yorkshire pudding (£8.95), half a duckling roasted with honey, served with an orange and Grand Marnier sauce (£11.95), and daily specials such as home-made lasagne (£6.95), chilli con carne (£7.50), and monkfish stroganoff (£11.45); the dining room is no smoking. Well kept Castle Eden, Otter Ale, Greene King Old Speckled Hen, and Wadworths 6X on handpump kept under light blanket pressure, quite a few malt whiskies, and 12 wines by the glass. From picnic-sets in front of the building, you can enjoy the flower-filled, sheltered garden – and the summer hanging baskets are lovely; there's also a wendy house. *(Recommended by Di and Mike Gillam, Denzil Taylor, Dennis Jenkin, Ewan and Sue Hewitt, Ann and Colin Hunt, John and Vivienne Rice)*

Heavitree ~ Tenant A Perring ~ Real ale ~ Bar food (all day Sat and Sun in summer) ~ Restaurant ~ (01647) 277223 ~ Children in eating area of bar and in family room ~ Open 11.30-3, 6-11; 11-11 Sat; 12-10.30 Sun; closed Mon Nov-Mar

LYDFORD SX5184 Map 1
Castle Inn 🏠
Village signposted off A386 Okehampton—Tavistock

The twin-roomed bar in this charming pink-washed Tudor inn has country kitchen chairs, high-backed winged settles and old captain's chairs around mahogany tripod tables on big slate flagstones. One of the rooms has low lamp-lit beams, a sizeable open fire, masses of brightly decorated plates, some Hogarth prints, and, near the serving counter, seven Lydford pennies hammered out in the old Saxon mint in the reign of Ethelred the Unready, in the 11th c. The bar area has a bowed ceiling with low beams, a polished slate flagstone floor, a collection of stallion posters, and a stained-glass door with the famous Three Hares; there's a snug with high-backed settles which is used by families. Good bar food might include lunchtime sandwiches (from £3.85), soup (£3.95), warm bacon and roquefort salad (£5.25), thai fishcakes with a sweet chilli dipping sauce (£5.85), steak and kidney pie (£6.75), wild mushroom risotto with nuts and red pepper sauce (£7.95), poached salmon salad (£8.50), and smoked chicken tagliatelle (£8.95); the restaurant is no smoking. Well kept Flowers IPA, Fullers London Pride, and Greene King Old Speckled Hen on handpump. Wednesday quiz evenings. The pub is next to the village's daunting, ruined 12th-c castle and close to a beautiful river gorge (owned by the National Trust; closed Nov-Easter); the village itself was one of the four strong-points developed by Alfred the Great as a defence against the Danes. *(Recommended by Mrs J H S Lang, Tony Walker, Peter Rogers, Ruth and Paul Lawrence, R M Corlett, Peter Meister, Jason Caulkin, P Rome, Pat and Tony Martin, Paul Boot, Chris and Fiona Whitton, Miss Diana Lewis)*

Free house ~ Licensee Lynn Hazelton ~ Real ale ~ Bar food (12-2.15, 6.30-9) ~ Restaurant ~ (01822) 820241 ~ Children in restaurant and family room ~ Open 11.30-11; 12-10.30 Sun; closed 25 Dec ~ Bedrooms: £41S/£62B

MARLDON SX8663 Map 1
Church House 🍴 ♀

Just W of Paignton

There's a good relaxed atmosphere in the spreading bar of this charming and attractive inn, and several different areas radiating off the big semicircular bar counter. The main bar has interesting windows, some beams, dark pine chairs around solid tables on the turkey carpet, and green plush-seated bar chairs; leading off here is a cosy little candlelit room with just four tables on the bareboard floor, a dark wood dado, and stone fireplace, and next to this is the attractive, dimly lit, no smoking restaurant with dried flowers in the big stone fireplace. At the other end of the building is a characterful room split into two parts with a stone floor in one bit and a wooden floor in another (with a big woodburning stove). Good, interesting bar food includes soup (£3.50; fish soup £5), sandwiches (from £3.50), braised beef with lemon and thyme potatoes (£8.50), lamb shank cooked with cumin and orange (£10), breast of chicken filled with feta and spinach (£10.50), whole lemon sole (£12.50), monkfish wrapped in bacon (£14), and puddings like chocolate bread and butter pudding or summer pudding (£3.50). Well kept Bass, Boddingtons, Flowers IPA , and Fullers London Pride with a guest such as Blackawton 44 Special or St Austell HSD on handpump, and 10 wines by the glass; piped music and skittle alley. There are three grassy terraces with picnic-sets behind. *(Recommended by Mr and Mrs C Roberts, P R and S A White, Alan and Paula McCully, B J Harding, David Whiteley, P Rome, Darly Graton, Graeme Gulibert)*

Whitbreads ~ Lease Julian Cook ~ Real ale ~ Bar food ~ Restaurant ~ (01803) 558279 ~ Children in eating area of bar and restaurant ~ Open 11.30-2.30, 5-11; 12-3, 6.30-10.30 Sun ~ Bedrooms: /£40B

NEWTON ABBOT SX8468 Map 1
Two Mile Oak ◖

A381 2 miles S, at Denbury/Kingskerswell crossroads

Run by a friendly young manageress, this old coaching inn has a relaxed atmosphere, a beamed lounge with several alcoves, a mix of wooden tables and chairs, and a fine winter log fire. The beamed and black-panelled bar is traditionally furnished, again with a mix of seating on the slate floor, lots of horsebrasses, and another good log fire. Well kept Bass, Flowers IPA, Greene King Abbot and Otter Ale tapped from the cask, and decent wines. Enjoyable bar food includes home-made soup (£3.25), filled baguettes (from £4.25), deep-fried breaded somerset camembert with peach chutney (£5.25), ploughman's (from

£5.75), smoked pigeon breast with a raspberry vinaigrette and pine kernels (£5.95), a medley of pork sausages (£6.25), local ham with eggs and sautéed potatoes (£6.50), pasta with a garlicky tomato, olive, and mushroom sauce (£6.95), roast shank of lamb with a rich red wine, mustard, mint and rosemary sauce or chicken supreme with a creamy Cornish tarragon sauce (£10.95), whole bass with lemon and truffle oil dressing (£14.95), and puddings such as banoffi pie, key lime chocolate pie or strawberry roulade (£3.45). Piped music, darts, and fruit machine. There are picnic-sets on the terrace where they hold summer barbecues, and a lawn with shrubs and tubs of flowers. *(Recommended by the Didler, Ian Phillips, JP, PP)*

Heavitree ~ Manager Karen May ~ Real ale ~ Bar food (12-2, 7-9) ~ (01803) 812411 ~ Children in lounge area ~ Live single or duo every other Fri ~ Open 11-11; 11-10.30 Sun; closed evenings 25 and 26 Dec

NEWTON ST CYRES SX8798 Map 1
Beer Engine ◀

Sweetham; from Newton St Cyres on A377 follow St Cyres Station, Thorverton signpost

As well as enjoying the consistently good own-brewed beers at this friendly old station hotel, you can also take them home with you: Rail Ale, Piston Bitter, and the strong Sleeper on handpump. There's a good bustling atmosphere, and the no smoking eating area of the spacious bar has partitioning alcoves, and windsor chairs and some cinnamon-coloured button-back banquettes around dark varnished tables on the brown carpet. Good bar food includes speciality sausages (£4.95), vegetarian dishes (from £4.95), chicken in barbecue sauce (£5.95), steak in their own ale pie (£6.50), and rump steak; roast Sunday lunch (£5.75 one course, £7.50 two courses). Darts, shove-ha'penny, dominoes, cribbage, chess, and Trivial Pursuits. The hanging baskets and window boxes are very pretty in summer, and in the large sunny garden, there are plenty of seats; popular summer barbecues. *(Recommended by G and A Wall, Bruce Bird, Cathy Robinson, John and Bryony Coles, Tony and Wendy Hobden, Ian Phillips, Jane and Adrian Tierney-Jones)*

Own brew ~ Licensee Peter Hawksley ~ Real ale ~ Bar food ~ Restaurant ~ (01392) 851282 ~ Children in eating area of bar ~ Open 11-11; 12-10.30 Sun

NOSS MAYO SX5447 Map 1
Ship

Off A379 via B3186, E of Plymouth

After eight months of renovations, this has now returned to its origins as a proper village inn. The location on a tidal inlet is very pretty, and visiting boats can tie up alongside – with prior permission; parking is restricted at high tide. Inside, the two thick-walled bars have a happy mix of dining chairs and tables on the wooden floors, log fires, bookcases, dozens of local pictures, newspapers to read, and a friendly, chatty atmosphere. Good food (which can be eaten anywhere in the pub) features much local produce, and includes soups such as white onion and pomerol mustard (£3.75), sandwiches (from £3.75; hot grilled baguettes from £4.75), smoked duck and orange salad with a lime dressing and roasted cashew nuts or moules marinières (£5.95), ploughman's (£6.50), roast vegetables on mixed herb pasta with a tomato and pesto sauce, or salmon and chive fishcakes with a light shellfish sauce (£6.95), steak and kidney pie (£7.25), cod tail deep-fried in beer batter with minted mushy peas (£8.50), braised shoulder of lamb with carrots, swede and mashed potato (£10.95), whole brill grilled with herb butter (£12.75), and oriental-style duck breast with stir-fried vegetables and Chinese egg noodles (£13.95). There are two no smoking areas. Well kept Exmoor Gold, Summerskills Tamar, Shepherd Neame Spitfire, Wadworths 6X and a guest such as Batemans or Everards Beacon on handpump, lots of malt whiskies, and quite a few wines by the glass. There are seats outside. *(Recommended by Mr and Mrs C Derry, Frances Capel, Stephen Archer)*

Free house ~ Licensees Lesley and Bruce Brunning ~ Real ale ~ Bar food (12-9.30) ~ Restaurant ~ (01752) 872387 ~ Children in eating area of bar and in restaurant until 7.30 ~ Open 11.30-11; 12-10.30 Sun

PETER TAVY SX5177 Map 1
Peter Tavy Inn
Off A386 nr Mary Tavy, N of Tavistock

Even in mid-winter, it is essential to arrive at this attractive old stone inn early, as it fills up quickly – especially at lunchtime. The low-beamed bar has high-backed settles on the black flagstones by the big stone fireplace (a good log fire on cold days), smaller settles in stone-mullioned windows, a snug, no smoking side dining area, and very friendly efficient service. Good bar food at lunchtime includes soup such as leek and potato (£2.25), baguettes or filled baked potatoes (from £3.95), baked avocado and prawns (£4.25), ham and egg (£5.50), roast beef and yorkshire pudding (£5.95), provençale vegetable pie (£6.25), and ploughman's (£6.75), with evening dishes like bacon and camembert parcels or seared scallop and bacon salad (£3.95), baked stuffed peppers with goats cheese (£6.95), boozy game casserole with stilton dumpling (£8.95), creole of seafood on spicy pineapple (£9.95), sweet and sour tuna on noodles (£10.95), game platter (ostrich, pheasant, wild boar, rabbit and venison, £12.95), and puddings like chocolate truffle torte, profiteroles or sticky toffee puddings (£3.50). Well kept Badger Best, Bass, Princetown Jail Ale, Summerskills Tamar Best, and a guest such as Mauldons Black Adder or Scattor Rock Devonian on handpump, kept under light blanket pressure; 30 malt whiskies, 10 wines by the glass, and organic cider, and pure apple juice; juke box, darts, and piped music. From the picnic-sets in the pretty garden, there are peaceful views of the moor rising above nearby pastures. *(Recommended by John Evans, Ann and Colin Hunt, D and S Ainsworth, Dr M W A Haward, Jacquie and Jim Jones, JP, PP)*

Free house ~ Licensees Graeme and Karen Sim ~ Real ale ~ Bar food (not 25 Dec) ~ Restaurant ~ (01822) 810348 ~ Children in restaurant ~ Open 12-2.30(3 Sat), 6.30(6 Sat)-11; 12-3, 6(6.30 winter Sun)-10.30 Sun; closed 25 Dec

POSTBRIDGE SX6780 Map 1
Warren House
B3212 1¼ miles NE of Postbridge

Remote on Dartmoor (and a valuable refuge after a walk), this friendly place has a lot of local character and is something of a focus for the scattered moorland community. The cosy bar has a fireplace at either end (one is said to have been kept almost continuously alight since 1845), and is simply furnished with easy chairs and settles under a beamed ochre ceiling, wild animal pictures on the partly panelled stone walls, and dim lighting (fuelled by the pub's own generator); there's a no smoking family room. Good no-nonsense home cooking includes locally made meaty or vegetable pasties, home-made soup, sandwiches and filled baked potatoes, good ploughman's, home-made rabbit pie (£6.20), home-made steak in ale pie (£6.70), home-made vegetable curry (£7), tenderloin of pork with wild mushroom sauce (£9.75), venison with a red wine sauce (£10.50), and home-made puddings such as chocolate truffle torte or lime posset. Well kept Badger Tanglefoot, Butcombe Bitter, Sharps Special, and Summerskills Tamar, with a guest like Lees Moonraker or Shepherd Neame Spitfire on handpump, farm cider, and malt whiskies. Darts, pool, cribbage, and dominoes; maybe piped local radio. *(Recommended by John and Vivienne Rice, Mrs J Ekins-Daukes, Anthony Longden, Ann and Colin Hunt, Charles Eatof, Dick and Madeleine Brown, P J Holdsworth)*

Free house ~ Licensee Peter Parsons ~ Real ale ~ Bar food (all day summer and on winter Sat and Sun) ~ Restaurant ~ (01822) 880208 ~ Children in family room ~ Open 11-11; 12-10.30 Sun; 11-3, 6-11 Mon-Thurs in winter

RACKENFORD SS8518 Map 1
Stag
Off A361 NW of Tiverton

Two brothers took over this fine thatched inn as we went to press; there are no noisy games machines or piped music to spoil the relaxed, chatty atmosphere, and they are keen to support local breweries and local food producers. The pub dates from 1196 making it perhaps Devon's oldest, and the bar is reached along a marvellous old cobbled entrance corridor between massive stone and cob walls: a couple of very high-backed old settles face each other in front of a huge fireplace with an ancient bressumer beam (and good log fire), and there are some other interesting old pieces of furniture as well as more modern seats, a very low dark ochre ceiling, a grand piece of oak making up the bar counter, and a narrow sloping side area with darts. A cottagey dining room leads off. Good bar food includes soup (£2.25), sandwiches (from £2.95), ploughman's (£4.25), ham and eggs (£4.75), tortellini with four different cheeses and a tomato and ricotta sauce (£4.95), steak and kidney pie (£6.95), daily specials such as aubergine parmigiano (£5.95), braised lamb shank (£6.95), and grilled fillet of bream (£7.95), and puddings like rhubarb crème brûlée or sticky toffee pudding (£2.75). Well kept Cotleigh Tawny and a couple of guest beers such as Barum Original or Otter Ale on handpump, and farm cider. *(Recommended by Richard Gibbs)*

Free house ~ Licensees Mike and Richard Mills-Roberts ~ Real ale ~ Bar food ~ Restaurant ~ (01884) 881369 ~ Children in eating area of bar and restaurant ~ Jazz last Weds of month ~ Open 11.30-3, 6-11; 12-4, 7-10.30 Sun ~ Bedrooms: £18.50/£21.50S

RATTERY SX7461 Map 1
Church House
Village signposted from A385 W of Totnes, and A38 S of Buckfastleigh

The craftsmen who built the Norman church were probably housed in the original building here, and parts of it still survive, notably the spiral stone steps behind a little stone doorway on your left. There are massive oak beams and standing timbers in the homely open-plan bar, large fireplaces (one with a little cosy nook partitioned off around it), windsor armchairs, comfortable seats and window seats, and prints on the plain white walls; the no smoking dining room is separated from this room by heavy curtains; Shandy the golden labrador is very amiable. Good bar food includes generously filled rolls and ploughman's with local cheeses (from £2.95), and daily specials such as chicken Wensleydale (£7.50), steak and stilton or fish pie (£8.95), chicken jambalaya (£9.25), and half a roast guinea fowl or fresh bass or lemon sole (£9.95). Well kept Dartmoor Best, Greene King Abbot, and Marstons Pedigree on handpump, lots of malt whiskies, and a decent wine list. Outside, there are peaceful views of the partly wooded surrounding hills from picnic-sets on a hedged courtyard by the churchyard. *(Recommended by Jacquie and Jim Jones, Ted George, Richard and Margaret Peers, Bob and Ann Westbrook, Peter and Jenny Quine, Dudley and Moira Cockroft, B J Harding, JP, PP)*

Free house ~ Licensees Brian and Jill Evans ~ Real ale ~ Bar food ~ No credit cards ~ (01364) 642220 ~ Children in eating area of bar and restaurant ~ Open 11-3, 6-11; 12-3, 7-10.30 Sun

SHEEPWASH SS4806 Map 1
Half Moon ♀ £ ⇌
Off A3072 Holsworthy—Hatherleigh at Highampton

This village pub takes up one whole side of the colourful village square – blue, pink, white, cream and olive thatched or slate-roofed cottages. Inside, the white walls of the neatly-kept carpeted main bar are covered in fishing pictures, there's solid old furniture under the beams, and a big log fire fronted by slate flagstones. Lunchtime bar snacks are traditionally simple and good and include sandwiches

(£1.50, toasties £2.25), home-made vegetable soup (£2.25), home-made pasties (£3.50), ploughman's (£3.95), home-cooked ham salad (£3.95), and home-made puddings (from £2). Well kept Courage Best, Marstons Pedigree, and a guest such as Ruddles Best on handpump (well kept in a temperature-controlled cellar), a fine choice of malt whiskies, and an extensive wine list; fruit machine, cribbage, dominoes, and separate pool room. This is still the place to stay if you love fishing as they have 10 miles of private fishing on the River Torridge (salmon, sea trout and brown trout) as well as a rod room, good drying facilities and a small shop stocking the basic necessities. *(Recommended by Dennis Jenkin, Bob and Ann Westbrook, Miss J F Reay, Charles Turner, Nigel and Olga Wikeley, R J Walden)*

Free house ~ Licensees Lee and Nathan Adey ~ Real ale ~ Bar food (12-1.45; no evening bar food (restaurant only)) ~ Restaurant ~ (01409) 231376 ~ Children in eating area of bar and restaurant ~ Open 11.30-2.30, 6-11; 12-2.30, 7-10.30 Sun ~ Bedrooms: £40B/£80B

SIDFORD SY1390 Map 1
Blue Ball ★ 🍺 🛏

A3052 just N of Sidmouth

Friendly and popular, this thatched old inn has been run by the same family (five generations in all) for nearly 90 years. The low, partly-panelled and neatly kept lounge bar has heavy beams, upholstered wall benches and windsor chairs, three open fires, and lots of bric-a-brac; the family room and part of the restaurant are no smoking. Bar food includes sandwiches (from £2.30), home-made soup (£2.75), local sausages (£3.75), ploughman's (from £4.50), caribbean vegetable casserole (£6.50), steak and kidney pudding (£7.75), grilled fillet of fresh salmon with a honey, mustard and dill sauce (£8.50), steaks (from £9.50), daily specials such as roast local topside of beef or fresh local plaice fillets (£6.95), and children's menu (from £2.75). Bass, Flowers IPA, Greene King Old Speckled Hen, Otter Ale, and a guest such as Falstaff or Robinsons on handpump, kept well in a temperature-controlled cellar, and a weekly choice of special wines plus their standard list; helpful staff. A plainer public bar has darts, dominoes, cribbage and a fruit machine; maybe piped music in the evening. Tables on a terrace look out over a colourful front flower garden, and there are more seats on a bigger back lawn – as well as in a covered area next to the barbecue; safe swing, see saw and play house for children. *(Recommended by Denzil Taylor, Mike Tucker, Mr and Mrs A Craig, PB, JB, R T and J C Moggridge, Moira and John Cole, S Palmer, Alan and Paula McCully, Geoffrey G Lawrance, David Peakall, Mrs M Grimwood, Paul R White, Rod Stoneman, P R and S A White, Mr and Mrs G Robson, Michael Buchanan, Lyn and Geoff Hallchurch, Joyce and Maurice Cottrell, David Carr, Eric Locker)*

Inn Partnership (Nomura) ~ Tenant Roger Newton ~ Real ale ~ Bar food (12-2(3 Sun), 6-9.30) ~ Restaurant ~ (01395) 514062 ~ Children in restaurant and family room ~ Occasional live entertainment ~ Open 10.30-11; 12-10.30 Sun ~ Bedrooms: £28(£40B)/£45(£70B)

SLAPTON SX8244 Map 1
Tower 🍴

Signposted off A379 Dartmouth—Kingsbridge

This atmospheric old place is a good all-rounder. There's a good choice of real ales, a decent wine list, particularly good food (for which we've given a Food Award this year), and a warm, friendly atmosphere. The low-ceilinged bar has armchairs, low-backed settles on the flagstones, and open log fires, and up to five well kept real ales such as Adnams Best, Badger Tanglefoot, Dartmoor Best, and Exmoor Bitter, with a guest such as Exmoor Gold or Wells Bombardier on handpump; farm cider and decent wines. Under the new chef, the good, imaginative food at lunchtime includes soups such as parsnip and cranberry or green bean and aubergine (£2.95), sandwiches (from £3.40), mushrooms sautéed with stilton and cream sauce (£4.25), warm ratatouille tartlet with basil dressed leaves (£4.95), local pork sausages with whole grain mustard mash and onion gravy (£5.95), lightly spiced crab cakes with a seafood nage (£6.95), and braised lamb shank with mash and a redcurrant and rosemary gravy (£7.95), with evening dishes such as home-made chicken liver pâté with spiced pears (£4.50), sautéed scallops with sweet chilli and crème fraîche (£6.95), poached guinea fowl with broad beans, garlic and pear couscous (£8.95), plaice fillets with tomato and chilli ham and spinach (£9.75), and crusted beef fillet with pepper sauce (£14.95), and puddings like chocolate and orange baked mousse, apricot and brandy bread and butter pudding or apple and toffee pie (£3.50); lots of interesting daily specials too using local game and fish. The dining room is no smoking; cribbage, dominoes, chess, backgammon, Scrabble, draughts, and piped music. There are picnic-sets on the neatly kept back lawn, which is overhung by the ivy-covered ruin of a 14th-c chantry. The lane up to the pub is very narrow. *(Recommended by the Didler, Roger Wain-Heapy, John Brightley, Brian and Bett Cox, Bob and Ann Westbrook)*

Free house ~ Licensees Nicola and Josh Acfield ~ Real ale ~ Bar food (12-2.30, 7-9.30; not winter Sun evening or Mon) ~ Restaurant ~ (01548) 580216 ~ Children in eating area of bar and restaurant ~ Live folk and jazz ~ Open 12-3, 6-11; 12-3, 7-10.30 Sun ~ Bedrooms: /£50S

SOURTON SX5390 Map 1
Highwayman ★

A386, S of junction with A30

You will be amazed at the sheer eccentricity of this pub's design. For 43 years the friendly owners have put great enthusiasm into the extraordinary décor, and although Mr and Mrs Jones's daughter and her husband now run the place, new features are still being added – this year, a fairy root and wishing tree. The porch (a pastiche of a nobleman's carriage) leads into a warren of dimly lit stonework and flagstone-floored burrows and alcoves, richly fitted out with red plush seats discreetly cut into the higgledy-piggledy walls, elaborately carved pews, a leather porter's chair, Jacobean-style wicker chairs, and seats in quaintly bulging small-paned bow windows; the ceiling in one part, where there's an array of stuffed animals, gives the impression of being underneath a tree, roots and all. The separate Rita Jones' Locker is a make-believe sailing galleon, full of intricate woodwork and splendid timber baulks, with white antique lace-clothed tables in the embrasures that might have held cannons. They sell only keg beer, but specialise in farm cider and organic wines, and food is confined to a range of meaty and vegetarian pasties (from £1.30) or platters and cheeses; service is warmly welcoming and full of character; old-fashioned penny fruit machine, and 40s piped music; no smoking at the bar counters. Outside, there's a play area in similar style for children with little black and white roundabouts like a Victorian fairground, a fairy-tale pumpkin house and an old-lady-who-lived-in-the-shoe house. You can take children in to look around the pub but they can't stay inside. The period bedrooms with four-posters and half-testers are attractive. A cycle route which incorporates the disused railway line now passes the inn, and there are bunk rooms available for walkers and cyclists. *(Recommended by Ann and Colin Hunt, the Didler, JP, PP, Dr M E Wilson)*

Free house ~ Licensees Buster and Rita Jones and S Thomson ~ Bar food (12-1.45, 7-10.15) ~ No credit cards ~ (01837) 861243 ~ Themed nights with live entertainment ~ Open 10-2, 6-10.30; 12-2, 7-10.30 Sun; closed 25 and 26 Dec ~ Bedrooms: /£35S(£50B)

SOUTH POOL SX7740 Map 1
Millbrook

Village off A379 from Frogmore, E of Kingsbridge

Even in mid-winter, this friendly, spotlessly kept place does get crowded, but that's hardly surprising as it is one of the smallest pubs in this *Guide*. The charming little back bar has handsome windsor chairs, a chintz easy chair, drawings and paintings (and a chart) on its cream walls, clay pipes on the beams, and fresh flowers; there's also a top bar. Good home-made bar food includes sandwiches, home-made soup, and ploughman's, kiln-roasted salmon with dill mayonnaise (£4.95), fresh crab and avocado (£5.95), grilled chicken, mozzarella and pesto or home-made crab cakes with curried cream sauce (£6.95), baked cod with cheesy mash and lemon butter (£7.95), halibut au poivre (£9.25), whole bass (£12.95), and rack of lamb with a redcurrant and red wine jus (£12.95). Well kept Bass, Fullers London Pride, Wadworths 6X, and a guest such as Badger Tanglefoot or Exmoor Hound Dog on handpump, and local farm cider; good, friendly service even when busy. Darts in the public bar in winter. You can sit outside even in poor weather as both the front courtyard and the terrace by the stream (where you can watch the Aylesbury ducks) are covered by canopies. Parking can be difficult. *(Recommended by B J Harding, Tracey and Stephen Groves, Roger Wain-Heapy, Mrs J Ekins-Daukes, Graham Johnson, S F Wakeham, P R and S A White, Peter Edwards, David Eberlin)*

Free house ~ Licensee Liz Stirland ~ Real ale ~ Bar food (not winter Sun evening) ~ No credit cards ~ (01548) 531581 ~ Children in family room ~ Open 11.30-2.30, 6(5.30 Sat)-11; 12-3, 6-10.30 Sun; 12-2.30, 6.30-11 in winter

SOUTH ZEAL SX6593 Map 1
Oxenham Arms ★ ♀ ⇌

Village signposted from A30 at A382 roundabout and B3260 Okehampton turnoff

A fine escape from the busy A30, this popular, friendly inn remains happily unchanged. It's a marvellous building with great character and a real sense of history, and was first licensed in 1477 – though it has grown up around the remains of a Norman monastery, built here to combat the pagan power of the neolithic standing stone that still forms part of the wall in the family room behind the bar (there are actually twenty more feet of stone below the floor). It later became the Dower House of the Burgoynes, whose heiress carried it to the Oxenham family. And Charles Dickens, snowed up one winter, wrote a lot of *Pickwick Papers* here. The beamed and partly panelled front bar has elegant mullioned windows and Stuart fireplaces, and windsor armchairs around low oak tables and built-in wall seats. The small family room (said to be no smoking, but one reader found quite a few ashtrays there) has beams, wheelback chairs around polished tables, decorative plates, and another open fire. Popular bar food includes home-made soup (£2.50), sandwiches (from £2.50), good ploughman's (£4.75), fish and chips (£5.50), nice local farm sausages with mustard and leek mash and onion gravy (£5.75), steak, kidney, mushroom and Guinness pie or daily curry (£6.25), daily specials such as cauliflower cheese (£4.95), lamb pie with sultanas or oriental chicken (£6.25), and salmon and broccoli mornay (£7.25), and children's menu (£2.95). The dining room is no smoking. Well kept Princetown IPA and Sharps Eden Ale on handpump or tapped from the cask, and an extensive list of wines including good house claret; darts, shove-ha'penny, dominoes, and cribbage. Note the imposing curved stone steps leading up to the garden where there's a sloping spread of lawn. *(Recommended by Nick Lawless, the Didler, Betsy Brown, Nigel Flook, Bernard Stradling, John and Sarah Perry, Richard and Margaret Peers, Basil Minson, Jacquie and Jim Jones, Tony and Wendy Hobden, Stephen and Jean Curtis, Dennis Jenkin, Ruth and Paul Lawrence, Jane and Adrian Tierney-Jones, Mrs Sylvia Elcoate, JP, PP, Peter Craske)*

Free house ~ Licensee James Henry ~ Real ale ~ Bar food ~ Restaurant ~ (01837) 840244 ~ Children in restaurant and family room ~ Open 11-2.30, 6-11; 12-2.30, 7-10.30 Sun ~ Bedrooms: £45B/£60B

The letters and figures after the name of each town are its Ordnance Survey map reference. *How to use the Guide* at the beginning of the book explains how it helps you find a pub, in road atlases or large-scale maps as well as in our own maps.

STAVERTON SX7964 Map 1
Sea Trout 🛏

Village signposted from A384 NW of Totnes

No matter what the weather is doing – torrential rain, flooded roads or brilliant sunshine, the appeal of this bustling and friendly place is such that you will always find a good crowd here. The neatly kept rambling beamed lounge bar has sea trout and salmon flies and stuffed fish on the walls, cushioned settles and stools, and a stag's head above the fireplace, and the main bar has low banquettes, soft lighting and an open fire. There's also a public bar with darts, pool, fruit machine, TV, table skittles, shove-ha'penny, dominoes, and juke box; the restaurant is no smoking. Good bar food includes home-made soup (£2.50), lunchtime sandwiches (from £3.50), mushrooms with garlic and cream and home-made bread (£3.65), ploughman's (from £4.50), pasta with spinach, roast onions, tomato and basil (£5.25), pork and apple sausages with onion gravy or steak and kidney pie (£6.25), lambs liver and bacon (£6.95), baked Brixham plaice (£7.95), steaks (from £8.95), and daily specials such as a changing curry, pork and bacon terrine with an apricot and seed mustard chutney (£4.50), grilled chicken breast on toasted brioche with slow roasted tomatoes, and a garlic and tomato dressing (£7.50), and confit of duck leg on red cabbage sautéed with chestnuts (£11.50); children's meals (from £2.85). Well kept Palmers Best, Bridport, Dorset Gold, and 200 on handpump, a decent range of wines, farm cider and local apple juices, and quite a few malt whiskies; efficient, helpful staff. There are seats under parasols on the attractive paved back garden. A station for the South Devon Steam Railway is not too far away. *(Recommended by Ron and Sheila Corbett, Lyn and Geoff Hallchurch, JP, PP, Joyce and Maurice Cottrell, Dr Paull Khan, Richard and Margaret Peers, John Wilson, Charles Turner, Jonathan Smith, the Didler, Richard Endacott, Beverley and Neil Gardner, Dennis Jenkin, Dudley and Moira Cockroft)*

Palmers ~ Tenants Nicholas and Nicola Brookland ~ Real ale ~ Bar food (till 9.45 weekends) ~ Restaurant ~ (01803) 762274 ~ Children in eating area of bar and restaurant ~ Open 11-3, 6-11; 12-4, 7-10.30 Sun ~ Bedrooms: £47.50B/£70B

STOCKLAND ST2404 Map 1
Kings Arms 🍴 🍷 🛏

Village signposted from A30 Honiton—Chard; and also, at every turning, from N end of Honiton High Street

There's always a good mix of customers in this bustling 16th-c pub because despite the emphasis on the good, enjoyable food, there's a proper locals' bar with well kept real ales, pub games, and live weekend music. The dark beamed, elegant dining lounge has solid refectory tables and settles, attractive landscapes, a medieval oak screen (which divides the room into two), and a great stone fireplace across almost the whole width of one end; the cosy restaurant has a huge inglenook fireplace and bread oven. Bar food is served at lunchtime only: sandwiches (from £1.75), home-made soup (£2.50), smoked mackerel pâté or vegetable mousse (£4), omelettes (from £4), various pasta dishes (£4.50), and steak and kidney pie or scrumpy pork (£5.50), there might be Portuguese sardines (£4), moules marinières or confit of duck with a plum sauce (£5), mushroom stroganoff or pasta carbonara (£7.50), supreme of guinea fowl or king prawn madras (£9.50), Cotley rack of lamb (£10.50), and puddings such as apple and treacle crumbly, crème brûlée or chocolate truffle torte (£3.50). In the evening, only the restaurant menu is available. Well kept Courage Directors, Exmoor Ale and Gold, and Otter Ale on handpump, over 40 malt whiskies (including island and west coast ones; large spirit measures), a comprehensive wine list, and farm ciders. At the back, a flagstoned bar has cushioned benches and stools around heavy wooden tables, and leads on to a carpeted darts room with two boards, another room with dark beige plush armchairs and settees (and a fruit machine), and a neat ten-pin skittle alley; dominoes, quiz machine, TV, and quiet mainly classical piped music. There are tables under cocktail parasols on the terrace in front of the white-faced thatched pub and a lawn enclosed by trees and shrubs. *(Recommended by Shirley Mackenzie, Pat and Sam Roberts, Pat and Robert Watt, Giles and Liz Ridout, Richard and Margaret Peers, Jenny and Chris Wilson, Muriel and Peter Gleave, Francis Johnston, Peter Burton)*

Free house ~ Licensees Heinz Kiefer and Paul Diviani ~ Real ale ~ Bar food (lunchtime only) ~ Restaurant ~ (01404) 881361 ~ Children in eating area of bar and restaurant ~ Live music Sat and Sun evenings and bank hols ~ Open 12-3, 6.30-11; 12-3, 6.30-10.30 Sun; closed 25 Dec ~ Bedrooms: £30B/£50B

STOKE FLEMING SX8648 Map 1
Green Dragon ♀
Church Rd

This is an interesting local with a relaxed atmosphere and quite a bit of character. It is run by Peter Crowther, the long-distance yachtsman, and there are cuttings about him and maps of his races on the walls. The main part of the flagstone and beamed bar has two small settles, re-upholstered bay window seats and stools, boat pictures, and maybe Electra or Maia the burmese cats or Rhea the relaxed german shepherd; down on the right is a wooden-floored snug with throws and cushions on battered sofas and armchairs, a few books (30p to RNLI), adult board games, and a grandfather clock. Down some steps is the Mess Deck decorated with old charts and lots of ensigns and flags, and there's a playbox of children's games; darts, shove-ha'penny, cribbage, and dominoes. Enjoyable home-made bar food includes freshly cooked filled baguettes, soup (£2.20), cottage pie or chicken livers sautéed in butter with apples, and finished with cider brandy and cream (£3.50), baked crab and mushrooms in a creamy anchovy sauce, topped with cheese (£4), spiced crevettes (£4.50), steak in ale or fish pies (£6.20), and daily specials such as thai crab cakes (£5.10), venison and cranberry pie (£6.90), kiln-roasted salmon (£7.50), and local rump steak (£9). Well kept Bass, Flowers IPA, Otter Ale, and Wadworths 6X on handpump (all except Bass kept under light blanket pressure), big glasses of good house wines, Addlestone's cider, Luscombe's slightly alcoholic ginger beer and organic apple and pear juices, and a decent range of spirits; you can take the beer away with you. There's a back garden with swings, a climbing frame and picnic-sets and a front terrace with some white plastic garden tables and chairs. The church opposite has an interesting tall tower. Parking can be tricky at peak times. *(Recommended by David Rule, Gavin May, Rona Murdoch, Dennis Jenkin, Charles Eatof, Eric Locker, Peter Edwards)*

Heavitree ~ Tenants Peter and Alix Crowther ~ Real ale ~ Bar food (12-2.30, 6.30-9(9.30 in summer)) ~ (01803) 770238 ~ Children in restaurant and snug ~ Occasional summer folk or Irish music ~ Open 11-3, 5.30-11; 12-3, 6(6.30 in winter)-10.30 Sun

STOKE GABRIEL SX8457 Map 1
Church House ★
Village signposted from A385 just W of junction with A3022, in Collaton St Mary; can also be reached from nearer Totnes

There's a lot of unspoilt character and plenty of history in this bustling local. The lounge bar has an exceptionally fine medieval beam-and-plank ceiling, a black oak partition wall, window seats cut into the thick butter-coloured walls, decorative plates and vases of flowers on a dresser, and a huge fireplace still used in winter to cook the stew. The mummified cat in a case, probably about 200 years old, was found during restoration of the roof space in the verger's cottage three doors up the lane – one of a handful found in the west country and believed to have been a talisman against evil spirits. Straightforward bar food includes a big choice of sandwiches and toasties (from £2.50; ham, cheese, pineapple and onion toastie £3.50), filled baked potatoes (from £3.50), ploughman's (from £4.25), steak and kidney in ale pie, chicken curry or stilton and leek bake (£5.95), and puddings (£2.95). Well kept Bass,Worthington Best, and a weekly guest ale on handpump, and quite a few malt whiskies. Darts and euchre in the little public locals' bar. There are picnic-sets on the little terrace in front of the building, and see if you can spot the priest hole, dating from the Reformation. No children. *(Recommended by Dr M E Wilson, Malcolm Taylor, Ruth and Paul Lawrence, Norman and Sarah Keeping, Dave Braisted, P R and S A White, Richard and Margaret Peers, Mr and Mrs E R Evans)*

Free house ~ Licensee T G Patch ~ Real ale ~ Bar food (11-2.30, 7-9.30) ~ (01803) 782384 ~ Open 11-3.30, 6-11; 11-11 Sat; 12-3.30, 7-10.30 Sun

STOKEINTEIGNHEAD SX9170 Map 1
Church House

Village signposted (not clearly) in Combeinteignhead E of Newton Abbot; or off A379 N of Torquay

The main bar to the right of the door in this 13th-c thatched inn has heavy beams, lots of copper and brass platters, kettles, and coffee pots in the inglenook fireplace and on the mantelpiece, a fine ornately carved huge settle and other smaller ones, rustic farmhouse chairs, a nice mix of tables including a big circular one, little lanterns, window seats, and a relaxed, informal atmosphere; a dining room leads off with an ancient stripped stone skeleton staircase with lots of little pictures around it; candles on the tables. Decent bar food includes sandwiches and ploughman's, home-made soup (£2.50), smoked salmon and trout roulade (£5.50), baked potato filled with bacon, onion and mushrooms with mango chutney and cheddar cheese glaze (£5.25), steak and kidney pie (£6.95), and hot green thai chicken curry or salmon and crab fishcake (£7.50). Well kept Adnams, Bass, and Greene King Abbot or Otter Ale on handpump, farm cider, and a decent range of whiskies. There's a simple public bar with darts, shove-ha'penny, cribbage, dominoes, fruit machine, TV, and quiet piped music. The neat back garden with dracaenas is on the way to the car park. *(Recommended by Nick Lawless, Richard and Margaret Peers)*

Heavitree ~ Managers J and C Wilson ~ Real ale ~ Bar food (12-2.15, 6.30-9.30) ~ (01626) 872475 ~ Children in eating area of bar and family room ~ Open 11-3, 5.30-11; 12-3, 6.30-10.30 Sun

STOKENHAM SX8042 Map 1
Tradesmans Arms 🍽

Just off A379 Dartmouth—Kingsbridge

This charming thatched village pub is the sort of place people always think of when friends want a recommendation. The little beamed bar has a warm, friendly atmosphere, plenty of nice antique tables and neat dining chairs – with more up a step or two at the back – window seats looking across a field to the village church, and a big fireplace; the no smoking room to the left of the door offers the same food as the bar. Good food at lunchtime includes snacks such as home-made soup (£2.75; fish soup with garlic flutes £3.25), sandwiches (from £2.65), and home-made pâté (£3.50), plus specials like home-made fishcakes with a spicy tomato sauce or mixed seafood in a white wine sauce topped with breadcrumbs and cheese (£5.50), venison stew (£6.75), and beef and mushroom casserole (£6.95); in the evenings, there might be prawns flamed in brandy with a garlic dip (£3.75), tartare of smoked salmon and puy lentils (£3.95), mussels provençale (£4.25), aubergine stuffed with roasted peppers and mushrooms, topped with breadcrumbs and cheese (£7.75), sauté of rabbit with fresh horseradish (£9.25), braised leg of barbary duck with orange and lemon sauce (£11.25), and fried halibut with lime and ginger sauce (£11.95), and puddings such as fresh pineapple and black pepper flamed in rum and served with coffee ice cream, apple and walnut puding or fresh lemon soufflé (from £2.95); Sunday roast lamb or beef (£6.95). Well kept Adnams Southwold and Broadside, and a guest such as Butcombe or Exmoor Ale on handpump, and quite a few malt whiskies. Dogs are welcome on a lead in the main bar area. There are some seats outside in the garden. *(Recommended by Mr and Mrs I Jones, Tracey and Stephen Groves, Roger Wain-Heapy, Mrs J Ekins-Daukes, Michael and Marianne Tann, Peter Edwards)*

Free house ~ Licensees John and Elizabeth Sharman ~ Real ale ~ Bar food (not Mon, Tues or Sat lunchtimes; not Sun or Mon evenings) ~ Restaurant ~ (01548) 580313 ~ Children in back room lunchtimes only ~ Open 12-3, 6.30-11; 6.30-11 Sat; 12-3 Sun; closed Sun evening, Mon, Tues and Sat lunch; but open full time bank hols

TIPTON ST JOHN SY0991 Map 1
Golden Lion
Pub signposted off B3176 Sidmouth—Ottery St Mary

New licensees have taken over this attractive village pub, and offer a friendly welcome and good food to their many customers. There's usually a roaring log fire, an attractive mix of furnishings, and well kept Bass, Greene King Old Speckled Hen, Otter Ale, and Wadworths 6X on handpump. Enjoyable bar food now includes home-made soup (£3.95), duck liver pâté with gooseberry chutney (£4.25), filled baked potatoes (£4.65), ploughman's, home-made steak and kidney pie, smoked turkey and tagliatelle carbonara or ham and eggs (all £4.95), cod in home-made beer batter (£6.50), fresh trout steak with a sun-dried tomato and tarragon butter (£6.95), escalope of salmon with dill and crème fraîche (£7.95), roasted rack of lamb with a rosemary and redcurrant jus (£10.45), 10oz rump steak with a brandy and wild mushroom sauce (£11.95), and Sunday roast (£6.95). The restaurant is no smoking; piped music, darts, fruit machine, and cribbage. Pleasant garden, and seats on the terrace. *(Recommended by Basil Minson, John and Vivienne Rice, Denzil Taylor, R J Walden, E G Parish, Christopher and Jo Barton, M J and C E Abbey, Barry Smith)*

Heavitree ~ Tenant David Ough ~ Real ale ~ Bar food ~ Restaurant ~ (01404) 812881 ~ Children in eating area of bar and restaurant ~ Open 11-3, 6-11; 11-11 Sat; 12-10.30 Sun ~ Bedrooms: /£40S

TOPSHAM SX9688 Map 1
Bridge ◄
2¼ miles from M5 junction 30: Topsham signposted from exit roundabout; in Topsham follow signpost (A376) Exmouth on the Elmgrove Road, into Bridge Hill

The fifth generation of the same family now helps out at this unspoilt and happily unchanging 16th-c pub. There are fine old traditional furnishings (true country workmanship, not just bought-in stuff) in the little lounge partitioned off from the inner corridor by a high-backed settle; log fire. A bigger lower room (the old malthouse) is open at busy times. The cosy regulars' inner sanctum keeps up to 10 real ales tapped from the cask: Batemans Yella Belly (their first organic bitter), Blackawton Westcountry Gold, Branscombe Vale Branoc and Summa That and their new Drayman's Bitter, Exe Valley Spring Beer, John Joule Victory Brew, Jollyboat Plunder, and Otter Ale; farm cider and elderberry wine; friendly service. Simple, tasty bar food such as pasties (£1.50), winter home-made soup (£2.60), sandwiches (£2.50), and ploughman's with home-cooked ham, smoked chicken, and smoked salmon (from £4.50); no noisy music or machines – just a chatty, relaxed atmosphere. There are riverside picnic-sets overlooking the weir. *(Recommended by the Didler, Hugh Roberts, David Hoult, Canon Michael Bourdeaux, Jane and Adrian Tierney-Jones, JP, PP, Tom McLean, Dr M E Wilson, Dr D E Granger)*

Free house ~ Licensee Mrs C Cheffers-Heard ~ Real ale ~ Bar food ~ No credit cards ~ (01392) 873862 ~ Children in room without bar ~ Open 12-2, 6(7 Sun)-10.30(11 Fri/Sat)

Passage House ♀

Ferry Road, off main street

In good weather, the wooden tables and chairs on the quiet shoreside terrace in front of this attractive waterside pub are a most pleasant place to enjoy a drink. Inside, the traditional bar has wall pews and bar stools, and is decorated with electrified oil lamps hanging from big black oak beams in the ochre ceiling; the lower dining area with its slate floor is no smoking. The lure for most is the good, fresh fish dishes; they have a fine choice of up to ten a day. Other bar food includes sandwiches (from £2.25), ploughman's (from £4.75), ham and eggs (£4.95), a pie of the day (£5.75), chicken curry (£5.95), liver and bacon (£6.25), and popular cod and fries (£6.75). Well kept Bass, Flowers IPA, Otter and Wadworths 6X on handpump, and good wines; piped music. As the car park is small, you can park on the quay and walk the 150 yards to the pub. *(Recommended by Basil Minson, John and Vivienne Rice, Pat and Dick Warwick, Richard and Margaret Peers, Mr and Mrs C R Little, David Carr)*

Heavitree ~ Manager Richard Davies ~ Real ale ~ Bar food (12-2.30, 7-9.30) ~ Restaurant ~ (01392) 873653 ~ Children in restaurant ~ Open 11-11; 12-10.30 Sun; 11-3, 5-11 weekdays in winter

TORCROSS SX8241 Map 1

Start Bay

A379 S of Dartmouth

Even on a wet day in mid-winter, this is an immensely popular dining pub, so it makes sense to get there early to be sure of a table. A local trawler catches the fish, a local crabber drops the crabs at the back door, and the landlord enjoys catching plaice, scallops, and bass: cod (medium £4.30; large £5.80; jumbo £7.90) and haddock (medium £4.40; large £5.90; jumbo £8), whole lemon sole (from £6.25), skate (£6.95), whole dover sole (in four sizes from £7.90), scallops (£8.50), brill (from £8.50), and whole bass (small £9.50; medium £10.50; large £11.50). Other food includes sandwiches (from £2.30), ploughman's (from £3.70), filled baked potatoes (from £2.80), vegetable lasagne (£5.50), gammon and pineapple (£6.90), steaks (from £8.60), puddings (£2.95), and children's meals (£3.90); they do warn of delays at peak times (and you will probably have to wait for a table); the sachets of tomato sauce or tartare sauce are not to everyone's taste. Well kept Bass and Flowers Original or Whitbreads Trophy on handpump, and maybe Heron Valley cider and fresh apple juice, and local wine from the Sharpham Estate. The unassuming main bar (which has a small no smoking area) is very much set out for eating with wheelback chairs around plenty of dark tables or (round a corner) back-to-back settles forming booths; there are some photographs of storms buffeting the pub and country pictures on its cream walls, and a winter coal fire; a small chatty drinking area by the counter has a brass ship's clock and barometer. The winter games room has darts and shove-ha'penny; there's more booth seating in a no smoking family room with sailing boat pictures. There are seats (highly prized) out on the terrace overlooking the three-mile pebble beach, and the freshwater wildlife lagoon of Slapton Ley is just behind the pub. *(Recommended by Charlie Harris, Alan Cowell, Ruth and Paul Lawrence, Michael Porter, Tony and Wendy Hobden, Carol Ackroyd, Peter McNamara, Alan Kilpatrick, Tracey and Stephen Groves, Eric Locker, Mr and Mrs Capp, John Brightley, Charles Eatof, Betsy and Peter Little)*

Whitbreads ~ Tenant Paul Stubbs ~ Real ale ~ Bar food (11.30(12 Sun)-2(2.15 Sun), 6-10) ~ (01548) 580553 ~ Children in family room ~ Open 11.30-11; 12-10.30 Sun; 11.30-2.30, 6-11 wkdys and Sat, and 12-3, 6-10.30 Sun in winter

---

Looking for a pub with a really special garden, or in lovely countryside, or with an outstanding view, or right by the water? They are listed separately, at the back of the book.

TOTNES SX8060 Map 1
Kingsbridge Inn ◀
Leechwell Street

Well worth the climb up the main street, this friendly place is the oldest pub in town. The low-beamed rambling bar is dimly lit, and has an elaborately carved bench in one intimate little alcove, comfortable plush seats and wheelbacks around rustic tables, broad stripped plank panelling, and bare stone or black and white timbering. A small area above the bar (usually reserved by diners) is no smoking. Enjoyable home-made bar food includes lunchtime sandwiches (from £2.95), filled baked potatoes (from £3.50), and ploughman's (from £4), as well as soup (£2.50), tagliatelle with mushroom and stilton sauce (£4.95), steak and kidney pie, liver and bacon, local sausages, and lasagne (all £6.95), and fish pie (£7.95), with evening extras such as steaks (from £8.95), duck with orange and green peppercorn sauce (£10.95), and shark steak with portuguese sauce (£11.25), and puddings like fruit crumble, chocolate torte or bread and butter pudding (£3.25). Well kept Bass, Cotleigh Tawny and Theakstons Old Peculier, with a couple of guests such as Badger K&B or Robinsons Old Tom on handpump; maybe piped music, but no noisy games machines. *(Recommended by Tony Baldwin, Paul R White, Mark Clezy)*

Free house ~ Licensees Michael Wright and Anne Collins ~ Real ale ~ Bar food (12-2, 6.30-9.30) ~ (01803) 863324 ~ Children in no smoking room ~ Live music, poetry readings and so forth every other Weds and Fri evenings ~ Open 11.30-3, 6-11; 12-3, 7-10.30 Sun; closed 26 Dec

TUCKENHAY SX8156 Map 1
Maltsters Arms 🍽 ♀ 🛏

Take Ashprington road out of Totnes (signed left off A381 on outskirts), keeping on past Watermans Arms

This is a lovely spot by a peaceful wooded creek, with tables by the water and free overnight moorings for boats; plenty of bird life and surrounding walks. The hard-working licensees continue to hold all sorts of events: regular jazz sessions, various courses such as RYA navigation, barbecues in good weather, and lots of outside summer musical concerts such as Handel's *Water Music* played in the middle of the river on their pontoon. They keep a smashing range of drinks including well kept Blackawton 44, Princetown Dartmoor IPA and two changing guest beers on handpump, 17 good wines by the glass, local cider, a serious bloody mary, and items in the freezer like buffalo grass vodka and various eau de vies. And the daily changing bar food also continues to draw customers, with lunchtime dishes such as creamy onion and saffron or yellow pepper and sweetcorn soup (£3.50), sandwiches (from £3.95), ploughman's (from £4.75), squid flash fried in balsamic vinegar (£4.95), smooth duck liver and orange pâté with a Grand Marnier dressing (£5.25), smoked salmon, mackerel and trout with a honey and mustard dressing (£5.75), cottage pie (£7.25), yam, spinach, mushroom and filo pie (£7.50), roast leg of lamb with rosemary gravy (£7.75), fillet steak with a creamy peppercorn and brandy sauce (£15.95), and grilled whole lemon sole with lemon and parsley butter (£17.50), with evening choices like fried herby salmon fishcakes with lemon, lime and dill dressing (£4.50), sautéed kidneys with onion, bacon and red wine (£5.25), spicy five bean chilli (£7.95), chicken supreme with creamy pesto sauce (£8.95), baked whole john dory with banana and balsamic vinegar (£9.95), and roast half Aylesbury duck with honey and five spice (£13.50), and puddings such as black forest crumble, chargrilled pineapple with butterscotch sauce or chocolate chip sponge pudding (£3.95); nice home-made bar nibbles, too. The long, narrow bar links two other rooms – a little snug one with an open fire, and plenty of bric-a-brac, and another with red-painted vertical seats and kitchen chairs on the wooden floor. Darts, shove-ha'penny, cribbage, dominoes, chess, backgammon, and TV for sports. There may be a minimum stay of two nights at weekends. *(Recommended by JP, PP,*

Jonathan Smith, P Rome, D Marsland, Peter Edwards, Malcolm King, Mike Gorton, Trevor
and Lynda Smith, Richard and Margaret Peers, Brian and Bett Cox, Catherine Pitt, MP,
Mrs J Street, John Evans, Mr and Mrs J French, Roger Wain-Heapy, Mr and Mrs M Cooper,
R Mathews, Mr and Mrs M Dalby, Roger Braithwaite, the Didler, Bernard Stradling,
Tracey and Stephen Groves, John and Elizabeth Thomason)

*Free house ~ Licensees Denise and Quentin Thwaites ~ Real ale ~ Bar food (12-3,
7-9.30) ~ Restaurant ~ (01803) 732350 ~ Children in separate family rooms ~ Jazz
1st and 3rd Fri of month; outside music in summer ~ Open 11-11; 12-10.30 Sun;
closed evening 25 Dec ~ Bedrooms: /£75S*

TWO BRIDGES SX6175 Map 1
Two Bridges Hotel
B3357/B3212 across Dartmoor

This is a popular and friendly meeting place, and as it is in a fine spot in the
middle of Dartmoor, well liked by walkers, too. The big L-shaped bar has a
relaxed, chatty atmosphere, brass-bound cask seats, brocaded built-in wall seats,
and captain's chairs on the turkey carpet, with upholstered settles and bentwood
chairs in the longer area; also, black beams and joists with pewter mugs and lots
of horsebrasses, interesting old photographs and all sizes of Royal prints all over
the walls, and some WWI-era photographs engraved on some windows. To order
food, you have to get a numbered table and pay first: soup (£3.50), filled baked
potatoes (from £3.95), sandwiches (from £4.10), west country cheese platter
(£5.50), a pasta dish or curry (£6.20), steak in ale casserole (£6.50), and sirloin
steak (£10.75). Well kept Boddingtons, Flowers IPA, and Princetown Jail Ale on
handpump served by courteous uniformed staff. A rather charming panelled
corridor with a fine wall clock and lovely Chris Chapman photographs leads to
an old-fashioned entrance lounge with comfortable button-back leather and other
settees and armchairs in front of a big roaring log fire. Outside, there are some
picnic-sets on grass with jackdaws hopping about; geese at the back. A fine old
bridge (floodlit at night) leads away from the inn over a quiet river. *(Recommended
by Charles Turner, John Brightley, Ann and Colin Hunt)*

*Free house ~ Licensee Lesley Davies ~ Real ale ~ Bar food ~ Restaurant ~ (01822)
890581 ~ Children in eating area of bar and restaurant ~ Pianist Fri/Sat evenings ~
Open 11-11; 12-10.30 Sun ~ Bedrooms: /£85B*

UGBOROUGH SX6755 Map 1
Anchor
Off A3121 – signed from A38 W of South Brent

Locals gather in the oak-beamed public bar of this bustling pub with its log fire in
the stone fireplace, and wall settles and seats around wooden tables on the
polished woodblock floor, while visitors tend to head for the comfortable
restaurant with its windsor armchairs (the lower area is no smoking). You can eat
from either the bar or restaurant menus and sit anywhere in the pub (apart from
Saturday night when there are no bar snacks in the restaurant): home-made soup
(£2.95), good burgers (from £2.95, including ostrich, venison and vegetarian),
omelettes (from £4.10), filled long rolls or hot melts (from £4.20; brie and
banana £4.50), ploughman's (from £4.25), stuffed aubergine (£5.45), steak and
kidney pie (£6.60), gammon and pineapple (£6.95), and daily specials; courteous
service. Well kept Bass, Suttons XSB and Knickadroppa Glory, and a couple of
guest beers on handpump or tapped from the cask; darts, cribbage, TV, and fruit
machine. There's a small outside seating area. *(Recommended by Stephen, Julie and
Hayley Brown, John Evans, Bob and Ann Westbrook, P R and S A White, Roger and Jenny
Huggins, John Wilson)*

*Free house ~ Licensee Sheelagh Jeffreys-Simmons ~ Real ale ~ Bar food ~
Restaurant ~ (01752) 892283 ~ Children welcome ~ Live entertainment most Fri
and Sat ~ Open 11-3, 5.30-11; 10-11.30 Sat; 11-3, 5.30-10.30 Sun ~ Bedrooms:
£30B/£50B*

UMBERLEIGH SS6023 Map 1

Rising Sun 🛏

A377 S of Barnstaple

This comfortable, friendly inn is ideal for anglers as they have five salmon and sea trout beats on the River Taw opposite, and plenty of stuffed fish and fishing memorabilia in the bar; lots of other outside activities too, making this a good base to stay. The bar is divided into two by a low stone wall with cushions on top; at one end are some brocaded stools and spindleback chairs around traditional tables on the flowery carpet, a small stone fireplace with a log-effect fire and hops above the hunting horn on the bressumer beam, and a cushioned window seat; piped music, darts, shove-ha'penny, and dominoes. The stone bar counter has a row of graded pewter tankards and lots of hops on the gantry, and serves well kept Bass, Clearwater Cavalier, Cotleigh Tawny, and Jollyboat Mainbrace Bitter on handpump, eight wines by the glass, Hancock's cider, and fruit smoothies. The other end of the room has high bar stools on the flagstones, a pine built-in wall bench and long cushioned wall seat by a big mural of the river valley, and a woodburning stove with logs stacked on either side; the River Room is no smoking. Good bar food includes lunchtime sandwiches (from £2.50) and ploughman's (from £4.95), as well as home-made soup (£2.95), fresh tagliatelle with mushroom and pesto sauce or home-made bread topped with grilled goats cheese and onion marmalade (£5.95), steak and kidney pudding (£7.95), game casserole with red cabbage and potato dumplings (£8.25), daily specials such as fresh linguini with cherry tomato, rocket and olives (£6.50), fresh mussel, prawn and pasta bake (£7.95), asian-style fresh tuna (£10.95), and home-made chocolate and armagnac mousse or poached pear with vanilla ice cream and caramel sauce puddings (£3.50). There are some green seats under parasols outside, and Umberleigh railway station is just a couple of hundred yards away, over the bridge. More reports please. (Recommended by Mrs L M Hardwick, George Atkinson, Pat and Robert Watt)

Free house ~ Licensees Charles and Heather Manktelow ~ Real ale ~ Bar food ~ Restaurant ~ (01769) 560447 ~ Children in eating area of bar ~ Impromptu music Mon evenings ~ Open 11-3, 6-11; 12-3, 7-10.30 Sun; closed 25 Dec ~ Bedrooms: £40B/£77B

WIDECOMBE SX7176 Map 1

Rugglestone £

Village at end of B3387; pub just S – turn left at church and NT church house, OS Sheet 191 map reference 720765

This unspoilt, tucked away local is named after the massive nearby granite boulder, which someone has calculated weighs 115 tons, and which people are said to be able to move easily using the church key – but not at all by brute force. The small bar has a strong rural atmosphere, just four small tables, a few window and wall seats, a one-person pew built into the corner by the nice old stone fireplace, and a rudimentary bar counter dispensing well kept Bass and Butcombe Bitter tapped from the cask; local farm cider and a decent little wine list. The room on the right is a bit bigger and lighter-feeling, and shy strangers may feel more at home here: another stone fireplace, beamed ceiling, stripped pine tables, and a built-in wall bench. There's also a little no smoking room which is used for dining; shove-ha'penny, cribbage, dominoes, and euchre. Good simple bar food includes home-made soup or meaty or vegetarian pasties (£2.45), filled baked potatoes (from £2.95), ploughman's (£4.20), cottage pie or a vegetarian dish of the day (£4.20), chicken pie (£4.40), local sirloin steak and onion in a roll (£4.45), beef in stout casserole with dumplings (£4.95), and home-made puddings such as treacle tart or fruit crumble (£2.95); friendly service. The cat is called Elbi, the two terriers, Tinker and Belle, and the young retriever Spring. Outside across the little moorland stream is a field with lots of picnic-sets (and some geese and chickens); old-fashioned outside lavatories. No children inside (though they

have constructed a large shelter with tables and chairs in the garden).
(Recommended by the Didler, Mr and Mrs Capp, R J Walden, Joy and Colin Rorke, JP, PP, J R Hawkes, Mike Gorton, John and Vivienne Rice, Mr and Mrs J McRobert, Bob and Ann Westbrook)

Free house ~ Licensees Lorrie and Moira Ensor ~ Real ale ~ Bar food ~ (01364) 621327 ~ Open 11-2.30(3 Sat), 6-11; 12-3, 6-10.30 Sun; evening opening 7 in winter

WINKLEIGH SS6308 Map 1
Kings Arms
Village signposted off B3220 Crediton—Torrington; Fore Street

On the edge of the little village square, this thatched pub is blossoming under its new regime. It has an attractive main bar with beams, some old-fashioned built-in wall settles, scrubbed pine tables and benches on the flagstones, and a woodburning stove in a cavernous fireplace; another woodburning stove separates the bar from the no smoking dining room. Good bar food includes home-made soup (£2.95), sandwiches (from £2.95), filled baguettes (from £3.95), chicken liver and brandy pâté (£4.50), whisky-cured smoked salmon (£4.95), roasted vegetables topped with goats cheese, roast courgettes with a neapolitan sauce and tagliatelle, ham and eggs or fish and chips (all £5.50), liver and bacon, chicken and spinach lasagne or steak and kidney pie (£6.50), salmon fillet with dill sauce (£7.95), whole bass with lemon parsley butter (£8.95), 10oz sirloin steak (£10.95), and puddings such as rich chocolate pot with clotted cream, sticky toffee pudding or blackberry and apple crumble (from £3). Well kept Bass, Brains Bitter and Butcombe Bitter on handpump, and decent wines; darts, cribbage, and dominoes. There are seats out in the garden. *(Recommended by R J Walden, Sandy Thomson, Ann and Colin Hunt)*

Free house ~ Licensees Heather Williams, Jamie Stuart and Pippa Hutchinson ~ Real ale ~ Bar food (all day) ~ (01837) 83384 ~ Children welcome ~ Open 11-11; 12-10.30 Sun; closed 25 Dec

WONSON SX6789 Map 1
Northmore Arms ♀ ◀
Off A382 ½ mile from A30 at Whiddon Down; turn right down lane signposted Throwleigh/Gidleigh. Continue down lane over hump back bridge; turn left to Wonson; OS Sheet 191 map reference 674903

This delightful secluded cottage is a real find, and all the more remarkable for being open all day. It's a friendly place with two small connected beamed rooms – modest and informal but civilised – with wall settles, a few elderly chairs, five tables in one room and just two in the other. There are two open fires (only one may be lit), and some attractive photographs on the stripped stone walls; darts, chess, dominoes and cribbage. Besides well kept ales such as Adnams Broadside, Cotleigh Tawny and Exe Valley Dobs, they have good house wines, and most enjoyable home-made food such as sandwiches (from £1.50; toasties from £1.95), garlic mushrooms (£2.65), ploughman's (£4.25), filled baked potatoes (from £4.25), ham and egg or liver and bacon (£4.75), roast lamb with garlic potatoes (£5.95), steak (£7.95), and puddings such as home-made treacle tart with clotted cream (£2.25); Sunday roast beef (£5.95); Tuesday curries (£6.95), and huge breakfasts. The ladies' lavatory is up steep steps. Tables and chairs sit precariously in the steep little garden – all very peaceful and rustic; excellent walking from the pub (or to it, perhaps from Chagford or Gidleigh Park). More reports please. *(Recommended by Lorna and Howard Lambert, Richard and Judy Winn)*

Free house ~ Licensee Mrs Mo Miles ~ Real ale ~ Bar food (12-9; 12-2.30, 7-9 Sun) ~ (01647) 231428 ~ Well behaved children away from bar ~ Open 11-11; 12-10.30 Sun ~ Bedrooms: /£30

WOODBURY SALTERTON SY0189 Map 1
Diggers Rest

3½ miles from M5 junction 30: A3052 towards Sidmouth, village signposted on right about ½ mile after Clyst St Mary; also signposted from B3179 SE of Exeter

Even though this thatched village pub is always busy (particularly at lunchtime, with retired customers), the friendly staff remain helpful and pleasant. The heavy beamed bar has a log fire at one end with an ornate solid fuel stove at the other, comfortable old-fashioned country chairs and settles around polished antique tables, a dark oak Jacobean screen, a grandfather clock, and plates decorating the walls of one alcove. The big skittles alley can be used for families in July and August; fruit machine. Well kept Bass and Sharps Doom Bar on ancient handpumps; sensibly placed darts and dominoes in the small brick-walled public bar. Bar food includes home-made soup (£2.05), sandwiches with home-cooked meats (from £2.95; local crab £3.95), home-made pâté (£3.85), filled baked potatoes (from £4.35), ploughman's (from £4.50), cold roast beef with chips or vegetable curry (£5.45), steaks (from £10.35), puddings (from £3.25), and Sunday roasts (£6.25). The terrace garden has views of the countryside. *(Recommended by Basil Minson, V N Stevenson, Paul R White, C Galloway, Betsy and Peter Little)*

Free house ~ Licensee Sally Pratt ~ Real ale ~ Bar food (12-1.45, 7-9.45) ~ Restaurant ~ (01395) 232375 ~ Children allowed away from main bar ~ Open 11-2.30, 6.30-11; 12-2.30, 7-10.30 Sun; closed evenings 25-26 Dec

WOODLAND SX7968 Map 1
Rising Sun

Village signposted off A38 just NE of Ashburton – then keep eyes peeled for Rising Sun signposts

On the edge of Dartmoor, this is a friendly, bustling inn with quite an emphasis placed on the good, interesting bar food. Changing frequently, the dishes might include sandwiches and ploughman's, home-made soup (£3.25), thai-style fishcakes with a vierge dressing or home-made pork and chicken liver pâté (£3.95), hazelnut and courgette bake with tomato sauce or a trio of local sausages with onion gravy (£6.50), fillet of gurnard marinated in spices and lime (£7.95), braised lamb shanks or tagliatelle with smoked salmon and prawns in a cream sauce (£8.95), breast of Gressingham duck with pickled plums (£10.95), and home-made puddings with clotted cream, such as sticky toffee pudding with butterscotch sauce, chocolate marquise, and raspberry cheesecake (£3.25); children's menu (£2.50; they can also have small helpings of some main course items), Sunday roast (£5.95), and popular pie nights with a choice of five pies, a pudding, a glass of wine, and coffee and fudge (£9.95). The dining area is no smoking. There's an expanse of softly lit red plush button-back banquettes and matching studded chairs, partly divided by wooden banister rails, masonry pillars and the odd high-backed settle. A forest of beams is hung with thousands of old doorkeys, and a nice part by the log fire has shelves of plates and books, and old pictures above the fireplace. Well kept Princetown Jail Ale and Dartmoor IPA, and Teignworthy Reel Ale on handpump; cheerful service. The family area has various toys (and a collection of cookery books). There are some picnic-sets in the spacious garden, which has a play area including a redundant tractor. More reports please. *(Recommended by Dr and Mrs A K Clarke, Brian, Dill, Jenni and Kate Hughes, Ian Phillips, D and H Broodbank, Richard and Margaret Peers, Colin and Sandra Tann)*

Free house ~ Licensee Heather Humphreys ~ Real ale ~ Bar food (12-2.15(3 Sun), 6-9.15) ~ Restaurant ~ (01364) 652544 ~ Children in eating area of bar and restaurant ~ Open 11-3, 6-11; 12-3, 7-10.30 Sun; closed Mon morning except bank hols and during July/Aug, and all day Mon in winter ~ Bedrooms: £28B/£53B

Lucky Dip

Besides the fully inspected pubs, you might like to try these Lucky Dips recommended to us and described by readers (if you do, please send us reports: www.goodguides.com).

Abbotsham [SS4226]
Thatched Inn: Extensively refurbished family pub, friendly staff, Bass, Butcombe, Courage Directors and John Smiths, attractive food inc good value Sun lunch, families welcome, mix of modern seats and older features; tables outside; handy for the Big Sheep *(Mr and Mrs I Bennett)*

Abbotskerswell [SX8569]
☆ *Court Farm* [Wilton Way; look for the church tower]: Attractive neatly extended 17th-c former farmhouse catering for Torbay's affluent retired folk, various rooms off long crazy-paved main beamed bar, partly no smoking, good mix of furnishings, Bass, Castle Eden, Flowers IPA and Fullers London Pride, farm cider, woodburners, good helpings of reasonably priced waitress-served food (can take a time when busy) from sandwiches to ostrich, steaks and bargain Sun lunch, half helpings for children, friendly helpful service; piped music; children in eating area, tables in pretty garden, open all day *(Andrew Hodges, Ian Mcintyre, LYM, John and Vivienne Rice, Mrs Sylvia Elcoate, Derek Allpass, John Wilson)*

Appledore [SS4630]
Beaver [Irsha St]: Great estuary views from raised area in well worn in harbourside pub, good value food (esp fish), friendly staff, well kept changing ales such as Bass, Butcombe, Flowers, decent house wines; can be smoky, pool in smaller games room; outdoor tables, children really welcome, disabled access *(Andy Marks)*
☆ *Royal George* [Irsha St]: Simple but good fresh food inc local fish in no smoking dining room with superb estuary views, cosy and unspoilt front bar (where dogs allowed), well kept ales such as Bass, Greene King Old Speckled Hen, Ind Coope Burton, decent wines, good friendly service, attractive pictures, fresh flowers; disabled access, picnic-sets outside, picturesque street sloping to sea *(Helen Hazzard)*

Ashprington [SX8156]
☆ *Watermans Arms* [Bow Bridge, on Tuckenhay road]: Bustling quarry-tiled heavy-beamed pub at the head of Bow Creek, high-backed settles and other sturdy furnishings, stripped stonework, log fire, wide food choice, comfortable and roomy inc children's, partly no smoking eating area, well kept Bass, Theakstons XB and a beer brewed for the pub, local wine and farm cider, darts, dominoes, cribbage; piped music, TV; children and dogs welcome, open all day, comfortable bedrooms, pretty flower-filled garden, more tables over road by creek *(John Evans, Trevor and Lynda Smith, Dr Phil Putwain, Mike and Mary Carter, Ellen Winter, J C Burley, Jonathan Smith, Catherine Pitt, LYM)*

Aveton Gifford [SX6947]
Taverners [Fore St]: Welcoming village local with good food inc home-made pizzas and sizzler steaks, real ales *(Geoff and Tricia Alderman, Joy and Colin Rorke)*

Axminster [SY2998]
Hunters Lodge [A35 nr B3165 junction]: Character 16th-c coaching inn, friendly and well run, good value bar and restaurant food inc carvery, pleasant staff, well kept Bass and Worthington; big garden with children's play area, well behaved dogs welcome *(I R Fourmy)*
Red Lion [Lyme St]: Friendly local with well kept Butcombe, at least three farm ciders, good cheap bar food, pleasant service *(R T and J C Moggridge)*

Axmouth [SY2591]
☆ *Ship* [Church St]: Comfortable and civilised, good fresh local fish and other food using their own herbs inc interesting vegetarian speciality, well kept Bass and Otter, good wine and coffee, lots of embroidered folk dolls, one room devoted to Guinness memorabilia, friendly staff and samoyeds, computer for customers, no smoking restaurant; skittle alley full of bric-a-brac, tables in attractive garden with long-established owl rescue home *(Dr and Mrs R Booth, LYM, David Peakall)*

Aylesbeare [SY0392]
Halfway [A3052 Exeter—Sidmouth, junction with B3180]: Comfortable convivial bar, lots of old wood, books, brasses, bric-a-brac and interesting sporting prints, enjoyable food in bar and restaurant inc generous carvery, well kept Bass, Otter and changing guest beers, quick friendly service; tables in garden, high views over Dartmoor, bedrooms *(P and J Shapley, Basil Minson)*

Bampton [SS9522]
Exeter [Tiverton Rd]: Well run long low stone-built pub under steep hill overlooking River Exe, several interconnecting rooms and large pleasant restaurant, huge choice of good food inc fish and carvery, reasonable prices, five or six well kept real ales inc Cotleigh and Exmoor tapped from the cask, friendly landlord, no piped music; tables out in front, bedrooms, open all day, fairly handy for Knightshayes Court *(Peter and Audrey Dowsett, Ian Phillips)*

Barnstaple [SS5533]
Panniers [Boutport St]: New Wetherspoons, fast efficient service, well kept beers and cider, low prices, simple appetising food all day, no smoking area, no piped music; no children *(Pat and Tony Martin)*
Reform [Reform St/Pilton Rd]: Quiet, friendly and civilised, brewing its own good Barum ales (Barum was the Anglo-Saxon name for the town) such as BSE, Original, Challenger and a real lager; bargain prices till 9 *(Tony Gayfer)*

Beer [ST2389]
Barrel of Beer [Fore St]: Small friendly family-run pub favoured for good range of real ales inc local ones, also reasonably priced straightforward food inc fresh fish; open all day *(Jeanne and Paul Silvestri)*

Belstone [SX6293]
Tors [a mile off A30]: Imposing stone building under friendly new local licensees, good choice

of reasonably priced generous food from good big baguettes up, well kept Flowers IPA, Sharps Doom Bar and Wadworths 6X, decent wines and malt whiskies, woodburner; bedrooms, attractive village well placed for N Dartmoor walks *(John and Vivienne Rice, Mark Griffiths, Tony and Wendy Hobden)*

Bere Ferrers [SX4563]
Old Plough [long dead-end rd off B3257 S of Tavistock]: Welcoming and attractive, with good value well prepared food, well kept changing mostly local real ales, stripped stone, low beam-and-plank ceilings, panelling, slate flagstones, old-fashioned furniture, woodburner, steps down to cosy restaurant; garden overlooking estuary *(Carole and John Smith)*

Berry Head [SX9456]
Berry Head Hotel: Large L-shaped pubby bar popular with Torquay businessmen, plenty of tables giving panoramic Torbay views, enjoyable food inc good carvery in room off, caring service, Dartmoor, Marstons Pedigree and Tetleys, unobtrusive piped music; children welcome *(Bob and Ann Westbrook)*

Bickleigh [SS9406]
☆ *Fishermans Cot*: Greatly extended thatched fishing inn with lots of tables on acres of turkey carpet attractively broken up with pillars, plants and some panelled parts, charming view over shallow rocky race below 1640 Exe bridge, more tables out on terrace and waterside lawn; emphasis on waitress-served food inc reasonably priced carvery, friendly efficient service, well kept Bass, Courage Best and Wadworths 6X; piped music; comfortable bedrooms looking over own terrace to river *(Ian Phillips, Joy and Colin Rorke, Alan Kilpatrick, BB)*

Bishop's Tawton [SS5630]
☆ *Chichester Arms* [signed off A377 outside Barnstaple; East St]: Friendly 15th-c cob and thatch pub with low bowed beams, large stone fireplace, old local photographs, plush banquettes, open fire, well priced good food from home-made soup and sandwiches to fine steaks and carvery, well kept Dartmoor Best, Ind Coope Burton and Tetleys, decent wines, games in family room, partly no smoking restaurant; picnic-sets on front terrace and in back garden; open all day *(N H E Lewis, LYM, Andy Marks)*

Bovey Tracey [SX8178]
Cromwell Arms [Fore St]: Popular friendly local with reasonably priced generous food inc good value Sun lunch, quick service, well kept well priced Marstons Pedigree and other beers, several areas with high-backed settles, no piped music *(Beverley and Neil Gardner)*

Brayford [SS7235]
☆ *Poltimore Arms* [Yarde Down; 3 miles towards Simonsbath]: Chatty and pubby old two-bar local in isolated spot, cheerful staff, good value food inc good Sun roast, well kept Cotleigh Tawny and Exmoor tapped from the cask, basic traditional furnishings, inglenook; maybe piped music, simple games room; children allowed in restaurant, picnic-sets in side garden;

no dogs inside *(LYM, Richard and Anne Ansell)*

Brendon [SS7547]
☆ *Rockford Inn* [Lynton—Simonsbath rd, off B2332]: Homely and friendly family-run inn well set for walkers (and fishermen) by East Lyn river, summer afternoon refreshments as well as generous food from sandwiches to fresh fish; well kept Cotleigh Tawny and Barn Owl and a guest beer, good choice of malt whiskies, darts, pool, shove-ha'penny, cribbage, dominoes; piped music; restaurant, children in eating areas, dogs welcome, folk night every 3rd Sat, bedrooms; open all day summer *(Brian and Peggy Green, LYM)*
Staghunters: Idyllic setting with garden by East Lyn river, welcoming licensees, traditional furnishings, popular substantial food from filled baguettes up inc fresh veg, well kept Wadworths 6X and Addlestone's cider, woodburner, family room with pool table, restaurant; walkers and dogs welcome, can get very busy, bedrooms *(Trevor and Lynda Smith)*

Bridestowe [SX5189]
Fox & Hounds [A386 Okehampton—Tavistock]: Friendly and well worn in moors-edge pub, good value generous food (all day at least in summer) inc good steaks, good range of real ales; bedrooms *(BB, Dr and Mrs Nigel Holmes, J Ingham)*

Bridford [SX8186]
☆ *Bridford Inn* [off B3193 Dunsford—Chudleigh]: Fine old pub carefully renovated, well kept local ales such as Scattor Rock, farm cider, wide choice of enjoyable sensibly priced lunchtime food from good sandwiches up, good welcoming service; well behaved dogs welcome, pretty views from tables outside *(Hugh and Peggy Holman, John and Vivienne Rice, BB)*

Brixham [SX9255]
Blue Anchor [Fore St/King St]: Warm and friendly harbourside pub with two or three well kept real ales, decent usual food inc local fish, nautical bar, two small dining rooms – one a former chapel, down some steps; open all day *(Bryan Robinson)*
Vigilance [Bolton St]: New Wetherspoons conversion of former shop, sizeable well furnished open-plan bar with no smoking area, good inexpensive food (inc good vegetarian range) and drink, no music, exemplary lavatories; nearby parking difficult *(David and Pam Wilcox)*

Broadclyst [SX9897]
☆ *Red Lion* [B3121, by church]: Peaceful old local with fine wisteria, long bar with heavy beams, cushioned window seats, some nice chairs around a mix of oak and other tables, flagstoned area with cushioned pews and low tables by old woodburner, collection of carpenters' planes, generous straightforward bar food inc children's and Sun roast, separate dining area with longer menu; well kept Bass, Fullers London Pride and Hardy Royal Oak; picnic-sets on front cobbles, more in small enclosed garden across quiet lane, not far from Killerton (NT – they own the pub too) *(James Flory, Stephen and Jean Curtis, Alan and Paula*

McCully, LYM, Ian and Nita Cooper)

Buckfastleigh [SX7366]

☆ *Dartbridge* [Totnes Rd, handy for A38]: Big bustling family pub, prettily placed opp Dart Valley Rly, good range of generous food (they keep good stilton), well kept Theakstons, above-average house wines, friendly service even under summer pressure; reasonable disabled access, tables in neatly kept roadside garden, 10 letting chalets *(John Evans, Dr and Mrs A K Clarke, John and Vivienne Rice)*

☆ *White Hart* [Plymouth Rd]: Simple but attractive comfortably carpeted open-plan bar with cheerful homely feel, woodburner one end, huge log fire the other, stone walls, lots of pictures, horsebrasses, plates, jugs and so forth; particularly well kept ales such as Ash Vine One Way Traffic, Greene King Abbot and Teignworthy Beachcomber, with a beer brewed for them by Teignworthy, also Sam's local farm cider, lots of pumpclips above bar, friendly landlord, decent home-made food in dining area and restaurant; dogs and children welcome – even have some toys; bedrooms, tables in pretty back courtyard with barbecues, open all day, cl Sun afternoon and Mon lunchtime *(Catherine Pitt, Jonathan Smith)*

Budleigh Salterton [SY0682]

Salterton Arms [Chapel St]: Well kept Bass, Branscombe Vale Branoc and Greene King Old Speckled Hen, wide range of reasonably priced food from sandwiches up, good value wines, helpful efficient staff, small open fires, upper dining gallery; children and dogs welcome, can get very busy summer; jazz winter Sun evenings, open all day wknds *(John Beeken, David Hoult, Betsy and Peter Little, LYM, Denzil Taylor)*

Burgh Island [SX6443]

Pilchard [300 yds across tidal sands from Bigbury-on-Sea; walk, or take summer Tractor – unique bus on stilts]: Great setting high above sea on tidal island with unspoilt cliff walks; not at all smart, but atmospheric, with ancient beams and flagstones, lanterns, nets and (when it's lit) blazing fire; Courage Best and Directors, basic food (all day summer, maybe nothing in winter though), piped music, dogs welcome (no children inside), some tables down by beach *(the Didler, JP, PP, LYM)*

Challacombe [SS6941]

☆ *Black Venus* [B3358 Blackmoor Gate—Simonsbath]: Doing well under current management, good varied home-cooked food inc choice of Sun roasts, fair prices, well kept Exmoor and Greene King Abbot, low 16th-c beams, pews, decent chairs, stuffed birds, woodburner and big open fire, separate games room, attractive big dining area (children over 5 allowed); seats in garden, attractive countryside; bedrooms *(Christopher Tull, BB, Don and Thelma Beeson)*

Chardstock [ST3004]

☆ *George* [off A358 S of Chard]: Extended thatched 15th-c inn with character furnishings and décor and ancient oak partition walls in massively beamed core, good log fires, good value food inc some interesting dishes, well kept

Courage Best and Fullers London Pride, friendly service; skittle alley, games bar, piped music; tables out in back loggia by sheltered cobbled courtyard, more in safely fenced grass area; children in eating area, bedrooms, good walks *(Esther and John Sprinkle, LYM, J Fowler, Ian Phillips, Andrew and Catherine Gilham, Paul R White)*

Chillington [SX7942]

☆ *Open Arms* [A379 E of Kingsbridge]: Roomy modernised open-plan turkey-carpeted bar with well kept ales such as Badger Tanglefoot, Bass, Beer Seller Mild, Exmoor and Wadworths 6X, good wines and choice of spirits, inexpensive hearty home-made food, good local atmosphere, back games room with pool *(John Brightley, BB, Tracey and Stephen Groves)*

Christow [SX8384]

☆ *Artichoke*: Pretty thatched local with open-plan rooms stepped down hill, low beams, some black panelling, flagstones, reliable food inc fish and game, big log fire (2nd one in no smoking end dining room), mainly Whitbreads-related ales; tables on back terrace, pretty hillside village nr Canonteign Waterfalls and Country Park *(BB, David and Elizabeth Briggs)*

Teign House [Teign Valley Rd (B3193)]: Attractive former farmhouse, open fire in beamed bar, good fresh food (all day) using local produce here and in family dining room (partly no smoking), well kept Devonian ale (brewed in the village), decent wines; cl Tues lunchtime *(Mrs B Davies)*

Chudleigh [SX8679]

Bishop Lacey [Fore St, just off A38]: Partly 14th-c church house with well kept Branscombe Vale, Flowers IPA, Fullers London Pride and a guest such as Princetown Jail, some tapped from casks in back bar, good value food, no smoking dining room; winter beer festival, open all day *(JP, PP, the Didler)*

Highwaymans Haunt [signed off A38]: Immaculate thatched pub, comfortable and friendly, with enjoyable food inc well appointed evening/Sun lunch carvery; no under-7s or dogs *(Ian Phillips)*

Old Coaching House [Fore St]: Bustling low-beamed rambling bars, tables cosily separated by low partitions, good service, decent food, real ales inc Bass and Teignworthy Reel Ale *(the Didler, JP, PP)*

Chudleigh Knighton [SX8477]

☆ *Claycutters Arms* [just off A38 by B3344]: Friendly and attractive 17th-c thatched two-bar village pub with wide choice of decent food from sandwiches to exotic dishes, well kept Bass and Marstons Pedigree, good service, stripped stone, interesting nooks and crannies, pleasant restaurant; tables on side terrace and in orchard *(LYM, D S Jackson, John and Vivienne Rice, A D Marsh, Alan and Paula McCully, John Wilson)*

Churchstow [SX7145]

Church House [A379 NW of Kingsbridge]: Generous good food from sandwiches to mixed grill and (Weds-Sat nights, Sun lunch) popular carvery in long character pub with heavy black beams (dates from 13th c), stripped stone, cushioned settles, back conservatory with floodlit well feature; well kept Bass, Fullers London Pride, Greene King Old Speckled Hen and changing guest ales, friendly efficient staff, no piped music; well behaved children and dogs welcome, tables outside (Richard and Margaret Peers, R and D Gray, Joy and Colin Rorke, LYM, J A Elllis, P R and S A White, Michael Porter)

Churston Ferrers [SX9056]

Churston Court [Church Rd]: Attractive Elizabethan former manor house in lovely setting next to village church nr Elbury Cove, nicely furnished bar, good food inc good fresh fish; bedrooms (Bob and Ann Westbrook)

Clayhidon [ST1615]

Merry Harriers: Recently reopened, welcoming new licensees concentrating on good restaurant food using local produce and seafood (already best to book at wknds), well kept beer, decent wines, good service, comfortable surroundings; large garden; good walking area (Patrick Darley, Nick and Lesley Warboys)

Clearbrook [SX5265]

☆ Skylark [off A386 Tavistock—Plymouth, edge of Dartmoor]: Roomy old Dartmoor-edge local doing well under experienced current licensees, welcoming atmosphere, wide choice of good value food from sandwiches up inc vegetarian dishes, good range of well kept real ales, simple furnishings, log fire, children's room; often busy with walkers; good Dartmoor and Plymouth Sound views, big back garden (Mike and Linda Boxall, Jacquie and Jim Jones)

Clovelly [SS3225]

New Inn [High St]: Attractive old inn halfway down the steep cobbled street, simple lower bar with friendly efficient service even when busy, good choice of inexpensive bar food, a real ale brewed for the pub; quiet piped music; bedrooms (Peter and Audrey Dowsett)

Red Lion [The Quay]: Rambling building worth knowing for its lovely position on curving quay, with character back bar, food inc fresh crab sandwiches and local fish (service can be slow), Dartmoor ale; pleasant, simple attractive bedrooms (R M Corlett)

Cockington [SX8963]

Drum [Cockington Lane]: Cheerfully bustling thatched and beamed tavern designed by Lutyens to match the quaintly touristy Torquay-edge medieval village, Dartmoor Bitter and Legend, roomy bar (can be smoky) and two family eating areas, quick service, Weds summer barbecues, winter skittle evenings and live music; piped music; open all day, tables on terrace and in attractive back garden by 500-acre park (JP, PP, Bob and Ann Westbrook)

Cockwood [SX9780]

☆ Ship [off A379 N of Dawlish]: Comfortable 17th-c inn overlooking estuary and harbour, partitioned beamed bar with ancient oven, decorative plates and seafaring prints and memorabilia, small no smoking restaurant with large open fire, good value food from open crab sandwiches up inc imaginative evening fish dishes and good puddings (freshly made so

takes time), well kept Bass and Greene King IPA and Abbot, friendly efficient staff; piped music; good steep-sided garden (Peter Salmon, John Beeken)

Coffinswell [SX8968]

☆ Linny [just off A380 at Kingskerswell]: Very pretty partly 14th-c thatched country pub in same friendly family for years, some concentration on wide choice of good generous food; cheerfully sociable big beamed bar, settles and other old seats, smaller areas off, well kept changing ales such as Jennings Sneck Lifter, Princetown Jail and Tetleys, cosy log fires, lots of twinkling brass, efficient service, no smoking area, children's room, upstairs restaurant extension (not always open); some tables outside, picturesque village (BB, Richard and Margaret Peers, Mr and Mrs C Roberts)

Colyford [SY2492]

White Hart [A3052 Exeter—Lyme Regis, by tramway stn]: Popular riverside pub with wide standard menu from sandwiches and ploughman's up, good fish choice, large main bar, changing real ales, wide choice of wine, children's games room, skittle alley, restaurant; trad jazz Sun night, tables in garden with boules (John and Kay Grugeon)

Croyde [SS4439]

Manor House Inn [St Marys Rd, off B3231 NW of Braunton]: Friendly local with well kept Flowers, quickly served decent bar food, separate restaurant area; bar billiards, darts, shove-ha'penny, skittles, attractive terraced garden – a good summer family pub (Mr and Mrs D J Nash)

☆ Thatched Barn [B3231 NW of Braunton; Hobbs Hill]: Lively rambling thatched pub nr great surfing beaches, with cheerful efficient staff, laid-back feel and customers to match (can get packed in summer); wide choice of generous food from sandwiches and baguettes up, well kept Bass, St Austell HSD and Tetleys, morning coffee, teas, cheerful young staff; restaurant, children in eating area, open all day; piped music may be a bit loud; bedrooms simple but clean and comfortable, tables outside (Mr and Mrs D J Nash, LYM, BKA, Steve Chambers, Andy Marks)

Culmstock [ST1014]

Culm Valley: Ancient pub in lovely spot by bridge in small village, simple décor, three open fires, friendly licensees and locals, enjoyable food from baked potatoes to steaks inc good vegetarian choice in bar and restaurant, well kept ales such as Bass, Badger Tanglefoot, Cotleigh Tawny and Exmoor, interesting village and former railway photographs, skittle alley; good tables under cocktail parasols out in front and some seating by the river, river walk to working wool museum (James Flory)

Dartington [SX7961]

Queens Arms [towards Totnes]: Straightforward Ushers pub with friendly service and good generous wholesome food; pretty flower-laden front terrace, handy for walks and cycle paths, open all day (Alan and Paula McCully)

White Hart Bar [Dartington Hall]: Simple

modern décor and open fires in the college's bar (open to visitors), good low-priced food, very special atmosphere sitting out in the famously beautiful grounds *(Dr and Mrs A K Clarke)*

Dartmouth [SX8751]

Dolphin [Market St]: Interesting building in picturesque part of town, good landlord, locally popular bar with reference books for crossword buffs, well kept real ales, cosy upstairs restaurant with good generous seafood; no children *(Charles Eatof, Mr and Mrs J French, I J and N K Buckmaster)*

☆ *Seven Stars* [Smith St]: Crowded beamed and panelled local, well priced and cooked popular food (can be a long wait), well kept ales such as Cottage Normans Conquest and Wadworths 6X, coal fire, end family area with sensible tables and settles; dogs welcome, maybe piped pop music, fruit machine; upstairs restaurant *(David and Elizabeth Briggs, BB)*

Denbury [SX8168]

☆ *Union* [The Green]: Spotless and comfortable low-beamed local on edge of old village green, same management as Anchor at Cockwood and similar good menu majoring on seafood, two eating areas, well kept Flowers Original, Greene King Old Speckled Hen and Wadworths 6X, good coffee, charming service; tables in garden by green, quietly pretty sheltered village *(Basil Minson, BB)*

Devonport [SX4555]

Pym Arms [Pym St]: Basic backstreet local with Princetown Jail and guest beers tapped from the cask, farm cider, no food; open all day Thurs-Sun *(JP, PP)*

Dittisham [SX8654]

☆ *Ferry Boat* [Manor St; best to park in village – steep but attractive walk down]: Very welcoming, in idyllic waterside setting, big windows making the most of it; good value food inc good range of baguettes and pies, real ale; nr little foot-ferry you call by bell, good walks *(Ken and Jenny Simmonds, Dr M E Wilson, Ken Flawn, LYM)*

Drewsteignton [SX7489]

☆ *Anglers Rest* [E of village; OS Sheet 191 map ref 743899]: Idyllic wooded Teign valley spot by 16th-c pack-horse bridge, lovely walks; much extended former tea pavilion, with tourist souvenirs and airy café feel, but has well kept Otter, Red Admiral and Sharps and reliable food (not Sun) inc good local cheese ploughman's, children's meals, apple cake and cream teas; friendly helpful service, log fire, waterside picnic-sets; cl winter evenings *(Dr P F A Watkins, LYM, JP, PP, Peter Meister)*

Dunsford [SX8189]

Royal Oak [signed from Moretonhampstead]: Generous home-cooked food and well kept changing ales in relaxed village inn's light and airy lounge bar, local farm ciders, well kept Greene King IPA and Abbot, woodburner; steps down to games room, provision for children; quiz nights, piped music; Fri barbecues in sheltered tiered garden, good value bedrooms in converted barn *(Joy and Colin Rorke, Dr P F A Watkins, LYM)*

East Budleigh [SY0684]

☆ *Sir Walter Raleigh* [High St]: Chattily convivial local nr interesting church in lovely village, neat and clean, with faultless service, decent food inc help-yourself salad bar and good Sun lunch, charming large no smoking dining room, well kept Flowers IPA, Marstons Pedigree and local brews, good house wine; no children; bedrooms *(Basil Minson, Dr M E Wilson, Pat and Robert Watt, LYM)*

East Down [SS5941]

☆ *Pyne Arms* [off A39 Barnstaple—Lynton nr Arlington]: Small and attractive, with spotless low-beamed bar, very wide choice of generous well cooked food till late evening, pleasant licensees, lots of nooks and crannies, individual furnishings inc high-backed curved settle, small no smoking galleried loft (where children allowed), well kept Bass and Worthington, good value house wines, flagstoned games area with unobtrusive juke box and TV; handy for Arlington Court, good walks *(LYM)*

East Prawle [SX7836]

Pigs Nose [Prawle Green]: Cheery low-beamed pub with welcoming new licensees doing enjoyable food from good ploughman's and sandwiches up, open fire, small selection of local beer and cider, easy chairs and sofa, pool, darts, small family area by kitchen; tables outside *(Roger Wain-Heapy)*

Exeter [SX9292]

☆ *Chaucers* [basement of C & A, High St]: Large dim-lit modern olde-worlde pub/bistro/wine bar down lots of steps, candles in bottles, well kept though very cool Bass and a beer brewed for the pub, good range of generous good value food inc adventurous dishes and afternoon bargains, quick friendly service, no smoking area, pleasant atmosphere; piped music *(Dr and Mrs A K Clarke, A Moore, Dr M E Wilson)*

Great Western [St Davids Hill]: Sociable public bar in large hotel, comfortably relaxed, with plenty of regulars, attractively priced honest food all day from sandwiches up (also a restaurant), daily papers, well kept Adnams, Bass, Fullers London Pride and local ales; peanuts in the shell, no music; bedrooms *(JP, PP, Richard Houghton, Tony and Wendy Hobden, Phil and Sally Gorton)*

Honiton [Paris St]: Elegant and friendly, with small choice of well kept real ales inc Bass, big helpings of good value tasty food *(Dr and Mrs A K Clarke)*

Hour Glass [Melbourne St]: Close to quay, thriving old city pub with beams, candles and lots of wood, Bass and Greene King Abbot, good house wine, enjoyable reasonably priced food, friendly helpful staff, cellar restaurant *(John and Vivienne Rice)*

Jolly Porter [St Davids Hill]: Attractive and airy, lively with students and locals, with big windows overlooking street, raised seating, well kept changing ales such as RCH Pitchfork, cheap plentiful food all day, bare boards, bric-a-brac and books, snooker room, family room; jazz Weds, open all day *(Catherine Pitt, JP, PP)*

Mill on the Exe [Bonhay Rd (A377)]: Good spot by weir with heated waterside terrace, bar comfortably done out with old bricks and timbers, recent extension into large airy river-view conservatory restaurant, good sensibly priced food, well kept St Austell Tinners and HSD, quick friendly service; children welcome *(BB, John and Vivienne Rice, Dr and Mrs A K Clarke)*

Prospect [The Quay]: Good waterfront spot, with comfortable upper river-view dining area (food from doorstep sandwiches up, service can be slow), well kept Bass and Wadworths 6X; lower beamed bar with games machines, piped music – live some evenings *(John and Vivienne Rice)*

☆ *Ship* [Martins Lane]: Pretty 14th-c pub with substantial comfortable furniture in bustling heavy-beamed bar, well kept Boddingtons, Flowers, Greene King Old Speckled Hen and Marstons Pedigree, farm cider, speedy friendly service, generously filled sandwiches only down here, enjoyable meals in upstairs restaurant; can get crowded, loud and smoky; handy for town centre and cathedral *(Dr M E Wilson, David Carr, Mr and Mrs C Roberts, LYM, Chris Parsons, P G Plumridge)*

Welcome [Canal Banks, off Haven Rd]: Old pub overlooking basin on Exeter Ship Canal, gas lighting and flagstones, very friendly old-school landlady, well kept Castle Eden or a guest beer such as RCH PG Steam, nostalgic 60s/70s juke box; has had free folk music Sun lunchtime *(the Didler)*

☆ *Well House* [Cathedral Yard, attached to Royal Clarence Hotel]: Big windows looking across to cathedral in congenial open-plan bar divided by inner walls and partitions, lots of interesting Victorian prints, good choice of well kept changing ales from good small breweries, quick service, popular bar lunches inc good sandwiches and salads, daily papers; Roman well beneath (can be viewed when pub not busy); piped music *(Mike Gorton, Hugh Roberts, BB, David Carr, Ian Phillips, P G Plumridge)*

Exminster [SX9487]

☆ *Swans Nest* [Station Rd, just off A379 on outskirts]: Huge choice of reasonably priced self-service food from sandwiches and children's dishes through salads and fresh fish to roasts and enticing puddings from long attractive carvery/buffet in very popular high-throughput pub, Bass and Dartmoor, helpful staff, well arranged and attractive rambling dining bar (great Christmas decorations) with no smoking areas; especially good for family groups with children, handy for M5 *(LYM, S F Wakeham, John Thomassen, Mr and Mrs P Hayward)*

Exmouth [SY0080]

Beach [Victoria Rd]: Woody interior in down-to-earth old quayside local, one room covered with shipping and lifeboat memorabilia and photographs, cast-iron-framed tables, Bass, Greene King Old Speckled Hen and Marstons Pedigree, food, welcoming service *(Dr M E Wilson)*

Beacon Vaults [The Beacon]: Warm and friendly, with three reasonably priced real ales, good value fresh food inc bargain specials *(Bryan Robinson)*

Grove [Esplanade]: Roomy panelled pub set back from beach with pleasant seafront garden and play area, well kept Bass, Boddingtons, Brakspears, Flowers, Greene King Abbot and Wadworths 6X (more on guest beer nights), decent house wines, good coffee, good value food inc plenty of local fish, friendly efficient service, lots of pictures, attractive fireplace at back; live music some nights *(Dr M E Wilson, Rita Horridge, David Hoult)*

Heavitree Arms [High St]: Split-level town-centre pub for all ages, buzzing atmosphere, well kept ales, nice wood fittings, cosy corners *(Dr M E Wilson)*

Exton [SX9886]

Puffing Billy: Newly renovated restaurant/dining pub with friendly management and wide choice of good inventive food inc seafood *(Peter Burton)*

Fairmile [SY0897]

Fairmile Inn [A30 Honiton—Exeter]: Refurbished two-bar pub with log fires, well kept ales inc Bass and Tetleys, pleasant staff, food from good value sandwiches up inc weekly OAP lunch, beamed inglenook dining room; quiz nights, tables in garden, good value simple bedrooms, big breakfast *(Philip Howes, K W Dabney)*

Frogmore [SX7742]

☆ *Globe* [A379 E of Kingsbridge]: Walls papered with maritime charts and hung with ship and yacht paintings, some built-in settles creating corner booths, mix of simple tables, open fire, well kept Exmoor Ale and Greene King Abbot, local farm cider in summer, country wines, bar food from sandwiches to steak inc children's, games and TV in flagstoned public bar; tables out on terraces, play area, creek view, plenty of walks, bedrooms; cl Mon lunchtime in winter *(Edmund Coan, Mrs J Ekins-Daukes, LYM)*

Georgeham [SS4639]

☆ *Rock* [Rock Hill, above village]: Good value food in well restored oak-beamed pub, well kept ales such as Cotleigh, Theakstons, Ushers Best and Wadworths 6X, local farm cider, decent wines, old red quarry tiles, open fire, pleasant mix of rustic furniture, lots of bric-a-brac, pleasant back conservatory great for children; piped music, darts, fruit machine, pool room; tables under cocktail parasols on front terrace, pretty hanging baskets *(Mr and Mrs I Bennett, BB)*

Gulworthy [SX4572]

Harvest Home: Welcoming landlord, St Austell HSD and Sharps real ales, good value real home cooking *(Dr and Mrs Nigel Holmes)*

Halwell [SX7853]

☆ *Old Inn* [A381 Totnes—Kingsbridge, junction with B3207]: Good atmosphere, warm welcome, chatty landlord, good value interesting food cooked by his Filipino wife, well kept RCH IPA, Premium and East St Cream; bedrooms *(D G T Horsford, Dudley and Moira Cockroft)*

Hartland [SS2524]

Hart [The Square]: Good value sound home cooking in two eating rooms attractively done out as cobbler's shop and (no smoking) village

shop, large popular public bar, friendly service
(Dr and Mrs David Smith)

Hartland Quay [SS2224]

☆ *Hartland Quay Hotel* [off B3248 W of
Bideford, down toll road (free Oct—Easter); OS
Sheet 190 map ref 222248]: Unpretentious and
relaxed old hotel in stunning cliff scenery,
rugged coast walks, real maritime feel with
fishing memorabilia and interesting shipwreck
pictures; efficient friendly service, small no
smoking bar, lots of tables outside – very
popular with holidaymakers; maybe well kept
Sharps Doom Bar (often keg beer only), basic
but generous food, dogs welcome, good value
bedrooms, seawater swimming pool; cl
midwinter *(Helen Hazzard, Mr and Mrs
McKay, Tony and Valerie Marshall, C P Scott-
Malden)*

Hexworthy [SX6572]

☆ *Forest Inn* [signed off B3357 Tavistock—
Ashburton, E of B3212]: Solid Dartmoor hotel
in fine surroundings, roomy plush-seated open-
plan bar and back walkers' bar, relaxing
atmosphere, real fire, daily papers; short choice
of good generous bar food, well kept local
Teignworthy ale inc a summer seasonal beer,
local cider, prompt service; good-sized
bedrooms, bunkhouse; fishing permits on sale,
good walking and horse riding *(Bruce Bird,
Denzil Taylor, LYM, Ann and Colin Hunt)*

Holbeton [SX6150]

Dartmoor Union [Fore St]: Friendly renovated
village pub, good food in comfortable bar or
candlelit back restaurant inc themed nights and
take-away fish and chips, local real ales inc
Skinners and St Austell; picturesque village
(G R Taylor, Carol Ackroyd, Peter McNamara)

Holcombe [SX9574]

Smugglers [Holcombe Dr]: Pleasant modern-
style pub locally and deservedly popular for
food from children's dishes to carvery; Bass and
other real ales, pool, bar billiards *(anon)*

Holne [SX7069]

☆ *Church House* [signed off B3357 W of
Ashburton]: Ancient welcoming country inn
well placed for attractive walks, open log fires
in both rooms, interesting building, honest well
cooked food from lunchtime sandwiches up,
children's helpings, no smoking areas, well kept
Dartmoor, Palmers and Wadworths 6X, Gray's
farm cider, country wines, decent house wines,
traditional games in public bar; well behaved
children in eating area; comfortable bedrooms
*(LYM, D and M T Ayres-Regan, Gill
Honeyman, Mr and Mrs J McRobert)*

Holsworthy [SS3408]

Kings Arms [Fore St/The Square]: 17th-c inn
with Victorian fittings, etched windows and
coal fires in three interesting traditional bars,
old pictures and photographs, 40s and 50s beer
advertisements, lots of optics behind ornate
counter, particularly well kept Bass and Sharps
Doom Bar, friendly locals; open all day, Sun
afternoon closure *(the Didler, JP, PP)*

Honiton [ST1500]

☆ *Red Cow* [High St]: Welcoming local, very busy
on Tues and Sat market days, scrubbed tables,
pleasant alcoves, log fires, well kept Bass,

Courage Directors and local Otter, decent
wines and malt whiskies, wide choice of good
value home-made food inc excellent sandwiches
and good puddings, fast service from friendly
Welsh licensees (may have Radio Wales), loads
of chamber-pots and big mugs on beams,
pavement tables; bedrooms *(Dr M W A
Haward, BB, John Oates, Dr Denise Walton)*

Hope Cove [SX6640]

Hope & Anchor: Simple seaside inn, friendly
and comfortable, with good open fire, kind
efficient staff, good value food, well kept
Wadworths 6X, reasonably priced wines,
flagstone floor, no piped music; children and
dogs welcome in family room, games room
with pool; good views from tables outside,
bedrooms *(Geoffrey and Karen Berrill, LYM,
June and Ken Brooks)*

Horsebridge [SX3975]

☆ *Royal* [off A384 Tavistock—Launceston]:
Quiet slate-floored rooms, no music or
machines, interesting bric-a-brac and pictures,
no smoking side room, extra dining room, Bass,
Sharps Doom Bar, Wadworths 6X and guest
beers, farm cider, bar billiards, cribbage,
dominoes, tasty food from baguettes and baked
potatoes to steak; no children in evening, tables
on back terrace and in big garden *(Dennis
Jenkin, Joan and Michel Hooper-Immins,
LYM)*

Ide [SX9090]

Huntsman [High St]: Straightforward local
with well kept Ringwood and good value food
from baguettes to home-made hot dishes,
friendly staff *(John and Vivienne Rice)*

☆ *Poachers* [3 miles from M5 junction 31, via
A30; High St]: Good welcoming atmosphere,
inventive reasonably priced generous food inc
good fish choice, well kept Branscombe Vale
Branoc and Otter, reasonably priced house
wines, prompt friendly service, sofas and open
fire; attractively decorated bedrooms
*(J Thomson, Mrs M A French, John and
Vivienne Rice)*

Ideford [SX8977]

☆ *Royal Oak* [2 miles off A380]: Friendly, dark
and cosy unspoilt thatched and flagstoned
village local, vast and interesting collection of
mainly marine memorabilia from Nelson to
World War II, well kept Flowers IPA and
Original, log fire, maybe occasional
sandwiches; maybe a vociferous jack russell *(the
Didler, Phil and Sally Gorton, JP, PP)*

Ilsington [SX7876]

Carpenters Arms: Unspoilt 18th-c local next to
church in quiet village, friendly licensees,
wholesome cheap food, well kept Bass and
guest beers on handpump or tapped from the
cask, log fire, parlour off main public bar; no
music, good walks *(Beverley and Neil Gardner,
E G Parish, Phil and Sally Gorton)*

Instow [SS4730]

☆ *Boat House* [Marine Parade]: Recently
refurbished airy high-ceilinged bar with huge
tidal beach just across lane, big old-fashioned
nautical paintings on stripped stone wall, well
kept Bass, Flowers IPA and a guest beer,
popular food from sandwiches to steaks inc

plentiful fish, open fire, good friendly service, lively family bustle – children welcome; piped music *(R J Walden, Mrs L M Hardwick, Lyn and Geoff Hallchurch, Andy Marks, LYM, Eamonn and Natasha Skyrme)*

Kenn [SX9285]

☆ *Ley Arms* [signed off A380 just S of Exeter]: Extended thatched pub in quiet spot nr church, polished granite floor in attractive beamed public bar, plush black-panelled lounge with striking fireplace, good wines, Bass and Flowers, bar food, efficient service, sizeable smartish restaurant side; piped music, no smoking family room, games area *(Dr and Mrs A K Clarke, LYM)*

Kennford [SX9186]

Seven Stars: Friendly little village pub with well kept beer, farm cider, interesting choice of food *(Dr and Mrs A K Clarke)*

Kenton [SX9583]

Devon Arms [Fore St; A379 Exeter—Dawlish]: Comfortable 16th-c beamed bar with old farm tools, animal photographs and hunting trophies, sound good value food from good sandwiches and soup up, Bass, Scattor Rock Teign Valley Tipple and Wadworths 6X, friendly helpful service, dining area; small back garden with play area, aviary and caged rabbits; bedrooms with own bathrooms *(Dennis Jenkin, John Beeken)*

Dolphin [Fore St]: Attractive pub with old black range and carved oak counter in public bar, beams, pews and settles in alcovey dining area, soft lighting, generous food inc fresh veg, Weds carvery and good puddings, well kept ales such as Charles Wells Eagle, Worthington Best and bargain Otter, reasonably priced wines, efficient welcoming service, no music; pretty village *(David and Elizabeth Briggs, Canon Michael Bourdeaux)*

Kilmington [SY2797]

☆ *Old Inn* [A35]: Thatched pub with pleasant local atmosphere, small character polished-floor front bar (dogs allowed here), back lounge with leather armchairs by inglenook fire, good value food inc local fish and good Sun lunch, well kept Boddingtons, Flowers IPA, Wadworths 6X and Worthington BB, traditional games, small no smoking restaurant; children welcome, two gardens *(Ian Phillips, A D Marsh, LYM, M Joyner, Mr and Mrs A Craig, R T and J C Moggridge)*

Kingsbridge [SX7344]

☆ *Crabshell* [Embankment Rd, edge of town]: Lovely waterside position, charming when tide in, with big windows and tables out on the hard, wide choice of bar food inc good fresh lunchtime shrimp or crab sandwiches; hot food (ambitious, concentrating on very wide choice of local fish and shellfish) may be confined to upstairs restaurant, with good views; quick friendly staff, Bass and Worthington, good farm cider, warm fire *(Ken Flawn, Mr and Mrs T A Bryan, BB)*

Kingskerswell [SX8767]

☆ *Barn Owl* [Aller Mills; pub signed just off A380 Newton Abbot—Torquay]: 16th-c converted farmhouse, large panelled bar with

ornamental plaster ceiling, other softly lit rooms with low black beams, flagstones, stripped stone and inglenook fireplace, lots of sportsmen and celebrity pictures, hayloft with Arsenal display; good young staff, decent interesting food in bar and restaurant, well kept Bass, Courage Best and Cotleigh Tawny, no smoking area; piped music and SkyTV sports; picnic-sets in small sheltered garden, bedrooms in adjoining Holiday Express *(LYM, Bob and Ann Westbrook, Simon Collett-Jones, John and Vivienne Rice, Mr and Mrs C Roberts, Mike and Mary Carter, Meg and Colin Hamilton, Derek Allpass, Andrew Hodges)*

☆ *Bickley Mill* [Stoneycombe, on road from Abbotskerswell to Compton and Marldon]: Rambling beamed rooms with lots of copper and brass, log fire, wide choice of food from sandwiches or baguettes up, real ale; piped music; children welcome, tables in courtyard, subtropical-style hillside garden, refurbished bedrooms *(Richard and Margaret Peers, Andrew Hodges, LYM)*

Kingswear [SX8851]

Royal Dart [The Square]: Friendly pub in fine setting by ferry and Dart Valley Railway terminal (great view of Dartmouth from balcony – not always open), good food inc seafood in bar and upstairs restaurant, Bass *(David Carr, Peter Meister)*

Ship [Higher St]: Tall and attractive old inn with interesting décor, quiet atmosphere, well kept Bass, nice wines, friendly service; one table with Dart views, a couple outside *(I J and N K Buckmaster, Betsy and Peter Little, Mr and Mrs J French)*

Knowle [SY0582]

Britannia [nr Budleigh Salterton]: Cheerful simple local with friendly licensees, surprisingly good food, well kept Bass, low drinks prices, log fire *(Dr M E Wilson)*

Lee [SS4846]

☆ *Grampus* [signed off B3343/A361 W of Ilfracombe]: Attractive and welcoming 14th-c pub short stroll from sea, simple furnishings, wide range of good simple home-made food, well kept real ales, woodburner, pool in family room, decent piped music, dogs welcome; two bedrooms, lots of seats in quiet sheltered garden, superb coastal walks *(BB, Trevor and Lynda Smith)*

Lewdown [SX4486]

Royal Exchange: Welcoming, with plenty of atmosphere, friendly and helpful licensees, good simple food inc good value steaks, well kept Courage; bedrooms *(Dr and Mrs Nigel Holmes)*

Loddiswell [SX7148]

☆ *Loddiswell Inn*: Neatly kept old village pub, warm and comfortable, with friendly licensees, log fire, good choice of freshly made generous food from snacks to fresh fish and other hot dishes using local produce, two well kept ales *(Bryan Robinson)*

Longdown [SX8691]

☆ *Lamb*: Attractive stone-built pub smartened up by new landlord, open-plan bar with good choice of real ales inc Badger IPA, wide choice of enjoyable food from good sandwiches up, settees in front alcove, dining area; tables outside *(John and Vivienne Rice)*

Luppitt [ST1606]

Luppitt Inn [back roads N of Honiton]: Unspoilt little basic farmhouse pub, friendly chatty landlady who keeps it open because she (and her cats) like the company; one room with corner bar and one table, another with fireplace and not much else – maybe lots of locally made metal puzzles on trial, Otter (also local) tapped from the cask, no food or music, lavatories across the yard; a real throwback, may be cl some lunchtimes *(the Didler, JP, PP)*

Luton [SX9076]

Elizabethan [Haldon Moor]: Popular low-beamed pub with nice atmosphere, huge range of good well presented food inc lots of pies and fresh local fish, luscious puddings (esp toffee and vanilla cheesecake), good choice of well kept beer and of reasonably priced house wines, friendly efficient staff *(L G Owen)*

Lydford [SX5184]

☆ *Dartmoor Inn* [A386]: Fair-sized dining pub (not a place for just a drink) with good creative food from good value ploughman's and well filled baguettes (bar food stops at 2 sharp) to appealing set meals, several peaceful rooms, attractive Shaker-style décor, well kept Bass and Fullers London Pride, good wines, helpful polite staff, good log fire, pool room; bedrooms, track straight up on to moor; cl Sun night, Mon *(Graham Brooks, Jacquie and Jim Jones, Mike Gorton)*

Lympstone [SX9984]

☆ *Globe* [off A376 N of Exmouth; The Strand]: Roomy dining area and bar, sensibly priced food from sandwiches to fresh fish, Bass, Flowers IPA and decent house wines, helpful friendly staff; children welcome, some live entertainment, open all day in summer *(LYM, John Wooll, Jacquie and Jim Jones, Chris Parsons, Dr M E Wilson, Canon Michael Bourdeaux, Basil Minson)*

Redwing [Church Rd]: Friendly two-bar local with Branscombe Vale Branoc, Greene King Abbot, Ushers and Charles Wells Bombardier, local farm ciders, good value food inc lots of local fish and good puddings, helpful efficient staff, small no smoking dining area with wild flowers; discreet piped music, live jazz Tues; pretty garden, unspoilt village with shore walks *(Peter Burton, John Beeken)*

Saddlers Arms [Exmouth Rd]: Useful good value roadside Country Carvery, warm and spacious, with Scottish Courage ales, friendly service; tables and play area in garden *(Geoffrey Hart)*

Lynmouth [SS7249]

☆ *Rising Sun* [Mars Hill, by harbour]: Wonderful position overlooking harbour, good immaculate bedrooms (one very small) in cottagey old thatched terrace stepped up hill; concentration on the hotel side and the attractive cosy no smoking restaurant (where residents come first – no supper bookings taken for others till 6.30), but they normally have well kept ales such as Courage Directors, Exmoor Fox and

Theakstons XB, good lunchtime bar food and a nice dog called Sophie; bedrooms, charming gardens up behind, children may be allowed in eating areas *(Mr and Mrs Matt Binns, Peter and Audrey Dowsett, Sally Anne and Peter Goodale, LYM, Keith and Margaret Kettell, Richard Rand, Colin Parker)*

Lynton [SS7249]

Hunters [Martinhoe, Heddon's Gate – which is well signed off A39 W of Lynton]: Popular for its glorious valley position in terrific NT walking country, enjoyable freshly prepared food from soup and baguettes to local seafood (may be a wait when crowded), cheerful young staff, real ale; garden with peacocks *(Diana Brumfit)*

Maidencombe [SX9268]

Thatched Tavern [Steep Hill]: Spotless hugely extended three-level thatched pub with lovely coastal views, well kept Bass, big family room, no smoking areas, well priced food inc local fish (can be a wait), restaurant; children allowed, nice garden with small thatched huts (dogs allowed out here but not in pub); pleasant bedrooms in annexe, good breakfast; small attractive village above small beach *(Bob and Ann Westbrook, P Rome)*

Marsh [ST2510]

☆ *Flintlock* [signed off A303 Ilminster—Honiton]: Comfortable 17th-c dining pub popular for wide choice of good varied reasonably priced food inc well cooked Sun lunches, friendly licensees, good range of well kept real ale and cider, nice décor with armoury and horsebrasses *(Brian and Bett Cox, D and M T Ayres-Regan)*

Mary Tavy [SX5079]

Royal Standard: Friendly new licensees in spotlessly comfortable traditional pub with lounge at one end and bar at the other, well kept Otter and guest beers, good generous home-made bar food inc good pies and pasties, open fire; dogs welcome *(Dr and Mrs Nigel Holmes, Robert and Sarah Lee, Jeanne and Paul Silvestri)*

Meavy [SX5467]

☆ *Royal Oak* [off B3212 E of Yelverton]: Pews, red plush banquettes, old agricultural prints and church pictures (the pub's owned by the parish), usual bar food from lunchtime sandwiches or baguettes up, well kept Bass, Princetown IPA and Jail Ale and a guest beer, friendly service, big fireplace in flagstoned locals' bar with dominoes and euchre; piped music; picnic-sets outside or on the green, no children *(Miss J E Winsor, Dennis Jenkin, LYM, David Rule)*

Merrivale [SX5475]

☆ *Dartmoor Inn* [B3357, 4 miles E of Tavistock]: Refurbished yet unchanging pub in tranquil spot with high Dartmoor views; generous reasonably priced lunchtime food inc good ploughman's, well kept ales inc Bass, Stones and one labelled for the pub, good choice of country wines, water from their 36-metre (120-ft) deep well, open fire, tables outside – very popular summer evenings; good walks, nr bronze-age hut circles, stone rows and pretty river *(Mayur Shah)*

Miltoncombe [SX4865]

☆ *Who'd A Thought It* [village signed off A386 S of Yelverton]: Attractive 16th-c black-panelled bar with interesting bric-a-brac, woodburner, barrel seats and high-backed winged settles, separate lounge, big dining conservatory with Plymouth Sound views, decent usual food, well kept Blackawton, Cornish Rebellion, Exmoor, Princetown Jail and Wadworths 6X; piped music, tables may be reserved for coach parties; children welcome, well planted garden with water feature (flaming torches may light your way from the car park on summer nights), more tables out in front; folk club Sun *(Ted George, LYM)*

Molland [SS8028]

London: Unspoilt and basic dim-lit Exmoor-edge pub, well worth tackling the narrow country lanes to get there; Bass, Cotleigh and Exmoor tapped from casks behind bar, good farm cider, good value straightforward bar food inc children's meals in big dining room and cosy evening restaurant, log fire, welcoming landlord, upper-crust locals; nice views from small front garden, next to wonderfully untouched church *(Shaun Pinchbeck, Richard and Anne Ansell)*

Morchard Bishop [SS7707]

London [signed off A377 Crediton—Barnstaple]: Open-plan low-beamed 16th-c coaching inn, big carpeted red plush bar with woodburner in large fireplace, big helpings of good home-made food in bar or small dining room, friendly engaging service, real ales inc Fullers London Pride and Sharps Doom Bar, pool, darts and skittles *(C J Fletcher, Peter Craske)*

Moretonhampstead [SX7585]

Bell [Cross St]: Friendly landlord, good coffee *(Ann and Colin Hunt)*

Plymouth [Court St]: Popular local, Bass and reasonably priced local ales, good mix of ages *(Brian and Genie Smart)*

Mortehoe [SS4545]

☆ *Chichester Arms* [off A361 Ilfracombe—Braunton]: Warmly welcoming young staff, lots of old village prints in busy plush and leatherette panelled lounge and comfortable no smoking dining room, wide choice of good value generous food (not Sun night or Mon, in winter, and not always available other days then) cooked by landlord inc local fish and meat and good veg and puddings, well kept ales inc local Barum Original, John Smiths and Ushers Best, reasonably priced wine, speedy service even on crowded evenings; pubby locals' bar with darts and pool, no piped music; skittle alley and games machines in summer children's room, tables out in front and in small garden, good walks *(Roger S Kiddier, Keith and Margaret Kettell, Gordon Stevenson, Pat and Tony Martin, Peter and Audrey Dowsett)*

☆ *Ship Aground* [signed off A361 Ilfracombe—Braunton]: Welcoming open-plan village pub with big family room, well kept Cotleigh ales, Hancock's cider in summer, decent wine, good selection of inexpensive bar food inc good

pizzas, big log fires, friendly service; massive rustic furnishings, interesting nautical brassware, friendly cross-eyed cat; pool, skittles and other games, piped music may obtrude; tables on sheltered sunny terrace with good views; piped music; by interesting church, wonderful walking on nearby coast footpath *(Mr and Mrs I Bennett, Peter and Audrey Dowsett, Richard Fendick, LYM)*

Smugglers Rest: Hotel with real ale such as Greene King Old Speckled Hen, friendly staff and good choice of generous inexpensive food in large plain bar; piped music, pool, fruit machine; bedrooms *(Peter and Audrey Dowsett)*

Muddiford [SS5638]

Muddiford Inn [B3230 Barnstaple—Ilfracombe]: Newly reopened family pub with friendly landlord, big garden, pleasant separate dining area, good range of inexpensive generous food inc children's helpings, Tetleys, open fire; may be piped music, renovations in the pipeline; garden with play area, handy for Marwood Gardens *(Peter and Audrey Dowsett)*

Newton Abbot [SX8671]

☆ *Olde Cider Bar* [East St]: Heady atmosphere fuelled by casks of eight interesting farm ciders and a couple of perries, with more in bottles, in unusual basic cider house, no-nonsense dark stools, barrel seats and wall benches, flagstones and bare boards, pre-war-style décor; good country wines, baguettes, heated pies and venison pasties etc, very low prices; small games room with machines *(JP, PP, Jonathan Smith, the Didler, Catherine Pitt)*

Newton Poppleford [SY0889]

Cannon [High St]: Interesting maritime décor, pleasant service, reasonably priced food inc speciality steaks and lunchtime bargain *(Pat and Robert Watt)*

Newton Tracey [SS5226]

Hunters [5 miles S of Barnstaple on B3232 to Torrington]: Friendly 15th-c pub with massive beams, four well kept ales, decent wines and malt whiskies, log fire, enjoyable food inc huge puddings and children's dishes, evening restaurant; skittle alley/games room, juke box and machines; tables outside, play area *(Andy Marks, Peter Bakker)*

North Bovey [SX7483]

☆ *Ring of Bells* [off A382/B3212 SW of Moretonhampstead]: Attractive bulgy-walled 13th-c thatched inn, well kept real ales such as Devonshire IPA and St Austell HSD, Gray's farm cider, games etc, good log fire, bar food inc good ploughman's and freshly prepared specials, restaurant; seats out by lovely tree-covered village green below Dartmoor; big bedrooms with four-posters – Dolly Parton stayed here *(John Crafts, LYM, Esther and John Sprinkle, Nick Lawless)*

North Molton [SS7933]

Sportsmans [Sandyway Cross, up towards Withypool]: Remote yet popular genuine country local fairly handy for Landacre beauty spot, with well kept Exmoor tapped from the cask, friendly atmosphere, good generous food *(Peter and Audrey Dowsett, Francis Johnston)*

Okehampton [SX5895]

Plymouth [West St]: Pretty pub with friendly helpful staff, local-feel bar (can be smoky) with surprisingly enterprising food, well kept mainly local ales tapped from the cask (May and Nov beer festivals), no smoking area, provision for children; open all day wknds *(R J Walden, Derek Allpass)*

Otterton [SY0885]

Kings Arms [Fore St]: Lively and comfortable open-plan family dining pub in charming village by Ladram Bay, good value straightforward home-made food from good hefty sandwiches and baked potatoes up inc children's helpings, well kept Flowers IPA and Otter, good service, TV and darts in lounge; dogs welcome, good skittle alley doubling as family room; bedrooms, beautiful evening view from picnic-sets in good-sized attractive back garden with play area *(Pat and Robert Watt, Richard Fendick, Chris Parsons, Dr P F A Watkins, A C and E Johnson, P A Legon)*

Paignton [SX8960]

Embassy [Colin Rd]: Welcoming licensees, pleasant staff, well kept beer, good home-made food inc daily fresh local fish and good value Sun lunch, nightly family holiday entertainment for the more mature; pretty floral displays, tables outside, handy for beach *(anon)*

Isaac Merritt [Torquay Rd]: Spacious open-plan Wetherspoons conversion of former shopping arcade, worth knowing for its low-priced food and drink all day; no music, no smoking area *(Andrew Hodges)*

Lime Tree [Dartmouth Rd]: Large L-shaped carpeted bar, comfortable seating, part panelling, red wallpaper, well kept Courage Directors, friendly staff, usual food (just three-course roast meals on Sun), no smoking area; open all day *(Mr and Mrs C Roberts)*

Ship [Manor Rd, Preston]: Large yet homely mock-Tudor pub with comfortable furnishings inc leather settees, soft lighting, well kept Bass and Worthington from very long bar, good generous low-priced food (dining areas on three floors), efficient service; a minute's walk from Preston beach *(Mr and Mrs C Roberts, Jo Miller)*

Parracombe [SS6644]

☆ *Fox & Goose* [off A39 Blackmoor Gate—Lynton]: Rambling pub with interesting photographs and lots of taxidermy, warmly welcoming helpful licensees, wide range of well priced freshly made good food using local ingredients, from sandwiches and hot filled rolls to barbecued fish steaks, well kept local ales, decent wines; children welcome *(David Jones, Miss S J Ebbutt, Miss E Holmes, P Hill)*

Plymouth [SX4755]

China House [Sutton Harbour, via Sutton Rd off Exeter St (A374)]: Conversion of Plymouth's oldest warehouse, listed for its super views day and night over harbour and Barbican; picnic-sets and benches on heated verandah, lofty spacious bar partitioned into smaller booth-like areas, great beams and flagstones, bare slate and stone walls, lots of nets, kegs and fishing gear – even a clinker-built boat; good log fire, well kept Bass, food from filled baguettes up; fruit machine, piped music; open all day from noon *(Lyn and Geoff Hallchurch, Shirley Mackenzie, Esther and John Sprinkle, B J Harding, LYM, Keith and Katy Stevens)*

Dolphin [Barbican]: Lively unpretentious local, good range of beers inc particularly well kept Bass and Worthington Dark tapped from the cask, coal fire; colourful green and orange décor, Beryl Cook paintings inc one of the friendly landlord; open all day *(JP, PP)*

Notte [Notte St]: Thriving atmosphere, single long bar (can get crowded) with barrel seats below windows, well kept Bass and Wadworths 6X tapped from the cask, wide range of enjoyable food inc seafood, polite welcoming service; free 50s/60s juke box *(Steve Whalley, Keith and Katy Stevens)*

Sippers [West Hoe Rd/Millbay Rd]: Small cleverly rebuilt Whitbreads pub, three levels, interesting nautical theme, cheerful polite young staff, well kept beer, good value food (not Mon night), triangular snooker table and bar billiards; open all day, shrub-lined garden with tables *(Keith and Katy Stevens, George Little, E G Parish)*

Thistle Park [Commercial Rd]: Welcoming pub nr National Maritime Aquarium, good range of well kept beers inc some from next-door Sutton brewery, tasty straightforward food all day, friendly landlady, interesting décor, children welcome; open all day, live music wknds *(the Didler, JP, PP)*

Portgate [SX4185]

☆ *Harris Arms* [Launceston Rd (old A30)]: Warmly friendly, bright and comfortable, good food inc superb South Devon steaks and mixed grill, well kept Bass and guest ales such as Sharps Doom Bar, prompt informal service with good attention to detail, wonderful view from dining room *(Dr and Mrs Nigel Holmes, Mr and Mrs Frank Greenwood, John and Sarah Perry)*

Postbridge [SX6579]

East Dart [B3212]: Central Dartmoor hotel by pretty river, cheery open-plan bar largely given over to promptly served usual food from filled rolls up, hunting murals and horse tack, friendly helpful service, well kept St Austell Tinners, Gray's cider, good fire, pool room; children welcome; bedrooms, some 30 miles of fishing *(John Brightley, Dennis Jenkin, BB)*

Prixford [SS5436]

New Ring o' Bells: Smart pub with good food choice, coal-effect gas fires; piped music may obtrude *(Peter and Audrey Dowsett)*

Ringmore [SX6545]

☆ *Journeys End* [signed off B3392 at Pickwick Inn, St Anns Chapel, nr Bigbury; best to park up opp church]: Atmospheric if unsmart old village inn with character panelled lounge, well kept changing ales such as Adnams Broadside, Badger Tanglefoot, Exmoor and Otter, some tapped from casks in back room, local farm cider, log fires; varied interesting food inc good fresh fish (helpful about special diets), friendly locals and staff, pleasant big terraced garden, sunny back add-on dining conservatory; children in basic family room; attractive setting nr thatched cottages, not far from the sea; bedrooms antique but comfortable and well equipped *(Mike and Wena Stevenson, Rona Murdoch, JP, PP, LYM, RB, the Didler, Steve Pocock, Dr R A Smye, Carol Ackroyd, Peter McNamara)*

Rockbeare [SY0295]

☆ *Jack in the Green* [off A30 bypass]: Emphasis on its two dining areas, good varied food, local fish and game, good vegetarian choice, delicious puddings, competitive prices, log fire in snug bar, well kept Bass, Cotleigh Tawny and Otter, interesting good value wines by the glass, friendly landlord, prompt service; tables out in courtyard, skittle alley *(Dr M E Wilson, Oliver and Sue Rowell, E V M Whiteway, J M and P M Carver, Mrs M A French, Lucien, Mrs Sylvia Elcoate, Betty Cloke)*

Salcombe [SX7338]

Fortescue [Union St, end of Fore St]: Sizeable five-room pub nr harbour, popular and welcoming, nautical theme throughout, lots of old local black and white shipping pictures, well kept Bass and Wadworths 6X, reliable food, quick pleasant service, relaxing atmosphere, good woodburner, big games room, no piped music; restaurant, terrace *(B J Harding, Keith and Katy Stevens)*

Victoria [Fore St]: Well placed, smartly attractive and tidy yet unpretentious, with bare-boards bar, comfortable lounge, cosy stone-walled dining room downstairs, copious imaginative good food cooked to order, jovial landlord and friendly courteous service, Bass, Courage and Worthington; maybe unobtrusive piped music, segregated children's room; bedrooms, terrace garden *(John Brightley)*

Sampford Peverell [ST0214]

☆ *Globe* [a mile from M5 junction 27, village signed from Tiverton turn-off; Lower Town]: Neat, spacious and comfortable, good range of generous home-made food from sandwiches to steaks inc fish and popular Sun lunch, well kept Bass and local guest beers; children allowed in eating area and family room, piped music, games in public bar, pool room, skittle alley; tables out in front, open all day; *(LYM, Dr and Mrs A K Clarke)*

Sandy Gate [SX9691]

Blue Ball [nr M5 junction 30, on Topsham rd]: Dining pub with limited but good rather upmarket food, good helpings, beams, old wood and tile floors, lovely settles, well kept Bass and well priced wine, no smoking section, hard-working young staff; good gardens inc good play area *(John and Vivienne Rice, Dr M E Wilson)*

Sandy Park [SX7087]

☆ *Sandy Park Inn* [A382 S of Whiddon Down]: Thatched country local with old-fashioned small bar, stripped old tables, built-in high-backed wall seats, big black iron fireplace, good food with copious veg here or in small cosy dining room, friendly staff, well kept ales such as Cotleigh Tawny, Hardy Country and Wadworths 6X, decent wines and farm cider; children in eating

area; simple clean bedrooms *(LYM, Philip Crawford, Mark Percy, Lesley Mayoh)*

Shaldon [SX9372]

☆ *Ferryboat* [Fore St]: Cosy and quaint little waterside pub, basic but comfortable, long low-ceilinged bar overlooking estuary with Teignmouth ferry and lots of boats, welcoming landlord and staff, Dartmoor, Greene King IPA and Old Speckled Hen, big helpings of good value varied home-made food, open fires, seafaring artefacts; tables on small sunny terrace across narrow road by sandy beach *(David Carr, John Beeken)*

London [The Green]: Friendly village pub with enjoyable food inc good crab baguettes, kind staff and well kept beer; children welcome, pretty waterside village *(Meg and Colin Hamilton)*

Shebbear [SS4409]

☆ *Devils Stone Inn* [off A3072 or A388 NE of Holsworthy]: Welcoming 16th-c tucked-away village pub with big oak-beamed bar, three other rooms, cheerful landlord, good range of beers, sensible food at sensible prices with bargain OAP helpings and children's dishes, helpful service, small restaurant area with huge inglenook log fire, large amiable pub dogs (visiting dogs welcome), family room; handy for Tarka Trail; garden with play area, simple bedrooms *(Alan and Heather Jacques, George Atkinson, C P Scott-Malden, LYM)*

Shiphay [SX8865]

☆ *Devon Dumpling* [Shiphay Lane, off A380/A3022 NW edge of Torquay]: Open-plan farmhouse pub, comfortable and clean, with plenty of space inc atmospheric cosy corners, aquarium and lots of decorations at Christmas; popular locally for good value generous straightforward food, pudding display by bar, well kept Boddingtons, Greene King Ruddles, Marstons Pedigree and Wadworths 6X, quick cheerful service; children in plainer upper barn loft, occasional live music, no dogs inside *(Mr and Mrs C Roberts)*

Sidbury [SY1595]

☆ *Hare & Hounds* [Putts Corner; A375 towards Honiton, crossroads with B3174]: Much-extended oak-panelled pub, roomy and relaxed lounge bar, wood-and-tiles tap room, two fine old chesterfields and more usual furnishings, stuffed birds, huge log fire; well kept changing ales such as Ash Vine, Coach House Dick Turpin, Fullers London Pride and two from Otter, very friendly staff, wide choice of quick inexpensive well cooked food inc perfect veg in bars and restaurant with popular Sun carvery; children's room, pool in side room, another with giant sports TV; big garden with play area, good views of valley below *(Peter and Audrey Dowsett, Dr M E Wilson, Pat and Dick Warwick, Michael Buchanan)*

Sidford [SY1390]

Rising Sun [School St]: Unpretentious and uncrowded two-bar village pub, friendly staff, three or four real ales, small menu inc genuine home cooking using local produce (like the blackberries they pick for the crumble) *(Bryan Robinson)*

Sidmouth [SY1089]

Bowd [junction B3176/A3052]: Big thatched family dining pub with sizeable garden, efficient food operation, Bass and Flowers Original, friendly staff, indoor and separate outdoor play areas; open all day *(Mrs Sylvia Elcoate, Michael Buchanan, LYM, Paul R White)*

☆ *Old Ship* [Old Fore St]: Partly 14th-c, with low beams, mellow black woodwork and panelling, sailing ship prints, good but not cheap food from open sandwiches to local fish, well kept Flowers Original, Wadworths 6X and a guest such as Youngs, prompt courteous service even when busy, friendly atmosphere; close-set tables but roomier raftered upstairs bar with family room, dogs allowed; in pedestrian zone just moments from the sea (note that around here parking is limited to 30 mins) *(John Beeken, BB, M Joyner, Chris Parsons, Chris Glasson)*

Silverton [SS9502]

☆ *Three Tuns* [Exeter Rd]: Wide choice of well prepared food inc fine vegetarian dishes in 17th-c or older inn's old-fashioned beamed bars or cosy restaurant (where children welcome), comfortable settees and period furniture, friendly obliging licensees, well kept local ales; tables in pretty inner courtyard, good value up-to-date bedrooms, good breakfast; handy for Killerton *(Sheila and Phil Stubbs)*

South Molton [SS7125]

Mill [off A361 at Bish Mill roundabout]: Neatly kept, with decent food inc children's, evening casseroles and steaks, well kept Cotleigh and guest ales, big games room (children allowed there and in dining room); pretty garden and walled terrace; cl Weds *(Mr and Mrs Kirkham, Mr and Mrs Pollock, Andy Marks)*

St Budeaux [SX4358]

Royal Albert Bridge [Saltash Passage]: 18th-c coaching inn in spectacular waterside spot with great Tamar and bridge views, lots of brassware and ship pictures, blazing log fire, Courage ale, good food range inc nice sandwiches, quick friendly and attentive service; tables out by water *(George Atkinson)*

Starcross [SX9781]

☆ *Atmospheric Railway* [The Strand]: Named for Brunel's experimental 1830s vacuum-powered steam railway here, with masses of intriguing associated memorabilia, prints and signs; Bass and Boddingtons, good farm cider, good choice of home-made food, log fire, family room, skittle alley; garden with tables and play area *(BB, C Galloway, Meg and Colin Hamilton)*

Sticklepath [SX6494]

Devonshire [off A30 at Whiddon Down or Okehampton]: Well used 16th-c thatched village inn next to foundry museum, easy-going low-beamed slate-floored bar with big log fire, longcase clock and friendly old furnishings, sofa in small snug, well kept St Austell ales tapped from the cask, farm cider, informal welcoming service, magazines to read, sandwiches, bookable Sun lunches and evening meals, hopeful pub dog, games room with piano and bar billiards; lively folk night 1st Sun in month, open all day Fri/Sat, bedrooms *(Nick Lawless,*

the Didler, JP, PP, Phil and Sally Gorton, LYM)

Stoke Fleming [SX8648]

Endsleigh [New Rd (A379)]: Relaxed atmosphere in comfortably smart modern bar of small hotel, good drinks range inc Shepherd Neame, newish owners doing good interesting food in seaview restaurant; roomy well equipped bedrooms *(G R Taylor)*

Stoke Gabriel [SX8457]

Castle [Barnhay]: Castle-shaped pub with big carpeted stripped-stone bar, real ales, low-priced food inc good choice of daily specials, friendly quick service *(Bryan Robinson)*

Stokeinteignhead [SX9170]

☆ *Chasers Arms*: Good food inc interesting dishes, imaginative veg and unusual puddings, in busy 16th-c thatched pub/restaurant (you can't go just for a drink, but they do bar snacks too and the style emulates a country pub); fine range of house wines, pleasant atmosphere, quick friendly service *(Richard and Margaret Peers, John and Marian Greenwood)*

Stokenham [SX8042]

☆ *Church House* [opp church, N of A379 towards Torcross]: Comfortable firmly run open-plan pub, hard-working landlord, good if not cheap food esp fresh local seafood, well kept ales inc Bass and Flowers Original, farm cider, good wines, no smoking dining room, unobtrusive piped music; front children's room with writing/drawing materials; attractive garden with enjoyably individual play area and fishpond *(I J and N K Buckmaster, Geoff and Tricia Alderman, Ruth and Paul Lawrence, LYM)*

Talaton [SY0699]

Talaton Inn [B3176 N of Ottery St Mary; off A30 at Fairmile]: Pretty outside, plainly modernised and spotless inside, new landladies doing good food from sandwiches and ploughman's up, pleasant service, Bass and local Otter Best *(Derek Harvey-Piper)*

Tavistock [SX4874]

Ordulph Arms [Pym St]: Large spacious bar with raised end dining area, good range of sensibly priced food, several real ales inc Flowers and local brews, friendly welcome *(M Joyner)*

Tedburn St Mary [SX8193]

☆ *Kings Arms* [off A30 W of Exeter]: Good choice of sensibly priced food (all day Sun) from sandwiches and interesting hot baguettes to unusual dishes in attractive old pub, open-plan but comfortable, with big log fire, beams and lots of brass, friendly welcome, well kept Bass, local farm cider, modern restaurant, end games area, children in eating area; bedrooms *(John and Vivienne Rice, LYM)*

Thorverton [SS9202]

☆ *Thorverton Arms*: Nicely appointed pub with wide range of well prepared bar food from sandwiches up inc children's, charming welcoming service, well kept Bass and Greene King Old Speckled Hen, good coffee, lots of country magazines, small restaurant; tables in flower-filled garden, pleasant village, enjoyable strolls by river *(Mrs Sylvia Elcoate)*

Thurlestone [SX6743]

Village Inn: Busy much refurbished pub owned by neighbouring smart hotel and emphasising wide food choice (cool cabinet, open kitchen behind servery, blackboards, etc); well kept Dartmoor, Palmers and Wadworths 6X, comfortable country-style furnishings, dividers forming alcoves; children and dogs catered for, darts, quiz nights, live music, handy for coast path *(Geoff and Tricia Alderman)*

Topsham [SX9688]

☆ *Globe* [Fore St; 2 miles from M5 junction 30]: Substantial traditional inn dating from 16th c, good solid furnishings and log fire in heavy-beamed bow-windowed bar, good interesting home-cooked food at reasonable prices, well kept Bass, Courage Best and Hancocks HB, decent reasonably priced wine, prompt friendly service, snug little dining lounge, good value separate restaurant, back extension; children in eating area, open all day; good value attractive bedrooms *(David Peakall, Andrew Woodgates, the Didler, LYM)*

☆ *Lighter* [Fore St]: Spacious and comfortably refurbished, with panelling and tall windows looking out over tidal flats, more intimate side room, well kept Badger Best, Tanglefoot and a beer brewed for the pub, friendly efficient staff, quickly served bar food inc local fish, open fire, good children's area; games machines, piped music; tables out in lovely spot on old quay, good value bedrooms *(Dr M E Wilson, Mike Tucker, Mrs Sylvia Elcoate, BB, David Carr, Charles Gysin, Hugh Roberts)*

Lord Nelson [High St]: Lots of sea prints and nautical memorabilia inc sails over big dining area, smaller side area up steps, wide choice of reasonably priced bar meals, very attentive friendly service, Bass and Flowers Original; maybe piped pop music *(the Didler, C J Farr, John Beeken)*

Steam Packet [Monmouth Hill]: Well priced bar food, several well kept ales, dark flagstones, scrubbed boards, panelling, stripped masonry, a lighter dining room; on boat-builders' quay *(the Didler, LYM)*

Torbryan [SX8266]

☆ *Old Church House* [most easily reached from A381 Newton Abbot—Totnes via Ipplepen]: Atmospheric early 15th-c inn by part-Saxon church, quaint bar on right with benches built into Tudor panelling, high-backed settle and big log fire, also rambling series of comfortable and discreetly lit lounges, one with a splendid inglenook fireplace; friendly helpful service, enjoyable food from soup and sandwiches through good one-price lunch board to guinea fowl, well kept Bass, Flowers IPA and Original, Marstons Pedigree, Wadworths 6X and a beer brewed for the pub, good choice of malt whiskies, decent wines; piped music; children welcome, well equipped bedrooms, roomy and immaculate *(Mr and Mrs Capp, Mrs Sylvia Elcoate, R T and J C Moggridge, LYM)*

Torquay [SX9265]

Cary Arms [Beach Rd]: Great sea and cliff views (it's reached by a dramatic drop into this secluded bay), cheerful service, decent straightforward food inc lots of sandwiches, well kept beers, pleasant piped music, tables on terrace; dogs and children welcome, bedrooms *(Beverley and Neil Gardner)*

Crown & Sceptre [Petitor Rd, St Marychurch]: Friendly two-bar local in 18th-c stone-built coaching inn, eight real ales inc guests, bar food, interesting naval memorabilia and chamber-pot collection, good-humoured landlord, jazz Tues and Sun, folk first Thurs of month, bands Sat *(the Didler, JP, PP)*

☆ *Hole in the Wall* [Park Lane, opp clock tower]: Ancient unpretentious low-beamed two-bar local nr harbour, consistently good value food, well kept Courage, Blackawton cider, friendly service, flagstones, lots of naval memorabilia, old local photographs, chamber-pots; open all day *(Joseph Cairns)*

London [Strand]: Vast Wetherspoons conversion of former NatWest bank overlooking harbour and marina, no smoking upper mezzanine bar, big local ship paintings and a couple of reproduction ship's figureheads, good value food all day, bargain coffee as well as usual real ales, no piped music; can be very busy *(George Atkinson, Andrew Hodges)*

Torrington [SS4919]

☆ *Black Horse* [High St]: Pretty twin-gabled inn dating from 15th c, overhanging upper storeys, beams hung with stirrups, solid furniture, oak bar counter, no smoking lounge with striking ancient black oak partition wall and a couple of attractive oak seats, oak-panelled restaurant with aquarium, enjoyable food inc OAP wkdy lunchtime bargains, well kept Courage Best and Directors and John Smiths and a changing guest beer, darts, shove-ha'penny, cribbage, dominoes; well reproduced piped music, friendly cat and dogs; open all day Sat, handy for RHS Rosemoor garden and Dartington Crystal *(D S Price, LYM)*

Totnes [SX8060]

King William IV [Fore St]: Warm and comfortably carpeted Victorian pub with refurbished settles and chairs in large open rooms, popular (esp with older people) for sensibly priced home-made food from sandwiches to bargain steak and huge mixed grill; Boddingtons, Flowers, Tetleys and Wadworths 6X, friendly service; bedrooms with own bathrooms *(Mr and Mrs C Roberts, C M Miles, J B Towers)*

Trusham [SX8582]

Cridford Inn [off B3193 NW of Chudleigh, just N of big ARC works]: Interesting 14th-c longhouse, Norman in parts, with Britain's oldest domestic window, lots of stripped stone, flagstones and stout timbers, pews and chapel chairs around kitchen and pub tables, big woodburner, well kept ales such as Scattor Rock Teign Valley, Charles Wells Bombardier and one brewed for the pub; usual food, cribbage, dominoes, Weds quiz night, children in no smoking eating area, piped music; tables out on raised front terrace *(John Wooll, Mrs Sylvia Elcoate, David Rule, LYM, Alan and Paula McCully)*

Turnchapel [SX4952]
☆ *Boringdon Arms* [off A379 via Plymstock and
Hooe; Boringdon Terr]: 18th-c pub at foot of
cliffs and built back into them, eight interesting
well kept ales such as Butcombe, Oakham JHB,
RCH Pitchfork and Sharps, farm cider, good
value freshly made food all day esp curries and
pies, cheerful landlord and welcoming staff,
roaring log fire in massive fireplace, RN, RM
and other nautical memorabilia, shelves of
bottled beers, occasional beer festivals; dogs
welcome, tables outside, shortish water-taxi
ride from central Plymouth; open all day,
reasonably priced bedrooms *(the Didler,
R J Walden, Dr B and Mrs P B Baker, JP, PP)*
New Inn [Boringdon Rd]: Friendly refurbished
waterside pub, great views across to Plymouth,
real ales such as Bass, Princetown Jail and
Sharps Doom Bar, wide choice of well priced
food inc local fish; piped music; open all day
wknds *(JP, PP)*

Ugborough [SX6755]
☆ *Ship* [off A3121 SE of Ivybridge]: Popular open-
plan dining pub extended from cosy 16th-c
flagstoned core, bright smartish bar, remarkably
wide choice of good restaurant food from lots
of fresh fish to ostrich, good fresh veg and tasty
puddings, good sandwiches too; well kept Bass
and Butcombe, tables outside *(B A Churley,
Mrs T A Bizat, Guy Vowles)*

Wembury [SX5349]
Odd Wheel [Knighton Hill]: Village pub with
largely home-made food from sandwiches to
seafood in big plush lounge, real ales inc
Courage, Princetown, Sutton and guest beers
tapped from the cask, traditional front games
bar; children's eating area, tiered garden with
play area, open all day Sat *(JP, PP)*

Westcott [ST0204]
Merry Harriers [B3181 S of Cullompton]:
Landlord cooks good wide-ranging food in bar
and (slightly higher price) attractive restaurant
inc fresh veg, delicious puddings; very
welcoming service by wife and daughter, big
log fire, good choice of beers and wines *(John
Close, Ken Flawn)*

Westleigh [SS4628]
☆ *Westleigh Inn* [½ mile off A39 Bideford—
Instow]: Excellent play area in big neat garden
overlooking Torridge estuary, inglenook log fire
and relaxed family atmosphere, food from
baguettes, baked potatoes and burgers up inc
children's meals and enjoyable Sun carvery,
well kept Bass, Courage Best, Marstons
Pedigree and Ushers Best; piped music and bar
billiards in one room, other no smoking; Tarka
Trail walks *(Mrs Jane Wyles, Richard Fendick,
Rita Horridge, LYM)*

Weston [ST1400]
Otter [signed off A30 at W end of Honiton
bypass]: Good log fire, heavy low beams,
candlelight, interesting mix of furnishings and
bric-a-brac, well kept Brains and Wadworths
6X, good value wines, usual food from
sandwiches up; children welcome – some toys
in second dining area, skittle alley, baby-
changing; tables on big lawn leading to River
Otter and its ducks and skipping-rocks, play

area *(Peter and Audrey Dowsett, N and S
Alcock, Esther and John Sprinkle, LYM,
E V M Whiteway)*

Whimple [SY0497]
☆ *New Fountain* [off A30 Exeter—Honiton;
Church Rd]: Attractive and civilised yet
extremely friendly beamed village pub with
cosy local atmosphere, good reasonably priced
food inc interesting dishes, well kept beers inc
Cotleigh and Teignworthy, woodburner *(LYM,
E V M Whiteway, Dr and Mrs A K Clarke)*
Thirsty Farmer: Large and rather grand (former
substantial private house), several smaller areas,
food from bar snacks to full meals, well kept
Whitbreads-related real ales, good service, log
fires, restaurant extension *(E V M Whiteway,
Dr and Mrs A K Clarke)*

Whitchurch [SX4972]
Whitchurch Inn [just S of Tavistock; Church
Hill]: Owned by the church, refurbished in
16th/17th-c style, good food and beer choice,
good wines *(Paul Redgrave, Jacquie and
Jim Jones)*

Widecombe [SX7176]
☆ *Old Inn* [B3387 W of Bovey Tracey]: Busy,
friendly and comfortable, with 14th-c
stonework, big log fires in both bars, olde-
worlde décor, some concentration on wide
choice of good value generous food (from well
filled granary rolls up) and prominent
restaurant area, well kept Courage and Ushers,
local farm cider, decent wines, good friendly
service, family room; in pretty moorland
village, very popular with tourist coaches; room
to dance on music nights, good big garden with
pleasant terrace; great walks – the one to or
from Grimspound gives spectacular views
*(LYM, Chris and Anna Rowley, Bob and Ann
Westbrook, Joy and Colin Rorke, Mark Percy,
Lesley Mayoh)*

Witheridge [SS8014]
Angel [The Square]: Airy and spacious, with
wide choice of good bar food esp sausages
(Bavarian chef), good drinks range, tea room
(Hazel Boundy)

Woodbury [SY0187]
☆ *White Hart* [3½ miles from M5 junction 30;
A376, then B3179; Church St]: Consistently
good value unpretentious local run by friendly
mother and son team, well kept Bass and
Worthington BB, decent wines, plain public
bar, comfortable quieter dining lounge, log fire;
attractive small walled garden with aviary,
skittle alley, nice spot by church in peaceful
village *(Dr M E Wilson)*

Woolacombe [SS4843]
Mill [Ossaborough rd, off B3343 (look for
flowerbed reading 'Mill Inn' on sharp bend 1½
miles E) and B3231]: Welcoming 17th-c
flagstoned former mill with chatty landlord,
interesting memorabilia, attractive layout; good
value no-nonsense food inc generous children's,
well kept Courage Directors, efficient friendly
service, large woodburner, pool table, children
welcome; tables in walled courtyard, play area
(Chris and Clare Wearne)

Wrafton [SS4935]
Williams Arms [A361 just SE of Braunton]:

Well run modernised thatched family dining pub giving children free rein, two big bars divided into several cosy areas, interesting wall hangings, wide bar food choice, unlimited self-service carvery in attractive separate restaurant, children's helpings, quick friendly helpful service, Bass and Courage, decent house wines; pool, darts, piped music, discreet TV; picnic-sets outside with play area and aviary *(Andy Marks, K R Harris)*

Yarcombe [ST2408]

Yarcombe Inn [A30 2 miles E of A303]: Attractive and welcoming 14th-c thatched local, good choice of generous food from popular hot open sandwiches and ploughman's up, cheerful licensee, separate dining room, nice little spotless front bar, well kept Dartmoor IPA; quiet piped music *(Ann and Colin Hunt, Dennis Jenkin)*

Yelverton [SX5267]

Rock [by roundabout on A386 half way between Plymouth and Tavistock]: Spacious extended pub with wide choice of food, friendly efficient service, good range of ales, ciders and wines, games room with big screen TV, good facilities for children; piped music; popular terrace with heaters, safe play area; open all day *(Jacquie and Jim Jones)*

Bedroom prices normally include full English breakfast, VAT and any inclusive service charge that we know of. Prices before the '/' are for single rooms, after for two people in double or twin (B includes a private bath, S a private shower). If there is no '/', the prices are only for twin or double rooms (as far as we know there are no singles). If there is no B or S, as far as we know no rooms have private facilities.

Dorset

New main entries this year are the Museum at Farnham (newly opened after refurbishment by top-notch licensees, will be a real star), the Saxon Arms at Stratton (a traditional thatched pub, but in fact brand new – another place with first-class hands at the helm), the Swan at Sturminster Newton (nice old coaching inn, very good new licensees here too), and, back in the Guide after a break, the well run Manor Hotel at West Bexington (yes it is a hotel, but its cellar bar is a cheerful holiday place). By contrast, five pubs here have been in all 20 editions of the Guide, ever since it started: the delightfully placed Spyway at Askerswell, the very traditional old Fox in Corfe Castle, the handsome Fleur-de-Lys at Cranborne (changing hands just as this edition went to press; fingers crossed for the future), the Pilot Boat in Lyme Regis (a popular food place), and the Shave Cross Inn (doing well under new licensees). Other pubs to watch here are the Anchor at Burton Bradstock (gaining a Food Award this year for its fresh fish), the Royal Oak in Cerne Abbas (enthusiastic new licensees also boosting local fresh fish, as well as making other improvements), the Anchor near Chideock (a really cheerful seaside pub), the New Inn at Church Knowle (nice to prowl around the cellar choosing your wine), the Fox at Corscombe (delightful food in charming surroundings), the Blackmore Vale in Marnhull (good value food including OAP bargains), the Langton Arms at Tarrant Monkton (good all round, a readers' favourite), and the gloriously unspoilt Square & Compass at Worth Matravers. From among all these, the Fox at Corscombe stands out as our Dorset Dining Pub of the Year. In the Lucky Dip at the end of the chapter, current pubs for the notebook are the Drovers at Gussage All Saints, Scott Arms at Kingston, White Horse at Litton Cheney, Loders Arms at Loders, Marquis of Lorne at Nettlecombe, Smugglers at Osmington Mills, Piddle at Piddletrenthide, Cricketers at Shroton, New Inn at Stoke Abbott, Greyhound at Sydling St Nicholas, Riverhouse at Upwey and Red Lion in Weymouth (all already inspected and approved by us). Drinks prices in the county are around the national average.

ANSTY ST7603 Map 2

Fox 🛏

Village well signposted in the maze of narrow lanes NW of Milton Abbas; pub signposted locally

This was once the home of Charles Hall who founded the Ansty Brewery in 1777. His granddaughter later married the Ansty head brewer who became a partner in the firm, thus forming Hall and Woodhouse. To this day Hall and Woodhouse (now trading under the name of Badger) have remained an independent family brewer and still own this building which actually became an inn in 1915. It's in a peaceful country spot and attracts a good mix of walkers, cyclists and locals who enjoy its pleasantly relaxed atmosphere. The carefully decorated high-ceilinged main bar has interesting photographs and pictures of the family history, patterned carpets, toby jugs, and of course, very well kept Badger Best and Tanglefoot on handpump; also eight wines by the glass. Another part has pool and a TV; piped music. Good, interesting bar food includes home-made soup or glazed goats cheese with home-dried tomatoes with a fresh herb dressing (£3.95), chicken liver parfait with toasted brioche and home-made chutney (£4.25), baguettes (£4.95), a medley of local sausages with roast onion gravy (£6.25), crispy cod in home-made beer batter (£8.95; very popular), fresh egg and spinach pasta with a parmesan and plum tomato sauce (£7.95), braised lamb shank on olive oil mash and roasted mediterranean vegetables (£8.95), daily specials such as bass with stir-fried vegetables or escalope of pork with fresh thyme and port jus (£7.95), and confit of aromatic duck leg with soy and sesame dressing (£9.95), puddings like orange and treacle tart, sticky toffee pudding or cheesecakes (£3.95), and a Sunday carvery with five roasts (£8.95 one course, £14.85 three courses). This is a nice place to stay. *(Recommended by Mrs June Victor, WHBM, Diana Brumfit)*

Badger ~ Tenants Philip and Shirley Scott ~ Real ale ~ Bar food (12-3, 6.30-9.30) ~ Restaurant ~ (01258) 880328 ~ Children in restaurant ~ Open 11-11.30; 12-11 Sun ~ Bedrooms: £70S(£45B)/£70B

ASKERSWELL SY5292 Map 2

Spyway ★ ♀

Village signposted N of A35 Bridport—Dorchester; inn signposted locally; OS Sheet 194 map reference 529933

The delightfully unspoilt little rooms at this simple country inn are cosily filled with old-fashioned high-backed settles, cushioned wall and window seats, and a vast collection of china teacups, harness and a milkmaid's yoke. The no smoking dining area has old oak beams and timber uprights, bright red chequered table cloths, and blue and white china. Promptly served reasonably priced bar food includes home-made soup (£3.75), several different ploughman's such as hot sausage and tomato pickle or home-cooked ham (from £4.50), home-made pies like steak and kidney, fish or chicken and mushroom (£4.95), casseroles, curries or chilli (from £5), steaks (from £7.50), and home-made puddings (£2.50). Very well kept Adnams, Branscombe Vale Branoc and Greene King Abbot and IPA on handpump, quite a collection of country wines, and 40 whiskies. Eggardon Hill, which the pub's steep lane leads up, is one of the highest in the region and there are marvellous views of the downs and to the coast from the back terrace and gardens (where you can eat on warm days). There are pleasant nearby walks along the paths and bridleways. *(Recommended by Ian Phillips, Dr and Mrs Nigel Holmes, Di and Mike Gillam, Paul R White, W W Burke, A K Day, Basil Minson, Denis and Dorothy Evans)*

Free house ~ Licensee Allan Dodds ~ Real ale ~ Bar food ~ Restaurant ~ (01308) 485250 ~ Children in restaurant and family room ~ Open 11-11; 11-3, 6-11 Sat; 12-3 Sun; closed Sun evening, Mon ~ Bedrooms: /£52S

BRIDPORT SY4692 Map 1

George

South St

This delightful Georgian house is a jolly good town pub with an enjoyable mix of customers. The two sizeable bars are divided by a coloured tiled hallway, and one is served by a hatch from the main lounge. There are nicely spaced old dining tables, country seats and wheelback chairs, big rugs on tiled floors, a mahogany bar counter, fresh flowers, and a winter log fire. Well kept Palmers IPA and Dorset Gold on handpump, and a decent wine list. Bar food includes sandwiches (from £2.75), quiche or home-made chicken liver or roasted trout and almond pâté (£4.50), vegetarian curry (£4.95) tagliatelle with tomato, blue cheese and mozzarella sauce or spinach, bacon and potato cakes or avocado and bacon salad (£5.25) and fresh plaice or haddock (£6.50). *(Recommended by DAV, Ian Phillips, Jean and Douglas Troup)*

Palmers ~ Tenants Jacqueline King and Ann Halliwell ~ Real ale ~ Bar food (breakfast only on Sun) ~ (01308) 423187 ~ Children in family room ~ Open 11-11(8.30am for coffee); 12-10.30(9.30am for coffee) Sun

BURTON BRADSTOCK SY4889 Map 1
Anchor 🍴

B3157 SE of Bridport

A real treat at this bustling little seafood pub – the sort of place that people go out of their way for – is the shellfish platter (£45 for two), and there are plenty more very good fresh fish dishes to choose from: Shetland mussels (£12.95), salmon (£13.95), scallops (£14.95), cod in parma ham (£15.95), brill (£17.95) and lobster thermidor (£24). Other dishes include peppered pork loin or lamb shanks (£12.95) and duck (£13.95). There's an additional lunchtime snack menu with lighter dishes such as soup (£3.95), steak and mushroom baguette (£4.95) and baked ham and egg, mackerel or salmon fishcakes (£6.95); puddings (£3.95). It's best to book well ahead at weekends. The lounge bar has pink plush cushioned wall seats and some fishy décor, and there's a public bar with big windows, more cushioned seats, usually a good crowd of locals and well kept Gibbs Mew Bishops Tipple, and Ushers Best and Spring Fever on handpump; the Scottish landlord keeps over 40 malt whiskies; darts, table skittles, bar billiards, TV, shove-ha'penny, cribbage and dominoes. The restaurant is no smoking. This is an attractive village. *(Recommended by Basil Minson, Brett Muldoon, Philip Bardswell)*

InnSpired ~ Lease J R Plunkett ~ Real ale ~ Bar food (till 9.30) ~ Restaurant ~ (01308) 897228 ~ Children in eating area of bar and restaurant ~ Open 11-3.30, 6-11; 11-11 Sat; 12-10.30 Sun

CERNE ABBAS ST6601 Map 2
New Inn 🛏

14 Long Street

Built as a guest house for the nearby Benedictine abbey, this stone-roofed old building then became a coaching inn in the mid 16th c. You'll still find the old pump and mounting block in the coachyard, behind which there is a big sheltered lawn with tables and a good play area. The comfortably relaxed L-shaped lounge bar has oak beams in its high ceiling, gleaming horsebrasses round a stone fireplace and seats in the stone-mullioned windows with a fine view down the main street of the attractive stone-built village. Good bar food includes home-made soup (£2.75), whitebait or Scottish smoked salmon (£4.20), ploughman's (£4.95), cod or plaice fillet (£5.75), steak or game pie (£6.95), venison casserole (£7.20), stuffed trout (£8.25) and duck breast (£9.65); the dining room is no smoking. Well kept Hardy Country, Royal Oak and Three Valleys on handpump and several malt whiskies; piped music. There are several walks from the village including walks up and around the prehistoric Cerne Abbas Giant chalk carving to nearby villages. *(Recommended by Prof Kenneth Surin, Alan and Hillie Johnson, Joan and Michel Hooper-Immins, JP, PP, Esther and John Sprinkle, Ian Phillips, Vivian T Green, Stephanie and Kamal Thapa)*

Eldridge Pope (Hardy) ~ Lease Dick and Ann Foad ~ Real ale ~ Bar food (not Mon evening Nov-Mar) ~ Restaurant ~ (01300) 341274 ~ Children welcome ~ Open 11-11; 12-10.30 Sun; closed 2.30-6 weekdays in winter ~ Bedrooms: £30S/£55B

Royal Oak 🍷

Long Street

Enthusiastic new licensees have made gentle improvements at this picturesque creeper-covered Tudor inn. They've smartened up the enclosed back garden with Purbeck stone terracing and decking, new furniture and outdoor heaters. The interior remains largely unchanged, its stone walls and ceilings still packed with an incredible range of small ornaments from local photographs to antique china, brasses and farm tools, with just a couple of nice new touches like candles and pots of herbs on the tables. The three flagstoned communicating rooms have sturdy oak beams, lots of shiny black panelling, an inglenook with an oven, and warm winter log fires. Five well kept real ales include Butcombe Bitter and Wadworths IPA with three guests such as Cottage Champflower and Full Steam Ahead and Greene King

Old Speckled Hen on handpump from the uncommonly long bar counter, as well as 10 or more wines by the glass, and over a dozen malt whiskies. The two chefs here are members of CARF (The Campaign for Real Food), try to use local produce where possible and have added more fresh local seafood to the specials board. The menu includes sandwiches (from £2.75), soup (£3.25), calamari or whitebait (£4.65), fish and chips (£5.95), lasagne (£6.95), half a dozen vegetarian dishes such as wild mushroom strudel (£7.25), lamb shank in plum, brandy and orange liqueur sauce (£7.55), poached salmon fillet with white wine and dill sauce (£8.45), fresh Portland crab salad (£8.95) and daily specials such as monkfish slices on pasta with coriander butter or king scallops (£8.75), cracked crab salad or bass with roasted fennel and peppers (£8.95), and puddings like strawberry cheesecake or bread and butter pudding (£2.90). *(Recommended by Paul Vickers, W W Burke, Stephen Bonarjee, the Didler, Stuart Paulley)*

Free house ~ Licensees David and Janice Birch ~ Real ale ~ Bar food (till 9.30 Mon-Sat) ~ (01300) 341797 ~ Children in eating area of bar ~ Folk Weds evening monthly ~ Open 11-3, 6-11; 12-3, 7-10.30 Sun

CHIDEOCK SY4292 Map 1
Anchor

Seatown signposted off A35 from Chideock

The very friendly family at this nicely situated seaside pub manage to keep a good welcoming atmosphere going even when it's bustling with the summer crowd. Part of its charm is the splendid situation – just a few steps from the cove beach and nesting dramatically beneath the 617ft Golden Cap pinnacle; the Dorset Coast path is nearby. Seats and tables on the spacious front terrace are ideally placed for the lovely sea and cliff views, but you'll have to get there pretty early in summer to bag a spot. Out of season, when the crowds have gone, the cosy little bars seem especially snug with warming winter fires, some sea pictures and lots of interesting local photographs, a few fossils and shells, simple but comfortable seats around neat tables, and low white-planked ceilings; the family room and a further corner of the bar are no smoking, and the cats are friendly. Good value bar food includes sandwiches (from £1.95), soup (£2.95), filled baked potatoes (from £3.65), ploughman's (from £4.45), burgers (£4.75), curry (£8.25), plaice (£8.45), and daily specials including fresh fish and lobster from the beach and puddings made by a local lady (£2.95). Well kept Palmers 200, IPA, and Bridport on handpump, under light blanket pressure in winter only, freshly squeezed orange juice, and a decent little wine list. Shove-ha'penny, cribbage, dominoes, and piped, mainly classical, music. There are fridges and toasters in the bedrooms where you make your own breakfast and enjoy the sea views. The hard-working and friendly licensees, who have run the Anchor for 15 years, also run the Ferry at Salcombe. *(Recommended by Linda Norsworthy, Dr and Mrs J Hills, Alan and Paula McCully, Dr David Cockburn, Peter Meister, Mike Tomkins, Robert Mitchell, Marianne and Peter Stevens, R and D Gray, DAV)*

Palmers ~ Tenants David and Sadie Miles ~ Real ale ~ Bar food (not Sun evening Nov-Mar) ~ (01297) 489215 ~ Well behaved children welcome ~ Jazz, folk and blues Sat evening, some summer Weds evenings ~ Open 11-11; 12-10.30 Sun; 11(12 Sun)-2.30, 6-11(7-10.30 Sun) winter; closed 25 Dec evening ~ Bedrooms: £25/£500

CHRISTCHURCH SZ1696 Map 2
Fishermans Haunt

Winkton: B3347 Ringwood road nearly 3 miles N of Christchurch

There are attractive views of the River Avon from the restaurant at this big, welcoming hotel which is not far from the New Forest. The open-plan, partly no smoking bar is very neat with tapestry upholstered chairs around tables, stools at a pine panelled bar counter, and a few pictures on brown wallpaper. At one end big windows look out on the neat front garden. Well kept Bass, Gales HSB and GB and Ringwood Fortyniner on handpump, and lots of country wines. Good value straightforward bar food includes sandwiches (from £2.50; toasties from £3), filled baked potatoes (from £4.25), and steak and kidney pie, scampi, lasagne or battered cod (£6.25). The quiet back garden has tables among the shrubs, roses and other flowers; disabled lavatories. *(Recommended by John and Vivienne Rice, Sue and Mike Todd, R T and J C Moggridge, W W Burke, Mr and Mrs A P Reeves, Andrew Daniels)*

Gales ~ Manager Kevin A Crowley ~ Real ale ~ Bar food ~ Restaurant ~ (01202) 477283 ~ Children in eating area of bar and restaurant ~ Open 10.30-2.30, 5-11; 10.30-11 Sat; 12-10.30 Sun ~ Bedrooms: £49.50B/£66B

CHURCH KNOWLE SY9481 Map 2
New Inn ♀
Village signposted off A351 just N of Corfe Castle

The fairly traditional menu at this partly thatched 16th-c pub includes sandwiches (from £3.75), popular home-made blue vinney soup (£3.75), ploughman's (from £5.50), steak and kidney pie (£7.75), and steaks (from £10.75), complemented by a good range of daily delivered fresh fish which might include moules marinières (£6.75), petits fruits de mer (£8.75) with john dory, turbot, halibut, bass and so on priced at the market rate each day. The pub is prettily set in a nice little village, and has been run by the same friendly licensees for 17 years. The two main bar areas are attractively furnished with farmhouse chairs and tables and lots of bric-a-brac on the walls, and there's a log fire at each end; the dining lounge has a good relaxed atmosphere. One area is no smoking. Well kept Flowers Original, Greene King Old Speckled Hen, and Wadworths 6X on handpump, farmhouse cider and organic apple juices. You can now browse their wine cellar which often includes interesting bin ends in their recently opened wine shack (they also do off sales from here), and they serve several wines by the glass (either 175 or 250 ml) as well as about a dozen malt whiskies; skittle alley (private hire only) and piped music. There are plenty of tables in the good-sized garden, which has fine views of the Purbeck hills. No dogs. There's camping in two fields at the back but you need to book beforehand; good disabled facilities. *(Recommended by W W Burke, Richard Siebert, DAV, Jayne and Peter Capp, Eric Locker, Mrs M K Leah, DWAJ)*

Inn Partnership (Nomura) ~ Tenants Maurice and Rosemary Estop ~ Real ale ~ Bar food (12-2.15, 6-9.30) ~ Restaurant ~ (01929) 480357 ~ Children welcome in family room ~ Open 11(12 Sun)-3, 6-11; evening opening 6.30 in winter; closed Mon evening Jan-March

COLEHILL SU0302 Map 2
Barley Mow
From roundabout junction of A31 Ferndown bypass and B3073 Wimborne road, follow Colehill signpost up Middlehill Rd, pass Post Office, and at church turn right into Colehill Lane; OS Sheet 195 map reference 032024

The cosy low beamed main bar at this fine old thatched drovers cottage has a good warming fire in the huge brick inglenook fireplace, attractively moulded oak panelling, some Hogarth prints and a relaxed dining atmosphere; the cat is called Misty. Generous helpings of home-made bar food include soup (£2.50), ploughman's (£5.25), steak and kidney pie (£6.75), mushroom crumble (£6.95), crab cakes (£7.95), cod fillet (£8.95), sirloin steak (£9.95), daily specials such as liver and onions (£6.95) and rack of lamb (£11.50), and puddings such as coffee fudge meringue or blackberry and apple pie (£3.25). Attentive staff serve well kept Badger Best, Tanglefoot and a seasonal ale on handpump, and a dozen fruit wines. The newly extended no smoking area is in keeping with the character of the place and has a log fire; piped music and fruit machine. It's particularly attractive in summer, when there are colourful tubs of flowers in front, and more flowers in hanging baskets set off vividly against the whitewash. At the back a pleasant, enclosed big lawn has a boules pitch and is sheltered by oak trees. There are good walks nearby. *(Recommended by Paul R White, WHBM, Ian Phillips)*

Badger ~ Manager Bruce Cichocki ~ Real ale ~ Bar food ~ (01202) 882140 ~ Open 11-3, 5.30-11; 12-3, 7-10.30 Sun

CORFE CASTLE SY9681 Map 2

Fox 🍺

West Street, off A351; from town centre, follow dead-end Car Park sign behind church

The licensees at this characterful old place expressed ironic surprise when we asked if they had a designatd no smoking area. It was the wrong question really as they run this well set old place as a very traditional pub, which means you can smoke here, they have old-fashioned hatch service, no piped music or games machines and children are allowed only in the garden. It's beautifully set with the evocative ruins of Corfe Castle rising up behind the pleasant suntrap garden (reached through a pretty flower-hung side entrance). Much of the pub is built from the same stone as the castle, it's particularly evident in an ancient fossil-dotted alcove and in the pre-1300 stone fireplace. The tiny atmospheric front bar has closely set tables and chairs, a romantic painting of the castle depicting it in its prime, other pictures above panelling, and old-fashioned iron lamps. An ancient well in the lounge bar has been glassed over and lit from within. Three to six well kept real ales might include Burton, Greene King Abbot, Fullers London Pride, Robinsons Old Tom, Wadworths 6X, and Youngs Special tapped from the cask. Bar food includes sandwiches (from £2.20), home-made soup (£2.30), filled baguettes (from £2.50), ploughman's (£4.10), ham and egg (£4.45), battered fresh cod (£5.45), and daily specials such as steak in Guinness pie (£5.45), chicken balti (£6.45), haddock in parsley sauce (£6.95) and rump steak (£8.90). The countryside surrounding this National Trust village is well worth exploring, and there's a local museum opposite. *(Recommended by Paul Vickers, Dr D E Granger, the Didler, Mr and Mrs Thomas, JP, PP, Dez and Jen Clarke)*

Free house ~ Licensees Graham White and Miss A L Brown ~ Real ale ~ Bar food (till 9.30 in summer) ~ (01929) 480449 ~ Open 11-3, 6.30-11; 12-3, 7-11 Sun; closed 25 Dec

Greyhound

A351

Despite its situation in a popular tourist village, they've managed to keep a good cheery local atmosphere at this bustling old pub. The garden is perfectly situated bordering the castle moat and has fine views of both the castle battlements and the surrounding Purbeck hills. The courtyard opens on to the castle bridge, and has lots of pretty climbing and flowering shrubs. Inside, the three pleasant small low-ceilinged areas of the main bar have mellowed oak panelling and lots of paintings, brasses, and old photographs of the town on the walls. Popular bar food includes filled rolls (from £1.75), filled baked potatoes (from £3.75; local crab £4.55), ploughman's (from £4.50), chilli (£6.50), steak in ale pie (£6.95), and daily specials such as thai-style crab and salmon fishcakes (£3.95), fried lambs kidneys with minted mash topped with crispy bacon (£7.95), confit of lamb shank with orange braised fennel, garlic mash and red wine jus (£9.50), baked bass or chargrilled swordfish (£11.50) and lobster (£18.25), and puddings such as local ice cream (£2.50) or summer pudding or chocolate mousse (£3.95). Alongside Adnams, Hampshire Strong and Ringwood Best four guests might include Ruddles, Greene King Old Speckled Hen and Timothy Taylor Landlord on handpump. The May beer festival is timed to coincide with the Civil War re-enactment at the castle. They have sensibly placed darts, winter pool, cribbage, dominoes, Purbeck shove-ha'penny on a 5ft mahogany board, TV, and piped music. The family room is no smoking. *(Recommended by Dez and Jen Clarke, Derek and Sylvia Stephenson, Esther and John Sprinkle, Klaus and Elizabeth Leist, Jeff Davies, W W Burke, the Didler, Martin and Jane Wright)*

Whitbreads ~ Lease Louisa Barnard ~ Real ale ~ Bar food (12-9 in summer; 12-2.30, 6-9 Mon-Fri in winter) ~ (01929) 480205 ~ Children welcome away from the bar ~ Live music Fri evening ~ Open 11-11; 12-10.30 Sun; (11-3, 6-11 Mon-Fri) winter ~ Bedrooms: /£50

If we know a pub does summer barbecues, we say so.

CORSCOMBE ST5105 Map 2

Fox 🍴 🍷 ◀

On outskirts, towards Halstock

Dorset Dining Pub of the Year

The menu at this picturesque old thatched pub is absolutely spot on. They source supplies carefully, and use the best local produce, free range and organic where possible. Dishes are traditionally imaginative combining well matched English and continental ingredients. There might be wild garlic soup (£4.50), tomato and basil risotto (£4.95), warm pigeon breast and bacon salad (£5.50), chicken in a creamy sauce with celery and red pepper sauce (£7.95), braised venison with juniper berries and red wine (£9.50), lamb shank with mustard mash (£13.25), halibut steak with tapenade crust or roast john dory with thyme and sea salt (£14.95), seared scallops with orange braised fennel (£16.50). They stick to the good old favourite puddings such as treacle tart, bread and butter pudding and meringues with clotted cream and make their own ice cream and sorbets (£3.25). It's in a lovely country spot with roses over the door, a friendly golden retriever, Bramble (who loves a bit of attention), his friend Cracker and his son called Rayburn (no other dogs are allowed), ducks and chickens. A flagstone room on the right has lots of beautifully polished copper pots, pans and teapots, harness hanging from the beams, small Leech hunting prints and Snaffles prints, Spy cartoons of fox hunting gentlemen, a long scrubbed pine table (a highly polished smaller one is tucked behind the door), and an open fire. In the left-hand room (partly no smoking) there are built-in settles, candles on the blue-and-white gingham tablecloths or barrel tables, an assortment of chairs, lots of horse prints, antlers on the beams, two glass cabinets with a couple of stuffed owls in each, and an L-shaped wall settle by the inglenook fireplace; darts, dominoes and backgammon. The no smoking dining room which is open at weekends and for winter breakfast has an Aga, pine cupboards, a welsh dresser, and lots of personal memorabilia. In summer, breakfast is taken in the conservatory with its maturing vine, orchids, and huge oak table. Well kept Exmoor Ale and Fullers London Pride and a summer guest like Exmoor Fox on handpump, a very good thoughtful wine list, local cider and home-made elderflower cordial, damson vodka, and sloe gin. There are seats across the quiet village lane on a lawn by the little stream, and this is a nice area for walks.

(Recommended by Mr and Mrs Bruce Jamieson, C J Langdon, Alan and Hillie Johnson, Jane Legate, Dr and Mrs J Hills, Marianne and Peter Stevens, Mike Tomkins, Ron Shelton, J Hale, Ewan and Sue Hewitt, Malcolm Taylor, John and Jane Hayter, Simon and Jane Williams, Michael Doswell, P J Keen, Miss G Irving, R Styles)

Free house ~ Licensees Martyn and Susie Lee ~ Real ale ~ Bar food (till 9.30 Fri, Sat) ~ Restaurant ~ (01935) 891330 ~ Well behaved children welcome ~ Open 12-3(3.30 Sat), 7-11; 12-4, 7-10.30 Sun; closed 25 Dec ~ Bedrooms: £60B/£65(£70B)

CRANBORNE SU0513 Map 2

Fleur-de-Lys 🛏

B3078 N of Wimborne

We're hoping that by the time the *Guide* has gone to press the new licensee at this 17th-c creeper clad inn may have made some gentle improvements. The pub is nicely set on the edge of Cranborne Chase, and has several historic associations. Hanging Judge Jeffreys stayed here, Thomas Hardy visited while writing *Tess of the D'Urbervilles*, and Rupert Brooke wrote a poem about the pub which takes pride of place above the fireplace. The oak-panelled lounge bar is attractively modernised, and there's a more simply furnished beamed public bar with well kept Badger Best and Tanglefoot on handpump, farm cider, and some good malt whiskies. Bar food (popular with the older set) includes home-made soup (£2.65), sandwiches (from £2.65), ploughman's (£4.50), nutty mushroom layer (£5.95), home-made steak pie (£6.45), chicken breast with a sauce of the day (£6.95), local trout (£7.95), and daily specials such chicken curry (£5.95), steak and kidney pudding (£6.45) and pork medallions (£9.95); puddings (£3.25), and children's menu (£3.15). Darts, dominoes, cribbage, fruit machine, TV, and piped music. A pair of ancient stone pillars in the car park are said to have come from the ruins of a nearby monastery. *(Recommended by Lynn Sharpless, Bob Eardley, B and K Hypher, Dennis Jenkin, R Halsey)*

Badger ~ Tenant Mr Foster ~ Real ale ~ Bar food (12-2, 6.30-9.15(7-8.45 Sun)) ~ Restaurant (evening only) ~ (01725) 517282 ~ Children in restaurant ~ Open 11-3, 6.30-11; 12-3, 7-10.30 Sun ~ Bedrooms: £30S(£35B)/£50S(£55B)

EAST CHALDON SY7983 Map 2
Sailors Return

Village signposted from A352 Wareham—Dorchester; from village green, follow Dorchester, Weymouth signpost; note that the village is also known as Chaldon Herring; OS Sheet 194 map reference 790834

Although in an isolated location, this well extended thatched pub is very popular, particularly in good weather when you can wander to the interesting little nearby church, enjoy a downland walk from the pub, or sit at benches, picnic-sets and log seats on the grass in front, and look down over cow pastures to the village. Lulworth Cove is nearby, and from nearby West Chaldon, a bridleway leads across to join the Dorset Coast Path by the National Trust cliffs above Ringstead Bay. The convivial flagstoned bar still keeps much of its original character while the newer part of the building has unfussy furnishings, old notices for decoration, and open beams showing the roof above. The dining area has solid old tables in nooks and crannies. Dependable, generously served bar food includes baguettes (£3.50), filled baked potatoes (from £4.95), and daily specials such as steak and kidney pie (£6.75), fish pie (£7.25), whole gammon hock (£8.25), whole local plaice (£8.95), and half a shoulder of lamb or pig roast (£9.25). Even when busy, service remains as good as ever. Well kept Flowers IPA and Ringwood and five guests such as Exmoor Gold, Hop Back Summer Lightning, Marstons Pedigree and Shepherd Neame Spitfire on handpump, country wines, and several malt whiskies; darts, TV, cribbage, dominoes and piped music. *(Recommended by Marjorie and David Lamb, Bryan and Betty Southwell, Pat and Robert Watt, Brian and Bett Cox, Klaus and Elizabeth Leist, Paul and Penny Rampton, Paul Vickers, Charlie Harris)*

Free house ~ Licensees Mike and Sue Pollard ~ Real ale ~ Bar food (all day in summer) ~ Restaurant ~ (01305) 853847 ~ Children in restaurant and summer marquee ~ Open 11-11; 12-10.30 Sun; 11-2.30, 6.30-11 winter; 12-2.30, 7-10.30 Sun winter; closed 25 Dec

EAST KNIGHTON SY8185 Map 2
Countryman 🍴 🍺 🛏

Just off A352 Dorchester—Wareham; OS Sheet 194 map reference 811857

This bustling pub is an enjoyable place to stay. There's a relaxing atmosphere in the neatly comfortable, long main bar with its mix of tables, wheelback chairs and relaxing sofas, and fires at either end. This room opens into several other smaller areas, including a no smoking family room, a games bar with pool and darts, and a carvery (£11.75 for a roast and pudding; not all day Monday or Tuesday lunchtime). Other enjoyable food includes sandwiches or filled rolls (from £2.45), home-made soup (£3), filled baked potatoes (from £3.95), omelettes (from £4.50), ploughman's (from £5.25), garlic and herb chicken breast or tomato and lentil lasagne (£7.95), a handful of daily specials such as sardines in garlic and chive butter (£4.95), sausages braised in red wine with horseradish mash (£7.75) and rack of lamb with wild mushroom and port sauce (£12.95) and home-made puddings like treacle tart or a steamed pudding of the day (from £3.45). Well kept Courage Best and Directors, Greene King Old Speckled Hen, Ringwood Best and Old Thumper on handpump, as well as farm cider, and a good choice of wines; piped music. There are tables and children's play equipment out in the garden as well as some toys inside (the family room is no smoking); dogs welcome. *(Recommended by Mike and Heather Watson, Miss G Irving, R Styles, Dr Paull Khan, Bruce Bird, Mr and Mrs M Boyd,*

W W Burke, Brian and Bett Cox, Stan Edwards, Julia and Richard Tredgett, Joyce and Maurice Cottrell, Rod Stoneman, Gary and Jane Gleghoth, Dr D E Granger)

Free house ~ Licensees Jeremy and Nina Evans ~ Real ale ~ Bar food (12-2, 6.30-9.30) ~ Restaurant ~ (01305) 852666 ~ Children welcome ~ Open 11-2.30, 6-11; 12-3, 6-11 Sun; closed 25 Dec ~ Bedrooms: £48B/£60B

EAST MORDEN SY9195 Map 2
Cock & Bottle ® ♀ ◖

B3075 between A35 and A31 W of Poole

You do need to book to be sure of a table at this popular dining pub. As well as lunchtime ploughman's (£5.50), changing bar food might include home-made pâté (£4.95), bouillabaisse (£4.95), brie and pancetta tartlett (£5.65), spicy crab cakes with a thai dipping sauce (£5.75), spinach and feta cheese filo parcels with spicy tomato coulis (£7.25), red thai chicken curry (£8.95), whole local plaice (£8.95), very good steak and kidney pudding or pigeon pie (£9.25), beef wellington (£15.25), puddings such as rum and raisin white chocolate tart or spotted dick (from £3.75), and children's dishes (£3.50). Most of the restaurant is no smoking. Well kept Badger Best, Tanglefoot and King and Barnes Sussex on handpump, and a good choice of decent house wines including half a dozen by the glass; cordial service (though when it's busy food can take a time to come). The refurbished interior is divided into several communicating areas (mostly laid out for dining) with heavy rough beams, some stripped ceiling boards, squared panelling, a mix of old furnishings in various sizes and degrees of antiquity, small Victorian prints and some engaging bric-a-brac. There's a good log fire, intimate corners each with just a couple of tables. Although the emphasis is on dining, there is a pubby wood floored public bar (with piped music, fruit machine and a sensibly placed darts alcove). This in turn leads on to yet another characterful dining room. They have some disabled facilities. There are a few picnic-sets outside, a garden area, and an adjoining field with a nice pastoral outlook. *(Recommended by R J Walden, W W Burke, Ruth and Paul Lawrence, Betsy Brown, Nigel Flook, Rod Stoneman, Mr and Mrs Thomas, Mr and Mrs S Oxenbury, Betsy and Peter Little, Lord Sandhurst, Howard and Margaret Buchanan, Malcolm Taylor, Dr Phil Putwain, Ian Phillips)*

Badger ~ Tenant Peter Meadley ~ Real ale ~ Bar food (12-2, 6(7 Sun)-9) ~ Restaurant ~ (01929) 459238 ~ Children in restaurant ~ Open 11-3, 6-11; 12-3, 7-10.30 Sun

EVERSHOT ST5704 Map 2
Acorn ♀ ⇌

Village signposted from A37 8 miles S of Yeovil

This prettily placed old coaching inn (immortalised as the Sow & Acorn in Thomas Hardy's *Tess of the D'Urbervilles*) is run along the same successful lines as its sister pub the Fox at Corscombe. It's a characterful old place with thoughtful touches and the sort of good solidly imaginative food that would earn a food award with more feedback from readers. As well as a very short pubby bar menu with filled baguettes (from £3.95), ploughman's (from £4.50), shepherd's pie (£4.50) and chilli (£5.95), more imaginative specials might include devilled kidneys or grilled sardines stuffed with chilli and ginger (£4.25), fried marinated pigeon breast (£4.50), scallops with bacon and vermouth or cream cheese and red pepper tagliatelle (£5.50), wild boar sausages with red cabbage or loin of lamb stuffed with black pudding (£8.25), bouillabaisse of squid and mussels (£8.50), seared salmon with saffron butter sauce or fried calves liver with a sage and onion sauce (£8.95), guinea fowl breast with roast garlic sauce (£9.50), roast duck breast with a blackcurrant sauce (£9.75), smoked haddock with dill and mustard sauce (£10.25), sirloin steak with green peppercorn sauce (£11.25), and puddings such as treacle tart, sticky toffee pudding, rhubarb and ginger crumble, crème brûlée (£3.50).The Hardy Bar has oak panelling and two carved Hamstone fireplaces done by local craftsmen, a fine oak carved and gilded sconce, pictures by local artists, re-upholstered chairs, and copies of the inn's deeds going back to the 17th c. Another lounge has a woodburning stove. The dining room and restaurant are no smoking. Well kept Fullers London Pride, Otter Bright and Palmers IPA and maybe Greene King Abbot on handpump, home-made elderflower cordial, damson vodka and sloe gin and an interesting wine list; pool, darts, skittle alley, dominoes, cribbage, backgammon, chess, and juke box. Outside, there's a terrace with dark oak furniture. This is a nice village with lots of good surrounding walks. *(Recommended by Marianne and Peter Stevens, Dr Paull Khan, P J Keen, Revd L J and Mrs Melliss, Michael Buchanan, S G N Bennett, Richard and Jean Green, Alan and Hillie Johnson)*

Free house ~ Licensees Martyn and Susie Lee ~ Real ale ~ Bar food (till 9.30 Fri/Sat) ~ Restaurant ~ (01935) 83228 ~ Children in eating area of bar ~ Open 12-3, 6.30-11(10.30 Sun) ~ Bedrooms: £55B/£75S(£80B)

FARNHAM ST9515 Map 2

Museum Hotel 🍴 🍷 🍺 🛏

Village signposted off A354 Blandford Forum—Salisbury

We expected great things of the Museum as soon as we learned it had been bought by the people who had made the Fox at Lower Oddington in Gloucestershire so special, and we haven't been disappointed: this remarkable place really is outstanding. They've spent 14 months transforming what from the outside is rather an odd-looking thatched building (built in the 17th c by General Pitt Rivers to offer accommodation and refreshment for his nearby museum), and the results were unveiled just in time for us to inspect it for this year's *Guide*. What stands out most is the top-class food – head chef Mark Treasure won a Michelin star at both his last two establishments – but you'll receive the same warmly individual welcome if all you want is a drink. Effortlessly civilised, the various areas have a bright, fresh feel, thanks both to the cheery yellow paint on the walls and the plentiful windows. The flagstoned bar has a big inglenook fireplace, light beams and good comfortably cushioned furnishings; all the tables have a little flower on. To the right is a dining room with plates on an antique dresser, while off to the left is a cosier hunt-themed room, with a very jolly 3-D tableau and a seemingly sleeping stuffed fox curled in a corner. Another room feels rather like a contemporary version of a baronial hall, soaring up to a high glass ceiling, with dozens of antlers and a stag's head looking down on to a long wooden table and church-style pews. It leads to an outside terrace with more wooden tables. The excellent promptly served bar food might include cauliflower, lemon and smoked salmon soup (£4.25), Denhay air-dried ham with aged balsamic vinegar, parmesan and wood sorrel (£4.95), grilled salmon salad with organic watercress and poached egg, smoked haddock fish pie with local Ashmore cheddar or toad in the hole with caramelised onions and thyme gravy (all £8.95), duck confit with potato purée, buttered spinach and roasted flat mushrooms (£9.50), and puddings such as white chocolate mousse with fresh raspberries (£3.95) or a delicious creamed rice pudding with oranges, praline and pistachio nuts (£4.25). Even dishes that sound familiar have some sort of unusual twist. Wherever possible they use organic produce, and make their own bread, jams, chutney and marmalades. The chef really goes to town in the attractive restaurant (booking is recommended). The choice of wines is excellent, and the three real ales come from independent local brewers: on our visit we found Golden Hill Exmoor Fox, Hopback Summer Lightning and Heritage Stonehenge. Very good attentive service: set up a tab and the efficient young staff will probably address you by name every time you go back to the bar. The bedrooms (some of which are in a stable block behind) have extras like home-made shortbread. *(Recommended by anon)*

Free house ~ Licensees Vicky Elliot and Mark Stephenson ~ Real ale ~ Bar food ~ Restaurant ~ (01725) 516261 ~ Well behaved children over 5 ~ Open 12-3, 6-11(7-10.30 Sun) ~ Bedrooms: /£65B

Places with gardens or terraces usually let children sit there – we note in the text the very few exceptions that don't.

FURZEHILL SU0102 Map 2

Stocks

Village signposted off B3078 N of Wimborne Minster

The good value two-course lunch on Tuesdays and Thursdays (£5.50) at this welcoming place is a favourite with older customers. Other good food is popular too and includes home-made soup (£2.95), lunchtime ciabatta sandwiches (from £3.95), home-made steak in ale pie (£7.95), home-made vegetable lasagne (£7.95), home-made curries (£7.95), steaks (from £7.95) and shoulder of lamb on the bone in minted gravy (£9.25); the restaurant is no smoking. The thatched part of this extended place has the most character: two long rooms divide into rather snug sections, each with an open fire – brick in one and stone in the other – plush wall and window seats and stools, and timbered ochre walls. A dining area leads off here, with lots of copper and earthenware, an area with nets and a crab pot, and a big wall mirror cleverly creating an illusion of even more space. There are other dining areas with more mirrors, solid farmhouse chairs and tables, low ceilings and soft lighting, and good New Forest black and white photographs, old prints, farm tools, hay sleds, and so forth – even a Rayburn range in one place; piped music. Well kept Ringwood Best and Fortyniner and a guest such as Charles Wells Bombardier on handpump; the original cellar had a tunnel that came out in Smugglers Lane. Darts. Out in front are some green plastic seats, and under a fairy-lit arbour by the car park at the back, solid teak furniture. *(Recommended by John and Vivienne Rice, B and K Hypher, Dr Phil Putwain)*

Scottish Courage ~ Manager T Balding ~ Real ale ~ Bar food (12-2, 6-9.30; all day Sun) ~ Restaurant ~ (01202) 882481 ~ Children welcome ~ Open 11-3, 5-11; 12-10.30 Sun

GODMANSTONE SY6697 Map 2

Smiths Arms

A352 N of Dorchester

There are only six tables in the quaint little bar of this tiny old-fashioned 15th-c thatched inn which measures just 12 by 4 metres and claims to be one of the smallest pubs in the country. Its unchanging interior is traditionally furnished with long wooden stools and chunky tables, antique waxed and polished small pews and an elegant little high-backed settle, all tucked against the walls. There are National Hunt racing pictures and some brass plates on the walls, and an open fire. Very well kept Wadworths 6X is tapped from a cask behind the bar; dominoes and cribbage. Simple but tasty home-made food might include sandwiches (from £1.95), giant sausage (£3.50), ploughman's (from £3.90), quiche or chilli (£4.95), and daily specials such as curried prawn lasagne or topside of beef and steak and kidney pie (£5.45) and puddings (£2). There are very pleasantly set seats and tables outside on a crazy-paved terrace and on the grassy mound by the narrow River Cerne. A nice walk leads over Cowdon Hill to the River Piddle. No children. *(Recommended by J Hale, David and Julie Glover, the Didler, Alan and Hillie Johnson)*

Free house ~ Licensees John and Linda Foster ~ Real ale ~ Bar food (12-3.30) ~ No credit cards ~ (01300) 341236 ~ Open 11-5.30; closed Dec-Feb

LYME REGIS SY3492 Map 1

Pilot Boat ♀

Bridge Street

This pleasantly bustling place is nicely set near the waterfront. The walls of its nautically themed bars are crowded with naval and maritime pictures and memorabilia from a notable collection of sailor's hat ribands to navy and helicopter photographs, lobster-pot lamps, sharks' heads, an interesting collection of local fossils, a model of one of the last sailing ships to use the harbour, and lots of local historical pictures. At the back, there's a long and narrow lounge bar overlooking the little River Lym. It's quite pubby with well kept Palmers Bridport, IPA and 200 on handpump, several wines by the glass, a skittle alley, cribbage and piped music. You can sit outside on the terrace, where the Duke of Monmouth declared himself king after capturing the town in 1685. Very reasonably priced (nearly qualifying for our bargain award) tasty bar food is served in generous helpings and includes home-made soup (£1.95), sandwiches (from £2.50), ploughman's or fresh crab (£3.95), popular cod and chips (£4.25), steak and kidney pie or avocado and sweetcorn bake (£6.50), pork and cider casserole (£6.95), local trout (£7.75), steaks (from £9.50) and a couple of daily specials such as chestnut and mushroom pie (£6.95) and venison casserole (£9.25). The dining area is no smoking. *(Recommended by Basil Minson, Joan and Michel Hooper-Immins, DAV, David Carr, Mike and Wendy Proctor, Prof Kenneth Surin, E G Parish, Bruce Bird, Derek, Hazel and Graeme Lloyd)*

Palmers ~ Tenants Bill and Caroline Wiscombe ~ Real ale ~ Bar food (12-10) ~ (01297) 443157 ~ Children welcome ~ Open 11-11; 12-10.30 Sun

MARNHULL ST7718 Map 2
Blackmore Vale

Coming S on B3092 (off A30 W of Shaftesbury), turn right just before church into Church Hill, which eventually leads into Burton Street

They've extended the no smoking dining area at this comfortably modernised place which has some good value meal options on the fairly traditional menu. A two-course pie meal – perhaps steak and ale, salmon and parsley or chicken and mushroom is just £7.95, the two-course Sunday roast £7.50, and on Tuesday and Thursday they do an OAP two-course menu for £3.75. There's also soup (£2.50), garlic mushrooms (£3.50), battered cod (£6), vegetable curry (£6.50), lamb steak in port and cranberry sauce (£6.75), chicken wrapped in ham and apricots (£8.75), and steaks (from £8). Customers bring in their own willow pattern china and blue glassware to display in the dining area which has honey coloured stone walls and a large open fire. The cosy smaller bar has settles and sofas, darts, pub games and equestrian prints as well as well kept Badger Best and a guest such as King and Barnes Sussex on handpump; piped music. One of the tables in the garden is thatched. *(Recommended by Stephen S Goodchild, Simon Mighall, Diana Brumfit)*

Badger ~ Tenants Nigel Dawe and Jill Collins ~ Real ale ~ Bar food ~ Restaurant ~ (01258) 820701 ~ Children welcome ~ Live entertainment bank hol Sun ~ Open 11.30-2.30, 6.30-11; 12-3, 7-10.30 Sun

PIDDLEHINTON SY7197 Map 1
Thimble

B3143

Buried amongst winding Dorset lanes, this pretty thatched pub is approached by a little footbridge over the River Piddle. The neatly kept, low-beamed bar is simpler than the exterior suggests, although nicely spacious so that in spite of drawing quite a lot of people in the summer, it never feels too crowded – service doesn't falter when it's busy either – remaining friendly and helpful. There's a handsome open stone fireplace, and a deep glassed over well. A wide choice of popular good value food might include home-made soup (£2.50), sandwiches (from £2.35), filled baked potatoes (from £3.05), local flavoured sausages (£3.80), ploughman's (from £3.85), battered cod (£5.55), spinach and ricotta cheese cannelloni (£5.65), steak and kidney pie (£6.35), sirloin steak (£10.10), with daily specials such as chilli (£5.95), game or beef, venison and ale pie (£6.35), salmon and stilton wellington in filo pastry (£6.70), bass (£7.65) and Sunday roast (£6.10).Well kept Badger Best and Tanglefoot, Hardy Country and Popes Traditional, and Ringwood Old Thumper on handpump, along with quite a few malt whiskies and farm cider. Darts, shove-ha'penny, dominoes, cribbage, and piped music. The flower-filled garden is an enjoyable place for lunch, and is attractively floodlit at night. *(Recommended by Dennis Jenkin, Mr and Mrs Thomas, Anthony Barnes, Pat and Robert Watt, Ewan and Sue Hewitt, Tony and Wendy Hobden, J G Roberts)*

Free house ~ Licensees N R White and V J Lanfear ~ Real ale ~ Bar food ~ Restaurant ~ (01300) 348270 ~ Children in eating area of bar ~ Open 12-2.30, 7-11(10.30 Sun); closed 25 Dec, evening 26 Dec

PLUSH ST7102 Map 2
Brace of Pheasants 🍽

Village signposted from B3143 N of Dorchester at Piddletrenthide

Once two cottages and the village smithy, this delightful 16th-c thatched pub is charmingly placed in a fold of hills surrounding the Piddle Valley. The comfortably airy beamed bar has good solid tables, windsor chairs, fresh flowers, a huge heavy-beamed inglenook at one end with cosy seating inside, and a good warming log fire at the other. The friendly black labrador is called Bodger, and the golden retriever Molly. Very good food includes goats cheese with caramelised pear (£4.25), thai crabcakes on stir-fried vegetables or twice baked parmesan and cheddar cheese soufflé (£4.75), chicken breast stuffed with prawns on light curry and mango cream sauce or pork tenderloin medallions with stilton and sherry sauce (£10.95), roast monkfish wrapped in bacon with rosemary and garlic (£12.25), with similarly appealing daily specials such as salmon and cod fishcakes with dill and orange sauce (£7.95), venison and orange pie (£8.25), and roast bass (£12.25), and home-made puddings such as chocolate and rum pot or raspberry and cream cheese tart (£3.75). The restaurant and family room are no smoking. Well kept Fullers London Pride and a guest such as Tisbury Stonehenge tapped from the cask. There's a decent-sized garden and terrace with a lawn sloping up towards a rockery. The pub lies alongside Plush Brook, and an attractive bridleway behind goes to the left of the woods and over to Church Hill. *(Recommended by Mike and Sue Loseby, GD, KW, Pat and Robert Watt, Joan and Michel Hooper-Immins, B, M and P Kendall, W W Burke, Mrs Hilarie Taylor, Capt and Mrs J Wagstaff, the Didler, Rod Stoneman, Peter and Anne-Marie O'Malley, Klaus and Elizabeth Leist, Phyl and Jack Street)*

Free house ~ Licensees Jane and Geoffrey Knights ~ Real ale ~ Bar food ~ Restaurant ~ (01300) 348357 ~ Children in family room ~ Open 12-2.30, 7-11(winter 10.30); 12-3, 7-10.30 Sun; closed winter Mon

PUNCKNOWLE SY5388 Map 2
Crown

Church Street; village signposted off B3157 Bridport—Abbotsbury; or reached off A35 via Chilcombe

This comfortable thatched and flint inn which is prettily set opposite a partly Norman church (and its rookery) was built in the 16th c as a home for the monks. The village, incidentally, is pronounced Punnell. The heavily beamed interior has log fires in big stone fireplaces and paintings by local artists for sale. There's a pleasantly informal mix of furnishings, darts and table skittles in the neatly kept rambling public bar, with a comfortable no smoking family room opening off. The welcoming stripped stone lounge bar has red plush banquettes and stools. Very reasonably priced decent bar food is quite a draw and includes sandwiches (from £1.60), home-made soup (£2.50), filled baked potatoes (from £3.70), mushroom and cashew nut pasta (£4.20), ploughman's (from £4.70), home-made steak, kidney and Guinness pie or chicken, cashew nut and red wine casserole (£6.50), gammon and pineapple (£6.95), salmon steak topped with orange and parsley butter (£8.95) and puddings such as syrup sponge pudding (£2.80). Well kept Palmers IPA, Bridport and 200 on handpump, and country wines, good friendly service. There's a nice view from the partly paved back garden, which has tables under two venerable fairy-lit apple trees. *(Recommended by Geoffrey G Lawrance, Pat and Tony Martin, Ian and Joan Blackwell, Lyn and Geoff Hallchurch, Alan and Hillie Johnson, Chris Mawson)*

Palmers ~ Tenant Michael Lawless ~ Real ale ~ Bar food ~ No credit cards ~ (01308) 897711 ~ Children in family room ~ Open 11-3, 6.30(7 in winter)-11; 12-3, 7-10.30 Sun; closed 25 Dec evening ~ Bedrooms: £23B/£46S(£42B)

SHAVE CROSS SY4198 Map 1
Shave Cross Inn ★

On back lane Bridport—Marshwood, signposted locally; OS Sheet 193 map reference 415980

The original timbered bar at this charming, partly 14th-c flint and thatch inn is a lovely flagstoned room, surprisingly roomy and full of character, with country antiques and an enormous inglenook fireplace. The no smoking dining area and restaurant are stylishly decorated with crimson walls, Renaissance drawings in red chalk and candles on the tables. They have three well kept real ales on handpump such as Adnams Broadside, Bass and Otter Ale, and several wines by the glass; piped music. Very good imaginative bar food includes home-made soup (£3.25), lunchtime baguettes (from £3.45), grilled sardines (£4.95), fresh salmon fishcakes (£5.75), confit of duck leg or wild mushrooms with a cream, herb and cheese sauce, smoked pigeon breast, ploughman's or home-made burger (£5.95), greek-style marinated pork, fresh haddock or vegetable risotto (£7.50), chicken breast with a stuffing of smoked mozzarella cheese and pesto wrapped in parma ham, or salmon fillet with lemon butter (£10.95) and duck breast with an orange and herb glaze or lamb cutlets with a redcurrant and red wine sauce (£13.95). The sheltered flower-filled garden with its thatched wishing-well and goldfish pool is very pretty. *(Recommended by R and D Gray, Michael Graubart and Valerie Coumont Graubart, Paul R White, Revd D Glover, Simon and Jane Williams, Brett Muldoon)*

Free house ~ Licensees Lisa and Nic Tipping ~ Real ale ~ Bar food (not Sun evening, Mon) ~ Restaurant ~ (01308) 868358 ~ Children in restaurant ~ Open 11.30-3, 7-11; 12-3, 7-10.30 Sun; closed winter Mon

SHERBORNE ST6316 Map 2
Digby Tap ◗ £

Cooks Lane; park in Digby Road and walk round corner

If you like your pubs down-to-earth and without frills then this old-fashioned town ale house – which is handy for the glorious golden stone abbey – will really appeal. A good mix of customers means there's a relaxed and friendly atmosphere in the genuinely simple stone-flagged main bar. There are several small games rooms with pool, cribbage, fruit machine, TV, and piped music. Both the food and beer are very reasonably priced. They keep four or five interesting real ales on handpump, working through around 20 different beers a week, most from local brewers such as Cottage, Exmoor, Goldfinch, Otter and Tisbury. Huge helpings of straightforward bar food, served lunchtime only, include good sandwiches or baguettes (from £1.75), filled baked potatoes (from £2.75) and lasagne, sausage casserole, liver and bacon and steak and mushroom pie (£3.95). There are some seats outside. *(Recommended by W W Burke, Andrew and Catherine Gilham, Dennis Jenkin, Revd A Nunnerley, Adrian and Gwynneth Littleton, Mick Simmons, Basil Minson, Stephen, Julie and Hayley Brown)*

Free house ~ Licensees Peter Lefevre and Nick Whigham ~ Real ale ~ Bar food (not evenings, not Sun) ~ No credit cards ~ (01935) 813148 ~ Children welcome in eating area of bar at lunchtime ~ Open 11-2.30, 5.30-11; 11-3, 6-11 Sat; 12-2.30, 7-10.30 Sun

STRATTON SY6593 Map 2
Saxon Arms ♀ ◗

Village signposted off A37 bypass NW of Dorchester; The Square

Like many Dorset pubs the Saxon Arms is thatched and made with traditional materials such as oak, flint and natural stone, but don't be fooled: it's brand new, built and opened shortly before this edition of the *Guide* went to press. We recommend it so quickly not simply for the unusual building, but because at their previous pub the hardworking Barretts were our Licensees of the Year; they're running things here in exactly the same way. The huge, bright open-plan room has plenty of space, with a fireplace and drinking area to the left, and a large no smoking dining section on the right. The floor is made with big flagstones, and there are smart curtains, fresh flowers on the light oak tables and comfortable cushioned settles. Among the photographs on the walls are scenes of the building's construction. Good bar food includes soup (£2.50), filled ciabatta (from £3.50), smoked mackerel with gooseberry and elderflower chutney (£4), ploughman's (£4.50), roasted vegetable lasagne (£6.50), steak, ale and mushroom pie (£7.75), rib-eye steak (£10.25) and daily specials such as fresh Portland crab salad (£7.95), fried scallops with smoked bacon and garlic butter (£4.95/£8.95) and roasted cod wrapped in air-dried ham (£8.50). Well kept Fullers London Pride, Palmers IPA, Saxon Gold and a guest such as Smiles Mayfly on handpump, about eight wines by the glass (very reasonably priced wine list), and a dozen malt whiskies; soft piped music, shove-ha'penny, cribbage, dominoes, table skittles. The chocolate labrador is called Ed. There are lots of tables outside, overlooking a clutch of similarly well constructed new buildings, including a village hall. *(Recommended by anon)*

Free house ~ Licensees Ian and Anne Barrett ~ Real ale ~ Bar food (11.30-2, 6.30-9; not 25 Dec) ~ (01305) 260020 ~ Children in eating area of bar ~ Open 11-2.30(3 Sat), 5.30-11; 12-3, 6.30-10.30 Sun; closed 25 Dec evening

STURMINSTER NEWTON ST7814 Map 2

Swan 🛏️

Town signposted off A357 Blandford—Sherborne, via B3092; Market Place

With particularly nice individually decorated bedrooms (which go down in price after you've stayed the first night), this popular 18th-c coaching inn is a good base for exploring the area. Traditional and very neatly kept, the busy beamed bar has a particularly interesting brick fireplace at one end, its tiny grate sitting incongruously next to an old safe. Close by is a comfortable green leatherette sofa, as well as wooden corner seats, a table with newspapers to read, and the odd stuffed fish or bird in glass cases. Elsewhere there's lot of exposed brickwork, including sturdy brick pillars dividing the room, plenty of panelling, and a good number of tables leading through into a couple of eating areas. As well as sandwiches, the very generously served good value bar food might include an elaborate curry, spinach and red pepper lasagne or a tasty chicken, gammon and leek pie (£6.95), and whole grilled plaice with prawns (£10.95); service may slow down at busier times, but is always polite and friendly. Like everything else at the bar, the well kept Badger Best and Tanglefoot have their prices displayed with admirable clarity; fruit machine, soft piped music. There are lots more tables on a terrace and lawn behind. The attractive building replaced an earlier one destroyed in a fire in 1729. *(Recommended by Pat and Robert Watt, Mrs Peachey)*

Badger ~ Tenants Roger and Marion Hiron ~ Real ale ~ Bar food ~ Restaurant ~ (01258) 472208 ~ Children in restaurant ~ Live music first Thurs every month, some bank hol Suns ~ Open 11-11; 12-10.30 Sun ~ Bedrooms: £44.95B/£59.95B

TARRANT MONKTON ST9408 Map 2

Langton Arms 🍺

Village signposted from A354, then head for church

A very good well balanced all-rounder, this charmingly set 17th-c thatched pub is doing very well at the moment. As well as two beer festivals a year, they have what they describe as a mini beer festival going on all the time, with well kept Ringwood Best and four quickly changing guests from lots of interesting little brewers such as Cottage, Cannon Royall, Moor and Tring on handpump. Very enjoyable bar food from a traditionally imaginative menu includes home-made soup (£2.95), deep-fried cod or four bean stew (£5.95), faggots in onion sauce (£6.50), fried lambs liver with bacon and sausage (£6.50), smoked trout salad or braised rabbit with tarragon and mustard (£6.95), chicken breast in oriental spices with peanut and chilli sauce or pigeon breast in cranberry and red wine sauce (£7.95) and puddings such as jam roly poly, treacle tart or local ice creams (from £3); Sunday roast (£6). The fairly simple beamed bar has a huge inglenook fireplace, settles, stools at the counter and other mixed dark furniture, and the public bar has a juke box, darts, pool, a fruit machine,

TV, cribbage, and dominoes; piped music. There's a no smoking bistro restaurant in an attractively reworked barn, a skittle alley that doubles as a no smoking family room during the day. The garden has a very good wood-chip play area, and there are good nearby walks. *(Recommended by Nick and Meriel Cox, Dr E Foreman, Ian Jones, Anthony Barnes, Dr D E Granger, PWV, TJ and JD Fitzgerald, Dr Paull Khan, Anne Turner, John Robertson, Christine and Neil Townend, Peter Salmon, Keith and Janet Eaton)*

Free house ~ Licensees Barbara and James Cossins ~ Real ale ~ Bar food (11.30-2.30, 6.30-9.30; 12-3, 6-9 Sun) ~ Restaurant ~ (01258) 830225 ~ Children welcome in family room and restaurant ~ Open 11.30-11; 12-10.30 Sun ~ Bedrooms: £50B/£70B

UPLODERS SY5093 Map 2
Crown
Village signposted off A35 E of Bridport

Readers are particularly impressed with the welcoming greeting and accommodating licensees at this homely, low-beamed village pub. They're also amazed at the generosity of the helpings of good value bar food: soup (£2.95), sandwiches (from £3.95), ploughman's, steak and kidney pudding or chicken and mushroom pie (£5.95), mushroom stroganoff or grilled haddock (£7.25), steaks (from £8.95), a couple of daily specials such as curry (£6.95) or bass (£10.95) and puddings such as spotted dick or rum and chocolate mousse (from £3.25). There are pictures by local artists on the red and gold flock wallpaper, and masses of polished bric-a-brac, including a shelf of toby jugs, an engaging group of model musicians and high-lifers on one window sill, more models on all the other surfaces – even on the sturdy balustrading that, with standing timber pillars, divides the pub into different parts. Its few black beams are liberally festooned with pewter and china tankards, copper kettles, horsebrasses and Service hats, and there's a bright log fire; piped music, dominoes, and cards. There are usually quite a few cheery locals around the bar (and regulars' colour snaps) drinking the well kept Palmers IPA, Dorset Gold and 200 on handpump. The no smoking dining area is down a few steps. There are tables out in an attractive two-tier garden, in quiet village surroundings. *(Recommended by Dr and Mrs Nigel Holmes, Galen Strawson, Mr and Mrs D A Cox)*

Palmers ~ Tenants John and Joan James ~ Real ale ~ Bar food (not Sun evening) ~ Restaurant ~ (01308) 485356 ~ Children over 5 ~ Open 11-3, 6-11; 12-3, 7-10.30 Sun; closed 25/26 Dec evening, 1 Jan

UPWEY SY6684 Map 2
Old Ship
Ridgeway; turn right off A354 at bottom of Ridgeway Hill into old Roman Rd

There's a pleasantly relaxed atmosphere in the attractive interconnected beamed rooms of this old wayside inn. There's a cosy open fire with horsebrasses along the mantelbeam, a mix of sturdy chairs and comfortable armchairs and some built-in wooden wall settles. Fresh flowers cheer up the solid panelled wood bar counter and tables, and there are china plates, copper pans and old clocks on the walls; piped music. Bar food includes soup (£2.95), sandwiches (£2.95), ploughman's (£4.95) and daily specials such as baked aubergine stuffed with chicken and feta cheese with a basil and tomato dressing (£9.95), daily fresh fish dishes (from £6.95; red snapper with a lemon and dill salad and caraway marmalade £10.25), duck breast with black cherries and brandy (£12.95) and peppered fillet with wholegrain mustard croquettes and balsamic jus (£13.95); vegetables are extra. Puddings might include toffee and walnut cheesecake or apple crumble (£3.50); the restaurant is no smoking. Well kept Bass, Greene King Old Speckled Hen, Ringwood Best and possibly a guest such as Courage Directors on handpump. There are colourful hanging baskets outside, and picnic-sets and umbrellas in the garden. *(Recommended by Alan and Hillie Johnson, Mr and Mrs G Robson, M G Hart)*

Inn Partnership (Nomura) ~ Tenants David Wootton, John and Simon Hana and Paul Harmer ~ Real ale ~ Bar food (12-2, 6.30(7 Sun)-9.30) ~ Restaurant ~ (01305) 812522 ~ Children welcome ~ Open 12-3, 6-11(7-10.30 Sun)

WEST BEXINGTON SY5387 Map 2

Manor Hotel 🛏

Village signposted off B3157 SE of Bridport; Beach Road

This well run and very relaxing old stone hotel is just a short stroll from the beach. You can see the sea from the smart no smoking Victorian-style conservatory, which has airy furnishings and lots of plants, from the bedrooms, and from the garden, where there are picnic-sets on a small lawn with flowerbeds lining the low sheltering walls; a much bigger side lawn has a children's play area. The bustling downstairs cellar bar (on the same level as the south-sloping garden) has small country pictures and good leather-mounted horsebrasses on the walls, red leatherette stools and low-backed chairs (with one fat seat carved from a beer cask) under the black beams and joists, as well as heavy harness over the log fire. Very good but not cheap bar food includes sandwiches (from £3.15), soup (£3.45), ploughman's (from £5.65), sausage and mash (£6.95), steak and kidney pie (£7.95), fish pie (£8.95), chicken stir fry (£10.95), skate (£11.95), and puddings like chocolate roulade or raspberry meringue (£3.95); good breakfasts. Well kept Hardy Country and Royal Oak on handpump, quite a few malt whiskies and several wines by the glass. Helpful courteous service. *(Recommended by Mr and Mrs D S Price, Revd D Glover, R Michael Richards, P J and Avril Hanson, David and Julie Glover)*

Free house ~ Licensees Richard and Jayne Childs ~ Real ale ~ Bar food (12-2, 6.30-10) ~ Restaurant ~ (01308) 897616 ~ Children welcome ~ Open 11-11; 12-11 Sun ~ Bedrooms: £57B/£100B

WORTH MATRAVERS SY9777 Map 2

Square & Compass 🍺

At fork of both roads signposted to village from B3069

For lovers of simple slightly idiosyncratic places, coming here is a delight. On a winter's evening with the rain lashing the windows, you wouldn't be that surprised if a smuggler, complete with parrot and wooden leg, suddenly materialised. During the 90 years that the Newman family have run this pub almost nothing has changed, it remains completely unspoilt, basic and unique. Well kept Ringwood Best, Badger Tanglefoot and an interesting changing guest such as Hop Back Thunderstorm are tapped from a row of casks and served to you in the hall through two serving hatches – there's no bar as such. A couple of rooms opposite have simple furniture on the flagstones, a woodburning stove, and a staunch band of friendly locals. Bar food is limited to pork and chilli or cheese and onion pie or pasties (£1.60), served any time when they're open; cribbage, shove-ha'penny and dominoes. There's also a free little museum displaying local fossils and artefacts, mostly collected by the current landlord and his father. This is a lovely peaceful hilltop setting, and on a clear day there's a fantastic view from benches in front of the pub, looking down over the village rooftops to the sea between the East Man and the West Man (the hills that guard the coastal approach) and the sun setting out beyond Portland Bill. Free-roaming hens, chickens and other birds may cluck happily around your feet. There are good walks from the pub but limited parking so it's perhaps best to park in the public car park 100 yards along the Corfe Castle road. *(Recommended by the Didler, Mike and Sue Loseby, Richard Siebert, Alan and Hillie Johnson, JP, PP, WHBM, Pete Baker, David Peakall, R M Corlett, Jeff Davies, Paul Vickers, Hazel and Michael Duncombe, Matt Britton, Alison Cameron, M S Catling, DAV, Ron Shelton)*

Free house ~ Licensee Charlie Newman ~ Real ale ~ Bar food ~ No credit cards ~ (01929) 439229 ~ Well behaved children ~ Open 12-3, 6-11; 12-11 Sat; 12-3(maybe 4 in summer), 7-10.30 Sun; closed Sun evening winter

---

Post Office address codings confusingly give the impression that some pubs are in Dorset, when they're really in Somerset (which is where we list them).

Lucky Dip

Besides the fully inspected pubs, you might like to try these Lucky Dips recommended to us and described by readers (if you do, please send us reports: www.goodguides.com).

Abbotsbury [SY5785]

Ilchester Arms [B3157]: Rambling stone inn done out as themed servants' quarters from cook's sitting room to potting shed, with appropriate bric-a-brac and old pine furniture, also prints of the famous swans; usual bar food from sandwiches or baked potatoes up, attractive no smoking conservatory restaurant, Courage Directors, Quay Weymouth JD and a guest such as Theakstons tapped from the cask; darts, winter pool, fruit machine, TV and piped music; children in eating areas, bedrooms, open all day *(Paul Vickers, LYM)*

Almer [SY9097]

☆ *Worlds End* [B3075, just off A31 towards Wareham]: Roomily rebuilt open-plan thatched family dining pub, beams, panelled alcoves and soft lighting, highest earner in the Badger chain, with their beers kept well, very wide choice of food all day (you can choose generous or smaller helpings), good quick service; open all day, picnic-sets out in front and behind, outstanding play area *(BB, Deborah and Ian Carrington)*

Benville Lane [ST5403]

Talbot Arms [off A356 NW of Dorchester]: Small village pub, hospitable landlord, very friendly staff, well kept local ales, good range of bar food; aviary, curiosity shop *(Richard and Anne Ansell)*

Bere Regis [SY8494]

Drax Arms [West St; off A35 bypass]: Comfortable village pub with cheerful helpful service, well kept Badger ales and farm cider, limited choice of good reasonably priced home-made food from sandwiches up, esp pies and casseroles, big open fire on left, small dining area; good walking nearby *(John and Joan Nash, Mr and Mrs J Brown, Stan Edwards)*

Blandford Forum [ST8806]

Crown [West St]: Best Western hotel, well furnished long bar used by locals as pub, well kept Badger from nearby brewery, good range of reasonably priced bar food; bedrooms *(Andrew Burke)*

Bournemouth [SZ0991]

Firefly & Firkin [Holdenhurst Rd]: Solid alehouse-style décor in former fire station, well kept beers, friendly service, reasonably priced food inc big filled baps to take away, regular live music *(anon)*

Goat & Tricycle [West Hill Rd]: Comfortable and friendly Wadworths pub with well kept beers inc guests such as Adnams Broadside and Archers Best, Cheddar Valley farm cider, lots of bric-a-brac inc hundreds of hats hung from ceiling, simple generous food *(Anthony Barnes)*

Bridport [SY4692]

Greyhound [East St]: Old pub smartly converted by Wetherspoons, with good choice of guest beers and food served until 9pm; polite friendly young staff, and young but well behaved customers in the evening *(Pat and Tony Martin)*

Burton Bradstock [SY4889]

Dove [Southover]: Recently refurbished thatched two-bar pub with some stripped stone, inglenook fireplace, wide choice of enjoyable food in bar and dining rooms, friendly service, well kept Adnams and Hardy Country, Thatcher's farm cider, darts, a few 1960ish theatrical photographs; busy in summer and can be smoky, piped nostalgic pop music; picnic-sets on steeply terraced back grass, rabbits and fancy fowl *(Pat and Robert Watt, BB, Mr and Mrs D S Price, DAV)*

Cerne Abbas [ST6601]

Red Lion [Long St]: Cottagey inn reopened in 2000 (but for sale as we go to press), partly 16th-c behind its Victorian façade, cosy areas leading off bar, popular food from soup and sandwiches up, well kept ales inc Hardy Royal Oak, decent wines, good local atmosphere, darts, shove-ha'penny and cribbage; skittle alley, neatly kept small and secluded flower-filled garden. *(Linda Norsworthy, R T and J C Moggridge, LYM)*

Charlton Marshall [ST9003]

☆ *Charlton Inn* [A350 Poole—Blandford]: Comfortably extended beamed pub with wide choice of good honest food from doorstep sandwiches up inc fresh fish and plenty of vegetarian dishes, very big helpings, particularly good veg, several carpeted country-style areas inc snug and plenty of dining tables, Badger Best and Tanglefoot, several wines by glass, quick service, no smoking area, unobtrusive piped music; small garden *(Diana Brumfit, WHBM, B and K Hypher, BB)*

Charmouth [SY3693]

Royal Oak [off A3052/A35 E of Lyme Regis]: Thoroughgoing gossipy local with well kept Palmers ales, friendly staff, traditional games inc darts, table skittles and bar billiards, bar snacks (not Tues), no TV or piped music *(Veronica Brown, Robert Gomme)*

Chickerell [SY6480]

Old Slaughterhouse [Bagwell Farm]: Good freshly made food in suprising surroundings, stripped brick, roaring fire, neat tables – and still some of the equipment used in this place's former days; big terrace with walled tent, on a working farm *(Howard and Margaret Buchanan)*

Turks Head [East St]: Busy stone-built village pub with huge helpings of freshly cooked food inc children's and wonderful puddings in spacious simply furnished eating area (former skittle alley), pleasant beamed bar with lots of old local photographs, pictures and decorative plates, cheerful service; children welcome, comfortable bedrooms, good breakfast *(Philip Bardswell)*

Chideock [SY4292]

George [A35 Bridport—Lyme Regis]: Thatched 17th-c pub, welcoming and relaxed, with neat rows of tables in simple front bar, plusher lounge, hundreds of banknotes on beams, lots of ephemera and bric-a-brac, big log fire, well kept Palmers, decent wines, enjoyable food inc fresh fish, family room and big restaurant (two no smoking areas); may be quiet piped music; tables in back garden with terrace, bedrooms *(Ailsa McLellan, Bruce Bird, Geoffrey G Lawrance, LYM)*

Corfe Castle [SY9681]

Bankes Arms [East St]: Big and busy, welcoming to families, with flagstones and comfortable traditional décor, subtle lighting, well kept Wadworths 6X, generous food, friendly service, restaurant; tables on terrace and in long garden with end play area overlooking steam railway; piped music, children and dogs welcome; bedrooms (no single-night bookings wknds), on attractive village square *(David and Carole Chapman)*

Dorchester [SY6890]

Blue Raddle [Church St]: Compact sidestreet local with small menu of good value lunchtime food, cheerful bustle then, well kept Greene King Abbot, Otter and two changing guest beers; maybe quiet piped jazz *(Ian and Joan Blackwell, the Didler)*

Kings Arms [High East St]: Well worn in hotel bar with well kept Bass, Courage Directors, Flowers Original and Tetleys, decent wines, well presented food from sandwiches up, pleasant helpful service, open fire; close associations with Nelson and Hardy's *Mayor of Casterbridge*; bedrooms (the Lawrence of Arabia suite and the Tutenkhamen have to be seen to be believed) *(the Didler, LYM, Dr David Cockburn, Alan and Hillie Johnson)*

Old Ship [High West St]: Unspoilt low-ceilinged local, warm and cosy, with generous cheap food, well kept Hardy Country and Royal Oak, friendly staff, comfortably worn back dining room *(Paul Reeve)*

Fiddleford [ST8013]

☆ *Fiddleford Inn* [A357 Sturminster Newton—Blandford Forum]: Comfortable and spacious, good generous quickly served food from sandwiches up in lounge bar, restaurant area and back family area, well kept Shepherd Neame Spitfire and Smiles Best, friendly service, three linked smartly refurbished areas, ancient flagstones and some other nice touches; unobtrusive piped music; big pleasant garden with play area *(M G Hart, John Coatsworth, B and K Hypher, LYM)*

Gillingham [ST8027]

☆ *Dolphin* [Peacemarsh (B3082)]: Popular dining pub with pleasant beamed bar for drinking (well kept Badger beers), good choice of particularly good value food all freshly cooked to order, regular themed menus, friendly staff, partly no smoking restaurant area; garden with climbing frame *(Mr and Mrs Thomas, R M Wickenden, BB)*

Gussage All Saints [SU0010]

☆ *Drovers*: Attractively placed country pub reopened by Ringwood, enlarged two-room bar redone in straightforward country style, well kept beer, good value food, plenty of friendly staff; tables on pretty front lawn with views across the Dorset hills *(LYM, W Ruxton, Paul Noble, B and K Hypher, Janet and Peter Race)*

Hinton St Mary [ST7816]

White Horse [just off B3092 a mile N of Sturminster]: Village local with unusual inglenook fireplace in cheery tiled bar, nicely set dining tables in extended lounge, reasonably priced food (booking advised Sun lunch), well kept John Smiths, Tetleys and changing guest beers, mulled wine, good landlord, darts; tables in flower garden *(Pat and Robert Watt)*

Horton [SU0207]

☆ *Drusillas* [Wigbeth]: Picturesque renovated 17th-c beamed pub, wide choice of food inc lots of fish, unusual dishes, OAP bargains, thatched dining extension, Boddingtons, Flowers IPA and Wadworths 6X, log fire, separate games bar with two pool tables; service may slow when very busy, piped pop music; children welcome, adventure playground *(Mr and Mrs Thomas, Eamonn and Natasha Skyrme, B and K Hypher)*

Kingston [SY9579]

☆ *Scott Arms* [West St (B3069)]: Busy holiday pub with rambling warren-like rooms, panelling, stripped stone, beams, open fires and some fine antique prints, attractive room overlooking garden, decent family extension, well kept Courage Directors and Ringwood Best, lots of wines, generous if not cheap standard food inc summer cream teas, no smoking dining area; darts, dominoes and fruit machine, piped music; well kept garden with superb views of Corfe Castle and the Purbeck Hills *(the Didler, W W Burke, Alan and Hillie Johnson, JDM, KM, Paul Thompson, Anna Blackburn, DAV, LYM, Joan and Michel Hooper-Immins, M G Hart, WHBM)*

Langton Herring [SY6182]

☆ *Elm Tree* [signed off B3157]: Old beamed pub, lots of copper, brass and bellows, cushioned window seats, windsor chairs, inglenook, and traditionally furnished extension, wide range of food from sandwiches up inc some interesting dishes (may be a long wait), Bass and Wadworths 6X, decent house wine; no dogs inside; pretty flower-filled sunken garden, track down to Coast Path which skirts Chesil lagoon *(Irene and Derek Flewin, Jean and Douglas Troup, Eric Locker, David and Michelle Bailey, LYM, Dennis Jenkin, GD, KW)*

Litton Cheney [SY5590]

☆ *White Horse*: Newish tenants in Palmers pub with three well kept ales, good home-made food using fresh local ingredients, pictures on stripped stone walls, country kitchen chairs in dining area, table skittles, friendly efficient staff; lovely spot on quiet lane into quaint village, picnic-sets on pleasant streamside front lawn *(BB, Ian Phillips, Mick Simmons, A E Furley)*

Loders [SY4994]

☆ *Loders Arms* [off A3066 just N of Bridport]: Well worn in local, welcoming and relaxed, log fire, Palmers real ales, good choice of house wines, good value changing food from huge baguettes to interesting main dishes, no smoking dining room, skittle alley; friendly great dane and elderly labrador, may be piped music; children in eating areas, pleasant views from tables in small back garden, pretty thatched village, open all day Sun *(LYM, Esther and John Sprinkle, Ian Phillips, Stephanie and Kamal Thapa, Colin and Janet Roe, DAV, D J Hayman)*

Lyme Regis [SY3492]

Cobb Arms [Marine Parade, Monmouth Beach]: Spaciously refurbished, with wide range of reasonably priced generous bar food, quick service even when busy, good value cream teas, well kept Palmers, decent wines, interesting ship pictures and marine fish tank; children welcome, open all day, tables on small back terrace, next to harbour, beach and coastal walk, bedrooms *(Bruce Bird)*

☆ *Royal Standard* [Marine Parade, The Cobb]: Right on broadest part of beach, with suntrap courtyard (own servery and wendy house); bar serving area dominated by pool table and piped pop, but has some fine built-in stripped high settles, and there's a quieter no smoking area with stripped brick and pine; well kept Palmers IPA, BB, 200 and Gold, helpful friendly staff, good value food inc sensibly priced sandwiches, plenty of local crab and fish, good cream teas, darts; children welcome *(Ian Phillips, Esther and John Sprinkle, BB)*

Marnhull [ST7718]

☆ *Crown* [about 3 miles N of Sturminster Newton; Crown Rd]: Part-thatched 17th-c dining pub, good value generous food, oak beams, huge flagstones, old settles and elm tables, window seats cut into thick stone walls, logs burning in big stone hearth, Badger Best and Tanglefoot, good service, small more modern lounge; skittle alley, may be piped music; tables in peaceful enclosed garden, children welcome *(S J and C C Davidson, LYM)*

Marshwood [SY3799]

Bottle [B3165 Lyme Regis—Crewkerne]: 16th-c thatched country local with big inglenook log fire in attractive low-ceilinged bar, small games bar, skittle alley; the enthusiastic licensees who made it a popular main entry for their unusual largely organic food and interesting real ales (even a craft shop) left in summer 2001, and we look forward to reports on the new regime; good spacious garden with camp site beyond, pretty walking country *(LYM)*

Milton Abbas [ST8001]

Hambro Arms [signed off A354 SW of Blandford]: In beautiful late 18th-c thatched landscaped village, good log fire, well kept Bass, Boddingtons and Tetleys, good generous food from sandwiches to steak inc fresh fish, prompt service, bright décor; darts, pool and TV in cosy back public bar, children in restaurant, no dogs, tables out on terrace, comfortable bedrooms *(Dennis Jenkin, LYM, GD, KW, S and D Moir, Geoffrey G Lawrance, R Halsey, Simon and Laura Habbishow)*

Mudeford [SZ1891]

☆ *Haven House* [beyond huge seaside car park at Mudeford Pier]: Much-extended and smartly refurbished, best in winter for old-fashioned feel in quaint little part-flagstoned core and

lovely seaside walks (dogs banned from beach May-Sept), good value food from good crab sandwiches up, cheerful service; very popular wknds and summer for position on beach with family cafeteria, tables on sheltered terrace; Whitbreads-related ales *(Derek and Sylvia Stephenson, John and Vivienne Rice, LYM)*

☆ *Ship in Distress*: Dining pub very popular for good fresh carefully cooked fish and seafood, and classy puddings, in restaurant (best to book) and bar – two rooms, one plain, one with hops, plants and nautical memorabilia; well kept Bass, Greenalls Original, Marstons Pedigree and Ringwood Best, good wine list, cosy atmosphere, friendly service (can slow at busy times) *(Betsy Brown, Nigel Flook, A D Marsh)*

Nettlecombe [SY5195]

☆ *Marquis of Lorne* [off A3066 Bridport—Beaminster, via W Milton]: Tucked away in lovely countryside, neat and comfortable panelled main bar, pleasant décor, two smarter dining areas, one no smoking, log fires, friendly atmosphere, new tenants doing enjoyable food from sandwiches up with some emphasis on fresh fish, well kept Palmers real ales, decent wines, public bar with cribbage, dominoes and table skittles; children in eating areas, may be classical piped music; comfortable bedrooms, big pretty garden with rustic-style play area *(Cathy Robinson, Mike Gorton, Denis and Dorothy Evans, Anthony Barnes, LYM)*

Okeford Fitzpaine [ST8011]

☆ *Royal Oak* [Lower St]: Well kept Ringwood Best, Wadworths 6X and weekly changing guest such as Exmoor Fox, farm cider, huge fireplace with copper-hooded stove in small traditional beamed and flagstoned front bar, no smoking green-painted L-shaped eating area with three very small cottagey interconnected rooms off, promising food from traditional pub dishes to more upmarket things, steps up to newly refurbished skittle alley, pool; quiz night, beer festival first wknd in July, tables on back lawn with play area, charming village *(W W Burke, BB)*

Osmington Mills [SY7381]

☆ *Smugglers* [off A353 NE of Weymouth]: Pretty part-thatched pub in fine position a short stroll up from the sea, with good cliff walks; much extended but done well, with cosy dark corners, log stove, shiny black panelling and nautical decorations; well kept Badger Best, Tanglefoot and a guest such as Firsty Ferret, quickly served generous food from good filled baps up, partly no smoking restaurant; discreet games area, piped music; children in eating areas, streamside garden with good play area and thatched summer bar, open all day summer, can be very crowded then (holiday settlement nearby); comfortable bedrooms, big breakfast, on Coast Path *(Paul Vickers, Mr and Mrs Thomas, LYM, the Didler, Pat and Tony Martin, Eric Locker, Alan and Ros Furley, R Huggins, D Irving, E McCall, T McLean, Esther and John Sprinkle)*

Parkstone [SZ0491]

Grasshopper [Bournemouth Rd]: Good generous

food inc carvery, reasonable prices, children welcome in new annexe *(Dr A Brookes)*

Piddletrenthide [SY7099]

☆ *European*: Friendly and unpretentious traditional oak-beamed pub locally favoured for good generous reasonably priced fresh food inc fine home-cooked ham and very good value lamb shanks (should book wknds), well kept Courage Directors and Ringwood Best, helpful cheery staff, log fire in attractive copper-hooded fireplace, willow-pattern china, stylish chairs; piped music; tables in neatly kept front garden, three bedrooms with own baths and good views *(Dennis Jenkin, Marianne and Peter Stevens, Francis Johnston, Mr and Mrs Philip Whiteley, BB)*

☆ *Piddle* [B3143 N of Dorchester]: Friendly plain-speaking landlord, emphasis on good food esp fish, with whole board of imaginative fish specials, most tables set for eating, but comfortable leatherette sofas in refurbished bar; good range of beers, children's room, dining room and pool room; spacious streamside garden with picnic-sets and play area; bedrooms planned; village and pub named after the river here *(David Keating, Ian Jones, BB)*

Poole [SZ0090]

Antelope [High St]: Local just off quay with recently refurbished restaurant, enjoyable food, five real ales, lots of RNLI photographs *(Keith and Katy Stevens)*

Beehive [Sandbanks Rd, Lilliput]: Good value food in large no smoking conservatory-style family eating area, friendly service, well kept beers; picnic-sets outside *(B and K Hypher)*

Blue Boar [Market Cl]: Comfortable, with good choice of real ales, wide choice of remarkably cheap food, lots of interesting nautical theme pictures and artefacts, cellar bar too; nearby parking can be difficult *(Peter and Audrey Dowsett)*

Crown [Market St]: Warm and friendly, with two linked bars, fairly priced plentiful food esp fresh fish, two-for-one bargains some days, four well kept ales inc Hardy Country and Royal Oak; unpretentious very helpful service *(Keith and Katy Stevens)*

Guildhall Tavern [Market St]: Good fresh food esp local fish in bright family dining pub (almost a French feel to it), well kept Ringwood, decent house wine, attentive welcoming service *(LYM, Steve Chambers, Joyce and Maurice Cottrell)*

☆ *Inn in the Park* [Pinewood Rd, off A338 towards Branksome Chine – via The Avenue]: Pleasantly decorated and cheerful small hotel bar popular with local residents and business people for well kept Adnams Broadside, Bass and Wadworths 6X and good value generous bar food (not Sun evening) from good 'sandwedges' (sandwiches with chips) up; polite young staff, attractive dining room (children allowed), log fire, tables on small sunny terrace; comfortable bedrooms, quiet pine-filled residential area above sea *(Pam Adsley, LYM)*

☆ *Portsmouth Hoy* [The Quay]: Enjoyable nautical theme, lots of interesting brassware and ships' insignia, bustling atmosphere, well kept ales inc Hardy Royal Oak, cheerful service, wide choice of usual food inc good value fish and chips special, nice back dining area, separate no smoking area; piped music, games machine; facing lively quay, handy for aquarium *(Dave Braisted)*

Rising Sun [Dear Hay Lane]: Refurbished largely as good value thai restaurant (booking recommended for well priced Sun buffet), Greene King Abbot and Ringwood Best, long bar with two smoking rooms one end, no smoking the other; adjacent pay and display parking *(W W Burke)*

Shah of Persia [Longfleet Rd/Fernside Rd (A35)]: Spacious roadhouse pleasantly redecorated with William Morris wallpaper and art deco lighting, lots of old posters and advertisements, well kept Hardy Country, Popes and Royal Oak and a guest such as Bass, wide choice of generous food (not Sat or Sun evening) from sandwiches and baguettes to mixed grill (occasional half-price bargains), big no smoking eating area, bright friendly service; piped music; new bedroom block *(B and K Hypher, Joan and Michel Hooper-Immins, Mr and Mrs Philip Whiteley)*

Portland Bill [SY6870]

Pulpit: Rather bare but comfortable and welcoming food pub in great spot nr Pulpit Rock, short stroll to lighthouse and cliffs; generous quickly served food inc Sun lunch, local shellfish and interesting puddings, Bass and Tetleys; piped music *(Joan and Michel Hooper-Immins)*

Powerstock [SY5196]

Three Horseshoes [off A3066 Beaminster—Bridport via W Milton]: Busy stone-and-thatch pub under new licensees (yet again), good fires and stripped panelling, well kept Palmers real ales, quite a few wines by the glass, children welcome in no smoking restaurant; open all day, bedrooms, lovely views towards the sea from tables in garden behind *(LYM)*

Preston [SY7082]

Spyglass [Bowleaze Coveway]: Busy family dining pub, great views over Weymouth from top of Furzy Cliff, wide choice of enjoyable food with plenty for children, Boddingtons, Courage Directors, Quay JD1742 and Ringwood Fortyniner; piped music may be loud; side adventure play area *(Joan and Michel Hooper-Immins)*

Shaftesbury [ST8622]

Half Moon [Salisbury Rd (A30, by roundabout)]: Busy and welcoming, with roomy restaurant area, good choice of food under new licensees, quick service; garden with adventure playground *(B and K Hypher, Marjorie and David Lamb)*

Ship [Bleke St]: Traditional 17th-c local, cosy and simple, with charmingly unmodernised architecture – black panelling, oak woodwork, handsome windows; well kept Badger Best and Tanglefoot, farm cider, separate eating area; shame about the piped music; pool and other games in public bar (crowded with young people wknd evenings), tables on terrace *(M and P Theodorou, LYM)*

☆ *Two Brewers* [St James St, 150 yds from bottom of Gold Hill]: Down steep famously photogenic Gold Hill, with friendly well divided open-plan turkey-carpeted bar, lots of decorative plates, very wide choice of reasonably priced popular fresh bar food (children's helpings of any dish), good puddings and Sun roasts, chatty landlord and good service, well kept Courage Best and Directors, Wadworths 6X and guest beers, good value wines, maybe quiet piped music in restaurant; picnic-sets in attractive good-sized garden with pretty views *(BB, Dave Irving, John and Joan Calvert)*

Shapwick [ST9302]

☆ *Anchor* [off A350 Blandford—Poole; West St]: Attractive décor, varnished pine tables on quarry tiles, cushioned chairs, warm atmosphere, good freshly cooked food changing monthly, three real ales, good wine list, good friendly staff, several small rooms with end dining room; piped music, occasional live; in heart of pretty thatched village, brightly painted tables in front, more on terrace behind, children welcome (small garden has play area); handy for Kingston Lacy *(Basil Cheesenham, Phil and Karen Kerkin, BB)*

Sherborne [ST6316]

☆ *Cross Keys* [Cheap St]: Comfortable and attractively refurbished market-centre local with run of small rooms, good sensible food, quick cheerful service, Bass and Courage; pot plants on each table, interesting display of postal history, postbox in corridor; talking fruit machine; open all day Sun, bowls for dogs, some seats outside *(Prof Kenneth Surin, R T and J C Moggridge)*

☆ *Skippers* [Horsecastles (A352 link rd)]: Extended pub with long stripped-stone bar partly laid for eating, immense choice of good generous food esp daily fresh fish, pleasant local bustle, jolly landlord, quick warm-hearted service in spite of crowds, well kept Wadworths IPA, JcB and 6X with a guest such as Butcombe, interesting pictures and bric-a-brac; tables outside *(Joan and Michel Hooper-Immins, Ewan and Sue Hewitt)*

Shroton [ST8512]

☆ *Cricketers* [off A350 N of Blandford (village also called Iwerne Courtney), follow signs]: Busy welcoming pub facing peaceful village green, bright divided bar with alcoves and cricketing memorabilia, good home-made food inc game, plenty of fish and good puddings (there may be a wait; booking advised Sun lunch), landlord informative about changing ales such as Butcombe, Shepherd Neame Spitfire and Ringwood True Glory served from pumps made into little cricket bats, pink and blue restaurant; big pool area, discreet piped music; pretty garden with tables and well stocked herb garden *(B and K Hypher, BB)*

Stoke Abbott [ST4500]

☆ *New Inn* [off B3162 and B3163 2 miles W of Beaminster]: 17th-c thatched pub very popular for generous competitively priced food inc fresh fish; beams, brasses, stripped stone alcoves on either side of one big log fireplace, another with

handsome panelling, no smoking dining room; friendly licensees and poodle, well kept Palmers ales, neat attractive garden with play area, nice setting in unspoilt quiet thatched village; children welcome, bedrooms; cl Mon in July/Aug *(LYM, Mr and Mrs A H Young, DAV)*

Stourton Caundle [ST7115]
Trooper: Two-bar village inn filled with ex-shepherd landlord's massive collection of shepherding and other country tools and equipment, more in skittle alley (where children allowed), with shepherds' huts outside; well kept ales inc Cottage and Exmoor, farm cider; cl Mon lunchtime *(anon)*

Studland [SZ0382]
Bankes Arms [off B3351, Isle of Purbeck; Manor Rd]: Very popular spot above fine beach, outstanding country, sea and cliff views from huge pleasant garden with masses of seating; comfortably basic, friendly and easy-going big bar with raised drinking area, substantial simple food (at a price) inc all day local fish, well kept beers such as Palmers, Poole, Wadworths 6X and unusual guest beers, local farm cider, attractive log fires, darts and pool in side games area; children welcome, just off Coast Path; can get very busy trippery wknds and in summer, parking can be complicated or expensive if you're not a NT member; big comfortable bedrooms *(Ron Shelton, Jeff Davies, Betsy and Peter Little, JDM, KM)*

Sturminster Marshall [SY9499]
Red Lion [N end of High St, opp church; off A350 Blandford—Poole]: Attractive and thriving flower-decked old-fashioned pub, open-plan, clean and pleasant, with low beams, good value food inc substantial interesting starters, bargain OAP two-course lunch, sandwiches on Sun too, friendly prompt service, well kept Badger ales, log fire, skittle alley doubling as family room *(Ron Shelton, Marjorie and David Lamb)*

Swanage [SZ0278]
Black Swan [High St]: Around eight changing well kept ales in small well worn in but very neatly kept bar with lots of brass, cheerful service, no music; separate dining room, big terrace *(the Didler, Bryan and Betty Southwell, Hazel and Michael Duncombe)*
Red Lion [High St]: Low beams, shelves and walls densely hung with hundreds of keys, mugs and lots of highly polished brass blow lamps, decent inexpensive food, well kept Flowers, Greene King Old Speckled Hen and Ringwood, prompt friendly staff, separate locals' bar; children's games in large barn, garden with partly covered back terrace *(Peter and Audrey Dowsett, the Didler, David and Carole Chapman)*

Sydling St Nicholas [SY6399]
☆ *Greyhound* [High St]: New licensees doing wide choice of particularly good food from filled crusty rolls to main dishes with plentiful properly cooked veg, good fish and delicious puddings, friendly family service, chatty locals, well kept Palmers and Youngs Special, long

brick bar counter, some stripped stonework and flagstones, pool, piped music; pleasant bistro-style flagstoned conservatory, restaurant; good tables in nice small garden with play area, very pretty village *(Cynthia and Stephen Fisher, Vivian T Green, Anthony Barnes, BB)*

Tarrant Keynston [ST9204]

True Lovers Knot: Village local with very friendly new owners, good food, well kept Badger ales, woodburner; big garden with play area, donkey and chickens *(Frank Smith)*

Three Legged Cross [SU0904]

Old Barn Farm [Ringwood Rd, towards Ashley Heath and A31]: Large quaint thatched Vintage Inn with good value usual food presented well, pleasant restaurant, friendly and attentive young staff, Bass and Worthington, decent wines; lots of tables on attractive front lawn by pond, some children's amusements, enormous dovecote; handy for Moors Valley Country Park *(Phyl and Jack Street, I R Fourmy)*

Tolpuddle [SY7994]

Martyrs [former A35 W of Bere Regis]: Good freshly cooked food in bar and busy attractively laid out restaurant, hard-working friendly staff, well kept Badger beers; well used by locals, children welcome, nice garden with ducks, hens and rabbits; quiet bypassed village *(Tony and Wendy Hobden, Martin and Jane Wright, Mr and Mrs R G Spiller, B and K Hypher)*

Upwey [SY6684]

☆ *Riverhouse* [B3159, nr junction A354]: Former Masons Arms, two cosy rooms, one no smoking, friendly and expert new licensees doing wide range of food from lunchtime baguettes through familiar dishes to mediterranean-style specialities, children's dishes, two well kept ales, good wine choice; disabled access, sizeable garden with play area *(anon)*

Wareham [SY9287]

Black Bear [South St]: Bow-windowed 18th-c hotel with old local prints and lots of brass in convivial well worn in lounge bar off through corridor, well kept Courage Directors and Hardy Country, good choice of keenly priced usual food inc vegetarian and children's, decent coffee, back restaurant, further room with TV; piped classical music; picnic-sets in pleasant flower-filled back yard, open all day; bedrooms *(David and Carole Chapman, D W Stokes, Joan and Michel Hooper-Immins, BB)*

Duke of Wellington [East St]: Small 18th-c pub, friendly, relaxing and civilised but unpretentious, with reliable food, Fullers London Pride and Ringwood beers, some original features; popular with family groups, open all day *(Dez and Jen Clarke)*

☆ *Kings Arms* [North St (A351, N end of town)]: Thriving traditional thatched town local, back serving counter and two bars off flagstoned central corridor, good value food (not Fri–Sun evenings) inc good choice of sandwiches and baguettes, friendly staff, well kept Whitbreads-related ales, garden *(LYM, R M Corlett)*

Quay Inn [The Quay]: Comfortable, light and airy stripped-stone bars in great spot right by the water, food from soup and sandwiches up,

open fire, well kept Whitbreads-related and other ales, children allowed away from main bar; picnic-sets out on quay; bedrooms, open all day summer, parking nearby can be difficult *(Dez and Jen Clarke, Paul Roughley, Julia Fox, Joyce and Maurice Cottrell)*

West Bay [SY4590]

Bridport Arms: Welcoming 16th-c thatched pub on beach of Bridport's low-key holiday village (was the Bridehaven pub in TV's *Harbour Lights*), generous good value food esp fish, cheerful service, well kept Palmers IPA, 200 and Gold, cosy lounge, big fireplace in basic flagstoned back bar, no music; paying public car park *(M Joyner, Joan and Michel Hooper-Immins)*

George [George St]: Red plush banquettes, mate's chairs, masses of shipping pictures, some model ships and nautical hardware, roomy L-shaped public bar with games and juke box, separate no smoking back restaurant; food inc lots of good value local fish from prawn and crab sandwiches up, well kept Palmers IPA and Gold, cheery service; tables outside, bedrooms *(Joan and Michel Hooper-Immins, BB)*

West Stour [ST7822]

Ship: Good value generous food, friendly newish licensees, well kept local beer, attractive furnishings, big log fire, intimate split-level restaurant; garden behind, comfortable bedrooms *(Pat and Robert Watt)*

Weymouth [SY6778]

Boot [High West St]: 18th-c pub nr harbour, warm and friendly, with beams and stone-mullioned windows, well kept Ringwood ales with a guest such as Adnams Broadside, farm cider, newish licensees doing good value snacks and straightforward lunches, decent house wine *(Bryan Robinson, Joan and Michel Hooper-Immins)*

Dorothy [Esplanade]: Real-ale pub converted from former café in outstanding seafront spot, great views from pavement tables; long bar, carpet and bare boards, local Quay Dorothy, Old Rott and Silent or Summer Knight, also interesting guest beers and Inch's cider, good value straightforward food inc crab sandwiches, friendly landlady, daily papers; children welcome, open all day, bedrooms (wknd bargains inc tour of Quay Brewery) *(the Didler, Richard Lewis)*

Kings Arms [Trinity Rd]: Friendly unspoilt two-bar quayside pub, lots of black beams and fishing prints, well kept Ringwood Best and Fortyniner and Wadworths 6X, good value food (not winter evening, may be a wait) from crab sandwiches to local fish *(Joan and Michel Hooper-Immins)*

Old Castle [Sudan Rd]: Newish licensees doing good value generous well presented food from sandwiches, ploughman's and baked potatoes to steaks, happy atmosphere; tables outside, close to beach *(Heidi Gale)*

☆ *Red Lion* [Hope Sq]: Lively unsmart bare-boards pub with four well kept beers such as Courage Best and Weymouth Organic Gold, quickly served cheap simple meals from good crab sandwiches up (not Fri-Sun evenings), interesting RNLI and fishing stuff all over the walls and ceiling (even two boats), open fires, daily papers, friendly family atmosphere, good staff; plenty of tables outside (more than inside), open all day in summer (food all day then too), opp smart touristy Brewers Quay complex in former brewery *(Joan and Michel Hooper-Immins, Jeff Davies, the Didler, Liz and John Soden, BB)*

Spa [Dorchester Rd, Radipole; off A354 at Safeway roundabout]: Large well run open-plan family pub, good helpings of interesting food with fresh veg, well kept Hardy Country, Popes and Royal Oak with a guest such as Courage Best, attentive friendly service, peaceful restaurant and back conservatory; good garden with play area *(Joan and Michel Hooper-Immins)*

Wellington Arms [St Alban St]: Homely calm oasis, panelled L-shaped bar with etched windows, good value lunchtime food (all day summer wkdys) from sandwiches to low-priced plain or fancy hot dishes and daily roasts, well kept Hardy Country, Popes and Royal Oak *(Joan and Michel Hooper-Immins)*

Wimborne Minster [SZ0099]

White Hart [Corn Market]: Old-fashioned low-beamed bar in pedestrian precinct a few steps from Minster, well kept Hardy Country and Royal Oak, coffee (but not tea), wide range of good fresh reasonably priced bar food from warm baguettes up in eating area, good friendly service *(Derek, Hazel and Graeme Lloyd)*

Wool [SY8486]

Ship [A352 Wareham—Dorchester]: Roomy open-plan thatched and timbered family pub, well decorated and furnished, with good choice of generous food inc children's in pleasant low-ceilinged main dining area, three smaller side rooms, friendly quick service, well kept Badger beers; shame about the piped music; picnic-sets overlooking railway in attractive garden with terrace, handy for Monkey World and Tank Museum, pleasant village *(Stan Edwards, B and K Hypher, W W Burke, Joan and Michel Hooper-Immins)*

Yetminster [ST5910]

White Hart [High St]: Lots of nooks and crannies in comfortable low-beamed stone and thatched village pub with enjoyable lunchtime food, well kept Bass and Oakhill real ales, friendly staff; well behaved children allowed, tables on back terrace, garden with play area *(Richard Fendick)*

'Children welcome' means the pub says it lets children inside without any special restriction. If it allows them in, but to restricted areas such as an eating area or family room, we specify this. Places with separate restaurants usually let children use them, hotels usually let them into public areas such as lounges. Some pubs impose an evening time limit – let us know if you find this:
www.goodguides.com

Essex

Quite a lot of comings and goings among the main entries here this year: the newcomers are the Three Willows at Birchanger (a good off-motorway food stop), the Whalebone at Fingringhoe (nicely redecorated, with very enjoyable food – but plenty of local action), the White Hart at Moreton (friendly and unassuming, with bargain lunches), the Sportsmans Arms at Nounsley (the filipino food is the surprise in this welcoming local – good beer, too), and the Mole Trap hidden away out in the country near Stapleford Tawney (a real country pub, with proper home cooking and beautifully kept beer). Other pubs on particularly good form here are the Cricketers at Clavering (imaginative food in this smart dining pub), the cheerful Sun in Feering (good beer and atmosphere, character service), the Square & Compasses at Fuller Street (imaginative food in this civilised and distinctive country local), the Green Man at Gosfield (good honest food), the White Hart in Great Yeldham (interesting food under new restaurateur-landlord), the cheerful Rainbow & Dove at Hastingwood (bargain food just off the M11), the Bell at Horndon-on-the-Hill (good all round, gaining a Food Award this year), the Shepherd & Dog at Langham (the sort of village local we all wish we had), and the Green Dragon at Youngs End near Braintree (a well run dining pub). From among all these, the pub that gains our title of Essex Dining Pub of the Year is the White Hart in Great Yeldham. The Bell in Castle Hedingham deserves a long service award: in every edition of the Guide since it first started 20 years ago, and in the same family throughout that time. In the Lucky Dip section at the end of the chapter, pubs we'd particularly recommend (virtually all inspected and approved) are the Alma in Chelmsford, Rose & Crown in Colchester, Theydon Oak at Coopersale Street, Marlborough Head and Sun in Dedham, Black Bull at Fyfield, Jolly Sailor at Heybridge Basin, Sutton Arms at Little Hallingbury, Ferry Boat at North Fambridge, Rose at Peldon, Cats at Woodham Walter and Rose & Crown in Wivenhoe. Drinks prices in the area are around the national average; the Punchbowl at Paglesham and Prince of Wales at Stow Maries had commendably low beer prices.

ARKESDEN TL4834 Map 5

Axe & Compasses ★ ♀

Village signposted from B1038 – but B1039 from Wendens Ambo, then forking left, is prettier

Set in a very pretty village, this rambling, thatched country pub has a welcoming and relaxed atmosphere. Dating back to the 17th c, the cosy carpeted lounge bar is the oldest part, and has beautifully polished upholstered oak and elm seats, easy chairs and wooden tables, a warming fire, and lots of gleaming brasses on the walls. A smaller quirky public bar (which can get a bit smoky) is uncarpeted, with cosy built-in settles and a dartboard. Home-made bar food includes sandwiches (from £2.50), soup (£3), chicken liver pâté (£3.95), prawn and smoked mackerel roulade (£4.95), battered plaice or steak and kidney pie (£7.95), stir-fried vegetables with creamy french mustard sauce in puff pastry or sautéed mushroom pancake with white wine, cream and parmesan (£7.95), sirloin steak (£11.95) and a tempting puddings trolley

(£3); more elaborate menu in no smoking restaurant. Well kept Greene King IPA, Old Speckled Hen and Ruddles County on handpump with a guest such as Greene King Black Baron or one by Bass, a very good wine list and over 20 malt whiskies; cheerful, helpful service. There are seats out on a side terrace with pretty hanging baskets; parking at the back, and a craft centre in the post office opposite. *(Recommended by MLR, Martin and Lois Sheldrick, Joy and Peter Heatherley, Peter Baggott, Jack Clarfelt, Mr and Mrs Thomas, Olive and Ray Hebson, Richard Siebert, Tina and David Woods-Taylor, Mrs M Thomas)*

Greene King ~ Lease Themis and Diane Christou ~ Real ale ~ Bar food (12-2, 6.45-9.30) ~ Restaurant ~ (01799) 550272 ~ Children in restaurant ~ Open 11.30-2.30, 6-11; 12-3, 7-10.30 Sun

BIRCHANGER TL5022 Map 5
Three Willows

Under a mile from M11 junction 8: A120 towards Bishops Stortford, then almost immediately right to Birchanger Village; don't be waylaid earlier by the Birchanger Services signpost!

Besides a wide choice of usual food from hot and cold sandwiches and filled baked potatoes up, what draws so many people here is the good choice of fresh simply cooked fish served generously with chunky chips and plain salads, at hard-to-beat prices: on our inspection visit, £6.95 for fish crumble, £7.95 for most fish including paella, £8.95 for grilled baby halibut. The roomily extended carpeted main bar is filled with dark chairs and tables laid for dining; above a puce dado, the buff and brown ragged walls have a plethora of cricketing prints, photographs, cartoons and other memorabilia – the pub's name refers to cricket bats of the last three centuries. Well kept Greene King IPA, Abbot and Triumph on handpump, decent house wines, friendly and very informal family service. A small public bar has pool and sensibly placed darts, and there's a fruit machine. It's advisable to book if you want to eat in their restaurant. There are picnic-sets out on a terrace with heaters and on the lawn behind, with a sturdy climbing frame, swings and a basketball hoop (you can hear the motorway out here). No children are allowed inside. *(Recommended by Stephen and Jean Curtis, David and Pauline Loom, Joy and Peter Heatherley)*

Greene King ~ Tenants Paul and David Tucker ~ Real ale ~ Bar food (12-2, 7-9, no food Sun evening) ~ Restaurant ~ 01279 815913 ~ Open 11.30-3, 6-11; 12-3, 7-10.30 Sun

BURNHAM-ON-CROUCH TQ9596 Map 5
White Harte   £
The Quay

Popular with boaty types in summer, this friendly old inn has a wonderful outlook over the yachting estuary of the River Crouch. You can hear the water lapping against its private jetty, and in winter, the enormous welcoming log fire fuels a cheerful atmosphere. Throughout the partially carpeted bars, with cushioned seats around oak tables, you'll find replicas of Royal Navy ships, and assorted nautical items such as a ship's wheel, a barometer, even a compass in the hearth. The other traditionally furnished high-ceilinged rooms have sea pictures on panelled or stripped brick walls. Straightforward bar food from a short menu includes sandwiches (from £1.90), soup (£2.40), seafood platter, vegetable lasagne, lamb cutlets or curry (£5), locally caught skate, plaice or cod (£7.20), and puddings such as apple crumble and fruit pies (£2.30). Well kept Adnams, Crouch Vale Best Bitter and Tolly on handpump; friendly prompt service. *(Recommended by George Atkinson, Joy and Peter Heatherley, Colin Parker, David Carr)*

Free house ~ Licensee G John Lewis ~ Real ale ~ Bar food ~ Restaurant ~ (01621) 782106 ~ Children welcome ~ Open 11-11; 12-10.30 Sun ~ Bedrooms: £19.80(£40S)(£45B)/£37(£55S)(£65B)

CASTLE HEDINGHAM TL7835 Map 5
Bell

B1058 E of Sible Hedingham, towards Sudbury

This fine old coaching inn has been run by the same family for well over 30 years. The unchanging beamed and timbered saloon bar has Jacobean-style seats and windsor chairs around sturdy oak tables, and beyond the standing timbers left from a knocked-through wall, some steps lead up to an unusual little gallery. Behind the traditionally furnished public bar, a games room has dominoes and cribbage. One bar is no smoking, and each of the rooms has a warming log fire; piped music. Straightforward bar food includes home-made soup (£2.75), beef or spicy beanburger (£3.50), ploughman's (£4.50), vegetarian chilli (£6.25), tandoori chicken kebabs or steak and Guinness pie (£6.50) and specials (including fish on Monday nights) such as liver and bacon casserole (£6); puddings such as treacle tart or apple and blackberry pie (from £2.50). Greene King IPA, Shepherd Neame Spitfire and a guest beer such as Fullers London Pride are tapped from the cask. The big walled garden behind the pub is a pleasant place to sit in summer and contains an acre or so of grass, trees and shrubs as well as a sandpit and toys for children; there are more seats on a small terrace. An acoustic guitar group plays on Friday evenings, they have live jazz on the last Sunday of the month, and there's a Sunday night pub quiz. The nearby 12th-c castle keep is worth a visit. *(Recommended by Richard Siebert, Mark Percy, Lesley Mayoh, Bill and Margaret Rogers, Ian Phillips)*

Grays ~ Tenant Penny Doe ~ Real ale ~ Bar food (12-(2.30 wknd)2, 7-(9 Sun and Mon)9.30) ~ (01787) 460350 ~ Children away from public bar ~ Traditional jazz last Sun lunchtime of month, acoustic guitar group Fri evening ~ Open 11.45-3, 6-11; 12-3, 7-10.30 Sun; closed 25 Dec

CHAPPEL TL8927 Map 5
Swan

Wakes Colne; pub visible just off A1124 Colchester—Halstead

Gas heaters mean that you can sit out in the sheltered suntrap cobbled courtyard even in what all too often passes for an English summer at this timbered old pub, when parasols, big overflowing flower tubs and French street signs lend it a continental feel. It's splendidly set, with the River Colne running through the garden leading its way down to an impressive Victorian viaduct below. Inside, the spacious and low-beamed rambling bar has standing oak timbers dividing off side areas, banquettes around lots of dark tables, one or two swan pictures and plates on the white and partly panelled walls, and a few attractive tiles above the very big fireplace (which is filled with lots of plants in summer). Fresh fish is their speciality, with daily catches bringing in trout grilled with almonds (£6.95), rock eel (£7.25, large £9), plaice (£7.95, large £10.95) and haddock (£7.95, large £10.95). Other good value and popular bar food includes filled baguettes or sandwiches (from £1.75), ploughman's (from £3.75), gammon with pineapple or home-made pies (from £5.95), sirloin steak (£10.95), and good puddings (from £3.25); simple children's menu. One of the restaurant areas is no smoking. Well kept Greene King IPA, Abbot and Ruddles County on handpump, a good choice of wines by the glass, and just under two dozen malt whiskies, served by cheery helpful staff; cribbage. Just a few minutes walk away is the Railway Centre (a must for train buffs). *(Recommended by Judy Wayman, Bob Arnett, Keith Fairbrother, B N F and M Parkin, Nigel and Olga Wikeley)*

Free house ~ Licensee Terence Martin ~ Real ale ~ Bar food (12-(3 wknds)2.30, 7(6.30 Sat)-(10 Sun)10.30) ~ Restaurant ~ (01787) 222353 ~ Children in eating area of bar and restaurant ~ Open 11-3, 6-11; 11-11 Sat; 12-10.30 Sun

CLAVERING TL4731 Map 5
Cricketers

B1038 Newport—Buntingford, Newport end of village

Readers are enthralled by the excellent imaginative food at this smart, comfortably modernised 16th-c dining pub (run by the parents of TV chef Jamie Oliver). It attracts a well heeled set, and prices are not cheap, but portions are generous. There can be a really lively atmosphere during busy lunchtimes, when you might have to wait for the freshly cooked bar food. As well as sandwiches (from £3.50), the seasonally changing menu might include chicken and pistachio nut terrine with leeks (£5.75), brochette of salmon and king prawns cooked in sesame oil with balinese chilli sambal (£6.85), steamed pancake filled with oriental vegetables in a sweet and sour sauce (£10.75), guinea fowl with apricot stuffing in a Cointreau gravy (£12.80) and a good fresh fish choice (especially on Tuesdays) such as bass with avocado and lime creamy sauce (£14.50); there's an enticing puddings trolley (£4.25); children's meals (£3.50), or they can have a half helping of some main meals. Service is friendly and professional. The spotlessly kept and roomy L-shaped beamed bar has standing timbers resting on new brickwork, and pale green plush button-backed banquettes, stools and windsor chairs around shiny wooden tables on a pale green carpet, gleaming copper pans and horsebrasses, dried flowers in the big fireplace (open fire in colder weather), and fresh flowers on the tables; one area is no smoking; piped music. Adnams, Tetleys and a guest on handpump; specialist teas. The attractive front terrace has picnic-sets and umbrellas among colourful flowering shrubs. Pretty and traditionally furnished bedrooms. *(Recommended by Terry Mizen, Maysie Thompson, Martin and Lois Sheldrick, Evelyn and Derek Walter, Mrs A Chesher, Robert Lester, Joy and Peter Heatherley, Mr and Mrs G P Lloyd, D Moore Brooks, Brian and Pat Wardrobe)*

Free house ~ Licensee Trevor Oliver ~ Real ale ~ Bar food (12-2, 7-10) ~ Restaurant ~ (01799) 550442 ~ Children must be well behaved ~ Open 10.30-3, 6-(10.30 Sun)11; closed 25 and 26 Dec ~ Bedrooms: £65B/£90B

COGGESHALL TL8224 Map 5
Compasses

Pattiswick; signposted from A120 about 2 miles W of Coggeshall

The attractive, spacious beamed bars of this friendly pub, surrounded by rolling countryside, are neatly kept and comfortable, with tiled floors and lots of brass ornaments. The atmosphere is welcoming and the staff friendly. Generous straightforward bar food includes sandwiches (from £3.95) and toasted baguettes (£5.95), garlic and pesto mushrooms (£6.50), ploughman's (from £6.95), toad in the hole, battered plaice or fisherman's pie (£8.95), and puddings such as lemon sorbet and baked vanilla cheesecake (from £3.95); three-course Sunday lunch (£12.95). More elaborate dishes are served in the adjacent, partly no smoking barn restaurant. Well kept Greene King IPA, Abbot and Ruddles County. In summer you can eat in the garden; there are seats on the lawns, and there's an adventure playground. *(Recommended by Gordon Neighbour, Charles Gysin, John Allen, Adrian White, Julie King, Andrew Hudson)*

Free house ~ Licensees Chris and Gilbert Heap ~ Real ale ~ Bar food (12-2, 7-9) ~ Restaurant ~ (01376) 561322 ~ Children in eating area of bar and restaurant ~ Open 11-3, 6.30-11; 12-3, 7-10.30 Sun

FEERING TL8720 Map 5
Sun ◼

Feering Hill; before Feering proper, B1024 just NE of Kelvedon

A real favourite with readers, who continually comment on the friendly, welcoming service and good atmosphere at this gabled inn, originally part of a 16th-c mansion. As many as 30 mostly unusual real ales pass through the six handpumps every week, and the wide choice of home-cooked food is based on the licensees' own favourite dishes. Standing timbers break up the several areas, with plenty of neatly matching tables and chairs, and green-cushioned stools and banquettes around the walls. Carvings on the beams in the lounge are reputedly linked with Catherine of Aragon, and there's a handsome canopy with a sun motif over the woodburning stove; newspapers, backgammon, chess, dominoes, fruit machine. The bar staff are happy to chat to you about their well kept real ales; a typical clutch might be Batemans Summer Swallow, Dark Horse Sunrunner, Fullers London Pride, Mauldons Suffolk Pride, Rawlinsons Rich Ruby Mild and Rebellion Gold Digger. They also keep one or two weekly changing farm ciders, and over 40 malt whiskies. Written up on blackboards over the fireplace, well presented good value bar food includes sandwiches (from £1.55), home-made soup (£2.20), baked potatoes (from £2.45), cumberland sausage (£3.70), ploughman's (from £4.25), and interesting specials (£4.95-£8) such as pork in lime and coconut, hare braised in brown ale and port or savoury peanut pie, and from time to time you can even try kangaroo, crocodile or ostrich meat (from £9.95); puddings such as fruit pie or rum and raisin crunch (from £2); children's menu. Behind the pub is a partly covered paved terrace with quite a few seats and tables; there are more in an attractive garden beyond the car park. They sometimes have barbecues on sunny weekends. Their Easter and August bank holiday beer festivals have a regional theme, when they'll stock ales from a particular county or area. (*Recommended by Colin Draper, Mrs V Brown, Michael and Jeanne Shillington, Peter Saville, Joy and Peter Heatherley*)

Free house ~ Licensees Charles and Kim Scicluna ~ Bar food (12-2, 6-10; 12-3, 6-9.30 Sun) ~ Restaurant ~ No credit cards ~ (01376) 570442 ~ Well behaved children in eating area of bar and restaurant ~ Open 12-3, 6-(10.30 Sun)11

FINGRINGHOE TM0220 Map 5
Whalebone

Follow Rowhedge, Fingringhoe signpost off A134, the part that's just S of Colchester centre; or Fingringhoe signposted off B1025 S of Colchester

The back garden, with gravel paths winding through the grass around a sizeable old larch tree, has picnic-sets with a peaceful valley view. Inside, the pub has been nicely redone, with local watercolours (for sale) on the yellow walls, fabric Roman blinds with swagged pelmets, neat wall lamps and a chandelier. Three room areas have been airily opened together, just leaving some timber studs, and there's a pleasant mix of chairs and cushioned settles around stripped tables on the unsealed bare boards. The main focus is the blackboard over the small but hot coal fire: an unexpected richness of changing specials, with starters such as roasted vegetable risotto, wild mushroom and chestnut soup, sautéed pigeon breast with port and pine kernels, and salmon and watercress pâté (all £4.50); main courses such as trout fillet with spinach and walnut mousseline and a redcurrant parfait, liver and bacon, and herby lamb currants with redcurrant gravy (all £9.50); and puddings such as spotted dick, hot lemon pudding and chocolate and hazelnut torte (all £4.50). The cooking is inventive, and the presentation is stylish. They also do a wide and interesting choice of lunchtime baked potatoes (£2.75), sandwiches and baguettes (from £2.95); and do a good breakfast, 10-11.30 am, and there's a good value set menu (two courses £7.95, three £9.95). Well kept Greene King IPA, Abbot and Old Speckled Hen and a guest such as Mauldons Eatanswill Old on handpump; good service; decent house wines and coffee, but piped music. (*Recommended by Jane Hunt, Jenny and Brian Seller*)

Free house ~ Licensee Vivien Steed ~ Real ale ~ Bar food (12-2.30, 6.30-9.30; all day Sun) ~ Restaurant ~ (01206) 729307 ~ Children in separate family room ~ Occasional plays, theme nights and music in the garden ~ Open 10-3, 5-11; 10-10.30 Sun

FULLER STREET TL7416 Map 5
Square & Compasses 🍽

From A12 Chelmsford—Witham take Hatfield Peverel exit, and from B1137 there follow Terling signpost, keeping straight on past Terling towards Great Leighs; from A131 Chelmsford—Braintree turn off in Great Leighs towards Fairstead and Terling

A welcoming atmosphere, cheery licensees and enjoyable, interesting food are some of the reasons that readers like this small, civilised country pub. The wide choice of home-made bar food ranges from filled rolls and sandwiches (from £2.75), soup (£3.60), ham and eggs (£7.25) and fish pie (£8.75) to regularly changing specials such as pigeon breast with crispy bacon croutons (£6.50), garlic sausages with bubble and squeak or goats cheese and red onion tart (£8.75), and fresh fish such as swordfish with roasted peppers (£13.50) or poached smoked haddock with razor clams (£11). Along with the stuffed birds, traps and brasses which adorn the L-shaped beamed bar, you'll find otter tails, birds' eggs and old photographs of local characters, many of whom still use the pub. Comfortable and well lit, this carpeted bar has a woodburner as well as a big log fire; shove-ha'penny, table skittles, cribbage, dominoes and a fruit machine. Very well kept Nethergate Suffolk County and Ridleys IPA tapped from the cask, decent French regional wines, good coffee. Disabled lavatories; carpeted dining room extension for private parties. Gentle country views from tables outside. *(Recommended by Roger and Pauline Pearce, John and Enid Morris, Peter Baggott, Tina and David Woods-Taylor, Charles and Pauline Stride, B N F and M Parkin, Paul and Ursula Randall, Bob and Maggie Atherton, Richard Siebert)*

Free house ~ Licensees Howard Potts and Ginny Austin ~ Real ale ~ Bar food (12-(3 wknds)2.15, 7-(10 Sat, 8.30 Sun)9.30) ~ Restaurant ~ (01245) 361477 ~ Well behaved children welcome in eating area of the bar ~ Open 11.30-3, 6.30-11; 12-3.30, 7-10.30 Sun

GESTINGTHORPE TL8138 Map 5
Pheasant

Village signposted from B1058

Food prices haven't changed since last year at this unassuming, welcoming country pub. There are fine views of the surrounding countryside from picnic-sets in the garden and, from a big cushioned bow window seat in the neatly kept lounge bar, you can look out over the quiet lane to gently rising fields. As well as a raised log fire, interesting old furnishings here include a grandfather clock, arts-and-crafts oak settle, and a pew. The oak-beamed public bar, with more ordinary pub furniture, has another log fire; darts, cribbage, dominoes and piped music. Good straightforward bar food includes soup (£2.95), sandwiches (from £3), filled baked potatoes (from £4), ham and eggs (£5.95), chilli con carne or barbecued chicken (£6.95), best end of lamb (£9.95), and rib-eye steak or duck (£10.95), with home-made puddings such as lemon tart and sticky toffee pudding (£3.50). A more elaborate restaurant menu is served throughout the pub. Well kept Adnams, Greene King IPA and Old Speckled Hen and maybe a guest such as Nethergate Umbel on handpump. *(Recommended by Ian Phillips)*

Free house ~ Licensee R Sullivan ~ Real ale ~ Bar food (12-2, 7-9; not Sun pm or Mon) ~ Restaurant ~ (01787) 461196 ~ Children welcome ~ Open 12-3(4 Sat), 6-11; 12-5, 7-10.30 Sun; closed Mon lunchtime

GOSFIELD TL7829 Map 5
Green Man 🍴 ♀

3 miles N of Braintree

This smart dining pub is especially popular for its help-yourself lunchtime cold table, where you can choose from a tempting selection of home-cooked ham and pork, turkey, tongue, beef and poached or smoked salmon, as well as game pie, salads and home-made pickles (from £6.95). There's a good choice of generous, mostly traditional English bar food including soups such as game with sherry (from £2.85), sandwiches (from £2.40), filled baked potatoes (from £2.60), soft roe on toast (£3.75), mixed grill (£7.25), calves liver and bacon or pork chops marinated in oil and mustard (£7.95), and chicken breast filled with crab, cream cheese and prawns (£8.95), as well as a decent selection of fresh fish such as trout baked with almonds (£7.50) or swordfish steak (£8.25); vegetarian dishes such as deep-fried vegetable platter are available on request (£6.25). Mouth-watering home-made puddings include fruit pies, pavlovas and treacle tart (£3), vegetables are fresh and the chips home-made. The landlady is welcoming and you can expect friendly, efficient service. There's a laid-back sociable atmosphere in the two little bars, which have well kept Greene King IPA and Abbot on handpump. Many of the decent nicely priced wines are by the glass; darts, pool, fruit machine and juke box. Booking is advisable even midweek if you want to eat here. *(Recommended by Richard Siebert, B N F and M Parkin, Richard and Margaret Peers, Bill and Pat Pemberton)*

Greene King ~ Lease Janet Harrington ~ Real ale ~ Bar food (12-2, 6.45-9, not Sunday evening) ~ Restaurant ~ (01787) 472746 ~ Well behaved children in restaurant and eating area of bar ~ Open 11-3, 6-11; 12-3, 7-10.30 Sun

GREAT YELDHAM TL7638 Map 5
White Hart 🍴 ♀

Poole Street; A1017 Halstead—Haverhill
Essex Dining Pub of the Year
There are 170 wines at this popular black and white timbered dining pub, including 10 by the glass. The food is what most people come here for, though; cooked by the landlord, the same ambitious menu is available in the bar or in the no smoking restaurant. At lunchtime you can enjoy sandwiches made from three types of home-baked bread (£4.95), starters such as soup (£3.75) or crispy ocean tempura with spicy chilli dip (£5.50), and main courses such as roast local pigeon with red cabbage (£6.95) or grilled rainbow trout with lemon and almond butter (£8.50). Meals on the more sophisticated evening menu might include four-cheese tart (£8.95), grilled skate wing with courgette spaghetti (£12.50) and crispy duck breast with roast apple and buttered spinach (£13.50); puddings such as bread and butter pudding or (a hot tip) sticky toffee pudding (from £4.50); Sunday roast (from £9.95); smaller helpings available for children. Booking is highly recommended; service can be slow at times. As well as Adnams Bitter, regularly changing real ales on handpump could be Tolly Mild and Poole Holes Bay Hog; they also stock organic fruit juices and cider. The main areas have stone and wood floors with some dark oak panelling especially around the fireplace; watch your head – the door into the bar is very low. There are pretty garden seats among a variety of trees and shrubs on the well looked after lawns. *(Recommended by Martin and Lois Sheldrick, Gordon Theaker, Peter Baggott, Marjorie and Bernard Parkin, Tina and David Woods-Taylor, Richard Siebert, Adrian White, Julie King, Ray and Jacki Davenport)*

Free house ~ Licensee John Dicken ~ Real ale ~ Bar food (12-2, 6.30-9.30) ~ Restaurant ~ (01787) 237250 ~ Children welcome ~ Open 11-3, 6-11; 12-3, 7-10.30 Sun

HASTINGWOOD TL4807 Map 5
Rainbow & Dove £

¼ mile from M11 junction 7; Hastingwood signposted after Ongar signs at exit roundabout
Quite a favourite with readers, this comfortable 17th-c rose-covered cottage makes for a relaxing break from the nearby motorway. There are cosy fires in the three homely little low-beamed rooms which open off the main bar area; the one on the left is particularly snug and beamy, with the lower part of its wall stripped back to bare brick and decorated with brass pistols and plates. A small function room is no smoking. The atmosphere is relaxed, even when it's busy. Enjoyable reasonably priced bar food includes sandwiches (from £2.25), baked potatoes (from £2.50), ploughman's (from £3.75), crab (£3.85), local sausages and mash (£4.25), turkey, ham and mushroom pie (£5), vegetable crumble (£5.75), and lots of fresh fish on a specials board such as skate wing, sea bream with mushroom sauce, pink trout with prawns and mushrooms, butterfish and swordfish (from £4.75). Well kept Courage Directors, Greene King IPA and a guest such as Youngs Special on handpump; piped music; it can get smoky. Hedged off from the car park is a stretch of grass with picnic-sets under cocktail parasols. *(Recommended by Joy and Colin Rorke, Tony Beaulah, B N F and M Parkin, Colin and Janet Roe, Mrs A Chesher, Patricia Beebe, Ian Phillips, Nigel and Olga Wikeley, Sally Anne and Peter Goodale, Michael Butler, Lynn Sharpless, Bob Eardley, Gordon Neighbour)*

Punch ~ Tenants Jamie and Andrew Keep ~ Real ale ~ Bar food (12-2.30, 7-9.30) ~
(01279) 415419 ~ Children in eating area of bar ~ Open 11.30-3, 6-11; 12-3, 7-10.30
Sun

HORNDON-ON-THE-HILL TQ6683 Map 3
Bell 🍺 🍷 🛏

M25 junction 30 into A13, then left into B1007 after 7 miles, village signposted from here

This medieval hall (a real sight in summer when it's covered with flowers) seems to
be doing better than ever, with readers singling out for comment the pleasant
atmosphere, beautifully presented food and obliging and knowledgeable staff. They
stock more than 100 well chosen wines from all over the world, including over a
dozen by the glass, and you can buy bottles off-sales. The heavily beamed bar has
some antique high-backed settles and benches, rugs on the flagstones or highly
polished oak floorboards, and a curious collection of hot cross buns hanging from a
beam. The popular menu, which changes twice a day, is available in the bar and no
smoking restaurant, and well cooked dishes might include sandwiches (from £4.95),
swede soup (£3.95), grilled asparagus with olives and lemon mayonnaise (£5.50),
yoghurt marinated cod with smoked tomato salsa or pot roast chicken with peas and
girolles (£11.95), grilled smoked rib-eye steak or cold red wine poached halibut
(£12.95), and puddings such as bramley apple and date ice cream or poached
rhubarb with ginger praline meringue (from £4 – readers recommend the lemon tart
with brandy snap); two-course set meal £13.95, three courses £15.95. They stock a
good range of well kept real ales, with changing guests such as Batemans XXXB,
Cottage Golden Arrow and Crouch Vale Brewers Gold joining Bass and Greene
King IPA on handpump; occasional beer festivals. On the last weekend in June, the
High Road outside is closed (by Royal Charter) for period-costume festivities and a
crafts fair. The beamed bedrooms are very attractive. (Recommended by John and Enid
Morris, Kevin Flack, Pat and Tony Martin, Richard Siebert, Bruce M Drew, Adrian White,
Julie King, Mrs A Mager, Thomas Neate, Joy and Peter Heatherley, Kay Vowles, Ian Phillips,
Len Banister)

Free house ~ Licensee John Vereker ~ Real ale ~ Bar food (12-1.45, 6.45-9.45; not
bank hol Mon) ~ Restaurant ~ (01375) 642463 ~ Children in eating area of bar and
restaurant ~ Open 11-2.30(3 Sat), 5.30(6 Sat)-11; 12-4, 7-10.30 Sun; closed 25 and
26 Dec ~ Bedrooms: /£65B

LANGHAM TM0233 Map 5
Shepherd & Dog 🍷

Moor Rd/High St; village signposted off A12 N of Colchester

'Excellent' is a word that keeps cropping when readers write to us about this
welcoming village pub. The spick and span L-shaped bar is made up of an engaging
hotch-potch of styles, with interesting collections of continental bottled beers and
brass and copper fire extinguishers, and there are usually books on sale for charity.
Made wherever possible from fresh local produce (all the meat is British), good
hearty home-cooked food which changes daily is chalked on boards around the bar,
and might include sandwiches (from £2.30), chicken satay or deep-fried brie with
gooseberry sauce (£3.95), beef stew with dumplings (£7.95), steaks (from £7.95),
butterfish marinated in lemon and oregano (£8.95), and puddings such as treacle
sponge and blackberry and rum tart (£3); Sunday roast (from £6.50). Well kept
Greene King IPA and Abbot with a weekly changing guest such as Nethergate
Suffolk County on handpump, and a short but thoughtful wine list; pleasant obliging
service. In summer, there are very pretty window boxes, and a shaded bar in the
enclosed side garden; tables outside. They now have regular (and very popular)
theme weeks and activity nights. (Recommended by Joy and Peter Heatherley, Peter Baggott,
Ian Phillips, B N F and M Parkin, Jenny and Brian Seller, Sarah Lomas, R J Walden)

Free house ~ Licensees Paul Barnes and Jane Graham ~ Real ale ~ Bar food (12-2, 6-
9.30) ~ Restaurant ~ (01206) 272711 ~ Children welcome ~ Folk jam sessions every
fourth Sun ~ Open 11-3, 5.30(6 Sat)-11; 12-3, 7-10.30 Sun; closed 26 Dec

LITTLE BRAXTED TL8314 Map 5

Green Man

Kelvedon Road; village signposted off B1389 by NE end of A12 Witham bypass – keep on patiently

Tucked away on an isolated lane, this pretty brick house is a great place to come for a quiet drink. The welcoming, cosy little lounge has an open fire and an interesting collection of bric-a-brac, including 200 horsebrasses, some harness, mugs hanging from a beam, and a lovely copper urn. Reasonably priced and enjoyably straightforward bar food includes sandwiches (from £2.20), good filled baguettes or baked potatoes (from £2.95), cottage pie (£3.25), haggis or ploughman's (from £5.25), and daily specials such as cheese and onion pudding (£4.75), tuna and sweetcorn pasta (£5.50), steak and ale pie (£6.95), and minted lamb casserole, with puddings such as bakewell or treacle tart, and fresh strawberries – grown by the barman – in summer (£2.95); friendly service. In the tiled public bar, well kept Ridleys IPA and Rumpus are served from handpumps in the form of 40mm brass cannon shells, along with several malt whiskies; darts, shove-ha'penny, cribbage, dominoes and fruit machine. The sheltered garden behind the pub has picnic-sets and a pond. *(Recommended by Derek and Sylvia Stephenson, M W Turner, Joy and Peter Heatherley)*

Ridleys ~ Tenant Tony Wiley ~ Real ale ~ Bar food (not Sun evening) ~ (01621) 891659 ~ Open 11.30-3, 6-11; 12-3, 7-10.30 Sun

LITTLE DUNMOW TL6521 Map 5

Flitch of Bacon 🛏

Village signposted off A120 E of Dunmow, then turn right on village loop road

Other people are discouraged from using mobile phones in this unchanging country pub, with its easy-going mix of locals and visitors gathering in the small timbered bar. It's simply but attractively furnished, with flowery-cushioned pews and ochre walls, and while quietly relaxing on weekday lunchtimes, in the evenings it can get quite bustling. From a short menu, the straightforward reasonably priced bar food might include sandwiches (from £2.30), liver and bacon with mash (£5.75), gammon steak (£6.25), smoked salmon and scrambled eggs (£6.75) and sirloin steak (£9), as well as puddings such as chocolate fudge cake (£2.50). Well kept Greene King IPA with a couple of guests such as Mighty Oak on handpump, several wines by the glass, and 10 or so malt whiskies; friendly hard-working licensees. They've now opened up a back room with french windows looking out on to the terrace. The pub has views across a quiet lane to a broad expanse of green, and has a few picnic-sets on the edge; the nearby church of St Mary is well worth a visit (the pub has a key). Basic, but clean and comfortable bedrooms. Handy for Stansted Airport. *(Recommended by John and Margaret Mitchell, Catherine Budgett-Meakin, Tony Beaulah, Richard Siebert, John and Anne McIver)*

Free house ~ Licensees David and Teresa Caldwell ~ Real ale ~ Bar food (not Sun evening) ~ No credit cards ~ (01371) 820323 ~ Children in eating area of bar and restaurant ~ Open 12-3, 6-(10.30 Sun)11 ~ Bedrooms: £40S/£55S

LITTLE WALDEN TL5441 Map 5

Crown ◗

B1052 N of Saffron Walden

In the low-beamed bar of this 18th-c low white cottage you can expect to find up to six very well kept real ales tapped from the cask by friendly, chatty staff. Alongside Adnams Bitter and Greene King IPA, there could be Adnams Broadside, Black Sheep Bitter and City of Cambridge Boathouse and Hobsons Choice. A warm, cosy atmosphere is helped along by a good log fire in the brick fireplace, bookroom-red walls, flowery curtains and a mix of bare boards and navy carpeting. Seats, ranging from high-backed pews to little cushioned armchairs, are spaced around a good variety of closely arranged tables, mostly big, some stripped. The small red-tiled room on the right has two little tables, and darts. Generously served bar food includes soup (£2.95), sandwiches (from £2.25), ploughman's (from £3.25), home-made lasagne (£6.95), steak and ale pie (£7.50), and changing daily specials on blackboards such as a vegetarian pasta dish (£6.25), pork with wine and stilton (£7.25), fish pie (£7.50) and lemon sole (£7.95), with puddings such as bread and butter pudding (from £2.95); piped local radio. The walk from the car park in the dark can be tricky. *(Recommended by Kevin Thorpe, Stephen, Julie and Hayley Brown, Catherine and Richard Preston, Peter Baggott, Joy and Peter Heatherley)*

Free house ~ Licensee Colin Hayling ~ Bar food (not Sun evening) ~ Restaurant ~ (01473) 625912 ~ Children welcome ~ Trad jazz Weds evening ~ Open 11-3, 6-11; 12-10.30 Sun; closed 26 Dec, evening Jan 1

MILL GREEN TL6401 Map 5

Viper 🍺 £

The Common; from Fryerning (which is signposted off north-east bound A12 Ingatestone bypass) follow Writtle signposts

This charmingly uncomplicated, friendly little pub is well worth a visit in summer, when its cottage garden is a mass of colour – the front of the pub itself is almost hidden by overflowing hanging baskets and window boxes. Two timeless cosy lounge rooms have spindleback seats, armed country kitchen chairs, and tapestried wall seats around neat little old tables, and there's a log fire. Booted walkers are directed towards the fairly basic parquet-floored tap room, which is more simply furnished with shiny wooden traditional wall seats, and beyond that there's another room with country kitchen chairs and sensibly placed darts; shove-ha'penny, dominoes, cribbage and a fruit machine. From an oak-panelled counter they serve very well kept Ridleys IPA and three weekly changing guests from breweries such as Nethergate and local Mighty Oak (who brew a warming winter ale, Vipers Venom, for the pub) on handpump, as well as farm cider. The simple bar snacks are served only at lunchtime, and include good sandwiches (from £2, toasted from £2.50), home-made soup (£2.50), hawaiian toast (£2.75), chilli (£3.25) and ploughman's (from £4.50). On bank holidays and some weekends, they serve filled baguettes with real ale sausages (£2.75). Cheerful service even when busy; no children in pub. Tables on the lawn overlook the tremendously well cared for garden. The friendly dog is called Ben. *(Recommended by Peter Baggott, John and Enid Morris, Pete Baker, Kay Vowles, Len Banister, Diana Brumfit)*

Free house ~ Licensees Roger and Fred Beard ~ Real ale ~ Bar food (12-2) ~ No credit cards ~ (01277) 352010 ~ Children in garden only ~ Open 12-3, 6-11; 12-3, 7-10.30 Sun

MORETON TL5307 Map 5

White Hart £

Village signposted off B184 just N of A414 roundabout

It's the unfailingly friendly and helpful service which produces such a pleasant atmosphere in this snug pub: a partly divided L-shaped lounge bar with one or two sturdy low beams, rusty orange cushions on wall seats, little elbow chairs and the inglenook seats by the log fire, rust-coloured velvet curtains, soft lighting, old-fashioned prints and lots of woodwork including some panelling. Well kept Adnams and Greene King IPA and Abbot on handpump, decent house wines, and unlimited coffee. Straightforward bar food includes soup (£2.50), sandwiches (from £2.95), ploughman's (from £3.95), spaghetti bolognese or breaded cod (£5.95) and specials such as home-made lasagne or vegetarian pasta bake (£4.95); bargain lunches Tues-Fri (one course £3.95, two £4.95 or three £5.95); there's an attractive small dining room with timbers in its stripped brick walls. A public bar on the right has pool and darts; there may be piped radio (on our inspection visit, it was turned down as we walked in – we didn't think our prickles were that obvious); TV, dominoes, fruit machine. There are picnic-sets out on a small back terrace, and on a grass area beyond the car park, clearly once an orchard, with a climber and crawler. *(Recommended by Ian Phillips, George Atkinson)*

Free house ~ Licensee Jim Dallas ~ Real ale ~ Bar food (11.30-3, 6.30-10.30, no food winter Mon) ~ Restaurant ~ (01277) 890228 ~ No children in bar after 9pm ~ Folk music Fri evening ~ Open 11-11; 12-10 Sun; 11-3, 6-11, closed Mon lunchtime winter

NOUNSLEY TL7910 Map 5
Sportsmans Arms 🍺

Village signposted off B1019 Hatfield Peverel—Maldon, then look for Sportsman Lane on right

The unusual feature in this friendly country local is the good value oriental food, cooked by the Filipino landlady: it might include chicken wings marinated in hoisin sauce and spices (£3.50) or stuffed tiger-tail prawns in filo pastry (£4), pork marinated in demerara sugar, garlic and herbs (£5.25), chunks of steak braised with a selection of indonesian spices and peppers (£5.50) or sweet and sour whole red snapper (£7.50), beside more traditional dishes such as sandwiches (from £1.75), filled yorkshire puddings (from £3.25 for sausage, onion and gravy to £4 for lamb and mango curry), ploughman's (£4.25) and 6oz rump steak (£6.75). The comfortably worn red plush bar has beams and standing timbers, quite a few repoussé brass platters and other brass ornaments, a couple of fireplaces, and a big TV; at the far end is a smallish dining area. The Adnams Broadside and Greene King IPA on handpump are particularly well kept; fruit machine, cribbage, dominoes and maybe piped country music. Off to the side is a big stretch of grass with lots of picnic-sets and a big play area with plenty of climbing frames and so forth. *(Recommended by Evelyn and Derek Walter)*

Punch ~ Licensees Mike and Mary Ann ~ Real ale ~ Bar food ~ Restaurant ~ 01245 380410 ~ Children in eating area of bar and restaurant ~ Open 11-3, 6-11; 12-4.30, 7-10.30 Sun

PAGLESHAM TQ9492 Map 5
Plough & Sail

East End; on the Paglesham road out of Rochford, keep right instead of heading into Church End

The big log fires inside this beautifully kept 17th-c dining pub are a welcome contrast to the bitter winds that bite in across the marshes in winter. Covered in white weatherboarding (like many of the older buildings around here), it's friendly and cosy inside, with pine tables and seats under its rather low beams, lots of brasses and pictures, and pretty flower arrangements. Good food includes sandwiches (from £2.75), soup (£2.75), ploughman's (£4.25), lasagne (£7.50) and steak and kidney pie (£7.95), with interesting daily specials such as field mushrooms topped with brie (£3.95), fresh prawns, crab and salmon on mixed leaves with balsamic dressing (£6.25), home-made curries (£6.95), and fresh fish such as fried skate or monkfish (from £8.95); home-made puddings such as fruit crumble and coconut and lime pudding with coconut ice cream (£3.25). The staff are friendly and attentive. Well kept Greene King IPA and and a guest such as Mighty Oak Burntwood on handpump; decent house wines; cribbage, dominoes and unobtrusive piped music. There are tables and an aviary in the attractive and neatly kept garden. It's in a pretty spot and so can get very busy on warm summer evenings. *(Recommended by George Atkinson)*

Free house ~ Licensee M Oliver ~ Real ale ~ Bar food (12-2, 7-9.30; 12-9 Sun) ~ Restaurant ~ (01702) 258242 ~ Children in eating area of bar ~ Open 11.30-(3.30 Sat)3, 6.30-11; 12-10.30 Sun

---

Anyone claiming to arrange or prevent inclusion of a pub in the *Guide* is a fraud. Pubs are included only if recommended by genuine readers and if our own anonymous inspection confirms that they are suitable.

Punchbowl

Church End; from the Paglesham road out of Rochford, Church End is signposted on the left

Well worth the long drive down country lanes, the cosy beamed bar of this pretty white weatherboarded pub is beautifully kept, with pews, barrel chairs and other seats, and lots of bric-a-brac. Enjoyable good value bar food includes rolls (from £2), sandwiches and filled baguettes (from £2.30), soup (£2.25), filled baked potatoes or prawn cocktail (£3.50), ploughman's (£4.25), vegetable jambalaya or battered haddock (£5.25), cajun chicken or gammon steak (£6.95), daily specials such as beef stroganoff or lamb with rosemary (£5.75), and good fresh fish such as grilled skate (from £6.95); puddings such as raspberry pavlova and bread pudding (from £2.75). Well kept Adnams, Bass, a changing Ridleys ale and a guest such as Fullers London Pride on handpump; piped music. There are some tables in the small garden, with a couple out by the quiet road. *(Recommended by Gordon Neighbour, George Atkinson)*

Free house ~ Licensees Bernie and Pat Cardy ~ Real ale ~ Bar food ~ Restaurant ~ (01702) 258376 ~ Children in restaurant ~ Open 11.30-3, 7- 11; 12-3, 7-10.30 Sun

STAPLEFORD TAWNEY TL5501 Map 5

Mole Trap ◖

Tawney Common, which is signposted off A113 just N of M25 overpass; OS Sheet 167 map reference 550013

It's a true sign of quality when a tucked-away pub pulls in plenty of people: tracking this one down on a weekday lunchtime inspection trip, along narrow country lanes to what seemed the back of beyond, we opened the door (mind your head as you go in!) to find it simply humming with customers. The smallish carpeted bar has black dado, beams and joists, brocaded wall seats, library chairs and bentwood elbow chairs around plain pub tables, and steps down through a partly knocked-out timber stud wall to a similar area; keeping those three coal fires blazing must be nearly a full-time job. There are a few small pictures, 3-D decorative plates, some dried-flower arrangements and (on the sloping ceiling formed by a staircase beyond) some regulars' snapshots, and also a few dozen beermats stuck up around the serving bar. The beers on handpump do change interestingly, and on our visit were Attleborough Wolf and Granny Wouldn't Like It; the piped radio was almost inaudible under the gentle wash of contented chatter. In the food line, the lamb curry is strongly tipped, and other home-made dishes include liver and bacon, chicken and ham pie, quiche or fresh fish (£5.50) and steaks (£6.95). There are some plastic tables and chairs and a picnic-set outside, and the cat we met is a friendly creature – in fact one of quite a tribe of resident animals, many rescued and most wandering around outside, including rabbits, more cats, a couple of dogs, hens, geese, a sheep, goats and horses. *(Recommended by Stephen Jeal, Eddie Edwards, LM)*

Free house ~ Licensees Mr and Mrs Kirtley ~ Real ale ~ Bar food (not Sun evening) ~ Restaurant ~ No credit cards ~ Children in eating area of bar ~ Open 11.30-3, 6.30-11; 12-3.30, 7-10.30 Sun; 12-3, 7-(10.30 Sun)11 winter

STOCK TQ6998 Map 5

Hoop ◖ £

B1007; from A12 Chelmsford bypass take Galleywood, Billericay turn-off

No children, fruit machines or piped music will prevent you from enjoying a well kept pint at this refreshingly unmodern village pub. As well as six changing real ales tapped from the cask or on handpump from breweries such as Adnams, Hop Back, Mighty Oak, Fullers, Youngs and Woodfordes, they serve changing farm ciders, perries and mulled wine in winter. The atmosphere in the cosy, bustling bar is inclusive and the staff are friendly. Traditional consistently good value bar food includes soup (£3), sandwiches (from £2), baked potatoes (from £2), omelettes (from £3), sausage pie (£4.50), home-baked ham and eggs or hotpot (£5), ploughman's (from £5.50) and various daily-delivered fresh fish (from £5) –

vegetables are extra. There's a coal-effect gas fire in the big brick fireplace, brocaded wall seats around dimpled copper tables on the left and a cluster of brocaded stools on the right; sensibly placed darts (the heavy black beams are pitted with stray flights), dominoes and cribbage. Prettily bordered with flowers, the large sheltered back garden has picnic-sets, a covered seating area, and an outside bar and weekend barbecues when the weather is fine. Over 21s only in bar; they hold a popular beer festival in May with up to 150 different real ales. The three collies are called Misty, Colly and Boots. *(Recommended by Sue and Bob Ward, T A S Halfhide, Kay Vowles, John and Enid Morris)*

Free house ~ Licensees Albert and David Kitchin ~ Real ale ~ Bar food (12-(8.30 Sun)9) ~ (01277) 841137 ~ Open 11-11; 12-10.30 Sun

STOW MARIES TQ8399 Map 5
Prince of Wales ✥

B1012 between S Woodham Ferrers and Cold Norton Posters

This welcoming laid-back marshland pub is good for real ale and fresh fish. The landlord is a real ale fanatic (with a monthly slot on a local radio station) and among five or six very well kept weekly changing real ales on handpump you might find Everards Tiger, Batemans Twin Towers, Cains Formidable, Crouch Vale SAS and Mordue Five Bridges; they also keep a range of Belgian draught and fruit beers, farm cider, and vintage ports. Enjoyable well cooked food with lots of fresh fish specials range from exotic fish such as saupe, mahimai and black barracuda (from £7.95) to greek-style pork chops (£5.45), as well as traditional bar food such as lunchtime rolls (from £2.45), ploughman's (from £4.45), chicken and mushroom or lamb and mint pie (£5.75), and puddings such as spotted dick and sticky toffee pudding (£2.50). Seemingly unchanged since the turn of the century, the cosy and chatty low-ceilinged rooms have in fact been renovated in a genuinely traditional style. Few have space for more than one or two tables or wall benches on the tiled or bare-boards floors, though the room in the middle squeezes in quite a jumble of chairs and stools. One room used to be the village bakery, and in winter the oven there is still used to make bread and pizzas. There are seats and tables in the back garden and, in the gap between the white picket fence and the pub's weather-boarded frontage, there's a terrace with herbs in Victorian chimney pots. They hold mediterranean barbecues every Sunday in summer, and occasional beer festivals with live music in the evenings. *(Recommended by Joy and Peter Heatherley, John and Enid Morris)*

Free house ~ Licensee Rob Walster ~ Real ale ~ Bar food (12-2.30, 7-9.30, 12-9.30 Sun) ~ (01621) 828971 ~ Children in garden and family room ~ Live music most bank hol wknds ~ Open 11-11; 12-10.30 Sun

WENDENS AMBO TL5136 Map 5
Bell ✥

B1039 just W of village

The extensive back garden with a new terrace at this jolly village local should be enough to keep children entertained with a big tree-sheltered lawn, wooden wendy house, proper tree swing, and a sort of mini nature-trail wandering off through the shrubs. They can have fun meeting the goats Reggie and Ronnie, and Gizmo the 14-stone bernese mountain dog. The small cottagey low-ceilinged rooms are spotlessly kept, with brasses on ancient timbers, wheelback chairs around neat tables, comfortably cushioned seats worked into snug alcoves, quite a few pictures on the cream walls, and a welcoming open fire. Bar food includes filled rolls (from £2.25), ploughman's (£4.25), home-made steak and kidney pie, filled yorkshire pudding or broccoli, tomato and pasta bake as well as specials (£6-£7) including a fresh fish and vegetarian option and home-made puddings such as apple pie, cherry trifle or spotted dick (£2.50); the dining room is no smoking. Well kept real ales include Adnams and a couple of guests on handpump; darts, cribbage, dominoes and piped music. *(Recommended by Joy and Peter Heatherley, S Horsley, Pam and David Bailey)*

Free house ~ Licensees David and Sheila Thorp ~ Real ale ~ Bar food (not Sun or Mon evenings) ~ Restaurant ~ (01799) 540382 ~ Children in restaurant ~ Thurs evening quiz ~ Open 1.30-3, 6-11; 11-11 Sat; 12-10.30 Sun; closed Sat and Sun afternoon in winter

YOUNGS END TL7319 Map 5
Green Dragon

A131 Braintree—Chelmsford, just N of Essex Showground

This busy dining pub has a good range of enjoyable bar food coupled with a pleasant pubby atmosphere. The restaurant area has an understated barn theme with stripped brick walls and a manger at one end, and a no smoking 'hayloft' part upstairs. Two bar rooms have ordinary pub furnishings, and there's a little extra low-ceilinged snug just beside the serving counter. The reasonably priced bar menu, served by cheerful staff, includes sandwiches (from £2, filled baguettes from £3), home-made soup (£2.75), baked potatoes (from £3), and ploughman's (from £4.50), filled baked potatoes, tiger prawns in filo pastry with plum sauce (£4.25), cottage pie topped with cheese (£5.50), sausages and mash (£7), curry of the day (£7.50), shoulder of lamb with wine, herbs and garlic (£10.50), or steaks (from £9.75) and daily specials (with a good choice of fish) such as smoked haddock and mozzarella fishcakes with tomato and basil sauce (£8.75) and roast duckling in orange sauce (£12), with puddings (from £3); fixed price set menu; smaller helpings available for children. At lunchtime (not Sunday) you can have bar food in part of the restaurant, where the tables are bigger than in the bar. Greene King IPA, Abbot and perhaps Ruddles County on handpump; unobtrusive piped jazz music. The neat back garden has lots of picnic-sets under cocktail parasols, a budgerigar aviary, climbing frame, and a big green play dragon. (*Recommended by Ian Phillips, Paul and Ursula Randall, George Atkinson*)

Greene King ~ Lease Bob and Mandy Greybrook ~ Real ale ~ Bar food (12-2.30, 6-9.30) ~ Restaurant ~ (01245) 361030 ~ Children under 10 in restaurant and eating area of bar till 8pm ~ Open 12-3, 5.30-11; 12-11 Sat; 12-10.30 Sun

Lucky Dip

Besides the fully inspected pubs, you might like to try these Lucky Dips recommended to us and described by readers (if you do, please send us reports: www.goodguides.com).

Ardleigh [TM0529]
☆ *Wooden Fender* [A137 – actually towards Colchester]: Friendly new licensees doing good choice of good value food, well kept Adnams, Greene King IPA and Abbot and a Mauldons seasonal beer, decent wines, open-plan but traditional beamed bar, log fires, children welcome in restaurant; may be piped music; pool in good-sized family garden (*George Atkinson, Steff Clegg, LYM*)
Ballards Gore [TQ9092]
Shepherd & Dog: Beamed pub with dark wood, parquet floor and lots of pictures, now doing good rather upmarket food, well kept ales such as Wadworths 6X and Wychwood Hobgoblin, pleasant seats out in front and on back lawn (*George Atkinson*)
Battlesbridge [TQ7894]
Barge [Hawk Hill]: Low white clapboarded local right by waterside antiques and craft centre, chatty bar on right, quieter eating areas on left – food all day (*BB*)
☆ *Hawk* [Hawk Hill]: Extensive Vintage Inn recently attractively refurbished, with rugs, settles and oak tables on flagstones, log fire,

hanging baskets, farm tools, dried hops, wide choice of food all day from separate servery inc interesting light lunches, well kept Bass and Tetleys, good wine list, daily papers; piped music, packed wknds with antiques enthusiasts visiting the centre here – service stays prompt despite the queue; open all day, children welcome, good tables out on front grass (*George Atkinson, BB*)
Billericay [TQ6893]
Duke of York [Southend Rd, South Green]: Pleasant beamed local with real fire, longcase clock, local photographs, upholstered settles and wheelback chairs, good value food in bar and modern restaurant, long-serving licensees, Greene King and occasional guest beers; maybe unobtrusive piped 60s pop music, monthly quiz night, fortnightly ladies' darts (*David Twitchett*)
Blackmore [TL6001]
Leather Bottle: Small, quiet and friendly two-bar pub, wide choice of reasonably priced food, up to four changing well kept ales; theme nights such as jazz, 70s, quizzes, garden behind (*Mark Morgan*)

Blackmore End [TL7430]

☆ *Bull* [off A131 via Bocking Church Street and Beazley End; towards Wethersfield]: Comfortable tucked-away dining pub, red plush built-in button-back banquettes, low black beams, further cottagey restaurant area, lots of blackboards for very wide choice from sandwiches to steak and set lunches, well kept Adnams, Greene King IPA and maybe a guest, decent wines; children welcome, cl Mon, picnic-sets outside *(Richard Siebert, LYM)*

Boreham [TL7509]

Six Bells [B1137]: Comfortable bar in thriving dining pub, good value freshly made straightforward food, cheerful efficient service even when busy, well kept Greene King IPA and Abbot and guest beers; play area in garden *(Paul and Ursula Randall)*

Buckhurst Hill [TQ4193]

Warren Wood [Epping New Rd]: Traditional friendly local looking over Epping Forest, good walks, well kept ales such as Adnams Broadside, Courage Best, Fullers London Pride and Ridleys IPA, good value straightforward lunchtime food (not Sun), back eating area, friendly fast service even to picnic-sets outside; piped music *(Ian Phillips, LM)*

Canewdon [TQ8994]

☆ *Anchor* [High St]: Congenial local atmosphere, low black beams and standing timbers, friendly landlord and staff, Greene King IPA and Abbot and a guest such as Youngs, wide choice of food inc interesting fish dishes and bargain two- and three-course meals, linked restaurant area; darts, games and TV in public bar, and juke box may jibe with lounge's piped music; disabled access, small garden with terrace and several aviaries, open all day *(George Atkinson, BB)*

Chelmsford [TL7006]

☆ *Alma* [Arbour Lane]: Attractively reworked by new owners, keeping local feel in flagstoned bar, with comfortable mix of furnishings around central fireplace in carpeted main area, cosy corner with leather sofa and armchair, shelves of books, interesting advertising posters, good unusual food (all day Sun) in bar and pleasant restaurant, real ales, decent wines; picnic-sets out on side terrace *(anon)*

Fox & Goose [A414 5 miles W]: Spaciously extended flower-decked roadside dining pub with generous quick food from sandwiches up, good service, comfortable banquettes, cheerful regulars, no smoking area *(LYM, M A and C R Starling)*

Horse & Groom [Roxwell Rd (A1060)]: Attractive mock-Tudor Chef & Brewer flagship family dining pub with good if not cheap food, well kept Courage Directors and Theakstons, decent wines, cheerful friendly staff, spacious bar, big pine tables in roomy no smoking dining area, country views from pleasant conservatory, unobtrusive piped music; tables outside *(D P and J A Sweeney)*

Queens Head [Lower Anchor St]: Recently refurbished vibrant backstreet local with three well kept Crouch Vale real ales, five changing guest beers such as Burton Bridge, Mauldons

and Oakham, summer farm cider, winter log fires, simple cheap generous lunchtime food from filled rolls to steak and ale pie etc; open all day from noon *(David Mansfield, Keith and Janet Morris)*

Chignall Smealy [TL6711]

Pig & Whistle: Attractively opened up, with beams, brasses and stripped brick, solid furniture and soft lighting, newish licensees doing good value generous food from sandwiches and light bar meals to restaurant dishes inc OAP midweek lunch, well kept Shepherd Neame ales, cheerful staff, partly no smoking restaurant; fruit machine, piped music; children welcome away from bar, tables out on terrace with wide views, climbing frame *(Mr and Mrs Youngs, Paul and Ursula Randall)*

Coggeshall [TL8522]

☆ *White Hart* [Bridge St]: Waiter-service dining pub with lots of low Tudor beams, antique settles among other more usual seats, prints and fishing trophies, wide choice of food from sandwiches up, well kept Adnams, decent wines and coffee; service may be slow; comfortable bedrooms *(BB, Kevin Flack, D B Molyneux-Berry)*

Colchester [TM0025]

Dragoon [Butt Rd (B1026)]: Welcoming unpretentious L-shaped local with distinct lounge and public ends, limited very cheap bar food (fry-up recommended), well kept Adnams and a guest beer, friendly staff *(Pete Baker)*

☆ *Rose & Crown* [East St]: Plush tastefully modernised Tudor inn, timbered and jettied, parts of a former gaol preserved in its rambling beamed bar, pew seats, well prepared original food, nice afternoon teas, good friendly staff and atmosphere, well kept Adnams Broadside, Tetleys and a good beer brewed for them, Sun bar nibbles; comfortably functional bedrooms, many in modern extension, with good breakfast *(Jenny and Brian Seller, Andrew Free, LYM)*

Coopersale Street [TL4702]

☆ *Theydon Oak* [off B172 E of Theydon Bois; or follow Hobbs Cross Open Farm brown sign off B1393 at N end of Epping]: Attractive weatherboarded dining pub with lots of hanging baskets, long convivial beamed bar with lots of brass, copper and old brewery mirrors, decorative antique tills, interesting old maps, well kept ales such as Black Sheep, Greene King IPA and Wadworths 6X, friendly staff, ample cheap quickly served food from sandwiches up inc plenty of bargain specials, Sun roasts and puddings cabinet; no piped music, popular with older lunchers – very busy in summer; no dogs, tables on side terrace and in garden with small stream (maybe ducks), wknd barbecues and separate play area *(Joy and Peter Heatherley, LM, George Atkinson, B J Harding, BB, Mrs A Chesher)*

Copthall Green [TL4200]

Good Intent: Open-plan roadside pub with plush wall banquettes, welcoming and efficient Italian landlord and family doing enjoyable bar food strong on pasta, ciabatta and pizzas, upstairs restaurant, well kept McMullens; shame about the piped radio; some picnic-sets outside *(Joy and Peter Heatherley)*

Coxtie Green [TQ5695]

White Horse [Coxtie Green Rd]: Cosy traditional local with good value food, friendly service, several real ales inc Fullers London Pride and guest beers, July beer festival; huge garden with play area *(Robert Lester)*

Dedham [TM0631]

Anchor [The Heath]: Character heavy-beamed Tudor inn, ornate bar, log fire, plenty of room, friendly service and atmosphere, well kept Adnams and Courage Directors, good coffee, decent food *(George Atkinson)*

☆ *Marlborough Head* [Mill Lane]: Handsome and civilised medieval timbered inn with pictures, log fires and beautiful carving in beamed central lounge, well kept Adnams, Courage Directors and Greene King IPA and Abbot, pleasant young staff, no smoking family room, lots of tables in dining bar (usual food, no sandwiches Sun evening); piped music; tables on terrace and in back garden, open all day wknds, comfortable bedrooms, charming village *(P Beeby, Joy and Peter Heatherley, Ian Phillips, Peter and Pat Frogley, Mr and Mrs Thomas, LYM)*

☆ *Sun* [High St]: Roomy and comfortably refurbished Tudor pub, cosy panelled rooms with log fires in splendid fireplaces, handsomely carved beams, well kept ales, decent wines, good varied food (not Sun evening), cheerful helpful staff; tables on back lawn, car park behind reached through medieval arch, wonderful wrought-iron inn sign; comfortable panelled bedrooms with four-posters, good walk to or from Flatford Mill *(Mr and Mrs David B Meehan, Mr and Mrs Ian Matthews, P Beeby, LYM)*

East Hanningfield [TL7601]

Three Horseshoes [signed from A130; The Tye, towards Danbury]: Simple opened-up beamed pub with plenty of tables, back restaurant, cosy and jolly atmosphere, friendly attentive landlady, usual bar food from good sandwiches up, Courage Directors; tables out on front gravel looking down green-lined village street *(George Atkinson)*

Windmill [The Tye]: Pleasant beamed bar, good standard food from baguettes to Sun roasts, several real ales inc Crouch Vale and a guest such as Wychwood Shires, good prompt service, restaurant Thurs-Sat evenings and Sun lunch; seats out on front terrace opp green (fairly busy road) *(George Atkinson)*

Easthorpe [TL9121]

☆ *House Without A Name* [village signed from A12]: 600 years old and a proper picture, cosy bar with heavy standing timbers and low beams recently reworked into good welcoming dining pub specialising in fresh seafood inc lobster and exotic fish (character Greek chef), well kept Adnams and Greene King, good wine list; tables in small garden *(Arthur Baker, LYM, Steff Clegg)*

Epping Forest [TQ3997]

Owl [Lippitts Hill, nr High Beach]: Big 1930s pub with beams and plates above bar, good cosy atmosphere, McMullens AK, Special Reserve and Gladstone, bar food; great Epping Forest views from cypress-shaded terrace, picnic-sets spread down to paddock with horses, pets corner (shame about the loudspeaker food announcements) *(Ian Phillips)*

Fyfield [TL5606]

☆ *Black Bull* [B184, N end]: Welcoming 15th-c pub with heavy low beams and standing timbers, comfortably modernised pubby bar, wide range of sensibly priced generous food from baguettes through traditional dishes to more spicy ones, no smoking country-style dining area, well kept Courage Directors, Greene King Ruddles and Marstons Pedigree, good service, open fire, traditional games; quiet piped music; tables outside, lots of flower-filled barrels, aviary with budgerigars and cockatiels *(LYM, Keith and Janet Morris, Colin and Janet Roe, Mrs A Chesher, Roy and Lindsey Fentiman, Beryl and Bill Farmer, Joy and Peter Heatherley, Ian Phillips)*

Goldhanger [TL9009]

Chequers [B1026 E of Heybridge; Church St]: Old beamed village pub looking across churchyard, good straightforward food inc fresh fish Fri and delicious puddings, well kept Ind Coope Burton and Tolly, cheerful staff, ingratiating cats; jazz and live music nights, good walks and bird-watching nearby *(George Atkinson)*

Great Bromley [TM0627]

Cross [Ardleigh Rd, just off A120 Colchester—Harwich]: Attractive old pub, plenty of atmosphere, good service from pleasant staff, food inc popular Sun carvery; open all day *(June and Rex Miller)*

Great Easton [TL6126]

☆ *Green Man* [Mill End Green; pub signed 2 miles N of Dunmow, off B184 towards Lindsell]: Cosy and congenial beamed bar dating from 15th c, interesting décor, lots of nooks and crannies, obliging service, good food, well kept ales such as Adnams, Greene King IPA and Ridleys, decent wine, conservatory; piped music; children welcome, barbecues in attractive garden by tennis court, pleasant rural setting *(Prof John and Mrs Patricia White)*

Swan [2 miles N of Dunmow, off B184 towards Lindsell]: Small cosy old pub in attractive village street, two clean and tidy traditional front rooms, country bygones, comfortable furnishings, warm atmosphere; friendly landlady, good range of simple food, real ales *(John Brightley)*

Great Horkesley [TL9732]

☆ *Rose & Crown* [Nayland Rd (A134)]: Old two-floored pub well worth knowing now for its good food; Greene King and other ales, three bars and restaurant *(John Prescott)*

Great Tey [TL8925]

Chequers [off A120 Coggeshall—Marks Tey]: Well kept comfortable old pub with good reasonably priced food inc daily fresh fish and good Sun roast, puddings and cheeses, efficient courteous service, well kept real ale, traditional games; children and dogs welcome, fine walled garden; quiet village, plenty of country walks *(B Phelvin)*

Great Wakering [TQ9387]

Exhibition [Exhibition Lane]: Pleasant terrace and garden area with waterfalls, small pond and gnomes, beamed interior with friendly staff, good value food esp fish, well kept ales such as Charles Wells Bombardier *(George Atkinson)*

White Hart [High St]: Attractive and hospitable beamed bar with cosy seating, friendly staff, good cheap generous food inc fish, well kept Ridleys IPA, lots of bric-a-brac, brasses and jugs; maybe piped local radio; seats in courtyard *(George Atkinson)*

Heybridge Basin [TL8707]

☆ *Jolly Sailor* [Basin Rd (B1026 E of Maldon)]: Friendly and unpretentious little local on popular boating estuary, simple furnishings, Adnams Broadside, Greene King IPA and maybe a guest beer, enjoyable food (not Sun-Tues evenings) from filled baguettes and baked potatoes to swordfish, lots of boating and marine pictures; piped music, games inc winter pool; children in dining room, open all day wknds and summer, tables on terrace by sea wall, shoreside walks *(George Atkinson, Claire Nielsen, David Carr, LYM)*

Old Ship [Lockhill]: Well kept Greene King IPA, Abbot and Old Speckled Hen, malt whiskies, good choice of standard food in bar with blond wooden furniture (window tables reserved for diners), more ambitious upstairs restaurant with estuary views, daily papers; well behaved dogs welcome, no children; seats outside, some overlooking water by canal lock – lovely views of the saltings and across to Northey Island, pretty window boxes; can be very busy, esp in summer when parking nearby impossible (but public park five mins' walk) *(Gavin May, Paul and Ursula Randall, R L Turnham)*

High Ongar [TL5603]

Foresters Arms [The Street]: Doing well under new licensees, good value wines, good choice of real ales tapped from the cask *(Bruce M Drew)*

Wheatsheaf [signed Blackmore, Ingatestone off A414 just E of Ongar]: New licensees in comfortable low-beamed pub with unusual intimate stalls in big front bay window, log fires each end, food (not Sun evening) from sandwiches up, real ales such as Flowers IPA and Greene King IPA; children in side room, charming big back garden, plenty of play space and equipment *(B N F and M Parkin, Ian Phillips, LYM)*

Kirby le Soken [TM2122]

Red Lion [B1034 Thorpe—Walton]: Attractive and pleasantly furnished 14th-c pub, friendly helpful service, good range of food inc imaginative dishes and good vegetarian choice in roomy bar, well kept Scottish Courage and guest ales; piped music can obtrude, predominantly young people in the evenings; big garden with play area and thatched eating area *(Chris Mawson)*

Layer de la Haye [TL9619]

Donkey & Buskins [B1026 towards

Colchester]: Old-fashioned country pub with good range of reasonably priced straightforward food in bar and dining room esp fresh fish and good Sun roasts, Greene King and Wadworths 6X, pleasant service; handy for Abberton Reservoir *(Gordon Neighbour, Jane Hunt)*

Leigh-on-Sea [TQ8385]

Crooked Billet [High St]: Homely old pub with waterfront views from big bay windows, local fishing pictures and bric-a-brac, bare boards, Adnams, Fullers London Pride and Ind Coope Burton, spring and autumn beer festivals, home-made lunchtime food (not Sun) inc seafood and vegetarian, friendly service; piped music, live music nights; open all day, side garden and terrace, more seats across road; pay-and-display parking by fly-over *(Ian Phillips, John and Enid Morris, George Atkinson, LYM)*

Little Baddow [TL7807]

☆ *Generals Arms* [The Ridge; minor rd Hatfield Peverel—Danbury]: Neatly kept, cheerful and pleasantly decorated, with good choice of enjoyable food inc lots of fish in long bar and modern restaurant, friendly service, well kept Adnams and guests such as Courage Directors, reasonably priced wines, quiet piped music; big lawn with tables and play area, open all day Sun *(Malcolm and Jennifer Perry, LYM)*

Little Clacton [TM1618]

Blacksmiths Arms [The Street]: Comfortable local with Fullers London Pride, Ind Coope Burton, Tetleys and Worthingtons from gleaming brass handpumps, friendly staff, woodburner in big hearth; discreet piped music; pretty garden *(Ian Phillips)*

Little Hallingbury [TL5017]

☆ *Sutton Arms* [Hall Green, S of village; A1060 Hatfield Heath—Bishops Stortford, 4 miles from M11 junction 8]: Pretty thatched cottagey pub with lovely hanging baskets, wide choice of decent generous home-made food from sandwiches and children's things to some more interesting dishes, friendly helpful staff, well kept beers such as Ind Coope Burton, Jennings, Tetleys and Charles Wells Bombardier, daily papers, extended beamed lounge bar on right, friendly if sometimes smoky smaller bar on left with big inglenook; fruit machine; a bit of a detour off M11, but can get very busy *(Steve Chambers, George Atkinson, BB)*

Little Waltham [TL7012]

☆ *Dog & Gun* [E of village, back rd Great Leighs—Boreham]: Long L-shaped timbered dining lounge recently refurbished in country style, new licensees doing good generous food from lunch snacks to enterprising but unpretentious restaurany dishes and civilised Sun family lunches, friendly atmosphere, well kept Bass and a changing guest beer, decent wine, suntrap conservatory; maybe piped music; good-sized garden with floodlit terrace, elegant pondside willow, unobtrusive climbing frame *(Paul and Ursula Randall, Peter Baggott)*

Loughton [TQ4297]

☆ *Gardeners Arms* [York Hill, just off A121 High Rd]: Country feel in traditional low-ceilinged pub with Adnams and Scottish Courage ales, two open fires, friendly service, good straightforward lunchtime bar food (not Sun) from sandwiches up with hot dishes all fresh-cooked (so can be delays), children in restaurant *(LYM, D R and A J Linnell)*

Maldon [TL8506]

Carpenters Arms [Gate St (behind Blue Boar)]: Convivial and welcoming, with well kept beer, inexpensive well cooked hearty food, friendly staff *(Kevin Flack)*

Manningtree [TM1031]

☆ *Crown* [High St]: Bustling 16th-c two-bar pub, lots of beams, old photographs, maps and fishing gear, open fire, well kept Greene King IPA, Abbot and Mild, bright cheerful staff, usual food inc interesting sandwiches and plenty for children, conservatory overlooking Stour estuary; picnic-sets in back yard, attractively priced bedrooms *(Rona Murdoch, Ian and Nita Cooper)*

Station Buffet [Manningtree Stn, out towards Lawford]: Clean and warm, with nostalgic early 1950s long marble-topped bar, three little tables and a handful of unassuming seats with adjoining eating area, well kept ales such as Adnams, Fullers London Pride and Greene King IPA, basic low-priced pubby food from good sandwiches up, friendly helpful service, no piped music *(Tony Hobden)*

Margaretting [TL6701]

Red Lion [B1002 towards Mountnessing]: Relaxed beamed local with good choice of enjoyable food from good fish and chips to more elaborate dishes in no smoking dining area, well kept Ridleys, efficient unrushed service, attractive floral displays; unobtrusive piped music; good wheelchair access, tables in front garden by road *(Joy and Peter Heatherley, Della Padfield)*

Margaretting Tye [TL6801]

White Hart: L-shaped bar with wide choice of good value promptly served straightforward food, well kept Adnams Broadside and Fishermans Mild, Greene King IPA and a guest beer such as Hogs Back TEA, friendly staff, back children's room; maybe piped music; attractive garden by quiet village green, barbecue, good walks *(Paul and Penny Rampton)*

Matching Tye [TL5111]

Fox [The Green]: Comfortable and attractive low-beamed 17th-c pub opp peaceful village green, wide choice of imaginative reasonably priced food, fine choice of real ales, large garden *(Mrs A Chesher)*

Mill Green [TL6401]

☆ *Cricketers*: Cheerful and popular dining pub in picturesque setting, plenty of tables out in front, interesting cricketing memorabilia, some farm tools, popular freshly cooked traditional food, well kept Greene King ales tapped from the cask, decent wines, no smoking area, friendly attentive service; children welcome, no music, cl winter Sun evenings *(M A and C R Starling)*

Mundon Hill [TL8601]

Roundbush: Massive range of very reasonably priced food; handy for walks by Blackwater

estuary *(Len Banister)*

Navestock Side [TQ5697]

Green Man: Large friendly village pub opp cricket field, Bass and Greene King IPA and Abbot, restaurant *(Robert Lester)*

Newport [TL5234]

Coach & Horses [Cambridge Rd (B1383)]: Enjoyable food, five real ales inc lots of guests, friendly landlord *(B N F and M Parkin)*

North End [TL6617]

Butchers Arms [A130 SE of Dunmow]: Doing well under welcoming current licensees, popular for wide choice of good food *(Tony Beaulah)*

☆ **North Fambridge** [TQ8597]

☆ *Ferry Boat* [The quay; village signposted from B1012 E off S Woodham Ferrers; keep on past railway]: Unpretentious 15th-c weatherboarded pub tucked down by the marshes, warmly welcoming chatty landlord, simple traditional furnishings, nautical memorabilia, log fire one end, woodburner the other, good value honest food from sandwiches up, well kept Shepherd Neame Bishops Finger, Master Brew and Spitfire, traditional games, children in family room and partly no smoking restaurant; piped music, fruit machine, TV; tables in garden with pond (ducks and carp), bedrooms in barn-like building behind, good lonely walks *(Gordon Tong, E D Bailey, David Carr, LYM)*

North Shoebury [TQ9286]

Angel [Parsons Corner]: Good bar food in attractive modern conversion of timbered and partly thatched former post office, Fullers London Pride, Greene King IPA and Abbot and an interesting guest such as Okells Manx, restaurant popular for business lunches *(George Atkinson)*

Old Harlow [TL4711]

Marquis of Granby [Market St]: Comfortable and friendly local with wide beer choice such as Benskins Best, Harviestoun Hijack, Marstons Pedigree, Old Mill Hallowe'en Surprise, Smiles, Tetleys and Woods Holy Cow, usual food, old gas cigar lighter on bar; pool, TV; attractive old tiled building *(Ian Phillips)*

Peldon [TL9916]

☆ *Rose* [junction unclassified Maldon road with B1025 Peldon—Mersea]: Cosy and very welcoming low-beamed bar with creaky close-set tables, some antique mahogany, chintz curtains and leaded lights, brass and copper, well kept Adnams, Flowers IPA and Wadworths 6X, decent wines, good food from separate counter from sandwiches to Prince of Wales's organic beef, no music; children welcome but not in the bar, restaurant Fri/Sat evening, big no smoking conservatory, spacious relaxing garden with geese, ducks and nice pond with water voles, play area; bedrooms, good breakfast *(D B Molyneux-Berry, Hazel Morgan, Gordon Neighbour, LYM)*

Pilgrims Hatch [TQ5795]

Black Horse [Ongar Rd (A128)]: Classic spacious beamed Vintage Inn, Bass, usual good quickly served food, lots of pictures, no smoking area; piped music; garden *(George Atkinson)*

Pleshey [TL6614]

☆ *White Horse* [The Street]: 15th-c beams and timbers, brightened up with cheerful tablecloths and flower posies, big back extension with two dining rooms, one no smoking (should book wknds), good range of enjoyable bar food from sandwiches to imaginative full meals (freshly made, so may take a while), well kept Youngs Bitter and AAA, decent wines; ubobtrusive piped music; luncheon club and theme nights, children welcome, tables out on terrace and in garden with small safe play area, pretty village with ruined castle *(Tony Beaulah, LYM, Paul and Ursula Randall)*

Rayleigh [TQ8090]

Olde Crown [High St]: Weatherboarded beamed pub with usual food from well priced sandwiches up, Theakstons XB, friendly staff, open fire; piped music *(George Atkinson)*

Rickling Green [TL5029]

Cricketers Arms [just off B1383 N of Stansted Mountfichet]: Beams, timbers and lots of cricketing memorabilia, wide choice of bar food esp fish and seafood, well kept Flowers IPA, Fullers ESB, Wadworths 6X and a guest beer tapped from the cask, good wines by the glass, open fires; piped music; picnic-sets in sheltered front courtyard, bedrooms (not cheap, breakfast extra; standard courtesy car) *(Kevin Thorpe, R T and J C Moggridge, Charles Gysin, Peter and Jean Hoare, LYM)*

Saffron Walden [TL5438]

Eight Bells [Bridge St; B184 towards Cambridge]: Large handsomely timbered Tudor pub under newish licensees, wide choice of enjoyable food in open-plan rambling bar and appealing partly no smoking medieval-theme tapestried restaurant, children allowed here and in family room with open fire, well kept Adnams, good wines, good friendly service; games machines; open all day, tables in garden, handy for Audley End, good walks *(LYM, John Brightley, Geoffrey and Brenda Wilson)*

Shalford [TL7229]

☆ *George* [B1053 N of Braintree]: Pleasantly refurbished sloping L-shaped bar with low beams, well spaced solid tables, decorative plates and brassware, needlework pictures, stencilled wall decorations, good fire in enormous fireplace, neat and friendly family service, good attractively priced food from sandwiches up, well kept Adnams Broadside and Greene King IPA and Abbot; lots of children wknds, tables on terrace *(BB)*

South Benfleet [TQ7786]

Hoy & Helmet [High St]: Rambling old beamed pub nr church, inglenook and nooks and crannies, Scottish Courage ales, standard food; piped music may be a bit intrusive; tables in pretty garden with terrace, lots of hanging baskets and flowers *(George Atkinson)*

Southend [TQ8885]

Last Post [Weston Rd]: Wetherspoons post office conversion, all the usual features, real ale choice, decent coffee, food all day, particularly low prices, friendly helpful service, no smoking area, no music; large conservatory, opens 10 *(George Atkinson)*

Stanford Rivers [TL5300]

☆ *Woodman* [Little End, London Rd (A113 S of Ongar)]: Weatherboarded roadside dining pub, well extended to ramble comfortably and attractively around central bar, with beams, log fire in big inglenook, lots of pictures and brasses, Shepherd Neame Bitter, Spitfire and Bishops Finger, food all day, efficient staff; piped music; open all day, big garden with country views, very good play area *(BB, George Atkinson)*

Stisted [TL7924]

☆ *Dolphin* [A120 E of Braintree, by village turn]: Well kept Ridleys tapped from the cask in heavily beamed and timbered properly pubby locals' bar on right, popular well priced straightforward food (not Tues or Sun evenings) inc steak bargains Sat evening, log fire, bright eating area on left (children allowed here); tables outside *(Pete Baker, LYM)*

Stock [TQ6998]

☆ *Bakers Arms* [Common Rd, just off B1007 Chelmsford—Billericay]: Busy open-plan low-beamed pub with smart banquettes, well kept Adnams Broadside, above-average home-made food, reasonable prices, attractive airy dining room with french windows to charming small garden, good pleasant service, no piped music *(David Twitchett)*

Bear [Mill Rd, just off B1007]: Recently refurbished, with civilised locals' front bar, well kept ales such as Adnams and Greene King Abbot, stained glass and bric-a-brac, cosy no smoking restaurant, children's room; nice back garden overlooking pond *(John and Enid Morris, BB)*

Thaxted [TL6130]

Farmhouse [Monk St]: Good friendly service, wide range of enjoyable food, well kept beer *(I D Greenfield)*

Swan [Bull Ring]: Attractively renovated Tudor pub opp lovely church, Adnams and Greene King, plenty of well spaced tables (but they take your credit card when you order food), good choice of well presented food, good-sized helpings, friendly staff, restaurant; piped music may obtrude; open all day, bedrooms *(Mrs W Boast, Charles Gysin)*

Theydon Bois [TQ4599]

☆ *Queen Victoria* [Coppice Row (B172)]: Cosy beamed and carpeted slightly old-fashioned lounge with roaring log fire, local pictures, mug collection, well presented quick straightforward good value food piled high from servery, good value Sun lunch, bright end dining area with interesting knick-knacks, smaller no smoking front bar, bigger back one, McMullens ales, decent house wines, very friendly accommodating staff; piped music can obtrude, very busy wknd lunchtimes; tables on terrace *(Joy and Peter Heatherley, H O Dickinson, George Atkinson, Keith and Janet Morris, Martin and Karen Wake)*

Sixteen String Jack [Coppice Row]: Simple pub on edge of Epping Forest, well kept McMullens; neat garden, dogs welcome *(Eddie Edwards)*

Thornwood Common [TL4704]

Carpenters Arms [nr M11/M25 junction]: Unspoilt pub with three bars, photographs and

other memorabilia from nearby North Weald
World War II fighter base, old farming and
wood-working tools and some breweriana,
several well kept ales inc Adnams Broadside,
good value enjoyable straightforward pub food
from baguettes and baked potatoes up
(David Twitchett)

Thorpe-le-Soken [TM1722]
Olive Branch [High St]: Wine bar/restaurant
rather than pub, but worth knowing for good
food in simple but careful setting; quiet piped
music *(Ian Glegg)*

Toot Hill [TL5102]
☆ *Green Man* [off A113 in Stanford Rivers, S of
Ongar, or A414 W of Ongar]: Still pleasantly
laid out much as a simply furnished country
pub with a long plush dining room, but now
best thought of as a restaurant both in price
and in style (meals rather than bar food); very
good wine list, Fullers London Pride, Youngs
Bitter and AAA; no under-10s, pretty front
terrace, tables in back garden *(LM, Keith and
Janet Morris, Len Banister, LYM, Ian Phillips,
Neil Hogg, Grahame McNulty, Martin and
Karen Wake, George Atkinson, R F Ballinger)*

Waltham Abbey [TL3800]
Volunteer [½ mile from M25 junction 26; A121
towards Loughton]: Good value generous
chinese food and other food from good
sandwiches and baguettes up in well run roomy
open-plan pub, popular with families; swift
service even when very busy, attractive
conservatory, McMullens Country and Mild;
piped music; some tables on side terrace, pretty
hanging baskets, nice spot by Epping Forest
*(Charles and Pauline Stride, Joy and Peter
Heatherley, BB, Tony Middis)*

West Bergholt [TL9627]
Treble Tile [Colchester Rd]: Good reasonably
priced food with extra evening choice in
casually furnished simple pub *(Ian Glegg)*

Wickham St Paul [TL8336]
☆ *Victory* [SW of Sudbury; The Green]: Spacious
family pub with fine range of good fresh food,
good beer choice, friendly efficient service even
when busy, view of village cricket green with
duck pond; unobtrusive piped music
(Ian Wilson, Peter Baggott)

Wivenhoe [TM0321]
Black Buoy [off A133]: 16th-c behind its more
recent façade, unpretentious open-plan partly
timbered bar, upper dining area glimpsing river
over roofs, wide choice of good generous food

(stops by 2) inc sandwiches, local fish and
interesting vegetarian dishes, well kept Adnams
and Flowers IPA, open fires; piped music;
pleasant village, own parking *(Meg and Colin
Hamilton, James Nunns, BB, Quentin
Williamson)*

☆ *Rose & Crown* [The Quay]: Unspoilt Georgian
pub on River Colne barge quay, low beams,
lots of ship pictures, scrubbed floors and log
fires, well kept Adnams Broadside with several
guests such as Friary Meux Best, Greene King
Abbot, Hampshire King Alfred and Robinsons
Frederics, good house wines, fine choice of
good food all day from fresh baguettes up
(next-door bakery), friendly and helpful young
staff, local and nautical books and maps, no
piped music; open all day Sun, lots of waterside
picnic-sets *(George Atkinson, Charles Gysin,
BB, John and Elizabeth Cox)*

Woodham Mortimer [TL8004]
Royal Oak [Chelmsford Road (A414
Danbury—Maldon)]: Comfortably toney décor
of pinks, greens and greys, corner banquettes, a
mix of chairs, stripped and sealed sturdy pub
tables with candles in bottles; has also had good
surprisingly stylish food for a main-road pub,
but the licensees and their équipe have just
moved to the Alma in Chelmsford and we've
not yet had reports on the new regime; Greene
King IPA and Abbot, decent house wines,
separate smartly pink restaurant; may be piped
music; tables on small side terrace and in the
garden behind, with playhouse and climbing
frame. *(BB)*

Woodham Walter [TL8006]
☆ *Cats* [back rd to Curling Tye and Maldon, from
N end of village]: Relaxed country cottage, low
black beams and timbering in timeless rambling
bar with interesting nooks and crannies, shelves
of china cats, well kept Greene King Abbot and
IPA and a guest beer, good doorstep
sandwiches, friendly service, no children or
piped music; pretty garden with farmland views
(Peter Baggott, LYM)

Writtle [TL6706]
Inn on the Green [The Green]: Spacious pub on
large attractive green, buoyant atmosphere, well
kept ales such as Courage Best and Directors,
Nethergate IPA and Old Growler, friendly well
dressed staff, good bar food, old
advertisements, sepia photographs; end games
area with pool and machines (popular with
young people) *(Colin Parker)*

Post Office address codings confusingly give the impression that some pubs are in
Suffolk, when they're really in Essex (which is where we list them).

Gloucestershire

This county exemplifies the reason for the time-honoured cry: 'Do not rely on an out-of-date Guide!' There are 52 main entries here this year. But only one of them has been in all 20 annual editions since the Guide started, and that one, the Village Pub at Barnsley, has changed out of all recognition. Several entries here are new this year, or pubs back in the Guide after a break: the Horse & Groom at Bourton-on-the-Hill doing well under its new landlady, the Craven Arms at Brockhampton (a friendly and spotless dining pub), the Hunters Hall at Kingscote (a fine old building, enjoyable food and thriving atmosphere), the Bell at Sapperton (entirely revamped, good food and wine, and great care on the beer side too), and the Old Corner Cupboard in Winchcombe (a handsome old pub, gently updated by enthusiastic new licensees). Other front-runners here this year are the Queens Arms at Ashleworth (good food and drink in charming surroundings), the welcoming Bear in Bisley, the Golden Heart at Brimpsfield (a fine all-rounder), the smart and foody New Inn at Coln St Aldwyns, the beautifully run Kings Arms at Didmarton, the cheerful and individualistic Five Mile House at Duntisbourne Abbots (good distinction between its drinking and eating sides), the Royal Oak at Gretton (friendly and enthusiastic new licensees), the Fox at Lower Oddington (a particular favourite with most readers), the Masons Arms at Meysey Hampton (good all round), the Carpenters Arms at Miserden (another most enjoyable all-rounder), the Black Horse at Naunton (thoroughly genuine, in lovely walking country), the New Inn at North Nibley (importing their own wines, as well as having good beers), the beautifully placed and very well run Butchers Arms at Sheepscombe, the smart yet relaxed Gumstool near Tetbury, and the charming little Farriers Arms at Todenham (the new landlord does imaginative food). Despite the high quality of the food in so many of these tried and tested favourites, it is a new entrant which carries off our title of Gloucestershire Dining Pub of the Year: the Bell at Sapperton. Traditionalists have some great old-fashioned pubs to try, most notably the Red Lion at Ampney St Peter, the Volunteer in Chipping Campden, and the beautifully sited Boat at Ashleworth Quay. In the Lucky Dip section at the end of the chapter, some pubs for the notebook are the Sherborne Arms at Aldsworth, Black Horse at Amberley, Crown of Crucis at Ampney Crucis, Stirrup Cup in Bisley, Twelve Bells in Cirencester, Green Dragon near Cowley, Ebrington Arms at Ebrington, Edgemoor at Edge, Crown at Frampton Mansell, Glasshouse Inn at Glasshouse, Fox at Great Barrington, Hobnails at Little Washbourne, Old Lodge at Minchinhampton, Weighbridge in Nailsworth, Wheatsheaf in Northleach, Falcon in Painswick, Boat at Redbrook, Queens Head in Stow-on-the-Wold and Horse & Groom at Upper Oddington. As we have already inspected the great majority of these, we can give them a firm recommendation. Drinks prices here are rather lower than the national average. Generally, pubs serving either Donnington or Hook Norton beers had the most attractive prices, but beers at the New Inn at North Nibley, Mill Inn at Withington, Olde Black Bear in Tewkesbury and Anchor at Oldbury-on-Severn were also relatively very cheap.

ALMONDSBURY ST6084 Map 2

Bowl 🛏

1¼ miles from M5, junction 16 (and therefore quite handy for M4, junction 20; from A38 towards Thornbury, turn first left signposted Lower Almondsbury, then first right down Sundays Hill, then at bottom right again into Church Road

Handy for the M5, this busy pub is a fine sight with the church next door, and its pretty flowering tubs, hanging baskets, and window boxes. The long neatly kept beamed bar has quite a mix of customers, blue plush-patterned modern settles, pink cushioned stools and mate's chairs around elm tables, horsebrasses on stripped bare stone walls, and big winter log fire at one end, with a woodburning stove at the other. With a sensible choice of small or large helpings for many dishes, bar food includes warm baguettes (from £3.60), grilled goats cheese and black olive salad (£4.50; main course £9.50), a bowl of mussels with a garlic and spring onion sauce (£4.50; main course £8.50), caesar salad with charred chicken, pancetta and parmesan (£4.75; main course £8.75), tagliatelle carbonara (£4.95; main course £8.50), crevettes in garlic and herb butter (£5.50; main course £10.50), steak and mushroom pie (£8.55), half lamb shoulder with a rosemary and redcurrant gravy (£8.95), calves liver with mash and onion gravy (£9.25), rib-eye steak (£11.25); there may be a wait at peak times. Well kept Bass, Bath Gem, Courage Best, Smiles Best, and maybe a guest such as Cottage Southern Bitter or Moles Best on handpump; piped music and fruit machine. The dog is called Corrie, and the black and white cat Jez. There are some picnic-sets across the quiet road. *(Recommended by Mr and Mrs J E C Tasker, Hugh Roberts, S H Godsell, B J Harding, Charles and Pauline Stride, Simon and Amanda Southwell, Joy and Peter Heatherley, Richard Fendick, Bob and Ann Westbrook, Roger and Jenny Huggins, R Mathews, Susan and Nigel Wilson, David Hoult)*

Free house ~ Licensee Mrs P Alley ~ Real ale ~ Bar food (till 10) ~ Restaurant ~ (01454) 612757 ~ Children in eating area of bar and restaurant ~ Open 11-3, 5(6 Sat)-11; 12-3.30, 7-10.30 Sun ~ Bedrooms: £39.50B/£64B

AMPNEY ST PETER SP0801 Map 4

Red Lion ◗

A417, E of village

The only unknown in this little roadside pub is who will be there when you arrive and what will be the topic of conversation. It's a great place for a friendly chat, with a fine mix of locals and visitors, splendidly traditional, and run by a charming, courteous landlord. A central stone corridor, served by a hatch, gives on to the little right-hand tile-floor public bar. Here, one long seat faces the small open fire, with just one table and a wall seat, and behind the long bench an open servery (no counter, just shelves of bottles and – by the corridor hatch – handpumps for the well kept Hook Norton Best and summer Haymaker, and maybe Flowers IPA). There are old prints on the wall, and on the other side of the corridor is a small saloon, with panelled wall seats around its single table, old local photographs, another open fire, and a print of Queen Victoria one could believe hasn't moved for a century – rather like the pub itself. There are seats in the side garden. *(Recommended by the Didler, R Huggins, D Irving, E McCall, T McLean, Peter and Audrey Dowsett, Giles Francis, JP, PP, Roger and Jenny Huggins)*

Free house ~ Licensee John Barnard ~ Real ale ~ No credit cards ~ (01285) 810280 ~ Children in the tiny games room ~ Open 6-10.30; 12-2.30, 6-10.30 Sat; 12-2.30, 7-10.30 Sun; closed weekday lunchtimes

ASHLEWORTH SO8125 Map 4

Queens Arms ⊕ ♀ ◗

Village signposted off A417 at Hartpury

The courteous licensees in this attractive low-beamed country pub have worked hard during their four years tenure to achieve their target of what a country village pub should be. They continue to add antiques to the civilised and immaculate décor, have a range of 15 real ales (with a rotating choice of 3), keep 10 wines by the glass, and use the best local produce for their popular home-made food. The comfortably laid out main bar, softly lit by fringed wall lamps and candles at night, has faintly patterned wallpaper and washed red ochre walls, big oak and mahogany tables and a nice mix of farmhouse and big brocaded dining chairs on a red carpet. Good, imaginative bar food includes lunchtime specials such as freshly baked baguettes (from £5.25), salad niçoise (£5.50), chicken, ham and leek pie (£6.50), South African sausage with tomato and onion gravy (£6.75), and grilled salmon with cherry tomatoes and a lemon thyme butter (£7.75), with evening dishes like chicken topped with mozzarella and capers, served with a marsala, mushroom and cream sauce or rack of spare ribs (£10.75), lamb noisettes with a garlic and rosemary stuffing with a red wine and wild mushroom sauce (£11.50), fresh monkfish and king scallops with a chilli, garlic and ginger dressing (£11.50), and wild boar with a rich fresh raspberry sauce (£12.95); puddings like cape brandy pudding (a South African speciality), raspberry crème brûlée or meringues with toffee cream and sugar bark (£3.95), and Sunday lunch (£6.95). The dining room is no smoking. The well kept real ales might include any of the following: Adnams Bitter and Broadside, Bass, Brains Bitter, Brakspears Bitter and Special, Donnington BB, Greene King Old Speckled Hen and IPA, Marstons Pedigree, Shepherd Neame Spitfire, Timothy Taylors Landlord, and Youngs Bitter and Special on handpump; a thoughtful wine list with some South African choices (the friendly licensees hail from there). Piped music, shove-ha'penny, cribbage, dominoes, and winter skittle alley. Two perfectly clipped mushroom shaped yews dominate the front of the building, and there are a couple of tables and chairs and old-fashioned benches in the back courtyard. *(Recommended by Roy and Lindsey Fentiman, B Knowles, Gill Waller, Tony Morriss, Bernard Stradling, Brian and Bett Cox, Di and Mike Gillam, Mrs A Vilsoen, Mr and Mrs P Slatter, Mike and Mary Carter, Rodney and Norma Stubington)*

Free house ~ Licensees Tony and Gill Burreddu ~ Real ale ~ Bar food (till 10 Fri/Sat) ~ Restaurant ~ (01452) 700395 ~ Well behaved children welcome ~ Open 12-3, 7-11(10.30 Sun); closed 25 Dec

ASHLEWORTH QUAY SO8125 Map 4
Boat ★

Ashleworth signposted off A417 N of Gloucester; quay signed from village

In an idyllic spot on the banks of the River Severn, this spotlessly kept, charming pub has been in the same family since it was originally granted a license by Charles II, and the charming landladies work hard at preserving its unique, gentle character. The little front parlour has a great built-in settle by a long scrubbed deal table that faces an old-fashioned open kitchen range with a side bread oven and a couple of elderly fireside chairs; there are rush mats on the scrubbed flagstones, houseplants in the window, fresh garden flowers, and old magazines to read; shove-ha'penny, dominoes and cribbage (the front room has darts). A pair of flower-cushioned antique settles face each other in the back room where Arkells BBB, RCH IPA, and Wye Valley Bitter, and guests from Bath Ales, Church End, Eccleshall, and Malvern Hills are tapped from the cask, along with a full range of Weston's farm ciders. They usually do good lunchtime rolls (from £1.30) during the week. This is a lovely spot on the banks of the River Severn and there's a front suntrap crazy-paved courtyard, bright with plant tubs in summer, with a couple of picnic-sets under cocktail parasols; more seats and tables under cover at the sides. The medieval tithe barn nearby is striking; some readers prefer to park here and walk to the pub. *(Recommended by Brian and Bett Cox, Di and Mike Gillam, P R and S A White, JP, PP, Derek and Sylvia Stephenson, the Didler, R E Davidson, R Huggins, D Irving, E McCall, T McLean, Pete Baker, Colin Parker, Ted George, Phil and Sally Gorton)*

Free house ~ Licensees Irene Jelf and Jacquie Nicholls ~ Real ale ~ Bar food (lunchtime only) ~ No credit cards ~ (01452) 700272 ~ Children welcome until 8pm ~ Open 11-2.30(3 Sat), 6-11; 12-3, 7-10.30 Sun; evening opening 7pm in winter; closed Mon and Weds lunchtimes Oct-Apr

AWRE SO7108 Map 4
Red Hart ◥

Village signposted off A48 S of Newnham

In a quiet spot between the River Severn and the Forest of Dean, this red-tiled 16th-c country pub has a friendly, relaxed atmosphere. The neat L-shaped bar, the main part of which has a deep glass-covered illuminated well, has an antique pine bookcase filled with cookery books, an antique pine display cabinet with Worcester china, and pine tables and chairs; there are plates on a delft shelf at the end, as well as a gun and a stuffed pheasant over the stone fireplace, and big prints on the walls; one area of the bar is no smoking, as is the restaurant. Good bar food includes sandwiches (from £3.50), home-made soup (£2.95), cajun chicken with caesar salad (£4.25), ploughman's (from £4.95), sausage and mash or a pie of the day (£6.95), a curry of the day (£7.25), and daily specials such as chargrilled tuna steak with rosemary hollandaise (£10.25), honey-roast salmon on black pasta with a pesto and white wine sauce (£10.50), and venison with an apple compote set on a port glaze (£11.95); puddings like home-made sticky toffee pudding or summer pudding (from £3.25). Well kept Bass and Fullers London Pride, plus changing guests such as Badger Tanglefoot, Freeminer Speculation or Goffs Jouster on handpump, several malt whiskies, and decent house wine; fruit machine and piped music. In front of the building are some picnic-sets. *(Recommended by Mike and Lynn Robinson, Clare and Paul Howes, Colin Parker, Guy Vowles, Lucien, David Jeffreys, S H Godsell)*

Free house ~ Licensee Jeremy Bedwell ~ Real ale ~ Bar food ~ Restaurant ~ (01594) 510220 ~ Children in eating area of bar until 8 ~ Open 12-3, 6.30-11; 12-3, 7-10.30 Sun

BARNSLEY SP0705 Map 4
Village Pub ⍩

A433 Cirencester—Burford

In the last few years this place which formerly truly lived up to its name has extended and put its emphasis much more on the food side. It's really now best thought of as an upmarket dining pub with prices to match. The low-ceilinged communicating rooms have oil paintings, plush chairs, stools, and window settles around polished candlelit tables, and country magazines and newspapers to read. Imaginative food includes lunchtime sandwiches (from £4.95; roast chicken breast, slow roast tomato and rocket £6), soup such as asparagus and parsley (£3.50), chicken liver parfait and celeriac remoulade (£5.25), marinated tuna steak, mint and pea couscous (£5.75), confit of duck leg with carrot and coriander puree (£9.50), escalope of pork with sage and onion potatoes (£10.50), roast monkfish with niçoise salad (£11), daily specials such as deep-fried lambs sweetbreads with aïoli (£5), crisp honey-glazed quail with soba noodles and lemon (£5.75), poached skate wing, mussels, clams, chorizo, and lemon vinaigrette (£11.50), and herb-crusted rack of lamb with minted peas (£13.75), and puddings like coconut tart mascarpone and lemon ice cream orange and chocolate brûlée or bramley apple crumble with clotted cream (£4.20); they bake their own bread daily. Well kept Hook Norton Bitter, Wadworths 6X, and a guest beer like Adnams Broadside, Hook Norton Old Hooky, Wadworths 6X, and a guest like Donnington SBA or Shepherd Neame Spitfire on handpump, local cider and apple juice, and malt whiskies. Shove-ha'penny, cribbage, dominoes, chess, and draughts. The sheltered back courtyard has plenty of tables, and its own outside servery. The pub is handy for Barnsley House Garden in the village. *(Recommended by Ann and Colin Hunt, Stuart Turner, R Huggins, D Irving, E McCall, T McLean, Jennifer Lamburn, Maysie Thompson, Dr and Mrs A S C Calder, Joanne Boissevain, Martin Webster, Hilary de Lyon, A L and L R Barnes, RJH, Richard and Margaret Peers, John Robertson)*

Free house ~ Licensees Tim Haigh and Rupert Pendered ~ Real ale ~ Bar food (12-2.30(3 Sat/Sun), 7-9.30(10 Fri/Sat) ~ (01285) 740421 ~ Children in eating area of bar ~ Open 11-3.30, 6-11; 11-4, 6-11 Sat; 12-4, 7-10.30 Sun; closed 25 Dec ~ Bedrooms: £55B/£70B

BISLEY SO9006 Map 4
Bear ◖ 🛏

Village signposted off A419 just E of Stroud

The easiest way to find this elegantly gothic 16th-c inn is to head for the church. There's a friendly welcome from the charming licensee, a good mix of locals and visitors, and the meandering L-shaped bar has a relaxed atmosphere, a long shiny black built-in settle and a smaller but even sturdier oak settle by the front entrance, and an enormously wide low stone fireplace (not very high – the ochre ceiling's too low for that); the separate no smoking stripped-stone area is used for families. Good home-made bar food includes soup (£3.25), tasty goats cheese toasties (£3.75), lots of filled french bread like spicy mushrooms, 4oz lamb steak with redcurrant jelly or prawns in lemon and garlic butter (from £4.50), sautéed potatoes and onions flavoured with smoked salmon and leek or chicken and bacon or burgers such as smoked haddock and caper with chilli and lime mayonnaise or sweet and sour pork (from £5.50), home-made pies and casseroles – moroccan spiced lamb, fish crumble, rabbit and vegetable, steak, kidney and Guinness (from £7.50), daily specials like tuna steak with warm caper and coriander vinaigrette, liver and bacon with onion gravy on bubble and squeak or pasta with wild mushrooms, bacon and a white wine and cream sauce, and puddings; small helpings for children, and good breakfasts. Well kept Bass, Flowers IPA, Tetleys, Wadworths 6X, and Wells Bombardier on handpump; friendly, helpful service. Darts, cribbage, and table skittles. A small front colonnade supports the upper floor of the pub, and the sheltered little flagstoned courtyard made by this has a traditional bench; the garden is across the quiet road, and there's quite a collection of stone mounting-blocks. The steep stone-built village is attractive. *(Recommended by Guy Vowles, P R and S A White, J A Cheverton, Keith and Katy Stevens, Mike and Lynn Robinson, Andrew and Ruth Triggs, Prof H G Allen, W Ruxton, R Huggins, D Irving, E McCall, T McLean, Paul Oneill, Mr and Mrs J Brown, Martin Jennings)*

Pubmaster ~ Tenants Simon and Sue Evans ~ Real ale ~ Bar food (not Sun evening) ~ (01452) 770265 ~ Children in family room ~ Open 11-2.30(3 Sat), 6-11; 12-3, 7-10.30 Sun ~ Bedrooms: /£40

BLAISDON SO7017 Map 4
Red Hart ◖

Village signposted off A4136 just SW of junction with A40 W of Gloucester; OS Sheet 162 map reference 703169

There's a good range of real ales and enjoyable food in this bustling pub, tucked away in the Forest of Dean. The flagstoned main bar has a thoroughly relaxing atmosphere – helped along by well reproduced piped bluesy music, and maybe Spotty the perky young jack russell – as well as cushioned wall and window seats, traditional pub tables, and a big sailing-ship painting above the good log fire. Well kept Hook Norton Best, Tetleys, and three guests such as Timothy Taylors Landlord, Uley Bitter, and Wickwar Brand Oak Bitter on handpump, and a decent wine list. On the right, an attractive two-room no smoking dining area with some interesting prints has good daily specials such as chicken satay with peanut sauce or moules marinières (£3.95), rack of ribs (£7.50), lemon chicken stir fry with noodles or trout fillets stuffed with spinach, almonds, lemon, and butter (£8.50), and joint of pork with a wholegrain mustard and honey gravy (£10.50); also, bar snacks like sandwiches, home-made soup (£2.75), ploughman's (£3.95), sausages and egg (£4.75), chicken curry or pasta with a tomato and basil sauce (£6.50), fresh grilled cod (£7.50), and sirloin steak with egg and bubble and squeak (£9.25). Piped music, shove-ha'penny, cribbage, dominoes, and table skittles. There are some picnic-sets out beside flowerbeds by the quiet road, and more in a pretty garden up behind where there's a barbecue area; pot-bellied pigs and ponies. Dogs welcome on a lead. *(Recommended by Clare and Paul Howes, Mike and Mary Carter, R Marshall, Colin Parker, Martin Jones)*

Free house ~ Licensee Guy Wilkins ~ Real ale ~ Bar food ~ Restaurant ~ (01452) 830477 ~ Children in eating area of bar and restaurant ~ Open 11.30-3, 6-11; 12-3.30, 7-10.30 Sun

BLEDINGTON SP2422 Map 4
Kings Head ★ ⑪ ♀ 🍴 🛏
B4450

This year, the room to the left of the bar in this upmarket 15th-c inn has been refurbished, and has drinking space for locals, benches on the new wooden floor, a woodburning stove, darts, cribbage, dominoes, TV, piped music, and a window looking out on to the green; on Sunday lunchtimes it is used by families. The main bar is full of ancient beams and other atmospheric furnishings (high-backed wooden settles, gateleg or pedestal tables), and there's a warming log fire in the stone inglenook (with a big black kettle hanging in it); the lounge looks on to the garden. At lunchtime, popular bar food includes sandwiches in granary or french bread (£3.95), couscous with grilled mediterranean vegetables and herb dressing or salads such as home-made gravadlax or goats cheese with bacon and onion (£5.95), steak in ale pie, thai chicken curry, grilled salmon and prawn fishcakes, toad-in-the-hole or lambs kidney in red wine, thyme and lavender (all £6.95), and fish and chips (£7.50). In the evening (the menu is served in the bar eating area of the restaurant) there might be bacon, black pudding and new potato salad topped with a poached egg (£4.95), smooth chicken liver parfait with white onion marmalade and a herb dressing (£5.95), shepherd's pie (£7.95), home-made ravioli filled with asparagus mousse on a rocket salad (£9.95), grilled swordfish, braised fennel and parsnip with a light butter sauce (£10.95), chump of English lamb, smoked potato rösti, caramelised carrots and a red wine jus (£11.95), rib-eye fillet steak on a bed of baby spinach, pomme alorniette and a marsala jus (£14.95), and a choice of three cheeses (£4.95). An antique bar counter dispenses well kept Hook Norton Best and Wadworths 6X with a couple of guests such as Archers Village, Goffs Jouster or Shepherd Neame Spitfire, an excellent extensive wine list, with 11 by the glass (champagnes also), 30 malt whiskies, organic apple juice and organic cider and perry. Part of the restaurant area is no smoking. There are seats in the back garden; aunt sally. At weekends, you are encouraged to stay two nights. The overwhelming majority of readers' reports, backed up by our own anonymous re-inspection this year, confirms the very high general appeal of this pub. However, scattered over the year we have had a handful of reports from readers who have not enjoyed themselves so much. We can't really guess at the reason for this, but should stress that it is a very small minority. *(Recommended by D J Hayman, John and Enid Morris, Nigel Woolliscroft, Mike Gorton, Richard Greaves, Rod Stoneman, Roger Braithwaite, Andrew Barker, Claire Jenkins, Jane McKenzie, John Bowdler, Jenny and Chris Wilson, Mike and Linda Hudson, Patricia A Bruce, K H Frostick, John Robertson, P Brown, Jonathan Smith, Steve Whalley)*

Free house ~ Licensees Nicola and Archie Orr-Ewing ~ Real ale ~ Bar food ~ Restaurant ~ (01608) 658365 ~ Children in restaurant ~ Open 11-2.30, 6-11 ~ Bedrooms: £45B/£60B

BOURTON-ON-THE-HILL SP1732 Map 4
Horse & Groom
A44 W of Moreton-in-Marsh

As well as being popular locally, this carefully renovated roadside inn offers a friendly welcome to visitors, too. The little high-beamed lounge bar, calm and attractive, has prints on the stripped-stone walls and settees and easy chairs around a large log fire, and there's a bigger public bar where you may find local regulars playing traditional pub games, and well kept Bass and Hook Norton on handpump. Good bar food includes sandwiches (£3), home-made pâté or home-made soup (£3.50), ploughman's (£4.80), filled baked potatoes (from £4.80), baguettes, omelettes, sausages and mash, ham and eggs, crab cakes or avocado and smoked salmon salad (all £5.80), and lemon sole (£9.80). The restaurant, with well spaced tables, is no smoking. The garden at the back has impressive views overlooking the countryside. *(Recommended by KN-R, J Hale, Francis and Deirdre Gevers-McClure)*

Free house ~ Licensee Linda Balhatchet ~ Real ale ~ Bar food (not Sun evening or

Mon) ~ Restaurant ~ (01386) 700413 ~ Children in eating area of bar and restaurant ~ Open 12-2.30(3 Sat), 7-11; 12-3, 7-10.30 Sun; closed Mon ~ Bedrooms: £60B/£75B

BOX SO8500 Map
Halfway Inn ♀

Edge of Minchinhampton Common; from A46 S of Stroud follow Amberley signpost, then after Amberley Inn turn right towards Box, then left along common edge as you reach Box; OS Sheet 162 map reference 856003; can also be reached from Brimscombe on A419 SE of Stroud

On the edge of the common, this extended tall house has light and airy open-plan upstairs bars around the central serving bar. There are simple rush seated sturdy blond wooden chairs around good wooden tables, a built-in wall seat and long pew, a woodburning stove, slightly naughty, well lit cartoons by Tim, bowls of lilies and other plants, and stripped wood floors. The bar has yellowy cream walls and ceiling, the dining area is mainly a warm terracota, there are windows with swagged curtains and views to the common, and an unusual pitched-roof area with a vast mirror and a big wrought-iron candalabra; it's all most inviting and attractive. Good, interesting bar food includes home-made soup (£3.25), cheese and herb fritters with plum chutney (£3.95), filled baguettes (from £3.95), ploughman's (£5.25), tian of crab and avocado (£5.25), roast pepper, spinach and goats cheese pancakes with pine nuts and tomatoes (£7.75), marinated chicken salad with ginger and sesame or haddock in beer batter with home-made tartare sauce (£7.95), pan-fried scallops and avocado and herb dressing salad (£8.25), slow-roasted duck leg with crispy bacon and orange and balsamic sauce or pork and leek sausages (£8.95), braised lamb shank with mustard mash and provençale vegetables (£9.95), and puddings such as dark chocolate and coffee charlotte with pistachio ice cream, raspberry crème brûlée or kirsch bavarois with nectarine compote and ginger and lime sauce (from £4.25). Well kept Archers Village, Bass, Hook Norton Best, and Wickwar BOB on handpump, kept under light blanket pressure, and very good wines. There are seats in the landscaped garden, and maybe giant Jenga and chess. *(Recommended by R Huggins, D Irving, E McCall, T McLean, Brian and Pat Wardrobe, Mary Kirman and Tim Jefferson, Andrew and Rosemary Reeves)*

Red Rose ~ Manager Michael Porter ~ Real ale ~ Bar food (12-9) ~ Restaurant ~ (01453) 832631 ~ Children welcome ~ Open 11-11; 12-10.30 Sun

BRIMPSFIELD SO9413 Map 4
Golden Heart ♀ ◀

Nettleton Bottom; A417 Birdlip—Cirencester, by start of new village bypass

This is a really enjoyable pub, both for its well kept beer and particularly good food, and although it can get quite busy, the staff are well organised and helpful. Inside, the main low-ceilinged bar is divided into three cosily distinct areas, with a roaring log fire in the huge stone inglenook fireplace in one, traditional built-in settles and other old-fashioned furnishings throughout, and quite a few brass items, typewriters, exposed stone, and wood panelling. A comfortable parlour on the right has another decorative fireplace, and leads into a further room that opens onto the terrace; two rooms are no smoking. Well presented, popular bar food includes sandwiches (from £2.75), home-made soup (£2.95), home-made pâté (£3.75), ploughman's (from £3.95), filled baked potatoes (from £4.50), mixed seafood mousse (£4.95), omelettes (£6.95), mushroom stroganoff (£7.50), hot chicken, bacon and avocado salad (£8.25), spaghetti bolognese (£8.50), poached fresh tuna steak with lemon mayonnaise (£9.25), kangaroo and black cherry casserole (£9.75), steaks (from £9.95), puddings like chocolate and rum log, rhubarb crumble or lemon and lime bavarois (£3.25), enjoyable Sunday roasts, and children's menu (£3.50). Well kept Archers, Marstons Pedigree and Timothy Taylors Landlord and Golden Best on handpump; decent wines. They hold beer festivals during the May and August bank holidays with live entertainment. There are pleasant views down over a valley from the rustic cask-supported tables on its suntrap gravel terrace, and good nearby walks. *(Recommended by Dr and Mrs James Stewart, Dorsan Baker, Charles Moncreiffe, R Huggins, D Irving, E McCall, T McLean, Stan and Hazel Allen, Guy Vowles, David Edwards, JP, PP, Neil and Anita Christopher, Leslie and Peter Barrett, Steve and Liz Tilley)*

Free house ~ Licensee Catherine Stevens ~ Real ale ~ Bar food (12-3, 6-10; 12-10 Sat and Sun) ~ Restaurant ~ (01242) 870261 ~ Children in eating area of bar and in family room ~ Open 11-3, 6-11; 11-11 Sat; 12-10.30 Sun ~ Bedrooms: £35S/£55S

BROAD CAMPDEN SP1637 Map 4
Bakers Arms ✑

Village signposted from B4081 in Chipping Campden

There are no noisy games machines or piped music to disturb the relaxed chatty atmosphere in this traditional village pub. The biggish room is divided into two, and the part with the most character is the tiny beamed bar with its pleasant mix of tables and seats around the walls (which are stripped back to bare stone), and inglenook fireplace at one end. The oak bar counter is attractive, and there's a big framed rugwork picture of the pub. Bar food includes lunchtime sandwiches (from £2.95), ploughman's (£3.95), and filled yorkshire puddings (£4.25), as well as home-made soup (£2.50), smoked haddock bake (£5.25), chicken curry (£5.50), cheese, leek and potato bake (£5.75), pie of the day or liver and bacon (£5.95), puddings (£2.75), and children's menu (£2.95). Well kept Donnington SBA, Hook Norton Best, Stanway Stanney Bitter, and Wells Bombardier on handpump. Darts, cribbage, dominoes. There are green tables under parasols by flower tubs on a couple of terraces and in the back garden, some seats under an arbour, and a play area. This is a tranquil village. *(Recommended by P R and S A White, Stuart Turner, Martin and Karen Wake, E V Walder, Richard Rand, Andrew and Ruth Triggs)*

Free house ~ Licensees Ray and Sally Mayo ~ Real ale ~ Bar food (all day in summer) ~ No credit cards ~ (01386) 840515 ~ Children welcome ~ Folk music 3rd Tues evening of month ~ Open 11.30-11; 12-10.30 Sun; 11.30-2.30, 4.45-11 weekdays in winter; closed 25 Dec, evening 26 Dec

BROCKHAMPTON SP0322 Map 4
Craven Arms ♀

Village signposted off A436 Andoversford—Naunton – look out for inn sign at head of lane in village; can also be reached from A40 Andoversford—Cheltenham via Whittington and Syreford

Deservedly popular, this attractive and friendly 17th-c inn is set in a pleasant gentrified hillside village with lovely views. There are low beams, thick roughly coursed stone walls and some tiled flooring, and though much of it has been opened out to give a sizeable (and spotlessly kept) eating area off the smaller bar servery, it's been done well to give a feeling of several communicating rooms; the furniture is mainly pine, with some wall settles, tub chairs and a log fire. Good bar food using fresh local produce includes home-made crab cakes with salsa (£4.75), home-made chicken liver pâté with home-made tomato chutney (£4.95), smoked salmon with dill mayonnaise (£4.95; main course £7.50), big ploughman's (from £4.95), cumberland sausage with onion and wine sauce (£6.95), mushrooms and nuts in ale under a puff pastry topping (£7.50), steak, mushroom and Guinness pie (£7.75), chicken supreme in stilton sauce or local trout stuffed with fresh herbs (£8.50), seared salmon with fresh lime and butter (£8.75), steaks (from £10.95), and home-made puddings like sticky toffee pudding, raspberry crème brûlée or apple crumble (from £3.50); good Sunday roasts. Well kept Fullers London Pride, Hook Norton Best and Wadworths 6X on handpump; friendly service. Shove-ha'penny. There are swings in the sizeable garden. *(Recommended by P R and S A White, Tom and Ruth Rees, Martin Jennings, Ian Dawson, Gary and Jane Gleghoth, Neil and Anita Christopher, John Brightley, Carol and Steve Spence, Dr and Mrs James Stewart, Jacquie and Jim Jones)*

Free house ~ Licensee Dale Campbell ~ Real ale ~ Bar food ~ Restaurant ~ (01242) 820410 ~ Children in eating area of bar and restaurant ~ Live entertainment Sun evening – jazz/quiz/barbecues ~ Open 11-3, 6-11; 12-3, 7-10.30 Sun

CHEDWORTH SP0511 Map 4

Seven Tuns

Village signposted off A429 NE of Cirencester; then take second signposted right turn and bear left towards church

The famous Roman villa is only a pleasant walk away from this little 17th-c pub, and there are other nice walks through the valley, too. The cosy little lounge on the right has a good winter log fire in the big stone fireplace, comfortable seats and decent tables, sizeable antique prints, tankards hanging from the beam over the serving bar, a partly boarded ceiling, and a relaxed, quiet atmosphere. The public bar on the left down a couple of steps has an open fire, and this opens into a no smoking dining room with another open fire; the skittle alley also acts as the games room with pool, darts, bar billiards, cribbage, and dominoes. Under the new licensee, bar food now includes sandwiches or baguettes (from £3.25; back bacon and fried mushrooms £3.50; Scotch sirloin steak £4.25), filled baked potatoes (£5.25), ploughman's (£5.50), ham and egg (£5.75), beef or vegetarian lasagne (£6.25), and daily specials such as soup (£2.95), oriental filo-wrapped prawn with soy dipping suace and prawn crackers (£5.25), home-made pies (£6.50), and fresh haddock in beer batter (£6.75); children's menu (£2.50), and roast Sunday lunch. Well kept Smiles Best, Youngs Bitter and seasonal ales, and local guests on handpump; lots of malt whiskies. Across the road is a little walled raised terrace with a waterwheel and a stream, and there are plenty of tables both here and under cocktail parasols on a side terrace. *(Recommended by Susan and Peter Davies, R Huggins, D Irving, E McCall, T McLean, Alastair Campbell, Trevor Owen, Nick and Meriel Cox, Lynn Sharpless, Bob Eardley, Patricia A Bruce)*

Smiles ~ Tenant Kevin Dursley ~ Real ale ~ Bar food (all day Mon-Sat; not Sun evening) ~ (01285) 720242 ~ Children welcome ~ Jazz/60s and 70s music evenings in summer ~ Open 11-11; 12-10.30 Sun; 11-3, 6-11 in winter

CHIPPING CAMPDEN SP1539 Map 4

Eight Bells ◀

Church Street (which is one way – entrance off B4035)

Part of the floor in the no smoking dining room of this handsome old inn has a glass inlet showing part of the passage from the church by which Roman Catholic priests could escape from the Roundheads. The heavy oak beams have massive timber supports, walls are of stripped stone, and there are cushioned pews and solid dark wood furniture on the broad flagstones, daily papers to read, and log fires in up to three restored stone fireplaces. Bar food includes lunchtime (not Sunday) filled baguettes, starters like vegetarian soup, chicken and leek terrine wrapped in smoked bacon with home-made chutney, twice baked cheese soufflé or fried lambs kidneys with savoy cabbage and bacon in a grain mustard sauce (£3.50-£5.50), main courses such as rock salmon in their own beer and yeast batter with home-made tartare sauce, beef and Guinness casserole with herb dumplings or baked breast of duck with garlic pomme purée finished with prunes and red wine (from £8.50), and home-made puddings like dark chocolate cheesecake with crème anglaise or lemon posset with raspberry coulis (£3.95); Sunday roast. Well kept Banks's Hanson's Bitter, Goffs Jouster, Hook Norton Old Hooky, and Marstons Pedigree, with a guest such as Wyre Piddle Piddle in the Hole on handpump from the fine oak bar counter; piped music, cribbage, and dominoes. Plenty of seats in the large terraced garden with striking views of the almshouses and church. Handy for the Cotswold Way walk to Bath. *(Recommended by John Bowdler, Moira and John Cole, Malcolm King, Steve Whalley, David Twitchett, Paul Boot, Stuart Turner, Pat and Roger Fereday, Martin Jones, Francis and Deirdre Gevers-McClure, Neil and Debbie Cook, Andrew and Ruth Triggs, Gordon, Kenette Wentner, R Davies, Di and Mike Gillam, J A and R M Ashurst)*

Free house ~ Licensee Neil Hargreaves ~ Real ale ~ Bar food (12-2(2.30 Fri-Sun), 6-9(6.30-9.30 wknds); no food Sun evening) ~ Restaurant ~ (01386) 840371 ~ Children welcome ~ Open 12-3, 5.30-11; 12-11 Sat; 12-10.30 Sun; closed 25 Dec ~ Bedrooms: £40B/£70B

Volunteer ◗

Lower High Street

As the lounge bar has been extended and re-carpeted and the front porch knocked down, the entrance into this friendly 18th-c pub is through a side door from the courtyard. There's a good mix of locals and visitors in the little bar by the street – which also has cushioned seats in bay windows, a log fire piled with big logs in the golden stone fireplace and hops, helmets and horse bits above it, proper old dining chairs with sage green plush seats and some similarly covered stools around a mix of tables, old army (Waterloo and WWI) paintings and bugles on the walls, with old local photographs on the gantry, and quite a few brass spigots dotted about. At lunchtimes (not Sunday), there's always a choice of roasts (£5.95), and enjoyable, home-made evening bar food such as soup (£2.50), warm garlic sausage salad topped with a poached egg (£4.95), home-roasted honey glazed ham with egg and chips (£5.75), crêpes filled with wild mushrooms topped with a spinach and cheese sauce or steak and kidney pie (£6.50), and calves liver and bacon with balsamic gravy (£7.50); at other times, there is warm goats cheese in puff pastry on leaf salad with lardons (£4.95), fresh chive battered cod (£5.75), chicken breast flamed with calvados and finished with cream and almonds (£8.50), roast English duck breast with orange and Cointreau sauce (£9.50), and 10oz rib-eye pepper steak (£10.50). Well kept North Cotswold Brewery Genesis, Stanway Stanney Bitter, and guests such as Fullers London Pride, Hook Norton Best, Wells Bombardier, and Wickwar Cotswold Way on handpump, and quite a few malt whiskies. There are picnic-sets in a small brick paved ivy courtyard with an arch through to the back garden with more picnic-sets. A door off here leads to the public bar with modern upholstered wing settles, juke box, darts, pool, fruit machine, cribbage, dominoes, and weekly quiz evenings, and tankards hanging from beams. They hold pig roasts and barbecues on bank holidays. *(Recommended by Colin Parker, Dr Paull Khan, E V Walder, Di and Mike Gillam, Steve Whalley, Don and Marilou Brooks)*

Free house ~ Licensee Hilary Mary Sinclair ~ Real ale ~ Bar food ~ (01386) 840688 ~ Children in eating area of bar ~ Open 11.30-3, 5(6 Sat)-11; 12-3, 7-10.30 Sun ~ Bedrooms: £27.50B/£55B

COLD ASTON SP1219 Map 4

Plough

Village signposted from A436 and A429 SW of Stow-on-the-Wold; beware that on some maps the village is called Aston Blank, and the A436 called the B4068

Already tiny, this 17th-c pub is made even smaller by the standing timbers that divide it into snug little areas. There are low black beams, a built-in white-painted traditional settle facing the stone fireplace, simple old-fashioned seats on the flagstone and lime-ash floor, and a happy mix of customers. As well as lunchtime sandwiches and traditional bar meals, the well liked bar food includes leek and gruyère tart (£6.95), salmon fishcake with parsley sauce and fine beans (£8.50), chicken breast with leek and bacon risotto (£9), breast of duck with roasted shallots, artichokes and pesto (£9.95), sirloin steak with stilton butter (£10.95), and home-made puddings. Well kept Donningtons Best and Hook Norton Best on handpump; darts and piped music. The small side terraces have picnic-sets under parasols, and there may be morris dancers out here in summer. There are plenty of surrounding walks but no boots are allowed in the pub. *(Recommended by Lynn Sharpless, Bob Eardley, Neil and Anita Christopher, Martin Jennings, Mrs N W Neill, E V Walder, Ann and Colin Hunt, Mr and Mrs B J P Edwards)*

Free house ~ Licensees Mr T Bignall and Miss L Newton ~ Real ale ~ Bar food (not Mon) ~ (01451) 821459 ~ Children welcome but must be well behaved ~ Open 11.45-2.30, 6.30-11; 12-3, 7-10.30 Sun; closed Mon (except bank hols)

The details at the end of each main entry start by saying whether the pub is a free house, or if it's tied to a brewery or pub group (which we name).

COLN ST ALDWYNS SP1405 Map 4

New Inn 🍴 ♟ 🛏

On good back road between Bibury and Fairford

Although most people come to this civilised inn to enjoy the particularly good (if not cheap) food, those wanting just a drink and a chat are made to feel just as welcome. The two neatly kept main rooms are attractively furnished and decorated, and divided by a central log fire in a neat stone fireplace with wooden mantelbeam and willow-pattern plates on the chimney breast; there are also low beams, some stripped stonework around the bar servery with hops above it, oriental rugs on the red tiles, and a mix of seating from library chairs to stripped pews. Down a slight slope, a further room has a coal fire in an old kitchen range at one end, and a stuffed buzzard on the wall. Sensibly, the menu offers a choice of helping size for several dishes: soup (£3.25; large helping £5.75), fried fillet of mackerel with a beetroot dressing or thai fishcakes with a sweet chilli dipping sauce (£4.50; main course £8.50), and caesar salad with a poached egg or satay chicken with a roasted peanut salad (£4.95; main course £9.50); also, fish and chips with mushy peas (£9), glazed bacon collar with root vegetables and parsley potatoes (£9.50), stir fry of sweet and sour pork with pineapple and spring onion (£11), daube of beef with creamed potatoes, smoked bacon and mushrooms or fried breast of chicken with mediterranean vegetable risotto and balsamic vinegar (£11.50), rib-eye steak with grilled field mushrooms and tomatoes (£13.50), and puddings like burnt lemon cream with raspberries, sticky toffee pudding with clotted cream or apple and cinnamon crumble (£4.50); vegetarian choices and children's meals. The restaurant is no smoking. Well kept Butcombe Best Bitter, Hook Norton Best, and Wadworths 6X on handpump, 8 good wines by the glass, and several malt whiskies. The split-level terrace has plenty of seats. The peaceful Cotswold village is pretty, and the riverside walk to Bibury is not to be missed. They like to be known as The New Inn At Coln. *(Recommended by A E Brace, J Hale, Tony Baldwin, John Bramley, Ann and Colin Hunt, R Huggins, D Irving, E McCall, T McLean, Lawrence Pearse, John Kane, M G Hart, Karen and Graham Oddey, Richard Rand, Mike and Mary Carter, Peter D B Harding, G T Brewster, S H Godsell; also in* The Good Hotel Guide*)*

Free house ~ Licensee Brian Evans ~ Real ale ~ Bar food (12-2.30, 7-9(9.30 Fri/Sat)) ~ Restaurant ~ (01285) 750651 ~ Children in eating area of bar; must be over 10 in restaurant ~ Open 11-11; 12-10.30 Sun ~ Bedrooms: £72S/£99B

CRANHAM SO8912 Map 4

Black Horse 🍺

Village signposted off A46 and B4070 N of Stroud; look out for small sign up village side turning

Tucked away down narrow lanes, this old-fashioned 17th-c pub is usually busy, even on a wet winter's day. A cosy little lounge has just three or four tables, and the main bar is quarry-tiled, with cushioned high-backed wall settles and window seats, and a good log fire. Served in generous helpings from a varied menu, the good, popular food might include sandwiches and toasties (from £2.25), ploughman's (£4.50), ham and eggs or niçoise salad (£5.95), faggots (£6.50), cottage pie or vegetable crumble (£6.95), toad-in-the-hole (£7.75), gloucester old spot pork chops (£7.95), cod with sun-dried tomatoes, olives and garlic (£8.25), steak and mushroom in ale pie or seafood casserole (£8.50), half a duck with apple sauce (£9.25), and half shoulder of lamb (£9.75). You can eat the same menu in the upstairs no smoking dining rooms (best to book at weekends). Very well kept Flowers Original, Hook Norton Best, Wickwar BOB, and guests such as Boddingtons or Marstons Pedigree on handpump, and country wines. Shove-ha'penny and piped music. Tables in the sizeable garden behind have a good view out over the steep village and wooded valley, and they keep chickens and rabbits; the jack russell is called Baxter and the cocker spaniel, Biscuit. *(Recommended by Ann and Colin Hunt, Pete Baker, Mike and Wendy Proctor, Mrs E A Bell, Martin Jennings, David and Phyllis Chapman, James Nunns, Gary and Jane Gleghoth)*

Free house ~ Licensees David and Julie Job ~ Real ale ~ Bar food (not Sun evening) ~ Restaurant ~ (01452) 812217 ~ Children welcome ~ Irish/folk music some Sun evenings; morris dancers in summer ~ Open 11.30-2.30, 6.30-11; 12-3, 7(8 in winter)-11 Sun

DIDMARTON ST8187 Map 2
Kings Arms ♀ 🍺

A433 Tetbury road

Thoughtful little touches in this attractively restored and decorated 17th-c coaching inn please readers very much. There's always a glass vase of large fresh flowers such as lilies on the bar, perhaps an unexpected bread basket with a proper pot of butter served with a bar meal, and generous glasses of wine from a bargain bin-end list. The knocked-through rooms work their way around a big central counter and have deep terracotta walls above a dark green dado, a pleasant mix of chairs on bare boards, quarry tiles and carpet, a big stone fireplace, and a nice old upright piano. Everything is neat and tidy, with good attention to detail. Good, enjoyable bar food includes soup (£2.95), baguettes (from £3.75; prawn with a lime and dill mayonnaise £4.50), chicken liver and mushroom pâté or ploughman's (£4.95), mild cajun fishcakes (£6.75), macaroni and goats cheese with sweet peppers, courgettes and mushrooms (£6.95), moules marinières with pommes frites or chicken tikka masala (£7.25), and shoulder of lamb, turnip and mint casserole (£7.50), with puddings such as bitter chocolate tart with coffee bean syrup and clotted cream or rhubarb streusel pie with vanilla ice cream (£4.50). Well kept John Smiths, Uley Bitter, and a couple of guests such as Bath Rare Hare or Smiles Best on handpump, a good wine list with half a dozen by the glass, farm cider in summer, and several malt whiskies; darts, cribbage, and dominoes. They have self-catering cottages in a converted barn and stable block. *(Recommended by Lyn and Geoff Hallchurch, S H Godsell, Tom and Ruth Rees, Gaynor Gregory, MRSM, KC, Lawrence Pearse)*

Free house ~ Licensees Nigel and Jane Worrall ~ Real ale ~ Bar food ~ Restaurant ~ (01454) 238245 ~ Children in eating area of bar and restaurant ~ Open 12-3, 6-11; 12-3, 7-10.30 Sun ~ Bedrooms: £45S/£80S

DUNTISBOURNE ABBOTS SO9709 Map 4
Five Mile House 🍺

Turn off A417 NW of Cirencester at 'Services, Duntisbourne Abbots'; from village turn off northbound bypass, turn immediately right to pass below bypass, then right down dead end

It's not an easy task to please both those who want an enjoyable meal out and others who are dropping in for just a drink and a chat. But the thoroughly old-fashioned feel in this delightful 300-year-old coaching inn is preserved by the landlord's tactful insistence that if you want to eat even a sandwich, you should move to one of the areas such as the lounge behind the left-hand snug or the dining room. The front room has a companionable bare-boards drinking bar on the right, with wall seats around the big table in its bow window and just one other table; on the left is a flagstoned hallway tap room snug formed from two ancient high-backed settles by a (new) woodburning stove in a tall carefully exposed old fireplace; newspapers to read. There's a small cellar bar (piped music on request down here – it's a perfect size for a group celebration), a back restaurant down steps, and a family room on the far side; cribbage and dominoes. The lounge and cellar bar are no smoking. Well kept Archers Village and Timothy Taylors Landlord, and a changing guest from breweries such as Cottage, Goffs, Wickwar, Wye Valley or Youngs on handpump (the cellar is temperature-controlled), interesting wines (strong on New World ones). Generous helpings of good, popular bar food (cooked by the landlord) include at lunchtime, open sandwiches (from £3.95), ploughman's (from £4.95), free range egg omelette (£5.95), home-cooked ham with eggs or deep-fried cod and chips (£6.95), and whole local trout with a prawn and lemon butter (£8.50), with evening dishes such as home-made soup (£3.25), home-made chicken liver pâté (£4.50), vegetable and seafood dimsum with a chilli and plum dip (£4.75), chicken breast fillet stuffed with stilton, wrapped in bacon and served with a mushroom and brandy cream sauce (£9.95), and daily specials like home-made faggots or hot avocado filled with apricots, figs, celery, apple and grapes and topped with toasted brie (£7.50), pork loin steaks glazed with honey and mustard (£9.50), and barbary duck breast with a mulled wine and orange glaze (£12.50); puddings such as white chocolate cheesecake, crème brûlée, treacle tart or fruit crumble (£3.50), children's helpings where possible, and roast Sunday lunch (£8.50). You may have to book some time ahead. Service is thoughtful and friendly. The gardens have nice country views. This quiet country lane was once Ermine Street, the main Roman road from London to Wales. *(Recommended by Roger and Jenny Huggins, R Huggins, D Irving, E McCall, T McLean, Phil and Sally Gorton, Miss S J Ebbutt, Neil and Anita Christopher, GL, JP, PP, Helen Eastwood, Sheila and Robert Robinson, Di and Mike Gillam, Lyn and Geoff Hallchurch, Andrew and Ruth Triggs, Patricia A Bruce, Giles Francis, K C and B Forman, Ann and Colin Hunt, Helen Gazeley, Guy Vowles)*

Free house ~ Licensees Jo and John Carrier ~ Real ale ~ Bar food (12-2.30, 6-9.30; not 25 Dec) ~ Restaurant ~ (01285) 821432 ~ Children welcome if well behaved ~ Monthly singsongs ~ Open 12-3, 6-11; 12-3, 7-10.30 Sun

DURSLEY ST7598 Map 2
Old Spot ⬤

By bus station

A lively bunch of locals and walkers and an interesting choice of real ales keep this unassuming white rendered old farmhouse as popular as ever. The front door opens into a deep pink little room with stools on shiny quarry tiles along its pine boarded bar counter, and old enamel beer advertisements on the walls and ceiling; there's a profusion of porcine paraphernalia. Leading off here there's a little room on the left with a bar billiards table, cribbage and dominoes, and the little dark wood floored room to the right has a stone fireplace. From here a step takes you down to a cosy Victorian tiled snug and (to the right) the no smoking meeting room. Well kept Uley Old Ric on handpump and changing guest beers from breweries such as Archers, Badger, Batemans, Bath, Exmoor, and Wickwar; several malt whiskies. Bar food includes sandwiches (from £2.75), filled baked potatoes (from £3.75), ploughman's (from £4.75), stir fries such as vegetarian or chicken (from £4.95), sausages such as lamb and mint or pork, leek and ginger, all served with red onion gravy (from £5.25), beef in ale pie (£5.50), smoked trout fillets (£5.15), and puddings (from £2.25). Pétanque in the pretty garden. *(Recommended by M G Hart, R Huggins, D Irving, E McCall, T McLean, G Coates, Rob Holt, Alan and Paula McCully, Colin Parker)*

Free house ~ Licensees Steve and Belinda Herbert ~ Real ale ~ Bar food (lunchtime only) ~ (01453) 542870 ~ Children in family room ~ Local musicians Weds evenings ~ Open 11-3, 5.30-11; 11-11 Sat; 12-10.30 Sun

EWEN SU0097 Map 4
Wild Duck ♀

Village signposted from A429 S of Cirencester

Quietly placed on the edge of a peaceful village, this civilised 16th-c inn has a high-beamed main bar with a nice mix of comfortable armchairs and other seats, paintings on the red walls, crimson drapes, a winter open fire, candles on tables, and magazines to read; the residents' lounge has a handsome Elizabethan fireplace and antique furnishings, and looks over the garden; piped music. Under a new team of chefs, bar food now includes spinach and gruyère cheese tart with a roast cherry tomato dressing (£4.95), ploughman's (£5.75), bacon and egg terrine with a dill and mustard mayonnaise (£5.95), chicken breast seasoned and grilled over fettucine with a pesto cream sauce or gorgonzola and walnut ravioli with a tomato and fresh oregano sauce (£6.95), roast chump of lamb with chorizo sausage, pilau rice and moroccan spiced gravy (£10.95), swordfish steak with coriander couscous, cashew nut and beansprout salad and sweet chilli sauce (£11.50), roast fillet of beef with rosemary and garlic on black pudding mash with burgundy wine sauce (£14.50), and puddings such as iced coconut and pawpaw parfait with lime or sticky toffee and apple pudding with cinnamon anglaise (from £3.95); Sunday roasts (£7.50). As well as Duckpond Bitter, brewed especially for the pub, well kept beers might include Archers Golden, Greene King Old Speckled Hen, Smiles Best, Theakstons Old Peculier, and Wells Bombardier on handpump, kept under light blanket pressure. Good wines, several malt whiskies, and shove-ha'penny. There are green painted cast-iron tables and seats in the neatly kept and sheltered garden. *(Recommended by R Huggins, D Irving, E McCall, T McLean, Nick and Meriel Cox, Di and Mike Gillam, Bernard Stradling, Susan and John Douglas, John Robertson, Gary and Jane Gleghoth, Charles and Pauline Stride, Colin Parker, Mr and Mrs G P Lloyd, Steve Chambers, Kevin Blake, P R and S A White, John Bramley, Christopher Harrowe)*

Free house ~ Licensees Tina and Dino Mussell ~ Real ale ~ Bar food (till 10pm) ~ Restaurant ~ (01285) 770310 ~ Children welcome ~ Open 11-11; 12-10.30 Sun ~ Bedrooms: £55B/£75B

FORD SP0829 Map 4
Plough
B4077

Set opposite a well known racehorse trainer's yard, this bustling and pretty stone pub has racing prints and photos on the walls in the beamed and stripped-stone bar, old settles and benches around the big tables on its uneven flagstones, and oak tables in a snug alcove; four welcoming log fires (two are log-effect gas), and dominoes, cribbage, shove-ha'penny, fruit machine, TV (for the races), and piped music. Enjoyable home-made bar food includes lunchtime baguettes (from £3.95), chilli carne (£5.95), cod in beer batter (£6.95), beef in red wine or pork in creamy mustard sauce (£8.95), and lamb cutlets with redcurrant jus (£9.95); they offer breakfasts for travellers on the way to the Gold Cup meeting at Cheltenham. They still have their traditional asparagus feasts every May-June, when the first asparagus spears to be sold at auction in the Vale of Evesham usually end up here. Well kept Donnington BB and SBA on handpump, and Addlestone's cider; polite, helpful service. There are benches in the garden, pretty hanging baskets, and a play area at the back. The Llama Farm and Cotswold Farm Park are nearby. *(Recommended by Tom Evans, Lyn and Geoff Hallchurch, Andrew and Ruth Triggs, Mike and Wena Stevenson, P and J Shapley, the Didler, Guy Vowles, Peter and Audrey Dowsett, Nick Lawless, JP, PP)*

Donnington ~ Tenant C Turner ~ Real ale ~ Bar food (not Sun evenings) ~ (01386) 584215 ~ Children welcome ~ Open 11-11; 12-10.30 Sun; closed 25 Dec ~ Bedrooms: £35S/£55S

GREAT RISSINGTON SP1917 Map 4
Lamb ♀ 🛏

Turn off A40 W of Burford to the Barringtons; keep straight on past Great Barrington until Great Rissington is signed on left

New licensees have taken over this partly 17th-c inn and have refurbished the rather civilised two-roomed bar. The walls are a warm peach colour, the cushioned seats are now covered in an orange and burgundy brocade with curtains to match, there are wheelback and tub chairs grouped around polished tables on the new beige carpet, and an open fire in the stone fireplace; some interesting things to look at include part of a propeller from the Wellington bomber that crashed in the garden in October 1943, a collection of old cigarette and tobacco tins (along a beam in the restaurant), photographs of the guide dogs the previous staff and customers have raised money to buy (over 20), a history of the village, and various plates and pictures. Enjoyable bar food now includes home-made soup (£3.25), sandwiches (from £3.25), filled baked potatoes (£4.50), lamb, rosemary and garlic sausages with gravy in a large yorkshire pudding (£5.50), a pasta dish of the day (£5.95), daily specials such as lamb curry, cod and chips or goulash (£5.50), red snapper (£8.50), mediterranean vegetable gateau (£8.95), and home-made puddings (£3); you can also eat from the more extensive menu in the partly no smoking restaurant (where there is another open fire). Well kept Hook Norton Best and a guest such as John Smiths or Wychwood Special on handpump, a decent wine list, and several malt whiskies; helpful service, piped classical music, darts, dominoes, and cribbage. You can sit out in the sheltered hillside garden or really take advantage of the scenery and walk (via gravel pits now used as a habitat for water birds) to Bourton-on-the-Water. *(Recommended by Andrew and Ruth Triggs, John and Jackie Chalcraft, Tony Walker, Michael and Jenny Back, Mike and Wena Stevenson)*

Free house ~ Licensees Paul and Jacqueline Gabriel ~ Real ale ~ Bar food ~ Restaurant ~ (01451) 820388 ~ Children welcome ~ Open 11.30-2.30, 6.30-11; 12-2.30, 7-10.30 Sun ~ Bedrooms: £35B/£55S(£60B)

GRETTON SP0131 Map 4
Royal Oak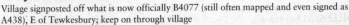

Village signposted off what is now officially B4077 (still often mapped and even signed as A438), E of Tewkesbury; keep on through village

The new welcoming licensees have injected real enthusiasm into this converted pair of old stone-built cottages. The series of bare-boarded or flagstone rooms has beams hung with tankards, hop bines and chamber-pots, old prints on dark ochre walls, a medley of pews and various chairs, candles in bottles on the mix of stripped oak and pine tables, and a friendly bustle. The no smoking dining conservatory has stripped country furnishings, and a broad view over the countryside. Good bar food includes baguettes, home-made soup (£3.25), duck and orange pâté or warm goats cheese salad (£3.95), fresh mussels with garlic, white wine, and cream (£4.25), spicy moroccan meatballs (£7.45), chicken with bacon, leek and mushroom sauce or braised knuckle of lamb (£8.45), honey and mustard pork hock (£8.95), steaks (from £9.45). Well kept Goffs Jouster and White Knight, Wadworths 6X, and a guest beer on handpump, and a decent wine list; piped music. They now hold a beer and music festival in June. From seats on the flower-filled terrace you can enjoy the fine views over the village and across the valley to Dumbleton Hills and the Malverns. There are more seats under a giant pear tree, a neatly kept big lawn running down past a small hen-run to a play area (with an old tractor and see-saw), and even a bookable tennis court. It's fun to watch the little trains on the private Gloucestershire—Warwickshire Railway at the bottom of the garden. *(Recommended by Bernard Stradling, Ted George, P and M Rudlin, Edward Jago, R J Herd, M Mainwaring)*

Free house ~ Licensee Myles Ball ~ Real ale ~ Bar food ~ Restaurant ~ (01242) 604999 ~ Children welcome ~ Local singers Weds evening ~ Open 12-3, 6-11; 12-4, 6-11 Sat; 12-4, 7-11 Sun

GUITING POWER SP0924 Map 4
Hollow Bottom

Village signposted off B4068 SW of Stow-on-the-Wold (still called A436 on many maps)

There's a good mix of customers in this snug 17th-c inn and a friendly, homely atmosphere. The comfortable beamed bar is full of racing memorabilia including racing silks, tunics and photographs (it is owned by a small syndicate that includes Peter Scudamore and Nigel Twiston-Davies), and there's a winter log fire in an unusual pillar-supported stone fireplace; the public bar has flagstones and stripped stone masonry and racing on TV. Enjoyable bar food is all home-made, and includes soups such as curried parsnip and apple or celery and stilton (£3.45), baguettes (from £4.25), chicken liver pâté with cumberland sauce (£4.45), filled baked potatoes (from £5.25), burgers or local sausages (£6.95), lasagne (£7.50), gammon and eggs (£7.95), calves liver (£10.95), steaks (from £12.95), grilled bass (£15.95), and puddings such as popular banoffi pie or mango cheesecake (£3.50); Sunday carvery. Well kept Greene King Old Speckled Hen, Hook Norton, and Wadworths 6X on handpump, and helpful, pleasant service; piped music. From the pleasant garden behind are views towards the peaceful sloping fields. Decent walks nearby. *(Recommended by Dr A Y Drummond, Terry Mizen, Michael and Jenny Back, Ted George, J S Baddiley, Gwen and Peter Andrews)*

Free house ~ Licensees Hugh Kelly and Charles Pettigrew ~ Real ale ~ Bar food (12-9.30) ~ Restaurant ~ (01451) 850392 ~ Children welcome ~ Live entertainment every 2nd Weds or Thurs ~ Open 11-11; 12-10.30 Sun ~ Bedrooms: £25B/£50B

KILKENNY SP0018 Map 4
Kilkeney Inn 🍴 ♀

On A436, 1 mile W of Andoversford, nr Cheltenham – OS Sheet 163 map reference 007187

Very much somewhere to come for a meal rather than a quick drink, this pleasant dining pub remains a popular place with many readers. As well as light lunches such as soup (£3.75), filled baguettes or ciabatta or ploughman's (£5.95), local sausages wrapped in bacon in a puff pastry parcel with onion gravy or spanish omelette (£6.95), a pasta of the day (£7.95), and poached fillet of smoked haddock on warm salad of potatoes and red onion with lemon cream (£7.95), there might be duck and liver terrine with brandy and green peppercorn on fresh brioche (£5.25), a medley of warm smoked fish (£6.75), duo of aubergine and pepper stuffed with tomato and double gloucester cheese (£9.95), chicken breast stuffed with leeks and sage with a sage and red wine cream sauce (£10.50), casserole of local venison and mushrooms with celeriac mash (£11.95), slow-roasted half shoulder of lamb with a provençale glaze (£13.25), supreme of duck roasted pink and carved onto chilli and coriander linguini in a cherry and vanilla glaze (£14.95), and puddings such as brandy and apricot bread and butter pudding, crème brûlée or meringue basket filled with damson and sloe gin ice cream with cinnamon and citrus syrup (from £3.95). Booking is recommended, especially at weekends. The extended and modernised bar, quite bright and airily spacious, has neatly alternated stripped Cotswold stone and white plasterwork, as well as gleaming dark wheelback chairs around the tables, and an open fire. Well kept Bass and Hook Norton on handpump and an interesting wine list. There's a comfortable no smoking dining conservatory. Attractive Cotswold views, and good parking. *(Recommended by Tom and Ruth Rees, Bernard Stradling, KN-R, M A and C R Starling, Gary and Jane Gleghoth, Denis and Dorothy Evans, Gordon Tong, A Jones, Ian Dawson, Guy Vowles)*

Free house ~ Licensees David and Liz Benson ~ Real ale ~ Bar food (all day at weekends) ~ Restaurant ~ (01242) 820341 ~ Well behaved children in eating area of bar ~ Jazz Fri evenings twice a month ~ Open 11.30-2.30, 6-11; 11.30-10.30 Sat; 12-10.30 Sun

KINGSCOTE ST8196 Map 4
Hunters Hall

A4135 Dursley—Tetbury

This civilised, creeper-covered old inn has held a continuous licence for 500 years. There is quite a series of bar rooms and lounges with fine high Tudor beams and stone walls, a lovely old box settle, sofas and miscellaneous easy chairs, and sturdy settles and oak tables on the flagstones in the lower-ceilinged, cosy public bar; piped music. An airy end room serves the enjoyable bar food which includes sandwiches (not Sunday lunch), home-made soup (£3.25), chicken and duck liver pâté with a red onion and orange chutney (£4.25), tian of prawns, mango and apple (£4.50), liver and bacon or steak, kidney and Guinness pie (£7.25), baked fillets of cod topped with a tomato and herb crust (£7.50), breaded cheese and risotto cake on provençale sauce (£8.25), baked supreme of chicken filled with brie and wrapped in bacon and carved on to a port wine sauce (£9.95), steaks (from £10.95), daily specials such as seafood chowder (£4.95), pasta in a mushroom, leek and herb cream (£7.95), roast loin of lamb carved on to a polenta crust (£9.75), and cajun-style grilled halibut on parsnip mash with mango coulis (£9.95); there's more space to eat in the no smoking Gallery upstairs; good breakfasts. Well kept Bass, Greene King Ruddles Best, Uley Hogs Head and a guest such as Smiles Best or Wickwar BOB on handpump; friendly, helpful staff. A back room – relatively untouched – is popular with local lads playing pool; darts, dominoes, cribbage, shove-ha'penny, and juke box. The garden has seats, and a new wooden fortress, play house, and swings for children.

(Recommended by S H Godsell, Charles and Pauline Stride, Steve Godfrey, Neil and Anita Christopher, R Huggins, D Irving, E McCall, T McLean, Revd A Nunnerley, Peter and Audrey Dowsett)

Old English Inns ~ Tenant Stephanie Ward ~ Real ale ~ Bar food ~ Restaurant ~ (01453) 860393 ~ Children welcome ~ Open 11-11; 12-10.30 Sun ~ Bedrooms: £50S/£75S

LITTLE BARRINGTON SP2012 Map 4
Inn For All Seasons 🍽 ♀
On the A40 3 miles W of Burford

The very good food enjoyed in a relaxed atmosphere continues to draw many customers to this civilised and comfortable old inn. The attractively decorated, mellow lounge bar has low beams, stripped stone, and flagstones, old prints, leather-upholstered wing armchairs and other comfortable seats, country magazines to read, and a big log fire (with a big piece of World War II shrapnel above it); maybe quiet piped classical music. They specialise in fresh Brixham fish: mussels (from £4), flash-fried squid (£5), thai fish curry (£9.50), wing of skate (£10), monkfish tail, whole bass or turbot fillet (from £12), and dover sole or whole lemon sole (from £14). Other non-fishy dishes include sandwiches, soup such as cream of broccoli and chicken (£3.75), grilled toulouse sausage with a creamy onion and mustard sauce (£4.60), cornish crab and king prawn pâté (£4.65), tagliatelle with a wild mushroom sauce (£7.50), chicken supreme wrapped in smoked bacon and cheddar cheese on a green peppercorn and ginger sauce (£8.95), grilled double saddle chop of lamb on minted mash and a mixed berry sauce (£9.95), Hereford rump steak (£11.95), and puddings such as hot walnut and syrup sponge with vanilla ice cream and Cotswold clotted cream (£3.75) or warm treacle tart with chocolate ice cream (from £3.75). Well kept Wadworths 6X, and Wychwood Shires XXX on handpump, a good wine list with 100 bin ends, and over 60 malt whiskies; cribbage and dominoes. The pleasant garden has tables and a play area, and there are walks straight from the inn. It's very busy during Cheltenham Gold Cup Week – when the adjoining field is pressed into service as a helicopter pad. *(Recommended by Nick Holmes, John Bramley, Mr and Mrs J McAngus, Peter and Audrey Dowsett, Tony and Rachel Schendel, Dr R J Rushton, Andrew and Ruth Triggs, Simon Collett-Jones, I D Greenfield, Pat and Tony Martin, Alastair Campbell, M A and C R Starling, Tony Walker, Richard Rand, Jim Bush, David and Brenda Tew)*

Free house ~ Licensees Matthew and Heather Sharp ~ Real ale ~ Bar food ~ Restaurant ~ (01451) 844324 ~ Children welcome ~ Open 11-2.30, 6-11; 12-2.30, 7-10.30 Sun ~ Bedrooms: £49.50B/£85B

LITTLETON-UPON-SEVERN ST5990 Map 4
White Hart 🍺
3½ miles from M4 junction 21; B4461 towards Thornbury, then village signposted

Several parts of this carefully restored pantiled pub are still as they were when it was built as a farmhouse in the 1690s. The three atmospheric main rooms have some fine furnishings such as long cushioned wooden settles, high-backed settles, oak and elm tables, and a loveseat in the big low inglenook fireplace; flagstones in the front, huge tiles at the back, and smaller tiles on the left, plus some old pots and pans, and a lovely old White Hart Inn Simonds Ale sign. By the black wooden staircase are some nice little alcove seats, there's a black-panelled big fireplace in the front room, and hops on beams. A no smoking family room, similarly furnished, has some sentimental engravings, plates on a delft shelf, and a couple of high chairs, and a back snug has pokerwork seats and table football; darts, cribbage, fruit machine, chess, backgammon and Jenga. Bar food includes sandwiches, home-made soup (£2.70), filled baguettes (from £3.50), ploughman's (from £4.25), broccoli and blue cheese tart or ham and eggs (£5.95), home-battered haddock, beef and cashew nut curry or salads like Italian pork with basil and tomato or turmeric creamed chicken (all £6.95), mushroom and nut stroganoff (£7.95), red snapper with chinese noodles (£8.25), puddings such as strawberry brûlée or summer pudding (£2.95), and roast

Sunday lunch (£6.95). Now that the pub is owned by Youngs, they keep Youngs Bitter, Special and Waggle Dance, and a guest such as Smiles Best on handpump. Picnic-sets on the neat front lawn with interesting cottagey flowerbeds, and by the good big back car park are some attractive shrubs and teak furniture on a small brick terrace. Several walks from the pub itself. *(Recommended by Matt Britton, Alison Cameron, Lyn and Geoff Hallchurch, Tom Evans, Mr and Mrs Thomas, George Little, Simon and Amanda Southwell, A C and E Johnson, Di and Mike Gillam)*

Youngs ~ Managers Howard and Liz Turner ~ Real ale ~ Bar food ~ (01454) 412275 ~ Children in restaurant ~ Open 12-2.30, 6-11.30; 11-11 Sat; 12-10.30 Sun ~ Bedrooms: £39.50B/£49.50B

LOWER ODDINGTON SP2325 Map 4

Fox 🍴 ♈

Near Stow-on-the-Wold

The licensees are still enthusiastically making improvements to this smart, very popular inn. A custom-built awning has been installed with outdoor heaters to cover the terrace in the newly planted cottage garden – this will enable customers to dine out on the chilliest of summer evenings. Improvements and new ideas have been added to the wine list and menu. A third bedroom with antiques has been opened, and a local artist and specialist painter has decorated the lavatories. The Red Room houses a collection of wine related antiques and corkscrews, and the other simply and spotlessly furnished rooms have fresh flowers and flagstones, an inglenook fireplace, hunting scene figures above the mantelpiece, a display cabinet with pewter mugs and stone bottles, daily newspapers, and hops hanging from the ceiling; dominoes, cribbage, backgammon, chess and cards. Served by staff in uniform shirts, the good, interesting food might include tomato and red pepper soup (£3.95), courgette and blue cheese risotto (£4.25), griddled ciabatta sandwiches (weekday lunchtimes only; from £4.50), baked sardines with lemon and herb butter (£5.25), super salmon fishcakes with a chive cream sauce, chicken, leek and mushroom pie, smoked haddock with spinach and a poached egg, and duck leg with shi-itake mushroom sauce, potato and parsnip mash (all £8.50), rib-eye steak (£10.75), daily specials such as roast shoulder of lamb with garlic, sage and cider sauce (£9.75) or griddled tuna loin with roasted peppers and aubergines (£11.50), and puddings like apple tart with calvados cream, plum and frangipane tart with plum sauce or white and dark chocolate iced terrine with Amaretti biscuits (£3.75); every Tuesday, they have special fish starters and main courses; Sunday roast sirloin of beef (£9.50). The wine list is excellent (they have daily and monthly specials), and they keep Badger Tanglefoot, Hook Norton Best, and a changing guest like Goffs Jouster or Shepherd Neame Spitfire on handpump. A good eight-mile walk starts from here (though a stroll around the pretty village might be less taxing after a fine meal). *(Recommended by D J Hayman, M O'Brien, Bernard Stradling, Pat and Roger Fereday, Stuart Turner, Roger Braithwaite, Eric Locker, G U Briggs, Andrew Barker, Claire Jenkins, Paul Boot, Peter Burton, John Kane, Karen and Graham Oddey, John Smither, R J Chenery, Charles Gysin, Mrs S White, M A and C R Starling, Derek and Sylvia Stephenson, Gary and Jane Gleghoth, Dr and Mrs James Stewart, Patricia A Bruce, Leslie and Peter Barrett, Francis and Deirdre Gevers-McClure, Kevin Poulter, Ian and Joan Blackwell, John Bramley)*

Free house ~ Licensees Sally and Kirk Ritchie ~ Real ale ~ Bar food (till 10pm) ~ Restaurant ~ (01451) 870888 ~ Children welcome if quiet and well behaved ~ Open 12-3, 6.30-11; 12-3, 7-10.30 Sun; closed 25 Dec, evenings 26 and 31 Dec, 1 Jan ~ Bedrooms: /£58B

MEYSEY HAMPTON SU1199 Map 4

Masons Arms

High Street; just off A417 Cirencester—Lechlade

It's not just locals and visitors who are made to feel welcome by the friendly staff in this 17th-c stonebuilt inn – hot dogs are offered a bowl of water. The longish open-plan bar has a bustling, chatty atmosphere, painted brick walls, carefully stripped beams with some hops, solid part-upholstered built-in wall seats with some matching chairs, good sound tables, a big inglenook log fire at one end, daily newspapers, and a few steps up to the no smoking restaurant. Well kept Bass, Hook Norton Best, and a couple of guests from Goffs or Hook Norton on handpump, and decent wines including several ports; dominoes, cribbage, and piped music. Well liked bar food includes sandwiches (from £1.95; filled baguettes from £3.95; hot bacon and mushroom £5.65), home-made soup (£2.45), filled baked potatoes (from £3.65), stilton and bacon mushrooms (£3.95), caesar salad with spicy chicken (£4.95), ploughman's (from £5.25), honey-roasted ham with two eggs (£5.65), liver and bacon in rich onion gravy (£6.35), steak and kidney pie (£6.55), spinach and mixed pepper tart (£6.95), tuna steak topped with prawns and dill butter (£7.65), duck breast grilled with oranges and lemons, flamed with Grand Marnier and topped with an orange sauce (£8.95), and sirloin steaks (from £9.75). *(Recommended by G W A Pearce, Rod Stoneman, Dennis Jenkin, Roger and Jenny Huggins, Simon Collett-Jones, Gwen and Peter Andrews, Andrew and Ruth Triggs, R Huggins, D Irving, E McCall, T McLean)*

Free house ~ Licensees Andrew and Jane O'Dell ~ Real ale ~ Bar food (not Sun evening) ~ Restaurant ~ (01285) 850164 ~ Children welcome until 9 ~ Open 11.30-2.45, 6-11; 12-4, 7-10.30 Sun; closed Sun evening in winter ~ Bedrooms: £40S/£60S

MISERDEN SO9308 Map 4
Carpenters Arms

Village signposted off B4070 NE of Stroud; also a pleasant drive off A417 via the Duntisbournes, or off A419 via Sapperton and Edgeworth; OS Sheet 163 map reference 936089

Run by a helpful, hard-working licensee, this friendly local is set in an idyllic Cotswold estate village. The two open-plan bar areas have low beams, nice old wooden tables, seats with the original little brass name plates on the backs and some cushioned settles and spindlebacks on the bare boards; also, stripped stone walls with some interesting bric-a-brac, and two big log fires; The small no smoking dining room has dark traditional furniture. The sizeable collage (done with Laurie Lee) has lots of illustrations and book covers signed by him. Well kept Goffs Jouster and Wadworths 6X on handpump, country wines, darts, cribbage, cards, and dominoes. Good bar food includes sandwiches, home-made soup (£3), chicken and bacon caesar salad (£4), honey-roast ham and egg (£6), cauliflower and leek bake (£6.50), pork chop topped with bacon and melted cheese or poached salmon steak (£6.75), home-made pie of the day (£6.95), and daily specials such as fresh vegetable curry with poppadums and mango chutney (£5.75), faggots in onion gravy or smoked haddock with lemon butter (£6.25), and quarter lamb shoulder slowly roasted in rosemary and honey (£8.50). There are tables out in the garden and occasional summer morris men. The nearby gardens of Misarden Park, open midweek summer, are well worth visiting. *(Recommended by Gary and Jane Gleghoth, Giles Francis, Keith Allen, Debbie and Neil Hayter, Ian Dawson)*

Free house ~ Licensee Johnny Johnston ~ Real ale ~ Bar food ~ Restaurant ~ (01285) 821283 ~ Children in eating area of bar and in restaurant until 9pm ~ Occasional country music ~ Open 11-2.30(3 Sat), 6-11; 12-3, 7-10.30 Sun

NAILSWORTH ST8599 Map 4
Egypt Mill 🍴 🛏

Just off A46; heading N towards Stroud, first right after roundabout, then left

This is a stylish conversion of a three-floor stonebuilt mill, which still has working waterwheels and the millstream flowing through. The brick-and-stone-floored split-level bar gives good views of the wheels, and there are big pictures and lots of stripped beams in the comfortable carpeted lounge, along with some hefty yet elegant ironwork from the old mill machinery. Although it can get quite crowded on fine weekends, it's actually spacious enough to feel at its best when it's busy – with good service to cope, and the atmosphere is almost bistro-ish; piped music. There's a civilised upstairs restaurant, and a no smoking area. Well kept Tetleys, Wadworths

6X, and a guest beer on handpump, and a wide choice of nicely presented good generous food such as lunchtime sandwiches (from £3), filled baguettes (from £3.80), omelettes (£5), and ploughman's (£5.50), as well as soup (£3.20), prawns on mediterranean couscous (£4.50), pasta and broccoli bake, fresh haddock and chips or home-made steak and kidney pudding (£7.95), chicken tikka (£8.95), steaks (from £11.95), fish from Cornwall such as lemon sole (£11.45), and puddings like bread and butter pudding or chocolate roulade (£4.50). The floodlit terrace garden by the millpond is pretty, and there's a little bridge over from the car park; no dogs. *(Recommended by Simon Collett-Jones, R Mathews, Charles and Pauline Stride, Christopher and Mary Thomas, Michael Doswell, P R and D Thomas, Ann and Colin Hunt, Neil and Debbie Cook)*

Free house ~ Licensee Stephen Webb ~ Real ale ~ Bar food ~ Restaurant ~ (01453) 833449 ~ Children in eating area of bar and restaurant ~ Open 11-3, 6.30(6 Sat)-11; 12-3, 6-11 Sun ~ Bedrooms: £49.50B/£75B

NAUNTON SP1123 Map 4
Black Horse ♀ 🛏

Village signposted from B4068 (shown as A436 on older maps) W of Stow-on-the-Wold

This busy old inn is very much enjoyed by readers for its genuinely welcoming atmosphere, friendly staff, and honest home cooking. The comfortable, neatly kept bar has black beams, stripped stonework, simple country-kitchen chairs, built-in oak pews, polished elm cast-iron-framed tables, and a warming open fire. Served by cheerfully efficient staff, bar food includes home-made soup (£3.30), baguettes (from £3.95), ploughman's (£5.50), home-made cottage pie or ham and egg (£7.25), steak and kidney pudding (£7.95), and good daily specials such as lancashire hotpot (£7.25), fillet of salmon in saffron sauce or chicken breast with stilton and bacon sauce (£7.50), home-made salmon and prawn fishcakes (£7.95), and rack of lamb (£7.95); the dining room is no smoking. Well kept and well priced Donnington BB and SBA on handpump, and sensibly placed darts, cribbage, dominoes, and piped music. Some tables outside, and good walks on the blowy hills. *(Recommended by E V Walder, John Bowdler, Pete Baker, Catherine and Richard Preston, James Oakley)*

Donnington ~ Tenant Martin David Macklin ~ Real ale ~ Bar food ~ (01451) 850565 ~ Children in eating area of bar and restaurant ~ Open 11.30-3, 6-11; 12-3, 7-10.30 Sun ~ Bedrooms: £25(£30B)/£45B

NORTH CERNEY SP0208 Map 4
Bathurst Arms ♀ 🛏

A435 Cirencester—Cheltenham

You'll soon make friends in this handsome, welcoming old place as the landlord likes to introduce his customers to each other – particularly if you are staying overnight. The beamed and panelled bar has a fireplace at each end (one quite huge and housing an open woodburner), a good mix of old tables and nicely faded chairs, old-fashioned window seats, and some pewter plates. There are country tables in a little carpeted room off the bar, as well as winged high-backed settles forming booths around other tables; one of the small dining rooms is no smoking. At lunchtime, bar food includes ploughman's (£5.50), a burger (£6.50), and home-made salmon fishcakes (£7.50), as well as soup (£2.95), chargrilled sardines with a fresh tomato compote (£3.95; main course £7.50), tart of baby leeks and wild mushrooms with a rocket salad (£7.50), fresh tagliatelle with a sun-dried tomato, basil and pine nut sauce or chilli prawns stir-fried with noodles, spring onions and peppers (£8.50), duck breast with braised red cabbage and redcurrant sauce (£9.50), fillet of beef with girolle mushrooms and red wine jus (£13.95), and puddings like sticky toffee pudding or rhubarb crumble (£3.50). Helpful, polite service. Well kept Bass, Hook Norton Best, Wadworths 6X, and a guest such as Archers or Arkells on handpump, and 11 good wines (including champagne) by the glass; piped music. The attractive flower-filled front lawn runs down to the little River Churn, and there are picnic-sets sheltered by small trees and shrubs; lots of surrounding walks. *(Recommended by Ann*

and Colin Hunt, Sarah Trayers, Lorna and Howard Lambert, Colin Parker, P and L Hope-Lang,
P R and S A White, J A Cheverton, Simon Collett-Jones, Dr and Mrs R E S Tanner, Dr and Mrs
Nigel Holmes, Peter and Anne-Marie O'Malley)

*Free house ~ Licensee Mike Costley-White ~ Real ale ~ Bar food ~ Restaurant ~
(01285) 831281 ~ Children welcome ~ Open 11-2.30, 6-11; 11-11 Sat; 12-10.30 Sun;
11-2.30, 6-11 Sat and Sun in winter; closed 25 Dec ~ Bedrooms: £45B/£65B*

NORTH NIBLEY ST7596 Map 4
New Inn 🍺

Waterley Bottom, which is quite well signposted from surrounding lanes; inn signposted from
the Bottom itself; one route is from A4135 S of Dursley, via lane with red sign saying Steep
Hill, 1 in 5 (just SE of Stinchcombe Golf Course turn-off), turning right when you get to the
bottom; another is to follow Waterley Bottom signpost from previous main entry, keeping
eyes skinned for small low signpost to inn; OS Sheet 162 map reference 758963; though this
is the way we know best, one reader suggests the road is wider if you approach directly from
North Nibley

After a walk at the weekend (when this tucked away, friendly country pub is open
all day), this is just the place for a relaxing drink. The lounge bar has cushioned
windsor chairs and varnished high-backed settles against the partly stripped stone
walls, and dominoes, cribbage, TV, and sensibly placed darts in the simple public
bar. Good home-made bar food includes sandwiches, good goose rillettes with
bread, coq au vin, steak and kidney pie or lentils and smoked sausage (all £5.50),
basil and parmesan-stuffed peppers (£6), cod and onion bake (£6.50), and salmon
fillet with fresh herbs (£9). Well kept Bath Gem Bitter, Cotleigh Tawny and WB (a
beer brewed specially for the pub), Greene King Abbot, and a guest such as Wickwar
Cotswold Way or York Yorkshire Terrier are dispensed from Barmaid's Delight (the
name of one of the antique beer engines) or tapped from the cask; they import their
own French wines. At the far end of the garden is a small orchard with swings and
slides, and there's a neatly kept terrace. No children. *(Recommended by PB, JB,
R Huggins, D Irving, E McCall, T McLean, Guy Vowles, JP, PP, Mike and Mary Carter,
Keith Allen, the Didler)*

*Free house ~ Licensees Jackie and Jacky Cartigny ~ Real ale ~ Bar food (not Mon
except bank hols) ~ (01453) 543659 ~ Live music Fri evening ~ Open 12-2.30, 6(7
Mon)-11; 12-11 Sat; 12-10.30 Sun; closed Mon lunchtime except bank hols*

OAKRIDGE LYNCH SO9103 Map 4
Butchers Arms

Village signposted off Eastcombe—Bisley road, E of Stroud, which is the easiest approach;
with a good map you could brave the steep lanes via Frampton Mansell, which is signposted
off A419 Stroud—Cirencester

Set above a particularly steep and twisty village, this white-painted pub has seats on
the neatly kept lawn looking down over the valley, and in summer the flowering tubs
and hanging baskets are very pretty. The spacious rambling bar has a few beams in
its low ceiling, some walls stripped back to the bare stone, old photographs,
comfortable, traditional furnishings like wheelback chairs around the neat tables on
its patterned carpet, and three open fires. Bar food includes burgers (from £3.95),
interestingly filled hot baguettes (£4.75), home-made cottage pie or cauliflower
cheese (£4.95), potato wedge dishes (from £5.50), omelettes (£5.95), brunch (£6.50),
fillet of haddock with celery sauce or beef, kidney, and mushroom in ale pie (£6.95),
and rib-eye steak (£9.50). Best to book at the weekend; the restaurant is no smoking.
Well kept Archers Best, Greene King Abbot, Tetleys Bitter, and Wickwar BOB on
handpump; a little room off the main bar has darts, a fruit machine and TV, and
there's a skittle alley. There are good walks in the valley along the old Thames &
Severn canal. *(Recommended by R Huggins, D Irving, E McCall, T McLean, Mike and Lynn
Robinson, Andrew and Ruth Triggs, Nick and Meriel Cox, Bernard Stradling)*

*Free house ~ Licensees Peter and Brian Coupe ~ Real ale ~ Bar food (not Sun evening;
restaurant shut Mon/Tues evenings) ~ Restaurant ~ (01285) 760371 ~ Children*

welcome away from main bar ~ Open 11-3, 6-11; 12-3, 7-10.30 Sun; closed 25 Dec, evening 26 Dec and 1 Jan

OLD SODBURY ST7581 Map 2
Dog

Not far from M4 junction 18: A46 N , then A432 left towards Chipping Sodbury

There's usually quite a mix of customers at this busy pub: drivers from the M4, cyclists and motorcyclists, and those dropping in after enjoying one of the many nearby walks. The two-level bar and smaller no smoking room both have areas of original bare stone walls, beams and timbering, low ceilings, wall benches and cushioned chairs, and open fires. From a huge menu, the choice of food might include fresh fish dishes like sole, plaice, halibut, cod, trout, scallops, shark or tuna, giant prawns, and several different ways of serving mussels and squid, as well as sandwiches (from £1.95), smoked mackerel pâté (£3.25), ploughman's (£4.50), cheese and onion flan (£5.50), vegetarian moussaka (£5.75), lasagne (£5.95), home-made steak and kidney pie or creamy seafood tagliatelle (£6.25), prawn curry, sweet and sour chicken or Mexican chilli-filled tacos (£6.95), steaks (from £6.95), puddings like home-made fruit pie, jam roly poly or rhubarb crumble (from £2.50), and children's meals (from £1.95). Well kept Marstons Pedigree, Wadworths 6X, Wickwar BOB, and a guest beer on handpump, several malt whiskies, and quite a few wines; good service. Dominoes, fruit machine, juke box, and skittle alley. Trophy, the border collie, likes playing football with customers. There's a large garden with lots of seating, a summer barbecue area, climbing frames, swings, slides, football net, and a bouncy castle most bank holidays. Beware, the pub asks customers to sign a credit card slip if they are running a tab, and it may not be easy to get an itemised bill afterwards, so ask when ordering. *(Recommended by Peter and Audrey Dowsett, Susan and Nigel Wilson, John and Enid Morris, Keith Allen, Christopher and Mary Thomas, Ian Phillips, Stephen, Julie and Hayley Brown, Mike and Mary Carter, Tom Evans, Joy and Peter Heatherley, David and Mary Webb, Mrs M Blundell, Mr and Mrs J French, Nigel and Sue Foster, R T and J C Moggridge, Graham and Lynn Mason)*

Whitbreads ~ Lease John and Joan Harris ~ Real ale ~ Bar food (11-10; 12-3, 7-9.30 Sun) ~ (01454) 312006 ~ Children welcome until 9 ~ Open 11-11; 12-3.30, 7-10.30 Sun ~ Bedrooms: £25/£40

OLDBURY-ON-SEVERN ST6292 Map 2
Anchor ◀

Village signposted from B4061

For 30 years, the hard-working licensees have kept consistently high standards at this spotless and friendly pub. The lounge has modern beams and stone, a mix of tables including an attractive oval oak gateleg, cushioned window seats, winged seats against the wall, oil paintings by a local artist, and a big winter log fire. Diners can eat in the lounge or bar area or in the no smoking dining room at the back of the building (good for larger groups) and the menu is the same in all rooms. All the food is home-made using local produce, attractively presented, and fairly priced, and although they don't do chips, they do offer dauphinois potatoes, new ones and baked, and Don Quixote (sliced and baked with cheese and onion). From the light menu, for those with smaller appetites or in more of a hurry, there might be home-made soup (£2.60), wholemeal bread with pâté, home-cooked beef and ham, sliced smoked chicken breast and fresh orange, and cheeses (from £3.50), and quite a few salads (from £4.50; prawn £5.95). There's also home-made faggots with onion gravy (£5.10), vegetable cassoulet (£5.95), pork and garlic sausages using local meat, or beef curry (£6.25), chicken italien or fresh salmon in a cream, crabmeat, prawn and white wine sauce (£6.95), and puddings like sticky toffee pudding with hot butterscotch sauce, banoffi pie or raspberry and apple crumble (from £2.95). Well kept Bass, Butcombe Bitter, and Theakstons Best and Old Peculier on handpump or tapped from the cask, all well priced for the area. Also over 75 malts, and a decent choice of good quality wines (12 by the glass); darts, shove-ha'penny, and cribbage;

they have wheelchair access and a disabled lavatory. There are seats in the pretty garden and lovely hanging baskets and window boxes, and the boules piste continues to draw in members – and spectators; plenty of walks to the River Severn and along the many footpaths and bridleways. St Arilda's church nearby is interesting, on its odd little knoll with wild flowers among the gravestones (the primroses and daffodils in spring are lovely). *(Recommended by George Little, Matt Britton, Alison Cameron, Mr and Mrs C Roberts, Christopher and Mary Thomas, Andy Gosling, Desmond Hall, Michael Doswell, James Morrell)*

Free house ~ Licensees Michael Dowdeswell, Alex de la Torre ~ Real ale ~ Bar food ~ Restaurant ~ (01454) 413331 ~ Children in restaurant only ~ Open 11.30-2.30, 6.30-11; 11.30-11 Sat; 12-10.30 Sun

PAXFORD SP1837 Map 4
Churchill 🍺

B4479, SE of Chipping Campden

Although much emphasis here is placed on the imaginative food, locals do still drop in for a drink, especially once the kitchens have closed at 9pm. The simply furnished atmospheric flagstoned bar has low ceilings, assorted old tables and chairs, and a snug warmed by a good log fire in its big fireplace; there's also a dining extension. Well kept Arkells 3B and Summer Ale, Hook Norton Best, and a guest such as Goffs Jouster or Shepherd Neame Spitfire on handpump, and 8 good wines by the glass; cribbage and dominoes. In the best pub tradition, they don't take bookings; your name goes on a chalked waiting list if all the tables are full. From a constantly changing menu, dishes might include spiced tomato and herb soup (£3), saffron marinated mackerel with cucumber sauce (£4.75), ox tongue, crisp sweetbreads, diced beetroot and cumberland sauce (£5), breast of pigeon with roast onion and celeriac purée (£5.25), honey-roast ham and egg (£6.50), john dory with red wine risotto, capers and spring onions in olive oil and tapenade (£8.50), lemon sole with a herb crust and sweet red pepper sauce or loin of rabbit filled with spiced aubergine lentils and mustard dressing (£10), braised lamb shank, casserole of haricot beans, thyme and chorizo sausage (£13), and puddings like sticky toffee pudding, passion fruit mousse with mango parfait and white chocolate sauce or panacotta with orange and nutmeg parfait (from £4); vegetables are extra, and vegetarian dishes are made to order. There are some seats outside; aunt sally. *(Recommended by Mr and Mrs Johnson, W W Burke, Leslie J Lyon, Martin Jones, Gwen and Peter Andrews, Bridget Griffin, David Hickson, Maysie Thompson, John and Christine Lowe, K H Frostick, Stephen and Judy Parish, Ian and Joan Blackwell, Stuart Turner, John and Enid Morris, Pat and Roger Fereday, Don Mather, Francis and Deirdre Gevers-McClure, John Evans, David Gregory)*

Free house ~ Licensees Leo and Sonya Brooke-Little ~ Real ale ~ Bar food ~ (01386) 594000 ~ Children in eating area of bar ~ Open 11.30-3, 6-11; 12-3, 7-10.30 Sun ~ Bedrooms: £40B/£70B

SAPPERTON SO9403 Map 4
Bell 🍴 🍷 🍺

Village signposted from A419 Stroud—Cirencester; OS Sheet 163 map reference 948033

Gloucestershire Dining Pub of the Year

After a year of renovations, this 250-year-old pub has an entirely new look. There are three separate, cosy rooms with a nice mix of wooden tables and chairs, country prints on stripped stone walls, log fires and woodburning stoves, fresh flowers, and newspapers and guidebooks to browse. Imaginative bar food, using local produce whenever possible and no frozen food at all (except ice cream), might include cold home-cooked ham, home-made piccalilli and a basket of hot crusty bread (£3.95), saffron and dolcelatte risotto cakes, tomato and garlic pulp (£4.25), welsh rarebit with red onion marmalade (£4.95), a platter of pork pie and cheese with home-made chutney and fruit (£5.95), roasted mushrooms with leeks, gorgonzola rarebit and a sweet pepper dressing (£8.95), slow honey-roast belly of pork with apple and mustard mash (£9.95), pine nut-crusted chicken breast filled with basil butter

(£10.95), and daily specials such as roast parsnip and curry soup (£3.25), spicy crab fritters with a coconut and mint dip (£5.95), warm salad of pigeon breast with black pudding and bacon (£7.95), roasted breast of duck with stir-fried noodles and home-made plum sauce or roasted hake steak on crushed chick peas with fresh basil oil and bacon lardons (£12.95), and home-made puddings like rhubarb and cinnamon crumble, chocolate and brandy mousse or Amaretto bread and butter pudding (£3.95); Sunday roast rib of Shorthorn beef (£9.95). A basket of home-made bread and butter accompanies every meal. Well kept Hook Norton Best, Uley Best and Old Spot and a guest such as Arkells Summer Ale or Bath Gem on handpump, up to 10 wines by the glass, champagne by the glass, and Weston's cider; cribbage and dominoes. Harry the springer spaniel likes to greet everyone. There are tables out on a small front lawn, and a partly covered back courtyard garden for eating outside. Good surrounding walks, and horses have their own tethering rail. *(Recommended by R Huggins, D Irving, E McCall, T McLean, John and Kay Grugeon, A S Kingsley, Guy Vowles, Keith Allen, Mark Gyde, Andrew J Carter, Giles Francis)*

Free house ~ Licensees Paul Davidson and Pat Le Jeune ~ Real ale ~ Bar food (not Mon except bank hols) ~ (01285) 760298 ~ Children in eating area of bar ~ Open 11-2.30, 6.30-11; 12-3, 7-10.30 Sun; closed Mon except bank hols

SHEEPSCOMBE SO8910 Map 4

Butchers Arms ♀

Village signed off B4070 NE of Stroud; or A46 N of Painswick (but narrow lanes)

This is the sort of friendly, relaxed pub where a good mix of customers mingles very happily in the chatty atmosphere – unspoilt by noisy games machines or piped music. They still have their popular policy of not reserving tables in the bar so casual diners and locals have a welcoming area in which to enjoy their drinks. The bar has log fires, seats in big bay windows, flowery-cushioned chairs and rustic benches, and lots of interesting oddments like assorted blow lamps, irons, and plates. Good lunchtime bar food includes home-made soup (£3.25), lots of filled rolls (from £3.50; bacon and egg £4.25; steak and mushrooms £4.95; chicken and bacon caesar salad topped with parmesan croutons (£4.75; main course £6.75), filled baked potatoes (from £4.75), home-made chicken liver pâté (£4.95), ploughman's (from £5.50), local beef and Guinness sausages with onion gravy or vegetable and nut hotpot bake (£6.50), and mixed game in a cranberry and red wine sauce topped with puff pastry (£7.75), with evening extras such as fresh local rainbow trout (£6.75), chicken simmered in a sherry, mushroom, onion and tomato sauce £8.75), and duck breast with an orange and Grand Marnier glaze (£11.95), and daily specials like salmon and haddock fishcakes with parsley and dill sauce (£6.75), braised lamb in a leek, mint and red wine sauce (£7.25), pork escalope topped with bacon, pineapple and melted cheese (£7.85), and grilled fresh monkfish medallions with a redcurrant dressing (£8.95). The restaurant and a small area in the bar are no smoking. Well kept Hook Norton Best, and two changing guests such as Wickwar Old Arnold or Wychwood Fiddler's Elbow on handpump, decent wines with several by the glass, and country wines; darts, cribbage, cards, and dominoes. The views are marvellous and there are teak seats below the building, tables on the steep grass behind, and a cricket ground behind on such a steep slope that the boundary fielders at one end can scarcely see the bowler. This is part of this pub's little Blenheim Inns group. *(Recommended by Brian, Dill, Jenni and Kate Hughes, Gary and Jane Gleghoth, Martin Jennings, Mike and Lynn Robinson, Bernard Stradling, Pat and Roger Fereday, David and Phyllis Chapman, Tom Evans, Guy Vowles, Bruce Bird, P R and S A White, Paul Oneill)*

Free house ~ Licensees Johnny and Hilary Johnston ~ Real ale ~ Bar food (12-2.30, 7-9.30) ~ Restaurant ~ (01452) 812113 ~ Children in eating area of bar and restaurant ~ Occasional morris men ~ Open 11.30-3, 6-11; 12-3.30, 7-10.30 Sun

---

Cribbage is a card game using a block of wood with holes for matchsticks or special pins to score with; regulars in cribbage pubs are usually happy to teach strangers how to play.

ST BRIAVELS SO5605 Map 4
George
High Street

The oldest part of this attractive white painted pub dates from medieval times and overlooks the 12th-c castle once used by King John as a hunting lodge; seats on a back flagstoned terrace enjoy the view. There's an ancient escape tunnel connecting the castle to the pub, and a ghost called George. The three rambling rooms have old-fashioned built-in wall seats, some booth seating, cushioned small settles, toby jugs and antique bottles on black beams over the servery, and a large stone open fireplace; a Celtic coffin lid dating from 1070, discovered when a fireplace was removed, is now mounted next to the bar counter. Enjoyable home-made bar food, with prices unchanged since last year, includes soup (£2.50), smoked salmon in a wine and dill sauce (£3.95), garlic tiger prawns (£4.95), vegetarian quiche or lasagne (£6.95), steak and kidney pie or curries (£7.95), chargrilled lamb steak with honey and mint sauce or venison casserole (£8.95), and pork tenderloin in mustard, cream and brandy sauce (£9.95). The dining room is no smoking; piped music. Well kept Adnams, Bass, Bath SPA, Marstons Pedigree, and RCH Pitchfork on handpump, and country wines. Lots of walks start nearby but muddy boots must be left outside; outdoor chess. (*Recommended by Colin Parker, Denys Gueroult, Desmond Hall, Keith Allen, LM, Mike and Lynn Robinson, Catherine and Richard Preston, Clare and Paul Howes, Mike and Mary Carter*)

Free house ~ Licensee Bruce Bennett ~ Real ale ~ Bar food ~ Restaurant ~ (01594) 530228 ~ Children in eating area of bar and restaurant if well behaved ~ Open 11-2.30, 6.30-11; 12-2.30, 7-10.30 Sun ~ Bedrooms: £35B/£45B

TETBURY ST8394 Map 4
Gumstool 🍴 ☆ 🛏
Part of Calcot Manor Hotel; A4135 W of town, just E of junction with A46

Although attached to a well thought of country hotel, this civilised dining bar does have a welcoming and informally relaxed atmosphere. There are some concessions to those wanting just a drink, but most people do come to enjoy the good, interesting food. The layout is well divided to give a feeling of intimacy without losing the overall sense of contented bustle, the lighting is attractive, and materials are old-fashioned (lots of stripped pine, flagstones, gingham curtains, hop bines) though the style is neatly modern. Beyond one screen there are a couple of marble-topped pub tables and a leather armchair by the big log fire; daily papers; well kept Bath Gem Bitter, Courage Best, Uley Hogshead, and Wickwar BOB on handpump, 60 malt whiskies, and a dozen interesting wines by the glass, spanning a wide price range. Several dishes on the menu sensibly come in two sizes: stilton and port rarebit on an apple, celery and grape salad (£4.75; generous £6.75), caramelised red onion tart with slow baked tomatoes, and taleggio on a rocket salad (£5.25; generous £7.50), devilled lambs kidney in pastry (£5.75; generous £8), and thai spiced crab cakes with cucumber and crème fraîche (£5.50; generous £8). They also offer soup (£3.25), a plate of local cheeses with celery, grapes and pickle (£5.50), gloucestershire old spot pork and beer sausages with spring onion mash and onion gravy (£8.50), smoked haddock fishcakes with lemon and dill (£8.80), breast of chicken with button mushrooms, bacon, caramelised red onions and a red wine sauce or slow-roasted duck salad with sweet and sour dressing, coriander and pickled Japanese ginger (£9), shepherd's pie with a garlic gratin crust (£9.30), chargrilled rib-eye steak with deep fried onions and tarragon shallot butter (£11), long braised lamb shank with pickled lemon, tomato and oregano (£11.25), and puddings like steamed lemon upside-down puddings with custard, spiced apple pie with cinnamon ice cream or crème brûlée (from £4); extra vegetables £1.50. To be sure of a table, you must book beforehand. Most of the restaurant is no smoking; piped music. The neat side lawn has a couple of picnic-sets; Westonbirt Arboretum is not far away. (*Recommended by Karen and Graham Oddey, John Kane, Geoff and Brigid Smithers, John Robertson, Ann and Colin Hunt, Donald Godden, A Jones, Bernard Stradling,*

Evelyn and Derek Walter, KC, KN-R, Rod Stoneman, Carol and Dono Leaman, Jason Caulkin)

Free house ~ Licensees Paul Sadler and Richard Ball ~ Real ale ~ Bar food (all day summer wknds) ~ Restaurant ~ (01666) 890391 ~ Children in eating area of bar ~ Open 12-2.30, 6-11; 12-11 Sat; 12-11 Sun; 12-2.30, 6-11 wknds in winter ~ Bedrooms: /£130B

TEWKESBURY SO8932 Map 4
Olde Black Bear

High Street (N end, just before the bridge)

Friendly new licensees have taken over this lovely timbered place, said to be the county's oldest pub. The fine, rambling ancient rooms are full of low heavy beams, lots of timbers, armchairs in front of open fires, bare wood and original tiled floors, plenty of pictures, bric-a-brac and photographs of Tewkesbury in the 1920s, a happy mix of tables and chairs, and fresh flowers. Fruit machine, and darts in the public bar; piped music. Well kept Courage Directors, Greenalls Bitter, Wadworths 6X, and a fortnightly guest on handpump or tapped from casks behind the bar in the main front room; quiz nights on Wednesday and Sunday. The enjoyable food includes lunchtime filled baguettes (from £2.40), soup (£2.95), deep-fried crunchy chicken with tomato and pepper dip (£3.25), burgers (from £3.75), ploughman's (from £4.75), sausages on cheddar mash with onion gravy (£4.95), beer battered fish and chips (£5.45), roasted tomato tortellini (£5.95), beef stew and dumplings (£6.25), steaks (from £7.95), and puddings such as sticky toffee pudding or blackberry and apple crumble (from £2.45); they hold monthly themed food evenings. Picnic-sets in the pleasant back garden overlook the River Avon; play area. *(Recommended by Colin Parker, Sue and Mike Todd, the Didler, Muriel and Peter Gleave, Alan and Paula McCully, Gordon Tong)*

Scottish Courage ~ Managers Darren and Wendy Rigby ~ Real ale ~ Bar food (12-9(8 Sun)) ~ Restaurant ~ (01684) 292202 ~ Children welcome away from bar ~ Open 11-11; 12-10.30 Sun

TODENHAM SP2436 Map 4
Farriers Arms ♀ ◖

Between A34 and A429 N of Moreton-in-Marsh

In an otherwise stone-built part of the world, this tucked-away country pub is the only brick building. The main bar has nice wonky white plastered walls, hops on the beams, lovely old polished flagstones by the stone bar counter and a woodburner in a huge inglenook fireplace. A tiny little room off to the side is full of old books and interesting old photographs. Under the new licensees, the good bar food now includes home-made soup (£2.95), grilled goats cheese on a pesto crouton with salad and sun-dried tomatoes (£3.25), sandwiches (from £3.25; 4oz sirloin baguette £7.85), ploughman's (£5.25), ham and eggs or home-made steak and kidney pie (£6.85), daily specials such as home-cured gravadlax (£3.75), home-made salmon fishcakes with a caper and lemon dressing (£6.95), a trio of local sausages with rich onion gravy or vegetable and goats cheese cannelloni (£7.95), seared tuna fillet with an avocado salsa (£8.75), barbary duck breast with parsnip mash and a redcurrant and port sauce (£10.25), and puddings (£3.25). Well kept Hook Norton Best, and a couple of guests such as North Cotswold Genesis or Wye Valley Butty Bach on handpump, and 11 wines by the small or large glass; darts, dominoes, aunt sally and piped music. There are a couple of tables with views of the church on a small terrace by the quiet little road. Please note, they no longer do bedrooms. *(Recommended by Ian and Nita Cooper, Martin Jones, Mike and Heather Watson, Roger Allen, Francis and Deirdre Gevers-McClure, Geoff Calcott, Miss A Keys, Mike Gorton)*

Free house ~ Licensees Sue and Steve Croft ~ Real ale ~ Bar food (not Mon evening) ~ Restaurant ~ (01608) 650901 ~ Children in eating area of bar and restaurant ~ Open 11-3, 6.30-11; 12-3, 6.30-10.30 Sun

WINCHCOMBE SP0228 Map 4
Old Corner Cupboard ◖

Gloucester Street

This attractive buttressed building, using golden stone stripped from Winchcombe Abbey many centuries ago, is flourishing under the friendly family that took it over recently. The comfortable stripped-stone lounge bar spreads back to a Tudor core with heavy black beams; there's also a little traditional hatch-service lobby, and a small side smoke room has a woodburning stove in a massive stone fireplace, some nice old furnishings, and a thriving local atmosphere (helped by darts, dominoes, shove-ha'penny, cribbage and maybe TV). The partly no smoking restaurant has gained some space without interfering with the building's structure. The enjoyable food is freshly made largely from local produce, and includes sandwiches (from £3.95), filled baguettes or baked potatoes (£4.75), starters such as soup (£3.95) and chicken liver pâté (£4.50), main dishes such as provençal nut wellington (£7), gammon and egg (£7.95) or steak and ale pie (£8.75), and dishes of the day such as liver and bacon (£6.95), roast pheasant in game sauce (£7.95) and bass with dill and vermouth sauce (£8.95); children's dishes are £3.50. Well kept Boddingtons, Flowers IPA and Original, Fullers London Pride and seasonal local Stanway ales such as Lords A'Leaping and Cotswold Gold on handpump, decent wines; soft piped music. Service is cheerful and helpful. There are tables in the garden behind, and the small quiet town is delightful. *(Recommended by John and Jackie Chalcraft, Martin Jennings, B A Dale)*

Whitbreads ~ Lease Alistair Macpherson and Mari Macpherson ~ Real ale ~ Bar food (12-2.30, 6-9.30; (not 25 Dec)) ~ Restaurant ~ (01242) 602303 ~ Children in eating area of bar and restaurant ~ Open 11-11

WITHINGTON SP0315 Map 4
Mill Inn

Village signposted from A436, and from A40; from village centre follow sign towards Roman villa (but don't be tempted astray by villa signs before you reach the village!)

The site of the original mill from which this mossy-roofed and friendly old stone inn takes its name is now an island in the pretty garden (where there are seats and tables), connected by a stone bridge; there are more seats on the main lawn. The beamed and flagstoned bar and other wooden floored rooms have little nooks and corners with antique high-backed settles, a bustling atmosphere, and large stone fireplaces; the old dining room is no smoking. Bar food includes soup (£2.95; large bowl £4.75), baguettes or filled baked potatoes (from £4), ploughman's or basket meals (from £4.25), leek and mushroom crumble (£5.95), chicken tikka masala or home-made steak in ale pie (£6.95), salmon and broccoli fishcakes (£6.75), pork and cider casserole (£7.25), and home-made apple pie or hot treacle sponge (£3.50); children's meals (from £2.75), and baby-changing facilities. Well kept Sam Smiths OB on handpump, a decent wine list, and quite a few malt whiskies; piped music, darts, and dominoes. This attractive village is surrounded by splendid walks. *(Recommended by Austin and Lisa Fleming, Mike and Wena Stevenson, Lyn and Geoff Hallchurch, Susan and Nigel Wilson, Dr and Mrs James Stewart, Lawrence Pearse, Martin Jennings, Neil Thompson, R Huggins, D Irving, E McCall, T McLean, Rod Stoneman, Anne and Leuan Williams, Ian Dawson, Maggie and Peter Shapland, Matt Britton, Alison Cameron, Dorsan Baker, Eddie Edwards)*

Sam Smiths ~ Managers Nathan Elvin and Robin Collyns ~ Real ale ~ Bar food ~ (01242) 890204 ~ Children welcome ~ Open 11.30-3, 6-11; 12-3, 6-10.30 Sun ~ Bedrooms: £45B/£55B

Please tell us if any Lucky Dips deserve to be upgraded to a main entry – and why. No stamp needed: The Good Pub Guide, FREEPOST TN1569, Wadhurst, E Sussex TN5 7BR or contact our web site: www.goodguides.com

WOODCHESTER SO8302 Map 4
Royal Oak ♀ 🍴

Church Road, North Woodchester; signposted off A46 on S edge of Stroud

The new licensees have made some changes here. The kitchen has been upgraded, a new dining room has been opened upstairs which makes the most of the valley view, they hold a quiz night on Mondays, tap dancing lessons on Saturday afternoon, and live music on Tuesdays and the last Friday of the month. The terrace has been extended and the hanging baskets are most attractive. The small simple local-feeling bar has a few highly varnished tables in the rather bright, small eating area on the left, and a few more towards the back; the massive fireplace has a welcoming log fire. Well kept Archers Best, Smiles Best, and Uley Old Spot and Bitter on handpump, a decent wine list, and good espresso or cappuccino; cribbage, dominoes, TV, and piped music. Using fresh local produce, bar food might include baguettes (from £3), goats cheese on salad (£3.95), cottage pie (£4.50), omelette and chips (£4.95), sausage and mash (£5), and rib-eye steak (£8.95), with daily specials such as carrot and parsnip soup (£3.50), home-made black pudding and chicken liver terrine with brioche (£5), mussels in a light curry cream sauce (£6), courgette, aubergine and stilton lasagne (£9.50), prawn and cod fishcakes with a mussel and watercress sauce (£11), grilled poussin with honey and sesame seeds on basmati rice (£11.50), and puddings like chocolate, prune and armagnac terrine or crème brûlée (£4). *(Recommended by Dr M E Wilson, Derek and Sylvia Stephenson, R Huggins, D Irving, E McCall, T McLean, James Morrell)*

Free house ~ Licensees Deborah Bates and Wendy Farrington ~ Real ale ~ Bar food (not Sun evening or Mon lunchtime) ~ Restaurant ~ (01453) 872735 ~ Children welcome ~ Live music last Fri of month; pianist Tues evening ~ Open 12-3, 5.30-11; 11-11 Sat; 12-10.30 Sun; closed Mon lunchtime

Lucky Dip

Besides the fully inspected pubs, you might like to try these Lucky Dips recommended to us and described by readers (if you do, please send us reports: www.goodguides.com).

Alderton [SP0033]
☆ *Gardeners Arms* [Beckford Rd, off B4077 Tewkesbury—Stow]: Attractive thatched Tudor pub keeping bar sensibly separate from bistro with good interesting food; pleasant atmosphere, well kept Hook Norton Best, Theakstons Best and XB and Wadworths 6X, above-average wines, log fire, good antique prints, high-backed settles among more usual seats; tables on sheltered terrace, well kept garden; children welcome *(LYM, Nigel Long, Michael and Christine Halls, Mr and Mrs J Williams)*

Aldsworth [SP1510]
☆ *Sherborne Arms* [B4425 Burford—Cirencester]: Cheerful wayside pub very popular for wide choice of good fresh food from baked potatoes and ploughman's up esp fish – can be booked solid on Sun even though much extended; log fire, beams, some stripped stone, smallish bar with big dining area and attractive no smoking conservatory, friendly obliging service and attentive landlord, several well kept ales such as Greene King IPA, Abbot and Ruddles County; games area with darts, lots of board games, fruit machine, piped music; pleasant front garden, lavatory for disabled *(Marjorie and David Lamb, Michael and Jenny Back, Robert and Patricia Battarbee, Alec Hamilton, BB, Michael Gray)*

Amberley [SO8401]
☆ *Black Horse* [off A46 Stroud—Nailsworth; Littleworth]: Civilised dining bar notable for its spectacular views; open fire and daily papers, conservatory, no smoking family bar, games room, usual food inc Mon-Thurs bargains, well kept ales such as Archers Best and Golden, Greene King Abbot, Ind Coope Burton, Marstons Pedigree and guests, farm cider, interesting murals; fine ladies', tables on back terrace with barbecue and spit roast area, more on lawn; open all day summer wknds *(Mrs E A Bell, LYM, B, M and P Kendall, R Huggins, D Irving, E McCall, T McLean, Peter and Audrey Dowsett, J Davidson, Stephen, Julie and Hayley Brown, Louise English)*

Ampney Crucis [SP0602]
☆ *Crown of Crucis* [A417 E of Cirencester]: Bustling rather hotelish food pub, good value food from sandwiches and good ploughman's up inc plenty of fish and nice puddings, attractive lemon and blue décor, split-level no smoking restaurant, Archers Village, Marstons Pedigree and Wadworths 6X, lots of tables out on grass by car park; children welcome, disabled facilities, comfortable modern bedrooms around courtyard, good breakfast; open all day *(PB, JB, Mr and Mrs J Brown, Andrew and Ruth Triggs, Mike and Linda Hudson, Lyn and Geoff Hallchurch,*

Matthew Last, Gloria Bax, R and J Robinson, Mr and Mrs J Evans, Mrs Mary Walters, LYM)

Andoversford [SP0219]

Royal Oak [signed just off A40; Gloucester Rd]: Cosy and attractive beamed village pub, lots of stripped stone, nice galleried dining room beyond big central open fire, well kept ales inc Goffs Jouster, reasonably priced food, obliging service; popular quiz night, tables in garden *(R Huggins, D Irving, E McCall, T McLean, BB)*

Apperley [SO8628]

☆ *Coal House* [Gabb Lane; village signed off B4213 S of Tewkesbury]: Airy bar notable for its splendid riverside position, with welcoming chatty landlord, Bass, Wadworths 6X and a guest ale such as Fullers London Pride, wide-ranging substantial enjoyable food from baguettes up, red plush seats; front terrace with Severn views, play area, moorings; walkers welcome *(BB, Martin Jennings, Mrs Mary Walters)*

☆ *Farmers Arms* [Lower Apperley (B4213)]: Spotless extended country local with polished wood, mix of chairs and chesterfields, old prints, beams and huge open fire, usual food inc fresh fish, separate thatched modern brewhouse producing their own Mayhems Oddas Light and Sundowner Heavy (though now owned by Wadworths), also Wadworths 6X, friendly staff and locals, piped music; children welcome, picnic-sets in neat garden with water feature, wendy house and play area *(M Joyner, LYM, Alan and Paula McCully, Claire Nielsen)*

Arlingham [SO7111]

Old Passage [Passage Rd]: Roomy pub with french windows to big garden extending down to River Severn, reasonably priced simple food, Marstons and John Smiths, small restaurant, very friendly landlord; games machines, service can slow; popular with summer campers *(BB, Mike and Lynn Robinson)*

Aust [ST5789]

Boars Head [½ mile from M48 junction 1; follow Avonmouth sign and keep eyes peeled for sign off]: Useful motorway break with nice mix of old furnishings, some stripped stonework, log fires, bar food from baguettes up inc Sun roast, children allowed in partly no smoking eating area, well kept Courage Best and Directors and Hardy Country, good house wines; piped music; pretty sheltered garden, dogs allowed on a lead *(R Mathews, Charles and Pauline Stride, Mr and Mrs Thomas, Peter Neate, LYM)*

Berkeley [ST6899]

Berkeley Arms [Market Pl]: Country town hotel with chintzy lounge, high-backed settles and games in unpretentious public bar, well kept local real ales; tables outside, bedrooms *(Dr and Mrs A K Clarke)*

Mariners Arms [Salter St; bottom of main rd through village]: Friendly and unspoilt beamed 15th-c pub, long and low, with well kept Bass, small range of good home-made food from sandwiches up, interesting photographs; tables outside *(Dr and Mrs A K Clarke)*

Bibury [SP1106]

☆ *Catherine Wheel* [Arlington; B4425 NE of Cirencester]: Open-plan main bar, quieter smaller back rooms, low beams, stripped stone, good log fires, no smoking dining area (children allowed), well kept Bass, Courage Best and Hardy Country, generous food from sandwiches up, traditional games; fruit machine, piped music; picnic-sets in attractive quiet and spacious garden with play area, famously beautiful village, handy for country and riverside walks; open all day, children welcome, refurbished bedrooms *(Peter and Audrey Dowsett, R Huggins, D Irving, E McCall, T McLean, Neil and Anita Christopher, Mike and Lynn Robinson, Andrew and Ruth Triggs, LYM)*

Swan [B4425]: Hotel in lovely spot on River Coln, roomy and very comfortable relaxing bar, reasonably priced food in nice adjoining brasserie, good service; tables out by pergola with masses of flowers, comfortable bedrooms *(Guy Vowles)*

Bishop's Cleeve [SO9529]

Farmers Arms [A435 N]: Pleasantly extended local, good choice of good value food, nice staff *(Mary and David Richards)*

Bisley [SO9006]

☆ *Stirrup Cup* [Cheltenham Rd]: Long rambling well furnished local doing well under current helpful licensees, good modestly priced food from sandwiches to generous Sunday roasts inc children's meals, well kept Hook Norton Best and Wadworths IPA and 6X, decent wines, friendly bustle, no music; dogs welcome *(Mike and Lynn Robinson, Prof H G Allen, Keith and Katy Stevens, M G Hart, Guy Vowles)*

Blockley [SP1634]

Crown [High St]: New regime (too recent for a firm rating) in golden stone Elizabethan inn with long interconnecting bar areas, open fires, food from sandwiches to meals in no smoking upstairs restaurant, well kept Bass and Hook Norton Best, decent wines; children in eating areas, has been open all day, tables in terraced coachyard surrounded by beautiful trees and shrubs, bedrooms *(M Borthwick, Mike and Mary Carter, LYM)*

☆ *Great Western Arms* [Station Rd (B4479)]: Peaceful and comfortable modern-style lounge, wide choice of promptly served good value home-cooked food, well kept Flowers, Hook Norton and Marstons Pedigree, friendly staff, no piped music, busy public bar with games room; attractive village, lovely valley view *(G W A Pearce, David Gregory)*

Bourton-on-the-Water [SP1620]

Coach & Horses [A429]: Welcoming licensees, a few tables in bar with settle by huge woodburner, above-average food with fresh interesting veg, well kept Hook Norton, separate restaurant; pleasant bedrooms in former stables, open all day *(Hilary Roberts)*

Duke of Wellington [Sherbourne St]: Generous enjoyable food in nicely furnished open-plan bar or cosy back dining room, friendly staff, well kept real ales, log fire; garden *(Ted George)*

Kingsbridge Arms [Riverside]: Large comfortable open-plan pub popular for pleasant village/river view from tables on terrace; well kept Bass and guests such as Caledonian Deuchars IPA and 80/-, good friendly atmosphere, interesting old prints and cartoons; piped music *(Ted George)*

Bream [SO6005]

Rising Sun [High St; Forest of Dean]: Large rambling pub with good Severn Estuary views, at least four real ales and Hoegaarden, good value food inc large filled yorkshire puddings *(Guy Vowles)*

Broadwell [SP2027]

Fox [off A429 2 miles N of Stow-on-the-Wold]: Attractive local opp broad green in nice village, generous straightforward food from good ploughman's up, well kept Donnington BB, SB and SBA, Addlestone's cider, stripped stone and flagstones, beams hung with jugs, log fire, darts, dominoes and chess, plain public bar with pool room extension, separate restaurant, maybe piped jazz; tables out on gravel, good big back garden with aunt sally, field behind for Caravan Club members; bedrooms *(George Atkinson)*

Brockweir [SO5401]

Brockweir Inn [signed just off A466 Chepstow—Monmouth]: Well placed Wye Valley walkers' pub (no muddy boots) with beams and stripped stonework, quarry tiles, sturdy settles, woodburner, snugger carpeted alcoves with brocaded seats, country décor, food inc sandwiches, well kept Adnams, Bass, Hook Norton Best, Smiles and Worthington BB, Stowford Press cider; upstairs restaurant, pool, machines and piped music in public bar, dogs allowed; conservatory, small garden with interesting covered terrace; open all day Sat, children in eating area; bedrooms *(Emma Kingdon, LYM, Colin Parker, Anne and Leuan Williams, Desmond Hall)*

Bussage [SO8804]

Ram: Well kept and sensitively extended Cotswold stone village pub, good valley view esp from new deck, good friendly atmosphere, generous helpings of good value wholesome food in entirely reworked dining area, pleasant flagstoned bar extension, several well kept ales, decent wines *(Dave Irving)*

Cerney Wick [SU0796]

Crown: Roomy, bright and cheerful lounge bar, comfortable conservatory extension, popular straightforward food inc good Sun roasts, well kept Whitbreads-related ales, friendly helpful staff, coal-effect gas fires, unobtrusive piped music, public bar with pool, darts, fruit machine; children welcome, good-sized garden with swings, small motel-style bedroom extension *(G W A Pearce, BB)*

Chalford [SO89023]

Old Neighbourhood [Chalford Hill]: Light and airy refurbishment, several areas, bare boards and solid tables, good generous food, welcoming easy-going atmosphere, wide range of real ales, open fire; play area, views from lovely big terrace and garden *(Dr and Mrs A K Clarke)*

Chedworth [SP0609]

Hare & Hounds [Fosse Cross, A429 N of Cirencester]: New management in interestingly furnished rambling dining pub, low beams, soft lighting, cosy corners, nice furnishings, two big log fires, small conservatory; well kept Arkells 2B, 3B and Kingsdown, good house wines; children welcome away from bar *(R Huggins, D Irving, E McCall, T McLean, LYM)*

Cheltenham [SO9422]

Belgian Monk [Clarence St]: Themed as Belgian-style bar with six helpfully described Belgian beers on tap, each served in its characteristic glass, lots more in bottles, good home-made soup, baguettes and largely Belgian food inc lots of seafood (the chips seem more English), hot chocolate etc, pleasant service; may be cl Sun *(Nick and Meriel Cox, Dave Irving, R T and J C Moggridge)*

Kemble Brewery [Fairview St]: Small backstreet Archers pub, all their beers inc Porter kept well at low prices, charming landlady, basic food; small back garden *(Colin Parker, Dave Irving, Guy Vowles)*

Mitres [Sandford St, off Bath Rd]: Unusual transformation by new owners, smart café-bar with good food choice, sensible wine list, Goffs Jouster real ale; events eg jazz in cellar bar, B&B in next-door cottage *(Guy Vowles)*

Montpellier Wine Bar [Bayshill Lodge, Montpellier St]: Wine bar not pub, but may have a real ale such as Timothy Taylors Landlord, and worth knowing for enterprising not cheap food from sandwiches up; open glass front leading out to pavement tables, SkyTV sports, interesting décor in well furnished downstairs restaurant with second bar *(Dave Irving, Martin and Karen Wake)*

Chipping Campden [SP1539]

☆ *Kings Arms* [High St]: Small hotel doing well under new management, enjoyable varied food, friendly staff and good log fire in comfortable old-fashioned bar; secluded back garden, open all day Sat, bedrooms *(Susan and John Douglas, LYM, K H Frostick)*

Lygon Arms [High St]: Stripped-stone bar with lots of horse pictures, open fires, well kept Hook Norton Best, Wadworths 6X and rarer guest beers, helpful service, enjoyable reasonably priced food till late evening in bar and small back dining room, raftered evening restaurant beyond shady courtyard with tables; children welcome, open all day exc winter wkdys; good bedrooms *(Klaus and Elizabeth Leist, Don and Marilou Brooks, David Gregory, LYM)*

☆ *Noel Arms* [High St]: Smart old place (Charles II stayed in 1651), polished oak settles, attractive old tables, armour, casks hanging from beams, tools and traps on stripped stone walls, well kept Bass and Hook Norton Best, decent food from sandwiches to some interesting dishes, no smoking restaurant, coal fire; piped music; children welcome, tables in enclosed courtyard, comfortable bedrooms *(LYM, Susan and John Douglas, Alain and Rose Foote, D P Brown)*

Chipping Sodbury [ST7282]

Squire [Broad St]: Three large rooms (inc a big

no smoking area), good range of freshly cooked food, pleasant atmosphere, good service, real ales; on broad old market street *(K R Harris)*

Cirencester [SP0201]

Golden Cross [Black Jack St, between church and Corinium Museum]: Popular backstreet 1920s local with good pubby atmosphere, simple very cheap generous food, well kept reasonably priced Arkells 2B and 3B, nice wine, friendly licensees, quick service, hanging jugs and beer mugs; pool, skittle alley, tables in back garden, open all day wknds, bedrooms *(R Huggins, D Irving, E McCall, T McLean, Dave Braisted, Peter and Audrey Dowsett)*

Slug & Lettuce [West Market Pl]: Flagstones, bare boards, lots of woodwork, wooden benches and chairs, good big tables, no smoking area, big log fires; well kept Courage ales, good coffee, wide choice of reasonably priced good food, civilised atmosphere though popular with young people, children welcome; piped pop music; tables in inner courtyard *(Duncan Cloud, Geoff and Brigid Smithers, LYM)*

Somewhere Else [Castle St]: Bistro-feel café/restaurant by day, lively bar (with tapas available) and more of a pub mood evenings, well kept Archers Best and Fullers London Pride *(R Huggins, D Irving, E McCall, T McLean)*

☆ *Twelve Bells* [Lewis Lane]: Lively well worn in backstreet pub with small low-ceilinged bar, small dining area with sturdy pine tables and rugs on quarry tiles, two cosy back rooms, coal fires, pictures for sale, clay pipe collection, particularly well kept changing beers such as Archers, Arkells, Castle Rock NPA and Woods Parish, friendly character landlord, impressive food esp fish (once you've deciphered the wallboard menu) lunchtime and early evening; small sheltered back garden with fountain *(Pete Baker, R Huggins, D Irving, E McCall, T McLean, Guy Vowles, Ian and Nita Cooper, Di and Mike Gillam, Mike Pugh, BB)*

Wheatsheaf [Cricklade St]: Friendly and roomy, cheap food until 4pm, several real ales, quick friendly service, no piped music; skittle alley, open all day *(Peter and Audrey Dowsett)*

Clearwell [SO5708]

Butchers Arms [High St]: Large attractive old stone-built dining pub with particularly well kept ales inc Smiles and Wadworths 6X, subdued red upholstery, dark woodwork, hops, big log fire, popular usual food; juke box; tables in neat back courtyard with pond and flowers *(Mike and Lynn Robinson, Keith Allen)*

☆ *Wyndham Arms* [The Cross]: Hotel's smart firmly run bar with burgundy plush seating, decorative beams, sombre patchwork pictures on stripped stone walls, big open fireplace; well kept Bass, good wines, lots of malt whiskies, good generous food in bar and restaurant (lunch stops at 2) inc Sun lunch with lots of hors d'oeuvres; attractive countryside nr Wye and Forest of Dean, comfortable spacious bedrooms in separate modern block, garden for residents (and supplies fresh veg) *(Clare and Paul Howes, Brian and Janet Ainscough, Andy and Sue Tye,*

LYM, A E Brace, Mr and Mrs Thomas)

Cleeve Hill [SO9826]

Rising Sun [B4632]: Worth knowing for the view over Cheltenham to the Malvern Hills from the terrace and lawn, esp as the evening lights come on; usual food, friendly staff, Greene King beers *(Ian Dawson, Di and Mike Gillam)*

Cliffords Mesne [SO6922]

Yew Tree [out of Newent, past Falconry Centre]: Enjoyable and enterprising if not cheap food (no sandwiches or rolls) in cosy very red-plush place on slopes of May Hill (NT), well kept ales such as Fullers London Pride, RCH Pitchfork and Shepherd Neame Spitfire, neat friendly staff, maybe pub dog; restaurant, children welcome, pool table in separate area, tables out on sunny terrace, play area; two bedrooms *(Dr A Y Drummond, Anne Drew, Michael and Jenny Back)*

Coates [SO9600]

☆ *Tunnel House* [follow Tarleton signs (right then left) from village, pub up rough track on right after railway bridge; OS Sheet 163 map ref 965005]: Idiosyncratic beamed country pub idyllically placed by interesting abandoned canal tunnel, very relaxed management style, mix of well worn armchairs, sofa, rustic benches, enamel advertising signs, stuffed mustelids, race tickets, real ales such as Archers Best, Greene King Old Speckled Hen, Smiles and Wadworths 6X, food increasingly popular wknds, Sunday barbecues, log fire, pub games, juke box; can be smoky; children welcome (plenty of room to run around outside, too), camping facilities *(Nick and Meriel Cox, R Huggins, D Irving, E McCall, T McLean, LYM)*

Codrington [ST7579]

☆ *Codrington Arms* [Wapley Rd; handy for M4 junction 18, via B4465]: Chain family dining pub dating partly from 15th c, several comfortable rooms, well spaced tables, wide choice of interesting food, quick friendly service, impressive housekeeping, well kept Bass, Courage Best and Hardy Country, good house wines, big log fire; piped music may obtrude; big garden with good views and play area *(Meg and Colin Hamilton, Gwen and Peter Andrews, Susan and John Douglas)*

Coleford [SO5813]

☆ *Dog & Muffler* [Joyford, best approached from Christchurch 5-ways junction B4432/B4428, by church – B4432 towards Broadwell, then follow signpost; also signposted from the Berry Hill post office cross-roads; beyond the hamlet itself, bear right and keep your eyes skinned: Very prettily set, with open-plan lounge, beamed and flagstoned back extension with games area (and juke box), pleasant back sun lounge dining room and verandah, well kept Sam Smiths and local Freeminers Speculation, cheerful helpful service, good value simple food inc cheap Sun lunch; well stapped picnic-sets in large attractive sheltered garden with good segregated play area, nice walks; children welcome, good value simple bedrooms *(Cath Beselle, Anne and Leuan Williams, Richard Butler, Marie Kroon, LYM)*

Colesbourne [SO9913]

Colesbourne Inn [A435 Cirencester—Cheltenham]: Gabled grey stone 18th-c coaching inn, beams, candlelight and log fires, spacious bar with heavy dark wooden chairs, settles and tables on bare boards, well kept Wadworths IPA, 6X and Farmers Glory, lounge with chintzy sofas and armchairs and big stripped stone fireplace, no smoking restaurant; traditional games, no dogs, piped music; views from attractive back garden and terrace, well appointed bedrooms in converted stable block (*LYM, Brian, Dill, Jenni and Kate Hughes, Jo Rees, John and Joan Wyatt, P R and S A White*)

Cowley [SO9614]

☆ *Green Dragon* [off A435 S of Cheltenham at Elkstone, Cockleford signpost]: New ownership for one-up two-bar country dining pub in nice spot, emphasis on food from sandwiches up, friendly if not always speedy service, beams, cream or stripped stone walls, log fires, fresh flowers and candles, tasteful dark furniture and fittings from Thompsons of Kilburn, pine boards or limestone composition floor, Courage Best, Hook Norton Best, Theakstons Old Peculier and Wadworths 6X, espresso machine; piped music may obtrude; children allowed in public bar, restaurant; big car park, two terraces, one heated, comfortable bedrooms off courtyard, good breakfast – good walking area (*Mrs J Rees, Mr and Mrs J Evans, Mr and Mrs P Eastwood, Leslie and Peter Barrett, R Huggins, D Irving, E McCall, T McLean, Gary and Jane Gleghoth, LYM, JP, PP, A and M Worth, Guy Vowles*)

Eastcombe [SO8904]

Lamb: Dignified stone building much extended by new licensees to take advantage of fine views towards Lypiatt Park, three or four well kept ales such as Youngs Special, Stowford Press cider, good imaginative inexpensive food, slightly Bohemian décor, roomy sparely furnished back dining room; lovely terrace (*Prof H G Allen, Christopher Mobbs, Miss W Reynolds, R Huggins, D Irving, E McCall, T McLean*)

Eastleach Turville [SP1905]

Victoria [off A361 S of Burford]: Unpretentious old-world local with friendly newish licensees doing wide choice of reasonably priced enjoyable food from sandwiches up, back dining extension off small pleasantly furnished beamed lounge, darts in big public bar, Arkells 2B and 3B, decent house wine, no piped music; pleasant front garden overlooking picturesque buildings opp, delightful village esp at daffodil time, popular with walkers; tight entrance to big car park (*Mrs Mary Walters, Peter and Audrey Dowsett, Marjorie and David Lamb, John Bowdler*)

Ebrington [SP1840]

☆ *Ebrington Arms* [off B4035 E of Chipping Campden or A429 N of Moreton-in-Marsh]: Unpretentious well worn traditional village local popular with walkers, low beams, stone walls, flagstones and inglenooks, decent simple food inc good sandwiches and popular fresh fish and chips, well kept Donnington SBA,

Hook Norton Best and a guest beer, pianola (no piped music or machines), traditional games; children welcome, no dogs at meal times, picnic-sets on sheltered terrace, handy for Hidcote and Kiftsgate, bedrooms (*Martin Jones, John Kane, David Gregory, LYM, Terry Mizen, Chris and Sandra Taylor, E V Walder, Guy Vowles, Mr and Mrs Richard Osborne*)

Edge [SO8509]

☆ *Edgemoor* [Gloucester Rd]: Tidy modernised dining place, ideal for grandma's birthday lunch, with wide choice of good value food inc fine home-made puddings, friendly landlord and quick helpful service, picture-window panoramic valley view, relaxing atmosphere, well kept Smiles, Uley Old Spot and Wickwar BOB, good coffee; no smoking area, children welcome, pretty terrace, good walks nearby; cl Sun evening (*LYM, Alun Jones, Mrs Sheela Curtis, Mrs E A Bell*)

Elkstone [SO9610]

☆ *Highwayman* [Beechpike; off northbound A417 6 miles N of Cirencester]: Rambling 16th-c warren of low beams, stripped stone, cosy alcoves, antique settles among more modern furnishings, big log fires, rustic decorations, well kept Arkells ales, good house wines, big back eating area (wide affordable choice inc vegetarian), quick friendly service; maybe quiet piped music; disabled access, good family room, outside play area (*the Didler, Peter and Audrey Dowsett, LYM*)

Epney [SO7611]

Anchor: Popular summer pub with good Severnside lawns, great riverbank walks; reasonably priced basic bar food from sandwiches and good ploughman's up, Boddingtons, big lounge bar, lots of sporting prints and photographs, good-sized public bar; skittle alley (*anon*)

Fairford [SP1501]

Bull [Market Pl]: Friendly beamed hotel, comfortably old-fashioned timbered bar with enormous choice of good value food, helpful service, well kept Arkells 3B and Kingsdown, two coal-effect gas fires, charming restaurant, no smoking areas; bedrooms small but fresh and bright, charming village, church has remarkable stained glass (*Peter and Audrey Dowsett, Guy Vowles*)

Fossebridge [SP0811]

Fossebridge Inn [A429 Cirencester—Stow-on-the-Wold]: Handsome Georgian inn with staid feel in much older civilised two-room bar at the back, pleasant old-fashioned furnishings with more modern side area, roaring log fires, popular food here or in dining area, Ind Coope Burton and Hook Norton Best; piped music; children welcome, tables out on streamside terrace and spacious lawn, comfortable bedrooms (*Giles Francis, R Huggins, D Irving, E McCall, T McLean, MRSM, LYM*)

Frampton Mansell [SO9102]

☆ *Crown* [off A491 Cirencester—Stroud]: Hard-working new licensees now doing all fresh food inc epic puddings, yet still a good villagey local feel; well kept Hardy ales, lovely views over village and steep wooded valley from stripped

stone flagstoned lounge bar with dark beam-
and-plank ceiling, attractive restaurant, public
bar with darts; children in eating area, teak
seats outside, decent bedrooms, good breakfast
*(R Huggins, D Irving, E McCall, T McLean, A
and G Rae, Giles Francis, LYM, Roger Everett,
Richard Fendick)*

Frampton on Severn [SO7407]

☆ *Bell* [The Green]: Welcoming Georgian dining
pub by huge village cricket green, good well
priced innovative lunchtime food inc interesting
choice of local sausages, helpings almost too
generous, log fire, pleasant staff, well kept real
ales inc interesting guests, steps up to L-shaped
family dining room, separate locals' bar with
pool; good back play area *(Jenny Garrett, Prof
H G Allen, Tom and Ruth Rees)*

Glasshouse [SO7121]

☆ *Glasshouse Inn* [first right turn off A40 going
W from junction with A4136; OS Sheet 162
map ref 710213]: Charming country tavern
with well kept ales such as Bass and Butcombe
tapped from the cask, beams and flagstones, log
fire in vast fireplace, good generous honest food
from thick sandwiches up, interesting
decorations, careful new extension subtly
furnished to keep the traditional mood; darts
and quoits, lovely hanging baskets, seats on
fenced lawn with interesting topiary inc yew
tree seat, fine walks in nearby Newent Woods
*(Mike and Mary Carter, Guy Vowles, Clare
and Paul Howes, LYM, Gill Waller, Tony
Morriss, the Didler)*

Gloucester [SO8218]

Black Swan [Southgate St]: Fine early Victorian
building handy for docks tourist attractions,
lots of tables in large comfortably smart room,
fireplace and chandelier giving character,
friendly service, good well priced standard food
(not Sun), six well kept mainly local ales; open
all day (Sun afternoon closure) tables outside,
bedrooms *(Gill Waller, Tony Morriss)*

☆ *Fountain* [Westgate St/Berkeley St]: Welcoming
and civilised L-shaped bar in 17th-c pub handy
for cathedral, plush seats and built-in wall
benches, cheap freshly made usual food inc
good range of curries, good helpful service, well
kept Brakspears, Boddingtons, Fullers London
Pride, Greene King Abbot and Wickwar BOB,
good range of whiskies, attractive prints,
handsome stone fireplace, log-effect gas fire;
tables in pleasant courtyard, good disabled
access, open all day *(BB, Sue and Mike Todd,
B M Eldridge, Jenny Garrett)*

Tall Ship [Southgate St, docks entrance]:
Extended Victorian pub by historic docks,
raised dining area with emphasis on wide
choice of enterprisingly cooked fresh fish, also
good sandwiches, ploughman's and daily
roasts, morning coffee and afternoon tea, well
kept Wadworths with a guest beer such as
Batemans XB; pool table tucked away down
one side, juke box; terrace, open all day *(John
Morgan, B M Eldridge)*

Great Barrington [SP2013]

☆ *Fox* [off A40 Burford—Northleach; pub
towards Little Barrington]: Charming spot in
summer, heated terrace and sizeable garden by

River Windrush (private fishing), orchard with
pond, river views from dining area; low-
ceilinged small bar with stripped stone and
simple country furnishings, Donnington BB and
SBA, farm cider, promptly served food from
sandwiches (not Sun) up – all day Sun and
summer Sat, not winter Mon night, restaurant
in former skittle alley; darts, shove-ha'penny,
cribbage, dominoes, juke box, fruit machine,
TV; open all day *(Michael and Jenny Back,
Andrew and Ruth Triggs, LYM, J Hale, Pete
Baker, E V Walder, Colin McKerrow, the
Didler)*

Greet [SP0230]

Harvest Home [B4078 N of Winchcombe]:
Well spaced tables, bay window seats, hop
bines on beams, food inc wkdy OAP lunches in
bar or big beamed pitched-roof side restaurant
(no smoking); sizeable garden, not far from
medieval Sudeley Castle *(LYM, R Mathews,
K H Frostick, John and Enid Morris, Martin
Jones)*

Gretton [SP0131]

Bugatti: Stylish and comfortable, personable
licensees, good interesting well served food with
good veg *(Jo Rees, Patricia A Bruce)*

Guiting Power [SP0924]

Farmers Arms [Fosseway (A429)]: Stripped
stone, mix of carpet and flagstones, well kept
Donnington BB and SBA, wide range of
unpretentious food from sandwiches up inc
children's dishes, good coal or log fire; skittle
alley, games area with darts, pool, cribbage,
dominoes, fruit machine; piped music; seats
(and quoits) in garden, good walks; children
welcome, bedrooms, lovely village *(the Didler,
LYM, Mike and Wena Stevenson, E V Walder,
Mrs D Stoner)*

Hillersland [SO5614]

Halfway House [B4432 Symonds Yat Rock—
Christchurch]: Cosy old recently reopened inn,
low beams festooned with hops, good value
home-made lunchtime food, evening bistro,
stripped pine and bric-a-brac; great views from
tables on lawns with swings, nice bedrooms
with own bathrooms in separate wing *(R
Marshall, Anne Drew, Clare and Paul Howes)*

Hinton Dyrham [ST7376]

☆ *Bull* [A46 towards Bath, then 1st right]: Good
new licensees in pretty 16th-c village pub, two
unspoilt bars each with log fires, beams and
stripped stone, good food (not Sun night), well
kept Bass and Wadworths IPA, 6X and Old
Timer, oak and elm settles in big public bar,
well equipped family room; big garden with
picnic-sets and play area *(John and Joan Nash)*

Hyde [SO8801]

☆ *Ragged Cot* [Burnt Ash; off A419 E of Stroud,
OS Sheet 162 map ref 886012]: 17th-c pub
under new ownership (sounding out customers
on what changes they'd like), beams and
stripped stone in rambling bar, log fire, good
value attractive bar food, good choice of well
kept real ales, good wine list, dozens of malt
whiskies, traditional games, no smoking eating
area; picnic-sets (and interesting pavilion) in
garden, comfortable bedrooms in adjacent
converted barn *(R Huggins, D Irving,*

E McCall, T McLean, Mike and Lynn
Robinson, LYM)

Kemble [ST9897]

☆ Thames Head [A433 Cirencester—Tetbury]:
Well served good food inc wide puddings
choice, well kept Arkells Bitter, 2B and 3B,
pleasant licensees and staff, stripped stone,
timberwork, cottagey back area with pews and
log-effect gas fire in big fireplace, country-look
dining room with another big gas fire, real fire
in front area; skittle alley, seats outside,
children welcome, good value four-poster
bedrooms (Lyn and Geoff Hallchurch,
I A Herdman, LYM)

Kerne Bridge [SO5819]

Inn on the Wye: Extended 18th-c inn with
comfortably dark bar surrounded by wine
bottles, Boddingtons, Flowers and Wadworths
6X, friendly staff, decent food inc Sun roast,
restaurant looking over River Wye to Goodrich
Castle; garden with picnic-sets and play area,
bedrooms with own bathrooms (Ian Phillips)

Lechlade [SU2199]

New Inn [Market Sq (A361)]: Big comfortable
lounge, good range of changing well kept ales
and very wide choice of generous well cooked
food, not expensive, friendly prompt service
even when busy, huge log fire, back restaurant,
front bar with games machine and TV; piped
music may obtrude; play area in big garden
extending to Thames, good walks; comfortable
bedrooms (Peter and Audrey Dowsett,
Mrs B Sugarman)

Red Lion [High St]: Comfortable local with
wide range of good value food inc good Sun
lunches, friendly service, well kept Arkells 2B
and 3B, restaurant with log fire (Peter and
Audrey Dowsett)

☆ Trout [A417, a mile E]: Low-beamed three-
room pub dating from 15th c, with some
flagstones, beams, stuffed fish and fishing
prints, spill-over bar out in converted
boathouse, big Thamesside garden with boules,
aunt sally; well kept Courage Best, John Smiths
and Wadworths 6X, popular well presented if
pricy food from ploughman's to steaks, no
smoking dining room, pleasant attentive
service, two fires; children in eating areas, jazz
Tues and Sun, no piped music, fishing rights;
maybe long waits in summer (open all day Sat
then), when very busy, with bouncy castle and
fairground swings; large car park (MDN,
A D Marsh, Peter and Audrey Dowsett, Simon
Collett-Jones, LYM, P R and S A White)

Little Washbourne [SO9933]

☆ Hobnails [B4077 Tewkesbury—Stow-on-the-
Wold]: Extensively refurbished around
attractive traditional front core with 15th-c
beams and log fire, two no smoking dining
rooms, wide range of food from huge filled
baps to restaurant dishes, helpful friendly
service, well kept Flowers Original, decent
wines, traditional games; children welcome
lunchtime, disabled facilities, tables on terrace,
extended play area and car park, bedroom
extension (Mike and Wena Stevenson, Joyce
and Maurice Cottrell, Mr and Mrs J Williams,
R Mathews, June and Mike Coleman,

B A Dale, LYM, Michael and Christine Halls)

Longford [SO8320]

Queens Head [Tewkesbury Rd]: Attractive
lounge and bar, partly no smoking restaurant
area, good lunches, slightly more upmarket
evening meals – good value; well kept real ales
such as Bass, Gales HSB, Hook Norton and
Wadworths 6X, friendly attentive service
(Peter Jones)

Longhope [SO6820]

Farmers Boy [Boxbush, Ross Rd; A40 outside
village]: Unpretentious two-room country pub
with friendly new licensees, well kept ales such
as Boddingtons, Smiles Best and Theakstons,
food inc two in one pies, OAP bargains Thurs,
heavy beams, log fire; piped music, separate bar
with big-screen TV and electric organ; pleasant
garden and terrace, may be cl Mon-Thurs
lunchtime in winter (Mike and Mary Carter,
BB, Christopher Tull)

Lower Swell [SP1725]

☆ Golden Ball [B4068 W of Stow-on-the-Wold]:
Sprucely unspoilt local with well kept
Donnington BB and SBA from the pretty
nearby brewery, good range of ciders and
perry, very friendly landlady, well presented
generous home-made food, log fire, games area
with fruit machine and juke box behind big
chimneystack, small evening restaurant (not
Sun evening), small garden with occasional
barbecues, aunt sally and quoits; maybe piped
classical music, no dogs or children, decent
simple bedrooms; pretty village, good walks
(the Didler, LYM)

Marshfield [ST7773]

☆ Catherine Wheel [High St; signed off A420
Bristol—Chippenham]: Plates and prints on
stripped stone walls, medley of settles, chairs
and stripped tables, open fire in impressive
fireplace, cottagey back family bar, charming
no smoking Georgian dining room, flower-
decked back yard; cheerful service, wide choice
of good if not cheap food (not Sun) inc
imaginative dishes, plenty of fish and generous
fresh veg, well kept Archers, Bass, Courage and
Wadworths 6X, farm cider, decent wines;
golden labrador called Elmer, darts, dominoes;
provision for children, unspoilt village (LYM,
Susan and John Douglas, Dr M E Wilson)

Minchinhampton [SO8500]

☆ Old Lodge [Nailsworth—Brimscombe – on
common fork left at pub's sign; OS Sheet 162
map ref 853008]: Relaxed and welcoming
dining pub owned by Smiles, small snug central
bar opening into bare-brick-walled room, no
smoking area, enjoyable food, well kept real
ales, friendly and efficient newish managers;
tables on neat lawn with attractive flower
border, looking over common with grazing
cows and horses; has been cl Mon (LYM,
James Morrell, R Huggins, D Irving, E McCall,
T McLean, PB, JB, Bernard Stradling)

Moreton-in-Marsh [SP2032]

Black Bear [High St]: Big unpretentious beamed
bar, stripped stone with hanging rugs and old
village pictures, well kept local Donnington
XXX, BB and SBA, basic public bar on right,
bare-boards separate dining room (not Sun

evening); piped radio may be obtrusive, games machine, TV and darts end; tables outside, bedrooms *(Joan and Michel Hooper-Immins, Ian and Nita Cooper, BB)*

☆ *Inn on the Marsh* [Stow Rd]: Good reasonably priced restaurant-style food in attractive candlelit dining conservatory, well kept Banks's, artist landlord, Dutch wife cooks excellent puddings; friendly young staff, comfortable armchairs and sofa, pink walls giving bistro look; bedrooms *(Mrs N W Neill)*
Swan [High St]: Friendly welcome in comfortable lounge with flowered wallpaper and old photographs, good choice of low-priced food inc pies and children's, well kept Boddingtons and Wadworths 6X, decent wine, staff friendly and efficient even when coachloads roll in on Tues market day; attractive restaurant *(Peter and Audrey Dowsett)*
Wellington [London Rd (A44 towards Chipping Norton)]: Friendly stone-built local with cheerful helpful staff, sensibly priced food from baguettes and baked potatoes inc children's dishes, well kept Hook Norton ales, settles and big TV in carpeted main bar; children welcome *(Ian and Nita Cooper)*
Nailsworth [ST8499]
George [Newmarket]: Traditional pub with good mature atmosphere and above-average food *(J H Bescoby)*

☆ *Weighbridge* [B4014 towards Tetbury]: Hard-working friendly licensees, three stripped stone rooms with antique settles and country chairs, beams hung with keys, rustic ironware, steps up to candlelit raftered loft, good choice of fresh food inc excellent two-in-one pies and some unusual traditional English dishes, well kept ales such as Theakstons, Uley and Wadworths 6X, good house wines, log fire; sheltered garden behind; open all day *(R Huggins, D Irving, E McCall, T McLean, LYM, Simon Collett-Jones, Tom and Ruth Rees, Bruce Adams)*
Newent [SO7225]
George [Church St]: Old coaching inn with friendly local feel in partly no smoking L-shaped bar, good value inexpensive lunchtime food from sandwiches up, big log fire, well kept Courage and local beers, restaurant; children welcome, bedrooms, nice location opp Shambles museum *(Gill Waller, Tony Morriss)*
Newland [SO5509]

☆ *Ostrich*: Partly 13th-c, new landlady keeping unspoilt character, plenty of atmosphere, unpretentious mix of furnishings, fine range of real ales such as Hook Norton Best, Monmouth Rebellion, RCH Pitchfork, Shepherd Neame Spitfire, Timothy Taylors Landlord and one brewed for them by Freeminer, candles on tables, big log fire, wide choice of good value food; small garden, dogs allowed on lead; no children, two bedrooms (nearby church clock strikes on the quarter) *(Phil and Heidi Cook, LYM)*
Northleach [SP1114]
Red Lion [Market Pl]: Handsome building in attractive village, good value usual food from good sandwiches to Sun roasts in

straightforward bar with good log fire, well kept Courage Directors, decent house wine, good coffee, very friendly staff and locals, restaurant; maybe unobtrusive piped music *(Jenny and Chris Wilson, Peter and Audrey Dowsett, Dr Colin Dourish)*

☆ *Wheatsheaf* [West End (Cheltenham rd)]: Recently reopened after transformation into smart dining pub, civilised atmosphere in three bright and clean flagstoned rooms, log fires, good food (veg extra), friendly service, well kept Hook Norton and Youngs or Wadworths 6X, good range of wines; lovely terraced garden, well equipped modern bedrooms *(Richard Greaves, Dr J J H Gilkes, Guy Vowles, R A Watson)*
Nympsfield [SO8000]

☆ *Rose & Crown* [The Cross; signed off B4066 Stroud—Dursley]: Bright well decorated stone-built village inn with good value generous food from great baguettes up, well kept Archers and Smiles, decent wines, friendly staff, daily papers, pink plush banquettes and lots of brass in pubby beamed bar with log fire, pews and other seats in large back bistro area; unobtrusive piped music, well behaved children allowed, picnic-sets in side yard and on sheltered lawn with good play area; bedrooms, handy for Cotswold walks *(BB, R Huggins, D Irving, E McCall, T McLean, Lawrence Pearse, Tom Evans, CMLM, Simon Collett-Jones, A and M Worth)*
Painswick [SO8609]

☆ *Falcon* [New St]: Sizeable old stone-built inn opp churchyard famous for its 99 yews; open-plan, largely panelled, with high ceilings, bare boards bar on right, mainly carpeted dining area with lots of prints on left, high bookshelves and shelves of ornaments by coal-effect fire, relaxing atmosphere, lots of wines by the glass, well kept Boddingtons and Wadworths 6X, with Hook Norton Best and Old Hooky in the public bar, good coffee, wide range of food from baguettes up, pleasant efficient service, daily papers, carpeted L-shaped dining area; bedrooms *(Di and Mike Gillam, John Brightley, Neil and Anita Christopher, John Holroyd, Martin Jennings, BB, Sue and Mike Todd)*
Parkend [SO6208]
Fountain [just off B4234]: Homely and welcoming, with assorted chairs and settles, real fire, old local tools and photographs, good freshly made usual food inc good range of curries, efficient landlord, well kept local Freeminer and guest beers; children welcome *(Pete Baker)*
Pillowell [SO6306]
Swan Cheesehouse [off B4234 Lydney—Parkend; Corner Rd]: Small carefully run pub, its bar food confined to ploughman's but with choice of several dozen unusual mainly local cheeses, good chutneys and pickles, also remarkable range of bottle-conditioned ales, and local and west country wines; attentive licensees, cheese/beer shop; no children or dogs, cl lunchtimes Mon/Tues and winter Weds *(Bernard Stradling)*

Poulton [SP1001]
Falcon [London Rd]: Clean and smart, with good choice of inexpensive food, well kept ales such as Arkells 3B, Hook Norton Best and Theakstons XB, friendly landlord, big fireplace; pretty village with ancient church *(Peter and Audrey Dowsett)*

Prestbury [SO9624]

☆ *Plough* [Mill St]: Welcoming well preserved thatched village local, good generous food in cosy and comfortable front lounge, service from corridor counter in basic but roomy flagstoned back tap room with grandfather clock and big log fire, consistently friendly service, well kept Flowers Original, Greene King Abbot and Tetleys tapped from the cask, delightful back garden *(Roger and Jenny Huggins, Dave Irving)*

Quenington [SP1404]
Keepers Arms [Church Rd]: Cosy and comfortable stripped-stone pub, traditional settles, bric-a-brac inc lots of mugs hanging from low beams, pleasant landlord, log or coal fires, decent food in both bars and restaurant, Boddingtons, no piped music; bedrooms, tables in garden *(Peter and Audrey Dowsett)*

Redbrook [SO5410]

☆ *Boat* [car park signed on A466 Chepstow—Monmouth, then 100-yard footbridge over Wye]: Beautifully set laid-back Wyeside walkers' pub, changing well kept ales such as Adnams Broadside, Jennings Cumberland, Theakstons Old Peculier, Wadworths 6X and Wye Valley tapped from casks, good range of country wines, decent coffee, usual food inc children's; rough home-built seats in informal garden with stream spilling down waterfall cliffs into duck pond, open all day wknds *(LYM, Richard C Morgan, LM, Dick and Madeleine Brown, Dave and Meg Richards, David Edwards, P Price, Mike and Lynn Robinson, Nick and Meriel Cox, Emma Kingdon, Colin Parker, P and M Rudlin)*

Redmarley [SO7631]
Rose & Crown [Playley Green; A417 just off M50 exit 2]: Generous helpings of good reasonably priced food from filled baps to Sun roasts in good-sized comfortable stripped stone lounge or big attractive restaurant (was skittle alley), quick cheerful service, good no smoking area, well kept Flowers Original and a guest beer, darts and pool in public bar; tables in garden, beautiful countryside *(W Welsford)*

Rodborough [SO8404]

☆ *Bear* [Rodborough Common]: Comfortably cosy and pubby beamed and flagstoned bar in smart hotel, friendly staff, pleasant window seats, welcoming log fire, hops hung around top of golden stone walls, interesting paintings, well kept ales inc Bass, good value food (bar and restaurant); children welcome, bedrooms *(C R Sanderson, R Huggins, D Irving, E McCall, T McLean)*

Sapperton [SO9403]
Daneway Inn [Daneway; off A419 Stroud—Cirencester]: Sleepy local worth tracking down for its tables on terrace and lovely sloping lawn in charming quiet wooded countryside near derelict canal with good walks and interesting

tunnel; amazing floor-to-ceiling carved oak fireplace, sporting prints, well kept Wadworths IPA, 6X and a guest such as Adnams, Weston's farm cider, food from filled baps up (may be a wait), small no smoking family room, traditional games in inglenook public bar; camping possible *(Dave Irving, Richard Fendick, Neil and Anita Christopher, Andrew and Ruth Triggs, Lyn and Geoff Hallchurch, Roger and Jenny Huggins, Tom McLean, Mike and Lynn Robinson, Keith Allen, Mandy and Simon King, Mrs Pat Crabb, Jonathan Smith, Ewan and Moira McCall, LYM)*

Selsley [SO8304]
Bell [B4066, just SW of Stroud]: Wide range of reasonably priced home-cooked bar food, good value ales such as Goffs Knight Rider, friendly landlord and staff in attractive little 17th-c village pub perched on hillside common overlooking Stroud, popular with Cotswold Way walkers *(Tom Evans)*

Shipton Oliffe [SP0218]
Frogmill [just off A40/A436 S of Andoversford]: Roomy yet cosy 17th-c stone-built coaching inn with large flagstoned bar, no smoking area, friendly service, enjoyable food, well kept Courage Directors; tables on streamside terrace with waterwheel, big play area, comfortable bedrooms *(Geoff Pidoux)*

Siddington [SU0399]

☆ *Greyhound* [Ashton Rd; village signed from A419 roundabout at Tesco]: Enjoyable atmosphere in two linked rooms full of copper, brass and bric-a-brac, two big log fires, interesting mix of tables and chairs, public bar with slate floor, darts and cribbage, extended function room doubling as skittle alley; decent straightforward bar food, well kept Badger Tanglefoot, Wadworths IPA and seasonal beers; seats out in well planted garden *(LYM, P R and S A White, Dave Irving, R T and J C Moggridge, Tom McLean, Roger and Jenny Huggins, Ewan and Moira McCall)*

Slad [SO8707]
Woolpack [B4070 Stroud—Birdlip]: Small unpretentious hillside village local with particularly friendly landlord, lovely valley views, several linked rooms with Laurie Lee photographs, some of his books for sale, good value food (not Sun evening) from sandwiches and baguettes to simple hot dishes, Weston's Old Rosie cider, well kept Bass and Uley Old Spot, log fire, games and cards *(Simon Collett-Jones, Tom Evans, Guy Vowles, Pete Baker)*

Snowshill [SP0934]

☆ *Snowshill Arms*: Handy for Snowshill Manor and for Cotswold Way walkers, with welcoming service, popular inexpensive food served quickly, well kept Donnington BB and SBA, spruce and airy carpeted bar, neat array of tables, local photographs, stripped stone, log fire; skittle alley, charming village views from bow windows and from big back garden with little stream and good play areas, friendly local feel midweek winter and evenings, can be very crowded other lunchtimes – get there early; children welcome if eating, nearby parking may be difficult *(LYM, Ian Dawson, Moira and*

John Cole, Jason Caulkin, Martin Jones, Martin Jennings)

Somerford Keynes [SU0195]

Bakers Arms: Homely partly stripped-stone local, wide choice of enjoyable food (booking recommended lunchtime esp Sun), reasonably priced well kept Courage Best and a couple of changing guest beers, two knocked-together rooms, dark wood tables (some kept for drinkers) on thick carpet; big garden, lovely Cotswold village *(R Huggins, D Irving, E McCall, T McLean)*

Stanton [SP0734]

☆ *Mount* [off B4632 SW of Broadway; no through road up hill, bear left]: Gorgeous spot up steep lane from golden-stone village, with views to Welsh mountains; heavy beams, flagstones and big log fire in original core, horseracing pictures and trappings and plenty of locals, roomy picture-window extensions, one no smoking; Donnington BB and SBA under light blanket pressure, farm cider, bar food (not Sun evening) from sandwiches up; open all day Sat and summer Sun, well behaved children allowed, tables outside *(P Price, KC, Ian Dawson, KN-R, John Brightley, Martin Dormer, John and Joan Calvert, Paul and Penny Rampton, Martin Jones, LYM, Terry Mizen, Dr A Y Drummond, Martin Jennings, D J Hayman)*

Staverton [SO9024]

House in the Tree [Haydon (B4063, W of Cheltenham)]: Pleasantly busy spick-and-span beamed pub, part thatched, with splendid choice of farm ciders, Fullers London Pride, Marstons Pedigree, Tetleys and Wadworths 6X, good value food in big dining lounge, more traditional public bar, inglenook log fire and interesting photographs; may get crowded wknds, plenty of tables in garden with good play area and pets corner *(Ian Phillips)*

Stow-on-the-Wold [SP1729]

☆ *Coach & Horses* [Ganborough (A424 N)]: Very wide choice of good generous sensibly priced food (all day summer Fri/Sat) inc popular Sun lunch in warmly welcoming beamed and flagstoned roadside pub alone on former coaching road, central coal fire, steps up to carpeted dining area with high-backed settles; friendly relaxed service, good value Donnington BB and SBA, no smoking area; popular skittle alley, children welcome, tables in garden, open all day Sun too *(Brian and Bett Cox, LYM, Mrs N W Neill, Joan and Michel Hooper-Immins, Mr and Mrs F J Parmenter)*

☆ *Queens Head* [The Square]: Good chatty old local with heavily beamed and flagstoned traditional back bar, high-backed settles, big log fire, horse prints, piped classical or opera, usual games, nice dogs; lots of tables in civilised stripped stone front lounge, good value straightforward fresh food (not Mon evening or Sun), well kept Donnington BB and SBA, mulled wine, friendly helpful service; children welcome, tables outside, occasional jazz Sun lunchtime *(LYM, Adrian and Gwynneth Littleton, the Didler, Neil Spink, D J Hayman)*

Royalist [Digbeth St]: Handsome 17th-c golden stone façade, recently much modernised inside but still some interesting ancient features (stonework, heavy beams in back room; parts of timber frame are around 1,000 years old); concentration now on spacious front dining room; well equipped bedrooms *(Alun Howells, BB)*

☆ *Talbot* [The Square]: Light, airy and spacious modern décor, brasserie/wine bar feel, plain tables and chairs on new wood block floor, modern prints, genteel relaxed atmosphere, continental-feel food, Wadworths 6X, daily papers, big log fire, bright friendly service even when busy; maybe piped radio; bedrooms nearby, open all day Sun *(Joan and Michel Hooper-Immins, George Atkinson, BB)*

Stroud [SO8504]

Golden Fleece [Nelson St, just E of centre]: Small old terrace pub, fairly dark inside, with well kept beer, daily papers, cheerfully musical décor, unobtrusive piped jazz, separate smaller upstairs room *(Dave Irving)*

Retreat [Church St (top end of High St)]: Bright and cheerfully trendy, with pink walls, polished wooden floors and tables, well kept Archers, remarkable choice of vodkas, imaginative lunchtime food, well behaved children welcome; can get crowded evenings, with a good sound system, no TV or machines *(Dave Irving)*

Teddington [SO9633]

Teddington Hands [3½ miles from M5 junction 9; Stow Rd]: Roomy and recently refurbished, good atmosphere, helpful friendly staff, Boddingtons, Marstons Pedigree and Shepherd Neame, good value generous food, no smoking area *(Martin Jennings)*

Tewkesbury [SO8932]

☆ *Bell* [Church St]: Interesting hotel bar with black oak beams and timbers, neat 17th-c oak panelling, medieval leaf-and-fruit frescoes, tapestries, armchairs and small tables; good food in bar and attractive evening restaurant, well kept Smiles and Theakstons, decent house wine, good coffee, friendly service, big log fire; garden above Severnside walk, nr abbey; bedrooms *(Roger Braithwaite, BB)*

Thornbury [ST6390]

Knot of Rope [High St]: Well appointed reputedly haunted town house, enjoyable food, good atmosphere, staff helpful with children, real ales *(K R Harris)*

Tockington [ST6186]

Swan: Clean, bright and spacious, with beams, standing timbers, bric-a-brac on stripped stone walls, log fire, friendly staff, Bass and Boddingtons, guests such as Greene King Triumph or Smiles tapped from the cask, country wines, reasonably priced food; piped music; tables in tree-shaded garden, quiet village *(Roger and Jenny Huggins)*

Tormarton [ST7678]

Compass [handy for M4 junction 18]: Busy extended off-motorway hotel/conference centre with choice of rooms inc cosy local-feeling bar open all day for wide choice of food, pleasant conservatory, friendly quick service, good wine choice, real ales inc Smiles, restaurant, children in eating areas; open all day, tables in garden, comfortable bedrooms *(LYM, S H Godsell, Ken Richards)*

Twyning [SO8737]

☆ *Fleet* [Fleet Lane, Twyning Green]: Superb setting at end of quiet lane, with good river views from roomy high-ceilinged bar, interesting nautical décor, snug styled as cosy kitchen with Aga, light and airy restaurant, good value standard food inc all-day baguettes, Whitbreads-related ales, pleasant staff; tables on terrace and lawn; disabled access, boat shop, stop on Tewkesbury—Bredon boat run, even own ferry across from Worcs bank (it's a long walk from the B4080) *(Martin Jennings, BB)*

Upper Oddington [SP2225]

☆ *Horse & Groom* [off A436 E of Stow-on-the-Wold]: Welcoming new licensees in 16th-c beamed pub given new light fresh bistro feel, plush carpeting, pale polished flagstones and some stripped stone, inglenook log fire, handsome antique settle among other more modern stripped pine chairs and tables, good choice of fresh interesting food, charming service, well kept Hook Norton Best and Wadworths 6X but on sparkler, good house wines; candles, may be soft piped classical music; attractive garden with rustic furniture on terrace and fine play area; children welcome, open all day summer, newly done pretty bedrooms with own bathrooms *(Tim Brierly, John Bramley, Christopher White, E J and M W Corrin, Pam and Gareth Turner, Jonathan Smith, K H Frostick, LYM, P and J Shapley, Richard Greaves, Dr and Mrs James Stewart, Simon Collett-Jones, Steve and Karen Holland, Ted George)*

Westonbirt [ST8690]

Hare & Hounds [A433 SW of Tetbury]: Substantial inn with well run turkey-carpeted bar at one end, comfortable and relaxed, with high-backed settles, food counter, Courage Best and Smiles Best, central log-effect gas fire, sporting prints; games in public bar on left, small tweedy more central cocktail bar; pleasant gardens, handy for Arboretum; good value bedrooms *(John Walley, BB, Meg and Colin Hamilton)*

Whitfield [ST6690]

White Horse [Buckover; A38/B4461, N of Bristol]: Appealing L-shaped bar with spectacular Severn valley view, welcoming

service, good choice of straightforward food from home-baked ham sandwiches up, well kept Brains *(S H Godsell, Charles and Pauline Stride)*

Whitminster [SO7708]

Fromebridge Mill [A38 nr M5 junction 13]: Large converted mill, lots of space and character in extended bar and dining areas, decent reasonably priced food from sandwiches and baked potatoes up inc carvery, friendly helpful staff; picnic-sets out behind overlooking weir, play area *(Neil and Anita Christopher, Charles and Pauline Stride, M G Hart)*

Wick [ST7072]

Rose & Crown [High St (A420)]: Busy and roomy Chef & Brewer, plenty of character, well kept beers such as Greene King Old Speckled Hen and Theakstons Best, daily papers, very wide food range (only main meals on Sun) *(Nigel Long, MRSM)*

Winchcombe [SP0228]

Bell [Gretton Rd]: Friendly and cosy local with full Donnington beer range well kept and reasonably priced, good lunchtime snacks inc freshly cut sandwiches *(Jonathan Smith, Colin Parker)*

White Hart [High St (B4632)]: Comfortable beamed and timbered stone-built inn with Swedish owners doing interesting food inc Fri lunchtime smorgasbord buffet, well kept ales such as Flowers, Marstons Pedigree and Stanway, decent wines, pleasant service; bedrooms spacious with good facilities *(Guy Vowles)*

Woodchester [SO8302]

☆ *Ram* [Station Rd, South Woodchester]: Attractively priced real ales such as Archers Best, John Smiths, Theakstons Old Peculier, Uley Old Spot and several interesting guest beers, in relaxed L-shaped beamed bar with nice mix of traditional furnishings, stripped stonework, bare boards, three open fires, darts, food from sandwiches to steaks, restaurant; children welcome, open all day Sat/Sun, spectacular views from terrace tables *(Stephen, Julie and Hayley Brown, R Huggins, D Irving, E McCall, T McLean, LYM)*

Wotton Under Edge [ST7593]

Swan [Market St]: Smart-looking hotel with pleasant big-windowed bar, sensibly priced food from sandwiches and baked potatoes up, friendly staff and dog, no piped music; bedrooms *(David and Kay Ross)*

Post Office address codings confusingly give the impression that some pubs are in Gloucestershire, when they're really in Warwickshire (which is where we list them).

Hampshire

Two classic pubs here have been in all 20 editions of the Guide: the charming little Harrow at Steep, in Ellen McCutcheon's family throughout that time – and for 50 years before then; and the White Horse, famous as the Pub With No Name, a favourite on the downs up above Petersfield. By contrast, four pubs here are new to the main entries this year (or back in these pages after a break): the Fox & Hounds at Crawley, reopened as a proper village pub (after a spell when it had been turned into a French restaurant), with really enjoyable food; the Trout at Itchen Abbas, nicely spruced up under newish tenants, and a pleasant place to stay; the Bush at Ovington, back on top form (though not cheap), an archetypal country pub in a lovely spot; and the Fleur de Lys at Pilley, the oldest pub in the New Forest, with enjoyable generous food. Other pubs doing specially well this year are the welcoming Sun at Bentworth (good all round, great beers), the attractively placed Red Lion at Boldre (hardworking new landlord), the well run Jolly Sailor right on the water at Bursledon, the unpretentious Flower Pots at Cheriton (brewing its own fine beers), the delightfully unspoilt Royal Oak in the heart of the New Forest at Fritham, the Royal Oak on the water (well, at high tide) at Langstone, the friendly Half Moon & Spread Eagle at Micheldever (good all round), the Ship at Owslebury (another nice all-rounder, particularly good for families in summer), the Trooper near Petersfield (a distinctive place, refreshingly different in some ways), the Coach & Horses at Rotherwick (up to eight real ales, enjoyable food), the Plough at Sparsholt (gaining a Food Award this year for its imaginative cooking), the Brushmakers Arms at Upham (always friendly and helpful, with enjoyable food), the Cartwheel at Whitsbury (a friendly bustle, decent food, good beer choice) and the Wykeham Arms in Winchester (first-class new licensees keeping this favourite pub at the top of the Hampshire tree). It's rare for us to give such a high accolade to a newcomer, but the food at the Fox & Hounds at Crawley has impressed us so much that it is our Hampshire Dining Pub of the Year. In the Lucky Dip section at the end of the chapter, places to look out for (the great majority inspected and approved by us) are the Ship at Bishop's Sutton, White Buck near Burley, Hampshire Bowman at Dundridge, Chestnut Horse at Easton, Crown at Everton, Jack Russell at Faccombe, Foresters Arms at Frogham, Old House At Home in Havant, Ship at Langstone, High Corner near Linwood, Angel in Lymington, Pilgrim at Marchwood, Castle of Comfort at Medstead, Trusty Servant at Minstead, Good Intent in Petersfield, Fish in Ringwood, Alice Lisle at Rockford, White Hart in Stockbridge, Cricketers Arms and Fox at Tangley, George at Vernham Dean and Red House in Whitchurch. Drinks prices here are rather higher than the national average, with a typical Hampshire pint of beer now breaking the £2 barrier. The Brushmakers Arms at Upham had the cheapest beer among our main entries, and the Peat Spade at Longstock and (brewing its own) the Flower Pots at Cheriton were also particularly good value.

ALRESFORD SU5832 Map 2

Globe ♀

The Soke, Broad Street (extreme lower end – B3046 towards Old Alresford); town signposted off A31 bypass

Civilised and rather smart, the main bar in this 17th-c pub has big winter log fires at each end – one with pretty cushions on a sofa in front of it – an attractive mix of wooden chairs and tables, fresh flowers and candles, old local photographs, and unusual pictures and objects of eastern art; the little restaurant is no smoking, and there's also a tented Garden Room which is popular for Sunday lunch. Good, interesting bar food includes home-made soups such as spinach and stilton or watercress (£3.25), sandwiches (from £3.50), pâté like stilton and walnut or chicken liver (from £4.25), anchovies provençale (£4.75), ploughman's (£4.95), wild mushroom and tarragon tagliatelle (£7.25), spicy chicken with mango and lime sauce (£8.50), thai fishcakes with noodles and chilli dipping sauce, lamb fillet with a red wine and port reduction and wild mushrooms, seared salmon with sweet pepper marmalade and crème fraîche raita or tenderloin of pork with brandy and melted cheese sauce (all £8.95), confit of duck with cranberry sauce (£9.50), and home-made puddings such as fresh fruit crumble, chocolate brownie caramel tart or sticky toffee pudding with hot toffee sauce (£4.25); Sunday roast sirloin of beef (£8.50). Well kept Brakspears Bitter, Courage Best and Directors, and Wadworths 6X on handpump, and 14 wines by the glass. In the garden, there are plenty of picnic-sets, and you can look over Alresford Pond, a sizeable stretch of water created in the 12th c and now a haven for wildlife. Nearby parking is limited; there's plenty about 100 metres away, at the bottom of truly named Broad St. The Georgian town is full of charm and character. *(Recommended by Jenny Cridland, Gordon Cooper, David Peakall, Ann and Colin Hunt, Margaret Ross, Simon Collett-Jones, Paul Thompson, Anna Blackburn, John Evans, Ian Phillips, Neil Rose)*

Unique Pub Co ~ Lease Marc Conway, Emma Duveen ~ Real ale ~ Bar food (all day summer Sat and Sun) ~ Restaurant ~ (01962) 732294 ~ Children welcome ~ Open 11-3, 6-11; 11-11 Sat; 12-10.30 Sun; 11-3, 6-11 winter Sat; 12-3, 7-10.30 Sun in winter

ARFORD SU8336 Map 2

Crown ◀

Arford Road; signposted off B3002 W of Hindhead

This unpretentious roadside house has a little bar with long cushioned brocaded wall benches and brocaded bar stools, a log fire in an old brick fireplace with horsebrasses around it, low ceilings, hops on a beam, and very nice service. At the far end are some steps up to an eating area with ochre walls, cushioned built-in wooden wall seats, candles on the tables, black and white photographs, small fairy paintings, well thumbed books, and another big old brick fireplace with more horsebrasses; one table is tucked away by the steps, and there are more steps down to a single snugged-in table. Well kept Adnams Bitter, Fullers London Pride, Greene King Abbot, and a guest such as Hogs Back TEA or Triple fff on handpump. Enjoyable bar food includes sandwiches (from £2.25), home-made soup (£3), ploughman's (from £4.25), filled baked potatoes (from £4.75), stuffies (baps with interesting fillings like prawn and crispy bacon or stilton, walnut and raisin, £5), home-cooked ham and egg (£6.50), chestnut loaf with salsa (£7.25), pie of the day (£7.50), marinated lamb chump chops (£10.50), steaks (from £11.25), daily specials, and puddings like home-made apple pie (£2.75); children's menu (£2.95). The restaurant is no smoking; piped music and dominoes. There are some picnic-sets in a dell by a tiny stream across the road, and lots of bird song. *(Recommended by Marianne and Peter Stevens, Sue and Bob Ward, Lynn Sharpless, Bob Eardley)*

Punch ~ Lease S Boorah and S Elsworth ~ Real ale ~ Bar food (till 10(9.30 Sun)) ~ Restaurant ~ (01428) 712150 ~ Children in eating area of bar and restaurant ~ Open 11-3, 6-11; 12-3, 7-10.30 Sun

BANK SU2807 Map 2
Oak ◗

Signposted just off A35 SW of Lyndhurst

After a good long walk from Brockenhurst, you will be ready to enjoy a pint of well kept Bass, Holdens Black Country Special, Otter Ale or Ringwood Best on handpump in this friendly 18th-c pub. There's a good bustling atmosphere and quite a mix of customers in the dimly lit L-shaped bar. On either side of the door in the bay windows are built-in green-cushioned seats, and on the right, two or three little pine-panelled booths with small built-in tables and bench seats. The rest of the bar has more floor space, with candles in individual brass holders on a line of stripped old and blond newer tables set against the wall on bare floorboards, and more at the back; some low beams and joists, fishing rods, spears, a boomerang, and old ski poles on the ceiling, and on the walls are brass platters, heavy knives, stuffed fish, and guns; a big fireplace. Cushioned milk churns along the bar counter, and little red lanterns among hop bines above the bar and country wines; piped music. Bar food (with prices unchanged since last year) includes sandwiches (from £1.80), soup (£3), filled baked potatoes (from £3.80), ploughman's (from £3.90), vegetable grill (£5.10), ham and egg (£5.35), steak and kidney pie (£5.95), king prawns (£7.90), and evening cajun chicken (£7.20), barbecue spare ribs (£7.40), and steaks (from £9.20). The side garden has picnic-sets and long tables and benches by the big yew trees. Dogs allowed if on a lead. More reports please. *(Recommended by W F C Phillips, M Joyner, Alan and Paula McCully)*

Free house ~ Licensees Nick and Sue Wateridge ~ Real ale ~ Bar food ~ (023) 8028 2350 ~ Children welcome ~ Open 11.30-2.30(3 Sat), 6-11; 12-3, 7-10.30 Sun

BEAUWORTH SU5624 Map 2
Milbury's ◗

Turn off A272 Winchester/Petersfield at Beauworth ¾, Bishops Waltham 6 signpost, then continue straight on past village

Plenty of walks surround this busy pub – the South Downs Way passes the door, the Wayfarers Walk is nearby, and there's a strenuous walk around Old Winchester Hill; the garden has fine views over rolling downland countryside. Inside, sturdy beams and panelling, stripped masonry, interesting old furnishings, and massive open fireplaces (with good winter log fires) offer reminders of the building's age, and there is a 600-year-old well with a massive 250-year-old treadmill – if you drop an ice cube into the spotlit shaft it takes eight full seconds to reach the bottom, which apparently means it is 300 feet deep. Well kept Cheriton Diggers Gold and Best, Hampshire Brewery Pride of Romsey, King Alfred's, Theakstons Old Peculier, and a beer named for the pub on handpump, Addlestones cider, 20 malt whiskies, and country wines. Decent bar food includes sandwiches, home-made soup (£2.95), deep-fried breaded mushrooms with garlic mayonnaise (£3.95), home-baked pizzas (from £5.65; not Sunday lunchtime), home-made lasagne (£5.95), home-made steak in ale pie, leek and stilton pancake with cream and cheese or fish in beer batter (£6.95), sirloin steak (£11.45), daily specials such as minted lamb casserole (£6.95), home-made chicken kiev (£7.25), and leg of lamb steak with a honey and rosemary sauce (£8.95); children's menu (from £2.95). One area is no smoking. The two black and white cats are called Neville and Nancy, and there's a golden labrador; fruit machine, skittle alley. The name of this pub was at first only a nickname, coming from the Millbarrow, a Bronze Age cemetery surrounding it, briefly famous back in 1833 when a Norman hoard of 6,000 silver coins was found here. *(Recommended by R J Walden, S G N Bennett, Jenny Cridland, Gordon Cooper, Mike and Maggie Betton, Mrs Thomas, Klaus and Elizabeth Leist, Ann and Colin Hunt, Richard Houghton, Tracey and Stephen Groves, Martin and Karen Wake, Mr and Mrs J French)*

Free house ~ Licensee Lenny Larden ~ Real ale ~ Bar food ~ (01962) 771248 ~ Children welcome ~ Open 12-11; closed 1 Jan ~ Bedrooms: £28.50/£40

BENTWORTH SU6740 Map 2

Sun ◖

Sun Hill; from the A339 coming from Alton the first turning takes you there direct; or in village follow Shalden 2¼, Alton 4¼ signpost

Down a narrow hidden lane just out of the village, this is a particularly friendly pub with a good welcome for all – and no noisy games machines or piped music to spoil the chatty atmosphere. There are high-backed antique settles, pews and schoolroom chairs, olde-worlde prints and blacksmith's tools on the walls, and bare boards and scrubbed deal tables on the left. An arch leads to a brick-floored room with another open fire and hanging baskets. The open fires in the big fireplaces in both the two little traditional communicating rooms are lit in winter which makes it all very cosy (and the thoughtful Christmas decorations are pretty). Tasty home-made bar food includes sandwiches (from £2.20), home-made soup (£2.95), ploughman's (£4.50), several vegetarian dishes such as avocado and stilton bake, nut roast or vegetable fajitas (from £5.25), sausage and mash with onion gravy (£5.95), salmon in white wine, chicken curry, steak and kidney pie or haddock bake with cheese (all £6.95), and home-made puddings such as apple crumble, chocolate mousse with Cointreau, and lemon cream pie (£2.95). They have around 8 real ales well kept on handpump such as Badger Champion, Brakspears Bitter, Bunces Pigswill, Cheriton Pots Ale, Courage Best, Fullers London Pride, and Ringwood Best; several malt whiskies. There are seats out in front and in the back garden, and pleasant nearby walks. *(Recommended by Martin and Karen Wake, Richard Houghton, Lynn Sharpless, Bob Eardley, Jenny and Chris Wilson, J Hale, Sue and Bob Ward, K Brewster, I Caldicott, Mark and Liz Wallace, Mr and Mrs D K MacDonald, the Didler)*

Free house ~ Licensee Mary Holmes ~ Real ale ~ Bar food ~ (01420) 562338 ~ Children in eating area of bar ~ Open 12-3, 6-11; 12-10.30 Sun

BOLDRE SZ3298 Map 2

Red Lion ★ ♀

Village signposted from A337 N of Lymington

Hard working and capable new licensees have taken over this popular New Forest pub. The four black-beamed rooms are filled with heavy urns, platters, needlework, rural landscapes, and so forth, taking in farm tools, heavy-horse harness, needlework, gin-traps and even ferocious-looking man-traps along the way; the central room has a profusion of chamber-pots, and an end room has pews, wheelback chairs and tapestried stools, and a dainty collection of old bottles and glasses in the window by the counter; there are some no smoking areas. There's a fine old cooking range in the cosy little bar. Good, if not particularly cheap, bar food includes home-made soup (£3.30), sandwiches (£3.75; club sandwich £5.75), home-made smoked haddock fishcakes with a white wine and cream sauce or pork and duck pâté (£5.20), ploughman's (£6), vegetable casserole (£7.20), calves liver and bacon (£8.60), beef and mushroom pie (£9.50), steaks (from £10.90), daily specials such as stilton chicken breast (£10.20), pigeon breast rossini (£10.90), or scallops with stir-fried vegetables laced with a thermidor sauce (£11.60), and puddings such as rhubarb crumble, red cherry cheesecake or whisky bread and butter pudding (£3.50). Well kept Courage Directors, and Thomas Hardy Royal Oak and Hardy Country on handpump, and an extensive wine list. In summer, the flowering tubs and hanging baskets are pretty, and there's a cart festooned with colour near the car park; seats in the back garden. This is a fine area for walking with 1,000 acres of Royden Wood Nature Reserve. No children. *(Recommended by Phyl and Jack Street, Sally and Aidan Vine, Martin and Karen Wake, Nigel and Anna Boden, A D Marsh, Lynn Sharpless, Bob Eardley, G L Carlisle, Alan and Paula McCully, Joan and Michel Hooper-Immins, Mrs Pam Mattinson, Basil Minson, Michael Buchanan, Martin Weinberg, John Davis)*

Eldridge Pope (Hardy) ~ Lease Vince Kernick ~ Real ale ~ Bar food (12-2.30, 6.30-9.30) ~ Restaurant ~ (01590) 673177 ~ Open 11-11; 12-10.30 Sun

BRAMDEAN SU6127 Map 2
Fox
A272 Winchester—Petersfield

Especially at lunchtime, there's a rather relaxed, civilised atmosphere in this popular, well run dining pub, and customers tend to be of a more mature age then. The open-plan and carefully modernised bar has black beams, tall stools with proper backrests around the L-shaped counter, and comfortably cushioned wall pews and wheelback chairs; the fox motif shows in a big painting over the fireplace, and on much of the decorative china. At least one area is no smoking. Much emphasis is placed on the good, rather pricy food, which at lunchtime includes sandwiches (from £2.75), soup (£2.95), pâté (£4.95), poached pear, blue cheese and crispy bacon salad (£5.95), king prawns with mayonnaise (£6.95), deep-fried fresh fillet of cod, home-made steak and kidney pie or chicken breast with a coarse-grain mustard sauce (£9.95), and grilled lamb cutlets (£9.95); evening choices such as mushrooms cooked with bacon and garlic (£4.95), chicken breast with asparagus in a boursin sauce (£11.95), roast rack of lamb with rosemary and garlic or half a roast duck with an orange gravy (£14.95), and lots of fresh fish such as grilled whole dover sole, grilled whole bass with salsa, tuna with herb butter, and monkfish tail with a tarragon sauce. Well kept Greene King Abbot on handpump. At the back of the building is a walled-in terraced area, and a spacious lawn spreading among the fruit trees, with a good play area – trampoline as well as swings and a seesaw. No children inside. *(Recommended by Colin and Janet Roe, Des and June Preston, Margaret Ross, John and Joan Calvert, Phyl and Jack Street, Betty Laker, Geoffrey and Brenda Wilson)*

Greene King ~ Tenants Ian and Jane Inder ~ Real ale ~ Bar food (not winter Sun or Mon evenings) ~ Restaurant ~ (01962) 771363 ~ Open 11-3, 6(6.30 in winter)-11; 12-3, 7-10.30 Sun; closed winter Mon evenings

BURITON SU7320 Map 2
Five Bells
Village signposted off A3 S of Petersfield

After enjoying one of the good nearby walks or a stroll through the pretty village, lots of customers get to this friendly country pub early to bag a table on the informal lawn that stretches back above the building; there are more seats on sheltered terraces. Inside, there are several interesting rooms, and the low-beamed lounge on the left, dominated by a big log fire, has period photographs on the partly stripped brick walls and a rather worn turkey carpet on oak parquet; the public side has some ancient stripped masonry, a woodburning stove, and old-fashioned tables; an end alcove has cushioned pews and board games. A good choice of popular bar food includes lunchtime baguettes (from £2.95), filled baked potatoes (from £3.95), and ploughman's (£4.95), as well as home-made soup (£3.25), ham and egg or mushroom risotto (£6.95), dijon chicken, slow-roasted lamb shank, grilled whole skate wing with lemon and capers or half roast duck with a rich berry fruit glaze (all £8.95), steaks (from £10.95), and home-made puddings such as bread and butter pudding, mint and vanilla crème caramel, and maple syrup and coconut tart (£3.25). Well kept Badger Best, Fursty Ferret, Sussex and Tanglefoot, and a guest such as Ballards Best on handpump, and decent wines with several by the glass. The three cats are called Trevor, Stan and Stella; darts, cribbage, dominoes, Trivial Pursuit, Scrabble, chess, backgammon, and piped music. The converted stables are self-catering cottages. *(Recommended by Ann and Colin Hunt, Val and Alan Green, Charles and Pauline Stride, Lynn Sharpless, Bob Eardley, Mike and Alison Stevens, Sheila Rowell, Geoffrey Johns, Ian Phillips, Phyl and Jack Street, Lord Sandhurst, John Davis, P R and S A White)*

Badger ~ Manager Bridget Slocombe ~ Real ale ~ Bar food (12-2(2.30 wknds), 6-10(9.30 Sun)) ~ Restaurant (Fri/Sat evenings and Sun lunch) ~ (01730) 263584 ~ Children in eating area of bar and restaurant ~ Live band every Weds ~ Open 11-2.30(3 Fri and Sat), 5.30-11; 12-3, 7-10.30 Sun

BURSLEDON SU4809 Map 2
Jolly Sailor ♀

2 miles from M27 junction 8; then A27 towards Sarisbury, then just before going under
railway bridge turn right towards Bursledon Station; it's best to park round here and walk as
the lane up from the station is now closed to cars

Apart from re-painting the outside of this waterside pub, more seating space has
been created and new outdoor heaters added for cooler weather; there are also tables
under the big yew tree or on the covered wooden jetty where you can look at the fine
yachts moored in the harbour. The airy front bar has ship pictures, nets and shells,
as well as windsor chairs and settles on the floorboards, and there are views of the
water from the window seat. The atmospheric beamed and flagstoned back bar,
with pews and settles by its huge fireplace, is a fair bit older. Enjoyable bar food
includes home-made soup (£3.35), sandwiches (from £3.95; crab and prawn with
lemon and dill mayonnaise £4.95), Greek salad (£4.85), cheese platter ploughman's
(£5.95), home-cooked ham with tomato salsa (£6.60), sausages with onion gravy
(£8.25), seafood pie (£8.95), minted lamb shoulder (£10.95), sirloin steak (£11.95),
and children's menu (£3.50), with daily specials such as stir-fried squid in honey and
mustard (£9.95), whole Torby sole with crispy prawns (£12.50), and swordfish
steak with aurora sauce (£12.25). The dining area is no smoking. Well kept Badger
Best, IPA, Golden Champion, Tanglefoot, and K&B Sussex, Gales HSB, and Gribble
Fursty Ferret on handpump, 8 wines by the glass, freshly squeezed juice, and country
wines; Jenga, Connect Four, and piped music. The path down to the pub (and of
course back up again) from the lane is steep. *(Recommended by LM, JP, PP, the Didler,
Ian Phillips, J A Cheverton, George Little, Roger and Pauline Pearce, Nigel and Sue Foster,
Ann and Colin Hunt, Lynne Prangnell, Tom and Ruth Rees, Betsy and Peter Little, Charles and
Pauline Stride)*

*Badger ~ Managers Adrian Jenkins and Jackie Cosens ~ Real ale ~ Bar food (12-9.30)
~ (023) 8040 5557 ~ Children in no smoking dining room ~ Open 11-11; 12-10.30
Sun; closed 25 Dec*

CADNAM SU2913 Map 2
White Hart

½ mile from M27 junction 1; A336 towards village, pub off village roundabout

As this comfortable pub is so close to the M27, it makes a good place for a break.
Most people come to eat, and served by efficient, friendly staff, there might be soup
(£3.50), quail pâté (£4.95), open sandwiches (from £4.95), grilled lambs liver and
onion gravy or home-made steak and kidney pie (£8.95), half a roast duck with a
cointreau and orange sauce (£11.25), whole Poole plaice (£10.95), scallops wrapped
in bacon around a timbale of rice with a spring onion and wine sauce (£12.50), and
Sunday roast half shoulder of lamb, beef and pork (£8.95). The spacious multi-level
dining lounge has good solid furnishings, soft lighting, country prints and
appropriate New Forest pictures and mementoes; one area is no smoking. Well kept
Flowers Original, Greene King Old Speckled Hen, Ringwood Best, and Whitbreads
Best on handpump, and quite a few wines by the glass from a thoughtful list; skittle
alley, piped music. There are seats in the garden where there is a fish pond; horses in
the next door paddock. More reports please. *(Recommended by Lynn Sharpless,
Bob Eardley, John and Vivienne Rice, R T and J C Moggridge, J M and P M Carver, John and
Joan Calvert, Philip Vernon, Kim Maidment, Darly Graton, Graeme Gulibert, Mrs Pam
Mattinson, W F C Phillips, Phyl and Jack Street, Mayur Shah, Simon and Laura Habbishow,
Mr and Mrs A Craig)*

*Whitbreads ~ Lease Peter and Shirley Palmer ~ Real ale ~ Bar food (12-2, 6-9.30(9
Sun) ~ (023) 8081 2277 ~ Children in eating area of bar ~ Open 11-3, 5.30-11; 12-3,
5.30-10.30 Sun*

Pubs with particularly interesting histories, or in unusually interesting
buildings, are listed at the back of the book.

CHERITON SU5828 Map 2
Flower Pots ★ ◥

Pub just off B3046 (main village road) towards Beauworth and Winchester; OS Sheet 185 map reference 581282

This is a smashing village local with no piped music or fruit machines, a wide mix of customers, and particularly well kept own-brewed beers. There are two little rooms and the one on the left feels almost like someone's front room, with pictures of hounds and ploughmen on its striped wallpaper, bunches of flowers, and a horse and foal and other ornaments on the mantelpiece over a small log fire; it can get smoky in here. Behind the servery there's disused copper filtering equipment, and lots of hanging gin-traps, drag-hooks, scaleyards and other ironwork. Good value straightforward bar food includes sandwiches (from £2; toasties from £2.20; big baps from £2.70), winter home-made soup (£2.80), filled baked potatoes (from £3.50), and hotpots such as lamb and apricot, chilli or beef stew (from £4.70); popular Indian dishes on Wednesday evenings. The menu may be restricted at weekend lunchtimes. From the Cheriton Brewhouse, they offer Diggers Gold, Pots Ale and Cheriton Best Bitter tapped from casks behind the bar. Darts in the neat extended plain public bar (where there's a covered well), also cribbage, shove-ha'penny and dominoes. On the pretty front and back lawns are some old-fashioned seats – very useful in fine weather as it can quickly fill up inside; they sometimes have morris dancers out here in summer. Near the site of one of the final battles of the Civil War, the pub once belonged to the retired head gardener of nearby Avington Park, which explains the unusual name. No children inside. *(Recommended by Bruce Bird, Lynn Sharpless, Bob Eardley, Chloe and Robert Gartery, Pamela and Merlyn Horswell, Charlie Harris, Simon J Barber, T G Thomas, Val and Alan Green, Peter Meister, S G N Bennett, Dave Holmes, Tony and Wendy Hobden, Francis Johnston, John Fahy, Sharon Holmes, Tom Cherrett, JP, PP, the Didler, Ann and Colin Hunt, Susan and John Douglas, Mr and Mrs J French, Ron Shelton, Charles and Pauline Stride, Michael and Robin Inskip, John Davis, Carol and Dono Leaman, Jenny Cridland, Gordon Cooper, Simon Collett-Jones, P R and S A White, Mark Percy, Lesley Mayoh)*

Own brew ~ Licensees Jo and Patricia Bartlett ~ Real ale ~ Bar food (not Sun evening or bank hol Mon evenings) ~ No credit cards ~ (01962) 771318 ~ Open 12-2.30, 6-11; 12-3, 7-10.30 Sun ~ Bedrooms: /£55S

CRAWLEY SU4234 Map 2
Fox & Hounds ⑪ ♀

Village signposted from A272 and B3420 NW of Winchester

Hampshire Dining Pub of the Year

This solidly constructed mock Tudor building is one of the most striking in a village of fine old houses. Each timbered upper storey successively juts further out, with lots of pegged structural timbers in the neat brickwork, and elaborately carved steep gable-ends. Restored recently and re-opened as a village pub, the beamed rooms are warmed by three log fires, there's a relaxed atmosphere, evening candlelight, a mix of attractive wooden tables and chairs, helpful and friendly staff, well kept Adnams, Butcombe, and Wadworths IPA, 6X, and seasonal ales on handpump, and interesting wines. Using fresh local produce, the very good bar food might include sandwiches, watercress soup (£3.95), chicken liver parfait with spicy chutney (£5), wild mushroom and sun-dried tomato risotto (£5.25), pork and leek sausages with bubble and squeak (£6.95), liver and bacon (£7.50), rabbit and partridge stew or chicken and coconut curry (£8.50), gateau of aubergine, courgette and dorset blue vinney cheese (£8.95), tuna niçoise or loin of pork with bean sprouts and spicy sauce (£9.95), grilled marlin with citrus marmalade (£12.75), rack of lamb with olive mash and black pudding or venison with a gooseberry sauce (£12.95), and chargrilled sirloin with caramelised onion and blue cheese (£13.50). Summer barbecues in the garden. *(Recommended by John and Joan Calvert, Madeleine and Keith Bright, Mr and Mrs A G Leece, Peter Jacobs, T Leeson, Mr and Mrs R Porter, Phyl and Jack Street)*

Free house ~ Licensees Richard and Kathryn Crawford ~ Real ale ~ Bar food (12-2, 6-9(9.30 Fri/Sat) ~ Restaurant ~ (01962) 776006 ~ Children welcome away from bar ~ Open 11-3, 6-11; 12-3, 6-10.30 Sun

DROXFORD SU6018 Map 2
White Horse 🍺 🛏

4 miles along A32 from Wickham

A good base for touring Hampshire, this rambling 16th-c inn is a neatly kept place with friendly licensees and locals. The atmospheric lounge bar is made up of several small cosy rooms – low beams, bow windows, alcoves, and log fires, while the public bar is larger and more straightforward: pool, darts, table skittles, TV, cribbage, dominoes, shove-ha'penny, and CD juke box. At lunchtime, decent bar food might include sandwiches (from £2), baguettes (from £2.50), filled baked potatoes (from £2.50), and ploughman's (from £3.75); there's also good home-made soup (£2.50), locally smoked fresh salmon pâté (£4), Portuguese sardines in garlic butter (£6.50), vegetable curry (£6.75), spicy cumberland sausages (£7.25), steaks (from £9), daily specials such as stuffed chicken breast (£7.50), duck breast (£9.50), and medallions of venison (£10.50), and children's menu (from £2.75). The dining room is no smoking. Well kept Greene King IPA, Abbot and Old Speckled Hen, Ruddles Best, and Wadsworths 6X on handpump; several malt whiskies. One of the cubicles in the gents' overlooks an illuminated well. There are tables in a secluded flower-filled courtyard comfortably sheltered by the building's back wings. *(Recommended by Dr Paull Khan, Lynn Sharpless, Bob Eardley, W W Burke, Tony and Wendy Hobden, Jenny Cridland, Gordon Cooper, A D Marsh, Esther and John Sprinkle, Ann and Colin Hunt, Charlie Harris, Ian Phillips, R M Corlett, Simon Collett-Jones)*

Morlands (Greene King) ~ Lease Paul Young ~ Real ale ~ Bar food (all day Sun; not 25/26 Dec, 1 Jan) ~ Restaurant ~ (01489) 877490 ~ Children in restaurant and family room ~ Open 11-11; 12-10.30 Sun ~ Bedrooms: £25(£40B)/£35(£50B)

EAST TYTHERLEY SU2927 Map 2
Star 🍴 🛏

Off B3084 N of Romsey, via Lockerley – turn off by railway crossing nr Mottisfont Abbey

The bar in this 16th-c dining pub has a mix of comfortable furnishings, log fires in attractive fireplaces, and horsebrasses and saddlery; there's a lower lounge bar, and a cosy and pretty no smoking restaurant. Good, interesting bar food (they tell us prices and choices have not changed since last year) includes open sandwiches or baguettes (£3.25), steak and kidney pie or chilli (£5.95), and daily specials such as fried duck liver on rye and caraway toast (£3.95), double baked goats cheese (£4.75), tiger prawn and scallop risotto (£4.95), pumpkin ravioli and bok choi (£7.90), liver and bacon (£7.95), monkfish and roasted carrot with chicken and black pudding (£12), and puddings like dark Belgian chocolate mousse or caramelised apple tart (from £3.50). You can eat the same menu in the bar or restaurant. Well kept Gales HSB, Ringwood Best, and a guest beer, several malt whiskies, and a thoughtful wine list with 10 by the glass. Chess, and a skittle alley for private functions. There are seats on the smartly furnished terrace, and a children's play area; The comfortable cottage-style bedrooms overlook the village cricket pitch. *(Recommended by Angela Cerfontyn, Lynn Sharpless, Bob Eardley, Prof H G Allen, A E Furley, A D Marsh, John and Joan Calvert, Ann and Colin Hunt, KC, Annette and John Derbyshire, Roger Sims, Val and Alan Green)*

Free house ~ Licensees Paul and Sarah Bingham ~ Real ale ~ Bar food ~ Restaurant ~ (01794) 340225 ~ Children welcome ~ Open 11-2.30, 6-11; 11-11 Sat; 12-10.30 Sun; 11-2.30, 6-11 Sat in winter; closed evening 25 Dec and 26 Dec ~ Bedrooms: £45S/£60S

EVERSLEY SU7861 Map 2
Golden Pot

Eversley Centre; B3272

The Monday evening rösti menu is as popular as ever at this little brick building – as is the other enjoyable food. There's a comfortable, easy-going atmosphere in the different spreading areas, bowls of lilies, candles in bottles on the tables, and one particularly snug part by the log-effect gas fire, with two armchairs and a sofa; piped music. The rösti have toppings such as melted cheese and two fried eggs (£6.50) or bratwurst and onion sauce (£6.75), and other dishes may include gnocchi tossed in olive oil with sage and parmesan or potted prawns (£4.50), smoked chicken salad with fresh mango and cajun croutons (£4.75), crab gravadlax or hot smoked salmon (£6.25), seared fresh tuna with coriander and a chilli dressing (£5.95), herby ratatouille (£8.95), red wine risotto with dolcelatte and rocket (£9.50), roast pork wrapped in parma ham with sage and a madeira sauce (£11.95), fishy main courses such as skate in black butter or monkfish with tomato sauce (from £11 to £14), and puddings like pear tartlette with clotted cream or white and dark chocolate pyramid with a rich Belgian truffle mousse (from £3.95). Well kept Badger **Tanglefoot**, Greene King IPA and Ruddles Best, Wadworths 6X, and maybe Wychwood Hobgoblin on handpump, and 12 wines by the glass; piped music. The pretty restaurant is no smoking. There are some picnic-sets in front by the car park with masses of colourful flowering pots, tubs, and window boxes. *(Recommended by KC, Martin and Karen Wake, Lynn Sharpless, Bob Eardley)*

Greene King ~ Lease Justin Winstanley ~ Real ale ~ Bar food (12-2.15, 6.30-9.15(9.30 Fri/Sat)) ~ Restaurant ~ (0118) 973 2104 ~ Pianist/vocalist/guitarist Mon evening ~ Open 11-3(3.30 Sat), 6(5 Fri)-11; 12-3.30, 7-10.30 Sun

FRITHAM SU2314 Map 2
Royal Oak

Village signed from exit roundabout, M27 junction 1; quickest via B3078, then left and straight through village; head for Eyeworth Pond

With lovely views and regular summer weekend barbecues in the neatly kept big garden (they have a marquee for bad weather), this charming cob and brick-built thatched pub is especially appealing in good weather; it's also part of a working farm, and there are animals at close quarters – plus ponies and pigs on the nearby green. The three bar rooms have a civilised and relaxed atmosphere, antique wheelback, spindleback, and other old chairs and stools with colourful seats around solid tables on the new oak flooring, prints and pictures involving local characters on the white walls, restored panelling and black beams, and two roaring log fires. Served by the friendly young licensees, the simple lunchtime food consists of freshly made soup (£3) and ploughman's with home-made pâté and quiche, and home cooked ham (£4), and sometimes home-made scotch eggs or sausage parcels. They do winter evening meals on one or two nights a week, and for parties by arrangement; well kept Ringwood Best, Fortyniner and True Glory tapped from the cask, and a guest such as Cheriton Diggers Gold; darts, and the back bar has quite a few books. Fine surrounding walks, and dogs are welcome. *(Recommended by the Didler, Pete Baker, Lynn Sharpless, Bob Eardley, Dennis Jenkin, Andy and Jill Kassube, George Atkinson, R J Walden, JP, PP, Ann and Colin Hunt)*

Free house ~ Licensees Neil and Pauline McCulloch ~ Real ale ~ Bar food (lunchtime – though see text) ~ No credit cards ~ (023) 8081 2606 ~ Children welcome ~ Occasional country music at weekends ~ Open 11-3, 6-11; 11-11 summer Fri, and all year Sat; 12-10.30 Sun

HAWKLEY SU7429 Map 2
Hawkley Inn ◀

Take first right turn off B3006, heading towards Liss 0.7 mile from its junction with A3; then after nearly 2 miles take first left turn into Hawkley village – Pococks Lane; OS Sheet 186 map reference 746292

At weekends, this is a popular spot for walkers to relax, and the pub is on the Hangers Way Path. It's an unpretentious country local with a chatty, friendly atmosphere and a good mix of customers, and the opened-up bar and back dining room have simple décor – big pine tables, a moose head, dried flowers, and prints on the mellowing walls; parts of the bar can get a bit smoky when it's busy, but there is a no smoking area to the left of the bar. A fine choice of half a dozen well kept real ales changes all the time, but might inlcude Ballards Trotton Bitter, Exmoor Gold, Goffs Fallen Knight, Kelham Island Pale Rider, RCH East Street Cream, and Sharps Doom on handpump, and their own cider. Promptly served, tasty bar food includes filled rolls, good soups such as stilton and celery or ham, tomato and watercress (£4.85), cheese, leek and potato pie (£7.95), Philippine lamb and olive stew (£8.25), beef stew (£8.50), and puddings such as spotted dick (£3.50). There are tables and a climbing frame in the pleasant garden *(Recommended by John Sedgwick, Martin and Karen Wake, the Didler, Francis Johnston, JP, PP, Lynn Sharpless, Bob Eardley, Dave Braisted, Len Banister, Pat and Tony Martin)*

Free house ~ Licensees E N Collins and A Stringer ~ Real ale ~ Bar food (not Sun evening) ~ (01730) 827205 ~ Well behaved children in eating area of bar until 8pm ~ Live music every second winter Sat ~ Open 12-2.30(3 Sat), 6-11; 12-3, 7-10.30 Sun

ITCHEN ABBAS SU5332 Map 2
Trout 🍴

4 miles from M3 junction 9; A34 towards Newbury, fork right on to A33, then first right into B3047

Just a few yards from the River Itchen and some lovely riverside walks, this brick-built village pub was where Charles Kingsley stayed and wrote *The Water Babies*; the pub was called the Plough, then. The comfortable carpeted lounge and chatty public bars have been attractively refurbished by the friendly new licensees, and the bedrooms are to be upgraded, with fishing and golfing breaks offered. Good bar food now includes home-made soup (£3.25), home-made duck pâté (£3.50), lunchtime ciabatta sandwiches (£3.95), black pudding on creamy mash with a red wine jus (£3.95), broccoli and stilton crumble (£5.95), fish and chips or steamed steak and mushroom pudding (£6.95), fillet of salmon with hollandaise (£7.95), bass with butter sauce, escolar with citrus dressing or sirloin steak with pepper sauce (all £8.95), and puddings such as chocolate fudge cake, strawberry cheesecake or banoffi pie (£3.95). Well kept Greene King IPA and Old Speckled Hen, Ruddles Best and County on handpump, a couple of dozen malt whiskies, and decent wines. Henry the cat likes to greet everyone; piped music, shove-ha'penny, cribbage, dominoes, and TV. There are seats in the sheltered side garden, which has also been prettily reworked. *(Recommended by Glen and Nola Armstrong, Mr and Mrs J Sale, E A Thwaite, Phyl and Jack Street, Mr and Mrs R W Allan)*

Greene King ~ Tenants Janet Graham and Gary Swan ~ Real ale ~ Bar food ~ (01962) 779537 ~ Children welcome ~ Open 12-2.30, 6-11; 12-11 Fri and Sat; 12-10.30 Sun; 12-2.30, 6-11 in winter ~ Bedrooms: £40S/£65S

LANGSTONE SU7105 Map 2
Royal Oak

High Street (marked as cul-de-sac – actually stops short of the pub itself); village is last turn left off A3023 (confusingly called A324 on some signs) before Hayling Island bridge

At high tide (when it looks its best), you can reach this charmingly placed pub by boat – landlubbers may be marooned if they don't consult the tide tables; from the terrace you can watch the goings-on in the adjacent harbour. Inside, the spacious and atmospheric flagstoned bar has windows from which you can see the ancient wadeway to Hayling Island (get here early to bag one of these), and simple furnishings like windsor chairs around old wooden tables on the parquet and ancient flagstones, and two winter open fires. Bar food includes soup (£2.95), bacon and mushroom melt (£3.95), steak in ale pie (£6.95), whole plaice (£7.50), salmon, thyme and lemon fishcakes or moules marinières (£7.95), butterfly chicken topped with bacon, cheese and creamy mushroom sauce, and popular sizzlers with steak, fish or chicken (£8.50); the dining area is no smoking. Well kept Boddingtons, Flowers Original, Gales HSB, and a guest such as Fullers London Pride or Greene King Old Speckled Hen on handpump, and decent wines; no noisy piped music or games machines. Morris dancers in summer; good coastal paths nearby.

(Recommended by Mike and Maggie Betton, Ann and Colin Hunt, Ian Phillips, Martin and Karen

Wake, Tony and Wendy Hobden, Val and Alan Green, Irene and Derek Flewin, Tracey and Stephen Groves, Esther and John Sprinkle, D P and J A Sweeney, Stephanie Smith, Leigh Hughes, John Davis)

Whitbreads ~ Manager Chris Ford ~ Real ale ~ Bar food (12-2.30, 6-9; snacks served all day) ~ Restaurant ~ (023) 9248 3125 ~ Children in eating area of bar and restaurant ~ Folk club 3rd Sun of month ~ Open 11-11; 12-10.30 Sun

LONGSTOCK SU3537 Map 2
Peat Spade

Village signposted off A30 on W edge of Stockbridge, and off A3057 Stockbridge—Andover

This attractive village is on the 44-mile Test Way long-distance path and there are bracing downland walks up around the Danebury hillfort path; the River Test is only about 100 yards away. The roomy and attractive squarish main bar is airy and high-ceilinged, with pretty windows, well chosen furnishings and a nice show of toby jugs and beer mats around its fireplace. A rather elegant no smoking dining room leads off, and there are doors to a big terrace; one area is no smoking. Good, interesting and well presented, the bar food might include sandwiches with home-made bread (£3.95), gazpacho or carrot and coconut soup (£4.10), caramelised onion and brie tartlet (£4.60), fresh anchovy fillets and smoked eel with a mild chilli sauce (£4.75), roasted onions stuffed with red pepper and their own free range eggs (£10.20), chicken stuffed with asparagus and a sweet lime dressing or loin fillet of escolar on glazed oranges with Cointreau sauce (£11.50), fillet of john dory with bean sprouts and a soy and sesame dressing or gressingham duck breast with girolle mushrooms and black cherry sauce (£13.50), and puddings such as peach and nut crumble with crème anglaise or summer fruit pudding with lemon crème compote (£4.25). Well kept Ringwood Fortyniner and Best, and Weltons Pridenjoy on handpump, and a decent wine list with several by the glass. As well as free range chickens, there are teak seats on the new terrace, with more in the not large but pleasant garden, and two cats and Mollie the diabetic dog (who is not allowed to be fed). *(Recommended by Ann and Colin Hunt, Lynn Sharpless, Bob Eardley, Miss Lisa Mead, Phyl and Jack Street, Margaret Ross, J Hale, John Robertson, Michael Smith, J M and P M Carver)*

Free house ~ Licensees Bernie Startup and Sarah Hinman ~ Real ale ~ Bar food (not Sun evening, not Mon) ~ Restaurant ~ No credit cards ~ (01264) 810612 ~ Children welcome ~ Open 11.30-3, 6-11; 12-3 Sun; closed Sun evening, all Mon, 25 Dec, 1 Jan ~ Bedrooms: £52.75B/£58.75B

MAPLEDURWELL SU6851 Map 2
Gamekeepers

3½ miles off M3 junction 6: A339 towards Basingstoke, then right signposted Old Basing, Hatch (A30 towards Hartley Wintney), then village and pub signed off on right; OS Sheet 185 map reference 686514

This neatly kept pub has dark beams, joists and standing timbers throughout, and a pleasant, relaxed atmosphere. The bar has brocaded heavy dark long seats and wheelbacks around tables prettily set with gingham tablecloths and candles in the eating part, hunting, fish, military, and country pictures on the partly stripped brick and partly cream and timber effect walls, and a log-effect gas fire in a slightly raised brick two-way fireplace; the flagstoned small part in the middle has wood panelling, horse tack and fox masks, and a large no smoking dining room with a glass-topped stone well with carp at the bottom. There's also a back bar with cushioned winged wooden settles and wheelbacks on the turkey carpet. Food is good and popular and includes filled baguettes (£4.95), spicy onion fritters with mango chutney and mint dips or black pudding and chorizo sautéed with apple and new potatoes (£5.25), green thai chicken salad (£5.95), mussels in white wine and cream (£6.25), mushroom stroganoff (£11.50), sugar-cured cod on a warm potato pancake with beetroot vinaigrette (£12.50), oven-roasted poussin breasts on a green mango and potato rösti with a wild mushroom jus (£13.25), and breast of gressingham duck with a light orange and black cherry sauce (£14.75); they have a lobster week in

May and a game week in November. Well kept Badger Best and Tanglefoot on handpump; piped music. The lasa apso dog is called Barney. There are picnic-sets on the terrace and back grassy area. More reports please. *(Recommended by M G Hart, Mrs M Webster)*

Badger ~ Tenants Shaun and Tracey Nother ~ Real ale ~ Bar food (12-2.15, 6.30-9.30; not Sun evening) ~ Restaurant ~ (01256) 322038 ~ Children in eating area of bar ~ Open 12-3, 6-11; 12-3, 7-10.30 Sun; closed winter Sun evenings

MICHELDEVER SU5138 Map 2
Half Moon & Spread Eagle

Village signposted off A33 N of Winchester; then follow Winchester 7 signpost almost opposite hall

This is an enjoyable country local with cheerful, attentive staff and a happy, relaxed atmosphere. The simply decorated and beamed bar has heavy tables and good solid seats – a nice cushioned panelled oak settle and a couple of long dark pews as well as wheelback chairs – and a woodburning stove at each end; a no smoking area with lighter-coloured furniture opens off. Good bar food includes sandwiches, gammon and egg (£6.50), lasagne (£6.95), cod in beer batter or fresh crab salad (£7.95), grilled local bass (£9.95), and surf and turf (£11.95); fresh local shellfish (when available), and daily specials. Well kept Greene King Abbot and IPA, and a guest such as Cheriton Pots Ale or Smiles Best on handpump; darts, pool, fruit machine, cribbage, and piped music. The landlord plays the saxophone, and they have an alsatian called Brew, and four cats. There are seats on a small sheltered back terrace, and some more widely spaced picnic-sets and a play area on the edge of a big cricket green behind; also, rabbits and chickens and a pony. This is a good starting point for exploring the Dever Valley (there are lots of good walks nearby). *(Recommended by Dr D E Granger, Phyl and Jack Street, Val and Alan Green, Dennis Jenkin, Charles Moncreiffe, Mike Gorton, Richard and Judy Winn)*

Greene King ~ Tenants Ray Douglas and Belinda Boughtwood ~ Real ale ~ Bar food (12-2, 6-9) ~ Restaurant ~ (01962) 774339 ~ Children welcome ~ Monthly live singer ~ Open 12-3, 6-11; 12-3, 7-10.30 Sun

NORTH GORLEY SU1611 Map 2
Royal Oak

Ringwood Road; village signposted off A338 S of Fordingbridge

This 17th-c thatched pub has a quiet, comfortable and neatly refurbished no smoking lounge on the left, though our own preference is for the busier main bar on the right: carpeted too, with pews, mate's chairs, a corner woodburning stove, old engravings and other pictures, with steps down to an attractive L-shaped eating area. This has a mix of dark pine tables and pleasant old-fashioned chairs, with big rugs on bare boards, and a further no smoking part with pine booth seating. There are french windows to a neatly kept sheltered back garden, with a play area. Bar food (with prices unchanged since last year) includes sandwiches (from £1.75; toasties £2.75), soup (£2.50), ploughman's (from £3.95), chicken curry, broccoli bake or lasagne (£5.75), steak and kidney in ale pie (£5.95), steaks (from £8.95), and puddings such as trifle, sticky toffee pudding or apple crumble (£2.75). Well kept Fullers London Pride, Greene King IPA, and Ringwood Best on handpump, decent wines, and several malt whiskies; sensibly placed darts, CD juke box, fruit machine, cribbage, dominoes, and skittle alley. Across the road is a big pond with ducks, and there are usually ponies roaming around. *(Recommended by John Branston, Colin and Sandra Tann, Dave Braisted, John Davis, Mr and Mrs T A Bryan, Mr and Mrs Thomas, MNF, R T and J C Moggridge)*

Whitbreads ~ Lease David Catt ~ Real ale ~ Bar food (12-2. 6.30-9) ~ Restaurant ~ (01425) 652244 ~ Children in eating area of bar ~ Open 11-11; 12-10.30 Sun; 11-3, 5-11 in winter

OVINGTON SU5531 Map 2
Bush

Village signposted from A31 on Winchester side of Alresford

New licensees have taken over this charming little cottage and have carefully refurbished the rooms, keeping the old-fashioned décor. The low-ceilinged bar has cushioned high-backed settles, elm tables with pews and kitchen chairs, masses of old pictures in heavy gilt frames on the walls, and a roaring fire on one side with an antique solid fuel stove opposite. Bar food is carefully sourced, using the best produce they can get: soup such as minted fresh pea or curried apple and cabbage (£4.40), home-made chicken liver pâté with brandy and port (£6.45), thai spiced crab cake with rocket salad (£6.60), tagliatelle with leek, cheese, sage and pink peppercorn sauce (£9.75), local trout fillets grilled with garlic, hazelnut and coriander butter (£11.80), roast ribs of Aberdeenshire beef with red wine and yorkshire pudding (£11.85), home-made wild mushroom and spinach lasagne (£11.90), venison casserole or fried halibut steak with lemon and dill butter (£13.50), and puddings; two rooms are no smoking. Well kept Wadworths IPA and 6X with guests such as Badger Tanglefoot or Red Shoot Tom's Tipple and Forest Gold on handpump, and several country wines and malt whiskies; cribbage, dominoes, and Scrabble. The friendly scottish springer spaniel is called Paddy. The pub is set in a lovely spot with seats in the garden behind which runs down to the River Itchen, and more on a tree-sheltered pergola dining terrace with a good-sized fountain pool. Nice walks nearby. *(Recommended by Michael and Ann Cole, John Evans, Ian Phillips, Susan and John Douglas, Mrs Rita Cox, Martin and Karen Wake, Margaret Ross)*

Wadworths ~ Managers Nick and Cathy Young ~ Real ale ~ Bar food (12-2.30, 7-9.30; not Sun evening) ~ (01962) 732764 ~ Well behaved children in family room ~ Open 11-3, 6-11; 12-2.30, 7-10.30 Sun

OWSLEBURY SU5123 Map 2
Ship

Whites Hill; village signposted off B2177 between Fishers Pond and Lower Upham; can also be reached from M3 junction 10 via Morestead, or from A272 2½ miles SE of A31 junction

What was the family room here has been refurbished, with pine tables and chairs on old pine floorboards, hops and wooden blinds, and is now a bustling, friendly restaurant. The old bars on the right of the front entrance have varnished black oak 17th-c ship's timbers as beams and wall props, sporting and naval mementoes, wheelback chairs around wooden tables, and a big central fireplace; on the left is a comfortable dining area. Good bar food at lunchtime includes filled baguettes, home-cooked ham and eggs (£6.75), steak and kidney pie or warm goats cheese salad with fig chutney (£6.95), thai prawn and crab cakes with hot chilli relish or calves liver sautéed in port with toasted brioche (£7.95), beef curry (£8.95), and steaks (from £10.50); also, home-made soup (£3.50), warm honey-glazed duck with oriental dressing (£5.25), spinach, mushroom and pepper parcel or pork with thyme, caramelised peaches and calvados (£9.95), lamb rosettes with brandy and mint sauce, cranberry and apricot compote (£10.25), and daily specials such as poached egg florentine (£4.25), giant tiger prawns with coriander butter (£6.95), locally made speciality sausage (duck and hoisin, wild boar, lamb and mint, £7.25), venison stew with red wine and bubble and squeak (£9.95), chargrilled butterfish with lemon cream sauce (£9.50), and braised shank of lamb with rosemary and red wine (£10.25); children's menu (£3.75). Well kept Cheriton Pots Ale, Greene King IPA and a couple of guests such as Bass or Flowers Original on handpump, and a decent wine list; cribbage, dominoes, piped music, and pétanque. Particularly in good weather, this is a fine place for families as they have a children's play area, a weekend bouncy castle, a pets corner, an aviary, and a summer marquee; both garden areas have fine views – one side looks right across the Solent to the Isle of Wight, the other gives a view down to Winchester. Lots of good surrounding walks. *(Recommended by R J Walden, Dennis Jenkin, P Price, John Fahy, Val and Alan Green, Lynn Sharpless, Bob Eardley, Michael and Robin Inskip, Dave Braisted, Alan and Paula McCully, Phyl and Jack Street, David Robson, Mrs S Cripps)*

Greene King ~ Lease Clive Mansell and Alison Carter ~ Real ale ~ Bar food (all day Sun) ~ (01962) 777358 ~ Children welcome ~ Occasional jazz ~ Open 11-3, 6-11; 11-11 Sat; 12-10.30 Sun; 11-3, 6-11 Sat in winter; closed winter Mon lunchtimes

PETERSFIELD SU7227 Map 2

Trooper ◀

From B2070 in Petersfield follow Steep signposts past station, but keep on up past Steep, on old coach road; OS Sheet 186 map reference 726273

You can be sure of a friendly welcome from the courteous and attentive licensee in this interesting pub, and this year he has opened up eight bedrooms (we'd expect this to be a nice place to stay, and look forward to reports from readers on that aspect). There's an island bar, tall stools by a broad edge facing big windows that look across to rolling downland fields, blond wheelback and kitchen chairs and a mix of tripod tables on the bare boarded or red tiled floor, little Persian knick-knacks here and there, quite a few ogival mirrors, big baskets of dried flowers, lit candles all around, fresh flowers, logs burning in the stone fireplace, and good piped music; newspapers and magazines to read. Most people do come to enjoy the good food, which might include soup with herby croutons (£3.50), garlic mushroom and prawn gratin (£4.95), grilled goats cheese and beef tomato on mixed leaves or bacon and avocado caesar salad (£5.95), mixed bean korma (£8.95), braised beef with dates and onions in a rich ale gravy (£9.95), their special slow roasted half shoulder of lamb with a rich honey and mint gravy (£10.95), breast of duck with orange and Grand Marnier sauce (£11.95), steaks (from £12.95), and fillet of cod with king prawns and lobster sauce (£14.95). The raftered restaurant is most attractive. Well kept Hook Norton Old Hooky, Ringwood Best, Timothy Taylors Landlord, and a guest such as Ballards on handpump, and decent house wines. There are lots of picnic-sets on an upper lawn and more on the partly covered sunken terrace which has french windows to the dining area. The horse rail in the car park ('horses only before 8pm') does get used. *(Recommended by Simon Collett-Jones, Steve McCathie, Wendy Arnold, Ann and Colin Hunt, Lynn Sharpless, Bob Eardley, Phyl and Jack Street)*

Free house ~ Licensee Hassan Matini ~ Real ale ~ Bar food ~ Restaurant ~ (01730) 827293 ~ Children welcome ~ Open 11-3, 6-11; 12-3 Sun; closed Sun evening, Mon ~ Bedrooms: £55B/£65B

WHITE HORSE ★ ◀

Priors Dean – but don't follow Priors Dean signposts: simplest route is from Petersfield, leaving centre on A272 towards Winchester, take right turn at roundabout after level crossing, towards Steep, and keep on for 4 miles or so, up on to the downs, passing another pub on your right (and not turning off into Steep there); at last, at crossroads signposted East Tisted/Privett, turn right towards East Tisted, then almost at once turn right on to second gravel track (the first just goes into a field); there's no inn sign; alternatively, from A32 5 miles S of Alton, take road by bus lay-by signposted Steep, then, after 1¾ miles, turn off as above – though obviously left this time – at East Tisted/Privett crossroads; OS Sheet 197 coming from Petersfield (Sheet 186 is better the other way), map reference 715290; the Pub With No Name (as most of its regulars know it – there's no inn sign)

It's the lovely relaxed atmosphere that readers enjoy so much at this fine old farmhouse. The two charming and idiosyncratic parlour rooms (candlelit at night) have open fires, various old pictures, farm tools, drop-leaf tables, oak settles, rugs, stuffed antelope heads, a longcase clock, and a couple of fireside rocking-chairs, and so forth; there's an attractive no smoking dining room with a big open fire. Up to 9 real ales on handpump (including the very strong and popular No Name Bitter), as well as Bass, Ballards Best, Bass, Fullers London Pride, Gales Butser, GB, and HSB, Ringwood Fortyniner, and a couple of guests. Dominoes, cribbage, chess, cards, and Jenga. Decent bar food includes home-made soup (£3.25), filled baked potatoes (from £3.95), sandwiches (from £3.50), ploughman's (£4.65), vegetarian dishes (from £5.95), steak and kidney pie (£6.95), steaks (from £8.95), and puddings like home-made bread and butter pudding (from £3.25). Rustic seats (which include chunks of tree-trunk) and a terrace outside; as this is one of the highest spots in the county it can be quite breezy; boules. If trying to find it for the first time, keep your eyes skinned – not for nothing is this known as the Pub With No Name – though there are now boards as you approach. Dogs are welcome. *(Recommended by Lynn Sharpless, Bob Eardley, Ann and Colin Hunt, Peter Meister, John Davis, Martin and Karen Wake, the Didler, Helen Sandelands, Charles and Pauline Stride, Paul S McPherson, Irene and Derek Flewin, JP, PP, Brian and Anna Marsden, Pat and Tony Martin, Giles Francis)*

Gales ~ Manager Janet Egerton-Williams ~ Real ale ~ Bar food (not Sun evening) ~ Restaurant ~ (01420) 588387 ~ Children in restaurant ~ Open 11-2.30, 6-11; 12-3, 7-10.30 Sun

PILLEY SZ3298 Map 2
Fleur de Lys
Village signposted off A337 Brockenhurst—Lymington

Originally, this old thatched place was a pair of foresters' cottages, and was established as an inn in 1096 – not surprisingly, this makes it the oldest pub in the New Forest. The lounge bar has heavy low beams, a collection of brass and copper ornaments, a huge inglenook log fire, and a handwritten list of landlords that goes back to 1498; the main bar and family room are no smoking. Generous helpings of good bar food include sandwiches, chips topped with garlic and cheese (£2.20), home-made soup (£3.25), ham and eggs (£5.50), local mixed game sausages, steak, kidney and mushroom pie, stuffed peppers or home-made fish pie (£7.95), rib of british beef or mediterranean fish stew (£8.95), salmon steak (£9.95). Well kept Flowers Original, Gales HSB, and Ringwood Best on handpump, decent wines, and country wines; friendly service. Piped music, fruit machine, cribbage, and dominoes. There are seats in the garden, a children's play area, and fine forest and heathland walks nearby. *(Recommended by Gavin May, John Davis, George Atkinson)*

Whitbreads ~ Lease Neil Rogers ~ Real ale ~ Bar food ~ (01590) 672158 ~ Children in family room ~ Open 11-2.30, 6-11; 12-3, 7-10.30 Sun; closed evenings 25 and 26 Dec ~ Bedrooms: /£50B

ROTHERWICK SU7156 Map 2
Coach & Horses 🔖
4 miles from M3 junction 5; follow Newnham signpost from exit roundabout, then Rotherwick signpost, then turn right at Mattingley, Heckfield signpost; village also signposted from B3349 N of Hook

In summer the hanging baskets and tubs here are especially pretty, and there are seats in the back garden. But there are plenty of customers in winter too, all keen to enjoy the warmly friendly welcome and roaring fire in the stripped brick fireplace. There are newspapers to read, oak chairs and other interesting furniture, and attractive pictures; one of the two small beamed front rooms is tiled, the other flagstoned. Enjoyable bar food at lunchtime includes sandwiches, freshly battered cod or a vegetarian dish (£6.95), home-made steak and kidney pudding (£7.45), and creamy chicken curry (£8.95), with evening choices such as soup (£2.95), duck and orange pâté (£3.95), garlic and chilli prawns (£4.95), escalope of pork with a creamy calvados sauce and garnished with spiced apple (£9.75), mignons of lamb with redcurrant, rosemary and thyme (£9.95), gressingham duck breast with an orange and redcurrant glaze (£11.65), and steaks (from £11.95). The eating areas are no smoking. Up to 8 well kept real ales on handpump at the servery in the parquet-floored inner area include Badger Best, IPA, Golden Champion, Tanglefoot, and K&B Sussex, and a couple of guests like Gribble Inn Fursty Ferret and Plucking Pheasant. The back garden has seats and pretty summer tubs and hanging baskets. *(Recommended by Simon Chell, Paul Vickers, Lynn Sharpless, Bob Eardley, Rod Hart, Julie and William H Ryan, KC, Nick and Meriel Cox, Richard and Margaret Peers, Margaret Ross, Susan and John Douglas, Ian Phillips, Martin and Karen Wake, Gordon Stevenson, Karen and Graham Oddey, Nick Corbett)*

Badger ~ Manager Mike Tyler ~ Real ale ~ Bar food (12-2.30, 6.30-9) ~ Restaurant ~ (01256) 762542 ~ Children in eating area of bar and restaurant ~ Open 11-11; 12-10.30 Sun

SOUTHSEA SZ6498 Map 2
Wine Vaults ◀

Albert Road, opposite Kings Theatre

This is a proper basic pub and a real ale drinker's haven. They keep up to a dozen beers on handpump, and have a double happy hour on any night from Monday to Thursday between 5.30 and 7.30 when the beers are cheaper (in fact on Monday it's £1.25 all night). If you arrive before 5.30 and are coming to eat, you get a free drink. There might be well kept Bass, Fullers London Pride, Greene King Ruddles County and Best, Hop Back Summer Lightning, Crop Circle and GFB, Itchen Valley Fagins, Marstons Pedigree, Ringwood Old Thumper and Fortyniner, and a beer named for the pub, Offyatrolli. The busy straightforward bar has wood-panelled walls, a wooden floor, and an easy-going, chatty feel; the raised back area is no smoking; pool, piped music, dominoes, chess, draughts, and backgammon. Bar food is good value and served in decent sized helpings, with sandwiches (from £1.95; not Sunday), filled baked potatoes (from £2.60), ploughman's (from £3.75), specials such as beef in ale casserole or spinach lasagne (£5.25), chicken and parmesan pasta bake or pork fajitas (£5.50), and avocado and brie salad (£5.75); friendly staff. Dogs are welcome. There are seats in the little garden, and a wooden gazebo. *(Recommended by Ann and Colin Hunt, Jason Caulkin, Phyl and Jack Street, A and J Evans, Howard James, Andy and Jill Kassube)*

Free house ~ Licensees Mike Hughes and J Stevens ~ Real ale ~ Bar food (12-9.30; not 25 Dec, 1 Jan) ~ (023) 9286 4712 ~ Children allowed away from bar but under 5s in upstairs pool room ~ Open 12-11; 12-10.30 Sun; closed 1 Jan

SPARSHOLT SU4331 Map 2
Plough ⅋ ♀

Village signposted off A272 a little W of Winchester

The popular food at this busy country dining pub is so good that we have given them a Food Award this year. It's all neatly kept, with friendly staff, and the main bar has a bustling atmosphere, an interesting mix of wooden tables and chairs, with farm tools, scythes and pitchforks attached to the ceiling; one area is no smoking. From quite a choice, the bar includes lunchtime sandwiches, baguettes such as prawn, tomato and chive mayonnaise (£5.75), marinated salmon salad with crusty bread (£8.50), chicken breast in lime and coriander with tomato and red onion salsa (£8.95), and tossed salad with strips of beef fillet in an oriental dressing (£9.50); also, three bean and vegetable casserole with pesto croûtes (£6.95), tagliatelle with mushrooms, rosemary and cream (£7.95), baised ham with celeriac mash and roasted vegetables (£8.50), roasted pork tenderloin wrapped in smoked bacon with apricot and ginger sauce (£11.95), and whole red snapper with shallots on a bed of roasted tomatoes (£13.95). To be sure of a table you must book beforehand. Well kept Wadworths IPA, 6X, Farmers Glory, and a seasonal guest on handpump, and an extensive wine list. There's a children's play fort, and plenty of seats on the terrace and lawn. *(Recommended by Mrs Rita Cox, Lynn Sharpless, Bob Eardley, R J Walden, Julian McCarthy, John and Joan Calvert, Phyl and Jack Street, Val and Alan Green, Hugh Roberts, John Wheeler)*

Wadworths ~ Tenants R C and K J Crawford ~ Real ale ~ Bar food (12-2, 6-9(9.30 Fri/Sat)) ~ (01962) 776353 ~ Children in eating area of bar ~ Murder mystery evenings March and Oct; Jazz 1st Sun in August ~ Open 11-3, 6-11; 12-3, 6-10.30 Sun; closed 25 Dec

STEEP SU7425 Map 2

Harrow

Take Midhurst exit from Petersfield bypass, at exit roundabout first left towards Midhurst, then first turning on left opposite garage, and left again at Sheet church; follow over dual carriageway bridge to pub

Unchanging and unspoilt, this country local has been run by the same family for 70 years. It's a charming place in an old-fashioned way and remains a favourite with its many customers. The cosy public bar has hops and dried flowers hanging from the beams, built-in wall benches on the tiled floor, stripped pine wallboards, a good log fire in the big inglenook, and maybe wild flowers on the scrubbed deal tables (and on the tables outside); dominoes and shove-ha'penny. Generous helpings of enjoyable home-made bar food include sandwiches, home-made scotch eggs (£2.80), wonderful, generous soups such as ham, split pea and vegetable (£3.70), huge ploughman's (from £4.70), home-made quiches (£7), and puddings such as delicious treacle tart or seasonal fruit pies (£3.50). Well kept Ballards Trotton Bitter and Best Bitter, Cheriton Diggers Gold, Pots or Village Elder, and Ringwood Best tapped from casks behind the counter, and local wine; polite and friendly staff, even when under pressure. The big garden is left free-flowering so that goldfinches can collect thistle seeds from the grass. The Petersfield bypass doesn't intrude on this idyll, though you will need to follow the directions above to find it. No children inside. *(Recommended by Keith and Katy Stevens, Ann and Colin Hunt, Tracey and Stephen Groves, Lynn Sharpless, Bob Eardley, Charles and Pauline Stride, the Didler, JP, PP, J Hale, Peter Meister, Irene and Derek Flewin, John Davis)*

Free house ~ Licensee Ellen McCutcheon ~ Real ale ~ Bar food (limited Sun evenings (not during winter)) ~ No credit cards ~ (01730) 262685 ~ Open 12-2.30, 6-11; 11-3, 6-11 Sat; 12-3, 7-10.30 Sun; closed winter Sun evenings

TICHBORNE SU5630 Map 2

Tichborne Arms

Village signed off B3047

There are pictures and documents on the walls in this neat thatched pub recalling the bizarre Tichborne Case (a mystery man from Australia claimed fraudulently to be the heir to this estate). The comfortable square-panelled room on the right has wheelback chairs and settles (one very long), a log fire in the stone fireplace, and latticed windows. On the left, there's a larger, livelier, partly panelled room used for eating. Bar food includes sandwiches (from £3.50), chicken, tarragon and mushroom pie (£7.25), steak and stilton in ale pie (£7.50), and crab salad (£9.50). Well kept Ringwood Best and Wadworths 6X with guests like Otter Ale, Ringwood True Glory, Robinsons, and Wells Bombardier tapped from the cask, country wines, and farm cider; sensibly placed darts, shove-ha'penny, cribbage, dominoes, and piped music; light-hearted Sunday evening quiz. There are picnic-sets outside in the big well kept garden, and plenty of surrounding walks. No children inside. *(Recommended by Lynn Sharpless, Bob Eardley, Ian Phillips, Danny Nicol, Geoff Palmer, Dr M E Wilson, the Didler, Ann and Colin Hunt, Mick Simmons, Phyl and Jack Street)*

Free house ~ Licensees Keith and Janie Day ~ Real ale ~ Bar food (12-1.45, 6.30-9.45; not 25 or 26 Dec) ~ (01962) 733 760 ~ Open 11.30-2.30, 6-11; 12-3, 7-10.30 Sun; closed evenings 25 and 26 Dec and evening 1 Jan

UPHAM SU5320 Map 2

Brushmakers Arms

Shoe Lane; village signposted from Winchester—Bishops Waltham downs road, and from B2177 (former A333)

No matter how busy this attractive old village pub is, the friendly licensee and his obliging staff always offer a warm welcome to all. The comfortable L-shaped bar is divided into two by a central brick chimney with a woodburning stove in the raised two-way fireplace, and there are comfortably cushioned wall settles and chairs, a variety of tables including some in country-style stripped wood, a few beams in the low ceiling, quite a collection of ethnic-looking brushes, and a crowd of chatty locals; also, a small snug. Well kept Bass, Ringwood Best, Wells Bombardier, and a beer named for the pub on handpump, decent wines by the glass, Addlestone's cider, and country wines. Generous helpings of enjoyable bar food include lunchtime snacks such as sandwiches (£3.75; filled hot croissants £4.25), filled baked potatoes or ploughman's (from £4.25), ham and egg (£5.25), and daily specials, as well as creamy vegetarian pasta, liver and bacon casserole, lasagne or chicken curry (all £5.95), mushroom and nut en croûte (£6.95), steak and kidney pudding or partridge with bacon and stilton (£7.95), salmon fillet with mustard and chive butter (£8.50), steaks (from £8.95), half leg of lamb in garlic and rosemary (£10.95), and home-made puddings (£3.50). Sensibly placed darts, dominoes, and fruit machine. The big garden is well stocked with mature shrubs and trees, and there are picnic-sets on a sheltered back terrace among lots of tubs of flowers, with more on the tidy tree-sheltered lawn. Good walks nearby. *(Recommended by Jenny Cridland, Gordon Cooper, Alan and Paula McCully, Lynn Sharpless, Bob Eardley, John and Joan Nash, Ann and Colin Hunt, R J Walden, John Davis, Val and Alan Green, P R and S A White)*

Free house ~ Licensee Tony Mottram ~ Real ale ~ Bar food ~ (01489) 860231 ~ Children in eating area of bar ~ Open 11-2.30(3 Sat), 5.30-11; 12-3.30, 7-10.30 Sun

WHERWELL SU3839 Map 2
Mayfly

Testcombe (i.e. not in Wherwell itself); A3057 SE of Andover, between B3420 turn-off and Leckford where road crosses River Test; OS Sheet 185 map reference 382390

To make the best of this busy pub, get here early to bag one of the tables beside the River Test and watch the swans, ducks and maybe plump trout, with a drink. Inside, the spacious, beamed and carpeted bar has fishing pictures and bric-a-brac on the cream walls above its dark wood dado, straightforward pub furnishings, two woodburning stoves, and bow windows overlooking the water; there's also a no smoking conservatory. Bar food comes from a buffet-style servery, and there are usually queues: home-made quiche (£4.90), a choice of cold meats (from £4.95), pies and casseroles, and chicken madras (£7.50); salads are an extra 80p a spoonful which can bump up prices a bit. Well kept Flowers Original, and Ringwood Best and Old Thumper on handpump, and country wines; fruit machine and piped music. *(Recommended by Charlie Harris, Pat and Robert Watt, J Hale, Betsy and Peter Little, Richard and Liz Dilnot, Alan and Ros Furley, Dr M E Wilson)*

Whitbreads ~ Managers Barry and Julie Lane ~ Real ale ~ Bar food (11.30-9.30) ~ (01264) 860283 ~ Children welcome ~ Open 10-11; 12-10.30 Sun

White Lion

B3420, in village itself

Before or after a visit to this friendly pub, it's worth strolling through the village, and there's a nice walk over the River Test and meadows to Chilbolton. The multi-level beamed bar has delft plates, sparkling brass, and fresh flowers, and well kept Adnams Best, Flowers Original, and Ringwood Best on handpump; the Village bar has an open fire, and there are two dining rooms – the lower one is no smoking. Good bar food includes lunchtime sandwiches and toasties (from £2.60) and baked potatoes (from £5), as well as ploughman's (£5), local sausages (£6), local mushrooms topped with tomatoes, herbs and onions (£6.25), and daily specials such as steak and mushroom pie or sweet and sour pork (£6.90), spinach and red pepper lasagne or giant haddock (£7), salmon and dill lasagne (£7.25), stuffed lemon sole (£7.45), rib-eye steak with pepper sauce (£8.80), duck with black cherry sauce (£9.25), and puddings (£3.20); Sunday roasts (worth booking for these). The two friendly black labradors are called Sam and Guinness; piped music. There are plenty of seats in the courtyard and on the terrace, and they hope to thatch the barn soon. More reports please. *(Recommended by Ann and Colin Hunt, John Davis, Lynn Sharpless, Bob Eardley, R Halsey, Brian Root, GLD)*

Inn Partnership (Nomura) ~ Lease Adrian and Patsy Stent ~ Real ale ~ Bar food (not 25 Dec) ~ (01264) 860317 ~ Well behaved children in restaurant ~ Folk 1st and 3rd Thurs of month ~ Open 10-2.30(3 Sat), 6(7 Mon/Tues)-11; 12-3, 7-10.30 Sun ~ Bedrooms: £32.50/£45

WHITSBURY SU1219 Map 2
Cartwheel ◀

Follow Rockbourne sign off A354 SW of Salisbury, turning left just before Rockbourne itself; or head W off A338 at S end of Breamore, or in Upper Burgate – we got mildly lost trying to find it direct from Fordingbridge!

Even though this cheerful local is rather out of the way, there are always plenty of customers – both locals and visitors. It's opened up inside, with pitched high rafters in one part, lower beams elsewhere, antlers, military prints, country pictures, what looks like a steam-engine's jockey wheel as a divider, and simple but comfortable cloth-cushioned wall seats and other chairs. There's a snug little room by the door, with a couple of tables either side of the fire; a small side room has darts, pool, fruit machine, dominoes, cribbage, Jenga, Scrabble, TV, and piped music. Generous food includes good sandwiches, roasted peppers filled with mushroom risotto (£5.95), fish pie, tuna steak with herb and caper butter or yorkshire pudding filled with roast beef and horseradish gravy (£6.25), and Tuesday home-cooked fish and chips which you can eat here or take away. Adnams Broadside, Bass, and Ringwood Best, with a couple of guests such as Shepherd Neame Spitfire or Wychwood Hobgoblin on handpump, in top condition, ciders, and maybe beer festivals around the second week in August; efficient service. The garden, sheltered by a shrubby steep slope, has weekly summer barbecues and a particularly good play area that children really enjoy. It's good walking country and dogs seem welcome. *(Recommended by Mr and Mrs Thomas, Lynn Sharpless, Bob Eardley, Dr D E Granger, Peter and Audrey Dowsett)*

Free house ~ Licensee Patrick James Lewis ~ Real ale ~ Bar food (not winter Mon evening) ~ (01725) 518362 ~ Children in eating area of bar and restaurant ~ Singing duo Fri evening every two months ~ Open 11-2.30(3 Sat), 6-11; 12-3, 7-10.30 Sun

WINCHESTER SU4829 Map 2
Wykeham Arms ★ 🍴 ♗ 🛏

75 Kingsgate Street (Kingsgate Arch and College Street are now closed to traffic; there is access via Canon Street)

Although new licensees have taken over this rather civilised but friendly inn, readers are quick to tell us that things are as good as ever. It remains an extremely popular place with a fine choice of drinks and food, and is a super place to stay. A series of stylish bustling rooms radiating from the central bar has 19th-c oak desks retired from nearby Winchester College, a redundant pew from the same source, kitchen chairs and candlelit deal tables and big windows with swagged paisley curtains; all sorts of interesting collections are dotted around. A snug room at the back, known as the Watchmakers, is decorated with a set of Ronald Searle 'Winespeak' prints, a second one is panelled, and all of them have a log fire; several areas are no smoking. Served by neatly uniformed, efficient staff, the very good food at lunchtime might include sandwiches (from £3; pork sausage with onion marmalade £3.95), home-made soup such as butternut squash (£3.25), cheese terrine (£5.25), vegetable lasagne (£5.50), haddock kedgeree (£5.75), lamb casserole (£6.25), thai chicken (£6.50), cassoulet (£6.75), and steaks (from £12.50), with evening dishes like salmon and dill terrine (£4.75), warm pigeon and bacon salad with grain mustard dressing (£5.25), garlic, wild mushroom and roasted pepper risotto with parmesan (£9.95), grilled fillets of red mullet marinated with chilli and garlic, served on warm couscous salad with red pepper coulis (£12.50), duck breast with bacon and a creamy wild mushroom sauce (£12.75), roast rack of Hampshire down lamb with garlic and rosemary-roasted vegetables and a port and redcurrant jus (£13.75), and puddings such as chocolate nemesis, raspberry and Benedictine bavarois or pecan pie (£4.50).

There's a fine choice of 20 wines by the glass (including sweet wines), and quite a few brandies, armagnacs and liqueurs. Also, well kept Bass, and Gales Bitter, Best, and HSB on handpump. There are tables on a covered back terrace, with more on a small but sheltered lawn. The lovely bedrooms in the pub are thoughtfully equipped, and the Saint George, a 16th-c annexe directly across the street (and overlooking Winchester College Chapel) has more bedrooms, a sitting room with open fire, a post office/general stores, and a Burgundian wine store; you can enjoy the good breakfasts either in your room there or at the pub. No children inside. *(Recommended by the Didler, Lynn Sharpless, Bob Eardley, Phyl and Jack Street, David and Nina Pugsley, Ann and Colin Hunt, L A E James, Peter and Audrey Dowsett, Gordon Prince, John Oates, Dr Denise Walton, Sean and Sharon Pines, Betsy and Peter Little, Mr and Mrs A H Young, R Michael Richards, Dennis Jenkin, Steve Whalley, Ian and Nita Cooper, Mr and Mrs Capp, Tracey and Stephen Groves, Alan and Paula McCully, David Peakall, P R and S A White, John Evans, G T Brewster; also in The Good Hotel Guide)*

Gales ~ Managers Peter and Kate Miller ~ Real ale ~ Bar food (12-2.30, 6.30-8.45; not Sun) ~ Restaurant ~ (01962) 853834 ~ Open 11-11; 12-10.30 Sun; closed 25 Dec ~ Bedrooms: £45S(£69.50B)/£79.50B

WOODGREEN SU1717 Map 2

Horse & Groom

Off A338 N of Fordingbridge, signposted from Breamore

The drive through the New Forest to get to this shuttered brick and flint house is lovely, and there are picnic-sets out on a little fenced front terrace and in the neat, spreading sheltered back garden. Inside, the set of smallish beamed rooms – with local nature pictures – rambles around the central servery, and there are darts, fruit machine, and TV in the simple locals' bar on the left, a log fire in a nice Victorian fireplace on the right, and a comfortable eating area; piped music. Reasonably priced bar food includes home-made soup (£2.95), sandwiches (from £2.95), filled baked potatoes (from £3.75), ploughman's (£4.95), fish and chips (£5.75), pasta with melting brie or florentine potato gratin (£5.95), steak and kidney pudding (£6.35), daily curry (£6.75), rack of lamb (£8.45), steaks (from £10.25), and home-made puddings such as cherry crème brûlée, bread and butter pudding or profiteroles with chocolate and brandy sauce (£3.45). Well kept Badger Best, IPA, Tanglefoot and Golden Champion, and a guest such as Ringwood Best on handpump; courteous, friendly service. *(Recommended by Dr D E Granger, Phyl and Jack Street, Lyn and Geoff Hallchurch, Ian Phillips, Lynn Sharpless, Bob Eardley, R J Walden, Klaus and Elizabeth Leist)*

Badger ~ Manager Colin Barter ~ Real ale ~ Bar food ~ Restaurant ~ (01725) 510739 ~ Children in eating area of bar and restaurant ~ Open 11-3, 6-11; 12-3, 7-10.30 Sun

---

Lucky Dip

Besides the fully inspected pubs, you might like to try these Lucky Dips recommended to us and described by readers (if you do, please send us reports: www.goodguides.com).

Alresford [SU5832]
Bell [West St]: Relaxing Georgian coaching inn with extended bar, smallish dining room, quickly served good value straightforward food inc children's helpings, well kept beers, friendly service, daily papers, log fire; attractive back courtyard, comfortably redone bedrooms *(Hazel and Michael Duncombe, Ann and Colin Hunt)*
Cricketers [Jacklyns Lane]: Large pub, cottagey eating area with good value straightforward food inc locally popular bargain wkdy lunches, well kept Flowers Original, friendly service, garden with play area *(Dr C S Shaw)*
Horse & Groom [Broad St; town signed off A31 bypass]: Open-plan carpeted bar with

beams, timbers and white-painted brickwork, nice bow window seats, well kept ales such as Bass, Fullers London Pride and Wadworths 6X, good choice of wines by the glass, enjoyable reasonably priced food inc good puddings, attentive service, back restaurant area (can get busy); piped music, occasional live, popular with a young crowd; children welcome, open all day Fri/Sat *(Lynn Sharpless, Bob Eardley, Hazel and Michael Duncombe, LYM)*
Ampfield [SU4023]
White Horse [A31 Winchester—Romsey]: Vastly extended open-plan Whitbreads dining pub, period-effect furniture, interesting décor, log fire, well kept ales (but served through sparkler) inc Ringwood, good choice of wines

by the glass, attentive service, Victorian prints and advertising posters in dining room; pub backs on to golf course and village cricket green; handy for Hillier arboretum, good walks in Ampfield Woods *(Lynn Sharpless, Bob Eardley, Phyl and Jack Street)*

Ashmansworth [SU4157]

Plough: Friendly no-frills pub in attractive village, Hampshire's highest; two quarry-tiled rooms knocked together, well kept Archers Village, Best and Golden and changing guest tapped from the cask, simple home-cooked food with good attentive service, log fire, no piped music; seats outside, good walks, handy for Highclere Castle *(the Didler, B Blaine)*

Axford [SU6043]

✩ *Crown* [Farleigh Rd (B3046)]: Busy smartish pub under new ownership, prints above dark panelling, good value generous food, well kept ales such as fff, Fullers London Pride and Greene King Abbot, good house wines, friendly prompt service, open fires, separate dining area; juke box in public bar; seats in pleasant garden with terrace, popular with walkers *(Lynn Sharpless, Bob Eardley, John and Vivienne Rice, Andy and Jill Kassube, Phyl and Jack Street)*

Battramsley [SZ3099]

✩ *Hobler* [A337 S of Brockenhurst]: Quirkily enjoyable bustling heavy-beamed pub with nice well used mix of furniture, lots of books and rustic bric-a-brac, matey atmosphere and friendly staff, good food from splendid bacon butties to bass, scallops and sizzle-your-own steaks, well kept Flowers Original, Wadworths 6X and a guest such as Gales HSB, dozens of malt whiskies and country wines, traditional games; piped music; spacious lawn with summer bar, very good play area and livestock paddock, good Forest walks; no children or mobile phones inside, jazz Tues, blues 2nd Thurs *(A D Marsh, Chris and Anna Rowley, David and Nina Pugsley, Dr and Mrs A K Clarke, LYM)*

Beaulieu [SU3902]

✩ *Montagu Arms* [almost opp Palace House]: Civilised hotel in attractive surroundings; separate more basic Montys bar/eaterie, open all day, with decent food, well kept Greene King and Ringwood Fortyniner, good wines, lots of malt whiskies; may be piped music; children welcome, picnic-sets out on front courtyard, comfortable bedrooms, good spot for walks *(Gavin May, LYM)*

Bentley [SU8044]

Bull [A31 Alton—Farnham dual carriageway, not in village itself]: Has been civilised and welcoming low-beamed respite from the trunk road, open all day, but no reports since April 2001 takeover, with extensive refurbishment and plans to build up restaurant side; news please *(LYM)*

Bighton [SU6134]

Three Horseshoes [off B3046 in Alresford just N of pond; or off A31 in Bishops Sutton]: Quiet old-fashioned village local with simple bare-boards stripped-stone public bar, solid-fuel stove in huge fireplace, small lounge with log fire, model cars, lorries and other transport-related decorations, well kept Gales HSB, BBB and seasonal beers, lots of country wines, basic food (not Weds evening), darts; piped music; children welcome, good walks nearby; cl Mon winter lunchtime *(the Didler, Lynn Sharpless, Bob Eardley)*

Bishop's Sutton [SU6031]

✩ *Ship* [B3047, former A31 on Alton side of Alresford – now bypassed]: Pleasantly relaxed, with friendly hard-working licensees, good unusual food inc tempting puddings, changing ales such as Hampshire King Alfred and Ringwood Best and Porter kept well by the landlady, good choice of wines by the glass, daily papers and other things to read, attractive small back dining room; tables in garden with a couple of thatched parasols; well behaved dogs and children welcome; handy for Watercress Line, good walks *(Sheila and Robert Robinson, LYM, Lynn Sharpless, Bob Eardley, Phyl and Jack Street)*

Bishop's Waltham [SU5517]

Barleycorn [Lower Basingwell St]: Georgian, with pleasant mix of dark oak and cream, some panelling, well kept Greene King ales inc Ruddles Best, log fire, friendly people, games in public bar, separate dining room – good value simple home-made food inc two-for-one lunch bargains Mon and Weds, children's dishes and good vegetarian choice; garden *(Val and Alan Green, Ann and Colin Hunt)*

✩ *Bunch of Grapes* [St Peters St]: Unspoilt simple village local run by the same family for a century; well kept Ushers inc a seasonal beer tapped from the cask, good chatty landlord and friendly locals, plenty of character, quaintly furnished snug off main room *(Val and Alan Green, Phil and Sally Gorton, Ann and Colin Hunt)*

White Horse [Beeches Hill, off B3035 NE]: Long bar in converted cottages, unspoilt and friendly, well kept Bass and Ringwood Best and Fortyniner, reasonably priced fresh and imaginative food, long-serving landlord, log fire; nr Northbrook Vineyard *(Val and Alan Green, Ron Shelton)*

Braishfield [SU3725]

✩ *Newport* [Newport Lane]: Very basic two-bar local, unsmart and unspoilt – quite a time warp; popular with older people at lunchtime (younger people evenings) for simple good value food inc huge cheap sandwiches and good value ploughman's, particularly well kept Gales HSB, Best and Butser, country wines, decent milky coffee, down-to-earth long-serving licensees; piped music, wknd singsongs; good garden with geese, ducks and chickens *(the Didler, Lynn Sharpless, Bob Eardley)*

Brockenhurst [SU3002]

Snakecatcher [Lyndhurst Rd]: Thriving well run pub with some emphasis on good if not cheap food from sandwiches to steaks cooked to order (so may be a wait), good Sat fish specials and children's food, interesting split-level bar and restaurant areas inc cosy part with log fire and easy chairs, well kept Hardy ales, nice choice of wines by the glass, good service, candles at night; two gardens, good walks nearby *(M Joyner, David and Carole Chapman, Michael Buchanan)*

Broughton [SU3032]

☆ *Tally Ho* [High St, opp church; signed off A30 Stockbridge—Salisbury]: Open-plan local with a real welcome for visitors, big plain modern flagstoned bar with darts (they don't mind walking boots), comfortable clean and uncluttered hunting-print lounge, good value fresh home cooking and good sandwiches, homely fire in each room, entertaining landlord, well kept Badger and Ringwood Best and True Glory, decent wines in two glass sizes, friendly staff, no piped music; children welcome, tables in charming secluded back garden, good walks *(Phyl and Jack Street, Geoffrey G Lawrance, Mary Kirman and Tim Jefferson, Lynn Sharpless, Bob Eardley, Brian and Anna Marsden, Margaret Ross)*

Burley [SU2003]

Burley Inn [The Cross]: Recent conversion of mock-Tudor building in New Forest village, good inventive food in bar and restaurant, Wadworths real ales; bedrooms *(anon)*

☆ *White Buck* [Bisterne Close; ¾ mile E, OS Sheet 195 map ref 223028]: Huge well run bar in 19th-c mock-Tudor hotel in lovely New Forest setting, emphasis on wide choice of reasonably priced good generous food, Gales Butser, HSB and GB and Ringwood Best, decent wines and country wines, good coffee, log fire, civilised banquettes, courteous efficient staff (but service may slow with the wknd crowds), thriving atmosphere, smart and attractive added end dining room (should book – but no bookings Sun lunchtime); may be quiet piped music, dogs welcome despite the carpets, hitching posts, pleasant front terrace and spacious lawn; good value well equipped bedrooms, superb walks towards Burley itself and over Mill Lawn *(BB, Harvey and Bramley, Derek and Sylvia Stephenson, W W Burke, Phyl and Jack Street, John H Smith, John Arthur, John and Joan Calvert)*

Cadnam [SU3013]

Coach & Horses [Southampton Rd]: Popular for wide choice of usual food from baguettes and baked potatoes up with some more elaborate dishes, OAP discounts on food and drink, friendly helpful efficient staff *(A D Marsh)*

Compass [Winsor, off Totton—Cadnam road at Bartley crossroads; OS Sheet 195 map ref 317143]: Popular bare-boards local off the beaten track, plain food from good bacon doorsteps to curry or British beef nights (most tables may be booked), good range of real ales inc Greene King Old Speckled Hen, occasional beer festivals, log fire; small side garden, Irish bands Thurs *(Geoff Pidoux, Phyl and Jack Street)*

☆ *Sir John Barleycorn* [Old Romsey Rd; by M27, junction 1]: Low-slung thatched Whitbreads Wayside Inn, attractive medieval fish on left with dim lighting, low beams and timbers, more of a chain-pub feel in extended part on right, real ales inc a guest such as Castle Eden, reasonably

priced wines, big helpings of good value food, helpful efficient service, two log fires, no smoking restaurant end; can be very busy; suntrap benches in front, eye-catching flowers *(A D Marsh, LYM, Dr and Mrs A K Clarke)*

Chalton [SU7315]

☆ *Red Lion* [signed E of A3 Petersfield—Horndean]: Pretty timbered thatched pub, Hampshire's oldest, with high-backed settles, heavy beams, panelling and ancient inglenook fireplace in cosy original core, well kept Gales Butser, Best and HSB, good wines and a good choice of other drinks, attentive smiling service; popular if less interesting modern no smoking family dining extension (no food Sun evening), piped music; pretty garden with downs views, nr Queen Elizabeth Country Park and Iron Age show farm and settlement, good walk to quaint St Hubert's Chapel, Idsworth *(Phyl and Jack Street, Pat and Tony Martin, Susan and John Douglas, Ann and Colin Hunt, Tony and Wendy Hobden, Gareth Davies, Roy Grove, LYM)*

Charter Alley [SU5957]

White Hart [off A340 N of Basingstoke]: Friendly village local, woodburner and no smoking area in lounge bar, skittle alley in simple public bar, wide choice of reasonably priced food in dining area, Greene King Abbot, Morrells and a guest ale such as Ash Vine *(J V Dadswell)*

Chilbolton [SU3939]

☆ *Abbots Mitre* [off A3051 S of Andover]: Wide choice of good generous food inc very good value OAP special in side lounge and attractive restaurant with small log fire, well kept ales such as Boddingtons, Flowers Original, Greene King Abbot and Old Speckled Hen and Ringwood, quick smartly dressed staff, separate front public bar and games room; a bit dark, but friendly, busy and roomy; garden with pleasant covered terrace, baskets and tubs of flowers, play area; open all day Sun, attractive village, riverside walks *(Phyl and Jack Street, Michael and Robin Inskip)*

Chilworth [SU4118]

☆ *Clump* [A27 Romsey Rd]: Busy extended dining pub, several connecting rooms off large central bar, warm homely décor, nice fireplaces, bookshelves, sofas, no smoking dining area with rustic french feel, spacious conservatory; wide choice of decent reasonably priced food with french influences, well kept Greene King Abbot and Old Speckled Hen and Ringwood, good choice of wines, attentive friendly service; unobtrusive piped music; open all day, large garden with barbecue *(Phyl and Jack Street, Emma Kingdon)*

Clanfield [SD7117]

Hogs Lodge [Gravel Hill]: Large well furnished pub well run by ex-landlord of Blacksmiths Arms, Donnington, Sussex; good generous food in bar and restaurant, well kept Gales ales, nice big garden with nice views *(Keith and Katy Stevens)*

Clanville [SU3149]

Red Lion: Updated 16th-c pub with enterprising food in bar, long conservatory and

Victorian-style added evening bistro (not Sun-Tues; also Sun lunch), no smoking areas, well kept real ales as at Stonehenge, friendly service *(anon)*

Crondall [SU7948]

☆ *Hampshire Arms* [Pankridge St]: Popular new chef at this unpretentious welcoming local, nicely presented fresh food from good value well filled baguettes (not Sun; home-baked bread) to enjoyable main dishes cooked to order so may be a wait, wider evening choice; well kept Greene King Old Speckled Hen and Ruddles, good house wines, pleasant service, cosy beamed main bar with huge fireplace, faded red velvet curtains, exposed brickwork, brasses, small conservatory restaurant with fresh flowers, candles and linen napkins, plain public bar with traditional games; boules *(Martin and Karen Wake, Alan Cowell)*

Crookham [SU7952]

George & Lobster [Crondall Rd]: Spaciously refurbished open-plan pub renamed by welcoming young licensees, good well presented food popular lunchtime with business people, good range of beers, pleasant restaurant *(Mr and Mrs J Brown)*

Damerham [SU1016]

☆ *Compasses* [signed off B3078 in Fordingbridge; East End]: Neatly refurbished small lounge bar divided by log fire from pleasant dining room with booth seating (children allowed here), pale wood tables and kitchen chairs, good food from sandwiches up esp soups and shellfish, marvellous cheese choice, Hop Back Summer Lightning, Ringwood Best, Wadworths 6X, a beer brewed for the pub and an interesting guest beer such as Centurion Ghost, good choice of wines by the glass, over a hundred malt whiskies, separate locals' bar with pool and juke box; big pretty garden by quiet village's cricket ground, downland walks, well equipped bedrooms *(Phyl and Jack Street, Mike and Tricia Kemp, BB, Mrs Ann Rix, Mr and Mrs Thomas, Andrew Kemp)*

Denmead [SU6611]

Forest of Bere [Hambledon Rd (B2150)]: Ancient flint-built village local with small cosy front lounge, real ales such as Bass, Friary Meux Best, Fullers London Pride and Ringwood, good choice of reasonably priced food from sandwiches to full meals, nice welcome from friendly regulars, darts and pool in lively back bar *(Ian Phillips)*

Harvest Home [Southwick Rd, Bunkers Hill]: Friendly and popular country local with long bar, eating area off, well kept Gales, good value food; increasingly suburban, but handy for Creech Wood walks *(Val and Alan Green)*

Downton [SZ2793]

Royal Oak [A337]: Wide food choice in neat partly panelled family pub, half no smoking, with well kept Whitbreads-related ales, decent wines, jovial atmosphere, friendly landlady, quick service; unobtrusive piped music; huge well kept garden with good play area *(K Carr-Brion, Mrs C M Sawyer)*

Droxford [SU6018]

Bakers Arms [High St]: Welcoming and roomy

bar and dining areas, attractive old brick pillars, blazing log fire, food inc several Sun roasts, Badger Tanglefoot and Ringwood; conservatory, children welcome, small play area *(Peter and Audrey Dowsett)*

Dummer [SU5846]

Queen [½ mile from M3 junction 7; take Dummer slip road]: Very handy for motorway, with beams, lots of softly lit alcoves, log fire, queen and steeplechase prints, well kept Courage Best, Fullers London Pride and Greene King Old Speckled Hen, food in bar and no smoking service-charge restaurant (they may keep your credit card; children allowed in restaurant); fruit machine, well reproduced piped music, no mobile phones; picnic-sets under cocktail parasols on terrace and in extended back garden *(KC, LYM, Ian Phillips, Malcolm Taylor, Tina and David Woods-Taylor, B N F and M Parkin, Simon Collett-Jones, Richard and Liz Dilnot)*

Dunbridge [SU3126]

Mill Arms [Barley Hill]: Friendly and cosily unpretentious, open-plan bars with stripped pine beams, sofas, open fire, conservatory restaurant, well presented food, real ales inc two brewed for the pub by Hampshire and Itchen Valley, late Sept beer festival, refurbished skittle alley; tables in pleasant two-level garden with wendy house, bedrooms *(Diana Brumfit, Phyl and Jack Street, Richard Houghton, Ann and Colin Hunt)*

Dundridge [SU5718]

☆ *Hampshire Bowman* [off B3035 towards Droxford, Swanmore, then right at Bishops W signpost]: Friendly and cosy though not smart, with great atmosphere and mix of customers (children, dogs and walkers welcome, usually some classic cars or vintage motorcycles); well kept Archers Village and Golden, Badger K & B Festive and Ringwood Best and Fortyniner tapped from the cask, decent house wines, country wines, home-made food inc quite a few vegetarian dishes (and Sun bar nibbles), sensible prices, efficient staff, battered corner armchair for non-smokers, gentle lurcher/collie cross; tables on spacious and attractive lawn, good downland walks *(Lynn Sharpless, Bob Eardley, Val and Alan Green, LYM, Ann and Colin Hunt)*

Durley [SU5116]

Farmers Home [Heathen St/Curdridge rd]: Good choice of popular food inc fresh fish and children's, big new restaurant area with seats in bays, well kept Bass, Boddingtons, Flowers Original and Ringwood Best, decent wine, log fire in pleasant small bar; may be piped radio; children welcome, big garden with good play area and pets corner, nice walks *(Phyl and Jack Street, Mr and Mrs A Craig, John and Joan Calvert)*

Robin Hood [Durley Street, just off B2177 Bishops Waltham—Winchester]: Well worn in two-room pub, far from smart but friendly, with surprisingly ambitious food, log fire, good cheerful service, Greene King ales, reasonably priced wines; darts and quiz evenings; back terrace and big pleasant garden with fine view and play area, good walks *(Val and Alan Green)*

East Boldre [SU3700]

☆ *Turf Cutters Arms* [Main Rd]: Relaxed and friendly dim-lit New Forest country local, lots of beams and pictures, elderly furnishings, two log fires, good freshly cooked food, Flowers Original, Wadworths 6X and a guest such as Gales HSB, several dozen malt whiskies; tables in garden, some good heathland walks; three big old-fashioned bedrooms, simple but comfortable *(Mr and Mrs L H Latimer, Phyl and Jack Street)*

East Meon [SU6822]

☆ *George* [Church St; signed off A272 W of Petersfield, and off A32 in West Meon]: Rambling and relaxing country pub doing well after refurbishment, heavy beams and inglenooks, four log fires, cosy areas around central bar counter, deal tables and horse tack; well kept Badger Best and Tanglefoot and a guest beer, decent wines, country wines, wide choice of substantial straightforward food, smart but friendly service; children welcome, good outdoor seating arrangements, quiz night Sun; small but comfortable bedrooms, good breakfast; pretty village with fine church, good walks *(Ann and Colin Hunt, LYM, Paul Evans, Susan and John Douglas, Danny Nicol, Brian and Anna Marsden)*

East Stratton [SU5339]

Northbrook Arms: Chatty flagstoned bar thoughtfully opened up, with well kept Gales, Ringwood and Otter, friendly licensees, reasonably priced generous food, kitchen tables, small side eating area, larger restaurant; picnic-sets on green opposite, idyllic setting, pretty thatched cottages; three bedrooms *(Lynn Sharpless, Bob Eardley, John and Kay Collman, Phyl and Jack Street)*

Easton [SU5132]

☆ *Chestnut Horse*: Comfortable upmarket rambling beamed dining pub dating from 16th c, friendly newish licensees doing good generous creative food (not cheap, and cooked to order so may be a wait), also Sun brunch from 10am, Bass, Courage Best, Itchen Valley and a beer brewed locally for the pub, decent but pricy wines, thriving atmosphere, efficient young staff, glowing log fire, pleasant dining room; small terrace with colourful flowers, lovely sleepy village, Itchen valley walks *(Cynthia and Stephen Fisher, Prof H G Allen, Phyl and Jack Street, Lynn Sharpless, Bob Eardley, Ron Shelton, Sheila and Robert Robinson, Des and June Preston)*

☆ *Cricketers* [off B3047]: Open-plan village local with well kept ales such as Bass, Becketts Amber, Itchen Valley Fagins, Otter and Ringwood Best, wide choice of good interesting piping hot food served promptly, enterprising hands-on newish landlord, friendly attentive service, small bright restaurant, good wine range; darts and shove-ha'penny one end, jazz duo Weds *(Lynn Sharpless, Bob Eardley, Mr and Mrs R W Allan, Ron Shelton)*

Ellisfield [SU6345]

Fox [Green Lane, Upper Common]: Village pub

with enthusiastic new licensees concentrating increasingly on food in main lounge bar with nicely laid tables and fresh flowers; one or two real ales, separate locals' bar, open fire, daily papers; pleasant garden, good walks (esp Bedlam Bottom to the W, lovely in spring) *(Phyl and Jack Street)*

Emery Down [SU2808]

☆ *New Forest* [village signed off A35 just W of Lyndhurst]: Good position in one of the nicest parts of the Forest, with good walks nearby; attractive softly lit separate areas on varying levels, each with its own character, nice pictures, two log fires, good reasonably priced food from generous filled baps up, well kept Flowers Original, Fullers London Pride, Greene King Old Speckled Hen and two Ringwood beers, wide choice of house wines, proper coffee, staff cope well with lively bustle; children allowed, small but pleasant three-level garden *(B and K Hyper, Dick and Madeleine Brown, LYM, Phyl and Jack Street, WHBM)*

Emsworth [SU7406]

Coal Exchange [Ships Quay, South St]: Compact comfortable Victorian local, cheerful service, good lunchtime food inc popular Sun lunch (open all day then), real fire each end, well kept Gales and a guest beer *(John Davis, Mr and Mrs T A Bryan, Ann and Colin Hunt)*

Lord Raglan [Queen St]: Welcoming and relaxing little Gales pub with long-serving landlord, log fire, good range of food esp fish, restaurant (must book summer wknds), live music Sun; children welcome if eating, pleasant garden behind overlooking sea *(Ann and Colin Hunt)*

Everton [SZ2994]

☆ *Crown* [Old Christchurch Rd, 3 miles W of Lymington]: Good interesting food cooked to order (so may be a wait), smallish bookable no smoking dining room off relaxing and informal traditional main bar, log fire, lots of jugs and china, well kept Bass, Ringwood and Whitbreads-related ales, friendly attentive service; lively separate public bar with pool, darts, table football, good juke box and welcoming chatty locals; no dogs, picnic-sets on front terrace and back grass, some good walks *(Peter Adams, WHBM, A D Marsh, Phyl and Jack Street)*

Ewshot [SU8150]

Windmill [Church Lane, off A287]: Small pub locally popular for good if not cheap food inc good Sun roast, welcoming licensees (he does the cooking), well kept Fullers London Pride, Ushers Best and Wadworths 6X, cellar bar, snug and dining room, green plush seating; enormous garden with putting green and Sun lunchtime barbecues *(Val and Alan Green, Ian Phillips)*

Faccombe [SU3858]

☆ *Jack Russell*: Smart yet comfortably homely bar with lots of pictures, enterprising reasonably priced food inc Fri/Sat theme nights (piped music to match), attractive dining conservatory, well kept beers inc a guest such as Fullers London Pride or Wyre Piddle in the Wind, helpful staff; disabled facilities, tables in lovely garden, nice setting opp village pond by flint church, bedrooms spotless and cheerful, good breakfast, good walks with rewarding views *(Phyl and Jack Street, Lynn Sharpless, Bob Eardley, Dick and Madeleine Brown)*

Fareham [SU5806]

Cob & Pen [Wallington Shore Rd, not far from M27 junction 11]: Pleasant pine furnishings, flagstones and carpets, Hook Norton Best and Ringwood ales, wide choice of good value straightforward food; large garden *(Val and Alan Green)*

Lord Arthur Lee [West St]: Wetherspoons pub/diner named for the local 1900s MP who presented Chequers to the nation, attractively priced well kept beers, food inc vegetarian choice *(Val and Alan Green)*

White Horse [North Wallington]: Smart friendly two-bar pub with Winchester ales from Portsmouth (see Winchester Arms entry there) *(Val and Alan Green)*

Fawley [SU4603]

☆ *Jolly Sailor* [Ashlett Creek]: Lively plushly modernised waterside pub with good value food inc Sun carvery and good vegetarian choice, Whitbreads-related and guest ales, hot drinks, friendly prompt service, restaurant, good liner pictures; piped music (live Fri/Sun), children welcome; by dinghy club overlooking busy shipping channel, handy for Rothschild rhododendron gardens at Exbury *(Charlotte Rae, LYM)*

Finchdean [SU7312]

George: Doing well under current licensees, decent food in lounge and smartened up public bar, good service *(Ann and Colin Hunt)*

Fordingbridge [SU1414]

George [Bridge St]: Friendly pub in lovely spot, wide choice of good value food inc good vegetarian dishes, Flowers and Gales HSB, helpful service, pleasant interior with spacious no smoking area; terrace and conservatory bar (children welcome here) facing River Avon and both attractively remodelled since it flooded them recently *(Dr and Mrs A K Clarke, John and Lynn Busenbark, Richard Burton)*

Freefolk [SU4848]

Watership Down [Freefolk Priors, N of B3400 – sharp lane uphill at W end of village]: Fine choice of well kept ales such as Archers Best, Berkeley Old Friend and Brakspears PA and Mild in genuine unaffected compact village pub, partly brick-floored, with functional furnishings, popular food inc good value Sun roasts (but even a sandwich may take time), no smoking conservatory; games area with plenty of old-fashioned slot machines and table football; piped music, Sun quiz night; nicely placed above grassy bank, attractive garden with play area and rabbit pen, pleasant walks *(T G Thomas, Mick Simmons)*

Frogham [SU1712]

☆ *Foresters Arms* [Abbotswell Rd]: Busy and well run extensively refurbished New Forest pub, flagstones and small woodburner, well kept Wadworths and guest ales, decent wines, reasonably priced straightforward food inc very popular Sun lunch, extended dining room;

children welcome, pleasant garden and front verandah; small camp site adjacent, good walks *(John and Joan Calvert, LYM)*

Froyle [SU7542]

Hen & Chicken [A31 Alton—Farnham]: 16th-c coaching inn with three attractive linked beamed rooms, inglenook log fire, usual bar food from sandwiches up, children's meals, Badger Best, Tanglefoot, Champion and K&B; children in eating area and restaurant, big garden with picnic-sets and play area, open all day *(B, M and P Kendall, I Caldicott, Ian Phillips, Phyl and Jack Street, M G Hart, LYM)*

Godshill [SU1715]

Fighting Cocks [B3078 Fordingbridge— Cadnam]: Generous good food inc beautifully cooked veg and good children's menu, well kept Flowers, Fullers London Pride, Gales HSB and Wadworths 6X, open fires, maps for walks – lovely New Forest setting; quiet piped music *(D P and J A Sweeney)*

Gosport [SZ5998]

Alverbank House [Stokes Bay Rd, Alverstoke]: Pleasant lounge with half a dozen well kept interesting changing ales in immaculate hotel set in woods at end of Walpole Park, over rd from promenade; good choice of food with plenty of veg, friendly staff, nice big garden with play area, Solent and Isle of Wight views; piped music; bedrooms very well appointed *(Val and Alan Green)*

☆ *Clarence* [Mumby Rd (A32)]: Partly 18th-c, incorporating a former chapel from the Isle of Wight, heavy furnishings, old books, prints and other pictures, good-sized no smoking area; wide choice of food in bar and upstairs restaurant, guest beers and ones from their own microbrewery (viewed through glass panels in bar and minstrel's gallery), log and coal fires, relaxed atmosphere, dogs welcome, no games or piped music but can be boisterous; medieval evenings, open all day *(Christina and Bob Buxey, Richard Houghton, Ann and Colin Hunt)*

Queens [Queens Rd]: Bare-boards pub whose landlady expertly keeps six or more changing strong ales with Badger Tanglefoot as a regular fixture, three areas off bar with coal fire in interesting carved fireplace; very quick service, maybe huge filled rolls and other simple food; sensibly placed darts, family area with TV, no piped music, quiz night Thurs; bedrooms, open all day Sat *(Ann and Colin Hunt)*

Hamble [SU4806]

King & Queen [3 miles from M27 junction 8; High St]: Lively seaside feel, welcoming staff, well kept beers inc Fullers London Pride, good value generous food inc interesting snacks, pine tables on bare boards; soft piped music; showers and laundry room for dirty sailors, tables on front gravel *(Val and Alan Green, Keith and Jill Cowell)*

Hambledon [SU6716]

☆ *Bat & Ball* [Broadhalfpenny Down; about 2 miles E towards Clanfield]: Extended dining pub opp seminal cricket pitch (matches most summer Sundays), plenty of cricket memorabilia, comfortable modern furnishings in three rooms and panelled restaurant, log fire; energetic landlord, well kept Gales ales, good interesting food from modestly priced snacks to fresh fish, lovely downs views *(LYM, W A Evershed, Tim Wellock, Val and Alan Green)*

Hannington [SU5355]

Vine: Spacious, friendly and lively, with reliable reasonably priced food inc Sun lunches, attractive dining conservatory, efficient service, evening restaurant (not Sun/Mon), well kept Badger beers, billiards room; may be piped music; terrace, big garden, nice spot up on downs, good walks *(Lynn Sharpless, Bob Eardley, Danny Nicol)*

Hardley [SU4304]

Forest Home [A362 Fawley rd]: Comfortably refurbished, with good value generous food, pleasant helpful staff, Fullers London Pride, Gales HSB and Greene King Old Speckled Hen; wheelchair access, disabled lavatory, garden with play area *(Mrs J Sykes, Dr M Owton)*

Hatherden [SU3450]

☆ *Old Bell & Crown*: Newish landlord doing imaginative food from quick lunchtime snacks to fresh fish and wild boar in roomy village pub, well kept Wadworths and guest ales, restaurant with no smoking part; pretty garden *(Dr Philip Wray)*

Havant [SU7106]

☆ *Old House At Home* [South St]: Much modernised low-beamed Tudor pub, nice rambling alcovey feel, two fireplaces in lounge, well kept Gales BBB, GB and HSB, welcoming licensees; piped music (live Sat – very popular with young people Fri/Sat night), back garden *(Ann and Colin Hunt, Val and Alan Green, D P and J A Sweeney, LYM)*

Parchment Makers [Park Road North]: Long Wetherspoons in former tax office, their usual food, up to 10 real ales, good service *(Ann and Colin Hunt, Val and Alan Green)*

Robin Hood [Homewell]: Relaxing old pub with low ceilings in rambling open-plan bar, well kept Gales ales tapped from the cask, reasonably priced food, open fire; sensibly placed darts, can get smoky *(Ann and Colin Hunt)*

Hayling Island [SU7098]

Inn on the Beach [Sea Front, South Hayling]: Largeish modern pub on shingle, roomy sunken bar, several real ales, friendly staff, good value food in dining area; some live music *(Guy Vowles)*

Hazeley [SU7459]

Shoulder of Mutton [Hazeley Heath]: Warmly friendly old dining pub, lots of regular lunchers for wide choice of generous home-made food from ploughman's to good steaks (no snacks just meals on Sun, when many tables are booked), efficient service, good fire in cosy lounge, no smoking area, well kept Courage ales; quiet piped music; attractive building, terrace and garden *(Mr and Mrs J Brown, W W Burke, R Lake, Mr and Mrs T A Bryan, Colin McKerrow)*

Hill Head [SU5402]

Osborne View [Hill Head Rd]: Roomy modern red plush clifftop pub with three stepped-back

levels and picture windows for stunning views to the Isle of Wight, well kept Badger Best, Tanglefoot and ales from the Gribble at Oving, efficient service, nautical prints and memorabilia, no music, food inc children's and evening restaurant; open all day, garden and beach access, nr Titchfield Haven bird reserve *(Michael and Robin Inskip, Ann and Colin Hunt, Val and Alan Green)*

Horndean [SU7013]

Ship & Bell [London Rd]: Comfortable and spacious pub/hotel adjoining Gales brewery, full range of their beers kept well, good range of wines, good standard food, quick friendly service, cheerfully relaxed bar with deep well, snug lounge with broad low steps up to dining room, interesting quotations and photographs; 14 bedrooms, nice walk to Catherington church *(Jenny and Chris Wilson, Phyl and Jack Street, Ann and Colin Hunt, Val and Alan Green)*

Horsebridge [SU3430]

☆ *John o' Gaunt* [off A3057 Romsey—Andover, just SW of Kings Somborne]: Small village pub very popular with walkers for good attractively priced food, well kept Itchen Valley Fagins, Palmers BB and Ringwood Best and Fortyniner, decent wines by the glass, friendly service, simple L-shaped bar, log fire, no piped music; pub black labrador, dogs welcome, picnic-sets out by mill on River Test, good walks *(Phyl and Jack Street, Lynn Sharpless, Bob Eardley)*

Hursley [SU4225]

Kings Head [A3090 Winchester—Romsey]: Large open-plan food pub, rather elegant décor, new licensees doing good value fresh food from temptingly filled baguettes to choice of steaks (old public bar now a dining area), well kept Fullers London Pride, decent wine; tables outside, skittle alley in cellar bar, bedrooms with own bathrooms planned *(Lynn Sharpless, Bob Eardley, J F M and M West)*

Hurstbourne Priors [SU4346]

Hurstbourne: Welcoming local, good value straightforward food, Hampshire King Alfreds and Wadworths 6X; bedrooms *(Dave Braisted, R T and J C Moggridge)*

Hurstbourne Tarrant [SU3853]

George & Dragon [A343]: Attractive whitewashed village pub with low beams and inglenook (log-effect gas fire), good value home-made food from baked potatoes up, eating area, real ales inc Boddingtons and Greene King IPA, friendly welcome, pool in back bar, friendly dog (others allowed if good); small secluded terrace, bedrooms, attractive village; cl Sun evening, Mon *(LYM, Jane Wright, Mandy Dancocks, JP, PP)*

Ibsley [SU1509]

Old Beams [A338 Salisbury—Ringwood]: Busy big black and white thatched chain pub, large main room divided by panelling and canopied log-effect gas fire, lots of varnished wooden tables and country-kitchen chairs under aged oak beams, small partly no smoking restaurant with own bar, no smoking buffet area and conservatory, Theakstons Best and XB, country wines; fruit machine and piped music; open all day (cl winter wkdy afternoons) *(the Didler,*

Paul R White, JP, PP, Mike and Heather Watson, LYM, Phyl and Jack Street)

Keyhaven [SZ3091]

☆ *Gun:* Busy yet cosy 17th-c pub looking over boatyard and sea to Isle of Wight, good choice of generous food using local produce; low beams, lots of nautical memorabilia, well kept beers such as Flowers, Greene King Old Speckled Hen, Marstons Pedigree and Ringwood True Glory, well over a hundred malt whiskies, bar billiards; children in back conservatory, garden with swings and fishpond *(Mayur Shah, Phyl and Jack Street, A D Marsh)*

Kingsclere [SU5258]

Crown [Newbury Rd]: Pleasantly reworked former school, long comfortable partly panelled lounge with central log fire, good reasonably priced food, striking no smoking hammer-beam dining room (another allows smokers), well kept Courage ales, attentive service, games in simpler public bar; children in family room, nearby downs walks *(Mark Percy, Lesley Mayoh, Phyl and Jack Street, LYM)*

Langstone [SU7105]

☆ *Ship* [A3023]: Waterside 18th-c former grain store, smart and well cared for, plenty of tables out on quiet quay, lovely view across to Hayling Island from roomy dimly lit nautical bar with upstairs dining room, fast friendly service, full Gales range kept well, good choice of wines by the glass, country wines, log fire, good generous food inc fresh fish and platters for two; most accept credit card; children's room, open all day, good coast walks *(D P and J A Sweeney, Irene and Derek Flewin, David and Carole Chapman, Jonathan Gibbs, Tony Hobden, Geoff Pidoux)*

Lee-on-the-Solent [SU5600]

☆ *Bun Penny* [Manor Way]: Carefully restored and extended, with low beams and flagstones, conservatory and restaurant, pleasant furnishings and bric-a-brac, two log fires (notices ask you to put on another log if you're cold), good choice of good food (and free peanuts), well kept Boddingtons, Flowers and Wadworths 6X, decent wines, daily papers, friendly efficient staff; garden, lots of flowers in summer *(Jess and George Cowley, Bryan McAlley, James Flory)*

Swordfish [Crofton Ave/Sea Lane, off Stubbington Lane]: Big comfortable pub notable for outstanding position with Solent views; big family room, tables on large lawn, steps down to sea path, usual pub food, Bass and Courage Best and Directors *(Esther and John Sprinkle)*

Wyvern [Common Barn Lane/Broom Way]: Neat and tidy Gales pub with cottagey frontage, naval fighter aircraft theme (hence the name), straightforward food, friendly service, well kept beers; pleasant walks nearby *(Val and Alan Green)*

Linwood [SU1910]

☆ *High Corner* [signed from A338 via Moyles Court, and from A31; keep on]: Big rambling pub very popular for its splendid New Forest position up a track, with extensive neatly kept lawn and lots for children to do; some

character in original upper bar, lots of back extension for the summer crowds, large helpings of good value food from sandwiches to steaks inc Sun carvery (nicely partitioned restaurant open all day Sun), well kept Whitbreads-related and other ales such as Wadworths 6X, decent wine, efficient service, no smoking verandah lounge; interesting family rooms, dogs welcome too, open all day Sat; bedrooms *(Kevin Flack, LYM, Geoff and Linda Dibble)*

Red Shoot [signed from A338 via Moyles Court, and from A31; go on up heath]: Nice New Forest setting, lots of space, some attractive old furniture and rugs on bare boards, large dining area with generous value food from good sandwiches up, friendly atmosphere and staff, six well kept ales inc Wadworths and Forest Gold or Toms Tipple brewed at the pub, children and dogs (and muddy boots) welcome; open all day wknds and summer, very touristy then (by big campsite and caravan park), can get smoky *(Uta and John Owlett, M Blatchly)*

Little London [SU6359]

Plough [Silchester Rd, off A340 N of Basingstoke]: Cosy unspoilt local with tiled floor, low beams, friendly landlord, limited food inc lots of baguettes, well kept Ringwood and changing guest beers, log fire, darts, bar billiards; attractive garden, handy for Pamber Forest and Calleva Roman remains *(J V Dadswell)*

Locks Heath [SU5006]

☆ *Jolly Farmer* [2½ miles from M27 junction 9; A27 towards Bursledon, left into Locks Rd, at end T-junction right into Warsash Rd then left at hire shop into Fleet End Rd]: Emphasis on wide choice of food from filled baps to steaks in extensive series of softly lit rooms with nice old scrubbed tables and a forest of interesting bric-a-brac and prints, coal-effect gas fires, no smoking area, well kept Flowers Original, Gales HSB and Greene King Old Speckled Hen, country wines, firm landlady, neat friendly staff; piped music, service charge for parties of over 8; two sheltered terraces, one with a play area; bedrooms *(Ann and Colin Hunt, Lynn Sharpless, Bob Eardley, Michael and Robin Inskip, Jenny Cridland, Gordon Cooper, Charles and Pauline Stride, LYM)*

Long Sutton [SU7447]

☆ *Four Horseshoes* [signed off B3349 S of Hook]: Unpretentious well kept open-plan black-beamed country local recently bought by its quietly helpful veteran licensees, good choice of home-made lunchtime food inc landlord's special cheese soup, full Gales range kept well, decent wines and country wine, log fire, daily papers, small glazed-in verandah with Sun carvery; picnic-sets on grass over road, boules pitch *(Phyl and Jack Street, BB, Chris and Anna Rowley)*

Longparish [SU4344]

☆ *Plough* [B3048, off A303 just E of Andover]: Open-plan carpeted dining lounge divided by arches, very wide food choice from sandwiches with chips to steaks, children's dishes, partly no smoking restaurant, well kept Boddingtons, Greene King Old Speckled Hen, Wadworths 6X and a guest such as Hampshire King Alfreds, country wines; piped music; children in eating areas, tables on terrace and in pleasant garden with pets corner, bedrooms *(Miss A G Drake, Ann and Colin Hunt, Lynn Sharpless, Bob Eardley, Mrs J Ekins-Daukes, John and Anne McIver, Geoffrey Kemp, R J Walden, Ian Jones, David and Ruth Shillitoe, Chris Mawson, Anthony Longden, LYM)*

Lower Froyle [SU7643]
Anchor [signed off A31]: Unassuming 14th-c traditional pub with roomy and brightly lit low-ceilinged bar and dining room, popular with older people lunchtime (esp Weds) for reasonably priced food inc sandwiches and fish, cheerful family service, well kept Hardy Royal Oak, decent malt whiskies; tables outside, bedrooms *(Ron Shelton)*

Lower Wield [SU6339]
☆ *Yew Tree* [off A339 NW of Alton, via Medstead or Bentworth]: Pricy country dining pub in nice quiet spot by village cricket pitch, small flagstoned bistro-style bar with good log fire and some imaginative bar dishes, friendly attentive service, Flowers IPA or fff Billericay Dicky tapped from the cask, good wines, expensive restaurant; tables out on front terrace and in garden, nearby walks *(Phyl and Jack Street, Martin and Karen Wake, J Hale, Norman and Sheila Sales, Louise English, LYM)*

Lymington [SZ3295]
☆ *Angel* [High St]: Bustling open-plan 17th-c coaching inn, dark oak furnishings to match the panelling and black beams, prints, photographs and so forth, wide choice of enjoyable food inc interesting dishes, well kept Bass and Courage Best, good communicative service; piped music; open all day, tables in attractive inner courtyard, bedrooms *(A D Marsh, LYM, Joan and Michel Hooper-Immins, Mr and Mrs A Craig, George Atkinson)*
Bosuns Chair [Station St]: Light and airy high-ceilinged rooms, enjoyable generous food inc fish cooked plainly or with options, friendly landlord, well kept Wadworths ales, popular with locals, Sun quiz night; garden with terrace, spacious comfortable bedrooms *(Gartlen and Wally Rogers)*
☆ *Chequers* [Ridgeway Lane, Lower Woodside – dead end just S of A337 roundabout W of Lymington, by White Hart]: Busy yachtsmen's local with polished boards and quarry tiles, attractive pictures, plain chairs and wall pews; generous good food in local fish, real ales such as Bass, Ringwood and Wadworths 6X, pleasant young staff, traditional games; maybe piped music; well behaved children allowed, tables and summer marquee in neat walled back family garden, attractive front terrace, handy for bird-watching at Pennington Marshes *(A D Marsh, Dick and Madeleine Brown, LYM, Phyl and Jack Street)*
☆ *Fishermans Rest* [All Saints Rd, Woodside]: Wide choice of good interesting food inc very popular Sun lunch, reasonable prices, well kept

Ringwood, decent wines, friendly staff, pleasant atmosphere, plenty of locals at bar; can get busy *(A D Marsh, Steve Chambers, John and Joan Calvert, Mr and Mrs R Buckley)*
Mayflower [Kings Saltern Rd]: Welcoming new licensees, cosy lounge, larger public bar, good reasonably priced food, well kept Gales ales, friendly black cat *(A D Marsh, Ann and Colin Hunt)*
Toll House [Southampton Rd (A337)]: Newly refurbished, with wide choice of good value food inc children's and Sun lunch, good friendly atmosphere, several real ales, pleasant efficient staff, oak beams; good-sized children's room, pleasant cottagey bedrooms *(A D Marsh, Phyl and Jack Street, Brian and Diane Mugford)*

Lyndhurst [SU2908]
Crown [High St]: Best Western hotel, cheerful log fire in cosy traditional panelled bar, stags' heads and antlers, obliging efficient staff, well kept Ringwood Best and Porter, good value well served food; bedrooms, fine forest walks *(A D Marsh, Shirley Mackenzie, George Atkinson, Phyl and Jack Street)*
Waterloo Arms [Pikes Hill]: 17th-c rambling thatched New Forest pub with low beams, pleasant furnishings, log fire, interesting beers tapped from the cask, good wine list, generous food, separate dining area; some children's amusements in large attractive back garden *(Pete and Josephine Cropper, W W Burke)*

Marchwood [SU3810]
☆ *Pilgrim* [Hythe Rd, off A326 at Twiggs Lane]: Homely yet immaculate décor in attractive thatched pub's long L-shaped bar with red plush banquettes, wide choice of consistently good value food, welcoming service, well kept Bass and Courage, cosy fire, separate more expensive restaurant; can be crowded, handy for Longdown Dairy Farm and Nature Quest; neat garden *(Phyl and Jack Street, John Hart, LYM, E W and S M Wills)*

Mattingley [SU7357]
Leather Bottle [3 miles from M3 junction 5; in Hook, turn right-and-left on to B3349 Reading Road (former A32)]: Wisteria-covered tiled pub with extension opening on to covered heated terrace, main bar with good inglenook log fires, cottagey black-beamed back bar with country pictures, Courage Best and Greene King Abbot, usual lunchtime bar food (more evening choice); fruit machine, ubiquitous piped music; pretty flowering baskets and tubs *(Karen and Graham Oddey, LYM, Ian Phillips)*

Medstead [SU6537]
☆ *Castle of Comfort* [signed off A31 SW of Alton; Castle St]: Genuinely traditional village pub, homely and cosily old-fashioned beamed lounge bar, well kept Ushers Best, Founders and a seasonal beer, good basic bar lunches inc soup and sandwiches, toasties and ploughman's, warmly friendly service, plush chairs, woodburner and small open fireplace, elderly dog, larger plain public bar with darts etc; sunny front verandah, more tables in neat side garden with fairy lights and play tree, nice walks *(Richard Butler, Marie Kroon, Phyl and*

Jack Street, BB, Roger Chacksfield, K Brewster, J V Dadswell)

Meonstoke [SU6119]

Bucks Head [just off A32 N of Wickham; Bucks Head Hill]: Landlord cooking good value substantial fresh food inc local game and good generous puddings for smallish dining lounge with dark red banquettes and good log fire, well kept Bass and Greene King IPA, decent wines, country wines, friendly staff (and cats), comfortable terracotta-coloured public bar with cosy fire (open all day Sun at least in spring and summer); pleasant walled garden, lovely village setting with ducks on pretty little River Meon, good walks (but they don't like cars left); bedrooms *(Ann and Colin Hunt, Lynn Sharpless, Bob Eardley, Val and Alan Green)*

Milford-on-Sea [SZ2891]

Smugglers [High St]: Big cheery pub well geared for holiday crowds, pleasant atmosphere, good blackboard choice of generous food from sandwiches to lots of fish, real ales; children welcome, side play area with boat to play on *(Miss J F Reay)*

Minstead [SU2811]

☆ *Trusty Servant* [just off A31 nr M21 junction 1]: Three opened-up rooms inc sizeable restaurant area, lots of character, wide choice of good generously served food from huge baguettes with chips to fresh fish and imaginative main dishes, well kept changing ales such as Flowers Original, Fullers London Pride and Ringwood Best, Thatcher's farm cider, country wines, very pleasant staff; may be pipe music; open all day, simple bedrooms, good breakfast, pretty New Forest village with wandering ponies and easy walks *(Alan and Paula McCully, DWAJ, D P and J A Sweeney, Dr M and Mrs G S Crawford, BB, Ann and Colin Hunt, Basil Minson)*

Monxton [SU3144]

Black Swan [High St]: Pretty extended pub among thatched rose-covered cottages, cosy lounge area with easy chairs and settee, two dining areas (one no smoking) off the main bar, wide range of good straightforward food from ample sandwiches or baked potatoes to steaks, Whitbreads-related beers, good quick service; tables in courtyard and garden with play area, barbecue and slow-flowing stream *(Margaret Ross, Phyl and Jack Street)*

Mortimer [SU6464]

Turners Arms [Fairfield Park, West End Rd, Mortimer Common]: L-shaped open-plan Brakspears pub with their beers inc Mild, full range of decent bar food inc OAP roast, friendly staff, log fire, no smoking restaurant; tables in garden *(Tony and Wendy Hobden)*

Mortimer West End [SU6363]

☆ *Red Lion* [Church Rd; Silchester turn off Mortimer—Aldermaston rd]: Country dining pub with good food inc interesting dishes, well kept Badger and other ales, friendly young hard-working licensees, lots of beams, stripped masonry, timbers and panelling, good log fire; quiet piped music; plenty of seats in pleasant garden with play area, and on small flower-filled front terrace; open all day, handy for

Roman Silchester *(LYM, Pat and Robert Watt, Adrian and Felicity Smith)*

Newtown [SU4764]

Swan [A339 2 miles S of Newbury, by junction with old A34]: Attractive old-world flagstoned Beefeater, friendly helpful staff, well kept real ales inc Badger Best and well chosen wine list, good varied bar snacks, old photographs *(Stephen and Judy Parish, R T and J C Moggridge)*

Travellers Rest [off A32 N of Wickham]: Uncomplicated two-bar country pub gently enlarged but still cosy, with warm welcome, three real ales inc Fullers London Pride, straightforward food, log fires, traditional furnishings, chatty local atmosphere; pretty back garden *(Ann and Colin Hunt, LYM)*

North Waltham [SU5645]

Fox [signed off A30 SW of Basingstoke; handy for M3 junction 7]: Comfortable two-bar village local in attractive spot, well kept Ushers Best and Founders, welcoming well organised service, wide choice of food inc lots of seasonal game (landlord an ex-gamekeeper) in bar and elongated dining area with log fire; quiet piped music, darts and juke box in public bar; children welcome, tables in garden, pleasant village *(Phyl and Jack Street)*

Oakhanger [SU7635]

Red Lion [off A325 Farnham—Petersfield]: Unpretentious and well worn in, surprisingly good food from snacks to more restauranty dishes esp seafood in side lounge, well kept Courage and an interesting guest ale such as local fff Moondance, thoughtful house wines, big log fire, welcoming helpful staff, proper separate public bar; tables in garden *(Glen and Nola Armstrong, Jonathan Hughes, Iain Robertson)*

Otterbourne [SU4623]

Old Forge [Main Rd]: Former restaurant pleasantly refurbished as Bass Vintage Inn, well organised, with their usual decent food, good service, Bass and Worthington, good atmosphere *(Phyl and Jack Street)*

Petersfield [SU7423]

☆ *Good Intent* [College St]: 16th-c core with low oak beams and well spaced good-sized pine tables, Fullers London Pride and other well kept ales, wide choice of decent food inc lots of unusual sausages, smart quiet, cosy family area *(Val and Alan Green, Phyl and Jack Street)*

Portsmouth [SU6606]

Churchillian [Portsdown Hill Rd, Widley]: Smallish open-plan dining pub, oak, cream and red carpet, big windows overlooking Portsmouth and Solent, usual food, real ales; quietish piped music; handy for Fort Widley equestrian centre and nature trail *(Val and Alan Green)*

Dolphin [High St, Old Portsmouth]: Spacious old timber-framed Hogshead with wide choice of food inc Sun roasts, good real ale range inc Ringwood 49er and Old Thumper, friendly staff, good log fire, cosy snug; video games; open all day Sat, children welcome in eating area, small terrace *(Keith and Katy Stevens, Ann and Colin Hunt, Andy and Jill Kassube, John Davis)*

Fleet & Firkin [King Henry I St, opp Guildhall]: Usual Firkin style with naval additions, roomy interior with first floor, friendly staff, large choice of real ales, simple bar food *(anon)*

George [Queen St, nr dockyard entrance]: Cosy and quiet one-room nautical pub with leather seats and panelling in front, more comfortably plush at back, real ales inc a cheap one brewed for the pub by Gales, friendly staff, log fire, covered well and Nelson pictures, separate food bar; handy for dockyard and HMS *Victory (Ann and Colin Hunt, R T and J C Moggridge)*

Sallyport [High St, Old Portsmouth]: Comfortable spick-and-span hotel, sympathetically modernised and still interesting, with thriving beamed bar, leather chesterfields, soft lighting, lots of naval prints, well kept chilled Bass, Gales HSB, Greene King Abbot and Marstons Pedigree, enjoyable reasonably priced bar food esp fish, efficient friendly staff, decent coffee, upstairs restaurant; comfortable bedrooms *(Alan Thomas, Steve Whalley, Ann and Colin Hunt, Neil and Anita Christopher)*

Ship Anson [Victory Rd, The Hard (opp Esplanade Stn, Portsea)]: Large well run pub open all day, with good value food, friendly locals, real ales; very handy for HMS *Victory* etc, car park a few mins' walk away *(Geoff Pidoux)*

Spice Island [Bath Sq]: Vast open-plan waterside Whitbreads pub, part dark and panelled in galleon style, part roomy modern bare-boards style, big windows and outside seats overlooking passing ships, well kept ales, food all day, family room (one of the few in Portsmouth), bright upstairs restaurant; can be very crowded *(Steve Whalley)*

☆ *Still & West* [Bath Sq, Old Portsmouth]: The star is for the position by the narrow harbour mouth, with big windows for great views even to the Isle of Wight; nautical décor, usual bar food, Gales HSB, IPA and a guest beer, upper partly no smoking restaurant; piped music may be loud, service can slow when busy; open all day, children welcome, picnic-sets out on terrace *(LM, Mark and Heather Williamson, Steve Whalley, Ann and Colin Hunt, LYM, Charlie Harris)*

Wellington [High St, off Grand Parade, Old Portsmouth]: Cosy open-plan pub with large Georgian bow window, nr seafront and historic square tower, relaxed chatty atmosphere, good bar food esp fresh fish, well kept Wadworths 6X and a beer brewed for the pub, generous wine, friendly experienced licensees, courteous old-fashioned service *(Steve Whalley, Ann and Colin Hunt)*

Winchester Arms [Winchester Rd]: Friendly two-bar local refurbished in style of old-fashioned London pub and brewing its own Winchester beers, relaxing atmosphere, log fires, bar food, no smoking area; tables in garden *(Val and Alan Green, Richard Houghton, Ann and Colin Hunt)*

Ringwood [SU1505]

☆ *Fish* [off A31 W of town]: New management doing interesting choice of well presented food, several quiet and cosy areas (some away from bar perhaps a bit dark), intriguing fishy decorations, good service and atmosphere, well kept Boddingtons, Brakspears, Flowers and Fullers, coffee and tea, log fire, no smoking eating area allowing children, no dogs; tables on riverside lawn with play area and budgerigar aviary, open all day *(T R and B C Jenkins, LYM, Geoffrey Hart)*

Inn on the Furlong [Meeting House Lane]: Long flagstoned bar, stripped brick and oak timbering, simple décor, full range of Ringwood beers from nearby brewery kept well, daily papers, good friendly service, cheap plentiful bar food, conservatory dining extension; open all day (Sun afternoon closure), live music some nights, Easter beer festival *(R T and J C Moggridge)*

London Tavern [Linwood Rd]: Pleasant family pub, enjoyable food inc Sun lunch *(Kerry Orman)*

Rockbourne [SU1118]

☆ *Rose & Thistle* [signed off B3078 Fordingbridge—Cranborne]: Attractive thatched 16th-c pub with good fresh home-made food inc home-made ice creams (best to book Sun lunch), well kept Marstons Pedigree, Ushers seasonal brews, Wadworths 6X and Youngers Scotch, good range of wines, pleasant service, civilised bar with antique settles, old engravings and good coal fire, traditional games, log fires in front restaurant with no smoking area; maybe piped classical music; children welcome, tables by thatched dovecot in neat front garden, charming tranquil spot in lovely village, good walks *(John Davis, Alan and Ros Furley, Mrs Ann Rix, LYM)*

Rockford [SU1608]

☆ *Alice Lisle*: Friendly modernised open-plan pub attractively placed on green by New Forest (can get very busy), emphasis on big conservatory-style family eating area with generous helpings of good food inc sandwiches, some interesting dishes and sensible children's menu; well kept Gales and guest beers, country wines, welcoming attentive staff, baby-changing facilities; garden overlooking lake with peacock and other birds, ponies wander nearby, children's play area, separate adults-only garden; handy for Moyles Court *(I R Fourmy, Geoffrey and Brenda Wilson, BB, Mr and Mrs J F Copping)*

Romsey [SU3521]

Abbey Hotel [Church St]: Comfortable plush and mahogany, good choice of reliable traditional food, welcoming efficient service, well kept Courage Best and Directors; bedrooms, opp Abbey *(Ron Shelton)*

☆ *Dukes Head* [Great Bridge Rd (A3057 towards Stockbridge)]: Attractive 16th-c dining pub festooned with flowering baskets in summer, picturesque series of interestingly decorated linked rooms, well kept Bass, Hampshire and Hardy ales, decent house wines, good coffee, rewarding choice of popular well presented food from fresh sandwiches up, inglenook eating places, log fires, candles at night; maybe quiet piped music; charming back garden with old tractor and rabbits *(Michael Buchanan,*

Jason Caulkin, David Wallington, Phyl and Jack Street, W W Burke, Ann and Colin Hunt, Jestyn Phillips)

Old House At Home [Love Lane]: Attractive 16th-c thatched pub with basic old-fashioned décor, good home-made food, well kept Gales and guest beers, long-serving licensee *(Mr and Mrs A Craig, Pat and Tony Cousins)*

Three Tuns [Middlebridge St; car park off A27 bypass]: Quaint old beamed local, small and friendly, with bright fires, huge helpings of good reasonably priced food (best to book on Sat), good choice of well kept real ales inc Flowers, Ringwood Best and Wadworths 6X, cheerful attentive staff; TV and fruit machine in public bar *(Mr and Mrs R W Allan, Derek Stafford)*

Rotherwick [SU7156]

☆ *Falcon* [4 miles from M3 junction 5; follow Newnham signpost from exit roundabout, then Rotherwick signpost, then turn right at Mattingley, Heckfield signpost; village also signposted from B3349 N of Hook]: Smart and lively country pub, newly refurbished, with comfortable bar and open-plan no smoking dining room, interesting food inc enjoyable specials and plenty of fresh fish, particularly well kept ales such as Archers Golden, Brakspears and Morrells Varsity, bright prompt service, log fire, darts, bar billiards; children welcome, big garden with swings and pasture views, good easy walks *(Mrs Hilarie Taylor)*

Rowlands Castle [SU7310]

☆ *Castle Inn* [Finchdean Rd]: Unspoilt Edwardian pub with tremendous atmosphere, flagstones and rugs, enormous dim-lit bar with central log fire, wide choice of good value food popular from sandwiches up, well kept Gales beers, friendly speedy young staff; children and dogs welcome, good provision for disabled, picnic-sets in big garden, pleasant village *(Phyl and Jack Street)*

Robin Hood [The Green]: Comfortable lounge bar with decent food inc wide choice of good value fish Thurs-Sun, three well kept ales, separate public bar, friendly landlord, dog and cat; pretty village *(Ann and Colin Hunt)*

Shawford [SU4624]

Bridge: Several large dining areas with decent food range inc good vegetarian choice, friendly service, real ales inc Courage Best and Directors, quietish piped music, silenced games machines, billiard room; garden with play area *(J S M Sheldon, Val and Alan Green)*

Shedfield [SU5613]

Samuels Rest [Upper Church Rd (signed off B2177)]: Neat and tidily refurbished Wadworths pub, rural theme, well kept IPA and a seasonal beer, decent food; silenced games machines and maybe piped radio in public bar; garden with terrace and boules *(Val and Alan Green)*

Wheatsheaf [A334 Wickham—Botley]: Busy and friendly little family-run local with small dining area, well kept ales tapped from the cask such as Itchen Valley, Mansfield and Ringwood Fortyniner, good value generous lunchtime food, decent wine, impromptu piano sessions in

public bar; garden, handy for Wickham Vineyard *(Ann and Colin Hunt, Val and Alan Green)*

Sherfield English [SU2822]

Hatchet [Romsey rd]: Traditional beamed pub, good varied food inc fish and children's dishes, Adnams, good wine choice, attentive staff, restaurant area; tables outside *(Emma Wright, Lesley Henry)*

Soberton [SU6116]

White Lion [School Hill; signed off A32 S of Droxford]: Cheerful take-us-as-you-find-us 16th-c country pub in nice spot by green, irregularly shaped public bar with built-in wooden wall seats and traditional games, well kept Greene King Old Speckled Hen, Wadworths 6X and a beer brewed for them by Hampshire, rambling no smoking eating area, decent house wine, sensible prices, no music, energetic beer mat retrieving collie called Spike; small sheltered pretty garden with suntrap fairy-lit terrace (and chickens); children in eating areas, open all day *(Val and Alan Green, LYM, Gareth Davies, Roy Grove, Brian and Anna Marsden, Dave and Jenny Francis)*

Sopley [SZ1597]

☆ *Woolpack* [B3347 N of Christchurch]: Rambling open-plan low-beamed bar, rustic furniture, woodburner and little black kitchen range, friendly service, food from filled rolls to steaks and Sun roasts, well kept Flowers Original, Ringwood Best and Wadworths 6X, no smoking conservatory; piped music; open all day, children in eating areas, picnic-sets on terrace, attractive garden with ducks on stream *(A E Furley, T J and J D Fitzgerald, Jean and Richard Phillips, LYM)*

Southampton [SU4212]

Cowherds [The Common]: Low-beamed Vintage Inn, recently refurbished, numerous friendly alcoves, tables in nice little bay windows, lots of Victorian photographs, carpets on polished boards, log fires, well kept Bass and Worthington, good wine choice, food inc some unusual dishes, restaurant; pleasant spot on common, tables outside with tie-ups and water for dogs (50p deposit on glasses taken outside – just across from university) *(Neil Rose, Stephen Savill)*

Crown [Highcrown St, Highfield]: Bustling warmly relaxed local, well kept Archers, Flowers Original, Fullers London Pride and Wadworths 6X, good value food, helpful staff, open fires; piped music; dogs allowed in main bar (giving country feel in the city), heated covered terrace, Sun quiz night, open all day *(Sharon Holmes, Tom Cherrett)*

Duke of Wellington [Bugle St]: Ancient timber-framed building on 13th-c foundations, bare boards, log fire, friendly relaxed atmosphere, well kept reasonably priced Adnams, Ringwood Best and guest beers, decent home-made standard food; very handy for Tudor House Museum *(Stephen and Jean Curtis, Bruce Bird)*

Giddy Bridge [London Rd]: Pleasant Wetherspoons, partly divided and not too big, upstairs area with balcony terrace, good staff, well kept ales such as local Itchen Valley

Wykehams Glory, sensibly priced food *(Val and Alan Green)*

Hogshead [Above Bar St]: Large typical Hogshead, five or more real ales (many more during beer festivals), farm cider, good value food, rather trendier upstairs bar; popular with students, piped music may be loud *(Val and Alan Green)*

Southampton Arms [Moorgreen Rd, West End; off B3035]: Friendly jolly local, quite big, with comfortable seats, cosy bar and attractive conservatory restaurant, reasonably priced food, Flowers and Ringwood ales *(Phyl and Jack Street)*

Southsea [SZ6499]

☆ *Eldon Arms* [Eldon St/Norfolk St]: Roomy, comfortable and quiet rambling bar with old pictures and advertisements, attractive mirrors, lots of enjoyable bric-a-brac and bookcases; changing well kept ales such as Elgoods and Morrells Oxford, decent wines, good changing range of promptly served food, sensibly placed darts; pool and fruit machine, restaurant, tables in back garden *(Val and Alan Green, Ann and Colin Hunt)*

Fuzz & Firkin [Albert Rd]: Good lively very spacious police-theme Firkin, usual bare boards and solid furnishings, friendly staff, well kept beer, decent food inc big filled baguettes; loud music and lots of young people Sat night *(Howard James)*

Southwick [SU6208]

Golden Lion [High St; just off B2177 on Portsdown Hill]: Unspoilt two-bar local with well kept Gales, also distinctive Suthwyk ales, brewed by local farm using its own barley which they malt themselves; friendly staff, good value homely food inc Sun lunch, pleasant restaurant; where Eisenhower and Montgomery came before D-Day, attractive village nr scenic walks *(anon)*

Stockbridge [SU3535]

☆ *Grosvenor* [High St]: Quietly luxurious atmosphere and quick cheerfully courteous service in pleasantly restrained and comfortable old country-town hotel's refurbished bar, decent food inc unusual sandwiches, well kept Greene King IPA, Abbot and Old Speckled Hen, country prints and log fire; inappropriate but muted piped music; big attractive garden behind; bedrooms good value *(R T and J C Moggridge, Ian Phillips, W W Burke, BB)*

☆ *White Hart* [High St; A272/A3057 roundabout]: New licensees doing good value food from soup and sandwiches to Sun lunch in welcoming divided bar, oak pews and other seats, attractive décor with antique prints, full range of Gales ales kept well, country wines, cheerful welcoming service; children allowed in comfortable beamed restaurant with blazing log fire, tables in garden; bedrooms *(Colin and Janet Roe, David and Ruth Shillitoe, Geoff Palmer, Phyl and Jack Street, LYM)*

Stratfield Turgis [SU6960]

☆ *Wellington Arms*: Elegant small country inn with relaxing armchairs and other individual furnishings in restful and attractively decorated tall-windowed two-room lounge bar, part with polished flagstones, part carpeted; wide choice of good if unpubby bar food, well kept Badger Best and Tanglefoot, orange juice pressed to order, open fire, magazines to read; garden, comfortable well equipped bedrooms *(Mrs S Moss)*

Swanmore [SU5816]

Hunters [Hillgrove]: Much-extended family dining pub, excellent for children, with big plain family room, wide choice of freshly made straightforward food inc lots of fish specials, and winding garden with secluded tables and several good play areas for different age groups, plenty under cover and even one for babies; also plush bar with lots of boxer pictures, bank notes, carpentry and farm tools, Charles Wells Bombardier and Gales HSB tapped from the cask, good house wine, country wines; very busy wknds *(Val and Alan Green, David and Carole Chapman)*

New Inn [Chapel Rd]: Friendly village pub with attentive licensees, Greene King ales, straightforward home cooking; games, darts, cricket team *(Val and Alan Green)*

☆ *Rising Sun* [Hill Pound; off B2177 S of Bishops Waltham]: Comfortable tile-hung pub, low beams, scrubbed pine, good log fires, good choice of well kept beers and of food inc interesting dishes (booking advised wknd), good reasonably priced wines, quick friendly service (new tenants), well separated extended dining area; pleasant garden with play area, handy for Kings Way long distance path – best to head W *(R Michael Richards, Jenny Cridland, Gordon Cooper, Val and Alan Green)*

Sway [SZ2898]

Hare & Hounds [Durns Town – just off B3055 SW of Brockenhurst]: Airy and comfortable New Forest family dining pub, lots of children, good range of food, well kept Flowers Original, Fullers London Pride and Ringwood Best; may ask to keep credit card at bar; picnic-sets and play frame in sizeable neatly kept garden, open all day Sat *(A D Marsh, LYM)*

White Rose [Station Rd]: Good food in bar and restaurant, friendly service, New Forest garden with pool; bedrooms *(Mr and Mrs D Moir)*

Tangley [SU3252]

☆ *Cricketers Arms* [towards the Chutes]: Tucked away in unspoilt countryside, character small front bar with tiled floor, massive inglenook, roaring log fire, bar billiards and friendly labrador called Pots, bistroish back flagstoned extension with a one-table alcove off, some good cricketing prints, attractively priced imaginative food inc fresh baguettes and mix-your-own evening pizzas, well kept Bass and Cheriton Pots tapped from the cask, hard-working landlord; tables on neat terrace *(J A Cheverton, LYM, I A Herdman)*

☆ *Fox* [crossroads S of village, towards Andover]: Cosy but lively little beamed and timbered pub with generous good value imaginative food inc fresh fish, generous veg and fine range of puddings, well kept Courage and guest ales, good choice of wines, two big log fires, newish licensees, prompt helpful service, two pleasant no smoking family dining rooms (*Phyl and Jack Street, J D G Isherwood*)

Titchfield [SU5305]

Bugle [High St, off A27 nr Fareham]: Roomy and comfortable family pub of some character, bay window, flagstones and blue carpet, popular good value generous bar food, friendly efficient service, well kept Boddingtons, Flowers IPA, Gales HSB and Wadworths 6X, restaurant in old barn behind; dogs welcome, attractive village handy for Titchfield Haven nature reserve, fine walk by former canal to coast; bedrooms (*John and Margaret Mitchell, Lynne Prangnell, Ann and Colin Hunt*)

Fishermans Rest [Mill Lane, off A27 at Titchfield Abbey]: Whitbreads pub/restaurant included for its riverside position opp Titchfield Abbey, tables out behind overlooking water; hearty food all day in eating area with close-set tables and no smoking family area, good choice of well kept ales inc Gales HSB, Flowers and Wadworths 6X, cheerful if not always speedy service, two log fires, daily papers, fishing memorabilia (*R T and J C Moggridge, Phyl and Jack Street, Val and Alan Green, Ann and Colin Hunt, LYM, Dave Braisted*)

Queens Head [High St; off A27 nr Fareham]: Ancient pub with welcoming licensees, cosy and friendly 1930s-feel bar with new collection of old local pictures, window seats and central brick fireplace, changing well kept ales such as Fullers London Pride and Greene King Old Speckled Hen, sparkling glasses, good value food esp fish cooked by landlord, attractive restaurant, a couple of cats; bedrooms, pleasant conservation village nr nature reserve and walks to coast (*Ann and Colin Hunt, Charles and Pauline Stride*)

☆ *Titchfield Mill* [A27, junction with Mill Lane]: Large popular Vintage Inn catering well for families in recently converted watermill, olde-worlde room off main bar, smarter dining room, upstairs gallery, stripped beams and interesting old machinery, reasonably priced food, well kept Bass and Worthington, neat attentive staff; piped music; open all day, nice terrace by mill stream with two waterwheels (*Ann and Colin Hunt, Phyl and Jack Street*)

Totford [SU5738]

Woolpack [B3046 Basingstoke—Alresford]: Friendly, warm and cosy pub/restaurant with well kept Gales HSB, Palmers IPA and local Cheriton Pots, stripped-brick bar, large dining room, decent food inc good Sun roast, open fire; may be piped radio; tables outside, lovely setting in good walking country; bedrooms (*Lynn Sharpless, Bob Eardley*)

Totton [SU3612]

Anchor [Eling Quay]: Much renovated pub included for lovely setting with tables out overlooking quayside green, yachts and church across water; well kept Bass, Fullers London Pride and Worthington, very wide range of good value usual food from sandwiches and baked potatoes up, children welcome; open all day, handy for NT Tidal Mill (*Ian Phillips, Nigel Cooper, Stephen Savill, R S Patrick, Phyl and Jack Street*)

Turgis Green [SU6959]

☆ *Jekyll & Hyde* [A33 Reading—Basingstoke]: Bustling rambling pub with nice mix of furniture, black beams and flagstones, some interesting prints particularly in back room, welcoming prompt service, well kept Badger Best and IPA and Wadworths 6X, stepped-up dining area with varied food from sandwiches up all day inc breakfast, children's helpings; lots of picnic-sets in good sheltered garden (some traffic noise), play area and various games; lavatories for the disabled (*KC, LYM*)

Twyford [SU4724]

Phoenix [High St]: Cheerful open-plan local with lots of prints, bric-a-brac and big end inglenook log fire, wide choice of sensibly priced generous food from sandwiches to steaks, friendly enthusiastic landlord, well kept Greene King with a guest such as Black Sheep, decent wines, back room with skittle alley, children allowed up one end lunchtime; quiet piped music; garden (*Lynn Sharpless, Bob Eardley, Val and Alan Green, Ann and Colin Hunt*)

Vernham Dean [SU3456]

☆ *George*: Rambling open-plan beamed and timbered pub spruced up under expert new management, inglenook log fire, good blackboard choice, well kept ales inc Marstons Pedigree, decent wines, no smoking eating area (children allowed); darts, shove-ha'penny, dominoes and cribbage; tables in pretty garden behind, lovely thatched village, fine walks (*LYM, the Didler, JP, PP, Phyl and Jack Street*)

Waltham Chase [SU5616]

Chase [B2177]: Comfortable seating like smart lounge, second room with extended no smoking eating area, good food from baguettes up, real ales such as Courage Best, Marstons and Timothy Taylors Landlord, reliable service; jazz nights (*Val and Alan Green, Keith and Jill Cowell, Ann and Colin Hunt*)

Well [SU7646]

☆ *Chequers* [off A287 via Crondall, or A31 via Froyle and Lower Froyle]: Low beams and panelling, cosy alcoves, pews and brocaded stools, 18th-c country prints and sepia photographs, roaring log fire, wide-ranging bar food from baguettes to steak, Sun roasts, well kept Badger IPA, Best and Tanglefoot, decent wines, restaurant; children welcome, open all day wknds, picnic-sets in back garden, vine-covered front arbour, nice spot (*Geoffrey G Lawrance, John Davis, Ann and Colin Hunt, Sue and Bob Ward, LYM, J Hale, Martin and Karen Wake, Simon Collett-Jones*)

West Meon [SU6424]

☆ *Thomas Lord* [High St]: Attractive village pub with good value generous food, enthusiastic new landlord, well kept Ringwood Best and Wadworths 6X, good selection of wines, collection of cricket club ties in spacious lounge, separate dining area, fresh flowers; crayons and paper for children, soft piped music; tables in garden (*Simon Collett-Jones*)

West Wellow [SU2919]

Rockingham Arms [off A36 Romsey—Ower at roundabout, signed Canada]: Beamed 19th-c pub down Forest-edge dead end, good choice of reasonably priced food, well kept Ringwood ales, good sensibly priced wine list, friendly atmosphere, open fire, comfortable restaurant, games in public bar; children welcome, very good play area in garden opening on to pretty heathland with roaming horses *(Ann and Colin Hunt, Mr Thomas, Stephen and Jean Curtis, Phyl and Jack Street)*

Weyhill [SU3146]

Weyhill Fair [A342, signed off A303 bypass]: Popular local with six well kept sensibly priced ales inc good varied guests, wide choice of good value food from filling baps to enjoyable puddings; spacious solidly furnished lounge with easy chairs around woodburner, old advertisements, smaller family room, no smoking area; children welcome, occasional live music, handy for Hawk Conservancy *(Iain Robertson, Phyl and Jack Street, BB)*

Whitchurch [SU4648]

☆ *Red House* [London St]: Comfortably modernised family-friendly bar with 14th-c beams, fireplace each end (one an inglenook with ancient flagstones in front), generous home-made food from home-baked rolls to good hot dishes inc interesting vegetarian ones, step up to no smoking restaurant area, well kept Cheriton Pots and a guest such as Ringwood True Glory, decent house wines, friendly service; attractive terrace with play area *(Tony and Wendy Hobden, Val and Alan Green, LYM, Lynn Sharpless, Bob Eardley)*

Wickham [SU5711]

Roebuck [Kingsmead; A32 towards Droxford]: Well appointed restauranty pub, two dining rooms (one no smoking), lots of prints and plates, library of books, even a white grand piano; Fullers London Pride and Gales Butser; conservatory *(Carol and Dono Leaman, A D Marsh)*

Winchester [SU4829]

Eclipse [The Square, between High St and cathedral]: Picturesque but decidedly unpretentious and well worn local, massive 14th-c beams and timbers, oak settles, well kept Flowers Original, Fullers London Pride, Hampshire King Alfred and Ringwood Old Thumper, well done generous lunchtime bar food inc interesting massive sandwiches and toasties; antique lavatories, no dogs, children in back area (no smoking lunchtime – front part can get smoky), seats outside, very handy for cathedral *(Dennis Jenkin, Mr and Mrs A H Young, Dave Braisted, LYM, Brian and Anna Marsden)*

Hyde [A333, continuing out of Jewry St]: Unspoilt 15th-c two-bar local with hardly a true right-angle, cosy and welcoming, sensible prices, particularly well kept Greene King ales *(Ann and Colin Hunt)*

King Alfred [Saxon Rd, Hyde]: Welcoming Victorianised pub with unfussy traditional décor, wood and opaque glass dividers, enjoyable food from lunchtime baguettes and baked potatoes to some enterprising dishes, Greene King ales inc Ruddles, good wine choice, friendly attentive staff; TV, pool, piped music; pleasant garden with boules and small animals *(Lynn Sharpless, Bob Eardley, Steve Marper, Mr and Mrs J Sale)*

Old Gaol House [Jewry St]: Good spacious Wetherspoons pub with large no smoking area, food all day at competitive prices, good choice of locally brewed beers, courteous staff; no piped music *(Tony Hobden)*

Percy Hobbs [Chapel Lane, Easton; Winchester exit of A31]: Big ranch-house style Brewers Fayre useful for long food service and very child-friendly, with well kept ales inc Fullers London Pride, pleasant alcoves, lots of tables outside; pervasive piped music and air conditioning *(Ian and Nita Cooper)*

Queen [Kingsgate Rd]: Roomy refurbished pub in attractive setting opp College cricket ground, dark dado, cricketing and other prints, bric-a-brac on window-sills, grandfather clock, newly reopened central fireplace, friendly hard-working licensees, well kept Greene King ales, decent wines, reasonably priced mainstream food from baguettes and baked potatoes to popular Sun lunch, disabled facilities; open all day Fri-Sun, neatly reorganised front terrace *(the Didler, Lynn Sharpless, Bob Eardley)*

☆ *Royal Oak* [Royal Oak Passage, off upper end of pedestrian part of High St opp St Thomas St]: Cheerful main area doubling as coffee bar, little rooms off (some raised), beams and bare boards, scrubbed tables, no smoking areas, good value quick food with ciabatta and roast veg leanings, up to ten or so real ales; piped music and several fruit machines; the cellar bar (not always open) has massive 12th-c beams and a Saxon wall which gives it some claim to be the country's oldest drinking spot *(the Didler, Val and Alan Green, David Peakall, Alan and Paula McCully, LYM, Ian and Nita Cooper)*

Wolverton [SU5558]

George & Dragon [Towns End; just N of A339 Newbury—Basingstoke]: Comfortable rambling open-plan oak-beamed pub, standing timbers, log fires, wide range of beers, decent wines, large menu, helpful service; no children in bar; pleasant large garden, skittle alley *(J V Dadswell)*

Herefordshire

Pubs on fine form here this year are the beautifully set Riverside at Aymestrey (very good food in nice surroundings), the Lough Pool at Sellack, flourishing with gentle improvements by a new licensee, the Stagg at Titley (very popular for its inventive fresh food), the Three Crowns at Ullingswick (a favourite for its combination of very good food with a simple no-nonsense homely atmosphere), the Carpenters Arms at Walterstone (a lovely untouched country haven), the Wellington at Wellington (entirely new to the Guide, nice food and drink in attractive surroundings), and the Butchers Arms out in the country near Woolhope (a special favourite, good all round). Pub food in the county really is exceptionally good nowadays: no fewer than six establishments have now gained our coveted Food Award. Against this stiff competition, our supreme accolade of Herefordshire Dining Pub of the Year goes this year to the Three Crowns at Ullingswick. In the Lucky Dip at the end of the chapter, pubs to note particularly this year are the Olde Tavern in Kington, Three Horseshoes at Little Cowarne, Saracens Head at Symonds Yat and Farmers Arms at Wellington Heath. Drinks prices, scarcely changing here this year, are well below the national average, with the Wye Valley beers from Hereford a good local buy – not to mention the county's famous ciders from Weston's and Bulmer's, and less-known good brands such as Dunkerton's.

AYMESTREY SO4265 Map 6

Riverside Inn 🍽 ♀ 🛏

A4110; N off A44 at Mortimer's Cross, W of Leominster

There are picnic-sets by a flowing river, and rustic tables and benches up above in a steep tree-sheltered garden as well as a beautifully sheltered former bowling green behind this idyllically situated black and white timbered inn. It's lovely out here in summer when big overflowing flower pots frame the entrances. In cooler months there's no shortage of warm log fires in the rambling beamed bar with its several cosy areas and good laid-back atmosphere. Décor is drawn from a pleasant mix of periods and styles, with fine antique oak tables and chairs, stripped pine country kitchen tables, fresh flowers, hops strung from a ceiling waggon-wheel, horse tack, a Librairie Romantique poster for Victor Hugo's poems, a cheerful modern print of a plump red toadstool. There's a big restaurant area, shove-ha'penny, cribbage and dominoes. Well kept own-brew ales on handpump include Kingfisher Ale, Jack Snipe and Red Kite; local farm cider in summer and decent house wines. The French chef provides a good mix of daily changing bar food which might include filled baguettes (from £3.75), soup such as leek and potato or fish (£3.25), wild mushrooms and garlic fried greens with crème fraîche (£8.95), monkfish and mussels in brandy cream sauce, rack of lamb with rosemary jus or duckling breast with savoy cabbage and bacon and bramble sauce (£13.95), a few lunchtime daily specials such as pork and leek sausages, lasagne or fish and chips (£5.95) and puddings such as home-made ice cream (from £3), crème brûlée or fresh lemon tart (£3.95) and a local cheese platter (£4.95). Residents are offered fly-fishing (they have fishing rights on a mile of the River Lugg), and a free taxi service to the start of the Mortimer Trail. It does get busy at weekends, so booking would be wise. (*Recommended by Guy Vowles, Margaret Ross, Gill Waller, Tony Morriss, Mr and Mrs A H Young, J Hale, John Whitehead, Pamela and Merlyn Horswell, Chris Flynn, Wendy Jones, Margaret and Andrew Leach, Kevin*

Thorpe, Prof John and Mrs Patricia White, Mike and Wena Stevenson, Denys Gueroult, Mike and Lynn Robinson, Mrs Ursula Hofheinz, Lady Freeland, Alan and Sheila Hart, Ian Jones, D Randall)

Own brew ~ Licensees Steve and Val Bowen ~ Real ale ~ Bar food ~ Restaurant ~ (01568) 708440 ~ Children over 8 in eating area of bar ~ Open 11-11; 12-10.30 Sun ~ Bedrooms: £25(£30S)(£30B)/£40(£50S)(£50B)

BRIMFIELD SO5368 Map 4
Roebuck 🍺 ♀ 🛏

Village signposted just off A49 Shrewsbury—Leominster

Each of the three rambling bars at this smart country dining pub has a different but equally civilised atmosphere. The quiet old-fashioned snug is where you might find locals drinking and playing dominoes, cribbage or shove-ha'penny by an impressive inglenook fireplace. Dark panelling in the 15th-c bar makes for a quietly relaxed atmosphere, and the Brimfield bar with a big bay window and open fire is light and airy. The brightly decorated cane furnished airy dining room is no smoking. All the food here is home-made, and where possible local produce is used. The innovative menu includes soup (£3.50), wild mushroom risotto or goats cheese and ratatouille en croûte (£5.25), steak and mushroom suet pudding or fish pie (£8.95), herbed salmon fillet with lemon and chervil hollandaise (£9.95), roast chicken breast with pearl barley, bacon and leek risotto and wild mushroom and red wine sauce (£11.95) and fillet steak stuffed with stilton and wrapped in bacon with a madeira sauce (£15.95). Equally imaginative daily specials might include pan roasted pigeon breasts with bacon and foie gras (£5.25) and grilled bass on lobster and chorizo paella with tomato and salmon sauce (£14.25). They have an interesting reasonably priced wine list, a carefully chosen range of spirits and well kept Tetleys and Woods Parish and a guest such as Archers Golden on handpump. There are seats out on the enclosed terrace, and readers tell us their dogs have been welcome. *(Recommended by David and Helen Wilkins, Paul Boot, Ralph and Gloria Maybourn, P J and Avril Hanson, Mike and Wena Stevenson, Mike and Lynn Robinson, W H and E Thomas, Walter and Susan Rinaldi-Butcher, Bill Reed, David Heath, Mr and Mrs A H Young, John Kane, John Whitehead, Gene and Kitty Rankin)*

Free house ~ Licensees David and Sue Willson-Lloyd ~ Real ale ~ Bar food ~ Restaurant ~ (01584) 711230 ~ Children in eating area of bar and restaurant ~ Open 11.30-3, 6.30-11; 12-3.30, 7-10.30 Sun ~ Bedrooms: £45B/£60B

CAREY SO5631 Map 4
Cottage of Content ♀

Village signposted from good road through Hoarwithy

This very pretty out-of-the-way medieval country cottage is charmingly set, with a little lane running past by a stream, picnic-sets on the flower-filled front terrace and a couple more on a back terrace looking up a steep expanse of lawn. Its atmospheric rooms have a pleasant mix of country furnishings – stripped pine, country kitchen chairs, long pews by one big table and a mix of other old-fashioned tables on flagstones and bare boards, and there are plenty of beams and prints; darts, cribbage, dominoes and TV. Imaginative well presented bar food is freshly prepared to order so there may be a wait. Changing blackboards might include soup (£2.50), home-made potted prawns (£4.50), marinated fresh anchovy fillets with potato salad (£4.75), fresh crayfish salad (£4.95), wild rice and mixed vegetable and orange risotto (£5.95), pie of the day (£6.95), thai fishcakes with mango and coconut dressing (£7.95), local beef fillet with port and anchovy sauce (£13.50), best end of local lamb with red wine, redcurrant and rosemary sauce (£12.50), and puddings such as citron tart, treacle tart and summer pudding (£2.95). Well kept Hook Norton Best on handpump, around 100 wines by the bottle, 40 malt whiskies and farm cider; attractive beamed bedrooms with sloping floors; continental breakfasts only. The samoyed dog is called Storm. Readers have found all tables laid for dining at weekends, when it is advisable to book. *(Recommended by the Didler, Ian Dawson, MDN,*

Denys Gueroult, Clare and Paul Howes, Anne and Leuan Williams, M J Brooks, Matt Britton, Alison Cameron)

Free house ~ Licensee Mike Wainford ~ Real ale ~ Bar food (till 9.30(10 Fri and Sat)) ~ Restaurant ~ (01432) 840242 ~ Children welcome ~ Open 12-2.30, 7(6 Sat)-11(10.30 Sun); closed 25 Dec lunchtime ~ Bedrooms: £35B/£48(£55B)

CRASWALL SO2736 Map 6
Bulls Head ◀

Hay-on-Wye—Llanfihangel Crucorney road along Golden Valley, via Longtown; OS Sheet 161 map reference 278360

It's well worth going out of your way to visit this remote stone-built pub which is in a peaceful spot between the Golden Valley and the Black Mountains. This is a great place for walks. It's the sort of pub where the friendly helpful landlord will happily knock up a plate of ham and eggs outside food service times, although during meal times the food is surprisingly imaginative. The bar, dating back some 200 years, is like a Welsh farmhouse kitchen, with many original features: low beams, flagstones, antique settles and elderly chairs, logs burning in an old cast-iron stove, sentimental 19th-c engravings that have clearly never seen the inside of an antiques shop. Well kept Wye Valley Butty Bach and a guest from a little brewer such as Dunn Plowman are tapped from the cask and served through a hatch; table skittles, cribbage and dominoes. Very generous helpings of well prepared inventive food are served in the partly no smoking dining area: chunks of generously filled home-baked bread (which they call huffers) with all sorts of fillings from smoked bacon and stilton to locally made sausages (£3.25-4.75), fried pigeon breast on haggis with game gravy (£7.95), very good rib-eye steak, grilled monkfish with fennel and lemon, brill with red pepper sauce or grilled monkfish with fennel and lemon (£9.95), hake with clams, mussels and langoustines (£10.95), and puddings such as fruit filled pavlova, sticky toffee pudding and rice pudding and blackberries (£3.50). There are tables outside, with a play area and room for camping. *(Recommended by JP, PP, Dr and Mrs P Johnston, David Edwards, Jayne and Peter Capp, John Brightley)*

Free house ~ Licensee Paul Chicken ~ Real ale ~ Bar food (11-3, 6-9.30) ~ (01981) 510616 ~ Open 11-11; 12-10.30 Sun; maybe cl lunchtime in winter ~ Bedrooms: £35B/£40(£45B)

DORSTONE SO3141 Map 6
Pandy

Pub signed off B4348 E of Hay-on-Wye

There's a notably friendly welcome from the very hospitable South African licensees at this ancient half-timbered pub. Said to be Herefordshire's oldest pub, it was built in 1185 by Richard de Brico to house workers constructing a chapel of atonement for his part in the murder of Thomas à Becket. The neatly kept homely main room (on the right as you go in), has heavy beams in the ochre ceiling, stout timbers, upright chairs on its broad worn flagstones and in its various alcoves, and a vast open fireplace with logs; a side extension has been kept more or less in character; no smoking area. The particularly chatty parrot is called Oscar and the hairy persian tom is Tootsie. Meals are prepared by the landlady, and may include South African dishes such as tomato bredie (a casserole of lamb, tomatoes and potatoes) and bobotie (£7.55), as well as stilton and broccoli or french onion soup (£2.95), filled baguettes (£3.50), crispy whitebait (£4.50), deep-fried mushrooms with garlic dip (£4.95), roast vegetables with feta, olives and parmesan with tagliatelle (£7.25), lamb and apricot casserole (£7.55) and Herefordshire rump steak (£10.95). Well kept Wye Valley Butty Bach and Dorothy Goodbodys and maybe a guest such as Tetleys on handpump, lots of malt whiskies, farm cider and chilled fruit juices; darts, quoits and piped music. Surrounded by pretty countryside, there are picnic-sets and a play area in the neat side garden. *(Recommended by Jacquie and Jim Jones, Sue Demont, Tim Barrow, Prof John and Mrs Patricia White, J Hale, Jim Abbott, Peter Meister, Muriel and Peter Gleave, Geoff Pidoux, David and Elizabeth Briggs, Pam and David Bailey)*

Free house ~ Licensees Paul and Marja Gardner ~ Real ale ~ Bar food ~ Restaurant ~ No credit cards ~ (01981) 550273 ~ Well behaved children welcome ~ Open 12-3, 6-11; 12-11 Sat; 12-3, 6.30-10.30 Sun; closed Monday lunchtime except bank hols

LEDBURY SO7138 Map 4

Feathers 🍴 ♀ 🛏

High Street, Ledbury, A417

Drinkers and diners mix comfortably in the rather civilised Fuggles bar at this elegantly striking Tudor timbered inn, with locals gathered at one end of the room or at stools by the long bar counter, cheerfully uninhibited by those enjoying the imaginative food and fine wines at the brasserie tables behind them. There are beams and timbers, hop bines, some country antiques, 19th-c caricatures and fowl prints on the stripped brick chimney breast (lovely winter fire), and fresh flowers on the tables – some very snug and cosy, in side bays. The food is not cheap, but good value considering its restaurant quality. A broad-ranging menu includes home-made soup (£4.25), chicken and red pepper terrine with cranberry and red currant sauce (£4.95), grilled goats cheese on spinach with dried cranberries and pistachio (£5.25), salmon and chive fishcakes (£7.95), couscous with roasted vegetables, chick peas and fresh herbs (£8.50), hake fillet with garlic lemon and caper butter (£9.95), gressingham duck breast with spiced plum and brandy compote (£13.95), seared lamb fillet with pepper and mustard crust on wilted greens (£14.50), a couple of daily specials such as grilled lambs liver on red onion and orange confit (£11.95) and puddings such as dark chocolate, lemon and pistachio pot or caramel apple and pear crumble (£4.50); friendly, attentive service. They do excellent afternoon teas in the more formal quiet lounge by the reception area, with comfortable high-sided armchairs and sofas in front of a big log fire, and newspapers to read. Well kept Bass, Fullers London Pride and Worthington and a guest such as Timothy Taylors Landlord on handpump; various malt whiskies, and farm cider. There is quite an emphasis on the hotel side of this operation, with its attractive timbered bedrooms, an indoor swimming pool and leisure spa. In summer abundant pots and hanging baskets adorn the garden at the back. *(Recommended by Jenny and Dave Hughes, Denys Gueroult, Dr P C Rea, Mike and Mary Carter, Patricia Beebe, David and Catherine Whiting, Mrs M Mills, Duncan Cloud, Peter Lloyd)*

Free house ~ Licensee David Elliston ~ Real ale ~ Restaurant ~ (01531) 635266 ~ Children welcome ~ Open 11-11; 12-10.30 Sun ~ Bedrooms: /£95B

LUGWARDINE SO5541 Map 4

Crown & Anchor ♀

Cotts Lane; just off A438 E of Hereford

A friendly relaxed atmosphere fills the several smallish and charming rooms at this attractive black and white timbered inn. There's a friendly local atmosphere in the bar, which is furnished with an interesting mix of pieces, and there's a big log fire. As well as decent wines, including a clutch of usefully priced bin ends, they have well kept Butcombe and Worthington Best and a guest such as Fullers London on handpump, and lots of malts. Good bar food might include two or three dozen sandwiches (from £2.50), home-made soup (£3), linguini with parmesan, basil and toasted pine nuts (£3.25), smoked salmon and sweet cucumber salad (£4.25), ploughman's (£5), battered cod (£6), at least eight vegetarian and a couple of vegan dishes such as aduki bean bake, lentil and ricotta moussaka and vegetable nut korma (£5.75), grilled trout with almonds and herb stuffing (£7.50), chicken supreme with smoked oysters in saffron cream sauce (£7.50), chargrilled Herefordshire sirloin steak (£11), a good choice of daily specials such as cassoulet (£7) and fried medallions of venison with shallots and red wine (£11), and puddings like sorbet with elderflower syrup and mixed berry crumble (£3.50). The main eating area is no smoking. In summer the pretty garden is filled with honeysuckle. The pub is surrounded by newish housing but in ancient times the Lugg flats round here – some of the oldest Lammas meadows in England – were farmed in strips by local farm tenants, and meetings with the lord of the manor were held here. *(Recommended by Lynn Sharpless, Bob Eardley, Hazel and Michael Duncombe, Denys Gueroult, Ian Phillips, George Atkinson, Darly Graton, Graeme Gulibert, Mike and Mary Carter, Christopher and Jo Barton)*

Enterprise ~ Lease Nick and Julie Squire ~ Real ale ~ Bar food (till 10(9.30 Sun)) ~ (01432) 851303 ~ Children welcome ~ Live jazz first Weds evening of month ~ Open 12-12; 12-10.30 Sun; closed 25 Dec

MUCH MARCLE SO6633 Map 4
Slip Tavern ♀

Off A449 SW of Ledbury; take Woolhope turning at village stores, then right at pub sign

The splendidly colourful gardens at this welcoming country pub overlook cider orchards that stretch out behind, and in October they celebrate Apple Day here with lots of apple and cider dishes. The cosy chatty bar, which is popular with older people at lunchtime but has a more villagey local atmosphere in the evening, has ladderback and wheelback upholstered chairs around black tables, and little country prints on neat cream walls. Well kept Hook Norton and Wadworths 6X on handpump, and a decent range of wines; very friendly service; no smoking area; table skittles, dominoes and piped music. A good choice of straightforward reasonably priced bar food includes filled rolls (from £1.90), soup (£2.30), deep-fried camembert (£3.45), ploughman's (£5.20), faggots (£5.75), cauliflower cheese (£5.95), lemon sole or home-made steak pie (£6.65), beef in ale (£7.45), pork fillet with pears (£7.95) and beef stroganoff (£8.65). There's more space for eating in the attractively planted conservatory, though it's best to book. Outside is a well separated play area. *(Recommended by Lucien, Mike and Mary Carter, Denys Gueroult, Chris Flynn, Wendy Jones, June and Mike Coleman, Patricia Beebe, Jenny and Dave Hughes)*

Free house ~ Licensee David Templeman ~ Real ale ~ Bar food ~ Restaurant ~ (01531) 660246 ~ Children in restaurant ~ Open 11.30-2.30, 6.30-11; 12-2.30, 7-10.30 Sun

ORLETON SO4967 Map 6
Boot

Just off B4362 W of Woofferton

The new landlord at this 16th-c partly black and white timbered pub was formerly a brewer at Hobsons, so you never know, he might start brewing here. In the meantime he's stocking well kept Hobsons Best and Town Crier and a local guest on handpump and local cider. Cheerful locals enjoy the traditional-feeling bar which has a relaxed pubby atmosphere, a mix of dining and cushioned armed wheelback chairs around a few old tables on the red tiles, hops over the counter and on some beams, a warming fire in the big fireplace with horsebrasses along the bressumer beam and a very high-backed settle. The lounge bar is up a couple of steps and has green plush banquettes right the way round the walls, mullioned windows, an exposed section of wattle and daub, and standing timbers and heavy wall beams. The small, pretty partly no smoking restaurant is on the left. Enjoyable bar food includes soup (£2.50), creamy stilton mushrooms (£3.75), garlic tiger prawns (£4.95), steak and kidney pie (£6.25), grilled plaice with grape and spring onion sauce (£7.25), chicken with lemon sauce (£7.50), and daily specials such as chicken curry or lamb casserole with dumplings (£5.95), loin of pork with rosemary and sherry sauce (£8.75) and creamed strips of sirloin (£10.50). Dominoes, cribbage. The garden has seats and a brick barbecue, a lawn with more seats under a huge ash tree and a fenced-in children's play area with their own tables and chairs, a wooden wendy house and swing. *(Recommended by Paul and Margaret Baker, John and Christine Lowe, John and Marian Greenwood, Mike and Lynn Robinson, Pamela and Merlyn Horswell, P and J Shapley)*

Free house ~ Licensee Duncan Brooks ~ Real ale ~ Bar food ~ Restaurant ~ (01568) 780228 ~ Children in eating area of bar and restaurant ~ Open 12-2.30(3 Sat), 6-11; 12-3, 7-10.30 Sun; cl Mon lunchtime winter

PEMBRIDGE SO3958 Map 6

New Inn

Market Square (A44)

This ancient place is beautifully set in the centre of an attractive black and white mini-town. Tables outside on the cobblestones between it and the former wool market overlook the church, which has an unusual 14th-c detached bell tower beside it. Inside, the three simple beamed little rooms of the venerably aged bar are comfortable and atmospheric, with their oak peg-latch doors and elderly traditional furnishings including a fine antique curved-back settle on the worn flagstones, and a substantial log fire. One room has sofas, pine furniture and books; the lounge is no smoking; darts, shove-ha'penny, and quoits. Well kept Black Sheep and Fullers London Pride and a guest such as Adnams on handpump; good friendly service. Good bar food is fairly straightforward and includes sandwiches (£2.75), ploughman's (£3.95), hot bacon sandwich (£4), stilton steak sandwich or cumberland sausages with yorkshire pudding (£5.95) and steak and mushroom pie, half a pint of prawns or fish and chips (£6.50). *(Recommended by N H E Lewis, R T and J C Moggridge, Moira and John Cole)*

Free house ~ Licensee Jane Melvin ~ Real ale ~ Bar food (till 9.30 Sat) ~ Restaurant ~ (01544) 388427 ~ Children in eating area of bar will 8 ~ Folk band third Thurs of the month ~ Open 11-3, 6-11; 12-3, 7-10.30 Sun; 12-2.30 winter; closed Mon-Weds first wk in Feb ~ Bedrooms: £20.50/£41B

RUCKHALL SO4539 Map 6

Ancient Camp ♀ ⇐

Ruckhall signposted off A465 W of Hereford at Belmont Abbey; from Ruckhall pub signed down private drive; can reach it too from Bridge Sollers, W of Hereford on A438 – cross Wye, then after a mile or so take first left, then left again to Eaton Bishop, and left to Ruckhall

This smart country pub was changing hands just as we went to press and the new licensees weren't available, but as it is a lovely place we felt inclined to give it the benefit of the doubt. Dramatic views from tables on the rose-fringed long front terrace look down sharply on a broad picturesque landscape, with the River Wye curling gently through the foreground. Sometimes you can see red kites circling above the valley. If you stay the night, ask for the room at the front which shares this view, and as the licensee owns a stretch of the river you could combine your stay with some fishing. The very civilised central beamed and flagstoned bar is simply but thoughtfully furnished with comfortably solid green-upholstered settles and library chairs around nice old elm tables. On the left, a green-carpeted room has matching sofas around the walls and kitchen chairs around tripod tables. On the right are simple dining chairs around stripped kitchen tables on a brown carpet, and stripped stonework; nice log fire. Please do let us know how you find the place now. *(Recommended by Mike and Mary Carter, Howard Gregory, Denys Gueroult, Pamela and Merlyn Horswell, Julia and Richard Tredgett, Richard and Stephanie Foskett)*

Free house ~ Real ale ~ No credit cards ~ (01981) 250449

SELLACK SO5627 Map 4

Lough Pool ★ ♀

Back road Hoarwithy—Ross-on-Wye

The new licensee at this lovely old black and white timbered country cottage is well known in the gastronomic world as a talented chef/licensee. He plans to build on the best aspects of this already well liked place and bring up the areas where it's been lagging. Many readers will be pleased to hear that as a starting point he's banished the piped music. Improvements to the kitchen should help plans to gear up the food by using fresh local and where possible organic produce, but at the same time keeping the menu nice and pubby in the bar, with a more elaborate imaginative choice in the re-decorated no smoking restaurant. There are now two guest beers such as Hook Norton and Wadworths 6X alongside well kept John Smiths and Wye Valley Bitter and Butty Bach on handpump, a good range of malt whiskies, local farm ciders and a well chosen reasonably priced wine list. The beamed central room has kitchen chairs and cushioned window seats around wooden tables (some now replaced by nicer ones) on the mainly flagstoned floor, sporting prints and bunches of dried flowers, and a log fire at each end. Other rooms lead off, with attractive individual furnishings and nice touches like the dresser of patterned plates. A good balanced bar menu includes soup (£3.25), black pudding fritters with beetroot relish (£4.25), ploughman's (£5.50), charcuterie (£4.50/£7.50), sausages, or steak and kidney pie (£6.25), spaghetti with tomato, basil and caper sauce (£6.95), battered cod with mushy peas and home-made tartare sauce (£9.50) and roast crispy duck with limes (£22 for two). There are plenty of picnic-sets on the neat front lawn, and pretty hanging baskets. *(Recommended by Matt Britton, Alison Cameron, Pat and Roger Fereday, Bernard Stradling, Andy and Sue Tye, Mike and Mary Carter, Ian Dawson, Peter and Audrey Dowsett, Lynn Sharpless, Bob Eardley, Peter Chester)*

Free house ~ Licensee Stephen Bull ~ Real ale ~ Bar food ~ Restaurant ~ (01989) 730236 ~ Children in eating area of bar and restaurant ~ Open 11.30-2.30, 6.30-11; 12-5(2 winter), 7-10.30 Sun; closed Sun eve in Nov-Feb

ST OWEN'S CROSS SO5425 Map 4
New Inn

Junction A4137 and B4521, W of Ross-on-Wye

Fine views from this unspoilt black and white timbered coaching inn stretch over rolling countryside to the distant Black Mountains. Inside, both the atmospheric locals' lounge bar and the no smoking restaurant have huge inglenook fireplaces, intriguing nooks and crannies, settles, old pews, beams, and timbers. Bar food, served in generous helpings, includes soup (£3.25), sandwiches (from £3.25), chicken liver pâté (£4.75), ploughman's (£4.75), lasagne or sausage and mash (£4.95), mushroom and asparagus pancake (£7.95), and daily specials such as swordfish steak with tomato and black olive tapenade or mediterranean vegetable roast (£7.95) and pork fillet in cider and dijon sauce (£8.95); friendly efficient service. Bass, Tetleys and Wadworths 6X on handpump, and a fair choice of malt whiskies; darts, shove-ha'penny, cribbage, dominoes, trivia and piped music. The three dobermans are called Baileys, Tia Maria and Ginnie. The big sunny garden with a few toys is enclosed for children and dogs. In summer the pub is festooned with award-winning colourful hanging baskets. *(Recommended by Martin and Karen Wake, Tom Evans, Pam and David Bailey)*

Free house ~ Licensee Nigel Donovan ~ Real ale ~ Bar food ~ Restaurant ~ (01989) 730274 ~ Children in eating area of bar and restaurant ~ Open 12-2.30(3 Sat, Sun), 6-11(7-10.30 Sun); closed 25 Dec ~ Bedrooms: £40S(£45B)/£70S(£80B)

STOCKTON CROSS SO5161 Map 4
Stockton Cross Inn

Kimbolton; A4112, off A49 just N of Leominster

You may need to book to be sure of a table at this beautifully kept little black and white timbered pub with its enjoyably old-fashioned local atmosphere. A comfortably snug area at the top end of the long heavily beamed bar has a handsome antique settle facing an old black kitchen range, and old leather chairs and brocaded stools by the huge log fire in the broad stone fireplace. There's a woodburning stove at the far end too, with heavy cast-iron-framed tables and sturdy dining chairs; there are more tables and chairs up a step in a small no smoking side area. Old-time prints, a couple of épées on one beam and lots of copper and brass complete the picture. Brains Reverend James, Wye Valley Butty Bach and an occasional guest such as Shepherd Neame Spitfire are well kept on handpump. The landlady's enterprising and enjoyable cooking might include soup (£3.25), fried goats cheese with plum sauce (£4.50), smoked duck breast with apple and thyme jelly (£4.95), hot tartlet filled with smoked salmon and haddock soufflé (£5.50), crêpe filled with vegetables, spinach, nuts and rice with mozzarella and tomato topping (£9.25), pork tenderloin filled with spinach wrapped in smoked bacon with white wine and cream sauce (£11.95), warmed seafood salad (£12.25) and bass fillet with parsley and tarragon butter (£15.55), with a few simpler daily specials such as lsasagne or cod and chips (£6.75), and tasty puddings such as bread and butter pudding, treacle tart or fresh fruit pavlova (£3.50). There are tables out in the garden, with maybe a fine summer show of sweet peas. *(Recommended by Denys Gueroult, Gordon Neighbour, P Fisk, Ian Phillips, Hazel and Michael Duncombe, Mike and Lynn Robinson)*

Free house ~ Licensee R Wood ~ Real ale ~ Bar food ~ Restaurant ~ (01568) 612509 ~ Children over 6 welcome ~ Open 12-3, 7-11(10.30 Sun); closed Mon evening

TITLEY SO3360 Map 6
Stagg 🍴 ♀
B4355 N of Kington

The main focus at this fairly simple-looking old place is decidedly on the two dining rooms, one quite big, the other intimate, and you will need to book to be sure of a table. The landlord/chef is a well informed enthusiast for local produce, and at any given time of year the menu reflects what is showing best locally, so you can be sure of good fresh interestingly cooked vegetables or salad. The more pubby blackboard menu includes sandwiches (from £3.50), ploughman's (£6.50), steak sandwich or crispy duck leg with cider sauce (£6.90) and smoked salmon and prawn risotto (£7.50), with more imaginative dishes on the printed restaurant menu (which you can eat from in the bar): pork tenderloin stuffed with black pudding mousse with apricot sauce (£9.90), rack of lamb with ratatouille (£12.50), turbot with samphire and bouillabaisse (£14.90), and beef fillet with red wine and shallots (£14). Puddings might include caramelised lemon tart with orange sorbet or passion fruit jelly with pannacotta (£3.90). The cheese board, tempting without being overfacing, has up to a dozen mainly local types. The wine list is nicely topped up with additional bin ends, and includes around ten good wines by the glass. A couple of well kept real ales on handpump come from brewers such as Brains, Hobsons and Tomas Watkins, and they keep a fine collection of malt whiskies. You need to know which are the right two weeks to enjoy their home-made sloe gin, as they get through the entire annual production of five litres in that short time. The bar, though comfortable and hospitable, is not large, and the atmosphere is civilised rather than lively; we have not yet heard from readers who have stayed here. There are tables out in the garden, and this is lovely countryside. *(Recommended by Tony Hall, Melanie Jackson, Richard and Stephanie Foskett, John Kane, Rob Whittle, David and Brenda Tew, Hywel Jones, Gemma Tucker, Mr and Mrs A H Young, Kate Whitfield, W H and E Thomas, Alan Whitfield, Stuart Turner)*

Free house ~ Licensees Steve Reynolds and Nicola Holland ~ Real ale ~ Bar food (12-2, 6.30-10(9 Sun)) ~ Restaurant ~ (01544) 230221 ~ Children welcome ~ Open 12-3, 6.30-11(7-10.30 Sun); closed Mon, first two wks Nov ~ Bedrooms: £40B/£60B

ULLINGSWICK SO5949 Map 4
Three Crowns 🍴 ♀
Village off A465 S of Bromyard (and just S of Stoke Lacy) and signposted off A417 N of A465 roundabout – keep straight on through village and past turn-off to church; pub at Bleak Acre, towards Little Cowarne

Herefordshire Dining Pub of the Year
What's nice about this place is that although you'll still find local farmers in the very homely welcoming bar, the standard of imaginative cooking is way above what you'd expect to find in a village local. Food is all cooked with real flair, using local and organic products as much as possible. As a consequence the seasonally changing menu is shortish but might include starters such as asparagus and pea broth with goats cheese and prosciutto, cheese and spinach soufflé, and warm duck liver mousse

with port glaze (all £4.95), main courses such as roast monkfish, scallop and langoustine with laverbread sauce and crispy seaweed, tagliatelle with asparagus, porcini and brown butter vinaigrette, and roast rack of lamb with béarnaise sauce (all £12.95), puddings such as lemon tart with confit orange or apple parfait (£3.95), and local cheeses (£3.95). They also do a two- and three-course lunch (£8/£10). The charmingly traditional interior has hops strung along the low beams of its smallish bar, a couple of traditional settles besides more usual seats, a mix of big old wooden tables with small round ornamental cast-iron-framed ones, open fires and one or two gently sophisticated touches such as candles on tables and napkins; half the pub is no smoking. They have well kept Hobsons Best and a stronger guest ale from a small local brewer on handpump, farm ciders, and up to 10 wines by the glass; cribbage. There are tables out on the attractively planted lawn, with good summer views.

(Recommended by Sir Nigel Foulkes, Mr and Mrs Macker, Gay Cheyne, Peter Burton, Mike and Lynn Robinson, Denys Gueroult, Colin Parker, Roger White, David Edwards, Neil and Margaret Meacher, Joanna and Paul Clark, Steve Furlong, Patricia Beebe, Rodney and Norma Stubington, Jenny and Dave Hughes)

Free house ~ Licensees Sue and Derrick Horwood and Brent Castle ~ Real ale ~ Restaurant ~ (01432) 820279 ~ Well behaved children welcome in eating area of bar ~ Open 12-2.30, 7-11; 12-3, 7-10.30 Sun; closed Tues and two wks after Christmas

UPTON BISHOP SO6527 Map 4
Moody Cow

2 miles from M50 junction 3 westbound (or junction 4 eastbound), via B4221; continue on B4221 to rejoin at next junction

The reliable freshly cooked and well presented food at this friendly bustling pub does draw in the crowds so you may need to book. The changing menu might include soup (£2.95), open ciabatta sandwiches (from £3.95), warm red onion tartlet with parmesan (£4.95), tempura king prawns with thai chilli sauce (£5.95), battered cod and chips (£6.95), sausage and mash (£7.95), chicken or king prawn jalfrezi, marinated pork fillet with rösti potato, chicken breast wrapped in bacon and stuffed with stilton with red wine sauce (£9.95), beef medallions with pink peppercorn sauce or half shoulder of lamb (£11.95), and puddings such as bread and butter pudding, good sticky toffee pudding or chocolate torte (£3.75) and cheese and biscuits with celery and walnuts (£5.95). Several separate snug areas angle in an L around the bar counter and have a pleasant medley of stripped country furniture, stripped floorboards and stonework, a few cow ornaments and naïve cow paintings, and a big log fire. On the far right is a biggish no smoking rustic and candlelit restaurant, with hop-draped rafters and a fireside area with armchairs and sofas. The far left has a second smaller dining area, just five or six tables with rush seats, green-stained woodwork, shelves of country china; piped music. Well kept Flower IPA, Hook Norton and Wadworths 6X on handpump. *(Recommended by LM, Neil and Anita Christopher, Jenny and Dave Hughes, Peter Burton, Colin Parker, Chris Flynn, Wendy Jones, Rob Holt, Guy Vowles, Mike and Mary Carter, J C Brittain-Long, Ian Jones)*

Free house ~ Licensee James Lloyd ~ Real ale ~ Bar food (12-2, 6.30-9.30; not Sun eve, Mon) ~ Restaurant ~ (01989) 780470 ~ Children in eating area of bar and restaurant ~ Open 12-2.30, 6.30-11; 12-3, 7-10.30 Sun; closed Mon lunchtime

WALTERSTONE SO3425 Map 6
Carpenters Arms

Village signposted off A465 E of Abergavenny, beside Old Pandy Inn; follow village signs, and keep eyes skinned for sign to pub, off to right, by lane-side barn

It's been in the same family for years, and you can see that this charming little stone cottage on the edge of the Black Mountains is run with real loving pride. This is the best sort of unspoilt country tavern, with its delightful old interior, and kindly welcoming landlady. Its genuinely traditional rooms have ancient settles against stripped stone walls, some pieces of carpet on broad polished flagstones, a roaring log fire in a gleaming black range (complete with pot-iron, hot-water tap, bread oven and salt cupboard), pewter mugs hanging from beams, and the slow tick of a clock. The snug main dining room has mahogany tables and oak corner cupboards, a big vase of flowers on the dresser – and a promising aroma of stock simmering in the kitchen. Another little dining area has old oak tables and church pews on flagstones. Home-made food might include sandwiches (from £1.60), soup (£3), farmhouse pâté (£3), prawn cocktail (£3.50), ploughman's (£4), scampi or plaice (£6), vegetarian lasagne, lamb korma or beef and Guinness pie (£6.50), chicken supreme with brandy and mushroom sauce (£8.50), pepper fillet steak (£12) and puddings (£3.50). Well kept Wadworths 6X and maybe one of their seasonal ales such as Summer Sault tapped from the cask; farm cider. The outside lavatories are cold but in character. *(Recommended by John Brightley, Jacquie and Jim Jones, Ivor and Shirley Thomas, Joyce and Maurice Cottrell)*

Free house ~ Licensee Vera Watkins ~ Real ale ~ Bar food ~ No credit cards ~ (01873) 890353 ~ Children welcome ~ Open 12-11

WELLINGTON SO4948 Map 6
Wellington ◖

Village signposted off A49 N of Hereford; pub at far end

Not the most promising building from the outside, this red brick Victorian pub has been appealingly reworked inside and brightened up a lot by its newish landlord. It has big high-backed dark wooden settles, a brick fireplace with a log fire in winter and fresh flowers in summer, and bric-a-brac such as elderly or antique cricket bats, other sporting equipment and farm and garden tools around the red-painted walls; there is stripped brickwork in the former stables, now a pleasant candlelit eating area. Hop bines decorate the bar, well kept ales such as Bass, Exmoor Fox, Hancocks HB, Hobsons, and Ridleys on handpump, Dutch Oranjeboom lager and farm cider; the public bar side has darts, board games and a piano. A good choice of enjoyable food includes home-made soup (£1.95), pâté of duck and orange (£2.45), sandwiches (from £2.50), big baguettes or baked potatoes (£3), pasta and mushroom au gratin (£5.95), turkey steak with lime, ginger and honey sauce (£6.95), lamb steak with minted gravy (£7.95), steaks (from £8.30); daily specials like grilled goats cheese on a sweet salad (£3.20), proper home-made pie of the day (£6.50), breast of pheasant with red wine and juniper sauce (£7.95), and poached bass with a prawn and mushroom sauce (£8.30); puddings such as treacle tart or banoffi pie (£2.95); Sunday lunch (£5.50); they hold a pot-luck 'dangerous dinner' on the first Tuesday of the month. The restaurant is no smoking. Service is friendly and interested; there may be quiet classical piped music. There are tables out in the garden behind, and an outside skittle alley. *(Recommended by Jestyn Phillips, Anne Morris)*

Free house ~ Licensee Chris Powis ~ Real ale ~ Bar food (12-2, 7-9.30) ~ Restaurant ~ (01432) 830367 ~ Well behaved children welcome ~ Open 12-2.30, 6(7 Sun)-11; closed Mon lunchtime

WEOBLEY SO4052 Map 6
Salutation ⊕ ♀ ⇌

Village signposted from A4112 SW of Leominster; and from A44 NW of Hereford (there's also a good back road direct from Hereford – straight out past S side of racecourse)

Even the bus shelter in this quaint little medieval village is black and white timbered, and this heavily beamed 500-year old hotel is one of the oldest buildings here. It's a quiet village in lovely lush countryside, so this is a nice place to stay, with well equipped comfortable bedrooms and breakfasts that won't leave you hungry. The two areas of the comfortable lounge – separated by a few steps and standing timbers – have a relaxed, pubby feel, brocaded modern winged settles and smaller seats, a couple of big cut-away cask seats, wildlife decorations, a hop bine over the bar counter, and logs burning in a big stone fireplace; more standing timbers separate it from the neat no smoking restaurant area, and there's a separate smaller parquet-floored public bar with sensibly placed darts, juke box, and a fruit machine; dominoes and cribbage. Very fairly priced bar food includes soup (£3.95), ratatouille filled grilled mushrooms (£4.95), lunchtime filled baguettes including warm chicken and red onion (from £5.10), lunchtime ploughman's (£5.25), daily roast or leek and mushroom strudel (£6.95), steak and stout pie (£7.25), salmon and coriander fishcakes or supreme of pheasant with mushrooms, red onions and thyme (£7.95), puddings such as lemon tart with raspberry coulis or hazelnut parfait with a rich chocolate sauce (£4.25); three-course Sunday lunch (£13.50); the restaurant is more elaborate and costs more. Well kept Hook Norton Best, Fullers London Pride and a guest such as Wye Valley Butty Bach on handpump, an extensive wine list with mainly new world bins, and a couple of dozen malt whiskies. There are tables and chairs with parasols on a sheltered back terrace. *(Recommended by Chris Flynn, Wendy Jones, MDN, Duncan Cloud, Hazel and Michael Duncombe, Mandy and Simon King, W H and E Thomas, John Davis, Prof John and Mrs Patricia White, Miss G Irving, R Styles, Ian Dawson, Mike and Wena Stevenson, Sue and Bob Ward, Jim Abbott, June and Mike Coleman, Mike and Lynn Robinson, Denys Gueroult, Ruth Levy, Tony Hall, Melanie Jackson, Chris Bartlett)*

Free house ~ Licensee Dr Mike Tai ~ Real ale ~ Bar food ~ Restaurant ~ (01544) 318443 ~ Children in eating area of bar, restaurant and conservatory ~ Open 11-11; 12-10.30 Sun ~ Bedrooms: £45S(£48B)/£69S(£72B)

WINFORTON SO2947 Map 6
Sun

A438 14 miles W of Hereford

This is very much a hands on place; they make their own bread, and smoke their own meats at this welcoming neatly kept little dining pub. Cheese fans will love its 10 different cheese ploughman's (£4.95), which are nicely spiked up by the landlady's good range of home-made chutneys (you can buy these by the jar to take home). The regularly changing menu might include butter bean, lemon and thyme pâté (£3.75), goats cheese and watercress tart (£4.50), smoked duck breast with berries (£4.95), turkey and wild mushroom pie (£7.20), aubergine and feta charlotte (£7.25), pigeon breasts with sesame and pine nut dressing (£9.90), and puddings such as gooseberry and elderflower fool or pecan and walnut tart with whisky ice cream (£4). There are two friendly beamed areas on either side of the central servery with an individual assortment of comfortable country-kitchen chairs, high-backed settles and good solid wooden tables, heavy-horse harness, brasses and old farm tools on the mainly stripped stone walls, and two log-burning stoves; no smoking area. Well kept Shepherd Neame Spitfire and Hook Norton and maybe a guest such as Greene King Abbot on handpump, and they keep several malt whiskies, and local cider; sensibly placed darts, cribbage, dominoes, maybe piped music. As well as sheltered tables and a good play area, the garden has an 18 hole pitch-and-putt/crazy golf course. *(Recommended by Nick and Meriel Cox, Cath Beselle, Ian Phillips, Dr Phil Putwain)*

Free house ~ Licensees Brian and Wendy Hibbard ~ Real ale ~ Bar food ~ Restaurant ~ No credit cards ~ (01544) 327677 ~ Children in eating area of bar and restaurant ~ Open 11.15-3, 6-11; 11.30-3, 7-11 Sun; closed Tues ~ Bedrooms: £32B/£52B

WOOLHOPE SO6136 Map 4
Butchers Arms 🍺

Signposted from B4224 in Fownhope; carry straight on past Woolhope village

They seem to have got just about everything spot on at this tucked away 14th-c country pub, from the lovely relaxed atmosphere generated by the friendly licensees, cheery staff and cosy interior, through to the generously served very well prepared enjoyable food. One of the spaciously welcoming bars has very low beams decorated with hops, old-fashioned well worn built-in seats with brocaded cushions, captain's chairs and stools around small tables, and a brick fireplace filled with dried flowers. The other bar, broadly similar though with fewer beams, has a large built-in settle and another log fire; there are often fresh flowers. Sliding french windows lead out to a little terrace with teak furniture, a few parasols and cheerful flowering tubs; there's also a tiny willow-lined brook. Freshly prepared bar food includes soup

(£2.95), whitebait (£4.25), leek and hazelnut terrine wrapped in vine leaves with wild berries (£4.95), ploughman's (from £4.75), mushroom biryani (£5.95), lasagne (£6.25), venison sausages and mash (£7.75), wild rabbit braised in cider, gammon steak or salmon fishcakes with creamy cheese sauce (£7.95) and rump steak (£8.95), and there are daily specials such as beef stroganoff or baked trout (£7.95), fish pie (£9.95) and pork loin with apple, cream and brandy sauce, pheasant breast with wild berry sauce or chicken breasts stuffed with cream cheese, garlic and chives (£10.95); generous puddings (from £2.95); the restaurant is no smoking. They have very well kept Hook Norton Best and Old Hooky and a guest such as Shepherd Neame Spitfire on handpump, local ciders, quite a few malt whiskies, and decent wines. The pub is just outside the village in a quietly relaxing spot, and the countryside around is really lovely – to enjoy some of the best of it, turn left as you come out of the pub and take the tiny left-hand road at the end of the car park; this turns into a track and then into a path, and the view from the top of the hill is quite something. *(Recommended by Martin Jennings, Lynn Sharpless, Bob Eardley, June and Mike Coleman, Lucien, Matt Britton, Alison Cameron, M Dean, Jenny and Dave Hughes, Greg Lacey, John Bowdler, R W Slawson, Philippa Lucas, Tony Gill, John Bailey, Mrs B Sugarman, Ian Jones)*

Free house ~ Licensees Sian and Mark Vallely ~ Real ale ~ Bar food (12-2.30, 6.30-9.30(10 Sat, 9 Sun)) ~ Restaurant ~ (01432) 860281 ~ Children welcome ~ Open 11.30-3, 6.30-11; 12-3, 7-10.30 Sun ~ Bedrooms: £30/£39

Crown ♀

In village centre

You can buy a very good value pint of local Wye Valley Bitter at this friendly well run old pub which is also very popular for its comprehensive choice of good value bar food (you may need to book). Other beers include well kept Smiles Best and a guest such as Timothy Taylors Landlord on handpump; decent wine list, and farm cider. As well as a dozen or so vegetarian dishes such as stilton, apple and walnut pasta bake, chestnut, onion and apple pie with cumberland sauce or courgette, mushroom and spinach lasagne (£6.70), the food includes home-made soup (£3.05), grilled sardines (£3.75), home-made crab cakes (£3.95), creamed smoked haddock pot (£4.95), lunchtime ploughman's (from £5.20), grilled bacon chop with plum sauce (£6.95), steak sandwich, steak, stout and mushroom pie or lamb, apricot and ginger casserole (£7.20), fish pie (£7.50), salmon steak with watercress sauce (£8.50), grilled fish of the day with white wine and mushroom sauce (£8.95), and lots of puddings such as blackcurrant torte, ginger and apple sponge, summer pudding or coffee and walnut gateau (£3.25). The neatly kept lounge bar has plush button-back built-in wall banquettes and dark wood tables and chairs. There's also an open fire, a timbered divider strung with hop bines, good wildlife photographs and little country pictures on the cream walls, and lots of attention to details such as flowers on tables. Heavy oak posts support a thick stone wall to the knocked through no smoking dining area; darts, shove-ha'penny, table skittles and quoits. In summer the pub is festooned with flowers, and there are picnic-sets on the neat front lawn. *(Recommended by Colin Parker, Guy Vowles, June and Mike Coleman)*

Free house ~ Licensees Neil and Sally Gordon ~ Real ale ~ Bar food (till 10) ~ Restaurant ~ (01432) 860468 ~ Children in eating area of bar and restaurant till 8 ~ Open 12-2.30, 6.30(7 Mon-Tues winter)-11; 12-3, 6(6.30 winter)-11 Sat; 12-3, 6.30(7 winter)-10.30 Sun; 7-11 Mon-Thurs, winter; closed evening 25 Dec

---

Post Office address codings confusingly give the impression that some pubs are in Herefordshire when they're really in Gloucestershire or even Wales (which is where we list them).

Lucky Dip

Besides the fully inspected pubs, you might like to try these Lucky Dips recommended to us and described by readers (if you do, please send us reports: www.goodguides.com).

Ashperton [SO6442]
Hopton Arms [A417]: Friendly staff and good food range from sandwiches to steak inc children's helpings in spotless pub; tables and play area in garden, bedrooms *(Mr and Mrs A Craig)*
Bodenham [SO5454]
Englands Gate [just off A417 at Bodenham turn-off, about 6 miles S of Leominster]: Locally popular for good variety of bar food at reasonable prices, well kept real ale *(Greta and Christopher Wells)*
Colwall [SO7342]
Crown [Walwyn Rd]: Two-bar village pub, attractive décor, daily papers, good honest food from sandwiches and ploughman's to popular Sun lunch friendly efficient service, well kept Butcombe, Marstons Pedigree and Timothy Taylors Landlord *(Mike and Mary Clark, Nick Bentley)*
Garway [SO4622]
Moon [Garway Common]: Good choice of well cooked food *(J A Goodrich)*
Hereford [SO5139]
Barrels [St Owens St]: Lively unpretentious two-bar local brewing its own good Wye Valley Hereford and Dorothy Goodbodys ales at attractive prices, also guest beers, farm ciders from Bulmer's, Stowford Press and Weston's, friendly staff, no food, side pool room with games, juke box and TV sports; open all day, live music at beer festival end Aug *(Mike Pugh, Richard Lewis, the Didler)*
Goodbodys [West St]: 16th-c black and white building, comfortable welcoming lounge with well kept local real ale, decent wines, tea and coffee, reasonable prices, good food from snacks up using local produce, upstairs restaurant *(Gill Waller, Tony Morriss)*
Green Dragon [Broad St]: Pleasant bars and decent buffet-style lunches in long-established central hotel; good value bargain breaks *(MDN)*
Victory [St Owen St, opp fire stn]: Pub decked out as galleon, front bar shaped like a ship, even a back crow's nest, and lots of shipping memorabilia; interesting collection of unusual ales inc Spinning Dog brewed at the pub (and yes, the dog really does spin when it chases its tail), also farm ciders, food early evening, real fire, back pool table and pub games; children welcome, open all day, some live music, tables outside *(Mike Pugh, Richard Lewis)*
Kington [SO3057]
☆ *Olde Tavern* [Victoria Rd, just off A44 opp B4355 – follow sign to Town Centre, Hospital, Cattle Mkt; pub on right opp Elizabeth Rd, no inn sign but Estd 1767 notice]: Wonderful time-warp old place, small plain parlour and public bar, dark brown woodwork, big windows, old settles and other antique furniture, china, pewter and curios; truly welcoming locals, well kept Ansells, gas fire, no music, machines or food; children welcome, though not a family pub; cl wkdy lunchtimes, outside gents' *(JP, PP, the*

Didler, Pete Baker, BB, Edward Jago)
Ledbury [SO6343]
Full Pitcher [The Wharf, Stretton Grandison; A449 SW, junction B4216]: Plush chain dining pub open all day for usual food, with no smoking area, three well kept ales such as Jennings Cumberland, friendly staff, farm tools etc; picnic-sets outside *(Ian and Nita Cooper)*
Leintwardine [SO4174]
☆ *Sun* [Rosemary Lane, just off A4113]: Redecorated but still basically unspoilt, three benches by coal fire in red-tiled front parlour off hallway, venerable landlady brings you well kept Woods tapped from the cask in her kitchen (and may honour you with the small settee and a couple of chairs by the gas fire in her sitting room); no food *(Pete Baker, BB, Kevin Thorpe)*
Leominster [SO4959]
☆ *Talbot* [West St]: Comfortable and hospitable old coaching inn in charming town, heavy beams and standing timbers, antique carved settles, fine log fires with 18th-c oak-panelled chimneybreasts, sporting prints; decent straightforward home-made bar food inc good sandwiches, well kept Ruddles, nice choice of wines, good coffee, warmly friendly long-serving staff, popular restaurant; piped music; good bedrooms and housekeeping *(LYM, Hazel and Michael Duncombe)*
Little Cowarne [SO6051]
☆ *Three Horseshoes* [off A465 S of Bromyard, towards Ullingswick]: Wide choice of good home cooking in quarry-tiled bar and spacious restaurant extension (lunchtime carvery) with no smoking conservatory, well kept ales such as Marstons Pedigree and Ruddles County, decent wines, log fire, mix of solid tables and chairs, friendly obliging licensees, disabled access; juke box, pool, darts and fruit machine; lovely country views from terrace and charming simple garden, quite unspoilt village; comfortable bedrooms *(Colin Parker, Sir Nigel Foulkes)*
Lyonshall [SO3355]
☆ *Royal George* [A480 S]: Unpretentious beamed and timbered village inn, clean and friendly, with good fresh food nicely served inc lots of unusual dishes and Sun lunch, well kept Bass, Boddingtons, Brains SA and Greene King Old Speckled Hen, six good value wines by the glass, small lounge bar and two pleasant partly no smoking dining areas off central servery, lots of clay pipes and old photographs, log fire; comfortable bedrooms, flower-filled garden *(George Atkinson, Norma and Keith Bloomfield, Colin Parker)*
Madley [SO4239]
Comet: New licensees for dining pub, same chef still doing good reasonably priced food *(Trevor Swindells)*
Mathon [SO7345]
Cliffe Arms [signed off B4220; or reached off A4103 via Cradley]: Pretty black and white heavy-beamed village pub, small slate-floored bar, dining area with woodburner, cushioned

pews and nice dining chairs, Adnams, Hobsons and Tetleys, good generous food (not Mon; not winter Sun evening) inc adventurous dishes, simple public bar with well lit pool, games, TV and juke box; may be service snags; children welcome, tables in sizeable streamside garden below Malvern Hills, cl Mon lunchtime *(Denys Gueroult)*

Mordiford [SO5737]
Moon [just off B4224 SE of Hereford]: In good spot by Wye tributary, walkers welcome; comfortable attractive lounge with roaring fire, good value food from filled baked potatoes to unusual specials, relaxed yet attentive service, real ales such as Marstons Pedigree, Tetleys and Wadworths 6X, local farm ciders, reasonably priced wines, front restaurant; back bar popular with young locals *(Martin Jennings, R T and J C Moggridge, Keith Allen)*

Orcop Hill [SO4728]
Fountain [off A466 S of Hereford]: Small village local with new licensees, basic but cosy bar with daily papers, big helpings of food in back dining room and restaurant inc fresh fish specials and cheap lunchtime deals, Marstons Pedigree and John Smiths; darts, piped music; tables in peaceful pretty front garden *(Mike and Lynn Robinson, Chris and Joan Woodward, J A Goodrich, BB)*

Ross-on-Wye [SO6024]
Crown & Sceptre [Market Pl]: Nice bustling atmosphere in open-plan pub, Archers, Greene King, Shepherd Neame and guests, lunchtime meals, coal fire; very busy wknds, bank hol beer festivals; tables outside, open all day *(JP, PP)*
Hope & Anchor [Riverside; coming from A40 W side, 1st left after bridge (Rope Walk)]: Big-windowed family extension looking out on gardens leading down to river, plenty of tables out here (and summer ice-cream bar and barbecues), thorough-going boating theme in well worn in cheery main bar, upstairs parlour bar and Victorian-style dining room, generous good value food inc sandwiches and good choice for children, well kept Banks's and Marstons Pedigree, farm cider, good house wine, attractive prices; open all day, can be crowded wknds *(LYM, Mike Sinclair, Keith Allen)*
Travellers Rest [Ledbury Rd, by M50 junction 4]: Large Beefeater with several rooms, wide choice of reasonably priced food, play area outside; can be very busy, piped music may be loud; bedrooms in Travel Lodge *(Peter and Audrey Dowsett)*

Shobdon [SO4062]
Bateman Arms: Venerable inn with relaxed local feel, two bars, well kept ales inc Woods, good range of enjoyable food using local supplies from club sandwiches up, friendly father and son; restaurant, bedrooms *(John Whitehead, Grahame McNulty)*

Symonds Yat [SO5615]
☆ *Saracens Head* [Symonds Yat E, by ferry, ie over on the Gloucs bank]: Riverside beauty spot next to 60p ferry, busy down-to-earth flagstoned bar popular with canoeists, mountain bikers and hikers, cheerful efficient staff, good range of well presented nourishing food from good value

sandwiches up, well kept Theakstons Best, XB and Old Peculier and Wye Valley, three farm ciders, pine tables, settles and window seats; cosy carpeted restaurant, games bar with pool, piped jazz and blues, SkyTV, lots of picnic-sets out on waterside terraces, live music Thurs; summer boat trips, nice bedrooms – good place to stay out of season *(Dave and Meg Richards, Keith Allen, Clare and Paul Howes, Ian Phillips, BB, Jane Taylor, David Dutton, Denys Gueroult)*
Wye Knot [B4164]: Simple and friendly, with Fullers London Pride and Wye Valley Golden and Hereford, enjoyable reasonably priced food *(Ian Phillips)*

Trumpet [SO6639]
☆ *Verzons* [A438]: Former hotel, newly reopened after extensive refurbishment as country inn with emphasis on fresh food; new owner has previously put two Gloucs dining pubs into the top rank for character and welcoming atmosphere *(anon)*

Walford [SO5820]
☆ *Mill Race* [B4234 Ross—Lydney]: Comfortable beamed bar, attentive friendly staff, good value food from sandwiches and filled baked potatoes to enterprising hot dishes, well kept Bass, good wine choice, restaurant through Norman arch; garden and play area *(Barry Smith, Andy Sinden, Louise Harrington)*

Wellington Heath [SO7141]
☆ *Farmers Arms* [off B4214 just N of Ledbury – pub signed right, from top of village; Horse Rd]: Big much modernised pub with good generous imaginative food, helpful, deft and friendly service, well kept ales such as Hancocks HB and Woods, good wines, plenty of comfortable plush banquettes, flame-effect gas fire, soft lighting from Tiffany-style lamps, a few big country prints; good walks *(BB, F Smyth, Dave Braisted, SYP, Ivan Gray, Paul Crook)*

Weobley [SO4151]
Marshpools [The Marsh, nr Ledgemoor]: Friendly country inn with good food, good well priced bedrooms *(K Tomlinson, A J Hartakies)*

Weston-under-Penyard [SO6323]
☆ *Weston Cross Inn*: Very pretty from outside, friendly new licensees doing good home-made food from basic bar snacks and ploughman's to wide choice of fine local meat and fresh fish; simple beamed bar with Boddingtons and Tetleys, Weston's cider, two back dining rooms; pool and TV; walkers welcome, views of picturesque village from tables on front lawn, more tables and play area behind *(Martin Jennings, Paula Cuthbert, BB)*

Whitney-on-Wye [SO2747]
Rhydspence [A438 Hereford—Brecon]: Very picturesque ancient black and white country inn right on Welsh border, with attractive old-fashioned furnishings, heavy beams and timbers in rambling spick-and-span rooms, enjoyable interesting food, if not cheap, using local produce, pretty dining room, Bass, Hook Norton Best and Robinsons Best, Dunkerton's farm cider, good wine choice, log fire; tables in attractive garden with fine views over Wye valley; comfortable bedrooms *(Denys Gueroult, Hazel and Michael Duncombe, LYM, Anne and Ieuan Williams)*

Hertfordshire

Just before we went to press one popular main entry here, the White Horse at Burnham Green, closed after a bad fire. While four other former main entries have moved out to the Lucky Dip section at the end of the chapter, several pubs here stand out as being on particularly good form these days: the friendly Irish-run Gibraltar Castle at Batford, the interesting Lytton Arms at Knebworth (good beers), the 16th-c Nags Head at Little Hadham (good reasonably price food, especially fish), the Boot at Sarratt (a friendly village-green pub, new to the main entries this year), and the George & Dragon at Watton-at-Stone (a county favourite, and our Hertfordshire Dining Pub of the Year; the licensees have just retired, but the former chef is a worthy successor). Two pubs deserve a special mention for keeping their place in the Guide *throughout its 20 years of publication: the distinctive old Brocket Arms at Ayot St Lawrence (under its landlord Toby Wingfield Digby ever since we started) and the Rose & Crown in St Albans (the American landlord's speciality big-deal sandwiches are much enjoyed here). Pubs showing well in the Lucky Dip section these days are the Bell at Benington, Black Horse in Chorleywood, Three Blackbirds at Flamstead, Rising Sun at Halls Green, Crown & Sceptre near Hemel Hempstead, and Fighting Cocks and Garibaldi in St Albans; we have inspected and approved all but two of these. Drinks prices in the county are a shade above the national average, but holding very steady this year; the Gibraltar Castle at Batford and White Horse in Hertford had the cheapest beers among the main entries.*

ALDBURY SP9612 Map 4
Greyhound

Stocks Road; village signposted from A4251 Tring—Berkhamsted, or reached directly from roundabout at E end of A41 Tring bypass

Tables outside this attractively placed pub face a picturesque village green complete with stocks and lively duckpond. Its handsome, Georgian frontage is especially stunning in autumn when the blazing leaves of its virginia creeper provide a brilliant counterpoint to the backdrop of bronzing Chiltern beechwoods (part of the National Trust owned Ashridge Estate). Some readers, though, recommend visiting in winter when the lovely warm fire and subtle lighting make it really cosy. Inside there's a buoyant and thriving atmosphere and service is smiling and efficient even when under pressure. There are some signs of the original earlier building – around the copper-hooded inglenook, for example; plenty of tables in the two rooms ramble off each side of the drinks and food serving areas. Badger Dorset Best, IPA, Tanglefoot and a Badger seasonal guest are kept well on handpump, and there's a weekday early evening happy hour (5-7pm). Generous bar food includes sandwiches from (£4.75), filled baked potatoes (£5.25), ham and eggs (£5.75), ploughman's (from £5.95), vegetable and bean chimichangas (£7.50) or battered haddock (£8.50) as well as specials such as scrambled egg, chorizo sausage and crispy black pudding (£5.95), home-made steak and ale pie (£7.95) or seafood platter (£8.50). The more elaborate evening specials board might include rib-eye steak with garlic, wine and thyme sauce (£11.95) and fresh halibut with prawns and saffron sauce (£14.95) with puddings like apple and clotted cream and toffee or banana mousse on a biscuit base

(£3.95). No smoking area, piped music, darts, fruit machine, TV, cribbage, dominoes. They don't mind well behaved dogs in the public bar, and plastic bags are kept near the entrance for muddy boots. Plenty of good walks nearby, for instance, around the monument to the canal mogul, the 3rd Duke of Bridgewater, up on the escarpment, and for the less energetic, the toll road through the Ashridge Estate is very attractive. *(Recommended by Derek and Sylvia Stephenson, George Atkinson, Tracey and Stephen Groves, Brian Root, Catherine and Richard Preston, Len Banister)*

Badger ~ Manager Jo Coletta ~ Real ale ~ Bar food (12-2.30, 7-10 Mon-Sat; 12-4 Sun; not Sun evening) ~ Restaurant ~ (01442) 851228 ~ Children away from bar ~ Open 11-11; 12-10.30 Sun; closed 25 Dec ~ Bedrooms: £60B/£75B

Valiant Trooper 🖪

Trooper Road (towards Aldbury Common); off B4506 N of Berkhamsted

The owner of this partly pink-painted and tiled pub is converting the restaurant into a more relaxed eating area, enhancing the friendly, traditional feel of the place. The first room, beamed and tiled in red and black, has built-in wall benches, a pew and small dining chairs around the attractive country tables, and a woodburning stove in the inglenook fireplace. In the middle bar, which has a wooden floor, there's some exposed brickwork and spindleback chairs – and signs warning you to 'mind the step'. The far room has nice country kitchen chairs around individually chosen tables, and a brick fireplace; decorations are mostly antique cavalry prints (rumour has it that the Duke of Wellington once met his officers here to discuss tactics). Bar food includes ciabatta sandwiches or filled baked potatoes (£3.50), ploughman's (from £4) and daily specials such as garlic mushrooms (£3.50), moules marinières (£4.50), roast vegetable lasagne (£7), steak and kidney pie (£7.50), duck with Pernod sauce (£9) or roast bass with garlic prawns (£10), with puddings such as sticky toffee pudding or white chocolate and raspberry torte (£3). The lounge bar is no smoking at lunchtime; pleasant obliging service. Well kept Fullers London Pride and Morrells Oxford Blue, with a couple of guests from brewers such as Adnams and Bass on handpump. Shove-ha'penny, dominoes, cribbage, bridge on Monday nights; dogs welcome. The enclosed garden has a play house for children. The village itself is fascinating, and handy for some of the very best Chilterns scenery – particularly nice views can be had from around the monument to the Duke of Bridgewater, and the woods close to the pub are very good for walking. *(Recommended by David and Ruth Shillitoe, V F Sullivan)*

Free house ~ Licensee Tim O'Gorman ~ Real ale ~ Bar food (12-(2.30 Sun)2, 6.30-9.15 Tues-Sat, they hope to serve food pm Sun-Mon by the time we go to press) ~ Restaurant ~ (01442) 851203 ~ Children in eating area of bar and restaurant, no under 14s in the smoking area ~ Open 11.30-11; 12-10.30 Sun

ARDELEY TL3027 Map 5
Jolly Waggoner

Village signposted off B1037 NE of Stevenage

This pleasant, cream-washed dining inn is peacefully set in a pretty tucked-away village. The comfortable bar, with a window overlooking the garden, has a relaxed and civilised atmosphere, with open woodwork and beams and a blazing fire in winter. Decorated with modern prints, the restaurant has been extended into the cottage next door. Using fresh local produce bar food includes sandwiches (from £2.85), soup (£4.50), ploughman's (£6) and a very popular omelette Arnold Bennett (£7.50), as well as changing specials such as tomato and mozzarella salad (£4.50), vegetable and pasta bake (£6.50), fresh crab (£8.50), chicken in wine, garlic and cream or salmon fillet on parmesan pasta (£10.50), calves liver with sage and butter or roquefort cheese and horseradish (£12) and puddings such as chocolate truffle torte, pineapple crème brûlée or lemon tart (£3.95); booking is essential for their Sunday lunch, and there's a £1 surcharge for credit cards where the bill is under £10. Well kept Greene King IPA tapped from the cask and Abbot on handpump, a decent range of wines and freshly squeezed orange juice in summer; maybe piped music.

There's a pleasant garden and terrace; Cromer Windmill is nearby. *(Recommended by Ian Phillips, Keith Tomalin, Catherine and Richard Preston, John Fahy)*

Greene King ~ Lease Darren Perkins ~ Real ale ~ Bar food (6.30-9.30, not Sun evenings or Mon exc bank hol lunchtime) ~ Restaurant ~ (01438) 861350 ~ Well behaved children over 7 welcome ~ Open 12-2.30(3 Sat), 6.30-11; 12-3, 7-10.30 Sun; closed Mon except bank hols, then cl Tues

ASHWELL TL2639 Map 5
Three Tuns
High St

This flower-decked 18th-c hotel has a pleasantly old-fashioned pubby atmosphere and is very popular with groups of hikers on summer weekends. The cosy lounge has an air of Victorian opulence, with its relaxing chairs, big family tables, lots of pictures, stuffed pheasants and fish, and antiques. The simpler more modern public bar has pool, darts, dominoes, a fruit machine, SkyTV and Greene King IPA, Abbot and a guest such as Everards Tiger on handpump, and there's a good choice of wines; piped music. Straightforward bar food includes sandwiches (from £2.25), filled baguettes (from £3.45), soup (£3.50), roll mop herrings or chicken liver pâté (£4.25), ploughman's (from £5.25), breaded scampi (£7.25), steaks (from £12.45), daily specials such as cauliflower bake (£7.95) or beef braised in a red wine, mushroom and garlic sauce (£8.75) and puddings including some home-made ones (from £3.50). There's boules in the substantial shaded garden, and one of the six bedrooms has a four-poster bed, and another its own dressing room. The village is attractive. *(Recommended by Moira and John Cole, Dr P C Rea, David and Ruth Shillitoe, Michael Porter, John and Christine Lowe, John and Moira Smyth, Ian Phillips, Gavin E Horner)*

Greene King ~ Tenants Claire and Darrell Stanley ~ Real ale ~ Bar food (12-2.30, 6-11; 12-9.30 Sat/Sun) ~ Restaurant ~ (01462) 742107 ~ Children welcome ~ Open 11-11; 12-10.30 Sun ~ Bedrooms: £35/£45(£55B)

AYOT ST LAWRENCE TL1916 Map 5
Brocket Arms
B651 N of St Albans for about 6 miles; village signposted on right after Wheathampstead and Mid Herts golf course; or B653 NE of Luton, then right on to B651

This peacefully set white-painted and tiled 14th-c brick pub is close to the house where George Bernard Shaw lived for over 45 years. Reputedly haunted by a monk from the local abbey who was tried and hanged here during the Reformation, it's a really atmospheric place. Two simple and very traditional low-ceilinged rooms have sturdy oak beams, a roaring fire in a big inglenook fireplace (with a woodburning stove in the back room); old-fashioned furnishings and magazines to read; darts, dominoes, cribbage and piped classical music. Adnams Broadside, Greene King IPA and Fullers London Pride on handpump, and a guest such as Ruddles County tapped from the cask; around a dozen wines by the glass. Lunchtime bar food includes sandwiches (from £2.50), soup (£3.50), filled baked potatoes (from £3.50), macaroni cheese (£4.75), home-made curries and chilli con carne (from £5), venison and duck sausages (£5.50), game pie (£6.50) with evening specials such as roast pheasant with red currant and port sauce (£13.50) and home-made puddings (from £3.50); there's an extended menu in the no smoking evening restaurant. It can get very crowded at weekends. The extensive south-facing suntrap walled garden is lovely in summer, with an outside bar and a children's play area. Just over the road are romantic remains of a medieval church (a late 18th-c local squire decided it spoilt his view and started knocking it down, until a furious Bishop of Lincoln called a halt). *(Recommended by Maggie and Peter Shapland, Giles Francis, J Hale, Martin and Lois Sheldrick, David and Ruth Shillitoe, Ian Phillips)*

Free house ~ Licensee Toby Wingfield Digby ~ Real ale ~ Bar food (12-2.30, 7.30-9.30, not pm Sun and Mon) ~ Restaurant ~ (01438) 820250 ~ Children welcome ~ Open 11-11; 12-11 Sun ~ Bedrooms: £60B/£80B

BATFORD TL1415 Map 5
Gibraltar Castle
Lower Luton Rd; B653, S of B652 junction

There's an interesting collection of militaria at this well run roadside pub, particularly at the end on the right as you go in, which has something of the feel of a hunting lodge; here the low beams found elsewhere give way to soaring rafters, and glass cases show off pristinely kept uniforms, bullets, medals and rifles. There's plenty to look at in the rest of the long carpeted bar, with its nice old fireplace, comfortably cushioned wall benches, and a couple of snugly intimate window alcoves, one with a fine old clock. Readers tend to be particularly struck by the welcoming atmosphere, friendly Irish landlord and polite staff. They serve well kept Fullers Chiswick, ESB, London Pride and seasonal brews on handpump, a good range of malt whiskies, well made Irish coffee, and a thoughtful choice of wines by the glass; piped music. Very tasty bar food might include club sandwiches or soup (from £2.95), potato or grilled haloumi cheese, salad, olives and pitta bread with Greek dips (£7.95), beef stroganoff or fisherman's pie (£8.95), sirloin steak with sautéed mushrooms and onions (£10.95), and puddings such as sticky toffee (£2.95); booking is recommended for their very popular, good value Sunday roast (£8.95). There are a few tables in front by the road, and pretty hanging baskets and tubs. On Tuesday evenings there's a live Cajun and Irish session. *(Recommended by Danny Nicol, Norma and Keith Bloomfield, Mrs Margaret Leale, Ian Phillips)*

Fullers ~ Tenant Derek Phelan ~ Real ale ~ Bar food (12-2.30, 6-9, not Sun evening) ~ (01582) 460005 ~ Children in eating area of bar ~ Live music Tues evening ~ Open 11-3, 5-11; 12-4, 6-10.30 Sun; closed 25 Dec evening

BRICKET WOOD TL1502 Map 5
Moor Mill £
Off Smug Oak Lane; turn at the Gate pub and entrance is a little further on the left; 2 miles from M1 junction 6, but a bit of a maze getting through Bricket Wood; Smug Oak Lane is off Lye Lane, on the far side, towards Colney Street and the A5183

This is a useful and unexpected retreat from the M25 or M1, where the pristine white-painted exterior of this well converted 18th-c mill looks much as it must have done in its prime. Inside, many of the original features remain intact: behind glass, down a little corridor leading to the bar, you can still see one of the huge mill wheels churning determinedly through the water. Displays on the wall reveal interesting bits of history, including a detailed cross-section of exactly how the mill used to work. The smallish bar has beams, brick walls and a flagstone floor, with a few wooden tables and chairs; a passageway leads to a wood-floored room with more tables. You'll find further indoor seating at the opposite end of the building and in a carpeted room upstairs which has a real fire; some areas are no smoking. In front of the building ducks and other birds wander around the millpond and there are masses of wooden picnic-sets (though you can hear the motorway from out here). On warm summer weekends they usually have a separate outside servery, with sandwiches and a few hot dishes. There's plenty of space for children to run around, as well as a massive fenced-off play area for under-9s, with quite a collection of slides, swings and so on. Flowers Original, Wadworths 6X and a guest such as Fullers London Pride on handpump; bar food, served all day, includes filled baguettes and baked potatoes (from £3.25), soup (£3.25), caramelised red onion and brie tart (£4.95), battered cod (£5.45), rib-eye steak (from £6.45) and minted rack of lamb with red wine and rosemary sauce (£10.45); puddings (from £3.25); fruit machines and maybe loudish piped music. *(Recommended by Ian Phillips)*

Out & Out ~ Manager Terry Bambury ~ Real ale ~ Bar food (12-10) ~ Restaurant ~ (01727) 875557 ~ Children welcome ~ Open 11-11; 12-10.30 Sun ~ Bedrooms: /£55.95B

COTTERED TL3129 Map 5
Bull
A507 W of Buntingford

Facing a row of pretty thatched cottages, this old tree-surrounded inn is popular for good helpings of thoughtfully presented bar food, including sandwiches (from £2.65), soup (£4.40), ploughman's (from £5), filled baked potatoes with good salad (from £5.50), steak, Guinness and stilton pie (£8), chicken in a cream, wine and garlic sauce (£11), and home-made puddings such as bread and brandy pudding, fruit crème brûlée or white chocolate cheesecake with a coffee and bitter orange sauce (£3.25); £1 surcharge for credit card bills under £10; friendly and obliging service. The airy relaxing low-beamed front lounge is attractively laid out and well looked after with antiques on a stripped wood floor and a good fire. A second bar has darts, a fruit machine, shove-ha'penny, cribbage and dominoes; unobtrusive piped music. Well kept Greene King IPA and Abbot on handpump and decent wines. There are benches and tables in the sizeable garden. *(Recommended by R L Turnham, John Fahy, Keith Tomalin, Peter and Joan Elbra, F J Lennox, Ian Phillips, Phil and Heidi Cook)*
Greene King ~ Lease Darren Perkins ~ Real ale ~ Bar food (12-2, 6.30-9; 7-9 Sun; not Tues evening) ~ Restaurant ~ (01763) 281243 ~ Well behaved children over seven if eating ~ Open 12-2.30(3 Sat), 6.30-11; 12-3, 7-10.30 Sun

HERTFORD TL3212 Map 5
White Horse ◀
Castle St

There's a fine choice of real ales at this friendly, unpretentious pub with generally up to 10 perfectly kept brews on at once. Especially impressive considering it's a tied house, the choice can be different every day, but you can expect to find beers such as Concertina Bengal Tiger, Earl Soham Gannet Mild, fff Moondance, H & H Guzzling Goose, Hopback Summer Lightning, Humpty Dumpty Little Sharpie and Woodfordes Wherry, alongside the Adnams and Fullers London Pride and ESB; they keep around 20 country wines. Very good value bar food includes filled baguettes (from £2.95), as well as hot dishes such as mushroom stroganoff (£3.50), curries and steak and kidney pie (£4.50) and thai fishcakes (£4.75). On Sunday they do a two-course lunch for £6, three courses for £7.50. Parts of the building are 14th c, and you can still see Tudor brickwork in the three quietly cosy no smoking rooms upstairs. Downstairs, the two main rooms are small and homely. The one on the left is more basic, with a bit of brewery memorabilia, bare boards, and a few rather well worn tables, stools and chairs; an open fire separates it from the more comfortable right-hand bar, which has a cosily tatty armchair, some old local photographs, beams and timbers, and a red-tiled floor. Service can be quite chatty, and though it's quite a locals' pub, visitors are made to feel welcome; shove-ha'penny, cribbage, dominoes. The pub faces the castle, and there's a bench on the street outside. *(Recommended by Pat and Tony Martin, Ian Arthur)*
Fullers ~ Tenant Nigel Crofts ~ Real ale ~ Bar food (lunchtime only) ~ (01992) 501950 ~ Children before 9pm in family room ~ Open 12-2.30, 5.30-11; 12-11 Sat; 12-10.30 Sun

KNEBWORTH TL2320 Map 5
Lytton Arms ◀
Park Lane, Old Knebworth, 3 miles from A1(M) junction 7; A602 towards Stevenage, 2nd roundabout right on B197 towards Knebworth, then right into Old Knebworth Lane; at village T-junction, right towards Codicote

There's a fine range of real ales in this Victorian gabled brick pub, built as an inn for the long-defunct Hawkes & Co brewery of Bishop's Stortford. Besides nine well kept guests from brewers such as Ringwood, Hop Back, Mighty Oak and Bass they serve Adnams Southwold, Bass, Fullers London Pride and Black Sheep Best on handpump, as well as Staropramen beer from Prague on draught, and up to 30 Belgian bottled beers. If you're not so keen on beer they've 50 malt whiskies, country wines, around four farm ciders, hot chocolate and herb teas, and in winter they serve hot gluhwein by the log fire (where they also roast chestnuts). Several solidly furnished simple big-windowed rooms, some panelled and each with a slightly different décor (railway memorabilia here, old Knebworth estate photographs there), amble around the big central servery, ending in a no smoking conservatory with orderly pale tables on its shiny brown tiles. Simple but well cooked bar food includes soup (£2.90), sandwiches (from £3), filled baked potatoes (from £4.10), ploughman's (from £4.95), mushroom and pepper stroganoff (£5.95), lasagne (£6.65), salmon fishcakes (£6.75) and ckicken curry (£6.95); friendly, welcoming service. There are picnic-sets and a giant chessboard on a terrace in front, and the back garden has a play area; dominoes and shove-ha'penny. The pub hosts beer festivals in spring and autumn. *(Recommended by Mr and Mrs M Dalby, Richard Lewis, BKA, Pat and Tony Martin, Derek and Sylvia Stephenson, Chloe and Robert Gartery)*

Free house ~ Licensee John Anderson Cliff Nye ~ Real ale ~ Bar food (12-2, 6.30-9.30, Sat 12-9, Sun 12-5) ~ (01438) 812312 ~ Children in family room and restaurant ~ Open Mon/Tues 11-3, 5-11, Weds-Sat 11-11; 12-10.30 Sun; Mon-Thurs 11-3, 5-11, Fri-Sat 11-11 winter

LITTLE HADHAM TL4322 Map 5
Nags Head

Hadham Ford; just S of A120 W of Bishops Stortford, towards Much Hadham

You can choose from around 20 fresh fish dishes every day in this sociable 16th-c country dining pub. Meat eaters and vegetarians shouldn't feel left out, though, as there are plenty of other dishes on the themed blackboards around the pub. Generous helpings of good reasonably priced bar food could include farmhouse grill (£5.75), poached skate in black butter, large battered cod, plaice or haddock or grilled bass (from £7.95), lots of good steak cuts (from £8.95) and seafood platter (£9.75), some of the ten vegetarian choices a day might be thai red curry, moussaka or roasted vegetable torte (from £5.25); puddings (from £3) such as sticky toffee pudding. The linked heavily black-beamed rooms feel cosy and there are old local photographs, guns and copper pans in the small bar on the right, which has well kept Greene King IPA, Abbot, Ruddles and a guest such as Marstons Pedigree tapped from the cask, decent house wines, and freshly squeezed orange juice. The atmosphere is warm and relaxing and staff are friendly and efficient. The no smoking restaurant is down a couple of steps (it's best to book for their good Sunday lunch). There are tables in a pleasant garden area, and Hopleys nursery specialising in unusual hardy perennials is just down the road; darts, fruit machine, TV. *(Recommended by Charles Gysin, B N F and M Parkin, MNF, Joy and Peter Heatherley)*

Greene King ~ Tenant Kevin Robinson ~ Real ale ~ Bar food ~ Restaurant ~ (01279) 771555 ~ Children in eating area of bar and restaurant ~ Open 11-2.30(3 Sat), 6-11; 12-3, 7-10.30 Sun

PERRY GREEN TL4317 Map 5
Hoops

Village signposted off B1004 Widford—Much Hadham

On a sunny day the peaceful garden of this obliging pub is a lovely place to spend a laid-back afternoon. Well established rose bushes line the path between the tables in front of the white-painted, tiled-roof house, and there are climbers, hanging baskets and a small, fenced-off pond. The building dates from the middle of the 17th c, and the bar has exposed brick walls, standing timbers, and plenty of tables squeezed in, several in a cosy no smoking dining area tucked behind an unusual copper hooded fireplace. There's a wide range of dishes on the blackboard menu ranging from sandwiches (from £2), filled baguettes (from £3.50), soup (£3.75), baked potatoes (from £3.75) and ploughman's (£4.60), to chicken madras (£8.50), fresh salmon poached in white wine and herbs with lemon and lime mayonnaise (£8.95), and elaborate sizzlers – prawn stir fry (£9.95) or fillet steak served on a sizzle plate

(£15.95); traditional Sunday lunch. The restaurant is no smoking and at busy times booking is recommended. Well kept changing real ales such as Adnams, Greene King IPA and Green Tye Wheelbarrow; piped music. The Henry Moore Foundation is opposite; there are guided tours in summer, by appointment only on (01279) 843333. *(Recommended by Kevin Thorpe, Maggie and Peter Shapland, Mrs P J Pearce)*

Green Tye ~ Lease Michael O'Connor ~ Real ale ~ Bar food (same as opening times) ~ Restaurant ~ (01279) 843568 ~ Children in restaurant ~ Occasional live music ~ Open 12-2.30, 6.30-11; 12-11 Sat; 12-10.30 Sun; Sat 12-2.30, 6-11 in winter

POTTERS CROUCH TL1105 Map 5
Holly Bush ◀

Off A4147

This beautifully kept country pub is an excellent place to come to read the papers and relax in delightful surroundings. The meticulously furnished bar has an elegantly timeless feel and it's not the kind of place where you'll find fruit machines or piped music. Everything is spotless, and shows unusually dedicated attention to detail. Thoughtfully positioned fixtures create the illusion that there are lots of different rooms – some of which you might expect to find in a smart country house. In the evenings neatly placed candles cast shadows over the mix of darkly gleaming varnished tables, all of which have fresh flowers and china plates as ashtrays. There are quite a few antique dressers, several with plates on, a number of comfortable cushioned settles, the odd plant, a fox's mask, some antlers, a fine old clock, carefully illuminated prints and pictures, and on the left as you go in there's a big fireplace. The long, stepped bar counter has particularly well kept Fullers Chiswick, ESB, London Pride and a seasonal beer on handpump, and the sort of old-fashioned till you hardly ever see in this hi-tech age. Service is calm and efficient even when they're busy. Straightforward bar food is served lunchtimes only (not Sun), from a menu that includes sandwiches (from £2.30, toasted from £2.70), burgers (from £3.65) filled baked potatoes (from £4.20), ploughman's (from £5), and chilli (£5.50). Behind the pretty wisteria-covered, white cottagey building the fenced-off garden with a nice lawn, handsome trees, and good wooden tables and chairs is a very pleasant place to sit in summer. Though the pub seems to stand alone on a quiet little road, it's only a few minutes from the centre of St Albans, and is very handy for the Gardens of the Rose; no dogs. *(Recommended by Mike Ridgway, Sarah Miles, BKA, Ian Phillips, Stan Edwards, Tracey and Stephen Groves)*

Fullers ~ Tenant R S Taylor ~ Real ale ~ Bar food (lunchtime, not Sun) ~ (01727) 851792 ~ Open 11.30-2.30, 6-11; 12-2.30, 7-10.30 Sun

REED TL3636 Map 5
Cabinet

High Street; village signposted from A10

Throughout the interior and in the sizeable gardens of this civilised dining pub there's a permanent exhibition for the sale of local sculptors' works. Children are allowed everywhere and the atmosphere is relaxed and welcoming. Good bar food on a changing blackboard might include sandwiches (from £2.25), soup (from £2.95), cumberland sausage and eggs (£4.65), chilli con carne (£5.65), pancakes filled with spinach, tomato, beans and cheese (£5.95), chargrilled chicken with herb and citrus butter (£7.85), and rib-eye steak (from £8.50); puddings (from £2.75); children's menu (£4.45). The emphasis is decidedly on the no smoking restaurant (with its more elaborate menu), which has stripped floors and a simple mix of wooden chairs and tables, a log fire in winter, and views over the back lawn. But in the evening locals do still gather in the cosy, friendly public bar, with its comfortable seating by the inglenook fireplace; piped music, darts, shove-ha'penny, dominoes, cribbage. In the adjoining snug there's a collection of board games (added to make it more appealing to families and children). Well kept Greene King Abbot and IPA and a couple of guests such as Adnams and Eccleshall Top Totty on handpump. On busy summer weekends they may open all day. *(Recommended by Catherine and Richard Preston, B, M and P Kendall, Peter and Joan Elbra, Olive and Ray Hebson, Keith and Janet Morris, Joy and Colin Rorke)*

Free house ~ Licensee Justin Scarborough-Taylor ~ Real ale ~ Bar food (12-2.15, 7-9.15; 12-9 bank hols) ~ Restaurant ~ (01763) 848366 ~ Children in eating area of bar and restaurant ~ Open 12-3(4 Sun), 6-11(10.30 Sun); 12-11 bank hols

SARRATT TQ0499 Map 5
Boot

The Green

There are cosy rambling rooms in this attractive tiled house facing the village green: comfortable cushioned benches along the part-panelled walls with carpet or dark flooring tiles, a fine early 18th-c inglenook fireplace with a good winter log fire, and a friendly welcome from the landlord. Bar food includes sandwiches (from £3.25), ploughman's (£4.75), and various home-made dishes such as smoked bacon and duck salad (£6.95), mediterranean vegetable bake (£7.65), steak and kidney pie (£7.65), fresh crayfish (£7.95) and lamb shank with rosemary and red wine sauce (£8.25); puddings such as spotted dick (£3.50); it's best to book if you want to eat in their new no smoking bistro style restaurant. Four well kept real ales might include Greene King IPA, Abbot and Ruddles County on handpump; sensibly segregated darts, cribbage, fruit machine, space game and piped music. It has an old-fashioned black wrought-iron bench and picnic-sets under a pair of pollarded century-old lime trees in front, and more seats on a pretty, sheltered lawn with roses, fruit trees and a weeping willow; there's also a children's play area. *(Recommended by Stan Edwards, W F Martin, John Hillman, Tracey and Stephen Groves)*

Free house ~ Licensee Richard Jones ~ Real ale ~ Bar food (lunchtime only) ~ Restaurant ~ 01923 262247 ~ Well behaved children in eating area of bar and restaurant ~ Open 11.30-3, 5.30-11; 12-10.30 Sun; closed 25 Dec evening

Cock

Church End: a very pretty approach is via North Hill, a lane N off A404, just under a mile W of A405

The latched door of this cosy cream-painted 17th-c country pub opens into a carpeted snug with a vaulted ceiling, original bread oven, and a cluster of bar stools. Through an archway, the partly oak-panelled cream-walled lounge has a lovely log fire in an inglenook, pretty Liberty-style curtains, pink plush chairs at dark oak tables, lots of interesting artefacts and pictures of cocks; piped music, and well kept Badger Best, IPA and Tanglefoot and a guest such as Badger K&B. Friendly staff serve generous helpings of bar food including sandwiches (from £2.95), baked potatoes (from £3.85), ploughman's (from £4.95), tasty wild boar or lincolnshire sausages and mash (£5.95), mediterranean seafood pasta (£6.50), chicken and asparagus pie or home-baked ham and eggs (£6.75) and daily specials such as crispy shredded beef topside (£8.25), toasted feta and aubergine with chilli dressing (£8.95) or grilled salmon with caper and watercress sauce (£9.50). The restaurant is in a nicely converted barn. At the front picnic-sets look out across a quiet lane towards the churchyard, and from the terrace at the back there are open country views, and tables under umbrellas on a pretty sheltered lawn; children's play area. *(Recommended by BKA, Mark Percy, Lesley Mayoh, Stan Edwards, David and Ruth Shillitoe, Jim Bush)*

Badger ~ Manager Dale John Tozer ~ Real ale ~ Bar food (12-2.30, 6-9.30) ~ Restaurant ~ (01923) 282908 ~ Children in eating area of bar and restaurant ~ Open 11-3, 5.30-11; 11-11 Sat; 12-10.30 Sun

---

The ◗ symbol shows pubs which keep their beer unusually well or have a particularly good range.

ST ALBANS TL1507 Map 5
Rose & Crown

St Michaels Street; from town centre follow George Street towards the Abbey, right just
before Abbey into Fishpool St, pub is near Kingsbury Watermill

You can get great speciality sandwiches at this relaxed and civilised Victorian town
pub. Served with potato salad, crisps and pickled cucumber on a granary or white
loaf or bap, there is a choice of varieties such as ham, peanuts, american cheese,
tomato and mayonnaise (£4.50), roast beef, onion, salami, swiss cheese and mustard
(£4.95), or turkey, salami, swiss cheese, lettuce, tomato and mayonnaise double-
decker toasted sandwich (£4.95) as well as from more traditional varieties (from £2).
A few other dishes include soup (£2.50), chilli (£5.25), vegetable stroganoff or
moussaka (£5.95). The traditional beamed public bars have unevenly timbered walls,
old-fashioned wall benches, chintzy curtains and cushions, and black cauldrons in a
deep fireplace (big fires in winter). This is where the welcoming American landlord
keeps his impressive collection of sports tickets and rugby and golfing memorabilia.
There's a no smoking area at lunchtime. Well kept Adnams, Courage Directors,
Tetleys and six fortnightly guests such as Hop Back Best and Timothy Taylors
Landlord on handpump; a dozen or so malt whiskies, fruit wines. Dominoes,
cribbage and darts which are sensibly set to one side. Lots of tables and benches
along the side and at the back in a pretty ivy-hung yard with shrubs and roses,
flower beds and attractive hanging baskets – a haven from the bustle up in the town.
The walk from the town centre down Fishpool Street is pretty. *(Recommended by
Ian Phillips, Kenneth and Sybil Court, Peter and Audrey Dowsett, BKA, Dr David Cockburn)*

*Inn Partnership (Nomura) ~ Tenant Neil Dekker ~ Real ale ~ Bar food (lunchtime
only, not Sun) ~ (01727) 851903 ~ Children in eating area of bar ~ Acoustic session
Mon evening, Irish folk Thurs evening ~ Open 11.30-3, 5.30(6 Sat)-11; 12-3, 7-10.30
Sun*

WATTON-AT-STONE TL3019 Map 5
George & Dragon ★ ⑪ ♀

Village signposted off A602 about 5 miles S of Stevenage, on B1001; High Street

Hertfordshire Dining Pub of the Year

Though the old licensees have just retired, this civilised country dining pub is still
very much the old firm as before. The chef has taken over as landlord and the staff
is largely unchanged. Good, beautifully presented dishes include sandwiches (from
£2.10), soup (£2.95) and ploughman's (£4.75) as well as more unusual dishes such
as prawn and mixed fish chowder (£5.75), chinese-style crispy duck (£7.45),
mediterranean tomato filled with cracked wheat, aubergine, haloumi and
mozzarella (£7.85), lemon sole poached in white wine, lemon and fresh herbs
(£8.75), roast chicken breast filled with sage leaves with marsala, sage and
mushroom cream sauce (£8.95) and daily specials like white anchovy fillets (£4.45),
braised beef with brandy and green peppercorn sauce (£6.85) or john dory with
chilli and spring onion butter (£8.25) and home-made puddings (£3.25); friendly,
professional service. The atmosphere is gently sophisticated, with kitchen elbow-
chairs around attractive old tables, dark blue cloth-upholstered seats in the bay
windows, an interesting mix of antique and modern prints on the partly timbered
ochre walls, and a big inglenook fireplace. A quieter room off the main bar has
spindleback chairs and wall settles cushioned to match the green floral curtains, and
a hunting print and old photographs of the village above its panelled dado. Proper
napkins, antiques and daily newspapers add to the smart feel. As well as a good
wine list they have well kept Greene King Abbot, IPA and Old Speckled Hen on
handpump, and several malt whiskies; fruit machine, and boules in the pretty
extended shrub-screened garden. The pub is handy for Benington Lordship
Gardens. *(Recommended by David and Pauline Loom, Bob and Maggie Atherton, Kenneth and
Sybil Court, Ian Phillips, BKA, John Branston, Mike Ridgway, Sarah Miles, Maysie Thompson,
Gordon Tong, Keith Tomalin, Peter and Marilyn Budden, David and Ruth Shillitoe, Enid and
Henry Stephens, Peter Burton, D B)*

Greene King ~ Tenant Jessica Tatlow ~ Real ale ~ Bar food (12-2, 7-10, not Sun evening) ~ Restaurant ~ (01920) 830285 ~ Children in eating area of bar and restaurant ~ Open 11-2.30, 6-11; 11-11 Sat; 12-3.30, 7-10.30 Sun; closed 25 Dec, pm 26 Dec

Lucky Dip

Besides the fully inspected pubs, you might like to try these Lucky Dips recommended to us and described by readers (if you do, please send us reports: www.goodguides.com).

Abbots Langley [TL0902]
Compasses [Tibbs Hill Rd]: Pleasantly modernised friendly and tidy local with good choice of good value food in bar or small dining area, well kept beers *(Stan Edwards, BKA)*

Amwell [TL1613]
☆ *Elephant & Castle* [signed SW from Wheathampstead]: Secluded and spacious floodlit grass garden behind low-beamed ancient pub with relaxed and welcoming local feel, great inglenook log fire, panelling, stripped brickwork, immensely deep covered well shaft in bar; good value hearty bar food (not Sun), well kept Marstons, friendly locals, good service; restaurant, children in eating area, *(LYM, Gordon Neighbour)*

Ashwell [TL2639]
☆ *Bushel & Strike* [off A507 just E of A1(M) junction 10, N of Baldock, via Newnham; Mill St opp church, via Gardiners Lane (car park down Swan Lane)]: Neat front dining bar with fresh flowers, hunting and coaching prints, local colour photographs, cheery prompt service, wide choice of food from nice sandwiches up, no smoking restaurant with 'conservatory' murals, sofas in back area, well kept Everards Tiger, Gales HSB and Greene King Old Speckled Hen, freshly squeezed fruit juice, hot toddies, mulled wine and half a dozen wines by the glass; tables on lawn and small terrace, maybe summer barbecues *(Norma and Keith Bloomfield, George Atkinson, LYM, Andy Black, David Peakall)*
Rose & Crown [High St]: Comfortable open-plan local with good bar food esp popular Tues fish night, 16th-c beams, lovely log fire, no smoking candlelit restaurant, well kept Greene King IPA and Abbot; darts and machines at plainer public end of L-shaped bar; tables in big pretty country garden *(Jenny and Dave Hughes, Phil and Heidi Cook)*

Benington [TL3023]
☆ *Bell* [Town Lane; just past Post Office, towards Stevenage]: Generous food from sandwiches to good main dishes, good service, well kept Greene King IPA, Abbot, Triumph and Old Speckled Hen in cheery partly 15th-c pub in very pretty village; hops with fairy lights hanging from low beams, sloping walls, flowers and candles on tables, unusual faded stag-hunt mural over big inglenook fireplace with woodburner, mix of old furnishings, aircraft memorabilia and enamel advertising signs, separate dining room; no children in bars, piped music, weekly folk night; big pleasant garden with country views, handy for

Benington Lordship *(Mike Ridgway, Sarah Miles, Martin Bishop, BB, Dave and Sue Thorneycroft)*

Berkhamsted [SP9807]
☆ *Boat* [Gravel Path]: Attractive canalside setting, waterside terrace, pleasant walks, well kept Fullers Chiswick, ESB, London Pride and a seasonal ale, good wines, bar food (not Fri-Sun evenings) from sandwiches up, friendly if not always speedy service, lunchtime no smoking area; fruit machine, sports TV, piped music; children welcome, open all day, no under-21s Fri/Sat nights *(BKA, D B, LYM, Dr P C Rea)*
Crown [High St]: Wetherspoons pub with good relatively cheap food, good choice of beers and wines, no smoking areas, no music *(Pat and Robert Watt)*
☆ *Old Mill* [A4251, Hemel end]: Huge efficient Chef & Brewer, well restored, with several rooms inc no smoking, all with well cared for furnishings, some surprisingly cosy and attractive, dark wood tables with candles, grandfather clock, two good fires; very wide blackboard choice of generous food from familiar to sohisticated, usually something available all day; well kept Theakstons Best and a guest beer, a dozen or so wines by the glass or half bottle, friendly staff, maybe piped jazz; fruit machines; tables outside, some overlooking unspectacular stretch of Grand Union Canal *(Pat and Robert Watt, BB, Linda Cooke)*
Rose & Crown [Gossoms End]: Particularly well kept real ale in small friendly local *(John Martin)*

Brickendon [TL3208]
☆ *Farmers Boy* [S of Hertford]: Roomy refurbished village pub in attractive spot nr green, wide choice of popular food all day from sandwiches up, friendly service, Adnams and Greene King, dining area; open all day, seats in back garden and over road *(Gordon Neighbour)*

Broxbourne [TL3707]
Crown [Old Nazeing Rd, nr station]: By canal junction, boating theme throughout, two real ales inc Everards Tiger, good value meals *(Quentin Williamson)*

Burnham Green [TL2516]
White Horse [off B1000 N of Welwyn]: This popular chain dining pub, with its attractive black-beamed core, raftered no smoking two-floor dining extension and pretty garden burned down in May 2001, and as we went to press there was no news of rebuilding/reopening date *(LYM)*

Bushey [TQ1395]
Swan [Park Rd; turning off A411]: Homely

atmosphere in rare surviving example of unspoilt single-room backstreet terraced pub, reminiscent of 1920s *(LYM, Pete Baker)*

Chapmore End [TL3216]

Woodman [off B158 Hertford—Wadesmill]: Small two-room village local by pond with well kept Greene King IPA and Abbot tapped from the cask, usual lunchtime food (not Sun) from sandwiches up, bare boards, simple furnishings; annual music festival; big back garden, small front one, pets corner and play area *(Ian Arthur)*

Chipperfield [TL0401]

Two Brewers [The Common]: Roomy open-plan knocked-through bar in country hotel, bow windows, two log fires, dark décor; good if not cheap food all day from sandwiches up, Scottish Courage ales, but no bar stools or bar-propping; provision for children, comfortable bedrooms *(LYM, Tracey and Stephen Groves, Andrew Scarr)*

Chorleywood [TQ0295]

☆ *Black Horse* [Dog Kennel Lane, the Common]: Very welcoming to families, walkers and even dogs (basket of dog biscuits on mantelpiece), nice seating under low dark beams in attractively divided traditional room with thick carpet, two massive log fires, good choice of well prepared food (not Mon) from sandwiches to good value Sun lunches (worth booking these), well kept Adnams, Flowers Original, Theakstons Best and Wadworths 6X, friendly landlord, no music; family area, separate bar with SkyTV; pretty setting, picnic-sets overlooking common *(Peter and Giff Bennett, Ian Phillips, Stan Edwards, David and Elaine Eaglen)*

Rose & Crown [Common Rd, not far from M25 junction 18]: Small cosy pub in cottage terrace, pretty setting facing common, good freshly made food, well kept beer, old-fashioned atmosphere *(Peter and Giff Bennett)*

Croxley Green [TQ0795]

Coach & Horses: Traditionally furnished, with large modern extension behind old front part facing green, usual food, Greene King and guest beers *(Iain and Joan Baillie)*

Cuffley [TL3002]

Plough [Plough Hill]: Well run, relaxing and welcoming, wide range of main courses inc OAP bargains, well spaced tables, good beer choice; garden tables under cocktail parasols *(B Gooding)*

Epping Green [TL2906]

Beehive [back rd Cuffley—Little Berkhamsted]: Cosy and popular local, comfortable beamed dining area, huge choice of good value generous fresh food esp fish, friendly service, Greene King ales; garden seats overlooking fields *(Brian Hillman, GLD, Lucien)*

Flamstead [TL0714]

☆ *Three Blackbirds* [High St (just off A5)]: Lively and welcoming low-beamed partly Tudor local, much modernised inside, but still with old dark wood and brickwork, pictures, brass, copper, lots of hops, two real fires, friendly efficient staff and chatty regulars, well kept Bass, Courage and John Smiths from central bar,

good value food from sandwiches to good Sun roasts, no smoking area; children's corner, dogs welcome (friendly pub dog), darts, pool, piped music, SkyTV; tables on terrace by car park behind, lots of flowers *(BB, George Atkinson, David and Ruth Shillitoe)*

Flaunden [TL0100]

☆ *Bricklayers Arms* [village signed off A41; from village centre follow Boxmoor, Bovingdon road and turn right at Belsize, Watford signpost]: Well refurbished cottagey country pub, low beams, timbered stub walls, well kept Fullers London Pride, Ringwood Old Thumper and maybe a guest such as Brakspears or Marstons Pedigree, decent wines, food from sandwiches to occasional South African specialities, friendly obliging service (can slow when busy), restaurant, children in eating areas; nice old-fashioned garden, nearby walks *(Peter Walters, David and Ruth Shillitoe, M J Brooks, Ian Phillips, Patrick Renouf, BKA, Lynn Sharpless, Bob Eardley, Keith Tomalin, LYM, Derek and Sylvia Stephenson, Tracey and Stephen Groves)*

Frithsden [TL0110]

☆ *Alford Arms* [from Berkhamsted take unmarked rd towards Potten End, pass Potten End turn on right, then take next left towards Ashridge College]: Good interesting food in secluded country local, sparkling fresh and clean, old-world atmosphere with helpful staff, step down to nicely furnished eating area with cosy alcoves, decent house wine; very popular, may have to book; darts, bar billiards, fruit machine; open all day Sat, in attractive countryside, picnic-sets out in front *(Linda Cooke, LYM, BKA)*

Graveley [TL2327]

George & Dragon [High St]: Well run old coaching inn, well kept Greene King ales, good value food inc imaginative dishes, extended restaurant *(Derek, Hazel and Graeme Lloyd)*

Waggon & Horses [High St]: Friendly former coaching inn with above-average food inc children's and good Sun roast, comfortable beamed and timbered lounge, big open fire, locals' snug by door, well kept Whitbreads-related ales; secluded attractive streamside back garden with terrace and summer barbecues, duckpond over road *(Derek, Hazel and Graeme Lloyd)*

Great Hormead [TL4030]

Three Tuns: Old timbered pub with wide range of good imaginative well presented food, small linked areas, big fireplace, large back conservatory extension *(John Brightley)*

Great Munden [TL3523]

☆ *Plough* [SW, towards Dane End]: Unique full-size working Compton theatre organ (from Gaumont, Finchley) in comfortable and lofty lounge extension built specially to house it; decent nicely presented food (Sun lunch with organ recital is worth booking), well kept Greene King IPA and Abbot, friendly landlord, pleasant staff, good facilities for the disabled; nearby walks *(LYM, Gordon Neighbour)*

Green Tye [TL4418]

Prince of Wales: Unpretentious and chatty traditional village local brewing its own Green

Tye ales such as Snowdrop and IPA, welcoming staff, simple lunchtime menu, coal fire; tables in garden *(Richard Houghton, Kevin Thorpe)*

Halls Green [TL2728]

☆ *Rising Sun* [NW of Stevenage; from A1(M) junction 9 follow Weston signs off B197, then left in village, right by duck pond]: Convivial 18th-c beamed country pub with good value generous food in bar or pleasant conservatory restaurant inc special evenings (booking recommended wknds), well kept Bass, Courage and McMullens ales, friendly informal service, big log fire in small lounge; good big family garden with terrace, summer barbecues, boules and play area *(Philip Bardswell, Derek, Hazel and Graeme Lloyd, Len Banister)*

Harpenden [TL1413]

Plough & Harrow [Southdown Rd]: Large open-plan pub with wide choice of food inc huge Sun lunches, real ales such as Courage Directors and Ruddles, decent wines, friendly licensees; Sun quiz night, good garden with big play area *(Mr Grant)*

Hatfield [TL2308]

Horse & Groom [Park St, Old Hatfield]: Welcoming old-fashioned town pub with well kept Courage, lots of old local photographs, tables outside *(Dr and Mrs A K Clarke)*

Red Lion [Great North Rd]: Big well equipped roadside pub with well kept beer, decent food, various games and welcoming service *(Dr and Mrs A K Clarke)*

Hemel Hempstead [TL0411]

☆ *Crown & Sceptre* [leaving on A4146, right at Flamstead/Markyate sign opp Red Lion]: Classic country pub, cheerful and friendly cosy communicating rooms, some oak panelling, antique settles among more usual seating, enjoyable food from sandwiches up, well kept Greene King IPA and Abbot and a guest such as Adnams or Marstons Pedigree, log fires; darts and dominoes, children and dogs welcome; back garden with chickens, ducks and scarecrow, heated front picnic-sets, good walks; open all day summer wknds *(LYM, Ian Phillips)*

Hertford [TL3212]

☆ *Old Cross Tavern* [St Andrew St]: Good choice of well kept ales, good home-made food, friendly olde-worlde feel with brass, china etc (recent conversion from antiques shop); small heated back terrace *(Colin Gardner, Ian Arthur)*

Hexton [TL1230]

☆ *Raven* [signed off B655]: Large plush 1920s family dining pub with four neatly furnished areas inc long tidy public bar (open fire, pool one end), big no smoking room, plenty of dining tables; wide range of good value food inc lots of starters and two children's menus, four well kept ales inc Boddingtons and Greene King Old Speckled Hen, friendly efficient service; children welcome, big garden with terrace, barbecue, well segregated play area *(Margaret and Roy Randle, Phil and Heidi Cook, Penny Miles)*

High Wych [TL4614]

Hand & Crown [signed off A1184 Harlow—Sawbridgeworth]: Red plush and turkey carpet,

small flagstoned end area, some timbering in puce walls, huge central feature fireplace dividing off restaurant area, wide choice of good value generous food from entertaining menu inc interesting baguettes and well cooked fresh veg, well kept Adnams and Greene King IPA and Abbot, plenty of whiskies, quick friendly service even when busy; piped music may obtrude a bit *(Mrs A Chesher, BB)*

Rising Sun: Cosy unspoilt local, serving hatch to carpeted lounge with coal or log fire, central area with Courage Best and guests such as Kitchen and Woodfordes Wherry tapped from casks behind the counter, friendly landlord and locals, bare-boards games room (children allowed) with darts and woodburner; no food, no mobile phones or pagers, no music; tables in small garden *(Kevin Thorpe, JP, PP, Pete Baker, the Didler)*

Hinxworth [TL2340]

☆ *Three Horseshoes* [High St; just off A1(M)]: Well run thatched, beamed and timbered 18th-c dining pub with good food (not Sun evening, Mon) inc unusual and children's dishes, pews in bar, steps up to no smoking high-ceilinged dining area, well kept Greene King IPA, Abbot and Ruddles, decent wines, friendly attentive staff, woodburner in big brick inglenook, soft lighting, no music; children welcome, good big garden with play area *(Anthony Barnes, George Atkinson, Ian Phillips)*

Lemsford [TL2112]

Crooked Chimney [Cromer Hyde Lane (B653 towards Wheathampstead)]: Big comfortable open-plan Vintage Inn dining pub with good if not cheap food inc children's helpings; central feature fireplace and two further log fires, enjoyable food, well kept ales, helpful staff; pleasant garden by fields, play area *(B N F and M Parkin, LYM)*

London Colney [TL1803]

Colney Fox [High St/Barnet Rd]: Roomy Vintage Inn, their usual good value food, pleasant décor, well kept Bass and Tetleys, quick service considering how busy it is; plenty of tables outside, lots of trees in spacious grounds *(George Atkinson)*

Newgate Street [TL3005]

Crown: Attractive flower-decked building with colourful garden, cosy inside, with friendly staff, good varied food esp fresh fish, well kept beers, good house wine; handy for walks in Northaw Great Wood *(Lucien, Mrs E E Sanders)*

Northaw [TL2802]

Two Brewers [Northaw Rd W/Judges Hill (B157)]: Several traditional snug areas, nice light dining room and garden with view of ancient parish church, enjoyable food from ploughman's to fish specialities, well kept Adnams Broadside, Benskins and Marstons Pedigree *(R F Ballinger)*

Nuthampstead [TL4034]

☆ *Woodman* [off B1368 S of Barkway]: Tucked-away thatched and weatherboarded village local, welcoming and well run, with plenty of character, well kept Adnams and Greene King beers, 17th-c beams and timbers, generous home-made food (not Sun evening) in bar and small restaurant extension, efficient friendly service, fresh flowers, sofa and other comfortable furnishings, inglenook log fire and another fire at opposite end, pool; interesting USAF memorabilia (nearby World War II airfield), inc a memorial outside; benches outside overlooking tranquil lane; bedrooms, open all day Sat *(BB, S Horsley)*

Oxhey [TQ1295]

Villiers Arms [Villiers Rd, off Pinner Rd nearly opp Bushey & Oxhey Stn]: Friendly backstreet pub, masses of bric-a-brac from old cigarette packets to sewing machines, sporting posters and local photographs, decent choice of beers, modest range of freshly cooked bar meals; parking can be difficult *(Stan Edwards)*

Piccotts End [TL0508]

Boars Head [just off A4146 N of Hemel]: Traditional two-bar local with old-fashioned welcoming landlord, popular straightforward food, Ind Coope Burton and Tetleys; pretty garden with picnic-sets under cocktail parasols *(Ian Phillips)*

Redbourn [TL1111]

Chequers [St Albans Rd (A5183), nr M1 junction 9]: Friendly flagstone-floored family dining pub, good value food, dark wood fittings, screened dining area, well kept ales, decent wines; pleasant garden *(John Ker)*

Sawbridgeworth [TL4814]

Gate [London Rd (A1184)]: 18th-c pub with good range of quickly changing well kept ales in lined glasses, plans for own microbrewery, bank hol beer festivals with live music, cheap fresh lunchtime food, roomy and relaxed front bar, back bar with pool and games; close to railway station *(Richard Houghton, JP, PP)*

Spellbrook [TL4817]

Three Horseshoes: Recently refurbished as spacious candlelit dining pub with good blackboard food choice *(Miss Elaine Pugh)*

St Albans [TL1407]

Blacksmiths Arms [St Peters St]: Hogshead real ale pub, Boddingtons, Wadworths 6X and guest beers, usual food, low prices; can be rather crowded Fri/Sat night *(anon)*

Boot [Market Pl]: Friendly old-fashioned city-centre pub opp clock tower, open-plan, with low beams and timbers, open fire, Adnams, Fullers London Pride, Marstons Pedigree and Tetleys, good choice of generous food all day till 8, good mix of customers; unobtrusive fruit machine and piped music *(John Brightley)*

Cock [St Peters St/Hatfield Rd]: Comfortably modernised and friendly town pub with well kept real ales and interesting history – it once had a floor of human bones, probably from second Battle of St Albans, 1461 *(LYM)*

Farmers Boy [London Rd]: Bustling bay-windowed pub with back brewery producing Verulam IPA, Farmers Joy and a monthly special such as Dark, also their own lager and ten continental bottled beers, lots of old prints on smoke-effect walls, real fire, back open kitchen serving straightforward food from sandwiches and baked potatoes up all day, helpful staff, two large friendly dogs; open all

day, plenty of tables out behind *(Richard Lewis, Tracey and Stephen Groves, the Didler)*

Farriers Arms [Lower Dagnall St]: Plain but welcoming little local in no-frills old part, well kept McMullens Country, AK Mild and Gladstone, bar food wkdys; customers' bicycles seem chained to all the lampposts in the area *(the Didler, JP, PP)*

☆ *Fighting Cocks* [Abbey Mill Lane; through abbey gateway – you can drive down]: Odd-shaped former abbey gatehouse, much modernised inside but still showing the sunken area which was a Stuart cockpit, some low and heavy beams, inglenook fires, and pleasant nooks, corners and window alcoves, a dozen well kept interesting ales, food too – nice lunchtime atmosphere, can be very busy evenings; maybe piped music; children welcome (good family room), attractive public park beyond garden, open all day *(the Didler, Meg and Colin Hamilton, Kevin Blake, Mr and Mrs M Dalby, Tracey and Stephen Groves, LYM, Richard Houghton)*

Fleur de Lys [French Row]: Interesting medieval building (though the best parts are now in a museum and it's much modernised), doing well under new management, with good range of customers, reasonably priced food; tables on terrace, open all day *(LYM)*

☆ *Garibaldi* [Albert St; left turn down Holywell Hill past White Hart – car park left at end]: Relaxed Fullers local with well kept Chiswick, London Pride and ESB and a guest such as Adnams, good low-priced wholesome lunchtime food (not Mon), good house wines in sensible measures, cheerful staff; children welcome, piped nostalgic pop music, open all day *(Antony Pace, Tracey and Stephen Groves, the Didler, MP, LYM)*

Great Northern [London Rd]: Well kept Courage Directors and Mauldons Great North Eastern in open-plan beamed and carpeted local, lots of train pictures, open fire, friendly staff; open all day, quiz nights *(Richard Lewis)*

Lower Red Lion [Fishpool St]: Bustling two-bar local, good chatty atmosphere, interesting range of well kept beers, home-made food, log fire, red plush seats and carpet; open all day Sat, tables in good-sized back garden, pleasant bedrooms *(Tracey and Stephen Groves, the Didler)*

Mermaid [Hatfield Rd]: Neat smart local, several pleasant seating areas inc quiet window seat, relaxed welcoming atmosphere, well kept beers inc interesting guests, wkdy bar lunches, darts; piped music, video screen; tables in garden, open all day *(Tracey and Stephen Groves, Richard Houghton)*

☆ *Plough* [Tyttenhanger Green; off A414 E]: Spacious and friendly village pub, polite prompt service, lovely longcase clock, good log fire, well kept Greene King and other ales, good value usual food, good collection of old beer bottles and other bric-a-brac, pleasant young staff; conservatory, big garden with play area *(Dr David Cockburn, LYM, Gordon Neighbour, the Didler)*

Portland Arms [Portland St/Verulam Rd]:

Relaxed local with friendly licensees, Fullers beers kept well, big open fire, good value home-made food; some live music *(MP)*

☆ *White Hart* [Holywell Hill]: Comfortable, civilised and interesting old hotel, two small bar areas opening into larger one with tables; antique panelling, handsome fireplaces and furnishings, relaxed atmosphere, helpful service, wide choice of food, real ales, good coffee; if it's not too busy the manager may show you the 16th-c murals; restaurant, bedrooms; limited back parking *(LYM, Joy and Colin Rorke)*

White Hart Tap [Keyfield; round corner from Garibaldi]: Small but friendly white-panelled pub, well kept Tetleys, good value lunchtime food; tables outside, open all day, live band Tues *(anon)*

White Lion [Sopwell Lane]: Traditional two-roomed local with well kept ales such as Adnams, Bass, Greene King Abbot and Oakhams JHB, enjoyable food, maybe a small late-summer beer festival, regular live blues; big back garden with play area *(MP)*

Stevenage [TL2324]

Chequers [High St]: Open-plan high-ceilinged Greene King pub, comfortable U-shaped bar, friendly staff, good value standard lunchtime bar food (not Sun) from sandwiches up inc Thurs night fish and chip bargains, rugby football memorabilia; busy wkdys, pool, juke box; well kept sunny courtyard *(Gordon Tong, R W E Farr)*

Therfield [TL3336]

☆ *Fox & Duck* [The Green; off A505 Baldock—Royston]: Pleasantly refurbished beamed village pub with cheerful atmosphere, rugs on old tiled floor, solid old-fashioned tables and chairs, dining room extension, good food inc adventurous dishes and seasonal game, well kept ales such as Greene King IPA and Ruddles and Theakstons, decent wines, courteous staff,

unobtrusive piped music; good children's garden with climbing frames, swings and tree house *(Joy and Colin Rorke, Susan and Nigel Wilson, Len Banister, R Grisenthwaite)*

Tring [SP9211]

☆ *Robin Hood* [Brook St]: Neat olde-worlde pub popular for good food esp fresh fish such as bass, brill or eels (wide choice, but they don't buy much of each, so the blackboard may change as you watch); half a dozen well kept Fullers and guest ales *(John Branston)*

Walkern [TL2826]

☆ *White Lion* [B1037]: Comfortably cottagey open-plan 17th-c pub, good log fire, Greene King IPA and Abbot, decent bar food, friendly staff, no smoking restaurant; children in eating areas, open all day, lots of outdoor distractions for children inc good play areas *(Ian Phillips, LYM, Mike Ridgway, Sarah Miles, B N F and M Parkin, Ian and Joan Blackwell, Penny Miles)*

Watford [TQ1196]

Moon Under Water [High St]: Wetherspoons with good choice of well kept real ales at low prices, decent good value food all day, no smoking area, no music; handy for Palace Theatre *(Stan Edwards)*

Westmill [TL3626]

Sword in Hand [village signed off A10 S of Buntingford]: 14th-c colour-washed pub in pretty village, beams and log fires, well kept Greene King IPA and Old Speckled Hen, food in bar and partly no smoking dining room; cl Sun evening and Mon, children welcome till 8, tables on attractive terrace and in side garden, play area inc football *(Maysie Thompson, Mike Ridgway, Sarah Miles, Klaus and Elizabeth Leist, Joy and Peter Heatherley, Enid and Henry Stephens, Gordon Tong, R R Thompson, LYM, Mark Blackburn, Jenny and Chris Wilson, Rosanna Ribolzi)*

Post Office address codings confusingly give the impression that some pubs are in Hertfordshire, when they're really in Bedfordshire or Cambridgeshire (which is where we list them).

Isle of Wight

The island has plenty of good family pubs, often with fine views; the Clarendon (Wight Mouse) at Chale is a fine example, with plenty for young children to do, but strong all round in pubbier matters. Interestingly, one of our main entries, the Bonchurch Inn in Bonchurch, is run by an Italian, while another, the cheerful Blacksmiths Arms near Carisbrooke has a German landlord (with some food and beers to match). Fresh fish is often a high point on the food side. For food, the Red Lion at Freshwater, the Seaview Hotel in Seaview and the New Inn at Shalfleet, all stand out. The New Inn's lovely fresh fish helps to earn it the title of Isle of Wight Dining Pub of the Year. The Spyglass in Ventnor, though its food is mainly standard pub cooking, does that so well that it earns a Food Award this year. The Crown at Shorwell is another place that's very popular indeed for a pub meal – a favourite all round. A special mention for consistency: the White Lion at Arreton and Clarendon at Chale have been in every edition of the Guide, *throughout its 20 years. In the Lucky Dip section at the end of the chapter, pubs to note particularly these days are the Fishermans Cottage on the beach at Shanklin, White Horse at Whitwell, and Bugle and Wheatsheaf in Yarmouth. Drinks prices on the island are rather higher than the national average, but there are interesting local beers to try from Goddards and Ventnor, and the choice of beers from the mainland is considerably wider than it used to be.*

ARRETON SZ5486 Map 2
White Lion
A3056 Newport—Sandown

It's the good straightforward reasonably priced food that, especially in summer, makes this cosy village pub such a popular destination. Besides sandwiches and baguettes (from £3.20), baked potatoes (from £4.75), mostly home-made dishes include spicy mushroom and tomato tagliatelle (£4.95), lasagne or chilli (£5.95), steak and kidney pie (£5.95), battered scampi (£6.45) or steaks (from £6.95), as well as specials such as gorgonzola and walnut pasta with green pesto sauce (£6.25), pork escalope in cream, paprika and pepper sauce (£7.45) and venison steak with port and forest fruit sauce (£10.25); no smoking restaurant and family room. The pleasant beamed lounge bar has shining brass and horse-harnesses on the partly panelled walls, and cushioned wheelback chairs on the red carpet; piped music, cribbage, dominoes, darts and fruit machine, TV. Well kept Badger Dorset Best, Fullers London Pride and maybe a summer guest such as Goddards Fuggle-Dee-Dum are served on handpump. You can sit out in front by the tubs of flowers; the pleasant garden has a small children's play area. *(Recommended by Alan Skull)*

Whitbreads ~ Lease Chris and Kate Cole ~ Real ale ~ Bar food (12-9) ~ Restaurant ~ (01983) 528479 ~ Children in family room and part of restaurant ~ Open 11-11; 12-10.30 Sun

---

If you see cars parked in the lane outside a country pub have left their lights on at night, leave yours on too: it's a sign that the police check up there.

BEMBRIDGE SZ6587 Map 2
Crab & Lobster

Foreland Fields Road, off Howgate Road (which is off B3395)

This clifftop pub, tucked away on a bluff above the shore, is an easy walk from the beach, and has great sea views from its terrace, garden and window seats. There's more room inside than you'd expect from the frontage, which is prettily bedecked with flower baskets in summer. The attractively decorated interior has a civilised, almost parlourish style, with lots of yachting memorabilia and old local photographs. The bar menu (which usually has quite a good choice of fresh local seafood specials) includes sandwiches (from £3.75), baked potatoes (from £3.95), ploughman's or baked avocado filled with crab (£4.95), spinach and stilton in puff pastry (£5.75), moules marinières (from £5.95), chicken curry or home-made lasagne (£5.95), fillet steak (£10.50) and half a local lobster (£11.50) with puddings such as spotted dick (£2.95); children's meals (£3.25); the restaurant is no smoking. Well kept Castle Eden, Flowers Original and Goddards Fuggle-Dee-Dum on handpump, decent house wines, country wines from the barrel, good coffee; piped music (even in the lavatories) and darts. It does get very popular (we've been told it's on coach trip itineraries) so best to get there early or late at lunchtime (the coaches tend to leave at 2pm). Good views from their new bedrooms – we look forward to hearing from readers who've tried them. *(Recommended by DHV, Mr and Mrs A Craig, Terry Mizen, Phil and Heidi Cook, Martin and Karen Wake, DP, D P and J A Sweeney)*

Whitbreads ~ Lease Adrian and Pauline Allan ~ Real ale ~ Bar food (12-2.30, 6-9.30) ~ Restaurant ~ (01983) 872244 – fax 01983 875349 ~ Children welcome ~ Open 11-11; 12-10.30 Sun ~ Bedrooms: /£60B

BONCHURCH SZ5778 Map 2
Bonchurch Inn

Bonchurch Shute; from A3055 E of Ventnor turn down to Old Bonchurch opposite Leconfield Hotel

Once the stables for a nearby manor house, the various buildings of this old stone pub are spread around a central courtyard. The furniture-packed Victorian bar, good for a leisurely drink, conjures up images of salvaged shipwrecks with its floor of narrow-planked ship's decking, and seats like the ones that old-fashioned steamers used to have. The welcoming landlord is Italian, and as well as sandwiches (from £2.70, toasted 30p extra), soup (£3), they serve pizza (from £4.50), nine different types of ploughman's and several Italian dishes like lasagne, risotto, spaghetti bolognese or cannelloni (from £6). Other dishes include chicken cordon bleu (£7.50), king prawn provençale or grilled halibut steak and sirloin steak (£8.50); for puddings they have ice creams and sorbets (£3). There's a separate entrance to the very simple no smoking family room which is a bit separate from the congenial atmosphere of the public bar, making this not the best place on the island for families. Courage Best and Directors are tapped from the cask, there are Italian wines by the glass, a few bottled French wines, and coffee; darts, bar billiards, shove-ha'penny, dominoes and cribbage. There's a separate sun lounge. They open the restaurant across the courtyard only for reservations in the evenings; the pub owns a holiday flat for up to six people (children must be over 7 years old). *(Recommended by J A Cheverton, Graham and Lynn Mason)*

Free house ~ Licensees Ulisse and Gillian Besozzi ~ Real ale ~ Bar food ~ Restaurant ~ (01983) 852611 ~ Children in separate family room and restaurant ~ Open 11-3, 6.30-11; 12-3, 7-10.30 Sun; closed 25 Dec ~ Bedrooms: /£70B

CARISBROOKE SZ4687 Map 2
Blacksmiths Arms 🍴

Park Cross, Calbourne Road; B3401 1½ miles W – and pub signed off Tennyson Trail

Run by a cheerful Bavarian landlord, this pretty brick and blue-painted roadside pub serves an interesting range of generous German food. Dishes such as frikadelle (mini burgers, £5.25), various schnitzels (from £7.95), rinderrolade (beef stuffed with German mustard, olives, bacon and onions, £8.50) and wild boar in red wine sauce (£8.95) all come with german-style potatoes and sauerkraut; club sandwiches and platters of up to half a dozen cheeses, or cooked and smoked meats are also available. More traditional English dishes include sandwiches (from £2.50), ploughman's (from £4.95), chicken and leek or steak and kidney pudding (£6.50), swordfish with lemon and herb butter (£7.50) and puddings such as home-made apple strudel and cheesecake (from £3.50); no credit cards; helpful polite service. As well as four or five changing real ales such as Badger Best, Black Dog and Fullers ESB and London Pride on handpump, there are deliveries from Munich of German draught and bottled beers and wines every few months. Set on a quiet hillside (and signposted off the Tennyson Trail) there are good views over the Solent from the simply built and furnished dining extension, and from tables in the smallish back garden, which has a play area with a bouncy castle. Inside, there's a slightly old-fashioned feel about the neatly kept front bars, and the upper bar is homely and cosy; table football. *(Recommended by J A Cheverton, Mike and Maggie Betton)*

Free house ~ Licensees Edgar and Donna Nieghorn ~ Real ale ~ Bar food (12-3, 6-10) ~ No credit cards ~ (01983) 529263 ~ Children in family room ~ Folk night Tues ~ Open 12-3, 6-11 wkdys; 11-(10.30 Sun)11wknds

CHALE SZ4877 Map 2
Clarendon (Wight Mouse) ♀ 🍴 🛏

In village, on B3399; also access road directly off A3055

Children are welcomed enthusiastically to this extremely popular, rambling family pub, and there's certainly plenty to keep them occupied. In the spacious back garden there's a toddlers' play area, swings, slides, bouncy castle, a junior adventure challenge, tricycles, a pets corner, and sometimes Punch and Judy shows. Even in the rain it has something to offer, with an indoor play area for under-12s (admission £1). Less energetic parents can sit and appreciate the lovely views out towards the Needles and Tennyson Downs, where the poet was inspired to write *Idylls of the King*. The original core of the pub is surprisingly traditional, with musical instruments, guns, pistols and so forth hanging over an open log fire. One end opens through sliding doors into a pool room with dark old pews, large antique tables, video game, juke box, darts, dominoes, fruit machine and pinball. At the other end there's a woody extension with more musical instruments, lots of china mice around a corner fireplace, decorative plates and other bric-a-brac, and even some oars from old lifeboats hanging from its high pitched ceiling; piped music; no smoking area. Seven well kept real ales include Fullers London Pride, Gales HSB, Greene King Old Speckled Hen, Marstons Pedigree and maybe a guest such as Ventnor Oyster Stout on handpump, an outstanding choice of around 365 whiskies, over 50 wines, and some uncommon brandies, madeiras and country wines. They've recently extended their bar menu which includes soup (£2.40), sandwiches (from £2.50, baguettes from £3), filled baked potatoes (from £2.50), ploughman's (from £4.25), pesto vegetable pancakes or home-made steak and kidney pie (£6.95), chicken fried with garlic and herbs (£7.95) and 8oz sirloin steak (£10.25), with daily specials such as barbecued spare ribs (£6.95) and bass (£7.95), and puddings such as cheesecake (from £2.75). Cheerful and efficient service; no smoking dining area. There's live music every evening and on Sunday lunchtimes. The bedrooms, some in adjoining former farm buildings, include three two-bedroom family suites. Though the Bradshaws (who ran the pub throughout its first 19 appearances in this *Guide*) have now handed over to the Plants, they still live next door, and it's fair to say that their spirit lives on in the place. *(Recommended by Danny Nicol, James Morrell, Dr and Mrs A K Clarke, Phil and Heidi Cook, Graham and Lynn Mason)*

Free house ~ Licensees Keith and Julia Plant ~ Real ale ~ Bar food (12-9.30) ~ Restaurant ~ (01983) 730431 ~ Children welcome ~ Live entertainment every night and Sun lunchtime ~ Open 11-11.45; 12-11 Sun ~ Bedrooms: /£78B

We now have a web site: www.goodguides.com

COWES SZ5092 Map 2

Folly

Folly Lane – which is signposted off A3021 just S of Whippingham

The maritime connections of this splendidly set pub go back a long way – the original building is based around a sea-going barge beached here in the early 1700s, and the roof evidently still includes part of its deck. Big windows in the bar and seats on a waterside terrace look out on to the boats on the river estuary; it gets understandably busy in summer. The nautically themed opened-out bar has a wind speed indicator, barometer and chronometer around the old timbered walls, as well as venerable wooden chairs and refectory-type tables, shelves of old books and plates, railway bric-a-brac and farm tools, old pictures, and brass lights. Straightforward bar food includes soup (£2.95), sandwiches (from £2.85), garlic mushrooms (£3.75), steak and kidney pie or half a barbecued chicken (£6.95), plaice (£9.95), 8oz sirloin steak (£10.95), shoulder of lamb (£12), and specials such as spinach and vegetable pancakes (£5.95), chicken curry (£6.95) and fresh fish (from £7.50). Flowers IPA and Original and in summer a guest such as Greene King Old Speckled Hen on handpump; no smoking area, pool, fruit machine, TV and piped music. There's a bouncy castle in the landscaped garden in summer. Watch out for the sleeping policemen along the lane if you're driving. If you're coming along the river they have moorings, a water taxi, long-term parking, and showers, and they even keep an eye on weather forecasts and warnings. *(Recommended by DHV, DP, Jason Caulkin)*

Whitbreads ~ Managers Andy and Cheryl Greenwood ~ Real ale ~ Bar food (12-9.30 (10 Sat)) ~ (01983) 297171 ~ Children in eating area of bar ~ Live entertainment Sat evenings and Thurs and Fri in summer ~ Open 11-11; 12-10.30 Sun

FRESHWATER SZ3487 Map 2

Red Lion 🍷

Church Place; from A3055 at E end of village by Freshwater Garage mini-roundabout follow Yarmouth signpost, then take first real right turn signed to Parish Church

Although this dining pub is tucked well enough out of the way to have kept a genuinely local atmosphere, the food is so popular that if you want to eat here it's a good idea to book ahead. Well cooked imaginative daily specials are listed on a big blackboard behind the bar, and might include clam chowder or bacon and lentil soup (£3), spicy coated sardines or crab and stilton stuffed mushrooms (£5.25), vegetable stir fry (£6.95), home-made fishcakes with parsley sauce or leek and chicken pie (£7.25), moules marinières (£7.95), pork steak with brandy and mushrooms (£8.75), rack of lamb with redcurrant gravy (£13.95) or whole lobster thermidor (£18.95); puddings might include chocolate and orange cheesecake, treacle sponge and whisky and walnut trifle (£3). Service can be a bit slow. The comfortably furnished open-plan bar has open fires, low grey sofas and sturdy country-kitchen style furnishings on mainly flagstoned floors, with bare boards at one end, and lots of local pictures and photographs and china platters on the walls. Well kept Flowers Original, Fullers London Pride, Goddards Special and Shepherd Neame Spitfire on handpump, and there's a good choice of wines including 16 by the glass; fruit machine and piped classical music. There are tables on a grassy area at the back (some under cover), behind which is the kitchen's herb garden, and a couple of picnic-sets in a quiet tucked-away square at the front, near the church; nearby good walks, especially around the River Yar. *(Recommended by R L Turnham, DAV, Mr and Mrs Flood, Philip Vernon, Kim Maidment, Tony and Wendy Hobden, Geoffrey Kemp, D P and J A Sweeney, Darly Graton, Graeme Gulibert, MDN)*

Whitbreads ~ Lease Michael Mence ~ Real ale ~ Bar food (12-2, 6.30-9) ~ (01983) 754925 ~ Children over 10 ~ Open 11.30-3, 5.30-11; 11-4, 6-11 Sat; 12-3, 7-10.30 Sun; closed 25 Dec evening

---

Please let us know of any pubs where the wine is particularly good.

ROOKLEY SZ5183 Map 2
Chequers
Niton Road; signposted S of village

A good place to keep children entertained, the large play area outside this former customs and excise house has a toboggan run and bouncy castle while inside there's a Lego table and colouring competitions in the large no smoking family room. The comfortable carpeted lounge bar is decorated with cottagey ornaments, and has a group of easy chairs and settees down at one end by the good winter log fire; from here there are inland views of rolling downland. The lively flagstoned public bar beyond retains its local character and is popular with young farmers; sensibly placed darts, fruit machine, TV, and maybe piped music. There's also a mother and baby room. Courage Best and Directors, Gales HSB, Greene King Old Speckled Hen, John Smiths and a guest such as Marstons Pedigree on handpump. Bar food includes soup (£2), sandwiches (from £2.20), baked potatoes (from £4.25), deep-fried brie with redcurrant jelly or moules marinières (£4.25), ploughman's (from £4.50), vegetable lasagne (£5.50), chicken curry (£5.95), rack of lamb (£7.95), roast duckling (£8.65) and steaks (from £9.75) and puddings (from £2.95); children's meals. *(Recommended by John Branston, Michael and Robin Inskip, R L Turnham)*

Free house ~ Licensees R G and S L Holmes ~ Real ale ~ Bar food (12-10) ~ (01983) 840314 ~ Children welcome ~ Open 11-11; 12-10.30 Sun

SEAVIEW SZ6291 Map 2
Seaview Hotel 🍽 ♀ 🛏
High Street; off B3330 Ryde—Bembridge

There are sea views from the continental-style terraces on either side of the path to the front door of this comfortably bustling hotel. Popular with locals, the nautical back bar is a lot pubbier than you might imagine from the outside with traditional wooden furnishings on the bare boards, lots of seafaring paraphernalia around its softly lit ochre walls, and a log fire. The civilised airier bay-windowed bar at the front has an impressive array of naval and merchant ship photographs, as well as Spy nautical cartoons for *Vanity Fair*, original receipts for Cunard's shipyard payments for the *Queen Mary* and *Queen Elizabeth*, and a line of close-set tables down each side on the turkey carpet. Using local ingredients wherever possible, good well presented generous bar food includes soup (£2.95), hot crab ramekin (£4.95), warm crispy duck and nut salad with tangy mango dressing (£6.50), spinach and ricotta puff with wholegrain mustard mash or pork and leek sausages and mash (£7.50), grilled swordfish steak with red wine reduction (£11.95), changing blackboard specials such as local crab and lobster, and puddings such as steamed treacle pudding with cream (£3.50) and iced lemon brûlée (£3.95); children's menu; the restaurant is no smoking. Service is generally good and the staff are friendly. Goddards and Greene King Abbot are kept on handpump, and there's a good wine list (the landlord used to be a director of Corney and Barrow wine merchants) and choice of malt whiskies; darts, cribbage, dominoes, shove-ha'penny and piped music. Some of the bedrooms have sea views. *(Recommended by Geoffrey Kemp, DP, J A Snell, Tony and Wendy Hobden, N J Franklin, MDN)*

Free house ~ Licensee N W T Hayward ~ Real ale ~ Bar food (12-2, 7-9.30) ~ Restaurant ~ (01983) 612711 ~ Children in eating area of bar and restaraunt, no under 5s in restaurant after 7.30pm ~ Open 11-(3 Sat)2.30, 6-11; 12-3, 7-10.30 Sun; closed three days at Christmas ~ Bedrooms: £65B/£75B

SHALFLEET SZ4189 Map 2
New Inn 🍽 ♀ 🍴
Main Road (A3054 Newport—Yarmouth)
Isle of Wight Dining Pub of the Year

The good fresh fish served at this welcoming former fishermen's pub is bought from the quay only a short walk away. A brief menu with sandwiches (from £2.95), filled baguettes from (£3.75) and ploughman's (from £5.25) is supplemented by changing blackboard specials (with up to 16 types of fish) which might include grilled sardines with garlic and black pepper butter (£3.95), mushrooms in white wine and stilton (£4.50), moules marinières (£4.95/£8.95), pork fillet with apple and cider sauce, chicken breast with honey and cream sauce or thai-style swordfish (£8.95), lobster salad (£11.95), and their famous fish platter for two (£45); it's a good idea to book. The partly panelled, flagstoned public bar has yachting photographs and pictures, a boarded ceiling, scrubbed deal tables, windsor chairs, and a roaring log fire in the big stone hearth, and the carpeted beamed lounge bar has more windsor chairs, boating pictures, and a coal fire. The snug is no smoking. Well kept Badger Best, Bass, Ventnor Golden and a couple of guests such as Goddards Fuggle-Dee-Dum and Jennings Cocker Hoop on handpump, and around 60 wines; piped music. *(Recommended by Renee and Dennis Ball, Michael and Robin Inskip, Mike and Maggie Betton, Penny and Peter Keevil, Mrs J A Uthwatt, MDN)*

Whitbreads ~ Lease Mr Bullock and Mr MacDonald ~ Real ale ~ Bar food (12-2.30, 6-9.30) ~ Restaurant ~ (01983) 531314 ~ Children away from main bar ~ Open 12-3, 6-(10.30 sun)11

SHORWELL SZ4582 Map 2

Crown

B3323 SW of Newport

This friendly old place is real favourite with readers and, despite its rural setting, one of the most popular pubs on the island. Summer crowds are drawn to its lovely, peaceful tree-sheltered garden, where picnic-sets and white garden chairs and tables overlook a little stream that broadens out into a wider trout-filled pool with prettily planted banks. There's a decent children's play area that blends in comfortably, and the pub has a truly welcoming attitude towards children. In the four friendly rooms that wander around its central bar there's a traditional atmosphere, and the staff are pleasant. The cosy beamed two-room lounge has blue and white china in an attractive carved dresser, old country prints on the stripped stone walls, other individual furnishings, a cabinet of model vintage cars, and a winter log fire with a fancy tilework surround. Black pews form bays around tables in a stripped-stone room off to the left, with another log fire; several areas are no smoking. The good range of tasty bar food includes sandwiches (from £2.25), soup (£2.50), good baked potatoes (from £3.75), ploughman's or pizzas (from £3.95), local crab cocktail or garlic mushrooms (£3.95), ham and egg or spicy vegetable schnitzel (£5.95), steaks (from £9.95) as well as specials such as home-made chicken and ham pie (£6.50), lamb shank with redcurrant gravy (£8.95) and local bass with citrus butter (£10.50); puddings (from £2.25), children's meals. Well kept Boddingtons, Flowers Original and Wadworths 6X, with a guest such as Badger Tanglefoot on handpump; piped music, darts and TV. *(Recommended by D P and J A Sweeney, Chris and Chris Ellis, P Price, Michael and Robin Inskip, Prof H G Allen, DHV, David and Carole Chapman, DAV, Terry Mizen, Mrs J A Uthwatt, David and Kay Ross)*

Whitbreads ~ Lease Mike Grace ~ Real ale ~ Bar food (12-2.30, 6-(9.30 Fri and Sat)9) ~ (01983) 740293 ~ Children welcome ~ Open 10.30-3, 6-11; 12-3, 6-10.30 Sun

VENTNOR SZ5677 Map 2

Spyglass 🍴

Esplanade, SW end; road down very steep and twisty, and parking can be difficult

If it's too wet to appreciate the view from the terrace of this marvellously positioned pub, perched above the sea wall, there's plenty to look at inside. Among the really interesting jumble of mainly seafaring memorabilia are wrecked rudders, ships' wheels, old local advertisements, rope makers' tools, stuffed seagulls, an Admiral Benbow barometer and an old brass telescope. The bustling mainly quarry-tiled interior is snug and pubby, and the atmosphere is buoyant; fruit machine, piped music. Generous helpings of good, reasonably priced bar food are promptly served and include sandwiches (from £2.75, baguettes from £3.75), filled baked potatoes (from £4.25), ploughman's and burgers (from £4.95), vegetable moussaka (£5.75), cottage pie (£5.95), tuna steak (£6.95), garlic prawns (£7.25), 8oz sirloin steak (£9.95) or tasty seafood platter (£10.95), and daily specials such as pork and mushroom cider casserole and crab and prawn gratin; puddings such as cherry or apple pie (from £2.75). They usually have well kept Badger Best and Tanglefoot, Ventnor Golden and possibly a guest on handpump. They don't mind dogs or muddy boots; no smoking area. On special occasions such as a lifeboat support week, there may be half a dozen or more guest ales tapped from the cask. *(Recommended by Darly Graton, Graeme Gulibert, Brian Root, Prof H G Allen, John Kirk, Michael Buchanan, R L Turnham, Sharon Holmes, Tom Cherrett, Keith Fairbrother)*

Free house ~ Licensees Neil and Stephanie Gibbs ~ Real ale ~ Bar food (12-2.15, 7-9.30(9 wknds) ~ (01983) 855338 ~ Children in family room ~ Live entertainment most nights ~ Open 10.30-11 (10.30 Sun); closed Mon-Fri 3-6.30 in winter ~ Bedrooms: /£50B

Lucky Dip

Besides the fully inspected pubs, you might like to try these Lucky Dips recommended to us and described by readers (if you do, please send us reports: www.goodguides.com).

Brading [SZ6086]
Bugle [High St (A3055 Sandown—Ryde)]: Big welcoming family place with good generous straightforward food inc children's, Fri curry night and Sun carvery, lots of tables in three roomy beamed areas, pretty floral wallpaper, quick friendly service, well kept Wadworths IPA; piped music; restaurant, supervised children's room with lots of games and videos, free lollipops for children, baby-changing in gents' as well as ladies', garden *(Ian and Nita Cooper, MDN)*
Brighstone [SZ4282]
Three Bishops [Main Rd]: Friendly bustling modern pub with good reasonably priced food, cheerful attentive service; large garden *(Michael and Robin Inskip)*
Calbourne [SZ4286]
Sun: Friendly helpful staff and decent generous food in old roadside pub, cosy no-frills bar, plain lower-level extension, extensive views across Brighstone Forest; subdued piped music *(June and Malcolm Farmer)*
Cowes [SZ4896]
Union [Watch House Lane]: Small Gales local with good atmosphere, cosy side room, good choice of beers inc interesting guest, good value food from fine crab sandwiches to generous well cooked nicely presented hot dishes; bedrooms *(Mr and Mrs M Dalby, Alan Skull)*
Downend [SZ5387]
Hare & Hounds [A3056]: Extended thatched family dining pub recently taken over by a chain, lots of beams and stripped brickwork, cosy alcoves in original part, more room in airy barn-type extension; open all day, wide views from terrace, nice spot by Robin Hill Country Park, which is a great place for children *(LYM)*
Havenstreet [SZ5690]
White Hart [Main Rd, off A3054 Newport—Ryde]: Cosy bar with lots of locomotive prints in ancient building, tidy and comfortable, well kept Badger ales, wide range of generous good value food (not Mon evening) inc good fresh

veg and splendid salads, friendly staff; interesting beer-bottle collection *(Mr and Mrs Gurr)*
Nettlestone [SZ6290]
Roadside Inn: Square town house recently reopened under very friendly new management, large airy comfortable bar, good food esp steak and kidney pudding, well kept real ales *(Dr and Mrs A K Clarke, Alan Skull)*
Niton [SZ5075]
Buddle [St Catherines Rd, Undercliff; off A3055 just S of village, towards St Catherines Point]: Extended former smugglers' haunt, heavy black beams, big flagstones, broad stone fireplace, no smoking areas, decent straightforward food inc seafood and griddle dishes (may be a wait), local farm cider, family dining room/games annexe, friendly dogs; well cared for sloping garden and terraces, good walks; open all day, some live jazz *(Chris and Chris Ellis, Tony and Wendy Hobden, LYM, Michael and Robin Inskip, Brian Root)*
Shanklin [SZ5881]
☆ *Chine* [Chine Hill]: Great clifftop setting, tastefully refurbished, with flagstones, beams, good food (can be a wait; not Sun evening or Mon), well kept local Goddards and a changing guest beer; some live music, bright family conservatory and small terrace overlooking beach and chine (which is illuminated at dusk) *(R L Turnham, D P and J A Sweeney, Gerry Hollington)*
☆ *Fishermans Cottage* [bottom of Shanklin Chine]: Unchanging thatched cottage in terrific beach setting, tucked into the cliffs, steep walk down beautiful chine, lovely beach walk to Luccombe; stripped stone and lots of bric-a-brac in low-beamed flagstoned bar, simple bar food, Courage Directors under light blanket pressure, local country wines, coffee all day; wheelchair access; children welcome, tables out on terrace, live entertainment Tues, Fri, Sat, cl Nov-early March *(Jason Caulkin, D P and J A Sweeney, P Price, Ian and Nita Cooper, Mr and*

Mrs J French, Keith Fairbrother, LYM)
Steamer [Esplanade]: Conversion of former
seafront hotel, good fun and great value, very
popular with holiday families; good range of
real ale inc local Ventnor Golden, enjoyable
food, fine sea views from balcony dining area;
singers and guitarists *(D P and J A Sweeney,
Mr and Mrs W Kidston)*
Ventnor [SZ5677]
Crab & Lobster [Grove Rd]: Comfortable old-
fashioned local with cask tables,
straightforward low-priced bar food lunchtime
and wknd evenings, well kept Ventnor and
guest ales, decent house wines, thoughtful
service; dogs allowed, open all day, bedrooms
(Lynn Sharpless, Bob Eardley)
☆ *Mill Bay* [Esplanade]: Seafront pub with light
airy décor, large conservatory, good choice of
reasonably priced generous food, Badger Best
and local Ventnor Gold, friendly service (and
very friendly dog called Caffrey); good live
music; big beachside terrace with play area
(D P and J A Sweeney, BB, R L Turnham)
Volunteer [Victoria St]: Small old-fashioned
local with interesting customers and involved
landlord, six well kept ales such as Badger,
Ringwood and Yates, reasonable prices, darts,
the local game of rings, no machines or juke
box, no food; open all day, quiz nights *(Darly
Graton, Graeme Gulibert)*
Whitwell [SZ5277]
☆ *White Horse* [High St]: Ancient pub with
welcoming young licensees, wide range of good
value home-made food inc good Sun lunch,
huge helpings, full range of Gales ales kept well,
cheerful quick service, well furnished big

interconnected beamed bars with popular no
smoking family dining extension, country
décor, horsebrasses, log fire; tables out on lawn
*(Prof H G Allen, Marc and Trish Steer, June
and Malcolm Farmer)*
Yarmouth [SZ3589]
☆ *Bugle* [The Square]: Old inn with low-ceilinged
panelled lounge, lively rather basic bar with
nautical memorabilia and counter like galleon
stern, usual food from well filled sandwiches
up, quick cheerful service, well kept
Whitbreads-related ales, restaurant, games
room with pool, children very welcome; piped
music can be rather loud, little or no nearby
parking; sizeable garden, summer barbecues,
good big airy bedrooms *(Dr and Mrs A K
Clarke, Michael and Robin Inskip, LYM)*
Kings Head [Quay St]: Cosy low-ceilinged
traditional pub opp car ferry, rather dark and
quaint, with well kept ales, good food inc well
prepared local fish, plush seats, friendly staff,
open fires, children's eating area, unobtrusive
piped music; can get crowded, public car park
some way off; bedrooms *(Michael and Robin
Inskip, Dr and Mrs A K Clarke)*
☆ *Wheatsheaf* [Bridge Rd, nr ferry]: Three
spacious rooms, light and airy no smoking
conservatory, well kept Brakspear, Goddards
Fuggle Dee Dum, Greene King Old Speckled
Hen and Wadworths 6X, cheerful staff, wide
choice of generous food all day inc fresh fish,
public bar with juke box and winter pool;
children welcome in most parts, open all day,
tables in garden *(Miss J F Reay, Ian and Nita
Cooper, DAV, D P and J A Sweeney, June and
Malcolm Farmer, LYM)*

Kent

Three good new entries here this year are the attractively reworked and updated Queens just outside Hawkhurst, the Chequers in Smarden (doing very well all round under friendly newish licensees) and the Swan at West Peckham (brewing lots of its own beers, and like the other two a good all-rounder). In contrast to this fresh blood, two pubs have been in the Guide every year since it started 20 years ago: the interesting old Three Chimneys near Biddenden, and the friendly and bustling Wheatsheaf at Bough Beech, still on top form. Other pubs doing particularly well this year here are the cheerfully unpretentious Gate Inn by the marshes at Boyden Gate (good all round), the untouched old Woolpack at Brookland, the Albion in Faversham (a favourite for food, drink and atmosphere), the Bottle House near Penshurst (interesting food, nice surroundings), the Dering Arms at Pluckley (good fish, a nice place to stay in), the pretty Rose & Crown by the woods near Selling (a good friendly all-rounder), the unspoilt Red Lion at Snargate, the Lord Raglan in Staplehurst (the landlord/chef went to the same school as your Editor – not that that's any recommendation, but his cooking and the unpretentiously civilised atmosphere most certainly are), the well run Beacon in Tunbridge Wells, and Sankeys there (rather wine-barish, but good beers as well as wines, plenty of atmosphere, and good seafood). For the second year running, the Albion in Faversham stands out as an admirable place for a special meal out, and is our Kent Dining Pub of the Year. In the Lucky Dip section at the end of the chapter, the Fountain at Cowden and Green Cross near Goudhurst both look very promising on the food side under their new licensees; we've inspected both and feel that they are headed towards the main entries. Other pubs to note in that section, also mostly already inspected and approved, are the Flying Horse at Boughton Aluph, Olde Beverlie in Canterbury, Chapter Arms at Chartham Hatch, Star & Eagle in Goudhurst, Artichoke at Hadlow, Golden Lion at Luddesdown, Golding Hop at Plaxtol, Rose & Crown at Pluckley, Coastguard at St Margaret's Bay, St Crispin at Worth and New Flying Horse in Wye. Average drinks prices in the county, rising more quickly than in most other places, are now significantly higher than the national average and have breached the £2 barrier for a pint of beer. The Swan at West Peckham, brewing its own, was one of the cheapest main entries (the other was the Queens outside Hawkhurst). Beers from the main local brewer Shepherd Neame were often cheaper than average, as were those from the smaller brewers Goachers and (from just over the Sussex border) Rother Valley.

BIDDENDEN TQ8538 Map 3
Three Chimneys ◧

A262, a mile W of village

Relaxed and civilised, this characterful old pub has a rambling, low oak beamed series of small, very traditional rooms with simple wooden furniture and old settles on flagstones and coir matting, some harness and sporting prints on the exposed brick walls, and good winter log fires. The simple public bar has darts, shove-ha'penny, dominoes and cribbage. As well as a good wine list, local Biddenden cider and several malt whiskies, the well kept Flowers Original, and Shepherd Neame Master Brew, Spitfire, and a seasonal beer are tapped straight from the cask. Imaginative, if not cheap, bar food includes soup (from £3.25), fresh marinated anchovy salad (£4.75), ploughman's (from £5.50), fresh crab cakes with a light thai dressing (£5.95), caramelised onion and goats cheese tartlet (£8.95), fried chicken breast with roasted vegetables (£11.95), confit of duck or leg of lamb with curried sweet roasted potato and wild rocket salad (£12.95), rib-eye steak (£13.95), roast cod on mustard mash (£15.95), and puddings such as lemon torte with plum compote and sticky toffee pudding (from £3.95). The quite civilised candlelit bare board restaurant has french windows opening onto the garden. There's a smart garden terrace area with plenty of tables and outdoor heaters for very pleasant dining. Every 4th Sunday in summer, they have classic car meetings. Sissinghurst gardens are just down the road. The licensees also own the Bell at Smarden. *(Recommended by Judy Robertson, J Hale, Darly Graton, Graeme Gulibert, David and Betty Gittins, Peter Meister, Colin and Janet Roe, the Didler, Alan and Heather Jacques, John Eggleston, Comus and Sarah Elliott, R E Davidson, K J Diamond, Mrs D Stoner, Keith Barker, Louise English, Kevin Thorpe, Pat and Tony Martin, JP, PP, John Evans, W K Wood, Meg and Colin Hamilton, M and B Writer)*

Free house ~ Licensees Craig and Jackie Smith ~ Real ale ~ Bar food ~ Restaurant ~ (01580) 291472 ~ Older children in eating area of bar ~ Open 11.30-2.30, 6-11; 12-3, 7-10.30 Sun

BOUGH BEECH TQ4846 Map 3

Wheatsheaf ♀ ◖

B2027, S of reservoir

There's a lovely bustling and friendly atmosphere in this fine old pub, and the landlady and her staff make both visitors and locals most welcome; there are also thoughtful touches like piles of smart magazines to read, nice nibbles, chestnuts to roast in winter, summer pimms and mulled wine in winter. The neat central bar and the long bar (with an attractive old settle carved with wheatsheaves, shove-ha'penny, dominoes, and board games) have unusually high ceilings with lofty oak timbers, a screen of standing timbers and a revealed king post. Divided from the central bar by two more rows of standing timbers – one formerly an outside wall to the building – is the snug, and another bar. Other similarly aged features include a piece of 1607 graffitti, 'Foxy Galumpy', thought to have been a whimsical local squire. There are quite a few horns and heads, as well as a sword from Fiji, crocodiles, stuffed birds, swordfish spears, and the only matapee in the south of England on the walls and above the massive stone fireplaces. The menu includes mozzarella and tomato crostini with rocket pesto, spiced chicken and plum sauce crostini, macaroni cheese and ploughman's (all £5.95), three cheese pasta with garlic bread or vegetable lasagne (£6.95), fillet of smoked haddock with spinach, mash and citrus sauce (£7.95), thai or indian curry, cold smoked chicken with grapefruit salad with citrus mayonnaise or lambs liver with bacon, black pudding and mash (all £8.95), and puddings like ginger pudding with brandy and ginger wine sauce, chocolate pecan tart or blackberry and apple pie. Well kept Butcombe Bitter, Fullers London Pride, Greene King Old Speckled Hen, Harveys Sussex, and Shepherd Neame Master Brew on handpump, good wines including local wine, and several malt whiskies. There's a rustic cottage, plenty of seats, and flowerbeds and fruit trees in the sheltered side and back gardens. The pub is thought to have started life as a hunting lodge belonging to Henry V. *(Recommended by Mr and Mrs D D Collins, Linda and Jim Webb, Martin and Karen Wake, Debbie and Neil Hayter, Sue Demont, Tim Barrow, John Robertson, Pat and Tony Martin, Derek Harvey-Piper)*

Whitbreads ~ Lease Elizabeth Currie ~ Real ale ~ Bar food (12-10) ~ (01732) 700254 ~ Children in eating area of bar ~ Folk and country Weds 8.30 ~ Open 11-11; 12-10.30 Sun

BOYDEN GATE TR2265 Map 3
Gate Inn ★ ♀ ◖

Off A299 Herne Bay—Ramsgate – follow Chislet, Upstreet signpost opposite Roman Gallery; Chislet also signposted off A28 Canterbury—Margate at Upstreet – after turning right into Chislet main street keep right on to Boyden; the pub gives its address as Marshside, though Boyden Gate seems more usual on maps

As well as being somewhere that really contributes to the local community, this fine old-fashioned pub is also a favourite with its many visitors from outside the area. It's been run by Mr Smith for 26 years now, and his cheerful and friendly personality is an important part of the bustling pubby atmosphere. The winter inglenook log fire serves both quarry-tiled rooms, and there are flowery-cushioned pews around tables of considerable character, hop bines hanging from the beam and attractively etched windows. Tasty bar food includes sandwiches (from £2; black pudding and bacon £3; filled baguettes from £2.95), quite a few burgers (from £2.60), home-made soup (£2.75), lots of filled baked potatoes (from £3.40), ploughman's (£4.50), home-made vegetable flan, grilled steak or spicy hotpots (£5.50), and puddings (from £2.50); they use organically grown local produce where possible, and you can generally buy local honey and free-range eggs. The eating area is no smoking at lunchtime. Well kept Shepherd Neame Bitter, Spitfire, and seasonal ales tapped from the cask, interesting bottled beers, a fine range of 17 wines by the glass, and country wines. Shove-ha'penny, dominoes and cribbage. On a fine evening, it's marvellously relaxing to sit at the picnic-sets on the sheltered side lawn listening to the contented quacking of what seems like a million happy ducks and geese (they sell duck food inside – 10p a bag), coots and moorhen; bat and trap. *(Recommended by Kevin Thorpe, Iain Robertson, Klaus and Elizabeth Leist, Mike Cowley, Helen Coster, David and Betty Gittins, Steve Rudge, Tracey Griffiths)*

Shepherd Neame ~ Tenant Christopher Smith ~ Real ale ~ Bar food (12-2, 6-9) ~ No credit cards ~ (01227) 860498 ~ Well behaved children in eating area of bar and family room ~ Open 11-2.30, 6-11; 12-4, 7-10.30 Sun

BROOKLAND TQ9724 Map 3
Woolpack £

On A259 from Rye, as you approach Brookland, take the first right turn where the main road bends left, just after the expanse of Walland Marsh; OS Sheet 189 map reference 977244

You can imagine smugglers sheltering at this Beacon Keeper's house from the winter marsh mists, and there's still plenty of old-fashioned character and atmosphere. The ancient entrance lobby has an uneven brick floor and black-painted pine panelled walls, and on the right, the simple but homely softly lit main bar has a good warming log fire and basic cushioned plank seats in the massive inglenook fireplace itself, a painted wood-effect bar counter hung with lots of water jugs, and some ships' timbers in the low-beamed ceiling that may date from the 12th c. On the quarry-tiled floor is a long elm table with shove-ha'penny carved into one end, other old and newer wall benches, chairs at mixed tables, and characterful photos of the locals (and perhaps their award winning sheep) on the walls. To the left of the lobby there's a sparsely-furnished little room, and an open-plan games room with central chimney stack, modern bar counter, and young locals playing darts or pool; dominoes, cribbage, shove-ha'penny, fruit machine, piped music and pub cat. Well kept Shepherd Neame Master Brew and Spitfire on handpump. The quite straightforward but most enjoyable bar food is particularly good value, and includes sandwiches (from £1.95), soup (£2.50), ploughman's (£4.25), cod and chips or vegetable lasagne (£4.75), chilli or home-made steak pie (£4.95), sirloin steak (£9.95), and daily specials like cauliflower cheese, liver and bacon, chicken and mushroom pie or whole grilled plaice (all £4.50), and lamb shank (£4.95); Sunday roast (£4.25). *(Recommended by Lynn Sharpless, Bob Eardley, Graham Brooks, John Davis, Peter and Joan Elbra, Simon and Sally Small, John and Lynn Busenbark, Pamela and Merlyn Horswell)*

Shepherd Neame ~ Tenants John and Pat Palmer ~ Real ale ~ Bar food ~ (01797) 344321 ~ Children in family room ~ Open 11-3, 6-11; 12-3, 7-10.30 Sun

CHIDDINGSTONE TQ4944 Map 3
Castle ♀

Village signposted from B2027 Tonbridge—Edenbridge

Records show there was a building called Waterslip House here in 1420, and this pub's stone foundations probably go back as far as that – so it could be where Anne Boleyn found shelter when she was stranded in a terrible blizzard on her way to nearby Hever. The rambling interior includes a handsome, carefully modernised beamed bar with well made settles forming booths around the tables, cushioned sturdy wall benches, an attractive mullioned window seat in one small alcove, and latticed windows; a couple of areas are no smoking. Bar food is usefully served all day, and includes open sandwiches or filled baked potatoes (from £4.15), filled baguettes (from £4.95), very hot chilli (£5.75), ploughman's (from £6.25), sausages (£5.95) and puddings (from £3.95); a decent children's menu, and children's facilities (bottle warmers and so forth). There's a very good wine list, well kept Harveys Best, Larkins Traditional (it's brewed in the village and in winter they have Porter too), and Youngs Ordinary on handpump, and a good range of malt whiskies; darts, shove-ha'penny, dominoes and cribbage. There are tables in front facing the church, and more in the pretty secluded vine hung garden. It's worth a walk around this National Trust village to look at the marvellously picturesque cluster of unspoilt Tudor houses, and the countryside around here is lovely. *(Recommended by M and B Writer, Anthony Longden, R E Davidson, Neil Rose, Michael and Ann Cole, James Nunns, Tina and David Woods-Taylor, J Hale, Patricia Beebe)*

Free house ~ Licensee Nigel Lucas ~ Real ale ~ Bar food (11-10.45; 12-10.15 Sun) ~ Restaurant ~ (01892) 870247 ~ Children welcome (not in public bar) ~ Open 11-11; 12-10.30 Sun

DARGATE TR0761 Map 3
Dove ⑭

Village signposted from A299

It's quite a surprise to find such imaginative restaurant-style food in a pub that is tucked away down a network of narrow lanes in a quiet hamlet. Changing daily, and using fresh seasonal local ingredients, the imaginative menu might include sandwiches (from £3.25), croque monsieur (£4.50), grilled sardines with virgin olive oil and garlic (£5), crab and spring onion risotto (£6), fresh crevettes with pickled ginger and herbs (£6.95), confit of duck with cherry tomato and wholegrain mustard dressing (£7.50), braised local free range chicken with oyster mushrooms and parsley (£14.50), breast of local duck with puy lentils flavoured with foie gras (£14.75), roast fillet of wild bass with crushed new potatoes and tapenade (£15.50), and puddings such as orange and passion fruit brûlée or baked chocolate pudding with crème anglais (£5); you must book. The charmingly unspoilt rambling rooms have photographs of the pub and its licensees throughout the century on the walls, a good winter log fire, and plenty of seats on the bare boards; piped music. They keep only Shepherd Neame Masterbrew on handpump.The sheltered garden has roses, lilacs, paeonies and many other flowers, picnic-sets under pear trees, a dovecot with white doves, a rockery and pool, and a swing. A bridlepath leads up from the pub (along the charmingly-named Plumpudding Lane) into Blean Wood. *(Recommended by Mr and Mrs Thomas, Richard Siebert, Norman Fox, Kevin Thorpe, David and Betty Gittins, Barry and Patricia Wooding, John and Elizabeth Thomason, John Davis, R E Davidson)*

Shepherd Neame ~ Tenants Nigel and Bridget Morris ~ Real ale ~ Bar food (not Sun afternoon, all day Mon or Tues evening) ~ (01227) 751360 ~ Children in eating area of bar ~ Open 11.30-3, 6-11.30; 12-3, 7-11 Sun

---

You can send us reports through our web site: www.goodguides.com

DEAL TR3752 Map 3
Kings Head £

Beach Street, just off A258 seafront roundabout

Just across the road from the promenade and the sea, this handsome three-storey Georgian inn has award-winning hanging baskets and window boxes, picnic-sets out on a broad front paved terrace area, and helpful, long-standing owners. A good mix of customers gathers in its four comfortable bar rooms which work their way round the central servery. The walls, partly stripped masonry, are interestingly decorated with marine architectural drawings, other maritime and local pictures and charts, and other material underlining connections with the Royal and Merchant navies, and another area has an interesting collection of cricket memorabilia. There are a couple of flame-effect gas fires; darts, fruit machine, and TV. A wide choice of good value food includes sandwiches (from £2.25), omelettes (from £3.95), filled baked potatoes (from £4.25), ploughman's (from £4.75), roast vegetable tart or chicken korma (£4.95), steak and kidney pie (£5.65), fish pie (£5.95), sirloin steak (£9.50), and daily specials such as fresh dressed crab (£6.95) or dover sole (from £9.95); two-course Sunday lunch (£8.95). Well kept Fullers London Pride, Shepherd Neame Master Brew and Spitfire, and a guest such as Bass, Courage Best or Greene King IPA on handpump; quiet piped music. Beware that traffic wardens here are vigilant; there's pay-and-display parking nearby. *(Recommended by Kevin Thorpe, Michael Tack, Hazel and Michael Duncombe, B J Harding, David Gregory)*

Courage (S & N) ~ Lease Graham Stiles and Shirley Rayner ~ Real ale ~ Bar food (11-2.30, 6-9) ~ (01304) 368194 ~ Children in eating area of bar ~ Open 10.30-11; 12-10.30 Sun ~ Bedrooms: £40B/£56B

FAVERSHAM TR0161 Map 3
Albion 🍴 ♉

Follow road through town and in centre turn left into Quay Lane; just before Shepherd Neame Brewery walkway over road turn right over bridge, bear right, first right into public car park

Kent Dining Pub of the Year

There's always such a cosmopolitan mix of customers at this splendid pub creating a good lively atmosphere – and although most people have come to enjoy the imaginative food, there's still a pubby feel around the spacious bar area, with drinkers perched comfortably on bar stools, taking in the working waterside views through big french windows. The light and airy open-plan bar is simply but effectively decorated with a mix of solid old pine furniture on wood and sisal flooring, pale pea green walls with nautical paraphernalia and old pine mirrors; piped music and dominoes. As well as lunchtime filled baguettes (from £3.50) and ploughman's (from £4.50), the very popular bar food, prepared by the French chef/licensee Patrick, might include hazelnut and roquefort terrine with cranberry marmalade (£4.50), fresh smoked mackerel with hard-boiled eggs and cherry tomatoes with mustard dressing (£4.55), ratatouille tartlet with a mixed leafy and nutty salad (£5.50), local sausages with melted onions (£7.25), pancake of spinach and mushroom with a creamy stilton sauce (£7.85), roast best-end of lamb with a garlic and herb crust and redcurrant sauce (£15.25), daily specials such as queen scallop with a dill, white wine and crème fraîche sauce with a warm brioche (£5.25), lamb and apricot moussaka with a greek yoghurt topping or a medley of wild mushroom risotto with a spinach and parmesan topping (£7.50), stuffed guinea fowl breast wrapped in bacon with red wine and wild mushrooms (£10.95), and baked bass fillet with lemon sauce and tomato, potato and basil confit (£13.25), and puddings such as dark chocolate pudding with a white chocolate and Amaretto sauce, apricot streusel with apricot and Cointreau sauce with greek yoghurt or fruit compote crème brûlée (from £3.95); best to book. Well kept Shepherd Neame Master Brew, Bishops Finger, Spitfire and seasonal ales kept under light blanket pressure, a decent French wine list, and friendly, efficient staff. There are picnic-sets out on the river walkway and you can stroll along the bank for about an hour;

disabled lavatories. *(Recommended by Mrs P G Newton, Tony Baldwin, E D Bailey, Rob Barthwick, Colin and Janet Roe, Gill and Keith Croxton, Pat and Tony Martin, David and Betty Gittins, J S M Sheldon, John Rahim, Angela Cerfontyn, John Davis, Grahame Brooks, Tina and David Woods-Taylor)*

Shepherd Neame ~ Tenants Patrick and Josephine Coevoet ~ Real ale ~ Bar food ~ (01795) 591411 ~ Children in eating area of bar ~ Open 11.30-3, 6.30(6 Sat)-11; 12-3, 7-10.30 Sun

FORDCOMBE TQ5240 Map 3
Chafford Arms
B2188, off A264 W of Langton Green

This tile-hung old pub is quite a sight in summer as it is festooned with flowers against a backdrop of cascading creepers and carefully tended shrubs and perennials. Most of the flowers are in front but there's a sheltered lawn behind with an attractive shrubbery and arbours, and a well nursed wych elm which still manages to hold the record as the largest wych elm in the British Isles. Inside, there's plenty of room between neat tables and comfortable seats on a turkey carpet, and an uncluttered décor. Full of sporting memorabilia and trophies, the quite separate public bar often gets much busier towards the close of the evening as the dining side winds down; darts, shove-ha'penny, cribbage, dominoes, TV, and fruit machine. Bar food includes sandwiches (from £2.65), soup (£2.95), ploughman's (£4.95), vegetarian quiche (£5.95), grilled trout or gammon steak (£7.95), and steaks (from £9.45). Well kept Larkins and Wadworths on handpump, local farm cider, and decent house wines. Just up the (steepish) lane is an archetypal village cricket green. *(Recommended by LM, John Davis, Roger and Pauline Pearce, E D Bailey, Geoffrey G Lawrance)*

Whitbreads ~ Lease Barrie Leppard ~ Real ale ~ Bar food (not Sun and Mon evening) ~ Restaurant ~ (01892) 740267 ~ Children welcome ~ Jazz 3rd Sun evening of month ~ Open 11.45-3, 6.30-11; 11-11 Sat; 12-4, 7-10.30 Sun

GROOMBRIDGE TQ5337 Map 3
Crown
B2110

By the time this book is published, new licensees will have taken over this quaint Elizabethan inn, but we are hoping that not too much will change. It is idyllically set at the end of a row of pretty cottages overlooking the steep village green, and there are picnic-sets in front on a sunny old brick terrace. Inside, several beamed rooms are charmingly snug, with locals crowded around the long copper-topped serving bar, and a jumble of bric-a-brac including old teapots, pewter tankards, and antique bottles. The walls, mostly rough yellowing plaster with some squared panelling and timbering, are decorated with small topographical, game and sporting prints, and a circular large-scale map with the pub at its centre. In winter, large logs burn in the big brick inglenook. The no smoking end room, normally for eaters, has fairly close-spaced tables with a variety of good solid chairs, and a log-effect gas fire in a big fireplace. Bar food has included sandwiches, good local sausages, vegetable and cashew nut curry, steak and mushroom pie, honey baked ham with chips, and roasted cod with a herb crust. Well kept Courage Directors, Harveys IPA, and Larkins on handpump, and local farm cider; shove-ha'penny, dominoes, cribbage and scrabble. Across the road is a public footpath beside the small chapel which leads, across a field, to moated Groombridge Place. *(Recommended by Joan and Andrew Life, Lynn Sharpless, Bob Eardley, Michael and Ann Cole, Ian Phillips, Peter Meister, John and Christine Lowe, Pat and Tony Martin, Tina and David Woods-Taylor, C E Barnes)*

Free house ~ Real ale ~ Bar food (not Sun evening) ~ Restaurant ~ (01892) 864742 ~ Children in restaurant and snug ~ Open 11-3, 6-11; 11-11 Sat; 12-10.30 Sun; 11-2.30, 6-11 Sat in winter ~ Bedrooms: £30/£40

HAWKHURST TQ7630 Map 3

Queens

Rye Road (A268 E)

First recorded as an inn in the 16th c, this handsome wisteria-covered Georgian-faced building is said to have been a haunt of the notorious Hawkhurst Gang, with all the usual tall tales of getaway tunnels and so forth. Much more civilised these days, the interior has been sensitively opened up and appealingly decorated in keeping with its age (though it's a shame that they've trendified its old name of Queens Head). By day, light filters in through creeper tendrils that threaten to cover the old sash windows, and at night it's candlelit. The cosy rooms have heavy low beams, are colour-washed in terracotta, sand or pea-green, and have a nice mix of old pine tables on bare boards. The main bar area is pleasantly chatty, with stools along the counter and a woodburning stove in a big brick inglenook. Down a step a dining area has a couple of plush sofas and chairs next to another fire. The pub was quite recently taken over by an accommodating Australian landlady and her two children, and as we went to press they were about to refurbish the spacious public bar (tucked away round to one side) as a 1920s-style wine bar; piped pop, fruit machine, pool. Particularly popular at lunchtime, bar food includes soup (£3.50), filled baguettes (from £4), ploughman's (£4.50), chicken and asparagus terrine or tomato mozzarella and rocket salad (£4.95), sausage and mash (£6.95), liver and bacon (£7.50), cod and smoked haddock fishcakes (£7.95), steak and mushroom pie (£8.75), avocado, prawn and smoked salmon salad (£8.95), red mullet fillets with avocado salsa on fettuccine with rocket salad (£10.50), a couple of daily specials, and puddings such as toffee crunch or raspberry cheesecake (£3.50). Well kept Adnams, Courage and Fullers London Pride on handpump. *(Recommended by Comus and Sarah Elliott, Jason Caulkin)*

Enterprise ~ Lease Janelle Tresidder ~ Real ale ~ Bar food (12-9(4 Sun)) ~ Restaurant ~ (01580) 753577 ~ Children in eating area of bar and restaurant ~ Jam night alternate Tues, live band Fri ~ Open 12-11(10.30 Sun) ~ Bedrooms: £45B/£65B

HODSOLL STREET TQ6263 Map 3

Green Man

Hodsoll Street and pub signposted off A227 S of Meopham; turn right in village

Handy for Eurostar, this friendly village pub has new licensees, and Mrs Hayward's son now does the cooking. There's a relaxing atmosphere in the big airy carpeted rooms which work their way round a hop-draped central bar, and neat tables are spaced tidily around the walls, with interesting old local photographs and antique plates, and a log fire at one end. Bar food includes a light lunchtime menu with sandwiches (from £2.95), filled baked potatoes (from £3.95), ploughman's (£4.50), wild boar sausages (£5.50), and ham and egg (£5.95), as well as home-made soup (£1.95), deep-fried breaded camembert with a redcurrant sauce (£3.75), garlic prawns (£5.50), stilton and roast pepper parcels (£8.25), chicken stuffed with prawns and wrapped in filo pastry (£9.25), pork fillet stuffed with black pudding (£9.75), smoked haddock with bombay potatoes and a poached egg or lamb shank (£9.95), and puddings like chocolate pavlova, banoffi pie or blackcurrant cheesecake (£3.25). Well kept Fullers London Pride, Marstons Pedigree, Youngs Bitter, and a guest such as Gales HSB on handpump, and a decent wine list; piped music. There are picnic-sets on a well tended lawn, an aviary and a goat, and pretty hanging baskets and flowering tubs; plenty of walks in the nearby North Downs. *(Recommended by Ian Phillips, Tina and David Woods-Taylor, B, M and P Kendall, Bill and Rachael Gallagher, Andrew Scarr, Chris and Sandra Taylor, Peter Meister)*

Whitbreads ~ Lease Jean Hayward ~ Real ale ~ Bar food ~ (01732) 823575 ~ Children welcome ~ Open 11-2.30, 6-11; 11-11 Fri and Sat; 12-10.30 Sun

---

Tipping is not normal for bar meals, and not usually expected.

HOLLINGBOURNE TQ8455 Map 3
Dirty Habit
B2163, off A20

Once a monastic house, this early 15th-c inn has a main bar with fairy lights threaded through a profusion of hops over the counter, some high bar chairs, heavy beams, and a long, very low beam leading to a panelled, dimly lit room: candles on sizeable tables, a very high-backed plush red cushioned settle with rather grand arms set opposite a big brown sofa, and a mix of dining chairs. Another little area has long settles, some chunky dining chairs, a brick fireplace, and newspapers on racks; a door from here leads up steps to a brick-tiered terrace with stone slab tables, green plastic chairs, statues, chimney pots filled with flowers, and a pergola. At the other end of the bar is a lighter room with more panelling, a relaxed, chatty atmosphere, a mix of chairs and tables, and a woodburning stove. Well kept Flowers Original, Greene King Old Speckled Hen, and Wadworths 6X or Farmers Glory on handpump, and home-made country wines; piped music. Enjoyable (if not cheap) bar food includes home-made soup (£3.75), baguettes (from £3.95), smooth chicken liver pâté (£4.50), ploughman's (from £4.75), spicy stuffed mussels (£5.50), curried vegetables or stir-fried chicken (£9.95), curried lamb and lentils (£10.95), bacon-wrapped chilli prawns, loin of pork with a spicy plum sauce glaze or a sizzle plate of monkfish with prawns and potatoes cooked in garlic butter (£11.95), scotch salmon fillets wrapped in filo pastry with chive butter (£12.50), and puddings (from £3.75). The pub is on the North Downs Way. *(Recommended by A W Lewis, Lynn Sharpless, Bob Eardley, Ian Phillips, Mike Tucker, Sally Anne and Peter Goodale, Mrs P G Newton, Kay Vowles, Alan and Heather Jacques, Dave Braisted)*

Free house ~ Licensee Kevin Bunney ~ Real ale ~ Bar food (12-2.45, 7-9.45) ~ (01622) 880880 ~ Children welcome ~ Jazz/rock/blues Mon evening ~ Open 11.30-3, 6.30-11; 12-3.30, 7-10.30 Sun

ICKHAM TR2257 Map 3
Duke William ♀
Village signposted off A257 E of Canterbury

Bigger than its little street front exterior suggests, this friendly and comfortable family-run pub has an open-plan carpeted bar that extends either side of the serving counter; the front part has a comfortably lived-in feel, helped by the big inglenook, all the brasses, copper and other bric-a-brac, longcase clock, and even gas lighting. There's more formal seating behind, with a rather smart air-conditioned restaurant area and then a well shaded no smoking Victorian-style conservatory which overlooks the attractive neatly kept garden and fields beyond. A wide choice of good home-made food includes sandwiches (from £1.90), baguettes (from £4.25), home-made soup (£3.50), ploughman's (from £5.50), quite a few pizzas (from £5.95), about a dozen different pasta dishes (from £5.45), steak and kidney pie or fried chicken with ginger and mixed spices (£6.95), prawn curry or chargrilled tuna with parmentiere potatoes (£9.95), and puddings from a trolley (£3.50). Well kept beers such as Adnams, Fullers London Pride, Shepherd Neame Masterbrew and Youngs Special on handpump, as well as 15 wines by the glass and freshly squeezed orange juice; darts, pool, shove-ha'penny, dominoes, fruit machine and juke box. *(Recommended by Kevin Thorpe, David and Betty Gittins, J S M Sheldon)*

Free house ~ Licensees Mr and Mrs A R McNeill ~ Real ale ~ Bar food (11-2, 6-10 (not Sun evening)) ~ Restaurant ~ (01227) 721308 ~ Children in restaurant and conservatory ~ Open 11-3, 6-11; 12-4, 7-10.30 Sun; closed Mon lunchtime (except bank hols)

We mention bottled beers and spirits only if there is something unusual about them – imported Belgian real ales, say, or dozens of malt whiskies; so do please let us know about them in your reports: www.goodguides.com

IDEN GREEN TQ8031 Map 3

Woodcock

Iden Green is signposted off A268 E of Hawkhurst and B2086 at W edge of Benenden; in village at crossroads by bus shelter follow Standen Street signpost, then fork left at pub signpost – beware that there is an entirely different Iden Green just 10 miles away near Goudhurst

There always seems to be a cheerful cluster of locals chatting happily to the friendly bar staff and jovial landlord at the bar counter of this unaffected little country pub. The small bar is snugly comfortable with exposed red brick walls, very low ceilings bearing down heavily on a couple of big timbers on its flagstone floor, as well as comfy sofa and armchairs by a warming woodburner, and chunky big old pine tables tucked snugly into little nooks. Real ales include well kept Greene King IPA, Abbot and Ruddles County, Harveys, and a guest like Rother Valley Level Best on handpump. Enjoyable bar food includes home-made leek and potato soup, pâté or tempura prawns (£3.95), filled baguettes (from £4), ham and egg (£5.50), fried lambs liver and bacon or steak, kidney, mushroom and ale pie (£7.95), sirloin steak (£9), rack of lamb with chilli, ginger and honey sauce (£10.95), duck breast with a black forest sauce or wing of skate with black butter and capers (£11.95), and puddings (£3.50); they have opened up an extra dining room this year. It can get very busy at weekends so you may need to book; darts, shove-ha'penny, fruit machine, and piped local radio. There are seats in the pretty side garden and the car park is across the road. *(Recommended by Grahame Brooks, Colin and Janet Roe, John McDonald, Ann Bond)*

Greene King ~ Lease Frank Simmons ~ Real ale ~ Bar food (12-2, 7-9) ~ Restaurant ~ (01580) 240009 ~ Children welcome ~ Open 11-11; 12-10.30 Sun

IGHTHAM TQ5956 Map 3

George & Dragon

The Street; A227 S of Borough Green

New licensees again for this wonky black and white timbered pub, built in 1515 for the Earl of Stafford, and there have been some refurbishments. The long main bar has a stripped wooden floor, a circular table with a mix of wooden dining chairs by the fireplace (there's another fireplace at the other end with a woodburning stove), plenty of high bar stools, leather sofas, and a good chatty atmosphere. The Duke of Northumberland was imprisoned in this room after the Gunpowder Plot was discovered. A very nice little end room is cottagey but simple with a pretty view through a sash window to the heart of this tiny village, and has heavy black beams, some big jugs in a corner display cupboard, and dried flowers in the brick fireplace; piped music. Food can now be eaten anywhere in the pub and might include sandwiches, home-made soup (£3), chicken liver pâté with spiced pear (£3.50), warm duck breast salad with chinese five-spice set onto roasted beetroot and apple (£4.50), haddock fillet and courgette in tempura batter with corn salsa or sausages made with ale, served with caramelised apples and red onion and thyme gravy (£7.50), steak and mushroom braise with olive oil mash or corn fed chicken breast with a dressing of yoghurt, honey, mustard and dill (£8), medallions of beef on spiced aubergine roundels with a white wine and cream sauce (£9.50), daily specials, and puddings; two-course Sunday lunch £8.50); part of the restaurant is no smoking. Well kept Shepherd Neame Master Brew and Spitfire and seasonal ales, decent wines, and friendly staff. Seats out on the back terrace; more reports please. *(Recommended by Ian Phillips)*

Shepherd Neame ~ Managers Charles Edgeter and Carole Slingo ~ Real ale ~ Bar food (all day; 12-3, 6-8(9 Mon) Sun) ~ Restaurant ~ (01732) 882440 ~ Children in eating area of bar and restaurant ~ Open 11-11; 12-10.30 Sun; closed evenings 25 and 26 Dec

IGHTHAM COMMON TQ5755 Map 3

Harrow ✿❢

Signposted off A25 just W of Ightham; pub sign may be hard to spot

There's little doubt that most people come to this civilised country dining pub to enjoy the imaginative food – but they do offer three real ales and the atmosphere is informal. Assorted country furniture stands on nice old brick flooring or black and white squared vinyl in two simply but attractively decorated rooms, both warmed by log fires in winter. The old-fashioned public bar is painted a cheerful sunny yellow above dark green dado, and there is appealing attention to detail such as daily papers, and fresh flowers and candles on the tables. Well presented, if not cheap, food includes dishes such as popular crab and ginger spring roll with sesame oil and a light soya sauce or mushroom medley vol-au-vent (£5.95), crispy duck with bubble and squeak and marmalade onion gravy, salmon and chive fishcakes with citrus sauce, roasted shank of lamb with couscous or venison and red wine sausages with shallots and red wine jus (all £8.95), cajun chicken (£9.95), and brochette of scallops, crevettes and sole with chilli, lime and coriander (£11.95). A decent sensibly priced wine list has plenty of good wines by the glass, and well kept ales include Greene King IPA, Abbot and a guest like Greene King Old Speckled Hen on handpump. A lush grapevine grows around the delightful little antiquated conservatory which leads off an elegant dining room laid with white cloths; piped music; tables and chairs on a pretty little pergola-enclosed back terrace. Very handy for Ightham Mote. *(Recommended by John McDonald, Ann Bond, Catherine and Richard Preston, Di and Mike Gillam, Michael Martin, Derek Thomas, Chris Reeve, Martin and Karen Wake, Tina and David Woods-Taylor, Guy Vowles, Nigel and Olga Wikeley, Ian Phillips, E D Bailey, JP, PP, Pat and Tony Martin)*

Free house ~ Licensees John Elton and Claire Butler ~ Real ale ~ Bar food (12-2.30, 6-9.30; not Sun evening or Mon) ~ Restaurant ~ (01732) 885912 ~ Children in restaurant ~ Open 12-3, 6-11; 12-3 Sun; closed Sun evening and Mon

LANGTON GREEN TQ5538 Map 3

Hare ✿❢ ♀

A264 W of Tunbridge Wells

With its pubby but comfortable atmosphere, this big Edwardian place is somewhere women feel as equally at home as men. The good, interesting food is what most customers are after: home-made soup (£3.75), stilton, celery and pecan nut tart with a raspberry dressing (£3.95), sandwiches (from £4.25; cumberland sausage topped with sticky caramelised red onion relish (£4.95), salmon and smoked haddock fishcakes with a tomato and spring onion salad or smoked ham, penne pasta and artichokes in a creamy pesto (£6.95), sardines with garlic and lemon butter (£7.25), meatloaf with parsley new potatoes and mushroom sauce (£7.95), cod fillet in a sesame crust with stir-fried vegetables and a sweet chilli and soy sauce or roast half shoulder of lamb with a rosemary and red wine sauce (£11.50), hare casserole with a leek and bacon mash (£12.95), and puddings like home-made apple pie, fruit crumble or sticky toffee pudding (from £3.95). There's a pleasant feeling of space throughout with lots of big windows and high ceilings in the knocked-through rooms, which have dark-painted dados below light walls, oak furniture and turkey carpets on stained wooden floors, old romantic pastels, and plenty of bric-a-brac (including a huge collection of chamber-pots). Old books, pictures and two big mahogany mirror-backed display cabinets crowd the walls of a big chatty room at the back which has lots of large tables (one big enough for at least 12) on a light brown carpet. From here french windows open on to a sheltered terrace with picnic-sets looking out on to a tree-ringed green. Well kept Greene King IPA and Abbot, and a couple of guests like Everards Tiger or Flowers Original on handpump, lots of wines by the glass, and over 40 malt whiskies; piped pop music in the front bar area, cribbage, and dominoes. *(Recommended by Derek Thomas, Dr David Cockburn, Peter Meister, Ian Phillips, Colin and Janet Roe, A W Lewis, Ken Arthur)*

Brunning & Price ~ Tenant Brian Whiting ~ Real ale ~ Bar food (12-9.30(9 Sun)) ~

Restaurant ~ (01892) 862419 ~ Well behaved children in restaurant ~ Open 11-11;
12-10.30 Sun

NEWNHAM TQ9557 Map 3
George

44 The Street; village signposted from A2 just W of Ospringe, outside Faversham

The spreading series of atmospheric rooms in this 16th-c pub has lots to look at:
dressers with teapots, prettily upholstered mahogany settles, dining chairs and
leather carving chairs around candlelit tables, table lamps and gas-type ceiling
chandeliers, and rugs on the waxed floorboards; hop bines hang from the beams and
there are quite a few pictures, open fires and fresh flowers. Under the new licensees,
good, well presented lunchtime food includes sandwiches or baguettes (from £1.95),
home-made soup (£2.75), moules marinières (£4.95), ploughman's (from £4.95),
goats cheese brushed with basil oil wrapped in smoked bacon and fried or local
bangers and mash (£5.95), mushroom stroganoff (£6.50), steak and kidney pudding
with onion gravy (£7.95), half shoulder of lamb with rosemary and red wine sauce
(£11.95), daily curries, and evening dishes like baked trout (£8.95), chicken breast
filled with king prawns with a cream, prawn and chive sauce (£10.95), honey-glazed
medallions of pork loin with a cider and grain mustard sauce (£12), and supreme of
guinea fowl with brandy, orange, tarragon, and crème fraîche (£12.95). Well kept
Shepherd Neame Master Brew, Spitfire, Bishops Finger, and seasonal beers on
handpump, 12 wines by the glass, and piped music. There are picnic-sets in a
spacious sheltered garden with a fine spreading cobnut tree, below the slopes of the
sheep pastures, and good nearby walks. More reports please. *(Recommended by Mr and
Mrs Thomas, R E Davidson, John and Elizabeth Thomason, Alan and Jan Summers)*

*Shepherd Neame ~ Tenant Marc Perins ~ Real ale ~ Bar food (12-2.30, 7-9.30) ~
Restaurant ~ (01795) 890237 ~ Children welcome ~ Occasional jazz/soul/blues ~
Open 11-3, 6.30-11; 12-4, 6.30-11 Sun; closed evening 25 Dec*

OARE TR0163 Map 3
Shipwrights Arms ◗

S shore of Oare Creek, E of village; coming from Faversham on the Oare road, turn right into
Ham Road opposite Davington School; or off A2 on B2045, go into Oare village, then turn
right towards Faversham, and then left into Ham Road opposite Davington School; OS Sheet
178 map reference 016635

They only sell beers brewed in Kent at this unchanging and characterful 17th-c inn.
Tapped from the cask, these might include Goachers Gold Star Ale, Mild, and
Shipwrecked, and Hot Daemon Dominator and Skrimshander; maybe strong local
farm cider. Three unspoilt little bars are dark and cosy, and separated by standing
timbers and wood part-partitions or narrow door arches. There's a medley of seats
from tapestry cushioned stools and chairs to black wood-panelled built-in settles
forming little booths, pewter tankards over the bar counter, boating jumble and
pictures, flags or boating pennants on the ceilings, several brick fireplaces, and a
woodburning stove. Bar food includes sandwiches (from £2.65), filled baked
potatoes (from £3.25), ploughman's (from £3.95), home-cooked ham and egg
(£4.75), chilli or mushroom stroganoff (£5.95), and puddings like treacle sponge
(from £2.75); part of the eating area is no smoking; piped music, shove-ha'penny,
cribbage and dominoes. An interesting approach to the pub is a walk from the
village through the tangle of boatyards, or you can moor a boat in the creek which
runs just below the Saxon Shore Way which is up a bank from the front and back
gardens of the pub. The setting is quite striking as the surrounding salt marshes are
designated areas of Special Scientific Interest and populated by rare birds.
*(Recommended by Kevin Flack, R E Davidson, Peter Holmes, the Didler, Kevin Thorpe, JP, PP,
Neil Spink, Richard Siebert, Dave Braisted, Stephen, Julie and Hayley Brown)*

*Free house ~ Licensees Derek and Ruth Cole ~ Real ale ~ Bar food (not Sun evening)
~ No credit cards ~ (01795) 590088 ~ Children in family room ~ Open 11-3, 6-11;
11-11 Sat; 12-10.30 Sun; 11-3, 6-11 Mon-Fri winter*

PENSHURST TQ5243 Map 3

Bottle House

Coldharbour Lane, Smarts Hill; leaving Penshurst SW on B2188 turn right at Smarts Hill signpost, then bear right towards Chiddingstone and Cowden; keep straight on

The neatly kept low beamed front bar in this friendly 15th-c pub has a well worn brick floor that extends to behind the polished copper-topped bar counter, and big windows look on to a terrace with climbing plants and hanging baskets around picnic-sets under cocktail parasols, and beyond to views of quiet fields and oak trees. The unpretentious main red-carpeted bar has massive hop-covered supporting beams, two large stone pillars with a small brick fireplace (with a stuffed turtle to one side), and old paintings and photographs on mainly plastered walls; quite a collection of china pot lids, which extend to the low ceilinged, no smoking dining room. Several cosy little areas lead off the main bar – all can be booked for private parties and can be smoking or non smoking; one room is covered in sporting pictures which extend to the ceiling. Good, interesting bar food includes home-made minestrone soup (£3.50), goose liver and sauternes mousseline (£4.50), spinach, roquefort and baby onion tartlet with tomato chutney (£4.75), thai spiced fishcake with chilli jam (£4.95), honey and mustard roasted ham with eggs (£7.95), wild mushroom stroganoff or spicy cajun chicken (£8.95), roasted wing of skate with lemon butter and capers (£10.95), fillet of beef wellington with a wild mushroom and madeira sauce (£14.95), and puddings like rum and white chocolate torte, hot cherry bakewell with calvados crème fraîche or individual passion fruit mousse (£3.50); two-course children's menu (£4.95). Well kept Harveys Best and Larkins on handpump, cider from Chiddingstone, and local wine; unobtrusive piped music. Dogs are welcome and there are good surrounding walks. *(Recommended by E D Bailey, R and S Bentley, Mr and Mrs S Oxenbury, J Hale, A E Brace, Susan and John Douglas, Carl and Jackie Cranmer, Chris Reeve, Mr and Mrs R G Lloyd)*

Free house ~ Licensees Gordon and Val Meer ~ Real ale ~ Bar food (till 10) ~ Restaurant ~ (01892) 870306 ~ Children welcome ~ Open 11-3, 6-11; 11-11 Sat; 12-10.30 Sun; closed 25 Dec

SPOTTED DOG 🍽

Smarts Hill; going S from village centre on B2188, fork right up hill at telephone box: in just under ½ mile the pub is on your left

Twenty miles of countryside stretch away before you from the tiered terrace of this quaint old tiled pub; there are seats on the front terrace under a large umbrella, and an outside heater. The neatly kept, low ceilinged, heavily beamed and timbered bar has some antique settles as well as wheelback chairs on its rugs and tiles, a cosy log fire in a fine brick inglenook fireplace, and attractive moulded panelling in one alcove. Under the new licensee, good bar food now includes sandwiches, soup (£3.95), grilled sardines with a thyme and lime dressing (£6.75), wild mushrooms with a saffron cream sauce on toasted brioche (£6.95), pasta with a cream of fennel and dill sauce (£9.50), fried tuna steak with an onion confit and oyster sauce (£9.95), fillet of cod baked with a herb crust (£10.50), breast of wood pigeon with a sesame and prune sauce (£10.95), lamb shank with a red onion and wine sauce (£11.75), and puddings such as tiramisu or syrup sponge (£3.95); the restaurant is no smoking. Well kept Adnams, Greene King Abbot, and Old Spotty which is brewed for the pub by Benskins on handpump, and an extensive wine list; piped music. *(Recommended by John Robertson, Derek Thomas, E D Bailey, Hazel and Michael Duncombe, Susan and John Douglas, Tina and David Woods-Taylor, Patricia Beebe, A E Brace, Martin Jennings)*

Free house ~ Licensee Shane O'Grady ~ Real ale ~ Bar food (12-2.30(4 Sat), 6-9.30; all day Sun) ~ Restaurant ~ (01892) 870253 ~ Children welcome ~ Open 12-3.30, 6-11; 12-11 Sat; 12-10.30 Sun; 12-3, 6-11 Sat in winter; closed 26 Dec, 1 Jan evening

---

It's very helpful if you let us know up-to-date food prices when you report on pubs.

PLUCKLEY TQ9243 Map 3
Dering Arms 🍴 ♀
Pluckley Station, which is signposted from B2077

The very good fish dishes continue to draw customers to this striking old building, originally built as a hunting lodge on the Dering Estate. As well as daily specials such as crab newburg or moules marinières (£4.95), salmon fishcakes with sorrel sauce (£10.95), fillet of black bream with marsh samphire and beurre blanc or grilled red mullet with tomato, chilli and rosemary olive oil (£12.95), monkfish with bacon, orange and cream sauce (£13.95), and scallops with basil spaghetti and saffron sauce (£14.95), there might be sussex smokies (£3.95), oysters from Ireland (£5.95), and tuna steak with garlic and lemon butter (£12.95), plus non-fishy choices like chicken livers sautéed with onions, bacon and mushrooms in a brandy and cream sauce (£3.95), pie of the day (£7.95), confit of duck with bubble and squeak potato cake and wild mushroom sauce or guinea fowl casseroled in sherry and tarragon sauce (£12.95), and rib-eye steak with cracked black pepper, brandy and cream (£13.95); puddings such as white chocolate mousse with orange and Cointreau coulis or fresh fruit salad with a warm caramel sabayon (from £3.50). The stylishly plain high-ceilinged bar has a variety of good solid wooden furniture on stone floors, and a roaring log fire in the great fireplace; dominoes, cribbage and shove-ha'penny. A smaller panelled bar with wood floors has similar dark wood furnishings. Well kept Goachers Gold Star, Real Mild Ale, Maidstone Porter, and seasonal ales on handpump, a very good extensive wine list, home-made lemonade, local cider and quite a few malt whiskies. The big simple bedrooms have old ad hoc furnishings. *(Recommended by Keith Barker, Peter Holmes, Lynn Sharpless, Bob Eardley, Dr E J C Parker, John McDonald, Ann Bond, Hilary Dobbie, Patricia Beebe, Louise English, Peter Meister, Alan and Gill Bull, John and Lynn Busenbark, Anthony Barnes, Michael Doswell)*

Free house ~ Licensee James Buss ~ Real ale ~ Bar food ~ Restaurant ~ (01233) 840371 ~ Children in restaurant and family room ~ Open 11.30-3, 6-11; 12-3, 7-11 Sun; closed 26-29 December ~ Bedrooms: £30/£40

RINGLESTONE TQ8755 Map 3
Ringlestone ♀ 🍺
M20 Junction 8 to Lenham/Leeds Castle; join B2163 heading N towards Sittingbourne via Hollingbourne; at water tower above Hollingbourne turn right towards Doddington (signposted), and straight ahead at next crossroads; OS Sheet 178 map reference 879558

The central bar in this historic inn – it was once a hospice for monks and eventually became an inn in 1615 – has farmhouse chairs, cushioned wall settles, and tables with candle lanterns on its worn brick floor, and old-fashioned brass and glass lamps on the exposed brick and flint walls; there's a woodburning stove and small bread oven in an inglenook fireplace. An arch from here through a wall – rather like the outside of a house, windows and all – opens into a long, quieter room with cushioned wall benches, tiny farmhouse chairs, three old carved settles (one rather fine and dated 1620), similar tables, and etchings of country folk on its walls (bare brick too). Regulars tend to sit at the wood-panelled bar counter, or liven up a little wood-floored side room; piped music (which can be obtrusive) and TV. Bar food includes a hot and cold lunchtime buffet (from £3.95), as well as soup (£4.35), liver and apple pâté or sausages (£6.35), beef, bacon and spinach lasagne (£7.65), vegetarian dishes (from £8.85), salads (from £9.50), lots of pies such as duck and damson or vegetable and nut (from £9.85), rump steak (£14.35), and puddings (£4.25). They do allow coach parties. Well kept Ringlestone (actually Whitbreads), Shepherd Neame Bishops Finger, Smooth, Spitfire and Master Brew, and Theakstons Old Peculier on handpump or tapped from the cask; two dozen country wines (including sparkling ones), local cider and fresh fruit cordials. The inn is surrounded by eight acres of land, including two acres of landscaped lawns, with shrubs, trees and rockeries, a water garden with four pretty ponds and cascading waterfalls, a charming fountain, and troughs of pretty flowers along the pub walls; plenty of seats. Well behaved dogs welcome. *(Recommended by Ian Phillips, Peter and Elizabeth May,*

Mike Gorton, Alan and Heather Jacques, B J Harding, Mandy and Simon King, Tina and David Woods-Taylor, Nigel and Olga Wikeley)

Free house ~ Licensees M Millington Buck and M Stanley ~ Real ale ~ Bar food (12-2, 7-9) ~ Restaurant ~ (01622) 859900 ~ Children welcome ~ Open 12-3, 6-11; 12-11(10.30 Sun) Sat; closed 25 Dec ~ Bedrooms: £97B/£107B

SANDGATE TR2035 Map 3
Clarendon

Head W out of Sandgate on main road to Hythe; about 100m after you emerge onto the seafront park on the road across from a telephone box on the right; just back from the telephone box is an uphill track

Set half way up a steep lane from the sea, this small, simple but friendly local has pretty summer hanging baskets and window boxes, and a few (somewhat rickety) benches at the front with a view of the water. Visitors will probably feel most comfortable in the big windowed lounge on the left – you can see the sea through one window, and occasionally, in the right conditions, the coast of France. There are a few impressions of the pub and a full display of the 1950s and 1970s Whitbread Inn sign miniatures as well as some period advertising; coal fires in both bars in winter. The straightforward, pubby, right hand bar (popular with locals) has a chatty atmosphere, and lots of old photographs of the pub and of Sandgate. Well kept Shepherd Neame Masterbrew and Spitfire, and seasonal ales on handpump from a rather nice Victorian mahogany bar and mirrored gantry, as well as 16 wines by the glass, 18 malts, and home-made sloe gin; shove-ha'penny, cribbage, dominoes, chess, backgammon, and draughts. Bar food includes sandwiches or baguettes (from £1.95; crab in season £3), filled baked potatoes (from £2.15), ploughman's (from £3.95), chicken or prawn curry, or steak, kidney, mushroom and ale pie (all £5.95), fish pie or seasonal crab salad (£6.25), and puddings like treacle sponge (£2.65); the dining room is no smoking. If you book they may serve food after 8.30. It's only 10 minutes from the Euro Tunnel. *(Recommended by R E Davidson, Ian Phillips, Kevin Thorpe, Peter Meister, John and Joan Calvert, Mike and Wendy Proctor, John Davis, Miss A G Drake)*

Shepherd Neame ~ Tenants Keith and Shirley Barber ~ Real ale ~ Bar food (till 8.30; not Sun evening) ~ No credit cards ~ (01303) 248684 ~ Well behaved children in dining area ~ Open 11.45-3, 6-11; 12-5 Sun; closed Sun evening

SELLING TR0456 Map 3
Rose & Crown

Signposted from exit roundabout of M2 junction 7: keep right on through village and follow Perry Wood signposts; or from A252 just W of junction with A28 at Chilham follow Shottenden signpost, then right turn signposted Selling, then right signposted Perry Wood

This is a smashing pub at any time of the year. In summer, there are outdoor heaters on the terrace so you can sit comfortably all evening and enjoy the fairy lit apple tree and award-winning cottagey back garden which is charmingly planted with climbers, ramblers and colourful cottage plants. The flowering tubs and hanging baskets in front are really lovely too, and there's also a neatly kept children's play area, lots of picnic-sets, bat and trap, and a small aviary. In winter, it's cosy and snug, with a blazing fire and very special Christmas decorations. But at any time, you can be sure of a friendly welcome from the attentive and genuinely welcoming licensees. Around the central servery there are pretty fresh flowers by each of the sturdy corner timbers, hop bines strung from the beams, and an interesting variety of corn-dolly work – there's more of this in a wall cabinet in one cosy side alcove, and much more again down steps in the comfortably cottagey restaurant. Apart from a couple of old-fashioned housekeeper's chairs by the huge log fire (replaced in summer by an enjoyably colourful mass of silk flowers interlaced with more corn dollies and so forth), the seats are very snugly cushioned. Good generously served bar food includes filled rolls (from £4), ploughman's (£4.75), steak and kidney pie (£5.95), chicken tikka masala or China Town platter (£7.90), fisherman's platter (£10), daily specials such as cod and haddock mornay (£7.50) or mushroom tortellini (£7.90), and lots of puddings on show in a cold cabinet down steps in a small family room: toffee apple tart, pecan and maple pie with local honey ice cream and Italian white chocolate (£2.95). Well kept changing ales such as Adnams Southwold, Goachers Mild, and Harveys Best, and a guest from Ales of Kent or Cottage on handpump, local cider, a good range of malts and decent wines in good measures; informal, helpful service; cribbage, shove-ha'penny, dominoes and piped music; the local TVR club meets here on the first Sunday lunchtime of the month. Dogs on leads are welcome in the bar and may even get a biscuit, and as the pub is set in the midst of 150 acres of natural woodland, this is good walking country. *(Recommended by Colin Parker, Adam Clegg, Kevin Thorpe, R E Davidson, Mr and Mrs Thomas, Patricia and Norman Pollard, Norman Fox, David and Betty Gittins, Colin and Sandra Tann, D J Roseveare)*

Free house ~ Licensees Richard and Jocelyn Prebble ~ Real ale ~ Bar food (not Sun or Mon evenings) ~ Restaurant ~ (01227) 752214 ~ Children in restaurant and family room ~ Open 11-3, 6.30-11; 12-3, 7-10.30 Sun; closed evening 25 Dec

SMARDEN TQ8842 Map 3

Chequers 🏠

Off A20 in Charing, via Pluckley; or off A274 at Standen just under a mile N of its junction with A262; The Street

During the two years that the friendly licensees have owned this 14th-c inn, they have worked hard to smarten the place up without losing too much character; they have certainly succeeded. What was the breakfast room is now a no smoking restaurant with lots of beams, an enormous fireplace, and a flagstoned floor. There's also a refurbished dining area with elegant reproduction tables and chairs, and a cosy, comfortable bar with a good relaxed atmosphere and plenty of chatty locals. New kitchens have been installed, and the garden has been landscaped, with a new walkway to the pond where there are fish and waterfowl, there's an arbour with climbing plants, and the terrace has attractive green metal tables and chairs on the new york stone. The charming bedrooms have also been refurbished and upgraded and now have their own bathrooms; there's even a four-poster, and they do huge breakfasts. Good bar food (not served on Saturday evening, only restaurant meals then) uses fresh local produce and might include home-made soup (£3.25), filled baguettes (from £3.95), garlic mushrooms (£4), ploughman's (£4.50), ham and egg or smoked salmon omelette (£6.95), spaghetti carbonara (£7.50), steak and kidney pudding (£10.95), lamb cutlets with minted gravy (£11.95), fresh fillet of salmon with king prawns and hollandaise sauce (£12.95), and home-made puddings like hot chocolate fudge cake, crème brûlée or cheesecakes (£3.95). Well kept Bass, Fullers London Pride, Harveys Best, and Greene King Ruddles County on handpump, several malt whiskies, and a decent wine list; piped music. The village is attractive. *(Recommended by Keith Barker, Tony and Wendy Hobden, Charlie Harris, Eddie Edwards, Iain Robertson, Colin and Janet Roe)*

Free house ~ Licensee Lisa Bullock ~ Bar food ~ Restaurant ~ (01233) 770217 ~ Children in eating area of bar and restaurant ~ Open 11-3, 6-11; 11-11 Sat ~ Bedrooms: £40B/£60B

SNARGATE TQ9928 Map 3

Red Lion ★ 🍺

B2080 Appledore—Brenzett

The last time this quite unspoilt village local was modernised was in 1890. The father-in-law of the current landlady bought it in 1911 and declared that nothing should be done to it, and to this day it remains delightfully frozen in time. Its three perfectly simple little rooms (and outdoor lavatories too), now lovingly run by his daughter-in-law and friendly granddaughter, still have their original cream tongue and groove wall panelling, a couple of heavy beams in a sagging ceiling and dark pine Victorian farmhouse chairs on bare boards. One charming little room, with a frosted glass wall through to the bar and a sash window looking out to a cottage garden, has only two dark pine pews beside two long tables, a couple more farmhouse chairs and a nice old piano stacked with books. Cheery groups of regulars catch up on local news, play toad in the hole or sample the very palatable Double Vision cider (from nearby Staplehurst) or well kept small brewery ales. As well as Goachers Light, there might be up to three guests from brewers such as Black Sheep, Hop Back, and Rother Valley tapped straight from casks on a low rack behind an unusual shop-like marble-topped counter, with little else behind to mark it as a bar other than a few glasses on two little shelves, some crisps and half a dozen spirit bottles. They don't serve food. Darts, shove-ha'penny, cribbage, dominoes, and table skittles. *(Recommended by R E Davidson, Mike Gorton, Susan and John Douglas, the Didler, Kevin Thorpe, JP, PP)*

Free house ~ Licensee Mrs Jemison ~ Real ale ~ No credit cards ~ (01797) 344648 ~ Children in family room ~ Open 12-3, 7-11; 12-3, 7-10.30 Sun

STAPLEHURST TQ7847 Map 3
Lord Raglan

About 1½ miles from town centre towards Maidstone, turn right off A229 into Chart Hill Road opposite Cross at Hand Garage; OS Sheet 188 map reference 785472

This unpretentious yet quite civilised country inn is run by a charming couple who have kept it simple, genuine and cosy. Everywhere you look its low beams are crammed with hops, and the mixed collection of comfortably worn dark wood furniture on quite well used dark brown carpet tiles and nice old parquet flooring is mostly 1930s; there's even a life-size effigy of Lord Raglan propped up in a chair in the corner. The interior is quite compact, with a narrow bar – you walk in almost on top of the counter and chatting locals – widening slightly at one end to a small area with a log fire in winter. In the other direction it works its way round to an intimate area at the back, with lots of wine bottles lined up on a low shelf. Small french windows lead out to an enticing little high-hedged terraced area with white plastic tables and chairs; there are wooden picnic-sets in the side orchard. Very generous helpings of bar food (cooked by the landlord) are nicely presented on willow pattern plates. Food is listed on blackboards behind the bar, and as well as a few pubby staples like sandwiches (from £2.50), filled baguettes (from £4.50, steak £5.95), ploughman's (£5.25), macaroni cheese with garlic bread (£5.50), and ham and egg (£5.95), there might be smoked duck and orange salad (£4.95), marinated anchovies with apple and potato salad (£5.25), shepherd's pie (£6.50), tagliatelle and red pepper sauce with aubergine (£7.50), pork fillet with apple and calvados sauce (£8.95), swordfish steak with lime butter, guinea fowl breast and red wine sauce, grilled bass, stir-fried beef fillet with peppers or king prawns with garlic and ginger (£9.95), and puddings such as banoffi pie, chocolate and coffee cheesecake or apple crumble (£3.50). There's a good wine list, and well kept real ales include Goachers Light, Harveys Best, and guest ales such as Rother Valley Level Best. No piped music or games machines here, just nice little conversational nooks. There is reasonable wheelchair access. *(Recommended by Colin and Janet Roe, Louise English, Peter Meister, Giles Francis, Comus and Sarah Elliott)*

Free house ~ Licensees Andrew and Annie Hutchison ~ Real ale ~ Bar food (12-2.30, 7-10) ~ (01622) 843747 ~ Children welcome ~ Open 12-3, 6-11; closed Sun; 25 and 26 Dec

STONE IN OXNEY TQ9427 Map 3
Crown

Off B2082 Iden—Tenterden

There's a good balance between locals gathered at the bar for a drink, and the dining area here. As well as a nice homely atmosphere, there's a big inglenook fireplace, two nice old dark wood pews and parquet flooring in the bar, and on the other side of the central servery the longish lounge has a red turkey carpet, well spaced dark wood pub tables, and two big bay windows with pretty views over a cornfield; piped music. Well kept Shepherd Neame Master Brew and two guests beers on handpump.

The black labrador is called Jack; pool in a small side bar, and pinball; pretty good disabled access to the lounge through the front door. Bar food might include filled baguettes (from £2.50), fried black pudding with chinese pickled cabbage, croutons and chutney dressing (£3.95), dressed scottish crab (£5.50), warm salad of duck breast with plum vinaigrette (£7.50), spiced pork kebab with a pepper and mushroom kebab (£8.95), half a boneless roast duck with blackcurrant sauce (£9.50), and puddings like plum crème brûlée or Eton mess (£2.95). More reports please. *(Recommended by John and Lynn Busenbark, Di and Mike Gillam, Colin and Janet Roe)*

Free house ~ Licensees Joe Cantor and Mandy Standen ~ Real ale ~ Bar food (not Sun evening Sun lunchtime Oct-April, Mon) ~ Restaurant ~ No credit cards ~ (01233) 758789 ~ Children in eating area of bar ~ Open 12-3, 6-11; 12-5 Sun; closed evening Mon/Sun

TOYS HILL TQ4751 Map 3
Fox & Hounds

Off A25 in Brasted, via Brasted Chart and The Chart

Although this down-to-earth country local has been run by the same cheery but firm licensee for over 30 years, Mrs Pelling told us as we went to press that she was considering leaving some time during the next year. There's little doubt that things would change if she does decide to retire. Bills at the moment are toted up on a piece of paper and change is given from an old-fashioned wooden till, and there are notices by the open fires warning against 'unofficial stoking'. You can sit comfortably on one of the well worn old sofas or armchairs which are scattered with cushions and throws, and when your eyes have adjusted to the dim lighting, read the latest *Country Life*, *Hello* or *Private Eye* or study the letters and press cuttings on the walls that describe the brewery campaign to upgrade the pub and Mrs Pelling's fight against it. Lunchtime bar food is at an absolute minimum with pre-wrapped filled rolls (from £1.50) and one or two simple dishes like ploughman's, cauliflower cheese or sausage and tomato pie (£4), and well stocked chocolate shelves. Well kept Greene King Abbot and IPA on handpump; darts, shove-ha'penny, cribbage and dominoes. The garden is lovely, with picnic-sets on a good area of flat lawn surrounded by mature shrubs. As you approach this peaceful retreat from the pretty village (one of the highest in the county) you will catch glimpses through the trees of one of the most magnificent views in Kent. There are good walks nearby, and it's handy for Chartwell and for Emmetts garden. *(Recommended by Pete Baker, Mike and Sue Loseby, Jenny and Brian Seller, Pat and Tony Martin, B, M and P Kendall, Bill and Rachael Gallagher)*

Greene King ~ Tenant Hazel Pelling ~ Real ale ~ Bar food (lunchtime only) ~ No credit cards ~ (01732) 750328 ~ Children in area with toys lunchtime only ~ Open 12-2.30(3 Sat), 6-11; 12-3, 7-10.30 Sun; closed 25 Dec

TUNBRIDGE WELLS TQ5639 Map 3
Beacon ♀

Tea Garden Lane; leaving Tunbridge Wells westwards on A264, this is the left turn off on Rusthall Common after Nevill Park

The pergola-covered wooden deck behind this Victorian pub has such marvellous sweeping hillside views that even on chilly days there are plenty of customers catching the sunset over Tunbridge Wells; volley ball, boules and rounders in summer. Inside, there's usually a good mix of customers chatting at the sweeping bar counter with its ranks of shiny bottles or sitting on the comfortable sofas by the fine old wood fireplace. The dining area and spreading bar run freely into each other with stripped panelling, lovely wood floors, ornately built wall units and glowing lamps giving a solidly comfortable feel. Good bar food includes soup (£3.25), lunchtime filled rustic bread or baked potatoes with interesting fillings such as roast turkey, fresh mango and orange, roasted vegetables and melted mozzarella or home-cured gravadlax and herb crème fraîche (£4.50-£6.95), bittersweet onion tart on pepper pastry with a light tomato and citrus vinaigrette (£5.25), thai spiced crab

cake with a warm lemon grass and ginger sauce (£6.25), home-made meatballs with
pasta shells and chunky tomato sauce (£6.95), fruity tiger prawn curry (£7.25),
salmon and hake fish croquettes with lemon and spinach sauce or bacon cutlet with
grain mustard cream, and herb mash (£7.75), and braised lambs neck fillet in a mint,
rosemary and redcurrant sauce (£9.95). Well kept Brakspears Special, Harveys Best
Bitter and Timothy Taylor's Landlord on handpump kept under light blanket
pressure, and 10 wines by the glass; shove-ha'penny, cribbage, dominoes.
*(Recommended by Mr and Mrs S Oxenbury, Colin and Janet Roe, Ian Phillips, Peter Meister,
Hilary Dobbie)*

*Free house ~ Licensee John Cullen ~ Real ale ~ Bar food (12-9 Fri, Sat and Sun) ~
Restaurant ~ (01892) 524252 ~ Children in eating area of bar and restaurant ~ Folk
club 2nd and 4th Mon of month ~ Open 11-11; 12-10.30 Sun*

Mount Edgcumbe Hotel ♀ ⇥

The Common

Most customers do come to this attractive tile-hung and weatherboarded hotel, set
on top of one of the several large rocky outcrops on the common, to enjoy the good
food, but the cheerful staff are quite happy to serve you a pint of well kept Harveys
Best or a glass of good wine from their extensive list if that's all you fancy; fresh
orange juice, too. As you enter the small cosy bar with lots of exposed brick and old
photographs of the town on the walls, there's a mini waterfall feature on the right,
with a few tables (candlelit at night) in an unusual grotto-like snug built into the
rock. In the evenings subdued wall lighting and the chatty buzz of customers make
for a welcoming atmosphere; piped music. The small two-room restaurant is most
attractive, with views out over the common, and tables out on a side terrace have a
similar outlook, reaching over the grass to the town beyond. Bar food includes filled
baguettes such as avocado, brie and tomato (£3.75), ploughman's (£4.50), roasted
mediterranean vegetables with fresh pesto or cream of mushroom and smoked garlic
soup (£4.75), moules frites (£6.45), and bangers and mash in rich onion gravy
(£6.50). There's also a three-course menu with a good choice of imaginative dishes.
You must book for Saturday evening. *(Recommended by Mrs S Clenshaw, James Galbraith)*

*Free house ~ Licensee Iain Arthur ~ Real ale ~ Bar food (12-2.30, 7-9.30; 12.30-7.30
Sun) ~ Restaurant ~ (01892) 526823 ~ Well behaved children welcome ~ Open 12-11;
12-10.30 Sun ~ Bedrooms: £65S/£90B*

SANKEYS ⊮ ♀

39 Mount Ephraim (A26 just N of junction with A267)

There's always a good, bustling atmosphere in this downstairs pub-cum-wine bar.
It's furnished with lots of closely spaced sturdy old pine tables and decorated with
old mirrors, prints, enamel advertising signs, antique beer engines and other bric-a-
brac (most of which has been salvaged from local pub closures); french windows
lead to a small suntrap terrace with teak tables and chairs under cocktail parasols.
Good, enjoyable food includes lunchtime baguettes, daily specials such as pasta
dishes (£7.50) or game or traditional English dishes (£8.50), plus a selection of
charcuterie (£5.50), baked goats cheese in puff pastry with pesto dressing (£6.50),
popular moules and frites (£7.50), fish and chips or salmon and leek fishcakes with
parsley sauce (£8.50), delicious cornish cock crabs (£14.50), fillet steak (£15), whole
lobster (£25), and puddings (£3.95); friendly, efficient staff. Well kept Harveys Best,
Larkins Traditional, and Timothy Taylors Landlord on tap, though most people
seem to be taking advantage of the superb wine list; they also have quite a choice of
unusual teas. You need to get there very early for a table in the bar; the restaurant is
no smoking. More reports please. *(Recommended by Dr David Cockburn, Philip Vernon,
Kim Maidment, Chris and Anna Rowley)*

*Free house ~ Licensee Guy Sankey ~ Real ale ~ Bar food (12-2.30, 7-9.30; not Sun) ~
Restaurant ~ (01892) 511422 ~ Children welcome ~ Live entertainment Sun evenings
~ Open 10-11; 12-10.30 Sun; closed 25 and 26 Dec*

ULCOMBE TQ8550 Map 3
Pepper Box ◀

Fairbourne Heath; signposted from A20 in Harrietsham; or follow Ulcombe signpost from A20, then turn left at crossroads with sign to pub

Views from the terrace here stretch over a great plateau of rolling arable farmland, and if you're in the garden, with its small pond, shrubs and flowerbeds, you may catch a glimpse of the deer that sometimes come up. It's a cosy old country inn, and the friendly, homely bar has standing timbers and low beams hung with hops, copper kettles and pans on window sills, some very low-seated windsor chairs and wing armchairs, and two armchairs and a sofa by the splendid inglenook fireplace with its warm log fire; the tabby tom is called Fred, and there are two more cats and a collie called Rosie. A side area is more functionally furnished for eating, and there's a very snug little no smoking dining room; piped music. Enjoyable bar food (not served on Saturday evening) includes quite a choice of sandwiches (from £3; bacon and egg £4.20; chinese chicken £4.50), home-made soup (£3.50), ploughman's (from £4.50), kent sausages and onion gravy (£6.50), braised beef and onions (£7), daily specials such as chicken satay (£4.80), sardines in garlic butter (£5), sautéed wild and button mushrooms (£5.20), vegetables in thai spices (£7.50), lambs liver and bacon with garlic mash (£9), chicken breast with wild mushroom and madeira sauce (£10), and salmon and monkfish in lemon cream sauce (£13). Very well kept Shepherd Neame Masterbrew, Bishops Finger, Spitfire and a seasonal guest tapped from the cask, and country wines; efficient, courteous service. No children inside.
(Recommended by Tina and David Woods-Taylor, R E Davidson, Mark Blackburn, Colin and Janet Roe, Comus and Sarah Elliott)

Shepherd Neame ~ Tenants Geoff and Sarah Pemble ~ Real ale ~ Bar food (not Sun or Mon evenings) ~ Restaurant ~ (01622) 842558 ~ Open 11-3, 6.30-11; 12-3, 7-11 Sun

WEST PECKHAM TQ6452 Map 3
Swan ◀

Off B2016, second turning left heading N from A26 (Swanton Road)

On one of those rare, perfect summer's evenings, it was a treat to find this little pub tucked away down country lanes. There are picnic-sets under parasols in front of the building and more on the charming cricket green opposite (where they offer picnics with a rug for £10); the nearby church is partly Saxon. Inside, it's light, airy, and open-plan, with rush-seated dining chairs and cushioned church settles around an attractive mix of refectory and other pale oak tables on the wood strip floor, lovely big bunches of flowers (one placed in the knocked-through brick fireplace), a few high rush-seated bar stools, hops and beams, some modern paintings at one end with black and white photographs of locals on the walls at the other end, and good Aztec-patterned curtains. It's quite a surprise to find seven or more own-brew real ales on handpump from their new microbrewery: on our inspection visit we had to choose between Black Swan, Ginger Swan, Parliament, Swan Blond, Swan Mild, Trumpeter and Whooper Swan. Enterprising bar food includes lunchtime baguettes (£2.95), home-made soup (£3.95), ploughman's (£5.50), sautéed squid and tiger prawn tails (£5.95), white cumberland stilton sausage with onion gravy (£8), stuffed aubergines (£8.25), cold poached salmon with chive and lime mayonnaise (£8.50), chicken dipped in cumin, coriander, chilli and brown sugar (£8.75), tenderloin of pork stuffed with chorizo with lemon grass and cardamom oil (£8.95), and puddings such as rhubarb and cinnamon crumble cake, bread and butter pudding or home-made ice creams (£3.50); friendly service, a good mix of customers, and piped music.
(Recommended by Simon and Sally Small, Robin Drummond, Eddie Edwards, Ken Arthur, LM, Chris and Anna Rowley, Kevin Thorpe)

Own brew ~ Licensee Gordon Milligan ~ Real ale ~ Bar food ~ (01622) 812271 ~ Children allowed if well behaved and eating ~ Live jazz/blues monthly Sun evening ~ Open 11-3(4 Sat), 6-11(9 Mon); maybe longer in summer; 12-4, 7-10.30 Sun

Lucky Dip

Besides the fully inspected pubs, you might like to try these Lucky Dips recommended to us and described by readers (if you do, please send us reports: www.goodguides.com).

Badlesmere [TR0154]
Red Lion [A251, S of M2 junction 6]: Attractive, spacious country pub where time stands still, up to six ales inc Fullers, Greene King and Shepherd Neame, local Theobald's farm cider, bar food (not Sun pm); pleasant garden, paddock for caravans and tents, summer beer and folk festivals, live music Tues and Fri pm, open all day Fri and wknds *(Kevin Thorpe)*

☆ **Barham** [TR2050]
Duke of Cumberland [The Street]: Welcoming open-plan country local, bare boards and flagstones, good value generous food, well kept ales, friendly service, open fire; bedrooms *(Peter Heaton)*

Bekesbourne [TR1856]
Unicorn [Bekesbourne Hill]: Well run country pub with good home-made food, friendly licensees, well kept Shepherd Neame and power-packed local cider *(R E Davidson, Howard Worton)*

☆ **Benenden** [TQ8033]
King William IV [The Street]: Compact low-ceilinged welcoming village local with rustic furnishings, smart lounge with small timbered-off dining area, nice range of reasonably priced food inc imaginative dishes, well kept Shepherd Neame ales, decent wines by the glass, good log fire, games in public bar; small garden *(Colin and Janet Roe, Gill Waller, Tony Morriss, LYM)*

Bishopsbourne [TR1852]
Mermaid [signed off A2]: Traditional welcoming unpretentious country local in same family for many years, simple food (not Sun evening) inc good filled rolls, well kept Shepherd Neame beers, small coal fire and darts in back public bar, no music or machines; lovely unspoilt Kentish village *(Kevin Thorpe)*

☆ **Boughton Aluph** [TR0247]
Flying Horse [Boughton Lees, just off A251 N of Ashford]: Interesting old pub with beams, shiny black panelling, stone-arched windows, two ancient glass-covered wells, big inglenook log fire, well kept Charles Wells Bombardier, Courage Best, Fullers London Pride and Greene King Old Speckled Hen and Ruddles, good wines, traditional games, food (maybe not Mon, limited Tues) from sandwiches up; piped music; open all day, children in back dining area, tables in spacious rose-filled garden, barbecues and bat and trap *(Ian Phillips, Colin and Janet Roe, Lynn Sharpless, Bob Eardley, R E Davidson, LYM)*

Boughton Street [TR0559]
☆ *White Horse* [nr M2 junction 7; The Street]: Carefully restored dark-beamed bars and timbered dining room, well prepared food all day inc early breakfast and good value carvery Thurs-Sat, well kept Shepherd Neame beers, decent wines, good tea and coffee, friendly service with a helpful welcome for children; tables in garden, good value bedrooms (back

ones quieter), good breakfast *(Colin and Sandra Tann, LYM)*

Brasted [TQ4654]
☆ *White Hart* [High St (A25)]: Roomy Vintage Inn with extension sun lounge and large no smoking eating area, happy bustling atmosphere, friendly young staff, substantial reasonably priced food from separate order counter, Battle of Britain bar with signatures and mementoes of Biggin Hill fighter pilots, well kept Bass and Tetleys, good choice of wine and fresh orange juice, hops on beams, daily papers, log fire; children welcome, big neatly kept garden with well spaced tables and play area; bedrooms, pretty village with several antique shops *(Hazel and Michael Duncombe, B J Harding, LM, K H Frostick, LYM, Christopher Maxse, Tina and David Woods-Taylor)*

Bredgar [TQ8860]
Sun [The Street]: Pleasant pub with Shepherd Neame ales, reasonably priced food; big garden with pond and fenced play area *(Ian Phillips)*

Brenchley [TQ6841]
Halfway House [Horsmonden Rd]: Welcoming staff and surroundings, wide choice of good value fresh food, good choice of beers and cider; dogs welcome *(Ken Arthur)*

Bridge [TR1854]
Plough & Harrow [High St]: Particularly well kept Shepherd Neame in small 17th-c two-bar local, coal fire and lots of sporting prints, good wine choice, darts and games in public bar; open all day Sat *(Roger Mardon)*
Red Lion [High St]: Cosy family-run traditional village pub with informal atmosphere, three well kept ales inc Courage Directors and a guest such as Adnams Broadside or Tolly Original, lots of wines by the glass, good genuine home-made food using local produce from doorstep sandwiches up; pleasant garden *(Roger Mardon, S Hawkins, A Clements)*
White Horse [High St]: Old dining pub opened up into comfortable single bar, huge fireplace, good fresh food from doorstep sandwiches up, well kept Bass and guest ales, interesting wines, friendly service, dining area and civilised restaurant; attractive village *(Roger Mardon)*

Broadstairs [TR3967]
Neptunes Hall [Harbour St]: Friendly early 19th-c two-bar local with Shepherd Neame beers, lunchtime snacks; no juke box or piped music though occasional live folk (daily during Aug folk festival), open all day *(Kevin Thorpe)*

Brook [TR0644]
Honest Miller [not far from M20 junction 10, via Willesborough Lees; The Street]: Friendly landlord, well kept changing ales such as Morrells and Youngs Special, good generous food inc elaborate ploughman's, cosy décor with handcrafted wooden tables, bar stools and so forth, pool tables; play area, interesting Norman church, good walking country *(Robert Gomme, Peter Holmes)*

Canterbury [TR1557]

☆ *Canterbury Tales* [The Friars, just off main St Peters St pedestrian area]: Popular pub/bistro, clean, airy and chatty, with well kept ales such as Adnams, Fullers London Pride, Greene King IPA and Shepherd Neame, enjoyable food from good sandwiches to trendier dishes, books, games and chess table, theatrical memorabilia (quick service if you're going to a play or concert), cheerful young well trained staff; may be piped jazz, busier with young people evening; live music Mon, jazz some Sun afternoons, open all day *(Dick and Madeleine Brown, Kevin Thorpe, John and Lynn Busenbark, Colin and Janet Roe)*

New Inn [Havelock St]: Traditional unspoilt Victorian local, elderly furnishings, bare boards, gas fire, good beermat collection, changing ales such as Burton Bridge, Fullers and Greene King, simple food, modern back conservatory; juke box popular with students, nearby parking difficult *(Kevin Thorpe)*

☆ *Olde Beverlie* [St Stephens Green; A290 from centre, then right at Tyler Hill/Univ sign]: Built 1570 with adjoining almshouses, open-plan rooms with beams, wattle and daub walls, flagstones, old prints, brasses, jugs etc, enjoyable food from good value interesting sandwiches up, Shepherd Neame ales and good wine choice, small restaurant; piped music; nicely restored walled courtyard garden with bat and trap *(Kevin Thorpe, David and Betty Gittins)*

Phoenix [Old Dover Rd]: Decent local with good value generous home cooking, well kept real ales such as Adnams and Greene King, friendly licensees *(David Field)*

Simple Simons [Church Lane, St Radigunds]: Step down into basic pub in 14th-c building, great beams, broad floorboards and flagstones, two woodburners, dim-lit upstairs banqueting hall, nine well kept ales such as Bass, Greene King Old Speckled Hen, Shepherd Neame and Theakstons XB and Old Peculier, impressive pump clip collection, simple lunchtime food, more studenty evening; good piped music, live blues Tues, jazz Thurs;, tables in courtyard, open all day *(Kevin Thorpe)*

Thomas Becket [Best Lane]: Cheerfully bustling beamed pub with rustic furnishings, hop bines, tankards and farm tools, good generous food from sandwiches to several daily roasts, real ales, friendly attentive staff, scrubbed tables and back eating area *(David and Betty Gittins)*

Thomas Ingoldsby [Burgate]: Big, wide and handsome Wetherspoons pub with good range of beer inc bargain Shepherd Neame, decent wines, good food choice, attractive prices, very friendly staff, lots of local interest around the walls; popular with young people *(Pat and Tony Martin)*

Capel [TQ6344]

☆ *Dovecote* [Alders Rd; SE of Tonbridge]: Attractive rustic pub in pleasant tucked-away hamlet, bare bricks, hop-hung beams, no smoking end with pitched ceiling, good food choice from good value ploughman's and baguettes up, Thurs bargain curry night, well kept beers tapped from the cask inc Harveys, King & Barnes and Larkins, Chiddingstone farm cider; tables outside, doves and big thatched dovecote in back garden *(LM, A W Lewis)*

Charing [TQ9551]

Bowl [Egg Hill Rd]: Popular 16th-c pub high on South Downs nr Pilgrims Way, well kept Fullers London Pride and three changing guest beers, simple food, games room with hexagonal pool table; big garden (room for camping and caravans), cl lunchtime Mon-Thurs, open all day Fri-Sun *(Kevin Thorpe)*

Charing Heath [TQ9249]

Red Lion: Friendly country pub now concentrating on good enjoyable food inc new carvery Sun lunch in large no smoking dining area, attractive front bar with Shepherd Neame Bitter and Spitfire *(Tony and Wendy Hobden)*

Chartham Hatch [TR1056]

☆ *Chapter Arms* [New Town St]: Attractive 18th-c dining pub overlooking orchards and doing well under new owners with fine track record, enjoyable food, Shepherd Neame and other real ales, decent wines, pleasantly relaxed service, good show of pictures; good Mon jazz night; tables in big garden, bedrooms planned *(John and Elizabeth Thomason, Dick and Madeleine Brown, Kath Libbert)*

Chiddingstone Causeway [TQ5247]

Greyhound [Charcott, off back rd to Weald]: Clean traditional local in quiet hamlet, very friendly and unpretentious, with interesting home cooking, nice crisp veg, well kept Flowers Original, Sun bar and table nibbles; barbecue and tables out in front *(Angela Gibson, Hilary Dobbie)*

Cobham [TQ6768]

☆ *Leather Bottle* [handy for M2 junction 1]: Ancient beamed and timbered pub with interesting woodwork and masses of Dickens prints reflecting his connections with the pub; much modernised inside, well kept Courage Best and maybe a seasonal guest beer such as Weltons Old Harry, friendly service, decent food from good toasties to mixed grills, restaurant; tables on big back lawn with play area, summer tuck shop and fishpond; quiet, pretty village; bedrooms *(LYM)*

Cowden [TQ4640]

☆ *Fountain* [High St; village usually signed off A264 and B2026]: Small unpretentious country local in pretty village, friendly new licensees doing a sensibly short choice of unusually good interesting food (with which they made their last pub the Kentish Horse at Markbeech a popular main entry), plain public bar with narrow cushioned wall benches, linoleum flooring, darts, local noticeboard, and two tables and chairs in small side room; small back carpeted beamed dining room with woodburner, just four tables and maybe a group of chatting locals; well kept Harveys, Larkins and guests, decent wines, walkers and dogs welcome, annual flower show *(Ken Arthur, Robin Drummond, BB)*

☆ *Queens Arms* [Cowden Pound; junction B2026 with Markbeech rd]: Unspoilt and warmly welcoming two-room country pub like something from the 1930s, with splendid landlady, well kept Brakspears, darts; may be cl wkdy lunchtimes (R E Davidson, Pete Baker, Kevin Thorpe, the Didler)

Darenth [TQ5671]

Chequers [down unsigned lane between A225 and B260 S of Dartford]: Traditional local with good choice of generous food (not Sun-Tues evening) inc good value Sun roast, well kept Courage Best and a guest beer, friendly staff, cheap drinks and crisps for children; can book tables in pleasant dining room, good view from sizeable back garden with small terrace (Kevin Flack, R T and J C Moggridge)

Deal [TR3655]

Chequers [Golf Rd (old coast rd to Sandwich)]: Now under same management as a Dover fish restaurant, with food from filled baguettes to wide choice of good fresh fish and seafood, Adnams Broadside, a German wheat beer and decent wines; adjoining chalet park (Guy Vowles)

Three Compasses [Beach St]: Well worth knowing for good food and atmosphere (Louise Sanford, Norman S Curtis)

Denton [TR2147]

Jackdaw [A260 Canterbury—Folkestone]: Imposing brick and flint Whitbreads Wayside Inn, open-plan bar recently decorated in cream and book-room red, up to five local real ales from Flagship or Kent Garden, large back restaurant, no music; children welcome, tables in pleasant garden, handy for nearby Battle of Britain museum at Hawkinge, open all day (Kevin Thorpe)

Dover [TR3141]

New Mogul [Chapel Pl, off York St South roundabout]: Traditional bare-boards two-bar local with constantly changing real ales tapped from the cask, good sandwiches, woodburner, old-fashioned pub games (no noisy machines or piped music); tables outside, open all day (anon)

Dungeness [TR0916]

Britannia [by old lighthouse]: The blockhouse appearance suits this unusual spot nr atomic power station and great wild beach: friendly and spotless inside, with good range of modestly priced food inc outstanding fresh local fish, smiling service, several well kept ales inc local Swale; handy for Romney Hythe & Dymchurch railway, RSPB reserve (Alan Cowell)

Dunks Green [TQ6152]

☆ *Kentish Rifleman*: Welcoming atmosphere in cosy early 16th-c two-bar local (the big stone-arched vaulted cellar may even be Roman); wide choice of good freshly cooked food, friendly service, well kept ales such as Fullers London Pride and Harveys, decent wine, plenty of character, no machines; dogs welcome; plenty of seats in unusually well designed garden behind (LM)

East Farleigh [TQ7452]

White Lion [Dean Street village, off B2010 SW of Maidstone]: This pub, a main entry in the 2001 edition, closed not long after it was published (LYM)

East Peckham [TQ6649]

Bush Blackbird & Thrush [Bush Rd; off A26/B2016 nr Hadlow]: Pretty 14th-c oak-beamed village pub, Shepherd Neame Bitter, Spitfire and seasonal beers tapped from the cask, enjoyable food and wine in refurbished lounge; good garden (the Didler)

Rose & Crown [Branbridges Rd]: Good value generous food inc fresh fish, quick service (Mrs E A Everard)

Egerton [TQ9047]

George [The Street]: Friendly two-bar 16th-c village pub, new licensees doing good range of reasonably priced food in bars and attractive restaurant, well kept Greene King, Hook Norton and Shepherd Neame ales; pretty setting, pleasant country view (Colin and Janet Roe)

Eynsford [TQ5365]

☆ *Malt Shovel* [Station Rd]: Neatly kept spacious old-fashioned dining pub handy for castles and Roman villa, dark panelling, generous freshly cooked food inc proper pies and curries and lots of good value fish and seafood (lobster tank), well kept Fullers, good choice of wine by the glass, friendly quick service, nice atmosphere; car park across busy road (Kevin Flack, Pat and Tony Martin)

Plough [Riverside]: Friendly riverside Beefeater recently refurbished in modern rustic style, good value food from bar snacks to restaurant meals, well kept beer and decent wines, log fires, good atmosphere, tables out by water (Kevin Flack)

Fairseat [TQ6261]

Vigo [A227]: Unspoilt, basic free house dating from 15th c with bare brick walls and open fire, well kept changing ales such as Goachers, Harveys, Ridleys and Youngs, no food; still has dadlums table in use (Kevin Thorpe)

Faversham [TR0161]

Anchor [Abbey St]: Smallish friendly two-bar local nr quay and station, several well kept Shepherd Neame ales, good quiet relaxed atmosphere, bare boards and individual furniture, hall with bench seats, low-priced food all day; a couple of picnic-sets outside, attractive old street (Tony and Wendy Hobden, the Didler)

Elephant [The Mall]: Picturesque flower-decked terrace town pub with well kept Greene King IPA and guest beers, thoughtful staff, simple but attractive furnishings on stripped boards, home-made food; summer barbecues, open all day (the Didler)

Sun [West St]: Roomy and rambling old-world 15th-c weatherboarded town pub with good unpretentious atmosphere in small well worn in low-ceilinged rooms, good value low-priced lunchtime food, well kept Shepherd Neame beers inc seasonal one from nearby brewery, good service; piped music; open all day, tables in pleasant back courtyard, interesting street (Tony and Wendy Hobden, the Didler, David and Betty Gittins)

Finglesham [TR3353]

☆ *Crown* [just off A258 Sandwich—Deal; The Street]: 16th-c country pub with wide choice of good value food in popular flagstoned inglenook dining area, Courage Best and Directors, Shepherd Neame and guest beers, good friendly service, stripped brickwork; children welcome, lovely garden, summer barbecues, caravan park *(Kevin Thorpe)*

Goudhurst [TQ7037]

☆ *Green Cross* [Station Rd (A262 W)]: Good interesting food, particularly fish and seafood, well kept Greene King IPA and Old Speckled Hen, Harveys and a guest such as Larkins, good wines, roomy and attractive back restaurant with good napkins, tablecloths etc, informal service; under the newish ownership the bar side (which has some bargain fish dishes) is still pretty basic, and when they have put more effort into that this pub could become a very popular main entry; bedrooms light and airy, good value; very handy for Finchcocks *(BB, Uta and John Owlett, Derek Thomas, Tina and David Woods-Taylor, Mrs Barbara Wheatley)*

☆ *Star & Eagle* [High St]: Striking medieval inn with settles and Jacobean-style seats in attractive heavily beamed open-plan bar, well kept Whitbreads-related ales, wide choice of decent food from filled baguettes up, polite efficient service, children welcome; tables out behind with pretty views, lovely character bedrooms, well furnished and comfortable, open all day *(Jean and Douglas Troup, LYM, Colin and Janet Roe, Pat and Tony Martin, K P Lovelock, Keith and Margaret Kettell)*

Hadlow [TQ6252]

☆ *Artichoke* [Hamptons, 4 miles SE of Plaxtol; OS Sheet 188 map ref 627524]: Dating from 13th c, with ancient low beams, high-backed wooden settles, some unusual wrought-iron glass-topped tables, huge welcoming inglenook log fire, gleaming brass, country pictures and bric-a-brac, friendly capable service, popular food inc good home-made pies, no smoking restaurant, well kept Adnams, Fullers London Pride, Greene King Abbot and Youngs Special, good range of spirits; children in eating area, seats outside inc pews in canopied front arbour, quiet rural setting; may keep credit card if you're running a tab; cl winter Sun evenings *(M Firth, Joan and Andrew Life, Sue Demont, Tim Barrow, BB, Martin Jennings)*

Herne Bay [TR1768]

Rose [Mortimer St]: Spick and span small traditional pub with simple but good freshly made lunchtime food, well kept Shepherd Neame; can get crowded and smoky wknds *(David and Betty Gittins)*

Hernhill [TR0660]

☆ *Red Lion* [off A299 via Dargate, or A2 via Boughton Street and Staplestreet]: Pretty Tudor inn by church and attractive village green, densely beamed and flagstoned, log fires, pine tables, no smoking upstairs restaurant, well kept Fullers London Pride and Shepherd Neame with a guest such as Marstons Pedigree, decent house wines, attentive staff, usual food; children welcome, garden with boules and good play area, bedrooms *(LYM, John Davis, Mr and Mrs Thomas)*

Horsmonden [TQ7040]

☆ *Gun & Spitroast* [The Heath]: Pleasantly furnished clean and polished 1930s pub on village green, friendly and welcoming, wide choice of sensibly priced interesting food, pretty inglenook dining room, obliging helpful staff, well kept ales inc Fullers London Pride and Harveys, log fire; dogs and walkers welcome, picnic-sets out behind with play area; has been cl Sun evening and Mon, three bedrooms *(Ian Phillips, Ken Arthur, Peter Salmon)*

Horton Kirby [TQ5668]

Fighting Cocks [The Street]: Country pub with comfortable saloon, good food inc take-away pizzas Mon; big riverside garden with goats, ducks, bat and trap, boules *(Kevin Flack)*

Ightham [TQ5956]

Chequers [The Street]: Refurbished pub very popular for simple home-made bar food inc well filled french bread *(Mike Tucker, Alan Cowell)*

Ightham Common [TQ5955]

Old House [Redwell, S of village; OS Sheet 188 map ref 591559]: Unspoilt and chatty two-room country local with no inn sign, bare bricks and beams, huge log fireplace filling one wall, basic furniture, four or five changing ales from all over, old cash register and small TV in side room; no food, music or machines, cl wkdy lunchtimes, opens 7 (later Tues) *(JP, PP, Kevin Thorpe)*

Ivy Hatch [TQ5854]

☆ *Plough* [off A227 N of Tonbridge]: More restaurant than pub, often fully booked, with wide choice of good food, fastidious French cooking, good neat thoughtful staff, impressive range of reasonably priced wines (and well kept Greene King IPA), attractive candlelit surroundings – upmarket in a friendly informal style; delightful conservatory and garden *(Derek Harvey-Piper, LYM, Derek Thomas, Di and Mike Gillam)*

Knockholt [TQ4658]

Three Horseshoes [Main Rd]: Two-bar pub refurbished by new licensees, good range of moderately priced food; new garden *(Philip J Heaps)*

Laddingford [TQ6948]

Chequers: Friendly village local with well kept ales such as Adnams, Boddingtons and Whitbreads, good food cooked by landlord (not Mon lunchtime), plenty for children; big garden, reasonably priced bedroom, Medway walks nearby *(A W Lewis)*

Lamberhurst [TQ6735]

☆ *Brown Trout* [B2169, off A21 nr entrance to Scotney Castle]: Popular dining pub specialising in briskly served fish, lots of steaks too, sauce and vinegar bottles on tables in biggish extension off small beamed bar, well kept Fullers London Pride and Harveys, fair choice of decent wines, friendly staff, good log fire, children in eating areas; can be very busy wknds; picnic-sets in large safe garden with play area, pretty window boxes and flower tubs in summer, open all day Sun and summer *(Mrs T A Bizat, Keith and Margaret Kettell, Ian Phillips, BB, W F C Phillips, Roy and*

Margaret Jones, K Chard, Meg and Colin Hamilton, Alan and Heather Jacques)
Elephants Head [Hook Green; B2169 towards T Wells]: Ancient rambling timber-framed country pub, well kept Adnams, Fullers London Pride and Harveys Best and Old, friendly staff, wide food choice, heavy beams, brick or oak flooring, big inglenook log fire, plush-cushioned pews etc; darts and fruit machine in small side area, quiet piped music; picnic-sets in big back garden with terrace and impressive play area (peaceful view), and by front green; nr Bayham Abbey and Owl House, popular with families wknds, quiz nights etc *(Ian Phillips, Meg and Colin Hamilton, LYM)*

Leigh [TQ5446]
Bat & Ball [High St]: Small village pub, pleasant landlord, good value generous home-cooked food esp pies (dining area one end), well kept Shepherd Neame beers inc a seasonal one and a guest such as Hook Norton Best, friendly staff and labrador called Guinness, no music, public bar with pool, darts and trophies; busy wknds, tables in garden *(Jilly Burrows, LM, Tony Hobden)*
☆ *Plough* [Powder Mill Lane/Leigh Rd, off B2027 NW of Tonbridge]: Attractive Tudor building recently well renovated by new owners with fine *Good Pub Guide* track record, emphasis on good food from traditional favourites to more adventurous dishes, well kept ales such as Greene King Old Speckled Hen and Harveys, friendly accommodating staff *(DWAJ, James Galbraith)*

Linton [TQ7550]
☆ *Bull* [A229 S of Maidstone]: New licensees in two-room bar with some carved settles as well as café-style chrome and wood furniture, fine old fireplace, well kept Shepherd Neame Bitter and Spitfire, decent if not cheap food (not Sun evening) from baguettes and sandwiches to steak and popular Sun roasts, sizeable attractive no smoking restaurant; children welcome, open all day wknds, lovely views from terrace behind, more tables in informal side garden *(Tina and David Woods-Taylor, B J Harding, Peter and Elizabeth May, Mike Tucker, LYM)*

Lower Hardres [TR1552]
☆ *Three Horse Shoes*: Old-fashioned country pub, Greene King and changing real ales such as Burton Bridge, Kent, Swale and Wychwood, good home cooking from baguettes to roasts (not Sun evening), friendly staff and locals, log fires and individualistic old furniture in both bars, Papas prints of Canterbury, plenty of old-fashioned board and card games, children and dogs welcome; no fruit machines or juke box, piped jazz, live jazz or blues Fri; tables in garden, cl Mon *(Kevin Thorpe, LYM)*

Luddesdown [TQ6667]
☆ *Cock* [Henley Street, N of village – OS Sheet 177 map ref 664672; off A227 in Meopham, or A228 in Cuxton]: Tucked-away early 18th-c country pub, homely bay-windowed lounge, quarry-tiled bar with pews, woodburner and traditional games inc bar billiards, log fires, well kept changing real ales such as Adnams Best and Broadside, Bass, Greene King Abbot

and Harveys, perhaps two farm ciders, modestly priced generous food (not Sun) from sandwiches up; open all day, no children allowed in, tables in big secure garden, boules *(Robert Gomme, Bill and Rachael Gallagher, Ian Phillips, Peter Meister, Nigel and Sue Foster, LYM)*
☆ *Golden Lion*: Friendly traditional pub in quiet downland village, big woodburner as well as open fire, well kept Fullers London Pride and Greene King Old Speckled Hen, good value simple fresh bar lunches particularly popular Sun roast, fast service, colourful candles in bottles, small conservatory; tables and play equipment in enclosed garden *(LM, LYM, John Branston)*

Maidstone [TQ7656]
Pilot [Upper Stone St (A229)]: Busy old roadside inn, home-made food (not Sun), well kept Harveys Bitter, Mild and seasonal ales, whisky-water jugs hanging from ceiling, darts and pool; tables outside, boules *(the Didler)*
Rifle Volunteers [Wyatt St/Church St]: Unspoilt quiet coaching inn with good home-made food, local Goachers Light, Mild and seasonal ales, tables outside *(the Didler)*

Markbeech [TQ4742]
Kentish Horse [off B2026 Hartfield—Edenbridge]: Attractive weatherboarded country pub under new licensees (too new for reader reports yet), well kept Harveys, Larkins Traditional and Wadworths 6X, long turkey-carpeted green-walled bar with good fire, small flagstoned games room with TV, pleasant restaurant with french windows to terrace and big garden with enclosed well equipped play area; children welcome, has been open all day *(LYM)*

Newnham [TQ9557]
☆ *Tapster* [Parsonage Farm, Seed Rd]: New pub in substantial former manor house with old tables and chairs on bare boards, quiet atmosphere, six interesting changing microbrews, own ciders and Syndale Valley English wines (also available in adjoining shop), keen helpful staff, good reasonably priced home-made food, huge log fire; dogs and children welcome, bedrooms *(Kevin Thorpe, R E Davidson, RWC)*

Oad Street [TQ8662]
Plough & Harrow [opp craft centre; handy for M2 junction 5]: Unpretentious olde-worlde local with brewery advertisements, jugs hanging from dark beams, careful lighting, well kept Shepherd Neame ales, limited but good inexpensive menu (not winter wkdy evenings); children welcome, picnic-sets in secluded back garden *(Ian Phillips)*

Old Romney [TR0325]
Rose & Crown [A259 opp church]: Simple village pub, peaceful and friendly, with well kept reasonably priced Greene King and other beers, good bar food, old local photographs; dogs welcome; well equipped chalet bedrooms, good breakfast *(I A Herdman, Eddie Edwards)*

Otford [TQ5359]
☆ *Bull* [High St]: Attractively laid out 15th-c Chef

& Brewer, several quietly spacious rooms, log fires in two enormous fireplaces, wide choice of good food all day inc interesting snacks, friendly staff; nice garden *(Kevin Flack, Emma Wright, Lesley Henry)*

☆ **Horns** [High St]: Cheerful and relaxed, 15th-c beams and timbers, big inglenook log fire, blue plush seats and wheelback chairs, neatly cottagey decorations, second room on left, attentive welcoming service, tables set for short choice of good generous well presented food from well filled sandwiches up (service can slow at busy lunchtimes), well kept Fullers London Pride and Harveys; no dogs *(W Ruxton, Thomas Neate, B, M and P Kendall)*

Painters Forstal [TQ9958]

☆ **Alma** [signed off A2 at Ospringe]: Homely and attractive weatherboarded village local, busy but neat and tidy, with good value food using local ingredients, well kept Shepherd Neame inc winter Porter, cheerful helpful service, comfortable large-ish dining lounge, small bare-boards public bar; maybe piped classical music; picnic-sets on lawn *(Bob and Val Collman, Tony Baldwin)*

Penshurst [TQ5243]

Leicester Arms [B2178]: Busy pub in charming village by Penshurst Place, cosy old bars and original dining room up steps, with country views and laughing green parrot, plainer back extension eating area with pianist Sat eve, generous food, well kept Fullers London Pride, Larkins and Wadworths 6X; lavatories down steps, but a disabled one in car park opp; children welcome, tables in back garden, bedrooms *(John Davis, Alan M Pring)*

☆ **Rock** [Chiddingstone Hoath; OS Sheet 188 map ref 497431]: Charmingly old-fashioned timber-framed pub, farmers and dogs in two spartan little beamed rooms, wonky brick floors, woodburner in inglenook; well kept Larkins, friendly staff, ring the bull; children and dogs welcome; front terrace, back garden, beautiful countryside nearby, cl Mon *(Ken Arthur, Kevin Thorpe)*

Pett Bottom [TR1652]

Duck [off B2068 S of Canterbury, via Lower Hardres]: Long cleanly refurbished bare-boards room with pine panelling and wine racks, well kept Greene King IPA and Abbot, wholesome generous food, decent wines, welcoming attentive service, open fire; piped music; children and dogs welcome, tables in sizeable garden, attractive spot, open all day *(Eddie Edwards, F J Robinson, LYM, M Matson)*

Plaxtol [TQ6054]

☆ **Golding Hop** [Sheet Hill (½ mile S of Ightham, between A25 and A227)]: Secluded country pub, good for families in summer with suntrap streamside lawn; small and simple inside, with well kept Flowers IPA on handpump, Daleside Gravesend Shrimpers, Otter and guest beers tapped from the cask, local farm ciders (sometimes even their own), limited basic bar food (not Mon evening), woodburner, portable TV for important sports events, bar billiards, game machine; well fenced play area *(Hugh Roberts, JP, PP, LYM, Pat and Tony Martin,*

Peter Meister, the Didler)

Pluckley [TQ9245]

Black Horse [The Street]: Attractive old house with open-plan bar, roomy back dining area, hops on beams, vast inglenook, cheery atmosphere, wide food choice (just roasts on Sun), well kept ales inc Fullers London Pride; piped music, fruit machine, children allowed if eating; picnic-sets in spacious informal garden by tall sycamores, good walks, open all day Fri-Sun *(Patricia Beebe, David and Betty Gittins, Di and Mike Gillam, Catherine and Richard Preston, BB, JP, PP)*

☆ **Rose & Crown** [Mundy Bois – spelled Monday Boys on some maps]: Welcoming quietly set pub very popular for good generous meals inc imaginative dishes and homely puddings in nicely furnished and cosy candlelit dining room, smallish saloon bar, separate public bar, good bar snacks esp notable baguettes, interesting sensibly priced wines and country wines, well kept Hook Norton Best and Shepherd Neame, farm cider, plenty of malt whiskies, helpful service; friendly dog *(A W Lewis, Annette and John Derbyshire, Colin and Janet Roe, Michael Doswell, I S Johnson)*

Ramsgate [TR3865]

Artillery Arms [West Cliff Rd]: Small chatty open-plan corner local with John Smiths and good range of adventurous changing guest ales, two farm ciders, doorstep sandwiches, straightforward two-level bar with artillery prints, cannons and stained-glass windows dating from Napoleonic era; juke box can be intrusive, downstairs darts and pool; quiz nights, open all day *(Kevin Thorpe)*

Rochester [TQ7467]

Coopers Arms [St Margarets St]: Jettied Tudor building behind cathedral, cosy and quaint inside, bustling local atmosphere, friendly staff, comfortable seating, generous cheap bar lunches, well kept Scottish Courage ales *(Steve Chambers, A W Lewis)*

Rolvenden [TQ8431]

☆ **Star** [High St]: Very friendly beamed pub, ochre walls and red ceilings, china and local pictures, enjoyable honest food inc proper pies, Greene King IPA, Abbot, Old Speckled Hen and Ruddles from hop-slung bar, decent house wines, games room with pool, machine and TV; tables and chairs on pretty flower-filled terrace with gate to sheep field *(BB, John Davis)*

Sandgate [TR2035]

Ship [High St]: Old-fashioned two-room local with well kept ales such as Greene King IPA, Harveys Best, Timothy Taylors Landlord and Theakstons Old Peculier tapped from the cask, farm cider, decent fairly priced wine, good value plain plentiful food, good service; not smart but warm and friendly, barrel seats and tables, lots of nautical prints and posters, sea views from seats out behind; piped radio, occasional live music *(John Davis, Colin and Janet Roe, Kevin Thorpe, R E Davidson, BB)*

Sandling [TQ7558]

Yew Tree [nestling under M20 just N of Maidstone; Grange Lane]: Comfortable and peaceful old local doing good freshly cooked competitively priced food (evenings too now), friendly efficient staff, well kept Shepherd Neame; pretty village with attractive church *(Nigel B Thompson)*

Sandwich [TR3358]

Admiral Owen [Strand St/High St]: Fine heavily beamed 15th-c inn opp ancient Stour toll bridge, log fires, open all day, Greene King ales and home-cooked food; medieval banquets, live music *(Kevin Thorpe)*

Red Cow [Moat Sole; 100 yds from Guildhall, towards Woodnesborough]: Carefully refurbished open-plan pub with eating area, old beams and pictures, changing ales such as Boddingtons, Fullers London Pride, and Greene King Abbot and Old Speckled Hen, good value food, good atmosphere, friendly staff, lovely log fire, old local pictures; soft piped music; guide dogs only, picnic-sets outside with garden bar and hanging baskets *(Kevin Thorpe)*

Sarre [TR2565]

☆ *Crown* [A28 Canterbury—Margate]: Bustling carefully restored pub with two attractive beamed bars, pictures of celebrity guests, good interesting bar lunches and evening restaurant dishes, well kept Shepherd Neame beers, decent house wines, friendly attentive staff, log fires; garden, open all day; bedrooms *(Iain Robertson, David Gregory, David and Betty Gittins)*

Seasalter [TR0864]

Jolly Sportsman [Faversham Rd]: Newish licensees doing particularly good upmarket food, very welcoming atmosphere, simple décor, decent wines *(Bruce Jamieson)*

Sevenoaks [TQ5555]

Bucks Head [Godden Green, just E]: Picturesque old local, picnic-sets out on front terrace by informal green and duckpond, well presented food from sandwiches up inc good puddings, welcoming service and atmosphere, cosy neatly kept bar and restaurant area, full Shepherd Neame range inc a seasonal beer kept well; children welcome away from bar, no dogs or muddy boots; quiet enclosed back garden with bird fountain and pergola, attractive country nr Knole *(Ken Arthur, B J Harding, LM)*

Shipbourne [TQ5952]

Chaser [Stumble Hill]: Attractive colonial-style hotel in lovely spot by village church and green, cheerful public bar welcoming walkers and dogs, with well kept Courage and Harveys, food from sandwiches (not cheap) to more sophisticated meals and decent wines in bistro-like end part with candles and stripped pine, and good high-vaulted restaurant; tables outside, comfortable bedrooms *(Meg and Colin Hamilton, Derek Thomas, Ken Arthur, Hugh Roberts)*

Sissinghurst [TQ7937]

Bull [The Street]: Enjoyable food in bar and big pleasant dark-beamed restaurant area, Harveys and other ales, good service, log fire, shelves of books and china; may be quiet piped music; neat quiet garden *(Jean Bowrage)*

Smarden [TQ8743]

☆ *Bell* [from Smarden follow lane between church and Chequers, then left at T-junction; or from A274 take unsignposted turn E a mile N of B2077 to Smarden]: Mid-17th-c pretty rose covered peg-tiled inn with striking chimneys, very pleasant mature garden, dim-lit snug low-beamed little rooms, ancient brick and flagstones or quarry tiles, pews and the like, warm inglenooks; no smoking room, end games area; simple bar food, Boddingtons, Flowers Original, Fullers London Pride, Greene King Old Speckled Hen, Harveys Best, Marstons Pedigree, Rother Valley Level Best and Shepherd Neame Bitter, local cider, country wines, winter mulled wine; simple bedrooms *(Peter and Elizabeth May, the Didler, R E Davidson, Peter Meister, JP, PP, Colin and Janet Roe)*

Flying Horse [Cage Lane (B2077)]: Good atmosphere in clean and friendly local, well kept Shepherd Neame ales inc seasonal, wholesome reasonably priced food *(Grahame McNulty)*

Sole Street [TR0949]

☆ *Compasses* [note – this is the Sole Street near Wye]: Unspoilt 15th-c country pub, easy-going low-ceilinged rambling bars with bare boards or flagstones, antique or reclaimed furnishings, massive brick bread oven, enamel advertisements, well kept Fullers ESB and London Pride and Shepherd Neame, Biddenden farm cider, fruit wines, well presented hearty food, cheery landlord; children welcome in extended garden room; bar billiards, piped music; big neatly kept garden with rustic tables, play area and various pets, good walks *(John and Elizabeth Thomason, R E Davidson, LYM, J V Dadswell)*

St Margaret's Bay [TR3844]

☆ *Coastguard*: Tremendous views to France from cheery and lively modernised seaside pub, cheap simple meals inc hefty helpings of good value fish and chips, good choice of well kept beer, decent house wines; children and dogs welcome, lots of tables on balcony with pretty hanging baskets and other plants, below NT cliff and nr Pines Garden *(Mrs S K Hamilton, LYM, R Waight, Kevin Flack, Mrs M A Hall, J Martin, A W Lewis, Gloria Bax)*

St Mary in the Marsh [TR0627]

Star [opp church]: Relaxed and remote down-to-earth pub, Tudor but very much modernised; friendly family service, well kept Shepherd Neame inc Mild and guest beers tapped from the cask, good food choice; tables in nice garden, good value attractive bedrooms with Romney Marsh views *(the Didler)*

Staple Street [TR0560]

Three Horseshoes [off A2 via Boughton Street, or A299, nr M2 junction 7]: Friendly and attractively unpretentious 17th-c brick and clapboard local with open fire, gaslight, interesting earthenware bottle collection, bare boards, well kept Shepherd Neame tapped from casks out at the back, Crippledick farm cider, good value simple food (not Sun or Mon lunchtime), no music; open all day Fri/Sat *(Kevin Thorpe)*

Stodmarsh [TR2160]

☆ *Red Lion* [High St; off A257 just E of Canterbury]: Good food inc chargrills, duck and game in well rebuilt pub, hops on beams, flagstones and bare boards, log fires, pine furniture, pictures and rustic bric-a-brac, friendly helpful landlord, well kept Greene King IPA and occasional guest beers such as Swale Kentish Pride tapped from the cask, farm cider, winter mulled wine, pub games; can get busy wknds, some live music; bedrooms, open all day, garden with bat and trap, nearby bird sanctuary *(Mrs S K Hamilton, A W Lewis)*

Stone Street [TQ5754]

☆ *Padwell Arms* [off A25 E of Sevenoaks, on Seal—Plaxtol by-road; OS Sheet 188 map ref 573546]: Small relaxed country local with long tables on front terrace overlooking orchards, more in nice back garden, good choice of genuinely home-cooked food using local produce (may stop promptly at 1.45pm), sensible prices, friendly staff, particularly well kept Badger, Hook Norton Old Hooky and lots of changing guest beers, two local farm ciders, open fires; dogs welcome, occasional live music and other events inc barbecues; good walks *(Hugh Roberts, Eddie Edwards, Pat and Tony Martin, the Didler, Robert Gomme)*

☆ *Snail*: Well run dining pub, with good food from ploughman's up, well kept Harveys, ad lib coffee, friendly staff, pleasant brasserie layout with some stripped stone, good atmosphere in bar part; attractive rambling garden *(LYM, M Firth, Derek Thomas)*

Stowting [TR1242]

☆ *Tiger* [off B2068 N of M20 junction 11]: Partly 17th-c country pub with good food using fresh local produce, attractive unpretentious furniture, candles on tables, rugs on bare boards, good log fire, friendly enthusiastic staff, well kept Everards Tiger, Fullers London Pride, Theakstons Best and Old Peculier and guest beers, well behaved children allowed; tables outside with occasional barbecues, good jazz Mon (cl Mon lunchtime) *(LYM, P Abbott)*

Sutton Valence [TQ8149]

Kings Head [North St]: Friendly and roomy, with good imaginative French country cooking in dining lounge, well kept Greene King IPA, separate public bar; on Greensand Way *(Colin and Janet Roe, Catherine and Richard Preston)*

Tenterden [TQ8833]

Eight Bells [High St]: Old building doing well under current management, traditional long bar, good value food inc interesting starters, very friendly efficient service, central courtyard glazed in as no smoking eating area; easy wheelchair access *(I S Johnson, W L Sleigh)*

White Lion [High St]: Recently tidily restored beamed 16th-c inn, open fires, books and fishing memorabilia, good service, generous popular food inc huge fish and chips, changing ales inc Bass, Caledonian 80/-, a Shepherd Neame seasonal beer and Worthington, smart back panelled restaurant; four-poster bedrooms, tables on terrace overlooking street, open all day *(Kevin Thorpe, Kevin Blake, K J Diamond)*

William Caxton [West Cross; top of High St]: Cosy and friendly 15th-c oak-beamed local, big inglenook log fire, wide choice of home-made food in bar or pleasant restaurant, Shepherd Neame beers inc seasonal; children welcome, tables in attractive front area, open all day, bedrooms *(the Didler)*

Woolpack [High St]: Striking-looking unpretentious 15th-c inn with several oak-beamed rooms inc family dining room, inglenook log fires, good generous home-cooked food, friendly quick service, well kept Boddingtons and Harveys, decent coffee, plenty of locals; open all day; comfortable bedrooms *(Colin and Janet Roe)*

Tonbridge [TQ6148]

Carpenters Arms [off A26 towards Golden Green; Three Elm Lane]: Nice balance of pub and restaurant, wide choice of enjoyable food inc unusual dishes, cheery attentive landlady; plenty of tables outside, wknd barbecues *(Mrs E A Everard)*

Chequers [High St]: New licensees doing wide choice of good value tasty food *(Mrs E A Everard)*

Tunbridge Wells [TQ5839]

Opera House [Mount Pleasant Rd]: Large Wetherspoons pub impressively restored to its 1900s opera-house layout (had been a bingo hall later), with original circle and stalls, stage lighting and ornate ceiling; Courage Directors, Theakstons Best and good range of guest beers, usual cheap Wetherspoons food, no smoking area, no piped music, silenced fruit machines, trivia; no children, can get crowded wknd evenings *(Dr David Cockburn, Kevin Blake)*

Royal Wells [Mount Ephraim]: Well lit, friendly and civilised hotel bar with comfortable settees and padded dining chairs, cosy corners, views over T Wells, well kept Shepherd Neame Bishops Finger and Porter, good value enterprising lunchtime brasserie menu, efficient staff, occasional live music; bedrooms *(BB)*

Toad Rock Retreat [Toad Rock signed off A264 W]: Clean roomy pub with good choice of home-made food inc children's, four real ales, good coffee, friendly service, open fire, separate pool and darts area, daily papers; soft piped classical music; wheelchair access, terrace and elevated garden, local walks *(Hazel Fail)*

Under River [TQ5551]

White Rock [SE of Sevenoaks, off B245]: Welcoming village pub with good mix of customers, small comfortable bar with hop-hung beams and back extension, good bar food, well kept Fullers London Pride, Harveys and Kent Admiral, no piped music; children welcome, picnic-sets on back lawn, handy for Greensand Way (walkers asked to use side door) *(LM, Derek Thomas)*

West Farleigh [TQ7152]

Tickled Trout [B2010 SW of Maidstone]: Black mark here is that they blatantly refuse to serve tap water; otherwise a pleasant dining pub, with well kept Whitbreads-related ales, massive choice of decent food inc good fish (can be slow if very busy), cheerful staff; colourful flowers and hanging baskets outside, Medway views (esp from big garden with play area), path down to river with good walks *(Simon and Sally Small, Colin and Janet Roe, Alan Cowell, LYM)*

Westbere [TR1862]
Old Yew Tree [just off A18 Canterbury—Margate]: Very heavily beamed early 14th-c pub, Courage Directors and Shepherd Neame, straightforward food from bar snacks to restaurant meals, cosy atmosphere, friendly staff; back garden *(Kevin Thorpe)*

Westerham [TQ4454]
Grasshopper [The Green]: Old village pub with friendly efficient staff, attractive choice of good food in bar and upstairs restaurant, well kept beers inc local Larkins, lots of bric-a-brac and Royal pictures in open-plan bar with three areas *(M Firth, Hazel and Michael Duncombe)*

Whitstable [TR1064]
Long Reach [Thanet Way]: Beefeater with wide range of reasonably priced food (can be a wait), children welcome, good décor and service *(Patricia and Norman Pollard)*
Royal Naval Reserve [High St]: Friendly, comfortable and cosy, with well kept Shepherd Neame, good reasonably priced fresh local fish, steps up to spotless and attractive dining room *(Di and Mike Gillam)*

Wickhambreaux [TR2258]
Rose [The Green]: Village-green pub dating from 14th c, three smallish rooms recently refurbished by new owners, stripped brick, beams and panelling, log fire in big fireplace, good home-cooked food, local real ales; garden with summer barbecues, hanging baskets *(Kevin Thorpe)*

Wingham [TR2457]
☆ *Red Lion* [Canterbury Rd]: Lovely jettied 14th-c inn, neatly modernised but cosy, old-fashioned

and gimmick-free, with attentive staff, well kept Flowers and Greene King, pleasant restaurant; bedrooms *(David and Betty Gittins, LYM)*

Worth [TR3356]
☆ *St Crispin* [signed off A258 S of Sandwich]: Stripped brickwork, bare boards, low beams, central log fire, real paraffin lamps, good value simple but interesting food from good cheap baguettes to well kept changing ales, some tapped from the cask, such as Brakspears SB, Gales HSB, Kitchen Brewery, Marstons Pedigree, Shepherd Neame and Charles Wells Bombardier, Belgian beers, local farm cider, restaurant; bedrooms (inc some chalet-style), charming big garden with barbecue, lovely village position *(W W Burke, Keith Jordan, Ted and Jan Whitfield, David and Betty Gittins)*

Wye [TR0546]
☆ *New Flying Horse* [Upper Bridge St]: Friendly and comfortably modernised 17th-c beamed inn, pleasantly light, with two or three rooms, wide choice of interesting fresh bar food, helpful service, well kept Shepherd Neame ales, inglenook log fires, bric-a-brac inc carousel horse; attractive good-sized garden with boules, pleasant bedrooms, good breakfast *(Alan and Jan Summers, David Kidd, R E Davidson, E A Thwaite)*

Yalding [TQ7050]
☆ *Walnut Tree* [B2010 SW of Maidstone]: Pleasant brightly lit beamed bar on several levels with inglenook and interesting pictures, friendly efficient staff, food from good baguettes to fresh fish, bargain OAP wkdy lunch, wide restaurant choice, well kept Harveys and Wadworths 6X; piped music not over-intrusive, live music Sun evening; bedrooms, attractive village, handy for Organic Garden *(Catherine and Richard Preston)*

Stars after the name of a pub show exceptional quality. One star means most people (after reading the report to see just why the star has been won) would think a special trip worth while. Two stars mean that the pub is really outstanding – many that for their particular qualities cannot be bettered.

Lancashire
(with Greater Manchester and Merseyside)

Richard Bowman, landlord of the Inn at Whitewell, has steered it into every annual edition of the Guide since it started 20 years ago – a proud record for this fine country inn. The only other establishment in this area to have featured every year is the grandly Victorian Philharmonic Dining Rooms in Liverpool, in fine fettle with its munificent restoration by Bass (or Six Continents, as we'll have to get used to calling them). To balance these old stagers are two new main entries, both of them most enjoyable food pubs: the Derby Arms out in the country near Longridge (in the same family for over a century), and the Red Lion at Mawdesley (straight in with a Food Award). Other pubs on top form here are the Black Dog at Belmont (no-nonsense real value), the thriving Stork at Conder Green, the friendly Black Horse at Croston (good beers, good value food), the nicely set rambling Cartford at Little Eccleston (brewing its own beers), the Marble Arch in Manchester (another pub that brews its own – distinctive beers, all organic and unfined), the Wheatsheaf at Raby (a nice all-rounder) and the Church Inn at Uppermill (a fine old moorside pub brewing very cheap beer). Our choice as Lancashire Dining Pub of the Year is the Red Lion at Mawdesley – a rare tribute for a pub making its first appearance in the Guide. Besides plenty of starred entries in both Manchester and Liverpool, pubs particularly worth noting in the Lucky Dip section at the end of the chapter are the Bay Horse at Bay Horse, Moorcock at Blacko, Lord Raglan up above Bury, Royal Oak in Garstang, Hest Bank Hotel at Hest Bank, Romper up above Marple, Royal Oak at Riley Green and Spread Eagle at Sawley. We have already inspected all but one of these, and can confirm that they are knocking loudly on the main-entry door. There are plenty of food bargains in the area, and drinks prices are far below the national average.

BELMONT SD6716 Map 7
Black Dog £ 🛏

A675

Built in 1750 as a working farm, this cosy pub was converted to an inn in 1825. It's been a much loved fixture in the *Guide* for the last 17 years, and has had the same welcoming licensees in all that time. It's a very friendly place that never seems to disappoint, and is particularly inviting on a cold winter evening, especially if you're tucked away in one of the various snug alcoves, one of which used to house the village court. The original cheery and traditional small rooms are packed with antiques and bric-a-brac, from railwaymen's lamps, bedpans and chamber-pots to landscape paintings. There are also service bells for the sturdy built-in curved seats, rush-seated mahogany chairs, and coal fires. An airy extension lounge with a picture window has more modern furnishings; darts, pool, shove-ha'penny, dominoes, cribbage, and fruit machine; softly piped classical music. Hearty bar food includes soup (£1.30, home-made winter broth £1.60), sandwiches (from £2, toasted from £2.30), peppered smoked mackerel (£3), quiche or ploughman's (from £4.30), broccoli, tomato, potato and three cheese bake (£4.80), seafood pizza (£5.30), well liked salads including the mighty 'landlord's' mix of chicken, ham, beef, pastrami, ox tongue and a pork pie (£6), and daily specials such as tuna steak in lime, coconut and ginger, venison in red wine or pork in white port and stilton sauce (£8); despite their very pubby policy of not taking bookings, it does tend to fill up quickly, so get there early for a table, and expect a wait when busy. The Holts Bitter and Mild on handpump are well kept and very good value. A small orchestra plays Viennese music on New Year's Day at lunchtime, and on several other evenings throughout the year. From two long benches on the sheltered sunny side of the pub, there are delightful views of the moors above the nearby trees and houses; a track leads from the village up Winter Hill and (from the lane to Rivington) on to Anglezarke Moor, and there are paths from the dam of the nearby Belmont Reservoir. Homely, reasonably priced bedrooms. *(Recommended by P Abbott, Brian Wainwright, Jim Abbott, Steve Whalley, Willie Bell, Mr and Mrs M Cross, Andy and Jill Kassube, Gordon Tong, Dr Paull Khan, Andy, Julie and Stuart Hawkins, MLR, John Robertson, Steve Atkinson, Lynn Sharpless, Bob Eardley)*

Holts ~ Tenant James Pilkington ~ Real ale ~ Bar food (12-2, 7-9; 12-3, 6.30-8 Sun) ~ Restaurant ~ No credit cards ~ (01204) 811218 ~ Children welcome ~ Open 12-4, 7-11(6.30-11 Sun) ~ Bedrooms: £32S/£42S

BISPHAM GREEN SD4914 Map 7
Eagle & Child 🍽 🍺

Maltkiln Lane (Parbold—Croston road, off B5246)

Stylishly furnished with good but understated pieces, the appealingly simple interior at this striking red brick pub consists of a civilised largely open-plan bar which is well divided by stubs of walls. There's coir matting in the no smoking snug and oriental rugs on flagstones in front of the fine old stone fireplaces. Nice old furnishings include a mix of small oak chairs around tables in corners, an oak coffer, several handsomely carved antique oak settles – the finest apparently made partly from a 16th-c wedding bed-head, and old hunting prints and engravings. The owner's family farm much of the land around Parbold, so there may be well hung meat from their various herds. Changing daily, good interesting home-cooked bar food might include soup (£2.80/£3.20), basil roast tomato and spinach tartlet (£3.50), wild mushroom risotto or grilled aubergines with couscous (£6.50), steak and ale pie (£6.80), braised lamb shank in coconut cream and lime (£9.50) and salmon supreme on rocket, honey roast apricot and lemon butter sauce (£9.80), and daily specials such as baked pollack fillet, wilted wild garlic leaves, prawns and lemon beurre blanc or grilled tuna steak with chorizo and balsamic vinegar (£9.50), and puddings such as caramel tart and kiwi fruit crème brûlée (£3.50). A good range of well kept beers includes Moorhouses Black Cat and Thwaites, with four or five changing guest ales from brewers such as Hanby, Hart, Jennings, Phoenix and Timothy Taylor, also changing farm cider, decent wines, some country wines and about 25 malt whiskies; maybe piped pop radio. The pub holds a popular beer festival over the second bank holiday in May, with live music in the evenings. Behind is a lovely wild garden with crested newts and nesting moorhens and Harry the dog is still around sometimes (no dogs allowed during food service). Watching players compete on the neat bowling green behind can be most relaxing, and the pub can provide bowls for anyone who wants to try the crowns which fool even the most experienced bowlers. *(Recommended by Paul Boot, Mr and Mrs S Mason, MLR, Michael Doswell, Stephen, Julie and Hayley Brown, Ray and Winifred Halliday, Revd D Glover, Jim Abbott, David Atkinson, John Fazakerley, Rob Fowell, Brian Kneale, Pat and Roger Fereday, Andy, Julie and Stuart Hawkins, Dr A and Dr A C Jackson, Walter and Susan Rinaldi-Butcher)*

*Free house ~ Licensee John Mansfield ~ Real ale ~ Bar food (12-2, 6-8.30(9 Fri, Sat);
12-8.30 Sun) ~ Restaurant ~ (01257) 462297 ~ Children away from bar area ~ Open
12-3, 5.30-11; 12-10.30 Sun; closed evening 25 Dec*

BLACKSTONE EDGE SD9716 Map 7
White House £

A58 Ripponden—Littleborough, just W of B6138

Readers love this imposing 17th-c building for its spectacular setting 1,300 feet
above sea level on the Pennine Way, and impressive views over the moors from its
lounge. Even in summer you may be greeted by swirling mists and wild moorland
winds, which make the cosy interior seem even more appealing. The bustling main
bar has a cheery atmosphere, with a turkey carpet in front of a blazing coal fire and
a large-scale map of the area (windswept walkers hardly know whether to head for
the map or the fire first). The snug Pennine Room opens off here, with brightly
coloured antimacassars on its small soft settees; there's also a dining extension. A
spacious room on the left has comfortable seating and a big horseshoe window
looking over the moors. The menu of generously served and enjoyably unpretentious
bar food includes soup (£2), sandwiches (from £3), cumberland sausage with egg
(£4.75), steak and kidney pie or vegetable quiche (£4.75), roast chicken breast (£5),
chilli, beef curry or lasagne (£5.50), steaks (from £7.50), puddings such as home-
made apple pie and sticky toffee pudding (from £2) and daily specials. Service is
prompt and friendly. Well kept real ales on handpump include Theakstons Best,
Black Sheep Special and one or two guests such as Exmoor Gold and Moorhouses
Pendle Witches Brew, also farm cider and malt whiskies; fruit machine. Muddy
boots can be left in the porch. *(Recommended by Dr C C S Wilson, Paul Fairbrother, Helen
Morris, Andy Gosling, Chloe and Robert Gartery, Graham and Lynn Mason, Derek and Sylvia
Stephenson)*

*Free house ~ Licensee Neville Marney ~ Real ale ~ Bar food ~ (01706) 378456 ~
Children welcome ~ Open 12-3, 6.30-11; 12-11 Sun*

CHIPPING SD6243 Map 7
Dog & Partridge ♀

Hesketh Lane; crossroads Chipping—Longridge with Inglewhite—Clitheroe

Parts of this spotlessly kept dining pub date back to 1515, but because of its
popularity it's been much modernised and extended since, with the eating space now
spreading over into a nearby stable (you may need to book). The comfortable main
lounge has small armchairs around fairly close-set low wood-effect tables on a blue
patterned carpet, brown-painted beams, a good winter log fire, and multi-coloured
lanterns. They have well kept Tetley Bitter and Mild with a weekly changing guest
such as Three B's Pinch Noggin on handpump, over 40 wines, and a good range of
malt whiskies; piped music. Lunchtime bar food (not Sun) includes soup (£2.30),
sandwiches (from £4, prawn £5), duck and orange pâté (£4), leek and mushroom
crumble (£7.50), steak and kidney pie or roast chicken with stuffing (£7.80), and
10oz sirloin steak (£11.25). Service is friendly and helpful. Smart casual dress is
preferred in the restaurant where you can eat in the evening and Sunday lunchtime;
dining areas are no smoking. The pub is in attractive countryside between Longridge
and Wolf Fell. *(Recommended by Margaret Dickinson, P Abbott, Steve Whalley)*

*Free house ~ Licensee Peter Barr ~ Real ale ~ Bar food (12-1.45 Mon-Sat) ~
Restaurant (7-9 Mon-Sat; 12-3, 3.30-8.30 Sun) ~ (01995) 61201 ~ Children welcome
~ Open 11.45-3, 6.45-11; 11.45-10.30 Sun*

If a service charge is mentioned prominently on a menu or accommodation terms,
you must pay it if service was satisfactory. If service is really bad you are legally
entitled to refuse to pay some or all of the service charge as compensation for not
getting the service you might reasonably have expected.

CONDER GREEN SD4556 Map 7

Stork £ 🛏

3 miles from M6 junction 33: A6 towards Lancaster, first left, then fork left; just off A588

Handy for the Lune estuary path, this rambling white-painted ancient inn is in a fine spot where the River Conder joins the Lune estuary, with tables outside looking out over the surrounding watery wastes. The bleak marshes on which it sits are made all the more eerie by the cries of waterfowl when the wind and tides are right, but bustling Glasson Dock is just a mile away, and the pub makes a handy break from Lancaster and the M6. Inside, one of the lived-in panelled rooms has a list of licensees going back to 1660, and there's a good fire; darts, pool, fruit machine, video game, juke box and piped music – can be obtrusive at times. Popular generously served bar food includes soup (£2.10), sandwiches (from £2.50), smoked chicken, lemon and basil pâté (£2.60), stilton and garlic mushrooms (£2.95), steak pie (£5.25), wild boar and apricot pie (£5.75), garlic and stilton chicken (£6.25), and daily specials such as stilton, sweet pepper, leek and sweet potato lasagne (£4.75), gammon and chicken pie in white wine sauce with wild mushroom and tarragon (£5.50), lamb rogan josh (£5.95) and grilled venison steak with red wine and rosemary sauce (£7.95); puddings such as caramel and apple pie or Baileys torte (£2.25). There may be quite a wait when busy. Well kept Boddingtons, Stork (brewed for the pub by Whitbreads), Timothy Taylors Landlord and maybe a guest on handpump; good coffee. Dogs welcome. *(Recommended by R T and J C Moggridge, Margaret Dickinson, J F M and M West, Tony Middis, Rob Fowell, David and Ruth Hollands, MLR, Michael Butler, R J Walden, Helen Flaherty, Roger and Debbie Stamp, Steve Whalley, John Clegg, Joy and Peter Heatherley, Michael Doswell, Dr Paull Khan)*

Free house ~ Licensee Tony Cragg ~ Real ale ~ Bar food (12-2, 6.30-9(9.30 Sat); 12-4, 4.30-9 Sun) ~ Restaurant ~ (01524) 751234 ~ Children welcome ~ Open 11-11; 12-10.30 Sun; closed 25 Dec ~ Bedrooms: £24.50S/£40S

CROSTON SD4818 Map 7

Black Horse ◖ £

Westhead Road; A581 Chorley—Southport

Very much at the heart of the community, this friendly Victorian village pub combines a good choice of well kept real ales, reliable home cooking and a warm welcome for locals and visitors alike. They hold beer festivals in April and October, and their usual beers include John Smiths, Theakstons Mild and Worthingtons and guests such as Black Sheep, Moorhouses Pendle Witch and Timothy Taylors on handpump. Very good value hearty bar food includes home-made soup (£1.75), sandwiches (from £2), ploughman's (£3.50), lasagne, steak and kidney pie or vegetable curry (£3.95), 6oz sirloin (£4.95), puddings (£2.15) with daily specials such as spicy tuna pasta bake (£3.50), minted lamb steak in red wine marinade or cajun chicken (£3.95), and a very popular Sunday roast (£4.25); children's and senior citizen's meals (£2.50). The dining area is no smoking. Furnished in keeping with the age in which it was built, the neatly kept bar has patterned carpets, attractive wallpaper, solid upholstered wall settles and cast-iron-framed pub tables, a fireplace tiled in the Victorian style and reproduction prints of that time (also a couple of nice 1950s street-scene prints by M Grimshaw), as well as darts, pool, cribbage, dominoes, fruit machine, satellite TV and piped music. The lounge extension with a woodburning stove is decorated in a gently relaxing style, in sympathy with the rest of the building. There are picnic-sets outside, and a good solid safely railed-off play area; the pub has its own crown bowls green and boules pitch and thriving teams (boules available from the bar). *(Recommended by John Fazakerley, R Mathews, George Little, Jim Abbott, Stephen, Julie and Hayley Brown, MLR, Mr and Mrs M Cooper, Kevin Thorpe)*

Free house ~ Licensee Graeme Conroy ~ Real ale ~ Bar food (12-2.30, 5.30-8.30; 12-7 Sun) ~ Restaurant ~ (01772) 600338 ~ Children in restaurant and eating area of bar till one hour after food service at night ~ Open 11-11; 12-10.30 Sun

DARWEN SD7222 Map 7
Old Rosins

Pickup Bank, Hoddlesden; from B6232 Haslingden—Belthorn, turn off towards Edgeworth opposite the Grey Mare – pub then signposted off to the right

It's worth the effort to find this isolated moorland inn and given its remote setting it's surprising how popular it is. Although there are lovely views over the moors and down into the wooded valley on clear days, the pubby atmosphere is arguably at its best on one of those foggy days when moorland mists obscure everything except the welcoming lights of the bar. Lots of mugs, whisky-water jugs and so forth hang from the high joists, while the walls are decorated with small prints, plates and old farm tools; a good log fire and comfortable red plush built-in button-back banquettes, stools and small wooden chairs around dark cast-iron-framed tables enhance the cosy feel. Reasonably priced bar food is served all day and includes soup (£1.95), sandwiches (from £2.50), black pudding (£2.70), salmon and haddock smokie (£3.95, large £6.95), meat pie (£4.75), cumberland sausage and mash (£5.25), chicken curry (£5.95), steak (£7) and daily specials such as king prawns with garlic (£4.95), lamb hotpot (£5.95) and puddings (from £2.75); good cheerful service. Well kept Jennings Bitter, Cumberland, Fell Runner and Sneck Lifter on handpump and plenty of malt whiskies; fruit machine and piped music. There are picnic-sets on the spacious crazy-paved terrace. *(Recommended by Andy and Jill Kassube, K C and B Forman, Dr Michael Allen, Michael Buchanan)*

Jennings ~ Managers John and Jess Griffiths ~ Real ale ~ Bar food (all day) ~ Restaurant ~ (01254) 771264 ~ Children welcome ~ Open 12-11(10.30 Sun) ~ Bedrooms: £52.50B/£65B

DOWNHAM SD7844 Map 7
Assheton Arms

From A59 NE of Clitheroe turn off into Chatburn (signposted); in Chatburn follow Downham signpost

This delightfully set dining pub takes its name from the family of Lord Clitheroe, who bought this stone-built village in 1558 and have preserved it in a traditional style ever since. A massive stone fireplace helps divide the separate areas of the rambling beamed bar which is cosiest in winter, and is furnished with olive plush-cushioned winged settles around attractive grainy oak tables, some cushioned window seats, and two grenadier busts on the mantelpiece. Window seats, and picnic-sets outside, look across to the church; part of the bar is no smoking. Bar food includes home-made ham and vegetable broth (£2.95), sandwiches (from £3.75, not Saturday evening or Sunday lunchtime), ploughman's (£4.50), chicken liver pâté (£4.75), courgettes with tomato, garlic, pesto and mozzarella (£6.75), chicken and mushroom pie (£6.95), venison, bacon and cranberry casserole (£7.95), grilled plaice with parsley butter (£8.95), and seafood specials such as grilled scallops with garlic butter and gruyère cheese (£6.50), half a dozen oysters (£6.95), grilled bream (£8.95) and monkfish with brandy, cream and peppercorns (£9.50); puddings and children's meals (£3.50); speedy service. Boddingtons or Castle Eden under light blanket pressure; decent wines by the glass or bottle; piped music. *(Recommended by P Abbott, Greta and Christopher Wells, Andy, Julie and Stuart Hawkins)*

Whitbreads ~ Lease David Busby ~ Real ale ~ Bar food (12-2, 7-10) ~ (01200) 441227 ~ Children welcome ~ Open 12-3, 7-11(10.30 Sun)

ENTWISTLE SD7217 Map 7
Strawbury Duck 🖛

Overshores Rd, by station; village signposted down narrow lane from Blackburn Rd N of Edgworth; or take Batridge Rd off B6391 N of Chapeltown and take pretty ¼ mile walk from park at Entwistle reservoir; OS Sheet 109 map reference 726177

Tables outside this traditional beamed and flagstoned country pub are perched high above a railway cutting, and a train ride from Blackburn or Bolton takes you along a little railway and through this cutting to a station next door. The cosy dimly lit L-shaped bar has Victorian pictures on its partly timbered, partly rough-stone walls, a variety of seats, stools, little settees and pews, a mounted gun, and one table made from an old church organ bellows. Bar food includes soup (£1.95), sandwiches (from £2.45), ploughman's (from £3.75), deep-fried cod or various pies such as steak and kidney or chicken and asparagus (£5.95) and 11oz T-bone steak (£9.75), and daily specials such as seared halibut with garden herb butter (£8.75), lamb fillet with rosemary jus (£9.25) and rump steak with stilton and garlic (£11.50); puddings (from £2.65); also children's dishes. Well kept Black Sheep, Boddingtons, Moorhouses Pendle Witches Brew and a couple of guests on handpump; fruit machine and piped music. The pub is tucked well away in a sheltered fold of the moors and is a popular base for Pennine walks (leave muddy boots in the porch). Accommodation has been refurbished recently, and rooms now have four-poster beds. *(Recommended by Andy and Jill Kassube, Catherine and Martin Snelling, P Abbott, Revd D Glover, Vicky and David Sarti)*

Free house ~ Licensee Lisa McEwan ~ Real ale ~ Bar food (12-9.30(8.30 Sun)) ~ Restaurant ~ (01204) 852013 ~ Children welcome ~ Live music Thurs evening ~ Open 11-11; 12-10.30 Sun ~ Bedrooms: £35S(£35B)/£45S(£45B)

FENCE SD8237 Map 7
Forest
Cuckstool Lane; B6248 Brierfield road off A6068

There's a pleasantly bustling atmosphere inside this civilised dining pub. A big open fire and subdued lighting create a cosy feel, with heavy panelling, lots of paintings, vases, plates and books. The open-plan bar has two rooms opening off it, and a side restaurant; no smoking area in conservatory dining room. Bar food includes soup (£2.65), a wide choice of interesting lunchtime sandwiches (from £3.95), thai king prawns in filo pastry with sweet chilli dip (£4.95), leek, potato and parmesan risotto with mozzarella (£7.50), lamb tagine with spicy couscous (£7.95), pork loin with madeira and mustard sauce or salmon and plaice in filo on a dill and cream sauce (£9.95), herb crusted noisette of lamb with red currant jus (£10.50), puddings (from £3.75). There is no children's menu but they will do small helpings of suitable dishes; you will need to book at the weekend. Ruddles, Marstons Pedigree and Theakstons Best with a guest such as Greene King Old Speckled Hen on handpump, a good choice of wines, friendly helpful service; unobtrusive piped music. *(Recommended by W K Woods, Louise English, I D Greenfield, Steve Whalley)*

Free house ~ Licensee Clive Seedall ~ Real ale ~ Bar food (12-2.30, 5.30-9.30; 12-9 Sun) ~ Restaurant ~ (01282) 613641/691673 ~ Children welcome ~ Open 12-11(10.30 Sun)

GARSTANG SD4845 Map 7
Th'Owd Tithebarn ★
Signposted off Church Street; turn left off one-way system at Farmers Arms

The big flagstoned terrace overlooking the Lancaster Canal at this creeper-covered converted tithe barn is a lovely spot for a drink in summer. Inside, the furnishings are reminiscent of a simple old-fashioned farmhouse kitchen parlour, with an antique kitchen range, a huge collection of agricultural equipment on the walls, stuffed animals and birds, and pews and glossy tables spaced out on the flagstones under the very high rafters – waitresses in period costume with mob-caps complete the vintage flavour. A 30-ft dining table in the middle of the restaurant caters for parties. Simple bar food and daily specials might include soup (£1.95), black pudding and salad (£2.25), filled baguettes (from £3.45), scampi, three cheese and broccoli bake or steak and kidney pudding (£5.95), salmon and garlic (£6.75), and puddings (£2.95); Flowers IPA and Tetleys on handpump, lots of country wines; fruit machine and piped music. As it's something of a tourist attraction, it can get very busy. *(Recommended by Abi Benson, Kevin Blake, Klaus and Elizabeth Leist)*

Mitchells ~ Manager Gordon Hutchinson ~ Real ale ~ Bar food (12-9(9.30 Sat)) ~ Restaurant ~ (01995) 604486 ~ Children in restaurant ~ Open 11-11; 12-10.30 Sun; 11-3, 6-11 winter; 12-3, 7-10.30 Sun winter

GOOSNARGH SD5839 Map 7

Horns ♀ ⇔

Pub signed from village, about 2 miles towards Chipping below Beacon Fell

The emphasis at this very friendly hotel – readers love staying here – in the foothills of the Pennines is on the enjoyable homely food which includes soup (£2.95), well presented sandwiches (from £3.25), ploughman's (£4.95), steak and kidney pie (£7.50), roast local pheasant or grilled gammon and egg (£7.95) and sirloin steak with mushrooms (£10.50), with daily specials such as vegetable bake (£7.75), roast of the day (£7.95), and baked hake (£8.50), all nicely served with freshly cooked, piping hot chips; home-made puddings might include home-made fruit pies or an excellent sticky toffee pudding (£3.95). A number of colourful flower displays add colour to the neatly kept snug rooms, all of which have log fires in winter. Beyond the lobby, the pleasant front bar opens into attractively decorated middle rooms; the dining rooms are no smoking. There's an extensive wine list with quite a few by the glass, and a fine choice of malt whiskies. Very good service from cheerful and helpful young staff; piped music. Nicely furnished, comfortable bedrooms. *(Recommended by R L Gorick, P J Holt, Margaret Dickinson, Vicky and David Sarti, Lynette and Stuart Shore, Charles and Pauline Stride, Simon Longe, Revd D Glover, Dave and Chris Watts)*

Free house ~ Licensee Mark Woods ~ Bar food (not Mon lunchtime) ~ Restaurant ~ (01772) 865230 ~ Children welcome ~ Open 11.30-3, 6.30-11; 11-11 Sat; 12-3, 6.30-10.30 Sun; closed Mon lunchtime except bank hols ~ Bedrooms: £55S(£55B) /£75S(£75B)

LITTLE ECCLESTON SD4139 Map 7

Cartford ♦ ⇔

Cartford Lane, off A586 Garstang—Blackpool, by toll bridge

This delightfully set old place is by a toll bridge over the River Wyre (tidal here), and holds fishing rights along 1½ miles; the scenery is not dramatic, but is peacefully engaging. The attractive rambling interior has oak beams, dried flowers, and an unusual layout on three different levels, with pleasantly uncoordinated cosy seating areas. Two levels are largely set for dining (the upstairs part is no smoking), and it's very popular with older lunchers on weekdays. Reasonably priced food includes soup (£1.95), sandwiches (from £2.70), pizzas (from £4.30, evenings only), home-made steak and mushroom pie (£4.85), lemon sole (£5.70), 10oz sirloin steak (£8.95) and blackboard specials such as beef vindaloo (£5.95), chicken with leek and stilton sauce, bass or red snapper (£6.95); puddings (£2.50). Unusually for a place that has such a following for its food, the Cartford is particularly strong on the beer side, drawing rather a different crowd on weekend evenings. Up to eight very well kept real ales on handpump include a couple from Hart (their own award winning microbrewery behind the pub with brewery tours by arrangement), Boddingtons, Fullers London Pride and up to four changing ales from interesting brewers such as Moorhouse, Phoenix and Rooster; decent house wines and several malt whiskies. Service is welcoming and helpful; log fire, pool, darts, dominoes, fruit machine, TV and piped music. There are tables out in a garden (not by the water), with a play area. *(Recommended by Harry Gleave, Dr B and Mrs P B Baker, Dr Paull Khan, Abi Benson)*

Free house ~ Licensees Andrew Mellodew and Val Williams ~ Real ale ~ Bar food (12-2, 6.30-9.30; 12-9 Sun) ~ (01995) 670166 ~ Children away from bar ~ Tues night quiz every other week ~ Open 12(11.30 Sat)-3, 6.30(7 winter Mon Thurs)-11; 12-10.30 Sun ~ Bedrooms: £35.95B/£48.95B

Waterside pubs are listed at the back of the book.

LIVERPOOL SJ4395 Map 7

Baltic Fleet ◧ £

Wapping

Just across the water from the Albert Dock, this well known Victorian pub has an authentic reek of maritime history. The friendly landlord boasts something of a seafaring ancestry too. His family (who have lived in this part of the world since the mid 19th c) were involved in the shipping trade to West Africa, and there are pictures of them dotted amongst the interesting old Mersey shipping prints inside. It's a fairly unusual triangular end of terrace building with nice big arched windows, brightly painted green, burgundy and white exterior, and apparently more entrances (eight) than any other pub in Liverpool. An abundance of interior woodwork and stout mahogany board floors lend to its nautical feel. There's also a good mix of old school furniture and dark wood tables, piped music and a TV. They have well kept very reasonably priced beers on handpump and served through a sparkler from the local brewer Passageway and maybe a guest, as well as about eight wines by the glass. Home-made lunchtime bar food includes soup (£2.75), sandwiches (from £2.95), cheese and onion quiche (£4.95) and home-made salmon fishcakes or beef and ale pie (made for the pub by the local butcher, from £4.95). In the evening, reasonably priced dishes include smoked salmon with brown bread (£2.95), aubergine and rosemary bake or sausages and mash with onion gravy (£4.95), smoked fish pie or chicken and sun-dried tomatoes with couscous (£5.95), and puddings such as apple crumble, bakewell tart or chocolate mousse (£2.50); popular Sunday roast (from £5.95). The small back room is no smoking. *(Recommended by the Didler, Stephen, Julie and Hayley Brown, Rob Fowell)*

Free house ~ Licensees Simon Holt and Julie Broome ~ Real ale ~ Bar food (12-2.30, 6-8.30; 12-3, 5.30-9.30 Fri; 11-3, 6.30-9.30 Sat; 12-4 Sun) ~ Restaurant ~ (0151) 709 3116 ~ Children in restaurant ~ Open 11.30-11; 11-11 Sat; 12-10.30 Sun

Philharmonic Dining Rooms ★

36 Hope Street; corner of Hardman Street

Not to be missed if you're in Liverpool, this recently spruced-up late Victorian gin palace is wonderfully opulent, from its smart marble façade to its elegant original fittings. The heart of the building is a mosaic-faced serving counter, from which heavily carved and polished mahogany partitions radiate under the intricate plasterwork high ceiling. The echoing main hall is decorated with stained glass including contemporary portraits of Boer War heroes such as Baden-Powell and Lord Roberts, rich panelling, a huge mosaic floor, and copper panels of musicians in an alcove above the fireplace. More stained glass in one of the little lounges declares 'Music is the universal language of mankind', and backs this up with illustrations of musical instruments; there are two plushly comfortable sitting rooms. Throughout the pub there's a good blend of customers, with theatre-goers, students, locals and tourists making up the happy bustle. Lavatory devotees may be interested to know that the famous gents' are original 1890s Rouge Royale by Twyfords: all red marble and glinting mosaics, in the eyes of some readers these alone earn the pub its star. Well kept Bass, Tetleys Bitter and Mild on handpump; friendly service; chess tables, fruit machine, TV and piped music. As we went to press they were refurbishing the kitchen and transforming the grand lounge into a smart restaurant which should be open by the time this *Guide* is in the shops – and which will change the tone for those who remember this as a place for a cheap lunchtime snack. *(Recommended by Steve Chambers, John A Barker, Stephen, Julie and Hayley Brown, the Didler, Lyn and Geoff Hallchurch, George Little, JP, PP)*

Bass ~ Manager Marie-Louise Wong ~ Real ale ~ (0151) 707 2837 ~ Open 12-11; 6.30-10.30 Sun

Pubs brewing their own beers are listed at the back of the book.

LONGRIDGE SD6039 Map 7
Derby Arms ♀
Chipping Road, Thornley; 1½ miles N of Longridge on back road to Chipping

This very welcoming old stone-built country pub has been run by the same family for over a century; the current licensee's great-grandmother was married from here in 1898. Though the thoughtful personal service stands out, it's particularly well liked for its very good food, excellently presented, and making splendid use of fresh local ingredients. A typical choice includes sandwiches, Bury market black pudding (£3.95), vegetarian hotpot (£6.95), roast chicken with bacon, stuffing and apple sauce (£7.50), an impressive steak and kidney pudding (£7.95), steaks (from £8.95), roast shank of lamb with redcurrant gravy (£9.95), and usually a wide choice of changing fish specials such as dressed crab (£5.75), fillet of fresh sea bream with a thai red curry sauce (£11.95), scallops in a cream and mushroom sauce or monkfish in batter (£12.95), and turbot with parma ham and asparagus (£14.50). Potatoes and vegetables come in separate dishes. They do various set menus, including a bargain Lancashire special, with three local dishes for £7.95; prompt, efficient and friendly waitress service. The main bar has something of a hunting and fishing theme, with old photographs commemorating notable catches, some nicely mounted lures above the comfortable red plush seats, and a stuffed pheasant that seems to be flying in through the wall. To the right is a smaller room with sporting trophies and mementoes, and a regimental tie collection, while off to the left are a couple of no smoking dining areas. Well kept Bass, Greenalls and Marstons Pedigree on handpump, and a good range of wines including several half-bottles and a dozen or so by the glass, particularly strong on South African. The gents' has dozens of riddles on the wall; you can buy a sheet of them in the bar (the money goes to charity). There are a few tables out in front, and another two behind the car park, enjoying fine views across to the Forest of Bowland. *(Recommended by R L Gorick, Miss Mary Roberts, Jean and Douglas Troup, Steve Whalley, Deborah Bamber)*

Free house ~ Licensee Mrs G M Walme ~ Real ale ~ Bar food (12-2.15, 6.30-9.30(6-10 Sat); 12-9.15 Sun) ~ Restaurant ~ (01772) 782623 ~ Children in restaurant ~ Open 12-3.30, 6-11; 12-10.30 Sun

LYTHAM SD3627 Map 7
Taps ◧ £
A584 S of Blackpool; Henry Street – in centre, one street in from West Beach

The bar at this spirited alehouse was so alive with enthusiastic chatter when we rang mid-afternoon to check a few details, the barman could hardly hear us speak. This is a place that really takes care of its customers. There's a view-in cellar that lets you admire the choice of well kept beers on offer, seat belts on the bar stools for while you're consuming it, and headrests in the gents which should keep you out of harm's way after sampling one too many. Alongside Boddingtons, weekly changing guests on handpump might include Batemans XXXB, Fullers London Pride, Taps (brewed for the pub by Titanic), Titanic Stout, Wadworths 6X and Wychwood Three Lions; there's also usually some country wines and a farm cider. The Victorian-style bare-boarded bar has a really friendly unassuming atmosphere, with plenty of stained-glass decoration in the windows, depictions of fish and gulls reflecting the pub's proximity to the beach, captain's chairs in bays around the sides, open fires, and a coal-effect gas fire between two built-in bookcases at one end. There's also a bit of a rugby theme, with old photographs and portraits of rugby stars on the walls; shove-ha'penny, dominoes and fruit machine. Good value straightforward home-made bar food includes sandwiches (from £1.50, hot roast beef £3.25), soup (£1.65), filled baked potatoes (from £1.95), curry (£3.50) and lasagne (£3.95). There are no meals on Sunday, but instead they have free platters of food laid out, with tasty morsels such as black pudding, chicken wings or minted lamb. There are a few seats outside. Parking is difficult near the pub – it's probably best to park at the West Beach car park on the seafront (it's free on Sunday), and walk. *(Recommended by Andy, Julie and Stuart Hawkins, Abi Benson, J F M and M West)*

Whitbreads ~ Manager Ian Rigg ~ Real ale ~ Bar food (lunchtime only; not Sun) ~ (01253) 736226 ~ Open 11-11; 12-10.30 Sun

MANCHESTER SJ7796 Map 7
Britons Protection ♀

Great Bridgewater St, corner of Lower Mosley St

As well as an interesting range of spirits, they now keep a magnificent 175 malt whiskies at this popular city drinker's pub. And if that's not enough to warm you up, and as something of a tribute to Manchester's notorious climate, the massive bar counter has a pair of heating pipes as its footrail. The licensees have been here for years and have kept up a really good social atmosphere in all that time and employ a proper career barman. The rather plush little front bar has a fine chequered tile floor, some glossy brown and russet wall tiles, solid woodwork and elaborate plastering. A tiled passage lined with battle murals leads to two inner lounges, one served by hatch, with attractive brass and etched-glass wall lamps, a mirror above the coal-effect gas fire in the simple art nouveau fireplace, and again good solidly comfortable furnishings. Besides well kept Jennings, Robinsons and Tetleys and a guest such as Coach House Honeypot on handpump, they have good wines. Reasonably priced bar food might include home-made soup (£1.45), sandwiches (from £2), ploughman's (£3.65), ham and egg (£3.95), unusual pies such as kangaroo, wild boar and ostrich (£4.75), and home-made daily specials (from £3.95); piped music. Busy at lunchtime, it's usually quiet and relaxed in the evenings, handy for Bridgewater Hall (and well known by many orchestral players) and the GMEX centre. There are tables out in the beer garden behind. *(Recommended by Brian and Anna Marsden, Kevin Blake, the Didler, GLD)*

Punch ~ Lease Peter Barnett ~ Real ale ~ Bar food (11-2.30, 6-7.30) ~ Restaurant ~ (0161) 236 5895 ~ Children in eating area of bar ~ Old Time Music Hall first Tues night of month, open house comedy club Weds night ~ Open 11-11; 12-10.30 Sun; closed 25 Dec

Dukes 92 £

Castle Street, below the bottom end of Deansgate

This cavernous old building has a wonderfully atmospheric setting by locks and under railway arches in the rejuvenated heart of old industrial Manchester. It originally housed stables for canal horses – today tables are set out by the canal basin which opens into the bottom lock of the Rochdale Canal – and it's all been very tastefully converted inside. Black wrought-iron work contrasts boldly with whitewashed bare plaster walls, the handsome bar is marble-topped, and an elegant spiral staircase leads to an upper room and balcony. Down in the main room the fine mix of furnishings is mainly rather Edwardian in mood, with one particularly massive table, elegantly comfortable chaises-longues and deep armchairs. Like its sister pub, the established Mark Addy, it offers an excellent choice of over three dozen cheeses and several pâtés – some quite unusual – served in huge helpings with granary bread (£3.80). Other bar food includes soup (£2.50), tagliatelle and roast vegetables or ham and leek pasta bake (£3.95), ciabatta (from £4.75), salmon and cod fishcakes, cajun chicken or moussaka (£4.95), mezze (£7.95) and oriental platter (£8.95). Well kept Boddingtons, Fullers London Pride, and a guest such as Timothy Taylors Landlord on handpump, along with the Belgian wheat beer Hoegarden, and quite a few Belgian fruit beers; decent wines and a large choice of malts, friendly staff; piped jazz. There's a permanent theatre in the function room where they show temporary exhibitions of local artwork, and on bank holiday weekends the forecourt may host jazz and children's theatre. *(Recommended by Stephen, Julie and Hayley Brown, P Abbott)*

Free house ~ Licensee Phil Lees ~ Real ale ~ Bar food (12-3, 5-8.30 Mon-Thurs; 12-6 Fri-Sun) ~ Restaurant ~ (0161) 839 8646 ~ Children welcome ~ Live bands outside in summer ~ Open 11-11; 12-10.30 Sun

Lass o' Gowrie ◀ £

36 Charles Street; off Oxford Street at BBC

At weekends during term time, this traditional tiled Victorian city centre pub is so alive with good-natured university students that you might have to drink your pint on the pavement outside, and piped pop music adds to the youthful buzz. At quieter times during the day, the music might be switched off to suit an older crowd of chatty locals. Seats around a sort of glass cage give a view of the brewing process in the cellar microbrewery where they produce their LOG35 and meaty LOG42. Alongside Boddingtons and Marstons Pedigree, six other well kept real ales on handpump change weekly but might include beers from brewers such as Deuchars, Durham, Phoenix, Greene King, Goose Eye and Picks, as well as Inch's Stonehouse cask cider; it might take some while to get served at busy periods. The simple but atmospheric long bar has gas lighting and bare floorboards and lots of exposed brick work. Hop sacks are draped from the ceiling, and the bar has big windows in its richly tiled arched brown façade. Very good value bar food includes sandwiches and baked potatoes (from £1) and daily specials such as vegetable lasagne and steak and ale pie (£4.10); efficient cheery service. The snug is no smoking at lunchtime when children are allowed there; fruit machine and satellite TV. *(Recommended by Sue Holland, Dave Webster, Andy, Julie and Stuart Hawkins)*

Own brew ~ Licensee Jamie Bell ~ Real ale ~ Bar food (11-6) ~ (0161) 273 6932 ~ Open 11-11; 12-10.30 Sun; closed 25 Dec

Marble Arch ◀ £

73 Rochdale Road (A664), Ancoats; corner of Gould Street, just E of Victoria Station

The sloping mosaic floor in the bar of this Victorian city ale house can be rather disconcerting after a few pints of their well kept own brew unfined organic real ales. From windows at the back of the pub you can look out over the brewery (tours by arrangement) where they produce the distinctive hoppy Cloudy Marble, Northern Quarter, Old Lag, Uncut Amber and the seasonal brew they serve here. They also keep a good choice of bottled beers, including some Belgian Trappist ones. Given the rather ordinary exterior the beautifully preserved interior is a lovely surprise. There's a magnificently restored lightly barrel-vaulted high ceiling, and extensive marble and tiling – the frieze advertising various spirits and the chimney breast above the carved wooden mantelpiece particularly stand out. The pub is furnished with leather sofas, cushioned settles and deep armchairs, and all the walls are stripped back to the glazed brick. Good value bar food includes soup (£1.85), lots of good sandwiches including roast vegetables and olives, and mexican chicken (£2.25/hot £2.60), burgers (£3), and a few daily specials such as sausages and mash, chilli or pasta tuna bake (£3.75) and pot-roast (£5.50). Games include bar billiards, a fruit machine, and pinball; juke box. The Laurel and Hardy Preservation Society meet here on the third Wednesday of the month and show old films. There's a little garden. *(Recommended by the Didler, JP, PP, Richard Lewis, Peter F Marshall)*

Own brew ~ Licensee Christine Baldwin ~ Real ale ~ Bar food (11.30-10(8 Fri), 12-4 Sat) ~ No credit cards ~ (0161) 832 5914 ~ Open 11.30-11.30; 12-11 Sat; closed Sunday

Royal Oak £

729 Wilmslow Road, Didsbury

Unchanging over the years, this lively end-of-terrace pub is well known for its famous vast array of cheeses, rarely served in less than a pound helping and with a substantial chunk of bread and extras such as pickled onions and sweet chutney (£3.50 for a choice of two cheeses); take-away bags are provided. Well kept Banks's Mild and Original, Marstons Bitter and Pedigree and a fortnightly changing guest beer such as Otter on handpump; efficient, friendly service. Antique theatre bills and so forth cover the walls of the busy bar, where local drinkers enjoy the cosy atmosphere. There are some tables and chairs outside, and in summer, lots of hanging baskets cheer up the simple exterior. *(Recommended by Mike and Linda Hudson, Stephen, Julie and Hayley Brown)*

Marstons (W & D) ~ Manager June Brunton ~ Real ale ~ Bar food (12-2.15 Mon-Fri only, not bank hols) ~ No credit cards ~ (0161) 434 4788 ~ Open 11-11; 12-10.30 Sun; closed 25 Dec evening

MAWDESLEY SD4914 Map 7
Red Lion ⦿

Heading N on B5246 from Parbold, turn right into Maltkiln Lane at Bispham Green signpost, then keep on, bearing right after 1.6 miles into Mawdesley High Street, and thence into New Street

Lancashire Dining Pub of the Year

The splendid food in the brightly painted conservatory is what draws so many people to this otherwise busily traditional village local. Even ordinary-sounding dishes are prepared with real flair, and the quality and presentation truly are outstanding. The choice might include ravioli with prosciutto, sun-dried tomatoes and mozzarella (£4.50), warm smoked salmon and anchovy salad with seed mustard vinaigrette (£5.50), roasted bell pepper with mediterranean vegetables and mozzarella melt or delicious salmon stuffed with prawns and spinach with a tomato and cheddar glaze (£9), bass with red pepper and basil vinaigrette (£9.50), roast Goosnargh duck with honey and star anise jus (£12), and saddle of wild boar with smoked bacon crackling and game sauce (£14); excellent puddings. At lunchtimes (not Sunday) they also do bar snacks such as sandwiches (from £3.25), and there are various set menus and themed events. Booking is recommended at weekends. The colourful décor in the dining room is quite a shock after the far more conventional bar, which has wooden tables, a brick bar counter, standing timbers, a few plants, a nice old clock, and a good chatty atmosphere; a separate public bar has a TV and fruit machine. Service is friendly and particularly helpful; the landlady first worked here as a barmaid 30 years ago, and the landlord works hard to make everyone feel at home. Well kept Theakstons Best and Websters, and several well chosen wines by the glass; piped music. There are tables in a courtyard behind, and more in front – surrounded by hanging baskets and flowering tubs. The two big lions standing guard by the main door are white, rather than red (and that's not a suggestion to the local Young Farmers!) *(Recommended by Michael Doswell, Paul Boot)*

Enterprise ~ Tenants Stella Thompson and Edward Newton ~ Real ale ~ Bar food (lunchtimes only, not Sun) ~ Restaurant ~ (01704) 822208/822999 ~ Children in restaurant ~ Jazz Sun afternoon monthly and Sun evening twice monthly in summer ~ Open 12-11(10.30 Sun)

MELLOR SJ9888 Map 7
Oddfellows Arms

Heading out of Marple on the A626 towards Glossop, Mellor is the next road after the B6102, signposted off on the right at Marple Bridge; keep on for nearly 2 miles up Longhurst Lane and into Moor End Road

An absence of piped music and games, and nice open fires, encourages a cosy chatty atmosphere in the low-ceilinged flagstoned bar at this pleasantly civilised old country pub. Although those just after a drink are made perfectly welcome, most people come here for the enjoyable food which includes soup (£2), sandwiches (from £2.25), mozzarella and tomato salad (£3.95), garlic tiger prawns on ciabatta bread (£4.45), peking duck (£4.95), salads (from £5.95), daily roast or various curries (£6.45), yoghurt marinated garlic chicken or cassoulet (£7.95), steaks (from £9.95), daily specials such as marinated goats cheese on ciabatta (£4.75), baked trout with lime leaves, chilli and white wine (£7.95), brill fillet with thyme-seasoned olive oil and warmed seafood salad (£10.95), cajun swordfish steak (£11.95), and puddings (£2.95). Well kept Adnams, Flowers IPA, Marstons Pedigree and a weekly changing guest such as Shepherd Neame Spitfire on handpump served with or without a sparkler; prompt friendly service. There's a small no smoking restaurant upstairs, and a few tables out by the road. Parking can be difficult when busy. *(Recommended by Revd D Glover, Mrs P J Carroll, Stephen, Julie and Hayley Brown, Dr W J M Gissane, David Hoult, Brian and Anna Marsden)*

Free house ~ Licensee Robert Cloughley ~ Real ale ~ Bar food (12-2.30, 6.30-9.30) ~ Restaurant ~ (0161) 449 7826 ~ Children welcome lunchtime and early evening ~ Open 12-3, 5.30-11; 7-10.30 Sun

NEWTON SD6950 Map 7
Parkers Arms
B6478 7 miles N of Clitheroe

In a delightful riverside setting and definitely one of the country's best summer drinking spots, the big front garden at this pretty cream and green painted pub is charmingly set in a bowl of tree-sheltered pastures between Waddington Fell and Beatrix Fell, and has lovely unspoilt views down over the River Hodder and its valley. It's a well run place with a friendly atmosphere, and red plush button-back banquettes, a mix of new chairs and tables, stuffed animals, prints and an open fire. Beyond an arch is a similar area with sensibly placed darts, cribbage, dominoes, fruit machine, TV and discreet piped music. Well kept Boddingtons, Flowers IPA and maybe a guest such as Black Sheep on handpump, with a good range of malt whiskies and around 50 wines. Generously served and well prepared bar food might include garlic mushrooms (£3.75), steak, kidney and ale pie (£5.95), mushroom stroganoff (£6.50), seafood pancake (£7.50), chicken à la king (£7.75), 10oz sirloin (£11.50), daily specials such as battered haddock (£6.75) and bass and prawn mornay (£9.95), and puddings (£3.25); well prepared hearty breakfasts; no smoking restaurant. The menagerie of pets including pygmy goats, rabbits, guinea pigs, hens, pheasants, parrots and two playful black labradors keeps children entertained; there's also a play area. *(Recommended by Mrs P J Carrol, Margaret Dickinson, Pat and Robert Watt, Karen Eliot, A Kitchen, Jim Abbott, Sue and Bob Ward, Mrs P J Carroll)*

Whitbreads ~ Lease Barbara Clayton ~ Real ale ~ Bar food (12-9 summer, 12-2.30, 6-9; 12-9 wknds in winter) ~ Restaurant ~ (01200) 446236 ~ Children in eating area of bar and restaurant ~ Open 11-11; 12-10.30 Sun; 11-2.30, 5-11 Mon-Fri in winter ~ Bedrooms: £38S/£50S

RABY SJ3180 Map 7
Wheatsheaf ◥
From A540 heading S from Heswall, turn left into Upper Raby Road, village in about a mile; The Green, Rabymere Road

There's a good mix of customers at this popular half-timbered and whitewashed country cottage, known in the quietly picturesque village as the Thatch. The nicely rambling rooms are simply furnished with an old wall clock and homely black kitchen shelves in the cosy central bar (it can get smoky), and a nice snug formed by antique settles built in around its fine old fireplace. A second, more spacious room has upholstered wall seats around the tables, small hunting prints on the cream walls, and a smaller coal fire. Good straightforward lunchtime bar food includes soup (£2.50), sandwiches including good rare beef and a very good range of toasties (from £2.65), ploughman's (£4.75), omelettes (£5.50), chicken breast with garlic and herbs (£5.95), steak and ale pie (£6), mixed grill (£6.40) and braised knuckle of lamb (£6.95), with daily specials such as pasta of the day (£4.15), roast of the day (£5.95) and poached salmon (£8.95). Expect to wait when busy. The spacious restaurant (with more elaborate evening menu) is in a converted cowshed that leads into a larger no smoking conservatory; piped music is played in these areas only. A good choice of up to eight real ales on handpump includes Cains, Greene King Old Speckled Hen, Tetleys, Theakstons Best, Old Peculier and XB, Thwaites Best and three or four weekly guests such as Dent Aviator, Triple fff Stairway to Heaven and Weetwood Old Dog, and a good choice of malt whiskies. There are picnic-sets on the refurbished patio and in the pleasant garden behind, with more seats out front.

(Recommended by D Bryan, John Watson, MLR, Pat and Tony Hinkins, MH, BD, Olive and Ray Hebson, Liz Bell, Michael Buchanan)

Free house ~ Licensee Thomas Charlesworth ~ Real ale ~ Bar food (lunchtime only) ~ Restaurant (evenings 6-9.15, Tues-Sat; not Sun and Mon) ~ (0151) 336 3416 ~ Children in eating area of bar, conservatory and restaurant ~ Open 11.30-11; 12-10.30 Sun

RIBCHESTER SD6435 Map 7
White Bull 🍺

Church Street; turn off B6245 at sharp corner by Black Bull

Set in an interesting Roman village by the River Ribble, this early 18th-c stone dining pub has an entrance porch supported by Tuscan pillars that have stood here or nearby for nearly 2,000 years. There are also remains of a Roman bath house scattered behind the pub, and there's a small Roman museum nearby. Inside, the spacious and attractively refurbished main bar has comfortable old settles, Victorian advertisements and various prints, and a stuffed fox in two halves that looks as if it's jumping through the wall. Most areas are set out for eating during the day, and in summer you can also eat out in the garden behind; the dining area is no smoking. Good reasonably priced bar food includes soup (£1.90), open sandwiches (from £3.45), spicy chicken pieces (£3.45), ploughman's, steak and kidney pie and meat or vegetable lasagne (£5.50), grilled lamb chops (£6.95), various steaks with a choice of toppings (from £7.95), specials such as braised beef with celery, herbs and beer sauce or poached salmon and tarragon omelette (£6.25) and puddings such as fruit crumble and bread and butter pudding (£2.65); children's menu. Well kept Boddingtons, Flowers and a couple of guests such as Black Sheep and Wadworths 6X on handpump, several wines, and a good range of malt whiskies; they also do coffees, tea, and hot chocolate. Service remains friendly and efficient even when it gets busy (it may be advisable to get there early or book); darts, TV, pool, juke box, and dominoes in the games room; piped music. This is a quiet village, and the clean and comfortable good value bedrooms here make this an enjoyable place to stay. *(Recommended by Rob Fowell, Robert and Margaret Whelband, Dr Paull Khan, JES, Pat and Dick Warwick)*

Whitbreads ~ Lease Neil Sandiford ~ Real ale ~ Bar food (11.30-2, 6.30-9.30;12-8 Sun; not Mon evening) ~ Restaurant ~ (01254) 878303 ~ Children in eating area of bar and restaurant ~ Open 11.30-3, 6.30-11; 12-10.30 Sun ~ Bedrooms: £30.50S/£40.50S(£46B)

STALYBRIDGE SJ9698 Map 7
Station Buffet 🍴 £

An impressive range of up to 20 guest ales a week passes through the eight handpumps on the marble-topped counter of this friendly classic Victorian platform bar, and they reckon to have sold over 3000 different brews since they opened again in 1996. Boddingtons, Flowers IPA and Wadworths 6X are on all the time, and such is their reputation for showcasing new real ales, they are approached all the time by interesting little microbreweries to stock the latest new brews. They also have farm cider, Belgian and other foreign bottled beers, and good beer festivals in early May and late November. Not smart but comfortably nostalgic, the bar has a welcoming fire below an etched-glass mirror, newspapers and magazines to read, old photographs of the station in its heyday and other railway memorabilia, and there's even a little conservatory. An extension along the platform leads into what was the ladies' waiting room and part of the station-master's quarters, with original ornate ceilings and a dining/function room with Victorian-style wallpaper; dominoes, cribbage, draughts. On a sunny day you can sit out on the platform. As well as good coffee and tea made freshly by the pot, there are cheap old-fashioned snacks such as black peas (50p), sandwiches (from £1.40), and three or four daily specials such as an all day breakfast, bacon casserole and a home-made pie with peas (£2-£3). They have candlelit folk evenings on Saturdays. *(Recommended by Bernie Adams, JP, PP, Mike and Wendy Proctor, the Didler, Peter Edwards, Richard Lewis, Tony Hobden, Paul Boot)*

Free house ~ Licensees John Hesketh and Sylvia Wood ~ Real ale ~ Bar food (12-9) ~ Restaurant ~ (0161) 303 0007 ~ Children welcome till 9pm ~ Candlelit folk music Sat evenings ~ Open 11-11; 12-10.30 Sun; closed 25 Dec

UPPERMILL SD9905 Map 7
Church Inn ⬛ £

From the main street (A607), look out for the sign for Saddleworth Church, and turn off up this steep narrow lane – keep on up!

This ancient pub manages to be smart and comfortable without losing any of the real local character that you'd expect from its remote setting alone on a steep moorland slope by an isolated church. They brew their own attractively priced Saddleworth ales here, including Saddleworth More, More Gold, Ayrtons, Bert Corner, Hopsmacker, Pete's Dragon and Shaftbender, with seasonal ales. The head brewer is obviously inspired by his output because if you're really lucky you'll catch him and his fellow morris dancers practising their moves in the garden. They also keep a couple of Scottish Courage guest beers on handpump, a good choice of wines, several malt whiskies and a farm cider. The big unspoilt L-shaped main bar has high beams and some stripped stone; one window at the end of the bar counter looks down over the valley, and there's also a valley view from the quieter no smoking dining room. The comfortable furnishings include settles and pews as well as a good individual mix of chairs, and there are lots of attractive prints, Staffordshire and other china on a high delft shelf, jugs, brasses and so forth. The quirkiness doesn't end with the morris men head here either. The horse-collar on the wall is worn by the winner of their annual gurning (or face-pulling) championship (part of the lively Rush Cart Festival, usually held over the August bank holiday), and handbells here are the church bellringers' practice set. There's a particularly warm welcome for both children and dogs (if the dogs dare to brave an ever-increasing army of rescued cats). A decent range of good value food includes soup (£1.65), sandwiches (from £2.95), pâté (£2.95), steak and ale pie (£5.25), half roast chicken (£5.25), mixed grill (£11.50) and daily specials such as a pasta dish (£5.25), hawaiian-style gammon (£5.75) and puddings such as trifle, chocolate fudge cake and jam roly poly (£2). Outside there are seats on a small terrace facing up towards the moors, with more out in a garden – and anything from rabbits, ducks and geese to horses and a couple of peacocks; occasional unobtrusive piped music. *(Recommended by Tony Hobden, JP, PP, Richard Lewis, K C and B Forman)*

Own brew ~ Licensee Julian Taylor ~ Real ale ~ Bar food (12-2.30, 5.30-9; 12-9 wknds) ~ Restaurant ~ (01457) 820902 ~ Children welcome ~ Open 12-11; 12-10.30 Sun

WHARLES SD4435 Map 7
Eagle & Child

Church Road; from B5269 W of Broughton turn left into Higham Side Road at HMS Inskip sign

Time stands still at this unchanging thatched ale house. There's a welcoming relaxed atmosphere, and even when it's not particularly cold, there should be a good fire burning in the intricate cast-iron stove. It's filled with the friendly landlord's marvellous collection of antique furniture, with the most interesting in the L-shaped bar, where a beamed area round the corner past the counter has a magnificent, elaborately carved Jacobean settle which originally came from Aston Hall in Birmingham, and carries the motto *exaltavit humiles*. There's also a carved oak chimneypiece, and a couple of fine longcase clocks, one from Chester, and another with a nicely painted face and an almost silent movement from Manchester. The plain cream walls are hung with modern advertising mirrors and some older mirrors, and there are a few exotic knives, carpentry tools and so forth on the plastered structural beams. Beers change all the time but might include Charles Wells Eagle and Mansfield Riding on handpump; darts in a sensible side area, pool, fruit machine, TV, friendly cat. One or two picnic-sets outside. *(Recommended by Kevin Blake, Ian and Nita Cooper)*

Free house ~ Licensee Brian Tatham ~ Real ale ~ (01772) 690312 ~ Open 7-11; 12-4, 7-10.30 Sun

WHITEWELL SD6546 Map 7
Inn at Whitewell ★★ 🍴 🍷 🛏

Most easily reached by B6246 from Whalley; road through Dunsop Bridge from B6478 is also good

Set deep in the Forest of Bowland, this enduringly popular hotel is surrounded by well wooded rolling hills set off against higher moors, and is perhaps most dramatically approached from Abbeystead. The hotel owns several miles of trout, salmon and sea trout fishing on the Hodder, and with notice they'll arrange shooting. All the spacious bedrooms are very well appointed with good bathrooms, CD players, and even some with their own peat fires in winter. The interior is impressively furnished: the old-fashioned pubby bar has antique settles, oak gateleg tables, sonorous clocks, old cricketing and sporting prints, log fires (the lounge has a very attractive stone fireplace), and heavy curtains on sturdy wooden rails; one area has a selection of newspapers, dominoes, local maps and guide books, there's a piano for anyone who wants to play, and even an art gallery. Although it gets very busy, it's spacious inside and out, so usually remains tranquil and relaxing. Well liked bar food includes soup (£3.20), open sandwiches (from £3.90), toasted walnut brioche (£5), seafood chowder (£5.50), grilled Norfolk kipper (£6.50), fish and chips (£7.80), fish pie (£8.40), warm spinach and ricotta tartlet (£9), fried lambs kidneys (£11), home-made puddings such as sticky toffee pudding and home-made honeycomb and butterscotch ice cream (£3.50) and hand-made farmhouse cheeses (from £3.50); the evening menu is slightly different. Very polite staff serve coffee and cream teas all day – you can buy jars of the home-made jam (from £1.50). Well kept Boddingtons and Marstons Pedigree on handpump, and around 180 wines – including a highly recommended claret. Down a corridor with strange objects like a stuffed fox disappearing into the wall is the pleasant suntrap garden, with wonderful views down to the valley. *(Recommended by Vicky and David Sarti, P Abbott, Paul Craddock, R L Gorick, Nigel Woolliscroft, Andy, Julie and Stuart Hawkins, Steve Whalley, Jenny and Chris Wilson, J F M and M West, Revd D Glover, Anthony Longden, K C and B Forman, Comus and Sarah Elliott, Mrs P J Carroll, Sue and Bob Ward, P J Holt: also in* The Good Hotel Guide*)*

Free house ~ Licensee Richard Bowman ~ Real ale ~ Bar food ~ Restaurant ~ (01200) 448222 ~ Children welcome ~ Open 11-3, 6-11; 12-2, 7-10.30 Sun ~ Bedrooms: £83B/£99B

YEALAND CONYERS SD5074 Map 7
New Inn

3 miles from M6 junction 35; village signposted off A6

The simply furnished little beamed bar on the left as you go into this homely ivy-covered stone building has a cosy village atmosphere, with a log fire in the big stone fireplace, cribbage and dominoes. On the right, two communicating no smoking cottagey dining rooms have dark blue furniture, shiny beams and an attractive kitchen range. Robinsons, Frederics and Hartleys XB and Robinsons seasonal beer on handpump, around 30 malt whiskies, winter mulled wine and home-made lemonade in summer; piped music can be obtrusive. When busy, there may be a wait for the good value bar food which includes soup (£2.60), sandwiches (from £2.95), satay mushrooms (£3.50), filled baked potatoes (from £3.60), filled baguettes (from £3.95), spicy mexican bean pot (£5.50), liver and onions (£5.95), stuffed mushrooms (£7.20), chicken breast with thyme and autumn fruits or pie of the day (£7.25), beef in beer (£7.95); puddings (from £2.95). A sheltered lawn at the side has picnic-sets among roses and flowering shrubs. There are plans to convert the old barn into bedrooms. *(Recommended by Mike Cowley, Helen Coster, Paul Boot, Tony Middis, Revd D Glover, Mike and Wendy Proctor, Roy and Margaret Jones, Gordon, Mike Tucker, Fred and Lorraine Gill, Roger Everett, P J Holt, Eric Locker, W K Wood, D Bryan)*

Robinsons ~ Tenants David and Jan Wrigley ~ Real ale ~ Bar food 11.30(12 Sun)-
9.30) ~ Restaurant ~ (01524) 732938 ~ Children welcome ~ Open 11-11; 12-10.30
Sun

Lucky Dip

Besides the fully inspected pubs, you might like to try these Lucky Dips recommended to us
and described by readers (if you do, please send us reports: www.goodguides.com).

Adlington [SD6114]
Bay Horse [Babylon Lane, Heath Charnock]:
Olde-worlde country pub, popular with
walkers, family atmosphere, enjoyable food
from baked beans on toast to full restaurant
meals, well kept Greenalls, decent wines, very
friendly landlady who'll try to cook what you
want even if it's not on the menu, log fires in
cosy bar; extensive crown bowling green
behind, open all day, children welcome, spotless
good value bedrooms, good hearty breakfast
(D L Woska, C Johnson)
Affetside [SD7513]
Pack Horse [Watling St]: Attractive neatly kept
moorland local on Roman road, snug pool
room, well kept Hydes ale, big helpings of
lunchtime bar food, restaurant; good walking
country *(P Abbott)*
Arkholme [SD5872]
Bay Horse [B6254 Carnforth—Kirkby
Lonsdale]: Attractive neatly kept old country
local, lovely inglenook, good pictures of long-
lost London pubs, popular food inc good value
sandwiches, well kept Bass, Boddingtons and
Wadworths 6X; own bowling green, charming
valley handy for Lune Valley walks *(Mr and
Mrs A Hills, Margaret Dickinson)*
Bacup [SD8623]
Queens [Yorkshire St]: Unspoilt, with back
main bar, homely front room on left with coal
fire, darts, cards, dominoes and shove-
ha'penny, friendly efficient service, well kept
John Smiths, pool on right *(Pete Baker)*
Barton [SD5137]
Fox [A6 N of Broughton]: Vintage Inn well
done as quaint traditional tavern, roomy
quarry-tiled bar, adages chalked on beams, logs
propping door open, emphasis on well
presented and tasty if not cheap food with
plenty of well spaced tables, helpful well trained
young staff, Bass beers, decent wines; opp good
plant nursery *(Margaret Dickinson)*
Bay Horse [SD4952]
☆ *Bay Horse* [just off A6 Galgate—Forton, S of
M6 junction 33]: Locally popular upmarket
dining pub down a quiet road, very good well
presented food from unusual sandwiches to
imaginative main courses inc fresh fish, booking
recommended; warm cosy atmosphere in
attractive red-painted bar with comfortable
cushioned wall-seats, well kept Everards
Beacon, Tetleys and Wadworths 6X, country
wines, lovely fires in bar and no smoking dining
room, relaxed atmosphere, helpful attentive
staff, piped music; peaceful garden *(Margaret
Dickinson, R L Gorick, Karen Eliot, BB)*
Belmont [SD6915]
Wrights Arms: Large but cosy, high on the

moors, enjoyable bar food such as hot beef
sandwiches and home-made meatballs, well
kept Tetleys, separate large restaurant;
children's play area behind *(Andy, Julie and
Stuart Hawkins)*
Birkenhead [SJ3289]
Crown [Conway St]: Multi-room town
alehouse with interesting tilework, up to a
dozen changing ales inc Cains, Greenalls and
Jennings, Weston's farm cider, good basic food,
low prices; open all day, cl Sun lunchtime *(the
Didler)*
Dispensary [Chester St]: Taken over and
renamed by Cains, with their beers, handsome
glass ceiling, good value lunchtime food; handy
for ferry *(the Didler)*
Stork [Price St]: Early 19th-c, beautifully cleaned
up without being spoilt; Threlfalls tiled façade,
four rooms around island bar, polished original
floor, old dock and ferry photographs, wkdy
lunches; open all day (not Sun) *(the Didler)*
Bispham [SD3140]
Old England [Red Bank Rd]: Thriving young
atmosphere; pool *(Abi Benson)*
Squirrel [Bispham Rd]: Low-priced food from
sandwiches to Toby carvery *(Abi Benson)*
Blackburn [SD6830]
Royal Oak [Royal Oak Ave/Pleckgate Rd
(B6233), nr A6119 ring rd]: Remarkably
peaceful surroundings considering nearby ring
road and town centre, spotless 18th-c pub with
good choice of beers and wines, welcoming
licensees, good value home cooking, proper
tablecloths, brass on beams *(William Ball)*
Blacko [SD8541]
☆ *Moorcock* [A682 towards Gisburn (and in fact
over the Yorkshire border)]: Beautifully placed
moorland dining pub, roomy and comfortable,
with big picture windows for breathtaking
views, tables set close for the huge range of
popular and often enterprising food inc lamb
from their own flock, excellent beef and some
German dishes, very friendly helpful staff,
decent wine, Thwaites Bitter and Mild under
top pressure; tables in hillside garden with
various animals, open all day for food Sun,
children and dogs welcome, bedrooms *(John
Watson, Steve Whalley, B Blaine, LYM)*
Blackpool [SD3035]
Bispham [Red Bank Rd]: Large very
comfortable lounge area, lively atmosphere,
simple good value bar food lunchtime and early
evening, well kept very well priced Sam Smiths
bitter *(Dr and Mrs A K Clarke, Abi Benson)*
Halfway House [St Annes Rd (A584), Squires
Gate]: Friendly Victorian-style John Barras pub,
well kept beer *(Dr and Mrs A K Clarke, Abi
Benson)*

No 3 [2 Whitegate Drive]: Large popular local, cosy seating in one part, good value upmarket food, larger more open area has wknd DJ *(Andy, Julie and Stuart Hawkins)*

Pump & Truncheon [Bonny St]: Real-ale pub opp police HQ, dark bare boards, blackboards with old jokes, good range of ales, lunchtime food, occasional beer festivals *(Dr and Mrs A K Clarke, Abi Benson)*

Saddle [Whitegate Dr, Marton]: Popular refurbished local with two rooms off small bar, lots of old prints and photographs, well kept ales inc Bass, good value food, good atmosphere; busy Easter beer festival with marquee extension *(Andy, Julie and Stuart Hawkins, Abi Benson)*

Bolton [SD7109]

Olde Man & Scythe [Churchgate]: Interesting old pub with cellar dating from 12th c, lively corridor-style drinking area, two quieter rooms popular for good value lunchtime food from sandwiches up, Flowers, Holts and Wadworths 6X, two or more farm ciders; handy for shopping area *(Andy and Jill Kassube)*

Spinning Mule [Nelson Sq]: Typical smart Wetherspoons, usual good choice of real ales and new world wines, decent coffee, reasonably priced food all day *(Andy and Jill Kassube)*

Broughton [SD4838]

☆ *Plough at Eaves* [A6 N through Broughton, 1st left about a mile after traffic lights]: Two very low-beamed carpeted bars, friendly and good value, with enjoyable food, well kept Thwaites ales, lots of malt whiskies, old-fashioned charm; darts, pool and other games, piped music; tables outside, well equipped play area *(Margaret Dickinson, LYM, Mike and Alison Leyland)*

Burnley [SD8728]

Ram [Burnley Rd, Cliviger]: One of the new breed of ultra-traditional Vintage Inns, with decent food, well kept Bass, good house wine range, log fires, no music or machines *(anon)*

Bury [SD8115]

☆ *Lord Raglan* [Mount Pleasant, Nangreaves; off A56/A666 N under a mile E of M66 junction 1, down cobbled track]: Welcoming friendly ivy-covered cottage row in lonely moorside location, with great views, and now brewing its own good Leydens Raglan Sleeve and Nanny Flyer; carefully made food from sandwiches to good meals using fresh ingredients inc a monthly diners' club, good service, good wines and interesting foreign bottled beers, lots of bric-a-brac in traditional front bar, big open fire in cosy back room, plainer blond-panelled dining room (where children allowed; crudités as you wait to go in) *(LYM, John and Sylvia Harrop, P Abbott)*

Carnforth [SD4970]

County Hotel [Lancaster Rd (A6)]: Neatly kept hotel, recently bought by Mitchells and well used by locals; reliable food from good sandwiches to restaurant meals *(Margaret Dickinson)*

Cheadle Hulme [SJ8787]

Hesketh [Hulme Hall Rd]: Comfortable open-plan pub with raised area one end, food servery the other end with good value piping hot food; well kept Marstons Pedigree, Theakstons Best and Old Peculier, friendly attentive service *(Mr and Mrs C Roberts)*

Chipping [SD6243]

Sun [Windy St]: Charming stone-built country local with three small snug rooms, food inc home-made pies, well kept Boddingtons (an underground stream cools the cellar), open fire, papers and magazines, pool, darts; attractive village *(Margaret Dickinson)*

Churchtown [SD4843]

☆ *Punch Bowl* [Church St, off A586 Garstang—St Michaels-on-Wyre]: Good choice of good food in attractive mock-Tudor beamed pub/restaurant with three small quaint bar rooms, panelling, stained glass, lots of stuffed animals, dining rooms; friendly staff, well kept Tetleys, good fires; disabled facilities, lovely village *(anon)*

Conder Green [SD4655]

Thurnham Mill Hotel [signed off A588 just S]: Former early 19th-c stone-built mill, comfortable beamed and flagstoned bar with good bar food, lots of whiskies, friendly staff and log fires, restaurant overlooking Lancaster Canal lock, tables out on terrace; comfortable bedrooms, good breakfast, open all day *(Lisa and Carl Henshaw)*

Cowling [SD5917]

Prince of Wales [Cowling Brow]: Consistently well kept Jennings ales and a guest beer, congenial surroundings, snug with coal fire, daily papers, friendly landlord *(Alison Mesher)*

Croston [SD4818]

Wheatsheaf [Town Rd]: Nice décor, hops and fresh flowers, stripped boards, generous food worth waiting for, well kept weekly guest beers, no smoking area *(Margaret Dickinson)*

Delph [SD9807]

Old Bell [Huddersfield Rd (A62)]: Former coaching inn, enjoyable restaurant food with seafood emphasis, good choice of beers such as Boddingtons and Timothy Taylors Landlord, friendly efficient service, comfortable bar, pleasant décor *(Roger Jones)*

☆ *Royal Oak* [off A6052 about 100 yds W of White Lion, turn up steep Lodge Lane and keep on up into Broad Lane]: Opp old moorland church in steep narrow winding lane, great views of surrounding valleys, real fires in three small rooms, comfortable solid furniture, appetising home-made food Fri-Sun evenings, particularly well kept ales such as Boddingtons, Moorhouses and Hook Norton Old Hooky, very friendly welcome; opens 7, cl lunchtime exc Sun *(Richard Houghton)*

Dunham Town [SJ7488]

Axe & Cleaver [School Lane]: Big 19th-c country house knocked into spacious open-plan family dining pub, good range of good plentiful (if not particularly cheap) food, well kept Scottish Courage ales, efficient friendly service, conservatory; piped music, air conditioning (can be too cool); garden with play area and maybe bouncy castle, handy for nearby Dunham Massey Hall *(Mrs P J Carroll, Mike and Wena Stevenson, R Davies)*

☆ *Vine* [Barns Lane, Dunham Massey]: Friendly and old-fashioned small-roomed local handy for the park, beamery and brass-topped tables, well kept cheap Sam Smiths, enjoyable food inc some interesting dishes; darts, quiet piped music, dogs welcome; plenty of tables in garden *(John Watson, Ian Phillips)*

Eccles [SJ7798]

Grapes [Liverpool Rd, Peel Green; A57 ½ mile from M63 junction 2]: Classic Edwardian local with superb glass and tiling, lots of mahogany, brilliant staircase, cheap Holts Bitter and Mild, fairly quiet roomy lounge and smoke room, pool room, vault with Manchester darts (can get quite loud and smoky), drinking corridor; open all day *(Pete Baker, the Didler)*

Lamb [Regent St (A57)]: Gorgeous untouched Edwardian three-room local with splendid etched windows, fine woodwork, tiling and furnishings, admirable trophies in display case; cheap well kept Holts Bitter and Mild, full-size snooker table; popular with older people *(GLD, the Didler)*

Royal Oak [Barton Lane]: Large unspoilt sidestreet local, several rooms, superb tilework, cheap Holts Bitter and Mild *(the Didler)*

Stanley Arms [Eliza Ann St/Liverpool Rd (A57), Patricroft]: Busy mid-Victorian corner local with cheap Holts Bitter and Mild, lunchtime sandwiches, popular front bar, hatch serving two back rooms, drinking corridor *(the Didler)*

White Lion [Liverpool Rd, Patricroft, a mile from M63 junction 2]: Classic welcoming Edwardian local, clean, tidy and popular with older people, with games in lively traditional public bar, tiled side drinking corridor with separate smoke room (wknd pianist) and quiet lounge off, great value Holts Bitter and Mild *(Pete Baker)*

Eccleston [SD5117]

Farmers Arms [Towngate (B5250, off A581 Chorley—Southport)]: Big friendly low-beamed pub/restaurant, wide choice of consistently good generous food all day, not cheap but good value; modernised but keeping character – black cottagey furniture, red plush wall seats, rough plaster covered with plates, pastoral prints, clocks and brasses; well kept Tetleys with a guest such as Brains SA, helpful service, darts; parking can be a problem when busy; good value bedrooms *(Derek Stafford)*

Edgworth [SD7316]

Black Bull [Bolton Rd, Turton]: Three-room pub with Jennings, Theakstons Bitter and Mild and guest beers such as Moorhouses Pendle Witches Brew or Charles Wells Bombardier, enjoyable food from sandwiches, baguettes and good home-made soup to hearty main dishes (all day wknds; not Mon), open fire, very friendly landlord, lovely summer floral displays; live music Thurs, Tues quiz night, moorside village, good walks *(Michael Buchanan)*

Egerton [SD7015]

Cross Guns [Blackburn Rd (A666)]: Good choice of sensibly priced bar food inc enjoyable hot sandwiches, children welcome in dining area, up to five real ales, friendly service *(Andy and Jill Kassube)*

Flag [Hardmans Lane/Arnold Rd]: Up to nine particularly well kept real ales, often inc local Bank Top; simple reasonably priced food *(Andy and Jill Kassube)*

Fence [SD8337]

Bay Horse [Wheatley Lane Rd, Higham]: Small and friendly, with well kept Marstons Pedigree, Theakstons and Charles Wells Bombardier, efficient service, good restaurant *(Alan J Morton)*

Fleetwood [SD3247]

North Euston [Esplanade, nr tram terminus]: Big comfortably refurbished bar in architecturally interesting Victorian hotel overlooking seafront, long railway connections; decent lunchtime food esp in coffee bar, wide range of well kept mainstream real ales, consistently good service, no smoking family area (till 7), seats outside; comfortable bedrooms, open all day *(Abi Benson)*

Garstang [SD4944]

Bradbeer Bar [Garstang Country Hotel & Golf Club; B6430 SJ]: Relaxed and spacious bar overlooking golfing greens, helpful well trained staff, huge woodburner, very good value imaginative food; tables outside, bedrooms *(Margaret Dickinson)*

Crofters [A6 bypass]: Comfortable neatly kept modern roadside hotel, pleasant roomy bar with good choice of reliable bar food, Mitchells ales; seats outside, bedrooms *(Margaret Dickinson)*

☆ *Royal Oak* [Market Pl]: Typical small-town inn, cosy yet roomy and comfortably refurbished, with attractive panelling, several eating areas inc charming snug, generous above-average food (all day Sun) inc imaginatively presented specials, small helpings of any dish for children or OAPs, pleasant staff, Hartleys and Robinsons, good value coffee; main bar can be smoky; restaurant, disabled access, comfortable bedrooms, open all day Sun *(Margaret Dickinson, Malcolm Taylor)*

Glasson [SD4456]

Victoria: Popular dining pub by harbour, reliable food inc lots of fresh fish, Mitchells beers, pleasant efficient staff *(Margaret Dickinson)*

Golborne [SJ5998]

Railway Hotel [High St]: Comfortable, friendly and unpretentious local brewing its own Hop House Bitter, other well kept beers; bedrooms, open all day *(Richard Houghton)*

Goosnargh [SD5537]

Bushells Arms [4 miles from M6 junction 32; turn right off A6 in Broughton, then left to Goosnargh in Whittingham]: The Bests who have made this neat largely no smoking dining pub so popular with readers, with consistently high standards over many years, left just as we were going to press – obviously too soon to say anything about the new regime; reports please *(LYM)*

Grapes [Church Lane]: Welcoming local with two low-beamed areas separated by big coal fire, lots of brass around this, collection of whisky-water jugs and old telephones, usual food inc sandwiches and good Sun roast, friendly staff, well kept changing ales such as Boddingtons, Harts Cleos Asp, Sarahs Hophouse, Tetleys Bitter and Mild and Theakstons Best, separate games room with darts and pool *(Steve Whalley, R L Gorick, Rona Murdoch)*

Greasby [SJ2587]

☆ *Greave Dunning* [Greasby Rd (off B5139)]: Extended pub with honest cheap food proving very popular under friendly new manager, good range of well kept beers, good service, cosy lace-curtained snugs off flagstoned locals' bar, lofty main lounge with upper food gallery *(Philip Hastain, Dawn Baddeley, LYM, E G Parish)*

Haggate [SD8835]

Horse & Hounds [Halifax Rd, Briercliffe; NE of Burnley]: Food inc good value huge baguettes with lots of chips, moor and valley views *(A Preston)*

Hawk Green [SJ9687]

☆ *Crown* [just S of Marple]: Wide choice of food in lively and spacious bar and well laid out restaurant in barn extension, very good value OAP lunch, well kept Robinsons, good friendly service; open all day Sun, handy for canal *(R Davies)*

Helmshore [SD7821]

White Horse [Holcombe Rd]: Big stone-built inn opened into large sympathetically modernised low-ceilinged lounge bar, the big tables set for dining but plenty of people just enjoying the well kept Boddingtons and Timothy Taylors Landlord; Irwell valley views from the front *(Steve Whalley)*

Hest Bank [SD4666]

☆ *Hest Bank Hotel* [Hest Bank Lane; off A6 just N of Lancaster]: Picturesque and welcoming three bar coaching inn, good for families, with wide range of good freshly made generous food (served all day) from sandwiches through fresh local fish and potted shrimps to busy all-day Sun carvery, also children's dishes, bargain set menus and special food nights, well kept ales such as Boddingtons, Robinsons, Timothy Taylors Landlord and a changing guest such as Good Honest't'ales Lady Godiva, decent wines, friendly efficient service, idiosyncratic cartoons of licensees, separate restaurant area, lively history, Weds quiz night; plenty of tables in garden beside Lancaster canal, attractive setting close to Morecambe Bay *(P A Legon, Margaret Dickinson, Andy and Jill Kassube, BB)*

Heywood [SD8510]

Wishing Well [York St (A58)]: Warm welcome, good cheap food from hot filled muffins and toasties to bargain main dishes, up to ten well kept real ales such as Phoenix *(Andy and Jill Kassube)*

Knott End-on-Sea [SD3548]

Bourne Arms [Bourne May Rd]: Large helpings of reasonably priced food inc Sun lunch, Boddingtons and Flowers IPA, interesting pictures and model boat; open all day, by seasonal Fleetwood passenger ferry *(Abi Benson)*

Leyland [SD5422]

Midge Hall [Midge Hall Lane]: Very popular for good value straightforward food from sandwiches and baked potatoes up, obliging friendly staff, Tetleys; children welcome, some live music, seats outside *(Margaret Dickinson)*

Limbrick [SD6016]

Black Horse [off A6 at Adlington; Long Lane]: Tastefully restored old-world up-and-down low-ceilinged stone-built pub, the first recorded in Lancs (1577); well kept Theakstons Best and XB, coal fires, friendly service, decent food; garden behind, handy for West Pennine country park, open all day *(Peter Heaton)*

Liverpool [SJ4395]

Cains Brewery Tap [Stanhope St]: Splendidly restored Victorian architecture with nicely understated décor, wooden floors, plush raised side snug, lots of old prints and breweriana, wonderful bar, flame-effect gas fire, newspapers; cosy relaxing atmosphere, friendly efficient staff, good well priced food, and above all four well kept attractively priced Cains ales with four guest beers from other small breweries; popular brewery tour ending here with buffet and singing; sports TV, open all day *(the Didler, JP, PP)*

Carnarvon Castle [Tarleton St]: Neat and welcoming city-centre pub next to main shopping area; long and narrow, with one main bar and back lounge, cabinet of Dinky toys, well kept Bass, Cains Bitter and Mild, lunchtime bar snacks; open all day, cl Sun *(the Didler, Dr and Mrs A K Clarke, John A Barker)*

Cracke [Rice St]: Attractively basic, bare boards, walls covered with posters for local events and pictures of local buildings, unusual Beatles diorama in largest room, juke box and TV, very cheap lunchtime food and Thurs curry night, well kept Cains, Marstons Pedigree and guest beers; popular mainly with young people; open all day, sizeable garden *(JP, PP, the Didler, Mr and Mrs S Mason)*

☆ *Dispensary* [Renshaw St; formerly the Grapes]: Small pub well refurbished by Cains in unpretentious Victorian style, lots of polished wood and glass inc marvellous etched windows, full range of their ales inc Dark Mild, Best and FX, also three or four interesting guest beers, bare boards, comfortable raised back bar, Victorian medicine bottles and instruments; decent wkdy food 12-7, friendly staff, open all day *(Edward Leetham, the Didler, George Little, MLR, Richard Houghton, John A Barker, Mark and Diane Grist, Rev John Hibberd)*

☆ *Doctor Duncan* [St Johns Lane]: Classic Victorian pub revived by Cains, their beers and guest ales kept well, enjoyable reasonably priced food till 7, friendly staff, no smoking area; open all day *(the Didler, Peter F Marshall)*

Everyman Bistro [Hope St, below Everyman Theatre]: Low-ceilinged tile-floor clattery basement, three well kept ales such as Black Sheep, Cains and Hanby Cascade, side room with well priced food inc wide and imaginative vegetarian choice and good school puddings, lights dimmed at 9; no smoking area *(G Coates, John A Barker)*

Excelsior [Dale St]: Good value Porterhouse food 11-6 (and breakfast from 9), Cains Bitter and Mild and guest beers; open all day, cl Sun *(the Didler)*

Globe [Cases St]: Welcoming well appointed traditional local, pleasant staff, well kept Cains Bitter and Dark Mild and Tetleys, good port, lunchtime filled baps, tiny sloping-floor back lounge, lots of prints of old Liverpool; open all day *(JP, PP, John A Barker, the Didler)*

Grapes [Mathew St]: Lively and friendly, with well kept Cains and Tetleys, good value lunchtime bar food, open-plan but pleasantly well worn cottagey décor (flagstones, old range, wall settles, no two chairs the same, gas-effect lamps); open all day, can get crowded Fri/Sat, cl Sun *(the Didler, John A Barker, JP, PP)*

Lion [Moorfields, off Tithebarn St]: Splendidly preserved ornate Victorian alehouse, etched glass and serving hatches in central bar, two small lounges off, unusual wallpaper, big mirrors, panelling and tilework, fine domed structure behind, well kept Lees, Timothy Taylor and Walkers, cheap lunchtime food; open all day *(the Didler)*

Midland [Ranelagh St]: Attractive and neatly kept Victorian pub with original décor, ornate lounge, long corner bar, nice etched glass and mirrors, Tetleys; can be noisy *(John A Barker, the Didler)*

Pacific [Temple St]: Modern bar with good well presented food such as dim sum starters and mussels in red thai stew, good service *(Mr and Mrs S Mason)*

Peter Kavanaghs [Egerton St, off Catherine St]: Well kept Cains, Greene King Abbot and guest beers in side-street local with plenty of character; open all day *(the Didler)*

Poste House [Cumberland St]: Small comfortable backstreet local with room upstairs, well kept Cains Bitter and Mild, good wkdy lunches, friendly licensees *(the Didler)*

Prince Arthur [Rice Lane]: Unspoilt Victorian alehouse, busy and friendly, well kept Walkers *(the Didler, JP, PP)*

☆ *Pump House* [Albert Dock]: Multi-level dock building conversion, good Mersey views, lots of polished dark wood, bare bricks, mezzanine and upper gallery with exposed roof trusses; marble counter with bulbous beer engines and brass rail supported by elephants' heads, tall chimney; wide choice of generous cheeses, some hot food, friendly efficient service; waterside tables, boat trips in season; keg beers, busy wknd evenings *(Margaret and Roy Randle)*

Roscoe Head [Roscoe St]: Three tiny unspoilt rooms, friendly, quiet and civilised, with outstandingly well kept Jennings and Greene King Old Speckled Hen, good value wkdy lunches, huge and growing tie collection; open all day *(the Didler)*

Ship & Mitre [Dale St]: Friendly gaslit local with very wide changing choice of well kept unusual beers served in over-sized lined glasses, good cheap basic lunches, pool, occasional beer festivals; open all day *(the Didler)*

Vernon Arms [Dale St]: Tap for Liverpool Brewery with six of their beers in top condition,

pleasant service, good value meals till 7; open all day, cl Sun *(the Didler)*

Vines [Lime St]: Big traditional pub, comfortable and friendly, with mosaic tilework, high-ceilinged room on right with stained glass; may not always have real ale, can get very busy *(the Didler, JP, PP)*

White Star [Rainford Gdns, off Matthew St]: Traditional basic local with well kept Cains and other beers such as Shepherd Neame, lots of woodwork, magnificent Bass mirror in back room, prints, White Star shipping line memorabilia, friendly service; SkyTV; open all day *(the Didler)*

Willowbank [Smithdown Rd, Toxteth]: Good straightforward food, well kept Cains and excellent range of guest beers, good selection of wines by the quarter-bottle *(Mr and Mrs S Mason)*

Longton [SD4726]

Dolphin [lane to Longton Marsh]: Busy family pub with good cheap food served 12-8 from sandwiches and baked potatoes to Sun roasts, pleasant speedy service; lots of tables out behind with good play area *(Margaret Dickinson)*

Lower Bartle [SD4833]

☆ *Sitting Goose* [off B5411 just NW of Preston; Lea Lane]: Attractive, neat country pub, very popular with older people for good value lunches, partly no smoking dining room, enthusiastic friendly licensees, good service, well kept Thwaites ales; conservatory, pleasant outdoor eating area overlooking trees and fields with adjacent play area *(P R and S A White, Margaret Dickinson)*

Lydgate [SD9704]

White Hart [Stockport Rd]: Tastefully refurbished inn overlooking Saddleworth Moor, brasserie bar with wide choice of good food from chicken and pesto sandwiches or home-made sausages up, Boddingtons and Lees, log fires, restaurant; bedrooms nice, pretty village *(anon)*

Lydiate [SD3604]

Scotch Piper [Southport Rd]: Medieval white-painted thatched pub with heavy black beams, thick stone walls, flagstone floors, Burtonwood Bitter and Top Hat and coal fire in front room, darts in middle room off corridor, carpeted back room, no food, music or machines; picnic-sets in large garden with aviary, hens, donkey and abundant flower baskets, open all day wknds *(Kevin Thorpe, the Didler)*

Manchester [SJ8284]

Ape & Apple [John Dalton St]: Uncharacteristically smart and open-plan Holts pub with their fantastic value beer kept well, comfortable seats in bare-boards bar with nice lighting and lots of old prints and posters, armchairs in upstairs lounge; good mix on busy wknd evenings (unusually for city centre, over-25s won't feel out of place), quieter lunchtime or midweek *(the Didler)*

Atlas [Deansgate, Castlefield end]: One of the first of the city's 'new' bars, and still one of the best: unique design to fit the railway arches, good modern food and lots of good beers, nice sitting out behind *(anon)*

Bar Centro [Tib St]: Continental-style two-floor café-bar, well kept Hydes and a couple of guest ales such as Boggart Clough and Phoenix Dark Moonlight, several continental draught beers, wide choice of creole and other food, daily papers, friendly helpful staff, frequent live music and DJs; open all day till late (1am Thurs-Sat), cl Sun *(Richard Lewis)*

Bar Fringe [Swan St]: Friendly continental café-style open-plan bar with appropriate glasses for six Belgian draught beers, well kept ales such as Bank Top Cliffhanger, Hydes Down The Hatch and Rudgate Ruby Mild, farm cider, friendly staff, food till 7, daily papers, cartoons, prints and bank notes, polished motorcycle hung above door; good music; tables out behind, open all day *(Richard Lewis, the Didler)*

☆ *Beer House* [Angel St, off Rochdale Rd]: Lively basic open-plan pub listed for its splendid range of well kept real ales, mainly unusual, inc monthly beer festivals – October's is a virtual transplant of Munich's Oktoberfest; also farm ciders and perry, several Belgian beers on tap, good range of bottled foreign beers, country wines, and cheap spirits doubles (wide choice); bare boards, friendly helpful staff and sleepy white alsatian, old local prints, robust cheap bar food lunchtime and Thurs/Fri evening inc bargain lunch (Mon), good curries and lots of cheeses, free chip muffins 5-6 Weds; darts, good CD juke box (may be loud), games machine, more comfortable upstairs bar with bar billiards, table footer and SkyTV, ceilidh band Tues; tables out behind, open all day *(Richard Lewis, the Didler, JP, PP, Ian Phillips)*

Castle [Oldham St, about 200 yards from Piccadilly, on right]: Unspoilt traditional front bar, small snug, full Robinsons range kept well from fine bank of handpumps, games in well worn back room, nice tilework outside; no food, children allowed till 7, blues Thurs, open all day (Sun afternoon closure) *(the Didler, Richard Lewis)*

Centro [Tib St]: Light and airy café-bar with tasteful wall coverings and pale wood furnishings, well kept ales such as Hydes Jekylls Gold and A Quick One, Slaters Top Totty and Moorhouses Gengas, several draught continental and US beers, cocktails, daily papers, food inc cajun, friendly staff, live music most nights; open all day till midnight (1am Thurs-Sat, cl Sun) *(Richard Lewis)*

Circus [Portland St]: Two tiny rooms, back one panelled with leatherette banquettes, very well kept Tetleys from minute corridor bar, friendly landlord, no music or machines; often looks closed but normally open all day wkdys (you have to knock) *(the Didler, JP, PP, Sue Holland, Dave Webster)*

City Arms [Kennedy St, off St Peters Sq]: Well kept changing beers such as Robinsons, Tetleys and Wadworths Old Timer, Belgian bottled beers, occasional beer festivals, popular bar lunches, quiet evenings; bare boards, wheelchair access but steps down to back lounge, open all day (cl Sat lunchtime, Sun) *(the Didler)*

Coach & Horses [Old Bury Rd, Whitefield;

A665 nr Besses o' the Barn Stn]: Multi-room coaching inn built around 1830, little changed, very popular and friendly, with well kept Holts, table service, darts, cards; open all day *(the Didler)*

Crescent [The Crescent (A6), Salford – opp Salford Univ]: Three 18th-c houses converted into beer house in 19th, unusual layout and homely unsmart décor, chatty buzzing local atmosphere, interesting guest ales, good value food, friendly staff, pool room, juke box; popular with students and university staff, open all day *(the Didler)*

Didsbury [Wilmslow Rd, Didsbury]: Attractively reworked Chef & Brewer, roomy yet with intimate alcoves and soft lighting inc candles, hop bines on oak beams, mixed old oak and pine furniture, well spaced tables, roaring log fire in stone fireplace, old Didsbury prints on dark panelling, old bottles and copper platters; well kept Marstons Pedigree, John Smiths and Theakstons, interesting hot dishes inc proper pies and good value steaks, also sandwiches, baked potatoes, topped ciabatta etc, Sun coffee and croissants, popular Sun lunch, daily papers, friendly efficient service; quiet piped music *(Dr and Mrs A K Clarke, Mr and Mrs C Roberts, Lisa Hulme, Frank Hill)*

Eagle [Collier St, off Greengate, Salford]: Old-fashioned backstreet local, absolutely no frills, well kept Holts Bitter and Mild at old-fashioned prices, bar servery to tap and passage with two smoke rooms (can indeed get smoky), old Salford pictures, very friendly manager, cheap filled rolls; open all day *(the Didler)*

Eagle & Child [Higher Lane, Whitefield]: Black and white pub set back from rd, with Holts Bitter and Mild; open all day *(the Didler)*

Egerton Arms [Gore St, Salford; A6 by station]: Several rooms, chandeliers, art nouveau lamps, excellent value Holts Bitter and Mild, also Boddingtons and Marstons; open all day *(the Didler)*

Goose on Piccadilly [Piccadilly]: Roomy and comfortable faux-Wetherspoons Bass pub, panelling, books and prints, good choice of reasonably priced food, even a bargain beer, friendly helpful staff (but if they say the Highgate Special is brewed in Rochdale, tell them it's actually from down in Walsall); open all day *(Richard Lewis)*

Grey Horse [Portland St, nr Piccadilly]: Cosy traditional Hydes local, welcoming and busy, with timbering, pictures and plates, well kept Bitter and Mild, some unusual malt whiskies, popular lunchtime food; no juke box or machines, open all day *(the Didler)*

Hare & Hounds [Shudehill, nr Arndale]: Long narrow bar linking front snug and comfortable back lounge (with TV), notable tilework, panelling and stained glass, well kept Holts, Lees and Tetleys, sandwiches, friendly staff; games and machine, piano singalongs, upstairs Fri folk club; open all day *(Pete Baker, the Didler, Richard Lewis)*

☆ *Jacksons Wharf* [Slate Wharf, Castlefield; across bridge from Barca]: Newish pub with masses of carved oak in amazing cathedral-like interior, pulpits on upper level, lovely views over canal quay, good range of beers and food *(Kevin Blake)*

Jolly Angler [Ducie St]: Unpretentious backstreet local, small and friendly, with well kept Hydes Bitter and Strong, coal fire, darts, pool and TV; informal folk singing Mon *(the Didler, Pete Baker, BB)*

Kings Arms [Bloom St, Salford]: Big busy old local, not smart and in a decayed area, but friendly, with ten or more well kept ales; small snug with a deep corridor and pinball machines; open all day, handy for Central station *(the Didler)*

☆ *Mark Addy* [Stanley St, off New Bailey St, Salford]: Unusual converted waiting rooms for boat passengers, barrel-vaulted red sandstone bays with wide glassed-in brick arches, cast-iron pillars and flagstones, amazing selection of cheeses and pâtés, well kept Boddingtons, Hero (brewed for them by Moorhouses) and guest beers, quite a few wines; flower-filled waterside courtyard, ducks on the stream *(LYM)*

Metropolitan [Lapwing Lane, Didsbury]: Huge welcoming dining pub, popular food inc Sun lunch, open fires, separate areas, gabled roof; lively wknd evenings *(anon)*

Moon Under Water [Deansgate]: Britain's biggest pub, Wetherspoons cinema conversion with entertainer stills, two bars, one very long, balcony seating (not always open), no smoking area; good range of real ales inc bargain pints, bustling atmosphere, friendly efficient staff, popular food all day inc deals for two *(Andy, Julie and Stuart Hawkins, Richard Lewis)*

☆ *Mr Thomas Chop House* [Cross St]: Long bustling Victorian city pub, bare boards and panelling by front bar, back eating area with crisp tilework, interesting period features inc wrought-iron gates, good very popular lunchtime food with innovative touches, efficient friendly staff, well kept Boddingtons, Timothy Taylors Landlord and a guest beer, decent wines, no smoking area; open all day *(the Didler, P Abbott, JP, PP, David Carr)*

New Grove [Bury New Rd, Whitefield]: Busy two-bar 1920s local with particularly well kept Holts Bitter and Mild; open all day *(the Didler)*

Old Monkey [Portland St]: Traditional Holts pub, built 1993 but you'd never guess from the etched glass and mosaic tiling; interesting memorabilia, warm hospitality, well kept cheap Bitter and Mild, low-priced food, upstairs lounge, wide mix of customers *(the Didler, Sue Holland, Dave Webster)*

Old Wellington [Cathedral Gates, off Exchange Sq]: Ancient pub reopened after move from Old Shambles Square during Arndale rebuild, original flagstones, panelling and 14th-c gnarled oak beams and timbers, new bar fittings; open-plan downstairs with small bar and appetising snacks in food area, partly no smoking restaurant upstairs, well kept Bass, afternoon tea; trendy piped music; tables out overlooking new Exchange Square *(BB, P Abbott, John Wooll, Doug Christian)*

Olde Nelson [Chapel St, Salford (A6 opp cathedral)]: Lots of brewery and whisky mirrors in drinking corridor linking front sliding-door snug and back lounge – more mirrors and brass here; Boddingtons, darts, dominoes, cards; live entertainment Sat *(Pete Baker, the Didler)*

☆ *Peveril of the Peak* [Gt Bridgewater St]: Three traditional rooms around central servery, lots of mahogany, mirrors and stained or frosted glass, splendidly lurid green external tilework; busy lunchtime but welcoming and homely evenings, with cheap basic lunchtime food (not Sun), very welcoming family service, log fire, well kept Scottish Courage ales, sturdy furnishings on bare boards, interesting pictures, pub games inc pool, table football, juke box; seats outside, children welcome, cl wknd lunchtimes *(the Didler, JP, PP, Sue Holland, Dave Webster, LYM)*

Plough [Hyde Rd (A57), Gorton]: Superb tiling, windows and gantry in basic local with TV and wooden benches in large public bar, two quieter back lounges, small pool room, Robinsons on electric cooling – handpumps kept for emergencies *(the Didler)*

Pot of Beer [New Mount St]: Small refurbished two-bar pub with bare boards, stripped bricks and timber, interesting changing guest beers some tapped from the cask in unusual stillage system (cask fronts projecting from temperature-controlled chamber), Thatcher's farm cider, continental beers inc Polish – generous good value food (wkdy lunchtimes) from there too, friendly licensees; open all day, cl Sun *(Richard Lewis, the Didler)*

Quay House [Salford Quays]: Beefeater and Travel Inn with solid new open-plan pub part, usual food all fairly cheap, good beer range; handy for the superb new Lowry – and for Old Trafford (so quite a jovial lunchtime atmosphere on United home match days); bedrooms *(John Wooll)*

☆ *Queens* [Honey St, Cheetham; off Red Bank, nr Victoria Stn]: Well preserved Empress Brewery tiled façade, well kept Phoenix Bantam, Timothy Taylors Landlord and guest beers from small British and Belgian breweries, Weston's farm cider, simple but often food all day, coal fire, bar billiards, backgammon, chess, good juke box; children welcome, quiz night Tues; unexpected views of Manchester across the Irk Valley and its railway lines from large back garden with good play area, worth penetrating the surrounding viaducts, scrapyards and industrial premises *(the Didler)*

Rain Bar [Gt Bridgewater St]: Good works conversion, lots of woodwork and flagstones, full range of Lees beers, good value food from 9am breakfast, daily papers, large upstairs bar too; no under-21s, terrace overlooking canal, open all day *(the Didler)*

Sand Bar [Grosvenor St]: Pair of Georgian houses with relaxed sometimes studenty series of varied areas, well kept changing ales such as Bass, Boddingtons, Coach House Gunmaker Mild, Lees Moonraker, Marstons Pedigree, Phoenix Bantam and Robinsons Frederics, lots of foreign bottled beers, decent wines, good value food esp vegetarian, seats from plain benches to comfortable armchairs, local artwork; pavement seating *(John Wooll)*

☆ *Sinclairs* [2 Cathedral Gates, off Exchange Sq]: Largely 18th-c low-beamed and timbered pub reopened after being dismantled, moved a short distance, and re-erected brick by brick, as part of the city centre reconstruction; cheap food, bargain Sam Smiths, friendly service, great atmosphere, upstairs bar with snugs and Jacobean fireplace; tables out by ultra-modern Exchange Square *(LYM, Doug Christian, JP, PP, the Didler)*

Smithfield [Swan St]: Open-plan family-run local with unusual well kept changing beers, several beer festivals, cheap food in back eating area from open kitchen servery, TV here, daily papers, friendly landlady; pool on front dais, games machine, juke box; open all day, bedrooms in nearby building *(Richard Lewis, the Didler, BB)*

Union [Liverpool St, Salford]: Down-to-earth local in industrial area, excellent value Holts Bitter and Mild and home-cooked food, impressive bar; open all day, Sun afternoon closure *(the Didler)*

White House [122 Gt Ancoats St]: Friendly local with big lounge and vault with pool table, well kept cheap Holts, Chesters Mild and guest beers *(the Didler)*

White Lion [Liverpool Rd, Castlefield]: Busy but friendly Victorian pub, tables for eating up one side of three-sided bar, home-made food all day till 10 inc good curries, separate steak and sausage menus and children's helpings, changing ales such as Boddingtons, Coach House Posthorse, Phoenix Arizona and Blizzard and Wadworths 6X, decent house wine, good tea, friendly service, real fire, lots of prints and Man Utd pictures, shelves of bottles and jugs; sports TV, disco Fri; children welcome, tables out among excavated foundations of Roman city overlooking fort gate, handy for Museum of Science and Industry and Royal Exchange Theatre, open all day *(Richard Lewis, the Didler)*

Marple [SJ9686]

☆ *Romper* [Ridge End, off A626 via Church Lane, following The Ridge signposts]: Beautifully placed dining pub above Peak Forest Canal in Goyt Valley, four softly lit knocked-through oak-beamed rooms, reliable generous food (all day Sun), well kept Jennings beers with Boddingtons as a guest, decent wines and lots of malt whiskies, efficient friendly staff; tables outside, opens noon *(P and M Rudlin, Mike and Wena Stevenson, LYM, Bob and Lisa Cantrell, Brian and Anna Marsden)*

Mawdesley [SD4915]

☆ *Robin Hood* [Blue Stone Lane (Croston—Eccleston road, N of village – keep going)]: Spotless comfortable open-plan dining pub with button-back wall banquettes, reproduction Victorian prints, decorative plates, stained-glass seat dividers, some stripped stone; good value generous home cooking with fresh veg and cheap children's helpings, small pretty upstairs restaurant, friendly staff coping well with the bustle, well kept Whitbreads-related and good

guest ales, decent wines, children's room; may be piped music, fruit machine; picnic-sets on neat side terrace, good fenced play area *(Margaret Dickinson)*

Mellor [SJ9988]

Moorfield Arms [Shiloh Rd; this is the Mellor near Marple, S of Manchester]: Wide choice of good imaginative food in sandblasted former chapel, high in the hills; three comfortable rooms, one with no smoking dining area, beams, stonework and original panelling, coal fire, well kept Marstons Pedigree, decent wine, good views all around; sunny garden *(Bob and Lisa Cantrell, Mike and Linda Hudson)*

Mellor Brook [SD6431]

Feildens Arms [Whalley Rd]: Extended and tastefully refurbished, busy bar, good reasonably priced food, friendly restaurant service *(Keith Barker)*

Morecambe [SD4565]

Chieftain [Pedder St]: Roomy yet cosy, with well kept Tetleys, good value lunchtime food inc good hot baguettes *(Andy, Julie and Stuart Hawkins)*

Oswaldtwistle [SD7226]

☆ *Britannia* [A677/B6231]: Attractive tastefully upgraded traditional core with log-burning ranges, dining area extended into adjoining barn, reasonably priced bar food with some emphasis on fresh fish, friendly service, well kept Thwaites Bitter; suntrap back terrace with moorland views and play area; food all day Sun, children in family restaurant *(Steve Whalley)*

Overton [SD4358]

Globe: Large and attractive, with good range of decent bar food, carvery, real ale, pleasant service, conservatory, safely fenced garden with play area, bedrooms; quiet spot, handy for Sambo's Grave at Sunderland Point *(Margaret Dickinson)*

Ship [Main St]: Victorian hotel recently refurbished and opened up, but keeping some handsome original features and famous egg collection; bar food, Thwaites real ale; no dogs, fruit machine and juke box in newly tiled lobby *(Kevin Thorpe)*

Padiham [SD7933]

☆ *Red Rock* [just N on Sabden Rd]: Unspoilt cottagey pub with lively chef/landlord doing short choice of good food cooked to order, three real ales, decent house wines, friendly service, several plants in beamed bar, log fire, separate dining room, occasional live music; large garden with lovely views and climbing frame, open all day wknds *(Michael and Deirdre Ellis, Tracey L Hartley, BB)*

Parbold [SD4911]

Wayfarer [A5209/Alder Lane]: Enjoyable food in peaceful civilised pub *(Brian Kneale)*

Pendleton [SD7539]

☆ *Swan With Two Necks*: Welcoming olde-worlde village pub below Pendle Hill, simply furnished and tidy, with good value generous home cooking, well kept Marstons Pedigree and Moorhouses Black Cat; large garden *(LYM, Steve Whalley)*

Preston [SD5330]

Black Horse [Friargate]: Thriving friendly

untouched pub in pedestrian street, full Robinsons ale range kept well, inexpensive lunchtime food, unusual ornate curved and mosaic-tiled Victorian main bar, panelling, stained glass, mosaic floor and two quiet cosy enclosed snugs off, upstairs 1920s-style bar; pictures of old town, lots of artefacts, good juke box; no children, open all day *(Pete Baker, Jonty MacRae-Campbell, the Didler)*

Eldon Hotel [Eldon St, Plungington]: Large Victorian local popular with university students, newish landlady has reopened the kitchen for hot and cold food; big-screen sports TV, quiz night Thurs, karaoke Fri *(Adrian Roberts)*

Fleece [39 Liverpool Rd, Penwortham Hill]: Well presented good value food, real ales, comfortable no smoking area; large garden with play area *(Margaret Dickinson)*

Grey Friar [Friargate]: Well managed Wetherspoons, with constantly changing range of well kept and well priced ales inc Milds and Porters, regular beer festivals, decent wines, chatty staff, good value food, no piped music; huge no smoking area, powerful air conditioning *(Jonty MacRae-Campbell, Jim and Maggie Cowell)*

Ramsbottom [SD7916]

Fishermans Retreat [Twine Valley Park, Bye Rd; signed off A56 N of Bury at Shuttleworth]: Surrounded by well stocked trout lakes, friendly rather than smart, with good value interesting and generous food with proper chips, well kept changing beers such as Dent, good choice of whiskies, welcoming service, busy restaurant; games room with two pool tables and games machines; open all day from 8am; plans for a hotel complex *(P Abbott, David and Ruth Shillitoe)*

Shoulder of Mutton [Lumb Carr Rd (B6214), Holcombe]: Popular traditional country pub with warm atmosphere, attractive lounge, nicely presented good value food, well kept guest beers, separate dining room; worth booking wknds, good walking area *(Jim Abbott, P Abbott)*

Riley Green [SD6225]

☆ *Royal Oak* [A675/A6061]: Cosy low-beamed three-room former coaching inn nr canal, reliably good food inc interesting specials, plenty of vegetarian and superb puddings, well kept Thwaites Bitter and Mild, friendly efficient service; ancient stripped stone, open fires, seats from high-backed settles to red plush armchairs, lots of nooks and crannies, turkey carpet, soft lighting, impressive woodwork, fresh flowers, interesting model steam engines; short walk from Leeds & Liverpool Canal, can be packed Fri night and wknds *(Catherine and Martin Snelling, BB)*

Ringley [SD7605]

Horseshoe [Fold Rd, Stoneclough; right off A667 at sign for Kidds Garden Centre]: Good creative food, wider choice evenings (with advance warning do game, seafood and imaginative vegetarian dishes); friendly landlord, cheap well kept Thwaites, three areas off main bar, open fire, interesting local

pictures, pleasant back garden; well behaved children lunchtime *(C H Reid, Ellis Heaton)*

Sabden [SD7737]

Pendle Witch [Whalley Rd]: Friendly recently refurbished open-plan pub in Victorian terrace, lots of witch-related ornaments, well kept Tetleys *(Steve Whalley)*

Sale [SJ7992]

Kings Ransom [Britannia Rd]: Large well furnished Edwardian pub on Bridgewater Canal, six separate areas inc big no smoking one, roaring fires, antique oil paintings, candlelight, well kept Boddingtons, Courage Directors, Ruddles County and two guest beers, annual beer festival, lots of malt whiskies, friendly efficient staff, good value food from good baked potatoes to carvery and interesting salads, also served Sun 4-7; tables out on pontoon, open all day *(Mike and Mary Carter, Doug Christian)*

Samlesbury [SD5929]

New Hall Tavern [nr M6 junction 31; Cuerdale Lane (B6230) off A677 opp Trafalgar Hotel]: Whitbreads and several guest beers, imaginative changing food prepared by landlady *(Jim and Maggie Cowell)*

Sawley [SD7746]

☆ *Spread Eagle*: Quiet upmarket 16th-c pub/restaurant, new chef doing splendid food inc good value wkdy set lunches and bargain early suppers (may be cl Sun evening), delicious velouté soup and very imaginative puddings, occasional themed evenings and dinner dances; comfortably sophisticated feel in light and airy lounge bar with well kept Black Sheep and Pendle Black Cat, several dozen malt whiskies, expanded list of well chosen wines, friendly efficient service, coal fire, comfortable green banquettes, lots of small round tables; food orders taken here for restauranty eating areas, inc soothing no smoking back dining room with big picture windows overlooking a pretty stretch of the River Ribble; watch out for ducks on the road, close to ruined abbey *(Steve Whalley, Mrs P J Carroll, Norman Stansfield, BB)*

Simonstone [SD7735]

☆ *Higher Trapp* [Sabden rd, off School Lane]: Attractive refurbished bar with relaxing views, well kept Boddingtons and Theakstons, food in bar and restaurant (all day Sun), no smoking areas, big conservatory; children welcome, comfortable bedrooms *(Margaret Dickinson)*

Skippool [SD3540]

River Wyre Hotel [Breck Rd(A585 just N of Poulton-le-Fylde)]: Impressively refurbished, with three comfortable areas (one no smoking, another child-free), keeping several open fires, things to look at, flower arrangements; wide choice of good interesting home-made bar food, real ale, good friendly service *(Paul Fairbrother, Helen Morris, Margaret Dickinson)*

Slyne [SD4765]

Slyne Lodge [Main Rd]: Clean well run hotel, very popular, well kept Jennings ales, caring helpful staff, good food in imaginative mediterranean-style dining room, open fire, welcoming bar, conservatory; terrace tables, bedrooms with own bathrooms *(Margaret Dickinson)*

Southport [SD3314]

Portland [Bedford Rd/Kew Rd, Birkdale]: Rustic minimalist décor, friendly staff, enjoyable food inc good ploughman's, unusual pub games; by attractive park *(anon)*

Thatch & Thistle [Norwood Rd (B5276, off A570)]: New pub, large but well divided, with food that's a cut above the norm, well kept Courage and Theakstons, real fires *(Michael Buchanan)*

Wetherspoons [Lord St]: Well placed, with good choice of food all day and well kept cheap beer *(P Abbott)*

Standish [SD5708]

Boars Head [A49/A5106 (Wigan Rd)]: Heavy low beams, log fires, cosy bays of curved wall seats, high wooden stools, sofa, two quieter rooms off; helpful staff, well kept Burtonwood and guest beers, occasional home-made wines; tables in flower-filled garden, bowling green, open all day Sat *(Brian Kneale)*

Stockport [SJ8889]

Alexandra [Northgate Rd]: Large backstreet pub with listed interior, reputedly haunted; Robinsons beers, pool room *(the Didler)*

Arden Arms [Millgate St, behind Asda]: Traditional and welcoming, with several room areas inc old-fashioned snug through servery, 1920s décor, fine old vault, brighter lounge area, great collection of working grandfather clocks, also Dinky toys; good value limited lunchtime bar food, well kept Robinsons *(Pete Baker, the Didler)*

Armoury [Shaw Heath]: Small unspoilt locals' bar, comfortable lounge, Robinsons Best and Hatters Mild, maybe Old Tom from a cask on the bar, lunchtime family room upstairs; open all day *(the Didler)*

Blossoms [Buxton Rd (A6)]: Busy traditional main-road local, very friendly, with well kept Robinsons Best and Hatters Mild, maybe Old Tom tapped from the cask; superb back room; open all day wknds *(the Didler, Bernie Adams)*

Florist [Shaw Heath]: Classic local, some alterations but still several separate rooms; Robinsons Best and Hatters Mild *(the Didler)*

Nursery [Green Lane, Heaton Norris; off A6]: 1930s pub tucked down cobbled lane in pleasant setting with bowling green behind, several rooms inc handsomely panelled lounge, good food inc very popular set Sun lunch (children welcome if eating), friendly efficient service, Hydes Bitter and Mild on electric pump, seasonal ale on handpump *(the Didler, R Davies)*

Queens Head [Little Underbank (can be reached by steps from St Petersgate)]: Long narrow late Victorian pub with delightful separate snug and back dining area; good bustling atmosphere, reasonable bar food, well kept Sam Smiths, daily papers, rare brass cordials fountain and old spirit lamps, old posters and adverts; no smoking area, some live jazz, open all day; famous narrow gents' *(the Didler, Bernie Adams)*

☆ *Red Bull* [Middle Hillgate]: Beamed and

flagstoned local, very friendly and well run, with very well kept Robinsons Best and Best Mild from nearby brewery, good value home-cooked bar lunches (not Sun), substantial settles and seats, open fires, impressive bar with lots of pictures, brassware and traditional island servery; quiet at lunchtime, can get crowded evening, open all day (Sun afternoon closure) *(LYM, the Didler)*

Swan With Two Necks [Princes St]: Classic panelled local, comfortable bar, back lounge and drinking corridor, skylight ceiling, Robinsons Mild and Bitter; handy for shops *(the Didler)*

Swinton [SD7602]

Morning Star [Manchester Rd, Wardley (A6)]: Busy Holts local, well kept ales, good value basic food wkday lunchtime, lively games-oriented bar, usually some Sat entertainment in lounge *(Pete Baker)*

Tarleton [SD4520]

☆ *Cock & Bottle* [off A59/A565 Preston—Southport; Church Rd]: Popular village dining pub with wide choice inc interesting starters, lots of game and fish; Thwaites Best Bitter and Mild, friendly helpful service, separate public bar *(Margaret Dickinson)*

Thornton Hough [SJ3080]

Thornton Hall Hotel [Neston Rd]: Good reasonably priced light meals in bar area, pleasant atmosphere, former grand country house in spacious grounds; bedrooms *(E G Parish)*

Thornton-Cleveleys [SD3342]

Gardeners Arms [Fleetwood Rd N]: Welcoming pub with good home cooking, regular live entertainment, two quiz nights a week *(Malcolm MacDonald, Abi Benson)*

Tavern at the Mill [Marsh Mill Village, Fleetwood Rd N]: Relaxing pub, food popular with all ages, children's area *(Abi Benson)*

Tockholes [SD6623]

Royal Arms [signed off A6062 S of Blackburn; Belmont Rd]: Well worth knowing for large garden, with play area and views from sheltered terrace, and good varied walks (nature trail opp); well worn in little rooms inside, one no smoking, with big open fires, old-fashioned décor, sandwiches and varied home cooking; Tetleys under top pressure, children welcome, may be piped popular classics; open all day Fri-Sun and summer *(John Fazakerley, LYM, Danny Litherland)*

Treales [SD4432]

Derby Arms: Reopened after major refurbishment, good food in bar and sizeable restaurant, well kept Boddingtons, Jennings and Theakstons *(A G Park)*

Tyldesley [SD6802]

Mort Arms [Elliott St]: Two-room pub popular with older locals, mahogany bar, etched glass and panels, comfortable lounge, very reasonably priced Holts Bitter and Mild, friendly landlord, crowds huddled around TV for Sat horseracing; open all day *(the Didler)*

Waddington [SD7243]

☆ *Lower Buck* [Edisford Rd]: Traditional moorland local reopened under friendly new licensees, well kept Black Sheep, Moorhouses Black Cat, Pride of Pendle and Premier, Rudgate Maelstrom and Timothy Taylors Landlord, popular basic home cooking, real fires, hatch-service lobby, front bar with built-in dresser, plain back room; pretty village *(BB, Alyson and Andrew Jackson)*

Weeton [SD3834]

Eagle & Child [Singleton Rd (B5260)]: Well kept rustic dining pub in byre-like style, low brick walls with old curved standing timbers, plenty of bric-a-brac, log fires; attractively served food from sandwiches and soup in tureens to imaginative main dishes, Scottish Courage ales, cafetière coffee, good wine list, 1950s nostalgic music, caring staff *(anon)*

West Bradford [SD7444]

Three Millstones [Waddington Rd]: Comfortable and attractive pub in quiet Ribble Valley village, good value food, well kept Courage Directors and Theakstons with plans for an on-site microbrewery, friendly service, open fire *(KC, P A Legon)*

Whittle-le-Woods [SD5721]

Sea View [Preston Rd (A6, not far from M61 junction 7)]: This friendly inland pub really does have a sea view (from upstairs); spacious but cosy and comfortable, with well kept

Courage Directors, Greene King Old Speckled Hen and Theakstons, good traditional reasonably priced food inc real chips, dining rooms (one no smoking), beams, horsebrasses and coach horns, big stone fireplace in extension; very busy Sat night, piped music *(Chloe and Robert Gartery, A Preston)*

Wigan [SD5805]

Springfield [Springfield Rd]: Large friendly unspoilt local with impressive woodwork, variety of rooms, Tetleys Bitter and Mild, usual food *(JP, PP, the Didler)*

Swan & Railway [Wallgate, opp Wigan NW Stn]: Traditional town pub that reverberates with passing trains, several rooms, high ceilings, mosaic tiling of swan and railway train, lovely swan stained-glass window, welcoming service, cheap basic lunchtime food (not wknds), Banks's ales, dominoes, TV *(Pete Baker)*

Wrea Green [SD3931]

☆ *Grapes* [Station Rd]: Busy but roomy open-plan Chef & Brewer with unusually imaginative food, pleasant clean dining area, well kept Boddingtons, Marstons Pedigree and Theakstons, good choice of wines by the glass, open fire, good service; tables out overlooking village green, picturesque church *(Abi Benson, M S Catling)*

Post Office address codings confusingly give the impression that some pubs are in Lancashire when they're really in Yorkshire (which is where we list them).

Leicestershire
and Rutland

Just one pub in this area has the unbroken record of appearing in every edition of the Guide *since it first appeared 20 years ago: it's the delightfully simple Cap & Stocking in Kegworth, still fetching its Bass by jug from the cellar. By contrast, four pubs here are newcomers to the* Guide, *or back after a break: the Olive Branch at Clipsham (a fine all-rounder under its young and enthusiastic new owners), the cheerful Bell at Gumley, the Old Brewery in Somerby (interesting beers, new owners doing a wider choice of food than when it last featured in these pages), and the Ram Jam Inn at Stretton (a very civilised break from the A1, with good food). Other pubs on top form here are the Nags Head in Castle Donington (beautifully presented imaginative food), the Bell at East Langton (good all round, and now brewing its own beer), the Old White Hart at Lyddington (much enjoyed for its food), the jovial Black Bull in Market Overton, the Nevill Arms at Medbourne (a favourite all-rounder, very good value), the restauranty Finches Arms nicely set at Upper Hambleton, and the Kings Arms at Wing (good all round, with very good food). From among all these the Finches Arms at Upper Hambleton emerges as our Leicestershire and Rutland Dining Pub of the Year. In the Lucky Dip section at the end of the chapter, pubs to note include the Holly Bush at Breedon on the Hill, Wheatsheaf at Greetham, Fox & Goose at Illston on the Hill, Coach & Horses at Kibworth Beauchamp, Black Horse in Market Bosworth, Cock at Peatling Magna, White Swan in Sileby, Bulls Head at Tur Langton, and Pear Tree and Wheatsheaf in Woodhouse Eaves. Beer prices in the area are close to the national average; several pubs brewing their own worked out much cheaper, as did the Rose & Crown at Hose and Swan in the Rushes in Loughborough. The good Grainstore beers from the pub of that name in Oakham can increasingly be found in other pubs now.*

BARROWDEN SK9400 Map 4
Exeter Arms ▦ 🍺

Main Street, just off A47 Uppingham—Peterborough

It's well worth a visit to this tranquil 17th-c coaching inn which is well placed in a pretty tucked away Rutland stone village for the Blencowe beers they brew in the lovely old free-standing barn behind. These are served from handpumps, alongside a guest such as Greene King IPA, and might include Beach Boys, Big Boys, Best Boys, Young Boys, and maybe seasonal brews such as Danny Boys, Choir Boys, Lover Boys and Fruity Boys. The simple long open-plan bar which stretches away either side of a long central counter is painted a cheery yellow and has a good friendly pubby atmosphere. It's quite straightforwardly furnished with wheelback chairs at tables at either end of the bar, on bare boards or blue patterned carpet. Freshly cooked bar food from the seasonally changing blackboard menu might include starters such as smoked fish platter, tomato and feta salad, grilled pear and brie (£3.50-£4), main courses such as chicken breast with asparagus and wine sauce (£8.50), grilled lemon sole, cod with roast pepper and garlic sauce and roast boned and stuffed quail with apple and tarragon sauce (£9), and puddings such as bread and butter or fruit crumbles (£3.50). Picnic-sets on a narrow terrace in front overlook the pretty village green and ducks on the pond, with broader views stretching away beyond, and there are more well spaced picnic-sets in a big informal grassy garden at the back; boules and horseshoe pitching. *(Recommended by DC, Norma and Keith Bloomfield, A C and E Johnson, Joan and Michel Hooper-Immins, Richard Cleaver, David Field, Richard Lewis, Jim Farmer, Mike and Sue Loseby, Kevin Thorpe, Derek and Sylvia Stephenson)*

Own brew ~ Licensees Pete and Elizabeth Blencowe ~ Real ale ~ Bar food (not Sun evening, Mon) ~ Restaurant ~ (01572) 747247 ~ Children welcome away from the bar and after 8pm only if eating ~ Blues band alternate Sun evenings, folk club alternate Mon evenings ~ Open 12-2ish(3 Sat, Sun), 6-11(7-10.30 Sun); closed Mon lunchtime ~ Bedrooms: £30S/£55S

BELMESTHORPE TF0410 Map 8
Blue Bell
Village signposted off A16 just E of Stamford

Originally three cottages that have been knocked through into one, this lovely old building is on two levels, so you peer down into the bar counter, and a slope winds down round the counter to another area with the same cottagey furniture they've used throughout. There's a very homely atmosphere, particularly in the first little beamed cottagey room, which has brocaded wing armchairs and a sofa around a low coffee table, gleaming brass platters, an open fire in a huge stone inglenook – which is open through to the games room – and lots of fresh flowers. Surprisingly imaginative bar food in helpings of just the right size includes sandwiches (£2.25), soup (£3.25), fried mushrooms with stilton sauce (£3.45), steak baguette (£5.25), ploughman's (£5.45), omelettes (£5.65), good tagliatelle with fresh tuna (£5.75), cajun spiced bean and root vegetable casserole (£8.75), lambs kidneys with sage chipolatas and madeira sauce (£9.45), and daily specials such as moules marinières (£5.95), trout with prawns, almonds and parsley lemon butter (£9.75), skate with caper butter sauce (£10.75) and beef stroganoff (£11.75). The pub has darts and pool; the landlord plays in both teams, and the landlady plays cribbage and dominoes. Keep an eye out for the naughty black labrador Rufus who is detrimental to stock levels as he steals crisps from behind the bar. Well kept Badger IPA, Bass, Greene King Old Speckled Hen and Ruddles County on handpump, a good choice of wines by the glass and mulled wine in winter. *(Recommended by Phil and Jane Hodson, M J Morgan, Anna Blowers, Judith Overton, Nina Blowes)*

Free house ~ Licensees Susan Bailey and Andrew Cunningham ~ Real ale ~ Bar food (not Sun evenings) ~ Restaurant ~ (01780) 763859 ~ Children in restaurant ~ Open 12-2.30, 6(5 Sat)-11; 12-10.30 Sun; closed 26 Dec and 1 Jan evening

BRAUNSTON SK8306 Map 4
Old Plough ♀
Village signposted off A606 in Oakham

The cosily traditional low beamed lounge at this rather genteel country pub has upholstered seats around cast-iron-framed tables and plenty of brass and other ornaments on the mantelpiece (there's a huge warming fire in winter). This leads into a modern no smoking dining conservatory, with a false ceiling made from parasols. The carpeted public bar has darts in winter; piped music. They have well kept local Grainstore Triple B and Ten Fifty and a couple of guests such as Shepherd Neame Bishops Finger, a well noted wine list, fruit punches in summer, and various teas and coffees. The main draw here is the seasonally changing menu which might include soup of the day (£2.75), crab cakes (£4.25), smoked salmon (£4.75), pork loin filled with apple and prune purée with port and prune jus (£9.25), swordfish with hollandaise sauce (£10.50), seared duck breast with a creamy ginger sauce on noodles (£12.50). Picnic-sets shelter among fruit trees in the garden, and there's a boules pitch and children's play area. This is a pretty village in the heart of Rutland. *(Recommended by Malcolm Taylor, Anthony Barnes, A C and E Johnson, Eric Locker, Dorsan Baker, Angus Lyon)*

Free house ~ Licensees David and Claire Cox ~ Real ale ~ Bar food (12-2.30, 7-9.30; 12-9.30) ~ Restaurant ~ (01572) 722714 ~ Children welcome ~ Open 11-3, 6-11; 11-11 Sat; 12-10.30 Sun ~ Bedrooms: £45B/£65B

CASTLE DONINGTON SK4427 Map 7
Nags Head ⑪ ♀
Hill Top; A453, S end

You will need to book a table at this civilised low-beamed dining pub. The emphasis is mainly on the imaginative beautifully presented food which is prepared using fresh local or French ingredients. The menu changes every day and includes lighter snacks and starters such as soup and baguette (£3.75), cajun chicken with tzatziki (£3.50), sausage and mash (£4.50), prawn pancake with mushroom and leek sauce (£4.75), tomato and mozzarella salad (£4.95), smoked salmon with toasted ciabatta (£6.95), and main courses such as beef, onion and red wine casserole (£9.95), baked cod with herb crust (£10.50), fried duck breast with curry oil and chicory (£11.95), grilled halibut with garlic and prawn sauce or roast rack of lamb with creamy leek polenta (£12.95) and sliced beef fillet with cajun spices with tzatziki dressing (£15.50). Puddings might include treacle oat tart, sticky toffee pudding, chocolate whisky trifle and cappuccino crème brûlée (£3.30). The little bar area as you enter is simplest, with quarry tiles, dark green dado and dark tables and wheelback chairs. A step takes you up into an intimate little dining room with simple pressed and punctured iron wall lamps and nice signed French prints on fresh cream walls, three chunky old pine candlelit tables on seagrass, and a little turkey rug in front of a pretty slate art deco fireplace. The other end of the bar takes you into a second much bigger and similarly decorated yellow-washed dining area, its well spaced tables giving it a more elegantly informal feel, and from here through an opening to the kitchen you can watch the chefs at work. You order at the bar and are then shown to your table by the waitress when your food is ready. Very attentive staff and conscientious landlord; well kept Banks's Mild, Marstons Pedigree and Mansfield on handpump, 20-30 malt whiskies and quite a few wines by the glass; handy for Donnington Race Track. *(Recommended by A C and E Johnson, the Didler, Marlene and Jim Godfrey, Peter Burton, Chris and Jo Nicholls, JP, PP, Peter and Jean Hoare, Darly Graton, Graeme Gulibert, Hugh A MacLean, Theo, Anne and Jane Gaskin, Paul Hopton)*

Marstons (W & D) ~ Tenant Ian Davison ~ Real ale ~ Bar food (Sun) ~ Restaurant ~ (01332) 850652 ~ Open 11.30-2.30, 5.30-11; 12-2.30, 7-10.30 Sun; closed 26 Dec, 1 Jan

CLIPSHAM SK9616 Map 8
Olive Branch ♀ ◀
Take B668/Stretton exit off A1 N of Stamford; Clipsham signposted E from exit roundabout

A stone-built country pub attractively set on a bend in the quiet village lane, this has picnic-sets out on a heated terrace, with more on the neat lawn sheltered in the L of its two low buildings. Reopened at the end of 1999 by new owners, it's been attractively reworked inside. There are dark joists and beams in the various smallish rambling room areas, a log fire in the stone inglenook fireplace, and an interesting mix of pictures, country furniture and books (many bought at antique fairs by one of the partners – ask if you see something you like, as much is for sale). The atmosphere is relaxed and friendly, and the emphasis is on Sean Hope's cooking (he was brought up in the village, and long before embarking on his professional cooking career elsewhere his first job was washing up here). In generous helpings and using much fresh local produce, it might include sandwiches (from £3.75), moules marinières (£4.95/£7.75), tempura battered tiger prawns with sweet chilli sauce (£5.25), stilton ploughman's (£5.50), sausage and mash (£7.75), rigatoni pasta with rocket, pine nuts, olive oil and parmesan (£9.25), grilled calves liver with herb mash and braised red cabbage (£9.50), fried salmon with creamed spinach and nutmeg (£9.75), roast monkfish with tomato and olive risotto and crispy braised fennel (£12.50). Puddings such as white chocolate cheesecake, sticky toffee pudding or caramelised lemon tart with raspberry coulis (£4.95) are particularly enjoyed, and a nice touch is the board of home-baked bread they bring for you to slice yourself. The young staff are friendly, efficient and helpful, and the Grainstore Olive Oil and Ten Fifty, with maybe a guest from Brewsters or Fenland, are kept well on handpump; they have a good blackboard choice of wines including interesting bin ends (some old clarets) and unusual sherries, and do freshly squeezed fruit juices. Two of the dining rooms are no smoking; there may be unobtrusive piped music. They have Saturday summer barbecues, and garden skittles. *(Recommended by Chris and Susie Cammack, James Muir, Mrs V Middlebrook, Alan and Gill Bull, RB, Mrs Kay Dewsbury, Mike and Sue Loseby, M J Morgan)*

Free house ~ Licensees Sean Hope, Ben Jones and Marcus Welford ~ Real ale ~ Bar food (not Sun evening) ~ Restaurant ~ (01780) 410355 ~ Children welcome ~ Open 12-3, 6-11; 12-11 Sat; 12-6 Sun; 12-3, 6-11 Sat winter; closed Sun evening

COTTESMORE SK9013 Map 7
Sun ⓨ ☓

B668 NE of Oakham

The emphasis at this 17th-c stonebuilt thatched village pub is on the good imaginative food which might include soup (£2.75), feta salad (£2.95), king prawns in garlic butter (£4.75), steak baguette (£5.95), grilled sardines or lasagne (£6.25), seared salmon fillet with lemon butter (£7.50), seafood tagliatelle (£7.95), roast duck (£10.95), and puddings such as chocolate sponge or apple crumble (£3.25). There are not many tables in the rooms off the bar, so it pays to get there early, or even book. As well as stripped pine furnishings, there's a winter fire in the stone inglenook, and pictures on the sunny yellow walls; piped music. Besides Adnams and Everards Tiger they have a guest beer such as Jennings Sneck Lifter on handpump, and also decent wines. Service is friendly and helpful. There are tables out in the garden; boules. *(Recommended by Mike and Sue Loseby)*

Everards ~ Tenant David Johnson ~ Real ale ~ Bar food (not Sun evening, Mon) ~ Restaurant ~ (01572) 812321 ~ Open 11.30-2.30, 6.30-11; closed 25, 26 Dec

EAST LANGTON SP7292 Map 4
Bell ◖ ▬ ⇦

The Langtons signposted from A6 N of Market Harborough; East Langton signposted from B6047

Readers speak very warmly of this friendly creeper-covered pub which is well liked for its cosy atmosphere, home brew beers, enjoyable food and comfortable accommodation. The long stripped-stone beamed bar is snug in winter with a good log fire and plain wooden tables. Their well kept Caudle ales are produced in a recently converted outbuilding and include Caudle Bitter and Bowler Strong Ale which are served alongside Greene King Abbot and IPA on handpump, with a couple of guests such as Bass and Adnams tapped straight from the cask (there's a £1 discount on a four pint pitcher). Good imaginative home-cooked food from a seasonally changing menu might include lunchtime sandwiches (from £2.25) generously served home-made soup (£2.95), hot filled baguettes (£3.95), goats cheese en croûte (£4.44), hazelnut and brown rice loaf (£7.95), fish and leek pie (£8.95), sausages of the season or liver and bacon casserole (£8.50), 8oz fillet (£13.50), and puddings (£3.25); Sunday carvery and weekday senior citizen's lunches, booking is advised at busy times; no smoking green-hued dining room. This is a nice place to stay as the bedrooms are very well appointed and service is particularly friendly.

There are tables out in the garden, and the attractive village is set in peaceful countryside. *(Recommended by Bernie Adams, Joan and Michel Hooper-Immins, Eric Locker, Robert and Catherine Dunster, Phil and Jane Hodson, Rona Murdoch, Comus and Sarah Elliott, Anthony Barnes, Duncan Cloud, Mike and Sue Losebey, Steve Whalley, Jim Farmer, A C and E Johnson, Dorsan Baker, Gerry Hollington, Angus Lyon, David Field, Derek and Sylvia Stephenson)*

Own brew ~ Licensee Alastair Chapman ~ Real ale ~ Bar food (till 10(9.30 Sun)) ~ Restaurant ~ (01858) 545278 ~ Children welcome ~ Open 11.30-2.30, 7(6 Fri, Sat)-11; 12-3, 7-10.30 Sun; closed 25 Dec ~ Bedrooms: £39.50B/£55B

EMPINGHAM SK9408 Map 4
White Horse

Main Street; A606 Stamford—Oakham

The open-plan carpeted lounge bar at this attractive and bustling old inn has a big log fire below an unusual free-standing chimney-funnel, lots of fresh flowers, and a very relaxed dining atmosphere. Bar food includes soup (£2.95), ciabatta with Italian cheeses (£3.95), moules marinières (£4.75/£7.65), seafood pancakes (£4.95/£8.65), lasagne (£7.65), sautéed lambs liver with bacon and onions and red wine sauce (£8.65), rack of lamb (£9.95), daily specials such as Rutland trout fillet with baby tomatoes, spring onion and fresh herb butter (£7.25), chicken korma (£7.45), duck breast with blueberry and blackberry port wine sauce (£8.65), and puddings such as lemon torte, pear and chocolate trifle or mulled berry summer pudding (£3.95); and they also do morning coffee and afternoon tea. The restaurant and the Orange Room are no smoking. Well kept Courage Directors and Ruddles County and a couple of guests such as Grainstore Triple B and Greene King Old Speckled Hen on handpump, and up to 10 wines by the glass; fruit machine and piped music. There are some rustic tables among urns of flowers outside. Bedrooms are in a converted stable block, and in case any of their residents get lucky with the fishing rod on nearby Rutland Water, they offer deep freezing facilities. *(Recommended by Mrs G Williams, Mike and Heather Watson, Roy Bromell, Mike and Wendy Proctor, Julie Dunne, Andrew Potts, B, M and P Kendall, Keith and Di Newsome, Malcolm Taylor, Phil and Jane Hodson, Mr and Mrs J E C Tasker, Joy and Peter Heatherley)*

Courage (S & N) ~ Lease Roger Bourne ~ Real ale ~ Bar food (12-2.15, 7.15-9.45(9.30 Sun)) ~ Restaurant ~ No credit cards ~ (01780) 460221 ~ Children in eating area of bar and restaurant ~ Open 10-11; 10-10.30 Sun ~ Bedrooms: £40B/£63B

EXTON SK9211 Map 7
Fox & Hounds

Signposed off A606 Stamford—Oakham

In days gone by this handsome old building was a busy refreshment stop for coachmen on the main route to Oakham. These days this quiet village makes a handy stop for walkers on the Viking Way. The civilised and comfortable high-ceilinged lounge bar has some dark red plush easy chairs as well as wheelback seats around lots of dark tables, maps and hunting and military prints on the walls, brass and copper ornaments, and a winter log fire in a large stone fireplace; piped music. The quite separate public bar has a livelier atmosphere, darts, pool, cribbage and dominoes. Friendly staff serve up to three well kept real ales on handpump such as Bass, Greene King IPA and Sam Smiths OBB. Well prepared generously served bar food includes sandwiches (from £2.50), soup (£2.75), lasagne or lamb chops with mint and apple sauce (£6.95) liver, bacon and onions or seafood pasta (£7.75), plaice and prawns or steak and kidney pie (£7.95), honey roasted local trout (£9.45), daily specials such as lamb curry, lincolnshire sausages or oxtail casserole (£6.25) and puddings (£3.50); maybe Sunday roast; no smoking dining room. There are seats among large rose beds on the well kept back lawn overlooking paddocks, and Rutland Water is only a couple of miles away. *(Recommended by Dr Paull Khan, Martin and Lois Sheldrick, Eric Locker, Angus Lyon, Mike and Sue Losebey, M J Morgan, Gordon Theaker, Norma and Keith Bloomfield, W H and E Thomas, Bill and Sheila McLardy, Gordon Neighbour, Mr and Mrs J Brown, J Hale, Phil and Jane Hodson)*

Free house ~ Licensees David and Jennifer Hillier ~ Real ale ~ Bar food ~ Restaurant ~ No credit cards ~ (01572) 812403 ~ Children in eating area of bar and restaurant ~ Open 11-3, 6(6.30 winter)-11; 12-3, 7-10.30 Sun ~ Bedrooms: £24/£38

GLOOSTON SP7595 Map 4
Old Barn

From B6047 in Tur Langton follow Hallaton signpost, then fork left following Glooston signpost

A heartily chatty young couple have taken over this extensively restored 16th-c pub, which is pleasantly approached down a winding narrow country lane. The lower beamed main bar has stripped kitchen tables, country chairs and an open fire; cribbage and dominoes. Four well kept real ales on handpump such as Adnams and Shepherd Neame Spitfire and a couple of guests such as Jennings Cumberland and Badger IPA. Bar food might include soup (£3.45), crab cocktail (£4.65), devilled kidneys (£9.75), vegetable stir fry (£7.95), grilled plaice (£11.95), roast rack of lamb with cherry and port sauce (£12.75), beef wellington (£14.75) and puddings such as crème brûlée or tiramisu (from £3.25); the dining area is no smoking. There are a few old-fashioned teak seats and picnic-sets in front. Breakfasts are good and the bedrooms are comfortable with French-style shower-and-wash cabinets that please most readers, though might perhaps best suit those with at least a modest degree of mobility; no dogs; more reports please. *(Recommended by Jim Farmer)*

Free house ~ Licensees Phillip John and Claire Lesley Buswell ~ Real ale ~ Bar food (not Mon lunchtime) ~ Restaurant ~ (01858) 545215 ~ Well behaved children in eating area of bar ~ Open 12-3, 6.30-11; 12-4, 7-10.30 Sun; closed Mon lunchtime ~ Bedrooms: /£55S

GUMLEY SP6790 Map 4
Bell

Off A6 Market Harborough—Kibworth, via Foxton; or off A5199 via Laughton; Main Street

Don't rush in too quickly: pause in the lobby to have a look at all the cricketing prints and cartoons and the miniature bat collection. The almost L-shaped bar on the right, with typical pub furnishings, has lots of hunting prints on its cream walls, game bird plates above the bar, china jugs and mugs and horsebrasses on some of its black beams and joists, more china on a delft shelf, and ornaments on the window sills, with maybe a big flower arrangement in the corner. The good value food includes sandwiches or soup (£2.50), beef casserole, spinach and brie lasagne or mushroom stroganoff (£7.95), chicken cooked in Southern Comfort (£10.95), monkfish with Pernod and cream (£11.95) and home-made puddings such as bread and butter pudding or sherry trifle (£2.75) and OAP lunches (£3.95). The dining room is no smoking. Well kept Boddingtons, Everards Tiger, Greene King IPA and a guest such as Archers Gold on handpump, cheerful service, perhaps quiet piped music (but no mobile phones). The pretty terrace garden behind is not for children or dogs. *(Recommended by J R Martin, Stephen, Julie and Hayley Brown, Jim Farmer, Eric Locker, David Field, John March, Gerry Dobson, Tim Wellock, George Atkinson)*

Free house ~ Licensee David Quelch ~ Real ale ~ Bar food ~ Restaurant ~ (0116) 2792476 ~ Children over 5, and not in garden ~ Open 11-3, 6-11; 12-6 Sun; closed Sun evening

HALLATON SP7896 Map 4
Bewicke Arms

On good fast back road across open rolling countryside between Uppingham and Kibworth; village signposted from B6047 in Tur Langton and from B664 SW of Uppingham

Gentle refurbishments at this ancient thatched inn have given the landlady the opportunity to put together a collection of memorabilia and some very old photographs of the ancient game of bottle kicking and hare pie tossing and its

associated parades and celebrations which take place outside the pub on Hare Pie
Bank every Easter Monday. Depending on Hallaton's victory or defeat in the last
competition the display will include either the bottles themselves, or a dummy bottle.
Some of the other nice old furnishings that readers might remember unfortunately
went missing during the refurbishments but there are still a couple of old-fashioned
settles, a wall bench, some big pine topped tables on the original old oak legs, and
log fires. Beers include well kept Bass, Flowers IPA and a guest from an independent
brewer such as Grainstore; fruit machine and piped music. Good reasonably priced
bar food includes soup (£3.50), sandwiches (from £3.50), hot avocado with stilton
and bacon (£4.95), hot goats cheese salad with strawberries (£4.75), breaded plaice
or roast pepper and tomato pasta (£6.95), thai vegetable curry, lasagne or steak and
mushroom pie (£7.95), duck breast with orange and ginger sauce (£9.25), rump
steak with tomatoes and mushrooms (£9.55) and puddings such as fresh fruit
pavlova or profiteroles with chocolate sauce (£3.95). This is a lovely place in
summer when you can sit out on the big terrace across the courtyard by the tea
room in the converted stable, and enjoy a home-baked cake while being entertained
by the congregation of ducks, rabbits, pigs, goats and sheep in the adjacent paddock
and lake; no dogs. *(Recommended by Eric Locker, Jim Farmer)*

*Mercury Taverns ~ Licensee Gail Spiers ~ Real ale ~ Bar food ~ Restaurant ~ (01858)
555217 ~ Children welcome ~ Open 12-3, 6-11; 12-10.30 Sun; 12-3, 7-10.30 Sun in
winter*

HOSE SK7329 Map 7
Rose & Crown
Bolton Lane

The more-or-less open-plan bar at this straightforward old free house in the sleepy
Vale of Belvoir has pool, darts, dominoes, cribbage, a fruit machine and piped
music. Four or five well kept real ales include Brains Mild, Greene King IPA and
Abbot and a guest or two from a microbrewery such as Jennings or Springhead.
There are no smoking areas in the restaurant and lounge bar. Big helpings of bar
food served by friendly attentive staff include soup (£1.95), spicy chicken dippers
(£2.95), filled baguettes (from £1.95), ham and egg (£4.50), broccoli and cream
cheese bake (£4.95), lasagne, chicken breast with white wine or chasseur sauce
(£5.50) and puddings such as treacle sponge or pecan pie (£2.50); Sunday lunch
(£4.95). There are tables on a fairy-lit sheltered terrace behind the building, and a
fenced family area at the back of the car park. *(Recommended by Derek and Sylvia
Stephenson, Brian Wainwright, Dr and Mrs J Hills, the Didler, Phil and Jane Hodson, A C and
E Johnson)*

*Free house ~ Licensees Brian and Janet Morley ~ Real ale ~ Bar food (not Mon (exc
bank hols), Tues, Sun evening) ~ Restaurant ~ (01949) 860424 ~ Children in eating
area of bar and restaurant ~ Open 12-2.30, 7-11; 12-3, 7.30-10.30 Sun; closed
lunchtime Mon-Weds in winter*

KEGWORTH SK4826 Map 7
Cap & Stocking ★ ◪

A mile or so from M1 junction 24: follow A6 towards Loughborough; in village, turn left at
chemists' down one-way Dragwall opposite High Street, then left and left again, into
Borough Street

The three rooms at this properly old-fashioned town local are an appealing
throwback to another age. They still serve Bass from an enamelled jug here, and the
brown paint and etched glass in the right-hand room make it seem little changed
since the 1940s. Each of the two determinedly simple but cosy front rooms has its
own coal fire, and a relaxing easy-going feel, and furnishings include big cases of
stuffed birds and locally caught fish, fabric-covered wall benches and heavy cast-
iron-framed tables, and a cast-iron range; cribbage, dominoes, trivia and piped
music. The back room has french windows to the pretty garden where there may be
floodlit boules and barbecues in summer. Well kept Bass, Hancocks HB and a guest

such as Wadworths 6X on handpump. Good value bar food includes filled rolls (from £1.40, hot beef and onion (£1.60), soup (£1.95), burgers (from £2.50), ploughman's and pizzas (from £4.60), chilli or vegetable curry (£5.25), tasty hungarian goulash (£5.95), beef stroganoff (£6.25) and daily specials such as thai chicken (£5.95) or beef in red wine (£6.25). It's very handy for the M1. *(Recommended by Martin and Jane Bailey, the Didler, Phil and Jane Hodson, B, M and P Kendall, Roger and Jenny Huggins, JP, PP, Pete Baker, Adam and Joan Bunting, L Davenport, Simon King, Darly Graton, Graeme Gulibert, Shaun Pinchbeck, Rona Murdoch, John Robertson, Mr and Mrs J McRobert, Keith Allen, MLR, Michel Hooper-Immins)*

Punch ~ Tenants Graham and Mary Walsh ~ Real ale ~ Bar food (11.30-2.15, 6.30(7 Sun)-8.45) ~ No credit cards ~ (01509) 674814 ~ Children welcome ~ Open 11.30-2.30(3 Sat), 6.30-11; 12-3, 7-10.30 Sun

LOUGHBOROUGH SK5319 Map 7
Swan in the Rushes ★ ◗ £
The Rushes (A6)

Usefully situated not far from the bustle of the town centre, this basic but rather civilised bareboard alehouse lives up well to Tynemills reputation for stocking a good range of beers and other drinks. Alongside Archers Golden, Marstons Pedigree and Tetleys, six changing guests might include Caledonian Deuchar IPA and Hop Back Summer Lightning. They also keep a good range of bottled beers from all over the world, over 30 malt whiskies, nine flavoured Polish vodkas, changing farm cider, perry, fruit wines and very good value soft drinks. There's a good mix of customers throughout the several neatly kept and simply furnished room areas, each with its own style. The most comfortable seats are in the left-hand bay-windowed bar (which has an open fire) and in the snug no smoking back family room. It can get very crowded, but service remains friendly and efficient. Very reasonably priced bar food includes filled baguettes (£2), baked potatoes (from £2.25), a choice of ploughman's (from £4.50), chilli (£4.50), and enjoyable home-made specials such as sausage and mash (£4.75), cottage pie, mushroom stroganoff or thai green curry (£4.95). Daily newspapers, dominoes and juke box; the function room doubles as a skittle alley. The simple bedrooms are clean and cosy; there are generous breakfasts, tables in an outside drinking area, and the M1 is not far. *(Recommended by Joan and Michel Hooper-Immins, Trish and Ian Avis, Andy and Ali, Ian Phillips, the Didler, JP, PP, A C and E Johnson, Pete Baker, Martin Wyss, Michel Hooper-Immins, Rona Murdoch)*

Tynemill ~ Manager Ian Bogie ~ Real ale ~ Bar food (12-2.30, 6-8.30; not Sat, Sun evenings) ~ (01509) 217014 ~ Children welcome in eating area of bar till 8pm or later if eating ~ Folk alternate Suns ~ Open 11-11; 12-10.30 Sun; closed 25 Dec ~ Bedrooms: /£30(£45S)

LYDDINGTON SP8797 Map 4
Old White Hart ⑪
Village signposted off A6003 N of Corby

It's the very good food that draws most customers to this really friendly old country inn. The menu and specials board change all the time, but might include home-made soups such as french onion, tomato and tarragon (£2.95), celery and parmesan tart (£3.95), fresh sardines on garlic and tomato toast (£4.25), lunchtime baguettes (from £4.95), sautéed sweetbreads glazed in honey and rosemary in puff pastry (£4.95), seared king scallops with cherry tomatoes and red onions on mixed leaves with balsamic dressing (£5.95), home-made chicken, bacon and herb pie, cod with herb crust and chive butter sauce or home-made sausages with fresh horseradish mash (£8.95), turbot in chive butter sauce (£11.95), half crispy duck with blackcurrant sauce (£13.95), and puddings such as lemon crème brûlée and hot sticky toffee pudding (£2.75). An original 17th-c window in the passage to the cosy bar is a discreet reminder that this pub was once part of the Burghley Estate.The softly lit low ceilinged bar has just three close-set tables in front of the warm log fire, with heavy bowed beams and lots of attractive dried flower arrangements. The bar opens into an attractive restaurant, and on the other side is a tiled-floor room with some stripped stone, cushioned wall seats and mate's chairs, and a woodburning stove; one restaurant is no smoking. Well kept Greene King IPA, Abbot and Triumph and a guest such as Timothy Taylors Landlord on handpump; piped music. There are picnic-sets in the safe and pretty walled garden which has twelve floodlit boules pitches – on Thursday you can listen to the church bell ringers. There are good nearby walks and the pub is handy for Bede House. *(Recommended by Ted George, Mike and Sue Loseby, Duncan Cloud, John A Barker, Eric Locker, A C and E Johnson, Rona Murdoch, Revd A Nunnerley, Stephen, Julie and Hayley Brown, Jim Farmer)*

Free house ~ Licensee Stuart East ~ Real ale ~ Bar food (12-2(2.30 Sun), 6-9; not Sun evening) ~ Restaurant ~ (01572) 821703 ~ Well behaved children welcome ~ Open 12-3, 6-11; 12-4, 7-10.30 Sun ~ Bedrooms: £45B/£65B

MARKET OVERTON SK8816 Map 7
Black Bull
Village signposted off B668 in Cottesmore

This very enjoyable old thatched stone-built pub is cheerfully run by its jovial landlord, and attracts lots of happy locals arriving in good time for a hearty lunchtime meal. There's a bustling friendly atmosphere in the low black-beamed bar with raspberry mousse walls, red plush stools and cushioned spindlebacks at dark wood pub tables, and flowers on the sills of its little curtained windows. A wide choice of changing good value food is listed on a big blackboard, straight in front of you as you go in, which might include filled ciabatta (from £3.75), starters such as cajun chicken with hot chilli dip, moules marinières, smoked haddock and prawn fishcakes with lemon sauce, potted crab (all £3.95), very reasonably priced lunchtime dishes such as liver and bacon, sizzling chicken, steak and kidney pudding, fish and chips (£6.95), and evening dishes such as roast zander – a freshwater fish – with potato, salmon and prawns with lemon and dill sauce (£9.95), steamed Nile perch (£10.95), fish mixed grill with hot garlic butter (£12.95), lamb shank (£14.95), home-made puddings such as tangy lemon cheesecake or crème brûlée (£3.25); no smoking area in main dining room; well kept Charles Wells Bombardier, Hook Norton Best, Marstons Pedigree, Ruddles and Theakstons Black Bull on handpump; piped music, darts, fruit machine, cribbage and dominoes. *(Recommended by Anthony Barnes, Eric Locker, Bill and Sheila McLardy, Stephen and Jean Curtis, Phil and Jane Hodson, Angus Lyon, RB)*

Free house ~ Licensees John and Val Owen ~ Real ale ~ Bar food (12-2, 6.30(7 Sun)-10) ~ (01572) 767677 ~ Children welcome ~ Open 11-2.30, 6-11; 12-3, 7-10.30 Sun; closed 25 Dec ~ Bedrooms: £30S/£45S

MEDBOURNE SP7993 Map 4
Nevill Arms 🍺
B664 Market Harborough—Uppingham

This imposing old mullion-windowed pub is set in the middle of a peacefully quaint village and reached by a footbridge over the duck-filled River Welland. It's a particularly nice place to stay with rooms in two neighbouring cottages and good breakfasts in the sunny conservatory, and the welcoming owners work hard to ensure you enjoy your visit. The appealing main bar has a cheery atmosphere, two winter log fires in stone fireplaces at either end of the room, chairs and small wall settles around its tables and a lofty, dark-joisted ceiling; piped music. A spacious back room by the former coachyard has pews around more tables (much needed at busy times), and some toys to amuse the children. In summer most people prefer eating at the tables outside on the grass by the dovecote. Five real ales tapped straight from the cask include Adnams, Fullers London Pride and Greene King Abbot with two changing guests such as Grainstore Cooking Bitter and Langton Caudle on handpump, and about two dozen country wines. Good value bar food includes sandwiches (from £2), hot filled panini with fillings such as mozzarella and tomato or brie and bacon (£3.95), ploughman's (£4), and blackboard specials such as toasted goats cheese with redcurrant sauce (£4.95), beef in garlic and ginger, pork in apple and plum or chicken in bacon and asparagus (£5.75). A wide choice of games includes darts, shove-ha'penny, cribbage, dominoes, table skittles, other board games and table football on request. The cat is called Truffles, and Cleo the great dane now has a son called Bertie to keep her company; other dogs are welcome. The church over the bridge is worth a visit. *(Recommended by Angus Lyon, Malcolm Taylor, Mike and Sue Loseby, Mrs B M Spurr, Joan and Michel Hooper-Immins, Eric Locker, Eileen Charles, Jim Farmer, Kevin Thorpe, Sue Holland, Dave Webster, JP, PP, David Field, Norma and Keith Bloomfield, R T and J C Moggridge)*

Free house ~ Licensees Nicholas and Elaine Hall ~ Real ale ~ Bar food ~ (01858) 565288 ~ Well behaved children welcome ~ Open 12-2.30, 6-11; 12-3, 7-10.30 Sun; closed 25 Dec, 1 Jan evenings ~ Bedrooms: £45B/£55B

NEWTON BURGOLAND SK3708 Map 4
Belper Arms ♀
Village signposted off B4116 S of Ashby or B586 W of Ibstock

Although this roadside pub is quite big and knocked through, its ancient features – heavy beams, changing floor levels and separate areas with varying floor and wall materials – all reflecting the various stages in its development, give it a cosy intimate feel. Parts are said to date back to the 13th c, and much of the exposed brickwork certainly looks at least three or four hundred years old. There's masses to look at, from a suit of old chain mail, a collection of pewter teapots and some good antique furniture, to the story of the pub ghost – Five to Four Fred – framed on the wall. A big central chimney, now freestanding, has a fire one side and a range on the other, with chatty groups of captain's chairs. Well kept Adnams and Marstons Pedigree on handpump, a guest or two such as Timothy Taylors Landlord, and ten wines by the glass; pleasant piped music. Freshly prepared bar food includes soup (£2.25), duck and orange pâté (£3.25), crab and salmon fishcakes with tomato and basil coulis (£3.50/£7), tiger trail prawns with red pepper, red onion and lime marinade (£3.95/£8), smoked chicken and pasta salad (£3.75/£7.50), steak and ale pie (£6.75), chicken breast marinated in lemon grass, chilli and garlic with lemon mayonnaise (£7.75), roast leg of lamb steak cooked with smoked bacon, baby onions, mushrooms and red wine (£8.50), and puddings such as sticky toffee, apple and cinnamon pancake and rum panna cotta (£2.75), as well as daily specials such as poached monkfish with coriander and cream sauce (£10.50), fried duck on red cabbage and rosemary jus (£11) and saddle of venison on mustard mash with sloe sauce (£11.75); three-course Sunday lunch (£10.25). Up a step on one side of the bar, the big square restaurant is no smoking. A rambling garden has boules, cricket nets and children's play area, and works its way round the pub to white tables and chairs on a terrace, and a steam-engine-shaped barbecue; campsite. *(Recommended by the Didler, Kevin Blake, JP, PP, Duncan Cloud, Anthony Barnes)*

Free house ~ Licensees Huw Price and Robert Judges ~ Real ale ~ Bar food ~ Restaurant ~ (01530) 270530 ~ Children in eating area of bar and restaurant ~ Open 12-3, 6-11; 12-11 Sat; 12-10.30 Sun

OAKHAM SK8508 Map 4
Grainstore
Station Road, off A606

Strategically positioned next to the staion, this three-storey Victorian grain warehouse was built so that loading trucks could pass right through the building. It was recently converted into a traditional tower brewhouse, with raw materials starting on the upper floor and the finished beer coming out on the bottom floor, and is run by Tony Davis who was head brewer at Ruddles. As soon as you arrive on the premises you get the feel of a working brewery, and you can see the vats of beer through glass doors in the functional open-plan bar. The interior is very simple with wide well worn bare floorboards, bare ceiling boards above massive joists (and noises of the workings above) which are supported by red metal pillars, a long brick-built bar counter with cast-iron bar stools, tall cask tables and simple elm chairs. Their fine beers (Grainstore Cooking, Steamin' Billy, Triple B, Ten Fifty and Mild) are served traditionally at the left end of the bar counter, and through swan necks with sparklers on the right. You can tour the brewery by arrangement, and they do take-aways. In summer they open huge glass doors on to a terrace stacked with barrels, and with picnic-sets; sporting events on TV, bar billiards, darts, giant Jenga and bottle-walking. They serve filled baguettes (£2) at lunchtime only; disabled access. *(Recommended by the Didler, Norma and Keith Bloomfield, Richard Lewis, Bernie Adams, A C and E Johnson, JP, PP, Stephen, Julie and Hayley Brown, Mike and Sue Loseby)*

Own brew ~ Licensee A H Davis ~ Real ale ~ Bar food ~ No credit cards ~ (01572) 770065 ~ Well behaved children welcome ~ Blues, jazz or folk first Sun of each month ~ Open 11-2.30, 5-11; 11-11 Fri, Sat; 12-10.30 Sun

OLD DALBY SK6723 Map 7
Crown ⊕

By school in village centre turn into Longcliff Hill

It's worth going to the trouble to find this tucked away, quite sophisticated creeper-covered former farmhouse. Three or four intimate little rooms have black beams, one or two antique oak settles, a mix of carvers and wheelback chairs, hunting and other rustic prints, open fires, and darts and cribbage; the snug is no smoking. Made from fresh local produce wherever possible, the choice of good imaginative food changes every three months, but might include soup or sandwiches (£3.95), caesar salad or watermelon and mozzarella (£4.50), cold vegetable terrine (£4.95), filled ciabatta (from £5.95), sausage and mash (£6.95), chicken, ham and mushroom pie (£7.50), lamb shank or chicken supreme with orange and cream sauce (£10.95), pork escalope filled with mozzarella and ham with apple and cider sauce (£11.25), roast loin of lamb stuffed with basil and garlic with cherry tomatoes, courgettes, layered potatoes and rosemary jus (£13.75), fillet steak on a crouton topped with pâtés with a red wine sauce (£17.50), and puddings such as key lime pie, summer pudding or hot apple lattice (£4.50); good service. The dining room has a pleasantly relaxed bistro feel. Outside, there is cast-iron furniture and rustic tables and chairs on the terrace, hanging baskets and urns of flowers, and steps lead down through the sheltered sloping lawn where you can practise your boules with the pub's two teams. Well kept Banks's and three changing guest ales such as Courage Directors, Morrels Varsity and Theakstons Old Peculier either on handpump or tapped straight from the cask, and two dozen or more malt whiskies; darts, boules. *(Recommended by Brian Skelcher, J M Parsons, Phil and Jane Hodson, Simon Chell, Mike and Sue Loseby, Eric Locker, the Didler, Angus Lyon, JP, PP, David and Helen Wilkins)*

Free house ~ Licensee Lynn Busby ~ Real ale ~ Bar food (not Sun evening or Mon lunchtime) ~ Restaurant ~ (01664) 823134 ~ Children over 5 at lunchtime, over 10 evenings ~ Open 12-3, 6-11(7.30-10.30 Sun); 12-2.30, 6.30-11(7.30-10 Sun) in winter; closed Mon lunchtime except bank hols

PEGGS GREEN SK4117 Map 7
New Inn £

Signposted off A512 Ashby—Shepshed at roundabout, then Newbold sign down Zion Hill

There's a lovely welcoming local feel at this quirky little place, with a cluster of regulars gathered round the old-fashioned booth bar catching up on the latest news. The cheery Irish licensees like to think of this village pub – now in the second generation of the same family – as an extension of their home. An incredible collection of old bric-a-brac covers almost every inch of the walls and ceilings of the two cosy tiled front rooms. The little room on the left, a bit like a kitchen parlour, has china on the mantelpiece above a warm coal fire, lots of prints and photographs and little collections of this and that, three old cast-iron tables, wooden stools and a small stripped kitchen table. The room to the right, which has quite nice stripped panelling and masses of the sort of bric-a-brac you can spend ages trawling through.

The little back lounge, with a stripped wooden floor, has a really interesting and quite touching display of old local photographs including some colliery ones. Food is served at fairly limited times so do check below. The very short menu includes filled cobs (£1.20), smoked haddock, irish stew with champ and toasted soda bread, beef and Guinness casserole and fish bake (£3.50), and faggots and peas which are the only dish on Monday evenings. Well kept Bass and Marstons Pedigree on handpump; piped music, dominoes and board games. *(Recommended by Bernie Adams, the Didler, JP, PP, Kevin Blake)*

Enterprise ~ Lease Maria Christina Kell ~ Real ale ~ Bar food (12-2; 6-8 Mon; not Tues-Sat evenings; not Sun) ~ No credit cards ~ (01530) 222293 ~ Well behaved children welcome ~ Open 12-2.30, 5.30-11; 12-3, 6.30-11(7-10.30 Sun) Sat

SADDINGTON SP6591 Map 4
Queens Head
S of Leicester between A50 and A6

There's a friendly informal atmosphere in the comfortably civilised bar of this welcoming dining pub. Bar food includes soup (£2.45), filled baguettes (from £2.95), fresh mussels (£3.95-£6.95), fish and chips (£6.95), and steak and ale pie or mushroom, leek and cheddar en croûte (£7.95); duck breast with redcurrant and orange sauce (£9.95), lamb shank (£11.95), home-made puddings including profiteroles, hot black cherry filled pancakes and apple crumble (£3.25); the bargain two-course meals for OAPs (£3.50, Monday to Friday) are hugely popular; prompt service. Although the emphasis is on dining, locals do pop in for the well kept Adnams, Everards Beacon and Tiger and a guest such as Greene King Abbot. There's also a good wine list and daily papers; piped music. The small no smoking conservatory restaurant looks across the valley to the reservoir, and tables in the long sloping garden also have lovely country views. *(Recommended by Gerry Dobson, Dez and Jen Clarke, Keith Allen, P Tailyour, Jim Farmer, Stephen, Julie and Hayley Brown)*

Everards ~ Tenant Simon Martin ~ Real ale ~ Bar food (12-2.30, 6.30-10; not Sun evening) ~ Restaurant ~ (0116) 240 2536 ~ Children over 5 ~ Open 12-3, 5.30(6 Sat)-11; 12-4, 7-10.30 Sun

SIBSON SK3500 Map 4
Cock
A444 N of Nuneaton

Without doubt, this thatched and timbered black and white pub has one of the prettiest exteriors in the *Guide*. Some parts date back as far as the 13th c, Dick Turpin is said to have sought refuge in its chimney in 1735, there was a cock pit in the garden until 1870, and up until just before the war it was owned by the Church, only gaining its Sunday licence in 1954. Proof of its age can still be seen in the unusually low doorways, ancient wall timbers, heavy black beams and genuine latticed windows of the spotlessly kept interior. An atmospheric room on the right has comfortable seats around cast-iron tables, and more seats built in to what was once an immense fireplace (fabled hideaway of the infamous highwayman). The room on the left has country kitchen chairs around wooden tables, and there's a no smoking dining area. Well kept Bass and M & B Brew XI on handpump; fruit machine and piped music. Generously served good value bar food includes home-made soup (£2.15), sandwiches – a very good beef one – (from £2.60), sautéed garlic mushrooms (£2.90), steak and kidney pie, battered cod, lasagne or ham and egg (£7.50), steaks (from £9.50), and daily specials such as chicken chasseur (£8.25), stuffed lambs hearts (£8.75), cajun tuna steak (£8.95) and baked bass with ginger and spring onion (£9.25); on Sunday lunchtime the only food is a three-course roast (£9.95). The restaurant was converted from a former stable block. A little garden and courtyard area has tables, summer hanging baskets and a flower filled dray cart in front. They have a caravan field (certified with the Caravan Club). *(Recommended by Geoffrey and Penny Hughes, Ian Phillips, JP, PP, Susan and John Douglas, Ian and Joan Blackwell)*

Punch ~ Lease Graham Lindsay ~ Real ale ~ Bar food (11.30-2, 6.30(6 Sat)-9.45 (7-9.30 Sun)) ~ Restaurant ~ (01827) 880357 ~ Children in eating area of bar and restaurant ~ Open 11.30-2.30, 6.30(6 Sat)-11; 12-3, 7-10.30 Sun; closed 25, 26 Dec evenings

SOMERBY SK7710 Map 4
Old Brewery 🍺 £

Off A606 Oakham—Melton Mowbray, via Cold Overton, or Leesthorpe and Pickwell; can also be reached direct from Oakham via Knossington; High Street

Although this popular place has been taken over by new licensees, they are still stocking the interesting range of good value award-winning beers which are brewed by Barrie Parish, the former licensee here. These include Baz's Bonce Blower, Poachers Ale and Special Bitter which are well kept alongside a couple of guests such as Bass and Fullers London Pride all on handpump. Groups can still book tours of the little brewery in the former stables, and they also have a beer festival in May. The comfortable L-shaped main bar has red plush stools and banquettes and plush-cushioned captain's chairs, a sofa in one corner, and a good log fire in the big stone fireplace; another bar has bays of button-back red seating. There's a cheerful relaxed atmosphere, with a much broader mix of customers than you might expect. The bar menu has been enlarged under the new licensees and now includes sandwiches (from £1.60), soup (£1.95), prawn cocktail (£3.25), chicken curry (£4.20), ploughman's (£4.25), spinach and mushroom lasagne or steak and kidney pie (£5.20), battered cod (£5.75), chicken with smoked cheese (£6.75) and 8oz sirloin (£7.75); no smoking area in restaurant. Pool, fruit machine, TV and piped music. A fenced-off area by the car park has white plastic tables and a climbing frame. *(Recommended by G Coates, JP, PP, O K Smyth, Richard Lewis, Phil and Jane Hodson, Rona Murdoch, Jim Farmer)*

Own brew ~ Licensees Wendy and Mick Farmer ~ Real ale ~ Bar food (till 9.30 Fri, Sat) ~ Restaurant ~ (01664) 454777 ~ Well behaved children in eating area of bar and restaurant ~ Live bands Sat evenings ~ Open 12-2.30, 6.30-11; 12-10.30 Sun ~ Bedrooms: /£40S

Stilton Cheese 🍺

High Street

This comfortable 16th-c pub offers a warm welcome and a wide choice of well cooked reasonably priced food – which is perhaps what you'd expect with three chefs in the family. The hop-strung beamed bar/lounge has a thriving relaxed atmosphere, lots of country prints on its stripped stone walls, a collection of copper pots, a stuffed badger and plenty of comfortable seats; shove-ha'penny, cribbage, dominoes and board games. There's a no smoking side restaurant up steps. Bar food might include stilton and cranberry parcels, fried whitebait or salmon and dill mousse (£3.50), sliced duck breast with ginger and orange sauce (£6.75), tuna steak with prawn béarnaise or monkfish provençale (£7.95), rack of lamb with a redcurrant glaze (£8.95), Rutland Water trout in prawn and caper butter (£9.95), and puddings such as walnut and ginger treacle tart, almond tart or tiramisu (£2.75). Well kept local Grainstore Ten Fifty, Marstons Pedigree and Tetleys and a guest such Timothy Taylors Landlord on handpump, a good choice of wines and about two dozen malt whiskies; good unruffled service. The patio area has wooden seating and outdoor heaters. *(Recommended by Joan and Michel Hooper-Immins, Eric Locker, Richard Lewis, Jim Farmer, Stephen, Julie and Hayley Brown, John Brightley)*

Free house ~ Licensees Carol and Jeff Evans ~ Real ale ~ Bar food (12-2, 6(7 Sun)-9) ~ Restaurant ~ (01664) 454394 ~ Children in eating area of bar and restaurant ~ Open 12-3, 6-11(7-10.30 Sun)

You can send us reports through our web site: www.goodguides.com

STRETTON SK9416 Map 8

Ram Jam Inn ♀ ⇌

Just off A1: heading N, look out for warning signs some 8 miles N of Stamford, turning off at big inn sign through service station close to B668; heading S, take B668 Oakham turn-off, inn well signed on left ¼ mile from roundabout

Not a pub, but an excellent A1 stand-in, this is a civilised and relaxing modern version of a Great North Road coaching stop, good for a few minutes' break, a snack or a meal at virtually any time of day, or a comfortable overnight stay. As you go in, the first part of the big stylish open-plan bar/dining area has terracotta-coloured walls decorated in one place with a spread of old bread boards, big ceramic tiles on the floor, bentwood chairs and café tables, and sofas in a cosy panelled alcove with daily papers and a standard lamp. The bar on the left here has Fullers London Pride and John Smiths on handpump, good house wines, freshly squeezed orange juice and fresh-ground coffee. This area spreads on back to a no smoking oak-boarded part with old prints and maps, more of the bentwood chairs, dining chairs, and (by a woodburning stove) another sofa and some wicker armchairs. On the right is a more formal dining layout, also no smoking, with well spaced solid tables and attractive Mediterranean photoprints by Georges Meris. Opposite the bar an open kitchen does imaginative if not cheap food from light snacks up, including soup (£3.50), pork terrine (£5.25), chicken ciabatta (£6.25), sausage and mash (£6.95), seafood pasta (£7.25), wild mushroom risotto (£7.95), braised lamb shank (£8.95), and interesting beautifully presented specials such as bouillabaisse with grey mullet fillet or seared scallops on a warm plaice mousse with open pepper ravioli and black sauce. The bread, baked on the premises, comes with proper butter, and puddings might be warm treacle tart, lime and basil cheesecake or chocolate and orange mousse (from £3.75); they also do cream teas (£3.95) and some rather appealing children's dishes (£3.95). The staff are friendly and flexible; there may be faint piped music. If you stay, they're very good at getting your breakfast on the table promptly. *(Recommended by Mike and Heather Watson, John Coatsworth, P Abbott, Mrs J Harry, Francis Johnston)*

Free house ~ Licensees Mike Littlemore and Mrs Margaret Cox ~ Real ale ~ Bar food (12-9.30) ~ Restaurant ~ (01780) 410776 ~ Children welcome in restaurant ~ Open 11-11; 12-10.30 Sun; closed 25 Dec ~ Bedrooms: £52.95B/£69.90B

THORPE LANGTON SP7492 Map 4

Bakers Arms ⓦ

Village signposted off B6047 N of Market Harborough

This thatched dining pub is tucked away in a small village and included in the *Guide* for its popular well presented meals which are made with fresh ingredients and might include grilled goats cheese with pink grapefruit and pink peppercorn dressing (£4.85), fried scallops with black pudding and orange dressing (£6.95), confit of neck of lamb with mash and baby vegetables (£12.50), baked bass with spiced sweet potatoes (£13.25), fillet steak topped with stilton crust with garlic mushrooms (£15.75), quite a few more fresh fish dishes on Thursday evenings, and puddings such as meringue and raspberry ripple ice-cream cake with fruit sauce (£3.75); booking is advisable and it's worth checking their opening times below carefully. Stylishly simple old-fashioned furnishings in the knocked through beamed cottagey interior include stripped pine tables on bareboard floors and turkey rugs, nice black and white photographs. Well kept Tetleys on handpump, an extensive wine list with five by the glass and winter mulled wine; good friendly service, and no games or piped music. There are picnic-sets in the garden. *(Recommended by David Field, Eric Locker, Simon G S Morton, Mike and Sue Loseby, Laurence)*

Free house ~ Licensee Kate Hubbard ~ Real ale ~ Bar food (12-2 Sat and Sun only; 6.30-9.30; not Sun evening, Mon) ~ Restaurant ~ (01858) 545201 ~ Pianist Fri evening ~ Open 6.30-11; 12-3, 6.30-11 Sat; 12-3 Sun; closed Mon, lunchtime Tues-Fri, Sun evening

UPPER HAMBLETON SK9007 Map 4

Finches Arms 🏮

Village signposted from A606 on E edge of Oakham

Leicestershire and Rutland Dining Pub of the Year

This well run stone dining pub is renowned for its very good imaginative freshly prepared food and warm welcome. The menu changes all the time but might include soup (£2.95), filled baguettes with really interesting fillings (from £3.95), parsley, shallot and onion tartlet with tomato and mustard seed salad (£4.25), goats cheese soufflé or antipasta (£4.95), grilled mackerel with lemon and stir-fried vegetables (£7.95), wild mushroom risotto in a savoy crêpe with tomato and basil sauce (£8.50), salmon fillet with asparagus and lemon butter (£9.25), chicken breast stuffed with jarlsberg and king prawns with stuffed tomatoes, sherry paprika cream (£9.95), sirloin steak with wild mushroom fondant and peppercorn and brandy sauce (£11.95), and puddings such as a home-made ice creams and sorbets in a brandy snap basket filled with fresh fruit, chocolate tart with vanilla cream and strawberries and blueberry crème caramel with blackberry ice cream (£3.95). The attractive bar and modern no smoking restaurant both have stylish cane furniture on wooden floors, and there are delightful river views over the expanse of Rutland Water (the twin village of Lower Hambleton is now somewhere below the reservoir) from the restaurant and hillside suntrap terrace; piped music. Well kept Greene King Abbot, Theakstons and Timothy Taylors Landlord on hand or electric pump. *(Recommended by Stephen, Julie and Hayley Brown, M J Morgan, Eric Locker, Mike and Sue Loseby, David Peakall, Anthony Barnes, Roy Bromell, Keith and Di Newsome, Sue Demont, Tim Barrow, Pamela Goodwyn, David Field, Peter H Stallard)*

Free house ~ Licensees Celia and Colin Crawford ~ Real ale ~ Bar food (12-2.30, 7-9.30; 12-3, 7-9 Sun) ~ Restaurant ~ (01572) 756575 ~ Children welcome ~ Open 11-11; 12-10.30 Sun ~ Bedrooms: £55B/£65S(£65B)

WING SK8903 Map 4

Kings Arms 🏮

Top Street, signed off A6003 S of Oakham

This genuinely friendly and relaxing early 17th-c inn scores top marks for its consistently good food, well kept ales and courteous and efficient service. Very enjoyable meals from a changing menu might include soup (£3.50), filled baguettes (from £4.25), ploughman's (£6.50), sausage and garlic mash with red wine jus (£7.50), fish stew (£7.95), battered haddock (£8.50), chicken supreme wrapped in bacon with stilton sauce (£9.90), roast bass on wild rocket with citrus dressing (£11.50) and fried monkfish medallions wrapped in parma ham on tomato and garlic sauce (£12.90). The bar has a traditional feel with wooden beams and a flagstone floor, as well as two large log fires, captain's chairs around pine and darker wood tables, old local photographs and a collection of tankards and old-fashioned whisky measuring pots; in the snug there are fishing rods and tackle; piped music. Well kept Batemans and Grainstore Cooking and a guest on handpump. The restaurant and comfortable neatly kept bedrooms are no smoking. There are seats, swings and slides in the sheltered garden, and a medieval turf maze is just up the road. *(Recommended by Duncan Cloud, Mrs E Rae, JP, PP, Jim Farmer, Stephen, Julie and Hayley Brown, Norma and Keith Bloomfield, Mike and Sue Loseby, Philip and June Caunt)*

Free house ~ Licensees Neil and Karen Hornsby ~ Real ale ~ Bar food (12-2, 6.30-9(8.30 Sun); not Mon lunchtime) ~ Restaurant ~ (01572) 737634 ~ Children welcome ~ Open 12-3, 6-11; 12-11(12-3, 6-11 winter) Sat; 12-10.30 Sun; cl Sun evening and Mon lunchtime in winter ~ Bedrooms: /£65B

Post Office address codings confusingly give the impression that some pubs are in Leicestershire, when they're really in Cambridgeshire (which is where we list them).

Lucky Dip

Besides the fully inspected pubs, you might like to try these Lucky Dips recommended to us and described by readers (if you do, please send us reports: www.goodguides.com).

Aby [TF4177]
Railway Tavern: Well kept Adnams, Everards Tiger and guest beers and home-made food in village pub's open bar; coal fire, railway memorabilia, games room *(JP, PP)*

Asfordby [SK7119]
Crown [Main St]: Pleasant mix of paintings, prints and posters, three changing well kept ales, lots of pump clips on beams, long back restaurant *(Phil and Jane Hodson)*

Ashby-de-la-Zouch [SK3516]
Thirsty Millers [Mill Lane Mews]: Brightly friendly old cottage pub with tales of tunnels to castle, no smoking dining area with big helpings of fresh food using local produce, plenty of salads and lighter food, well kept real ales, good generous house wines, good service, civilised atmosphere; unusual lavatories seem designed for the stature-challenged *(Charmaigne Taylor, Mr and Mrs P Eastwood)*

Barnsdale [SK9008]
☆ *Barnsdale Lodge* [just off A606 Oakham—Stamford]: Extensive conservatory dining bar with good choice of generous attractively presented food, charming décor, comfortable sitting-roomish coffee lounge, cream teas, friendly attentive staff, real ales such as Greene King Old Speckled Hen and Ruddles and Tetleys; prices on the high side; bedrooms comfortable and attractive, with good breakfast; adjacent antiques centre and handy for Barnsdale Gardens *(BB, O K Smyth, M J Morgan, Peter H Stallard)*

Barrow upon Soar [SK5717]
Navigation [off South St (B5328)]: Extended split-level pub based on former barge-horse stabling, attractive and comfortable, with lovely canal view from small back terrace with moorings; good value home-made food (may be limited winter) inc interestingly filled baguettes (only these Sun lunchtime), unusual bar top made from old pennies, central open fire, friendly staff, family room; several well kept ales such as Marstons Pedigree and Tetleys, good prices, skittle alley; maybe piped music, SkyTV *(Phil and Jane Hodson, Bernie Adams)*

Belton [SK4420]
Queens Head [off A512/A453 between junctions 23 and 24, M1; Long St]: Welcoming former coaching inn with two pleasant bars and large dining room, good service, above-average food, well kept Bass, three wines of the month; bedrooms, attractive village *(John and Sylvia Harrop)*

Billesdon [SK7202]
Queens Head [Church St]: Beamed and partly thatched local with wide range of good well priced home cooking, well kept Everards and a guest ale such as Adnams, decent wines, comfortable lounge bar with warm log fire, unspoilt public bar, small conservatory eating area and upstairs restaurant, friendly staff; can get smoky; children welcome, pretty stone village *(Christopher and Jo Barton, Jim Farmer,*

Anthony Barnes)
Bitteswell [SP5385]
Man at Arms [The Green]: Popular for quickly served cheap generous food inc lunchtime bargains for two, L-shaped bar with long front bar, small snug and big eating area, well kept ales, friendly service *(Ted George)*

Botcheston [SK4805]
Greyhound [Main St, off B5380 E of Desford]: Traditional village pub with welcoming service, good freshly made food inc bargain lunches, children's food, evening specials and Sun carvery, well kept beer, small restaurant *(Bernie Adams)*

Branston [SK8129]
Wheel [Main St]: Two cosy and comfortable bars in 18th-c real village pub, good solid food inc game, log fires, friendly atmosphere, well kept John Smiths, splendid countryside nr Belvoir castle *(Nigel Hopkins)*

Braunston [SK8306]
Blue Ball [Cedar Street; off A606 in Oakham]: Thatched dining pub with series of rooms inc no smoking room and small conservatory, beams, woodburner and country pine, food from good baguettes up inc children's helpings, well kept Marstons Pedigree and John Smiths, good choice of wines; dominoes, shove-ha'penny, piped music; children welcome, open all day Sun *(Pat and Roger Fereday, Alan Wilcock, Christine Davidson, Jim Farmer, LYM)*

Breedon on the Hill [SK4022]
☆ *Holly Bush* [A453 Ashby—Castle Donington]: Comfortably plush, with low black beams, lots of brass, sporting plates etc, well kept Marstons Pedigree and Tetleys, fine choice of wines by the glass, freshly made real food (not Sun) inc substantial baguettes, restaurant (may be fully booked Sat, cl Sun), decent coffee, no smoking area, quick friendly staff, good atmosphere; piped music; some tables outside, two nice bedrooms with own bathrooms; interesting village with Anglo-Saxon carvings in hilltop church above huge limestone face *(JP, PP, John and Sylvia Harrop, BB, Dr C D and Mrs S M Burbridge)*

Burrough on the Hill [SK7510]
Stag & Hounds [Main St, off B6047 S of Melton Mowbray]: Relaxed and popular, taken over by local postmaster to save it as a village amenity; good value food, well kept Greene King IPA and guest beers, open fires, dining room; children allowed, garden with play area *(John Jenkins, LYM, Jim Farmer)*

Catthorpe [SP5578]
Cherry Tree [Main St, just off A5 S of M1/M6/A14 interchange]: Welcoming and attractive country local with welcoming new licensees; cosy, clean and warm, with good value food from wide choice of good sandwiches and baguettes up, well kept Bass, Hook Norton Best and an interesting guest beer, quick service, dark panelling, lots of plates

and pictures, maybe elderly dog sprawled by woodburner at cosy end; hood skittles, maybe piped radio; cl Mon/Tues lunchtimes *(George Atkinson, Bernie Adams)*

Croxton Kerrial [SK8329]

Peacock [A607 SW of Grantham]: 17th-c former coaching inn with good value generous home cooking in long bar and small restaurant inc fine choice of puddings, pleasant service, Castle Rock ales, decent wines, hops on beams, real fire partitioned off at one end, some bric-a-brac; piped music, pool; well behaved children welcome, skittle alley, picnic-sets in garden *(A C and E Johnson)*

Desford [SK4703]

Lancaster [Station Rd]: Extended village local with decent food from sandwiches and baguettes to steaks, Courage Directors and Everards Tiger, Mild and Beacon; large conservatory *(Ian Phillips, Gerry Dobson)*

Earl Shilton [SP4697]

Branagans [A47]: Former King William IV well revamped, two comfortable lounges, one with TV and celebrity photographs, another no smoking and music-free, also bare-boards bar with singer photographs, darts, machines and TVs; well kept Bass, Marstons Pedigree and guest beers (OAP happy prices at times), good home-made food from sandwiches up inc OAP bargains and entertaining children's menu, good friendly service; open all day, disabled access *(Bernie Adams)*

Foxton [SP6989]

Bridge 61 [Foxton Locks, off A6 3m NW of Market Harborough (park by bridge 60/62 and walk)]: In good setting at foot of long flight of canal locks, spartan flagstones and pine furniture, quickly served food, lots of canalia and boating relics, Everards and a guest ale, games and family room; gift and provision shop next door *(Dave Braisted)*

Shoulder of Mutton [Main St, off A6 N of Market Harborough]: Cheerful service, lots of pine tables and chairs, well kept Marstons Pedigree and Tetleys, wide choice of reasonably priced food from sandwiches to sizzler steaks (less choice Sun), big woodburner, small restaurant; piped music; friendly dogs and cats, picnic-sets on big front lawn *(Ian and Nita Cooper)*

Great Bowden [SP7488]

Red Lion [Main St]: Open-plan lounge bar (can be smoky), Marstons Pedigree and Tetleys, keen and friendly new licensees doing short choice of interesting modern British cooking in smart dining room on right; carefully reworked garden *(Rona Murdoch)*

Great Dalby [SK7414]

Royal Oak [B6047 S of Melton Mowbray]: Low-beamed and timbered 17th-c village pub with farm tools, good popular bar food inc wide evening choice and Sun lunch, quick service, Tetleys on sparkler (beers not cheap); tables in garden with play area *(W H and E Thomas)*

Great Glen [SP6597]

Old Greyhound [A6 Leicester—Mkt Harboro]: Refurbished (again), with decent range of food,

Adnams Broadside and Greene King Abbot, friendly service, back bar with settles and elderly sofas *(Rona Murdoch)*

☆ *Yews* [A6]: Welcoming and attractively refurbished roomy Chef & Brewer, spreading series of softly lit and relaxing separate areas, wide range of enjoyable food, well kept Courage Best and Marstons Pedigree, good house wines, young helpful staff, coal fires; piped music; good disabled access and facilities, big attractive garden with terrace; open all day *(Anthony Barnes, Doug and June Miles, BB, Mr and Mrs D Moir)*

Greetham [SK9214]

Plough [B668 Stretton—Cottesmore]: Tied to Grainstore of Oakham, with their beers inc a Mild and a seasonal beer kept well, interesting home-made food (baguettes sold by the inch), friendly helpful licensees and staff, coal-effect gas fire dividing cosy lounge from eating area, lots of prints and really exhilarating variety of pub games; games machine, tables out behind (with quoits), open all day Fri-Sun *(Richard Lewis, Bernie Adams)*

☆ *Wheatsheaf* [B668 Stretton—Cottesmore]: Comfortable and welcoming L-shaped communicating rooms, country prints and plates on dining room walls, odd pivoted clock, roaring woodburner, wide choice of good value generous food served till 11 from filled rolls through bargain specials to lots of chargrills, well kept Boddingtons and Tetleys, attentive service, pool and other games in end room; soft piped music; picnic-sets on grass by back car park beside little kingfisher stream (running under pub, it keeps the cellar cool); bedrooms in annexe *(Michael and Jenny Back, Mr and Mrs J Brown, BB)*

Hallaton [SP7996]

Fox [North End]: Comfortable very English country pub with welcoming Spanish landlord adding an imaginative continental touch to the good value menu (also Sun carvery); well kept Marstons Pedigree and Tetleys, good value wine inc half-bottles; children welcome, tables out by village duckpond *(O K Smyth)*

Halstead [SK7505]

Salisbury Arms [Oakham Rd]: Good food (same menu and landlord as Bewicke Arms in Hallaton) in friendly well kept pub's bar or restaurant, which has great views; well kept Bass, log fire, two boules pitches *(Jim Farmer, P Gibb)*

Hathern [SK5032]

Three Crowns [Wide Lane, just off A6]: Busy three-room village local with real fires, Bass, M&B Mild and guest beers, inc Wicked Hathern ales from new local microbrewery; skittle alley, nice garden *(the Didler)*

Heath End [SK3621]

☆ *Saracens Head* [Heath End Lane; follow Calke Abbey coach signs from main rd]: Basic unspoiled two-room farm pub by Staunton Harold Reservoir visitor centre, handy for Calke Abbey; well kept Bass served by jug from the cask, great value filled rolls and toasties, helpful friendly long-serving licensees, cosy coal fires in lounge and tiled-floor bar; picnic-sets on nice grass area, popular with walkers and cyclists *(the Didler, Bernie Adams, JP, PP)*

Hemington [SK4528]

Jolly Sailor [Main St]: Welcoming heavily beamed village local with well kept Bass, Greene King Abbot, M&B Mild, Mansfield, Marstons Pedigree and four guest ales, summer farm cider, good range of malt whiskies and other spirits, good big fresh rolls; good open fire each end, big country pictures, brasses, blow-torches and bric-a-brac, table skittles; beautiful hanging baskets and tables outside; open all day *(the Didler, JP, PP)*

Hose [SK7329]

Black Horse [Bolton Lane]: Friendly little two-room local with four or five well kept real ales such as Brains SA Dark Mild, reasonably priced ambitious food, quarry tiles, darts, open fire, amicable landlord *(Andy and Ali, Darly Graton, Graeme Gulibert, Phil and Jane Hodson, JP, PP, the Didler)*

Houghton on the Hill [SK6703]

Old Black Horse [Main St (just off A47 Leicester—Uppingham)]: Extensively refurbished Everards dining pub, very hospitable, with their beers and guests such as Adnams and Burton Bridge Stairway to Heaven, good value well presented food (no hot food Mon lunchtime), friendly helpful staff, partly no smoking bare-boards dining area; big attractive garden with boules *(George Atkinson)*

Illston on the Hill [SP7099]

☆ *Fox & Goose* [Main St, off B6047 Mkt Harboro—Melton]: Welcoming and idiosyncratic unspoilt chatty local, plain but comfortable, with interesting pictures and assorted oddments, well kept Everards Beacon, Tiger, Original and a guest beer, table lamps, good coal fire; no food, no bedrooms sometimes available *(LYM, Dez and Jen Clarke, Kevin Thorpe)*

Kegworth [SK4826]

Britannia [London Rd]: Good value food, inc bargain Sun lunch 12-9 *(Mrs P Withers)*

Red Lion [a mile from M1 junction 24, via A6 towards Loughborough; High St]: Very traditional brightly lit village local with four plainish rooms around small servery, well kept ales such as Adnams, Banks's Mild, Black Sheep, Caledonian IPA, Fullers London Pride and Marstons Pedigree, limited choice of good wholesome food, good prices; assorted furniture, coal and flame-effect fires, delft shelf of beer bottles, daily papers, darts; picnic-sets in small back yard, garden with play area, open all day *(CMW, JJW, the Didler, JP, PP, BB)*

☆ *Station Hotel* [Station Rd towards West Leake, actually just over the Notts border (and its postal address is in Derbyshire!)]: Busy well refurbished pub with bare brick and woodwork, coal fires, two rooms off small bar area, well kept Bass, Courage Directors, Worthington and guest beers, upstairs restaurant with good home cooking; big back lawn, play area; simple good bedrooms, sharing bathroom *(JP, PP, the Didler)*

Kibworth Beauchamp [SP6893]

☆ *Coach & Horses* [A6 S of Leicester]: Turkey-carpeted local with welcoming and unobtrusively helpful staff, good home-made food, heartening log fire in huge end inglenook, relaxed atmosphere, good range of well kept beers inc Ansells and Bass, decent wines, china and pewter mugs on beams, cosy candlelit restaurant *(Duncan Cloud, Jim Farmer, Eric Locker, BB)*

Kibworth Harcourt [SP6894]

☆ *Three Horse Shoes* [Main St]: Village pub with good choice of competitively priced food inc game and popular family Sun lunch, children welcome with half helpings, well kept Marstons Best and Pedigree with a guest such as Everards Tiger, friendly landlord, comfortable and spacious plush seating, side eating areas; piped music, children welcome; tables on attractive back terrace *(Duncan Cloud, LYM)*

Kilby [SP6295]

Dog & Gun [Main St, off A50 S of Leicester]: Welcoming and relaxed landlord, attentive staff, consistently well kept ales inc Bass, good choice of good fairly priced food inc speciality plate-sized yorkshire puddings and good fish, good wine choice, coal fire, lovely white cat called Webster; popular, can get busy — booking advised *(P Tailyour)*

Kilby Bridge [SP6197]

Navigation [A50 S of Leicester]: Fine canalside position with waterside garden, nice old tiled-floor front bar, big dining area, generous straightforward meaty food, well kept Ansells and Greene King Old Speckled Hen, good coffee; piped music, fruit machines, busy bookable restaurant; children welcome, no dogs *(Rona Murdoch)*

Kirby Bellars [SK7117]

Flying Childers [A607 W of Melton Mowbray]: Big open-plan family dining pub with no smoking and family areas, massive range of usual Tavern Table food all day, puddings cabinet, well kept Banks's and Marstons, good wine choice, side pool and games room; children very welcome, indoor play barn, picnic-sets outside, open all day *(Richard Lewis, Phil and Jane Hodson)*

Kirby Muxloe [SK5104]

Castle Hotel [Main St]: Extended Chef & Brewer with usual Ruddles, Courage Best and Directors and Marstons Pedigree, decent wines, log fire, candles on tables; based on 17th-c farmhouse, garden running down to ruined castle's moat *(Ian Phillips, Gerry Dobson)*

Royal Oak [Main St]: Unassuming 1960s exterior, comfortable inside, with good atmosphere, full Everards range kept well, good food in bar and sizeable restaurant area inc fish specialities (some caught by landlord), good value early lunch and wide range of filled baguettes; friendly service, good wine list, handy for nearby 15th-c castle ruins; piped music *(Gerry Dobson, James Widdowson, Jane Elvidge)*

Knipton [SK8231]

Red House [signed off A607 Grantham—Melton Mowbray]: Handsome refurbished Georgian hunting lodge, generous interesting food, well kept Marstons, John Smiths and a guest beer, good friendly landlord, hunting prints in busy lounge with open fire, sizeable restaurant with attractive conservatory, traditional games in public end; open all day, comfortable bedrooms, terrace with ornamental pool, lovely views over pretty village nr Belvoir Castle *(Miss Joan Morgan, LYM, Bernie Adams)*

Knossington [SK8008]

Fox & Hounds [off A606 W of Oakham; Somerby Rd]: Unspoilt small beamed village pub, very welcoming, with coal fire in cosy comfortable lounge, well kept Courage with guests such as Bass and Boddingtons, huge choice of malt whiskies, reasonably priced food inc unusual dishes, small restaurant (best to book), darts, pool room for younger customers; can be smoky; summer barbecues in big garden *(Rona Murdoch)*

Langham [SK8411]

Noel Arms [Bridge St]: Beams, flagstones and lots of pictures in long pleasant low-ceilinged bar/dining area, generous good value standard food, well kept Greene King Abbot, Mansfield and Marstons Pedigree, friendly service, central log fire; piped music, well behaved dogs allowed; picnic-sets on front terrace *(George Atkinson, Anthony Barnes, LYM)*

Leicester [SK5804]

Ale Wagon [Rutland St/Charles St]: The first pub tied to Hoskins & Oldfields, with up to eight of that small brewery's good interesting ales from Mild to fruit beers, also a couple of guest beers and Weston's perry; good knowledgeable service (tasters offered), basic two-room 1930s interior; open all day, handy for station *(the Didler, Joan and Michel Hooper-Immins)*

Café Bruxelles [High St]: Continental feel in former bank, tall Victorian bar gantry, ornate domed ceiling with painted scenes between gold filigree plasterwork, back area done out as Belgian café with more plasterwork, check oilcloth tablecloths, old labels and coloured tiles on walls, quick friendly service, well presented food inc Belgian snacks, ciabattas and fixed-price meals, lots of unusual bottled beers and several continentals on draught, coffees, good budget wines, small downstairs bar; jazz Mon night, more studenty evenings *(Rona Murdoch)*

Gateway [The Gateway]: Tynemill conversion of old hosiery factory (ladies' underwear on show), bare boards except in no smoking area, five changing ales (one at bargain price) such as Caledonian Deuchars IPA, Ossett, Ridleys Old Bob and Rudgate Ruby Mild, good range of sandwiches and hot dishes till 8 (6 Sun) inc good vegetarian/vegan range, friendly knowledgeable service; piped music, TV; quiz Sun, open all day *(Rona Murdoch, Claire Dunn, Rod Weston, the Didler)*

Globe [Silver St]: Reopened after careful refurbishment, improving the layout but keeping the old-fashioned feel with lots of woodwork in rooms off central bar, charming more peaceful upstairs dining room, wrought-iron gas lamps, good service, Everards real ales, usual food cooked to order; children allowed in some parts *(LYM, Rona Murdoch, Peter H Stallard)*

Granby [Granby St]: Large spaciously comfortable John Barras pub, lots of wood and artefacts, nice furnishings and décor, cheap food, friendly staff, well kept Courage Directors; open all day *(Richard Lewis, Michael Tack)*

Hat & Beaver [Highcross St]: Basic two-room local handy for Shires shopping centre, good well filled rolls, Hardys & Hansons Best, Best Mild and Classic; TV *(the Didler)*

Hind [London Rd (opp stn)]: Dark wood décor, well kept Ansells, Marstons Pedigree and several guest beers, good choice of malt whiskies, friendly staff and atmosphere, lunchtime food, interesting centrepiece clock; darts, games machine, juke box; open all day *(SLC, Richard Lewis)*

Hogshead [Market St]: Long thin Whitbreads alehouse, bare boards and flagstones, panelling, old local photographs, up to ten changing real ales, bottled beers, lots of country wines, no smoking area, friendly young staff, daily papers; all day food, open all day *(Gerry Dobson, Joan and Michel Hooper-Immins, Richard Lewis, the Didler, John A Barker)*

Last Plantagenet [Granby St]: Light and airy Wetherspoons cinema conversion, good choice of well kept beers inc a bargain special, occasional beer festivals, decent cheap food, no smoking area and some booths at the back, lots of prints; open all day, disabled facilities *(Richard Lewis)*

Marquis of Wellington [London Rd]: Carefully restored, with splendid gold and black Edwardian exterior, horsey and old Leicester prints on high panelling, bare boards, soft lighting, well kept Everards ales inc seasonal from long marble counter, reasonably priced usual food, good friendly service, flame-effect gas fire, big windows; piped music, big-screen TV, fruit machine; open all day, disabled access and facilities, colourful heated back courtyard with murals and attractive plants *(Duncan Cloud, G Coates, Richard Lewis, SLC)*

Queen of Bradgate [High St]: Largeish, with dark paint and attractive lighting, decent food inc tempting snacks *(John A Barker)*

Swan & Rushes [Oxford St/ Infirmary Sq]: Recently refurbished and reopened, good choice of real ales inc Oakham JHB and four guest beers, fine range of Belgian beers, enjoyable food *(the Didler)*

Vaults [Wellington St]: Very basic concrete-floored cellar bar with interesting quickly changing microbrews, some tapped from the cask by knowledgeable landlord – a great place for beers; friendly staff, filled rolls, Sunday cheeses, low ceiling with iron pillars (can get smoky), tall settles forming booths, stripped brick walls with old signs rather reminiscent of a railway station; open all day Fri-Sun, cl Mon-Thurs lunchtime, may be entrance fee for Sun live bands *(the Didler, John A Barker)*

Loughborough [SK5319]

Albion [canal bank, about ¼ mile from Loughborough Wharf]: Down-to-earth little old canalside local with emphasis on well kept

Mansfield Bitter and Riding Dark Mild, Sam Smiths OB and guests such as Shepherd Neame; friendly owners, cheap straightforward home-made food, coal fire; children welcome, occasional barbecues, budgerigar aviary in pleasant big courtyard *(the Didler, Christopher Hartley)*

Tap & Mallet [Nottingham Rd]: Fairly plain pub distinguished by five or six changing microbrews, farm cider, occasional beer festivals; back garden, open all day Sat/Sun *(the Didler, JP, PP)*

Lutterworth [SP5484]

Fox [Rugby Rd; very handy for M1 junction 20]: Comfortable dining chairs in lounge, wholesome food, welcoming new licensees, well kept Whitbreads-related ales, good coffee, helpful service, two good open fires; video game, maybe discreet piped music; tables in garden *(P Tailyour, Bruce M Drew, M W Turner)*

Market Bosworth [SK4003]

☆ *Black Horse* [Market Pl]: 18th-c, with several beamed rooms, wide choice of good value interesting fresh food inc good vegetarian choice, friendly attentive service, well kept Greene King IPA, Marstons Pedigree, John Smiths and Tetleys, good house wines and coffee, cosy village bustle, log fire, two charming labradors; restaurant; tables outside – nice setting next to almshouses in centre of attractive village not far from Bosworth Field *(Peter Fearn, Ian Phillips, Heather Couper, John Brightley)*

Market Harborough [SP7388]

Three Swans [High St]: Comfortable and handsome coaching inn renovated as conference hotel, with beams and old local prints in plush and comfortable panelled front bar and comfortable no smoking back lounge, wide range of food from well priced sandwiches up, fine conservatory (also no smoking) and attractive suntrap courtyard, decent wines, well kept Courage Directors and Theakstons Best or XB, good coffee, friendly helpful staff, more formal upstairs restaurant; piped music; good new bedrooms in extension *(Joan and Michel Hooper-Immins, Jim Farmer, Gerry Dobson, George Atkinson, Ian and Joan Blackwell)*

Mountsorrel [SK5714]

Swan [Loughborough Rd, off A6]: Old flagstones, red banquettes, short choice of good food cooked to order (so can be quite a wait), small dining area in side room, well kept Ruddles and Theakstons Old Peculier, wide choice of bottled beers and of good wines by the glass, log fires, good landlady; can get smoky, outside lavatories; small walled back garden leading down to canalised River Soar; bedrooms *(Rona Murdoch, A C and E Johnson, Jim Farmer)*

Newbold Verdon [SK4402]

Windmill [Brascote]: Friendly pub with good food inc choice of Sun roasts, pleasant service *(Stan and Dorothy Garner)*

North Kilworth [SP6183]

Swan [A427]: Pleasantly refurbished village pub, two rooms linked by arch, decent food inc good baguettes, friendly landlord, Tetleys; Irish folk music *(Dave Braisted)*

Oakham [SK9306]

Normanton Park [off A606 E, S of Rutland Water nr Empingham]: Refreshingly informal waterside hotel's Sailing Bar with good choice of food, well kept Greene King Old Speckled Hen and Ruddles and Tetleys; bedrooms, fine views, Rutland Water walks straight from extensive gardens *(BB, M J Morgan, Peter H Stallard)*

Wheatsheaf [Northgate]: Neat and friendly down-to-earth three-room 17th-c local nr church, full Everards range, good basic pub food, open fire; pleasant back garden *(Angus Lyon, Norma and Keith Bloomfield)*

☆ *Whipper In* [Market Pl]: Friendly stone-built coaching inn with creaky boards, oak-beamed and panelled lounge opening into spotless and attractive bistro area, good interesting food (if not cheap) from sandwiches up, real ales, decent wines; comfortable bedrooms *(W H and E Thomas, LYM, Phil and Jane Hodson)*

Peatling Magna [SP5992]

☆ *Cock* [off A50 S of Leicester]: Thriving village local with two rooms, horsey pictures and plates above coal-effect gas fire and on beams, cushioned wall benches, plush stools, cosy log fire, neat country dining area, good value generous food (will do special orders on 48 hours' notice; two sittings for Sun lunch), well kept Courage Directors and John Smiths, decent house wines, friendly staff, lots of events, discounted beer and free nibbles (wkdys 5-7pm); cl wkdy lunchtimes *(B R Pain, Gerry Dobson, LYM)*

Peatling Parva [SP5889]

Shires [Main St]: Good food in large comfortable no smoking conservatory dining room, special food nights and wknd carveries, friendly service, real ale; shame about the piped music; big garden *(Dr and Mrs R E S Tanner)*

Queniborough [SK6412]

Horse & Groom [School Lane]: Lounge packed at lunchtime for the wide choice of enjoyable food from baguettes to cheap traditional and more exotic dishes, well kept Greene King Old Speckled Hen and Tetleys; pool in small back public bar *(Howard and Margaret Buchanan)*

Quorndon [SK5616]

Fox [High St]: Newly refurbished in pleasant old-world style, almost hotelish comfort, well kept Bass, decent food all day, log fires, good landlady; sizeable back garden with tables *(Alan and Paula McCully, Keith Routley, P A Jones)*

☆ *White Hart* [High St (A6)]: One of very few pubs which are Grade I listed, very carefully refurbished to keep original character, and doing well under friendly new licensees; good home cooking inc unusual dishes, well kept Banks's Mild, Greene King IPA, Ind Coope Burton and interesting guest beers, log fires, Victorian family dining room with handsome stove; tables out behind with boules *(P A Jones)*

Redmile [SK8036]

Olde Windmill [Main St, off A52 Grantham—Nottingham]: Comfortable lounge and dining

room, well kept Boddingtons and Wadworths 6X, good house wines, good value home-made food *(Paul S McPherson, W and P J Elderkin)*
Peacock [off A52 W of Grantham; at crossroads follow sign for Belvoir Castle, Harlby, and Melton]: Attractive stone dining pub with four beamed pubby rooms, open fires, pews, stripped country tables and chairs, the odd sofa and easy chair, some stripped golden stone, old prints, chintzy curtains, spacious conservatory-style area; well kept Boddingtons, Flowers IPA, Timothy Taylors Landlord and Whitbreads, no smoking area, dominoes, piped music, good bedrooms; tables outside, peaceful setting nr Belvoir Castle *(Simon Chell, Bob and Maggie Atherton, LYM, Martin and Penny Fletcher, Paul Boot)*

Seaton [SP9098]
George & Dragon [Church Lane, off B672 Caldecott—S Luffenham]: Two-bar pub in unspoilt village, good views of famous viaduct, well kept Greene King IPA, Marstons Pedigree and Theakstons Best, generous attractively priced food cooked to order, helpful friendly prompt service; juke box (may obtrude in public bar); pool; tables outside, very clean lavatories *(Michael and Jenny Back, Rona Murdoch, Jim Farmer)*

Shawell [SP5480]
White Swan [Main St; village signed off A5/A427 roundabout – turn right in village; not far from M6 junct 1]: Attractive 17th-c beamed and panelled pub, open fire, good range of food from baguettes through some unusual specialities to good Sun lunch, well kept Banks's and Marstons Pedigree, service chatty and helpful even when busy, no smoking restaurant; tables out in front, cl lunchtime exc Sun *(Rona Murdoch)*

Shearsby [SP6290]
Chandlers Arms [Fenny Lane, off A50 Leicester—Northampton]: Comfortable village pub with brocaded wall seats, wheelback chairs, flowers on tables, house plants, swagged curtains, candlemaker pictures, Marstons Bitter and Pedigree and Fullers London Pride, no smoking bar on left, wide food choice; may be piped music; tables in secluded raised garden *(P Tailyour, Duncan Cloud; BB)*

Sileby [SK6015]
☆ *White Swan* [Swan St]: Bright, cheerful and relaxed, with imaginative attractively priced food (not Sun evening or Mon lunchtime) from snacks up inc wkdy bargains, well kept Marstons Pedigree, nice house wines, good service, comfortable and welcoming dining lounge, small tasteful book-lined restaurant (booking needed) *(Bridget Smith, Jim Farmer)*

South Croxton [SK6810]
☆ *Golden Fleece* [Main St]: Large, clean and friendly, with enjoyable good value fresh food from good baguettes up in proper bar with some sofas, dark corners and attractive separate restaurant, good service, well kept ales such as Bass, M&B Mild, Marstons Pedigree and Timothy Taylors Landlord, log fire; big TV; lovely area *(Jim Farmer, Ian Phillips, Michael Dilks)*

Sutton Cheney [SK4100]
☆ *Hercules* [off A447 3 miles S of Market Bosworth]: Attractive old local with darts and dominoes in cheerful long bar, frequently changing well kept guest ales and two brewed for the pub, good choice of bar lunches (not Mon), evening restaurant (not Mon; also Sun lunch), friendly staff (landlord was a Wolves footballer), open fire; piped music; Sun quiz night, children welcome, cl Mon lunchtime *(LYM, Bernie Adams)*

Swinford [SP5779]
Chequers [handy for M1/M6/A14 interchange; High St, opp church]: Recent light and airy refurbishment, pine boards and lots of local pictures, attentive friendly service, good food choice, Ansells ales with a guest such as Elgoods Golden Newt; skittles, piped music, machines *(George Atkinson)*

Swithland [SK5413]
☆ *Griffin* [Main St; between A6 and B5330, between Loughborough and Leicester]: Good value local, with well kept Everards, decent straightforward food from sandwiches up (not Sun-Tues evenings), friendly staff, pleasant décor in two cosy arch-linked rooms with old-fashioned woodburners; hallway has memorabilia about footballer landlord Alan Birchinell, back skittle alley; gardens by stream, nice setting *(LYM, Pete Baker)*

Syston [SK6311]
Hobby Horse [Glebe Way]: Popular Tom Cobleigh family pub with beams, panelling and stripped brick, country memorabilia, lots of areas inc upper gallery, good choice of food inc generous children's, friendly helpful staff, well kept Courage Directors and Marstons Pedigree; picnic-sets and play area outside, open all day *(Richard Lewis)*

Thornton [SK4607]
Bricklayers Arms [S of M1, junction 22; Main St]: Traditional old village local with roaring fire and old photographs in beamed bar, Everards Tiger, Beacon and Mild and Greene King Old Speckled Hen, friendly landlord and good staff, good value food, cosy restaurant; piped radio, quiz nights; large back garden with play area, handy for reservoir walks *(Bernie Adams)*

Tilton on the Hill [SK7505]
Salisbury Arms [Oakham Rd, off B6047]: Recently refurbished, lots of nooks and crannies, good blackboard menu, well kept Bass and Marstons Pedigree, restaurant; open country views, two boules pitches *(Melv Tebbett)*

Tinwell [TF0006]
Crown [Crown Lane]: Cosy and convivial village local, wide choice of good food, truly helpful landlord, real ales *(Christopher and Jo Barton)*

Tugby [SK7600]
Fox & Hounds [A47 6 miles W of Uppingham]: Enjoyable generous food, good atmosphere, well kept beer; large outdoor area for children *(Steven Toon)*

Tur Langton [SP7194]
☆ *Bulls Head* [Shangton Rd]: Pleasantly refurbished, keeping unspoilt village feel in bar

with open fire and darts, good choice of freshly made good food inc interesting starters, wide vegetarian choice and midweek bargains in quaint separate restaurant off lounge, well kept ales such as Adnams, Bass and Marstons Pedigree, friendly helpful service (but may be a wait when busy), decent wine list; tables in garden *(Arthur Baker, P Gibb, Eric Locker, Jim Farmer, Rona Murdoch, Melv Tebbett)*

Twyford [SK7210]

Saddle [Main St; off B6047 E of Leicester]: Friendly family-run local with comfortable L-shaped knocked-through bar, well kept Mansfield and John Smiths, open fire, reasonably priced usual food, charming little beamed dining area; pool, piped music and TV in games end; *(Rona Murdoch)*

Uppingham [SP8699]

Falcon [High St East/Market Sq]: Civilised town-centre hotel with plenty of character in oak-panelled bar and comfortable lounge, light and airy, with skylights and big windows over market sq, pleasant light lunches and afternoon teas, well kept Courage Directors, good coffee, nice open fire, serious dailies and fashionable magazines; bedrooms, back car park (can get full) *(W H and E Thomas, Norma and Keith Bloomfield, George Atkinson)*

Walton on the Wolds [SK5919]

Anchor [Loughborough Rd]: Long rambling open-plan pub popular lunchtime with businessmen for good straightforward food (but no credit cards); friendly and unpretentious local evening atmosphere, well kept ales such as Exmoor Gold, Timothy Taylors Landlord and a seasonal beer from Marstons; tables outside, nice village *(Norma and Keith Bloomfield, Phil and Jane Hodson)*

Whitwell [SK9208]

☆ *Noel Arms* [Main Rd]: Wide choice of good food (till 10) from good value ploughman's and bacon baguette to fish and delicious puddings, in spaciously extended light pine restaurant and smart carpeted bar with lower side room, well kept Courage and Marstons Pedigree, charming quick service, suntrap tables outside with play area, occasional barbecues; piped music, can get busy; handy for Rutland Water, children welcome; bedrooms *(LYM, Peter H Stallard)*

Wing [SK8903]

Cuckoo [Top St]: Smart and friendly thatched open-plan pub, good value generous food (not Tues, and beware, they may leave the 'Food' board outside after they've stopped serving) inc authentic curries, well kept Bass, Marstons Pedigree and interesting guest beers, great licensees, nice log fires, midsummer beer festival, cuckoo clock, darts and pool at one

end, dining area with small fish tank the other; children and dogs welcome, wknd live music, plenty of tables in tidy garden *(JP, PP, Stephen, Julie and Hayley Brown, Phil and Jane Hodson, Bernie Adams)*

Woodhouse Eaves [SK5214]

☆ *Pear Tree* [Church Hill; main street, off B591 W of Quorndon]: Attractive upper flagstoned food area with pitched roof and pews forming booths, open kitchen doing enjoyable food (not Sun night) from sandwiches up, welcoming staff; sympathetically refurbished lower pub part with conservatory, log fire, well kept Greene King Abbot, Ind Coope Burton, Marstons Pedigree and Tetleys, good choice of malt whiskies, decent wines; children welcome, open all day bank hol wknds, picnic-sets and summer bar outside, good nearby walks *(David and Helen Wilkins, Ian and Jane Irving, Brian and Genie Smart, A C and E Johnson, JP, PP, LYM, Keith Routley)*

☆ *Wheatsheaf* [Brand Hill; beyond Main St, off B591 S of Loughborough]: Plush and busy open-plan beamed country pub, smart customers, good interesting home-cooked food from sandwiches up, Greene King Abbot, Hook Norton Best and Marstons Pedigree, decent wines, pleasant service, log fire, upstairs restaurant; floodlit tables outside, dogs welcome but no motor-cyclists or children *(JP, PP, the Didler, A C and E Johnson, Ruth Cooper, LYM)*

Wymeswold [SK6023]

Hammer & Pincers [East Rd (A6006)]: Clean, bright and spaciously extended country dining pub with pine furniture in four or five rooms on several levels, good value generous home-cooked food, well kept Bass, Ruddles County, Marstons Pedigree, Theakstons Best and XB and guest beers, friendly service; tables on terrace and in neat garden *(C H and B J Owen)*

Three Crowns [45 Far St]: Snug village pub with good welcoming atmosphere, good value food, well kept Adnams, Marstons, Tetleys and usually a local guest beer, pleasant character furnishings in beamed bar and split-level lounge, couple of dogs *(the Didler, A C and E Johnson)*

Wymondham [SK8518]

Berkeley Arms [Main St]: Immediate welcome in attractive old stone building, two cosy bars done up with new furnishings, enjoyable individual food at attractive prices from fresh crusty bread sandwiches up, good choice of beers such as Adnams, Marstons Pedigree and Tetleys, good coffee; restaurant *(John and Anne Latham, Steven and Sally Knight, Anthony Barnes)*

People don't usually tip bar staff (different in a really smart hotel, say). If you want to thank a barman – dealing with a really large party say, or special friendliness – offer him a drink. Common expressions are: 'And what's yours?' or 'And won't you have something for yourself?'

Lincolnshire

New main entries here this year, or pubs back in the Guide after a break of
some years, are the friendly Castle Inn at Castle Bytham (very generous good
value food, good beers), the interesting 16th-c Lea Gate Inn near Coningsby
(nice food here, too) and the Red Lion at Newton (an excellent buffet as well
as regular hot dishes). Another three places have been in every edition of the
Guide throughout its 20 years: the Beehive in Grantham with its unique living
beehive inn-sign, the Wig & Mitre in Lincoln (carving out a name for itself
even back then with its all-day food – and still very popular under its same
landlady Valerie Hope), and the altogether grander George of Stamford (seems
to get better and better – now as then Ivo Vannocci at the helm). Other pubs
on top form are the Welby Arms at Allington (a good dining pub), the
Chequers at Gedney Dyke (good imaginative food, especially fish), the Black
Horse at Grimsthorpe (perhaps most popular as a dining pub, but good all
round – gains a Place to Stay Award this year), the Blue Cow at South
Witham (brewing its own beers, liked too for food and its family atmosphere)
and the Mermaid at Surfleet (good attractively priced food). The Chequers at
Gedney Dyke, a particular favourite for a good meal out, gains our accolade
of Lincolnshire Dining Pub of the Year. The Cider Centre at Brandy Wharf is
not to be missed if you have any interest in that queen of English drinks. In
fact drinks prices in the area are close to the national average, with beer at the
Mermaid at Surfleet and Victoria in Lincoln (a fine pub) particularly cheap,
and beers from Batemans the county's main brewer always worth looking out
for. In the Lucky Dip section at the end of the chapter, pubs to look out for
(most already inspected and vouched for by us) include the Red Lion at East
Kirkby, Finch Hatton Arms at Ewerby, Bell at Halton Holegate, Masons Arms
in Louth, Massingbird Arms at South Ormsby and Cross Keys at Stow.

ALLINGTON SK8540 Map 7
Welby Arms ◗

The Green; off A1 N of Grantham, or A52 W of Grantham

Readers are full of praise for this well run, friendly village local and, set in a quiet
village in pleasant countryside, it's a handy respite from the A1. Cheerful obliging
waitresses serve really good home-cooked food (readers have commented on their
good, crunchy chips), which might include soup (£2.95), filled baguettes and
ploughman's (from £3.75, lunchtime only), garlic mushrooms (£3.95), fried brie
wedges (£4.25), battered haddock (Tues-Fri, £6.45), fish pie (£7.95) and brie and
bacon chicken (£8.95), and puddings like cherry cheesecake and boozy tiramisu
(£2.95). Booking, especially at weekends, is advisable, and they like you to eat in the
back dining lounge rather than the bar. The atmosphere is traditionally welcoming
and the landlord likes to chat to his customers. The large bar area is divided by a
stone archway, has black beams and joists, log fires (one in an attractive arched
brick fireplace), red velvet curtains and comfortable burgundy button-back wall
banquettes and stools. The civilised dining lounge looks out on to tables in a
sheltered walled courtyard with pretty hanging baskets in summer; no smoking.
Bass, John Smiths, Timothy Taylors Landlord and up two guests such as Greene

King Abbot and Fullers London Pride served through a sparkler but kept \
decent wines and a good range of country wines; piped music, cribbage and \
dominoes. There are picnic-sets on the front lawn. *(Recommended by Michael and \
Back, JP, PP, MLR, Stephen and Jean Curtis, Mike and Penny Sanders, the Didler, Tony Gayfer, \
C and R Bromage, Kevin Thorpe, F J Robinson, Peter F Marshall, Mrs K L Heath, Prof John and \
Mrs Patricia White, Phil and Jane Hodson, Bill and Sheila McLardy, H Bramwell, Margaret and \
Roy Randle, Peter and Jean Hoare)*

*Free house ~ Licensees Bob and Josie Dyer ~ Real ale ~ Bar food (12-2, 6.30-9.30, 6-9 \
Sun) ~ Restaurant ~ (01400) 281361 ~ Children in eating area of bar and restaurant ~ \
Open 12-2.30(3 Sat), 6-11; 12-3, 6-10.30 Sun ~ Bedrooms: £48S/£60S*

ASWARBY TF0639 Map 8
Tally Ho ♀ 🛏

A15 S of Sleaford (but N of village turn-off)

This handsome, civilised place was built as a farm manager's house for the estate in
the 17th c and became an inn in early Victorian times. The bar is more or less
divided in two by an entrance lobby stacked full with logs, giving the feel of two
little rooms, each with their own stripped stone fireplace, candles on a nice mix of
chunky old pine tables and small round cast-iron-framed tables, big country prints
on cream walls and big windows; daily papers, piped music. Real ales, appreciated
by thirsty locals standing round the bar, include well kept Bass and Batemans XB
and a guest such as Brewsters Serendipity on handpump and good house wines. The
generous bar food includes soup (£2.75), lincolnshire sausage (£4.75), ploughman's
or filled french bread (£4.95), blackboard specials which might be four cheese tartlet
or smoked mackerel pâté (£3.85), mediterranean vegetable lasagne (£6.25), lambs
liver and bacon in red wine gravy, salmon and spinach fishcakes or beef and ale pie
(£6.95), chicken pieces in pepper and orange sauce (£7.15), rump steak (£10.50);
carefully prepared home-made puddings might include lemon crumble and
blackberry sponge (£2.75). Booking might be necessary if you want to eat in the
attractive pine-furnished restaurant. Among the fruit trees at the back there are
tables. The bedrooms are in a neatly converted back block, formerly the dairy and a
barn. Over the road, the pretty estate church, glimpsed through the stately oaks of
the park, is worth a visit. *(Recommended by Ken and Jenny Simmonds, P F Thomson,
Richard Cole, M J Morgan, Philip and June Caunt, Ted and Jan Whitfield, Mike and Maggie
Betton, Derek and Sylvia Stephenson, L M Parsons, Anthony Barnes)*

*Free house ~ Licensee Christine Robertson ~ Real ale ~ Bar food (12-2.30, 6.30-10) ~
Restaurant ~ (01529) 455205 ~ Children welcome ~ Open 12-3, 6-(7-10.30 Sun)11;
closed 26 Dec ~ Bedrooms: £35B/£50B*

BARNOLDBY LE BECK TA2303 Map 8
Ship ♀

Village signposted off A18 Louth—Grimsby

Although this genteel pub, filled with such an amazing collection of Edwardian and
Victorian bric-a-brac that it feels a bit like a museum, has changed hands, the new
landlord says he doesn't intend to make any real changes. Comfortable dark green
plush wall benches with lots of pretty propped up cushions face tables, many booked
for dining, and there are heavily stuffed green plush Victorian-looking chairs on a
green fleur de lys carpet. Heavy dark-ringed drapes and net curtains swathe the
windows, throwing an opaque light on the beautifully laid out nostalgic collection of
half remembered things like stand-up telephones, violins, a horn gramophone,
bowler and top hats, old rackets, crops and hockey sticks, a lace dress, stuffed birds
and animals, and grandmotherly plants in ornate china bowls. Only the piped music
is slightly incongruous. Good bar food could include mushrooms with cream and
garlic sauce (£3.45), scotch salmon and prawns (£4.95), beef madras or vegetarian
lasagne (£6.95), halibut steak with herb and garlic butter (£9.95) and mixed grill
(£10.95) and daily specials (with lots of good fresh fish from Grimsby) such as
vegetable stir fry or stilton and mushroom crêpe (£6.95), lemon sole with salmon

and prawns in a cheese sauce, fresh dressed crab or lamb steak with port sauce (£10.95) and puddings such as chocolate and brandy fudge cake or white chocolate crème brûlée (£2.95). Well kept Courage Directors, Castle Eden and Marstons Pedigree on handpump, and an extensive wine list with plenty by the glass. There are a few picnic-sets under pink cocktail umbrellas outside at the back, next to big hanging baskets suspended from stands. *(Recommended by P Norton, Keith Topliss, DC)*

Free house ~ Licensee Carl Broughton ~ Real ale ~ Bar food (12-2, 7-9.30) ~ Restaurant ~ (01472) 822308 ~ Children welcome ~ Open 12-3, 6.30-11; 12-3, 6.30-10.30 Sun

BRANDY WHARF TF0197 Map 8
Cider Centre
B1205 SE of Scunthorpe (off A15 about 16 miles N of Lincoln)

Reputedly only one of three in the country, this canal-side cider tavern has more than 60 varieties of cider. There are up to 15 on draught, 8 tapped from casks while the rest are kept in stacks of fascinating bottles and small plastic or earthenware kegs on shelves behind the bar (they also keep country wines and mead). The friendly landlord is happy to talk about cider and on request will open up his small museum and show you his collection of over 900 different cider bottles and jugs from around the country. The simple main bar has wheelback chairs and brown plush wall banquettes, cheery customer photographs and a good little coal fire. The dim-lit lounge bar has all sorts of cider memorabilia and humorous sidelights on cider-making and drinking – look out for the foot of 'Cyril the Plumber' poking down through the ceiling. Generous, good value bar food includes sandwiches (£2.20, £2.60 toasted), burgers (from £3.20), ploughman's (from £3.60), pork and cider sausages (from £3.60), broccoli and cream cheese bake (£5.65) and chicken curry or chilli (£5.80) with wonderful real chips; piped British folk music. The pub is set next to a canal in four acres of orchard and meadow, and a simple glazed verandah looks onto the river where there are moorings and a slipway. There's also a caravan site; quite a few appropriate special events. No children inside but there's plenty to do in the orchard which also has tables and chairs; the whole place is no smoking. *(Recommended by M J Morgan, John and Sylvia Harrop, JP, PP, Mike and Lynn Robinson, Andy and Jill Kassube, the Didler, Bernie Adams)*

Free house ~ Licensee Ian N Horsley ~ Bar food (12-2, 7-9.45, not Tues lunchtime, not winter Mon) ~ No credit cards ~ (01652) 678364 ~ Open 12-3, 7-11; 12-(3 winter)4, 7-10.30 Sun; closed Mon lunchtime winter; closed Christmas to New Year

CASTLE BYTHAM SK9818 Map 8
Castle Inn ◖
Village signposted off A1 Stamford—Grantham, or off B1176 N of Stamford; High Street

The thriving village atmosphere and cheerfully welcoming service (everyone's 'dearie', 'sweetie', 'my darling') put a smile on your face almost as soon as you step through the door here. The bar, cosily lit with table lamps and soft wall lights, has some small dark brown plush button-back banquettes and a mix of other seats, lots of brass and copper toasting forks, tongs, candlesticks, jugs and pots gleaming around the log fire, horsebrasses on the black beams and joists, and a few farm tools, antlers and heavy horse tack on the stripped stone walls. Bow windows look down over the village (which is attractive) to rolling countryside beyond. Robust home cooking is a high point. The menu includes soup (£2.95), sandwiches (from £3.25), hot smoked mackerel with horseradish sauce (£3.95), crispy thai-style prawns (£4.25), chicken curry or steak and kidney pie with suet crust (£6.25), ham and mushroom tagliatelle (£6.50), grilled lamb cutlets (£7.50), salmon in asparagus and lobster sauce (£8.25), and puddings (£3.50). Main dishes come with six or seven carefully cooked vegetables – their sauté potatoes are particularly good. Well kept real ales such as Adnams Best, Boddingtons, Oakham JHB and Shepherd Neame Bishops Finger on handpump; efficient cheerful service even on very busy nights; may be piped pop music. A back dining area on the left, with regency striped pink wallpaper and a collection of china and other pigs, is no smoking, and their Christmas decorations can be rather special. There are metal tables on a little terrace, and they have CCTV for parked cars. *(Recommended by Michael and Jen... Ray and Winifred Halliday, RB)*

Free house ~ Licensees Gary and Jill Ward ~ Real ale ~ Bar food (12-2, 6.30-10) ~ Restaurant ~ (01780) 410504 ~ Children in restaurant ~ Open 12-2, 6.30-11(10.30 Sun); closed Mon

CONINGSBY TF2458 Map 8
Lea Gate Inn

Leagate Rd (B1192, ¾ mile NW)

Before the fens were drained this 16th-c place stood by one of the perilous tracks through the marshes, and outside the door you can still see the small iron gantry that used to hold a lamp to guide travellers safely along their way. Inside is pleasant and friendly, with three separate cosy and softly lit areas linked together around the corner bar counter, attractively furnished with a variety of tables and chairs including antique oak settles with hunting-print cushions and two great high-backed settles making a snug around the biggest of the fireplaces. Another fireplace has an interesting cast-iron fireplate depicting the Last Supper above it; there are heavy black beams supporting ochre boards, and a collection of bottles in one cabinet. Promptly served good value bar food includes soup (£2.25), nicely presented sandwiches (from £2.50), garlic mushrooms (£2.95), ploughman's (£4.95), lincolnshire sausages (£5.25), vegetarian dishes such as pasta pepper bake (£6.95), smoked chicken breast or plaice stuffed with prawns in a wild mushroom and wine sauce (£7.95), and steaks (from £9.50), with specials such as game pie (£7.95) and fresh bass (£10.95), and good home-made puddings; children's meals. Well kept Marstons Pedigree, John Smiths, Theakstons XB and a guest such as Charles Wells Bombardier on handpump; piped jazz or pop music, fruit machine. There are tables outside, and an enclosed play area. We have not yet heard from readers who have stayed in the newish bedroom block. *(Recommended by the Didler, JP, PP, Bill and Sheila McLardy, Phil and Jane Hodson, Michael and Jenny Back)*

Free house ~ Licensee Mark Dennison ~ Bar food (12-2, 6.30-9.30) ~ Restaurant ~ (01526) 342370 ~ Children away from main bar, no under 5s after 9pm ~ Open 11.30-3(3.30 Sat), 6.30(6 Sat)-11; 12-3, 6-10.30 Sun; closed last week in Oct ~ Bedrooms: £47.50B/£60B

CORBY GLEN SK9924 Map 8
Woodhouse Inn

A151, between A1 and Bourne

Look out for the long wood carving of the Battle of Britain in this 19th-c stone-built country pub. The licensee here served as an RAF officer attached to the Italian Air Force in Sardinia for nearly a decade and on Friday nights they fire up a Sardinian woodburning brick-built oven in the garden, and serve an unusual Mediterranean carvery (£7.95). Bar food (which is served only at lunchtime) is limited to filled baguettes (£3.95) or their three-course meal which changes daily (their restaurant serves a mixture of traditional English and Mediterranean dishes). The open-plan interior works its way around a centralish stone counter, and is quite simply decorated, with a beige turkey carpet, pink walls, mixed dark wood tables and a variety of chairs; there are french windows opening onto a carefully planted garden with a terrace and lawn. The corridor to the gents' has an exceptional collection of fighter jet prints, each signed and dedicated to the landlord. Theakstons Best and XB and an occasional guest beer on handpump; piped easy listening. We'd like to hear readers' opinions on whether this place is now too much of a restaurant to be included. *(Recommended by Phil and Jane Hodson, Kevin Thorpe, M J Morgan, Peter Burton)*

Free house ~ Licensees Mike and Linda Pichel-Juan ~ Real ale ~ Bar food (lunchtime only) ~ Restaurant ~ (01476) 550316 ~ Well behaved children welcome ~ Open 12-2.30, 7-11; 12-3, 7-10.30 Sun ~ Bedrooms: £37.50B/£45B

DYKE TF1022 Map 8

Wishing Well ◀

21 Main Street; village signposted off A15 N of Bourne

This bustling big black and white village inn seems to be doing well under its new landlady. Well kept Everards Tiger and Greene King Abbot are served alongside three regularly changing guests such as Timothy Taylors Landlord and Brains SA on handpump. The popular, good value bar food includes soup (£2.80), sandwiches (from £2.80), starters such as prawn cocktail and chicken wings (from £4), home-made lasagne or steak and ale pie (£6.50), breaded scampi (£6.95) and steaks (from £7.95) with puddings such as apple pie or carrot cake (from £2.50). The no smoking restaurant has been refurbished. There's a wishing well at the end of the long, rambling bustling front bar – as well as lots of heavy beams, dark stone, brasswork, candlelight and a cavern of an open fireplace. The carpeted lounge area has a chesterfield settee, green plush button-back low settles and wheelback chairs around individual wooden tables. The quite separate public bar, smaller and plainer, has sensibly placed darts, pool, fruit machine, video game and piped music. There's a small conservatory and tables and a play area in the garden. *(Recommended by John Curtis, Phil and Jane Hodson, M J Morgan, MLR, Richard Lewis, Dr Paull Khan, Sue and Bob Ward, JP, PP, Peter H Stallard)*

Free house ~ Licensee Theresa Gallagher ~ Real ale ~ Bar food (12-2, 6-9) ~ Restaurant ~ (01778) 422970 ~ Children in eating area of bar and restaurant, over fives only evenings ~ Open 11-2.30, 6-11; 12-2.30, 7-10.30 Sun ~ Bedrooms: £35B/£50B

GEDNEY DYKE TF4125 Map 8

Chequers ⑪ ♀

Village signposted off A17 Holbeach—Kings Lynn

Lincolnshire Dining Pub of the Year

A few feet below sea level, this friendly Fenland pub continues to impress readers with its good, imaginative food. The speciality here is the really fresh fish and seafood specials such as seared monkfish with herb crumb and coriander relish, seabass fillet with beurre blanc sauce and cromer crab salad. Other fairly priced and attractively presented food includes sandwiches (from £2.75), home-made soup (£3.50), warm potato and black pudding salad (£4.95), pigeon breast with leek and potato purée in cider sauce (£8.95), haunch of local venison (£11.50), 6oz fillet of local beef (£11.95) and good home-made puddings (£3.50); roast Sunday lunch. Well kept Adnams Bitter, Greene King Abbot, and a guest such as locally brewed Dixons Old Honesty on handpump, decent wine list with about 10 by the glass, elderflower pressé and apple juice. The fairly simple interior is spotlessly kept, with an open fire in the bar, a rather old-fashioned restaurant area at one end, and, overlooking a garden with picnic-sets, there's a no smoking dining conservatory; piped music. *(Recommended by Mr and Mrs J Brown, Mike and Bridget Cummins, June and Malcolm Farmer, W K Wood, O K Smyth, Barbara Wensworth, MLR, Tony Middis, Peter and Jean Hoare, Roger Everett, June and Ken Brooks, Phil and Jane Hodson, Val and Alan Green, Mrs Thomas, JP, PP, Dr G E Martin)*

Free house ~ Licensees Simon and Linda Rattray ~ Real ale ~ Bar food (not 25 Dec) ~ (01406) 362666 ~ Children welcome ~ Open 12-2, 7-11(10.30 Sun)

GRANTHAM SK9135 Map 7

Beehive £

Castlegate; from main street turn down Finkin Street opposite St Peter's Place

Now under a new licensee, this unpretentious pub's claim to fame is its remarkable pub sign – a hive full of living bees, mounted in a lime tree. It's been here since at least 1830, and probably the 18th c, making this one of the oldest populations of bees in the world. The comfortably straightforward L-shaped bar is partly divided by a wall and fireplace and has a bustling, friendly atmosphere, with tables on bare boards. Three well kept real ales on handpump might include beers from brewers such as the local Newby Wyke, Bass and Everards on handpump. It's popular with students. Good value bar food includes sandwiches (from £1.50), burgers (from £1.75), filled baked potatoes (£2.50), scampi or gammon and egg (£3.50) and 8oz rump steak (£4.95); two meals for £5.50 Saturday lunchtime. Fruit machine, juke box, pool, SkyTV, piped music. *(Recommended by the Didler, JP, PP, Phil and Jane Hodson, Richard Lewis, Derek and Sylvia Stephenson)*

Free house ~ Licensee Tina Hayward ~ Real ale ~ Bar food (12-2.30, 5.30-7.30, 12-4 only Sun) ~ Restaurant ~ (01476) 404554 ~ Children welcome ~ Karaoke Sun evening ~ Open 11.30-11; 12-10.30 Sun

GRIMSTHORPE TF0422 Map 8
Black Horse ⏧ ♀ 🛏

A151 W of Bourne

This handsome grey stone coaching inn continues to impress us with its beautifully cooked and presented bar food, and it's recently increased its already excellent wine list. The food from a changing menu (of a standard and style rare for this part of the world) includes dishes such as soup of the day (£2.75), baked goats cheese, ratatouille and pesto (£4.95), oak-smoked salmon (£6), spinach risotto (£9.50), mackerel fillets with orange braised vegetables and fish velouté (£10.95), stuffed guinea fowl leg with sage mash (£11.25) and puddings such as rhubarb brûlée or poached clementines with rice pudding and caramel sauce; three-course Sunday lunch (£13.95). Their no smoking restaurant does more elaborate food. The neatly kept narrow bar, with oak flooring and homely wallpaper, has stools along an oak timbered counter on one side, and intimate tables on the other. There's also a cosy window seat, a nice round oak table, a coal fire in a stripped stone fireplace, lamps and fresh flowers. They serve well kept Black Horse Bitter and Grimsthorpe Castle (both brewed for the pub by Oldershaws); piped music. *(Recommended by M J Morgan, Janet and Peter Race, W J Allen, Peter Burton, Robin and Diana Rumsam, Peter and Anne-Marie O'Malley, M J Brooks, R C Wiles; also in The Good Hotel Guide)*

Free house ~ Licensees Brian and Elaine Rey ~ Real ale ~ Bar food (12-2, 7-9.30) ~ Restaurant ~ (01778) 591247 ~ Children in eating area of bar ~ Open 11.30-2.30, 6.30(6 Sat)-11; 12-3, 7-10.30 Sun ~ Bedrooms: £50B/£69B

LINCOLN SK9771 Map 8
Victoria ◗ £

6 Union Road

Tucked away in a back street behind the castle this quaint, early Victorian local is a proper ale house. No pretensions here and few concessions to comfort but the chatty, buoyant atmosphere more than makes up for that. The simply furnished little tiled front lounge has a coal fire and pictures of its namesake, Queen Victoria. It attracts a good mix of ages and is always bustling especially at lunchtime and later on in the evening. The good range of well kept real ales includes Batemans XB, Everards Original and Timothy Taylors Landlord with up to five guests from brewers such as Oldershaws and Black Sheep as well as foreign draught and bottled beers, and around twenty country wines. Limited but good value lunchtime food includes filled cobs (from £1.20, huge bacon ones, £2.75), toasted sandwiches (£1.95), all-day breakfast and basic home-made hot dishes such as beef stew, sausage and mash, chilli or curry (£3.75), ploughman's (£4); Sunday roast (£5). You can sit in the small conservatory or in the gravelled side garden which has good views of the castle. They hold beer festivals the third week in June and the first week in December. *(Recommended by JP, PP, David Carr, Barbara Wensworth, the Didler, MLR, Andy and Jill Kassube, Mike and Lynn Robinson, Stephen, Julie and Hayley Brown, Chris and Elaine Lyon, Adrian and Felicity Smith, Richard Lewis)*

Tynemill ~ Manager Neil Renshaw ~ Real ale ~ Bar food (12-2.30; 11-2 Sat; 12-2 Sun) ~ Restaurant ~ (01522) 536048 ~ Jazz or folk first Sun of month ~ Open 11-11; 12-10.30 Sun

Wig & Mitre ★ ♀

30-32 Steep Hill; just below cathedral

This handy, popular pub, between the castle and the cathedral, is open from 8am till midnight every day of the year and is the type of place where you can feel comfortable just popping in for a coffee. The building dates from the 14th c and there are plenty of period features. There's a real buzz in the simpler beamed downstairs bar which has exposed stone walls, and pews and Gothic furniture on oak floorboards, and comfortable sofas in a back carpeted area. Upstairs, the civilised dining room is light and airy with views of the castle walls and cathedral, shelves of old books, and an open fire, and is decorated with antique prints and more modern caricatures of lawyers and clerics, with plenty of newspapers and periodicals lying about. They serve food all day, although it's by no means cheap. There's a full breakfast menu (English breakfast £7.50), and various other menus which between them might include sandwiches (from £3.95), soup (£4.50), baked cheese soufflé with spinach and mushrooms (£6.75), roast mediterranean vegetable and goats cheese tart (£9.50), roast duck with red thai curry sauce (£14.75), monkfish medallions with tiger prawns and black pasta with a herb butter sauce (£15.50), and fillet steak on bacon and potato rösti with mushroom duxelle and port wine sauce (£16.95), as well as puddings such as steamed lemon sponge and chocolate and hazelnut moussecake with crème fraîche (£4.50), and a cheeseboard (£4.95). Besides well kept Marstons Pedigree and Morrells Varsity on handpump, they have an excellent selection of over 95 wines, many of them available by the glass and lots of liqueurs and spirits; they serve freshly squeezed orange juice and have a proper espresso machine. *(Recommended by David Carr, Lucien, Hugh A MacLean, Mike and Lynn Robinson, David and Ruth Hollands, Stephen, Julie and Hayley Brown, Steve Chambers, Richard Lewis, Mike and Heather Watson, Mike and Maggie Betton, Torrens Lyster, Adrian and Felicity Smith, Patricia Beebe, JP, PP)*

Free house ~ Licensees Paul Vidic and Valerie Hope ~ Real ale ~ Bar food (8-11) ~ Restaurant ~ (01522) 535190 ~ Children in eating area of bar and restaurant ~ Open 8-12

NEWTON TF0436 Map 8

Red Lion

Signed from A52 E of Grantham; pub itself also discreetly signed off A52

Readers like the impressive daily help-yourself cold buffet and the carvery roasts on Saturday evening and Sunday lunchtime at this welcoming old pub. It's comfortable and civilised inside with old-fashioned seating, partly stripped stone walls with old tools and stuffed creatures. Aside from a good range of steaks (from £9.95), bar food could include root vegetables in tomato gravy (£5.95), vegetable curry (£6.50), battered haddock or steak pie (£7.95), gammon steak, salmon or trout (£8.95) with specials such as salmon fishcakes (£6.95); senior citizens two-course meal (£6.95). The dining room is partly no smoking. Well kept Batemans XB and a guest such as Abbot Ale on handpump, friendly service; may be piped music, fruit machine. The pub runs two squash courts which can be used by non-members. A neat, sheltered back garden has some seats on the grass and on the terrace and there's a good children's play area. The nearby countryside is ideal for walks and, according to local tradition, this village is the highest point between Grantham and the Urals. *(Recommended by John Curtis, Andy and Jill Kassube, JP, PP, Natalie and Alan Strange, Mr and Mrs G S Pink, M J Morgan)*

Free house ~ Licensee Mr Blessett ~ Real ale ~ Bar food ~ (01529) 497256 ~ Very well behaved children away from bar ~ Open 12-2.30, 6(7 Mon)-11; 12-2.30, 7-10.30 Sun

---

Please tell us if the décor, atmosphere, food or drink at a pub is different from our description. We rely on readers' reports to keep us up to date. No stamp needed: The Good Pub Guide, FREEPOST TN1569, Wadhurst, E Sussex TN5 7BR.

SOUTH WITHAM SK9219 Map 8
Blue Cow ✦

Village signposted just off A1 Stamford—Grantham

Not content with brewing its good own beer this old stone-walled country pub also does enjoyable bar food, well liked by families as well as beer fans. You enter past a little water feature on lit steps down to the cellar. Two bars inside are served by a central counter. One dark-beamed room has nice hardwood Indonesian tables, bentwood chairs, wickerwork and panelling and prettily curtained windows. The second has shiny flagstones and dark blue flowery carpet, big black standing timbers and beams and partly stripped stone walls. As well as sandwiches which are served all day, a good choice of bar food includes soup (£3.50), cheese and garlic stuffed, crumbed mushrooms (£3.80), malaysian chicken satay (£4.25), steak and Guinness pie (£6.45), leek, potato and courgette pancake (£6.85), steaks (from £9.25), lamb with spinach and mild nutmeg sauce (£9.85), and changing daily blackboard specials such as sea food curry and cajun chicken; no smoking restaurant; piped music; darts, TV, cribbage, table skittles and dominoes. The well kept own-brew beers on handpump are Thirlwells Best, Cuddy and Blue Cow. There are tables out on a pleasant terrace by the garden. We still haven't heard from anyone who has stayed here, but they will even stable your horse overnight. (*Recommended by Anthony Barnes, Derek and Sylvia Stephenson, Mr and Mrs M Doherty, Phil and Jane Hodson, Kevin Thorpe, JP, PP, Stephen, Julie and Hayley Brown, the Didler, Richard Lewis, David and Ruth Hollands, Joan and Michel Hooper-Immins*)

Own brew ~ Licensees Dick and Julia Thirlwell ~ Real ale ~ Bar food (12-2.30, 6-9.30) ~ Restaurant ~ (01572) 768432 ~ Children welcome ~ Open 12-11 ~ Bedrooms: £40S/£45S

STAMFORD TF0207 Map 8
Daniel Lambert ✦

St Leonards Street

This roadside pub is named after a 19th-c prison warden who weighed more than 52 stone when he died suddenly during an overnight stop in Stamford. The simply decorated smallish bar makes a nice down-to-earth pubby alternative to our other much smarter main entry here. There's a big picture of Daniel Lambert and other bits and pieces about him, a log fire in winter, and maroon plush stools and chairs on a green carpet. They have well kept Adnams, Courage Directors, Tetleys and Timothy Taylors Landlord and a guest such as Black Sheep on handpump, as well as eight wines by the glass. Bar food includes sandwiches (from £2.50), soup (£2.75), hot filled baguettes (from £3.25), stilton and Guinness pâté (£3.75), burgers (from £4.25), three cheese and pasta broccoli bake (£5.75), chicken in a honey and mustard sauce or deep-fried scampi (£6.95), steaks (from £10.50), daily specials such as sausage and mash (£4.50) and puddings such as jam roly poly and toffee cream pie (from £3.25); no smoking restaurant; fruit machine, cribbage, dominoes and piped music. The tidy, thoughtfully planted little terraced back garden has aluminium tables and chairs and, with its subtle lighting, looks nice at night. Daniel Lambert is buried in St Martin's churchyard and you can see items of his clothing (he measured 9 ft 4 in round the body) in the Stamford Museum in Broad Street. (*Recommended by the Didler, Richard Cleaver*)

Free house ~ Licensees Mr and Mrs Welsh ~ Real ale ~ Bar food (not Sun and Mon evenings) ~ Restaurant ~ (01780) 755991 ~ Children in eating area of bar and restaurant ~ Open 12-2.30, 6-11; 11.30-11 Sat; 12-3, 7-10.30 Sun

George of Stamford ★ 🍽 ♊ 🛏

71 High St, St Martins

This very attractive old coaching inn in the heart of the town has retained its character despite having every modern comfort. Built in 1597 for Lord Burghley, it includes parts of a much older Norman pilgrim's hospice – and a crypt under the cocktail bar that may be 1000 years old. There's a variety of seats in its smart, but relaxed rooms ranging from sturdy bar settles through leather, cane and antique wicker to soft settees and easy chairs, while the central lounge has sturdy timbers, broad flagstones, heavy beams, and massive stonework; there's supposed to be a ghostly face in the wooden panelling in the London room which appears if you look hard enough. The Garden Lounge has well spaced furniture on herringbone glazed bricks around a central tropical grove. You can get snacks at the bar such as filled ciabattas (from £3.95), soup (from £4.25), chicken liver pâté with hot bread (£5.95) and a daily pudding (£3.50) but our food award is for the informal Garden Lounge restaurant which serves not cheap but very good food with a continental lean (one of the licensees is Italian). Dishes might include gruyère fritters (£5.95), moules marinières (£6.95), chargrilled lambs liver (£10.50), dressed crab or escalope of salmon (£11.95), spaghetti with half a lobster (£14.95) and puddings (£4.95). Well kept Adnams Broadside, Ruddles Best and Fullers London Pride on handpump, but the best of all are the wines, many of which are Italian and good value with about 18 by the glass; there's also freshly squeezed orange juice, filter, espresso or cappuccino coffee; friendly and very professional staff. There's waiter drinks service in the cobbled courtyard at the back which is lovely in summer, with comfortable chairs and tables among attractive plant tubs and colourful hanging baskets; there's also a neatly maintained walled garden, with a sunken lawn where croquet is often played. *(Recommended by Michael Sargent, Mike and Sue Loseby, Janet and Peter Race, Lynn Sharpless, Bob Eardley, R C Wiles, Anthony Barnes, Steve Chambers, Maysie Thompson, David Carr, Stephen, Julie and Hayley Brown, Gordon Neighbour, the Didler, Chris and Liane Miller, Paul Hopton; also in* The Good Hotel Guide*)*

Free house ~ Licensees Chris Pitman and Ivo Vannocci ~ Real ale ~ Bar food (11-11) ~ Restaurant ~ (01780) 750750 ~ Children welcome ~ Open 11-11; 12-10.30 Sun ~ Bedrooms: £55S(£78B)/£115B

SURFLEET TF2528 Map 8
Mermaid

Just off A16 N of Spalding at bridge over River Glen

Some of our readers come every month to this genuine old-fashioned dining pub and, although much of it looks unchanged since the 70s, it's still absolutely pristine and fresh looking inside. A small central glass-backed bar counter complete with original Babycham décor serves two high-ceilinged rooms, which have huge netted sash windows, green patterned carpets, beige Anaglypta dado, brass platters, navigation lanterns and horse tack on cream textured walls, and a mixture of banquettes and stools. Well kept Adnams Broadside and John Smiths and a couple of guests like Batemans XXX and Hook Norton Old Hooky. Two steps down, the restaurant is decorated in a similar style. You may need to book for the big helpings of enjoyable bar food. Served on very hot plates, the traditional menu has been the same for 13 years and includes soup (£2.25), garlic mushrooms(£2.95), cottage pie, liver and bacon or seafood platter (£6.25), steaks (from £9.50) and a couple of daily specials like minted lamb casserole (£6.25) or rack of lamb (£8.75) and puddings like cheesecake (£2.50); on Sunday they do a three-course lunch (£8.95). The service is friendly and helpful and this is the type of place where you can feel comfortable lingering. There's a pretty garden with seats for a hundred and a children's play area which is safely walled from the river which runs beside the pub. *(Recommended by Michael and Jenny Back, Mike and Penny Sanders, Beryl and Bill Farmer, Phil and Jane Hodson)*

Free house ~ Licensee C D Wilcox ~ Real ale ~ Bar food (11.30-2, 6.30-9.30; 12-2, 7-9 Sun) ~ Restaurant ~ (01775) 680275 ~ Children over 5 in restaurant ~ Open 11.30-3, 6.30-11; 12-3, 7-10.30 Sun; closed 26 Dec, 1 Jan

---

'Children welcome' means the pub says it lets children inside without any special restriction. If it allows them in, but to restricted areas such as an eating area or family room, we specify this. Some pubs may impose an evening time limit.

WOODHALL SPA TF1963 Map 8
Abbey Lodge
Tattersall Rd (B1192 Woodhall Spa—Coningsby)

The discreetly decorated bar at this family-run roadside inn has Victorian and older furnishings, as well as pictures showing its World War II connections with RAF Coningsby – Squadron 617 which is based at the former airfield opposite and still holds reunion dinners here. They serve well kept Bass, Worthington and a guest such as Greene King IPA on handpump; friendly atmosphere and staff. The straightforward bar menu includes sandwiches (from £1.75), soup (£2.75), pâté with cumberland sauce (£4.25), deep-fried crispy vegetables (£4.95), ploughman's (£5.25), lamb lasagne (£5.50), poached cod with prawns (£7.25) and steaks (from £9.75) as well as specials such as beef or vegetarian chilli (£6.25), with quite a few puddings such as marshmallow and butterscotch sundae or jam sponge (£2.75). *(Recommended by JP, PP, Walter and Susan Rinaldi-Butcher, Bill and Sheila McLardy, Hugh A MacLean)*

Free house ~ Licensee Annette Inglis ~ Real ale ~ Bar food (Sat 6.30-10) ~ Restaurant ~ (01526) 352538 ~ Open 11-2.30, 6.30(6 Sat)-11; closed Sun

---

Lucky Dip

Besides the fully inspected pubs, you might like to try these Lucky Dips recommended to us and described by readers (if you do, please send us reports: www.goodguides.com).

Alford [TF4576]
Half Moon [West St (A1004)]: Well run local with good choice of well kept ales and food from sandwiches to particularly good fish dishes, attractive dining area, decorous lounge, spacious L-shaped bar, back games area; children welcome (adaptable menu for them), nice fairy-lit back garden with barbecues *(Derek, Hazel and Graeme Lloyd, John and Sylvia Harrop, BB)*
☆ *White Horse* [West St (A1004)]: Comfortably plush low-ceilinged pub, well kept Mansfield and guest beers, good value fresh-cooked food in bar and restaurant, polite staff; clean bedrooms, good breakfast *(Mike and Lynn Robinson, LYM, M J Winterton)*
Aubourn [SK9262]
☆ *Royal Oak*: Good generous straightforward food in pleasantly decorated two-room lounge bar with open fire, well kept Batemans XB and XXXB, Sam Smiths, and a guest beer on handpump, friendly service, back games room; nice garden *(Mrs Sheila MacPhail)*
Barkston [SK9341]
Stag [Church St]: Beamed pub with good home-made food inc flexible children's dishes in left-hand dining bar with mixed tables and chairs, well kept Everards Tiger and Beacon and a guest beer, good wine choice, friendly helpful staff, pool, darts and TV in second bar, small back conservatory; picnic-sets out in front and in big back garden *(Richard Lewis)*
Billingborough [TF1134]
Fortescue Arms [High St]: Cosy traditional atmosphere, beams, big log fire, country bygones, good value well prepared food esp home-made pies and good veg, bar dining area and restaurant, well kept Ansells, Bass, Ind Coope Burton and a guest beer, decent wines,

friendly attentive staff; tables under apple trees in big garden, attractive village *(John Curtis)*
Boston [TF3244]
Carpenters Arms [Witham St]: Lively traditional bare-boards local, well kept Bass, Batemans Mild and XB and guest beers, enterprising home-cooked lunchtime food inc good cheap rolls; bedrooms reasonably priced *(the Didler, JP, PP)*
Eagle [West St, towards stn]: Basic cheery local with well kept Batemans, Castle Rock, Timothy Taylors Landlord and three guest beers at low prices, cheap food, children in eating area lunchtime; Mon folk club, live music Sat, open all day Sat *(BB, the Didler, JP, PP)*
Ropers Arms [Horncastle Rd]: Batemans corner local in nice spot by river and windmill, quiet and unassuming – gets lively for big screen TV football Sun; some live entertainment; open 2-11, all day wknds and summer *(the Didler, JP, PP)*
Castle Bytham [SK9818]
Fox & Hounds [High St]: Beams, stripped stone and plush seating, log fire, lots of brass and ornaments, wide food choice from baguettes and baked potatoes to fish and steaks, well kept changing ales such as Banks's Original, Grainstore Cooking, Marstons Pedigree and Oakham JHB, good choice of malt whiskies, friendly staff and locals; piped music; children welcome, garden with play area *(Richard Lewis)*
Chapel St Leonards [TF5572]
Ship [Sea Rd]: Comfortable old local just outside Skegness, welcoming chatty landlord, open fires, well kept Batemans Mild, XB, XXXB and a seasonal beer, traditional games; tables outside *(the Didler, Phil and Jane Hodson, JP, PP)*

Cleethorpes [TA3008]

No 2 Refreshment Room [Station Approach]: Tiny basic 60s-throwback bar almost on platform, Mansfield Mild, John Smiths Magnet and usually a good guest beer from a small brewery, no food; open all day *(the Didler, JP, PP)*

☆ *Willys* [Highcliff Rd; south promenade]: Open-plan bistro-style seafront pub with café tables, tiled floor and painted brick walls; brews its own good beers, also well kept Batemans and guest beers and good value basic lunchtime home cooking; friendly staff, quiet juke box, panoramic Humber views; popular November beer festival, open all day *(the Didler, JP, PP, Keith Wilson)*

Coleby [SK9760]

☆ *Bell* [village signed off A607 S of Lincoln, turn right and right into Far Lane at church]: Friendly dining pub with three linked rooms each with a log fire and low black joists, well kept Bass, Flowers Original and Tetleys, wide choice of home-made bar food all day (not Mon) inc tempting puddings, friendly staff, foreign number-plate collection, restaurant; picnic-sets outside, handy for Viking Way walks, open all day (cl afternoon Jan/Feb); good value bedrooms, massive breakfast *(Richard Lewis, LYM, Judy Pearson, Mr and Mrs G S Pink, P J and Avril Hanson, M Dean)*

Colsterworth [SK9224]

Fox [A1]: Recently reopened, with plenty of rooms, wide choice of food all day inc children's menu, Sun lunchtime carvery, Boddingtons, Courage Directors and Tetleys, side games room with pool, darts, TV and juke box; children welcome, frequent Fri/Sat discos or bands *(Richard Lewis)*

Donington on Bain [TF2382]

☆ *Black Horse* [Main Rd; between A153 and A157, SW of Louth]: Relaxed atmosphere and pleasant layout, with low-beamed snug back bar and softly lit inner room (with murals of carousing Vikings) off main village bar, log fires, bar food from filled baked potatoes to steaks, Ruddles Best and John Smiths; no smoking restaurant, games room off public bar, juke box or piped music; children very welcome, picnic-sets in back garden, on Viking Way *(Mike and Maggie Betton, Mike and Lynn Robinson, LYM)*

East Kirkby [TF3362]

☆ *Red Lion* [Fen Rd]: Lots of chiming clocks, jugs, breweriana and interesting old tools (some for sale behind), well kept Bass, Worthington and a guest beer, good value standard food, friendly staff, open fire, family room, traditional games; wheelchair access, tables outside (and more machinery), camping; handy for Air Museum *(the Didler, Phil and Jane Hodson, Derek and Sylvia Stephenson, Dave Braisted, JP, PP)*

Eastgate [TF1019]

Waggon & Horses: Good value dining pub recently refurnished with pine furniture, wide food choice freshly cooked to order, Bass and a guest beer; quiet piped music; open all day *(Michael Hicks)*

Ewerby [TF1247]

☆ *Finch Hatton Arms* [Main St]: Handsome, well decorated and plushly furnished mock-Tudor pub with wide choice of good value food inc fresh fish and Sun lunch, well kept ales inc a guest beer, coal fire, smart dining room, comfortable back locals' bar; bedrooms *(BB, Richard Cole, Bill and Sheila McLardy)*

Folkingham [TF0733]

Greyhound [Market Pl]: Enormous 17th-c coaching inn with Georgian façade, light and airy series of rooms, lots of antiques, crafts and collectables for sale, good bar lunches, perhaps real ales such as Bass; open 9.30-5; plans for bedrooms *(M J Morgan, Peter H Stallard)*

Frognall [TF1610]

☆ *Goat* [Spalding Rd (B1525, off A16 NE of Mkt Deeping)]: Friendly pub with low beams and stripped stone, enjoyable food (all day Sun) esp home-made pies, also children's, particularly well kept Adnams Best and three interesting guest beers such as Tring Side Pocket and Normans Secret Hop, log fires, two dining rooms (one no smoking) where children welcome, helpful landlord; maybe piped music; good wheelchair access, big garden with terrace and play equipment, separate area for under-5s *(Michael and Jenny Back, Derek and Sylvia Stephenson, Phil and Jane Hodson)*

Gainsborough [SK8189]

Eight Jolly Brewers [Ship Court, Silver St]: Bustling unpretentious pub with beams, bare bricks and brewery posters, up to eight well kept well priced changing ales and one brewed for them by Highwood, quieter bar upstairs, simple lunchtime food (not Sun), friendly staff and locals; folk club, open all day Fri-Sun *(JP, PP, the Didler, Richard Lewis)*

Grantham [SK9135]

☆ *Angel & Royal* [High St]: Hotel with remarkable worn 13th-c carved stone façade, splendidly restrained décor, medieval oriel window seat in upstairs plush-seated bar on left, massive inglenook in friendly high-beamed main bar opp, tapestries, well kept Greene King Ruddles County and two guest beers, good bar food; open all day Fri/Sat, bedrooms in comfortable back extension *(David Carr, JP, PP, LYM, Phil and Jane Hodson, the Didler, Richard Lewis)*

Blue Bull [Westgate]: Cosy two-bar refurbished local, lots of brass, ornaments, pictures and stuffed fox, well kept Marstons Pedigree and quickly changing guest beers such as local Newby Wyke and Oldershaws, Belgian bottled beers, quite a few ciders, papers and beers, magazines, partly no smoking dining room with good reasonably priced home-cooked food (not Sun or Mon evenings), traditional games, juke box; handy for station *(Richard Lewis, the Didler)*

Blue Pig [Vine St]: Two-room Tudor pub, beams, panelling, stripped stone and flagstones, friendly bustle, well kept Castle Eden, Flowers Original and changing guests such as Grainstore Harvest, Wadworths 6X and Yorkshire Terrier, helpful staff, good simple lunchtime bar food, open fire, daily papers, lots of prints and bric-a-brac; piped music, games machine; tables out behind, open all day *(David Carr, Richard Lewis, the Didler, JP, PP)*

Chequers [Market Pl]: Recently re-opened and smartened up, with comfortable seating, lots of pictures, friendly hard-working landlady, four real ales; no food *(Richard Lewis)*

Dr Thirstys [Westgate]: Newly converted shop popular with younger people, lots of polished wood, breweriana and inn-signs, long back lounge with pool, good food choice, two well kept Batemans ales and Tetleys; piped music, games machines; partly covered side garden, open all day *(Richard Lewis)*

Hogshead [Market Pl]: Polished boards or flagstones, barrels, panelling and stripped brick, light and airy with plenty of standing area, back part with armchair and settee by open fire, more seats upstairs, several well kept ales (dozens in Oct beer festival), Belgian bottled beers, farm ciders, good menu, friendly helpful staff, old local prints; piped music, games machines; open all day *(Richard Lewis)*

Muddle Go Nowhere [Barrowby Rd; W edge, nr A1/A52]: Large comfortable Tom Cobleigh family pub, lots of beams, woodwork and bare brick, country décor with range fireplaces, no smoking areas, generous food inc Sun roasts, well kept John Smiths Magnet and Theakstons Cool Cask, XB and Old Peculier, quick friendly service; outside and inside play areas inc new play barn, baby changing and disabled facilities, Mon quiz night, open all day *(Richard Lewis, R C Vincent)*

Nobody Inn [Watergate]: Friendly bare-boards open-plan local with well kept Everards Tiger and lots of guest beers such as Barnsley IPA, Newby Wyke White Squall, Oldershaws Old Boy and cheap Sam Smiths OB; back games room with pool, table footer, good juke box, SkyTV; open all day *(Richard Lewis, the Didler)*

☆ *Tollemache* [St Peters Hill/Catherine Rd]: Roomy and popular L-shaped Wetherspoons, unusual in being good for families yet having a proper pub atmosphere; interesting choice of well kept ales, good generous food choice inc generous children's bargains, efficient friendly service, usual high-standard décor with big lower-level family no smoking area, leather settee and armchairs by open fire, old books, local pictures and Co-op memorabilia; attractive big terrace with fountain and play area, open all day, handy for Belton House *(Richard Lewis, Pat McGurk)*

Grimsby [TA2609]

Corporation [Freeman St]: Well kept Bass and Worthington in traditional town pub with nice back lounge – original panelling, leather seats, old Grimsby shipping photographs; second lounge, lively public bar with games and TV *(Pete Baker)*

Old Coach House [Bethlehem St]: Friendly Irish-theme pub with the beers you'd expect, enjoyable food such as sausages and colcannon with onion gravy *(Dr and Mrs A K Clarke)*

Halton Holegate [TF4165]

☆ *Bell* [B1195 E of Spilsby]: Unchanging pretty

village local, simple but comfortable and consistently friendly, with wide choice of decent home-made food inc Sun lunches and outstanding fish and chips, well kept Batemans XB, Mansfield Old Baily and Tetleys, Lancaster bomber pictures, pub games, maybe piped music; children in back eating area (with tropical fish tank) and restaurant *(Michael and Jenny Back, the Didler, LYM, Derek and Sylvia Stephenson, JP, PP)*

Heckington [TF1444]

☆ *Nags Head* [off A17 Sleaford—Boston; High St]: Two-room 17th-c village pub with huge inglenook fireplace, wall banquettes, well kept Bass, Tetleys and perhaps a guest beer, generous home-made food from sandwiches up, no smoking upstairs dining room, darts, pool, shove-ha'penny, fruit machine, juke box, TV and piped music; children welcome, open all day, Sun quiz night, fortnightly live entertainment, picnic-sets and play area in garden (beyond dogs' yard), bedrooms *(B N F and M Parkin, Beryl and Bill Farmer, Dr Paull Khan, LYM)*

Heighington [TF0369]

Turks Head [High St]: Friendly welcome for strangers, well kept beer, nice food *(anon)*

Holbeach [TF3524]

Lion [Spalding Rd]: Enjoyable low-priced home-made food served piping hot, well kept Adnams Broadside, Marstons Pedigree, John Smiths and Tetleys, very friendly helpful landlord, coal fire, massive beams in neat no smoking end restaurant area; juke box, fruit machines *(Michael and Jenny Back)*

Horncastle [TF2669]

Admiral Rodney [North St]: Comfortable hotel with wide range of well kept beers and wines, helpful staff, sensibly priced food inc satisfying carvery in courtyard restaurant, no smoking area; bedrooms, good parking *(Gordon B Thornton)*

Hough-on-the-Hill [SK9246]

Brownlow Arms [High Rd]: This 16th-c building is no longer a pub, now a restaurant-with-rooms (worth knowing for good interesting restaurant-quality food inc special wkdy meal offers, relaxing lounge with sofas and comfortable chairs, friendly efficient service, good value pretty bedrooms, good breakfast); peaceful picturesque village handy for Belton House *(Mike and Maggie Betton, David and Ruth Hollands)*

Irnham [TF0226]

Griffin [Bulby Rd]: Small old stone-built village pub noted for three well kept changing guest beers, with up to three dozen in early July beer festival (lots of room for tents and caravans); big open fire in lounge, back snug, restaurant, friendly staff; nice village setting *(Richard Lewis, M J Morgan)*

Kirkby on Bain [TF2462]

Ebrington Arms [Main St]: Generous good value food inc cheap Sun lunch, five or more well kept changing ales from small breweries far and wide, prompt welcoming service, daily papers, low 16th-c beams, two open fires, nicely set out dining areas each side, copper-topped tables, wall banquettes, jet fighter and racing car pictures; games area with darts, restaurant, maybe piped Irish music; beer festivals Easter and Aug bank hols, wheelchair access, tables out in front, swings on side lawn, camp site behind, open all day *(the Didler, P A Legon, Richard Lewis)*

Lincoln [SK9871]

Bull & Chain [Langworthgate]: Excellent licensees in popular unpretentious local with comfortable banquettes, decorative plates, cheap food (all day Sun), Bass and John Smiths, good darts team, dominoes; children welcome, juke box, machines; big garden overlooking tennis court, not far from cathedral *(Mr and Mrs G Baker, David Carr)*

Cornhill Vaults [Exchange Arcade]: Unusual vaulted underground pub with cheap well kept Sam Smiths, freshly made bar lunches inc unusual sandwiches, pool table in separate area, friendly service; juke box after 3, live music evenings *(the Didler, JP, PP)*

Golden Eagle [High St]: Cheerfully busy basic two-bar town pub, wide choice of well kept and very attractively priced changing ales such as Batemans, Everards, Fullers and Timothy Taylors, good choice of country wines, good value lunchtime food; open all day Fri/Sat *(the Didler, JP, PP, Andy and Jill Kassube)*

Green Dragon [Waterside North/Broadgate]: Noble waterside Tudor building – carved 16th-c façade gave its homelier name 'The Cat Garret'; downstairs bar with character timbers, beams, flagstones, stripped brickwork and lots of prints, upper bar too at lunchtime, quick bar food, well kept Everards, friendly staff, open fire, daily papers; good piped music, frequent live nights *(LYM, Richard Lewis)*

☆ *Jolly Brewer* [Broadgate]: Busy art deco real ale pub with some items of special interest, real fire, thriving atmosphere and enthusiastic owners, well kept Bass, Theakstons XB and four guests, good well priced lunches inc Sun roasts; games machines and juke box, can be crowded wknd evenings; tables in good outside area, open all day *(the Didler, JP, PP)*

Morning Star [Greetwellgate]: Unpretentious well scrubbed local handy for cathedral, friendly atmosphere, good value lunches esp Fri specials, well kept reasonably priced Bass, Greene King Ruddles Best and a guest beer, coal fire, aircraft paintings, nice outside area; piano night Sat, open all day exc Sun *(the Didler, JP, PP)*

☆ *Queen in the West* [Moor St; off A57 nr racecourse]: A good few well kept changing ales such as Bass, Marstons Pedigree, Theakstons XB and Old Peculier and reasonably priced simple bar lunches in busy and welcoming old backstreet pub below cathedral; military prints and miniatures in well decorated lounge, interesting sporting prints in public bar with TV, darts, games; open all day Fri/Sat *(the Didler, JP, PP)*

Sippers [Melville St; opp bus stn]: Popular two-bar lunchtime pub with good food (not wknd evenings), Courage Directors, Greene King Old Speckled Hen, Marstons Pedigree and guest beers, very friendly licensees; quieter evenings,

cl Sun lunchtime *(the Didler, JP, PP)*

Strugglers [Westgate]: Friendly refurbished local with well kept Bass, Marstons Pedigree and a guest such as Fullers London Pride, coal fire in small back snug; open all day Fri-Sun *(the Didler)*

Little Bytham [TF0118]

☆ *Willoughby Arms* [Station Rd, S of village]: Good generous straightforward food, well kept Batemans XB and (brewed in back barn, bedrooms being converted above) Newby Wyke Deep and Lord Ancaster, with guests such as Church End Old Pal, Grainstore Winter Nip and Wye Valley Dorothy Goodbodys Winter Tipple, also frequent folk and beer festivals; friendly staff, big log fire and lots of prints in beamed stripped stone lounge, side dining room, games room with TV; good piped music, live music in cellar bar wknds; pleasant back garden overlooking fields, open all day wknds *(Richard Lewis, Steve and Jan Charlton, RB)*

Long Sutton [TF4222]

Crown & Woolpack [High St, off bypass A17 Kings Lynn—Holbeach]: Good generous cheap home cooking (well filled baguettes only, Mon-Weds) in basic lively local with panelled back dining room, good Sun lunch (must book), Bass and Worthington BB, roaring fire, dominoes; piped music, outside lavatories *(Michael and Jenny Back)*

Louth [TF3387]

Kings Head [Mercer Row]: Large unfussy bar, well kept beer, good range of good value bar food inc roasts and traditional puddings *(the Didler, JP, PP)*

☆ *Masons Arms* [Cornmarket]: Light and airy, with plush seats, big sunny bay window, good mix of different-sized tables, panelled back bar, friendly landlord and family, well kept full Batemans range, Marstons Pedigree and guest beers such as Ushers Spring Fever and Woodfordes Nog, farm cider, decent coffee, good home-made food from big hot sandwiches up, good upstairs dining room (remarkable art deco former masonic lodge meeting room); piped radio; good bedrooms, open all day exc Sun *(David and Ruth Hollands, A J Jones, JP, PP, the Didler, Geoffrey G Lawrance, John and Sylvia Harrop, BB)*

Olde Whyte Swanne [Eastgate]: Popular and friendly, ancient low beams, comfortable front bar with open fire, decent soup, Bass and guest beers *(JP, PP, the Didler, P J and Avril Hanson)*

Wheatsheaf [Westgate]: Cheerful well kept early 17th-c inn, real fires in all three bars, Bass, Boddingtons and Flowers, decent lunchtime food; can be crowded; tables outside, open all day Sat and summer Sun *(the Didler)*

Woolpack [Riverhead Rd]: 18th-c wool merchant's house popular for good home cooking (not Sun or Mon evenings) and Batemans ales inc a Mild, Marstons Pedigree and guest ales; bar, lounge, snug, two real fires; cl Mon lunchtime, open all day Sat *(the Didler, Mike and Lynn Robinson)*

North Kelsey [TA0401]

Butchers Arms [Middle St; off B1434 S of Brigg]: Busy refurbished village local, opened up but not too modern, low ceilings, flagstones, bare boards, dim lighting, with five well kept Highwood beers (brewed by owner on his farm), good value cold lunches, enthusiastic cheerful service, woodburner; pub games, no juke box, tables outside, opens at 4 wkdys, open all day wknds *(the Didler, JP, PP)*

Norton Disney [SK8859]

☆ *St Vincent Arms* [Main St, off A46 Newark—Lincoln]: Attractive and welcoming village pub with well kept Batemans XXXB or Marstons Pedigree and maybe guest beers, open fire, good cheap generous plain food from sandwiches up inc beautifully cooked veg, pleasant landlord, appropriately decorated adults' dining room; tables and big adventure playground out behind *(Sue and Bob Ward, the Didler, JP, PP, Andy and Jill Kassube)*

Old Bolingbroke [TF3565]

Black Horse: Recently reopened and refurbished, enjoyable foor from chip butties and sandwiches to big steaks, well kept Greene King Abbot and Old Speckled Hen *(Mike and Lynn Robinson)*

Revesby [TF2961]

Red Lion [A155 Mareham—Spilsby]: Traditional local with a welcome for visitors, good range of reasonably priced home-made food in bar and restaurant *(JP, PP, Simon and Carol Hadwick)*

Rippingale [TF0927]

Bull [just off A15 Bourne—Sleaford; High St]: Fresh and spotless, with welcoming American landlady, attentive service, good varied reasonably priced food using local produce in bar and nice restaurant, wide range of well kept ales, good wine selection, no smoking areas, no piped music; tables in garden with big play area *(Gordon B Thornton)*

Rothwell [TF1599]

☆ *Nickerson Arms* [off B1225 S of Caistor]: Attractive heavy-beamed old pub reopened by new owners, civilised bar divided by arches and warm central coal fire, spacious dining area, enjoyable food, well kept Batemans and other ales; darts and dominoes, may be piped music; tables outside *(LYM, Wilson Keith)*

Scampton [SK9579]

Dambusters [High St]: Beams, hops and masses of RAF and other World War II memorabilia, good food (not Sun/Mon evenings), pleasant nostalgic atmosphere, well kept Greene King IPA, Abbot and Ruddles and guest beers, log fire; adjoining post office *(Gordon B Thornton)*

Silk Willoughby [TF0542]

Horseshoe [A15 S of Sleaford]: Worth knowing for consistently good food – good value, too *(John Curtis)*

Skegness [TF5660]

☆ *Vine* [Vine Rd, off Drummond Rd, Seacroft]: Unspoilt extended hotel based on late 18th-c country house, calm and comfortable well run bar overlooking drive and own bowling green, imposing antique seats and grandfather clock in turkey-carpeted hall, juke box in inner oak-panelled room; three well kept Batemans ales, good value food using local produce in bar and

restaurant, friendly staff, tables on big back sheltered lawn with swings; good reasonably priced bedrooms, peaceful suburban setting not far from beach and bird-watching *(JP, PP, BB, Ted and Jan Whitfield, the Didler)*

Skendleby [TF4369]

☆ *Blacksmiths Arms* [off A158 about 10 miles NW of Skegness]: Some concentration on good imaginative generous food in big busy back restaurant extension, very generous one-price main courses, also old-fashioned two-room bar, cosy and quaint, with view of cellar, deep 17th-c well, well kept Batemans XB and XXXB tapped from the cask, friendly staff, open fire *(JP, PP, the Didler, Val and Alan Green)*

Sleaford [TF0645]

Carre Arms [Mareham Lane]: Hotel with sizeable pub part, good choice of generous light lunches and of evening restaurant meals, decent wines, helpful landlady; bedrooms *(Bill and Sheila McLardy)*

South Ormsby [TF3775]

☆ *Massingbird Arms* [off A16 S of Louth]: Homely refurbished 17th-c pub, very helpful and obliging landlord, well kept John Smiths Magnet and a guest beer, interesting freshly cooked food all day, tea and coffee, Sun lunch, restaurant Thurs-Sun evenings; good value bedrooms, open all day *(the Didler, JP, PP, Martin Dormer)*

South Thoresby [TF4077]

☆ *Vine* [about a mile off A16 N of Ulceby Cross]: Large village inn with small pub part – tiny passageway servery, steps up to three-table lounge, wide choice of good food from thai fishcakes to Aberdeen Angus steaks in nicely panelled no smoking dining room, well kept Batemans XB and a guest such as Fullers London Pride, first-class choice of malt whiskies, good value wines, separate pool room; bedrooms, tables in pleasant garden *(the Didler, JP, PP)*

Stamford [TF0207]

Green Man [Scotgate (A606/B1081)]: Bare boards or flagstones, stripped brickwork, well kept ales such as Grainstore Ten Fifty, Iceni Mild, Kitchen Tubby Tangerine, Outlaw Optic and Theakstons Best, open fire, welcoming regulars, lunchtime food (not Sun), pub games, SkyTV in back room; beer festivals Easter and late summer; unusual alley to garden, bedrooms *(Richard Lewis, the Didler, Richard Houghton)*

Lord Burghley [Broad St]: Busy old pub with several rooms, stripped stone, good atmosphere and service, well kept Bass, Fullers London Pride and Greene King IPA, farm cider, food (not Sun evening) inc good steak and kidney pie and steamed puddings; pleasant small walled garden, open all day *(the Didler)*

Periwig [Red Lion Sq/All Saints Pl]: Gallery above narrow split-level bar, well kept Courage Directors, Oakham JHB, John Smiths and Theakstons XB, well filled good value baguettes, baked potatoes, ploughman's and salads (not Sun), chequered tablecloths in bistro-style eating area; unobtrusive piped music; open all day *(the Didler)*

St Peters [St Peters St]: 18th-c, with upstairs

cloisters and downstairs bars, busy local atmosphere, well kept Marstons Best and Pedigree and several guest beers tapped from the cask, good choice of wines by the glass, eclectic back bistro food, quiet music, friendly staff; open all day Fri/Sat, cl wkdy lunchtimes, parking some way off *(the Didler, Lynn Sharpless, Bob Eardley, Peter H Stallard)*

Stow [SK8882]

☆ *Cross Keys* [B1241 NW of Lincoln]: Modernised and extended, with pleasant dining areas and emphasis on interesting prettily presented food inc delicious black pudding and hazelnut speciality, unusual vegetarian choices, cheap lunchtime specials and good puddings, well kept ales such as Everards, Greene King Old Speckled Hen and Theakstons Best and Old Peculier through sparkler, good range of wines, quick friendly service, big woodburner; may be piped music; Saxon minster church just behind; cl Mon lunchtime *(Hugh A MacLean, BB, Chris and Elaine Lyon, Mr and Mrs J Brown, Lucien)*

Surfleet Seas End [TF2728]

Ship [Reservoir Rd; off A16 N of Spalding]: Unspoilt 17th-c riverside pub, flagstone bar, open fires, well kept Everards Original, Beacon and Tiger and a guest beer, good home-cooked meals inc interesting recipes esp fresh fish (delicious seafood platter needs 24 hrs' notice), no smoking dining room; bedrooms, may be cl wkdy lunchtime *(M J Morgan)*

Susworth [SE8302]

Jenny Wren [East Ferry Rd]: Good rather upmarket food at reasonable prices inc lots of seafood in large dining area overlooking River Trent, lots of panelling, stripped brickwork, low beams and brasses, various nooks and crannies, three well kept real ales, big open fire, polite service; some tables out by water *(JP, PP, Chris and Elaine Lyon)*

Tealby [TF1590]

☆ *Kings Head* [Kingsway, off B1203 towards bottom of village]: Mossy-thatched and beamed pub in quiet Wolds village famous for its cottage gardens, handy for Viking Way walk; generous food inc sandwiches and meaty home-made pies (very popular lunchtime with older people), Fri-Sun fish nights, well kept Bass, Stones and Worthingtons, farm cider, pleasant service; restaurant, wheelchair access, picnic-sets in attractive garden *(Martin Dormer, the Didler, Ellen Weld, David London, BB)*

Tetford [TF3374]

White Hart [East Rd, off A158 E of Horncastle]: New licensees in early 16th-c pub with interesting layout, old-fashioned settles, slabby elm tables and red tiled floor in pleasant quiet inglenook bar, no smoking snug, basic games room, lots of whiskies, usual food; seats and swings on sheltered back lawn, simple bedrooms *(the Didler, JP, PP, LYM)*

Uffington [TF0607]

Gainsborough [Main Rd]: Former Gainsborough Lady, reopened spring 2001 after refit by former landlord of Black Horse at Elton, interesting lunchtime bar food from sandwiches up, evening restaurant with no smoking area, Adnams, Banks's, Bass, Greene King IPA and guest ales, good choice of wines by the glass; children welcome in eating area at lunchtime, cl Sun evening and Mon *(anon)*

Welton Hill [SK9872]

Farmers Arms [A46 Lincoln—Market Rasen]: Well run with hearty helpings of good freshly made food *(M Clark, Mr and Mrs A P Padbury)*

Woolsthorpe [SK8435]

☆ *Chequers* [Main St; the one nr Belvoir, signed off A52 Grantham—Nottingham]: Attractively refurbished and extended village pub in sight of Belvoir Castle, with good freshly made food in bar and restaurant inc interesting lunches and local game, well kept ale, friendly service, warmly local winter atmosphere (roaring fires, dominoes), lots of events esp Fri in big entertainments area, own cricket ground; tables outside, boules; bedrooms *(June and Malcolm Farmer, BB)*

Rutland Arms [off Sedgebrook Rd N of village]: Comfortable family pub in quiet spot below Belvoir Castle, by disused Grantham Canal (7-mile restored towpath walk from town); popular reasonably priced generous food in bars and restaurant, well kept Bass and a couple of guests such as Brewsters Sludge Gut and John Smiths, friendly long-serving landlord, lounge with some high-backed settles, hunting prints, brasses and bric-a-brac, open fire; video juke box, darts and pool in annexe, muddy boots allowed here; big lawn with good play area, field for caravans and camping, open all day wknds *(Richard Lewis, Bernie Adams)*

Stars after the name of a pub show exceptional character and appeal. They don't mean extra comfort. And they are nothing to do with food quality, for which there's a separate knife-and-fork symbol. Even quite a basic pub can win stars, if it's individual enough.

Norfolk

*Pubs showing particularly well here this year are the chatty and pubby Kings
Arms in Blakeney and the White Horse there (a nice place to stay), the cosy
Jolly Sailors at Brancaster Staithe (new licensees settling in very well), the
restauranty but very friendly White Horse by the marshes there, the smart old
Hoste Arms in Burnham Market, the Ratcatchers at Cawston (good all round,
particularly on the food side), the individualistic Saracens Head near
Erpingham, the Kings Head at Letheringsett (back in the Guide after a break –
particularly good for families), the Fat Cat in Norwich (an amazing range of
well kept real ales), the Ferry Inn at Reedham (another pub welcomed back to
the Guide after an absence, in a lovely spot and doing well all round), the Rose
& Crown at Snettisham (a special favourite, very good on all counts), the
Lifeboat at Thornham (full of atmosphere), and the Three Horseshoes at
Warham (a classic old-fashioned country pub). Making the most of its coastal
position for its fresh seafood, even samphire from the foot of its garden, the
White Horse at Brancaster Staithe is our Norfolk Dining Pub of the Year. The
interesting Adam & Eve in Norwich, under a very cheery new landlady this
year, is the only Norfolk pub with an unbroken record of featuring in all 20
editions of the Guide. Pubs doing well in the Lucky Dip section at the end of
the chapter, most of them already inspected by us and jostling for space
among the main entries, are the Chequers at Binham, Manor in Blakeney,
Three Swallows at Cley next the Sea, Ugly Bug at Colton, Feathers in Holt,
Olde Buck at Honingham, Scole Inn at Scole, Crown at Stanhoe, Chequers at
Thompson, Dukes Head at West Rudham and Bird in Hand at Wreningham.
This is not a cheap area. Drinks prices are generally rather higher than the
national average; Darbys at Swanton Morley and the Fat Cat in Norwich
stood out for their cheap beer.*

BAWBURGH TG1508 Map 5
Kings Head

Pub signposted down Harts Lane off B1108, which leads off A47 just W of Norwich

The four sunny yellow linked rooms at this cosy old pub have low beams, some
standing timbers, a warming log fire in a large knocked-through canopied fireplace,
a woodburner in the attractive inglenook in the end room, and comfortable
upholstered seats and banquettes. Quite a choice of enjoyable bar food might include
soup with home-made bread (£2.95), sandwiches or baguettes (from £3), cajun
squid rings with thai mango salad (£3.95), smoked chicken with marinated cherry
tomatoes and salad (£4.50), smoked salmon and dill pasta (£7.50), steak and kidney
pudding (£7.95), red snapper with buttered spinach and smoked salmon sauce
(£11.50), Caribbean fish stew (£12.50), fillet steak on a wild mushroom potato cake
with cider, whole grain and stilton sauce (£14.50). Helpings are generous; no
smoking restaurant. Well kept Adnams Bitter, Courage Directors, Greene King IPA,
Woodfordes Wherry and a guest such as Nethergate Swift Spring Ale on handpump
and a dozen wines by the glass; cribbage, dominoes and piped music. There are
rustic tables and benches on the gravel outside and a garden with outdoor heaters on
the terrace and herbaceous plants. *(Recommended by C W Dix, Jamie and Sarah Allan,*

Stephen, Julie and Hayley Brown, Lynn Sharpless, Bob Eardley, Lesley Kant, Anthony Barnes, Michael Butler, Kelly Lewis, Pete Beasley)

Free house ~ Licensee Anton Wimmer ~ Real ale ~ Bar food (12-2(2.30 Sun), 7-10) ~ Restaurant ~ (01603) 744977 ~ Children in eating area of bar and restaurant ~ Solo musician every 2nd Mon ~ Open 11(9 coffee)-11; 12(9 coffee)-10.30 Sun; closed 25 Dec evening

BLAKENEY TG0243 Map 8
Kings Arms ◀

West Gate St

Friendly locals chat happily at this low-ceilinged bustling18th-c pub. The three simply furnished, knocked-through pubby rooms have some interesting photographs of the licensees' theatrical careers, other pictures including work by local artists, and what can only be the smallest cartoon gallery in England in a former telephone kiosk. Look out for the brass plaque on the wall that indicates a flood level mark; two small rooms are no smoking – as is the airy garden room; darts, shove-ha'penny, and dominoes. Very well kept Greene King Old Speckled Hen, Marstons Pedigree, Websters Yorkshire, and a couple of guests such as Adnams and Woodfordes Wherry are on handpump or tapped straight from the cask. Generously served bar food includes sandwiches, filled baked potatoes, crab ploughman's, moules in cream and wine (£4.50), home-made pies (the fish one is tasty), casseroles, and pasta dishes (from £5.50), fresh cod, plaice and haddock (£5.95), and sirloin steak; enjoyable breakfasts. The large garden has lots of tables and chairs and a separate, well equipped children's area. *(Recommended by Peter and Pat Frogley, Peter and Anne-Marie O'Malley, P G Plumridge, MDN, A E Brace, Paul and Ursula Randall, Di and Mike Gillam, M J Morgan, Simon Pyle, R Macfarlane, Nigel Woolliscroft, Kevin Macey, Patricia Beebe, Klaus and Elizabeth Leist, Dr C A Brace, Keith and Chris O'Neill, Val and Alan Green, John Robertson, B N F and M Parkin, Kevin Thorpe)*

Free house ~ Licensees John Howard and Marjorie Davies ~ Real ale ~ Bar food (12-9.30(9 Sun)) ~ (01263) 740341 ~ Children welcome ~ Open 11-11(10.30 Sun) ~ Bedrooms: /£55S

White Horse ♀ ☞

4 High Street; off A149 W of Sheringham

This nice little hotel is a friendly, happy place with quite a mix of sailing folk, holiday-makers, and locals. The chatty long main bar is predominantly green with a Venetian red ceiling, and restrained but attractive décor – including framed watercolours by a local artist; one small eating area is no smoking. Well kept Adnams, Bass, and Woodefordes on handpump, and a wide choice of reasonably priced wines with 11 by the glass (wine tastings in spring and winter); cribbage. Good bar food includes sandwiches (from £2.50; dressed crab £3.25), home-made soup (£2.95; tasty cockle chowder £3.75), deep-fried local whitebait (£3.95), cheese and vegetable pie (£5), battered plaice (£6.25), and daily specials such as garlic grilled sardines (£3.50), grilled goats cheese salad (£4.25), roast mediterranean vegetable and brie flan (£6.25), pork cassoulet or lamb tagine (£6.50) and grilled grey mullet and salsa verde (£6.95). The conservatory restaurant is attractive. Tables out in a suntrap courtyard and pleasant paved garden. The bedrooms are well equipped, if not very large. *(Recommended by Paul and Ursula Randall, Peter and Pat Frogley, Peter and Anne-Marie O'Malley, Minda and Stanley Alexander, MDN, T Simon Couzens, Eric Locker, Kevin Macey, E M and H P N Steinitz, M J Morgan, SA, J, A D Cross, Val and Alan Green, J F M and M West, Pamela Goodwyn)*

Free house ~ Licensees Daniel Rees and Dan Goff ~ Real ale ~ Bar food (12-2, 6-9) ~ Restaurant ~ (01263) 740574 ~ Children in family room ~ Open 11-3, 6(5.30 Sat)-11; 12-3, 6-10.30 Sun; closed 2 wks in Jan ~ Bedrooms: £40B/£80B

We now have a web site: www.goodguides.com

BLICKLING TG1728 Map 8
Buckinghamshire Arms
B1354 NW of Aylsham

This handsome Jacobean inn is attractively placed at the gates to Blickling Hall and owned by the National Trust. The small front snug is simply furnished with fabric-cushioned banquettes, while the bigger lounge has neatly built-in pews, stripped deal tables, and Spy pictures. Enjoyable bar food includes baguettes, baked potatoes and ploughman's on request, soup (£2.95), deep-fried whitebait with lemon mayonnaise (£4.25), mediterranean crumble (£5.50), sausage and herb or steak and kidney pies (£5.95), crab mornay (£6.25), home-made rabbit pie or home-made lasagne (£6.50), grilled cod with lemon butter (£6.95), puddings such as banoffi pie or treacle tart (£3.25), and Sunday roast (£6.25). Well kept Greene King Abbot and IPA, and Woodfordes Wherry on handpump, local cider, and a good range of wines; cribbage and dominoes. Lots of tables on the big lawn, and they serve food from an out-building here in summer; perhaps all-day opening in summer if it's busy or there's an event on at the Hall; minimum of two nights booking at the weekend. *(Recommended by Ian and Nita Cooper, Peter and Pat Frogley, Mike and Sue Loseby, Ian Phillips, Dave Braisted, Stephen, Julie and Hayley Brown, W K Wood, Di and Mike Gillam, Mike and Bridget Cummins, Mike and Karen England, John Wooll)*

Free house ~ Licensees Robert Dawson-Smith and David Brooks ~ Real ale ~ Bar food ~ Restaurant ~ (01263) 732133 ~ Well behaved children in restaurant ~ Open 11-3, 6.15-11; 11-3, 7-10.30 Sun; closed 25 Dec ~ Bedrooms: /£60(£60S)

BRANCASTER STAITHE TF7743 Map 8
Jolly Sailors
Main Road (A149)

Doing well under its new licensees, this cheerfully run pub is nicely set on the edge of thousands of acres of National Trust dunes and salt flats, which makes it a real treat for birdwatchers as this is prime birdwatching territory. The simple but stylish old-fashioned pub has three small rooms, a log fire, and a good mix of seats; prompt friendly service, even when busy. Generous helpings of enjoyable bar food from a changing menu that usually has several local fish dishes might include sandwiches (from £2.50; fresh crab £4.25), hot sausage and onion baguette (£3.95), goats cheese and spinach tartlet (£3.95), garlic king prawns (£5.50), brie and roast vegetables (£6.95), cajun chicken breast or battered cod (£7.95), Brancaster baked crab salad (£8.95), swordfish steak (£9.50), grilled bass (£9.95), rib-eye steak topped with garlic prawns (£11.95), and home-made puddings such as jam roly poly, rhubarb crumble and cheesecake (£3.25); the attractive restaurant is no smoking. Well kept Greene King IPA, a beer brewed for the pub by Wolfe and Woodfordes Wherry on handpump, and decent wines; piped music. There are sheltered tables in the nice garden with a terrace, enclosed play area. *(Recommended by Keith Williamson, Nigel Woolliscroft, John Beeken, Mike and Wendy Proctor, Eric Locker, M J A Switzer, Pat and Clive Sherriff, Di and Mike Gillam, Ian Arthur, Tracey and Stephen Groves)*

Free house ~ Licensees Darren Humphrey and Wendy Darrington ~ Real ale ~ Bar food (12-4, 5-9.30(8.30 Sun)) ~ Restaurant ~ (01485) 210314 ~ Children welcome ~ Open 11-11; 12-10.30 Sun

White Horse 🍽 ♀ 🛏
A149 E of Hunstanton
Norfolk Dining Pub of the Year

The mussels, samphire, cockles and oysters they serve at this seaside pub are all collected from the bottom of the garden which gives onto saltings and a sea channel. Given the unassuming exterior of this place you'd never guess what was in store for you inside, let alone the lovely views. It's an airy open-plan bistro-style inn with big windows, solid stripped tables with country chairs and pews on the mainly stripped wood floors, and cream walls packed with interesting local black and white photographs. Stools line a handsome counter manned by friendly young staff, and there's a particularly easy-going relaxed atmosphere here. You get the lovely views of the Norfolk Coastal Path, tidal marsh and Scolt Head Island beyond from tables (laid for eating) by great picture windows round to the side and back of the bar. The airy dining conservatory with sun deck and terrace enjoys the same view. One dining area is no smoking. Well kept Adnams, Greene King IPA and Abbot, Woodfordes Wherry and a guest such as Black Sheep on handpump, 20 malt whiskies and about a dozen wines by the glass from an extensive and thoughtful wine list; bar billiards. The menu changes twice a day and is extremely good. At lunchtime it might include home-made soup (from £2.50), moules marinières (£4.65/£8.50), toasted goats cheese with oven roasted plum tomatoes and pesto dressing (£4.95), seared scallops with wilted red chard and caper oil (£7.75), pork and leek sausages (£7.95), battered whiting (£8.15), braised ling with chick pea and red chard cream (£9.50) and fried chicken breast with wild mushroom cream (£9.75). Evening dishes may be a touch more expensive: grilled bass with roasted plum tomato or rib-eye steak with warm tomato and onion salad (£12.95) and grilled halibut with house-made squid ink linguini, spinach and tomatoes (£13.25). Very well designed bedrooms each have their own outside terrace and view. *(Recommended by J and D Boutwood, John and Sylvia Harrop, John Wooll, Mrs Pamela Westley, Tracey and Stephen Groves, Keith Sale, M J Morgan, O K Smyth, M J A Switzer, J P Marland, Angela and Andrew Webster, Mr and Mrs B Golding, Brenda Crossley, Mike and Sue Loseby)*

Free house ~ Licensees Cliff Nye and Kevin Nobes ~ Real ale ~ Bar food (not Sat evening) ~ Restaurant ~ (01485) 210262 ~ Children welcome ~ Live folk or Irish Fri evening ~ Open 11-11; 12-10.30 Sun; closed 25 Dec evening ~ Bedrooms: £60B/£90B

BURNHAM MARKET TF8342 Map 8
Hoste Arms ⓦ ♀ ⛺

The Green (B1155)

This civilised but informally smart 17th-c hotel is a fine example of how good food, accommodation and a little town local can be offered in one place. The boldly decorated bars are nice and pubby with massive log fires and are enjoyed by a friendly muddle of gentry, farmers, fishermen and shoppers. The panelled bar on the right has a series of watercolours showing scenes from local walks, there's a bow-windowed bar on the left, a nice sitting room, a little art gallery in the staircase area, and well kept Greene King IPA and Abbot and Woodfordes Wherry and Nelson's Revenge on handpump, a good wine list with plenty of big names including champagne by the glass, a decent choice of malt whiskies, and freshly squeezed orange juice. Imaginative, highly enjoyable food includes sandwiches, soup (£3.25), sticky pork salad with mango and Namm Jim dressing (£4.95), tempura black pudding with poached egg and devilled sauce (£5.25), dressed Cromer crab with chicory and french bean salad (£5.95), fried lambs liver with mustard mash or grilled red mullet with pasta tossed in a herb cream (£6.95), seared tuna with oriental vegetables and hoi sin sauce (£9.95), whole lemon sole with crushed potatoes and soft herb butter emulsion (£11.75), honey glazed duck breast, celeriac purée and provençale sauce (£12.25), and crisp fried bass on fennel, wild rice and sweet pea dressing (£13.75). A pleasant walled garden at the back has tables on a terrace. *(Recommended by Nigel Woolliscroft, M J Morgan, R J Walden, J Hale, R C Wiles, David Heath, M J A Switzer, Colin Draper, David and Anne Culley, Peter Rozee, Keith and Jill Wright, Pat and Roger Fereday, Gordon Stevenson, A D Cross, Patricia Beebe, DF, NF, David Pugh, Tony Middis, David Rule, Michael and Ann Cole, David Field, Abi Benson, Nick Lawless, Tracey and Stephen Groves, Peter and Pat Frogley, MDN, Roy Bromell, John Davis; also in* The Good Hotel Guide)

Free house ~ Licensees Paul and Jean Whittome and Joanne Race ~ Real ale ~ Bar food ~ Restaurant ~ (01328) 738777 ~ Children welcome away from bar area ~ Open 11-11; 12-10.30 Sun ~ Bedrooms: £66S/£90B

BURNHAM THORPE TF8541 Map 8
Lord Nelson ◀

Village signposted from B1155 and B1355, near Burnham Market

Predating the birth of Nelson by some 100 years, this very enjoyable pub was originally named the Plough and was renamed in honour of its most famous customer who was born in this village. It's no surprise to find lots of pictures and memorabilia of him lining the walls, and they have an unusual rum concoction called Nelson's Blood. The characterful little bar has well waxed antique settles on the worn red flooring tiles and smoke ovens in the original fireplace, and an eating room has flagstones, an open fire, and more pictures of the celebrated sailor; there's one no smoking room. There's no bar counter – you order your pint of well kept Greene King IPA or Abbot or Woodfordes Wherry at the table, and they are then tapped from the cask in a back stillroom and brought to you by the very friendly staff. Very good bar food includes prawn cocktail (£4.10), English breakfast, ploughman's or lunchtime filled baguettes (from £4.95), breaded plaice (£5.50), grilled lamb chops with red wine and rosemary (£8.75) and daily specials such as home-made chicken liver and wild mushroom pâtés (£4.30), crab and beetroot salad (£4.50), pork and leek sausages and mash (£7.95) and seared hake in chilli and herb butter (£8.95); shove-ha'penny, dominoes, draughts, and cards. There's a good sized play area in the very big garden. *(Recommended by DF, NF, the Didler, Dr David Cockburn, John Wooll, Giles and Liz Ridout, Anthony Barnes, Nigel Woolliscroft, Kevin Thorpe, Abi Benson, Tracey and Stephen Groves, M J A Switzer, Mike and Wendy Proctor, Roger Purkiss, Sarah Lynch, DJH, Paul and Ursula Randall, Barbara Wensworth)*

Greene King ~ Lease Lucy Stafford ~ Real ale ~ Bar food (12-2.30, 6.30-9) ~ Restaurant ~ (01328) 738241 ~ Children welcome in family room ~ Open 11-3, 6-11; 12-3, 6-10.30 Sun; closed Mon, Tues in winter

CAWSTON TG1422 Map 8
Ratcatchers 🍴 ♀

Eastgate, S of village – on B1149 from Norwich turn left towards Haveringland at crossroads ½ mile before the B1145 Cawston turn

The name of this warmly welcoming dining pub is supposed to have originated at the turn of the century when the building was first converted to an inn, and the local ratcatcher was the first person to stay here. These days the very atmospheric cosy L-shaped beamed bar has an open fire, nice old chairs and a fine mix of walnut, beech, elm and oak tables, a quieter and cosier candlelit dining room on the right, and a conservatory. There are no smoking areas throughout the pub. The very good food is probably some of the best in the area, so it's as well to book to be sure of a table. The menu includes smoked mackerel (£4.45), fried whitebait (£4.90), shell on prawns (£4.95), ploughman's (£5.85), sausage and mash (£5.95), cottage pie (£6.75), indonesian stir fry (£7.75), beef and ale or fish pie (£8.20), peppered chicken (£9.85), and daily specials such as lemon sole or wild salmon with thai prawns (£11.95) and roast guinea fowl with fresh herbs and wild mushrooms, bacon and juniper sauce (£8.95). Well kept Adnams Best, Greene King IPA and a beer named for the pub (brewed for them by Hancocks) on handpump, a good wine list with half a dozen by the glass; dominoes, cribbage, and piped music. There are tables on the terrace by special outside heaters for dining in cooler weather. *(Recommended by Di and Mike Gillam, John Beeken, Tony Middis, Sally Anne and Peter Goodale, Ian Phillips, Sheila and Brian Wilson, W W Burke)*

Free house ~ Licensees Peter and Denise McCarter ~ Real ale ~ Bar food (12-2, 6.15-9.45) ~ Restaurant ~ (01603) 871430 ~ Children welcome ~ Open 11.45-3, 5.45(6.30 Sun)-11

Real ale to us means beer which has matured naturally in its cask –
not pressurised or filtered.

ERPINGHAM TG1732 Map 8

Saracens Head ⏣ ♟ 🛏

At Wolterton – not shown on many maps; Erpingham signed off A140 N of Aylsham, keep on through Calthorpe, then where road bends right take the straight-ahead turn-off signposted Wolterton

Standing rather eccentrically in the middle of a field, this gently civilised place is very popular with readers. The two-room bar looks out on a charming old-fashioned gravel stableyard with picnic-sets and is simple and stylish, with high ceilings, terracotta walls, and red and white striped curtains at its tall windows – all lending a feeling of space, though it's not actually large. There's a mix of seats from built-in leather wall settles to wicker fireside chairs as well as log fires and flowers on the mantelpieces. There's a pretty little four-table parlour on the right in cheerful nursery colours, and another big log fire. Well kept Woodfordes Blickling and Adnams or Greene King Abbot on handpump; decent malt whiskies. The wine list is really quite interesting, with some shipped direct from a French chateau. It's almost essential to book for the imaginative bar food, served in a relaxed and informal atmosphere, which might include starters such as parsnip and spring onion soup, red onion and goats cheese tart or venison rissoles with sun dried tomatoes and cream (from £3.95), main courses such as baked avocado with apple and goats cheese (£8.95), local sausages, black pudding and venison liver with tomato and basil pearl barley (£9.25), venison medallions with wild mushrooms and marsala (£12.50) and fried scallops with rosemary and cream (£12.95), and puddings such as rich chocolate pot with orange jus, brown bread and butter pudding or mulled wine and red fruit pudding (£3.50); remarkably good value two-course weekday lunch (£5.50), monthly themed feasts, and enjoyable breakfasts. *(Recommended by Pamela Goodwyn, R M Corlett, P R Morley, Miss G Irving, R Styles, Bob Arnett, Judy Wayman, E M and H P N Steinitz, Susan and Nigel Wilson, Denys Gueroult, Judy Wayman, Bob Arnett, Kevin Thorpe, the Hon Mrs Fennell, Minda and Stanley Alexander, D P Brown, Neil Powell, John Wooll, Lynn Sharpless, Bob Eardley, David Twitchett, John and Angela Main, B N F and M Parkin, S Watkin, P Taylor, Ian and Nita Cooper, J F M and M West, Tony and Gill Powell, DF, NF; also in* The Good Hotel Guide*)*

Free house ~ Licensee Robert Dawson-Smith ~ Real ale ~ Bar food ~ Restaurant ~ (01263) 768909 ~ Well behaved children in eating area of bar and restaurant ~ Open 11.30-3, 6-11; 12-3, 7-10.30 Sun; closed 25 Dec ~ Bedrooms: £40B/£60B

HEYDON TG1127 Map 8

Earle Arms

Village signposted from B1149 about midway between Norwich and Holt

Hardly changed since the 1630s, this special little village with its simple but pretty green lined with charming cottages and houses is the sort of place film companies always pick out as a location. The two carpeted rooms at this yellow-painted brick pub remain unspoilt and mainly unchanged too. They open off a small lobby with a handsomely carved longcase clock, and are individually furnished and decorated, with pretty rosehip wallpaper over a stripped dado, china on shelves, deep tiled-floor cupboards with interesting bric-a-brac, attractive prints and good log fires; one has hatch service. Dominoes, darts, cribbage, fruit machine, and piped music. Bar food might include vegetarian couscous (£5.50), steak and kidney pudding (£5.90), cod provençale (£6.10) and duck with orange and Cointreau sauce (£7.10). Well kept Adnams Bitter, Woodfordes Wherry and a guest such as Batemans XXXB on handpump. There are picnic-sets in a small and prettily cottagey back garden, and on the front wall above the colourful flower borders is what looks like a figurehead of possibly Ceres the Mother Earth symbol. *(Recommended by Mike and Sue Loseby, John Wooll)*

Free house ~ Licensee Andrew Harrison-Taylor ~ Real ale ~ Bar food (not Sun, Mon evenings) ~ Restaurant ~ No credit cards ~ (01263) 587376 ~ Children welcome ~ Open 12-3, 6-11; 12-3, 7-11 Sun

HORSEY TG4522 Map 8
Nelson Head
Signposted off B1159 (in series of S-bends) N of Gt Yarmouth

Nicely set in National Trust land, this simple country pub is not always easy to find as the sign is often hidden by trees in summer. Horsey Windmill and the beach are just down the road and it's the nearest pub to Horsey Mere so attracts a mix of customers from ramblers to birdwatchers and yachtsmen all enjoying its two homely unpretentious little rooms. It's furnished with straightforward but comfortable seats (including four tractor-seat bar stools), bits of shiny bric-a-brac, small local pictures for sale, a good fire and geraniums on the window sill, with Woodfordes Wherry and (of course) Nelsons Revenge on handpump. Bar food includes ploughman's (£4.25), vegetarian tagliatelle (£5.50), ham and egg (£5.95) sirloin steak (£9.25), and daily specials such as home-made steak in ale pie (£5.95), chilli or seafood pie (£6.95), and Italian chicken (£7.25). The garden has picnic-sets and an outside marquee, and dogs are allowed. *(Recommended by Cathy Robinson, Lawrence Bacon, Jean Scott, W W Burke, Mike and Wendy Proctor, George Atkinson)*

Free house ~ Licensee Reg C Parsons ~ Real ale ~ Bar food ~ No credit cards ~ (01493) 393378 ~ Children in eating area of bar and family room ~ Open 12-3, 6(7 winter)-11(7-10.30 Sun)

ITTERINGHAM TG1430 Map 8
Walpole Arms ◖
Village signposted off B1354 NW of Aylsham

The impressive menu at this attractive red brick dining pub changes daily. There's a lighter snack menu with dishes such as cauliflower and leek cheese (£4.50), pork pie or chicken waldorf on toasted ciabatta (£4.75) and ham and eggs (£6), and a more inventive contemporary menu with things like roast asparagus on watercress with a soft egg and smoked trout or potato pancake with sweet pickled herrings and cucumber yoghurt (£5.25), sausage, bubble and squeak (£7.25), saltimbocca (£9.25), roast cod with noodles, bok choi and crab broth (£9.50), rib-eye steak and béarnaise sauce (£11) and puddings such as a greek tart with yoghurt, lemon curd, honey and sunflower seeds, apricot, banana and strawberry crumble or tatin of peaches with ice cream, almonds and raspberry sauce (£4.50). The biggish open-plan bar has a good bustling friendly atmosphere, little windows, stripped brick walls, a dark navy carpet, heavy timber props for the stripped beam and plank ceiling and well spaced heavy unstripped tables including two long glossy planked dark ones. You probably won't hear the faint piped music over the sound of contented chat. As well as Adnams Bitter and Woodfordes Wherry and a guest such as Greene King Old Speckled Hen they have a decent wine list; dominoes, cribbage, fruit machine. It's tucked away in the country so although the garden is largely uncultivated, picnic-sets out here are a pleasant place to sit in summer. *(Recommended by John Wooll, Peter and Jean Hoare, Lynn Sharpless, Bob Eardley, the Hon Mrs Fennell, Stephen, Julie and Hayley Brown, Di and Mike Gillam)*

Free house ~ Licensee Keith Reeves ~ Real ale ~ Bar food ~ Restaurant ~ (01263) 587258 ~ Children in eating area of bar and restaurant ~ Open 11-3, 6-11; 12-3, 7-10.30 Sun

LARLING TL9889 Map 5
Angel ◖ 🛏
A11 S of Attleborough

This very neatly kept pub has been run by the same friendly family since 1913. The comfortable 1930s-style lounge on the right has cushioned wheelback chairs, a nice long cushioned and panelled corner settle, some good solid tables for eating off and some lower ones, squared panelling, a collection of whisky-water jugs on the delft shelf over the big brick fireplace which houses a big woodburner, a couple of copper kettles, and some hunting prints; there are two dining rooms (one of which is no smoking). Reliable bar food includes sandwiches and toasties (from £2.50; the bacon and banana is popular), soup (£2.50), home-made pâté (£3.95), creamy mushroom pot (£3.95), ploughman's or omelettes (£4.95), home-made burgers (from £5.25), ham and egg (£6.95), broccoli and cream cheese bake (£6.95), lamb balti (£6.95), fish crumble (£7.95), steaks (from £9.95), daily specials such as home-made steak and kidney pie (£6.95) and battered cod (£7.25), and home-made puddings (from £2.95). Well kept Adnams Best and guests from local brewers like Iceni, Orkney and Wolf on handpump, and over 100 malt whiskies. The quarry-tiled black-beamed public bar has a good local atmosphere, with darts, dominoes, juke box and fruit machine; piped music. A neat grass area behind the car park has picnic-sets around a big fairy-lit apple tree, and a safely fenced play area. Peter Beale's old-fashioned rose nursery is nearby. *(Recommended by Anthony Barnes, A E Brace, Stephen, Julie and Hayley Brown, John Robertson, MDN, K H Frostick, G Coates, Ian Phillips, Mike and Karen England, Laura and Stuart Ballantyne, Tony W Dickinson, Dave Braisted)*

Free house ~ Licensee Andrew Stammers ~ Real ale ~ Bar food (12-2, 6.30-9.30; 12-2.30, 6.30-10 Fri, Sat) ~ Restaurant ~ (01953) 717963 ~ Children welcome ~ Duos and karaoke Thurs ~ Open 10-11; 12-10.30 Sun ~ Bedrooms: £30B/£50B

LETHERINGSETT TG0538 Map 8
Kings Head

A148 just W of Holt

Families are particularly welcome at this very enthusiastically run pub in the heart of the Glaven Valley. There's lots of children's activities including a play castle, living willow tunnel, toys, bikes and games, and a children's menu with a better choice than usual. This is an energetic place with a good live music line-up (see below for times). The carpeted bar has metal-legged tables, a couple of armchairs and log fires, with various interesting prints, pictures and other items, including a signed poem by John Betjeman, on the walls. There's also a small plush lounge, and a separate games room with darts, pool, shove-ha'penny, dominoes, cribbage, fruit machines, and piped music. Reasonably priced bar food includes sandwiches (from £2.95), soup (£2.95), ploughman's (from £5.45), vegetarian lasagne (£6.45), scampi (£7.45) and mixed grill (£11.95). Well kept Greene King Abbot and three guests such as Greene King IPA, Woodfordes Ketts Rebellion and Wolf Wolf in Sheeps Clothing on handpump, a dozen malt whiskies, and good service. The spacious lawn has plenty of tables, and is quite attractive on a sunny day. The pub is in a very pleasant setting, in grounds well back from the road, opposite a church with an unusual round tower, and not far from an interesting working water mill. Dogs allowed. *(Recommended by Tony W Dickinson, S Horsley, Sue and Mike Todd, R C Vincent, M J Morgan)*

Free house ~ Licensees David and Pamela Watts ~ Real ale ~ Bar food (12-9) ~ (01263) 712 691 ~ Children welcome ~ Live music Sat evening Sept-June, Sun afternoons June-Sept ~ Open 11-11; 12-10.30 Sun

MUNDFORD TL8093 Map 5
Crown 🍺 £

Crown Street; village signposted off A1065 Thetford—Swaffham

Set in a pretty village, this attractive 17th-c posting inn makes a good lunchtime stop if you're visiting nearby Thetford Forest. The beamed lounge bar has a huge open fireplace in a flint wall, captain's chairs around highly polished tables, interesting local advertisements and other memorabilia, and a friendly bustling atmosphere. If the pub is full, a spiral iron staircase with *Vanity Fair* cartoons beside it leads up to the club room, an elegant restaurant and the garden. There are more heavy beams in the separate red-tiled locals' bar on the left, which has cast-iron-framed tables, another smaller brick fireplace with a copper hood, sensibly placed darts, cribbage, dominoes, fruit machine, TV, juke box, and a screened-off pool table. Well kept Courage Directors, Theakstons, Woodfordes Wherry and a couple of guests from Iceni and Nethergate on handpump, and over 50 malt whiskies. Very helpful staff serve tasty bar snacks such as sandwiches (from £2.25), filled baguettes (from £4.15), home-made soup (£2.95), burgers (from £3.75), local herby sausage (£5.25), honey fried chicken (£5.75), local trout (£6.45), fillet of cod in tomato and mustard seed batter (£7.25), and daily specials such as roast pepper and tomato tagliatelle (£5.50), poached skate wing with green onion and cheddar cream (£8.75) and T-bone with brandy and cracked peppercorn cream (£12.95); children's helpings of most meals. *(Recommended by Michael and Ann Cole, Christopher Turner, Mrs J L Crutchfield, R J Walden, Stephen, Julie and Hayley Brown, Ian Phillips, Bill and Sheila McLardy, Mike and Karen England, Anthony Barnes, Dr Paull Khan, Nigel Hopkins, Keith and Janet Morris, Minda and Stanley Alexander)*

Free house ~ Licensee Barry Walker ~ Real ale ~ Bar food (12-3, 7-10) ~ Restaurant ~ (01842) 878233 ~ Children welcome ~ Open 11-11; 12-10.30 Sun ~ Bedrooms: £35B/£55B

NORWICH TG2308 Map 5
Adam & Eve ♀ £

Bishopgate; follow Palace St from Tombland, N of cathedral

Well situated in the town centre and near the cathedral, this characterful place is the oldest pub in Norwich, and is thought to date back to at least 1249 – though the striking Dutch gables were added in the 14th and 15th c. The little old-fashioned bars quickly fill at lunchtime with a good mixed crowd of people, and there are antique high-backed settles (one handsomely carved), cushioned benches built into partly panelled walls, and tiled or parquet floors; the snug room is no smoking at lunchtime; piped music. Enjoyable, good value bar food under the cheery new landlady includes sandwiches, granary baps or filled french bread (from £2.55), cheese and ale soup with with pastry top (£3.75), ploughman's (from £4.50), chilli or chicken curry (£4.75), ham and egg (£4.85), daily specials such as home-made ratatouille (£3.85), king prawns in garlic sauce (£5.25), crispy chicken in batter with a spicy dip (£4.85), a roast of the day with yorkshire pudding (£4.95), and puddings like home-made spicy bread and butter pudding (from £2.70). Well kept Adnams Bitter, Greene King IPA, Charles Wells Bombardier and Theakstons Old Peculier, and a guest such as Adnams Broadside on handpump, a wide range of malt whiskies, about a dozen decent wines by the glass, Addlestone's cider and freshly squeezed orange juice. There are wooden picnic-sets in front of the pub and very pretty summer tubs and hanging baskets. *(Recommended by Tina and David Woods-Taylor, Patricia Beebe, Charles and Pauline Stride, Steve Chambers, the Didler, MJVK, Pat and Clive Sherriff, Dr David Cockburn, Simon Pyle, Michael Tack, W W Burke)*

Unique Pub Co ~ Licensee Rita McCluskey ~ Real ale ~ Bar food (12-7; 12-2.30 Sun) ~ (01603) 667423 ~ Children welcome in snug ~ Open 11-11; 12-10.30 Sun; closed 25, 26 Dec, 1 Jan

Fat Cat ◀

West End St

Orkney, the Isle of Skye and Dublin are just a few of the remoter places that supply beers to this traditional alehouse. They keep a remarkable 26 real ales at any one time, and they're all in excellent condition. About half are on handpump, while the rest are tapped from the cask in a still room behind the bar – big windows reveal all. They also keep four draught Belgian beers (two of them fruit), draught lagers from Germany and the Czech Republic, up to 15 bottled Belgian beers, 15 country wines, and local Norfolk cider. Open all day, this is a classic town pub, with a good mix of customers and a lively bustling atmosphere at some times of the day, and tranquil lulls in the middle of the afternoon. The no-nonsense furnishings include plain scrubbed pine tables and simple solid seats, lots of brewery memorabilia, bric-a-brac and stained glass. Bar food consists of a dozen or so rolls at lunchtime (60p; not Sunday). There are tables outside. *(Recommended by David Twitchett, Ian Phillips, the Didler, Keith and Katy Stevens, Tracey and Stephen Groves)*

Free house ~ Licensee Colin Keatley ~ Real ale ~ No credit cards ~ (01603) 624364 ~ Open 12(11 Sat)-11; 12-10.30 Sun

REEDHAM TG4101 Map 5
Ferry Inn

B1140 Beccles—Acle; the ferry here holds only two cars but goes back and forth continuously till 10pm, taking only a minute or so to cross – fare £2.75 per car, 25p foot passengers

You can get to this splendidly placed Broads pub by boat – either by the working chain ferry (see above) or on a holiday hire boat (if you eat in the pub, they give you free mooring and showers); there are plenty of well spaced tables on the terrace overlooking the water. Inside, the long front bar has big picture windows, comfortable banquettes and some robust rustic tables carved from slabs of tree-trunk; the secluded back bar has antique rifles, copper and brass, and a fine log fire. Good food includes home-made soup (£2.60), jumbo mushroom topped with ratatouille (£5.95), home-made curry (£6.25), home-made pie of the day (£6.50), lasagne (£6.25), home-cured gammon with pineapple (£6.95), steaks (£11.25), daily specials such as roast sirloin (£5.95), kiln smoked salmon steak with hollandaise (£7.65) and puddings (£2.75); good fresh vegetables. The restaurant and family room are no smoking. Well kept Adnams Bitter and Broadside and Woodfordes Wherry and a guest such as Shepherd Neame Spitfire on handpump, quite a few malt whiskies, country wines, and good cheerful staff; piped music. The woodturner's shop next door is worth a look. *(Recommended by Mr Alcuin, Sue and Bob Ward, John Wooll, Miss J Durbridge, W Shakeshaft, Anthony Barnes)*

Free house ~ Licensee David Archer ~ Real ale ~ Bar food (12-2 (cold food till 2.30), 6.30-9) ~ Restaurant ~ (01493) 700429 ~ Children in restaurant and family room till 9pm ~ Folk twice weekly ~ Open 11-3, 6.30(6 Sat)-11; 12-10.30 Sun

Railway Tavern ▰

Just off B1140 Beccles—Acle; in the Beccles direction the little chain ferry stops at 10pm

Set just above the railway station, this attractive and rather imposing listed Victorian brick building is popular with locals for its friendly atmosphere and well kept Humpty Dumpty beers which are brewed just up the road by the former licensee. Of the six brews there are usually two on in the pub, served alongside a couple of interesting microbrewery guests such as Iceni Fine Soft Day and Nethergate Suffolk County. The pub hosts a beer festival in mid April and mid September with up to 50 beers on in a week – it's such a popular event they put on extra trains. The fairly simple but nicely pubby lounge has a high ceiling, dark wood tables and chairs on a turkey carpet, high netted and swagged windows, and red leatherette stools and a couple of tractor seats at the red velvet studded bar, behind which is an impressive range of about 70 malt whiskies. The much simpler very pubby public bar has bare boards, darts, pool and TV; piped music. Bar food usually includes soup (£2.70), fried whitebait with lemon mayonnaise (£3.80), steak and kidney pudding or home-made burgers (£5.90), fish and chips (£6.50), beef and ale pie (£6.90), but the menu moves up a notch or two from Thursday to Saturday when they also have a very good range of fresh fish from Lowestoft, such as juniper marinated herrings on buttered leeks with red pepper mayonnaise (£3.90), provençale mussels (£4.90), bacon-wrapped monkfish on leek mash (£9.50), thai spiced marlin on spring greens (£11.90) and fried red snapper on steamed curly kale with mornay sauce and roast tomatoes (£12.50). It's best to book at weekends. There's a pretty gravelled courtyard and garden at the back, and white metal chairs on a terrace at the front overlook the station. *(Recommended by Anthony Barnes, Alan Thomas, Bob Arnett, Judy Wayman, Kevin Thorpe)*

Free house ~ Licensee James Lunn ~ Real ale ~ Bar food (12-2, 6-9(9.30 Fri-Sun)) ~ Restaurant ~ (01493) 700340 ~ Children welcome ~ Folk first and third Weds ~ Open 11-3, 6-11; 11-11 Sat; 12-10.30 Sun ~ Bedrooms: £30S/£50S(£60B)

REEPHAM TG0922 Map 8
Old Brewery House
Market Square; B1145 W of Aylsham

Overlooking an old-fashioned town square, this Georgian hotel has a big high-ceilinged bar with a good pubby atmosphere, a nice mix of oldish pub tables, lots of farming and fishing bric-a-brac and old enamel advertisements on its pale ochre walls, a piano and a dark green dado. A step down from this main seating area takes you to a tiled-floor serving part with well kept Adnams, Green King Abbot, local Reepham, and a guest such as Ruddles County on handpump, and several malt whiskies. There's also a red-carpeted lounge leading off, with dark panelling and sturdy brocaded armchairs; piped music. Under the new licensees, generous helpings of bar food include sandwiches (from £2.95), soup or prawn cocktail (£2.95), ploughman's (£4.95), sausage and mash (£5.25), chilli or tagliatelle carbonara (£5.50), ratatouille bake (£5.95), fish pie (£5.25) and beef and ale pie (£6.50). The dining room and new conservatory are no smoking. *(Recommended by Marjorie and Bernard Parkin, Maggie and Peter Shapland)*

Free house ~ Licensee David Peters ~ Real ale ~ Bar food ~ Restaurant ~ (01603) 870881 ~ Children welcome ~ Live entertainment most Fri evenings ~ Open 11-11(12 Sat); 12-10.30 Sun ~ Bedrooms: £47.50B/£75B

RINGSTEAD TF7040 Map 8
Gin Trap
Village signposted off A149 near Hunstanton; OS Sheet 132 map reference 707403

This reliable carefully run village local has a copper kettle, carpenters' tools, cartwheels, and bottles hanging from the beams in the lower part of the well kept chatty bar, toasting forks above the woodburning stove, a lots of gin traps ingeniously converted to electric candle-effect wall lights, and captain's chairs with cast-iron-framed tables on the green-and-white motif carpet; part of this bar is no smoking. A small no smoking dining room has over 100 chamber-pots suspended from the ceiling, and high-backed pine settles; you can book a table in here. Well kept Adnams Best, Greene King Abbot, Woodfordes Nog, and Gin Trap Bitter brewed by Woodfordes for the pub, and a guest on handpump. Good bar food includes lunchtime sandwiches (£2.75) and ploughman's (from £3.75), as well as nut cutlet (£5), lasagne (£6), steak and kidney pie (£6.25), scampi (£6.75), steaks (from £9.25), home-made vegetarian quiche (£6), daily fish specials such as cod, plaice or salmon (from around £6) and half a roast chicken with trimmings (£7); home-made puddings such as Jamaican bread and butter pudding and fruit crumbles (£3). A handsome spreading chestnut tree shelters the car park, and the back garden has seats on the grass or small paved area and pretty flowering tubs. The pub is close to the Peddar's Way; hikers and walkers are welcome, but not their muddy boots. There's an art gallery next door, boules in the very old brewhouse barn and self-catering accommodation. *(Recommended by Bill and Pat Pemberton, John Beeken, O K Smyth, Hazel and Michael Duncombe, M J Morgan, Ian Phillips, John and Angela Main, Chris Mawson, M J A Switzer, Willie Bell, M Joyner, Paul and Margaret Baker, Tracey and Stephen Groves, Michael Tack, Keith and Chris O'Neill)*

Free house ~ Licensees Brian and Margaret Harmes ~ Real ale ~ Bar food ~ No credit cards ~ (01485) 525264 ~ Children welcome away from main bar and not too late ~ Open 11.30-2.30, 6.30-11; 12-2.30, 6.30-10.30 Sun

SNETTISHAM TF6834 Map 8
Rose & Crown 🍴 ♀ 🛏
Village signposted from A149 Kings Lynn—Hunstanton Rd, just N of Sandringham

There's massive confirmation in our postbag this year that the licensees of this ancient white pub are making their philosophy really work: they aim to make you feel thoroughly at home from the moment you arrive until the end of a memorably satisfying visit. Freshly cooked seasonal bar food using local produce where possible is from a changing menu which might include lunchtime dishes such as smoked gammon and pearl barley broth (£3.50), toasted filled foccacia (£4.95), fried sardines with pak choi salad (£5.50) and beef, Guinness and mushroom casserole or portuguese-style salt cod with roast peppers, aïoli and parmesan (£8.50), with evening dishes such as roasted red pepper and tomato soup with vanilla oil (£3.50), greek tapas with pitta bread (£5.75), roast chicken breast with spinach polenta and crab and lime bisque (£10.95), grilled black bream with asian leaves, strawberry stilton and toasted pecan nuts (£13.25), and daily specials such as braised lamb shank and chorizo and bean stew with sweet potato chips (£9.95), additional vegetables (£1.50); they have a pudding chef so expect these to be good, and where practical they will do small helpings of menu items for children. The interior has been very thoughtfully put together, with several separate areas each with its own character: an old-fashioned beamed front bar with black settles on its tiled floor, and a great log fire; another big log fire in a back bar with the landlord's sporting trophies and old sports equipment; a no smoking bar with a colourful but soothing décor and white linen tablecloths (this room is favoured by people eating); and another warmly decorated room, nice for families, with painted settles and big old tables. Some lovely old pews and other interesting furniture sit on the wooden floor of the dining room, and there are shelves with old bottles and books, and old prints and watercolours. Well kept Adnams Bitter and Broadside, Bass, Greene King IPA and maybe a guest such as Fullers London Pride on handpump, quite a few wines by the glass and freshly squeezed orange juice. The colourful enclosed garden has picnic-sets among herbaceous borders and flowering shrubs, and two spectacular willow trees; also a great wooden fort, swings, a playhouse and chipmunks. The bedrooms are most attractive. Well behaved dogs welcome. *(Recommended by John and Sylvia Harrop, Mike and Wena Stevenson, Mr and Mrs T Christian, M Dean, JMC, Eric Locker, Nick Lawless, DF, NF, John Wooll, Bob and Sue Hardy, Keith Sale, David and Anne Culley, Jim Cowan, Jane Scarrow, Alan and Ros Furley, Ian Phillips, Tracey and Stephen Groves, Gordon Cooper, Jenny Cridland Ramsey, J M and P M Carver, Mike Ridgway, Sarah Miles, M J Morgan)*

Free house ~ Licensee Anthony Goodrich ~ Real ale ~ Bar food (12-2(till 2.30 wknds), 7-9(9.30 Fri, Sat)) ~ Restaurant ~ (01485) 541382 ~ Children in eating area of bar, restaurant, and family room ~ Open 11-11; 12-10.30 Sun ~ Bedrooms: £50B/£80B

STIFFKEY TF9743 Map 8

Red Lion

A149 Wells—Blakeney

They don't mind walking boots in one of the fairly spartan well used bars at this traditional roadside pub so it's worth a detour inland if you're walking the coastal path. Although simple the bars are quite atmospheric. The oldest parts have a few beams, aged flooring tiles or bare floorboards, big open fires, a mix of pews, small settles and a couple of stripped high-backed settles, a nice old long deal table among quite a few others, and oil-type or lantern wall lamps. The smallest is painted red. They have well kept Greene King IPA and Woodfordes Wherry and a couple of guests such as Elgoods Black Dog and Greene King Abbot on handpump or tapped from the cask, as well as Adnams wines, and Stowford Press cider; darts, dominoes, cribbage, and board games. The back restaurant leads into a no smoking conservatory, and there are wooden seats and tables out on a back gravel terrace, with more on grass further up beyond. There's a pretty steam with ducks and swans across the road, and some pleasant walks from this unspoilt village. Good value bar food might include goats cheese salad (£4.95), steak and kidney pie or pork and leek sausages (£6.95), ham salad or fresh sole or plaice (£7.95) and sea trout (£8.50). *(Recommended by M J Morgan, M J A Switzer, Judy Wayman, Bob Arnett, DJH, Nigel Woolliscroft, Kevin Macey, Sue Demont, Tim Barrow, John Prescott, Lee Melin, Peter and Pat Frogley, David Field, MDN, P G Plumridge, Brian and Halina Howes)*

Free house ~ Licensee Matthew Rees ~ Real ale ~ Bar food ~ (01328) 830552 ~ Children welcome away from bar area ~ Open 12-3, 6-11

STOW BARDOLPH TF6205 Map 5
Hare Arms ♀

Just off A10 N of Downham Market

The sort of place you wish for as a local, this neatly kept creeper-covered pub has a timelessly traditional village atmosphere. The welcoming bar is decorated with old advertising signs and fresh flowers, with plenty of tables around its central servery, and a good log fire; maybe two friendly ginger cats and a sort of tabby. This bar opens into a spacious heated and well planted no smoking conservatory. Bar food includes sandwiches (from £2.50), ploughman's (£6.75), mushroom stroganoff (£7.25), steak and mushroom pie, turkey breast wrapped in bacon with creamy mustard sauce, spare ribs, chestnut and parsnip bake or spinach and mixed pepper tart (£7.50), swordfish steak with black bean sauce or red snapper fillet with garlic butter (£8.95) and steaks (from £10.75). Well kept Greene King IPA and a couple of guests such as Badger Tanglefoot and Ruddles County on handpump a decent range of wines, and quite a few malt whiskies; maybe cockles and whelks on the bar counter; fruit machine. The pretty garden has picnic-sets under cocktail parasols and wandering peacocks and chickens. *(Recommended by Judy Pearson, R C Vincent, J F M and M West, John Wooll, Brian Root, Jonathan Tong, Anthony Barnes, David Rule, Ian Phillips, Tracey and Stephen Groves, Michael and Ann Cole)*

Greene King ~ Tenants David and Trish McManus ~ Real ale ~ Bar food (12-2, 7-10) ~ Restaurant ~ (01366) 382229 ~ Children in conservatory and family room ~ Open 11-2.30, 6-11; 12-2.30, 7-10.30 Sun; closed 25, 26 Dec

SWANTON MORLEY TG0117 Map 8
Darbys 🍺

B1147 NE of Dereham

Nicely pubby, there's a good, bustling atmosphere and fine mix of both locals and visitors in this creeper-covered brick pub. It's a careful conversion of two derelict farm cottages, and has a long bare-boarded country style bar with a comfortable lived in feel, lots of gin-traps and farming memorabilia, a good log fire (with the original bread oven alongside), tractor seats with folded sacks lining the long, attractive serving counter, and fresh flowers on the big stripped pine tables; maybe papers to read. A step up through a little doorway by the fireplace takes you through to the no smoking dining room. The children's room has a toy box and a glassed-over well. Enjoyable bar food includes filled baguettes (from £3.40), stilton and port pâté (£4.25), garlic and stilton mushrooms (£4.75), fried trout or battered cod (£6.50), salmon fillet with dill butter cream sauce (£7.95), steak and mushroom pudding (£8.75) and pigeon breast with red wine and mushroom sauce (£9.50). Around eight well kept real ales include Adnams Best and Broadside, Badger Tanglefoot, Greene King IPA, Woodfordes Wherry and a couple of guests such as Greene King Abbot, King and Barnes Sussex and Theakstons Old Peculier on handpump. A labrador and border collie might be around; darts, dominoes, cribbage, board games, and piped music. The garden has a really good play area. The bedrooms are in carefully converted farm buildings a few minutes away (they usually run a free (pre-booked) taxi service to and from the pub for residents), and there's plenty to do if you're staying as the family also own the adjoining 720-acre estate, and can arrange clay pigeon shooting, golf, fishing, nature trails, and craft instruction. *(Recommended by Michael and Jenny Back, Ian Pendlebury, E D Bailey, Ian Phillips, MDN)*

Free house ~ Licensees John Carrick and Louise Battle ~ Real ale ~ Bar food (12-2.15, 6.30-9.15; 12-9.45 Sat, Sun, and Fri in summer) ~ (01362) 637647 ~ Children in family room ~ Open 11.30-3, 6-11(11.30-11 Fri in summer); 11.30-11 Sat; 12-10.30 Sun

---

Though we don't usually mention it in the text, most pubs will now make coffee or tea – always worth asking.

THORNHAM TF7343 Map 8
Lifeboat

Turn off A149 by Kings Head, then take first left turn

The genuinely characterful main bar (they call it the Smugglers) at this rambling old white-painted stone pub is atmospherically lit with antique paraffin lamps suspended amongst an array of traps and yokes from its great oak beamed ceiling. It's cosily furnished with low settles, window seats, pews, and carved oak tables on the rugs on the tiled floor, and decorated with masses of guns, swords, black metal mattocks, reed-slashers and other antique farm tools. A couple of little rooms lead off here, and all in all there are five open fires. There are no games machines or piped music, though they still play the ancient game of 'pennies' which was outlawed in the late 1700s, and dominoes. As it can get pretty busy here during high days and holidays it is more relaxing and enjoyable away from these peak times. Very well prepared bar food includes soup (£3.50), chicken liver and garlic pâté or sardine fillets with thai spices (£4.50), filled baguettes (from £4.95), ploughman's (£5.75), spinach and mozzarella lasagne (£7.95), salmon and dill fishcakes (£8.50), pork with date, prune and port wine sauce or roast monkfish tail with lime and couscous crust (£10.95), daily specials such as warm chorizo, black pudding and smoked chicken salad with plum chutney (£4.50), Brancaster mussels (£7.95), baked hake fillet with pesto fettuccine (£8.95), and puddings such as fresh fruit crumble or sticky toffee pudding (£3.65). Well kept Adnams, Bass, Greene King IPA and Abbot, Woodfordes Wherry, and a guest such as Greene King Old Speckled Hen on handpump and several malt whiskies. Up some steps from the busy verdant conservatory is a sunny terrace with picnic-sets, and further back is a children's playground with fort and slide. The pub faces half a mile of coastal sea flats, most of the bedrooms have sea views, and there are lots of lovely surrounding walks. *(Recommended by Mike and Wendy Proctor, Hazel and Michael Duncombe, Mike and Sue Loseby, the Didler, Ian Phillips, Ian Arthur, Charlie Harris, John Wooll, Roger Purkiss, Sarah Lynch, O K Smyth, Bruce Bird, Peter Rozee, David Humeniuk, John Robertson, Derek and Sylvia Stephenson, Brian Root, Nick Lawless, June and Malcolm Farmer, Bill and Pat Pemberton, Nigel Woolliscroft, Keith Fairbrother, M J Morgan; also in* The Good Hotel Guide*)*

Free house ~ Licensee Charles Coker ~ Real ale ~ Bar food (12-2.30, 6-9.30) ~ Restaurant ~ (01485) 512236 ~ Children welcome ~ Open 11-11; 12-10.30 Sun ~ Bedrooms: £54B/£78B

TITCHWELL TF7543 Map 8
Manor Hotel 🛏

A149 E of Hunstanton

There are wonderful views over the salt marshes to the sea from the seats by the picture windows in the bar of this comfortable hotel which is handily placed for lunch after enjoying one of the many nearby walks or birdwatching on the Titchwell RSPB reserve opposite. The tranquil lounge has magazines, an open fire, and a good naturalists' record of the wildlife in the reserve. The pretty no smoking restaurant leads into a conservatory which opens onto the sheltered neatly kept walled gardens. As well as daily specials (which are probably the best value) such as Italian meatballs, baked crab thermidor or thai-style crispy duckling with pancakes (all around £6), the good food might include lunchtime sandwiches or baguettes, home-made soup (£3.50), grilled goats cheese brushed with garlic and herbs (£4.50), bean and basil risotto with buttered spinach or crispy cod in beer batter (£8.50), a medley of local fish with pasta or poached breast of chicken in a tomato and chive sauce (£10), cajun spiced grey mullet with a lime and coriander dressing (£10.95), and grilled whole lemon sole with herb butter (£13.50); children's helpings (£6). Greene King IPA and Abbot on handpump. There's a championship golf course only moments away. *(Recommended by M J A Switzer, M J Morgan, Peter and Pat Frogley; also in* The Good Hotel Guide*)*

Free house ~ Licensees Ian and Margaret Snaith ~ Real ale ~ Bar food ~ Restaurant ~ (01485) 210221 ~ Children welcome ~ Open 12-2, 6-11(10.30 Sun) ~ Bedrooms: £45B/£90B

TIVETSHALL ST MARY TM1686 Map 5

Old Ram ♀ ⛺

A140 15 miles S of Norwich, outside village

The very sizeable interior of this much extended dining pub soon fills up with customers, and with food served all day from 7.30am it is a useful place to know. The spacious country styled main room has a turkey rug on rosy brick floors, lots of stripped beams and standing timbers, antique craftsmen's tools on the ceiling, a huge log fire in the brick hearth and a longcase clock. It's ringed by smaller side areas, one has bright red walls, and the no smoking dining room has striking navy walls and ceiling, swagged curtains and an open woodburning stove. This leads to a second comfortable no smoking dining room and gallery; unobtrusive fruit machine, TV, cribbage, dominoes, and piped music. The sheltered flower-filled terrace is very civilised with outdoor heaters, cushioned seats and big green parasols. Bar food includes soup (£3.25; with a sandwich £5.95), tomato and goats cheese tartlet on a pesto sauce (£4.25), king prawns in garlic butter (£4.95), chargrilled burgers (from £6.50), sausage and mash (£7.95), steak and mushroom pie or mushrooms en croûte with sage sauce (£8.50), chicken curry (£8.95), grilled skate (£9.95), fried bass with fennel pâté and sweet pepper sauce (£12.95), steaks (from £11), and puddings such as toffee meringue gateau or crème brûlée (£3.50). They also offer an Over Sixty Club Menu with main courses at £5.95. Well kept Adnams, Woodfordes Wherry and a couple of guests such as Fullers London Pride and Hancocks on handpump, around two dozen wines by the glass, carafe or bottle, freshly squeezed orange juice and fresh fruit milkshakes. Comfortable beamed bedrooms; no dogs. *(Recommended by Stephen, Julie and Hayley Brown, Steve Chambers, J F M and M West, Beryl and Bill Farmer, Ian and Nita Cooper)*

Free house ~ Licensee John Trafford ~ Real ale ~ Bar food (7.30am-10pm) ~ Restaurant ~ (01379) 676794 ~ Children in eating area of bar and restaurant ~ Open 11-11; 12-10.30 Sun; closed 25, 26 Dec ~ Bedrooms: £51.95B/£70B

UPPER SHERINGHAM TG1441 Map 8

RED LION

B1157; village signposted off A148 Cromer—Holt, and the A149 just W of Sheringham

The two modest but charming little bars at this simple, relaxing flint cottage have stripped high-backed settles and country-kitchen chairs on the red tiles or bare boards, plain off-white walls and ceiling, a big woodburning stove, and newspapers to read; the snug is no smoking. Good bar food might include home-made soup (£2.95), home-made pâté (£4), stilton-stuffed mushrooms (£4), sweet and sour chicken (£6.50), lasagne (£6.95), vegetable curry, lambs liver in port and orange gravy (£6.75), thai red chicken curry (£7.25), steak and kidney pie (£7.25), and fresh fish such as whole plaice, crab thermidor, halibut, tuna (all £8.50). Well kept Greene King IPA, and Woodfordes Wherry on handpump, with over 30 malt whiskies and decent wines; dominoes and cribbage. *(Recommended by Stephen, Julie and Hayley Brown, David and Julie Glover, S Watkin, P Taylor, Peter and Pat Frogley, Minda and Stanley Alexander, Lord Sandhurst, P R Morley, Roy and Margaret Jones, John Davis)*

Free house ~ Licensee Sue Prew ~ Real ale ~ Bar food (12-2, 6.30-9) ~ Restaurant ~ No credit cards ~ (01263) 825408 ~ Children in eating area of bar ~ Open 11.30-11.30; 12-11.30 Sun; 11.30-3, 6.30-11 winter ~ Bedrooms: £20/£40

WARHAM TF9441 Map 8

Three Horseshoes ♠ ⛺

Warham All Saints; village signposted from A149 Wells-next-the-Sea—Blakeney, and from B1105 S of Wells

It's best to arrive at this unspoilt old-fashioned country pub early as they don't take bookings and it is a popular place. Parts of the building date back to the 1720s, and the simple interior with its gas lighting looks little changed since the 1920s. There's a genuinely pubby atmosphere in the three rooms which have stripped deal or mahogany tables (one marked for shove-ha'penny) on a stone floor, red leatherette settles built around the partly panelled walls of the public bar, and open fires in Victorian fireplaces; an antique American Mills one-arm bandit is still in working order (it takes 5p pieces; there's a 1960s one that takes 1p pieces), there's a big longcase clock with a clear piping strike, and a twister on the ceiling to point out who gets the next round. Good hearty English bar food is very reasonably priced and might include leek and potato or crab soup (£2.70), parsnip and butterbean bake (£4.80), neck of lamb hotpot (£5.80), beef and rabbit pie or cheese baked crab (£6.20), garlic lamb pie (£7), steak and kidney pie (£7.80), and plenty of steamed puddings such as spotted dick or lemon drizzle pudding (£2.70); half helpings for children; service can slow up at peak times. Well kept Greene King IPA, Woodfordes Wherry, and a weekly guest such as Buffys Polly's Folly on handpump or tapped from the cask, good home-made lemonade, and local summer cider. The dining room is no smoking. Darts, cribbage, and dominoes, and one of the outbuildings houses a wind-up gramophone museum – opened on request. There are rustic tables out on the side grass. *(Recommended by John Beeken, John Wooll, Lynn Sharpless, Bob Eardley, Tracey and Stephen Groves, Kevin Thorpe, Roger Purkiss, Sarah Lynch, Anthony Longden, David Field, Mike and Wendy Proctor, MDN, Angela and Andrew Webster, Peter and Pat Frogley, Lesley Kant, R Macfarlane, DJH, Pam and David Bailey, the Didler, Philip and Susan Philcox, Patrick and Ann Healy, Minda and Stanley Alexander)*

Free house ~ Licensee Iain Salmon ~ Real ale ~ Bar food (12-2, 6.30-8.30) ~ No credit cards ~ (01328) 710547 ~ Children welcome in family room ~ Open 11.30-2.30, 6-11; 12-3, 6-10.30 Sun; closed 25, 26 Dec ~ Bedrooms: £24/£48(£52S)

WELLS-NEXT-THE-SEA TF9143 Map 8
Crown £

The Buttlands

This unspoilt little black and white hotel is attractively set at the end of an elegant green surrounded by quiet and attractive Georgian houses. The pubby front bar has bowed beams, and well kept Adnams, Bass, and a guest such as Woodfordes Wherry on handpump and several malt whiskies. Two quieter back rooms have some interesting pictures on the wall over the roaring log fire, including several big Nelson prints and maps showing the town in the 18th and 19th centuries; piped music. A neat conservatory has small modern settles around the tables. Enjoyable bar food includes lunchtime sandwiches (from £1.70), soup (£2.25), gressingham duck and pork terrine with cherries marinated in brandy (£4.95), tagliatelle with Italian meat sauce (£5.25), steak in ale cobbler (£5.95), sirloin steak (£10.50), and daily specials such as fresh crab (£5.95), feta cheese tartlet (£6.50), sausages and onion gravy or lamb chops with redcurrant, garlic and coriander glaze (£6.95), venison casserole with cranberries (£8.75), and puddings such as blackcurrant brûlée or chocolate truffle (£2.95). *(Recommended by John Wooll, Keith and Chris O'Neill, Denys Gueroult, Ted and Jan Whitfield, John Robertson, Jim Cowan, Jane Scarrow, John and Angela Main, John and Sylvia Harrop, Cathy Robinson)*

Free house ~ Licensee Wilfred Foyers ~ Real ale ~ Bar food ~ Restaurant ~ (01328) 710209 ~ Children in eating area of bar and restaurant ~ Open 11-2.30, 6-11; 12-2.30, 7-10.30 Sun ~ Bedrooms: £55S/£69S

WINTERTON-ON-SEA TG4919 Map 8
Fishermans Return 🍺 🛏

From B1159 turn into village at church on bend, then turn right into The Lane

Thought to be about 300 years old, this brick and flint wood panelled inn has been run by the same hospitable licensees for the last 25 years. There's a lovely sandy beach nearby, and it's particularly pleasant on a sunny day with attractive wrought-iron and wooden benches on a pretty front terrace with nice views, and more seats in the sheltered garden. Children will be kept occupied by the pond and pets corner which has ornamental chickens and bantams. The cosily attractive white-painted lounge bar has vases of fresh flowers, neat brass-studded red leatherette seats and a winter log fire. The panelled public bar has low ceilings and a glossily varnished nautical air; two rooms are no smoking. Bar food includes toasties (from £2), cottage pie (£4.25), ploughman's (£4.50), fish pie (£5) chilli or battered cod (£6.25) and daily specials such as sun-dried tomato and fresh salmon pâtés (£4.50), chicken breast in lime and coriander (£7.25), braised lamb shank in rhubarb and ginger or baked bass with a herb crust (£9.75), and puddings such as baked black cherry cheesecake or strawberry and apple crumble. Well kept Greene King Abbot and Triumph, Woodfordes Wherry and Great Eastern Ale, and two guests on handpump, decent wines, around 30 malt whiskies, and James White's cider; darts, dominoes, cribbage, pool, fruit machine, and juke box. The characterful bedrooms, up the steep curving stairs, have low doors and uneven floors. *(Recommended by Dave Braisted, Mike and Wendy Proctor, Klaus and Elizabeth Leist, John Wooll, Mike and Sue Loseby, Ian Phillips, MJVK, Tony W Dickinson, James Rouse, Carol Horne, Mr and Mrs C M Pearson)*

Free house ~ Licensees John and Kate Findlay ~ Real ale ~ Bar food ~ (01493) 393305 ~ Children in family room ~ Open 11-2.30, 6.30-11; 11-11 Sat; 12.10.30 Sun ~ Bedrooms: /£65B

WOODBASTWICK TG3315 Map 8
Fur & Feather 🍺
Off B1140 E of Norwich

You are virtually guaranteed a really good pint at this converted thatched cottage as it is the tap for Woodfordes brewery which is right next door and they usually have all seven of their beers on at the same time. Although the interior isn't the cosiest you'll find this is more than made up for by the very welcoming atmosphere and friendly staff. Bar food is pretty good here too, with the rooms set out in the style of a dining pub. There might be soup (£2.30), home-made chicken liver pâté (£4.25), ploughman's (£6.75), leek and butter bean crumble or home-made meat loaf with a brandy and pepper sauce (£7.25), salmon and prawn tagliatelle or steak and kidney pudding (£7.95), and children's meals (£3.25); friendly, helpful staff. The restaurant and part of the bar are no smoking; piped music and cribbage. There are tables out in the very pleasant garden, and the pub forms part of a very attractive estate village; no dogs. *(Recommended by Klaus and Elizabeth Leist, Mike and Wendy Proctor, Nick Lawless, Nick and Meriel Cox, Pat and Clive Sherriff, Jonathan and Gillian Shread, Steve Thomas, Bruce Bird, Tony W Dickinson, Anthony Barnes, David and Julie Glover, the Didler, JDM, KM, Ian Phillips)*

Woodfordes ~ Tenants John and Jean Marjoram ~ Real ale ~ Bar food ~ Restaurant ~ (01603) 720003 ~ Children in restaurant ~ Open 12-3, 6-11(7-10.30 Sun)

Lucky Dip

Besides the fully inspected pubs, you might like to try these Lucky Dips recommended to us and described by readers (if you do, please send us reports: www.goodguides.com).

Acle [TG3910]
Kings Head [The Street]: Large and comfortable, good choice of ales inc well kept Greene King IPA, good generous home-made food esp choice of Sun roasts in restaurant *(Colin Gardner)*
Banningham [TG2129]
Crown [Colby Rd]: Consistently friendly welcome, interesting choice of good value well presented food, well kept beer, decent wines *(Ken and Barbara Turner)*
Barford [TG1107]
Cock [B1108 7 miles W of Norwich]: Recently reopened after attractive interior refurbishment, well kept beers inc good local Blue Moon Sea of Tranquillity and Hingham High, friendly

landlord and chef, good interesting food *(Mrs Lindsay Hunt)*
Binham [TF9839]
☆ *Chequers* [B1388 SW of Blakeney]: Long beamed bar with coal or log fires each end, one in inglenook, sturdy plush seats, well kept Adnams Best, Greene King IPA and Abbot, Nethergate and Woodfordes Wherry, decent house wines, landlord cooks using local produce, very popular Sun lunch, good rolls and sandwiches, small no smoking dining area, prompt cheerful service, good coal fires each end, some nice old prints, no piped music (but may be sports TV); picnic-sets out in front and on grass behind, open all day, two bedrooms, interesting village with huge priory church

*(Kevin Thorpe, Shaun and Diane, John Wooll,
R C Vincent, BB, John Beeken, Graham and
Jill Wood, Paul and Ursula Randall, P and
D Carpenter)*

Blakeney [TG0243]

☆ *Manor* [The Quay]: Attractive hotel in own
grounds with civilised, comfortable and
peaceful pub part, popular esp with older
people for good enterprising generous waitress-
served bar food, not expensive, inc well filled
crab sandwiches and attractive puddings; well
kept Adnams Best and Broadside and
Boddingtons, decent house wines, friendly
helpful staff, straightforward bar, separate
lounge, conservatory, good value restaurant;
sunny tables outside with room for children to
run around, good bedrooms; opp wildfowl
reserve and sea inlet *(R Davies, Stephen
Watson, Paul and Ursula Randall, John
Beeken, Kevin Macey, Keith and Chris O'Neill)*

Brancaster [TF7743]

Ship [A149]: Comfortable and relaxing old
country inn doing well under current landlady,
her sister cooking good value food, good choice
of well kept beers, big coal fires, obliging staff,
restaurant with plans for improvement; three
comfortable bedrooms, good breakfast,
restored garden *(M J Morgan)*

Burnham Market [TF8342]

Lord Nelson [Creake Rd]: Smartened up by
new licensees, with emphasis on good food –
landlady has a good restaurant track record;
tables outside *(LYM, A D Cross)*

Caister-on-Sea [TG5211]

Ship [Victoria St, off Tan Lane]: Busy local
notable for its riot of magnificent hanging
baskets and spectacular flower tubs and other
less likely containers on front terrace and small
back garden; modern furnishings, spacious
family room (with pool table closed off at
lunch), well kept Greene King IPA and Old
Speckled Hen, decent house wines, heaps of
good value satisfying food inc cheap fresh local
fish, coal fire; nostalgic piped pop music, big
screen TV and games machines in side areas, no
dogs; not far from long sandy beach
(Tony W Dickinson, L Beales, BB)

Castle Rising [TF6624]

Black Horse: Comfortable and spotless
Beefeater family dining pub by church and
almshouses in pleasant unspoilt village, good
furnishings inc sofas, casual reliable food,
mainly Whitbreads-related ales, friendly
unhurried service, long hours; children
welcome, own menu and play packs; no dogs,
pleasant tables out under cocktail parasols, play
area *(John Wooll)*

Cley next the Sea [TG0443]

George & Dragon [High St, off A149 W of
Sheringham]: Attractive Edwardian inn popular
with salt-marsh birdwatchers, locals' bar,
lounge and dining area, sombre décor with St
George artefacts, wide choice of generous food
inc good sandwiches (local crab), well kept
Greene King IPA, Abbot and a seasonal ale;
sizeable garden over road with boules pitch;
bedrooms *(DF, NF, Kevin Macey, Eric Locker,
Paul and Ursula Randall, MDN, LYM, M J A*

*Switzer, Tracey and Stephen Groves, Stephen
Hughes)*

☆ *Three Swallows* [Holt Rd, Newgate Green; nr
church]: Plain but chummy take-us-as-you-find-
us village local on quiet lane facing green,
banquettes around long high leathered tables,
roaring fire, steps up to second eating area,
good log fire in no smoking stripped pine
dining room, good value generous quickly
served home-made food from sandwiches (good
crab) to fresh fish, well kept Adnams and
Greene King IPA from unusual richly carved
bar, decent wines; dogs welcome, wandering
tabbies; barbecues in big attractive garden with
croquet, budgerigar aviary, surprisingly
grandiose fountain, wooden climbing frame
and goat pen, with church tower as glorious
backdrop; simple, clean but comfortable
bedrooms, good breakfast; handy for the salt
marshes, open all day summer *(M J Morgan,
R Hale, E M and H P N Steinitz, Shaun and
Diane, S Carlisle, BB, S Watkin, P Taylor,
MDN, David Lovegrove, Kevin Macey)*

Cockley Cley [TF7904]

☆ *Twenty Churchwardens* [off A1065 S of
Swaffham]: Cheerful no-frills village pub in
converted former school, small, clean and
welcoming, with three linked beamed rooms,
well kept Adnams and Elgoods, Weston's farm
ciders, good coffee, courteous landlord, chatty
barmaid, helpful bustling waitresses, limited but
good bar food inc bargain home-made pies,
darts alcove *(Brian Horner, Brenda Arthur,
Peter and Pat Frogley)*

Colkirk [TF9126]

☆ *Crown* [Village signposted off B1146 S of
Fakenham; and off A1065]: The friendly
licensee who made this unpretentiously
comfortable country pub a popular main entry,
with his well kept Greene King ales and a guest
such as Everards, lots of wines by the glass and
wide choice of tasty food in the no smoking
dining room, retires as this edition is published,
so no news yet of his successor; reports, please
(LYM)

Coltishall [TG2719]

☆ *Kings Head* [Wroxham Rd (B1354)]:
Refurbished riverside pub largely laid out for
eating, good choice of good imaginative food
esp fish, also bargains lunches, children's meals
and pretty puddings, well kept Adnams,
Marstons Pedigree, Woodfordes Wherry and
guest beers, decent wines, quick cheerful
service, no smoking area, open fire, several
stuffed fish inc a 50lb pike (personable
chef/landlord competes in international fishing
contests); cheap comfortable bedrooms,
moorings nearby *(Sheila and Brian Wilson,
Mrs H J Chapman, Mr and Mrs R Bromley)*

☆ *Red Lion* [Church St (B1354)]: Modernised
family pub, decent straightforward generous
food inc good puddings, friendly helpful
service, good range of well kept beers inc
Weasel brewed for them by Woodfordes,
several attractive split-level rooms esp cellar
bar, restaurant; away from water but pleasant
setting, tables out under cocktail parasols by
fountain, good play area *(Tony W Dickinson)*

Colton [TG1009]

☆ *Ugly Bug* [well signed once off A47]: Surprisingly big and still growing pub out in the country, snugly old-fashioned layout with built-in banquettes, turkey carpet, red velvet curtains, old enamel advertisements, well kept changing ales such as Fullers London Pride and Greene King Abbot, good food with particularly good chips in bar and restaurant, evening choice wider, sensible choice of wines, good atmosphere and service; piped music; children in conservatory with bar billiards, terrace and big garden with koi carp in pretty lake; two comfortable bedrooms *(Bill and Sheila McLardy, BB, W W Burke)*

Cromer [TG2142]

Red Lion [off A149; Brook St]: Substantial Victorian seafront hotel, stripped-flint carpeted lounge with screened areas, old bottles and chamber-pots, well kept Adnams, M&B Butlers and McMullens Gladstone, friendly staff, pleasant old-fashioned atmosphere (rather like that of the town itself); very wide range of bar food inc children's, restaurant with lots of fresh seafood; tables in back courtyard; bedrooms comfortable, splendid sea views *(Jamie and Sarah Allan)*

Denver Sluice [TF6101]

☆ *Jenyns Arms* [signed via B1507 off A1122 Downham Mkt bypass]: Extensive well laid out roadhouse-style pub in fine spot by spectacular hydraulic sluices controlling Great Ouse, tables out by water, well kept ales such as Greene King IPA and Old Speckled Hen, M&B Mild and Worthington, generous usual food (not Sun evening) from good sandwiches to roasts and tempting puddings, friendly, helpful and efficient staff; children welcome, big light and airy games area with pool, piped music; bedrooms *(Bruce Bird, BB, Judy Pearson, Michael and Jenny Back)*

Dereham [TF9913]

Bull [High St]: Beamed Georgian pub with biggish bar and side rooms (one no smoking at lunchtime), central open fire, good value substantial food from sandwiches up, Greene King IPA and Abbot, reasonably priced house wines, quick cheerful helpful service; usually open all day, tables in yard behind *(Ian Phillips, John Wooll)*

☆ *George* [Swaffham Rd]: Welcoming panelled bar, clean and comfortable, with alcove seating, well kept ales inc Adnams, Bass and Woodfordes Wherry and Nelsons Revenge, good bar food choice esp vegetarian and fish, friendly attentive service; bedrooms good *(Simon Pyle)*

Phoenix [Church St]: Much modernised market-town hotel with good value food from bar meals to bargain filling lunches in small pleasant restaurant, decent wines, large busy public bar, quick pleasant service; bedrooms *(John Wooll)*

Diss [TM1180]

☆ *Greyhound* [off B1077; St Nicholas St]: Handsome high moulded Tudor beams in comfortable lounge, well kept Greene King and Woodfordes Wherry, good value generous food from real sandwiches up, friendly staff, big

brick fireplace; children in eating area, games in public bar *(P G Plumridge, LYM)*

Docking [TF7637]

Pilgrims Reach [High St]: Emphasis on imaginative food in quiet restaurant, starters from that menu available as imaginative bar food in warm and comfortable small bar (can be busy), well kept Adnams Bitter and Broadside and their good wines, friendly chef/landlord, children's room; tables on attractive sheltered back terrace *(O K Smyth)*

Railway Inn [Station Rd]: Doing well under newish licensees, with ongoing renovations, wide choice of enjoyable food from doorstep sandwiches up, quick friendly service, well kept real ales inc local microbrews, lounge bar and compact restaurant, fresh flowers, some rail posters (station closed 50 years ago), smaller chummy public bar with pool in annexe; usually open all day *(John Wooll, Mark Sheard, Mike and Wendy Proctor)*

Downham Market [TF6103]

☆ *Crown* [Bridge St]: 17th-c coaching inn, all steps, nooks and crannies, with good log fire in small homely oak-panelled flagstoned bar, 635 Pathfinder bomber squadron photographs, well kept Theakstons, speedy service, good food Thurs-Sun (stops sharply at 2) in attractively presented veg, can be eaten in restaurant; picnic-sets in coach yard, comfortable bedrooms cantilevered out over it, big breakfast *(Andy and Carol, Bill and Sheila McLardy)*

East Harling [TL9986]

Nags Head [Market St (B1111)]: Plush seats in neat bars, recently extended dining area with no smoking tiled-floor part (children allowed here), wide range of good interesting food from new kitchen, prompt friendly service, Adnams, Wadworths 6X and Whitbreads; juke box; big garden with boules and aviary; not far from Snetterton *(Ian Phillips)*

East Winch [TF6916]

Carpenters Arms [A47]: Friendly atmosphere and staff, Greene King IPA, Abbot and Old Speckled Hen and a guest beer, enjoyable food inc special offers, well managed no smoking restaurant *(R C Vincent)*

Erpingham [TG1931]

Spread Eagle [A47]: Brick-built local with cheerful friendly staff, a true welcome for children and dogs (even from the pub cat), snug bar with comfortable sofa, good value food from sandwiches to Sun roasts and school puddings, Adnams Best, Fullers London Pride, Greene King IPA and Woodfordes Nelsons Revenge, pool table; children and dogs welcome, live music Sun lunchtime and Sat; neat garden *(Kevin Thorpe, Sue Grossey)*

Fakenham [TF9229]

Bull [Bridge St (B1146 S of centre)]: Unpretentious bare-boards pub, warm and welcoming, brewing its own good Blanchfield Best, Black Bull Mild and Raging Bull, log-effect gas fire, lots of farm tools, interesting old photographs, side rooms with pool and video games; tables outside, open all day Thurs-Sat at least in summer *(Ian Phillips, Dr David Cockburn)*

Henry IV [Greenway Lane]: Friendly and helpful Hungry Horse family dining pub, interesting décor, good value food inc Sun roasts, Greene King real ales; unobtrusive TV *(R C Vincent)*

Wensum Lodge [Bridge St]: Roomy bar in extensive modern hotel built around mill conversion, two beamed restaurant areas (one no smoking), generous food from sandwiches to some interesting hot dishes and good puddings, attentive service, Greene King IPA, conservatory, restaurant; tables outside with riverside lawn, comfortable bedrooms *(John Wooll, Anthony Barnes, LYM)*

Foulden [TL7799]

White Hart [White Hart St]: Friendly old pub with plain country furnishings, separate snug, pleasant newish licensees, home-made food inc Sun lunch, Greene King IPA and Abbot; cl Sun evening, side garden with play area, bedrooms in converted outbuildings, handy for Oxburgh Hall (NT) *(Rita Scarratt)*

Framingham Earl [TG2603]

Railway Tavern [Norwich Rd (B1332)]: Modern food pub under friendly management, with good choice of beers, generous home-cooked food from sandwiches to good vegetarian dishes and steaks *(Pat and Clive Sherriff)*

Garboldisham [TM0081]

Fox [A1066 Thetford—Diss, junction with B1111]: This sympathetically updated and rambling old pub, with original beams, old pews and massive woodburner, has been a popular main entry for its enjoyable food including unusual sandwiches (also a no smoking restaurant), good beers and nice service; we have no news yet of the new outfit which is taking over, so reports please *(LYM)*

Gayton [TF7219]

☆ *Crown* [B1145/B1153]: Attractive flower-decked pub, well kept and comfortable without being flashy, with some unusual old features; friendly relaxed atmosphere, wkdy lunchtime salad buffet and interesting evening meals, well kept Greene King IPA, XX Mild and Abbot, limited but good wine choice, pleasant staff, games room; tables in sheltered garden *(Judy Wayman, Bob Arnett, Anthony Barnes, LYM)*

Geldeston [TM3991]

☆ *Locks* [off A143/A146 NW of Beccles; off Station Rd S of village, obscurely signed down long rough track]: Remote drinking pub alone at the navigable head of the River Waveney, virtually unchanged in several decades, ancient candlelit core with brick walls, tile floor, big log fire, well worn assorted chairs and tables, Woodfordes ales tapped from casks, friendly informal service; big extension for summer crowds and wknd music nights, summer evening barbecues, meadow camping; may be cl winter wkdys *(LYM, the Didler)*

Great Bircham [TF7632]

Kings Head [B1155, S end of village (called and signed Bircham locally)]: Rather grand-looking Edwardian country inn, Italian landlord, unassuming lounge bar (two room areas), mix of high and low tables suiting both diners and

drinkers, open fire, a few Italian food specialities, no smoking dining area, well kept Adnams, Bass and Greene King IPA, malt whiskies, decent wines; somnolent alsatian, Brandy; big side lawn with picnic-sets and play things, attractive village with decent art gallery; Houghton Hall nearby, as is striking windmill *(M J Morgan, LYM, John and Angela Main, John Wooll)*

Great Cressingham [TF8401]

☆ *Windmill* [Water End, off A1065 Swaffham—Brandon]: Roomy family pub with three beamed bars, partitioned nooks and crannies, huge log fireplace, good value popular food, friendly prompt service, well kept Adnams Best and Broadside, Bass, Greene King IPA and a beer brewed for them by Bass, decent wines, lots of prints, posters and farm tools, stripped brick and tiled floors, conservatory; piped music, games room with pool, SkyTV, live music; well kept big garden, dogs allowed *(Kevin Thorpe)*

Gunton Station [TG2535]

Suffield Arms [off A149 Cromer—N Walsham; Station Rd]: Isolated Greene King local doing well under amiable current landlord, decent pubby food (new restaurant extension built on its bowling green), well kept Greene King; lots of tables in garden *(David Twitchett)*

Harpley [TF7825]

Rose & Crown [off A148 Fakenham—Kings Lynn; Nethergate St]: Modest good value home cooking inc fresh veg, unusual vegetarian dishes, good puddings and children's meals in small comfortable lounge and dining room, well kept Greene King IPA and Tetleys, decent wine, helpful service; high chairs provided; good tables in attractive garden with play equipment inc an unusual tyre arrangement, quietly attractive village *(John Wooll, R C Vincent, Tom Gondris)*

Hickling [TG4022]

Pleasure Boat: Spacious modern bar and fair-sized dining room in great spot – the only building on a short dyke at quiet end of Hickling Broad, lots of birds, a mix of sailors, birdwatchers and walkers, even a tiny beach; good parking and moorings *(Prof H G Allen)*

Holt [TG0738]

☆ *Feathers* [Market Pl]: Interesting locals' bar comfortably extended around original panelled area with open fire, busy on Sat market day, attractive entrance/reception area with antiques, friendly staff, good value promptly served generous food, well kept Greene King IPA and Abbot, decent wines; bedrooms spacious and comfortable *(Mr and Mrs J Brown, B N F and M Parkin, Chris Mawson, Peter H Stallard)*

Honingham [TG1011]

☆ *Olde Buck* [just off A47]: Ancient pub with four beamed rooms, some emphasis on very good range of consistently enjoyable good value food inc huge sandwiches, lunchtime bargains and nice puddings; well kept Greene King IPA and Flowers IPA, welcoming attentive service *(Jestyn Phillips, Michael Butler, Mrs Judy Gowing)*

Hunstanton [TF6842]
Marine Bar [part of Marine Hotel, St Edmunds Terr]: Small bar packed with tables, bustling local atmosphere, prompt welcoming service, wide range of attractively priced quick food all day, good beer choice, lots of china, bric-a-brac and 50s advertisements; tables under cocktail parasols out on attractive lower fairy-lit terrace, Thurs quiz night; bedrooms, holiday flat *(Michael Tack)*

Hunworth [TG0635]
☆ *Blue Bell* [signed off B roads S of Holt]: Modest country local with some settees in comfortable L-shaped bar, cheerful landlord, Adnams Bitter, Greene King Abbot and IPA, Woodfordes Wherry and guest beers, good value bar food from soup and sandwiches up, no smoking flagstoned dining room; children welcome, pleasant garden with summer bar service and play area *(Judy Wayman, Bob Arnett, Michael and Jenny Back, LYM)*

Kenninghall [TM0485]
Red Lion [B1113 S of Norwich; East Church St]: Well restored, with stripped beams, small panelled snug, stable-style restaurant area, open fires, good food with good vegetarian choice, Adnams, Greene King and guest ales; now has bedrooms *(Sue Anderson, Phil Copleston)*

Kings Lynn [TF6019]
Freebridge Farm [Clenchwarton Rd, West Lynn]: Brewers Fayre family dining pub with good value food, quick smart service, well equipped indoor and outdoor play areas; bedrooms in adjoining Travel Inn *(R C Vincent, Julie Vincent)*
London Porterhouse [London Rd]: Small, friendly and lively local with good mix of customers and well kept Greene King IPA and Abbot tapped from the cask; open all day Fri-Sun *(the Didler)*
Olde Maydens Heade [Tuesday Market Pl]: Large refurbished Scottish Courage pub popular for OAP bargains at lunchtime carvery, efficient service; shame about the piped music *(Mrs A Chesher, B N F and M Parkin)*
Tudor Rose [St Nicholas St (just off Tuesday Market Place – main square)]: Lively 15th-c town pub with well kept Adnams Broadside, Badger Tanglefoot, Bass, Batemans XB and Timothy Taylors Landlord, good choice of other drinks and usual food from sandwiches up, no smoking upstairs restaurant; sensibly priced bedrooms *(John Wooll, R C Vincent, M Joyner, Peter H Stallard, LYM)*
Wildfowler [Gayton Rd, Gaywood]: Useful Big Steak pub, smart but comfortable and relaxed even when busy, popular food inc children's (fun packs for them), good choice of wines in big glasses, fast friendly service, real ales such as Marstons Pedigree, separate non-food adult area (can be smoky) *(R C Vincent)*

Langham [TG0041]
Bluebell [Holt Rd]: Spotlessly refurbished, with cheerful welcoming Norfolk licensees, good value quickly served home-made food inc popular OAP wkdy lunches, well kept real ales, no smoking eating area; good disabled access and facilities, quiz night; charming garden with apple trees, bluebells then roses, set well away

from road looking up to church tower *(Mr and Mrs R A Barton, Peter and Pat Frogley, Keith and Chris O'Neill)*

Lenwade [TG1018]
Bridge Inn [Fakenham Rd]: Clean and friendly, with good choice of well cooked food, attentive staff, well kept real ales, short choice of moderately priced wines; bedrooms *(Dr Ashley Duthie)*

Lyng [TG0617]
Fox & Hounds [The Street]: Sociable old pub on River Wensum, beams, flagstones and open fire in roomy comfortable lounge, welcoming licensees doing good reasonably priced food inc local game, seafood and children's dishes, real ales such as Buffys Mild, Greene King, Marstons and Woodfordes Wherry, chess and backgammon, restaurant with no smoking area, public bar with pool and juke box, weekly live music; interesting pottery opp *(Brian W Kirby, D Pettet)*

Mundesley [TG3136]
Seaview House Hotel [Paston Rd]: Side entrance to welcoming bar well used by locals, good food; bedrooms *(Pamela Goodwyn)*

Neatishead [TG3421]
White Horse [The Street]: Warm and welcoming multi-roomed pub popular with boaters, lots of old Broads pictures, welcoming family service, well kept ales, popular food inc very wide choice of good pies *(W A Evershed)*

Newton [TF8315]
George & Dragon [A1065 4 miles N of Swaffham]: Distinctive roadside pub, unhurried atmosphere popular with older people, good value food inc generous Sun lunch and popular puddings (advisable to book), friendly service, good choice of beers, several small dining areas; children allowed only if eating, pleasant garden with play area, handy for Castle Acre Priory *(R C Vincent)*

Northrepps [TG2439]
Parsons Pleasure [Church St]: Converted tithe barn with good food (not Sun in winter), not over-elaborate, in lively and friendly bar and attractive restaurant, well kept Greene King IPA and Abbot; bedrooms with own bathrooms, nr church in peaceful village *(David Twitchett, Di and Mike Gillam, Paul and Ursula Randall)*

Norwich [TG2408]
Coach & Horses [Thorpe Rd]: Tap for the Chalk Hill brewery, with their own Bitter, CHB, Dreadnought, Flint Knappers and Old Tackle, also guests such as Boddingtons and Timothy Taylors, reasonably priced food 12-9 (8 Sun), also breakfast with limitless coffee; bare-boards L-shaped bar with open fire, lots of prints, back dining area, friendly staff; picnic-sets out in front *(the Didler, Richard Lewis, Tony Hobden)*
Gibraltar Gardens [Heigham St]: Partly 16th-c timbered riverside pub, vast hall separated by central fireplace, several real ales, fairly wide choice of enjoyable home-cooked food, friendly staff, no smoking area; children welcome, waterside garden – busy on warm days, barbecues *(Paul Mallett, Sue Rowland, Mary Morris)*

Rose [Rupert St/Trinity St]: Pleasant main bar, real ales such as Adnams and Chalk Hill, good choice of wines by the glass, freshly cooked food with interesting variations on standard menu; tables outside *(Anthony Barnes)*

Steam Packet [Crown Rd, behind Anglia TV]: Popular and friendly two-bar Adnams pub, no smoking at lunchtime, open all day; great for music (you should see the landlord's kick-dancing routine) *(the Didler)*

Old Hunstanton [TF6842]

Ancient Mariner [part of L'Estrange Arms Hotel, Golf Course Rd]: Large bar, relaxed and cheerful, done up with lots of dark wood, bare bricks and flagstones, several little areas inc upstairs gallery, pleasant furnishings, good value usual food, four well kept ales inc Adnams and Broadside and Bass, unusually good wines by the glass, open fires, papers and magazines; hotel has good restaurant and nice bedrooms, long garden down to dunes, play area *(John Wooll, Pat and Derek Westcott, David Pugh, M J A Switzer)*

Neptune: Former no-nonsense local recently refurbished, with decent food in dining area, Adnams, Greene King IPA and Abbot and a guest beer such as Wolf Granny Wouldn't Like It, friendly staff; three bedrooms with own bathrooms *(Ian Arthur)*

Poringland [TG2800]

Dove [Bungay Rd]: Friendly and cosy local with cheap food, well kept beer *(Comus and Sarah Elliott)*

Royal Oak [B1332 5 miles S of Norwich]: Good atmosphere in neatly modernised local with some emphasis on well kept real ales – at least three, up to eight at wknds; comfortable banquettes in timber-effect bays, log-effect gas fire, pub games inc cards and dominoes; tables outside *(Stewart Parvin, BB)*

Pulham Market [TM1986]

Crown [Harleston Rd]: Beautiful low thatched white pub by church overlooking green, heavy beams, unusual mix of pictures, very welcoming landlady, plentiful well cooked food, well kept beer, good service even when very busy *(David Twitchett)*

Rollesby [TQ4416]

Horse & Groom [A149]: Busy open-plan renovated lounge bar attached to motel, with wide choice of good generous home-made food esp interesting fish dishes and seafood, good friendly service, Boddingtons, decent wines, separate restaurant menu; good disabled facilities, well equipped bedrooms *(J B Thackray, Janet and Peter Race, Miss J Durbridge, W Shakeshaft)*

Roydon [TM0980]

White Hart [A1066 just W of Diss]: Roomy and attractive partly 15th-c pub, brasses on beams, good value generous well cooked food, changing beers such as Marstons, restaurant *(Gordon Neighbour)*

Salthouse [TG0743]

Dun Cow [A149 Blakeney—Sheringham]: Extensively refurbished well run pub looking over salt marshes, good bar food inc six sorts of burger and some fresh fish, well kept Adnams,

Greene King and other ales, open fires, stripped beams and cob walls; children welcome, blues nights, big attractive walled garden with sheltered courtyard, figs and apples, separate family garden with play area, good walks and birdwatching nearby (sightings blackboard) *(S Watkin, P Taylor, Steve Thomas, Kevin Macey, Eric Locker, M J Morgan)*

Scole [TM1478]

☆ *Crossways* [Bridge Rd]: Pleasant atmosphere in unpretentious 16th-c inn with impressive fireplaces, friendly staff, good food choice, well kept Adnams and Greene King Abbot, unusually good wines, good restaurant, children's room; dogs welcome (they have a cat and dog), bedrooms *(Eddie Edwards)*

☆ *Scole Inn* [off A140 bypass just N of A143; Ipswich Rd]: Stately old coaching inn of outstanding architectural interest, with a real sense of history, antique settles, old oak chairs and tables, impressive inglenook log fires, old prints and collectables and other old-fashioned features in lounge and bare-boards public bar used by locals; decent bar food from baguettes up, more elaborate menu in large no smoking restaurant inc good vegetarian dishes, well kept Adnams, Courage Directors and summer guest beers, friendly staff; cribbage, dominoes, piped music; children and dogs welcome, open all day, comfortable bedrooms in former stable block *(LYM, Steve Chambers, Pat and Clive Sherriff, Eddie Edwards)*

Sculthorpe [TF8930]

☆ *Sculthorpe Mill* [inn signed off A148 W of Fakenham, opp village]: Sympathetically converted 18th-c mill popular in summer for its spacious streamside garden with play area; dim-lit civilised beamed bar with several rooms, open fire, decent house wines, real ales such as Adnams, John Smiths and Theakstons, bar food, restaurant; children in eating areas, open all day wknds and summer, comfortable bedrooms *(John Wooll, David and Catherine Whiting, John Beeken, S Watkin, P Taylor, DJH, Ian Phillips, M J Morgan, LYM)*

Sea Palling [TG4226]

Hall Inn: Roomy and pleasant old bar, fairly unspoilt, with low-beamed dining area off, Adnams and Sam Smiths, decent food, friendly efficient service; picnic-sets on front lawn, 10 mins from beach *(John Wooll)*

Sheringham [TG1543]

Robin Hood [Station Rd]: Good value generous food and efficient service in seaside family pub, children very welcome *(John Wooll)*

South Wootton [TF6422]

Farmers Arms [part of Knights Hill Hotel, Grimston Rd (A148/A149)]: Olde-worlde conversion of barn and stables, wide choice of reasonably priced food all day in bar and restaurant, Scottish Courage ales with a guest such as Marstons Pedigree, good wines, abundant coffee, friendly efficient service; children welcome, open all day; comfortable motel bedrooms, health club *(John Wooll)*

Stanhoe [TF8036]

☆ *Crown* [B1155 towards Burnham Mkt]: Cosy and friendly Elgoods local, short choice of good value home cooking inc excellent game (food may stop early on quiet evenings), well kept Elgoods Cambridge, decent wine and coffee, convivial ex-RAF landlord and wife, small bright traditional bar with interesting nooks and corners, central log fire, one beam studded with hundreds of coins; well behaved children welcome, tables on side lawn, lots of fancy fowl (and chicks) outside; caravan site, s/c cottage available *(BB, John Wooll, Tracey and Stephen Groves, C H and B J Owen, O K Smyth)*

Swaffham [TF8109]

George [Station St]: Comfortable market-town hotel with well kept old-fashioned bar, wide choice of reasonably priced decent food, Greene King IPA and Abbot, friendly fast service; children welcome; bedrooms *(R C Vincent, W W Burke, Penny Miles)*

Thetford [TL8782]

Dolphin [Old Market St]: Pleasant décor, friendly atmosphere, efficient service, well kept Bass and Greene King IPA, simply cooked well presented food; quietish piped music *(Mike and Karen England)*

Thompson [TL9296]

☆ *Chequers* [Griston Rd, off A1075 S of Watton]: Long, low and picturesque 15th-c thatched dining pub with good interesting food in series of olde-worlde quaint rooms, Adnams, Fullers London Pride, Greene King IPA and local Wolf, good modestly priced wine list, friendly service, low beams, inglenooks, some stripped brickwork, antique tools and traps; games machines; tables outside, new bedroom block *(LYM, Kelly Lewis, Pete Beasley, Mike and Karen England, Marjorie and Bernard Parkin, Pam and David Bailey)*

Thornham [TF7343]

Kings Head [Church St/High St (A149)]: Pretty old pub with lots of hanging baskets, roomy low-beamed bars with banquettes in well lit bays, Greene King IPA and Abbot, Marstons Pedigree and Tetleys, good food inc local fish, no smoking dining room, friendly Northern landlord, open fire; dogs allowed; well spaced tables on back lawn with barbecues, three homely and comfortable bedrooms (one now with own bath), pleasant walks *(G J Hill, M J Morgan, Nick Lawless)*

Tibenham [TM1389]

Greyhound [The Street]: Recently taken over by the people who made the Fox at Garboldisham a popular main entry; one to watch *(anon)*

Titchwell [TF7543]

Briarfields [Main Rd]: Good substantial bar food, well kept Adnams, moderately priced house wines and friendly service in hotel's newly refurbished back bar and lounge; terrace overlooking salt marshes, telescope and bird-sightings book; bedrooms comfortable and well appointed – a nice place to stay *(O K Smyth)*

Three Horseshoes [A149]: Generous bar food, well kept Adnams and Woodfordes Wherry and friendly service in refurbished bar with rough walls, exposed wood, beams and struts, log fires; family room, restaurant, play area in garden with great view over RSPB reserve; peaceful pleasantly furnished bedrooms, handy

for beach *(M J A Switzer)*

Trunch [TG2834]

Crown [Front St]: Friendly new licensees doing wide range of real ales, plans for tea rooms *(Craig Camidge)*

Walpole St Andrew [TF5017]

Princess Victoria [off A17 W of A47 junction; Market Lane]: 17th-c pub carefully restored keeping character, good value fresh food, well kept real ale, log fires, friendly if not always speedy service, lots of bric-a-brac for sale; beware, they won't serve tap water *(Marion Turner)*

Watton [TF9100]

Willow House [High St]: Hotel and restaurant with good pubby atmosphere in its two bars, well kept Adnams and a guest such as Greene King Old Speckled Hen, reasonably priced bar food *(Mike and Karen England)*

Welney [TL5293]

Lamb & Flag [Main St]: Well kept Elgoods Cambridge and Old Smoothy, enjoyable bar food and substantial meals; handy for wildfowl reserve *(MDN)*

West Beckham [TG1339]

☆ *Wheatsheaf* [off A148 Holt—Cromer; Church Rd]: Gently renovated separate beamed areas, roaring log fire in one part, a smaller coal one in another, comfortable chairs and banquettes, enormous black cat, well kept Bass and several Woodfordes ales, good wine choice, local country wines, generous food (not Sun evening; may be a wait) from sandwiches up, two no smoking dining rooms; darts, bar billiards, shove-ha'penny, dominoes, piped music; children welcome, partly terraced front garden with restored gipsy caravan *(Philip and Susan Philcox, S Watkin, P Taylor, LYM)*

West Rudham [TF8127]

☆ *Dukes Head* [A148 Fakenham—Kings Lynn]: 17th-c, with three attractively homely rooms, relaxed mix of locals and visitors, short choice of good generous home-made food from sandwiches up using local ingredients inc fish and game, well kept Adnams, Shepherd Neame and Woodfordes Wherry, decent wines, good coffee, friendly landlord, helpful service, log fires, newspapers and plenty of books, interesting cricketing prints; no dogs, good disabled access *(John Wooll, David and Brenda Tew, BB)*

West Walton [TF4713]

☆ *King of Hearts* [N of Wisbech; School Rd]: Comfortably refurbished dining pub with wide choice of good genuine food in smartly furnished bar and restaurant, good hot buffet (as much as you want), quick friendly service copes well even with big parties and special diet needs, full Elgoods range and a guest beer, lots of decorative china, no smoking area; holds key for lovely next-door church *(Michael and Jenny Back)*

Weston Longville [TG1115]

Parson Woodforde [signed off A1067 Norwich—Bawdswell in Morton]: Clean and spacious beamed pub with well kept Adnams Extra, Wolf Golden Jackal and Woodfordes Wherry, lots of alcoves, two huge fireplaces, willing service, big restaurant; tables on terrace, flower-filled back garden *(Neil and Anita Christopher, Anthony Barnes)*

☆ *Bell* [Blakeney Rd]: Big welcoming open-plan local with new Danish landlord cooking wide choice of interesting food inc some Danish dishes, Adnams Best and Bass, good wines; carpeted no smoking conservatory, picnic-sets on lawn and small garden behind *(BB, John Wooll, Peter and Pat Frogley, Kevin Macey)*

Woodton [TM2993]

Kings Head [Hempnall Rd]: Good food, four real ales and six wines by the glass, friendly prompt service, two-room bar and separate restaurant *(Anthony Barnes)*

Wreningham [TM1698]

☆ *Bird in Hand* [just off B1113 E of Wymondham (Norwich Rd, outside village)]: Thriving dining pub, roomy and tastefully refurbished with cosy alcoves, wide choice of decent reasonably priced food from sandwiches up inc unusual vegetarian dishes, well presented Sun lunch and OAP midweek lunches, well kept Adnams and Woodfordes ales, good friendly service, local bygones and Lotus car photographs, Victorian-style panelled restaurant; quiet piped pop music; picnic-sets in neatly kept garden *(Bob Arnett, Judy Wayman, BB, Pat and Clive Sherriff, John Wooll)*

Wymondham [TG1101]

☆ *Green Dragon* [Church St]: Very picturesque heavily timbered jettied 14th-c inn, bulky beams, log fire (Tudor mantelpiece), well kept Flowers IPA, friendly relaxed service, good food from sandwiches to attractively priced main dishes, small back bar, bigger no smoking turkey-carpeted dining area, some interesting pictures; children and dogs welcome; bedrooms, nr glorious 12th-c abbey church *(the Didler, BB, Michael Butler, Mike and Penny Sanders)*

Post Office address codings confusingly give the impression that some pubs are in Norfolk when they're really in Suffolk (which is where we list them).

Northamptonshire

Some fairly intensive inspecting in the county this year whittled down our final shortlist to just one new main entry: the George at Great Oxendon, interesting if not cheap food in civilised and nicely individual surroundings. Other pubs on particularly good form here these days are the welcoming Windmill at Badby (good food), the George & Dragon at Chacombe (good interesting food), the good value Red Lion at Crick (a handy M1 pub), the Falcon at Fotheringhay (particularly popular for its food), and the Star at Sulgrave (a nice all-rounder). As a place for a special meal out, the Falcon at Fotheringhay earns our title of Northamptonshire Dining Pub of the Year. As a matter of interest, not one of this county's current main entries featured in the first edition of this Guide, 20 years ago; all are relatively recent additions. The Lucky Dip section at the end of the chapter includes the possible next generation: current stars there, most of them already inspected and approved by us, are the New Inn at Abthorpe, Olde Coach House at Ashby St Ledgers, Queens Head at Bulwick, Eastcote Arms at Eastcote, Royal Oak at Eydon, Dusty Fox at Harlestone, Red Lion at Hellidon, Griffins Head at Mears Ashby and Boat at Stoke Bruerne. Drinks prices in the county are generally close to the national average; the White Swan at Woodnewton, under its new licensee, had the cheapest beer price we found (for a pint of Batemans).

BADBY SP5559 Map 4
Windmill 🍴 🛏

Village signposted off A361 Daventry—Banbury

From businessmen to walkers there's a friendly welcome for everyone at this well run, old thatched inn. The atmosphere is relaxed and civilised in the two chatty beamed and flagstoned bars which have cricketing and rugby pictures, simple country furnishings in good solid wood, and an unusual white woodburning stove in an enormous white-tiled inglenook fireplace. There's also a cosy and comfortable lounge, and pleasant modern hotel facilities for staying guests (an unobtrusive modern extension is well hidden at the back). Good, generous bar food is served promptly by good-natured efficient staff and might include soup (£2.75), sandwiches (from £2.75 to £6.25 for tasty triple-decker ones), potato skins with yoghurt and mint dip (£3.75), crispy whitebait (£4.50), filled jacket potatoes (from £4.50), ploughman's (£5.50), aubergine stuffed with rice and nuts (£6.25), venison burgers with creamy peppercorn sauce (£8.25), fresh crab salad (£9.25), 8oz sirloin steak (£10.50), monkfish provençale (£11.25), duck breast with lime, mango, chilli and ginger glaze (£11.50); puddings (from £3.50). The pleasant restaurant is no smoking. Well kept Bass, Boddingtons, Flowers Original and Wadworths 6X on handpump; dominoes, quiet piped music. *(Recommended by Dr P C Rea, John McDonald, Ann Bond, John Kane, Anthony Barnes, Ian Phillips, George Atkinson, Dennis John Boddington, Howard and Margaret Buchanan, Karen and Graham Oddey, Mr and Mrs S J Spademan, Martin and Penny Fletcher, Robin and Sheila Pitt)*

Free house ~ Licensees John Freestone and Carol Sutton ~ Real ale ~ Bar food ~ Restaurant ~ (01327) 702363 ~ Children in eating area of bar and restaurant ~ Open 11.30-3(4 Sat), 5.30-11; 11.30-4, 7-11 Sun ~ Bedrooms: £52.50B/£69B

CHACOMBE SP4943 Map 4

George & Dragon 🍴

2½ miles from M40 junction 11: A361 towards Daventry, then village signposted on right; Silver Street

The relaxed atmosphere and imaginative food at this peaceful, well-run inn set in a pretty village make it a good respite from the nearby M40. The neat, spacious bar has comfortable seats, beams, flagstones, and logs burning in a massive fireplace, and Courage Directors, Theakstons XB and Best plus a guest such as Wadworths 6X on handpump; fruit wines. The wide range of food from a fortnightly changing blackboard is not cheap; well prepared dishes might include baked potatoes (from £3.40), sandwiches (from £3.65, filled baguettes from £4.95), black pudding salad (£4.95), mussels in garlic cream (£5.75), cheese and mixed vegetable pie or baked, stuffed peppers (£7.95), faggot, sausage and onion casserole (£8.50), fillet steak (£14.95) and good fish dishes such as monkfish and salmon kebabs, poached cod with tomato, onion and basil sauce or fried shark steak (£10.95); puddings such as tangy lemon mousse and chocolate fudge cake (£3.45). Staff are friendly and accommodating. Afternoon teas and cold snacks; no smoking area in restaurant; darts, dominoes and piped music. *(Recommended by Stuart Turner, B H Andrews, Mike and Mary Carter, Karen Eliot, JES, Tom Evans, Barrie and Teresa Hopwood, R T and J C Moggridge, Charles Moncreiffe, W W Burke, Martin and Penny Fletcher, W Ruxton, J M Pitts, M A and C R Starling, Jenny and Brian Seller)*

Free house ~ Licensee Ray Bennett ~ Real ale ~ Bar food (12-2, 7-9.30) ~ Restaurant ~ (01295) 711500 ~ Children welcome ~ Open 12-11(10.30 Sun) ~ Bedrooms: £42.50B/£60B

CHAPEL BRAMPTON SP7266 Map 4

Brampton Halt

Pitsford Road; off A5199 (was A50) N of Northampton

This attractive red brick Victorian station master's house stands alone by the little Northampton & Lamport Railway. Inside, one low-ceilinged area with a woodburning stove has wash drawings of steam trains; by the bar counter, a high-raftered dining area has dagging shears and other agricultural bygones; there's Victorian-style floral wallpaper throughout, with matching swagged curtains, and sturdily comfortable furniture. A visit here makes part of a good day out for the family. There are train rides at weekends with additional bank holiday and Santa specials, and the Nene Valley Way – a 14-mile walk and cycle-way – runs along an adjacent converted old track through pretty countryside. Straightforward bar food includes sandwiches (from £2.95), ploughman's (£4.95), ham and eggs or various burgers such as chicken, beef or spicy bean (£5.95), bacon and stilton salad or scampi (£5.95) and sirloin steak (£8.95); puddings (£2.95). Well kept Adnams, Everards Old Original and Tiger, Fullers London Pride and a guest such as Greene King IPA on handpump; decent wines; friendly service; trivia, maybe piped music. They may stay open all day at weekends when the weather's fine. There are a few tables in a small sun lounge. *(Recommended by Bernie Adams, Michael Tack, Stephen, Julie and Hayley Brown, Duncan Cloud, Ian Phillips, Gerry Dobson, Dave Braisted)*

Free house ~ Licensees Roger and Caroline Thom ~ Real ale ~ Bar food (lunchtimes all week, 7-9 Fri and Sat, winter times may be different) ~ (01604) 842676 ~ Well behaved children in eating area of bar ~ Open 12-2.30, 5.30-11; 12-11 Sat; 12-4, 7-10.30 Sun; 12-3.30, 5.30-11 winter Sat

CLIPSTON SP7181 Map 4

Bulls Head 🍺

B4036 S of Market Harborough

The hundreds of coins that gleam from the black beams in this ancient village inn are part of a tradition started by US airmen based nearby during World War II – they used to leave their money wedged in the cracks of the ancient woodwork, waiting for their return when they could buy their next drink. Nowadays they serve well kept Bass, Worthingtons, Marstons Pedigree, Greene King Old Speckled Hen, and a guest such as Abbot Ale on handpump and they've an amazing choice of over 550 malt whiskies (though we've heard that this may be reduced when the landlord stops collecting blended whiskies). The bar is divided into three cosily dim areas leading down from the servery, with comfortable seats, sturdy small settles and stools upholstered in red plush, a grandmother clock, some harness and tools, and a log fire. There's a dining area in the room at the back with oak settles, high-backed chairs and a grandfather clock keeping time; the walls are hung with china meat platters. Bar food includes home-made soup (£2.95), sandwiches and baked potatoes (from £3.25), breaded mushrooms (£3.50), battered haddock (£4.95), vegetable stir fry, home-made pies or 10oz gammon steak (£6.95), specials such as lemon sole (£9.50) or roast duckling with orange and ginger glaze (£9.95) and puddings (£3.75); children's menu (£2.50). One of the bars and part of the restaurant are no smoking; table skittles, darts, TV, fruit machine, dominoes, piped music and newspapers. Slightly saucy pin-ups decorate the gents'. Outside, a terrace has a couple of white tables under cocktail parasols. *(Recommended by Rona Murdoch, John Bramley, Phil and Jane Hodson, Debbie Dexter, Mike and Sue Loseby, George Atkinson, Grahame McNulty, Brian and Anna Marsden, Comus and Sarah Elliott, R T and J C Moggridge, Duncan Cloud, Ian Phillips, Dr D J and Mrs S C Walker, Graham and Lynn Mason, E J and M W Corrin)*

Free house ~ Licensees George, Sue and Joe Price ~ Real ale ~ Bar food (11.30-2, 6.30-9.30; not Mon lunchtime) ~ Restaurant ~ (01858) 525268 ~ Children welcome ~ Open 11.30-3, 5.30-11; 12-3, 7-10.30 Sun; closed Mon lunchtime exc bank holidays ~ Bedrooms: £29.50S/£45S

CRICK SP5872 Map 4
Red Lion ★ £
A mile from M1 junction 18; A428

Readers are continually impressed by the good value, generous food and relaxed, welcoming atmosphere at this dark sandstone, old thatched pub. Served by friendly staff, lunchtime snacks include sandwiches (from £1.10), ploughman's (from £2.60), and hearty main courses such as chicken and mushroom pie, leek and smoky bacon bake, plaice or vegetable pancake rolls (all £3.95); in the evening they offer a wider range of dishes including rainbow trout or roast duck (£6.50) and steaks (from £9) as well as puddings such as lemon meringue pie (from £2); Sunday roast (£4.25). The snug low-ceilinged bar has lots of comfortable seating and a tiny log stove in a big inglenook. Four well kept changing beers might be Marstons Pedigree, Greene King Old Speckled Hen, Theakstons Best and Websters Yorkshire on handpump. There are a few picnic-sets under cocktail parasols on grass by the car park, and in summer you can eat on the terrace in the old coach yard which is sheltered by a Perspex roof; lots of pretty hanging baskets. An added bonus is that it's only a mile from the M1. *(Recommended by Dr B and Mrs P B Baker, Ian Phillips, Karen Eliot, Mandy and Simon King, G P Kernan, David and Ruth Shillitoe, Sheila Rowell, Geoffrey Johns, June and Ken Brooks, Kevin Blake, Humphry and Angela Crum Ewing)*

Wellington ~ Lease Tom and Paul Marks ~ Real ale ~ Bar food (not Sun evening) ~ (01788) 822342 ~ No children under 14 in evenings ~ Open 11.15-2.30, 6.15-11; 12-3, 7-10.30 Sun

EAST HADDON SP6668 Map 4
Red Lion ★ ⇌
High St; village signposted off A428 (turn right in village) and off A50 N of Northampton

One of our smarter entries, where the neat lounge bar of this elegant and substantial golden stone hotel is furnished with some attractive antique furniture. Along with oak panelled settles, white-painted panelling, library chairs and a mix of oak, mahogany and cast-iron-framed tables, there are recessed china cabinets, old prints and pewter, and little kegs, brass pots, swords and so forth hung sparingly on a couple of beams. They serve very well kept real ales such as Adnams Broadside, Charles Wells Bombardier and Marstons Pedigree on handpump, and decent wines; piped music. Popular (though not cheap) bar food from a daily changing menu might include soups (£3.50), sandwiches (£4), home-made terrine with cumberland sauce (£7), couscous, apple and celery strudel or herring fillets in sweet tomato marinade (£9), home-made fishcakes with tomato and basil sauce (£10) and lamb noisettes in a rich wine sauce (£11) with puddings from the trolley (£4). There's a more elaborate menu in the pretty no smoking restaurant which overlooks the garden; good breakfasts. The walled side garden is a pleasant place to enjoy coffee after a meal, with lilac, fruit trees, roses and neat little flowerbeds; it leads back to the bigger lawn, which has well spaced picnic-sets. There are more tables under cocktail parasols on a small side terrace, and a big copper beech shades the gravel car park. *(Recommended by Stuart Turner, Martin and Lois Sheldrick, Ian Phillips, David Mansfield, Martin and Penny Fletcher, Maysie Thompson)*

Charles Wells ~ Lease Ian Kennedy ~ Real ale ~ Bar food (12-2, 7-9.30, not Sun evening) ~ Restaurant ~ (01604) 770223 ~ Children in eating area of bar and restaurant ~ Open 11-2.30, 6-11; 12-2.30, 7-10.30 Sun; closed 25 Dec ~ Bedrooms: £60S/£75S

FARTHINGSTONE SP6155 Map 4
Kings Arms ◗

Off A5 SE of Daventry; village signposted from Litchborough on former B4525 (now declassified)

They sell a good selection of British cheeses at the bar of this handsome gargoyled 18th-c stone pub. Listed up on a board you can take them away or, if you ask the landlord, he may make a platter up for you on a weekday evening (from £5.30); also for sale are local crafts, wines and olive oil. There's a huge log fire in the small timeless flagstoned bar which has comfortable, homely sofas and armchairs near the entrance; whisky-water jugs hanging from oak beams, and lots of pictures and decorative plates on the walls. A games room at the far end of the bar has darts, dominoes, cribbage, table skittles and board games. Hook Norton is kept alongside three guests such as Adnams Broadside, Brakspear Special and Woodfordes Wherry. Bar food (they stick quite rigidly to their limited food times) might include soup (£2.75), filled baguettes (from £3.75), filled yorkshire puddings (£5.30), macaroni and lentil bake (£6.55), ginger pork (£6.95) and salmon fillet with mustard and dill sauce (£7.55) with puddings such as raspberry meringue (£3.25); decent wines and fruit wines, and informal service; no credit cards. Readers recommend sitting in the well cared for sheltered garden when the weather is nice; the outside gents' has an interesting newspaper-influenced décor. The village is picturesque with good walks nearby (including the Knightley Way). Do check the limited opening and food serving times below before you head out to visit this pub. *(Recommended by R M Corlett, Pete Baker, Tom Evans, John McDonald, Ann Bond, Howard and Margaret Buchanan, George Atkinson)*

Free house ~ Licensees Paul and Denise Egerton ~ Real ale ~ Bar food (only Sat and Sun lunchtime) ~ No credit cards ~ (01327) 361604; fax same ~ Children welcome ~ Open 7-11; 12-3, 7-11 Sat; 12-3, 7-10.30 Sun; closed Mon and Weds, lunchtime Mon-Fri

FOTHERINGHAY TL0593 Map 5
Falcon ★ ⑪ ♀

Village signposted off A605 on Peterborough side of Oundle

Northamptonshire Dining Pub of the Year

This civilised dining pub is a good place to come for a special occasion and readers only have good things to say about their well presented, inventive food. Their set lunch menus (two courses £11, three courses £14.75) are very good value considering the standard of their cooking and might include thai-style chicken noodle and coconut soup, followed by spinach, parmesan and mascarpone tart with white onion cream rounded off with sticky toffee pudding with rum and raisin ice cream. Or you can choose from the seasonally changing bar menu where there might be starters such as baked goats cheese with roast cherry tomatoes, basil oil and foccacia (£5.75), crispy duck spring rolls with spiced asian coleslaw and sweet and sour dressing (£6), main courses such as roast polenta with parmesan and herbs (£9.50), calves liver with olive oil mash, bacon, spinach and red wine shallot sauce (£13.50), corn-fed chicken breast with fondant potato in a wild mushroom and tarragon cream sauce (£13.75) and roast monkfish with black pudding, tomato salsa and fried leeks (£15.50) with puddings such as chocolate pecan tart with home-made pecan ice cream (from £4.50). Understandably popular, it's a good idea to book; friendly, polite service. The comfortable lounge has cushioned slatback armchairs and bucket chairs, winter log fires in a stone fireplace, fresh flower arrangements, and a hum of quiet conversation. The pretty conservatory restaurant is usually busy with diners, and if the weather's nice the terrace is a particularly enjoyable place to eat. Locals gather in the much smaller tap bar with darts; the dining room and conservatory are no smoking. Well kept Adnams and Greene King IPA, and a couple of guests such as Fullers London Pride and Theakstons on handpump, and good wines including a champagne by the glass. The vast church behind is worth a visit, and the ruins of Fotheringhay Castle, where Mary Queen of Scots was executed, are not far away. *(Recommended by Martin and Penny Fletcher, Howard and Margaret Buchanan, Marion Turner, Maysie Thompson, Philip and Susan Philcox, Steve Chambers, Terry Mizen, Martin and Lois Sheldrick, Mike and Sue Loseby, Eric Locker, David and Mary Webb, B, M and P Kendall, Derek and Sylvia Stephenson, Michael Sargent, D P Brown)*

Free house ~ Licensees Ray Smikle and John Hoskins ~ Real ale ~ Bar food (12-2.15, 6.30-9.30) ~ Restaurant ~ (01832) 226254 ~ Children welcome ~ Open 12-2.30, 6-10.30; 12-2, 7-10 Sun

GREAT OXENDON SP7383 Map 4

George ♀ 🛏

A508 S of Market Harborough

Rather gaunt-looking on its bank high over the main road, this turns out to be really cosy and convivial inside. A great deal of care has gone into the furnishings and décor, from the welcoming lobby with its overstuffed chairs, former inn-sign, and lavatories entertainingly decked out with rather stylish naughty pictures, through the attractive prints and engravings in the two opened-together rooms of the main beamed bar, to the Portmeirion plates, and the turkey-carpeted no smoking conservatory overlooking the shrub-sheltered garden. There's a comfortable mix of chairs with the odd cushioned pew, and a thriving atmosphere boosted by good staff who clearly enjoy their work. Food, very popular with older lunchers despite the somewhat daunting prices, includes home-made soup (£2.95), filled rolls (from £4.25), moules marinières (£5.25), grilled haddock (£7.95), honey-roast lamb shank (£8.95), and duck, chorizo and butter bean casserole (£9.65). We can particularly recommend the tender and tasty steak baguette (£7.25), nicely served with little sautéed new potatoes and a well dressed salad, and the specials such as grilled haddock or wild mushrooms with sun-dried tomato and pesto pasta (£7.65) and pot-roasted pheasant or tarragon salmon (£8.95). Well kept Adnams and Bass on handpump, a decent choice of good wines by the glass, daily papers on sticks, a big log fire (with a nice club fender); maybe piped easy-listening classical music. *(Recommended by George Atkinson, Stephen, Julie and Hayley Brown, I C Millar, Gerry Dobson)*

Free house ~ Licensees Nan and Allan Wiseman ~ Bar food (12-2, 7-10) ~ Restaurant ~ (01858) 465205 ~ Children in eating area of bar and restaurant ~ Open 11.30-3, 6(7 Sat)-11; 12-3 Sun; closed Sun evening ~ Bedrooms: /£59.50S

We accept no free drinks or payment for inclusion. We take no advertising, and are not sponsored by the brewing industry – or by anyone else. So all reports are independent.

HARRINGWORTH SP9298 Map 4
White Swan ✐

Seaton Road; village SE of Uppingham, signposted from A6003, A47 and A43

Set in a pretty village with a famous 82-arch railway viaduct, this limestone Tudor inn still shows signs of its coaching days in the blocked-in traces of its carriage-entry arch. There's a pleasantly calming atmosphere and the staff are friendly and efficient. The neatly kept central bar area has good solid tables, a hand-crafted oak bar counter with a mirror base and an attractive swan carving on its front, an open fire, and pictures relating to the World War II airfield at nearby Spanhoe among a collection of old village photographs (in which many of the present buildings are still recognisable). The roomy and welcoming lounge/eating area has comfortable settles, while a quieter no smoking dining room has a collection of old jugs, craft tools, dried flower arrangements and locally painted watercolours. Cooked by a Spanish chef, good, varied bar food includes sandwiches (from £2.50), soup (£2.95), hot baguettes (from £3), home-made chicken liver pâté or grilled goats cheese with sun-dried tomatoes and black olives (£3.95), asparagus, mushroom and brie pancakes or grilled chicken stuffed with onion and mushrooms and topped with stilton, (£6.95), venison sausages, bubble and squeak and onion gravy (£7), braised lamb knuckle with rosemary, orange and redcurrant sauce (£8.95) and steaks (from £8.95) with puddings such as strawberry jam sponge pudding and hot chocolate brownies (£2.95). Well kept Greene King IPA and Ruddles County and maybe a guest such as Wadworths 6X on handpump. Darts and piped music; tables outside on a little terrace. *(Recommended by Nigel Williamson, David and Mary Webb, Mike and Sue Loseby, Angus Lyon, Joan and Michel Hooper-Immins)*

Free house ~ Licensees John and Carol Harding ~ Real ale ~ Bar food (12-2, 7-10(9 Sun)) ~ Restaurant ~ (01572) 747543 ~ Children in eating area of bar and restaurant ~ Fri music night twice a month ~ Open 11.30-2.30, 6.30-11; 12-3, 7-10.30 Sun ~ Bedrooms: £40S/£55S

OUNDLE TL0487 Map 5
Mill

Barnwell Rd out of town; or follow Barnwell Country Park signs off A605 bypass

You can watch the stream race below the building through a big glass panel by the entrance of this well restored mill. The Domesday Book records a mill on this site, and the waterwheel, which dates from the early 17th c, did not stop turning till 1930. A ground floor bar (open in the evening only) has red leatherette button-back built-in wall banquettes against its stripped-stone walls. Bar food is available in the upstairs Trattoria which has stalls around tables with more banquettes in bays, stripped masonry and beams, another race feature, and small windows which look down over the lower millpond and the River Nene; large no smoking area; piped music. As well as quite a few tex-mex dishes such as chilli tacos (£8.55) and fajitas (from £11.95), the wide range of bar food might include soup (£2.95), filled baguettes and baked potatoes (from £3), salmon and prawn roll (£4.95), lasagne or vegetable balti (£7.95), smoked fishcakes (£8.95) and steaks (from £9.95), daily specials such as sweet and sour vegetables (£6.95) and pesto salmon (£9.95); puddings might include crumble and cheesecake (£3.50); large selection of liqueur coffees. Changing beers might include Bass, Fullers London Pride and Greene King Ruddles and Old Speckled Hen. There are picnic-sets under cocktail parasols on a grassy area at the side. *(Recommended by Michael Tack, George Atkinson)*

Free house ~ Licensees Neil Stewart and Peter Bossard ~ Real ale ~ Bar food (12-2, 6.30-9; 12-5, 6.30-9 Sat and Sun) ~ Restaurant ~ (01832) 272621 ~ Children in eating area of bar and restaurant ~ Open 11-3, 6.30-11; 11-11 Sat; 12-10.30 Sun; 11-3, 6.30-11 winter Sat and Sun

Ship 🍺 £

West Street

The heavily beamed lounge bar of this companionable, bustling local is made up of three rooms that lead off the central corridor on the left. Up by the street there's a mix of leather and other seats, with sturdy tables and a log fire in a stone inglenook, and down one end a panelled no smoking snug has button-back leather seats built in around it. Well kept Bass, Oakham JHB, Shepherd Neame Spitfire and Hop Back Summer Lightning on handpump, a good range of malt whiskies, cappuccino and espressos, cocktails Weds, Fri and Sat evening. Very good value bar food from a changing blackboard menu might include soup (£2.50), sandwiches (from £2.50), chicken liver pâté (£4), ham, egg and chips (£4.50), steak and ale pie (£5.50) and lunchtime specials such as barnsley lamb chop or home-made seafood pie (£4.95); puddings might include raspberry meringue or home-made fruit crumble (£2.50). Smiling, efficient service. The tiled-floor public side has darts, dominoes, fruit machine and juke box. The wooden tables and chairs outside on the series of small sheltered terraces are lit at night. Several of the clean and comfortable bedrooms are in a recent extension. *(Recommended by R T and J C Moggridge)*

Free house ~ Licensees Andrew and Robert Langridge ~ Real ale ~ Bar food (till 3 Sun) ~ Restaurant ~ (01832) 273918 ~ Children in eating area of bar till 9.30pm ~ Disco every first Weds and live jazz last Sun of month ~ Open 11-11, 12-10.30 Sun; 11-1 25 Dec ~ Bedrooms: £25(£30S)/£40(£50S)(£60B)

SULGRAVE SP5545 Map 4

Star 🛏

E of Banbury, signposted off B4525; Manor Road

This hospitable, creeper-covered stonebuilt inn is the type of place where you pop in for a drink and end up staying all evening, writes one reader. There's certainly plenty to see in the neatly kept airy bar of this former farmhouse – look out for the stuffed backside of a fox, seeming to leap into the wall, a hare's head fitted with little antlers to make it resemble a miniature stag, and a kangaroo with an Ozzie hanging-corks hat. Newspaper front pages record events such as Kennedy's assassination, the death of Churchill and the first successful hole in the heart operation, and a blackboard displays an obscure fact of the day. The part by the big inglenook fireplace (with a paper skeleton on its side bench) has polished flagstones, the other part a red carpet, and furnishings are mainly small pews, cushioned window seats and wall benches, kitchen chairs and cast-iron-framed tables. Generous helpings of enjoyable, traditional English seasonal dishes from the blackboard menu might include soup (£3.75), whitebait with thai sauce (£4.75), prawns wrapped in filo pastry (£4.95), good cheese and potato pie (£8.75), home-made steak and kidney sausages and mash, poached smoked haddock or beef goulash (£9.75), and home-made puddings such as lime and ginger cheesecake and bakewell tart (£3.75); no smoking back restaurant. Well kept Hook Norton Best, Old Hooky and Generation and a monthly changing guest beer such as Fullers London Pride on handpump. There's a very warm welcome from the friendly staff and landlord, and one or two very regular locals; alley skittles, cribbage, dominoes; tables outside, some under a covered trellis. Well maintained, comfortable bedrooms. The pub is on the road to George Washington's ancestral home and is handy for Silverstone. *(Recommended by Mike and Sue Loseby, Martin and Penny Fletcher, D P Brown, Susan and John Douglas, Jack Clarfelt, Gwyneth and Salvo Spadaro-Dutturi, Ian Phillips, George Atkinson, J G Roberts)*

Hook Norton ~ Tenant Andrew Willerton ~ Real ale ~ Bar food (12-2, 6.30-9.30, 12-4 Sun) ~ Restaurant ~ (01295) 760389 ~ Open 11-2.30, 6-11; Sun and bank holidays 12-5; closed 25 Dec ~ Bedrooms: £40S/£65S

Bedroom prices are for high summer. Even then you may get reductions for more than one night, or (outside tourist areas) weekends. Winter special rates are common, and many inns cut bedroom prices if you have a full evening meal.

WOODNEWTON TL0394 Map 5

White Swan

Main Street; back roads N of Oundle, easily reached from A1/A47 (via Nassington) and A605 (via Fotheringhay)

This friendly country pub has just been taken over by new licensees so more reports please on whether we should continue to include it. The unremarkable frontage hides a surprisingly capacious interior where the main focus is on the dining area. All the starters on the short bar menu are £2.50 and include soup and deep-fried cajun mushrooms while mains such as ploughman's, gammon steak, battered cod or sirloin steak are £4.99. More elaborate blackboard specials might include chicken stuffed with stilton in a port sauce (£8.99), barbary duck breast with black cherry sauce (£9.99) and fresh seabass (£10.99) with puddings such as dime bar toffee crunch pie (£2.50). The restaurant is no smoking; cheerful, attentive service. The other end has a woodburner and space for drinkers with well kept Fullers London Pride and Batemans and a guest on handpump; maybe local radio. There are tables and a boules pitch on the back lawn (league matches Tuesday evenings).
(Recommended by Stephen, Julie and Hayley Brown, Mike and Sue Loseby, Anthony Barnes, Eric Locker, David and Mary Webb)

Free house ~ Licensees Susan and David Hydon ~ Real ale ~ Bar food (12-1.45(2.30 Sun), 7(6 Fri)-9, not Mon or evenings Sun) ~ Restaurant ~ (01780) 470381; fax 01780 470422 ~ Children in restaurant ~ Open 12-2.30(3 Sat), 7(6 Fri)-11; 12-3, 7-10.30 Sun; closed Mon

Lucky Dip

Besides the fully inspected pubs, you might like to try these Lucky Dips recommended to us and described by readers (if you do, please send us reports: www.goodguides.com).

Abthorpe [SP6446]
☆ *New Inn* [signed from A43 at 1st roundabout S of A5; Silver St]: Tucked-away partly thatched real country local, rambling take-us-as-you-find-us dim-lit bars, beams, stripped stone, inglenook log fire, masses of pictures and old family photographs, attractively priced home cooking (not Sun/Mon) inc good cheap crab sandwiches, well kept Hook Norton Best, Old Hooky and Double Stout, a guest such as Greene King Abbot, good choice of malt whiskies, hospitable landlord, lots of old family photographs etc; nice big garden with goldfish, rabbits and aviary, quiet village *(BB, Christopher Hayle)*

Apethorpe [TL0295]
Kings Head [Kings Cliffe Rd]: Roomy stone-built pub bought by residents of attractive conservation village, comfortable lounge with log fire, changing ales such as Fullers London Pride, Marstons Bitter and Pedigree and Wadworths 6X, good coffee, obliging landlord and staff, arch to big dining area with wide choice of good food inc fish, separate bar food menu (not Mon); cosy bar with pool; children welcome, picnic-sets in small courtyard *(David and Mary Webb, Mrs Jane Basso, M J Morgan)*

Ashby St Ledgers [SP5768]
☆ *Olde Coach House* [4 miles from M1 junction 18; A5 S to Kilsby, then A361 S towards Daventry; village also signed off A5 N of Weedon; Main St]: Back on form under cheerful current landlord and staff, rambling softly lit rooms with high-backed winged settles on polished black and red tiles, old kitchen tables, harness and hunting pictures, big log fire, half a dozen or so well kept ales such as Caledonian Golden Promise, Everards Old Original, Flowers Original and Smiles Golden, good choice of decent wines (generous measures), front games room, varied well prepared food; big-screen TV, piped music; seats out among fruit trees and under a fairy-lit arbour, barbecues, play area, disabled access, interesting church nearby – see the skeleton; comfortable bedrooms, open all day Sat *(Susan and John Douglas, LYM, G Coates, E J and M W Corrin, Robert and Catherine Dunster, Simon King, Martin and Penny Fletcher, D P Brown)*

Ashton [TL0588]
Chequered Skipper [the one NE of Oundle, signed from A427/A605 island]: Handsome thatched pub on chestnut-tree green of attractive elegant estate village, light and airy rebuilt open-plan café/bar with tables left and right, changing real ales such as Fenland Doctors Order, Mauldons Mole Trap, Oakham JBH and Tetleys, reasonably priced food (not Mon) from baked potatoes and ciabattas to restaurant main courses, young helpful friendly staff *(Michael and Jenny Back)*

Aynho [SP5133]
☆ *Cartwright Arms* [Croughton Rd]: Friendly former posting inn, good home-made food in neatly modernised beamed lounge and bar, well kept Hook Norton Best and Theakstons XB, helpful friendly staff, reasonably priced restaurant, a few tables in pretty corner of former coachyard; bedrooms comfortable and

attractive, nice village *(George Atkinson, BB)*

☆ *Great Western Arms* [B4031 W, towards Deddington]: Unpretentious welcoming creeper-covered pub by what used to be station on main Oxford—Banbury rail line, good generous cheap food in roomy informal dining areas, clubby lounge with log fire, well kept Hook Norton Bitter and Mild, pleasant staff, interesting GWR memorabilia inc lots of steam locomotive photographs; small games area with darts and bar billiards, children's room; enclosed garden by Oxford Canal with moorings, flower-decked back courtyard *(Pete Baker, Sue Demont, Tim Barrow)*

Badby [SP5559]

☆ *Maltsters Arms* [The Green]: Long beamed room with light wood furniture, roaring fire each end, good reasonably priced food inc some unusual dishes, well kept ales inc interesting guest beers, friendly attentive service, hood skittles; may be soft classical piped music; garden with terrace and new seats, well placed for walks on nearby Knightley Way; bedrooms *(George Atkinson)*

Barnwell [TL0484]

☆ *Montagu Arms* [off A605 S of Oundle, then fork right at Thurning, Hemington sign]: Attractive unspoilt stone-built pub in pleasant streamside village, two bars with low beams, flagstones or tile and brick floors, not smart but warm, cosy and welcoming; well kept Adnams Bitter and Broadside and Flowers IPA and Original, good choice of interesting hearty food running up to swordfish, good puddings, log fire, neat back dining room; games room off yard, big garden with good well equipped play area, barbecue and camping; open all day wknd, comfortable bedrooms in separate block *(BB, Michael and Jenny Back)*

Brixworth [SP7470]

Coach & Horses [Harborough Rd, just off A508 N of Northampton]: Welcoming old stone-built village inn nr Pitsford reservoir, good helpful staff, generous food from good sandwiches to popular Sun lunches, well kept Adnams and Frankton Bagby Barnstormer, decent house wine, friendly helpful service, beams and lots of pictures, no smoking restaurant; piped music *(George Atkinson)*

Bugbrooke [SP6757]

Wharf Inn [The Wharf; off A5 S of Weedon]: Spotless pub in super spot by canal, generous food in raised eating area and big restaurant, well kept Frog Island real ales, hard-working new landlord, good friendly service, weekly quiz nights and monthly jazz; plenty of tables on waterside lawn *(Ted George, Gerry Dobson)*

Bulwick [SP9694]

☆ *Queens Head* [just off A43 Kettering—Duddington]: Shortish choice of good interesting beautifully served food from sandwiches and unusual starters or snacks to popular Sun roasts and imaginative puddings in neat and unpretentious partly beamed bar, small fire each end, well kept ales such as Adnams, Fullers London Pride, Greene King, Hancocks HB and Marstons Pedigree, warm

but not over-effusive welcome; live folk music Mon, when menu may be limited *(BB, Anthony Barnes, Eric Locker)*

Collingtree [SP7555]

☆ *Wooden Walls of Old England* [1¼ miles from M1 junction 15; High St]: Friendly new family running tidy low-beamed thatched local, model galleon and some other nautical memorabilia (underlining the meaning of the name), well kept real ales, freshly cooked enjoyable food, good service, open fire; children welcome, lots of picnic-sets and play area in nice back garden *(BB, Kevin Macey)*

Cranford St John [SP9277]

Red Lion [3 miles E of Kettering just off A14]: Good range of good value generous food in welcoming and attractive two-bar stone pub, well kept Ind Coope and Tetleys, decent house wine, good-humoured service; pleasant garden, quiet village *(Meg and Colin Hamilton)*

Eastcote [SP6753]

☆ *Eastcote Arms* [Gayton Rd; village signposted from A5 3 miles N of Towcester]: Friendly village pub, new tenants keeping up the pleasantly unpretentious feel (regulars may come with their barn owl), traditional furnishings with two flame-effect fires, floral dado wallpaper, cottagey curtains, fresh flowers; well kept ales such as Adnams, Bass, Fullers London Pride, Greene King IPA and Youngs, decent wines and malt whiskies, enjoyable honest food inc good Sun lunch, no smoking dining room; unobtrusive piped music; picnic-sets and other tables out behind with roses, geraniums and so forth around the neat lawn, peaceful village *(Susan and John Douglas, Gerry Dobson, Peter Batty, LYM, George Atkinson)*

Evenley [SP5834]

☆ *Red Lion* [The Green]: Small friendly beamed local very popular lunchtime for enjoyable food from good sandwiches to plenty of grills, fish and vegetarian, also Sun lunches, Banks's, Marstons Pedigree and a guest such as Morrells Varsity, decent coffee and choice of wines, attentive service, inglenook, some flagstones, cricketing books and other memorabilia; piped music; opp attractive village green, tables out on lawn *(George Atkinson, Marjorie and David Lamb)*

Eydon [SP5450]

☆ *Royal Oak* [Lime Ave; village signed off A361 Daventry—Banbury, and from B4525]: Attractively refurbished old-fashioned 17th-c local, polished flagstones, thriving informal atmosphere, enjoyable food in several pleasantly decorated rooms, Hook Norton Best, Theakstons Black Bull and Timothy Taylors Landlord, welcoming efficient service *(Lucy Pellerin, LYM, Richard Joyce, R Jones)*

Farthinghoe [SP5339]

Fox [just off A422 Brackley—Banbury; Baker St]: Quiet village local with stone fireplace, floors part tiled and part carpet, big helpings of enjoyable food from good baguettes up, friendly licensee happy to do smaller ones for elderly, Charles Wells ales; garden *(Mr and Mrs Hugh Spottiswoode)*

Flore [SP6460]

Royal Oak [A45 W of M1 junction 16; High St]: Stone-built pub with two linked bars, lots of wood, gas fire, woodburner, friendly staff, limited choice of fresh food (not Mon/Tues evening or Sun), well kept Bass and a guest beer, good coffee, amiable dog called Biscuit, no mobile phones; darts, hood skittles and machines in separate area; picnic-sets in garden with barbecue and play area, pretty hanging baskets (*CMW, JJW*)

Gayton [SP7054]

Eykyn Arms [High St]: Cheerful stone-built pub keeping much of its original style, plush lounge with naval memorabilia, roomy bar with large keyring collection, lots of village prints and photographs, side conservatory with Princess Diana photographs, well kept Charles Wells ales, usual food inc good sandwiches; pool, darts, dominoes, hood skittles, TV; picnic-sets out on terrace (*CMW, JJW*)

Queen Victoria [High St]: Smartly refurbished village pub, several areas off central bar, light panelling, beams, lots of pictures and woodburner, wide choice of decent food from baguettes up, Theakstons XB and Youngers; piped music (*LYM, Gerry Dobson, George Atkinson*)

Grafton Regis [SP7546]

☆ *White Hart* [A508 S of Northampton]: Thatched pub in thatched village, several linked rooms, good home-made bar food (not Sun evening) inc several good soups, also bookings-only restaurant with open fire – very popular for flamboyant chef's good reasonably priced imaginative cooking; well kept Greene King IPA and Abbot, lots of decent wines by the glass, helpful service, pensive african grey parrot; piped music; good-sized garden (food not served there); cl Mon exc bank hols (*CMW, JJW, Alan Sutton, BB, R M Corlett*)

Great Addington [SP1159]

Hare & Hounds [Main St]: Small L-shaped pub very popular for good value lunchtime food (worth booking), very friendly staff (*David and Mary Webb*)

Great Billing [SP8162]

Elwes Arms [High St]: Thatched stone-built 16th-c village pub, wide choice of good value food inc tempting Sun lunch, three well kept real ales; darts, fruit machine, TV, may be piped music, Thurs and Sun quiz nights, no dogs; children welcome, wheelchair access, garden with play area (*CMW, JJW*)

Great Brington [SP6664]

☆ *Fox & Hounds/Althorp Coaching Inn* [off A428 NW of Northampton, nr Althorp Hall]: Attractive thatched stone-built pub with fine log fires in quaint low-beamed flagstoned bar with lots of bric-a-brac, Greene King IPA and Abbot and several interesting guest beers, decent wines, bar food (not Mon-Weds or Sun evening) from pricy baguettes up; games room down steps, piped music (live Tues/Weds); children welcome, open all day wknds and summer, tables in attractive courtyard and side garden with play area (*George Atkinson, Stephen, Julie and Hayley Brown, John Evans,*

Martin and Penny Fletcher, LYM)

Great Houghton [SP7958]

Old Cherry Tree [Cherry Tree Lane; a No Through Road off A428 just before the White Hart]: New licensees at early 19th-c pub, several rooms, stripped stone, low beams and dark panelling, wide range of good value food from good toasties up, well kept Charles Wells Eagle and Bombardier and Greene King Old Speckled Hen, friendly service; piped music, no dogs; picnic-sets in good back garden, quiet village spot (*Anthony Barnes, George Atkinson, Michael Tack, CMW, JJW*)

Greens Norton [SP6649]

Butchers Arms [High St]: Large comfortably refurbished lounge, four well kept real ales, some emphasis on wide choice of good value food, service attentive if not quick; separate bar, games room with darts, pool, machines and TV, piped pop music; disabled access, picnic-sets out in front, pretty village nr Grafton Way walks (*Richard Burton, CMW, JJW*)

Hackleton [SP8055]

White Hart [B526 SE of Northampton]: Comfortable welcoming 18th-c country pub with dining area down corridor, stripped stone and brickwork, illuminated well, brasses and artefacts, soft lighting, fresh flowers, good value generous fresh food inc local produce, well kept Fullers London Pride and Greene King IPA and Ruddles, split-level flagstoned bar with flame-effect fire, pool and hood skittles; quiz Sun; garden with picnic-sets and perhaps small bouncy castle, open all day (*CMW, JJW, Mr Biggs*)

Harlestone [SP7064]

☆ *Dusty Fox* [A428, Lower Harlestone]: Former Fox & Hounds attractively reworked as Vintage Inn, relaxed atmosphere, small front bar and lounge, nice furnishings, hops on beams, local photographs, expanded mainly no smoking dining area, barn redone in conservatory style; enjoyable food all day from separate servery, some nouvelle-ish dishes, Bass and Fullers London Pride, decent wines, friendly speedy service; some tables outside, open all day (*Alan Sutton, Tim and Ann Newell*)

Harrington [SP7779]

Tollemache Arms [High St; off A508 S of Mkt Harboro]: Handsome and civilised beamed Tudor pub, well kept Charles Wells Eagle and Bombardier, cheap house wines, open fires, friendly and obliging service, food in bar and candlelit restaurant, small back garden with country views; children welcome, clean and attractive bedrooms, quiet stone-built village (*M J Morgan*)

Hellidon [SP5158]

☆ *Red Lion* [Stockwell Lane, off A425 W of Daventry]: Small wisteria-covered inn in beautiful setting by green of unspoilt village, clean, cosy and comfortable, good value food inc good Tues/Weds OAP lunch, well kept Bass, Hook Norton Best and Worthington BB, two farm ciders, very helpful chatty staff, softly lit new stripped stone dining area with hunting prints, comfortable lounge, two friendly retrievers by woodburner in bar, games room with hood skittles; tables outside, good bedrooms, pleasant walks nearby *(Dr Alan Sutton, George Atkinson)*

Isham [SP8874]

Lilacs [Church St/Mill St]: Unspoilt three-room country local, well kept Greene King ales, good value honest food (not Sun); very popular lunchtime with OAPs inc superb chips, no smoking lounge, big games room with pool, darts and skittles; tables outside *(CMW, JJW, Howard and Margaret Buchanan, Mr and Mrs Nick Kingsley)*

Monk & Minstrel [Kettering Rd]: Former Red Lion rebranded, large U-shaped bar and restaurant area, wide choice of generous decent food (not Sun evening), two or three real ales, good choice of other drinks, real fire, daily papers; children welcome, games machines, quiet piped music, quiz night *(CMW, JJW)*

Islip [SP9879]

☆ *Woolpack* [Kettering Rd, just off A14, by bridge into Thrapston]: Comfortable old inn, very popular lunchtime for wide choice of good food inc interesting dishes, armchairs and prints in spacious beamed and stripped-stone lounge, Adnams, Bass, Greene King IPA and Abbot and Marstons Pedigree, cafetière coffee, friendly licensees and staff, woodburner, Sun restaurant lunch; bedrooms *(David and Mary Webb)*

Kilsby [SP5671]

George [A5; on dead end road]: Big pub doing well under chatty hard-working landlady, attractive high-ceilinged oak-panelled lounge with hunting prints and plush seating, interesting changing well kept ales, good value home-made food from soup and rolls to Sun lunch, large nicely furnished dining room, separate public bar; piped music, darts and pool; no dogs, pleasant garden *(George Atkinson, Ted George)*

Kislingbury [SP6959]

Old Red Lion [High St, off A45 W of Northampton]: Ambitious fresh food inc lots of fish on Fri, steaks, game, even ostrich and kangaroo, also Sun lunch (and Sun meat raffle), well kept Bass and Greene King IPA, good choice of other drinks, friendly service, bar, lounge/restaurant (lower part no smoking) and games room; SkyTV, piped music, Tues quiz night; picnic-sets on terrace with swings and slide *(R M Corlett, Ted George, CMW, JJW)*

Litchborough [SP6353]

Old Red Lion [Banbury Rd, just off former B4525 Banbury—Northampton]: Attractive sandstone village local opp church and little green, well kept ales inc Banks's, Marstons Pedigree and Morrells Varsity, welcoming Irish landlord, no food but peanuts and olives on the bar, daily papers, flagstones, beams, wall settles, log fire in great deep inglenook; no piped music, fruit machine in corridor, games room for pool and skittles; picnic-sets in small neat garden *(Susan and John Douglas, CMW, JJW)*

Little Brington [SP6663]

☆ *Old Saracens Head* [4½ miles from M1 junction 16, first right off A45 to Daventry; also signed

off A428; Main St]: Alcoves in roomy lounge, lots of pictures, books and odds and ends, even a red telephone box, well kept Fullers London Pride, Jennings Cumberland and Thwaites Reward, good food choice, good log fire (when it's lit), games bar, extended no smoking restaurant area; maybe piped music; tables in neat back garden, handy for Althorp House and Holdenby House *(George Atkinson, Gerry Dobson, BB)*

Lowick [SP9780]

☆ *Snooty Fox* [signed off A6116 Corby—Raunds]: Attractive two-room lounge with handsome 16th-c beams, log fire in huge stone fireplace, neat dining tables, enjoyable food from baguettes up, real ales such as Batemans Hop Bine, Greene King IPA, Hook Norton Best and Worthingtons, restaurant; piped music, service can sometimes slow; floodlit picnic-sets out on front lawn *(George Atkinson, Michael and Jenny Back, Eric Locker, LYM, Ted George)*

Mears Ashby [SP8466]

☆ *Griffins Head* [Wilby Rd]: Pleasantly refurbished country pub with smart front lounge and cosy back locals' bar, small dining room with no smoking area, friendly courteous service, good straightforward food from sandwiches to good value Sun roasts, very popular generous OAP lunches Mon-Fri, bargain midweek suppers, attractive views and hunting prints, well kept Everards ales inc Mild with a guest such as Brewsters Belly Dance (from Belvoir), huge fireplace; games room with darts, skittles and machine, piped music; children welcome, seats out in small garden, on edge of attractive thatched village *(Mary Morris, Eric Locker, Anthony Barnes, George Atkinson)*

Milton Malsor [SP7355]

Greyhound [2¼ miles from M1 junction 15, via A508]: Big busy Chef & Brewer, well refurbished in olde-worlde mode, lots of nooks and crannies, 15th-c beams, old pictures and china, pewter-filled dresser, candlelit pine tables; good log fire, wide choice of food all day from filled rolls up, well kept John Smiths, Theakstons Best, Old and XB, good range of wines; the top-notch manager who added to all this an attractively relaxed atmosphere and very good service has now moved on; piped jazz or classical music; open all day, well behaved seated children welcome, spreading front lawn with duck/fish pond *(LYM)*

Nassington [TL0696]

Black Horse [Fotheringhay Rd – 2½ miles S of A1/A47 interchange W of Peterboro]: Civilised 17th-c beamed and panelled dining pub in nice village, splendid big stone fireplace, panelling, easy chairs and small settees in two rooms linked by bar servery, well kept real ales, good varied wine list, very attentive service; attractive garden, open all day summer wknds *(LYM, Brian Wainwright, Peter H Stallard)*

Nether Heyford [SP6558]

☆ *Old Sun* [pub signed off A45 just W of M1 junction 16; Middle St]: Family-run 18th-c stone-built pub packed with brassware, railway memorabilia and advertising signs; three beamed bars, rugs on parquet, red tiles or flagstones, big log fire, homely restaurant, good cheap home-made lunchtime food from sandwiches to limited hot dishes, more choice evenings and Sun, Banks's, Greene King Ruddles Best and a wknd guest beer, friendly relaxed service, hood skittles; quiet piped music; picnic-sets in yard with dovecote, flowers and shrubs among old farm equipment *(CMW, JJW, Gerry Dobson, George Atkinson)*

Newnham [SP5859]

Romer Arms [The Green]: Stained pine panelling, mix of flagstones, quarry tiles and carpet, log fire, light and airy back conservatory, friendly attentive service, good generous home cooking inc some unusual dishes and popular Sun lunch (no snacks then), Courage Directors and Greene King IPA and Abbot; games room, piped music, opens noon or so, picnic-sets in back garden looking over fields, small attractive village *(George Atkinson)*

Northampton [SP7962]

Bold Dragoon [High St, Weston Favell; off A4500 Wellingborough Rd]: Worth knowing for wide range of well kept reasonably priced beers; conservatory restaurant, terrace and garden *(Gerry Dobson)*

Britannia [3¾ miles from M1 junction 15; Old Bedford Rd (off A428)]: Rambling recently refurbished pub with massive beams, mix of flagstones and carpet, attractive 18th-c kitchen, three real ales, decent food from baguettes up, no smoking area, conservatory; may be piped music, Tues quiz night; picnic-sets by River Nene *(CMW, JJW, LYM, Dr Alan Sutton)*

Malt Shovel [Bridge St (approach rd from M1 junction 15); best parking in Morrisons opp back entrance]: Long pine and brick bar opp Carlsberg Brewery, up to 13 changing beers inc a Mild, most from small breweries, Belgian bottled beers, lots of whiskies, farm cider, country wines, occasional beer festivals, daily papers, good value home-made usual food from hot baguettes up lunchtime and early evenings, not Sun (can take a while), breweriana; piped music, darts, some live music; picnic-sets on small back terrace *(CMW, JJW, Bruce Bird)*

Wig & Pen [St Giles St]: L-shaped Mansfield pub, fair choice of cheapish lunchtime food, four real ales, real fire; TV, machines, piped music, entertainment most nights – popular with young people; tables on heated back terrace, open all day *(CMW, JJW)*

Old [SP7873]

☆ *White Horse* [Walgrave Rd, N of Northampton between A43 and A508]: Wide choice of enjoyable sensibly priced food from good low-priced baguettes to interesting main dishes and popular Sun lunch, thriving atmosphere in cosy and comfortable lounge with good log fire, lots of pictures and plates, friendly service, well kept Banks's and Marstons Pedigree, decent wines, good coffee, restaurant, unusual theme nights; piped radio; lovely garden overlooking 13th-c church *(Mary Morris, Gerry Dobson)*

Orlingbury [SP8572]

Queens Arms [signed off A43 Northampton—

Kettering, A509 Wellingborough—Kettering; Isham Rd]: Stone-built pub, large comfortable airy lounge with banquettes, stools and side no smoking area, wide choice of good if not cheap fresh food, evening restaurant, up to eight well kept beers, good atmosphere; maybe piped pop music; nice garden with play area *(CMW, JJW, Gerry Dobson, J V Dadswell)*

Ravensthorpe [SP6670]

Chequers [Chequers Lane]: Spotless refurbished beamed pub with wide range of good value bar food inc good well priced Sun lunch (worth booking this), well kept Fullers London Pride and several interesting guest beers, good service, restaurant (Weds-Sat); TV, fruit machine, piped music, monthly quiz night; open all day Sat, quiet garden with terrace and play area *(Gerry Dobson, R M Corlett)*

Roade [SP7551]

Cock [just off A508 S of M1 junction 15]: Enjoyable well presented lunchtime bar food, Marstons Pedigree, Theakstons and guest beers, cheerful staff, plates, horsebrasses, flame-effect gas fire; piped music; children in lounge bar *(Dr Alan Sutton)*

Rothwell [SP8181]

Rowell Charter [Sun Hill (A6)]: Ancient pub with two open fires, friendly service, unusual range of up to eight consistently well kept beers, sensible prices, decent food *(Stephen, Julie and Hayley Brown)*

Rushton [SP8482]

Thornhill Arms [Station Rd]: Pleasantly refurbished rambling pub prettily set opp attractive village's cricket green, wide choice of good value food from sandwiches up in neatly laid out dining area and smart high-beamed back restaurant, welcoming helpful service, well kept ales, open fire *(Michael and Jenny Back, Graham and Lynn Mason)*

Sibbertoft [SP6782]

☆ *Red Lion* [Welland Rise, off A4303 or A508 SW of Mkt Harboro]: Cosy and civilised dining pub, lounge tables set for generous standard food with good veg selection, big tables and comfortably cushioned wall seats, well kept Bass, Everards Tiger and a guest beer, decent wines, good friendly service, magazines, attractive beamed restaurant, covered tables outside; cl Mon/Tues lunchtimes, two self-contained holiday flats *(Stephen, Julie and Hayley Brown, Gerry Dobson)*

Silverstone [SP6643]

Royal Oak [Brackley Rd (A43)]: New licensees doing good choice of reasonably priced food in good-sized bar with central coal-effect fire, room off, Grand Prix memorabilia, Bass and Fullers London Pride; children welcome, quiz night Thurs, may be piped pop *(CMW, JJW)*

Southwick [TL0192]

Shuckburgh Arms [Main St]: Small genuinely old stone and thatch pub, low ceilings, cosy unspoilt atmosphere, substantial simple food, attentive landlady, well kept Adnams, Fullers London Pride and Wadworths 6X; tables and play area in garden *(John Brightley)*

Stoke Bruerne [SP7450]

☆ *Boat* [3½ miles from M1 junction 15 – A508

towards Stony Stratford then signed on right;
Bridge Rd]: Busy pub in nice spot by beautifully
restored lock opp British Waterways Museum
and shop; cheerful landlord and friendly staff,
little character flagstoned bar by canal, pleasant
central-pillared back lounge without the views
(children allowed in this bit), tables by towpath;
well kept Banks's, Marstons Best and Pedigree
and guests such as Thwaites, skittle alley; bar
snacks, no smoking restaurant (not Mon
lunchtime) and all-day tearooms, pub open all
day summer Sats, canal boat trips *(G W A
Pearce, George Atkinson, Derek Harvey-Piper,
LYM, David Mansfield)*

Thorpe Mandeville [SP5344]
Three Conies [off B4525 E of Banbury]: More
reports please on the new regime at this stone-
built 17th-c dining pub, with some
concentration on fish (and fishy décor in no
smoking dining room), flagstoned bar, cheerful
modern colours, well kept Hook Norton beers;
children welcome, tables on terrace and
spacious back lawn *(LYM)*

Towcester [SP6948]
Monk & Tipster [Watling St East]: Former
Watling Well, recently reopened after careful
refurbishment with bigger eating area
(Christopher Hayle)
Saracens Head [Watling St W]: Substantially
modernised coaching inn with interesting
Pickwick Papers connections, steps up from
cobbled entrance to panelled bar on right with
carpets on pine boards, comfortable lounge,
Victorian dining room, Charles Wells Eagle and
Bombardier with a guest such as Courage
Directors, neat staff, bar food; gents' down
steep steps; well equipped bedrooms *(LYM,
Gerry Dobson, Christopher Hayle)*

Upper Benefield [SP9789]
Wheatsheaf [Upper Main St]: Attractive
country pub in pleasant rural area, good value
varied food in bar and restaurant, friendly
owners, good choice of beers, fine house wines
(Mrs E E Sanders)

Wadenhoe [TL0083]
☆ *Kings Head* [Church Street; village signposted
(in small print) off A605 S of Oundle]: New
licensees in beautifully placed two-bar 17th-c
country pub, picnic-sets on sun terrace and
among trees on big stretch of grass by River
Nene, pretty village; solid pine furniture, good
snack menu, have had more elaborate winter
and evening dishes, well kept Adnams Bitter
and Broadside and Marstons Pedigree, good
selection of books, no smoking areas, beamed
dining room, games room; children in eating
areas, has been cl Mon lunchtime *(Patricia
Beebe, Michael Tack, J Hale, LYM)*

Walgrave [SP8072]
Royal Oak [Zion Hill, off A43
Northampton—Kettering]: Old ironstone
building with five well kept real ales, wide
choice of food inc interesting dishes, friendly
efficient service, bar and dining lounge split
into smaller areas, no smoking area, good
coffee, piped pop may be intrusive; children
welcome, tables outside, play area *(CMW,
JJW, Edward Pearce)*

Weedon [SP6458]
Narrow Boat [Stowe Hill (A5 S)]: Very popular
in summer for spacious terrace and big garden
overlooking canal, barbecues; plain décor with
canal prints, low bar tables, high-raftered back
restaurant extension with canal views, enjoyable
food from ciabatta sandwiches to popular good
value Sun lunch, friendly helpful service, well
kept Charles Wells ales, open fire; fruit
machine, skittles, quiet piped music; bedrooms
in back motel extension, narrowboat hire next
door *(LYM, George Atkinson, Mary Morris)*
Plume of Feathers [Bridge St/West St, Weedon
Bec, off A5/A45]: Beams, stripped brickwork,
pine furniture, candles and old books, very
reasonably priced food cooked to order (not
Sun evening), largely no smoking dining area,
attentive service, three well kept real ales inc
Charles Wells Eagle and Greene King IPA; quiz
night, can get smoky when busy, piped music
(some live), TV, pool, hood skittles and games
machines; children welcome, picnic-sets and
play area in garden, canal and walks nearby
(CMW, JJW)

Welford [SP6480]
Shoulder of Mutton [High St (A50)]: Neat and
tidy low-ceilinged pub nr canal marina, partly
divided by standing timbers and arches, plenty
of tables and wheelback chairs, copper and
brass, usual food inc children's, real ales such as
Bass, Fullers London Pride and Greene King
Ruddles Best, good house wines and coffee,
friendly service; piped music; skittle room,
exemplary lavatories, good back garden with
play area; cl Thurs *(Duncan Cloud,
Gerry Dobson, BB)*

Welton [SP5866]
☆ *White Horse* [High St; off A361/B4036 N of
Daventry]: Friendly two-bar beamed village
pub, cosy dining areas inc one no smoking,
energetic young landlord doing good value food
from light lunches and imaginative fish and
vegetarian dishes to plenty of meaty meals,
changing well kept ales such as Greene King
Old Speckled Hen and Theakstons Black Bull,
with guests such as Everards Perfick and one
from Frog Island, decent house wines, attentive
licensees, big open fire, public bar with
woodburner, darts, table skittles and pool
room; attractively lit garden with play area,
terrace and barbecue *(Peter Phillips, Dr and
Mrs A K Clarke)*

West Haddon [SP6272]
Pytchley [High St]: No-nonsense home-made
food inc Sun lunch in bar and dining room,
good helpings, well kept beers inc Theakstons
XB, good friendly service; 17 bedrooms *(Mary
Morris)*
Sheaf [about 3 miles from M1 junction 18;
A428 towards Northampton, West End]: Cosy
upstairs lounge and restaurant, beams and log
fire, Bass and Worthington; friendly service,
reasonably priced straightforward food *(Gerry
Dobson)*

Yardley Gobion [SP7644]
Coffee Pot [High St (off A508)]: Charming
roomy village local with well kept ales such as
Caledonian Deuchars, Fullers London Pride and

Tetleys, flame-effect fires each end of low-beamed L-shaped bar, assorted furniture, stripped brick, boards and carpet, cheerful staff, landlord does good value food, children in dining room; games room with pool, fruit machine, piped music, TV, live music most wknds, challenging quiz nights, no dogs; back garden with play area *(CMW, JJW, Dr Alan Sutton)*

Yardley Hastings [SP8656]
Red Lion [High St, just off A428 Bedford—Northampton]: Thatched stone-built pub with good value nicely presented food (not Sun/Mon evenings) inc good Sun roast, particularly well kept Charles Wells ales with a guest such as Adnams, good range of soft drinks and attractively priced coffee, efficient service, several rooms inc cosy lounge with lots of pictures, interesting brass and copper, artificial flowers, garden; no children, piped music *(CMW, JJW, George Atkinson)*

'Children welcome' means the pub says it lets children inside without any special restriction. If it allows them in, but to restricted areas such as an eating area or family room, we specify this. Places with separate restaurants usually let children use them, hotels usually let them into public areas such as lounges. Some pubs impose an evening time limit – let us know if you find this:
www.goodguides.com

Northumbria
(County Durham,
Northumberland and
Tyneside)

In this large area there are four pubs which have kept their place in every annual edition of the Guide since the first, 20 years ago. They are the formidably ancient Lord Crewe Arms at Blanchland (welcoming, a lovely building), the unspoilt Jolly Fisherman in Craster, the Rose & Crown at Romaldkirk (doing particularly well these days, good food and a fine all-rounder), and the Olde Ship in Seahouses, packed with seafaring memorabilia, and run throughout that time by Alan and Jean Glen. Other pubs doing specially well here this year are the enjoyably old-fashioned Rat at Anick (great views, good beer – a newcomer to the Guide), the County in Aycliffe (very good food – another new entry), the charmingly simply Dipton Mill Inn at Diptonmill (brews its own beer), the well run and welcoming Feathers in Hedley on the Hill (imaginative good value food, especially interesting vegetarian ones), and the Seven Stars in Shincliffe (very popular for its good food and thriving local atmosphere). Among all these places, enthusiasm for the really good food at the County in Aycliffe is running particularly high among readers: though it is very rare for us to give this accolade to a new entry, it is our Northumbria Dining Pub of the Year. Pubs in the Lucky Dip section at the end of the chapter that merit special attention are Foxtons in Berwick-upon-Tweed, the Angel in Corbridge, Tankerville Arms at Eglingham, General Havelock at Haydon Bridge, Apple at Lucker, Bridge Hotel in Newcastle, Ship at Newton-by-the-Sea, Wooden Doll in North Shields, Tynemouth Lodge in Tynemouth and Anchor at Whittonstall. Drinks prices in the area are comfortably below the national average.

ALLENDALE NY8355 Map 10
Kings Head £ 🍺

Market Place (B6295)

Now a Jennings house, this welcoming old coaching inn is set in the rambling square of a very attractive little town and gets particularly busy on market days. The spacious bar/lounge has a big log fire, straightforward pub furnishings, some interesting bric-a-brac and decent bar food such as soup (£1.60), sandwiches (from £1.75), fish and chips, lasagne or beef and ale pie (£4.95), tomato and garlic tagliatelle (£5.25), venison sausage (£5.95), chicken breast stuffed with ham with a cream cheese sauce (£6.95), game pie (£7.95), sirloin steak (£10.95), and puddings.

Half a dozen real ales include Jennings Bitter, Cockerhoop, Cumberland and Sneck Lifter and a couple of guests such as Greene King Abbot and Timothy Taylors Landlord on handpump, all kept well in a temperature-controlled cellar; 75 malt whiskies. Darts, dominoes, and piped pop music; quoits on clay pitches in the back garden. There are good walks in the area, and the road through the valley is a fine scenic drive. *(Recommended by Ted Tomiak, Barbara Wensworth, Mike and Lynn Robinson)*

Jennings ~ Tenants Tracy Thompson and Lenny Slater ~ Real ale ~ Bar food (12-2.30, 6.30-9) ~ Restaurant ~ (01434) 683681 ~ Children welcome ~ Folk/blues most Fri or Sat evenings ~ Open 11-11; 12-10.30 Sun; closed 25 Dec evening ~ Bedrooms: £24B/£45B

ALLENHEADS NY8545 Map 10
Allenheads Inn £ 🛏

Just off B6295

Every available space on the walls, ceilings, and bar of this cheerfully run pub is covered by thousands of collectibles, and in the loosely themed rooms you can find stuffed animals, mangles, old radios, typewriters, long silenced musical instruments, an engine-room telegraph, brass and copper bygones, a plastic lobster, a four-foot wooden chicken, brooms, birdcages and even shoes – the list is endless and it's all clean and enthusiastically well cared for. The games room (with darts, pool, and antique juke box) has perhaps the most effervescent collection, and the car club discs and number plates on the panelling verify the fact that members of a classic car club try to persuade their vehicles to wend their way up here. By the licensees' own admission there's too much to dust it very often; the naval room and the dining room are no smoking. Under the new licensees, they do huge helpings of good value straightforward pubby food such as sandwiches (from £1.65), vegetarian chilli (£4.50), cod (£5), beef or chicken curry (£5.25), steak or chicken pie (£5.50), and puddings (from £2); also maybe special offer of two steaks and a bottle of wine (£15). Well kept Ind Coope Burton and Tetleys, and two guest beers such as Marstons Pedigree and Timothy Taylors Landlord on handpump; decent coffee, real fire, piped music. Readers report the bedrooms to be warm and comfortable. There are tables outside, flanked by more hardware – the sorts of machinery that wouldn't fit inside. The pub is on the Sustrans C2C cycle route. *(Recommended by Kevin Thorpe, Mike and Lynn Robinson, Ted Tomiak, B, M and P Kendall)*

Free house ~ Licensee Stephen Wardle ~ Real ale ~ Bar food (till 10) ~ Restaurant ~ No credit cards ~ (01434) 685200 ~ Children in eating area of bar and dining room ~ Open 12-4, 7-11; 12-11(12-4, 7-11 winter) Sat; closed 25 Dec ~ Bedrooms: £25B/£43B

ANICK NY9665 Map 10
Rat 🍺

Village signposted NE of A69/A695 Hexham junction

Quite a throw-back, this is what pubs should have been like some 50 years ago (but usually weren't). Warm, cosy and softly lit, it has a coal fire blazing in a blacked kitchen range, and lots to look at: antique floral chamber-pots hanging from the beams, china and glassware, maps and posters, framed sets of cigarette cards, and quite a lot of Laurel and Hardy memorabilia from figurines to a signed photograph. Furnishings keep up the relaxed traditional mood, with brocaded chairs around old-fashioned pub tables. Enjoyable straightforward home-made lunchtime bar food served very generously includes sandwiches (from £2.95), soup (£1.95), ploughman's (£3.95), steak and kidney pudding, gammon and so forth with blackboard specials such as tagliatelle carbonara (£6.95), chicken breast in garlic butter or leek and stilton (£7.95), pork fillet with peach, honey and black pepper sauce, fried tuna in tomato, garlic and basil sauce or seared swordfish steak with mango chutney (£8.95) and half roast duck in Cointreau and orange sauce (£10.50). They do puddings such as sticky toffee, banana and amaretti cheesecake, and apple and raspberry crumblecake. Besides the two small eating areas, a conservatory gives lovely views of the north Tyne valley, shared by the tables out on the terrace and in a charming garden, with dovecote, statues and even flowers sprouting unexpectedly from boots. Well kept ales on handpump such as Greene King Old Speckled Hen, Mordue Workie Ticket, Ruddles and a guest or two such as John Smiths and Theakstons Old Peculier; attentive landlady (with a wry sense of humour), friendly helpful staff; daily papers and magazines. *(Recommended by Dr Graham Thorpe, Chris Rounthwaite, Mike and Lynn Robinson, John Foord, Michael Doswell)*

Free house ~ Licensees Joan and Donald D'Adamo ~ Real ale ~ (01434) 602814 ~ Children in eating area of bar and restaurant ~ Open 11-3, 6-11; 12-3, 7-10.30 Sun

AYCLIFFE NZ2722 Map 10
County 🍴 🍷 🍺
The Green; just off A1(M) junction 59, by A167

Northumbria Dining Pub of the Year

Driving past, you could easily mistake this white pub, with its name emblazoned on the walls in big fancy script, as the sort of roadside local best left to the business of neighbourhood wakes, wedding receptions and pigeon club suppers. The reality is very different. Top-notch cooking by its young ex-factory hand chef/landlord (in the process of buying the place as we went to press) now brings diners from far and wide, including heads of government gnawing away at the BSE crisis over a good piece of local beef. A sensibly limited choice of reasonably priced bar food served at lunchtime and in the early evening (until the bistro opens) might include a choice of soups (£3), open sandwiches (£4.50), prawn cocktail (£3.95), sausage and mash or cajun chicken (£7), battered cod (£7.40) and seared salmon with chargrilled vegetables and prawn couscous (£10). Though the ingredients are good solid largely local produce, the style of cooking is light and deft (and all is cooked fresh, so there might be a bit of a wait). The evening bistro menu (best to book) is more elaborate, including dishes such as crab and prawn risotto with lobster sauce (£5.60), warm salad of black pudding, chorizo and spiced apple topped with a soft poached egg (£6.20), grilled leg of lamb steak with mediterannean vegetable and mint couscous topped with cucumber raita (£13.45) and halibut steak with welsh rarebit crust, pesto new potatoes and tomato salad (£13.95). Puddings are a high point, and might include lime and lemon cheesecake (£3.95), chocolate torte with Grand Marnier crème anglaise (£4.50) and a regional cheese selection (£5.95). Furnishings in the extended bar and bistro are fresh and modern, definitely geared to grown-up dining, and the minimalist décor gives a light and airy feel, but there's no mistaking the friendly and civilised mood brought by a happy mix of expectation and contentment. Four real ales on handpump include Charles Wells Bombardier, John Smiths Magnet and a couple of guests from brewers such as Daleside and Hambleton, and a good choice of wines by the glass; service too is good. There may be piped music. The green opposite is pretty. *(Recommended by D Stephenson, M Borthwick, Jenny and Dave Hughes)*

Scottish Courage ~ Tenant Andrew Brown ~ Real ale ~ Bar food (12-2, 6-9.30) ~ Restaurant ~ (01325) 312273 ~ Children welcome ~ Open 12-3, 5.30(6.30 Sat)-11; 12-3, 7-10.30 Sun

BELFORD NU1134 Map 10
Blue Bell
Market Place; village signed off A1 S of Berwick

There's a nice civilised welcome and attentive service at this substantial old coaching inn which makes a welcome refuge from the busy A1. The comfortable lounge bar has upholstered seats on the turkey carpet, coaching prints on the walls and a warming log fire, and the counter was taken from the Theatre Royal in Newcastle; piped music. A good variety of bar food includes sandwiches and soup, warm salad of goats cheese with tomato salsa and pine kernels (£3.95), dressed crab with spinach and mozzarella or garlic king prawns with lemon mayonnaise (£4.25), tomato, feta and basil omelette (£4.45), steak and kidney pie (£6.85), quorn and aubergine balti (£7.25), game pie (£7.55), baked Scottish salmon with black pepper and paprika or chicken tikka massala (£7.95) and puddings (£3.75); the restaurants are no smoking. There's an extensive wine list and well kept John Smiths and Theakstons on handpump, darts, pool, table skittles, hood skittles, cribbage, dominoes, juke box and fruit machine and a large garden. *(Recommended by Christine and Neil Townend, David Carr, KN-R, Frank Davidson, Michael Doswell, Chris Rounthwaite, Dr Paull Khan)*

Free house ~ Licensee Paul Shirley ~ Real ale ~ Bar food ~ Restaurant ~ (01668) 213543 ~ Children welcome ~ Live band or disco Fri, Sat night ~ Open 12-2, 6.30(7 Sun)-11 ~ Bedrooms: £44B/£84S(£92B)

BLANCHLAND NY9750 Map 10
Lord Crewe Arms

This lovely old stone village is separated from the rest of the world by several miles of moors, rabbits and sheep. Set in the heart of the village, this fine old inn was originally part of the 13th-c guest-house of a Premonstratensian monastery – the attractive walled garden (where you can eat) was formerly the cloisters – before it became home for several distinguished families after the dissolution in 1536. Its tremendous age is evident everywhere. The very atmospheric narrow bar is housed in an unusual stone barrel-vaulted crypt, its curving walls being up to eight feet thick in some places. Plush stools are lined up along the bar counter and next to a narrow counter down the opposite wall, and there are a couple of built in wood banquettes at one end. Whitbread Castle Eden on handpump; darts. Upstairs, the quietly welcoming Derwent Room has low beams, old settles, and sepia photographs on its walls, and the Hilyard Room has an massive 13th-c fireplace once used as a hiding place by the Jacobite Tom Forster (part of the family who had owned the building before it was sold to the formidable Lord Crewe, Bishop of Durham). Good bar food includes soup (£2), very good filled crispy rolls (from £3.25), ploughman's (£4.60), tagliatelle with creamy wild mushroom sauce and parmesan (£5.25), smoked salmon, prawns and tuna salad (£6), brie and broccoli pastry bake (£7.50), sirloin steak (£10.50), and puddings (£3.75). *(Recommended by Anthony Longden, Andy and Jill Kassube, Hazel and Michael Duncombe, Jenny and Dave Hughes, Eric Larkham, B, M and P Kendall, Mike and Lynn Robinson)*

Free house ~ Licensees A Todd, Peter Gingell and Ian Press, Lindsey Sands ~ Real ale ~ Bar food ~ Restaurant ~ (01434) 675251 ~ Children welcome ~ Open 11-11; 12-10.30 Sun ~ Bedrooms: £80B/£110B

CARTERWAY HEADS NZ0552 Map 10
Manor House Inn ♀ ◖

A68 just N of B6278, near Derwent Reservoir

The changing well balanced menu at this popular stone house has a gently contemporary feel. Home-made dishes are very well prepared and might include spinach and mushroom soup (£2.40), spicy mushrooms with rosemary and tomato (£3.25/£6.50), king prawns in lemon and dill butter (£4.95/£9.95), mediterranean vegetables with goats cheese en croûte (£7.50), chicken breast stuffed with crayfish and chives (£9.95), calves liver, black pudding, onions and rocket and garlic mash (£11.95), beef fillet with claret and juniper (£14.95), puddings such as honey and ginger sponge, raspberry and vanilla panna cotta or fig and almond cake with Baileys and butterscotch sauce (£3.25) and local cheese and biscuits (£3.95); part of the restaurant – which has a large collection of jugs – is no smoking. The locals' bar has an original wooden-boarded ceiling, pine tables, chairs and stools, old oak pews, and a mahogany counter. The comfortable lounge bar has a woodburning stove. Picture windows give fine southerly views over moorland pastures. Well kept Charles Wells Bombardier, Courage Directors, Theakstons Best, and a guest from a local brewer like Mordue or Northumberland on handpump, draught scrumpy, over 60 malt whiskies, and decent wines with about eight by the glass; darts, dominoes and piped music (only in the bar). There are rustic tables out on a small side terrace and lawn. Bedrooms are clean and comfortable and the breakfasts are good. *(Recommended by Chris Rounthwaite, Andy and Jill Kassube, J F M and M West, MLR, Jenny and Dave Hughes, Michael Doswell)*

Free house ~ Licensees Moira and Chris Brown ~ Real ale ~ Bar food (12-2.30, 7-9.30(9 Sun)) ~ Restaurant ~ (01207) 255268 ~ Well behaved children welcome ~ Open 11-3, 5.30-11; 11-11 Sat; 12-3, 6.30-10.30 Sun; closed 25 Dec evening ~ Bedrooms: £33B/£55B

CHATTON NU0628 Map 10
Percy Arms
B6348 E of Wooler

The attractively lit and neatly kept bar at this pleasant stone pub has horse bits and brasses on beams, maps and country pictures on the walls, green stripy upholstered wooden wall seats, and cushioned farmhouse chairs and stools. Through a stone arch is a similar room with a woodburning stove. They keep Theakstons on electric pump and the piped music is fairly unobtrusive. The public bar has darts, pool, dominoes, fruit machine, video game and juke box. The panelled dining room with its pretty plates on a delft shelf is most attractive. Under new licensees, bar food includes soup (£1.95), lunchtime baguettes (from £2.95, steak £5.95), soup or potato wedges (£2.95), prawn cocktail (£4.45), steak and kidney pie, battered haddock or mushroom and pepper stroganoff (£5.95), steamed chicken with lime and tarragon sauce (£7.75), grilled lamb cutlets (£8.95), fried duck breast with orange and Grand Marnier sauce (£9.95) and puddings such as chocolate and hazelnut roulade or sherry trifle (£2.50). There are picnic-sets on the small front lawn above the village road. Residents have the use of a sauna, sunbed, keep fit equipment and 12 miles of private fishing, where there may be salmon, sea trout or stocked rainbow trout. No dogs in public areas. *(Recommended by Jack and Heather Coyle, H H Liesner, Mr and Mrs M Cross, Chris Rounthwaite, Jonathan D Harrison, Joy and Peter Heatherley, Dr Paull Khan, Mrs J Booth, Darly Graton, Graeme Gulibert)*

Free house ~ Licensee Paul Trett ~ Real ale ~ Bar food (12-2.30, 6.30-9.30) ~ Restaurant ~ (01668) 215244 ~ Children welcome ~ Live music Fri evening, quiz night Thurs ~ Open 11-3, 6-11; 12-3, 6-10.30 Sun ~ Bedrooms: £25S/£50B

CRASTER NU2620 Map 10
Jolly Fisherman £
Off B1339, NE of Alnwick

This is quite a simple local but readers really enjoy its very friendly unpretentious atmosphere, and they particularly love the crabmeat, whisky and cream soup they are famous for (£2.75) and the highly praised well filled crab sandwiches (£2.50). Other simple bar snacks include burgers (from £1.60), sandwiches (from £1.75) and home-made Craster kipper pâté (£2.50). There are lovely views over the harbour and out to sea from the big picture windows or the little garden, and there's a nice mix of locals and visitors in the atmospheric bar. The snug by the entrance is popular with workers from the harbour or the kippering shed opposite. Well kept Tetleys and Theakstons on handpump, and a range of malt whiskies. Darts, pool, dominoes, cribbage, fruit machine and juke box. The pub can get crowded on sunny days, but unlike places in similar settings never begins to feel like a tourist attraction. There's a lovely clifftop walk to Dunstanburgh Castle. *(Recommended by Pat and Tony Martin, the Didler, Joy and Peter Heatherley, David Carr, Chris Rounthwaite, Mike and Lynn Robinson, Adam and Joan Bunting, Comus and Sarah Elliott, John Allen, Phil and Sally Gorton, Christine and Malcolm Ingram, Chloe and Robert Gartery, Mike and Wendy Proctor, Michael Doswell)*

Pubmaster ~ Lease W P Silk ~ Real ale ~ Bar food (12-8; 11-2.30, 6-8 winter) ~ Restaurant ~ No credit cards ~ (01665) 576218 ~ Children welcome ~ Open 11-11; 12-10.30 Sun; 11-3, 6-11(10.30 Sun) winter

DIPTONMILL NY9261 Map 10

Dipton Mill Inn 🍴 £

Dipton Mill Road; off B6306 S of Hexham at Slaley, Blanchland and Dye House, Whitley Chapel signposts and HGV route sign

The friendly landlord at this little two-roomed pub really knows his ales and is a brewer in the family-owned Hexhamshire Brewery, hence the good choice of their well kept beers: Hexhamshire Shire Bitter, Devil's Water, Devil's Elbow and Whapweasel; they also keep Tetleys Bitter, two dozen malt whiskies and Weston's Old Rosie cider. The pub is tucked away and not easy to find in a little hamlet by steep hills in a peaceful wooded valley – there are plenty of easy-walking footpaths nearby. You can take a seat on the sunken crazy-paved terrace by the restored mill stream, or in the attractively planted garden with its aviary. Inside, the snug little bar has a very relaxed and friendly atmosphere, dark ply panelling, red furnishings and open fires. Very reasonably priced generous helpings of food are freshly prepared by the landlady and include minestrone soup (£1.65), sandwiches (from £1.60), ploughman's from a very good choice of nine cheeses (£3.75) and salads (£4.50), with specials such as cheese and tomato flan, ratatouille and couscous (£4.50), mince and dumplings or haddock baked with tomato and basil or steak and kidney pie (£5.15) and puddings like syrup sponge and custard or apple crumble (£1.65). The back games room has darts, bar billiards, shove-ha'penny and dominoes. *(Recommended by John Foord, Mike and Lynn Robinson, J G Thorpe, Gill Waller, Tony Morriss, Ted Tomiak, Phil and Sally Gorton, Richard Lewis)*

Own brew ~ Licensee Geoff Brooker ~ Real ale ~ Bar food (12-2.30, 6.30-8.30) ~ (01434) 606577 ~ Children welcome ~ Open 12-2.30, 6-11; 12-4.30, 7-10.30 Sun; closed 25 Dec

DUNSTAN NU2520 Map 10

Cottage ♀

Village signposted off B1339 Alnmouth—Embleton

Set in a quiet village not far from the sea by an outstanding stretch of the Northumberland coast, this large dining pub looks as if it was once a low row of cottages. An extensive low-beamed carpeted bar area is quite handsomely laid out, with stools, small chairs and wall banquettes around dimpled copper tables, some panelling and stripped brickwork, soft lighting, and quite a bit of bric-a-brac including a fine model sailing ship on the mantelpiece of the substantial brick fireplace; piped music. Generous helpings of bar food might include soup (£2.25), cullen skink (£4.25), spinach and ricotta cannelloni (£7.65), game and port pie (£8.45), fisherman's platter (£9.50), steaks from (£11.50) and daily specials such as beef bourguignon (£5.95) and Mexican chicken (£6.50). Well kept Charles Wells Bombardier and Wylan Cottage on handpump, and a good choice of reasonably priced wines; neatly dressed helpful young staff. You can eat in the bar, or in a pleasant well planted no smoking back conservatory with café furnishings on its tiled floor; there's also a comfortable beamed medieval-theme restaurant. It can be very quiet midweek out of season. A games area has pool, darts, a fruit machine and TV. Outside, there are white plastic tables and chairs on a flowery terrace by the conservatory, with some tables in a sheltered arbour; these look out on quite a stretch of lawn. The modern bedrooms overlook the garden. *(Recommended by MLR, Jonathan D Harrison, Roy and Lindsey Fentiman, Mr and Mrs T Christian, M S Catling)*

Free house ~ Licensee Zoe Finlay ~ Real ale ~ Bar food (12-2.30, 7-9.30) ~ Restaurant ~ (01665) 576658 ~ Children welcome ~ Open 11-3, 6-12; 12-3, 7-11 Sun ~ Bedrooms: £35B/£63B

GREAT WHITTINGTON NZ0171 Map 10
Queens Head 🍴 ◀

Village signposted off A68 and B6018 just N of Corbridge

The two beamed rooms at this simple but civilised stone inn are comfortably furnished and neatly decorated with some handsome carved oak settles among other more modern furnishings, a mural above the fireplace near the bar counter, old prints and a collection of keys, and log fires. A fairly wide ranging menu served by courteous helpful staff includes lunchtime sandwiches (£3.50) and ploughman's (£4.50), as well as more elaborate dishes such as smoked chicken and hazelnut salad (£4.95), home-made seafood ravioli with cheese sauce or smoked salmon and tiger prawn mille feuille with lime and fennel salsa (£5.95), honey-roast gammon with dijon mustard mash and peppercorn sauce (£8.95), honey-fried chicken on noodles with ginger and lemon marmalade or cod fillet with spinach and herb crust (£10.95), roast duck breast on spiced cabbage with ginger and balsamic glaze (£12.95), two or three daily specials such as trout fillet with roasted fennel (£9.95) and puddings such as nougat ice cream on fruit coulis or chocolate mousse with coffee anglaise (£3.50); the restaurant is no smoking. Well kept Black Sheep Best, Hambleton Bitter and Queens Head Bitter (brewed for them by Hambleton) on handpump, 30 malt whiskies, and decent wines; maybe unobtrusive piped music. There are six picnic-sets on the small front lawn, and the surrounding partly wooded countryside is pretty. *(Recommended by Jenny and Dave Hughes, Mike and Lynn Robinson, Peter Mueller, Michael Doswell, Mr and Mrs R Peacock, GSB, Chris Rounthwaite, RJH)*

Free house ~ Licensee Ian Scott ~ Real ale ~ Bar food ~ Restaurant ~ (01434) 672267 ~ Children in eating area of bar and restaurant ~ Open 12-2.30, 6-11; 12-3, 7-10.30 Sun; closed Mon except bank holidays

GRETA BRIDGE NZ0813 Map 10
Morritt Arms ♀

Hotel signposted off A66 W of Scotch Corner

You'll want to visit this characterfully civilised country inn to see the rather jolly larger than life Dickensian mural which runs round the walls of the delightfully pubby bar. It was painted in 1946 by J V Gilroy who is more famous for his old Guinness advertisements, six of which are also displayed on the walls here. The bar is named after Charles Dickens, who stayed here in 1838 on his way to start his research for *Nicholas Nickleby*. There are also big windsor armchairs and sturdy plush-seated oak settles clustered around traditional cast-iron-framed tables, and big windows that look out on the extensive lawn. Flowers brighten up the rooms, and there are open fires; piped music. Well kept Black Sheep, Tetleys, Theakstons and Timothy Taylors Landlord on handpump, quite a few malt whiskies, a very extensive wine list with about two dozen by the glass; cheerful staff. There's a proper old shove-ha'penny board, with raisable brass rails to check the lie of the coins, pool, cribbage and dominoes. Freshly cooked enjoyable bar food includes filled baguettes (from £2.75), soup or chicken liver pâté (£3.25), sausages and mash or vegetable lasagne (£5.95), steak and kidney pie or braised lamb shank (£6.50) and scampi or ploughman's (£6.95). There's a slightly more elaborate menu in the adjacent no smoking bistro which has just been refurbished with wood floors and wrought iron, and hung with paintings and prints – by local artists – which you can buy. There are some picnic-sets in the attractively laid out and fairly large garden, teak tables in a pretty side area looking along to the graceful old bridge by the stately gates to Rokeby Park, and swings, slide and rope ladder at the far end. *(Recommended by R L Gorick, Dr Paull Khan, Brian and Janet Ainscough, Susan and John Douglas, Mr and Mrs J E C Tasker, Derek and Sylvia Stephenson, Mr and Mrs M Doherty)*

Free house ~ Licensees Peter Phillips and Barbara Johnson ~ Real ale ~ Bar food (12-3, 6-9) ~ Restaurant ~ (01833) 627232 ~ Children welcome ~ Open 11-11(10.30 Sun) ~ Bedrooms: £59.50B/£83.50B

HALTWHISTLE NY7166 Map 10

Milecastle Inn ◀

Military Rd; B6318 NE – OS Sheet 86 map reference 715660

There's a cosy welcome at this remotely set 17th-c pub which is very handy if you're visiting Hadrian's Wall – you will need to arrive early as it can get very busy. The snug little rooms of the beamed bar are decorated mainly with brasses, horsey and local landscape prints and attractive dried flowers, and two winter log fires; at lunchtime the small comfortable restaurant is used as an overflow. Bar food includes lunchtime sandwiches (from £2.50) and ploughman's (£4.75), soup (£2.25), smoked duck breast with apricot coulis (£4.50), chicken kiev (£6.95), steak and kidney pie (£6.25), seafood crêpes or game pie (£6.95) and daily specials such as sausage and cider casserole (£5.50) and wild boar and duckling pie (£7.25). Three well kept real ales might include Jennings Cockerhoop, Northumberland Castles Bitter and Tetleys on handpump, a fair collection of malt whiskies, and a good wine list. Walkers welcome (but no rucksacks allowed). No games or music. There are some tables and benches outside in a sheltered walled garden with a dovecote. *(Recommended by Michael Buchanan, B, M and P Kendall, Paul Thompson, Anna Blackburn, Jenny and Dave Hughes, Phil and Sally Gorton, Paul Fairbrother, Helen Morris, Mike and Wendy Proctor)*

Free house ~ Licensees Ralph and Margaret Payne ~ Real ale ~ Bar food (12-2, 6.30-9.30) ~ Restaurant ~ (01434) 321372/320682 ~ Children over 5 in eating area of bar and restaurant ~ Open 12-3, 6.30-11; closed Sun evening Nov-Mar

Wallace Arms

Rowfoot, Featherstone Park – OS Sheet 86 map reference 683607

The five interlinked rooms at this rambling former farmhouse have simple furnishings, unpretentious decorations and a good bustling atmosphere. The small beamed main bar has dark oak woodwork, some stripped stone, comfortable seats, and a good log fire; the side games room has another fire (also pool, shove-ha'penny, table skittles, dominoes, trivia and piped music). Good value bar food includes soup (£2.15), filled baguettes (from £3.25), ploughman's (£3.95), vegetable lasagne (£5), chicken kiev (£5.60) and steak and ale pie (£5.80). Two well kept ales from Big Lamp on handpump, and 36 malt whiskies. Picnic-table sets outside on both sides of the quiet lane have lovely fell views, and there's a play area and quoits at the back. A nice walk from the pub is the South Tyne Trail which runs along the former Alston railway line; access for disabled people is fairly easy. *(Recommended by Michael Buchanan, Ted Tomiak)*

Free house ~ Licensees Mr and Mrs Blackburn ~ Real ale ~ Bar food ~ No credit cards ~ (01434) 321872 ~ Children welcome ~ Open 12-3, 6-10.30; 12-11 Sat; 12-10.30 Sun; closed Tues

HEDLEY ON THE HILL NZ0859 Map 10

Feathers 🍴

Village signposted from New Ridley, which is signposted from B6309 N of Consett; OS Sheet 88 map reference 078592

The landlady's interest in vegetarian food is reflected in five or so tempting vegetarian dishes at this delightful old stone pub. The menu changes twice a week and given the standard of the imaginative cooking is very good value. There might be lettuce, mange tout and mint soup (£3.25), caesar salad (£3.95), goats cheese and red onion tart or spiced chick pea, sweet potato and vegetable tortilla (£6.25), salmon steak with lemon and parsley butter or pork casserole with apricots and spices (£6.50), lamb casserole with fresh pesto and tomatoes or sun-dried tomato, olive and roast pepper risotto (£7.50) and puddings such as pear and ginger pudding or whisky and honey ice cream (£3.25). There's still a good pubby atmosphere in the three well kept turkey-carpeted traditional bars, with beams, open fires, stripped stonework, solid brown leatherette settles and old black and white photographs of local places and country folk working the land. Well kept Boddingtons, Mordue

Workie Ticket and two guest beers from brewers such as Big Lamp and Black Sheep on handpump; they hold a mini beer festival around Easter with over two dozen real ales which ends with a barrel race on Easter Monday; decent wines, and around 30 malt whiskies. Darts, shove-ha'penny, table skittles, cribbage, and dominoes. From picnic-sets in front you can watch the world drift by. *(Recommended by John Foord, Mike and Lynn Robinson, Gwyneth and Salvo Spadaro-Dutturi, GSB, Michael Doswell, Ted Tomiak, Phil and Sally Gorton, Karen and Graham Oddey, RJH)*

Free house ~ Licensee Marina Atkinson ~ Real ale ~ Bar food (not lunchtimes or Mon except bank holidays) ~ No credit cards ~ (01661) 843607 ~ Children in eating area of bar and family room till 9pm ~ Open 6-11; 12-3, 6-11 Sat; 12-3, 7-11 Sun; closed wkday lunchtimes except bank holidays and 25 Dec

LANGLEY ON TYNE NY8160 Map 10
Carts Bog Inn
A686 S, junction B6305

The welcoming clean and tidy main black-beamed bar at this isolated moorside pub has a big log fire in the central stone fireplace, local photographs and horsebrasses, and windsor chairs and comfortably cushioned wall settles around the tables. It rambles about, with flagstones here, carpet there, mainly white walls with some stripped stone. A side lounge (once a cow byre) with more wall banquettes has pool, darts, dominoes and piped music; quoits pitch. Good freshly made food includes sandwiches (from £2.25), ploughman's or battered cod and a good choice of daily specials such as Caribbean fruit and vegetable curry, peppercorn pork, chicken breast in lemon and tarragon sauce, local lamb and apricot casserole or beef teriyaki (all £5.85); tasty puddings include chocolate fudge cake and apple crumble (£2.10). Well kept Theakstons Best, Yates and a guest such as Jennings on handpump, and around 30 malt whiskies; good friendly service. There are views over the silvery dry stone walls of high hilly sheep pastures from tables in the garden. *(Recommended by Richard Butler, Marie Kroon, Ted Tomiak, Peter and Anne-Marie O'Malley)*

Free house ~ Licensees Neil and Alison Wishart ~ Real ale ~ Bar food (12-2.30, 7-9.30) ~ No credit cards ~ (01434) 684338 ~ Children in restaurant and family room ~ Open 12-3, 7-11(10.30 Sun)

MATFEN NZ0372 Map 10
Black Bull
Village signposted off B6318 NE of Corbridge

A profusion of summer hanging baskets, shrubs and bedding plants gives a cheerful welcome at this striking creeper-covered long stone inn which is set by the green of an attractive out-of-the-way 18th-c estate village; there are plenty of seats on a terrace overlooking the green. There's a comfortable local dining-out atmosphere in the extended turkey-carpeted bar, which has windsor chairs around dark pub tables, lots of steeplechasing pictures and red plush banquettes. A side room has more plush banquettes, and attractive 1940s *Picture Post* photographs. Generous helpings of bar food from sandwiches or soup (£2.25) up are served with good fresh vegetables, and might include duck liver pâté with cumberland sauce (£3.95), fillet of haddock (£5), home-made steak, mushroom and ale pie (£5.50), large filled yorkshire pudding (£5.95), trout fillet with lemon butter (£6.50), sirloin steak (£11.92), and daily specials like hot beef sandwich (£3.75), thai chicken (£6.25), roast rack of lamb (£6.95), gammon steak (£5.95), guinea fowl with thyme gravy (£6.25); the comfortable restaurant is no smoking at lunchtime. Charles Wells Bombardier, Theakstons Black Bull and maybe a summer guest all kept under light blanket pressure; 20 malt whiskies, log fires; a separate games bar has juke box, TV, fruit machine, sensibly placed darts, pool and dominoes; no dogs. *(Recommended by John Foord, Jim and Maggie Cowell, Chris Rounthwaite, Dr Paull Khan)*

Free house ~ Licensees Colin and Michele Scott ~ Real ale ~ Bar food ~ Restaurant ~ (01661) 886330 ~ Children in games room and restaurant ~ Open 11-3, 6-11; 11-11 Sat; 11-10.30 Sun ~ Bedrooms: £35B/£65B

NEW YORK NZ3370 Map 10
Shiremoor Farm ★

Middle Engine Lane/Norham Road; from A19 going N from Tyne Tunnel, right into A1058 then next left signposted New York, then left at end of speed limit (pub signed); or at W end of New York A191 bypass turn S into Norham Road, then first right (pub signed)

This smartly relaxed and enjoyable pub is an award winning conversion of a group of derelict farm buildings. Its spacious interior is furnished with a charming mix of interesting and extremely comfortable furniture, a big kelim on the broad flagstones, warmly colourful farmhouse paintwork on the bar counter and several other tables, conical rafters of the former gin-gan, a few farm tools, and good rustic pictures such as mid-West prints, big crisp black and white photographs of country people and modern Greek bull sketches. Gentle lighting in several well divided spacious areas cleverly picks up the surface modelling of the pale stone and beam ends. There's a very busy chatty atmosphere, and a good mix of customers. Bar food includes sandwiches (£1.65), pork balti (£4.95), scampi or ricotta and spinach cannelloni with tomato sauce and mozzarella (£5.45), roast salmon fillet on creamed ginger leeks (£5.95), fried chicken breast coated with stilton, garlic and prawn sauce (£7.95), medallions of beef fillet with pepper sauce (£9.95), and puddings like pecan pie or sticky toffee pudding (£2.75). Well kept Theakstons Best, Timothy Taylors Landlord, Mordue Workie Ticket and a guest such as Batemans XXXB and decent wines by the glass. The no smoking granary extension is good for families. There are picnic-sets on neat grass at the edge of the flagstoned farm courtyard, by tubs and a manger filled with flowers. *(Recommended by Chris Rounthwaite, David Carr, Mike and Lynn Robinson)*

Free house ~ Licensees C Hornsby and C W Kerridge ~ Real ale ~ Bar food (12-10) ~ Restaurant ~ (0191) 257 6302 ~ Children welcome ~ Open 11-11; 12-10.30 Sun

NEWCASTLE UPON TYNE NZ2563 Map 10
Crown Posada 🍺

31 The Side; off Dean Street, between and below the two high central bridges (A6125 and A6127)

Perhaps one of the most architecturally interesting pubs in Newcastle, this marvellously unspoilt old pub is the second oldest in the city, and was once the haunt of ships' masters and chief engineers. A golden crown adds grandeur to an already imposing carved stone façade – as do the magnificent pre-Raphaelite stained-glass windows. Inside there's a lot of architectural charm such as an elaborate coffered ceiling, stained glass in the counter screens, a line of gilt mirrors each with a tulip lamp on a curly brass mount (matching the great ceiling candelabra) and Victorian flowered wallpaper above the brown dado; below this are fat heating pipes – a popular footrest when the east wind brings the rain off the North Sea. It's a very long and narrow room making quite a bottleneck by the serving counter, and beyond that, a long soft green built-in leather wall seat is flanked by narrow tables. Half a dozen well kept real ales from brewers such as Bass, Jennings and Mordue on handpump; lunchtime sandwiches with a packet of crisps (£1). Friendly barmen, chatty customers; fruit machine and an old record player that provides background music when the place is quiet. Best to visit during the week when regulars sit reading the papers in the front snug; at the weekend it's usually packed. No children. A few minutes' stroll to the castle. *(Recommended by Richard Lewis, Giles Francis, David Carr, John Allen, Mike and Lynn Robinson, the Didler, Eric Larkham, John A Barker, Edward Watson)*

Free house ~ Licensee Malcolm MacPherson ~ Real ale ~ No credit cards ~ (0191) 232 1269 ~ Open 11(12 Sat)-11; 7-10.30 Sun; closed Sun lunchtime

---

Ideas for a country day out? We list pubs in really attractive scenery at the back of the book – and there are separate lists for waterside pubs, ones with really good gardens, and ones with lovely views.

NEWTON-ON-THE-MOOR NU1605 Map 10
Cook & Barker Arms 🛏

Village signposted from A1 Alnwick—Felton

Although the food at this busy stone inn is very popular there's still a good pubby atmosphere in the relaxing and unfussy long beamed bar which has stripped, partly panelled walls, brocade-seated settles around oak-topped tables, framed banknotes and paintings by local artists on the walls, brasses, a highly polished oak servery, and a coal fire at one end with a coal-effect gas fire at the other; another room has tables, chairs, an old settle, and darts (popular with locals), and the games room has scrubbed pine furniture and french windows leading on to the terrace; the top bar area is no smoking. Well kept rotating ales on handpump include Black Sheep and Timothy Taylors Landlord and a couple of guests such as Charles Wells Eagle and Badger Best, quite a few malt whiskies, an extensive wine list, and over 20 wines by the glass. Imaginative changing bar food might include pea and mint soup (£2.25), tomato, avocado and mozzarella with olives and basil (£4.25), seafood tapas (£6.80), thai fishcake with roasted green vegetables (£6.95), braised lamb shank with sage mash and puy lentils or duck and orange sausages with a shallot marmalade (£7.25), king scallops and ragoût of courgettes and garlic with gruyère (£7.95), roast loin of pork with greens, black pudding and rosemary mash (£8.95) and puddings (£3.75). *(Recommended by Adam and Joan Bunting, Joy and Peter Heatherley, Jenny and Dave Hughes, Mike and Wendy Proctor, Karen and Graham Oddey, Katherine Ward, Jack and Heather Coyle, Mike and Lynn Robinson, Stephen and Jean Curtis, Jim Bush)*

Free house ~ Licensee Phil Farmer ~ Real ale ~ Bar food (12-2, 6-9) ~ Restaurant ~ (01665) 575234 ~ Children welcome ~ Open 11-3, 6-11; 12-3, 6-10.30 Sun ~ Bedrooms: £37.50B/£70B

RENNINGTON NU2119 Map 10
Masons Arms 🛏

Stamford Cott; B1340 NE of Alnwick

There's a relaxed atmosphere in the comfortably modernised beamed lounge bar at this very well run village pub. There are wheelback and mate's chairs around solid wooden tables on the patterned carpet, plush bar stools, lots of brass, pictures and photographs on the walls. The dining rooms (one is no smoking) have pine panelling and wrought-iron wall lights. Quickly served good value food includes lunchtime sandwiches, home-made soup (£2.15), home-made Craster kipper pâté (£4.25), fried haddock (£5.75), pork and chive sausage (£5.75), steaks (from £12.45) and daily specials such as lamb and rosemary casserole (£6.75) and salmon thermidor or venison and beef casserole (£6.95); Sunday lunch is popular. Courage Directors and McEwans 80/- on handpump; shove-ha'penny, dominoes, darts and piped music. There are sturdy rustic tables on the little front terrace, surrounded by lavender. The comfortable, spotlessly clean bedrooms in the adjacent stable block are just the place from which to explore the nearby Northumbrian coast. Please note, children are not allowed to stay overnight. *(Recommended by Michael Wadsworth, Graham and Ann Smith, Joy and Peter Heatherley, Frank Davidson, Chris Rounthwaite, D S Jackson, Mr and Mrs R Head, Comus and Sarah Elliott, David Cooke)*

Free house ~ Licensees Frank and Dee Sloan ~ Real ale ~ Bar food ~ Restaurant ~ (01665) 577275 ~ Children in family room and restaurant ~ Open 12-2, 6.30-11; 12-2.30, 6.30-10.30 Sun ~ Bedrooms: £27.50B/£55B

ROMALDKIRK NY9922 Map 10
Rose & Crown ★ 🍽 ♀ 🛏

Just off B6277

Still on tremendously good form, this immaculately kept 18th-c coaching inn goes from strength to strength year after year, with continual care and attention given to the details that mark this place out from other pubs. The cosy beamed traditional bar has old-fashioned seats facing the warming log fire, a Jacobean oak settle, lots of brass and copper, a grandfather clock, and gin-traps, old farm tools, and black and white pictures of Romaldkirk on the walls. The smart Crown Room, where bar food is served, has more brass and copper, original etchings of game shooting scenes and farm implements. The hall is hung with wine maps and other interesting prints and a photograph of the Hale Bopp comet over Romaldkirk church that was taken by a guest; no smoking oak-panelled restaurant. As well as making their own marmalades, jams, chutneys and bread, they also change the very imaginative bar menu weekly. It is very popular so you will need to book. In addition to lunchtime baps (from £3.35) and ploughman's (£5.50), excellent food might include home-made soup (£2.95), baked cheddar soufflé with green herb sauce (£4.50), fried black pudding with leek and bacon risotto and balsamic jus (£4.95), sautéed chicken livers with roasted pepper brioche and salad (£7.95), confit of duck leg with spiced red cabbage and red wine jus (£9.50), baked smoked haddock with wilted spinach, poached egg and hollandaise (£10.50), steak, kidney and mushroom pie (£8.50), fried pigeon with root rösti, onion confit and juniper berry sauce (£10.95) and puddings such as sticky toffee pudding or walnut and syrup tart (£3.25). Well kept Black Sheep and Theakstons Best on handpump; good, friendly service. Tables outside look out over the village green, still with its original stocks and water pump. The village is close to the superb Bowes Museum and the High Force waterfall, and has an interesting old church. The recently decorated charming bedrooms have fresh flowers, hair dryers, and trouser presses – and on the top floor are three rooms (two are suites and one has a sitting area) with hi-fi systems. *(Recommended by Peter and Wynne Davies, Susan and John Douglas, H H Liesner, Kevin Thorpe, J C Burley, Jenny and Dave Hughes, Ian and Jacqui Ross, David Kidd, Sue and Geoff Price, Robert Barnes, John Shields, Chloe and Robert Gartery, Stephen P Edwards, David and Heather Stephenson, R L Gorick, Geoff and Tricia Alderman; also in* The Good Hotel Guide*)*

Free house ~ Licensees Christopher and Alison Davy ~ Real ale ~ Bar food (12-1.30, 6.30-9.30) ~ Restaurant ~ (01833) 650213 ~ Children welcome, must be over 6 in restaurant ~ Open 11-3, 5.30-11; 12-3, 7-10.30 Sun; closed 24-26 Dec ~ Bedrooms: £62B/£86B

SEAHOUSES NU2232 Map 10
Olde Ship ★ 🍴 🛏

Just off B1340, towards harbour

A recent very interesting addition to the treasure-trove of genuine seafaring memorabilia at this nice stone harbour hotel is the nameboard from the paddle steamer *Forfarshire*, which was the ship that Grace Darling went to rescue in 1838. There's also a model of the *Forfarshire*, and the story of the rescue. In fact the entire characterful bar is a tribute to the sea and seafarers – even the floor is scrubbed ship's decking. There are lots of shiny brass fittings, sea pictures and model ships (including a fine one of the North Sunderland lifeboat and a model of Seahouses' lifeboat *The Grace Darling*), as well as ship's instruments and equipment, and a knotted anchor made by local fishermen. It's gently lit by stained-glass sea picture windows and an open fire in winter. One clear window looks out across the harbour to the Farne Islands, and as dusk falls you can watch the Longstones lighthouse shine across the fading evening sky; the low-beamed Cabin room is no smoking. A short but balanced changing bar menu might include minestrone soup (£2.60), roast lamb, liver and onion casserole or fish stew (£6.50), and puddings such as chocolate trifle or banoffi pie (£3.15). A good choice of real ales takes in Bass, Ruddles Best and Theakstons Best, Greene King Old Speckled Hen and possibly a couple of guests such as Black Sheep or Courage Directors on handpump, and over two dozen malt whiskies; dominoes and piped music. There are pews surrounding barrel tables in the back courtyard, and a battlemented side terrace with a sun lounge looks out on the harbour; putting and quoits. An anemometer is connected to the top of the chimney. You can book boat trips to the Farne Islands Bird Sanctuary at the harbour, and there are bracing coastal walks, particularly to Bamburgh, Grace Darling's birthplace. The pub is not really suitable for children. *(Recommended by Comus and Sarah Elliott, Barbara Wilder, Andy Meaton, the Didier, Roger Purkiss, Sarah Lynch, Gill Waller, Tony Morriss, Peter and Hazel Fawthrop, Mr and Mrs Maurice Thompson, J V Dadswell,*

Mike and Lynn Robinson, Roger Everett, S Watkin, P Taylor, David Carr, KN-R, Pat and Tony Hinkins)

Free house ~ Licensees Alan and Jean Glen ~ Real ale ~ Bar food ~ Restaurant ~ (01665) 720200 ~ Children in family room till 9.30 ~ Open 11-11; 12-10.30 Sun ~ Bedrooms: £39S/£78B

SHINCLIFFE NZ2941 Map 10

Seven Stars 🍽 ⇐

High Street North; A177 a mile or so S of Durham

The relaxed and comfortably welcoming interior of this early 18th-c village inn is quite civilised but still largely unspoilt, so although the food here is very good there's still a nice local atmosphere. The lounge bar has a coal fire in its handsome Victorian fireplace, with a pair of big Staffordshire dogs on the mantelpiece below a big mirror, old brewery advertisements, copper kettles hanging from the beams, and cushioned wall banquettes and stools around cast-iron-framed tables. Very enjoyable imaginative bar food from a changing menu might include home-made soup (£3.50), salad of calamari and monkfish or New Zealand mussels marinated in oriental spices with tempura batter (£5.50), wild mushroom, spinach and ricotta pancake (£9.50), fried salmon escalope on spring onion, lemon and crab risotto (£10.50), chicken breast stuffed with toulouse sausage and black pudding (£11.50). Well kept Marstons Pedigree and a couple of guests such as Charles Wells Bombardier and Courage Directors on handpump, 25 malt whiskies, friendly staff; chess, draughts, dominoes and piped music. The candlelit dining room and half the lounge are no smoking. Parking can be a problem but it's just 10 minutes' or so drive from central Durham, with fairly frequent buses passing the door. Pretty window boxes, creepers, and seats out at the end of the attractive village street. *(Recommended by R M Corlett, Jenny and Dave Hughes, Mike Ridgway, Sarah Miles, Peter Burton, Michael Doswell, B and J Shurmer, Ted Tomiak)*

Free house ~ Licensees Nigel and Deborah Gadd ~ Real ale ~ Bar food (12-2.30, 6-9.30) ~ Restaurant ~ (0191) 384 8454 ~ Children in eating area of bar and restaurant ~ Open 12-11 ~ Bedrooms: £40S/£50S

STANNERSBURN NY7286 Map 10

Pheasant ⇐

Kielder Water road signposted off B6320 in Bellingham

Kielder Water is just up the road from this very nice old village pub; the traditionally comfortable lounge is partly stripped stone and partly panelled. The separate public bar is similar but simpler and opens into a games room with darts, pool, and dominoes; piped music. There's a good mix of visitors and locals in the evening when the small no smoking dining room can get crowded. The landlord here is particularly friendly and helpful. Enjoyable bar food includes game and mushroom pie (£6.95), garlic chicken breast salad (£7.95), roast lamb with redcurrant jus (£8.50), seafood pasta (£8.95), fillet steak with peppercorn and cream sauce (£13.50) and a couple of daily specials such as seafood pasta or game and mushroom pie (£8.95). Well kept Black Sheep, Greene King Old Speckled Hen, Theakstons and Timothy Taylors Landlord on handpump, around 34 malt whiskies and quite a nice reasonably priced wine list. It's in a peaceful valley with picnic-sets in the streamside garden, a pony paddock behind, and quiet forests all around. *(Recommended by Jonathan and Carolyn Lane, Comus and Sarah Elliott)*

Free house ~ Licensees Walter and Irene Kershaw ~ Real ale ~ Bar food ~ Restaurant ~ (01434) 240382 ~ Children welcome till 9.30 ~ Open 11-3, 6-11; 12-3, 7-10.30 Sun; closed Mon and Tues Jan-Feb ~ Bedrooms: £40B/£60B

Most pubs in this book sell wine by the glass. We mention wines if they are a cut above the average. Please let us know of any good pubs for wine.

THROPTON NU0302 Map 10
Three Wheat Heads 🏠
B6341

This stonebuilt 17th-c village hotel is set in the heart of Coquetdale. The carpeted bar on the right and the pleasant and roomy dining area have good fires (there's a fine tall stone fireplace), wheelback chairs around neat rows of dark tables, more heavily cushioned brocaded seats, comfortable bar stools with backrests, and an elaborate longcase clock; darts and dominoes. Bar food might include soup (£2.50), garlic mushrooms (£3.95), fresh battered cod (£5.25), steak and mushroom pie (£6.85), grilled tuna with lemon and dill butter (£7.95), fried lambs kidneys with dijon and stilton sauce (£8.95), sirloin steak (£10.50) and puddings (£2.50); the café style restaurant is no smoking. Well kept John Smiths and Marstons Pedigree on handpump; piped music. There are lovely views towards Simonside Hills from the attractive garden, which has a play area and dovecote. *(Recommended by Ted Tomiak, David and Heather Stephenson, Pat and Tony Martin, KN-R, John Foord, R Richards)*

Pubmaster ~ Lease Danny Scullion ~ Real ale ~ Bar food ~ Restaurant ~ (01669) 620262 ~ Children welcome ~ Open 11-3, 6-11; 11-11 Sat; 11-10.30 Sun ~ Bedrooms: £39B/£59B

WARENFORD NU1429 Map 10
Warenford Lodge
Off A1 3 or 4 miles S of Belford

You'll need to keep your eyes open to find this slightly quirky stone house as it has no pub sign outside, and do check their limited opening times before you set out. It's well worth the trip though for the attractively presented home-made food which might include soup with Turkestan bread (£2.80), kipper pâté (£3.50), wild mushroom risotto (£4.25), cannelloni (£6.20), battered cod (£6.50), poached salmon fillet with lime butter (£6.90), fish soup (£8.50), lamb shank with fruit jelly on celeriac, garlic and rosemary mash (£9.90) and a couple of daily specials such as lamb kofta curry (£7.20) and sea trout stuffed with crabmeat (£7.90). A decent selection of wines and malt whiskies, and a good choice of teas. Quite simple sixties décor makes the bar look quite modern but it's actually fairly old, with cushioned wooden seats around pine tables, some stripped stone walls, and a warm fire in the big stone fireplace; steps lead up to an extension which now has comfortable dining tables and chairs, and a big woodburning stove. *(Recommended by H H Liesner)*

Free house ~ Licensee Raymond Matthewman ~ Bar food (12-1.30(not wkdays), 7-9.30) ~ Restaurant ~ (01668) 213453 ~ Children in eating area of bar and restaurant ~ Open 7-11; 12-2, 7-11 Sat and Sun; closed Mon(Mon-Weds in winter) and wkday lunchtimes

Lucky Dip
Besides the fully inspected pubs, you might like to try these Lucky Dips recommended to us and described by readers (if you do, please send us reports: www.goodguides.com).

Acomb [NY9366]
Miners Arms [Main St]: Charming small 18th-c pub, up to seven real ales, good coffee, comfortable settles, huge fire in stone fireplace, advertising mirrors, brass plates, children in dining room; garden behind, may be cl winter lunchtimes, open all day Sun and summer *(Mike and Lynn Robinson)*
Alnmouth [NU2511]
☆ *Saddle* [Northumberland St (B1338)]: Unpretentious stone-built hotel rambling through several areas inc spacious dining area, wide choice of generous pubby food, well kept

real ales such as Greene King Old Speckled Hen and Theakstons Best, games room with ping pong as well as pool etc, no smoking restaurant; unobtrusive piped music; children welcome, open all day Sat, tables outside, comfortable bedrooms, attractive beaches, good coastal walks *(Jack and Heather Coyle, LYM)*
Aycliffe [NZ3024]
Blacksmiths Arms [Preston-le-Skerne; off A167 on Aycliffe—Gt Stainton rd]: Spotless two-bar country pub with well kept changing beers from small breweries far and wide, low prices Sun evening, may be free beer and wine tasting

Fri, simple lunchtime food from sandwiches up, eclectic evening dishes using local meat and organic veg, good Sun lunch; peacocks, ducks and guinea fowl in neat back garden *(Michael Doswell)*

Bamburgh [NU1835]

Lord Crewe Arms [Front St]: Small hotel prettily set in charming coastal village dominated by Norman castle; back hotel bar with log fire, more modern side bar with hunting murals (children and dogs allowed here), Bass and Stones under light blanket pressure, decent basic food inc lunchtime sandwiches and much fried food, no smoking restaurant (not always open); short walk from splendid sandy beach, bedrooms comfortable if creaky, good breakfast esp kippers (may be piped pop music); winter opening may be restricted *(LYM, Barbara Wilder, Andy Meaton, Jonathan and Carolyn Lane, Carol and Dono Leaman, Mike and Lynn Robinson, David Carr, Robin and Glenna Etheridge)*

Victoria [Front St]: Pleasantly refurbished, good bar food, interesting brasserie, well kept beer, caring young staff; comfortable bedrooms, lovely setting *(Comus and Sarah Elliott)*

Barnard Castle [NZ0516]

Old Well [The Bank]: Emphasis on pleasant no smoking dining area (well behaved children allowed here), big helpings of good food cooked by daughter from sandwiches and baked potatoes through good fish and chips to gourmet evenings, welcoming helpful staff, well kept Courage and Tetleys, decent wines; terrace over town walls, comfortable bedrooms *(David and Kay Ross)*

Beamish [NZ2254]

☆ *Shepherd & Shepherdess*: Very useful for its position nr outstanding open-air heritage museum, and very popular for good range of quick fairly priced straightforward food, standard layout with tables around walls, but comfortable, with good service, well kept Stones and Worthingtons, decent wines, coal fires; can get crowded, piped music; children welcome, tables and play area with glass-fibre monsters out among trees; has been open all day *(LYM, David Carr, Mike and Lynn Robinson)*

Belsay [NZ1079]

☆ *Highlander* [A696]: Well run dining pub with good range of food in extensively refurbished side bar and open-plan dining area, nice plain wood tables, reasonable prices, good welcoming service, well kept Scottish Courage ales, good log fires, unobtrusive piped music, separate locals' bar; open all day *(John Oddey, Joy and Peter Heatherley)*

Berwick-upon-Tweed [NT9953]

☆ *Barrels* [Bridge St]: Convivial pub, homely feel despite bistro style, with thorough-going nautical décor, car memorabilia and interesting pine furniture inc old school desks in lounge, attractive prices, well kept Boddingtons, Marstons Pedigree and guests such as Hambleton Stud and Hanby Premium and Rainbow Chaser, imaginative food inc tapas, munchies, snacks and main dishes, friendly accommodating staff; may be piped heavy R&B or good juke box, live music eg August bank hol blues festival; open all day *(Gill Waller, Tony Morriss, Comus and Sarah Elliott, P Abbott, Steve Williams)*

☆ *Cantys Brig* [B6461 towards Paxton]: Rather modern attractive bar with eating area and yachting décor, friendly landlord, wife cooks good reasonably priced enterprising fresh food inc local fish and haggis, efficient service, McEwans and Theakstons real ales, open fire, interesting modern pictures in smart dining room up spiral stairs, overlooking River Whiteadder; tables out on lawn running down to it; may be cl some evenings *(C J Cox, A Monro, P Abbott)*

☆ *Foxtons* [Hide Hill]: Cheerful welcoming two-floor bar with slightly frenchified bistro atmosphere, wide choice of good imaginative food, well kept changing ales such as Caledonian 80/- and Timothy Taylors Landlord (happy hour 5.30-6.30), good range of wines and whiskies, friendly service; side restaurant; busy, so worth booking evenings *(C J Cox, A Monro, Darly Graton, Graeme Gulibert)*

☆ *Rob Roy* [Dock View Rd/Dock Rd, Spittal (Tweedmouth)]: Quiet and cosy seaview restaurant pub with good fresh local fish and outstanding speciality fish soup, dark fishing-theme rustic bar with roaring fire and polished wood floor, pleasant dining room, friendly landlord; keg beers but decent wines and good fresh coffee; bedrooms *(Paul S McPherson, P Abbott)*

Birtley [NZ2756]

Millhouse [Blackfell; handy for A1 southbound, just S of Angel, off A1231 Sunderland/Washington slip rd]: Extended pub with olde-barn décor, alcoved eating areas, Theakstons Best and XB, no smoking restaurant (food all day inc lunch and early-supper bargains) *(Jenny and Dave Hughes)*

Moulders Arms [Peareth Terr]: Busy pleasantly refurbished local by church in old part of village, substantial reasonably priced straightforward food (till 10 evenings) inc children's, well kept changing ales such as Camerons, quick service; garden *(Jenny and Dave Hughes)*

Boulmer [NU2614]

Fishing Boat: Straightforward pub, clean, friendly and spacious, with low-priced Belhaven beers, food inc good crab sandwiches; some tables outside, those at the back overlooking the sea – nice spot *(David Cooke)*

Byrness [NT7702]

Byrness Hotel [A68 Otterburn—Jedburgh]: Pleasant border hotel by the last stage of the Pennine Way; Theakstons ales, good food and decent service; camping free if you don't use the shower *(Steve Jennings)*

Carlbury [NZ2115]

Carlbury Arms [just off A67 just E of Piercebridge]: Busy dining pub locally popular for good choice of reasonably priced food (may take a while), well kept John Smiths Magnet or Theakstons *(Francis Johnston)*

Consett [NZ1151]

Grey Horse [Sherburn Terr]: Brews its own

Derwent Rose beers in former back stables, often named in connection with the steel works here which closed in 1980, such as Red Dust, Steel Town and The Works, also one named for Paddy the pub dog; lots of malt whiskies, very friendly licensees, good range of customers, occasional beer festivals, open all day *(Eric Larkham)*

Corbridge [NY9964]

☆ *Angel* [Newcastle Rd]: Small 17th-c hotel with attentive happy staff, good value bar food and a well kept real ale in well worn in plush and panelled lounge and locals' back bar, fresh imaginative food in restaurant; bedrooms *(John Foord, LYM, Chris Rounthwaite, Graham and Lynn Mason)*

☆ *Black Bull* [Middle St]: Roomy unpretentious pub, old-fashioned and low-ceilinged, with good value generous food, well kept Whitbreads-related and guest ales, reasonably priced wines, large no smoking restaurant; stone-floored bar with traditional settles, mix of comfortable chairs, roaring fire, friendly attentive staff, good atmosphere even on crowded Fri/Sat night; open all day *(John Foord, Mike and Lynn Robinson)*

Dyvels [Station Rd]: Unassuming, informal and relaxing, with particularly well kept Bass, Black Sheep and a guest beer, reasonably priced food, friendly landlord and attentive staff; tables in pleasant area outside, open all day Sat and summer Sun, cl winter wkdy lunchtimes, decent bedrooms *(John Foord)*

☆ *Robin Hood* [East Wallhouses, Military Rd (B6318 5 miles NE)]: Unpretentious pub popular for generous wholesome food inc good steak baguettes (choice widest in good-sized candlelit back restaurant); beamed lounge with blazing fires, lots of bric-a-brac and interesting carved settles, great views from bay window, quick friendly service even when busy, daily papers; Greene King Old Speckled Hen, Marstons Pedigree and Tetleys, piped music *(Paul Fairbrother, Helen Morris, Chris Rounthwaite, Michael Doswell)*

☆ *Wheatsheaf* [Watling St/St Helens St]: Newly refurbished, with new chef doing wide choice of good food inc seasonal game in pleasantly decorated dining lounge and big conservatory restaurant, well kept Theakstons and guest beers, good choice of wines and malt whiskies, good service; pub games, piped music, some picnic-sets outside; bedrooms *(Jim and Maggie Cowell, Jack and Heather Coyle, LYM)*

Cotherstone [NZ0119]

☆ *Fox & Hounds* [B6277]: Simple 200-year-old country inn, relaxed and comfortable beamed bar with log fire, various alcoves and recesses, local photographs and country pictures, two restaurant rooms, one no smoking; popular home-made food, Black Sheep Best and Yorkshire Square; bedrooms, children welcome, pretty spot overlooking village green, good nearby walks *(Comus and Sarah Elliott, Sue and Geoff Price, Kevin Thorpe, LYM, Jenny and Dave Hughes, Mike and Lynn Robinson, Paul and Ursula Randall)*

Crawcrook [NZ1363]

Rising Sun [Bank Top]: Recently well refurbished, with cheerful staff, well kept ales Boddingtons, Castle Eden, Mordue Workie Ticket and two or three guest beers from long bar, huge choice of popular food in dining area with conservatory, steps up to lounge, separate pool room; neatly kept garden, open all day *(John Foord)*

Crookham [NT9138]

Blue Bell [Pallinsburn; A697 Wooler—Cornhill]: Small bar and smart comfortably carpeted L-shaped dining area with enjoyable home-made food from good crab and other sandwiches to lots of fish and huge steaks, friendly atmosphere, efficient service, well kept McEwans 80/- *(John Allen, Brian and Lynn Young, Michael Doswell, Christopher Beadle, C A Hall)*

Darlington [NZ2915]

☆ *No 22* [Coniscliffe Rd]: Its own well kept Village ales (brewed by Hambleton) and several recherché guest beers, enthusiastic landlord, wide range of good lunchtime food, good service, friendly atmosphere, unusual vaulted wood ceiling; open all day, cl Sun *(C A Hall, Richard Lewis, A York)*

Old Yard Tapas Bar [Bondgate]: Despite name, has well kept John Smiths Magnet and Theakstons Cool Cask and Old Peculier in front bar; friendly staff, mediterranean-style food in dining areas; open all day (Sun afternoon closure) *(Richard Lewis)*

Quaker Coffee House [Mechanics Yard, High Row (narrow passage by Binns)]: Small and narrow, with cellar-bar feel from dim lighting and bare bricks, well kept unusual beers such as Castle Eden Nimmos XXXX, Hambleton Nightmare and Village White Boar, Ridleys Five Rings and Springhead Roundhead Gold, friendly staff, daily papers and magazines, upstairs daytime restaurant with good choice of food and wines; open all day (not Sun lunchtime) *(Richard Lewis)*

Tanners Hall: Large open-plan Wetherspoons with nice furnishings, old local prints, well kept beers inc interesting guests, good wine choice, good menu inc bargain specials, friendly staff; tables outside, open all day *(Richard Lewis)*

Tap & Spile [Bondgate]: Leased by Castle Eden, with their beer and others such as Gales HSB, Theakstons Black Bull and Woods Wonderful, Weston's Old Rosie cider, lunchtime food, bare boards and brickwork, friendly staff and locals, darts, games machines, folk and quiz nights; open all day *(Richard Lewis)*

Durham [NZ2742]

Court Inn [Court Lane]: Good generous food all day (not Sun) inc late-evening bargains, well kept ales such as Bass, Ruddles County and Youngs Special, interesting wine offer, big L-shaped room bustling in term-time with students and teachers, helpful outside price list; seats outside *(C A Hall, John Fazakerley)*

Duke of Wellington [A167 S of Nevilles Cross]: Busy but spacious Victorian-style local with easily guessable nickname, useful for wide

range of hearty good value generous food inc
Sun lunch, plentiful veg, well kept Bass,
Worthington and a guest beer, efficient friendly
service, pleasant separate restaurant; children
welcome *(John Watson, M Borthwick)*

☆ *Victoria* [Hallgarth St (A177 nr Dunelm
House)]: Down-to-earth cosy unpretentious
local, three small and attractive panelled rooms
packed with Victoriana, well kept Hodges
Original, Marstons Pedigree, McEwans 80/-
and a guest beer, lots of malt whiskies,
welcoming landlord and staff, wonderful crisps,
no juke box or TV, coal fires in bar and back
room; good value bedrooms *(the Didler, MP,
Mr and Mrs Maurice Thompson)*

Ebchester [NZ1055]

☆ *Derwent Walk* [Ebchester Hill (B6309
outside)]: Friendly pub by the Gateshead—
Consett walk for which it's named, walkers
welcome, fine views, wide choice of good
generous home-made food with plenty of fresh
veg, full Jennings range kept well and a guest
such as Adnams, good wine range, good log fire
(James Brown, John Allen)

Eggleston [NY9924]

☆ *Three Tuns* [Church Bank]: Attractive
welcoming local by broad sloping Teesdale
village green, log fire and some interesting
furniture in relaxing traditional bar, boms mots
on beams, generous straightforward food (not
Sun evening) in big-windowed back room, Castle
Eden and an occasional guest beer, helpful
service; children welcome, tables on terrace and
in garden *(LYM, Sue and Geoff Price)*

Eglingham [NU1019]

☆ *Tankerville Arms* [B6346 Alnwick—Wooler]:
Pleasant long stone village pub with enjoyable
food using local ingredients from sandwiches to
interesting main dishes and Sun roasts, friendly
obliging service, well kept Black Sheep, Greene
King Ruddles and Mordue Workie Ticket,
decent choice of wines, malt whiskies and of
teas and coffees, black joists, some stripped
stone, plush banquettes, captain's chairs and
turkey carpet, coal fires each end, snug no
smoking lounge; dominoes, piped music;
children welcome, garden tables *(C A Hall,
Michael Doswell, A D McLaren, Joy and Peter
Heatherley, Jack and Heather Coyle, Carol and
Dono Leaman, Chris Rounthwaite, LYM,
Darly Graton, Graeme Gulibert)*

Embleton [NU2323]

☆ *Dunstanburgh Castle*: Enjoyable dining room
meals at bar prices inc game and fresh fish in
comfortable hotel attractively placed nr
magnificent coastline, nice bright bar with
young enthusiastic staff, several malt whiskies
and well priced wines; keg beers; bedrooms
clean and well furnished *(D S Jackson, Frank
Davidson)*

Etal [NT9339]

☆ *Black Bull* [off B6354 SW of Berwick]: Pretty
white-painted cottage, the only thatched pub in
Northumberland, spacious unpretentious open-
plan lounge bar with glossily varnished beams,
well kept Stones and Tetleys, 30 malt whiskies,
farm cider, usual bar food from sandwiches up;
children in eating area, games room with darts,

dominoes, pool, TV, juke box and piped music;
open all day Sat, a few picnic-sets out in front;
nice spot nr castle ruins and light railway *(Brian
and Lynn Young, Mike and Lynn Robinson,
Hilary Edwards, Michael Doswell, LYM, Chris
Rounthwaite, Angus Lyon)*

Falstone [NY7287]

Blackcock: Cosy and friendly old-fashioned
hikers' local, open fires, good value usual food
inc baguettes, baked potatoes and big filled
yorkshire puddings (beware, may stop serving
early if busy), well kept changing ales such as
Boddingtons, Castle Eden and their own cheap
Blackcock, attractive décor; dogs welcome,
children allowed in pool room, quiet juke box;
bedrooms, handy for Kielder Water *(Comus
and Sarah Elliott, Phil and Sally Gorton, Jack
and Heather Coyle)*

Gateshead [NZ2657]

Angel View [Low Eighton; A167, just off A1]:
Named for exceptional view of Angel of the
North nearby; sympathetically refurbished
hotel, several small attractively furnished areas,
good value bar food from sandwiches to steaks,
helpful friendly staff, restaurant; bedrooms
*(Mike and Lynn Robinson, Jenny and Dave
Hughes)*

Waggon [Galloping Green Rd, Eighton Banks]:
Extended and refurbished local, good value
generous straightforward food from sandwiches
and baked potatoes to Sun lunch, comfortable
airy eating areas inc conservatory overlooking
old Bowes Railway, well kept beers, friendly
prompt service *(M Borthwick)*

Haltwhistle [NY7064]

Black Bull [Market Sq]: Friendly locals,
particularly well kept ales such as Jennings and
Northumberland, also ones brewed at the pub,
real fires, no music or food *(Andy and Jill
Kassube)*

Hartlepool [NZ5132]

Jacksons Wharf [Marina Way/The Highlight]:
New but looks 18th-c, with attractive maritime
interior, decent straightforward food (beware
the incendiary madras curry), well kept
Camerons; next to Historic Quay Museum
(David Carr)

Haydon Bridge [NY8364]

☆ *General Havelock* [A69]: Current owners doing
good bar food inc imaginative dishes in civilised
and individually furnished dining pub, open
fires, well kept changing beers such as Black
Sheep Best and Big Lamp Prince Bishop,
welcoming service, enterprising cooking using
fresh local ingredients in smart Tyne-view
stripped stone restaurant, good wines by the
glass, children welcome; tables on terrace
(J G Thorpe, John Oddey, LYM)

Hexham [NY9464]

Tap & Spile [Battle Hill/Eastgate]: Open-plan
with central bar, half a dozen quickly changing
well kept ales, country wines, good filling
lunchtime food, open fire, expert friendly
service; children welcome, no dogs, regular live
music, open all day *(John Foord, Hazel and
Michael Duncombe, Richard Lewis)*

High Force [NY8728]

☆ *High Force Hotel* [B6277 about 4 miles NW of

Middleton-in-Teesdale]: Beautifully placed high-moors hotel, named for England's highest waterfall nearby and doubling as mountain rescue post, with basic décor to suit; brews its own good value hoppy Teesdale Bitter, Cauldron Snout and Forest; also Theakstons and good choice of bar food (and of malt whiskies), helpful service, friendly atmosphere; quiz night Fri, usually open all day summer but may be cl quiet lunchtimes; children very welcome, comfortable bedrooms, pleasant garden *(LYM, Kevin Thorpe, Mrs Roxanne Chamberlain)*

Holwick [NY9027]

Strathmore Arms [back rd up Teesdale from Middleton]: Quiet and cosily welcoming unspoilt country pub in beautiful scenery just off Pennine Way, good home cooking at attractive prices, Theakstons Best and Black Bull with a guest such as Greene King Ruddles, log fire, darts, piano; bedrooms and camp site, open all day *(Jack and Heather Coyle, Kevin Thorpe, Sue and Geoff Price, Geoff and Angela Jaques)*

Holy Island [NU1241]

Crown & Anchor: Straightforward pub with good beer and quickly served food inc excellent sandwiches, cheerful landlord, good décor inc interesting rope fancy-work *(Peter Lewis)*

☆ *Ship* [Marygate; causeway passable only at low tide, check times on (01289) 330733]: Nicely set summer pub, spotless bar with eating area off, beamery, wooden furniture, bare boards, panelling, maritime/fishing memorabilia and pictures; good value straightforward food (may be a wait even for sandwiches) esp local crab and fish, well kept real ales in summer such as Border Blessed, Holy Island and Sacred Kingdom, good choice of whiskies, friendly service; no dogs, even in garden; three comfortable Victorian-décor bedrooms, may close for a while Jan/Feb *(Mike and Di Saxby, Gill Waller, Tony Morriss, Pat and Tony Martin, Neil and Anita Christopher, John Brightley, Roger Everett, Mr and Mrs M Rouse)*

Horsley [NZ0966]

Lion & Lamb [B6528, just off A69 Newcastle—Hexham]: Popular reasonably priced generous food (not Sun evening) from sandwiches to enjoyable cooked meals inc Mon steak night and bargains for two Tues/Weds, well kept changing ales such as Castle Eden, Durham Magus, Fullers London Pride and Shepherd Neame Spitfire, cafetière coffee, good service, two main rooms, small smart restaurant, stripped stone, flagstones, panelling, untreated tables and chairs; Tyne views from attractive garden with roomy terrace and play area; open all day *(Mike and Lynn Robinson)*

Houghton-Le-Spring [NZ3450]

Chilton Moor Country Pub [Chilton Moor]: Good value generous food inc fresh fish; keg beer *(Jenny and Dave Hughes)*

Kenton Bankfoot [NZ2068]

☆ *Twin Farms* [Main Road]: Sir John Fitzgerald pub recently built in elegant period rustic style with recycled stone, timbers etc, several areas,

nooks and crannies off central bar, good food from sandwiches through unusual snacks to interesting main dishes and meals in well run restaurant, well kept Mordue Workie Ticket, Timothy Taylors Landlord and two guest beers, well chosen wines, real fire, courteous efficient service, families welcome; piped music, machines; disabled facilities, open all day *(Eric Larkham, Robin Hilton, John Oddey)*

Longframlington [NU1301]

☆ *Granby*: Attractive and comfortably modernised family-run two-room bar with wide choice of good generous food, Worthingtons real ale, good collection of malt whiskies, decent wines, welcoming service, restaurant; bedrooms in main building good (but it's a busy road), with big breakfast *(R Richards, Jack and Heather Coyle, B D Jones, LYM)*

Lowick [NU0139]

☆ *Black Bull* [Main St (B6353, off A1 S of Berwick-upon-Tweed)]: Friendly bustle in nicely decorated country local with comfortable main bar, small back bar, big back dining room popular for good choice of decent food inc take-aways, well kept McEwans 80/-, good welcoming service; three attractive bedrooms, on edge of small pretty village *(Kevin Thorpe, Joel Dobris, C A Hall)*

Lucker [NU1631]

☆ *Apple*: Warmly welcoming smartly refurbished stone pub (doubles as post office), surprisingly good food from inventively filled baguettes and enterprising light lunches to creative evening meals and good Sun lunch, thoughtful children's dishes or half-price small helpings; John Smiths, well priced wines and good coffee, friendly chatty staff, small new restaurant extension; piped music *(C J Cox, A Monro, Michael Doswell)*

Netherton [NT9807]

Star [off B6341 at Thropton, or A697 via Whittingham]: Unspoilt local in superb remote countryside, spartan but clean, many original features, well kept Castle Eden tapped from the cask and served in small entrance lobby, large high-ceilinged room, welcoming landlady and regulars; no food, music or children; open evenings and Sun lunch *(RWC, Kevin Thorpe, the Didler, Phil and Sally Gorton)*

Newburn [NZ1665]

☆ *Keelman* [Grange Rd, by Tyne Riverside Country Park]: Shares attractive granite-built former 19th-c pumping station with Big Lamp Brewery, their full range at attractive prices; high ceiling, lofty windows, wooden gallery, no smoking area, obliging staff, waitress-served good straightforward bar food (not Sun evening) inc early evening specials and children's (a very popular family place in summer); fruit machine, piped music; brewery visits; open all day, tables outside, bedrooms in new block, handy for walks *(Kevin Thorpe, Mike and Lynn Robinson, John Foord)*

Newcastle upon Tyne [NZ2464]

Bacchus [High Bridge East, between Pilgrim St and Grey St]: Two sizeable rooms with fine old mirrors, panelling, solid red leather seating and plenty of standing room, also quieter corners, six well kept local Mordue Workie Ticket, Tetleys, Theakstons Best and three guest beers, wide choice of cheap hot lunches (not Sun); piped music; open all day, cl Sun lunchtime unless Newcastle United playing at home *(Eric Larkham, the Didler, John Foord, Ted Tomiak, GSB)*

Blackie Boy [Groat Market]: Great old-fashioned atmosphere, narrow bar gets very crowded (but room to move in front entrance), good range of cheap lunchtime food, Theakstons beers; TV, fruit machine; open all day *(Mike and Lynn Robinson)*

Bodega [Westgate Rd]: Bare-boards Edwardian drinking hall worth a look for the well restored colourful walls and ceiling with two magnificent original stained-glass domes; well kept Mordue Geordie Pride (sold here as No 9) and other mainly local beers tapped from the cask, lunchtime food; juke box or piped music (can be obtrusive), machines, TV, Tues quiz night, busy evenings (and if Newcastle Utd at home or on TV); open all day, next to Tyne Theatre *(Mike and Lynn Robinson, the Didler, Eric Larkham)*

☆ *Bridge Hotel* [Castle Sq, next to high level bridge]: Big friendly high-ceilinged room divided into several areas leaving plenty of space by the bar with replica slatted snob screens, well kept ales such as Black Sheep, Boddingtons, Mordue Workie Ticket and guest beers, decent lunchtime food, magnificent fireplace, great views of river and bridges from back windows; sports TV, piped music, fruit machines, very long-standing Mon folk club upstairs; tables on flagstoned back terrace overlooking section of old town wall, open all day *(Mike and Lynn Robinson, the Didler, Eric Larkham, John A Barker, David Carr, LYM)*

Chillingham [Chillingham Rd, Heaton]: Two big rooms, fine panelling and furnishings, well kept Black Sheep, Mordue Workie Ticket, Theakstons and guest beers, occasional beer festivals, good cheap food lunchtime and (not wknd) early evening; piped music or juke box in bar with TV and pool room with two tables and darts; children in quieter lounge (Weds quiz night), open all day *(Mike and Lynn Robinson, Eric Larkham, Stuart and Alison Wallace)*

Cluny [Lime St (no inn sign; entrance at top of cobbled way down to Ouseburn, by Byker city farm)]: Bar/café in well refurbished 1870s warehouse, reasonably priced food all day (all home-made so may be a wait), Banks's Best, Big Lamp Premium and Prince Bishop, guest beers and continental ones, display space for paintings, sculptures and craft works by artists with studios in same complex; piped music, live performances; open all day (cl Mon afternoon) *(Eric Larkham, John Foord)*

Cooperage [The Close, Quayside]: One of city's most ancient buildings, stripped stone bar with pool and juke box, cosy beamed lounge, good waterfront setting; Bass, Fullers London Pride, Greene King Old Speckled Hen and a changing Mordue beer (good prices Mon, Thurs and till 9 Fri/Sat), hearty fresh sensibly priced lunchtime food, disabled facilities; quiz night

Tues, cl Sun, upstairs night club Mon (student night) and Thurs-Sat *(the Didler, LYM, David Carr, Eric Larkham)*

Duke of Wellington [High Bridge West, between Grey St and Bigg Mkt]: Small well run L-shaped Victorian-style pub with many dozens of pictures commemorating the Iron Duke and Waterloo, well kept Ind Coope Burton, Marstons Pedigree, Tetleys and up to four guest beers, occasional beer festivals, hot and cold lunchtime sandwiches and baked potatoes (not Sun); juke box, machines, TV, very busy match days; open all day (cl Sun afternoon) *(Eric Larkham, John A Barker)*

Egypt Cottage [City Rd]: Small, good thorough refurbishment, enjoyable food (not wknd evenings), Greene King Ruddles Best, Workie Ticket and another Mordue beer and Theakstons Cool Cask; open all day *(Eric Larkham)*

Fitzgeralds [Grey St]: Handsomely refurbished Victorian pub in elegant street on fringe of Bigg Market, lots of levels and alcoves (two short sets of steps between entrance, main area and lavatories), discreet lighting, red mahogany and polished brass, Black Sheep, Mordue Workie Ticket and two guest beers, wide range of good value lunchtime food (not Sun) inc freshly baked baguettes; can get very busy, piped music, machines; cl Sun am *(Eric Larkham, John A Barker)*

Forth [Pink Lane]: Comfortable and recently brightened up, with lounge area behind main bar, well kept Adnams Best and Bass, lunchtime food inc Sun; piped music, juke box, TV, Sun quiz night *(Eric Larkham)*

Free Trade [St Lawrence Rd, off Walker Rd (A186)]: Great atmosphere in artfully basic split-level pub with awesome river and bridge views (plans for a tall block of flats on the far bank), well kept Marstons Pedigree and Mordue Five Bridges, Geordie Pride and Workie Ticket, distinctive atmosphere, good wkdy early lunchtime sandwiches, real fire, cricket radio, free CD player, quiz Weds; steps down to lavatories; high-standard gents' graffiti, tables out on terrace a bit like a Buddhist pebble garden (or sit on grass overlooking Tyne), open all day *(Ted Tomiak, Mike and Lynn Robinson, Eric Larkham)*

Globe [Barker St]: Large lively bar, smaller comfortable lounge, hot and cold sandwiches, baked potatoes, Bass, Stones, Theakstons Black Bull and a guest beer; open all day, tables out by car park *(Eric Larkham)*

Hotspur [Percy St]: Light and airy open-plan Victorian pub, friendly and well furnished, with big front windows and decorated mirrors, well kept Courage Directors, McEwans 80/-, Theakstons Best and Old Peculier and guest beers, farm cider, lots of bottled Belgian beers, good value wine; machines, big-screen sports TV, piped music, upstairs ladies'; open all day, sandwiches and hot snacks all day till 9; can get packed, esp pre-match *(John A Barker, Eric Larkham)*

New Bridge [Argyle St]: Large recently refurbished comfortable bar, separate areas and alcoves, nice old photographs, enjoyable home-made lunchtime food inc telephone take-aways, two changing well kept ales – usually local; darts, piped music, Weds quiz night; open all day, view of Millennium Bridge from side entrance *(Eric Larkham)*

Newcastle Arms [St Andrews St]: Open-plan pub on fringe of China Town, well kept Black Sheep, Fullers London Pride and one or two guest beers, occasional mini beer festivals, friendly staff, decent food till 6 inc sandwiches, interesting old local photographs; piped music, big-screen sports TV, gets very busy esp on match days; open all day (cl Sun afternoon) *(Mike and Lynn Robinson, Eric Larkham)*

Old George [Cloth Market, down alley past Pumphreys]: Former coaching inn with splendid panelling, beams and attractive fireplace; well kept Bass and Stones, good lunches *(Mike and Lynn Robinson)*

Ouseburn Tavern [Shields Rd, Byker]: This pub, the original Tap & Spile and long a *Guide* favourite, has sadly closed to make way for a supermarket *(LYM)*

Quayside [The Close]: Former Beefeater in Tyneside warehouse, now reworked as a floodlit Wetherspoons, various areas and levels, food all day till 10, Theakstons Best and three guest beers, various special offers; open all day, tables out in central courtyard *(Eric Larkham)*

Queens Arms [Simpson Terr, Shieldfield]: Small pub well under welcoming new landlord, Caledonian IPA and often a second beer, Courage Directors and Theakstons Best, two coal fires, happy hour 6-8; popular Weds student night, open all day Fri-Sun *(anon)*

Ship [Stepney Bank]: Traditional local beside Byker city farm, little changed in 30 years; particularly well kept Boddingtons and Castle Eden Bitter and Nimmos XXXX, unusual toasted sandwiches (normally all day), very friendly locals, pool and juke box in lounge, darts and TV in bar; seats outside and picnic-sets on green opp, open all day *(Mike and Lynn Robinson, Eric Larkham, John Allen)*

Tilleys [Westgate Rd]: Next to Tyne Theatre and nr performing arts college, so interesting mix of customers; large old-fashioned bar with scores of classic film stills, good lunchtime soup, ploughman's with up to 16 cheeses and six pâtés, full Jennings beer range, keen friendly manager and staff; big TV, juke box, machines, pool table in the small mirrored snug, can get very busy with students; open all day (not Sun lunchtime unless Newcastle playing at home) *(Mike and Lynn Robinson, John A Barker, Eric Larkham)*

Tyne [Maling St]: Single-room pub at confluence of Ouseburn and Tyne, Black Sheep, Durham Magus and seasonal beers, exotic hot or cold sandwiches all day, band posters; free CD juke box, fruit machine, sports TV, live music Sat afternoon, Weds/Sun evening, lavatories up stairs; fairy-lit garden (loudspeakers out here too) under an arch of Glasshouse Bridge, barbecues Sun lunch, early Fri evening; open all day, can get very full *(Mike and Lynn Robinson, Eric Larkham)*

Tyne Theatre [Westgate Rd]: Pit Bar, with separate street entrance but hidden in bowels of beautiful Victorian theatre, has whitewashed brick and pine panelling, lots of photographs of theatres, sandwiches and snacks, TV for soccer and soaps, welcoming staff and regulars – like a cosy living room without the couch; separate Bistro Bar (no street entrance) now has well kept and reasonably priced Bass and Stones *(Eric Larkham)*

Union Rooms [Westgate Rd]: Popular two-storey Wetherspoons in lavishly restored high-ceilinged Victorian gentlemen's club, lovely stairway, stained glass, marble and pillars, lots of pictures in several areas off two large bars, good reasonably priced beer choice, farm cider, usual food all day, friendly staff, no music, disabled facilities; can get busy and smoky, but there are no smoking areas (and no mobile phones Fri/Sat night); open all day *(Richard Lewis, Eric Larkham)*

Newfield [NZ2033]

☆ *Fox & Hounds* [Stonebank Terr]: Cosy and friendly rather than smart, and well worth knowing for good attractively priced food; decent wines, changing real ales, welcoming landlords *(Tony Hall, Melanie Jackson, Angela Smurthwaite)*

Newton-by-the-Sea [NU2424]

☆ *Ship* [The Square, Low Newton]: Good plain local, formerly owned by the church but now National Trust, quaintly tucked into top corner of courtyard of old cottages facing spectacular seascape above beach, new licensees doing good generous lunchtime snacks such as crab stotties and sandwiches, also reasonably priced fish suppers (must book), coffee, tea, well kept Border Farne Island and Northumberland Main Seam and Secret Kingdom, pool table; queues can build on hot days; children welcome (but cl 5-7), picnic-sets out on green *(Geoffrey and Penny Hughes, John Foord, Gill Waller, Tony Morriss, Comus and Sarah Elliott, Mike and Lynn Robinson, Michael Doswell, Darly Graton, Graeme Gulibert, David Cooke)*

North Shields [NZ3467]

Brewers Fayre [Royal Quays, Coble Dene Rd]: Well organised for families, with decent food and drink *(Mrs M Hogg)*

☆ *Magnesia Bank* [Camden St]: Big well run refurbished Victorian pub overlooking Tyne, well kept Durham, Mordue and guest beers in lined glasses, vast choice of cheerful home-made lunchtime food, friendly staff, open fire; quiet piped pop music, TV, machines; children welcome, tables outside, open all day, live music Thurs and Sun often featuring members of Lindisfarne *(Mike and Lynn Robinson, Jack and Heather Coyle, Eric Larkham)*

☆ *Tap & Spile* [Tynemouth St]: Doing well under current management, well kept Bass, Fullers London Pride, Theakstons Black Bull and lots of quickly changing changing beers, Weston's Old Rosie cider, good home-cooked food inc children's helpings all day till early evening, quiet comfortable lounge on right, bar with darts, TV and occasional live music, pub greyhound (likes his beer); open all day *(Eric Larkham)*

☆ *Wooden Doll* [Hudson St]: Jennings pub doing well under enthusiastic new licensees, full range of their beers kept well, enjoyable food inc fresh fish priced by size, helpful welcoming service, largely no smoking eating area, high view of fish quay and outer harbour, informal mix of furnishings in bare-boards bar, lots of paintings by local artists for sale; disabled facilities, children welcome till 8, some live music, open all day Sat *(John Oddey, Michael Doswell, Eric Larkham, LYM, Mike and Lynn Robinson)*

Piercebridge [NZ2116]

George [B6275 just S of village, over bridge]: Atttractively placed rambling old inn refurbished throughout by new licensees (too recent for us to give a full rating), usual bar food, riverside restaurant and garden, provision for children, bedrooms; open all day, reports please *(LYM)*

Ponteland [NZ1871]

☆ *Badger* [Street Houses; A696 SE]: Well done olde-worlde reworking of 18th-c house by main road garden centre, relaxing well furnished rooms and alcoves, flagstones, carpet or bare wood, timbered ceilings, stripped stone, brick and timbering, real fires, three Bass-related ales, decent wines, good-sized helpings of reasonably priced food (most people here for this – can get busy Sun lunchtime), helpful efficient uniformed staff; quiet piped music; good disabled access and facilities *(John Foord, Karen and Graham Oddey, M Borthwick, Beryl and Bill Farmer)*

Rennington [NU2118]

Horseshoes: Flagstoned pub, clean, comfortable and friendly, with good helpings of enjoyable fresh honest food, real ales, good service; children welcome, tables outside, attractive village well placed for coast *(Stephen Auster)*

Riding Mill [NZ0161]

☆ *Wellington* [A695 just W of A68 roundabout]: Large 17th-c Chef & Brewer, carefully refurbished in tune with its age, beams, two big log fires and mix of tables and chairs, some upholstered, some not; interesting menu from ciabatta sandwiches up inc good vegetarian choice and nice puddings, Courage Directors and Theakstons Bitter and Black Bull, good shortish wine choice, friendly welcome and service; piped classical music, can get busy; disabled access, children welcome, play area and picnic-sets outside, pretty village with nearby walks and river *(Andy and Jill Kassube, Michael Doswell)*

Rochester [NY8497]

Redesdale Arms [A68 3 miles W of Otterburn]: Rebuilt (after 1993 explosion and fire in which two readers lost all their luggage and *Good Pub Guide* but escaped with their lives), with interesting prints in pretty terracotta-pink room, welcoming staff, well kept beer, good food choice inc Sun carvery and outstanding crabcakes; comfortable bedrooms *(Peter and Anne-Marie O'Malley)*

Romaldkirk [NY9922]

☆ *Kirk*: Cosy and very friendly local, well worn but clean, with wide choice of interesting good value food (not Tues), well kept Castle Eden and a guest such as Black Sheep, good coffee and log fire, 18th-c stonework, paintings for sale; darts, piped popular classics; picnic-sets out by green of attractive moorland village, doubles as PO *(Kevin Thorpe)*

Rothbury [NU0602]

☆ *Newcastle Hotel*: Small solid Victorian hotel in imposing spot at end of green, comfortably refurbished lounge with separate dining area, second bar, Tetleys and two guest ales, friendly service and entertaining locals, good plentiful carefully prepared food inc high teas 3.30-5.30 Apr-Oct, toasties only winter Sun pm; good value comfortable bedrooms, open all day, handy for Cragside (NT) *(Michael Wadsworth, John Brightley, John Foord)*

Ryton [NZ1564]

Ryton Park Hotel [Holburn Lane, Ryton Park]: Pleasant staff, Theakstons real ale, good bar food running up to steaks, separate restaurant; bedrooms *(Jenny and Dave Hughes)*

Seaton Sluice [NZ3477]

Kings Arms [West Terrace]: Reasonably priced home-made food all day, usual Scottish Courage beers *(Mike and Lynn Robinson)*

☆ *Waterford Arms* [A193 N of Whitley Bay]: Dining pub with food all day, double doors between restaurant and homely bar, tables here likely to be laid for food too (esp fish), Greene King Old Speckled Hen, Jennings Cocker Hoop, Marstons Pedigree and Worthingtons; games area with juke box, pool etc, live entertainment Thurs/Fri; children welcome, open all day, simple good value bedrooms, nice cliff walks *(Peter Burton, LYM, David Carr)*

Sedgefield [NZ3629]

Hardwick Arms [North End]: Bar and lounge with restaurant, attractively priced food, friendly service even on busy race days, live music Sun and Weds; bedrooms *(Eric Larkham)*

Shincliffe [NZ2941]

Rose Tree [Lower Shincliffe, A177 S of Durham]: Clean and comfortable local by River Wear, with friendly helpful staff, wide range of good value substantial food, well kept Bass and Theakstons; children welcome, tables outside *(John Watson)*

Slaley [NY9757]

Rose & Crown: Good home-made food from sandwiches to restaurant meals inc good value Sun lunch, four well kept real ales, good choice of malt whiskies, welcoming service, comfortable dark-beamed lounge hung with lots of mugs and jugs, public bar with darts, fruit machine, juke box; tables outside, bedrooms attractive and well equipped *(Eric Larkham)*

Travellers Rest [B6306 S of Hexham]: Large open-plan country pub, dating from 18th c but redone, with beams, flagstones and polished wood floors, comfortable high-backed settles forming discrete areas; enjoyable food (not Sun evening) from lunchtime sandwiches to interesting cooked dishes in bar and evening restaurant, four well kept ales; tables outside with well equipped adventure play area behind, three bedrooms, open all day *(Eric Larkham, Andy and Jill Kassube)*

South Shields [NZ3766]
Alum Ale House [Ferry St (B1344)]:
Unpretentious and relaxed 18th-c pub handy
for ferry, big bars with real fire, pictures and
newspaper cuttings, well kept Banks's,
Camerons, Marstons and a beer brewed for
them by Durham, good value basic lunchtime
bar food; piped music, machines, some live
music; children welcome, open all day
(Eric Larkham)
Railway [Mill Dam/Coronation St]: Well kept
Scottish Courage and guest ales in brightly lit
two-roomed pub with shipping theme in bar,
spiral stairs up to lounge *(Eric Larkham)*
Riverside [Commercial Rd]: Well kept Timothy
Taylors Landlord and other quickly changing
beers, farm cider, sandwiches, good service;
upstairs lavatories; open all day (Sun afternoon
closure) *(Eric Larkham)*
Steamboat [Mill Dam/Coronation St]: Masses
of interesting nautical bric-a-brac, friendly
landlord, five well kept ales, sandwiches;
usually open all day, nr river and market place
(Eric Larkham)
Stanley [NZ1953]
Harperley Hotel [Harperley Country Park, 1½
miles W of Stanley]: Good home cooking inc
bargain three-course restaurant lunch and
evening carvery, well kept Courage Directors
and Jennings or Greene King; extensive
grounds, good walks *(Mike and Lynn
Robinson, M Borthwick, Anne and David
Robinson, Jack and Heather Coyle)*
Stannington [NZ2279]
☆ *Ridley Arms* [just off A1 S of Morpeth]:
Recently pleasantly refurbished and extended,
with good value honest varied food all day in
several areas off main bar, pleasant and cosy in
relaxed rustic style, friendly attentive staff, well
kept Whitbreads-related ales and a guest such
as Mordue Workie Ticket, quiet lounge,
restaurant *(LYM, Michael Doswell, M
Borthwick)*
Stockton on Tees [NZ4419]
Sun [Knowles St]: Particularly well kept Bass at
tempting price in friendly town local; folk night
Mon, open all day *(the Didler)*
Tudhoe [NZ2636]
Green Tree: Good sensibly priced home-cooked
food inc good value Sun lunch, well kept real
ale in lined glasses, friendly family service,
elegant no smoking dining room *(C A Hall)*
Tynemouth [NZ3668]
☆ *Tynemouth Lodge* [Tynemouth Rd (A193), ½
mile W of Tynemouth Metro stn]: Genuine-
feeling friendly little Victorian-style pub
(actually older), very popular for particularly
well kept Bass, Belhaven 80/-, Caledonian
Deuchars IPA, occasional guest beers and farm
ciders, decent wines, cheap lunchtime filled
rolls, coal fire, keen and friendly landlord; quiet
on wkdy afternoons, can be packed evenings;
no dogs or children; open all day, tables in back
garden *(LYM, Adrian Don, Eric Larkham)*
Wall [NY9269]
☆ *Hadrian* [on Hexham—Bellingham/Rothbury
Rd]: Two-room beamed lounge with wide
choice of generous food inc speciality pies, well

kept Jennings Cumberland and Worthingtons,
good house wine, interesting reconstructions of
Romano-British life, woodburner, quick
pleasant service, no smoking bar and airy
dining room; children welcome, unobtrusive
piped music, games in public bar; neat garden,
roomy comfortable bedrooms – back ones
quieter, with good views *(D P Brown, Michael
Doswell, Phil and Heidi Cook, Mike and Lynn
Robinson, BB)*
Warden [NY9267]
Boatside [½ mile N of A69]: Extended dining
pub with pretty country-style interior
redecorated in light warm colours, interesting
bric-a-brac and World War II memorabilia,
restaurant and smaller dining room, good range
of bar food using fresh ingredients, friendly
attentive service, Courage Directors and
Theakstons; small neat enclosed garden,
arractive spot by Tyne bridge *(Michael
Doswell)*
Wark [NY8677]
Battlesteads: Low-beamed two-room bar with
dark blue banquettes, dark panelling and floral
wallpaper, stuffed fish over open fire,
restaurant beyond; good value imaginative
home-made food from sandwiches to lots of
grills and popular Sun lunch, welcoming Dutch
landlady, Battlesteads Bitter and Theakstons,
good coffee; bedrooms *(Michael Doswell, Phil
and Sally Gorton)*
Warkworth [NU2506]
☆ *Hermitage* [Castle St]: Rambling pub with
interesting quaint décor, old range for heating,
well kept Jennings and John Smiths, good
generous food from sandwiches to interesting
dishes cooked to order inc fresh local fish, good
service, friendly dry-humoured landlord and
staff, dining area and small plush upstairs
restaurant; bedrooms, tables out in front,
attractive setting *(BB, Michael Wadsworth, Jack
and Heather Coyle, Stephen and Jean Curtis)*
Masons Arms [Dial Pl]: Welcoming and
comfortable thriving local, quick friendly
service, good generous food inc good fish
choice and bargain lunch, well kept Courage
Directors, Newcastle Exhibition and Youngers,
good coffee, local pictures; dogs allowed,
attractive back flagstoned courtyard *(Mike and
Lynn Robinson, Jack and Heather Coyle)*
Sun [Castle Terr]: 17th-c hotel handy for castle
(useful parking) in attractive village not far
from sea, friendly helpful staff, well kept
Theakstons, ample food inc local fish in homely
comfortable bar; children welcome, bedrooms
with good views *(R Davies)*
Weldon Bridge [NZ1399]
Anglers Arms [signed just off B6344 nr A397
junction]: Welcoming pub in splendid location,
comfortable traditional lounge bar, old prints,
grandfather clock, old china and stuffed fish;
good generous bar food inc lunchtime
sandwiches, hot beef baguettes and memorable
cheese platter, good value more upmarket
restaurant, Border Special, Courage Directors
and a guest beer; tables in good garden with
play area, bedrooms *(Bruce Jamieson, the Very
Rev Stephen Platten)*

West Moor [NZ2770]
George Stephenson [Great Lime Rd; northern outskirts of Newcastle]: Nicely refurbished, with friendly staff, good choice of interesting changing northern ales such as Durham, Northumberland and Wylam, frequent bargains; good live music Weds, Thurs and Sat, Mon quiz night, open all day *(Mike and Lynn Robinson)*

Whalton [NZ1382]
Beresford Arms: Tudoresque décor in attractive dining pub particularly popular with older people for genuine straightforward home cooking at reasonable prices; friendly helpful staff (but beware 25p charge for tap water), well kept real ales, pretty village *(Jack and Heather Coyle, Chris Rounthwaite)*

Whitley Bay [NZ3572]
Fitzgeralds [South Parade]: Character pub with lovely glasswork, big main room, raised dining area, smaller more intimate snug, five or six well kept changing beers, plentiful basic food, good friendly staff; can get very busy evenings, live music Weds, DJ Thurs-Sat; open all day (cl Sun afternoon), children well catered for *(Keith Jacob)*

Whittonstall [NZ0857]
☆ *Anchor* [B6309 N of Consett]: Spotless stone-built beamed dining pub recently well reworked, comfortable banquettes in L-shaped lounge and dining area with high-raftered pitched roof, attractive rag-rolling above pine dado, interesting old north east photographs and facsimile posters, huge choice of good generous food from sandwiches through unusual hot dishes to popular Sun lunch, well kept Courage Directors and a guest such as Greene King Ruddles, good coffee, service efficient and friendly even under pressure; piped music; nice countryside *(Jack and Heather Coyle, Michael Doswell, Mike and Lynn Robinson)*

Wooler [NT9928]
Tankerville Arms [A697 N]: Pleasant hotel bar in tastefully modernised old building, good choice of homely food inc local produce (small helpings on request), Border Farne Island, Marstons Pedigree and Theakstons Best, very helpful service, smart restaurant (with maybe local folk music Sun lunchtime); bedrooms, pleasant setting, nice garden *(John Brightley, Mike and Lynn Robinson, Stephen and Jean Curtis, Darly Graton, Graeme Gulibert)*

Wylam [NZ1265]
Boathouse [Station Rd; across Tyne from village]: Warm and comfortable two-room pub with up to nine well kept ales inc one brewed for them by the new local Wylam Brewery, good choice of malt whiskies, wkdy sandwiches and wknd bar meals, roaring coal fire; children welcome, Sat afternoon impromptu folk/blues sessions, open all day *(Mike and Lynn Robinson, John Foord, Eric Larkham)*

Real ale may be served from handpumps, electric pumps (not just the on-off switches used for keg beer) or – common in Scotland – tall taps called founts (pronounced 'fonts') where a separate pump pushes the beer up under air pressure. The landlord can adjust the force of the flow – a tight spigot gives the good creamy head that Yorkshire lads like.

Nottinghamshire

One pub here, the Olde Trip to Jerusalem in Nottingham, has been in each year's edition of the Guide *since it started 20 years ago; always worth seeing for the intriguing way it's built into the caverns below the castle. Nottingham itself has many more fine pubs, and a growing collection of really interesting new bars such as the Via Fossa (see the Lucky Dip section at the end of the chapter for more). The Lincolnshire Poacher is a particular favourite, with more than a dozen handpumps, good individual food, and friendly atmosphere and service; it's typical of the area's small Tynemill chain, and if you like the sound of our description of this one you'll almost certainly like any of the others elsewhere. Fellows Morton & Clayton, brewing its own beers, is another Nottingham favourite. Outside the city, pubs on top form include the chatty Victoria in Beeston (good imaginative food, masses of good beers and whiskies), the carefully run Dovecote in the interesting medieval village of Laxton, the French Horn at Upton (very good bar food) and the good value Three Horse Shoes in Walkeringham (a riot of flowers in summer). The Caunton Beck at Caunton does good food all day, and the Martins Arms at Colston Bassett also has good food. For its cheerful combination of good food with a buzzy and properly pubby atmosphere, the Victoria in Beeston is our Nottinghamshire Dining Pub of the Year (it's another Tynemill pub). In the Lucky Dip section, pubs to note are the Beehive at Maplebeck and Star at West Leake (two favourite unspoilt country pubs), and the Mail Coach in Newark, Limelight and Sir John Borlase Warren in Nottingham, Market Hotel in Retford and Stratford Haven in West Bridgford. Beer prices in the county are comfortably below the national average; by far the cheapest we found was the beer brewed at Fellows Morton & Clayton.*

BEESTON SK5338 Map 7
Victoria 🍴 ▨
Dovecote Lane, backing on to railway station
Nottinghamshire Dining Pub of the Year
Carefully converted from an almost derelict railway hotel, this friendly pub is popular for its imaginative food (with around 10 vegetarian choices a day) and good choice of real ales. The 12 changing well kept ales might include Everards Tiger, Ossett Silver King, Batemans XB, Burton Bridge Summer Ale, Whim Hartington IPA, Castle Rock Hemlock, Dark Star Cascade and Hook Norton Best on handpump; also, two traditional ciders, over a hundred malt whiskies, 20 Irish whiskeys, and half a dozen wines by the glass. The lounge and bar back on to the railway station, and picnic-sets in a pleasant area outside (with new heaters) overlook the platform where trains pass just feet below. The three downstairs rooms in their original long narrow layout have simple solid traditional furnishings, very unfussy décor, stained-glass windows, stripped woodwork and floorboards (woodblock in some rooms), newspapers to read, and a good chatty atmosphere; dominoes, cribbage, piped music. From a daily changing blackboard menu the popular, reasonably priced bar food (served in the no smoking dining area) might include sandwiches (from £1.40) as well as vegetarian dishes such as bombay pizza (£5.95), stuffed vine leaves with mozzarella and peppers or asparagus, taleggio and

chive tart (£4.95) or mediterranean platter (£6.95) and other dishes such as lincolnshire sausages and mash (£5.95), pork kebabs (£6.50), seared salmon fillet with cajun spices (£7.95), italian lamb meatballs (£6.95) and grilled monkfish and pancetta parcels (£10.50); puddings such as plum tart with amaretto ice cream and hot bananas with dark rum and ice cream (£2.95-£3.50). *(Recommended by Andy and Ali, Dr and Mrs J Hills, Keith Allen, Darly Graton, Graeme Gulibert, Tony Hobden, Richard Lewis, Mike and Wena Stevenson, the Didler, Malcolm Taylor, JP, PP, Peter and Jean Hoare, Shaun Pinchbeck, James and Laura Newton, R M Taylor, Simon King, MP, Mr Nicholson)*

Tynemill ~ Manager Natasha Averre ~ Real ale ~ Bar food (12-(8 Sun)9) ~ (0115) 925 4049 ~ Children in eating area of bar till 8pm ~ Open 11-11; 12-10.30 Sun

CAUNTON SK7460 Map 7
Caunton Beck 🍽 ♀

Main Street; village signposted off A616 Newark—Ollerton

Served from 8am till 10.30pm, the enjoyable food at this spacious, civilised place is really appreciated by readers. As well as sandwiches (from £4.95) and English breakfast (£6.50) the monthly changing menu (not cheap) might include thai chicken broth (£4.95) and tiger prawn tempura (£6.95), roast guinea fowl with black pudding, onion and thyme compote (£11.95), fillet of sea bream with black pasta and crab and basil butter (£13.50), roasted red onion tart with red pepper dressing and deep-fried beans (£9.50) as well as puddings such as champagne jelly set with summer berries or chilled coconut rice pudding with caramelised pineapple and blackcurrant sorbet (£3.95). They do good value two- and three-course set meals (not Saturday evening). Almost new, but not new-looking, the pub was reconstructed, using original timbers and reclaimed oak, around the skeleton of the old Hole Arms. Scrubbed pine tables and country-kitchen chairs, low beams and rag-finished paintwork make for a relaxed feel. There are tables out on delightful terraces with lots of flowers and plants. Well kept Banks's, Marstons Pedigree and Timothy Taylors Landlord on handpump, good house wines including a choice of half bottles, freshly squeezed orange juice; welcoming service, daily papers and magazines, no music. *(Recommended by Phil and Jane Hodson, Chris and Elaine Lyon, Mr and Mrs J Glover, B, M and P Kendall, Derek and Sylvia Stephenson, David and Ruth Hollands, Darly Graton, Graeme Gulibert, Joy and Peter Heatherley, E D Bailey, Dr G E Martin)*

Free house ~ Licensees Julia Allwood and Paul Vidic ~ Real ale ~ Bar food (8am-10.30pm) ~ Restaurant ~ (01636) 636793 ~ Children in eating area of bar and restaurant ~ Open 8am-12 midnight

COLSTON BASSETT SK7033 Map 7
Martins Arms 🍽 ♀ ◀

Village signposted off A46 E of Nottingham; School Lane, near market cross in village centre

You should probably visit this smart, civilised place in a restauranty frame of mind, as prices are quite a bit higher than you'd usually expect to find in a country dining pub. And beware that you may have to hand over your credit card before you choose from the imaginative, extensive menu served by neatly uniformed staff. Well cooked, contemporary dishes might include soup (£3.95), sandwiches (from £3.95, speciality ones such as stilton rarebit with watercress, apple and grapes from £6.95), twice baked cheese soufflé or warm squid salad with new potatoes and chorizo (£6.95), roasted vegetable frittata with gruyère or gnocchi pasta with spicy minced lamb in cheese sauce (£10.95), steak and mushroom pie with herb mash (£13.95), roulade of chicken stuffed with crabmeat (£13.95), and delicious puddings such as chocolate bread and butter pudding with toffee ice cream or trio of lemons with summer fruits (from £4.95) or English cheeses (£6.95). A bad point is that they may make you pay for mineral water if you want a glass of water with your food. Antique furnishings, hunting prints and warm log fires in the Jacobean fireplaces give an upmarket air to the comfortable bar, and there's a proper snug. A good choice of well kept real ales on handpump might include Bass, Black Sheep, Greene King IPA and Marstons Pedigree, and up to four guests such as Black Dog Special and Woodfordes Wherry; a good range of malt whiskies and cognacs, and an interesting wine list; cribbage and dominoes. The elegant restaurant is smartly decorated with period fabrics and colourings. There are tables out in the sizeable attractive lawned garden, which backs on to estate parkland; in summer you can play croquet out here. Readers recommend Colston Bassett Dairy just outside the village, which sells its own stilton cheese. *(Recommended by Derek and Sylvia Stephenson, Ian Phillips, Roger A Bellingham, Mandy and Simon King, Hugh Roberts, Phil and Jane Hodson, Mrs M D Dimarino, JP, PP, the Didler, Darly Graton, Graeme Gulibert, Richard Butler, Marie Kroon, A C and E Johnson)*

Free house ~ Licensees Lynne Strafford Bryan and Salvatore Inguanta ~ Real ale ~ Bar food (12-2, 6-10; not Sun evenings) ~ Restaurant ~ (01949) 81361 ~ Children over 14 in restaurant and garden ~ Open 12-3, 6-11; 12-3, 7-10.30 Sun; closed 25 Dec evening

ELKESLEY SK6975 Map 7
Robin Hood
High Street; village well signposted just off A1 Newark—Blyth

Close to the A1, this friendly village local makes a good lunch stop. The roomy carpeted dining lounge is comfortably furnished with pictures, some copper pans and a small collection of horse bits. Enjoyable, well presented changing bar food might include sandwiches (from £2.10), starters such as spaghetti and mussels with red chilli, parsley, garlic and lemon (£4), grilled chicken liver salad (£4.20), and main courses such as ploughman's (£4.65), salmon and cod fishcake with lemon butter and chive sauce (£4.20), chicken curry (£5), gammon and eggs (£7.50) and blackboard specials such as thai seafood hotpot (£4.20), duck leg with port and redcurrant jus (£8.50) or beef fillet with roasted shallots and red wine sauce (£13.50); prompt, friendly service. There's also a plain but neatly kept public bar, with pool, TV and fruit machines; unobtrusive piped music. Boddingtons on handpump and a guest such as Flowers IPA under light blanket pressure. The garden (which is moderately well screened from the A1) has picnic-sets and a play area. *(Recommended by Gordon Tong, Michael Butler, Tony Gayfer, John and Sylvia Harrop, Comus and Sarah Elliott, Rita and Keith Pollard, Mr and Mrs J Glover, Mr and Mrs J E C Tasker, Michael Buchanan, D L Parkhurst)*

Whitbreads ~ Lease Alan Draper ~ Real ale ~ Bar food (not Sun evening) ~ Restaurant ~ (01777) 838259 ~ Children in eating area of bar ~ Open 11.30-2.30, 6.30-11; 12-3, 7-10.30 Sun

KIMBERLEY SK5044 Map 7
Nelson & Railway ◖ £
1 mile from M1 junction 26; at exit roundabout take A610 to Ripley, then signposted Kimberley, pub in Station Road

Since this cheery two-roomed Victorian pub is directly opposite the Hardys & Hansons brewery it's not surprising that the Kimberley Bitter, Classic and seasonal ales on handpump are so well kept. A real hub of village life, it even has its own amateur dramatic society. There's a mix of Edwardian-looking furniture in the friendly beamed bar and lounge, with interesting brewery prints and railway signs on the walls. Darts, alley and table skittles, dominoes, chess, cribbage, Scrabble, fruit machine and juke box. There are tables and swings out in a good-sized cottagey garden. Straightforward bar food includes soup (£1.30), sandwiches (from £1.30; hot rolls from £1.60), garlic chicken goujons (£2.65), ploughman's (£4.55), breaded scampi, chicken tikka masala or gammon and egg (£4.95), mushroom stroganoff (£4.65) and specials including home-made pie of the day (£4.95), and seafood dishes such as grilled swordfish (£6.45); puddings (£1.85) and children's meals (£1.65); Sunday lunch (£3.95 adults, £2.95 children); the dining room is no smoking at meal times; attentive service. Its name comes from a shortening of its original title the Lord Nelson Railway Hotel, in the days when it stood yards away from two competing railway stations. *(Recommended by MLR, Pete Baker, Peter F Marshall,*

Bernie Adams, Dr and Mrs J Hills, Tom Evans, JP, PP, Richard Lewis, Andy Gosling, the Didler, Shaun Pinchbeck)

Hardys & Hansons ~ Tenant Harry Burton ~ Real ale ~ Bar food (12-2.30, 5.30-9; 12-6 Sun) ~ (0115) 938 2177 ~ Children in eating area of bar and restaurant ~ Open 11.30(11 Sat)-11; 12-10.30 Sun ~ Bedrooms: £22B/£37B

LAXTON SK7267 Map 7

Dovecote

Signposted off A6075 E of Ollerton

This popular, well run red brick house is next to three huge medieval open fields and this is one of the only parts of the country still to be farmed using this historic method. Every year in the third week of June the grass is auctioned for haymaking, and anyone who lives in the parish is entitled to a bid – and a drink. The visitor centre behind the pub explains it all. Inside there's a welcoming atmosphere and service is friendly and competent. The central room has brocaded button-back built-in corner seats, stools and chairs, and a coal-effect gas fire, and opens through a small bay (which was the original entrance) into another similar room. Around the other side, a simpler room with some entertaining Lawson Wood 1930s tourist cartoons leads through to a pool room with darts, fruit machine, dominoes and piped music; no smoking area. Good value, straightforward, well liked bar food includes home-made soup (£2.20), sandwiches (from £3), mushroom stroganoff or vegetable lasagne (£5.75), sweet and sour battered chicken (£6.20), steak and kidney pie (£5.90), and specials such as duck slices in orange sauce (£6.40), fresh cod or haddock (£5.85) and 10oz fillet steak stuffed with stilton (£10.50). Mansfield Bitter and two guest ales such as Everards Beacon and Charles Wells Bombardier. There are wooden tables and chairs on a small front terrace by a sloping garden which has a disused white dovecote and a children's play area. They've got two new rooms and a site for six caravans with lavatories and showers. *(Recommended by Kevin Thorpe, CMW, JJW, JP, PP, John and Sylvia Harrop)*

Free house ~ Licensees Stephen and Betty Shepherd ~ Real ale ~ Bar food ~ (01777) 871586 ~ Children in eating area of bar and restaurant ~ Open 11.30-3, 6.30-11; 12-3, 7-10.30 Sun ~ Bedrooms: £35B/£40B

NOTTINGHAM SK5640 Map 7

Fellows Morton & Clayton ◖ £

54 Canal Street (part of inner ring road)

This carefully converted old canal building pub brews its own beers, Samuel Fellows and Post Haste, and from a big window in the quarry-tiled glassed-in area at the back you can see the little brewery. They also have well kept Fullers London Pride, Timothy Taylors Landlord and Mallard on handpump. There's a really buzzy atmosphere in the softly lit bar which has dark red plush seats built into alcoves, wooden tables, more seats up two or three steps in a side gallery, and bric-a-brac on the shelf just below the glossy dark green high ceiling; a sympathetic extension provides extra seating. Piped pop music, fruit machine, big TV, and daily newspapers on a rack. From the large terrace outside which has seats and tables there are views of the canal. Popular, good value bar food includes home-made soup (£1.75), local cheeses with bread (£3.50), filled baguettes (from £4.25), chicken and pasta bake, steak and kidney pie and 5oz rump steak (£5.95), battered haddock (£5.95), and a couple of daily specials such as roast beef (£4.25) and tortellini with creamy spinach sauce (£4.95), with puddings such as crêpes suzette, cheesecake and profiteroles (£2.95-£4.95); swift, friendly service. It's popular with local workers at lunchtime and a younger set in the evening when it can get smoky. Nottingham station is just a short walk away. *(Recommended by JP, PP, SLC, Rona Murdoch, the Didler, Richard Lewis, David Carr, Derek and Sylvia Stephenson)*

Own brew ~ Licensees Les Howard and Keely Willans ~ Real ale ~ Bar food (11.30-9.30) ~ Restaurant ~ (0115) 950 6795 ~ Children in restaurant ~ Open 11-11; 12-10.30 Sun

Lincolnshire Poacher ◖

Mansfield Road; up hill from Victoria Centre

Particularly well liked by readers at the moment, this homely, bustling town pub is known for its perfectly kept real ale, friendly service and reasonably priced food. Thirteen handpumps serve around eight changing guest ales from brewers such as Brains, Castle Rock and Enville alongside Fullers London Pride, Batemans XB and XXXB, Caledonian Deuchars IPA and Archers Gold; also good ciders, and around 85 malt whiskies and 10 Irish ones. Apart from sandwiches (from £1.50, served all day), tasty daily specials might include lincolnshire sausages and mash or home-made steak and kidney pie (£5.25), grilled tuna steak (£5.50), lasagne (£4.95) and goats cheese ravioli (£4.75); no chips. The traditional big wood-floored front bar has wall settles and plain wooden tables, and is decorated with breweriana; it opens on to a plain but lively room on the left, from where a corridor takes you down to the chatty panelled back snug – newspapers to read; cribbage, dominoes, cards, backgammon, piped music; no smoking area at lunchtime. Be warned it can get very busy in the evenings when it's popular with a younger crowd. A conservatory overlooks tables on a large terrace behind. *(Recommended by Stephen, Julie and Hayley Brown, David Carr, Tony and Wendy Hobden, the Didler, Rona Murdoch, JP, PP, R M Taylor, Mrs Rita Cox, Roger and Jenny Huggins, P Price, Comus and Sarah Elliott)*

Tynemill ~ Manager Paul Montgomery ~ Real ale ~ Bar food (12-3(4 Sun), Tues-Thurs 5-8, not 26 Dec and 1 Jan) ~ (0115) 9411584 ~ Open 11-11; 12-10.30 Sun; closed 25 Dec

Olde Trip to Jerusalem ★ £

Brewhouse Yard; from inner ring road follow The North, A6005 Long Eaton signpost until you are in Castle Boulevard then almost at once turn right into Castle Road; pub is up on the left

The name of this deceptively normal-looking pub is a reference to the 12th-c crusaders who used to meet on this site on the way to the Holy Land. Built into caverns burrowing into the sandstone rock below the castle, the panelled walls of the unique upstairs bar – thought to have served as cellarage for an early medieval brewhouse which stood here – soar narrowly into the dark rent above. Also mainly carved from the rock, the chatty downstairs bar has leatherette-cushioned settles built into the dark panelling, tables on flagstones, and more low-ceilinged rock alcoves; also a no smoking parlour/snug and two more caves open to the public. Very well kept real ales include Hardys & Hansons Kimberley Best, Best Mild, Classic and their Cellarman's Cask (brewed every two months or so), and Marstons Pedigree on handpump; friendly staff. Very good value bar food includes soup (£1.20), sandwiches (from £2.49), burgers (from £1.99), sausage and mash (£3.99), cheese, leek and potato bake (£4.49), giant filled yorkshire pudding, liver and onions, steak and ale pie, cod and chips, scampi (£4.99), rump steak (£6.99), and puddings (from £1.99); fruit machine and ring the bull game; seats outside. *(Recommended by David Carr, Rona Murdoch, Susan and Nigel Wilson, Keith and Janet Morris, Kevin Blake, James Nunns, JP, PP, R M Taylor, Richard Butler, Marie Kroon, SLC, Tony and Wendy Hobden, the Didler, Keith Allen, Richard Lewis, Peter F Marshall)*

Hardys & Hansons ~ Manager Claire Underdown ~ Real ale ~ Bar food (11(12 Sun)-6) ~ (0115) 9473171, fax 0115 9501185 ~ Children in eating area of the bar till 6 ~ Open 11-11; 12-10.30 Sun

Vat & Fiddle ◖

Queens Bridge Rd, alongside Sheriffs Way (nr multi-storey car park)

Serving good Castle Rock beers from the brewery next door, this plain brick pub is well regarded by real ale lovers. Here, around five good Castle Rock beers, mostly quite full-bodied and often including a Stout, are served in top condition on handpump as well as an equal number of guests from brewers such as Batemans and Caledonian; occasional beer festivals. The very straightforward bar has quite a strong 1930s feel. Its simple interior has cream and navy walls and ceiling, varnished pine tables and bentwood stools and chairs on parquet and terrazzo flooring, plain blue curtains and some brewery memorabilia. Lunchtime bar food from a short menu includes soup (£1.95), rolls (from £1.40), chilli (£2.95), ratatouille (£2.95) and Hemlock sausage and mash (£3.50). There are picnic-sets on a front terrace by the road and more on a back terrace. The station is a short walk away. *(Recommended by SLC, Richard Lewis, JP, PP, David Carr, R M Taylor, Derek and Sylvia Stephenson, the Didler)*

Tynemill ~ Managers Julian Grocock and N Trafford ~ Real ale ~ Bar food (12-3, not evenings) ~ (0115) 985 0611 ~ Open 11-11; 12-10.30 Sun

Via Fossa

Canal Street (on corner of inner ring road)

Wandering around the various galleries and balconies of this huge converted warehouse, you get the feeling that you are looking up or down on to different sections and rooms on a film set. Imagine a surreally romantic interpretation of a medieval castle with big winding staircases, dark red passages, organ pipes and ecclesiastical woodwork in a chapel, a massive clock that seems to be tumbling off the wall, iron chandeliers, royal portraits in oils, roaring fires in stone fireplaces, intricately carved panelling – and then some decadent 90s twists such as zebra print upholstery on asymmetrical furniture against sea-green walls. A wall of french windows opens on to a big tiered terrace next to the canal, and there are more smart wood tables out on a heavily planted first-floor terrace with the same view. Good bar food, served by friendly staff, includes soup (£2.95), open sandwiches (from £4.25), steak and red onion tortilla wrap (£4.45), red thai chicken curry (£6.25), fish and chips (£5.75), and in the evening more elaborate dishes might include moules marinières (£3.75), wild boar sausages with mash (£7.45), moroccan lamb kebabs (£9.95) and fried salmon (£7.65) with puddings such as chocolate fudge cake and banoffi slice (from £3.50). The well reproduced piped pop has more presence than just background music. The monastic-style antiqued lavatories are fun, with their rows of butler's sinks for hand-washing. Well kept Courage Directors, John Smiths and Tetleys served at several counters dotted around; decent wines; daily papers. *(Recommended by Kevin Blake, Dave Braisted, the Didler, Keith and Katy Stevens, JP, PP)*

Scottish Courage ~ Manager Rob Fletcher ~ Real ale ~ Bar food (11-10) ~ Restaurant ~ (0115) 947 3904 ~ DJs at weekends and occasional jazz bands ~ Open 11-11; 12-10.30 Sun

UPTON SK7354 Map 7
French Horn

A612

Picnic-sets on the big sloping back paddock of this popular dining pub look out over farmland, and the front is decorated with attractive flower displays in summer. Readers are as enthusiastic as ever about the good food here and most of the tables are laid for eating, even on weekday lunchtimes. The wide choice of bar food includes soup (£2.50), sandwiches (from £2.95, baguettes from £3.85), baked potatoes (from £4.25) and ploughman's (from £4.50) which are served only at lunchtime. Other dishes might be fried goats cheese (£3.95), crab claws with white wine and fish velouté (£4.95), chicken and cashew nut stir fry (£7.50), English lamb saddle with mustard, thyme and redcurrant sauce (£12.50), potato and leek bake (£6.95) or Scottish salmon with tomatoes and mozzarella (£9.25) followed by puddings such as bread and butter pudding or blackcurrant cheesecake (£3.10); booking is usually necessary if you want to eat here. There's a nicely relaxed atmosphere in the neat and comfortable open-plan bar with cushioned captain's chairs, wall banquettes around glossy tables, and watercolours by local artists (some may be for sale). Well kept Adnams and Courage Directors and a guest such as Greene King IPA on handpump; piped music. *(Recommended by John and Christine Lowe, Pat and Tony Martin, Dave Braisted, Phyl and Jack Street, Bill and Sheila McLardy, JP, PP, D L Parkhurst, Jim Cowan, Jane Scarrow, Mike and Sue Loseby)*

Pubmaster ~ Tenant Joyce Carter ~ Real ale ~ Bar food (12-2, 6-9, 12-10 Sun) ~ Restaurant ~ (01636) 812394 ~ Children welcome ~ Jazz alternate Sun evenings ~ Open 11-11; 12-10.30 Sun

WALKERINGHAM SK7792 Map 7
Three Horse Shoes
High Street; just off A161, off A631 W of Gainsborough

In summer the rather ordinary frontage of this pleasant village pub is transformed into a blaze of colour by the licensees' spectacular hanging baskets and flower displays. The 9,000 plants they use complement the slight austerity of the simple old-fashioned décor inside. They've a wide choice of good value food and they have plans to extend their snack menu. Enjoyable dishes might include soup (£1.50), mushrooms and ham in creamy garlic sauce or home-made pâté (£3.25), pork medallions in a white wine, mustard and cream sauce (£7.75), home-made steak and kidney or mushroom, cheese, leek and nut pie (£6.25), grilled plaice or liver, bacon and sausage casserole (£5.95) and specials such as braised steak with red wine and mushrooms (£7.50). In the welcoming bar you'll find well kept Bass, Stones, Worthington Best and a guest beer such as Batemans XXXB on handpump. Darts, dominoes, fruit machine, video game, and piped music. Outside there are seats among the flowers and a Japanese-style millennium garden beside the top car park. *(Recommended by JP, PP, P J White, Chris and Elaine Lyon, Marlene and Jim Godfrey, Mike and Sue Loseby)*

Free house ~ Licensee John Turner ~ Real ale ~ Bar food (not Sun evening) ~ Restaurant ~ (01427) 890959 ~ Children welcome ~ Open 11.30-3, 7-11; 12-3, 7-10.30 Sun

---

Lucky Dip

Besides the fully inspected pubs, you might like to try these Lucky Dips recommended to us and described by readers (if you do, please send us reports: www.goodguides.com).

Awsworth [SK4844]
Gate [Main St, via A6096 off A610 Nuthall—Eastwood bypass]: Friendly old traditional local with Hardys & Hansons Best and Mild, coal fire in lounge, small pool room; nr site of once-famous railway viaduct – photographs in passage *(the Didler, JP, PP)*
Hogs Head [quite handy for M1 junction 26, via A610/A6096; Main St]: Friendly neatly kept family-run pub with huge helpings of fresh traditional food inc two-for-one bargains and very popular Sun carvery, well kept beers inc Bass, Hardys & Hansons and Timothy Taylors Landlord, restaurant; clean modern bedrooms *(anon)*
Bagthorpe [SK4751]
Dixies Arms [2 miles from M1 junction 27; A608 towards Eastwood, then first right on to B600 via Sandhill Rd, then first left into School Rd; Lower Bagthorpe]: Well kept real ales in quaint 18th-c beamed and tiled-floor local, entrance bar with tiny snug next to bar, small part-panelled parlour with great recently restored fireplace, tables, chairs and wall bench in longer narrow room with toby jugs and darts, friendly landlord and labrador, unobtrusive fruit machine and rarely used juke box; jazz or folk Sat, quiz night Sun, big garden with wknd barbecues, play area and football pitch, own pigeon, gun and morris dancing

clubs; open 2-11, all day wknds *(Anne de Gruchy, JP, PP, the Didler)*
Bingham [SK7039]
Horse & Plough [A52]: Well renovated former betting shop (and once a chapel), low beams, flagstones and stripped brick, prints and old brewery memorabilia, well kept Belvoir Star, Courage Directors, Charles Wells and three guest beers, good wine choice, upstairs restaurant with polished boards, hand-painted murals and good food from open kitchen; under same management as Horse & Groom in Nottingham, open all day *(the Didler)*
Bleasby [SK7149]
Waggon & Horses [Gypsy Lane]: Comfortable banquettes in carpeted lounge, open fire in character bar, Banks's and Marstons Pedigree, reasonably priced fresh lunchtime food from snacks up, Fri fish and chips night, chatty landlord; piped music; back lobby with play area and comfortable chairs to watch over it, tables outside, small camping area behind *(the Didler)*
Blyth [SK6287]
Angel [Bawtry Rd]: Cheerful much-modernised coaching inn with partly no smoking lounge/dining area, well kept Hardys & Hansons Best, nice coal fire, assorted furniture, usual food served on Sun too (rare around here); piped music, smaller public bar and pool

room; children welcome, garden with play area, simple bedrooms *(CMW, JJW, LYM)*

Bramcote [SK5037]

White Lion [just off A52 W of Nottingham; Town St]: Full Hardys & Hansons range kept well in popular end-terrace local, bar serving two split-level adjoining rooms, tables in garden behind *(Alan and Eileen Bowker)*

Burton Joyce [SK6443]

☆ *Wheatsheaf* [A612 E of Nottingham]: Well refurbished Chef & Brewer, several softly lit and fairly individually furnished rooms around a central bar, antiques and grandfather clock, lots of wine bottles scattered around; very wide choice of decent food, well kept Courage Directors and Theakstons Best and XB, log and coal fires; piped music, maybe classical; good garden areas, good disabled access and facilities *(BB, Kevin Blake)*

Car Colston [SK7242]

Royal Oak [The Green, off Tenman Lane (off A46 not far from A6097 junction)]: Largeish 18th-c pub opp one of England's biggest village greens, woodburner in main room, unusual vaulted brick ceiling in second room, good choice of reasonably priced food inc children's, Mansfield and Marstons Pedigree, decent coffee, good soft drinks choice, fresh flowers and pot plants; piped music; picnic-sets on roomy back lawn, open all day Sun, cl Mon lunchtime *(CMW, JJW)*

Carlton-on-Trent [SK7964]

Great Northern [Ossington Rd; village signed just off A1 N of Newark]: Large busy local next to railway line, comfortable and welcoming, with lots of railway memorabilia, toys in large family room; Mansfield Riding, local Springhead and guest ales, decent if limited food inc good fish and chips, small dining area, good service; garden with play area *(Derek and Sylvia Stephenson, JP, PP)*

Caythorpe [SK6845]

Black Horse [Main St, off A6097 NE of Nottingham]: 300-year-old country local, recently extended but unspoilt and uncluttered, run by same family for many years; microbrewery producing its own good Dover Beck ales, guests such as Bass and Black Sheep, enjoyable food (not Sun, and may be no food for strangers if there's pressure on the kitchen) inc imaginative sandwiches, good fresh fish Weds-Fri, Mon curry night, small bar, larger tap room across yard, real fire; opp pottery, handy for Trent walks *(the Didler, CMW, JJW, Alan and Eileen Bowker, Norma and Keith Bloomfield)*

Clarborough [SK7383]

Gate [Smeath Lane]: Open-plan pub in attractive spot by Chesterfield Canal, good value food esp fish and chips, all freshly cooked (so can be a wait if busy), Adnams, Mansfield and Stones, good choice of other drinks, open fire, friendly service, no smoking area, restaurant overlooking waterside garden; piped music, moorings available *(CMW, JJW, Mike and Sue Loseby)*

Collingham [SK8361]

Kings Head [High St]: Modernised Georgian

building, three real ales inc Timothy Taylors Landlord, ad lib coffee, bar sandwiches, good food with unusual touches and properly cooked veg in restaurant *(Darly Graton, Graeme Gulibert)*

Cotgrave [SK6435]

Rose & Crown [Main Rd, off A46 SE of Nottingham]: Comfortably refurbished, with Boddingtons and guest beers such as Greene King Abbot and Old Speckled Hen, good simple food *(Norma and Keith Bloomfield, Richard Butler, Marie Kroon)*

Cottam [SK8179]

Moth & Lantern: Several comfortable areas inc conservatory, pleasant décor, wide choice of good value food inc children's, John Smiths and Tetleys, friendly helpful staff; pool, juke box, TV and games machine; play area, pets corner, bedrooms *(Richard Lewis)*

Cropwell Bishop [SK6835]

Lime Kiln [Kinoulton Rd (off A46 E of Nottingham)]: Friendly two-bar pub with wide choice of generous fresh food inc children's (can be a wait), well kept Courage Directors, good choice of wines and soft drinks, hunting trophies, small dining room, family conservatory with budgerigars; fruit machine, quiet piped music, TV; terrace and garden *(CMW, JJW)*

Cuckney [SK5671]

Greendale Oak [High Croft]: Good range of reasonably priced well cooked and served food (not wknd evenings) from sandwiches up, some OAP bargains, helpful licensees, swift service even when very busy midweek lunchtime, roomy L-shaped bar with banquettes, chamber-pots, Davy lamps, coins and banknotes on beams, two real ales, good coffee, popular evening restaurant; quiet piped music, games machine, children if eating, no dogs; bedrooms *(CMW, JJW, Hugh A MacLean)*

Dunham [SK8174]

Bridge Inn [Main St]: Nr toll bridge, real fire, Springhead and two guest beers, enjoyable food, friendly landlord and locals, L-shaped room with lots of artefacts, beams, brass ornaments; piped music; well behaved children welcome, wheelchair access, tables outside, open all day Sun *(Richard Lewis)*
White Swan [A57 Retford—Lincoln; Main St]: Pleasant local with two comfortable lounge areas, wide choice of usual food (breakfast too), well kept Stones, Tom Woods Old Timber and Worthingtons at attractive prices, decent wines, friendly staff; large grass area, caravan site, sizeable new fishing pond *(Richard Lewis)*

East Stoke [SK7549]

Paunchfote Arms [A46/Moor Lane]: Comfortable if not cheap, with enjoyable food from soup and baguettes up in lounge dining area and restaurant, Bass and Marstons Pedigree, pictures for sale; piped music, theme nights *(CMW, JJW)*

Eastwood [SK4846]

Foresters Arms [Main St, Newthorpe]: Proper two-room village inn, clean and cosy, with Hardys & Hansons on electric pump, relaxing lounge, TV and old local photographs in bar, darts, dominoes and skittles, piano sing-along wknds; nice garden, occasional barbecues *(the Didler, JP, PP)*

Epperstone [SK6548]

Cross Keys [Main St]: Friendly old small two-bar village pub, locally popular for hearty home-cooked food (not Sun or Mon) inc cheap OAP lunch Tues-Fri; well kept Hardys & Hansons beers, cheerful if not always speedy service; pretty village, pleasant countryside *(CMW, JJW)*

Farnsfield [SK6456]

Red Lion [Main St, off A614]: Roomy refurbished village pub, comfortable banquettes, pictures and brass, friendly obliging service, popular food (not Sun/Mon evenings) inc children's and Mon-Sat OAP roast lunches, fair prices, several Mansfield ales, decent wines, open fire, restaurant; piped music, TV, fruit machine; picnic-sets and swings in garden *(CMW, JJW)*

Hickling [SK6929]

Plough [Main St]: Welcoming new licensees in interesting old pub, two levels and several rooms extended around old cottage, armchairs and settees in largest room, very cosy snug, four real ales such as Bass, Charles Wells Bombardier and Wadworths 6X, wide choice of food, several open fires; fruit machine, maybe quiet piped music; children welcome, garden with barbecue and fenced-off water feature, nice spot by Grantham Canal basin (locally navigable), towpath walks *(CMW, JJW)*

Hockerton [SK7156]

Spread Eagle [A617 Newark—Mansfield]: Spacious and neatly kept open-plan pub with very friendly landlord, good reasonably priced straightforward food, well kept Mansfield ales with a guest such as Greene King Abbot, attractive mix of furnishings inc church pews, decorative china *(Phil and Jane Hodson)*

Huthwaite [SK4560]

Woodend Inn [Chesterfield Rd, N of village]: Former miners' local done up as Brewers Fayre dining pub, comfortable, good value bar meals *(Peter and Audrey Dowsett)*

Kimberley [SK5044]

Stag [Nottingham Rd]: Relaxing and friendly 16th-c local run by devoted landlady, low beams, dark panelling and settles, well kept Boddingtons, Greenalls Bitter and Mild, Marstons Pedigree and a guest beer; attractive back garden with play area, cl wkdy lunchtime (opens 5; 2 Sat, 12 Sun) *(JP, PP, the Didler)*

Kirkby in Ashfield [SK5056]

Countryman [Park Lane (B6018 S)]: Lively traditional atmosphere in upgraded former miners' local, attractive bas relief murals of shooting scenes in cottagey beamed lounge bar, decorative plates and mining memorabilia, well kept Bass, Theakstons and usually two guests, beer festivals, good value generous bar food (not Sun, Mon evening), public bar with pool; popular with walkers, play area, good live folk, rock and blues Fri; open all day *(Kevin Blake, the Didler)*

Duke of Wellington [Church St]: Plush beamed

lounge with lots of pictures, pool and TV in pleasant bar, friendly staff, well kept Mansfield beers, good cheap food; tables outside *(Kevin Blake)*

Wagon & Horses [Chapel St]: Three-room local with plates showing mining area in beamed bar, character landlord, well kept Hardys & Hansons ales, good value food till early evening; quiz nights, own football team *(Kevin Blake)*

Lambley [SK6245]

Robin Hood & Little John [Main St]: Welcoming old-fashioned village local, well kept Banks's, Mansfield and Marstons Pedigree, roaring log fires, lunchtime food from hearty sandwiches to changing hot dishes, cards and dominoes in heavy-beamed public bar, heavyweight pub dog called Eadie; popular with walkers *(Brian and Halina Howes)*

Low Marnham [SK8070]

Brownlow Arms: Dating from 16th c but largely rebuilt after 1993 fire, boat-shaped bar with quietly friendly and chatty rooms off either side, lots of beams, panelling and bric-a-brac, good choice of freshly made food (so may be a wait; not Mon lunchtime), two real ales, real fire, piano in one room, ice-cream fridge in another; children and dogs welcome, disabled access, picnic-sets on terrace *(CMW, JJW)*

Lowdham [SK6646]

Old Ship [nr A612/A6097; Main St]: Traditional beamed country local with dining area in extended split-level lounge/bar, attractive area with big round tables, lots of pictures, plates, copper and brass, open fire, separate public bar; well kept real ales such as Marstons Pedigree and John Smiths, occasional guest beers, above-average food, friendly service; quiz nights, pleasant walks nearby *(Kevin Blake)*

Worlds End [Plough Lane]: Small, clean and friendly old beamed village pub with log fire at one end of long room, dining area the other, fresh flowers, some original features, very reasonably priced straightforward food using local produce (may be a wait), small-helping OAP lunches; piped music; good window boxes, picnic-sets in garden; may sometimes be closed for private parties *(Mrs M Duckworth, CMW, JJW)*

Maplebeck [SK7160]

☆ *Beehive* [signed down pretty country lanes from A616 Newark—Ollerton and from A617 Newark—Mansfield]: Cosy and unspoiled beamed country tavern in nice spot, excellent landlady, tiny front bar, rather bigger side room, traditional furnishings, open fire, free antique juke box, well kept local Maypole and Rudgate ales, good cheese or ham rolls, tables on small terrace with flower tubs and grassy bank running down to little stream, play area with swings, barbecues; may be cl wkdy winter lunchtimes, very busy other wknds and bank hols *(the Didler, LYM, Anna, Dr B and Mrs P B Baker, Bernie Adams, JP, PP)*

Morton [SK7251]

Full Moon [Main St; back rd SE of Southwell]: 16th-c local in out-of-the-way hamlet not far from River Trent, wide choice of good value standard food inc good fish and vegetarian, children's dishes, lots of puddings, OAP bargain lunch and very popular Sun lunch, four well kept ales inc local Caythorpe, energetic congenial landlord, polite service, comfortable L-shaped lounge; children welcome; piped music, pool and TV in games room, no dogs (pub has persian cat), lots of events; big garden with terrace, picnic-sets, play area *(Dr B and Mrs P B Baker, D A F Bewley, JP, PP, the Didler, CMW, JJW)*

Newark [SK8054]

Fox & Crown [Appleton Gate]: Bare-boards but comfortable Tynemill pub, nooks and corners inc no smoking back family areas, stone or wood floors, big brewery mirrors and other breweriana, well kept ales such as Batemans XXXB, Belvoir Beaver, Caledonian Deuchars IPA, Everards Tiger, Hook Norton Best and Marstons Pedigree, Inch's cider, dozens of malt whiskies, continental draught and bottled beers, flavoured vodkas, good choice of wines, freshly made food from sandwiches up, friendly efficient staff; good wheelchair access, occasional live music, open all day *(Richard Lewis, the Didler, Ian Phillips)*

☆ *Mail Coach* [London Rd, nr Beaumond Cross]: Friendly open-plan Georgian local, pleasant décor in three candlelit separate areas, lots of pictures, big fire, well kept Boddingtons, Flowers IPA and guest beers such as Barnsley and Springhead, enjoyable home-made lunchtime food inc some unusual dishes, pleasant staff; pub games, jazz, blues or folk wknds; tables outside *(Kevin Blake, the Didler)*

Newcastle Arms [George St]: Thriving traditional Victorian local with well kept Mansfield Home Bitter and Mild, Ruddles Best, Charles Wells Bombardier and several bottled beers, friendly landlord; TV in lounge with racing prints, games in public bar, tables outside *(Richard Lewis, the Didler)*

☆ *Old Malt Shovel* [North Gate]: Welcoming and comfortably opened-up, with enjoyable food from doorstep sandwiches to some Portuguese dishes, fresh veg, well kept Adnams Broadside, Greene King Abbot, Theakstons XB, Timothy Taylors Landlord and a good one brewed for them by Rudgate, open fire, choice of teas, lots of books and bottles on shelves, cheerfully laid-back atmosphere and service; evening restaurant Weds-Sun; pub games, wheelchair access *(Derek and Sylvia Stephenson, the Didler)*

Old Post Office [Kirk Gate]: Roomy conversion of former main PO keeping lots of old features inc delivery van which children can eat inside, telegraph poles and telephone box, split-level bar with comfortable gallery and all-day café/bistro area, enjoyable food inc take-aways, or just drop in for a coffee, or well kept Bass, Courage Directors, Fullers London Pride, Greene King IPA or Theakstons; daily papers, pleasant courtyard with plenty of tables out under cocktail parasols, lots of flowers *(Ian Phillips, Kevin Blake, Judy Pearson)*

Rutland Arms [Barnby Gate]: Dating from 17th c though much modernised, beams, alcoves, different levels, old kitchen range and bric-a-brac, lunchtime food, well kept Mansfield beers; SkyTV sports; bedrooms, fine courtyard *(Kevin Blake)*

Sir John Arderne [Market Pl/Church St]: Comfortable Wetherspoons, well kept beers with bargain prices, good choice of wines, friendly service, good menu, no smoking areas; open all day *(Richard Lewis)*

Wing [Bridge St, just off Market Pl]: Tucked-away character local nr church, well kept Theakstons Best, XB and Old Peculier, games room; tables outside *(the Didler)*

Newstead [SK5252]

Station Hotel [Station Rd]: Busy basic red-brick village local opp station on Robin Hood rail line, bargain well kept Barnsley Bitter and Old Tom Mild, old railway photographs; no food Sun (nor rail service then) *(the Didler, JP, PP)*

Nottingham [SK5640]

☆ *Bell* [Angel Row, off Market Sq]: Bustling friendly low-beamed 15th-c pub, back bar now carefully restored and extended, two smaller timbered and panelled front bars, Bass, Black Sheep, Brains SA and guest beers such as Belvoir Beaver, Mansfield, Marstons Pedigree, John Smiths and Springhead Roaring Meg from extraordinarily deep sandstone cellar, ancient stairs to attractive calmer raftered room with nice window seats used as lunchtime family restaurant for good value simple well presented lunchtime food; good value wines; trad jazz Sun lunchtime (rolls only then), Mon and Tues evenings; open all day, cl Sun afternoon *(Keith and Katy Stevens, JP, PP, Andy and Ali, the Didler, LYM, Richard Lewis, R M Taylor)*

Canal House [Canal St]: Striking new bare-brick and parquet alehouse conversion of wharf building by Tynemill, little indoors canal basin with a couple of boats by the bar and a bridge to further seating area, well kept changing beers such as Castle Rock Hemlock and Timothy Taylors Landlord with a continental lager, good upstairs restaurant and second bar, attractive waterside terrace; live music, student nights, open all day *(the Didler, Richard Lewis)*

Coopers Arms [Porchester Rd, Thornywood]: Solid Victorian local with three unspoilt rooms, Home Mild and Bitter, Theakstons XB; small family room in skittle alley; cl Weds lunchtime *(JP, PP, the Didler)*

Falcon [Canning Circus/Alfreton Rd]: Traditional intimate unspoilt two-room corner local, Adnams, Boddingtons and Tetleys, daily papers, good upstairs restaurant *(the Didler, JP, PP)*

Forest [Mansfield Rd]: Tynemill pub – same small group as Lincolnshire Poacher – with two smallish basic rooms knocked together, prints and beer posters on wood panel and tiled walls, well kept Castle Rock Hemlock, Greene King Abbot, Woodfordes Wherry and a guest such as Batemans, low prices, varied food inc Mexican and enjoyable vegetarian dishes *(Rona Murdoch, Roger and Jenny Huggins, Darly Graton, Graeme Gulibert)*

Fox & Crown [Church St/Lincoln St, Old Basford]: Pleasantly refurbished open-plan local, back microbrewery producing its own Alcazar Vixens Vice, Brush Bitter, New Dawn and Maple Magic winter ale, brewery tours Sat; wide choice of pizzas and other dishes inc sandwiches, helpful staff and Canadian landlord; good piped music, games machines, Tues quiz night, SkyTV sports; tables out behind, open all day *(Richard Lewis, the Didler, JP, PP)*

Goose [Ambleside, Gamston; off A6011, E edge of city]: Comfortable newish family pub attractively done, with beams, bare bricks, different levels and areas, old prints and artefacts inc replica of antiquated living room hearth, no smoking family dining area, indoor and outdoor play areas, wide choice of food inc children's and OAP bargains, well kept Hardys & Hansons Best, Classic, Best Mild and a changing special such as Pedlers Pride, decent wines, friendly helpful staff; piped music, games machines; open all day *(Richard Lewis)*

Horse & Groom [Radford Rd, New Basford]: Popular and well run partly open-plan local next to former Shipstones brewery, with their name over door and other memorabilia; nice snug, changing well kept ales such as Bass, Belvoir Star, Gales HSB, Charles Wells Bombardier and Whim Hartington, good value fresh food from sandwiches up, daily papers, jazz, folk, blues or skiffle nights Fri in converted back stables; open all day *(the Didler, JP, PP, David Atkinson, Darly Graton, Graeme Gulibert)*

☆ *Limelight* [Wellington Circus, nr Playhouse]: Extended convivial bar and restaurant attached to Playhouse theatre, well kept Adnams, Batemans XB, Courage Directors, Marstons Pedigree, Theakstons XB and guests inc a Mild, reasonably priced food from rolls to full meals (not Sun lunchtime), pleasant efficient staff, theatre pictures, maybe live celebrities (also good mix of customers inc nearby lawyers), occasional modern jazz, attractive continental-style outside seating area; open all day, live blues and jazz *(JP, PP, Derek and Sylvia Stephenson, Kevin Blake, the Didler, A C and E Johnson)*

Lion [Lower Mosley St, New Basford]: Well managed pub with good prices, up to ten well kept ales inc local Mallard from one of city's deepest cellars (glass viewing panel – and can be visited at quiet times), farm cider, wide choice of good wholesome food inc doorstep sandwiches, open-plan bare bricks and boards, log fire, daily papers, live folk, jazz and blues Fri-Sun; summer barbecues, open all day *(the Didler, JP, PP, David Atkinson)*

Peacock [Mansfield Rd]: Warm candlelit Victorian pub, well kept Mansfield, Timothy Taylors Landlord and guest beers from small breweries, pleasant bar, lounge with bell-push table service, food inc big pies; licensed for backgammon, open all day *(Patrick Renouf)*

Pit & Pendulum [Victoria St]: Split-level bar given gothic haunted house décor, with exemplary lighting, some good furniture inc tables with old coins and treasure maps; John Smiths, lunchtime food, cellar bar, lavatories through false bookcase, open all day *(Kevin Blake)*

Plough [St Peters St, Radford]: Licensees (formerly of Castle Rock Brewery) planning their own Nottingham Brewing Co microbrewery behind here *(the Didler)*

Portland Arms [Portland Rd]: Well kept beers, lunchtime food inc Sun roast, Notts Forest memorabilia, games and sports TV; can get smoky; open all day wknds *(the Didler)*

Punchbowl [Porchester Rd, Mapperley]: Recently comfortably refurbished, with wide choice of beers inc guests such as Fullers London Pride *(Richard Greenwood)*

Salutation [Hounds Gate/Maid Marion Way]: Whitbreads Hogshead with up to a dozen or more changing ales (at a price) and lots of bottled beers, speedily served usual food inc two-for-one bargains, ancient back part with beams, flagstones and well worn cosy corners, plusher modern front lounge, helpful staff; can get busily noisy *(Rona Murdoch, Roger and Jenny Huggins, R M Taylor, BB, Keith and Katy Stevens, Susan and Nigel Wilson, JP, PP)*

☆ *Sir John Borlase Warren* [Ilkeston Rd/Canning Circus (A52 towards Derby)]: Several connecting individual rooms attractively redone in light colours with matching settees and low tables, interesting Victorian decorations, fittings and prints, candles in saucers, enjoyable lunchtime food, no smoking eating area (can get smoky elsewhere when the students are in at night), very friendly staff, Courage, Marstons Pedigree and a guest beer such as Leatherbritches tapped from the cask; children welcome (not Fri/Sat evenings), tables in attractively lit back garden with barbecues *(JP, PP, David Carr, Rona Murdoch, Roger and Jenny Huggins, MP)*

Nuthall [SK5144]

Three Ponds [Kimberley Rd (B600, away from city), off A610 nr M1 junction 26]: Friendly and tastefully refurbished family dining pub with wide range of good value food till 8 inc OAP and off-peak bargains, Hardys & Hansons Best, Best Mild and Classic, good coffee, good staff; piped music and games machines, mostly no smoking; children in family room, big back garden with play area, open all day *(CMW, JJW)*

Orston [SK7741]

Durham Ox [Church St]: Welcoming country local opp church, well kept Home, Marstons Pedigree, John Smiths, Theakstons and a guest beer, wine fresh from sensible small bottles, good value beef, ham and other rolls (no hot food); comfortable split-level open-plan bar with interesting RAF/USAF memorabilia, collection of whisky bottles; tables outside (and hitching rail for ferrets as well as for horses) *(JP, PP, Phil and Jane Hodson, the Didler, R M Taylor)*

Papplewick [SK5450]

Griffins Head [B683/B6011]: Refurbished under newish licensees, cottagey room off central bar, locals' bar, attractive candlelit

raftered dining area, decent food, well kept
Theakstons; tables outside, barbecues, handy
for Newstead Abbey *(Kevin Blake)*

Radcliffe on Trent [SK6439]

Black Lion [A52]: Friendly bar, big
comfortable lounge, good choice of food from
beef cobs to full meals, well kept Home Bitter
and three or four guest beers; big garden and
play area, Oct charity steam fair *(the Didler)*

Ravenshead [SK5554]

Hutt [A60 Nottingham—Mansfield]: Recently
refurbished Chef & Brewer, character softly lit
rooms, alcoves and intimate areas, good food
choice inc unusual dishes, well kept Courage
Directors, Theakstons XB and an occasional
guest beer; open all day *(Kevin Blake)*

Retford [SK7080]

☆ *Market Hotel* [off West Carr Rd, Ordsall;
follow Leisure Centre signs from A620, then
just after industrial estate sign keep eyes
skinned for pub sign on left]: Owned by same
family for 40 years, with particularly good
choice of well kept ales (up to 40 in autumn
beer festival), comfortable plush banquettes,
generous good value straightforward food (not
Sun evening) friendly helpful service; very busy
Fri/Sat night, jazz 3rd Sun in month, open all
day Sat *(Richard Lewis, JP, PP, LYM, Mike
and Sue Loseby, Derek and Sylvia Stephenson)*

Selston [SK4553]

Horse & Jockey [just off M1 junction 27]:
Three carefully refurbished main rooms on
three levels, cosy snug off lower bar area,
beams, flagstones and coal fire in cast-iron
range, Bass, Greene King Abbot, Timothy
Taylors Landlord and other ales on handpump
or in jugs direct from the cellar casks, decent
lunchtime food (not wknds), bar billiards in top
room; open all day Sat *(the Didler, JP, PP)*

Skegby [SK5060]

Forest [Forest Rd]: Comfortable open-plan pub
where locals go for a civilised evening out, with
wonderful collection of plates naming every
mine in Notts; friendly staff, Home and
Mansfield ales, quick efficient service; quiet
piped music; busy wknds *(Peter and Audrey
Dowsett)*

South Leverton [SK7881]

Plough [Town St]: Tiny unchanging pub
doubling as morning post office, basic trestle
tables and benches, real fire, Greene King
Ruddles Best and a guest beer, traditional
games, tables outside; open 2-11 (all day Sat,
12-4, 7-10.30 Sun) *(the Didler, JP, PP, Mike
and Sue Loseby)*

Southwell [SK6953]

☆ *Bramley Apple* [Church St (A612)]: Helpful
friendly service, good value lunchtime food inc
fresh fish and very crisp veg, generous Sun
lunch, well kept Mansfield and a good guest
beer, good atmosphere, attractively worked
Bramley apple theme, eating area screened off
by stained glass; comfortable bedrooms *(David
Carr, BB, M J Brooks, Peter and Jean Hoare)*
Old Coaching House [Church St]: Well
refurbished, beams and old-world nooks
around central bar, up to six changing well
kept ales, roaring coal fires, bar billiards, shove-

ha'penny and other traditional games; tables on
terrace, may be cl wkdy lunchtimes, open all
day wknds *(the Didler, JP, PP)*

Stoke Bardolph [SK6441]

Ferry Boat [off A612 in Burton Joyce;
Riverside]: Large Millers Kitchen family dining
pub in lovely spot overlooking River Trent,
waterside picnic-sets, sheep, ducks, geese and
swans opposite, several comfortable largely no
smoking areas, lots of wood, copper, brass and
ornaments, good choice of good value food inc
wkdy lunchtime loyalty discounts for OAPs,
two real ales, fair choice of wines, attentive
service, daily papers (inc framed sheets in
gents'); fruit machine, quiet piped music, Tues
quiz night; open all day *(CMW, JJW)*

Sutton in Ashfield [SK5059]

King & Miller [Kings Mill Rd E]: Comfortable
family pub, play areas inside and out, alcove
tables, huge range of reasonably priced food,
warm welcome, decent wines, Hardys &
Hansons beers *(Andy and Jill Kassube)*
Travellers Rest [Huthwaite Rd]: Friendly
panelled local with pictures, shelves of bric-a-
brac, attractive fireplace, well kept Mansfield
beers, good value lunchtime food, darts, pool
and TV in separate bar *(Kevin Blake)*

Thurgarton [SK6949]

Red Lion [Southwell Rd (A612)]: Bright and
cheery 16th-c inn, recently extended in front,
with good unusual freshly cooked food (all day
Sat, Sun and bank hols) inc fresh fish in roomy
split-level beamed bars and restaurant, well
kept Mansfield and Marstons Pedigree, flame-
effect fire, unobtrusive fruit machine; children
welcome, well spaced tables and dogs on leads
in attractive big garden *(CMW, JJW,
David and Ruth Hollands, Kevin Blake,
W and P J Elderkin)*

Underwood [SK4751]

Red Lion [Church Lane; off B600, nr M1
junction 27]: 17th-c village pub with good
value family food inc OAP lunches, smartly
refurbished spacious open-plan bar with open
fire, pictures and some cushioned settles, well
kept Boddingtons, Marstons Pedigree and guest
beers, penny arcade machine, no piped music;
children welcome, picnic-sets and large
adventure playground in big garden with
terrace, attractive setting; open all day Fri-Sat
(Anne de Gruchy, the Didler)

Upton [SK7354]

Cross Keys [A612]: Rambling heavy-beamed
bar with lots of alcoves, central log fire,
interesting bric-a-brac and medley of
furnishings, three real ales, decent wines,
enterprising food choice inc sandwiches and
Sun lunch; may be piped music, Sun folk night;
children in back extension with carved pews or
upstairs restaurant; opp British Horological
Institute *(LYM, Phil and Jane Hodson, CMW,
JJW, Darly Graton, Graeme Gulibert)*

Watnall Chaworth [SK5046]

☆ *Queens Head* [3 miles from M1 junction 26:
A610 towards Nottingham, left on B600, then
keep right; Main Rd]: Cosy and tastefully
extended three-room old pub with wide range
of good value food, well kept Home Bitter and

Mild, Theakstons XB and Old Peculier and a guest beer, efficient friendly service; intimate snug, dining area, beams and stripped pine, coal fires; fruit machine, piped music; picnic-sets in spacious and attractive back garden with big play area; open all day Fri/Sat (the Didler, JP, PP)

Wellow [SK6766]

☆ Olde Red Lion [Eakring Rd, just off A616 E of Ollerton]: Low-beamed and panelled 16th-c pub by green with towering maypole which gives its name to the local brewery that brews good Lions Pride for the pub, alongside well kept changing beers such as Robinsons Old Stockport, Ruddles Best and Shepherd Neame Spitfire; quick friendly service, good value fresh food from sandwiches to Sun roasts, no smoking restaurant and dining area, no piped music; children welcome, picnic-sets outside (LYM, Eric Locker, Dr and Mrs J Hills)

West Bridgford [SK5838]

Southbank [Trent Bridge]: Under same ownership as Fellows Morton & Clayton; bright and airy refurbishment extended into former insurance offices, polished wood floors, local Mallard, Timothy Taylors Landlord and a guest beer, good food choice; handy for cricket ground and Nottingham Forest FC (the Didler)

☆ Stratford Haven [Stratford Rd, Trent Bridge]: Busy and chatty Tynemill pub (former pet shop), five distinct areas in long G-shape, bare boards, lots of brewery pictures, good atmosphere, well kept changing ales such as Adnams Broadside, Caledonian Deuchars IPA, Castle Rock Hemlock, Marstons Pedigree and a Mild, farm ciders, good choice of whiskies and wines, good home-cooked food, daily papers, tables outside; can get crowded and smoky (there is a small no smoking snug); handy for cricket ground and Nottingham Forest FC, open all day (Patrick Renouf, the Didler, A C and E Johnson, R M Taylor, JP, PP)

Test Match [Gordon Sq, West Bridgford]: Handsome art deco, with revolving door, high ceiling and sweeping staircase (to the lounge and lavatories); big cricketing prints, some signed bats, full range of Hardys & Hansons beers (Brian and Halina Howes)

Willow Tree [Rufford Way/Stamford Rd]: 1970s pub refurbished in partly divided traditional style, well kept Bass, Worthington

and a guest such as Fullers London Pride (Alan and Eileen Bowker)

West Leake [SK5226]

☆ Star [Melton Lane, off A6006]: Comfortable oak-panelled dining lounge with good central log fire (enjoyed by Cracker the ginger tom), pewter mugs, china, pictures and attractive table lamps, traditional beamed and quarry-tiled country bar on left with wall settles, plenty of character and traditional games, good value home-made food inc cheap steaks, well kept Bass and two or three changing ales such as Cains Dr Duncans IPA and Robinsons Best, good choice of malt whiskies, good coffee, welcoming licensees and friendly helpful service, no piped music or machines; children in eating area, picnic-sets on front terrace (quiet spot) and in garden with play area (CMW, JJW, LYM, the Didler, Richard and Jean Green, JP, PP, Michael and Jenny Back)

West Markham [SK7272]

Mussel & Crab [Sibthorpe Hill; B1164 nr A1/A57/A638 roundabout N of Tuxford]: Former roadside family dining pub reworked by new owners as fish restaurant, two roomy dining areas (beams and stripped stone, or more flamboyant pastel murals), welcoming attentive staff, enjoyable food with plenty of choice on vast array of blackboards besides fish and seafood fresh daily from Brixham, real ale, decent wines; picnic-sets on terrace, play area, views over wheatfields (Dr P D Smart)

Widmerpool [SK6429]

Pullman [1st left off A606 coming towards Nottingham from A46 junction; Kinoulton Lane]: Popular family dining pub in well converted and extended station building, generous Sun carvery, good vegetarian dishes, real ale (Darly Graton, Graeme Gulibert)

Worksop [SK5879]

Mallard [Station, Carlton Rd]: Listed station building noted for its quickly changing beers from small breweries and wide range of foreign bottled beers; coal fire, traditional games; wheelchair access, seats outside, parking in station pay and display, open all day (Sun afternoon closure) (JP, PP, Richard Houghton, Tony Hobden)

White Lion [Park St]: Wetherspoons, smaller than usual, nicely done, with no smoking area, food all day, real ales such as Timothy Taylors Landlord, Theakstons and Shepherd Neame Spitfire; tables out on terrace (Tony Hobden)

Real ale to us means beer which has matured naturally in its cask – not pressurised or filtered. We name all real ales stocked. We usually name ales preserved under a light blanket of carbon dioxide too, though purists – pointing out that this stops the natural yeasts developing – would disagree (most people, including us, can't tell the difference!)

Oxfordshire

Quite a clutch of pubs in this favoured county have kept their place in every annual Guide since it started 20 years ago: the lovely old Lamb in Burford, a classic, excellent all round; the restauranty Sir Charles Napier on the escarpment above Chinnor (still run in her inimitable style by Julie Griffiths), the impressively preserved medieval White Hart at Fyfield (the Howard family have had it all that time), the Turf Tavern tucked down its alley in Oxford, and the Lamb at Shipton-under-Wychwood. Balancing these old stagers is a notable batch of new entries this year: the Blewbury Inn at Blewbury (good food, lovely warm atmosphere), the Horse & Groom at Caulcott (an enjoyable all-rounder, with good beer), the Anchor in Henley (a comfortably old-fashioned antidote to the town's smart affluence), the Rising Sun at Highmoor (an attractive dining pub in a nice spot), the Isis Tavern by the river in Oxford, and the White Swan at Wigginton (the new landlord's cooking has earned him our Food Award in his first few months here). Other pubs on top form this year are the restauranty Boot at Barnard Gate, the Merrymouth at Fifield (good cooking, interesting ancient pub), the cheerful Plough at Finstock (a nice all-rounder), the Falkland Arms at Great Tew (an idyllic country pub), the Five Horseshoes in the Chilterns beech woods at Maidensgrove (good food), the Royal Oak at Ramsden (good food in a friendly and pubby atmosphere), the peaceful Home Sweet Home at Roke (a civilised and traditional dining pub), the Bell at Shenington (a nice village pub with good home cooking), the well run Talk House at Stanton St John, the friendly and attractive Stags Head at Swalcliffe, and the bustling Trout at Tadpole Bridge on the Thames (new no smoking dining room and bedrooms). With a good choice of places for a special meal out in this county, the Lamb in Burford gains the top title of Oxfordshire Dining Pub of the Year. In the Lucky Dip section, current favourites are the Bell at Adderbury, Crown at Church Enstone, Bear & Ragged Staff in Cumnor, Unicorn in Deddington, Trout at Godstow, Bear and Rose & Crown in Oxford, Crown at Pishill, Bishop Blaize and Moody Cow at Sibford Gower and White Hart at Wytham (all but one of these already inspected and approved by us). Food is generally not cheap in the county, and drinks prices here are high, with a pint of beer commonly costing around 15p more than the national average. The local Hook Norton beers are well worth looking out for, usually bringing a welcome touch of sanity to your drinks bill.

BANBURY SP4540 Map 4
Reindeer £
47 Parsons Street, off Market Place

The chatty licensees and staff go to great lengths to make visitors feel at home in this old-fashioned town pub and in winter the atmosphere is made even more welcoming by two roaring log fires. The long front room has heavy 16th-c beams, very broad polished oak floorboards scattered with rugs, a magnificent carved overmantel for one of the fires, and traditional solid furnishings. Ask them to show you the Globe

Room – an attractively proportioned room, where Cromwell held court before the Battle of Edgehill, with original wonderfully carved 17th-c panelling. Arrive early for their straightforward lunchtime bar food which includes soup (£2.10), doorstep or hot sandwiches (from £2.30), home-made stilton and port pâté (£2.95), filled baked potatoes (from £3.20), ploughman's (from £3.50), home-made quiche (£3.60), chilli con carne (£3.80) and chicken and mushroom pie (£4.85) with daily specials such as avocado and prawn bake or stilton pasta (£3.25) and puddings (from £2.10); all day breakfast (£3.10). Well kept Hook Norton Best, Old, Mild, and Generation and guests such as Timothy Taylors Landlord and Crouch Vale SAS on handpump, country wines, 30 Irish whiskies, good coffee, and even snuffs and clay pipes for the more adventurous; shove-ha'penny, cribbage, dominoes and piped music. A smaller back room up steps is no smoking at lunchtime. The little back courtyard has picnic-sets under parasols, aunt sally, and pretty flowering baskets; no under-21s (but see below). *(Recommended by Geoff Pidoux, Iain R Hewitt, P M Hewitt, Steve Whalley, Ted George, Amanda Eames, CMW, JJW, the Didler)*

Hook Norton ~ Tenants John and Hazel Milligan ~ Real ale ~ Bar food (11-2, sandwiches and pies all day) ~ (01295) 264031 ~ Children in Globe Room lunchtime only if eating ~ Open 11-11; closed Sun, bank hol Mon, 25 Dec

BARNARD GATE SP4010 Map 4

Boot

Village signposted off A40 E of Witney

At this handy stop from the A40 there are more than 100 items of celebrity footwear. The stone-tiled dining pub has stout standing timbers and stub walls with latticed glass breaking up the main area, there's a huge log fire, and nice solid country tables and chairs on bare boards. Good (though not cheap) food includes tasty lunchtime sandwiches (from £5.75), and main meals such as tortellini filled with gorgonzola, walnut and artichoke (£8.45), oak roast salmon salad (£8.95), green thai chicken curry (£10.75), steak and Guinness pie (£10.95) and monkfish with vermouth and mustard sauce (£11.95); puddings; part of the restaurant is no smoking. Well kept Hook Norton Best on handpump, and decent wines. The tables out in front are out of earshot of the nearby road. *(Recommended by Geoff Pidoux, D and M T Ayres-Regan, Stuart Turner, Philip and Ann Board)*

Traditional Freehouses ~ Manager Andrew Lund-Yates ~ Real ale ~ Bar food (12-2.30, 7-9.30; 12-9.30 Sat, 12-9 Sun) ~ Restaurant ~ (01865) 881231 ~ Children in eating area of bar and restaurant ~ Piano Mon evening and Sun lunch ~ Open 11-3; 11-11 Sat; 11-10.30 Sun

BINFIELD HEATH SU7478 Map 2

Bottle & Glass ★

Village signposted off A4155 at Shiplake; in village centre fork right immediately after Post Office (signposted Harpsden) and keep on for half mile

Converted from three farm cottages in the 15th c, this pretty thatched black and white timbered pub has a cheery, sociable atmosphere. Good, home-made bar food written on blackboards (roasts only on Sun) might include lunchtime sandwiches (£3.75), a satisfying ploughman's or garlic mushrooms on toast or chicken and liver pâté (£5.50), quiche (£7.25), vegetarian or seafood pasta (£7.50), beef and apricots in red wine (£9.25), steaks (£11.75), and puddings such as bakewell tart and orange cheesecake (from £3.75); swift service. The neatly kept low beamed bar has a fine fireplace, scrubbed ancient tables, a bench built into black squared panelling, spindleback chairs on the attractive flagstones, and a window with diamond-scratched family records of earlier landlords. The smaller, laid-back side room is similarly decorated; shove-ha'penny, dominoes. Well kept Brakspears Bitter, and seasonal Old or Special on handpump, and quite a few malt whiskies. Dogs on leads and children are welcome in the lovely big garden which has old-fashioned wooden seats and tables under little thatched roofs (and an open-sided shed like a rustic pavilion). *(Recommended by Mr and Mrs T A Bryan, the Didler, Paul Vickers)*

Brakspears ~ Tenants Mike and Anne Robinson ~ Real ale ~ Bar food (12-1.45, 7-9.30; not Sun evening) ~ Restaurant ~ (01491) 575755 ~ Open 11-3.30, 6-11; 12-3.30, 7-10.30 Sun

BLEWBURY SU5385 Map 2
Blewbury Inn ♀
London Road (A417)

The enthusiastic and very likeable young couple who now run this small downland village inn have already given it a warmly friendly neighbourly feel. He's French, and is in charge of the kitchen, producing some bold flavours and combinations. The choice might include wild onion and organic cider soup (£4.10), wild boar terrine with grilled onion bread (£5), five spice chicken strips with green peppers (£5.10), roast turkey with savoy cabbage, chorizo and potato gnocchi in cranberry and citrus jus (£10.50), cod with spinach, grilled queen scallop and potato anglaise with parsley and tomato beurre blanc (£11.20) or lamb fillet medallions with pesto mash with white and broad bean cassoulet in oregano jus (£13.50); puddings such as raspberry crème brûlée with blackcurrant sorbet (£5). The bar on the left has an attractive wood-effect floor (we'd guess its choice has something to do with the landlady's work as marketing manager of a flooring firm), a tremendous mix of simple furnishings from a blue director's chair to a big box settles, and French art and period advertising posters on the dusky red walls, with a good log fire. They have good house wines, as well as well kept Hook Norton Best, Timothy Taylors Landlord and a guest such as Shepherd Neame Spitfire on handpump. The carpeted dining room has wheelback chairs around pub tables, and just one or two carefully chosen plates and pictures on its stencilled cream walls above a green dado. Once a month it's given over to 'club nights', with themed dinners for regulars, but even then they really go out of their way to make complete strangers feel welcome and part of things; small bedrooms. *(Recommended by Drs E J C Parker)*

Free house ~ Licensees Franck and Kally Peigne ~ Bar food (lunchtimes only) ~ Restaurant ~ (01235) 850496 ~ Children welcome ~ Open 12-3, 6-11; 12-3 Sun; closed Sun evening, all day Mon ~ Bedrooms: £40S/£50S

BROADWELL SP2504 Map 4
Five Bells
Village signposted off A361 N of Lechlade, and off B4020 S of Carterton

The neatly kept garden of this snug former coaching inn, run by chatty licensees, is ablaze with colour in the summer while in winter you can appreciate the two big, warming log fires inside. It can get very busy in the spotlessly kept, well furnished series of rooms which have a pleasant mix of flagstones and carpeting, low beams, antique pistols, and plates and rural pictures on the walls. The sizeable dining room to the right of the lounge and the small conservatory (both no smoking) overlook the spacious garden – where they play aunt sally, and grow some of the vegetables used in the kitchen. Well liked, reasonably priced bar food includes sandwiches (from £1.75), soup (£2.50), and dishes such as stilton mushrooms (£3.75), cajun prawns (£3.95), hearty ham, egg and chips (£4.50), fish and chips (£4.95), salmon and prawn gratin or chicken breast in wine and mushrooms (£6.25), almond roast or gammon and pineapple (£6.50), steaks (from £9.95) and puddings such as ginger pudding (from £2.95); well cooked vegetables in separate tureens; it's advisable to book for Sunday lunch. Well kept Bass with a guest beer such as Archers Village on handpump, and decent house wine. The public bar has darts, dominoes and piped music. Wheelchair access. The friendly brown labrador is called Toby; look out for the pot holes in the track leading to the pub. *(Recommended by Marjorie and David Lamb, P R and S A White, K H Frostick, KN-R, Peter and Audrey Dowsett, Nick Lawless, Phil and Jane Hodson, Mr and Mrs J Evans)*

Free house ~ Licensees Trevor and Ann Cooper ~ Real ale ~ Bar food (12-1.45, 7-9; not Sun evening or all day Mon) ~ Restaurant ~ (01367) 860076 ~ Well behaved children if eating, not in conservatory or bar, not Sat evening ~ Open 11.30-2.30, 7(6.30 Sat)-11; 12-3, 7-10.30 Sun; closed Mon ~ Bedrooms: /£50S

BUCKLAND SU3497 Map 4

Lamb ♀ ⛺

Village signposted off A420 NE of Faringdon

The emphasis in this rather smart 18th-c stone dining pub, set in a tranquil village, is on the food. At restaurant quality as well as prices, good bar food might include weekday sandwiches (from £2.50), home-made soups (from £3.60), sautéed herring roes (£3.95), baked seafood pancake (£5.95), scrambled eggs with smoked salmon and prawns or ploughman's (£6.25), and tagliatelle carbonara (£8.50) with evening dishes such as monkfish and prawn ragoût (£12.50), rump steak (£16.50) and fried dover sole (£17.95); puddings such as sticky date and toffee pudding and baked banana with rum (from £4.25); three-course Sunday lunch (with coffee and petits fours) is £20.50. Opening off a hallway, and divided in two by dark painted timbers, the neatly civilised little bar has plush blue furnishings, potted plants around the windows, and a few carefully chosen sheep and lamb pictures and models around the cream-painted walls. On a piano are newspapers to read, and examples of their own chutneys and jams. Hook Norton Best, Wadworths 6X and a guest such as Adnams Broadside, a dozen or so wines by the glass, and carefully mixed pimms or bucks fizz; very obliging service; piped music. There are a couple of white plastic tables on a terrace, and a good few wooden picnic-sets in the very pleasant tree-shaded garden; good walks nearby. *(Recommended by Simon Collett-Jones, Sue Demont, Tim Barrow, Graham Johnson)*

Free house ~ Licensees Paul and Peta Barnard ~ Real ale ~ Bar food (12-2, 7-9.30, no food 25, 26 Dec and evening 1 Jan) ~ Restaurant ~ (01367) 870484 ~ Children welcome ~ Open 11-3, 5.30-11; 11-3, 7-10.30 Sun ~ Bedrooms: £47.50B/£59.50B

BURCOT SU5695 Map 4

Chequers

A415 Dorchester—Abingdon

This attractive thatched pub has been taken over by the man who used to run the Boars Head in Ardinton. Inside, the smartly comfortable lounge is surprisingly spacious with beams, an open fire, well kept Brakspears and guests such as Bass and Arkells 3B on handpump; also some good whiskies, unusual liqueurs, sherry from the wood, and a large collection of miniatures in display cabinets; shove-ha'penny, cribbage, dominoes. The regularly changing menu could include soup (£3), baked field mushrooms (£3.50), ciabattas (from £3.75), sautéed chicken livers, bacon and pine nuts (£4.25), herb risotto with capsicums (£7), roasted duck leg and baked pear (£8.75) or tempura of scallops with chilli jam (£10.50), with puddings such as caramel mousse (from £3.50); friendly service. They have their own decent little no smoking art gallery. The neatly kept roadside lawn comes alive in summer, with lots of colourful pots, hanging baskets, and bedding plants, tables and chairs among roses and fruit trees, and a vegetable patch at the lower end where they grow their own salad and herb produce; there are more seats on the terrace (lit at night). *(Recommended by G S B G Dudley, Geoff Pidoux)*

Free house ~ Licensee Mark Stott ~ Real ale ~ Bar food (not Sun or Mon evening) ~ Restaurant ~ (01865) 407771 ~ Children welcome ~ Open 12-3, 6-11; closed Sun and Mon evening (though they plan to open then in future)

BURFORD SP2512 Map 4

Lamb ★★ ⑪ ♀ ◧ ⛺

Sheep Street; A40 W of Oxford

Oxfordshire Dining Pub of the Year

This consistently popular, classic 15th-c Cotswold stone inn impresses readers with its courteous service, well cooked food and timeless atmosphere – one reader writes that it's still as good as when he visited it fifty years ago. The roomy beamed main lounge is charmingly traditional, with distinguished old seats including a chintzy high winged settle, ancient cushioned wooden armchairs, and seats built into its stone-mullioned windows, bunches of flowers on polished oak and elm tables, oriental rugs on the wide flagstones and polished oak floorboards, and a winter log fire under its fine mantelpiece. Also, a writing desk and grandfather clock, and eye-catching pictures, shelves of plates and other antique decorations. The public bar has high-backed settles and old chairs on flagstones in front of its fire. It's best to get there early if you want a table in the bar where enjoyable (though not cheap) daily changing bar food includes sandwiches or filled baguettes (from £3.50), home-made soup (£3.75), ploughman's (£5.75), coarse veal and quail pâté (£5.95), sautéed chicken livers with bacon and caramelised onions (£7.50), fresh grilled sardine fillets with creamed spinach sauce or wild mushroom risotto (£7.95) and lamb and mint sausages (£9); on Sundays there are proper roasts but no bar meals. They stick quite rigidly to food service times; the peaceful formal restaurant is no smoking. Well kept Hook Norton Best, Wadworths 6X and a guest such as Badger IPA are dispensed from an antique handpump beer engine in a glassed-in cubicle (you'll be given the choice between straight glass or handle when you order); good wines. A pretty terrace leads down to small neatly-kept lawns surrounded by flowers, flowering shrubs and small trees, and the garden itself is a real suntrap enclosed as it is by the warm stone of the surrounding buildings. *(Recommended by Chris Richards, K H Frostick, Nigel Williamson, Alan Clark, Jason Caulkin, Lynn Sharpless, Bob Eardley, Steve Whalley, Nigel Woolliscroft, Denis and Dorothy Evans, B A Littlewood, Maysie Thompson, R Huggins, D Irving, E McCall, T McLean, Simon and Laura Habbishow, Mr and Mrs A H Young, Geoff Pidoux, Andrew and Ruth Triggs, Michael Smith, R Michael Richards, Esther and John Sprinkle, Angela Cerfontyn, John and Enid Morris, Angus Lyon, John Bramley, John Evans, Ben and Sheila Walker, Joyce and Maurice; also in* The Good Hotel Guide*)*

Free house ~ Licensee Richard de Wolf ~ Real ale ~ Bar food (lunchtime only; not Sun) ~ Restaurant (evenings; Sun lunch) ~ (01993) 823155 ~ Children welcome ~ Open 11-2.30, 6-11; 12-3, 7-10.30 Sun; closed 25 and 26 Dec ~ Bedrooms: £70B/£115B

Mermaid

High St

The handsome Tudor-style frontage of this very busy pub juts out onto the broad pavement of this famously picturesque sloping Cotswold street. Slightly set back from the main bustle, there's a lovely cottagey feel inside; mullioned bay windows in the handsome Tudor façade invite you into the attractive long and narrow bar with its beams, polished flagstones, brocaded seats in bays around the single row of tables down one side, and pretty dried flowers. The inner end, with a figurehead over the fireplace and toby jugs hanging from the beams, is panelled, the rest has stripped stonework; there's an airy dining room and a no smoking upstairs restaurant. Generous bar food (which you order from a desk and computer opposite the bar) might include lunchtime snacks such as soup (£3.85), filled baguettes (£3.95; hot from £4.95) and meals such as mushroom omelette (£5.50), corned beef hash with melted cheese (£5.95), battered cod (£6.95) and chicken and asparagus pie (£7.50) with evening dishes such as hot chicken strips with curry sauce (£8.95) and guinea fowl with white wine and mushrooms (£13.95). The friendly staff cope well with the crowds. Well kept Greene King IPA, Old Speckled Hen and Ruddles on handpump; fruit machine and piped music. There are picnic-sets under cocktail parasols. *(Recommended by Ian Phillips, Steve Whalley, Geoff Pidoux, Martin Jones, D George, Geoffrey and Penny Hughes, Phil and Jane Hodson)*

Morlands (Greene King) ~ Lease John and Lynda Titcombe ~ Real ale ~ Bar food (11.30-3, 6-9.30, 11-11 Sat and Sun) ~ Restaurant ~ (01993) 822193 ~ Children over 5 years in restaurant ~ Open 11(10.30 Sun-)11; closed evening 25 Dec

---

People don't usually tip bar staff (different in a really smart hotel, say). If you want to thank them – for dealing with a really large party say, or special friendliness – offer them a drink.

CAULCOTT SP5024 Map 4
Horse & Groom 🍺

Lower Heyford Road (B4030)

Creeper-covered and partly thatched, this 16th-c cottage is much modernised inside. Its cheerful licensees (he does the cooking) give it a warmly welcoming feel, helped along by the blazing fire in the big inglenook with masses of pump clips under its long bressumer beam. An L-shaped red-carpeted room angles around the servery, with plush-cushioned settles, chairs, stools and a few dark tables at the low-ceilinged bar end, a baseball cap collection and framed racehorse cigarette cards. The far end, up a shallow step, is set for dining, with lots of decorative jugs hanging on black joists, a big antique print and some decorative plates. The food majors on a wide variety of O'Hagan speciality sausages, and also includes sandwiches (from £2.90), home-made soup (£2.95), baked potatoes (from £3.10), deep-fried camembert (£3.95), ham, egg and chips (£5.75), mushrooms in cream and garlic (£6.25), king prawns in garlic and brandy or fried cajun chicken (£8.75), and steaks (from £9.75); specials such as salmon steak with lemon and dill sauce or duck breast with fresh cranberries and port sauce (£9.50). Well kept Hook Norton Best on handpump, with quickly changing interesting guest beers (on our inspection visit, Lichfield Noahs Dark, and – from Tipperary – honeyed Dwan Irish Gold and Pictish Fraoch), and decent house wines. There is a small side sun lounge, with picnic-sets under cocktail parasols on a neat side lawn. *(Recommended by David Campbell, Vicki McLean, George Atkinson, D C T and E A Frewer)*

Free house ~ Licensees Chris and Celestine Roche ~ Real ale ~ Bar food ~ Restaurant ~ (01869) 343257 ~ Children in eating area of bar and restaurant ~ Open 11-3, 6-11; 12-3, 7-10.30 Sun

CHALGROVE SU6396 Map 4
Red Lion

High St (B480 Watlington—Stadhampton)

The local church has owned this traditional pub since it first appeared in written records in 1637, and probably a good bit longer as some of the timbers date back to the 11th c. The picnic-sets in front are attractively floodlit at night and inside there's a smartly contemporary twist to its décor. All the walls are painted a crisp white which contrasts strikingly with the simple dark furnishings, the windows have neatly chequered green curtains and fresh flowers, and there's an old woodburner and a log fire. Across from the fireplace is a painting of the landlady's aunt, and there are a few carefully collected prints and period cartoons. There's quite an emphasis on the food, and changing menus might include soup (from £3.25), filled baguettes (from £3.50), goats cheese tartlet with shallot purée or grilled asparagus with bacon and balsamic vinegar (£4.50), spicy meatballs with tomato sauce and linguini (£5.95) and warm tuna niçoise salad (£6.95) with more elaborate evening dishes such as roasted poussin spatchcock with lime and ginger and hot potato salad (£8.50); puddings such as dark chocolate soufflé with home-made shortbread (£3.50); restricted menu Monday and Tuesday lunchtime; children's menu (£3.50) or they can have smaller portions of main meals. Well kept Brakspears, and Fullers London Pride and one of their seasonal ales on handpump, and a decent wine list (they will generally open a bottle of wine and buy back the remainder if you don't finish it); pleasant service. The back dining room (sometimes used for functions) is no smoking; piped music, cribbage, dominoes, shove-ha'penny and darts in the tiled public bar. They play aunt sally in the good big garden behind, which has a pergola and play equipment. There are some notable medieval wall paintings in the church; the partly thatched main street of the village is pretty. *(Recommended by R J Chenery)*

Free house ~ Licensees Jonathan and Maggi Hewitt ~ Real ale ~ Bar food (not Sun and Mon evening) ~ Restaurant ~ (01865) 890625 ~ Children in eating area of bar ~ Open 12-3, 6-11; 12-3, 7-10.30 Sun; closed a few days between 25 Dec and 1 Jan

CHECKENDON SU6684 Map 2

Black Horse

Village signposted off A4074 Reading—Wallingford; coming from that direction, go straight through village towards Stoke Row, then turn left (the second turn left after the village church); OS Sheet 175 map reference 666841

For many decades this classic country local has been in the same family. Tucked away in fine walking country and popular with walkers and cyclists, it won't disappoint those who like their pubs basic and secluded. There's a refreshingly relaxed atmosphere in the back still room, where well kept Brakspears and a few local guests such as West Berkshire Good Old Boy or Mr Chubbs are tapped from the cask. The room with the bar counter has some tent pegs ranged above the fireplace, a reminder that they used to be made here; a homely side room has some splendidly unfashionable 1950s-look armchairs, and there's another room beyond that. They keep pickled eggs and usually do fresh filled rolls (from £1.45). There are seats out on a verandah and in the garden. *(Recommended by the Didler, Adrian and Felicity Smith, LM, Pete Baker, Paul Vickers)*

Free house ~ Licensees Margaret and Martin Morgan ~ Real ale ~ No credit cards ~ (01491) 680418 ~ Well behaved children welcome ~ Open 12-2(3 Sat and Sun), 7-11(10.30 Sun); closed evening 25 Dec

CHINNOR SU7698 Map 4

Sir Charles Napier 🍽 ♀

Spriggs Alley; from B4009 follow Bledlow Ridge sign from Chinnor; then, up beech wood hill, fork right (signposted Radnage and Sprigg Alley) then on right; OS Sheet 165 map reference 763983

In all the years we've known it this has always been more stylish restaurant than pub, but we have always convinced ourselves that it can still just about squeeze into our elastic definition of a pub on the strength of its small, friendly bar, even though most of its customers are heading for the larger restaurant. As well as Wadworths 6X or IPA tapped from the cask, you can choose between champagne on draught, an enormous list of exceptionally well chosen wines by the bottle (and a good few half-bottles), freshly squeezed juice, Russian vodkas and quite a few malt whiskies. The bar menu includes dishes such as delicious coconut and lime soup (£5), grilled quail with spiced lentil salad (£5.75), noodles with crab and ginger (£6.75), poached smoked salmon with couscous, roast pheasant with celeriac purée and braised cabbage or gnocchi with tomato sauce and parmesan (£9.50); puddings such as crème brûlée and chocolate parfait (£6). Service is not included. Sunday lunch in summer is served in the crazy-paved back courtyard with rustic tables by an arbour of vines, honeysuckle and wisteria (lit at night by candles in terracotta lamps). There may be quite a wait when busy. Piped music is well reproduced by the huge loudspeakers, and there's a good winter log fire. The croquet lawn and paddocks by the beech woods drop steeply away to the Chilterns, and there's a boules court out here too. *(Recommended by Patricia Purbrick, G S B G Dudley, J Hale, Mrs Jackie Williams, K C Quin, Bob and Maggie Atherton)*

Free house ~ Licensee Julie Griffiths ~ Real ale ~ Bar food (lunchtime; not Sun evening or all Mon) ~ Restaurant (evening) ~ (01494) 483011 ~ Children must be over 7 in evening ~ Open 12-2.30, 6.30-12; 12-3.30 Sun; closed Sun evening and Mon

CHIPPING NORTON SP3127 Map 4

Chequers 🍺

Goddards Lane

'A drinkers pub with good food' is how one reader accurately sums up this unpretentious local. Its three softly lit beamed rooms which are nicely old-fashioned – no frills, but clean and comfortable, with plenty of character – have log fires and low ochre ceilings, friendly efficient service, and a lively evening atmosphere. Besides very well kept Fullers Chiswick, London Pride, ESB and seasonal brews on handpump (unusual to have the full Fullers range around here), they have nice house wines and good espresso and cappuccino coffee; cribbage, dominoes, shove-ha'penny, and board games. Along with home-made soup (£2.50), lunchtime sandwiches (from £2.45) and ploughman's (£4.95), imaginative bar meals include three or four thai dishes such as mixed bean mussamen or vegetable stir fry (£6.75), around three vegetarian dishes which could include roasted vegetable lasagne (£6.45) while other dishes might be mushrooms filled with garlic and stilton (£3.95), salmon fillet with cajun spices (£7.95) or roasted lamb shoulder with mint gravy (£8.95); puddings such as home-made chocolate tart and baked vanilla cheesecake (from £2.95). The no smoking restaurant at the back (quiet piped music), was converted from an old barn adjacent to the courtyard. It's very handy for the town's Victorian theatre. *(Recommended by Geoff Pidoux, Chris Richards, Richard Greaves, Andy and Jill Kassube, George Atkinson, Stuart Turner, Gordon, Di and Mike Gillam, R S Greaves, P L Haigh, Mrs N W Neill, KN-R)*

Fullers ~ Tenant Josh Reid ~ Real ale ~ Bar food (12-2.30, 6-9; 12-5 Sun; not Sun evening) ~ Restaurant ~ (01608) 644717 ~ Children in eating area of bar ~ Open 11-11; 12-10.30 Sun

CLIFTON SP4831 Map 4
Duke of Cumberlands Head ♀ ⇔
B4031 Deddington—Aynho

This quietly welcoming pub, only a short walk from the canal, continues to satisfy our readers. Although the emphasis is on food drinkers are not neglected and there's a good choice of wines, well kept Adnams Southwold, Hook Norton Best, and Wadworths 6X on handpump and more than 30 malt whiskies. Most of the tables are in the spacious if rather reserved lounge with a lovely log fireplace; there are more in the cosy yellow-painted no smoking room. Enjoyable bar food includes lunchtime sandwiches (not Sun), soup such as courgette and mint (£3.50), baked, smoked goats cheese wrapped in smoked trout (£5), smoked trout salad (£8), spinach and ricotta cannelloni or mediterranean casserole (£8.50), wild boar steak with apple, cream and cider sauce (£10), steak (from £13) and puddings such as cherry and almond tart or raspberry and apple crumble (£3.50). You can get smaller portions of several of the meals; decent breakfasts. There are tables out in the garden. By the time this book comes out they should have finished redecorating. *(Recommended by Sir Nigel Foulkes, S H Godsell, Anthony Barnes, Paul Craddock, Martin and Penny Fletcher, John Bowdler, George Little, Michael Hasslacher, Mrs Joy Griffiths, David Green, Susan and John Douglas)*

Free house ~ Licensee Nick Huntington ~ Real ale ~ Bar food (12-2, 6.30-9(9.30 Fri and Sat)) ~ Restaurant (not Mon and Tues evening) ~ (01869) 338534 ~ Children welcome ~ Open 12-2.30(3 Sat), 6.30-11; 12-3 Sun; closed 2nd week in Oct 2001 ~ Bedrooms: £35S(£45B)/£60S(£70B)

CUDDESDON SP5903 Map 4
Bat & Ball ⇔
S of Wheatley; if coming from M40 junction 7 via Gt Milton, turn towards Little Milton past church, then look out for signpost; in village centre

This pub is well worth visiting even if you've no particular love of cricket, and every inch of wall-space is covered with cricketing programmes, photographs, porcelain models in well lit cases, score books, cigarette cards, pads, gloves and hats, and signed bats, bails and balls. The immaculately kept L-shaped bar has beams and low ceilings, comfortable furnishings, a partly flagstoned floor, and a good relaxed atmosphere. Served by obliging staff, enjoyable bar food includes soup (£3.55), enjoyable filled baguettes such as chicken and bacon (from £4.45), ploughman's (£6.95), and daily specials such as whole grilled sole (£10.95) or guinea fowl with black pudding and mash (£11.95), with puddings such as banana and toffee crème brûlée (£3.95). The restaurant is no smoking; in the evenings most of the tables are laid out for eating. Well kept Banks's LBW, Marstons Pedigree and a changing guest on handpump as well as a decent wine list; cribbage, dominoes and piped music. A very pleasant terrace at the back has seats, aunt sally, and good views over the Oxfordshire plain. You can buy sweets from jars behind the bar. *(Recommended by Paul Craddock, Jim Bush, Steve and Liz Tilley, Barbara Wensworth, Humphry and Angela Crum Ewing, Ron Harris, Geoff Pidoux, J V Dadswell)*

Cains ~ Tenant Tony Viney ~ Real ale ~ Bar food (12-2.45, 6.30-9.45) ~ Restaurant ~ (01865) 874379 ~ Well behaved children welcome ~ Open 11-11; 12-10.30 Sun ~ Bedrooms: £49S/£60S

CUXHAM SU6695 Map 2
Half Moon
4 miles from M40 junction 6; S on B4009, then right on to B480 at Watlington

You can buy local eggs, honey and chutney in the bar of this thatched country pub which once again has a new licensee. They use local ingredients wherever possible and all the cooking herbs are picked from the garden overlooked by a gazebo, covered in roses, clematis and honeysuckle in summer. The three comfortable low-beamed bar areas have open fires, with rather country cottage-style furnishings, books and prints. From a daily changing menu bar food might include sandwiches (from £3.50), potato pancake with smoked trout and pickled beetroot or home-made soup (£4), baked salmon with panzanella salad and wilted pea vine, or grilled calves liver with smoked bacon and cheddar pancake (£9) and steak (from £9.95) with puddings such as vanilla and Greek yoghurt cheesecake with baked peach (£4). Well kept Brakspears Bitter and Special and maybe one of their seasonal ales on handpump; piped music. There are seats sheltered by an oak tree on the back lawn, and a climbing frame. Across the road, a stream runs through the quiet village. *(Recommended by Paul Vickers)*

Brakspears ~ Tenant Kieron Daniels ~ Real ale ~ Bar food (12-2.30, 6.30-9.30) ~ Restaurant ~ (01491) 614110 ~ Children welcome ~ Open 11.30-2.30(12-3 Sat), 5.30-11; 12-10.30 Sun

EXLADE STREET SU6582 Map 2
Highwayman ♥ 🛏
Signposted just off A4074 Reading—Wallingford

Mostly 17th-c, but with some parts dating back another 300 years or so, this rambling inn is a friendly place to visit. The two beamed rooms of the bar have quite an unusual layout, with an interesting variety of seats around old tables and even recessed into a central sunken inglenook; an airy no smoking conservatory dining room has more seats (mainly for eating) and overlooks the garden. As well as home-made soup (£3.95) and lunchtime sandwiches (from £4.50) regularly changing, enjoyable (though not cheap) bar food could include roast sirloin baguette (£6.25), smoked chicken and pancetta salad (£6.75), sausage and mash (£7.95) and seared salmon with orange (£8.95). Well kept Black Sheep, Theakstons and a guest on handpump, several malt whiskies, decent wines, freshly squeezed orange juice, champagne and kirs, and home-made crisps on the bar. The attractive garden has tables and fine views over the attractive surrounding wooded countryside. They have an à la carte restaurant; the bedrooms have been refurbished. *(Recommended by the Didler, Paul Vickers, Simon Chell, Nick Holmes, JP, PP, DHV, Phyl and Jack Street, Sue Demont, Tim Barrow, LM)*

Free house ~ Licensee Charles Edmundson-Jones ~ Real ale ~ Bar food (12-2.30, 7-9.30) ~ Restaurant ~ (01491) 682020 ~ Over 5s in restaurant ~ Occasional music evenings ~ Open 12-3, 6-11; 11-11 Sat; 12-10.30 Sun ~ Bedrooms: £55S/£70S

The knife-and-fork award distinguishes pubs where the food is of exceptional quality.

582 *Oxfordshire*

FIFIELD SP2318 Map 4

Merrymouth

A424 Burford—Stow

Readers are full of praise for the interesting food and well trained staff at this isolated family-run 13th-c stone pub. It has a civilised but warmly welcoming atmosphere in the simple but comfortably furnished L-shaped bar, with nice bay-window seats, flagstones, horsebrasses and antique bottles hanging from low beams, some walls stripped back to the old masonry, and an open fire in winter; backgammon, dominoes and piped classical music. The freshly made bar food might include sandwiches (from £2.50, beef baguette £5.25), soup (£2.95), mushrooms cooked in whisky (£3.95), braden rösti (£4.75), spicy chick pea casserole (£6.95), steak and kidney pie (£7.50), chicken in celery, mushroom, onion and yoghurt sauce (£7.95), chargrilled steaks (from £7.95), and daily specials such as stilton and walnut pâté (£4.25), butterbean and mushroom bake (£6.95), tasty guinea fowl (£8.95), barbary duck breast (£9.75) and lemon sole (£10.50), with home-made puddings such as raspberry and marshmallow meringue and bread pudding with whisky sauce (from £3.50). Well kept Hook Norton Best, Wychwood Hobgoblin and maybe a guest such as Wadworths 6X on handpump, good wines including three by the glass; except for six tables in the bar the pub is no smoking. There are tables on a terrace and in the back garden (there maybe a little noise from fast traffic on the road); dogs on leads welcome. The bedrooms are well cared for and quaint. The Domesday Book mentions an inn on this site and its name comes from the Murimuth family, who once owned the village in which it is set. *(Recommended by Cliff Blakemore, Mrs N W Neill, Valerie and Graham Cant, D J Lewis, H Standing, D P Brown, Robert Gomme, J C Burgis, Bernard Stradling, B A Dale, Colin McKerrow)*

Free house ~ Licensees Andrew and Timothy Flaherty ~ Real ale ~ Bar food ~ Restaurant ~ (01993) 831652 ~ Well behaved children welcome in eating area of bar ~ Open 12-3, 6-(11 Sat)10.30; 12-3, 7-10 Sun; closed Sun evening in winter ~ Bedrooms: £45S/£65B

FINSTOCK SP3616 Map 4

Plough 🛏

The Bottom; just off B4022 N of Witney

This thatched pub is very much the hub of the village, and the friendly brothers who run it with such care are what makes it so special. Nicely split up by partitions and alcoves, the long low-beamed rambling bar is comfortable and relaxed, with an armchair by the open log-burning stove in the massive stone inglenook, and tiles up at the end by the servery (elsewhere is carpeted), and walls decorated with rosettes the licensees have won at Crufts, and other doggy-related paraphernalia. There are tables (and aunt sally) in the good sizeable garden with several heavily scented rare specimen roses. Good bar food includes home-made soup (£2.70), generous sandwiches (from £4.10), specials such as popular steak, stout, stilton and mushroom pie (£10.35), herb-crusted rack of lamb with port and redcurrant gravy (£10.66), monkfish kebabs in a creamy leek sauce (£10.86) and delicious home-made puddings such as rhubarb and strawberry crumble (from £3.05). A comfortable low-beamed stripped-stone dining room is on the right. Adnams Broadside, Brakspears Bitter and Ted & Bens Organic Beer, Hook Norton Best and maybe a guest on handpump or tapped from the cask, summer farm cider, and a special bloody mary. A separate games area has bar billiards, cribbage, and dominoes. There are plenty of good walks in the attractive countryside. Their llasa apso is called Jumbo, and other dogs are welcome in the garden (on a lead) and in the public bar. *(Recommended by Stuart Turner, Geoff Pidoux, Martin and Karen Wake, R T and J C Moggridge, Patricia Beebe, Simon and Laura Habbishow)*

Free house ~ Licensees Keith and Nigel Ewers ~ Real ale ~ Bar food (12-2, 7-9.30) ~ Restaurant ~ (01993) 868333 ~ Children welcome away from bar ~ Occasional bands ~ Open 12-3, 6-(10.30 Sun)11; 12-2.30, 6-11 Sat in winter; closed evening 1 Jan ~ Bedrooms: /£50S

FYFIELD SU4298 Map 4
White Hart
In village, off A420 8 miles SW of Oxford

Don't be fooled by the humble façade of this relaxed pub – it has an impressive medieval interior. The bustling main room is a grand (and draughty) hall with soaring eaves, huge stone-flanked window embrasures and an attractive carpeted upper gallery. The cosy low-ceilinged side bar has an inglenook fireplace with a **huge** black urn hanging over the grate, and a framed history of the pub, on the wall, makes a pleasant contrast. The priests' room and barrel-vaulted cellar are no smoking dining areas. As well as bar food they serve well kept Hook Norton Best, Theakstons Old Peculier, Wadworths 6X and a guest such as Fullers London Pride on handpump or tapped from the cask, and country wines; darts, shove-ha'penny, dominoes, cribbage, and piped music. It's well worth wandering out through the heavy wooden door to the rambling, sheltered and flowery back lawn, which has a children's playground. Built for Sir John Golafre to house priests who would pray for his soul, it's been run for four hundred years by St John's College, Oxford. *(Recommended by Geoff Pidoux, Kevin Blake, T G Thomas, Susan Dente, Darly Graton, Graeme Gulibert, Ian Jones, James House, Susan and John Douglas)*

Free house ~ Licensees John and Sherry Howard ~ Real ale ~ Bar food (till 10pm,) ~ Restaurant ~ (01865) 390585 ~ Children welcome away from main bar ~ Open 12-3, 6(10.30 Sun)-11; closed 25 and evening 26 Dec

GREAT TEW SP3929 Map 4
Falkland Arms 🍺
Off B4022 about 5 miles E of Chipping Norton; The Green

Set in an attractive, peaceful village of untouched golden-stone thatched cottages this is a real classic of a country pub. The partly panelled bar has high-backed settles and a diversity of stools around plain stripped tables on flagstones and bare boards, one, two and three-handled mugs hanging from the beam-and-board ceiling, dim converted oil lamps, shutters for the stone-mullioned latticed windows, and a fine inglenook fireplace with a blazing fire in winter. The bar counter is decorated with tobacco jars and different varieties of snuff which you can buy; dominoes and Jenga. Up to seven well kept ales include Wadworths Henry's Original and 6X and guests such as Badger Tanglefoot and Timothy Taylors Landlord, 60 malt whiskies, 16 country wines, and farm cider. Well presented lunchtime bar food includes soup (£2.95), filled baguettes (from £3.50), ploughman's (£5.95), steak and kidney pie, bangers and mash or a vegetarian dish (from £6.50), with more sophisticated evening restaurant meals (booking necessary) such as chicken breast on cabbage and bacon with tarragon gravy (£7.95), bream fillets with lime, chilli and coriander (£8.50), and slow cooked lamb shank with rosemary and garlic (£9); home-made puddings include sharp lemon tart with orange sorbet and sticky toffee pudding (from £3.50). The dining room is no smoking. You have to go out into the lane and then back in again to use the lavatories. There are tables outside in front of the pub, with picnic-sets under umbrellas in the garden behind – where there's a dovecote; they hold an annual summer beer festival. Small good value bedrooms (no under 14s). *(Recommended by Karen and Graham Oddey, K H Frostick, the Didler, Kevin Blake, Paul Boot, Geoff Pidoux, JP, PP, Ian Patrick, Mrs Jackie Williams, Mrs Mary Walters, Dean Riley, Martin and Karen Wake, Ian Phillips, Kevin Thorpe, Alec Hamilton)*

Wadworths ~ Managers Paul Barlow-Heal and S J Courage ~ Real ale ~ Bar food (lunchtime) ~ Restaurant ~ (01608) 683653 ~ Children in restaurant lunchtimes only ~ Live folk Sun night ~ Open 11.30-2.30, 6-11; 11.30-11 Sat; 12-10.30 Sun; 11.30-3, 6-11 Sat in winter; 12-3, 7-10.30 Sun in winter ~ Bedrooms: £40S/£65S(£80B)

Bedroom prices include full English breakfast, VAT and any inclusive
service charge that we know of.

HENLEY SU7882 Map 4

Anchor ◀

Friday Street; coming in over bridge, first left towards A4155 then next right

Cosy and relaxing, this homely old-fashioned local is a refreshing contrast to the gloss and style of this rich little town. Informally run by a friendly and obliging landlady, it has a well worn in mix of elderly traditional pub furnishings in its two main rooms, with throw rugs, scatter cushions, chintz curtains, some venerable wall boarding and dim lighting adding to the cottagey feel. The beams in the dark ochre ceiling are thickly hung with chamber-pots, steins, whisky-water jugs, copperware and so forth, and there are interesting pictures: mainly local river photographs in the left room, a mix of antique sporting, ship and comical prints on the right, which has darts, bar billiards, a piano and TV. Generous bar food includes an impressive choice of sandwiches (from £3), baked potatoes (from £4.50) and baguettes (from £5) as well as main dishes (from £6.50) such as steak and ale pie, stroganoff, seafood mornay, rack of ribs and thai or indian curry. Well kept Brakspears PA and SB on handpump, and a good range of malt whiskies and of wines by the glass. A simply furnished back dining room has lots of rowing photographs, and a cage with a chatty cockatiel and budgerigar; behind is a charming informal terrace surrounded by lush vegetation and hanging vines. The friendly chocolate labrador is called Ruger. On your way to the lavatories you may have to thread your way through bicycles leaning in the lobby; and may find a washing machine in the ladies'. *(Recommended by the Didler, Simon Collett-Jones, Lynn Sharpless, Bob Eardley, JP, PP)*

Brakspears ~ Tenant G A Ian-Savage ~ Bar food (12(4 winter Sun)-2.30, 7-9, not Sun evening in winter, not 25 Dec) ~ (01491) 574753 ~ Well behaved children away from main bar ~ Open 11-11; 12-10.30 Sun; closed after 2pm 25 Dec

HIGHMOOR SU6984 Map 2

Rising Sun

Witheridge Hill, signposted off B481; OS Sheet 175 map reference 697841

Recently reworked as a dining pub, this pretty black and white building has an airy, civilised feel. There are seats around a few simple tables in a smallish carpeted area on the right, by the bar, with some bar stools too, and a big log-effect stove in a big brick inglenook fireplace. The main area spreading back from here has shiny bare boards and a swathe of red carpeting, with well spaced tables, attractive pictures on cream or dark salmon walls, and a side bit with a leather settee, low games table and shove-ha'penny, liar dice, chess and so forth. There's some emphasis on the food side, which might include jalapeño peppers with yoghurt and mint dip (£4.25), baguettes (£4.85), ploughman's (from £4.95), spicy sausages (£5.75), vegetable, chicken or prawn thai stir fry (£6.85), moules marinières or breaded lemon sole (£7.45) and steaks (from £10.45) with specials such as crab cakes with chilli sauce or chicken liver pâté (£4.25), roast pork knuckle and mash or penne pasta with creamy pesto sauce (£7.25) and roast lamb shoulder with redcurrant and rosemary sauce (£9.25); puddings such as blackberry pancakes (from £3.25). Well kept Brakspears PA and SB on handpump, good pleasant service; may be unobtrusive piped pop music. There are picnic-sets on a fairy-lit terrace and on grass among trees; it's a nice quiet spot, by a rough sloping green. *(Recommended by Mr Tucker)*

Brakspears ~ Licensees Bill and Beryl Farrell ~ Real ale ~ Bar food (12-2.30, 7-9.30; 12-2.30, 6.30-9.15 Sun) ~ Restaurant ~ (01491) 641455 ~ Children welcome ~ Open 11-3, 6-11; 12-3, 6.30-10.30 Sun

HOOK NORTON SP3533 Map 4

Gate Hangs High ♀

Banbury Rd; a mile N of village towards Sibford, at Banbury—Rollright crossroads

A useful stop on the way to Upton House or Broughton Castle, this tucked away country pub tends to fill up quickly, especially at weekends. The bar has joists in the long, low ceiling, a brick bar counter, stools and assorted chairs on the carpet, and a gleaming copper hood over the hearth in the inglenook fireplace. Well kept Hook Norton Best and another from their brewery on handpump, a good wine list, and a range of malt whiskies; dominoes. In summer, there are spectacular flowering tubs and wall baskets around the picnic-sets in front of the pub and the broad back lawn is a nice place for a drink, with holly and apple trees, swings for children to play on and fine views. There's quite an emphasis on the bar food with sandwiches (from £2.50), soup (£2.95), and changing dishes such as chicken in a brandy cream sauce (£8.95), pork loin with apricot stuffing (£9.25), steak (£10.50) and halibut with watercress sauce (£11.50); home-made puddings. You'll need to book for Sun lunch. Five miles south-west of the pub are the Bronze Age Rollright Stones – said to be a king and his army who were turned to stone by a witch. *(Recommended by Sir Nigel Foulkes, Iain R Hewitt, Marjorie and David Lamb, C L Kauffmann, Geoff Pidoux, Martin Jennings, Stephen, Julie and Hayley Brown, Eric George, R Lake)*

Hook Norton ~ Tenant Stuart Rust ~ Real ale ~ Bar food (not Sun evening) ~ Restaurant ~ (01608) 737387 ~ Children in eating area of bar and restaurant ~ Open 11.30-3, 6.30-11; 12-3, 7-11 Sun; closed 25 Dec

Pear Tree ⚑

Village signposted off A361 SW of Banbury

Barely 100 yards away from the Hook Norton brewery, this agreeable little pub has the full range of their ales on handpump including very well kept Hook Norton Best, Old Hooky, Generation, Mild, seasonal ales and country wines. The chatty knocked together bar area has country-kitchen furniture on the nicely timbered floor, some long tables, a well stocked magazine rack, and open fires. With more and more people coming for the good food, it can get very cramped; dominoes, indoor and outdoor chess, and Jenga. Generous bar food from a short menu includes soup (£2.95), sandwiches (from £3.25), filled baked potatoes (from £4.25) and ploughman's (from £5.25), ham and eggs or chicken curry (£5.95), home-made fish or beef pie (£6.50) and puddings such as apple flan and custard (£2.75); children's meals (£3.50). There's an aunt sally in the attractive, sizeable garden which has plenty of seats. *(Recommended by Mike Gorton, Geoff Pidoux, the Didler, Robert Gomme, Martin and Penny Fletcher, Andy and Jill Kassube, Steve Whalley, Tom Evans, John Bowdler, Iain R Hewitt, K H Frostick, Mike and Wena Stevenson, Dick and Madeleine Brown, Stephen, Julie and Hayley Brown, Alette and Russell Lawson)*

Hook Norton ~ Tenant J Sivyer ~ Real ale ~ Bar food (not Sun evening) ~ (01608) 737482 ~ Children in eating area of bar ~ Open 11.30-2.30(4 Sat), 6-11; 12-4, 7-10.30 Sun ~ Bedrooms: £35S/£50S

Sun ⚑ 🛏

High Street

Facing the church in a prime site in a pretty village, this popular pub has a buoyant and laid-back local atmosphere which is perhaps most noticeable in the flagstoned front bar, with its huge log fire, hop-strung beams, and one table reserved for games. Behind the central servery a cosy carpeted room with comfortable banquettes and other seats leads into the attractive no smoking green-walled restaurant. Tasty bar food includes home-made soup (£2.95), very good filled baguettes (from £3.25), ploughman's (from £5.50), smoked chicken and strawberry salad or olive ciabatta with cajun chicken (£5.95), steak and Hook Norton pie (£6.50), fried chicken in a mild curry sauce (£7.95), duck confit with red cabbage and sautéed potatoes (£8.75) and peppered 6oz fillet steak (£8.95). Well kept Hook Norton Best, Best Mild, Generation and Old Hooky on handpump, good value wines including nine by the glass; friendly service. Tables out on a back terrace; good wheelchair access and disabled facilities. *(Recommended by Sir Nigel Foulkes, John Bowdler, Amanda Eames, Richard Greaves, Steve Whalley, Iain R Hewitt, Pete Baker, Andy and Jill Kassube, John Bramley, Geoff Pidoux, Dr W J M Gissane, R S Greaves, Sue and Jim Sargeant, Tim and Ann Newell, Roger Braithwaite)*

586   Oxfordshire

Hook Norton ~ Tenants Richard and Jane Hancock ~ Bar food ~ Restaurant ~
(01608) 737570 ~ Open 11.30-(3 Sat)2.30, 6-11; 12-3, 7-10.30 Sun; closed 25 Dec ~
Bedrooms: £30B/£50B

LEWKNOR SU7198 Map 4
Olde Leathern Bottel

Under a mile from M40 junction 6; just off B4009 towards Watlington

Set in a charming village near the M40, this laid-back country pub has two bar
rooms with heavy beams in the low ceilings, rustic furnishings, open fires, and an
understated décor of old beer taps and the like. The no smoking family room is
separated only by standing timbers, so you won't feel segregated from the rest of the
pub. Bar food includes lunchtime sandwiches (from £2.10), ploughman's (£4.95),
baked potatoes (from £4.95), chicken balti or mozzarella penne (£6.95), king
prawns in filo pastry (£7.95) and steaks (from £8.95) with specials such as caribbean
chicken or mediterranean bake (£6.95); puddings such as treacle sponge (£2.95).
Well kept Brakspears Bitter, Special, and winter Old on handpump; dominoes and
piped music. Alongside the car park, the attractive sizeable garden is a nice place to
unwind and children like the play area too. (Recommended by T R and B C Jenkins,
Marjorie and David Lamb, Andy Gosling, P Price, Tim and Ann Newell)

Brakspears ~ Tenant Mr L S Gordon ~ Real ale ~ Bar food (12-2, 7-9; 12-2, 6-10 Fri
and Sat) ~ (01844) 351482 ~ Children in family room ~ Open 11-2.30(3 Sat), 6-11;
11-3, 7-10.30 Sun

MAIDENSGROVE SU7288 Map 2
Five Horseshoes 🍴 ♀

W of village, which is signposted from B480 and B481; OS Sheet 175 map reference 711890

Set on a lovely common high up in the Chiltern beechwoods and close to good local
walks, this highly regarded 17th-c brick pub has a separate bar set aside for walkers
(and their boots). Readers are full of praise for the imaginative bar food here which
includes lunchtime dishes such as home-made soup (£3.85; their popular stilton soup
£4.35), ploughman's (£5.45), filled baked potatoes (from £6.50), pancakes with
fillings such as smoked chicken and mushroom in a creamy sauce or spicy thai
vegetables (from £6.95), warm smoky bacon and stilton salad (£6.95), braised lamb
shank with provençale sauce (£9.95), and daily specials. Also, the à la carte menu
can be taken at any time: chargrilled vegetables (£5.95), prawn and crab ravioli or
tagliatelle with provençale sauce (£7.50), pork fillet in honey and mustard sauce with
deep-fried vegetables (£10.95), rack of lamb with minted apricot sauce (£14.50) and
halibut with a herb crust (£15.50) with home-made puddings such as warm citrus
sponge or cookies and fudge cheesecake (from £4.50). On Sundays in winter they do
set meals (£15.95) and in summer they hold barbecues. The atmosphere in the
rambling main bar is really welcoming. Furnished with mostly modern wheelback
chairs around stripped wooden tables (though there are some attractive older seats
and a big baluster-leg table), it has a proper log fire in winter; the low ceiling in the
main area is covered in bank notes from all over the world, mainly donated by
customers. Well kept Brakspears PA, SB and seasonal ales on handpump, and a
dozen wines by the glass, including champagne. There are fine views from the
sheltered back garden which has a rockery and some interesting water features. Look
out for the red kites which now patrol the surrounding countryside – if you're as
lucky as one reader, you might even be able to spot one from your table in the
extended restaurant. (Recommended by Adrian and Felicity Smith, S and H Tate-Lovery,
Desmond Hall, Michael Porter, T R and B C Jenkins, Miss E J Jesson, M Borthwick,
Derek Thomas, John and Barbara Main, Barbara Wilder, Andy Meaton, Jayne and Peter Capp,
Paul Hopton)

Brakspears ~ Tenants Graham and Mary Cromack ~ Real ale ~ Bar food ~ Restaurant
~ (01491) 641282 ~ Children welcome in top bar ~ Open 11-2.30, 6-11; 12-9 Sun;
closed 26 Dec

MURCOTT SP5815 Map 4
Nut Tree ♀
Off B4027 NE of Oxford, via Islip and Charlton-on-Otmoor

In front of this neatly thatched pub, run by new licensees, there's an unusual collection of gargoyles, each loosely modelled on one of the local characters. While there's still a quiet part for those only wanting a drink, quite a bit of space, especially at lunchtime, is given over to diners. The civilised beamed lounge has a long polished bar with brasses, antiques and pictures all round, and a winter log fire; there's also a small back partly no smoking conservatory-style restaurant. From a daily changing menu bar food might include sandwiches (from £3.50), soup (£3.95), smoked chicken with mixed peppers (£5.75), crayfish tail salad (£5.95), tortellini stuffed with ricotta and spinach (£8.95), caribbean parrot fish with orange and caper sauce (£11.95) and steaks (from £11.95); puddings (from £4.50). They serve Batemans XB and Hook Norton Best as well as two guests such as Adnams Broadside and Timothy Taylors Landlord on handpump, a fair number of malt whiskies, and a decent range of wines with several by the glass. There are usually ducks on the pond at the front, pretty hanging baskets and tubs in summer, and plenty of other animals including peacocks, rabbits and a donkey; also aunt sally in the well kept garden. Roundhead soldiers used to come here when Cromwell had his headquarters at nearby Boarstall. *(Recommended by Mr and Mrs T A Bryan, J Hale, Mrs M Reid)*

Free house ~ Licensees Mr Sparks and Mr Wood ~ Real ale ~ Bar food (12-2, 6.30-9.30) ~ Restaurant ~ (01865) 331253 ~ Children in restaurant ~ Open 12-3, 6.30-11; 12-3, Sun

OXFORD SP5203 Map 4
Isis Tavern
Off Donnington Bridge Road (between A4144 Abingdon Road and A4158 Iffley Road); park in Meadow Lane, walk over bridge, then turn left and walk 300 yds along towpath); no car access

As most customers get here by boat, this is busiest in summer, but is well worth knowing too as a quiet winter bolt hole, beside a water-meadow nature reserve and just along from pretty Iffley Lock, with plenty of geese, ducks, swans and coots on the water. Around the central bar servery is a pleasantly informal medley of furnishings on the turkey carpet, including a couple of little settees by a log fire, but the mood is set by the forest of mainly nautical bric-a-brac hanging from the high ceiling – anything from nets and buoys to full-size boats. A similar mass of stuff covers the walls, among it some fine old photographs of racing yachts and one or two attractive model boats. Vying for attention are big menu boards, listing food such as baguettes (from £3.95), buttered vegetable kebab (£3.95), ploughman's (£4.55), steak and ale pie (£5.95), moules marinières (£6.25), salmon steak (£7.25) and marinated mango chicken or rump steak (£8.95). Well kept Morrells Oxford and Oxford Blue on handpump and a guest such as Hardy Royal Oak; friendly service; daily papers; sensibly placed well lit darts and bar billiards in one corner, shove-ha'penny, chess, dominoes, cribbage, maybe piped pop music and TV. There are picnic-sets out on a terrace and in the garden, which has a massive yew tree among other trees and shrubs, and outdoor heaters; swings, slide, aunt sally by arrangement, even a traditional bowling alley. *(Recommended by anon)*

Morrells ~ Manager David Burley ~ Real ale ~ Bar food (11.30-9; 12-8 Sun) ~ Restaurant ~ (01865) 247006 ~ Children in eating area of bar and restaurant ~ Open 11-11; 12-10.30 Sun

Kings Arms £
40 Holywell St

Bustlingly full of students, dons and tourists who, on fine evenings, spill out onto the pavement opposite the Sheldonian theatre (where the students graduate), this pub dates back to the 16th c. Inside, there's a big rather bare main room, with a no smoking coffee room just inside the Parks Road entrance, and several cosy and comfortably worn-in side and back rooms, each with a different character and customers. An extra back room has a sofa and more tables and there's a tiny room behind that. They still keep a dictionary for the crossword buffs in the Dons Bar, with its elderly furnishings and tiled floor, mix of old prints and photographs of customers, and sympathetic lighting; daily newspapers, fruit machine, video game and cribbage. Well kept Youngs Bitter, Special and one of their seasonal ales with guests such as Smiles Best and Wadworths 6X on handpump, a fine choice of wines with over 15 by the glass, and up to 20 malt whiskies. Promptly served, the decent, good value bar food includes home-made soup (£1.95), filled baked potatoes (from £3.65), burgers, spaghetti bolognese or three bean chilli (£4.25), filled ciabattas (£4.50), lasagne or fish and chips (£5.25), beef pie in stout and mushroom gravy (£6.50) and sirloin steak (£7.95). Cold snacks are served all day, and on Sundays they open at 10.30 for breakfast and coffee. *(Recommended by Dick and Madeleine Brown, Rona Murdoch, Margaret and Roy Randle, Mr and Mrs G Owens, I D Greenfield, Kevin Blake, R Huggins, D Irving, E McCall, T McLean, S J and C C Davidson)*

Youngs ~ Manager David Kyffin ~ Real ale ~ Bar food (11.30-9.30) ~ (01865) 242369 ~ Children in eating area of bar and family room till 8pm ~ Open 10.30-11; 10.30-10.30 Sun

Turf Tavern 🍺

Tavern Bath Place; via St Helen's Passage, between Holywell Street and New College Lane

Much the same as when Hardy described them in *Jude the Obscure*, the little dark-beamed and low-ceilinged rooms of this pretty place are usually overflowing with a mix of customers, who come for the infectious lively atmosphere and the range of well kept ales on handpump. Alongside Archers Golden, Boddingtons and Deuchars IPA, these might include Brakspears Bee Sting, Charles Wells Summer Solstice, Flowers Original, Harviestoun Waverley, RCH Pitchfork, Robinsons Frederics, Tisbury Stonehenge and Titanic Captain Smith. They also stock Belgian beers, a few country wines and a couple of farm ciders; video game. Reasonably priced, straightforward bar food served by friendly young staff includes baguettes (from £2.90), filled baked potatoes (from £3), sausage and mash (£4.25), lasagne (£4.75), fish and chips (£4.95) and steak and ale pie (£5.35) with specials such as vegetable stroganoff (£4.95) and blackened cajun chicken (£5.15); the top food area is no smoking. On long summer evenings it's especially nice to sit out on the tables in the three attractive walled-in flagstoned or gravelled courtyards (one has its own bar); in winter, they have gas heaters to huddle around. As it's very popular with students in the evening, you may have problems finding a seat. *(Recommended by David Peakall, Catherine Pitt, T R and B C Jenkins, the Didler, R Huggins, D Irving, E McCall, T McLean, Eric Locker, Rona Murdoch, Kevin Blake, Jonathan Smith, Dick and Madeleine Brown, Geoff Pidoux, Nigel Woolliscroft, Andrew Barker, Claire Jenkins, Stephanie Smith, Gareth Price, S J and C C Davidson, Jim and Maggie Cowell, Philip and Ann Board, Paul Hopton)*

Laurel Pub Company ~ Manager Darren Kent ~ Real ale ~ Bar food (12-7.30) ~ (01865) 243235 ~ Children in eating area of bar ~ Open 11-11; 12-10.30 Sun

RAMSDEN SP3515 Map 4
Royal Oak 🍷 🍺 🛏️

Village signposted off B4022 Witney—Charlbury

Good food, enthusiastic staff and a proper pubby atmosphere in the traditional beamed bar of this unpretentious village inn make it a long term favourite with quite a few of our readers. The basic furnishings are comfortable, with fresh flowers, bookcases with old copies of *Country Life* and, when the weather gets cold, a cheerful log fire. Popular, bar food might include home-made soup (£3.25), chicken liver and Cointreau pâté (£3.75), ploughman's or club sandwiches (£4.95; lunchtime only, not Sunday), pie of the week (£6.50), stilton, leek and mushroom with puff pastry in white wine sauce (£6.50), fresh crab and smoked salmon fishcakes and steamed steak and kidney pudding (£10.95) and steaks (from £10.50); on Thursday evenings they do rump steak, a glass of wine and home-made pudding (£12.50); roast Sunday lunch. The dining room is no smoking. Well kept real ales on handpump include Archers Golden, Hook Norton Best and Old Hooky and occasional guests such as West Berkshire Good Old Boy; enjoyable house wines. There are tables and chairs in the courtyard and garden. The cosy bedrooms are in separate cottages. *(Recommended by Rainer Zimmer, Nick Lawless, Suzanne Baylis, Franklyn Roberts, L G Owen, Christine Harmer-Brown, Angus Lyon, Vicky and Matt Wharton, Geoff Pidoux, Stuart Turner, Peter Dolan)*

Free house ~ Licensee Jon Oldham ~ Real ale ~ Bar food (12-2.30, 7-10) ~ Restaurant ~ (01993) 868213 ~ Children in restaurant ~ Open 11.30-3, 6.30-11; 12-3, 7-10.30 Sun; closed 25 Dec ~ Bedrooms: £35S/£55S

ROKE SU6293 Map 2
Home Sweet Home
Village signposted off B4009 Benson—Watlington

The two smallish bar rooms of this traditional, rather smart pub have a pleasant, relaxed atmosphere. There's a lovely large log fire, heavy stripped beams, leather armed chairs on the bare boards, a great high-backed settle with a hefty slab of a rustic table in front of it, and a few horsey or game pictures such as a nice Thorburn print of snipe on the stone walls. On the right, a carpeted room with low settees and armchairs and an attractive corner glass cupboard, leads through to the restaurant. A wide choice of good, popular bar food includes sandwiches, toasties, and club sandwiches (from £2.55), home-made soup (£2.95), lots of ploughman's (from £4.25), filled baked potatoes (from £4.75), and daily specials such as fresh cod in light beer batter (£5.95), warm crab and saffron tart (£6.45), steak and kidney pudding (£7.95), and cajun chicken (£8.25), and home-made puddings such as boozy prune tart or vanilla and chocolate cheesecake (£3). Well kept Brakspears on handpump, and a good choice of malt whiskies; welcoming, efficient staff. The low-walled front garden is ideal for eating on a sunny day; there are lots of flowers around the tables out by the well. *(Recommended by Iain and Joan Baillie, Nick Holmes, Marjorie and David Lamb)*

Free house ~ Licensees Jill Madle, Peter & Irene Mountford ~ Real ale ~ Bar food (12-2, 6-9(9.30 Sat)) ~ Restaurant ~ (01491) 838249 ~ Well behaved children welcome ~ Open 11-3, 6-11; closed Sun evening

SHENINGTON SP3742 Map 4
Bell
Village signposted from A422 W of Banbury

Handy for Upton House, this 17th-c pub is part of a row of golden stone cottages in a charming village. Readers like the generous portions of food (cooked by the landlady) which, from a short menu, might include kipper pâté and toast (£3.50), almond and celery bake, prawn and salmon quiche or home-cooked ham salad (£6.25), lasagne (£6.75), chicken in tarragon sauce (£7.50), salmon in watercress sauce or lamb and mint casserole (£7.95) as well as sandwiches (from £2.40); puddings such as rhubarb crumble or sticky toffee pudding (£2.95). There's a laid-back atmosphere in the heavy-beamed and carpeted lounge with cushioned wall and window seats, vases of flowers on the tables, and horsebrasses and an old document on the cream walls; the wall in the flagstoned area on the left is stripped to stone and decorated with heavy-horse harness, and the right side opens into a little pine-panelled room (popular with locals) with decorated plates; cribbage, dominoes, coal fire. Well kept Hook Norton Best on handpump. Tables at the front look across to the green, and there are seats in the small attractive back garden. The west highland terrier is called Lucy and the labrador, Daisy. There are good surrounding walks. *(Recommended by Sir Nigel Foulkes, John Kane, Martin Jones, K H Frostick, George Atkinson, Geoffrey and Penny Hughes, John Bramley, DC, Iain R Hewitt, John Bowdler)*

Free house ~ Licensee Jennifer Dixon ~ Real ale ~ Bar food (not Mon lunchtime) ~ Restaurant ~ (01295) 670274 ~ Children in eating area of bar ~ Open 12-2.30(3 Sat), 6.30-11; 12-4, 7-10.30 Sun; closed Mon lunchtime ~ Bedrooms: £20/£40B

SHIPTON-UNDER-WYCHWOOD SP2717 Map 4
Lamb ♀ 🛏

Off A361 to Burford

This friendly pub is handy for many of the Cotswold attractions, and the beamed bar is a good place to unwind after a hard day's sightseeing. Furnishings include a fine oak-panelled settle, a nice mix of solid old farmhouse-style and captain's chairs on the wood-block floor, polished tables, cushioned bar stools, pictures (including a circular map of the area) on old partly bared stone walls, newspapers on rods to read, and an open fire. Greene King Ruddles County and Hook Norton Best are served from handpumps on an oak bar counter; also several malt whiskies, and a good wine list (champagne by the glass). Bar food includes soup (£3.25), smoked haddock and chive tartlets (£4.50), chargrilled tuna with black pepper butter (£8.95), pork medallions with apple and brandy (£9.95), and calves liver with Pernod and onions (11.95), with puddings such as chocolate and Cointreau truffle cake (£3.95); popular lunchtime carvery (£6.95-£9.95). The restaurant is no smoking; best to reserve a table at weekends. We should say that readers' enthusiasm has tended to wax and wane a bit, perhaps depending on staff changes. There are seats in the garden. *(Recommended by Michael Hyde, Mike and Penny Sutton, Maysie Thompson, Mrs S Spevack, Mrs A Jones, Stuart Turner, John Kane, Paul Boot, Andrew and Ruth Triggs, Geoff Pidoux, Phyl and Jack Street, Graham Johnson, John Bowdler, David and Ruth Shillitoe)*

Old English Inns ~ Real ale ~ Bar food ~ Restaurant ~ (01993) 830465 ~ Children in eating area of bar ~ Open 11-11; 12-10.30 Sun ~ Bedrooms: £60S/£75B

Shaven Crown 🛏

Elizabeth I is said to have used parts of this imposing building as a hunting lodge, and in the 14th c it was a hospice for the monastery of Bruern. There's a magnificent double-collar braced hall roof, lofty beams and a sweeping double stairway down the stone wall, and the beamed bar has a relief of the 1146 Battle of Evesham, as well as seats forming little stalls around the tables and upholstered benches built into the walls. The courtyard is a tranquil place to sit on a sunny day, and is pleasantly lit up at night when gas heaters allow you to soak up the atmosphere without shivering. Bar food includes soup (£3.10), sandwiches (from £3.50), chicken livers with yorkshire pudding or deep fried camembert (£4), ploughman's (£6.50), steak, ale and kidney pie or poached salmon with white wine and parsley sauce or lentil burger (£7.95), half duck with orange and cinnamon sauce (£9.95) and puddings such as dark chocolate and rum mousse or treacle tart (£3.50); children's helpings, and Sunday lunch; service is friendly and efficient. Well kept Hook Norton Best and a guest such as Abbot Ale on handpump, and several wines by the glass; shove-ha'penny, dominoes and cribbage. As well as in the courtyard, there are old-fashioned seats set out on the stone cobbles and crazy paving, with a view of the lily pool and roses; the pub has its own bowling green. *(Recommended by E J and M W Corrin, Andrew and Ruth Triggs, Stuart Turner, Andrew Birkinshaw, Marjorie and David Lamb)*

Free house ~ Licensees Robert and Jane Burpitt ~ Real ale ~ Bar food (12-2, 5.30-9.30) ~ Restaurant ~ (01993) 830330 ~ Children welcome away from main bar ~ Open 12-2.30, 5-11; 12-11 Sat; 12-10.30 Sun ~ Bedrooms: £55B/£85.95B

SOUTH STOKE SU5983 Map 2
Perch & Pike

Off B4009 2 miles N of Goring

This little brick and flint dining pub is just a field away from the Thames. The relaxing bar has comfortable seats, low beams, open fires, a nice assortment of tables, well kept Brakspears Bitter, Old and Special and a guest on handpump, and around a dozen malt whiskies. Enjoyable home-made bar snacks include home-made soups such as tomato and basil, triple-decker sandwiches (from £3.50) while main dishes could be sausage and mash or beer battered haddock. The more elaborate menu served in the small no smoking restaurant could include starters (£4.95-£7.85) such as confit of duck leg or grilled goats cheese with avocado, and main courses like rack of lamb with herb crust or beef fillet with wild mushrooms and daily fish specials such as roast marlin with parmesan mash (£8.95-£16.95); puddings. The window boxes are pretty, there are seats out on the large flower-bordered lawn, and more on a new Cotswold stone terrace. *(Recommended by Adrian and Felicity Smith, Chris Glasson, Barbara Wensworth, Ian Phillips)*

Brakspears ~ Tenants Jason Hursey and Alan Laycock ~ Real ale ~ Bar food (12-2.30, 7-9.45) ~ Restaurant ~ (01491) 872415 ~ Children in restaurant ~ Open 11-3, 6-11; 12-3, 7-10.30 Sun

STANTON ST JOHN SP5709 Map 4
Star

Pub signposted off B4027; village is signposted off A40 heading E of Oxford (heading W, you have to go to the Oxford ring-road roundabout and take unclassified road signposted to Stanton St John, Forest Hill etc); bear right at church in village centre

This friendly pub is a lovely warm place to visit on a cold winter's day. An attractive extension on a level with the car park has rugs on flagstones, pairs of bookshelves on each side of an attractive inglenook fireplace, old-fashioned dining chairs, an interesting mix of dark oak and elm tables, shelves of good pewter, terracotta-coloured walls with a portrait in oils, and a stuffed ermine; down a flight of stairs are little low-beamed rooms – one has ancient brick flooring tiles and the other quite close-set tables. A good range of bar food includes sandwiches (£2.40), soup (£2.40, soup and sandwich £4.25), filled baked potatoes (from £2.95), ploughman's (from £3.95), chicken liver pâté (£3.95), spinach and mushroom strudel, battered haddock or steak and ale pie (£6.95), cajun catfish or chicken kiev (£7.95) and puddings (£3.15). Well kept Wadworths IPA and 6X and one of their other ales on handpump, and country wines. The family room is no smoking. The walled garden has seats among the rockeries and children's play equipment. *(Recommended by Marjorie and David Lamb, R T and J C Moggridge, Geoff Pidoux, Canon Michael Bourdeaux, Kevin Blake, Mrs M Blundell, Paul Hopton)*

Wadworths ~ Manager Michael Urwin ~ Real ale ~ Bar food (12-2, 6.30-9.30, not Sun evening) ~ (01865) 351277 ~ Children in family room ~ Open 11-2.30, 6.30-11; 12-2.30, 7-10.30 Sun

Talk House ♀ ⇔

Wheatley Road (B4027 just outside village)

The tables in the sheltered courtyard of this peacefully set 17th-c pub are set around an impressive fountain. There's a pleasant atmosphere in the various capacious rooms, which have lots of oak beams, flagstoned and tiled floors, stripped original stonework, simple but solid rustic furnishings, and attractive pictures and other individual and often light-hearted decorations. While most of the tables are set for dining, there's enough room for those just wanting a sociable drink. The good bar food is on the pricy side and, as well as lunchtime baguettes (£5.50), includes home-made soup (£3.50), grilled mediterranean vegetables (£4.95), aromatic duck (£5.50), wild boar terrine with tomato and apricot chutney (£5.75), steak and mushroom pie or scotch salmon steak (£9.95), pork loin fillet with sausage and leek stuffing (£13.95) and fillet steak (£14.95), with tasty vegetarian dishes such as wild mushroom stroganoff or sun-dried tomato and pesto tagliatelle (£8.95); puddings such as hot chocolate fudge cake (£3.95). Well kept Greene King Old Speckled Hen, Fullers London Pride and Hook Norton on handpump, good house wines, several malt whiskies and coffee. *(Recommended by Geoff Pidoux, Martin Jennings, Darly Graton, Graeme Gulibert)*

Mercury Taverns ~ Manager Anne-Marie Carlisle-Kitz ~ Real ale ~ Bar food (12-2, 7-9.30(10 Fri and Sat); 12-9 Sun) ~ Restaurant ~ (01865) 351648 ~ Children welcome ~ Live band on first Sun of the month ~ Open 12-3, 5.30-11; 12-10.30 Sun ~ Bedrooms: /£49.50B

SWALCLIFFE SP3737 Map 4

Stags Head

Bakers Lane, just off B4035

Tables in front of this charmingly picturesque, old thatched village pub look down over a peaceful, steeply winding little lane opposite the church. Behind is a series of neatly terraced gardens with palm trees, a small fountain, several tables under a pergola, and a sensibly segregated play area. The landlord is friendly and it's snug and welcoming inside; in the evening all the tables have candles. There's a big woodburner at the end of the low-beamed bar and next to it a standard lamp, and high-backed wooden pews and cushioned seats beside the stone walls. Lots of little jugs hang from the ceiling, and the 'head' of a Master of Foxhounds rather than the fox. A lighter room has lots more tables, and a tiled fireplace, along with newspapers to read, plenty of books, and lists of various local events and activities. As well as lunchtime dishes such as baguettes (from £3.95) and roast ham, egg and chips or battered haddock (£5.95), bar food might include brie and bacon melt (£4.25), pasta with stilton and artichoke (£8.50), tuna steak with warm red pepper and tomato salsa (£8.75), apple and marsala pork (£9.95) and pot roasted lamb shoulder (£10.95) with quite a few spicy dishes such as lamb tikka masala (£8.95) and lime and chilli chicken (£9.50); puddings might include white chocolate truffle tart and their unusual chocolate chilli cake (from £3.50) as well as their boozy home-made ice creams; children's menu (£3.95). Well kept Brakspears, Hook Norton, and a guest from a brewery such as Wychwood; good changing wine list, with six by the glass, and a generous, well made bloody mary. They have two dogs and two cats. Piped easy listening, darts, shove-ha'penny, cribbage and two dominoes teams. *(Recommended by Amanda Eames, John Kane, Mrs Mary Walters, Mr and Mrs R A Buckler)*

Free house ~ Licensees Ian and Julia Kingsford ~ Real ale ~ Bar food (12-2.15, 7-9.30; not Mon) ~ Restaurant ~ (01295) 780232 ~ Children welcome ~ Open 11.30-2.30(3 Sat), 6.30-11; 12-3, 7-10.30 Sun; 12-4 and closed in the evening on Sun winter; closed Mon

TADPOLE BRIDGE SP3300 Map 4

Trout

Back road Bampton—Buckland, 4 miles NE of Faringdon

The well kept garden of this peacefully set Thames-side pub is pretty in summer with small fruit trees, attractive hanging baskets, and flower troughs. It's good for walkers and families, there are moorings for boaters, and you can fish on a two-mile stretch of the river (the pub sells day tickets). The cheerful, bustling atmosphere is helped along by the friendly staff. Made using local produce, well presented bar meals might include home-made soup such as tomato and pesto (£3.25), chicken and game pâté with red onion marmalade (£4.75), cumberland sausage and mash (£7.50), smoked bacon steak (£8.50), vegetable lasagne (£8.75), baked mullet (£11.95) and roast lamb loin with couscous (£14.95). The small L-shaped original bar has plenty of seats on flagstones and this year they serve home-made sloe gin, cherry plum brandy and elderflower cordial as well as real ales such as Archers Village, Fullers London Pride and a couple of guests on handpump; comprehensive wine list, several malt whiskies. Darts, dominoes, cribbage and other board games, and piped music. Reports, please, on their new no smoking dining room and bedrooms. *(Recommended by Peter and Audrey Dowsett, P R and S A White, David Humphreys, John Evans, Herbert and Susan Verity, Paul Craddock, A D Marsh, Mr and Mrs C Crichton)*

Free house ~ Licensee Christopher J Green ~ Real ale ~ Bar food (till 3 Sun, not Sun evening except bank hol wknds) ~ Restaurant ~ (01367) 870382 ~ Children welcome ~ Open 11.30-3, 6-11; 12-3, 7-10.30 Sun; closed Sun evening in winter, 25-29 Dec and 1st week in Feb ~ Bedrooms: £55S/£80B

Pubs close to motorway junctions are listed at the back of the book.

THAME SP7005 Map 4
Swan ◧
9 Upper High Street

'Quirky' is how the landlady describes the décor of this civilised 16th-c hotel – tables in the main bar are either crates, trunks or a butcher's block, and there's an assortment of well worn armchairs and comfortable old sofas, several grouped together around the stone fireplace. Though nothing seems to match it all blends together perfectly. Brightly painted tiles cover the bar counter and the wall behind, and there are beams, timbers, faded rugs, old-fashioned saucy seaside postcards and a handsome clock. Cushioned sofas meander along a passageway, then down a step is an odd but cosy low-ceilinged room with paintings of erstwhile locals on the walls. Well kept Brakspears, Hook Norton and a guest on handpump. Service is exceptionally friendly and attentive. Good home-made bar food such as sandwiches (from £2.65), soup (£3.50), swordfish cake (£5.50), lamb and mushroom hotpot or vegetable and cheese bake (£5.95), fried calamari or barbecued beef kebabs (£6.50), their popular steak sandwich (£6.95), and puddings such as chocolate mousse cake (£4.50). The upstairs restaurant still has its medieval ceiling. Piped classical music, newspapers to read, good cappuccino, dominoes, cribbage, shut the box, chess, backgammon. There are a few tables at the back, in a small shopping arcade. It can get very busy in the evening and parking is quite tricky on market days. *(Recommended by James Chatfield, Tim and Ann Newell)*

Free house ~ Licensee Sue Turnbull ~ Real ale ~ Bar food (12-2.30, 7-9) ~ Restaurant ~ (01844) 261211 ~ Children welcome away from bar till 8 ~ Open 11-11; 12-10.30 Sun; closed 25 and 26 Dec ~ Bedrooms: £50S/£95B

WATLINGTON SU6894 Map 4
Chequers
3 miles from M40 junction 6; take B4009 towards Watlington, and on outskirts of village turn right into residential road Love Lane which leads to pub

The pretty garden of this tucked away pub has picnic-sets under apple and pear trees, sweet peas, roses, geraniums, begonias, and rabbits. Readers enjoy the nicely presented bar food which includes sandwiches and toasties (from £2.50), prawns in filo pastry or deep-fried camembert (£4.90), lentil and aubergine moussaka (£6), steak and kidney pie or chicken curry (£7.50), steaks (from £10.50), fried calves liver (£11.50) or grilled dover sole (£14.50); specials such as polynesian chicken (£9.50) or lamb shank in red wine with leek mash (£11.50) and puddings such as treacle tart (from £4); it's a good idea to book for their good Sunday lunch. The rambling bar has a low panelled oak settle and character chairs such as a big spiral-legged carving chair around a few good antique oak tables, a low oak beamed ceiling darkened to a deep ochre by the candles which they still use, and red-and-black shiny tiles in one corner with rugs and red carpeting elsewhere; steps on the right lead down to an area with more tables. A conservatory with very low hanging vines looks out over the garden. Well kept Brakspears Pale Ale, Special and seasonal ales on handpump, a decent little wine list. The cheese shop in Watlington itself is worth a visit and in spring, the nearby Watlington woods are a mass of bluebells. *(Recommended by Howard Dell, Barbara Wilder, Andy Meaton, John Branston)*

Brakspears ~ Tenants John and Anna Valentine ~ Real ale ~ Bar food ~ Restaurant ~ (01491) 612874 ~ Children in family room ~ Open 11.30-2.30, 6-11; 12-3, 7-10.30 Sun; closed 26 Dec

WIGGINTON SP3833 Map 4
White Swan ⑪
Village signposted off A361 SW of Banbury

This small tucked-away stone-built pub has not much more than half a dozen tables, but the new landlord's cooking is a big draw here. Booking in the evenings is already advisable, and though it was quiet on our anonymous lunchtime inspection visit we anticipate trade will build up quickly here as word gets around. We swithered over unusual and tempting sandwiches (from £3.25) such as black pudding with mango, stilton with pear, or tuna melt, then plumped for two dishes of the day. Swordfish (like tuna, all too easy to dry out) was grilled just right, nicely cooked and still succulent. Liver and bacon (£7.95) was a far cry from your coarse café variety: with its rich gravy this was full of flavours and – very rare for this dish – even looked pretty. At the end of March, this came with genuine new potatoes, nicely cooked string beans, carrots and calabrese, and a clever mix of little bits of sauté potatoes with red pepper and onion in a savourous pan reduction. For such individual cooking, the food came remarkably quickly. Other dishes could include soup (£2.95), feta and olive salad (£3.95), smoked salmon, tomato and mozzarella pancakes (£4.95), corned beef hash (£6.50) and pork spare ribs (£7.25), with specials such as rabbit in cider and mustard (£8.95), and guinea fowl, lemon sole or duck breast in strawberry sauce (£11.95); puddings such as chocolate bread pudding (£2.95). We sat at a table on old flooring tiles by a hot inglenook log fire opposite the bar counter (which has well kept Hook Norton Best, Best Mild and Double Stout on handpump); down a step from here is a simply decorated carpeted area with neat tables and wheelback chairs, and the main blackboard over another huge fireplace. Service is quietly pleasant; relaxed chatty atmosphere; piped Dean Martin on our visit. There are a few picnic-sets out on a little terrace and patch of lawn behind. *(Recommended by Stuart Turner, Andrew J Carter, George Atkinson, M Benjamin)*

Hook Norton ~ Tenants Stephen and Karen Coutts-Williams ~ Real ale ~ Bar food (12-2.30, 6-10) ~ Restaurant ~ (01608) 737669 ~ Children welcome ~ Open 12-3, 6-11; 12-4, 7-11 Sun

WOODSTOCK SP4416 Map 4
Feathers 🍴 🛏

Market St

We continue to include this formal but unstuffy Cotswold stone hotel because readers really like the old-fashioned Courtyard Bar at the back. With oils and watercolours on its walls, stuffed fish and birds (don't miss the live parrot, too), and a central open fire, it opens on to the beautiful sunny courtyard with a small water feature, and attractive tables and chairs among geraniums and trees. Well presented (though certainly not cheap) food from a short bar menu might include mediterranean fish soup or wild mushroom, asparagus and truffle oil risotto (£5.95), smoked chicken, crispy bacon and avocado salad (£6.95), smoked salmon with lime crème fraîche (£7.95) and rare roast beef baguette (£8.50); puddings (from £4.95); the restaurant is no smoking. Well kept (if pricy) Wadworths 6X on handpump, decent house wine, a good choice of malt whiskies, summer home-made lemonade and pimms, freshly squeezed orange juice and afternoon teas; excellent service; piped music. Get there early for a table. *(Recommended by John Bramley, John and Enid Morris, Derek Thomas, Kenneth Booth, John Bowdler, Patricia Beebe, Andrew Barker, Claire Jenkins)*

Free house ~ Licensees Messrs Pendril, Bate and Shelton ~ Real ale ~ Bar food (12.30-2.30, 6.30-8; not Sat evenings) ~ Restaurant ~ (01993) 812291 ~ Children welcome ~ Open 10-(10.30 Sun)11; closed to non-residents evening 25 Dec ~ Bedrooms: £115B/£135B

WOOTTON SP4419 Map 4
Kings Head 🍴

Chapel Hill; off B4027 N of Woodstock

Although you can choose to eat in the bar or garden instead of the spacious, formal restaurant, this attractive 17th-c Cotswold stone house is somewhere you'd come for a treat rather than a casual lunch. The food is good (though not cheap) and all home-made – they even make their own bread and ice cream. Dishes range from soup (£3.95), warm duck salad with puréed plum sauce or seared pigeon breast with caramelised shallots (£4.95) to chargrilled pork medallions with honey and basil cream sauce or mediterranean vegetables and couscous (£10.95), steaks (from

£10.95) and pink roasted duck breast with apple and thyme (£12.95), roasted rack of English lamb with five peppers (from £15.50); puddings such as caramelised citrus tart (£4.95). No smoking in the restaurant. Ruddles Best and Wadworths 6X on handpump, and a good wine list with quite a few by the glass. The civilised and relaxing beamed no smoking lounge bar has a nice mix of old oak settles and chairs around wooden tables, comfortable armchairs and chintzy sofas, an open log fire, and old prints and ceramics on the pale pink walls. Although they are allowed in the restaurant, this is not really a place geared towards children; no children's meals. *(Recommended by Mike and Mary Carter, Jason Caulkin, LM, Alan Clark, O Richardson, Sir Nigel Foulkes, Martin and Karen Wake, Geoff Pidoux, John Bowdler)*

Free house ~ Licensees Tony & Amanda Fay ~ Real ale ~ Bar food (not Sun evening) ~ Restaurant ~ (01993) 811340 ~ Well behaved children over 12 in restaurant ~ Open 11-11; 12-3 Sun; closed Sun evening ~ Bedrooms: £65B/£90B

Lucky Dip

Besides the fully inspected pubs, you might like to try these Lucky Dips recommended to us and described by readers (if you do, please send us reports: www.goodguides.com).

Adderbury [SP4635]
☆ *Bell* [High St; just off A4260, turn opp Red Lion]: Unpretentious largely unspoilt beamed village local with chiming grandfather clock, some panelling, relaxed atmosphere, generous good fresh food, well kept Hook Norton inc seasonal ales; homely front room with armchairs and sofa by huge log fire, sewing machines and standard lamp, smaller back music room with two pianos, old settles, and folk nights 1st and 3rd Mon of month; candlelit restaurant *(Geoff Pidoux, BB, Pete Baker, Giles Francis)*
☆ *Red Lion* [The Green; off A4260 S of Banbury]: Smartly civilised but welcoming, with big inglenook, panelling, high stripped beams and stonework, cosy no smoking back dining room up steps, good food, full Wadworths range kept well, several wines by the glass, daily papers, games area on left; piped music; children in eating area, tables out on well kept terrace, comfortable bedrooms, open all day summer *(Michael and Jenny Back, Iain R Hewitt, LYM, Geoff Pidoux)*

Alvescot [SP2704]
Plough [B4020 Carterton—Clanfield]: Friendly partly 17th-c beamed village pub popular at lunchtime for wide choice of good value food inc Sun lunch (must book), quick service, well kept Wadworths and a guest beer, decent wines, good coffee, old maps and plates, log fire (but cool and pleasant on hot days), dining extension; quiet piped music, separate public bar with bar billiards and TV; colourful hanging baskets *(Marjorie and David Lamb, Nigel and Anna Boden)*

Ardington [SU4388]
☆ *Boars Head* [signed off A417 Didcot—Wantage]: Civilised dining pub, simple but smart country décor in low-beamed two-room bar, plainer no smoking extension, adventurous if pricy food, well kept Arkells 3B, Brakspears and a guest beer, good wines; darts, shove-ha'penny, cribbage, dominoes, board games, TV and piped music; children welcome, cl Sun evening, peaceful attractive village *(Dick and Madeleine Brown, Jenny and Chris Wilson, R Halsey, Simon Collett-Jones, Angela and Andrew Webster, J Hale, LYM, Peter B Brown)*

Ashbury [SU2685]
Rose & Crown [B4507/B4000; High St]: Smart, roomy and comfortable open-plan beamed bar, part of hotel, with highly polished woodwork, settees, pews and oak tables and chairs, traditional pictures, good choice of unpretentious sensibly priced food, well kept Arkells, friendly helpful staff, bar billiards in room off, charming restaurant; bedrooms, attractive village nr Ridgeway *(Peter and Audrey Dowsett)*

Asthall [SP2811]
☆ *Maytime* [off A40 at W end of Witney bypass, then 1st left]: Comfortably genteel dining pub with very wide choice of good value well served meals inc plenty for vegetarians (just set lunch on Sun), some bar snacks, slightly raised plush dining lounge neatly set with tables (best ones down by fire may be booked for overnight guests), airy conservatory restaurant (children allowed behind screen), Morrells and Wadworths 6X, decent wines, prompt service, interesting pictures, small locals' bar with flagstones and log fire; piped music; in tiny hamlet, nice views of Asthall Manor and watermeadows from garden, attractive walks, quiet comfortable bedrooms around charming back courtyard *(BB, Mrs D Rawlings, Lucien)*

Bampton [SP3103]
Elephant & Castle [Bridge St (A4095 W end)]: Homely and friendly feel in three rooms off bar, stripped stone, interesting mix of furniture inc fine sideboard, well kept and well priced real ales such as Adnams, Archers Village and Vale Wychert, darts, dominoes, cards *(Pete Baker)*
Romany [Bridge St; off A4095 SW of Witney]: 17th-c local, unpretentious and well worn in, with partly stripped stone walls, log fire, well kept Archers Village, Bass and guest beers from ancient pre-Norman cellars, low-priced food from sandwiches to Sun lunch, no smoking restaurant; darts, cribbage, dominoes, fruit

machine, TV and piped music; picnic-sets in big back garden with good play area and aunt sally (G U Briggs, LYM, Paul Hopton)

Beckley [SP5611]

Abingdon Arms [signed off B4027; High St]: Handsome old pub with extensive pretty garden dropping away into orchard, and floodlit terrace; attractively refurbished lounge and smaller public bar, well kept Brakspears, food from sandwiches up, good walks (John Roots, Geoff Pidoux, David Clifton, LYM)

Bessels Leigh [SP4501]

Greyhound: Roomily refurbished family dining pub, comfortable and cheerful, with lots of no smoking rooms, varied good value food from baguettes to Sun carvery, well kept beers, decent wine, friendly helpful staff, open fires, children's room with lots of toys; piped music, sometimes lunchtime pianist; open all day, play area outside (Tony Baldwin, Geoffrey and Carol Thorp, Peter and Audrey Dowsett, Geoff Pidoux)

Bix [SU7285]

Fox [A4130]: Classic unassuming roadside local, two unspoilt oak-floored rooms, Brakspears (BB, the Didler, JP, PP, Richard Butler, Marie Kroon)

Bletchingdon [SP5017]

Blacks Head [Station Rd; B4027 N of Oxford]: Traditional village pub, cosy stripped-stone lounge with woodburner, dining area and newish conservatory behind; limited choice of home-cooked food (veg are extra), well kept Flowers IPA, Marstons Pedigree and Youngs Special, locals' bar with darts, cards and dominoes; pleasant garden with aunt sally, long-standing Thurs folk nights (Pete Baker, R Huggins, D Irving, E McCall, T McLean)

Blewbury [SU5385]

Load of Mischief [South St (off A417)]: Comfortable pub/restaurant with Greene King Morlands, friendly staff, good food in bar (which can be smoky) or dining room; may be soft piped music; tables on small attractive back terrace (Howard Dell)

☆ *Red Lion* [Nottingham Fee – narrow turning N from A417]: Beamed tiled-floor downland village pub, well kept Brakspears, enjoyable food from soup and sandwiches to duck and venison, big log fire, cribbage, dominoes, no piped music, restaurant (children allowed); tables in nice back garden, bedrooms, pretty surroundings (Howard Dell, Dick and Madeleine Brown, LYM, Michael Clough)

Bloxham [SP4235]

☆ *Elephant & Castle* [off A361, fairly handy for M40 junction 1; Humber St]: Relaxed and unchanging, with striking 17th-c stone fireplace in simple but elegant public bar, strip wood floor, big winter log fire in comfortable lounge; darts, bar billiards, dominoes, cribbage, fruit machine, and shove-ha'penny on a hardy board over a century old; well kept Hook Norton Best, Old Hooky, Generation and seasonal ales, a monthly guest beer, farm cider (guests in summer), around 30 malt whiskies, straightforward promptly served lunchtime bar food, low prices; children welcome, open all

day Sun, sunny flower-filled courtyard, maybe wknd barbecues; imposing Cotswold village (A E Brace, GSB, LYM)

Boars Hill [SP4802]

Fox [between A34 and B4017; Fox Lane]: Clean and attractive family-friendly refurbished Chef & Brewer in pretty wooded countryside, interesting rambling rooms on different levels, huge log fireplaces, poems on the wall, wide choice of reasonably priced food, well kept ales, decent wine, polite service, day's paper framed in gents'; may be soft piped classical music or jazz; restaurant, pleasant raised verandah, charming big sloping garden with play area, open all day (Dick and Madeleine Brown, Geoff Pidoux)

Bodicote [SP4537]

Plough [Goose Lane/High St; off A4260 S of Banbury]: Quaint and dark 14th-c pub with well kept Archers Best, Theakstons XB and Old Peculier and guest beers, country wines, wide choice of well cooked straightforward food, good friendly service; old beams, pictures and brasses, dining area (the Didler, Iain R Hewitt)

Brize Norton [SP3007]

Chequers [Station Rd]: Roomy open-plan pub with wide choice of food inc OAP lunches, friendly staff, pleasant atmosphere, RAF theme (KN-R)

Bucknell [SP5525]

Trigger Pond [handy for M40 junction 10; Bicester Rd]: Neat stone-built pub opp the pond, good fresh home cooking inc old-fashioned puddings (must book Sun lunch), nice atmosphere, well kept changing ales such as Adnams, Badger Best and Tanglefoot and Hook Norton Best; piped music; pleasant terrace and garden (Mrs Marion Evans)

Burford [SP2512]

Angel [Witney St]: Long heavy-beamed dining pub in attractive ancient building, reopened with brasserie and doing well under new landlord (M and P Theodorou, LYM)

Bull [High St]: Handsome ancient building well reconstructed a decade ago, chatty front bar on left, steps down to comfortable and relaxing beamed and panelled dining lounge, three big log fires, well kept Greene King Ruddles County and Theakstons, good choice of wines by the glass, usual food from sandwiches up; piped music; children welcome, open all day, tables out in front or back through old coach entry, comfortable bedrooms (LYM, Ted George, Andrew and Ruth Triggs, Phil and Jane Hodson)

Cotswold Arms [High St]: Good sensibly priced food, beautiful stonework, pleasant efficient service (Klaus and Elizabeth Leist, Geoff Pidoux)

☆ *Royal Oak* [Witney St]: Neat 17th-c local tucked away from summer crowds, Wadworths beers, wide range of simple food, beams and stripped stone, great collection of beer mugs and steins, pine tables and chairs, antlers over log-effect gas fire, bar billiards, back dining room; tables out on terrace, sensibly priced bedrooms off garden behind (Simon Collett-Jones, Peter and Audrey Dowsett)

Chadlington [SP3222]

☆ *Tite* [off A361 S of Chipping Norton, and B4437 W of Charlbury; Mill End, slightly out of village – at garage turn towards Churchill, then left at playground]: Civilised and welcoming food-oriented local with good if not cheap home-made food from good choice of sandwiches and starters through unusual main dishes to lovely puddings, wider choice in evenings, vine-covered restaurant evenings and Sun lunchtime, well kept ales such as Archers and Wychwood, good house wines, friendly efficient service, big log fire in huge fireplace, settles, wooden chairs, prints, rack of guide books, daily papers, pink-painted walls; piped classical music, children welcome, cl Mon exc bank hols; superb garden full of shrubs, some quite unusual, with stream running under pub – path from car park winds through it; plenty of tables outside, good walks nearby *(BB, John and Janet Davey, Geoff Palmer)*

Charlbury [SP3519]

☆ *Bell* [Church St]: Attractive civilised bar in small 17th-c hotel, flagstones, stripped stonework and huge open fire, welcoming service, short choice of good interesting bar lunches (not Sun) from sandwiches up, well kept Hook Norton and Wadworths, wide choice of malt whiskies, decent if pricy restaurant; children in eating area, comfortable quiet bedrooms, good breakfast *(Mike and Mary Carter, M and P Theodorou, LYM)*

☆ *Bull* [Sheep St]: Very good bistro-style atmosphere and surroundings, restaurant on left and freshly furnished dining bar on right with armchairs and magazines, interesting range of well presented good generous food, well kept Greene King IPA, good wines and coffee, jovial landlord; cl Mon *(BB, Rod Cookson, Martin and Karen Wake, Janet and Philip Shackle)*

Charney Bassett [SU3794]

Chequers: Popular and friendly 18th-c two-room village-green local, spacious rambling interior, enjoyable sensibly priced food (may be snacks only, Sat lunchtime), well kept ales such as Greene King and Wadworths 6X, good service; pool, piped music; small garden, children welcome, has been cl Mon *(Pete Baker, R M Sparkes, M Shepherd, Vanessa Clark, Kate Parry, Paul Bevan)*

Checkendon [SU6682]

Four Horseshoes [off A4074 Reading—Wallingford]: Attractive partly thatched local, traditional furnishings, better-than-average food inc Sun lunchtime in stripped-floor dining lounge (children allowed), well kept Brakspears, good simple wine list, friendly landlord, locals' bar with pool and maybe piped music; big garden with picnic-sets and wknd lunchtime barbecues, super hanging baskets, good walks *(Howard Dell, LM)*

Chipping Norton [SP3126]

☆ *Oxford House* [Horsefair]: Good British and Italian food from new Italian landlord, who had built his previous pub (the Fox at Westcott Barton) into a popular *Guide* main entry *(David Campbell, Vicki McLean)*

Chislehampton [SU5998]

Coach & Horses [B480 Oxford—Watlington, opp B4015 to Abingdon]: Small comfortable two-bar 16th-c pub, homely but civilised, with good choice of well prepared food in sizeable dining area (polished oak tables and wall banquettes), well kept ales inc Flowers and Hook Norton, big log fire, good cheerful service; well kept terraced gardens overlooking fields by River Thame, comfortable bedrooms in back courtyard *(Nick Parslow, Iain Robertson)*

Christmas Common [SU7193]

☆ *Fox & Hounds* [signed from B480/B481]: This formerly basic cottage-pub nr the Chilterns viewpoint of Watlington Hill has just been well done up as a dining pub, with good food from an open kitchen to go with its beams, ancient flooring tiles, bow windows and big inglenook log fire; well kept Brakspears Bitter, Special and winter Old, tables outside *(LYM)*

Church Enstone [SP3724]

☆ *Crown* [Mill Lane; from A44 take B4030 turn off at Enstone]: New licensees' son doing good fresh food from filled baguettes up, pleasant cottagey bar, good-sized light modern dining area and conservatory, log fire in brass-fitted stone fireplace, beams and stripped stone, well kept ales such as Hampshire King Alfred, Hook Norton Best and Wadworths 6X, decent wines by the glass; may be piped music; four spotless bedrooms *(Geoff Pidoux, Mike and Wena Stevenson, Keith Jacob, Lynn Sharpless, Bob Eardley, W Ruxton, Geoff Palmer, Terry Mizen, LYM, Mrs C A Baggaley)*

Church Hanborough [SP4212]

☆ *Hand & Shears* [opp church; signed off A4095 at Long Hanborough, or off A40 at Eynsham roundabout]: Attractively done pub/restaurant, long gleaming bar, steps down into spacious back eating area, another small dining room, wide choice of good brasserie-style food from simple bar dishes to fish and grills inc good thai curries, attentive young staff, well kept Boddingtons, Fullers London Pride and Hook Norton Best, decent wines, open fires, good atmosphere, smartish customers; soft piped music *(LM, Geoff Pidoux, BB, Paul Craddock)*

Clifton Hampden [SU5495]

☆ *Barley Mow* [towards Long Wittenham, S of A415]: Interesting and attractively refurbished thatched Chef & Brewer, very low ancient beams, oak-panelled family room, Scottish Courage ales, good choice of food all day inc good range of fish, well trained staff who like to please, log fire, restaurant; piped music; tables on pleasant terrace and in well tended waterside garden with doves and fancy fowls, short stroll from the Thames; bedrooms, open all day *(David Humphreys, Nick Holmes, LYM)*

☆ *Plough* [A415]: Thatched pub, unusual in being Turkish-run and entirely no smoking, with low beams, soft lighting and panelling, antique furniture on tiled floor, wide range of mainly restaurany food all day (but sandwiches too), well kept Courage Best and Directors and John Smiths, good wines, light and airy restaurant;

open all day, children in eating areas, tables outside, bedrooms in converted building across courtyard *(Gill and Keith Croxton, the Didler, Tom and Ruth Rees, Geoff Pidoux, Alistair Forsyth, LYM)*

Combe [SP4115]
Cock [off A4095 at Long Hanborough; The Green]: Spick and span classic country pub facing green in charming village, two pleasant bars, friendly landlord and helpful staff, Morrells beers, food from good home-made soup and baguettes up *(Dick and Madeleine Brown)*

Cothill [SU4699]
Merry Miller: Large comfortably olde-worlde pub/restaurant based on 17th-c granary, stripped stone and flagstones, wide choice of good generous food inc sandwiches, some interesting dishes and children's helpings, unusual bar nibbles, friendly efficient staff, well kept Badger Tanglefoot, good choice of wines, log fires; disabled access *(D C T and E A Frewer)*

Crawley [SP3412]
☆ *Lamb* [Steep Hill; just NW of Witney]: Recently extended 17th-c stone-built pub, several levels inc unspoilt old beamed bar, no smoking family area and restaurant, good value varied food, quick service, welcoming young licensees, well kept ales such as Hook Norton Best and Marstons Pedigree, decent wines, log fire in big fireplace, cricketing décor; quiet piped music; views from tables on terraced lawn behind, pretty village *(Mike and Mary Carter, Peter and Audrey Dowsett)*

Crowell [SU7499]
Shepherds Crook [B4009, 2 miles from M40 junction 6]: Honest traditional pub tastefully refurbished with stripped brick, timber and flagstones, imaginative changing food inc good fresh fish and local meat and game, carpeted raftered dining area, well kept beers such as Archers Gold, Batemans XXXB, Bathams, Hook Norton and Timothy Taylors Landlord, decent wines, friendly straight-talking landlord, no music or machines; views from tables out on green *(Torrens Lyster, H R Hodges)*

Cumnor [SP4603]
☆ *Bear & Ragged Staff* [signed from A420; Appleton Rd]: Busy comfortably rambling dining pub refurbished with lots of kitsch bric-a-brac, no smoking area, well kept Morrells Oxford, Graduate, Varsity and a changing guest beer, reasonably priced food (service can slow), friendly young staff; children in eating areas, open all day Sun in summer *(LYM, Malcolm and Jane MacDonald, Mr and Mrs K McCulloch, David Humphreys, Jim Bush, Colin and Maureen Butterworth, Kevin Blake, Dick and Madeleine Brown, D C T and E A Frewer, Sue Demont, Tim Barrow)*
Vine [Abingdon Rd]: Busy and restauranty modernised pub with wide choice of enjoyable food from baguettes to Sun family lunches (must book these), extended back dining area, no smoking area in conservatory, three well kept guest ales, good wine range; picnic-sets in attractive back garden *(B and F A Hannam)*

Deddington [SP4631]
Crown & Tuns [New St]: Unsmart and convivial local, three small bars, welcoming long-serving landlord and regulars, well kept and priced Hook Norton, games room with pool *(David Campbell, Vicki McLean)*
☆ *Deddington Arms* [off A4260 (B4031) Banbury—Oxford; Horse Fair]: Welcoming beamed and timbered hotel with mullioned windows, done up in more modern style, with much ochre paintwork and bar table area extended into former end games area; good imaginative food, four well kept ales inc Wadworths 6X, good choice of wines by the glass, friendly efficient staff; open all day, children in eating area, busy spacious restaurant, comfortable chalet bedrooms around courtyard, attractive village with lots of antiques shops *(LYM, Garry Lucas, Dr and Mrs J R C Wallace, Michael Sargent, Gordon Tong)*
☆ *Unicorn* [Market Pl]: Busy and friendly 17th-c inn, nicely redecorated modernised bar, inglenook fireplace, very big helpings of usual food inc inexpensive set lunch in oak-beamed restaurant, three real ales, morning coffee, pleasant service – quick without making you feel rushed; cobbled courtyard leads to lovely walled back garden, with smartly matching tables, chairs and deckchairs; bedrooms *(Arthur Baker, George Atkinson, George Little, Mr and Mrs Hugh Spottiswoode, BB, Geoff Pidoux)*

Denchworth [SU3791]
☆ *Fox* [off A338 or A417 N of Wantage; Hyde Rd]: Picturesque old thatched village pub with two good log fires and plush seats in low-ceilinged comfortable connecting areas, very welcoming attentive service, good attractively priced food from sandwiches to popular Sun carvery, Greene King IPA, Abbot and Morlands Original, good house wines and coffee, coal fire, some paperbacks, small beamed restaurant; may be piped pop music; pleasant sheltered garden, peaceful village *(Marjorie and David Lamb, Peter and Audrey Dowsett, David Humphreys, BB)*

Dorchester [SU5794]
☆ *George* [just off A4074 Maidenhead—Oxford; High St]: Handsome timbered building with fine old furnishings in civilised beamed bar, roaring log fire, enjoyable but pricy food from sandwiches to some interesting main dishes (just roast and sandwiches Sun lunchtime), well kept Brakspears and a guest beer, good wines; open all day, children in restaurant, bedrooms *(LYM, Ray and Jacki Davenport)*
Plough [Abingdon Rd]: Small one-man pub, low-priced home cooking by the friendly landlord, good atmosphere, pub games inc aunt sally, pictures and prints for sale, well kept Morlands; may be quiet piped classical music *(anon)*

Ducklington [SP3507]
☆ *Bell* [off A415, a mile SE of Witney; Standlake Rd]: Pretty thatched pub with colourful hanging baskets, big stripped stone and flagstoned bar with scrubbed tables,

woodburner (and glass-covered well), old local photographs, farm tools and log fires, hatch-served public bar, well laid out big back restaurant (its beams festooned with bells); well kept Greene King Old Speckled Hen and Ruddles, good house wines, wide choice of reasonably priced food all home-made (not Sun eve), friendly service, cards and dominoes, no piped music; folk night 1st Sun of month, regular events such as morris dancing or raft races; small garden behind with play area, bedrooms *(Peter and Audrey Dowsett, Lucien, BB, Pete Baker)*

Duns Tew [SP4528]
White Horse [off A4260 N of Kidlington]: 16th-c beamed pub in attractive village, roomy bar and pretty dining extension, stripped bricks and stonework, rugs on flagstones, oak timbers and panelling, enormous inglenook, settles and homely stripped tables, daily papers, smaller quieter room, good service, enjoyable food, well kept beers inc Hook Norton Best and Wadworths 6X, decent wine list; disabled access, bedrooms in former stables *(Gary Wright, LYM)*

East Hagbourne [SU5288]
Fleur de Lys [Main Rd]: Attractive black and white timbered building, with one clean and tidy single bar – half drinking place with cards and darts (lots of trophies in cabinet), half lounge with more emphasis on food; interesting if not large choice, fresh and good value, also well kept Greene King ales, good welcoming service, quite a few stuffed fish; ceilidhs 3rd Weds, tables out behind *(Pete Baker)*

East Hendred [SU4588]
☆ *Wheatsheaf* [signed off A417; Chapel Sq]: Attractive 16th-c black and white timbered village pub with high-backed settles in quarry-tiled inglenook bar, booth seating up steps, well kept Greene King beers, usual food from sandwiches up, dominoes, shove-ha'penny; piped music; open all day wknds, tables in colourful back garden *(Peter and Jean Hoare, Marjorie and David Lamb, David Humphreys, LYM)*

Eaton [SP4403]
☆ *Eight Bells* [signed off B4017 SW of Oxford]: Hospitable unspoilt Tudor local, two small low-beamed bars, wide range of food, well kept Greene King IPA and Morlands Original with a guest such as Badger Best, open fires, friendly informal service, piano, farm tools, horse tack and brasses, dining room (children allowed here) off cosy lounge; quiz night Sun, no dogs, tables in front garden with aunt sally, tethering rail for horses, nice walks *(LYM, Ian Jones, R W Reah)*

Enslow [SP4818]
Rock of Gibraltar [off A4095 about 1½ miles SW of Kirtlington]: Tall building with modern dining extension overlooking canal (and lorry park opposite), upper conservatory with even better view, well kept Hook Norton, pleasant friendly staff, beams, stripped stone, bright narrowboat paintwork, cycles on ceiling; piped pop music; lots of picnic-sets under cocktail parasols in pretty waterside garden *(LM, Geoff Pidoux)*

Enstone [SP3724]
Harrow [A44 Chipping Norton—Woodstock]: Lively and attractive family-friendly village pub, wide choice of enjoyable home-made food in large back dining room, well kept Morrells Oxford Blue, welcoming service *(Angus Lyon)*

Epwell [SP3540]
Chandlers Arms [Sibford Rd, off B4035]: Chatty and unspoilt two-roomed 16th-c local in attractive out-of-the-way village, friendly landlord, well kept Hook Norton ales, limited choice of good food; pleasant quiet garden *(John Brightley)*

Ewelme [SU6491]
Shepherds Hut [off B4009 about 5 miles SW of M40 junction 6; High St]: Cosy beamed pub popular for good choice of fresh food (worth booking wknds) inc lovely puddings, charming landlady, quick cheerful service, well kept Greene King Morlands, decent coffee, rowing memorabilia, Formula 1 photographs, pot plants, darts, small restaurant; may be piped music, fruit machine; children welcome, tables and swing in small pleasant garden *(Mr and Mrs M Evans)*

Faringdon [SU2895]
Bell [Market Pl]: Well worn in bar with red leather settles, inglenook fireplace with 17th-c carved oak chimney-piece, interesting faded mural in inner bar, well kept ales inc Wadworths 6X, bar food and restaurant; fruit machine in lobby, children and dogs allowed; tables out among flowers in cobbled back coachyard, bedrooms *(LYM, CMW, JJW)*
Plough [Coxwell; A420, 1½ miles SW towards Swindon]: Wide choice of reasonably priced food inc Sun lunch, good range of beers such as Arkells and Wadworths 6X, decent wine, ex-jockey landlord; children in dining conservatory, skittles, no dogs *(Ian Phillips)*

Filkins [SP2304]
Five Alls [signed off A361 Lechlade—Burford]: Comfortable Cotswold stone pub, now part of a small upmarket local group, with concentration on imaginative choice of good if not cheap food in rambling bar and nicely furnished restaurant, helpful staff, well chosen house wines, well kept Bass and Wychwood Hobgoblin, good coffee, daily papers, no piped music, bookable tables; plenty of tables on terrace and neat lawns, garden chess, attractive well equipped bedrooms, nice village *(Ted George, M J and C E Abbey, Peter and Audrey Dowsett, Mr and Mrs J Evans)*

Godstow [SP4809]
☆ *Trout* [off A34 Oxford bypass northbound, via Wytham, or A40/A44 roundabout via Wolvercote]: Creeper-covered medieval pub, much extended and commercialised as big tourist draw – not spoilt and nicely done, but can sometimes get swamped by visitors; fires in three huge hearths, beams and shiny ancient flagstones, furnishings to suit, attractive pictures, roomy dining area, back children's area; decent food all day inc good big pies, well kept Bass and Worthington, good New World wines, winter mulled wine, friendly quick service, quiet piped music; charming in summer

with lovely flagstoned heated terrace by a stream full of greedily plump perch, peacocks in the grounds, Godstow abbey ruins opp *(LYM, Bill Sykes, Peter and Audrey Dowsett, Geoff Pidoux, Gordon, P R and S A White)*

Goring [SU6080]

☆ *Catherine Wheel* [Station Rd]: Good value food inc lots of fish, well kept Brakspears BB, Mild, SB and Old, also Ted & Bens Organic, maybe taster samples, Stowford Press cider, decent wine, good informal atmosphere, very friendly landlord, staff and locals, two cosy bars, good log fire, restaurant; notable door to gents'; nice courtyard and garden, handy for Thames Path, attractive village *(Catherine Pitt, Jonathan Smith, Sue and Mike Todd, A D Marsh)*

☆ *John Barleycorn* [Manor Rd]: Endearing and well run low-beamed cottagey local in pretty Thames village, prints in cosy little lounge bar, good choice of well priced generous home-made food in adjoining eating area, well kept Brakspears, pool in end room, friendly helpful service; bedrooms clean and simple *(the Didler, Derek Harvey-Piper)*

Goring Heath [SU6678]

☆ *King Charles Head* [off A4074 NW of Reading – OS Sheet 175 map ref 664788]: Charming small-roomed rambling country pub, civilised furnishings and décor, wide choice of good value generous traditional GM-free food (all day Sat/Sun), popular Sun lunch and lots of thai dishes, well kept Badger Best, Tanglefoot and K&B, log fire, relaxed atmosphere, friendly prompt service, daily papers; may be soft piped classical music; open all day wknds, lots of picnic-sets in big garden, idyllic woodland setting, good walks nearby *(Simon Collett-Jones, LYM, Lucy Kirkman, Susan and John Douglas)*

Great Haseley [SP6301]

Old Plough [handy for M40 junction 7; Rectory Rd]: Small and friendly with welcoming licensees, lunchtime bar snacks and good evening food esp steaks, well kept beer, helpful staff; quiet area *(Mrs A Pantin)*

Hailey [SP3414]

Bird in Hand [Whiteoak Green; B4022 Witney—Charlbury]: Greatly extended old Cotswold pub, smart yet relaxed and friendly; popular for reasonably priced food inc good fish in lounge or attractive restaurant, quick friendly service, well kept Boddingtons, Courage Directors and Marstons Pedigree, lots of wood, well chosen pictures, subdued lighting (inc candles on tables) and large open fire, nice views, unobtrusive piped music; comfortable quietly set cottage-style bedrooms, huge car park *(Nigel and Sue Foster, Angus Lyon, Mike and Mary Carter)*

Hailey[SU6485]

Lamb & Flag [B4022 a mile N of Witney; Middletown]: Charming pub with good range of reliable food prepared to order, attentive service, well kept Greene King beers inc Old Speckled Hen *(Marjorie and David Lamb)*

☆ *King William IV* [the different Hailey nr Ipsden, off A4074 or A4130 SE of Wallingford]:

Attractive 16th-c pub in charming peaceful countryside, some concentration on wide choice of good generous food, friendly service, full Brakspears range, beams, bare bricks and tiled floor, big log fire, well kept traditional furnishings and fittings, extended dining room; super views from front terrace *(the Didler, Wendy Arnold, JP, PP, Colin McLachlan, LYM)*

Headington [SP5407]

Butchers Arms [Wilberforce St; off London Rd by Oxford UFC, past housetop shark, then first left and first right]: Welcoming backstreet local with long narrow seating area, good value wkdy lunchtime food, well kept Fullers beers, lots of sports trophies and memorabilia, games corner with darts, bar billiards and sports TV, pleasant garden with barbecues *(Pete Baker)*

Henley [SU7682]

Bird in Hand [Greys Rd]: Quiet and pleasant local with well kept Brakspears, Fullers London Pride, Wychwood and a guest beer such as Hook Norton or West Berkshire, friendly landlord; aviary in big garden behind *(Jonathan Smith)*

Old Bell [Bell St]: Well kept Brakspears PA, Old and Mild in homely and attractive heavily beamed front bar with wall-length window filled with pot plants, good food in back dining room *(Comus and Sarah Elliott, the Didler)*

Three Horseshoes [Reading Rd]: Good value food from doorstep sandwiches to daily specials, tables outside *(D Mackinder)*

Three Tuns [Market Pl]: Heavy beams and panelling, two rooms opened together around old-fashioned central servery with well kept Brakspears, straightforward generous home-cooked food all day; separate games bar with juke box and fruit machine, no children; floodlit back terrace *(JP, PP, LYM, the Didler)*

Highmoor [SU6984]

☆ *Dog & Duck* [B481 N of Reading, off A4130 Henley—Oxford]: Cosy and cottagey low-beamed country pub with chintzy curtains, floral cushions, lots of pictures; relaxing bar on left, dining room on right, log fire in each, smaller dining room behind, fine choice of good generous food inc good vegetarian dishes, hard-working young licensees, well kept Brakspears PA, SB and Old; tables in garden *(the Didler)*

Kelmscot [SU2499]

Plough [NW of Faringdon, off A417 or A4095]: Pretty pub under new licensees, in lovely spot nr upper Thames – good river walks; log fire, beams and flagstones in small stripped-stone bar, well kept Archers, Flowers Original and Wadworths 6X, two simple back dining lounges; piped music, darts, shove-ha'penny, cribbage, dominoes, dogs allowed in public bar; pretty garden, picnic-sets under cocktail parasols out in front *(M W Schofield, LYM)*

Kidlington [SP4914]

Kings Arms [The Moors, off High St (not the Harvester out on the Bicester Rd)]: Welcoming unpretentious two-bar local with enjoyable wkdy lunchtime food from sandwiches to a few basic hot meals and good value daily roast, well kept Greene King IPA, Ind Coope Burton and a guest beer; occasional barbecues in courtyard *(Pete Baker)*

Kingston Bagpuize [SU4098]

Hinds Head [Witney Rd]: Quiet and unpretentious small country pub, two recently refurbished bars with good reasonably priced food, well kept beers, good service; play area *(Nick Holmes)*

Langford [SP2402]

☆ *Bell* [off A361 N of Lechlade]: Congenial country restaurant/pub with two rooms off tiny bar, pleasantly low-key simple but smart décor, big log fire, books and magazines, fresh flowers, evening candles, sensibly short choice of enjoyable reasonably priced food inc wkdy steak bargains, some stylish dishes and good veg, welcoming staff, Hook Norton and Marstons Pedigree, good wines, proper coffee, no piped music *(P R and S A White, Michael Gray, D Bouch, Mrs Linda Ferstendik)*

Long Wittenham [SU5493]

☆ *Machine Man* [Fieldside; back lane parallel to main road, off A415 SE of Abingdon]: Plain largely 19th-c building, friendly unpretentious bar with good mix of customers, well kept Black Sheep, Greene King Triumph, Rebellion Smuggler, West Berkshire Good Old Boy and four changing guest beers, decent malt whiskies and wines (half a dozen by the glass), enjoyable hearty food inc choice of fish; darts (taken seriously here), fruit machine, piped music; dogs and children welcome; bedrooms, aunt sally outside *(Franklyn Roberts, LYM, David Humphreys, Margaret and Roy Randle, Nick Holmes)*

Plough [High St]: Enjoyable sensibly priced food in friendly low-beamed refurbished lounge with lots of brass, games in public bar, inglenook log fires, Ushers ales, good service, games and children's room; Thames moorings at bottom of long spacious garden, bedrooms *(Marjorie and David Lamb)*

Longworth [SU3899]

☆ *Blue Boar* [Tucks Lane]: Cosy thatched country local with plenty of character, two good log fires and unusual décor (skis on beams etc), scrubbed tables, and piped music; good value food inc unusual dishes and speciality evenings, well kept Bass and Morrells, friendly quick service, hot coal fires; quiet village *(Peter and Audrey Dowsett, Howard James, Richard Pinnington)*

Lower Assendon [SU7484]

Golden Ball [B480]: Attractive 16th-c pub, cosy and rustic traditional interior with beams and half-height panelling, wide-ranging good food, log fire, well kept Brakspears, good choice of house wines; garden behind *(Simon Collett-Jones, the Didler)*

Marsh Baldon [SU5699]

Seven Stars [the Baldons signed off A4074 N of Dorchester]: Good interesting generous food inc splendid steak and kidney pie (no sandwiches; only lunchtimes some Sat lunchtimes) in big open room, decent wines, good coffee; on attractive village green *(anon)*

Marston [SP5209]

☆ *Victoria Arms* [Mill Lane]: Attractive grounds by River Cherwell inc spacious terrace, good play area, punt moorings and hire; full Wadworths range and guest beers inc Bavarian ones kept well, generous good food (not Sun evening in winter) from chunky sandwiches up inc children's dishes, friendly attentive staff, lots of tables in civilised main room and smaller ones off, real fires; very busy wknd lunchtimes and summer, soft piped music, children and dogs allowed; lavatory for disabled; beware sleeping policemen *(Geoff Pidoux, BB, Alette and Russell Lawson)*

Middle Assendon [SU7385]

☆ *Rainbow* [B480]: Pretty and cottagey country local in peaceful setting, unspoilt low-beamed divided bar, welcoming landlord, good choice of unpretentious but tasty food cooked by landlady, well kept Brakspears; tables on front lawn *(Mr and Mrs McKay, Keith and Margaret Kettell)*

Middleton Stoney [SP5323]

Jersey Arms [Ardley Rd (B430/B4030)]: Small 19th-c stone-built hotel, low and rambling, with relaxing atmosphere in cosily upmarket traditional bar, beams and panelling, dark tables and chairs, good log fire in big fireplace, good range of interesting home-made food from well filled baguettes up, efficient service, a well kept real ale, good wine list and coffee; piped music, restaurant popular for business lunches; garden, comfortable bedrooms *(Dennis John Boddington)*

New Yatt [SP3713]

Saddlers Arms: Small welcoming pub with good choice of generous food inc fresh fish in bar or light and airy dining conservatory, prompt service, chatty licensee, occasional unusual beers; friendly dogs *(Marjorie and David Lamb)*

North Hinksey [SP4905]

☆ *Fishes* [off A420 just E of A34 ring road; N Hinksey Lane, then pass church into cul de sac signed to Rugby club]: Comfortable and tranquil, with helpful licensees, good choice of good value food (not Sun evening) inc some imaginative dishes, well kept Morrells Varsity and Graduate, decent house wines, Victorian-style open-plan lounge and pleasant no smoking family conservatory; traditional games, soft piped music; big streamside garden with good play area and two aunt sally pitches *(Dick and Madeleine Brown, Dr Roger Crisp)*

Northmoor [SP4202]

Red Lion [B4449 SE of Stanton Harcourt]: Refurbished 15th-c stone-built village pub, heavily beamed bar and small dining room off, welcoming log fire, good choice of reasonably priced food inc good value Sun lunch, well kept real ales, cheerful landlord; no dogs; garden *(Geoff Pidoux)*

Oxford [SP5106]

☆ *Bear* [Alfred St/Wheatsheaf Alley]: Intimate low-ceilinged and partly panelled 16th-c rooms, not over-smart and often packed with students; thousands of vintage ties on walls and beams, simple lunchtime food most days inc sandwiches (kitchen may be cl Weds), well kept changing ales such as Adnams, Fullers London Pride and Hancocks HB from centenarian handpumps on recently renewed pewter bar counter, no games machines; upstairs ladies'; tables outside, good all day summer *(LYM, Catherine Pitt, Jonathan Smith, Tim and Ann Newell, Paul Deane, R Huggins, D Irving, E McCall, T McLean, Paul Hopton)*

Eagle & Child [St Giles]: Busy pub with nice panelled front snugs, tasteful stripped-brick modern back extension with no smoking conservatory, well kept Greene King Abbot and Old Speckled Hen, Marstons Pedigree, Tetleys and Wadworths 6X, plentiful quickly served food, newspapers, events posters; tourists head for the tiny mid-bars full of actors' and Tolkien/C S Lewis memorabilia; piped music *(Andy and Jill Kassube, Helen Ridley, BB, Chris Glasson, Eirlys Roberts, Paul Hopton)*

Grapes [George St]: Traditional pub, some original features, lots of theatrical posters and memorabilia, bar snacks, well kept Morrells *(Kevin Blake)*

Harcourt Arms [Cranham Terr]: Friendly local with some character, pillars dividing it, good value snacks inc cheap sandwiches and baked potatoes, well kept Fullers, well reproduced piped jazz, good choice of board games *(Pete Baker)*

Hobgoblin [St Aldates]: Good atmosphere, three well kept Wychwood ales and up to four guest beers such as Burton Bridge, Enville, Heather, Moor or RCH; open all day, inexpensive food till 6pm, wkday student discount till 8, special beer price Tues *(Jonathan Smith, Catherine Pitt, Paul Hopton)*

Lamb & Flag [St Giles/Banbury Rd]: Attractive old pub owned by nearby college, big windows over street, well kept real ales, good value well served food, cheerful service; can be packed with students, back rooms with exposed stonework and panelled ceilings have more atmosphere *(Chris Glasson)*

☆ *Rose & Crown* [North Parade Ave]: Good well priced lunchtime home cooking inc Sun roasts and particularly well kept Adnams and Ind Coope Burton in friendly and unspoilt old local; decent wine, prompt service from enthusiastic and concerned bearded landlord and wife; reference books for crossword buffs, no piped music, machines or mobile phones, jazz piano Tues; traditional small rooms, pleasant back yard with motorised awning and huge gas heater – children not allowed here or inside unless with friends of landlord *(Franklyn Roberts, Chris Glasson, BB, Torrens Lyster, Paul Hopton)*

Three Goats Heads [Friars Entry, St Michaels St]: Two friendly, individual and attractive bars, relaxed downstairs (with bare boards, TV, fruit machine and piped music – can be loud), more formal up; well kept cheap Sam Smiths, good choice of quick generous food, dark wood, booths and political prints *(Margaret and Roy Randle)*

Wharf House [Butterwyke Pl/Speedwell St]: Refreshingly good simple drinkers' pub, bare boards, knowledgeable, friendly and helpful landlord, well kept Hook Norton Old Hooky and RCH Pitchfork, guests such as Uley Old Spot and Wickwar BOB, two farm ciders, masses of bottled German and Belgian beers with their proper glasses, pub dog; open all day Sat *(Jonathan Smith, Catherine Pitt)*

☆ *White Horse* [Broad St]: Bustling and studenty, sandwiched between bits of Blackwells bookshop; single small narrow bar with snug one-table raised back alcove, mellow oak beams and timbers, ochre ceiling, beautiful view of the Clarendon building and Sheldonian, good lunchtime food (the few tables reserved for this), well kept Tetleys-related ales and Wadworths 6X, Addlestone's cider, friendly licensees *(Stephanie Smith, Gareth Price, BB)*

White House [Botley Rd]: Plenty of atmosphere, good well presented food, well kept Greene King Abbot, Tetleys and Wadworths 6X; handy for railway station *(Margaret and Roy Randle)*

Pishill [SU7389]

☆ *Crown* [B480 Nettlebed—Watlington]: Lovely wisteria-covered ancient building with black beams and timbers, deep burgundy paintwork, log fires and candlelight, relaxed atmosphere, good home-cooked food (not Sun or Mon evenings) from filled baguettes to hearty but modern and imaginative dishes, well kept Brakspears, Flowers Original and a guest beer, prompt friendly service; children allowed Sun lunchtime in restaurant, pleasant bedroom in separate cottage, picnic-sets on attractive side lawn, pretty country setting – lots of walks *(JP, PP, Gordon Prince, the Didler, LYM, Michael Porter, Chris Richards, Susan and John Douglas, David and Joan Mason)*

Play Hatch [SU7476]

Crown: Good choice of interesting and attractively presented if not cheap food in spacious rambling olde-worlde 16th-c pub, very popular with families; two bars and several rooms inc barn extension restaurant and big no smoking conservatory, well kept Brakspears PA, SB and Old tapped from the cask, decent wines, good service; play area outside *(James Edge)*

Shoulder of Mutton: Small low-ceilinged country pub well worth knowing for good food from hot filled rolls to main dishes inc interesting pies and Sun lunch (must book), fine oak settle screening fire, friendly landlord, Greene King ales; well kept garden with old-fashioned roses, real well *(Eric Locker)*

Radcot [SU2899]

Swan [A4095 2½ miles N of Faringdon]: Sheltered and attractive Thames-side garden, with boat trips from pub's camping-ground opp (lift to bring wheelchairs aboard); wide choice of affordable food inc good value sandwiches and afternoon teas, well kept Greene King (not so cheap), log fire, lots of stuffed fish, piped music, pub games; children in eating area; bedrooms clean and good value, with good breakfast *(LYM, Peter and Audrey Dowsett)*

Rotherfield Peppard [SU7081]

Red Lion [Peppard Common]: Unspoilt

traditional ochre-ceilinged village pub with good mix of diners and drinkers, well kept Brakspears and an organic beer, good value nice food, daily papers, cribbage *(Mr and Mrs T A Bryan, Christopher Turner)*

Shilton [SP2608]

☆ *Rose & Crown* [off B4020 S of Burford]: Mellow, attractive and popular 17th-c low-beamed stone-built village local opp pond in pretty village, small beamed bar with tiled floor, woodburner and inglenook, small carpeted dining area, good choice of reasonably priced home-made food from sandwiches and toasties up (should book for Sun roasts), well kept Greene King beers inc Old Speckled Hen and Ruddles, quick friendly service; soft piped music, darts *(Marjorie and David Lamb, Dr and Mrs A K Clarke, G W A Pearce)*

Shiplake Row [SU7478]

White Hart [off A4155 W of Shiplake]: Relaxed and friendly, with three connecting rooms mainly set for good choice of food (just roasts Sun lunchtime), well kept Brakspears, decent house wines, log fires; interestingly planted back garden, nice location, fine views, good walks *(Simon Collett-Jones)*

Shrivenham [SU2488]

Prince of Wales [High St; off A420 or B4000 NE of Swindon]: Congenial stone-built pub with spotless low-beamed carpeted lounge, pictures, lots of brasses, log fire, wholesome generous food inc Sun roasts, small dining area, cheerful thoughtful landlord kind to children, well kept Wadworths and Charles Wells Bombardier, no piped music; side bar with darts and fruit machine, no dogs, can be smoky; garden *(Peter and Audrey Dowsett, Mike Ridgway, Sarah Miles)*

Sibford Gower [SP3537]

☆ *Bishop Blaize* [Burdrop]: Friendly old-fashioned stone-built beamed pub dating from 17th c, nicely kept bar spreading through several levels, good value food inc lots of home-made pies (kitchen shuts at 2), well kept Hook Norton Best and a guest such as Hampshire or Vale, decent wines, cheerful landlord, efficient service, unpretentious décor with cartoons; picnic-sets and play area in big attractive south-facing hillside garden, grand views, good walks *(Lisa Tallis, John Brightley, Guy Vowles)*

☆ *Moody Cow* [signed off B4035 Banbury—Shipston on Stour; Temple Mill Rd]: Pretty and cottagey thatched dining pub, formerly the Wykham Arms, taken over by landlord of its eponym at Upton Bishop in Herefs, refurbished and renamed, with emphasis on wide choice of good value if not cheap meals inc upmarket dishes in attractive partly no smoking restaurant, comfortable open-plan low-beamed stripped-stone lounge, nice pictures, table made from glass-topped table, inglenook tap room, good service, well kept Banks's, Hook Norton and a guest ale, good coffee, good if pricy house wines, dominoes; children welcome; country views from big well planted garden, lovely manor house opp; has been cl Mon lunchtime *(Guy Vowles, John Brightley, LYM, Iain R Hewitt)*

South Moreton [SU5588]

☆ *Crown* [off A4130 or A417 E of Didcot; High St]: Cheerful open-plan rambling old village pub with superbly kept Wadworths and guest beers, some tapped from the cask, decent coffee, good fresh genuine home-made food inc plenty of fresh fish, faultless friendly service, spotless housekeeping; children allowed, discount scheme for OAPs; piped music, Mon quiz night; small garden *(Margaret Ross, Marjorie and David Lamb)*

Sparsholt [SU3487]

Star [Watery Lane]: Comfortable old local with cheerful relaxed atmosphere, horse-racing talk, log fire, attractive pictures, daily papers, well kept beers inc a guest, enjoyable freshly made food; subdued piped music; back garden, pretty village *(David Humphreys, Marjorie and David Lamb)*

Steeple Aston [SP4725]

Red Lion [off A4260 12 miles N of Oxford]: Colin Mead, the long-serving landlord who with his wife Margaret made this little stone-built pub a civilised and very individual classic, retired in summer 2001, so fingers crossed for the comfortable beamed and partly panelled bar, evening no smoking restaurant and suntrap front terrace; is it too much to hope that the new people will have such good food, well kept beers, and great range of malt whiskies, brandies and wines? *(LYM)*

Steventon [SU4791]

☆ *Cherry Tree* [B4017 (High St); village signed off A34 S of Abingdon via A4130]: 18th-c pub with well kept Wadworths IPA and 6X and changing guests such as Red Shoot Toms Tipple and Tisbury Archibald Beckett, decent wines, generous well priced food inc sophisticated dishes and good vegetarian choice, open-plan beamed areas around island bar, flagstones and bare boards, mix of furniture inc heavily carved settles and brocaded dining chairs, dark green walls, open fires, old prints and stuffed creatures; fruit machine, may be unobtrusive piped music in public bar; tables out on terrace *(BB)*

☆ *North Star* [Stocks Lane, The Causeway, central westward turn off B4017]: Tiled passage leading to unchanging unspoilt main bar with built-in settles forming snug, steam-engine pictures, interesting local horsebrasses and other brassware; open fire in parlourish lounge, simple dining room; Greene King Morlands ales tapped from casks in a side room, cheap wkdy lunchtime bar food, cribbage; tables on side grass, front gateway through living yew tree *(JP, PP, the Didler, Pete Baker, LYM)*

Stoke Lyne [SP5628]

☆ *Peyton Arms* [off B4100]: Largely unspoilt stone-built pub with well kept Hook Norton beers (full range) tapped from casks behind small corner bar in sparsely decorated front snug, very friendly landlord and locals, log fire, hops hanging from beam, bigger refurbished room with darts, dominoes and cribbage, charity book store, may be filled cobs; well behaved children and dogs welcome, pleasant garden with aunt sally; cl Mon/Tues lunchtimes (*Rona Murdoch, Pete Baker, Wendy Muldoon, JP, PP, the Didler*)

Stoke Row [SU6784]

Cherry Tree [off B481 at Highmoor]: New licensees in unspoilt low-beamed village local, one room like someone's parlour, well kept Brakspears BB, Mild and SB tapped from casks in back stillage room, well priced sandwiches and soup, log fire; families welcome in lounge and back games room (with pool), swings in good garden (*the Didler, JP, PP, Dick and Madeleine Brown*)

☆ *Crooked Billet* [Nottwood Lane, off B491 N of Reading – OS Sheet 175 map ref 684844]: Rustic pub layout with heavy beams, flagstones, antique pubby furnishings and great inglenook log fire, but in practice a restaurant – good, with wide choice of well cooked interesting meals (not cheap), attentive service, well kept Brakspears tapped from the cask (no bar counter), decent wines, relaxed homely atmosphere – like a French country restaurant; children welcome, occasional live music, big garden by Chilterns beechwoods (*the Didler, LYM, J Hale, JP, PP, Dr and Mrs R E S Tanner*)

☆ *Grouse & Claret* [Kingwood Common; a mile S of Stoke Row, signed Peppard and Reading, OS Sheet 175 map ref 692825]: Well run 18th-c dining pub with a wide range of good freshly made food from filled baguettes up inc imaginative specials and outstanding puddings, pleasant traditional interior with cosy nooks, drinkers made welcome by friendly helpful staff, Brakspears PA and Fullers London Pride, good wine choice; piped music; attractive terrace (*Michael Porter, Sheila Keene, Darren and Jane Staniforth*)

Stoke Talmage [SU6799]

Red Lion [signed from A40 at Tetsworth]: Basic old-fashioned country local, very friendly and cheerful; sociable bare-boards public bar with well kept Hook Norton and lots of changing guest beers from small corner servery, chatty landlord, open fire, prints, posters, darts, shove-ha'penny and other games, carpeted modern lounge; tables under cocktail parasols in pleasant garden, cl lunchtime Mon–Thurs (*the Didler, Pete Baker, JP, PP, Torrens Lyster*)

Stonor [SU7388]

☆ *Stonor Arms*: Elegant upmarket 18th-c village inn with comfortable flagstoned bar, rowing and cricket memorabilia, log fires, good food from soup and sandwiches to sophisticated dishes at appropriate prices (canapés with drinks, petits fours with good coffee), welcoming young staff, well kept Luxters real ale, decent wines, daily papers and magazines, lovely conservatory; walled garden, good bedrooms (*J F M and M West*)

Sunningwell [SP4900]

Flowing Well [just N of Abingdon]: Doing well under current management, with good plentiful enterprising food from baguettes to restaurant meals, remarkable collection of rare rums, real ales, good choice of wines by the glass, good

young staff; garden with picnic-sets under cocktail parasols (*Dick and Madeleine Brown*)

Swerford [SP3731]

☆ *Masons Arms* [A361 Banbury—Chipping Norton]: Attractively reworked with pale panelling, stripped stone and wood flooring, pine furniture and easy chairs, lots of copper and brass, log fires, smart yet relaxed friendly atmosphere, daily papers, wide range of good generous food inc game and fish in bar and valley-view restaurant, well kept Hook Norton and a guest such as Highgate Mild; attractive small terrace and big north-facing garden (can be breezy) with play area, comfortable bedrooms (*Iain R Hewitt, Arthur Baker, Stuart Turner, Robert Gomme, David Campbell, Vicki McLean, Ted George*)

Swinbrook [SP2811]

☆ *Swan* [back rd a mile N of A40, 2 miles E of Burford]: Softly lit little beamed and flagstoned 16th-c pub prettily set by a bridge over the Windrush, gently smartened up, with antique settles, sporting prints and woodburner in friendly flagstoned tap room and back bar (now mainly laid for dining); good attractively presented food (all day wknd) inc interesting specials, Greene King ales, farm ciders, cheery laid-back service, traditional games, magazines, no piped music; seats by the lane and in small side garden; the nearby churchyard has the graves of the Mitford sisters (*Simon Collett-Jones, LYM, J Hale, Iain R Hewitt, Geoff Pidoux, Matthew Shackle*)

Swinford [SP4309]

Talbot [B4044 just S of Eynsham]: Oldish beamed pub with interesting choice of good value generous fresh food, well kept Arkells, friendly staff, long bar with some stripped stone and naval memorabilia, log-effect gas fire, games room; tables in garden (some traffic noise), pleasant walk along lovely stretch of the Thames towpath (*Chris Glasson*)

Sydenham [SP7201]

☆ *Crown* [off B4445 Chinnor—Thame]: Relaxed low-beamed village local in picturesque village, open fires in long narrow bar, small garden with roses and climbing frame, views of lovely church; has been very popular for wholesome good value pub food and well kept Morrells Best and Varsity with a guest such as Adnams, but the licensees changed in summer 2001 and we have no news yet of the new regime; children welcome, may be quiet piped music, dominoes, darts and quiz nights (*BB, Howard Dell, Laura Barbrook, Jane and Andy Rankine, Lesley Bass*)

Thame [SP7005]

Bird Cage [Cornmarket]: Quaint black and white beamed and timbered pub refurbished in bistro style, good menu (late-night diners' club Weds-Sat), well kept ales, espresso machine, friendly staff, open fires; piped music (*LYM, Tim and Ann Newell*)

Thrupp [SP4815]

☆ *Boat* [off A4260 just N of Kidlington]: Unpretentious and relaxing stone-built local in lovely surroundings by canal, good value decent food with fresh veg, quick friendly service, well kept Morrells, decent wine, coal fire, old canal

pictures and artefacts, bare boards and stripped pine, no piped music; good folk nights 2nd and 4th Sun, occasional theatre; restaurant, nice garden behind with plenty of tables, some in shade *(Pete Baker, P and J Shapley, Sue Demont, Tim Barrow, Geoff Pidoux, R Huggins, D Irving, E McCall, T McLean)*
Jolly Boatman [Banbury Rd]: Extended basic pub with enjoyable cheap food, well kept ales, pleasant staff, eating area and conservatory overlooking canal; children allowed *(Geoff Pidoux)*

Toot Baldon [SP5600]
Crown [off A4074 or B480; past green]: Nice beamed and flagstoned stone-built pub which as we write is closed, in a planning stalemate over proposals by Fullers to extend the dining side *(LYM)*

Wantage [SU4087]
☆ *Royal Oak* [Newbury St]: Very friendly and popular two-bar local with lots of ship photographs and naval bricabrac, several well kept ales such as Bass, Wadworths IPA and beers brewed for the pub by West Berkshire, landlord who really knows his beers (and is generous with tasters); lunches Fri-Sat; table football, darts, cribbage; has been cl Mon-Thurs lunchtimes, bedrooms *(BB, Dick and Madeleine Brown, JP, PP, the Didler)*
Shoulder of Mutton [Wallingford St]: Friendly and chatty local, old-fashioned and unchanging, coal fire and racing TV in bar, passage to two small snug back rooms, well kept Greene King Morlands Original, popular food; tables outside, bedrooms *(JP, PP, Pete Baker, the Didler)*

West Hendred [SU4489]
☆ *Hare* [A417]: Civilised and welcoming dining pub, very popular for generous good interesting food served till late evening, efficient friendly staff, good choice of wines; pleasant garden *(David Humphreys)*

Westcott Barton [SP4325]
Fox [Enstone Road; B4030 off A44 NW of Woodstock]: Spacious yet cosy stone-built village pub, low beams and flagstones, pews and high-backed settles, well kept Greene King Abbot, Hook Norton, John Smiths and guest beers, log fires, usual food from sandwiches through pasta to steaks, small no smoking restaurant (children allowed here); piped music; open all day Thurs-Sun, pleasant garden with water feature, play area and peaceful view *(LYM)*

Weston-on-the-Green [SP5318]
Ben Jonson [B430 nr M40 junction 9]: New management in thatched country pub, comfortable dark wood settles in welcoming beamed lounge bar, food inc lunchtime sandwiches with chips and salad, well kept Fullers London Pride and Wadworths 6X, good house wine, friendly service, discreet pool room; usually open all day, children very welcome; big sheltered garden with occasional barbecues *(G J Hodson, D C T and E A Frewer)*

Wheatley [SP5905]
Sun [Church Rd]: Small, quaint and friendly,

with good bar food, well kept reasonably priced Flowers and Ind Coope Burton; pleasant garden *(Geoff Pidoux)*

Witney [SP3510]
Angel [Market Sq]: Popular 17th-c town local, extended but unchanging, several well kept ales inc Hook Norton Old Hooky, wide choice of attractively priced food, homely surroundings and hot coal fire, quick friendly service even when packed; pool room, coffee bar; parking nearby can be difficult *(Peter and Audrey Dowsett, Sue and Mike Todd)*
☆ *Three Horseshoes* [Corn St, junction with Holloway Rd]: Attractive 16th-c stone-built pub with heavy beams, flagstones, log fires, simple well polished old furniture, separate dining room, friendly welcome, good home-made food inc some unusual dishes and good choice for vegetarians, well kept Greene King Abbot and Morlands Original and a guest beer *(George Cowie, Robin Sweet)*

Wolvercote [SP5009]
Plough [First Turn/Wolvercote Green]: Lots of comfortably well worn in pubby linked areas, armchairs and Victorian-style carpeted bays in main lounge, good varied food esp soups and fresh seafood in flagstoned dining room and library (children allowed here), well kept Morrells Oxford, Varsity and Oxford Blue, decent wines, traditional snug, good-sized public bar with pool and machines; picnic-sets on front terrace looking over rough meadow to canal and woods *(BB, R T and J C Moggridge, Simon Pyle)*
Red Lion [Godstow Rd]: Big no smoking dining extension, good choice of cheap food, friendly landlady, older part with lots of photographs, prints and memorabilia, five coal fires; quiet piped music; garden with play area *(Peter and Audrey Dowsett)*

Woodstock [SP4416]
☆ *Black Prince* [A44 N]: Subtly lit timbered and stripped-stone 18th-c pub with old-fashioned furnishings, armour, swords, big fireplace, reasonably priced enjoyable food from traditional to Tex-Mex in bar and dining room, well kept Hook Norton, Theakstons Old Peculier and guest beers, fast friendly service, children allowed; Mon quiz night, occasional live music; tables out in attractively reworked garden by small river (plans for music inc classical out here), nearby right of way into Blenheim parkland *(Geoff Pidoux, David Campbell, Vicki McLean)*
Queens Own [Oxford St (A44)]: Small stone building dating from 17th c, unpretentious long narrow bar done up with bare boards, stripped stone, beamery, antique settles, elderly tables, hops on beams and candles; welcoming service, wide range of homely well priced food inc real chips (all day Sat/Sun), well kept Ushers Best and Founders, country wines, magazines and daily papers; discreet piped music, lively Mon quiz night; children welcome, attractive small back walled courtyard garden *(J A Cheverton, Klaus and Elizabeth Leist, Kevin Blake, Rona Murdoch)*
☆ *Star* [Market Pl]: Big beamed town pub with

friendly atmosphere, decent food all day from sandwiches up inc good value home-made pies, lunchtime salad bar and popular family Sunday lunches, well kept beers, bare boards, some stripped stone, daily papers, open fires; piped music, quiz machine, TV; bedrooms clean and spacious, good breakfast *(Geoff Pidoux, BB, Mel and Billie Tinton, John Bowdler, M and P Theodorou)*

☆ *Woodstock Arms* [Market St]: 16th-c heavy-beamed stripped-stone local, good value straightforward home-made food inc good vegetarian choice, friendly prompt service, log-effect gas fires in splendid stone fireplaces, well kept Morrells ales, decent wine, commendable housekeeping; tables out in yard, bedrooms *(MP, Kevin Blake)*

Woolstone [SU3089]

☆ *White Horse* [village signed off B4507]: Plushly refurbished partly thatched 16th-c pub with steep Victorian gables, two big open fires in spacious beamed and part-panelled room with air of highly polished well cared-for antiquity, quickly served food inc several vegetarian dishes, friendly laid-back staff and black labrador, well kept Wadworths 6X and a guest such as Hook Norton Best, decent wines, lots of whiskies, good coffee, log fire; quiet piped music; children allowed in eating area, sheltered garden, four charming good value bedrooms, big breakfast, secluded interesting village handy for White Horse and Ridgeway walkers *(Dr and Mrs A Hepburn, BB)*

Wootton [SP4320]

☆ *Killingworth Castle* [Glympton Rd; B4027 N of Woodstock]: Striking three-storey 17th-c coaching inn, good local atmosphere, well kept Greene King ales, decent house wines, generous freshly made food, friendly service, long narrow main bar with pine furnishings, parquet floor, candles and log fire, bar billiards, darts and shove-ha'penny in smaller games end, pleasant garden; jazz Weds, folk Fri; bedrooms *(Geoff Pidoux, Pete Baker, Gordon)*

Wroxton [SP4142]

☆ *North Arms* [Mills Lane; off A422 at hotel, pub at back of village]: Pretty thatched stone pub nicely placed in peaceful corner of lovely village, with attractive quiet garden; good varied food, well kept real ale, log fire, nice wooden furnishings, character restaurant; unobtrusive piped music *(LYM, K H Frostick)*

White Horse [A422]: Pleasant open-plan interior, enthusiastic efficient managers, log fires, good fresh reasonably priced food using local produce from lunchtime baguettes up, well kept ales, good wine choice; tables in garden with terrace and play area *(Mr and Mrs Hugh Spottiswoode, Mr and Mrs D Field, R J Chenery, Iain R Hewitt, J J and B Dix)*

Wytham [SP4708]

☆ *White Hart* [off A34 Oxford ring rd]: High-backed settles and log fire in handsome partly panelled flagstoned bar, small no smoking lounge (children allowed here), well kept Adnams Best, Bass and Greene King Old Speckled Hen, all-day salad bar, other food from sandwiches to mixed grill; open all day, pretty garden with summer barbecues, unspoilt preserved village *(Eric Locker, Peter and Audrey Dowsett, Dick and Madeleine Brown, Don and Marilou Brooks, Geoff Pidoux, Martin and Karen Wake, LYM)*

Yarnton [SP4711]

Red Lion [Cassington Rd]: Welcoming local with good range of cheap straightforward food, well kept Greene King IPA, pleasant service *(R T and J C Moggridge)*

The Post Office makes it virtually impossible for people to come to grips with British geography, by using a system of post towns which are often across the county boundary from the places they serve. So the postal address of a pub often puts it in the wrong county. We use the correct county – the one the pub is actually in. Lots of pubs which the Post Office alleges are in Oxfordshire are actually in Berkshire, Buckinghamshire, Gloucestershire or Warwickshire.

Shropshire

Showing just how much things change from year to year, only one pub in the county – the Royal Oak at Cardington – has kept its place in every year's Guide since it started 20 years ago. And this year there are no fewer than four new entries here: the Six Bells in Bishop's Castle (a second pub brewing its own beers in this lucky town), the Cookhouse at Bromfield (very good food in up-to-the-minute surroundings), the Old Gate at Heathton (a friendly dining pub with a nice garden), and the Malthouse in Ironbridge (a good relaxed and welcoming all-rounder). Other pubs on fine form here this year are the Castle Hotel in Bishop's Castle (one of those friendly hotels that's also nice just for a drink or a snack), the Bear in Bridgnorth (a good all-rounder, particularly enjoyable food), the friendly Burlton Inn (a favourite, good all round and gaining a Stay Award this year), the bustling and chatty Unicorn in Ludlow (good home cooking), the Hundred House at Norton, and the Wenlock Edge Inn on Wenlock Edge (much loved by a great variety of readers, a smashing pub). With a good choice of places for a special meal out here, the Burlton Inn at Burlton tops the chart and is our Shropshire Dining Pub of the Year. In the Lucky Dip section at the end of the chapter, pubs to note particularly are the Railwaymans Arms in Bridgnorth, Sun at Clun, Coalbrookdale Inn at Coalbrookdale, Boat at Coalport, Sun at Corfton, Lion at Hampton Loade (very nice indeed, but may close this winter), Pound at Leebotwood, Ragleth at Little Stretton, Red Lion at Llanfair Waterdine, Church Inn in Ludlow, Crown at Munslow, Coach & Horses and Three Fishes in Shrewsbury and Stiperstones Inn at Stiperstones. Drinks prices in the county are comfortably below the national average, with most of our main entries having a good interesting choice of real ales, and several brewing their own (very pocket-friendly for customers). Beers from the small local brewer Hobsons are quite widely available here at attractive prices.

BISHOP'S CASTLE SO3289 Map 6
Castle Hotel
Market Sq, just off B4385

Standing right at the top of the town, this substantial early 18th-c Georgian stone coaching inn is festooned with pretty hanging baskets in summer, has a couple of picnic-sets by flowering tubs in front, and more in the reworked back garden, which now has two terraces on either side of a large formal raised fish pond, pergolas and climbing plants, and stone walls; the views are very pretty. Inside, it's neatly kept with a relaxed, civilised atmosphere, a good mix of customers, and a warm welcome from the landlady. On the right is a clubby small beamed and panelled room glazed off from the entrance, with old local prints and sturdy leather chairs on its muted carpet; on the left a bigger room has maroon plush wall seats and stools, big Victorian engravings, a coal fire and nice table-lamps; no piped music but they do have shove-ha'penny, dominoes, cribbage, and TV. Enjoyable bar food includes sandwiches (from £2.40), soup (£2.80), ploughman's (£4.50), roasted vegetable flan (£5.50), a hearty fry up £5.95), vegetable cannelloni stuffed with spinach and ricotta cheese and a tomato sauce (£6.45), and steak and kidney pie (£8.25), with evening dishes like smoked trout and smoked salmon pâté (£4.75), cheese, leek and mushroom sausages (£7.95), peppered lamb fillet with mint and caper sauce (£8.50), venison sausages in red wine (£8.75), rump steak with port and stilton sauce (£8.95), and good puddings such as chocolate squidgy cake, hot sticky toffee pudding and strawberry meringues (£3.30); well cooked vegetables. There is a no smoking dining room in the evening and on Sunday lunchtime. Well kept Bass, Black Sheep, Hobsons, and local Six Bells Big Nev's on handpump, and over 50 malt whiskies. The very spacious and comfortable bedrooms are attractively decorated, with antique furniture; good breakfasts. The friendly basset hound is called Wellington. *(Recommended by Kevin Thorpe, Anthony Barnes, Richard and Barbara Philpott, Darly Graton, Graeme Gulibert, Rona Murdoch, Steve Whalley, Derek and Sylvia Stephenson, G Coates, Roger White, John Whitehead)*

Bass ~ Licensees David and Nicky Simpson ~ Real ale ~ Bar food ~ (01588) 638403 ~ Children in eating area of bar ~ Open 12-2.30, 6.30(6 Sat)-11; 12-2.30, 7-10.30 Sun ~ Bedrooms: £35B/£60S

Six Bells 🍺

Church Street

Since a brewery was re-established at this cheerfully unpretentious former coaching inn in 1997, it's quickly gained a reputation for its excellent beers, some of which you'll find stocked by other pubs in the area. Big Nev's is most people's favourite, with Marathon, Cloud Nine and Brew 101 the other regular brews. The beers aren't the pub's only draw: there's a good chatty feel in the two simple rooms, and though it's all fairly no-frills, the atmosphere is very relaxed and welcoming. One bar is really quite small, with plenty of locals tucked around the fireplace or on benches around plain wooden tables; the second, bigger room has bare boards, another fireplace, and lots of board games (they have regular Scrabble nights). Bar food might include sandwiches (from £2), soup (£2), asparagus with melted butter or pancakes stuffed with brie, spinach and mushrooms (£3.50), fidget pie (£5), filo basket filled with ginger stir-fried vegetables (£7), medallions of lamb with tarragon, parsley and red wine sauce (£8), grilled halibut with asparagus and cream sauce (£9), and good home-made puddings; they use organic suppliers wherever possible. The lounge is no smoking at meal times. They keep farm cider, and a wide range of country wines. You can arrange tours of the brewery. *(Recommended by Kevin Thorpe, the Didler, Derek and Sylvia Stephenson, Richard Houghton, Darly Graton, Graeme Gulibert)*

Own brew ~ Licensees Neville and Colin Richards ~ Real ale ~ Bar food (not Sun evening or Mon except bank holidays) ~ No credit cards ~ (01588) 630144 ~ Children welcome ~ Folk every third Fri Sept-Jun ~ Open 12-2.30, 5-11; 12-11 Sat; 12-10.30 Sun; closed Mon lunchtimes and winter Tues, Weds

Three Tuns 🍺

Salop Street

Across the yard from this bustling, well converted pub is the four-storied Victorian brewhouse where each stage of the brewing process descends from floor to floor within the unique tower layout (it's a Grade 1 listed building). Well kept Three Tuns XXX, Offa, Sexton, a seasonal ale and the odd guest beer such as Adnams on old-fashioned handpump, with bottled Clerics Cure, Little Tun and Bellringer; they do home-brew kits and carry-out kegs, sales by the barrel or cases of Clerics Cure – phone for details. The no-frills beamed rooms are very simply furnished with low backed settles and heavy walnut tables, chatty locals, and newspapers to read. An annual beer festival takes place in July with morris dancers in the yard. Good bar food includes filled baguettes, fish soup (£3.50), various home-made pâtés (£4), grilled goats cheese with onion marmalade or pork and ale sausages (£6.50), steak in ale pie (£7.50), daily fresh fish (around £8), good organic steaks (£9.50), and puddings (£3.25); they use locally produced vegetables. Cribbage, shove-ha'penny, dominoes, backgammon and cards. There's a small garden and terrace. *(Recommended by Pat and Tony Martin, Kevin Thorpe, Karen and Graham Oddey, the Didler,*

Malcolm Taylor, Rona Murdoch, John Sandilands, Darly Graton, Graeme Gulibert, Rob Holt, Steve Whalley, Gene and Kitty Rankin)

Own brew ~ Licensee Jan Cross ~ Real ale ~ Bar food (12-2.30, 7-9.30; not Sun evening in winter) ~ (01588) 638797 ~ Children in family room ~ Jazz Sun evening in winter; occasional live music in function room ~ Open 12-3.30, 5-11; 12-10.30(11 Sat) Sun ~ Bedrooms: £45B/£75B

BRIDGES SO3996 Map 6
Horseshoe

Near Ratlinghope, below the W flank of the Long Mynd

A real oasis in these deserted hills, this attractive old place has very pleasantly positioned tables outside by the little River Onny, and the pub is handy for walks on the Long Mynd itself and on Stiperstones. The comfortable bar has interesting windows, a good log fire, well kept Adnams Bitter, Shepherd Neame Spitfire, Timothy Taylors Landlord, and Worthington on handpump, as well as several malt whiskies, and farm and bottled cider; a small dining room leads off from here; darts and piped music. Bar food (with prices unchanged since last year) includes soup (£1.60), sandwiches (from £1.80, triple-decker toastie with bacon, pâté, tomato and cucumber £2.80), ploughman's (£4.50), all day breakfast (£5.35), cod and chips or gammon and egg or pineapple (£5.95) and extra dishes (slightly more expensive) such as fresh fish, casseroles and pasta; puddings (from £2.10). *(Recommended by Dr Bob Bland, Karen and Graham Oddey, John and Diana Niblett, Peter Meister, Nigel Woolliscroft, Anthony Barnes, Kevin Thorpe, G Coates, Di and Mike Gillam)*

Free house ~ Licensee Colin Waring ~ Real ale ~ Bar food (12-3, 6-9; all day Jun-Aug; not over Christmas) ~ (01588) 650260 ~ Children welcome ~ Open 12-3, 6-11; 11-11 Sat; 12-10.30 Sun; closed 25 Dec

BRIDGNORTH SO7293 Map 6
Bear ◧

Northgate (B4373)

At lunchtime, a good crowd of locals and visitors gathers to enjoy the interesting daily specials in this attractive cream-painted former coaching inn: chive and wild mushroom risotto with fresh parmesan topping (£5), blue cheese soufflé with sautéed potatoes (£5.20), mushroom and chicken crêpes with cream sauce (£5.80), seared tuna steak on thai-style salad with ginger dressing or exotic stir-fried pineapple chicken with toasted cashews (£6), and salmon and ginger fishcakes on creamed spinach with tomato coulis (£6.20); they also offer sandwiches (from £1.60), soup (£2.50), ploughman's or ham and egg (£4.25), and rump steak (£5.75), and Thursday evening gourmet dinners when the lounge is transformed into a restaurant with table service. Booking is essential for this; juke box, dogs welcome. There are two unpretentious carpeted bars: on the left of the wide entrance hall, brocaded wall banquettes, small cushioned wheelback chairs, whisky-water jugs hanging from the low joists, gas-type wall lamps; on the right, rather similar furnishings, with the addition of a nice old oak settle and one or two more modern ones, more elbow chairs, a few brasses, and local memorabilia from antique sale and tax notices to small but interesting photographs of the town. From here, french windows open on to a small sheltered lawn with picnic-sets. There's a comfortable and friendly bustle, helped along by well kept ales on handpump from the central servery, including Bathams Best, Boddingtons, Hobsons, Holdens, and a guest such as Salopian Golden Thread or Timothy Taylors Landlord, and several wines by the glass. *(Recommended by Gill Waller, Tony Morriss, Jean and Richard Phillips, Roger White, SLC, Derek and Sylvia Stephenson)*

Free house ~ Licensee Mrs Juanita Gennard ~ Real ale ~ Bar food (lunchtime only (except Thurs evening); not Sun) ~ No credit cards ~ (01746) 763250 ~ Children in eating area of bar ~ Open 11(10.30 Sat)-2.30(3 Sat), 5-11; 12-3, 7-10.30 Sun ~ Bedrooms: £35S/£52B

BROMFIELD SO4877 Map 6
Cookhouse ♀
A49 2 miles NW of Ludlow

Once the home of Clive of India (and until recently the Clive Arms), this handsome brick house looks from the outside like an immaculately maintained Georgian home, so it's a real shock to discover the astonishing conversion inside. Everywhere has been brightly modernised in a smartly contemporary – almost minimalist – fashion; the only area still keeping anything of a period feel is the back bar, itself something of a surprise after the look of the rest of the place. During the day the focus is on the café-bar style dining room, rather like a funky canteen, with modern light wood tables, and a big open kitchen behind a stainless steel counter at one end. A door leads through into the bar, sparse but neat and welcoming, with round glass tables and metal chairs running down to a sleek, space-age bar counter with fresh flowers, newspapers and spotlights. Then it's down a step to the cosier, high-ceilinged back room, where traditional features like the huge brick fireplace, exposed stonework, and soaring beams and rafters are delightfully juxtaposed with wicker chairs, well worn sofas and new glass tables. An attractive secluded terrace has tables under cocktail parasols and a fish pond. Very good well presented bar food includes soup (£3.95), various salads (from £4.95), tart of mediterranean vegetables and sun-dried tomato custard (£5.25), lunchtime fish and chips or bangers and mash (£5.95), tagliatelle with roasted vegetables topped with goats cheese, sweet and sour chicken on egg-fried rice or slow-roasted lamb shank with spring vegetables, rosemary and thyme jus and lime pickle potatoes (all £6.95), and Sunday roasts (£6.95); children's helpings. You can get two courses for £10.50. Well kept Hobsons on handpump, and the good wine list includes eight by the glass; there's a good choice of coffees and teas. Some areas are no smoking. Friendly service; piped music. *(Recommended by Guy Vowles, Gordon Tong)*

Free house ~ Licensee Paul Brooks ~ Real ale ~ Bar food (11-3, 6-10) ~ Restaurant ~ (01584) 856565 ~ Children welcome ~ Open 11-11; 12-10.30 Sun

BURLTON SJ4626 Map 6
Burlton Inn 🍴 🍺 🛏
A528 Shrewsbury—Ellesmere, near junction with B4397

Shropshire Dining Pub of the Year
This is a smashing place, very well run by the particularly friendly and helpful licensees, and with smart new bedrooms (we have given them a Stay Award this year) and popular, imaginative food. Everything in the three fresh-feeling cottagey connecting rooms seems meticulously arranged and cared for, from the flower displays in the brick fireplace or beside the neatly curtained windows, to the piles of *Country Living* and interior design magazines left seemingly casually in the corner. There are a few racing prints, spurs and brasses on the walls, and open fires in winter; dominoes and cribbage. Good bar food such as home-made soup (£3.25), chicken liver and mushroom pâté with a red onion and apple marmalade (£5.25), a trio of Italian cold meats with sharp apricot chutney (£5.50), hot prawn pot with a cream and wine sauce topped with parmesan and gruyère (£5.95), steak and kidney in ale pie (£7.50), ricotta, feta and vine leaf tart with a tomato and basil relish (£8.75), thai salmon topped with crème fraîche and sesame-dressed leaves (£9.50), fettuccine with scallops and smoked salmon in a cream and white wine sauce (£12.50), and steaks (from £12.50), with daily specials like grilled haloumi cheese with tomato on a ciabatta croûte and mediterranean salad (£8.50), fresh dressed crab with cucumber and dill mayonnaise (£8.95), supreme of chicken stuffed with goats cheese and honey glazed or fresh fillet of grilled plaice topped with anchovy butter (£9.50). They have up to a dozen home-made puddings such as white chocolate cheesecake with a sharp raspberry coulis, sticky toffee pudding, crème caramel or apricot egg custard tart (£3.75); cheerful service. Well kept Banks's and three guests such as Batemans XXXB, Jennings Cocker Hoop, and Woods Shropshire Lad on handpump. There are tables on a small lawn behind, with more

on a strip of grass beyond the car park, and smart wooden furniture on the pleasant terrace. The pub sign is a reminder of the days when this was known as the Cross Keys; dogs welcome. *(Recommended by Sue and Bob Ward, S Horsley, Richard and Barbara Philpott, Tim Lawrence, Mrs P J Carroll, David Heath, John Sandilands, Mr and Mrs F Carroll)*

Free house ~ Licensee Gerald Bean ~ Real ale ~ Bar food (12-2, 6.30-9.45(7-9.30 Sun); limited menu Mon lunchtime) ~ (01939) 270284 ~ Well behaved children in eating area of bar ~ Open 11-3, 6-11; 12-3.30, 7-10.30 Sun; closed bank hol Mon lunchtimes; evening 25 Dec, 26 Dec ~ Bedrooms: £45B/£70B

CARDINGTON SO5095 Map 4
Royal Oak ◀

Village signposted off B4371 Church Stretton—Much Wenlock, pub behind church; also reached via narrow lanes from A49

New licensees had just taken over this splendid old place as we went to press and were still finding their feet. The pub has been licensed as a pub for longer than any other in Shropshire, and there's plenty of character in the rambling, low-beamed bar with its roaring winter log fire, cauldron, black kettle and pewter jugs in its vast inglenook fireplace, old standing timbers of a knocked-through wall, and red and green tapestry seats solidly capped in elm; dominoes and maybe piped music. Bass, Hobsons, Marstons Pedigree and a guest such as Woods Shropshire Lad or Wye Valley Butty Bach are kept under light blanket pressure on handpump, and there's enjoyable simple home-made bar food. At lunchtime this includes soup or filled baguettes (from £3), good cauliflower cheese (£3.75), ploughman's (from £4.50), very tasty fidget pie (£4.75), with a few more evening choices such as mango chicken (£6.75), vegetable lasagne, lamb shank with minted gravy or salmon supreme (£7.50), steaks (from £8.50), and puddings like chocolate sponge pudding or home-made apple pie (from £2.50). A comfortable no smoking dining area has exposed old beams and studwork. Tables in the rose-filled front courtyard have lovely views over hilly fields, and a mile or so away – from the track past Willstone (ask for directions at the pub) – you can walk up Caer Caradoc Hill which looks over scenic countryside. *(Recommended by David Field, John Brightley, Peter Meister, Malcolm Taylor, MP, Carolle Roberts, Dr Bob Bland, John Whitehead)*

Free house ~ Licensee Alan White ~ Real ale ~ Bar food (12-2, 7-8.30; not Sun evening) ~ Restaurant ~ (01694) 771266 ~ Children in restaurant and eating area of bar during meal times ~ Open 12-3, 7-11(10.30 Sun); closed Mon except bank holidays

CRESSAGE SJ5904 Map 6
Cholmondeley Riverside ♀

Off A458 SE of Shrewsbury, slightly before Cressage itself if coming from Shrewsbury

There are superb views down to a pretty meandering stretch of the River Severn from tables in the big conservatory here or from seats in the perfectly positioned garden. Spacious and comfortable, the civilised bar has a variety of stripped pine and oak church pews, cushioned settles and tables dotted around the central servery, with a mix of country prints, plates and tapestries on the walls; piped music. Good bar food might include lunchtime baguettes, home-made soup (£3.25), carpaccio of beef fillet with olive oil and parmesan shavings or ceviche of salmon with chilli, coriander and lime (£4.95), brochette of king prawns grilled in garlic and parsley butter (£5.95), field mushroom stuffed with spinach, topped with grilled hollandaise sauce (£7.50), honey-roast ham in cumberland sauce (£8.95), chicken breast with a mushroom, dijon mustard and cream sauce or salmon fishcakes with hollandaise sauce (£9.25), marinated noisette of local lamb with rosemary gravy (£9.95), and grilled gressingham duck breast with a port, spring onion and ginger sauce (£10.50). You can eat from either menu throughout the building; booking is advised at weekends. Well kept Marstons Best and Pedigree, and Woods Shropshire Lad on handpump, and an excellent choice of interesting wines; champagne by the glass, and a special bloody mary. French windows lead out to the garden; coarse fishing on the river costs £4 a day, though it's free if you're staying. *(Recommended by Mike and Wendy Proctor, Dr Bob Bland, Mrs R Farmer, Liz Bell, MP, Mr and Mrs W D Borthwick, R P and P F Edwards, Paul Boot, John Whitehead, Phil and Heidi Cook, Patricia A Bruce, SLC, Nigel Woolliscroft, M Joyner, David and Michelle Bailey, Dick and Madeleine Brown, JES, O K Smyth)*

Free house ~ Licensees John Radford and John P Wrigley ~ Real ale ~ Bar food (12-2.15, 6.30-10) ~ Restaurant ~ (01952) 510900 ~ Children welcome ~ Open 10-3, 6.30(6 Sat)-11; 12-3, 7-10.30 Sun; closed 25 Dec ~ Bedrooms: £50B/£65B

HEATHTON SO8192 Map 4
Old Gate ◖

Off B4176 W of Wombourn; heading W, fork left via Halfpenny Green

The out-of-the-way location doesn't stop this welcoming creeper-clad pub drawing the crowds, particularly on a Saturday evening, when if you're planning to eat it's well worth booking a table. Readers with children have especially enjoyed their meals here; one family tells of appealingly decorated children's helpings, and the occasional free chocolate bar or ice cream. Friendly staff may greet you at the door – and remember your name after just one visit. The building dates from around 1600, and has a busily traditional feel; everything has a slight reddish tinge, and there are plenty of tables packed into the two small main rooms, along with plush seats, lots of bric-a-brac, two open fires, and the odd idiosyncratic touch like a model bird or balloons hanging from the ceiling. The wide choice of freshly prepared food includes niçoise salad (£7.95), spicy chicken stir fry (£8.95), fried pork loin in oyster mushroom and cream sauce (£9.95), salmon on roast vegetables (£10.95), roast shoulder of lamb on root vegetables (£11.95), grilled plaice with garlic and herb butter (£12.95), and excellent home-made puddings (£3.80). Well kept Enville, Greene King Abbot and Timothy Taylors Landlord from the tiny bar counters; also draught cider. A small lawn behind has picnic-sets and play equipment, and is very colourful in summer. The two golden retrievers are called Biffo and Cromwell. *(Recommended by John and Gillian Scarisbrick, Ian S Morley, Joy and Peter Heatherley)*

Punch ~ Lease Jamie Atkins ~ Real ale ~ Bar food (12-2, 6.30-9) ~ Restaurant ~ (01746) 710431 ~ Children welcome ~ Open 12-2.30, 6.30-11; 11-3, 7-10.30 Sun; closed Mon

HOPTON WAFERS SO6476 Map 6
Crown

A4117 Kidderminster—Ludlow

The emphasis in this well restored and attractive creeper-covered inn remains on the wide range of food – though they do keep four real ales, and have 8 wines by the glass. Using only fresh ingredients, the frequently changing and interesting bar food might include sandwiches, soup (£3.25), smoked mackerel and sweet pepper pâté (£3.95), flash fried pigeon breast with smoked bacon on balsamic dressed leaves (£4.75), goats cheese tartlet on caramelised leeks and red onions (£7.95), breast of chicken with garlic, cream and herb sauce glazed with stilton (£8.75), confit of crispy duck with orange and brandy sauce (£9.75), medallions of pork tenderloin with mushrooms, cream, white wine and french mustard (£9.95), shank of lamb in an apricot, grain mustard, mint and rosemary sauce (£10.45), and puddings like summer pudding with mint and orange crème fraîche, treacle tart with custard, and raspberry crème brûlée (£3.75). It's worth noting that on Sunday there are no light lunches. The cosy cream painted beamed bar has a large inglenook fireplace and purpose built dark wood furniture, oil paintings, and fresh flowers. The restaurant is no smoking, and is closed on Sunday evening and all Monday; piped music and cribbage. Well kept Banks's Bitter, Marstons Pedigree, Timothy Taylors Landlord, and Woods Parish on handpump. Outside, the terrace areas have tables under cocktail parasols, and there's a pleasant streamside garden with tubs of bright flowers and a duck pond. *(Recommended by Mr and Mrs E Borthwick, Dr and Mrs P Johnston, Mike and Mary Carter, Hugh Bower, Dr T E Hothersall, David and Helen Wilkins)*

Free house ~ Licensee Alan Matthews ~ Bar food (12-2.30, 6-9.30) ~ Restaurant ~ (01299) 270372 ~ Children must be well behaved and away from bar ~ Open 12-3, 6-11(10.30 Sun) ~ Bedrooms: £48B/£75S(£70B)

IRONBRIDGE SJ6704 Map 6

Malthouse ♀

The Wharfage (bottom road alongside Severn)

Opposite the river, this is a big busy barn of a place, very nicely decorated, and with a really laid-back feel despite the buzz and lively bustle. The walls are covered with changing works by local artists, and there's live music every Wednesday-Sunday evening – mostly jazz, but also funk, latin and world music. Spotlessly clean, the spacious bar is broken up by pine beams and concrete pillars, and has lots of scrubbed light wooden tables with candles; piped music. Good bar food includes soup (£2.25), ham and pistachio terrine (£3.95), thai-style fishcakes on spicy tomato and soy sauce (£6.95), fresh cod in beer batter (£7.25), chicken, cashew and sweet potato curry (£7.50), and three-cheese frittata with asparagus and slow-dried cherry tomato salad and rosemary pesto (£7.95); children's menu, and good Sunday roasts. Fresh fish is delivered from Brixham, but most other ingredients are firmly local: the pork comes from the woods opposite. Well kept Boddingtons, Courage Directors, Flowers Original and Wadworths 6X on electric pump, and a wide choice of wines, several by the glass; friendly service from efficient young staff. The atmosphere is quite different in the restaurant (most of which is no smoking), and the bedrooms are all individually decorated. There are a few tables in front. The enthusiastic young licensees also run the Habit in Bridgnorth and plan further openings. *(Recommended by John Whitehead, Dr Bob Bland, M Joyner)*

Free house ~ Licensees Alex and Andrea Nicoll ~ Real ale ~ Bar food ~ Restaurant ~ (01952) 433712 ~ Children welcome ~ Live music Weds-Sun evenings ~ Open 11-11; 12-10.30 Sun; closed 25 Dec ~ Bedrooms: £49B/£59B

LONGVILLE SO5393 Map 4

Longville Arms

B4371 Church Stretton—Much Wenlock

The two spacious bars in this welcoming, relaxed inn have stripped beams and original stone, and the lounge bar on the left has dark plush wall banquettes and cushioned chairs, with some nice old tables. The room on the right has new oak panelling, and there's a new no smoking dining room with disabled access. From a smallish menu, the tasty bar food includes soup (£1.95), home-made pâté (£2.95), deep-fried whitebait with a yoghurt mint dip (£3.25), mushroom and mixed pepper tagliatelle (£5.50), lasagne (£5.95), chicken breast in a mushroom, prawn and white wine sauce (£7.50), supreme of fresh salmon en croûte (£8.50), steaks (from £9.95), daily specials, and puddings (£2.50). Well kept Courage Directors, Charles Wells Bombardier, and a guest such as Bass or Greene King Old Speckled Hen with a guest on handpump, and several malt and Irish whiskies; darts, pool, dominoes and piped music. There are picnic-sets in a terraced side garden, and a play area. *(Recommended by Ray and Winifred Halliday, C P Scott-Malden, John Whitehead, Jill Bickerton, R T and J C Moggridge, Paul and Margaret Baker, Ron Shelton, Mrs M Edwards, Abi Benson, Gene and Kitty Rankin)*

Free house ~ Licensees Chris and Wendy Davis ~ Real ale ~ Bar food (12-2.30, 7-9.30) ~ Restaurant ~ (01694) 771206 ~ Children in eating area of bar and restaurant ~ Open 12-3, 7-11; 12-4, 6-11 Sat ~ Bedrooms: £30S/£46S

If you have to cancel a reservation for a bedroom or restaurant, please telephone or write to warn them. A small place – and its customers – will suffer if you don't. And recently people who failed to cancel have been taken to court for breach of contract.

LUDLOW SO5175 Map 4
Unicorn 🍴

Corve St, off main road to Shrewsbury

Even when this 17th-c inn is really busy – which it often is – the staff manage to cope with the rush with friendly efficiency; best to get there early. The appetising range of food remains one of the main draws: home-made soup (£2.75), chicken liver pâté (£4.25), pasta, artichoke and blue cheese bake or home-cooked ham with parsley sauce (£6.75), lamb cutlets with onion and rosemary sauce (£7.25), mediterranean-baked vegetables with brie and garlic bread (£8.25), beef in ale with herb dumplings (£8.50), bacon-wrapped chicken and creamy mushroom sauce (£8.95), mixed grill (£9.25), steaks (from £9.25), bass with pink peppercorn sauce (£12.25), half a roast duck with cumberland sauce (£13.25), and home-made puddings (£3.50); friendly and obliging service. There's a good social buzz in the solidly beamed and partly panelled bar, with a mix of friendly locals and visitors, and a huge log fire in a big stone fireplace; the timbered, candlelit restaurant is no smoking. Well kept Flowers IPA and Wadworths 6X on handpump; cribbage and dominoes. Outside, tables shelter pleasantly among willow trees on the pretty little terrace right next to the modest River Corve. This is a picturesque town. Please note, they no longer do bedrooms. *(Recommended by Dennis Jenkin, Karen and Graham Oddey, MP, Patricia A Bruce, Mr and Mrs M Cross, P G Plumridge, Sue Holland, Dave Webster, Mandy and Simon King, Ron Shelton, Ray and Jacki Davenport, Charles Moncreiffe, DAV, Mike and Mary Carter, James Morrell, Mr and Mrs A H Young, Bruce Bird, Di and Mike Gillam, JES, Anthony Barnes, M Joyner, Stan and Hazel Allen, Dr and Mrs P Johnston, Gene and Kitty Rankin, David Twitchett)*

Free house ~ Licensees Alan and Elisabeth Ditchburn ~ Real ale ~ Bar food (12-2.15, 6(7 Sun)-9.15) ~ Restaurant ~ (01584) 873555 ~ Children in eating area of bar and restaurant ~ Open 12-2.30(3.30 Sat), 6-11; 12-3.30, 7-10.30 Sun; closed 25 Dec

MUCH WENLOCK SO6299 Map 4
George & Dragon 🍺

High St

Very popular locally, this unassuming town pub has around 2,000 jugs hanging from the beams in the cosily atmospheric rooms, as well as old brewery and cigarette advertisements, bottle labels and beer trays, and George-and-the-Dragon pictures; there are furnishings such as antique settles among more conventional seats, and a couple of attractive Victorian fireplaces (with coal-effect gas fires). At the back, the quieter snug old-fashioned rooms have black beams and timbering, little decorative plaster panels, tiled floors, a big mural as well as lots of smaller pictures (painted by local artists), and a little stove in an inglenook. They keep four real ales on handpump and get through around 300 different ones a year: Hook Norton Best, Everards Beacon and Tiger, Hobsons Town Crier, and Salopian Golden Thread; country wines, and cranberry, elderflower, and ginger pressé. Enjoyable bar food might include sandwiches (from £2.25), filled baked potatoes (from £2.95), ploughman's (from £3.75), welsh rarebit with diced apple, celery and walnuts (£3.95), stilton and walnut pâté (£4.25), home-made leek and mushroom bake (£7.25), good home-baked ham with parsley sauce (£7.75), breast of chicken in an apricot, mead and cream sauce (£7.95), and puddings such as home-made bread and butter pudding or hot fruit crumble (£2.75); the restaurant is no smoking. *(Recommended by JES, John Oates, Dr Denise Walton, John Whitehead, Di and Mike Gillam, Pat and Tony Martin, Kevin Thorpe, Nigel Woolliscroft, Dr Bob Bland, O K Smyth)*

Free house ~ Licensee Barry Blakeman ~ Real ale ~ Bar food (not Sun evening or Weds) ~ Restaurant ~ No credit cards ~ (01952) 727312 ~ Children in eating area of bar and restaurant ~ Open 12-2.30, 6(7 Sun)-11; closed Weds lunchtime

---

Pubs staying open all afternoon at least one day a week are listed at
the back of the book.

Talbot 🛏

High Street

Dating back in part to 1360, this comfortable place was originally part of Wenlock Abbey and today a delightful little coach entry leads off High Street to green seats and tables in an attractive sheltered courtyard, and the entrance to the bar. Inside, there are several neatly kept areas with comfortable green plush button-back wall banquettes around tables, low ceilings, and two big log fires in inglenooks; the walls are decorated with prints of fish and brewery paraphernalia, and there are art deco-style lamps and gleaming brasses. Well kept Bass, and a guest from Batemans or Woods on handpump, and several malt whiskies; pleasant and polite staff. Good bar food might include soup (£2.95), sandwiches (from £2.95), filled baked potatoes (from £4.25), omelettes (from £5.95), poached salmon with white wine and mushroom sauce (£8.45) and daily specials such as smoked haddock pasta bake (£6.95) and shropshire pie (pork, leeks, cider and cheese, £7.50). *(Recommended by M Joyner, Alan and Paula McCully, John Whitehead)*

Free house ~ Licensees Mark and Maggie Tennant ~ Real ale ~ Bar food (12-2, 7-9.30(8.30 Sun)) ~ Restaurant ~ (01952) 727077 ~ Children welcome ~ Open 11-3, 6-11; 12-3, 7-10.30 Sun; closed 25 Dec ~ Bedrooms: £45B/£90B

NORTON SJ7200 Map 4

Hundred House 🍴 ♀ 🛏

A442 Telford—Bridgnorth

Of course the attractively presented, good food in this popular family-run inn is a major draw, but the very well established cottagey gardens are worth a visit in themselves, with old-fashioned roses, trees, and herbaceous plants, and a very big working herb garden that supplies the kitchen. The neatly kept interior, prettied up with lots of dried and fresh flowers, herbs and hops, is divided into several separate areas, with old quarry tiles at either end and modern hexagonal ones in the main central high beamed part. Steps lead up past a little balustrade to a partly panelled eating area where stripped brickwork looks older than that elsewhere. Handsome fireplaces have log fires or working Coalbrookdale ranges (one has a great Jacobean arch with fine old black cooking pots), and around sewing-machine tables are a variety of interesting chairs and settles with some long colourful patchwork leather cushions; the main dining room is no smoking. Enjoyable bar food includes home-made soup (£3.95), chicken liver pâté with cream and brandy (£4.95), pork sausages with onion gravy (£6.95), charlotte of carrot wrapped in courgette with roast shallots and tomato coulis (£8.50), steak and kidney pie or chargrilled chicken with sweet red pepper coulis, mint yoghurt and fennel salad (£8.95), and daily specials such as assiette of ham terrine with cured duck breast (£7.95), braised lamb casserole (£11.95), local sirloin steak (£12.95), chargrilled salmon fillet with tarragon cream sauce (£13.95), chargrilled swordfish loin with tomato salsa and smoked paprika mayonnaise (£14.95), and home-made puddings such as hot chocolate pudding or raspberry crème brûlée (from £4.95). Well kept Heritage Bitter (brewed for them by a small brewery: light and refreshing and not too bitter), with three or four guests such as Batemans XB, Everards Tiger, Highgate Saddlers, and Robinsons Bitter on handpump, an extensive wine list with house wines by the carafe, half carafe, and big or small glass, farm cider and lots of malt whiskies; pretty bedrooms.

(Recommended by Pat and Sam Roberts, John Sandilands, R C Wiles, Mike and Wendy Proctor, Gill and Keith Croxton, Paul Boot, Mike and Mary Carter, Stephanie Smith, Leigh Hughes, Mr and Mrs G Owens, A J Bowen, Trevor and Lynda Smith; also in The Good Hotel Guide)

Free house ~ Licensees The Phillips Family ~ Real ale ~ Bar food (12-2.30, 6-10(7-9 Sun)) ~ Restaurant ~ (01952) 730353 ~ Children in eating area of bar and restaurant ~ Open 11-2.30, 6-11; 11-11 Sat; 11-3, 7-10.30 Sun ~ Bedrooms: £75B/£99B

SHREWSBURY SJ4912 Map 6
Armoury 🍴 ♟

Victoria Quay, Victoria Avenue

By the time this book is published, the area in front of this former warehouse will have been pedestrianised and there will be tables out there for summer dining. You can take boats out on the River Severn, escorted past rows of weeping willows by swans and gently quacking ducks – it does get busy, particularly at weekends. Big arched windows overlooking the river light up the single airy room which is packed with old prints, documents and other neatly framed ephemera, with glass cabinets showing off collections of explosives and shells as well as corks and bottle openers, and one entire wall covered with copiously filled bookshelves. There's a mix of good heavy wooden tables, chairs and high-backed settles, interspersed by the occasional green-painted standing timber, and colonial fans whirring away on the ceiling. Tables at one end are laid out for eating, with a grand stone fireplace at the other end. An eye-catching range of varied drinks served from behind the long bar counter includes well kept Boddingtons, Wadworths 6X, Woods Shropshire Lad, and up to five changing guests on handpump, as well as a good wine list with several by the glass, around 70 malt whiskies, a dozen different gins, lots of rums and vodkas, a wide choice of brandies, and some unusual liqueurs. Alongside soup (£3.95), sandwiches (from £3.25) and ploughman's (£5.75), bar food includes chilli crab and potato cakes with cucumber and coriander yoghurt (£3.95), chicken liver and smoked bacon pâté with a pineapple and onion chutney (£4.25), cumberland sausage with horseradish mash and red wine gravy (£6.95), lambs liver with mashed sweet potato, crispy smoked bacon and stilton gravy (£7.45), crispy pancake filled with oyster mushrooms, spring greens and ginger served on stir-fried lemon and spinach noodles (£8.25), cold poached salmon fillet with asparagus mousse (£8.50), rib-eye steak with peppercorn sauce (£12.50), and puddings such as treacle tart or chocolate chip sponge (£4.25). The pub doesn't have its own parking but they sell vouchers for parking up nearer the Quarry. *(Recommended by I D Greenfield, Dr Bob Bland, M Joyner, SLC, MP, John Brightley, Karen and Graham Oddey, John A Barker, Mrs P Wilson)*

Brunning & Price ~ Managers Jill Mitchell and Eugene Millea ~ Real ale ~ Bar food (12-2.30, 6-9.30; 12-9.30(9 Sun)Sat) ~ (01743) 340525 ~ Children till 9pm ~ Open 12-11(10.30 Sun); closed 25 and 26 Dec

WENLOCK EDGE SO5796 Map 4
Wenlock Edge Inn ★ 🍴 🛏

Hilltop; B4371 Much Wenlock—Church Stretton, OS Sheet 137 map reference 570962

It's always heartening to come across a pub that receives such warm enthusiasm from so many readers, and over so many years. There are few pubs that offer a welcome as genuine, and the friendly landlord and his family go out of their way to get visitors involved in the bar room chat, with the cosy feel perhaps at its best on story-telling night (the second Monday in the month at 8pm) when the right hand bar is packed with locals telling tales, some true and others somewhat taller. There's a big woodburning stove in an inglenook and a shelf of high plates in the right hand bar, which leads into a little dining room. The room on the left has pews that originate from a Methodist chapel in Liverpool, a fine oak bar counter, and an open fire; the dining room is no smoking. Very popular and all home-made, the reasonably priced bar food using organic produce where possible includes soups such as the house favourite, tomato and sweet red pepper (from £2.75), garlic mushrooms in sherry and crème fraîche (£3.95), fishy starters such as fresh salmon cakes, hot smoked salmon or pickled herrings (from £3.95), organic bean and vegetable bake, steak and mushroom pie or chicken and apricot flan (£6.95), local leg of lamb with garlic and mint (£7.50), haddock, cod or plaice fried in butter (from £7.50), roast breast of duck with morello cherry sauce (£8.90), organic steaks (from £9.90), and puddings such as bakewell tart, hot chocolate fudge pudding or raspberry and apple crumble (from £3.40); good breakfasts. Well kept local

Hobsons Best and Town Crier on handpump, interesting whiskies, decent wines by the glass and bottle, and lots of unusual non alcoholic drinks such as old-fashioned lemonade, ginger beer, raspberry and ginger brew, fruit cordials and a good choice of coffees. No music – unless you count the chimes of mini Bertha the fusee clock (Big Bertha is away having a major overhaul); dominoes, and books and charts on Chinese horoscopes. There are some tables on the front terrace, and more on a side terrace; also, a herb garden and wildlife pond, and water is drawn from their own 190 ft well. There are lots of walks through the National Trust land that runs along the Edge. Bedrooms are cosy and well appointed. *(Recommended by John Whitehead, Mike and Wena Stevenson, M W Schofield, David Field, M Joyner, Dennis Jenkin, RJH, Ron and Val Broom, Karen and Graham Oddey, G T Brewster, David and Helen Wilkins, R M Corlett, T A Smith, Lynn Sharpless, Bob Eardley, Les Brown, Ian and Denise Foster, David and Michelle Bailey, Ray and Winifred Halliday, Jean and Douglas Troup, Anthony Barnes, A C Duke, Sue Holland, Dave Webster, JES, Malcolm Taylor, Ben and Sheila Walker, Ron Shelton; also in* The Good Hotel Guide*)*

Free house ~ Licensees Stephen and Di Waring ~ Real ale ~ Bar food (not Mon except for residents) ~ Restaurant ~ (01746) 785678 ~ Children in eating area of bar and restaurant ~ Open 11.30-2.30, 6.30-11; 12-2.30, 6.30-10.30 Sun; closed Mon lunchtime, 24-26 Dec ~ Bedrooms: £45S/£70S

WENTNOR SO3893 Map 6

Crown

Village and pub signposted (not very clearly) off A489 a few miles NW of junction with A49

From picnic-sets and old-fashioned teak garden seats on the neat back lawn here, there's a fine view of the Long Mynd. This has been an inn ever since it was built in 1640, and there are beams, standing timbers, a good log fire, some nice big prints, and a collection of china and cut glass; much of the main bar area is laid for eating, and one end has a snug area with two new sofas, pictures and a dresser filled with Portmeirion 'Botanic Garden' china. As well as sandwiches (from £2.25) and soup (£2.40), bar food might include grilled goats cheese (£3.95), cottage pie (£4.95), smoked salmon and dill quiche (£5.50), curry (£6.50), tarragon chicken (£8.95), and fillet steak (£13.45); the cosy beamed restaurant is no smoking. Well kept Hobsons Best, Greene King Old Speckled Hen, Salopian Shropshire Gold and Worthington Best on handpump, decent wines and a good choice of malt whiskies; piped music. *(Recommended by Guy Vowles, C Osborn, Malcolm Taylor, Stan and Hazel Allen)*

Free house ~ Licensees Simon and Joanna Beadman ~ Real ale ~ Bar food ~ Restaurant ~ (01588) 650613 ~ Children must be well behaved ~ Open 12-3, 7-11; 12-11 Sat; 12-10.30 Sun ~ Bedrooms: £27S/£53B

WHITCHURCH SJ5345 Map 7

Willey Moor Lock ◗ £

Actually just over the Cheshire border, the pub is signposted off A49 just under 2 miles N of Whitchurch

It's not surprising there's such a good view of the colourful narrowboats on the Llangollen Canal from this perfectly placed pub, as it used to be the lock keeper's cottage, and you have to cross a little footbridge over the canal and its rushing sidestream to get to it. Neatly kept by a welcoming landlady, the low beamed rooms attract a good mix of customers, with brick-based brocaded wall seats, stools and small chairs around dimpled copper and other tables, a large teapot collection and a decorative longcase clock, and two winter log fires. Alongside well kept Theakstons Best, there might be Hanby All Seasons, and Weetwood Eastgate on handpump, with a choice of around 30 malt whiskies. Straightforward bar food includes sandwiches (from £2.25), filled baked potatoes (£3.20), minced beef and onion pie or ratatouille (£3.95), chicken curry (£4.75), lasagne (£5.25), battered cod (£5.50), gammon or mixed grill (£7.50) and puddings such as spotted dick or toffee apple crumble pie (from £1.75). Fruit machine, piped music, and several dogs and cats. There are tables under cocktail parasols on a terrace, and a children's play area in the garden. *(Recommended by Mike and Wena Stevenson, Sue Holland, Dave Webster, Rob Fowell, Mr and Mrs J Underwood, SLC)*

Free house ~ Licensee Elsie Gilkes ~ Real ale ~ Bar food (12-2, 6-9.30(9 Sun, Mon)) ~ (01948) 663274 ~ Children welcome away from bar ~ Open 12-2.30(2 winter), 6-11; 12-3(2.30 winter), 7-10.30 Sun; closed 25 Dec

WISTANSTOW SO4385 Map 6

Plough ☜

Village signposted off A49 and A489 N of Craven Arms

This is the home of the very tasty Woods beers – all brewed in the separate older building right by the pub: Woods Parish, Special, the strong Wonderful and seasonal ales on handpump; they also keep Addlestone's and Weston's cider, and quite a few cognacs. The building is nothing prepossessing internally or externally but is simply furnished, with high rafters, cream walls and mahogany furniture on a russet turkey carpet, and welsh dressers, and oak tables and chairs to give the modernised bar a more homely feel; friendly service. Popular English cooking includes dishes such as home-made soup (£2.95), welsh rarebit on garlic bread (£3.75), grilled goats cheese salad (£4.10), filled baguettes (£5), cider baked ham with parsley sauce or lamb and rosemary casserole (£6.95), large pork chop topped with cheese and grain mustard (£7.35), steak and kidney pie (£7.50), breast of chicken cooked with honey, ginger and apricots (£8.75), smoked haddock on a bed of spinach, topped with a poached egg (£8.95), and puddings like bread, butter and marmalade pudding, poached pears with butterscotch sauce or crème brûlée (£3.30); on Sundays, they only do two roasts, and a fish and vegetarian choice. The games area has darts, pool, juke box, and fruit machine. There are some tables under cocktail parasols outside.
(Recommended by Dr R F Fletcher, John Whitehead, D W Stokes, Mr and Mrs D T Deas, Colin Parker, Mr and Mrs C Roberts, Sue Holland, Dave Webster, R T and J C Moggridge)

Own brew ~ Tenant Denis Harding ~ Real ale ~ Bar food (not Sun or winter Mon evenings) ~ Restaurant ~ (01588) 673251 ~ Children in eating area of bar ~ Open 11.30-2.30, 6.30-11; 12-2.30, 7-10.30 Sun; 12-2, 7-11 in winter

Lucky Dip

Besides the fully inspected pubs, you might like to try these Lucky Dips recommended to us and described by readers (if you do, please send us reports: www.goodguides.com).

Atcham [SJ5409]
Mytton & Mermaid: Comfortable and friendly, with good range of usual food; bedrooms, nice setting opp entrance to Attingham Park (NT) *(Joan and Tony Walker)*
Bridgnorth [SO7193]
Black Horse [Bridge St, Lowtown]: Several well kept changing ales such as Banks's in long thin welcoming pub with comfortable low-beamed oak-panelled lounge bar, plenty of wines and country wines, darts in simpler public bar, restaurant (not Sun); piped music; tables outside, good disabled access, open all day wknds, bedrooms *(G Coates)*
Habit [E Castle St]: Bistro atmosphere and pleasant décor, good unusual nicely presented food (all day Sun) attractively served; nr top of Cliff Railway *(M Joyner)*
Halfway House [Cleobury Rd]: Heavily black-beamed bar with settles, wheelback chairs and big fireplace, some interesting ancient wall decoration, friendly staff and good pubby atmosphere, good value food, well kept local ales such as Woods Shropshire Lad, several

dozen malt whiskies, pleasant back dining conservatory; garden with barbecue, comfortable bedrooms – they organise activity holidays *(Dr Phil Putwain)*
Poachers Pocket [Mill St]: Surprising amount of decorations inc naughty (but not crude) jokes in family pub with excellent food, lively motivated young staff, well kept Banks's; piped music may obtrude *(Chris Glasson)*
☆ *Punch Bowl* [B4364 towards Ludlow]: Comfortably refurbished beamed and panelled 17th-c country pub, spacious and clean, with some interesting prints, good generous bar food inc fresh veg, good Sun carvery (best to book), friendly attentive service, well kept beers inc Marstons Pedigree, decent wines; piped music; bedrooms, superb views *(John Whitehead, Mr and Mrs M Browning)*
☆ *Railwaymans Arms* [Severn Valley Stn, Hollybush Rd (off A458 towards Stourbridge)]: Good interesting more or less local ales inc a Mild in converted waiting-room at Severn Valley steam railway terminus, bustling on summer days; coal fire, station nameplates,

superb mirror over fireplace, tables out on platform; may be simple summer snacks, children welcome, wheelchair access; the train to Kidderminster (another bar there) has an all-day bar and bookable Sun lunches *(Pat and Tony Martin, P and M Rudlin, the Didler, JP, PP, Nigel Woolliscroft, Gill Waller, Tony Morriss, LYM)*

Shakespeare [West Castle St]: Character black and white building, keeping charm inside with partly divided separate areas; friendly, with straightforward food inc good value locally popular Sun lunch; children welcome *(Gill Waller, Tony Morriss)*

Brockton [SO5894]

☆ *Feathers* [B4378]: Interesting restauranty food in stylish country dining pub (the landlord seems to think rather too stylish for our *Guide*) with comfortable seats in attractively decorated beamed rooms (two no smoking) and delightful conservatory, Banks's and Morrells Varsity under light blanket pressure; children allowed, cl wkdy lunchtimes and Mon *(Malcolm Taylor, Paul Boot, Dr Bob Bland, P Fisk, LYM)*

Broseley [SJ6701]

Pheasant [Church St]: Country dining pub carefully restored with small friendly bar, oak floors, antique furniture and old paintings, traditional home cooking, real ales, good wines, log fires; two bedrooms, plans for more *(Mr and Mrs P Lally)*

Bucknell [SO3574]

Baron of Beef [Chapel Lawn Rd; just off B4367 Knighton Rd]: Big log fire in front bar, spotless pleasantly refurbished back lounge with fresh flowers, interesting prints, rustic memorabilia inc grindstone and cider press, good bar food inc enterprising vegetarian dishes, largish upstairs restaurant with own bar and popular wknd carvery, well kept Greene King IPA, Hobsons and Woods Governors, farm cider, decent house wines, good welcoming service; games room with pool and darts, occasional live entertainment; big garden with play area *(John Whitehead, June and Mike Coleman)*

Calverhall [SJ6037]

Old Jack [New St Lane]: Thriving village pub with friendly staff, good range of food in bar and separate dining area, well kept beer, sensible wine list, beams and button-back banquettes *(M Joyner)*

Cleobury Mortimer [SO6775]

Kings Arms [A4117 Bewdley—Ludlow]: Warmly decorated open-plan bar with pews, bare boards and well spaced tables, good log fire, beamed dining area stretching beyond island servery, usual bar food from soup and sandwiches up, friendly attentive service, well kept Hobsons Best and Town Crier and a guest beer; piped music; open all day, children welcome, garden with water feature, reasonably priced bedrooms *(DHV, Karen and Graham Oddey, LYM)*

Clun [SO3081]

☆ *Sun* [High St]: Tudor beams and timbers, some sturdy antique furnishings and interesting prints, enormous open fire in flagstoned public bar, friendly helpful service, good generous

reasonably priced food in larger carpeted lounge bar, well kept ales inc Banks's Bitter and Mild, Hobsons and Woods Shropshire Lad; children allowed in eating area, tables in sheltered well planted back garden with terrace; nice bedrooms, lovely village *(C H and B J Owen, DC, David and Helen Wilkins, David Field, the Didler, John Whitehead, BB, Martin and Karen Wake, Kevin Thorpe)*

Coalbrookdale [SJ6704]

☆ *Coalbrookdale Inn* [Wellington Rd, opp Museum of Iron]: Long flight of steps up to handsome dark brick 18th-c pub, simple, cheerful and bustling tiled-floor bar with local pictures, six or seven well kept changing ales such as Adnams, Brains, Enville Mild, Everards Tiger, Fullers London Pride, Greene King Abbot and Charles Wells Bombardier from square counter also serving rather smaller room set more for the huge platefuls of good value often imaginative food (not Sun) from sandwiches to steaks; good log fire, farm cider, country wines, good mix of people, piano, remarkable bottled beer collection, no piped music; dogs welcome, opens noon *(R T and J C Moggridge, Phil and Heidi Cook, the Didler, BB, Dr Bob Bland)*

Coalport [SJ6903]

☆ *Boat* [Ferry Rd, Jackfield; nr Mawes Craft Centre, over footbridge by chinaworks museum]: Cosy 18th-c quarry-tiled bar recovered after flood closure, coal fire in lovely range, good food inc local free-range pork, game and cheeses and good value Sun lunch, well kept Banks's Bitter and Mild, Camerons and Marstons Pedigree, Weston's farm cider, darts; summer barbecues on big tree-shaded lawn, in delightful part of Severn Gorge, newly replaced footbridge making it handy for Coalport China Museum *(Dr Bob Bland, BB, the Didler, M Joyner)*

Shakespeare [High St]: Simple friendly cream-washed timbered pub by pretty Severn Gorge park, handy for china museum, with large quantities of good value quickly served home-made food, well kept Banks's *(Gill Waller, Tony Morriss, BB)*

Corfton [SO4985]

☆ *Sun* [B4368 Much Wenlock—Craven Arms]: Friendly and well worn in country local with well kept Corvedale Normans Pride, Secret Hop and Divine Inspiration from brewery behind (tours available) as well as other well kept ales, reasonably priced food from generous baps to bargain Sun lunch inc children's, fish and lots of vegetarian, pleasant lounge with interesting prints, lively beamed bar, and dining room with no smoking area, beer bottle collection and covered well; tables on terrace and in good-sized garden with good play area; piped music; open all day, tourist information, particularly good disabled access throughout *(BB, Michael and Jenny Back, Dr and Mrs P Johnston)*

Cressage [SJ5903]

Eagles [A458 Shrewsbury—Bridgnorth]: Friendly staff, enjoyable generous food, Courage Directros and John Smiths *(Dave Braisted)*

Eardington [SO7192]
Swan [Knowle Sands]: Friendly and attractive
recently renovated dining pub, good beer
choice, good value food, prompt helpful service
(David Cosham)
Edgerley [SJ3517]
Royal Hill [off A5 at Nesscliffe, via Wilcot and
Pentre, then towards Melverley rather than
Edgerley]: 17th-c brick-built country local
overlooking River Severn, worn tiled corridor
behind tall settles forming snug around coal fire,
parlour-like carpeted lounge with easy chairs,
rocking chair and electric fire, back bar with
two well kept Salopian beers and Worthington,
no food exc Sun rolls and (busy) Thurs night
fish and chips; children welcome, garden, cl
winter wkdy lunchtimes *(Kevin Thorpe)*
Ellerdine Heath [SJ6122]
Royal Oak: Genuine happy quarry-tiled
country local, well kept reasonably priced local
ales such as Hanby Drawwell, Hobsons Best
and Salopian, simple choice of good value food
(not Tues) from sandwiches up; may be lots of
children, pool room, TV, piped music; play
area, open all day Sat *(John Morgan)*
Halfway House [SJ3411]
Seven Stars [A458 Shrewsbury—Welshpool]:
Spotless and unspoilt, like a private house; very
small bar with two high-backed settles by the
gas fire, well kept cheap Burtonwood Best and
Mild tapped from casks in the friendly owner's
kitchen area, no food or music *(the Didler,
Kevin Thorpe, JP, PP)*
Hampton Loade [SO7586]
☆ *Lion*: Warm and welcoming stripped stone inn
tucked away down pot-holed lane on
Kidderminster side of village (lengthy detour if
approached from other side), in very attractive
spot overlooking River Severn; would be main
entry but pub's future uncertain, and may close
due to lesser winter trade; open fires, friendly
efficient staff, particularly attentive landlord
chats with everyone, good unusual food inc
generous Sun lunch, well kept Hook Norton
Best and one or two guest beers usually inc
local Enville, fine wines and country wines, two
bars, lounge, two dining rooms behind smaller
bar with log fire, restaurant for booked meals;
if anything the well worn in interior adds to the
cosy feel; very busy in summer or when Severn
Valley Railway has wknd steam spectaculars
(quaint ferry crossing to station), quiet
otherwise; well-behaved children welcome if
eating lunchtime (or if booked to dine evening),
dogs welcome, picnic-sets outside, good day-
ticket fishing; cl Mon exc bank hols, cl wkdy
lunchtimes Oct-Apr exc Christmas *(BB, Gill
Waller, Tony Morriss, Nigel Woolliscroft,
David Edwards, Dave Braisted)*
Highley [SO7483]
Ship [Severnside]: Well kept Bass, handy for
Severn Way walks (and Severn Valley Railway)
(Dave Braisted)
Hodnet [SJ6128]
☆ *Bear* [Drayton Rd (A53)]: Busy but relaxed
16th-c pub with good range of reasonably
priced well presented food from sandwiches up,
Scottish Courage ales, friendly helpful service;

sofas and easy chairs in foyer, roomy
refurbished bar with good solid furnishings and
log fire, restaurant with corner alcove and
glass-tile floor over unusual sunken garden in
former bear pit; open all day, children welcome
(high chairs and child-size cutlery), six good
value comfortable bedrooms, opp Hodnet Hall
gardens and handy for Hawkstone Park *(Louis
and Jeanne Grein)*
Ironbridge [SJ6703]
Golden Ball [Newbridge Rd/Wesley Rd, off
Madeley Hill]: Friendly partly Elizabethan local
at the top of the town, with helpful landlord,
well kept mainstream and more local beers,
competitively priced substantial food inc good
vegetarian choice, real fire, pleasant terraced
walk down to river; children welcome,
comfortable bedrooms *(Gill Waller, Tony
Morriss, Martin Jennings, MLR)*
Meadow [Buildwas Rd]: Popular and
welcoming Severnside dining pub done up with
old-fashioned beamery, cigarette cards, tasteful
prints and brasses; wide choice of good value
generous fresh food inc imaginative specials in
lounge and downstairs restaurant, smart
welcoming service, well kept Greene King Old
Speckled Hen, decent wines; piped music may
obtrude; pretty waterside garden *(Mrs M
Maguire, John Whitehead, Hugh A MacLean)*
Robin Hood [Waterloo St]: Five comfortable
and attractive connecting rooms with various
alcoves inc barrel-vaulted dining room, lots of
gleaming brass and old clocks, well kept
changing ales such as Banks's Mild, Bass,
Fullers London Pride, Golden Oval, Yorks
Stonewall and Rauch, Stowford Press and
Weston's Old Rosie ciders, friendly service,
good value standard food inc sandwiches; seats
out in front, nice riverside setting by new road
bridge, handy for museums complex;
bedrooms, good breakfast *(Stephanie Smith,
Leigh Hughes)*
Leebotwood [SO4798]
☆ *Pound* [A49 Church Stretton—Shrewsbury]:
Attractive, spotless and comfortable beamed
and thatched 16th-c pub, well presented good
value generous food from sandwiches to fresh
fish and local carvery roasts in bar and big well
laid-out no smoking restaurant, well kept ales
inc John Smiths, Marstons Pedigree and Woods
Shropshire Lad, good wine list (occasional
tastings), friendly efficient staff; tables in garden
*(C H and B J Owen, MDN, John Whitehead,
TOH)*
Leighton [SJ6105]
Kynnersley Arms: Simple Victorian building
built on the remains of a corn mill, armchairs
and settees in back area with glass panel
showing mill machinery in cellar, coal fire in
main area, separate dining alcove, pool table,
very friendly landlady, cheap simple food; good
walks nearby *(John Brightley)*
Little Stretton [SO4392]
☆ *Green Dragon* [village well signed off A49]:
Well kept Tetleys, Wadworths 6X, Woods
Shropshire Lad and quickly changing guest
beers, reasonably priced food from good
interesting baguettes up, cheap house wine,

malt whiskies, helpful staff, children in eating area and restaurant; tables outside, handy for Cardingmill Valley (NT) and Long Mynd *(LYM, Nigel Woolliscroft, DAV)*

☆ *Ragleth*: Neatly kept bay-windowed lounge, walkers and dogs welcome in brick-and-tile-floored bar with huge inglenook, wide range of enjoyable home-made food from good ham sandwiches to steaks inc great value hotpot, quick service, plain-speaking landlord, well kept Hobsons Town Crier and usually a guest beer such as Wye Valley Rock, Stowford Press cider, decent house wine, children welcome, back restaurant; tables on lawn by tulip tree *(Stephanie Smith, Leigh Hughes, MDN, Martin and Karen Wake, Kevin Thorpe, Dave Braisted, Dr Bob Bland, LYM)*

Llanfair Waterdine [SO2476]

☆ *Red Lion* [signed from B4355; turn left after bridge]: Spotless old inn nicely set nr good stretch of Offa's Dyke path, emphasis on dining from good interesting if not cheap bar food to inventive restaurant meals, heavy-beamed largely no smoking turkey-carpeted rambling lounge bar with cosy alcoves and woodburner, small black-beamed and flagstoned tap room, interesting well kept ales, cordials, tiny back conservatory looking down to River Teme (the Wales border); children in restaurant (must be over 8); picnic-sets in lovely garden *(R P and P F Edwards, Mike and Wena Stevenson, Mr and Mrs K Pritchard, Dr Phil Putwain, LYM, Helen Maynard, Karen and Graham Oddey, Sue Demont, Tim Barrow)*

Llanyblodwel [SJ2423]

Horseshoe [signed off B4936]: Black and white timbered Tudor inn in lovely riverside spot, plenty of outside seats, a mile of fly-fishing; basic low-beamed front bar with old black range in inglenook fireplace, built-in settles, lots of brass and china, well worn in rooms rambling off, food (not Sun evening or Mon) from lunchtime baguettes up, oak-panelled dining room, Bass and Worthington and a range of malt whiskies; darts, pool, cribbage, dominoes, fruit machine, piped music; children in eating area, bedrooms, cl Mon lunchtime exc bank hols *(John Kane, LYM, Geoff and Angela Jaques)*

Loppington [SJ4729]

Dickin Arms [B4397]: French chef has been doing good interesting food for this straightforward two-bar country local's dining room; open fire, Bass, Wadworths and Youngers; babies and dogs welcome, play area outside, pretty village *(Lorna and Howard Lambert)*

Ludlow [SO5175]

Charlton Arms [Ludford Bridge]: Friendly pub overlooking River Teme and the town; airy rooms, good mix of customers, relaxed atmosphere, super range of well kept beers mostly from small local breweries, good value food inc home-made soup and Sun roasts, hard-working licensees; bedrooms clean, waterside garden, open all day wknds *(Derek and Sylvia Stephenson, Dr and Mrs P Johnston, Ian Stephens)*

☆ *Church Inn* [Church St, behind Butter Cross]: Banquettes, prints and paintings, welcoming prompt service, good value straightforward bar food (ploughman's or popular roast lunch only, Sun), well kept Courage Directors, Hook Norton and local summer guest ales, no smoking restaurant; quiet piped music, little parking nearby; children welcome, open all day, comfortable bedrooms, good breakfast *(James Morrell, P G Plumridge, Dave Braisted, B D Jones, LYM)*

Feathers [Bull Ring]: Superb timbered building, striking inside too with Jacobean panelling and carving, fine period furnishings; you'll probably be diverted to a less distinguished side café-bar for the good sandwiches and other decent bar food, or a casual drink – well kept Woods real ales; pleasant attentive service, nice restaurant, good parking; comfortable bedrooms, not cheap *(Kevin Thorpe, D W Stokes, LYM, Gene and Kitty Rankin)*

Madeley [SJ6904]

All Nations [Coalport Rd]: Spartan but friendly one-bar pub, licensee's family brewing its own distinctive cheap pale ale since the 1930s – but up for sale as we go to press; good value lunchtime sandwiches, handy for Blists Hill *(Kevin Thorpe, Pete Baker, the Didler, Gill Waller, Tony Morriss)*

Market Drayton [SJ6734]

Gingerbread Man [Adderley Rd, northern outskirts]: Large Tom Cobleigh family pub done up country-style, lots of beams and wood, no smoking areas, good value decent food inc bargains and good children's menu, friendly slick service, well kept Boddingtons and Theakstons, disabled access; play areas indoors and out, open all day *(M Joyner, John Whitehead, E G Parish)*

Marshbrook [SO4489]

Station Hotel [over level crossing by B4370/A49, S of Church Stretton]: Warm and roomy refurbished pub, well kept Boddingtons, Flowers and Woods ales from high-gloss carved bar, reasonably priced food from warm baguettes to good interesting main dishes, quick service, real ales; unobtrusive piped music *(R K Whitfield, John Whitehead)*

Morville [SO6794]

Acton Arms [A458 Bridgnorth—Shrewsbury]: Friendly and relaxed two-bar pub, spotless and nicely furnished, with well kept Banks's and Marstons Pedigree, well prepared enjoyable food, sensibly priced wines, good service; big attractive garden *(John Whitehead, B Melling, Chris Glasson)*

Much Wenlock [SO6299]

Gaskell Arms [High St (A458)]: 17th-c beams, brasses, pubby décor and big brass-canopied log fire dividing the two rooms; good value food using local produce inc good Sun lunch in busy bars and old-fashioned restaurant with white linen and uniformed waitresses, well kept Courage Directors, John Smiths and Theakstons, banknote collection; subdued piped music, fruit machine in lobby; bedrooms *(John Whitehead, David and Anne Culley, R M Corlett)*

Wheatland Fox [High St]: 17th-c inn with thriving bustle, oak beams and panelling, two smallish bars and neat dining room, wide choice of good reasonably priced well presented food, five interesting real ales, friendly staff; comfortable bedrooms, good breakfast (Carolyn and Trevor Golds, Mr and Mrs M Browning, BB)

Munslow [SO5287]

☆ Crown [B4368 Much Wenlock—Craven Arms]: Tudor beams, broad flagstones and cosy nooks and crannies in split-level lounge, good log fire, another in traditional snug, microbrewery producing their own Butchers Best with a guest such as Hobsons Town Crier, generous food from baguettes up, stripped stone eating area, friendly landlady, several dogs; piped music; children welcome, attractive bedrooms, tables outside (Sue Holland, Dave Webster, John Brightley, Mike Pugh, DC, Dr R J Rushton, David Edwards, Anthony Barnes, H Connor, Kevin Thorpe, Ray and Jacki Davenport, LYM)

Nesscliffe [SJ3819]

Old Three Pigeons [A5 Shrewsbury—Oswestry]: Dating from 16th c, with two well worn in bar areas, brown sofas, mix of tables, log fires, brasses, four changing ales, log fires, dining room with wide range of food inc bargains for two; juke box (not always switched on); children welcome, some tables outside, grounds with Russian tank and lots of other used military hardware, ducks and swans on lake, very well stocked bird garden; opp Kynaston Cave, good cliff walks (J S M Sheldon, LYM)

Norbury [SO3692]

Sun [OS Sheet 137 map ref 363928]: Ancient welcoming place opp church in remote village; lovely simple building, open fire, low beams and lots of gleaming brass, good basic food inc soup and sandwiches, well kept beer; fine walks inc unusual route up to the Stiperstones (Dr Bob Bland)

Northwood [SJ4633]

Horse & Jockey: Low-beamed country pub with simple décor, lots of horse and jockey memorabilia, fox brushes over bar, jovial landlord and staff, nice fire, wide choice of popular straightforward food inc OAP bargains and good children's dishes in plain dining area; children and dogs welcome, play area (Sue and Bob Ward)

Oswestry [SJ2929]

Fox [Church St/Cross St]: Ancient black and white timbered façade, little local entrance bar down a step, attractive low-beamed and panelled main room with dark oak furniture, good plain décor, fox theme, well kept Marstons Pedigree, nice bar meals, open fire (Nigel Woolliscroft)

Picklescott [SO4399]

☆ Bottle & Glass [off A49 N of Church Stretton]: Warmly welcoming unspoilt early 17th-c country local tucked away in delightful spot below N end of Long Mynd, pleasant quarry-tiled bar and lounge/restaurant, two log fires, friendly proficient owners, well kept Woods

real ales, good value food esp home-made pies; quiet in winter, busy summer – wise to book for food then, esp Sun lunch; bedrooms (DC, John Whitehead, Jill Bickerton)

Pulverbatch [SJ4202]

☆ White Horse [off A49 at N end of Dorrington]: Rambling country pub, black beams and heavy timbering, masses of gleaming brass and copper, willow-pattern plates and pewter, open coalburning range, fabric-covered high-backed settles and brocaded banquettes, attractive country pictures, well kept Flowers Original, Wadworths 6X and Whitbreads Trophy, decent wines, over 100 malt whiskies, friendly service, enjoyable food; seats in front loggia (Dr Bob Bland, LYM)

Queens Head [SJ3427]

Queens Head [just off A5 SE of Oswestry, towards Nesscliffe]: Emphasis on good value food (all day Fri and wknds) from speciality sandwiches inc good steak baguettes to lots of fish and steaks, well kept reasonably priced Theakstons Best, XB and Old Peculier with a guest such as Woods, pleasant helpful staff, two fairly well worn dining areas with roaring coal fires, nice conservatory; garden by restored Montgomery Canal, country walks (John Whitehead, DAV)

Ryton [SJ4803]

Fox [the one nr Dorrington, S of Shrewsbury]: Smart but relaxed country pub with comfortable lounge bar and dining area, friendly new licensees doing good range of tasty home-made food, well kept Bass and good range of other ales, no smoking restaurant; hill views (David and Jill Head)

Selattyn [SJ2633]

Cross Keys [B4579 NW of Oswestry]: Unspoilt 17th-c village local in glorious remote countryside, low-priced Banks's Bitter and Mild, two small rooms, games room with pool and large screened-in porch (children allowed here), no music or machines – just chat, led by friendly landlord; usually no food (may be good sandwiches); folk music Thurs, attractive split-level garden, cl wkdy lunchtimes (Kevin Thorpe, D W Stokes, JP, PP)

Shifnal [SJ7508]

Oddfellows [High St]: Bistro-style pub with wide range of interesting sensibly priced food in four linked rooms, Timothy Taylors beer, tables outside (M Joyner)

White Hart [High St]: Good value friendly timbered 17th-c pub, quaint and old-fashioned, separate bar and lounge, comfortable but without frills, good range of interesting changing well kept ales, promptly served home-made food inc fresh veg, welcoming staff (Gill Waller, Tony Morriss)

Shrewsbury [SJ4912]

Albert [Smithfield Rd]: Two-room pub with well kept Banks's Bitter, Original and Pipkin and Mansfield Dark; fruit machine (SLC)

Boat House Inn [New St/Quarry Park; leaving centre via Welsh Bridge/A488 turn into Port Hill Rd]: Comfortably modernised Whitbreads Hogshead in lovely position by footbridge to Severn park, river views from long lounge bar, tables out on sheltered terrace and rose lawn; well kept changing ales such as Boddingtons, Greene King Old Speckled Hen, a local Salopian beer and guests such as Fullers London Pride and Timothy Taylors Landlord, friendly helpful staff, good range of standard food, bare boards, low ceilings, darts in smaller bar; children welcome, summer barbecues, popular with young people evening; open all day *(Dr Bob Bland, LYM)*

☆ *Coach & Horses* [Swan Hill/Cross Hill]: Welcoming little unspoilt Victorian pub, panelled throughout, with main bar, cosy little side room and back dining room, good value food inc daily roasts and some unusual dishes, well kept Bass, Goodalls Gold (brewed for pub by Salopian) and a guest such as Smiles, relaxed atmosphere, prompt helpful service even when busy, interesting prints, wide mix of customers; pretty flower boxes outside *(Pete Baker, Richard and Barbara Philpott, JP, PP, John Whitehead, David and Pam Wilcox, the Didler)*
Cromwells [Dogpole]: Smallish dim-lit pubby bar, warm and cosy, well kept Theakstons Best and a seasonal guest such as Batemans Autumn Fall, good value fresh food from baguettes to good game or steak and kidney pies, pleasant staff, decent wines, restaurant (same menu) raised garden and terrace behind; piped music; open all day Sat; nice bedrooms sharing bathrooms *(Dr Bob Bland, SLC)*
Dolphin [A49 ½ mile N of stn]: Refurbished early Victorian pub now with its own Dolphin ales from back brewhouse, changing guest beers, foreign bottled beers and perhaps farm ciders, friendly staff, two small gas-lit rooms; cl lunchtime Mon-Sat but opens 3 Fri/Sat *(the Didler, John A Barker)*
Loggerheads [Church St]: Small pub done out in old style, back panelled smoke room with scrubbed-top tables, high-backed settles and real fire, three other rooms with lots of prints, flagstones and bare boards, quaint linking corridors, food all day Mon-Sat till 6, friendly staff and locals, well kept Banks's Bitter, Mild, Camerons Strongarm and a guest such as Bass, darts, dominoes, poetry society *(the Didler, JP, PP)*

☆ *Three Fishes* [Fish St]: Extensively refurbished heavy-beamed timbered and flagstoned pub, no mobile phones and no smoking throughout – very clean and fresh; well kept changing ales such as Adnams Extra, Brakspears, Fullers London Pride, Gales HSB and Salopian Minsterley, lunchtime food, lots of interesting photographs, prints and bric-a-brac, friendly quick service; open all day, cl Sun *(John A Barker, M Joyner, Dr Bob Bland, JES, LYM, the Didler, G Coates)*

Stiperstones [SJ3600]
☆ *Stiperstones Inn* [signed off A488 S of Minsterley; OS Sheet 126 map ref 364005]: Very helpful friendly service, simple fresh food all day inc local whinberry pie, welcoming little modernised lounge bar with comfortable

leatherette wall banquettes, lots of brassware on ply-panelled walls, well kept Boddingtons, Flowers IPA and Woods Parish, decent wine, very low prices, real fire, darts in plainer public bar, maybe unobtrusive piped music; restaurant, tables outside; clean basic cheap bedrooms (small dogs welcome), good breakfast, open all day; good walking (they sell maps) *(Elizabeth Paton-Smith, John and Diana Niblett, Steve Whalley, BB)*

Telford [SJ7011]
Crown [Market St, Oakengates (off A442, handy for M54 junction 5)]: Bright bare-boards pub with up to ten changing real ales from small breweries inc Hobsons Best as a regular, frequent beer festivals, lots of foreign bottled beers, helpful knowledgeable staff, friendly locals, basic front bar, tables and barrels in side room, no smoking back room (not after 8 Thurs-Sat), darts and pool, coal fire; live music Thurs; tables outside *(John Morgan, G Coates)*

Upper Farmcote [SO7792]
☆ *Lion o' Morfe* [off A458 Bridgnorth—Stourbridge]: Country pub with good very reasonably priced food, well kept beer, log fire in plush lounge, coal fire in traditional public bar, carpeted pool room, conservatory; attractive garden spreading into orchard *(John and Gillian Scarisbrick, LYM)*

Wellington [SJ6511]
Cock [Holyhead Rd]: Former coaching inn popular for its real ale bar, with half a dozen changing well kept beers usually from small breweries, farm cider, large pine tables and big fireplace, also comfortable no smoking lounge; open all day Thurs-Sat, bedrooms *(James Windsor)*

Weston Heath [SJ7713]
Countess Arms [A41 S of Newport]: Newish purpose-built two-level pub with well kept Banks's Original, Boddingtons, Greene King Old Speckled Hen, Marstons Pedigree, 30 wines by the glass, wide choice of good interesting largely modern food reasonably priced (and served from 11), efficient unhurried service, great feeling of space; children's area, barbecue, disabled facilities, open all day till midnight *(David and Jill Head, Pat and Sam Roberts)*

Woofferton [SO5269]
Salwey Arms [A456/B4362 S of Ludlow]: Pleasant old-fashioned pub popular for wide choice of good food from fine sandwiches up; well kept Bass and Tetleys *(M S Catling)*

Yorton [SJ5023]
Railway: Same family for over 60 years, friendly and chatty mother and daughter, unchanging atmosphere, simple cosy bar with coal fire, big comfortable lounge with fishing trophies, well kept Wadworths 6X, Woods Parish, Special and Shropshire Lad on handpump, a guest beer tapped from the cask, simple sandwiches if you ask, pub games – no piped music or machines *(Sue and Bob Ward, the Didler)*

Somerset

We include Bristol in this county, as well as Bath. Bath has one of the chapter's newcomers this year: the Star, a remarkably unspoilt old tavern. The other newcomers are the attractive old Lamb in Axbridge (a different landlord since it was last in the Guide, doing very well all round these days) and the Who'd A Thought It in Glastonbury (another good interesting all-rounder, nice to stay at). At the other end of the scale are two pubs which have been in all 20 editions of the Guide, since it started: the happily unchanging and old-fashioned Tuckers Grave at Faulkland, and the Three Horseshoes, a pleasant country pub at Langley Marsh. The foot and mouth crisis has hit pubs in the west of the county particularly hard this last year; and the lovely Royal Oak at Winsford had an extra dose of misfortune, with a third thatch fire – they fear that their insurers will now rule out their open fires. Other pubs on fine form here this year are the Globe at Appley (much enjoyed for good food in a happy atmosphere), the cheerful Square & Compass near Ashill (popular home cooking), the Ring o' Bells at Compton Martin (a nice country all-rounder, with helpful staff), the Strode Arms at Cranmore (much loved for its good food and atmosphere), the interesting Waggon & Horses near Doulting (good food and wines), the Inn at Freshford (good food in a lovely spot), the utterly unspoilt Rose & Crown at Huish Episcopi (well over a century in the same family), the well run Kingsdon Inn (good all round), the Royal Oak at Luxborough (quite a favourite, and nice to stay in), the very well run Notley Arms at Monksilver (kind to families), the friendly and old-fashioned Halfway House at Pitney (lots of good beer, nice simple food), the olde-worlde Swan at Rowberrow, the Montague Inn at Shepton Montague (nice new landlady and new chef doing good imaginative food), and the Rose & Crown at Stoke St Gregory (a friendly all-rounder). The Blue Ball at Triscombe has also been doing very well, but we haven't yet seen it in its latest guise: the licensees have turned the former pub into their home, and have put a lot of energy into reworking an adjacent 15th-c building as the pub part. From among the county's top-notch food pubs, our title of Somerset Dining Pub of the Year goes to the new team in the Montague Inn at Shepton Montague. In the Lucky Dip section at the end of the chapter, pubs to note particularly this year are the Brewery Tap and Commercial Rooms in Bristol, Gardeners Arms in Cheddar, Carew Arms at Crowcombe, Crown at Exford, Hungerford Arms at Farleigh Hungerford, Farmers Arms near Frome, Bull at Hardway, Stag at Hinton Charterhouse, Ring o' Roses at Holcombe, Old Crown at Kelston, Pilgrims Rest at Lovington, Queens Head in Milborne Port and Royal Oak at Over Stratton. Drinks prices in the area are close to the national average, with pubs getting their beers from west country brewers such as Butcombe, Cotleigh, Exmoor, RCH and Teignworthy often scoring on price.

Bedroom prices normally include full English breakfast, VAT and any inclusive service charge that we know of. Prices before the '/' are for single rooms, after for two people in double or twin (B includes a private bath, S a private shower).

APPLEY ST0621 Map 1
Globe ⊕

Hamlet signposted from the network of back roads between A361 and A38, W of B3187 and W of Milverton and Wellington; OS Sheet 181 map reference 072215

Even on dismal winter evenings, customers are happy to brave snowy conditions to enjoy the good food in this 15th-c country pub. Generously served, dishes might include sandwiches, home-made soup (£2.75; smoked haddock and bacon chowder £5.25), mushrooms in cream, garlic and horseradish (£3.95), a light cold egg pancake filled with prawns, celery and pineapple in marie rose sauce (£6.50), home-made steak and kidney in ale pie (£7.25), thai vegetable curry (£7.50), lamb curry with mint, yoghurt and coriander (£7.75), steaks (from £9.25), chicken breast stuffed with lemon grass, chilli and ginger (£9.75), half a crispy roast duckling with red onion, orange and madeira sauce (£11.75), daily specials such as beef stroganoff (£8.25), grilled fillet of pork with fresh sage, shallot, seed mustard, cream and white wine (£9.95), fresh whole lemon sole or fresh crab salad (£10.95), and puddings such as white chocolate and Malteser ice cream or bread and butter pudding (£3.25); Sunday roast (£5.95) and children's meals (from £3.75). The simple beamed front room has benches and a built-in settle, bare wood tables on the brick floor, and pictures of magpies, and there's a further room with easy chairs and other more traditional ones, open fires, a collection of model cars, and *Titanic* pictures; alley skittles and pool. The restaurant is no smoking. A stone-flagged entry corridor leads to a serving hatch from where Cotleigh Tawny and guests such as Palmers IPA or John Smiths are kept on handpump; summer farm cider. Seats, climbing frame and swings outside in the garden; the path opposite leads eventually to the River Tone. The lavatories are outside. (*Recommended by Martin Dormer, A and J Evans, S G N Bennett, James Flory, Brian and Bett Cox, Richard and Margaret Peers, the Didler, George R Ayres, Mark Wilkinson*)

Free house ~ Licensees A W and E J Burt ~ Real ale ~ Bar food ~ Restaurant ~ (01823) 672327 ~ Children welcome ~ Open 11-3, 6.30-11; 12-3, 7-10.30 Sun; closed Mon except bank holidays

ASHILL ST3116 Map 1
Square & Compass

Windmill Hill; off A358 NW of junction with A303, OS Sheet 193 map reference 310166

Apart from the removal of a wall separating the bar and eating area, little has changed at this bustling and unassuming country pub. There's always a cheerful welcome from the friendly licensees, and the bar has simple comfortable furnishings, an open fire, and well kept Exmoor Ale and Gold and a guest from local breweries like Ash Vine and Branscombe. Enjoyable bar food (with prices unchanged since last year) includes home-made soup (£2.50), good sandwiches (from £2.95), ploughman's (£4.95), lasagne, spinach and ricotta cannelloni or steak and kidney pie (£5.95), pork tenderloin with apples and cider (£6.50), lamb with a honey and mustard glaze, chicken with stilton and bacon or trout and almonds (£7.50), steaks (from £7.50), and puddings such as apple pie or bread and butter pudding (£2.50). Dominoes and piped music; the cats are called Daisy and Lilly. There's a terrace outside and a garden with picnic-sets, sweeping views over the Blackdown Hills, and a children's play area. (*Recommended by Mr and Mrs Anthony Trace, Rev Michael Vockins, Mr and Mrs C Roberts, Bernard Blake, Graham and Rose Ive, Ian Phillips*)

Free house ~ Licensees Chris and Jane Slow ~ Real ale ~ Bar food (12-3, 7-9.30) ~ (01823) 480467 ~ Children welcome ~ Open 12-3, 6.30-11; 12-3, 7-10.30 Sun; closed evening 25 Dec

---

We mention bottled beers and spirits only if there is something unusual about them – imported Belgian real ales, say, or dozens of malt whiskies; so do please let us know about them in your reports: www.goodguides.com

AXBRIDGE ST4255 Map 1
Lamb
The Square; off A371 Cheddar—Winscombe

Set in a notably attractive market square and facing a striking medieval house, this ancient place has a big rambling bar full of heavy beams and timbers, cushioned wall seats and small settles, an open fire in one great stone fireplace, and a collection of tools and utensils including an unusual foot-operated grinder in another. Well kept Butcombe Bitter and Gold, and Wadworths 6X on handpump from a bar counter built largely of bottles, and local cider. Enjoyable bar food includes sandwiches (from £2.50), brie wedges with cranberry sauce or whitebait (£3.75), ploughman's (£4.75), bangers and mash (£5.50), vegetable curry (£5.65), beef in Guinness pie (£6.75), boozy chicken (£8.95), daily specials such as mushroom and pepper pot (£3.95), stilton stuffed mushrooms (£4.25), and seafood lasagne (£5.95), and treacle pudding or blackberry and apple crumble (£2.65). Though the sheltered back garden's not big, it's prettily planted with rock plants, shrubs and trees. (Recommended by KC, Trevor Anderson, Alan and Paula McCully)

Butcombe ~ Manager Mr Ogborne ~ Real ale ~ Bar food (12-2.30, 6.30-9(9.30 Sat)) ~ (01934) 732253 ~ Children in eating area of bar ~ Open 11.30-11; 12-10.30 Sun ~ Bedrooms: /£40(£50B)

BATCOMBE ST6838 Map 2
Three Horseshoes 🍴 ♀ 🍺
Village signposted off A359 Bruton—Frome

Almost as soon as this honey stone, slate-roofed pub opens, customers flock in, looking forward to the good, interesting food – but drinkers do not feel out of place. The longish narrow main room has a civilised but relaxed atmosphere, cream-painted beams and planks, ivy-stencils and attractive artificial ivy, fruit and flower decorations, a few naïve cow and farm animal paintings on the lightly ragged dark pink walls, some built-in cushioned window seats and stripy-cushioned solid chairs around a nice mix of old tables, candles in black spiral holders, two clocking-in clocks, and a woodburning stove at one end with a big open fire at the other; there's a plain tiled room at the back on the left with more straightforward furniture. Changing daily, the food might include home-made soup (£3.50), pheasant and pistachio terrine, fried chicken livers with an orange and redcurrant dressing or goats cheese salad with pine nuts and pesto (all £4.95), smoked duck salad with a honey and balsamic dressing (£5.50), grilled toulouse sausages with mash and onion gravy (£8.95), penne mixed with olives, roasted peppers, tomatoes and basil (£9.95), breast of chicken on coriander and cumin couscous with roasted garlic and sun blush tomatoes (£11.50), sirloin steak with bacon, mushroom and onion jus, salmon fillet wrapped in parma ham with capers and minted crème fraîche or guinea fowl with a wild berry jus (all £12.95), venison wellington (£16.95), and puddings such as cold coffee and amaretti soufflé, summer pudding or iced chocolate parfait (£3.95). The stripped stone dining room is pretty, and the conservatory is no smoking. Well kept Bass, Butcombe and Wadworths 6X with a guest such as Fullers London Pride on handpump, and decent wines by the glass. The back terrace has picnic-sets, with more on the grass, and a big well equipped play area. The pub is on a quiet village lane by the church which has a very striking tower. More reports please.
(Recommended by Dr Penny North, Dr Peter Rudd, Pat and Robert Watt, Mr and Mrs A H Young, Ian Phillips, John A Barker)

Free house ~ Licensees Mr and Mrs Lethbridge ~ Real ale ~ Bar food (till 10pm Fri/Sat) ~ Restaurant ~ (01749) 850359 ~ Children welcome ~ Open 12-3, 6.30-11; 12-3, 7-10.30 Sun

---

Most pubs in the *Guide* sell draught cider. We mention it specifically only if they have unusual farm-produced 'scrumpy' or specialise in it. Do please let us know about any uncommon draught cider you find in a pub: www.goodguides.com

BATH ST7464 Map 2

Old Green Tree ◀

12 Green St

This may be a small pub, but it is big in character. There are no noisy games machines or piped music to spoil the chatty, friendly atmosphere, and the three little oak-panelled rooms include a comfortable lounge on the left as you go in, its walls decorated with wartime aircraft pictures in winter and local artists' work during spring and summer, and a no smoking back bar; it can get pretty packed at peak times, and the big skylight lightens things up attractively. Lunchtime bar food includes soup (£3), popular smoked trout open sandwich, tasty salads or bangers and mash (£5), and daily specials such as home-made pâté, authentic spicy dishes, coq au vin, Italian lamb, and vegetarian curry (also £5). Well kept Bath SPA, RCH Pitchfork, Wickwar Brand Oak Bitter, and guests such as Cottage Southern Bitter, Hop Back Summer Lightning, and Oakhill Black Magic Stout on handpump, several malt whiskies, a nice little wine list with helpful notes and 12 wines by the glass, winter hot toddies, a proper pimms, and good coffee; chess, backgammon, shut the box, Jenga. The gents', though good, are down steep steps. No children.
(Recommended by Catherine Pitt, Roger Wain-Heapy, Mike Pugh, David Carr, the Didler, Simon and Amanda Southwell, Derek and Sylvia Stephenson, Dr and Mrs A K Clarke, Pete Baker, Alan J Morton, Phil and Sally Gorton, Jonathan Smith, M V Ward, Andrew and Catherine Gilham)

Free house ~ Licensees Nick Luke and Donna Murphy ~ Real ale ~ Bar food (lunchtime) ~ No credit cards ~ Jazz Sun, Celtic and folk Tues ~ Open 11-11; 12-10.30 Sun

Star ◀

The Paragon, junction with Guinea Lane

In quiet steep streets of undeniably handsome if well worn stone terraces, yet handy for the main shopping area, this old pub gives a strong sense of the past. It may have been modernised, but if so at least 50 years ago. Four (well, more like three and a half) small linked rooms are served from the single bar, separated by sombre panelling with glass inserts, and furnished with traditional leatherette wall benches and the like – even one hard bench that the regulars call Death Row. The lighting's dim, and not rudely interrupted by too much daylight (most of the windows were blocked in years ago). With no machines or music, chat's the thing here – or perhaps cribbage if you dare take on the adept locals, on the green baize tables in one of the back rooms. Particularly well kept Bass is tapped from the cask, and they have Abbey Bellringer, Batemans XXXB, Greene King Old Speckled Hen, and Thwaites Daniel's Hammer. Simple bar snacks include filled rolls (from £1.60; served throughout opening hours during the week), plus Friday and Saturday lunchtime hot dishes such as sausages and mash with a choice of horseradish, garlic or butter mashed potatoes or liver and bacon (£4.50), and minted lamb shank (£6.50), and Sunday lunchtime bar nibbles (quail eggs, chopped sausage, chicken wings and so forth). Shove-ha'penny, cribbage and dominoes, and Tuesday evening quiz. No children inside, coal fires, friendly service. *(Recommended by Dr and Mrs A K Clarke, Catherine Pitt, the Didler, Phil and Sally Gorton, Jonathan Smith, Pete Baker, Roger Wain-Heapy, Mr and Mrs S Carter, David Carr)*

Punch ~ Manager Terry Langley ~ Real ale ~ Bar food (See text) ~ (01225) 425072 ~ Open 12-2.30, 5.30-11; 12-11 Sat; 12-3, 7-10.30 Sun; closed evening 25 Dec

BLAGDON ST5059 Map 2

New Inn

Park Lane/Church Street, off A368

You can look down over fields to the wood-fringed Blagdon Lake and to the low hills beyond from seats at the back of this old-fashioned pub. Inside, the two interesting rooms have ancient beams decorated with gleaming horsebrasses and a few tankards, some comfortable antique settles – one with its armrests carved as dogs – as well as little plush armchairs, mate's chairs and so forth, and big logs burning in both stone inglenook fireplaces; one area is no smoking. Good bar food includes soup (£2.50), sandwiches (from £2.50), ploughman's or ham and eggs (£5.95), vegetarian lasagne (£6.15), daily specials such as chilli or chicken curry (£6.15), and steak and kidney or chicken and mushroom pie (£6.75), and Sunday roast; the main dining area is also no smoking. Well kept Butcombe and Wadworths IPA and 6X on handpump; piped music. *(Recommended by Ken Flawn, Roger and Jenny Huggins, Mr and Mrs B J P Edwards, Robert Huddleston)*

Free house ~ Licensee Pat McCann ~ Real ale ~ Bar food (not Mon) ~ (01761) 462473 ~ Children in restaurant but no babies ~ Open 11-2.30, 6.30-11; 12-3, 6.30-10.30 Sun; closed Mon

BRADLEY GREEN ST2538 Map 1
Malt Shovel

Pub signposted from A39 W of Bridgwater, near Cannington; though Bradley Green is shown on road maps, if you're booking the postal address is Blackmoor Lane, Cannington, BRIDGWATER, Somerset TA5 2NE; note that there is another different Malt Shovel on this main road, 3 miles nearer Bridgwater

Nicely tucked away in a remote hamlet, this pleasant, friendly pub has a beamed, homely main bar with window seats, some straightforward elm country chairs and sturdy modern winged high-backed settles around wooden tables, various boating photographs, and a black kettle standing on a giant fossil by the woodburning stove. There's also a little snug with white walls and black beams, a solid oak bar counter with a natural stone front, and red tiled floor. Tasty home-made bar food includes lunchtime sandwiches (£2.95) and ploughman's (from £4), as well as filled baked potatoes (from £4.50), steak and kidney pie (£6.50), daily specials such as home-made pâté or home-made soup (£2.50), deep-fried whitebait (£2.95), pasta and spinach mornay (£5.95), somerset pork or beef bourguignon (£6.50), breaded scampi (£7.50), scallops à la crème (£9.50), and steaks (from £9.50), and puddings like fruit tarts and pies, cheesecakes, and mousses. The restaurant and family room are no smoking. Well kept Butcombe Bitter, Exmoor Fox, and two guests from Cotleigh, Cottage or RCH on handpump, farm cider, and a fair choice of malt whiskies, and wines by the glass; sizeable skittle alley, dominoes, cribbage, and piped music. The family room opens on to the garden, where there are picnic-sets, a fishpond, and an aviary. No dogs inside. West of the pub, Blackmore Farm is a striking medieval building. *(Recommended by Ian Phillips, Maysie Thompson, Tom Evans, Kate and Peter Bird, Comus and Sarah Elliott, Brian and Anna Marsden)*

Free house ~ Licensees R and F Beverley & P and S Monger ~ Real ale ~ Bar food ~ Restaurant ~ (01278) 653432 ~ Children in restaurant and family room ~ Open 11.30-3, 6.30-11; 12-3, 7-10.30 Sun; evening opening 7 in winter; closed winter Sun evenings ~ Bedrooms: £26.50B/£38B

CASTLE CARY ST6332 Map 2
George 🛏

Market Place; just off A371 Shepton Mallet—Wincanton

The cosy beamed front bar in this thatched coaching inn has a massive black elm mantelbeam over the log fire that is said to be over 1,000 years old, as well as a bow window seat, a cushioned high-backed settle by the fire, and just six or seven tables; piped music. An inner no smoking bar, separated by a glazed partition from the inn's central reception area, has a couple of big landscapes, some pictures made from butterfly wings, and a similarly decorous but busy feel. Under the new licensees, bar food now includes filled baps or sandwiches (from £2.45), home-made soup (£2.80), filled baked potatoes (from £3.60), ploughman's (£4.95), home-made pâté (£3.50), fried chicken liver on a toasted crouton with a creamy red wine and mushroom sauce (£4.75), beetroot and citrus salad (£7.95), pork loin steak topped with onions, honey and grilled cheese (£8.45), chicken breast stuffed with blue cheese on pasta with a wild mushroom sauce (£8.65), steaks (from £8.85), and oven-roasted salmon with onion marmalade (£9.20); the restaurant is no smoking. Well kept Otter Ale and Wadworths 6X and a couple of guests such as Butcombe Bitter and Courage Directors on handpump, decent house wines with several by the glass, and a fair range of malt whiskies and other spirits. *(Recommended by Philip and June Caunt, Christopher and Mary Thomas, Simon and Laura Habbishow, Tony Gayfer, Dave Irving, KC, Dennis Jenkin, Michael and Ann Cole, M G Hart, David and Pauline Brenner)*

Old English Inns ~ Managers Len and Jayne Cartwright ~ Real ale ~ Bar food (12-2.30, 6-9.30) ~ (01963) 350761 ~ Children welcome ~ Open 10.30-11; 12-10.30 Sun ~ Bedrooms: £50B/£75B

CATCOTT ST3939 Map 1
Crown

Village signposted off A39 W of Street; at war memorial turn off northwards into Brook Lane and keep on

Once a cider house, this friendly pub is on a quiet country lane in a farming community. To the left of the main door is a pubby little room with built-in brocade-cushioned settles, a church pew and red leatherette stools around just four rustic pine tables, a tall black-painted brick fireplace with dried flowers and a large cauldron, and working horse plaques; around the corner is a small alcove with a really big pine table on its stripped stone floor. Most of the pub is taken up with the roomy, more straightforward dining area with lots of wheelback chairs around tables, and small 19th-c fashion plates on the cream walls – and it's obviously here that people come to enjoy the popular food. From the specials lists, there might be brie fritters with hot cherry sauce (£3.45), chicken goujons in breadcrumbs, sesame seeds, chilli and lemon and served with a pineapple and coriander salsa (£3.85), pork tenderloin with lime, coconut milk, and ginger (£8.45), cod supreme topped with a parsley, pine nut and parmesan crust, with watercress sauce (£8.75), fillet steak with brandy, cream and green peppercorn sauce (£12.95), and puddings such as baked white chocolate and black cherry cheesecake, plum and walnut crumble or lime, mascarpone and amaretti biscuit parfait (£2.95); from the menu, bar food includes sandwiches (from £1.70), soup (£2.10), filled baked potatoes (from £3.55), parsnip and tomato bake or home-made steak and kidney pie (£5.75), poached salmon with cream dill sauce (£7.95), steaks (from £9.25), and children's dishes (from £2.65). Well kept Butcombe Bitter and Smiles Best, and a guest such as Greene King Abbot or Shepherd Neame Spitfire on handpump or tapped from the cask, and piped old-fashioned pop music; fruit machine. The original part of the pub is white-painted stone with black shutters and is pretty with window boxes and tubs. Out behind are picnic-sets and a play area for children with wooden equipment. *(Recommended by Jenny and Chris Wilson, Comus and Sarah Elliott)*

Free house ~ Licensees C R D Johnston and D Lee ~ Real ale ~ Bar food (11.30-2, 6(7 Sun)-10) ~ Restaurant ~ (01278) 722288 ~ Children welcome ~ Open 11.30-2.30, 6-11; 12-3, 7-10.30 Sun; closed 25 Dec

CHURCHILL ST4560 Map 1
Crown

Skinners Lane; in village, turn off A368 at Nelson Arms

With up to eight real ales tapped from the cask, it is not surprising that this unspoilt little stone-built cottage is so popular. Changing regularly, there might be Bass, Church End Stout Coffin, Palmers IPA, and RCH Hewish IPA, P G Steam, and Old Slug Porter; country wines. The small and local stone-floored and cross-beamed room on the right has a wooden window seat, an unusually sturdy settle, and built-in wall benches; the left-hand room has a slate floor, and some steps past the big log fire in a big stone fireplace lead to more sitting space. Enjoyable bar food (they tell us prices and examples have not changed since last year) includes home-made soups like carrot and coriander or leek and potato (from £2.20), excellent rare beef sandwich (£2.50), ploughman's, chilli con carne, quiche or faggots (£3.95), and various casseroles (from £4.95); some of the meat comes from their own farm. They can be busy at weekends, especially in summer. There are garden tables on the front and a smallish but pretty back lawn with hill views; the Mendip Morris Men come in summer. Good walks nearby. *(Recommended by Mr and Mrs F J Parmenter, Tom Evans, Joy and Peter Heatherley, Ian Phillips, Jonathan Smith, Matt Britton, Alison Cameron, George Cowie, KC, Guy Vowles, the Didler, Jane and Graham Rooth, Paul Hopton)*

Free house ~ Licensee Tim Rogers ~ Real ale ~ Bar food (lunchtime) ~ No credit cards ~ (01934) 852995 ~ Children in eating area of bar ~ Open 12-11

CLAPTON-IN-GORDANO ST4773 Map 1
Black Horse

4 miles from M5 junction 19; A369 towards Portishead, then B3124 towards Clevedon; in N Weston opp school turn left signposted Clapton, then in village take second right, maybe signed Clevedon, Clapton Wick

In summer, the little flagstoned front garden here is exceptionally pretty, with a mass of flowers in tubs, hanging baskets and flowerbeds; there are some old rustic tables and benches, with more to one side of the car park and a secluded children's play area. Paths from the pub lead up Naish Hill or along to Cadbury Camp. Inside, the partly flagstoned and partly red-tiled main room has winged settles and built-in wall benches around narrow, dark wooden tables, window seats, a big log fire with stirrups and bits on the mantelbeam, and amusing cartoons and photographs of the pub. A window in an inner snug is still barred from the days when this room was the petty-sessions gaol; high-backed settles – one a marvellous carved and canopied creature, another with an art nouveau copper insert reading East, West, Hame's Best – lots of mugs hanging from its black beams, and plenty of little prints and photographs. There's also a simply furnished room just off the bar (where children can go), with high-backed corner settles and a gas fire; darts, dominoes, cribbage, shove-ha'penny, and piped music. Simple bar food includes filled baguettes such as bacon and brie (£3.95), ploughman's, and hot dishes like broccoli and cream cheese bake, chilli con carne or steak and kidney pie (from £4.40). Well kept Bass, Courage Best, Smiles Best, and Websters Green Label on handpump or tapped from the cask, and Thatcher's farm cider. *(Recommended by the Didler, Comus and Sarah Elliott, Tom Evans, Susan and Nigel Wilson, Matt Britton, Alison Cameron, June and Ken Brooks, A C and E Johnson, Kevin Blake, Colin and Janet Roe, Ian Phillips)*

Inntrepreneur ~ Tenant Nicholas Evans ~ Real ale ~ Bar food (not evenings, not Sun lunchtime) ~ No credit cards ~ (01272) 842105 ~ Children in family room ~ Live music Mon evening ~ Open 11-3, 6-11; 11-11 Fri and Sat; 12-3, 7-10.30 Sun

COMBE HAY ST7359 Map 2
Wheatsheaf

Village signposted from A367 or B3110 S of Bath

Particularly in good weather, this is a smashing place to be. There are three dovecotes built into the walls, tables on a spacious terraced lawn overlooking the lovely valley, church, and ancient manor stables, and award-winning flowers; plenty of good nearby walks, too. Inside, the pleasantly old-fashioned rooms have low ceilings, warm burgundy walls, brown-painted settles, pews and rustic tables, a very high-backed winged settle facing one big log fire, old sporting and other prints, and quite a few earthenware jugs. Popular bar food includes home-made soup (£3.50), ploughman's (from £5.25), glazed ham (£5.90), smoked chicken and ham terrine or home-made lasagne (£6.50), home-made vegetarian nut roast with madeira sauce, venison sausages and pork and wild mushroom sausages with an onion and cranberry sauce, home-made steak and kidney pie or sautéed tiger prawns in garlic butter and dill (all £8.50), and breast of wood pigeon and mushroom tossed in a madeira jus on a crisp vegetable rösti (£11.50); the restaurant is no smoking. Well kept Bath Gem, Courage Best and Greene King Old Speckled Hen tapped from the cask, several malt whiskies, and decent wines; shove-ha'penny, dominoes and cribbage. *(Recommended by Roger Wain-Heapy, E H and R F Warner, Dr and Mrs A K Clarke)*

Free house ~ Licensee Pete Wilkins ~ Real ale ~ Bar food (12-2, 6.15-9.30) ~ (01225)
833504 ~ Children welcome ~ Open 11-3, 6-11; 12-4, 7-10.30 Sun; closed 25 and 26
Dec and 1 Jan ~ Bedrooms: £50S/£75S

COMPTON MARTIN ST5457 Map 2
Ring o' Bells 🍺

A368 Bath—Weston

Although many people do come to this attractively placed pub to enjoy the good
food, drinkers are just as warmly welcomed by the friendly landlord and his staff,
and the beer is particularly well kept. The cosy, traditional front part of the bar has
rugs on the flagstones and inglenook seats right by the log fire, and up a step is a
spacious carpeted back part with largely stripped stone walls and pine tables.
Popular, reasonably priced bar food includes sandwiches (from £1.50; toasties from
£2.25; BLT in french bread £2.95), soup (£1.95), filled baked potatoes (from £2.75),
good omelettes (from £3.25; not Sundays), stilton mushrooms (£3.50), ploughman's
(from £3.25), ham and eggs (small £3.60, large £4.40), lasagne, mushroom, broccoli
and almond tagliatelle or beef in ale (£4.95-£5.25), generous mixed grill (£9.75),
daily specials like various fresh fish dishes (from £5.25), home-made pies or curries
(£5.50), somerset pork (£5.95), salmon en croûte (£6.50), and puddings (£2.25);
best to get here early to be sure of a seat. On handpump or tapped from the cask,
there might be Butcombe Bitter and Gold, Wadworths 6X and a weekly guest beer
from perhaps Bath, Shepherd Neame or Youngs; local ciders, and malt whiskies. The
public bar has darts, cribbage, dominoes, and shove-ha'penny; table skittles. The
family room is no smoking, and has blackboards and chalks, a Brio track, and a
rocking horse; they also have baby changing and nursing facilities, and the big
garden has swings, a slide, and a climbing frame. The pub is not far from Blagdon
Lake and Chew Valley Lake, and is overlooked by the Mendip Hills. *(Recommended
by Tom Evans, Nigel Long, David Carr, Comus and Sarah Elliott, Hugh Roberts, Michael
Doswell, Roger and Jenny Huggins)*

*Free house ~ Licensee Roger Owen ~ Real ale ~ Bar food (till 10pm Fri and Sat) ~
Restaurant ~ (01761) 221284 ~ Children in family room ~ Open 11.30-3(3.30 Sat),
6.30-11; 12-3.30, 7-10.30 Sun*

CRANMORE ST6643 Map 2
Strode Arms ★ 🍽 ♀

West Cranmore; signposted with pub off A361 Frome—Shepton Mallet

This old former farmhouse is run by people who care about their customers whether
they are regulars or visitors – and there are plenty of each. The rooms have charming
country furnishings, fresh flowers (and pretty dried ones), pot plants, a grandfather
clock on the flagstones, remarkable old locomotive engineering drawings and big
black and white steam train murals in a central lobby, good bird prints, newspapers
to read, and lovely log fires in handsome fireplaces. The same menu for the popular
food is used in both the bar and restaurant, though sandwiches (from £2.75),
ploughman's (from £4.75), and baked potatoes (£4.95) are only served in the bar.
Daily specials include smoked trout, prawn and spinach terrine (£4.75), cheese,
potato and onion pasties (£6.25), cottage pie (£6.85), fresh fish (from £8), sugar-
baked ham with parsley sauce (£8.25), and puddings such as lime and ginger crunch
flan, raspberry, pear and almond crumble or fresh strawberry roulade (from £3);
there's also soup (£3), scallops and bacon (£6.25), ham and eggs (£6.75), spaghetti
with a fresh tomato and basil sauce (£7.25), home-made pies (£7.50), smoked
haddock and cod fishcakes (£8.25), wild boar steak grilled with an apple and honey
crust (£8.75), and steaks (from £9.85). Half the restaurant and half the bar area are
no smoking; friendly service. Well kept Oakhill Best, Wadworths 6X and IPA, and a
guest from Hook Norton, Skinners or Wychwood on handpump, an interesting
choice of wines by the glass from a thoughtful menu, and lots more by the bottle,
and quite a few liqueurs and ports. The pub is an attractive sight in summer with its
neat stonework, cartwheels on the walls, pretty tubs and hanging baskets, and seats

under umbrellas on the front terrace; more seats in the back garden. On the first Tuesday of each month, there's a vintage car meeting, and the East Somerset Light Railway (which we hope is still open by the time this book is published) is not far away. *(Recommended by Tom Evans, Brian and Bett Cox, Lynn Sharpless, Bob Eardley, Gaynor Gregory, Ian Phillips, J F M and M West, Andy Sinden, Louise Harrington, Mr and Mrs Thomas, Phil and Sally Gorton, John Close, Alan and Paula McCully, Revd A Nunnerley, M G Hart, Mark and Heather Williamson, Peter Burton)*

Free house ~ Licensees Rodney and Dora Phelps ~ Real ale ~ Bar food (till 10pm Fri and Sat) ~ Restaurant ~ (01749) 880450 ~ Children in restaurant ~ Open 11.30-2.30, 6.30-11; 12-3, 7-10.30 Sun; closed Sun evening Oct-Mar

DOULTING ST6445 Map 2
Waggon & Horses ♀

Doulting Beacon, 2 miles N of Doulting itself; eastwards turn off A37 on Mendip ridge N of Shepton Mallet, just S of A367 junction; the pub is also signed from the A37 at the Beacon Hill crossroads and from the A361 at the Doulting and Cranmore crossroads

It's rather special that this attractive 18th-c inn holds some remarkable classical music and other musical events during the spring and autumn, that take place in a big raftered upper gallery reached by a flight of imposing external stone steps to one side of the building; there can also be few pubs where the piano is a carefully tuned Steinway grand. The rambling bar has studded red leatherette seats and other chairs, a homely mix of tables including antiques, and paintings and drawings everywhere. Two rooms are no smoking. Interesting daily specials might include moules marinières (small £4.50, large £8.50), cauliflower cheese (£6.90), hake steaks galician style, a delicate stew of monkfish, fennel and leeks or seafood kebabs (£9.20), roast wild duck with an orange and Grand Marnier sauce or poached salmon with a spinach, sorrel and tarragon sauce (£9.50), and pot-roasted wild goose in a vintage port sauce (£10.90). From the menu, there might be sandwiches (from £2), soup (small £3.20, large £4.90), spicy bean casserole or omelettes using their own free range eggs (£6.90), ham and eggs or lasagne (£6.90), steaks (from £10.50), chicken breast topped with ham, cheese and tomato (£10.90), and puddings such as steamed ginger and lemon pudding, crème brûlée or treacle tart (from £3.90). Well kept Ushers Best and Founders and seasonal ales on handpump, a small, carefully chosen wine list, cocktails, and friendly service; chess, dominoes, and skittle alley. The big walled garden (with summer barbecues) is lovely: elderly tables and chairs stand on informal terracing, with picnic-sets out on the grass, and perennials and flowering shrubs intersperse themselves in a pretty and pleasantly informal way. There's a wildlife pond, and a climber for children. Off to one side is a rough paddock with a horse (horses are one passion of Mr Cardona, who comes from Colombia and who has bred an Olympic horse, Sir Toby) and a goat called Dennis, and various fancy fowl, with pens further down holding many more in small breeding groups – there are some really quite remarkable birds among them, and the cluckings and crowings make a splendidly contented background to a sunny summer lunch. They often sell the eggs, too. *(Recommended by Mr and Mrs Thomas, Michael and Ann Cole, Susan and Nigel Wilson, MRSM)*

InnSpired ~ Lease Francisco Cardona ~ Real ale ~ Bar food ~ Restaurant ~ (01749) 880302 ~ Children allowed but must be well behaved and quiet ~ Classical concerts and some jazz ~ Open 11.30-2.30, 6-11; 12-3, 7-11 Sun; closed 25 Dec

DOWLISH WAKE ST3713 Map 1
New Inn

Village signposted from Kingstone – which is signposted from old A303 on E side of Ilminster, and from A3037 just S of Ilminster; keep on past church – pub at far end of village

New licensees again for this neat village pub, but happily it remains a friendly place with enjoyable food and good beer. The bar has dark beams, old-fashioned furnishings that include a mixture of chairs, high-backed settles, and attractive sturdy tables, and a woodburning stove in the stone inglenook fireplace. Bar food now includes home-made soup (£2.50), soft roes on toast (£2.95), sandwiches (from £2.95), pâté or stuffed mushrooms (£3.25), filled baked potatoes (from £3.50), whitebait (£3.95), ploughman's (from 4.65), ham and egg (£4.95), chilli (£5.50), mediterranean pasta bake (£5.95), fish bake (£6.95), duck a l'orange (£8.95), steaks (from £8.95), daily specials such as red pepper and mushroom lasagne or mignons of lamb (from £6.95), and puddings like home-made treacle tart, spotted dick or lemon brûlée (from £2.25). Well kept Butcombe Bitter, Fullers London Pride, and Wadworths 6X on handpump, a decent choice of whiskies, and Perry's cider. This comes from just down the road, and the thatched 16th-c stone cider mill is well worth a visit for its collection of wooden bygones and its liberal free tastings (you can buy the half-dozen different ciders in old-fashioned earthenware flagons as well as more modern containers; it's closed on Sunday afternoons). In a separate area they have darts, shove-ha'penny, dominoes, cribbage, bar billiards, table skittles as well as alley skittles. The family room is no smoking and looks out on the pleasant back garden which has flowerbeds and a children's climbing frame. There's a rustic bench, tubs of flowers and a sprawl of clematis in front. *(Recommended by Gaynor Gregory, G U Briggs, Revd A Nunnerley, Peter Salmon, Douglas Allen, Hugh Roberts, Richard and Jean Green, Mr and Mrs M Dalby, S G N Bennett, Dennis Jenkin, Theo, Anne and Jane Gaskin, Ian Phillips, Pat and Tony Martin, Alan and Paula McCully, Graham Brooks, Michael Doswell, Susan and Nigel Wilson)*

Free house ~ Licensees Rebecca Gray and Alan Toms ~ Real ale ~ Bar food ~ (01460) 52413 ~ Children in family room ~ Open 11-3, 6-11; 12-3, 7-10.30 Sun

EAST LYNG ST3328 Map 1
Rose & Crown
A361 about 4 miles W of Othery

Firmly run by Mr Mason, this busy pub has a pretty back garden (largely hedged off from the car park) with plenty of seats and lovely rural views. Inside, the open-plan beamed lounge bar has a winter log fire (or a big embroidered fire screen) in a stone fireplace, a corner cabinet of glass, china and silver, a court cabinet, a bow window seat by an oak drop-leaf table, copies of *Country Life*, and impressive large dried flower arrangements. Well liked bar food includes sandwiches (from £2), soup (£2.40), ploughman's (from £3.95), ham and egg (£4.50), omelettes (from £5), steaks (from £10), roast duckling with orange sauce (£12), puddings like home-made treacle tart or fruit crumble (£3), and daily specials such as mushroom and vegetable stroganoff, steak and Guinness casserole or pork chop with mustard sauce; the dining room is no smoking. Well kept Butcombe Bitter and Gold, and Hardy Royal Oak on handpump; skittle alley and piped music. *(Recommended by Brian and Bett Cox, Alan and Paula McCully, James Flory, Richard and Margaret Peers)*

Free house ~ Licensee Derek Mason ~ Real ale ~ Bar food ~ Restaurant ~ (01823) 698235 ~ Children in eating area of bar ~ Open 11-2.30, 6.30-11; 12-3, 7-10.30 Sun ~ Bedrooms: £30S/£50S

EAST WOODLANDS ST7944 Map 2
Horse & Groom ♀ ◀
Off A361/B3092 junction

Set on the edge of the Longleat estate, this is a small, civilised place. The pleasant little bar on the left has stripped pine pews and settles on dark flagstones, well kept Branscombe Vale Branoc, Butcombe Gold, Greene King IPA, and Wadworths 6X tapped from the cask, and an extensive wine list with several by the glass. The comfortable lounge has a relaxed atmosphere, an easy chair and settee around a coffee table, two small solid dining tables with chairs, and a big stone hearth with a small raised grate. Well liked bar food includes home-made soup (£2.75), sandwiches or baguettes (from £1.40), stir-fried duck breast with honey and ginger (£4), ploughman's (from £4.25), liver and bacon, ham with parsley sauce or stilton and asparagus tagliatelle (£6.10), oriental spring roll with noodles in black bean sauce, poached smoked haddock with curried potatoes and poached egg or roasted garlic hake (£6.50), noisette of lamb in rich red pepper sauce (£8.25), sirloin steak (£9.50), and puddings like chocolate marble cheesecake, fruit fool or orange and chocolate ginger crunch crème (from £3.40). The restaurant is no smoking. Cribbage, shove-ha'penny, and dominoes. There are picnic-sets in the nice front garden by five severely pollarded limes and attractive troughs and mini wheelbarrows filled with flowers; more seats behind the big no smoking dining conservatory. *(Recommended by Lyn and Geoff Hallchurch, Brian and Genie Smart, the Didler, MRSM)*

Free house ~ Licensees Rick Squire and Kathy Barrett ~ Real ale ~ Bar food (11.30-2, 6.30-9; not Sun evening or Mon) ~ Restaurant ~ (01373) 462802 ~ Children in restaurant ~ Open 11.30-2.30, 6.30-11; 12-3, 7-10.30 Sun; closed Mon lunchtime

EXFORD SS8538 Map 1
White Horse 🍺
B3224

The River Exe runs past this biggish, three-storey creepered place with its half-timbered top storey, and the attractive village is particularly pretty in summer. The more-or-less open-plan bar has windsor and other country kitchen chairs, a high-backed antique settle, scrubbed deal tables, hunting prints, photographs above the stripped pine dado, and a good winter log fire. Well kept Exmoor, Ale, Gold and Stag, Greene King Old Speckled Hen, and Marstons Pedigree on handpump, and over 80 malt whiskies. Enjoyable bar food (with prices unchanged since last year) includes soup (£1.95), sandwiches (from £1.95; baguettes from £2.95), ploughman's (from £3.75), sausage, egg, beans, and chips (£4.55), cauliflower cheese (£5.45), home-made lasagne (£5.75), home-made steak and kidney pie (£5.95), daily specials such as game pie (with whatever the chef has, £5.95), gammon and pineapple (£6.25), half a roast chicken (£7.45), and whole lemon sole (£9.25), puddings like gooseberry pie or bread and butter pudding (£2.75), and Sunday carvery (£5.75); friendly service. The restaurant and eating area of the bar are no smoking; fruit machine, TV, cribbage, dominoes, and winter darts. *(Recommended by Trevor and Lynda Smith, Drs E J C Parker, Jane and Adrian Tierney-Jones, Peter and Audrey Dowsett)*

Free house ~ Licensees Peter and Linda Hendrie ~ Bar food (11.30-2.30, 6-9.30) ~ Restaurant ~ (01643) 831229 ~ Children welcome ~ Open 11-11 ~ Bedrooms: £35B/£60B

FAULKLAND ST7354 Map 2
Tuckers Grave £
A366 E of village

Readers are always delighted to return to this warmly friendly basic cider house after many years, and find that absolutely nothing has changed. It still claims the title of Smallest Pub in the *Guide*, and the flagstoned entry opens into a teeny unspoilt room with casks of well kept Bass and Butcombe Bitter on tap and Thatcher's Cheddar Valley cider in an alcove on the left. Two old cream-painted high-backed settles face each other across a single table on the right, and a side room has shove-ha'penny. There's a skittle alley and tables and chairs on the back lawn, as well as winter fires and maybe newspapers to read. Food is limited to sandwiches and ploughman's at lunchtime. There's an attractive back garden. *(Recommended by Pete Baker, Dr M E Wilson, the Didler, Phil and Sally Gorton, Peter Winter-Hart, R T and J C Moggridge, R Huggins, D Irving, E McCall, T McLean, David Carr)*

Free house ~ Licensees Ivan and Glenda Swift ~ Real ale ~ Bar food ~ No credit cards ~ (01373) 834230 ~ Children in family room ~ Open 11-3, 6-11; 12-3, 7-11 Sun

---

People named as recommenders after the main entries have told us that the pub should be included. But they have not written the report – we have, after anonymous on-the-spot inspection.

FRESHFORD ST7960 Map 2
Inn at Freshford
Village signposted off B3108 – OS Sheet 172 map reference 790600

This is a lovely spot by the River Frome and there are seats in the pretty garden, as well as walks to the Kennet & Avon Canal. Inside is comfortably modernised, and the bar has plenty of atmosphere, interesting decorations, and a particularly friendly, helpful landlord. Well kept Bass, Courage Best, Marstons Pedigree, and Wadworths 6X on handpump, and reliable, tasty bar food that might include home-made soup (£2.95), sandwiches (from £3.25), ploughman's (from £4.95), thai-style vegetable curry or ratatouille (from £5.95), steak in ale pie (£6.25), half a dozen fresh fish specials (from £7.95), and daily specials such as duck breast with Cointreau and orange sauce, shoulder of lamb with a mint and cranberry sauce, and guinea fowl supreme with cider and apple sauce (from £7.95). The restaurant is no smoking. *(Recommended by Susan and Nigel Wilson, R T and J C Moggridge, Meg and Colin Hamilton, Michael Doswell, Roger and Jenny Huggins, W F C Phillips)*

Latona Leisure ~ Manager John Williams ~ Real ale ~ Bar food (12-2, 6-9) ~ Restaurant ~ (01225) 722250 ~ Children welcome ~ Open 11-3, 6-11; 12-3, 7-10.30 Sun

GLASTONBURY ST5039 Map 2
Who'd A Thought It 🛏
Northload Street (off A39/B3151 roundabout)

Attractively reworked a few years ago, this makes nice use of mellow reclaimed brick, relaid flagstones and pine panelling. Above an old-fashioned range are hung fly-fishing rods and a gun, and the walls (and even the ceiling of the no smoking eating area) are profusely decorated with blue and white china, lots of photographs including aerial ones of old Glastonbury, and bygones from a shelf of earthenware flagons and another of old bottles to venerable enamel advertising signs. There are several linked areas, friendly, light and airy, with black beams and joists, coal fires, and a mix of furnishings from built-in pews to stripped country tables and chairs; one room shows a well uncovered in the 1980s. A good range of freshly prepared and nicely presented honest food includes soup (£2.65), sandwiches (from £2.95), filled baguettes (from £3.25), goats cheese on roasted vegetables (£3.75/£5.95), beef or spinach and stilton lasagne (£6.25), pie and roast of the day (£6.50), fried tuna or swordfish (£6.95) and puddings (£2.95). Well kept Palmers IPA, Gold and 2000 on handpump, good value wines, pleasant staff and daily papers. The lavatories are worth a look (the gents' has all you don't need to know, from what to do in a gas attack to a history of England from the Zulu Wars to World War II, the ladies' is more Beryl Cook). The outside of the pub is attractive. *(Recommended by David Carr, A J Smith, David and Audrey Sprague, C Woodward, Brian and Anna Marsden)*

Palmers ~ Tenant David Morgan ~ Real ale ~ Bar food (12-2, 6-10; 12-2.30, 6-9.30 Sun) ~ (01458) 834460 ~ Children in the well room ~ Open 11-2.30, 5-11(11-11 Fri, Sat); 12-2.30, 6-10.30 Sun; closed 25 Dec evening ~ Bedrooms: £40B/£58B

HALLATROW ST6357 Map 2
Old Station
Wells Road (A39, close to junction with A37 S of Bristol)

The forest of clutter hanging from the ceiling in this popular pub includes anything from sombreros and peaked caps to kites, from flags to fishnets, from ceramic charcoal stoves to sailing boats, from parasols to post boxes. Entertaining nonsenses abound, like the kilted dummy girl and the wall of car grills. The rather handsome island bar counter has well kept Ash Vine Challenger, Bass, Moles Best, Otter and Wickwar Brand Oak on handpump, and a mix of furnishings includes a sofa, high chairs around big cask tables, and small settles and dining or library chairs around more orthodox tables. The new landlord felt he was too busy to give us any information on the several times we contacted him, but food has included home-made soup, home-made pâté, deep-fried prawn and crab fritters, beef or vegetable curry, steak and kidney pie or lasagne, and rack of lamb with a rosemary and redcurrant sauce. Piped radio, fruit machine. Behind is a no smoking railway carriage restaurant (photographs in the bar show the hair-raising difficulty of getting it here). The garden alongside has picnic-sets under cocktail parasols, and spreads back to a well equipped play area, with a recreation ground beyond. More reports on the new regime, please. (Recommended by Alan and Paula McCully, Susan and Nigel Wilson, Comus and Sarah Elliott, Roger and Jenny Huggins, Cliff Blakemore, Julia and Richard Tredgett, David Whiteley)

Brains ~ Manager Gordon Beck ~ Real ale ~ Bar food ~ (01761) 452228 ~ Children in eating area of bar and restaurant ~ Open 11-3, 5(6 Sat)-11; 12-3, 7-10.30 Sun ~ Bedrooms: £31B/£45B

HUISH EPISCOPI ST4326 Map 1
Rose & Crown
A372 E of Langport

One reader was delighted to arrive here on a Saturday lunchtime to find what seemed to be a local farmers' market in the front room where you could nose around and buy things. The atmosphere and character remain determinedly unpretentious and welcoming, and Mrs Pittard's family have been here for well over 130 years. There's no bar as such – to get a drink (prices are very low), you just walk into the central flagstoned still room and choose from the casks of well kept Teignworthy Reel Ale and a couple of local guest beers such as Branscombe Vale Summa That, Butcombe Bitter, Smiles Bitter or several farm ciders (and local cider brandy). This servery is the only thoroughfare between the casual little front parlours with their unusual pointed-arch windows; genuinely friendly locals. Food is home-made, simple and cheap: generously filled sandwiches (from £1.80), broccoli and stilton or tomato and lentil soup (£2.60), good filled baked potatoes (from £2.60), ploughman's (£3.80), spinach lasagne or cottage pie (£5.75), pork, apple and cider cobbler, spicy chicken and vegetable pie or steak in ale pie (all £5.95), and puddings like home-made apple pie or sherry trifle; good helpful service. Shove-ha'penny, dominoes and cribbage, and a much more orthodox big back extension family room has pool, darts, fruit machine, and juke box; skittle alley and popular quiz nights. They hope to have a no smoking room soon. There are tables in a garden outside, and a second enclosed garden with a children's play area. George the dog will welcome a bitch but can't abide other dogs, though Bonny the welsh collie is not so fussy. The local folk singers visit regularly, and on some summer weekends you might find the pub's cricket team playing out here (who always welcome a challenge); good nearby walks, and the site of the Battle of Langport (1645) is close by. (Recommended by Ian and Joan Blackwell, Andrew and Catherine Gilham, Ian Phillips, C J Mullan, Stephen, Julie and Hayley Brown, Pete Baker, Phil and Sally Gorton, Kevin Thorpe, Theo, Anne and Jane Gaskin, Veronica Brown, the Didler)

Free house ~ Licensee Mrs Eileen Pittard ~ Real ale ~ Bar food (12-2, 5.30-8; sandwiches throughout opening hours) ~ No credit cards ~ (01458) 250494 ~ Children welcome ~ Open 11.30-2.30, 5.30-11; 11.30-11 Fri and Sat; 12-10.30 Sun

KINGSDON ST5126 Map 2
Kingsdon Inn
At Podimore roundabout junction of A303, A372 and A37 take A372, then turn right on to B3151, right into village, and right again opposite Post Office

After (or before) a visit to nearby Lytes Cary (National Trust) or the Fleet Air Arm Museum, this pretty little thatched cottage is a popular place for lunch. It's bustling and friendly with three charmingly decorated, low-ceilinged rooms, and on the right are some very nice old stripped pine tables with attractive cushioned farmhouse chairs, more seats in what was a small inglenook fireplace, a few low sagging beams, and an open woodburning stove with colourful dried and artificial fruits and flowers on the overmantel; down three steps through balustrading to a light, airy room with cushions on stripped pine built-in wall seats, curtains matching the scatter cushions, more stripped pine tables, and a winter open fire. Another similarly decorated room has more tables and another fireplace. At lunchtime, good, reasonably priced food includes home-made soup (£2.90), deep-fried whitebait or ploughman's (£4.20), grilled goats cheese salad with walnut dressing (£4.40), leek, stilton and walnut pie or lambs liver, bacon and onions (£5.50), and chicken breast in a cider and cream sauce or haddock and prawn mornay (£5.90), with evening dishes like crab and prawn mornay (£4.80), smoked duck and orange salad (£5.20), spicy singapore noodles (£7.80), wild rabbit in dijon mustard sauce (£8.90), pork tenderloin with apricots and almonds (£9.90), roast rack of lamb with port and redcurrant sauce (£11.90), monkfish in a tomato, herb and garlic sauce (£12.90), fillet steak with pepper sauce (£13.90), and puddings such as sticky ginger pudding with ginger ice cream or whisky and coffee pavlova (£3.30); two dining areas are no smoking. Well kept Cotleigh Barn Owl, Fullers London Pride, Otter Bitter, and a guest from Butcombe or Cottage on handpump, decent wines, and 20 malt whiskies. Picnic-sets on the grass. *(Recommended by Richard and Jean Green, Peter and Audrey Dowsett, Pat and Robert Watt, Ian Phillips, Stephen Brocklebank, Martin and Karen Wake, Sheila and Phil Stubbs, Brian and Anna Marsden)*

Free house ~ Licensees Leslie and Anna-Marie Hood ~ Real ale ~ Bar food (till 10) ~ Restaurant ~ (01935) 840543 ~ Well behaved children away from main bar; under 12s to leave by 8pm ~ Open 11.30-3, 6-11; 12-3, 7-10.30 Sun

LANGLEY MARSH ST0729 Map 1
Three Horseshoes ◖

Village signposted off B3227 from Wiveliscombe

This red sandstone country pub is tucked away in the Somerset hills. It has a back bar with low modern settles and polished wooden tables, dark red wallpaper, planes hanging from the ceiling, banknotes papering the wall behind the bar counter, a piano, and a local stone fireplace. Well kept Fullers London Pride, Palmers IPA, and a guest such as Harveys Best or Ridleys ESX Best tapped from the cask, and farm cider. Genuinely home-made, good value food includes filled rolls (from £2.25), soup (£2.50), pizzas (from £3.95; can take away as well), chilli and chick pea hotpot (£3.95), lamb in Pernod (£5.25), good steak and kidney pie (£5.50), and daily specials such as aduki bean and vegetable stew (£3.95), chilli tacos (£5.50), pheasant breasts cooked in cider and cream (£6.25), and cod fillet in cheese and wine sauce (£7.25); no chips or fried food and most vegetables come from the garden. The no smoking dining area has antique settles and tables and benches, and the lively front room has sensibly placed shove-ha'penny, table skittles, darts, dominoes, and cribbage; separate skittle alley, and piped music. You can sit on rustic seats on the verandah or in the sloping back garden, with a fully equipped children's play area; in fine weather there are usually vintage cars outside. By the time this book is published, a barn at the back of the pub will have been converted into a self-catering cottage (no children or dogs). More reports please. *(Recommended by the Didler, Mr and Mrs R Woodman)*

Free house ~ Licensee John Hopkins ~ Real ale ~ Bar food (not winter Mon) ~ Restaurant ~ (01984) 623763 ~ Well behaved children away from bar area ~ Occasional folk music ~ Open 12-2.30, 7-11(10.30 Sun); closed winter Mon

LUXBOROUGH SS9837 Map 1
Royal Oak ★ ⑪ ◖ 🛏

Kingsbridge; S of Dunster on minor roads into Brendon Hills – OS Sheet 181 map reference 983378

Since taking over, Mr and Mrs Barrow have put a lot of hard work and enthusiasm into this country inn. They've made a lot of improvements, especially to the bedrooms, and readers have been quick to tell us how much they have enjoyed staying here – it's ideal for exploring Exmoor. There's always a friendly welcome, and the atmospheric bar rooms have beams and inglenooks, good log fires, flagstones in the front public bar, a fishing theme in one room, a real medley of furniture, and a thriving atmosphere; two characterful dining rooms (one is no smoking). Well kept real ales such as Bass, Cotleigh Tawny, Exmoor Gold, Palmers 200, a guest beer, and a beer named for the pub called Acorn on handpump, local farm cider, several malt whiskies, and a thoughtful wine list. Highly enjoyable bar food includes home-made soup (£2.95), sandwiches (from £3.50), thai salmon and crab fishcakes with a tomato and coriander salsa (£5.95), chargrilled vegetables with lemon couscous and yellow pepper pesto or chargrilled breast of chicken on spring greens tossed with smoked bacon with a tomato and mustard seed dressing (£9.50), steaks (from £9.50), honey and soy glazed duck with stir-fried noodles and plum sauce (£10.25), charred fillet of halibut with a Gentleman's Relish butter (£12.75), and puddings (£3.25); really good breakfasts. Pool, dominoes, cribbage, and shove-ha'penny – no machines or music. Tables outside, and lots of good surrounding walks. *(Recommended by Lynn Sharpless, Bob Eardley, Lorna and Howard Lambert, the Ransley family, Julia and Richard Tredgett, Geoff and Linda Dibble, James Flory, Mr and Mrs R Hill, Nigel Woolliscroft, R M Corlett, Phil and Heidi Cook, Mr and Mrs E W Howells, F W Cane, Kevin Martin, D A Price, Neil Rose, Robert Connor, Matt Britton, Alison Cameron, Hugh Roberts, Julie Gilbert, A and J Evans, the Didler, Jenny Grimshaw, Peter and Audrey Dowsett)*

Free house ~ Licensee Cecil Barrow ~ Real ale ~ Bar food ~ Restaurant ~ (01984) 640319 ~ Children in eating area of bar and restaurant ~ Folk every 2nd Fri evening ~ Open 11-2.30, 6-11; 12-2.30, 7-11 Sun ~ Bedrooms: £45B/£65B

MELLS ST7249 Map 2

Talbot 🍴 🍷 🛏

W of Frome; off A362 W of Buckland Dinham, or A361 via Nunney and Whatley

Although much emphasis is placed on the good, imaginative food in this rather smart place, there is a 15th-c tithe barn with a high beamed ceiling which locals head for to enjoy the well kept Butcombe and Fullers London Pride tapped from the cask. Taken in the restaurant, the lunchtime food might include home-made soup (£3.95), ham and eggs (£7.65), hot ratatouille and cheese flan, various omelettes, ploughman's, griddled bratwurst sausages with garlic mash and onion gravy or baked mushrooms stuffed with stilton and walnuts (all £7.50), and daily specials like chicken curry (£7.95), sweet and sour stir-fried duck (£8.25), and beef casserole (£8.95); evening dishes such as steamed asparagus in puff pastry (£5.50), grilled scallops (£7.25), fillet of pork stuffed with leek and stilton (£13.50), breast and confit leg of Gressingham duck marinated in ginger, plum sauce and lime (£13.95), lots of fresh daily delivered fish (from around £9.95), and puddings (£4.25); they also offer a two-course menu (£9.95). The licensee is friendly and helpful, and the attractive main room has stripped pews, mate's and wheelback chairs, fresh flowers and candles in bottles on the mix of tables, and sporting and riding pictures on the walls, which are partly stripped above a broad panelled dado, and partly rough terracotta-colour. A small corridor leads to a nice little room with an open fire; piped music, table skittles, TV, cribbage and dominoes. Sunday roast, and nice breakfasts; good wines, and well chosen staff. There are seats in the cobbled courtyard. The village was purchased by the Horner family of the 'Little Jack Horner' nursery rhyme and the direct descendants still live in the manor house next door. The inn is surrounded by lovely countryside and good walks. *(Recommended by Jane and Graham Rooth, S G N Bennett, Kevin Flack, Richard Fendick, Susan and Nigel Wilson, Philip Pedley, John Coatsworth, Geoff and Brigid Smithers, Chris and Liane Miller, Roger Wain-Heapy, S H Godsell)*

Free house ~ Licensee Roger Stanley Elliott ~ Real ale ~ Bar food ~ Restaurant ~ (01373) 812254 ~ Children welcome ~ Open 12-2.30(3 Sat), 6.30-11; 12-3, 7-10.30 Sun; closed evening 25 Dec ~ Bedrooms: £45B/£75B

People don't usually tip bar staff (different in a really smart hotel, say). If you want to thank them – for dealing with a really large party say, or special friendliness – offer them a drink.

MONKSILVER ST0737 Map 1
Notley Arms ★ ⑩
B3188

As popular as ever, this bustling, friendly pub does tend to fill up quickly with customers keen to enjoy the good, reasonably priced food – and in proper pub fashion, they don't take reservations, so you do have to get there pretty promptly. The beamed and L-shaped bar has small settles and kitchen chairs around the plain country wooden and candlelit tables, original paintings on the black-timbered white walls, fresh flowers, a couple of woodburning stoves, and maybe a pair of cats. Bar food includes sandwiches (from £2.75), home-made soup (£2.75), very good ploughman's (from £3.95), home-made tagliatelle with ham, mushrooms, cream and parmesan cheese (£4.75), warm stilton flan with balsamic pear (£5.50), fresh asparagus and parmesan feuilletté or bacon, leek and cider pudding (£5.75), beef in ale pie (£7.75), fresh cod fillet with shrimp butter (£8.25), sirloin steak (£8.95), puddings such as strawberry cheesecake, brown bread ice cream or banana and pecan nut cake with toffee sauce (from £2.75), and winter roast Sunday lunch; very good cheerful staff. Well kept Exmoor Ale, Smiles Best, Wadworths 6X, and maybe Youngs Special on handpump, and country wines; cribbage, dominoes, chess, Scrabble, trivia, table tennis (in alley), and alley skittles. Families are well looked after, with colouring books and toys in the bright no smoking little family room. There are more toys outside in the immaculate garden, running down to a swift clear stream. *(Recommended by Mr and Mrs J M Lefeaux, Christine and Neil Townend, Richard Rand, John Bramley, Don and Thelma Beeson, W H and E Thomas, John Close, Pat and Tony Martin, M G Hart, David Biggins, W W Burke, Dr David Cockburn, J Roy Smylie, Kevin Flack, Mr and Mrs Thomas, the Didler, Peter and Audrey Dowsett)*

Inn Partnership (Nomura) ~ Lease Alistair and Sarah Cade ~ Real ale ~ Bar food (no food for 2 wks end Jan-beg Feb) ~ (01984) 656217 ~ Children in family room ~ Open 11.30-2.30, 6.30-11; 12-2.30, 7-11(10.30 in winter) Sun; closed 25 Dec

NORTH CURRY ST3225 Map 1
Bird in Hand
Queens Square; off A378 (or A358) E of Taunton

Liked by locals and visitors, the busy but cosy main bar here has pews, settles, benches, and old yew tables on the flagstones, and original beams and timbers; log fires in inglenook fireplaces. Bar food includes baked mushrooms stuffed with crab and prawns (£4.95), moules marinières (£5.25), baked aubergine, courgette and peppers in a pesto sauce on pasta (£6.75), venison steak in redcurrant, orange and port sauce or halibut in orange, Cointreau and dill sauce (£10.95), rack of lamb with red wine and mint sauce (£11.95), and home-made puddings such as crème brûlée, sticky toffee pudding or dark and white chocolate mousse (£3.75); roast Sunday lunch. More formal dining is available in the separate restaurant area with conservatory. Well kept Badger Tanglefoot, and Otter Ale with perhaps Exmoor Ale or Hop Back Summer Lightning on handpump, and Rich's farm cider; piped music. Summer barbecues on the terrace. *(Recommended by Ian Phillips, J Davidson, C F D Moore, Andrew and Catherine Gilham, James Flory)*

Free house ~ Licensee James Mogg ~ Real ale ~ Bar food (not Mon) ~ Restaurant ~ (01823) 490248 ~ Children welcome ~ Open 12-2.30(5.30 Fri), 7-11; 12-4, 7-11(10.30) Sat; closed Mon lunchtime

NORTON ST PHILIP ST7755 Map 2
George ★ 🛏
A366

It is worth visiting this exceptional building to take in the fine surroundings of a place that has been offering hospitality to locals and travellers for over 700 years. The central Norton Room, which was the original bar, has really heavy beams, an oak panelled settle and solid dining chairs on the narrow strip wooden floor, a variety of 18th-c pictures, an open fire in the handsome stone fireplace, and a low wooden bar counter. Well kept Wadworths IPA, 6X, and a guest on handpump, decent wines with a good choice by the glass, and pleasant service. As you enter the building, there's a room on the right with high dark beams, squared dark half-panelling, a broad carved stone fireplace with an old iron fireback and pewter plates on the mantelpiece, a big mullioned window with leaded lights, and a round oak 17th-c table reputed to have been used by the Duke of Monmouth who stayed here before the Battle of Sedgemoor – after their defeat, his men were imprisoned in what is now the Monmouth Bar. The Charterhouse Bar is mostly used by those enjoying a drink before a meal: a wonderful pitched ceiling with trusses and timbering, heraldic shields and standards, jousting lances, and swords on the walls, a carved oak mirror above the fine old stone fireplace, high backed cushioned heraldic-fabric dining chairs on the big rug over the wood plank floor, an oak dresser with some pewter, and heavy brocaded curtains in mullioned windows. Lunchtime bar food includes sandwiches, home-made soup (£3.95), mushroom and stilton pepper pot (£4.45), cumberland sausage (£6.95), steak in ale pie or vegetable roulade (£7.95), chicken breast in a coarse mustard sauce (£8.95), and fresh local trout topped with lemon butter (£10.45); in the evening, there might be mussels in white wine, cream and garlic sauce or honey-glazed wood pigeon (£5.95), stuffed peppers (£7.95), salmon and prawn fishcakes on a tarragon sauce (£9.95), duck breast on a wild berry sauce (£10.45), steaks (from £10.95), and medallions of pork tenderloin with a pear and shallot sauce (£11.95). The no smoking dining room – a restored barn with original oak ceiling beams, a pleasant if haphazard mix of early 19th-c portraits and hunting prints, and the same mix of vaguely old-looking furnishings – has a good relaxing, chatty atmosphere. The bedrooms are very atmospheric and comfortable – some reached by an external Norman stone stair-turret, and some across the cobbled and flagstoned courtyard and up into a fine half-timbered upper gallery (where there's a lovely 18th-c carved oak settle). A stroll over the meadow behind the pub (past the picnic-sets on the narrow grass pub garden) leads to an attractive churchyard around the medieval church whose bells struck Pepys (here on 12 June 1668) as 'mighty tuneable'. *(Recommended by the Didler, Jane and Graham Rooth, R Huggins, D Irving, E McCall, T McLean, Ann and Colin Hunt, David Carr, Hugh Roberts, John Robertson, Dave Braisted)*

Wadworths ~ Managers David and Tania Satchel ~ Real ale ~ Bar food (12-2.30, 7-9.30) ~ Restaurant ~ (01373) 834224 ~ Children in restaurant ~ Open 11-2.30, 5.30-11; 11-11 Sat; 12-3, 6.30-10.30 Sun ~ Bedrooms: /£80B

PITNEY ST4428 Map 1

Halfway House 🍺

Just off B3153 W of Somerton

A fine range of up to 10 real ales, with six regulars tapped from the cask, are kept in this friendly, old-fashioned pub: Butcombe Bitter, Cotleigh Tawny, Hop Back Summer Lightning, and Teignworthy Reel Ale, with guests such as Archers Golden, Hop Back Crop Circle, and RCH Pitchfork. They also have 20 or so bottled beers from Belgium and other countries, Wilkins's farm cider, and quite a few malt whiskies. There's a bustling, chatty atmosphere and a fine mix of customers, and the three rooms all have good log fires, and a homely feel underlined by a profusion of books, maps and newspapers; dominoes, cards and chess. Good simple filling food includes sandwiches (from £2.25; the smoked salmon and the turkey with walnut seasoning are very tasty), soup (£2.50), filled baked potatoes (from £2.95), and a fine ploughman's with home-made pickle (from £3.95). In the evening they do about half a dozen home-made curries (from £7.50). There are tables outside. *(Recommended by Andrew and Catherine Gilham, Pat and Tony Martin, James Flory, R J Walden, the Didler, Ian Phillips, Peter Winter-Hart, Theo, Anne and Jane Gaskin, Jane and Adrian Tierney-Jones, Hugh Roberts)*

Free house ~ Licensees Julian and Judy Lichfield ~ Real ale ~ Bar food (not Sun) ~ (01458) 252513 ~ Well behaved children welcome ~ Open 11.30-3, 5.30-11; 12-3.30, 7-10.30 Sun

ROWBERROW ST4558 Map 1
Swan
Village signposted off A38 ¼ mile S of junction with A368

In a quiet village with nice surrounding walks, this spacious olde-worlde pub has low beams, some stripped stone, warm red décor, comic hunting and political prints, an ancient longcase clock, and a good chatty atmosphere; huge log fires, darts, table skittles, and shove-ha'penny. Enjoyable, freshly cooked food at lunchtime includes toasties (£3.95), macaroni cheese (£4.05), faggots and mash (£4.25), bacon and mushroom omelette (£4.45), minted lamb chops (£5.25), chilli (£5.65), and sugar-glazed ham in parsley sauce (£5.75); in the evening, there might be smoked haddock and salmon fishcakes, braised lamb shank or trout in Pernod (£8.95), and venison steak in port, stilton and walnut sauce, stuffed lemon sole with prawns and cream cheese or duck, bacon, brandy and orange pie (all £9.95). Well kept Bass, Butcombe Bitter and Gold, and a guest beer on handpump, and Thatcher's cider; careful well managed service. There are picnic-sets by a pond in the attractive garden, and a tethering post for horses. No children inside. *(Recommended by Hugh Roberts, Mr and Mrs F J Parmenter, Comus and Sarah Elliott, Ken Flawn, MRSM)*

Butcombe ~ Managers Elaine and Robert Flaxman ~ Real ale ~ Bar food (not Sun evening in winter) ~ (01934) 852371 ~ Open 12-3, 6-11; 12-3, 7-10.30 Sun

RUDGE ST8251 Map 2
Full Moon 🍴 🍺
Off A36 Bath—Warminster

There are fine views from this unspoilt 17th-c inn across the valley to Salisbury Plain and Westbury White Horse. Inside, there's a lot of character and a gently upmarket atmosphere, and the two rooms on the right have low white ceilings with a few black beams, a built-in settle by the bar, wheelbacks and slatback chairs around cast-iron framed tables, a woodburning stove in an inglenook fireplace with riding boots on the mantelbeam, and original shutters by the cushioned window seats. The flagstoned tap room has old stripped pine tables, there's a small private no smoking dining room with polished furniture and a skittle alley, and a formal back no smoking restaurant that looks out over the pretty gardens (plenty of seats); shove-ha'penny and cribbage. This is very much an old-style local at lunchtime and early evening, but later on and at weekends, the emphasis is on the very good food: open sandwiches, freshly made soup with their own breads (£3.50), pear, penne and walnut salad with raspberry vinaigrette (£4.50), red onion tart (£4.95), breast of lightly smoked duck with winter fruit chutney (£5.25), aubergine and wild mushroom gateau with a rich pepper coulis (£8.95), steaks (from £9.50), breast of chicken with a lime and coriander dressing and sweet pepper compote (£9.75), tenderloin of pork with fresh sage on caramelised red onions with a mild mustard sauce (£11.50), tuna with pesto and balsamic vinegar (£12.95), and a medley of seafood on spinach tagliatelle or shoulder of slowly braised lamb (£13.95). Two-course Sunday lunchtime carvery (£9.95). Well kept Bass, Butcombe Bitter, and a beer called Moonshine named for the pub on handpump, local ciders, and several malt whiskies. More reports please. *(Recommended by Peter D B Harding, Steve Whalley, M G Hart, WHBM)*

Free house ~ Licensees Chris and Patrick Gifford ~ Real ale ~ Bar food ~ Restaurant ~ (01373) 830936 ~ Children in restaurant lunchtime and early evening ~ Open 12-11; 12-11 Sat; 12-10.30 Sun ~ Bedrooms: £45B/£60B

SHEPTON MONTAGUE ST6731 Map 2
Montague Inn 🍴 🍷 🛏
Village signposted just off A359 Bruton—Castle Cary

Somerset Dining Pub of the Year

The new landlady has made quite an impression on this country pub. The rooms are simply but tastefully furnished with stripped wooden tables, kitchen chairs and a log fire in the attractive inglenook fireplace, the no smoking candlelit restaurant has linen tablecloths, and the food under the new chef is very good indeed. Using the best local produce, there might be home-made soup (£4), sandwiches (from £4), filled baguettes (from £5), warm rigotte cheese with olive oil and spices on a cool orange salad (£5), ploughman's, glazed vegetarian onion quiche or a plate of antipasti (all £6), Baltimore crabcake (£7), mille feuille of mediterranean vegetables or steamed somerset belly of pork (£11), seafood mixed grill, stuffed corn-fed chicken breast or local lamb noisettes on local greens, topped with a light blue vinney soufflé and apple cider jus (all £14), and home-made puddings such as fruit crumbles or crêpes, chocolate marquise or panacotta with marinated baby figs (all £4.50); generous and delicious breakfasts, and particularly good, cheerful service. Well kept Butcombe Bitter and Greene King IPA on handpump, and fine wines. The pretty back garden and terrace have good views. More reports please. *(Recommended by Richard and Jean Green, Martin and Karen Wake, John Robertson)*

Free house ~ Licensee Pat Elcock ~ Bar food ~ Restaurant ~ (01749) 813213 ~ Children in family room ~ Open 12-2.30, 6.30-11; 12-2.30, 7-10.30 Sun; closed winter Mon ~ Bedrooms: /£70B

SOUTH STOKE ST7461 Map 2
Pack Horse

Village signposted opposite the Cross Keys off B3110, leaving Bath southwards – just before end of speed limit

Now into its sixth century, this former priory and three-gabled stone house has a central alleyway that runs through the middle that is still a public right of way to the church, and used to be the route along which the dead were carried to the cemetery; it stops along the way at a central space by the serving bar with its well kept Courage Best, Ushers Best and Wadworths 6X on handpump, farm cider, and malt whiskies. The ancient main room has a good local atmosphere, a log fire in the handsome stone inglenook, antique oak settles (two well carved) and cushioned captain's chairs on the quarry-tiled floor, some Royalty pictures, a chiming wall-clock, a heavy black beam-and-plank ceiling, and rough black shutters for the stone-mullioned windows (put up in World War I). There's another room down to the left (with less atmosphere). There's quite a choice of reasonably priced bar food such as home-baked baguettes (from £2.15), soup (£2.55), filled baked potatoes (from £3.55), ploughman's (from £4.55), ham and eggs (£4.95), daily specials such as home-made stilton and vegetable parcels (£6.75), steak and kidney pie, sherry chicken or pork in cider (£6.95), lamb fillet (£7.25), Scottish salmon fillet with lemon grass and coriander sauce (£8.95), and Scottish Angus steaks (from £8.95). Rather fine shove-ha'penny slates are set into two of the tables, dominoes, piped music, and winter quiz evenings. The spacious back garden has seats and pretty roses; boules. *(Recommended by John Mason, M G Hart, Roger and Jenny Huggins, John Bowling)*

InnSpired Inns ~ Tenants Garth Evans and Nikki Evans ~ Real ale ~ Bar food (12-2, 6-9; 12-6 Sun) ~ Restaurant ~ (01225) 832060 ~ Children welcome ~ Open 11.30-2.30, 6-11; 11-11 Sat; 12-10.30 Sun

SPARKFORD ST6026 Map 2
Sparkford Inn

High Street; just off A303 bypass W of Wincanton

With the Fleet Air Arm Museum at Yeovilton and Haynes Motor Museum both nearby, this homely old coaching inn is a useful stop for lunch, and it can get pretty busy, especially if a coach arrives before you – though staff cope admirably. There's a rambling series of rather low-beamed, dimly lit rooms with good dining chairs around a nice mix of old tables in varying sizes, a colour scheme leaning towards plummy browns and dusky pinks, and plenty of worthwhile prints and other things to look at – including an intricate old-fashioned scrapbook screen; piped music. Well liked bar food includes sandwiches (from £2.65), home-made soup (£2.75), ploughman's (£4.95), creamy garlic mushrooms (£4.30), filled baked potatoes (from £4.50), home-cooked ham and egg (£5.95), carrot slice with cranberry sauce (£5.95), cottage pie (£6.45), beef and Guinness or chicken and leek casseroles or smoked haddock and bacon (£6.95), a very popular lunchtime carvery (£6.50), and home-made puddings (£3.15); the restaurant is no smoking. Well kept Bass, Black Sheep, Butcombe Bitter, and Greene King Old Speckled Hen on handpump. Tables outside, with a decent play area, and pretty tubs of flowers. *(Recommended by Andrew and Catherine Gilham, Ian Phillips, Dr M E Wilson, Colin Draper, Kevin Flack, Christopher and Mary Thomas, Richard and Margaret Peers, R J Walden, Mr and Mrs Gordon Turner, Guy Consterdine, Laura Wilson, Esther and John Sprinkle, Ian and Nita Cooper, J F and G J Wheeler, Jayne Capp)*

Free house ~ Licensee Paul Clayton ~ Real ale ~ Bar food ~ Restaurant ~ (01963) 440218 ~ Children welcome ~ Open 11-11; 12-10.30 Sun ~ Bedrooms: £35B/£49.50B

STANTON WICK ST6162 Map 2
Carpenters Arms ♀ 🛏
Village signposted off A368, just W of junction with A37 S of Bristol

Set in peaceful countryside, this long and low tile-roofed inn was converted from a row of old miners' cottages. The Coopers Parlour on the right has one or two beams, seats around heavy tables with fresh flowers, and attractive curtains and plants in the windows; on the angle between here and the bar area there's a fat woodburning stove in an opened-through corner fireplace. The bar has wood-backed built-in wall seats and some red fabric-cushioned stools, stripped stone walls, and a big log fire. Diners are encouraged to step down into a snug inner room (lightened by mirrors in arched 'windows'), or to go round to the sturdy tables angling off on the right; most of these tables get booked at weekends. Good bar food includes sandwiches (from £4.75; fillet steak and fried onions £7.50), fried sardines with orange and coriander butter (£4.95), Scottish salmon fishcakes with provençale sauce (£5.25; main course £8.95), crispy duck and baby spinach leaf salad with potato and bacon croutons (£5.95), steak and mushroom in ale pie (£7.95), stir fry of mediterranean vegetables and wild mushrooms with soy sauce and balsamic vinegar (£8.95), roast cod fillet on green and red pepper salsa or thai chicken curry (£9.95), medallions of pork tenderloin with sweet sherry, bacon, mushrooms and cream (£10.95), knuckle of lamb with fried shredded leek and spiced redcurrant sauce (£11.95), and steaks (from £12.75). Well kept Bass, Butcombe Bitter, Courage Best, and Wadworths 6X on handpump, a decent wine list, and several malt whiskies; fruit machine and TV. There are picnic-sets on the front terrace and pretty flowerbeds. *(Recommended by June and Ken Brooks, D Marsland, Richard Fendick, E H and R F Warner, Richard Kitson, Richard Kennell, Christopher and Mary Thomas, Roy and Lindsey Fentiman, J Osborn-Clarke, John and Beryl Knight, Ron Shelton)*

Buccaneer Holdings ~ Manager Simon Pledge ~ Real ale ~ Bar food (12-2, 7-10) ~ Restaurant ~ (01761) 490202 ~ Children in eating area of bar and restaurant ~ Pianist Fri/Sat evenings ~ Open 11-11; 12-10.30 Sun ~ Bedrooms: £59B/£79B

STOGUMBER ST0937 Map 1
White Horse £
From A358 Taunton—Williton, village signposted on left at Crowcombe

Set opposite the church in a quiet village square, this pleasant whitewashed pub has changed little since one reader last saw it 40 years ago. The neatly kept long bar room has plenty of locals, cushioned captain's chairs around heavy wooden tables, old village photographs with more recent ones for comparison, warm winter fires, and unobtrusive piped jazz and folk music. Bar food includes sandwiches and home-made soup (£2), filled baked potatoes (from £3), ham and egg or omelettes (£3.50), lasagne (£5.50), chicken curry (£5), steak and kidney pudding (£6.50), 10oz steak (£9), and puddings (£2.50). Well kept Cotleigh Tawny and maybe Bath Gem or Exmoor Fox on handpump. There's a no smoking dining area, a games room with darts, fruit machine, and dominoes, and skittle alley. The garden is quiet except for rooks and sheep in the surrounding low hills. The West Somerset Steam Railway is nearby and the restored railway halt is worth a visit. *(Recommended by Ian Phillips, Hugh Roberts, John Bramley, Joan and Michel Hooper-Immins, Roger and Jenny Huggins, Kevin Flack, Dr David Cockburn, Gene and Kitty Rankin)*

Free house ~ Licensees Graham Roy, Edith Boada ~ Real ale ~ Bar food ~ (01984) 656277 ~ Children in eating area of bar and restaurant ~ Open 11.30-2.30, 6-11; 12-3, 7-10.30 Sun ~ Bedrooms: £27B/£40B

STOKE ST GREGORY ST3527 Map 1
Rose & Crown ⊕ ♀ ⊨

Woodhill; follow North Curry signpost off A378 by junction with A358 – keep on to Stoke, bearing right in centre

As well as being a friendly place for an enjoyable meal or drink, this country cottage is a comfortable and popular place to stay, and has been run for 22 years by the same hard-working licensees. The bar is decorated in a cosy and pleasantly romanticised stable theme: dark wooden loose-box partitions for some of the interestingly angled nooks and alcoves, lots of brasses and bits on the low beams and joists, stripped stonework, and appropriate pictures including a highland pony carrying a stag; many of the wildlife paintings on the walls are the work of the landlady, and there's an 18th-c glass-covered well in one corner. Using fresh local produce, fresh fish from Brixham, and their own eggs, the bar food at lunchtime might include sandwiches in home-made granary bread (from £2.50), ploughman's (£4.20), ham and egg or omelettes (£5), grilled liver and bacon, scrumpy chicken or gammon and pineapple (£6.50), vegetarian dishes such as nut roast chasseur or stir-fry vegetables (£7.50), grilled skate wings (£8), steaks (from £9), and puddings (£2.75); evening dishes are similar (but cost a bit more) with extras such as prawn stir fry (£7.50) and excellent grilled 8oz rib-eye steak (£9), and they also offer a three-course meal for £13.50 with more elaborate dishes like stuffed burgundy snails, lobster soup, roast duckling with cherry or roast rack of lamb. Plentiful breakfasts, and a good three-course Sunday lunch (£8.25). The attractive dining room is no smoking. Well kept Hardy Royal Oak, and guests like Black Sheep, Exmoor Ale or Hardy Royal Oak on handpump, Thatcher's farm cider, and a good wine list; unobtrusive piped classical music and dominoes. Under cocktail parasols by an apple tree on the sheltered front terrace are some picnic-sets; summer barbecues and a pets corner for children. The pub is in an interesting Somerset Levels village with willow beds still supplying the two basket works. *(Recommended by Ian Phillips, J Davidson, Anne Ashurst, KC, Karen Eliot, Theo, Anne and Jane Gaskin, David Griffin, Brian and Bett Cox, Mike and Wena Stevenson, Tony Lunn, Miss S Simmons, Brian A Smith, B and K Hypher, Peter Burton, Mr and Mrs Thomas, Andy Sinden, Louise Harrington, John and June Hayward, Sue and David Arnott, Keith Mould)*

Free house ~ Licensees Ron and Irene Browning ~ Real ale ~ Bar food ~ Restaurant ~ (01823) 490296 ~ Children welcome ~ Open 11-2.30, 7-11; 12-3, 7-10.30 Sun ~ Bedrooms: £25(£35B)/£38(£50B)

TRISCOMBE ST1535 Map 1
Blue Ball ⊕ ♀

Village signposted off A358 Crowcombe—Bagborough; turn off opposite sign to youth hostel; OS Sheet 181 map reference 155355

By the time this book is published, Mr Groves will have moved in here, and shifted the pub into the first floor of a lovely 15th-c thatched stone-built former coaching stables. This long, low building slopes gently down on three levels, each with its own woodburning stove, and cleverly divided into seating by hand-cut oak partitions; all the work has been carried out with old-fashioned craftsman's skills, and although new, the bar looks many years old, and there is plenty of space. Well kept Cotleigh Tawny, Otter Ale and Head, and a guest such as Timothy Taylors Landlord or Youngs Special on handpump; there are 400 wines on the list and they will open any under £20 for just a glass; old cognacs and armagnacs, farm ciders, and freshly squeezed orange juice. As well as lunchtime filled baguettes (from £4.50), thai chicken salad (£4.95, main course £8.95), and fish and chips (£5.50), there might be home-made soup (£3.50), chicken liver and madeira parfait (£4.95), tea-smoked duck breast salad with francatelli sauce (£5.50), moules marinières (£5.95), slow braised belly of pork with soy, ginger and garlic (£6.50), seared scallops with chilli, garlic and coconut (£6.95; main course £13.95), pasta with fried courgette sauce, garlic and marjoram (£7.95), moroccan beef and apricot tagine (£8.95), local chicken breast with asparagus sauce (£9.75), steaks (from £9.75), quantock duck breast with port and redcurrant sauce (£11.50), and puddings such as rich chocolate and mascarpone tart, sticky toffee pudding or warm treacle and lemon tart (£3.75). They have two tortoisehell cats, whippets, and a lurcher. The decking at the top of the woodside, terraced garden makes the most of the peaceful views. More reports please. *(Recommended by Robin Fawcett, John and Joan Calvert, Brian and Bett Cox, Simon Watkins, Nick and Lesley Warboys, CMJ, James Flory, Gethin Lewis, Carole Macpherson, Gene and Kitty Rankin)*

Free house ~ Licensee Patrick Groves ~ Real ale ~ Bar food ~ Restaurant ~ No credit cards ~ (01984) 618242 ~ Well behaved children welcome ~ Open 12-2.30(3 Sun), 7-11(10 Sun); closed 25 Dec, evenings 26 Dec and 1 Jan

WELLS ST5545 Map 2

City Arms

High St

In England's smallest city, this 16th-c building was originally a jail but became a pub in 1810. There are usually several locals enjoying a pint which gives a relaxed and chatty feel, and the courteous, helpful staff offer a warm welcome to all. To reach the pub, you walk through a charming cobbled courtyard with white metal seats and tables, trees and flowers in pots, and an attractive side verandah. Inside, it's rather like a cellar bar with arched doorways and double ballaster-shaped pillars, green-cushioned mate's chairs, a nice old black settle, a Regency-style settee and a couple of well worn, homely sofas, and a plush pink sturdy wall settle; up a step is a similar room with pictures and Wills Grand National cigarette cards on the walls, big tables and solid chairs, and beyond that, a separate bar with neat sturdy brocaded settles forming booths around tables; plenty of Victorian and Victorian-style engravings. One area is no smoking. Good bar food might include sandwiches, vegetable soup (£2.95), chicken liver and cognac pâté (£3.75), fresh roast sardines with pesto dressing (£3.95; large £7.50), sausage and mash (£4.95), cauliflower cheese with ham (£5.50), spicy chilli (£6.25), quorn korma (£6.95), devilled kidneys or somerset smokies (smoked haddock and spinach baked in a creamy sauce topped with potatoes and cheese, £7.25), home-made steak and kidney pudding (£7.95), steaks (from £8.95), roasted halibut steak with an orange and Pernod sauce (£12.95), and interesting daily specials. They keep six real ales on handpump such as Adnams Best, Butcombe Gold, Cotleigh Tawny, Greene King Abbot, Palmers IPA, and Timothy Taylors Landlord, as well as farm ciders; piped pop music. There's a fine open-beamed upstairs restaurant. *(Recommended by Joan and Michel Hooper-Immins, JCW, Eric Locker, Richard Fendick, Peter Meister, Pat and Tony Martin, Lynn Sharpless, Bob Eardley, Peter Smith, Brian and Anna Marsden, Gene and Kitty Rankin)*

Free house ~ Licensees Brian and Sue Marshall and Jim Hardy ~ Real ale ~ Bar food (all day until 10(9.30 Sun)) ~ Restaurant ~ (01749) 673916 ~ Children welcome ~ Open 10-11; 12-10.30 Sun

WINSFORD SS9034 Map 1

Royal Oak ♀ ⇔

In Exmoor National Park, village signposted from A396 about 10 miles S of Dunster

Sadly, this very pretty thatched inn suffered another fire and had to close for a few months, but by the time this book is published everything will be up and running – though they may not be allowed any more open fires. It is in fine surroundings with good nearby walks (up Winsford Hill for magnificent views, or over to Exford), and they do a useful guide to Exmoor National Park identifying places to visit. The attractively furnished and cosy lounge bar has a cushioned big bay-window seat from which you can look across the road towards the village green and foot and packhorse bridges over the River Winn, tartan-cushioned bar stools by the panelled counter (above which hang horsebrasses and pewter tankards), the same cushions on the armed windsor chairs set around little wooden tables, and a splendid iron fireback in the big stone hearth; plenty of locals create a chatty, relaxed atmosphere. Another similar bar offers more eating space with built-in wood-panelled seats creating booths, fresh flowers, and country prints; there are several pretty and comfortable lounges. Bar food includes home-made soup (£3.50), sandwiches (with salad and crisps, from £4.50), grilled goats cheese with roasted tomatoes and olives, with a garlic and fresh basil dressing (£4.75), ploughman's (from £5.95), braised venison sausages and mash with a rich onion gravy (£8.25), steak and kidney pudding or baked smoked haddock (£8.50), local game casserole (£8.95), sirloin steak (£13.50), and home-made puddings (£2.95). Well kept Cotleigh Barn Owl and Harrier, and Exmoor Ale on handpump; shove-ha'penny, cribbage, and dominoes. *(Recommended by Jane and Adrian Tierney-Jones, Comus and Sarah Elliott, David and Ruth Hollands, A and J Evans, Tom Evans, Diana Brumfit, Matt Britton, Alison Cameron, Peter and Giff Bennett, Mr and Mrs S Kerry Bedell)*

Free house ~ Licensee Charles Steven ~ Real ale ~ Bar food ~ Restaurant ~ (01643) 851455 ~ Children in eating area of bar and restaurant ~ Open 11-2.30, 6-11; 12-3, 6-11 Sun ~ Bedrooms: £86B/£105B

WITHYPOOL SS8435 Map 1
Royal Oak ♀ 🛏
Village signposted off B3233

R D Blackmore stayed in this village inn while writing *Lorna Doone*. The beamed lounge bar has a fine raised log fireplace, comfortably cushioned wall seating and slat-backed chairs, and stags' heads, stuffed fish, several fox masks, sporting prints and paintings and various copper and brass ornaments on its walls. The locals' bar (named after the barman Jake who has been here for over 25 years) has some old oak tables, and plenty of character. Bar food includes sandwiches, soup (£3.70), fried chicken livers with crispy pancetta, shallots, croutons and aged balsamic vinegar (£4.50), salmon fishcakes with chilli jam, lemon and lime mayonnaise (£5.50), home-cooked ham with double egg and chips (£6.50), tenderloin of tamworth pork with bubble and squeak and calvados sauce or stir-fried egg noddles with pomadori tomatoes, buffalo mozzarella and ripped herbs (£7.50), braised lamb shank with boulangère potato, onion loaf and minted mushy peas (£8.80), and local sirloin of beef (£13). Well kept Exmoor Ale and Stag on handpump, quite a few malt whiskies, a decent wine list, and farm cider. It can get very busy (especially on Sunday lunchtimes), and is popular with the local hunting and shooting types; cribbage, dominoes, and shove-ha'penny; piped music in the restaurant only. There are wooden benches on the terrace, and just up the road, some grand views from Winsford Hill. The River Barle runs through the village itself, with pretty bridleways following it through a wooded combe further upstream. *(Recommended by Gethin Lewis, Sally Anne and Peter Goodale, DAV, Sue Demont, Tim Barrow, Jane and Adrian Tierney-Jones, Peter and Audrey Dowsett)*

Free house ~ Licensee Gail Sloggett ~ Real ale ~ Bar food (12-2, 6.30-9.30) ~ (01643) 831506 ~ Children in top bar and restaurant only ~ Open 11-3, 6-11; 12-3, 6-11 Sun ~ Bedrooms: £38(£53B)/£92B

WOOKEY ST5145 Map 2
Burcott
B3139 W of Wells

The two simply furnished small front bar rooms in this neatly kept and friendly little roadside pub are connected but different in character. There's a square corner bar counter in the lounge, fresh flowers at either end of the mantelpiece above the tiny stone fireplace, Parker-Knollish brocaded chairs around a couple of tables, and high bar stools; the other bar has beams (some willow pattern plates on one), a solid settle by the window and a high backed old pine settle by one wall, cushioned mate's chairs and fresh flowers on the mix of nice old pine tables, dried flowers in a brass coal scuttle, old-fashioned oil-type wall lamps, and a hunting horn on the bressumer above the fireplace. A little room on the right has darts, shove-ha'penny, cribbage and dominoes, neat built-in wall seats, and small framed advertisements for Schweppes, Coke, Jennings and Oakhill, and there's a roomy back restaurant with black joists, stripped stone walls and sea-green check tablecloths. Tasty bar food includes home-made soup (£2.25), sandwiches (1½ rounds, from £2.75; toasties from £2.15; open baguettes £3.95), filled baked potatoes (from £3.45), stuffed mushrooms (£3.75), ploughman's (from £4.45), home-cooked ham and eggs or vegetable and cashew nut bake (£5.25), home-made steak in ale pie (£6.25), mexican-style king prawns (starter £6.50, main course £12.50), chicken topped with leeks and mushrooms in a white wine cream sauce (£8.95), salmon fillet topped with prawns (£10.45), steaks (from £10.50), and daily specials. Well kept Cotleigh Barn Owl, Sharps Doom Bar, and a guest such as Greene King Abbot or Timothy Taylors Landlord on handpump, and several wines by the glass. The sizeable garden is well spread and has picnic-sets and plenty of small trees and shrubs, and there's a paddock beyond. The window boxes and tubs at the front are pretty in summer. More reports please. *(Recommended by Hugh Roberts, Philip Bardswell, Alan and Paula McCully, Ian and Nita Cooper)*

Free house ~ Licensees Ian and Anne Stead ~ Real ale ~ Bar food (12-2, 6.30-9.30; not Sun evening) ~ Restaurant ~ (01749) 673874 ~ Children in restaurant and family room ~ Open 11.30-2.30(3 Sat), 6-11; 12-3, 7-11 Sun; closed 25 Dec, 1 Jan

---

Lucky Dip

Besides the fully inspected pubs, you might like to try these Lucky Dips recommended to us and described by readers (if you do, please send us reports: www.goodguides.com).

Abbots Leigh [ST5473]
George [A369, between M5 junction 19 and Bristol]: Popular and friendly main-road dining pub with huge choice of attractively presented food from snacks up, real ales inc Marstons Pedigree, two log fires; no children, good-sized enclosed garden *(LYM, Simon and Amanda Southwell, J Osborn-Clarke, D B Davies)*
Ashcott [ST4336]
Ashcott Inn [A39 W of Glastonbury]: Attractively homely stripped-stone beamed bar, mix of pleasantly old-fashioned and newer furniture, gas-effect log fire in inglenook, usual food from sandwiches up (all day in summer), partly no smoking restaurant, Butcombe and a guest beer, decent wines; quiet piped music; skittle alley, tables on terrace and in pretty garden with adventure play areas *(Peter and Audrey Dowsett, Ian Phillips, G Coates, Richard and Margaret Peers, Comus and Sarah Elliott, LYM)*
Pipers [A39/A361, SE of village]: Large welcoming beamed lounge, well kept ales such as Butcombe, Greene King Old Speckled Hen, Oakhill, John Smiths, Tetleys, Wadworths and Youngers, prompt pleasant service, woodburner, leather armchairs, pictures for sale, wide choice of good reasonably priced food from sandwiches to steaks inc children's in prettily set no smoking beamed dining area; unobtrusive piped music; pleasant roadside

garden *(Christopher and Mary Thomas)*
☆ *Ring o' Bells* [High St; follow Church and Village Hall signs off A39 W of Street]: Neatly kept comfortably modernised local, steps up and down making snug areas (at least for the able-bodied), well kept local Moor Withy Cutter and two interesting guest beers, Wilkins's farm cider, wide choice of good value wholesome home-made food inc unusual dishes and sturdy puddings, separate no smoking stripy pink dining room, decent wines, chatty landlord and helpful service, inglenook woodburner; piped pop music; skittle alley, fruit machines; attractively planted back garden with play area, camping *(G Coates, BB, MP, Richard Fendick)*
Backwell [ST4767]
New Inn [West Town Rd (A370 W of Bristol)]: Small pub/restaurant, clean and friendly, with impressive choice of very good reasonably priced food inc great range of fresh fish and good puddings; good service and atmosphere, no music *(J Osborn-Clarke)*
Bath [ST7565]
Bell [Walcot St]: Lively and student musicians' pub, with up to nine well kept changing ales from breweries such as Abbey, Bath, Butcombe, Courage, Fullers, RCH and Wadworths, good cheap rolls, friendly efficient service; frequent free music *(Jonathan Smith, Dr and Mrs A K Clarke)*

Coeur de Lion [Northumberland Pl; off High St by W H Smith]: Tiny single-room pub in charming flower-filled flagstoned pedestrian alley, cosy and friendly little bar, well kept changing ales, log-effect gas fire, good mulled wine at Christmas, lunchtime filled rolls in summer – perhaps Bath's prettiest pub, esp in summer; open all day *(LYM, Dr and Mrs A K Clarke, the Didler)*

Crystal Palace [Abbey Green]: Cheerfully busy modernised bar, sheltered courtyard with lovely hanging baskets, heated conservatory; good value freshly prepared straightforward food (not Sun evening) inc lunchtime snacks, speedy friendly service, well kept ales, log fire; fruit machines, video game, pinball, piped music *(David Carr, LYM)*

Devonshire Arms [Wellsway]: Well worn in local, very cheap good food *(Dr and Mrs A K Clarke, Meg and Colin Hamilton)*

☆ *George I* [Mill Lane, Bathampton (off A36 towards Warminster or A4 towards Chippenham)]: Popular creeper-covered canalside pub, attractive no smoking family dining room overlooking water, wide choice of enjoyable if not cheap food inc baguettes and fish, good log fires, Bass, Courage Directors and Wadworths 6X, quick friendly service; tables on quiet terrace, safe and spacious, with garden bar (interesting seats in front yard, but traffic noise there); can get crowded, esp wknds *(Meg and Colin Hamilton, Matt Britton, Alison Cameron, GSB, Dr and Mrs A K Clarke, Claire Nielsen)*

☆ *Hop Pole* [Albion Buildings, Upper Bristol Rd]: Tastefully refurbished and revitalised by Bath Ales, with their beers and a guest kept well, good value lunchtime food (not Mon) inc popular Sun lunches, friendly atmosphere, traditional settles, no smoking area, no juke box or pool; skittle alley, garden with boules *(Dr and Mrs A K Clarke, Colin and Peggy Wilshire, Richard Houghton)*

Olde Farmhouse [Lansdown Rd]: Pleasant setting on hill overlooking Bath, well kept Abbey Bellringer (from neighbouring microbrewery), Butcombe and Wadworths, real fire, maybe filled cobs, L-shaped parquet-floor bar with wall seats, panelling, stained-glass lamps and bar gantry, big jazz pictures; juke box, big-screen TV; jazz some evenings, open all day *(the Didler, G Coates)*

Pig & Fiddle [Saracen St]: Small busy pub tied to Ash Vine, with their full range kept well at sensible prices from island bar, maybe guests such as Abbey and Bath, friendly service, two big open fires, clocks set to different time zones, good value home-made food, upper restaurant area, takeaways too; very lively at night (lots of students), good if loud piped music; seats on big front terrace *(Dr and Mrs A K Clarke, Jonathan Smith, Catherine Pitt, Derek and Sylvia Stephenson)*

Porter [George St/Miles's Buildings]: Lively and informal, with well kept Abbey Bellringer, Marstons Pedigree and Smiles, wide choice of other drinks, largely organic and entirely vegetarian food inc vegan dishes, games room

with two pool tables, music area with its own bar and DJs or live bands (admission charge only on comedy nights) *(anon)*

Pulteney Arms [Daniel St]: Small, with well kept Bass, Smiles, Wadworths 6X and a guest tapped straight from the cask, good chip baps and other food, jugs and lots of rugby posters and Bath RFC memorabilia; unobtrusive piped music or juke box; pavement tables *(Pete Baker, Dr and Mrs A K Clarke)*

Rising Sun [Grove St]: Friendly and relaxed small pub with well kept Ushers ales, attractively priced food inc sandwiches or rolls, darts, skittle alley *(Richard Pierce)*

Sam Weller [Upper Borough Walls]: Well kept Bass and Wadworths 6X, good food cooked to order inc all-day breakfast, no smoking area, friendly young staff, lively mix of customers *(Dr and Mrs A K Clarke)*

Slug & Lettuce [York Hotel, George St]: Modern bar, comfortable, opulent and welcoming, with well kept ales from striking spun aluminium pumps *(Dr and Mrs A K Clarke, MDN)*

Bathford [ST7966]

Crown [Bathford Hill, towards Bradford-on-Avon, by Batheaston roundabout and bridge]: Spacious and attractively laid out, several distinct but linked areas inc no smoking garden room, good log fire, interesting fairly priced food, well kept real ales, decent wines; families welcome, tables on terrace, nice garden *(Meg and Colin Hamilton, LYM)*

Beckington [ST8051]

Woolpack [off A36 Bath—Warminster]: Well refurbished old inn with attractive no smoking lounge, flagstoned bar with log fire, enjoyable if pricy food (no smoking dining room – children allowed here and in conservatory), well kept Courage and other ales, decent wines; comfortable bedrooms, open all day *(Mr and Mrs A H Young, LYM)*

Binegar [ST6149]

Horse & Jockey: Welcoming local with real ales inc Wadworths, local Thatcher's farm cider, good value generous food esp pizzas; skittle alley – busy on bowls nights *(Mike Crewes)*

Bishops Lydeard [ST1629]

Bird in Hand [Mount St]: Small comfortable village local with pleasant welcoming staff, well kept Greene King Abbot and Otter, simple food; garden *(John A Barker)*

Blackford [ST4147]

Sexeys Arms [B3139 W of Wedmore]: Pleasant village pub dating from 1400s, friendly landlord well up in local history, enjoyable meals; picnic-sets in garden *(Richard Fendick)*

Blagdon [ST5059]

Queen Adelaide [High St]: Quiet clean one-bar pub in lovely spot overlooking Blagdon Lake, traditionally decorated, plenty of candlelit tables, wide choice of well cooked generous food (not cheap but good value), well kept Bass, coal-effect gas fire *(Alan and Paula McCully)*

Bleadon [ST3357]

Queens Arms [Celtic Way]: Comfortable

traditional 16th-c local doing well under friendly and efficient new licensees, well kept Badger Tanglefoot, Bass, Palmers BB and Thumper and RCH PG Steam from casks behind bar, plenty of character, convivial atmosphere, nicely cooked fresh food from usual dishes to imaginative specials, woodburners in tap room and dining room; may be unobtrusive piped music, Sun quiz night *(Hugh Roberts, Keith Mould, Kate and Peter Bird, Jude Lloyd)*

Bradford-on-Tone [ST1722]
White Horse: Welcoming, well furnished and neatly kept stone-built local in quiet village, enjoyable reasonably priced food in bar and restaurant, well kept Cotleigh and Juwards ales, decent wines; well laid out side garden, skittle alley *(Ben and Sheila Walker, Christine and Neil Townend)*

Brent Knoll [ST3350]
Red Cow [2 miles from M5 junction 22; right on to A38, then first left into Brent St]: Vast choice of good value food from filled rolls to Sun lunch, well spaced tables in smartly spotless largely no smoking dining lounge (children allowed), family room, service normally helpful and quick (may slow when very busy), well kept beers such as Bass, Fullers London Pride and Greene King Old Speckled Hen; no dogs inside, skittle alley, tables outside *(Chris Mawson, Mr and Mrs F J Parmenter, BB, Dennis Jenkin, Graham Brooks, Peter and Audrey Dowsett)*

Bridgetown [SS9233]
Badgers Holt: Neat simply furnished bar, Bass, open fire, quick service, well served food inc cheap Sun roast, restaurant; tables on small terrace *(Peter and Audrey Dowsett)*

Bristol [ST5773]
Alma [Alma Vale Rd, Clifton]: Cheerful town pub well refurbished without losing character, real ales such as Greene King Abbot, Theakstons XB and Wadworths 6X, good plain cheap food, friendly service, no music; popular upstairs theatre Tues-Sat – best to book *(Simon and Amanda Southwell, Dr M E Wilson)*
Avon Packet [Coronation Rd, Southville]: Cheerful old-fashioned pub with well kept real ale, big garden useful for children; handy for SS Great Britain *(Dr and Mrs A K Clarke)*
Bag o' Nails [St Georges Rd, Hotwells]: Small shop front for cosy but airy room, well worn benches and small tables along its length, bare boards, soft gas lighting, inglenook seat by gas fire, glazed portholes into cellar, old local pictures, well kept Bass, Burton Bridge, Wye Valley and three changing ales such as Adnams Oyster Stout, RCH East Street Cream and Smiles Best from long bar, lots of bottled beers, friendly interesting landlord, helpful staff, good soup and sandwiches; piped jazz, port and stilton nights 2nd and 4th Weds *(Brian and Halina Howes, Jonathan Smith, Catherine Pitt, Mike Pugh, Ian and Nita Cooper, Paul Hopton)*
Baileys Court [Baileys Cout Rd, Bradley Stoke]: Well converted enormous farmhouse, lots of drinking areas, large indoor play area,

lots of outdoor attractions too *(Dr and Mrs A K Clarke)*
Bell [Alfred Pl, Kingsdown]: Small cosy local, well kept RCH Pitchfork and East St Cream, Wickwar BOB and a guest beer, lunchtime sandwiches and toasties, friendly landlady, peaceful at lunchtime, candlelit at night; open all day Sat *(Catherine Pitt, Jonathan Smith)*
☆ *Brewery Tap* [Upper Maudlin St/Colston St]: Tap for Smiles brewery, small and busy – get there early for a seat; their beers kept well and sensibly priced, also unusual continental bottled ones, interesting unpretentious décor, good chatty atmosphere even when packed, log fire in no smoking room, food inc filled rolls, no piped music; cl Sun lunchtime *(the Didler, Simon and Amanda Southwell, David Kilham, Jonathan Smith, Dr and Mrs A K Clarke, Jane and Graham Rooth, Paul Hopton)*
Bridge [Passage St]: Neat tiny one-bar city pub nr floating harbour, good friendly service, lots of film stills, well kept Bath and Courage Best, popular lunchtime snacks *(Jonathan Smith, the Didler, Paul Hopton)*
Chateau [Park St]: Big busy Smiles pub with their ales kept well, Victorian feel, lots of pictures, open fires, roomy back conservatory, good home-made lunchtime food (many tables reserved Sat), more limited evening *(Simon and Amanda Southwell, Jonathan Smith)*
☆ *Commercial Rooms* [Corn St]: Vast Wetherspoons establishment, its thriving atmosphere and impressive building setting it apart from the typical chain pub; lofty domed ceiling, snug cubicles along one side, gas lighting, comfortable quieter no smoking room with ornate balcony; reasonable prices, wide changing choice of good real ales, food all day inc super granary bread sandwiches; good location, very busy wknd evenings *(David Kilham, Alan and Paula McCully, Brian and Halina Howes, Simon and Amanda Southwell, D J and P M Taylor, David Carr)*
Cottage [Baltic Wharf, Cumberland Rd]: Converted customs house on southern bank of Floating Harbour, nr Maritime Heritage Centre, with fine views of Georgian landmarks from terrace; comfortable, roomy and civilised, with generous home-made food all day, well kept Flowers IPA, Smiles Best and Wadworths 6X; may be piped music; open all day, access through sailing club or on foot along waterfront *(Ian and Nita Cooper, Ian Phillips)*
Fleece & Firkin [St Thomas St, off Redcliff St and Victoria St]: Lively atmosphere in lofty dim-lit 18th-c hall stripped back to striking stonework and flagstones, basic furniture, well kept Smiles, lunchtime food (not Sun) inc big filled baps, pleasant staff, live music Weds-Sat, children wknds *(LYM)*
Highbury Tavern [St Michaels Hill, Cotham]: Almost opp Highbury Vaults (see below), with some similar food and welcoming atmosphere but otherwise different: five lagers, Smiles beer, big-screen TV, may be disco music and light projectors, jazz and quiz nights *(Simon and Amanda Southwell)*
Highbury Vaults [St Michaels Hill, Cotham]:

Busy with students and teachers, nice series of small rooms with old-fashioned furniture and prints; now tied to Youngs, with their beers and guests inc Smiles, cheap bar food (not Sat/Sun evenings), bar billiards, dominoes, cribbage; attractive back terrace with heated arbour, open all day, children welcome *(Catherine Pitt, the Didler, Paul Hopton, LYM)*

☆ *Hope & Anchor* [Jacobs Wells Rd, Clifton]: Character bare-boards 18th-c pub with lively studenty atmosphere, hop bines, large shared pine tables, well kept changing ales such as Butts Barbus Barbus, Bath SPA, Goffs Jouster and Black Knight and Smiles Holly Hops, fast pleasant service, reliable substantial cheap food inc lots of sandwiches, interesting dishes and sumptuous ploughman's – very popular lunchtime; can get crowded and smoky late evening, pub cat; disabled access, summer evening barbecues on good back terrace with interesting niches, occasional live music *(David Kilham, Catherine Pitt, Jonathan Smith, Lindsay Harford, Hugh Roberts, G Coates, Debbie Wall, Simon and Amanda Southwell, Jane and Graham Rooth, Paul Hopton)*

Horts City Tavern [Broad St]: Big, enjoyable food inc huge choice of sandwiches served quickly in two main bars and eating area, well kept Bass, Courage Best and several interesting ales from small breweries, friendly helpful service, some panelling, old pictures and bookshelves, other more modern areas, pool in games area; open all day, beer festivals, special offers and events or music most nights (till 1am Fri/Sat) *(Simon and Amanda Southwell, Ian and Nita Cooper)*

Kings Head [Victoria St]: Old and well refurbished, keeping original features, lots of polished brass and wood, small 'tramcar' snug, well kept ales inc Courage, friendly atmosphere, splendid mirrored bar back and interesting gas pressure gauge; cl Sat lunchtime, open all day Weds-Fri *(the Didler, Di and Mike Gillam, Brian and Halina Howes)*

Llandoger Trow [off King St/Welsh Back]: By docks, interesting as the last timber-framed building built here, and making the most of its picturesque past in very cosy collection of cleverly lit small alcoves and rooms with original fireplaces and carvings; reasonably priced simple bar food, draught sherries, eclectic array of liqueur coffees, friendly staff, good mix from students to tourists *(David and Kay Ross, Joe Wheeler, D J and P M Taylor)*

Nova Scotia [Baltic Wharf, Cumberland Basin]: Unspoilt old pub on S side of Floating Harbour, views to Clifton and Avon Gorge, good range of real ales inc Bass and a guest such as Youngs Special, good value food inc filling baguettes, wooden seats, some nautical touches *(Sue Demont, Tim Barrow)*

Old Fish Market [Baldwin St]: Ground floor of imposing red and cream brick building converted to roomy and airy Fullers pub, good mural showing it in 1790s along one wall, lots of wood inc rather ornate counter, parquet floor, lunchtime food inc sandwiches and home-baked pies, well kept ales inc London

Pride, good coffee, daily papers; quiet piped music *(David and Kay Ross, Simon and Amanda Southwell)*

Penny Farthing [Whiteladies Rd, Clifton]: Panelled pub with late Victorian bric-a-brac inc penny-farthing, armchairs opp bar, lots of table seating, real ales such as Adnams Broadside, Badger Tanglefoot, Bass, Butcombe and Wadworths IPA and 6X racked behind bar, very reasonably priced home-made food lunchtime and evening, friendly helpful staff; can get very busy evenings *(Simon and Amanda Southwell, Ian Phillips)*

Post Office Tavern [Westbury Hill, Westbury-on-Trym]: Well kept ales such as Bass, Butcombe, Fullers London Pride, Otter and several more, friendly service and good menu esp pizzas in converted post office with lots of interesting and appropriate memorabilia, good-sized no smoking lounge *(Matt Britton, Alison Cameron, Jonathan Smith)*

Prince of Wales [Stoke Lane (A4018), Westbury-on-Trym]: Comfortable and busy local with strong sports following, well kept ales such as Bass, Black Sheep, Courage Best, Fullers London Pride, Shepherd Neame, Smiles Best and Websters, welcoming landlord, popular lunchtime bar food; large garden with play area and boules *(Jonathan Smith)*

Reckless Engineer [Temple Gate, opp Temple Meads stn]: Friendly staff, wide range of customers and of well kept beer inc Smiles, bright wooden interior with raised seating area, pump clips on ceiling, interesting posters; piped music, games machines; open all day *(Catherine Pitt)*

Red Lion [Worrall Rd, Clifton]: Comfortable club-like lounge with open fire, larger bar with highly carved dresser separating off small pool area, several farm ciders such as Blackthorn, Cheddar Valley, Thatcher's and Thornton's, also Butcombe Bitter; rolls and sandwiches *(Ian Phillips)*

Three Brooks [Bradley Stoke District Centre]: Large modern pub, useful if you're passing, with helpful uniformed staff, relaxed atmosphere, wide range of food, well kept beers, coffee always available; some live entertainment, tables outside, play area *(Dr and Mrs A K Clarke, Roger and Jenny Huggins)*

Van Dyck Forum [Fishponds Rd]: Wetherspoons shop conversion, so less ornate than some; good range of cheap well kept real ales, friendly helpful staff, no music; open all day *(Dr and Mrs A K Clarke)*

Victoria [Chock Lane, Westbury-on-Trym]: Wadworths pub down quiet lane, warm and friendly, with well kept IPA, 6X, Old Timer and a couple of guests such as Adnams Broadside, wide choice of fresh food *(Jonathan Smith)*

Brompton Regis [SS9531]

☆ *George*: 17th-c ex-farmhouse in quiet village, warmly welcoming and attentive chef/landlord, very wide choice of reasonably priced home-made food, three real ales, organic wines, woodburners, skittle alley; may be quiet piped music, no juke box or machines, Exmoor views from garden by churchyard, dogs welcome, good walks *(John A Barker, Peter and Audrey Dowsett)*

Brushford [SS9225]

☆ *Carnarvon Arms*: Well equipped sporting hotel with own stabling, fishing and shooting, roomy bar with well kept Cotleigh Tawny from long counter, occasional guest beers, wide range of spirits and liqueurs, friendly staff, good home-cooked bar food inc notable daily specials; good wheelchair access, homely comfort in bedrooms *(Mr and Mrs J M Lefeaux)*

Buckland Dinham [ST7551]

☆ *Bell* [High St]: Attractive 16th-c pub with narrow beamed main bar, pine furnishings inc booth settles, interesting décor, woodburner in huge inglenook; wide choice of generous straightforward food, well kept ales inc Butcombe, quite a few malt whiskies, friendly landlord, children allowed in comfortable partly no smoking two-level dining room; cribbage, dominoes, piped music; sheltered garden with boules and side terraces, field with small wendy house and play area *(George Atkinson, Else Smaaskjaer, Kay Smith, LYM, Roger and Jenny Huggins, Susan and Nigel Wilson)*

Burnham-on-Sea [ST3049]

Dunstan House [Love Lane]: Large thoughtfully divided seating area in converted hotel, concentration on wide choice of competitively priced food from sandwiches up, Bass, Dartmoor and RCH ales, efficient service, conservatory looking over well equipped play area – very popular in summer *(MP)*

Butleigh [ST5233]

☆ *Rose & Portcullis*: Welcoming old country pub, good reasonably priced food inc good vegetarian choice and scrumptious puddings in bars and restaurant, well kept Courage Directors; tables in pretty back garden *(Richard Fendick)*

Cannington [ST2539]

Friendly Spirit [Brook St]: Usual food, friendly atmosphere, well kept beers *(Chris and Anna Rowley)*

Kings Head [High St (off A39)]: Vast blackboard choice of enjoyable food, friendly licensees, decent beers and wines; bedrooms *(Chris and Anna Rowley)*

Chard [ST3208]

Choughs [High St]: Attractive 16th-c building (supposedly haunted by Judge Jeffreys) with friendly family service, farm cider, daily papers, cheap usual food *(Veronica Brown)*

Hornsbury Mill [Hornsbury Hill (A358 N)]: Pleasant well run restaurant with rooms rather than pub, but also does snacks in comfortable bar (tidy dress); charming setting by big pond with ducks, natural fountains and turning mill wheel – good for children; bedrooms *(anon)*

Cheddar [ST4653]

☆ *Gardeners Arms* [Silver St]: Friendly and old-fashioned 16th-c beamed pub with wide choice of enjoyable freshly made food from lunchtime sandwiches and baguettes to interesting main dishes, local beers inc Butcombe, good choice of reasonably priced wine, log fire, nice atmosphere, interesting old local photographs;

children welcome, garden *(Mr and Mrs D C Groves, Christopher and Mary Thomas, R Pring)*

Chew Magna [ST5763]

Bear & Swan [South Parade]: Good food such as crab omelette and roast partridge (book well ahead wknds), good service *(Angus and Rosemary Campbell)*

☆ *Pony & Trap* [New Town; back rd to Bishop Sutton]: Small gently refurbished tucked-away pub with very friendly licensees, relaxing atmosphere, flagstones and antiques, well kept Butcombe and Ushers, good coffee, good value straightforward generous food, attentive service, daily papers (ballpoint pens for crosswords); quiet piped music, children's room, good views at the back; good walks, delightfully rural hillside setting near Chew Valley Lake *(Richard Fendick, F J Willy, Michael Doswell)*

Clevedon [ST4071]

Moon & Sixpence [The Beach]: Substantial seafront Victorian family dining pub with good choice of generous usual food (puddings free to OAPs), quick sympathetic service, balconied mezzanine floor with good view of magnificently restored pier and over to Brecon Beacons, well kept real ale, choice of wines, no smoking area; piped 60s music *(Richard Fendick, David Carr, Tom and Ruth Rees)*

Regent [Hill Rd]: Recently refurbished and now locally popular, with simply furnished light and roomy bistro bar looking out on Victorian shopping street, Badger Best and Tanglefoot and King & Barnes Old, wide wine choice, generous light meals, more choice in downstairs restaurant *(JCW)*

Congresbury [ST4363]

Old Inn [Pauls Causeway, off main rd]: Low-beamed tucked-away family local, smartened up without being spoilt, deep-set windows with pretty curtains, huge fireplaces, one with ancient stove opening to both bar and no smoking dining area, well kept ales inc Bass and Youngs Special tapped from the cask, wide range of good value food (not Sun or evenings in winter); tables in back garden *(Alan and Paula McCully)*

Plough [High St (B3133)]: Old-fashioned flagstoned local with welcoming new landlady, three seating areas off main bar, two log fires, old prints, farm tools and sporting memorabilia; welcoming staff, well kept Bass, Butcombe, Worthington BB and interesting guest beers, lunchtime sandwiches, darts, table skittles, shove-ha'penny and cards; small garden with boules, aviary and occasional barbecues *(Dr Hugh White, Hugh Roberts)*

Prince of Wales [A370 ½ mile from village]: Small, cosy and comfortable, with olde-worlde stripped brickwork, beamery and door frames, lots of brass and china, good sensible furniture, wide choice of good value food inc very popular bargain two-course lunch (or supper Mon-Thurs), good ice creams, low-priced real ales inc Oakhill, friendly professional service, separate dining room; tables in garden *(K R Harris, Tom Evans)*

☆ *White Hart* [signed from A38 Bristol—
Bridgwater, or off A370 Bristol—Weston, from
bottom of Rhodiate Hill; Wrington Rd]: Family
favourite for wide choice of generous tasty
home-made food inc good Sun roasts and
puddings, full range of Badger beers and a guest
kept well, welcoming landlady, good service,
fires each end, low beams, old pictures, brasses
and bric-a-brac, solid furnishings, light bright
conservatory dining extension, pleasant
children's room, small locals' bar, no piped
music; good-sized garden with terrace, Mendip
views, big play area and attractive aviary
*(Tom Evans, S H Godsell, Jonathan Smith,
Christopher and Mary Thomas, Kate and Peter
Bird)*

Corfe [ST2319]

☆ *White Hart* [B3170 S of Taunton]: Friendly
licensees, son cooks good food worth waiting
for, priced in snack or full meal size, also
sandwiches, ploughman's and unusual home-
made ice creams; lounge with small stools,
attractive small no smoking dining room, good
choice of real ales with guests such as Fullers
London Pride; children welcome *(John Close,
David and Teresa Frost)*

Crewkerne [ST4409]

White Hart [Market Sq, opp Post Office]:
15th-c, cosy, quiet and peaceful, comfortable
plain wooden furniture, fresh food and veg,
wide choice of beers and spirits, efficient jolly
staff *(anon)*

Cross [ST4155]

New Inn [A38 Bristol—Bridgwater, junction
A371]: Pleasant and friendly pub, well kept
Wadworths 6X, wholesome reasonably priced
food, fine views; games room upstairs *(Alan
and Paula McCully)*

Crowcombe [ST1336]

☆ *Carew Arms*: Friendly 17th-c beamed village
inn, unspoilt and original, large log fire in
lively old-fashioned flagstoned public bar with
hunting trophies, quieter carpeted lounge,
skittle alley; well kept Badger Tanglefoot,
Butcombe or Exmoor, Lane's farm cider,
enjoyable straightforward food inc good
choice of sandwiches and baguettes,
welcoming helpful landlord; folk nights, good
value comfortably refurbished bedrooms, fine
hill views from garden, nice spot at foot of
Quantocks *(Alan and Paula McCully, Dr
David Cockburn, the Didler, Phil and Sally
Gorton, R M Corlett, Richard and Jean
Green)*

Curry Rivel [ST3925]

Olde Forge [Church St]: Small welcoming bar,
attractive décor, mugs on beams, well kept
John Smiths and a monthly guest beer, good
usual food, pleasant service, light and bright
beamed dining room with local artists' work
for sale; quiet piped music *(Christopher and
Mary Thomas)*

Dinnington [ST4013]

Rose & Crown: Good atmosphere in attractive
unspoilt and welcoming country local with
good value home cooking, well kept Butcombe,
Teignworthy and Charles Wells Bombardier
(John A Barker)

Ditcheat [ST6236]

☆ *Manor House* [signed off A37 and A371 S of
Shepton Mallet]: Pretty village pub, unusual
arched doorways connecting big flagstoned bar
to comfortably relaxed lounge and dining area,
charming staff, well kept Butcombe tapped
from the cask, limited food (not cheap),
interesting wines, open fires, skittle alley, tables
on back grass *(Lyn and Geoff Hallchurch, BB,
Alan and Paula McCully, John A Barker)*

Drayton [ST4024]

Drayton Arms [off A378 nr Curry Rivel;
Church St]: Pleasant pub with decent food inc
bargain lunch Weds *(Theo, Anne and Jane
Gaskin)*

Dulverton [SS9127]

Rock House [Jury Rd]: Good range of real ales
such as Boddingtons, Branscombe Vale Branoc,
Cotleigh Golden Eagle, Flowers Original,
Golden Hill Exmoor and Whitbreads, cheap
food, pool room, no piped music *(Peter and
Audrey Dowsett)*

Dunster [SS9943]

Dunster Castle Hotel [High St]: Popular well
appointed hotel bar with well kept Bass and
other real ales, friendly staff, wide choice of
sensibly priced enjoyable food in eating area
and dining room from good sandwiches to Sun
lunch; bedrooms with own bathrooms, useful
car park *(David Biggins, W H and E Thomas,
H O Dickinson, Chris and Anna Rowley)*

Luttrell Arms [High St; A396]: Hotel in
interesting 15th-c timber-framed abbey
building, back bar with high beams hung with
bottles, clogs and horseshoes, stag's head and
rifles on walls above old settles and more
modern furniture, big log fires, ancient glazed
partition dividing off small galleried and
flagstoned courtyard, quiet garden with Civil
War cannon emplacements, well kept Bass and
Exmoor Gold; comfortable bedrooms *(DAV,
LYM, H O Dickinson)*

East Coker [ST5412]

☆ *Helyar Arms* [off A37 or A30 SW of Yeovil;
Moor Lane]: Well decorated spotless and
roomy open-plan lounge, low beams,
woodburner, lots of brass and pictures, dark-
stained traditional furnishings, world map with
pushpins for visitors; good atmosphere despite
considerable extensions, good generous food,
well kept Bass, Boddingtons and Flowers,
reasonably priced wines, sparkling old-
fashioned high-raftered dining room, friendly
helpful staff; no dogs, comfortable bedrooms
with own bathrooms, attractive setting
(Dennis Jenkin)

Easton [ST5047]

Easton Inn [A371 NW of Wells]: Pretty pub
with new chef doing good imaginative food in
roomy back dining room inc plenty of fish,
game and themed food evenings, relaxed bar
with settees, daily papers and real ale
(occasional beer festivals); good tables on
terrace and new lawn, lovely views over the
Levels *(Mr and Mrs D C Groves, Richard
Fendick)*

Emborough [ST6151]

Old Down: Recently reopened after extensive

refurbishment, real ales inc local ones and Bass tapped from the cask, restaurant-quality food at low prices; bedrooms *(Mike Crewes)*

Evercreech [ST6538]

Bell [Bruton Rd (B3081)]: Stone-built pub with enjoyable home-made food from sandwiches and baguettes to thai and several fish dishes, Adnams and Butcombe, cafetière coffee, several high-ceilinged linked rooms, watercolours above panelled dado, mix of solid furnishings, woodburner and log-effect gas fire; quiet piped music; quiet village handy for Bath & West Showground *(Pat and Robert Watt, B and K Hypher)*

Exford [SS8538]

☆ *Crown* [The Green (B3224)]: Civilised country hotel, one small bar mainly for drinkers, another for the generous food from good ploughman's to beautifully presented imaginative main dishes with lots of veg, well kept ales such as Exmoor Fox and Gold and Flowers, good choice of wines by the glass, big log fire, friendly helpful service, hunting memorabilia and ancient firearms, close-set but comfortable tables, no piped music; attractive streamside garden, good bedrooms *(Dick and Madeleine Brown)*

Failand [ST5171]

Failand Inn [B3128 Bristol—Clevedon]: Simply furnished country pub, popular for good straightforward reasonably priced food in ample helpings, with comfortable dining extension, friendy efficient service, well kept Courage; 60s piped music *(Tom Evans, Richard and Judy Winn)*

Farleigh Hungerford [ST8057]

☆ *Hungerford Arms* [A366 Trowbridge—Norton St Philip]: Relaxed and friendly local atmosphere, well kept Bass, Courage Best, Otter Bitter and Bright and Wadworths 6X, maybe Thatcher's cider, sensibly priced food, pleasant staff, good solid furnishings inc snug alcoves, pink walls, stained glass and hunting prints, heavy dark beams, carved stone fireplaces, steps down to no smoking restaurant with nice country view inc Hungerford Castle ruins, children allowed here and in family room; darts, fruit machine; back terrace with same view, open all day wknds *(Michael Doswell, Pat and Dick Warwick, LYM, Meg and Colin Hamilton, Hugh Roberts, George Atkinson)*

Farmborough [ST6660]

New Inn [Bath Rd (A39)]: Large welcoming pub/restaurant (formerly the Farmborough) with enjoyable food, Morrells real ale *(A B Clarke)*

Fitzhead [ST1128]

Fitzhead Inn [off B3227 W of Taunton]: Quiet tucked-away country pub with quite a spacious feel for such a small place, well kept ales such as Cotleigh Tawny, Exmoor, Fullers London Pride, Hook Norton and Tisbury Natterjack (masses of beer mats on ceiling), farm cider, decent wines, singing chef doing good food from bar food to more elaborate evening dishes; casual service, piped music can obtrude *(LYM, Mark Wilkinson)*

Frome [ST7749]

☆ *Farmers Arms* [Spring Gardens, out northwards towards Oldford]: Child-friendly little riverside pub with young chef doing good interesting food from crispy won tons to good fish choice, friendly landlord, log fire, plenty of games; pretty raised garden, open all day *(Peter D B Harding, Claire Nielsen, Meg and Colin Hamilton)*

Glastonbury [ST4938]

George & Pilgrims [High St]: 15th-c inn with magnificent carved stone façade, interesting front bar with heavy tables, handsome stone fireplace (flame-effect gas fire) and traceried stained-glass bay window; rest of pub more ordinary; well kept Bass and Wadworths 6X, decent food, helpful staff, children in buffet and pleasant upstairs restaurant, occasional live music; good clean bedrooms *(LYM, David Carr)*

Hardway [ST7134]

☆ *Bull* [off B3081 Bruton—Wincanton at brown sign for Stourhead and King Alfred's Tower; Hardway]: Pretty and welcoming beamed country dining pub, popular locally esp with older people wkdy lunchtimes for wide choice of reliably good generous food inc fresh veg in comfortable bar and character dining rooms, friendly obliging service, well kept Butcombe and a guest beer, farm cider, log fire; unobtrusive piped music, sell paintings and meringues; tables and barbecue in rose garden over road, bedrooms *(Dinah and Henry Ellis, Mavis and Robert Harford, Richard Kitson)*

Hatch Beauchamp [ST3020]

☆ *Hatch Inn* [old village rd, not bypass]: Cheerfully welcoming carpeted lounge bar, lots of copper and brass, attractive bow-window seats and log fire, well priced waitress-served food here and in dining area, well kept ales such as Bass, Courage Directors and Fullers London Pride, farm ciders, simple separate village bar with games, skittle alley across yard; good value bedrooms *(BB, Andrew and Catherine Gilham, F J Davis, Peter and Audrey Dowsett)*

Hinton Charterhouse [ST7758]

☆ *Rose & Crown* [B3110 about 4 miles S of Bath]: Roomy open-plan partly divided nicely panelled bar with well kept Bass, Butcombe and Smiles tapped from casks, wide choice of good value generous home-made food inc plenty of fish and vegetarian, hard-working and amiable young owners, Rugby memorabilia, ornate stone fireplace, magazines to read, restaurant, skittle alley; open all day Sat *(BB, Meg and Colin Hamilton)*

☆ *Stag* [B3110 S of Bath; High St]: Attractively furnished ancient pub with well kept ales such as Bass and Butcombe, smiling service, log fire, well cooked good value food, nicely furnished stripped-stone dining area, no piped music; children allowed in well thought out eating area, away from bar but not isolated; tables outside, has been open all day *(Dr M E Wilson, Michael and Daphne Tighe, LYM)*

Holcombe [ST6649]

☆ *Ring o' Roses* [A367 S of Radstock]:

Extensively renovated 17th-c country pub in lovely setting, emphasis on consistently good food in comfortable bar and large beamed restaurant, Oakhill Best or Mendip Gold, charming attentive service; log fire, daily papers, afternoon teas; nice views from small garden, children and dogs welcome, comfortable bedrooms, good breakfast *(Susan and Nigel Wilson, Philip Crawford)*

Holton [ST6827]

☆ *Old Inn* [off A303 W of Wincanton]: Charming rustic 16th-c pub, quiet and friendly, with beams, ancient flagstones, log fire, hundreds of key fobs, nice bric-a-brac, big open woodburner, plump cat; pleasant service, Butcombe and Wadworths 6X, good interesting attractively priced food in bar and restaurant (must book Sun lunch); walking-sticks for sale, tables outside, sheltered garden up steps *(BB, James Nunns)*

Ilchester [ST5222]

Bull [The Square]: Unpretentiously welcoming, informal service, reasonably priced food inc inventive vegetarian dishes, well kept local beers such as Butcombe *(Mr and Mrs T A Bryan, Sue and Mike Todd)*

Kelston [ST7067]

☆ *Old Crown* [Bitton Rd; A431 W of Bath]: Four small friendly traditional rooms with hops on beams, carved settles and cask tables on polished flagstones, logs burning in ancient open range, two more coal-effect fires, well kept Butcombe and guest beers such as Bass, Smiles and Wadworths 6X tapped from the cask, Thatcher's cider, low-priced generous bar food (not Sun or Mon evenings), small restaurant (not Sun), no machines or music; children in eating areas, open all day wknd, picnic-sets under apple trees in sunny sheltered back garden *(Susan and Nigel Wilson, LYM, Mr and Mrs Thomas, Mr and Mrs S Carter, Michael Doswell)*

Kilve [ST1442]

Hood Arms [A39 E of Williton]: Woodburner in bar, cosy little plush lounge, no smoking restaurant, popular bar food (no sandwiches), friendly attentive service; skittle alley, tables on sheltered back terrace by garden; nice bedrooms – back are quietest *(Gordon Stevenson, LYM, Gene and Kitty Rankin)*

Knapp [ST3025]

Rising Sun: This handsome 15th-c longhouse, a popular main entry, has now closed for conversion to a private house *(LYM)*

Leigh upon Mendip [ST6947]

Bell [Leigh St]: Friendly L-shaped local bar, good value food in bar and restaurant, Bass, Butcombe and Wadworths IPA and 6X; garden *(Alan and Eileen Bowker)*

Limington [ST5322]

Lamb & Lark [off A37 from S end of Ilchester]: Well appointed old two-room village pub with good range of well cooked interesting reasonably priced food, entertaining helpful landlord, well kept Butcombe and Greene King Old Speckled Hen; tables outside, pub ram in field over road *(John A Barker)*

Litton [ST5954]

Kings Arms [B3114, NW of Chewton Mendip

on A39 Bath—Wells]: Interesting partly 15th-c pub rambling back under low heavy beams from big hall with polished flagstones, nice old-fashioned settles, huge fireplace, large family room; new management, with food from sandwiches up, real ales such as Bass, Courage Best, and Wadworths 6X; neat streamside gardens with good play equipment *(LYM)*

Long Ashton [ST5570]

Angel [Long Ashton Rd]: Two-level lounge bar attractively hung with pewter tankards, well kept Courage Best and Smiles, comfortable seating and blazing log fire, local memorabilia inc old balloon prints, fresh flowers, front smoking room and two other rooms (children allowed there), usual food from baked potatoes and baguettes up; tolerable piped music; tables in quiet courtyard *(Simon and Amanda Southwell, JCW, Lyn and Geoff Hallchurch)*

Long Sutton [ST4625]

☆ *Devonshire Arms* [B3165 Somerton—Martock, just off A372 E of Langport]: Tall gabled stone inn with settees on right, partly no smoking restaurant area on left, lots of sporting and country prints, well kept Theakstons Best, quite a few wines by the glass, friendly staff, bar food from sandwiches up, cream teas, homely flagstoned back bar with darts and TV; piped music, and perhaps rather too many mobile phones; children in eating areas, open all day, bedrooms *(Revd A Nunnerley, Dr and Mrs Michael Smith, LYM)*

Lovington [ST5930]

☆ *Pilgrims Rest* [B3153 Castle Cary—Keinton Mandeville]: Keen landlord cooks very good value imaginative bistro food from fresh local ingredients (so may be a wait), daily fresh fish, well kept ales inc local Cottage, good wines, welcoming landlady and labrador called Sooty, pleasant décor in keeping with the old building, flagstones, big log fire, intimate candlelit evening restaurant; cl Tues lunchtime and Mon *(Anne Westcott, Mrs J Kent, Peter Winter-Hart)*

Lower Weston [ST7266]

Weston [Newbridge Rd]: Former Sportsman, taken over and extensively refurbished as large chain pub, good range of real ales, no smoking area *(A B Clarke)*

Midford [ST7560]

☆ *Hope & Anchor* [Bath Rd (B3110)]: Cosy and clean, with welcoming service, good attractively presented interesting food inc imaginative puddings in bar and flagstoned restaurant end, well kept Bass, Butcombe and Smiles, good Spanish wines, proper coffee, friendly service, log fire; tables outside, pretty walks along River Frome *(Joy and Peter Heatherley, Gaynor Gregory, Lyn and Geoff Hallchurch, Roger Wain-Heapy)*

Milborne Port [ST6718]

☆ *Queens Head* [A30 E of Sherborne]: Attractively refurbished, friendly licensees and staff, good food inc speciality curries and bargain nights such as Weds carvery and Thurs steaks, beamed lounge, good range of well kept ales such as Greene King Old Speckled Hen, Smiles and Wadworths 6X, farm ciders, friendly service, games in public bar, skittle alley, quiet roomy restaurant; live music nights, children welcome away from bars, tables in sheltered courtyard and garden with play area, three cosy good value bedrooms *(Pat and Robert Watt, LYM, Brian Chambers, Dominic Jamieson)*

Montacute [ST4916]

☆ *Kings Arms* [Bishopston]: Friendly and hard-working new licensees, enjoyable food from good sandwiches up in refurbished bars and no smoking restaurant, blazing log fires, stripped 16th-c hamstone walls, Courage Directors and Greene King Old Speckled Hen, good house wines and coffee, cheerful staff; spotless lavatories, children welcome, pleasant garden, small bedrooms in modern extension *(James Nunns, W W Burke, Dennis Jenkin, Mrs Pam Mattinson, Sir Richard FitzHerbert, Shirley Mackenzie)*

Nailsea [ST4670]

Blue Flame [West End]: Small traditional local, several intriguing rooms, well kept ales such as Bass, Fullers London Pride and Smiles tapped from the cask, Thatcher's farm cider, filled rolls, cosy open fires, great mix of all ages; pub games, children's room, sizeable informal garden *(the Didler, Jonathan Smith, A C and E Johnson, Paul Hopton)*

Moorend Spout [Union St]: Low-priced freshly made food (not Sun evening) and Bass and other ales in neatly kept early 18th-c beamed local with tables on terrace and pleasant lawn with fish pond; children welcome in restaurant, nostalgic piped music, live music Sun *(Richard Fendick)*

Old Farmhouse [B3130 towards Wraxall]: Attractive, welcoming and spotless, with scrubbed tables, school benches and dried flowers in converted old barn, stripped boards and flagstones; wide choice of good home-made food, well kept Bass and guests such as Badger, friendly service; good for children, beautiful garden with good play area and barbecues on cobbled terrace, Sun quiz night *(Alan and Paula McCully)*

Nether Stowey [ST1939]

Rose & Crown [St Mary St]: Local bustle in former 16th-c posting inn, well kept Cotleigh, Cottage, Moor and guest beers, farm cider, enjoyable food, separate public bar, restaurant (not Mon/Tues); bedrooms, open all day *(the Didler)*

North Perrott [ST4709]

Manor Arms [A3066 W of Crewkerne; Middle St]: Attractively modernised 16th-c inn on pretty village green, beams and mellow stripped stone, good value imaginative freshly made meals rather than snacks inc plenty of fish and fresh veg in clean and tidy bar and cosy restaurant, no smoking area, well kept Boddingtons, Butcombe and Smiles, good wine choice, good coffee, hard-working licensees, inglenook log fire; bedrooms (those in the inn may be warmer than the former stable block), pleasant garden with adventure play area *(Stephen S Goodchild)*

Norton St Philip [ST7755]

Fleur de Lys [High St]: 13th-c stone cottages

joined centuries ago for many-roomed black-beamed flagstoned village local, cosy family atmosphere, busy friendly staff, huge fireplace, good value tasty home-made food from good choice of baked potatoes up, good fresh veg, well kept Bass, Oakhill Best, Wadworths 6X and Worthingtons; children very welcome, skittle alley *(Bob and Sue Hardy, M G Hart, the Didler, Meg and Colin Hamilton, Dr M E Wilson, Susan and Nigel Wilson)*

Over Stratton [ST4315]

☆ *Royal Oak* [off A303 via Ilminster turn at South Petherton roundabout]: Well run thatched family dining pub, attractive and welcoming, flagstones and thick stone walls, prettily stencilled beams, scrubbed pine kitchen tables, pews, settles etc, log fires and rustic décor; fine choice of competitively priced popular food, no smoking restaurant, well kept Badger Best, Golden Champion and Tanglefoot, efficient friendly service; open all day Aug, tables outside with barbecues and good play areas for toddlers and older children inc an assault course with trampolines *(Ian Phillips, John A Barker, LYM, P Gilpin, Guy Consterdine)*

Panborough [ST4745]

☆ *Panborough Inn* [B3139 Wedmore—Wells]: Large well run 17th-c inn comfortably restored after fire damage, wide range of generous and imaginative good value food, several attractive rooms, inglenook, beams, gleaming brass and copper, fresh and dried flowers, well kept Butcombe and a guest beer, friendly chatty licensees; small restaurant, skittle alley, live music Fri, quiet views from tables in front terraced garden *(Jenny and Brian Seller, BB, Alan and Paula McCully, Richard Fendick, Kate and Peter Bird)*

Porlock [SS8846]

Ship [High St]: Picturesque thatched partly 13th-c pub smartened up under new owners, well kept Cotleigh Barn Owl, Courage Best and guest beers such as Cottage and Hop Back, low beams, flagstones and big inglenook log fires, back dining room, pub games and pool; children very welcome, sunny garden, nearby nature trail to Dunkery Beacon, bedrooms *(LYM, G Coates, Jane and Adrian Tierney-Jones)*

Porlock Weir [SS8547]

☆ *Ship* [separate from but run in tandem with neighbouring Anchor Hotel]: Prettily restored old inn noted for its wonderful setting by peaceful harbour, with tables in terraced rose garden and good walks (but no views to speak of from bars); busy Mariners Bar with friendly staff, well kept ales such as Exmoor and Ushers, roaring fire, usual food; piped music, dogs welcome, back family room; attractive bedrooms *(Trevor and Lynda Smith, Roger and Jenny Huggins, H O Dickinson, Kevin Flack, LYM, R M Corlett, Peter and Audrey Dowsett)*

Portishead [ST4777]

Albion [Old Bristol Rd]: Hungry Horse dining pub popular for filling food from sandwiches up, L-shaped carpeted bar with two log fires, brasses, beamery, bric-a-brac and old photographs, Greene King IPA and Abbot, restaurant; some tables out on front lawn *(Tom Evans)*

Phoenix [Victoria Sq, just off High St]: Thriving local open all day, small and cosy, well kept Marstons Pedigree, just crisps and such *(Tom Evans)*

☆ *Poacher* [High St]: Popular with regular older lunchers for wide range of freshly cooked food with real veg, well kept Courage, Smiles Best and a guest beer such as Wychwood Hobgoblin (may be chosen by customer ballot), friendly helpful staff, new no smoking restaurant area; cl Sun pm *(Tom Evans, K R Harris)*

Windmill [Nore Rd]: Great views over Severn to Wales from former windmill tower and extensions, newly reworked as roomy and spotless well furnished pub on three levels, good generous food particularly popular with older lunchers but available all day, well kept Greene King Old Speckled Hen, Smiles and Wadworths 6X, sensible prices; new garden, open all day *(Tom Evans)*

Ridgehill [ST5462]

Crown [Crown Hill/Regis Lane; off B3130 2 miles S of Winford]: Deep in the country, large pub pleasantly redone in rustic style with attractive furniture inc upholstered settles in small comfortably cluttered beamed rooms; enjoyable usual food from good sandwiches up, well kept Bass and Wadworths IPA and 6X, friendly staff, family area, log fire in delightful old fireplace, lovely valley views from window tables and tables on pleasant terrace *(Ian Phillips)*

Rode [ST8153]

Bell [Frome Rd]: Smart, spotless and roomy, nicely balanced choice of good food, newish licensees with good track record, well trained friendly staff *(Ted George)*

Rodney Stoke [ST4850]

Rodney Stoke Inn [A361 Wells—Weston]: Good range of imaginative well presented food in bar and back evening restaurant, well kept beer, good wine, skittle alley; tables out on terrace, camp site *(Richard Fendick, Ken Flawn, Michael and Jeanne Shillington)*

Shirehampton [ST5376]

George [High St]: Large welcoming town pub, dark oak panelling, interesting stairs and nooks and crannies *(Dr and Mrs A K Clarke)*

Lifeboat [High St]: Bar made from a lifeboat, lots of charts and maritime photographs *(Dr and Mrs A K Clarke)*

Somerton [ST4828]

☆ *Globe* [Market Pl]: Chatty and bustling old stone-built local with log fire, good interesting reasonably priced home-made bar food, attentive landlord and friendly staff, well kept ales inc Bass, Boddingtons and Butcombe, good choice of wine, two spacious bars, dining conservatory, back pool room; no music, skittle alley, tables in garden *(Graham and Elizabeth Hargreaves, Ian Phillips, Theo, Anne and Jane Gaskin)*

Staple Fitzpaine [ST2618]

☆ *Greyhound* [off A358 or B3170 S of Taunton]: Interesting rambling country pub back in

private hands, antique layout, flagstones and inglenooks, pleasant mix of settles and chairs, log fires throughout; well kept changing ales such as Badger Tanglefoot, Exmoor, Fullers London Pride and Otter, good freshly made food, friendly service, relaxing sophisticated atmosphere; good bedrooms *(Andrew Barbour, Brian and Bett Cox, LYM)*

Star [ST4358]

Star [A38 NE of Winscombe]: Unpretentious roadside pub, good mix of tables, huge inglenook fireplace, big fish tank, well kept Bass, decent food inc good fish and chips, friendly service, enthusiastic Sun lunchtime raffle (bar nibbles then); country views from picnic-sets in field behind *(Alan and Paula McCully)*

Stathe [ST3729]

Black Smock: Good choice of well presented reasonably priced food all home-made (so may be a wait if busy), friendly efficient licensees, well kept Butcombe, good local atmosphere; bedrooms clean and comfortable, good fishing nearby *(Neil Dunlop)*

Stratton-on-the-Fosse [ST6554]

White Post Inn [A367 S of Midsomer Norton, by B3139 roundabout]: Comfortable Victorian pub with several rooms, popular and friendly; well kept Bass and Butcombe tapped from casks behind the bar, limited good food; varied live entertainment, open all day *(the Didler)*

Tarr [SS8632]

Tarr Farm [Tarr Steps; OS Sheet 181 map ref 868322]: Nicely set for river walks, lovely views from gardens front and back, cosy inside with four smallish rooms, huge tables made from slabs of wood, well kept Exmoor and Flowers, nice wine, good value bar food, good cream teas (log fires in tea room), charming evening restaurant, no piped music; has been open all day (hours curtailed 2001 during foot and mouth outbreak) *(Peter and Audrey Dowsett)*

Taunton [ST2525]

☆ *Hankridge Arms* [Hankridge Way, Deane Gate (nr Sainsbury); very handy for M5 junction 25]: 16th-c former farm restored a few years ago as well appointed old-style Vintage Inn in modern shopping complex, pleasant atmosphere and service, good choice of reasonably priced generous enjoyable food inc some interesting dishes in bar and restaurant, Badger Best, Champion and Tanglefoot, log fire; quiet piped music; plenty of tables outside *(Ian Phillips, David and Sarah Johnson, Jonathon and Jane Still, Dr and Mrs A K Clarke)*

Masons Arms [Magdalene St]: Genial traditional town pub popular with local businessmen, good changing range of particularly well kept ales such as Bass, Exe Valley and Juwards, reasonably priced quick home-made food (not Sun but served late other evenings), comfortably basic furnishings, pool table, no music; pin-ups in gents', good bedrooms *(Peter L Skinner, Douglas Allen, Ian Phillips)*

Vivary Arms [Middleway, Wilton; across Vivary Park from centre]: Pretty pub with good value distinctive freshly made food inc good soup and plenty of fish, in snug plush lounge and small dining room; prompt friendly service, relaxed atmosphere, real ales such as Smiles Best, John Smiths and Charles Wells Bombardier, decent wines, no music; bedrooms with own bathrooms in Georgian house next door, easy street parking *(Ian Phillips)*

Thurloxton [ST2730]

☆ *Maypole* [A38 Taunton—Bridgwater]: Several attractively refurbished areas, wide choice of generous fresh food using local produce from filled baps up, quick friendly obliging service, well kept Whitbreads-related and other ales such as Wadworths 6X, biggish no smoking area, log fire; soft piped music, skittle alley; enclosed garden, peaceful village *(Dr and Mrs A K Clarke, Mrs P Gummer, P Gilpin)*

Timberscombe [SS9542]

Lion [Church St]: Exmoor-edge former coaching inn dating from 15th c, three rooms off comfortable flagstoned main bar, log fires, hearty food from baked potatoes and hot dogs to giant mixed grill, Butcombe, Addlestone's cider, friendly staff; piped music; bedrooms *(Joan and Michel Hooper-Immins, Peter and Audrey Dowsett)*

Tintinhull [ST4919]

Lamb [Vicarage St]: Refurbished village pub with friendly helpful staff, wide range of food inc bargain lunches (must book for new no smoking restaurant), well kept ales such as Greene King Ruddles Best and County, good choice of other drinks, nice garden; handy for Tintinhull Manor (NT) *(D J Hayman, Theo, Anne and Jane Gaskin)*

Trudoxhill [ST7443]

White Hart [off A361 SW of Frome]: Beams, stripped stone, friendly atmosphere, mainly table seating with a couple of easy chairs by one of the two log fires, enjoyable food inc good baguettes and off-peak bargains, real ales, Thatcher's farm cider, country wines; children in eating area, restaurant, no dogs, picnic-sets in flower-filled sheltered side garden *(the Didler, LYM, Hugh Roberts)*

Tytherington [ST7645]

Fox & Hounds: 17th-c, with roomy and tidy L-shaped stripped-stone bar, small no smoking dining area, well kept Bass, Butcombe and a guest beer tapped from the cask, farm ciders, generous interesting food inc some German dishes (welcoming German landlord); tables outside, comfortable bedrooms with own bathrooms, good breakfast *(A L and L R Barnes)*

Upton Noble [ST7139]

☆ *Lamb* [Church St; off A359 SW of Frome]: Small 17th-c stripped-stone village local with warmly welcoming efficient staff, well kept Butcombe, Flowers, Greene King Old Speckled Hen and Wadworths 6X, good home-made food, comfortable lounge bar, lovely view from no smoking restaurant; darts, pool etc in public bar, two dogs; big garden, cl Mon lunchtime *(Michael and Rosalind Dymond)*

Wadeford [ST3110]

Haymaker: Good choice of interesting home-

made food with fresh veg, plenty of vegetarian dishes, good helpings and reasonable prices, friendly atmosphere and pleasant décor, obliging service, Whitbreads-related ales, nicely set out restaurant, separate games room; bedrooms *(Lyn and Geoff Hallchurch, D S Price, D Pettet, David and Teresa Frost)*

Wambrook [ST2907]

☆ *Cotley Inn* [village signed off A30 W of Chard; don't follow the small signs to Cotley itself]: Stone-built pub in quiet spot with plenty of surrounding walks; smart but unpretentious, with simple flagstoned entrance bar opening on one side into small plush bar, two-room no smoking dining area (children allowed here), several open fires, Otter and Wadworths 6X; pool, piped music, skittle alley; seats and play area in garden, good bedrooms *(LYM, Colin and Janet Roe, Theo, Anne and Jane Gaskin)*

Wells [ST5545]

Crown [Market Pl]: Old coaching inn just S of cathedral, partly no smoking bistro on right with well presented food and friendly service, L-shaped public bar on left with magnificent fireplace behind the bar, Butcombe and Oakhill tapped from the cask (and maybe piped music), back espresso/wine bar starting with continental breakfast; William Penn connection, seats in back courtyard; bedrooms *(M J A Switzer, B and K Hypher, Anthony Barnes)*

☆ *Fountain* [St Thomas St]: Comfortable dining pub, wkdy lunchtime bargains, fresh fish, crisp veg, interesting ice creams and puddings in unpretentious carpeted downstairs bar with roaring log fire, or popular upstairs restaurant (worth booking wknd, good Sun lunch); quick service, well kept Ushers Best, Founders and Puck, farm cider, good choice of wines with Spanish emphasis, good coffee; can get very full wknd lunchtimes, may be piped music; right by cathedral – popular with choir, and you may even be served by a Vicar Choral); children welcome *(Hugh Roberts, Mr and Mrs C Roberts, David Biggins, Peter Meister, J F M and M West, Peter Smith, Veronica Brown, John Hillman)*

West Harptree [ST5557]

☆ *Blue Bowl* [B3114, out of village towards Chew Lake]: Extended stone-built country dining pub with lots of tables in engaging series of separate rooms, good well priced food from sandwiches to steaks inc children's dishes, good choice of well kept ales such as Butcombe, Courage Best and Wadworths 6X, friendly helpful landlord and staff, restaurant; well behaved children allowed, tables on back terrace and spacious enclosed lawn, good bedrooms *(Wendy Jones, John and Jan Fenner, BB)*

West Horrington [ST5948]

☆ *Slab House* [B3139 NE]: Attractive and well kept, bright in summer and cosy in winter, with roaring fire, paintings, china and old clocks, wide choice of good generous food from sandwiches to imaginative dishes in bar and small upmarket restaurant area, quick welcoming service, well kept Flowers Original; discreet piped music; spotless lavatories, tables out on terrace and lawns, play area

(Richard Fendick, J and M Marshall, Denis and Mary Turner)

West Huntspill [ST3044]

Crossways [A38 (between M5 exits 22 and 23)]: Informal and well worn in, with variety of places to sit inc a family room, interesting decorations and log fires, up to eight well kept real ales, notable local farm cider, decent wines, sensibly priced food (may be a wait), no piped music; skittle alley and pub games, picnic-sets among fruit trees in quite a big garden *(R J Walden, Ted George, E D Bailey, B J Harding, LYM, Steve Whalley, David Carr, Kevin Macey, Hugh Roberts, C Aspinall, B A Dale, Richard Kennell, Alan and Paula McCully, Geoff and Tricia Alderman)*

West Monkton [ST2628]

Monkton Inn: Comfortable country pub, spacious bar broken up into cosy and attractive areas, enjoyable food from new French/Italian chef/landlord, welcoming quick service, good farm cider; lots of tables in garden with play area, peaceful spot *(Anthony Forester-Bennett)*

Weston-Super-Mare [ST3261]

Claremont Vaults [Birnbeck Rd; seafront, N end]: Large well used dining pub included for wonderful views down the beach or across the bay, helped by floor being raised about a foot; Bass, Tetleys and Worthington, decent wine, friendly obliging service; quiet piped music *(Peter and Audrey Dowsett, Richard Fendick, Ian Phillips)*

Off The Rails [Station]: Tiny platform bar with real ales such as Hewish IPA and Sharps Doom Bar, properly steaming tea urn, cast-iron-framed tables, stools and banquettes; cafeteria and bookstall squeezed in too *(Ian Phillips)*

☆ *Woolpack* [St Georges, just off M5 junction 21]: Olde-worlde 17th-c coaching inn with friendly relaxing atmosphere, good varied well priced food inc some sophisticated dishes and good fish choice, pleasant window seats and library-theme area, well kept and attractively priced Oakhill with guests such as Shepherd Neame, keen efficient service, small but attractive restaurant; skittle alley *(Comus and Sarah Elliott)*

Wheddon Cross [SS9238]

☆ *Rest & Be Thankful* [junction A396/B3224, S of Minehead]: Spotless comfortably modern two-room bar with buffet bar and no smoking restaurant, wide range of generous home-cooked food inc children's, friendly and helpful speedy service even when busy, well kept ales such as Bass, Exmoor, Greene King Old Speckled Hen and Ushers Best, two good log fires, huge jug collection, aquarium and piped music; communicating games area, skittle alley, tables out in courtyard, public lavatory for the disabled, no dogs inside; bedrooms *(LYM, Dennis Jenkin)*

Winsley [ST7961]

Seven Stars [B3108 W of Bradford-on-Avon (pub just over Wilts border)]: Big stripped-stone open-plan restaurant pub with good food from well presented ploughman's up, snug alcoves, log-effect gas fires, Ushers ales (though not a place for a drop-in drink); picnic-sets out on terrace, attractive village *(PB, JB, MRSM)*

Witham Friary [ST7440]

Seymour Arms [signed from B3092 S of Frome]: Welcoming unspoilt local, two rooms served from central hatch, well kept Ushers Best and a guest beer, Rich's local farm cider; darts, cards, dominoes – no juke box or machines; attractive garden *(the Didler)*

Wiveliscombe [ST0827]

Bear [North St]: Home-cooked food, good range of well kept local beers (wknd brewery visits, beer festival with music and morris dancers), farm ciders, very attentive friendly landlord; play area, good value bedrooms *(the Didler)*

Wookey Hole [ST5347]

Wookey Hole Inn: Usefully placed family pub, four changing real ales and eight Belgian beers, enjoyable realistically priced food, nice staff; jazz Sun lunchtime, pleasant garden, bedrooms *(Mark Hey)*

Wraxall [ST4872]

Old Barn [just off Bristol Rd (B3128)]: Traditionally done barn conversion with oak beams, flagstones, fresh flowers on scrubbed tables, lots of well kept beers such as Bass, Butcombe, Moles, Smiles and Uley tapped from the cask, friendly atmosphere, pretty terrace with DIY barbecue (bring your own food or buy here) *(Jonathan Smith)*

Wrington [ST4762]

Plough [2½ miles off A370 Bristol—Weston, from bottom of Rhodiate Hill]: Friendly pub with good new landlord, plentiful tasty food, well kept Smiles and Youngs, pleasant no smoking dining area; pretty front and side garden, open all day *(Alan and Paula McCully)*

Bedroom prices normally include full English breakfast, VAT and any inclusive service charge that we know of. Prices before the '/' are for single rooms, after for two people in double or twin (B includes a private bath, S a private shower). If there is no '/', the prices are only for twin or double rooms (as far as we know there are no singles). If there is no B or S, as far as we know no rooms have private facilities.

Staffordshire

One pub here has been in every year's Guide since it started 20 years ago: the remarkable Yew Tree at Cauldon, packed with interesting things, and run throughout that time by the inimitable Alan East. Other pubs doing well here this year are the appealingly simple George at Alstonefield, the Watts Russell Arms there (new licensees doing well in this 18th-c walkers' pub), the Burton Bridge Inn in Burton upon Trent (brewing its own interesting ales), the rambling old Black Lion in the pretty conservation village of Butterton, the Queens at Freehay near Cheadle (good food at this civilised newcomer to the Guide), the ancient Holly Bush at Salt (enjoyable food using local produce), the friendly and comfortable Greyhound at Warslow (the welcoming landlord's made this quite a favourite) and the Olde Royal Oak at Wetton (a nice all-rounder, well placed for walkers). The title of Staffordshire Dining Pub of the Year unusually for us goes to a new entry: the Queens at Freehay near Cheadle. Some pubs to note particularly in the Lucky Dip section at the end of the chapter are the Moat House at Acton Trussell, Coopers Tavern in Burton upon Trent, Den Engel in Leek, Olde Dog & Partridge in Tutbury and Mainwaring Arms at Whitmore. Drinks prices in the area are well below the national average – and nowhere so far below as in the Yew Tree at Cauldon, which has bargains in the spirits line as well as its remarkably cheap beers. In this area many pubs don't open till noon, and quite a few don't open at all on weekday lunchtimes.

ALSTONEFIELD SK1355 Map 7
George
Village signposted from A515 Ashbourne—Buxton

Attracting a good mix of locals, campers and hikers, in fine weather there's a pleasant atmosphere outside as well as inside this agreeably simple stone pub. In a peaceful farming hamlet, by the village green, the stone seats beneath the pub sign are a nice place to sit and watch the world go by. The unchanging straightforward low beamed bar has a collection of old photographs and pictures of the Peak District, and pewter tankards hanging by the copper-topped bar counter; warm coal fire in winter. The spacious no smoking family room has plenty of tables and wheelback chairs. Well kept Burtonwood Bitter and Top Hat and a guest on handpump; darts, dominoes and piped music. Straightforward, good value bar food (which you order at the kitchen door) includes sandwiches (£2.10), soup (£2.25), ploughman's (from £4.75), meat and potato pie (£5.85), quiche (£6.30), chicken breast, lasagne or breaded plaice (£6.50) and a couple of daily specials; home-made puddings such as apple bakewell or fudge and walnut pie (£2.60). The big sheltered stableyard behind the pub has a pretty rockery with picnic-sets. You can arrange with the landlord to camp on the croft; no dogs or muddy boots. *(Recommended by Anthony Barnes, the Didler, Rob Fowell, John and Christine Lowe, Dr W J M Gissane, Catherine and Richard Preston, Eric Locker, Kevin Thorpe, Peter F Marshall, David Edwards, Colin Parker, Mike and Wendy Proctor, Nigel Woolliscroft, L Davenport)*

Burtonwood ~ Tenants Richard and Sue Grandjean ~ Real ale ~ Bar food ~ (01335) 310205 ~ Children in family room ~ Open 11-3, 6-11; 11-11 Sat; 12-10.30 Sun; closed 25 Dec

Watts Russell Arms

Hopedale

New licensees have taken over this 18th-c shuttered stone house, set outside the village in a deep valley of the Peak District National Park. Close to Dovedale and the Manifold it's inevitably popular with walkers and on weekends it gets very busy. The cheerful beamed bar has brocaded wall banquettes and wheelback chairs and carvers, an open fire below a copper hood, a collection of blue and white china jugs hanging from the ceiling, bric-a-brac around the roughcast walls, and an interesting bar counter made from copper-bound oak barrels; no smoking area. Straightforward bar food includes filled baps (from £2.50), soup (£2.75) filled baked potatoes (from £3.75), english breakfast, home-made chilli con carne, dish of prawns or breaded plaice (£5.95), ploughman's (£6.25), sirloin steak (£10.95) and daily specials such as vegetarian pasta bake and lamb in red wine and plum sauce (£7.95). Well kept Black Sheep, Timothy Taylors Landlord and a guest such as Adnams Regatta on handpump, about a dozen malts, decent range of soft drinks; piped music. Outside there are picnic-sets under red parasols on the sheltered tiered little terrace, and garden. They hope to have a restaurant by winter 2001. *(Recommended by Mike and Wendy Proctor, Rob Fowell, the Didler, Carol and Steve Spence)*

Free house ~ Licensees Bill and Julia Kiely ~ Real ale ~ Bar food ~ (01335) 310271 ~ Children over 6 ~ Open 12-2.30(3 Sat, Sun), 7-(10.30 Sun)11; closed Mon lunchtime in winter

BURTON UPON TRENT SK2423 Map 7

Burton Bridge Inn ◖ £

24 Bridge St (A50)

Most people come to this straightforward, bustling brick local for the very well kept Burton Bridge ales brewed on the premises. They might include Bitter, Porter, Festival, and their monthly changing Gold Medal Ale as well as a guest from a brewery such as Woodfordes on handpump; they also have around 25 whiskies and over a dozen country wines. The simple little front bar leads into an adjacent room with another bar area and a no smoking oak panelled lounge with the bar counter separating the two areas. The bar has wooden pews, plain walls hung with notices and awards and brewery memorabilia, and the lounge has oak beams, a gas effect fireplace and old oak tables and chairs. Good but basic, filling bar snacks include cobs (from £1.10, hot roast pork or beef £2.30), filled baked potatoes (from £2.30), giant yorkshire puddings with fillings such as sausage, ratatouille or faggots and mash (from £2.80) and tasty oatcakes filled with cheese (£3); the panelled upstairs dining room is open at lunchtime only. A blue-brick patio overlooks the brewery in the long old-fashioned yard at the back. Book well in advance if you want to use their skittle alley. *(Recommended by P Price, the Didler, C J Fletcher, Rob Fowell, Ted and Jan Whitfield, Theo, Anne and Jane Gaskin, Pete Baker)*

Own brew ~ Licensee Kevin McDonald ~ Real ale ~ Bar food (lunchtime only, not Sun) ~ No credit cards ~ (01283) 536596 ~ Children welcome ~ Open 11.30-2.15, 5.30-11; 12-2, 7-10.30 Sun; closed bank hol Mon lunchtime

BUTTERTON SK0756 Map 7

Black Lion

Village signposted from B5053

If it's too wet to thoroughly appreciate the views over the Peak District National Park, there are plenty of interesting things to look at in the neat rambling rooms of this friendly unspoilt 18th-c stone inn. One welcoming bar has a low black beam-and-board ceiling, lots of brassware and china, a fine old settle curling around the walls, well polished mahogany tables, and a good log fire. Off to the left are red plush button-back banquettes around sewing-machine tables and Victorian prints, while an inner room has a fine old kitchen range. Generous, popular bar food might include soup (£2.50), creamy garlic mushrooms (£3.25), broccoli and brie rösti (£6), steak and ale pie, chicken curry or cod and prawn crumble (£6.50), steaks (from £9) and roast lamb shank with port and rosemary sauce (£9.75), with specials such as pork and beef goulash or texas chilli (£7.50); puddings might include strawberry jam sponge (£2.75). Well kept real ales on handpump could be Theakstons Best, Marstons Pedigree and Hartington Bitter along with a guest such as Charles Wells Bombardier; several malt whiskies. Darts, bar billiards, dominoes, cribbage, table skittles, and separate well lit pool room; piped music. Outside picnic-sets and rustic seats on a prettily planted terrace look up to the tall and elegant spire of the local church of this pretty conservation village. *(Recommended by Mike and Wendy Proctor, Rita and Keith Pollard, Nigel Woolliscroft, the Didler, E G Parish, John Brightley, Dr Paull Khan, Rob Fowell, Carol and Steve Spence, Sue Holland, Dave Webster)*

Free house ~ Licensees Tim and Lynn Lowes ~ Real ale ~ Bar food (12-(2.30 Sat and Sun), 7-9) ~ (01538) 304232 ~ Children in eating area of bar and restaurant ~ Open 12-2.30(3 Sat and Sun), 7-11(10.30 Sun); closed Mon lunchtime ~ Bedrooms: £35B/£55B

CAULDON SK0749 Map 7
Yew Tree ★★ £
Village signposted from A523 and A52 about 8 miles W of Ashbourne

Don't be put off by the rather plain appearance of this roadside local, tucked between enormous cement works and quarries and almost hidden by a towering yew tree, inside is an Aladdin's cave of treasure – a veritable museum's worth of curiosities all lovingly collected by the lively landlord himself. The most impressive pieces are perhaps the working Polyphons and Symphonions – 19th-c developments of the musical box, often taller than a person, each with quite a repertoire of tunes and elaborate sound-effects; take plenty of 2p pieces to work them. But there are also two pairs of Queen Victoria's stockings, ancient guns and pistols, several penny-farthings, an old sit-and-stride boneshaker, a rocking horse, swordfish blades, and even a fine marquetry cabinet crammed with notable early Staffordshire pottery. Soggily sprung sofas mingle with 18th-c settles, plenty of little wooden tables and a four-person oak church choir seat with carved heads which came from St Mary's church in Stafford; above the bar is an odd iron dog-carrier (don't ask how it works!). As well as all this there's an expanding set of fine tuneful longcase clocks in the gallery just above the entrance, a collection of six pianolas (one of which is played most nights), with an excellent repertoire of piano rolls, a working vintage valve radio set, a crank-handle telephone, a sinuous medieval wind instrument made of leather, and a Jacobean four-poster which was once owned by Josiah Wedgwood and still has the original wig hook on the headboard. The very cheap, simple snacks include hot pork pies (70p), meat and potato pies, chicken and mushroom or steak pies (85p), hot big filled baps and sandwiches (from £1), quiche, smoked mackerel or ham salad (£3.40) and home-made puddings (£1-£1.50). Well kept beers – also very reasonably priced – include Bass, Burton Bridge and Titanic Mild on handpump or tapped from the cask, and there are some interesting malt whiskies such as overproof Glenfarclas; spirits prices are very low here, too. Piped music, darts, shove-ha'penny, table skittles (taken very seriously here), dominoes and cribbage. Dovedale and the Manifold Valley are not far away. *(Recommended by Mike and Wendy Proctor, Ann and Colin Hunt, Gavin E Horner, Adrian and Felicity Smith, Helen Sandelands, Tim Lawrence, Rob Fowell, Sue Holland, Dave Webster, the Didler, Brian and Anna Marsden, Bernie Adams, Karen and Graham Oddey, Nigel Woolliscroft, Paul Boot, DC, S J and C C Davidson)*

Free house ~ Licensee Alan East ~ Real ale ~ Bar food (11-9.30 most days) ~ No credit cards ~ (01538) 308348 ~ Children in Polyphon room ~ Folk music first Tues in month ~ Open 10-3, 6-11; 12-3, 7-10.30 Sun

If you enjoy your visit to a pub, please tell the publican. They work extraordinarily long hours, and when people show their appreciation it makes it all seem worth while.

CHEADLE SK0342 Map 7

Queens at Freehay

A mile SE of Cheadle; take Rakeway Road off A522 (via Park Avenue or Mills Road), then after a mile turn into Counslow Road

Staffordshire Dining Pub of the Year

This pub seemed to us a bit smaller than the Yates's last one (the Izaak Walton at Cresswell) – but that could easily be because most of their old customers seem to have followed them here, and been topped up by a whole lot of new ones. Certainly, the thriving atmosphere goes well with the surroundings: the comfortable lounge bar is attractively decorated with small country pictures, its pretty curtains matching the cushions. It opens through an arch into a light and airy dining area, with neatly spaced tables. It's the food that is the main thing here: mainly familiar sorts of dishes, nothing too far out, but all cooked carefully with good flavours, and nicely presented. The menu might include lunchtime snacks such as filled baked potatoes (from £2.50), crusty rolls (from £3.25), local black pudding with crispy bacon and cheddar or duck and noodle stir fry (£3.95) with other dishes such as spinach and ricotta cannelloni, fisherman's bake or fish and chips (£7.95), chicken filled with stilton and bacon in mild mustard sauce or mini lamb joint with mash and red wine gravy (£8.95), with blackboard specials such as home-made game pie or fresh local rainbow trout with lemon and butter (£8.95), roast duck with port and cranberry sauce (£9.95) or poached halibut with white wine, cream and grapes (£10.95); puddings such as hot chocolate fudge cake and treacle and walnut tart (from £2.95). Well kept Marstons Pedigree on handpump; quick attentive service. *(Recommended by Mike and Wendy Proctor, John and Gillian Scarisbrick, Bernard Stradling)*

Free house ~ Licensees Graham and Ann Yates ~ Bar food (12-2(2.30 Sun), 6(6.30 Sun)-9.30) ~ Restaurant ~ 01538 722383 ~ Well behaved children in eating area of bar and restaurant ~ Open 12-2.30, 6-11; 12-3, 6.30-10 Sun; closed 25 and 26 Dec, evening 1 Jan

ECCLESHALL SJ8329 Map 7

George ♀ ◖

Castle Street; A519 S of Newcastle-under-Lyme, by junction with B5026

Brewed by the owners' son, Andrew, the five Slaters beers that are served here – Bitter, Original, Top Totty, Organ Grinder and Premium – are the main reason to come to this 18th-c inn. They also keep a guest beer from another small local brewer, good wines by the glass and about 30 malt whiskies. The snug beamed bar has a pubby atmosphere with a part-carpeted, part-York stone floor, brocaded seats, and an open fire in a big brick inglenook with an attractively carved oak bressumer beam. A wide choice of bar food includes soup (£2.50), sandwiches (£2.50, baguettes £3.45), peking style crispy duck (£4.25), steaks (from £7.95), roasted filo pastry parcel, game pie or florentine style salmon steak (£8.95) and fried chicken breast with creamy mushroom sauce (£9.25); bistro restaurant; cribbage, dominoes and piped music. *(Recommended by Sue Holland, Dave Webster, E G Parish, John Whitehead, MLR, Rob Fowell, Margaret Ross)*

Own brew ~ Licensees Gerard and Moyra Slater ~ Real ale ~ Bar food (12-2, 7-9, all day Sat and Sun) ~ Restaurant ~ (01785) 850300 ~ Children in eating area of bar and restaurant ~ Open 11-11; 12-10.30 Sun ~ Bedrooms: £55B/£70B

LONGDON SK0714 Map 7

Swan With Two Necks ◖

Off A51 Lichfield—Rugeley; coming from Lichfield turn right into Brook Road

The cosy atmosphere in this pleasant pub is helped along on cold winter days by five warming coal fires. There's a chatty atmosphere in the long quarry-tiled bar which is divided into three room areas, with low beams (very low at one end), a restrained décor, and house plants in the windows; two-room carpeted restaurant. The garden has picnic-sets and swings and an outdoor summer servery. As well as a very generous helping of cod and chips (small £6.50, large £7.50), other food on the menu includes soup (£1.90), lunchtime sandwiches (from £2.10), sausage and egg or lunchtime ploughman's (£4.20), seafood platter or pies such as beef, ale and mushroom or chicken, ham and leek or stuffed chicken breast (£5.90), beef stroganoff, venison steak or fresh salmon and asparagus (£6.20) and rack of spring lamb (£7.20); limited menu on Sunday evening. Real ales on handpump include Ansells, Ind Coope Burton and a changing guest such as Timothy Taylors Landlord; decent wines and kir, friendly helpful service; piped music. *(Recommended by Gill Waller, Tony Morriss, Paul and Margaret Baker, John Whitehead, DAV, Rob Fowell, D C Abberley)*

Punch ~ Lease Jacques and Margaret Rogue ~ Real ale ~ Bar food (12-1.45, 7-9.15(8.45 Sun)) ~ Restaurant ~ (01543) 490251 ~ Children over 10 welcome in eating area of bar and restaurant ~ Open 12-2.30(3 Sat), 7-11; 12-3, 7-10.30 Sun

ONECOTE SK0555 Map 7
Jervis Arms
B5053, off A523 Leek—Ashbourne

This cheerful 17th-c pub caters well for families with a pets corner with pigmy goats, slides and swings, two family rooms (one is no smoking) with high chairs and a mother and baby room. The irregularly shaped cosy main bar has white planks over shiny black beams, window seats, wheelback chairs, two or three unusually low plush chairs, beer pump clips and bottles and a big stone fireplace. As well as well kept Bass and Titanic Best they have up to eight changing guests in summer from brewers such as Abbeydale, Shefford, Sarah Hughes, Timothy Taylor and Whim on handpump and under light blanket pressure; they've a fair range of malt whiskies. Bar food such as soup (£1.60), sandwiches (from £2), breaded lobster (£2.75), filled baked potatoes or ploughman's (from £4.95), steak and kidney pie (£4.95), minted lamb (£6.95) and puddings (£2.50); children's menu (from £2.25); one of the dining rooms is no smoking. Darts, dominoes, cribbage, fruit machine, piped music and occasional TV. A spacious converted barn behind the pub has self-catering accommodation. *(Recommended by Rob Fowell, P Price, DAV, Peter Dale)*

Free house ~ Licensee Pete Hill ~ Real ale ~ Bar food (12-2, 7-10(9.30 Sun)) ~ (01538) 304206 ~ Children in eating area of bar ~ Open 12-3, 7(6 Sat)-11; 12-10.30 Sun

SALT SJ9527 Map 7
Holly Bush
Village signposted off A51 S of Stone (and A518 NE of Stafford)

Readers are enthusiastic about the home-made bar food at this white painted thatched house set in a pretty village, and you should arrive early if you want to eat here as it fills up very quickly. The menus are prepared from as much fresh local produce as possible, and include sandwiches (from £1.75, triple deckers £2.95), filled baked potatoes (from £2.25) breaded mushrooms or pâté (£3.25), steaks (from £5.95), poached plaice (£7.25), steak and ale pie or greek lamb (£7.95), and daily changing specials such as grilled black pudding with poached egg (£3.25), fresh scottish mussels steamed in cider with cream and onion sauce (£5.95), wild mushroom stroganoff (£6.25), cod with a herb and goats cheese crust (£8.45), and duck breast in green peppercorn and sherry sauce (£10.50); home-made puddings (from £2.75); Sunday roasts. The oldest part of the building dates back to the 14th c, and has a heavy beamed and planked ceiling (some of the beams are attractively carved), a salt cupboard built in by the coal fire, and other nice old-fashioned touches such as an antique pair of clothes brushes hanging by the door, attractive sporting prints and watercolours, and an ancient pair of riding boots on the mantelpiece. Around the standing-room serving section several cosy areas spread off, including a modern back extension which blends in well, with beams, stripped brick work and a small coal fire; there are comfortable settees as well as more orthodox seats. Well kept Bass, Boddingtons and Courage Directors on handpump, friendly and efficient service, maybe piped nostalgic pop music; darts, shove-ha'penny, cribbage, backgammon, Jenga, fruit machine. The big back lawn has rustic picnic-sets and a busy dovecote; they may have traditional jazz and a hog roast in summer as well as a fireworks display on 5 November. *(Recommended by Rob Fowell, Stan and Hazel Allen, Kerry Law, Angela Westwood, Andy Gosling, June and Mike Coleman, John and Gillian Scarisbrick, Phil and Jane Hodson, Joy and Peter Heatherley, Brian and Anna Marsden, Jim Bush)*

Free house ~ Licensee Geoffrey Holland ~ Real ale ~ Bar food (12-2, 6-9.30) ~ (01889) 508234 ~ Children in eating area of bar ~ Open 12-3, 6-11; 12-11 Sat; 12-10.30 Sun

WARSLOW SK0858 Map 7
Greyhound 🏠

B5053 S of Buxton

The genial landlord at this slated stone pub goes out of his way to make sure his punters feel welcome. Cosy and comfortable inside, the beamed bar has long cushioned oak antique settles (some quite elegant), houseplants in the windows and cheerful fires. The home-made, well cooked bar food in large helpings includes lunchtime sandwiches (from £2.25), soup (£2.30), spicy thai fishcakes or ginger creel prawns (£3.50), and a choice of around 20 main meals which include lunchtime ploughman's (from £5.50), steak, mushroom and ale pie, spinach and red pepper lasagne or creamy chicken curry (£6.75), pork fillet in a brandy and cream sauce, tuna and pasta florentine or game pie (£7); children's meals. Well kept Marstons Pedigree, Worthingtons and a guest beer such as Charles Wells Bombardier or Black Sheep on handpump. In the side garden there are picnic-sets under ash trees, with rustic seats out in front where window boxes blaze with colour in summer. The simple bedrooms are clean and comfortable; good breakfasts. The pub is surrounded by pretty countryside and is handy for the Manifold Valley, Dovedale and Alton Towers. The licensees also run the Devonshire Arms in Hartington. *(Recommended by Derek and Sylvia Stephenson, Mike and Wendy Proctor, Nigel Woolliscroft, Bernard Stradling, Karen and Graham Oddey, Rob Fowell, E G Parish, Stephen Jeal)*

Free house ~ Licensees David and Dale Mullarkey ~ Real ale ~ Bar food ~ (01298) 84249 ~ Children welcome ~ Live music Sat evenings, not bank or school holidays ~ Open 12-2.30, 7-11; 12-3, 7-10.30 Sun; closed lunchtime Mon (except bank holidays) and Tues ~ Bedrooms: £17.50/£35

WETTON SK1055 Map 7
Olde Royal Oak

Village signposted off Hulme End—Alstonefield road, between B5054 and A515

Set in lovely National Trust walking country, this aged white-painted and shuttered stone village house has a welcomingly inclusive, timeless atmosphere. The relaxing bar serves well kept Black Sheep, Jennings Cumberland and and Ruddles County on handpump and you can taste Anklecracker, an ale brewed especially for them by Titanic as a tribute to the official world toe wrestling championship that takes place here during the first week of July; around 35 whiskies. The bar has black beams – hung with golf clubs – supporting the white ceiling boards, small dining chairs sitting around rustic tables, a piano surrounded by old sheet music covers, an oak corner cupboard, and a coal fire in the stone fireplace; this room extends into a more modern-feeling area which in turn leads to a carpeted sun lounge looking out on to the small garden; piped music, darts, TV, cribbage and dominoes. Generous, promptly served bar food includes soup (£2.20), prawn cocktail (£3.50), ploughman's (£5.25), battered cod or steak and Guinness pie (£5.95), scampi (£5.25), lasagne or leek and stilton bake (£5.95) and puddings like chocolate sponge pudding or cherry cheesecake (from £1.95); Sunday roast (£5.25). Behind the pub is a croft suitable for caravans and tents, and Wetton Mill and the Manifold Valley are nearby. *(Recommended by Kevin Blake, Adrian and Felicity Smith, Sue Holland, Dave Webster, the Didler, Nigel Woolliscroft, Mike and Wendy Proctor, Eric Locker)*

Free house ~ Licensees Kath and Brian Rowbotham ~ Real ale ~ Bar food ~ (01335) 310287 ~ Children in family room ~ Entertainment Sat night ~ Open 12-3, 7-11(10.30 Sun) ~ Bedrooms: /£43S

Lucky Dip

Besides the fully inspected pubs, you might like to try these Lucky Dips recommended to us and described by readers (if you do, please send us reports: www.goodguides.com).

Abbots Bromley [SK0724]
Royal Oak: Traditionally furnished old inn, usual main menu from sandwiches to steaks with imaginative blackboard dishes, generous helpings, well kept Mansfield, Marstons Pedigree and a guest beer, decent wine, efficient friendly service, open fire, comfortable and attractive dining lounge (worth booking) *(Geoff and Tricia Alderman)*
Acton Trussell [SJ9318]
☆ *Moat House* [signed from A449 just S of Stafford; handy for M6 junction 13]: Busy timbered canalside food place, partly dating from 1320, attractive grounds with picnic-sets overlooking Staffs & Worcs Canal; comfortable oak-beamed bar with big open fireplace and armchairs, nice décor, sophisticated bar food inc good fresh fish and produce from the family's farm, well kept Banks's Bitter and Original and Marstons Pedigree, good wine list, efficient service, no smoking restaurant; fruit machine, piped music; children welcome, open all day wknds, bedrooms *(Karen Eliot, Rob Fowell, Paul and Margaret Baker, Graham and Lynn Mason, Alan Thomas, Mike and Wendy Proctor, Brian and Anna Marsden, LYM, L Davenport, Peter and Elizabeth May)*
Alrewas [SK1714]
William IV [William IV Rd, off main st]: Warm and friendly, with good specials changing weekly – separate raised bookable eating area; no food Sun-Weds evenings *(Paul McGonnell)*
Brewood [SJ8808]
Admiral Rodney [Dean St]: Recently highly Victorianised, with secluded alcoves, well kept Holt, Plant & Deakins ales, generous reasonably priced food, friendly service, games room; can get very busy *(Mike and Wena Stevenson)*
Burton upon Trent [SK2423]
Alfred [Derby St]: Tied to local small Burton Bridge brewery, their full range kept well from central bar serving two spartan rooms, good beer-oriented food too; pool in back, friendly landlord, lots of country wines; open all day Fri/Sat, cheap bedrooms *(the Didler)*
☆ *Coopers Tavern* [Cross St]: Traditional counterless back tap room with notably well kept Bass, Hardys & Hansons Classic and Best and Marstons Pedigree straight from imposing row of casks (no serving counter), barrel tables, cheap nourishing lunchtime hot filled cobs, pie and chips etc (not Sun), homely front parlour with piano and coal fire, very friendly staff; tap room can get smoky; impromptu folk nights Tues *(the Didler, LYM, Pete Baker)*
Derby Inn [Derby Rd]: Unspoilt friendly local with cosy panelled lounge, great collection of railway memorabilia in long narrow bar, Marstons Pedigree, local veg, eggs and cheese for sale; sports TV, open all day Fri/Sat *(the Didler, C J Fletcher)*
Devonshire Arms [Station St]: Now tied to Burton Bridge, with a good range of their ales

and of continental bottled beers, decent lunchtime food, lots of snug corners; open all day Fri/Sat *(the Didler)*
Roebuck [Station St]: Comfortable Victorian-style alehouse opp former Bass and Ind Coope breweries, Greene King Abbot, Ind Coope Burton, Marstons Pedigree and Tetleys with several guest beers, enjoyable cheap food inc add-it-up dishes (you choose the ingredients), friendly staff, prints and artefacts; piped music; open all day wkdys, decent bedrooms *(the Didler, Joan and Michel Hooper-Immins)*
Thomas Sykes [Anglesey Rd]: In former stables and waggon shed of ex-Everards brewery (latterly Heritage Brewery Museum), two high-ceilinged rooms with stable fittings and breweriana, wood benches, cobbled floors, well kept Bass and Marstons Pedigree on handpump and guest beers tapped from the cask, fine pump clip collection, good cheap basic food; outside gents'; open all day Fri *(the Didler, C J Fletcher)*
Chorley [SK0711]
Malt Shovel [off A51 N of Lichfield via Farewell]: Friendly village local esp popular with older people, central partly stripped brick bar, comfortable lounge, proper bare-boards public bar with darts, dominoes and cards, well kept Ansells Bitter and Mild, Tetleys and a guest beer, real fires; organist 1st Sat of month *(Pete Baker)*
Clifton Campville [SK2510]
☆ *Green Man* [Main St]: Neatly kept low-beamed 15th-c village pub with inglenook and chubby armchair in public bar, airy modernised lounge, welcoming efficient service, well kept Adnams Broadside, Marstons Pedigree and Tetleys, good value food from huge hot baguettes to well priced Sun lunch and lots of puddings, piped music in games area; children in back family room, garden with play area *(Michael and Jenny Back, LYM)*
Codsall [SJ8603]
Codsall Station [Chapel Lane/Station Rd]: New pub in listed station buildings carefully restored by Holdens, good range of their beers kept well inc one brewed for the pub, lots of railway memorabilia, reasonably priced food; open all day wknds *(Gill Waller, Tony Morriss)*
Consall [SK0049]
☆ *Black Lion* [Consall Forge, OS Sheet 118 map ref 000491; best approach from Nature Park, off A522, using car park ½ mile past Nature Centre]: Traditional country tavern tucked away in rustic old-fashioned canalside settlement, by steam railway, enjoyable food inc good fish choice and some interesting dishes, good coal fire, well kept Marstons Best and Pedigree, friendly landlady; piped music; children (but not muddy boots) welcome; busy wknds, good walking area *(LYM, Mike and Wendy Proctor)*
Copmere End [SJ8029]
☆ *Star* [W of Eccleshall]: Classic simple two-room country local, particularly well kept Bass and

Chalk Hill Dreadnought, beautifully presented freshly made food (not Sun evening) from sandwiches up inc fine puddings and popular Sun lunch, very friendly service, log fire, children welcome; open all day Sat, picnic-sets in beautiful back garden full of trees and shrubs, overlooking mere – good walks *(Nigel Woolliscroft)*

Cresswell [SJ9739]

☆ *Izaak Walton* [off A50 Stoke—Uttoxeter]: Early Victorian dining pub recently reopened after period refurbishment with prints and panelling, several small rooms and larger upstairs area, wide food choice all day from sandwiches and filled rolls to steaks and mixed grill, Mon/Tues bargains, Bass and two guest beers; well behaved children welcome, disabled facilities (but some steps), pleasant back garden, open all day *(LYM, June and Mike Coleman)*

Dilhorne [SJ9743]

Red Lion [A521 Cheadle—Blyth Bridge, opp turn to village at Boundary]: Cosy traditional long bar with lots of brass and lamps, friendly staff, well kept Marstons Pedigree and Wadworths 6X, good value food from soup and baguettes to huge steaks and bargain Sun lunch in small unpretentious dining room; piped music; on ridge overlooking the wooded Cheadle Hills with plenty of country walks, handy for Foxfield Steam Railway *(Tim Wellock)*

Eccleshall [SJ8328]

Badger [Green Lane]: Friendly staff, well kept sensibly priced ales such as Titanic, good food, quick smiling service, tables outside; well maintained comfortable bedrooms, quite handy for M6 *(Simon Harris)*

Enville [SO8286]

Cat [A458 W of Stourbridge]: Mainly 17th-c, with four friendly and relaxing areas rambling around central bar, cheerful fire, landlord helpful with the very wide choice of well kept ales inc local Enville, mulled wine, quickly served generous food from imaginative sandwiches to unusual specials, popular upstairs restaurant, games room; cl Sun, popular with walkers – on Staffordshire Way *(Gill Waller, Tony Morriss, the Didler)*

Foxt [SK0348]

☆ *Fox & Goose*: Three-room pub with pre-film *Titanic* memorabilia and lots of sewing machines, four well kept ales inc one brewed for the pub, Addlestone's cider, short choice of well cooked generous bar food (no puddings), wider choice in upmarket restaurant, friendly chatty service *(R T and J C Moggridge, DC)*

Gnosall [SJ8221]

Navigation [Newport Rd]: Pleasant two-bar pub overlooking Shrops Union Canal, reasonably priced usual food, well kept Courage, friendly service, dining conservatory *(Mike and Wena Stevenson)*

Great Chatwell [SJ7914]

Red Lion: Popular country pub, well kept ales such as Banks's, Boddingtons, Everards Beacon and Tiger, Flowers IPA and Mansfield, wide food range (not Mon) from good sandwiches up, puddings cabinet, plenty of friendly staff, dining room, games room down passage;

children welcome, with good play area, aviaries, rabbits and pony, cl wkdy lunchtimes, open all day wknds *(Michael and Jenny Back)*

Hanley [SJ8747]

Coachmakers Arms [Lichfield St]: Unpretentious friendly town local, three small rooms and drinking corridor, well kept Bass and Worthington, well filled cobs, popular darts, cards and dominoes, skittles *(the Didler, Sue Holland, Dave Webster, Pete Baker)*

Golden Cup [Old Town Rd]: Friendly local with imposing Edwardian façade and bar fittings, Bass and Greene King Ruddles County; open all day (cl Sun afternoon), can be busy wknds, nice garden *(the Didler)*

Hardings Wood [SJ8354]

Bluebell: Old boaters' tavern between Macclesfield and Trent & Mersey Canals, half a dozen or more real ales from small breweries, filled rolls, busy front bar, quieter back room *(Edward Leetham)*

Hartshill [SJ8745]

Jolly Potters [Hartshill Rd (A52)]: Outstanding Bass in four-room local, gently smartened-up but largely unspoilt, with classic central bar, corridor to public bar (with TV) and three small homely lounges; very welcoming to strangers *(the Didler, Sue Holland, Dave Webster, Pete Baker)*

High Offley [SJ7725]

Anchor [off A519 Eccleshall—Newport; towards High Lea, by Shrops Union Canal, Bridge 42; Peggs Lane]: Unchanging basic canal pub in same family for over a century, two plain rooms behind partition, well kept Marstons Pedigree and Wadworths 6X tapped into jugs, Weston's farm ciders, may be lunchtime sandwiches; outbuilding with small shop and semi-open lavatories, seats outside, caravan/campsite; cl Mon-Thurs winter *(Nigel Woolliscroft, Mike and Wena Stevenson, the Didler)*

Hulme End [SK1059]

Manifold Valley Hotel [B5054 Warslow—Hartington]: Comfortable 18th-c country pub nr river, spacious lounge bar with open fire, four well kept real ales, wide choice of generous popular food from superb stilton sandwiches to Sun lunch, separate dining room; children and cyclists welcome; bedrooms in converted stone smithy off secluded back courtyard, disabled facilities *(BB, DC)*

Kidsgrove [SJ8354]

Blue Bell [Hardings Wood Rd]: Unpretentious traditional ale house with two bar areas, small no smoking area, four or five well kept and interesting changing ales, Belgian beers, farm cider, friendly landlord and customers; may be cl wkdy lunchtimes *(Mike and Wendy Proctor, Nigel Woolliscroft)*

Kinver [SO8483]

White Hart [High St]: Rambling old building with usual bar food, Banks's and a guest beer, tables on terrace *(Dave Braisted)*

Knighton [SJ7527]

Haberdashers Arms: Simple 19th-c country local in attractive spot, well kept Banks's, Marstons Pedigree and guest beers, sandwiches;

often open all day, big garden *(Nigel Woolliscroft)*

White Lion [B5415 Woore—Mkt Drayton]: Roomy unpretentious bar, friendly licensees and staff, three open fires, well kept Bass and guests, good generous home-made food (not Mon), cosy dining area, conservatory and restaurant; large adventure playground *(John Worthington)*

Leek [SJ9856]

☆ *Den Engel* [St Edward St]: Belgian-style bar in high-ceilinged former bank, over 40 beers from there, bottled and draught, changing real ales, upstairs restaurant with continental dishes inc Flemish beer-based specialities (Fri/Sat lunch, Weds-Sat night, bar food Sun night); piped classical music, very busy Fri/Sat evening, has been cl Mon, Tues and Thurs lunchtimes *(the Didler, Mike and Wendy Proctor, Richard Lewis)*

☆ *Swan* [St Edward St]: Comfortable and friendly old three-room pub with good cheap lunchtime food, pleasant helpful staff, no smoking lounge, well kept Bass and guest ales, occasional beer festivals, lots of malt whiskies, choice of coffees; downstairs wine bar; folk club, seats in courtyard *(Mike and Wendy Proctor, Sue Holland, Dave Webster, the Didler)*

☆ *Wilkes Head* [St Edward St]: Basic convivial three-room local dating from 18th c (still has back coaching stables), tap for well kept Whim ales and tied to them, also interesting guest ales; welcoming regulars and dogs, friendly landlord happy to chat, lunchtime rolls, home-made stilton for sale, good choice of whiskies, farm cider, pub games, gas fire; children allowed in one room (but not really a family pub), fair disabled access, tables outside, open all day *(Pete Baker, the Didler, G Coates)*

Lichfield [SK1109]

Queens Head [Queen St]: Marstons alehouse-theme pub with their own and well kept guest beers, bare boards and comfortable old wooden furniture, short but interesting range of well-cooked daily specials and self-choice counter of unusual cheeses with sour-dough bread or muffins, huge helpings (doggy bags provided) at very reasonable prices; friendly staff *(C J Butler, Gill Waller, Tony Morriss)*

Longsdon [SJ9554]

Wheel [Leek Rd (A53)]: Beamed pub with blazing fire, neat eating area extension and upstairs restaurant, good choice of generous food, charming efficient staff, well kept Courage Directors *(Mr and Mrs C Roberts)*

Newcastle-under-Lyme [SJ8445]

Old Brown Jug [Bridge St]: Good pub food lunchtimes and early Fri evening, keen new landlord had been cooking free curries Thurs evening, well kept Mansfield Riding, Marstons Pedigree and a monthly guest beer; Weds jazz night *(anon)*

Norbury Junction [SJ7922]

Junction [off A519 Eccleshall—Newport via Norbury]: Nice canalside spot, good range of reasonably priced home-made food in bar and carvery restaurant, well kept Banks's, friendly efficient service *(Mike and Wena Stevenson)*

Oaken [SJ8602]

Foaming Jug [Holyhead Rd; A41 just E of A464 junction]: Welcoming and interesting olde-worlde open-plan pub, wide choice of good mid-priced food, good service, well kept Bass beers, good wine choice, plenty of jugs on show; piped music; children welcome, well kept small garden *(Myke and Nicky Crombleholme, Mrs D Hardy)*

Penkhull [SJ8644]

☆ *Greyhound* [Manor Court St]: Relaxed traditional two-room pub in surprisingly villagey hilltop setting, food (not Sun/Mon evenings) inc particularly good value filling snacks, well kept Marstons Pedigree and Tetleys; children in eating area, picnic-sets on back terrace, open all day Fri-Sun *(LYM, Sue Holland, Dave Webster, Nigel Woolliscroft)*

Marquis of Granby [St Thomas Pl]: Well kept Banks's and Marstons Pedigree in popular village local *(Nigel Woolliscroft)*

Reaps Moor [SK0861]

Butchers Arms [off B5053 S of Longnor]: Isolated moorland pub, lots of atmosphere in several distinct areas, good value food inc Sun lunch, Marstons Pedigree and a guest beer; free camping for customers *(the Didler)*

Rocester [SK1039]

Red Lion [High St]: Marstons Best and Pedigree at attractive prices, huge choice of generous food with chips and peas, 1930s piped music *(Brian and Genie Smart)*

Rolleston on Dove [SK2427]

Spread Eagle [Church Rd]: Attractive old village pub with good range of well kept Bass-related ales, good value food all day, small restaurant with fresh fish, popular Sun carvery; pleasant garden, nice village *(M Borthwick)*

Shenstone [SK1004]

Plough & Harrow [Pinfold Hill, off A450]: Real country pub with enjoyable food, Bathams beer and friendly service even at busy times *(C J Butler)*

Shraleybrook [SJ7850]

☆ *Rising Sun* [3 miles from M6 junction 16; from A500 towards Stoke take first right turn signposted Alsager, Audley; in Audley turn right on B5500]: Relaxed and well worn in, with well kept changing ales such as Fullers London Pride, Robinsons Old Stockport and Youngs Special, simple generous cheap food inc pizzas, omelettes and plenty of vegetarian dishes; beams, timbering, shiny black panelling, two log fires, friendly staff; children and well behaved dogs welcome, piped music or juke box (may be loud), TV room, folk nights 2nd and 4th Thurs; good disabled access (but bar counter is high), open all day Fri-Sun and bank hols, play area, camping in two paddocks; has been cl winter lunchtimes Mon-Thurs, with talk of plans for conversion to flats *(Richard Lewis, LYM, Rob Fowell, Sue Holland, Dave Webster, G Coates)*

Stoke-on-Trent [SJ8745]

Staff of Life [Hill St]: Character city local, welcoming even when packed, unchanging layout of three rooms and small drinking corridor, well kept Bass ales *(Pete Baker,*

Sue Holland, Dave Webster, the Didler)
Stourton [SO8585]

☆ *Fox* [Bridgnorth Rd]: Comfortable, friendly and peaceful, with good value food from hot baguettes and other bar dishes to interesting cooking for bistro and conservatory (or tables outside), lovely log fires, Bathams beer; pretty village, nr Kinver Country Park walks *(Mr and Mrs P Hulme)*
Tatenhill [SK2021]

☆ *Horseshoe* [off A38 W of Burton; Main St]: Civilised tiled-floor bar, cosy no smoking side snug with woodburner, two-level restaurant and back family area, good value food (all day Sat) from sandwiches to steaks inc children's, well kept Marstons ales, good wine range, quick polite service; pleasant garden, good play area *(LYM, M Borthwick, C J Fletcher)*
Tean [SK0138]

Dog & Partridge [Uttoxeter Rd]: Good imaginative bar food, very reasonably priced, in pleasant conservatory restaurant; straightforward bar *(Dr T E Hothersall)*
Teanford [SK0040]

Ship: Small local with good food choice, all home-made, in lounge bar and friendly separate dining room/bistro, well kept real ales *(Mike and Wendy Proctor, John and Gillian Scarisbrick)*
Thorncliffe [SK0360]

Mermaid [2 miles NE at N edge of the Morridge; pub named on OS Sheet 119]: Isolated moorland pub now run by landlord with fine track record, good bar food, friendly atmosphere, old well and mermaid pictures, panoramic views from restaurant (Fri/Sat night, good Sun lunch) *(Mike and Wendy Proctor)*
Tutbury [SK2028]

☆ *Olde Dog & Partridge* [High St; off A50 N of

Burton]: Handsome and well managed Tudor timbered inn, largely given over to big and attractively laid out carvery; early-eater and lunch bargains inc good carvery and impressive puddings range, friendly service, second small restaurant, well kept Marstons Pedigree and a guest beer, good wine choice; comfortable bedrooms in separate block *(LYM, Eric Locker, David Green, John and Christine Lowe)*
Uttoxeter [SK0933]

Vaults [Market Pl]: Bass and Marstons Pedigree in unpretentious three-room local, handy for stn; large bottle collection *(the Didler)*
Wheaton Aston [SJ8412]

Hartley Arms [Long St (Canalside, Tavern Bridge)]: Roomy and restful, decent food inc interesting dishes, well kept Banks's beers, quick friendly service; tables outside, pleasant spot just above canal, nice long view to next village's church tower *(Mike and Wena Stevenson)*
Whitmore [SJ8141]

☆ *Mainwaring Arms* [3 miles from M6 junction 15 – A53 towards Mkt Drayton]: Popular old place of great character, rambling interconnected oak-beamed rooms, stone walls, four open fires, antique settles among more modern seats; well kept Bass, Boddingtons, Marstons Pedigree, wide range of foreign bottled beers and ciders, friendly service, seats outside, children in eating area, no piped music; open all day Fri/Sat, picturesque village *(George Little, Nigel Woolliscroft, E G Parish)*
Wombourne [SO8792]

☆ *Vine* [High St]: Tastefully modernised and extended Vintage Inn, good interesting food all day served piping hot, well kept Bass and a guest such as Greene King Old Speckled Hen; unobtrusive piped music *(Maureen DuMont)*

'Children welcome' means the pub says it lets children inside without any special restriction. If it allows them in, but to restricted areas such as an eating area or family room, we specify this. Places with separate restaurants usually let children use them, hotels usually let them into public areas such as lounges. Some pubs impose an evening time limit – let us know if you find this:
www.goodguides.com

Suffolk

Several of our entries here seem to have gone on to supercharger this year: really enthusiastic reports from readers, and signs that the top echelon of Suffolk pubs are pulling out all the stops to win new friends. The current stars are the Queens Head at Bramfield (great atmosphere and imaginative food, now largely organic), the simple and friendly Victoria at Earl Soham (brews its own good beers), the civilised Red Lion at Icklingham (lots of fresh fish), the Angel in Lavenham (a real favourite), the timeless old Kings Head at Laxfield (new licensees earning it a Star Award this year), the cosy little Star at Lidgate (nice mediterranean cooking), the Brewers Arms at Rattlesden (lovingly prepared imaginative food in a relaxed atmosphere), the cheerful and interesting Crown at Snape (good imaginative food here too), the Crown in Southwold (Adnams' flagship, so the beers and wines are excellent – and the stylish food's good, too), the civilised Angel at Stoke-by-Nayland (a great all-rounder, flourishing under its new owners), the nicely individualistic Moon & Mushroom at Swilland (great beers, good food and atmosphere), and the relaxing Rose at Thorington Street (nice fresh fish). Three other pubs deserve special praise for their consistency over the years: the Butt & Oyster at Pin Mill near Chelmondiston (a great spot), the Ship at Dunwich (cheap food including local fish) and the very welcoming Jolly Sailor in Orford have all featured in every single annual edition of the Guide *since it started 20 years ago. Despite stiff opposition, particularly from the Angel at Stoke-by-Nayland and Crown in Southwold, the Queens Head at Bramfield is developing its food side so rewardingly that, for the second year running, it earns the prize of Suffolk Dining Pub of the Year. This is not generally a cheap area, with drinks prices a little higher than the national average. The local Adnams is the general beer of choice in the county, full of flavour and often featuring as the cheapest on a pub's list. The much newer St Peters are also well worth looking out for, with some very iinteresting beers; the charming brewery itself, at South Elmham, is also worth visiting (see Lucky Dip section at the end of the chapter). In that section, some rising stars are the Crown at Buxhall, Bell at Cretingham, Ferry Boat at Felixstowe Ferry, Fox & Goose at Fressingfield, Old Chequers at Friston, Brewery Tap in Ipswich, Bell at Middleton, Harbour and Lord Nelson in Southwold, Maybush at Waldringfield and Kings Head at Yoxford.*

BILDESTON TL9949 Map 5
Crown 🍴
104 High St (B1115 SW of Stowmarket)

Inevitably for such an old pub this very pretty old black and white timbered 15th-c coaching inn has its fair share of ghost stories, there's a lady in grey, a gentleman in a tricorn hat and two children in Victorian dress. As we went to press new licensees were planning to make some changes to the décor in the pleasantly comfortable bar which has dark beams, an inglenook fireplace (a smaller more modern one has dried flowers), wooden tables, armchairs and wall banquettes, at the moment upholstered to match the floral curtains in the latticed windows. Bar food includes soup (£2.50), sandwiches (from £2.75), vegetable stroganoff (£5.50), tuna steak (£6.75), steak in ale or chicken with wild mushroom sauce (£6.95) and puddings such as sticky toffee pudding or profiteroles (£3.25); part of the dining room is no smoking. Well kept Adnams and a couple of guests tapped from the cask. Darts, fruit machine and piped music. The courtyard area has wrought-iron furniture and parasols, and the big attractive back garden has more seats among shrubs and trees. Quiet, comfortable bedrooms. *(Recommended by Ian Phillips, George Cowie, Rupert Sanderson)*

Free house ~ Licensees Pat Lansbury and L Stringer ~ Real ale ~ Bar food ~ Restaurant ~ (01449) 740510 ~ Children welcome ~ Live bands wkends, quiz night alt Tues ~ Open 12(11 Sat)-3, 6-11 ~ Bedrooms: £45.83S/£64.63S

BRAMFIELD TM4073 Map 5
Queens Head 🍴

The Street; A144 S of Halesworth

Suffolk Dining Pub of the Year

Over half the dishes on the menu at this deservedly popular old pub have received an organic authentification. Although much emphasis is placed on the imaginative food, there are plenty of drinking locals, and friendly, helpful licensees to create a relaxed, bustling atmosphere. The high-raftered lounge bar has scrubbed pine tables, a good log fire in its impressive fireplace, and a sprinkling of farm tools on the walls; a separate no smoking side bar has light wood furnishings; one side of the pub is no smoking. They use mainly organic fruit and vegetables and some meat, and delicious dishes might include sandwiches, potato and fresh lovage or celery soup (£3.25), dates wrapped in bacon on a mild mustard sauce (£4.15), ceviche of fresh mackerel and sardine fillets (£4.25), mushroom and fresh herb omelette with exotic leaf, bean and apple salad (£5.50), chicken, leek and bacon crumble or steak, kidney and mushroom in ale pie (£7.25), local venison and wild boar sausages with onion gravy (£7.95), lamb shank in red wine with garlic mash (£13.95), daily specials such as grilled goats cheese on a roast beetroot and walnut salad (£4.50) and whole fresh red snapper baked in a parcel with orange and garlic (£9.95), and home-made puddings like rhubarb crumble ice cream, wild strawberry sorbet, chocolate and Cointreau pot or sticky toffee pudding (from £2.95). They keep a good English cheeseboard (£3.75), and good bread comes with nice unsalted butter. Good, polite service (real linen napkins), well kept Adnams Bitter and Broadside, half a dozen good wines by the glass, home-made elderflower cordial, and local apple juices and organic wines and cider. *(Recommended by Tracey and Stephen Groves, Pat and Tony Martin, June and Perry Dann, Comus and Sarah Elliott, Simon Cottrell, A C and E Johnson, P F Whight, Stephen, Julie and Hayley Brown, Toby Holmes, Pat and Roger Fereday, Pamela Goodwyn, Bruce Jamieson, Stephen R Holman, Peter Frost, Neil Powell, Sally Anne and Peter Goodale, John Beeken, MDN, Keith and Jill Wright, Frederic Chadburn)*

Adnams ~ Tenants Mark and Amanda Corcoran ~ Real ale ~ Bar food (12-2, 6.30-10(7-9 Sun)) ~ (01986) 784214 ~ Children in eating area of bar ~ Open 11.45-2.30, 6.30-11; 12-3, 7-10.30 Sun; closed 25 Dec evening, 26 Dec

BROME TM1376 Map 5
Cornwallis 🍴 ☍ 🛏

Rectory Road; after turning off A140 S of Diss into B1077, take first left turn

Although very much a hotel, the beamed and timbered 16th-c bar at the core of this largely 19th-c country house has all the virtues that you'd want in a civilised country pub. A step up from the tiled-floor serving area, through heavy timber uprights, takes you to a stylishly comfortable carpeted area which is attractively furnished with a good mix of old and antique tables, some oak settles alongside cushioned library chairs, a glazed-over well, and a handsome woodburning stove. Alongside Adnams, St Peters Best and a guest such as Adnams Broadside on handpump, they have a carefully chosen wine list with 20 by the glass, organic local juices, bottled beers and champagne. A nicely planted Victorian-style side conservatory has coffee-lounge cane furniture, and there's an elegant restaurant. The shortish imaginative bar menu changes every two months, but might include potato soup with deep fried goats cheese (£4.50), saffron marinated mackerel with rocket and basil salad and red pepper dressing (£4.95), haddock, parsley and pea risotto with mint pesto (£5.95), roast salmon fillet with bubble and squeak, cucumber and caper berry pickle (£8.95), steak and kidney pudding (£9.75), sautéed calves liver with braised shallots, buttered kale and pancetta (£10.50), lamb steak and braised green lentils with garlic and rosemary root vegetables (£11.95) and puddings such as bitter chocolate tart or vanilla, nasturtium and rosewater mousse (£3.95). The hotel is grandly approached down a tree-lined drive and set in 20 acres of grounds with magnificent topiary, wandering ducks and a very attractive water garden. *(Recommended by Ian Phillips, David Twitchett, Stephen, Julie and Hayley Brown, Mike and Wendy Proctor)*

Free house ~ Licensees Jeffrey Ward and Richard Leslie ~ Real ale ~ Bar food (12-9) ~ Restaurant ~ (01379) 870326 ~ Children welcome ~ Open 11-11; 12-10.30 Sun ~ Bedrooms: £79.50B/£99.50B

BUTLEY TM3651 Map 5

Oyster

B1084 E of Woodbridge

Nothing really changes from year to year at this cheerful little family run country pub. There's a medley of stripped pine tables, stripped pews, high-backed settles and more orthodox seats, a pair of good coal fires in fine Victorian fireplaces, and a spinning dial hanging below one of the very heavy beams for deciding who'll buy the next round – the Adnams Bitter, Broadside Extra and their seasonal beers on handpump are well kept. They will turn the piped music off if asked; darts and dominoes. Bar food includes sandwiches (from £2.75), soup (£3.50), ploughman's (£5.50), vegetable lasagne, moussaka and broccoli pasta bake (£5.95), local ham in parsley sauce (£7.95) and puddings (£3.50). The back garden has picnic-sets and solid wooden tables and chairs, with budgerigars in three aviaries. *(Recommended by David Carr, Pat and Tony Martin, Dr and Mrs P Johnston)*

Adnams ~ Tenant Mr Hanlon ~ Real ale ~ Bar food ~ Restaurant ~ (01394) 450790 ~ Children welcome ~ Folk Sun evening ~ Open 12-3, 6-11; 12-11 Sat; 12-3, 7-10.30 Sun

CAVENDISH TL8046 Map 5

Bull

High Street (A1092 Long Melford—Clare)

Set in an especially pretty village, this attractive 16th-c pub is run by a welcoming, genuinely helpful licensee. There's a lively bustling atmosphere in the open-plan beamed interior, heavy standing timbers, fine fireplaces, and a good mix of diners and locals enjoying a drink; one room is no smoking. Besides sandwiches (from £1.95) and ploughman's (from £4.25), a very big choice of daily specials chalked up all round the pub on blackboards might include smoked salmon stuffed with prawns or tiger prawns in filo with a dip (£5.95), various curries (from £7.95), baked lamb shank with greek herbs, tortellini stuffed with prawns with a wine, cream and mascarpone sauce (£8.95), breaded veal escalope topped with ham and mozzarella with a tomato and oregano sauce (£10.95), a good mixed grill (£11.95) and steaks (from £12.95); fish is delivered fresh daily, and might include grilled haddock or cod (£6.95), skate (£9.95), and Torbay sole (£11.95); home-made puddings like tiramisu, cheesecakes or crumbles (from £3.50). Well kept Adnams Bitter, Broadside and a seasonal ale, and several wines by the glass. There are tables in the garden and they have summer barbecues. The pub has a car park. *(Recommended by David Gregory, R F Ballinger, Nick Holmes, David Clifton)*

Adnams ~ Tenant Gavin Crocker ~ Real ale ~ Bar food ~ Restaurant ~ (01787) 280245 ~ Children in eating area of bar and restaurant ~ Open 10.30-3, 6-11; 12-3, 7-10.30 Sun

CHELMONDISTON TM2038 Map 5
Butt & Oyster
Pin Mill – signposted from B1456 SE of Ipswich

There are fine views of ships coming down the River Orwell from Ipswich, lines of moored black sailing barges, and woods beyond from the bay windows inside this very simple old bargeman's pub. The half-panelled timeless little smoke room is pleasantly worn and unfussy, with model sailing ships around the walls and high-backed and other old-fashioned settles on the tiled floor, and ferocious beady eyed fish made by a local artist gaze at you from the walls. Adnams Best and Broadside, Tolly Cobbolds Bitter, Original and Mild and a fortnightly changing guest beer such as Marstons Pedigree on handpump or tapped from the cask, and decent wines; shove-ha'penny, shut the box, cribbage and dominoes. Straightforward but good value bar food includes soup (£2.95), filled baguettes (from £3.95), tiger prawns in filo pastry (£4.75), half a pint of shell-on prawns (£4.95), vegetable curry (£6.45), Lowestoft cod and chips (£6.95), steak and ale pie (£7.95), fillet steak (£10.95) and puddings (£2.95). Readers especially enjoy visits here during the annual Thames Barge Race (end June/beginning July). *(Recommended by George Atkinson, Nigel Murray, Ian Phillips, Comus and Sarah Elliott, David Carr, Keith Fairbrother, Linda Norsworthy, Mike and Mary Carter, the Didler, Pamela Goodwyn, Mr Alcuin, Alan Thomas, James Nunns)*

Pubmaster ~ Tenant Steve Lomas ~ Real ale ~ Bar food (12-2.30, 6.30-9.30; 12-9.30 Sun) ~ (01473) 780764 ~ Children welcome ~ Open 11-11; 12-10.30 Sun

COTTON TM0766 Map 5
Trowel & Hammer 🍽 ♀
Mill Rd; take B1113 N of Stowmarket, then turn right into Blacksmiths Lane just N of Bacton

The spreading series of quiet rooms at this civilised wisteria-covered pub have fresh flowers, lots of beamery and timber baulks, a big log fire (as well as an ornate woodburning stove at the back), and plenty of wheelbacks and one or two older chairs and settles around a variety of tables. Much emphasis is placed on the highly enjoyable, fairly priced food, and it's probably best to book. The menu changes daily but might include tomato and basil soup (£2.50), assiette of squid, goujons of cod and whitebait with tartare sauce (£3.95), sweet cured herrings in honey and mustard mayonnaise (£4.25), smoked salmon with chive crème fraîche (£4.75), walnut and gorgonzola filled pasta with smoked cheddar shavings or fish pie (£6.95), medallions of salmon with thai-style noodles and spicy tomato sauce (£7.55), pork steak with stilton and walnut sauce (£7.95), fried king scallops with creamy basil sauce and pasta or grilled monkfish with spinach and creamy chive and saffron sauce (£8.95), duck breast with wild cherry and orange sauce (£9.75), polite, helpful staff. Well kept Adnams, Greene King IPA and Abbot, and a guest from a brewer like Mauldons and Nethergate Bitter on handpump or tapped from the cask, an interesting wine list and lots of unusual spirits; pool, fruit machine and piped music. A pretty back garden has lots of roses and hollyhocks, neat climbers on trellises, picnic-sets and a recently renovated swimming pool. *(Recommended by Mike and Mary Carter, George Atkinson, Paul and Margaret Baker, Ian Phillips, George Cowie, Anthony Barnes, Pamela Goodwyn, Stephen P Edwards, Mike and Wendy Proctor)*

Free house ~ Licensees Simon amd Jonathan Piers-Hall ~ Real ale ~ Bar food (12-2, 6-9(10 Fri, Sat)) ~ Restaurant ~ (01449) 781234 ~ Well behaved children in eating area of bar ~ Open 12-3, 6-11; 12-11 Sat; 12-10.30 Sun

DENNINGTON TM2867 Map 5
Queens Head £
A1120

The helpful licensee and his staff will make sure you receive a warm welcome at this picturesque Tudor pub which is prettily set on the village green by the church. It was owned for centuries by a church charity, and the arched rafters in the steeply roofed part of the bar are reminiscent of a chapel. The main L-shaped room has carefully stripped wall timbers and beams, a handsomely carved bressumer beam, comfortable padded wall seats on the partly carpeted and partly tiled floor, well kept Adnams Bitter and Mauldons Mole Trap on handpump, served from the brick bar counter, and piped classical music. It's all neatly kept and full of happy customers. Reasonably priced bar food includes sandwiches (from £2.20), fried whitebait or chicken liver and garlic pâté (£3.75), smoked salmon and prawn rolls (£4.25), ploughman's (£4.50), chicken and mushroom lasagne or beef curry (£4.95), soft cheese and garlic stuffed mushrooms (£5.95), steak and mushroom pie (£6.50), lemon sole stuffed with crab and seafood sauce (£6.75), pork tenderloin with chinese spices (£7.95), vegetables and chips might be extra. There are seats on a side lawn, attractively planted with flowers, and sheltered by some noble lime trees, and the pub backs on to Dennington Park where there are swings and so forth for children. *(Recommended by Eric Locker, R J Walden, Michael Sargent, Pamela Goodwyn, Martin and Lois Sheldrick, Comus and Sarah Elliott, Charles and Pauline Stride, Terry Mizen, June and Perry Dann, Ian Phillips, Mr and Mrs M Hayes)*

Free house ~ Licensees Ray and Myra Bumstead ~ Real ale ~ Bar food (12-2, 6.30-9) ~ Restaurant ~ (01728) 638241 ~ Children in family room, must be over 7 Sat evening ~ Open 11.30-2.30, 6.30-11; 12-3, 6.30-10.30 Sun

DUNWICH TM4770 Map 5

Ship ★ ◧ £ ⇌

St James Street

Dunwich today is such a charming little place it's hard to imagine that centuries ago it was one of England's busiest ports. Since then fairly rapid coastal erosion has put most of the village under the sea, and there are those who claim that on still nights you can sometimes hear the old church bells tolling under the water. Readers enjoy staying at this charming old brick pub, and there's plenty to do nearby: the Dunwich Museum almost next door is certainly worth a visit, the RSPB reserve at Minsmere is close by, and there are plenty of surrounding walks. The cosy main bar is traditionally furnished with benches, pews, captain's chairs and wooden tables on its tiled floor, a woodburning stove (left open in cold weather) and lots of sea prints and nautical memorabilia; fruit machine, dominoes and cribbage. There's a good bustling atmosphere, especially at lunchtime, but the friendly, helpful staff and licensee manage to cheerfully cope with the crowds and make everyone feel welcome. Very well kept Adnams Bitter and Broadside and a guest from a brewer such as Mauldons on handpump at the handsomely panelled bar counter. There's a conservatory, an attractive sunny back terrace, and a large garden with well spaced picnic-sets and an enormous fig tree. They serve simple fresh fish and home-made chips, with the fish straight from boats at the beach (£5.70 lunchtime, £7.25 in the evening). The lunchtime menu includes home-made soup (£1.95), sausage and chips (£4.30), potato and onion bake or ploughman's (£4.75) and pork and bean stew (£5.25); with stilton and walnut pâté (£4.75), sausages or ratatouille (£6.95), fried cod or plaice (£7.25), fish crumble (£8.25) and duck breast with orange sauce (£10.25) in the evening. The restaurant is no smoking. *(Recommended by David Kidd, Nigel Woolliscroft, Eric Locker, Tina and David Woods-Taylor, M J Morgan, Eddie Edwards, Keith Fairbrother, Brian Wainwright, Keith and Margaret Evans, MDN, Peter and Anne-Marie O'Malley, Adrian and Gwynneth Littleton, Michael Sargent, Tracey and Stephen Groves, John Beeken, David Peakall, Peter and Pat Frogley, P G Plumridge, Stephen, Julie and Hayley Brown, Anthony Barnes, Denys Gueroult, Cathy Robinson, A C and E Johnson, KN-R, Pamela Goodwyn, David Field, Simon and Sally Small, Neil P; also in* The Good Hotel Guide*)*

Free house ~ Licensees Stephen and Ann Marshlain ~ Real ale ~ Bar food (not 25 Dec) ~ Restaurant ~ (01728) 648219 ~ Children in restaurant and family room ~ Open 11-3.30, 6-11; 12-3.30, 7-11 Sun; closed 25 Dec evening ~ Bedrooms: £45S/£55S

Please let us know of any pubs where the wine is particularly good.

EARL SOHAM TM2363 Map 5

Victoria ◀

A1120 Yoxford—Stowmarket

There's an easy going, friendly local atmosphere at this charmingly unpretentious little village pub. The traditional bar is fairly basic with stripped panelling, kitchen chairs and pews, plank-topped trestle sewing-machine tables and other simple scrubbed pine country tables with candles, tiled or board floors, an interesting range of pictures of Queen Victoria and her reign, a piano and open fires. The interesting range of own-brewed ales here is produced from the microbrewery by the previous licensees: Victoria Bitter, a mild called Gannet, and a stronger ale called Albert are well kept on handpump. Good value home-made bar food includes sandwiches (from £1.75), soup (£2.50), ploughman's (from £3.75), tasty corned beef hash (£3.50), vegetarian pasta dishes (£4.25), pork and pineapple or lamb curry (£5.50), beef casserole (£6.25), and a winter Sunday roast (£6.25). Cribbage and dominoes; seats out in front and on a raised back lawn. The pub is close to a wild fritillary meadow at Framlingham and a working windmill at Saxtead. *(Recommended by Pat and Tony Martin, Comus and Sarah Elliott, J F M and M West, A C and E Johnson, M J Morgan, Ian Phillips, T G Thomas, Kevin Thorpe)*

Own brew ~ Licensee Paul Hooper ~ Real ale ~ Bar food (12-2.30, 6-10) ~ No credit cards ~ (01728) 685758 ~ Children in eating area of bar ~ Folk music Tues ~ Open 11.30-3, 6-11; 12-3, 7-10.30 Sun

ERWARTON TM2134 Map 5

Queens Head ♀ ◀

Village signposted off B1456 Ipswich—Shotley Gate; pub beyond the attractive church and the manor with its unusual gatehouse (like an upturned salt-cellar)

The best tables at this unassuming and relaxed 16th-c pub are by the window which looks out over fields to the Stour estuary. The friendly bar has bowed black oak beams in the shiny low yellowing ceiling, comfortable furnishings, a cosy coal fire, and several sea paintings and photographs. Adnams Bitter and Broadside and Greene King IPA are very well kept on handpump, and they have a decent wine list with several half bottles, and a wide choice of malt whiskies. Good value very tasty bar food includes sandwiches, home-made soup (£2.95), ploughman's (£5.50), vegetable lasagne, home-made moussaka or beef and ale casserole (£7.50), chicken breast in Pernod and prawn sauce (£7.95), breaded prawns with lemon and cajun dip (£8.50), steak, kidney and mushroom pudding (£7.95), steaks (from £9.50) and daily specials such as crab salad (£6.95), red lentil curry (£7.25) and seafood stroganoff, or partridge casserole (£7.95); no smoking area in restaurant. Darts, bar billiards, shove-ha'penny, cribbage, dominoes and piped music. The gents' has a fascinating collection of navigational maps. There are picnic-sets under summer hanging baskets in front. Handy for Erwarton Hall with its peculiar gatehouse. *(Recommended by Tony and Shirley Albert, Ian Phillips, MDN, George Atkinson)*

Free house ~ Licensees Julia Crisp and B K Buckle ~ Real ale ~ Bar food ~ Restaurant ~ (01473) 787550 ~ Children in restaurant ~ Open 11-3, 6.30-11; 12-3, 7-10.30 Sun; closed 25 Dec

FRAMSDEN TM1959 Map 5

Dobermann ◀ ⏢

The Street; pub signposted off B1077 just S of its junction with A1120 Stowmarket—Earl Soham

A central open fire separates the two spotlessly kept areas of this charmingly restored open plan thatched pub. This is a lively little place with a good friendly welcome, dog prints, photographs of show rosettes won by the owner's dogs all over the white walls and maybe Puss Puss the cat. There are pale stripped beams in the very low ceilings, a big comfy sofa, a couple of chintz wing armchairs and a mix of other chairs and plush-seated stools and winged settles around polished rustic tables. Good bar food in generous helpings includes sandwiches (from £2), soup (£3.50), ploughman's (from £4.95), steak (from £8.95) and daily specials such as asparagus (£2.95), mexican chicken (£8.25) and trout cooked in white wine with toasted almonds. Well kept Adnams Bitter and Broadside, and a guest such as Mauldons Mole Trap on handpump; efficient service. Cribbage, dominoes, and piped radio. They play boules outside, where there are picnic-sets by trees and a fairy-lit trellis, and lots of pretty summer hanging baskets and colourful window boxes; no children. *(Recommended by Alan Cowell, Alan and Judith Gifford, Mr Norbury, Mrs Hughes, Pat and Tony Martin, Comus and Sarah Elliott, J Hale, Mike Ridgway, Sarah Miles, S Marshall)*

Free house ~ Licensee Susan Frankland ~ Real ale ~ Bar food ~ Restaurant ~ No credit cards ~ (01473) 890461 ~ Open 12-3, 7-11(10.30 Sun); closed Mon ~ Bedrooms: /£50S

GREAT GLEMHAM TM3361 Map 5
Crown ♀ ◗ 🛏

Between A12 Wickham Market—Saxmundham and B1119 Saxmundham—Framlingham

Dogs and wellies are welcome at this attractive pub which is set in a particularly pretty village. The interior is beautifully kept, with sofas on rush matting in the big entrance hall; an open-plan beamed lounge has wooden pews and captain's chairs around stripped and waxed kitchen tables, local photographs and paintings on cream walls, fresh flowers, and some brass ornaments; log fires in two big fireplaces. Well kept Greene King IPA and Old Speckled Hen are served from old brass handpumps, and decent bar food includes sandwiches (from £2.95), soup (£3.25), baked potatoes (from £4.25), ham and eggs (£4.75), ploughman's (£4.95) and daily specials such as whitebait (£4.25), butterfly prawns with lemon mayonnaise (£4.95), mushroom and spinach lasagne or beef rissoles (£6.95), steak and kidney pie or salmon steak with lime and chives (£7.95), and sirloin steak (£9.95); children's menu (£2.95). Dominoes and cribbage. A tidy, flower-fringed lawn, raised above the corner of the quiet village lane by a retaining wall, has some seats and tables under cocktail parasols; disabled access. *(Recommended by Comus and Sarah Elliott, Pamela Goodwyn, Norman and Sheila Sales, David Field)*

Free house ~ Licensees Barry and Susie Coote ~ Real ale ~ Bar food ~ (01728) 663693 ~ Children welcome ~ Open 11.30-3, 6.30-11; 12-3, 7-10.30 Sun; closed Mon (except bank holidays)

HARTEST TL8352 Map 5
Crown

B1066 S of Bury St Edmunds

One reader told us they received their friendliest welcome ever at this very well run pink-washed pub where drinkers and diners are made to feel equally at home. It's by the church (bell-ringing practice is on Thursday evenings) on a fine village green, and has seats on the big back lawn set among shrubs and trees; more seats on the sheltered side courtyard, and a children's play area. There's plenty of space in the very pleasant interior, you can sit anywhere in either the bar, two no smoking dining areas or conservatory. Enjoyable bar food includes home-made soup (£2.50), sandwiches (from £2.75), home-made chicken liver pâté (£4.25), ploughman's (£5), baguettes or omelettes (from £5.50), fresh fillet of cod or haddock (£7.75), home-made lasagne (£8), chicken breast on tagliatelle with tomato and basil sauce (£8.50), and steaks (from £10); popular Sunday lunch (£13.50 for three courses). They have special Monday evening menus (from £9.50 for three courses), a Wednesday pie menu (£9 for two courses), and a very good value Friday fish meal (£9 (£11 evenings) for three courses). Greene King IPA, Abbot, and Old Speckled Hen on handpump, kept under light blanket pressure, decent house wines, and quick, very helpful black-tie staff; quiet piped music. *(Recommended by David Kidd, MDN, David Gregory, Pamela Goodwyn, Mandy and Simon King, D P Brown)*

Greene King ~ Tenants Paul and Karen Beer ~ Real ale ~ Bar food (12-2, 6.30-9.15) ~ Restaurant ~ (01284) 830250 ~ Children in eating area of bar and restaurant ~ Open 11-2.30, 6-11; 12-3, 6-10.30 Sun; closed Sun evenings Jan-Feb

HORRINGER TL8261 Map 5

Beehive ♀

A143

It's a shame we don't get more reports about this jolly nice cottagey pub, although the ones we do get are all from very contented readers. There's a gently civilised atmosphere in the rambling little rooms which have some very low beams, carefully chosen dining and country kitchen chairs on coir or flagstones, one or two wall settles around solid tables, picture-lights over lots of 19th-c prints, and stripped panelling or brickwork. Food from the daily changing imaginative menu is very good, and might include tomato and roast pepper soup (£3.95), shellfish chowder (£4.50), chicken, coriander and ginger terrine with lime dressing (£4.95), braised chicken in red wine, garlic and thyme jus or salmon escalope with herb mustard gratin (£9.95), braised lamb shank with redcurrant reduction (£10.50) and puddings such as ginger crème brûlée, pecan tart or warm chocolate chip coffee sambuca cake (£3.95). Well kept Greene King IPA and a changing beer such as Greene King Abbot on handpump, and decent changing wines with half a dozen by the glass. An attractively planted back terrace has picnic-sets and more seats on a raised lawn. Their dog Muffin is very good at making friends, although other dogs are not really welcome. *(Recommended by F J Lennox, Pat and Tony Martin, Derek Thomas, Geoffrey and Brenda Wilson, Pamela Goodwyn, Mike and Mary Carter, Paul Boot, David Kidd, Hazel Morgan, David Twitchett)*

Greene King ~ Tenants Gary and Dianne Kingshott ~ Real ale ~ Bar food (not Sun evening) ~ Restaurant ~ (01284) 735260 ~ Children welcome ~ Open 11.30-2.30, 7-11; 12-2.30, 7-10.30 Sun; closed 25, 26 Dec

HUNDON TL7348 Map 5

Plough 🛏

Brockley Green – nearly 2 miles SW of village, towards Kedington

There are five acres of particularly lovely landscaped gardens with fine views of the Stour valley surrounding this remotely set pub. A very pleasant terrace has good wooden furniture under a pergola, there's an ornamental pool and croquet and putting. Inside, the neatly kept knocked-through carpeted bar has plenty of old standing timbers, low side settles with Liberty-print cushions, pine kitchen chairs and sturdy low tables on the patterned carpet, lots of horsebrasses on the beams, and striking gladiatorial designs for Covent Garden by Leslie Hurry, who lived nearby. Home-made bar food includes lunchtime sandwiches and ploughman's, soup (£2.95), smoked mackerel pâté (£4.25), home-made prawn quiche (£7.75), lasagne (£6.95), vegetable korma (£7.75), salmon and lemon sole crumble or steak and onions topped with a savoury scone (£7.95), pot roasted minted lamb (£8.75), breast of chicken wrapped in bacon with a mushroom and tomato sauce (£8.95), and steaks (from £10.75); Sunday roasts (£7.75). Well kept Greene King IPA, Woodfordes Wherry and a guest beer such as Shepherd Neame Spitfire on handpump; quite a few wines, 30 malt whiskies and organic soft drinks; piped music. Parts of the bar and restaurant are no smoking. It's a certified location for the Caravan Club, with a sheltered site to the rear for tourers, and if you stay in the pub the comfortable bedrooms have good views. There are two friendly resident labradors. More reports please. *(Recommended by Richard Gibbs)*

Free house ~ Licensees David and Marion Rowlinson ~ Real ale ~ Bar food (till 9.30 Mon-Sat) ~ Restaurant ~ (01440) 786789 ~ Open 11(12 winter)-2.30, 5-11; 12-3, 7-10.30 Sun ~ Bedrooms: £45S(£55B)/£65S(£75B)

The letters and figures after the name of each town are its Ordnance Survey map reference. *How to use the Guide* at the beginning of the book explains how it helps you find a pub, in road atlases or large-scale maps as well as in our own maps.

ICKLINGHAM TL7872 Map 5
Red Lion 🍴

A1101 Mildenhall—Bury St Edmunds

This civilised 16th-c thatched dining pub is the perfect place for a pleasant drink at the bar followed by a relaxing Sunday lunch. Get there a bit earlier (or book) for a table in the nicer beamed open-plan bar which has a big inglenook fireplace and is attractively furnished with a nice mixture of wooden chairs, big candlelit tables and turkey rugs on the polished wood floor. A simpler area behind a knocked through fireplace has dark wood pub tables on carpets; piped classical music. There's quite an emphasis on the popular enjoyable bar food which includes home-made soup (£3.55), home-made pâté (£3.65), local sausages with mash and onion gravy (£6.25), lambs liver and bacon (£7.95), pork chops with apple and cider sauce or warm fillet of chicken and crispy pasta salad (£8.95) and over a dozen changing fish dishes such as mackerel with caper butter (£9.95), ling fillet with tomato soup and cheese (£10.95), mixed grill (£11.85) and bass with chilli butter (£15.95). Well kept Greene King IPA and Abbot on handpump, lots of country wines and fruit presses, and winter mulled wine. In front (the pub is well set back from the road) picnic-sets with colourful parasols overlook the car park and lawn, and at the back more seats on a raised terrace face the fields – including an acre of the pub's running down to the River Lark, with Cavenham Heath nature reserve beyond; giant outside Jenga; handy for West Stow Country Park and the Anglo-Saxon Village. *(Recommended by Pat and Robert Watt, Andrew Scarr, J F M and M West, R M Harrold, P R and A M Caley, Mrs A Scott, Stephen, Julie and Hayley Brown, Nick and Meriel Cox, Ian Phillips, Martin and Lois Sheldrick)*

Excalibur ~ Lease Jonathan Gates and Ian Hubbert ~ Real ale ~ Bar food (12-2.30, 6-10; 12-2, 7.15-9.30 Sun) ~ Restaurant ~ (01638) 717802 ~ Children welcome ~ Open 12-2.30, 6-11; 12-2, 7.15-10.30 Sun

LAVENHAM TL9149 Map 5
Angel ★ 🍴 ♀ ▰ 🛏

Market Pl

This carefully renovated Tudor inn is one of the most liked pubs in the *Guide*. As well as being an excellent place to eat and stay it also remains popular with locals popping in for just a drink and a chat. The long bar area, facing on to the charming former market square, is light and airy, with a buoyantly pubby atmosphere, plenty of polished dark tables, a big inglenook log fire under a heavy mantelbeam, and some attractive 16th-c ceiling plasterwork (even more elaborate pargeting in the residents' sitting room upstairs). Round towards the back on the right of the central servery is a no smoking family dining area with heavy stripped pine country furnishings. The very good food can be eaten in either the bar or restaurant, and might include starters such as sweet potato and ginger soup (£3.50), game terrine with cumberland sauce (£4.95), half a dozen fresh oysters (£5.50), snacks such as pork pie and pickles or ploughman's (£4.95) and main courses such as steak and ale pie (£7.95), grilled salmon fillet with prawn and lemon sauce, lamb chops grilled with onion and rosemary gravy (£8.95), pot roast guinea fowl with apple and ginger sauce (£9.25), and puddings such as strawberry meringue roulade, steamed syrup sponge pudding or raspberry crème brûlée. Well kept Adnams Bitter, Greene King IPA and Abbot, and Nethergate Bitter on handpump, quite a few malt whiskies, and several decent wines by the glass or part bottle (you get charged for what you drink). They have shelves of books, dominoes, and lots of board games; classical piped music. There are picnic-sets out in front overlooking the square, and white plastic tables under cocktail parasols in a sizeable sheltered back garden; it's worth asking if they've time to show you the interesting Tudor cellar. *(Recommended by the Didler, John Wooll, Dr M E Wilson, David Twitchett, Charles and Pauline Stride, Derek and Sylvia Stephenson, Charles Gysin, Giles and Liz Ridout, David Carr, Mr and Mrs M Hayes, MDN, Paul Boot, Patricia Beebe, Pamela Goodwyn, Miss G Irving, R Styles, David Kidd, Ian Phillips, Mrs D Fiddian, Pam and David Bailey, Andy Gosling, Richard Siebert, David Gregory, Paul S McPherson, Maysie Thompson, David and Ruth Hollands)*

Free house ~ Licensees Roy Whitworth and John Barry ~ Real ale ~ Bar food (12-2.15, 6.45-9.15) ~ Restaurant ~ (01787) 247388 ~ Children in eating area of bar and restaurant ~ Classical piano Fri evenings ~ Open 11-11; 12-10.30 Sun; closed 25-26 Dec ~ Bedrooms: /£70B

Swan ★ 🛏

High St

It's well worth a visit to this lovely timbered Elizabethan hotel to look at the interior of one of Lavenham's famously attractive buildings. It actually incorporates several fine half-timbered buildings, including an Elizabethan house and the former Wool Hall. It's quite smart and does have all the trimmings of a well equipped hotel (and not a cheap one), but buried in its heart is the peaceful little tiled-floor bar with leather chairs, a set of handbells that used to be employed by the local church bell ringers for practice, and memorabilia of the days when this was the local for the US 48th Bomber Group in the Second World War (many Americans still come to re-visit old haunts). From here armchairs and settees spread engagingly through a network of beamed and timbered alcoves and more open areas. Overlooking the neat, sheltered courtyard garden is an airy Garden Bar. Well kept Adnams and Greene King IPA. A fairly short bar food menu includes home-made soup (£3.50; soup and a sandwich £7), sandwiches (from £3.50; toasted bagel with smoked salmon and cream cheese £4.50; plum tomato, buffalo mozzarella, basil and pine nut dressing on focaccia bread £5.95), ploughman's (£7), salads such as grilled tuna fish with french beans and tomato olive oil dressing or sautéed potatoes, mushrooms, black pudding, crispy bacon, red onion and poached egg (from £7.50), sausage with onion mash and real ale chutney (£8), and grilled salmon, spinach and mash, and lemon fish cream or grilled minute steak (£9.50); good morning coffee and afternoon tea. There is also a lavishly timbered no smoking restaurant with a minstrel's gallery.
(Recommended by the Didler, David Carr, F J Lennox, David and Ruth Hollands, Giles and Liz Ridout, Patricia Beebe, Derek Thomas, George Atkinson)

Heritage Hotels ~ Manager Francis Guildea ~ Real ale ~ Bar food ~ Restaurant ~ (01787) 247477 ~ Children welcome ~ Open 11-2.30, 6-11; 11-3, 7-10.30 Sun ~ Bedrooms: £79B/£158B

LAXFIELD TM2972 Map 5
Kings Head ★ 🍺

Behind church, off road toward Banyards Green

A reader visiting here after a ten year interval told us that this thatched 15th-c house hasn't changed at all in that time. There's gentle timeless atmosphere in the charming, old-fashioned front room which has a high-backed built-in settle on the tiled floor and an open fire. Two other equally unspoilt rooms have pews, old seats, scrubbed deal tables, and some interesting wall prints. There's no bar – the well kept Adnams Bitter, Broadside, and Regatta, Earl Soham Low House (named for the pub after its local nickname), Gannet Mild and a couple of guests from brewers such as Greene King IPA and Mauldons are tapped from the cask. Tasty bar food now includes sandwiches, baked banana with stilton (£2.50), pork and leek sausages with mash and onion gravy (£5.50), steak in ale pie (£6.50), and puddings such as apple and rhubarb crumble or lemon and lime syllabub (£2.95). The old bowling green forms the major part of the garden, and is surrounded by benches and tables; there's an arbour covered by a grape and hop vine, and a small pavilion for cooler evenings.
(Recommended by A C and E Johnson, Mr and Mrs Thomas, Rev John Hibberd, R J Walden, J Hale, Neil Powell, Mrs Kay Dewsbury, the Didler, Phil and Sally Gorton, Ian and Nita Cooper, J F M and M West, Comus and Sarah Elliott, Stephen R Holman, Kevin Thorpe, Richard Siebert, Stephen, Julie and Hayley Brown)

Free house ~ Licensees George and Maureen Coleman ~ Real ale ~ Bar food ~ Restaurant ~ No credit cards ~ (01986) 798395 ~ Children in restaurant and family room ~ Impromptu trad music all day Tues ~ Open 11-3, 6-11; 11-11 Tues; 12-4, 7-10.30 Sun; opens at 12 in winter

LEVINGTON TM2339 Map 5
Ship

Gun Hill; village signposted from A14, then follow Stratton Hall sign

Although a recent fire destroyed the thatch on this charming old pub which is prettily set next to a little lime-washed church, they will be open again by the time this book is in the shops – in fact they had to delay the opening because the building is listed and they were obliged to wait for the October harvest of the Norfolk reed used for the job. They salvaged the entire contents so there's still quite a nautical theme inside with lots of ship prints and photos of sailing barges, and a marine compass set under the serving counter in the middle room, which also has a fishing net slung over it. As well as benches built into the walls, there are a number of comfortably upholstered small settles, some of them grouped round tables as booths, and a big black round stove. The dining room has more nautical bric-a-brac, beams taken from an old barn, and flagstones; two no smoking areas. Bar food includes salmon fishcakes (£6.25), sausage and bacon pie, king prawns in garlic butter, lamb casserole (£6.50) and steak and kidney pudding (£6.95). Well kept Adnams Broadside and Bitter, Greene King Abbot and IPA, and a beer named for the pub on handpump or tapped from the cask; dominoes. If you look carefully enough, there's a distant sea view from the picnic-sets in front. No children inside. (*Recommended by Ian Phillips, June and Malcolm Farmer, Giles and Liz Ridout, J F M and M West, Charles and Pauline Stride, Mike and Mary Carter, David Carr, Derek Harvey-Piper, MDN, Ian and Nita Cooper*)

Pubmaster ~ Tenants William and Shirley Waite ~ Real ale ~ Bar food (not Sun-Tues evenings) ~ Restaurant ~ (01473) 659573 ~ Open 11.30-3, 6-11; 12-3, 7-10.30 Sun; closed evenings 25-26 Dec

LIDGATE TL7257 Map 5
Star 🍴 ♀

B1063 SE of Newmarket

With its delightful mix of traditional English and Mediterranean influences, there's a lovely relaxed atmosphere and very good food at this most attractive little village pub. It's run by a charmingly friendly Spanish landlady, but its small main room still has lots of English pubby character, with handsomely moulded heavy beams, a good big log fire, candles in iron candelabra on good polished oak or stripped pine tables, bar billiards, dominoes, darts and ring the bull, and just some antique Catalan plates over the bar to give a hint of the Mediterranean. Besides a second similar room on the right, there's a cosy simple dining room on the left. The easy going atmosphere, and the changing bar menu with crisp and positive seasons in some dishes, speak more openly of the South. There might be mediterranean fish soup or prawns in garlic (£4.50), a Catalan salad (£5.90), Spanish omelette, grilled cod or venison sausages, (£6.50), lasagne or roast lamb in garlic and wine (£11.50), stuffed quail in honey or monkfish marinière (£12.50), parrillada – seafood stew (£14.50), puddings such as strawberry cream tart or chocolate roulade (£4); lunchtime two-course menu £10.50. Greene King IPA, Abbot, Old Speckled Hen on handpump, and enjoyable house wines; darts, bar billiards, dominoes, ring the bull and maybe unobtrusive background music. There are tables on the raised lawn in front and in a pretty little rustic back garden. (*Recommended by Michael Sargent, Frank and Margaret Bowles, R C Wiles, Stephen P Edwards, B N F and M Parkin, Mr and Mrs E R Evans, David Field, Martin and Lois Sheldrick, Sally Anne and Peter Goodale*)

Greene King ~ Lease Maria Teresa Axon ~ Real ale ~ Bar food (not Sun evening) ~ Restaurant ~ (01638) 500275 ~ Children in eating area of bar and restaurant ~ Open 11-3, 5(6 Sat)-11; 12-3, 7-11 Sun; closed evening 25 Dec, 1 Jan

---

Children – if the details at the end of an entry don't mention them, you should assume that the pub does not allow them inside.

ORFORD TM4250 Map 5
Jolly Sailor £
Quay Street

Built in the 17th c mainly from wrecked ships' timbers, this unspoilt old favourite
once had a reputation as a smugglers' hangout. These days it makes a good base for
walkers, fishermen and birdwatchers, and you can be sure of a genuinely cheery
friendly welcome. The several snugly traditional rooms are served from counters and
hatches in an old-fashioned central cubicle. There's an unusual spiral staircase in the
corner of the flagstoned main bar – which also has 13 brass door knockers and other
brassware, local photographs, and a good solid fuel stove; a small room is popular
with the dominoes and shove-ha'penny players, and has draughts, chess and
cribbage. Chatty and friendly staff serve well kept Adnams Bitter and Broadside on
handpump and big helpings of good straightforward bar food such as local battered
fish – cod, eel, flounder – and chips, home-made steak pie or lasagne, home-cooked
ham and egg, local seasonal pheasant, and daily roasts (all £5.25); the dining room is
no smoking. There are lovely surrounding coastal walks and plenty of outside
pursuits; several picnic-sets on grass at the back have views over the marshes. No
children or credit cards. (Recommended by Comus and Sarah Elliott, Diana Brumfit, Paul
Hathaway, Dr M E Wilson, MDN, Peter and Pat Frogley, Mr and Mrs S Oxenbury, Keith
Fairbrother, Graham Jones, David and Brenda Tew, Kevin Thorpe, Tracey and Stephen Groves,
David Carr, Peter D B Harding)

Adnams ~ Tenant Philip Attwood ~ Real ale ~ Bar food (not Mon-Thurs evenings
Nov-Easter; possibly not some lunchtimes in Nov) ~ No credit cards ~ (01394)
450243 ~ Open 11.30-2.30, 7-11; 12-2.45, 7-10.30 Sun; closed evenings 25, 26 Dec ~
Bedrooms: /£40

RATTLESDEN TL9758 Map 5
Brewers Arms 🍴
Signposted on minor roads W of Stowmarket, off B1115 via Buxhall or off A45 via Woolpit

This solidly built 16th-c village local is popular for its good, interesting food which is
served in a relaxed and friendly pubby atmosphere. The pleasantly simple beamed
lounge bar on the left has book-lined walls, individually chosen pictures and bric-a-
brac. It winds back through standing timbers to the main eating area, which is partly
flint-walled, has a magnificent old bread oven and new more comfortable seating;
piped music. As well as sandwiches and light lunches, the very good imaginative
menu might include tomato and basil soup (£3.25), stuffed garlic mushrooms
(£3.95), smoked salmon with raspberry dressing (£4.95), filo layer of stir-fried
vegetables with sweet and sour leeks, steak pudding or prawn curry (£8.95),
marinated shank of lamb with port and mint gravy (£10.95), Gressingham duck
with black cherry sauce (£11.95), roast bass fillet on minted pea purée (£12.95), and
puddings such as toffee sponge pudding, chilled coffee mousse with almond praline
or apple pie (from £3.50). The restaurant is no smoking. Very welcoming and
friendly service, and well kept Greene King Abbot, IPA and Old Speckled Hen and
maybe a guest such as Gales HSB on handpump and kept under light blanket
pressure; decent wines. French windows open on to a garden edged with bourbon
roses; boules. (Recommended by Mrs Kay Dewsbury, David Kidd, Charles and Pauline Stride,
Roy and Margaret Jones, Mrs A Scott, Pamela Goodwyn, Stephen, Julie and Hayley Brown, JMC,
Ian Phillips)

Greene King ~ Tenant Jeffrey Chamberlain ~ Real ale ~ Bar food (not Sun evening,
Mon) ~ Restaurant ~ (01449) 736377 ~ Children over 5 in eating area of bar ~ Open
12-3, 6.30-11; 12-3, 8-10.30 Sun; closed Mon

Looking for a pub with a really special garden, or in lovely countryside, or with
an outstanding view, or right by the water? They are listed separately, at
the back of the book.

REDE TL8055 Map 5
Plough 🍴 ♟

Village signposted off A143 Bury St Edmunds—Haverhill

There's a genuinely warm welcome from the jovial licensee at this lovely pink washed, partly thatched pub. The traditionally simple cosy bar has copper measures and pewter tankards hanging from low black beams, decorative plates on a delft shelf and surrounding the solid fuel stove in its brick fireplace, and red plush button-back built-in wall banquettes; maybe piped pop music. Very enjoyable and consistently good bar food includes calves liver with onion jam and red wine sauce, crab au gratin or poussin stuffed with goats cheese and garlic (£8.95), black cherry guinea fowl on mashed potato with black cherry jus (£9.95) and grilled bass stuffed with spinach and chilli (£13.95). This is a lovely spot, sometimes the only sound is birdsong from the aviary or surrounding trees, or perhaps the cooing from the dovecote. There are picnic-sets in front and pheasants strutting across the lawn in the sheltered cottagey garden at the back. *(Recommended by Martin Jones, Patricia Beebe, P F Whight, J Hale)*

Greene King ~ Tenant Brian Desborough ~ Real ale ~ Bar food (not Sun evening) ~ Restaurant ~ (01284) 789208 ~ Children in eating area of bar and restaurant ~ Open 11-3, 6.30-11; 12-3, 6.30-10.30 Sun

SNAPE TM3959 Map 5
Crown 🍴 ♟ 🛏

B1069

Just a stone's throw from Snape Maltings, this popular unspoilt inn is well worth a visit in its own right. It offers a really warm welcome from courteous staff, very good food and is a really comfortable place to stay. The attractive rooms are furnished with striking horseshoe-shaped high-backed settles around the big brick inglenook, spindleback and country kitchen chairs, and nice old tables on some old brick flooring. An exposed panel shows how the ancient walls were constructed, and there are lots of beams in the various small side rooms. The dining room is no smoking. From the imaginative menu, there might be chick pea, chorizo and tomato soup (£2.95), coarse game pâté (£4.50), smoked salmon and potato cake with chive crème fraîche (£5.25), smoked duck breast with chutney and salad (£5.50), salmon and dill fishcakes with lime tartare sauce (£8.50), steak and kidney pudding or chicken breast filled with brie and sun-dried tomatoes with a tomato coulis (£8.95), rack of lamb with red wine and mint gravy (£10.95), Sunday roast (£8.50), and home-made puddings such as sticky toffee pudding or crème brûlée (£3.75). Well kept Adnams Bitter, Broadside and a seasonal ale on handpump, and a good thoughtful wine list with 8 by the glass (including champagne). There are tables and cocktail parasols in the pretty roadside garden. The bedrooms are full of character with beamed ceilings, sloping floors and doorways that you may have to stoop through; good generous breakfasts. No children. *(Recommended by MDN, Phil and Heidi Cook, Joy and Peter Heatherley, Lynn Sharpless, Bob Eardley, Tracey and Stephen Groves, D J Hayman, Norman and Sheila Sales, Mr and Mrs S Oxenbury, Martin Jennings, David Carr, Comus and Sarah Elliott, M A and C R Starling, R C Wiles, Neil Powell, Anthony Barnes)*

Adnams ~ Tenant Diane Maylott ~ Real ale ~ Bar food ~ Restaurant ~ (01728) 688324 ~ Open 12-3, 6-11(7-10.30 Sun); closed 25 Dec, 26 Dec evening ~ Bedrooms: /£65B

Golden Key

Priory Lane

Still clocking up their years here, Mr and Mrs Kissick-Jones who are Adnams's longest serving tenants, have been at this cheerfully civilised inn for nearly 25 years now. The low-beamed stylish lounge has an old-fashioned settle curving around a couple of venerable stripped tables on the tiled floor, a winter open fire, and at the other end, some stripped modern settles around heavy Habitat-style wooden tables on a turkey carpet, and a solid fuel stove in the big fireplace. The cream walls are hung with pencil sketches of customers, a Henry Wilkinson spaniel and so forth; a brick-floored side room has sofas and more tables. Well kept Adnams, Broadside and Old Ale, as well as a decent wine list, and about a dozen malt whiskies. Unfussy, but very well executed home-cooking might include filled rolls (from £2.25), soup (£3.95), prawns in filo pastry with chilli dip (£4.75), mushrooms with stilton (£5.25), sausage, egg and onion pie or smoked haddock quiche (£6.95), vegetable lasagne, broccoli cheese and potato bake or steak, mushroom and Guinness pie (£7.95), honey roast ham (£8.95), loin lamb chops (£9.95) and puddings such as hot lemon cake or sticky toffee pudding (£3.75); one dining room is no smoking. There are plenty of white tables and chairs on a terrace at the front near the small sheltered flower-filled garden. *(Recommended by Martin and Lois Sheldrick, M W Turner, Tracey and Stephen Groves, Lynn Sharpless, Bob Eardley, Phil and Heidi Cook, Neil Powell, Richard Siebert, Joy and Peter Heatherley, Paul Bailey, David Carr, Comus and Sarah Elliott)*

Adnams ~ Tenants Max and Suzie Kissick-Jones ~ Real ale ~ Bar food (12-2.30, 6-9.30) ~ Restaurant ~ (01728) 688510 ~ Children in eating area of bar and restaurant ~ Open 12-3, 6-11(7-10.30 Sun) ~ Bedrooms: £45B/£65B

Plough & Sail 🍴 ♀

Snape Maltings Riverside Centre

There's a light and airy feel at this busy extended pub. Four different areas include the original part with its log fires, sofas and settles, the bar where the Adnams Bitter, Broadside and seasonal ales are well kept on handpump, and two restaurants, one with a mezzanine which is actually under the eaves and has a balcony overlooking the bustle below. There's a nice mix of customers and the atmosphere is relaxed and friendly. Bar food includes soup (£3.75), chicken liver and lemon pâté with onion marmalade and toasted brioche (£4.25), grilled goats cheese on toasted focaccia with rosemary and parsley dressing (£4.75), asparagus and stilton cream filo pastry tart (£5.15), spinach and ricotta cannelloni (£7.95), fried lambs liver with onion, bacon and mash (£8.75), duck breast with mango compote (£9.15) and baked pork fillet on coarse grain mustard mash with peach and plum compote (£9.45), and puddings such as summer fruits pudding or black cherry tart (£4.25). The big enclosed flower-filled courtyard has teak tables and chairs under parasols where you can sit with a drink and a newspaper before enjoying a concert at the Snape Maltings concert hall on site. *(Recommended by David Carr, Anthony Barnes, June and Perry Dann, Charles and Pauline Stride, T G Thomas, Tracey and Stephen Groves, George Atkinson, Pamela Goodwyn, R C Wiles)*

Free house ~ Licensees G J C and G E Gooderham ~ Real ale ~ Bar food (12-2.30(12-3 Sat, Sun), 7-9(9.30 Fri, Sat)) ~ Restaurant ~ (01728) 688413 ~ Children in restaurant ~ Folk and fish and chips evening alternate winter Thurs ~ Open 11-3, 5.30-11; 11-11 Sat; 12-4, 7-10.30 Sun; 11-3, 5.30-11 winter Sat, 12-3, 7-10.30 Sun in winter

SOUTHWOLD TM5076 Map 5
Crown ★ 🍴 ♀ 🍽

High Street

The elegant beamed main bar at this rather smart old hotel has a stripped curved high-backed settle and other dark varnished settles, kitchen chairs and some bar stools, pretty, fresh flowers on the mix of kitchen pine tables, newspapers to read, a carefully restored and rather fine carved wooden fireplace, and a relaxed atmosphere; the small no smoking restaurant with its white cloths and pale cane chairs leads off. The smaller back oak-panelled locals' bar has more of a traditional pubby atmosphere, red leatherette wall benches and a red carpet; the little parlour on the left is also no smoking; shove-ha'penny, dominoes and cribbage. This is Adnams's flagship pub so there's a particularly carefully chosen wine list from a choice of 250, with a monthly changing choice of 20 interesting varieties by the glass or bottle, as well as the full range of Adnams beers which are perfectly kept on handpump, and quite a few malt whiskies. Very popular changing bar food from a stylish menu includes butternut and parmesan soup (£3.20), six oysters with red wine and shallot reduction (£8.10), tapas (£8.50 for two), fresh fish in a watermelon curry with aubergine and yoghurt (£9.50), confit of duck leg with grilled aubergine and crushed potatoes (£9.75), grilled lemon sole with roasted new potatoes and caper mayonnaise (£10.25), roast loin of lamb with creamy parmesan risotto (£10.95), and puddings such as banana cheesecake with lemon icing (£3.95), chocolate nut torte with berry compote and honey mascarpone (£4.10), and Neals Yard cheese (£4.25). There are a few tables in a sunny sheltered corner outside. *(Recommended by J F M and M West, Margaret Heath, Ian and Jane Irving, Stephen, Julie and Hayley Brown, Susan and John Douglas, Stephen P Edwards, John Wooll, David Peakall, Tracey and Stephen Groves, Evelyn and Derek Walter, Joy and Peter Heatherley, MJVK, Comus and Sarah Elliott, Ian Phillips, R C Wiles, Richard Siebert, Mike and Sue Loseby, Steve and Liz Tilley, Tina and David Woods-Taylor, G T Brewster, Steve Chambers, the Didler, R J Walden, David Kidd, Peter Burton, Geoffrey and Brenda Wilson, Nigel Woolliscroft)*

Adnams ~ Tenant Michael Bartholomew ~ Real ale ~ Bar food (12-2, 7-9.30) ~ Restaurant ~ (01502) 722275 ~ Children over 5 in restaurant ~ Open 10.30-3, 6-11; 12-3, 6-10.30 Sun ~ Bedrooms: £57B/£82B

STOKE-BY-NAYLAND TL9836 Map 5
Angel 🍴 🍷 🛏

B1068 Sudbury—East Bergolt; also signposted via Nayland off A134 Colchester—Sudbury

Despite new ownership, the management team at this stylishly elegant dining pub is intact and keeping things well up to scratch. It's a good all-rounder with remarkably good food, well kept real ales and a relaxed and friendly atmosphere; it's a nice place to stay overnight. The comfortable main bar area has handsome Elizabethan beams, some stripped brickwork and timbers, a mixture of furnishings including wing armchairs, mahogany dining chairs, and pale library chairs, local watercolours and older prints, attractive table lamps, and a huge log fire. Round the corner is a little tiled-floor stand-and-chat bar – with well kept Adnams Bitter, Greene King IPA, Abbot and a guest such as their Ruddles County on handpump, and a thoughtful wine list. One no smoking room has a low sofa and wing armchairs around its woodburning stove, and Victorian paintings on the dark green walls. Attractively presented and generously served, the imaginative food includes home-made soup (£2.95), griddled fresh sardines in oregano (£4.75), deep-fried cambazola with cranberry sauce (£4.75), steamed mussels in white wine and cream (£4.75), fresh dressed crab with home-made mayonnaise (£5.95), roast ballotine of duckling with a cassis sauce (£6.95), steak and kidney pudding (£7.25), chicken and king prawn brochette with yoghurt and mint dip (£9.75), grilled fresh skate wing (£9.95), brochette of scallops wrapped in bacon (£11.50) and honey-glazed roast rack of lamb (£11.50); home-made puddings such as dark chocolate gateau or raspberry bavarois (£3.75). You may have to book well ahead at weekends. There are cast-iron seats and tables on a sheltered terrace. *(Recommended by Barbara Wilder, Andy Meaton, Adrian and Gwynneth Littleton, Ian Phillips, MDN, Pamela Goodwyn, C L Kauffmann, David Twitchett, Derek Stafford, Hazel Morgan, Richard Siebert, Peter and Pat Frogley, Stephen and Jean Curtis, Alan Clark, Lynn Sharpless, Bob Eardley, Anthony Longden, David Gregory, John and Enid Morris, J F M and M West, Peter and Marilyn Budden)*

Horizon Inns ~ Manager Michael Everett ~ Real ale ~ Bar food ~ Restaurant ~ (01206) 263245 ~ Children in family room and restaurant if over 8 ~ Open 11-2.30, 6-11; 12-3, 6-10.30 Sun; closed 25, 26 Dec, 1 Jan ~ Bedrooms: £50B/£65B

SWILLAND TM1852 Map 5
Moon & Mushroom 🍴

Village signposted off B1078 Needham Market—Wickham Market, and off B1077

They keep only independent East Anglian beers such as Buffys Hopleaf and Norwich Terrier, Nethergates Umbel, Wolf Bitter and Coyote and Woodfordes Norfolk Nog and Wherry, all tapped straight from casks racked up behind the long counter at this cosy little place. It's run by cheerful, genuinely helpful people and there's a good mix of chatty customers – all of which creates a bustling but relaxed atmosphere. The homely interior is mainly quarry tiled with a small coal fire in a brick fireplace, old tables (with lots of board games in the drawers) arranged in little booths made by pine pews, and cushioned stools along the bar. An unusual touch is the four hearty hotpots in the no smoking dark green and brown painted cottagey dining room through a small doorway from the bar. These are served to you from Le Creuset dishes on a warming counter and might include coq au vin, pork with peppers, minted lamb, pheasant au vin (all £6.55). You then help yourself to a choice of half a dozen or so tasty vegetables. Another couple of dishes might include ploughman's (£4.25), halibut mornay and stilton and pasta bake (£5.95), with proper home-made puddings like raspberry and apple crumble, bread and butter pudding and toffee and ginger pudding with butterscotch sauce (£2.95). This is still a real local so food service ends quite early. They have about 10 decent wines by the glass and 20 malt whiskies. You approach the pub through an archway of grapevines and creepers, and a little terrace in front has flower containers, trellis and nice wooden furniture under parasols. No children inside. *(Recommended by George Atkinson, J F M and M West, Keith Fairbrother, Charles and Pauline Stride, Comus and Sarah Elliott, Pat and Tony Martin, Pamela Goodwyn, Mr and Mrs M Hayes, E D Bailey)*

Free house ~ Licensees Clive and Adrienne Goodall ~ Real ale ~ Bar food (12-2, 6.30-8.15; not Sun, Mon) ~ No credit cards ~ (01473) 785320 ~ Open 11-2.30, 6-11; 12-2.30, 7-10.30 Sun

THORINGTON STREET TM0035 Map 5
Rose

B1068 Higham—Stoke by Nayland

It's the smiling welcome from the cheery landlady and her daughter, the properly pubby atmosphere and the nice mix of customers, that readers really enjoy at this welcoming village pub. The building is partly Tudor, and has been knocked through into a single longish partly divided room, with old beams, pine tables and chairs, and enough pictures, prints and brasses to soften the room without overdoing the décor. Among them are old photographs of the landlady's family who were in the fishing trade. Food is not over-fancy, but good and well thought out. Frequent fresh fish deliveries mean fish and seafood are particularly tasty: fish and chips (£5.95), whole baby squid, dover and torbay sole, whole plaice, jumbo haddock, skate wing, and mussels, lobsters, oysters, crab and mediterranean prawns (£7.95-£12.95). Other dishes might include sandwiches (from £2.20), home-made soup (£3.95), ploughman's (from £3.75), lunchtime lasagne, chilli or quiche (£5.95), chicken goujons in sesame seeds with garlic mayonnaise (£7.95), steaks (from £8.95) and puddings such as pineapple upside-down cake, popular melt-in-the-mouth meringues filled with fruit and cream, and blackberry and apple pie (£2.50). The top end of the restaurant is no smoking. Well kept Adnams, Greene King Abbot and IPA, Woodfordes Wherry, and a guest beer on handpump, and decent wines; dominoes, cribbage, cards, dice, and piped music. The fair-sized garden has picnic-sets and summer barbecues, and overlooks the Box valley. *(Recommended by ML, Charles and Pauline Stride, Ian Phillips, MDN, M A and C R Starling, Keith Fairbrother, J F M and M West)*

Free house ~ Licensee Kathy Jones ~ Real ale ~ Bar food ~ Restaurant ~ No credit cards ~ (01206) 337243 ~ Children welcome ~ Open 12-3, 7-11(10.30 Sun); closed Mon

TOSTOCK TL9563 Map 5
Gardeners Arms

Village signposted from A14 (former A45) and A1088

Reliably good, this charmingly unspoilt pub is run by a jovial landlord and has a bustling villagey atmosphere. The cosily smart lounge bar has heavy low black beams and lots of carving chairs around decent sized black tables and a warming fire, and in the lively tiled public bar there's darts, pool, shove-ha'penny, dominoes, cribbage, juke box, and an unobtrusive fruit machine; regular quiz nights. Very well kept Greene King Abbot, IPA and seasonal beers on handpump. Very enjoyable, good value bar food includes sandwiches (from £1.60; toasties £3.50), ploughman's (from £4.50), gammon and eggs (£6.75), and daily specials such as steak and kidney pie or vegetable enchilada (£6.50), moroccan lamb tagine with minted couscous (£7.25), chinese king prawn and ginger stir fry on noodles (£8.25); the dining area is no smoking. There's a pleasantly sheltered lawn with picnic-sets among roses and other flowers. *(Recommended by George Atkinson, Derek R A Field, Mike and Mary Carter, Comus and Sarah Elliott, Catherine and Richard Preston, Mr and Mrs G Robson, Mrs Kay Dewsbury, Mr and Mrs M Hayes, Roy and Margaret Jones, Pippa Daniels, Ian Phillips)*

Greene King ~ Tenant Reg Ransome ~ Real ale ~ Bar food (not Mon, Tues evening, Sun lunchtime) ~ Restaurant ~ (01359) 270460 ~ Children in restaurant ~ Open 11.30(11 Sat)-2.30, 7-11; 12-3, 7-10.30 Sun

WALBERSWICK TM4974 Map 5
Bell

Just off B1387

The very lovely interior of this unpretentious old place has brick floors, well worn flagstones and oak beams that were here 400 years ago when the sleepy little village was a flourishing port. The characterful, rambling bar is traditionally decorated with curved high-backed settles, tankards hanging from oars above the bar counter, and a woodburning stove in the big fireplace; a second bar has a very large open fire. Enjoyable changing bar food might include carrot and coriander soup (£2.95), fried chicken livers in sherry (£4.25), battered cod, haddock or plaice (£5.95), mushroom stroganoff (£6.95), grilled salmon with gravadlax sauce (£7.95), beef stroganoff (£8.25), fillet steak with pork and pâté (£11.50), and home-made puddings (£3). Well kept Adnams Bitter, Broadside and Regatta on handpump, darts, shove-ha'penny, cribbage and dominoes, with boules outside. There are two resident boxer dogs, and dogs are welcome. To really make the most of the setting, it's worth taking the little ferry from Southwold, and then enjoying the short walk along to the pub. This is a nice spot close to the beach, and the seats and tables on the sizeable lawn here are sheltered from the worst of the winds by a well placed hedge. Most of the bedrooms look over the sea or river. *(Recommended by John Wooll, Comus and Sarah Elliott, David Peakall, Ian Phillips, the Didler, Richard Siebert, MDN, Jilly Burrows, Tracey and Stephen Groves, T G Thomas, G K Smale, A C and E Johnson, MJVK, Penny Miles, Howard James, Richard Pinnington)*

Adnams ~ Tenant Sue Ireland Cutting ~ Real ale ~ Bar food ~ Restaurant ~ (01502) 723109 ~ Children in eating area of bar and family room ~ Open 11-3, 6-11; 12-10.30 Sun(12-3.30, 7-10.30 winter) ~ Bedrooms: £60S/£70S(£90B)

WESTLETON TM4469 Map 5
Crown 🍴 🍷 🍺 🛏

B1125 Blythburgh—Leiston

You'll still find horses in the stables at this extended coaching inn and smugglers' haunt (and there are the usual tales of a tunnel going under the road, and surfacing by the pulpit in the church opposite). The parlour room has a sanded wooden floor, a mix of old settles (one dated 1780), pews, nice old chairs, and old barrel tables, and a log fire. Henry James mentioned the red quarry-tiled floor in the main bar, which also has country chairs and attractive stripped tables, good local photographs and farm tools, and there's a carpeted no smoking dining conservatory. Though these surroundings are unpretentious, the atmosphere tends to the upmarket. You can eat formally or informally from the imaginative daily changing menu which might include lunchtime open sandwiches with home-made bread (from £3.95) or ploughman's (£5.25), and other beautifully presented dishes such as white onion and ham hock soup with goats cheese (£3.50), crisp brie and shredded honey, lemon and chilli chicken legs on sweet and sour cucumber salad (£4.75), spring onion and smoked haddock potato cake with tartare sauce (£4.95), fried fillets of local plaice

(£5.95), saffron risotto topped with aubergines, red pepper and spiced courgettes (£8.25), roast pork belly with smoked bacon, mash and onion jus (£9.95), fried fillet of local long-lined cod or fried salmon fillet on warm gooseberry chutney, spiced baked courgettes, prawns and caper juices (£10.50), braised lamb shank with rosemary, celeriac and carrot mash with spiced braised red cabbage (£10.75), and home-made puddings such as rhubarb and Grand Marnier ice cream, baked American vanilla cheesecake with fresh raspberries and pressed chocolate and amaretto mousse soufflé cake with a light chocolate mousse (£3.95). Well kept on handpump, the half dozen or so real ales include Adnams, Nethergate County, St Peters Organic, Tindalls Suffolk and a guest such as Fullers London Pride; 90 malt whiskies, and a carefully chosen wine list. Dominoes, cribbage, shove-ha'penny, darts, bar skittles, bar quoits, and quiet piped light modern music (classical in the restaurant and only music by people who have stayed here). The pretty garden has plenty of seats (the ones on the floodlit terrace are warmed by outside heaters), a pets corner with pot bellied pigs, budgies and ducks, and Sunday afternoon pig roasts during the summer school holidays. Good walks nearby. *(Recommended by Robert and Catherine Dunster, Pamela Goodwyn, Comus and Sarah Elliott, Tracey and Stephen Groves, R and P Baker, Michael and Ann Cole, M J Morgan, David Field, Richard Siebert)*

Free house ~ Licensees Richard and Rosemary Price ~ Real ale ~ Bar food (12-2.15, 7-9.30) ~ Restaurant ~ (01728) 648777 ~ Children welcome ~ Open 11-3, 6-11; 12-3, 7-10.30 Sun; closed 25 and 26 Dec ~ Bedrooms: £59.50B/£69.50B

WINGFIELD TM2277 Map 5

De La Pole Arms 🍴 🍺

Church Road; village signposted off B1118 N of Stradbroke

This beautifully restored village inn which is tucked away off the beaten track in lovely countryside is one of only three St Peters pubs. They stock all the St Peters beers on handpump and their entire range of over a dozen bottled beers. The deliberately simple yet elegant décor is very traditional with interesting bric-a-brac, comfortable traditional seating, and no distraction by noisy games machines or piped music. Very good bar food, served by courteous, friendly staff, might include soup (£3.95), a bowl of mussels or prawns (£6.95), cheese, spinach and ham bake (£7.50), steak and stout pie (£7.95), cold seafood platter (£8.95), baked halibut (£9.25), grilled skate wings (£9.50), and puddings such as apple crumble and custard, mango and orange mousse and chocolate and rum pots (£3.95); the restaurant is no smoking. *(Recommended by Tom Gondris, W K Wood, R C Wiles, Pat and Tony Martin, Roger Everett, MDN, A C and E Johnson, J F M and M West, Julie and Bill Ryan)*

St Peters ~ Tenant Sally Prior ~ Real ale ~ Bar food ~ Restaurant ~ (01379) 384545 ~ Children in eating area of bar and restaurant ~ Open 11-3, 6-11; 12-3 Sun; closed Sun evening and Mon

Lucky Dip

Besides the fully inspected pubs, you might like to try these Lucky Dips recommended to us and described by readers (if you do, please send us reports: www.goodguides.com).

Aldeburgh [TM4656]
Mill [Market Cross Pl, opp Moot Hall]: Friendly, with reasonably priced food cooked to order inc local fish, good service, well kept Adnams ales, decent coffee (a lunchtime tipple of choice here), locals' bar, cosy no smoking beamed dining room with *Gypsy Queen* model, sea view; cream teas July/Aug (open all day then, can get rather full); fruit machine; open all day Fri/Sat, bedrooms *(anon)*
White Hart [High St]: Friendly and individual refurbished Victorian local (go for the seats on the right), good choice of well kept ales inc

Adnams, remarkable range of spirits, good value hearty lunchtime sandwiches and ploughman's, open fire; folk and Irish music nights; open all day, comfortable bedrooms *(Mr and Mrs David Spillane, Tracey and Stephen Groves)*
Alderton [TM3441]
Swan [The Street]: Comfortable and relaxed, with good food *(John Martin)*
Aldringham [TM4461]
☆ *Parrot & Punchbowl* [B1122/B1353 S of Leiston]: Neatly kept beamed pub with good food inc local fish from downstairs servery,

dining-room meals Fri-Sun (must book then), lots of decent wines, well kept Adnams and Greene King IPA, no piped music; children welcome, dogs allowed; pleasant sheltered garden with own servery and a couple of swings, nice craft centre opp *(BB, Jim McBurney)*

Bardwell [TL9473]

Six Bells [village signed off A143 NE of Bury; keep straight through village, then fork right into Daveys Lane off top green]: Comfortably modernised low-beamed restauranty pub dating from 16th c, well kept Adnams or Marstons Pedigree, decent wines, coal-effect fire in big fireplace; wide choice of bar meals with more elaborate evening dishes, restaurant with no smoking conservatory, children welcome, garden with play area and wendy house; attractive pine-furnished bedrooms in separate building, cl Mon-Weds lunchtimes exc bank hols *(Martin Jennings, Charles and Pauline Stride, Pamela Goodwyn, LYM, W H and E Thomas, M J Morgan)*

Barham [TM1451]

Sorrel Horse [Old Norwich Rd]: Cheerful and attractive pink-washed pantiled 17th-c country pub, nicely refurbished bar with magnificent log fire, lots of beams, lounge and two dining areas off, particularly well kept Tolly ales, ample good value food inc interesting specials, prompt friendly service; good garden with big play area and barbecue, stables opp; children welcome, well placed for walks *(Ian and Nita Cooper, J F M and M West)*

Barton Mills [TL7173]

☆ *Bull* [by A11 (due to be dual carriageway, so access may change), close to Five Ways roundabout nr Mildenhall]: Reopened after reworking, big log fire in quarry-tiled new main bar, attractive rambling original bar and dining area, Adnams Bitter and Broadside, Greene King IPA and a beer brewed for the pub; bedrooms being refurbished *(BB, Ian Phillips)*

Beyton [TL9363]

White Horse [signed off A14 and A1088; Bury Rd]: Busy dining pub on village green, friendly staff, well kept Greene King Abbot *(Comus and Sarah Elliott)*

Blaxhall [TM3657]

Ship [off B1069 S of Snape; can be reached from A12 via Little Glemham]: Welcoming new Dutch landlord (grew up near here) in low-beamed traditional pub, attractive country setting, log fire, unassuming dining lounge, well kept Tolly and Marstons Pedigree, piped music, pool in public bar; children in eating area, self-catering cabins available; has been cl Mon lunchtime *(LYM, Joy and Alistair Shaw)*

Brandeston [TM2460]

Queens Head [The Street, towards Earl Soham]: Unpretentiously attractive open-plan country local, leather banquettes and old pews, well kept Adnams Broadside and a seasonal ale, decent food (not Sun evening) inc great sausages, family room; shove-ha'penny, cribbage, dominoes, piped music; bedrooms, campsite, big neat garden with good play area *(LYM, David Jones, David Kidd, Pamela Goodwyn)*

Brent Eleigh [TL9447]

Cock [Lavenham Rd (A1141)]: Unspoilt thatched pub with piano in clean and cosy snug, benches, table and darts in second small room, coal fires, lots of old photographs of local villages, no food beyond crisps and pickled eggs, Adnams, Greene King IPA or Abbot and Nethergate Mild; nice garden, attractive inn-sign, bedrooms *(Kevin Thorpe, the Didler, Phil and Sally Gorton)*

Bury St Edmunds [TL8564]

Angel [Angel Hill]: Thriving long-established country-town hotel with good food inc beautifully presented starters in elegant Regency restaurant and terrace rooms, helpful friendly service, well kept Adnams in rather plush bar, cellar grill room; bedrooms comfortable *(P F Whight)*

Cupola House [The Traverse]: Interesting building with grand central staircase to upstairs no smoking bar, experienced new landlord doing good value honest food, charming service, ad lib coffee *(MDN)*

Linden Tree [Out Northgate St/Station Hill]: Good bustling yet relaxed atmosphere and wide choice of generous cheap food from good baguettes up in pleasant family dining pub with stripped pine bar, friendly quick service, well kept Greene King ales, decent wines in two glass sizes, freshly squeezed orange juice, popular no smoking conservatory restaurant (worth booking), good well kept garden *(Mr and Mrs T B Staples, J F M and M West)*

Nutshell [Traverse, Abbeygate St]: Quaint and attractive corner pub, perhaps the country's smallest inside, with particularly well kept Greene King IPA and Abbot, friendly landlord, lots of odd bric-a-brac inc mummified cat; cl Sun and Holy Days *(the Didler, Mike and Wendy Proctor)*

Old Cannon [Cannon St]: Fairly new pub/restaurant with good imaginative generous food inc thai, brewing its own beers such as Cannon Best and Gunners Daughter, also Adnams and good wine choice by the glass, unusual décor with two large polished copper brewing kettles by the bar, and what looks like a floorless upper room complete with suspended furnishings above *(Martin Coe)*

Buxhall [TM0057]

☆ *Crown* [signed off B1115 W of Stowmarket, then left at Rattlesden sign; Mill Rd]: Welcoming low-beamed country pub with open fire and small round tables, standing timbers separating no-smoking main dining room with pews, big tables and candles, good choice of sensibly priced home-made food using local produce, friendly service, well kept Greene King IPA, Ruddles County, XX Mild and Badger K&B and a guest such as Woodfordes Wherry, decent wines, games in light and airy public bar; children allowed if eating, pleasant garden with heated terrace and play area, cl Sun evening and Mon *(BB, Derek R A Field)*

Charsfield [TM2556]

Three Horseshoes [off B1078]: Warmly welcoming village pub with enthusiastic landlord, up to six well kept ales inc Greene

King and Woodfordes, fine choice of wines, generous reasonably priced fresh and imaginative food in dining area and small restaurant, daily paper, games; tables in garden *(Keith Sale, Sue Harvey)*

Chelsworth [TL9848]

Peacock [B1115 Sudbury—Needham Mkt]: New landlord doing well in attractive and prettily set old dining pub, cosy pubby décor, lots of Tudor brickwork and exposed beams, enjoyable food, well kept real ales, big inglenook log fire, well spaced comfortable tables; nice small garden, comfortable bedrooms, pretty village *(Desmond Keane, LYM)*

Chillesford [TM3852]

Froize [B1084 E of Woodbridge]: The Shaws have now leased this pleasantly decorated pub, which had been a great place for Alistair Shaw's enterprising fish cooking, his wife Joy's hospitality, and good real ales, to a company; initially he was still to be found in the kitchen, to ease the transition, and some very good meals resulted, but we need more reports on the new regime before we can give a firmer recommendation; bedrooms, tables out on terrace, play area *(LYM, Charles and Pauline Stride, Pamela Goodwyn, Bruce Jamieson)*

Clare [TL7645]

☆ *Bell* [Market Hill]: Large timbered inn with comfortably rambling bar, splendidly carved black beams, old panelling and woodwork around the open fire, side rooms (one with lots of canal and other prints), well kept Nethergate ales inc Mild (this is the brewer's local), also others such as Greene King IPA, decent wines, friendly helpful staff, usual food from sandwiches up inc children's in dining conservatory opening on to terrace; darts, pool, fruit machine; bedrooms off back courtyard, open all day Sun, very special village, lovely church *(Paul S McPherson, Richard and Valerie Wright, Pat and Tony Martin, LYM, George Atkinson)*

☆ *Swan* [High St]: Straightforward village local, early 17th-c but much modernised, lots of copper and brass and huge log fire, public bar with World War II memorabilia and another fire (dogs allowed here), friendly landlord, reasonably priced food from huge bargain huffers up; no children; lovely flower tubs out behind *(Nick Holmes, BB, R J Walden, A J Lennox)*

Creeting St Mary [TM1155]

Highwayman [A140, just N of junction with A14]: Much extended and improved, emphasis on food inc interesting dishes and popular Sun lunch, three changing ales such as Adnams and Woodfordes Wherry, decent wines, extension gallery overflow; tables on back lawn *(Ian and Nita Cooper)*

Cretingham [TM2260]

☆ *Bell* [The Street]: Comfortable village pub mixing striking 15th-c beams, timbers and glorious log fire in big fireplace with more modern renovations and furnishings, Adnams and changing guest beers, good generous food inc children's, attentive landlord; no smoking lounge and restaurant with Sun lunch, traditional games in public bar, family room; charming beamed bedrooms, good breakfast, may open all day in summer, seats out in rose garden and on front grass *(LYM, J F M and M West, John and Patricia White)*

Eastbridge [TM4566]

Eels Foot [off B1122 N of Leiston]: Light modern furnishings in cheerfully basic country pub with well kept Adnams, darts in side area, wide choice of usual food, neat back dining room; walkers, children and dogs welcome, tables and swings outside, pretty village handy for Minsmere bird reserve and heathland walks; open all day in summer for coffee and cream teas, live music some Sats, impromptu music Thurs *(LYM, Eddie Edwards, Jonathan and Ann Tross, Tina and David Woods-Taylor, June and Perry Dann)*

Felixstowe [TM3035]

White Horse [Church Rd]: Friendly refurbished pub with nicely presented inexpensive food from sandwiches and large ploughman's to popular Sun lunch, pleasant staff, very helpful landlord, no smoking dining room; tables outside, play area *(Jackie Deale)*

Felixstowe Ferry [TM3337]

☆ *Ferry Boat*: Cottagey 17th-c pub tucked between golf links and dunes nr harbour and Martello tower, great for walks by sea; extended and much modernised as family pub, good value food inc fresh fish, well kept Adnams and Greene King IPA and Old Speckled Hen, friendly service, good log fire; tables outside, busy summer wknds – can be very quiet other times *(Klaus and Elizabeth Leist, Ian Phillips, June and Malcolm Farmer, LYM, Jackie Deale)*

Victoria: Welcoming child-friendly riverside pub, good generous food emphasising local seafood, well kept Adnams and Greene King ales, briskly efficient friendly service, sea views from upstairs dining area *(Pamela Goodwyn, Ian Phillips, Dr Roger Turner)*

Fressingfield [TM2677]

☆ *Fox & Goose* [Church Rd]: Restful 16th-c country inn by churchyard and duckpond (and still owned by the Church), beautiful timbering, small cosy side bar and separate simple but pretty dining room, appealingly different upmarket pub food inc good fishcakes and gorgeous tangy citrus tart, attentive service, Adnams Best, wine from local Oakhill vineyard, no music or machines *(Comus and Sarah Elliott, Ray and Jacki Davenport)*

Friston [TM4160]

☆ *Old Chequers* [just off A1094 Aldeburgh—Snape]: Welcoming and civilised dining pub with simple but stylish country pine furnishings, light and airy décor, good if not cheap interesting food inc fish, game and Sun carvery, well kept Adnams, good wines and whiskies, friendly staff; good walk from Aldeburgh *(P F Whight, Pamela Goodwyn, Mrs P J Pearce, LYM, Martin and Lois Sheldrick)*

Groton [TL9541]

Fox & Hounds: Welcoming old pub, locally popular for food inc good pies and salmon;

beautiful dispersed village (Massachusetts connection) with fine church and old mulberry tree *(Klaus and Elizabeth Leist)*

Hadleigh [TM0242]

Ram [Market Pl]: Pleasantly unassuming two-bar pub facing Georgian corn exchange, very friendly, with good food at bargain price, well kept Greene King IPA and Abbot, quick service *(Ian Phillips)*

Haughley [TM0262]

☆ *Kings Arms* [off A45/B1113 N of Stowmarket; Old St]: Good atmosphere in 16th-c timbered pub with airy 1950s back part now refurbished to match in something of a gaol theme, nice mix of drinking and dining, wide choice of good value home-made food, friendly helpful staff, well kept Adnams Broadside and Greene King Abbot, decent wines, busy public bar with games, log fire; piped music; tables and play house in colourful back garden *(Quentin Williamson, BB)*

Holbrook [TM1636]

Compasses [Ipswich Rd]: Clean, tidy and spaciously refurbished, well kept ales inc a guest such as Adnams, friendly attentive staff, big log fire, fairly priced food in bar and restaurant; garden with play area *(Michael Hyde, Alan Thomas)*

Huntingfield [TM3473]

Huntingfield Arms [The Street]: Neat and unpretentious, overlooking green, light wood tables and chairs, beams and stripped brickwork, decent food inc good salads and fresh fish, well kept Adnams and Greene King, friendly service, restaurant, games area with pool beyond woodburner *(Neil Powell)*

Icklingham [TL7772]

☆ *Plough* [The Street]: Welcoming service, well kept Adnams, Greene King IPA and a couple of guests such as Ind Coope Burton and Greene King Old Speckled Hen, good range of home-made food, friendly atmosphere, lots of cricketing memorabilia and books; subdued piped music; big garden with play area *(Bruce M Drew)*

Ipswich [TM1744]

☆ *Brewery Tap* [Cliff Rd]: Ground floor of early 19th-c building nestling under vast Tolly brewery, looking over road to docks; their beers kept well, decent food inc good baguettes all day (not Sun/Mon evenings), cheerful prompt helpful service, traditional games, children's room, brewery tours twice weekly; piped music (not in no smoking room on right); open all day, wheelchair access *(Keith Fairbrother, Charles and Pauline Stride, Mike and Mary Carter, LYM, Jenny and Brian Seller)*

Golden Lion [Cornhill]: Cheerful service in busy Wetherspoons, low-priced beers, bargain meals for two *(Klaus and Elizabeth Leist)*

Kersey [TL9944]

Bell [signed off A1141 N of Hadleigh; The Street]: Quaint flower-decked Tudor building in picturesque village, low-beamed bar with tiled floor and log fire divided from lounge by brick and timber screen, prompt service, well kept Adnams, decent house wines, food in bar and restaurant; open all day (afternoon teas),

children allowed, sheltered back terrace with fairy-lit side canopy *(J and D Boutwood, Pamela Goodwyn, MDN, LYM, David Gregory)*

Lavenham [TL9149]

Cock [Church St]: Welcoming and attractive thatched village pub, quiet at lunchtimes, basic bar, plush lounge, separate family dining room, Adnams and Greene King IPA and XX Mild on handpump, Abbot tapped from the cask, good wine choice, quick service, cheap food inc pies, fish and red-hot curry *(the Didler, Sue and Bob Ward, David Carr, Mr and Mrs D Drake)*

Great House [Market Pl]: Good bar lunches in a lovely setting, excellent service, fine choice of wines, polished French restaurant; bedrooms not cheap but very good *(Nick Holmes, I D Barnett)*

Layham [TM0240]

☆ *Marquis of Cornwallis* [Upper St (B1070 E of Hadleigh)]: Beamed 16th-c pub popular lunchtime with businessmen and retired locals for nicely prepared generous food inc good ploughman's and fresh veg, plush lounge bar, friendly atmosphere, well kept beers such as Marstons Pedigree, good wines and coffee; good valley views, popular bird table and picnic-sets in extensive riverside garden, open all day Sat in summer; bedrooms handy for Harwich ferries *(Keith Fairbrother)*

Lindsey [TL9744]

White Rose: This attractive thatched and timbered country dining pub closed in autumn 2000, with plans for conversion to a private house *(LYM)*

Lindsey Tye [TL9846]

Red Rose: Friendly and relaxed, with imaginative good value food from refurbished kitchen, well kept beer *(David Goodfellow)*

Long Melford [TL8645]

☆ *Bull* [Hall St (B1064)]: Medieval former manorial great hall, now a hotel (and not cheap), with beautifully carved beams in old-fashioned timbered front lounge, log fire in huge fireplace, antique furnishings (and games machine), daily papers; more spacious back bar with sporting prints; good range of bar food from sandwiches to one-price hot dishes inc imaginative salads and fresh fish, no smoking restaurant, well kept Adnams Best, Greene King IPA and Nethergate, friendly staff (when you find them); children welcome, courtyard tables, open all day Sat/Sun; comfortable bedrooms *(Michael and Ann Cole, Maysie Thompson, David Twitchett, George Atkinson, LYM, D S Cottrell)*

☆ *Cock & Bell* [Hall St]: Attractive pub with roomy and comfortable carpeted bar and dining area, welcoming service, enjoyable good value food and wine, well kept Courage Best and Directors and Greene King IPA, pleasant service *(Alan Jones)*

Crown [Hall St]: Dark green ceiling and walls show off carefully chosen prints and nicely placed furniture, dusky pink banquettes on one side, big log fire, well kept Bass and Greene King IPA and Old Speckled Hen, obliging service, reasonably priced generous food; quiet and pleasant piped music; well equipped bedrooms, huge breakfast *(Len Banister, David Gregory, LYM)*

Lowestoft [TM5390]

Jolly Sailors [Pakefield St/Wilson Rd, off A12]: Generous well prepared food esp fish, bargain OAP Mon/Tues lunches and popular all-day Sun carvery in big busy partly no smoking bar and much-booked restaurant; well kept Adnams, Boddingtons and Woodfordes Wherry, helpful uniformed staff, sweeping sea view from front part, no smoking family garden room; handy for beach and quaint Pakefield church *(J F M and M West)*

Market Weston [TL9777]

☆ *Mill* [Bury Rd (B1111)]: Well opened up, combining restaurant and pub without clashes; good interesting fresh food using local produce inc popular Sun lunch, well kept Adnams, Greene King IPA and an Old Chimneys beer from the village brewery, enthusiastic effective service; children welcome, theme nights *(Derek R A Field)*

Middleton [TM4367]

☆ *Bell* [off B1125 Leiston—Westleton; The Street]: Charming little traditional pub, part thatched and beamed, in pretty setting nr church; woodburner in comfortable lounge, well kept Adnams ales tapped from the cask, good simple food inc children's, attractive prices, keen and lively landlord; darts and open fire in public bar (dogs allowed), small back dining room, picnic-sets in garden, camping; maybe piped radio, folk nights some wknds, opening times may vary; handy for RSPB Minsmere and coast *(MDN, Tracey and Stephen Groves, Jonathan and Ann Tross, Comus and Sarah Elliott, D J Morgan, June and Perry Dann)*

Mildenhall [TL7174]

Bell [High St]: Well kept Courage Best and Directors in 18th-c inn's spacious beamed bar, open fires, friendly obliging service, good value generous food; comfortable bedrooms *(Ian Phillips)*

Monks Eleigh [TL9647]

☆ *Swan* [B1115 Sudbury—Stowmarket]: Innovative fresh home-made food inc seasonal game and several fish dishes in comfortably modernised lounge bar, real ales inc Adnams and Greene King, good value wines, friendly efficient service, open fire, pleasant dining extension; bedrooms *(Dr T and Mrs J Walker)*

Needham Market [TM0855]

Limes [High St]: Welcoming and lively, with well kept Greene King IPA, Abbot and good choice of guest beers, plenty of friendly locals, wide choice of sensibly priced popular food, nicely served, jazz nights; bedrooms *(John Davis)*

Lion [Ipswich Rd/Lion Lane]: Mossy-tiled roomy local with wide range of usual food (not Sun evening), friendly staff, Adnams, Boddingtons and Greene King IPA, soft lighting; picnic-sets and play area in big garden *(Ian Phillips)*

Newbourne [TM2643]

Fox [The Street]: New landlord in pleasant 17th-c pub, enjoyable food using fresh local produce, well kept Tolly tapped from the cask, cosy unspoilt oak-beamed drinking area around log fire, nice golden retriever (Hector), separate family room, dining extension; pretty hanging baskets, lots of tables out in attractive garden with pond, musical evenings *(Charles and Pauline Stride, Pamela Goodwyn)*

Orford [TM4250]

Crown & Castle: Well established hotel recently taken over by experienced new management, interesting if not cheap bar food inc good ploughman's and fresh crab, refurbishments in the current stripped-down and polished-up fashion, busy dining room; pleasant bedrooms in garden block *(MDN, J F M and M West)*

Kings Head [Front St]: Bright cheerful feel in airily refurbished beamed lounge bar overlooking churchyard, well kept Adnams ales, good coffee, reasonably priced food inc sandwiches and the noted local smokery products, decent wines, friendly staff and locals, attractive restaurant; live music Fri, attractive character bedrooms with own bathrooms *(MDN, M J Morgan, Dr D J and Mrs S C Walker, LYM)*

Polstead [TL9938]

☆ *Cock* [signed off B1068 and A1071 E of Sudbury, then pub signed; Polstead Green]: Interesting reasonably priced food (not Sun evening) from good value big lunchtime rolls up, welcoming landlady, well kept ales such as Adnams Broadside, Greene King IPA and Woodfordes Wherry, good coffee (with warmed shortbread), good choice of wines, black beams and timbers, dark pink walls, woodburner and open fire, random mix of unassuming furniture, plenty of locals, evening barn restaurant; piped music; children welcome, picnic-sets out overlooking quiet green, side play area, cl Mon *(BB, Pamela Goodwyn, MDN, Glyn and Janet Lewis)*

Preston [TL9450]

Six Bells [just NE of Lavenham; The Street]: New licensees yet again in gently refurbished ancient manor-owned pub with central bar between tartan-carpeted dining end and good-natured games end; friendly service, simple generous food, good relaxed atmosphere, real ales inc Greene King, decent wines; tables out on grass, quiz nights *(MDN)*

Ramsholt [TM3041]

☆ *Ramsholt Arms* [Dock Rd, off B1083]: Lovely isolated spot, with picture-window nautical bars overlooking River Deben; good log fire, well kept Adnams and guests such as Timothy Taylors Landlord and Woodfordes Wherry, several wines by the glass, good staff, no smoking restaurant, summer afternoon terrace bar (not Sun); longish steep walk down from car park, busy summer wknds; children welcome, comfortable spacious bedrooms with stunning view, yacht moorings nearby *(LYM, J Hale, Comus and Sarah Elliott, Keith Fairbrother, Pamela Goodwyn)*

Saxtead Green [TM2665]

☆ *Old Mill House* [B1119; The Green]: Roomy dining pub across green from working windmill, beamed carpeted bar, neat country-look flagstoned restaurant extension, brick servery, wooden tables and chairs, pretty curtains, popular reasonably priced freshly made food inc good puddings and nightly carvery, well kept Adnams, Courage Best and Directors and Shepherd Neame Spitfire, decent wines; children very welcome, discreet piped music; sizeable garden, pretty back terrace, good play area *(LYM, Ian and Nita Cooper)*

Shotley Gate [TM2434]

☆ *Bristol Arms* [end of B1456; Bristol Hill]: Unusual dining pub, superb estuary views from dining room with well prepared standard food inc tempting fresh fish, polite service, good value wines; bar has Adnams, Greene King Abbot and local Harwich ales, some interesting spirits, lots of nautical memorabilia, also cuddly toys and canteens of cutlery for sale, and off-licence cut-price drinks inc uncommon whiskies and liqueurs; some picnic-sets out overlooking water *(Ian Phillips, J F M and M West, P F Whight)*

Shottisham [TM3144]

Sorrel Horse [Hollesley Rd]: Simple thatched two-bar pub in tucked-away village, well kept Tolly ales tapped from the cask, reasonably priced straightforward food lunchtime and early evening, friendly service, good fire; quiz nights some Sats, tables on green in front *(the Didler)*

South Cove [TM4981]

Five Bells [B1127 Southwold—Wrentham]: Hospitable and spacious creeper-covered pub with stripped pine, three Adnams ales, wide choice of good value food inc wkdy OAP bargains and generous Sun lunch, welcoming licensees; tables out in front, play area, several dogs, large caravan park in back paddock *(George Atkinson, David Field)*

South Elmham [TM3389]

☆ *St Peters Brewery* [St Peter S Elmham; off B1062 SW of Bungay]: Very attractive bar and restaurant attached to tucked-away brewery in medieval manor buildings, good food, lovely country setting, black swans on pond in front; interesting brewery tour: imaginative range of ales, using water from 200-ft bore hole, hand capping and labelling; open all day Fri/Sat and summer bank hols, 12-7 Sun; booking advised *(David Field, Dr D J and Mrs S C Walker, Stephen, Julie and Hayley Brown, Comus and Sarah Elliott)*

Southwold [TM5076]

☆ *Harbour Inn* [Blackshore, by the boats; from A1095, right at Kings Head – pass golf course and water tower]: Tiny low-beamed front bar, back bar with lots of nautical bric-a-brac (even ship-to-shore telephone and wind speed indicator), upstairs dining area, lots of atmosphere, well kept Adnams Bitter and Broadside, coal fires, solid old furnishings, real fish and chips and other food from good baguettes up, quick service; darts, table skittles, folk nights; open all day, tables outside with play area and ducks *(MJVK, LYM, Comus and Sarah Elliott, G K Smale, Howard James, Richard Pinnington)*

Kings Head [High St]: Cheerful and lively extended dining pub bustling with family parties, lots of maroon and pink plush, very wide choice of reliable home-made food from filled rolls up inc good fish specials, well kept Adnams, good house wines, no smoking area; comfortable family/games room with well lit pool table; jazz some Sun nights, decent bedrooms *(Ian and Jane Irving, Alan Thomas, Tim and Ann Newell, John Wooll, MJVK, BB)*

☆ *Lord Nelson* [East St]: Bustling cheerful easy-going seaside local with perfectly kept Adnams Mild, Bitter, Extra, Broadside and Old, decent wines, good generous basic lunchtime food freshly made from sandwiches up, low prices, quick attentive service, air cleaner; low ceilings, panelling and tiled floor, spotless light wood furniture, lamps in nice nooks and crannies, Lord Nelson memorabilia and super soda-syphon collection, no music, sheltered back garden; disabled access (not perfect, but they help), children welcome away from main bar *(Alan Thomas, Colin and Dot Savill, Dr D J and Mrs S C Walker, Comus and Sarah Elliott, the Didler, BB, John Davis, Howard James, Richard Pinnington)*

Red Lion [South Green]: Big windows looking over green to sea, pale panelling, ship pictures, brassware and copper; pleasant prompt service, well kept Adnams Bitter, Broadside and Mild, good value food inc good fish, family room, tables outside; right by the Adnams retail shop; bedrooms small but comfortable *(BB, Joy and Peter Heatherley, Comus and Sarah Elliott, Dr D J and Mrs S C Walker, Dr and Mrs Nigel Holmes)*

☆ *Sole Bay* [East Green]: Homely Victorian local moments from sea, opp brewery (and the Sole Bay lighthouse), lots of polished seafaring memorabilia, light wood café-style furnishings, basic inexpensive lunchtime food (not Sun in winter) inc children's, full Adnams range particularly well kept, good house wines, decent coffee, welcoming landlord and friendly dogs; unobtrusive piped music, darts, TV, can be smoky; conservatory with cockatoos, tables on side terrace *(Comus and Sarah Elliott, MDN, Tim and Ann Newell, P G Plumridge, LYM, Michael Hyde, T G Thomas, Tracey and Stephen Groves, Ian and Jane Irving, Mike and Wendy Proctor)*

☆ *Swan* [Market Pl]: Smart hotel not pub, but has relaxed comfortable back bar with well kept Adnams and Broadside, full range of their bottled beers, fine wines and malt whiskies, good bar food (not cheap, but worth it) inc enormous open sandwiches, friendly staff, chintzy and airy front lounge; good bedrooms inc garden rooms where (by arrangement) dogs can stay too *(Terry Mizen, Joy and Peter Heatherley, LYM, R M Harrold, Stephen P Edwards)*

Spexhall [TM3780]

Huntsman & Hounds [Stone St]: 17th-c pub with beams and standing timbers, usual pub furnishings, cosy village atmosphere, helpful friendly staff, good generous freshly made food inc fresh veg (OAP lunch Tues), well kept

Adnams ales, decent house wines, attractive prices, central log fire, darts, restaurant area; tables in garden with pond, bedrooms *(June and Perry Dann)*

Theberton [TM4365]

Lion [B1122]: Friendly and cosy village pub, comfortable banquettes, lots of old local photographs, pictures, copper, brass and plates, fresh flowers, good value freshly made pub food inc children's, welcoming licensees, Adnams and several guest beers such as Badger IPA, Elgoods and Woodfordes Wherry, amiable spotted dog most evenings; piped radio, cribbage, separate part with darts, pool and TV, jazz 1st Sun of month, maybe flowers for sale; garden with picnic-sets, small terrace and camp site *(Comus and Sarah Elliott)*

Thornham Magna [TM1070]

Four Horseshoes [off A140 S of Diss; Wickham Rd]: Handsome thatched pub open all day, with attractive dim-lit rambling well divided bar, very low heavy black beams, mix of chairs and plush banquettes, country pictures and farm tools, logs burning in big fireplaces, inside well; pleasant staff, Adnams, Courage Directors, Greene King Old Speckled Hen and Charles Wells Bombardier, food (all day Sun) inc OAP bargains, no smoking areas; piped music, fruit machine and TV; bedrooms, picnic-sets on big sheltered lawn, handy for Thornham Walks and thatched church with ancient frescoes and fine retable *(Mrs E A Shortland-Jones, LYM, Ian Phillips, Ian and Nita Cooper, BB, E D Bailey, Mike and Wendy Proctor)*

Thorpeness [TM4759]

☆ *Dolphin*: Smartly refurbished and restored, attractive and stylish almost Scandinavian décor, light and bright, with good choice of enjoyable food, well kept Adnams and Marstons Pedigree, good wine range, helpful relaxed staff; dogs welcome in public bar; comfortable bedrooms *(Kathy and Chris Armes, Anthony Barnes, Pamela Goodwyn)*

Trimley St Martin [TM2736]

Hand in Hand [High Rd]: Attractive and welcoming extended village local, good generous home cooking from Spanish omelettes to game and tender steaks, decent wine, quick polite service, good atmosphere, pleasant dining rooms *(Charles and Pauline Stride, Jackie Deale, P F Whight)*

Waldringfield [TM2844]

☆ *Maybush* [The Quay, Cliff Rd]: Beautifully placed estuary-side pub down narrow country lane, sailing memorabilia inc Giles cartoons in large airy rooms, some concentration on wide

range of generous well priced and well cooked food inc plenty of fish and good puddings, very friendly quick service even on busy summer lunchtimes, real ales such as Adnams; sizeable verandah with good views over River Deben and its bird-haunted sandbanks *(Mike and Mary Carter, Pamela Goodwyn, Simon and Sally Small, David Carr, Howard James, Richard Pinnington)*

Wangford [TM4679]

Angel [signed just off A12 by B1126 junction; High St]: Handsome 17th-c village inn with well spaced tables in light and airy bar, usual food from sandwiches to Sun roasts, Adnams, Greene King Abbot and Woodfordes Wherry, children in no smoking dining room; open all day, comfortable new bedroom wing *(LYM)*

Woodbridge [TM2749]

Bull [Market Hill]: Neatly kept 16th-c inn with front blinds and window boxes, cosy little bar and other small beamed rooms, wide choice of good value food, well kept Adnams, accommodating landlady and friendly staff; small but comfortable bedrooms, good breakfast *(George Atkinson)*

Old Mariner [New St]: Olde-worlde, with good value food, well kept beer, good staff; jazz and folk Thurs *(Comus and Sarah Elliott)*

Olde Bell & Steelyard [New St, off Market Sq]: Unusual olde-worlde pub under new management, steelyard still overhanging the street, good friendly mix of drinking and dining in bar, well kept Greene King, short but varied blackboard choice of home-made food from good filled baguettes up, good service *(David Carr, Keith Fairbrother)*

Yoxford [TM3968]

Griffin [High St]: Friendly 14th-c local with good cosy and pleasantly unsmart atmosphere, log fires, good value generous food using local supplies inc generous bargain lunch and children's, well kept Adnams and a couple of changing guest beers, attentive staff, medieval feasts in log-fire restaurant decorated to match; quiz night Thurs, two pub cats; comfortable beamed bedrooms, good breakfast *(Comus and Sarah Elliott, Paul and Penny Rampton, Adrian and Gwynneth Littleton)*

☆ *Kings Head* [A12]: Recently reopened by enthusiastic hard-working licensees, no smoking throughout so all fresh and clean, four very well kept changing ales from far and wide, continental bottled beers and German wheat beer; food already good value, inc interesting cheeses and local meat, and plans to develop this *(John O'Leary, Comus and Sarah Elliott)*

> Post Office address codings confusingly give the impression that some pubs are in Suffolk when they're really in Norfolk or Cambridgeshire (which is where we list them).

Surrey

This is a very pricy county for the pub lover. Drinks prices are well above the national average, and it's now virtually impossible to find a pint of beer here for under £2. Food's not cheap, either, with it getting hard to find even a ploughman's at much under £5, for instance. So the search for real quality becomes paramount. Two pubs here, the unspoilt and good value Dolphin at Betchworth and the Plough at Blackbrook (a great choice of wines by the glass), earn praise for their long record of consistency, featuring in the Guide every year since it started 20 years ago. Two others are new to this edition: another Betchworth pub, the Red Lion (a smart dining pub), and the cottagey old-fashioned Donkey at Charleshill (nice balance between drinking, chatting and eating). After winnowing out quite a number of pubs from the county this year, ones showing particularly well are the friendly and nicely placed Cricketers just outside Cobham, the civilised and attractive Withies at Compton, the well run Anglers Retreat in Laleham (thriving atmosphere, fish specialities), the Skimmington Castle up on Reigate Heath (lots of character, nice spot), the wonderfully un-Surrey Scarlett Arms at Walliswood (they stopped doing the rabbit pie when the ferret died), and the Jolly Farmer at Worplesdon (a smart dining pub) – the Jolly Farmer takes our title of Surrey Dining Pub of the Year. In the Lucky Dip section at the end of the chapter, pubs showing particularly well this year are the Drummond Arms at Albury, William IV at Albury Heath, Swan in Ash Vale, Plough at Coldharbour, Marneys in Esher, White Bear at Fickleshole, Kings Arms at Ockley, White Horse at Shere, Volunteer at Sutton Abinger, Botley Hill Farmhouse near Warlingham, Inn at West End and Old Crown in Weybridge. There are quite a few reliable Vintage Inns in the area, generally reworked (or even built from new) as very olde-worlde pubs with well drilled service and decent food all day: good examples in Chertsey, Farleigh, Weybridge and Wotton.

ABINGER COMMON TQ1145 Map 3
Abinger Hatch

Off A25 W of Dorking; follow Abinger signpost, then turn right towards Abinger Hammer

Although this friendly pub, run by a brother and sister team, is generally quiet on weekday lunchtimes, it becomes a cheerful bustle at weekends with walkers, cyclists, and families – but staff cope admirably with the rush. There's plenty of old-fashioned cosy character, with heavy beams, flagstones, big log fires, and simple homely furnishings, including pews forming booths around oak tables in a side carpeted part. Quite a range of reasonably priced, straightforward food includes soup (£2.45), filled rolls (from £2.60), whitebait with paprika (£3.95), ploughman's (from £4.25), vegetable kiev (£5.95), curry of the day or ham and eggs (£6.25), hot seared salmon with prawn and butter sauce (£8.75), 10oz sirloin steak (£10.25), and children's meals (from £3.25); on Tuesday evenings they do a fish and chip supper (£3.50) and on Friday evenings, steak and chips (£4.99); roast Sunday lunch (£5.75). The restaurant is no smoking. Up to half a dozen real ales on handpump such as Abinger Hatch Best (brewed for the pub by the local Weltons brewery), Adnams, Badgers IPA and Tanglefoot, Fullers London Pride, and Harveys Best, with winter mulled wine, farm cider and over 20 malt whiskies. Wisteria tumbles over its tiled roof, a big fig tree grows in front, and the village church stands just across the green. Set on a neat stretch of side grass sheltered by beech and rose hedges, picnic-sets under fir trees tempt out patrols of friendly ducks. There are attractive walks among the surrounding rolling hills. *(Recommended by James Nunns, Derek Harvey-Piper, Jenny and Brian Seller, Tony Scott, Dick and Madeleine Brown, J S M Sheldon, Edward Longley)*

Free house ~ Licensees Jan and Maria Walaszkowski ~ Real ale ~ Bar food (not Sun or Mon evenings) ~ Restaurant ~ (01306) 730737 ~ Children in eating area of bar and restaurant ~ Open 11.30-3, 5-11; 11-11 Sat; 12-10.30 Sun

BETCHWORTH TQ2149 Map 3

Dolphin

The Street

This is a genuine, friendly and surprisingly unspoilt village pub, popular with walkers and lunchers alike. The homely neatly kept front room has kitchen chairs and plain tables on the 400-year-old scrubbed flagstones, and the carpeted back saloon bar is black-panelled with robust old-fashioned elm or oak tables. There are three warming fires, and a nice chiming longcase clock. The enjoyable good value bar food is generously served, and includes sandwiches (from £2), home-made soup (£2.25), mussels in garlic (£4.20), ploughman's (from £4.45), vegetable or beef lasagne (£6.15), steaks (from £8.40), daily specials, and puddings such as jam roly poly or bread pudding (£2.15); best to get there early or book a table beforehand. Well kept Youngs Bitter, Special and AAA, and two seasonal guests on handpump, with up to 18 wines by the glass; silenced fruit machine, darts, cribbage and dominoes. There are some seats in the small laurel-shaded front courtyard and picnic-sets on a lawn by the car park, opposite the church and on the back garden terrace. Parking can be very difficult in summer. No children inside. *(Recommended by John Davis, D P and J A Sweeney, Mike Gorton, Don Mather, Chris Richards, Roger and Jenny Huggins, Mark Percy, Lesley Mayoh, DWAJ, Mike Tomkins, Martin and Penny Fletcher, Tina and David Woods-Taylor, Keith Bell, Ian Phillips, Dennis Jenkin, G T Brewster, J Hale)*

Youngs ~ Managers George and Rose Campbell ~ Real ale ~ Bar food (12-2.30, 7-10) ~ (01737) 842288 ~ Open 11-3.30, 5.30-11; 11-11 Sat; 12-10.30 Sun

Red Lion ♀

Turn off A25 W of Reigate opp B2032 at roundabout, then after 0.3 miles bear left into Old Road, towards Buckland

Much changed in the last three years or so, this is now a civilised dining pub – indeed, almost more restaurant-with-rooms than pub. The light and airy bar, with a log-effect gas fire and pictures above its panelled dado, has plenty of tables, with steps down to a stylish new long flagstoned room, and a dining room, candlelit at night, which strikes some readers as Tuscan in mood. The good food, served generously, includes sandwiches (from £3.85), home-made soup (£3.95), deep-fried camembert with cumberland sauce (£4.75), pâté with chutney (£4.95), ploughman's (£5.25), good steak and kidney pudding or roast vegetable risotto (£7.95), minted shoulder of lamb (£9.50), steaks (from £10.95), and daily specials such as parma ham and mascarpone tartlet with an exotic citrus dressing (£5.95) or salmon with a cajun crust and mint yoghurt (£10.95). There's particular praise for puddings (£4.25), like sticky toffee pudding or raspberry cream tartlet; Sunday lunch is particularly popular. The dining room is no smoking. Well kept Adnams, Fullers London Pride and Greene King Old Speckled Hen or Ringwood Best on handpump, good house wines, and charmingly enthusiastic and helpful waitress service. There may be piped pop music. Outside are plenty of picnic-sets on a lawn with a play area, and in good weather tables set for dining on a rose-trellised terrace. The garden backs on to the village cricket green, and you don't notice the road at the front, as it's set well below the pub in a tree-lined cutting. We have not yet had reports from readers on the bedrooms, in a separate new block. *(Recommended by C and R Bromage, John Evans, Mike and Heather Watson, Chris and Anna Rowley, Derek Harvey-Piper, G T Brewster, Susan and John Douglas, Mike Gorton)*

Free house ~ Licensees Simon Monsi and John Bateman ~ Real ale ~ Bar food (all day wkdys; 12-4, 5.30-10(8.45 Sun) Sat) ~ Restaurant ~ (01737) 843336 ~ Children welcome ~ Open 11-11; 12-10.30 Sun; closed 31 Dec-2 Jan ~ Bedrooms: £75S/£85S

BLACKBROOK TQ1846 Map 3
Plough ♀

On byroad E of A24, parallel to it, between Dorking and Newdigate, just N of the turn E to Leigh

In summer, the white frontage of this neatly kept, comfortable pub is quite a sight with its pretty hanging baskets and window boxes; there are new tables and chairs on the terrace, and a children's Swiss playhouse furnished with little tables and chairs in the secluded garden. Inside, the partly no smoking red saloon bar has fresh flowers on its tables and on the window sills of its large linen curtained windows, and down some steps, the public bar has brass-topped treadle tables, a formidable collection of ties, old saws on the ceiling, and bottles and flat irons; piped music, shove-ha'penny, and cribbage. As well as reasonably priced and enjoyable lunchtime bar snacks such as taramasalata or hummous with pitta bread (£3.25), local sausages (£3.95), filled baked potatoes (from £3.95), ploughman's (£4.75), and toasted bagels (from £4.95), there are daily specials such as spinach, mushroom and sweetcorn chowder (£2.75), tartlet of ratatouille and gruyère (£3.75), terrine of game with cranberry sauce (£3.95), vegetable paella (£5.95), deep-fried fillets of cod or lasagne (£6.95), roast bacon-wrapped breast of guinea fowl on couscous with orange and lemon sauce (£9.45), and steaks (from £11.95), and puddings such as apple and cranberry pie, spiced bread and butter pudding or strawberry meringue sundae (£3.45); they hold four popular curry evenings a year. Well kept Badger Best, Old Ale, and Tanglefoot, Gribble Inn Fursty Ferret, and Badger K & B Sussex on handpump, 16 wines by the glass, and several ports; friendly and efficient service from smartly dressed staff. The countryside around here is particularly good for colourful spring and summer walks through the oak woods. The pub usually hosts an atmospheric carol concert the Sunday before Christmas. More reports please. *(Recommended by Jenny and Brian Seller, D B Molyneux-Berry, Chris Richards, Ian Phillips, Derek Harvey-Piper, G T Brewster)*

King & Barnes (Badger) ~ Tenants Chris and Robin Squire ~ Real ale ~ Bar food (not Mon evening) ~ (01306) 886603 ~ Children welcome until 9pm ~ Open 11-2.30 (3 Sat), 6-11; 12-3, 7-10.30 Sun; closed 25 and 26 Dec, 1 Jan

CHARLESHILL SU8944 Map 2
Donkey

B3001 Milford—Farnham near Tilford; coming from Elstead, as soon as you see pub sign, turn left

This old-fashioned beamed cottagey pub places quite an emphasis on the good food, though still offering a welcome to those wanting just a drink. The bright saloon has lots of polished stirrups, lamps and watering cans on the walls, and prettily cushioned built-in wall benches, while the lounge has a fine high-backed settle, highly polished horsebrasses, and swords on the walls and beams. Enjoyable food includes home-made soup (£2.95), sandwiches (from £3), ploughman's or thai fishcakes (£4.95), fresh cornish crab (£5.95), stilton and asparagus en croûte (£8.95), calves liver and bacon or chicken with mozzarella and pesto (£10.95), lobster thermidor (£15.50), daily specials such as rack of lamb with a garlic and herb crust (£13.95) or whole bass with dill and butter sauce (£16.50), and puddings such as chocolate fudge cake or banoffi pie (£3.95); there's a no smoking conservatory. Well kept Greene King Abbot and Old Speckled Hen on handpump; piped music. The garden is very attractive with plenty of seats, there's a new terrace, a big fairy-lit fir tree, and a wendy house for children; the two friendly donkeys are called Pip and Daisy. *(Recommended by Mrs M Hewitt, Sue and Mike Todd, J J L Richards, Edward Longley, John and Joyce Snell)*

Greene King ~ Licensees Lee and Helen Francis ~ Real ale ~ Bar food (not Sun evening) ~ Restaurant ~ (01252) 702124 ~ Children welcome ~ Open 11-3, 6-11; 12-3 Sun; closed Sun evening

COBHAM TQ1060 Map 3
Cricketers

Downside Common; 3¾ miles from M25 junction 10; A3 towards Cobham, 1st right on to A245, right at Downside signpost into Downside Bridge Rd, follow road into its right fork – away from Cobham Park – at second turn after bridge, then take next left turn into the pub's own lane

It's particularly pleasant sitting outside this friendly pub in summer, either in front at one of the many tables overlooking the village green, or behind in the charming neatly kept garden, with its standard roses, dahlias, bedding plants, urns and hanging baskets. Inside, the roomy open-plan interior has plenty of atmosphere, with a good log fire, and crooked standing timbers – creating comfortable spaces – supporting heavy oak beams so low they have crash-pads on them. In places you can see the wide oak ceiling boards and ancient plastering laths. Furnishings are quite simple, and there are horsebrasses and big brass platters on the walls; the stable bar is no smoking. Enjoyable bar food includes a huge choice of salads such as home-made quiche of the day (£4.35), ploughman's (£5.50), avocado, tomato, and mozzarella (£5.75), provençale vegetable wellington (£5.95), and home-made salmon coulibiac (£6.55), plus hot dishes like cottage pie or steamed mussels with soy sauce (£5.95), pork and leek sausages with onion gravy (£6.25), steak, mushroom and Guinness pie or home-made chicken curry (£6.95), grilled fillet of fresh salmon with tarragon butter (£7.25), sugar-baked ham with peaches (£8.50), and children's menu (£3.95); prompt service. It's worth arriving early to be sure of a table – especially on Sunday. Well kept Courage Best, Greene King Old Speckled Hen, Theakstons Best, Wadworths 6X, and Youngs Bitter on handpump, and several wines by the glass. Dogs welcome. (Recommended by Mrs J L Crutchfield, Kevin Williams, Gee Cormack, Gordon Prince, Geoffrey Kemp, G T Brewster, Stephanie Smith, Leigh Hughes, B, M and P Kendall, Edward Longley, Susan and John Douglas, Martin and Karen Wake)

Inntrepreneur ~ Tenant Wendy Luxford ~ Real ale ~ Bar food (12-2, 6.30-10) ~ Restaurant ~ (01932) 862105 ~ Children in Stable bar ~ Open 11-2.30, 6-11; 12-3, 7-10.30 Sun

COMPTON SU9546 Map 2
Withies

Withies Lane; pub signposted from B3000

After a walk up the lane to Polsted Manor and Loseley Park, this popular 16th-c pub is a fine place for a meal or a socialising drink with friends. It's especially attractive inside, with low beams in the little bar, some fine 17th-c carved panels between the windows, and a splendidly art nouveau settle among the old sewing machine tables; there's a log fire in a massive inglenook fireplace. From the short, unchanging choice of straightforward bar food, there is soup (£3.50), filled baked potatoes (from £4), smoked salmon pâté or ploughman's (£4.25), sandwiches (from £4.25; fresh crab when available £4.90), cumberland sausages with mash and onion gravy (£4.90), and seafood platter (£9.50). You can also choose from the more elaborate (and more expensive) restaurant menu, which draws in a well heeled local set. Well kept Bass, Fullers London Pride, Greene King IPA and Badger K & B Sussex on handpump; helpful, friendly service. The immaculate garden, overhung with weeping willows, has tables under an arbour of creeper-hung trellises, more on a crazy-paved terrace and several under old apple trees. The neat lawn in front of the steeply tiled white house is bordered by masses of flowers. (Recommended by LM, J Hale, John Evans, Derek Harvey-Piper, G T Brewster, Debbie and Neil Hayter, M J Bastin, Dennis Jenkin, Mrs M Blundell, Martin and Karen Wake, Jenny and Brian Seller, Kevin Williams, Gee Cormack, Mrs J L Crutchfield, Mrs Jane Basso)

Free house ~ Licensees Brian and Hugh Thomas ~ Real ale ~ Bar food (12-2.30, 7-10) ~ Restaurant ~ (01483) 421158 ~ Children welcome ~ Open 11-3, 6-11; 12-3 Sun; closed Sun evening

DUNSFOLD TQ0036 Map 3

Sun

Off B2130 S of Godalming

Symmetrical arched double porches sheltering neat twin bottle-glass bow windows lead you into the old but basic interior of this elegantly brick-fronted pub, with a friendly old-fashioned atmosphere, scrubbed pine furniture and a log fire in an inglenook. A good mix of locals and visitors gather in the bar to enjoy the well kept ales including Badger K&B Sussex, Friary Meux Best, and Marstons Pedigree on handpump, and the decent wine list. Decent bar food includes sandwiches (from £2.40), soup (£3.50), ploughman's (from £5.25), daily specials such as marinated lamb shank (£8.95), escalope of veal (£10), fresh fish at the weekend (from £11), and puddings (£3.75); cottagey restaurant. Darts, table skittles, cribbage, dominoes and shove-ha'penny. There are seats on the terrace and more overlooking the quiet village green. More reports please. *(Recommended by S G N Bennett, Michael Sargent, Susan and John Douglas, KC)*

Greaves Bros Leisure ~ Lease Ian Greaves ~ Real ale ~ Bar food (12-2.15, 7-10) ~ Restaurant ~ (01483) 200242 ~ Well behaved children in restaurant and eating area of bar ~ Live music once a month ~ Open 11-3, 6-11; 12-4, 7-10.30 Sun

ELSTEAD SU9143 Map 2

Woolpack

The Green; B3001 Milford—Farnham

Customers tend to return to this bustling, friendly pub again and again, which is always a good sign. Most people do come to eat, and served quickly by helpful staff, the menu might include home-made soup (£3.50), hot breaded camembert with port and cranberry sauce or home-made trout and horseradish pâté (£4.95), roasted aubergine and pepper salad topped with herbed yoghurt and parmesan (£5.75), king prawns in filo pastry with sweet chilli sauce (£5.95), spinach and cottage cheese lasagne (£7.50), lamb curry or hawaiian chicken (£7.95), home-made cod and prawn or chicken and ham pie (£8.50), pork fillet medallions in mango, brandy and a touch of chilli (£10.95), kingfish in orange, wine and thyme sauce (£11.95), steaks (from £11.95), calves liver in sage and orange butter (£12.50), and home-made puddings (£3.50). Weaving shuttles and cones of wool hang above the high-backed settles in the long airy main bar with fireplaces at each end, and there's a weaving loom in the big room leading off from here. As well as window seats there are spindleback chairs around plain wooden tables, and decorations include lots of country prints, scales and brass measuring jugs; the fireplace with its wooden pillars and lace frill is unusual. Well kept Fullers London Pride and Greene King Abbot are tapped from the cask, there's a decent wine list, and a cheery atmosphere. Dominoes, cribbage and fruit machine. A family room leads to the garden with picnic-sets. *(Recommended by Graham Osborne, Ian Phillips, David Peakall, Lynn Sharpless, Bob Eardley, Gordon Stevenson, Michael Sargent, Geoffrey Kemp, Lady Muir, Edward Longley)*

Punch ~ Lease S A Askew ~ Real ale ~ Bar food (12-2, 7-9.45(9 Sun)) ~ Restaurant ~ (01252) 703106 ~ Children in restaurant and function room ~ Open 11-2.30, 6-11; 11-11 Sat; 12-10.30 Sun; closed 25 Dec evening, all day 26 Dec

HASCOMBE TQ0039 Map 3
White Horse

B2130 S of Godalming

Tucked away in a pretty village among lovely rolling wooded country lanes on the Greensand Way, this picturesque old rose-draped inn is a popular stop for walkers. Inside, there's a cheerful bustle among the simple but atmospheric rooms. The cosy inner beamed area has a woodburning stove, hops hanging from the beams, and quiet small-windowed alcoves that look out on to the garden; there's also a conservatory with light bentwood chairs and peach coloured décor. Generously served good bar food includes sandwiches (from £4), good proper ploughman's (from £4.95), home-made burgers (£7), asparagus and sun-dried tomato risotto (£7.95), half roast guinea fowl (£8.95) and chargrilled steak (£10.50); best to get there early for a table at lunchtime, especially at weekends. Well kept Adnams Best, Badger Tanglefoot, and Bass on handpump, and a sizeable wine list; friendly service from helpful staff. Darts, shove-ha'penny and dominoes. There are several tables on the spacious sloping back lawn, with more on a little terrace by the front porch. In autumn, you can combine a trip here with a walk among the beautifully coloured trees and shrubs in nearby Winkworth Arboretum. More reports please. *(Recommended by Michael Sargent, LM, Susan and John Douglas, Gordon Stevenson, John Davis, S G N Bennett)*

Punch ~ Lease Susan Barnett ~ Real ale ~ Bar food (12-2.20, 7-10) ~ Restaurant ~ (01483) 208258 ~ Children in eating area of bar and separate family room ~ Open 11-3, 7-11; 11-11 Sat; 12-10.30 Sun; closed 25 Dec

LALEHAM TQ0568 Map 3
Anglers Retreat

5 miles from M25 junction 13; A30 E, then at roundabout turn on to A308 (signposted Kington, Sunbury), then at roundabout after another 1.3 miles turn right on to B377; in Laleham turn right on to B376 (Staines Road)

As this carefully extended, popular pub is close to Laleham Abbey which used to be the seat of the Lucan family, it previously had the somewhat ill-fated name of the Lucan Arms. There are good solid furnishings, big windows, and pale panelling with neat wrought-iron light fittings – and more wrought iron in the partitions which separate the open-plan bar area into three or four distinct sections; a couple of coal fires on cold days. A big well stocked marine tropical aquarium is set into one wall, and there's an even bigger one in the smart no smoking restaurant area (which is often full – it's best to book). As well as winter soup (£3.95), filled baguettes (from £5.95), vegetarian dishes (£6.95), cajun chicken pasta (£7.45), and steaks (from £9.95), they specialise in fresh fish such as red snapper, skate wing, tuna, halibut, and cod (from £9); puddings (£3.95), and Sunday roasts (£6.95). Brakspears PA, SB and a seasonal ale on handpump, decent wines, prompt friendly service; unobtrusive piped music, fruit machine. There are tables out in front, with bright hanging baskets and flower tubs, and the back garden has a play area. The River Thames is quite close by. *(Recommended by Ian Phillips, Shirley Lunn, Sue and Jim Parkyn, Mayur Shah, Ian Jones)*

Brakspears ~ Tenant Sean Alderson ~ Real ale ~ Bar food (12-2.30, 6-9.30; 12-9 Sat and Sun) ~ Restaurant ~ (01784) 440990 ~ Children in restaurant ~ Sun night pub quiz ~ Open 11-11; 12-10.30 Sun

LEIGH TQ2246 Map 3
Plough

3 miles S of A25 Dorking—Reigate, signposted from Betchworth (which itself is signposted off the main road); also signposted from South Park area of Reigate; on village green

Handy for Gatwick airport, this pretty tiled and weatherboarded cottage is attractively set by the village green. On the right is a very low beamed, cosy, white walled and timbered dining lounge, and on the left, a simple more local pubby bar with a good bow window seat and an extensive choice of games: darts, shove-ha'penny, dominoes, table skittles, cribbage, fruit machine, Jenga, backgammon, or shut the box. Well kept Badger Best, Tanglefoot, Sussex, and winter Old Ale on handpump; piped music. Nicely presented food ranges from bar snacks including a huge range of sandwiches (from £2.50), soup (£3.25), tuna melt (£3.50), filled baked potatoes (from £4.25) and ploughman's (£4.75), to main meals such as penne tossed in leek, cream and goats cheese sauce (£6.95), smoked haddock on spinach, topped with cheese sauce (£9.50), chicken breast with leeks and stilton cream (£9.50), honey-glazed duck breast with a mixed berry sauce (£11.95), steaks (from £10.95) and puddings such as pavlova or apple pie (from £3.50); decent wine list (all bottles are available by the glass as well). There are picnic-sets under cocktail parasols in a pretty side garden (fairy-lit in the evening) and pretty hanging baskets. Parking nearby is limited. *(Recommended by G T Brewster, DWAJ, Ian Phillips, D P and J A Sweeney, Mr and Mrs T A Bryan, Hugh Roberts)*

King & Barnes (Badger) ~ Tenant Sarah Bloomfield ~ Real ale ~ Bar food (12-2.30, 7-10 Mon-Fri, 12-10 wknds) ~ Restaurant ~ (01306) 611348 ~ Children in restaurant ~ Open 11-11; 12-10.30 Sun

MICKLEHAM TQ1753 Map 3
King William IV 🍽 🍺

Byttom Hill; short but narrow steep track up hill just off A24 Leatherhead—Dorking by partly green-painted restaurant – public car park down here is best place to park; OS Sheet 187 map reference 173538

Cut into a steep hillside – it's quite a climb up – this unusually placed pub has panoramic views from its snugly atmospheric plank-panelled front bar. The more spacious back bar is quite brightly lit, with kitchen-type chairs around its cast-iron-framed tables, log fires, fresh flowers on all the tables, and a serviceable grandfather clock. Enjoyable bar food might include weekday sandwiches, ploughman's (from £5.25), filled baked potatoes (from £5.50), brie and leek in filo pastry with apricot purée, steak, kidney and mushroom pie or seafood pie (£8.25), tandoori chicken (£8.95), chargrilled tuna fish (£9.25), rump steak (£10.25), and puddings such as hot chocolate fudge cake or fruit crumble (£3.75); the choice is more limited on Sundays and bank holidays, and they don't take bookings in summer. Well kept Adnams Best, Badger Best, Hogs Back TEA and a guest such as Ringwood Fortyniner on handpump; quick and friendly service; light piped music. At the back, the lovely terraced garden is neatly filled with sweet peas, climbing roses and honeysuckle and plenty of tables (some in an extended open-sided wooden shelter with gas heaters); a path leads straight up through woods where it's nice to walk after lunch – quite a few walkers do come here. No children inside. *(Recommended by John Crafts, Ian Jones, D P and J A Sweeney, John Davis, Donald and Nesta Treharne, J S M Sheldon, Ian Phillips, Mr and Mrs D D Collins, Mrs J L Crutchfield, Charlie Harris, Mike and Heather Watson, Mike and Lynn Robinson, John Evans, J Wright, Mrs M Blundell, Kevin Williams, Gee Cormack, Marion Turner)*

Free house ~ Licensees Chris and Jenny Grist ~ Real ale ~ Bar food (12-2, 7-9.30) ~ (01372) 372590 ~ Open 11-3, 6-11; 12-3, 7-10.30 Sun; closed 25 Dec, evening 31 Dec

PIRBRIGHT SU9454 Map 2
Royal Oak 🍺

Aldershot Rd; A324S of village

They take their beer very seriously here, with up to 10 at once on handpump, and over 150 guests a year from all over the country supplementing the particularly well kept Becketts Original, Flowers IPA and Original, local Hogs Back TEA and Rebellion IPA; four beer festivals are held at regular intervals, and they also have a good range of wines by the glass and bottle. A rambling series of snug side alcoves has heavy beams and timbers, ancient stripped brickwork, and gleaming brasses set around the three real fires, and furnishings include wheelback chairs, tapestried wall seats, and little dark church-like pews around the trim tables; a bar extension overlooks the pretty flower-filled back garden and is joined onto the existing no smoking dining area. Served by helpful staff, bar food includes soup (£2.95), filled baguettes (from £3.50), salmon and watercress terrine (£3.95), ploughman's (from £5.95), pie of the day (from £6.95; luxury fish pie £7.95), spinach, ricotta and goats cheese cannelloni (£7.95), steaks (from £10.95), and puddings (£3.45); five Sunday roasts (£7.25). Children are allowed to sit at four tables in the dining area if eating with their parents, and it's best to arrive early for a table. The front gardens are very colourful and look particularly attractive on fine evenings when the fairy lights are switched on. The big back garden leads down to a stream, and is less affected by noise from passing traffic; there may be barbecues and spit-roasts out here in summer. Good walks lead off in all directions, and the licensees are usually happy to let walkers leave their cars in the car park – if they ask first. *(Recommended by Dr J D Bassett, KC, Gordon Stevenson, Nigel and Olga Wikeley, Simon Good, D P and J A Sweeney, Edward Longley, R Lake, Shirley Lunn, Jayne and Peter Capp)*

Laurel Pub Company ~ Manager John Lay ~ Real ale ~ Bar food (12-2, 6.30-9.30 Mon-Fri, 12-9 wknds) ~ (01483) 232466 ~ Children allowed while food is served ~ Quiz night last Mon of month ~ Open 11-11; 12-10.30 Sun

REIGATE HEATH TQ2349 Map 3
Skimmington Castle

3 miles from M25 junction 8: through Reigate take A25 Dorking (West), then on edge of Reigate turn left past Black Horse into Flanchford Road; after ¼ mile turn left into Bonny's Road (unmade, very bumpy track); after crossing golf course fork right up hill

It's well worth the journey to find this rather remote – though often busy – quaint old country pub. The bright main front bar leads off a small central serving counter with dark simple panelling. There's a miscellany of chairs and tables, shiny brown vertical panelling, a brown plank ceiling, well kept Greene King IPA, Wadworths 6X, Youngs Special and a guest such as Adnams Broadside on handpump, with several wines by the glass, and cask conditioned cider. The cosy back rooms are partly panelled too, with old-fashioned settles and windsor chairs; one has a big brick fireplace with its bread-oven still beside it – the chimney is said to have been used as a highwayman's look-out. There's another small room down steps at the back; shove-ha'penny, cribbage, dominoes, ring the bull, board games, and piped music. Good popular bar food includes soup and sandwiches (from £2.85, smoked salmon £3.95), ploughman's (from £4.50), fresh breaded haddock (£6.25), pork in cider pie (£6.50), roast chump of lamb with couscous (£8.50), beef wellington (£10.50), daily specials such as moules marinières (£5.50), venison steak (£8.95), and monkfish wrapped in seaweed (£10.50), and puddings (£2.95); to be sure of a table, you must book ahead. There are nice views from the crazy-paved front terrace and tables on the grass by lilac bushes, with more tables at the back overlooking the meadows and the hillocks. There's a hitching rail outside for horses, and the pub is handy for ramblers on the North Downs. *(Recommended by Chris Gillings, Edward Longley, Derek Harvey-Piper, John Davis, Gordon Stevenson, Ian Phillips, Zelda Tolley, Mike Gorton, R T and J C Moggridge, Joy and Peter Heatherley)*

Pubmaster ~ Tenants Anthony Pugh and John Davidson ~ Real ale ~ Bar food (12-2.15, 7-9.30; 12-2.30, 7-9 Sun) ~ (01737) 243100 ~ Children welcome ~ Folk second Sun of month ~ Open 11-3, 5.30(6 Sat)-11; 12-10.30 Sun; closed evenings 25 and 26 Dec and 1 Jan

WALLISWOOD TQ1238 Map 3
Scarlett Arms

Village signposted from Ewhurst—Rowhook back road; or follow Oakwoodhill signpost from A29 S of Ockley, then follow Walliswood signpost into Walliswood Green Road

'Very un-Surrey' is how a reader described this pub, and we know exactly what he meant. It's an unspoilt and charming country cottage with three neatly kept, communicating rooms, and low black oak beams, deeply polished flagstones, simple but perfectly comfortable benches, high bar stools with backrests, trestle tables, country prints, and two roaring winter log fires, one in a huge inglenook. Well kept Badger Tanglefoot, K&B and Mild on handpump; darts, cribbage, shove-ha'penny, table skittles, dominoes and a fruit machine in the small room at the end; piped music. Straightforward bar food includes sandwiches (from £3.25), ploughman's (£4.75), pizzas (also to take away, from £5.25), sausage or ham, egg and chips (£6.50), steak and kidney pie (£6.75), steaks (from £10.50), daily specials, and puddings (from £3.25). On a sunny day, you can sit on the peaceful benches out the front, or on old-fashioned seats and tables with umbrellas in the pretty well tended garden. There are lots of walks nearby. No children. *(Recommended by Jonathan Stewart, Anna Pointer, Kevin Thorpe, Howard Dell, G T Brewster, Sue and Mike Todd, Klaus and Elizabeth Leist, Susan and John Douglas)*

King & Barnes (Badger) ~ Tenant Jess Mannino ~ Real ale ~ Bar food (12-2, 6.30-9.30) ~ No credit cards ~ (01306) 627243 ~ Open 11-2.30, 5.30-11; 12-3, 7-10.30 Sun

WORPLESDON SU9854 Map 3
Jolly Farmer 🍴 🍺

Burdenshott Road, off A320 Guildford—Woking, not in village – heading N from Guildford on the A320, turn left at Jacobs Well roundabout towards Worplesdon Station; OS Sheet 186 map reference 987542

Surrey Dining Pub of the Year

In an attractive rural setting, this is a smart and roomy dining pub, though there is still a proper bar, with comfortable modern furnishings and a fresh décor integrated well with the beams and woodwork. You can eat here, or in a dining extension with stripped brickwork and well spaced tables. The food is in fact a major attraction, running from soup (£4) and large open sandwiches (from £5, though they'll happily make more standard-size normal ones on request) to garlic prawns (£6), cashew nut roast or crab cakes (£6.80), lots of pasta dishes (around £7.50), rack of lamb (£16.50), and steak au poivre (£16.95), with some emphasis on fresh fish such as tasty kedgeree (£7.20), calamari (£7.80), chargrilled swordfish with salsa fresca (£13.80), and scallops wrapped in bacon with cream and Cointreau sauce or monkfish provençale (£15.80). They don't turn their nose up at chips, which are good here. Puddings are worth leaving room for, and might include fresh fruit brûlées, crème caramel and bread and butter pudding (£4.25). Well kept changing ales on handpump such as Bowmans, fff Moondance, Fullers London Pride and Sharps Doom Bar on handpump, decent wines, and warmly attentive service. There are picnic-sets under cocktail parasols in a good-sized sheltered garden with flowers and fruit trees. The car park is shared with Whitmore Common, which has scope for pleasant walks. *(Recommended by Mrs Hilarie Taylor, Derek Harvey-Piper, Betty Laker, Ian Phillips, MDN, Julia and Tony Gerhold, KC, Edward Longley, J S M Sheldon, R Lake)*

Free house ~ Licensees Mr and Mrs Ponsonby ~ Real ale ~ Bar food (not Sun or Mon evenings) ~ Restaurant ~ (01483) 234658 ~ Children allowed away from bar area ~ Open 11.30-3, 6-11; 12-3 Sun; closed Sun evening

---

Post Office address codings confusingly give the impression that some pubs are in Surrey when they're really in Hampshire or London (which is where we list them). And there's further confusion from the way the Post Office still talks about Middlesex – which disappeared in 1965 local government reorganisation.

Lucky Dip

Besides the fully inspected pubs, you might like to try these Lucky Dips recommended to us and described by readers (if you do, please send us reports: www.goodguides.com).

Albury [TQ0547]
☆ *Drummond Arms* [off A248 SE of Guildford; The Street]: Comfortable and civilised panelled alcovey bar, conservatory (children allowed here) overlooking pretty streamside back garden with fountain and covered terrace, some emphasis on food, several well kept real ales, attentive helpful staff; piped music; bedrooms, attractive village, pleasant walks nearby *(J S M Sheldon, Edward Longley, G T Brewster, LYM, DAV, MDN)*
Albury Heath [TQ0646]
☆ *William IV* [Little London, off A25 Guildford—Dorking – OS Sheet 187 map ref 065468]: Welcoming newish management in bustling local and walkers' pub, old-fashioned low-beamed flagstoned bar with big log fire, home-made food from sandwiches up (good hot salt beef ones), real ales such as Badger Best, Fullers London Pride, Greene King Abbot, Wadworths 6X and local Hogs Back, simple café-style dining area, close-packed tables in upstairs restaurant; shove-ha'penny and cards, children welcome, attractive front garden with long wall seat *(LYM, Edward Longley, G T Brewster, D P and J A Sweeney, Don Mather, J S M Sheldon, MDN)*
Ash [SU8951]
Standard of England [Ash Hill Rd]: Friendly local, good food, lots of community activity *(Sandra Fell)*
Ash Vale [SU8952]
☆ *Swan* [Hutton Rd, off Ash Vale Rd (A321) via Heathvale Bridge Rd]: Big homely Chef & Brewer on the workaday Basingstoke Canal, cheerful helpful staff, broad good value menu, well kept Courage Best, Greene King Old Speckled Hen, Wadworths 6X and changing guest beers; can be very busy, piped classical music; children welcome, garden, well kept terraces and window boxes, open all day *(David and Kay Ross, Mr and Mrs J Brown, Dr and Mrs P Beck, Edward Longley)*
Banstead [TQ2559]
Mint [Park Rd, off High St towards Kingswood]: Comfortably opened up with several nicely decorated areas, very popular at lunchtime for good value generous food (not Sun evening) from sandwiches up, prompt courteous service, good choice of well kept ales inc Bass, garden with play area *(Jenny and Brian Seller, Derek Thomas, MRSM)*
Bisley [SU9459]
Hen & Chickens [Guildford Rd]: Modernised local with Tudor beams and plenty of atmosphere, well kept beers inc Courage Best, quickly served well cooked food, pleasant efficient management; no children in the bar, small garden *(anon)*
Bletchingley [TQ3250]
Prince Albert [Outwood Lane]: Good sensibly priced fresh food (but you may have a 20-min wait even for sandwiches) in attractive cosy beamed pub, several nooks and corners, motor

racing pictures, well kept Wadworths 6X and a local beer, thriving atmosphere, smallish restaurant with accent on good fresh fish; tables on terrace and in small pretty garden *(Dick and Madeleine Brown, J S M Sheldon, Catherine and Richard Preston)*
☆ *William IV* [3 miles from M25 junction 6; Little Common Lane, off A25 on Redhill side of village]: Quaint quiet old country pub down pretty lane, tile-hung and weatherboarded, with comfortable little back dining room, good choice of good food and of well kept ales such as Fullers London Pride, Harveys Best, Pilgrims Progress and Youngs Special, good wines, good atmosphere, lots of bric-a-brac, helpful friendly service; two-level garden with summer barbecues *(Mr and Mrs R G Lloyd, LYM)*
Bramley [TQ0044]
☆ *Jolly Farmer* [High St]: Sociable and welcoming, very popular for wide choice of generous fresh usual food, changing well kept ales such as Bass, Badger Best, Hogs Back TEA, Hop Back Summer Lightning and Pilgrim Crusader, Czech Budvar and Warsteiner on tap, proper coffee, welcoming service, two log fires, beer mat and banknote collections, big restaurant; comfortable bedrooms *(LYM, MDN)*
Brockham [TQ1949]
Royal Oak [Brockham Green]: Nice spot opp fine church on charming village green below North Downs, nr River Mole; simple but pleasant, with murals in comfortable lounge/dining area, bare boards and log fire on other side, well kept beers such as Adnams, Gales HSB, Greene King Old Speckled Hen, Harveys and Wadworths 6X (Aug beer festival), food from sandwiches up, local pictures for sale; children and dogs welcome (pub has a boxer), open all day, good garden with play area *(Catherine and Richard Preston, Susan and John Douglas)*
Capel [TQ1740]
Crown [signed off A24 at Beare Green roundabout; The Street]: Pleasantly rustic old beamed village pub by interesting church, cosy and comfortable ochre-walled small-roomed bar areas and partly no smoking restaurant, well kept ales inc Marstons Pedigree, friendly staff, generous food from warm baguettes up; piped radio, pool in two-level public bar, dogs welcome *(Howard Dell, C and R Bromage)*
Chertsey [TQ0466]
Crown [London St (B375)]: Friendly and relaxed Youngs pub with button-back banquettes in traditionally renovated high-ceilinged bar, tall and very sonorous longcase clock, well kept ales, nicely presented no-nonsense food from doorstep sandwiches and baked potatoes up, courteous attentive staff; neatly placed darts, discreet fruit machines; children welcome, garden bar with conservatory, tables in courtyard and garden with pond; smart 30-bedroom annexe

(Tony and Wendy Hobden, Ian Phillips)

Golden Grove [Ruxbury Rd, St Anns Hill (nr Lyne)]: Busy local with low beams, bare boards and stripped wood, cheap straightforward home-made food from sandwiches up (not Sat-Mon evenings) in pine-tabled eating area, well kept ales inc Ind Coope Burton, Fullers London Pride and Theakstons, cheerful service, coal-effect gas fire; piped music, fruit and games machines; big garden with friendly dogs, a grape-laden vine hangs over the picnic tables in summer, play area, wooded pond *(Ian Phillips)*

☆ *Kingfisher* [Chertsey Bridge Rd]: Recent brick-by-brick relocation of old west country building to make attractive Vintage Inn dining pub beautifully placed by busy bridge and Thames lock, warm medley of furnishings in lots of small intimate areas, old woodwork and careful lighting, enjoyable food from sandwiches to some interesting main dishes (may be a longish wait on busy Sat afternoon), well kept Bass, Fullers London Pride and Hancocks HB, good wine choice, attentive helpful service, good log fire, riverside garden by road; familes welcome if eating, otherwise no under-21s *(Jenny and Brian Seller, Geoffrey Kemp, Mayur Shah, D P and J A Sweeney, Ian Phillips, Dr M E Wilson, James Nunns)*

Chiddingfold [SU9635]

Crown [The Green (A283)]: Picturesque old inn in attractive surroundings, well worth a visit for its fine carving, Elizabethan plaster ceilings, massive beams, lovely inglenook log fire and tapestried panelled restaurant; enjoyable but not cheap food from sandwiches up in simpler side bar, three Badger beers; children allowed, tables out on verandah, has been open all day, good bedrooms *(David and Kay Ross, LYM, Eddie Edwards)*

☆ *Rams Nest* [Petworth Rd (A283 S)]: 18th-c inn, well restored in traditional style, hops on beams, big log fires, relaxing atmosphere, pews and high-backed settles, cosy reading area with easy chairs, books and magazines; lots of antique furnishings, well rounded choice of good generous food, well kept real ales, good value wines, friendly service, pool, seemly piped music; children allowed in back restaurant, garden with covered terrace, wendy house and play area; good newish bedrooms in separate block *(Gerry and Wendy Fry, Miles Halton)*

Chilworth [TQ0346]

☆ *Villagers* [Blackheath; off A248 across the level crossing, SE of Guildford]: Attractive woodland pub, good walks all around (shown on table-mats); small flagstoned room with big fireplace suiting walkers and dogs, main carpeted bar with beams, timbers and pews, neat little adjoining dining room, well kept Courage Best, Fullers London Pride, Greene King Old Speckled Hen, Hogs Back TEA, decent wines, pleasant young staff, food from big sandwiches to plenty of fish and popular family Sun lunch (best to book then); unobtrusive piped music; sheltered back terrace, steps up to good-sized lawn, short path through trees to cricket green; children in eating areas, open all day wknds *(Colin Wetherley-Mein, Martin and Karen Wake, Susan and John Douglas, LYM, Eddie Edwards, Gordon Stevenson, G T Brewster, MDN)*

Chipstead [TQ2757]

☆ *Ramblers Rest* [Outwood Lane (B2032)]: Picturesque collection of partly 14th-c buildings, extensive range of different drinking areas with different atmospheres, panelling, flagstones and low beams, wide range of well kept ales inc Flowers, Fullers London Pride, Marstons Pedigree and Wadworths 6X, good generous freshly made modern food (not cheap), family restaurant; big pleasant garden behind, attractive views, decent walks nearby; piped music; open all day inc Sun, no dogs *(BB, Gordon Stevenson, DWAJ, Tony Scott, G T Brewster, J S M Sheldon)*

Well House [Chipstead Lane, off A23 just W of Coulsdon; nearer Mugswell or Kingswood]: Partly 14th-c, cottagey and comfortable, with lots of atmosphere, decent straightforward food (not Sun evening) from massive sandwiches up, friendly staff, log fires in all three rooms, well kept Bass and other ales; dogs allowed; attractive garden with well reputed to be mentioned in Domesday Book (loudspeaker food announcements though), delightful setting *(Jenny and Brian Seller, LYM)*

White Hart [Hazelwood Lane]: Open-plan bar with cheap well presented food from sandwiches up, real ale such as Bass, Fullers London Pride, Greene King IPA and Hancocks HB, cheery staff; pleasant walled garden, maybe summer bouncy castle *(Ian Phillips)*

Claygate [TQ1563]

Foley Arms [Hare Lane]: Solid Victorian two-bar Youngs local, real fires, good reasonably priced lunches from proper sandwiches through omelettes to mixed grill, real ales; open all day, attractive garden with play area *(G R Taylor)*

Cobham [TQ1059]

☆ *Plough* [Plough Lane, towards Downside]: Cheerful black-shuttered local with comfortably modernised low-beamed lounge bar partly divided by L-shaped settles, huge log fire dividing it from restaurant area, Courage Best and Directors, Wadworths 6X and Charles Wells Bombardier, decent house wines, helpful staff, pine-panelled snug with darts, good choice of good value quickly served lunchtime food from sandwiches up; tables outside *(LYM, John Davis, Martin and Karen Wake, James Nunns)*

Coldharbour [TQ1543]

☆ *Plough* [village signed in the network of small roads around Leith Hill]: Friendly two-bar pub well placed for good walks, brewing their own Leith Hill beers, with well kept guests such as Badger Tanglefoot, Hogs Back TEA, Ringwood Old Thumper, Timothy Taylors Landlord and Theakstons Old Peculier, also country wines and Biddenden farm cider and perry, bar food, prompt service, stripped light beams and timbering, big open fire on right, no smoking restaurant; children welcome in newly converted barn, picnic-sets out in front and in terraced garden with fish pond and waterlilies; open all day wknds, plans for bedrooms with own bathrooms *(LYM, Mike and Lynn Robinson, Peter Meister, Sally Causer, K Hulme, Stephanie Smith, Leigh Hughes, Ian Phillips, Chris Richards, Chris Reeve, Mrs P J Pearce, John Branston, G T Brewster)*

Compton [SU9546]
Harrow [B3000 towards Godalming off A3]: Good choice of expensive well presented home-made food from sandwiches and filled baked potatoes up, well kept Greene King IPA and Abbot and Hogs Back TEA; children welcome, open all day, cl Sun evening; bedrooms *(Mrs Hilarie Taylor, Edward Longley, R J Hayward, LYM)*

Cranleigh [TQ0539]
Three Horseshoes [High St]: Friendly village local, well kept King & Barnes, lunchtime snacks; can get very busy evenings, open all day *(Stephen S Goodchild)*

Dorking [TQ1649]
☆ *Cricketers* [South St]: Bustling little Fullers local, very neat and tidy, with solidly comfortable furniture, cricketing memorabilia on stripped brick walls, cheap no-nonsense food (not Fri/Sat evening or Sun lunch), well kept Chiswick, London Pride and ESB, low prices, helpful friendly service, nice suntrap back terrace with barbecues; open all day *(Jonathan Stewart, Anna Pointer, LYM)*

Eashing [SU9543]
Stag [Lower Eashing (just off A3 Guildford/Godalming bypass, southbound only)]: Attractive and tranquil 17th-c beamed pub, interesting furnishings inc plenty of sofas in several smart but cosy traditional interconnecting rooms, well kept local beer, several wines by the glass, attentive chatty staff, log fire, pictures of landlord's work as stunt man, mainly restauranty food; tables in pleasant streamside garden with terrace *(Julia and Tony Gerhold, Tina and David Woods-Taylor, Edward Longley)*

East Clandon [TQ0651]
☆ *Wishing Well* [just off A246 Guildford—Leatherhead; The Street]: Rambling dining pub with masses of hanging baskets, small spotless connecting rooms, food from ploughman's through omelettes, quiches, pies and pasta up freshly made by landlady (so may be a wait), big inglenook log fire, fine old elm bar counter, well kept Hogs Back TEA and Marstons Pedigree, attentive welcoming service; children welcome, tables in quiet garden, handy for two NT properties; no dogs, boots or overalls, cl Mon *(LYM, Mike and Heather Watson, Dr Barry Newman, C and R Bromage, P J Keen)*

Effingham [TQ1253]
Plough [Orestan Lane]: Welcoming commuter-belt Youngs local with consistently well kept ales, honest home cooking inc enjoyable Sun lunch, good wine choice, two coal-effect gas fires, beamery, panelling, old plates and brassware in long lounge, no smoking

extension; popular with older people – no dogs, children, music or machines, attractive garden with play area; convenient for Polesdon Lacey (NT) *(D B Molyneux-Berry, Mrs M Blundell, Barrie Drewitt)*
Sir Douglas Haig [off A246 Leatherhead—Guildford]: Large open-plan beamed pub with armchairs, sofa, books and TV one end, mix of old and new tables and chairs at the other, bar food from sandwiches to steaks, well kept Bass, Fullers London Pride, Gales BB and HSB, good choice of coffees; piped music and machines may obtrude, TV, can be smoky; children in eating area, open all day, tables on attractive terrace and back lawn, decent bedrooms *(Jenny and Brian Seller, Stephen, Julie and Hayley Brown, LYM)*

Egham [TQ0171]
☆ *Beehive* [Middle Hill]: Small friendly local, well kept changing ales such as Brakspears, Fullers London Pride, Gales Trafalgar and Hopback Summer Lightning, beer festivals, good quick reasonably priced home-made vegetarian and other food in small dining area, polite service; nice garden with picnic-sets and play area *(Ian Phillips)*
Crown [High St]: Busy simply furnished local settling down after chain takeover, four or five changing ales such as Courage, Fullers and Greene King, usual food, coal fires; juke box or piped music, TV, pool in public bar; charming back walled garden with lively aviary and pretty pond *(Ian Phillips)*
Foresters Arms [North St]: Welcoming backstreet pub with reasonably priced food in separate dining area, well kept Courage Best and guests such as Brakspears and Greene King IPA, friendly landlord, pool table *(Ian Phillips)*

Englefield Green [SU9772]
☆ *Fox & Hounds* [Bishopsgate Rd; off A328 N of Egham]: Popular Old Monk pub in good setting backing on to riding stables on edge of Windsor Great Park, short walk from Savile Garden, tables on pleasant front lawn and back terrace; well kept Brakspears, Courage Directors and Fullers London Pride, enjoyable bar food, more costly restaurant, two good log fires, daily papers; piped music, no children; open all day wknds and July-Sept, picnic-sets outside, good big new car park *(Roger Everett, Simon and Laura Habbishow, Mike and Jennifer Marsh, J S M Sheldon, LYM, Ian Phillips, J Hale)*
Sun [Wick Lane, Bishopsgate]: Unassuming welcoming local, well kept Bass, Courage Best, Greene King Abbot and Shepherd Neame Spitfire, decent wines, reasonable prices, daily papers, roaring log fire in back conservatory, biscuit and water for dogs, usual food inc good sandwiches, rolls and Sun lunch; quiet garden with aviary, handy for Savile Garden and Windsor Park *(Ian Phillips, LM)*

Epsom [TQ2060]
Albion [High St]: Hogshead with decent food, plenty of guest and bottled beers *(Justin Hulford)*
Barley Mow [Pikes Hill]: Friendly and attractively refurbished Fullers local,

deceptively big and keeping many old features, with well kept ales, decent food (not Sun evening), conservatory and sizeable garden – very busy on warm summer evenings; open all day *(Justin Hulford)*

Derby Arms [Downs Rd, Epsom Downs]: Popular and reliable Vintage Inn dining pub, busy and friendly, with wide choice of reasonably priced food in homely bar and added restaurant, helpful service, pleasantly homely décor, log fires, no smoking area; open all day Sun, nice tables outside, good views *(Mrs G R Sharman, Kevin Williams, Gee Cormack)*

Esher [TQ1566]

☆ *Marneys* [Alma Rd, Weston Green]: Attractive low-ceilinged cottagey pub in charming spot overlooking church, duck pond, green and golf course, well kept Courage Best and Directors, good interesting food reflecting Norwegian landlord's national cuisine, quick service by friendly uniformed staff, family dining area, decent wines; very small – can get crowded; tables outside *(Lynne Leighton Hare, Ian Wilson, John Crafts)*

☆ *Prince of Wales* [West End Lane; off A244 towards Hersham, by Princess Alice Hospice]: Well run Victorian Chef & Brewer, attractive period décor, cosy candlelit corners, open fires, turkey carpets, old furniture, prints and photographs; massive choice of generous reasonably priced food, well kept Courage Best, Greene King Old Speckled Hen and Theakstons, good wine choice, quick friendly staff, daily papers, family area; big garden, nr green and pond *(Mr and Mrs J French, Mrs M Blundell, D B Molyneux-Berry, James Nunns)*

Ewell [TQ2262]

Spring [London Rd]: Popular recently extended and refurbished pub, modern approach to traditional comfort, spacious and airy, with friendly efficient service, low-priced bar food inc Sun roast, real ales such as Bass and Worthingtons, decent wine choice, restaurant; TV and machines not obtrusive, Tues quiz night; garden with barbecues *(Kevin Williams, Gee Cormack)*

Farleigh [TQ3659]

☆ *Harrow* [Farleigh Common, off B269 Limpsfield—Warlingham]: Well run Vintage Inn, reliably enjoyable food with some individuality, Bass, Hancocks HB, Worthingtons and lots of wines by the glass from large horseshoe bar, well trained staff, several rooms inc large no smoking area, old farm tools and machinery *(John Branston, Jim Bush)*

Farnham [SU8445]

☆ *Fox* [Frensham Rd, Lower Bourne]: New licensees continuing the enterprising reasonably priced food (all day wknds) here, pleasant bistro atmosphere, Greene King Old Speckled Hen and Ruddles Best, good value wines, deep crimson décor with heavy curtains, prints, some stripped brickwork, nice blend of wooden furniture and raised back area; picnic-sets and small adventure playground outside *(Martin and Karen Wake)*

Spotted Cow [Bourne Grove, Lower Bourne (towards Tilford)]: Welcoming country local with wide choice of home-made food inc lots of fresh fish, well kept Adnams, Courage and Hogs Back TEA, decent wine, witty landlord, attentive friendly service, reasonable prices; play area in big garden, nice surroundings *(Dr J D Bassett, M Borthwick)*

Fickleshole [TQ3960]

☆ *White Bear* [Featherbed Lane/Fairchildes Lane; off A2022 Purley Rd just S of A212 roundabout]: Rambling interestingly furnished partly 15th-c family country pub with lots of small rooms, flagstone floors, friendly service, well kept Flowers IPA and Fullers London Pride and ESB, plenty of food from good sandwiches up (and Kettle crisps), OAP lunches Thurs, restaurant; fruit machine, video game, piped music; children welcome, jazz Weds, open all day Sat; play area in sizeable garden, lots of picnic-sets with white-painted bear on front terrace *(LYM, LM, Jim Bush)*

Forest Green [TQ1240]

☆ *Parrot* [nr B2126/B2127 junction]: Rambling country pub with attractive furnishings and secluded extended restaurant, well kept Courage Directors, Fullers London Pride, Hogs Back TEA, John Smiths and Wadworths 6X, good food, helpful Scottish landlady, good cheerful service even when crowded, end locals' bar with open fire, interesting bric-a-brac and pool; piped music; children welcome, open all day; plenty of tables in garden by cricket green, good walks nearby *(W F Kent, Alan Thomas, LYM, G T Brewster)*

Frensham [SU8341]

Holly Bush: Bright and friendly pub nr Frensham Ponds, Greene King and other ales, good value generous home food from toasted sandwiches to daily roast *(Gordon Stevenson)*

Friday Street [TQ1245]

Stephan Langton [signed off B2126, or from A25 Westcott—Guildford]: Busy country local, comfortable bar, red-painted and parlour-like lounge, well kept Bass, Fullers London Pride, Harveys and Youngs Special, half a dozen wines by the glass, bar food (may be a wait), no smoking area in restaurant; darts, shove-ha'penny, cribbage, dominoes and piped music, children in snug or restaurant only; plenty of tables in front courtyard, more on back tree-surrounded steam-side terrace, peaceful spot, surrounded by good walks, open all day summer *(J S M Sheldon, Mike and Lynn Robinson, LYM, LM, John Branston)*

Godalming [SU9743]

Kings Arms & Royal [High St (A3100)]: Friendly series of partitioned rooms in 18th-c coaching inn (Tsar's Lounge worth seeing if it's not booked for a function), enjoyable bar food, obliging service; bedrooms, nice garden beyond car park *(BB, Klaus and Elizabeth Leist)*

Gomshall [TQ0847]

Compasses [A25]: Plain bar (open all day) and much bigger neatly comfortable no smoking dining area, good value food from sandwiches and baked potatoes to steak, good children's menu, well kept Fullers London Pride with several guest beers, good value house wines, pleasant efficient service; piped music, live Fri; open all day, children welcome, pretty garden sloping down to roadside mill stream, peaceful bedrooms *(R T and J C Moggridge, Mike and Lynn Robinson, Tony and Wendy Hobden, Mike Tomkins, John and Margaret Mitchell, LYM)*

Guildford [SU9949]

Olde Ship [Portsmouth Rd (A3100 S)]: Three distinct areas around central bar, ancient beams, flagstones, log fire in big fireplace, candles and comfortable mix of furniture, no smoking zone (no mobile phones either), part with tables and chairs, well kept Greene King, good range of fairly priced food inc good pizzas, decent wines, obliging service; no music *(Tony and Wendy Hobden, Edward Longley)*

Hambledon [SU9639]

Merry Harriers [off A283]: Homely and casually old-fashioned country local popular with walkers, very quiet wkdy lunchtimes; lovely inglenook log fire, dark wood and red décor, dark pine bar, pine tables, impressive collection of chamber-pots hanging from beams, well kept ales such as Hogs Back TEA and Hop Back Crop Circle, farm cider, reasonably priced fresh simple food from sandwiches up; pool room, folk night 1st Sun of month; big back garden, picnic-sets in front and over road – caravan parking *(S G N Bennett, Phil and Sally Gorton)*

Holmbury St Mary [TQ1144]

Royal Oak: Well run, warm and cheery 17th-c beamed coaching inn in pleasant spot by green and church, relaxing atmosphere, good helpings of popular fresh food, well kept ales such as Greene King IPA, friendly efficient service, log fire, some tables on front lawn; bedrooms, good walks *(Gordon Stevenson, Mike and Heather Watson, R Lake)*

Horley [TQ2842]

Olde Six Bells [quite handy for M23 junction 9, off Horley turn from A23; Church Rd – head for the church spire]: Ancient stone-roofed Vintage Inn – part of heavy-beamed open-plan bar was probably a medieval chapel, and some masonry may date from 9th c; local atmosphere, reasonably priced food inc good snacks, Bass, Fullers London Pride and Hancocks HB, log fires, upstairs raftered dining room, conservatory, two friendly black cats; tables out by bend in River Mole, meadow opposite; open all day wkdys *(LYM, Ian Phillips)*

Horsell [SU9859]

Cricketers [Horsell Birch]: Friendly local with neatly kept bar and extended eating area, carpet and shiny boards, good choice of reasonably priced straightforward food (all day Sun and bank hols) with very good veg, Brakspears, Courage Best, Greene King Old Speckled Hen and Wadworths 6X; children well catered for; big well kept garden, and seats out in front overlooking village green *(Ian Phillips)*

Laleham [TQ0469]

Three Fishes [Staines Rd (B376)]: Nice spot nr Thames, good bar food, well kept Fullers London Pride, nice contrast between bright conservatory with big pine tables and smaller darker alcoves; restaurant *(D P and J A Sweeney)*

☆ *Three Horseshoes* [B376 (Shepperton Rd)]: Smart and plushly modernised, but dating from 13th c, with flagstones, heavy beams, log-effect fires, cosy areas off central serving area, big no smoking conservatory, interesting history; new manageress, big helpings of popular food from sandwiches up, well kept Courage Best, Fullers London Pride and guests such as Greene King Old Speckled Hen, decent generous wines, efficient service; TV, piped music; lots of picnic-sets on terrace, open all day *(LYM, Simon Collett-Jones, D P and J A Sweeney, John Davis, Gordon Prince, Ian Jones)*

Leatherhead [TQ1656]

Dukes Head [High St]: Busy and friendly town pub, enjoyable honest food from separate servery, beams, timbers, nice furnishings and open fire, good coffee, small front bar with pool and games machine; piped music; handy for riverside walks *(DWAJ)*

Limpsfield Chart [TQ4251]

Carpenters Arms [Tally Rd]: Much modernised open-plan pub in delightful setting by village common, lovely walks, easy reach of Chartwell; well kept Bass, Greene King IPA, Friary Meux, Fullers London Pride and Wadworths 6X, decent coffee, nice range of throughtfully prepared home-made food, efficient service, well worn-in furnishings, darts one end (dogs welcome), eating area the other; garden *(Ian Phillips, Hazel and Michael Duncombe)*

Mickleham [TQ1753]

Running Horses [Old London Rd (B2209)]: Friendly refurbished 16th-c beamed village pub below Box Hill, well kept Friary Meux, Greene King Abbot, Hogs Back TEA and Youngs, quick cheerful service even when packed with impatient walkers, big log fire and smaller coal-effect one, comfortable and attractive dining extension/conservatory, no children; opp church, nice view from pretty courtyard garden *(Ian Phillips, G T Brewster, A D Marsh)*

Mogador [TQ2452]

Sportsman [from M25 up A217 past 2nd roundabout, then Mogador signed; edge of Banstead Heath]: Interesting and welcoming low-ceilinged local, quietly placed on Walton Heath, a magnet for walkers and riders; well kept ales, enjoyable popular food, darts, bar billiards; dogs welcome if not wet or muddy; tables out on common, on back lawn, and some under cover *(Jenny and Brian Seller)*

Newdigate [TQ2042]

Surrey Oaks [off A24 S of Dorking, via Beare Green; Parkgate Rd]: Light and airy main lounge off snug flagstoned low-beamed core with inglenook woodburner, well kept Adnams, Fullers London Pride and unusual guest beers, Aug bank hol beer festival, bar food (not Sun/Mon evenings) from filled baguettes up; pool in games room, piped music; children in partly no smoking eating areas, good big garden with terrace, rockery, water feature, play area and pets corner *(Jenny and Brian Seller, C and R Bromage, Alan and Paula McCully, John Beeken, G T Brewster, LYM)*

Ockley [TQ1439]

☆ *Cricketers* [Stane St (A29)]: Pretty 15th-c stone-built village local with Horsham slab roof, flagstones, low beams, inglenook log fires, farm tools, shiny pine furniture, friendly helpful licensees, good value honest generous food from sandwiches to Sun roast, well kept ales such as Fullers London Pride and Ringwood Best, country wines, small attractive dining room with cricketing memorabilia; maybe piped radio, darts area; seats in delightful back garden with duck pond and play area *(Don Mather, Lady Muir, John Davis, LYM)*

☆ *Kings Arms* [Stane St (A29)]: Comfortably old-fashioned 17th-c country inn with inglenook log fire, heavy beams and carved woodwork, generous imaginative fresh food in bar and small restaurant, well kept Flowers and a seasonal beer, decent wines, good welcoming service; discreetly placed picnic-sets in immaculate big back garden, bedrooms with beautifully fitted bathrooms *(Derek Harvey-Piper, Kevin Williams, Gee Cormack, Stephen S Goodchild)*

Old School House [Stane St]: Fine school house attractively converted to popular and enjoyable dining pub, good value generous food from sandwiches up inc fresh pasta and fish, friendly attentive service, well kept King & Barnes, good wines, wonderful log fire *(S and D Moir, G T Brewster)*

Outwood [TQ3245]

☆ *Bell* [Outwood Common, just E of village; off A23 S of Redhill]: Attractive extended 17th-c country dining pub, olde-worlde beamed bar and sparser restaurant area, good choice of well kept ales such as Harveys and Youngs, quick cheerful young staff, good value food inc bargain lunches, log fires; children and dogs welcome, piped music may obtrude; summer barbecues and cream teas, has been open all day; pretty fairy-lit garden with country views, handy for windmill *(G T Brewster, Craig Pickard, LYM, Klaus and Elizabeth Leist)*

Peaslake [TQ0845]

☆ *Hurtwood* [off A25 S of Gomshall]: Small comfortable pre-war country hotel in fine spot for walkers (no muddy boots inside, though), well kept Courage Best, Fullers London Pride and local Hogs Back TEA, also good coffee, wine list and malt whiskies, good well priced bar food, friendly helpful service, no piped music, sizeable interesting restaurant; bedrooms *(Ian Phillips, BB, Jenny and Brian Seller, G T Brewster)*

Pirbright [SU9455]

Cricketers [The Green]: Friendly welcoming local, pleasant service, good home cooking, well kept Ind Coope Burton *(Shirley Mackenzie)*

Puttenham [SU9347]

Good Intent [The Street/Seale Lane]: Beamed country local, short choice of bar food (not Sun/Mon evenings) from sandwiches up, Weds fish and chips night, changing well kept ales such as Adnams, Brakspears and Youngs, Inch's farm cider, log fire, pool, old photographs of the pub; dogs allowed, no children, open all day wknds *(John Davis, Martin and Karen Wake)*

Reigate [TQ2450]

Nutley Hall [Nutley Lane]: Friendly, sparsely furnished pub with good unusual food *(G T Brewster)*

Ripley [TQ0556]

Anchor [High St]: Tudor inn in new hands again, enjoyable updated food such as ciabatta 'sandwiches' and thai dishes, lively local feel in old-fashioned cool dark low-beamed connecting rooms, well kept real ales, good service, games in public bar; tables in coachyard *(BB, Derek Harvey-Piper, M J Brooks)*

Jovial Sailor [Portsmouth Rd]: Enjoyable food all day, very popular on Sun – lots of children then; piped music aimed to suit the customers *(Shirley Mackenzie)*

Seven Stars [Newark Lane (B367)]: Wide choice of generous food inc good Sun lunches, Benskins and Greene King IPA and Abbot, good friendly service, attractive garden behind *(D P and J Á Sweeney)*

Runfold [SU8747]

Princess Royal [off A31 just NE of Farnham]: Large comfortable 1920s pub with good value straightforward food, good range of beers and house wine, friendly service, inglenooks, dining conservatory – very busy with families Sun lunchtime; picnic-sets and play area behind *(A D Marsh)*

Sendmarsh [TQ0455]

Saddlers Arms [Send Marsh Rd]: Low-beamed local, open fire, no smoking area, toby jugs, brassware etc, new licensees doing shorter choice of more conventionally priced food (finishes promptly at 2pm), well kept Tetleys-related ales with a guest such as Wadworths 6X; quiet piped music, machines in separate bar; tables outside *(Kevin Williams, Gee Cormack)*

Shackleford [SU9345]

Cyder House [Pepperharrow Lane]: Cottagey pub recently refitted with lots of mellow pine, cosy atmosphere, dining room and separate children's room with toys and small furniture; wide choice of enjoyable food from ciabatta sandwiches to imaginative starters and hot dishes, chatty friendly staff, good range of well kept ales such as Badger Tanglefoot and Hogs Back TEA, decent house wines, log fires, interesting bric-a-brac; fruit machine in back room, may be piped pop music; picnic-sets on back lawn, nice village setting *(Martin and Karen Wake, Susan and John Douglas)*

Shamley Green [TQ0343]

☆ *Red Lion* [The Green]: Smartly done-up dining pub with neat décor, dark polished furniture, rows of books, open fires, local cricketing photographs, enjoyable if pricy food all day from sandwiches and good ploughman's to steaks, children's helpings and unusual puddings, well kept Flowers, Greene King Abbot, Youngs and farm cider, good choice of wines, cafetière coffee, friendly staff, smart restaurant; open all day, children welcome, sturdy tables in nice garden; bedrooms *(David and Kay Ross, LYM, Edward Longley, Gordon Stevenson, LM)*

Shepperton [TQ0867]

Red Lion [Russell Rd]: Roomy, quiet and welcoming old wisteria-covered two-bar local across rd from Thames, plenty of tables on terrace among fine displays of shrubs and flowers, more on lawn over road (traffic noise); well kept Brakspears, Courage Best, Fullers London Pride and Charles Wells Bombardier, quick service, interesting prints, red-cushioned seating, generous usual food in bars and restaurant *(James Nunns)*

Thames Court [Shepperton Lock, Ferry Lane; turn left off B375 towards Chertsey, 100yds from Square]: Huge recently rebuilt Vintage Inn well placed by Thames, generous usual food from snacks upwards all day, well kept Bass and maybe Fullers London Pride, galleried central atrium with separate attractive panelled areas up and down stairs, two good log fires, daily papers, friendly service; children welcome, attractive riverside tree-shaded terrace with big gas radiant heaters *(Stephanie Smith, Leigh Hughes, Mayur Shah)*

Shere [TQ0747]

☆ *White Horse* [signed off A25 3 miles E of Guildford; Middle St]: Striking half-timbered medieval Chef & Brewer, extensively enlarged but still full of character and welcoming, with several rooms off the small busy bar (inc rather dark but good-sized children's area), uneven floors, massive beams, Tudor stonework, oak wall seats, two log fires, one in a huge inglenook, enjoyable food all day from chunky sandwiches up, well kept beers such as Courage Best and Hogs Back TEA, lots of wines by the glass, efficient service; tables outside, beautiful village *(R Lake, LYM, Mrs G R Sharman, Susan and John Douglas, DWAJ, Edward Longley, Kevin Flack, Mike and Lynn Robinson, G T Brewster, MDN)*

Staines [TQ0471]

Bells [Church St]: Recently extended traditional local, mature and relaxed, with well kept Youngs Bitter and Special, decent wines, new kitchen doing prompt home-made lunchtime food from good sandwiches up, friendly staff, cosy furnishings, central fireplace; darts, cribbage, games machine, maybe piped music – not evenings; plenty of seats in big garden with terrace *(Simon Collett-Jones, Tony Middis, Shirley Lunn)*

Old Red Lion [Leacroft]: Roomy and comfortable, with helpful landlord, well kept Courage Best, Fullers London Pride and Youngs, games area; open all day Sat *(R Huggins, D Irving, E McCall, T McLean)*

☆ *Swan* [The Hythe; south bank, over Staines

Bridge]: Splendid Thameside setting, with moorings, tables on riverside verandah, big conservatory, several distinctly different areas to suit a mix of customers inc a young-things music room, fairly peaceful upstairs restaurant, and calm chatty corridor, enjoyable traditional food, cheerful service, well kept Fullers ales; can be very busy Sun lunchtime and packed with the under-30s on summer evenings; comfortable bedrooms *(LYM, R Huggins, D Irving, E McCall, T McLean, Shirley Lunn, Simon Collett-Jones)*

Sunbury [TQ1068]

Flower Pot [Thames St, Lower Sunbury; handy for M3 junction 1, via Green St off exit roundabout]: Quiet and pleasant 18th-c inn with nice local feel, well kept ales such as Fullers London Pride, Greene King IPA and Abbot and Youngs, good choice of wines by the glass, attentive cheerful young staff, good home-made food in bar and small restaurant; simple comfortable bedrooms *(D P and J A Sweeney)*

Magpie [Thames St]: Lovely Thames views from upper bar and small terrace by boat club, good food from ploughman's up, well kept Boddingtons, Greene King and Marstons Pedigree, decent wines, efficient antipodean service, no smoking areas; jazz in lower bar Mon; bedrooms *(D P and J A Sweeney, Paul Thompson, Anna Blackburn)*

Sutton Abinger [TQ1046]

☆ *Volunteer* [Water Lane; just off B2126 via Raikes Lane, 1½ miles S of Abinger Hammer]: Three well modernised low-ceilinged linked traditional rooms, antique military prints, big rugs on bare boards or red tiles, good choice of food, not cheap but worth it, from baguettes to fresh fish, no smoking area, Badger IPA, Best, Golden Champion and Tanglefoot, decent wines, welcoming service, roaring fire, homely medley of furnishings; restaurant, children welcome away from bar; nice country setting, good tables out on flowery terrace and suntrap lawns stepped up behind, open all day summer wknds, good walks *(G T Brewster, D B Molyneux-Berry, James Nunns, LYM, C and R Bromage, Mike and Heather Watson, Mrs Hilarie Taylor)*

Tadworth [TQ2354]

Blue Anchor [Dorking Rd (B2032)]: Busy, warm and homely Vintage Inn, with log fires and candles, cheerful helpful staff, well kept Bass, Fullers London Pride and Worthington, decent wine, vast helpings of food – very popular so may be a wait; piped music or juke box *(Stephanie Smith, Leigh Hughes, Mrs G R Sharman, Jenny and Brian Seller)*

Dukes Head [A217 opp Common and woods]: Pleasantly and surprisingly basic considering the area, with well kept Friary Meux, Wadworths 6X and a guest such as Robinsons *(P A Legon)*

Tatsfield [TQ4156]

Old Ship [Westmore Green]: Big bar with lots of interesting pictures and bric-a-brac, Greene King IPA and Youngs, prompt courteous service, enjoyable mix of food from good range of sandwiches and baguettes to fresh fish, small restaurant with log fire; pretty setting on green opp duck pond, play area in big garden with good value holiday barbecues *(LM, Jenny and Brian Seller)*

Thames Ditton [TQ1567]

☆ *Fox on the River* [Queens Rd, signed off Summer Rd]: Spacious but cosy Vintage Inn in delightful spot, lots of tables on attractive Thameside terrace and lawn overlooking Hampton Court grounds, good bar food from sandwiches and ploughman's to more inventive dishes with proper veg, well kept reasonably priced Bass and Tetleys, good choice of wines by the glass, friendly helpful staff, lively mix of customers, log fire, flagstones, river pictures, popular restaurant; moorings, open all day *(Tom and Ruth Rees, Sue and Mike Todd, A D Marsh, Tony Scott, David and Carole Chapman)*

George & Dragon [High St]: Pleasant atmosphere, good value food, friendly service, well kept Bass and Courage Best, family room; quiet piped music; open all day *(R A Watson)*

Greyhound [Hampton Court Way, Weston Green]: Popular and attractive, under promising new regime, Whitbreads-related ales with a guest such as Youngs Special, food inc Sun lunch; former golf club-house, now cut off from course by road, but still has something of the feel, with big pine tables in airy rooms; very busy after Twickenham internationals *(B Phelvin)*

Thorpe [TQ0268]

Rose & Crown [Sandhills Lane, Thorpe Green]: Good roomy Chef & Brewer, sympathetically renovated without faux-rustic antiquity; good changing home-made food, good atmosphere, real ales such as Courage Best and Directors, Morlands Old Speckled Hen and Theakstons XB, good choice of wines by the glass, pleasant attentive staff, daily papers, piped classical music; can get crowded; nice gardens and good outdoor children's area *(Ian Phillips)*

Virginia Water [SU9969]

☆ *Rose & Olive Branch* [Callow Hill]: Small unpretentious pub with emphasis on wide choice of good home-made food inc lots of fish and unusual speciality pies (busy Fri night, best to book then), real ales such as Greene King IPA and Abbot, decent wines, friendly helpful service, matchbox collection; quiet piped music; children allowed lunchtime, attractive garden, good walks *(Ken and Joyce Hollis, Ian Phillips, Simon Collett-Jones, Guy Charrison)*

Walton-on-Thames [TQ0966]

Anglers [Riverside, off Manor Rd]: Roomy refitted pub on Thames towpath (renamed Slug & Lettuce in recent years), a few peaceful tables outside (local by-law prevents their evening use); Courage and Greene King beers, plentiful food, plenty of bare-boards floor area, large first-floor river-view family room (facing bungalows opposite); moorings, boat hire next door *(Mayur Shah, the Didler)*

Weir [off Sunbury Lane]: Wide range of good food from sandwiches up, Badger Best and

Tanglefoot, traditional décor, masses of pictures, candles on tables, attractive family room done as part-panelled library looking over water, smartly dressed staff; lots of picnic-sets crowded on to big terrace with good view over river and weir (and steel walkway); open all day Sun, lovely towpath walks *(Mayur Shah)*

Warlingham [TQ3759]

☆ *Botley Hill Farmhouse* [B269 towards Limpsfield]: Busy more or less open-plan dining pub, lots of low-ceilinged interlinked rooms up and down steps, soft lighting, spreading turkey carpet, quite closely set tables, big fireplace with copper and blacked pans above the log fire in one attractive flagstoned room, restaurant with overhead fishing net and seashells, small no smoking area; good if not cheap food inc lots of fish and seafood, well kept ales such as Greene King IPA, Abbot and Triumph, Pilgrims and Shepherd Neame Spitfire, good house wines; children welcome, cream teas, wknd entertainments (may be loud live bands outside), tables on terrace, neat garden with play area, ducks and aviary *(Jenny and Brian Seller, BB, Mr and Mrs R G Lloyd, Tina and David Woods-Taylor, A D Jenkins)*

☆ *White Lion* [Farleigh Rd (B269)]: Uunspoilt and bustling old local with Tudor fireplace snugged in by high-backed settles, friendly dark-panelled rooms, very low beams, sensibly priced food from sandwiches up, well kept Bass, Fullers London Pride, Hancocks HB and guest beers, prompt service; may be piped music in eating area; tables out in back garden *(Michael and Ann Cole, B, M and P Kendall, Jim Bush, LYM)*

West Byfleet [TQ0460]

Yeoman [Old Woking Rd]: Nicely decorated family dining pub, a treat for pre-teens; friendly staff turn down the piped music if you ask *(Shirley Mackenzie)*

West Clandon [TQ0452]

☆ *Bulls Head* [A247 SE of Woking]: Friendly and comfortably modernised 16th-c country local, very popular esp with older people lunchtime for reliably good value home-made food from sandwiches, ploughman's and baked potatoes to steak, small lantern-lit front bar with open fire and some stripped brick, old local prints, raised rather canteenish back inglenook dining area, efficient service, Courage Best, Greene King Old Speckled Hen and Marstons Pedigree, good coffee, no piped music, games room with darts and pool; lots of tables and good play area in garden, convenient for Clandon Park, good walking country *(DWAJ, R Lake, Shirley Mackenzie)*

☆ *Onslow Arms* [A247 SE of Woking]: Rambling partly 17th-c country pub, pricy but good and convivial; dark nooks and corners, heavy beams, flagstones, warm seats by inglenook log fires, soft lighting, lots of brass and copper; eight well kept ales, decent wines, nicely presented sandwiches, carvery-style hot-lamp bar food servery (not Sun evening), partly no smoking dining room (popular Sun lunches), great well lit garden; children welcome, open all day *(LYM, G W A Pearce)*

West End [SU9461]

☆ *Inn at West End* [Guildford Rd (A322, S of M3 junction 3)]: Former Wheatsheaf, perked up and renamed by new licensees, good food in bar and extended bistro-style restaurant, friendly professional service, well kept beers, good wines inc champagne by the glass; conservatory, picnic-sets in large garden behind *(Dr P C Rea, Guy Consterdine)*

West Horsley [TQ0753]

☆ *King William IV* [The Street]: Welcoming and comfortable local, red plush banquettes in neatly secluded areas, very low beams, enjoyable bar and restaurant food cooked to order (so may be a wait), well kept Courage Best, Directors and John Smiths, good coffee, attentive staff, log fires; good disabled access, darts area, piped radio; small garden, gorgeous hanging baskets *(Mike and Heather Watson, Gordon Prince, John Evans, J S M Sheldon, P J Keen)*

Weybridge [TQ0965]

Badgers Rest [Oatlands Chase]: Hotel well refurbished (with bare brick and very realistic beams) as warm and welcoming Vintage Inn, already very popular with older people lunchtime for wide choice of good food from sandwiches up, well kept Bass and Worthington, very helpful staff; seven or eight linked rooms with tables for varying numbers, separate food counter, back area for smokers; tables on front lawn; immaculate bedrooms *(W W Burke, James Nunns)*

Grotto [Monument Hill]: Straightforward pub with good thai food, Courage, Greene King IPA and Ruddles County *(James Nunns)*

Minnows [Thames St/Walton Lane]: Vintage Inn, usual pleasantly old-fangled décor and food from good value open sandwiches up, well kept Bass and Tetleys, freshly squeezed orange jouce, generous filter coffee, friendly very attentive staff; round picnic-sets on decking set into front lawn *(LM)*

☆ *Old Crown* [Thames St]: Friendly and well run old-fashioned three-bar pub, warm and comfortable, very popular lunchtime for good platefuls of reasonably priced straightforward food from sandwiches up esp fresh Grimsby fish (served evening too), good specials; well kept Courage Best and Directors, John Smiths, Youngs Special and a guest such as Charles Wells Bombardier, no smoking family lounge and conservatory, no music or machines but may be sports TV in back bar; children welcome, suntrap streamside garden *(D WAJ, Ian Phillips, Jonathan Gibbs, J S M Sheldon, Minda and Stanley Alexander)*

Prince of Wales [Cross Rd/Anderson Rd off Oatlands Drive]: Congenial and attractively restored, with relaxed country-local feel, reasonably priced generous bar food inc interesting dishes and Sun lunch with three roasts (but may be a long wait even for just baguettes), well kept ales such as Adnams, Boddingtons, Fullers London Pride, Tetleys and Wadworths 6X, ten wines by the glass,

friendly service, coal-effect gas fires, imaginative menu in stripped pine restaurant down a couple of steps (candlelit bistro feel there at night) *(James Nunns, Minda and Stanley Alexander)*

Windlesham [SU9264]

Brickmakers [Chertsey Rd]: Popular dining pub with flagstones and pastel colours for bistro feel, wide range of freshly made food, cheerfully busy bar, well kept Brakspears, Courage Best, Fullers London Pride and Marstons Pedigree, good choice of wines, welcoming service, log fire, conservatory, no music; well behaved children allowed, attractive garden with boules and barbecues (live music some summer Suns), lovely hanging baskets *(B and K Hypher, John Davis, Simon Collett-Jones)*

Half Moon [Church Rd]: Lively and welcoming extended local, good range of well kept ales, good value straightforward food inc popular family Sun lunch and fresh veg, good service, modern furnishings, log fires, interesting World War II pictures; children welcome, piped music, silenced fruit machine; huge well kept garden popular with families *(Robert Hay)*

Surrey Cricketers [Chertsey Rd (B386)]: Warm welcome, lots of neat small tables on bare boards, huge choice of good generous food inc seafood, Fullers London Pride, Greene King Old Speckled Hen and Wadworths 6X, many more seats in separate skittle alley; garden *(Mr and Mrs T A Bryan, Gordon Prince, Ian Phillips)*

Witley [SU9439]

White Hart [Petworth Rd]: Tudor beams, good oak furniture, log fire in cosy panelled inglenook snug where George Eliot drank, welcoming landlord, Shepherd Neame ales with a guest such as Marstons Pedigree, public bar with usual games, restaurant; piped music; seats outside, lots of pretty hanging baskets etc, play area *(Michael Sargent, LYM)*

Woking [TQ0058]

Litten Tree [Constitution Hill]: Hotel renamed and made over into modern pub with well priced interesting food in bar and restaurant, Bass, Courage Directors and a beer brewed for this chain, friendly helpful staff; good bedrooms *(Ian Phillips)*

Wetherspoons [Chertsey Rd]: Well converted with lots of intimate areas and cosy side snugs, good range of food all day, reasonably priced beers inc interesting guest ales *(Tony Hobden)*

Wood Street [SU9550]

Royal Oak [Oak Hill]: Brightly lit pub with well kept Hogs Back and several interesting guest beers, moderately priced food with lots of fresh veg and good home-made puddings, friendly service *(Edward Longley, Gordon Stevenson)*

White Hart [White Hart Lane; off A323 just W of Guildford]: Country local dating from 16th c, good range of plentiful wholesome food from snacks up in big dining area, interesting well kept beers, good range of malt whiskies, helpful young landlord; picnic-sets in garden, peaceful spot *(Mrs Hilarie Taylor)*

Woodmansterne [TQ2760]

Woodman: New landlord in late 19th-c village pub, unpretentiously enlarged, with good range of reasonably priced food in good dining area (only roast on Sun), Bass and Fullers London Pride; garden with play area *(Jenny and Brian Seller, Stephanie Smith, Leigh Hughes, Kevin Williams, Gee Cormack)*

Worcester Park [TQ2166]

Plough [Malden Rd/Church Rd, Old Malden]: Harvester dining pub based on ancient pub, little snug in pleasant bar, friendly staff, decent food and house wines, Tetleys *(Ian Phillips)*

Wotton [TQ1247]

☆ *Wotton Hatch* [A25 Dorking-Guildford]:

Attractive neatly kept Vintage Inn family dining pub, largely no smoking rambling rooms around 17th-c core, interesting furnishings, good choice of generous food (all day Thurs-Sun and summer) from hearty sandwiches up, well kept Bass and Fullers London Pride with a guest such as Hancocks HB, decent wines, freshly squeezed orange juice, prompt service; gentle piped music, no dogs; impressive views from neat garden, open all day *(Ian Phillips, Mrs G R Sharman, Derek and Maggie Washington, Roger and Jenny Huggins, Alan and Paula McCully, M G Hart, Dick and Madeleine Brown, LYM, John Crafts, C and R Bromage, Piotr Chodzko-Zajko)*

Sussex

Quite a change-around here this year, with half a dozen pubs from last year's edition no longer in the main entries, and as many newcomers replacing them. The pubs to welcome this year are the ancient George in the lovely village of Alfriston, the friendly Old Oak at Arlington (former almshouses, a nice all-rounder), the Basketmakers Arms in Brighton (surprisingly good food and wine in this cheery local), the Coach & Horses prettily placed at Compton (a nice balance between drinking and eating), the Shepherd & Dog tucked below the downs at Fulking, the Duke of Cumberland Arms at Henley (new landlord doing enterprising food in this idyllic country pub), and the unpretentious Sussex Ox at Milton Street (a good beautifully placed all-rounder). Alongside these newcomers are four pubs which have been in every edition of the Guide *since it started 20 years ago: the cheerful Black Horse at Byworth (good food and drink in a lovely relaxed atmosphere), the Star just outside Heathfield (plenty of atmosphere, decent food, helpful staff, nice garden), the Three Cups near Punnetts Town (a fine country local – let's hope that its owners Greene King keep it that way) and the Mermaid in Rye (a handsome ancient inn with a nice back bar). Other pubs here on top form this year are the unchanging Rose Cottage at Alciston, the Fountain at Ashurst (attractive renovations, and cooking that this year gains it our Food Award), the unspoilt cottagey Cricketers Arms at Berwick (quite a favourite), the Six Bells at Chiddingly (lots of individuality, bargain food), the Tiger at East Dean (a nice all-rounder on a lovely village green), the friendly old Three Horseshoes in Elsted (lovely garden), the Griffin at Fletching (another all-round favourite), the Woodmans Arms at Hammerpot (hard-working landlord doing well), the George & Dragon at Houghton (nice pub, lovely views), the Queens Head at Icklesham (good all round), the pleasantly laid-back Snowdrop in Lewes, the Halfway Bridge Inn near Lodsworth (good imaginative food), the Horse Guards at Tillington (one of our most popular southern dining pubs), the Keepers Arms at Trotton (proper home cooking in this friendly country pub), and the Giants Rest at Wilmington (charming atmosphere, good food). For a special meal out, our top shortlist would be the Fountain at Ashurst (particularly for its imaginative dishes of the day), the Griffin at Fletching, the Badgers near Petworth and the Horse Guards at Tillington, with very good food too at the Jolly Sportsman at East Chiltington. Of all these, the Fountain, flourishing under its enthusiastic young landlords, is our Sussex Dining Pub of the Year. As well as so many good main entries in Sussex, the Lucky Dip section at the end of the chapter is unusually strong. Particularly appealing these days are the Spotted Cow in Angmering, Gardeners Arms at Ardingly, Colonnade and Cricketers in Brighton, Rainbow Trout at Broad Oak (the one down towards Rye), Hatch at Colemans Hatch, George & Dragon near Coolham, Old Vine at Cousley Wood, Cricketers at Duncton, Royal Oak at East Lavant, Woolpack at Fishbourne, Swan at Fittleworth, Lamb at Ripe, Cock at Ringmer, White Horse at Sutton, Five Bells at West Chiltington, Cat at West Hoathly, Lamb at West Wittering and Dorset Arms at Withyham. Drinks prices in the area have held fairly steady this year, but even so are clearly higher than the national average, with a typical Sussex pint now costing at least £2. For pocket relief, turn to the Golden Galleon near Seaford: the beer brewed at the pub is very cheap. Harveys is now the only big Sussex brewer. You may come across a beer called King & Barnes Sussex, but it's now brewed down in Dorset by Badger (we call it Badger K&B – the K&B Mild is brewed for Badger by their Gribble Inn at Oving).*

ALCISTON TQ5005 Map 3

Rose Cottage

Village signposted off A27 Polegate—Lewes

In summer, this bustling country cottage is very pleasant with ducks and chickens in the back garden, and gas heaters for cooler evenings; the charming little village (and local church) are certainly worth a look. Inside, there are cosy winter log fires, and half a dozen tables with cushioned pews under quite a forest of harness, traps, a thatcher's blade and lots of other black ironware, with more bric-a-brac on the shelves above the stripped pine dado or in the etched-glass windows; in the mornings you may also find Jasper the parrot (it can get a little smoky for him in the evenings); it's best to arrive early to be sure of a seat. There's a lunchtime overflow into the no smoking restaurant area. Made from fresh local produce wherever possible (fresh fish comes from a fisherman at Eastbourne, eggs from their own chickens, and venison from the landlord's brother-in-law), hearty bar food includes pâté (£3.25), ploughman's (from £4.75), lincolnshire sausages (£5.25) and rib-eye steak (£7.50), with daily specials such as beef and ale pie (£6.75), chicken in white wine and mushroom sauce (£7.50), good vegetarian dishes (around £7.50), wild rabbit in cream and mustard sauce or whole local plaice with lemon and parsley butter (£7.95), venison braised in port and Guinness (£8.50), whole grilled bass with pickled ginger and soy sauce (£9.95), and roast Sunday lunch (£7.50); very good home-made puddings like home-grown rhubarb crumble, treacle tart or hot chocolate fudge brownie (£3.25). Well kept Harveys Best, winter Old, and a guest such as Rother Valley Level Best on handpump, decent wines including a 'country' of the month and six by the glass (or half litre), winter mulled wine, summer pimms and sangria, and Biddenden farm cider; the landlord, whom we have known now for many years, is quite a character; darts, dominoes, cribbage, and maybe piped classical music. House martins and swallows continue their annual custom of nesting above the porch, seemingly unperturbed by the people going in and out beneath them. The small paddock in the garden has ducks and chickens. Nearby fishing and shooting. *(Recommended by Martin and Karen Wake, Catherine and Richard Preston, Mark Weber, R and S Bentley, B, M and P Kendall, Peter Meister, Bruce Bird, MDN, Christopher Turner, John Beeken, David Carr, Colin and Janet Roe, the Didler, Val and Alan Green, Ann and Colin Hunt, Sally Anne and Peter Goodale)*

Free house ~ Licensee Ian Lewis ~ Real ale ~ Bar food (till 9.30 (exc Sun)) ~ Restaurant ~ (01323) 870377 ~ Children welcome in restaurant and eating area of bar but must be over 6 in evening ~ Open 11.30-3, 6.30-11; 12-3, 7-10.30 Sun; closed 25 and 26 Dec ~ Bedrooms: /£50S

ALFRISTON TQ5203 Map 3

George 🛏

High Street

Opposite the intriguing façade of the Red Lion, this 14th-c timbered inn oozes age – just the place to take visitors from overseas. The long main bar has massive low beams hung with hops, appropriately soft lighting, and a log fire (or summer flower arrangement) in a huge stone inglenook fireplace that dominates the room, with lots of copper and brass around it. Sturdy stripped tables have settles and chairs around them, and there's a thriving atmosphere, thanks to the jovial current landlord and his hard-working staff. The popular home-made bar food at lunchtime includes sandwiches (from £3.50), soup (£3.95), flat mushroom with goats cheese and smoky bacon (£4.95), mushroom stroganoff (£5.50), ploughman's or home-made steak and kidney pie (£6.25), sweet and sour prawns (£6.50), and battered cod (£6.95), with evening dishes like seafood platter (£5.95), carpaccio of beef fillet (£6.50), goats cheese and frangipane pithivier with sweet chilli sauce (£9.95), roasted duck breast with spiced plums (£12.95), lemon sole stuffed with prawns and paprika with a light saffron sauce (£13.95), and steaks (from £13.95). If you stay, breakfasts here are good, too. Well kept beers such as Greene King Abbot, Old Speckled Hen and Ruddles County, and a guest such as Everards Tiger on handpump, decent wines; piped music, table skittles, cribbage, dominoes, backgammon, and Jenga. Besides the cosy candlelit restaurant, there's a garden dining room; or you can sit out in the charming flint-walled garden behind. The lovely village is a tourist honey-pot; you can escape the crowds on a fine riverside walk down to Cuckmere Haven, and two long-distance paths (South Downs Way and Vanguard Way) cross in the village. *(Recommended by Charlie Harris, John and Lynn Busenbark, Francis Johnston, Michael and Ann Cole)*

Greene King ~ Tenant Kate Crouch ~ Real ale ~ Bar food (12-2.30, 7-9(10 Sat and Sun)) ~ Restaurant ~ (01323) 870319 ~ Children welcome away from main bar ~ Classical guitarist Sat evening ~ Open 12-11; 12-10.30 Sun; 12-3, 6-11 in winter; closed 25 and 26 Dec ~ Bedrooms: £40B/£60B

AMBERLEY SO8401 Map 3
Black Horse
Off B2139

Handy for the South Downs Way, this very pretty pub has a main bar with high-backed settles on flagstones, beams over the serving counter festooned with sheep and cow bells, traps and shepherds' tools, and walls decorated with lots of old local prints and engravings; there are plenty of pictures too and some unusual teapots in the similar but more comfortable saloon bar; log fires at either end of the main bar and two in the restaurant. Under the new licensee, the decent straightforward bar food includes sandwiches (£4.55), and main meals (£5.95-£8.95) such as lasagne, chicken diane, broccoli and pasta bake, various curries, yorkshire pudding filled with steak in ale casserole, and scampi; Sunday roast, and a Tuesday three-course lunch (£5). Well kept Friary Meux, Ind Coope Burton and a guest such as Greene King Old Speckled Hen on handpump, and several malt whiskies. Fruit machine and piped music. There are seats in the garden; dogs welcome. You can walk along the banks of the River Arun, and the open air Amberley Industrial Museum is nearby. *(Recommended by Bruce Bird, Peter Meister, Ian Phillips, R Halsey, Ian Rankin, Cathy Robinson)*

Pubmaster ~ Tenant Gary Tubb ~ Real ale ~ Bar food (all day) ~ (01798) 831552 ~ Well behaved children welcome ~ Open 11-11; 12-10.30 Sun

Bridge
B2139

With pretty summer hanging baskets, this attractive old white painted place is well liked for it food. The comfortable and relaxed bar has a couple of cushioned window seats and a mix of wooden chairs by a few tables along one side, a group of crimson velveteen bucket seats around a table at one end with a button-backed brown sofa beside them, soft lighting from candles, and a tiled bar gantry. A small cosy room with similar seats leads off the bar, and a delft shelf and beam with brass, copper, and lots of bottles leads to the attractively furnished two-roomed dining area. Under the new licensee, changing bar food might include sandwiches, soup (£3.95), ploughman's (£4.50), chicken liver pâté with cumberland sauce (£4.95), thai fishcakes with chilli jam (£5.95; main course £11.95), steak and kidney pie or leek and stilton crêpes (£7.75), deep-fried beer battered cod (£8.95), sausages with onion gravy and mash (£9.95), steaks (from £10.25), duck breast with plum sauce, braised half shoulder of lamb with redcurrant and mint jus, pork fillet with apple confit and port sauce or chargrilled sirloin steak with pepper sauce (all £11.95). Flowers Original, Fullers London Pride, Harveys Sussex, and Youngs on handpump; piped music. There are white plastic seats and tables in front of the pub, with more in a little side garden. *(Recommended by J Davidson, David Holloway, Nick and Meriel Cox, Patrick Renouf, Bruce Bird, Ian Jones, Ian Phillips)*

Free house ~ Licensee Lee Hastings ~ Real ale ~ Bar food (12-2.30, 7-9.30; 12-4 Sun; closed Sun evening) ~ Restaurant ~ (01798) 831619 ~ Children welcome ~ Open 11-11; 12-10.30 Sun

Sportsmans

Crossgates; Rackham Rd, off B2139

A bedroom extension has been built on to this village pub, and as we went to press, the bars were about to be refurbished. But a strong reason for a visit here, is to enjoy the panoramic views from inside the bars and conservatory, and from the decked terrace at the back. Well kept Miserable Old B****r (brewed for the pub by Brewery on Sea, and named after a charity fund-raising club that's based here), plus Fullers London Pride, Morrells Graduate, and Youngs Special on handpump, and scrumpy cider. The brick floored public bar has a hexagonal pool table, fruit machine, darts, cribbage, dominoes and giant Jenga, and the pretty little red-tiled conservatory is engagingly decorated with old local bric-a-brac. Bar food includes changing dishes from the blackboard such as sandwiches, mushroom and courgette stroganoff (£6.95), pasta carbonara, chicken and leek pie or lamb korma (£7.25), sausages with red wine gravy (£7.95), and poached fillet of bass with bean sprouts, noodles and a mango and avocado salsa (£9.95). More reports please. *(Recommended by J A Snell, John Fahy, Charlotte Rae, Peter D B Harding, Dennis Jenkin)*

Free house ~ Licensees Jenny and Chris Shanahan ~ Real ale ~ Bar food ~ (01798) 831787 ~ Children in eating area of bar ~ Open 11-2.30(3 Sat), 6-11; 12-3, 7-10.30 Sun ~ Bedrooms: £45S/£60S

ARLINGTON TQ5407 Map 3
Old Oak

Caneheath, off A22 or A27 NW of Polegate

Everyone – including dogs – is made most welcome in these 17th-c former almshouses. The open-plan, L-shaped bar has heavy beams, well spaced tables and comfortable seating, log fires, and a calm, relaxed atmosphere. Well kept Badger Best, Harveys Best, and a guest such as Adnams Regatta or Fullers London Pride tapped from the cask, and several malt whiskies; piped music. Good bar food at lunchtime includes filled baguettes (from £4.50), ploughman's (£4.90), filled baked potatoes (from £5.75), macaroni cheese (£6.25), salads with home-cooked meats (from £6.50), and lasagne (£6.75), with evening dishes like hot mushrooms with stilton (£3.50), green lipped mussels in garlic (£3.75), cajun chicken (£7.75), grilled lamb steak with a redcurrant and rosemary sauce (£8.50), steaks (from £9.25), and daily specials like fresh cod in batter or various curries (£6.25), steak and kidney pudding (£6.40), grilled whole plaice filled with prawns (£7.50), and breast of chicken with stilton and mushroom sauce (£8.25); friendly service. The basset hound is called Hetty. Seats in the peaceful garden, and Abbotswood nature reserve is nearby. *(Recommended by J H Bell, Michael and Ann Cole, R M Warner)*

Free house~ Licensee Ian Nicoll ~ Bar food (Sun or Mon evenings) ~ Restaurant ~ (01323) 482072 ~ Children in restaurant ~ Occasional live entertainment Sun evening ~ Open 11-3, 6-11; 12-3, 7-10.30 Sun

---

We checked prices with the pubs as we went to press in summer 2001. They should hold until around spring 2002 – when our experience suggests that you can expect an increase of around 10p in the £.

ASHURST TQ1716 Map 3
Fountain 🍴 🍺
B2135 S of Partridge Green

Sussex Dining Pub of the Year

The main dining area in this welcoming 16th-c country pub has now been restored, and during building works, old plaster and panelling have been removed to show ancient brickwork and add to the pub's impressive collection of heavy oak beams. The neatly kept and charmingly rustic tap room on the right has a couple of high-backed wooden cottage armchairs by the log fire in its brick inglenook, two antique polished trestle tables, and fine old flagstones; there are more flagstones in the opened-up snug with heavy beams, simple furniture, and its own inglenook fireplace. Well kept Adnams, Fullers London Pride, Harveys Best and Shepherd Neame Bitter with a guest such as Ringwood Best or Shepherd Neame Spitfire on handpump; freshly squeezed apple juice from their own press in September (proceeds to a children's charity), and decent wines; cribbage, dominoes, shove-ha'penny, and an oak-beamed skittle alley that doubles as a function room. Good popular food includes lunchtime sandwiches (from £3.95), ploughman's (£5.50), and home-cooked ham with free range egg (£6.50), plus salads such as grilled goats cheese with sunflower seeds (from £7.50), steak, mushroom and ale pie or popular smoked haddock and prawns in a cheese sauce (£7.95), evening steaks (from £12.50), puddings like sticky toffee pudding, blackberry and apple pie or hot chocolate fudge cake (£3.95), and imaginative daily specials such as local pheasant and partridge casserole, leek, red onion and parmesan strudel, braised organic beef with mushrooms and shallots, fresh roasted bream stuffed with fennel and orange, or mahi mahi with a roasted pepper and dill dressing (from around £8.95). Service is pleasant and attentive. The prettily planted garden (including raised herb beds for the kitchen) is developing well, and there are plenty of tables on the wooden decking, a growing orchard, and a duck pond. No children inside. *(Recommended by R Edwards, Avril Burton, Ben Whitney and Pippa Redmond, David and Sue Lee, Mrs Sally Kingsbury, Mr and Mrs Thomas, Bruce Bird, Karen Eliot, C A Hall, John Davis, David Holloway, Tony and Wendy Hobden)*

Free house ~ Licensees Mark and Chris White ~ Real ale ~ Bar food (12-2, 6.30-9.30; sandwiches only Sun and Mon evenings) ~ Restaurant ~ No credit cards ~ (01403) 710219 ~ Folk music 2nd Weds evening of month ~ Open 11.30-2.30, 6-11; 12-3, 7-10.30 Sun

BARNHAM SU9604 Map 3
Murrell Arms £
Yapton Rd

Quite unspoilt and old-fashioned, this has been run by the Cuttens for over 35 years. Over that time, they have collected hundreds of jugs, mugs, china plates and old bottles that are jammed together along delft shelves, little prints, pictures and old photographs cover the walls, agricultural artefacts hang from the ceiling, and there's an elderly grandfather clock, a collection of old soda syphons, an interesting Cox's change machine and Crystal Palace clock, and some old horsebrasses. The saloon bar has some nice old farmhouse chairs, a very high-backed settle by the piano, a mix of tables (including a fine circular Georgian one) with candles in bottles on its partly turkey carpeted, very old dark wood parquet floor, and a huge polished half-barrel bar counter. To get to the cheerful public bar, you walk past the stillage room where the barrels of Gales HSB, BBB and a changing guest are stored; lots of country wines and two open fires. The simple tiny snug over a half wall (the only place where really well behaved children are tolerated) has an enormous bell wheel from the church on the ceiling; darts. Straightforward bar food includes cockles and mussels (85p), ploughman's (from £1.75), tasty bacon hock with crusty bread (£3.50), and a couple of daily specials such as liver and bacon casserole, boiled belly of pork with parsley sauce or lambs kidneys (£3.50). From the car park, you walk through a pretty flower-filled courtyard with a large cider press on one side, and fine ancient wooden benches and tables under a leafy grape vine on the other – note the huge bellows on the wall; there are picnic-sets on a cottagey little enclosed garden up some steps. *(Recommended by Stephanie and Kamal Thapa, Ann and Colin Hunt, John Fahy)*

Gales ~ Tenant Mervyn Cutten ~ Real ale ~ Bar food (not Thurs evening) ~ No credit cards ~ (01243) 553320 ~ Well behaved children in snug ~ Folk Thurs evening and last Sun of month ~ Open 11-2.30, 6-11; 11-11 Sat; 12-10.30 Sun

BERWICK TQ5105 Map 3
Cricketers Arms
Lower Rd, S of A27

This is a smashing little pub, formerly two flint cottages, and set in a quiet village close to the downs. The three little similarly furnished rooms have simple benches against the half-panelled walls, a pleasant mix of old country tables and chairs, burgundy velvet curtains on poles, a few bar stools, and some country prints; quarry tiles on the floors (nice worn ones in the middle room), two log fires in little brick fireplaces, a huge black supporting beam in each of the low ochre ceilings, and (in the end room) some attractive cricketing pastels; some of the beams are hung with cricket bats. Service remains helpful and friendly – even when it's busy. Good straightforward bar food includes home-made soup (£3.25), pâté (£4.50), filled baguettes (from £4.50), local pork and herb sausages or ploughman's (from £4.95), gammon and egg, a vegetarian dish or local cod in batter (£6.95), steaks (from £9.50), daily specials (from £6.95), and puddings (£3.25); they hold themed food evenings in winter. Well kept Harveys Best and a seasonal ale tapped from the cask, and decent wine; darts, shove-ha'penny, cribbage, and an old Sussex coin game called toad in the hole. The old-fashioned cottagey garden is lovely on a sunny day with little brick paths, mature flowering shrubs and plants, and lots of picnic-sets in front of and behind the building. The wall paintings in the nearby church done by the Bloomsbury group during WWII are worth a look. *(Recommended by Kevin Thorpe, MDN, Peter and Joan Elbra, Peter Meister, the Didler, John Beeken, Ian Phillips, R D Henshaw, Tina and David Woods-Taylor, David Carr, Ann and Colin Hunt)*

Harveys ~ Tenant Peter Brown ~ Real ale ~ Bar food (12-2.15, 6.30-9; all day wknds) ~ (01323) 870469 ~ Children in family room; under 5s under strict parental control ~ Open 11-3, 6-11(all day July/Aug); 11-11 Sat; 12-10.30 Sun; closed 25 Dec

BILLINGSHURST TQ0830 Map 3
Blue Ship ◗
The Haven; hamlet signposted off A29 just N of junction with A264, then follow signpost left towards Garlands and Okehurst

Tucked away down a remote country lane, this charmingly unpretentious pub is an idyllic spot for a summer evening visit, when you can relax at the tree-shaded side tables or by the tangle of honeysuckle around the front door, and contentedly take in the air of peaceful simplicity. Dogs and their walkers are welcome (must be kept on leads; no muddy boots), and there's a play area for children. Inside, the cosy beamed and brick-floored front bar has a blazing fire in the inglenook fireplace, scrubbed tables and wall benches, and hatch service dispensing well kept Badger Best and K&B on handpump, and farm cider. A corridor leads to a couple of small carpeted rooms with dark wood tables and chairs, old prints and fresh flowers, where children can sit – one is no smoking. Darts, bar billiards, shove-ha'penny, cribbage, dominoes and table skittles (on request). It can get crowded with a pleasant mix of customers, particularly at weekends; there may be a playful cat. Reasonably priced traditional bar food includes sandwiches (from £2.25), ploughman's (from £4.10), macaroni cheese (£4.50), cheese-on cottage pie (£4.85), ham and eggs (£5.70), steak and onion pie (£6.50), and puddings such as treacle sponge or blackcurrant and apple pie (£2.75). *(Recommended by Kevin Thorpe, the Didler, John Davis, Di and Mike Gillam, Ian Phillips, Susan and John Douglas)*

King & Barnes (Badger) ~ Tenant J R Davie ~ Real ale ~ Bar food (not Sun or Mon evenings) ~ No credit cards ~ (01403) 822709 ~ Children in two rooms without bar ~ Open 11-3, 6-11; 12-3.30, 7-10.30 Sun

BLACKBOYS TQ5220 Map 3
Blackboys Inn
B2192, S edge of village

After a walk along the Vanguard Way footpath or in the Woodland Trust opposite, the garden of this pretty 14th-c weatherboarded house is a pleasant place to relax. There's masses of space and rustic tables overlooking the pond, with more on the front lawn under the chestnut trees. Inside, a string of old-fashioned and unpretentious little rooms has dark oak beams, bare boards or parquet, antique prints, copious curios (including a collection of keys above the bar), and a good log fire in the inglenook fireplace. Decent food includes home-made soup (£3), ploughman's or filled baked potatoes (from £3.95), steak butty (£4.50), ham and eggs (£4.95), home-made pie (£6.50), steaks (from £9.95), daily specials such as moules marinières (£5.50), king prawns with garlic, chilli and lemon grass (£9.95), and salmon niçoise (£11.50), and puddings like home-made summer pudding or banoffi pie (from £3.95). There are more elaborate restaurant meals (served throughout the pub) such as smoked salmon papillote (£5.95), mediterranean vegetable risotto (£9.95), roast fillet of lamb with wild mushrooms and a rosemary and thyme reduction (£12.50), and chilli fish (£14.95). The restaurant and dining areas are no smoking; obliging, efficient service even when busy. Well kept Harveys Best, Pale Ale, and a monthly guest on handpump; darts, fruit machine and juke box. *(Recommended by Ann and Colin Hunt, the Didler, Jenny and Brian Seller, Tessa Burnett, Tina and David Woods-Taylor, Michael and Ann Cole, Derek Thomas, R J Walden)*

Harveys ~ Tenants Edward and Claire Molesworth ~ Real ale ~ Bar food (12-2.15, 6.30-9.30; not Sun evenings) ~ Restaurant ~ (01825) 890283 ~ Children in restaurant ~ Open 11-3, 6-11; 12-3, 7-10.30 Sun; closed 1 Jan

BRIGHTON TQ3105 Map 3
Basketmakers Arms £
Gloucester Road – the E end, near Cheltenham Place; off Marlborough Place (A23) via Gloucester Street

Run for 15 years by a local character, this bustling and cheerful backstreet local is popular with Saturday shoppers, and has a relaxed, friendly atmosphere, well kept Gales Bitter, GB, HSB, and seasonal ales, and good wines by the large glass. The two small rooms have brocaded wall benches and stools on the stripped wood floor, lots of interesting old tins all over the walls, cigarette cards on one beam with whisky labels on another, and some old photographs and posters; piped jazz and polite staff. Good value enjoyable bar food includes lots of sandwiches (from £1.95; brie and avocado £2.75; hot salt beef on granary £3.25), particularly good home-made meaty and vegetarian burgers (£2.50), baked potatoes with fillings such as avocado, shrimp and mayonnaise or beef, chilli and yoghurt (£2.95), ploughman's (£3.50), and specials such as cod in beer batter or fried tuna with garlic and coriander salad or sausage and mash with cabbage and onion gravy (£3.95). *(Recommended by the Didler, Richard Houghton, Stephanie and Kamal Thapa)*

Gales ~ Tenants P and K Dowd, A McIlwaine, A Mawer ~ Real ale ~ Bar food (12-2.30, 5.30-8.30; 12-3.30 Sat; 12-4 Sun; not Sat/Sun evenings) ~ Children in eating area of bar until 8pm ~ Open 11-11; 12-10.30 Sun; closed 26 Dec

BURPHAM TQ0308 Map 3
George & Dragon ◀
Warningcamp turn off A27 outside Arundel: follow road up and up

Built in 1736, this popular dining pub is in an attractive setting at the end of the village between the partly Norman church (which has some unusual decoration) and cricket ground; just a short walk away are splendid views down to Arundel Castle and the river. The attractive setting aside, bar food remains the biggest draw with most of the tables getting booked up in advance, so it certainly pays to phone the pub before visiting. As well as snacks such as filled baked potatoes (from £3.25), filled baguettes (from £5.50), and ploughman's, the very good food might include moules marinières (£5.95), chicken and asparagus or steak and horseradish pie (£6.20), seafood platter (crab, prawns, smoked salmon, mackerel, and poached salmon, £6.95 or £12.50), glazed gammon steak with sugar and mustard or half pheasant (£7.95), shank of lamb with mint and apricot sauce (£8.50), calves liver with bacon and onion gravy (£8.95), and home-made puddings such as chocolate and nut brownie, raspberry mousse or bananas in rum and coffee (£4.25). Be warned – they stick rigidly to their food service times; friendly efficient service from charming young staff. The neatly kept, spacious open-plan bar has good strong wooden furnishings, lots of interesting prints, well kept Arundel Best, Harveys Best, and Brewery on Sea Spinnaker, and a guest such as Cotleigh Tawny or Fullers London Pride on handpump, and a decent wine list; piped music. From this remote hill village of thatch and flint, there are plenty of enjoyable surrounding walks. *(Recommended by Sue Demont, Tim Barrow, R T and J C Moggridge, Ian Phillips, Roger and Debbie Stamp, Diana Brumfit, J Davidson, John Beeken, DF, NF, Ann and Colin Hunt)*

Scottish Courage ~ Tenants James Rose and Kate Holle ~ Real ale ~ Bar food (12-2, 7-9.45; not Sun evening) ~ Restaurant ~ (01903) 883131 ~ Well behaved children (preferably over 8) in eating area of bar and restaurant ~ Open 11-2.30, 6-11; 12-3, 7-10.30 Sun; closed Sun evening Oct-Easter

BURWASH TQ6724 Map 3
Bell

A265 E of Heathfield

This is a pretty village, and the pub with its colourful summer hanging baskets and tubs fits it well; picnic-sets look across the busy road to the church and charming cottage-lined lane opposite. Inside, there's a good quietly chatty atmosphere and usually a couple of cheerful locals sitting at the high-backed bar stools by the counter. The relaxed L-shaped bar to the right of the main door has built-in pews and a mix of seats with brocaded cushions, all sorts of ironwork, bells and barometers on its ochre Anaglypta ceiling and dark terracotta walls, and a good winter log fire. Well kept Greene King IPA, Ruddles Best and County, and a guest such as Batemans XB or Harveys Best on handpump, and a range of malt whiskies and decent wines. Darts, shove-ha'penny, ring the bull, table skittles, cribbage, dominoes, TV and unobtrusive piped music. Generous helpings of enjoyable home-made bar food include sandwiches, roast vegetable lasagne (£5.50), fruity chicken curry (£5.95), fresh skate wing in caper butter, fresh griddled tuna or braised lamb shank with minted gravy (£7.95), fillet steak plain or with a creamy peppercorn sauce (£10.95), and puddings like blackberry and apple crumble, bananas in hot butterscotch sauce or bread and butter pudding (£2.75). The no smoking restaurant is to be redecorated this year. Car park at the back; dogs welcome. *(Recommended by Joan and Andrew Life, Jenny and Brian Seller, C E Barnes)*

Greene King ~ Lease Colin and Gillian Barrett ~ Real ale ~ Bar food (not Sun evenings) ~ Restaurant ~ (01435) 882304 ~ Children welcome ~ Open 11-3.30, 6-11; 11-11 Sat; 12-10.30 Sun; closed evenings 25 and 26 Dec ~ Bedrooms: /£45

BYWORTH SU9820 Map 2
Black Horse

Signposted from A283

You can be sure of a warm welcome from the cheerful licensees in this thoroughly old-fashioned pub, and the combination of good food and well kept beers in a relaxed atmosphere makes for a most enjoyable visit. The simply furnished though smart bar has pews and scrubbed wooden tables on its bare floorboards, and open fires; the no smoking back dining room has lots of nooks and crannies and a tented curtain to keep out the draughts. Reasonably priced bar food includes sandwiches (from £3.25), good ploughman's (from £4.75), daily specials such as slow-roasted lamb shanks with garlic, honey and redcurrants (£6.95), lamb steak with ginger and apricot sauce, crab cakes, chicken with wholegrain mustard, brandy and tarragon sauce or chestnut pâté en croûte (all £7.25), monkfish with salsa verde (£7.50), and puddings (from £2.95). Well kept Arundel Gold, Cheriton Pots Ale, Marstons Pedigree, and a guest beer on handpump kept under light blanket pressure. Bar billiards, shove-ha'penny, cribbage, dominoes, and piped music. The particularly attractive garden is at its best (and most popular) in summer: tables on a steep series of grassy terraces, sheltered by banks of flowering shrubs, look across a drowsy valley to swelling woodland, and a small stream runs along under an old willow by the more spacious lawn at the bottom; dogs are welcome on a lead. *(Recommended by John Davis, Bruce Bird, M J Bastin, J Hale, Jean-Bernard Brisset)*

Cockerel Inns ~ Managers Rob Wilson and Teri Figg ~ Real ale ~ Bar food (not evening, Mon lunchtime) ~ Restaurant ~ (01798) 342424 ~ Well behaved children in restaurant ~ Open 11-2.30(3 Sat), 6-11; 12-3, 7-10.30 Sun

CHARLTON SU8812 Map 3
Fox Goes Free

Village signposted off A286 Chichester—Midhurst in Singleton, also from Chichester—Petworth via East Dean

As Goodwood Racecourse is not far away, this cheerful old pub does get busy on race days; it's also handy for the Weald and Downland Open Air Museum. The first of the dark and cosy series of separate rooms is a small, carpeted bar with one table, a few very mixed chairs and an open fireplace. Standing timbers divide a larger beamed bar which has old and new elm furniture, a huge brick fireplace with a woodburning stove, a couple of elderly armchairs, red tiles and carpet, and brasses and old local photographs on the yellowed walls. A dining area with hunting prints looks over the garden and the South Downs beyond. The no smoking family extension is a clever conversion from horse boxes and the stables where the 1926 Goodwood winner was housed; darts, cribbage, dominoes, fruit machine, and piped music. Well kept Ballards Best, Bass, Fox Goes Free (brewed for the pub by Tetleys), Ringwood Best and a guest such as Hop Back Summer Lightning on handpump, pimms and sangria by the jug in summer, farm cider and several wines by the glass. Good, interesting bar food might include sandwiches, avocado stilton bake (£3.75), crab and asparagus bake or mushrooms stuffed with goats cheese (£4.75), king prawns fried in garlic or smoked chicken, duck and walnut salad (£5.75), ratatouille or wild mushroom filo slice (£6.75), fish pie (£6.95), pigeon, apple and calvados (£8.50), red sea bream fillet in bacon and white wine or cod steak on roasted peppers with a parmesan crust (£9), venison steak with redcurrant and port (£9.50), duck breast with roquefort and red wine (£11), and puddings (£3.25). The attractive secluded garden is the best place to sit in summer, with several terraces, plenty of picnic-sets among fruit trees, and a notable downland view; the barbecue area can be booked. The friendly jack russell is called Wiggles and the black cat, Guinness. *(Recommended by Ann and Colin Hunt, Debora Rolph, D R and A J Linnell, John Davis, Prof S Barnett, John and Sherry Moate, Pat and Derek Westcott, Martin and Karen Wake)*

Free house ~ Licensee Oliver Ligertwood ~ Real ale ~ Bar food (12-2.30(3.30 Sat, 4 Sun), 6.30(6 Sat/Sun)-10.30(10 Sun)) ~ Restaurant ~ (01243) 811461 ~ Children in restaurant and family room ~ Live music Weds evening ~ Open 11-3, 6(5 Fri)-11; 11-11 Sat; 12-10.30 Sun; closed 4-5.30 Sat(6 Sun) in winter ~ Bedrooms: £35(£40S)/£50(£55S)

CHIDDINGLY TQ5414 Map 3
Six Bells ★ £

Village signed off A22 Uckfield—Hailsham

You can be sure of a friendly welcome from the cheerful landlord in this old-fashioned pub, whether you are a regular or a visitor, and there's always a colourful mix of customers. Solid old wood furnishings include pews and antique seats, log fires, lots of fusty artefacts and interesting bric-a-brac, and plenty of local pictures and posters. A sensitive extension provides some much needed family space; dominoes and cribbage. It can get very busy, and the Sunday lunchtime jazz in particular attracts a lot of people. Another big draw is the remarkably low-priced bar food, straightforward but tasty, with dishes such as filled baguettes, soup (£1.50), steak and kidney pie (£2.70), ploughman's or baked potatoes (from £3.50), lasagne or stilton and walnut pie, chilli or chicken curry (£3.90), lemon peppered haddock (£4.95), hock of ham (£5.95), and puddings such as treacle tart or banoffi pie (£2.50). Well kept Courage Directors, Harveys Best, and Charles Wells Bombardier on handpump. Outside at the back, there are some tables beyond a big raised goldfish pond, and a boules pitch; the church opposite has an interesting Jefferay monument. Vintage and Kit car meetings outside the pub every month. This is a pleasant area for walks. *(Recommended by Mrs A Chesher, Charlie Harris, Mike Gorton, Ann and Colin Hunt)*

Free house ~ Licensee Paul Newman ~ Real ale ~ Bar food (11.30-2.30, 6-10) ~ (01825) 872227 ~ Children in family room ~ Live music Sat evening and Sun lunchtime ~ Open 11-3, 6-11; 12-10.30 Sun

CHIDHAM SU7804 Map 2
Old House At Home

Off A259 at Barleycorn pub

Handy for Chichester and with plenty of surrounding walks, this bustling country pub is a popular place for a meal. The homely bar has timbering and low beams, windsor chairs around the tables, long seats against the walls, and a welcoming log fire. Under the new licensee, good, popular bar food might include home-made soup (£3.55), deep-fried brie with honey and orange dressing (£4.50), devilled whitebait (£4.95), ploughman's (from £4.95), daily specials such as mixed vegetable crostini (£4.95), sausage and mash or roasted mediterranean vegetables (£5.95), gigotte of lamb (£7.95), chargrilled chicken in caesar salad or baked whole bass (£8.95), black bream with garlic and herbs (£9.95), puddings (£3.95), and Sunday roast (£6.95). The eating area is no smoking. Well kept Bass, Friary Meux, Fullers London Pride, Greene King Abbot, and Wadworths 6X on handpump, and wine by the small or large glass. *(Recommended by I D Greenfield, Mrs Angela Bromley-Martin, Ian Phillips, Paul Boot, D B Wood, R J Walden, John Davis, J Hale, Pat and Tony Martin, Lyn and Geoff Hallchurch, Richard Hoare, J A Snell, Ann and Colin Hunt, Tony and Wendy Hobden, Brian and Genie Smart, Pat and Tony Hinkins, B and F A Hannam)*

Free house ~ Licensee Bob Carruthers ~ Real ale ~ Bar food (12-2, 6-9) ~ (01243) 572477 ~ Children in eating area of bar until 8pm ~ Open 11.30-2.30(3 Sat), 6-11; 12-3.30, 7-10.30 Sun

COMPTON SU7714 Map 2
Coach & Horses ◀

B2146 S of Petersfield

Going back much further than its coaching days – to the 15th c, in fact – this is now a good mildly upmarket local, kept spick and span by its friendly Belgian landlady. With attractively wooded hilly countryside nearby, it caters well for walkers, with a log fire at each end of the roomy front public bar. The charming little plush beamed lounge bar serves partly as a relaxing ante-room to the attractive restaurant, but also has well presented consistently appetising bar food cooked by the landlord. This might include sandwiches or filled baguettes (from £2.50), home-made soup (£3.10), crab cannelloni (£5.50), ham and eggs (£5.95), chicken, mushroom and tarragon pie (£7.65), baked aubergine and chargrilled peppers topped with buffalo mozzarella or home-made salmon fishcakes with spicy tomato sauce (£7.75), bacon hock with mustard mash (£7.85), duck leg confit with caramelised onions (£8.45), steaks (from £10.95), grilled bass (£11.95), and puddings such as brioche bread and butter pudding with apricots and brandy, chocolate tart with Belgian chocolate or icky sticky toffee pudding (£3.95). Well kept Cottage Wessex Steam, fff Altons Pride, Fullers ESB, Palmers 200, and Ringwood Fortyniner on handpump, attentive staff; old-fashioned juke box, bar billiards, cribbage and dominoes. There are tables out by the square in front, and a small secluded back garden; it's a pleasant village, not far from Uppark (NT). *(Recommended by B M O'Connell, Karen and Graham Oddey)*

Free house ~ Licensees David and Christiane Butler ~ Real ale ~ Bar food ~ Restaurant ~ (023) 9263 1228 ~ Children welcome ~ Open 11.30-2.30(3 Sat), 6-11; 12-3, 7-10.30 Sun

COWBEECH TQ6114 Map 3
Merrie Harriers
Village signposted from A271

Friendly, welcoming new owners have taken over this pleasantly unassuming white-clapboarded village inn. The beamed and panelled bar has a traditional high-backed settle by the brick inglenook, as well as other tables and chairs, and unobtrusive piped music. Well liked bar food includes garlic mushrooms or whole stuffed red pepper (£3.95), lunchtime ploughman's (from £4.95) or home-cooked ham and eggs (£5.25), broccoli and cauliflower cheese (£6.95), home-made steak in ale pie (£7.95), tuna steak with lemon and fresh ginger or fresh chilli, lime and coriander chicken (£8.95), fillet steak (£12.95), and home-made puddings. Well kept Harveys Best and a guest such as Shepherd Neame Spitfire or Charles Wells Bombardier on handpump. The brick-walled and oak-ceilinged back restaurant is no smoking. There are rustic seats in the terraced garden. *(Recommended by Mrs K Batchelor, Ron Harris, R J Walden, Mr and Mrs Thomas, Nigel and Olga Wikeley, J H Bell, Colin and Janet Roe)*

Free house ~ Licensees Lucy and Jeff Kirkham ~ Real ale ~ Bar food ~ Restaurant ~ (01323) 833108 ~ Children in restaurant ~ Open 11.30-2.30, 6-11; 12-3, 7-10.30 Sun; closed 25 Dec

CUCKFIELD TQ3025 Map 3
White Harte ● £
South Street; off A272 W of Haywards Heath

Unless you arrive at this pretty, partly medieval tile-hung pub by about 12.15 on a weekday, all the tables will have been taken up with those keen to enjoy the good value lunchtime food. They tell us prices have not changed since last year, which makes the straightforward meals even more of a bargain: sausage and chips (£3.80), ploughman's (from £3.90), and five or so home-cooked specials such as casseroles, pies like chicken and mushroom, fish, or steak and kidney, turkey breast in mushroom sauce, smoked haddock bake, or stilton and celery quiche (all £4.50); roasts (£4.90). The comfortable beamed lounge has a mix of polished floorboards, parquet and ancient brick flooring tiles, standing timbers, a few local photographs, padded seats on a slightly raised area, and some fairly modern light oak tables and copper-topped tables. Furnishings in the public bar are sturdy and comfortable with a roaring log fire in the inglenook, maybe the friendly cat, and sensibly placed darts. Well kept Badger Best and K&B and a guest beer on handpump; piped music, fruit machine, and shove-ha'penny. *(Recommended by DWAJ, Ian Phillips, John Shepherd)*

Badger ~ Tenant Ted Murphy ~ Real ale ~ Bar food (lunchtime; not Sun) ~ No credit cards ~ (01444) 413454 ~ Children in eating area of bar lunchtime only ~ Open 11-3, 6-11; 12-3, 7-10.30 Sun

DANEHILL TQ4128 Map 3
Coach & Horses
From A275 in Danehill (S of Forest Row), take School Lane towards Chelwood Common

Set in attractive countryside, this cottagey pub has a relaxed, friendly atmosphere, and a mix of chatty customers. There's a little public bar to the right with half-panelled walls, simple furniture on highly polished wooden floorboards, a small woodburning stove in the brick fireplace, and a big hatch to the bar; darts. The main bar is on the left with plenty of locals crowding around the wooden bar counter or sitting at the high wooden bar stools enjoying the well kept Harveys Best, and a couple of a guests such as Adnams Best or Badger Best on handpump. Drinks are stacked in a nice old-fashioned way on shelves behind the bar, and there's just one table on the stripped wood floor here. A couple of steps lead down to a half-panelled area with a mix of wheelbacks and old dining chairs around several characterful wooden tables on the fine brick floor, a large lantern in the tiny brick fireplace, and some large Victorian prints; candles and flowers on the tables. Down another step to the dining area with stone walls, a beamed vaulted ceiling, baskets and hops hanging from other beams, and a woodburning stove; through a lovely arched doorway is a small room with just a couple of tables; piped jazz. Served by friendly staff, the enjoyable bar food includes snacks such as sandwiches (from £3.75; steak with tomato and lettuce £4.95), filled baked potatoes (from £4.50), and grilled focaccia with onion, anchovy, olive and emmenthal cheese or grilled ciabattas with pesto, mozzarella and tomato (£4.95), plus home-made soup (£3.95), seared squid with pancetta (£4.95), citrus-marinated black tiger prawns (£5.95), lamb and mint sausages with colcannon mash and mustard sauce or a proper fish pie (£7.95), leek and gruyère tart (£8.50), rack of lamb with tomato and coriander tabouleh (£9.95), daily specials such as thai green vegetable curry with coconut relish (£8.50) or chicken breast filled with mascarpone and thyme cream (£9.95), and puddings such as summer fruit and white chocolate strudel, chocolate and orange tart or apple and calvados pancakes (£3.95); a good wine list. There's a big attractive garden with plenty of seats, and fine views of the South Downs. More reports please. *(Recommended by Nigel Ward, Michael and Ann Cole, G J C Moss)*

Free house ~ Licensee Ian Philpots ~ Real ale ~ Bar food (till 9.30 Fri and Sat; not Sun evening exc bank hol wknds) ~ Restaurant ~ (01825) 740369 ~ Well behaved children welcome ~ Open 11.30-3, 6-11; 12-4, 7-10.30 Sun; closed evenings 25 and 26 Dec and 1 Jan

EAST CHILTINGTON TQ3715 Map 3
Jolly Sportsman ⑪ ♀

2 miles N of B2116; Chapel Lane – follow sign to 13th-c church

For a really special meal out, this tucked away civilised Victorian dining pub is just the place to head for. Changing all the time, the imaginative food might include mediterranean tomato soup (£3.90), cornish crab, shrimp and herb polenta (£4.95), seared scallop, smoked salmon, cucumber and crème fraîche (£5.25), poached skate wing, salmon caviar and chives (£10.25), baked whole bass, seaweed and butter sauce (£12.95), gressingham duck with plum and ginger compote (£13.45), roast guinea fowl with Saint George mushrooms (£13.25), and puddings such as raspberry champagne jelly with panna cotta, apricot, walnut, ginger and toffee pudding or blueberry and almond tart with vanilla sauce (£4.85); two-course, daily changing lunch (£10). A couple of chairs by the fireplace are set aside for drinkers in the chatty little bar with stripped wood floors and a mix of furniture, but most people head for the smart but informal no smoking restaurant with contemporary light wood furniture, and modern landscapes on pale yellow painted brick walls. Well kept Jennings Bitter and a guest beer on handpump, a remarkably good wine list, farm cider, up to 30 malts, summer fruit cocktails and good sherries; Scrabble. There are rustic tables and benches under gnarled trees in a pretty cottagey front garden, and the large back lawn with a children's play area looks out towards the South Downs; good walks nearby. *(Recommended by Mrs Rita Cox, Michael Sargent, John Beeken, Ken Arthur)*

Free house ~ Licensee Bruce Wass ~ Real ale ~ Bar food (till 10pm Fri/Sat; till 3pm Sun) ~ Restaurant ~ (01273) 890400 ~ Children welcome ~ Open 12-3, 6-11; 12-4 Sun; closed Sun evening, all day Mon (exc bank holidays)

EAST DEAN TV5597 Map 3
Tiger ♀

Pub (with village centre) signposted – not vividly – from A259 Eastbourne—Seaford

To be sure of a seat – inside or out – you must get to this justifiably popular, old-fashioned local early. It's an idyllic spot by a secluded sloping village green lined with similar low cottages, and the outside is brightened up with flowering climbers and window boxes in summer. Inside, the smallish rooms (candlelit at night) have low beams hung with pewter and china, polished rustic tables and distinctive antique settles, and old prints and so forth. Well kept Harveys Best with guests such as Adnams Best, Flowers Original or Gales HSB on handpump, and a fair choice of wines with several interesting vintage bin-ends and 10 by the glass. Good bar food from a sensibly short list might include delicious french fish soup (£4.25), 20 different enjoyable ploughman's (£4.95; they keep 14 different cheeses), home-made oven-baked bruschetta (£5.95), lasagne (£6.25), mediterranean vegetable filo parcel with chive and lemon crème fraîche (£6.50), fresh dressed local crab salad, thai-style crab cakes with chilli dipping sauce or rich beef burgundy casserole (£6.95), ragoût of venison or half roast pheasant on dauphinois potatoes (£8.95), and whole fresh local lobster (£10.95); their meat comes from the very good local butcher who wins awards for his sausages. At lunchtimes on hot days and bank holidays they usually have only cold food. Being on the South Downs Way, it's naturally popular with walkers and the lane leads on down to a fine stretch of coast culminating in Beachy Head. No children inside. (Recommended by Mark Percy, Lesley Mayoh, Ann and Colin Hunt, Martin and Karen Wake, Michael and Ann Cole, Catherine and Richard Preston, Bill and Rachael Gallagher, DF, NF, G T Brewster, Mike Gorton, Ian Phillips, John Davis, Mrs M Thomas)

Free house ~ Licensee Nicholas Denyer ~ Real ale ~ Bar food ~ No credit cards ~ (01323) 423209 ~ Morris dancers on bank holidays, mummers 26 Dec ~ Open 11-3, 6-11; 11-11 Sat; 12-10.30 Sun

ELSTED SU8119 Map 2
Three Horseshoes ◖

Village signposted from B2141 Chichester—Petersfield; also reached easily from A272 about 2 miles W of Midhurst, turning left heading W

In summer, the lovely garden of this popular 16th-c pub is very special: free-roaming bantams, plenty of tables, pretty flowers, and marvellous views over the South Downs. Inside, the snug little rooms in winter provide a cosy refuge from the cold night air, when candlelight and enormous log fires illuminate the ancient beams and flooring, antique furnishings and attractive prints and photographs. Enjoyable bar food includes home-made soup (£3.95), a generous ploughman's with a good choice of cheeses (£5.95), prawn mayonnaise wrapped in smoked salmon (£6.95), wild mushroom risotto (£7.95), chicken and sage pie or braised lamb with apples and apricots in a tomato chutney sauce (£8.95), steak and kidney in ale pie (£9.50), fresh seasonal crab and lobster, and home-made puddings such as raspberry and hazelnut meringue and chocolate truffle torte (£3.95). Well kept changing ales racked on a stillage behind the bar counter might include Ballards Best, Cheriton Pots, Timothy Taylors Landlord and a couple of guests such as Hop Back Summer Lightning and Ringwood Fortyniner; summer cider; friendly service; dominoes. (Recommended by Martin and Karen Wake, Ann and Colin Hunt, John Beeken, Tracey and Stephen Groves, Bruce Bird, John Davis, Peter Meister, Paul and Penny Dawson, Paul Boot)

Free house ~ Licensees Andrew and Sue Beavis ~ Real ale ~ Bar food (not winter Sun evenings) ~ (01730) 825746 ~ Well behaved children in eating area of bar and restaurant ~ Open 11-2.30, 6-11; 12-3, 7-10.30 Sun; closed Sun evening in winter

FAIRWARP TQ4626 Map 3
Foresters Arms

Set back from B2026, N of northern Maresfield roundabout exit from A22

This cheerful local is handy for the Vanguard Way and Weald Way at the south end of Ashdown Forest. Inside, there's a woodburning stove in a big stripped stone fireplace, a comfortable lounge bar, well kept Badger Best, Golden Champion, Tanglefoot and K&B on handpump, and farm cider. Bar food includes filled baguettes, home-made soup (£3.50), garlic mushrooms or pâté (£4.25), whitebait (£4.50), roasted peppers or lasagne (£6.95), lambs liver and mash (£7.95), breast of chicken with mango (£8.95), 10oz sirloin steak (£11.25); good popular Sunday lunch, and efficient service. Cribbage, dominoes, and piped music. There are tables and benches among interesting plants outside in the garden, pretty award-winning hanging baskets, and a patio seating area. *(Recommended by Joan and Andrew Life, David Peakall, R J Walden, Peter Meister, Colin and Janet Roe, J H Bell, G T Brewster)*

Badger ~ Tenant Colin Boyd ~ Real ale ~ Bar food (12-2, 6-9) ~ Restaurant ~ (01825) 712808 ~ Children in eating area of bar and restaurant ~ Open 11-11; 12-10.30 Sun; 12-3, 6-11 in winter

FIRLE TQ4607 Map 3

Ram

Village signposted off A27 Lewes—Polegate

Families are particularly welcome in this no-frills, properly traditional 17th-c village pub, and there is now a microwave for heating baby food (which is on sale here), a children's menu, nappy-changing facilities, toys and games, and they were installing play equipment in the garden as we went to press. Walkers are also welcome as this is by a fine stretch of the South Downs, and muddy boots are happily tolerated. The atmosphere throughout the well worn bars is genuinely friendly and relaxed, with winter log fires, comfortable seating and soft lighting; the snug is no smoking, and there's quite a mix of customers. Well kept Harveys Best, Old Scrapie (brewed for the pub by Ringwood), a guest such as Cains IPA on handpump, and farm cider; darts, shove-ha'penny, cribbage and toad in the hole. The gents' has a chalk board for graffiti, and there are tables in a spacious walled garden behind. They have an elderly ginger cat called Orange, and a comical goose. Bar food includes soup (£3.50), filled baguettes (£5), filled baked potatoes (£5.50), ploughman's (£6.50), ricotta and spinach cannelloni (£7), battered cod (£7.50), chilli (£8), half a roast chicken (£9.50), daily specials, and puddings (£3); three sizes of children's meals (from £3), and cream teas. Be warned, it can get very busy – especially at weekend lunchtimes. Nearby Firle Place is worth visiting for its collections and furnishings, and Glyndebourne is not far away. *(Recommended by John Beeken, Kevin Thorpe, the Didler, BKA, Susan May, Ann and Colin Hunt, Dr David Cockburn, D S Cottrell)*

Free house ~ Licensees Michael Wooller, Keith Wooller, Nikki Bullen ~ Real ale ~ Bar food (12-9) ~ (01273) 858222 ~ Children welcome in snug and family room ~ Folk 2nd Mon and 1st Weds of month ~ Open 11.30-11; 12-10.30 Sun; closed evening 25 Dec ~ Bedrooms: £50B/£80B

FLETCHING TQ4223 Map 3

Griffin ★ ⑪ ♀ ⇦

Village signposted off A272 W of Uckfield

In a pretty spot on the edge of Sheffield Park, this civilised old inn has tables in the lovely back garden with fine rolling Sussex views, and more seats on a sheltered gravel terrace where they may have spit roasts; plenty of space for children. Inside, the beamed and quaintly panelled bar rooms have a good bustling atmosphere, blazing log fires, old photographs and hunting prints, straightforward furniture including some captain's chairs, china on a delft shelf, and a small bare-boarded serving area off to one side. A snug separate bar, now called the Club Room, has sofas, pool, a juke box, and TV. Popular, imaginative bar menu (using as much local organic produce as possible) includes pumpkin, honey and ginger soup (£4.50), local ewes cheese and parsley mousse terrine with sun-dried tomato dressing (£5.50), hot ciabatta sandwiches (thai marinated breast of chicken £5.50, tuna niçoise £5.95), spicy lamb meatballs with minted yoghurt on tagliatelle or leek, gruyère and goats cheese tart (£6.95), steak and kidney pudding with parsley mash or slow-cooked lamb shanks (£8.50), fried marinated salmon on noodles with bok choi (£9.50), pot-roasted local pheasant with bacon and puy lentils (£9.95), confit of duck with honey and cloves on a potato and celeriac rösti (£10.50), and puddings such as rhubarb and ginger crumble, chocolate and cognac flan, and seasonal fruit brûlée (£4.95). There's a more elaborate (and expensive) restaurant menu. At busy times you can expect a long wait for food. Well kept Badger Tanglefoot and K&B, Hardy Country,

Harveys Best, and Rother Valley Level Best on handpump, and a fine wine list with several (including champagne) by the glass. Some of the bedrooms in the converted coach house have four-poster beds and a fireplace. *(Recommended by Brian and Janet Ainscough, Colin and Janet Roe, Susan and John Douglas, Jenny and Brian Seller, BKA, C L Kauffmann, Comus and Sarah Elliott, Keith and Janet Eaton, Christopher Wright, John Davis, Martin and Karen Wake, Mike and Mary Carter, John and Lynn Busenbark, Mr and Mrs S Oxenbury, Derek Thomas, J Hale, Derek Harvey-Piper, John Robertson, J H Bell, Louise English, Chris Richards, Richard Siebert; also in* The Good Hotel Guide*)*

Free house ~ Licensees N Pullan, J Pullan and John Gatti ~ Real ale ~ Bar food ~ Restaurant ~ (01825) 722890 ~ Children in eating area of bar and restaurant ~ Live music Fri evening and Sun lunchtime ~ Open 12-3, 6-11; 12-11 Sat; 12-3, 7-10.30 Sun; 12-3, 6-11 Sat in winter; closed 25 Dec ~ Bedrooms: /£75S(£85B)

FULKING TQ2411 Map 3
Shepherd & Dog

From A281 Brighton—Henfield on N slope of downs turn off at Poynings signpost and continue past Poynings

Very popular with walkers – a path leads straight up to the South Downs Way – this charmingly atmospheric little pub used to sell illicit liquor to thirsty shepherds on their way to Findon sheep fair. The partly panelled cosy bar still has shepherds' crooks and harness on the walls, as well as antique or stoutly rustic furnishings around the log fire, and fresh flowers on the tables. A changing range of well prepared bar food might include sandwiches (from £2.95), home-made soup (£3.25), filled baked potatoes (from £4.95), a plate of locally smoked salmon (£5.95), a wide choice of ploughman's, with a good selection of carefully picked cheeses (£5.95), a vegetarian dish like aubergine bake (£6.50), big summer salads (around £8.25), steak and kidney pie (£6.95), salmon fillet (£9.75), sirloin steak (£12.95), daily specials such as mini tartlets filled with spinach, sun-dried tomato and goats cheese (£4.75), green lipped mussels (£5.25), home-made shepherd's pie (£7.25) or rack of barbecue spare ribs (£7.95), and home-made puddings like banoffi pie (£3.50). Try and get there early, especially if you want a prime spot by the bow windows, as all year round the pub can get crowded; service can slow down at the busiest times (summer weekends, maybe). Well kept Badger Best, Tanglefoot and seasonal changing Golden Ferret on handpump; dominoes, and toad in the hole. There are good views across to the sweeping downs from the series of pretty planted grassy terraces, some fairy-lit, as well as a little stream running down through the garden. *(Recommended by Marion Turner, LM, John Davis, Lady Muir, Kevin Blake, David Holloway, Ann and Colin Hunt)*

Badger ~ Manager G M Chapman ~ Real ale ~ Bar food (12-3, 6-9.30; 12-9.30 Sat; 12-9 Sun) ~ (01273) 857382 ~ Children welcome ~ Open 11-11; 12-10.30 Sun

HAMMERPOT TQ0605 Map 3
Woodmans Arms

Pub visible and well signposted on N (eastbound) side of A27 just under 4 miles E of A284 at Arundel; heading W on A27 the turn is about ½ mile beyond the pub

Don't be put off by the busy A27 – once you're inside this delightful 16th-c pub, the traffic noise fades into oblivion. The friendly landlord offers an excellent welcome and works hard to make the best of his pub; they have won the Arun in Bloom competition, Loo of the Year, and recently came second for Gales's Best Kept Cellar. The brick-floored entrance area has a cosy armchair by the inglenook's big log fire, lots of brass, pictures by local artists for sale, and old photographs of regulars. On the right a carpeted dining area with candles on the tables has wheelback chairs around its tables, and cheerfully cottagey decorations; on the left a small no smoking room has a few more tables. Some of the beams are so low they are strung with fairy lights as a warning. Well presented honest home-made food includes soups such as vegetable or mushroom (£2.95), sandwiches (from £2.95), broccoli and stilton bake or lasagne (£6.25), very good sweet and sour pork (£6.75), nice steak and kidney pie or ham and eggs (£6.95), home-made curry (£7.35), fresh local fish on Fridays, extra mature sirloin steak with port and stilton sauce (£10.50), and two Sunday roasts (£6.95). Well kept Gales GB, HSB, Butser Bitter and a guest such as Fullers London Pride or Timothy Taylors Landlord on handpump, and country wines. Cribbage and piped music. The yellow labrador is called Tikka. The garden here – despite some road noise – is charming, with picnic-sets and tables on a terrace (they have mobile outside heaters for chillier weather), under a fairy-lit arbour and on small lawns among lots of roses and tubs of bright annuals. This is good walking country, and the enthusiastic landlord has been known to hand out free maps of a good circular walk from the pub – best to phone ahead if you are a sizeable party. *(Recommended by Bruce Bird, Lawrence Pearse, R and S Bentley, Ann and Colin Hunt, Joan and Michel Hooper-Immins, Dennis Jenkin, Alan Cowell, J Davidson)*

Gales ~ Tenants Malcolm and Ann Green ~ Real ale ~ Bar food (not Sun evening) ~ Restaurant ~ (01903) 871240 ~ Well behaved children in restaurant ~ Folk every 2nd Sun evening ~ Open 11-3, 6-11; 12-3.15, 7-10.30 Sun

HARTFIELD TQ4735 Map 3
Anchor 🍺

Church Street

The original bar in this 15th-c pub has heavy beams, old advertisements and little country pictures on the walls above the brown-painted dado, houseplants in the brown-curtained small-paned windows, and a woodburning stove. Another bar has flagstones, more old beams, a dining area with good tables and chairs, and huge logs burning in an old inglenook fireplace. Well kept Bass, Flowers IPA and Original, Fullers London Pride, and Harveys Best on handpump. Bar food includes sandwiches or toasties (from £2.25; avocado and prawn £3.75), home-made soup (£3), filled baked potatoes (from £4.25), ploughman's (from £4.50), vegetable and noodle stir fry (£4.75), home-made pork and walnut pâté with cumberland sauce, local sausages or omelette Arnold Bennett (£5), home-cooked ham and egg (£5.25), smoked haddock fritters (£6.75), tuna fishcakes with cheese sauce or beef and vegetable stir fry (£7), tandoori chicken kebab (£7.75), sirloin steak (£11), and puddings like crème caramel or chocolate and rum mousse (from £3); quick friendly service. Darts in a separate lower room; shove-ha'penny, cribbage, dominoes, and piped music. The front verandah soon gets busy on a warm summer evening. There's a play area in the popular garden. *(Recommended by Kevin Thomas, Nina Randall, Alan Cowell, Michael and Ann Cole, K H Frostick, LM)*

Free house ~ Licensee Ken Thompson ~ Real ale ~ Bar food (12-2, 6-10) ~ Restaurant ~ (01892) 770424 ~ Children welcome ~ Open 11-11; 12-10.30 Sun; closed evening 25 Dec ~ Bedrooms: /£50S

HEATHFIELD TQ5920 Map 3
Star

Old Heathfield – head East out of Heathfield itself on A265, then fork right on to B2096; turn right at signpost to Heathfield Church then keep bearing right; pub on left immediately after church

This friendly old place has been an inn ever since it was built in 1328 as a resting place for pilgrims on their way along this high ridge across the Weald to Canterbury. There's a good welcome for both locals and regulars and a relaxed, chatty atmosphere in the L-shaped beamed bar, reached up some well worn brick steps, with a log fire in the inglenook fireplace, panelling, built-in wall settles and window seats, and just four or five tables; a doorway leads into a similarly furnished smaller room; the tables are candlelit at night. Chalked up on boards, a decent choice of bar food includes ploughman's (£5.50), home-made pies or cold meats with bubble and squeak (£7.25), mussels in saffron (£7.50), local cod in beer batter or fresh crab (£8.95), pan-fried smoked salmon (£9.95), marinated duck breast (£10.50), and winter game dishes; efficient, courteous service. Well kept Harveys Best, Shepherd Neame Best Bitter, and a guest such as Jennings Snecklifter on handpump, some malt whiskies and farm cider; bar billiards and shove-ha'penny. The prettily planted sloping garden with its rustic furniture has lovely views of rolling oak-lined sheep pastures – Turner thought it fine enough to paint. Dogs on leads are welcome. *(Recommended by Joan and Andrew Life, Lucien, Jenny and Brian Seller, Mrs J Ekins-Daukes, Alan Cowell)*

Free house ~ Licensees Mike Chappell and Fiona Airey ~ Real ale ~ Bar food (12-2.15(2.30 wknds), 7-9.30) ~ Restaurant ~ (01435) 863570 ~ Well behaved children welcome ~ Open 11.30-3, 5.30-11; 12-3, 7-10.30 Sun

HENLEY SU8925 Map 2
Duke of Cumberland Arms
Village signposted just off A286 S of Fernhurst; N of Midhurst; if coming from Midhurst, take 1st turn into village, then keep bearing right; OS Sheet 186 map reference 894258

This pretty little tucked-away stone-built cottage, covered with wisteria, has one of the most unusual pub gardens in the region. On a slope, it's lush and quite big, with lilacs and other shrubs, and willows by a stream running down through a series of three ponds once used for the pre-industrial iron industry here, but now stocked with trout (which you'll find on the menu). Gnarled old benches and more modern seats out here give lovely views over Black Down and the wooded hills south of Haslemere. Inside are just two unpretentious little low-ceilinged rooms, with a log fire in each, gas lamps on white-painted panelled walls, simple seats around scrubbed rough oak tables, and a few wood carvings, plates, old framed documents, and stuffed birds and animals. Friendly new licensees are doing enjoyable food such as home-made soup (£3.50), filled rolls (using bread made especially for them, from £3.50), well liked chicken liver pâté (using a 70-year-old recipe, £4), several ploughman's (from £4.50), fresh oysters (£6), popular seafood cocktail (smoked salmon wrapped around smoked trout, prawns and crab, £6.50), daily changing pasta dishes (from £7), late breakfast (£7.50), sun-dried tomato and mushroom risotto or chicken sautéed with black pudding, button mushrooms, and shallots with a red wine jus (£8.95), fresh fish dishes (they use a fisherman who phones every day to tell them what he has caught that day; from around £10.50), a whole roast joint (you order it in advance and it comes served on a big board with roast potatoes and vegetables all around it, from £12.50), and puddings like fruit crumble, lemon tart or cheesecakes (from £4). Well kept Adnams Broadside, Ballards Best, Gales Bitter and HSB and Hop Back Summer or Winter Lightning tapped from the cask, and farm ciders; no piped music or games. The young white boxer is called Arnie. *(Recommended by Miles Halton, Ian Phillips)*

Free house ~ Licensee Gaston Duval ~ Real ale ~ Bar food ~ Restaurant ~ (01428) 652280 ~ Children welcome lunchtime; over 5 in evening ~ Open 11-3, 6-11; 12-3, 7-10.30 Sun; closed 25 Dec

HORSHAM TQ1730 Map 3
Black Jug
31 North St

Even when this lively town pub is really busy, the friendly staff remain obliging and quick, serving the good food promptly while still managing a warm welcome for customers. The airy open-plan turn-of-the-century-style room has a large chatty central bar, a nice collection of heavy sizeable dark wood tables, comfortable chairs on a stripped wood floor, cream walls crammed with interesting old prints and photographs above a dark wood panelled dado, and a warm terracotta ceiling. A spacious no smoking conservatory has similar furniture and lots of hanging baskets; piped music. Well kept Courage Directors, Harveys Best, Greene King Old Speckled Hen, Marstons Pedigree, and Wadworths 6X on handpump, 30 malt whiskies, a good wine list with 14 by the glass, and eight chilled vodkas from Poland and Russia. Densely written on a blackboard, the interesting bar food includes soup (£3.25), filled baguettes or open sandwiches (from £3.50), chicken liver and green peppercorn pâté with orange marmalade (£4.50), ploughman's or grilled field mushrooms filled with stilton and chives (£4.75), deep-fried risotto cakes with mozzarella, sun-dried tomatoes and red onion with a spring onion and tomato garnish (£5.95), baked smoked haddock on spinach topped with creamy cheese sauce (£6.75), steakburger topped with bacon and cheese (£7.95), chicken supreme on roasted vegetables with a pesto drizzle (£9.95), wild boar steak with an apple and potato cake with a rich cognac sauce (£11.95). There are quite a few tables sheltered under a pagoda outside on a back flower-filled terrace, and they have outdoor heaters. More reports please. *(Recommended by Mrs Romey Heaton)*

Brunning & Price ~ Lease Sam Cornwall-Jones ~ Real ale ~ Bar food (12-10) ~ Restaurant ~ (01403) 253526 ~ Children in eating areas until 6pm ~ Open 11-11; 12-10.30 Sun; closed 26 Dec

HOUGHTON TQ0111 Map 3
George & Dragon
B2139 W of Storrington

The views are a big draw to this fine, mostly Elizabethan timbered building, with tables in the garden looking down past a hardy walnut tree and a wishing well towards the Arun valley; there are plenty of good surrounding walks, and to reach the South Downs Way, turn left off the side road to Bury. Inside, there's a pleasant atmosphere in the rambling heavy-beamed bar, which though comfortably modernised, still has points of interest such as a formidable fireplace, clockwork roasting-spit motor, and gourds given a glowing patina by rubbing with goosefat. Attractive antique tables lead into a back extension; the restaurant is no smoking. A wide choice of good reasonably priced food ranges from soup (£2.50), sandwiches (from £3.75) and ploughman's (£4.95), to liver and onions or sausages and mash (£6.45), steak, kidney, and Guinness pie (£6.95), grilled local trout, whole bacon hock or 8oz rump steak (£7.45), rack of lamb (£11.95), and puddings such as fruit crumble and crème brûlée (£3); they offer a weekday, over-50s bargain two-course set lunch (£6.45). Well kept Courage Best and Directors, and maybe Fullers London Pride on handpump, half a dozen malts, several wines by the glass, and service which is normally good and prompt (there may be the odd hitch on a really busy Saturday); piped music. Charles II stayed here after fleeing from the Battle of Worcester, in 1651. *(Recommended by Tony and Wendy Hobden, J H Bell, A D Marsh, Prof S Barnett, Miss J F Reay)*

SFI ~ Managers Paul and Julie Brooker ~ Real ale ~ Bar food (12-2.30, 6-9.30; all day Sat and Sun) ~ Restaurant ~ (01798) 831559 ~ Children welcome ~ Open 11-3, 6-11; 11-11 Sat; 12-10.30 Sun

ICKLESHAM TQ8716 Map 3
Queens Head ♀ ◀
Just off A259 Rye—Hastings

There's a fine choice of drinks at this well run handsome pub, with 16 wines by the glass (many in small or large sizes), well kept Daleside Shrimpers, Greene King IPA and Abbot, and guests such as Fullers ESB, Hampshire Pride of Romsey, and Harveys Old on handpump, and Biddenden cider. The open-plan areas work round a very big serving counter which stands under a vaulted beamed roof, the high beamed walls and ceiling of the easy-going bar are lined with shelves of bottles and covered with farming implements and animal traps, and there are well used pub tables and old pews on the brown patterned carpet. Other areas (two are no smoking) are popular with diners and have big inglenook fireplaces. Generously served, enjoyable bar food includes sandwiches (from £2.45), home-made soup such as lentil and bacon or sweet potato and watercress (£3.25), home-made pâté (£3.95), soft herring roes on toast (£4.25), ploughman's (£4.50), home-cooked ham and egg (£5.50), broccoli and cauliflower cheese (£5.95), curry of the day or steak and mushroom in ale pie (£6.95), steaks (from £9.95), and home-made daily specials such as wild mushroom risotto (£5.75), chicken breast in stilton and apricot sauce (£6.95), lots of fresh fish (£7-£10), scallops in wine, cream and bacon sauce (£9.95), and puddings such as fruit crumble or banoffi pie (from £2.75); prompt service from friendly efficient staff. Shove-ha'penny, dominoes, fruit machine, and piped music. Picnic-sets look out over the vast, gently sloping plain of the Brede valley from the little garden, and there's an outside children's play area, and boules. Good local walks. *(Recommended by John Davis, Ron Harris, J H Bell, Alan Thomas, Simon and Sally Small, John and Christine Lowe, Keith and Chris O'Neill, Susan and John Douglas, Lucien, David Carr, Ken Arthur, Martin and Karen Wake, Mark Lewis, R J Walden, Richard Fendick)*

Free house ~ Licensee Ian Mitchell ~ Real ale ~ Bar food (12-2.45, 6.15-9.45; all day Fri-Sun; not 25/26 Dec) ~ (01424) 814552 ~ Well behaved children in eating area of bar until 8.30pm ~ Live jazz/blues/folk/classical Tues evenings ~ Open 11-11; 12-10.30 Sun; closed evening 25 Dec

KINGSTON NEAR LEWES TQ3908 Map 3
Juggs ◨

The Street; Kingston signed off A27 by roundabout W of Lewes, and off Lewes—Newhaven road; look out for the pub's sign – may be hidden by hawthorn in summer

Quaint inside and out, this tile-hung rose-covered cottage can be reached on a walk over the downs from Lewes. There are a good many close-set rustic teak tables on the sunny brick terrace, a neatly hedged inner yard has more seating under cocktail parasols, and a timber climber and commando net. Inside, furniture ranges from an attractive little carved box settle, Jacobean-style dining chairs and brocaded seats in the rambling beamed bar to other settles and more neatly orthodox tables and chairs in a small no smoking dining area, under the low-pitched eaves on the right. The cream or stripped brick walls are hung with flower pictures, battle prints, a patriotic assembly of postcards of the Lloyd George era, posters, and some harness and brass. Bar food (with prices unchanged since last year) includes ploughman's (£4.25), open sandwiches (from £4.95), haddock and chips (£5.95), home-made steak and kidney pudding (£8.95), steaks (from £9.95) and daily specials (around £6.95). On Sunday lunchtime food is limited to a cold buffet. One of the family rooms is no smoking. Service remains speedy and efficient (aided by a rather effective electronic bleeper system to let you know when meals are ready), even when very busy; the bar can get smoky at times. Well kept Harveys Best, and a couple of guests such as Adnams and Fullers London Pride on handpump. Log fires, dominoes and shove-ha'penny. *(Recommended by Tony Scott, John Davis, Mr and Mrs Thomas, Mike and Lynn Robinson)*

Free house ~ Licensees Andrew and Peta Browne ~ Real ale ~ Bar food (12-2, 6-9) ~ Restaurant ~ (01273) 472523 ~ Children in separate family room ~ Open 11-11; 12-10.30 Sun; 11-3, 6-11 in winter

LEWES TQ4110 Map 3
Snowdrop ◨

South Street; off Cliffe High Street, opposite S end of Malling Street just S of A26 roundabout

Particularly at lunchtime, there's a good mix of customers of all ages and types in this bustling but laid-back pub. It takes on an unusual maritime theme including figureheads, ship lamps and assorted bric-a-brac, and upstairs there's more seating, a second pool table and bar billiards, a sunset sea mural, and a star chart painted on the blue ceiling; in the evenings, there's more of a cosmopolitan crowd and different styles of music, both live and on the juke box. Mainly vegetarian and using organic produce where possible, the good, interesting food might include sandwiches (from £1.70; filled baguettes from £2; filled pittas from £2.20), various soups (£2.50), lots of pizzas (from £4.75), tacos with refried beans, salsa, salad and sour cream, goats cheese, spinach, onion and tomato tart (all £5.50), four different curries (£6), and puddings such as chocolate sponge pudding, baked mango and strawberry cheesecake, and vegan chocolate cake (£2.50). Four well kept real ales such as Harveys Best, Hop Back Summer Lightning, Ringwood Old Thumper, and seasonal Harveys guest beer on handpump, good coffee and friendly staff. There are seats in two spacious outside areas beneath the cliffs. *(Recommended by John Beeken, Ann and Colin Hunt, Keith and Janet Morris, Kevin Thorpe, Catherine and Richard Preston)*

Free house ~ Licensee Reuben May ~ Real ale ~ Bar food (12-3, 6(7 Sun)-9) ~ No credit cards ~ (01273) 471018 ~ Children in eating area of bar ~ Live jazz Mon evening, local bands Sat evening ~ Open 11-11; 12-10.30 Sun

LODSWORTH SU9223 Map 2
Halfway Bridge Inn ★ ♀ ◖

Just before village, on A272 Midhurst—Petworth

The barn next to this warmly friendly and smartly civilised pub has now been converted into attractive bedrooms, all with exposed beams and original woodwork; one has disabled access. The three or four rooms are comfortably furnished with good oak chairs and an individual mix of tables, and they use attractive fabrics for the wood-railed curtains and pew cushions. Down some steps, the charming no smoking country dining room has a dresser and longcase clock; one of the log fires is contained in a well polished kitchen range, and paintings by a local artist line the walls. A good range of drinks includes well kept beers such as Cheriton Pots Ale, Fullers London Pride, Gales HSB, and guests such as Becketts Old Town Bitter, Harveys Old, and Charles Wells Bombardier on handpump, rather special local cider, and a thoughtful little wine list with a changing choice by the glass; dominoes, cribbage, shove-ha'penny, backgammon, Jenga, bagatelle, and mah jong. Changing regularly, the interesting food includes lunchtime open sandwiches (from £4.50; roast pork with redcurrant jelly and melted stilton £4.95), tagliatelle of leeks with a sweet pepper and cream sauce (£4.75), fish soup with gruyère, rouille and croutons (£4.95), risotto fishcakes with parsley sauce (£5.25), cumberland sausage with grain mustard mash and onion gravy (£5.95), wild mushroom coulibiac with soured cream (£8.50), steak, kidney, mushroom and Guinness pudding (£8.95), home-made confit of duck with root vegetable purée and garlic, thyme and honey sauce (£9.25), herb-crusted cod fillet with boulangère potatoes (£9.50), pheasant supreme stuffed with cranberries and chestnuts and wrapped in bacon (£9.95), 8oz fillet of English beef au poivre (£14.75), and puddings such as banana toffee pie, crumble of the day, and baked chocolate and orange cheesecake (£3.50); popular Sunday roasts. The friendly jack russell is called Ralph, and the two jack-russell crosses, Chip and Bonzo (they all wear obligatory 'please don't feed me' badges). At the back there are seats on a small terrace. *(Recommended by John Davis, Sue Demont, Tim Barrow, A Gardiner, B, M and P Kendall, John and Joan Calvert, Mrs J L Crutchfield, Tracey and Stephen Groves, Ann and Colin Hunt, Jackie Webb, Martin and Karen Wake, R E Davidson, R T and J C Moggridge, M J Bastin, Bob Gardiner, J H Bell, Michael Bayne, Julie and Bill Ryan)*

Free house ~ Licensees Simon and James Hawkins ~ Real ale ~ Bar food (12-2(2.30 wknds), 7-10) ~ Restaurant ~ (01798) 861281 ~ Children over 10 in restaurant ~ Occasional jazz Sun evening in summer ~ Open 11-3, 6-11; 12-3, 7-10.30 Sun ~ Bedrooms: £45B/£75B

LURGASHALL SU9327 Map 2
Noahs Ark

Village signposted from A283 N of Petworth; OS Sheet 186 map reference 936272

An inn since it was built in 1537, this was given its present name with reference to the narrow causeway over the formerly marshy ground at its front. The two neatly furnished bars have fresh flowers or warm log fires (one in a capacious inglenook) depending on the season, well kept Greene King IPA, Old Speckled Hen and Ruddles County on handpump, and several well polished trophies. The family room is decorated like the inside of an ark; darts, dominoes, cribbage and piped music. Well liked bar food includes soup (£3.25), sandwiches (from £3.95), filled baked potatoes (£4.50), melted goats cheese with artichokes and red peppers (£5), very popular hot wraps filled with crispy duck, cucumber and hoisin sauce or chilli beef strips with onions and sour cream (£5.95), ploughman's (from £4.50), aubergine and sweet potato fritters (£5), wild boar and apple sausages or home-made beef burgers (£6.50), ostrich with artichoke and juniper jus, fillet of sole with prawns on coconut and coriander sauce or steaks (£12.50), and puddings such as nutty chocolate torte or toffee banana crumble (£3.50). Splendid flowering baskets in summer. *(Recommended by Ann and Colin Hunt, John Evans, Derek Harvey-Piper, R Lake)*

Greene King ~ Tenant Bernard Joseph Wija ~ Real ale ~ Bar food (12-2.30, 7-9.30) ~ Restaurant ~ (01428) 707346 ~ Children in restaurant and family room ~ Open 11-3, 6-11; 12-3, 7-10.30 Sun

MILTON STREET TQ5304 Map 3
Sussex Ox

Off A27 just under a mile E of Alfriston roundabout

The friendly, hands-on new licensees have worked hard to restore and carefully extend this attractive country pub, with its magnificent downs views. There's a smallish beamed bar with a brick floor and roaring log fire in a woodburning stove, a good no smoking family room, and a separate restaurant. Well kept Harveys Best and Old, and two guests such as Ballards Best, Hop Back Summer and Winter Lightnings, or Youngs on handpump; organic apple juice, Biddenden cider, and English wines; piped music, darts, and dominoes. Well liked, unpretentious bar food includes filled rolls and baked potatoes, home-made soup (£3.25), ploughman's (from £4.75), roasted vegetable and ricotta cheese flan (£5.75), three different home-made burgers (from £6), sussex pie (£6.75), barbecue chicken (£6.95), steaks (£7.25), and puddings such as home-made meringues or banoffi pie (£3.50); children's menu (£3.50; they also do a picnic in a box for them); enthusiastic helpful staff. There's an elderly jack russell and collie, a big lawn and marvellous play area, and lots of good walks; the pub does get busy at weekends. *(Recommended by Michael and Ann Cole)*

Licensees Doug and Jeannie Baker ~ Real ale ~ Bar food (11-2, 6-9) ~ Restaurant ~ (01323) 870840 ~ Children in restaurant and family room ~ Open 11-3, 6-11; 12-3, 7-10.30 Sun

NUTHURST TQ1926 Map 3
Black Horse ◀

Village signposted from A281 at Monks Gate 2 miles SE of Horsham

Dating back to the 16th c, this country inn has seats on the front terrace with more in the woodland streamside garden behind; plenty of surrounding walks. The main bar has big Horsham flagstones, an inglenook fireplace, and well kept Harveys Best, Fullers London Pride and Weltons Pride 'n' Joy on handpump; quite a few historical photographs). The restaurant and snug are no smoking. Straightforward bar food includes filled baguettes (£5.25), ploughman's (£5.95), basket meals (£7.95), and daily specials; cribbage and piped music. More reports please. *(Recommended by R J Walden, Phil and Jane Hodson, John Davis, Mr and Mrs Thomas, Susan May, Jean-Bernard Brisset)*

Free house ~ Licensee Karen Jones ~ Real ale ~ Bar food (12-2.30, 6.30-9) ~ Restaurant ~ (01403) 891272 ~ Children in eating area of bar and restaurant ~ Monthly Sunday lunchtime jazz ~ Open 11-3(3.30 Sat), 6-11; 12-3.30, 7-11 Sun

OFFHAM TQ4012 Map 3
Blacksmiths Arms

A275 N of Lewes

Run by a friendly landlord, this neatly kept, old red brick cottage continues to serve consistently good, interesting food. At one end of the gleaming central counter in the open-plan bar is a huge inglenook fireplace with logs stacked at one side, and at the other is the airy dining area; most of the close-set tables are laid for eating. Nice old prints of London, some Spy prints and several old sporting prints decorate the walls above shiny black wainscoting. As well as bar snacks such as ploughman's (from £4.65), filled baked potatoes (£5.50), and ham and eggs (£5.95), there might be soup (£3.50), thai marinated prawns on red onion, mango and coriander salsa (£4.95), rabbit, pork and duck pâté with balsamic gooseberry jam (£5.25), chinese spiced crabmeat tartlet with ginger, lime and sesame dressed salad (£5.50), vegetable curry (£6.75), home-made lasagne (£7.50), steak and kidney pie (£7.95), fresh fish dishes like scallops, sardines, lemon sole, monkfish and so forth (from £8.95), escalope of pork with sweet and sour sauce, calves liver roasted with a sage and thyme crust with redcurrant lyonnaise sauce or wild bass steak roasted with peppers, red onions and coriander with a ginger and lime syrup (all £9.25), guinea fowl with apricot and plum pot roast (£9.50), and puddings such as home-made fruit pie, coconut and dark chocolate brûlée with home-made macaroons or caramelised apple tart (£3.75); careful efficient service. Well kept Harveys Best on handpump. French windows open onto a tiny little brick and paved terrace with a couple of flowering tubs and picnic-sets under umbrellas; beware of the dangerous bend when leaving the car park; spotless disabled lavatories. No children inside. *(Recommended by LM, Sarah Large, P Rome, Ken Arthur, G T Brewster, Peter Craske)*

Free house ~ Licensee Jean Large ~ Real ale ~ Bar food (not Sun evening) ~ Restaurant ~ (01273) 472971 ~ Open 11.30-3, 6.30-11; 12-3 Sun; closed Sun evening

OVING SU9005 Map 2
Gribble Inn ◗

Between A27 and A259 just E of Chichester, then should be signposted just off village road; OS Sheet 197 map reference 900050

There's a peaceful cottagey feel in the several linked rooms of this busy 16th-c thatched pub. Although owned by Badger, the eight real ales are brewed here and can often be found in other pubs owned by the brewery: Fursty Ferret, Gribble Ale, K&B Mild, Porterhouse, Pigs Ear, Plucking Pheasant, Reg's Tipple, and winter Wobbler on handpump; also 20 country wines, and farm cider. The chatty bar has lots of heavy beams and timbering, and old country-kitchen furnishings and pews. Half the dining room is no smoking, and all of the family room. Good bar food at lunchtime includes toasties (from £4.25), open sandwiches (from £3.50), platters (£4.95), home-cooked ham and eggs (£6.25), and home-made burger or mixed grill (£6.95); there's home-made soup (£2.50), also coconut brie with home-made cranberry and port sauce (£4.50), broccoli and cream cheese pasta or home-made bacon and onion suet roly poly (small helping £5.75, big helping £7.25), cod in beer batter (£7.25), home-made steak and kidney pudding or tuna steak with asparagus and cheese sauce (£7.95), and steaks (from £8.25). Shove-ha'penny, cribbage, dominoes, fruit machine and a separate skittle alley. There's a covered seating area, and more chairs in the pretty garden with apple and pear trees. Dogs on leads welcome in bar. *(Recommended by Laura Wilson, Joan and Michel Hooper-Immins, Ann and Colin Hunt, Tony and Wendy Hobden, Peter and Audrey Dowsett, Keith and Margaret Kettell, Dave Braisted, Geoff Pidoux, Ian Phillips, P R and S A White, J Davidson, Karen Eliot, Esther and John Sprinkle, Alan Kilpatrick, Veronica Brown, Mr and Mrs J Brown)*

Own brew ~ Managers Brian and Cynthia Elderfield ~ Real ale ~ Bar food (12-2.30, 6-9.30) ~ Restaurant ~ (01243) 786893 ~ Children in family room ~ Trad jazz 1st Tues of month ~ Open 11-3, 5-11; 12-3, 7-10.30 Sun; closed evening 25 Dec

PETT TQ8714 Map 3
Two Sawyers ◗

Pett Rd; off A259

Now that this cheery old country local is the brewery tap to the Old Forge Brewery, you will find their range of beers on handpump: Cuddle, Forge Bitter and Pett Progress, with seasonal guests like Black Pett, Brothers Best, Santa Forge, and Summer Eclipse, and guests from other breweries, too; also Gunthorpe's Double Vision farm cider. They use meat from their own farm for the beef, mushroom and ale pie (£6.75), steaks, and half shoulder of lamb in port and redcurrant sauce (£9.35). Other bar food such as filled rolls (from £2.45; steak baguette £4.20), soup (£2.50), ploughman's (from £4.20), all day breakfast (£5.85), vegetarian cannelloni (£6.65), some unusual specials like wild boar (£11.95), and crocodile (£12.95), home-made puddings (from

£2.75), and children's menu (£11.95). The meandering low-beamed rooms are simply but genuinely put together, with black band saws on cream walls, handsome iron wall lamps and stripped tables on bare boards in its two simple bars, and dark wood pub tables and cushioned banquettes in a tiny low-ceilinged snug, with a very old painted flint wall on one side; a sloping passage leads down to a low-beamed carpeted restaurant; fruit machine, cribbage, dominoes, and piped music. An iron gate leads from a pretty suntrap front brick courtyard to a quiet back garden with shady trees, a few well spaced picnic-sets, children's play area and boules. *(Recommended by Lucien, the Didler, John Davis, Iain Robertson, Michael and Ann Cole, E G Parish)*

Own brew ~ Licensees Clive Soper, John and Karen Perkins ~ Real ale ~ Bar food (all day in summer) ~ Restaurant ~ (01424) 812255 ~ Children in restaurant until 8pm ~ Local groups and bands Fri evenings ~ Open 11-11(12 Fri/Sat); 11-11 Sun ~ Bedrooms: £35/£40

PETWORTH SU9719 Map 2

Badgers ⊗ ♀

Coultershaw Bridge; just off A285 1½ miles S

If you want a special meal out, then this popular dining pub with its stylish furnishings and sophisticated yet relaxed atmosphere is the place to head for. Although there is a small chatty drinking area with a couple of tables, bar stools and an attractive antique oak monk's chair by the entrance, the space around the island bar servery is devoted to dining tables – well spaced, with an attractive mix of furniture from old mahogany to waxed stripped pine. White walls bring out the deep maroon colour of the high ceiling, and charming wrought-iron lamps, winter log fires, stripped shutters for the big Victorian windows, and a modicum of carefully chosen decorations including a few houseplants and dried flower arrangements complete the graceful décor. Besides the good if not cheap restaurant menu, the changing choice of attractively presented enjoyable bar food might include sandwiches (from £3.50), ploughman's (from £4.95), bubble and squeak or sausage and mash (£6.95), caesar salad (£7.50), beef stroganoff (£10.95), pheasant with rösti (£11.95), and a good choice of fish such as salmon papillote or coquilles St Jacques (£15.95). Well kept Badger Best and Harveys Best on handpump, with a good range of well chosen house wines and a fine list by the bottle; maybe faint piped music (the dominant sound is quiet conversation). A terrace by a waterlily pool has stylish metal garden furniture under parasols, and some solid old-fashioned wooden seats. No motorcyclists. *(Recommended by Mr Battersby, Ken Arthur, Patricia Beebe, John Beeken, Mrs Roxanne Chamberlain)*

Free house ~ Licensee Miss Arlette ~ Real ale ~ Bar food ~ Restaurant ~ (01798) 342651 ~ Children over 5 away from bar ~ Open 11-3, 5.30(7 Sat)-11; 12-3, 7-10.30 Sun; closed Sun evenings in winter ~ Bedrooms: /£70B

PUNNETTS TOWN TQ6220 Map 3

Three Cups

B2096 towards Battle

The licensees are losing their tenancy in early summer 2002 and we are keeping our fingers crossed that the brewery doesn't do anything too drastic to what has always been a very neighbourly and unassuming country pub. The peaceful and friendly long low-beamed bar has attractive panelling, comfortable seats including some in big bay windows overlooking a small green, and a log fire in the big fireplace under a black mantelbeam dated 1696. A partly no smoking back dining room leads out to a small covered terrace with rather well worn seats in the garden beyond. Decent bar food has included sandwiches, ploughman's, omelettes, steak in ale pie or seafood lasagne, sirloin steak, and several home-made daily specials such as rabbit pie or devilled kidneys. Well kept Greene King IPA, Harveys Best, and a guest such as Wadworths 6X on handpump; darts, shove-ha'penny, cribbage, dominoes and piped music. The pub dogs Monty and Lettie and Molly the cat welcome other dogs (on a lead). Nice surrounding walks. *(Recommended by Peter Meister, W Ruxton, Lucien, John Beeken)*

Greene King ~ Tenants Colin and Barbara Wood ~ Real ale ~ Bar food (12-2.15, 6.30-9.15) ~ (01435) 830252 ~ Children welcome ~ Open 11.30-3, 6.30-10.30; 11.30-11 Sat; 12-10.30 Sun; closed Sun evenings in winter

RUSHLAKE GREEN TQ6218 Map 3
Horse & Groom
Village signposted off B2096 Heathfield—Battle

In an attractive setting by the large village green, this bustling local is a popular place for both a drink and a chat or a leisurely meal. On the right is the heavily beamed dining room with guns and hunting trophies on the walls, plenty of wheelback chairs around pubby tables, and a log fire. The little L-shaped bar has more low beams – watch your head – and is simply furnished with high bar stools and bar chairs, red plush cushioned wall seats and a few brocaded cushioned stools, and a brick fireplace with some brass items on the mantelpiece; horsebrasses, photographs of the pub and local scenes on the walls, and fresh flowers. A small room down a step has jockeys' colours and jockey photographs and watercolours of the pub, and hops on the ceiling. Good, constantly changing bar food might include soup (£3.50), goats cheese, aubergine and red onion tart (£6.50), chicken breast stuffed with roasted almonds with spinach and pepper sauce (£7.50), steak in ale pie (£7.95), mixed tagliatelle with seared smoked salmon and cherry tomatoes (£8.25), seared swordfish with niçoise salad (£8.75), steamed turbot with samphire and mushroom sauce (£9.50), half local lobster (£10.50), and puddings like squidgy chocolate meringue, fruit crumble or summer pudding (£3.95). Well kept Harveys Best, Shepherd Neame and a guest beer on handpump, 5 wines and champagne by the glass. Picnic-sets in the slowly maturing rustic garden with pretty country views. The licensees also own the Star in Old Heathfield. *(Recommended by Ken Arthur, Colin and Janet Roe)*

Free house ~ Licensees Mike and Sue Chappel ~ Real ale ~ Bar food (12-2.30, 7-9.30) ~ Restaurant ~ (01435) 830320 ~ Children in eating area of bar and restaurant ~ Open 11.30-3, 5.30-11; 11.30-4, 6-11.30 Sat; 12-4, 7-11 Sun

RYE TQ9220 Map 3
Mermaid ♀ ⟳
Mermaid Street

The sign outside this lovely black and white timbered hotel says 'rebuilt in 1472', and the cellars are two or three centuries older than that. The smashing little bar at the back is where those in search of a light lunch and a drink tend to head for, and there's a mix of quite closely set furnishings such as Victorian gothic carved oak chairs, older but plainer oak seats and more modern ones in character, and a massive deeply polished bressumer beam across one wall for the huge inglenook fireplace; three antique but not ancient wall paintings show old English scenes. Well kept (if not cheap) Greene King Old Speckled Hen and Marstons Pedigree on handpump, and a short choice of bar food includes filled baguettes (from £5), braised meatballs with tomato sauce on pasta, cumberland sausage with mash and onion gravy or moules marinières (all £6.50), baked fish pie (£7.50), cold poached fillet of salmon (£8.50), and puddings such as strawberry shortbread or individual fruit tarts with chantilly cream (£5); children's meals (£4.50). The lounge and the smart (expensive) restaurant are no smoking. Good wine list, chess, cards and TV. Seats on a small back terrace overlook the car park – where morris dancing teams may vie with each other on some bank holiday weekends. *(Recommended by Susan and John Douglas, Dave Irving, the Didler, John and Lynn Busenbark, David Carr, Kevin Flack, Noel Watts, Emma Kingdon, Paul S McPherson, Louise English)*

Free house ~ Licensees Robert Pinwill and Mrs J Blincow ~ Real ale ~ Bar food (11-6 in summer) ~ Restaurant ~ (01797) 223065 ~ Children in eating area of bar and restaurant ~ Open 12-11(10.30 Sun) ~ Bedrooms: £70B/£140B

If you know a pub's ever open all day, please tell us.

SALEHURST TQ7424 Map 3
Salehurst Halt ♀

Village signposted from Robertsbridge bypass on A21 Tunbridge Wells—Battle Rd

Almost next door to the attractive 14th-c church, this bustling little local is run by charming, friendly licensees. The L-shaped bar has a pleasant chatty atmosphere, good plain wooden tables and chairs on flagstones at one end, a cushioned window seat, beams, a little open brick fireplace, a time punch clock, olde worlde pictures, and fresh flowers; lots of hops on a big beam divide this from the beamed carpeted area with its mix of tables, wheelback and farmhouse chairs, and a half wall leads to a dining area. Enjoyable home-made food at lunchtime includes sandwiches (from £3), pasta with feta cheese and capers (£4.95), home-made burgers (from £5.50), and spicy mexican chicken, steak and mushroom pie or home-baked ham with egg (all £5.95); more elaborate choices might be duck liver pâté (£3.95), moules marinières or sizzling tiger prawns (£4.95), spicy vegetable parcel (£7.95), beef in ale pie or cider chicken (£8.95), duck à l'orange or monkfish in tomato, garlic, oregano and olive oil (£10.95), and puddings like spotted dick, cider apple crumble or banoffi pie (from £2.95). Well kept Harveys Best on handpump, and good wines. It can get very busy at weekends, and service may slow down then. The small garden has terraces and picnic-sets and the window boxes and tubs are very pretty. *(Recommended by Colin and Janet Roe, Jason Caulkin, Ian Phillips)*

Free house ~ Licensees Vicky and Ozker Hassan ~ Real ale ~ Bar food ~ Restaurant ~ (01580) 880620 ~ Children welcome ~ Open 12-3, 7-11; closed Mon (except bank holidays)

SCAYNES HILL TQ3623 Map 3
Sloop ◗

Freshfield Lock; at top of Scaynes Hill by petrol station turn N off A272 into Church Rd, keep on for 1½ miles and then follow Freshfield signpost

After a visit to Sheffield Park Gardens or the Bluebell Steam Railway, this pleasantly set country pub is a good spot for lunch. The long saloon bar has wheelbacks and other chairs around pubby tables, a warmly friendly atmosphere, well kept Greene King IPA, Abbot, Dark Mild, Ruddles County, and a couple of guests such as Black Sheep Bitter, Gales HSB or Charles Wells Bombardier on handpump, and a decent wine list with 8 by the glass; there are benches in the old-fashioned brick porch. Good home-made bar food includes soups such as stilton and broccoli or vegetable with garlic croutons (£3.95; popular New Hampshire fish stew £6.95), roast peppers filled with onion, mushroom and bacon, topped with cheese (£4.50), lunchtime ploughman's (£4.95), vegetable lasagne or home-made steak, stout and mushroom pie (£6.95), liver and bacon with onion gravy (£7.95), maple and mustard chicken, pheasant braised in blackcurrant and winter ale (£8.95), steaks (from £9.95), grilled whole bass with olives, garlic and tomato (£11.95), daily specials such as devilled kidneys (£6.95), marlin tagliatelle with tomato and brie (£8.95), sautéed venison in port, thyme and honey (£9.95), and fillet of beef stroganoff (£10.95), and puddings such as home-made apple crumble, crème brûlée or bread pudding with maple and cream (£3.50); best to book. Good service from chatty, welcoming staff. The basic but airy public bar has restored woodwork, settles and cushioned stools on the bare boards, and railway memorabilia on the walls; bar billiards (in a small room leading off the bar), piped music, darts, shove-ha'penny, cribbage and dominoes. There are lots of tables in the sheltered garden. *(Recommended by Ken Arthur, Martin and Jane Wright, Susan and John Douglas, John Branston, R J Walden, Roger and Pauline Pearce)*

Greene King ~ Tenant Nigel S Cannon ~ Real ale ~ Bar food (12-2.15, 6.30-9.15 Mon-Sat, 12-8.30 Sun) ~ (01444) 831219 ~ Children in eating area of bar ~ Live music 1st Fri of month ~ Open 12-3, 6-11; 12-10.30 Sun

---

Prices of main dishes usually include vegetables or a side salad.

SEAFORD TV4899 Map 3

Golden Galleon ♀ ◖

Exceat Bridge; A259 Seaford—Eastbourne, near Cuckmere

What was the conservatory in this bustling pub is now the brewery and on full view for customers. A new Italian pizza oven has been installed and pizzas are served Monday to Saturday evenings (from £4.50). As well as the half a dozen or so Cuckmere Haven beers brewed on site by the landlord's brother-in-law (including an old-fashioned cask conditioned stout), there might be guests such as Harveys Armada, Palmers Dorset Gold, and Shepherd Neame Spitfire on handpump or tapped from the cask; also farm ciders, good wines by the glass, a decent choice of malts, continental brandies, Italian liqueurs, and cappuccino or espresso coffee. Most people, however, come for the food: sandwiches, home-made soup (£3.25), tuna fish and butter beans with capers, onions, garlic and parsley (£3.95), ploughman's (from £4.75), their own smoked salmon (£5.50), filled baked potatoes (from £5.50), lots of salads (from £6.25), fish of the day in crispy batter (£6.95), halloumi bake (£7.95), stincotto (large pork joint cooked on the bone with wine and herbs, £10.95), steaks (from £11.45), daily specials such as lasagne (£7.95), mushrooms, red onion and leeks in ale gravy in puff pastry (£8.95), Italian platter (£9.75), and half shoulder of lamb slowly roasted in minted gravy (£10.95), and puddings (£3.25). The spreading main bar with high trussed and pitched rafters creating quite an airy feel is the only place where smoking is allowed; the river room becomes a restaurant on Sunday lunchtime. The pub is perfectly set for several attractive walks – along the river, down to the sea or inland to Friston Forest and the downs, and there are fine views towards the Cuckmere estuary and Seven Sisters Country Park from tables in the sloping garden. On sunny weekends it can get particularly busy. *(Recommended by Dr David Cockburn, Tina and David Woods-Taylor, P Rome, Enid and Henry Stephens, Dave Braisted, Ann and Colin Hunt, E G Parish)*

Own brew ~ Licensee Stefano Diella ~ Real ale ~ Bar food (12-3, 6-9(9.30 Fri and Sat)) ~ (01323) 892247 ~ Children away from bar ~ Open 11-11; 12-10.30 Sun; closed Sun evenings (from 4pm) in winter

SINGLETON SU8713 Map 2

Fox & Hounds

Just off A286 Midhurst—Chichester; heading S into the village, the main road bends sharp right – keep straight ahead instead; if you miss this turn, take the Charlton road, then first left

This is a consistently enjoyable and pretty 16th-c village pub – one reader has been coming here for 30 years. The partly panelled main bar has cream paintwork, a polished wooden floor, daily papers and books to borrow, and a good winter log fire. There's a second bar with green settles and another fire, a third flagstoned room on the left, and a further no smoking seating area off a side corridor. Good honest generous food includes home-made soup (£3.25), open sandwiches (from £4.50), an excellent cheese platter with good ripe cheeses laid out attractively, and pickles and chutneys provided in separate pots (£5.50), pasta of the day or nut roast (£7.50), liver and bacon or steak in ale pie (£7.75), gammon with mustard, mushrooms and melted cheese (£7.95), rump steak (£8.50), and daily specials such as beef stew with herby dumplings (£7.75) or smoked haddock with a poached egg (£8.50); service is prompt and cheerful. Well kept Ballards Best, Bass and Hancocks HB on handpump, decent wines by the glass, coffee with free refills; no music or machines. There are tables on an attractive small back terrace, and beyond that a big walled garden with colourful flowerbeds and fruit trees. The Weald & Downland Open Air Museum is just down the road, and Goodwood Racecourse is not far away. *(Recommended by Ann and Colin Hunt, Tony and Wendy Hobden, P R and S A White, Prof S Barnett, Dennis Jenkin)*

Enterprise ~ Lease Tony Simpson and Vicki Wright ~ Real ale ~ Bar food (12-2, 6.30-9) ~ (01243) 811251 ~ Children in family room ~ Open 11.30-3, 6-11; 12-3, 7-10.30 Sun

TILLINGTON SU9621 Map 2
Horse Guards 🍴 ♀ 🛏
Village signposted off A272 Midhurst—Petworth

Under the friendly new licensees, this prettily-set 18th-c dining pub remains somewhere for a special meal out. The neatly kept cosy beamed front bar has some good country furniture, a log fire and a lovely view beyond the village to the Rother Valley from a seat in the big black-panelled bow window. A wide choice of enjoyable and imaginative (if not cheap) food includes lunchtime bar snacks such as sandwiches (from £4.95), ploughman's (from £5.95), tortilla wraps filled with cajun chicken or strips of beef with peppers and sour cream, pasta with salmon and broccoli or popular goats cheese tart (£6.95), ham and egg with bubble and squeak (£7.25), and ballotine of foie gras with fruit chutney (£8.95); in the evening, more elaborate dishes might include crêpes with smoked salmon and chive cream (£7.50), coquilles St Jacques or leek and crayfish terrine with sauce aigre-doux and truffled watercress dressing (£7.95), lobster cocktail with lemon and dill mayonnaise (£8.50), risotto with fine herbs, deep-fried shallots and parmesan (£9.95), chicken breast stuffed with mushrooms with a ragoût of forest mushrooms laced with madeira (£12.50), fillet of beef with sauce béarnaise and pont-neuf (£16.95), bass with orange and fennel (£17.95), and puddings like chocolate tart with clotted cream, summer fruit pudding or glazed lemon tart with raspberry sorbet (£4.25); good Sunday roast beef with yorkshire pudding (£9.95); when you book a table, you will be asked whether you wish a smoking or no smoking area. The good wine list has 16 by the glass; well kept Fullers London Pride and Youngs Special on handpump. Darts and cribbage. There's a terrace outside, and more tables and chairs in a sheltered garden behind. The 800 year old church opposite is worth a look.
(Recommended by Ann and Colin Hunt, John Evans, Keith and Margaret Kettell, Sally Anne and Peter Goodale, J Hale, Lord Sandhurst, Michael and Ann Cole, Ian Jones, Sue Demont, Tim Barrow, Derek Thomas, Gordon Theaker, J A Snell, Alan Thomas, J H Bell, Tina and David Woods-Taylor, Peter B Brown)

Free house ~ Licensee Paul Brett ~ Real ale ~ Bar food (12-2, 7-10) ~ Restaurant ~ (01798) 342332 ~ Children in eating area of bar; must be over 6 in evening ~ Open 11-3, 6-11; 12-3, 7-10.30 Sun ~ Bedrooms: £65B/£82B

TROTTON SU8323 Map 2
Keepers Arms
A272 Midhurst—Petersfield; pub tucked up above road, on S side

The friendly licensees continue to restore this 18th-c country pub. A new bar counter has been built using a huge slab of elm, and a raised dining area created, and the front terrace has been rebuilt so 40 people can comfortably sit there. The beamed L-shaped bar, with timbered walls and some standing timbers, has original flooring tiles, with parquet floor elsewhere. There are sofas by the big log fire, and the walls are decorated with some unusual pictures and artefacts that reflect the Oxleys' previous long years of travelling the world. The wheelback chairs and dark pub tables continue to give way to a more interesting medley of old or antique seats, with oak refectory tables and the like, and the dining tables are decorated with pretty candelabra, and bowls of fruit and chillis. Good home-made food includes open sandwiches, soup (£3.50), fine cheese and salami platters that several people can share (£5), crispy duck with hoisin sauce, cucumber and spring onion in puff pastry (£9), proper fish pie with cod, prawns, smoked salmon and squid (£9.50), chargrilled ostrich medallion with a wild cranberry and balsamic jus (£10.50), and puddings such as home-made treacle tart (£3.50); in winter they have a special game pie with venison, pheasant, partridge, and wild duck (£8.50), and in summer (by appointment only), a fresh seafood platter with lobster, dressed crab, crab claws, giant crevettes, atlantic prawns, langoustine, and oysters (£18.50 per person); the restaurant is no smoking. A good relaxed civilised atmosphere, well kept Ballards Best and Nyewood Gold and Cheriton Pots on handpump, decent wines including English champagne, and organic spirits; maybe relaxed piped music (there's a musically decorated piano). *(Recommended by Bruce Bird, Val and Alan Green, Cathy Robinson, Martin and Karen Wake, Ann and Colin Hunt, Prof S Barnett, Derek Harvey-Piper)*

Free house ~ Licensees Steve and Jenny Oxley ~ Real ale ~ Bar food ~ Restaurant ~ (01730) 813724 ~ Children welcome ~ Dinner jazz and acoustic guitar occasionally ~ Open 11(12 Sat)-3, 6.30-11; 12-3 Sun; closed Sun evening, all Mon except bank hol lunchtime

WEST ASHLING SU8107 Map 2
Richmond Arms ◀

Mill Lane; from B2146 in village follow Hambrook signpost

Close to an attractive mill and pond, this small out-of-the-way village pub has a relaxing, friendly atmosphere. The main bar is dominated by a central servery and has a 1930s feel, with its long wall benches, library chairs, and black tables; there's a dark wooden dado with a cream wall in one part and wallpaper in the other, wooden ducks on the picture rails and pictures on the walls, and an open fire in the stripped brick fireplace. Well kept Greene King IPA, Abbot, one of their seasonal ales and Harveys on handpump. Under the new landlady, decent home-made bar food includes sandwiches and soup (from £2.50), filled baguettes (from £3.50), ham and egg (£5.95), steak and kidney pie (£6.95), steaks (from £7.95), and daily specials such as mushroom and red pepper stroganoff or smoked haddock and mozzarella fishcakes (£5.95), and sausage and mash and onion gravy or spicy meatballs with pasta and a tomato and chilli sauce (£6.95). Darts, pool, cribbage, fruit machine, and a skittle alley. There's a pergola, and some picnic-sets by the car park. *(Recommended by Mrs Sally Kingsbury, Ann and Colin Hunt, Dr D E Granger)*

Greene King ~ Tenant Doris Westlake ~ Real ale ~ Bar food (12-2(2.30 wknds), 7-9) ~ (01243) 575730 ~ Children welcome ~ Open 11-2.30, 5.30-11; 11-11 Sat; 12-10.30 Sun; 11-3, 5.30-11 Sat in winter

WILMINGTON TQ5404 Map 3
Giants Rest

Just off A27

Watched over by the impressive chalk-carved Long Man of Wilmington, at the foot of the South Downs, this comfortable Victorian pub is run by charming, friendly licensees. The long wood floored bar and adjacent open areas, one with a log fire, are simply furnished with old pews and pine tables (each with their own bar game or wooden puzzle), and serve well kept Harveys Best, Hop Back Summer Lightning, and Timothy Taylors Landlord on handpump; orange and grapefruit juice squeezed in front of you, and decent wines. From a changing blackboard, well presented and very reasonably priced bar food includes soup (£3), bacon and mushrooms in garlic (£4.50), ploughman's (from £5), local sausages (£5.50), a warm salad of halloumi cheese, tomato and basil (£6), macaroni cheese (£7), salmon fishcakes with lemon mayonnaise or beef in beer pie (£7.50), chicken in a creamy leek and stilton sauce or home-cooked ham with home-made chutney and bubble and squeak (£8.50), trout fillet with crème fraîche, walnut and horseradish sauce (£9), lamb off the bone in asparagus sauce (£9.50), and puddings such as home-made strawberry rhubarb pie or upside-down apple and ginger pudding (£3.50). There's a sizeable no smoking area. Plenty of seats in the good-sized front garden. *(Recommended by Ian Phillips, Sue Demont, Tim Barrow, Simon Pyle, Robert Heaven, John Beeken, T R and B C Jenkins, R J Walden)*

Free house ~ Licensees Adrian and Rebecca Hillman ~ Real ale ~ Bar food ~ (01323) 870207 ~ Children in family areas ~ Open 11-3, 6-11; 11-11 Sat; 12-10.30 Sun

---

'Children welcome' means the pub says it lets children inside without any special restriction; readers have found that some may impose an evening time limit – please tell us if you find this: www.goodguides.com

WINEHAM TQ2320 Map 3
Royal Oak
Village signposted from A272 and B2116

This delightfully old-fashioned place never changes – there are no fruit machines, piped music or even beer pumps, the food sticks to snacks, and children are restricted to the garden. Inside is simply furnished, logs burn in an enormous inglenook fireplace with a cast-iron Royal Oak fireback, and there's a stuffed stoat and crocodile, a collection of jugs, ancient corkscrews decorating the very low beams above the serving counter, racing plates, tools and a coach horn on the walls; maybe a nice tabby cat, and views of quiet countryside from the back parlour. Well kept Harveys Best and Marstons Pedigree tapped from the cask in a still room; darts, shove-ha'penny, dominoes, cribbage. Bar snacks are limited to home-made winter soup (£2), sandwiches (from £2, smoked salmon £2.50), and ploughman's (from £4.50); courteous service – the pub has been in the same family for over 50 years. It can get very busy at weekends and on summer evenings. The charming frontage has a lawn with wooden tables by a well. More reports please. *(Recommended by Phil and Sally Gorton, John Davis)*

Inn Business ~ Tenant Tim Peacock ~ Real ale ~ Bar food (11-2.30, 5.30-10.30) ~ No credit cards ~ (01444) 881252 ~ Open 11-2.30, 5.30(6 Sat)-11; 12-3, 7-10.30 Sun

---

Lucky Dip

Besides the fully inspected pubs, you might like to try these Lucky Dips recommended to us and described by readers (if you do, please send us reports: www.goodguides.com).

Alfriston [TQ5103]
☆ *Star* [High St]: Fascinating façade decorated with fine medieval carvings, striking figurehead red lion on the corner; stolid quiet heavy-beamed bar with medieval sanctuary post, fine antique furnishings, big log fire in Tudor fireplace, some no smoking areas, helpful service; Bass, limited simple though not cheap bar food, restaurant; comfortable bedrooms in up-to-date part behind, open all day summer *(the Didler, Sally Anne and Peter Goodale, Charlie Harris, David Carr, Norman Fox, LYM)*
Angmering [TQ0704]
☆ *Spotted Cow* [High St]: Beautifully presented generous food (very popular wkdy lunchtimes with older people) from imaginative sandwiches up, well kept Badger K&B, Courage Best and Directors, Greene King Old Speckled Hen and a guest such as Youngs Special, good choice of wines by the glass, attentive service, smuggling history, sporting caricatures, cool and roomy in summer, two log fires winter; restaurant, no smoking conservatory, big garden with boules and play area; open all day summer wknds (very busy then), monthly Sun afternoon jazz, lovely walk to Highdown hill fort *(Mrs Sally Kingsbury, John Beeken, R Edwards, Bruce Bird, Tony and Wendy Hobden)*
Ardingly [TQ3429]
☆ *Gardeners Arms* [B2028 2 miles N]: New management in neatly refurbished olde-worlde dining pub, keeping up its reputation for reliable fresh home-made food and quick cheerful service even when crowded, big inglenook log fire, well kept Badger and Harveys, morning coffee and tea, attractive decorations; may be soft piped music, no

children; well spaced tables out among small trees, handy for Borde Hill and Wakehurst Place *(B J Harding, M Borthwick, Michael Porter, Mr and Mrs D Moir)*
Oak [Street Lane]: Beamed 14th-c dining pub handy for show ground, good reasonably priced menu, Harveys and Shepherd Neame Spitfire, prompt friendly service, lots of brass and lace curtains, magnificent old fireplace, bright comfortable restaurant extension; tables in pleasant garden, reservoir walks *(Martin and Jane Wright, C and R Bromage)*
Arlington [TQ5407]
☆ *Yew Tree* [off A22 nr Hailsham, or A27 W of Polegate]: Neatly modernised two-bar village local very popular for hearty home cooking inc delicious puddings (smaller helpings can be arranged), well kept Harveys ales, log fires, efficient cheery service (but book well ahead for Fri in summer); subdued piped music, darts, maybe eggs for sale; conservatory, good big garden and play area, by paddock with farm animals *(BB, Tina and David Woods-Taylor, Miss A G Drake, John Beeken)*
Arundel [TQ0107]
St Marys Gate [London Rd, by cathedral]: Long comfortable open-plan bar, alcoves, lots of horse-racing caricatures, generous good value home-made food from sandwiches up, well kept Badger Best and Tanglefoot, friendly staff coping well with the bustle, no smoking restaurant area one end, TV in small back room; unobtrusive piped music; picnic-sets on pleasant back terrace, quiet good value bedrooms *(Tony Hobden)*
☆ *Swan* [High St]: Recently taken over by Gales, with their Butser, GB and HSB and a guest such as Fullers London Pride; smartly refurbished

open-plan L-shaped bar with attractive woodwork and matching fittings, beaten brass former inn-sign hanging on wall, friendly efficient young staff, good choice of food from baguettes and baked potatoes to restaurant meals; piped music can get loud – small side room a bit quieter; restaurant, good bedrooms, open all day *(John Davis, Bruce Bird, Pat and Tony Martin, Veronica Brown, LYM, Ann and Colin Hunt, Tony and Wendy Hobden, Keith and Margaret Kettell)*

Ashurstwood [TQ4237]

Maypole [Maypole Rd]: Basic well worn in country local with helpful friendly staff and regulars, well kept real ale, decent sandwiches; informal garden *(Dr D E Granger)*

Balcombe [TQ3033]

☆ *Cowdray Arms* [London Rd (B2036/B2110 N of village)]: Roomy main-road pub filling quickly at lunchtime for good value choice of well prepared and presented food from sandwiches to some interesting dishes, good helpings, polite attentive service, wide range of well kept ales such as Black Sheep, Greene King IPA, Abbot and Tanners Jack and Harveys, occasional beer festivals, roomy L-shaped bar and spacious no smoking restaurant with conservatory; children welcome, garden with good play area *(DWAJ, KC, Ian Phillips, Tony and Wendy Hobden)*

Balls Cross [SU9826]

Stag [signed off A283 N of Petworth]: Welcoming 17th-c country pub with flagstones and log fires, good food, well kept Badger ales; pleasant back garden, bedrooms, good walks *(Roger and Debbie Stamp, R J Walden, J A Snell)*

Barcombe [TQ4114]

☆ *Anchor* [Barcombe Mills]: Peacefully set in lawns by winding River Ouse (rowing boat hire), with cream tea and cold drink kiosk and wknd barbecues, and lots of quiet walks; two bars, recovered now from the floods, and two no smoking dining areas (children welcome), food from sandwiches and baked potatoes to more elaborate main dishes, well kept Badger Best and Tanglefoot, Harveys Best and a guest beer, decent wines, traditional games; open all day, bedrooms *(Stephanie and Kamal Thapa, LYM)*

Battle [TQ7416]

Senlac [Station Rd/Battle Hill]: Well decorated pub with attractive bistro, good food, friendly caring service *(E G Parish)*

Beckley [TQ8523]

Rose & Crown [Northiam Rd (B2088)]: Character coaching inn, welcoming and unspoilt, cosy eating area with log fire, simple choice of very generous good freshly prepared food, Adnams Broadside, Harveys and three guest beers changing weekly, friendly service; children welcome, good views from garden with swing *(Gill Waller, Tony Morriss, Colin and Janet Roe)*

Billingshurst [TQ0825]

Olde Six Bells [High St (A29)]: Picturesque partly 14th-c flagstoned and timbered pub with well kept Badger ales, cheerful landlord, inglenook fireplace, pretty roadside garden *(Tony Beaulah, LYM)*

Binsted [SU9806]

☆ *Black Horse* [Binsted Lane; about 2 miles W of Arundel, turn S off A27 towards Binsted]: Pretty 17th-c local with ochre walls and open fire in big comfortable bar, bar food inc generous sandwiches and well presented freshly cooked specials, wider range in back conservatory restaurant, well kept Courage Directors, Gales HSB, Harveys Best and Hop Back Summer Lightning, darts and bar billiards one end, shelf of sweetie jars, greyhound racing trophies; piped music; tables on terrace, idyllic garden, views over valley; bedrooms *(R T and J C Moggridge, Bruce Bird, BB)*

Boarshead [TQ5332]

Boars Head [Eridge Rd, off A26 bypass]: Good friendly service and good value fresh food in attractive old unspoilt pub, quiet spot *(Michael and Ann Cole)*

Bolney [TQ2623]

Bolney Stage [off A23 just N of A272]: Polished timbered dining pub locally popular for wide range of good handsomely presented food, prompt friendly service; handy for Sheffield Park and Bluebell Railway *(Ron and Sheila Corbett)*

Bosham [SU8003]

Anchor Bleu [High St]: Lovely waterside position in attractive village earns its *Guide* place, sea and boat views, little terrace outside massive wheel-operated bulkhead door to ward off high tides (cars parked on seaward side often submerged); plenty of potential inside, open all day *(Dave Braisted, LYM, Ann and Colin Hunt, Geoffrey and Brenda Wilson, Tony and Wendy Hobden)*

Berkeley Arms [just outside old village]: Good atmosphere, cheerful landlord and staff, lounge with eating area, well kept Gales, public bar *(Ann and Colin Hunt)*

White Swan [A259 roundabout]: Well refurbished, with two bar areas and large dining room (children allowed here), sociable landlord, good choice of beers such as Hop Back Summer Lightning and Crop Circle, John Smiths and Youngs, good value beer, usual bar food from toasties and baked potatoes up, also restaurant dishes, log fire *(Ann and Colin Hunt, Tony and Wendy Hobden)*

Brighton [TQ3104]

Bath Arms [Union St/Meeting House Lane, The Lanes]: Several high-ceilinged rooms with panelling and old fireplaces, lots of old photographs and cartoon prints, pleasant atmosphere, attentive staff, good value bar food from sandwiches up, real ales such as Brakspears seasonal, Courage Best and Directors, Greene King Abbot, Highgate Saddlers and Theakstons, decent coffee, New World wines *(Ian Phillips)*

☆ *Colonnade* [New Rd, off North St; by Theatre Royal]: Small nicely preserved Victorian bar, with red plush, shining brass, gleaming mirrors, interesting pre-war playbills and lots of signed theatrical photographs, white gloves and canes in top hats peeking over plush curtains, good friendly service even when very busy, perhaps limited snacks inc good salt beef sandwiches (free seafood or roast potato nibbles Sun lunchtime instead), particularly well kept Bass, Boddingtons and Harveys (early evening wkdy happy hour), good choice of good value wines, tiny front terrace; next to Theatre Royal, they take interval orders – and performers like it *(Sue Demont, Tim Barrow, Ian Phillips, W W Burke, Alan Thomas, BB, R T and J C Moggridge, Keith Routley)*

☆ *Cricketers* [Black Lion St]: Compact and bustling down-to-earth town pub, very well run, with ageing Victorian furnishings and lots of interesting bric-a-brac – even a stuffed bear; well kept Bass, Boddingtons, Courage Directors and Greene King Old Speckled Hen tapped from the cask, good coffee, friendly staff, usual well priced lunchtime bar food with fresh veg in upstairs bar, restaurant (where children allowed) and covered ex-stables courtyard bar; piped music; open all day *(Ian Phillips, LYM, R T and J C Moggridge, Tony and Wendy Hobden, Kevin Blake)*

☆ *Evening Star* [Surrey St]: Very popular for half a dozen or more well kept interesting changing (mostly local) ales inc their own good Skinners brews; enthusiastic landlord (may let you sample before you buy), changing farm ciders and perries, good simple lunchtime food, old-fashioned local atmosphere, well worn but clean bare boards, simple furnishings, good mix of customers, railway memorabilia; unobtrusive piped music, live music nights *(Bruce Bird, Sue Demont, Tim Barrow, R T and J C Moggridge)*

Font & Firkin [Union St, The Lanes]: Cleverly converted circular church (still has pulpit and bell pulls, alongside Sunday comedians and other live entertainment), sturdy old furnishings, some tables up on narrow balcony around cupola base, pleasant service, decent food inc good value Sun roasts, real ales; good loud music, can be packed with young people at night *(BB, Dr and Mrs A K Clarke)*

George [Trafalgar St]: Three linked rooms (the front ones are the best) off main bar, nice mix of furnishings on stripped floor, several big mirrors and nice etchings, mix of youngish customers, well kept Boddingtons, Flowers IPA and Harveys, lots of wines by the glass, freshly squeezed fruit juice, inexpensive popular vegetarian/vegan food all day, pleasant staff, daily papers; piped pop music; children welcome, small heated back courtyard under marquee *(BB, Ian Phillips)*

Great Eastern [Trafalgar St]: Long narrow bar with lots of books and bric-a-brac, nice mix of old furnishings on wood-strip floor, chatty relaxed atmosphere, decent food 12-4, real ales, friendly staff, thoughtful wine list, cheap spirits, good coffee; quiet piped music *(BB)*

☆ *Greys* [Southover St, Kemp Town]: Buoyant atmosphere in very small basic open-plan corner local with two or three rough and ready tables for eating – must book, strongly recommended for limited choice of good food lunchtime and Tues-Thurs evening, Belgian chef with some adventurous original recipes; very

friendly staff, well kept Flowers, Fullers London Pride, uncommon guest beers and Belgian bottled beers, well chosen and reproduced piped music, interesting live music Sun lunchtime (more during Brighton Festival) *(Richard Houghton, BB)*

Hand in Hand [Upper St James's St, Kemptown]: Busy friendly local brewing its own Kemptown beers, also Badger Best and Tanglefoot, Stowford Press cider, good value snacks such as sandwiches, pies and pizzas wkdy lunchtimes, Sun roast potatoes, good service, dim-lit bar with tie collection and newspaper pages all over walls *(Brian and Halina Howes, Gill Waller, Tony Morriss)*

Sir Charles Napier [Southover St]: Friendly Gales pub, cosy and busy, with well kept HSB and other ales, plenty of food, lots of interesting local memorabilia, quaint terrace; some live music, quiz nights, morris dancing *(Stephanie and Kamal Thapa)*

Sussex [East St]: Busy and well run, with traditional L-shaped pubby bar, good basic food from sandwiches up, well kept real ales, good choice of wines by the glass, pleasant staff; piped music; open all day, tables out in the square *(Dr and Mrs A K Clarke)*

Victory [Duke St]: Friendly local with lovely tiled façade and etched windows, long benches and medley of chairs and tables on bare boards, open fire in cosy snug, nautical memorabilia, Courage Best and Directors, good value bar food (not Sun/Mon) *(Brian and Halina Howes)*

Broad Oak [TQ8220]

☆ *Rainbow Trout* [A28/B2089, N of Brede]: Well run olde-worlde pub with wide range of well cooked generous food esp fish served by pleasant waitresses in attractive bustling low-beamed bar and big no smoking restaurant extension; gets very crowded but plenty of room for drinkers, with well kept Boddingtons, Flowers and Fullers London Pride, decent wines; tables out on large lawn *(E G Parish, Phil and Sarah Kane, Glenn and Louise Hamilton)*

Brownbread Street [TQ6715]

☆ *Ash Tree* [off A271 (was B2204) W of Battle; 1st northward rd W of Ashburnham Pl, then 1st fork left, then bear right into Brownbread Street]: Tranquil country local tucked away in isolated hamlet, cosy beamed bars with nice old settles and chairs, stripped brickwork, two inglenook fireplaces, evening candlelight, well kept Greene King Old Speckled Hen and Harveys Best, bar food (may only do their good main dishes at busiest times eg Sun lunch), cheerful service; simple games room on left with darts, pool, fruit machine, juke box, bar billiards; children in eating area, pretty garden with picnic-sets, open all day *(LYM, James Nunns)*

Bucks Green [TQ0732]

Fox [A281 Horsham—Guildford]: Ancient open-plan inglenook bar, wide choice of enjoyable food esp fish, well kept Badger beers inc K&B, decent wines by the glass, friendly helpful staff, restaurant area; play area *(Alistair Forsyth)*

Burwash [TQ6724]

☆ *Rose & Crown* [inn sign on A265]: Low-beamed timbered local tucked away down lane in pretty village, pleasant staff, well kept Harveys, decent wines, good log fire, good value varied food in bar and attractive restaurant; tables out in small quiet garden, limited nearby parking *(Derek Harvey-Piper, BB, R M Warner)*

Bury [TQ0113]

☆ *Squire & Horse* [Bury Common; A29 Fontwell—Pulborough]: Welcoming landlady and good Australian chef/landlord, some concentration on wide changing range of good home-made food in big sectioned dining area (sandwiches too), well kept ales such as Fullers London Pride, Harveys and guests, smart friendly staff, spotless bar and restaurant with fresh flowers, Sun bar nibbles; tables in pretty outside area, cl Sun evening, Mon *(M E C Comer, M O S Hawkins, Ann and Colin Hunt, Fiona and Keith Warton, John Davis, C and G Fraser)*

Buxted [TQ4923]

☆ *White Hart* [Station Rd (A272)]: Neatly kept roadside pub doing well under experienced new licencees, main bar divided by timbering, big brick fireplace, hops and some horsebrasses, red leatherette seats, left-hand dining bar, lots of interesting food, well kept Greene King Old Speckled Hen and Harveys, cheery chatty feel with efficient friendly staff and quite a few locals, big bright and airy dining conservatory with fairy-lit plants and light wooden furniture on wood-strip floor; maybe piped pop music; pleasant garden with plenty of seats *(RDK, BB, Michael and Ann Cole, Ken Arthur)*

Catsfield [TQ7213]

White Hart [A269]: Well kept Harveys, enjoyable honest food; good walking country *(Francis Johnston)*

Chailey [TQ3919]

Five Bells [A275 9 miles N of Lewes]: Promising new regime (they've got rid of the pool table, juke box and machines), interesting choice of home-made food, real ales, big log fire, good service; picnic-sets in big garden with play area *(anon)*

Chelwood Gate [TQ4129]

Red Lion [A275, S of Forest Row junction with A22]: Good quickly served bar food from sandwiches and baked potatoes to imaginative specials in main bar, smaller room and restaurant, well kept Shepherd Neame ales and decent wines, friendly attentive staff, small coal fire; children welcome, delightful big sheltered side garden with well spaced tables, more out in front – handy for Ashdown Forest walks *(C and R Bromage, John Beeken, BB)*

Chichester [SU8605]

Coach & Horses [St Pancras]: Comfortably refurbished open-plan pub, clean and friendly, well kept Ballards and Greene King ales, good lunchtime bar food from open side kitchen, bar nibbles Sun, quick service; quiet piped music; attractive back terrace *(Peter and Audrey Dowsett, Ann and Colin Hunt, Bruce Bird)*

Dolphin & Anchor [West St]: Wetherspoons in former hotel opp cathedral, good value food inc good range of curries, six low-priced real ales, cheerful young well trained staff; no children, very busy with young people Sat night, doorman and queues to get in; pleasant back terrace, open all day *(Veronica Brown, Klaus and Elizabeth Leist, J A Snell)*

Fountain [Southgate]: Attractive front bar with bric-a-brac, wide food choice from sandwiches and baguettes to good hot dishes ordered from counter in no smoking dining room (eat anywhere), well kept Badger Best and Tanglefoot, friendly efficient staff, afternoon teas, second bar, fruit machines; open all day, live music Tues and Sat, quiz night Thurs *(Ann and Colin Hunt, Sue and Mike Todd, Tony and Wendy Hobden)*

Nags Hotel [St Pancras]: Lots of panelling and old books, log fires, substantial good food in bar and recently pleasantly refurbished eating area inc evening and Sun lunch carvery, friendly staff, thriving local atmosphere, well kept Boddingtons, Flowers Original, Fullers London Pride, Greene King Old Speckled Hen and Wadworths 6X; piped music, live some nights *(John Davis, Ann and Colin Hunt)*

Park Tavern [Priory St, opp park]: Comfortably relaxing local with well kept Gales and Greene King Abbot, nice eating area specialising in hot lunchtime baguettes, also sandwiches, baked potatoes and limited cooked meals, cheerful service; attractive spot opp Priory Park *(Ann and Colin Hunt, Tony Hobden, R T and J C Moggridge)*

Punch House [East St]: Smartened up after recent fire; handy for shoppers, friendly service, decent coffee *(Ann and Colin Hunt)*

Toad [West St]: Enjoyable conversion of redundant church to real ale pub, multi-level seating around big central bar, good value straightforward food till 6, Hardy beers, decent coffee; music and constant videos, good mix of customers inc lively young people at night; open all day, opp cathedral *(Ann and Colin Hunt, Veronica Brown, David and Carole Chapman, Geoff Pidoux)*

Chilgrove [SU8116]

☆ *Royal Oak* [off B2141 Petersfield—Chichester, signed Hooksway down steep hill]: Welcoming and smartly simple two-room country tavern in charming spot, beams, brick floors, country-kitchen furnishings, huge log fires, sensibly priced home-made standard food, well kept real ales inc Arundel Best, games; has been cl Mons; provision for children, attractive seats outside, good walks *(Ann and Colin Hunt, Prof S Barnett, LYM)*

White Horse [off B2141, Petersfield—Chichester]: More smart restaurant than pub, good lunches (not as expensive as evening), remarkable list of outstanding wines, punctilious service; idyllic downland setting with small flower-filled terrace and big pretty garden, lots of fine walks *(Phyl and Jack Street, RDK)*

Climping [TQ0001]

Black Horse : Friendly and unpretentious family-run Irish pub, good value food from home-made soup and huge ploughman's up, real ales; skittle alley, walk to beach *(Michael Sargent)*

Cocking [SU8717]
Blue Bell [A286 S of Midhurst]: Pleasant country local refurbished by new licensees, enjoyable food, well kept Greene King ales, roaring log fires; good walks – just off South Downs Way *(Prof S Barnett, Dave Braisted, Ann and Colin Hunt)*

Colemans Hatch [TQ4533]
☆ *Hatch* [signed off B2026, or off B2110 opp church]: Quaint and attractive weatherboarded Ashdown Forest pub dating from 1430, big log fire in beamed bar, small back restaurant with another log fire, good interesting food from baked potatoes, giant ploughman's and filled ciabatta bread to bass and steak, well kept Harveys, freshly pressed local apple juice, good friendly mix of customers inc families; front terrace and beautifully kept big garden *(B St C Matthews, Mr and Mrs S Oxenbury, LYM, Michael and Ann Cole)*

Colgate [TQ2232]
Dragon [Forest Rd]: Cosy and unpretentious, with friendly service, well kept Badger ales inc K&B, good value food inc interesting sandwiches; big garden, pleasant and secluded – good for children *(R A Watson, Mrs Angela Bromley-Martin, G T Brewster)*

Coolham [TQ1423]
☆ *George & Dragon* [pub signed just off A272]: Cheery local atmosphere in heavy-beamed bar with enormous inglenook fireplace, unpretentious furnishings, well kept Badger ales inc K&B, enjoyable and generous home-made food from sandwiches to steak, helpful staff, traditional games inc bar billiards; fruit machine, TV, can get pretty busy; children welcome in eating areas, well spaced tables out in big attractive orchard garden, open all day wknds *(R J Walden, John Davis, Tony Beaulah, Ian Phillips, LYM, Theo, Anne and Jane Gaskin)*
Selsey Arms [A272/B2139]: Several bar areas, open fires, good food from filled rolls and baked potatoes up, well kept Fullers London Pride and Charles Wells Bombardier, friendly considerate service even when quite busy; charming garden behind *(C and R Bromage)*

Cousley Wood [TQ6533]
☆ *Old Vine* [B2100 Wadhurst—Lamberhurst]: Good dining pub with lots of old timbers and beams, wide range of generously served modestly priced decent food inc good fish, good house wines, four well kept ales, pleasant waitresses and barmaids; rustic pretty restaurant on right, pubbier bare-boards or brick-floored area with woodburner by bar; credit cards impounded if you run a bar bill; a few tables out behind *(Jason Caulkin, Ben Whitney and Pippa Redmond, Mrs Pamela Cooper, Comus and Sarah Elliott, BB)*

Crawley [TQ2636]
Snooty Fox [Haslett Ave, opp Three Bridges Stn]: Comfortable recently refurbished Big Steak pub, real ales inc Tetleys, decent value food, no smoking area *(Tony Hobden)*

Cripps Corner [TQ7721]
White Hart : Comfortable and friendly country pub, wide choice of good food inc good value OAP menu Mon-Thurs, cheerful quick service, no smoking eating area, Harveys, sensibly priced wines; maybe discreet piped music; garden *(Mrs Anne Booth)*

Crockerhill [SU9207]
Winterton Arms [just off A27 Chichester—Fontwell]: Beamy old pub, not smart but attractive, with public bar and two lacy dining rooms, good fresh food, pleasant service, well kept Fullers London Pride, open fire *(Val and Alan Green)*

Dallington [TQ6619]
Swan [Woods Corner, B2096 E]: Country local with new young chef/landlord doing enjoyable food, candles at night in bare-boards low-beamed bar, and in simple carpeted back dining room with far views to Beachy Head, well kept Harveys Best and Wadworths 6X, decent house wines, good coffee; may be piped music, strangers may not always feel entirely welcome; steps down to smallish garden *(BB)*

Dell Quay [SU8302]
Crown & Anchor [off A286 S of Chichester]: Modernised 15th-c pub in splendid spot overlooking Chichester Harbour on site of Roman quay, can be packed at wknds; well kept Courage Best and Directors and Theakstons XB, cheery smartly dressed staff, food all day from sandwiches up esp plenty of fresh local fish (can be a wait); marina views from garden and comfortable bow-windowed lounge bar, panelled public bar with unspoilt fireplace (dogs welcome), restaurant *(Dave Braisted, Ann and Colin Hunt, DF, NF, David H T Dimock, BB, Jose Boyer)*

Donnington [SU8502]
Blacksmiths Arms [Left off A27 on to A286 signed Selsey, almost immediate left on to B2201]: Reworked with minimalist décor and rather upmarket food from new kitchen, real ales such as Greene King Abbot, Buckland Bitter and Winchester Old Cathedral, friendly service; big garden with play area, plenty of picnic-sets, and a summer dining marquee and barbecues *(Laura Wilson, Esther and John Sprinkle, Ian Rankin, LYM)*

Duncton [SU9617]
☆ *Cricketers* [set back from A285]: Charming country pub taken over by friendly new landlord, open-plan bar with standing timbers, big inglenook log fire, a good mix of furnishings inc cushioned settles, wildlife pictures, pleasant dining room (children allowed here) down a couple of steps, well kept ales such as Archers Golden and Youngs, good choice of wines by the glass; idyllic garden behind with picnic-sets and attractive arbour, skittle alley, rope swing *(Ann and Colin Hunt, Nigel and Olga Wikeley, A R Hawkins, Sheila Rowell, Geoffrey Johns, LYM, Bruce Bird, David H T Dimock)*

Eartham [SU9409]
George [signed off A285 Chichester—Petworth, from Fontwell off A27, from Slindon off A29]: Big popular pub smartly refurbished in light

wood, comfortable lounge, attractive pubbier public bar with games, old farm tools and photographs, popular food from baguettes and baked potatoes to fish, steaks and interesting pies, well kept Gales Best, Butser, HSB, and maybe a guest beer, log fire, cheerful service, no smoking restaurant; piped music; children welcome in eating areas, pretty garden and surroundings, open all day summer wknds *(LYM, Ann and Colin Hunt, Mrs Jill Silversides, Barry Brown)*

Easebourne [SU8922]

Olde White Horse [off A272 just NE of Midhurst]: Cosy pub pleasantly refurbished under new licensees, large mainly bare-boards bar with several distinct areas inc fireside armchairs and small no smoking dining area, Greene King IPA, Abbot and Old Speckled Hen, sensibly priced bar food inc speciality sandwiches and Thurs OAP lunch; tables on back grass and in courtyard *(E M and H P N Steinitz, LYM, Tony and Wendy Hobden)*

East Ashling [SU8207]

Horse & Groom : Good popular food and friendly service in relaxing pub with particularly good value real ales; some tables outside *(P R and S A White, Ann and Colin Hunt)*

East Dean [SU9012]

☆ *Hurdlemakers* [signed off A286 and A285 N of Chichester – OS Sheet 197 map ref 904129]: Unpretentious village pub with good value generous food in softly lit L-shaped bar, well kept ales such as Adnams, Badger and Wadworths, friendly efficient staff, a helpful welcome for wet walkers and children; comfortable bedrooms, self-serve breakfast, charming spot on South Downs Way by peaceful green of quiet village, with rustic seats and swing in pretty walled garden *(Ann and Colin Hunt, LYM)*

East Lavant [SU8608]

☆ *Royal Oak* [signed off A286 N of Chichester; Pook Lane]: Peaceful dining pub with well cooked restauranty food, well kept Badger ales, country wines, friendly service, plain furnishings, rugs on bare boards and flooring tiles, two open fires and a woodburner, racing prints; attractively planted gardens inc secluded terrace with bookable tables, good walks; cl Sun pm and Mon *(Ann and Colin Hunt, Mrs Angela Bromley-Martin, John Davis, Debora Rolph, LYM)*

East Preston [TQ0702]

Fletcher Arms [opp stn]: Thriving family pub with half a dozen well kept ales such as Adnams Broadside, Fullers London Pride and Ringwood Best, good bar food (not Sun evening), friendly atmosphere, some unusual bric-a-brac, local photographs, lots of events; big well kept garden with pets corner, play area and barbecues *(Bruce Bird, Tony Hobden)*

Elsted [SU8119]

Elsted Inn [Elsted Marsh]: Unpretentious country pub with new licensees (who took over too recently for us to give a firm rating), cheery buzz in two small bars, nice country furniture, wooden floors, original shutters, old railway photographs, three log fires, traditional games, well kept ales such as Ballards, Cheriton Pots and Fullers London Pride; lovely enclosed downs-view garden with big terrace and summer barbecues, well appointed adjacent bedroom block *(LYM)*

Eridge Station [TQ5434]

Huntsman: Unpretentious pub with surprisingly good enterprising home-made food, friendly service, well kept Badger K & B beers, some interesting wines, farm cider; also good for walkers and their dogs *(Ken Arthur)*

Fairlight Cove [TQ8712]

Cove Continental [Waites Lane]: Friendly, with good sensibly priced local beers inc Pett Progress, may be freshly cooked whelks on bar *(Glenn and Louise Hamilton)*

Faygate [TQ2134]

Frog & Nightgown [Wimland Rd]: Unchanged single-room country local, relaxed and old-fashioned but clean, comfortable and friendly, with well kept Fullers London Pride, Harveys and a guest beer, good fire, bird prints, sofa and chaise-longue; friendly dog, no food, some live music; seats in big quiet garden, nice scenery *(C and R Bromage, R A Watson)*

Felpham [SZ9599]

Thatched House [Limmer Lane]: Local with sensibly priced good home-made food, well kept Gales, nice service, pool in public bar, pleasant smaller lounge *(R T and J C Moggridge)*

Fernhurst [SU9028]

☆ *Red Lion* [The Green; off A286, 3 miles S of Haslemere]: Heavy-beamed old pub tucked quietly away by green nr church, friendly staff, good value food inc interesting specials, attractive layout and furnishings, well kept real ales from local breweries, good wines, no smoking area, good relaxed atmosphere; children welcome, pretty garden *(Graham Godden, BB)*

Ferring [TQ0902]

Tudor Close [Ferringham Lane, S Ferring]: Thatched former barn, imposing intricately carved fireplace, ornate lamp stands, high rafters, no smoking gallery dining area, good choice of enjoyable reasonably priced home-made food (not Sun evening or Mon), well kept Courage, Gales BB and Wadworths 6X, good-natured helpful service, no piped music; peaceful seats outside *(Michael and Ann Cole)*

Findon [TQ1208]

☆ *Gun* [High St]: Civilised low-beamed village pub, recently renovated, large pine-floored part no smoking dining area, traditional main bar, good attractively presented food from lunchtime sandwiches to modern light and main dishes, quick service, well kept ales such as Courage Directors, Fullers London Pride, Gales HSB, Harveys Best and Badger K & B; attractive sheltered lawn, pretty village in horse-training country below Cissbury Ring *(Tony Hobden, Avril Burton, LYM)*

Fishbourne [SU8404]

Bulls Head [Fishbourne Rd (A259 Chichester—Emsworth)]: Interesting and relaxing old building with fair-sized main bar, full Gales range kept well, unusual guest beers, friendly efficient service, good varied main courses often using local produce (not Sun evening), log fires, no smoking area, children's area, restaurant, fine new downstairs lavatories; skittle alley, boules pitch *(Ann and Colin Hunt, J A Snell, Mrs Jane Basso)*

☆ **Woolpack** [Fishbourne Rd W; just off A27 Chichester—Emsworth]: Big comfortably refurbished open-plan pub with enthusiastic friendly landlord, a nice variety of seats inc settees, smart dining and no smoking area, good thai food, well kept Adnams Best, Fullers London Pride, Greene King IPA, Youngs Bitter and Special and guest microbrews; dogs welcome, big garden with barbecues and spit-roasts, various events inc live music *(J A Snell, Ann and Colin Hunt, Tony and Wendy Hobden, Bruce Bird, Keith and Katy Stevens)*

Fittleworth [TQ0118]

☆ **Swan** [Lower St]: Prettily placed 14th-c inn with big inglenook log fire in unpretentious low-beamed lounge, good home-made food in attractive panelled side room with landscapes by Constable's deservedly less-known brother George, well kept Boddingtons, friendly attentive service; piped music, games inc pool in public bar; well spaced tables on big sheltered back lawn, good walks nearby; children in eating area, comfortable bedrooms, open all day Thurs-Sat *(LYM, Brian Turner, R G Glover, Julie and Bill Ryan, Mrs M Alderton)*

Fletching [TQ4223]

☆ **Rose & Crown** [High St]: Well run unpretentious 16th-c village pub locally popular for good home-made food with fresh veg in bar and small restaurant, friendly attentive service, real ales, beams, inglenooks and log fires, tables in pretty garden *(Comus and Sarah Elliott, RDK)*

Frant [TQ5835]

Abergavenny Arms [A267 S of T Wells]: Large mock-Tudor main-road pub, comfortably well worn, with half a dozen well kept ales such as Hardys & Hansons Classic, wide choice of reasonably priced popular food inc ploughman's, log fire, bar billiards; children welcome *(Val and Alan Green)*

Graffham [SU9217]

Foresters Arms: Big helpings of enjoyable food in friendly smallish traditional two-room country pub, country sports pictures, well kept Gales HSB, big log fire, no music, daily papers and magazines, small pretty no smoking restaurant (can be fully booked); walkers welcome, may be crowded wknds; tables in big garden, bedrooms *(David Cosham)*

☆ **White Horse**: Friendly licensees doing good food in spotless family pub with good South Downs views from conservatory, small dining room, terrace and big garden; good range of well kept ales, log fires, walkers welcome *(Mr and Mrs H Dabinett, John and Pat Horne, Mrs C Powell, J A Snell)*

Halland [TQ4916]

Black Lion [A22/B2192]: Decent waitress-served food from wide price range inc children's in bar and restaurant; disabled facilities,

bedrooms with own bathroom *(Abi Benson)*

Halnaker [SU9008]

☆ **Anglesey Arms** [A285 Chichester—Petworth]: Welcoming service and quickly cooked genuine food esp steaks and fish in unpretentious bar with traditional games, well kept real ales, good wines (some direct Spanish imports); simple but smart candlelit dining room with stripped pine and flagstones (children allowed), tables in garden *(Ann and Colin Hunt, John Davis, LYM)*

Hassocks [TQ3015]

Pilgrims Goose [A273 N]: Several welcoming areas, decent food, log fires, good choice of wines; pleasant garden *(Pamela Goodwyn)*

Hastings [TQ8209]

☆ **First In Last Out** [High St, Old Town]: Congenial and chatty beer-drinkers' pub – even the cat is a character, holding his central armchair against all comers; open-plan bar attractively divided by settles, pews forming booths, posts and central raised log fire, good reasonably priced Crofters and Cardinal brewed here with a couple of guest ales, farm cider, friendly landlord, no games or juke box; interesting simple lunchtime food, free Sun cockles; small back terrace, parking nearby difficult *(Peter Meister)*

☆ **Stag** [All Saints St]: Early 17th-c former smugglers' pub among crooked Tudor buildings on high pavement (up a few steps), low beams, bare boards, stout furniture, lots of pictures, no frills; well kept full Shepherd Neame range, plenty of malt whiskies, ex-fireman landlord, friendly long-serving staff, some fascinating stories; wknd bar food inc occasional bargain barbecues, fish suppers Weds, steeply terraced garden behind *(the Didler, Hazel and Michael Duncombe, Kevin Blake)*

Henfield [TQ2116]

White Hart [High St (A281)]: 16th-c village pub with interesting tiled roof, comfortable L-shaped lounge and big no smoking area, lots of panelling, tools hanging from low beams, horsebrasses, paintings, prints, photographs and fresh flowers, log fire, large popular dining area with good choice of home-cooked food inc vegetarian and tempting puddings, hard-working licensees, friendly efficient service, well kept Badger, Harveys Best and Shepherd Neame; children welcome, garden with terrace and play area *(Jenny and Brian Seller, Ron Shelton)*

Hermitage [SU7505]

☆ **Sussex Brewery** [A259, by Thorney Island turn]: Thriving stripped-brick bar with sawdust and bare boards, immense log fire and flagstoned alcove (this bit food-free Fri/Sat night), well kept Badger and other real ales, good food choice inc local fish, cheerful young staff, no smoking red plush dining room up a few steps, no machines or piped music; can get crowded; small walled garden, open all day Sat *(Ann and Colin Hunt)*

Herstmonceux [TQ6312]

Welcome Stranger [Church Rd]: Unspoilt single-room pub in same family for nearly a century, well kept Harveys Bitter and Old and a guest beer from small serving hatch; cl wkdy lunchtimes *(the Didler, Phil and Sally Gorton)*

Heyshott [SU8918]

Unicorn [off A286 S of Midhurst]: Very friendly small country local prettily placed by village green, well kept Ballards Best, Bass and a beer brewed for the pub, good interesting generous bar food, cheerful service even when busy, attractive restaurant; children allowed, reasonable disabled access, garden with barbecue, handy for South Downs Way *(Ann and Colin Hunt, Francis Johnston, J A Snell)*

Hooe [TQ6809]

☆ *Lamb* [A259 E of Pevensey]: Prettily placed Bass Vintage Inn, extensively refurbished with some character and charm, arches and lots of stripped brick and flintwork, one snug area around huge log fire and lots of other seats, big tables, very wide choice of generous popular food inc good sandwiches and baguette range, children's dishes, well kept Bass and Harveys, quick friendly service *(Gill and Keith Croxton)*

Horsted Keynes [TQ3828]

Crown [The Green]: Comfortable congenial local, huge fire, well kept beer, good reasonably priced food, helpful landlord; children welcome, tables outside looking over green *(Michael and Ann Cole, Mrs V Brown, Martin and Jane Wright)*

Green Man [The Green]: Traditional village inn in attractive spot facing green, spotless but not too modernised, with bare boards and hop bines, well kept Greene King IPA and Abbot and Harveys Best, good value generous home-made food from ploughman's and baguettes to restaurant dishes, bistro dining room; lots of plastic tables on forecourt, handy for Bluebell Line *(Tony and Wendy Hobden, LM, Gill Waller, Tony Morriss)*

Station Buffet: Traditional buffet bar on Bluebell Line, well kept Harveys Best, good value food inc cornish pasties *(the Didler)*

Ifield [TQ2437]

Plough: Ancient local in pleasant spot nr 13th-c church, well kept Badger beers, traditional food, good atmosphere, friendly staff, comfortably refurbished saloon with lots of brass and wood, games in small public bar; tables out in front, handy for local Barn Theatre *(anon)*

Isfield [TQ4417]

Laughing Fish: Welcoming and simply modernised village local with well kept Greene King IPA and Harveys Best, and Old, good honest home-made lunchtime food (not Sun/Mon); children welcome, tables in small garden with entertaining enclosed play area, right by Lavender Line *(Tony and Wendy Hobden, BB, the Didler, P and L Taylor)*

Jevington [TQ5601]

☆ *Eight Bells*: Busy and well run two-bar pub, wood and tiled floors, wide choice of good value generous home-made food from ploughman's up, friendly service, well kept Adnams Broadside and Harveys Best; piped music; tables under cocktail parasols on front terrace, large attractive downs-view garden, lovely village, outstanding area for walking (walkers welcome), South Downs Way, Weald

Way and 1066 Trail all nearby *(John Beeken, Pam Adsley, Alan Thomas, Catherine and Richard Preston)*

Kingsfold [TQ1636]

Dog & Duck [A24 Dorking—Horsham, nr A29 junction]: Cosy old country pub under friendly new management, well kept King & Barnes ales, good value nicely presented food inc good sandwiches and popular lunches, attentive service, open fires *(R A Watson)*

Wise Old Owl [A24 Dorking—Horsham, nr A29 junction]: 1930s pub well reworked as Vintage Inn, decent food and wines, Bass, daily papers, friendly staff *(Ian Phillips)*

Kirdford [TQ0126]

Half Moon [opp church, off A272 Petworth—Billingshurst]: Prettily set 17th-c tile-hung cottage, a main entry highly praised for its fresh fish in previous editions, but taken over summer 2000 and turned into a (good) thai restaurant; simple partly quarry-tiled bars, open fire in beamed eating area, tables in pretty back garden and out in front *(Cathy Robinson, LYM, Mike Gorton, John and Diana Niblett, Marion Turner)*

Lavant [SU8508]

Earl of March [A286, Mid Lavant]: Roomy village pub very popular lunchtime for cheap generous food from sandwiches up, well kept Bass, Cottage Golden Arrow, Ringwood Old Thumper and changing guest beers from small breweries, Weston's Old Rosie cider, no smoking area by servery, naval memorabilia, bric-a-brac and prints, games and puzzles, no piped music; children and dogs welcome, live music Thurs; good views from garden, good local walks *(Lyn and Geoff Hallchurch, Tony and Wendy Hobden, Ann and Colin Hunt)*

Hunters [Midhurst Rd (A286)]: Roomy and comfortable, nicely divided into separate areas, with wide choice of attractively presented and reasonably priced bar food inc some exotic dishes, good service, well kept beer, lots to look at, pleasant restaurant; large pretty garden, bedrooms *(Prof S Barnett, Ann and Colin Hunt)*

Lewes [TQ4110]

Black Horse [Western Rd]: Nice two-bar local with well kept Harveys and other ales such as Brakspears, Fullers and Wadworths 6X, bar food, friendly service *(the Didler)*

Brewers Arms [High St]: Smartly kept pub dating from 1540, back lounge bar, usual food inc good value cooked lunches, well kept Harveys and a guest beer, games room, list of landlords since 1744 in public bar *(the Didler, Tony and Wendy Hobden)*

John Harvey [Harveys Brewery, Cliffe High St]: New tap adjoining Harveys brewery, all their beers tapped from the cask kept perfectly, nice lunchtime snacks, interestingly different crisps; good upstairs restaurant, innovative without being pretentious *(Anne and Tim Locke)*

☆ *Lewes Arms* [Castle Ditch Lane/Mount Pl – tucked behind castle ruins]: Charming unpretentious corner local built into castle mound, small front bar with larger lounge and eating area off, particularly well kept Harveys and Greene King Abbot, good orange juice, very reasonably priced simple but unusual lunchtime food, friendly service, daily papers, local pictures, no music – great place for conversation; comically small garden, so people migrate to pavement and street *(John Beeken, Anne and Tim Locke)*

Rainbow [High St]: Comfortable softly lit lounge with decent food, well kept Flowers and Wadworths 6X, friendly service, daily papers and magazines, attractive terrace; trendy spot for young people evenings, sometimes with bouncers *(Anne and Tim Locke)*

Lindfield [TQ3425]

☆ *Bent Arms* [High St]: New licensees doing decent food, antique and art deco furnishings and stained glass, good choice of well kept ales, farm cider, prompt friendly service, children in restaurant and eating area; back flower garden, bedrooms *(LYM, Klaus and Elizabeth Leist)*

Litlington [TQ5201]

☆ *Plough & Harrow* [between A27 Lewes—Polegate and A259 E of Seaford]: Spotless and attractively extended flint pub doing well under new landlord, cosy beamed front bar and dining area done up as railway dining car (children allowed here), well kept Badger IPA, Best and Tanglefoot, decent wines by the glass, good home cooking; back lawn with children's bar, aviary and pretty views; has had live music Fri *(John Beeken, S J Barney, LYM)*

Littlehampton [TQ0202]

☆ *Arun View* [Wharf Rd; W towards Chichester, opp railway stn]: Roomy and comfortable 18th-c inn in lovely spot right on harbour with river directly below windows, well kept Boddingtons and other ales much appreciated by locals, wide choice of reasonably priced well cooked bar food from fresh sandwiches to good fish, diligent friendly service, restaurant strong on local fish (wise to book), flower-filled terrace overlooking busy waterway; summer barbecues evenings and wknds; bright good value bedrooms *(Miss J F Reay, John Davis, Hazel and Michael Duncombe, A H Ross)*

Dew Drop [Wick St]: Pleasant two-bar local with well kept Gales Best and HSB and a guest such as Ringwood XXXX Porter, lots of fruit wines, friendly landlady *(Jonathan Smith)*

Littleworth [TQ1920]

☆ *Windmill* [pub sign on B2135; village signed off A272 southbound, W of Cowfold]: Small spotless local with log fires in compact but cosy beamed lounge and panelled flagstoned public bar; simple but good bar food (not Sun eve winter) inc interesting specials, well kept Badger beers, welcoming helpful landlord (can arrange monastery tours), good service, bric-a-brac large and small inside and out, darts, dominoes, cards and bar billiards; no music; children welcome, peaceful and attractive side garden *(Bruce Bird)*

Lodsworth [SU9223]

Hollist Arms [off A272 Midhurst—Petworth]: Cheerful recently reworked pub welcoming children throughout, well kept real ales, enjoyable food from good value generous baguettes up; nice garden, attractive village spot

(Ann and Colin Hunt, J Hale)

Lower Beeding [TQ2225]

Crabtree [Brighton Rd]: 16th-c pub with fine inglenook log fire in beamed Belloc bar, well kept Badger beers inc K&B, usual food *(LYM, Commander H S Taylor, Mr and Mrs Thomas, G T Brewster)*

Loxwood [TQ0431]

Onslow Arms [B2133 NW of Billingshurst]: Well refurbished local with lively young staff, well kept Badger K & B ales, good house wines, lovely old fireplaces, big helpings of plain food (service can be slow), take-away pizzas; picnic-sets in garden sloping to river and nearby newly restored Wey & Arun canal, good walks and boat trips *(Bruce Bird, Tony and Wendy Hobden)*

Marehill [TQ0618]

White Horse [A283 E of Pulborough]: Fullers London Pride, Greene King and Lancing ales, good ample food from triple-decker sandwiches to full meals, two open fires; tables in garden, handy for RSPB Pulborough Brooks reserve *(Ron Shelton, B and F A Hannam)*

Mayfield [TQ5827]

Carpenters Arms [Fletching St]: Comfortably unpretentious local, pleasant décor and atmosphere, wide choice of food from sandwiches to fresh-grilled fish, well kept Harveys, good landlord, traditional games, no music *(Colin and Janet Roe)*

☆ *Middle House* [High St]: Handsome 16th-c timbered inn in pretty village, L-shaped beamed locals' bar with massive fireplace, well kept Fullers London Pride, Greene King Abbot, Harveys Best and a guest beer such as Old Forge Petts Progress, local cider, decent wines, quiet lounge with leather chesterfields around log fire in ornate carved fireplace, generous enjoyable food from home-made sausages and mash to three-course Weds jazz menu, panelled no smoking restaurant, friendly service; piped music; afternoon tea in terraced back garden with lovely views, slide and play house; children welcome, open all day *(Susan and John Douglas, R M Warner, Mike and Heather Watson, Dave Braisted, LYM, David and Betty Gittins, Sue White, R J Walden)*

☆ *Rose & Crown* [Fletching St]: Pretty weather-boarded old inn with wide food choice from lunchtime toasties through well priced specials to tuna, steak and good puddings, cosy little low-beamed front rooms, big inglenook, well kept Greene King Abbot and Old Speckled Hen and Harveys Best, maybe home-made elderflower cordial, friendly staff, shove-ha'penny; piped music; children welcome, attractive bedrooms, tables outside; open all day Sat *(LYM, J Graveling)*

Midhurst [SU8821]

Wheatsheaf [Wool Lane/A272]: Attractive and relaxing low-beamed and timbered 16th-c local with good value generous food inc very good sandwich choice, very friendly staff, well kept Ballards Old Ale and King & Barnes beers; open all day *(Ann and Colin Hunt)*

Newick [TQ4121]

☆ *Bull* [A272 Uckfield—Haywards Heath]:

Attractive old rambling pub, welcoming, comfortable and peaceful for a midweek lunch, lots of beams and character, good value generous food inc interesting cooking, fresh Newhaven fish and OAP lunches in sizeable eating area, inglenook log fires, welcoming attentive service, well kept ales such as Courage Directors, Harveys, Marstons Pedigree and Theakstons; no music, booking advised wknds *(BB, RDK)*

Nutley [TQ4426]

William IV [Fords Green (A22)]: Roomy pub with friendly helpful young staff, generous cheap food, well kept beer; garden with play area *(Ken Arthur)*

Partridge Green [TQ1919]

Green Man [Jolesfield]: Good well presented food with Mediterranean influence inc unusual tapas-style starters in bar and restaurant, good-sized helpings, cheerful and helpful young staff *(Avril Burton, R D Henshaw)*

Patching [TQ0806]

Horse & Groom [former A27 Worthing—Arundel]: Large and attractive family pub, welcoming service, open fire, well kept Badger beers inc seasonal, good value restaurant with imaginative choice, good fresh veg, succulent steaks and children's menu; good garden *(Tony and Wendy Hobden, Bruce Bird)*

Pett [TQ8713]

Royal Oak: Well run friendly pub (remembered rather surprisingly by some readers as a Temperance Inn), roomy bars, well kept real ales, good generous well presented food in separate dining area *(Lucien, Gill Waller, Tony Morriss)*

Petworth [SU9721]

☆ *Well Diggers* [Low Heath; A283 towards Pulborough]: Picturesquely cluttered low-ceilinged stripped stone bar almost a museum of the rural 1920s, long tables in stylishly simple dining room, very good if not cheap food esp fish using fresh ingredients, friendly landlord, well kept Ballards and Youngs, decent wines, no music or machines; plenty of tables on attractive lawns and terraces, lovely views *(Patrick Hall, LYM)*

Playden [TQ9121]

Peace & Plenty [A268/B2082]: Unpretentious pub with woodburner in big inglenook, food all day in two dining areas, well kept Greene King IPA, Abbot and Triumph, children allowed; tables in pretty garden (some traffic noise), open all day *(Keith and Chris O'Neill, Karen Eliot, Mr and Mrs J French, LYM)*

Poynings [TQ2612]

Royal Oak [The Street]: Well kept Courage Directors, Greene King Old Speckled Hen and Harveys, decent generous food inc fish (may be a wait even for sandwiches), large beamed bar around central servery, no smoking area, fox masks and woodburner; big attractive garden with barbecue and summer marquee *(Simon Collett-Jones, Ian Phillips)*

Pulborough [TQ0518]

Oddfellows Arms [Lower St]: 17th-c, with stripped stonework, flagstones and low beams, Badger K&B, Flowers and Fullers London

Pride, generous freshly made straightforward food, open fire dividing off public area with darts and bar billiards; open all day Tues-Sat, garden with play area *(Tony and Wendy Hobden)*

Ringmer [TQ4412]

☆ *Cock* [Uckfield Rd – blocked-off section of rd off A26 N of village turn-off]: Very welcoming country pub, heavy 16th-c beams and flagstones in main bar with big inglenook log fire, pleasant modernised rooms off inc no smoking lounge, back restaurant, well kept Harveys Best and a seasonal beer, Fullers London Pride and a guest such as Rother Valley, huge blackboard choice of enjoyable reasonably priced food, good service, lovely flower arrangements; children allowed in overflow eating area; quiet piped music; tables on small terrace and in big sloping fairy-lit garden with shrubs, fruit trees and lots of spring flowers *(Michael and Ann Cole, Martin and Jane Wright, Lucien, LYM, Mr and Mrs J French, John Davis, Tony and Wendy Hobden)*

Ripe [TQ5010]

☆ *Lamb* [signed off A22 Uckfield—Hailsham, or off A27 Lewes—Polegate via Chalvington; Church Lane]: Interestingly furnished partly panelled rooms around central servery, masses of attractive antique prints and pictures, nostalgic song-sheet covers, automotive memorabilia, Victorian pin-ups in gents'; wide choice of generous sound food inc fish and children's, friendly courteous landlady, changing well kept ales such as Bass, Fullers London Pride, Harveys and Rother Valley Spirit Level, good range of reasonably priced wines, several open fires; pool room, TV; pleasant sheltered back garden with play area and barbecues *(BB, John Beeken, Kevin Thorpe)*

Robertsbridge [TQ7323]

Ostrich [Station Rd]: Well refurbished, with enjoyable food, Badger K&B, Harveys BB and guest beers, games room; tables in attractive garden, bedrooms *(the Didler)*

Rudgwick [TQ0833]

Kings Head [Church St]: Attractively refurbished local with wide choice of standard lunchtime food, good separate evening Thai restaurant, well kept Fullers London Pride, Harveys, King & Barnes and Wadworths 6X; by fine old church in pretty village *(Stephen S Goodchild)*

Rusper [TQ2037]

Star [off A264 S of Crawley]: Beamed coaching inn, interesting décor and pleasant atmosphere, friendly service, good range of real ales, good well priced food, open fires *(R A Watson)*

Rye [TQ9220]

Olde Standard [High St]: Welcoming and interesting cosy local with lots of beams and stripped brick, well kept beers inc one from local Old Forge, good value generous food, darts, log-effect gas fire; piped music; open all day *(Kevin Thorpe, Alan Thomas)*

Union [East St]: Nice old pub with lots of Civil War memorabilia inc weaponry, wide choice of good home-cooked food, real ale, good wines, children welcome *(Kevin Thorpe)*

Ypres Castle [Gun Garden; steps up from A259, or down past Ypres Tower]: New landlord for this traditional straightforward local with its simple no smoking dining room, several well kept ales, home-made food inc local fish, traditional games; may be piped music; children welcome, fine views from picnic-sets on sizeable lawn, open all day *(Gill Waller, Tony Morriss, Kevin Thorpe, John Davis, LYM)*

Rye Harbour [TQ9220]

Inkerman Arms: Friendly and cosy unpretentious local nr nature reserve, good food inc fresh local fish and old-fashioned puddings, well kept Whitbreads-related ales and one from local microbrewery, interesting painted frieze; boules *(Gill Waller, Tony Morriss)*

Seaford [TV4898]

Old Boot [off High St]: Well kept beer, friendly service, pleasant décor, relaxing atmosphere, good food *(Bill and Rachael Gallagher)*

Selham [SU9320]

Three Moles: Small old-fashioned pub tucked away in woodland village, quietly relaxing atmosphere, friendly landlady, well kept Badger K&B, Ballards Mild, Skinners Betty Stogs and guest beers, plenty of board games; no food, monthly singsongs; nice walks, open all day wknds *(Roger and Debbie Stamp, Bruce Bird, Sue Demont, Tim Barrow)*

Selmeston [TQ5006]

Barley Mow [A27 Eastbourne—Lewes]: Homely pub recently taken over by friendly and experienced licensees of nearby Eight Bells, Jevington; good value interesting home-made food in bar and restaurant, good house wine, well kept beer; small garden *(Andy Sinden, Louise Harrington)*

Shoreham-by-Sea [TQ2105]

☆ *Red Lion* [Upper Shoreham Rd, opp church]: Modest dim-lit low-beamed and timbered 16th-c pub with settles in snug alcoves, good value well presented food (bacon and onion pudding recommended), changing ales such as Morrells Varsity and Oxford Blue and RCH Pitchfork, decent wines, farm cider, friendly efficient staff, log fire in unusual fireplace, another open fire in no smoking dining room; piped music may obtrude; pretty sheltered garden, good downs views and walks *(Tony and Wendy Hobden, John Davis, John Beeken, Eddie Edwards)*

Shortbridge [TQ4521]

☆ *Peacock* [Piltdown; OS Sheet 198 map ref 450215]: Comfortable and welcoming rebuilt beamed and timbered bar, big inglenook, very generous nicely presented bar food served piping hot inc good vegetarian and fish, well kept Harveys and Wadworths 6X, pleasant service, restaurant; shame about the piped music (they will turn it down), children may be much in evidence; sizeable garden *(Kevin Selby, Lynne Willcock, BB, E A Thwaite, Michael and Ann Cole, RDK)*

Sidlesham [SZ8598]

Anchor [Selsey Rd]: Courage Best and Directors

and Greene King Old Speckled Hen, friendly staff, decent usual food inc wkdy OAP lunches, plenty of tables; nice terrace, handy for wildlife centre, open all day *(Laura Wilson)*

Slindon [SU9708]

Newburgh Arms [School Hill]: Congenial, comfortable and relaxed beamed bar, well cared for furnishings, big log fire, sizeable dining area with rows of tables, enjoyable food inc bargain two-course lunch, interesting specials and nice choice of home-made puddings, well kept Badger Best, lots of country wines, friendly service; piped music; good area for downs walks, pretty hanging baskets in summer *(Tony Scott, Gill and Keith Croxton, Tony Hobden)*

☆ *Spur* [Slindon Common; A29 towards Bognor]: Popular, roomy and attractive 17th-c pub, welcoming atmosphere, two big log fires, pine tables, good choice of interesting good value food changing daily, well kept Courage Directors and Greene King Ruddles, cheerful efficient staff, large elegant restaurant, games room with pool and darts; friendly dogs; children welcome, pretty garden *(John Davis, Ian and Jane Irving, Ann and Colin Hunt, Ken and Angela Smith, Derek Harvey-Piper)*

South Harting [SU7819]

Ship [North Lane (B2146)]: Welcoming unpretentious17th-c local, informal and unspoilt, with dimly lit bar, roaring log fire, old photographs, well kept Mansfield Old Baily, Palmers and Ushers, good wine by the glass, good choice of good value food from sandwiches up at rather close-set tables, unobtrusive piped music, friendly staff and dogs, simpler public bar (dominoes, maybe chestnuts to roast by its log fire); nice setting in pretty village *(Prof S Barnett, Ann and Colin Hunt)*

White Hart [B2146 SE of Petersfield]: Rugs on polished wood, gleaming brasses and copper, interesting old photographs, big log fire, well spaced tables, efficient friendly young staff, well kept ales such as Flowers, Fullers London Pride and Greene King IPA, wide food choice from very generous unusual sandwiches to Sun roasts and interesting blackboard specials, restaurant, separate public bar; well behaved dogs allowed, walkers and children welcome (toys in well integrated games/family room); good garden behind for them too, with spectacular downs views, handy for Uppark *(John Davis, Lyn and Geoff Hallchurch, David and Barbara Davies, Ian Mcintyre)*

Stedham [SU8522]

☆ *Hamilton Arms* [School Lane (off A272)]: Proper English local but decorated with Thai artefacts and run by friendly Thai family, basic pub food but also interesting Thai bar snacks and popular restaurant (cl Mon); pretty hanging baskets, seats out by quiet lane, village shop in car park, good walks nearby *(Barbara Wensworth)*

Steyning [TQ1711]

Chequer [High St]: Timber-framed Tudor pub with labyrinthine bars, good range of well kept Whitbreads-related beers, wide choice of generous usual food from good sandwiches and snacks up, friendly service (normally prompt – if not, check) *(John Davis, Prof S Barnett, J M and P M Carver)*

Stoughton [SU8011]

☆ *Hare & Hounds* [signed off B2146 Petersfield—Emsworth]: Friendly and leisurely airily modernised pub below downs with reliably good home-made food (can take a while) in airy pine-clad bar and restaurant, big open fires, changing well kept ales such as Badger Golden Champion, Bass, Fullers London Pride, Gales HSB, Hop Back GFB and a beer brewed for the pub by Hampshire, back darts room; children in eating areas, tables on pretty front terrace and in back garden; nr Saxon church, good walks nearby *(Brian and Anna Marsden, LYM, Prof S Barnett, Ann and Colin Hunt)*

Sutton [SU9715]

☆ *White Horse* [The Street]: Charming traditional country pub in quiet little hamlet nr Bignor Roman villa, island servery separating bare-boards bar from two-room dining area, simple décor and furnishings, enjoyable food from sandwiches to local game and fish; Brewery on Sea, Courage Directors, Charles Wells Bombardier, Youngs and a guest such as Badger Golden Champion, log fire, friendly staff; tables in garden up behind, good value bedrooms, comfortable and well equipped *(Dave Braisted, John Davis, Mr and Mrs David B Meehan, J Davidson, BB, Mrs M Miln, C L Kauffmann, Bruce Bird)*

Telham [TQ7714]

Black Horse [A2100 Battle—Hastings]: Small low-beamed pub with good varied sensibly priced food, friendly landlord, Shepherd Neame beers, log fires, no piped music, canal maps and plaques; spring folk/jazz festival *(Lucien)*

Thakeham [TQ1017]

White Lion [off B2139 N of Storrington; The Street]: This popular 16th-c two-bar village local closed in late 2000, with plans for conversion to a private house *(LYM)*

Turners Hill [TQ3435]

Crown [East St]: Spacious dining pub, different levels (one with pitched rafters), good choice inc Sun lunch, log fire, pleasant décor with pictures etc, well kept ales such as Greene King Old Speckled Hen and Tetleys, decent wines, helpful service, soft piped music, tables outside, pleasant valley views from back garden; children welcome; two bedrooms *(BB, RDK)*

Upper Beeding [TQ1910]

Rising Sun [Shoreham Rd (A2037)]: Homely old pub just off South Downs Way, well laid out inside, with cosy side rooms, character nooks and crannies and soft lighting; good value home-made food from good ploughman's to imaginative dishes, well kept Boddingtons, Ind Coope Burton, Flowers, Fullers London Pride and Marstons Pedigree, welcoming staff, unobtrusive piped music, pleasant garden *(John Beeken)*

Wadhurst [TQ6131]

☆ *Best Beech* [Mayfield Lane (B2100 a mile W)]: Well run dining pub, pleasant dim-lit bar on left with wall seats, quiet but individual décor and

coal fire, cosy eating area with lots of pictures and china on right, well done fresh bar food (not Sun evening) from sandwiches to particularly good steaks, well kept Harveys and other ales, quick service; back restaurant, good value bedrooms, good breakfast *(BB)*

Greyhound [B2099]: Neatly kept village pub with current licensees doing enjoyable home-made food and set Sun lunch in restaurant or pleasant beamed bar with big inglenook log fire, well kept Bass, Greene King Old Speckled Hen, Harveys and Youngs Special, decent wines by the glass, games area with bar billiards, no piped music; tables in well kept and attractive sheltered bar garden; bedrooms *(BB, Neil Rose, R Hale)*

Warbleton [TQ6018]

☆ *Warbil in Tun*: Welcoming and pretty extended dining pub with good value food esp meat (helpful ex-butcher landlord), good puddings, well kept reasonably priced Harveys Best, good coffee, relaxed civilised atmosphere, beams and red plush, huge log fireplace, no music; tables on roadside green, attractive tucked-away village *(Michael and Ann Cole)*

Washington [TQ1212]

Frankland Arms [just off A24 Horsham—Worthing]: Whitbreads Wayside Inn, roomy and welcoming, with wide choice of food all day from warm baguettes to good puddings, well kept Flowers Original, Fullers London Pride and Wadworths 6X, decent wine choice, log fires, pleasant prompt service; big bar and smaller comfortable dining area, games area with pool and darts, disabled facilities; tables in neat garden, quiet spot yet busy wknds *(John Davis, John Beeken)*

West Chiltington [TQ0918]

☆ *Elephant & Castle* [off A283 or B2139 E of Pulborough; Church St]: Open-plan local with plenty of character, stripped stone, dark wood furniture, turkey carpet and flagstones, open fire, good value generous freshly made straightforward food plus some South African dishes, well kept Badger ales, fresh flowers, friendly helpful South African landlord, no music; public bar with darts, children welcome, good terraced garden with play area, aviary, ducks and geese, behind ancient church in attractive village *(BB, Ian Wilson, Mr and Mrs Thomas, Martin and Penny Fletcher)*

☆ *Five Bells* [Smock Alley, off B2139 SE]: Well kept ales inc a Mild from Badger or Harveys and four guests from small breweries, annual beer festival, farm cider, enthusiastic welcoming licensees, good value fresh food (not Sun evening), log fire, beams and panelling, old photographs, unusual brass bric-a-brac, distinctive conservatory dining room; no piped music, peaceful garden with terrace *(Bruce Bird, Peter D B Harding, Nicholas Pope)*

West Dean [SU8512]

Selsey Arms [A286 Midhurst—Chichester]: Smart and roomy no smoking dining lounge with added tables, wide range of tasty good value food from simple bar snacks to generous restauranty main dishes, well kept Courage Best, Marstons Pedigree and Goodwood, good value wine, welcoming newish licensees, good cheerful service, log fire, lots of horse-racing pictures and memorabilia, public bar with games room *(Ann and Colin Hunt, Tony and Wendy Hobden)*

West Hoathly [TQ3632]

☆ *Cat* [signed from A22 and B2028 S of E Grinstead; North Lane]: Relaxing and polished pub/restaurant, fresh flowers and candles, beams and panelling, two roaring log fires, well kept Harveys Best and Hardy Royal Oak, decent wines, home-made food from upmarket sandwiches up, smiling service; piped classical music, no children, dogs or muddy boots; tables out on small terrace with quiet view of church *(Dr D E Granger, Derek Harvey-Piper, Martin and Karen Wake, John Davis, LYM, John Fahy, Alan Cowell)*

Vinols Cross Inn [Hammingden Lane/North Lane; towards Sharpthorne]: Down-to-earth pub with several blackboards of good straightforward food from prodigious sandwiches up, well kept Greene King IPA and Abbot, Harveys and Wadworths 6X, good cheery service, some interesting furniture; also sells English cheeses *(Jim Bush, Jenny and Brian Seller)*

West Itchenor [SU8001]

Ship [The Street]: Large panelled pub in good spot nr Chichester Harbour, good long walk from W Wittering; wide range of beautifully presented food in bar and restaurant, well kept Courage Directors, Greene King Old Speckled Hen and a beer brewed for the pub, two roaring fires, lots of bric-a-brac inc many chamber-pots, seats made from old boat, children in eating area, tables outside; said to be able to get supplies for yachtsmen (nearest shop is two miles away) *(Glenn and Louise Hamilton)*

West Wittering [SZ8099]

☆ *Lamb* [Chichester Rd; B2179/A286 towards Birdham]: 18th-c country pub under cheerful new management, several rooms neatly knocked through with tidy furnishings, rugs on tiles, blazing fire, well kept Badger ales with Gribble guests, decent wines, wide choice of reasonably priced food from separate servery, quick service, good Sun bar nibbles; dogs on leads allowed, tables out in front and in small sheltered back garden – good for children, with outside salad bar on fine days; busy in summer *(Ann and Colin Hunt, P R and S A White, J A Snell, BKA, BB, Christine and Geoff Butler)*

Winchelsea [TQ9017]

☆ *New Inn* [German St; just off A259]: Variety of solid comfortable furnishings in bustling rambling beamed rooms, Georgian décor, some emphasis on food inc good fresh fish (sandwiches too), well kept Greene King IPA and Abbot and Harveys, decent wines and malt whiskies, quick friendly service, log fire; separate public bar with darts, children in eating area, pretty bedrooms (some sharing bathrooms), delightful setting *(J H Bell, LYM, Keith and Janet Morris)*

Wisborough Green [TQ0526]

Cricketers Arms [Loxwood Rd, just off A272

Billingshurst—Petworth]: Attractive open-plan old local under new management from summer 2000, very low beams, bare boards and timbering, two big woodburners, pleasant mix of country furniture, five or six real ales, robust food from sandwiches up, no smoking stripped brick dining area on left, cheerful service; piped music may obtrude; tables out on terrace and across lane from green *(Stephen S Goodchild, Lucien, LYM)*

Three Crowns [Billingshurst Rd (A272)]: Big clean and polished open-plan bar stretching into dining room, stripped bricks and beams, wide choice of good usual bar food from sandwiches, baguettes and big ploughman's up inc children's and good value meals for smaller appetites, generous hot dishes and popular Sun lunch, well kept ales such as Ballards, quick attentive service, no smoking restaurant, games room; sizeable back garden *(DWAJ, Tony and Wendy Hobden)*

Withyham [TQ4935]

☆ *Dorset Arms* [B2110]: Bustling 16th-c pub in pleasant countryside, genuine atmosphere inc sturdy tables and simple country seats on wide oak floorboards, good log fire in Tudor fireplace, well kept Harveys PA, Best and Mild, decent wines inc local ones; best to book for landlady's good home cooking, pretty no smoking restaurant; darts, dominoes, shove-ha'penny, cribbage, fruit machine, piped music; white tables on brick terrace by small green *(Comus and Sarah Elliott, DWAJ, Robert Gartery, G T Brewster, Peter and Joan Elbra, LYM, Mr and Mrs D D Collins)*

Woodmancote [SU7707]

Woodmancote Arms [the one nr Emsworth]: Comfortable and relaxing village pub with new licensees, enjoyable food from bar snacks (log fire in eating area) to meals in pretty and unpretentious restaurant, well kept Courage Directors, decent wines; large games room for pool and darts *(Tony and Marion Spillard, Ann and Colin Hunt)*

Worthing [TQ1403]

Castle Tavern [Newland Rd]: Revived as free house under friendly new licensees, well kept Harveys Best, Hop Back GFB and Summer Lightning, Shepherd Neame Bishops Finger and a couple of unusual guest beers such as Arundel, fff, Skinners or Wolf, good local atmosphere, good choice of attractively priced home-made food inc Sun roasts (not Sun/Mon evenings); live music Mon and Sat, open all day Fri/Sat *(Bruce Bird, Tony and Wendy Hobden)*

Coach & Horses [Arundel Rd, Clapham (A27 W)]: Spotless 17th-c coaching inn with friendly new licensees, lots of brass and china, real fire, good bar food (can order ahead by phone) in pleasant well furnished extended dining area, cosy second back bar, well kept Fullers London Pride, Youngs Special and guests such as Adnams Best and Broadside, Greene King Abbot or Timothy Taylors Landlord, decent coffee; piped music; children welcome, Tues quiz night, occasional live music, well kept garden with lots of tables *(Tony and Wendy Hobden, Bruce Bird)*

George & Dragon [High St, Old Tarring]: Good lunchtime food, well kept Hop Back Summer Lightning and guest beers and friendly efficient service in airy lounge of extended 17th-c pub, beams and panelling, bric-a-brac, brass platters and old photographs, no music, no smoking dining area; dogs allowed (not in attractive garden) *(Bruce Bird, Harvey and Bramley)*

Hare & Hounds [Portland Rd, just N of Marks & Spencer]: Friendly bustling extended pub with well kept ales such as Flowers, Fullers London Pride, Greene King Old Speckled Hen, Marstons Pedigree and Youngs from central brass and oak bar, good choice of reasonably priced straightforward food (not Fri-Sun evenings) from sandwiches up, wide range of customers inc plenty of regulars, pleasant staff, tented courtyard, occasional jazz; no car park but three multi-storeys nearby *(Val and Alan Green, Tony and Wendy Hobden)*

Selden Arms [Lyndhurst Rd, between Safeway and hospital]: Friendly Northern licensees concentrating on well kept changing beer range such as Ballards, Ringwood and Wolf, lunchtime bar food and wknd specials, real fire; open all day *(Bruce Bird)*

Vine [High St, W Tarring]: Neatly kept friendly local in nice spot away from the day trippers, current landlord doing good home-made food (not Sun evening), well kept Badger beers inc Gribble brews with a guest such as Hop Back Summer Lightning, farm cider; occasional live music; tables in back courtyard *(Bruce Bird, R T and J C Moggridge)*

Yapton [SU9704]

Lamb [Bilsham Rd (B2132)]: Child-friendly olde-worlde pub with good friendly service, Greene King Abbot, Harveys Best and a guest such as Brains SA, log fire, good value food with plenty of veg inc Sun roast, attractive no smoking dining room with fine collection of aircraft or railway decorative plates; plenty of picnic-sets in big garden with chickens, ducks (eggs for sale), goats and wonderful play area *(Miss H Orchard, Tony and Wendy Hobden, Glenn and Gillian Miller)*

Maypole [signed off B2132 Arundel rd; Maypole Lane]: Recently refurbished country pub with well kept Badger K & B and Ruddles, two log fires in cosy lounge, reasonably priced generous food inc Sun roasts, welcoming staff; skittle alley, seats outside, on good circular walk from Buxted *(R T and J C Moggridge, Bruce Bird)*

Stars after the name of a pub show exceptional quality. One star means most people (after reading the report to see just why the star has been won) would think a special trip worth while. Two stars mean that the pub is really outstanding – many that for their particular qualities cannot be bettered.

Warwickshire
(with Birmingham
and West Midlands)

One pub here has the distinction of having featured in every edition of the Guide since it started 20 years ago: the aptly named Crooked House at Himley, a real curiosity. By contrast, four pubs are new to the main entries (or back in these pages after a break of quite a few years). The Falcon at Hatton is an attractively reworked and interesting dining pub, fairly handy for the motorway; the Red Lion at Long Compton is a welcoming all-rounder, with a fine old rambling bar; the lively Garrick in Stratford-upon-Avon fits in well with both the town's age and its theatrical traditions; and the carefully restored Bell in Welford-on-Avon is a rewarding all-rounder. Other places here currently on top form are the Bell at Alderminster (imaginative food in this enthusiastically run dining pub), the stylish and upmarket Fox & Goose at Armscote (its imaginative food earning it a Food Award this year), the handsome old Kings Head at Aston Cantlow (another place climbing into the Food Award category now), the attractive Fox & Hounds at Great Wolford (good all round under its new licensees), the smart Howard Arms at Ilmington (a good dining pub, gaining a Place to Stay Award this year), and the cheerful Green Dragon at Sambourne. For its sense of occasion and good if not cheap food, the Fox & Goose at Armscote gains the title of Warwickshire Dining Pub of the Year. Drinks prices vary widely in the area, being generally very low in and around the great West Midlands conurbation. Outside this area, drinks prices are generally slightly higher than the national average. In the Lucky Dip section at the end of the chapter, pubs showing well this year are the Herons Nest at Knowle, George at Lower Brailes, Butchers Arms at Priors Hardwick, Blue Boar at Temple Grafton, Tilted Wig and Zetland Arms in Warwick and Bulls Head at Wootton Wawen.

ALDERMINSTER SP2348 Map 4
Bell 🍴 ♀

A3400 Oxford—Stratford

The licensees put in a huge effort to keep this comfortably smart dining pub flourishing by putting on lots of parties, food festivals, and classical and light music evenings throughout the year. There's some emphasis on the freshly cooked to order food from an imaginative menu which changes monthly. There might be soup (£3.50), filled baguettes (from £4.25), brie, bacon, garlic and mushroom tart (£4.50), pâté with cumberland sauce (£5.75), fisherman's crêpe with lobster and prawn sauce au gratin (£6.25), potato, leek, mushroom and stilton bake with tomato and sage sauce (£6.95), pie of the week or fishcakes with dill sauce (£8.95), stir-fried spiced duck breast with wilted greens and potato rösti (£10.95) and home-made puddings such as dark chocolate, almond and brandy torte, coffee and walnut cheesecake or blackcurrant sorbet (from £4). The communicating areas of the neatly kept spacious bar have plenty of stripped slatback chairs around wooden tables on the flagstones and wooden floors, little vases of flowers, small landscape prints and swan's-neck brass-and-globe lamps on the cream walls, and a solid fuel stove in a stripped brick inglenook. Two changing real ales might be Greene King Abbot and Ruddles County under light blanket pressure, alongside a good range of wines and champagne by the glass, freshly squeezed juice and cocktails. They have high chairs, and readers with children have felt particularly welcome. A conservatory and terrace overlook the garden and Stour Valley. *(Recommended by John Bowdler, Joan Crane, Eileen White, Dr Alan Sutton, Stuart Turner, L G Owen, Duncan Slater, Basil Minson, Simon G S Morton, John Bramley, Iain R Hewitt, Angela Cerfontyn, Brian Skelcher, Mr and Mrs Hugh Spottiswoode, Moira and John Cole, K H Frostick, Roy Bromell, Catherine and Richard Preston, Jack Clarfelt, Michael and Jeanne Shillington, Roger Braithwaite)*

Free house ~ Licensees Keith and Vanessa Brewer ~ Real ale ~ Bar food ~ Restaurant ~ (01789) 450414 ~ Children welcome ~ Open 12-2.30, 7-11(10.30 Sun) ~ Bedrooms: £25(£35S)(£45B)/£45(£55S)(£60B)

ARMSCOTE SP2444 Map 4
Fox & Goose 🍽

Off A3400 Stratford—Shipston

Warwickshire Dining Pub of the Year

Décor at this stylishly transformed pretty village pub, although quite contemporary, still has a pubby feel, with bright crushed velvet cushions and coverings on wooden pews and stools, big mirrors on the walls (a warm red colour in the small bar, cream in the larger eating area), polished floorboards, some smart curtains, and lots of black and white pictures of animals. A stuffed fox stalks a goose above the dining room's woodburning stove, and there's a log fire in the flagstoned bar. Outside, the garden has an elegant deck area overlooking a big lawn with tables, benches and fruit trees. Service is charming and helpful. Listed on a chalkboard menu, the very good imaginative food might include sandwiches with salad (£4.25), whisky-flavoured gravadlax or smoked goose salad with raspberry dressing (£4.95), saffron risotto cakes on spinach with caramelised tomatoes (£8.95), tuna niçoise (£9.95) and seared monkfish with home-made linguini or chicken stuffed with feta cheese and sun-dried tomatoes with sweet tomato and butter sauce (£10.50), fried calves liver and bacon with bubble and squeak in a red wine jus (£11.50), and puddings such as sticky toffee, rhubarb and apple crumble and lemon tart (£3.95). Well kept Brakspears and a couple of guests such as Hook Norton and Charles Wells Bombardier on handpump, mulled wine in winter, jugs of pimms in the summer, and well chosen wines. Piped jazz. Several of the neighbouring houses boast splendid roses in summer. We have not yet heard from anyone staying in the new bedrooms, but they look really nice (with great bathrooms). *(Recommended by Stuart Turner, Norman and June Williams, Mrs L Price, Robert and Catherine Dunster, E V Walder, E Prince, John Bramley, Lisa Perry, Roger Braithwaite, Michael and Jeanne Shillington)*

Free house ~ Licensee Sue Gray ~ Real ale ~ Bar food ~ Restaurant ~ (01608) 682293 ~ Children in restaurant ~ Open 12-3, 6-11(10.30 Sun); closed 25, 26 Dec, 1 Jan ~ Bedrooms: £40B/£75B

ASTON CANTLOW SP1359 Map 4
Kings Head 🍽

Village signposted just off A3400 NW of Stratford

There's a new food award this year for the very good often inventive food at this carefully restored beautifully timbered black and white Tudor pub. Meals are freshly prepared, from a menu that changes very regularly but which might include soup (£3.45), red onion and goats cheese tart with pesto crust (£4.95), crispy oriental duck salad with sesame and blackberry dressing (£5.45), chicken liver parfait with fig and apple chutney (£5.75), fried pigeon breast with endive and pine nut salad and stilton dressing (£5.95), salmon and leek fishcakes with saffron crème fraîche (£9.45), spiced chick pea fritters with tzatziki and marinated vegetables (£9.25), chicken breast stuffed with wild mushrooms and apricots with tarragon cream sauce (£9.95), grilled venison steak with crushed new potatoes, parsnips and apple with cranberry jus (£10.95), and puddings such as chocolate and butter pudding or caramelised cranberry and orange brûlée (£4.25). The pub is a charming sight, with its wisteria and colourful hanging baskets. Inside, the clean and comfortable village bar on the right is a nice mix of rustic surroundings with a civilised gently upmarket atmosphere, a low beamed ceiling, wooden settles around its massive inglenook log fireplace and flagstones. The chatty quarry-tiled main room has attractive window seats and oak tables. Well kept Greene King Abbot, M&B Brew XI and a couple of guests such as Fullers London Pride and Shepherd Neame Spitfire on handpump, decent wines and piped jazz. The pub is not far from Mary Arden's house in Wilmcote which is well worth a visit. *(Recommended by Mr and Mrs Gordon Turner, Stan and Hazel Allen, John Kane, Peter Meister, C P Scott-Malden, Sue Holland, Dave Webster, Susan and John Douglas, June and Mike Coleman, Alun Howells, David Gregory, Martin Jennings, Joy and Peter Heatherley, Brian and Carole Polhill)*

Whitbreads ~ Lease Paul Hales ~ Real ale ~ Bar food (12-2.30, 7-10(9 Sun)) ~ Restaurant ~ (01789) 488242 ~ Children welcome ~ Open 11-11; 12-10.30 Sun; 11-3, 5.30-11 Mon-Thurs in winter; closed 25 Dec evening

BERKSWELL SP2479 Map 4
Bear

Spencers Lane; village signposted from A452 W of Coventry

This picturesque 16th-c timbered pub is a successful example of the Chef & Brewer formula country pub. The traditional interior has comfortably snug low-beamed areas, alcoves, nooks and crannies as well as panelling, bric-a-brac and prints, piped music, roaring log fires in winter and air conditioning in summer. In one place the heavy timbers show the slope of the catslide eaves. The emphasis is very much on dining. A snack menu includes doorstep sandwiches (from £2.95) and filled rustic rolls or baked potatoes (from £3.85), and various blackboards list a huge range of daily specials such as soup (£2.60), hot chicken liver and bacon salad or seafood paellla (£4.05), moules provençaux (£4.55), beef and Theakstons pie (£5.95), pasta with asparagus (£6.95), fisherman's pie (£7.95), prawn and scallop linguini (£9.05), thai green curry (£9.95), beef stroganoff (£13.25), and puddings such as orange and lemon truffle, baked white chocolate tart or apple and pecan pie (from £2.95). Well kept Courage Directors, Theakstons Best and a couple of guests such as Charles Wells Bombardier and Badger on handpump; decent house wines all served by the glass; piped music. There are tables behind on a tree-sheltered back lawn. It's a shame they shortened its original name, the Bear and Ragged Staff, which referred to the Earl of Warwick. The village church is well worth a visit. *(Recommended by Alun Howells, Brian Skelcher, June and Mike Coleman, Brian and Genie Smart, D P Brown, Peter and Audrey Dowsett, Susan and John Douglas, John Brightley)*

Scottish Courage ~ Managers Nick and Jackie Lancaster ~ Real ale ~ Bar food (11-10 Mon-Sat, 12-9.30 Sun) ~ (01676) 533202 ~ Children in restaurant ~ Open 11-11; 12-10.30 Sun

BIRMINGHAM SP0586 Map 4
Fiddle & Bone

4 Sheepcote Street; opposite National Indoor Arena South car park

Music plays quite a leading role at this remarkable conversion of an airy schoolhouse which was started several years ago by two members of the City of Birmingham Symphony Orchestra when they couldn't find a pub in Birmingham they really liked. There's a cheerful and lively atmosphere, with live bands on the big stage at the end of the lofty main bar every evening and weekend lunchtimes playing jazz, blues, soul, classical, and folk, or there's good piped music at other times. Their website, www.fiddle-bone.co.uk includes a list of forthcoming gigs and festivals. The decorations are fun, with various musical instruments hanging from the ceiling or the walls, and along the bar counter trombones have been ingeniously converted into lights. Spotless varnished light pine tables with cushioned benches form little booths along each side of the bare-boards room, and a staircase in the middle leads down to the restaurant and a flagstoned bar area with a lighter café-bar feel. There are lots of picnic-sets outside here, but you get a better view of the boats on the adjacent canal through the windows of another bar upstairs. Well kept Courage Everards Tiger, Marstons Pedigree, Theakstons Best and a couple of guests such as Adnams or Theakstons Old Peculier under light blanket pressure, and unusual schnapps; efficient helpful staff. Good bar food, with most things available all day, includes sandwiches (from £2.50), filled baked potatoes (£2.95), all day breakfast (£4.75), steak and ale pie, gammon steak or vegetarian lasagne (£5.25) and an eat as much as you like buffet (£5.95). It's close to the Sea Life Centre, and a waterbus stops just outside. *(Recommended by Alan and Hillie Johnson, Ian and Nita Cooper, David Carr, Catherine Pitt, Ian Phillips, Jack Barnwell, Sue and Geoff Price)*

Free house ~ Licensee Ian Davies ~ Real ale ~ Bar food (11(12 Sun)-10) ~ Restaurant ~ (0121) 200 2223 ~ Children in eating area of bar ~ Live music every night and wkend lunchtimes ~ Open 11-11; 12-10.30 Sun

Tap & Spile 🍺 £

Gas St/Brindley Wharf

This nicely placed pub has an authentic wharfside pubby feel. The bar looking out on the revivified Gas Street canal basin has an attractive back-to-basics yet quite cottagey décor, with stripped brickwork, bare boards and reclaimed timber, old pine pews and settles, and lots of prints. Small interconnecting rooms lead off on three levels and are busy but not overcrowded. One has a complete kitchen range. Eight well kept ales on handpump include Adnams, Bass, Batemans XB, Everards Tiger, Fullers London Pride, Greene King Old Speckled Hen, Highgate Mild and Hook Norton Old Hooky; also proper farm cider and fruit wines. Very reasonably priced bar food includes soup (£2.20), filled baguettes (from £2.65, hot from £3.50), fish and chips or steak pie (£4.25), roasted vegetable lasagne, sausage and mash or gammon steak (£4.50), scampi (£4.75) and puddings such as chocolate fudge cake or hot pudding of the day (£2.15); piped music, darts, fruit machine and dominoes. There are some picnic-sets out by the water in summer; no children. *(Recommended by David Carr, Mr and Mrs Nick Kingsley, Dave Braisted, Lawrence Bacon, Jean Scott, Ian Phillips, Tony and Wendy Hobden)*

Unique Pub Co ~ Manager James Forbes ~ Real ale ~ Bar food (12-7.30(5.30 Fri-Sun)) ~ (0121) 632 5602 ~ Open 12-11(10.30 Sun); closed 25, 26 Dec

BRIERLEY HILL SO9187 Map 4

Vine 🍺 £

Delph Road; B4172 between A461 and (nearer) A4100

This warmly welcoming no-nonsense pub is well and truly West Midlands in character, with its friendly down-to-earth landlord and staff. It's known in the Black Country as the Bull & Bladder, from the good stained-glass bull's heads and very approximate bunches of grapes in the front bow windows. It's a popular place, full of local characters, and can get crowded in the warmly welcoming front bar which has wall benches and simple leatherette-topped oak stools; the extended and refurbished snug on the left has solidly built red plush seats, and the back bar has brass chandeliers as well as darts, dominoes and fruit machine. As it's the tap for the next-door Bathams brewery you can expect the Bitter and Mild, and Delph Strong in winter to be in very good condition, and they are very reasonably priced. Simple but good fresh lunchtime snacks are very good value, too: samosas (65p), sandwiches (from £1), pasta bake and salad (£2) and curry, faggots and peas, or steak and kidney pie (£2.50). *(Recommended by the Didler, Theo, Anne and Jane Gaskin, Dave Braisted)*

Bathams ~ Manager Melvyn Wood ~ Real ale ~ Bar food (lunchtimes Mon-Fri only) ~ No credit cards ~ (01384) 78293 ~ Children in eating area of bar and family room ~ Open 12-11; 12-10.30 Sun

COVENTRY SP3379 Map 4
Old Windmill £
Spon Street

Known locally as Ma Brown's after a former landlady, this friendly and unpretentious timber-framed 15th-c inn stands on its original site – unlike the rest of the buildings in the street, which are an interesting collection of evacuee survivors from the blitz. The nicely battered interior is full of character: one of the rambling series of tiny cosy old rooms is little more than the stub of a corridor, another has carved oak seats on flagstones and a woodburner in a fine ancient inglenook fireplace, and another has carpet and more conventionally comfortable seats. There are exposed beams in the uneven ceilings, and a back room preserves some of the equipment used when Ma Brown brewed here. Well kept Banks's, Charles Wells Bombardier, Courage Directors, Greene King Old Speckled Hen, Marstons Pedigree and a frequently changing guest, usually from an independent brewer, all kept under light blanket pressure; fruit machine and juke box. Straightforward good value food passed out straight from the kitchen door includes filled toasties (£1.80), filled baked potatoes (from £1.75), liver and onions, cottage or steak pie (£3.50), gammon steak (£3.75), stuffed peppers (£3.90), and an OAP special (£2.50); part of the dining area is no smoking. The pub is popular with students, extremely busy on Friday and Saturday evenings, and handy for the Belgrade Theatre. *(Recommended by Peter and Audrey Dowsett, Stephen, Julie and Hayley Brown, John A Barker, Roger and Jenny Huggins, Nigel Espley, Liane Purnell, Giles Francis, Alan and Hillie Johnson)*

Unique Pub Co ~ Lease Lynne Ingram ~ Real ale ~ Bar food (12-2.30) ~ Restaurant ~ No credit cards ~ (024) 7625 2183 ~ Children in restaurant if eating ~ Folk first Tues of month ~ Open 11-11; 12-10.30 Sun

DUNCHURCH SP4871 Map 4
Dun Cow
A mile from M45 junction 1: on junction of A45 and A426

At the heart of a pleasant village with nice antique shops, this extensive mainly Georgian coaching inn is very popular for the reasonably priced food. Get there early for a table during normal meal times, and you may have to queue to order from the shortish menu, but as they serve food all day you might prefer to pick a quieter time. Bar food includes soup (£2.35), lunchtime sandwiches and chips (from £3.60), sausage and cheddar mash (£4.95), baked roquefort cheesecake (£5.95), beef, mushroom and ale pie or scampi (£6.25), fish and chips (£6.35) and rump steak (£8.15). The pleasant and spotlessly kept interior has been well preserved, with lots of traditional features like welcoming open fires, rugs on the wooden and flagstone floors, exposed oak beams and country pictures, farmhouse furniture and bric-a-brac. Well kept Bass and Tetleys on handpump and a reasonable choice of wines by the glass; no smoking area and piped music. Outside there are tables in the pretty coachyard and on a sheltered side lawn. *(Recommended by George Atkinson, Roger and Jenny Huggins, Colin Mason, Alain and Rose Foote)*

Vintage Inns ~ Manager Florrie D'Arcy ~ Real ale ~ Bar food (12-10(9.30 Sun)) ~ (01788) 810305 ~ Children welcome ~ Open 11-11; 12-10.30 Sun ~ Bedrooms: £42.50B/£52.50B

Cribbage is a card game using a block of wood with holes for matchsticks or special pins to score with; regulars in cribbage pubs are usually happy to teach strangers how to play.

EDGE HILL SP3747 Map 4
Castle
Off A422

It's worth popping into this beautifully positioned crenellated octagon tower for a look at its interesting architecture. It's a folly that was built in 1749 by a Gothic Revival fanatic to mark the spot where Charles I raised his standard at the start of the Battle of Edge Hill. The big attractive garden (with aunt sally) has glimpses down through the trees of the battlefield, and it's said that after closing time you can hear ghostly sounds of the battle; there's even been the apparition of a cavalry officer galloping by in search of his severed hand. There are arched doorways, and the walls of the warm and cosy lounge bar have the same eight sides as the rest of the main tower, decorated with maps, pictures and a collection of Civil War memorabilia. In the public bar there are old farm tools as well as darts, pool, cribbage, dominoes, fruit machine, piped music and well kept Hook Norton ales and a couple of guests such as Greene King Abbot and Shepherd Neame Spitfire on handpump, country wines, farm cider and around 30 malt whiskies. Simple bar food includes sandwiches (from £2.95), ploughman's (£4.75), chicken curry or spinach and feta goujons (£5.50), lasagne (£6.10), steak and kidney pudding and cajun chicken (£6.95) and mixed grill (£7.15). Upton House is nearby on the A422, and Compton Wynyates, one of the most beautiful houses in this part of England, is not far beyond. *(Recommended by Brian and Anna Marsden, George Atkinson, Susan and John Douglas, Paul and Margaret Baker, D P Brown, Nigel and Sue Foster, Mayur Shah, Colin Parker, Angus Lyon, MJVK, John Brightley, Michael Smith, Alan Cowell, Humphry and Angela Crum Ewing, Iain R Hewitt, Rona Murdoch)*

Hook Norton ~ Lease N J and G A Blann ~ Real ale ~ Bar food ~ (01295) 670255 ~ Children welcome ~ Open 11.15-3, 6-11; 11-11 Sat; 12-10.30 Sun ~ Bedrooms: £35B/£55B

FIVE WAYS SP2270 Map 4
Case is Altered ◀▣

Follow Rowington signposts at junction roundabout off A4177/A4141 N of Warwick, then right into Case Lane

You can be sure of a warm welcome from the cheery staff and regulars at this delightful white cottage where little has changed over the three centuries that it's been licensed to sell beer. There's no food, no children or dogs, and no noisy games machines or piped music. The small and simple main bar has a fine old poster showing the Lucas Blackwell & Arkwright brewery (now flats) and a clock with its hours spelling out Thornleys Ale, another defunct brewery; there are just a few sturdy old-fashioned tables, with a couple of stout leather-covered settles facing each other over the spotless tiles. From this room you reach the homely lounge (usually open only weekend evenings and Sunday lunchtime) through a door lit up on either side. A door at the back of the building leads into a modest little room, usually empty on weekday lunchtimes, with a rug on its tiled floor and an antique bar billiards table protected by an ancient leather cover (it takes pre-decimal sixpences). Well kept and very reasonably priced Brains Dark Mild, Greene King IPA and Hook Norton and a guest ale at weekends from a small local brewer are served by rare beer engine pumps mounted on the casks that are stilled behind the counter. Behind a wrought-iron gate is a little brick-paved courtyard with a stone table under a chestnut tree. *(Recommended by Pete Baker, the Didler, Brian Skelcher, John Brightley, Susan and John Douglas)*

Free house ~ Licensee Jackie Willacy ~ Real ale ~ No credit cards ~ (01926) 484206 ~ Open 12(11.30 Sat)-2.30, 6-11; 12-2, 7-10.30 Sun; closed 25 Dec evening

You can send us reports through our web site: www.goodguides.com

GREAT WOLFORD SP2434 Map 4
Fox & Hounds ★ ⑪ ◖

Village signposted on right on A3400 3 miles S of Shipston on Stour

New licensees at this inviting 16th-c stone pub are running it along the same successful lines as the previous owners which means that although its main draw is still the imaginative bar food there's also a very good range of real ales and a welcoming pubby atmosphere. The cosy low-beamed old-fashioned bar has a nice collection of chairs and candlelit old tables on spotless flagstones, old hunting prints on the walls, and a roaring log fire in the inglenook fireplace with its fine old bread oven. A small tap room serves well kept Hook Norton and around five changing beers which might include Adnams Broadside, Cottage Champflower and Great Western and Timothy Taylors Landlord on handpump, and over 200 malt whiskies. Alongside straightforward meals such as sandwiches (from £3.75), soup (£2.95) and ploughman's (from £6.95), imaginative daily specials might include fresh sardines stuffed with onions and basil with provençale sauce (£3.75), roasted mediterranean vegetable salad (£5.25), caesar salad (£5.75/8.95), salmon fillet poached on local asparagus with hollandaise (£9.95), cornish lemon sole topped with prawns, garlic and mascarpone (£11.50), fried guinea fowl on bacon and lyonnaise potatoes with a plum and herb compote (£10.95), baked potato skins filled with tomato and cream cheese and puréed potatoes topped with mozzarella with tomato coulis (£8.25), and puddings such as lavender crème brûlée or elderflower and rhubarb fool (from £4.50). There's a well on the terrace outside. They don't serve breakfast if you stay here. *(Recommended by Stuart Turner, John Bowdler, L G Owen, John Bramley, Phil and Sarah Kane, Mrs N W Neill, Kenette Wentner, John Kane, David Field, Mike Gorton, Sir Nigel Foulkes, Iain R Hewitt, A and G Rae, David R Crafts, John and Enid Morris, Alun Howells, George Atkinson, the Didler, Ted George)*

Free house ~ Licensees Wendy Veale and John Scott-Lea ~ Real ale ~ Bar food (12-2.30, 7-9) ~ Restaurant ~ No credit cards ~ (01608) 674220 ~ Well behaved children welcome ~ Jazz Sun evening ~ Open 12-3, 6-11; closed Mon ~ Bedrooms: £35B/£55B

HATTON SP2467 Map 4
Falcon

4.6 miles from M40 junction 15; A46 towards Warwick, then left on A4177, and keep on past Hatton; Birmingham Road, Haseley

Very handy for Warwick, this well reworked old pub has five calm and relaxing open plan rooms working their way around a central island bar. Lots of stripped brickwork, low beams, tiled and oak-planked floors tell of the building's internal age, with a couple of dark blue walls, nice prints and old photographs, arrangements of pretty fresh flowers, big turkey rugs and a nice mix of stripped and waxed country tables and various chairs adding a smart touch. A big barn-style back dining area is no smoking. A wide choice of interesting food includes lunchtime sandwiches (from £2.95), soup (£3.50), pâté with beetroot and mango chutney (£4.50), crispy duck salad with hoisin (£4.95), wild mushroom stroganoff (£6.95), calves liver on potato and onion rösti with port sauce (£7.50), beef, garlic and black peppercorn stew with roasted root vegetables (£8.50) and duck breast with orange sauce (£9.25). Well kept Banks's Bitter and Original, Hook Norton Best, M&B Brew XI, Marstons Pedigree and a guest such as Otter on handpump. A well separated games room has darts, fruit machine and a TV, and there are picnic-sets out on lawns at the side and behind. *(Recommended by Brian Skelcher, Di and Mike Gillam, Bob and Laura Brock, Susan and John Douglas, Michael and Jeanne Shillington)*

Peacock Inns ~ Manager John Sedgewick ~ Real ale ~ Bar food (12-3, 7-9(6-9.30 Sat); 12-3 Sun; not Sun evening) ~ Restaurant ~ (01926) 484737 ~ Children welcome in the no smoking area ~ Open 11.30-11; 12-10.30 Sun

---

If we know a pub has an outdoor play area for children, we mention it.

HIMLEY SO8791 Map 4
Crooked House ★ £

Pub signposted from B4176 Gornalwood—Himley, OS Sheet 139 map reference 896908; readers have got so used to thinking of the pub as being near Kingswinford in the Midlands (though Himley is actually in Staffs) that we still include it in this chapter – the pub itself is virtually smack on the county boundary

It's worth a visit to this remotely set and wonky old brick house for its novelty value, as, believe it or not, you're really likely to lose your sense of balance as you walk in. When subsidence caused by mine workings underneath here threw the pub 15 degrees out of true they propped it up, rehung the doors and straightened the floors. The result leaves your perceptions spinning in a way that can really feel like being at sea. Inside on one table a bottle on its side actually rolls 'upwards' against the apparent direction of the slope, and for a 10p donation you can get a big ball-bearing from the bar to roll 'uphill' along a wainscot. There's a friendly atmosphere in the old rooms, and at the back is a large, level and more modern extension with local antiques. Very reasonably priced Banks's Bitter and Original, Marstons Pedigree and a beer named for the pub on hand or electric pump; dominoes, fruit machine and piped music. Good value bar food includes soup (£1.85), thai prawns (£2.95), lasagne (£4.95), bangers and mash (£5.25), chicken tikka masala (£5.75), steak and kidney pie (£5.95), and puddings such as apple pie or bread and butter pudding (£2.50). The conservatory is no smoking at food times, and there's a spacious outside terrace. It can get busy here in summer with coach trips. *(Recommended by the Didler, Ian Phillips)*

Banks's (W & D) ~ Manager Gary Ensor ~ Real ale ~ Bar food (12-2, 6-8.30; 12-5 Sun; not Sun evening) ~ (01384) 238583 ~ Children in eating area of bar ~ Open 11.30(11 Sat)-11; 12-10.30 Sun; 11.30-2.30, 6-11 Mon-Fri in winter

ILMINGTON SP2143 Map 4
Howard Arms 🍽 ♀ 🛏

Village signposted with Wimpstone off A34 S of Stratford

The stylishly simple interior of this smart golden-stone dining inn is light and airy, and attractively painted a warm golden colour that works well with the rugs on broad polished flagstones, a few good prints and hearty open fires. A couple of tables stand in a big inglenook screened from the door by an old-fashioned built-in settle, and a snug area off here is no smoking. Freshly prepared food from an imaginative menu that changes two or three times a week might include soup (£3.50), baked fresh sardines with lemon and garlic butter or brie, red leicester and cream cheese tart (£5), beef, ale and mustard pie (£8.50), salmon and chive cakes with prawn and tomato butter (£9), lemon and rosemary marinated chicken supreme with couscous and olives (£9.50), fried duck breast with stewed apples and cider cream sauce (£11), thai marinated red mullet (£12) and home-made puddings such as cappuccino mousse with shortbread biscuit, warm treacle tart or lemon crème brûlée with brandy snap tuile (from £4). Well kept Everards Tiger, North Cotswold Genesis and a guest such as Shepherd Neame Spitfire, organic juices and over a dozen wines by the glass; shove-ha'penny. The garden is lovely in summer with fruit trees sheltering the lawn, a colourful herbaceous border and tables on a neat gravel terrace. It's nicely set beside the village green, and there are lovely walks on the nearby hills (as well as strolls around the village outskirts). *(Recommended by Alan and Hillie Johnson, K H Frostick, E V Walder, Martin Jennings, Stuart Turner, Christopher Harlowe, Mrs M K Leah, Peter and Audrey Dowsett, John Kane, John Bowdler, Ken Arthur, George Atkinson, John Bramley, R Lake, Maysie Thompson, Hugh Bower, Martin Jones, Sue Holland, Dave Webster, Brian Skelcher; also in* The Good Hotel Guide*)*

Free house ~ Licensees Rob Greenstock and Martin Devereux ~ Real ale ~ Bar food (not Sun evening) ~ Restaurant ~ (01608) 682226 ~ Children in eating area of bar till 7.30 only if eating ~ Open 11-3, 6-11; 12-3, 7-10.30 Sun ~ Bedrooms: £45B/£74B

LAPWORTH SP1970 Map 4
Navigation

Old Warwick Rd S of village (B4439 Warwick—Hockley Heath); by Grand Union Canal, OS Sheet 139 map reference 19170

This bustling local really comes into its own in summer when it stays open all day to make the most of its pretty canalside setting, and locals and canal-users sit right out by the water or on a back terrace – there's outside hatch service. There's always a happy bustling atmosphere in the friendly flagstoned bar, and service is cheery and efficient even when it's busy. It's decorated with some brightly painted canal ware and cases of stuffed fish, has high-backed winged settles, seats built around its window bay and a coal fire in its high-mantled inglenook. Another quieter room has tables on its board-and-carpet floor, and a modern extension is nicely done with rugs on oak floors, cast-iron tables and bentwood chairs and delightful views over the sheltered flower-edged lawn, and on down to the busy canal behind. Bar food, in remarkably generous helpings, includes sandwiches (from £2.95), chicken balti (£6.95), vegetarian quiche or goats cheese salad (£7.25), battered cod (£7.50), pork loin with mustard and cider sauce or salmon and crab fishcakes with white wine and dill sauce (£8.95), chicken breast wrapped in bacon and stuffed with brie with a creamy barbecue sauce (£9.25), and fillet steak with pepper sauce or redcurrant jus (£11.95). Very well kept Bass, M&B Brew XI, Highgate Dark Mild and a daily changing guest such as Timothy Taylors Landlord on handpump, farm cider and lots of malt whiskies; fruit machine. The pub and gardens are prettily lit at night. *(Recommended by Di and Mike Gillam, Peter Brueton, Keith Allen, Peter Meister, Brian and Anna Marsden, Keith Jacob, Simon Cole, Lyn and Geoff Hallchurch, Piotr Chodzko-Zajko, John Evans, Jim Bush)*

Bass ~ Lease Andrew Kimber ~ Real ale ~ Bar food (12-2(3 Sun), 6-9) ~ (01564) 783337 ~ Children welcome ~ Open 11-11; 12-10.30 Sun; 11-2.30, 5.30-11 Mon to Fri in winter

LITTLE COMPTON SP2630 Map 4
Red Lion

Off A44 Moreton-in-Marsh—Chipping Norton

There's a pleasant villagey atmosphere at this attractive 16th-c stone local which is in a handy spot for exploring the Cotswolds. The simple but civilised and comfortable low-beamed lounge has snug alcoves, and a couple of little tables by the log fire. The plainer public bar has another log fire, and darts, pool, cribbage, dominoes, fruit machine and juke box. Donnington BB on handpump and an extensive wine list; good service. The good bar food here is so popular that you may need to book (especially at weekends). Good value bar food includes soup (£2.75), chicken liver pâté (£3.95), filled baguettes (from £3.25), ploughman's (£4.50), filled baked potatoes (from £4.25), breaded plaice (£5.50), tagliatelle niçoise (£6.25) and daily specials such as creamy devilled mushrooms (£4.25), seafood pie (£7.95) and fried pork loin with pink peppercorn sauce (£9.25); no smoking dining area. No dogs – even in the garden, where there are tables and a children's play area. *(Recommended by H O Dickinson, Mike and Mary Carter, Mr and Mrs P Eastwood, R T and J C Moggridge, Ted George, George Atkinson, Stuart Turner, Gordon Prince, Martin Jennings)*

Donnington ~ Tenant David Smith ~ Real ale ~ Bar food ~ Restaurant ~ (01608) 674397 ~ Children in eating area of bar and restaurant ~ Open 12-2.30, 6-11; 7-10.30 Sun ~ Bedrooms: £30/£40

LONG COMPTON SP2832 Map 4
Red Lion

A3400 S of Shipston-on-Stour

This attractive former coaching inn has been well refurbished, to make the most of its old features without introducing too much olde-worlde clutter. The roomy lounge bar has brown panelling and stripped stone, with a lot of old local photographs and other pictures and a high delft shelf with antique bottles. In its rambling corners there are old-fashioned built-in settles among pleasantly assorted and comfortable old seats and tables on the flagstones, and there are good log fires. Good value food includes sandwiches (from £1.95), soup (£2.60), warm smoked trout (£3.50), ploughman's (from £4.40), chilli (£6.15), cashew nut paella (£6.25), steak and kidney pie (£6.75) and daily specials such as grilled sardines (£3.95), leek and stilton sausages and mash (£6.75), salmon fishcakes on noodles with sweet chilli sauce and coriander (£8.25) and fried pork tenderloin with calvados, apples and cream (£8.50). Well kept Adnams, Courage Directors, Hook Norton and Websters on handpump; the landlord is warmly welcoming and attentive, and his staff are efficient and helpful. The simple public bar has pool; unobtrusive piped music. There are tables out in the garden, with a play area. *(Recommended by Stuart Turner, George Atkinson)*

Free house ~ Licensee Jenny Parkin ~ Real ale ~ Bar food ~ Restaurant ~ (01608) 684221 ~ Children welcome ~ Open 11-2.30, 6-11; 12-3, 7-10.30 Sun

MONKS KIRBY SP4683 Map 4
Bell 🍽 ♀

Just off B4027 (former A427) W of Pailton; Bell Lane

There's an enjoyably comfortable blending of warm Mediterranean hospitality, tasty Spanish food and traditional pubby surroundings at this timbered and flagstoned old pub. An extensive tapas menu has everything from griddled fresh sardines to meatballs (£4.25-£5.25), while the printed menu includes a hugely tempting range of Spanish and fish dishes as well as some English dishes: battered squid or chorizo in white wine and garlic (£4.25), seafood cocktail (£4.50), moules marinières (£4.65), scallops cooked with white wine, tomato, lemon juice and bread crumbs (£4.95), battered cod or spaghetti carbonara (£7.95), grilled tuna (£9.75), half a roast duck with plum sauce (£11.25), grilled shark with garlic and lemon juice (£11.75), halibut cooked in tomato, white wine and cream with prawns and vegetables (£12.25), seafood paella (£12.75), shellfish with tomatoes and cream cooked in lobster sauce or beef stroganoff (£12.95), half a lobster and chicken baked in white wine and cream sauce (£14.75), bass cooked in white wine and shellfish sauce (£15.75) and lots of steak cuts (from £13.75). The dark beamed and flagstoned interior although old is fairly straightforward with a no smoking dining area and piped music. In addition to well kept Boddingtons and Flowers Original on handpump there's a very good wine list, ports for sale by the bottle and a good range of brandies and malt whiskies. A simple little back terrace has rough-and-ready rustic woodwork, geese and chickens and lawns extending to a pretty little view across a stream to a buttercup meadow. *(Recommended by Susan and John Douglas, Sir Michael McLintock, Mike and Penny Sutton, Stephen, Julie and Hayley Brown, Nigel Plested, Mr and Mrs D Griffin)*

Free house ~ Licensee Paco Garcia Maures ~ Real ale ~ Bar food (12-2.30, 7-10.30; not Mon lunchtime) ~ Restaurant ~ (01788) 832352 ~ Children welcome ~ Open 12-2.30, 7-11; closed Mon lunchtime, 26 Dec, 1 Jan

SAMBOURNE SP0561 Map 4
Green Dragon

A435 N of Alcester, then left fork onto A448 just before Studley; village signposted on left soon after

The three pleasantly atmospheric communicating rooms at this very enjoyable village-green pub have low beams, rugs on flagstones, little elbow chairs and more upright ones, some small settles, open fires and piped music plus well kept Bass, Hobsons and M & B Brew XI on handpump. In summer the shuttered and timbered façade is prettily bedecked with colourful hanging baskets, and there are picnic-sets and teak seats among flowering cherries in a side courtyard by the car park, and bowls. Very generous helpings of tasty food include a big range of sandwiches (from £2.50), soup (£2.95), grilled goats cheese with mixed leaves and thyme dressing or tomato and mozzarella salad (£4.50), parma ham with melon (£5.50), steak, ale and mushroom pie, roast stuffed peppers or mixed bean chilli (£6.50), fish of the day

(£6.95), pork filled with mushroom, herb and madeira sauce (£7.95) and confit of duck in red wine and mushroom sauce (£10.95). The bedrooms are neatly decorated and well equipped. *(Recommended by Michael and Jeanne Shillington, Jean and Richard Phillips, John Bramley, June and Ken Brooks, David and Barbara Knott, Mike Gorton, Brian and Janet Ainscough, Mike and Mary Carter, Terry Mizen, Graham and Lynn Mason)*

Bass ~ Lease Phil Burke ~ Real ale ~ Bar food (12-2, 6.30-10; not Sun) ~ Restaurant ~ (01527) 892465 ~ Children in eating area of bar ~ Open 11-3, 6-11; 12-4, 7-10.30 Sun ~ Bedrooms: £48B/£60B

SEDGLEY SO9193 Map 4
Beacon ★ ◖

129 Bilston Street (no pub sign on our visit, but by Beacon Lane); A463, off A4123 Wolverhampton—Dudley

The beautifully aromatic Sarah Hughes beers here – Dark Ruby, Pale Amber and Surprise Bitter – are brewed in a building at the back of this unspoilt own-brew brick pub, and you can arrange to tour the brewery. The front door of this old place opens straight into a plain quarry-tiled drinking corridor, and the original Victorian layout means you may find a couple of locals propped up against the wall by the stairs, chatting to the waistcoated barman leaning in the doorway of his central serving booth. You can easily imagine a Victorian traveller tucked up in the little room on the left by the imposing green tiled marble fireplace with its big misty mirror, the door closed for privacy and warmth, a drink handed through the glazed hatch, while the cat (Sally) sleeps on under the wall settle. The dark woodwork, turkey carpet, velvet and net curtains, heavy mahogany tables, old piano and little landscape prints all seem unchanged since those times. A simpler room on the right, with a black kettle and embroidered mantel over a blackened range, has a stripped wooden wall bench. The corridor runs round into a very big dark-panelled smoking room with particularly long red leather wall settles down each side, gilt-based cast-iron tables, a big blue carpet on the lino floor, and dramatic sea prints. Round a corner, the conservatory is genuinely for plants, and has no seats. The only food they serve is cheese and onion cobs (80p). A children's play area in the garden has a slide, climbing frame and roundabout. *(Recommended by the Didler, Kevin Thorpe)*

Own brew ~ Licensee John Hughes ~ Real ale ~ No credit cards ~ (01902) 883380 ~ Children in family room ~ Open 12-2.30, 5.30-10.45(11 Fri); 11.30-3, 6-11 Sat; 12-3, 7-10.30 Sun

SHUSTOKE SP2290 Map 4
Griffin ◖ £

5 miles from M6 junction 4; A446 towards Tamworth, then right on to B4114 and go straight through Coleshill; pub is at Furnace End, a mile E of village

There's always a good mixed crowd, even mid-week, in the welcoming low-beamed L-shaped bar at this charmingly unpretentious and very friendly country local. Two stone fireplaces (one's a big inglenook) have warming log fires, and it's furnished with a nice old-fashioned settle and cushioned café seats (some quite closely packed), sturdily elm-topped sewing trestles, lots of old jugs on the beams, beer mats on the ceiling and fruit machine. A fine feature here is the interesting range of up to 10 real ales including Highgate Mild, Marstons Pedigree and Theakstons Old Peculier, interesting guests such as RCH Pitchfork One, and a couple from their own microbrewery which produces the very palatable Church End, Choir Boy, Cuthberts, Old Pal, Vicars Ruin or perhaps Pews Porter, all from a servery under a very low heavy beam; country wine, mulled wine and hot punch. Very good value tasty lunchtime bar food includes pie and chips, broccoli bake or lasagne (£5) and cod, chips and mushy peas (£5.50); you may need to arrive early to get a table. The conservatory is popular with families, and outside are old-fashioned seats and tables on the back grass, a children's play area, and a large terrace with plants in raised beds. *(Recommended by Colin Fisher, J V Dadswell, DAV)*

Own brew ~ Licensee Michael Pugh ~ Real ale ~ Bar food (not evenings or Sun) ~ No credit cards ~ (01675) 481205 ~ Well behaved children in family room and in conservatory ~ Open 12-2.30, 7-11(7-10.30 Sun); closed 25, 26 Dec evening

STRATFORD-UPON-AVON SP2055 Map 4
Garrick ♀

High Street

The name of this very attractive ancient pub originates from 1769 when the actor David Garrick visited Stratford and inaugurated the Stratford Festival. The small, heavily timbered and often irregularly shaped rooms are full of secluded corners and have high ceiling beams, some walls stripped back to bare stone and others heavily plastered with posters, and long upholstered settles and stools made from barrels on bare boards. The small air-conditioned dining room at the back of the house centres on an open fire with a conical brass hood. Well kept Flowers IPA, Greene King Abbot, Wadworths 6X and a guest such as Hook Norton Old Hooky on handpump, a fruit machine, piped music and a TV. Very friendly helpful staff serve generous helpings of sensibly priced bar food – sandwiches are served all day – such as soup (£2.45), bruschetta (£2.65), sandwiches (from £3.25), fish and chips (£5.95), roast vegetable filo tart (£6.25), vegetable lasagne (£6.45), fish pie (£7.45), fried chicken with garlic and chablis sauce (£7.95) and puddings such as treacle sponge or apple crumble (£3.55). *(Recommended by Michael Dandy, Bill Sykes, Ted George, Ted and Jan Whitfield, Kevin Blake, Alan and Hillie Johnson, Canon Michael Bourdeaux)*

Laurel Pub Company ~ Licensee Vicky Lang ~ Real ale ~ Bar food (12-9) ~ (01789) 292186 ~ Children in restaurant ~ Open 11-11; 12-10.30 Sun

WARMINGTON SP4147 Map 4
Plough £

Village just off B4100 N of Banbury

Very traditional and understated, this little village local is well placed in a delightful village a few yards up a quiet lane from a broad sloping green with duck pond and ducks. It looks especially pretty in the autumn, when the creeper over the front of the stone building turns a striking crimson. There's a nicely relaxed and cheery atmosphere in the unpretentious pubby bar which is dominated by a big fireplace and its copper hood and has old photographs of the village and locals, an old high-backed winged settle, cushioned wall seats and lots of comfortable art deco elbow chairs and library chairs. Well kept Greene King Abbot and IPA, Hook Norton Best, Marstons Pedigree and a guest such as Greene King Ruddles County on handpump, and several malt whiskies; darts, dominoes, cribbage and piped pop music. Straightforward but tasty food includes sandwiches (from £1.50), soup (£2.50), ploughman's (from £4.50), steak and kidney pie or cottage pie (£4.95), scampi (£5.50) and ham, egg and chips (£5.95). Very friendly licensee and staff. *(Recommended by Chris and Jo Nicholls, Sue Holland, Dave Webster)*

Free house ~ Licensee Denise Linda Willson ~ Real ale ~ Bar food (12-2, 6.30-8.30; not Sun, Tues evenings) ~ No credit cards ~ (01295) 690666 ~ Children in eating area of bar ~ Open 12-3, 5.30-11; 7-10.30 Sun; closed 25 Dec evening

WELFORD-ON-AVON SP1452 Map 4
Bell

Off B439 W of Stratford; High Street

About three years ago this comfortable 17th-c brick pub was renovated by the current licensees. They removed the carpets to expose original flagstone floors, stripped black paint from the low ceiling beams to reveal the original woodwork, put in antique or period style furniture, and with the reinstated inglenook fireplace they now have three real fires. Each of the five different areas has its own character, from the cosy red painted bar to the light and airy green-washed terrace room.

Popular bar food includes soup (£2.45), fried brie with ginger and apricot compote (£3.95), sandwiches (from £3.95), ploughman's (£4.95), breaded plaice or lasagne (£6.95), pork with whole grain mustard (£7.25), beef casserole (£7.75), minted lamb curry or home-made pies (£7.95) and puddings such as steamed chocolate pudding (£3.95). Well kept Boddingtons, Flowers Original, Hobsons, Wadworths 6X and a guest such as Shepherd Neame Spitfire on handpump; malt whiskies; piped music, shove-ha'penny, table skittles and dominoes. In summer the creeper covered exterior is hung with lots of colourful baskets, and there are seats in the pretty secluded garden area and back courtyard. The riverside village, with its church and thatched black and white cottages, is pretty. *(Recommended by A and G Rae, Peter Lloyd, Roger Everett, Tony Walker, Brian and Bett Cox, June and Mike Coleman, B A Dale)*

Whitbreads ~ Lease Colin and Teresa Ombler ~ Real ale ~ Bar food (12-2.30, 7-9.30(10 Fri, Sat)) ~ Restaurant ~ (01789) 750353 ~ Children welcome ~ Open 11.30-3, 6.30(6 Fri, Sat)-11; 12-2.30, 7-10.30 Sun; closed 25 Dec evening

Lucky Dip

Besides the fully inspected pubs, you might like to try these Lucky Dips recommended to us and described by readers (if you do, please send us reports: www.goodguides.com).

Alveston [SP2356]
Ferry [Ferry Lane; end of village, off B4086 Stratford—Wellesbourne]: New French and Italian licensees doing well in comfortable open-plan dining pub, enjoyable imaginative food esp fish, fresh pasta and lunchtime baguettes, well kept beers, good house wines, low-key décor, log fire; nice spot, path along River Avon *(Michael and Jeanne Shillington, LYM)*

Amblecote [SO9085]
Robin Hood [Collis St]: Small informal open-plan local, well kept Bathams, honeyed Enville, Everards Beacon and Tiger and two guest beers, farm ciders, good value food in dining area, friendly staff, children allowed till 8.30 if eating; monthly quiz night, comfortable bedrooms *(Nigel Espley, Liane Purnell)*

Ardens Grafton [SP1153]
☆ *Golden Cross* [off A46 or B439 W of Stratford, OS Sheet 150 map ref 114538; Wixford rd]: Recently nicely revamped as restaurant dining pub, with good choice of generous well presented interesting food in flagstoned bar or comfortable dining room with well spaced tables, themed food nights, well kept Bass, Flowers IPA and Hook Norton, welcoming efficient service, log fire; wheelchair access, tables in charming garden, nice views *(June and Mike Coleman, Don Mather)*

Atherstone [SP3097]
Bull [A5, just S at Witherley turn-off]: Prompt efficient service, food from generously served rolls to good restaurant meals, well kept beer; bedrooms *(Neil Ravenscroft)*
Kings Head [Old Watling St]: Nicely decorated open-plan canalside pub with obliging licensees, well kept beers, good food range; garden with play area *(Bernie Adams)*

Avon Dassett [SP4049]
Prince Rupert [off A41 Banbury—Warwick; aka the Avon]: Pleasant décor and dining room, relaxing atmosphere, freshly cooked food, Hook Norton, John Smiths and a guest beer, Civil War memorabilia; wet and muddy walkers welcome – floors can cope; attractive small village *(Martin Jennings)*

Baginton [SP3375]
Old Mill [Mill Hill]: Smart Chef & Brewer conversion of old watermill nr airport (and Lunt Roman fort), with gardens leading down to the River Sower; uniformed staff, Scottish Courage beers, good wine choice, heavy beams and timbers in roomy main bar, restaurant; bedrooms *(Pete Yearsley, LYM)*

Barford [SP2660]
Joseph Arch [A429, handy for M40]: Two well kept changing ales, good malt whiskies and enjoyable food in pub named for founder of agricultural workers' union (born and died nearby) *(John L Evans)*

Barston [SP2078]
Bulls Head [from M42 junction 5, A4141 towards Warwick, first left, then signed down Barston Lane]: Attractive partly Tudor village local, oak-beamed bar with log fires and Buddy Holly memorabilia, comfortable lounge with pictures and plates, dining room, friendly relaxed service, good value basic food inc good fresh fish, well kept Bass, M&B Brew XI and Tetleys, secluded garden, hay barn behind *(Pete Baker, Brian Skelcher)*

Barton [SP1051]
☆ *Cottage of Content* [pub signed off B4085, just S of Bidford-on-Avon]: Cosy and quaint traditional flagstoned low-beamed bar with solid fuel stove in inglenook, easy-going atmosphere and plenty of locals, good simple home-cooked bar food, well kept Whitbreads-related real ales, piped music, restaurant; picnic-sets in front of the pretty house, touring caravan site with good play area behind; day fishing on River Avon here, though no nearby moorings *(BB, M Bertelsmann)*

Bearley [SP1760]
Golden Cross [Bearley Cross, A3400 N of Stratford]: Clean and well ordered pub/restaurant, nicely cooked generous food in small restaurant or lovely old timbered bar with open fireplaces and soft lighting, well kept

Whitbreads-related ales, helpful welcoming staff *(David Gregory, David Green)*

Birmingham [SP1783]

Abraham Derby [Airport departure lounge]: Popular bar with Abraham Derby machinery theme, several well kept Bass-related beers with a guest such as Marstons Pedigree, friendly staff, food; open all day *(Richard Lewis)*

☆ *Bellefield* [Winson St, Winson Green]: Unspoilt friendly sidestreet local with beautiful Victorian tile pictures, ornate ceiling, Georgian smoking room; Everards Mild, Tiger and Old Bill and guest beers, interesting bottled beers and occasional beer festivals; good value West Indian home cooking, pub games, music; open all day, terrace for children *(the Didler)*

Old Joint Stock [Temple Row W]: Fullers ale and pie house in former bank, their ales from big Victorian-style central bar, good value food, pillared walls, lofty ceiling, upper balcony seating; popular with office workers *(Ian and Joan Blackwell)*

Poachers Pocket [Cole Hall Lane, Stetchford]: Former 18th-c farmhouse by wetlands country park in residential district, stripped pine and quarry tiles in small linked rooms, old range in raftered kitchen, darts and magnificent inglenook in front sitting room, TV and fruit machine in central bar, two reasonably priced real ales, pleasant service, airy and roomy dining area in former back stables and barn with lots of memorabilia; sturdy seats and tables out on fancily paved terrace *(Susan and John Douglas)*

Prince of Wales [Alcester Rd, Moseley]: Good unspoilt bare-boards local, hatch service to snug, two quiet and comfortable back parlours (one frozen in 1900), ochre walls, lively chatty atmosphere, well kept Ansells Bitter and Mild, Ind Coope Burton, Marstons Pedigree and Tetleys, wide choice of good cheap food, fast service even when packed *(Keith Jacob, Dr Stephen Decent)*

Shakespeare Ale House [Airport departure lounge]: Well kept Bass ales, panelling and smoke-effect pub décor; food *(Richard Lewis)*

Spread Eagle [Warwick Rd, Acocks Green]: Pleasing and well managed Wetherspoons with very good young staff, wide changing choice of well kept and priced real ales, usual food all day inc bargains for two *(J W Busby)*

White Swan [Bradford St, Digbeth]: Unfussy but clean and comfortable friendly local with serving hatch to corridor, big bar, fire in small back lounge, ornate tilework, charming staff, good fresh rolls, well kept Ansells Bitter and Mild and Tetleys *(Pete Baker)*

Woodman [Albert St]: Little-changed Victorian pub with unusual juke box (mainly 60s and Irish) in friendly and lively L-shaped main bar, hatch service to relaxing back smoke room with superb tiling and coal fire, particularly good fresh warm baguettes, well kept Ansells Mild, Tetleys and a guest beer, friendly unhurried service *(Pete Baker, the Didler)*

Bloxwich [SJ9902]

Turf [Wolverhampton Rd; aka Tinky's]: Unspoilt local, with two serving hatches to central corridor, large waiting-roomish tiled bar with heating pipe under settles, tiny back parlour with chairs around tiled fireplace, unusual padded wall settles with armrests in left-hand smoking room, original etched windows and fittings, Wm Morris curtains and wallpaper, cheap local Holdens Mild and XB or Golden Glow; no food or music, outside lavatories *(Giles Francis, Kevin Thorpe, the Didler)*

Cherington [SP2836]

Cherington Arms: Newish licensees doing good interesting food, well kept Hook Norton, good value wines *(Sue and Jim Sargeant)*

Church Lawford [SP4576]

Old Smithy [Green Lane]: Much extended thatched and beamed 16th-c dining pub with dark woodwork in L-shaped lounge on various levels, good range of food cooked to order from separate servery, well kept Bass, Greene King IPA and Abbot, Judges and (brewed next door) Frankton Bagby, good friendly service; games room, conservatory; no dogs, children welcome, garden with slide *(Alain and Rose Foote, Alan and Hillie Johnson, R Huggins, D Irving, E McCall, T McLean)*

Coventry [SP3379]

Browns [Earl St, between Council House and Herbert Art Gallery]: Tempting range of freshly cooked hearty food at one reasonable price all day in big stylish modern café-bar, many different types of seating area inc terrace, decent wines, chilly beers (not cheap); live music upstairs some nights, open 9am-11pm (1am Fri/Sat, 10-7 Sun) *(Nigel Espley, Liane Purnell)*

Flying Standard [Trinity St]: Well laid out Wetherspoons, popular for its attractively priced drinks; food all day *(Nigel Espley, Liane Purnell)*

Nursery [Lord St]: Informal and cosily basic Victorian local popular for its well kept ales inc a Mild, changing guest beers and beer festivals Jun and Dec; lots of local rugby memorabilia, pleasant back terrace, open all day *(John Brightley, Charles Eatof)*

Town Wall [Bond St, behind Coventry Theatre]: Compact unspoilt Victorian pub, with engraved windows, open fire in small T-shaped lounge, simple bar with TV for big sports events, tiny clubby snug and flower-filled back yard; well kept Bass and M&B Brew XI, good value home-cooked food inc generous doorstep sandwiches *(John Brightley)*

Dudley [SO9390]

☆ *Bottle & Glass* [Black Country Museum, Tipton Rd]: Splendid reconstruction of old Black Country alehouse in extensive open-air working Black Country Museum (well worth a visit for its re-created assortment of shops, gaslit cinema with Charlie Chaplin shorts, fairground, school, barge wharf and tram system); friendly staff in period clothes, well kept Holdens Bitter and Mild ('Lager? We don't sell any of that modern stuff!'), good chunky filled rolls and smokies, wall benches, sawdust on old boards, woodburner; children welcome in two separate rooms off passage *(LM)*

Rag & Mop [Sedgley Rd]: No-frills Black Country pub with well kept Banks's, generous home-made food, low prices, coal fire (G P Kernan)

Easenhall [SP4679]

☆ Golden Lion [Main St]: Cottagey 16th-c inn in same family since 1931, attractively decorated comfortable lounge, low beams, dark panelling, settles and inglenook log fire, good value generous food inc self-service lunches (two plate sizes), good Sun carvery and good fresh veg, efficient welcoming service even when busy, Boddingtons, Flowers Original and Theakstons Best, decent wines, good coffee; spacious attractive garden with terrace, barbecue, pet donkey; well equipped bedrooms in new wing, attractive village (Roy Bromell, Carol and David Havard, John Brightley)

Eathorpe [SP3868]

☆ Plough [car park off B4455 NW of Leamington Spa]: Big helpings of good food inc some bargain meals in long neat split-level lounge/dining area with toning walls, carpets and table linen, good friendly chatty service, good coffee, huge piranha in tank; cl some wkdys (John Brightley, DC)

Ettington [SP2749]

☆ Chequers [A422 Banbury—Stratford]: Comfortable and welcoming restaurant-style 'pub' with imaginative food served by attentive smartly dressed waiters, Adnams, Hook Norton and a guest beer such as Fullers London Pride, extensive wine list, no smoking area; piped music; neat back garden. (Mr and Mrs Hugh Spottiswoode, LYM, J and D Whiting, John Bramley, Iain R Hewitt)

Houndshill House [A422 towards Stratford; aka Mucky Mongrel]: Civilised dining pub with welcoming landlord and enjoyable traditional food in pleasant surroundings, very popular with families and OAPs; well kept Scottish Courage ales, stripped stone and beams, good service, tables in big attractive garden with play area well away from buildings, good views from front; children welcome, good well equipped bedrooms (Jack Barnwell, J A and R M Ashurst)

Gaydon [SP3654]

Malt Shovel [just off M40 junction 12, across B4100; Church Rd]: Unusual panelled bar with big stained-glass window at one raised end, small lounge area with sofas and easy chairs, open bar with beams, barrels, stone jars and fish tank with shubunkins, good value standard food, Flowers IPA and well kept Batemans, filter coffee, newish licensees and welcoming service; maybe loud piped heavy metal (Sue and Bob Ward)

Halesowen [SO9683]

Waggon & Horses [Stourbridge Rd]: Welcoming local, refurbished but entirely unpretentious, noted for well kept Bathams, a house beer and up to a dozen or so interesting changing ales from small independent brewers – staff well informed about them; no food, open all day (the Didler, Gill Waller, Tony Morriss)

Hampton in Arden [SP2081]

White Lion [High St; handy for M42 junction 6]: Unpretentious inn with beamed lounge, real fire, nautical décor inc navigation lights, welcoming staff, quick food (not Sun) from sandwiches to steaks inc children's, well kept Bass, M&B Brew XI and John Smiths, decent wine, public bar with cribbage and dominoes, back dining room; bedrooms, attractive village, handy for NEC (Brian and Lynn Young, LYM)

Hampton Lucy [SP2557]

☆ Boars Head [Church St, E of Stratford]: Homely décor in low-beamed two-bar local next to lovely church, log fire, lots of brasses, well kept ales such as Church End, Hook Norton and Shepherd Neame Spitfire, prompt friendly service, well presented straightforward food (not Sun evening); picnic-sets in neat and attractive secluded back garden, pretty village nr Charlcote House (Brian Skelcher, Tony Walker, Susan and John Douglas, Nigel and Sue Foster, Peter Meister)

Harbury [SP3759]

☆ Shakespeare [just off B4451/B4452 S of A425 Leamington Spa—Southam; Mill St]: Popular and comfortable dining pub with interesting layout of linked low-beamed rooms, stripped stonework, big central inglenook log fire, horsebrasses, good choice of freshly cooked sensibly priced food (not Sun/Mon evenings), well kept Flowers IPA, Fullers London Pride and Timothy Taylors Landlord, good hospitable service (landlady has great memory for customers); pleasant conservatory, darts in separate pool room, children welcome, tables in back garden with aviaries (Michael and Jenny Back, Nigel and Sue Foster, Alan and Hillie Johnson, Neil and Anita Christopher, BB, John Bramley)

Henley-in-Arden [SP1568]

Bird in Hand [A34 towards Solihull]: Wide choice of good value food from baguettes up inc bargain two-course lunches; fine range of well kept ales such as Everards, Flowers IPA and Wadworths 6X, good wine list, friendly attentive service, open-plan bar and eating area; pretty conservation town with good churches (Brad Featherman, Gill and Keith Croxton, S and D Moir)

Iron Cross [SP0551]

Queens Head [A435 Evesham—Alcester]: Lively traditional pub, clean and comfortable, with warmly welcoming staff, wide range of real ales inc Fat Gods brewed at the pub, good home-made food range inc bargain specials and good Sun lunch, lots of antiques and plenty to look at; open all day (Mrs B Jewell)

Kenilworth [SP2871]

☆ Clarendon House [High St]: Comfortable and civilised bar/brasserie, sofas and daily papers in partly panelled bar, well kept Greene King IPA, Abbot, Triumph and guest beers, decent wines, friendly efficient service, daily papers, good imaginative food from generous sandwiches and baguettes up, interesting specials, reasonable prices, joky complaints dept (well with blown-up skeleton 'complainer'); unobtrusive 1930s-style piped music; open all day (Adrian White, Julie King, Joan and Tony Walker, R T and J C Moggridge, Colin Mason)

Knowle [SP1876]

Black Boy [off A4177 about 1½ miles S]: Wide choice of modestly priced food in bungalow dining pub, much extended but keeping canalside feel, friendly staff, well kept Everards Tiger; plenty of tables outside, play area *(Dave Braisted, Dr and Mrs A K Clarke)*

☆ *Herons Nest* [Warwick Rd S]: Attractively reworked former hotel by Grand Union Canal, dining tables in several individual rooms inc no smoking areas, some flagstones and high-backed settles, hops on beams, interesting décor, open fires, wide choice of good value home-cooked food inc children's helpings, well kept Bass and Tetleys, good choice of wines, friendly staff; plenty of tables in garden with moorings, bedrooms *(Pete Yearsley, Bill Sykes, John Beeken, Jack Barnwell)*

Lapworth [SP1670]

Boot [B4439, by Warwickshire Canal]: Waterside dining pub done up in cool modern upmarket rustic style, raised dining area (food confined to here on busy Sat night, but may take up all tables at other times), roaring fire, good atmosphere, food (not cheap) from good baguettes to steaks and fish, well kept beers such as Greene King Old Speckled Hen and Wadworths 6X, decent wines (big glasses), smartly enthusiastic young staff, daily papers, lots of board games, cartoons; piped nostalgic pop music; good lavatories, nice garden, pleasant walks *(Susan and John Douglas, John Brightley, Joyce and Maurice Cottrell)*

Leamington Spa [SP3165]

Hogshead [Warwick St]: Spotless little open-plan pub with some character, bric-a-brac and good atmosphere, raised no smoking area with sofas as well as chairs, bare boards and brickwork in main area, fine range of well kept changing ales, good value straightforward food, good helpful staff; can get busy wknds *(Ted George)*

Leek Wootton [SP2868]

Anchor [Warwick Rd]: Firmly run bookable dining lounge very popular (esp with older people) for wide choice of good value generous fresh hot food (all day Sat, not Sun), well kept Bass and a guest beer, decent wine, lots of very close-set tables, overflow into smaller bar; picnic-sets in pleasant garden behind *(Roger Braithwaite, Tony Walker, John Bramley, Alan and Hillie Johnson, John Whitehead)*

Lighthorne [SP3355]

☆ *Antelope* [Old School Lane, Bishops Hill; a mile SW of B4100 N of Banbury]: Attractive 17th-c stone-built dining pub in very pretty uncrowded village setting, two comfortable and clean bars (one old, one newer) with Cromwellian theme, separate dining area, wide choice of good reasonably priced food inc old-fashioned puddings, well kept Flowers IPA and Wadworths 6X, faultless friendly service; piped music, but turned down on request; little waterfall in banked garden *(Hugh Bower)*

Long Itchington [SP4165]

Blue Lias [Stockton Rd, off A423]: Well placed on Grand Union Canal, with friendly efficient staff, enjoyable reasonably priced food *(anon)*

☆ *Harvester* [off A423 S of Coventry; The Square]: Unpretentious welcoming two-bar village local with 60s feel, quiet, neat and tidy, with efficiently served very cheap food from sandwiches to good steaks, three well kept Hook Norton and a guest ale, friendly landlord, fish tank in lounge bar, cosy relaxed restaurant; nothing to do with the chain of the same name *(Pete Baker, J V Dadswell)*

Two Boats [A423 N of Southam, by Grand Union Canal]: Lively canal views from waterfront seating area and alcove window seats, well kept Hook Norton and changing ales such as Greene King Abbot, Marlow Rebellion and Worthingtons, welcoming staff, generous cheapish food, rather a social club feel (even to the pleasant 60s piped music, live music Fri/Sat); open all day *(BB, Sue Demont, Tim Barrow)*

Lower Brailes [SP3039]

☆ *George* [B4035 Shipston—Banbury]: Handsome old stone-built inn with good freshly made food inc game in season, smart country-style flagstoned restaurant, local feel in roomy flagstoned front bar with dark oak tables, nice curtains and inglenook log fire, darts, panelled oak-beamed back bar with soft lighting and green décor, half a dozen well kept Hook Norton ales, welcoming landlord; provision for children, live music most Sat and Mon evenings and Sun afternoon; aunt sally in sizeable neatly kept sheltered garden with terrace and covered area, comfortable bedrooms, lovely village, open all day *(Pete Baker, Sue and Jim Sargeant, John Bowdler, Martin Jennings, LYM)*

Lowsonford [SP1868]

☆ *Fleur de Lys* [off B4439 Hockley Heath—Warwick]: Prettily placed old canalside pub, half no smoking and friendly but not cheap, log fires, lots of beams, well kept Flowers Original, Fullers London Pride, Greene King Old Speckled Hen and a guest such as Wychwood Fiddlers Elbow, decent wines inc many by the glass, enjoyable bar food; children in family room, waterside garden, open all day *(Brian and Anna Marsden, R Mathews, Ray and Jacki Davenport, LYM, Michael Smith)*

Loxley [SP2552]

☆ *Fox* [signed off A422 Stratford—Banbury]: Cheerful pub very popular evenings for wide range of good value fresh homely cooking; very neat and clean, with panelling, a few pictures and plates, settles, brocaded banquettes, pleasant dining area, friendly landlord and cat, five well kept ales such as Bass, Greene King Abbot and Hook Norton; piped music; tables in good-sized garden behind, sleepy village handy for Stratford *(R J Herd)*

Monks Kirby [SP4683]

Denbigh Arms [Main St]: 17th-c pub under welcoming new management, beams, old photographs and interesting 18th-c pew seating, no smoking family room, big helpings of enjoyable food from sausage and chips through curries to giant steaks, Theakstons Best and XB and three guest beers; upstairs folk club 2nd Sun of month; play area *(Roger and Jenny Huggins, John Brightley, Alan and Hillie Johnson)*

Napton [SP4560]

Folly [off A425 towards Priors Hardwick; Folly Lane, by locks]: Beamed canalside pub in lovely spot by Napton locks, three bars on different levels, attractive mix of furnishings inc huge farmhouse table in homely front bar, generous food esp good home-made pies, good service by very friendly staff, well kept ales such as Brewsters Marquis and Hook Norton, two big log fires, pool in back games room; good big lawn with play area, wishing well and fine views (also all-day summer shop and small agricultural museum); very busy wknds, but winter hours may be curtailed *(Gill and Keith Croxton)*

Napton Bridge Inn [Southam Rd (A425), Napton Bottom Lock]: Big busy unpretentious canal pub, recently refurbished, clean and bright, with pine panelling, open fires and old tables and chairs in three smallish rooms, friendly hard-working staff, wide range of enjoyable food running up to good choice of steaks, well kept Flowers Original, Tetleys and guest ales, good house wine, magazines, lots of canal and water pictures, no smoking dining area overlooking water; piped music, no dogs, children welcome, garden behind *(George Atkinson, Carol and David Havard)*

Nether Whitacre [SP2392]

Dog [Dog Lane, off B4098 Coventry—Tamworth]: 16th-c pub with several low-beamed areas, masses of bric-a-brac, wide choice of well priced food (may be a wait when busy), Bass, M&B Brew XI and a guest beer; children welcome, garden *(Alan and Hillie Johnson)*

Netherton [SO9387]

☆ *Old Swan* [Halesowen Rd (A459 just S of centre)]: Friendly and traditional, doing well under committed newish landlord, with good cheap beer brewed at the pub, also Greene King Old Speckled Hen and occasional guest beers, widening choice of cheap food inc Sun lunches, nice old solid fuel stove, fine mirrors, decorative swan ceiling, matching extension *(LYM, Nigel Espley, Liane Purnell)*

No Mans Heath [SK2808]

Four Counties [B5493 Tamworth—Ashby]: Homely and immaculate, with very friendly long-serving licensees, interesting brass and other ornaments, witty pictures, lovely stained glass, limited but enjoyable food inc popular Sun lunch, five real ales such as Everards Original, Ind Coope Burton and Marstons Pedigree, roaring fires; small no smoking dining room *(Bernie Adams)*

Northend [SP3952]

Red Lion [off B4100 Warwick—Banbury; Bottom St]: Recently reopened with concentration on impressive and imaginative food (already booked up wknds); well kept M&B Brew XI, Timothy Taylors Landlord and a guest beer, decent wines, bright lighting *(Michael and Jeanne Shillington, Cliff Bennett)*

Offchurch [SP3565]

Stags Head [Welsh Rd, off A425 at Radford Semele]: Low-beamed thatched village pub with enjoyable food in bar and restaurant inc good value two-course lunch, friendly service, well kept Bass and Flowers Original; quiet piped music; tables in good-sized garden with play area *(John Brightley, Steve and Sue Griffiths, Tony Walker)*

Old Hill [SO9685]

Waterfall [Waterfall Lane]: Down-to-earth local, very friendly staff, consistently well kept and well priced Bathams, Enville, Hook Norton, Marstons and three or four interesting guest beers, farm cider, country wines, cheap plain home-made food from good filled rolls to Sun lunch and special snacks Fri, tankards and jugs hanging from boarded ceiling; piped music, children welcome, back garden with play area; open all day wknd *(Dave Braisted, the Didler)*

Oldbury [SO9888]

Waggon & Horses [Church St, nr Savacentre]: Ornate Victorian tiles, copper ceiling and original windows in busy town pub with several well kept changing ales, wide choice of generous food inc lots of puddings in bar and bookable upstairs bistro, decent wines, friendly efficient service even when busy, lively comfortable lounge with tie collection, side room with high-backed settles and big old tables, open fire, Black Country memorabilia; opens noon *(the Didler)*

Oxhill [SP3149]

Peacock: Nice atmosphere, very welcoming even when busy; good range of food *(MJVK)*

Preston Bagot [SP1765]

Crabmill [B4095 Henley-in-Arden—Warwick]: Comfortably upmarket timbered dining pub (even a uniformed parking attendant) recently expensively reworked with sofas and coffee tables in stylish two-level lounge, Flowers and Marstons Pedigree from steely modern bar, decent wines, elegant table settings in roomy candlelit low-beamed dining area, lots of nooks and crannies, food from bar meals to modern restaurant cooking, quick young staff; rows of picnic-sets in big garden with play area, open all day *(Susan and John Douglas, LYM)*

Priors Hardwick [SP4756]

☆ *Butchers Arms* [off A423 via Wormleighton or A361 via Boddington, N of Banbury; Church End]: Upmarket restaurant in pleasantly reworked 14th-c building, oak beams, flagstones, panelling, antiques and soft lighting (soft voices, too – a refined low murmur); huge choice of very well cooked and presented food (not cheap but worth it) inc fixed price lunches, small bar with inglenook log fire used mainly by people waiting for a table (also simple public bar); keg beer but good wines, very friendly Portuguese landlord, punctilious service, country garden *(Mr and Mrs Hugh Spottiswoode, K H Frostick, BB, H W Clayton)*

Priors Marston [SP4857]

☆ *Holly Bush* [follow Shuckburgh sign, then first right by phone box]: Golden stone pub, small rambling rooms, beams and stripped stone, old-fashioned pub seats, blazing log fire one end, central woodburner, friendly helpful service, well kept Flowers IPA, Hook Norton Best and Marstons Pedigree, good food from interesting soups and good range of baguettes up, large restaurant; large friendly dog, darts, pool, games machines, juke box, piped music; children welcome, tables in sheltered garden, pretty village, bedrooms *(George Atkinson, John Bramley, Di and Mike Gillam, John Brightley, Alan and Hillie Johnson, LYM, James Nunns)*

Rushall [SK03001]

Manor Arms [Park Rd, off A461]: Old low-beamed pub by Rushall Canal, with several rooms in contrasting styles; no bar (pumps fixed to the wall, shelves of bottles around them), big inglenook fireplace, generous helpings of good simple fresh pub food, well kept Banks's Bitter and Original; can get crowded early at wknds; waterside garden, by Park Lime Pits nature reserve *(Keith and Ann Arnold, Steve Jennings)*

Shilton [SP4084]

Shilton Arms [B4065 NE of Coventry]: Pleasant village pub with good range of good value food (all day Sun), enormous helpings, three real ales, decent house wine, no smoking section; garden with play area *(CMW, JJW, Mike and Wendy Proctor)*

Shipston-on-Stour [SP2540]

☆ *Black Horse* [Station Rd (off A3400)]: 16th-c thatched pub with interesting ornaments and inglenook coal fire in spotless low-beamed bar, homely and relaxed; reasonably priced carefully cooked food inc wkdy OAP bargain lunches, well kept Chadwicks Best, Marstons Pedigree and Ruddles, friendly staff and locals, small dining room; back garden with terrace and barbecue *(John Robertson)*

Old Mill [Mill Rd]: A hotel, but used as a pub by locals, also popular for lunch and dinner (good Italian dishes – Italian landlord); bedrooms *(K H Frostick)*

☆ *White Bear* [High St]: Massive settles and cheerful atmosphere in traditional front bar with good log fire, well kept Bass and Marstons Pedigree, decent wines, friendly staff, interesting food in bar and simply furnished no smoking back bistro with several small rooms (live music here instead Sun night); tables in small back yard and benches on street; bedrooms simple but clean, with huge breakfast, open all day *(Sue and Jim Sargeant, George Atkinson, LYM, Michael and Jeanne Shillington)*

Snitterfield [SP2159]

Foxhunter [Smiths Lane/School Rd; off A46 N of Stratford]: Small, clean, comfortable and attractive, keen young management, banquettes and hunting pictures in L-shaped bar/lounge, wide range of well presented and reasonably priced food cooked to order, real ales inc Hook Norton; maybe piped music; children allowed, tables outside *(Martin Jennings)*

Southam [SP4161]

☆ *Old Mint* [Coventry St (A423 towards Banbury)]: Impressive 14th-c building with heavy beams and plenty of character, some concentration on good reasonably priced food, well kept ales such as Bass and Fullers London Pride, friendly service, log fire, front opened up as games room; pleasant back courtyard *(LYM, Rona Murdoch)*

Stockton [SP4365]

Boat [A426 Southam—Rugby]: Child-friendly open-plan canalside pub with simple cheerful décor inc colourful tiled tables and real fires, good value generous food, well kept Greene King IPA, friendly service, no smoking eating areas; piped music may obtrude rather; lots of tables out overlooking water *(M C and S Jeanes, Ian and Nita Cooper)*

Crown [High St]: Well run and friendly village pub, two log fires, brasses and copper pans, assorted furniture inc armchairs and settee, at least six real ales (some unusual) kept well by Irish landlord, good reasonably priced straightforward home-made food inc sandwiches and vegetarian; pool, darts and other games one end, piped music or juke box; restaurant in ancient barn *(Ted George)*

Stonnall [SK0703]

Old Swann [off A452; Main St]: Wide choice of home-made lunchtime food from sandwiches up inc bargain OAP meals, big dining extension (booking advised Sun), cold Bass, M&B Brew XI and Worthingtons *(Jack Barnwell)*

Royal Oak [just off A452 N of Brownhills]: Popular and welcoming refurbished beamed local, well kept ales such as Bass, Greene King Old Speckled Hen and Ruddles County, Charles Wells Bombardier and Wadworths 6X, farm cider, jovial attentive landlord, enjoyable food inc bargain midweek lunch in bar and evening restaurant, also Sun lunch; no music *(A and M Worth)*

Stourbridge [SO8984]

Seven Stars [Brook Rd, nr stn]: Well organised and sympathetically extended Victorian pub with impressive high ceiling, decorative tiles and ornate carving in period bar, good food inc huge starters and all-day cold snacks in lounge eating area or larger restaurant on left, well kept changing ales such as Bathams, Courage Directors and Theakstons Best; comfortably bustling atmosphere, friendly regulars, nice staff; open all day *(the Didler)*

Stratford-upon-Avon [SP2055]

Dirty Duck [Waterside]: 16th-c Whitbreads Wayside Inn nr Memorial Theatre – still attracts actors, lots of signed RSC photographs; Flowers IPA, Greene King Old Speckled Hen and Wadworths 6X, quick friendly service, open fire, bustling public bar (little lounge seating for drinkers), children allowed in small dining area, prices on the high side; attractive small terrace looking over riverside public gardens – which tend to act as summer overflow; properly the Black Swan *(LYM, Brian Skelcher, Theo, Anne and Jane Gaskin, M Joyner, Alan Thomas, Dr Alan Sutton, Ted and Jan Whitfield, Francis and Deirdre Gevers-McClure, Kevin Blake, Richard Lewis)*

Falcon [Chapel St]: Attractive Tudor building with big fireplace in quiet panelled bar, other rooms inc lighter more modern ones, well kept Flowers, friendly staff, restaurant; may be piped music; bedrooms (quieter but more functional in modern wing) *(Mike Ridgway, Sarah Miles, Alan Thomas)*

Jester [Cox's Yard, Bridgefoot]: Part of tourist

complex, brewing its own good Cox's Jester and Juggler, long light and airy bar with friendly staff, bar food, play area, roomy riverside terrace; brewery tours available, open all day, good disabled facilities *(Richard Lewis)*

Lamplighter [Rother St, opp United Reform Church; handy for Friday Market]: Homely and civilised, with small bar, lounge/snug and larger side area off square central servery, nice mix of wooden chairs and settles around oblong and round table, alcoves, pillars, stripped brick and some flagstones, lots of show business pictures, guns on walls and beams, good cheap food, well kept Marstons and other beers, friendly staff; TV, games machines *(Richard Lewis)*

Pen & Parchment [Bridgefoot, by canal basin]: Whitbreads Hogshead with Shakespeare theme in L-shaped split-level lounge and snug, beams, bare boards and balusters, small alcoves and no smoking area, big open fire in old fireplace, prompt service, blackboards showing up to 10 often interesting changing ales, decent food and special drinks offers, also ciders and wines; occasional beer festivals (may not attract your favourite sort of person then); tables out among shrubs and ivy, pretty hanging baskets, good canal basin views; busy road *(Ted George, Richard Lewis, Alan Thomas)*

Queens Head [Ely St]: Comfortable L-shaped bar with beams and decorated bare brickwork, interesting artefacts, good choice of well kept beers, log fire, cheerful long-serving staff, lunchtime food; big sports TVs *(Richard Lewis)*

Windmill [Church St]: Cosy old pub with town's oldest licence, beyond the attractive Guild Chapel; low beams, quarry-tiled front bar, bare boards in main one, wide choice of good value food, well kept real ales inc interesting guests, friendly efficient staff, good civilised mix of customers, carpeted dining area; tables outside *(Kevin Blake, Sue Holland, Dave Webster, Alan Thomas)*

Stretton-on-Fosse [SP2238]

Plough [just off A429]: Welcoming 17th-c village pub, small bar and larger lounge, jugs and mugs on oak beams, Ansells Bitter and Mild and Tetleys, attentive staff, good changing food inc OAP meals (booking suggested), good-sized fireplace, small attractive candlelit dining room on right; darts, bedrooms at nearby farm under same ownership *(K H Frostick, June and Mike Coleman)*

Temple Grafton [SP1255]

☆ *Blue Boar* [a mile E, towards Binton; off A422 W of Stratford]: Recently extended country dining pub with beams, stripped stonework and log fires, cheerful attentive staff, well kept ales such as Brakspears Hooray Henley, Greene King Old Speckled Hen, Hook Norton and Theakstons XB, usual bar food from baked potatoes up, more elaborate dishes in comfortable restaurant (past glass-top well with golden carp) with no smoking section, good wine choice, traditional games in flagstoned side room; children welcome, open all day summer wknds, picnic-sets outside, pretty flower plantings; comfortable well equipped

bedrooms inc some new ones *(Brian and Bett Cox, Theo, Anne and Jane Gaskin, Don Mather, Stan and Hazel Allen, LYM, Ian Phillips)*

Tipton [SO9592]

Pie Factory [Hurst Lane, Dudley Rd towards Wednesbury; A457/A4037]: Used to be a nicely barmy clutter of esoteric ancient meat-processing equipment, strings of model hams, even an office staffed by pigs; all that's now much toned down, but still worth knowing for good value hearty food inc children's and lots of pies, well kept beers; piped music, pool, TV; some live music, children welcome, open all day, food all day Sun *(D P and J A Sweeney, LYM)*

Rising Sun [Horseley Rd, off A461]: Several well kept changing ales such as RCH Pitchfork and a Mild, farm cider, great range of malt whiskies, thriving atmosphere; Aug bank hol beer festival *(the Didler)*

Upper Brailes [SP3039]

☆ *Gate*: Attractive and tidily old-fashioned low-beamed village pub, sizeable part-panelled bar, smaller lounge with stripped stone, old bread oven and lots of brass, welcoming landlord, well kept Hook Norton beers with a guest such as Elgoods Golden Newt, big log fire, well priced food from a simple menu, games room; children if well behaved; tables in extensive back garden with wendy house, pretty hillside spot *(Michael and Jenny Back)*

Upper Gornal [SO92921]

Britannia [Kent St]: Dating from 18th c and once a slaughterhouse; now a Bathams local, with their cheap Best and Mild kept superbly and authentic Black Country atmosphere, especially in back room originally laid out for table drinks service; open all day Sat *(the Didler)*

Walsall [SP0198]

Green Dragon [High St]: Old-fashioned town pub, three floors with plenty of varnished wood, engraved glass, brown ceilings and wooden floors, huge helpings of low-priced food, Banks's ales *(Dave Braisted)*

Lyndon House [Upper Rushall St]: Good atmosphere, well kept beer *(C J Butler)*

Tap & Spile [John St]: Victorian backstreet local, formerly the New Inn (aka Pretty Bricks), with well kept Theakstons, Charles Wells Bombardier and several changing guest beers, good value generous food (occasional curry club), welcoming staff, real fires; non-invasive music *(C J Butler, Keith and Ann Arnold)*

White Lion [Sandwell St]: Good atmosphere, good range of well kept real ales inc a guest beer, well priced lunchtime food; games room, open all day Sat *(C J Butler)*

Warwick [SP2865]

Crown [Coventry Rd]: Welcoming town pub, well kept real ales (happy hour gives extra half for each pint); bedrooms *(Joy and Peter Heatherley, Dr and Mrs A K Clarke)*

Old Fourpenny Shop [Crompton St, nr racecourse]: Friendly, cosy and comfortable split-level M&B pub with five well kept changing guest beers, welcoming licensees, simple lunchtime bar food, cheerful service, restaurant, no piped music; bedrooms *(Nigel and Sue Foster)*

Racehorse [Stratford Rd]: Large comfortable family dining pub, cheerful and bustling, with good value generous food all day inc children's and OAP bargains, well kept Everards Tiger and guest beers, no smoking areas inc back conservatory (children welcome); open all day *(Ian and Nita Cooper)*

Rose & Crown [30 Market Pl]: Cheerfully and interestingly decorated unpretentious three-room town pub, well kept Bass, M&B Brew XI and Highgate Dark Mild, traditional games, limited low-priced food from sandwiches up; piped nostalgic pop music; children welcome, open all day *(Peter Meister, Pete Baker, LYM)*

☆ *Tilted Wig* [Market Pl]: Roomy and airy, somewhere between tearoom and pub, big windows on square, stone-effect floor on left, bare boards on right, carpet behind, brocaded banquettes and kitchen chairs around pine tables, some stripped stone and panelling, well kept Ansells, Marstons Pedigree and Tetleys, good fairly priced Australian wines, wide choice of good reasonably priced home-made bistro food (not Sun evening) from sandwiches and baguettes up, lively bustle, quick friendly service, two coal-effect fires; SkyTV, piped music may be loud; tables in garden, live jazz and folk Sun evening, open all day, comfortable well appointed bedrooms *(JES, BB, Jenny and Chris Wilson, Jim and Maggie Cowell, Peter Meister)*

☆ *Zetland Arms* [Church St]: Pleasant and cosy town pub with short choice of cheap but good bar food (not wknd evenings), well kept Marstons Pedigree and Tetleys, decent wine in generous glasses, friendly quick service, neat but relaxing small panelled front bar with toby jug collection and sports TV, comfortable larger L-shaped back eating area with small conservatory, interestingly planted sheltered garden; children may be allowed; bedrooms, sharing bathroom *(LYM, Martin Jennings, Jim and Maggie Cowell, Alan and Hillie Johnson, John Bramley)*

Weston-under-Wetherley [SP3669]

Bull [B4453 Leamington Spa—Rugby]: Cosy village pub, generous good value tasty food in lounge and restaurant area, very friendly staff *(Andrew Johnson)*

Willenhall [SO9698]

Kipper House [Upper Lichfield St]: Enjoyable family pub with bare boards, cream walls, high ceilings, dark wood furniture, and dark snug end bit; good choice of reasonably priced food, two well kept Ushers ales, friendly locals, pool, TV; disabled access, open all day Fri/Sat *(G Coates)*

Willey [SP4984]

☆ *Sarah Mansfield* [just off A5, N of A427 junction; Main St]: Hospitable and welcoming, lots of dining tables in two comfortable and spotlessly refurbished rooms mainly given over to eating, beams and polished flagstones, stripped masonry, cosy corners, open fire, small bar area, wide range of food from sandwiches

and baked potatoes up, attentive young staff, up to four well kept ales such as Hancocks HB; pool table at back, maybe piped local radio *(George Atkinson)*

Willoughby [SP5267]

Rose [just off A45 E of Dunchurch]: Friendly small partly thatched beamed pub with emphasis on good value straightforward food from filled rolls to tender Sun carvery, OAP lunches Tues and Thurs, tiled bar, carpeted lounge, evening restaurant, Courage Directors and John Smiths, cheerful staff, games room, seats out in front, garden with play area; cl Mon and Weds lunchtimes, Tues music night *(George Atkinson)*

Wilmcote [SP1657]

☆ *Mary Arden* [The Green]: Cheerful atmosphere, beams, pine boards, comfortable seats around good-sized tables, glass-topped well and woodburner, good choice of reasonably priced food, friendly young staff, well kept Hook Norton Best and Charles Wells Bombardier from long counter; tables on terrace overlooking Palmers Farm (formerly mistakenly known as Mary Arden's house), more in back garden, very attractive village; comfortable bedrooms *(Steve Chambers, S J and C C Davidson, J and D Whiting)*

Withybrook [SP4384]

☆ *Pheasant* [B4112 NE of Coventry, not far from M6, junction 2]: Big busy dining pub with lots of dark tables, plush-cushioned chairs, friendly efficient service, very wide choice of generous food inc good value specials and good vegetarian choice, Scottish Courage ales, good coffee, blazing log fires; piped music; children welcome, tables under lanterns on brookside terrace *(Mr and Mrs J E C Tasker, LYM, Adrian White, Julie King)*

Wixford [SP0954]

Fish [B4085 Alcester—Bidford]: Roomy L-shaped bar and snug, beams, polished panelling, carpets over flagstones, stuffed fish, reasonably priced bar food; corridor to lavatories is quite an art gallery *(Tony Walker)*

☆ *Three Horseshoes* [off A46 S of Redditch, via A422/A435 Alcester roundabout, or B439 at Bidford]: Roomy and nicely renovated, with consistently good generous food from bar meals up inc fresh fish, interesting choice (esp wknds, when it can get crowded), nice puddings, helpful service, good range of well kept mainly Whitbreads-related ales, bric-a-brac from blowtorches to garden gnomes; pleasant seating areas outside *(Peter Lloyd, M J and C E Abbey)*

Wollaston [SO8884]

Unicorn [Bridgnorth Rd]: Cosy and unpretentious former brewhouse, unspoilt L-shaped bar and lounge with lots of brasses and knick-knacks, small back snug, well kept Bathams *(Gill Waller, Tony Morriss)*

Wolverhampton [SO9198]

☆ *Combermere Arms* [Chapel Ash (A41 Tettenhall rd)]: Back to its proper name after briefly Irished spell as Kearneys, old-fashioned friendly local with three small cosy rooms, well kept Banks's and guest beers, decent wines, very welcoming staff, food inc bargain sandwiches and good value Sun lunch, bare boards and quaint touches, bar billiards; quiz Tues, small secluded garden with terrace and summer live music *(George and Anne Davidow, Mrs D Hardy, David and Sarah Jones)*

☆ *Great Western* [Sun St, behind BR station – left down subway under railway, turn right at end]: Vibrantly popular (esp before a Wolves match), well run and down to earth, with particularly well kept Bathams and Holdens, many old railway photographs and other memorabilia, traditional front bar, other rooms inc separate no smoking bar, very promptly served good inexpensive unpretentious lunchtime food (not Sun) from hot and cold cobs up; SkyTV; open all day, roomy back conservatory, tables in yard with good barbecues *(Gill Waller,*

Tony Morriss, Pete Baker, the Didler)
Wootton Wawen [SP1563]
☆ *Bulls Head* [just off A3400 Birmingham—Stratford]: Smart and attractive black and white dining pub with low Elizabethan beams and timbers, comfortable chairs, rugs setting off good flagstones, well kept Banks's, Claverley and Marstons Pedigree, good wines, enjoyable, though not cheap, food inc several fresh fish (extra charge for veg), friendly unhurried service; pews in more austere tap room with dominoes, shove-ha'penny; children welcome, open all day Sun, tables on pleasant terrace – handy for Stratford Canal walks *(Alun Howells, LYM, John Bramley, Lisa and Carl Henshaw, David and Ruth Shillitoe, Ian Phillips)*

'Children welcome' means the pub says it lets children inside without any special restriction. If it allows them in, but to restricted areas such as an eating area or family room, we specify this. Places with separate restaurants usually let children use them, hotels usually let them into public areas such as lounges. Some pubs impose an evening time limit – let us know if you find this: www.goodguides.com

Wiltshire

The Haunch of Venison in Salisbury, a marvellously well preserved old town tavern, appeared in our first edition 20 years ago, and has been in every year since, always under the same licensees Antony and Victoria Leroy. Two other pubs have also figured in every edition: the rambling old White Hart at Ford (great atmosphere, restauranty at night), and the Lamb at Hindon (popular for its interesting food). By contrast, another five pubs are new to this edition (though most have figured in years past): the interesting old Waggon & Horses at Beckhampton (new landlord doing well, lots of wines by the glass), the Smoking Dog in Malmesbury (nice front bars, popular back bistro), the Vine Tree at Norton (perked up nicely under enthusiastic new licensees), the Royal Oak at Wootton Rivers (a pleasant dining pub), and the civilised Bell at Wylye (gently upmarket food, good beers). Other pubs currently doing particularly well here are the Talbot at Berwick St John (flourishing under expert new licensees), the Cross Guns near Bradford-on-Avon (bustling good value dining pub), the restauranty Three Crowns at Brinkworth, the friendly Horseshoe at Ebbesbourne Wake (a particular favourite, with good home cooking and well kept beers), the Angel at Heytesbury (imaginative food in its pretty little dining room, a nice place to stay), the handsome old Grosvenor Arms at Hindon (food getting high praise under the newish chef), the canalside Barge at Seend (a nice all-rounder), and the Pear Tree at Whitley (an imaginative dining pub with a terrific choice of wines by the glass). From the fine choice of places here for a special meal out, the very well managed White Hart at Ford takes our title of Wiltshire Dining Pub of the Year. In the Lucky Dip section at the end of the chapter, pubs to watch are the Crown at Broad Hinton, Bridge Inn at Horton, Malet Arms at Newton Tony, Swan at Wilton (the little village, not the town), Poplars at Wingfield and White Horse at Winterbourne Bassett. Wiltshire drinks prices are very close to the national average, with Wadworths or one of the smaller local breweries such as Archers, Tisbury, Stonehenge or Moles tending to give better value than beers from the bigger combines.

ALVEDISTON ST9723 Map 2

Crown 🛏

Village signposted on left off A30 about 12 miles W of Salisbury

Happily, after several licensee changes over the last few years, this lovely 15th-c thatched inn, peacefully set in a very pretty spot, has been taken over by the very hard-working former assistant manager who plans to settle things down by making his stay here a long one. There's a cosy atmosphere in the three charming low-beamed and partly panelled rooms, which have deep terracotta paintwork, two inglenook fireplaces and dark oak furniture. Imaginative and very fairly priced food given its quality includes soup, sandwiches or baguettes (£3.25), warm salad of bacon, sauté potatoes and gruyère cheese (£4.75), with daily specials such as scallops with lime and coriander sauce (£5.25), butter bean casserole with herb crumb topping (£6.95), braised leg of lamb stuffed with feta, vine leaves, olives and mint, roast cod on pecorino mash with saffron cream sauce or pork loin medallions on sage and onion rösti with cider sauce (£8.95), and sole fillet roulade with lobster mousse and dill cream (£9.95). One of the dining areas is no smoking. Well kept Ringwood Best, Wadworths 6X, Charles Wells Bombardier and guests such as Badger Tanglefoot, Greene King Old Speckled Hen and Shepherd Neame Spitfire on handpump; darts, cribbage, dominoes and piped music. The attractive garden is nicely broken up on different levels around a thatched white well, with shrubs and rockeries among neatly kept lawns; it faces a farmyard with ponies and other animals, and there's a play area; good value bedrooms. *(Recommended by Dr and Mrs Michael Smith, Douglas and Ann Hare, Simon and Laura Habbishow, WHBM, Blaise Vyner)*

Free house ~ Licensee Paul Waite ~ Real ale ~ Bar food (12-2, 7-9.30(9 Sun)) ~ (01722) 780335 ~ Children in restaurant ~ Open 11.30-2.30, 6-11; 12-2.30, 7-10.30 Sun; closed 25 Dec ~ Bedrooms: £25S/£47.50S

AXFORD SU2370 Map 2
Red Lion
Off A4 E of Marlborough; on back road Mildenhall—Ramsbury

This pretty flint-and-brick pub has fine views over a valley from picture windows in its beamed and pine-panelled bar. The bar has a pleasant mix of comfortable cask seats and other solid chairs on a parquet floor, and you can buy the paintings by local artists which hang on the walls; the restaurant and bar eating area are no smoking. Well kept Hook Norton and Wadworths 6X and an occasional guest such as Wadworths seasonal ales on handpump, and a good choice of sensibly priced wines by the glass. Blackboard specials change every now and then but might include home-made chicken liver pâté (£4.25), fresh crab and avocado salad (£4.95), home-made nut roast with tomato and basil sauce (£8.25), guinea fowl in cream, chive and sherry sauce (£10.75), T-bone steak (£14.50), and lots of fish such as whole fresh plaice (£9.75), monkfish tails baked with rosemary and garlic (£12.50) and mixed fried seafood platter with garlic and olive oil (£14.95). Other food includes bar snacks such as sandwiches (from £1.95), soup (£2.75), ploughman's (from £4.25), home-cooked Wiltshire ham (£5.25), and steak and kidney pie (£6.95); service can be slow when busy. The sheltered garden has picnic-sets under cocktail parasols, swings, and lovely views. *(Recommended by MDN, Angus and Rosemary Campbell, Stephen Savill, D B, K A Bishop, Sheila and Robert Robinson, Julie and Bill Ryan)*

Free house ~ Licensees Mel and Daphne Evans ~ Real ale ~ Bar food (12-2, 7-10) ~ Restaurant ~ (01672) 520271 ~ Children welcome ~ Open 11-3, 6.30-11; 12-3.30, 7-10.30 Sun; closed Sun evening in winter

BECKHAMPTON SU0868 Map 2
Waggon & Horses
A4 Marlborough—Calne

Always a cheerful sight to coachmen coming in from what was notorious as the coldest stretch of the old Bath road, this attractive old thatched ex-coaching inn is still a welcoming stop. The open-plan bar is welcoming with its beams in the shiny ceiling where walls have been knocked through, large, shiny wood floors, mustard walls, old-fashioned high-backed settle on one side of the room, with a smaller one opposite, leatherette stools, and comfortably cushioned wall benches. Bar food includes home-made soup (£1.95), sandwiches (from £2.95), beef and stilton pie (£5.95), fillet steak (£8.95), daily specials such as peppers stuffed with mushroom risotto (£6.25), chicken breast topped with stilton and ham or lamb shoulder with minted gravy (£6.95) and puddings such as hot chocolate fudge pie or home-made sherry and peach trifle (£2.95). Well kept Wadworths IPA, 6X, Farmers Glory and their seasonal beer on handpump and over a dozen wines by the glass; piped music, darts, pool, dominoes, fruit machine, juke box and TV. Silbury Hill – a prehistoric mound – is just towards Marlborough, and Avebury stone circle and the West Kennet long barrow are very close too. *(Recommended by Tim and Isobel Smith, Brian and Pat Wardrobe, Mrs Roxanne Chamberlain, Sheila and Robert Robinson, Tony Beaulah, Dave Braisted)*

Wadworths ~ Manager Doug Shepherd ~ Real ale ~ Bar food (not Sun evening) ~ (01672) 539418 ~ Children in restaurant ~ Open 11-2.30, 5.30(6 Sat)-11; 12-3, 7-10.30 Sun; closed 25 Dec evening

BERWICK ST JAMES SU0639 Map 2
Boot

B3083, between A36 and A303 NW of Salisbury

There's a contented cosy atmosphere, a huge winter log fire in the inglenook fireplace at one end, sporting prints over a smaller brick fireplace at the other, and houseplants on the wide window sills in the bar at this attractive flint and stone pub. The flagstoned bar which has well kept Bass and Wadworths IPA and 6X on handpump, a few well chosen house wines, half a dozen malts and farm cider is partly carpeted, with a mix of tables, cushioned wheelback chairs, and a few bar stools by the counter. A charming small back no smoking dining room has a nice mix of dining chairs around the three tables on its blue Chinese carpet, and deep pink walls with an attractively mounted collection of boots. It's a pity we don't get more reports about the very good bar food here, as they use as much local produce as possible, vegetables may come from the garden in season, and a good imaginative menu makes it the sort of place we'd expect to qualify for a food award: soup (£3.95), fried camembert with raspberry coulis, seafood salad with lemon and dill mayonnaise or breaded butterfly prawns with sweet chilli sauce (£5.50), fresh fish of the day, twice baked goats cheese soufflé with creamy cheese sauce, chilli or lasagne (£7.95), fried lambs kidneys on apple rösti with cider jus or beef in stilton stew (£8.95), chicken in a white wine, tomato, garlic and black olive sauce with linguini (£10.25), warm salad of smoked pigeon breasts and sautéed potatoes with rémoulade sauce (£10.50) and 10oz sirloin steak (£12.95). Service is very friendly and helpful; maybe unobtrusive piped jazz. The sheltered side lawn, very neatly kept with pretty flowerbeds, has some well spaced picnic-sets. *(Recommended by Howard and Margaret Buchanan, KC, S and H Tate-Lovery, J Monk, Charles Moncreiffe, David R Crafts)*

Wadworths ~ Tenant Kathie Duval ~ Real ale ~ Bar food (12-2.30, 6.30-9.30(7-9 Sun)) ~ Restaurant ~ (01722) 790243 ~ Children welcome ~ Open 12-3, 6-11(7-10.30 Sun); closed Mon lunchtime, 25, 26 Dec evening

BERWICK ST JOHN ST9422 Map 2
Talbot ♀

Village signposted from A30 E of Shaftesbury

Harvey the cat has featured in most of the last 10 editions of the *Guide*, but this is his first time at this lovely old village pub, just taken over by the former owners of the Cott at Dartington and other Devon institutions. This is a smaller place than their previous pubs, and they are loving the much more hands-on approach they can take here. Very enjoyable freshly prepared bar food from a daily changing blackboard menu might include vegetable and pearl barley broth (£3.50), grilled goats cheese (£4.75), mixed mushroom risotto (£5.95), moussaka and feta cheese salad or sausage and mash (£6.50), rabbit casserole on grainy mustard mash (£6.75), steak and kidney pudding (£6.95), with more substantial evening dishes such as thai crab cakes with coriander and sweet tomato dressing or wild mushroom tartlet with beetroot and apple salsa (£4.75), duck casserole with black pudding, juniper and orange (£9.95), halibut steamed on a prawn risotto with asparagus and lemon butter (£12.50), fillet steak with roasted onions and red wine sauce (£15.50), and puddings such as apple and almond pudding, chocolate brandy mousse and rhubarb and ginger fool (£3.75). Well kept Bass, Butcombe and Wadworths 6X on handpump, farm cider, fresh juices, and a fine choice of wines. The single long, heavily beamed bar is simply furnished with cushioned solid wall and window seats, spindleback chairs, a high-backed built-in settle at one end, and tables that are candlelit in the evenings. There's a huge inglenook fireplace with a good iron fireback and bread ovens, and nicely shaped heavy black beams and cross-beams with bevelled corners. *(Recommended by D J and J R Tapper, Dr and Mrs Michael Smith)*

*Free house ~ Licensees David and Susan Grey ~ Real ale ~ Bar food ~ Restaurant ~
(01747) 828222 ~ Children welcome ~ Open 12-2.30, 6.30-11; 12-4 Sun; closed Sun
evening, and Mon except bank holidays*

BOX ST8369 Map 2

Quarrymans Arms

Box Hill; coming from Bath on A4 turn right into Bargates 50 yds before railway bridge, then
at T-junction turn left up Quarry Hill, turning left again near the top at grassy triangle; from
Corsham, turn left after Rudloe Park Hotel into Beech Rd, then third left on to Barnetts Hill,
and finally right at the top of the hill

This low stone building which is ideally situated for cavers, potholers and walkers
was once the local of the Bath stone miners which explains a lot of the mining
related hardware dotted around the interior. They now run interesting guided trips
down the mine. Good food, a warm welcome and sweeping valley views are the
other rewards waiting for you at the end of the sinuous drive down a warren of lanes
to get here. While many people come for the varied enjoyable bar food, one pleasant
modernised room with an open fire, interesting quarry photographs and
memorabilia covering the walls, is entirely set aside for drinking the well kept
Butcombe, Moles and Wadworths 6X on handpump, and a guest or two from West
Country breweries such as Abbey and Bath, good wines, over 60 malt whiskies, and
10 or so vintage cognacs. As well as soup and sandwiches (both £2.50), good bar
food might include stilton and asparagus pancake (£3.75), camembert parcels
(£4.50), moules marinières (£5.25), lasagne (£7.25), home-made curries or pies
(£7.95), various stir fries (£8.25), pork medallions (£9.45), rack of lamb (£11.50),
barbary duck (£12.50) and lots of fish such as bass, barracuda, mackerel and tuna;
good prompt service. Cribbage, dominoes, fruit machine, shove-ha'penny, football,
boules, cricket and piped music. An attractive outside terrace has picnic-sets.
*(Recommended by Sally Anne and Peter Goodale, Jonathan Smith, Joy and Peter Heatherley, Lyn
and Geoff Hallchurch, Ian Phillips, Catherine Pitt)*

*Free house ~ Licensees John and Ginny Arundel ~ Real ale ~ Bar food (12-3, 6-10.30)
~ Restaurant ~ (01225) 743569 ~ Children welcome ~ Open 11-3, 6-11; 11-11.30
Sat; 12-10.30 Sun ~ Bedrooms: /£45*

BRADFORD-ON-AVON ST8060 Map 2

Cross Guns

Avoncliff; pub is across footbridge from Avoncliff Station (road signposted Turleigh turning
left off A363 heading uphill N from river in Bradford centre, and keep bearing left), and can
also be reached down very steep and eventually unmade road signposted Avoncliff – keep
straight on rather than turning left into village centre – from Westwood (which is signposted
from B3109 and from A366, W of Trowbridge)

In summer – when it can get quite busy – most people sit outside this family-run
dining pub on the numerous seats in the pretty floodlit and terraced gardens with
fabulous views over the wide river Avon, and the maze of bridges, aqueducts (the
Kennet & Avon Canal) and railway tracks that wind through its quite narrow gorge.
A couple of the plain sturdy oak tables in the bar are set aside for drinkers, but
otherwise, the rest of the bar is given over to diners, with a core of low 17th-c
mate's chairs, stone walls, and a 16th-c inglenook with a smoking chamber behind
it. A remarkable range of drinks includes well kept Bass, Millworkers Token
(brewed for the pub), Worthingtons and a guest such as Greene King Old Speckled
Hen on handpump, about 100 malts, 25 country wines, and around 50 cocktails
(including non-alcoholic ones); darts, table skittles, TV and piped music. Bar food
includes sandwiches (from £1.80), home-made soup (£3), filled baked potatoes
(from £3.50), salads (from £5), steak and ale pie (£6.95), local trout (£7.95),
mushroom stroganoff or half roast duck with orange sauce (£8), 16 oz rump steak
(from £8.95), and daily specials such as cumberland sausage ring and onion gravy or
sweet and sour vegetables (£6.95), salmon fishcakes with tarragon sauce or minted
lamb chops with redcurrant jelly (£7.95), puddings (£3.50). A Tannoy system

announces meal orders to outside tables; booking is advisable. There may be long waits for food, when busy. Walkers are very welcome, but not their muddy boots. Having seen the crowds, passengers on the Bristol to Weymouth railway line might be tempted to alight at the platform opposite and cross the aqueduct that leads to the pub. *(Recommended by P R and S A White, Charles and Pauline Stride, Bill Sykes, Sue Demont, Tim Barrow, Ian Phillips, Roger Wain-Heapy, W F C Phillips, Lyn and Geoff Hallchurch, Denis Christian, Ann and Colin Hunt, Keith Fairbrother)*

Free house ~ Licensees Jenny and Ken Roberts ~ Real ale ~ Bar food (12-10) ~ Restaurant ~ (01225) 862335/867613 ~ Children in eating area of bar and restaurant ~ Open 10-12; closed 25, 26 Dec evening ~ Bedrooms: £30/£50(£60B)

Dandy Lion

35 Market St

If there isn't one of their evening poetry readings happening when you visit this thriving town pub, or if the happy mix of customers and friendly staff doesn't provide enough entertainment, there will at least be a daily aphorism chalked on a board, newspapers to read and nostalgic piped pop music to distract you, The pleasantly relaxed long main bar here has big windows on either side of the door with a table and cushioned wooden armchairs by each, nice high-backed farmhouse chairs, old-fashioned dining chairs, and a brocade-cushioned long settle on the stripped wooden floor (there's a couple of rugs too), sentimental and gently erotic pictures on the panelled walls, an overmantel with Brussels horses and fairy-lit hops over the bar counter. At the back and up a few steps, a snug little bare-boarded room has a lovely high-backed settle and other small ones around sturdy tables, a big mirror on the mulberry walls, and a piano. Good reasonably priced bar food at lunchtime includes sandwiches or filled baguettes (from £2.95), home-made soup (£3.25), toasted bagels (£3.75), five pasta dishes (from £3.95), filled baked potatoes (£4.50), basque-style mussels or field mushrooms with garlic, herbs, tomato and capsicum baked with cheese and cream (£5.25), fresh local trout (£5.50), and rump steak (£8.25); in the evening, extra dishes include home-made gravadlax and smoked trout (£4.50), kleftiko (£8.50), speciality 'hot stone' dishes you cook yourself (from £9.95) and daily specials such as smoked trout and prawns with pasta and brandy cream sauce or warm chicken, brie and cranberry bap (£5.25), grilled plaice (£6.95), lamb cutlets with mint and mushroom sauce (£8.95) and duck with orange and Grand Marnier sauce (£9.95), and puddings such as hot cherries in brandy and iced lemon parfait (from £3.50). Well kept Butcombe and Wadworths IPA, 6X , JCB on handpump, and good coffee. The upstairs restaurant is candlelit at night and has an area with antique toys and baskets of flowers. The pub is especially popular with a younger crowd at weekends. *(Recommended by Dr M E Wilson, Joy and Peter Heatherley, Susan and Nigel Wilson, Richard Pierce, Sue Demont, Tim Barrow)*

Wadworths ~ Tenant Jennifer Joseph ~ Real ale ~ Bar food ~ Restaurant ~ (01225) 863433 ~ Children in eating area of bar and restaurant ~ Open 10.30-3, 6-11; 11.30-2.30, 7-10.30 Sun

BRINKWORTH SU0184 Map 2
Three Crowns 🍴 ♀

The Street; B4042 Wootton Bassett—Malmesbury

The well varied and quite restauranty menu at this friendly village pub covers an entire wall, and while meals are not cheap, the generous helpings certainly offer good value for money. As well as lunchtime snacks such as filled rolls (lunchtime only, from £3.45), and heartily filled baked potatoes or proper ploughman's (from £6.40), dishes might include steak and kidney pie (£9.45), chicken en croûte filled with prawns, Boursin cheese and basil with madeira, mushroom and cream sauce (£12.85), pork tenderloin medallions with cheese dumplings and cherry wine sauce (£13.35), fruit stuffed quail on a pâté crouton with port sauce (£14.30), halibut poached in white wine and with coconut milk, lime and chilli with crispy leeks (£15.95); all main courses are served with half a dozen fresh vegetables. Most people choose to eat in the elegant no smoking conservatory, and as this is a popular place you do need to get here early. It's nicely set across a lane from a church, with a lovely traditional feel in all of its little enclaves, with big landscape prints and other pictures on the walls, some horsebrasses on the dark beams, a dresser with a collection of old bottles, tables of stripped deal (and a couple made from gigantic forge bellows), big tapestry-upholstered pews and blond chairs, and log fires. Although food is certainly the priority, there's a good range of real ales such as Archers Best, Boddingtons, Castle Eden, Fullers London Pride and Wadworths 6X on handpump, just over 90 wines, with at least 10 by the glass, and mulled wine in winter; sensibly placed darts, shove-ha'penny, dominoes, cribbage, chess, fruit machine, piped music. There's a light and airy garden room and a terrace with outdoor heating to the side of the conservatory. The garden stretches around the side and back, with well spaced tables, and looks over a side lane to the church, and out over rolling prosperous farmland. *(Recommended by Evelyn and Derek Walter, Andrew Shore, Gill and David Morrell, Susan and Nigel Wilson, Mrs Thomas, Comus and Sarah Elliott, Joyce and Maurice Cottrell, Gordon and Carole Barnett)*

Whitbreads ~ Lease Anthony Windle ~ Real ale ~ Bar food (12-2, 6-9.30; not 25 Dec) ~ Restaurant ~ (01666) 510366 ~ Well behaved children welcome ~ Open 11-3.30, 6-11; 12-4, 6.30-10.30 Sun

CHICKSGROVE ST9729 Map 2
Compasses 🍴 ♟ 🛏

From A30 5½ miles W of B3089 junction, take lane on N side signposted Sutton Mandeville, Sutton Row, then first left fork (small signs point the way to the pub, in Lower Chicksgrove; look out for the car park)

While the reliably good food at this pleasantly relaxed old thatched house may be snappily modern, the welcoming atmosphere in the bar remains reassuringly traditional, with old bottles and jugs hanging from beams above the roughly timbered counter, farm tools and traps on the partly stripped stone walls, and high-backed wooden settles forming snug booths around tables on the mainly flagstone floor. As well as soup (£3.95) and sandwiches (from £3.45), enjoyable meals from an imaginative changing menu might include popular goats cheese and pesto rustic loaf or bacon and onion tartlet (£4.95), scallops with mustard, cream and sun-dried tomato (£7.50), steak and kidney pie (£7.95), fried wild mushrooms with apple cream sauce and noodles (£8.95), braised leg of lamb with garlic, tomato and rosemary, sausage and mash or fried shark steak with fruit salad (£9.95), venison fillet with sweet cream sauce (£10.95), pigeon breast with wild mushrooms (£13.95), braised crocodile in cajun spices (£15.45), and puddings such as lemon cheesecake and pineapple in gin and Pimms (£3.75); all meals are served with a good choice of vegetables. Welcoming bar staff serve well kept Bass, Chicksgrove Churl (brewed for the pub by Wadworths), Wadworths 6X and maybe a guest such as Tisbury Stonehenge or Adnams Best on handpump, and six wines by the glass; cribbage, dominoes, bagatelle and shove-ha'penny. The quiet garden and flagstoned farm courtyard are very pleasant places to sit, and there's a nice walk to Sutton Mandeville church and back via Nadder Valley. Be warned, they close on Tuesdays after bank holiday Mondays. *(Recommended by Martin and Karen Wake, Dr and Mrs Nigel Holmes, Stephanie and Kamal Thapa, Dr David Cockburn, David and Natalie Towle, Adrian and Gwynneth Littleton, Ann and Colin Hunt, M G Hart, Dr and Mrs Michael Smith)*

Free house ~ Licensee Jonathan Bold ~ Real ale ~ Bar food (not Sun evenings) ~ Restaurant ~ (01722) 714318 ~ Well behaved children welcome ~ Open 12-3, 6-11; 12-3, 7-10.30 Sun; closed Mon except bank holidays, then cl Tues ~ Bedrooms: £40S/£55S

CORSHAM ST8670 Map 2
Two Pigs ◗
A4, Pickwick

The unique atmosphere in this truly traditional little drinker's pub (no food or under 21s) is always chatty and friendly and is perhaps at its liveliest on a Monday night, when live blues draws a big crowd into the very narrow and dimly lit stone-floored bar. The admirably old-fashioned feel owes much to the charismatic landlord, who has amassed a zany collection of bric-a-brac in the thirteen or so years he's been in charge, including enamel advertising signs on the wood-clad walls, pig-theme ornaments, old radios. He also knows a thing or two about beer, and alongside Hop Back Summer Lightning and Stonehenge Pigswill on handpump you can expect to find a couple of well kept changing guests such as Branscombe Value Bitter and Teignworthy Beachcomber; also a range of country wines. A good mix of customers gathers around the long dark wood tables and benches, and friendly staff provide good prompt service; piped blues. A covered yard outside is called the Sty. Beware of their opening times – the pub is closed every lunchtime, except on Sunday. *(Recommended by Catherine Pitt, Dr M E Wilson, Jonathan Smith, Dr and Mrs A K Clarke)*

Free house ~ Licensees Dickie and Ann Doyle ~ Real ale ~ No credit cards ~ (01249) 712515 ~ Blues Mon evening ~ Open 7-11; 12-2.30, 7-11 Sun

CORTON ST9340 Map 2
Dove ♀ ⇌

Village signposted from A36 at Upton Lovell, SE of Warminster; this back road on the right bank of the River Wylye is a quiet alternative to the busy A36 Warminster—Wilton

The attractively furnished main bar at this charming cottagey country pub is focused on a big central fireplace, with a huge winter log fire giving it a warmly homely feel. There is a mix of carpeting, flagstones and oak flooring, with some good pictures, a mix of chairs and cushioned wall seats, and dining tables in areas off (the rectangular room off can be a bit clattery when it's full); the conservatory is no smoking; piped music. Good inventive well presented food at very sensible prices includes daily-changing lunchtime snacks such as interestingly filled baguettes (£4.50), grilled goats cheese with red onion and apple chutney (£5), ploughman's (£5.25), steak and kidney pie (£5.95), baked creamy haddock filled crêpes with cheese sauce (£6.95), sausage and mash (£7.25) and fruity beef curry (£7.50). More sophisticated evening meals might include hare and pink peppercorn terrine (£5), pear poached in white wine with parma ham (£5.75), pork loin chop with prune chutney and cider sauce (£10.95), seared bass with crab risotto (£13), calves liver and lambs kidneys with caramelised shallots and madeira sauce (£13.25) and home-made puddings (£3.50). Three well kept weekly changing real ales on handpump might be from brewers such as Butcombe, Shepherd Neame and Wadworths, good wines by the glass, attentive friendly staff, daily papers. The stone building is pretty with climbing roses in summer, is set back from the road by a front courtyard, and has tables on the neatly kept back lawn; occasional summer barbecues. *(Recommended by Sue Demont, Tim Barrow, Roger Purkiss, Sarah Lynch, Roderick Baker, David R Crafts, Julie and Bill Ryan)*

Free house ~ Licensee William Harrison-Allan ~ Real ale ~ Bar food (12-2.30, 7-9.30(9 Sun)) ~ Restaurant ~ (01985) 850109 ~ Children in eating area of bar and restaurant ~ Open 12-3(3.30 Sat), 6.30-11; 12-4, 7-10.30 Sun ~ Bedrooms: £45S/£65S

DEVIZES SU0061 Map 2
Bear ♀ ◗ ⇌
Market Place

You can buy beer in splendid old-fashioned half-gallon earthenware jars from Wadworths brewery which is only a stone's throw from this imposing old coaching inn. The relaxed chatty atmosphere in the big main carpeted bar with its black winged wall settles and muted red cloth-upholstered bucket armchairs around oak tripod tables is made cosier in winter by roaring log fires. Separated from the main bar by some steps and an old-fashioned glazed screen, a room named after the portrait painter Thomas Lawrence (his father ran the establishment in the 1770s) has dark oak-panelled walls, a parquet floor, shining copper pans on the mantelpiece above the big open fireplace, and plates around the walls; part of it is no smoking. Decent, reasonably priced bar food includes home-made soup (£2.95), sandwiches (from £2.75), filled baked potatoes or baguettes (from £3.95), ploughman's or omelettes (from £4.50), ham, egg and chips (£4.75), fish and chips (£5.75), daily specials such as beef in beer casserole with dumplings (£4.95), fish of the day (£5.25) and home-made puddings (£2.95); there are buffet meals in the Lawrence Room – you can eat these in the bar too. On Saturday nights they have a good value set menu in the restaurant. Well kept Wadworths IPA and 6X and a guest on handpump, over a dozen wines by the glass, a good choice of malt whiskies, and freshly squeezed juices from an old-fashioned bar counter with shiny black woodwork and small panes of glass. In spite of the double glazing, you can hear noise from the traffic outside some of the bedrooms; good breakfasts. This place has provided shelter to distinguished guests as diverse as King George III and Dr Johnson. *(Recommended by the Didler)*

Free house ~ Licensee Keith Dickenson ~ Real ale ~ Bar food (11-2.30, 7-9.30) ~ Restaurant ~ (01380) 722444 ~ Children in eating area of bar and restaurant ~ Open 10-11; 12-10.30 Sun; closed 25 and 26 Dec ~ Bedrooms: £60B/£88B

EBBESBOURNE WAKE ST9824 Map 2

Horseshoe 🍺 🛏

On A354 S of Salisbury, right at signpost at Coombe Bissett; village is around 8 miles further on

Highly praised for its good home-cooking, well kept ales and friendly service, this unspoilt, welcoming old country pub which is delightfully set off the beaten track in fine hilly downland seems to have found the magic formula for keeping customers happy. It's not surprising really, given how accommodating the very cheerful landlord is. There are fresh home-grown flowers on the tables in the beautifully kept bar with lanterns, farm tools and other bric-a-brac crowded along its beams, and an open fire; a conservatory extension seats 10 people. Enjoyable traditional bar food (add about a pound to each dish if you're visiting in the evening when there will be a couple more heavier weight items) includes soup (from £3.50), a hearty ploughman's (£4.95), sausage and mash or lasagne (£7.95), locally made faggots, oak smoked trout salad, a choice of super home-made pies or liver and bacon casserole (£8.25), and excellent home-made puddings such as sticky zesty lemon crunch, peach shortcake, summer pudding and brandy snap basket (£3.75). Well kept Ringwood Best and Wadworths 6X and guests such as Adnams Broadside, Butcombe, Stonehenge Pigswill and Wadworths IPA tapped from the row of casks behind the bar, farm cider, country wines, and several malt whiskies. Booking is advisable for the small no smoking restaurant, especially at weekends when they can fill up quite quickly. The barn opposite is now used as a gymnasium; good walks nearby. There are three goats in a paddock at the bottom of the garden, and a couple of playful dogs; good breakfasts if you're staying. *(Recommended by Dr and Mrs Michael Smith, the Didler, Adrian and Gwynneth Littleton, D R Wilson, Mrs A M Viney, Dr and Mrs Nigel Holmes, MP, Tom Clay, Brian and Diane Mugford, Di and Mike Gillam, Martin Weinberg, Dr and Mrs David Smith, Graham Sumner, Jayne and Peter Capp)*

Free house ~ Licensees Anthony and Patricia Bath ~ Real ale ~ Bar food (not Sun or Mon evenings) ~ Restaurant ~ (01722) 780474 ~ Children in eating area of bar and restaurant ~ Open 12-3, 6.30-11(7-10.30 Sun); closed 25 Dec ~ Bedrooms: £35B/£50B

All main entries have been inspected anonymously by the Editor or Deputy Editor. We accept no payment for inclusion, no advertising, and no sponsorship from the drinks industry – or from anyone else.

FONTHILL GIFFORD ST9232 Map 2
Beckford Arms 🛏

Off B3089 W of Wilton at Fonthill Bishop

This unchanging pleasant old inn is set on the edge of a fine parkland estate with a lake and sweeping vistas. The smartly informal rooms have a light and airy feel, with stripped bare wood, a parquet floor and a pleasant mix of tables with church candles. In winter, a big log fire burns in the lounge bar that leads into the light and airy back garden room with a high pitched plank ceiling and picture windows looking on to a terrace. Locals tend to gather in the straightforward public bar with darts, fruit machine, pool, TV and piped music. Made from local produce wherever possible, very enjoyable bar food includes sandwiches (from £3.50, filled baguettes from £4.95), soup (£3.75), toasted goats cheese (£4.75), ploughman's (from £5.95), sausage and mash or feta, black olive and plum tomato salad (£7.95), prawn and salmon fishcakes with basil and lime reduction or thai chicken curry (£8.95) and several additional evening dishes such as fried chicken breast with tarragon cream (£9.95) and lamb cutlets with mint mash and red onion gravy (£10.95); some of the fruit and vegetables are picked fresh from the garden. Well kept Greene King Abbot, Hop Back Best, Timothy Taylors Landlord and a weekly guest such as Shepherd Neame Spitfire on handpump. This place is well run by friendly licensees and their staff, and bedrooms are good value. *(Recommended by Lyn and Geoff Hallchurch, John and Angela Main, Tony Gayfer)*

Free house ~ Licensees Karen and Eddie Costello ~ Real ale ~ Bar food (12-2, 7-9.30(10 Sat)) ~ (01747) 870385 ~ Children in family room ~ Open 12-11; 12-10.30 Sun; closed 25 Dec ~ Bedrooms: £35S/£65B

FORD NT9538 Map 2
White Hart ★ ⑪ ♀ 🍺 🛏

A420 Chippenham—Bristol; follow Colerne sign at E side of village to find pub

Wiltshire Dining Pub of the Year

Unfaltering over the years, the continuing popularity of this fine stone country inn apparently stems from its ability to be all things to all people. Ideal for a weekend country break for those who want to treat themselves to good food and a comfortable night's sleep, the cosy bar also draws a younger crowd of locals in the evening, who make the most of the good range of beer and other drinks on offer. Set in stunning countryside, the grounds are wonderful in summer, when peacocks strut around the garden and you can sit on the terrace by the trout stream that babbles under a little stone bridge; there are good walks in the hills beyond the pub, too. There are heavy black beams supporting the white-painted boards of the ceiling, tub armchairs around polished wooden tables, small pictures and a few advertising mirrors on the walls, and an ancient fireplace (inscribed 1553); pool on a circular table, dominoes, TV, board games and piped music. They keep fine wines (including about eight by the glass), farm cider, a dozen malt whiskies, and up to eight well kept (if not cheap) real ales on handpump or tapped from the cask such as Bybrook White Hart, Courage Directors, Theakstons, Wadworths 6X and a couple of guests such as Burton Bridge Bitter and Thomas Hardy Royal Oak; friendly and helpful service. You will need to book for the very enjoyable, interesting food, which might include lunchtime bar snacks such as good soups like celery or lentil, mushroom and tarragon (£2.95), filled baguettes (from £3.95), ploughman's (from £4.75), provençale vegetables and polenta (£5.25), smoked duck breast with potato salad, hazelnut dressing and crispy vegetables or lambs liver and bacon with mash and onion gravy (£6.25), thai chicken curry (£6.50) and grilled salmon with lemon butter (£6.95), and a more elaborate evening menu with dishes ranging from duck confit with caramelised pineapple and fried pak choi (£5.95) to roast soy marinated chicken breast with noodles and stir-fried vegetables in oyster sauce (£11.95) and grilled turbot fillet on buttered spinach with scallop, asparagus and saffron risotto and chive cream sauce (£17.50); three-course set lunch menu (£13.95). All bedrooms are spacious and well equipped; excellent breakfasts, and a secluded swimming pool for residents (the peacocks can make for an unusual dawn chorus). *(Recommended by Sally Anne and Peter Goodale, Mr and Mrs McKay, Joy and Colin Rorke, Frank Willy, Jonathan Smith, J Osborn-Clarke, Guy Vowles, Lyn and Geoff Hallchurch, Susan and Nigel Wilson, Richard Pierce, Dave Irving, M G Hart, Neil and Debbie Cook, John Robertson, Brian and Bett Cox, David and Nina Pugsley, Les Brown, Betsy Brown, Nigel Flook, Dr and Mrs A K Clarke, B J Harding, Gill and David Morrell, MDN, Mr and Mrs C Littleton, Alan J Morton, Graham and Rose Ive, Mr and Mrs D J Hook, Andrew Shore, James A Walker, JFM and M West)*

Eldridge Pope (Hardy) ~ Managers Peter and Kate Miller ~ Real ale ~ Bar food (12-2, 7-9.30(10 Fri, Sat; 9 Sun)) ~ Restaurant ~ (01249) 782213 ~ Children in the pool room and buttery ~ Open 11-3, 5-11; 12-3, 7-10.30 Sun; closed 25 Dec evening ~ Bedrooms: £64B/£84B

GREAT HINTON ST9059 Map 2
Linnet

3½ miles E of Trowbridge, village signposted off A361 opp Lamb at Semington

The new licensee at this attractive old brick pub has shifted the emphasis towards the imaginative freshly prepared bar food which now includes soup (£3.50), duck pancakes with cucumber salsa and plum sauce (£4.95), warm smoked trout and prawn fishcake on lime leaf and chive sauce (£5.25), puff pastry parcel of tomatoes, mozzarella and roasted artichokes on sautéed spinach with tomato and sage sauce (£9.75), roast salmon fillet on lemon and chive polenta cake with langoustine and sorrel sauce (£10.25), lamb loin on redcurrant and mint risotto with madeira and rosemary sauce (£12.25) and puddings such as orange and roasted hazelnut sponge with lemon curd cream or apple and cinnamon bread and butter pudding with rum anglaise (from £4.25). The little bar to the right of the door has a blue-green carpet and lots of photographs of the pub and the brewery, there are bookshelves in a snug end part and the cosy restaurant is candlelit at night. Well kept Wadworths IPA and 6X on handpump, 22 malt whiskies and quite a few wines. In summer, the flowering tubs and window boxes with seats dotted amongst them are quite a sight. *(Recommended by Michael Doswell, Lyn and Geoff Hallchurch, Dr M E Wilson, Mr and Mrs J P Keates)*

Wadworths ~ Tenant Jonathan Furby ~ Real ale ~ Bar food ~ Restaurant ~ (01380) 870354 ~ Children in restaurant ~ Open 12-3, 6-11; 12-3, 7-10.30 Sun; closed Mon

HEYTESBURY ST9242 Map 2
Angel 🍴 ♀ 🍺 🛏

High St; just off A36 E of Warminster

This peacefully set 16th-c inn is situated in a quiet village street just below the Salisbury Plain, and is a very pleasant place to stay, with imaginative bar food, well kept ales, and above all, impeccable service ensuring that customers are well looked after. The spacious homely lounge on the right, with well used overstuffed armchairs and sofas and a good fire, opens into a charming back dining room which is simple but smart with a blue carpet, blue-cushioned chairs and lots of prints on the white-painted brick walls. On the left, a long beamed bar has a convivial evening atmosphere, a woodburner, some attractive prints and old photographs on its terracotta-coloured walls, and straightforward tables and chairs. The dining room opens on to an attractive secluded courtyard garden. Good food includes home-made soup (£3.50), filo prawns with sweet chilli mayonnaise (£5.50), filo basket with oyster mushrooms, spinach, feta and pink peppercorns (£5.75), sausage and mash (£6.50), game and vegetable pie (£6.95), braised lamb shank (£9.75), butterfly pork loin on baby spinach and oyster mushrooms with puy lentils (£10.95), roast salmon fillet with parmesan risotto and crispy leeks (£11.75), roast saddle of venison on red cabbage braised in orange and mixed spice (£14.75), puddings such as sticky toffee pudding with butterscotch sauce and devon cream, warm frangipane and raspberry tart (£3.50), and English cheeses (£3.75). A good choice of very well kept beers includes Marstons Pedigree, Ringwood Best and Timothy Taylors Landlord on handpump; also around a dozen wines by the glass. Bedrooms are either new or recently refurbished. *(Recommended by David R Crafts, Lynn Sharpless, Bob Eardley, Alex Cleland, Jim Cook, Hugh Roberts, Chris Richards, John Robertson, Ian Phillips, Susan and Nigel Wilson, Michael Doswell, M G Hart, Ann and Colin Hunt, Sue Demont, Tim Barrow, Julie and Bill Ryan)*

Free house ~ Licensee Jeremy Giddings ~ Real ale ~ Bar food (12-2, 7-9.30) ~ Restaurant ~ (01985) 840330 ~ Children welcome ~ Open 11.30-3, 6.30-11; 12-3, 7-10.30 Sun ~ Bedrooms: £40B/£50B

HINDON ST9132 Map 2
Grosvenor Arms 🍴 ♀ 🛏
B3089 Wilton—Mere

New licensees have cosied up this this 18th-c coaching inn by painting the traditional pubby bar red, decorating it with Victorian prints and artefacts and bringing in a nice mix of old tables and chairs. The candlelight, lovely log fire and fresh flowers help, and there are flagstones. Off the entrance hall is a civilised no smoking lounge with grey panelling, armchairs, settees, a cushioned antique settle and country magazines. The long dining room has been smartened up with cream paint and big photographs of the surrounding area, and a huge window lets you view the goings on in the kitchen. There's some concentration on good freshly made well presented food which changes daily but might include gazpacho soup (£3.95), grilled open sandwiches (£4.50), sausage and mash (£6.95), smoked haddock fishcakes with fresh bean salad and red pepper coulis (£7.50), tagliatelle with langoustine and scallops (£8), grilled pork cutlet with braised fennel (£8.95), sirloin steak with rocket and parmesan salad and creamed celeriac; vegetables (£1.95), and puddings such as praline parfait with raspberry coulis or orange and rosemary cheesecake (£4.50). Well kept Bass and Wadworths 6X and a guest such as Tisbury Stonehenge on handpump, good house wines including about a dozen by the glass, daily papers. There are good teak chairs around tables under cocktail parasols and big flowering tubs in the back courtyard, which is very prettily lit at night. *(Recommended by Betsy and Peter Little, John Evans, Capt and Mrs J Wagstaff, Mr and Mrs A H Young, Mike Gorton, A and G Evans, Sue Demont, Tim Barrow, Lady Greig, W W Burke, Ian Phillips)*

Free house ~ Licensee Penny Simpson ~ Real ale ~ Bar food ~ Restaurant ~ (01747) 820696 ~ Children in eating area of bar and family room ~ Open 11-11; 12-3 Sun; closed Sun evening ~ Bedrooms: £45.50B/£60B

Lamb
B3089 Wilton—Mere

The most enjoyable places to sit in this unchanging, solid old hotel are probably the two slate-floored lower sections of the roomy long bar. There's a long polished table with wall benches and chairs, blacksmith's tools set behind a big inglenook fireplace, and at one end a window seat (overlooking the village church) with a big waxed circular table, spindleback chairs with tapestried cushions, a high-backed settle and brass jugs on the mantelpiece above the small fireplace; there are lots of tables and chairs up some steps in a third bigger area. Very good, though not cheap bar food might include soup (£3.95), ploughman's (£4.50), lasagne, wild mushroom tagliatelle, garlic chicken or steak and kidney pie (£8.25), roast salmon with creamed leeks (£8.50), poached monkfish with scallops and vermouth (£8.95), steaks (from £9.50), lamb shank (£9.95) and puddings (£3.95); the Sunday roast is good value, and they usually serve cream teas throughout the afternoon. The restaurant is no smoking. Four real ales include Wadworths 6X alongside two constantly changing guests such as Oakhill Best and Stonehenge Pigswill, there are just under a dozen wines by the glass, and the range of whiskies includes all the malts from the Isle of Islay; friendly service can be slow when busy. There are picnic-sets across the road (which is a good alternative to the main routes west); limited parking. Dogs welcome in bar. *(Recommended by John Evans, Mike Gorton, B D Jones, Joy and Colin Rorke, W W Burke, David Peakall, Peter and Audrey Dowsett, B, M and P Kendall, C L Kauffmann, V N Stevenson, Mrs J H S Lang, Ian Phillips, Guy Vowles)*

Free house ~ Licensee Cora Scott ~ Real ale ~ Bar food (12-2.30, 7-10) ~ Restaurant ~ (01747) 820573 ~ Children welcome ~ Open 11-11; 12-10.30 Sun ~ Bedrooms: £45B/£75B

KILMINGTON ST7736 Map 2
Red Lion £ 🏠

Pub on B3092 Mere—Frome, 2½ miles S of Maiden Bradley; 3 miles from A303 Mere turn-off

This 15th-c ivy covered country pub is owned by the National Trust. The comfortably cosy low ceilinged bar is pleasantly furnished with a curved high-backed settle and red leatherette wall and window seats on the flagstones, photographs on the beams, and a couple of big fireplaces (one with a fine old iron fireback) with log fires in winter. A newer no smoking eating area has a large window and is decorated with brasses, a large leather horse collar, and hanging plates. Simple very good value bar food is served at lunchtime only and includes soup (£1.80), sandwiches (from £2.20, toasted £2.70), filled baked potatoes (from £2.70), cornish pasties (from £3.65), ploughman's (from £3.95), steak and kidney pie or lamb and apricot pie (£4.45), creamy fish pie (£4.50), meat or vegetable lasagne (£5.95), and maybe one or two daily specials; last orders for food at 1.50pm. Well kept Butcombe and Butts Jester and a guest such as Timothy Taylors Landlord on handpump, farm cider, various pressés such as elderflower, citrus, limeflower and lemongrass and ginger, and monthly changing wines. Sensibly placed darts, dominoes, shove-ha'penny and cribbage. There are picnic-sets in the big attractive garden, where Kim the labrador is often to be found. It's popular with walkers – you can buy locally made walking sticks, and a gate leads on to the lane which leads to White Sheet Hill, where there is riding, hang gliding and radio-controlled gliders. Stourhead Gardens are only a mile away. No dogs at lunchtime. *(Recommended by Gordon Prince, W F C Phillips, WHBM, B, M and P Kendall, Roger Wain-Heapy, KC, John Evans, Mike Gorton)*

Free house ~ Licensee Chris Gibbs ~ Real ale ~ Bar food (12-1.50; not 25, 26 Dec) ~ No credit cards ~ (01985) 844263 ~ Well behaved children in eating area of bar till 9pm ~ Open 11.30-2.30, 6.30-11; 12-3, 7-10.30 Sun ~ Bedrooms: £25/£35

LACOCK ST9168 Map 2
George 🏠

Set in a beautifully preserved National Trust village and licensed continuously since the 17th c, this very unspoilt and homely old pub is renowned for the unfalteringly friendly welcome from the long-serving landlord and his staff. Another famous talking point here is the three-foot treadwheel set into the outer breast of the magnificent central fireplace. This used to turn a spit for roasting, and was worked by a specially bred dog called, with great imagination, a turnspit. There's a marvellously relaxing atmosphere in the comfortable low beamed bar, with upright timbers in the place of knocked-through walls making cosy corners, candles on tables (even at lunchtime), armchairs and windsor chairs, seats in the stone-mullioned windows and flagstones just by the counter; piped music. The well kept Wadworths IPA, JCB and 6X are very reasonably priced, and there's a decent choice of wines. It does get busy here so it's a good idea to book for the generously served enjoyable bar food which might include sandwiches (from £1.95), filled baguette (from £3.75), lasagne, beef and beer pie, broccoli and cream cheese bake or ham salad (£6.95), and home-made puddings such as lemon cheesecake and sticky banana and toffee pudding (£4.25); fresh vegetables and real chips. The barn restaurant is no smoking. There are picnic-sets with umbrellas in the back garden, as well as a play area with swings, and a bench in front that overlooks the main street. The bedrooms (very highly praised by readers) are up at the landlord's farmhouse, with free transport to and from the pub. It's a nice area for walking. *(Recommended by Stephen and Jean Curtis, Bob and Val Collman, J Osborn-Clarke, Joan and Michel Hooper-Immins, Mrs Pat Crabb, Jenny and Chris Wilson, Roger Wain-Heapy, Mrs Thomas, Richard and Liz Dilnot, David and Nina Pugsley, P R and S A White, Mike and Mona Clifford, R Huggins,*

D Irving, E McCall, T McLean, Roger and Jenny Huggins, Geoff Palmer, Peter and Audrey Dowsett)

Wadworths ~ Tenant John Glass ~ Real ale ~ Bar food (12-2, 6-9.30) ~ Restaurant ~ (01249) 730263 ~ Children in eating area of bar and restaurant ~ Open 11-2.30, 5-11; 10-11 Sat; 12-10.30 Sun

Red Lion

High Street; village signposted off A350 S of Chippenham

The interior of this imposing National Trust owned Georgian inn has been gently refurbished this year. The cream painted airy long bar is now subtly divided into cosy areas by open handrails, and has new characterfully distressed heavy dark wood tables and chairs with tapestry covers to go with the dark wood distressed dado. There are turkey rugs on the partly flagstoned floor, a fine old log fire at one end, aged looking paintings, and branding irons hanging from the ceiling. The snug is now much cosier with comfortable new leather armchairs. Bar food includes soup (£2.75), sandwiches (from £3), whitebait (£3.95), ploughman's (from £5.50), scampi (£7.95), 8oz rump steak (£9.95), daily specials such as pie of the day or spinach and goats cheese strudel (£5.95), chicken roulade or pork, sherry and mushroom casserole (£6.95), salmon steak (£7.95), and puddings (£2.95); the top dining area is no smoking. Wadworths IPA, JCB, 6X and one of their seasonal beers on handpump, and several malt whiskies; fruit machine and piped music. It can get busy, and towards the latter half of the evening it's especially popular with younger people. Close to Lacock Abbey and the Fox Talbot Museum. *(Recommended by Mike and Mona Clifford, Trevor Owen, R Huggins, D Irving, E McCall, T McLean)*

Wadworths ~ Manager Chris Chappell ~ Real ale ~ Bar food (12-2, 6-9(6.30-8.30)) ~ (01249) 730456 ~ Well behaved children welcome ~ Open 11(11.30 Sat)-11; 12-10.30 Sun; 11-2.30, 6-11 wkdys in winter ~ Bedrooms: £55B/£75B

Rising Sun

Bewley Common, Bowden Hill – out towards Sandy Lane, up hill past Abbey; OS Sheet 173 map reference 935679

The three little rooms at this cheery unpretentious pub have been knocked together to form one simply furnished atmospheric area, with a mix of old chairs and basic kitchen tables on stone floors, stuffed animals and birds, country pictures, and open fires. Very well kept Moles Best, Molecatcher, Molennium and Tap Bitter plus one of their seasonal ales and maybe a guest such as Abbey Bellringer on handpump, farm cider and friendly service from welcoming staff. Darts, shove-ha'penny, cribbage and board games. Generously served good home-made food includes baguettes (from £3.25), ploughman's (£5.50), ham, egg and chips (£6), battered cod and chips or pasta with tomato sauce (£6.50), crispy duck pancakes, spinach and pepper tart or stir-fried vegetables (£7) and particularly popular stir fries such as beef teriyaki or thai chicken curry (£8.50). The surrounding countryside is lovely, and the views from the two-level terrace, looking right out over the Avon valley some 25 miles or so, are among the most splendid in the country; it's a particularly attractive sight around sunset. *(Recommended by Dr B and Mrs P B Baker, Pat and Tony Martin, Richard Pierce, Mrs Mary Walters)*

Free house ~ Licensee Sue Sturdy ~ Real ale ~ Bar food (12-2, 7-9(9.30 Fri) Sat; not Sun-Tues evening) ~ (01249) 730363 ~ Children welcome away from bar till 9pm ~ Live music every Weds and every other Sun from 3pm ~ Open 11.30-3, 6-11; 12-10.30 Sun; closed 26 Dec evening, 1 Jan

Ideas for a country day out? We list pubs in really attractive scenery at the back of the book – and there are separate lists for waterside pubs, ones with really good gardens, and ones with lovely views.

LIMPLEY STOKE ST7861 Map 2
Hop Pole

Coming S from Bath on A36 take B3108 at traffic lights signed Bradford on Avon, turn right off main road at sharp left-hand bend before the railway bridge, pub is 100 yds on right (car park just before on left)

They manage to maintain a good balance between drinking and dining at this friendly and unhurried cream stone monks' wine lodge (with its name deeply incised on the front wall). A cheerful bunch of locals gathers in the cosy dark-panelled room on the right – this area can get very crowded when the pub is busy – with red velvet cushions on settles in its alcoves, some slat-back and captain's chairs on its turkey carpet, lantern lighting, a log fire and Bass, Butcombe, Courage Best and a changing guest such as Fullers London Pride on handpump, five malt whiskies; darts, shove ha'penny, bar billiards, cribbage, dominoes, TV and piped music. The roomier left-hand lounge (with an arch to a cream-walled inner room) is mostly laid for diners, and also has dark wood panelling and a log-effect gas fire. A wide choice of bar food (you may need to book) includes filled baps (from £2.50), deep-fried brie in cranberry sauce (£3.95), home-made pies (from £6.45), local trout (£8.75), Scotch salmon (£8.95), daily specials such as broccoli and stilton bake (£6.25), salmon and crab fishcakes (£8.75), grilled bass with cumin crust and red onion marmalade (£9.25), thai-style monkfish (£9.75), beef wellington (£12.25), Sunday roasts (from £6.25) and children's meals (from £2.95). The restaurant is no smoking. An attractive enclosed garden behind has rustic benches, a terrace and pond, and boules. This is just a short stroll from the Kennett & Avon canal, and makes a good base for waterside walks. *(Recommended by Roger Wain-Heapy, Dr M E Wilson, DAV)*

Latona Leisure ~ Managers Bob and Mich Williams ~ Real ale ~ Bar food (12-2, 6.30-9.15) ~ Restaurant ~ (01225) 723134 ~ Well behaved children in restaurant and family room ~ Open 11-2.30, 6-11; 12-3, 7-10.30 Sun; closed 25 Dec

LITTLE CHEVERELL ST9853 Map 2
Owl 🍺

Low Rd; just off B3098 Westbury—Upavon, W of A360

The peaceful and neatly traditional bar at this splendidly cosy little village local has terracotta walls, a pleasant jumble of furnishings including plenty of chairs, stools, high-backed settles and tables and agricultural tools and split-cane fishing rods on the walls. There are fresh flowers on the tables, local papers and guides to read, a gently ticking clock, two or three stuffed owls behind the bar, horse tack (showing the landlady's equestrian interests – Coker, her beer-drinking horse, is stabled next door), and a piano which separates the main area from a snugger room at the back. All the food is cooked by Miss Boast herself, listed on changing blackboards, and might include soup (£3.25), pâté (£3.95), ploughman's (£5.50), chicken curry or sausage and mash (£6.95), scampi (£7.95), chicken with garlic, mushroom and cream (£8.95), poached salmon with hollandaise sauce (£9.95), magret of duck in black cherry, honey and brandy sauce (£10.50), and home-made puddings such as banoffi pie or lemon brûlée (£3.50); roast lunches (£6.95) or ploughman's only at Sunday lunchtime. Alongside well kept Wadworths 6X there are three changing guest ales on handpump such as Butcombe, Fullers London Pride and Stonehenge Pigswill, plus 15 malts; shove-ha'penny, cribbage and board games. The pub is set in a particularly peaceful spot, and at the back, the lovely tall ash and willow lined garden reverberates with the sound of wood pigeons cooing, with rustic picnic-sets on a long lawn that runs down over two levels to a brook, and a terrace above here with plastic tables and chairs. No children inside. *(Recommended by Susan and Nigel Wilson, Theo, Anne and Jane Gaskin, Pat and Robert Watt, Ron Shelton, Lyn and Geoff Hallchurch, Brian and Anna Marsden)*

Free house ~ Licensee Pia Maria Boast ~ Real ale ~ Bar food (12-2, 6-9) ~ Restaurant ~ (01380) 812263 ~ Open 11.30-2.30, 6-11; 12-3, 7-10.30 Sun; cl Mon, Sun evening in winter

LOWER CHUTE SU3153 Map 2
Hatchet

The Chutes well signposted via Appleshaw off A342, 2½ miles W of Andover

For many, the enchanted appearance and unchanging friendly local atmosphere make this timeless 16th-c thatched cottage one of the most archetypically attractive pubs in the county. Especially low beams look down over a lovely mix of captain's chairs and cushioned wheelbacks set around oak tables, and there's a splendid 17th-c fireback in the huge fireplace, with a big winter log fire in front. Good bar food includes sandwiches or baguettes (from £2.95, steak £4.95), home-made soup (£3.25), garlic mushrooms (£3.95), ploughman's (£4.95), thai vegetable stir fry (£5.75), liver and bacon (£5.95), lasagne or steak and stout pie (£6.25), moules marinières (£6.50) and a popular salmon, halibut and prawn wellington (£6.95). Thursday night is curry night when you can eat as much as you like (£6.50); no smoking restaurant. Well kept ales on handpump include Fullers London Pride, Greene King IPA and Wadworths 6X, and there's a range of country wines; friendly staff. Cribbage, dominoes and piped music. There are seats out on a terrace by the front car park, or on the side grass, as well as a children's sandpit. *(Recommended by Alan and Gill Bull, Mrs J H S Lang, David Whiteley, David and Ruth Shillitoe, the Didler, Lynn Sharpless, Bob Eardley)*

Free house ~ Licensee Jeremy McKay ~ Real ale ~ Bar food (12-2.15, 6.30-9.45) ~ Restaurant ~ (01264) 730229 ~ Children in restaurant ~ Open 11.30-3, 6-11; 12-4, 7-10.30 Sun ~ Bedrooms: /£45S

MALMESBURY ST9287 Map 2
Smoking Dog

High Street

This double-fronted mid-terrace 17th-c pub has a good friendly local atmosphere in its two smallish front bars, with flagstones, dark woodwork, cushioned bench seating, big pine tables and a blazing log fire, and well kept Adnams, Archers, Brains Bitter, Revd James and SA with a guest such as Fullers London Pride on handpump. It's popular with young people in the evenings. A flagstoned corridor with local notices on the walls leads to a bare-boards back bistro. The food is interesting, attractively presented and good value, and includes soup (£3.25), filled baguettes (from £4.25, steak £5.25), grilled mushroom with goats cheese or spicy chicken pâté (£4.95), baked avocado with brie, rosemary and almonds on pepper and tomato sauce (£9.95), roast duck breast with red wine, cloves and honey (£13.95), daily specials such as trout with almond stuffing (£9.95) and baked talapia with red peppers, onion, chilli and garlic (£12.95), and puddings such as warm pear and almond tart or banana and passion fruit pavlova (from £3.75). The friendly staff are helpful, and kind to children (they keep Scrabble, dominoes and so forth). Steep steps lead up to half a dozen tables in a small back garden with pleasant views out over the town. *(Recommended by P M Grasby, Catherine Pitt, Mike Ridgway, Sarah Miles)*

Brains ~ Manager Ricky Mattioli ~ Bar food (12-2, 7-9.30) ~ Restaurant ~ (01666) 825823 ~ Children in eating area of bar and restaurant ~ Open 11.30-11; 12-10.30 Sun

NETHERHAMPTON SU1029 Map 2
Victoria & Albert ◀

Just off A3094 W of Salisbury

The new licensee at this charmingly traditional thatched cottage turned over 30 different real ales on four handpumps in his first three months here, and he plans to continue clocking them up at this rate by sourcing beers from all over the country from brewers such as fff, Fullers, Morlands and Woldham. The black beamed bar is filled with gleaming brassware, a good mix of individual tables and nicely cushioned old-fashioned wall settles on the ancient polished floor tiles, and has piped music and board games. Pubby bar food includes soup (£3), filled baguettes or ploughman's

(£3.95), battered cod and chips (£5.95), home-made pies (£7.95) and puddings such as apple pie or crumbles (£3.25). The restaurant is no smoking. There's hatch service for the sizeable garden behind, with well spaced picnic-set and a big weeping willow. Handy for Wilton House (and Nadder Valley walks). *(Recommended by Jayne and Peter Capp, Dorsan Baker, David and Elizabeth Briggs, Lynn Sharpless, Bob Eardley, R Mathews, Tracey and Stephen Groves, Dr and Mrs A K Clarke, David and Kay Ross, Dr David Cockburn)*

Free house ~ Licensee Bob Drew ~ Real ale ~ Bar food (11.30-2.30, 7-9; not Sun evening) ~ Restaurant ~ (01722) 743174 ~ Children in snug and restaurant ~ Open 11-11; 12-10.30 Sun

NORTON ST8884 Map 2
Vine Tree ♀

4 miles from M4 junction 17; A429 towards Malmesbury, then left at Hullavington, Sherston signpost, then follow Norton signposts; in village turn right at Foxley signpost, which takes you into Honey lane

Very enthusiastic new licensees have really pulled this civilised dining pub (housed in an attractively converted 18th-c mill house, and seemingly much more remote than its proximity to the motorway would suggest) well back up to its old good standards. A lively atmosphere fills the three smallish rooms which open together with sporting prints, a mock-up mounted pig's mask (used for a game that involves knocking coins off its nose and ears), lots of stripped pine, candles in bottles on the tables (the lighting's very gentle), and some old settles. From a seasonally changing menu, and using local ingredients where possible, a wide range of enjoyable food might include soup (£3.25), moules marinières (£4.95), locally smoked duck breast and apple salad with raspberry dressing (£5.50), local speciality sausages (£8.75), fishcakes with roasted red pepper sauce (£8.95), fried squid stuffed with seafood risotto, with green lip mussels and fresh mussel cream or roast cod with steamed baby vegetables and saffron sauce (£12.95), daily specials such as grilled plaice with citrus butter (£10.95) and fried scallops and bass fillets with asparagus and parmesan gratin and balsamic shallot dressing (£13.95), and puddings such as white and dark chocolate torte or passion fruit cheesecake with black cherry ice cream (£4.50). Best to book, especially at weekends; one dining area is no smoking. Well kept Archers Village, Wychwood Fiddlers Elbow, Youngs, a guest and around 10 wines by the glass; piped music. There are picnic-sets in a two acre garden which includes a pretty walled terrace with a lion fountain and urns of flowers, a well fenced separate play area with a fine thatched fortress and three boules pitches; dogs welcome. They are hoping to convert some outbuildings into six bedrooms. *(Recommended by Mr and Mrs J R Lewis, Dr M E Wilson, A R Ainslie, Miss A Kerr-Wilson, Miss M W Hayter, R Huggins, D Irving, E McCall, T McLean)*

Free house ~ Licensees Charles Walker and Tiggi Wood ~ Real ale ~ Bar food (12-2.30, 7-9.30; 12-9.30 Sun) ~ Restaurant ~ (01666) 837654 ~ Children welcome, but not too late in the restaurant ~ Open 11.30-2.30, 6-11; 12-10.30 Sun; closed 25 Dec evening

PITTON SU2131 Map 2
Silver Plough ♀

Village signposted from A30 E of Salisbury (follow brown tourist signs)

The black beams in the comfortable front bar of this country dining pub are strung with hundreds of antique boot-warmers and stretchers, pewter and china tankards, copper kettles, toby jugs, earthenware and glass rolling pins, painted clogs, glass net-floats, and coach horns and so forth. Seats on the turkey carpet include half a dozen red-velvet-cushioned antique oak settles (one elaborately carved beside a very fine reproduction of an Elizabethan oak table), and the timbered white walls are hung with Thorburn and other gamebird prints, original Craven Hill sporting cartoons, and a big naval battle glass-painting. The back bar is simpler, but still has a big winged high-backed settle, cased antique guns, substantial pictures, and – like the front room – flowers on its tables. The wide range of home-made food might include lunchtime sandwiches (from £4.50) and ploughman's (£5.75), teriyaki beef or pasta with bacon and mushroom sauce (£6.50), sausage and yorkshire pudding (£6.75), stir-fried chicken, chilli and oriental vegetables with noodles (£7.25), roasted peppers with ratatouille and tomato coulis, feta and hazelnut or hot chicken salad (£7.50) and fillet steak (£14.95); The restaurant is no smoking. Well kept Badger Best, IPA and Tanglefoot and another from the brewery under light blanket pressure, a fine wine list including ten by the glass and some well priced and carefully chosen bottles, a good range of country wines, and a worthy choice of spirits. There's a skittle alley next to the snug bar; cribbage, dominoes and shove-ha'penny. A quiet lawn has picnic-sets and other tables under cocktail parasols, and there are good downland and woodland walks nearby. *(Recommended by R J Walden, Adrian and Gwynneth Littleton, Ian Phillips, S and D Moir, Patrick and Helen Dunn)*

Badger ~ Manager Adrian Clifton ~ Real ale ~ Bar food (12-2, 7(6 Sun)-9) ~ Restaurant ~ (01722) 712266 ~ Children in eating area of bar ~ Open 11-3, 6-11; 12-3, 6-10.30 Sun; closed 25, 26 Dec evening

POULSHOT ST9559 Map 2
Raven 🍺

Village signposted off A361 Devizes—Seend

This splendidly tucked away, classic country pub is prettily set across from the village green. Two intimate black-beamed rooms are well furnished with sturdy tables and chairs and comfortable banquettes, with well kept Wadworths IPA, JBC and 6X on electric pump, and there's an attractive no smoking dining room. Prepared by the friendly landlord, enjoyable generously served bar food includes cream of leek soup (£2.90), smoked salmon pâté (£3.65), roast topside of beef, chicken korma or lamb cooked with apricots (£7.65), moussaka (£8.35), seafood crumble (£8.90) and sirloin steak with pink peppercorn and cream sauce (£11.40), and puddings such as home-made redcurrant and raspberry cheesecake or apple and blackcurrant crumble (£3.10). The gents' is outside. *(Recommended by Charles and Pauline Stride, Pat and Tony Martin, Mr and Mrs J Brown, J Hale)*

Wadworths ~ Tenants Philip and Susan Henshaw ~ Real ale ~ Bar food ~ Restaurant ~ (01380) 828271 ~ Children in restaurant ~ Open 11-2.30, 6.30-11; 12-3, 7-10.30 Sun

ROWDE ST9762 Map 2
George & Dragon 🍴 ♀

A342 Devizes—Chippenham

A particular highlight at this attractive old dining pub is the impressive choice of very beautifully prepared fish which is delivered fresh from Cornwall. The quality and price of the meals are what you would expect of an upmarket restaurant, and the seasonally changing thoughtful menu combines traditional English dishes with snappier continental cooking. Fish dishes might include carpaccio of tuna with parmesan shavings (£6), fried squid with lemon, garlic and parsley or crab soup (£7/£12), warm salad of scallops and bacon (£8/£16), grilled skate with herb butter (£10), monkfish with green peppercorns, brandy and cream (£16), and whole grilled lobster (£28.50). Other enticing meals made from well chosen fresh ingredients might include provençale fish soup with rouille, gruyère and garlic croutons (£5), serrano ham with figs (£7), game risotto or cheese soufflé baked with parmesan and cream (£9), pasta with lamb roasted with garlic, wine and juniper (£11) and puddings such as lemon tart or chocolate orange liqueur roulade with caramelised oranges (£4.50); two-course lunch (£10); no smoking dining room. Service is usually helpful, but one or two readers have felt that there could sometimes be more smiles. Tastefully furnished with plenty of dark wood, the bar has a log fire with a fine collection of brass keys by it, while the bare-floored dining room has quite plain and traditional feeling tables and chairs, and is close enough to the bar to retain a pleasant chatty atmosphere. Three changing well kept real ales on handpump might be from breweries such as Bath, Butcombe and Goffs, and there's also local farm cider and continental beers and lagers; shove-ha'penny, cribbage and dominoes. In summer, a lovely walk along the nearby Kennett & Avon Canal provides a good appetiser (or indeed, a digestif). *(Recommended by Mrs G Delderfield, E H and R F Warner, David Whiteley, John and Vivienne Rice)*

Free house ~ Licensees Tim and Helen Withers ~ Real ale ~ Bar food (12-2, 7-10; not Sun or Mon) ~ Restaurant ~ (01380) 723053 ~ Children in restaurant till 9pm ~ Open 12-3, 7-(10.30 Sun)11; closed Mon lunchtime, 25 Dec, 1 Jan

SALISBURY SU1429 Map 2
Haunch of Venison

1 Minster Street, opposite Market Cross

This marvellous old pub was constructed over 650 years ago as the church house for St Thomas's, just behind. Inside, there are massive beams in the ochre ceiling, stout red cushioned oak benches built into its timbered walls, genuinely old pictures, a black and white tiled floor, and an open fire; a tiny snug opens off the entrance lobby. A quiet and cosy panelled upper room has a small paned window looking down on to the main bar, antique leather-seat settles, a nice carved oak chair nearly three centuries old, and a splendid fireplace that dates back to the building's early years; behind glass in a small wall slit is the smoke-preserved mummified hand of an unfortunate 18th-c card player. Well kept Courage Best and Directors and Wadworths 6X are served on handpump from a unique pewter bar counter, with a rare set of antique taps for gravity-fed spirits and liqueurs; over 80 malt whiskies, decent wines (including a wine of the week), and a range of brandies; chess. Bar food includes vegetable soup (£3.50), sandwiches (from £3.50), salmon and dill fishcake with basil mayonnaise (£4.95), venison sausage and mash or venison stew and cheese cobbler (£6.95), venison steak with mash and red wine jus (£9.95), and puddings (from £3.50); set menu (£6.95). The restaurant is no smoking but the bar can get a little smoky, and at times service can veer towards the inattentive. *(Recommended by the Didler, Dorsan Baker, Tom Clay, Ann and Colin Hunt, Mr and Mrs A P Reeves, Steve Chambers, Richard Rand, Mr and MrsC M Pearson, Dr David Cockburn)*

Scottish Courage ~ Lease Antony and Victoria Leroy ~ Real ale ~ Bar food (12-2.30; 6.30-9.30(10 Sat); not Sun evening) ~ Restaurant ~ (01722) 321062 ~ Children in eating area of bar and restaurant ~ Open 11-11; 12-10.30 Sun

New Inn

New Street

This ancient and creaky timbered town centre inn is one of only a handful of pubs that are completely no smoking throughout. Charming staff provide friendly, courteous service, and an inglenook fire in the largest room keeps the atmosphere warm and cosy; there are heavy old beams, horsebrasses, timbered walls, and a panelled dining room, with quiet cosy alcoves. Bar food is served throughout the pub, and includes soup (£2.45), sandwiches (from £3.25), camembert with crusty bread (£3.95), ploughman's (£4.95), bean and potato goulash (£5.95), beef and mushroom pie (£6.95), fresh local trout (£8.95), chicken breast cooked with mushrooms in white wine and cream sauce (£9.95), pork tenderloin done in cider and apricots (£9.95), and puddings (from £3.25). Well kept Badger Dorset Best, Golden Champion and Tanglefoot on handpump, and decent house wines; maybe piped Radio 2. Tables out in the sizeable pretty walled garden look up to the spire of the nearby cathedral. The back bedrooms are quieter; no cooked breakfast. *(Recommended by Ian Phillips, Dr M E Wilson, Mr and MrsC M Pearson, Tony and Wendy Hobden, Ms B Sheard, Alan J Morton, Brian and Anna Marsden, Ann and Colin Hunt, Lucy Bloomfield)*

Badger ~ Tenant John Spicer ~ Real ale ~ Bar food (12-2.30, 6(7 Sun)-9.30) ~ (01722) 327679 ~ Children in restaurant, eating area of bar and family room ~ Open 11-3, 6(7 Sun)-11; 11-11 Sat; 11-3, 6-11 Sat in winter; closed 25, 26 Dec ~ Bedrooms: £39.50B/£55B

Old Ale House ◖ £

Crane Street, off High Street opp New Street; public car park in Mill Road

This buzzing town pub is related to the Old Ale Houses in Truro and Falmouth (Cornwall), and is a fairly close copy of their style and atmosphere. A surprising mix of customers of all ages and types gathers in the long open-plan bar which is divided into sections by stout standing timbers and partly panelled stub walls, and has a real hotch-potch of old sofas, seats and tables, with cosy lighting and quite an entertaining clutter of casks, old cigar and cigarette boxes and country pictures. In one place, red hand and boot prints march across the ceiling, and there's a working red telephone box at one end. Bar food includes chinese spring rolls (£2.95), filled baguettes (from £3.45), filled baked potatoes (from £3.75), all day breakfast or battered cod (£4), sausage and mash (£4.10), mushroom and cheddar bake (£4.35), pie of the week (£4.95), 8oz gammon steak (£5.55), chicken topped with bacon and cheese (£5.95) and ribs and chips (£6.10). Well kept Gales HSB, Marstons Pedigree, Ringwood Best and Wadworths 6X with a guest from a local brewer such as Stonehenge on handpump; dispensers of peanuts and chocolate peanuts; darts, cribbage, dominoes, TV, fruit machines and a juke box and piped pop that some readers may find a bit loud. A little back courtyard has a few picnic-sets. *(Recommended by Tony Hobden)*

Free house ~ Licensees Patrick Barker and Sarah Jones ~ Real ale ~ Bar food (12-3 only) ~ No credit cards ~ (01722) 333113 ~ Children welcome till 6pm ~ Live music Thurs evening ~ Open 11-11; 12-10.30 Sun; closed 25 Dec

SEEND ST9461 Map 2

Barge

Seend Cleeve; signposted off A361 Devizes—Trowbridge, between Seend village and signpost to Seend Head

Particularly lovely in summer, the neatly kept waterside garden at this popular pub is an ideal spot for watching the bustle of boats on the Kennet and Avon Canal. Old streetlamps allow you to linger there after dark and moorings by the humpy bridge are very handy for thirsty bargees. For colder days, the bar has a big log fire, friendly and relaxed atmosphere, unusual barge theme décor, and intricately painted Victorian flowers which cover the ceilings and run in a waist-high band above the deep green lower walls. A distinctive mix of attractive seats includes milkchurns and the occasional small oak settle among the rugs on the parquet floor, while the walls have big sentimental engravings. The watery theme continues with a well stocked aquarium, and there's also a pretty Victorian fireplace, big bunches of dried flowers, and red velvet curtains for the big windows; fruit machine and piped music. The wide choice of good generously served bar food includes soup (£2.50), coarse pâté (£4.50), lunchtime ploughman's (£5.25), Wiltshire ham and eggs (£6.95), steak, kidney and ale pie or roast yellow peppers filled with goats cheese and beef tomatoes with pesto dressing (£7.50), scampi (£8), seared tuna steak with caper, lemon and garlic dressing (£12.50), with daily specials such as wild mushroom and truffle oil tart (£4.50), spicy thai fishcakes (£5.50), pork tenderloin wrapped in bacon with whole grain mustard (£10.50) and bass with chilli and lime (£14.50). In the evening, meals are served with fresh vegetables and a couple of additional dishes are a bit more restauranty; the restaurant extension is no smoking. They recommend booking for meals, especially at weekends. Well kept Badger Tanglefoot, Wadworths IPA and 6X, and a guest beer such as Butcombe on handpump, lots of malts and mulled wine in winter; cheery service from uniformed staff. Barbecues outside on summer Sundays. At the busiest times you may find queues to get in the car park. Dogs are welcome. *(Recommended by Roger and Pauline Pearce, Jenny and Dave Hughes, Pat and Tony Martin, Geoff Palmer, Paul Thompson, Anna Blackburn, W F C Phillips, Charles and Pauline Stride, Nigel and Olga Wikeley, Roger Wain-Heapy, Ian Phillips, P R and S A White, David Whiteley)*

Wadworths ~ Tenant Christopher Moorley Long ~ Real ale ~ Bar food (12-2, 7-9.30(10 Fri and Sat)) ~ Restaurant ~ (01380) 828230 ~ Children welcome ~ Open 11-3, 6-11; 11-11 Sat; 12-10.30 Sun; 11-3, 6-11 Mon-Sat in winter; 12-4, 7-10.30 Sun in winter

SEMLEY ST8926 Map 2

Benett Arms ♀

Turn off A350 N of Shaftesbury at Semley Ind Estate signpost, then turn right at Semley signpost

The charismatically friendly landlord, Joe Duthie, has been at this delightful village inn, set in a lovely spot right on the Dorset border, nearly a quarter of a century, and in that time his friendly welcome has got cheerier and more entertaining and the atmosphere throughout the pub even warmer and happier. Two cosy and hospitable rooms are separated by three carpeted steps, and are furnished with one or two settles and pews, a deep leather sofa and chairs, hunting prints, carriage lamps for lighting, a pendulum wall clock, and ornaments on the mantelpiece over the log fire; there's a thatched-roof servery in the stone-floored bar, and a dark panelling dado in the carpeted upstairs area. Freshly prepared bar food includes sandwiches (from £2.20), soup (£2.95), ploughman's (£5.25), ham and salami with olives, sausage and mash or calamari (£5.95), steak and kidney pie or gravadlax with dill sauce (£6.95), duck confit with orange marmalade (£7.50), venison, orange and juniper casserole (£8.95), local trout (£9.95), gammon in cider or half a roast duckling (£10.95), 8oz fillet steak cooked in sherry (£14.95), and puddings such as sherry trifle and apple charlotte (from £3.25). Four real ales on handpump might include Adnams, Brakspears and a guest, also farm cider, four chilled vodkas, 18 malt whiskies, lots of liqueurs, and a thoughtfully chosen wine list, including a good few by the glass; friendly chatty staff. Cribbage and TV, but no machines or music. There are seats outside. Well behaved dogs welcome. They recently added a pond to the village green, and Mr Duthie hopes to see ducks nesting there soon. *(Recommended by Matthew Last, Lynn Sharpless, Bob Eardley, Betsy Brown, Nigel Flook, Jayne and Peter Capp, J Hale)*

Enterprise ~ Lease Joe Duthie ~ Real ale ~ Bar food (11-3, 6.30-10) ~ Restaurant ~ (01747) 830221 ~ Children in eating area of bar and restaurant ~ Open 11-11; 12-10.30 Sun; closed 25, 26 Dec ~ Bedrooms: £31S/£48B

SHERSTON ST8585 Map 2

Rattlebone ♀

Church St; B4040 Malmesbury—Chipping Sodbury

This lively old inn takes its name from a local hero who died fighting King Canute in the Battle of Sherston in 1016. There's a good pubby atmosphere throughout the several spotless rambling rooms, with pink walls, pews and settles, country kitchen chairs around a mix of tables, big dried flower arrangements, lots of jugs and bottles hanging from the low beams, and plenty of little cuttings and printed anecdotes. In the public bar there's a hexagonal pool table, darts, table football, Connect Four, shove-ha'penny, fruit machine, cribbage, dominoes, TV and juke box; also alley skittles. One nice touch here is that you can have a very reasonably priced meal from the pubby lunchtime menu which includes good filled jumbo baps (from £2.95), filled baked potatoes (from £3.50), ploughman's (from £3.95), ham, egg and chips (£5.25), and deep-fried plaice with chips (£5.50), or you can eat from the more sophisticated menu which includes wild mushroom and dijon mustard tagliatelle (£4.25), puff pastry tart with mozzarella, basil and tomatoes (£4.50), chicken and leek pie (£7.50), lamb shank with country vegetable jus (£9.50), salmon fillet with capers and smoked butter (£9.75). If there's nothing to your liking on either of those menus they also have daily specials, usually including quite a lot of fresh fish, such as cod and salmon thai fishcakes (£8.95) and bass with baby vegetables (£10.95). Sunday roast (£7.95), and puddings such as bread and butter pudding with clotted cream or lemon and vanilla cheesecake (£3.50); part of the dining area is no smoking. Well kept Smiles Best, Youngs Triple A, Bitter and Special and a seasonal brew from Youngs on handpump, over 50 malt whiskies, half a dozen rums, decent wines including about 15 by the glass, and fruit wines. The smallish garden is very pretty with flowerbeds, a gravel terrace, and picnic-sets under umbrellas. There are four boules pitches, and the Sherston carnival week concludes with a festival of boules at the pub on the second Saturday in July. It's handy for the M4 and Westonbirt Arboretum. *(Recommended by Christopher and Mary Thomas, Mike and Mona Clifford, Joy and Peter Heatherley, Andrew Shore, Charles and Pauline Stride, Ann and Colin Hunt, Mike Pugh, Betsy and Peter Little)*

Youngs ~ Managers Neil Coombs and Claire Graham ~ Real ale ~ Bar food (12-2, 7-9.30(10 Sun)) ~ Restaurant ~ (01666) 840871 ~ Children away from main bar servery ~ Open 12-11(10.30 Sun); closed evening 25 Dec

WHITLEY ST8866 Map 2
Pear Tree 🍽 ♀

Off B3353 S of Corsham, at Atworth 1½, Purlpit 1 signpost; or from A350 Chippenham—Melksham in Beanacre turn off on Westlands Lane at Whitley 1 signpost, then left and right at B3353

A sympathetically constructed extension at this very well run attractive honey-coloured stone farmhouse has given them a bright spacious garden room and a new kitchen. There's smart new teak furniture on the terrace, which looks over carefully maintained gardens that are prettily lit at night to show up features like the ruined pigsty. The front bar has cushioned window seats, some stripped shutters, a mix of dining chairs around good solid tables, a variety of country pictures and a Wiltshire regiment sampler on the walls, a little fireplace on the left, and a lovely old stripped stone one on the right. The popular big back restaurant (candlelit at night) has green dining chairs, quite a mix of tables, and a pitched ceiling at one end with a quirky farmyard theme – wrought-iron cockerels and white scythe sculpture. While the charming licensees and first-class staff will make you feel more than welcome if all you want is a pint of well kept Bass, Wadworths 6X or the guest, or maybe one of the 27 or so decent wines available by the glass, the food is the main reason for coming here. Beautifully presented dishes include provençale fish soup with cheese croûte and aïoli (£5.25), grilled ciabatta with smoked chicken, watercress and mayonnaise (£5.95), smoked salmon and paprika fishcakes with rocket salad (£7.50), pork and leek sausages with horseradish mash and red wine gravy (£8.25), sautéed skate with vegetable salad and tomato confit vinaigrette (£11.50), rib-eye steak with sautéed mushrooms and rich veal jus (£12.95), with daily specials such as watercress and potato soup (£3.40), braised guinea fowl with creamy parmesan and mange tout risotto (£12.20), and puddings such as honey and rhubarb parfait on champagne sauce, lemon and lime curd ice cream on a lime sauce, or almond and apricot tart with a compote of apricots (from £4.75). The good value set lunch menu is very popular (two-course £9.95, three-course £12.25), and it's best to book in the evening. There are picnic-sets on the terrace, and boules. *(Recommended by Lord Sandhurst, Susan and Nigel Wilson, Lyn and Geoff Hallchurch, Diana Brumfit, Catherine Pitt, Mr and Mrs A H Young, Andrew Shore, Michael Doswell, J H Bescoby, Jonathan Smith, Sue Demont, Tim Barrow, John and Jane Hayter)*

Free house ~ Licensees Martin and Debbie Still ~ Real ale ~ Bar food (12-2(2.30 Sun), 6.30-9(10 Fri, Sat)) ~ Restaurant ~ (01225) 709131 ~ Children in restaurant ~ Open 11-3, 6-11; 12-3, 7-10.30 Sun

WOODBOROUGH SU1159 Map 2
Seven Stars ♀

Off A345 S of Marlborough: from Pewsey follow Woodborough signposts, then in Woodborough bear left following Bottlesford signposts

There's a pleasant blend of the traditional English pub with a strong gallic influence from the French licensee at this thatched red brick house. There's quite a continental leaning in the daily changing bar food which might include french onion soup (£2.95), filled baguettes (from £3.75), ploughman's (from £4.25), moules farçies, provençaux or marinières or croque monsieur (£4.75), crevettes sautéed in garlic butter or smoked duck breast (£5.75), aubergine provençale (£7.25), local sausages with garlic mash and onion gravy (£7.95), spicy squid basquaise or chicken breast with camembert in red wine sauce (£9.75), jugged hare (£10.75), seafood pot au feu or sirloin steak with red wine and onions (£12.75) and puddings such as tarte tatin, home-made sorbets and chocolate fondant (£3.95); they receive regular deliveries from France, and smaller helpings are available for children. The bar is traditionally furnished with polished bricks by the bar counter, hunting prints, attractively moulded panelling, a hot coal fire in the old range at one end, a big log fire at the other, a pleasant mix of antique settles and country furniture, cast-iron-framed tables and cosy nooks here and there; maybe sophisticated piped music. Well kept Badger Best, Stonehenge Pigswill and Wadworths 6X on handpump, and an exemplary wine list (including plenty of French), and interesting bin ends. There are seven acres of riverside gardens, and an alsatian, a white west highland terrier and a black cat constitute the friendly menagerie. Please note, the pub shuts on Tuesdays following bank holiday Mondays. *(Recommended by Dennis Jenkin, Karen and Graham Oddey, Phyl and Jack Street, Ellen Winter, Marshall and Ruth May, Mrs G Delderfield, Chantal Patel)*

Free house ~ Licensees Philippe Cheminade and Kate Lister ~ Real ale ~ Bar food ~ Restaurant ~ (01672) 851325 ~ Well behaved children in restaurant ~ Open 12-3, 6-11; 12-3 Sun; closed Sun evening and all day Mon except lunchtimes on bank holidays, then cl Tues

WOOTTON RIVERS SU1963 Map 2
Royal Oak ♀

Village signposted from A346 Marlborough—Salisbury, from A345 Marlborough—Pewsey, and B3087 E of Pewsey

This attractive thatched and timbered village, with the Kennet and Avon Canal passing through at one end, is well worth exploring, particularly the 13th-c church which houses the curious George V Coronation clock. Then head for this beamed 16th-c thatched pub for their popular, extensive range of bar food. They do seem to be more interested in diners than drinkers, and it's advisable to book for an evening meal (when some customers may be quite smartly dressed). As well as lunchtime sandwiches (from £3.50) and ploughman's (from £5.50), the choice might include soup (£2.75), Cornish crab soup (£3.75), baked goats cheese on sweet pepper salad with anchovies (£5.50), filled ciabatta (£6), scampi (£7.75), grilled salmon or grilled chicken breast with cajun spices (£8.50), seafood salad (£10.50), several steaks (from £13), and daily specials like chilli (£6.50), steak and Guinness pie (£8.50) and grilled lamb cutlets with port and redcurrant sauce (£10.50); puddings include sherry trifle, hot chocolate fudge cake and stem ginger with cream (from £3.75). The friendly L-shaped dining lounge has slat-back chairs, armchairs and some rustic settles around good tripod tables, a low ceiling with partly stripped beams, partly glossy white planks, and a woodburning stove. The timbered bar is comfortably furnished, and has a small area with board games, darts, pool, fruit machine and juke box. Well kept Wadworths JCB and 6X and a guest ale such as Fullers London Pride kept under light blanket pressure, or tapped straight from the cask, interesting whiskies, and a good wine list (running up to some very distinguished vintage ones); service may slow at busy times. There are tables under cocktail parasols in the back gravelled yard. *(Recommended by Stephen Savill, Trevor Owen, Mrs June Wilmers)*

Free house ~ Licensees John and Rosa Jones ~ Real ale ~ Bar food (12-2.30, 7-9.30) ~ Restaurant ~ (01672) 810322 ~ Children in eating area of bar and restaurant ~ Open 10-3.30, 6-11; 10-4, 6-11.30 Sat; 12-4, 6-11 Sun ~ Bedrooms: £20(£25S)/£40(£45S)

WYLYE SU0037 Map 4
Bell ◀

Just off A303/A36 junction; High Street

There's a civilised unhurried atmosphere at this cosy little 14th-c country pub. The neatly kept and black-beamed front bar has one of the inn's three winter log fires, and sturdy rustic furnishings that go well with the stripped stonework and neat timbered herringbone brickwork. The comfortably carpeted no smoking restaurant with pristine white linen has a more sophisticated feel. Very well cooked bar food using fresh ingredients includes sandwiches (from £3.50), soup (£3.50), greek salad

(£4.95), duck liver terrine (£5.95), ploughman's (£6.95), tagliatelle bolognese (£6.95), sausages and celeriac mash (£7.50), good upmarket changing daily specials such as vegetable terrine (£4.95), smoked salmon mousse with caviar (£5.95), roast loin of pork with apple sauce (£8.95) and trio of salmon, bass and monkfish with couscous and tomato and basil sauce (£12.95) and puddings such as local strawberries and cream or gooseberry crumble (£4.95). Four well kept real ales are sourced from all over the country and come from brewers such as Cains, Harviestoun, Hook Norton and Ringwood. They keep a good range of country wines and about seven wines by the glass including one from a local vineyard; piped music, cribbage and daily papers. There are seats outside on a pleasant walled terrace and in a back garden. The pub is nicely set in a peaceful village, and is very handy for Stonehenge; there are fine downland walks near here. *(Recommended by Mrs Pam Mattinson, Colin and Janet Roe, Mark Sheard, Michael and Ann Cole, Charles Moncreiffe, Phil and Sally Gorton, Denis Dutton, Charles Gysin)*

Free house ~ Licensees Keith and Linda Bidwell ~ Real ale ~ Bar food (12-2(2.30 Sun), 6-9.30(7-9 Sun)) ~ Restaurant ~ (01985) 248338 ~ Seated children welcome in dining room ~ Open 11.30-2.30, 6-11; 12-3, 7-10.30 Sun ~ Bedrooms: £30B/£45S(£60B)

Lucky Dip

Besides the fully inspected pubs, you might like to try these Lucky Dips recommended to us and described by readers (if you do, please send us reports: www.goodguides.com).

Aldbourne [SU2675]
☆ *Blue Boar* [The Green (off B4192)]: Relaxed and nicely furnished, with homely feel, farm tools, boar's head and flame-effect woodburner in Tudor area, extensive more modern back lounge/dining area popular for good choice of inexpensive food from generous sandwiches up, fresh veg; three well kept Wadworths ales, good choice of wines and soft drinks, polite service; darts, quiet piped music; children welcome, neatly kept small back country garden, seats out facing pretty village green nr church *(CMW, JJW, Peter and Audrey Dowsett)*

Bishops Cannings [SU0364]
☆ *Crown* [Chandlers Lane; off A361 NE of Devizes]: Welcoming and unassuming refurbished two-bar local with wide choice of good value generous food, well kept Wadworths IPA and 6X, decent wines, upstairs dining room; dogs welcome, tables in garden behind, next to handsome old church in pretty village, walk to Kennet & Avon Canal *(Lyn and Geoff Hallchurch, Marjorie and David Lamb)*

Bishopstone [SU0725]
White Hart [Butts Lane; the one nr Salisbury]: Attractively refurbished, with enjoyable good value food inc interesting specials and OAP wkdy bargains. Flowers Original and Wadworths 6X, attentive friendly well dressed staff, log fire, pleasant atmosphere, roomy restaurant, games area with pool; garden with play area *(Dr and Mrs Michael Smith, David and Elizabeth Briggs)*

Bradford-on-Avon [ST8261]
Barge [Frome Rd]: Child-friendly pub nice for summer, with relaxing canalside garden, well priced food inc lunchtime baguettes, friendly landlord; sensibly priced bedrooms *(Claire Nielsen)*

☆ *Beehive* [Trowbridge Rd, Widmore]: Friendly and simple old-fashioned pub on outskirts, old playbills, cricketing prints and cigarette cards, up to eight well kept ales mainly from small local brewers, some tapped from the cask, traditional food esp substantial sandwiches (some hot) with baskets of chips, good range of wines; children and dogs welcome, resident cats, service can slow on busy summer wknds; attractive good-sized canalside back garden, barbecues *(Pete Baker, Dr M E Wilson)*
Three Horseshoes [Frome Rd, by big car park nr station]: Good friendly licensees and staff, well kept mostly local beers, good generous food, cosy furnishings, plenty of nooks and corners; small restaurant, tables and chairs on terrace *(Ted George, Dr M E Wilson)*

Broad Hinton [SU1076]
☆ *Crown* [off A4361 about 3 miles S of Swindon]: Open-plan slightly old-fashioned village inn, good interesting food (freshly made, so may be a wait) in roomy and comfortably plush eating area (children like the fish tank), well kept Arkells ales, good range of wines, welcoming helpful uniformed staff, no smoking area; may be piped music; unusual gilded inn sign, attractive and sheltered spacious garden with fishpond and play area; bedrooms *(Mrs Rosemary Bayliss, LYM, Trevor Owen, Nick and Meriel Cox, CMW, JJW, Brian and Pat Wardrobe)*

Bulford [SU1643]
Rose & Crown [High St]: Friendly and pleasant, with reasonably priced food inc sizzler dishes, Greene King IPA and Abbot *(James Nunns)*

Castle Combe [ST8477]
Salutation [The Gibb; B4039 Acton Turville—Chippenham, nr Nettleton]: Surprisingly large old pub with choice of beamed seating areas inc

comfortable lounge and locals' bar, huge handsome fireplace, separate raftered thatched and timbered restaurant; jovial landlord, Whitbread-related ales, good choice of wines, enjoyable food inc fresh Cornish fish; open all day, pretty garden with pergola *(MRSM)*

Charlton [ST9588]

☆ *Horse & Groom* [B4040 towards Cricklade]: Wide choice of good generous food in civilised and relaxing bar, old firearms, farm tools and log fire, simpler right-hand bar with hops on beams, friendly staff, well kept Archers and Wadworths, farm cider, decent wines; restaurant (good value Sun lunch), tables outside; dogs welcome, comfortable bedrooms *(Gill and David Morrell, R Huggins, D Irving, E McCall, T McLean, LYM)*

Cherhill [SU0370]

Black Horse: Popular beamed oak-panelled dining pub, linked areas crowded with tables for wide range of very good value generous food (two evening sittings), prompt service, friendly landlord, no smoking area, huge fireplace, four Ushers ales; children welcome *(Dr M E Wilson)*

Chilmark [ST9632]

☆ *Black Dog* [B3089 Salisbury—Hindon]: Comfortably modernised 15th-c beamed pub with enjoyable food, well kept ales such as Bass, Hook Norton and Wadworths 6X, good value house wines, friendly staff, good local atmosphere (regulars turn up on horseback), armchairs by lounge log fire, fossil ammonites in the stone of the attractive dining room; dogs welcome, tables out by road *(Pat and Robert Watt, Mr and Mrs G Robson, LYM, Kevin Flack, John and Marian Greenwood)*

Chilton Foliat [SU3270]

Wheatsheaf [E of junction B4001/B4192]: Old-fashioned genuine village local with welcoming landlady, comfortable beamed lounge, separate dining room, well kept Greene King and Wadworths 6X, good value decent food from well filled sandwiches up, open fire; dogs welcome, pool room, very quiet piped music; big garden *(Denis Dutton, Dick and Madeleine Brown)*

Christian Malford [ST9678]

☆ *Mermaid* [B4069 Lyneham—Chippenham, 3½ miles from M4 junction 17]: Long cheerful bar pleasantly divided into areas, good food worth waiting for inc some interesting dishes and super ploughman's, well kept ales such as Bass, Fullers London Pride, Wadworths 6X and Worthingtons BB, decent whiskies and wines, some attractive pictures; bar billiards, darts, fruit machine, piped music (live blues Thurs), may be a bit smoky; tables in garden, bedrooms *(BB, Mr and Mrs F J Parmenter, Richard Pierce, Alan Wilson)*

Clyffe Pypard [SU0776]

Goddard Arms: Unpretentious 16th-c village pub with log fire and raised dining area in split-level main bar, small sitting room with another fire and two old armchairs, down-to-earth chatty and welcoming licensees, well kept Wadworths 6X and guests such as Flowers IPA and Greene King Abbot, good value

straightforward freshly made food, back skittle alley with prints, paintings, sculptures, second-hand books and records for sale (busy music nights, and pool room off, with darts, cribbage etc); no cards taken; open all day wknds, sculpture garden, bedrooms, tiny pretty thatched village in lovely countryside *(Pete Baker, CMW, JJW)*

Coate [SU0462]

New Inn: Nice unspoilt village pub, very friendly, old tables on tile floors, Wadworths ales tapped from the cask *(the Didler)*

Collingbourne Ducis [SU2453]

Blue Lion [High St]: Not smart but welcoming, with wide choice of reasonably priced usual food, well kept Flowers Original, Ringwood and Wadworths 6X, decent wines, quick chatty service, big log fire, Victorian-style furnishings, no piped music, separate back bar with pool, restaurant; pretty village *(R T and J C Moggridge)*

☆ *Shears* [Cadley Rd]: Popular racing-country pub doing well under new landlord, good fresh imaginative food in bar and restaurant, generous helpings and reasonable prices, well kept beers; good value bedrooms *(A W Moulds)*

Coombe Bissett [SU1026]

☆ *Fox & Goose*: Spacious neatly kept open-plan pub by delightful riverside village green, good value food inc fine puddings, Badger Best, K&B and Tanglefoot, decent coffee, welcoming staff, rustic refectory-style tables, coal fires, old prints, hanging chamber-pots, evening restaurant; can be very busy wknds, piped music (classical at lunchtime); children catered for, picnic-sets on terrace and in garden with play area, good wheelchair access *(Lyn and Geoff Hallchurch, Ian Phillips)*

Corsham [ST8769]

Great Western [Station Rd]: Comfortable local with friendly landlord and staff, well kept local ales inc Abbey, Bath, Moles and Wadworths, darts in separate bar *(Jonathan Smith)*

Hare & Hounds [Pickwick]: New licensees in attractive local, fire in comfortable lounge area, main bar with piped music and discreet sports TV, third room with alcove seating and pool, bar food, Bass; Dickens said to have based *Pickwick Papers* characters on regulars he met here *(George Atkinson)*

Methuen Arms [High St]: Cosy old-world hotel, formerly a priory, good food in bar and pricier restaurant, Bass, Wadworths 6X and occasional guest beers, good local atmosphere, sombre lounge bar; skittle alley, tables in attractive courtyard with outside staircase and dovecote in wall, comfortable bedrooms *(BB, Catherine Pitt)*

Pack Horse [High St]: Nice little local, lively at times (occasional karaoke), with new licensees, food and three guest beers (often Courage Directors) in small bar area; open all day *(Catherine Pitt)*

Crockerton [ST8642]

Bath Arms [just off A350 Warminster—Blandford]: Attractive old dining pub, good reasonably priced food, two or three real ales inc one brewed for the pub, plenty of tables in several rooms and picnic-sets in garden *(Richard Fendick)*

Crudwell [ST9592]

Plough [A429 N of Malmesbury]: Nice timeless local feel, friendly service, quiet lounge, dining area with comfortable well padded seats and more in elevated part; remarkably wide range of briskly served good value food, well kept ales such as Bass, Boddingtons, Greene King Old Specked Hen and Wadworths 6X, open fires, bar with darts and juke box, pool room; pleasant side garden *(R Huggins, D Irving, E McCall, T McLean, Lyn and Geoff Hallchurch, David and Ruth Hollands)*

Derry Hill [ST9570]

Lansdowne Arms [Church Rd]: Pleasant relaxed atmosphere in attractively refurbished Victorian pub, soft lighting, lots of candles, well kept Wadworths and a guest beer, good choice of good value wines by the glass, interesting reasonably priced food, open fire, restaurant; garden with good play area, handy for Bowood *(Peter B Brown)*

Devizes [SU0161]

Moonraker [Nursteed Rd]: Large comfortable 1930s pub with enjoyable food, well kept Wadworths IPA and 6X, good whiskies (expert Scottish landlord), friendly service *(Richard Pierce)*

Queens Head [Dunkirk Hill]: Well kept Moles beers, usual food at attractive prices *(Dr B and Mrs P B Baker)*

Donhead St Andrew [ST9124]

Forester [off A30 E of Shaftesbury, just E of Ludwell; Lower St]: Small traditional thatched pub with plenty of character, very friendly owners, enjoyable food from sandwiches up, well kept beers inc Ringwood Best, Greene King and Smiles, armchairs by inglenook fireplace, separate restaurant area; small garden with a few plastic tables on tiny terrace and picnic-sets on lawn, nice views, lovely village *(Martin and Karen Wake)*

East Knoyle [ST8830]

Seymour Arms [The Street; just off A350 S of Warminster]: Roomy creeper-covered stone-built black-beamed pub, quietly welcoming and comfortable, with rambling more or less L-shaped bar areas, cosy part with high-backed settle by log fire, good freshly made generous food from huge granary baguettes to interesting specials using local produce, well kept Wadworths IPA, 6X and Farmers Glory, friendly Welsh landlady, two well behaved dogs; may be piped music; tables in garden with play area, good value bedrooms *(Roger and Pauline Pearce, W Ruxton, Sue and Len Lewis, BB, Lyn and Geoff Hallchurch)*

Easton Royal [SU2060]

Bruce Arms [Easton Rd]: Fine old unspoilt local, nicely basic, with scrubbed pine tables, brick floor, well kept Butts, Wadworths 6X and guest ales, Pewsey organic cider, good rolls made to order; open all day Sun *(the Didler)*

Farleigh Wick [ST8064]

Fox & Hounds [A363 Bath—Bradford]: Well extended welcoming low-beamed rambling bar

with easy mix of drinkers and eaters, highly polished old oak tables and chairs, gently rural decorations, Bass and Marstons Pedigree; attractive garden *(Meg and Colin Hamilton, Mrs J H S Lang, Mr and Mrs A H Young, Lyn and Geoff Hallchurch, MRSM)*

Fovant [SU0128]

Pembroke Arms [A30 W of Salisbury]: Cheerful two-roomed local with three fires, interesting World War I museum in saloon bar, also pig bric-a-brac (landlady's an aficionado – there's a live one outside); good food with ironic emphasis on sausages but plenty for vegetarians, well kept Flowers and Ringwood Best, good service, room with revolving hexagonal pool table; comfortable bedrooms, good breakfast, neat and tidy side garden, close to regimental badges cut into the hillside *(Richard and Liz Dilnot, Ann and Colin Hunt, Wendy Norman)*

Giddeahall [ST8574]

☆ *Crown* [A420 Chippenham—Ford; keep eyes skinned as no village sign]: Interesting Tudor pub with character furnishings in attractive rambling beamed bars, log fire, enjoyable food (platters recommended), warmly welcoming licensees, no piped music; comfortable bedrooms *(LYM, Peter and Audrey Dowsett)*

Heddington [ST9966]

☆ *Ivy*: Thatched 15th-c village pub with good inglenook log fire in plain L-shaped bar, heavy low beams, timbered walls, well kept Wadworths 6X tapped from the cask, good simple home-made food (not Sun-Weds evenings) inc fish, back children's room, sensibly placed darts, dog and cat; open all day wknds, seats outside the picturesque house, attractively set hamlet *(Pete Baker, Phil and Sally Gorton, the Didler, Dr B and Mrs P B Baker, LYM)*

Heytesbury [ST9242]

Red Lion [High St]: Friendly and comfortable, with nice quiet atmosphere, good straightforward food, well kept real ales; good bedrooms *(Ann and Colin Hunt)*

Highworth [SU1891]

Freke Arms [Swanborough; B4019, a mile W on Honnington turning]: Airy and friendly, smart but relaxed, four rooms on different levels, well kept ales inc Arkells 2B and 3B, food inc good sandwiches and straightforward hot dishes (nothing expensive), quick service, no piped music; small garden with play area, nice views *(Peter and Audrey Dowsett)*

☆ *Saracens Head* [High St]: Comfortable and relaxed rambling bar, good-humoured licensees, friendly service, several distinct interesting areas around great central chimney block, wide choice of good value straightforward bar food (limited Sun) inc OAP bargains and children's, well kept Arkells 2B and 3B; piped music, public bar with TV; children in eating area, tables in sheltered courtyard, open all day wkdys; comfortable bedrooms *(LYM, Nigel and Sue Foster, Peter and Audrey Dowsett)*

Hodson [SU1780]

☆ *Calley Arms* [not far from M4 junction 15, via

Chiseldon; off B4005 S of Swindon]: Relaxed and welcoming big bar with raised no smoking dining area, good well priced food (not Sun/Mon evenings), cheerful prompt thoughtful service, well kept Wadworths ales with a guest, dozens of malt whiskies, farm ciders, country wines, darts and open fire one end; children welcome, picnic-sets in garden with dovecote, plenty of good walks *(Sheila and Robert Robinson, M G Hart)*

Holt [ST8561]

Toll Gate [Ham Green; B3107 W of Melksham]: Homely warm décor with sofas and armchairs around log fire, changing ales such as Abbey Bellringer, Butcombe, Exmoor Gold and Moles, farm cider, coffee with home-made biscuits, some emphasis on adventurous choice of beautifully presented food in upstairs restaurant; two cats, and a goat in the back garden *(Catherine Pitt, P R and S A White, Peter J Harrison)*

Honeystreet [SU1061]

Barge: Friendly unspoilt pub by Kennet & Avon Canal, charming almost 18th-c atmosphere in bar, back room with murals and painted ceiling devoted to crop circles, well kept Ushers, usual food from sandwiches up, good prices, log fires; pleasant garden, bedrooms – nice setting and good downland walks *(Lyn and Geoff Hallchurch, Bill Sykes, N Chambers)*

Horton [SU0463]

☆ *Bridge Inn* [off A361 Devizes—Beckhampton]: Experienced new landlady doing enjoyable food in spacious pub by Kennet & Avon canal, four well furnished areas with carpets or flagstones, dark wood and warm colours, cheerful efficient service, Wadworths IPA and 6X tapped from the cask, decent wines, log fire, prompt service, good restaurant; disabled lavatories, tables in garden *(Susan Cadel, K Murray-Morrison)*

Hurdcott [SU1633]

Black Horse [signed off A338 N of Salisbury]: Pretty black and white pub, new landlord/chef doing good generous food, Wadworths 6X, quick welcoming service, small restaurant; no machines, dogs on leads and children allowed away from bar, tables in pretty garden *(David and Elizabeth Briggs)*

Kington St Michael [ST9077]

Jolly Huntsman [handy for M4 junction 17]: Roomy, with scrubbed tables, old-fashioned settees, pleasant rather dark décor, good range of well kept changing ales, open fire, dining end (would make a good no smoking area) with enjoyable fresh-cooked food from an interesting menu, welcoming helpful staff; maybe sports TV; two cheap bedrooms *(Dave Irving, Mr and Mrs F J Parmenter)*

Langley Burrell [ST9375]

Brewery Arms [The Common]: Refurbished local with enjoyable food from good ploughman's to some imaginative dishes and well priced three-course meals (should book wknds), well kept beers, some tapped from the cask, good coffee *(Richard Pierce, Lyn and Geoff Hallchurch)*

Lea [ST9586]

Rose & Crown: Smart Victorian dining pub

with red and white tiles by bar, comfortable sofas by big open fire, attractive dining areas off with old prints and dark red walls, helpful family-friendly staff, well kept Arkells 2B, 3B and a seasonal ale; unobtrusive piped music *(Mike Ridgway, Sarah Miles)*

Little Somerford [ST9784]

Saladin: Recently reopened by new owners as smart but cosy family dining pub, comfortable armchairs, chesterfield and log fire, enjoyable food with choice of snacky or restauranty menus, well kept real ales, several Belgian beers, decent wines, pleasant knowledgeable service *(R Huggins, D Irving, E McCall, T McLean, John and Lee Faber, Dr and Mrs J Hicks)*

Lockeridge [SU1467]

☆ *Who'd A Thought It* [signed off A4 Marlborough—Calne just W of Fyfield]: Welcoming village pub with good sensibly priced well presented food inc very popular OAP lunch, well kept Wadworths, good wine choice, caring landlord, log fire, family room – good for children; pleasant back garden with play area, delightful quiet scenery, lovely walks *(Sheila and Robert Robinson, Stephen Savill, Jenny and Brian Seller, Mrs June Wilmers, Tony Baldwin)*

Longbridge Deverill [ST8740]

George [A350/B3095]: Extended village pub, spacious and relaxed even when busy, good reasonably priced food, well kept Gales, good service, restaurant *(Dave Braisted)*

Lower Woodford [SU1136]

Wheatsheaf [signed off A360 just N of Salisbury]: New management in prettily set 18th-c dining pub, miniature footbridge over indoor goldfish pool, vast food choice, well kept Badger Best, IPA and Tanglefoot; piped music; children welcome, good disabled access, baby-changing, good big tree-lined garden with play area *(I D Barnett, Lynn Sharpless, Bob Eardley, Martin Weinberg, Tracey and Stephen Groves, LYM)*

Ludgershall [SU2650]

Queens Head [High St]: Friendly local with open fire, good choice of cheap home-made food, well kept Hampshire Strongs Best with a guest such as Wadworths 6X, friendly service *(R T and J C Moggridge)*

Ludwell [ST9122]

Grove Arms [A30 E of Shaftesbury]: Attractive décor, three changing beers such as Banbury Old Vic, good varied food, polite young staff, spotless housekeeping, restaurant; small children may be much in evidence *(P J Keen)*

Malmesbury [ST9287]

Kings Arms [High St]: Popular well worn in 16th-c town pub with two bars, warm and friendly atmosphere, low prices, popular food from sandwiches and other bar snacks to fresh crabs and ambitious meals in pleasant restaurant, Flowers IPA and a guest such as Mighty Oak, lots of wines by the glass; nice courtyard garden, jazz last Sat of month, comfortable bedrooms *(Dr and Mrs R E S Tanner)*

☆ *Suffolk Arms* [Tetbury Hill, S of junction with B4014]: Huge helpings of good value food and cheerful efficient service in knocked-through bar and big no smoking panelled dining room; well kept Wadworths IPA and 6X and a changing guest beer, log fire; children welcome *(R Huggins, D Irving, E McCall, T McLean, Robert Gartery, LYM)*

Manton [SU1668]
Oddfellows Arms [High St, signed off A4 Marlborough—Devizes]: Good village local, for both drinkers and diners alike; roomy comfortable bar with lots of nooks and crannies and relaxing atmosphere, cheerful willing service, generous helpings of good value imaginative food inc fish and plenty of vegetarian, well kept Wadworths inc a seasonal beer, country wines; children welcome, big garden *(Lyn and Geoff Hallchurch, Sheila and Robert Robinson, Myra and Roy Jackson)*

Marlborough [SU1869]
☆ *Sun* [High St]: Well worn in old-fashioned 15th-c pub with heavy sloping beams, wonky floors, dim lighting, log fire, benches built into black panelling, food from sandwiches to steaks, ales such as Bass and Wadworths 6X, daily papers, no smoking dining area; piped music may be loud; simple bedrooms, small back courtyard *(KN-R, Trevor Owen, Ian Phillips, LYM, Sheila and Robert Robinson, Rona Murdoch, Pat and Tony Martin, Stephen Savill, Betsy and Peter Little)*

Marston Meysey [SU1297]
Old Spotted Cow [off A419 Swindon—Cirencester]: Big well laid out open-plan Cotswold stone pub, good value generous food, well kept Flowers IPA, Wadworths 6X and an interesting guest beer, decent wines, welcoming licensees, comfortable chairs, raised stone fireplace, plants and pictures; bar billiards, darts, board and children's games, fruit machine, quiet piped music; open all day wknds, spacious garden with picnic-sets on terrace and lots of play equipment *(R Huggins, D Irving, E McCall, T McLean, Peter and Audrey Dowsett)*

Mildenhall [SU2069]
☆ *Horseshoe*: Newish management keeping relaxed traditional feel in three attractive partly partitioned rooms and small no smoking dining room, good value varied well presented food, well kept Archers, Wadworths and Worthingtons, decent sensibly priced wines, friendly efficient service, pristine lavatories; bedrooms, picnic-sets out on grass, lovely setting in good walking country *(Mrs Pat Crabb, Tim and Isobel Smith, Trevor Owen)*

Monkton Farleigh [ST8065]
Kings Arms: Attractive ancient building under new landlord, good home-made food inc interesting dishes in bar and no smoking tapestried restaurant with huge inglenook, Ushers ales, farm cider, unusual wines; darts, bar billiards, Fri live music; rustic tables in front partly flagstoned courtyard, aviaries in back garden *(Lyn and Geoff Hallchurch, Mike, Sue, Natalie and Verity Clay, Susan and Nigel Wilson, Miss M W Hayter)*

Newton Tony [SU2140]
☆ *Malet Arms* [off A338 Swindon—Salisbury]:

Very popular nicely placed local opp footbridge over chalk stream, good food inc fresh seafood in cosy bar and separate side restaurant, well kept ales such as Ringwood Best, Stonehenge Heelstone, Wadworths 6X and Wickwar BOB, pleasant mix of customers (busy even midweek, let alone Sat night), efficient cheerful staff; attractive quiet village *(Dr and Mrs Nigel Holmes, David and Elizabeth Briggs, Howard and Margaret Buchanan, Francis Johnston, Miss E Holmes, P Hill, David Whiteley)*

Nomansland [SU2517]
Lamb [Forest Rd]: Attractive old-fashioned building in lovely New Forest setting on Hants border, wide choice of good value bar food inc lots of puddings, good range of beers inc Ringwood, good welcoming service; friendly donkeys, good walks *(Adrian and Mandy Bateman)*

North Newnton [SU1257]
Woodbridge [A345 Upavon—Pewsey]: Blazing log fire, collection of old maps, prints on walls, well kept Wadworths IPA, 6X, Farmers Glory and seasonal guest, summer farm cider, friendly efficient service, bar food; piped music, no dogs; pleasantly furnished bedrooms (three with own bathroom); plenty of tables and play area (not much for older children) in expansive garden backing on to River Avon, space for tents or caravans, fly fishing passes available *(Betsy and Peter Little, Patricia A Bruce, Bruce Bird, LYM, Ian Phillips)*

North Wroughton [SU1482]
Check Inn [Woodland View (A4361 just S of Swindon)]: Welcoming single bar with various comfortable areas inc children's, half a dozen well kept interesting changing ales in oversized lined glasses, lots of Czech and German bottled beers, farm cider, good food choice, log fire, pictures for sale; pub games, quiet piped music, TV, fruit machines; disabled access, garden bar (can pitch tent, motorway noise), open all day Fri-Sun *(CMW, JJW, Richard Lewis)*

Nunton [SU1526]
☆ *Radnor Arms* [off A338 S of Salisbury]: Pretty ivy-clad village pub very popular for wide-ranging good value food inc fish and local game, friendly helpful staff, well kept Badger inc Tanglefoot; three pleasantly decorated and furnished linked rooms inc cheerfully busy yet relaxing bar and staider restaurant; log fires, very friendly labrador; can get rather crowded, booking essential at wknds; attractive garden popular with children *(Mrs Ann Rix, R J Walden, David and Elizabeth Briggs)*

Odstock [SU1426]
Yew Tree [off A338 S of Salisbury]: Pretty thatched and low-beamed country dining pub, very busy wknds, with big blackboard choice of wholesome food, good range of real ales, welcoming unpretentious atmosphere, efficient service; good walks *(Dr and Mrs Michael Smith)*

Ramsbury [SU2771]
Bell [signed off B4192 NW of Hungerford, or A4 W]: Cleanly opened-up beamed and bay-windowed pub with food from good if not cheap lunchtime sandwiches to more elaborate

dishes, especially in the evening, no smoking restaurant, Wadworths IPA, 6X and may be a guest beer, two woodburners; piped blues and jazz; picnic-sets on raised lawn *(Sheila and Robert Robinson, Gordon Prince, Alistair Forsyth, LYM)*

Crown & Anchor [Crowood Lane/Whittonditch Rd]: Friendly and relaxed beamed village pub, popular for good value carefully done simple food, well kept Bass, Tetleys and usually a guest beer, good house wine, open fires, pool in public bar; no piped music, children welcome, garden with terrace *(Susan and Ewan Robbie, Mr and Mrs P Smith)*

Salisbury [SU1429]

Wyndham Arms [Estcourt Rd]: Basic modern corner pub with small cosy room opp bar, friendly atmosphere, reasonably priced good Hop Back beers (originally brewed here until their popularity needed larger premises over at Downton), inc GFB, Best, Crop Circle, Summer Lightning and winter Entire Stout, country wines, simple bar food *(Kent Barker)*

Seend [ST9460]

Bell [Bell Hill (A361)]: Four-room refurbished pub with cosy settees in lounge, attentive cheerful service, well kept Wadworths IPA and 6X, good food from sandwiches to steaks in bars and attractive upstairs dining room with good views; pubby locals' bar, no music *(Pat and Tony Martin, Lyn and Geoff Hallchurch, Dr and Mrs A K Clarke, Geoff Palmer)*

Three Magpies [Sells Green – A365 towards Melksham]: Unspoilt partly 18th-c pub with well kept Wadworths IPA and 6X, Stowford Press cider, local country wines, wide range of usual food from good value ploughman's up; big garden with play area *(Pat and Tony Martin, Jenny and Dave Hughes, M Borthwick)*

Semington [ST9259]

☆ *Lamb* [The Strand; A361 Devizes— Trowbridge]: Cheerfully pubby and busy series of rooms with helpful friendly service, good choice of popular food inc some interesting dishes, well kept Butcombe, Ringwood Best and Shepherd Neame Spitfire, decent wines, good coffee, woodburner and log fire, children in eating area, tables out in colourful walled garden; helpful to wheelchairs, cl Sun evening *(Mr and Mrs J P Keates, LYM, Michael and Rosalind Dymond)*

Somerset Arms [A350 2 miles S of Melksham]: Cosy 16th-c coaching inn, heavy-beamed long bar, real and flame-effect fires, high-backed settles, plenty of tables, lots of prints and brassware, wide range of good value food in bar and restaurant inc some imaginative dishes (the cheerful service can sometime slow), Badger beers, good coffee; piped music; pleasant garden behind, short walk on busy road from Kennet & Avon Canal *(Roger and Pauline Pearce, Charles and Pauline Stride, K R Harris, K H Frostick)*

Sherston [ST8586]

☆ *Carpenters Arms* [Easton (B4040)]: Cosy beamed pub with good choice of reasonably priced food inc children's and lots of fresh fish, Whitbreads-related ales tapped from the cask,

small rooms with shiny tables on carpeted floors, log fire, friendly efficient staff, small restaurant; TV in locals' bar, no piped music; tables in pleasant garden *(Peter and Audrey Dowsett, R Huggins, D Irving, E McCall, T McLean)*

South Marston [SU1987]

Carpenters Arms [just off A420 E of Swindon]: Spaciously extended with lots of seating areas, good value generous food (may be a wait) inc OAP wkdy lunch and popular Sun roasts, well kept Arkells 2B and 3B, friendly staff, blazing coal fire, pleasant olde-worlde décor with old Swindon photographs; pool room, quiet piped music, quiz night Mon; play area and animals in big back garden, new bedroom wing *(CMW, JJW, Peter and Audrey Dowsett)*

Carriers Arms [Highworth Rd]: Vast choice of well presented usual food (not Sun evening, and may be a wait) in enjoyably compact bar, larger lounge or restaurant, pleasant décor, friendly licensees, Ushers ales, decent wine; juke box, fruit machine *(Lyn and Geoff Hallchurch, CMW, JJW)*

South Wraxall [ST8364]

Long Arms [Upper S Wraxall, off B3109 N of Bradford on Avon]: Busy and friendly cosily refurbished country local with wide-ranging good value food inc good Sun lunch and OAP lunches Tues-Fri, well kept Bass and Wadworths, good range of wines by the glass, log fire, two dogs; pretty garden *(Miss M W Hayter, Susan and Nigel Wilson)*

Steeple Langford [SU0437]

Rainbows End [off A36 E of A303 junction]: Attractive pub with large comfortable bar, good varied home-made food, friendly welcome, three changing well kept beers such as Hop Back Old Red Devil; nice lake and valley views from sunny conservatory and terrace, picnic-sets on lawn *(Richard Fendick)*

Stockton [ST9738]

Carriers [just off A36 Salisbury—Warminster, or follow Wylye sign off A303 then turn right]: Enjoyable food in homely softly lit bar with family photographs, lots of good horse tack around log fire, regimental shields, fishing memorabilia, pretty dining extension, courteously old-fashioned service, well kept Wadworths 6X and a beer brewed for them by Tisbury, decent wine; piped music, friendly young alsatian; bedrooms, sunny roadside seats, pretty village pub in Wylye valley *(Pat and Robert Watt, BB)*

Stourton [ST7734]

☆ *Spread Eagle* [Stourhead signed off B3092 N of junction with A303 just W of Mere]: NT pub in lovely setting at head of Stourhead lake (though views from pub itself not special), front bar with open fire, settles and country décor, cool and spacious civilised back dining rooms popular mainly with older people; decent food, Bass and Wadworths 6X, friendly waitress service, tables in back courtyard; bedrooms *(Pat and Dick Warwick, LYM, J F and G J Wheeler)*

Swindon [SU1485]

Beehive [Prospect Hill]: Well hidden character local, plain and unaffected, lively mix from students to older people with a faintly bohemian streak, well kept Morrells, simple lunchtime food, Irish folk nights *(Simon Moffat)*

Glue Pot [Emlyn Sq]: Tap for Archers Brewery, with their ales kept well, maybe a guest such as Brains, good soft drinks choice, high-backed settles around pine tables, lunchtime snacks inc good value ploughman's, friendly locals; can get a bit smoky, pub games; tables on terrace – in Brunel's Railway Village; open all day (cl Sun afternoon) *(CMW, JJW)*

Savoy [Regent Circus]: Bustling Wetherspoons in excellently converted cinema, seven real ales, decent food (Thurs evening curry club), affordable prices, split-level seating areas, books and film memorabilia, comfortable atmosphere, decent wine, quick friendly service; popular with all ages (no children), no music, some no smoking areas, open all day *(Peter and Audrey Dowsett, CMW, JJW, Richard Pierce)*

Victoria [Victoria Rd]: Good local atmosphere, decent food and real ale, plenty of life and character *(Simon Moffat)*

Trowbridge [ST8557]

Sir Isaac Pitman [Castle Pl]: Large two-level Wetherspoons well done out in elm-coloured wood, comfortable alcoves, no smoking area, good choice of beer, popular food, attractive prices, pleasant service *(Dr M E Wilson)*

Upavon [SU1355]

☆ *Antelope* [High St; A345/A342]: Quietly friendly, with good home cooking in bar and pretty back restaurant, log fire, five well kept real ales, small bow-windowed games area with darts, bar billiards and local RAF memorabilia *(the Didler, LYM, Diana Brumfit)*

Upper Woodford [SU1237]

Bridge Inn: Roomy and popular softly lit pub (was used by Madonna on honeymoon), friendly staff, good range of speedily served food inc ploughman's with lots of bread (handy for ducks in attractive riverside garden across road), well kept Flowers and Wadworths 6X, pretty setting; best to book wknds *(David and Elizabeth Briggs, Richard Fendick)*

Upton Lovell [ST9440]

Prince Leopold: Civilised dining pub with imaginative food in nicely decorated candlelit restaurant, real ales such as Ringwood and Young Tom, decent good value wines, cheerful staff; tables in small attractive garden by Wylye trout stream, comfortable quiet bedrooms *(Richard Fendick)*

Upton Scudamore [ST8647]

Angel: Old whitewashed village pub redone as big dining pub, good bar and restaurant food with some interesting combinations, friendly attentive service (can slow when it's busy – best to book), real ales inc Butcombe and Wadworths 6X, good wine choice, stylish modern décor; terrace tables, comfortable well equipped bedrooms – even have CD players *(Claire Nielsen, Susan and Nigel Wilson, Lyn and Geoff Hallchurch)*

Wanborough [SU2083]

Black Horse [2 miles from M4 junction 15; Callas Hill (former B4507 towards Bishopstone)]: Former country local now thoroughly redeveloped in rustic style, but still warmly welcoming, with particularly helpful landlord, enjoyable lunchtime food from sandwiches to good value Sun roast, well kept competitively priced Arkells Bitter, 2B and 3B, good generous coffee, no piped music, darts; picnic-sets in informal elevated garden with play area, caravan parking in adjoining field, lovely downland views *(Comus and Sarah Elliott, Tom Evans)*

Cross Keys [Burycroft, Lower Wanborough]: Hugely extended village pub with solid wood floor, alcoves and bric-a-brac, well kept ales, good choice of food, back restaurant *(anon)*

Harrow [High St; nr M4 junction 15]: Pretty thatched pub with low-beamed two-level refurbished bar, big stone fireplaces, pine panelling, settles and bay window alcoves, stuffed animals, well priced ales such as Brakspears, Greene King Old Speckled Hen, Hook Norton Old Hooky and Youngs Special, good fresh food inc Sun roast (free bar nibbles then), simple beamed and flagstoned stripped stone dining room with another open fire; tables on small terrace *(R Huggins, D Irving, E McCall, T McLean, Comus and Sarah Elliott, CMW, JJW, Lynda Payton, Sam Samuells)*

New Calley Arms [Ham Rd]: Four real ales, good choice of soft drinks, lunchtime food inc filled rolls, real fire in bar, lounge on one side, darts and games machine the other; dogs allowed, picnic-sets in small garden *(CMW, JJW)*

Plough [High St, Lower Wanborough]: Long low thatched stone pub with three old-world rooms, huge centrepiece log fire in one, another more or less for evening dining; good down-to-earth atmosphere, real ales inc Archers Village, Bass and Wadworths 6X, good interesting home-made food (not Sun), friendly efficient staff, bar billiards; open all day Sat *(Comus and Sarah Elliott, R Huggins, D Irving, E McCall, T McLean)*

Shepherds Rest [Foxhill, out towards Baydon; from A419 through Wanborough turn right]: Remote and unassuming Ridgeway pub popular with walkers and local racing people (decorations to match), half a dozen well kept ales such as Black Sheep, Fullers London Pride and Timothy Taylors Landlord, wide food choice in long lounge and dining extension, log fire, lots of pictures, pool room; piped music, very busy in summer; picnic-sets and play area outside, children welcome, camping behind with shower etc *(Nigel and Sue Foster)*

Westbrook [ST9565]

Westbrook Inn [A3102 about 4 miles E of Melksham]: Good range of home-cooked food in unpretentious neatly refurbished village pub with friendly staff, relaxed atmosphere and Wadworths real ales; large no smoking dining room, pretty garden *(LYM, K R Harris)*

Wilcot [SU1360]

☆ *Golden Swan* [signed off A345 N of Pewsey, and in Pewsey itself]: Very pretty old steeply thatched pub in nice rural setting nr Kennet & Avon Canal, unpretentiously welcoming and well worn in, lots of china hanging from beams of two small rooms, well kept Wadworths IPA and 6X and in winter Old Timer, welcoming licensees, nice old retriever and playful cats, basic good value home-made bar food (not Sun evening or Mon), dining room, games room with bar billiards; rustic tables on pretty front lawn, field with camping, occasional folk and barbecue weekends, children welcome; good value simple bedrooms, not smart but big and airy *(LYM, Tim and Isobel Smith)*

Wilton [SU2661]

☆ *Swan* [the village S of Gt Bedwyn]: Warm and friendly simple pub with stripped pine tables and bright unusual décor, wide variety of tasty good value food made by landlady all day inc doorstep sandwiches, home-made sausages, exotic dishes and Sun roast – good for family lunches; welcoming landlord, well kept changing ales such as Fullers London Pride, Thwaites and Wadworths 6X, pool; children welcome, garden with small play area, picturesque village with windmill, handy for Crofton Beam Engines *(John H Smith, Brian and Anna Marsden, Lyn and Geoff Hallchurch, Keith Allen)*

Wingfield [ST8256]

☆ *Poplars* [Shop Lane]: New licensees doing very well in attractive and friendly country local, now very popular lunchtimes for good value interesting food; well kept Wadworths ales, pleasant service, enjoyable atmosphere, no juke box or machines; own cricket pitch *(Dr M E Wilson, Meg and Colin Hamilton, LYM, Lyn and Geoff Hallchurch)*

Winterbourne Bassett [SU0975]

☆ *White Horse* [off A4361 S of Swindon]: Attractively restored 1920s pub in lovely countryside, pleasant modern dining conservatory, very wide choice of good fresh generous food (may be a wait if busy) inc several fish dishes and good Sun roast, cheerful efficient service, well kept Wadworths and occasional guest beers, good wine list and coffee, huge goldfish in tank on bar; seats outside, pleasant setting *(Tony Baldwin, Trevor Owen, Lyn and Geoff Hallchurch, Sheila and Robert Robinson, CMW, JJW, Geoff Palmer)*

Woodfalls [SU1920]

Woodfalls Inn [The Ridge]: Sofas and daily papers in much updated L-shaped bar, small dining room, conservatory, enjoyable food, well kept beers such as Courage Best and Directors, Fullers and Gales HSB, friendly staff; bedrooms, nr New Forest *(Dr and Mrs A K Clarke)*

Wootton Bassett [SU1082]

Sally Pusseys [A420 just off M4 junction 16]: Crowded at lunchtime for generous unpretentious food from baguettes and baked potatoes to plenty of fish and Sun carvery, helpful friendly staff, well kept Arkells 2B, 3B and Kingsdown, good coffee, spacious bar/dining lounge with hops on beams and lots of pictures, good-sized lower restaurant; maybe piped 10cc, James Taylor etc; picnic-sets in sizeable garden *(J H Bescoby, K R Harris, Stephen Savill, Darren and Jane Staniforth, CMW, JJW)*

Woodshaw [Garraways, Woodshaw; handy for M4 junction 16]: Three carpeted levels, good value food (not Sun evening) cooked by landlord, three Arkells ales from central bar, decent wines, good choice of soft drinks, friendly landlady, fresh flowers, dining one end, darts and TV the other, framed cigarette cards; quiet piped music, two fruit machines; garden with picnic-sets and play area, attractive window boxes and hanging baskets *(CMW, JJW)*

Please keep sending us reports. We rely on readers for news of new discoveries, and particularly for news of changes – however slight – at the fully described pubs. No stamp needed: The Good Pub Guide, FREEPOST TN1569, Wadhurst, E Sussex TN5 7BR or send your report through our web site: www.goodguides.com

Worcestershire

Several new entries here this year (two of them back in the Guide *after a break): the cheerful, unusual and good value Little Pack Horse in Bewdley, the Old Chequers at Crowle (a useful off-motorway dining pub), and the Crown & Trumpet in Broadway – a good straightforward accompaniment to that village's highly polished beauty. In contrast to these, the extraordinarily well preserved medieval Fleece at Bretforton has been in every edition of the* Guide *since its first publication 20 years ago. Other pubs doing specially well here this year are the Farmers Arms at Birtsmorton (an archetypal English country pub), the Bear & Ragged Staff at Bransford (earning a Food Award this year), the Fox & Hounds in Bredon (consistently enjoyable food), the Boot at Flyford Flavell (a friendly dining pub flourishing under its newish licensees), the lively King & Castle on the Severn Valley Railway platform in Kidderminster (gains a Beer Award this year), and the Anchor at Welland (earning both a Food Award and a Beer Award now). The Monkey House at Defford deserves a special word: a real rarity, a roadside cider house run much as it has always been by the family who have had it for 140 years. Although there may be more elaborate cooking elsewhere, the combination of good food and service with a nice friendly atmosphere makes the Anchor at Welland our Worcestershire Dining Pub of the Year. Current stars in the Lucky Dip section at the end of the chapter are the Fountain at Clent, Three Kings at Hanley Castle, Bell & Cross at Holy Cross, Crown at Kemerton, Brandy Cask in Pershore, Bellmans Cross at Shatterford, Peacock near Tenbury Wells and Ship in the town, and Coventry Arms at Upton Snodsbury; the Talbot at Knightwick is always worth trying, too. Drinks prices in the county are comfortably below the national average, particularly at the King & Castle in Kidderminster; beer at the Farmers Arms at Birtsmorton and Bear & Ragged Staff at Bransford is also attractively priced.*

BEWDLEY SO7875 Map 4
Little Pack Horse ◀

High Street

No longer part of the O'Rourke chain, this ancient low-beamed heavily timbered pub is nestled in the quiet back streets of a historic riverside town. Cosily pubby and bustling inside and nicely warmed by a woodburning stove in winter, it's home to masses of intriguing bric-a-brac, old photographs and advertisements, and a pleasant mix of old furnishings; piped music. As well as tasty pies (which you can take away) with some unusual fillings such as salmon, prawn and parsley, mediterranean vegetable and kidney bean or potato, leek and cauliflower (from £5.15) and lunchtime sandwiches (from £3), good value well presented food could include soup (£1.95), chicken liver and brandy pâté (£2.95), moroccan vegetable and chick pea couscous (£4.95) mushroom, spinach and sweetcorn stroganoff (£5.25), cumberland sausage, mash and mushy peas (£5.70), cajun seasoned roast chicken (£6.15) and steaks (from £9.95); more elaborate evening menu. They serve around three well kept ales which could include Ind Coope Burton, Ushers Best and a guest on handpump. Service is cheerful and efficient. *(Recommended by June and Ken Brooks,*

Chris Kent, Dr and Mrs P Johnston, Celia Gould, David Wernick, P and M Rudlin, Peter Chaning-Pearce)

InnSpired ~ Tenant Michael Stewart Gaunt ~ Bar food (12-2, 6-9.15; 12-8 Sun, not Mon evening) ~ (01299) 403762 ~ Children in family room and garden ~ Open 12-3, 6-11; 12(10.30 Sun)-11wknds and bank holidays; closed 25 Dec evening

BIRTSMORTON SO7935 Map 4
Farmers Arms 🍺 £

Birts Street, off B4208 W of Birtsmorton

Readers continue to describe this well run black and white timbered local as an archetypal English pub. Run by a friendly mother and daughter team, service is friendly and the atmosphere pleasantly relaxed. The big room on the right, which has a no smoking area, rambles away under low dark beams, with some standing timbers, and flowery-panelled cushioned settles as well as spindleback chairs; on the left an even lower-beamed room seems even more cosy, and in both the white walls have black timbering; darts in a good tiled area, shove-ha'penny, cribbage, and dominoes. Sociable locals gather at the bar for the well kept Hook Norton Best and Old Hooky and a weekly guest from a brewer such as Cannon Royall on handpump. The reasonably priced, straightforward home-made bar food includes sandwiches (from £1.60), soup (£1.90), ploughman's (from £2.80), macaroni cheese (£3.30), fish and chips (£4.55), chicken and vegetable curry (£4.50), lasagne (£4.95), steak and kidney pie (£5.50), gammon steak (£6.75) and mixed grill (£8.50); puddings such as apple pie or steamed treacle pudding (from £1.90). There are seats out on the large lawn. The pub's opening hours vary according to the number of customers. There are plenty of good walks nearby. (Recommended by Derek and Sylvia Stephenson, P and M Rudlin, Martin Jennings, Dave Braisted, A C and E Johnson, Mike and Mary Carter, Ian and Nita Cooper)

Free house ~ Licensees Jill and Julie Moor ~ Real ale ~ Bar food (12-2, 6-9.30) ~ No credit cards ~ (01684) 833308 ~ Children in eating area of bar ~ Open 11-2.30, 6-11; 12-4, 7-10.30 Sun

BRANSFORD SO7852 Map 4
Bear & Ragged Staff 🍽 ♀

Off A4103 SW of Worcester; Station Rd

It's probably best to book a table if you want to eat at this stylish but welcoming place, especially now that it's earned our Food Award; there's quite an emphasis on the dining side, with proper tablecloths, linen napkins, and fresh flowers on the tables. Changing bar food might include soup (£3.25), lunchtime filled rolls (from £3.95), five-cheese tortellini baked in tomato sauce (£5.65), cajun spiced salmon fillet or grilled chicken breast with potato scones (£6.50), duck confit with creamy mash and red wine sauce (£6.75) and specials such as avocado, crab and tomato pancake (£5.50), roast shallot and woodland mushroom tart (£8.95) and roast monkfish in parma ham (£12.95) with puddings such as thai spiced poached pear with caramelised pineapple or rhubarb tart with crunchy hazelnut topping (£3.75). There are fine views over rolling country from the cheerful interconnecting rooms (one room in the restaurant is no smoking) as well as some seats by an open fire and well kept Bass and Highgate Special on handpump; a good range of wines (mainly New World ones), lots of malt whiskies, and quite a few brandies and liqueurs; cribbage, dominoes, and piped music. (Recommended by Denys Gueroult, Norman and June Williams, Mrs D Whitby, George Atkinson)

Free house ~ Licensees Lynda Williams and Andy Kane ~ Real ale ~ Bar food ~ Restaurant ~ (01886) 833399 ~ Children welcome in eating area of bar and restaurant till 9pm ~ Jazz 1st Sun evening of month ~ Open 12-2.30, 6-11; 12-2.30, 7-10.30 Sun

---

We say if we or readers have seen dogs or cats in a pub.

BREDON SO9236 Map 4
Fox & Hounds

4½ miles from M5 junction 9; A438 to Northway, left at B4079, then in Bredon follow signpost to church and river on right

In an attractive setting next to a church down a lane leading to a river, this pretty thatched pub looks best in summer when it's bedecked with brightly coloured hanging baskets. Served by friendly and efficient staff, readers continue to enjoy the attractively presented bar lunches, which might include home-made soup (£3.25), ploughman's and sandwiches (from £4.95), lasagne, cauliflower and broccoli gratin, mexican chilli beef (£6.75), salmon and crab fishcakes (£6.95), jumbo king prawns (£10.25), 8oz sirloin steak (£10.95) and beef and bacon bourguignon (£11.95). The restaurant menu (which you can eat in the bar) includes dishes such as pork fillet with onion marmalade (£9.75), roast duck or rack of lamb with rosemary and honey (£11.95), and puddings (from £3.50); Sunday roast. There's a welcoming atmosphere in the comfortably modernised carpeted bar, with dressed stone pillars and stripped timbers, a central woodburning stove, upholstered settles, wheelback, tub, and kitchen chairs around attractive mahogany and cast-iron-framed tables, dried grasses and flowers, a toy fox dressed in hunting scarlet, and elegant wall lamps. A smaller side bar with assorted wooden kitchen chairs, wheelbacks, and settles, has an open fire at each end. Well kept Banks's Bitter, Marstons Pedigree and Greene King Old Speckled Hen on handpump, several malt whiskies and wines by the glass; piped music. No smoking in restaurant and part of the bar; some of the picnic-sets are under Perspex. *(Recommended by Derek and Sylvia Stephenson, W H and E Thomas, Moira and John Cole, June and Mike Coleman, Bob and Ann Westbrook, Martin Jennings, Colin Parker, Simon Watkins, Bruce Bird, M Joyner, Gordon Tong)*

Whitbreads ~ Lease Mike Hardwick ~ Real ale ~ Bar food ~ Restaurant ~ (01684) 772377 ~ Children welcome ~ Open 11.30-2.30, 6.30ish-11; 12-10.30 Sun

BRETFORTON SP0943 Map 4
Fleece ★★ £

B4035 E of Evesham: turn S off this road into village; pub is in centre square by church; there's a sizeable car park at one side of the church

In summer, when it gets very busy, they make the most of the extensive orchard at this memorably atmospheric old pub, with seats on the goat-cropped grass that spreads around the beautifully restored thatched and timbered barn, among the fruit trees, and at the front by the stone pump-trough. There's also an adventure playground, an aviary, and an enclosure with geese and goats; there are more picnic-sets in the front courtyard. What makes this place so fascinating, though, is the stunningly unspoilt medieval building. Before becoming a pub in 1848 it was a farm owned by the same family for nearly 500 years. In 1977 it was bequeathed to the National Trust by the great granddaughter of the original landlord, and many of the furnishings such as the great oak dresser that holds a priceless 48-piece set of Stuart pewter are heirlooms that have remained here since its time as a farmhouse. Its fine country rooms have massive beams and exposed timbers, worn and crazed flagstones (scored with marks to keep out demons), and plenty of oddities such as a great cheese-press and set of cheese moulds, and a rare dough-proving table; a leaflet details the more bizarre items. There's a fine grandfather clock, ancient kitchen chairs, curved high-backed settles, a rocking chair, and a rack of heavy pointed iron shafts, probably for spit roasting, in one of the huge inglenook fireplaces – there are three warming winter fires. The room with the pewter is no smoking. Straightforward bar food (which can be slow to arrive owing to limited kitchen facilities) is ordered through a hatch and includes sandwiches (from £1.95), ploughman's (from £3.95), vegetable kiev (£4.50), steak and kidney or chicken and leek pie (£5.25), lamb chops (£5.85), steak (£7.25), specials such as broccoli and cheese quiche (£4.60) and lamb and mint suet pudding (£5.25); puddings such as sticky toffee pudding (from £2.20); Sunday roast (£4.75); children's meals (£2.75). Cannon Royall Buckshot, M & B Brew XI, Hook Norton Bitter, Uley Old Spot and

Wyre Piddle on handpump, over a dozen country wines and farm cider. Darts, cribbage, dominoes, shove-ha'penny. There may be morris dancing and they hold the village fete and annual asparagus auctions at the end of May, an annual beer festival in July and the village Silver Band fete on August bank holiday Monday. *(Recommended by Steve Chambers, the Didler, Susan and John Douglas, Stuart Turner, Helen Sandelands, Mike and Wena Stevenson, Mike and Heather Watson, John Brightley, KN-R, Michael Smith, Matt Williams, Michael and Jenny Back, Joan and Michel Hooper-Immins, Colin and Judith Roberts, Martin Jennings, John Kane, Ian and Nita Cooper, Hugh Roberts)*

Free house ~ Licensee Graham Brown ~ Real ale ~ Bar food (11.45-2, 6.30-9) ~ (01386) 831173 ~ Children welcome ~ Open 11-3, 6-11; 11-11 Sat; 12-10.30 Sun

BROADWAY SP0937 Map 4
Crown & Trumpet ◖

Church Street

From local farmers and hikers to tourists, this lovely golden stone pub warmly welcomes a good range of customers. The cosily unpretentious beamed and timbered bar has dark high-backed settles and a blazing log fire; quiz night on Thursdays, Saturday sing-along duo, and darts, bar billiards, shove-ha'penny, cribbage, dominoes, and ring the bull at one end, fruit machine and piped music; also, Evesham quoits. Well kept Black Sheep Bitter, Flowers Original, Hook Norton Old Hooky, Greene King Old Speckled Hen and tasty local Stanway Bitter on handpump, hot toddies and mulled wine in winter, and summer pimms and kir. Straightforward good value bar food includes soup (£2.45), faggots and mushy peas, steak and kidney pie or beef cooked in a local plum sauce (£5.45), 10oz rump steak (£8.95), daily specials (£3.95-£6.95); asparagus menu (from £5.45), and Sunday roast; quick, friendly, efficient service; seats out on the front terrace. *(Recommended by Derek and Sylvia Stephenson, Di and Mike Gillam, Andrew and Ruth Triggs, David Green, Ted George, Mr and Mrs G Owens)*

Free House ~ Licensee Andrew Scott ~ Real ale ~ Bar food (12-2, plus 6-9 Sat and Sun) ~ Children in eating area of bar ~ Sat evening entertainment ~ Open 11(2.30 in winter)-3; 11-11 Sat; 12-11 Sun ~ Bedrooms: /£55S(£60B)

CROWLE SO9256 Map 4
Old Chequers ♀

2.6 miles from M5 junction 6; A4538 towards Evesham, then left after 0.6 miles; Crowle Green

Handy for the motorway, this smoothly run much-modernised dining pub rambles extensively around an island bar, with plush-seated mate's chairs around a mix of pub tables on the patterned carpet, some brass and copper on the swirly-plastered walls, lots of pictures for sale at the back, and a coal-effect gas fire at one end (there's central heating too). A big square extension on the right, with shinily varnished rustic timbering and beamery, has more tables. Popular generous food (all home-made) includes good value imaginative light lunches such as soup (£2.25), grilled black pudding topped with bacon, tomato and cheese, chicken liver in cream and brandy, smoked haddock and prawns in cheese sauce or grilled goats cheese with roasted vegetables (£5.75) with other dishes such as mushroom stroganoff or sweet potato pancakes (£5.95), thai chicken curry or chicken boursin (£9.75), lamb cutlets with redcurrant, mint and orange sauce (£11) and fresh fish such as grilled lemon sole with lemon butter, bass with olive and parmesan mash or monkfish wrapped in parma ham with curried mayonnaise (£11); puddings such as crème brûlée (from £3.25). Service is prompt and friendly; well kept real ales such as Archers, Banks's and Camerons on handpump, good value house wines. There are picnic-sets out on the terrace behind, among shrubs and small fruit trees – a pleasant spot, with pasture beyond. Disabled access. *(Recommended by June and Mike Coleman, Ian Jones, Martin Jennings, Stuart Paulley, Brian and Pat Wardrobe, John Bowdler)*

Free house ~ Licensees Steven and Ian Thomas ~ Real ale ~ Bar food (12-1.45, 7-9.45, not Sun evening) ~ Restaurant ~ (01905) 381275 ~ Children in eating area of bar at lunchtime ~ Open 12-2.30, 7(10.30 Sun)-11; closed 25 and 26 Dec

DEFFORD SO9143 Map 4
Monkey House

A4104 towards Upton – immediately after passing Oak public house on right, there's a small group of cottages, of which this is the last

One of the few remaining absolutely traditional cider houses, this pretty black and white thatched cottage has been run by a member of the landlord's wife's family for the last 140 years. You'll have to look carefully to spot it as the only hint from the outside that it is actually a pub is a notice by the door saying 'Licensed to sell cider and tobacco'. Its name is taken from the story of a drunken customer who, some years ago, fell into bramble bushes and swore that he was attacked by monkeys. Very cheap Bulmer's Medium or Special Dry cider is tapped from barrels and poured by jug into pottery mugs (some locals have their own) and served from a hatch beside the door. As a concession to modern tastes, beer is sold in cans. They don't do food (except crisps and nuts), but you can bring your own. In the summer you could find yourself sharing the garden with Anna the bull terrier, Tapper the jack russell, and hens and cockerels that meander in from an adjacent collection of caravans and sheds; there's also a pony called Mandy. Alternatively you can retreat to a small and spartan side outbuilding with a couple of plain tables, a settle and an open fire; darts and dominoes. *(Recommended by the Didler, Pete Baker)*

Free house ~ Licensee Graham Collins ~ No credit cards ~ (01386) 750234 ~ Open 11-2.30, 6-10.30; 12-2.30, 7-10.30 Sun; closed 25 Dec

FLYFORD FLAVELL SO9754 Map 4
Boot

½ mile off A422 Worcester—Alcester; sharp turn into village beside Flyford Arms, then turn left into Radford Road

A real favourite with some of our readers, this Georgian fronted country pub dates (in part) back to the 13th c. The heavily beamed and timbered back part is mainly a dining area now (part is no smoking), with a log fire in the big fireplace, and plates on its walls. Its lower end, divided by a timbered part wall, has a glass-topped well and leads into a modern conservatory with brocaded dining chairs and swagged curtains. The recently refurbished little beamed front bar has hunting prints, elbow chairs, and inglenook seats by the small log fire; on its left are darts and a well lit pool table. With around seven vegetarian dishes a day, the good choice of reasonably priced food could include soup (£1.95), sandwiches and baguettes (from £2.75), home-made faggots (£5.50), sun-dried tomato penne or leek and potato bake (£6.75), cod in beer batter (£7.25), beef, Guinness and mushroom pie, half a gressingham duck or sirloin steak (£9.95), saddle of lamb (£10.95); puddings such as home-made treacle and orange tart (£2.75). It's very popular with older people for lunch. *(Recommended by June and Mike Coleman, Martin Jennings, Gordon, W H and E Thomas, Richard Kitson, Theo, Anne and Jane Gaskin)*

Free house ~ Licensee Sue Hughes ~ Real ale ~ Bar food (12-2, 6.30(6 Sat)-10; 12-2, 7-9.30 Sun) ~ Restaurant ~ (01386) 462658 ~ Children in eating area of bar and restaurant ~ Open 12-3, 6.30-11; 11.30-3, 6-11 Sat; 12-6, 7-10.30 Sun; not Sun afternoon winter; closed 25 Dec evening ~ Bedrooms: £45S/£55S

FORHILL SP0575 Map 4
Peacock ◖

2 miles from M42 junction 2; A441 towards Birmingham; after roundabout 1st right (sharp) into Ash Lane just before garage by highish canal bridge, left into Stonehouse Lane, left at T-junction, right at next T-junction (into Lea End Lane); pub at junction Lea End Lane and Icknield St. Can also be reached from junction 3

As this edition comes out, the spacious knocked-through beamed rooms of this quietly set pub have a pleasantly relaxed atmosphere. It has an attractive mix of country chairs, pews and tables on flagstone and quarry tiled floors, standing timbers, cream or stripped brick walls simply decorated with a couple of prints, fresh blue curtains in big leaded windows and a couple of fires including a woodburning stove in a big inglenook. The dining area, with a big serving hatch showing the working kitchen, has some attractive decorations including a striking peacock print and a big stone greyhound by its fireplace. But in January, it's likely to be reworked, possibly substantially, as part of the Chef & Brewer chain. Do let us know what you think of the changes. As we go to press the bar meals (no sandwiches) include soup, chilli or battered cod, braised minted half shoulder of lamb with redcurrant and rosemary jus, and daily specials such as roast turkey or halibut fillet on fennel with lemon butter, with home-made puddings like bread and butter pudding. Up to now they have had at least five well kept real ales on handpump, such as Courage Directors, Enville, Hobsons Best, Moorhouses Black Cat, Theakstons Best and Old Peculier; country wines. There are picnic-sets on a back terrace, and more on front grass under a striking Scots pine and other trees; fruit machine. *(Recommended by Alan and Paula McCully, Jean and Richard Phillips, Susan and John Douglas, Comus and Sarah Elliott, Dick and Madeleine Brown, Patricia Beebe)*

Scottish Courage ~ Manager Stephan Wakeman ~ Real ale ~ Bar food (12-6 only) ~ Restaurant (evening) ~ (01564) 823232 ~ Children in restaurant ~ Open 12(10.30 Sun)-11

KEMPSEY SO8548 Map 4
Walter de Cantelupe ♀

Main Road; 3¾ miles from M5 junction 7: A44 towards Worcester, left on to A4440, then left on to A38 at roundabout

Run by a friendly and enthusiastic chef/landlord, this unpretentious roadside inn even sells jars of his home-made chutney. Boldly decorated in red and gold, the bar area has an informal and well worn in mix of furniture, an old wind-up HMV gramophone and a good big fireplace. The dining area has various plush or yellow leather dining chairs, an old settle, a sonorous clock, and candles and flowers on the tables. As well as tasty Black Pear from the nearby Malvern Hills brewery, well kept real ales on handpump include Highgate Special and Timothy Taylors Landlord with a guest such as Black Sheep Bitter. There's a good choice of wines by the glass (they import direct from Italy and have regularly changing bin ends as well as English wines from a local vineyard). Using lots of local produce, the bar menu includes dishes such as home-made soup with locally baked bread (£2.75), sandwiches (from £3), stilton, port and walnut pâté (£4.25), a nicely presented generous ploughman's (£4.70), roasted mediterranean vegetables with couscous salad (£6), fennel, red onion and mushroom stroganoff (£6.50), steak and Guinness pie (£6.80), lemon and oregano pork with lemon mayonnaise (£7.25), and smoked haddock with creamed spinach and poached egg (£8.50); puddings; Sunday lunch; no smoking dining area; cribbage and table skittles. You can sit out in the pretty walled garden at the back; the friendly labrador is called Monti. *(Recommended by M Joyner, Pat and Tony Martin, Susan and Nigel Wilson, R Mathews, Peter Burton, Chris Flynn, Wendy Jones, Mr and Mrs J E C Tasker, Nick Lawless, June and Mike Coleman, W H and E Thomas, Mike and Mary Carter, David and Nina Pugsley, Shaun Pinchbeck, Brian and Anna Marsden, Richard and Judy Winn)*

Free house ~ Licensee Martin Lloyd Morris ~ Real ale ~ Bar food (12-2, 6-9) ~ Restaurant ~ (01905) 820572 ~ Children under 12 in eating area of bar till 8.15pm ~ Open 11.30-2.30(3 Sat), 5.30-11; 12-3, 6-10.30 Sun; 12-10.30 July and Aug Sun; closed Mon except bank holidays, 25, 26 and 31 Dec, 1 Jan and 3rd wk in Jan ~ Bedrooms: £30B/£50B

KIDDERMINSTER SO8376 Map 4
King & Castle ⚑ £

Railway Station, Comberton Hill

Set on the terminus of Britain's most lively private steam railway, this intriguing re-creation of a classic station refreshment room conjures up the feel of a better-class Edwardian establishment that has relaxed a little to embrace more informal modern ways. The genial landlady and friendly staff cope well with the bank holiday and railway gala day crowds (when it can be very difficult to find a seat). The atmosphere is lively and sometimes noisily good-humoured and it can get rather smoky. Furnishings are solid and in character (even to the occasional obvious need for a touch of reupholstery), and there is the railway memorabilia that you would expect. With steam trains right outside, some railway-buff readers are quite happy to start and end their journeys right here; others have used a Rover ticket to shuttle between here and the Railwaymans Arms in Bridgnorth (see Shropshire chapter). Either way you can take your pint outside on to the platform and watch the trains steam by. Well kept Bathams, Tetleys and two guests such as Berrow, Cottage or Wyre Piddle on handpump (with at least one at bargain price), Addlestone's farm cider. A wide choice of straightforward, good value bar food includes filled rolls (£1.50), filled baked potatoes (from £2.65), ploughman's or omelettes (£4.65), scampi or breaded plaice (£4.95), cajun chicken (£4.95) and weekend specials such as chilli (£3.95) and lasagne (£4.75); children's meals (from £2.50). *(Recommended by Gill Waller, Tony Morriss, P and M Rudlin, Bernie Adams, Pat and Tony Martin, R C Vincent)*

Free house ~ Licensee Rosemary Hyde ~ Real ale ~ Bar food (12-2(2.30 Sat and Sun), 6-8 Fri and Sat, 7-9 Sun) ~ No credit cards ~ (01562) 747505 ~ Children welcome if seated ~ Open 11-3, 5-11; 11-11 Sat; 12-10.30 Sun; closed 25 Dec evening

OMBERSLEY SO8463 Map 4
Crown & Sandys Arms ♀ 🛏

Coming into the village from the A4133, turn left at the roundabout in middle of village, and pub is on the left

Quite different from the way it used to be, this pretty Dutch-gabled inn is now firmly in the current trend of very food-oriented bistro pubs: it's even sponsored by Moët et Chandon, the champagne firm. One big open plan bar has pub tables and settles on flagstone floors, a long granite counter, lots of fresh flowers, and wine themed pictures (the landlord is a wine merchant). The limestone-floor conservatory leads out to a Japanese-style terrace. As you'd imagine, the wine list is good with wines by the glass, and they have well kept Adnams Broadside, Greene King Abbot Ale and Marstons Pedigree with a guest such as Woods Parish on handpump. Ambitious, well presented food (which you can eat in the bar) could include lunchtime dishes such as sandwiches (£3.95), filled baguettes (from £5.25), fishcakes (£6.95), wild boar and game casserole with honey, cider and sage (£7.95), vegetarian lasagne (£9.95) and fillet steak with shropshire blue cheese and smoky bacon (£16.95), with more elaborate evening dishes such as monkfish and scallops cooked in parmesan cream sauce (£6.95), malaysian chicken curry (£9.95) and roasted lamb shank with bubble and squeak in rosemary gravy (£11.95) with specials such as marinated swordfish (£11); sweets such as chocolate and banana bread and butter pudding (£4.95). Leading from the garden, there's a large new garden with wooden benches. *(Recommended by Chris Flynn, Wendy Jones, Martin and Pat Grafton, Alun Howells, Alan J Morton, Shaun Pinchbeck, Trevor Owen, John Whitehead, Mike and Wendy Proctor)*

Free house ~ Licensee Richard Everton ~ Real ale ~ Bar food (12-2.30, 6-10; 12-2.30, 6-9.30 Sun) ~ Restaurant ~ (01905) 620252 ~ Children welcome ~ Occasional summer events ~ Open 11.30-3, 5-11; 11.30-11 Sat; 12-10.30 Sun ~ Bedrooms: £55S/£65S

Kings Arms 🍽

One room in this big black-beamed and timbered Tudor pub has Charles II's coat of arms moulded into its decorated plaster ceiling – a trophy from his reputed stop here in 1651. The various wood floored cosy nooks and crannies in the comfortably informal rambling rooms are spotlessly kept and full of stuffed animals and birds, rustic bric-a-brac and fresh flowers, and there are four open fires. The imaginative menu changes every six weeks or so, and the well presented dishes might include soup (£3), fresh sardines with paprika or black pudding, crispy bacon and quail egg salad (£5.25), roasted peppers with goats cheese and basil pesto (£9.25), home-made steak and kidney pie or local pork and apple sausages with butternut squash and sage mash (£9.50), crispy roast half duck with orange and watercress (£12), and puddings such as rhubarb tart and chocolate and praline brûlée (£4), alongside a good range of mainly fresh fish daily specials such as octopus grilled in cajun butter (£5.95), home-made salmon and crab fishcakes (£9.75), whole crab thermidor (£11.50), plaice with cracked pepper butter and asparagus (£12), bass with crispy green beans (£13.50), and if you really want to push the boat out a seafood platter for two (£50); even the snacks are served with linen napkins. For some readers, service was a bit lacking in vitality earlier this year; we hope it's now recovered its usual style. Well kept Banks's Bitter, Marstons Pedigree, Morrells Varsity and maybe a guest on handpump. A tree-sheltered courtyard has tables under cocktail parasols, and colourful hanging baskets and tubs in summer, and there's also a terrace. *(Recommended by P and J Shapley, Alan and Paula McCully, Mrs D Smallwood, K R Harris, Basil Minson, JCW, Mike and Mary Carter, Muriel and Peter Gleave, Ian Jones, John Whitehead, Alun Howells, Denys Gueroult, Nigel Long, Chris Flynn, Wendy Jones, David and Ruth Shillitoe)*

Free house ~ Licensee D Pendry ~ Real ale ~ Bar food (12-2.15, 6.30-10) ~ Restaurant ~ (01905) 620142 ~ Well behaved children over 8 in eating areas ~ Jazz in garden some Suns in summer ~ Open 12-2.30, 6-11; 12-10.30 Sun

PENSAX SO7269 Map 4
Bell 🍺

B4202 Abberley—Clows Top, SE of the Snead Common part of the village

Picnic-sets in the back garden of this homely roadside mock-Tudor pub look out over rolling fields and copses to the Wyre Forest. They serve around five changing well kept real ales which could include Archers Golden, Enville Best, Hobsons, Hook Norton and Timothy Taylors Landlord. The L-shaped main bar has a restrained traditional décor, with long cushioned pews on its bare boards, good solid pub tables, and a woodburning stove. Beyond a small area on the left with a couple more tables is a more airy dining room with french windows opening on to a wooden deck that on hot days can give a slightly Californian feel; it has a log fire for more British weather; no smoking dining room. Besides sandwiches (from £3.50), regularly changing straightforward bar food might include filled baked potatoes and omelettes (from £4.50), home honey-cured ham and egg (£6) and rump steak (£8.95). *(Recommended by Geoffrey and Penny Hughes, Celia Gould, David Wernick, Gill Waller, Tony Morriss, Dr B and Mrs P B Baker, Greg Lacey, Jim Haworth)*

Free house ~ Licensees John and Trudy Greaves ~ Real ale ~ Bar food (12-2, 6-9; 12-4 Sun) ~ (01299) 896677 ~ Children in eating area and family room ~ Open 12-2.30, 5-11; 12-10.30 Sun; closed Mon lunchtime except bank holidays

WELLAND SO7940 Map 4
Anchor 🍽 🍺

Drake Street; A4104 towards Upton

Worcestershire Dining Pub of the Year

This pretty, fairy-lit Tudor cottage is much enjoyed by readers for its attentive staff and well made bar food (it now gains a Food Award), and this year its good beers also earn it our Beer Award. The welcoming L-shaped bar has country prints on the walls, some armchairs around chatty low tables, and more sitting-up chairs around eating-height tables. Beyond is a spreading comfortably furnished dining area, nicely set with candles, pink tablecloths and napkins. Besides soup (£2.95), filled baked potatoes (from £3.99), omelette or a variety of ploughman's (from £3.99), an extensive choice of changing food on blackboards by the bar might include garlic and herb-smoked mackerel (£3.99), mushrooms, bacon and black pudding (£4.10), steak, kidney and ale pie (£6.99), pork loin stuffed with apple in stilton sauce, garlic mushroom and mascarpone cheese lattice pie (£7.95), trout fillet with lemon and herb butter (£9.05) and half roast duck with orange and Cointreau (£13.99); tempting puddings (from £2.99). Six well kept changing beers such as Charles Wells Bombardier, Church End Anchor Bitter, Hook Norton Anchor Best and Malvern Hills Black Pear on handpump; shove-ha'penny, cribbage, chess, dominoes and maybe unobtrusive piped music. Handy for the Three Counties Showground, it has a field for camping with tents or caravans with electric hook-up points. In summer the front is festooned with colourful hanging baskets, with a passion flower and roses climbing the walls. There are picnic-sets on the lawn, with flower borders and a big old apple tree. Their two new bedrooms have garden views (we have not yet heard from readers who have stayed in them). *(Recommended by J H C Peters, Derek and Sylvia Stephenson, Bernard Stradling, Alan and Paula McCully, Ian Phillips, Margaret Marriott)*

Free house ~ Licensees Colin and Caroline Barrett ~ Real ale ~ Bar food ~ Restaurant ~ (01684) 592317 ~ Children in restaurant ~ Open 11.45-3, 6.45(6.30 Sat)-11; 12-3 (7-10.30 for bookings only) Sun ~ Bedrooms: £30B/£50B

WYRE PIDDLE SO9647 Map 4
Anchor
B4084 WNW of Evesham

From the big airy back bar of this friendly 17th-c pub you can watch the peaceful comings and goings on the River Avon. Served by courteous, helpful staff, readers have good things to say about the reasonably priced, generously served bar food. Cooked fresh to order, the menu changes around every two weeks but could include soup (£2.75), lunchtime sandwiches (from £3.25), chicken, mushroom and brandy pâté (£3.95), curried beef and mushroom pasty (£6.95), vegetable burgers (£7.25), venison sausage, steak and mushroom casserole (£7.50), cold game pie (£7.95), sicilian chicken and pork in masala wine sauce (£8.50), scottish salmon fillet with dill and vermouth sauce (£9.75); specials could be chicken balti (£7.25) with puddings such as bakewell tart and chocolate fudge cake (£3); Sunday roast (£7.95). The friendly and well kept little lounge has a good log fire in its attractively restored inglenook fireplace, comfortably upholstered chairs and settles, and two beams in the shiny ceiling. The dining area has an open fire, rugs on stripped wood floors and wooden tables and chairs. Well kept Boddingtons, Flowers Original, Marstons Pedigree and a monthly guest under light blanket pressure, 8 wines by the glass, 10 malts and country wines; fruit machine and piped music. There are seats on the spacious back lawn that runs down to the water; beyond there are views spreading out over the Vale of Evesham as far as the Cotswolds, the Malverns and Bredon Hill. *(Recommended by F Smyth, Helen Eastwood, Mike and Linda Hudson, Theo, Anne and Jane Gaskin, Jenny and Bill Heilbronn, Martin Jennings, Stuart Turner, Mr and Mrs A H Young, Brian and Bett Cox, Terry Mizen, Shaun Pinchbeck)*

Whitbreads ~ Lease Michael Senior ~ Real ale ~ Bar food ~ Restaurant ~ (01386) 552799 ~ Children in eating area of bar and restaurant ~ Open 11-2.30, 6-11; 12-3, 6-11 Sat; 12-3, 7-10.30 Sun; closed 25 Dec evening, 26 Dec

Lucky Dip
Besides the fully inspected pubs, you might like to try these Lucky Dips recommended to us and described by readers (if you do, please send us reports: www.goodguides.com).

Badsey [SP0742]
Wheatsheaf [E of Evesham; High St]: Doing well under current licensees, well kept ales such as Greene King Old Speckled Hen and Wadworths 6X, good New World wines in good-sized glasses, well prepared food inc unusual dishes, partly no smoking restaurant off small lounge, separate public bar; bedrooms, some new *(Martin Jennings)*
Baughton [SO8741]
Jockey [A4104 Pershore—Upton]: Emphasis on good generous restaurant food (also thick country sandwiches), good friendly service, well kept ales such as Adnams Broadside, Banks's and Malvern Hills Black Pear, decent wines,

smart unfussy furnishings *(Derek and Sylvia Stephenson, Brian and Bett Cox, Peter Dingley, Pat and Tony Martin)*
Belbroughton [SO9277]
Olde Horse Shoe [High St]: Well run, with decent food from hot pork baguettes to good Sun lunch, Bass, friendly staff, log fire; walkers welcome *(David Edwards, Mike and Mary Carter)*
Bournheath [SO9474]
☆ *Gate* [handy for M5 junction 3; Dodford Rd]: Attractive country dining pub with wide choice of attractively priced good food inc lots of vegetarian, Mon Mexican night, lunchtime and early evening bargains, well kept Smiles Best

and Heritage, quick friendly service even though busy, restaurant; nice garden *(G Coates)*

Bredon [SO9236]

Royal Oak [Main Rd]: Roomy and relaxed carpeted bar with open fire, Banks's, Marstons Pedigree and a guest beer, nice choice of well presented food (not Sun evening, Mon/Tues) in bar and dining room, friendly staff; pool, darts, skittle alley, barbecues *(Derek and Sylvia Stephenson)*

Broadway [SP0739]

☆ *Collin House* [follow Willersey sign off A44 Broadway bypass roundabout, into Collin Lane]: Small country hotel, not a pub, but worth knowing for wide choice of good interesting freshly done food inc traditional puddings; attractive bar, very relaxed and civilised, good log fires, no machines or piped music (but no sandwiches or ploughman's either); nice restaurant not overpriced (wise to book), good wines, proper coffee, pleasant staff; tables outside; comfortable bedrooms *(N H White)*

Horse & Hound [High St]: Spacious pub useful for food all day, open fire, Whitbreads-related ales with guests such as Goffs Jouster or Hook Norton Old Hooky, good choice of wines by the glass, Sunday papers *(E V Walder, Christopher and Jo Barton)*

Lygon Arms [High St]: Stately but expensive Cotswold hotel in strikingly handsome ancient building, interesting old rooms rambling away from the attractive oak-panelled bar; good imaginative food in adjoining brasserie/wine bar, tables in prettily planted courtyard, well kept gardens; children allowed away from bar; bedrooms smart and comfortable; open all day in summer *(LYM, Bernard Stradling)*

Charlton [SP0145]

Gardeners Arms [the one nr Pershore; Strand]: Straightforward local on green of pretty thatched village, huge helpings of moderately priced fresh food, welcoming atmosphere and service, lots of tables in lounge, spartan public bar with darts, Whitbreads-related ales, decent choice of wines; quiet piped music *(Don Goodwin, Brian and Bett Cox)*

Claines [SO8558]

☆ *Mug House* [Claines Lane, off A449 3 miles W of M5 junction 3]: Fine views from ancient country tavern in unique churchyard setting by fields below the Malvern Hills, extensively refurbished but keeping atmosphere with low doorways and heavy oak beams, well kept Banks's Bitter and Mild, good generous snacks (not Sun), children allowed in snug away from servery *(LYM, Dave Braisted, A C and E Johnson)*

Cleeve Prior [SP0849]

Kings Arms [Bidford Rd (B4085)]: Unspoilt 16th-c beamed pub off the tourist track, well run and comfortable, with good imaginative food at reasonable prices, well kept Wadworths 6X and a guest beer, friendly helpful family service, no smoking dining room, no piped music; children welcome *(Mr and Mrs Richard Osborne)*

Clent [SO9279]

☆ *Fountain* [Odnall Lane]: Spotlessly well run small country dining pub in lovely walking territory, central open fires, warm welcome, good food from sandwiches to restaurant dishes inc good range of fresh properly cooked fish (worth booking wknds), quick friendly staff, well kept Banks's, Marstons Pedigree and a guest beer, wines served in cut glass, choice of ciders and teas; few no smoking tables; bedrooms being converted in outbuildings *(Debbie Shepherd, W H and E Thomas, Mr and Mrs P Hulme, June and Mike Coleman)*

Clifton upon Teme [SO7261]

Lion: Civilised and comfortable former coaching inn, with friendly staff and licensee, good choice of drinks inc well kept Banks's and guest beers, wide choice of food, central log fire in big beamed bar, separate dining area; tables outside, attractive beamed bedrooms, pretty village *(Trevor Owen)*

Colwall [SO7440]

Wellington [A449 Malvern—Ledbury]: Small and comfortable, good food with Italian touches – seafood, duck and venison all recommended; good service *(Jenny and Bill Heilbronn)*

Cutnall Green [SO8768]

Chequers [Kidderminster Rd]: Has been clean and comfortable country pub with beamed bar, well kept Marstons Pedigree and a guest, scrubbed tables, stylish green and cream décor, interesting if not cheap french-style food, picnic-sets out in front; was for sale 2001 *(Ian Shorthouse)*

☆ *Live & Let Live* [A442 Kidderminster—Droitwich]: Picturesquely cottagey creeper-covered pub, small, busy and unpretentious, with first-rate service, Bass and Tetleys, wide range of good reasonably priced home-made food from lots of sandwiches and interesting light meals to Sun roasts in no smoking timbered dining room or popular open-sided summer marquee; charming small garden *(Richard and Diane Sabell)*

Dodford [SO9372]

Dodford Inn [Whinfield Rd]: Very friendly unpretentious country pub in extensive grounds, quiet spot overlooking wooded valley, lots of footpaths; relaxed peaceful atmosphere, very reasonably priced home cooking inc plenty of snacks, well kept Greenalls and guest beers, garden with terrace and play area; camp and caravan site *(Richard Houghton, Bernie Adams)*

Doverdale [SO8665]

Honey Bee [off A449 Kidderminster—Worcester]: Former Ripperidge Inn, now majoring on honey – lots of beehives outside, inc some working ones at a safe distance, also a demonstration glass-paned one in a window, honey-making equipment, honeys for sale; good range of enjoyable food, Boddingtons, Theakstons and a beer brewed for the pub, settee and easy chairs by fire, lots of dining tables, plenty of staff; good disabled access and facilities, pleasant surroundings *(Dave Braisted, June and Mike Coleman)*

Drayton [SO9076]

Robin Hood [off B4188]: Comfortable early 19th-c dining pub with inglenook log fire, low beams and lovely stained glass in large lounge, handsome wooden furniture, cheerful landlady and friendly efficient service, well kept Ansells, Ind Coope Burton and several guest beers, good value varied food esp curries and vegetarian dishes, regulars' pictures in cosy bar; garden with trampoline and pets corner, attractive surroundings, good walks; open all day wknds *(Bernie Adams)*

Dunhampstead [SO9160]

☆ *Firs* [just SE of Droitwich, towards Sale Green – OS Sheet 150 map ref 919600]: Pretty dining pub, with flower-filled terrace, small grassy garden, lots of hanging baskets, comfortable no smoking dining conservatory; good food from doorstep sandwiches up (hot dishes freshly made so can be a wait), well kept Banks's and Marstons, welcoming service, friendly dogs, flowers on tables; fairly quiet wkdy lunchtimes, booking advised wknd; nice spot not far from canal *(M J and C E Abbey, LYM)*

Eldersfield [SO8131]

☆ *Greyhound* [signed from B4211; Lime St (don't go into Eldersfield itself), OS Sheet 150 map ref 815314]: Unspoilt two-bar country local with good inexpensive proper country cooking (not Mon), well kept Ansells, Tetleys, Theakstons, Wadworths 6X and a couple of guest beers such as Butcombe, friendly young licensees and welcoming regulars, surprisingly modern lavatories with interesting mosaic in gents', pretty garden and room for children to play in *(the Didler, Derek and Sylvia Stephenson)*

Elmley Castle [SO9841]

☆ *Old Mill* [signed off A44 and A435, not far from Evesham]: Good value lunchtime specials, well kept Whitbreads-related ales, good choice of wines, attractive bar and separate restaurant, children allowed in eating area, helpful efficient landlady and friendly staff; former mill house with lovely secluded garden looking over village cricket pitch to Bredon Hill, good walks; comfortable well equipped bedrooms in converted granary *(Martin Jennings, Tony Middis, Guy Vowles, LYM, MRSM)*

Evesham [SP0344]

Green Dragon [Oat St, towards library off High St]: 16th-c coaching inn, formerly part of monastery, brewing own Asum and Gold (glass panel shows brewery); small dining lounge, big comfortable public bar, back pool room and skittle alley, old well in corridor, friendly staff, attractive prints, cheap food, quiet at lunchtime; evening piped music, maybe TV, live music, bouncers; good value bedrooms, good breakfast *(Pete Baker)*

Fairfield [SO9475]

Swan [B4091; marked PH on OS map]: Friendly typical Banks's pub, good value straightforward food inc hot pork sandwiches *(Dave Braisted)*

Far Forest [SO7175]

Horse & Jockey: Enjoyable food, welcoming staff, good choice of beers and wines; truly child-friendly *(Simon and Fiona Mitchell)*

Plough [A4117 Bewdley—Ludlow, just W of junction with A456]: Bright and cosy beamed dining area, largely no smoking, popular lunchtime with older people for wide-ranging good value nicely cooked food; quick friendly service, small bar with well kept Bass, M&B Mild and a guest beer, woodburner, lots of brass and china; children over 5 allowed if eating, subdued piped pop music; plenty of picnic-sets on neat lawn, good walks *(P and M Rudlin)*

Feckenham [SP0061]

☆ *Lygon Arms* [B4090 Droitwich—Alcester]: Energetic, experienced and very hospitable new licensees building up good choice of home-cooked food esp fresh fish, well kept Boddingtons, Greene King Old Speckled Hen and Wadworths 6X, plans for conservatory *(Peter Williams, Martin Jennings)*

Finstall [SO9869]

Cross [Alcester Rd]: Pine-panelled lounge and small timbered snug in local perched high above road, with good value bar food and well kept Whitbreads-related ales; seats on sheltered lawn *(LYM, Dave Braisted)*

Flyford Flavell [SO9754]

☆ *Flyford Arms* [Old Hill]: Light and airy refurbishment, lots of cricket pictures, good range of well served food inc bargain two-course meal and particularly good vegetarian dishes, wider evening restaurant choice, Tetleys and a beer labelled for the pub, friendly helpful staff, back dining room; bedrooms *(Dave Braisted, Martin Jennings, Rod Stoneman, Debbie Wall)*

Great Witley [SO7566]

Hundred House [Worcester Rd]: Busy much-modernised coaching inn and former magistrates' court, friendly quick service, well kept Bass, long choice of decent moderately priced food; handy for ruined Witley Court and remarkable church *(M A and C R Starling)*

Hanbury [SO9663]

Eagle & Sun [B4090 Droitwich rd]: Neatly laid out, with Banks's Bitter, Marstons Pedigree and other beers, good value food inc good carvery; nice spot by canal and wharf *(Martin Jennings)*

Vernon Arms [B4090]: Newish licensees doing simple food at exceptionally low prices, Bass ales; camp site, annual steam fair *(Dave Braisted)*

Hanley Castle [SO8341]

☆ *Three Kings* [Church End, off B4211 N of Upton upon Severn]: Unspoilt and unchanging classic country local, friendly and well worn in, with huge inglenook and hatch service in little tiled-floor tap room, consistently well kept Butcombe, Thwaites and usually three guest beers from small breweries, farm cider, dozens of malt whiskies, two other larger rooms, low-priced homely food (not Sun evening – singer then; be prepared for a maybe longish wait other times), seats of a sort outside; family room, bedroom *(the Didler, Gill Waller, Tony Morriss, Pat and Tony Martin, Colin Parker, LYM)*

Hanley Swan [SO8142]

Swan [B4209 Malvern—Upton]: Relaxed

traditional pub by green with big duck pond, varied reasonably priced food running up to steaks and good value Sun lunch, well kept Theakstons Best and XB, decent wine, prompt friendly service, comfortable spacious lounge with hunting trophies, old guns and cow-bells, nice locals' bar (TV news), small attractive restaurant evenings and Sun lunch; tables on lawn, big play area *(BB, Jenny and Dave Hughes)*

Holy Cross [SO9278]

☆ *Bell & Cross*: Unspoilt early 19th-c machine-free pub, new owners keeping it largely unaltered but doing good freshly made interesting food, several small parlour-like rooms off central corridor, tiny bar counter in one with well kept Banks's and a guest such as Marstons Pedigree, decent wines, friendly helpful staff; darts, full noticeboard; attractive good-sized garden *(Pete Baker, Jane and Neil Kendrick)*

Kemerton [SO9437]

☆ *Crown* [back rd Bredon—Beckford]: Welcoming 18th-c pub with refreshingly modern light furnishings in bustling L-shaped lounge bar, consistently good interesting country cooking from sandwiches up inc plenty of fish and enjoyable puddings, well kept Bass and Boddingtons, quietly friendly helpful staff, daily papers; pretty garden, upmarket village worth a look around, good walks over Bredon Hill *(Moira and John Cole, Di and Mike Gillam, Martin Jennings, Bernard Stradling, Colin Parker, Jeff and Miriam Hancock)*

Kidderminster [SO8376]

Boars Head [Worcester St]: Interesting bar lunches (not Sun), central servery for cosy snug and basic bar, heated covered courtyard with bottle bar for busy nights – can be lively evenings *(Gill Waller, Tony Morriss)*

Old Waggon & Horses [Ismere (A451 towards Stourbridge)]: Solid former carriers' pub with etched windows and hatch-style bar front in quarry-tiled public bar, cosy L-shaped lounge and dining room with knick-knacks, interesting menu with good vegetarian choice, thai meals on Sun *(Gill Waller, Tony Morriss)*

Kinnersley [SO8643]

New Royal Oak [off A38 S of Worcester]: Welcoming pub with horse-racing memorabilia in cosy bar, Bass and Beowulf Heroes; short changing choice of very imaginative, enjoyable food inc generous starters in separate conservatory restaurant *(Miss A G Drake, Colin Parker)*

Knightwick [SO7355]

☆ *Talbot* [Knightsford Bridge; B4197 just off A44 Worcester—Bromyard]: Nicely placed 14th-c inn of considerable character, interesting furnishings and good pictures in opened-up heavily beamed bar; though quite a favourite of ours, it's not quite consistent enough for the main entries, but when on form is hard to beat, with a good choice of well cooked if not cheap food inc unusual dishes and delicious puddings using fresh local ingredients, decent wines, and their own ales (also using their own farm produce); children and well behaved dogs

welcome, posher restaurant (same menu), tables served outside, comfortable character bedrooms (some over back public bar which has games and juke box), own fishing on the Teme; open all day *(Muriel and Peter Gleave, Pat and Tony Martin, Mike Pugh, Gill Waller, Tony Morriss, P Fisk, Guy Vowles, Christopher Harrowe, Trevor Owen, Colin Parker, Mike and Wendy Proctor, Arnold Tasker, Dr Thomas S Low-Beer, LYM)*

Leigh Sinton [SO7850]

Royal Oak [Malvern Rd]: Good food and reasonably priced wine list, with plenty of locals *(anon)*

Lindridge [SO6769]

Nags Head [A443 E of Tenbury Wells]: Good value generous straightforward food, well kept Marstons, good welcoming service, pleasant Teme valley views inc hop yard *(Geoffrey and Penny Hughes)*

Long Bank [SO7674]

Running Horse [A456 W of Bewdley]: Large well kept Chef & Brewer, well kept Courage Best, Theakstons and a guest beer, very wide food choice from sandwiches and baked potatoes up inc lots of fish, beams and log fires, pleasant atmosphere; disabled facilities, large garden and terrace, big fenced play area (no children inside now) – and there are horses alongside *(June and Mike Coleman)*

Longdon [SO8336]

Hunters Inn [B4211 S, towards Tewkesbury]: Attractive décor and relaxed atmosphere, comfortable furnishings, beams, flagstones, log fires, brass, copper and bric-a-brac, beamed dining area; pleasant if not always speedy service, generous food from sandwiches up inc children's dishes, real ales, decent wines, good views *(David and Catherine Whiting, Bernard Stradling, LYM)*

Lower Broadheath [SO8356]

Bell [Bell Lane/Martley Rd]: Friendly village local, Banks's Bitter and Mild, decent food, helpful staff, pool etc; outside play area *(Trevor Owen)*

Lulsley [SO7455]

☆ *Fox & Hounds* [signed a mile off A44 Worcester—Bromyard]: Tucked-away country pub with smallish parquet-floored bar stepping down into neat dining lounge, pretty little restaurant on left, good food from unusual soups and excellent steak baguette to interesting main dishes, well kept Bass and a local beer, decent wines, open fire; picnic-sets in quiet and colourful enclosed side rose garden *(BB, Chris Flynn, Wendy Jones)*

Malvern [SO7641]

Malvern Hills Hotel [opp British Camp car park, Wynds Point; junction A449/B4232 S]: Welcoming hotel in fine position high in the hills, popular for good value filling bar food; well kept Greene King Old Speckled Hen, Hobsons, Malvern Hills, Woods Shropshire Lad and a guest beer, good polite service, plush panelled lounge bar with open fire, more expensive restaurant; tables outside, bedrooms small but comfortable, open all day *(M Joyner, Keith and Katy Stevens, P and M Rudlin)*

Newland [SO7948]
Swan [Worcester Rd (A449)]: Good food esp thai and malay dishes, good beer choice inc locals, Shepherd Neame Spitfire and Wadworths 6X, nice licensees, delightful quiet and homely atmosphere; pleasant garden *(P Quickfall)*

Ombersley [SO8463]
Cross Keys [A449, Kidderminster end]: Small refurbished beamed pub with comfortable front bar, conservatory restaurant, good generous food esp daily fresh fish, well kept beers such as Boddingtons, Hook Norton and Wadworths *(W H and E Thomas, Nigel Long)*

Pershore [SO9445]
☆ *Brandy Cask* [Bridge St]: Own-brewed generously hopped Brandysnapper, John Baker and Whistling Joe at attractive prices, also Courage Directors, Ruddles Best and a guest such as Ushers Founders, Aug beer festival, freshly made food from sandwiches to steaks inc imaginative salads and some interesting dishes in properly pubby bar (can get smoky) and quaintly decorated no smoking brasserie, quick friendly helpful service; well behaved children allowed; long attractive garden down to river (keep a careful eye on the children), with terrace and koi pond *(Martin Jennings, Derek and Sylvia Stephenson, Gill Waller, Tony Morriss, Pat and Tony Martin, the Didler, Tom Evans, Dr and Mrs Jackson)*

Pound Green [SO7678]
New Inn [B4194 NW of Bewdley]: Attractive pub rambling out from old central core, quiet nooks and corners, friendly efficient staff, good atmosphere, good food in bar and dining room, well kept beer with usually two guests; live music nights *(P and M Rudlin)*

Shatterford [SO7981]
☆ *Bellmans Cross* [Bridgnorth Rd (A442)]: Big attractively refurbished pub/restaurant with imaginative beautifully presented bar food (team of French chefs), good French food in tasteful restaurant, Bass and guest beer, thoughtful wine list, friendly helpful service *(Mike and Mary Carter, Theo, Anne and Jane Gaskin)*

Red Lion [Bridgnorth Rd (A442)]: Immaculate olde-worlde pub straddling the Shropshire boundary, with gleaming copper and brass, lively coal fire, wide choice of good generous well presented food in smart partly no smoking restaurant extension, also good bar food from sandwiches up, reasonably priced Banks's Best and Woods Shropshire Lad, good atmosphere, very friendly staff, fine views; well behaved children welcome, disabled facilities *(June and Mike Coleman)*

Sneachill [SO9053]
Nightingale: Roomy Bass Vintage Inn with some character and interesting old photographs, friendly attentive young service, well kept real ale, sensible choice of good ample food *(John Whitehead)*

Stoke Pound [SO9667]
☆ *Queens Head* [Sugarbrook Lane, by Bridge 48, Worcester & Birmingham Canal]: Big plush air-conditioned waterside dining pub with good generous straightforward food inc good value eat-as-much-as-you-can carvery and lots of puddings (Sun lunch very popular, booking advised), Scottish Courage ales, pleasant helpful staff; piped music may obtrude, rather close-set tables; waterside terrace, camping site, good walk up the 36 locks of the Tardebigge Steps, quite handy for Avoncroft buildings museum *(Bill Sykes, Theo, Anne and Jane Gaskin)*

Stoke Prior [SO9468]
☆ *Country Girl* [B4091 S of Bromsgrove; Sharpway Gate]: Attractive country pub, clean and welcoming, with comfortable lounge, rustic brickwork, light oak beams, farm tools, soft lighting, good generous food inc enterprising vegetarian specials, efficient service, well kept Whitbreads-related and other ales such as Wadworths 6X, unobtrusive piped music; enclosed garden, walks on Dodderhill Common *(Mr and Mrs Gordon Turner)*

Stoke Wharf [SO9468]
Navigation [Hanbury Rd (B4091)]: Friendly pub nr Worcs & Birmingham Canal, still with the feel of its Davenports days (though that brewery is long gone); popular for good food inc (by prior arrangement) fantastic seafood platter, also Thurs paella night *(Dave Braisted)*

Stoke Works [SO9365]
Boat & Railway [Shaw Lane]: Old-fashioned canalside Banks's pub, popular and unpretentious, with good lunchtime snacks, pretty hanging baskets *(Dave Braisted)*

Tenbury Wells [SO5968]
☆ *Fountain* [Oldwood, A4112 S]: Quaint 17th-c low timbered pub, recently redone open-plan black-beamed lounge with huge shark tank, fishy and other bric-a-brac and country pictures, coal-effect gas fire, big dining room beyond, quickly served home-cooked food mixing traditional and unusual, served with their own herb oil, real ales brewed for the pub, decent wines by the glass, good whisky choice, friendly service, no smoking area; open all day, disabled facilities, children's play barn, picnic-sets on big side lawn with boules and lots of play equipment *(Alan Boucker, BB)*

☆ *Peacock* [A456 about 1½ miles E – so inn actually in Shrops]: Attractive 14th-c roadside dining pub with relaxed yet buoyant atmosphere in several separate rooms, heavy black beams, big log fire in front lounge, comfortable kitchen chairs and ex-pew settles; good attractively presented food from baguettes to enterprising light and main dishes, lots of fresh veg, good friendly service, real ales such as Hobsons, good wines by the glass, back family room, charming bistro; exemplary ladies', picnic-sets on terrace, lovely setting by River Teme, good bedrooms *(P and J Shapley, Basil Minson, LYM, Chris Flynn, Wendy Jones, Mr and Mrs C Millward)*

☆ *Ship* [Teme St]: Small L-shaped bar with lots of dark wood inc fine Elizabethan beams, little hunting prints and other pictures, well kept Ansells and guests such as Hobsons Best, decent wines, good coffee, good imaginative food inc fresh fish and Sun lunch, reasonable prices, thoughtful and genuine smiling service, bright no smoking dining room with fresh flowers; piped music; picnic-sets in coach yard and on neat sheltered back lawn, comfortable bedrooms *(Guy Vowles, Norma and Keith Bloomfield, K and B Barker, Richard and Barbara Philpott, BB)*

Tibberton [SO9057]
Speed the Plough [nr M5 junction 6; Plough Rd, off A4538]: Friendly local with well kept beers, good steaks, no music, amiable cat *(Dave Braisted)*

Upton Snodsbury [SO9454]
☆ *Coventry Arms* [A422 Worcester—Stratford]: Hunting prints, fox masks, horse tack and racing gossip in welcoming beamed country inn with cottagey armchairs among other seats, coal fire, well kept Bass, Boddingtons, Marstons Pedigree and Greene King Old Speckled Hen, lots of malt whiskies and ports, cheerful efficient service, good choice of enjoyable food inc good value lunches – two comfortable dining rooms, back conservatory with well spaced cane tables; spacious pleasant lawn (some traffic noise) with well equipped play area; bedrooms attractively decorated *(W H and E Thomas, BB, George Atkinson)*
French House: Two roomy bars thoroughly Frenchified with hundreds of wine bottles racked on ceiling, French signs and ornaments inc Napoleon statue, two grandfather clocks, even a useable mock guillotine; good value French food, cheerful staff, good choice of wines, well kept John Smiths and Theakstons Best, French piped music *(Dave Braisted, Ian and Denise Foster, June and Mike Coleman)*

Upton upon Severn [SO8540]
Little Upton Muggery [Old St, far end main st]: Basic pub with thousands of mugs on the ceiling, good value generous food inc good home-made vegetarian choice (may be a wait), well kept Ushers Best and Founders, friendly helpful service, simple furnishings, open fires, pool in third room *(M Joyner, Rona Murdoch)*
☆ *Olde Anchor* [High St]: Picturesque rambling 16th-c pub, neat, tidy and chatty, with helpful service, old-fashioned furnishings, black timbers propping its low beams, sparkling copper, brass and pewter, good fire in unusual central fireplace; well kept Courage Directors, Theakstons and Charles Wells Bombardier, usual food; small back terrace, some tables out in front, open all day summer, can get crowded evenings then *(LYM, Rona Murdoch)*
Plough [Waterside]: Newly refurbished pub in

good Severnside spot (summer pleasure cruises), with tables outside, helpful staff, Banks's beers, decent sensibly priced food, family area *(Trevor Owen)*

Weatheroak Hill [SP0674]
☆ *Coach & Horses* [Icknield St – coming S on A435 from Wythall roundabout, filter right off dual carriageway a mile S, then in village turn left towards Alvechurch; not far from M42 junction 3]: Roomy and friendly country pub brewing its own good Weatheroak beers, also good well kept choice of others from small breweries; plush-seated low-ceilinged two-level dining bar, tiled-floor proper public bar, bar food inc lots of baguettes and bargain fish and chips, also modern restaurant with well spaced tables; plenty of seats out on lawns and upper terrace; piped music; children allowed in eating area *(Ian and Nita Cooper, Peter and Jenny Quine, Pete Baker, Dr and Mrs A K Clarke, LYM)*

West Malvern [SO7645]
Brewers Arms [The Dingle]: Refurbished country local down steep path from the road, with welcoming landlord, well kept Banks's-related beers, enjoyable food (not Mon lunchtime), good atmosphere esp Tues folk nights; small garden *(Dr Stephen Decent)*

Whittington [SO8752]
Swan [just off M5 junction 7]: Brightly painted country-style bar with lots of pews, changing imaginative reliably good value food, friendly well trained young staff coping well with the bustle, well kept Banks's and Marstons Pedigree, decent wine, log fire; children welcome, garden with play area *(Chris Flynn, Wendy Jones)*

Wildmoor [SO9675]
Wildmoor Oak [a mile from M5 junction 4 – 1st left off A491 towards Stourbridge; Top Rd]: Busy local with Bass and Everards Tiger, reasonably priced food in bar (no children) and new restaurant; small terrace and garden *(Ian Shorthouse)*

Wolverley [SO8279]
Live & Let Live: Recently much refurbished, with good choice of good value food, Tetleys, big front conservatory *(Dave Braisted)*

Worcester [SO8454]
Severn View [Newport St]: Attractive black and white timbered pub, roomy and comfortable, with helpful staff, good bar food, open fireplaces; bedrooms, views of river beyond main road *(E G Parish)*

Post Office address codings confusingly give the impression that some pubs are in Worcestershire, when they're really in Gloucestershire, Herefordshire, Shropshire, or Warwickshire (which is where we list them).

Yorkshire

*Eight pubs here have real staying power, marking up an entry in every year's
Guide since it started 20 years ago. They are the proudly unspoilt gaslit White
Horse in Beverley, the nicely placed Buck at Buckden, the Fauconberg Arms at
Coxwold (new licensees doing imaginative food), the handsome yet relaxed
Olde White Harte in Hull, the beautifully preserved Whitelocks in Leeds
(cheap food and beer), the Queens Arms at Litton (a lovely spot for walkers),
the very civilised Yorke Arms at Ramsgill, and the Old Bridge in Ripponden
(Ian Beaumont who had owned it since our first edition has just retired, but
the new licensee has been managing it for 17 years). Alongside these old
stagers, newcomers to this edition (including pubs back after a break) are the
Black Bull in Boroughbridge (responding well to a friendly new landlord), the
Wyvill Arms at Constable Burton (carefully sourced imaginative food), the
Durham Ox at Crayke (interesting bar, good inventive cooking), the Kings
Head in Masham (good all round, with helpful staff), the prettily set Golden
Lion in Osmotherley (another good all-rounder), the White Swan in Pickering
(a civilised small hotel with a very welcoming bar and good food), and the Bay
Horse at Terrington (on fine form under its newish landlord). Pubs which
currently stand out here for a special meal are the Crab & Lobster at Asenby,
the Abbey Inn at Byland Abbey (its new bedrooms are a big success), the Fox
& Hounds at Carthorpe (the attentive staff will open any wine bottle even if
you want just a glass), the Blue Lion at East Witton (earns a star this year for
its all-round quality), the spotless nicely placed Plough at Fadmoor, the smart
General Tarleton at Ferrensby, the fine old Star at Harome (a very inventive
young chef/landlord), the impeccably run Angel at Hetton, the Charles
Bathurst at Langthwaite (such good food is quite a surprise in the bleak
surroundings – and it's a nice place to stay), the unpretentious Sandpiper in
Leyburn, the smartly refurbished Wellington at Lund, the civilised Black Bull
at Moulton (handy for the A1), the upmarket Yorke Arms at Ramsgill (a nice
spot for a stay), the very friendly Hare at Scawton, the splendidly run Three
Acres at Shelley, the Fox & Hounds at Starbotton (hearty cooking to suit this
little walkers' inn), the Jefferson Arms at Thorganby (the landlady's Swiss
husband does good röstis, good bedrooms too), and the Sportsmans Arms at
Wath in Nidderdale (the long-serving landlord's cooking combines with the
surroundings to make this an enjoyable place to stay). And among the new
entries mentioned above, the Durham Ox and Wyvill Arms look set to join
these top dining pubs. From among this rich choice, we name the Blue Lion at
East Witton Yorkshire Dining Pub of the Year. Many other Yorkshire pubs
have a deep hold on readers' and our own affections, for other reasons.
Among these, ones on specially good form these days are the Birch Hall at
Beck Hole (a smashing little cross between pub and sweetie shop), the family-
run Royal Oak at Dacre Banks (a rewarding all-rounder), the beautifully set
and well run Horse Shoe at Egton Bridge, the friendly George tucked up in the
dales at Hubberholme, the Chequers at Ledsham (a friendly break from the
A1, brewing its own good beers), the charming Laurel looking down to the
sea in Robin Hood's Bay, the well run Golden Lion in Settle (good all round),*

the friendly Fat Cat in Sheffield (lots of real ales, bargain food), the Wombwell Arms at Wass (new licensees doing very well), and in York the Maltings and Tap & Spile (largely for their great beers). As if the choice was not wide enough already, the Lucky Dip section at the end of the chapter adds to the list of hot prospects: current stars there are the Rose & Crown at Bainbridge, Kaye Arms on Grange Moor, Gray Ox at Hartshead, Racehorses in Kettlewell, Red Lion at Langthwaite, Gold Cup at Low Catton, White Horse just outside Rosedale Abbey, Devonshire Cat and Hillsborough in Sheffield, Tan Hill Inn miles from anywhere on Tan Hill, and Olde Starre, Royal Oak and York Arms in York. Drinks prices are well below the national average, with Sam Smiths the Tadcaster brewer setting a fine low-price example, and excellent value too at the New Barrack in Sheffield and (both brewing their own) the Sair in Linthwaite and the Fat Cat in Sheffield.

ALDBOROUGH SE4166 Map 7

Ship 🛏

Village signposted from B6265 just S of Boroughbridge, close to A1

Opposite an ancient church, this friendly and attractive old pub is handy for the A1. The heavily beamed bar has some old-fashioned seats around heavy cast-iron tables, and lots of copper and brass on the walls, and a coal fire in the stone inglenook fireplace. Good bar food at lunchtime (they tell us prices have not changed since last year) includes a wide choice of sandwiches (from £2.25; bacon and avocado £4.50; open tuna with melted cheese £5.25), soup (£2.50), ploughman's (£4.75), giant yorkshire pudding with roast beef (£5.50), steak and kidney pie or home-made lasagne (£5.75), lamb cutlets with mint (£6.25), gammon and egg (£7.50), steaks (from £8.25), and good daily specials such as liver and bacon (£5.50), queen scallops (£5.75), pork chop with apple fritter (£7.50), and smoked haddock with broccoli (£8.95); the evening restaurant menu is more elaborate; good breakfasts and friendly brisk service. Well kept Greene King Ruddles Best, John Smiths, and Tetleys Bitter on handpump, and quite a few malt whiskies; piped music. There are seats on the front terrace. The Roman town with its museum and Roman pavements is nearby. *(Recommended by Janet and Peter Race, Christine and Malcolm Ingram, Roger A Bellingham, GSB, Charles and Pauline Stride, Brian and Janet Ainscough, Greta and Christopher Wells)*

Free house ~ Licensee Duncan Finch ~ Real ale ~ Bar food (not Sun evening) ~ Restaurant ~ (01423) 322749 ~ Children in eating area of bar and in restaurant but must be well behaved ~ Open 12-2.30(3 Sat), 5.30-11; 12-3, 7-10.30 Sun ~ Bedrooms: £32S/£45S

APPLETREEWICK SE0560 Map 7

Craven Arms 🍺

Village signposted off B6160 Burnsall—Bolton Abbey

One reader was rather pleased to find himself caught in this creeper-covered 17th-c pub in deep snow – there are roaring fires (one in an ancient range) to warm the small cosy rooms, and good beer and food. Attractive settles and carved chairs are spread among more usual seats, beams are covered with banknotes, and there are harness, copper kettles and so forth, and a warm atmosphere. Bar food includes home-made soup (£2.10), sandwiches (from £2.35), ploughman's (£4.40), cumberland sausage and onion sauce (£5.50), home-made steak and kidney pie (£5.40), grilled ham and eggs (£6.30), and steaks (from £9.10); the little no smoking dining room is charming. Well kept Black Sheep Bitter and Special, Tetleys Bitter, and Theakstons Best and Old Peculier on handpump, and several malt whiskies; darts, cribbage, and dominoes – no music or noisy games machines. From picnic-sets in front, you look south over the green Wharfedale valley to a pine-topped ridge;

there are more seats in the back garden, and plenty of surrounding walks. Adjoining the pub is an attractive self-catering barn converstion. *(Recommended by Anthony Longden, A J Bowen, Mrs R A Cartwright)*

Free house ~ Licensee Linda Nicholson ~ Real ale ~ Bar food (not Tues evening) ~ (01756) 720270 ~ Children welcome ~ Open 11.30-3, 6.30-11; 12-3, 7-10.30 Sun; closed Tues evening in winter

ASENBY SE3975 Map 7

Crab & Lobster 🍴 ♀ 🛏

Village signposted off A168 – handy for A1

A new dining pavilion has been added to this newly thatched, very popular pub. It is created on a nautical theme with an authentic 1950s diving suit hanging from the ceiling surrounded by sails, tuna fish floats, flags and a capstan, and there are Edwardian sofas, big tropical plants, and a lovely handcrafted bar. The gardens have seen some changes, and have bamboo and palm trees lining the paths, and there's now a gazebo at the end of the walkways; seats on a mediterranean-style terrace. The rambling, L-shaped bar has quite a bit of character, with a fishing net attached to the beams holding shells and so forth, and an interesting jumble of seats from antique high-backed and other settles through settees and wing armchairs heaped with cushions, to tall and rather theatrical corner seats and even a very superannuated dentist's chair; the tables are almost as much of a mix, and the walls and available surfaces are quite a jungle of bric-a-brac, with standard and table lamps and candles keeping even the lighting pleasantly informal. Very good imaginative food might include rabbit terrine with celeriac and apple rémoulade and chutney or french bean salad with grilled goats cream, sour cream and hazelnuts (£5.50), mussels with shallots, garlic, thyme, white wine and cream (£5.95), salmon and dill rilletes with sweet potato pancake and grilled asparagus or lunchtime fish club sandwich (not Sunday; £6.50), baked queen scallops, garlic and gruyère (six £6.95, nine £9.95), egg pasta, artichokes, chargrilled vegetables, parmesan and pesto (£9.50), posh fish and chips with minted mushy peas (£12.50), crisp duck confit, black pudding, toffee apples and oranges (£12.95), thai green fish curry with coconut rice, nan bread and pickles (£13.50), moroccan-style tagine of salmon, monkfish and king prawns (£14.50), beef fillet, horseradish and parsnip purée, shallots, stilton and port glaze (£16.50), and puddings such as white chocolate mousse, lemon crème puff, rhubarb, and lemon curd ice cream or sticky toffee pudding, butterscotch sauce and fudge ice cream (£4.50). Well kept Bass, Black Sheep, Timothy Taylors Landlord, and Worthingtons on handpump, and good wines by the glass from an interesting wine list; well reproduced piped music. The opulent bedrooms are in the surrounding country house which has three acres of mature gardens, a tennis court and 180 metre golf hole with full practice facilities. *(Recommended by Jenny and Dave Hughes, Edward and Deanna Pearce, Mrs V Middlebrook, Susan and John Douglas, Kevin Blake, H Bramwell, Janet and Peter Race, A Kerr, Brian and Pat Wardrobe, Tim and Sue Halstead, David and Ruth Hollands, Steve Whalley, Mrs E E Sanders)*

Free house ~ Licensees David and Jackie Barnard ~ Real ale ~ Bar food (all day) ~ (01845) 577286 ~ Children welcome ~ Jazz Sun ~ Open 11-11; 12-11 Sun ~ Bedrooms: £80B/£100B

AYSGARTH SE0088 Map 10

George & Dragon

Off A684

Although this 17th-c coaching inn is popular with locals (and there are plenty of photographs of them enjoying themselves), there's a welcome for visitors, too. The small, cosy and attractive bar usually has a warm open fire with a dark wooden mantelpiece, built-in cushioned wooden wall seats and plush stools around a few pubby tables, tankards, jugs, and copper pots hanging from the thick beams, portraits of locals by the landlord on the panelled walls, and high bar stools by the decorative wooden bar; well kept Black Sheep Bitter, John Smiths, and Theakstons

Best on handpump. There's also a polished hotel lounge with antique china. Decent bar food includes home-made soup (£2.95), chicken and ham pâté (£4.25), seafood crêpe (£4.50), bangers and mash with apple sauce and rich gravy (£7.50), liver and bacon (£7.95), steak in ale pie or cod fillet with a fresh lemon and caper butter sauce (£8.50), home-made salmon and prawn fishcakes with parsley and sweetcorn sauce or roast leg of lamb with garlic mash (£8.95), steaks (from £11.95), and daily specials such as crispy duck pancakes (£4.95) or lemon chicken with soy noodles (£9.25); children's dishes (£3.50). Piped music, TV, dominoes, cribbage, and two golden retrievers, Douglas and James. Outside on the paved beer garden are some picnic-sets and tubs of pretty flowers, and the surrounding scenery of Upper Wensleydale is lovely. *(Recommended by Christine and Neil Townend, R Macfarlane, Janet and Peter Race, Trevor and Lynda Smith, Mr and Mrs K M Hezelgrave , P Abbott, John Close, Walter and Sue Anderson, Mike and Maggie Betton, Jayne and Peter Capp)*

Free house ~ Licensees Neil and Alison Vaughan ~ Real ale ~ Bar food (12-2, 6-9) ~ Restaurant ~ (01969) 663358 ~ Children welcome ~ Open 11-11; 12-10.30 Sun ~ Bedrooms: £35S/£59S

BECK HOLE NZ8202 Map 10

Birch Hall

Off A169 SW of Whitby, from top of Sleights Moor

The focal point (and tourist attraction) of the village, this pub-cum-village shop is unique and charming. There are two rooms with the shop selling postcards, sweeties and ice creams in between, and hatch service to both sides. Furnishings are simple – built-in cushioned wall seats and wooden tables (spot the one with 136 pennies, all heads up, embedded in the top) and chairs on the floor (flagstones in one room, composition in the other), some strange items such as French breakfast cereal boxes and a tube of Macleans toothpaste priced 1/3d, and well kept ales such as Black Sheep Bitter, Theakstons Black Bull, and guests from local breweries on handpump; several malt whiskies. Bar snacks like butties (£1.80), super locally-made pies (£1.20), and home-made scones and cakes including their lovely beer cake (from 70p); friendly, welcoming staff; dominoes. Outside, an ancient oil painting of nearby Thomasson Foss waterfall hangs on the pub wall, there are benches out in front, and steep steps up to a little steeply terraced side garden with some ducks and a moorland view. This is a lovely spot with marvellous surrounding walks – you can walk along the disused railway line from Goathland; part of the path from Beck Hole to Grosmont has been surfaced with mussel shells. *(Recommended by Alan and Paula McCully, Keith and Di Newsome, Pat and Tony Martin, the Didler, Kevin Thorpe, Chris Flynn, Wendy Jones)*

Free house ~ Licensee Colin Jackson ~ Real ale ~ Bar food (available during all opening hours; not 25 Dec) ~ No credit cards ~ (01947) 896245 ~ Children in small family room ~ Open 11-11; 12-10.30 Sun; 11-3, 7.30-11 in winter, 12-3, 7.30-10.30 Sun in winter; closed winter Mon evenings

BEVERLEY TA0340 Map 8

White Horse £

Hengate, close to the imposing Church of St Mary's; runs off North Bar

Dating from around 1425, this fine unspoilt pub has a carefully preserved Victorian feel – quite without frills; it is known locally as 'Nellies'. The basic but very atmospheric little rooms are huddled together around the central bar, with brown leatherette seats (high-backed settles in one little snug) and basic wooden chairs and benches on bare floorboards, antique cartoons and sentimental engravings on the nicotine-stained walls, a gaslit pulley-controlled chandelier, a deeply reverberating chiming clock, and open fires – one with an attractively tiled old fireplace. Well kept and very cheap Sam Smiths OBB on handpump. Very good value, simple food includes sandwiches (from £1.50; not Saturday), home-made yorkshire pudding and gravy (£2.50), filled baked potatoes (from £3), home-made mince and onion pie, chicken curry or liver and onions (all £3.50), mushroom and nut fettuccine, home-made meaty or vegetarian lasagne or gammon and egg (£4.25), and puddings such as home-made fruit pie or chocolate sponge (£1.95); Sunday roast (£4.25). A separate games room has pinball, dominoes, TV, fruit machine, juke box, and two pool tables – these and the no smoking room behind the bar are the only modern touches. John Wesley preached in the back yard in the mid-18th c. *(Recommended by Paul and Ursula Randall, the Didler, Pete Baker, Kevin Thorpe, Christine and Neil Townend, Shaun Pinchbeck, Don and Shirley Parrish, Arby)*

Sam Smiths ~ Manager John Etherington ~ Real ale ~ Bar food (lunchtime only; not Mon) ~ No credit cards ~ (01482) 861973 ~ Children welcome away from bar until 8pm ~ Live folk Mon, jazz Weds, folk 1st Sun lunchtime of month ~ Open 11-11; 12-10.30 Sun; closed evening 25 Dec

BLAKEY RIDGE SE6799 Map 10
Lion 🍺 🛏

From A171 Guisborough—Whitby follow Castleton, Hutton le Hole signposts; from A170 Kirkby Moorside—Pickering follow Keldholm, Hutton le Hole, Castleton signposts; OS Sheet 100 map reference 679996

As this isolated 16th-c inn is open all day, it makes a useful stop for thirsty walkers – there are plenty of surrounding walks, and stunning views, and at 1355 ft above sea level, this is said to be the 4th highest pub in England. The beamed and rambling bars have warm open fires, a few big high-backed rustic settles around cast-iron-framed tables, lots of small dining chairs, a nice leather settee, and stone walls hung with some old engravings and photographs of the pub under snow (it can easily get cut off in winter). Bar food includes sandwiches (from £2.75), ploughman's (£4.95), giant yorkshire pudding and gravy (£2.25), home-cooked ham and egg, vegetable lasagne or home-made steak and mushroom pie (£6.75), chicken in mushroom and cream sauce (£7.25), steaks (from £9.45), puddings like spotted dick or apple pie (£2.95), and children's meals (£3.50). Both restaurants are no smoking. Well kept Greene King Old Speckled Hen, John Smiths, and Theakstons Best, Old Peculier, Black Bull and XB on handpump; piped music. *(Recommended by Geoff and Angela Jaques, R Mathews, S and D Moir, Bob and Lisa Cantrell, GD, KW)*

Free house ~ Licensee Barry Crossland ~ Real ale ~ Bar food (12-10(10.30 Fri/Sat)) ~ Restaurant ~ (01751) 417320 ~ Children welcome ~ Live music monthly Thurs ~ Open 11-11(12 summer Sat); 12-10.30 Sun ~ Bedrooms: £17.50(£32B)/£50(£58B)

BOROUGHBRIDGE SE3967 Map 7
Black Bull 🛏

St James Square; B6265, just off A1(M)

Under a friendly new landlord, this attractive 13th-c inn has been looking after people travelling between Scotland and England for many centuries. The main bar area, with a big stone fireplace and brown leather seats, is served through an old-fashioned hatch, and there's a cosy and attractive snug with traditional wall settles. Well liked bar food includes home-made soup (£2.25), sandwiches (from £2.75; ciabatta rolls from £4.95), crab and salmon fishcakes with sun-dried tomato sauce (£3.75), omelettes (from £3.95), pork and chive sausages in onion gravy (£4.75), pasta with mushrooms, onions and peppers in cream sauce with parmesan (£5.65), pie of the day (£5.95), thai sweet and sour chicken with oriental vegetables and noodles (£6.95), steaks (from £12.50), and puddings such as glazed home-made lemon tart with candied orange zest and an orange scented cream sauce or dark chocolate and brandy mousse with home-made blackcurrant bombe (from £2.95). Well kept Black Sheep Bitter, John Smiths, and a guest such as Fullers London Pride or Charles Wells Bombardier on handpump, enjoyable wines (with nine by the glass), quite a few malt whiskies, and proper coffee – and they do afternoon teas. Service is friendly and attentive, the two borzoi dogs are called Charlie and Sadie, and the two cats Mimi and Cyny; dominoes and quiz nights, and the local mummers perform here half a dozen times a year. The comfortable bedrooms are in a more modern wing. *(Recommended by Michael Doswell, Joy and Peter Heatherley, the Didler, Sharon Holmes, Tom Cherrett, Geoffrey and Penny Hughes, Joe Green, C W Dix)*

Free house ~ Licensees Anthony and Jillian Burgess ~ Real ale ~ Bar food (12-2, 6-9.30; all day Sat) ~ Restaurant ~ (01423) 322413 ~ Children welcome ~ Open 11-11; 12-10.30 Sun ~ Bedrooms: £40.50S/£54S

BRADFIELD SK2392 Map 7
Strines Inn

From A57 heading E of junction with A6013 (Ladybower Reservoir) take first left turn (signposted with Bradfield) then bear left; with a map can also be reached more circuitously from Strines signpost on A616 at head of Underbank Reservoir, W of Stocksbridge

A pub since 1771, this isolated moorland inn was originally built as a manor house in 1275, although most of the building dates from the 16th c. The main bar has a welcoming atmosphere, black beams liberally decked with copper kettles and so forth, quite a menagerie of stuffed animals, homely red-plush-cushioned traditional wooden wall benches and small chairs, and a coal fire in the rather grand stone fireplace; there's a good mixture of customers. A room off on the right has another coal fire, hunting photographs and prints, and lots of brass and china, and on the left, a similarly furnished room is no smoking. Tasty bar food includes home-made soup (£2.50), sandwiches (from £1.70; toasties from £2; hot pork £2.60), filled baked potatoes (from £3.25), garlic mushrooms (£3.95), filled giant yorkshire puddings (£5.95), liver and onions (£6.25), spicy bean casserole (£6.75), 10oz rump steak (£8.95), daily specials such as home-made quiche (£5.50), pasta in bacon, tomato and basil sauce (£5.95), cajun-style chicken breast (£6.95), and tuna in lemon pepper butter (£8.95), and puddings like maple and pecan tart or Bailey's and toffee cheesecake (£2.95). Well kept Camerons Strongarm, Lichfield Steeplejack, Mansfield Ridings Bitter, and Marstons Pedigree on handpump, several malt whiskies, and good espresso or cappuccino coffee; dominoes, cribbage, and piped music. The children's playground is safely fenced in (and far enough away from the pub not to be too noisy), and they have a summer bouncy castle. From the picnic-sets are fine views, and there are some rescued animals – goats, geese, hens, sheep, and several free-roaming peacocks; well behaved dogs welcome. The bedrooms have four-poster beds and one has an open log fire. *(Recommended by the Didler, Jim Bush, A Preston, Paul Craddock, Jeremy Butcher, Suzanne Hosworth, Keith Fairbrother)*

Free house ~ Licensee Jeremy Stanish ~ Real ale ~ Bar food (all day in summer) ~ (0114) 285 1247 ~ Well behaved children welcome until 9pm ~ Open 10.30-11; 10.30-10.30 Sun; 10.30-3, 6-11 weekdays in winter; closed 25 Dec ~ Bedrooms: £40B/£65B

BREARTON SE3261 Map 7
Malt Shovel ⚲ ♀ ◀

Village signposted off A61 N of Harrogate

As they don't take bookings (but there is a waiting list system) in this especially popular, 16th-c village pub, you do have to arrive at opening time to be sure of a seat. Several heavily-beamed rooms radiate from the attractive linenfold oak bar counter with plush-cushioned seats and a mix of tables, an ancient oak partition wall, tankards and horsebrasses, both real and gas fires, and paintings by local artists (for sale) and lively hunting prints on the walls. Quite a choice of decent, reasonably priced bar food might include sandwiches, mussels in white wine, garlic and herbs (£3.95), good ham and blue wensleydale tart, nut roast with pesto cream sauce or ploughman's (£5.25), steak in ale pie (£6.25), sausages and mash or pheasant, rabbit and hare pie (£6.50), seafood au gratin, liver, bacon and black pudding or warm chicken salad with lemon dressing (£6.95), tuna with warm potato salad and lemon and caper dressing (£7.95), chargrilled steaks (from £8.50), and puddings such as apple and bramble crumble or sticky toffee pudding (£2.75). Well kept Black Sheep Bitter, Daleside Nightjar, and Durham Magus, and two guests such as Goose Eye Brontë or Rudgate Ruby Mild on handpump, real cider, 30 malt whiskies, and a small but interesting and reasonably priced wine list (they will serve any wine by the glass); they serve their house coffee (and a guest coffee) in cafetières. Darts, shove-ha'penny, cribbage, and dominoes. You can eat outside on the small terrace on all but the coldest of days as they have outdoor heaters; there are more tables on the grass. This is an attractive spot off the beaten track, yet handy for Harrogate and Knaresborough. *(Recommended by Barbara Wensworth, Carol Ackroyd, Peter McNamara, Mr and Mrs R Milhinch, Robert and Susan Whitehead, Geoffrey and Brenda Wilson, H Bramwell, Patricia A Bruce, B, M and P Kendall, Shaun Pinchbeck, Andy and Jill Kassube, Michael Doswell, Peter and Anne-Marie O'Malley, Mrs V Middlebrook, Les Brown, Pat and Tony Martin, Michael and Rosalind Dymond)*

Free house ~ Licensee Leslie Mitchell ~ Real ale ~ Bar food (not Sun evening, not Mon) ~ No credit cards ~ (01423) 862929 ~ Children welcome ~ Open 12-2.30, 6.45-11; 6.30-10.30 Sun; closed Mon

BUCKDEN SD9477 Map 7
Buck ♀
B6160

Particularly on Sunday lunchtime, this attractive creeper-covered stone pub cleverly manages to combine its smart Sunday lunch customers with its muddy-booted fell walkers, and make everyone feel just as comfortable and welcome. The modernised and extended open-plan bar has upholstered built-in wall banquettes and square stools around shiny dark brown tables on its carpet – though there are still flagstones in the snug original area by the serving counter; local pictures, hunting prints, willow-pattern plates on a delft shelf, and the mounted head of a roebuck on bare stone above the log fire. Served by uniformed staff, good bar food includes home-made soup (£3.25), black pudding parfait with wholegrain mustard dressing and toasted brioche (£4.20), breaded fishcake with deep-fried leek and tartare sauce (£4.85), sandwiches (from £4.95), bass and red pepper terrine (£5.20), pork and leek sausage with cider and onion gravy, bacon chops with provençale tomato or smoked chicken and bacon caesar salad (all £7.25), fresh pasta with pepperoni, tomato sauce and gruyère (£7.50), salmon en croûte with Boursin cheese and chive and prawn beurre blanc (£8.95), and steaks; the dining area and restaurant are no smoking. Well kept Theakstons Best, Old Peculier, Black Bull, and XB on handpump, 30 malt whiskies, and decent wines; piped music, dominoes, and fruit machine. Seats on the terrace enjoy good surrounding moorland views. *(Recommended by Terry Mizen, Gethin Lewis, Ann Williams, Tony Hughes, WAH, John Robertson, Maggie and Peter Shapland, Malcolm and Jane MacDonald, Trevor and Lynda Smith, P and J Shapley, Mr and Mrs J E C Tasker)*

Free house ~ Licensee Nigel Hayton ~ Real ale ~ Bar food (12-5, 6.30-9(9.30 Fri/Sat; 8.30 Sun)) ~ Restaurant ~ (01756) 760228 ~ Children in family room; must be over 7 in restaurant ~ Open 11-11; 12-10.30 Sun; closed 2nd and 3rd wk Jan ~ Bedrooms: £39B/£78S

BURNSALL SE0361 Map 7
Red Lion 🍴 ♀ 🛏
B6160 S of Grassington, on Ilkley road; OS Sheet 98826 map reference 033613

In fine weather, seats on the back terrace, lit by old gas lamps, have fine views, and from more seats on the front cobbles (and from most of the bedrooms) you can see the River Wharfe; fishing permits for 7 miles of river. Inside, the bustling main bar has attractively panelled walls (hung with old photographs of local fell races), sturdy wall seats, windsor armchairs, oak benches, and rugs on the stripped floor. The carpeted, no smoking front dining area, served from the same copper-topped counter through an old fashioned small-paned glass partition, has a log fire; dominoes. Highly enjoyable food might include lunchtime snacks such as sandwiches (from £3.75; open sandwiches or rustic bread with smoked ham, brie and red onion marmalade £6.25), goats cheese in filo pastry with mango chutney and sorrel salad (£5.25), a plate of cheeses and charcuterie (£6.95), and cannelloni stuffed with wild mushrooms, spinach and feta cheese topped with a roast tomato and garlic sauce (£9.50), as well as cream soup (£2.95), salad of poached free range eggs, lardons of bacon, garlic croutons, and crispy leeks (£6.25), duck liver parfait (£6.50), tartlet of leek and goats cheese with rocket salad (£9.50), pot roast pork with roasted shallots, apple sauce and rösti potato (£11.75), venison with fried polenta, wild mushrooms and green peppercorn sauce (£12.75), roast duckling with leg confit, apple tart and sticky onions (£14.95), and puddings like white chocolate and rosemary brûlée, glazed lemon tart with raspberry sauce and crème anglaise, and banana sticky toffee pudding with banana and rum ice cream (from £4.95). Well kept Greene King Old Speckled Hen, Theakstons Best and Black Bull, and Timothy Taylors Landlord on handpump, several malt whiskies, and a very good wine list with around 11 by the glass. They also perform civil marriage ceremonies here. *(Recommended by Mandy and Simon King, Nigel Long, Greta and Christopher Wells, Michael Doswell, Neil Woodhead, Karen and Graham Oddey, Frank and Margaret Bowles, Bill and Pat Pemberton, Andrew McElligott, Mike and Wena Stevenson, A J Bowen)*

Free house ~ Licensee Elizabeth Grayshon ~ Real ale ~ Bar food (12-2.30(3 Sun), 6-9.30) ~ Restaurant ~ (01756) 720204 ~ Children welcome ~ Open 11.30-11; 12-10.30 Sun ~ Bedrooms: £50B/£100B

BYLAND ABBEY SE5579 Map 7

Abbey Inn 🍴 🛏

The abbey has a brown tourist-attraction signpost off the A170 Thirsk—Helmsley

The hauntingly beautiful abbey ruins opposite this carefully renovated inn are all that is left of what was at one time the largest ecclesiastical building in Europe. The charming bedrooms enjoy the marvellous abbey views (which are elegant and floodlit at night), and there is plenty of room on the terrace and in the garden. The two no smoking characterful front rooms also look out at the abbey, and have big fireplaces, oak and stripped deal tables, settees, carved oak seats, and Jacobean-style dining chairs on the polished boards and flagstones, various stuffed birds, little etchings, and china cabinets, and some discreet stripping back of plaster to show the ex-abbey masonry. The Library has lots of bookshelves and a large single oak table (ideal for a party of up to 10 people), and the big back room has lots of rustic bygones; piped music. Very good varied food at lunchtime might include home-made soup (£3), sandwiches (from £3.95), ploughman's (£6.50), broccoli and almond mousse and parma ham with a red onion marmalade (£6.75), ramekin of aubergine and goats cheese with a basil and tomato vinaigrette (£7.50), pork steak with a bramble and ginger glaze or super beef in ale pie (£7.95), wild boar sausages on a bed of cheese and herb mash with cumberland sauce (£8.95), shoulder of lamb (£12), with evening dishes such as chicken liver and ginger parfait with chilli and orange chutney (£4.75), a brochette of crevettes fried in lemon grass and garlic butter with home-made garlic mayonnaise (£7), chicken breast braised in coriander and garlic on a thai salad with peanut sauce (£9.50), roasted monkfish on cheese and herb mash with deep-fried anchovies and chilli olive oil (£13), and fillet of English beef with a red wine jus and sweet potato spaghetti (£16.50). Well kept Black Sheep Bitter and Tetleys on handpump, and an interesting wine list with 8 by the glass. The grey tabby cat is called Milly. *(Recommended by Michael Doswell, June and Ken Brooks, R F Grieve, H Bramwell, Mike and Mary Carter, Walter and Susan Rinaldi-Butcher, Peter and Anne-Marie O'Malley, David and Helen Wilkins, P Hansford, Keith and Di Newsome, Steve and Sue Griffiths, Jenny and Dave Hughes, Mr and MrsC M Pearson; also in* The Good Hotel Guide*)*

Free house ~ Licensees Jane and Martin Nordli ~ Real ale ~ Bar food (not Sun evening or Mon lunchtime) ~ Restaurant ~ (01347) 868204 ~ Children in eating area of bar and restaurant ~ Open 12-3, 6.30-11; 12-4 Sun; closed Sun evening and Mon lunch ~ Bedrooms: /£70B

Real ale may be served from handpumps, electric pumps (not just the on-off switches used for keg beer) or – common in Scotland – tall taps called founts (pronounced 'fonts') where a separate pump pushes the beer up under air pressure. The landlord can adjust the force of the flow – a tight spigot gives the good creamy head that Yorkshire lads like.

CARLTON SE0684 Map 10
Foresters Arms 🍴 ♟ 🛏

Off A684 W of Leyburn, just past Wensley; or take Coverdale hill road from Kettlewell, off B6160

By the time this book is published, the long-standing licensee will probably have left this charming inn, set in a pretty village at the heart of the Yorkshire Dales National Park. We are keeping our fingers firmly crossed that whoever takes over will manage to keep the relaxed pubby atmosphere for drinkers, while still offering very good imaginative food. There are open log fires, low beamed ceilings, well kept Black Sheep Bitter and Special, and John Smiths on handpump, a fine choice of wines by the glass or carafe from a restaurany list, and up to 50 malt whiskies. Light bar lunches have included roast black pudding with dijon vinaigrette (£5.95), fish soup or baked sweet onion and coverdale cheese and onion tart (£6.50), ham and eggs (£7.95), king prawn and smoked bacon salad (£8.25), seafood risotto (£8.50), with evening bar dishes such as sun-dried tomato and herb risotto (£3.95), mussels with garlic and herb butter (£6.95), fillet of sea bream on onion marmalade with white wine sauce or pork fillet with mustard and mushroom sauce (£9.95), and puddings such as baked date, almond and armagnac tart, crème brûlée or chocolate tart with coffee bean sauce (from £3.95). The partly no smoking restaurant specialises in good fresh fish; piped music, darts, and dominoes. There are some bench seats outside among tubs of flowers; lovely views. *(Recommended by Alan J Morton, Malcolm and Jennifer Perry, Jackie Webb, Terry Mizen, Dr C C S Wilson, Comus and Sarah Elliott, Karen Eliot, Janet and Peter Race, Mr and Mrs K M Hezelgrave , Martin and Karen Wake)*

Free house ~ Licensee B Higginbotham ~ Real ale ~ Bar food (not Sun evening or Mon and Tues lunchtime) ~ Restaurant ~ (01969) 640272 ~ Well behaved children in eating area of bar; must be over 12 in restaurant in evening ~ Open 12-3, 6.30-11; 12-3, 7-10.30 Sun; closed all Mon and Tues lunchtime ~ Bedrooms: £40S/£75S

CARTHORPE SE3184 Map 10
Fox & Hounds 🍴 ♟

Village signposted from A1 N of Ripon, via B6285

With friendly, attentive staff, a fine wine list, and particularly good, enjoyable food, it is not surprising that this neatly kept, extended dining pub is doing so well; to be sure of a table it's best to book (particularly at weekends). Served by well trained staff, the interesting dishes might include a choice of home-made soups (£2.65), black pudding with caramelised apple and onion marmalade (£3.95), smoked trout fillets with horseradish sauce (£4.45), chicken breast filled with coverdale cheese in a creamy sauce (£8.95), poached Scottish salmon with hollandaise sauce (£9.25), roast rack of lamb on a blackcurrant crouton with redcurrant gravy (£11.95), and half a roasted gressingham duckling with orange sauce, parsley and thyme stuffing and apple sauce (£12.95), with daily specials like fresh salmon fishcakes (£3.95), duck filled filo pastry parcels with plum sauce (£4.95), steak and kidney pie (£7.95), prawn curry (£8.95), baked haddock with a crispy crumb crust (£9.25), and braised lamb shank with root vegetable purée or whole dressed fresh Whitby crab (£9.95), and puddings such as white chocolate cheesecake with a dark chocolate ice cream or sticky ginger sponge pudding with ginger wine and brandy sauce (£3.75). They do offer sandwiches, and three-course Sunday lunch (£11.95; children £6.95). There are some theatrical memorabilia in the corridors, and the cosy L-shaped bar has quite a few mistily evocative Victorian photographs of Whitby, a couple of nice seats by the larger of its two log fires, plush button-back built-in wall banquettes and chairs, plates on stripped beams, and some limed panelling; piped light classical music. An attractive high-raftered no smoking restaurant leads off with lots of neatly black-painted farm and smithy tools. Well kept John Smiths Bitter on handpump, and from their extensive list they will open any wine for you just to have a glass. *(Recommended by John Coatsworth, Mr and Mrs J E C Tasker, Adam and Joan Bunting, Mrs Jane Wyles, June and Ken Brooks, Gethin Lewis, Pat and Tony Martin, Michael Doswell, Peter Burton, Mr and Mrs M Pettit)*

Free house ~ Licensees Howard and Bernadette Fitzgerald ~ Real ale ~ Bar food (not Mon) ~ Restaurant ~ (01845) 567433 ~ Children welcome ~ Open 12-2.30, 7-11(10.30 Sun); closed Mon; 1st full week of New Year

CONSTABLE BURTON SE1791 Map 10
Wyvill Arms ⊗ ♀
A684 E of Leyburn

The gardens behind this creeper-covered ex-farmhouse have been landscaped, and there is now a herb and vegetable garden, and several large wooden benches with large white parasols for outdoor dining. Inside, the bar is decorated with teak and brass, with mirrors along the back of the bar, wine racks, and ornate shelving, and a bar counter which came from a bank 30 years ago. There's a mix of seating (including a 1695 mop-hair engraved-back chair won by the licensee's grandfather in a boxing match), a finely worked plaster ceiling with the Wyvill family's coat of arms, and an elaborate stone fireplace. The second bar, where food is served, has semi-circled, upholstered alcoves, a seventies juke box with music for all ages, and old oak tables; the reception area of this room includes a huge chesterfield which can seat up to eight people, another carved stone fireplace, and an old leaded church stained-glass window partition. Both rooms are hung with pictures of local scenes, most of which are prints done by the local artist, Peter Alice. Using locally supplied produce, the enjoyable home-made food includes light lunches such as soup (£2.45), scrambled egg and smoked salmon (£3.75), mediterranean risotto (£5.45), duck leg with a pear and ginger sauce (£5.75), omelettes (from £5.95), and steak and mushroom pie or gammon and eggs (£7.45), as well as marinated charred ribs with barbecue sweet and sour sauce (£4.25), spicy meatballs (£4.45), salmon and crab fishcake with a poached egg and a tangy sauce (£5.25), thai-style vegetable stir fry (£6.95), steak and onion pie (£7.95), grilled breast of chicken with leek, bacon and stilton sauce or lemon sole with chilli and red pepper butter (£8.95), fillet of pork with an apple and mint sauce and juniper butter (£9.95), braised knuckle of pork with sauerkraut, roasted garlic potatoes and a pork jus or monkfish tails wrapped in parma ham on a bed of spinach with a shi-itake red wine emulsion (£10.95), and steaks (from £12.95). Well kept Black Sheep, Boddingtons, John Smiths Bitter, and Theakstons Best on handpump, and a thoughtful wine list; cribbage and dominoes. The white bull terrier is called Tricky. *(Recommended by Jonty Willis, Pete Sturgess, Richard Greaves, Mrs E A Lamb, Mr and Mrs K M Hezelgrave)*

Free house ~ Licensee Nigel Stevens ~ Real ale ~ Bar food ~ Restaurant ~ (01677) 450581 ~ Children welcome ~ Open 11-3, 6-11; 12-3, 7-10.30 Sun; closed Mon Jan-Mar unless bookings or B&B ~ Bedrooms: £34B/£56B

COXWOLD SE5377 Map 7
Fauconberg Arms ★ ♀
Off A170 Thirsk—Helmsley, via Kilburn or Wass; easily found off A19, too

Under the new licensees, the restaurant here is being refurbished (and is now no smoking), and the front part will become a comfortable area with sofas, for drinks before a meal or coffee afterwards. The two cosy knocked-together rooms of the lounge bar have carefully chosen furniture – most of it is either Mouseman or the work of some of the other local craftsmen, or cushioned antique oak settles and windsor high-backed chairs and oak tables; there's a marvellous winter log fire in an unusual arched stone fireplace, and gleaming brass. For those wanting an informal drink and chat, there's also an old-fashioned back locals' bar; darts, dominoes, cribbage, fruit machine, TV, and piped music. Good bar food now includes home-made soup (£2.95), interestingly filled baguettes and brioche (from £4.50), chicken and mint roulade with mango and chilli salsa or potted wensleydale cheese with rhubarb chutney (£4.95), tagliatelle napoletana or smoked chicken breast with curried mayonnaise (£6.95), whitby cod in beer batter (£7.95), trio of game sausages with bubble and squeak and red onion marmalade (£8.95), duck with onion and ginger confit and tomato and chilli jam (£11.95), and puddings such as chocolate mousse, pistachio brûlée or lemon tart (£4.50); roast Sunday lunch (£7.25). Well kept John Smiths, and Theakstons Cask and Best on handpump, and an extensive wine list. This is a delightful, unchanging village with attractive tubs of flowers on the cobbled verges of the broad street, and the inn itself is named after Lord Fauconberg, who married Oliver Cromwell's daughter Mary. *(Recommended by Michael Butler, Michael Doswell, Mr and Mrs P Dix, Mrs Jane Wyles, Peter Walker, Walter and Susan Rinaldi-Butcher, Edward and Deanna Pearce)*

Free house ~ Licensees Stefan Przybylski and Julie Gough ~ Real ale ~ Bar food (12-9) ~ Restaurant ~ (01347) 868214 ~ Children welcome ~ Open 11-11; 12-10.30 Sun ~ Bedrooms: £35B/£60B

CRAY SD9379 Map 7
White Lion ◗

B6160, Upper Wharfedale N of Kettlewell

This former drovers' hostelry is the highest pub in Wharfedale (at 1,100 ft up by Buckden Pike), and the surrounding countryside is superb; in fine weather, you can sit at picnic-sets above the very quiet steep lane or on the great flat limestone slabs in the shallow stream which tumbles down opposite. Inside, the simply furnished bar has a traditional atmosphere, seats around tables on the flagstone floor, shelves of china, iron tools and so forth, a high dark beam-and-plank ceiling, and a warming open fire; there's also a no smoking dining room. Decent bar food at lunchtime (they tell us prices have not changed since last year) includes sandwiches or home-made soup (£2.75), filled giant yorkshire puddings (from £2.95), cumberland sausage (£5.95), and lasagne (£6.25), with more elaborate evening meals such as chicken and smoked bacon salad with herb vinaigrette (£3.25), vegetable curry (£6.95), poached local trout with almond butter (£7.95), and pork fillet with an apricot, redcurrant, and port sauce (£8.95). If you eat early in the evening (5.15-6.16), you get a 20% discount. Well kept Black Sheep, Moorhouses Pendle Witches Brew, Roosters, and Timothy Taylors Landlord on handpump; dominoes, cribbage, and ring the bull. *(Recommended by the Didler, Chris and Elaine Lyon, Dr A and Dr A C Jackson, Ann Williams, Tony Hughes, Derek and Sylvia Stephenson, Andy and Jill Kassube, Mr and Mrs J E C Tasker)*

Free house ~ Licensees Kevin and Debbie Roe ~ Real ale ~ Bar food ~ (01756) 760262 ~ Children in family room ~ Open 11-11; 12-10.30 Sun; closed 25 Dec ~ Bedrooms: /£45(£55S)

CRAYKE SE5670 Map 7
Durham Ox ⓦ

Off B1363 at Brandsby, towards Easingwold; West Way

The Fosse Way passes through this village, but this pub is quite a stumbling-block; once sat down to such an enjoyable lunch, you may decide that's the end of your walk. The old-fashioned lounge bar has venerable tables and antique seats and settles on the flagstones, pictures and photographs on the dark red walls, interesting satirical carvings in its panelling (which are Victorian copies of medievel pew ends), polished copper and brass, and an enormous inglenook fireplace with winter log fires (flowers in summer). In the bottom bar is a framed illustrated acount of the local history (some of it gruesome) dating back to the 12th c, and a large framed print of the original famous Durham Ox which weighed 171 stones. Some of the panelling here divides off a bustling public area which has a good lively atmosphere and more traditional furnishings. Consistently good food includes home-made soups with home-made bread (£3.95), sandwiches (from £4.95; with chips and salad), duck leg confit or yorkshire black pudding terrine with a port reduction and pickled walnuts (£4.95), main courses such as seared calves liver, beetroot mash, grilled pancetta, shallot and red wine jus or seared fillet of bass with warm spring onion, new potato and caper salad and balsamic vinegar (£12.95), sautéed loin of venison, haggis mashed potato, swede fondant and whisky sauce (£14.95), daily specials, a cheeseboard with home-made fruit cake, chutneys and local cheeses (£3.95 for two choices, £5.95 for the full cheeseboard), and delicious puddings such as coffee bean scented crème brûlée with a white chocolate water ice (£4.95). Well kept John Smiths, Tetleys, and Theakstons XB on handpump, with maybe a guest such as Charles Wells Bombardier; piped music (some feel it unnecessary), fruit machine, and dominoes. There are seats outside on a terrace and in the courtyard, and the comfortable bedrooms are in converted farm buildings (we'd be grateful for any reports on these); disabled access. The tale is that this is the hill which the Grand Old Duke of York marched his men up; the view from the hill opposite is wonderful. *(Recommended by Greta and Christopher Wells, Andrew Nesbit, Walter and Susan Rinaldi-Butcher, Marlene and Jim Godfrey)*

Free house ~ Licensee Michael Ibbotson ~ Real ale ~ Bar food ~ Restaurant ~ (01347) 821506 ~ Children in eating area of bar until 9 ~ Open 12-3, 6-11; 11-11 Sat; 12-10.30 Sun; 12-3, 6-11 Sat in winter; closed 31 Dec ~ Bedrooms: £70B/£80B

CROPTON SE7588 Map 10
New Inn ♨ ⇦

Village signposted off A170 W of Pickering

One reader was so keen to try all the own-brewed beers in this comfortably modernised and popular village inn, that he stayed the night: Two Pints, Backwoods, Honey Gold, King Billy, and Scoresby Stout which they keep well on handpump, and a guest such as Thwaites. The airy lounge has Victorian church panels, terracotta and dark blue plush seats, lots of brass, cricketing memorabilia, and a small open fire. A local artist has designed historical posters all around the no smoking downstairs conservatory. Decent var food includes soup (£2.95), sandwiches (from £2.95), garlic prawns (£3.95), ploughman's (£5.95), lasagne (£6.25), steak and mushroom in ale pie or broccoli lasagne (£6.50), chicken curry (£6.95), pork chop glazed with barbecue sauce (£8.95), and fillet steak topped with pâté (£13.95). The elegant no smoking restaurant is furnished with genuine Victorian and early Edwardian pieces. Darts, pool, dominoes, fruit machine, and piped music, There's a neat terrace, a garden with a pond, and a gift shop. *(Recommended by Geoff and Angela Jaques, Alan and Paula McCully, Kevin Thorpe, Pat and Tony Martin, C A Hall, Steve Whalley, GD, KW, Miss G Irving, R Styles, Dr Paull Khan, Peter and Anne-Marie O'Malley, Karen and Steve Brine, M J Morgan)*

Own brew ~ Licensee Sandra Lee ~ Real ale ~ Bar food (12-2, 6.30-9.30) ~ Restaurant ~ (01751) 417330 ~ Children welcome ~ Live entertainment monthly ~ Open 11-11; 12-10.30 Sun ~ Bedrooms: £35B/£62B

DACRE BANKS SE1962 Map 7
Royal Oak ♨

B6451 S of Pateley Bridge

As this 18th-c stone pub is very much a family concern, you can be sure of a warm welcome. It's basically open-plan, and the two comfortable lounge areas (one is no smoking) have interesting old photographs and poems with a drinking theme on the walls, an open fire in the front part, and well kept Rudgate Viking, and guests like Black Sheep Bitter, Daleside Old Legover, and Timothy Taylors Landlord on handpump. Generous helpings of well liked bar food include snacks such as sandwiches (from £2.75; filled baguettes from £4.50), filled baked potatoes (from £3.50), and ploughman's (£5.50), plus home-made soup (£2.50), stilton and port pâté or black pudding with apple chutney (£3.50), garlic mushrooms in ham and brandy cream sauce (£3.75), roast rib of beef with yorkshire pudding (£5.95), goats cheese and pepper parcels on a tomato and spring onion sauce (£6.50), steak and mushroom pie (£6.95), medallions of pork fillet in dijon mustard sauce (£7.95), salmon fillet in butter with garlic and Dublin Bay prawns (£8.95), roast rack of lamb with a passion fruit, redcurrant and port glaze (£9.25), and 10oz sirloin steak (£12); hearty breakfasts. The restaurant is no smoking. Darts, pool, cribbage, dominoes, and piped music. There are lovely views from the seats on the terrace and from the big garden; boules. *(Recommended by Dr and Mrs Nigel Holmes, S Horsley, Jim Abbott, John Robertson, A J Bowen, Simon Longe, Derek and Sylvia Stephenson, C W Dix, Dr Paull Khan,*

P Abbott, Howard Gregory, Michael and Rosalind Dymond, Lawrence Pearse, Graham and Lynn Mason)

Free house ~ Licensee Stephen Cock ~ Real ale ~ Bar food ~ Restaurant ~ No credit cards ~ (01423) 780200 ~ Children in eating area of bar until 9 ~ Open 12(11.30 Sat)-3, 5-11; 12-3.30, 7-10.30 Sun ~ Bedrooms: £30B/£50S

EAST WITTON SE1586 Map 10
Blue Lion ★ ⑪ 🛏️

A6108 Leyburn—Ripon

Yorkshire Dining Pub of the Year

This is a consistently first-class inn, deservedly popular, and there's always a good mix of customers keen to enjoy the top quality drinks, imaginative food, and courteous, friendly welcome – many customers choose to stay overnight. The big squarish bar has high-backed antique settles and old windsor chairs and round tables on the turkey rugs and flagstones, ham-hooks in the high ceiling decorated with dried wheat, teazles and so forth, a delft shelf filled with appropriate bric-a-brac, several prints, sporting caricatures and other pictures on the walls, a log fire, and daily papers; the friendly labrador is called Archie. Changing regularly, the excellent food might include sandwiches, home-made soup (£3.40), caesar salad with pancetta and chargrilled chicken (£4.95), thai-style crab fishcake with chilli jam (£5), corned beef hash with a fried egg (£5.25), fresh mussels baked with white wine, garlic and aromatics topped with a herb crust (£5.50), smoked wild boar sausage with bubble and squeak and red wine sauce (£5.75), fresh tagliatelle tossed with cep sauce and finished with parmesan (£8.50), steak and kidney pudding or sautéed escalope of guinea fowl with a tomato and spinach compote (£10.95), braised leg of lamb with flageolet beans and herb mash (£11.75), and poached fillet of smoked haddock on new potatoes, topped with a poached egg and toasted with gruyère (£12.25); lovely puddings and good breakfasts; no snacks on Sunday lunchtime. Well kept Black Sheep Bitter and Riggwelter, and Theakstons Best and Old Peculier, and decent wines with quite a few by the glass. Picnic-sets on the gravel outside look beyond the stone houses on the far side of the village green to Witton Fell, and there's a big, pretty back garden. *(Recommended by Tim and Sue Halstead, P Abbott, Susan and John Douglas, Trevor and Lynda Smith, Brian and Janet Ainscough, Roger Purkiss, Sarah Lynch, the Didler, Keith and Jill Wright, Greta and Christopher Wells, Jane Taylor, David Dutton, Walter and Sue Anderson, Mr and MrsC M Pearson, Jim Abbott, Mrs Jane Wyles, George Little, Philip and Susan Philcox, Terry Mizen, Mike and Maggie Betton, Mrs V Middlebrook, Darly Graton, Graeme Gulibert, N J Worthington, S L Tracy, Nigel Brewitt, Mr and Mrs J E C Tasker, Mike and Bridget Cummins, Keith Barker, Louise English, Martin and Karen Wake, Matthew Wright, Peter and Anne-Marie O'Malley, M J Morgan)*

Free house ~ Licensee Paul Klein ~ Real ale ~ Bar food ~ Restaurant ~ (01969) 624273 ~ Children in eating area of bar and restaurant ~ Open 11-11; 12-10.30 Sun ~ Bedrooms: £53.50S/£69S(£79B)

EGTON BRIDGE NZ8005 Map 10
Horse Shoe 🛏️

Village signposted from A171 W of Whitby; via Grosmont from A169 S of Whitby

Even on a wet late autumn night, this charmingly placed inn has a good, bustling atmosphere, and on a fine day, there's always a quite a crowd enjoying the lovely setting, with comfortable seats on a quiet terrace and lawn beside a little stream (where there are ducks); attractive gardens with pretty roses, mature redwoods and geese and bantams, and fishing is available on a daily ticket from Egton Estates. Plenty of surrounding walks, too. Inside, the bar has old oak tables, high-backed built-in winged settles, wall seats and spindleback chairs, a big stuffed trout (caught near here in 1913), pictures on the walls, and a warm log fire; the restaurant is no smoking. Generous helpings of well liked bar food include lunchtime sandwiches (from £2.60; lemon chicken and sun-dried tomato in a hot baguette £4.40), and dishes such as soup (£2.50), stilton mushrooms (£3.60), home-made chicken liver pâté (£3.80), gammon topped with egg and pineapple or fish pie (£7.60), tortellini stuffed with ricotta cheese, served with mediterranean olive sauce (£7.70), chicken breast with a red wine, mushroom and bacon sauce (£7.80), whole lamb shank braised with a rosemary and red wine sauce and minted mash (£8.60), sirloin steak (£12.50), daily specials such as green lip mussels in white wine and dill (£4.80) or honey-roast duck breast with berry and cassis sauce (£10.20). Well kept John Smiths and Theakstons Best, and guests from local breweries like Black Dog and Durham on handpump, and malt whiskies; darts, dominoes, and piped music. A different way to reach this beautifully placed pub is to park by the Roman Catholic church, walk through the village and cross the River Esk by stepping stones. Not to be confused with a similarly named pub up at Egton. *(Recommended by Christopher Hayle, Bill and Pat Pemberton, Mike and Wendy Proctor, Richard Cole, R Mathews, P J and Avril Hanson, Susan Sullivan)*

Free house ~ Licensees Tim and Suzanne Boulton ~ Real ale ~ Bar food (not 25 Dec) ~ Restaurant ~ (01947) 895245 ~ Children in restaurant and family room ~ Open 11.30-3(4 winter Sat), 6.30-11; all day bank holidays; 12-4. 7-10.30 Sun; closed 25 Dec ~ Bedrooms: £30S/£40(£50S)

FADMOOR SE6789 Map 10
Plough 🍴 ♀

Village signposted off A170 in or just W of Kirkbymoorside

Overlooking the quiet village green, this beautifully kept pub remains as popular as ever for its smashing food and welcoming staff. The elegantly simple little rooms have rugs on seagrass, richly upholstered furnishings, and yellow walls, well kept Black Sheep and Timothy Taylors Landlord on handpump, and an extensive wine list. Quickly served, the ample helpings of food might include sandwiches, smoked bacon and swiss cheese tartlet (£4.75), spinach, parma ham and pine nut salad (£5.50), chicken caesar salad (£5.95), sweet and sour king prawns with sweet chilli and ginger dressing (£6.50), fresh mussels (£6.75), seared king scallops on black pudding and orange sauce (£7.50), grilled venison steak on a damson risotto with red wine and grain mustard sauce (£13.75), whole bass stuffed with herbs, chinese five spice, chilli and garlic (£14.75), and puddings such as marmalade and almond sponge with custard, passion fruit and vanilla parfait, and hot chocolate brownies with hot chocolate sauce and crunchie ice cream (£3.50). The restaurant is no smoking. They have an extensive wine list with blackboard additions, and well kept Black Sheep and Timothy Taylors Landlord; shove-ha'penny, dominoes, and piped music. There's a new terrace this year. *(Recommended by Jenny and Dave Hughes, Rachel and Katie Swinden, Greta and Christopher Wells, Walter and Sue Anderson, Geoff and Sylvia Donald, Peter and Anne-Marie O'Malley, Alan and Paula McCully, Geoff and Angela Jaques, Michael Doswell)*

Holf Leisure Ltd ~ Licensee Catherine Feather ~ Real ale ~ Bar food (12-1.45, 6.30-8.45; not Tues) ~ Restaurant ~ (01751) 431515 ~ Children welcome until 9 ~ Open 12-2.30, 6.30-10.50; 12-2.30, 7-10.30 Sun; closed Tues

FERRENSBY SE3761 Map 7
General Tarleton 🍴 ♀ 🛏

A655 N of Knaresborough

Sophisticated, highly enjoyable food draws customers to this comfortable and rather smart 18th-c coaching inn. The beamed and carpeted bar has brick pillars dividing up the several different areas to create the occasional cosy alcove, some exposed stonework, and neatly framed pictures on the white walls; there's a mix of country kitchen furniture and comfortable banquettes, a big open fire, and a door leading out to a pleasant tree-lined garden with smart green tables. The imaginative bar food includes grilled goats cheese on home-made brioche with an olive and tomato salsa or parfait of chicken livers and foie gras with confit duck, chorizo, bacon lardons and various leaves, dressed with a walnut and balsamic dressing (£4.50), provençale fish soup on a shi-itake mushroom risotto with plum sugar dressing (£4.95), deep-fried garlic salted baby squid with a light salad and asian dressing (£5.95), toasted walnut bread with cream cheese, bacon and smoked salmon, and mango chutney (£6.75), award-winning sausages with mash and a rich red onion gravy (£7.95), fish hors d'oeuvres (£11.95; makes a great starter for two), chargrilled haunch of venison with creamed celeriac, wild mushrooms and a red sauce and juniper berry cream (£12.95), daily specials such as baked salmon and goats cheese en croûte with mange tout and caviar cream (£9.50), fresh red snapper on a vine-ripened tomato tart with olive oil potatoes, herb salad and pesto (£10.95) or goosnargh duck breast with chargrilled potatoes, walnuts, prunes and watercress with a red wine sauce and drizzled with honey (£12), and puddings like sticky toffee pudding, a trio of iced parfaits with a trio of sauces, and warm rich chocolate brownie with chocolate fudge sauce (from £3.75). Well kept Black Sheep Best, Tetleys and Timothy Taylors Landlord on handpump, and over 20 good wines by the glass. The courtyard eating area (and restaurant) are no smoking. Good bedrooms with their own separate entrance. *(Recommended by Malcolm and Jennifer Perry, R Mathews, Pierre and Pat Richterich, M Firth, Janet and Peter Race, Mrs and Mrs Philip Titcombe, H Bramwell, Michael Doswell, Mr and Mrs J E C Tasker, Lesley Bass, Peter and Anne-Marie O'Malley, Roger A Bellingham)*

Free house ~ Licensees John Topham and Stephen Mannock ~ Real ale ~ Bar food (12-2.15, 6-9.30) ~ Restaurant ~ (01423) 340284 ~ Children welcome ~ Open 12-3, 6-11(10.30 in winter); closed 25 Dec ~ Bedrooms: £74.95B/£84.90B

FLAMBOROUGH TA2270 Map 8
Seabirds

Junction B1255/B1229

Handy for visiting the seabird colonies at Bempton Cliffs, this straightforward village pub offers a friendly welcome to regulars and visitors. The public bar has quite a shipping theme, and leading off here the comfortable lounge has a whole case of stuffed seabirds along one wall, as well as pictures and paintings of the local landscape, and a woodburning stove. Bar food at lunchtime includes sandwiches, soup (£1.95), giant yorkshire pudding filled with onion gravy (£2.85), omelettes (from £4.95), leek and mushroom crumble (£6.15), and haddock mornay (£6.75), with evening dishes such as hot and spicy marinated Whitby creel prawns in breadcrumbs (£4.95), chicken kiev (£7.95), and steaks (from £11.15), with daily specials like fresh local crab, liver, bacon and sausage casserole, tagliatelle with rich tomato, seafood and cream sauce or roast duck breast on a bed of celeriac mash with marmalade sauce (from around £5.50). Best to book for Sunday lunchtime. Well kept John Smiths and a weekly changing guest on handpump, and a decent wine list. Friendly, hardworking staff; dominoes and piped music. There are seats in the sizeable garden, and you can eat out here in fine weather. *(Recommended by Eric Locker, C and R Bromage, Paul Craddock)*

Free house ~ Licensee Jean Riding ~ Real ale ~ Bar food (not Sun evening) ~ Restaurant ~ (01262) 850242 ~ Well behaved children in restaurant ~ Open 11.30-3, 7(6.30 Sat)-11; 12-3, 8-10.30 Sun; closed Mon evening in winter

GOOSE EYE SE0340 Map 7
Turkey

High back road Haworth—Sutton-in-Craven, and signposted from back roads W of Keighley; OS Sheet 104 map reference 028406

You can visit the microbrewery in this friendly pub and see where they brew their four real ales – they ask for a donation for Upper Wharfedale Fell Rescue – Turkey Bitter, Lost John's, Dow Cave, and Black Shiver, plus a guest such as Greene King Abbot on handpump, and 40 whiskies. There are various cosy and snug alcoves, brocaded upholstery, and walls covered with pictures of surrounding areas; the restaurant is no smoking. Generous helpings of decent bar food include home-made soup (£2.10), sandwiches (from £3.50), giant yorkshire pudding with roast beef and gravy (£4), home-made pie (£5.80), steaks (from £6.20), home-made daily specials (£5.40), and puddings (from £2.40); Sunday lunch (£5.80); children's meals (£3.20);

noticeable piped music. A separate games area has pool, fruit machine, cribbage and dominoes. (Recommended by Geoffrey and Brenda Wilson, B, M and P Kendall, Andy and Jill Kassube, Dr B and Mrs P B Baker, Dr C C S Wilson)

Free house ~ Licensees Harry and Monica Brisland ~ Real ale ~ Bar food (not Mon; all day Sun) ~ Restaurant ~ No credit cards ~ (01535) 681339 ~ Children in eating area of bar and in restaurant until 9 ~ Open 12-3(4.30 Sat), 5.30(7 Sat)-11; 12-10.30 Sun; closed Mon lunch except bank holidays

HAROME SE6582 Map 10
Star ⊕ ♀
Village signposted S of A170, E of Helmsley

For those not wanting to drive home after a delicious meal in this pretty 14th-c thatched inn, you can now stay in one of the two bedrooms in their nearby thatched 15th-c cottage. The interior of the pub is charming, with a dark bowed beam-and-plank ceiling, well polished tiled kitchen range, plenty of bric-a-brac, interesting furniture (this was the first pub that 'Mousey Thompson' ever populated with his famous dark wood furniture), two wonderful log fires, daily papers and magazines, and a no smoking dining room; the coffee loft in the eaves is popular. For the excellent, inventive food, fish is delivered daily from Hartlepool, they grow their own herbs and some vegetables, use local hen, duck, and guinea fowl eggs, and three types of honey from the village; they also offer 15 British cheeses. Changing daily, the dishes might include sandwiches, spring green soup with smoked bacon dumplings (£2.95), terrine of boiled gammon with a fried quail egg, spiced pineapple pickle, and mustard seed dressing (£4.95), shallow-fried kipper croquettes with tartare velouté, flat parsley, and anchovy salad (£5.50; main course £9.95), a plate of marinated spring vegetables with cauliflower purée and roast almond cream (£5.95), grilled queen scallops with avocado fritters and smoked bacon (£7.95; main course £12.95), breast of corn-fed guinea fowl with celeriac purée, fairy ring mushrooms, tarragon and dry sherry (£10.95), warm salad of locally reared duck with wild turnip rösti and raisin stuffing (£12.50), roast loin of suckling pig with cider potato, sage, and black pudding stuffing, and cider brandy sauce (£13.50), fillet of brill with a deep-fried scampi fritter, pea purée, and cherry tomato ketchup (£13.95), and puddings like baked ginger parkin with rhubarb ripple ice cream and hot spiced syrup, sticky plum pudding with cognac custard and apple brandy compote or caramelised fresh lemon tart with a sauce of raspberries (from £4.50); good, helpful service. Well kept Black Sheep, John Smiths, Theakstons Best, and a guest like Black Sheep Riggwelter on handpump, farm ciders, freshly squeezed juices, home-made rhubarb schnapps or bramble vodka, and quite a few wines by the glass from a fairly extensive wine list. There are some seats and tables on a sheltered front terrace with more in the garden with fruit trees and a big ash behind. They have a village cricket team. (Recommended by Richard Kennell, B, M and P Kendall, Peter Walker, Peter Burton, Walter and Susan Rinaldi-Butcher, R F Grieve, Peter and Anne-Marie O'Malley, Roger S Kiddier, Shaun Pinchbeck, Marlene and Jim Godfrey, Kevin Blake, Walter and Sue Anderson, Greta and Christopher Wells, Keith and Margaret Kettell, Peter Lewis, Mrs and Mrs Philip Titcombe)

Free house ~ Licensees Andrew and Jacquie Pern ~ Real ale ~ Bar food (11.30-2, 6.30-9.30; 12-6 Sun; not Sun evening, not Mon) ~ Restaurant ~ (01439) 770397 ~ Children welcome ~ Open 11.30-3, 6.15(6 Sat)-11; 12-10.30 Sun; closed Mon; 1 wk Nov; 3 wks Jan ~ Bedrooms: £45B/£90B

HEATH SE3519 Map 7
Kings Arms
Village signposted from A655 Wakefield—Normanton – or, more directly, turn off to the left opposite Horse & Groom

There are seats along the front of this old-fashioned pub facing the green, which is surrounded by stone merchants' houses of the 19th c; picnic-sets on a side lawn, and a nice walled flower-filled garden. Inside, the gas lighting adds a lot to the atmosphere, and the original bar has a fire burning in the old black range (with a long row of smoothing irons on the mantelpiece), plain elm stools and oak settles built into the walls, and dark panelling. A more comfortable extension has carefully preserved the original style, down to good wood-pegged oak panelling (two embossed with royal arms), and a high shelf of plates; there are also two other small flagstoned rooms, and the conservatory opens on to the garden. Good value bar food includes sandwiches (from £1.50), home-made soup (£1.75), vegetable curry (£3.75), omelettes (from £3.50), lamb casserole, home-made lasagne or battered haddock (£4.75), puddings (£2.25), and children's meals (£2.55). As well as cheap Clarks Bitter, they also serve guests like Clarks Festival, Tetleys Bitter, and Timothy Taylors Landlord on handpump. *(Recommended by Derek and Sylvia Stephenson, the Didler, Alan Kilpatrick, M Joyner)*

Wakefield Pub Co ~ Manager Alan Tate ~ Real ale ~ Bar food (12-2, 6-9.30; 12-8.30 Sun) ~ (01924) 377527 ~ Children in eating area of bar and restaurant ~ Open 11.30-3, 5.30-11; 11.30-11 Sat; 12-10.30 Sun

HECKMONDWIKE SE2223 Map 7
Old Hall

New North Road; B6117 between A62 and A638; OS Sheet 104 map reference 214244

This interesting, historic building was once the home of Nonconformist scientist Joseph Priestley. It was built in the 15th c, though the outer walls were replaced by stone in the 16th c, and inside there are lots of old beams and timbers, latticed mullioned windows with worn stone surrounds, brick or stripped old stone walls hung with pictures of Richard III, Henry VII, Katherine Parr, and Joseph Priestley, and comfortable furnishings. Snug low-ceilinged alcoves lead off the central part with its high ornate plaster ceiling, and an upper gallery room, under the pitched roof, looks down on the main area through timbering 'windows'; one area is no smoking. Bar food includes filled rolls (from £2.75), a pie of the day, vegetable lasagne, chicken curry or chilli con carne (all £4.95), good beer-battered haddock (£6.25), gammon and egg (£6.95), rump steak (£7.45), and puddings such as fruit crumbles or pies (£1.95). Well kept (and cheap) Sam Smiths OB on handpump; fruit machine, piped music, and maybe sports or music quizzes on Tuesday night and a general knowedge one on Thursday evening. *(Recommended by Michael Butler, Bernie Adams, John Knighton, Marlene and Jim Godfrey)*

Sam Smiths ~ Manager Robert Green ~ Real ale ~ Bar food (12-2, 6-9; 12-4.30 Sun) ~ (01924) 404774 ~ Children welcome ~ Open 11-11; 12-10.30 Sun

HETTON SD9558 Map 7
Angel ★ ⑪ ♀

Just off B6265 Skipton—Grassington

This particularly well run place remains a firm favourite with many of our readers. The car park is usually full by 11.45, but despite its popularity, the bar staff greet everyone on arrival and remain efficient and welcoming throughout; they now take bookings and use a blackboard to chalk up a waiting list. The first class, imaginative food is what customers have come to enjoy (though the range of drinks is excellent, too): home-made black pudding with crisp pancetta and braised puy lentils (£4.95), grilled goats cheese on toasted ciabatta with a black olive and tomato salsa (£5.25), little moneybags (seafood baked in a crisp pastry bag with lobster sauce, £5.50), home-cured and air dried beef with rocket, parmesan and virgin oil (£6.50), local cornfed chicken breast wrapped in air dried ham on a bed of celeriac and tarragon chicken jus (£11.95), roast breast of goosnargh duckling with corn syrup and ginger, garnished with spring onions and shi-itake mushrooms or seared fillet of bass on a crisp tomato tart, rocket salad, drizzled with pesto (£13.95), roast loin of yorkshire dales lamb and seared kidneys with creamed spinach and roast garlic (£14.50), daily specials such as cream of roast butternut squash soup (£3.50), queen scallops baked in garlic butter and gruyère (£4.95; main course £7.50), award winning pork sausage with rich onion gravy (£7.95), poached fillet of smoked haddock, spinach, slow roast tomatoes, and hollandaise sauce (£8.25), Italian antipasti (£9.25), and puddings like chocolate brownie cheesecake, crème brûlée or warm bread and butter pudding (from £4.50). Well kept Black Sheep Bitter, Tetleys, and Timothy Taylors Landlord and Golden Best on handpump, 300 wines (with 25 by the glass, including champagne), and a good range of malt whiskies. The four timbered and panelled rambling rooms have lots of cosy alcoves, comfortable country-kitchen chairs or button-back green plush seats, Ronald Searle wine snob cartoons and older engravings and photographs, log fires, and in the main bar, a Victorian farmhouse range in the big stone fireplace; the snug and bar lounge are no smoking (as is the main restaurant). Wooden seats and tables under colourful sunshades on the terrace. *(Recommended by Mike and Bridget Cummins, Dr David Cockburn, Brian Kneale, WAH, Mandy and Simon King, Steve Whalley, John and Christine Lowe, Revd D Glover, RJH, Mr and Mrs J E C Tasker, Paul Boot, Peter Burton, Geoffrey and Brenda Wilson, Greta and Christopher Wells, P Abbott)*

Free house ~ Licensees Denis Watkins and John Topham ~ Real ale ~ Bar food (12-2.15, 6-9) ~ Restaurant ~ (01756) 730263 ~ Well behaved children welcome ~ Open 12-3, 6-10.30(11 Sat); closed 1 week Jan

HUBBERHOLME SD9178 Map 7

George

Village signposted from Buckden; about 1 mile NW

The road through this little village is the highest in the Dales, reaching 1,934 ft, and this unspoilt old inn is near the ancient church where J B Priestley's ashes are scattered (this was his favourite pub). The two neat and cosy rooms have genuine character: heavy beams supporting the dark ceiling-boards, walls stripped back to bare stone and hung with antique plates and photographs, seats (with covers to match the curtains) around shiny copper-topped tables on the flagstones, and an open stove in the big fireplace. Good, wholesome bar food at lunchtime includes filled yorkshire puddings (from £2.60), filled rolls (£2.95), ploughman's (£4.95), tagliatelle with chicken and asparagus in a cream sauce (or minus the chicken; £6.50), gammon and eggs (£6.90), and halibut steak in herb butter (£8.95), with evening dishes such as brie wedges with a fruity dip (£4.20), prawn cocktail (£5.25), steak and kidney pie or vegetable moussaka (£6.95), steaks (from £8.95), and breast of duck in a raspberry and red wine sauce or dales lamb chops in rosemary and garlic gravy (£9.95), and daily specials like somerset pork (£8.95) or lamb shank in red wine sauce (£9.95). Very well kept Black Sheep Bitter and Special, and Tetleys on handpump; darts, dominoes, cribbage, and backgammon. There are seats and tables outside looking over the moors and River Wharfe – where they have fishing rights. *(Recommended by MJVK, Kevin Thorpe, John Robertson, Nigel Long, Walter and Susan Rinaldi-Butcher, Mike and Maggie Betton, Adrian and Felicity Smith, Shaun Pinchbeck, Dr and Mrs Jackson, Ann Williams, Tony Hughes, David Dutton, Jane Taylor)*

Free house ~ Licensees Jenny and Terry Browne ~ Real ale ~ Bar food (12-2, 6.30-8.45) ~ (01756) 760223 ~ Children in eating area of bar ~ Open 11.30-3, 6-11; 12-3, 6.30-10.30 Sun; closed 2nd 2 wks Jan ~ Bedrooms: £28(£37S)(£40B)/£42(£56S)(£60B)

HULL TA0927 Map 8

Minerva 🍺

Park at top of pedestrianised area at top of Queen's St and walk over Nelson St or turn off Queen's St into Wellington St, right into Pier St and pub is at top; no parking restrictions wknds, 2-hour stay Mon-Fri

As the front of this handsome pub faces the River Humber, you can sit outside, and on the piers on each side, and watch the boats in the bustling marina. The several rooms ramble all the way round a central servery, and are filled with comfortable seats, quite a few interesting photographs and pictures of old Hull (with two attractive wash drawings by Roger Davis) and a big chart of the Humber; one room is no smoking during mealtimes. A tiny snug has room for just three people, and a back room (which looks out to the marina basin) houses a profusion of varnished woodwork; two coal fires in winter. They hold three beer festivals a year – at Easter, mid-July, and whenever the Sea Shanty Festival is on – August/September. Otherwise, they keep Tetleys, Timothy Taylors Landlord, and a changing guest from maybe Abbeydale, Barnsley or Oakham on handpump. Good sized helpings of straightforward bar food such as filled baked potatoes (from £2.50), baguettes (from £2.75), salad platters (from £4.25), home-made steak in ale pie or lasagne (£4.45), popular huge battered haddock (£4.85), barbecue chicken (£5.25), and puddings (£2.25); daily specials, Sunday roast (£4.45), and Wednesday curry nights. The lounge is no smoking when food is being served. Dominoes, cribbage, fruit machine, TV, and piped music. *(Recommended by Peter F Marshall, the Didler, Pat and Tony Martin, Brian and Pat Wardrobe, David Carr)*

Punch ~ Managers Eamon and Kathy Scott ~ Real ale ~ Bar food (not Fri/Sat/Sun evenings) ~ (01482) 326909 ~ Children in eating area of bar if eating ~ Open 11-11; 12-10.30 Sun; closed 25 Dec

Olde White Harte ★ £

Off 25 Silver Street, a continuation of Whitefriargate (see previous entry); pub is up narrow passage beside the jewellers' Barnby and Rust, and should not be confused with the much more modern White Hart nearby

This is a fine place for eating Hull cheese (an 18th-c euphemism for enjoying a great deal to drink – the town was known then for its very strong ales). The curved copper-topped counter serves well kept Banks's, Hull Bitter, Marstons Pedigree, McEwans 80/- and Theakstons Old Peculier on handpump; friendly staff. The six bars have some fine features. The downstairs one has attractive stained-glass windows that look out above the bow window seat, carved heavy beams support black ceiling boards, and there are two big brick inglenooks with a frieze of delft tiles; shove-ha'penny, fruit machine, table skittles, cribbage, and dominoes. Straightforward bar snacks plus daily specials. It was in the heavily panelled room up the oak staircase that in 1642 the town's governor Sir John Hotham made the fateful decision to lock the nearby gate against Charles I, depriving him of Hull's arsenal; it didn't do him much good, as in the Civil War that followed, Hotham, like the king, was executed by the parliamentarians. There are seats in the courtyard, and outside heaters. *(Recommended by Richard Lewis, the Didler, Peter F Marshall, David Carr)*

Scottish Courage ~ Lease Brian and Jenny Cottingham ~ Real ale ~ Bar food (not evenings) ~ Restaurant ~ No credit cards ~ (01482) 326363 ~ Children in eating area of bar and restaurant ~ Open 11-11; 12-10.30 Sun

KETTLESING SE2256 Map 7
Queens Head ♀ ◖

Village signposted off A59 W of Harrogate

The landlord's kindness and helpfulness extended, on one occasion, to arranging for a mechanic to make a minor car repair to a customer's vehicle while they enjoyed a meal. There's a good atmosphere in the L-shaped carpeted main bar, and lots of quite close-set elm and other tables around its walls, with cushioned country seats. It's decorated with Victorian song sheet covers, lithographs of Queen Victoria, little heraldic shields, and a delft shelf of blue and white china. Nicely presented good value food, very popular on weekday lunchtimes with older people, includes a special three-course lunch (£6.95), plus filled yorkshire puddings (from £2.75), sandwiches (from £2.95; fillet steak £3.50; super hot chicken and bacon £3.95), home-made soup (£2.75), omelettes (£4.50), and home-made battered haddock (£5.95), with evening dishes such as chicken liver pâté with port and smoked bacon (£3.95), grilled lamb or pork chops (£7.95), steaks (from £10.50), and daily specials like wild boar and apple sausage, salmon fillet with a herb crust and parsley butter (£6.95), chicken breast with mushrooms, bacon and red wine sauce (£8.95), lemon sole with a tomato, caper and lemon butter (£9.50), and medallions of beef with peppercorn sauce (£11.50); three-course Sunday lunch (£8.95). The atmosphere is quietly chatty (there may be unobtrusive piped radio), and there are coal or log fires at each end. A smaller bar on the left, with built-in red banquettes, has cricketing prints and cigarette cards, coins and banknotes, and in the lobby there's a life-size portrait of our present Queen; piped music, dominoes, and table skittles. Well kept Black Sheep Bitter, Theakstons Old Peculier and a quickly changing guest from local breweries such as Roosters on handpump, good house wines, and quick service. There are benches out in front, by the quiet village lane. More reports please. *(Recommended by B, M and P Kendall, Patricia A Bruce, F J Robinson, Hugh A MacLean)*

Free house ~ Licensee Glen Garbutt ~ Real ale ~ Bar food (11.30-1.45, 6.30-9.45) ~ Restaurant ~ (01423) 770263 ~ Children welcome anywhere during week, in back room weekends ~ Open 11-11; 12-10.30 Sun ~ Bedrooms: £52.87B/£76.37B

KIRKBYMOORSIDE SE6987 Map 10
George & Dragon
Market place

This 17th-c coaching inn has a good bustling atmosphere on Wednesdays, when this pretty, small town has its market day. The pubby front bar has leather chesterfields as well as the brass-studded solid dark red leatherette armchairs set around polished wooden tables, dark green walls and panelling stripped back to its original pitch pine, horsebrasses hung along the beams, newspapers to read, and a blazing log fire; piped music. There's also an attractive beamed bistro, and a no smoking restaurant. Well presented, enjoyable bar food at lunchtime includes good sandwiches, soup (£2.50), wild mushroom and chicken liver parfait (3.50), thai crab cakes with oriental vegetables (£3.95), smoked haddock croquettes with a warm lentil sauce (£5.50), spicy couscous baklava with sour cream and cucumber dressing (£5.45), and roasted knuckle of pork with a sharp plum sauce or marinated chicken on a sizzling platter and home-made paratha bread (£6.95). Well kept Black Sheep Bitter, Tetleys, and a guest beer on handpump, and a good wine list. There are seats under umbrellas in the back courtyard and a surprisingly peaceful walled garden for residents to use. The bedrooms are in a converted cornmill and old vicarage at the back of the pub. *(Recommended by Shaun Pinchbeck, Walter and Sue Anderson, Peter and Anne-Marie O'Malley, Alan and Paula McCully, Canon David Baxter, M J Bastin, S and D Moir, Comus and Sarah Elliott, Steve and Sue Griffiths, Susan and Nigel Wilson, Robert and Susan Whitehead, M J Morgan)*

Free house ~ Licensee Elaine Walker ~ Real ale ~ Bar food (12-2.15, 6.30-9.15) ~ Restaurant ~ (01751) 433334 ~ Children in eating area of bar and restaurant ~ Open 10-11; 12-10.30 Sun ~ Bedrooms: £49S/£79B

KIRKHAM SE7466 Map 7
Stone Trough
Kirkham Abbey

Several beamed and cosy rooms in this welcoming inn have warm log fires, a friendly atmosphere, and well kept Black Sheep Bitter, Tetleys, Timothy Taylors Landlord, and a guest such as Greene King Old Speckled Hen, Marstons Pedigree, and Theakstons Old Peculier on handpump; 8 wines by the large glass. Changing regularly, the well presented and very good bar food might include home-made soup (£3.50), sandwiches (from £3.50; home-roast rib of beef £3.95), pork, chicken and apricot terrine wrapped in bacon with tomato chutney and toasted brioche (£4.50), salad of mediterranean vegetables with chorizo, feta cheese and olives (£4.75), bangers and mash with real ale onion gravy (£6.50), smoked haddock fishcakes with lemon butter sauce and home-made chips (£6.75), farfalle pasta with wild mushrooms, tarragon and brandy, topped with parmesan shavings (£6.95), slow roast shoulder of lamb with redcurrant and rosemary gravy on herb mash (£8.25), chargrilled salmon escalope with sliced new potatoes, spinach and leeks in a white wine and cream sauce (£8.50), rib-eye steak with a roast garlic and thyme butter (£10.95), and puddings such as chocolate sponge with bitter chocolate sauce, caramelised banana and pecan cheesecake and fresh fruit tart with raspberry coulis (from £3.95). They stop serving bar food earlyish in the evening so the no smoking restaurant (which has a fire in an old-fashioned kitchen range) can take over; the cat is called Crumble. Pool, fruit machine, dominoes, shove-ha'penny, and piped music; TV in the pool room. From the seats outside, there are lovely views down the valley, and the inn is handy for Kirkham Abbey and Castle Howard. More reports please. *(Recommended by Mrs Dickinson, Shaun Pinchbeck, Mrs K McManus)*

Free house ~ Licensees Sarah and Adam Richardson ~ Real ale ~ Bar food (12-2, 6.30-7.30(8.30 Sun)) ~ Restaurant ~ (01653) 618713 ~ Well behaved children welcome ~ Open 12-2.30, 6-11(12 summer Sat); 11.45-11(10.30 in winter) Sun; closed Mon except bank holidays; 25 Dec

LANGTHWAITE NY9902 Map 10
Charles Bathurst 🍴 🍺 🛏

Arkengarthdale, a mile N towards Tan Hill; generally known as the CB Inn

To make the most of the very good, imaginative food here, you should stay overnight in comfortable and extra pretty bedrooms. This is a lovely – if bleak – spot, with wonderful views over Langthwaite village and Arkengarthdale, and there are plenty of surrounding walks; walkers and their well behaved dogs are welcome. Appropriately stolid from the outside, but warmly welcoming inside, this converted cottage has been knocked through to make a long bar with clean and uplifting décor, light pine scrubbed tables, country chairs and benches on stripped floors, plenty of snug alcoves, and a roaring fire. The island bar counter has well kept Black Sheep Bitter and Riggwelter, John Smiths and and a guest like Theakstons Best on handpump, and a short but interesting list of wines; piped music, darts, pool, TV, cribbage and dominoes. Using local ingredients and cooked by the licensee, the impressive food might include filled baguettes (from £3.25; hot tomato, mushroom and mozzarella £3.65), tuscan bean soup or liver and orange pâté (£3.85), smoked herring and sweet pepper salad with avocado (£3.95), thai spare ribs (£4.25), steak and kidney pie (£7), dry smoked loin of bacon with dijon glaze (£7.20), smoked cod fishcake with poached egg and hollandaise (£7.60), locally shot game pie (in season, £8.75), fresh dressed crab with minted new potatoes (£9.30), and shank of local lamb with lentil cake and juniper jus, grilled fillet of bass on baby leaf spinach and gruyère sauce or guinea fowl, boned and stuffed, with lime, ham and madeira jus (£10.50). At busy times of year you may need to book a table; the dining room is no smoking. Service is quick and attentive. *(Recommended by Chris and Fiona Whitton, Jane Gilbert, Geoffrey and Brenda Wilson, John Coatsworth, Mr and Mrs Maurice Thompson, A S and P E Marriott)*

Free house ~ Licensees Charles and Stacy Cody ~ Real ale ~ Bar food ~ Restaurant ~ (01748) 884567 ~ Children welcome ~ Open 11-11; 3-11 Mon-Thurs during Dec-Feb; 12-10.30 Sun ~ Bedrooms: /£60B

LASTINGHAM SE7391 Map 10
Blacksmiths Arms 🍺

Off A170 W of Pickering at Wrelton, forking off Rosedale road N of Cropton; or via Appleton or Hutton-le-Hole

A friendly new licensee has taken over this litle pub, set opposite a lovely Saxon church in an attractive village. They've carefully refurbished throughout but there's still a cosily old-fashioned beamed bar with a log fire in an open range, traditional furnishings, well kept Black Sheep Bitter and Theakstons Best and Black Bull on handpump. Enjoyable home-made bar food includes soup (£2.50), wholemeal hoagies or filled baguettes (from £3.25), broccoli pancakes with cheese sauce or stir-fried vegetables in a filo pastry parcel (£6.55), roast beef with yorkshire pudding (£6.75), lamb and mint pie (£7.25), fish pie (£7.50), chicken dijon (£7.95), fresh baked salmon with tiger prawns (£8.75), half a honey roast duck with tangy orange sauce (£9.65), and puddings such as lemon sponge, Tia Maria tower with kiwi fruit or sticky toffee pudding (£3.25); the dining room is no smoking. Darts, cribbage and dominoes. The surrounding countryside is lovely and there are tracks through Cropton Forest. *(Recommended by Mrs K L Heath, John Foord, Peter Lewis, Dr Paull Khan, S and D Moir)*

Free house ~ Licensee Craig Miller ~ Real ale ~ Bar food (12-2.30, 7-9.15) ~
Restaurant ~ (01751) 417247 ~ Children welcome ~ Open 12-3, 7-11(10.30 Sun) ~
Bedrooms: /£50B

LEDSHAM SE4529 Map 7
Chequers

Claypit Lane; a mile W of A1, some 4 miles N of junction M62

Doing particularly well, this friendly stone-built village pub has welcoming licensees who make everyone feel at home. The old-fashioned little central panelled-in servery has several small, individually decorated rooms leading off, with low beams, lots of cosy alcoves, newspapers to read, a number of toby jugs, log fires, and a good bustling atmosphere. Enjoyable bar food includes home-made soup (£2.95), sandwiches (from £4.25), chicken liver pâté (£3.95), home-made steak and mushroom pie or sausage and mash (£8.95), warm pastry tartlet filled with roasted mediterranean vegetables (£9.35), chicken breast with mango, pink grapefruit and orange (£10.35), daily specials such as goats cheese salad (£3.95), vegetable stir fry (£10.45), and pork loin medallions (£10.95), and puddings such as bread and butter pudding or creamy wedge of cheesecake (from £3.45), ploughman's (£4.85), scrambled eggs and smoked salmon (£5.50), home-made steak and mushroom pie (£7.25), generous grilled gammon and two eggs (£7.95), daily specials such as lamb trio with mint and raspberry or chicken cordon bleu (£9.45), calves liver lyonnaise (£9.75), turbot in white wine and prawn sauce (£10.35), and sirloin steak with wild mushroom sauce (£10.45). They brew their own Brown Cow Best Bitter and Simpsons No 4, and keep John Smiths and Theakstons Best on handpump. A sheltered two-level terrace behind the house has tables among roses, and the hanging baskets and flowers are very pretty. *(Recommended by Mr and Mrs T B Staples, E A Thwaite, B, M and P Kendall, Philip and June Caunt, R J Herd, J C Burley, the Didler, Richard Cole, Malcolm and Jennifer Perry, R T and J C Moggridge, IHR, Shaun Pinchbeck, R M Corlett, George Little, Michael Jefferson, Pat and Tony Martin, Neil and Anita Christopher, Greta and Christopher Wells, Jenny and Dave Hughes)*

Own brew ~ Licensee Chris Wraith ~ Real ale ~ Bar food (12-9.15; not Sun) ~
Restaurant ~ (01977) 683135 ~ Children in restaurant ~ Open 11-11; closed Sun

LEEDS SE3033 Map 7
Whitelocks ★ £

Turks Head Yard; alley off Briggate, opposite Debenhams and Littlewoods; park in shoppers' car park and walk

Not many city centre pubs remain as splendidly preserved as this bustling place. It has hardly changed since 1886, and the long and narrow old-fashioned bar has polychrome tiles on the bar counter, stained-glass windows and grand advertising mirrors, and red button back plush banquettes and heavy copper-topped cast-iron tables squeezed down one side. And although it might be best to get here outside peak times as it does get packed, the friendly staff are quick and efficient. Good, reasonably priced bar food includes giant yorkshire puddings (from £1.95), sandwiches (from £2.45), and tasty shepherds's pie, home-made steak and potato pie or vegetable or meaty lasagne (£2.45); after 8pm, they only serve sandwiches. Well kept Greene King Old Speckled Hen and Ruddles, John Smiths, and Theakstons Best, XB and Old Peculier on handpump. At the end of the long narrow yard another bar is done up in Dickensian style. *(Recommended by Ted and Jan Whitfield, D B, Alan J Morton, the Didler, Janet and Peter Race, Dr David Cockburn, David Carr, Edward Leetham, Andy and Jill Kassube, Mike Ridgway, Sarah Miles)*

Scottish Courage ~ Manager Toby Flint ~ Real ale ~ Bar food (all day) ~ Restaurant ~
(0113) 245 3950 ~ Children in top bar at lunchtime ~ Open 11-11; 12-10.30 Sun

---

You can send us reports through our web site: www.goodguides.com

LEVISHAM SE8391 Map 10

Horseshoe

Pub and village signposted from A169 N of Pickering

Set at the top of a lovely unspoilt village and surrounded by plenty of walks, this neatly kept, traditional pub makes a good spot for lunch; there are picnic-sets on the attractive village green. The bar has brocaded seats, a log fire in the stone fireplace, bar billiards, and well kept Theakstons Best, XB and Old Peculier on handpump, quite a few malt whiskies, and reasonably priced food such as home-made soup, sandwiches, home-made chicken liver pâté, ploughman's, sausages with rich red wine and onion gravy, and steak and kidney in ale pie; the dining room is no smoking. Bar billiards, dominoes, and piped music. More reports please.
(Recommended by Geoff and Angela Jaques, Brian and Pat Wardrobe, Kathryn Gradwell)

Free house ~ Licensees Brian and Helen Robshaw ~ Real ale ~ Bar food (not winter Mon) ~ No credit cards ~ (01751) 460240 ~ Children in eating area of bar and restaurant ~ Open 11-3, 6-11; 12-3, 6-10.30 Sun; closed winter Mon ~ Bedrooms: £28/£56S

LEYBURN SE1191 Map 10

Sandpiper 🍴

Just off Market Place

This is an enjoyable little 17th-c stone cottage, whether you are dropping in for a quick drink (which in good weather can be had at white cast-iron tables on the front terrace amidst the lovely hanging baskets and flowering climbers), or planning a more leisurely meal. The bar has a couple of black beams in the low ceiling, antlers, and a few tables and chairs, and the back room up three steps has attractive Dales photographs. Down by the nice linenfold panelled bar counter there are stuffed sandpipers, more photographs and a woodburning stove in the stone fireplace; to the left is the no smoking restaurant. At lunchtime, the good food might include sandwiches (from £2.10; steak with coleslaw £4.25), sausage and mash (£5.60), smoked chicken and caesar salad (£5.95), omelettes (from £6.25), chicken in red wine with button onions, mushrooms, and black bacon (£6.75), and crispy duck leg salad with oriental dressing (£9.50); in the evening there might be game terrine with warm brioche (£4), seared scallop with a celeriac purée (£6.50), pasta with wilted greens and feta (£8.75), pot roasted rabbit with wild mushrooms (£8.95), grilled tuna with caramelised shallots (£10.75), moroccan spiced lamb with couscous (£10.95), and roasted salmon salad with lemon (£6.95). Puddings like raspberry and almond tart with clotted cream, crème brûlée or sticky toffee pudding with butterscotch sauce (from £3.30). Well kept Black Sheep Bitter, Dent Aviator, and Theakstons Bitter on handpump, around 100 malt whiskies, and a decent wine list; piped music. *(Recommended by Alan J Morton, Janet and Peter Race, Margaret and Roy Randle, Ted Tomiak, P Abbott, Darly Graton, Graeme Gulibert, Carol and Dono Leaman, Mr and Mrs K M Hezelgrave, Jack and Heather Coyle, Terry Mizen, Jim Abbott, Louise English)*

Free house ~ Licensees Jonathan and Michael Harrison ~ Real ale ~ Bar food (lunchtime) ~ Restaurant ~ (01969) 622206 ~ Children in eating area of bar but must leave restaurant by 8pm ~ Open 11.30-3, 6.30-11; 12-2.30, 7-10.30 Sun; closed Mon (except bank holidays) ~ Bedrooms: /£55S(£60B)

LINTHWAITE SE1014 Map 7

Sair 🍺

Hoyle Ing, off A62; 3½ miles after Huddersfield look out for two water storage tanks (painted with a shepherd scene) on your right – the street is on your left, burrowing very steeply up between works buildings; OS Sheet 110 map reference 101143

The large choice of own-brewed ales on handpump continues to draw in customers to this unspoilt and old-fashioned pub: Linfit Bitter, Dark Mild, Special, Gold Medal, Cascade, Special, Old Eli, Leadboiler, Autumn Gold, and the redoubtable Enochs Hammer; occasionally they replace Cascade with Swift, Ginger Beer,

Janet St Porter, Smoke House Ale, Springbok Bier or Xmas Ale. Weston's farm cider and a few malt whiskies; weekend sandwiches. The four rooms are furnished with pews or smaller chairs on the rough flagstones or carpet; there are bottle collections, beermats tacked to beams, and roaring log fires; one room is no smoking. The room on the left has shove-ha'penny, dominoes, and cribbage; piano players welcome. There are more seats in front of the pub this year, and a striking view down the Colne Valley. The Huddersfield Narrow Canal is being restored, and the section through Slaithwaite is now open; in the 3½ miles from Linthwaite to the highest, deepest, and longest tunnel in Britain, are 25 working locks and some lovely countryside. More reports please. *(Recommended by the Didler)*

Own brew ~ Licensee Ron Crabtree ~ Real ale ~ Bar food ~ (01484) 842370 ~ Children welcome in 3 rooms away from bar ~ Open 7(5 Fri)-11; 12-11 Sat; 12-10.30 Sun

LINTON SE3946 Map 7
Windmill

Leaving Wetherby W on A661, fork left just before hospital and bear left; also signposted from A659, leaving Collingham towards Harewood

The small beamed rooms have walls stripped back to bare stone, polished antique oak settles around copper-topped cast-iron tables, pots hanging from the oak beams, a high shelf of plates, and log fires; the conservatory is no smoking. Attractively presented, tasty food includes lamb and rosemary sausages (£6), mussels in tomato and bacon sauce (£6.95), lamb with mint and honey (£7), good salmon (£8.95), chicken and feta cheese (£8.95), and good mixed grill (£10.50); two-course Sunday lunch (£6.25). Well kept John Smiths, Theakstons Best and a couple of guest beers on handpump; piped music. The pear tree outside was planted with seeds brought back from the Napoleonic Wars and there is a secret passage between the pub and the church next door. *(Recommended by Piotr Chodzko-Zajko, J C Burley, S Watkin, P Taylor, Howard and Margaret Buchanan, Donald and Margaret Wood)*

Scottish Courage ~ Lease Janet Rowley and John Littler ~ Real ale ~ Bar food (not Sun evening) ~ Restaurant ~ (01937) 582209 ~ Children in eating area of bar and restaurant ~ Jazz monthly ~ Open 11-11; 12-10.30 Sun; 11-3, 5-11 in winter

LITTON SD9074 Map 7
Queens Arms

From B6160 N of Grassington, after Kilnsey take second left fork; can also be reached off B6479 at Stainforth N of Settle, via Halton Gill

Ideally situated for walkers (there are plenty of surrounding walks – a track behind the inn leads over Ackerley Moor to Buckden, and the quiet lane through the valley leads on to Pen-y-ghent), this attractive white-painted building has stunning views over the fells from picnic-sets in front, and from the two-level garden. The main bar on the right has a good coal fire, stripped rough stone walls, a brown beam-and-plank ceiling, stools around cast-iron-framed tables on the stone and concrete floor, a seat built into the stone-mullioned window, and signed cricket bats. The left-hand room has been turned into an eating area with old photographs of the Dales around the walls. The family room is no smoking. Decent bar food includes home-made soup (£2.50), sandwiches (from £3.50), filled baked potatoes (from £4.50), home-made rabbit pie (£6.90), gammon and egg (£7.20), home-made game pie (£8.90), daily specials such as battered haddock or roast beef (£6.95), chicken with stilton and smoked bacon or halibut with a fresh seafood sauce (£9.20), mushroom and Quorn stroganoff (£8.95), local pheasant (£9.60), and puddings like apricot bread and butter pudding or apple and almond pie (from £3). Well kept Black Sheep and Tetleys on handpump; darts, dominoes, shove-ha'penny, cribbage, and piped music. *(Recommended by Edmund Coan, B, M and P Kendall, Phil Heys, Greta and Christopher Wells)*

Free house ~ Licensees Tanya and Neil Thompson ~ Real ale ~ Bar food ~ (01756) 770208 ~ Children in family room ~ Open 12-3, 7-11; 11.30-3, 6.30-11(10.30 Sun) Sat; closed Mon (open bank holidays), Jan ~ Bedrooms: /£58S

LUND SE9748 Map 8
Wellington 🍽 ♀
Off B1248 SW of Driffield

As well as enjoying the very good bar food at lunchtime in this smartly refurbished pub, you can now extend this to the newly opened area at the back in the evening – though the main bar remains a haven for drinkers only, then. The most atmospheric part is the cosy Farmers Bar, a small heavily beamed room with an interesting fireplace and some old agricultural equipment; the neatly kept main bar is much brighter, with a brick fireplace and bar counter, well polished wooden banquettes and square tables, dried flowers, and local prints on the textured cream-painted walls; one part is no smoking. Off to one side is a plainer flagstoned room, while at the other a York-stoned walkway leads to a room with a display case showing off the village's Britain in Bloom awards. At lunchtime, the interesting choice of food might include soup (£3.25), caesar salad with parmesan shavings and garlic croutons (£3.95), country pâté with crab apple and herb jelly (£4.95), sandwiches (from £4.95), quiche of fresh asparagus, spring onion and mature cheddar (£7.95), roasted peppers stuffed with roast vegetables and mediterranean-style couscous with sweet and sour sauce or smoked haddock fishcakes with mild curried apple sauce and home-made chips (£8.95), and chicken, banana and almond korma with nan bread (£9.50), and evening dishes like red onion and shallot tarte tatin topped with toasted goats cheese (£4.75), filo pastry swag bag of mushrooms, bacon and brie (£4.95), beef in Guinness with prunes and root vegetables (£9.45), mixed seafood thermidor (£10.95), veal cutlet fried with lemon and fresh rosemary on roast garlic mash (£13.95), and puddings such as chocolate sponge with chocolate sauce, hazelnut lemon meringue with a lemon zappy sauce or orange and Grand Marnier mousse (from £3.50). Well kept Black Sheep, John Smiths, and Timothy Taylors Landlord with a changing guest on handpump, and a good wine list with a helpfully labelled choice by the glass. Briskly efficient service from uniformed staff; piped music, darts, pool, TV, fruit machine, cribbage and dominoes. A small courtyard beside the car park has a couple of benches. *(Recommended by Colin Draper, June and Ken Brooks, Shaun Pinchbeck, T A Foy)*

Free house ~ Licensees Russell Jeffery and Sarah Warburton ~ Real ale ~ Bar food (not Sun evening or Mon) ~ Restaurant (Tues-Sat evenings) ~ (01377) 217294 ~ Children in eating area of bar lunchtime only ~ Open 12-3, 6.30-11(10.30 Sun); closed Mon lunchtime

MASHAM SE2381 Map 10
Kings Head 🛏
Market Square

In a good market square position, this welcoming inn has been refurbished, upstairs and downstairs. The two opened-up rooms of the bar have traditional pine tables and chairs on the wood-stripped floor, a roaring fire in the imposing fireplace, a big clock (from Masham Station), and well kept Theakstons Best, Cool Cask, Black Bull, and Old Peculier, and several wines by the glass. Good, enjoyable bar food includes home-made soup (£2.95), ciabatta sandwiches or tortilla wraps (from £3.25), black pudding stack or prawn bayou (£3.45), grilled goats cheese on toasted ciabatta (£3.95), ham and eggs (£4.45), bangers with buttered mash and onion gravy (£5.25), pasta with wild mushroom sauce (£6.25), steak and stilton pie (£6.45), honey and peppercorn chicken or prawn and smoked salmon salad (£7.45), daily specials such as chicken breast stuffed with swiss cheese, mozzarella and spinach on a bed of roasted vegetables and gruyère sauce (£10.95), mahi mahi supreme wrapped in courgettes on spring cabbage with mushrooms and chilli (£12.95), and puddings like banoffi pie, strawberry daiquiri cheesecake or chocolate muffin cake (from £3.25); helpful friendly service. The restaurant is no smoking; piped music. There are picnic-sets in front of the building, with more on the back terrace, and pretty, award-winning hanging baskets and window boxes. *(Recommended by Janet and Peter Race, Francis Johnston, James Nunns, Ian Arthur, R M Corlett, John Coatsworth, Simon and Laura Habbishow, Jenny and Dave Hughes)*

Scottish Courage ~ Manager Philip Capon ~ Real ale ~ Bar food (12-3, 6-10; all day Sat, Sun, bank holidays) ~ Restaurant ~ (01765) 689295 ~ Children welcome ~ Open 11-11; 12-10.30 Sun ~ Bedrooms: £56.95B/£78.90B

MIDDLEHAM SE1288 Map 10
Black Swan

Market Pl

In a rather steep and pretty village, this 17th-c stone inn has a good mix of customers with plenty of walkers and lads from the local stables – the pub is in the heart of racing country. The immaculately kept heavy-beamed bar has high-backed settles built in by the big stone fireplace, racing memorabilia on the stripped stone walls, and horsebrasses and pewter mugs; well kept Black Sheep Bitter, John Smiths Bitter and Theakstons Best, Old Peculier, and XB on handpump, several malt whiskies and a decent little wine list. Bar food (they tell us prices have not changed since last year) includes lunchtime sandwiches (from £1.95), filled baked potatoes (from £2.95), and ploughman's (from £3.95), as well as home-made soup (£1.95), battered haddock (£5.95), vegetable lasagne (£5.25), lasagne or chicken with a creamy spicy, coconut sauce (£5.50), and evening gammon with pineapple (£7.95), steaks (from £10.25), and children's dishes (£2.95). Darts, dominoes and piped music. There are tables on the cobbles outside and in the sheltered back garden. Good walking country. More reports please. *(Recommended by Mike and Mary Carter, John Sleigh, B, M and P Kendall, Greta and Christopher Wells, Mrs Jane Wyles, Terry Mizen)*

Free house ~ Licensees George and Susan Munday ~ Real ale ~ Bar food ~ Restaurant ~ (01969) 622221 ~ Children welcome until 9 ~ Open 11-3.30, 6-11; 12-3, 6.30-10.30 Sun; closed evening 25 Dec ~ Bedrooms: £28S/£50B

MOULTON NZ2404 Map 10
Black Bull 🍽

Just E of A1, 1 mile E of Scotch Corner

Particularly handy for the A1, this decidedly civilised place makes an excellent stop for lunch or dinner. The bar has a lot of character – as well as a huge winter log fire, fresh flowers, an antique panelled oak settle and an old elm housekeeper's chair, built-in red-cushioned black settles and pews around the cast iron tables (one has a heavily beaten copper top), silver-plate Turkish coffee pots and so forth over the red velvet curtained windows, and copper cooking utensils hanging from black beams. A nice side dark-panelled seafood bar has some high seats at the marble-topped counter. Good lunchtime bar snacks include lovely smoked salmon in sandwiches (£3.25), on a plate (£5.50), and in pâté (£5.75); they also do very good home-made soup served in little tureens (£2.75), fresh plump salmon sandwiches (£3.25), chicken, bacon and avocado baguette, ploughman's or bangers and mash (£4.95), linguini with tomato sauce, pancetta and parmesan (£5.25), queenie scallops in garlic with wensleydale and thyme crumb (£5.75), carpaccio of peppered rump with caper and cornichon salad or smoked haddock, walnut and gruyère quiche (£5.95), warm salad of asparagus, pancetta, parmesan and quails eggs (£6), and puddings such as hot orange liqueur pancakes or crème brûlée (£3.50). In the evening (when people do tend to dress up), you can also eat in the polished brick-tiled conservatory with bentwood cane chairs or in the Brighton Belle dining car. Good wine, a fine choice of sherries, and around 30 malt whiskies, and 30 liqueurs. There are some seats under trees in the central court. *(Recommended by Mr and Mrs J Glover, Marlene and Jim Godfrey, Mr and Mrs J E C Tasker, Ivor and Shirley Thomas, Jenny and Dave Hughes, Anthony Longden, Greta and Christopher Wells, John Close)*

Free house ~ Licensees Mrs Audrey and Miss S Pagendam ~ Bar food (lunchtime, not Sun) ~ Restaurant (evening) ~ (01325) 377289 ~ Children welcome if over 7 ~ Open 12-2.30, 6-10.30(11 Sat); 12-2 Sun; closed Sun evening and 24-26 Dec

---

We say if we know a pub has piped music.

MUKER SD9198 Map 10
Farmers Arms
B6270 W of Reeth

Well placed for both nearby rewarding walks and interesting drives up over Buttertubs Pass or to the north, to Tan Hill and beyond, this is a friendly, unpretentious local with no noisy games or piped music and a chatty, traditional atmosphere. The cosy bar has a warm open fire and is simply furnished with stools and settles around copper-topped tables. Straightforward bar food includes lunchtime baps (from £2.35) and toasties (£2.50), as well as soup (£2), jumbo sausage (£4.95), home-made steak pie (£5.75), mediterranean vegetable bake (£5.95), grilled rainbow trout (£6.50), steaks (from £8.75), daily specials, puddings, and children's meals (from £3.20). Castle Eden Nimmo's XXXX, John Smiths, and Theakstons Best and Old Peculier on handpump; darts and dominoes. They have a self-catering studio flat to rent. *(Recommended by Gareth and Toni Edwards, Mr and Mrs K M Hezelgrave, Catherine and Richard Preston, B, M and P Kendall, Christine and Neil Townend, P T Sewell, Gwyneth and Salvo Spadaro-Dutturi, Jim Abbott, P Abbott, Charlie Watson)*

Free house ~ Licensees Chris and Marjorie Bellwood ~ Real ale ~ Bar food ~ No credit cards ~ (01748) 886297 ~ Children welcome ~ Open 11-3, 7-11; 12-3, 7-10.30 Sun

NEWTON ON OUSE SE5160 Map 7
Dawnay Arms
Village signposted off A19 N of York

One of the obvious draws to this attractive black-shuttered inn is the neat, sloping lawn that runs down to the River Ouse, where there are moorings; plenty of seats on the terrace. Inside, on the right of the entrance is a spacious room with a good deal of beamery and timbering and plush wall settles and chairs around wooden or dimpled copper tables. To the left is another airy room with plush button-back wall banquettes built into bays and a good log fire in the stone fireplace; lots of brass and copper. Good bar food includes sandwiches, soup (£2.50), home-made pâté (£3.25), confit duck (£4.50), salmon, crab and prawn thermidor (£8.95), chicken parcels stuffed with pork and apple, wapped in bacon (£9.95), casseroled pheasant breasts wrapped in bacon (£11.95), and several vegetarian choices; they also offer an early bird menu (5.30-7pm, Monday to Friday; two courses £4.95, three courses £5.95). The restaurant is no smoking. Well kept Flowers Original, Greene King Old Speckled Hen, and Tetleys on handpump, and around 90 malt whiskies; fruit machine and piped music. Benningbrough Hall (National Trust) is five minutes' walk away. More reports please. *(Recommended by F J Robinson, Jenny and Dave Hughes, Edward and Deanna Pearce, Bob and Sue Hardy)*

Free house ~ Licensees Alan and Richard Longley ~ Real ale ~ Bar food ~ Restaurant ~ (01347) 848345 ~ Children in eating area of bar ~ Open 12-3, 5.30(6 Sat)-11; 12-3, 7-10.30 Sun

NUNNINGTON SE6779 Map 7
Royal Oak 🍴
Church Street; at back of village, which is signposted from A170 and B1257

Very neatly kept and attractive, this busy little pub is very much somewhere to enjoy good food served by friendly and efficient staff, rather than a place for a casual drink: sandwiches, home-made vegetable soup with lentils and bacon (£3.40), chicken liver pâté with home-made chutney (£4.15), stuffed mushrooms with stilton pâté (£4.40), seafood hors d'oeuvres (£4.95), ploughman's (£6.95), vegetable lasagne (£7.95), salmon and prawn tagliatelle, steak and kidney casserole or chicken breast in orange and tarragon sauce (£8.95), crispy roast duckling (£11.50), and sirloin steak (£12.95). The restaurant is no smoking. Well kept Tetleys, Theakstons Old Peculier, and a guest beer on handpump. The bar has carefully chosen furniture such as kitchen and country dining chairs or a long pew around the sturdy tables on the turkey carpet, and a lectern in one corner; the high black beams are strung with earthenware flagons, copper jugs and lots of antique keys, one of the walls is stripped back to the bare stone to display a fine collection of antique farm tools, and there are open fires. Handy for a visit to Nunnington Hall (National Trust). More reports please. *(Recommended by Mrs Jane Wyles, Walter and Sue Anderson, Peter Burton)*

Free house ~ Licensee Anthony Simpson ~ Real ale ~ Bar food (not Mon) ~ Restaurant ~ (01439) 748271 ~ Children in family room ~ Open 12-2.30, 6.30-11; 12-2.30, 7-10.30 Sun; closed Mon

OSMOTHERLEY SE4499 Map 10
Golden Lion 🍺
The Green, West End; off A19 N of Thirsk

On the green of the small pretty village, this old stone-built inn has two or three good tables out in front looking across to the market cross. Inside, the roomy beamed bar on the left, simply furnished with old pews and just a few decorations on its white walls, has a pleasantly lively atmosphere, with a good welcome for even soggy walkers (this is the start of the 44-mile Lyke Wakes Walk, on the Cleveland Way, and quite handy for the Coast to Coast Walk). On the right, a similarly unpretentious eating area, brightened up with fresh flowers, has good value generous food, with familiar dishes prepared and presented with real care and bags of taste. The choice might include sandwiches (from £2.50), home-made soup (£3.25), home-made rough chicken liver pâté with onion and apricot relish (£4.95), meaty or vegetarian lasagne or popular home-made beefburger (£5.50), white crab with brown crab mayonnaise (£6.50), home-made steak and kidney pie with a suet crust (£6.95), salmon fishcakes with spinach and creamy sorrel sauce (£8.50), chargrilled poussin with rosemary and garlic (£8.75), pork wrapped in parma ham and sage with a marsala sauce (£10.95), and puddings such as well liked chocolate cake, a middle eastern orange cake with marmalade cream, or raspberry ripple cheesecake (£3.75); good home-made chips. Well kept Hambleton Bitter and North Yorkshire Fools Gold on handpump, good coffee, and swift friendly service. They hope to open bedrooms soon. *(Recommended by Michael Butler, John and Deborah Tacon, P Abbott, Dr Bob Bland, Lady Greig, Mr and Mrs Maurice Thompson)*

Free house ~ Licensee Christie Connelly ~ Real ale ~ Bar food (during all opening hours) ~ Restaurant ~ (01609) 883526 ~ Children welcome ~ Open 12-3.30, 6-11; 12-11(10.30 Sun) Sat; closed evening 25 Dec

PENISTONE SE2402 Map 7
Cubley Hall
Mortimer Road; outskirts, towards Stocksbridge

There are four acres of gardens around this handsome place – originally a grand Edwardian country house – with plenty of seats under umbrellas, a good children's playground, and distant views. Inside, there's panelling, elaborate plasterwork, and mosaic tiling, plush furnishings in the spreading bar and two snug rooms leading off, and a roomy conservatory. A wide choice of bar food, usefully served all day, includes home-made soup (£1.90), sandwiches (from £2.35), garlic mushrooms (£2.45), burgers (from £2.75), popular pizzas (from £3.95), home-made lasagne (£5.85), home-made steak in ale pie (£5.95), chicken and bacon risotto or rack of ribs (£6.95), chargrilled tuna with a warm salad of vine tomatoes and pesto infused couscous (£8.95), steaks (from £8.95), puddings such as steamed chocolate and orange pudding and vanilla custard or spiced apple and pear crumble (£2.95), and children's menu (£2.50. Well kept Greene King Abbot, Ind Coope Burton, Tetleys, and a guest beer like Fullers London Pride on handpump, and a decent wine list with half a dozen by the glass. One room is no smoking; piped music, fruit machine, and TV. This is often busy with weekend wedding receptions. *(Recommended by A Preston, G Dobson, Derek and Sylvia Stephenson)*

Free house ~ Licensees John Wigfield and David Slade ~ Real ale ~ Bar food (all day; till 10 Fri/Sat) ~ Restaurant ~ (01226) 766086 ~ Children welcome ~ Open 11.30-11(10.30 Sun) ~ Bedrooms: £53B/£69B

PICKERING SE7983 Map 10
White Swan ♀ ☛

Market Place, just off A170

This former coaching inn is on a winning streak these days. As well as its flourishing gently upmarket hotel side, with very comfortable recently reworked bedrooms, it has a charming country atmosphere in its small and civilised front bar, with panelling, dark plush cushions and a log fire; the snug, with another fire, is no smoking. They use as much carefully sourced local produce as possible, which at lunchtime might run from sandwiches (from £4.75; yorkshire rarebit with pear chutney and watercress salad £4.95; chicken breast with guacamole, bacon and lemon dressing £5.50), home-made soup (£3.95), creamed mushrooms with garlic and dry cured bacon (£4.10), chicken liver pâté (£4.25), grilled swaledale goats cheese or yorkshire rarebit (£4.95) through whitby crab or grilled sausages with mash and onion gravy (£6.95), ploughman's (£7.25), lambs liver (£7.80), salmon fishcakes with lemon sauce (£7.95), to chargrilled sirloin steak (£10.95), with more elaborate or heartier evening dishes such as assiette charcuterie with parmesan and lemon (£6.95), potted whitby lobster and crab with watercress and mustard seed salad (£7), marinated vegetables with fresh herb salad and polenta (£10), parma ham-wrapped pork fillet with porcini stuffing, baby leeks, thyme potatoes and pan juices (£13.50), roast rack of spring lamb with chargrilled courgettes, olive oil mash and mint sauce (£14.25), and roast monkfish with tomato and coriander curry and green sauce (£14.50), and puddings such as lemon tart with lime and mascarpone ice cream, rich chocolate cake with clotted cream and macerated cherries or crème brûlée with apple crisps and chantilly cream (from £3.50). The same menu is available (with a small surcharge) in the small and attractive no smoking dining room. If you stay, the breakfast is good. Well kept Black Sheep Bitter and Special and a local guest beer on handpump, nine good house wines (by two sizes of glass) and an impressive wine list, good coffee, friendly helpful staff. There's a busy but comfortable family room. *(Recommended by Peter and Anne-Marie O'Malley, Janet and Peter Race, Sir Richard FitzHerbert, Alan and Paula McCully, Sylvia and Tony Birbeck, Mrs C Monk, John Foord; also in* The Good Hotel Guide)

Free house ~ Licensees Marion and Victor Buchanan ~ Real ale ~ Bar food (12-4, 5-6.30; 12-5, 7-9 Sun) ~ Restaurant ~ (01751) 472288 ~ Children in eating area of bar and restaurant ~ Open 10.30-3, 6-11; 10-11 Mon and Sat; 12-5, 7-10.30 Sun ~ Bedrooms: /£100B

PICKHILL SE3584 Map 10
Nags Head ⊕ ♀

Take the Masham turn-off from A1 both N and S, and village signposted off B6267 in Ainderby Quernhow

This is a smashing place to take a break from the A1, and it has been run for nearly 30 years, with professional enthusiasm, by the Boynton brothers. The busy tap room on the left has beams hung with jugs, coach horns, ale-yards and so forth, and masses of ties hanging as a frieze from a rail around the red ceiling. The smarter lounge bar has deep green plush banquettes on the matching carpet, and pictures for sale on its neat cream walls, and another comfortable beamed room (mainly for restaurant users) has plush button-back built-in wall banquettes around dark tables, and an open fire. From a varied menu, the much enjoyed food includes sandwiches, fresh crab bisque (£2.95), marinated squid with tomato salad (£3.95), mushrooms filled with pâté and smoked bacon on a bed of red cabbage (£4.50), hors d'oeuvres (£4.95), carrot and coriander tart with roasted fennel and Pernod sauce (£7.95), supreme of chicken filled with spinach, gruyère and sun blushed tomatoes, crusty-topped rabbit and pheasant pie or salmon, halibut and prawn crumble (£9.95), roast pork fillet with a herb crust and calvados sauce (£10.95), roast rack of English lamb with honey and soy sauce (£11.50), and puddings such as zebra chocolate mousse pots or almond crème brûlée (£3.50). The library-themed restaurant is partly no smoking. Well kept Black Sheep Bitter, Hambleton Bitter, John Smiths, and

Theakstons Black Bull on handpump, a good choice of malt whiskies, and several vintage armagnacs, wines by the glass, and bin ends. One table is inset with a chessboard, and they also have cribbage, dominoes, shove-ha'penny, and faint piped music. There's a front verandah, a boules and quoits pitch, and 9-hole putting green. *(Recommended by Alan J Morton, Mr and Mrs J E C Tasker, Michael Doswell, J G Thorpe, Andy and Jill Kassube, Richard Cole, Mr and Mrs T B Staples, Roger Everett, B, M and P Kendall, John Ker, Sue and Geoff Price, Paul and Margaret Baker)*

Free house ~ Licensees Edward and Raymond Boynton ~ Real ale ~ Bar food (12-2, 6-9.30) ~ Restaurant ~ (01845) 567391 ~ Well behaved children welcome until 7.30pm ~ Open 11-11; 12-10.30 Sun ~ Bedrooms: £40B/£60B

POOL SE2445 Map 7
White Hart

Just off A658 S of Harrogate, A659 E of Otley

A Vintage Inn and therefore given the careful management controls, similar in many respects to others in the chain, but this friendly place has been carefully reworked, and the décor suits it well. The four rooms have a relaxing atmosphere, a restrained country appearance, a pleasant medley of assorted old farmhouse furniture on the mix of stone flooring and carpet, and two log fires; only one area is for smokers. At lunchtime, the enjoyable food includes home-made soup (£2.35), sandwiches (from £3.60), fried sticky chicken and tiger prawns (£4.25), sausages and cheddar mash (£4.95), macaroni cheese and spinach (£5.95), beef and mushroom pie (£6.25), and baked rainbow trout with parsley butter (£7.50); in the evening, there might be caesar salad (£2.95), salmon and broccoli fishcakes (£4.75), seafood salad (£6.95), minted lamb loin with savoury cheese pudding (£8.25), and steaks (from £8.15); Sunday roasts (£6.25). Well kept Bass and Tetleys on handpump, and all wines on the list sold in two sizes of glass; piped music and fruit machine. There are tables outside, and although the road is quite busy, this is pleasant walking country. *(Recommended by Ray and Winifred Halliday, R Mathews, Greta and Christopher Wells, Michael Butler, Janet and Peter Race)*

Vintage Inns ~ Manager David Britland ~ Real ale ~ Bar food (12-10(9.30 Sun)) ~ Restaurant ~ (0113) 202 7901 ~ Children in eating area of bar ~ Open 11-11; 12-10.30 Sun

RAMSGILL SE1271 Map 7
Yorke Arms ★ ⑪ ♀ 🛏

Take Nidderdale road off B6265 in Pateley Bridge; or exhilarating but narrow moorland drive off A6108 at N edge of Masham, via Fearby and Lofthouse

There's no doubt that this is a civilised place to enjoy a first rate meal and a lovely place to stay – but walkers dropping in for a beer are made just as welcome by the friendly, courteous staff. The bars have fresh flowers and polish smells, two or three heavy carved Jacobean oak chairs, a big oak dresser laden with polished pewter and other antiques, and open log fires. Exceptionally good, imaginative food includes oyster mushroom and fine herb risotto (£5.75), black pudding cooked in brioche, poached smoked haddock and mustard sauce or mousse of roquefort with beetroot sorbet (£7.50), fried langoustine niçoise (£7.95), baked butternut squash, spinach and goats cheese, and tomato fondue (£11.50), salmi of duck, artichoke, potato purée, breast of duck and sauce bigarade or basil crusted loin of lamb, tomato and aubergine, roasted kidney and saffron (£13.95), roast fillet of turbot, tomato bordelaise, salsify, and potato croquettes (£15.95), daily specials like mediterranean fish salad (£5.50), fillet of brill, crab hollandaise, green beans, and straw potatoes (£13.50), and fried calves liver, sweet potato purée and red onion confit (£14.50), and puddings such as chocolate parfait, compote of cherries, and warm chocolate cake or panna cotta, roasted apricots and almonds (from £5.50). Well kept Black Sheep Special and Shepherd Neame Spitfire on handpump, a fine wine list with up to a dozen by the glass, and a good choice of brandies, malt whiskies, liqueurs, and fresh juices; piped music. They prefer smart dress in the no smoking restaurant in the evening. You can walk up the magnificent if strenuous moorland road to Masham, or perhaps on the right-of-way track that leads along the hill behind the reservoir, also a bird sanctuary. Please note, the bedroom prices include dinner, bed and breakfast. *(Recommended by Mrs C Monk, Mrs Jane Wyles, Alyson and Andrew Jackson, I D Greenfield, Michael and Rosalind Dymond, Mr and MrsC M Pearson, Greta and Christopher Wells, Tracey and Stephen Groves, John Close, Karen and Graham Oddey, Pierre and Pat Richterich, David and Ruth Hollands; also in* The Good Hotel Guide*)*

Free house ~ Licensees Bill and Frances Atkins ~ Real ale ~ Restaurant ~ (01423) 755243 ~ Children in family room ~ Open 11-3, 6-11; 12-3, 6-11 Sun ~ Bedrooms: £90B/£105B

RIPLEY SE2861 Map 7
Boars Head 🍽 ♀ 🍺 🛏

Off A61 Harrogate—Ripon

In a delightful estate village, this comfortable hotel has a friendly bar, still very much used by locals – which contributes to the relaxed atmosphere. There's a separate entrance to reach it, though you can walk through the public rooms if you wish; it's a long flagstoned room with green checked tablecloths and olive oil on all the tables, most of which are arranged to form individual booths. The green walls have jolly little drawings of cricketers or huntsmen running along the bottom, as well as a boar's head (part of the family coat of arms), a couple of cricket bats, and well kept Black Sheep, Theakstons Best and Old Peculier, their intriguing Crackshot – brewed to their own 17th-c recipe by Daleside – and a guest such as Daleside Old Leg Over or Dent Aviator on handpump; an excellent wine list (with 10 or so by the glass), and a good choice of malt whiskies. Particularly good, interesting bar food includes sandwiches, home-made soup (£3.25), glazed goats cheese with cherry tomatoes and asparagus (£4; main course £8), cured venison with balsamic dressing and shaved parmesan (£4.25; main course £8.50), marinated pork steak on a purée of carrot and swede or seared salmon fillet on a tomato and herb couscous with watercress dressing (£8.95), roast duck breast on black bean noodles and hoisin sauce (£9.95), and puddings such as coffee crème brûlée topped with vanilla pod ice cream or sticky toffee pudding and butterscotch sauce (£3.50). Part of the bar is no smoking; piped music. Some of the furnishings in the hotel came from the attic of next door Ripley Castle, where the Ingilbys have lived for over 650 years. A pleasant little garden has plenty of tables. They are kind to children and dogs. *(Recommended by Janet and Peter Race, P Abbott, C W Dix, Jenny and Chris Wilson, Mrs Jane Wyles, Patricia A Bruce, Geoff and Anne Field, Jim Abbott; also in* The Good Hotel Guide*)*

Free house ~ Licensee Sir Thomas Ingilby ~ Real ale ~ Bar food (12-2.30(2 winter), 6.30-10(9.30 winter)) ~ Restaurant ~ (01423) 771888 ~ Children welcome ~ Open 11-11; 12-10.30 Sun; 11-3, 5-11in winter ~ Bedrooms: £99B/£120B

RIPPONDEN SE0419 Map 7
Old Bridge ♀

Priest Lane; from A58, best approach is Elland Road (opposite Golden Lion), park opposite the church in pub's car park and walk back over ancient hump-backed bridge

Having managed this civilised 14th-c pub for 17 years, Mr Eaton Walker and his wife have now taken over the ownership of it. It's in a lovely setting by the medieval pack horse bridge over the little River Ryburn, and the three communicating rooms (one of which is no smoking) are each on a slightly different level. There are oak settles built into the window recesses of the thick stone walls, antique oak tables, rush-seated chairs, a few well chosen pictures and prints, a big woodburning stove, and a relaxed atmosphere; fresh flowers in summer. Good, popular bar food includes a well liked weekday lunchtime cold meat buffet which always has a joint of rare beef, as well as spiced ham, quiche, scotch eggs and so on (£8.95 with a bowl of soup and coffee); also, sandwiches, home-made soup (£2.50), duck terrine in sweet plum pickle or salmon, prawn and dill pâté (£3.95), meat and potato pie with pickled red cabbage or salmon and leek pasta bake (£5), thai chicken curry, courgette, apple and brie lasagne (£5.25), fish pie (£5.50), and puddings like apple and cinnamon oat tart, lemon cream pie or banana and toffee pancakes (£2.75). Well kept Black Sheep Special, Moorhouses Bitter, and Timothy Taylors Best, Landlord, and Golden on handpump, 30 malt whiskies, a good choice of foreign bottled beers, and interesting wines with at least a dozen by the glass. More reports please. (*Recommended by Mike Ridgway, Sarah Miles, Adrian and Felicity Smith, R T and J C Moggridge, Peter Burton*)

Free house ~ Licensees Tim and Lindsay Eaton Walker ~ Real ale ~ Bar food (12-2, 6.30-9.30; not Sat or Sun evening) ~ (01422) 822595 ~ Children in eating area of bar until 8 ~ Open 12-3, 5.30-11; 12-11 Sat; 12-10.30 Sun

ROBIN HOOD'S BAY NZ9505 Map 10
Laurel 🍺

Village signposted off A171 S of Whitby

At the bottom of a row of fishermen's cottages at the heart of one of the prettiest and most unspoilt fishing villages on the northeast coast is this charming little pub. The friendly beamed main bar is neatly kept, bustles with locals and visitors, and is decorated with old local photographs, Victorian prints and brasses, and lager bottles from all over the world; there's a roaring open fire. Bar food consists of summer sandwiches and winter soup. Well kept John Smiths and Theakstons Old Peculier and Black Bull on handpump; darts, shove-ha'penny, dominoes, cribbage, and piped music. In summer, the hanging baskets and window boxes are lovely. They have a self-contained apartment for two people. (*Recommended by Bill and Pat Pemberton, Norma and Keith Bloomfield, Geoff and Angela Jaques, Steve Whalley, Mike and Wendy Proctor, GD, KW, Richard Cole*)

Free house ~ Licensee Brian Catling ~ Real ale ~ No credit cards ~ (01947) 880400 ~ Children in snug bar only ~ Open 12-11; 12-10.30 Sun

SAWLEY SE2568 Map 7
Sawley Arms ♀

Village signposted off B6265 W of Ripon

Mrs Hawes has firmly run this smart place for over 33 years now. The neatly kept small turkey-carpeted rooms have log fires and comfortable furniture ranging from small softly cushioned armed dining chairs and settees, to the wing armchairs down a couple of steps in a side snug; maybe daily papers and magazines to read, piped music. Two small rooms (and the restaurant) are no smoking. Good, genuinely home-made bar food includes interesting soups with croutons (£3), lunchtime sandwiches (from £4.30), salmon mousse or stilton, port and celery pâté (£4.95), steak pie (£6.70), curried chicken breast (£7.75), daily specials such as ham, spinach and almond pancakes with tomato coulis (£4.95), lamb casserole or roast duckling quarter with orange curaçao sauce (£6.75), and smoked haddock on spinach with a cheese glaze (£8.50), and puddings such as madeira truffle or rich fruit cake with cheese (from £3.50). Good house wines and piped music. The award-winning flowering tubs, baskets and gardens are lovely. There are two stone cottages in the grounds to rent. Fountains Abbey (the most extensive of the great monastic remains – floodlit on late summer Friday and Saturday evenings, with a live choir on the Saturday – is not far away. More reports please. (*Recommended by Janet and Peter Race, Jason Caulkin, Mrs Jane Wyles*)

Free house ~ Licensee Mrs June Hawes ~ Bar food (not Sun or Mon evenings) ~ Restaurant ~ (01765) 620642 ~ Well behaved children allowed if over 9 ~ Open 11.30-3, 6.30-10.30; 12-3 Sun; closed Sun and Mon evenings ~ Bedrooms: /£65B

Food details, prices, timing etc refer to bar food – not to a separate restaurant if there is one.

SCAWTON SE5584 Map 10
Hare 🍴

Village signposted off A170 Thirsk—Helmsley, just E of Sutton Bank

'Excellent in all aspects' is how several readers describe this warmly friendly, low-built pub, said to date back in part to Norman times. The bars are comfortably modernised without losing their cosy and unspoilt feel, and have rag rugs on flagstones and carpet, stripped pine tables, an old-fashioned range and a woodburner, lots of bric-a-brac, a settee, simple wall settles, a seat in the bow window, and a comfortable eating area; in the innermost part there's a heavy old beam-and-plank ceiling; shove-ha'penny, cribbage, and dominoes. Attractively presented, the imaginative food is first rate, and there is genuine concern for your enjoyment from the helpful staff: home-made soup (£2.50), game terrine with home-made piccalilli (£4.50), slices of smoked duck with warm smoked bacon and sherry vinegar reduction or good crab tart topped with gruyère cheese and a red pepper marmalade (£4.95), smoked haddock fishcakes or well liked brie and pear chutney in filo pastry with a compote of cherry tomato, basil and aubergine (£7.95), confit of duck with black pudding, onion mash and redcurrant and red wine jus or wild boar sausages with beetroot mash and onion gravy (£8.95), beef wellington with madeira sauce (£10.95), rack of local lamb with rosemary sauce, prime local sirloin steak or whole fried bass with chilli jam (£12.95), and puddings such as trio of chocolate puddings, sublime caramelised lemon tart with raspberry sauce or very popular assiette of 6 puddings (from £3.50); the chips are exceptional. The two dining rooms are no smoking. Service is friendly (as are the two dogs); well kept Theakstons, and Timothy Taylors Landlord on handpump; piped music. A big garden behind has tables, and the pub is attractive with roses against its cream walls and green woodwork, and its pair of inn-signs with attractive naïve hare paintings; handy for Rievaulx Abbey. *(Recommended by Walter and Susan Rinaldi-Butcher, Pat and Tony Martin, Janet and Peter Race, Peter Burton, P Hansford, Mrs V Middlebrook, David and Helen Wilkins, P J and Avril Hanson, Mr and Mrs J E C Tasker, Alyson and Andrew Jackson, Michael Doswell)*

Free house ~ Licensee Graham Raine ~ Real ale ~ Bar food (12-2.30, 6.30-9.30) ~ Restaurant ~ (01845) 597289 ~ Children welcome ~ Open 12-3.30(4 Sat), 6.30 (6 Sat)-11; closed Mon lunchtime

SETTLE SD8264 Map 7
Golden Lion

B6480, off A65 bypass

This is the sort of delightful place that customers return to. It's a nicely old-fashioned market town inn with a good mix of customers, and a friendly and cheerful pubby atmosphere. The bar has an enormous fireplace, comfortable settles and plush seats, brass, and prints and Chinese plates on dark panelling; a surprisingly grand staircase sweeps down into the spacious high-beamed hall bar. Good, enjoyable bar food (which can also be eaten in the restaurant at lunchtime) might include various tapas like salmon fishcakes, chicken satay or vegetable kebabs (£2.75), sandwiches (from £3.25; hot ciabatta sandwiches from £4.10; chicken and avocado topped with melted cheese and crispy bacon £4.45), filled baked potatoes (£4.25), ploughman's (£5.95), caesar salad (£6.25), daily specials such as cullen skink (£3.50), lamb, vegetable, rosemary and apricot pudding or delicious east indies chicken (£6.95), salmon steak with fresh noodles and tomato salsa (£7.45), and pheasant breast wrapped in bacon or mini joint of lamb cooked slowly in a sweet mint marinade (£8.95). Well kept Thwaites Bitter, Chairmans, and a seasonal guest beer on handpump, and decent wines with at least 7 by the glass. The lively public bar has pool, fruit machine, dominoes, TV, and piped music; the black and white cat is called Luke. *(Recommended by Don and Marilou Brooks, Margaret Dickinson, DC, Janet and Peter Race, Carol and Dono Leaman, Pat and Tony Martin, Pat and Robert Watt, Dr M E Wilson, Simon Longe, Tracey and Stephen Groves)*

Thwaites ~ Tenant Phillip Longrigg ~ Real ale ~ Bar food (12-2.30, 6-10; 12-10 Sat

and Sun) ~ Restaurant ~ (01729) 822203 ~ Children welcome ~ Open 11-11; 12-10.30 Sun ~ Bedrooms: £25(£33B)/£50(£62B)

SHEFFIELD SK3687 Map 7
Fat Cat ◀ £

23 Alma St

A huge draw to this well run pub is the big choice of well kept real ales on handpump. They keep around 10 ales, including their own, and have a popular Brewery Visitor's Centre (you can book brewery trips (0114) 249 4804) with framed beer mats, pump clips, and prints on the walls. As well as their own-brewed and cheap Kelham Island Bitter, Pale Rider, another Kelham Island beer, and Timothy Taylors Landlord, there are seven interesting guest beers on handpump from breweries like Coach House, Cropton, Durham, Glentworth, Lloyds, Titanic, and so forth, plus continental and British bottled beers, a Belgian draught beer, fruit gin, country wines, and farm cider. Incredibly cheap, enjoyable bar food includes sandwiches, lentil soup (£1.30), ploughman's, spinach pasta, courgette and potato pie, pork casserole or quiche (all £2.50), and puddings such as rhubarb crumble or jam roly poly (£1); well liked Sunday lunch (£3). There's always a good, friendly bustle and a wide mix of customers from far and wide, and the two small downstairs rooms have brewery-related prints on the walls, coal fires, simple wooden tables and cushioned seats around the walls, and jugs, bottles, and some advertising mirrors; the one on the left is no smoking; cribbage and dominoes, and maybe a not-so-fat-cat wandering around. Steep steps take you up to another similarly simple room (which may be booked for functions) with some attractive prints of old Sheffield; there are picnic-sets in a fairylit back courtyard. *(Recommended by CMW, JJW, Terry Barlow, Roger Purkiss, Sarah Lynch, the Didler, Richard Lewis, David Carr, Mike and Wendy Proctor, Giles Francis, John A Barker)*

Own brew ~ Licensee Stephen Fearn ~ Real ale ~ Bar food (12-2.30, 6-7.30; not Sat or Sun evening, not 1 Jan) ~ No credit cards ~ (0114) 249 4801 ~ Children in upstairs room (if not booked up) ~ Open 12-3, 5.30-11; 12-3, 7-10.30 Sun; closed 25 and 26 Dec

New Barrack ◀ £

601 Penistone Rd, Hillsborough

There's always a lively crowd of customers in this sizeable but friendly pub, which is not surprising since they have live music three times a week and a choice of nine real ales. Served by knowledgeable staff, the well kept beers on handpump might include regulars such as Abbeydale Moonshine, Barnsley Bitter, John Smiths Magnet, and Wentworth WPA and four guests beers; also, five continental draught lagers, 40 continental bottled beers, and 60 malt whiskies. The comfortable front lounge has red leather banquettes, old pine floors, an open fire, and collections of decorative plates and of bottles, and there are two smaller rooms behind, one with TV and darts – the family room is no smoking. Cribbage, dominoes, and piped music. The good value simple food is all freshly made and might include sandwiches (from £1.30; steak £4.50), chicken casserole cooked in cider, mushroom roast with sunflower and sesame seeds with pumpkin and saffron sauce, and baked aubergines with cheese, tomato, garlic, fresh basil and caper stuffing (all £4.25); on the first Wednesday of the month, they hold a tapas evening, and on the other three, they have a curry or middle eastern evening (£4.95); good value Sunday lunch. Daily papers and magazines to read; maybe quiet piped radio. There are tables out behind. Local parking is not easy. More reports please. *(Recommended by CMW, JJW, Richard Lewis, David Carr, Roger Purkiss, Sarah Lynch, the Didler)*

Free house ~ Licensee James Birkett ~ Real ale ~ Bar food (12-2.30, 6-8(8.30 Thurs, Fri); not Sat or Sun evening) ~ No credit cards ~ (0114) 234 9148 ~ Children in family room ~ Folk Mon evening, jazz Tues evening, blues Sat evening ~ Open 12-11; 12-10.30 Sun

SHELLEY SE2112 Map 7

Three Acres 🍴 ♟ 🍺 🛏

Roydhouse (not signposted); from B6116 heading for Skelmanthorpe, turn left in Shelley (signposted Flockton, Elmley, Elmley Moor) and go up lane for 2 miles towards radio mast

Thoroughly deserving of all its awards, this civilised former coaching inn is especially popular for its exceptional food. The roomy lounge bar has a relaxed, friendly atmosphere, tankards hanging from the main beam, button-back leather sofas, old prints and so forth, and maybe a pianist playing light music. Imaginative and highly enjoyable, the bar food includes sandwiches or filled baguettes (from £2.95; smoked breast of chicken with asparagus and sun-dried tomato mayonnaise £3.75), french onion soup baked with a gruyère crouton (£3.50), chicken liver parfait on toasted brioche with caramelised onions or moules marinières (£4.95), lovely potted shrimps (£6.95), sheeps milk cheese ravioli with tomatoes and basil (£5.95), toasted lemon chicken with garlic and lemon mayonnaise (£6.25), locally smoked salmon with free range scrambled eggs or fried noodles with seared tofu, vegetables and cashew nuts (£8.95), braised oxtails with horseradish mash or steak, kidney and mushroom pie (£9.95), brochette of tandoori king prawns, monkfish and baby squid on roast aubergine and tomato with sauce raita (£11.95), fresh dressed cornish crab or chargrilled peppered rib-eye steak (£14.95), and puddings such as sticky toffee banana pudding with toffee sauce, chocolate marquise with white chocolate ice cream or sticky lemon tart with lemon curd ice cream (£4.95); they only serve snacks on Saturday lunchtime in the bar. There's a specialist delicatessen next door. Well kept Adnams Bitter, Mansfield Bitter, Marstons Pedigree, and Timothy Taylors Landlord on handpump, over 50 whiskies, exceptional (if not cheap) choice of wines, with 10 by the glass, and freshly squeezed orange juice. This is a nice place to stay and the breakfasts are particularly good. There are fine views across to Emley Moor, occasionally livened up by the local hunt passing. *(Recommended by Peter and Giff Bennett, George and Jeanne Barnwell, Paul Craddock, Revd D Glover, Hugh Roberts, Alan J Morton, Mike Tucker, Dr James Oliver, Keith and Katy Stevens, W K Wood, Stephen, Julie and Hayley Brown)*

Free house ~ Licensees Neil Truelove and Brian Orme ~ Real ale ~ Bar food (not Sat lunch) ~ Restaurant ~ (01484) 602606 ~ Children in eating area of bar and restaurant ~ Open 12-3, 6-11(10.30 Sun) ~ Bedrooms: £55B/£75B

SINNINGTON SE7485 Map 10

Fox & Hounds 🛏

Village signposted just off A170 W of Pickering

The good, interesting food continues to draw customers to this neat 18th-c coaching inn, set in a pretty village. The clean and welcoming beamed bar has nice pictures and old artefacts, a woodburning stove, and comfortable wall seats and carver chairs around the neat tables on its carpet. The curved corner bar counter has well kept Black Sheep Special and Camerons on handpump and a good choice of malt whiskies. The menu is the same in both the bar and no smoking restaurant: lunchtime sandwiches and warm ciabattas, home-made soup (£2.95, sunblushed tomato and mozzarella tart (£4.25), duck and pistachio pâté (£4.75), fried battered haddock with mushy peas (£6.45), smoked bacon escalope topped with melted cheese and herb crust (£7.45), sautéed chicken breast with a cream, bacon and mushroom sauce (£7.95), chargrilled pork steak with sweet pepper and apple marmalade (£7.85), seared salmon fillet with a lime, dill and cream sauce with a hint of ginger (£8.25), wild mushroom and calabrese risotto with white truffle oil and a parmesan biscuit (£8.45), king prawn and monkfish green thai curry (£9.95), and fillet of lamb rolled in fresh parsley and garlic with lemon zest couscous and an apricot salsa (£12.75). There's a separate no smoking stables bar; piped music, dominoes, and darts. Dogs are welcome, pleasant chatty service, and if you're staying, the breakfasts are good. Picnic-sets out in front. More reports please. *(Recommended by IHR, Mr and Mrs S Oxenbury, Colin and Dot Savill, David and Ruth Hollands, Alan and Paula McCully, H E Wynter, M J Morgan, M Borthwick)*

Free house ~ Licensees Andrew and Catherine Stephens ~ Real ale ~ Bar food (12-2, 6.30-9) ~ Restaurant (evening) ~ (01751) 431577 ~ Children in eating area of bar and in restaurant before 8 ~ Open 12-2.30, 6(6.30 Sun and in winter)-11(10.30 Sun) ~ Bedrooms: £44S(£54B)/£60S

STARBOTTON SD9574 Map 7
Fox & Hounds 🍴 ⏴

B6160 Upper Wharfedale road N of Kettlewell; OS Sheet 98 map reference 953749

As well as being an enjoyable place to stay, this warmly friendly and prettily placed little Upper Wharfedale village inn has a good crowd of chatty locals (though visitors are made very welcome, too) and offers imaginative food and well kept real ales. The bar has traditional solid furniture on the flagstones, a collection of plates on the walls, whisky jugs hanging from the high beams supporting ceiling boards, and a big stone fireplace (with an enormous fire in winter). To be sure of a seat, it's best to get here early as the food is so popular: lunchtime baguettes and ploughman's, soup with home-made brown bread (£3), stilton, sun-dried tomato and sweet roast pecan salad or blue cheese soufflé with tomato and onion salad (£3.75), mixed bean and apple casserole or lamb and mint burger in a bap (£6.75), steak and mushroom pie (£7.25), chicken, leek and mushroom crumble (£7.50), bacon steaks with cumberland sauce (£7.75), moroccan-style lamb (£8.75), and home-made puddings such as chocolate ginger pudding with chocolate fudge sauce, brown sugar chestnut meringues, and sticky toffee pudding (£3); hard-working, cheerful staff. Well kept Black Sheep Bitter, Theakstons Old Peculier, and Timothy Taylors Landlord on handpump, and around 60 malt whiskies. Dominoes, cribbage, and well reproduced, unobtrusive piped music. Seats in a sheltered corner enjoy the view over the hills all around this little hamlet. *(Recommended by Pierre and Pat Richterich, Malcolm and Jennifer Perry, the Didler, Martin and Karen Wake, Chris and Elaine Lyon, Tracey and Stephen Groves, Charlie Watson, Philip and Susan Philcox, Greta and Christopher Wells, Mr and Mrs P Dix)*

Free house ~ Licensees James and Hilary McFadyen ~ Real ale ~ Bar food ~ (01756) 760269 ~ Children in eating area of bar ~ Open 11.30-3, 6.30-11; 12-3, 7-10.30 Sun; closed Mon (except bank hol lunch) and Jan-mid Feb ~ Bedrooms: /£55S

SUTTON UPON DERWENT SE7047 Map 7
St Vincent Arms 🍺

B1228 SE of York

This is very much a family-run affair with a genuine pubby atmosphere, no noisy games or piped music, and up to 8 well kept real ales on handpump. Tapped from the cask or on handpump, the beers might include Banks's Bitter, Fullers London Pride, ESB, Chiswick, and a seasonal beer, John Smiths, Timothy Taylors Landlord, and Charles Wells Bombardier; also a range of malt whiskies, and very reasonably priced spirits. Enjoyable bar food includes sandwiches (from £1.80), home-made soup (£2.20), filled baked potatoes (from £2), home-made chicken liver pâté with onion marmalade (£4), smoked haddock topped with welsh rarebit (£4.50), lasagne (£7), steak and kidney pie (£7.50), king prawns in Pernod (£9.50), steaks (from £10.50), daily specials such as cumberland sausage and mash (£5.20), vegetable stir-fry (£5.50), and chicken stuffed with apricots or pork stroganoff (£8.50), and puddings such as treacle tart (£2.35). One eating area is no smoking. The parlour-like, panelled front bar has traditional high-backed settles, a cushioned bow-window seat, windsor chairs and a gas-effect coal fire; another lounge and separate dining room open off. There are seats in the garden. The pub is named after the admiral who was granted the village and lands by the nation as thanks for his successful commands – and for coping with Nelson's infatuation with Lady Hamilton. *(Recommended by Paul and Ursula Randall, Shaun Pinchbeck, J C Burley, Tony Gayfer, Greta and Christopher Wells)*

Free house ~ Licensee Phil Hopwood ~ Real ale ~ Bar food ~ Restaurant ~ (01904) 608349 ~ Children welcome ~ Open 11.30-3, 6-11; 12-3, 7-10.30 Sun

TERRINGTON SE6571 Map 7
Bay Horse

W of Malton; off B1257 at Hovingham (towards York, eventually sigposted left) or Slingsby (towards Castle Howard, then right); can also be reached off A64 via Castle Howard, or via Welburn and Ganthorpe

In an unspoilt village on one of the rolling old coach roads that make the most of the Howardian Hill views, this charming country pub has a cosy lounge bar with country prints and a good log fire, a handsome dining area and back family conservatory with old farm tools, well kept Black Sheep and Timothy Taylors Landlord on handpump, and 80 malt whiskies. Tasty bar food includes home-made soup (£2), sandwiches (from £2.30; filled baguettes from £2.55), deep-fried king prawns with a tomato and herb dip (£3.95), smoked salmon and prawn parcels stuffed with cream cheese (£4.50), pies such as steak and kidney (£6.50) and game (£6.95), ham and eggs (£7.95), daily specials like cheese and broccoli bake, italian-style chicken, lemon sole with peppercorn dressing or swordfish steak (from around £6), and puddings like sticky toffee pudding or cheesecakes (£2.65). On Thursday evenings they hold a steak and wine night (£14.95 per couple). The present restaurant is to be refurbished, and there are plans to add a second dining area. The traditional public bar has darts, shove-ha'penny, and dominoes. There are tables out in a small but attractively planted garden. *(Recommended by Edward and Deanna Pearce, Peter and Anne Hollindale, Pat and Tony Martin)*

Free house ~ Licensee Michael Wilson ~ Real ale ~ Bar food (not Sun evening) ~ Restaurant ~ (01653) 648416 ~ Children in eating area of bar and restaurant ~ Open 12-3, 6.30-11(10.30 Sun)

THORGANBY SE6942 Map 7
Jefferson Arms 🍴 🛏

Off A163 NE of Selby, via Skipwith

The rösti menu in this friendly pub is very popular with customers, and is prepared by Mrs Rapp's husband who is Swiss. A rösti is a speciality with grated, fried potatoes: with swiss pork sausages in onion sauce or spinach, cheese and fried egg (£5.80), with ham and cheese gratinated and a fried egg, grilled lamb croquettes with herb oil and onion or with tuna, prawns, black olives, tomatoes and cheese (all £6.40), and pork in a cream of mushroom sauce (£7.90). Also, sandwiches (from £2.60; filled baguettes from £3.20), fluffy omelette filled with ham, cheese or mushrooms (£5.40), home-made ostrich burger (£6.40), vegetable lasagne (£6.80), haddock in beer batter with home-made chips (£6.90), chicken breast in a light creamy curry sauce with peaches (£9.90), halibut steak with herbs and butter (£10.90), and puddings such as hot chocolate fudge cake or lemon sponge pudding (from £3); the restaurant is no smoking. The spacious main bar is relaxed and stylish, with brick pillars and bar counter, dark wooden cushioned pews, several big mirrors on the green fleur-de-lys pattered walls, and a couple of decorative chairs. A delightful little beamed lounge is more comfortable still, full of sofas and armchairs, as well as fresh flowers and potted plants, a fireplace with logs beside it, an antique telephone, and a pile of *Hello!* magazines. The long narrow no smoking conservatory is festooned with passion flowers. Well kept Black Sheep Bitter and John Smiths on handpump, and a thoughtful wine list; piped music, dominoes, chess and backgammon. There are tables in a porch area, and more in a side garden with roses and a brick barbecue. It's a nice, peaceful place to stay. *(Recommended by June and Malcolm Farmer, Paul and Ursula Randall, Darly Graton, Graeme Gulibert, Derek and Sylvia Stephenson, Shaun Pinchbeck, J C Burley, Mr and Mrs M Hayes, Mr and Mrs Hugh Wood)*

Free house ~ Licensee Margaret Rapp ~ Real ale ~ Bar food ~ Restaurant ~ (01904) 448316 ~ Children in eating area of bar ~ Open 12-3, 6-11; 12-10.30 Sun; closed Mon, closed Tues lunchtime ~ Bedrooms: £35S/£55S

It's against the law for bar staff to smoke while handling food or drink.

THORNTON WATLASS SE2486 Map 10

Buck 🍺 🛏

Village signposted off B6268 Bedale—Masham

Some refurbishment this year for this popular inn, but the long-standing licensees (now at the helm for 15 years) make sure it remains a genuine local with their own cricket team (the pub not only borders the village cricket green – one wall is actually the boundary) and quoits team, and live music every other week. The pleasantly traditional right-hand bar has upholstered old-fashioned wall settles on the carpet, a fine mahogany bar counter, a high shelf packed with ancient bottles, several mounted fox masks and brushes (the Bedale hunt meets in the village), a brick fireplace, and a relaxed atmosphere; piped music. Good, popular food at lunchtime might include sandwiches, home-made soup (£2.75), tasty Masham rarebit (wensleydale cheese with local ale topped with bacon), smoked haddock fishcake or feta cheese and olive salad (£4.25), tandoori king prawns (£5.75), lasagne or steak and kidney pie (£7.75), aubergine, chick pea and tomato curry or deep fried whitby cod (£7.95), mediterranean lamb (£8.25), stir-fried chicken in black bean sauce (£8.95). Well kept Black Sheep Bitter, John Smiths, Tetleys, Theakstons, and guests from local breweries on handpump, and around 40 malt whiskies. The beamed and panelled no smoking dining room is hung with large prints of old Thornton Watlass cricket teams; a bigger bar has darts and dominoes. The sheltered garden has an equipped children's play area and there are summer barbecues – both quite a draw for families. *(Recommended by Mr and Mrs K M Hezelgrave , Doug Christian, Mrs Jane Wyles, Rod and Christine Hodkinson, John Close, RB, Mark Sandford, Ian and Brenda Paterson, Janet and Peter Race, Mr and Mrs J E C Tasker, Geoffrey and Brenda Wilson)*

Free house ~ Licensees Michael and Margaret Fox ~ Real ale ~ Bar food (12-2, 6.15-9.30) ~ Restaurant ~ (01677) 422461 ~ Children welcome ~ Jazz Sun lunchtime twice a month ~ Open 11-11; 11-midnight Sat; 12-10.30 Sun; closed evening 25 Dec ~ Bedrooms: £40S/£55(£60B)

WASS SE5679 Map 7

Wombwell Arms 🍷 🛏

Back road W of Ampleforth; or follow brown tourist-attraction sign for Byland Abbey off A170 Thirsk—Helmsley

Helpful and friendly new licensees have taken over this bustling pub, and readers are quick to show their enthusiam. It's an enjoyable place to stay, the food is very good indeed, and there's a relaxed, welcoming atmosphere. The little central bar is spotlessly kept and cosy, and the three low-beamed dining areas are comfortable and inviting and take in a former 17th-c granary. The imaginative food might include lunchtime sandwiches (from £3.75; hot or open ones from £4.95; not Sunday), home-made soups like spicy lentil, cauliflower and almond or curried parsnip (£2.95), garlic mushrooms topped with wensleydale cheese (£3.45), smoked salmon mousse (£4.65), aubergine tagine with spicy dumplings (£6.25), whitby cod with a crisp and cheese topping or steak, Guinness and mushroom pie (£7.95), local rabbit cooked with cider, apples and cream or lamb cutlets with chargrilled mediterranean vegetables (£8.95), salmon fillet in vodka, lime and watercress sauce (£9.25), chicken breast stuffed with stilton and sweet peppers and wrapped in bacon (£9.75), half pheasant with orange and brandy sauce (£9.95), and puddings (from £3.70). The restaurant is no smoking. Well kept Black Sheep Bitter, Timothy Taylors Landlord, and a guest such as Cropton Two Pints or Hambleton Goldfield on handpump, decent malt whiskies, and a carefully chosen wine list; cribbage, dominoes, and board games. *(Recommended by Peter and Anne-Marie O'Malley, Janet and Peter Race, Chris and Elaine Lyon, Peter Burton, R S and A Talbot, Christine and Neil Townend, R F Grieve, P and J Shapley, Mrs Jane Wyles, GD, KW, Mr and Mrs J E C Tasker, David and Helen Wilkins, Steve and Sue Griffiths, Richard Cole, Margaret and Brian Sanderson)*

Free house ~ Licensees Andy and Sue Cole ~ Real ale ~ Bar food (11.30-9.30) ~ Restaurant ~ (01347) 868280 ~ Children in restaurant ~ Open 11.30-11; 12-10.30 Sun; 12-2.30, 6.30-11winter Mon-Sat; 12-3, 7-10.30 Sun in winter ~ Bedrooms: £38B/£55B

WATH IN NIDDERDALE SE1467 Map 7
Sportsmans Arms 🍴 ☘ 🛏️

Nidderdale road off B6265 in Pateley Bridge; village and pub signposted over hump bridge
on right after a couple of miles

To make the most of a visit to this civilised restaurant-with-rooms, it's best to stay
overnight in one of the extremely comfortable and well equipped bedrooms. Most
people come to enjoy the superb food, but there is a welcoming bar where locals do
drop in for just a drink, and the long-standing licensee and his unassuming and
genuine staff will make everyone welcome. Using the best local produce – game from
the moors, fish delivered daily from Whitby, and Nidderdale lamb, pork and beef –
the carefully presented and prepared delicious food might include lunchtime
sandwiches, fresh soup (£3.50), warm goats cheese on roasted peppers with walnut
oil (£4.95), special hors d'oeuvres (from £5.50), smoked salmon rösti, crème fraîche,
and balsamic vinegar (£5.90), loin of pork with green peppercron and dijon sauce
(£9.90), breast of chicken on risotto with wild mushroom sauce (£10.50),
Scarborough woof in a tomato and basil crust (£11), Whitby cod with rarebit,
tomato and caper sauce (£11.50), monkfish provençale or grilled sirloin steak in a
stilton and olive sauce (£13.50), and puddings such as baked rice with prunes soaked
in rum, rich double chocolate roulade or sticky toffee pudding (from £4). The
restaurant is no smoking. There's a very sensible and extensive wine list, a good
choice of malt whiskies, several Russian vodkas, and Theakstons on electric pump;
open fires, dominoes. Benches and tables outside. As well as their own fishing on the
River Nidd, this is an ideal spot for walkers, hikers, and ornithologists, and there are
plenty of country houses, gardens, and cities to explore. *(Recommended by RJH,
Christine and Geoff Butler, Michael and Rosalind Dymond, Ivor and Shirley Thomas, Christine
and Malcolm Ingram, Mrs R A Cartwright, David and Susan Grey, Mrs C Monk, Geoff and
Angela Jaques, Patricia A Bruce, Mandy and Simon King, Janet and Peter Race, B, M and
P Kendall, P R Morley, Greta and Christopher Wells; also in* The Good Hotel Guide*)*

*Free house ~ Licensee Ray Carter ~ Real ale ~ Bar food ~ Restaurant ~ (01423)
711306 ~ Children in restaurant ~ Open 12-2.15, 7-11; closed 25 Dec ~ Bedrooms:
£45B/£70B*

WHITBY NZ9011 Map 10
Duke of York 🍺

Church Street, Harbour East Side

There's plenty of atmosphere in this lively pub with its splendid view over the
harbour entrance and the western cliff. The welcoming and comfortable beamed
lounge bar has decorations that include quite a bit of fishing memorabilia – though
it's the wide choice of good value fresh local fish on the menu itself which appeals
most: there might be fresh crab or prawn sandwiches (£2.95), large fillet of fresh cod
or fresh crab salad (£5.95), as well as other sandwiches (from £2.50; filled baguettes
from £3.95), vegetable lasagne (£4.95), steak in ale pie or chilli (£5.50), and
puddings. Well kept Black Sheep, Courage Directors, and John Smiths on
handpump, decent wines, lots of malt whiskies, hot winter mulled wine, and chilled
summer sangria, and quick pleasant service even when busy; piped music, TV, and
fruit machine. The pub is close to the famous 199 Steps that lead up to the abbey.
*(Recommended by Christopher Hayle, Peter F Marshall, Janet and Peter Race, David and Ruth
Hollands, the Didler, Mike and Mary Carter)*

*Unique Pub Co ~ Lease Lawrence Bradley ~ Real ale ~ Bar food (12-9; not 25 Dec) ~
No credit cards ~ (01947) 600324 ~ Children in restaurant until 9 ~ Live
entertainment Sun evenings ~ Open 11-11; 12-10.30 Sun; closed 25 Dec ~ Bedrooms:
/£30(£45B)*

Planning a day in the country? We list pubs in really attractive
scenery at the back of the book.

WIDDOP SD9333 Map 7
Pack Horse

The Ridge; from A646 on W side of Hebden Bridge, turn off at Heptonstall signpost (as it's a sharp turn, coming out of Hebden Bridge road signs direct you around a turning circle), then follow Slack and Widdop signposts; can also be reached from Nelson and Colne, on high, pretty road; OS Sheet 103 map reference 952317

Considering its isolation high up on the moors, this traditional walkers' pub is remarkably popular. The bar has warm winter fires, window seats cut into the partly panelled stripped stone walls that take in the moorland view, sturdy furnishings, and well kept Black Sheep Bitter and Special, Greene King Old Speckled Hen, and Thwaites Bitter on handpump, around 130 single malt whiskies, and some Irish ones as well, and decent wines; efficient service. Bar food includes home-made soup (from £1.95), filled baguettes (from £3.50), ploughman's (£3.95), home-made steak and kidney pie or vegetable bake (£4.95), steaks (from £7.95), and specials such as various curries (£6.95), fresh local trout (£8.95), and local seasonal game; two-course weekday lunchtime special (£5.95). The restaurant is only open on Saturday evenings. There are seats outside. *(Recommended by MJVK, Dr C C S Wilson, P Taylor, Greta and Christopher Wells, Neil Woodhead)*

Free house ~ Licensee Andrew Hollinrake ~ Real ale ~ Bar food ~ Restaurant ~ (01422) 842803 ~ Children welcome ~ Open 12-3, 7-11; 12-11 Sun; closed weekday winter lunchtimes and Mon Oct to Easter ~ Bedrooms: £28S/£44B

YORK SE5951 Map 7
Maltings 🍺 £

Tanners Moat/Wellington Row, below Lendal Bridge

Run by a larger-than-life character, this lively small pub is much loved by real ale drinkers – not just for the beers, but for its friendly, chatty atmosphere and entirely contrived, tricksy décor (which may not go down well with everyone). It is strong on salvaged somewhat quirky junk: old doors for the bar front and much of the ceiling, enamel advertising signs for the rest of it, what looks like a suburban front door for the entrance to the ladies', partly stripped orange brick walls, even a lavatory pan in one corner. There are six or seven particularly well kept changing ales on handpump, such as Black Sheep, Crouch Vale SAS, Enville White, Roosters Outlaw Stars and Stripes, Timothy Taylors Ram Tam, and York Brideshead, with frequent special events when the jovial landlord adds many more. He also has two or three continental beers on tap, up to four farm ciders, a dozen or so country wines, and more Irish whiskeys than you normally see. Decent well priced generous lunchtime food (get there early for a seat) might include sandwiches (from £2.10), very popular truly home-made chips (£2) with chilli or spaghetti bolognese (£2.50), in a giant butty (£3), and haddock (£4.50), and beef in ale pie or stilton and leek bake (£4.95). The day's papers are framed in the gents'; fruit machine and maybe piped radio. Nearby parking is virtually impossible; the pub is very handy for the Rail Museum. *(Recommended by Richard Lewis, Sue Holland, Dave Webster, Eric Larkham, the Didler, Chris and Elaine Lyon, Amie Taylor, Andy and Jill Kassube, N J Worthington, S L Tracy, David Carr, P Abbott)*

Free house ~ Licensee Shaun Collinge ~ Real ale ~ Bar food (12-2 weekdays, 12-4 weekends; not evenings) ~ No credit cards ~ (01904) 655387 ~ Children tolerated but must be well behaved ~ Blues Mon, folk Tues ~ Open 11-11; 12-10.30 Sun

Tap & Spile 🍺 £

Monkgate

Don't be put off by the unprepossessing exterior of this late-Victorian brick building. Inside, the front lounge has wooden furnishings on the stripped wooden floor, some panelling, a bookcase, a back bar, and a lounge area with a raised games area: darts, fruit machine, TV, dominoes, and piped music. But it's the friendly atmosphere, and fine choice of around 8 well kept real ales on handpump, that draws in the customers. Changing almost daily, there might be Arundel Best, Black Sheep Bitter, Courage Directors, Everards Tiger, Hambleton Nightmare, Harviestoun Brooker's Bitter & Twisted, Roosters Yankee, and Theakstons Mild; also, farm cider, and 20 country wines. The big split-level bar has a front area with leather seating, lots of books on big bookshelves, cricketing Spy cartoons, a cosy open fire, and a raised back area with pool, darts, fruit machine and TV; dominoes and piped music. Straightforward bar food includes sandwiches or toasties (£2.50; hot baguettes £2.95), home-made soup (£1.95), filled baked potatoes (£2.95), filled giant yorkshire puddings, steak in ale pie, pork with apples, honey and cider, cottage pie or haddock with lemon sauce (all £4.50), daily specials, and puddings (£1.95). The outside terrace has seats under parasols and outside heaters for cooler weather; there are more seats in the garden. *(Recommended by the Didler, Eric Larkham, David Carr, Canon Michael Bourdeaux, Paul and Ursula Randall, Ian Baillie, Greta and Christopher Wells, P Abbott)*

Local Heroes Pub Co ~ Manager Andy Mackay ~ Real ale ~ Bar food (12-3; not evenings) ~ (01904) 656158 ~ Children in eating area of bar ~ Various live entertainment Sun evening ~ Open 11.30-11; 12-10.30 Sun

---

Lucky Dip

Besides the fully inspected pubs, you might like to try these Lucky Dips recommended to us and described by readers (if you do, please send us reports: www.goodguides.com).

Aberford [SE4337]
Swan [best to use A642 junction to leave A1]: Useful high-throughout dining pub, vast choice of good value generous food from good sandwiches to bargain carvery and display of puddings, lots of black timber, prints, pistols, cutlasses, stuffed animals and hunting trophies, well kept Boddingtons, Flowers, Tetleys and Timothy Taylors, generous glasses of wine, friendly and amusing uniformed staff, upstairs evening restaurant; children welcome, bedrooms *(H Bramwell)*
Acaster Malbis [SE5945]
Ship [Moor End]: Comfortably worn riverside inn, very busy in summer (caravan sites nearby), two-level bar with dark beams and brasses, decent food from sandwiches and baguettes, well kept Timothy Taylors Landlord, efficient friendly service, attractive garden with play area; bedrooms clean and comfortable *(Mr and Mrs C Roberts)*
Ainderby Steeple [SE3392]
☆ *Wellington Heifer* [A684, 3 miles from A1]: Very wide choice of enjoyable fresh food inc good Sun lunch served quickly, cheerfully and generously in long low-ceilinged bar, two-level lounge and dining room, log fires, good beer range; discounts for local B&B visitors *(Carol and Dono Leaman, Mike and Maggie Betton)*
Ainthorpe [NZ7008]
☆ *Fox & Hounds* [Brook Lane]: Charmingly traditional moorland pub with wide choice of well presented fresh food inc interesting dishes and good puddings, reasonable prices, grand open fire, well kept Black Sheep and Theakstons, good friendly service; open all day, good bedrooms *(Tim and Catherine Jones, Mr and Mrs M Bashford, Mr and Mrs C J Pink)*
Aislaby [SE8508]
Huntsman [Main Rd, off A171 W of Whitby]: Extended beamed pub with lots of pictures, cosy seating, wide choice of good value food

inc superb sandwiches, fish, local produce, good vegetarian range and children's dishes, very efficient friendly staff, well kept Camerons and Marstons, decent wines; piped music, busy wknds and holidays; children welcome, bedrooms *(Edward Leetham)*
Allerthorpe [SE7847]
☆ *Plough* [Main St]: Clean and airy two-room lounge bar with friendly welcome, snug alcoves, hunting prints, World War II RAF and RCAF photographs, open fires, wide choice of good sensibly priced food, well kept Greene King Old Speckled Hen, Marstons Pedigree, Theakstons Best and Tetleys, decent house wines, well served coffee, restaurant; games extension with pool, piped music or juke box etc; pleasant garden, handy for Burnby Hall *(Greta and Christopher Wells, Paul and Ursula Randall, LYM)*
Allerton Bywater [SE4227]
Boat [Main St]: Busy pub brewing its own refreshing Boat ales such as Boatburger wheat beer, good value food for the heartiest appetites, friendly staff (landlord an ex Rugby League player, appropriate mementoes); pity area, garden by Aire & Calder Canal, open all day Sun and summer *(Andy and Jill Kassube, Phil and Anne Smithson)*
Ampleforth [SE5878]
☆ *White Swan* [East End]: Recently reworked but keeping traditional country atmosphere, with beams, bare boards (a striking tartan carpet in one no smoking dining room), a variety of seating areas inc nooks and corners, enjoyable food from lunchtime sandwiches (not Sun) and thoughtful children's dishes to enterprising dishes and unusual specials (such as a carve-yourself roast duck with a jug of delicious orange sauce), well kept John Smiths, Timothy Taylors Landlord and Tetleys, lots of malt whiskies, decent wines, good friendly service even on very busy Sat night; plenty of tables on

back terrace, open all day Sun *(Liz Clayton)*

Appleton Roebuck [SE5542]

Shoulder of Mutton [Chapel Green]: Cheerful and attractive unpretentious bar overlooking village green, wide choice of good value food inc cheap steaks in bar and restaurant, well kept Sam Smiths on all four handpumps, quick friendly service; can be crowded with caravanners summer; bedrooms *(Mr and Mrs C Roberts, Beryl and Bill Farmer)*

Appleton-le-Moors [SE7388]

Moors [off A170 E of Kirkby Moorside]: Traditional stone-built village pub refurbished throughout by new owners, old-fashioned no smoking beamed bar with high-backed settle built in by log fire in old range, real ale, wide choice of food in no smoking dining room, pool room (smoking allowed); new bedrooms in former back barn, tables in walled garden, moors walks straight from the pub *(anon)*

Arncliffe [SD9473]

☆ *Falcon* [off B6160 N of Grassington]: Basic well worn country tavern, ideal setting on moorland village green, no frills, Youngers tapped from cask to stoneware jugs in central hatch-style servery, generous plain lunchtime and early evening sandwiches and snacks, open fire in small bar with elderly furnishings and humorous sporting prints, airy back sunroom (children allowed here lunchtime) looking on to pleasant garden; run by same family for generations – they take time to get to know; cl winter Thurs evenings; plain bedrooms (not all year), good breakfast and evening meal – real value *(Kevin Thorpe, Ann Williams, Tony Hughes, LYM, the Didler)*

Arthington [SE2644]

Wharfedale [A659 E of Otley]: Recently refurbished, warm and comfortable, mix of tables, chairs and banquettes in open-plan carpeted bar, intimate alcoves, soft lighting, Yorkshire landscapes, good food range, well kept ales inc Black Sheep, several wines by the glass, separate restaurant *(Michael Doswell)*

Askrigg [SD9591]

Crown [Main St]: Pleasant neatly kept no-frills local, several separate areas off main bar with blazing fires inc old-fashioned range, relaxed atmosphere, cheap generous home-cooked food inc good value Sun lunch and good puddings choice, Black Sheep, Dent and Theakstons XB from swan necks, helpful welcoming staff; has doubled as James Herriot's 'Drovers Arms'; children and walkers welcome, tables outside *(Mr and Mrs J McRobert, P Abbott, Walter and Sue Anderson, Terry Mizen)*

Kings Arms [signed from A684 Leyburn—Sedbergh in Bainbridge]: Early 19th-c coaching inn in popular village, three old-fashioned bars with photographs of filming here of James Herriot's *All Creatures Great and Small*, interesting traditional furnishings and décor (shame they don't always light the log fire), well kept ales such as Black Sheep, John Smiths, Theakstons Best and XB, good choice of wines by the glass and of malt whiskies, wide food choice (may be a wait when busy), no smoking waitress-served grill room and set-priced

restaurant; bedrooms, independent holiday complex behind *(Walter and Sue Anderson, Martin and Karen Wake, Catherine and Richard Preston, P Abbott, Mrs Jane Wyles, Mike and Wena Stevenson, Mrs S E Griffiths, Gareth and Toni Edwards, LYM, Mike Ridgway, Sarah Miles, Norman Fox, John Close, Dr and Mrs Nigel Holmes, Godfrey and Sue Barker)*

Bainbridge [SD9390]

☆ *Rose & Crown*: Ancient inn overlooking moorland village green, old settles in old-fashioned beamed and oak-panelled front bar with big log fire, well kept John Smiths and Thwaites, good coffee, enjoyable food from good value baguettes up in bar and restaurant (service stops 2 sharp); children welcome, busy back extension popular with families (pool, juke box etc); open all day, bedrooms *(Jim and Maggie Cowell, Pat and Robert Watt, Mrs Jane Wyles, Norman Fox, P Abbott, Greta and Christopher Wells, Jim Abbott, Geoffrey and Brenda Wilson, Suzanne McCarthy, LYM)*

Bardsey [SE3643]

☆ *Bingley Arms* [Church Lane]: Ancient pub smartly decorated to match, good home-made fresh food inc interesting dishes and early-supper bargains, spacious lounge divided into separate areas inc no smoking, huge fireplace, well kept Black Sheep, John Smiths and Tetleys, good wines, pleasant speedy service, smaller public bar, picturesque upstairs brasserie; charming quiet terrace with interesting barbecues inc vegetarian *(John and Christine Lowe, Christine and Neil Townend, LYM, John and Helen Rushton)*

Barkisland [SE0520]

New Rock: Modest hilltop pub popular for incredibly cheap well cooked food (evenings only), Moorhouses Pendle Witches Brew and Tetleys *(Herbert and Susan Verity)*

Bessacarr [SE6101]

Hare & Tortoise [Bawtry Rd (A638)]: Former surgeon's house redone as relaxed and civilised Vintage Inn, varying-sized antique tables in small rooms off bar, sensibly priced food all day, friendly and efficient young staff, good drinks choice, log fire *(Stephen Woad)*

Beverley [TA0339]

Corner House [Norwood]: Warm and welcoming, attractive pastel décor, pews, easy chairs and sofas, friendly staff, good fresh food (inc Sun breakfast from 10), well kept beer, wide range of fresh fruit juices, hot beverages *(Abigail Tack)*

Tap & Spile [Flemingate]: Well done Tap & Spile in ancient building, friendly service and laid-back atmosphere, well kept changing ales such as Black Sheep and Palmers, Weston's farm cider, huge choice of country wines, decent basic food, no smoking room; lovely view of Minster *(Paul and Ursula Randall)*

Woolpack [Westwood Rd]: Small welcoming local in former 19th-c cottage pair, well kept ales such as Burtonwood and Hop Back Summer Lightning, decent wines by the glass, limited food, tiny snug, not much bigger lounge, very friendly service, simple spotless furnishings, no pretensions, brasses, teapots, prints and maps *(Paul and Ursula Randall)*

Bilbrough [SE5346]

Three Hares [off A64 York—Tadcaster]: Firmly run quietly upmarket dining pub with good individually prepared food (so not quick), minimalist décor, Black Sheep, Timothy Taylors Landlord and a guest beer from end bar with sofas and log fire, good value wines; has been cl Mon *(Shaun Pinchbeck, LYM, Mr and Mrs C Roberts)*

Bingley [SE1039]

Brown Cow [Ireland Bridge; B6429 just W of junction with A650]: Genuine and unpretentious, open-plan but snugly divided, with easy chairs, toby jugs, lots of pictures, panelling; well kept Timothy Taylors Bitter, Best, Landlord and winter Ram Tam, good reasonably priced food from sandwiches to steaks, no smoking restaurant; maybe piped music, jazz Mon; children welcome, tables on sheltered terrace, pleasant spot *(Nigel and Sue Foster, LYM)*

Star [York St]: Tucked-away local well worth finding for particularly well kept Tetleys Bitter and Mild *(J Reed-Purvis)*

Birstall [SE2126]

Black Bull [from Bradford towards Dewsbury turn right at parish church into Church Lane]: Old building opp part-Saxon church, dark panelling and low beams, upstairs former courtroom (now a function room, but they may give you a guided tour), Whitbreads-related ales with maybe an interesting guest such as Ossett Special, good cheap home-made food inc bargain early meals and good value Sun lunch, old local photographs; recent small extension; jazz nights Thurs *(Edward Leetham, Derek and Sylvia Stephenson, Michael Butler, Bernie Adams)*

Bishop Burton [SE9939]

Altisidora [A1079 Beverley—York]: Good value family food pub open all day, comfortable alcoves inc raised no smoking area off low-beamed modernised lounge, wide choice of enjoyable food, Marstons Pedigree and three other ales, welcoming helpful staff; nr pretty pond in lovely village green *(LYM, Andy Marks, Mr and Mrs F J Parmenter)*

Bishop Monkton [SE3366]

Lamb & Flag [off A61 Harrogate—Ripon]: Small pub with decent menu, real ales, sparkling brasses and other knick-knacks; good-sized back garden, pretty village *(Margaret Dickinson, Walter and Sue Anderson, H Bramwell)*

Masons Arms [St Johns Rd]: Cosy carpeted bar with real ale, open fire and dark wood furnishings, neat restaurant, good enterprising cooking inc flame grills; bedrooms, pretty village overlooking beck *(Mrs Jane Wyles)*

Bishop Wilton [SE7955]

Fleece [just off A166 York—Bridlington; Pocklington Rd]: Recently refurbished with concentration on good food (booking suggested), open-plan but partly divided, nice atmosphere, efficient staff *(P R Morley)*

Bishopthorpe [SE5947]

Marcia [Main St]: Welcoming and immaculate

village pub with good choice of reasonably priced freshly cooked food, generous helpings, wide range of beers, wines and spirits, friendly staff, family room; soft piped music; clean and comfortable bedrooms, tables in back garden, pleasant village, picturesque riverside walk from York *(D J Kay)*

Bolton Abbey [SE0754]

Devonshire Arms: Comfortable and elegant hotel in marvellous position, good if pricy food from sandwiches up in attractively furnished brasserie bar with modern paintings, well kept Greene King Ruddles County, John Smiths and Theakstons Black Bull, good wines, smiling staff, tables in garden; handy for the priory, walks in the estate and Strid River valley; smart restaurant, helicopter pad; good bedrooms *(Mrs Jane Wyles)*

Boroughbridge [SE3967]

Three Horseshoes [Bridge St]: Spotless unspoilt 1930s pub/hotel run by same family from the start, character landlord, friendly locals, huge fire in lounge, darts, dominoes and cards in public bar (not always open), original features inc slide-down glass bar shutters, good plain home cooking from sandwiches to steaks in bars and restaurant, well kept Camerons Strongarm and Tetleys, splendidly tiled ladies'; bedrooms, open all day Sun *(Pete Baker, Kevin Thorpe, the Didler, Phil and Sally Gorton)*

Bradford [SE1633]

☆ *Cock & Bottle* [Barkerend Rd, up Church Bank from centre; on left a few hundred yds past cathedral]: Carefully restored Victorian décor, well kept John Smiths and Tetleys, deep-cut and etched windows and mirrors enriched with silver and gold leaves, stained glass, enamel intaglios, heavily carved woodwork and traditional furniture, saloon with a couple of little snugs (one often with Christian counselling) and a rather larger carpeted music room, open fire in public bar *(BB, the Didler)*

☆ *Fighting Cock* [Preston St (off B6145)]: Busy bare-floor alehouse by industrial estate, particularly well kept Timothy Taylors Landlord and ten or more changing ales such as Black Sheep, Exmoor Gold, Sam Smiths and Theakstons, also farm ciders, foreign bottled beers, food inc all-day doorstep sandwiches, coal fires; low prices *(the Didler, A Boss)*

New Beehive [Westgate]: Edwardian inn popular with musicians, artists, bohemians and students, lots of rooms inc good pool room, huge range of beers, gas lighting, candles and coal fires; no food Sun, live music below (open till 1am Fri/Sat); nice back courtyard, bedrooms *(the Didler)*

Shoulder of Mutton [Kirkgate]: Notable for its fine suntrap garden; cosy inside, with decent fresh lunchtime food (not Sun), well kept cheap Sam Smiths *(the Didler)*

Brandesburton [TA1247]

☆ *Dacre Arms* [signed off A165 N of Beverley and Hornsea turn-offs]: Brightly modernised comfortably bustling pub popular for wide choice of generous good value food from lunchtime sandwiches (not wknds) to steaks, inc OAP specials and children's; well kept Black Sheep, Courage Directors, Tetleys and Theakstons Old Peculier tapped from the cask, children welcome, darts, restaurant; open for food all day wknds *(Andy Marks, Bill and Sheila McLardy, LYM)*

Bridlington [TA1867]

Hook & Parrot [Esplanade]: Modern pub well done out in olde-worlde nautical style, lots of old lamps, snug alcoves, reasonably priced Scottish Courage beers, lunchtime food; pool, TV etc in separate bar *(Kevin Blake)*

Pavilion Bar [Jeromes, Esplanade]: Wicker chairs, modern art, huge lamps, lots of glass and iron pillars in former Floral Hall Theatre, well kept Marstons Pedigree and John Smiths, food lunchtime and early evening; play area, small stage for entertainment *(Kevin Blake)*

Brighouse [SE1323]

Red Rooster [Brookfoot; A6025 towards Elland]: Homely stone-built alehouse with well kept Roosters Yankee and quickly changing interesting ales from all over, brewery memorabilia, open fire, separate areas inc one with books to read or buy, no food, no machines *(the Didler)*

Brompton [SE9582]

Cayley Arms [A170 W of Scarborough]: Welcoming uncluttered pub in pretty village, friendly helpful staff, good freshly cooked generous food inc good choice of fish and local shellfish, reasonable prices, well kept ales inc Theakstons; garden *(Greta and Christopher Wells, Beryl and Bill Farmer, Peter Burton)*

Village Inn [off A684 just N of Northallerton; Water End]: Huge collection of china, tankards, teapots, cows and jugs; wide range of hearty good value food pleasantly served in long cosy narrow room, good range of beers and whiskies; well appointed bedrooms in motel wing behind, attractive countryside *(Doug Christian)*

Burley Woodhead [SE1545]

Hermit: Small pub, recently sympathetically renovated and extended, oak panelling and beams, comfortable built-in seats, bay window seat with Wharfedale views, well kept Courage Directors, John Smiths and Magnet, Tetleys and Theakstons Best, good value food, restaurant; no machines or juke box *(Stephen Denbigh, John and Lis Burgess)*

Burn [SE5928]

Wheatsheaf [A19 Selby—Doncaster]: Welcoming, with good value usual food, John Smiths, Timothy Taylors Landlord, Tetleys and a guest microbrew, eclectic décor inc assorted saws, hops, model lorries, galleon, big rocking horse; pool room, small garden *(Neil and Anita Christopher)*

Burnt Yates [SE2561]

☆ *Bay Horse* [B6165 6 miles N of Harrogate]: Friendly 18th-c dining pub with wide range of bar food inc outstanding steaks and some choice vegetarian dishes, log fires, low beams, brasses, hunting pictures; well kept real ales such as Rudgate Ruby Mild, courteous staff, pleasant restaurant (booking advised); maybe piped music; bedrooms in motel extension

(Tim and Ann Newell, Jim Abbott)

New Inn [Pateley Bridge Rd]: Candlelit pub with good atmosphere, lots of antiques, nicely panelled back room, well prepared traditional food, good reasonably priced wines, well kept Theakstons *(Mrs Jane Wyles, Sue Holland, Dave Webster)*

Burton Agnes [TA1063]

Blue Bell [Main Rd]: Small white-fronted pub with limited choice of good food from good doorstep sandwiches up, separate dining room, pleasant service; piped music; handy for Burton Agnes Hall and Norman manor house *(anon)*

Burton Leonard [SE3364]

Hare & Hounds [off A61 Ripon—Harrogate]: Well organised country pub with good local following for wide choice of reasonably priced good generous food inc interesting dishes and popular steak and kidney pie, warm, comfortable and spotless beamed bar with paintings, copper and brass, sofas in cosy coffee lounge, well kept ales such as Black Sheep, Tetleys, Theakstons and Timothy Taylors Landlord, decent wines, very friendly attentive staff even when busy, pleasant spacious restaurant; children welcome if eating, no games or juke box *(H Bramwell, Geoff and Anne Field)*

Calder Grove [SE3017]

Navigation [just off M1 junction 39; A636 signposted Denby Dale, then 1st right – Broad Cut Rd]: Good motorway break – cheery waterside local full of canalia, with well kept ales such as Bass and Eastwood Black Stump and Nettlethrasher, low prices, good simple food; tables outside with play area, walks by Calder & Hebble Canal *(Phil and Anne Smithson, LYM)*

Campsall [SE5414]

Old Bells [High St]: Well kept real ales, cheap food, friendly staff; handy diversion from A1 *(Comus and Sarah Elliott)*

Carlton Husthwaite [SE5077]

Carlton Inn: Cosy and pleasantly modernised dining pub with good varied food (even Sun evening) with super veg, bargain lunches, fine choice for three-course candlelit dinner (booking advised), cheerful efficient service, well kept Youngers *(Walter and Susan Rinaldi-Butcher, R and J Bateman)*

Cawood [SE5737]

☆ *Ferry* [King St (B1222 NW of Selby), by Ouse swing bridge]: Unspoilt but neatly kept 16th-c inn, welcoming comfortable rooms, massive inglenook, stripped brickwork, bare boards, well kept Marstons, Timothy Taylors Landlord and local guest beers tapped from the cask, good reasonably priced food; cl wkdy lunchtimes; tables out on flagstone terrace and grass by fascinating River Ouse swing bridge, good value modest bedrooms with bathrooms *(Janet and Peter Race, R E and E C M Pick)*

Clifton [SE1622]

☆ *Black Horse* [Towngate/Coalpit Lane; off Brighouse rd from M62 junction 25]: Smart yet cosily charming dining pub very popular for wide choice of good generous food from interesting ciabatta sandwiches and other snacks to restaurant meals inc good value set dinners; comfortable oak-beamed bars, very good service, well kept Whitbreads-related and other beers such as Black Sheep and Tetleys, decent wines, open fire; comfortable bedrooms, pleasant village *(Michael Butler, Mike Ridgway, Sarah Miles, Andy and Jill Kassube)*

Cloughton [SE9798]

Falcon [A171 out towards Whitby]: Stone-built pub dating from 18th c, on edge of Staintondale moor, views to sea; big open-plan bar with welcoming real fire, good value food inc fine seafood salad in pleasant dining area (no booking, but worth the wait for a table), cheerful service, well kept Bass, pleasant staff; good bedrooms with own bathrooms *(Eric Locker, Walter and Sue Anderson)*

Hayburn Wyke Hotel [just N of Cloughton Newlands]: Warmly friendly very black and white L-shaped bar smartened up under new owners, great position nr NT Hayburn Wyke, spectacular Cleveland Way coastal path and Scarborough—Whitby path/bicycle trail, lots of tables outside; well kept Black Sheep, Theakstons and guest beers, good value food in eating area and restaurant inc wknd carvery, pleasant informal service; well behaved children welcome, unobtrusive play areas, comfortable bedrooms, good breakfast *(M Borthwick, Mr and Mrs L H Latimer)*

Cloughton Newlands [TA0196]

☆ *Bryherstones* [Newlands Rd, off A171 in Cloughton]: Several interconnecting rooms, well kept Timothy Taylors beers, over 50 whiskies, cosy local atmosphere (dogs seem welcome), good reasonably priced generous food in separate eating area, welcoming service; pool room, quieter room upstairs; children welcome, delightful surroundings; cl Mon lunchtime *(Louise Delaine, Walter and Sue Anderson)*

Coley [SE1226]

☆ *Brown Horse* [Lane Ends, Denholme Gate Rd (A644 Brighouse—Keighley, a mile N of Hipperholme)]: Very popular lunchtime for long-serving licensees' good sensibly priced traditional food (not Sat evening), prompt smart staff, well kept Timothy Taylors Landlord and Theakstons, decent house wines, open fires in three bustling rooms, golfing memorabilia, pictures, delft shelf of china and bottles, pipe collection, no smoking restaurant and small light back conservatory overlooking garden *(Robert Gartery, Geoffrey and Brenda Wilson)*

Colton [SE5444]

☆ *Old Sun* [off A64 York—Tadcaster]: Attractive 17th-c beamed local, friendly new landlady and chef/landlord from Bangkok, authentic food from there alongside familiar dishes, low doorways, old settles and banquettes, sparkling brasses, well kept Courage Directors and John Smiths, decent wines, log fires, welcoming staff; picnic-sets out in front *(J C Burley, Andrew and Ruth Triggs)*

Cracoe [SD9760]

☆ *Devonshire Arms* [B6265 Skipton—Grassington]: Low shiny black beams

supporting creaky white planks, little stable-type partitions, solidly comfortable furnishings, polished flooring tiles with rugs here and there, old pictures, helpful management, good value food, well kept Jennings beers; darts, dominoes, cribbage, piped music; children in eating areas, picnic-sets on terrace with well kept flowerbeds, more seating on lawn, recently refurbished bedrooms, open all day *(Mr and Mrs P Dix, I D Greenfield, WAH, LYM)*

Crakehall [SE2490]

Bay Horse [A684 2 miles NW of Bedale]: Good imaginative carefully presented food, Black Sheep and good house wines, helpful service, welcoming fires, cheerful locals; fine setting on green *(Janet and Peter Race)*

Cross Hills [SE0045]

Old White Bear [Keighley Rd]: Enterprising local brewing its own Old Bear Best and occasional seasonal beers (also Boddingtons), wide choice of good reasonably priced home cooking, five welcoming rooms, beams and open fires, pub games; piped music, games machine, TV *(J Reed-Purvis, Dr B and Mrs P B Baker, Richard Lewis)*

Dalehouse [NZ7818]

Fox & Hounds [Dalehouse Bank, off A174 at Staithes]: Small spotless country pub with fox and hounds theme throughout, busy local front bar, very friendly attentive staff, well kept Theakstons, good usual home-made food from children's dishes through good choice of fresh fish to steaks, no smoking side room *(David Field)*

Deighton [SE6243]

White Swan [A19 N of Escrick]: Popular local dining pub with consistently good value food from sandwiches and ploughman's up inc good vegetarian choice, welcoming service, two comfortable bars, separate restaurant, good choice of wines by the glass; seats outside (some traffic noise), pretty floral decorations *(P R Morley, Roger A Bellingham, Keith and Di Newsome)*

Dewsbury [SE2523]

Huntsman [Walker Cottages, Chidswell Lane, Shaw Cross – pub signed]: Cosy converted cottages alongside urban-fringe farm, low beams, lots of brasses and agricultural bric-a-brac, friendly locals, wide choice of well kept beers inc Black Sheep and John Smiths, roaring fire, small no smoking front extension; no food evening or Sun/Mon lunchtime, busy evenings *(Michael Butler)*

Leggers [Robinsons Boat Yard, Savile Town Wharf, Mill St E (SE of B6409)]: Friendly if basic wharfside hayloft conversion with up to six real ales inc Sunset beers brewed here such as Marriot Mild and Canal No 5, their own cider, reasonably priced lunchtime food and filled rolls all day, real fire, helpful staff, daily papers and magazines, low beams, lots of old brewery and pub memorabilia; pool and games machines; open all day *(the Didler, Richard Lewis, Andy and Jill Kassube)*

☆ *West Riding Licensed Refreshment Rooms* [Station, Wellington Rd]: Busy three-room early Victorian station bar with well kept ales such as

Black Sheep, Durham White Velvet, Roosters Special and Timothy Taylors Landlord, also one from Anglo Dutch (a local microbrewery they partly own); farm ciders, good value interesting wkdy lunchtime food inc vegetarian, popular midweek curry or pie nights, daily papers, friendly staff, coal fire, no smoking area till 6, lots of steam memorabilia; juke box may be loud, jazz nights; disabled access, open all day *(the Didler, N J Worthington, S L Tracy, Andy and Jill Kassube, Richard Lewis)*

Doncaster [SE5703]

Corner Pin [St Sepulchre Gate W, Cleveland St]: Refurbished two-room corner local, well kept beers inc guests such as Barnsley and local Glentworth, plush lounge, old prints, good value traditional food from fine hot sandwiches up, bar with darts, games machine and TV; open all day *(the Didler, Richard Lewis, N J Worthington, S L Tracy)*

Hogshead [Hall Gate]: Large brightly decorated open-plan pub with good choice of well kept microbrewery beers, friendly staff, usual menu, light wood tables and chairs, armchairs and sofa by fireplace; tables out behind, open all day, can get very busy evenings *(Richard Lewis)*

Leopard [West St]: Lively and friendly, with superb tiled façade, lunchtime food, well kept John Smiths, Glentworth Lightyear and a changing guest beer such as Wychwood Dr Thirstys; lounge with lots of bric-a-brac, children's games and juke box (some classic 80s tracks), bar area with pool, darts, TV and machine; open all day, good live music upstairs, disabled access; can get very busy, close to railway stn *(Richard Lewis, the Didler)*

Salutation [South Parade, towards race course]: Bustling 18th-c Tetleys Festival Alehouse with plenty of beams and comfortable seating, good choice of well kept beers inc rarities, low-priced food all day, side games room; back TV area, quiet juke box; open all day, tables out behind *(Richard Lewis, N J Worthington, S L Tracy)*

Tut 'n' Shive [W Laith Gate]: Well kept Black Sheep and other ales, farm cider, popular food, attractive prices, enthusiastic landlord and friendly staff, bare boards, flagstones and panelling (even old doors pressed into service as wall/ceiling coverings), lots of pump clips, dim lighting; pin table, good juke box, games machine, big-screen SkyTV sports, quiz and music nights; open all day *(Richard Lewis)*

Downholme [SE1198]

Bolton Arms [off A6108 Leyburn—Richmond]: Cosy two-bar village pub with lots of pictures, old advertisements and Royal Scots Greys memorabilia; great views from conservatory dining room, interesting food cooked to order, well kept Theakstons, decent wines; two spacious bedrooms sharing bathroom *(Mrs C V Harden)*

Easingwold [SE5270]

George [Market Pl]: Trim market town hotel popular with older people, comfortable quiet corners even when busy, well kept Black Sheep, Theakstons and guest beers, good food in bar and restaurant inc Whitby fish, pleasant staff; bedrooms *(Margaret Dickinson, Greta and Christopher Wells, Janet and Peter Race)*

East Keswick [SE3644]

Travellers Rest [A659 N of Leeds]: Genial landlord, good value food inc children's helpings and good choice of sandwiches, Black Sheep and Tetleys, good views, extra dining area upstairs; play area, handy for Harewood House *(M Joyner)*

East Witton [SE1586]

☆ *Coverbridge Inn* [over ½ mile on road to Middleham]: Homely and welcoming unspoilt old Dales pub with two small character bars, massive helpings of good home-made food in eating area, well kept Theakstons; open all day, bedrooms – handy for walkers *(Anna, LYM)*

Egton Bridge [NZ8005]

☆ *Postgate* [signed off A171 W of Whitby]: Relaxed two-bar moorland village local, cheerful landlord, useful bar meals inc good fish choice, some unusual dishes and children's, well kept Theakstons, beams, ochre walls and dark panelling, quarry tiles, rustic bric-a-brac, old coal-fired kitchen range, traditional games in public bar, small restaurant; tables on sunny flagstoned terrace, has been open all day, bedrooms *(LYM, Phil and Heidi Cook, Colin McKerrow)*

Elland [SE1121]

Barge & Barrel [quite handy for M62 junction 24; Park Rd (A6025, via A629 and B6114)]: Large welcoming old-fashioned pub brewing several of its own good real ales, changing guest beers, pleasant staff, huge helpings of cheap lunchtime food (not Weds), family room (with air hockey); piped radio; seats by industrial canal, open all day *(John Marshall, the Didler, Richard Houghton)*

Ellerby [NZ8015]

Ellerby Hotel [just off A174 Whitby rd; Ryeland Lane]: Quiet small hotel with good pub atmosphere, imaginative bar meals from usual pies to unusual meat and fish dishes, very welcoming staff, well kept beer; good restaurant; bedrooms comfortable and well priced, with enormous breakfast *(Walter and Sue Anderson, Derek Stafford)*

Elslack [SD9249]

☆ *Tempest Arms* [just off A56 Earby—Skipton]: Enjoyable food stop, with cheerful service, quietly decorated linked areas, stripped stonework, log fire, wide choice from sandwiches to Aberdeen Angus steaks, Jennings ales with a guest such as Adnams, lots of wines by the glass, restaurant; piped music; tables outside largely screened from the road; children welcome, bedrooms, open all day *(Mike and Mary Carter, Patrick Renouf, WAH, Andy and Jill Kassube, Dudley and Moira Cockroft, LYM)*

Embsay [SE0053]

☆ *Elm Tree* [Elm Tree Sq]: Popular well refurbished open-plan beamed village pub with settles and old-fashioned prints, log-effect gas fire, no smoking dining room, good honest hearty home-made food lunchtime and from 5.30 inc good-sized children's helpings, friendly helpful service, well kept changing ales such as Fullers London Pride, Greene King Abbot,

Marstons Pedigree, Timothy Taylors Landlord, Wadworths 6X and one brewed for the pub, games area; busy wknds esp evenings; comfortable good value bedrooms, handy for steam railway *(M S Catling, Dudley and Moira Cockroft)*

Escrick [SE6442]

Black Bull [E of A19 York—Selby]: Wide choice of food inc popular cheap Sun lunch and early supper bargains in relaxed and unpretentious open-plan pub divided by arches and back-to-back fireplaces, flagstones one side, mix of wooden tables with benches, stools and chairs, small helpings for children and OAPs, good friendly service, well kept John Smiths, Tetleys and Theakstons, back dining room *(Roger A Bellingham, Mrs B Garmston)*

Farndale East [SE6697]

☆ *Feversham Arms* [Church Houses, next to Farndale Nature Reserve]: In lovely daffodil valley (very busy then), two unspoilt but bright flagstoned rooms, lots of brass, jugs and plates, fox masks, stuffed stoat, coal fire in old kitchen range; well kept Tetleys, good value straightforward home-made food, smart beamed and stripped-stone restaurant, friendly family service; very popular wknds; nice small garden, good bedrooms, big breakfast *(I J Thurman, Mr and Mrs C J Pink)*

Farnley Tyas [SE1612]

☆ *Golden Cock* [signed off A629 Huddersfield—Sheffield]: Spacious and smartly comfortable, with wide range of good adventurous food, also good choice of sandwiches (not cheap) and popular Sun lunch, welcoming landlord, efficient cheerful service, Tetleys Mild and a guest such as Timothy Taylors, good wine choice; pleasant hill village *(A Preston)*

Finghall [SE1890]

Queens Head [off A684 E of Leyburn]: Warm, comfortable and roomy, with friendly helpful staff, reasonably priced good food, well kept Johns Smiths and Theakstons with a guest such as Marstons Pedigree, good wine range, large back Dales-view restaurant; open all day, wheelchair access, disabled facilities, no dogs *(John Richards, Pete Sturgess)*

Firbeck [SK5688]

Black Lion [New Rd]: Newish licensees putting emphasis on enjoyable food in tall pleasantly modernised old village pub, reasonable prices, two small rooms off bar, walls covered with hundreds of interesting photographs, well kept ales such as Barnsley and Timothy Taylors Landlord, pleasant back restaurant extension; two bedrooms, attractive village nr Roche Abbey *(Peter F Marshall, Richard Cole)*

Flamborough [TA2270]

North Star [N Marine Rd]: Sizeable hotel with comfortable but pleasantly pubby bar and eating area, decent choice of enjoyable bar food inc game and fresh fish, no smoking restaurant; tables in pleasant garden with goldfish pond, comfortable bedrooms *(Paul Craddock)*

Gargrave [SD9354]

Anchor: Useful spacious family place with wide range of real ales and simple reasonably priced food inc children's, pleasant service, restaurant,

canalside tables and good play area; lots of amusements, piped music; bedrooms in modern wing *(WAH, LYM)*

Giggleswick [SD8164]

Black Horse [Church St]: Hard-working newish landlord in quaint 17th-c village pub crammed between churchyard and pretty row of cottages, smart décor, enjoyable food in bar or intimate dining room, well kept real ales inc Timothy Taylors, reasonable prices, coal fire *(MJVK, Jon Blythe)*

Harts Head [Belle Hill]: Cheerful and convivial, locally popular and very busy at wknds, with wide choice of tasty food in bar and restaurant, well kept beers and good wine list *(Walter and Susan Rinaldi-Butcher)*

Old Station [A65 Settle bypass]: Handy stop for generous straightforward home-made food in L-shaped bar with brasses, railway prints and dining end, friendly staff, well kept John Smiths and Tetleys Mild and Bitter, no smoking restaurant; bedrooms *(MJVK)*

Goathland [NZ8301]

Inn on the Moor [Mill Green Way]: Rambling place, good food in restaurant, decent wine; good value bedrooms, excellent breakfast *(LM)*

Golcar [SE0816]

Scapehouse [off A62 (or A640) up W of Huddersfield]: Roomy and well run, with good value changing menu, well kept Jennings ales, friendly staff, built-in settles, wooden tables and stools, interesting pews in end alcove, real fire, huge map in passage, separate dining room *(H K Dyson)*

Grange Moor [SE2215]

☆ *Kaye Arms* [A642 Huddersfield—Wakefield]: Firmly recommended as very good family-run restaurary pub, civilised and busy, with imaginative proper food, courteous efficient staff, exceptional value house wines, hundreds of malt whiskies, no smoking room; handy for Yorkshire Mining Museum; cl Mon lunchtime *(G Dobson, A Preston, Michael Butler, LYM)*

Grassington [SE0064]

☆ *Black Horse* [Garrs Lane]: New licensees in comfortable and cheerful open-plan pub, very popular in summer, with well kept Black Sheep Bitter and Special, Tetleys and Theakstons Best and Old Peculier, food from good sandwiches up inc children's, modern furnishings, open fires, darts in back room, small attractive restaurant; sheltered terrace, bedrooms comfortable, well equipped and good value *(the Didler, BB, P Abbott, Hazel and Michael Duncombe)*

☆ *Devonshire* [The Square]: Handsome old hotel with good window seats and tables outside overlooking sloping village square, interesting pictures and ornaments, beams and open fires, good range of well presented generous food from sandwiches to good Sun lunch in big dining room, pleasant family room, cheerful chatty staff and nice mix of locals and visitors, well kept Black Sheep Best and Timothy Taylors Landlord, decent wines; bedrooms *(LYM, Jenny and Brian Seller, George Atkinson)*

Foresters Arms [Main St]: Unpretentious and

friendly old coaching inn with Black Sheep and other changing ales, good value bar food lunchtime and evening, pool; reasonably priced bedrooms *(the Didler)*

Great Ayton [NZ5611]

☆ *Royal Oak* [off A173 – follow village signs; High Green]: Wide range of generous good food, well kept Courage Directors and Theakstons, helpful friendly staff, unpretentious bar with good fire in huge inglenook, beam-and-plank ceiling, bulgy old partly panelled stone walls, traditional furnishings inc antique settles, long dining lounge (children welcome), separate restaurant; pleasant views of elegant village green from bay windows; comfortable bedrooms *(LYM, Paul Fairbrother, Helen Morris, Geoff and Angela Jaques)*

Great Ouseburn [SE4562]

☆ *Crown* [off B6265 SE of Boroughbridge]: Cheerful village pub emphasising wide choice of good sensibly priced food (all day Sat) from baguettes to some interesting dishes and big steaks, well kept Black Sheep, John Smiths, Theakstons and a local guest beer, lots of Edwardian pictures and assorted bric-a-brac, largely no smoking eating areas; may be piped music; well behaved children welcome, tables in garden with sunny terrace and play area, cl wkdy lunchtimes, open all day wknds and bank hols *(Alan J Morton, Janet and Peter Race, LYM)*

Green Hamerton [SE4657]

☆ *Bay Horse* [York Rd; off A59 York—Harrogate]: Welcoming bar with log fire, good home-made food from soup and fresh sandwiches up, well kept Timothy Taylors Landlord, good wine choice; pleasant bedrooms in converted stables *(Thomas Hoyle, Douglas Smith)*

Greenhow Hill [SE1164]

Miners Arms [B6265 Pateley Bridge—Grassington]: Welcoming young landlord/chef doing good value generous restaurant food, well kept Scottish Courage and Black Sheep ales, decent wines, cheerful service, relaxed atmosphere, beams and brasses, woodburner; quiet piped music, anteroom with pool and darts; children welcome, bedrooms, has been cl Mon *(Howard Gregory, Ellen and Tom Hunt, P R Morley)*

Grenoside [SK3394]

☆ *Cow & Calf* [3 miles from M1 junction 35; Skew Hill Lane]: Three neat and friendly connected rooms, one no smoking, high-backed settles, stripped stone, brass and copper hanging from beams, plates and pictures, good value hearty fresh food (not Sun evening) inc sandwiches and children's, well kept low-priced Sam Smiths OB, tea and coffee, friendly attentive service; quiet piped music, music quiz nights; family room in block across walled former farmyard with picnic-sets; splendid views over Sheffield, disabled access, open all day Sat *(CMW, JJW, LYM, DC)*

Grewelthorpe [SE2376]

☆ *Crown* [back rd NW of Ripon]: Open fire in cosy two-room bar, good generous food inc

interesting dishes, reasonable prices, well kept ales such as Black Sheep, John Smiths, Old Mill and Theakstons, simple décor, games room with bar billiards, back restaurant; picnic-sets out in front, pleasant small village, good walks nearby *(Dorsan Baker)*

Grinton [SE0598]

Bridge Inn [B6270 W of Richmond]: Cosy unpretentious riverside inn in lovely spot opp Cathedral of the Dales, two well used bars, very friendly service, good range of good value simple well prepared food from decent sandwiches to good steaks, well kept Black Sheep Special, Greene King Old Speckled Hen, John Smiths Best, Tetleys and a guest beer, decent wines, nice restaurant area; attractive tables outside, front and back; bedrooms with own bathrooms, dogs welcome, open all day, good walks *(James Nunns, B, M and P Kendall)*

Gunnerside [SD9598]

Kings Head [B6270 Swaledale rd]: Small open-plan flagstoned local in pretty riverside Dales village, good value simple home-made food, well kept ales such as Black Sheep, Theakstons and one brewed locally for the pub, old village photographs, children welcome; unobtrusive piped music; seats out by bridge, good walks nearby, open all day *(Gareth and Toni Edwards, Lawrence Pearse, Catherine and Richard Preston, Jim Abbott)*

Halifax [SE0924]

☆ *Shears* [Paris Gates, Boys Lane; OS Sheet 104 map ref 097241]: Hidden down steep cobbled lanes among tall mill buildings, dark unspoilt interior, well kept Timothy Taylors Landlord and Golden Best and a guest beer, welcoming expert landlord (not Tues), friendly staff; very popular for good cheap lunchtime food from hot-filled sandwiches to home-made pies, curries, casseroles etc; sporting prints, local sports photographs, collection of pump clips and foreign bottles; seats out above the Hebble Brook *(Pat and Tony Martin, the Didler)*

☆ *Shibden Mill* [Shibden, just NE]: Cottagey and welcoming riverside pub dating back to 17th c, doing well under new management; smart inside, with good interesting well presented bar lunches from sandwiches up, popular restaurants (downstairs one has beams and wonky walls), Black Sheep, guest beers and one brewed for the pub, good wine; hidden away in valley bottom, a picture when floodlit *(Greta and Christopher Wells, Dr and Mrs L Wade)*

Three Pigeons [Sun Fold, South Parade; off Church St]: Welcoming, with six or seven well kept changing ales such as Black Sheep, Moorhouses, Riverhead and Timothy Taylors, simple lunchtime food from sandwiches and burgers to interesting dishes, log fire; handy for Eureka! museum *(Michael Williamson, Andy and Jill Kassube, B C Hammond)*

Hampsthwaite [SE2659]

Joiners Arms [about 5 miles W of Harrogate; High St]: Smartly welcoming pub, spotless and nicely updated, large recent back dining extension in keeping with the beams and stripped stone, good food from hot sandwiches to popular Sun lunch, friendly electronically speeded service, well kept Ruddles and John Smiths, decent wines; attractive village *(Michael Butler, D W Stokes)*

Harden [SE0838]

Malt Shovel [Wilsden rd, off B6429]: New regime since summer 2000 in handsome dark stone building, three neat black-beamed rooms with blue plush seats, horse tack and bric-a-brac, some fine panelling, open fire, decent sensibly priced all-day bar food inc baguettes and baked potatoes, well kept Tetleys, dominoes; piped music; open all day summer Thurs-Sun, children in eating area, tables in pretty garden, lovely streamside spot *(Paul Craddock, LYM, Geoffrey and Brenda Wilson)*

Harewood [SE3245]

Harewood Arms [A61 opp Harewood House]: Busy hotel, former coaching inn, three attractive, comfortable and spaciously relaxing lounge bars, dark green décor, decent food from sandwiches up (also breakfast and bacon and sausage sandwiches served till 11.30, and afternoon teas), friendly service, well kept ales inc cheap Sam Smiths OB, decent house wines, good coffee, Harewood family memorabilia; bedrooms *(Geoffrey and Brenda Wilson, Hugh A MacLean, John and Sylvia Harrop)*

Harrogate [SE3155]

☆ *Drum & Monkey* [Montpellier Gdns]: Not a pub but well worth knowing for enjoyable downstairs fish bar with splendid seafood, eat at long bar or pub-style tables, good French wines; bustling, chatty and friendly – must book evenings *(Michael and Rosalind Dymond, Derek Stafford)*

Gardeners Arms [Bilton Lane (off A59 either in Bilton itself or on outskirts towards Harrogate)]: Small stone-built house converted into good old-fashioned local, totally unspoilt with tiny bar and three small rooms, tiled floors, panelling, old prints and little else; very cheap well kept Sam Smiths OB, coal fire; tables in nice garden, lovely peaceful setting *(the Didler, Kevin Thorpe)*

New Inn [B6162 towards Harlow Carr]: Refreshingly unpretentious and good value, Timothy Taylors Landlord, simple food inc good choice of proper sandwiches and ploughman's, friendly helpful service, spacious no smoking area in comfortable bar; handy for Harlow Carr Gardens *(Peter and Anne Hollindale)*

Harthill [SK4980]

Beehive [Union St]: Two-bar village pub with chef/landlord doing wide choice of enjoyable well priced food (not Mon lunchtime) inc proper pies and Sun lunch (then no bar snacks), three well kept ales inc Timothy Taylors, good choice of wines and soft drinks; games room with pool, fruit machine, piped pop music; children welcome, picnic-sets in attractive garden, walks nearby *(G P Kernan, CMW, JJW)*

Hartshead [SE1822]

☆ *Gray Ox* [not very far from M62 junction 25]: Recently attractively refurbished dining pub with flagstones, farm tools and country

pictures, four areas inc no smoking room, good choice of generous tasty food from good sandwiches to upmarket main dishes and very popular Sun lunch (all afternoon), well kept Black Sheep, Timothy Taylors Landlord, Tetleys and Theakstons, long wine list, helpful attentive staff; open all day Sun, nice spot *(Derek and Sylvia Stephenson, Pat and Tony Martin, Marlene and Jim Godfrey)*

Hawes [SD8789]

Crown [Market Pl]: Traditional market town local, lively and welcoming, with good range of good value quickly served substantial bar food, well kept Theakstons Best, XB and Old Peculier, quick service, coal fire each end; walkers welcome, children allowed away from bar; seats out on cobbled front forecourt *(Karen Eliot)*

Fountain [Market Pl]: Warmly friendly inn, bright open bar and lounge, lots of posters from local operatic society's past productions, decent food, helpful staff, real ales inc Black Sheep Special and Riggwelter and Boddingtons, enjoyable quickly served bar food; maybe piped radio; bedrooms *(George Atkinson)*

White Hart [Main St]: Cosy bustle in old-fashioned local (esp wknd and Tues market day), quieter on left, wide choice of good value food in bar and restaurant, warm fire, well kept Black Sheep and Theakstons, welcoming service, darts and dominoes; occasional craft fairs, good value bedrooms *(Jim Abbott, Mrs S E Griffiths, Catherine and Richard Preston, P Abbott)*

Hebden Bridge [SE0027]

Hare & Hounds [Billy Lane, Wadsworth]: Welcoming local licensees, roaring fire, well kept Timothy Taylors Landlord, Best and Golden Best, generous reasonably priced straightforward food (not Mon evening or winter Tues evening), various bric-a-brac, well behaved children welcome, no music; tables on terrace with lovely views, plenty of good walks; cl wkdy lunchtimes, open all day wknds, well appointed bedrooms *(MJVK, Norman Stansfield, Bruce Bird)*

White Lion [Bridge Gate]: Solid stone-built inn with hospitable landlord, comfortable bar and country-furnished bare-boards dining lounge, good choice of reasonably priced good generous food all day, well kept Boddingtons and Timothy Taylors Landlord; bedrooms comfortable *(MJVK, Mike Ridgway, Sarah Miles)*

Helmsley [SE6184]

Royal Oak [Market Pl]: Three attractively refurbished and comfortable rooms with some antiques, substantial food with good veg, welcoming landlord, quick service even though busy, Camerons Bitter and a Banks's seasonal beer; pool, piped music, TV; picnic-sets outside, open all day, good bedrooms *(John Foord)*

Hepworth [SE1606]

Butchers Arms [off A616 SE of Holmfirth; Towngate]: Friendly L-shaped bar, jovial landlord, dark beams, partly panelled stone walls, pine tables on light wood floor, large log fire in dining room, well kept Marstons

Pedigree, Theakstons XB and Timothy Taylors Landlord, enjoyable food inc popular lunchtime buffet; pictures for sale, pool and darts one end, dogs welcome; open all day Fri/Sat, good animal sculpture nearby (Stephen, Julie and Hayley Brown)

Heslington [SE6350]

Deramore Arms [Main St, nr Univ]: Friendly well kept traditional local, warm welcome, wide choice of real ales inc Timothy Taylors Landlord, beer festivals, good value straightforward food inc Sun indian night; games machines, TV, quietish juke box; on peaceful village green (Dr and Mrs A K Clarke, A York)

High Hoyland [SE2710]

Cherry Tree [Bank End Lane; 3 miles W of M1 junction 38]: Clean and attractive stone-built village pub, low beams, brasses, cigarette card collections, friendly staff, good range of beers inc John Smiths and Tetleys, open fire, small popular restaurant (best to book, esp Sun lunch); lovely views over Cannon Hall Country Park from front (Greta and Christopher Wells)

Holme-on-Spalding-Moor [SE8137]

Cross Keys [Moor End]: Impressive cheap food from huge filled rolls up inc good vegetarian choice, real ale inc Worthington, welcoming helpful service (John Murray)

Holmfirth [SD1508]

Fox House [B6106 Dunford Rd – just over S Yorks border]: Bass Vintage Inn with wide choice of good value food from sandwiches up, reasonable prices, several big old rooms, friendly staff (Eric Locker)

Rose & Crown [Victoria Sq]: Friendly family-run pub with tiled floor, several rooms, good range of real ales (the Didler)

Horbury [SE3018]

Boons [Queen St]: Lively, chatty and comfortably unpretentious, with local Clarks, John Smiths and two or three guest beers kept well, simple lunchtime food now, some flagstones, bare walls, Rugby League memorabilia, back tap room with pool; very popular, can get crowded (Michael Butler)

Horton in Ribblesdale [SD8172]

☆ *Crown* [B6479 N of Settle]: Clean and pleasant straightforward low-ceilinged bar with dark woodwork, lots of brass and good fire, good value home cooking, very well kept ales such as Theakstons Old Peculier, welcoming helpful staff, open fire; simple good value bedrooms, good bunkhouse – a haven for walkers (Steve Jennings)

Golden Lion: Unpretentious village pub with generous well served bar food, flagstoned bar (SkyTV), comfortable lounge and games room; good value bedrooms, cheap bunkhouse (Bob and Lisa Cantrell)

Huddersfield [SE1416]

Head of Steam [Station, St Georges Sq]: Busy atmosphere, railway memorabilia, model trains, cars, buses and planes for sale, pies, sandwiches, baked potatoes and good value Sun roasts, no smoking eating area, friendly staff, hot coal fire, well kept changing ales such as B&T R101, Cottage S&D, Highgate Dark,

Hop Back Summer Lightning, Slaters and Tetleys, lots of bottled beers, farm ciders, Gales fruit wines; open all day (David Carr, Andy and Jill Kassube, Richard Lewis)

Nags Head [New Hey Rd, Ainley Top; handy for M62 junction 24, by A643]: Long comfortably olde-worlde bar useful for good value food from quickly served hot-filled baguettes up, carvery in converted barn, well kept Scottish Courage ales (Andy and Jill Kassube)

Old Court Brew House [Queen St]: High-ceilinged former court, bright, airy and not too crowded, original plasterwork and fittings such as gas lamps, long bar, armchairs and sofas; a Whitbreads pub with half a dozen of their ales kept well, also three or four brewed here – the top of the brew copper, surrounded by glass, sticks up through the floor; games machines, food; open all day (David Carr)

☆ *Rat & Ratchet* [Chapel Hill]: Bare-boards two-room local brewing its own beer (changing each month) alongside big changing collection of well kept guest ales, two more comfortable rooms up steps, basic well cooked cheap bar food inc outstanding sandwiches and popular Weds curry night; ambiance more pleasant than you might guess from outside, open all day (from 3.30 Mon/Tues) (the Didler)

Hull [TA0927]

Bay Horse [Wincolmlee]: Popular corner local, Batemans' only local pub here, their beers kept well, good value food, rugby connections; open all day (the Didler, J Mumby)

Green Bricks [Humber Dock St]: Early 19th-c inn overlooking marina, usually open all day, lunchtime and early evening meals, Bass and a related beer, seating outside (David Carr)

☆ *Olde Black Boy* [High St, Old Town]: Sympathetically refurbished pub in Old Town conservation area, little black-panelled low-ceilinged front smoke room, lofty 18th-c back vaults bar with leather seating, two rooms upstairs (one with pool), good value food lunchtime (not Sun) and late afternoon (not wknds), also Sun breakfast, friendly service, well kept ales such as McEwans 80/-, Roosters Racer, Tetleys and Wychwood Old Devil, about 20 country wines, interesting Wilberforce-related posters etc, old jugs and bottles; darts, piano (live music Thurs), games machine; children allowed, open all day (the Didler, BB, Richard Lewis)

Olde Blue Bell [alley off Lowgate; look out for huge blue bell over pavement]: Friendly traditional three-room 17th-c local with well kept cheap Sam Smiths OB, good value simple lunchtime food, remarkable collection of bells; open all day exc Sun afternoon (the Didler, BB)

Tap & Spile [Spring Bank]: Usual bare boards and brick but comfortable banquettes in no smoking area; framed brewery posters, eight real ales, Old Rosie farm cider, country wines, reasonably priced food; piped music, fruit machine; small back terrace (the Didler)

Hutton-le-Hole [SE7090]

Crown [The Green]: Bustling friendly local overlooking pretty village green with wandering sheep, huge helpings of good simple food, friendly service, well kept real ale, lots of whisky-water jugs; children welcome *(Walter and Sue Anderson)*

Ilkley [SE1346]

Cow & Calf [Hangingstone Rd (moors rd towards Hawksworth)]: Enjoyable home cooking, good bedrooms *(Colin McKerrow)*

Ingleton [SD6973]

☆ *Wheatsheaf* [High St]: 17th-c coaching inn with long bar serving well kept Black Sheep Best and Riggwelter and Moorhouses, changing good value food prepared to order from fresh ingredients, from nicely filled maize-flour baps up, quick friendly service, real fire, dining room; walkers and children welcome, big garden with hawks, handy for Ingleborough *(Sue Board, Catherine and Martin Snelling)*

Keighley [SE0641]

Boltmakers Arms [East Parade]: Split-level open-plan local with affable landlord, particularly well kept Timothy Taylors Landlord, Best, Golden Best and guest beers; open all day *(the Didler, Peter F Marshall)*

Dalesway [Bradford Rd, Sandbeds]: Newish Brewers Fayre popular for good children's areas outside and (small charge) inside, lots of tables, friendly welcome, usual food, reasonable service *(WAH)*

Globe [Parkwood St]: Refurbished local by Worth Valley steam railway track, wkdy lunches, Tetleys and Timothy Taylors Landlord, Best and Golden Best; open all day *(the Didler)*

Kettlewell [SD9772]

☆ *Kings Head*: Lively and cheerful old character local away from centre, flagstones and log fire in big inglenook, well kept ales such as Black Sheep and Theakstons, good value food, helpful courteous service; pool room, bedrooms *(B, M and P Kendall, BB, P Abbott, Edmund Coan)*

☆ *Racehorses* [B6160 N of Skipton]: Comfortable and civilised, with very friendly attentive service, enjoyable home-made usual food from good value crusty cobs to good Sun carvery, well kept ales inc Theakstons XB and Old Peculier, good choice of wines, log fires; dogs welcome in front bar, tables on attractive terrace, well placed for Wharfedale walks, good bedrooms with own bathrooms *(Nigel Long, BB, Tracey and Stephen Groves, Rita and Keith Pollard, Malcolm and Jennifer Perry, Jim Abbott, Trevor and Lynda Smith)*

Kilham [TA0665]

Star [Church St]: Quaint old pub in pretty village, warm fires in three of the four small rooms, welcoming landlord and staff, well kept John Smiths, Theakstons and a beer, decent fairly priced food in bar and popular flagstoned barn restaurant, darts, dominoes *(Ian S Morley, Edward Pearce)*

Kilnsey [SD9767]

☆ *Tennants Arms*: Good range of good food esp steaks, well kept Black Sheep, Tetleys and Theakstons Best and Old Peculier, open fires, friendly staff, several rooms, interesting decorations; piped music; beautiful Wharfedale setting, with views of spectacular overhanging

crag from restaurant; comfortable immaculate bedrooms all with private bathrooms, good value; good walks *(Mike Tucker)*

Kirkby Malham [SD8960]

Victoria: Pleasantly understated Victorian décor, good friendly service, good value food, well kept Theakstons and good wine choice; attractive good value bedrooms, lovely village with interesting church – quieter than nearby Malham though busy with walkers at lunchtime *(Liz and John Soden)*

Kirkby Overblow [SE3249]

☆ *Star & Garter* [off A61 S of Harrogate]: Cosy old-fashioned pub, friendly, roomy and relaxing, very popular lunchtime with older people for generous good value food inc imaginative specials, good vegetarian choice and Sun lunch, well kept Camerons and Tetleys, decent wines, huge log fires, bluff no-nonsense Yorkshire landlord, consistently good service, dining room for evening meals; open all day, nice village setting *(Peter and Anne Hollindale, H Bramwell)*

Knapton [SE5652]

Red Lion [Main St]: Small well run village local, a welcome for strangers, well kept John Smiths, strong horse-racing traditions; limited food *(P Abbott)*

Knaresborough [SE3557]

☆ *Blind Jacks* [Market Pl]: Former 18th-c shop now a charming multi-floor traditional tavern, with simple but attractive furnishings, brewery posters etc, well kept Black Sheep, Hambleton White Boar and Nightmare Stout, Timothy Taylors Landlord and changing guest beers, farm cider and foreign bottled beers; well behaved children allowed away from bar, open all day from noon, cl Mon till 5.30 *(the Didler, LYM)*

Langthwaite [NZ0003]

☆ *Red Lion* [just off Reeth—Brough Arkengarthdale rd]: Homely unspoilt 17th-c pub, individual and relaxing, in charming Dales village with ancient bridge; basic cheap nourishing lunchtime food, well kept Black Sheep Bitter and Riggwelter and John Smiths, country wines, tea and coffee; well behaved children allowed lunchtime in very low-ceilinged side snug, quietly friendly service; the ladies' is a genuine bathroom; good walks all around, inc organised circular ones from the pub – maps and guides for sale *(Greta and Christopher Wells, Catherine and Richard Preston, James Nunns, LYM, Philip and Susan Philcox)*

Leeds [SE3033]

☆ *Adelphi* [Hunslet Rd]: Well restored handsome Edwardian tiling, woodwork and cut and etched glass, several rooms, impressive stairway; particularly well kept Tetleys Bitter, Mild and Imperial (virtually the brewery tap), prompt friendly service, good spread of cheap food at lunchtime, crowded but convivial then; live jazz Sat *(the Didler)*

Angel [Angel Inn Yard]: Handsomely restored old inn, enjoyable food from good hot and cold sandwiches up in peaceful upstairs lounge bar with small comfortable no smoking area, good service, Sam Smiths and mixed clientele downstairs; shame about the piped music; heated tables outside *(Marlene and Jim Godfrey)*

Duck & Drake [Kirkgate, between indoor mkt and Parish Church]: Big no-frills pub with a dozen or more well kept reasonably priced ales inc local brews such as Hambleton, Old Mill, Rooster and Timothy Taylors, farm ciders, basic furniture and beer posters and mirrors; simple substantial lunchtime food from filled rolls to Sun lunches, friendly staff, games room with hot coal fire and Yorkshire doubles dartboard as well as pool etc; juke box, big-screen sports TV, quiz nights, live music Sun, Tues and Thurs nights; open all day *(the Didler, Richard Lewis, Pete Baker)*

☆ *Garden Gate* [Whitfield Pl, Hunslet]: Ornate but thoroughly down-to-earth Victorian pub with various rooms off central drinking corridor, well worth a look for its now near-unique style and intricate glass and woodwork; Tetleys Bitter and Mild foaming with freshness, farm cider, no food; open all day, can be boisterous evenings *(the Didler, BB)*

Grove [Back Row, Holbeck]: Well preserved 1930s pub, four rooms off drinking corridor, Courage Directors, John Smiths, Theakstons XB, Youngers No 3 and guest beers; open all day (cl 4-7 wknds) *(the Didler)*

Highland [Cavendish St]: Victorian pub tucked behind offices and flats, good choice of sandwiches, Tetleys Bitter and Mild *(the Didler)*

Hogshead [Gt George St, opp Infirmary]: Spacious open-plan pub, bare boards, barrels, partitions, old Leeds prints, some upstairs seating, very wide choice of changing well kept ales inc unusual ones, pub food from filled rolls to pies, friendly efficient staff, relaxing atmosphere, newspapers to read; piped music, open all day *(Richard Lewis)*

Palace [Kirkgate]: Up to ten or so well kept Tetleys-related and changing guest beers, good value lunchtime food from sandwiches up inc two-for-one bargains in no smoking dining area, polished wood, unusual lighting from electric candelabra to mock street lamps, friendly helpful staff, may be bargain wine offers; games end with pool, TV, good piped music; tables out in front and in small heated back courtyard, open all day *(Richard Lewis, Michael J Gittins)*

Scarborough [Bishopgate St, opp stn]: Tetleys Festival Alehouse with ornate art nouveau tiled curved frontage, bare boards, barrel tables, lots of wood, ten or so interesting changing real ales in fine condition, good prices, farm cider, wide choice of cheap wkdy lunchtime food inc occasional special offers, friendly helpful staff, music-hall posters; very busy lunchtime and early evening, machines, TV; open all day *(Richard Lewis, Ted and Jan Whitfield)*

Tap & Spile [top end of Merrion Centre, Merrion Way]: Tiles and flagstones, stripped stone walls, prints of old Leeds, well kept changing ales inc local favourites such as Hambleton, Old Mill and Timothy Taylors Landlord, lunchtime food; pool (this part can

get smoky), TV, piped music; open all day, cl Sun *(Mike Fehle)*

Viaduct [Lower Briggate]: Peaceful pub which actively caters for disabled customers; pleasantly furnished long narrow bar, lots of wood, well kept Tetleys-related and guest ales esp Milds, popular lunchtime food, friendly helpful staff, no smoking area; attractive back garden, open all day exc Sun afternoon *(the Didler, Richard Lewis)*

☆ *Victoria* [Gt George St, just behind Town Hall]: Ornate bustling early Victorian pub with grand etched mirrors, impressive globe lamps extending from the majestic bar, imposing carved beams, booths with working snob-screens, smaller rooms off; well kept Tetleys inc Mild and several well chosen guest beers, friendly smart bar staff, reasonably priced food in luncheon room with end serving hatch, no smoking room; open all day *(the Didler, Ted and Jan Whitfield, David Carr)*

Wetherspoons [City Station, North Concourse]: Light and airy arched bar, glazed panelling and stone floors, bright colours, IKEA-look furnishings, tables out on concourse, six well kept beers, good menu inc sandwiches, pastries etc and take-aways (ditto coffee), daily papers, friendly helpful staff; open all day (breakfast from 7) *(Richard Lewis)*

Whip [alley off Boar Lane, parallel to Duncan St]: Particularly well kept Ansells Mild, Ind Coope Burton, Tetleys Mild, Bitter and Imperial; traditional feel, friendly helpful staff, lively mixed customers; tables in courtyard *(the Didler)*

Linton in Craven [SD9962]

☆ *Fountaine* [just off B6265 Skipton—Grassington]: Extended traditional pub charmingly set among ancient buildings on neat green running down to little stream; up to seven real ales on handpump, usual food all day from sandwiches up, darts and dominoes; open all day, children in no smoking family room and restaurant *(John Robertson, Karen and Graham Oddey, B, M and P Kendall, Mandy and Simon King, Terry Mizen, J C Burley, Greta and Christopher Wells, Malcolm and Jennifer Perry, LYM)*

Low Catton [SE7053]

☆ *Gold Cup* [signed off A166 in Stamford Bridge or A1079 at Kexby Bridge]: Three neatly comfortable linked rooms, open fires each end, plush seats, good solid tables, some decorative plates and brasswork, new conservatory extension, reliable no nonsense bar food inc good choice for small appetites, no smoking restaurant with pleasant views, well organised friendly service, well kept John Smiths and Tetleys, back games bar with pool, dominoes, and fruit machine; open all day wknds, cl Mon lunch exc bank hols, garden with good play area, paddock with goats, ponies, fishing rights on the adjoining Derwent *(LYM, P R Morley, H Bramwell)*

Low Marishes [SE8277]

School House: Fine isolated pub, beams hung with all sorts of unusual bric-a-brac, well kept Black Sheep, local Hambleton and Tetleys, welcoming landlord and pub dog, simple menu, eating area, games room with pool, new conservatory, no music; charming garden, well on front terrace, interesting church opp, bedrooms planned *(Kevin Thorpe)*

Low Row [SD9897]

Punch Bowl [B6270 Reeth—Muker]: Plain cheery family bar and games area, well kept Theakstons Best, XB and Old Peculier and a guest such as Castle Eden, rows of malt whiskies, decent house wines, wide choice of good value generous food inc enormous cheap baguettes, log fire; piped music; great Swaledale views from terrace with quoits pitches below; popular tea room 10-5.30 with home-made cakes, small shop, bicycle and cave lamp hire, folk music Fri; open all day in summer, good basic bedrooms sharing bathrooms, also bunkhouse, big breakfast *(James Nunns, Gareth and Toni Edwards, Mr and Mrs Maurice Thompson, Lawrence Pearse)*

Lower Dunsforth [SE4465]

☆ *Angler*: Modern pub by river, recently taken over by new chef/landlord with fine track record, good stir fries, lots of fish, well kept Black Sheep, John Smiths and a guest beer, very good choice of wines by the glass, friendly staff and relaxed atmosphere; no smoking dining area, tables on terrace, fishing and moorings, bedrooms planned *(anon)*

Malham [SD8963]

☆ *Listers Arms* [off A65 NW of Skipton]: Easy-going open-plan lounge, busy wknds, relaxed attitude to children and dogs, attractive good value bar food inc unusual sandwiches, well kept changing ales such as Black Sheep, Ind Coope Burton and Wadworths 6X, continental beers, lots of malt whiskies, well worn-in furnishings and fittings, roaring fire, restaurant famous for steaks (good wine list); games area with pool and maybe piped music; seats outside the substantial creeper-covered stone inn overlooking small green, more in back garden – nice spot by river, ideal for walkers; bedrooms *(Mr and Mrs J McRobert, Jason Caulkin)*

Malton [SE7972]

Royal Oak [Town St, Old Malton]: Charming spotless pub, friendly helpful service, good guest beers, good value quickly served standard food inc Whitby seafood platter; tables in sunny garden, children welcome, handy for Eden Camp *(Margaret Dickinson)*

Marsden [SE0412]

☆ *Riverhead* [Peel St, next to Co-op; just off A62 Huddersfield—Oldham]: Basic own-brew pub in converted grocer's, spiral stairs down to microbrewery producing good range of interesting beers named after local reservoirs (the higher the reservoir, the higher the strength) inc Mild, Stout and Porter, farm cider, friendly service and locals, unobtrusive piped music, no food (maybe sandwiches) or machines; wheelchair access, cl wkdy lunchtimes, open all day wknds, nice stop after walk by canal or on the hills *(the Didler, H K Dyson)*

Marton cum Grafton [SE4263]

☆ *Olde Punch Bowl* [signed off A1 3 miles N of

A59]: Interesting well presented food in attractive old pub with comfortable and roomy heavy-beamed open-plan bar, open fires, brasses, framed old advertisements and photographs; Tetleys and Theakstons, decent wines, no piped music, welcoming service, restaurant; children welcome, good play area and picnic-sets in pleasant garden *(Greta and Christopher Wells, LYM)*

Masham [SE2381]

☆ *Black Sheep Brewery* [Crosshills]: Modern bistro-style drinking area, smart but welcoming and fun, on top floor of maltings which now houses the brewery – not a pub, but likely to appeal to *Guide* readers, together with a brewery visit; pleasant functional décor, upper gallery, good imaginative varied food all day inc nice puddings, excellent service, some worthwhile beery tourist trinkets, and of course the Baa'r has well kept Black Sheep Bitter, Special, Riggwelter and Yorkshire Square; interesting brewery tour, good family facilities inc play area; cl 5 Mon and late winter Sun evenings, can be very busy *(Howard Gregory, Susan and Nigel Wilson, John Coatsworth, Janet and Peter Race)*

Meltham [SE0910]

Will's o' Nat's [Blackmoorfoot Rd, NW of village off B6107]: Reopened after alterations and new colour scheme, flagstoned bar, wood floor room off, good new landlord, Black Sheep, Timothy Taylors Landlord and Tetleys, very reasonably priced food in carpeted dining area; handy for walkers on Colne Valley and Kirklees circular walks and for Blackmoorfoot reservoir (birdwatching) *(LYM, H K Dyson)*

Middleham [SE1288]

☆ *White Swan* [Market Pl]: Old flagstoned and oak-beamed village hotel with open fires and good pubby atmosphere in entrance bar, good choice of interesting food in bar and homely dining room inc vegetarian, early evening bargains and good cheeses, well kept Black Sheep Riggwelter, Hambleton, John Smiths and Theakstons; comfortable bedrooms, attractive setting *(Darly Graton, Graeme Gulibert, Juliet Howard, Shane Lee)*

Middlesmoor [SE0874]

☆ *Crown* [top of Nidderdale rd from Pateley Bridge]: Remote inn with beautiful view over stone-built hamlet high in upper Nidderdale, warmly welcoming landlord and family, simple well presented generous food inc good sandwiches, particularly well kept Black Sheep and Theakstons, rich local atmosphere, blazing log fires in cosy spotless rooms, homely dining room, tables in small garden; good value simple bedrooms *(Jim Abbott, Greta and Christopher Wells, D W Stokes, Trevor and Diane Waite)*

Mirfield [SE2041]

Hare & Hounds [Liley Lane (B6118 S)]: Recently refurbished, with wide choice of good value food from lunchtime sandwiches to interesting main dishes, friendly efficient service, pleasant atmosphere, decent wines, no smoking eating area; can get very busy; tables outside, views towards Huddersfield *(Andy and Jill Kassube, M Borthwick)*

Monk Fryston [SE5029]
Crown [Main St, opp Monk Fryston Hall]:
Village pub well run by welcoming new
licensees, well kept Mansfield and Marstons
Bitter, Pedigree and Fever Pitch, limited choice
of good food with fresh veg, attractive prices
(Peter F Marshall)

North Grimston [SE8468]
Middleton Arms: Comfortable locally popular
dining pub nicely placed on edge of Yorkshire
Wolds, good generous food at nicely laid tables,
well kept Tetleys, friendly staff; lovely garden
*(Colin and Dot Savill, Eric Locker,
M J Morgan)*

North Newbald [SE9136]
☆ *Tiger* [off A1034 S of Mkt Weighton; The
Green]: Proper village pub of considerable
character, on big green surrounded by rolling
hills, handy for Wolds Way walking; roaring
fire, good home-made food from fine
sandwiches up, OAP lunches, consistently well
kept ales such as Black Sheep, John Smiths,
Timothy Taylors Landlord and Tetleys, games
room; open all day *(Mike and Alison Leyland,
LYM, C A Hall)*

North Rigton [SE2749]
Square & Compass [Rigton Hill]: Roomy
comfortably modernised bar, lounge and
restaurant area, pleasant staff, good value usual
food inc good specials, Boddingtons and other
ales *(T R and M Abram)*

Northallerton [SE3794]
Golden Lion [High St]: Good atmosphere in
large recently refurbished Forte ex-coaching
inn, two big public bars, good inexpensive food
in attractive eating area, well kept beers inc
Hambleton and John Smiths, good coffee;
bedrooms *(Doug Christian)*

Norwood Green [SE1427]
☆ *Olde White Beare* [signed off A641 in Wyke, or
off A58 Halifax—Leeds just W of Wyke]:
Large 17th-c building well renovated and
extended, with several attractive rooms, beams,
brasses, good personal service, well kept
Whitbreads-related and guest beers such as
Timothy Taylors, good choice of usual food in
bar and handsome restaurant in former barn
inc bargain early suppers and popular Sun
lunch; tables outside front and back, barbecues
*(George Little, Adrian and Felicity Smith, Pat
and Tony Martin)*

Nosterfield [SE2881]
☆ *Freemasons Arms*: Cosy pub with friendly and
civilised open-plan bar and dining areas, two
log fires, beams, pews and flagstones, well kept
Black Sheep, Timothy Taylors Landlord and
Ram Tam and Tetleys, short choice of good food (not Mon evening), smiling
service, Empire theme with interesting curios
and World War I relics; tables outside, very
pleasant surroundings *(Ian S Morley)*

Oakworth [SE0138]
☆ *Grouse* [Harehills, Oldfield; 2 miles towards
Colne]: Comfortable, interesting and spotless
old pub packed with bric-a-brac, gleaming
copper and china, lots of prints, cartoons and
caricatures, dried flowers, attractively
individual furnishings; locally very popular for

well presented good home-made lunchtime bar
food (not Mon) from soup and sandwiches up,
charming evening restaurant, well kept
Timothy Taylors, good range of spirits,
entertaining landlord, courteous service; fine
surroundings and Pennine views *(Chris and
Clare Wearne, Mrs M G Brook)*

Oldstead [SE5380]
☆ *Black Swan* [Main St]: Unpretentious spotless
inn in beautiful surroundings with pretty valley
views from two big bay windows and picnic-
sets outside, reasonably priced good standard
food, well kept Theakstons, friendly landlord;
children welcome, bedrooms in modern
extension facing back car park *(Alan Sutton,
BB)*

Osmotherley [SE4597]
Queen Catherine [West End]: Good family
pub, welcoming atmosphere, roomy modern
décor, popular reasonably priced food, Tetleys
and a guest beer *(Michael Butler)*
Three Tuns [South End, off A19 N of Thirsk]:
Now restaurant-with-rooms rather than pub,
stylish and individual upmarket food in a bistro
atmosphere, faux Rennie Mackintosh décor
mixing local sandstone with pale oak panelling
and furniture, no real ales; children welcome,
comfortable and tasteful bedrooms, open all
day, good nearby walks *(Walter and Susan
Rinaldi-Butcher, LYM, Roger Everett, Greta
and Christopher Wells, Michael Butler,
Malcolm and Jean Ray, David and Ruth
Shillitoe)*

Ossett [SE2719]
☆ *Brewers Pride* [Low Mill Rd/Healey Lane, off
B6128]: Warmly friendly basic local brewing its
own beers, well kept guest beers too, cosy front
room and bar both with open fires, brewery
memorabilia, small games room, good food
choice Fri/Sat, generous Sun bar nibbles; quiz
night Mon, country & western Thurs; open all
day wknds, big back garden with local
entertainment summer wknds, nr Calder &
Hebble Canal *(the Didler)*
Victoria [Manor Rd, just off Horbury Rd]:
Plain exterior concealing cosy back restaurant
with washroom theme and wide range of good
value evening food, popular Sun carvery, well
kept Tetleys and a guest beer such as Greene
King, decent wines, friendly service, small bar
(may be piped music); cl lunchtime Mon-Thurs,
no lunchtime food Fri/Sat *(Mike Ridgway,
Sarah Miles, Michael Butler)*

Otley [SE2045]
Rose & Crown [Bondgate]: Comfortable
traditional beamed stone-built pub with
friendly welcoming staff, cosy bar and small
restaurant, well kept ales inc guests, good range
of reasonably priced home-made food (not
Fri/Sat evenings) from generous baguettes up;
can be busy lunchtime *(Michael J Gittins)*
Summer Cross [East Busk Lane/Pool Rd
(A659)]: Attractive modern refurbishment,
enjoyable sensibly priced food, OAP discount
wkdys *(Marlene and Jim Godfrey)*

Outlane [SE0817]
Nont Sarahs [A640 Huddersfield—Rochdale]:
Four-room high moorland local with wide

views from back dining area's big windows, panelled main bar, good helpings of decent usual food inc early evening specials, John Smiths and Theakstons, children's room full of toys; open all day *(Michael Butler)*

Pickering [SE7984]

Bay Horse [Market Pl]: Heavy-beamed open-plan plush bar with bay windows, old local prints and shining brasses, big fire, well kept ales such as Greene King Abbot, generous good value food, pleasant service, big back public bar with games and inglenook, upstairs restaurant with good wknd carvery *(John Foord, BB, Alan and Paula McCully)*

Black Swan [Birdgate]: Clean and comfortable hotel dating from 16th c, polite attentive staff, good food, well kept John Smiths and Theakstons XB, broad low-beamed bar with well furnished back dining part, quietly plush middle area with bric-a-brac on beams; shame about the games machines, juke box in lively top end may be loud; bedrooms, good breakfast *(Michael Butler, Peter and Anne-Marie O'Malley, Alan and Paula McCully)*

Redmire [SE0591]

☆ *Kings Arms* [Wensley—Askrigg back road]: Tucked away in attractive village, simple bar with wall seats around cast-iron tables, oak armchair, woodburner, decent bar food, no smoking restaurant, well kept Black Sheep, John Smiths, Theakstons and a guest beer, over 50 malt whiskies; pool, dominoes, cribbage, quoits; children welcome, seats in pretty garden with Wensleydale view, fishing nearby, handy for Castle Bolton *(Mrs S E Griffiths, J Flanders, Jeremy Butcher, Suzanne Hosworth, Catherine and Richard Preston, Gareth and Toni Edwards, Richard Greaves, LYM, Pete Sturgess)*

Reeth [SE0499]

☆ *Black Bull* [B6270]: Friendly village pub in fine spot at foot of broad sloping green, traditional dark beamed and flagstoned L-shaped front bar cosy at night, Timothy Taylors Landlord and Theakstons inc Old Peculier, reasonably priced food inc good vegetarian options and some imaginative dishes, open fires, helpful staff, children welcome; piped music in pool room; tables outside, comfortable bedrooms with lovely Dales views, good breakfast *(Catherine and Richard Preston, Jane Taylor, David Dutton, R M Corlett, LYM, James Nunns)*

Buck: Comfortably modernised, with good varied well priced food in bar and restaurant, sensible prices, good atmosphere, efficient service even when busy – it's very popular with hikers; bedrooms, good breakfast *(R M Corlett, Geoffrey and Brenda Wilson)*

Ribblehead [SD7880]

☆ *Station Hotel* [B6255 Ingleton—Hawes]: Immaculate walkers' pub, very isolated but warm and friendly, by Ribblehead Viaduct – ideal for railway enthusiasts, with interesting murals based on its history; kind licensees, good log fire in woodburner, well kept Black Sheep Special and Theakstons, low-priced wine, huge helpings of decent food from sandwiches to steaks, dining room; open all day in season,

good value simple bedrooms and next-door bunkhouse, good wholesome breakfast *(T A Smith, Jenny and Chris Wilson, R C Vincent, Jenny and Brian Seller)*

Ripon [SE3171]

One-Eyed Rat [Allhallowgate]: No-frills bare-boards pub emphasising real ales such as Ash Vine Challenger, Black Sheep, Cains Triple Hop, Rudgates Well Blathered, Timothy Taylors Landlord and Woodfordes Wherry, Biddenden farm cider, lots of country wines (no food); cigarette cards, framed beer mats, bank notes and old pictures; bar billiards, no juke box, tables in pleasant outside area *(P Abbott, Jenny Garrett)*

Ripponden [SE0319]

Beehive [Hob Lane, off Cross Wells Rd]: Small hillside pub with welcoming landlord, well kept Black Sheep and Timothy Taylors Landlord, consistently good modestly priced food inc fresh fish, separate restaurant *(Herbert and Susan Verity)*

Besom Brush [Oldham Rd]: Two-room pub with well kept Timothy Taylors Landlord and Tetleys, good reasonably priced home cooking (lunchtime and early evening, not wknd) inc bargains for two, friendly very helpful staff (good with wheelchairs), conservatory *(Pat and Tony Martin, Alan Stocks)*

Robin Hood's Bay [NZ9505]

Victoria [Station Rd]: Clifftop Victorian hotel overlooking bay, well kept changing ales such as Camerons and Marstons Pedigree, quick friendly service, wide choice of fresh food, good views from garden, solid period décor in bar, large airy green-walled family room; tidy bedrooms, good well served breakfast *(Dr Roger Turner)*

Roecliffe [SE3766]

Crown: Thriving pub under newish licensees, well kept Black Sheep, good choice of well presented good value food, good service; lovely village *(Janet and Peter Race, Colin McGuire)*

Rosedale Abbey [SE7395]

☆ *Milburn Arms* [off A170 W of Pickering]: New licensees in neat beamed L-shaped bar with log fire, four well kept ales such as Black Sheep, Greene King Old Speckled Hen and Tetleys, wide choice of generous food from lunchtime sandwiches to steak, no smoking restaurant, children welcome; piped music, traditional games; comfortable bedrooms, huge breakfast, nice village below moors *(Greta and Christopher Wells, Stuart Lake, LYM)*

☆ *White Horse* [300 yds up Rosedale Chimney Bank Rd – entering village, first left after Coach House Inn]: Cosy and comfortable farm-based country inn in lovely spot above the village, friendly landlord and staff, character bar with elderly maybe antique furnishings, lots of stuffed animals and birds, well kept ales such as Black Sheep, Theakstons Best and Old Peculier and a weekly guest beer, quite a few wines and good choice of malt whiskies, good generous home-made food from sandwiches and ploughman's to mixed grill, great views from terrace (and from restaurant and bedrooms); children allowed if eating, occasional jazz nights, open all day Sat; attractive bedrooms – a nice place to stay, good walks *(Peter Lewis, Paul Fairbrother, Helen Morris, LYM)*

Rotherham [SK4292]

Rhinoceros [Bridgegate]: Welcoming Wetherspoons in former old shop, traditional interior, good value hearty food all day, cheerful competent staff, good changing choice of well kept ales *(Nigel Sherriff)*

Runswick Bay [NZ8217]

☆ *Royal* [off A174 NW of Whitby]: Super setting tucked into cliffs, lovely views over fishing village and sea from welcoming big-windowed plain front lounge and terrace, limited choice of good value food inc huge helpings of fresh local fish, well kept Black Sheep (served without sparkler on request), good service, bustling nautical back bar, family room with TV and darts; steep walk down from top car park, or use expensive village car park; bedrooms *(Keith and Janet Morris, BB)*

Sandsend [NZ8613]

Hart [East Row]: Good helpings of good food from fine crab sandwiches up in shoreside pub with log fire in character downstairs bar, friendly staff and well kept Camerons bitter; pleasant garden *(Greta and Christopher Wells, Eric Locker)*

Saxton [SE4736]

Greyhound [by church in village, 2½ miles from A1 via B1217]: Charming unchanging Grade II local by church in attractive quiet village, well kept cheap Sam Smiths OB tapped from the cask, three small unspoilt rooms on linking corridor, old prints, open fires and settles, masses of china plates; TV in room on right, no food; a couple of picnic-sets in side yard with attractive hanging baskets, open all day wknds *(Kevin Thorpe, LYM, Kevin Blake)*

☆ *Plough* [not far from A1, off B1217 towards Towton; Headwell Lane]: Smart but friendly and quaint, with big dining room and front lounge, huge changing blackboard choice of good interesting freshly made food (not Sun evening) inc plenty of fish and beautiful puddings, friendly staff, well kept Theakstons, good choice of house wines, good coffee, blazing smokeless fire; seats outside, cl Mon; pleasant stone village with magnificent church *(Ian S Morley)*

Scaling Dam [NZ7412]

Grapes [Guisborough Rd (A171, opp reservoir)]: Large open-plan pub with beamed original core, red plush banquettes, open fire, spacious restaurant, usual food, fish specialities and carvery Sun lunch, Tetleys, welcoming landlord; may be piped 60s music; bedrooms *(Phil and Heidi Cook)*

Scarborough [TA0588]

Golden Ball [Sandside, opp harbour]: Seafront pub with good harbour and bay views, panelled bar with nautical memorabilia, lunchtime food (not Sun), well kept low-priced Sam Smiths OB; basic family lounge, tables outside *(Eric Larkham, Kevin Blake)*

☆ *Hole in the Wall* [Vernon Rd]: Unusual long chatty local on three levels, well kept ales such as Durham, Shepherd Neame and Theakstons

BB, XB and Old Peculier and good changing guest beers, country wines, good cheap home-made lunchtime food (not Sun); sometimes piped music but no machines *(Eric Larkham, Shaun Pinchbeck, Kevin Blake, A Boss, the Didler)*

Indigo Alley [N Marine Rd]: Trendy open-plan pub with good range of real ales such as Hop Back, Roosters and as a regular Daleside, also Leffe on tap, no food or machines, piped music – live Tues-Thurs and Sun; open till midnight Fri/Sat in summer *(Eric Larkham, Wendy Muldoon)*

Raffels [Falsgrave Rd/Belgrave Cres]: Smart stylish pub (once a gentleman's club), lots of chandeliers, leather sofas, portraits, velvet curtains and game trophies, large front bar and separate plush restaurant, well kept Theakstons *(Kevin Blake)*

Scarborough Arms [North Terr]: Cosy and comfortable mock-Tudor pub, walls decorated with weaponry, good value filling meals (not Sun evening), well kept Marstons, John Smiths Bitter and Magnet and a guest beer, darts, pool; good outside seating, open all day *(A Boss, Eric Larkham)*

Tap & Spile [Falsgrave Rd]: Former White Horse reworked with authentic lived-in feel in its three rooms (one no smoking), interesting changing well kept ales, efficient good-humoured staff, home-made food *(the Didler)*

Scotton [SE3359]

Guy Fawkes Arms [Main St]: Helpful and friendly landlord, good bar food (not Tues), wider restaurant choice, well kept John Smiths and Tetleys *(R S and A Talbot)*

Settle [SD8264]

Royal Oak [Market Pl (B6480, off A65 bypass)]: Market-town inn with new licensees doing good value generous food, well kept Black Sheep and Timothy Taylors Landlord, willing service, roomy and congenial partly divided open-plan panelled bar, comfortable seats around brass-topped tables, restaurant, no smoking area; children welcome, bedrooms with own bathrooms *(Bill and Steph Brownson, Brian Horner, Brenda Arthur, Janet and Peter Race, LYM)*

Sheffield [SK3687]

Bankers Draft [Market Pl]: Clean and tidy Wetherspoons conversion of a former Midland Bank, bars on two roomy well kept floors, standard food all inc bargains, good range of sensibly priced real ales, no smoking areas; open all day *(CMW, JJW, Richard Lewis, Catherine Pitt, John A Barker)*

Blue Ball [Main Rd, Wharncliffe Side]: Large modern comfortably carpeted open-plan Tom Cobleigh pub, lots of wood, step up to no smoking dining area, inexpensive food inc four Sun roasts and lots of fresh properly cooked veg, two real ales, attentive service; pool table partitioned off, fruit machine, quiet piped music; open all day *(CMW, JJW)*

Cask & Cutler [Henry St; Shalesmoor tram stop right outside]: Well refurbished small corner pub, six changing guest beers and bottled Belgians, frequent beer festivals, farm ciders and perry, plans for its own microbrewery, coal fire in no smoking bar on left, friendly licensees, dog and cat, appropriate posters, lunchtime food inc popular cheap Sun lunch (booking advised), daily papers, pub games; open all day Fri/Sat, cl Mon lunchtime, wheelchair access, tables in nice back garden *(the Didler, Richard Lewis)*

☆ *Devonshire Cat* [Wellington Street]: New sister venture to Fat Cat (see main entries), bright and airy contemporary continental-feel café/bar with polished light wood, some bare boards, no smoking area, good value food, staff knowledgeable about the dozen well kept real ales, some tapped from the cask in glazed stillage (and one brewed for the pub), lots of bottled beers, two farm ciders, tea and coffee; open all day *(John A Barker, the Didler)*

Frog & Parrot [Division St/Westfield Terr]: Bare boards, lofty ceiling, huge windows, comfortable banquettes up a few steps, lively studenty café-bar atmosphere in evenings, friendly staff, interesting beers brewed on the premises (one fearsomely strong) and others such as Boddingtons, Kelham Island Easy Rider and Marstons Pedigree, lots of malt whiskies and vodkas, good range of food inc pizzas; may be loud juke box (but you don't notice it after a couple of Roger & Outs), games machine; open all day *(LYM, John A Barker)*

Gardeners Rest [Neepsend Lane]: Smartly rejuvenated pub with friendly beer-enthusiast landlord, Timothy Taylors Landlord, Mild and Porter, up to four guest beers from one changing brewery, Belgian beers on tap and in bottle, no smoking room, lunchtime food, bar billiards (free Mon), sky and water photographs; live music Tues/Thurs/Sat, quiz Sun; disabled facilities, conservatory and back garden overlooking river, open all day *(the Didler, Richard Lewis, Richard Houghton)*

Hallamshire [West St by tram stop]: Comfortable and friendly Tetleys Festival Ale House with handsome marble-tiled façade, carpeted side lounge off main bar, polished dark pine, nice semi-alcove layout, lots of brewery and Sheffield prints, jugs and bric-a-brac, Bass, Marstons Pedigree, Tetleys and a guest such as Greene King Abbot, decent range of wines, good food choice 11-7; open all day *(Richard Lewis, John A Barker)*

☆ *Hillsborough* [Langsett Rd/Wood St; by Primrose View tram stop]: Hotel feel despite the friendly welcome and all the changing well kept ales at attractive prices inc rarities, landlord happy to chat about them, enjoyable low-priced early-evening food (not Sun) from baguettes up, bare-boards bar, lounge, no smoking room with fire, daily papers; piped music, TV; views to ski slope from picnic-sets on big back terrace with barbecues; bedrooms with own bathrooms, covered parking, real ale bar open only Thurs-Sun evenings *(Richard Houghton, CMW, JJW, the Didler)*

Hogshead [Orchard St]: Light and airy café feel by day, with modern art and unusual bright modern décor, five changing real ales tapped from the cask such as Black Sheep, Fullers or Greene King, plenty of bottled Belgians, country wines, malt whiskies, farm cider, four levels with downstairs patisserie and settees upstairs; disabled facilities, open all day *(Catherine Pitt)*

Kings Head [Poole Rd, off Prince of Wales Rd, Darnall; not far from M1 junctions 33/34]: Cheap enjoyable freshly made wkdy lunchtime food (evenings by arrangement), three real ales inc Marstons Pedigree, friendly hard-working staff, comfortable lounge, lots of plants, brass and copper; big-screen TV, maybe quiet piped music; tables in small back Spanish-style yard with small water feature and maybe bouncy castle, bedrooms now *(CMW, JJW)*

New Crown [Handsworth Rd (B6200 – was A57)]: Friendly local with three real ales, good helpings of good straightforward food lunchtime (not Sun) and wkdy early evenings inc OAP bargains, darts, TV and games machine in second bar, restaurant; piped music, karaoke Weds, disco Fri and Sun; open all day *(CMW, JJW)*

Noahs Ark [Crookes]: Friendly recently refurbished pub, popular with students, with long-serving landlord, up to eight real ales, huge range of simple cheap filling food (not Sun evening) all freshly prepared (so may be a wait) inc early evening bargains; dominoes, pool, TV, quiet piped music; disabled facilities, open all day exc Sun *(CMW, JJW)*

Old Grindstone [Crookes/Lydgate Lane]: Victorian pub reopened under new management, Tetleys and guest beers from Kelham Island or Black Sheep, good value food inc students' bargains, obliging service, daily papers, raised no smoking area; games area with pool, machines etc, TV, piped pop music; open all day, jazz Mon *(Peter F Marshall, CMW, JJW)*

Red Deer [Pitt St]: Small cosy backstreet local surrounded by Univ buildings, wide choice of good value lunchtime food, well kept Bass, Greene King Abbot and Old Speckled Hen, Marstons Pedigree, Timothy Taylors Landlord, Tetleys and three changing guest beers, pleasant raised back area *(the Didler, John A Barker)*

Red House [Solly St]: Small backstreet pub with charming landlady (and her big stray dog), panelled front room, back snug, comfortable chairs and banquettes, delft shelf of china, well kept ales such as Adnams, Greene King IPA and Jennings, good value wkdy lunchtime food, main bar with pool, darts and cards; occasional folk music *(John A Barker, Pete Baker)*

Red Lion [Charles St, nr stn]: Welcoming central bar serving separate traditional rooms, ornate fireplaces and coal fires, attractive panelling and etched glass; cosy and comfortable, well kept Stones and Theakstons, good simple lunchtime food, small back dining room, pleasant conservatory *(John A Barker, Pete Baker, N J Worthington, S L Tracy, the Didler)*

Rutland Arms [Brown St]: Jolly place handy for the Crucible (and station), good wine and six or seven cheap beers inc Marstons Pedigree and Stones, plentiful good value food lunchtime and very early evening, handsome façade; tables in prettily kept outdoor area *(the Didler)*

Staffordshire Arms [Sorby St, Pitsmoor (A6135)]: Well run convivial local with Banks's, Stones and Worthingtons, sandwiches, some seats by bar opening into larger space, cosy snug; two snooker rooms, quiz nights, wknd entertainment; open all day exc Sun *(Bernie Adams)*

Walkley Cottage [Bole Hill Rd]: Chatty 1930s pub popular for good choice of good value food (not Sun evening, may be more limited Mon) inc generous Sun roast, up to seven real ales, farm cider, good coffee and soft drinks choice, friendly black cat and Max the cocker spaniel (not during food service times); piped music, games room with pool, machines, darts and SkyTV, quiz night Thurs; children welcome, views from picnic-sets in small back garden with swings, lovely hanging baskets *(CMW, JJW)*

Sicklinghall [SE3648]

☆ Scotts Arms [Main St]: Nice layout with low beams, old timbers, log fire in double-sided fireplace, good blackboard food choice, well kept Theakstons Best, XB and Old Peculier, good coffee, range of wines, good cheerful unhurried service, daily papers; may be piped classical music; big garden with play area *(Derek Stafford, LYM)*

Simonstone [SD8791]

Game Tavern [Simonstone Hall]: Comfortable and tastefully furnished lounge bar attached to country house hotel, carefully cooked food inc good hotpot, well kept Theakstons, hunting trophies, fantastic views, a warm welcome for walkers; good bedrooms *(Paul Aston, Jim Abbott)*

Skerne [TA0455]

Eagle [Wansford Rd]: Fine unspoilt village pub, small front parlour and basic bar either side of hall, low-priced well kept Camerons brought on tray from cellar (ask to see the rare Victorian cash-register beer dispenser), coal fire, friendly landlord and chatty local atmosphere, darts; no food, cl wkdy lunchtimes *(Kevin Thorpe, Pete Baker, the Didler)*

Skipton [SD9852]

Black Horse [High St]: Bustling and friendly beams-and-stripped-stone coaching inn opp castle, popular with cavers, climbers and Saturday-market people; good choice of usual food served quickly, Scottish Courage real ales, huge log-effect gas fire in big stone fireplace; open all day, children welcome, play barn and small outdoor play area, bedrooms with own bathrooms *(WAH)*

Narrow Boat [Victoria St]: Town pub nr canal, up to half a dozen well kept ales from small breweries, lots of bottled Belgians, good plain lunchtime food, welcoming staff, two-level bar (smoking confined to upper gallery), home-made chutney and mustard for sale; jazz Tues, quiz Weds; open all day *(Dr B and Mrs P B Baker, Mr and Mrs P Eastwood)*

Red Lion [Market Sq]: Well furnished and bustling (next to the market), with decent reasonably priced food servery, Boddingtons and

Castle Eden, cheerful staff *(George Atkinson)*

☆ Woolly Sheep [Sheep St]: Dates from 17th c, two beamed bars off flagstoned passage, exposed brickwork, stone fireplace, lots of sheep prints and old photographs, old plates and bottles, full Timothy Taylors range kept well, good value changing food inc good home-made puddings and plenty for children, prompt friendly service, roomy comfortable dining area; spacious pretty garden, six bedrooms *(John Fazakerley, Mr and Mrs Justin Beament, Peter and Anne Hollindale)*

Sledmere [SE9365]

Triton [junction B1252/B1253 NW Gt Driffield]: Simple 18th-c inn in attractive spot, high-backed settles in small bar, good log fire, well kept Tetleys, simple generous bar food (not Mon lunchtime); games and juke box in public bar, children welcome; bedrooms *(LYM)*

Sleights [NZ8606]

Plough [Coach Rd]: Pleasant two-bar stone-built pub with emphasis on food; good views, well kept John Smiths and Theakstons *(M Borthwick)*

Snaith [SE6422]

☆ Brewers Arms [Pontefract Rd]: Good beers – Traditional, Nellie Dean, Bullion, Old Curiosity, and Willows Wood – brewed at this converted mill, bright friendly open-plan bar, carpeted conservatory-style dining area, straightforward food from good sandwiches to steaks and Sun carvery with OAP lunches Mon-Thurs; piped music may obtrude; children in eating areas, bedrooms *(Michael Butler, LYM)*

Sneaton [NZ8908]

Sneaton Hall [Beacon Way; B1416 S of Whitby]: Small country hotel with comfortable old-fashioned bar, good changing choice of well cooked food, elegant restaurant, good Sun lunch, lovely views to Whitby abbey, very friendly staff, dominoes; tables on terrace, garden with quoits; bedrooms *(M Borthwick)*

South Dalton [SE9645]

Pipe & Glass [West End; just off B1248 NW of Beverley]: Friendly dining pub in charming secluded setting, with large attractive conservatory restaurant overlooking Dalton Park (must book wknds), some high-backed settles, old prints, log fires, beams and bow windows; Theakstons and simple food in stripped-stone beamed bar; quiet piped music; children welcome, tables in garden with splendid yew tree, three comfortable bedrooms with good huge breakfast *(LYM, Kevin Thorpe, Mrs B Dennison)*

Sowerby [SE4381]

George [just S of Thirsk; Front St]: Attractive two-bar Georgian pub with newish chef doing good food esp fresh fish, good vegetarian repertoire, decent house wines, Tetleys-related real ales, helpful informal service, restaurant; handsome village *(Edward and Deanna Pearce)*

Sprotbrough [SE5302]

☆ Boat [2¼ miles from M18 junction 2; Nursery Lane]: Interesting roomy stone-built ex-farmhouse with lovely courtyard in charming quiet spot by River Don, three individually furnished areas, big stone fireplaces, latticed windows, dark brown beams, lots of old photographs, very wide choice of good value generous usual food (no sandwiches), well kept John Smiths, farm cider, prompt helpful service; piped music, fruit machine, no dogs; big sheltered prettily lit courtyard, river walks; restaurant (Tues-Sat evening, Sun lunch); open all day summer Sats *(Michael Butler, LYM, GSB)*

Stanbury [SE0037]

☆ *Old Silent* [Hob Lane]: Very popular neatly rebuilt moorland dining pub with several interconnecting rooms, stone floors, mullioned windows and open fires, conservatory, friendly restaurant, games room, juke box; big choice of enjoyable straightforward food from good sandwiches to some interesting specials with fresh veg, friendly attentive staff, well kept Theakstons; bedrooms *(BB, Greta and Christopher Wells, Norman Stansfield, Dr Wallis Taylor)*

Stokesley [NZ5209]

☆ *White Swan* [West End]: Very friendly country pub with great range of cheeses, home-made pickle and several pâtés for ploughman's, well kept Captain Cook ales brewed at the pub and interesting changing guest beers, welcoming staff, well worn in but clean, comfortable and tidy split-level panelled bar, hat display, friendly ridgeback called Bix and little black dog called Titch; midweek live blues and jazz *(Greta and Christopher Wells, C A Hall, Val Stevenson, Rob Holmes, Mr Broad)*

Stutton [SE4841]

Hare & Hounds: Stone-built pub with cosy low-ceilinged rooms, very popular with readers under its former landlord; refurbished under new manager, with well kept Sam Smiths OB, decent wine, revamped menu (not Sun evening), well behaved children in restaurant; may be piped music; cl Mon, lovely long sloping garden with playthings *(Tim and Sue Halstead, LYM)*

Tan Hill [NY8906]

☆ *Tan Hill Inn* [Arkengarthdale rd Reeth—Brough, at junction Keld/W Stonesdale rd]: Wonderfully remote old stone pub on Pennine Way – Britain's highest, nearly five miles from the nearest neighbour, basic, bustling and can get overcrowded, full of bric-a-brac and pictures inc good old photographs, simple sturdy furniture, flagstones, ever-burning big log fire (with prized stone side seats); well kept Theakstons Best, XB and Old Peculier (in winter the cellar does chill down – whisky with hot water's good then), big helpings of comforting food inc popular yorkshire pudding, sandwiches too; children and dogs welcome, open all day at least in summer; bedrooms, inc some with own bathrooms in newish extension; often snowbound, with no mains electricity (juke box powered by generator); Swaledale sheep show here last Thurs in May *(LYM, John Close, Lawrence Pearse, Kevin Thorpe, Gwyneth and Salvo Spadaro-Dutturi, David Dutton, Jane Taylor, Geoffrey and Brenda Wilson, Steve Jennings)*

Thixendale [SE8461]

Cross Keys [off A166 3 miles N of

Fridaythorpe]: Unspoilt welcoming country pub in deep valley below the rolling Wolds, single cosy L-shaped room with fitted wall seats, relaxed atmosphere, four or five well kept ales such as Castle Eden, Jennings and Theakstons, sensible home-made food all from blackboard; large pleasant garden behind, popular with walkers, handy for Wharram Percy earthworks *(Margaret Dickinson, the Didler)*

Thoralby [SE0086]

George: Relaxed Dales village local catering happily for walkers and visitors too, welcoming new licensees May 2000, huge helpings of main courses and puddings, well kept Black Sheep and John Smiths, choice of red wines, darts, dominoes; not smoky even on a busy Fri night *(Richard Dean)*

Thorganby [SE6942]

Ferryboat: Take real pride in their well kept beer – Roosters and a rotating guest such as Fullers London Pride or Rudgate; friendly staff, children allowed in conservatory, lovely garden by River Derwent *(David Butterworth)*

Thornton [SE0933]

☆ *Ring o' Bells* [Hill Top Rd, off B6145 W of Bradford]: Spotless 19th-c moortop dining pub very popular for wide choice of well presented good home cooking inc fresh fish, meat and poultry specialities, superb steaks, good puddings, bargain early suppers, separate-sittings Sun lunch (best to book), well kept Black Sheep Bitter and Special and Theakstons, crisp efficient service, pleasant bar, popular air-conditioned no smoking restaurant and pleasant conservatory lounge; wide views towards Shipley and Bingley *(Derek and Sylvia Stephenson, Walter and Susan Rinaldi-Butcher)*

Thornton Dale [SE8383]

New Inn [The Square]: Recently renovated keeping beams and old-world charm, well kept Black Sheep, John Smiths and Timothy Taylors, enjoyable food inc popular imaginative evening meals; attractive roomy bedrooms with own bathrooms, good breakfast, pretty village *(Michael Butler)*

Thornton in Lonsdale [SD6976]

☆ *Marton Arms* [just NW of Ingleton]: Big welcoming beamed bar opp attractive church, ancient stripped stone walls festooned with caving pictures (for sale), roaring log fire, good relaxed atmosphere, plain pine furniture, up to 15 well kept ales, farm cider, over 150 malt whiskies, martinis to make your hair stand on end, good value generous food from sandwiches to kangaroo, efficient friendly service even when busy; bar billiards room; children welcome, marvellous Dales views from garden; open all day wknds, cl winter wkdys, pleasant spacious annexe bedrooms (one equipped for disabled), good breakfast, great walking country *(Andy and Jill Kassube, Paul and Diane Burrows)*

Thornton-le-Clay [SE6865]

☆ *White Swan* [off A64 York—Malton; Low St]: Comfortably old-fashioned beamed dining pub, homely and peaceful, with genial attentive landlord, good freshly cooked well thought-out food inc imaginative dishes, fresh fish and late suppers, well kept Black Sheep and a guest beer, decent wines, good log fire, shining brasses, children welcome, plenty of board games, good view from impeccable ladies'; well chosen piped music; tables on terrace, neatly kept grounds with duck pond, herb garden and rescued donkeys, attractive countryside nr Castle Howard; cl Mon lunchtime *(Nicholas Pawley, Sarah Turnbull, Mrs K McManus)*

Thorpe Hesley [SK3796]

Travellers [Smithy Wood Rd, just off A629 Cowley Hill towards Chapeltown at M1 junction 35]: Homely early Victorian two-bar pub with no smoking dining room/ conservatory, two well kept real ales, decent food (not Sun/Mon evenings) with fresh veg, stuffed birds, brass, pictures and fresh flowers; piped music, high chairs for children; big garden with play area and pets corner, woodland walks nearby *(CMW, JJW)*

Thorpe Salvin [SK5281]

Parish Oven [Church St/Worksop Rd]: Spacious beamed pub with old cooking range in partly no smoking dining room, good choice of cheap food inc takeaways and Sun roast, John Smiths or Theakstons and a guest ale, TV and pool, amusements in children's room (children's parties can be arranged); garden with picnic-sets and play area *(CMW, JJW)*

Threshfield [SD9863]

Old Hall Inn [B6160/B6265 just outside Grassington]: Three knocked-together rooms, high beam-and-plank ceiling with lots of chamber-pots, cushioned wall pews, tall well blacked kitchen range, usual food, John Smiths, Theakstons, and Timothy Taylors Bitter or Landlord, darts, dominoes; piped music; neat garden with aviary, good base for Dales walks – two s/c cottages; children in eating area, cl Mon winter *(WAH, LYM)*

Tickhill [SK5993]

Royal Oak [Northgate]: One long room with central bar, very popular lunchtime with OAPs for decent food (not Sun evening) inc fresh fish, Black Sheep and other real ales; quiet piped music, TV, quiz nights; garden with play area *(CMW, JJW)*

Topcliffe [SE4076]

Angel [off A1, take A168 to Thirsk, after 3 miles follow signs for Topcliffe; Long St]: Big place carefully and comfortably done up in series of separately themed areas inc an attractive and softly lit stripped-stone faux-Irish bar, also billiards room and two dining rooms, wide choice of reasonably priced food inc some interesting dishes and lots of fish, John Smiths, Tetleys and Theakstons, decent wines; unobtrusive piped music; tables outside *(Susan and John Douglas, Val Stevenson, Rob Holmes)*

Tosside [SD7755]

Dog & Partridge: Homely village pub recently reopened by friendly local licensees, decent sandwiches and some home-made hot dishes *(Margaret Dickinson)*

Ulley [SK4687]

Royal Oak [2 miles from M1 junction 31 – Turnshaw Rd, off B6067 in Aston]: Friendly and cosy stone-built dining pub in lovely countryside by church, popularly priced bar food served till late inc children's and choice of Sun roasts, well kept cheap Sam Smiths OB, largely no smoking stable-theme beamed dining lounge with rooms off, good family room; quiet piped music; some picnic-sets outside with play area, can get packed on warm summer evenings, esp Sat *(CMW, JJW)*

Upper Hopton [SE1918]

Freemasons Arms [B6118 NE of Huddersfield]: Enjoyable reasonably priced Italian food, well kept ales such as Black Sheep, Old Mill and Timothy Taylors Landlord, superb views down over Huddersfield from front conservatory *(Derek and Sylvia Stephenson)*

Wakefield [SE3320]

Fernandes Brewery Tap [Avison Yard, Kirkgate]: Top floor of 19th-c malt store converted to tap for Fernandes microbrewery, their beers and guests kept well, good breweriana collection, welcoming atmosphere; cl Mon-Thurs lunchtime, open all day Fri-Sun *(the Didler)*

Henry Boons [Westgate]: Well kept Clarks (from next-door brewery), Black Sheep, Tetleys and Timothy Taylors in two-room bare-boards local, friendly staff, breweriana; side pool area, machines, live bands; open all day *(Richard Lewis, the Didler)*

Redout [Horbury Rd, Westgate]: Busy traditional city pub, four rooms off long corridor, Rugby League photographs, well kept Tetleys Bitter and Mild and Timothy Taylors Landlord, pub games *(the Didler)*

Talbot & Falcon [Northgate]: Popular Tetleys Festival Alehouse with friendly long bar, panelling and lots of prints, back lounge, wide choice of well kept ales largely from small breweries, foreign bottled beers, good choice of reasonably priced food, quick service; good juke box, TV, games machines; open all day *(Richard Lewis, Derek and Sylvia Stephenson)*

Wagon [Westgate End]: Busy friendly local specialising in well kept ales mainly from interesting small breweries inc at least two from Durham, lunchtime food, log fire, reasonable prices; side pool table, games machine, juke box; benches outside, open all day *(the Didler, Richard Lewis)*

Wakefield Labour Club [Vicarage St]: Shed-style club, small and inviting – all welcome, visitors can just sign in; wide changing choice of real ales from small breweries, farm cider, Belgian beers; cl lunchtime Mon-Thurs *(the Didler)*

Wales [SK4783]

Duke of Leeds [Church St]: Quiet and comfortable 18th-c stone-faced village pub kept spotless by chatty 3rd-generation landlord, well kept Boddingtons, Brains, Castle Eden and Greene King Abbot, good value generous food (not Mon/Tues lunchtimes) inc lunchtime children's dishes (may be a wait when busy), good soft drinks range, long no smoking lounge and smaller room where smoking allowed, no smoking dining areas, lots of brass and copper, pictures for sale, table fountains, flame-effect gas fire; may be quiet piped music; no credit cards taken, nearby walks *(CMW, JJW)*

Walkington [SE9937]

☆ *Ferguson-Fawsitt Arms* [East End; B1230 W of Beverley]: Mock-Tudor bars in 1950s style, doing well under helpful and welcoming newish management; good choice of good value food inc carvery from airy no smoking flagstone-floored food bar, very popular lunchtime with older people, friendly cheerful service, Courage Directors and John Smiths, decent wine; tables out on terrace, games bar with pool table; delightful village *(June and Ken Brooks, Mr and Mrs F J Parmenter, Andy Marks, LYM)*

Warley [SE0524]

Maypole [village signed off A646 just W of Halifax]: Friendly farmhouse-style refurbishment, country furniture on flagstons, three rooms with two majoring on food – enormous good value choice from substantial lunchtime bar snacks to imaginative evening meals inc seafood, well kept beers such as Boddingtons and Greene King Old Speckled Hen, good choice of wines *(Pat and Tony Martin)*

Warley Town [SE0524]

Maypole: Good food and service and nice bustle in traditional old village pub, garden with pleasant seating area; local bands in summer *(T Gibson)*

Weaverthorpe [SE9771]

Star [Main St]: Two comfortable bars with log fires, wide choice of good food inc game (may be a wait), well kept Camerons and a guest beer such as Yorkshire Last Drop, exceptionally welcoming staff, restaurant; nice bedrooms, good breakfast, quiet village setting; cl wkdy lunchtimes *(C A Hall)*

Wentbridge [SE4817]

Blue Bell: Several communicating rooms, beams, stripped stone, farm tools and other bric-a-brac, solid wooden tables, chairs and settles; wide choice of good value quick generous food inc interesting dishes, small helpings of some, friendly efficient service, well kept Tetleys and Timothy Taylors Landlord, long wine list; family room, good view from garden *(Hazel and Michael Duncombe, Roy and Lindsey Fentiman)*

West Burton [SE0186]

☆ *Fox & Hounds* [on green, off B6160 Bishopdale—Wharfedale]: Clean and cosy unpretentious local on long green of idyllic Dales village, friendly newish landlord doing wide choice of good value generous home-made food inc children's and good puddings, well kept Black Sheep and Theakstons Old Peculier, residents' dining room, children and dogs welcome; nearby caravan park; good modern bedrooms, lovely walks and waterfalls nearby *(R F B Wivell, D M Hall, Abi Benson)*

West Tanfield [SE2678]

☆ *Bruce Arms* [A6108 N of Ripon]: Thriving dining pub with good rather upmarket food inc interesting dishes in intimate log-fire bar or restaurant, friendly service *(Janet and Peter Race, Mrs Jane Wyles, LYM)*

☆ *Bull* [Church St (A6108 N of Ripon)]: Open-plan but the feel of two smallish rooms, comfortable pub furniture, popular food all day inc good generous sandwiches, well kept Black Sheep ales, decent wines, welcoming service, small restaurant; children allowed away from bar; tables in attractive garden behind sloping steeply to river *(Jim and Maggie Cowell, BB)*

West Witton [SE0688]

☆ *Wensleydale Heifer* [A684 W of Leyburn]: Comfortable inn with good generous food from sandwiches through good value early suppers Weds and Sun to fish and game, low-ceilinged small interconnecting areas in genteel front lounge, big attractive bistro, separate smart restaurant, good log fire, attractive prints, pleasant décor, excellent service, no music; small bar with decent wines, well kept Black Sheep, John Smiths and Theakstons Best, and another fire; nice big bedrooms (back ones quietest), good big breakfast *(John and Sheila Lister, Paul Aston)*

Whitby [NZ8911]

Tap & Spile [New Quay Rd]: Well decorated three-room bare-boards local, no smoking area, good value bar food inc good local fish and chips noon-7, half a dozen well kept ales, country wines, farm ciders, traditional games; frequent folk nights, open all day *(the Didler)*

Whixley [SE4458]

Anchor [New Rd]: Warm and friendly village local, good value well cooked food, bargain carvery lunch particularly popular with OAPs, friendly helpful efficient service, well kept John Smiths and Tetleys, several rooms, coal fire in small lounge, eccentric teapots on every surface, sunny conservatory *(Janet and Peter Race, H Bramwell, Keith and Di Newsome)*

Wigglesworth [SD8157]

Plough [B6478, off A65 S of Settle]: New licensees doing enjoyable food inc good Sun lunch, little rooms off bar, some spartan yet cosy, others smart and plush, inc no smoking panelled dining room and snug, separate pleasant conservatory restaurant with panoramic Dales views, real ales; attractive garden, good bedrooms *(Jean and Douglas Troup)*

Worsall [NZ3909]

Ship [Low Worsall, off B1264 SW of Yarm]: Extended pub, recently very smartly refurbished, with good choice of well presented good food inc interesting dishes, friendly staff *(Mr and Mrs M Bashford)*

Wykeham [SE9783]

Downe Arms [A170 Scarborough—Pickering]: Good choice of generous good value food from baguettes up (just the baguettes as roast meat as Sunday bar snacks) in comfortable bar and separate barn-style dining room, stripped pine and cottagey furnishings, John Smiths and Theakstons, good service, family room, pool; piped music may be a bit obtrusive; play area, bedrooms *(M Borthwick)*

York [SE5951]

Ackhorne [St Martins Lane, Micklegate]: Fine changing range of well kept ales from Roosters and other small breweries, farm cider, maybe perry, country wines, foreign bottled beers, good coffee, beams, leather wall seats, old prints, bottles and jugs, carpeted snug one end, good value food (not Mon evening or Sun) from good choice of sandwiches up, friendly interested staff, open fire, daily papers, traditional games, silenced games machine; Sun quiz night; open all day, tables out behind *(Sue Holland, Dave Webster, Richard Lewis, the Didler, Roger A Bellingham, Eric Larkham)*

☆ *Black Swan* [Peaseholme Green (inner ring road)]: Marvellous timbered and jettied Tudor building, nice black-beamed back bar with vast inglenook, cosy panelled front bar with little serving hatch, crooked-floored hall with fine period staircase; low-priced usual food from baked potatoes and baguettes up, well kept Worthington Best and guests such as Bass and York Yorkshire Terrier, several country wines; piped music; useful car park *(Bob and Laura Brock, Paul and Ursula Randall, the Didler, Richard Lewis, Mr and Mrs Jon Corelis, Mike Ridgway, Sarah Miles, Kevin Blake, David Carr, J V Dadswell, P Abbott, LYM)*

☆ *Blue Bell* [Fossgate]: Warmly welcoming Edwardian pub with good choice of well kept ales, tiny tiled-floor front bar with roaring fire, panelled ceiling, stained glass, bar pots and decanters, corridor to back smoke room not much bigger, hatch service to middle bar, lively local atmosphere, lunchtime sandwiches on counter; open all day, can get very busy *(Eric Larkham, Richard Lewis, the Didler, Sue Holland, Dave Webster, Pete Baker)*

First Hussar [opp Viking Hotel, North St]: Basic stripped-brick and bare-boards décor in three smallish rooms, military prints and memorabilia, no smoking snug, many well kept changing ales such as Adnams Fisherman, Black Sheep, Celebration Premium, Jennings Cumberland, Ridleys Big Tackle, Robinsons Frederics and York Yorkshire Terrier and Wet 'n' Wild, Weston's Old Rosie cider, friendly staff, cheap lunchtime food inc nice sandwiches and simple hot dishes, magazines; may be piped radio, darts, machines, Weds blues night, quiz nights; children welcome, tables outside, open all day *(Richard Lewis, Eric Larkham)*

Golden Ball [Cromwell Rd/Bishophill]: Unspoilt 1950s feel, small, quiet and homely; no piped music or TV, no food but good fish and chip shop next door *(Mr and Mrs Jon Corelis)*

Golden Lion [Church St]: Big comfortable open-plan T & J Bernard pub done up in bare-floored Edwardian style (in fact first licensed 1771), beams, plenty of lamps, lots of prints; friendly efficient staff, real ales such as Boddingtons, Fullers London Pride, Lees Plum Pudding, John Smiths and Theakstons Best and Old Peculier, plenty of bottled beers, wide choice of cheap quick generous food all day, good choice of wines by the glass; fruit machine, piped music; open all day *(Richard Lewis, C A Hall, Phil and Jane Hodson)*

Hansom Cab [Market St]: Crowded dark-panelled bar, long and narrow, with wall seats, wing chairs, side alcoves, plenty of tables, interesting ceiling (like a glass pyramid surrounded by plants), cheap quick food counter, well kept Sam Smiths; children allowed lunchtime *(Susan and Nigel Wilson, Mr and Mrs C Roberts, Eric Larkham)*

☆ *Hole in the Wall* [High Petergate]: Rambling open-plan pub handy for Minster, beams, stripped masonry, lots of prints, turkey carpeting, plush seats, well kept Mansfield beers, good coffee, cheap food noon onwards inc generous Sun lunch, prompt friendly service; juke box, games machines, piped music not too loud, live some nights; open all day *(Ian Baillie, Richard Lewis, LYM)*

Last Drop [Colliergate]: Old building restored by York Brewery in traditional style as their first tied pub, half a dozen of their own beers with a well kept guest such as Exmoor Gold, good menu from sandwiches and baked potatoes to some beer-linked specialities, friendly staff, bare boards, big barrels and comfortable seats; open all day, can get very busy lunchtime *(Richard Lewis)*

☆ *Lendal Cellars* [Lendal]: Split-level ale house down steps in broad-vaulted 17th-c cellars carefully spotlit to show up the stripped brickwork, stone floor, interconnected rooms and alcoves, very well kept Adnams, Boddingtons, Castle Eden and Marstons Pedigree, farm cider, country wines, foreign bottled beers, cheerful staff, children allowed for good plain food 11.30-7(5 Fri/Sat); good piped music, popular with students; open all day *(Richard Lewis, Eric Larkham, Ian Baillie, the Didler, LYM)*

Masons Arms [Fishergate]: Unchanged 1930s local, two fires in panelled front bar with blow lamps and pig ornaments, good range of beers inc guests, generous interesting home-made food, friendly service; comfortable bedrooms with own bathrooms, tables out in front and on back riverside terrace *(Eric Larkham)*

Minster Tavern [Marygate]: Small Edwardian pub, three rooms (one no smoking) off central corridor, warm and friendly atmosphere, fires and woodburners, well kept Bass, John Smiths and two guest beers, sandwiches; piped music; tables out behind *(Eric Larkham, Richard Lewis)*

☆ *Olde Starre* [Stonegate]: City's oldest licensed pub, with 'gallows' sign across York's prettiest street, original panelling and prints, green plush wall seats, several other little rooms off porch-like lobby, well kept John Smiths Bitter and Magnet and Theakstons Best, XB and Old Peculier from long counter, good value separate food servery; piped music, fruit and games machines; open all day, children welcome away from bar, flower-filled garden and courtyard with Minster glimpsed across the rooftops *(Mr and Mrs Jon Corelis, Dave Braisted, David Carr, John Fazakerley, Greta and Christopher Wells, Mike Ridgway, Sarah Miles, Eric Larkham, LYM)*

Punch Bowl [Stonegate]: Family-run local with masses of hanging baskets, small panelled rooms off corridor, friendly helpful service, wide range of good generous lunchtime food from sandwiches up (no smoking area by servery), well kept Bass and Worthingtons;

piped music, games machines; open all day, good value bedrooms *(Eric Larkham, George Atkinson, Sue Holland, Dave Webster)*

Red Lion [Merchantgate, between Fossgate and Piccadilly]: Low-beamed rambling rooms with plenty of atmosphere, some stripped Tudor brickwork, relaxed old-fashioned furnishings, well kept Scottish Courage ales, bar food, good juke box or piped music; tables outside *(Greta and Christopher Wells, LYM)*

Roman Bath [St Sampsons Sq]: Roman bath remains down steps from this cheerfully busy but spacious bar are worth seeing (£1, child 50p); good quick friendly service, well kept John Smiths, straightforward well prepared food *(Peter and Anne Hollindale)*

☆ *Royal Oak* [Goodramgate]: Unspoilt three-room black-beamed 16th-c pub (remodelled in Tudor style 1934) with warm welcoming atmosphere, cosy corners with blazing fires, good value generous home-made usual food (limited Sun evening) inc home-baked bread served 11.30-7.30, speedy service from cheerful bustling young staff, reliably well kept Greene King Abbot, Ind Coope Burton and other changing ales, wines and country wines, good coffee; prints, swords, busts and old guns, no smoking family room; handy for Minster and open all day, can get crowded *(Richard Lewis, Eric Larkham, Paul and Ursula Randall, BB, Kate, George Atkinson)*

Snickleway [Goodramgate]: Snug and comfortable little old-world pub, cheerful landlord, well kept Greene King Old Speckled Hen and John Smiths, fresh well filled sandwiches and a good value hot dish lunchtimes, lots of antiques, copper and brass, good coal fires, cosy nooks and crannies, unobtrusive piped music, prompt service,

dwindling cartoons in gents' *(Kevin Blake, Paul and Ursula Randall)*

Spread Eagle [Walmgate]: Refitted and comfortably brightened up under new owners, though still keeping some character; Banks's and related ales, bar food, tables out behind *(LYM, Eric Larkham)*

Waggon & Horses [Gillygate]: Small calm traditional pub, lots of horse tack, blacksmith equipment and sepia photographs, quick helpful service, good fire, reasonably priced decent straightforward food, right-hand dining room; back car park *(A York)*

Wellington [Alma Terr]: Quiet and welcoming early Victorian local with two bars and pool room off central corridor, coal fire, cheap Sam Smiths OB; tiny neat back yard with lots of flower baskets *(the Didler)*

☆ *York Arms* [High Petergate]: Snug and cheerful little basic panelled bar (beware the sliding door), big modern back lounge, cosier partly panelled no smoking parlour full of old bric-a-brac, prints, brown-cushioned wall settles, dimpled copper tables and an open fire; quick helpful service, well kept Sam Smiths OB, good value simple food lunchtime to early evening (not Sun-Tues), no piped music; by Minster, open all day *(Eric Larkham, BB, I Mann, Richard Lewis, A York, P Abbott, C A Hall)*

York Brewery Tap [Toft Green, Micklegate]: Upstairs lounge at York Brewery, with their own Brideshead, Stonewall, Terrier and Last Drop in top condition, also bottled beers; friendly staff happy to talk about the beers, lots of breweriana, comfortable settees and armchairs, magazines and daily papers; no food, brewery tours, shop; open all day, annual membership fee £3 unless you live in York *(Richard Lewis, the Didler)*

London
Scotland
Wales
Channel Islands

London

New entries here this year are the Cross Keys in Endell St, a likeable and unpretentious little hideaway (Central London); the Duke of Cambridge in North London, pricy but rewarding, both for its very good food and for its unusual real ales (the pub is wholly organic); and the Colton Arms in Greyhound Road, a real surprise for London, with its interesting furnishings and relaxed out-of-London feel, and the equally surprising Portobello Gold, enterprising and rather exotic, with that great rarity for London pubs – bedrooms (both West London). In contrast to these are quite a number of pubs which have kept their place in the Guide every year since its first edition 20 years ago. In Central London pride of place goes to the splendidly old-fashioned and unchanging Lamb & Flag just off Covent Garden, then as now in the hands of Adrian and Sandra Zimmerman. Other time-tested Central London pubs which have kept their place Guide after Guide are the extraordinary art nouveau Black Friar, the unusual cubicled Cittie of York (a great favourite, doing very well these days), the Lamb with its authentic Victorian décor and buoyant atmosphere, the civilised Museum Tavern (food all day), the Olde Mitre charmingly hidden away in Ely Place, and the Red Lion in Waverton Street, charmingly unpretentious despite its Mayfair surroundings. Other pubs with such a long-term record of consistent quality are, in East London, the almost Dickensian Grapes on the river in Limehouse; in North London, the cheerfully old-fashioned Holly Bush in Hampstead village, and the Spaniards Inn up on the Heath; in South London, the George in Southwark, a remarkably preserved 17th-c galleried coaching inn; and in West London, the Dove, a prime riverside pub. Other more recent additions to the Guide that are on specially fine form these days are the buzzing Eagle (good food from its open kitchen), the Jerusalem Tavern (a general favourite now), the old-fashioned Nags Head tucked away between Harrods and Hyde Park Corner, the matey little Seven Stars, and the welcoming Star in its mews just off Belgrave Square (all Central); the lively riverside Prospect of Whitby (East); the Flask, a true Hampstead local (North); the riverside Cutty Sark (lots of atmosphere), the action-packed Fire Station (good food), and the busy but civilised White Cross, further upstream on the Thames (South); and the White Horse in West London, with excellent beer and wines and enjoyable food. It is now entirely possible to head for a London pub for a special meal out. Besides places already picked out for this, others with really good food are the Anglesea Arms in Wingate Road, the Atlas and the Havelock Tavern (all West London). Our overall choice of London Dining Pub of the Year is the wholly organic Duke of Cambridge, St Peter's Street, North London. The Lucky Dip section at the end of the chapter follows a slightly different order to the main entries, in that named outer London suburbs come last, after the Central, East, North, South and West numbered postal districts. In that section, pubs of special note are the Chandos, Fox & Hounds, Grouse & Claret, Mad Bishop & Bear, Princess Louise, Salisbury and Scarsdale Arms (Central); the Barley Mow (East); the Head of Steam and Orange Tree (North); the Bell, Old Thameside, Rebatos and Trafalgar (South); and in

Outer London the Old Jail (Biggin Hill). Drinks prices are abhorrently high in London, now averaging close to £2.20 a pint. The two Sam Smiths pubs (Olde Cheshire Cheese and Cittie of Yorke) bring a touch of Yorkshire sanity to London prices, and Wetherspoons pubs always have bargain beers. London's two brewers, Fullers and Youngs, are generally less expensive than 'outsider' beers.

CENTRAL LONDON Map 13

Albert

52 Victoria Street, SW1; ⊖ St James's Park

Always busy – especially on weekday lunchtimes and after work – the huge open plan bar of this fine Victorian pub has a wonderfully diverse mix of customers, from tourists and civil servants to even the occasional MP (the division bell is rung to remind them when it's time to get back to Westminster). There's a surprisingly airy feel thanks to great expanses of heavily cut and etched windows along three sides, as well as good solid comfortable furniture, an ornate ceiling, and some gleaming mahogany. Service from the big island counter is generally swift and efficient (particularly obliging to people from overseas), with Courage Best and Directors, Theakstons Best and a guest like Greene King Abbot on handpump. The separate food servery is good value, with sandwiches (readers particularly enjoy the roast beef), soup (£2.25), salads (from £3.50) and several home-cooked hot dishes such as cottage pie, fish and chips, sweet and sour chicken and vegetable lasagne (all £4.95); usefully, there's something available all day. The upstairs restaurant does an eat-as-much-as-you-like carvery, better than average (all day inc Sunday, £14.95); it may be worth booking ahead. The handsome staircase that leads up to it is lined with portraits of former Prime Ministers. Piped music, fruit machine. Handily placed between Victoria and Westminster, the pub is one of the great sights of this part of London (if rather dwarfed by the faceless cliffs of dark modern glass around it). *(Recommended by Stephen Bonarjee, Sue Demont, Tim Barrow, Brian Kneale, Tony and Wendy Hobden, Meg and Colin Hamilton, Mayur Shah, Joel Dobris)*

Scottish Courage ~ Managers Roger and Gill Wood ~ Real ale ~ Bar food (11-10.30, 12-10 Sun) ~ Restaurant ~ (020) 722 27606 ~ Children in eating area of bar and restaurant ~ Open 11-11; 12-10.30 Sun; closed 25 Dec

Archery Tavern 🍺

4 Bathurst St, W2, opposite the Royal Lancaster hotel; ⊖ Lancaster Gate

Taking its name from an archery range that occupied the site for a while in the early 19th c, this nicely maintained Victorian pub is a good bet for visitors to this side of Hyde Park. There's plenty of space, and all sorts of types and ages can be found chatting quietly in the several comfortably relaxing, pubby areas around the central servery. On the green, pattern-papered walls are a number of archery prints, as well as a history of the pub and the area, other old prints, dried hops, and quite a few plates running along a shelf. Well kept Badger Best, IPA, Sussex and Tanglefoot on handpump, with a guest like Gribble Ale. A big back room has long tables, bare boards, and a fireplace; darts, a big stack of board games, fruit machine, piped music. Served all day, bar food includes sandwiches (from £1.75), fishcakes (£5.25), and daily specials such as chicken, leek and stilton pie (5.75); they do breakfasts on weekend mornings. There's lots more seating in front of the pub, under hanging baskets and elaborate floral displays, and some nicely old-fashioned lamps. A side door leads on to a little mews, where the Hyde Park Riding Stables are based. *(Recommended by Chris Richards, Tracey and Stephen Groves, Sue Demont, Tim Barrow)*

Badger ~ Tenant Nigel Ingram ~ Real ale ~ Bar food (12-9.30) ~ (020) 7402 4916 ~ Children welcome ~ Open 11-11; 12-10.30 Sun

Argyll Arms ◖

18 Argyll St, W1; ⊖ Oxford Circus, opp tube side exit

A useful retreat from the crowds of neighbouring Oxford Street, this bustling
Victorian pub is much as it was when built in the 1860s. The most atmospheric and
unusual part is the three cubicle rooms at the front; all oddly angular, they're made
by wooden partitions with distinctive frosted and engraved glass, with hops trailing
above. A long mirrored corridor leads to the spacious back room, with the food
counter in one corner; this area is no smoking at lunchtime. Chalked up on a
blackboard, the choice of meals includes good sandwiches and filled baguettes (from
£3.95), sausage and mash or fish and chips (£5.75), and steak and kidney pie,
vegetable cannelloni or a daily roast (£5.95). Well kept Adnams, Fullers London
Pride, Greene King IPA and Tetleys on handpump; also Addlestone's cider, malt
whiskies, and freshly squeezed orange and pineapple juice. Friendly, prompt and
efficient staff; two fruit machines, piped music (louder in the evenings than at lunch,
and very loud indeed at times). Open during busier periods, the quieter upstairs bar
overlooks the pedestrianised street – and the Palladium theatre if you can see
through the foliage outside the window; divided into several snugs with comfortable
plush easy chairs, it has swan's neck lamps, and lots of small theatrical prints along
the top of the walls. The gents' has a copy of the day's *Times* or *Financial Times* on
the wall. The pub can get very crowded (and can seem less distinctive on busier
evenings), but there's space for drinking outside. *(Recommended by John Fazakerley,
George Atkinson, Joel Dobris, Richard Rand, Mayur Shah, Ian Phillips, Stephen, Julie and Hayley
Brown, the Didler)*

*Bass ~ Managers Mike Tayara and Regina Kennedy ~ Real ale ~ Bar food (11(12
Sun)-3.30) ~ Restaurant ~ (020) 7734 6117 ~ Children welcome in restaurant at
lunchtime ~ Open 11-11; 12-8 Sun; closed 25 Dec*

Bishops Finger ♀

9-10 West Smithfield, EC1 – opposite Bart's Hospital; ⊖ Farringdon

Not huge, but comfortable and smartly civilised, this swish little place is in a verdant
square beside Smithfield Market. The well spaced out room has bright yellow walls
(nicely matching the fresh flowers on the elegant tables and behind the bar), big
windows, carefully polished bare boards, a few pillars, and comfortably cushioned
chairs under a wall lined with framed prints. Well kept Shepherd Neame Master
Brew, Bishops Finger, Spitfire and seasonal brews on handpump, with a wide choice
of wines (eight by the glass), and several ports and champagnes; friendly service.
Good food from an open kitchen beside the bar includes tasty ciabatta sandwiches
filled with things like goats cheese, pesto and beef tomato (from £3.35), vegetable
specials like warm goats cheese salad (£4.95), various different types of sausage, with
mash (from £5.95), and several daily changing hot dishes. There are a couple of
tables outside. *(Recommended by Mike Gorton, Jim Bush, Joel Dobris)*

*Shepherd Neame ~ Manager Angus Mclelland ~ Real ale ~ Bar food (12-2.30, 6-9) ~
(020) 7248 2341 ~ Well behaved children during the day in eating area of bar ~ Open
11-11; closed Sat, Sun, bank holidays, 24 Dec*

Black Friar

174 Queen Victoria Street, EC4; ⊖ Blackfriars

The highlight of this busy place is the unique décor, which includes some of the best
fine Edwardian bronze and marble art-nouveau work to be found anywhere. The
inner back room has big bas-relief friezes of jolly monks set into richly coloured
Florentine marble walls, an opulent marble-pillared inglenook fireplace, a low
vaulted mosaic ceiling, gleaming mirrors, seats built into rich golden marble recesses,
and tongue-in-cheek verbal embellishments such as Silence is Golden and Finery is
Foolish. See if you can spot the opium smoking-hints modelled into the fireplace of
the front room. You'll see the details more clearly if you come on a Saturday
lunchtime, when the pub isn't so crowded as during the week. Well kept Adnams,

Fullers London Pride and Greene King IPA on handpump; fruit machine. A limited range of lunchtime bar food includes filled rolls (from £2.95), baked potatoes (from £3.50), and a couple of daily changing hot dishes such as sausage and mash or pasta (£5.25). The pub is bigger inside than seems possible from the delightfully odd exterior, but in the evenings does get busy: lots of people spill out onto the wide forecourt in front, near the approach to Blackfriars Bridge. If you're coming by Tube, choose your exit carefully – it's all too easy to emerge from the network of passageways and find yourself on the other side of the street or marooned on a traffic island. *(Recommended by Dr David Cockburn, the Didler, JP, PP, Dr M E Wilson)*

Bass ~ Manager Mr Becker ~ Real ale ~ Bar food (12-2.30) ~ (020) 7236 5474 ~ Open 11.30-11; 12-3 Sat; closed Sat evening, Sun and bank holidays

Cittie of Yorke ◖

22 High Holborn, WC1; find it by looking out for its big black and gold clock; ⊖ Chancery Lane

Like a vast baronial hall, the main back bar of this unique pub takes your breath away when seen for the first time. Vast thousand-gallon wine vats rest above the gantry, big bulbous lights hang from the soaring high raftered roof, and the extraordinarily extended bar counter stretches off into the distance. It does get packed at lunchtimes and in the early evening, particularly with lawyers and City folk, but it's at busy times like these when the pub seems most magnificent. Most people tend to congregate in the middle, so you may still be able to bag one of the intimate, old-fashioned and ornately carved booths that run along both sides. The triangular Waterloo fireplace, with grates on all three sides and a figure of Peace among laurels, used to stand in the Grays Inn Common Room until barristers stopped dining there. Well kept Sam Smiths OB on handpump (appealingly priced at around a pound less than the typical cost of a London pint); friendly service from smartly dressed staff, fruit machine and piped music in the cellar bar. A smaller, comfortable wood-panelled room has lots of little prints of York and attractive brass lights, while the ceiling of the entrance hall has medieval-style painted panels and plaster York roses. Served from buffet counters in the main hall and cellar bar, bar food includes sandwiches (from £3.25), and half a dozen hot dishes such as steak and kidney pie or pasta with mushroom and white wine sauce (£4.50). A pub has stood on this site since 1430, though the current building owes more to the 1695 coffee house erected here behind a garden; it was reconstructed in Victorian times using 17th-c materials and parts. *(Recommended by Rona Murdoch, Stephanie Smith, Gareth Price, the Didler, Derek Thomas, Sarah Meyer, Ted George, Catherine Pitt, Mr and Mrs Jon Corelis, R Huggins, D Irving, E McCall, T McLean, Jim Bush, Tracey and Stephen Groves)*

Sam Smiths ~ Manager Stuart Browning ~ Real ale ~ Bar food (12-9) ~ (020) 7242 7670 ~ Open 11.30-11; closed Sun, bank holidays

Cross Keys ◖ £

Endell Street, corner with Betterton Street, WC2; ⊖ Covent Garden

Prettily tucked behind a little group of trees, with picnic-sets out on the cobbles under them, this small pub is refreshingly un-Londonish. The service is truly friendly and personal as well as efficient, and the single compact room has a comfortably relaxed and chatty feel. The serving counter along one side has some interesting early Beatles memorabilia above it, and the other dark walls, lined with an elderly dark brown button-back leather banquette, are packed with prints, engravings, photographs and oil paintings (as well as a huge gilt mirror, behind a couple of potted palms in chamber-pots and a row of fin de siècle lamps in the shape of elegant ladies). In the soft lighting you can hardly make out the original function of much of the bric-a-brac hanging densely below the high ceiling and its raj fans, though the diver's helmet and French horns are plain enough. Besides an impressive range of sandwiches (£1.95-£2.50), they do filled baked potatoes (£2.95), burgers (£3.95) and a few home-made dishes served piping hot. Well kept Courage Best and Directors, Marstons Pedigree and a guest beer on handpump; fruit machine. There is a small upstairs bar, which may be closed for a private function; the gents' is down in the basement. *(Recommended by Kevin Blake)*

Unique Pub Co ~ Tenant John Devlin ~ Real ale ~ Bar food (12-2.30, not evenings) ~ (020) 7836 5185 ~ Open 10.30-11; 12-10.30 Sun; closed 25 Dec evening

Dog & Duck ◖

18 Bateman Street, on corner with Frith Street, W1; ● Tottenham Court Rd/Leicester Square

You need to move fast to bag a table at this pint-sized corner house; the busy main bar really is tiny, though at times it manages to squeeze in a surprisingly large number of people. There are some high stools by the ledge along the back wall, and further seats in a slightly roomier area at one end. On the floor by the door is a mosaic of a dog, tongue out in hot pursuit of a duck, and the same theme is embossed on some of the shiny tiles that frame the heavy old advertising mirrors. The unusual little bar counter serves very well kept Fullers London Pride, Greene King IPA, Timothy Taylors Landlord, and a guest such as Adnams Broadside; also Addlestone's cider. There's a fire in winter, and newspapers to read; piped music (can be loud these days). On busier evenings they open a snug upstairs bar, though in good weather especially, most people tend to spill onto the bustling street outside. A real Soho landmark, the pub is said to be where George Orwell celebrated when the American Book of the Month Club chose *Animal Farm* as its monthly selection. Ronnie Scott's Jazz Club is near by. Note they don't allow children. *(Recommended by Mike Gorton, Roger and Jenny Huggins, Ted George, Tracey and Stephen Groves, R Huggins, D Irving, E McCall, T McLean, Mark Stoffan)*

Bass ~ Manager Alison Wernet ~ Real ale ~ (020) 7494 0697 ~ Open 12-11; 5-11 Sat; 6-10.30 Sun; closed Sat, Sun lunchtimes, 25 Dec

Eagle ⊕ ⅄

159 Farringdon Rd, EC1; opposite Bowling Green Lane car park; ● Farringdon/Old Street

As ever, the distinctive mediterranean-style meals here have delighted readers over the last year, but there's also been much praise for the atmosphere – it buzzes with life, and despite the emphasis on eating, always feels chatty and pubby. Made with the finest quality ingredients, the food still ranks among the very best you'll find in any London pub, effortlessly superior to those in the welcome imitators that have sprung up all over the city. Typical dishes might include Florentine pea soup (£4.50), poached ham hock with chick peas, spinach and chives, marinated rump steak sandwich, or linguini with crab, lemon, garlic, chilli and parsley (£8.50), roast spring chicken with celeriac, celery and cream or shoulder of lamb with chilli, caraway seeds, couscous and dried fruits (£9.50), and grilled tuna with an Italian herb and olive oil sauce (£11.50); they also do Spanish and goats milk cheeses (£6), and Portuguese custard tarts (£1). Though they don't take credit cards, they do accept debit cards. On weekday lunchtimes especially, dishes from the blackboard menu can run out or change fairly quickly, so it really is worth getting here as early as you possibly can if you're hoping to eat. The open kitchen forms part of the bar, and furnishings in the single room are simple but stylish – school chairs, a random assortment of tables, a couple of sofas on bare boards, and modern paintings on the walls (there's an art gallery upstairs, with direct access from the bar). Quite a mix of customers, but it's fair to say there's a proliferation of young media folk (the *Guardian* is based just up the road). It gets particularly busy in the evening (and can occasionally be slightly smoky then), so this isn't the sort of place you'd go for a quiet dinner, or a smart night out. Well kept Charles Wells Bombardier and IPA on handpump, good wines including a dozen by the glass, good coffee, and properly made cocktails; piped music (sometimes loud). There are times during the week when the Eagle's success means you may have to wait for a table, or at least not be shy about sharing; it can be quieter at weekends. *(Recommended by R Huggins, D Irving, E McCall, T McLean, Joel Dobris, Richard Siebert, Anna and Martyn Carey, Stephen, Julie and Hayley Brown, Ian Phillips, P Abbott)*

Free house ~ Licensee Michael Belben ~ Real ale ~ Bar food (12.30-2.30(3.30 Sat,

Sun), 6.30-10.30; not Sun evening) ~ Restaurant ~ (020) 7837 1353 ~ Children in eating area of bar ~ Open 12-11(5 Sun); closed Sun evening, bank holidays, one week at Christmas

Grapes

Shepherd Market, W1; ✪ Green Park

The old-fashioned dimly lit bar of this chatty place has a nicely traditional atmosphere, with plenty of stuffed birds and fish in glass display cases, wooden floors and panelling, comfortable plush seats, and a snug little alcove at the back. On sunny evenings smart-suited drinkers spill out onto the square outside. A good range of six or seven well kept (though fairly pricy) beers on handpump usually takes in Boddingtons, Brakspears, Flowers IPA, Fullers London Pride, Marstons Pedigree, and Wadworths 6X; fruit machine. They no longer do any bar food. Service can slow down a little at the busiest times – it's much quieter at lunchtimes. Shepherd Market is these days one of central London's best kept secrets, full of civilised places to eat, though it's not so long ago that it enjoyed a rather murkier reputation. *(Recommended by Ian Phillips, John Fazakerley, Tracey and Stephen Groves)*

Free house ~ Licensees Gill and Eric Lewis ~ Real ale ~ Open 11-11; 12-10.30 Sun; closed 25 Dec, restricted hours some bank holidays

Grenadier

Wilton Row, SW1; the turning off Wilton Crescent looks prohibitive, but the barrier and watchman are there to keep out cars; walk straight past – the pub is just around the corner; ✪ Knightsbridge

Tucked away in a tranquil part of Knightsbridge, it's hard to believe this snugly characterful little place is so close to Hyde Park Corner. It's one of London's most special pubs, patriotically painted in red, white and blue as a reminder of the days when it was the mess for the officers of the Duke of Wellington. His portrait hangs above the fireplace, alongside neat prints of Guardsmen through the ages. The bar is tiny (some might say cramped), but you should be able to plonk yourself on one of the stools or wooden benches, as despite the Grenadier's charms it rarely gets too crowded. Well kept Courage Best and Directors, Greene King Old Speckled Hen and Marstons Pedigree from handpumps at the rare pewter-topped bar counter; service is friendly and chatty, if occasionally a little slow. On Sundays especially you'll find several of the customers here to sample their famous bloody marys, made to a unique recipe. Bar food includes bowls of chips (£2) and nachos (£3.50) – very popular with after work drinkers – and good sausage and mash (£5.55) or hot steak sandwiches (£6.25); Sunday roast (£11.25). There's an intimate (and not cheap) back restaurant. The single table in the peaceful mews outside is an ideal spot to dream of the day you might be able to afford one of the smart little houses opposite. A well documented poltergeist gives the Grenadier claim to be the capital's most haunted pub. *(Recommended by Mayur Shah, Tracey and Stephen Groves, David Peakall, Guy Consterdine)*

Scottish Courage ~ Manager Patricia Smerdon ~ Real ale ~ Bar food (12-3, 6-9.30(9 Sun)) ~ Restaurant ~ (020) 7235 3074 ~ Children in eating area of bar ~ Open 12-11(10.30 Sun)

Guinea

Bruton Place; ✪ Bond Street, Green Park, Piccadilly, Oxford Circus

Not to be confused with the quite separate upscale Guinea Grill which takes up much of the same building (uniformed doormen will politely redirect you if you've picked the entrance to that by mistake), this cosy little pub can nevertheless impress with its lunchtime bar food: their tasty steak and kidney pie (Mon-Fri, £6) has won several awards, and for some people is the main reason for coming. Their impressive ciabattas (from £4.95) have also drawn praise. Like the Grenadier above, it's hidden away in a smart mews, and is pretty much standing room only. Three cushioned wooden seats and tables are tucked to the left of the entrance to the bar, with a couple more in a snug area at the back, underneath a big old clock. Most people tend to lean against a little shelf running along the side of the small room, or stand outside in the street, where there are another couple of tables. Well kept Youngs Bitter, Special and seasonal brews from the striking bar counter, which has some nice wrought-iron work above it. The look of the place is appealingly simple, with bare boards, yellow walls, old-fashioned prints, and a red-planked ceiling with colonial-style fans, but the atmosphere is chatty and civilised, with plenty of suited workers from Mayfair offices. Parts of the building date back to the 17th c, when the street provided stabling for the big houses nearby. *(Recommended by Derek Harvey-Piper, the Didler, Thomas Shortt)*

Youngs ~ Manager Carl Smith ~ Real ale ~ Bar food (12.30-2.30 wkdays only) ~ (020) 7409 1728 ~ Open 11-11; 6.30-11 Sat; closed Sat lunchtime, Sun

Jerusalem Tavern ★ ◖

55 Britton St, EC1; ⊖ Farringdon

Now a firm favourite with readers – and deservedly so – this carefully restored old coffee house is one of only a very few pubs belonging to the small, Suffolk-based St Peter's Brewery. Darkly atmospheric and characterful, it's a vivid re-creation of an 18th-c tavern, seeming so genuinely old that you'd never guess the work was done only a few years ago. The highlight is the full range of the brewery's delicious beers: depending on the season you'll find St Peter's Best, Fruit beer, Golden Ale, Grapefruit, Strong, Porter, Wheat beer, Winter, and Spiced Ales, all tapped from casks behind the little bar counter. The full range is usually available in their elegant, distinctively shaped bottles (you may already have come across these in supermarkets); the Organic bitter is particularly well liked by readers. If you develop a taste for them – and they are rather addictive – they sell them to take away. There's been a pub of this name around here for quite some time, but the current building was developed around 1720, originally as a merchant's house, then becoming a clock and watchmaker's. It still has the shop front added in 1810, immediately behind which is a light little room with a couple of wooden tables and benches, a stack of *Country Life* magazines, and some remarkable old tiles on the walls at either side. This leads to the tiny dimly lit bar, which has a couple of unpretentious tables on the bare boards, and another up some stairs on a discreetly precarious balcony. A plainer back room has a few more tables, as well as a fireplace, and a stuffed fox in a case. There's a relaxed, chatty feel in the evenings – though as the pub becomes more popular it's getting harder to bag a seat here then, and it can feel crowded at times. Blackboards list the simple but well liked lunchtime food: soup, good big sandwiches in various breads (from £4.50), and a couple of changing hot dishes like bangers and mash (£5) or steak and ale pie (£6.50). Prompt, polite service. A couple of tables outside overlook the quiet street. Note they don't allow children, and it's closed at weekends. The brewery has another main entry at Wingfield in Suffolk. *(Recommended by the Didler, John Fazakerley, Neil Rose, Colin Draper, Catherine Pitt, Sue Demont, Tim Barrow, Ian Phillips, Mike Gorton, Giles Francis, Richard Lewis, SLC, Derek Thomas, Stephen, Julie and Hayley Brown, JP, PP, Charlie Pierce)*

St Peters ~ Manager George Wortley ~ Real ale ~ Bar food (12-4 Mon-Fri) ~ (020) 7490 4281 ~ Open 11-11; closed wknds, Christmas week

Lamb ★ ◖

92-94 Lamb's Conduit Street, WC1; ⊖ Holborn

Well liked for its unique appearance, this old favourite feels much as it would have done in Victorian times. It's famous for the cut-glass swivelling 'snob-screens' all the way around the U-shaped bar counter; sepia photographs of 1890s actresses on the ochre panelled walls, and traditional cast-iron-framed tables with neat brass rails around the rim very much add to the overall effect. Consistently well kept Youngs Bitter and Special and changing guests like Smiles Best on handpump, and around 40 different malt whiskies. Lunchtime bar food such as sandwiches, lambs liver and bacon or sausage and mash (£5.25), fish and chips (£5.50), and steak and ale pie (£5.95); popular Sunday roasts (£5.95). Shove-ha'penny, cribbage, dominoes; no machines or music. A snug room at the back on the right is no smoking, and there are slatted wooden seats in a little courtyard beyond. It can get very crowded, especially in the evenings. Like the street, the pub is named for the Kentish clothmaker William Lamb who brought fresh water to Holborn in 1577. Note they don't allow children. *(Recommended by Derek Thomas, Joel Dobris, Tracey and Stephen Groves, the Didler, Robert Davis, Ted George, R Huggins, D Irving, E McCall, T McLean, LM, Stephen, Julie and Hayley Brown)*

Youngs ~ Manager Michael Hehir ~ Real ale ~ Bar food (12-2.30, 6-9(not Sun evening)) ~ (020) 7405 0713 ~ Open 11-11; 12-4, 7-10.30 Sun

Lamb & Flag ◀

33 Rose Street, WC2, off Garrick Street; ⊖ Leicester Square

Tucked down a narrow lane close to Covent Garden, this atmospheric old place can be empty at 5pm and heaving by 6. There's a real mix of tourists and after work drinkers most evenings, and even in winter you'll find an overflow of people drinking and chatting in the little alleyways outside. It's had an eventful and well documented history: Dryden was nearly beaten to death by hired thugs outside, and Dickens described the Middle Temple lawyers who frequented it when he was working in nearby Catherine Street. The low-ceilinged back bar has high-backed black settles and an open fire, and in Regency times was known as the Bucket of Blood from the bare-knuckle prize-fights held here. Access throughout has been improved in recent years; the more spartan front bar now leads easily into the back, without altering too much the snug feel of the place. Well kept Charles Wells Bombardier, Courage Best and Directors, Marstons Pedigree, Youngs Special and maybe a couple of guest beers on handpump; like most pubs round here, the beer isn't cheap, but on weekdays between 11 and 5 you should find at least one at quite an attractive price. Also, a good few malt whiskies. Bar food, lunchtimes only, includes a choice of several well kept cheeses and pâtés, served with hot bread or french bread (£3.50), as well as doorstep sandwiches (from £3.50), sausage, chips and beans (£3.50), and hot dishes like cottage pie (£4.25) and roast beef or lamb (£5.95). The upstairs Dryden Room is often quieter than downstairs, and has jazz every Sunday evening; there's a TV in the front bar. *(Recommended by Catherine Pitt, Derek Thomas, Mike Gorton, Jonathan Smith, Joel Dobris, the Didler, JP, PP, Andrew and Catherine Gilham, Eric Larkham, R Huggins, D Irving, E McCall, T McLean, Roger and Jenny Huggins, Ian Phillips, Ted George)*

Free house ~ Licensees Terry Archer and Adrian and Sandra Zimmerman ~ Real ale ~ Bar food (12-3) ~ Restaurant ~ No credit cards ~ (020) 7497 9504 ~ Children in eating area of bar ~ Jazz Sun evenings ~ Open 11-11; 12-10.30 Sun; closed 25 Dec, 1 Jan

Lord Moon of the Mall

16 Whitehall, SW1; ⊖ Charing Cross

Within easy walking distance of many of central London's most famous sights, this well converted former bank is a reliable pitstop for sightseers and visitors – and it's more individual than some of the Wetherspoons pubs. The impressive main room has a splendid high ceiling and quite an elegant feel, with smart old prints, big arched windows looking out over Whitehall, and a huge painting that seems to show a well-to-do 18th-c gentleman; in fact it's Tim Martin, founder of the Wetherspoons chain. Once through an arch the style is recognisably Wetherspoons, with a couple of neatly tiled areas and bookshelves opposite the long bar; fruit machines, trivia. They usually have seven or eight real ales, with the regulars usually Fullers London Pride, Greene King Abbot, Shepherd Neame Spitfire, and Theakstons Best. The good value bar food – served all day – is from the standard Wetherspoons menu: soup (£2.75), sandwiches (from £3.10), and hot dishes like cottage pie (£4.90), spinach and red pepper lasagne (£5.45), and chicken balti (£5.95). The terms of the licence rule out fried food. The back doors are now only used in an emergency, but were apparently built as a secret entrance for the bank's account holders living in Buckingham Palace (Edward VII had an account here from the age of three); an area by here is no smoking. As you come out of the pub Nelson's Column is immediately to the left, and Big Ben a walk of ten minutes or so to the right. Note they don't allow children. *(Recommended by Mark Stoffan, Sue Demont, Tim Barrow, John Fazakerley, Ted George, Mr and Mrs A H Young, Roger and Jenny Huggins)*

Wetherspoons ~ Manager Gary Cowams ~ Real ale ~ Bar food (11-10; 12-9.30 Sun) ~ (020) 7839 7701 ~ Open 11-11; 12-10.30 Sun; closed 25 Dec

Moon Under Water 🍺

105 Charing Cross Rd, WC2; ⊖ Tottenham Court Rd/Leicester Square

When Wetherspoons converted the former Marquee club into a pub they sensibly eschewed any pseudo-traditional fittings and went for something just a bit more modern. The result is remarkable: big and brash, it's a perfect central London meeting point, attracting an intriguing mix of customers, from Soho trendies and students to tourists and the local after-work crowd. The carefully designed main area is what used to be the auditorium, now transformed into a cavernous white-painted room stretching far off into the distance, with seats and tables lining the walls along the way. It effortlessly absorbs the hordes that pour in on Friday and Saturday evenings, and even when it's at its busiest you shouldn't have any trouble traversing the room, or have to wait very long to be served at the bar. There are normally up to ten very nicely priced real ales on handpump: Courage Directors, Fullers London Pride, Greene King Abbot, Shepherd Neame Spitfire, Theakstons Best, and several rapidly changing more unusual guests; they have regular real ale festivals and promotions. Also quite a range of coffees, most of which you can buy to take away. Served all day, the good value food is the same as at other Wetherspoons pubs – filled baps (from £3.10), mediterranean pasta bake (£5.65), steak and chips (£6.99) and so on; friendly service. The former stage is the area with most seats, and from here a narrower room leads past another bar to a back door opening on to Greek St (quite a surprise, as the complete lack of windows means you don't realise how far you've walked). A couple of areas – including the small seating area upstairs – are no smoking. Essentially this is a traditional pub that just happens to have a rather innovative design, so it's worth a look just to see the two combined; if you find it's not quite your style, at the very least it's a handy shortcut to Soho. They don't allow children. *(Recommended by Mark Stoffan, Ian Phillips, Ted George, BKA)*

Wetherspoons ~ Manager Nicola Harper ~ Real ale ~ Bar food (11-10; 12-9.30 Sun) ~ (020) 7287 6039 ~ Open 11-11; 12-10.30 Sun

Museum Tavern 🍺

Museum Street/Great Russell Street, WC1; ⊖ Holborn or Tottenham Court Rd

Unspoilt and quietly civilised, this old-fashioned Victorian pub is directly opposite the British Museum. The single room is simply furnished and decorated, with high-backed wooden benches around traditional cast-iron pub tables, and old advertising mirrors between the wooden pillars behind the bar. A decent choice of well kept beers usually takes in Charles Wells Bombardier, Courage Directors, Greene King Abbot and IPA, and Theakstons Best and Old Peculier; even for this area they're not cheap. They also have several wines by the glass, a choice of malt whiskies, and tea, coffee, cappuccino and hot chocolate. Lunchtime tables are sometimes hard to come by, but unlike most other pubs in the area it generally stays pleasantly uncrowded in the evenings. In late afternoons especially there's a nicely peaceful atmosphere, with a good mix of locals and tourists. Available all day from a servery at the end of the room, straightforward bar food might include pie or quiche with salads (£5.75), ploughman's, sausage and mash in yorkshire pudding (£5.75), and fish and chips (£6.45). It gets a little smoky when busy. There are a couple of tables outside under the gas lamps and 'Egyptian' inn sign. Karl Marx is supposed to have enjoyed the occasional glass here. Note they don't allow children. *(Recommended by Michael Butler, Sue Demont, Tim Barrow, Mark Stoffan, Howard England, Len Banister, Stephen, Julie and Hayley Brown, Joel Dobris, Mike Gorton, Simon Collett-Jones)*

Scottish Courage ~ Manager Tony Murphy ~ Real ale ~ Bar food (12-10) ~ (020) 7242 8987 ~ Open 11-11(10.30 Sun); closed 25 Dec

Nags Head ◧

53 Kinnerton St, SW1; ⊖ Knightsbridge

A favourite with many readers (and certain celebrities these days), this quaint little gem is one of the most unspoilt pubs you're likely to find in the whole of London, let alone so close to the centre. Hidden away in an attractive and peaceful mews minutes from Harrods, you could be forgiven for thinking you'd been transported to an old-fashioned local somewhere in a sleepy country village, right down to the friendly regulars chatting around the unusual sunken bar counter. It rarely gets too busy or crowded, and there's such a snugly relaxed and cosy feel it's sometimes hard to leave. The small, panelled and low-ceilinged front area has a wood-effect gas fire in an old cooking range (seats by here are generally snapped up pretty quickly), and a narrow passage leads down steps to an even smaller back bar with stools and a mix of comfortable seats. The well kept Adnams is pulled on attractive 19th-c china, pewter and brass handpumps. There's a 1930s What-the-butler-saw machine and a one-armed bandit that takes old pennies, as well as rather individual piped music, often jazz, folk or show tunes from the 1920s-40s. There are a few seats and a couple of tables outside. Bar food (usefully served all day, though not really the pub's main draw) includes sandwiches (from £3.50), ploughman's or plenty of salads (from £4.95), sausage, mash and beans, chilli, or steak and mushroom pie (all £4.95), and various roasts (£5); there's a £1.50 surcharge added to all dishes in the evenings, and at weekends. Service is polite and efficient rather than friendly. Many readers will be delighted to learn they have a fairly hard line policy on mobile phone use. *(Recommended by Giles Francis, the Didler, Chris Richards, James Nunns, Pete Baker, Tracey and Stephen Groves, Mayur Shah, Penny Miles)*

Free house ~ Licensee Kevin Moran ~ Real ale ~ Bar food (12-9.30) ~ No credit cards ~ (020) 7235 1135 ~ Children in eating area of bar ~ Open 11-11; 12-10.30 Sun

O'Hanlons ◧

8 Tysoe St, EC1; ⊖ Angel, but some distance away

Handy for Sadlers Wells, this genuinely Irish pub is a proper, traditional local, perhaps a bit scruffy for more particular tastes, but to others friendly and surprisingly alluring – and worth a detour for the excellent range of beers produced in Mr O'Hanlon's small brewery over the river. Some of these – notably the delicious Blakeleys Number One – have found their way into a few other pubs around the south (if you're further away, their award-winning wheat beer can sometimes be found in Safeway), but this is the finest place to sample the full range, which varies according to the season. One winter ale, Myrica, is made from bog myrtle and honey. Highlights are their Maltsters Weiss, Firefly, Red Ale, and Dry Stout; they may also have a guest or two such as Fullers London Pride. The long basic bar has bare boards and stained yellow walls, assorted prints and posters, newspapers to read, a signed rugby ball in a case, and comfortably cushioned furnishings; there are a couple of cosy armchairs tucked away in an oddly angular little alcove. The TV is used for rugby, but no other sports. A narrow corridor with a big mirror lined with yellowing cuttings about the beer or other London brewers leads to a lighter back room that's open during busy periods. Served only on weekdays, a short choice of good home-made food might include things like monkfish, smoked salmon, prawn and dill terrine (£5.50), spring lamb, fresh mint, and mixed pepper meatloaf (£5.50), and in winter Irish stew (£5.50); in winter they may also do Sunday lunch, with a choice of roasts. The atmosphere is notably relaxed, and the look of the place fits in with that perfectly. An Irish folk band plays every Thursday evening. There are a couple of tables outside. *(Recommended by the Didler, Sue Demont, Tim Barrow, Tracey and*

Stephen Groves, Ted George, SLC, Stephen, Julie and Hayley Brown, Richard Lewis)

Free house ~ Licensee Patrick Mulligan ~ Real ale ~ Bar food (not Sat, Sun) ~ (020) 7278 7630 ~ Children welcome ~ Irish folk Thurs evening ~ Open 11-11; 12-10.30 Sun; closed bank hol Mons

Old Bank of England ♀

194 Fleet St, EC4; ✆ Temple

Don't be fooled by the rather austere Italianate exterior; the opulent bar at this splendidly converted old building rarely fails to impress first and even second time visitors. Three gleaming chandeliers hang from the exquisitely plastered ceiling high above the unusually tall island bar counter, and the green walls are liberally dotted with old prints, framed bank notes and the like. Though the room is quite spacious, screens between some of the varied seats and tables create a surprisingly intimate feel, and there are several cosier areas at the end, with more seats in a quieter galleried section upstairs. Up to the mid-1970s this was a subsidiary branch of the Bank of England, built to service the nearby Law Courts; it was then a building society until Fullers transformed it into their flagship pub in 1995. The mural that covers most of the end wall looks like an 18th-c depiction of Justice (one effusive reader compares it with the Sistine Chapel), but in fact features members of the Fuller, Smith and Turner families. Well kept Fullers Chiswick, ESB, London Pride and seasonal brews on handpump, and around 20 wines by the glass; efficient service from neatly uniformed staff. Good generously served bar food includes soup (£2.75), deep-filled sandwiches (from £3.50), ploughman's, several pies like chicken and mushroom or venison and wild boar (£5.95), mini lamb burgers in pitta bread (£7.25), fish and chips (£7.50), and grilled swordfish (£7.95); they do cream teas in the afternoon. The dining room is no smoking (and you don't have to eat to sit there). Maybe piped classical music. It can get busy after work. Note they don't allow children. In winter the pub is easy to spot by the Olympic-style torches blazing outside; the entrance is up a flight of stone steps. Pies have a long if rather dubious pedigree in this area; it was in the vaults and tunnels below the Old Bank and the surrounding buildings that Sweeney Todd butchered the clients destined to provide the fillings in his mistress Mrs Lovett's nearby pie shop. *(Recommended by Howard England, Ted George, John and Christine Lowe, Dr and Mrs A K Clarke, the Didler, Joel Dobris, JP, PP, Ian Phillips, Charles Gysin)*

Fullers ~ Manager Hayley Gill ~ Real ale ~ Bar food (12-8) ~ (020) 7430 2255 ~ Open 11-11; closed wknds

Olde Cheshire Cheese

Wine Office Court; off 145 Fleet Street, EC4; ✆ Blackfriars

Over the years Congreve, Pope, Voltaire, Thackeray, Dickens, Conan Doyle, Yeats and perhaps Dr Johnson have stopped in the dark, unpretentious little rooms of this 17th-c former chop house. Genuinely historic, and full of character, it's one of London's most famous old pubs, but it doesn't feel as though it's on the tourist route. The almost unending profusion of small bars and rooms has bare wooden benches built in to the walls, sawdust on bare boards, and, on the ground floor, high beams, crackly old black varnish, Victorian paintings on the dark brown walls, and big open fires in winter. A particularly snug room is the tiny one on the right as you enter, but perhaps the most atmospheric bit is the Cellar bar, down steep narrow stone steps that look like they're only going to lead to the loo, but which in fact take you to an unexpected series of cosy areas with stone walls and ceilings, and some secluded corners. There's plenty of space, so even though it can get busy during the week (it's fairly quiet at weekends) it rarely feels too crowded. Lunchtime bar food includes hot toasted panini (£2.95), ploughman's (£4.25), and steak and ale pie, lasagne or various daily specials (£4.25); they may do a few bar snacks in the evening. Well kept Sam Smiths OB on handpump, as usual for this brewery, extraordinarily well priced (almost £1 less than other beers can cost at more expensive London pubs); friendly service. Some of the Cellar bar is no smoking at lunchtimes. In the early 20th-c the pub was well known for its famous parrot that for over 40 years entertained princes, ambassadors, and other distinguished guests. When she died in 1926 the news was broadcast on the BBC and obituary notices appeared in 200 newspapers all over the world; she's still around today, stuffed and silent, in the restaurant on the ground floor. *(Recommended by LM, Mark Stoffan, Ted George, the Didler, SLC, Howard England, P Abbott, JP, PP, Anthony Longden)*

Sam Smiths ~ Manager Gordon Garrity ~ Real ale ~ Bar food (12-9; not wknds) ~ Restaurant (Sunday) ~ (020) 7353 6170/4388 ~ Children in restaurant ~ Open 11.30-11; 11.30-3, 5.30-11 Sat; 12-3 Sun; closed Sun evening

Olde Mitre £

13 Ely Place, EC1; the easiest way to find it is from the narrow passageway beside 8 Hatton Garden; ⊖ Chancery Lane

The only complaint we hear of this carefully rebuilt little tavern is that it's so hard to find; however many times you visit, you still have to think about how to get there. But it more than repays the effort, standing out not just for its distinctive character and history, but also for the really exceptional service and welcome; the landlord clearly loves his job, and works hard to pass that enjoyment on to his customers. The cosy dark panelled small rooms have antique settles and – particularly in the back room, where there are more seats – old local pictures and so forth. It gets good-naturedly packed between 12.30 and 2.15, filling up again in the early evening, but by around 9 becomes a good deal more tranquil. An upstairs room, mainly used for functions, may double as an overflow at peak periods. Well kept Adnams, Bass, and Tetleys on handpump; notably chatty staff; darts. Bar snacks are limited to really good value toasted cheese sandwiches with ham, pickle or tomato (£1.75). There are some pot plants and jasmine in the narrow yard between the pub and St Ethelreda's church. Note the pub doesn't open weekends. The iron gates that guard one entrance to Ely Place are a reminder of the days when the law in this district was administered by the Bishops of Ely; even today it's still technically part of Cambridgeshire. *(Recommended by Dr Bob Bland, Richard Rand, Sue Demont, Tim Barrow, JP, PP, the Didler, John Fazakerley, SLC)*

Punch ~ Manager Don O'Sullivan ~ Real ale ~ Bar food (11-9.15; not wknds) ~ No credit cards ~ (020) 7405 4751 ~ Open 11-11; closed wknds, bank holidays

Red Lion ◼

Waverton Street, W1; ⊖ Green Park

In one of Mayfair's quietest and prettiest corners (though feeling distinctly un-London), this smart old place has a comfortably civilised air, even on busy weekday evenings when it's full of suited after-work drinkers. It can get busy at lunchtimes too, when there's a very nice buzzing atmosphere. The main L-shaped bar has small winged settles on the partly carpeted scrubbed floorboards, and London prints below the high shelf of china on its dark-panelled walls. Well kept Courage Best and Directors, Greene King IPA, and Theakstons Best on handpump, and they do rather good bloody marys (with a daunting Very Spicy option); also a dozen or so malt whiskies. Bar food, served from a corner at the front, includes sandwiches (from £3), ploughman's (£4.50), sausage and mash (£4.75), cod and chips, half rack of grilled pork ribs or cajun chicken (all £6.95), and specials such as mushroom stroganoff. Unusually for this area, they serve food morning and evening seven days a week. The gents' usually has a copy of *Private Eye* at eye level (it used to be the *Financial Times*). *(Recommended by Joel Dobris, Ian Phillips, Mandy and Simon King, Mayur Shah)*

Scottish Courage ~ Manager Greg Peck ~ Real ale ~ Bar food (12-2.30, 6-9.30) ~ Restaurant ~ (020) 7499 1307 ~ Children in eating area of bar and restaurant ~ Open 11.30-11; 6-11 Sat; 12-3, 6-10.30 Sun; closed Sat am, 25,26 Dec, 1 Jan

---

Tipping is not normal for bar meals, and not usually expected.

Red Lion ◖

Duke of York Street, SW1; ✪ Piccadilly Circus

For many people this is central London's most perfectly preserved Victorian pub, the mirrors so dazzling, and the gleaming mahogany so warm, that it's hard to believe they weren't put in yesterday. Other notable architectural features squeezed into the very small rooms include the crystal chandeliers and cut and etched windows, and the striking ornamental plaster ceiling. There's a minuscule upstairs eating area and a few front tables where diners have priority downstairs to enjoy the simple lunchtime snacks such as pork pie (£1.50), sausage rolls (£1.80), cornish pasty (£2.50), and sandwiches (£2.80) or filled baguettes (£3.50). Well kept Adnams, Bass, Fullers London Pride, Ind Coope Burton, and Tetleys on handpump, and friendly, efficient service. It can be very crowded at lunchtime (try inching through to the back room where there's sometimes more space); many customers spill out onto the pavement, in front of a mass of foliage and flowers cascading down the wall. No children inside. (Recommended by Ian Phillips, Mike Gorton, the Didler, DC)

Bass ~ Manager Michael Brown ~ Real ale ~ Bar food (12-4) ~ No credit cards ~ (020) 7321 0782 ~ Open 11.30(12 Sat)-11; closed Sun; bank holidays

Seven Stars   £

53 Carey St, WC2; ✪ Holborn (just as handy from Temple or Chancery Lane, but the walk through Lincoln's Inn Fields can be rather pleasant)

This unspoilt little pub facing the back of the Law Courts has changed hands since our last edition. Built in 1602, it hasn't altered too much since the last century, and though there's not much space (at times it's standing room only – and that can mean outside), it's full of character and genuine charm. To get to the tiny old-fashioned bar, you enter the door underneath a profusion of hanging baskets, marked General Counter. On the walls are lots of caricatures of barristers and judges, and posters of legal-themed British films; as there's not much space there aren't too many furnishings, though the two cosy little rooms have plenty of shelves for drinks or leaning against. The new landlady has written a book about pub food, and has placed a greater emphasis on eating than there was before; that also means there are slightly more tables than previously (when most eating had to be done standing up). A short daily changing blackboard might include a choice of three sandwiches such as mature English cheddar (£3.50) or smoked goose and spinach leaves (£4.50), half a dozen oysters (£5.50), and a couple of hot dishes like welsh rarebit (£4), corned beef hash (£5.50), or beef and ale stew (£5.50). Adnams Best, Broadside and maybe a guest like Charles Wells IPA on handpump; they also serve vintage port with fruit cake. Stairs up to the lavatories are very steep – a sign warns that you climb them at your own risk. (Recommended by Simon Collett-Jones, the Didler, Richard Rand, JP, PP, LM, Ian Phillips)

Free house ~ Licensee Roxy Beaujolais ~ Real ale ~ Bar food (11-11) ~ (020) 7242 8521 ~ Open 11-11; 12-11 Sat; closed Sun

Star ◖

Belgrave Mews West, SW1, behind the German Embassy, off Belgrave Sq; ✪ Knightsbridge

Recent television documentaries have suggested all sorts of intriguing goings-on at this simple, traditional place over the years, including the plotting of the Great Train Robbery. It's another of those timeless places that seems distinctly un-London, with a pleasantly quiet and restful local feel outside peak times – as well as a nice welcome and particularly well kept Fullers beers. A highlight in summer is the astonishing array of hanging baskets and flowering tubs outside, much more impressive than average. The small entry room, which also has the food servery, has stools by the counter and tall windows; an arch leads to a side room with swagged curtains, well polished wooden tables and chairs, heavy upholstered settles, globe lighting and raj fans. The back room has button-back built-in wall seats, and there's a similarly furnished room upstairs. Good value straightforward lunchtime bar food might include sandwiches, ploughman's, and a couple of hot dishes like sausage, chips and beans (£4.95), with evening meals such as vegetable lasagne (£5.50) and chargrilled tuna steak (£6.95). Fullers Chiswick, ESB, London Pride and seasonal beers on handpump. It can get busy at lunchtime and on some evenings, with a good mix of customers. *(Recommended by Dr M Owton, John Fazakerley, the Didler, Len Banister, JP, PP, Joel Dobris)*

Fullers ~ Manager T J Connell ~ Real ale ~ Bar food (12-2.30,6(6.30 Sat, 7 Sun)-9) ~ (020) 7235 3019 ~ Children welcome ~ Open 11.30-11; 11.30-3, 6.30-11 Sat; 12-3, 7-10.30 Sun

Westminster Arms ▣

Storey's Gate, SW1; ⊖ Westminster

The main draw at this unpretentious and friendly Westminster local – very handy for the abbey and the Houses of Parliament – is the choice of real ales, which generally includes Adnams Broadside, Bass, Brakspears PA, Gales IPA, Greene King Abbot, Theakstons Best, Westminster Best brewed for them by Charringtons, and a monthly changing guest; they also do decent wines, and a dozen or so malt whiskies. Usually packed after work with government staff and researchers, the plain main bar has simple, old-fashioned furnishings, with proper tables on the wooden floors and a good deal of panelling; there's not a lot of room, so come early for a seat. Most of the food is served in the downstairs wine bar (a good retreat from the ground floor bustle), with some of the tables in cosy booths; typical dishes include filled rolls (from £3.50), lasagne or steak and kidney pie (£6), and fish and chips or scampi (£6.50). Piped music in this area, and in the more formal upstairs restaurant, but not generally in the main bar; fruit machine. There are a couple of tables and seats by the street outside. They ring the Division Bell to prompt MPs to get back across the road to vote. *(Recommended by the Didler, Kevin Flack, Mike Gorton, Ian Phillips, Jonathan Smith, JP, PP, Lynn Sharpless, Bob Eardley)*

Free house ~ Licensees Gerry and Marie Dolan ~ Real ale ~ Bar food ~ Restaurant (weekday lunchtimes (not Weds)) ~ (020) 7222 8520 ~ Children in restaurant ~ Open 11-11(6 Sat); 12-6 Sun; closed 25-26 Dec

EAST LONDON Map 12

Grapes

76 Narrow Street, E14; ⊖ Shadwell (some distance away) or Westferry on the Docklands Light Railway; the Limehouse link has made it hard to find by car – turn off Commercial Road at signs for Rotherhithe tunnel, then from the Tunnel Approach slip road, fork left leading into Branch Road, turn left and then left again into Narrow Street

One of London's most characterful riverside pubs, in a peaceful spot well off the tourist route, this warmly welcoming 16th-c tavern was used by Charles Dickens as the basis of his 'Six Jolly Fellowship Porters' in *Our Mutual Friend*: 'It had not a straight floor and hardly a straight line, but it had outlasted and would yet outlast many a better-trimmed building, many a sprucer public house.' Not much has changed since, though as far as we know watermen no longer row out drunks from here, drown them, and sell the salvaged bodies to the anatomists as they did in Dickens' day. The back part is the oldest, with the small back balcony a fine place for a sheltered waterside drink; steps lead down to the foreshore. The partly-panelled bar has lots of prints, mainly of actors, some elaborately etched windows, and newspapers to read. Well kept Adnams, Ind Coope Burton and Marstons Pedigree on handpump, a choice of malt whiskies, and a decent wine list. Bar food such as soup (£2.75), sandwiches (from £2.95), bangers and mash (£4.95), home-made fishcakes with caper sauce (£5.25), dressed crab (£6.95), and a generous Sunday roast (no other meals then, when it can be busy); hard-working bar staff. Booking is recommended for the good upstairs fish restaurant, which has fine views of the river. Shove-ha'penny, table skittles, cribbage, dominoes, chess, backgammon, maybe piped classical or jazz; no under 14s. Note they don't open Saturday lunchtimes. The pub was a favourite with Rex Whistler who came here to paint the river; the results are really quite special. *(Recommended by Bob and Maggie Atherton, David Peakall, Susan and John Douglas)*

Punch ~ Manager Barbara Haigh ~ Real ale ~ Bar food ~ Restaurant ~ (020) 7987 4396 ~ Open 12-3, 5.30-11; 7-11 Sat; 12-3, 7-10.30 Sun; closed Sat lunchtime, some bank holidays

Prospect of Whitby

57 Wapping Wall, E1; ✪ Wapping

With such a lively history it's no wonder this entertaining old pub does rather play on its pedigree; the tourists who flock here lap up the colourful tales of Merrie Olde London, and only the most unromantic of visitors could fail to be carried along by the fun. Pepys and Dickens were both frequent callers, Turner came for weeks at a time to study its glorious Thames views, and in the 17th c the notorious Hanging Judge Jeffreys was able to combine two of his interests by enjoying a drink at the back while looking down over the grisly goings-on in Execution Dock. The pub is an established favourite on the evening coach tours, but is usually quieter at lunchtimes. Plenty of bare beams, bare boards, panelling and flagstones in the L-shaped bar (where the long pewter counter is over 400 years old), while tables in the courtyard look out towards Docklands. Well kept Courage Directors and Greene King Old Speckled Hen on handpump (at tourist prices), and quite a few malt whiskies; basic bar meals such as ploughman's (£4.75), steak and ale pie or pasta bolognese (£5.75) are served all day, with a fuller menu in the upstairs restaurant. One area of the bar is no smoking; fruit machine, golf game. Built in 1520, the pub was for a couple of centuries known as the Devils' Tavern thanks to its popularity with river thieves and smugglers. *(Recommended by R Huggins, D Irving, E McCall, T McLean, Mike Gorton, Simon Collett-Jones, Richard Siebert, Susan and John Douglas, Ian Phillips)*

Scottish Courage ~ Manager Christopher Reeves ~ Real ale ~ Bar food (all day) ~ Restaurant ~ (020) 7481 1095 ~ Children welcome ~ Open 11-11; 11-10.30 Sun; closed 25 Dec

NORTH LONDON Map 13

Chapel 🍴 ♀

48 Chapel St, NW1; ✪ Edgware Rd

Well known for its excellent food, this cosmopolitan, much-modernised pub is relaxed and civilised at lunchtimes; in the evenings the quality of meals remains the same, but it all gets a little bit louder. The menu changes every day, but might include things like spinach and nutmeg soup (£3.50), goats cheese, tomato and oyster mushroom tart (£8), roast chicken stuffed with sun-dried tomatoes and peppers (£9.50), roasted john dory with artichoke and anchovy sauce or roast guinea fowl breasts with sage (£12.50), and puddings such as an excellent tarte tatin (£3.50). Light and spacious, the cream-painted main room is dominated by the open kitchen; furnishings are smart but simple, with plenty of plain wooden tables around the bar, and more in a side room with a big fireplace. It fills up quite quickly, so you may have to wait to eat during busy periods. In summer, tables on the terrace can be busy with chic local workers enjoying a break. Prompt and efficient service from helpful staff, who may bring warm walnut bread to your table while you're waiting. In the evening trade is more evenly split between diners and drinkers, and the music can be quite noticeable then, especially at weekends. Adnams and Greene King IPA on handpump (both rather expensive, even for London), a good range of interesting wines (up to half by the glass), cappuccino and espresso, and a choice of teas such as peppermint or strawberry and vanilla. *(Recommended by Sebastian Power, Len Banister)*

Bass ~ Tenant Lakis Hondrogiannis ~ Real ale ~ Bar food (12-2.30, 7-10) ~ (020) 7402 9220 ~ Children welcome ~ Open 12-11; 12-3, 7-11 Sun

Compton Arms ♀

4 Compton Avenue, off Canonbury Rd, N1; ⊖ Highbury & Islington

A very nice, well run tiny local hidden away up a peaceful mews – nothing too spectacular, or particularly unusual, but with the bonus of a very pleasant and relaxing crazy paved terrace behind. The unpretentious low-ceilinged rooms are simply furnished with wooden settles and assorted stools and chairs, with local pictures on the walls; free from games or music (though there is a TV), it has a very personable, village local feel. Well kept Greene King Abbot, IPA and seasonal brews on handpump, and around a dozen wines by the glass; friendly service. Good value bar food includes sandwiches (from £2.25), soup, changing daily specials (£3.95), five vegetarian dishes (£4.50), and half a dozen different types of sausage served with mashed potato and home-made gravy (£4.50); Sunday roasts (£5.25). At the back are benches and tables among flowers under a big sycamore tree; there's a covered section so you can still sit out if it's raining, and maybe heaters in winter. *(Recommended by Tracey and Stephen Groves, Joel Dobris, Sue Demont, Tim Barrow)*

Greene King ~ Manager Paul Fairweather ~ Real ale ~ Bar food (12-3, 6-9; not Tues evening) ~ (020) 7359 6883 ~ Children in back room till 8 ~ Open 12-11

Duke of Cambridge 🍴 ♀ ◀

30 St Peter's St, N1; ⊖ Angel, though some distance away

London Dining Pub of the Year
London's first completely organic pub, this very well refurbished cornerhouse caused quite a stir when it first appeared, but has now comfortably settled into its role of right-on gastropub – so successfully that its owners have opened similar ventures in other parts of town. Don't be fooled into thinking it's at all faddy: the food and drink here are excellent, the extra attention put into sourcing everything simply meaning standards end up higher. The one downside is that so do the prices, particularly for the drinks, but it's worth the extra to enjoy choices and flavours you simply won't find anywhere else. There are four organic real ales on handpump, not cheap but tasty (though we haven't yet personally verified the claim that organic drinks are less likely to cause a hangover): from London's small Pitfield Brewery Eco Warrior and Singhboulton (named for the pub's two owners), St Peters Organic Ale, and Shoreditch Organic Stout. They also have organic draught lagers and cider, organic spirits, and a very wide range of organic wines, many of which are available by the glass; the full range of drinks is chalked up on a blackboard, and also includes good coffees and teas, and a spicy ginger ale. The big, busy main room is simply decorated and furnished, with lots of chunky wooden tables, pews and benches on bare boards, a couple of big metal vases with colourful flowers, daily papers, and carefully positioned soft lighting around the otherwise bare dark blue walls. The atmosphere is warmly inviting, with the constant sound of civilised chat from a steady stream of varied customers, many of whom do fit the Islington stereotypes: on our last visit, conversations on neighbouring tables revolved around the latest TV commissions and Italian Renaissance art. No music or games machines. Another blackboard lists the changing choice of well presented food: things like pumpkin, pear and celery soup (£4.50), chicken liver pâté (£6), four-cheese risotto with leek (£7), moroccan vegetable stew (£8), roast pheasant with bean and bacon cassoulet and thyme jus (£12), fried hake with portuguese potato and pepper stew (£12.50), and pear and almond tart (£6.50); children's helpings. A note explains that though they do all they can to ensure their game and fish have been produced using sustainable methods, these can't officially be classed as organic. They take credit cards. A corridor leads off past a few tables and an open kitchen to a couple of smaller candlelit rooms, more formally set for eating; there's also a small side terrace. The company's other pubs are the Crown in Victoria Park, and the Pelican in Ladbroke Grove. *(Recommended by Joel Dobris, Peter and Jean Hoare)*

Free house ~ Licensees Geetie Singh and Esher Boulton ~ Real ale ~ Bar food (12.30-3, 6.30-10.30(9 Sun); not Mon am) ~ (020) 7359 3066 ~ Children welcome ~ Open 12(5 Mon)-11; 12-10.30 Sun

Flask ♀ £

14 Flask Walk, NW3; ⊖ Hampstead

Just around the corner from the Tube, but miles away in spirit, this distinctive old local
is still a popular haunt of Hampstead artists, actors, and local characters. The snuggest
and most individual part is the cosy lounge at the front, with plush green seats and
banquettes curving round the panelled walls, a unique Victorian screen dividing it from
the public bar, an attractive fireplace, and a very laidback and rather villagey
atmosphere. A comfortable orange-lit room with period prints and a few further tables
leads into a more recent but rather smart dining conservatory, which with its plants,
prominent wine bottles and neat table linen feels a bit like a wine bar. A couple of
white iron tables are squeezed into the tiny back yard. Well kept Youngs Bitter, Special
and seasonal brews on handpump, around 20 wines by the glass, and decent coffees –
they have a machine that grinds the beans to order. Bar food might include sandwiches
(from £2), soup, and daily changing specials like chicken casserole, lamb curry or
spiced minced beef pie with a cheese and leek mash topping (from £5.50). A plainer
public bar (which you can only get into from the street) has leatherette seating,
cribbage, backgammon, lots of space for darts, fruit machines, trivia, and big screen
SkyTV. Friendly service. A noticeboard has news from their darts and cricket teams.
There are quite a few tables outside in the alley. The pub's name is a reminder of the
days when it was a distributor of the mineral water from Hampstead's springs.
(Recommended by P Price, the Didler, Mr and Mrs Jon Corelis, JP, PP, Len Banister)

*Youngs ~ Manager John Cannon ~ Real ale ~ Bar food ~ Restaurant ~ (020) 7435
4580 ~ Children in conservatory ~ Open 11-11; 12-10.30 Sun*

Holly Bush

Holly Mount, NW3; ⊖ Hampstead

Back to more regular opening after a fair amount of behind-the-scenes work over the
last year or so, this cheery old local is the kind of place that's especially appealing in
the evenings, when there's a good mix of chatty locals and visitors, and a timeless
feel to the atmospheric front bar. Under the dark sagging ceiling are brown and
cream panelled walls (decorated with old advertisements and a few hanging plates),
open fires, and cosy bays formed by partly glazed partitions. Sadly, health and safety
regulations prevent them lighting the real Edwardian gas lamps in the traditional
way. Slightly more intimate, the back room, named after the painter George
Romney, has an embossed red ceiling, panelled and etched glass alcoves, and ochre-
painted brick walls covered with small prints and plates. Well kept Adnams Bitter
and Broadside, Benskins and Fullers London Pride on handpump, and a good wine
list; friendly service. Bar food includes soup (£3), cumberland sausage and mash
(£6.75), fish pie (£7.75), and beef, Guinness and mushroom pie (£8.50); weekend
roasts (£9.50). On fine days there may be tables on the pavement outside. The stroll
up to the pub from the tube station is delightful, along some of Hampstead's most
villagey streets. *(Recommended by the Didler, Mr and Mrs Jon Corelis)*

*Punch ~ Manager Rupert Baird-Murray ~ Real ale ~ Bar food (12.30-4, 6.30-10.30
Mon-Fri, 12.30-10.30 Sat, 12.30-9.30 Sun) ~ No credit cards ~ (020) 7435 2892 ~
Children in eating area of bar and restaurant ~ Open 12-11(5 winter); 12-11 Sat; 12-
10.30 Sun*

Olde White Bear

Well Road, NW3; ⊖ Hampstead

Very close to the Heath, this villagey and almost clubby neo-Victorian pub pulls off
the rare trick of making all sorts of different types of people feel relaxed and at
home. Friendly and traditional, the dimly lit main room has lots of Victorian prints
and cartoons on the walls, as well as wooden stools, cushioned captain's chairs, a
couple of big tasselled armed chairs, a flowery sofa, handsome fireplace and an
ornate Edwardian sideboard. A similarly lit small central room has Lloyd Loom
furniture, dried flower arrangements and signed photographs of actors and

playwrights. In the brighter end room there are elaborate cushioned machine tapestried pews, and dark brown paisley curtains. The choice of beers on handpump usually takes in Adnams, Greene King Abbot, Fullers London Pride, Marstons Pedigree and Youngs; also 10 or so malt whiskies. Served all day, bar food includes good elaborate sandwiches (from £3.50), ploughman's (£4.95), Japanese tempura prawns £4.95), a daily pasta dish (£5.45), pork and leek sausages (£5.95), cod in beer batter or beef and Guinness pie (£6.55), and sirloin steak (£8.95); Sunday roasts (£6.55). There are a few tables in front, and more in a new courtyard behind. Cards, chess, TV, Thursday quiz nights. Parking may be a problem – it's mostly residents' permits only nearby. *(Recommended by the Didler, JP, PP)*

Vanguard ~ Lease Jason Rudolph and Christopher Ely ~ Real ale ~ Bar food (12-10(9.30 Sun)) ~ (020) 7435 3758 ~ Open 11-11; 12-11 Sat; 12-10.30 Sun

Spaniards Inn ◖

Spaniards Lane, NW3; ⊖ Hampstead, but some distance away, or from Golders Green station take 220 bus

Lots of historic and literary connections at this very busy former toll house: Keats supposedly wrote 'Ode to a Nightingale' in what's still one of London's finest pub gardens, highwayman Dick Turpin is said to have been born here, and it's thought to have been named after the Spanish ambassador to the court of James I (who had a private residence here). The garden is arranged in separate seeming areas by judicious planting of shrubs, with slatted wooden tables and chairs on a crazy-paved terrace opening on to a flagstoned walk around a small lawn, with roses, a side arbour of wisteria and clematis, and an aviary. It can get crowded out here in summer, when the pub is a popular stop for visitors and tourists. Inside, the low-ceilinged oak-panelled rooms of the attractive main bar have open fires, genuinely antique winged settles, candle-shaped lamps in pink shades, and snug little alcoves. Well kept Adnams Broadside, Bass, Fullers London Pride, and a changing guest on handpump – though in summer you might find the most popular drink is their big jug of pimms; piped classical music, newspapers, fruit machine, trivia. You can get something to eat all day; at lunchtimes filled baguettes (£4.25) and hot dishes like vegetable lasagne (£6.50), and cottage pie or chilli (£6.95), and in the evenings a wider choice including various salads (from £7.95), fish and chips, mushroom risotto or sausages and mash (£7.95), and rib-eye steak (£10.95). On Sundays they may just do a roast. The food bar is no smoking. Some recent reports have criticised the prices and service. The pub is very handy for Kenwood, and indeed during the 1780 Gordon Riots the then landlord helped save the house from possible disaster, cunningly giving so much free drink to the mob on its way to burn it down that by the time the Horse Guards arrived the rioters were lying drunk and incapable on the floor. Parking can be difficult – especially when people park here to walk their dogs on the heath. *(Recommended by Ian Phillips)*

Bass ~ Manager Mike Bowler ~ Real ale ~ Bar food (12-10) ~ (020) 8731 6571 ~ Children welcome ~ Open 11-11; 12-10.30 Sun

Waterside

82 York Way, N1; ⊖ Kings Cross

Kings Cross isn't the most appealing part of London for visitors, so this handily positioned pub is a useful place to know about if you're passing through. An unexpected treat is the relaxing outside terrace overlooking the Battlebridge Basin, often busy with boats. The building is a pastiche of a 17th-c cider barn, with stripped brickwork, latticed windows, genuinely old stripped timbers in white plaster, lots of dimly lit alcoves, spinning wheels, milkmaids' yokes, and horsebrasses and so on, with plenty of rustic tables and wooden benches. Fullers London Pride and changing guests like Adnams or Batemans XXXB on handpump; bar food (served all day Mon-Fri) is mostly pizzas. Pool, table football, fruit machine, big screen TV for sports, and sometimes loudish juke box. No dogs inside. *(Recommended by Stephen, Julie and Hayley Brown)*

Whitbreads ~ Manager John Keyes ~ Real ale ~ Bar food (11-10 Mon-Fri, 12-6 Sat, 12-4.30 Sun) ~ (020) 7713 8613 ~ Children in eating area of bar till 7pm ~ Open 11-11; 12-11 Sat; 12-10.30 Sun; closed 25, 26 Dec, 1 Jan

SOUTH LONDON Map 12

Alma ♀

499 York Road, SW18; ✆ Wandsworth Town

Though this unexpectedly stylish local feels rather smart, the furnishings are mostly quite simple: a mix of chairs and cast-iron-framed or worn wooden tables around the brightly repainted walls, and a couple of sofas, with gilded mosaics of the Battle of the Alma and an ornate mahogany chimney-piece and fireplace adding a touch of elegance. The popular but less pubby dining room has a fine turn-of-the-century frieze of swirly nymphs; there's waitress service in here, and you can book a particular table. Youngs Bitter, Special and seasonal brews from the island bar counter, along with maybe Smiles Bitter and good house wines (with around 20 by the glass), freshly squeezed juices and fruit smoothies, good coffee, tea or hot chocolate; newspapers out for customers. Even when it's very full – which it often is in the evenings – service is careful and efficient. Good, imaginative bar food (with something available all day), might include sandwiches, soups like roasted fennel and parsnip (£3.50), fresh asparagus with chicory, rocket and parmesan (£4.50), whole wheat pancakes with rocket pesto, artichoke hearts, sweet roast peppers and mozzarella (£6.75), marinated beef stir fry with noodles and mange tout (£7.50), smoked haddock fishcake with watercress and chard salad and chive sauce (£7.85), spicy lamb brochette with minted couscous and sweet red pepper coulis (£8.25); they do lunchtime specials like caramelised onion tartlet or provençale salad for £5.50. Much of the meat is organic, and comes from their own farm in Dorking. The menu may be limited on Sunday lunchtimes. If you're after a quiet drink don't come when there's a rugby match on the television, unless you want a running commentary from the well heeled and voiced young locals. Pinball, dominoes. Charge up their 'smart-card' with cash and you can pay with a discount either here or at the management's other pubs, which include the Ship at Wandsworth (see below). Travelling by rail into Waterloo you can see the pub rising above the neighbouring rooftops as you rattle through Wandsworth Town. *(Recommended by the Didler, Mayur Shah, JP, PP, Ian Phillips)*

Youngs ~ Tenant Charles Gotto ~ Real ale ~ Bar food (12-10, 12-4 Sun, not Sun evening) ~ Restaurant ~ (020) 8870 2537 ~ Children welcome ~ Open 11-11; 12-10.30 Sun; closed 25 Dec

Anchor

34 Park St – Bankside, Southwark Bridge end; ✆ London Bridge

A warren of dimly lit, creaky little rooms and passageways, this atmospheric old riverside pub is ideally placed for visits to Tate Modern and the Globe theatre – there's a model of the original in the bar. The current building dates back to about 1750, when it was built to replace an earlier tavern, possibly the one that Pepys came to during the Great Fire of 1666. 'All over the Thames with one's face in the wind, you were almost burned with a shower of fire drops,' he wrote. 'When we could endure no more upon the water, we to a little ale-house on the Bankside and there staid till it was dark almost, and saw the fire grow.' Today's view of the river and the City from the Anchor's busy front terrace is hard to beat; there are plenty of tables to enjoy the scene. The main bar has bare boards and beams, black panelling, old-fashioned high-backed settles, and sturdy leatherette chairs; even when it's invaded by tourists it's usually possible to retreat to one of the smaller rooms. Courage Directors, Marstons Pedigree and Wadworths 6X on handpump; they also do jugs of pimms, and mulled wine in winter. Cribbage, dominoes, three fruit machines, and occasionally rather loud piped music. Bar food (the subject of rather mixed reports over the last year) includes filled baguettes (from £3.50), soup, baked potatoes (£3.95), and five changing hot dishes like steak and ale pie, or chicken with a mustard and porter sauce (all around £5.50); they do a Sunday roast in the upstairs restaurant. Parts of the bar and restaurant are no smoking; other areas can get smoky at times. The new manager has introduced Thameside barbecues in summer, until 10pm if it's sunny. Morris dancers occasionally pass by. Round the corner, the Clink is good on the area's murky past. *(Recommended by the Didler, Joel Dobris, Stephen, Julie and Hayley Brown, George Atkinson, JP, PP, Ian Phillips, Kevin Flack, Eric Larkham)*

Scottish Courage ~ Manager Darren Woodhead ~ Real ale ~ Bar food (12-6(barbecue open till 10pm if sunny)) ~ Restaurant ~ (020) 7407 1577 ~ Children welcome ~ Open 11-11; 12-10.30 Sun

Bulls Head ♀ £

373 Lonsdale Road, SW13; ⇌ Barnes Bridge

It's live music that puts this imposing Thameside pub on the map: every night for the last 40 years top class jazz and blues groups have performed here. You can hear the music quite clearly from the lounge bar (and on peaceful Sunday afternoons from the villagey little street as you approach), but for the full effect and genuine jazz club atmosphere it is worth paying the admission to the well equipped music room. Bands play 8.30-11 every night plus 2-4.30pm Sundays, and depending on who's playing prices generally range from £4 to around £10. There's a big, simply furnished and decorated bar with photos of the various musicians who've played here, as well as a couple of cosier areas leading off, and an island servery with Youngs Bitter, Special and seasonal beers on handpump, over 80 malt whiskies, and a very good range of well chosen wines – 142 at the last count, with 30 by the glass. A short range of good value bar food might include things like soup (£1.60), ciabatta sandwiches (from £2.60), and main courses such as steak and kidney pie or roasts (around £4.50); service is efficient and friendly. Dominoes, cribbage, shove-ha'penny, Scrabble, chess, cards, TV and fruit machine. *(Recommended by Derek Thomas, Jenny and Chris Wilson, Mike Tomkins, Tony Middis)*

Youngs ~ Tenant Dan Fleming ~ Real ale ~ Bar food (11.30-2.15, 6-10.15) ~ Restaurant ~ (020) 8876 5241 ~ Children welcome during the day ~ Jazz and blues every night ~ Open 11-11; 12-10.30 Sun; closed 25 Dec

Crown & Greyhound

73 Dulwich Village, SE21; ⇌ North Dulwich

Big enough to absorb everyone without too much difficulty, this place caters well for children, offering Lego and toys to play with, as well as children's meals and baby changing facilities. A pleasant garden has lots of picnic-sets under a chestnut tree, and a play area with sandpit. It's worth a look inside for the décor: the most ornate room is on the right, with elaborate ochre ceiling plasterwork, fancy former gas lamps, Hogarth prints, fine carved and panelled settles and so forth. It opens into the former billiards room, where kitchen tables on a stripped board floor are set for eating. A big conservatory looks out on the garden. A central snug leads to the saloon with upholstered and panelled settles, a coal-effect gas fire in the tiled fireplace, and Victorian prints. Well kept Ind Coope Burton, Tetleys and Youngs on handpump, along with a monthly changing guest like Adnams or Greene King Old Speckled Hen; they have a wine of the month, and open at 10 for morning coffee. Changing every day, the lunchtime choice of bar meals might include big doorstep sandwiches (from £2.75), soup (£2.20), and a range of specials like chicken in mustard sauce, spinach and potato pie, lamb in red wine or cod mornay (all £6.25). Best to arrive early for their popular Sunday carvery, they don't take bookings. The family room is no smoking. Fruit machine, TV. Known locally as the Dog, the pub was built at the turn of the century to replace two inns that had stood here previously, hence the unusual name. Busy in the evenings, but quieter during the day, it's handy for walks through the park, and for the Dulwich Picture gallery. *(Recommended by Sue Demont, Tim Barrow, Ian Phillips)*

Bass ~ Manager Bernard Maguire ~ Real ale ~ Bar food (12-2, 6-9) ~ Restaurant (evenings only) ~ (020) 8299 4876 ~ Children in restaurant and family room ~ Open 11-11; 12-10.30 Sun

Cutty Sark

Ballast Quay, off Lassell Street, SE10; ⇌ Maze Hill, from London Bridge, or from the river front walk past the Yacht in Crane Street and Trinity Hospital

Fine summer evenings draw the crowds to the waterside terrace across the narrow cobbled lane from this attractive late 16th-c white-painted house, which enjoys good views of the Thames and the Millennium Dome. The view is perhaps better from inside, through the big upper bow window – itself striking for the way it jetties out over the pavement. Despite recent changes the atmospheric bar still has an old-fashioned feel, with flagstones, rough brick walls, wooden settles, barrel tables, open fires, low lighting and narrow openings to tiny side snugs; some readers easily imagined smugglers and blackguards with patches over their eyes at every turn. Well kept Bass, Fullers London Pride, Greene King Old Speckled Hen and a guest such as Harveys on handpump, a good choice of malt whiskies, and a decent wine list. An elaborate central staircase leads to an upstairs area; fruit machine, juke box. Served in a roomy eating area, generous bar food includes popular filled baguettes (from £3.75), steak and ale pie, fish and chips or liver and bacon (all £6.25), and mixed grill (£8.95); Sunday roasts. You can usually get food all day on weekdays. Service can slow down at busy times. The pub can be very busy with young people on Friday and Saturday evenings. They have jazz festivals two or three times a year. *(Recommended by R Huggins, D Irving, E McCall, T McLean, the Didler, B J Harding, Richard Rand, Michael Stanworth, Kevin Flack, LM)*

Free house ~ Licensee Arthur Hughs ~ Real ale ~ Bar food (12-9(5 Sat, Sun)) ~ (020) 8858 3146 ~ Children upstairs ~ Open 11-11; 12-10.30 Sun; closed 25 Dec evening

Fire Station 🍴 🍺

150 Waterloo Rd, SE1; ⊖ Waterloo

Best known for the imaginative food served from the open kitchen in the back dining room, this remarkable conversion of the former LCC central fire station is the favoured choice for the area's after-work drinkers. It's hardly your typical local, but it does a number of traditionally pubby things better than anyone else nearby. The décor in the two vibrantly chatty rooms at the front is something like a cross between a warehouse and a schoolroom, with plenty of wooden pews, chairs and long tables (a few spilling onto the street), some mirrors and rather incongruous pieces of dressers, and brightly red-painted doors, shelves and modern hanging lightshades; the determinedly contemporary art round the walls is for sale, and there's a table with newspapers to read. Well kept Adnams Broadside, Brakspears, Youngs, and a beer brewed for them by Hancocks on handpump, as well as a number of bottled beers, variously flavoured teas, several malt whiskies, and a good choice of wines (a dozen by the glass). They serve a short range of bar meals between 12 and 5.30, which might include several interestingly filled ciabattas (from £4.45), and a daily pasta dish (£6.50), but it's worth paying the extra to eat from the main menu. Changing daily, this has things like tagliatelle with a cheese, leek, pea and asparagus sauce, with rocket and parmesan (£9.95), chicken breast stuffed with mozzarella, sun-blushed tomato and sage risotto with pesto dressing (£11.95), marinated pork fillet with celeriac and bacon mash and rhubarb jus (£12.25), tandoori seared tuna fillet with sag aloo, raita, aubergine chutney and curry oil (£12.50), and puddings such as peach and almond tart with custard sauce; some dishes can run out, so get there early for the best choice. They also do a simpler set menu between 5.30 and 7.30 (£10.95 two courses, £13.50 three). You can book tables. Piped modern jazz and other music fits into the good-natured hubbub; there's a TV for rugby matches. Those with quieter tastes might find bustling weeknights here a little too hectic (it can get noisy then) – it's calmer at lunchtimes and during the day. At the busiest times in the bar, it's a good idea to keep your belongings firmly to hand. The pub is very handy for the Old Vic, Waterloo Station and the Imperial War Museum a bit further down the road. *(Recommended by Sue Demont, Tim Barrow, Dave Braisted, David Peakall, Richard Lewis, Gill Waller, Tony Morriss, Kevin Flack, Mandy and Simon King, P Abbott, Derek Thomas, Lynn Sharpless, Bob Eardley, Richard Siebert, Mayur Shah)*

Regent ~ Manager Peter Nottage ~ Real ale ~ Bar food (11-5.30) ~ Restaurant ~ (020) 7620 2226 ~ Children welcome ~ Open 11-11; 12-10.30 Sun; closed 25, 26 Dec, 1 Jan, Easter wknd

Founders Arms

Hopton Street (Bankside); ✆ Blackfriars, and cross Blackfriars Bridge

Out on a broad stretch of the riverside walkway, this bustling modern pub enjoys splendid views of the Thames, St Paul's, and the Millennium Bridge, either from the big waterside terrace, or the sparkling, spacious glass-walled bar. If you're inside, the lighting is nice and unobtrusive so that you can still see out across the river at night. Close to Shakespeare's Globe and handy for Tate Modern, it can get busy, particularly on weekday evenings, when it's popular with young City types for an after-work drink. Well kept Youngs Bitter, Special and seasonal brews from the modern bar counter angling along one side. Served pretty much all day, the enjoyable bar food includes food such as sandwiches (from £3.55; paninis from £4.25), soup (£3.50), cumberland sausages and mash or roast chicken and avocado salad (£6.85), fresh haddock in beer batter (£6.95), steak and ale pie (£7.95), pan-seared scallops on egg noodles with cucumber relish (£10.50), daily specials, and puddings like apple flan or chocolate domino (£3.50); roast Sunday lunch (£7.95); good, neat and cheerful service. One raised area is no smoking; piped music, and two fruit machines. No children inside. *(Recommended by Val and Alan Green, the Didler, JP, PP, Eric Larkham, Joel Dobris, Ian and Nita Cooper)*

Youngs ~ Managers Mr and Mrs P Wakefield ~ Real ale ~ Bar food (12-9) ~ (020) 7928 1899 ~ Open 11-11; 12-10.30 Sun

George ★ ◖

Off 77 Borough High Street, SE1; ✆ Borough or London Bridge

Preserved by the National Trust, this splendid looking place is probably the best example of a 17th-c coaching inn you're likely to come across, but it's not just the history that stands out: it has a good atmosphere too, and a wide range of beers. The tiers of open galleries look down over a bustling cobbled courtyard with plenty of picnic-sets, and maybe morris men and even Shakespeare in summer. Noted as one of London's 'fair inns for the receipt of travellers' as early as 1598, it was rebuilt on its original plan after the great Southwark fire in 1676, then owned for a while by Guys Hospital next door. What survives today is only a third of what it once was; the building was 'mercilessly reduced' as E V Lucas put it, during the period when was it owned by the Great Northern Railway Company. Inside is unspoilt and atmospheric, the row of no-frills ground-floor rooms and bars all containing square-latticed windows, black beams, bare floorboards, some panelling, plain oak or elm tables and old-fashioned built-in settles, along with a 1797 'Act of Parliament' clock, dimpled glass lantern-lamps and so forth. The snuggest refuge is the room nearest the street, where there's an ancient beer engine that looks like a cash register. Two rooms are no smoking at lunchtimes. They usually have eight well kept real ales on at once, from a range including Boddingtons, Fullers London Pride, Greene King Abbot and Old Speckled Hen, and a beer brewed for them, Restoration; mulled wine in winter, several teas and coffees. Lunchtime bar food might include filled baked potatoes (from £3), soup (£3.25), filled rolls or baguettes (from £3.50), sausage and mash or roast vegetable lasagne (£5.25), and steak, mushroom and Guinness pie (£5.45). A splendid central staircase goes up to a series of dining rooms and to a gaslit balcony; darts, trivia. Service can slow down at busy times. Unless you know where you're going (or you're in one of the many tourist groups that flock here during the day in summer) you may well miss it, as apart from the great gates there's little to indicate that such a gem still exists behind the less auspicious looking buildings on the busy high street. *(Recommended by Richard Lewis, Neil Rose, John Beeken, Sue Demont, Tim Barrow, P Abbott, Mike Tomkins, Giles Francis, Robert Davis, Derek Thomas, Kevin Flack, Mike Gorton, Nigel and Sue Foster, Ian Phillips, the Didler, Ted George, JP, PP, LM)*

Whitbreads ~ Manager George Cunningham ~ Real ale ~ Bar food (12-3 (4 wknds)) ~ Restaurant ~ (020) 7407 2056 ~ Children welcome ~ First Fri of month English folk ~ Open 11-11; 12-10.30 Sun

Horniman

Hays Galleria, Battlebridge Lane, SE13; ⊖ London Bridge

A few changes at this spacious pub since our last edition; there's a new manager, and the décor has changed quite a bit, creating a lighter, more minimalist atmosphere. Happily, one thing that hasn't altered is the splendid views of the Thames, HMS *Belfast* and Tower Bridge from the picnic-sets outside. Inside, there's plenty of polished wood, various comfortable carpeted areas, a few sofas, and well spread out tables. There's a set of clocks made for tea merchant Frederick Horniman's office showing the time in various places around the world. Fewer real ales than before, now just Adnams and Fullers London Pride, but still a choice of teas and coffees. Bar food includes big sandwiches (£3.95), and hot dishes like macaroni cheese or beef hotpot (£4.95). Fruit machine, TVs, unobtrusive piped music. The pub is at the end of the visually exciting Hays Galleria development, several storeys high, with a soaring glass curved roof, and supported by elegant thin cast-iron columns; various shops and boutiques open off. It's busy round here in the daytime, but quickly goes quiet as the evening draws on. They don't allow children. *(Recommended by Mike Ridgway, Sarah Miles, Ian Phillips, Mark Stoffan)*

Bass ~ Manager Chris Howard ~ Real ale ~ Bar food (12-9) ~ (020) 7407 1991 ~ Open 11-11(10.30 Sun); closed Dec 25, 1 Jan

Market Porter ◀

9 Stoney Street, SE1; ⊖ London Bridge

Open between 6.30 and 8.30am for workers and porters from Borough Market opposite to enjoy a drink at the start of the day, this busily pubby place is worth a stop for its splendid range of well kept beers, one of the most varied in London. The eight ales on handpump usually include Courage Best and Harveys Best, and rapidly changing guests you're unlikely to have heard of before – let alone come across in this neck of the woods: readers have recently enjoyed Batemans Dicky Finger, Ben and Ted's Organic Bitter, Old Kent Pull Pitch, Oliver Hare Mad March Hare, Swale Old Stroker, and brews from the nearby London Bridge Brewery. They usually get through 20 different beers each week. The main part of the atmospheric long U-shaped bar has rough wooden ceiling beams with beer barrels balanced on them, a heavy wooden bar counter with a beamed gantry, cushioned bar stools, an open fire, and 1920s-style wall lamps. Sensibly priced simple lunchtime bar food includes sandwiches, and hot dishes such as fish and chips wrapped in newspaper (£5.50), steaks (£8.45), and Sunday roasts. Obliging, friendly service; darts, fruit machine, TV, and piped music. A cosy partly panelled room has leaded glass windows and a couple of tables. Part of the restaurant (which has an additional couple of real ales) is no smoking. The company that own the pub – which can get a little full at lunchtimes (it's quiet in the afternoons) – have various other pubs around London; ones with similarly unusual beers (if not quite so many) can be found in Stamford St and Seymour Place. *(Recommended by Ted George, the Didler, Richard Lewis, JP, PP, John A Barker, Ian Phillips, Sue Demont, Tim Barrow, Joel Dobris)*

Free house ~ Licensee Anthony Heddigan ~ Real ale ~ Bar food (12-2.30 only) ~ Restaurant ~ (020) 7407 2495 ~ Children in eating area of bar till 6pm, wknds only ~ Open 6am-8.30am, then 11-11; 11-11 Sat; 12-10.30 Sun

---

If we know a pub has an outdoor play area for children, we mention it.

Ship ♀

41 Jews Row, SW18; ⇌ Wandsworth Town

Hidden away in an otherwise undistinguished part of Wandsworth, this smartly busy riverside pub is a delightful spot in fine weather, with lots of picnic-sets on the extensive terrace, pretty hanging baskets and brightly coloured flowerbeds, small trees, and an outside bar; a Thames barge is moored alongside. Every day in summer, and at winter weekends, there's a barbecue out here, serving very good home-made burgers and sausages, marinated lamb steaks, goats cheese quesidillas, and even cajun chicken and lobster; it's all weather, with plenty of covered areas if necessary. The food inside is particularly appealing, as at the Alma above (under the same management) relying very much on free-range produce, much of it from Mr Gotto's farm; the menu might include poached pear, prosciutto and taleggio cheese (£4.45), spring onion pancake with home-cured gravadlax (£4.95), leek, pea and baby corn risotto with whole field mushrooms and shredded basil (£7.25), lemon and garlic corn-fed chicken with chilli rice and wilted spinach (£8.95), pan-fried darne of salmon with chinese leaves, creamed potatoes and parsley and pesto sauce (£8.90), fillet of pork with potato gratin, green beans and stilton sauce (£9.50), and barbary duck breast with fresh mango and cassis gravy (£11.50). You can book tables (except at Sunday lunchtimes). Only a small part of the original ceiling is left in the main bar – the rest is in a light and airy conservatory style; wooden tables, a medley of stools, and old church chairs on the floorboards, and a relaxed, chatty atmosphere. One part has a Victorian fireplace, a huge clock surrounded by barge prints, an old-fashioned bagatelle, and jugs of flowers around the window sills. The basic public bar has plain wooden furniture, a black kitchen range in the fireplace and a juke box. Well kept Youngs Bitter, Special and seasonal brews and Smiles Bitter on handpump, plus freshly squeezed orange and other fruit juices, a wide range of wines (a dozen or more by the glass) and a good choice of teas and coffees. Service is friendly and helpful. The pub's annual firework display draws huge crowds of young people, and they also celebrate the last night of the Proms. In summer the adjacent car park can fill up pretty quickly. *(Recommended by Steve Chambers)*

Youngs ~ Tenant C Gotto ~ Real ale ~ Bar food (12-10.30(10 Sat)) ~ Restaurant ~ (020) 8870 9667 ~ Children in restaurant ~ Open 11-11; 12-10.30 Sun; closed 25 Dec

White Cross ♀

Water Lane; ⊖/⇌ Richmond

On a sunny day the paved garden in front of this popular Thameside pub feels a little like a cosmopolitan seaside resort; the plentiful tables overlooking the water are sheltered by a big fairy-lit tree (identified by Kew Gardens as a rare Greek whitebeam), and in summer there's an outside bar. The setting is perfect, delightful in summer, and with a certain wistful charm in winter as well. Inside, the two chatty main rooms have something of the air of the hotel this once was, as well as comfortable long banquettes curving round the tables in the deep bay windows, local prints and photographs, an old-fashioned wooden island servery, and a good mix of variously aged customers. Two of three log fires have mirrors above them – unusually, the third is underneath a window. A bright and airy upstairs room has lots more tables and a number of plates on a shelf running round the walls; a couple of tables are squeezed onto a little balcony. Youngs Bitter, Special and seasonal beers on handpump, and a good range of 15 or so carefully chosen wines by the glass; friendly service. From a servery at the foot of the stairs, lunchtime bar food includes good sandwiches (from £2.50), salads (from £5.45), a variety of sausages (£6.25), and good daily changing home-made dishes such as pasta (£6.25) or mixed game pie (£6.50). No music or machines – the only games are backgammon and chess. Boats leave from immediately outside to Kingston or Hampton Court. Make sure when leaving your car outside that you know the tide times – it's not unknown for the water to rise right up the steps into the bar, completely covering anything that gets in the way. *(Recommended by Mike Tomkins, Bob and Maggie Atherton, Ian Phillips, David and Nina Pugsley, Mrs E A Everard, Mayur Shah)*

Youngs ~ Managers Ian and Phyl Heggie ~ Real ale ~ Bar food (12-4; not evenings) ~ (020) 8940 6844 ~ Children in family room ~ Open 11-11; 12-10.30 Sun

Windmill ♀

Clapham Common South Side, SW4; ⊖ Clapham Common/Clapham South

A painting in the Tate by J P Herring has the Windmill in the background, shown behind local turn-of-the-century characters returning from the Derby Day festivities. It hasn't changed that much since, and is a big, bustling, Victorian pub, spacious enough to serve all the visitors to neighbouring Clapham Common. The comfortable and smartly civilised main bar has plenty of prints and pictures on the walls, real fires, and a mix of tables and seating; smaller areas open off, and however busy it gets you can generally find a quiet corner. Bar food such as sandwiches and baguettes (from £3.50), steak and ale pie, chargrilled burgers and salads (£5.50); service is prompt and friendly. Well kept Youngs Bitter, Special and seasonal beers and Smiles Bitter on handpump, with a good choice of wines by the glass and plenty more by the bottle. Cribbage, dominoes, fruit machine, piped music, TV. The bedrooms are comfortable and well equipped; it's worth checking the prices, as they can be a bit cheaper at weekends. *(Recommended by Ian Phillips)*

Youngs ~ Managers Peter and Jennifer Hale ~ Real ale ~ Bar food (12-2.30, 7-10) ~ Restaurant ~ (020) 8673 4578 ~ Children in eating area of bar ~ Open 11-11; 12-10.30 Sun ~ Bedrooms: £97.50B/£105B

WEST LONDON Map 13
Anglesea Arms 🍺

15 Selwood Terrace, SW7; ⊖ South Kensington

Though the leafy front patio of this genuinely old-fashioned pub can seem like the place to be on a warm evening, it's really rather nice inside, managing to feel both smart and cosy at the same time. Despite the surrounding affluence, the elegantly characterful bar has a very friendly and chatty atmosphere, as well as central elbow tables, a mix of cast-iron tables on the bare wood-strip floor, wood panelling, and big windows with attractive swagged curtains; at one end several booths with partly glazed screens have cushioned pews and spindleback chairs. The traditional mood is heightened by some heavy portraits, prints of London, and large brass chandeliers. A very good choice of real ales might include Adnams Bitter and Broadside, Brakspears Bitter and Special, Fullers London Pride, and a guest like Harveys Sussex or Youngs; they also keep a few bottled Belgian beers, and several malt and Irish whiskies. Downstairs has been converted into a separate eating area, in recognition of the pub's growing popularity for good food; it still has its Victorian fireplace. The menu includes lunchtime baguettes, soup (£3.50), chicken liver pâté (£4.75), salmon fishcakes (£5.25), cumberland sausages and mash (£6.90), beer battered fish and chips or roasted vegetables glazed with harissa and topped with grilled goats cheese (£7.95), daily fish specials such as skate wings with black butter and capers or grilled whole plaice with lemon butter (£9.95), and rib-eye steak (£12.95); good all-day Sunday roasts. Service is friendly and helpful. The pub is very popular with well-heeled young people, but is well liked by locals too; perhaps that's because many of the locals are well-heeled young people. *(Recommended by John Fazakerley, the Didler, Joel Dobris, Ian Phillips, Mark Percy, Lesley Mayoh, Richard Siebert)*

Free house ~ Licensees T W Simpson, E Whittingham, B McGill ~ Real ale ~ Bar food (12-3, 6.30-10; 12-10 Sat; 12-9.30 Sun; not 25 Dec) ~ Restaurant ~ (020) 7373 7960 ~ Children in eating area of bar ~ Open 11-11; 12-10.30 Sun

---

We mention bottled beers and spirits only if there is something unusual about them – imported Belgian real ales, say, or dozens of malt whiskies; so do please let us know about them in your reports: www.goodguides.com

Anglesea Arms ⑪ ♀

35 Wingate Road, W6; ⊖ Ravenscourt Park

One of the best known of London's gastropubs (despite its out-of-the-way location), and with good reason: the food really is top notch. Changing every lunchtime and evening, the inventive menu might include several starters like goats curd, courgette and oregano tart (£4.50), catalan-style chorizo, garlic and eel gratin (£4.95), and pigeon, foie gras and chicken liver terrine with brioche and onion marmalade (£5.25), and half a dozen or so main courses such as wilted wild garlic leaf and morel risotto (£7.25), stuffed saddle of rabbit 'cock a leekie' (£7.50), chargrilled chump of lamb (£9.75), and delicious red mullet on saffron mash with mediterranean vegetables (£9.95); good puddings, and some unusual farmhouse cheeses (£4.50). The bustling eating area leads off the bar but feels quite separate, with skylights creating a brighter feel, closely packed tables, and a big modern mural along one wall; directly opposite is the kitchen, with several chefs frantically working on the meals. You can't book, so best to get there early for a table, or be prepared to wait. A couple of readers have found it rather smoky. It feels a lot more restaurantly than, say, the Eagle, though you can also usually eat in the bar: rather plainly decorated, but cosy in winter when the roaring fire casts long flickering shadows on the dark panelling. Neatly stacked piles of wood guard either side of the fireplace (which has a stopped clock above it), and there are some well worn green leatherette chairs and stools. Courage Best, Fullers London Pride, Greene King Old Speckled Hen and Marstons Pedigree on handpump, with a wide range of carefully chosen wines listed above the bar. Several tables outside overlook the quiet street (not the easiest place to find a parking space). *(Recommended by P Abbott, Derek Thomas, Richard Siebert, B, M and P Kendall)*

Scottish Courage ~ Lease Dan and Fiona Evans, René Rice ~ Real ale ~ Bar food (12.30-2.45, 7.30-10.45; 1-3.30, 7.30-10.15 Sun) ~ Restaurant ~ (020) 8749 1291 ~ Children in eating area of bar and restaurant ~ Open 11-11; 12-10.30 Sun; closed 24 Dec-1 Jan

Atlas ⑪ ♀

16 Seagrave Rd, SW6; ⊖ West Brompton

Once the kind of place that deserved a fleeting visit at best, the Atlas has been transformed by two brothers (one of whom used to be a chef at the Eagle) into an unexpectedly rewarding food pub. The imaginative meals have quickly gained quite a reputation, and there's a nicely buzzing atmosphere in the evenings. Tables are highly prized, so if you're planning to eat – and most people do – arrive early, or swoop quickly. Listed on a blackboard above the brick fireplace, and changing every day, the shortish choice of excellent meals might include cauliflower and saffron soup with parmesan crostinis (£3.50), fresh marinated anchovies on bruschetta with cucumber relish (£6), calves liver risotto with onion, carrot and sage (£7.50), grilled tuscan sausages with roast shallots, baked polenta, porcini and field mushrooms (£8), moroccan chicken with sweet potatoes and couscous salad (£8.50), pan-fried lemon sole with puy lentils and salsa verde (£11), and grilled rib-eye steak with spiced black beans (£11.50); they sometimes have a nice chocolate cake, or good cheeses. The long knocked-together bar has been nicely renovated without removing the original features; there's plenty of panelling and dark wooden wall benches, with a mix of school chairs and well spaced tables. Smart young locals figure prominently in the mix, but there are plenty of locals too, as well as visitors to the Exhibition Centre at Earls Court (one of the biggest car parks is next door). Charles Wells Bombardier, Fullers London Pride, and Greene King IPA on handpump, and a well chosen wine list, with a changing range of around ten by the glass; friendly service. The piped music is unusual – on various visits we've come across everything from salsa and jazz to vintage TV themes. Down at the end is a TV, by a hatch to the kitchen. At the side is a narrow yard with lots of tables and colourful plants (and heaters for winter). *(Recommended by Derek Thomas)*

Free house ~ Licensees Richard and George Manners and Piers Baker ~ Real ale ~ Bar food (12-3, 7-10.30(10 Sun)) ~ (020) 7385 9129 ~ Children in eating area of bar till 7pm ~ Open 12-11(10.30 Sun); closed 24 Dec-2 Jan

Bulls Head

Strand-on-the-Green, W4; ⊖ Kew Bridge

In a lovely riverside setting, this well worn and cosy pub has a comfortably traditional feel, its pleasant little rooms rambling through black-panelled alcoves and up and down steps. Old-fashioned benches are built into the simple panelling, and small windows look past attractively planted hanging flower baskets to the river just beyond the narrow towpath. Well kept Courage Directors, Theakstons Best and Old Peculier, and Wadworths 6X on handpump. Well liked home-made bar food, served all day, includes filled baguettes (£4.99), changing hot dishes like spinach and ricotta cannelloni, chicken tikka or beef and ale pie (£5.99), and Sunday roasts (£6.99); the food area is no smoking. A games room at the back has darts, fruit machine and trivia. The pub isn't too crowded even on fine evenings, though it can get busy at weekends, especially when they have a raft race on the river. As we went to press they were still waiting for a refurbishment; when it happens – and some feel it's already a little overdue – the pub may be closed for a few weeks, so it may be best to check they're open before making a special journey. The original building served as Cromwell's HQ several times during the Civil War, and it was here that Moll Cutpurse overheard Cromwell talking to Fairfax about the troops' pay money coming by horse from Hounslow, and got her gang to capture the moneybags; they were later recovered at Turnham Green.The nearby City Barge is even older than the Bulls Head, and just as nice – it can be hard choosing between them. *(Recommended by Ian Phillips, Mike and Mary Carter, Bob and Maggie Atherton)*

Scottish Courage ~ Manager Bob McPhee ~ Real ale ~ Bar food (12-3.30, 6.30-10; 12-7 Sun) ~ (020) 8994 1204 ~ Children in conservatory ~ Open 11-11; 12-10.30 Sun

Churchill Arms ⬛

119 Kensington Church St, W8; ⊖ Notting Hill Gate/Kensington High St

Imagine a bustling, cheery local, with a genuinely welcoming landlord, staff who fill your beer right to the top of the glass, and really excellent food; hard to find at the best of times, let alone in London, but it pretty much sums up the appeal of this chatty place. It always seems jolly and lively, but they really go to town on Halloween, St Patrick's Day and Churchill's birthday (30 November), when you'll find special events and decorations, and more people than you'd ever imagine could feasibly fit inside. The vibrant atmosphere owes a lot to the friendly Irish landlord, who works hard and enthusiastically to give visitors an individual welcome. One of his hobbies is collecting butterflies, so you'll see a variety of prints and books on the subject dotted around the bar. There are also countless lamps, miners' lights, horse tack, bedpans and brasses hanging from the ceiling, a couple of interesting carved figures and statuettes behind the central bar counter, prints of American presidents, and lots of Churchill memorabilia. Well kept Fullers Chiswick, ESB, London Pride, and seasonal beers on handpump, with a good choice of wines. The pub can get crowded in the evenings – even early in the week it's not really a place to come for a quiet pint; it can get a bit smoky too. The spacious and rather smart plant-filled dining conservatory may be used for hatching butterflies, but is better known for its big choice of really excellent Thai food, such as a very good, proper Thai curry, or duck with noodles (all around £5.50). Service in this part – run separately from the pub – isn't always as friendly as in the pub. You should also be able to get lunchtime sandwiches (from £1.95), ploughman's (£2.50), and Sunday lunch. Fruit machine, TV; they have their own cricket and football teams. *(Recommended by Giles Francis, LM, Susan and John Douglas)*

Fullers ~ Manager Jerry O'Brien ~ Real ale ~ Bar food (12-2.30, 6-9.30; not Sun evening) ~ Restaurant ~ (020) 7727 4242 ~ Children welcome ~ Open 11-11; 12-10.30 Sun; closed 25 Dec evening

Colton Arms

187 Greyhound Road, W14; ✇ Barons Court

Next to the Queens Club tennis courts and gardens, this pub kept so lovingly by its long-serving landlord has a very un-London feel. The atmosphere is that of a relaxed and welcoming village local in one of the smarter shire counties. The main U-shaped front bar has a log fire blazing in winter, highly polished brasses, a fox's mask, hunting crops and plates decorated with hunting scenes on the walls, and a remarkable collection of handsomely carved 17th-c oak furniture. That room is small enough, but the two back rooms are tiny; each has its own little serving counter, with a bell to ring for service. Well kept Courage Best and Directors on handpump (when you pay, note the old-fashioned brass-bound till); no food. Pull the curtain aside for the door out to a charming back terrace with a neat rose arbour. *(Recommended by Susan and John Douglas)*

Unfortunately, as we decided to include this new entry at the very last minute, we were unable to contact the pub to check details before we went to press.

Dove

19 Upper Mall, W6; ✇ Ravenscourt Park

Said to be where 'Rule Britannia' was composed, this old-fashioned Thamesside tavern has a delightful tiny back terrace, where the main flagstoned area, down some steps, has a few highly prized teak tables and white metal and teak chairs looking over the low river wall to the Thames reach just above Hammersmith Bridge. If you're able to bag a spot out here in the evenings, you'll often see rowing crews practising their strokes. By the entrance from the quiet alley, the front bar is cosy and traditional, with black wood panelling, and red leatherette cushioned built-in wall settles and stools around dimpled copper tables; it leads to a bigger, similarly furnished room, with old framed advertisements and photographs of the pub. Well kept Fullers London Pride and ESB on handpump. Bar food includes filled baguettes (from £3.50), main courses like lasagne, cod and chips or steak and kidney pudding (£5.95), and steaks (from £8.25). No games machines or piped music. It's not quite so crowded at lunchtimes as it is in the evenings. A plaque marks the level of the highest-ever tide in 1928. Note they don't allow children. *(Recommended by Martin and Karen Wake, D J and P M Taylor, Mike Tomkins, B, M and P Kendall, the Didler, JP, PP, Andy Gosling)*

Fullers ~ Manager M L Delves ~ Real ale ~ Bar food (12-2.30(4 Sun), 6.30-9) ~ (020) 8748 5405 ~ Open 11-11; 12-10.30 Sun; closed 25, 26 Dec

Havelock Tavern 🍴 ♀

Masbro Road, W14; ✇ Kensington(Olympia)

A blue-tiled cornerhouse in an unassuming residential street, this out-of-the-way place is worth tracking down for its excellent quality food. Changing every day, the menu might include things like spiced red bean and bacon soup with coriander and crème fraîche (£4), rabbit rillettes with gherkins, toast and chutney (£5.50), warm feta, courgette, red onion and tomato tart (£6.50), cod fishcake with spinach, tomato aïoli and lemon (£8), poached gammon with yellow split peas, green peppercorns and mint (£8.50), and roast sirloin of beef with polenta, savoy cabbage and anchovy and lemon butter (£10.50); you can't book tables, and they don't take credit cards. On our last visit they had an unusual way of spotting where you were sitting – upon ordering we were given a vase of fresh flowers marked with the table number. Until 1932 the building was two separate shops (one was a wine merchant, but no one can remember much about the other), and it still has huge shop-front windows along both street-facing walls. The L-shaped bar is plain and unfussy: bare boards, long wooden tables, a mix of chairs and stools, a few soft spotlights, and a fireplace; a second little room with pews leads to a small paved terrace, with benches, a tree, and wall climbers. Well kept Brakspears, Marstons Pedigree and Wadworths 6X on handpump from the elegant modern bar counter, and a good range of well chosen wines, with around 10 by the glass; mulled wine in winter, and home-made elderflower soda. Service is particularly friendly and attentive, and the atmosphere relaxed and easy-going; no music or machines, but plenty of chat from the varied range of customers. Dominoes, Scrabble and other board games. Though evenings are always busy (you may have to wait for a table then, and some dishes can run out quite quickly), it can be quieter at lunchtimes, and in the afternoons can have something of the feel of a civilised private club. On weekdays, parking nearby is metered. *(Recommended by Susan and John Douglas, Bob and Maggie Atherton, Patrick Renouf)*

Free house ~ Licensees Peter Richnell, Jonny Haughton ~ Real ale ~ Bar food (12.30-2.30(3 Sun), 7-10(9.30 Sun)) ~ No credit cards ~ (020) 7603 5374 ~ Children welcome ~ Open 11-11; 12-10.30 Sun; closed Easter Sun, Christmas

Portobello Gold ♀

95 Portobello Road, W11; ✆ Notting Hill Gate

Sitting in the back dining room of this enterprising pub feels a long way from trendy Notting Hill, and almost like being on holiday somewhere warm and sunny; covering one wall is a mural of an exotic-seeming bay, there's a profusion of plants and trees, and comfortable wicker chairs, stained wooden tables, and a cage of vocal canaries all add to the exotic, outdoor effect. In the old days – when we remember this being a Hells Angels hangout – this was the pub garden, and in summer they may still open up the roof. The walls here and in the smaller, brightly painted front bar are covered with changing displays of art and photography, and there's a cheerfully laid-back, almost bohemian atmosphere; the bar also has a nice old fireplace, cushioned pews, and daily papers. The Gold was the first place in the UK to serve oyster shooters (a shot glass with an oyster, salsa, horseradish, Tabasco and lime), and they still have something of an emphasis on oysters and seafood; the salt and pepper sit appealingly in oyster shells. The monthly changing menu might typically include big ciabattas, cajun jumbo shrimp, caesar salad with chicken or anchovies or fried squid (£5.95), half a dozen Irish rock oysters (£6.50), sausage and mash (£6.50), mexican fajitas, and poached scotch salmon (£9.75); they do a good pecan pie. On Sunday, roasts are served until 8pm. You can eat from the same menu in the bar or dining room (part of which is no smoking). They take credit cards. Opening at 10 for coffee and fresh pastries, the bar has well kept Courage Directors and a guest such as Greene King Old Speckled Hen or Shepherd Neame Spitfire, as well as a Pitfield cask-conditioned lager, a couple of draught Belgian beers, a good selection of bottled beers from around the world, and a wide range of interesting tequilas and other well sourced spirits; the wine list is good, with around 15 available by the glass, and they also have a cigar menu and various coffees. Polite, helpful young staff; piped music, chess, backgammon; no games machines. A new oyster bar is planned. They also plan to move their upstairs Internet café next to the pub, and even introduce a couple of terminals to a discreet corner of the bar; already the bedrooms can be set up with free Internet access. The landlord has compiled a database of what's sold in each of the surrounding antique shops, for those who'd like their browsing slightly more focused. There are a couple of tables and chairs on the pretty street outside, which like the pub, is named in recognition of the 1769 battle of Portobello, fought over control of the lucrative gold route to Panama. A lively stall is set up outside during the Notting Hill Carnival. Parking nearby is metered; it's not easy to bag a space. We have not yet heard from readers staying here. *(Recommended by David Azam)*

Unique Pub Co ~ Managers Michael Bell and Rob Jameson ~ Real ale ~ Bar food (12-5, 7-11) ~ Restaurant ~ (020) 7460 4900 ~ Children welcome till 8pm ~ Open 10-11(10.30 Sun); closed Christmas ~ Bedrooms: £55B/£80B

All *Guide* inspections are anonymous. Anyone claiming to be a *Good Pub Guide* inspector is a fraud, and should be reported to us with name and description.

White Horse ♀ ◀

1 Parsons Green, SW6; ⊖ Parsons Green

Busy, friendly and meticulously run, this splendidly organised pub has earned lots of praise from readers over the last year, not least for its continued emphasis on an impressively eclectic range of drinks. Seven perfectly kept real ales include Adnams Broadside, Bass, Harveys Sussex, Highgate Mild, Roosters Ranger (brewed to their specification) and changing guests like Dark Star Spiced Vice and Roosters Yankee; they also keep 15 Trappist beers, 45 other foreign bottled beers, a dozen malt whiskies, and a broad range of good, interesting and not overpriced wines. Every item on the menu, whether it be scrambled egg or raspberry and coconut tart, has a suggested accompaniment listed beside it, perhaps a wine, or maybe a bottled beer. They're keen to encourage people to select beer with food in the same way you might do wine, and organise regular beer dinners where every course comes with a recommended brew. The often inventive bar food might include sandwiches (from £4), ploughman's (with some unusual cheeses, £5), chicken liver and foie gras parfait (£5.25), cucumber sushi with Hoegaarden tempura prawns (£6.75), salmon fishcakes with tarragon mayonnaise or arancini with mozzarella, chargrilled vegetables and pesto dressing (£7.75), beer battered cod and chips (£8.25), and pan-fried sea bass with thai green curry, sticky rice and bok choy (£12.75). There's usually something to eat available all day; at weekends there's a good brunch menu, and in winter they do a very good Sunday lunch. The stylishly modernised U-shaped bar has plenty of sofas, wooden tables, and huge windows with slatted wooden blinds, and winter coal and log fires, one in an elegant marble fireplace. The pub is usually busy (sometimes very much so, with an obvious part of the mix the sort of people that once earned the pub its hated nickname, the Sloaney Pony), but there are usually enough smiling, helpful staff behind the solid panelled central servery to ensure you'll rarely have to wait too long to be served. All the art displayed is for sale; they have a small gallery upstairs, with bi-monthly exhibitions. The back restaurant is no smoking. On summer evenings the front terrace overlooking the green has something of a continental feel, with crowds of people drinking al fresco at the white cast-iron tables and chairs; there may be Sunday barbecues. They have monthly beer festivals (often spotlighting regional breweries), as well as lively celebrations on American Independence Day or Thanksgiving. *(Recommended by the Didler, Ian Phillips, D P and J A Sweeney, Tracey and Stephen Groves, LM, JP, PP, Derek Thomas, Richard Rand)*

Bass ~ Manager Mark Dorber ~ Real ale ~ Bar food (12-10.30(sandwiches only 4-6)) ~ Restaurant ~ (020) 7736 2115 ~ Children in eating area of bar and restaurant ~ Open 11-11; 12-10.30 Sun; closed 24-27 Dec

White Swan

Riverside; ⇄ Twickenham

Reassuringly traditional, this unpretentious 17th-c riverside house is built on a platform well above ground level, with steep steps leading up to the door and to a sheltered terrace, full of tubs and baskets of flowers. Even the cellar is raised above ground, as insurance against the flood tides which wash right up to the house. Across the peaceful almost rural lane is a little riverside lawn, where tables look across a quiet stretch of the Thames to country meadows on its far bank past the top of Eel Pie Island. The friendly bar has bare boards, big rustic tables and other simple wooden furnishings, and blazing winter fires. The photographs on the walls are of regulars and staff as children, while a back room reflects the landlord's devotion to rugby, with lots of ties, shorts, balls and pictures; backgammon, cribbage, piped blues or jazz. Well kept Charles Wells Bombardier, Greene King IPA, Marstons Pedigree and Shepherd Neame Spitfire on handpump, with around 10 wines by the glass; mulled wine in winter. In summer there's a weekday lunchtime buffet, taking in everything from cheese and ham to trout and smoked salmon, while other bar food includes sandwiches (from £2.50), soup (£3), and winter lancashire hotpot or calves liver (£6). Evening meals are only served in summer. They have an annual raft race on the river the last Saturday in July, barbecues on summer weekends, and an enthusiastic Burns Night celebration. The pub can get busy at weekends and some evenings. It's a short stroll to the imposing Palladian Marble Hill House in its grand Thames-side park (built for a mistress of George II). *(Recommended by Mike Tomkins, Peter Meister)*

Massive Ltd ~ Licensees Steve and Kirsten Roy ~ Real ale ~ Bar food ~ (020) 8892 2166 ~ Children welcome ~ Folk Weds evening Nov-Apr ~ Open 11-11; 12-10.30 Sun; 11-3, 5.30-11(10.30 Sun) winter

Windsor Castle

114 Campden Hill Road, W8; ✪ Holland Park/Notting Hill Gate

A wonderful draw whatever the season, this unchanging place is cosy in winter with its time-smoked ceilings and dark wooden furnishings, and lovely in summer thanks to the big tree-shaded garden behind. There are lots of sturdy teak seats and tables on flagstones out here – you'll have to move fast to bag one on a sunny day – as well as a brick outside bar, and quite a secluded feel thanks to the high ivy-covered sheltering walls. They have outside heaters so you can sit out all year round. Inside, the series of tiny unspoilt rooms all have to be entered through separate doors, so it can be quite a challenge finding the people you've arranged to meet – more often than not they'll be hidden behind the high backs of the sturdy built-in elm benches. A cosy pre-war-style dining room opens off, and soft lighting and a coal-effect fire add to the appeal. Served all day, bar food includes things like filled ciabattas (from £4.50), ploughman's (£4.50), oyster mushroom and pepper pasta (£5.75), steamed mussels (£6.25), fish and chips, and various sausages with mash and onion gravy (£7.25); they do a choice of roasts on Sunday (£9.95), when the range of other dishes is more limited. Adnams, Bass and Fullers London Pride on handpump, along with decent house wines, various malt whiskies, and maybe mulled wine in winter. No fruit machines or piped music. Usually fairly quiet at lunchtime – when several areas are no smoking – the pub can be packed some evenings, often with (as they think) Notting Hill's finest. *(Recommended by Giles Francis, Ian Phillips, Sue Demont, Tim Barrow)*

Bass ~ Manager Carole Jabbour ~ Real ale ~ Bar food (12-10) ~ (020) 7243 9551 ~ Open 12-11(10.30 Sun); closed 25, 26 Dec

Lucky Dip

Besides the fully inspected pubs, you might like to try these Lucky Dips recommended to us and described by readers (if you do, please send us reports: www.goodguides.com).

CENTRAL LONDON
EC 3
Walrus & Carpenter [Monument St/Lovat Lane]: Two contrasting bars, particularly well kept Youngs beers *(Dr and Mrs A K Clarke)*

EC1
Bleeding Heart [Bleeding Heart Yard, off Greville St]: Unpretentious traditional pub, quieter than many, with well kept Adnams ales and imaginative range of wines by the glass *(Sue Demont, Tim Barrow)*
Butchers Hook & Cleaver [W Smithfield]: Conversion of former bank, attractive décor, nice mix of chairs inc some button-back leather armchairs, wrought-iron spiral stairs to pleasant mezzanine, decent waitress-served food inc lots of pies and wkdy breakfast from 7.30am, full Fullers range kept well, friendly staff, good mix of customers, relaxed atmosphere; big-screen sports TV; open all day *(BB, SLC)*
City Pride [Farringdon Lane]: Comfortable

two-room Fullers pub with cheap fresh food all day inc sandwiches, well kept London Pride and ESB, decent wines by the glass, friendly bustle, efficient smiling service, quieter extra seating upstairs *(Ian Phillips)*
Leopard [Seward St]: Unfortunately this fine traditional pub closed in 2001, victim of a major redevelopment *(LYM)*
Pheasant [Goswell Rd]: Bare-boards bar and sofa lounge area, with well kept ales such as Adnams (no longer a Firkin pub); SkyTV, no wknd food *(Giles Francis, LYM)*
Sir John Oldcastle [Farringdon Rd]: Large Wetherspoons pub, very popular lunchtime *(SLC)*

EC2
49 Gresham Street [Gresham St]: Edwardian-style Fullers pub and cellar bar in big modern office block, their beers kept well, good food inc hot and cold sandwiches, filled baps, hot dishes *(Ian Phillips, Mike and Mona Clifford)*

51 Gresham Street [Gresham St]: Another purpose-built pub, busy downstairs, quieter up (exc Fri evening), prompt service; Sam Smiths OB, the area's cheapest pint *(Jim Bush)*

City Tup [Gresham St]: Unusual for this area in being a ground-floor pub with an upstairs gallery; known as the Baa, with pleasant atmosphere, Courage Best and Directors and a guest such as Charles Wells Bombardier, choice of food; piped music may be loud *(Ian Phillips)*

☆ *Dirty Dicks* [Bishopsgate]: Traditional City cellar (now a Whitbreads Hogshead) with bare boards, brick barrel-vaulted ceiling, interesting old prints inc one of Nathaniel Bentley, the original Dirty Dick; good choice of real ales, wine racks overhead, decent food inc open sandwiches, baguettes and reasonably priced hot dishes, pleasant service, loads of character – fun for foreign visitors *(LYM, JP, PP, the Didler)*

George [Great Eastern Hotel, Liverpool St]: Good classy American-tavern atmosphere in magnificent room, beautifully done up; usual keg beers, good plain food at high prices (beware 12.5% service charge on top) *(Joel Dobris, Mr and Mrs Jon Corelis)*

Hamilton Hall [Bishopsgate; also entrance from L'pool St Stn]: Big busy Wetherspoons pub, flamboyant Victorian baroque décor, plaster nudes and fruit mouldings, chandeliers, mirrors, upper mezzanine, good-sized upstairs no smoking section (not always open, though – can get crowded and smoky downstairs), comfortable groups of seats, reliable food all day from well filled baguettes up, well kept Scottish Courage and guest beers, decent wines, good prices; fruit machine, video game but no piped music; open all day – and of course the lavatories are free, unlike Railtrack's extortionate ones nearby *(Ian Phillips, Richard Lewis, LYM)*

Old Dr Butlers Head [Masons Ave]: 17th-c City pub with beams, bare boards, dark wood, cream paint, small-paned windows, a few small tables around big irregularly shaped room, raised back area with old leather and dark wood benches (and bar billiards); Adnams, Boddingtons, Brakspears, Fullers London Pride and Marstons Pedigree, quick service, lunchtime food, upstairs bar *(James Nunns)*

Pacific Oriental [Bishopsgate]: Light airy bar with pastel walls, light wood furniture on polished tiles, big glass panels showing microbrewery producing their own Pils, Bishops and Weiss, decent wines, oriental bar food 3-9.30 in back dining area, upstairs restaurant with no smoking area; SkyTV, piped music; children allowed, open all day *(Richard Lewis)*

EC3

East India Arms [Fenchurch St]: Archetypal city gents' pub with well kept Youngs, good service even with the lunchtime crowds *(Ian Phillips)*

Lamb [Grand Ave, Leadenhall Mkt]: Old-fashioned stand-up bar with spiral stairs to light and airy upper no smoking carpeted lounge bar overlooking market's central crossing, plenty of tables and corner servery strong on cooked meats inc hot sandwiches, well kept Bass, Youngs and a guest beer, engraved glass, plenty of ledges and shelves; also basement bar with shiny wall tiling and own entrance *(JP, PP, the Didler, Dr and Mrs A K Clarke)*

Liberty Bounds [Trinity Sq]: Large busy two-floor Wetherspoons in former bank, good range of well priced beers; fairly handy for Tower of London *(Dr and Mrs A K Clarke, Eddie Edwards)*

Minories [Minories, opp Tower of London]: Newish pub in railway arches, nr Tower of London; lots of separate seating areas, well kept ales *(Dr and Mrs A K Clarke)*

Swan [Ship Tavern Passage, off Gracechurch St]: Busy businessmen's pub with narrow flagstoned bar, larger upstairs room, unspoilt Victorian panelled décor, good friendly service, generous lunchtime sandwiches, particularly well kept Fullers; no music or machines in main bar *(Dr and Mrs A K Clarke)*

EC4

Hatchet [Garlick Hill]: Convivial small City pub, main bar with small back lounge, Greene King IPA and Abbot, basic low-priced hot meals *(Ian Phillips)*

Old Bell [Fleet St, nr Ludgate Circus]: Fine old intimate tavern (rebuilt by Wren as commissariat for his workers on nearby church), lively atmosphere, some tables tucked away to give a sense of privacy; well kept Bass and a guest beer, good sandwiches *(BB, the Didler, JP, PP)*

☆ *Punch* [Fleet St]: Warm, comfortable, softly lit Victorian pub, not too smart despite superb tiled entrance with mirrored lobby; dozens of *Punch* cartoons, ornate plaster ceiling with unusual domed skylight, good bar food, Bass and guest beers such as Marstons and Wadworths *(the Didler)*

SW1

☆ *Antelope* [Eaton Terr]: Stylish panelled local, rather superior but friendly; bare boards, lots of interesting prints and old advertisements, well kept ales such as Adnams, Fullers London Pride, Marstons Pedigree and Tetleys, good house wines, sandwiches, baked potatoes, ploughman's and one-price hot dishes; surprisingly quiet and relaxed upstairs wkdy lunchtimes, can get crowded evenings; open all day, children in eating area *(Franki McCabe, JP, PP, LYM, the Didler)*

☆ *Buckingham Arms* [Petty France]: Congenial Youngs local with lots of mirrors and woodwork, unusual long side corridor fitted out with elbow ledge for drinkers (and SkyTV for motor sports), well kept ales, decent simple food, reasonable prices, service friendly and efficient even when busy; handy for Buckingham Palace, Westminster Abbey and St James's Park, open all day *(LYM, the Didler)*

Colonies [Wilfred St]: Friendly and comfortable open-plan split-level pub with surprisingly local feel, good typical lunchtime food from good sandwiches up, Courage Best and Directors and

Theakstons Best, African bric-a-brac; very popular with Palace St civil servants *(Stephen Bonarjee)*

☆ Fox & Hounds [Passmore St/Graham Terr]: Small cosy bar with well kept ales such as Adnams, Bass, Greene King IPA and Harveys, friendly landlady and staff, narrow bar with wall benches, big hunting prints, old sepia photographs of pubs and customers, some toby jugs, hanging plants under attractive skylight in back room, bar food, coal-effect gas fire; piano replaced by shorter-keyboard organ (not such a tight fit – you can now reach the bottom octave); coal-effect gas fire; can be very busy Fri night, quieter wkdy lunchtimes *(the Didler, Tracey and Stephen Groves)*

Gallery [Lupus St]: Opp Pimlico Underground and handy for the original Tate, with attractive Old Master reproductions, snug layout, Bass, Courage Best, Greene King Abbot and Shepherd Neame Spitfire, decent food *(Stephen Bonarjee)*

☆ Grouse & Claret [Little Chester St]: Solidly built pastiche of discreetly old-fashioned tavern just off Belgrave Sq, smart but welcoming and very well run, with attractive furnishings inc plush little booths, well kept ales such as Boddingtons, Brakspears, Greene King IPA, Wadworths 6X and Youngs Special, games area, decent bar food inc good hot baps; basement wine bar with three-course lunches, swish upstairs restaurant; children in eating area, open all day weekdays, cl Sun evening and bank hols *(Dr and Mrs A K Clarke, BB)*

Jugged Hare [Vauxhall Bridge Rd/Rochester Row]: Fullers Ale & Pie pub in converted colonnaded bank with balustraded balcony, chandelier, prints and busts; their ales kept well, friendly efficient service, decent food, no smoking back area; fruit machine, unobtrusive piped music *(John Fazakerley, BB, Dr and Mrs A K Clarke)*

☆ Morpeth Arms [Millbank]: Roomy Victorian pub handy for the original Tate, some etched and cut glass, old books and prints, photographs, earthenware jars and bottles, well kept Youngs ales, good range of food from sandwiches up, good choice of wines, helpful well organised staff; busy lunchtimes, quieter evenings, seats outside (a lot of traffic) *(the Didler, BB, Sue Demont, Tim Barrow, Howard England, Joel Dobris)*

☆ Orange Brewery [Pimlico Rd]: Many readers will be sorry to hear that this friendly pub has stopped brewing its distinctive beers – now just Adnams, Courage Best and Directors, Theakstons Best, Charles Wells Bombardier and a changing guest; simple panelled bar, all day food inc various pies or sausages, no smoking eating area; juke box; some seats outside *(Richard Rand, Peter Meister, LM, Paul Thompson, Anna Blackburn, Howard England, LYM)*

☆ Paxtons Head [Knightsbridge]: Peaceful classy Victorian pub, attractive period décor and furnishings inc gas lamps and Victorian etched glass and mirrors from Paxton's Crystal Palace; large central bar, decent steaks and so forth in upstairs restaurant, nice little cellar overflow bar *(JP, PP, the Didler)*

☆ Red Lion [Crown Passage, behind St James's St]: Nice unpretentious early Victorian local tucked down narrow and increasingly smart passage nr Christies, panelling and leaded lights giving a timeless feel, friendly relaxed atmosphere, decent lunchtime food inc fresh proper sandwiches, real ales such as Adnams and Courage Directors, reasonable prices; unobtrusive piped music *(Tina and David Woods-Taylor, Chris Glasson, BB)*

☆ Wetherspoons [Victoria Station]: Warm, comfortable and individual, a (relatively) calm haven above the station's bustle, with cheap ever-changing real ales inc interesting guest beers, wide choice of reasonably priced decent food all day, prompt friendly service, good furnishings and housekeeping – and great for people-watchers, with glass walls and tables outside overlooking the main concourse and platform indicators *(Sue Demont, Tim Barrow)*

SW3

Crown [Dovehouse St]: Particularly well kept ales inc Adnams, shortish choice of lovingly prepared good value unpretentious food, friendly staff, no piped music *(Brian Barder)*

☆ Henry J Beans [Kings Rd]: Spacious bar with decent wines, pricy but splendid range of whiskies, other spirits, lagers and bottled beers, good value burger-style bar food; well spaced tables, fine collection of enamelled advertising signs, keen young staff, the biggest sheltered courtyard garden of any central London pub, with its own summer pimms bar; open all day, provision for children *(Ian Phillips, LYM)*

Hour Glass [Brompton Rd]: Small recently redecorated pub, well kept Fullers, good value food all sessions (not Sun) from speciality toasted sandwiches and baguettes to straightforward hot dishes, efficient friendly young staff; sports TV, can be a bit smoky; pavement tables, handy for V&A and other nearby museums *(LM)*

W1

☆ Audley [Mount St]: Classic top-notch city pub, opulent red plush, High Victorian mahogany and engraved glass, clock hanging in lovely carved wood bracket from ornately corniced ceiling, well kept Courage Best and Directors from long polished bar, good food and service, good coffee, upstairs panelled dining room; open all day *(LYM, Dr M E Wilson)*

Beehive [Homer St, just off Edgware Rd]: Small hidden-away country-feel pub with unfussy décor, wonderful pictures of Victorian London, friendly helpful landlady *(Sue Demont, Tim Barrow)*

Carpenters Arms [Seymour Pl]: Chatty chaps' local run by same company as the Market Porter (see main entries), with good real ales, always three unusual ones; bare boards, helpful friendly staff, decently priced usual food; can get busy early evening, TV, piped music *(Mark Stoffan, BB)*

Clachan [Kingly St]: Wide changing range of

ales inc Timothy Taylors Landlord and above-average food in comfortable well kept pub behind Libertys, ornate plaster ceiling supported by two large fluted and decorated pillars, comfortable screened seating areas, smaller drinking alcove up three or four steps; can get very busy *(Sue Demont, Tim Barrow, George Atkinson)*

Cock [Great Portland St]: Large corner local with enormous lamps over picnic-sets outside, Victorian tiled floor, lots of wood inc good carving, some cut and etched glass, high tiled ceiling, ornate plasterwork, velvet curtains, coal-effect gas fire; popular lunchtime food in upstairs lounge with coal-effect gas fire each end, well kept cheap Sam Smiths OB *(the Didler)*

Devonshire Arms [Denman St]: Small bustling bare-boards bar, small upstairs lounge, good value food all day, welcoming friendly staff, well kept Courage Best and Directors, interesting mix of customers *(Chris Glasson)*

Fullers Ale Lodge [Avery Row]: Sidestreet local with well kept London Pride and ESB; cl Sun *(the Didler)*

George & Dragon [Cleveland St]: Well kept Greene King ales, hearty food such as pies or filled yorkshire pudding *(Bob and Laura Brock)*

King & Queen [Foley St]: Rare Adnams pub, their beers kept well, friendly landlord; quiet wknds *(Sue Demont, Tim Barrow)*

Mash 2 [Gt Portland St]: Very California, great place for a brew and a pizza; light and airy, five popular if not cheap beers brewed here, food 11.30-4 (all day Sun; service charge in restaurant), friendly staff *(Joel Dobris, Richard Lewis)*

☆ *Masons Arms* [Upper Berkeley St/Seymour Pl]: Old-fashioned roomy cornerhouse with interesting history, lots of panelling, convincing flame-effect fires and a few private nooks, such as cosy booth once used as a discreet retreat for gentry; well kept Badger beers, friendly service, nice old prints; fruit machine, loudish piped music *(Mark Stoffan, BB)*

☆ *Old Coffee House* [Beak St]: Masses of interesting bric-a-brac, unusually wide choice of decent lunchtime food (not Sun) in upstairs food room full of prints and pictures, well kept Courage Best and Directors and Marstons Pedigree; fruit machine, piped music; children allowed upstairs 12-3, open all day exc Sun afternoon; very popular with wknd shoppers and tourists *(LYM, David Blackburn, Kevin Blake)*

Running Footman [Charles St]: Bow window, dark panelling, ochred ceiling with painting of the eponymous footman, Courage Directors and Theakstons; one of those small London pubs that manages to feel comfortable even when it's crowded *(Dr M E Wilson)*

Waxy O'Connors [Rupert St]: Small ordinary street entry to surprising 3D maze of communicating areas filled with gothic plethora of reclaimed woodwork; lagers and stouts, friendly young staff, food good if you have the money; a lively crowd of young up-front people *(Dr M E Wilson)*

Windmill [Mill St]: Gilt plaster cherubs, welcoming civilised atmosphere, clean and pleasant dining areas (no smoking downstairs, smoking up), Youngs ales, some emphasis on wines *(James Nunns, Ian Phillips)*

Woodstock [Woodstock St; off Oxford St nr Selfridges]: Small, cosy and busy, with well kept Courage Directors and Greene King Abbot, wide range of strong imported beers, welcoming landlord and staff, satisfying lunchtime food (can be rather crowded then), pleasant open fire, humorous notices, no noisy music *(Chris Glasson)*

W2

Cow [Westbourne Park Rd]: Several real ales, good food in bar and civilised almost formal upstairs restaurant *(Guy Vowles)*

☆ *Mad Bishop & Bear* [Paddington Stn]: Up the escalator from concourse in new part of station, nice clone of classic city pub (or do we mean airport pub?) with cream and pastel décor, ornate plasterwork, fancy mirrors and lamps inc big brass chandeliers, parquet, tiles and carpet, leather snugs, lots of wood and prints, full Fullers beer range kept well from long counter, good wine choice, smartly dressed staff, wide choice of good value food from breakfast (7.30 on) to Sun roasts, big no smoking area; loudish piped music; open all day, tables out overlooking concourse *(Richard Lewis, I A Herdman, Dr M E Wilson, BB)*

☆ *Victoria* [Strathearn Pl]: Interesting and well preserved corner local, lots of Victorian Royal and other memorabilia, *Vanity Fair* cartoons and unusual little military paintings, two cast-iron fireplaces, wonderful gilded mirrors and mahogany panelling, brass mock-gas lamps above bar, bare boards and banquettes, relaxed atmosphere, friendly attentive service, well kept Fullers Chiswick, London Pride, ESB and Red Fox, good choice of wines by the glass, well priced food counter; upstairs has leather club chairs in small library/snug (and, mostly used for private functions now, replica of Gaiety Theatre bar, all gilt and red plush); quiet piped music; pavement picnic-sets *(LYM, Simon Collett-Jones)*

W8

☆ *Scarsdale Arms* [Edwardes Sq]: Busy Georgian Chef & Brewer in lovely leafy square, keeping a good deal of character, with stripped wooden floors, two or three fireplaces with good coal-effect gas fires, lots of knick-knacks, ornate bar counter; well kept ales such as Courage and Greene King Old Speckled Hen, decent wines, back food servery with reasonably priced food; tree-shaded front courtyard with impressive show of flower tubs and baskets, open all day *(LYM, Joel Dobris, Alan J Morton)*

WC1

Duke of York [Roger St]: Quietly placed and unpretentious, with Formica-top tables and café chairs on patterned lino, and emphasis on surprisingly good interesting modern food; cool and welcoming young atmosphere (big Andy

Warhol-style pictures), real ales such as Greene King Old Speckled Hen and Ind Coope Burton, helpful staff *(Joel Dobris, BB)*

☆ *Princess Louise* [High Holborn]: Etched and gilt mirrors, brightly coloured and fruity-shaped tiles, slender Portland stone columns, lofty and elaborately colourful ceiling, attractively priced Sam Smiths from the long counter, quieter plush-seated corners, simple bar snacks, upstairs lunchtime buffet; even the Victorian gents' has its own preservation order; crowded and lively during the week, usually quieter late evening, or Sat lunchtime; open all day, cl Sun *(the Didler, Kevin Blake, Stephen R Holman, Stephen, Julie and Hayley Brown, LYM, JP, PP)*

Rugby [Great James St]: Sizeable corner pub with well kept Shepherd Neame ales, usual food, good service *(Joel Dobris, the Didler)*

Swan [Cosmo Pl]: Half a dozen well kept real ales from old polished wood bar (they do trios of samplers for the price of a pint), good value generous chain-pub food from sandwiches up all day, dark old-fashioned refurbishment with plenty of old photographs; piped pop music may obtrude; seats out in pedestrian alley *(Sue and Bob Ward, Howard Dell, LYM)*

WC2

☆ *Chandos* [St Martins Lane]: Open all day from 9 (for breakfast), very busy downstairs bare-boards bar with snug cubicles, quieter (exc Fri evening) and more comfortable upstairs with opera photographs, low wooden tables, panelling, leather sofas, orange, red and yellow leaded windows; well kept cheap Sam Smiths OB, air conditioning (but can get packed and smoky early evening), prompt cheerful mainly antipodean service, basic food from sandwiches to Sun roasts; darts, pinball, fruit machines, video game, trivia and piped music; children upstairs till 6; note the automaton on the roof (working 10-2 and 4-9) *(Ted George, Susan and Nigel Wilson, John Fazakerley, Mark Stoffan, LYM, Jim Bush)*

Freedom Brewing Co [Earlham St]: Roomy café-bar below new Thomas Neal shopping precinct, bare boards, plain moulded pale plywood furniture, long stainless steel servery, viewing windows to copper kettles of microbrewery producing its own distinctive if high-priced Pilsner, Pale Ale, Wheat, Soho Red, Organic and Dark, usual bar food, good wine choice, friendly helpful staff – resident German brewer happy to answer questions; may be loud piped pop music, flat panel videos or SkyTV; open all day *(Richard Lewis, BB)*

Marquis of Granby [Chandos Pl]: Small and narrow, with cosy parlour-like areas each end through arched wood-and-glass partitions, well kept Adnams, Marstons Pedigree and guest ales; open all day *(the Didler, Ted George)*

Nags Head [James St/Neal St]: Etched brewery mirrors, red ceiling, mahogany furniture, some partitioned booths, lots of old local prints, popular lunchtime food counter, friendly staff, three well kept McMullens ales – unusual here; piped music, games machine, often crowded;

open all day *(Richard Lewis)*

☆ *Porterhouse* [Maiden Lane]: New London outpost of Dublin's Porterhouse microbrewery, shiny three-level (and multi-million-pound) structure full of stairs, galleries and copper ducting and piping, some nice design touches, their own interesting if pricy unpasteurised draught beers inc Porter and two Stouts (they do a comprehensive tasting tray), also their TSB real ale and a guest such as Brakspears O Be Joyful, good choice of wines by the glass, reasonably priced food 12-9 from soup and open sandwiches up with some emphasis on rock oysters, sonorous openwork clock, neatly cased bottled beer displays; piped music, Irish bands Weds-Fri and Sun, sports TV in gents'; open all day, tables on front terrace *(Richard Lewis, Catherine Pitt, BB)*

Round House [Garrick St/New Row]: Well kept ales such as Batemans Dream, Courage Directors, Fullers London Pride, Greene King IPA, Harviestoun Wee Stoater and Theakstons Best, Belgian bottled beers and decent wines, nice fittings with lots of wood, daily papers and magazines, wide choice of food from sandwiches up all day, friendly helpful staff; open all day *(Richard Lewis)*

☆ *Salisbury* [St Martins Lane]: Floridly Victorian with plenty of atmosphere, theatrical sweeps of red velvet, huge sparkling mirrors and cut glass, glossy brass and mahogany; wide food choice from simple snacks to long-running smoked salmon lunches and salad bar (even doing Sun lunches over Christmas/New Year), well kept Tetleys-related ales, decent house wines, friendly service, no smoking back room *(BB, Kevin Blake, the Didler, Mark Stoffan, Dr M E Wilson)*

Shakespears Head [Africa House, Kingsway]: Busy London atmosphere in typical Wetherspoons with their usual ales, wines and varied food, charming staff *(Val and Alan Green)*

Sherlock Holmes [Northumberland St; aka Northumberland Arms]: Particularly fine collection of Holmes memorabilia, inc complete model of his apartment; well kept Boddingtons, Flowers IPA, Fullers London Pride and Wadworths 6X, usual furnishings, friendly staff, upstairs restaurant; busy lunchtime *(James Nunns, BB)*

Ship & Shovell [Craven Passage]: Badger Best, Champion and Tanglefoot kept well, reasonably priced food, pleasant décor inc interesting prints, mainly naval (to support a fanciful connection between this former coal-heavers' pub properly called Ship & Shovel with Sir Cloudesley Shovell the early 18th-c admiral); there's a second cosier bar across the alley *(Bob and Laura Brock, M Hickman, the Didler)*

EAST LONDON
E1

Captain Kidd [Wapping High St]: Thames views from large open-plan nautical-theme pub in renovated Docklands warehouse stripped back to beams and basics, good choice of hot

and cold food all day inc several puddings, Sam Smiths keg beers, obliging bow-tied staff, lively bustle; sports TV; chunky tables on roomy back waterside terrace *(Susan and John Douglas, R Huggins, D Irving, E McCall, T McLean)*
Dickens Inn [St Katharines Way]: Splendid position above smart docklands marina, oddly Swiss-chalet look from outside with its balconies and window boxes, interesting stripped-down bare boards, baulks and timbers interior, several floors inc big pricy restaurant extension, popular with Theakstons Old Peculier; popular with overseas visitors, seats outside *(Bob and Maggie Atherton, the Didler, LYM)*
☆ *Town of Ramsgate* [Wapping High St]: Interesting old-London Thamesside setting, with restricted but evocative river view from back floodlit terrace and wooden deck; long narrow bar with squared oak panelling, well kept ales Fullers London Pride, usual bar food inc hot baguettes; games, TV for rugby matches, unobtrusive piped music; open all day *(Ian Phillips, LYM, Richard Siebert)*
White Swan [Alie St]: Unobtrusive pub with well kept Shepherd Neame beers, reasonably priced pub lunches, young welcoming staff; maybe quiet TV *(Neil Hardwick)*

E14
☆ *Barley Mow* [Narrow St]: Steep steps down into converted dockmaster's house, clean and comfortable, with Victorian-style wallpaper over dark panelled dado, lots of sepia Whitby photographs, candles and ship's lanterns, reasonably priced food from sandwiches to hearty imaginative dishes, well kept Brains, Greene King IPA, Ind Coope Burton and Tetleys, partly panelled conservatory with stained-glass french windows; big heaters for picnic-sets on spacious if breezy terrace with great views over two Thames reaches, swing-bridge entrance to Limehouse Basin and mouth of Regents Canal, still has electric windlass used for hauling barges through; children and dogs welcome, car park with CCTV *(Ian Phillips, Susan and John Douglas)*

NORTH LONDON
N1
Albion [Thornhill Rd]: Low ceilings, snug nooks and crannies inc cosy back hideaway, some old photographs of the pub, open fires, some gas lighting, no smoking area, good range of real beers, reasonably priced straightforward food with plenty of specials, friendly service, interesting Victorian gents'; flower-decked front courtyard, big back terrace with vine canopy *(BB, Aidan Wallis, Sue Demont, Tim Barrow)*
Angel [High St, opp Angel tube stn]: Large, light and airy open-plan Wetherspoons with feel of a comfortable continental bar, busy but relaxing, friendly staff, good choice of well kept beers (some bargains), usual food; no smoking areas, silenced games machine, no music, open all day *(Richard Lewis)*
Island Queen [Noel Rd]: Welcoming character pub handy for Camden Passage antiques area, well kept Bass and Fullers London Pride and

good value wines from elegant island bar, fresh often unusual food, friendly welcome; pool, children welcome *(LYM, Tracey and Stephen Groves)*
Wenlock Arms [Wenlock Rd]: Friendly and popular open-plan pub, central bar serving 10 or so well kept changing ales from small breweries, always inc a Mild, also farm cider and perry, foreign bottled beers, snacks inc good salt beef sandwiches, coal fires, darts; piped music; open all day, modern jazz Tues, trad Fri, piano Sun lunch *(Richard Lewis)*

N6
☆ *Flask* [Highgate West Hill]: Comfortable Georgian pub, mostly modernised but still has intriguing up-and-down layout, sash-windowed bar hatch, panelling and high-backed carved settle tucked away in snug lower area (but this nice original core open only wknds and summer); usual food (limited Sun) all day inc salad bar, changing beers such as Adnams, Greene King Abbot and Old Speckled Hen and Youngs, coal fire; very busy Sat lunchtime, well behaved children allowed, close-set picnic-sets out in attractive heated front courtyard *(the Didler, Ian Phillips, LYM, Len Banister, Kevin Macey, Susan and John Douglas)*
Prince of Wales [Highgate High St]: Small well preserved local, said to be haunted, with well kept ales, decent wine, coal fires, wide range of wkdy bar food; tables on small terrace *(Dr and Mrs A K Clarke)*
Victoria [North Hill, Highgate]: Five well kept real ales, daily-changing good food, good value wines *(Lorna and Howard Lambert)*

N10
Fantail & Firkin [Muswell Hill Broadway]: Well kept ales in unusual surroundings of converted church *(anon)*

N19
Old Crown [Highgate Hill]: Old-fashioned pub with good choice of well kept real ales *(Dr and Mrs A K Clarke)*

N20
☆ *Orange Tree* [Totteridge]: Spacious pub by duckpond, good value standard food served efficiently even on busy wknds, well kept ales inc guest beers (the red wines can get a trifle over-warm), friendly service, plush décor but welcoming to children (and walkers, who leave boots in porch); tables outside, pleasant surroundings – still a village feel *(Piotr Chodzko-Zajko, Neil Ruckman, Steve Chambers, LYM)*

N21
Kings Head [The Green, nr Winchmore Hill stn]: Recently spaciously done up in olde-worlde style, log fire dividing off eating area with enjoyable food, friendly staff; plans for moving the food upstairs to a restaurant *(Mrs W Boast)*

NW1
☆ *Euston Flyer* [Euston Rd, opp British Library]:

Spacious and comfortable open-plan pub opp British Library, full Fullers range kept well, decent food inc vast baps with chips, friendly service – still quick and attentive when it's crowded; plenty of light wood, tile and wood floors, smaller more private raised areas, flying machines with Latin tags as décor, big doors open to street in warm weather; unobtrusive piped music, busy with young people evenings; open all day, cl 8.30 Sun *(Ted George, Richard Lewis)*

☆ Head of Steam [Eversholt St]: Large busy Victorian-look bar up stairs from bus terminus and overlooking it, lots of rail memorabilia, also Corgi collection, unusual model trains and buses and magazines for sale; nine interesting well kept ales (also take-away), most from little-known small breweries, monthly themed beer festivals, Weston's farm cider and perry, lots of bottled beers and vodkas, simple cheap bar meals, kind service, no smoking area, downstairs restaurant; TV, bar billiards, security-coded basement lavatories; open all day *(Richard Lewis, Catherine Pitt, the Didler, BB, Mark Stoffan, Susan and John Douglas, Sue Demont, Tim Barrow, Jonathan Smith)*

Unicorn [Camden Rd]: After a spell as the Pickled Newt, back to its busy jolly self, with several well kept real ales *(Dr and Mrs A K Clarke)*

NW3

Duke of Hamilton [New End]: Undemanding traditional family-run Fullers pub, good value, with London Pride, ESB and a seasonal beer; open all day, suntrap terrace, next to New End Theatre *(the Didler, Kevin Macey)*

☆ Old Bull & Bush [North End Way]: Attractively decorated in Victorian style, comfortable sofa and easy chairs, nooks and crannies, side library bar with lots of bookshelves and pictures and mementoes of Florrie Ford whose song made the pub famous; friendly landlord, prompt attentive service, good food bar inc tender filled bagels and good Sun specials, reasonable prices, decent wines and mulled wine, restaurant with no smoking area; good provision for families, pleasant terrace *(BB, Kevin Blake, Sarah Meyer)*

NW5

☆ Lord Palmerston [Dartmouth Park Hill]: Reliably good reasonably priced contemporary food, Courage Best and Directors and lots of lagers, interesting arty locals; well planted conservatory and prize-winning garden *(Joel Dobris)*

NW8

☆ Crockers [Aberdeen Pl]: Magnificent original Victorian interior, full of showy marble, decorated plaster and opulent woodwork; relaxing and comfortable, with well kept ales inc Bass, friendly service, decent food inc good Sun roasts; tables outside *(the Didler, LYM)*

SOUTH LONDON
SE1

Bunch of Grapes [St Thomas St]: Good atmosphere, well kept Youngs *(BKA)*

Globe [Bedale St/Green Dragon Ct]: Dark Victorian interior in heart of Borough Market, good choice of real ales *(the Didler)*

☆ Hole in the Wall [Mepham St]: Welcoming no-frills drinkers' dive in railway arch virtually underneath Waterloo Stn – rumbles and shakes when trains go over; not a place for gastronomes or comfort-lovers but well worth knowing for its dozen well kept changing ales and nearly as many lagers, also good malts and Irish whiskeys; loudish juke box, pinball and games machines; basic food all day (cl wknd afternoons) *(James Nunns, Chris Glasson, LYM)*

Kings Arms [Newcomen St]: Comfortable and elegant, with well kept Courage ales, cheap food, friendly service, some fine mid-Victorian features *(Ian Phillips, Dr and Mrs A K Clarke)*

☆ Old Thameside [Pickfords Wharf, Clink St]: Good 1980s pastiche of ancient tavern, two floors, hefty beams and timbers, pews, flagstones, candles; splendid river view upstairs and from charming waterside terrace by replica of Drake's *Golden Hind*; well kept Tetleys and Marstons Pedigree with guests such as Adnams and Fullers, friendly staff, all-day salad bar, lunchtime hot buffet; pool down spiral stairs, piped music; nr Clink Museum, open all day but cl 3 at wknds, cl bank hols *(Kevin Flack, Dave Braisted, LYM, Susan and John Douglas, Val and Alan Green, Eric Larkham)*

Pommelers Rest [Tower Bridge Rd]: Unusual for a Wetherspoons pub in having a large family room (no smoking); their usual food all day, fast efficient cheerful service, well kept Adnams, Shepherd Neame Spitfire, Theakstons Best and guest beers such as Freeminers Iron Brew *(Ian and Nita Cooper)*

Royal Oak [Tabard St]: Traditional local standing out for its full range of well kept Harveys ales; open all day *(BKA)*

Ship [Borough Rd]: Busy, long and narrow, with good atmosphere, well kept Fullers, good food, friendly staff; a local for the RPO *(the Didler)*

Wheatsheaf [Stoney St]: Borough Market local, dark-panelled and basic, with wholesome cheap lunchtime food, well kept Courage Best and four unusual guest beers such as Harts No Balls, Lidstones Session BB and Milton Electra and Cyclops, farm cider, friendly staff, interesting local prints; TV, piped music, separate games bar; will lose its top floor to railway viaduct widening; open all day, cl Sun *(Richard Lewis, the Didler, David Butterworth)*

SE10

Admiral Hardy [College Approach, Greenwich Mkt]: Large smart open-plan pub with Courage Best, Greene King Old Speckled Hen, Shepherd Neame Spitfire and a guest such as Flagship from Chatham, short choice of generous well prepared lunchtime food *(Tony and Wendy Hobden)*

Ashburnham Arms [Ashburnham Grove]: Friendly Shepherd Neame local with good pasta and other food (not Sat-Mon evenings), quiz night Tues; pleasant garden with barbecues *(the Didler)*

Richard I [Royal Hill]: Quiet and friendly no-nonsense traditional two-bar local with well kept Youngs, bare boards, panelling, good range of traditional food inc outstanding sausages, good staff, no piped music; tables in pleasant back garden with barbecues, busy summer wknds and evenings *(the Didler)*

☆ *Trafalgar* [Park Row]: Attractive and substantial 18th-c building with splendid river view, fine oak-panelled rooms inc pleasant dining room, efficient staff welcoming even when busy (can get packed Fri/Sat evenings, may have bouncer then), good atmosphere, well prepared usual food inc speciality whitebait, real ales inc Theakstons, good house wines; handy for Maritime Museum, may have jazz wknds *(Mark Stoffan, Kevin Flack, Bruce M Drew)*

SE13

Watch House [Lewisham High St]: Usual Wetherspoons style, good value special offers; disabled facilities *(Alan M Pring)*

SE16

☆ *Mayflower* [Rotherhithe St]: Friendly and cosy riverside local with black beams, high-backed settles and open fire, good views from upstairs dining room and atmospheric wooden jetty, well kept Bass and Greene King IPA and Abbot, decent bar food (not Sun night), friendly staff; children welcome, open all day; in unusual street with lovely Wren church *(the Didler, Susan and John Douglas, LYM)*

SE17

Beehive [Carter St]: Unpretentious but stylishly run bare-boards pub/bistro with charming island bar, photographs of former Prime Minister in bar, modern art in candlelit dining room, good choice of home-made food all day from sandwiches to steaks, well kept Courage Best and Directors and Fullers London Pride, remarkably wide range of wines; friendly service from smartly bow-tied staff; piped music, two TVs; tables outside *(Pete Baker, BB)*

SE19

Occasional Half [Anerley Hill]: Roomy high-ceilinged pub with reasonably priced bar food inc bargain meals for two, no smoking area till 7, several real ales such as Hancocks HB and occasional beer festivals; huge TV screen, Tues quiz night, some tables out by road, handy for Crystal Palace *(Ian and Nita Cooper)*

SE26

☆ *Dulwich Wood House* [Sydenham Hill]: Youngs pub in Victorian lodge gatehouse complete with turret, well kept ales, decent wines, attractively priced straightforward food (cooked to order so may be a wait) popular at lunchtime with local retired people, friendly service; steps up to entrance; lots of tables in big pleasant back garden with old-fashioned street lamps and barbecues *(Alan M Pring)*

SW2

Crown & Sceptre [Streatham Hill/South Circular junction]: Ornate Wetherspoons, imposing yet warm and friendly, good traditional décor, sensible-sized areas inc no smoking, well kept reasonably priced ales inc some unusual ones, good value well organised food, good service *(the Didler)*

SW8

☆ *Bell* [Wandsworth Rd, nr South Bank University]: High-ceilinged Victorian pub transformed into new open-kitchen dining pub nr South Bank University, big picture windows, modern décor but mixed old furnishings inc comfortable green sofas; good value well flavoured and attractively presented food inc Sun roasts, Courage Best and Directors, good choice of wines by glass, attentive friendly service, civilised atmosphere, daily papers – relaxed at lunchtime, quite funky in evenings, with loudish dance music, maybe piped jazz at other times; lavatories up steps *(Susan and John Douglas, BB)*

☆ *Rebatos* [South Lambeth Rd]: Lots of Spanish customers, real Spanish feel, consistently good authentic food in front tapas bar and pink-lit mirrored back restaurant – great atmosphere, frequent evening live music *(Sue Demont, Tim Barrow, Derek Thomas, BB)*

Royal Albert [St Stephens Terr, off S Lambeth Rd]: Large relaxing book-lined back room, armchairs, sofas, tables of varying heights, nice lighting, well kept ales such as Flowers IPA, Greene King Abbot and Marstons Pedigree; front bar with piped music, TV and games; quiet back terrace *(Sue Demont, Tim Barrow, BB)*

SW11

Battersea Boathouse [Groveside Ct, Lombard Rd]: Stylish, airy and attractive riverside bar and restaurant with comfortable mix of furnishings from settees and easy chairs to intimate or more partyish dining tables, Adnams and maybe other real ales such as Fullers London Pride and Youngs, wide choice of spirits and of good wines by the glass, small no smoking area, daily papers and board games; has had good food from sandwiches to interesting bistro dishes with some emphasis on fish, but no news yet on changed management earlier this year; maybe soft piped jazz; big waterside terrace opp Chelsea Harbour, open all day wknd *(Susan and John Douglas)*

Eagle [Chatham Rd]: Attractive and friendly old backstreet pub, real ales such as Flowers IPA, Fullers London Pride and Tetleys, helpful landlord; peaceful and relaxed unless rugby on big-screen TV, pub dog; paved back garden and seats in front *(Sue Demont, Tim Barrow, Ian Phillips)*

Prince Albert [Albert Bridge Rd]: Large lavishly decorated Victorian pub opp Battersea Park;

lively and friendly, with real ales and games *(A J Clark)*

SW15

Coat & Badge [Lacy Rd]: Large rustic-effect pine bar, well kept real ales, maybe a wheat beer on tap, interesting wines, popular food, buoyant atmosphere *(Guy Vowles)*
Halfway House [Priests Bridge]: Friendly local named for its position between what used to be the Richmond market gardens and the former Covent Garden market they served; well kept Flowers Original tapped from the cask, sensibly priced food all day all week, helpful staff; Tues quiz night, Thurs live bands; handy for Beverley Brook trail *(Jenny and Brian Seller)*

SW17

Leather Bottle [Garratt Lane]: Partly panelled split-level Youngs pub, their full beer range kept well, good wine choice, blackboard food, friendly young staff; lots of picnic-sets in garden *(LM)*

SW18

Old Sergeant [Garratt Lane]: Unspoilt local with long-serving landlord, well kept Youngs Bitter, Special and seasonal beers, wkdy lunches; open all day *(the Didler)*

SW19

Rose & Crown [Wimbledon High St]: Comfortably modernised old local with well kept Youngs Bitter and Special, friendly service, decent generous food from back servery at sensible prices, open fires, set of Hogarth's proverb engravings, roomy U-shaped bar with open fire and green plush seats in alcoves; conservatory, tables in former coachyard *(LYM, MRSM)*

WEST LONDON
SW6

Duke of Cumberland [New Kings Rd, Parsons Green]: Huge lavishly restored Edwardian pub, attractive decorative tiles and interesting panel fleshing out his life; well kept Youngs Bitter and Special, cheerful at wknd lunchtimes, relaxed for wkdy lunchtime food (no food Fri-Sun evenings) *(BB, the Didler)*
Pharaoh & Firkin [Fulham High St]: Huge pub with Egyptian theme, welcoming staff, well kept beer; bustling young atmosphere evenings *(Dr and Mrs A K Clarke)*
Salisbury [Sherbrooke Rd/Dawes Rd]: Made over as trendily simple two-level bar with bare boards, sofas and bays of green plush banquettes, Fullers London Pride and Charles Wells Bombardier, bank of unobtrusive pop videos above bar; separate cocktail bar and upmarket dark red restaurant with good imaginative modern cooking esp fish, exemplary service; one of a very small chain of trendy places which now also part-owns the Groucho Club *(Susan and John Douglas)*

W4

☆ *City Barge* [Strand on the Green]: Small panelled riverside bars in picturesque partly 15th-c pub (this original part reserved for diners lunchtime), also airy newer back part done out with maritime signs and bird prints; usual bar food (not Sun) inc fish and chips worth waiting for, well kept Courage Directors and Wadworths 6X, back conservatory, winter fires, some tables on towpath – lovely spot to watch sun set over Kew Bridge *(LYM)*

W6

☆ *Brook Green* [Shepherds Bush Rd]: Large Victorian Youngs pub, comfortably up-to-date seating but much of its original character kept in 1999 renovations inc noble high ceilings, ornate plaster, chandeliers, coal fire; good choice of reasonably priced enjoyable home-made food with proper veg, well kept ales, friendly atmosphere, good mix of customers; 15 bedrooms *(Pete Baker, Patrick Renouf)*
Latymers [Hammersmith Rd]: Bustling café/bar with lots of steel and glass, well kept Fullers ales, Thai food *(Chris Glasson)*
☆ *Stonemasons Arms* [Cambridge Grove]: Excellent food in trendy gastropub, main courses such as fried celery-crushed ostrich fillet, confit of duck with potato, leek and nutmeg gratin, and stuffed aubergine with couscous, all around £10 mark; plain décor, lots of modern art, open kitchen, ceiling fans; mostly young customers evenings, loudish piped music *(Susan and John Douglas, BB)*
☆ *Thatched House* [Dalling Rd]: Youngs dining pub with their full beer range, and emphasis on particularly good modern food – though local drinkers still come; stripped pine, modern art, big armchairs, good wine list, welcoming staff and regulars, conservatory; no music; open all day wknds *(Susan and John Douglas, Jestyn Thirkell-White)*

W7

Fox [Green Lane]: Friendly recently redecorated open-plan 19th-c pub in quiet cul de sac nr Grand Union Canal, well kept real ales, good value wholesome food from sandwiches to home-made hot dishes inc Sun roasts, dining area, panelling and stained glass one end, wildlife pictures and big fish tank, farm tools hung from ceiling; darts end, garden, occasional wknd barbecues, towpath walks *(Colin and Peggy Wilshire, Ian Phillips, LM)*

W8

☆ *Britannia* [Allen St, off Kensington High St]: Peaceful and very friendly two-bar local little changed since the 60s, debonair and relaxed, with good value fresh home-cooked lunches, well kept Youngs, helpful long-serving landlady, no music; attractive indoor back 'garden' (no smoking at lunchtime), friendly dog and cat; open all day *(Giles Francis, the Didler)*

W9

Truscott Arms [55 Shirland Rd]: Pleasant local, well kept changing ales from splendid row of 10 handpumps, jazz nights *(the Didler)*
☆ *Warrington* [Warrington Cres]: Handsome and

comfortable Victorian gin palace with decorative woodwork and tiles, luscious mirrors, arches and alcoves (said once to have been a brothel – hence the murals); thriving friendly bustle, well kept full Fullers range with a guest such as Brakspears, small coal fire, imposing staircase up to good Thai restaurant, lunchtime Thai bar food too; good tables on big back terrace, nr Little Venice *(the Didler, Alec Hamilton)*

W14

Albion [Hammersmith Rd]: Popular corner pub with particularly well kept Courage Directors, Theakstons Best and guest beers such as Lees Scorcher and Nethergate Wild Fox, real fire, prints, panelling and beams, spiral stairs to comfortable upper lounge, good food choice, friendly staff; open all day *(Richard Lewis)*
Britannia Tap [Warwick Rd]: Small narrow Youngs pub, kept well (as are the beers), with welcoming landlord, sensible food, Sun bar nibbles *(the Didler)*
Frigate & Firkin [Blythe Rd, Olympia]: Lots of wood, brewing memorabilia, bare boards, good choice of reasonably priced food, friendly staff, well kept Ind Coope Burton, Tetleys and guest beers; open all day, picnic-sets by pavement, maybe live music *(Richard Lewis)*
Old Parrs Head [Blythe Rd]: Attractively restored Victorian façade, tidy and cosy inside, with lots of memorabilia, good Thai food, little candlelit back dining room *(John Brightley, Susan and John Douglas)*
Warwick Arms [Warwick Rd]: Early 19th-c, with lots of old woodwork, comfortable atmosphere, friendly regulars (some playing darts or bridge), good service, well kept Fullers beers from elegant Wedgwood handpumps, limited tasty food (not Sun evening), sensible prices, no piped music; open all day, tables outside, handy for Earls Court and Olympia *(the Didler)*

OUTER LONDON
BARNET [TQ2496]
☆ *King William IV* [Hadley Highstone, towards Potters Bar]: Snug well tended local doing well under friendly new management, old-fashioned inside and out, with good atmosphere, nooks and corners, some antique Wedgwood plates over fireplaces (real fires), good home-made lunchtime food inc good fresh fish Fri (back restaurant), well kept ales such as Hook Norton and Tetleys; flower-framed front terrace *(Kevin Macey, David and Ruth Shillitoe)*
☆ *Olde Mitre* [High St]: Small early 17th-c local (remains of a famous coaching inn), bay windows in low-ceilinged panelled front bar with fruit machines, three-quarter panelled back area on two slightly different levels, bare boards, lots of dark wood, dark floral wallpaper, open fire, pleasant atmosphere, friendly service, well kept Tetleys and changing guests such as Adnams and Marstons Pedigree; open all day *(Catherine Pitt, LYM)*
Olde Monken Holt [High St]: Well run, with good home-made food all day, well kept

Courage Best and Directors, friendly landlord, pleasing olde-worlde interior; nice setting, handy for Hadley Wood Common *(Kevin Macey)*

BIGGIN HILL [TQ4159]
☆ *Old Jail* [Jail Lane]: Ancient building which was a mainstay for Battle of Britain RAF pilots, with lots of RAF pictures and plates on walls, beams, some painted brickwork, oak floorboards, two large bar areas, one with a snug, friendly service, welcoming atmosphere, well kept Bass, Fullers London Pride, Greene King IPA, Harveys and a guest such as Charles Wells Bombardier, good value quickly served food cooked by the landlord; attractive garden *(Mr and Mrs D D Collins, M and B Writer, B, M and P Kendall, LM)*

BRENTFORD [TQ1777]
Brewery Tap [Catherine Wheel Rd]: Panelled local with three neatly kept rooms, good range of well kept Fullers beers, good value lunchtime blackboard specials, welcoming landlord and staff; open all day *(LM)*

BROMLEY [TQ4167]
Five Bells [Bromley Common]: Comfortable and relaxing, chatty atmosphere (locals and students), wide choice of popular lunchtime food inc notable home-made steak pie, real ale *(Alan M Pring)*

CARSHALTON [TQ2864]
Fox & Hounds [High St]: Old timbered and flagstoned pub with upper part projecting on pillars, well kept changing ales such as Benskins, Fullers London Pride, Greene King Old Speckled Hen, Ind Coope Burton, Marstons Pedigree and Ridleys Five Rings, straightforward food; pool *(Ian Phillips)*
Racehorse [West St]: Proper two-bar pub with part of lounge laid for dining, well kept Courage Best and Directors and Greene King IPA, Abbot and Ruddles, good chunky sandwiches and wide choice of honest food esp fish, good quick service, friendly atmosphere, welcome absence of false airs and graces *(Ian Phillips, Jenny and Brian Seller)*

CHEAM [TQ2463]
Harrow [High St]: Recently reopened and already popular for good value food inc bargain steaks, pleasant service; piped music not too loud *(DWAJ)*

CHELSFIELD [TQ4963]
☆ *Bo-Peep* [Hewitts Rd]: Traditional pub dating from 16th c, magnificent Tudor fireplace, lots of brasses, no smoking sheep-theme beamed dining room, wide choice of popular food from good soup and sandwiches up, Courage and Tetleys, friendly service; lots of tables outside *(A E Brace, B, M and P Kendall, Alan M Pring)*

CHESSINGTON [TQ1763]
☆ *North Star* [Hook Rd (A243 N of M25 junction 9)]: Busy Bass family dining pub,

popular with older people wkdy lunchtime for good value food from sandwiches and baked potatoes to bargain steak or mixed grill; several areas, good log fire, good friendly service and atmosphere; quiet piped music *(DWAJ)*

CHISLEHURST [TQ4469]

Crown [School Rd]: Decent food inc lots of well prepared fish in several dining areas, broad range of customers, well kept Shepherd Neame beers; tables out overlooking green *(B, M and P Kendall)*

COCKFOSTERS [TQ2796]

Cock & Dragon [Chalk Lane/Games Rd]: Roomy, with mix of tables, pews and leather chesterfields, usual bar food and good Thai dishes served quickly, good range of wines and malt whiskies, restaurant, no piped music; handy for Trent country park *(Amanda Eames, Kevin Macey)*

COWLEY [TQ0582]

Paddington Packet Boat [High Rd/Packet Boat Lane]: Large two-bar Fullers pub nr Grand Union Canal, old but much modernised, with Chiswick, London Pride and ESB, wide choice of decent food, good staff; pleasant terrace *(Tony Hobden)*

CROYDON [TQ3365]

☆ *Princess Royal* [Longley Rd]: A Croydon oasis, like a small sociable country pub, with particularly well kept Greene King IPA, Abbot, Dark Mild and a seasonal or guest ale, good home-cooked food throughout opening hours, log fire; piped music *(Iain Gordon)*

CUDHAM [TQ4459]

Blacksmiths Arms [Cudham Lane S]: Decent generous reasonably priced food from sandwiches and baguettes up, well kept Courage Best and Directors and Shepherd Neame Spitfire, good coffee, quick friendly service and bar staff; nearly always busy yet plenty of tables, with no smoking area, cheerfully well worn cottagey atmosphere, soft lighting, blazing log fires, low ceiling; big garden, pretty window boxes, handy for good walks *(LM, B J Harding, B, M and P Kendall)*

DOWNE [TQ4464]

George & Dragon [High St]: Open-plan beamed pub popular with families, wide choice of good value blackboard food from sandwiches and baked potatoes to Sun lunch *(Alan M Pring)*

HAMPTON [TQ1370]

Dukes Head [High St]: Friendly open-plan local with good home-made bar lunches from fresh sandwiches up (not Sun), and interesting full meals evenings (not Sun) and Sun lunchtime, inc popular Weds steak night, well kept Courage Best, Gales HSB, John Smiths and a guest such as Wadworths 6X, small dining room; dogs welcome subject to approval of

resident golden retrievers Ben and Tessa, small pleasant terrace with good value barbecues *(Gordon Prince)*

HAMPTON COURT [TQ1668]

Kings Arms [Hampton Court Rd, by Lion Gate]: Oak panels and beams, stripped-brick lounge with bric-a-brac and open fire one end, public bar the other, pleasant relaxed atmosphere, well kept if not cheap Badger beers, good choice of wines by the glass, usual food, efficient service; piped music may obtrude; children welcome, open all day, picnic-sets on hedged front terrace with camellias in tubs *(Susan and John Douglas, Martin and Karen Wake, Simon Collett-Jones, John Crafts, LYM)*

HAREFIELD [TQ0590]

Coy Carp [Copperhill Lane]: Former Fisheries Inn recently well done out in olde-worlde Vintage Inn style, their usual well cooked food all day, good range of wines, Bass beers; lovely spot by Grand Union Canal *(D P and J A Sweeney)*

HARLINGTON [TQ0878]

White Hart [High Street S]: Large carefully redesigned two-bar Fullers dining pub, good bustling atmosphere, alcoves with good solid furniture, enjoyable interesting food with more sophisticated evening choice (service may slow when very busy), well kept London Pride and ESB; piped music *(Dr and Mrs A K Clarke, Tom Evans)*

HARROW [TQ1586]

Castle [West St]: Well worn in Fullers local in picturesque part, fine range of their ales, vast choice of good cheap food from generous sandwiches and starters to steaks, daily papers, several rooms inc classic lively traditional bar and big sedate back lounge with log-effect fires, wall seats, variety of prints; steep steps to street, nice garden *(Ian Phillips, Dr and Mrs A K Clarke)*

ILFORD [TQ4386]

Great Spoon of Ilford [Cranbrook Rd]: Friendly and relaxing Wetherspoons, real ales such as Courage Directors, Fullers London Pride and Hop Back Summer Lightning, good mix of ages; food all day *(Robert Lester)*
Red House [Redbridge Lane E; TQ4188]: Large multi-level Beefeater steak house with Adnams and Boddingtons, enjoyable food, waterfall and coloured lights; adjoining Travelodge *(Robert Lester)*

ISLEWORTH [TQ1675]

London Apprentice [Church St]: Large Thames-side Chef & Brewer furnished with character and worth knowing for its position and attractive waterside terrace; bar food, upstairs restaurant (open all Sun afternoon), well kept Scottish Courage beers; children welcome, open all day; popular wknds with rugby fans *(LYM, W W Burke, Chris Glasson)*

KENLEY [TQ3259]

☆ *Wattenden Arms* [Old Lodge Lane; left (coming from London) off A23 by Reedham Stn, then keep on]: Popular dark-panelled traditional 18th-c country local nr glider aerodrome, well kept Bass, Hancocks HB and Fullers London Pride, good value straightforward lunchtime food from good sandwiches and steak sandwiches up, friendly prompt service, lots of interesting patriotic and World War II memorabilia inc RAF photographs; one end can get smoky; a welcome for walkers, picnic-sets on small side lawn *(LM, LYM)*

KESTON [TQ4164]

Greyhound [Commonside]: Friendly service, decent food, trendily minimalist décor and furnishings; pleasant garden *(Alan M Pring)*

KINGSTON [TQ1869]

Gazebo [Riverside Walk/Kings Passage; alley off Thames St by Superdrug – or from Kingston Bridge]: Revamped to appeal to younger customers, with trendy food; worth knowing for terrific river view upstairs, with lots of seats on balcony and terrace *(Anon)*

NORWOOD GREEN [TQ1379]

☆ *Plough* [Tentelow Lane (A4127)]: Attractive old-fashioned low-beamed décor, cheerful villagey feel in cosy main bar and two rooms off inc family room; well kept Fullers ales inc Chiswick, welcoming efficient service, decent cheap lunchtime food (no roasts on Sun), flame-effect gas fire; can get crowded wknds; disabled facilities, occasional barbecues in lovely garden with play area, even a bowling green dating from 14th c, open all day, quite handy for Osterley Park *(Jenny and Brian Seller)*

PINNER [TQ1289]

Queens Head [High St]: Traditional pub dating from 16th c, welcoming bustle, interesting décor, good value fresh food inc sandwiches, well kept changing ales such as Marstons Pedigree and Youngs Special, friendly staff and landlord, no music or machines; useful car park *(Antony Pace, Mayur Shah)*

PONDERS END [TQ3695]

Navigation [Wharf Rd]: Beefeater food pub in converted 1920s pumping station, access through industrial estate but in fields by canal; usual food, Boddingtons, Marstons Pedigree and Wadworths 6X, waterside picnic-sets, play area *(Ian Phillips)*

PURLEY [TQ3161]

Foxley Hatch [Russell Hill Rd]: Wetherspoons conversion, warmly friendly local atmosphere, Theakstons and other well kept ales inc at least two changing guests, decent food all day, low prices, good staff, no music, no smoking area, disabled facilities *(Jim Bush, David Phipps)*

RICHMOND [TQ1874]

Britannia [Brewers Lane]: Homely, cosy and relaxed local attracting more mature regulars than some other Richmond pubs, welcoming efficient staff, good value food esp generous lunchtime sandwiches; nice upstairs room *(Mayur Shah, Bill and Vera Burton)*

Orange Tree [Kew Rd]: Newly refurbished, with fine plasterwork, a more roomy and airy feel than previously, well kept Youngs from central bar, good food, friendly service, sports TV; open all day, pleasant tables outside *(Mayur Shah, LYM)*

SELSDON [TQ3562]

Sir Julian Huxley [Addington Rd]: New Wetherspoons shop conversion, good choice of cheap real ales and other special drinks offers, usual reasonably priced food all day *(Jim Bush)*

SURBITON [TQ1867]

Lamb [Brighton Rd]: Popular and friendly if hardly smart, particularly well kept beers inc maybe an interesting guest (landlord is a real ale enthusiast), food, darts, cribbage, garden *(Tim Hurrell)*

Wagon & Horses [Surbiton Hill Rd]: Roomy traditional family local with four bar areas, friendly landlord and staff inc full-time pot-boy, well kept Youngs and decent wine by the glass, no piped music, good Thai food in mezzanine eating area leading to grapevine terrace *(Tom and Ruth Rees)*

SUTTON [TQ2562]

Belmont [Brighton Rd, Belmont]: Fairly modern, with comfortable bar, interesting décor, well kept Fullers London Pride, reasonably priced carvery/restaurant, good service; handy for Banstead Heath walks *(Jenny and Brian Seller)*

TEDDINGTON [TQ1671]

Tide End Cottage [Broom Rd/Ferry Rd, nr bridge at Teddington Lock]: Cosy and friendly low-ceilinged pub in Victorian cottage terrace, lots of river, fishing and rowing memorabilia and photographs in two little rooms united by big log-effect gas fire; good reasonably priced straightforward bar food from sandwiches and café-type meals to huge Sun roasts served 12-5 (can get busy then), well kept Greene King IPA; sports TV in part-tented back bar; no river view, but some tables on back terrace *(LM, Dr and Mrs A Hepburn)*

TWICKENHAM [TQ1473]

Turks Head [Winchester Rd, St Margarets; behind roundabout on A316]: Recently refurbished Fullers pub, extended in same panelled style, new landlord and staff and some concentration on food (not cheap), well kept ales; manic on rugby days; stand-up comics Mon/Sat in hall behind *(LM, BB)*

UXBRIDGE [TQ0584]

☆ *Load of Hay* [Villier St, off Cleveland Rd opp Brunel University]: Small local popular for wide choice of good value freshly made generous food, good long-serving landlady, well kept interesting changing beers, thoughtful choice of teas, impressive fireplace in no smoking back part used by diners, more public-bar atmosphere nearer serving bar, another separate bar, local paintings; dogs welcome, flower-filled back garden, covered area with mature vine *(Anthony Longden)*

WALLINGTON [TQ2863]
Dukes Head [Manor Rd]: Reworked Youngs pub/hotel, bars divided into several friendly rooms, log fire, decent food from sandwiches to chargrills, Bitter and Special; air-conditioned bedrooms, views over pleasant green *(Ian Phillips)*

WOODFORD GREEN [TQ4091]
☆ *Three Jolly Wheelers* [Chigwell Rd (A113)]: Large, friendly and comfortable Vintage Inn, attractively done out in old-world style with individual furnishings and old oak, Bass and other ales, good food from sandwiches to steaks all day in bar and restaurant, no smoking area, newspapers framed in gents'; large garden, masses of hanging baskets *(Neil Spink, Joy and Colin Rorke)*

Scotland

The five Scottish places which have been in every edition of the Guide throughout its first 20 years typify something particular to Scotland. All are more or less smart hotels, doubling in a typically Scottish way as good places to drop in for a drink or a pub meal, and in that sense performing the role that in England or Wales would normally be taken by a pub. They are the Loch Melfort Hotel in its lovely spot by the sea at Arduaine (new licensees this year), the Riverside Inn at Canonbie (just taken over from the Phillipses, who had been running it since the Guide started), the smart Crinan Hotel in its enviable position where the Crinan Canal joins the sea (run by Nicolas Ryan throughout the time we have known it; good food), Burts Hotel in Melrose (Graham and Anne Henderson, now helped by their children, have been in charge there for all these years; it's a fine all-rounder), and the Killiecrankie Hotel near Pitlochry (smart yet relaxed, with imaginative food; lovely grounds and scenery). The towns and cities are the best place to find more thorough-going pubs in Scotland; our six Edinburgh entries are fine examples, with the classic Abbotsford doing particularly well these days; the Prince of Wales in Aberdeen has very good beers and bargain food; Glasgow has plenty of lively pub action in interesting buildings; the neat and attractive Fishermans Tavern in Broughty Ferry is doing well all round; the Fox & Hounds in Houston brews its own good beers; the bustling Four Marys in Linlithgow is great for real ales, but has plenty of interest too (and bargain food); the Oban Inn in Oban (back in these pages after a break) is on fine fettle as a good-natured harbourside local; the Ferry Boat in Ullapool is another fine harbour pub, with good beers, a nice bar, and comfortable bedrooms. For food, the main excitement is generally out in the country or in the smaller settlements, where more and more Scottish pubs and inns are taking real trouble to cook the good local fish and meats with imagination and flair. Excellent examples are the beautifully placed Applecross Inn at Applecross (on particularly good form, with a fine new chef, and a lot of careful improvements to the inn itself), the Byre at Brig o' Turk, the Cawdor Tavern at Cawdor (masses of interesting whiskies in this nice pub, too), the Drovers at East Linton, the Seafood Restaurant and Bar in St Monance, the comfortable and informally stylish Wheatsheaf at Swinton (a particular favourite), and the Morefield Motel on the edge of Ullapool (what an unlikely place in which to find such good fish and seafood). Despite this hot competition, the consistent excellence of the Wheatsheaf at Swinton earns it our title of Scotland Dining Pub of the Year. Other pubs on fine form here this year are the Galley of Lorne at Ardfern (nice new licensees), the cottagey Badachro Inn at Badachro (a fine all-rounder in a glorious waterside spot), the quirkily ultra-Scottish Inverarnan Inn at Inverarnan, the Old Inn at Gairloch (a new entry to the Guide, newish owners doing a handsome range of beers and enjoyable food), the nicely placed Swan at Kingholm Quay (another new entry), the cosy Crown by Portpatrick's harbour, another very enjoyable all-rounder, and the Lion & Unicorn at Thornhill (nice bar meals, plenty of character). In the Lucky Dip section at the end of the chapter, we have listed pubs under their postal counties (not always identical to the new administrative areas). Current notables in this section are, in Aberdeenshire, the Boat at Aboyne; in Argyll, the Bridge of Orchy Hotel; in Inverness-shire, the Old Forge at Inverie and Royal in Kingussie; in Morayshire, the Crown & Anchor in Findhorn; in Perthshire, the Loch Tummel Inn; in Roxburghshire, the Border at Kirk Yetholm; and on the Islands, the Ardvasar Hotel and Stein Inn on Skye, and the Polochar Inn on South Uist. Drinks prices in Scotland are rather above typical English levels. Places where we found beer much cheaper than the Scottish average were the Counting House in Glasgow, Old Inn at Gairloch, and Fishermans Tavern in Broughty Ferry.

ABERDEEN NJ9305 Map 11
Prince of Wales 🍺 £
7 St Nicholas Lane

You're sure to receive a cheering welcome at this old tavern, set at the very heart of the city's shopping centre, with Union Street almost literally overhead. The cosy flagstoned area in the middle of the pub makes the city's longest bar counter, and it's a good job too; some lunchtimes there's standing room only, with a real mix of locals and visitors creating a friendly bustling feel. It's furnished with pews and other wooden furniture in screened booths, while a smarter main lounge has some panelling and a fruit machine. A fine range of particularly well kept beers includes Bass, Caledonian 80/-, Inveralmond, Isle of Skye, Theakstons Old Peculier and guests such as a beer named for the pub, other beers from Inveralmond, and maybe Oakham JHB or Orkney Dark Island on handpump or tall fount air pressure; good choice of malt whiskies. Popular and generously served home-made lunchtime food includes lentil soup (£1.60), filled baguettes (from £3), baked potatoes (£3.50), macaroni cheese (£4), home-made steak and ale pie (£4.40), and deep-fried breaded haddock (£4.60); friendly staff. On Sunday evening fiddlers provide traditional music. *(Recommended by Christine and Neil Townend, M Dean, the Didler)*

Free house ~ Licensees Peter and Anne Birnie ~ Real ale ~ Bar food (lunchtime only (may start doing evening)) ~ (01224) 640597 ~ Children in eating area of bar ~ Folk music Sun evening ~ Open 11-12; 12.30-11 Sun

APPLECROSS NG7144 Map 11
Applecross Inn 🍽
Off A896 S of Shieldaig

The drive to this welcoming inn over the pass of the cattle (Beallach na Ba) is one of the highest in Britain, and a truly exhilarating experience. The alternative route, along the single-track lane winding round the coast from just south of Shieldaig, has equally glorious sea loch and then sea views nearly all the way. More popular than you might expect from the loneliness of the setting, you'll usually find it has a number of cheerful locals in the newly refurbished bar with its woodburning stove, newly exposed stone walls, and upholstered pine furnishings on the stone floor; there's also a new no smoking dining area with lavatories for the disabled and with baby changing facilities. Usually available all day, the very good, enjoyable bar food under the new chef might include sandwiches, rocket, sweet chilli and parmesan or slow roasted tomato and onion soups (£2.25), haggis flambed in Drambuie, topped with cream (£3.95), local prawns in hot garlic butter or home-made macaroni cheese (£5.95), squat lobster thai curry or fresh haddock in crispy batter with home-made tartare sauce (£6.95), king scallops in garlic butter with lemon and crispy bacon (£8.95), lots of daily specials, and home-made puddings such as vanilla panna cotta with red berry compote or chocolate and rosemary mousse (£2.95). You must book for the no smoking restaurant. Pool (winter only), TV, and juke box (unless there are musicians in the pub); a good choice of around 50 malt whiskies, and efficient, welcoming service. There's a nice garden by the shore with tables. The bedrooms have been refurbished this year and all have a sea view; marvellous breakfasts. *(Recommended by Dr D E Granger, Lorna Baxter, John Winstanley, Peter F Marshall, Simon Chell, Olive and Ray Hebson, Michael Buchanan, Mark and Diane Grist, Ian Jones, Joan Thorpe)*

Free house ~ Licensee Judith Fish ~ Bar food (12-9; not 25 Dec or 1 Jan) ~ Restaurant ~ (01520) 744262 ~ Children welcome until 8.30pm ~ Traditional ceilidhs Fri evening ~ Open 11-12(11.30 Sat); 12.30-11 Sun; closed 1 Jan ~ Bedrooms: £25/£50(£60B)

ARDFERN NM8004 Map 11
Galley of Lorne
B8002; village and inn signposted off A816 Lochgilphead—Oban

Seats on the sheltered terrace and in the cosy main bar here share marvellously peaceful views of the sea, loch, and yacht anchorage. Ideally placed across from Loch Craignish and imbued with a relaxing atmosphere, it has a log fire, old highland dress prints and other pictures, big navigation lamps by the bar counter, an unfussy assortment of furniture, including little winged settles and upholstered window seats on its lino tiles, and a good mix of customers. Under the friendly new licensee, good bar food now includes home-made soup (£2.25; soup and a sandwich £4.50), sandwiches with home-made bread (from £2.50), haggis with whisky and cream (£3.65), ploughman's (from £4.95), spicy tagliatelle with basil and white wine (£5.95), home-made steak in Guinness pie or moules marinières (£6.50), fresh daily fish dishes like whole lemon sole or plaice (from around £7.95), steaks (from £11), and puddings such as cloutie dumpling (£2.50); children's menu (£1.95), and a spacious restaurant (which they may make no smoking). Quite a few malt whiskies, and they are considering offering real ales; darts, pool, dominoes, fruit machine, TV and piped music. *(Recommended by Mr and Mrs R M Macnaughton, Mrs K Charnley, Mike and Sue Loseby, Dr G E Martin)*

Free house ~ Licensee John Dobbie ~ Bar food (12-2, 6.30-8.30) ~ Restaurant ~ (01852) 500284 ~ Children welcome ~ Open 11-2.30, 5-12; 11-12 Sat; 11-11 Sun; closed 25 Dec ~ Bedrooms: £45B/£70B

ARDUAINE NM7910 Map 11
Loch Melfort Hotel 🛏
On A816 S of Oban and overlooking Asknish Bay

Wooden seats on the front terrace of this welcoming cream-washed Edwardian hotel have a magnificent view over the wilderness of the loch and its islands; a pair of powerful marine glasses allow you to search for birds and seals on the islets and the coasts of the bigger islands beyond. The airy, modern Skerry bar and bistro has been refurbished by the new licensees, and now has a nautical theme with charts, sailing photographs and so forth on the walls; big picture windows look out over the small rocky outcrops from which the room takes its name. Enjoyable food includes soup (£2), sandwiches, toasties or filled baguettes or ciabatta (from £2.75), smoked mackerel pâté (£3.75), filled baked potatoes (from £3.75), ploughman's (£5.50), pasta with tomato, basil, mushrooms, spinach and crème fraîche or vegetable ratatouille (£5.75), Morecambe Bay potted shrimps (£5.95), cutlets of Speyside lamb with rosemary and caper wine gravy (£8.50), Aberdeen Angus steak (£12.50), daily specials, puddings (£3), and children's menu (£3.50). The main restaurant is no smoking, and there's a good wine list and choice of malt whiskies. The comfortable bedrooms also enjoy sea views, and breakfasts are good. Passing yachtsmen are welcome to use the mooring and drying facilities, and hot showers. It's a short stroll from the hotel through grass and wild flowers to the rocky foreshore, where the friendly licensees keep their own lobster pots and nets. From late April to early June the walks through the neighbouring Arduaine woodland gardens are lovely. More reports please. *(Recommended by Lorna Baxter, John Winstanley, Peter F Marshall)*

Free house ~ Licensees Nigel and Kyle Schofield ~ Bar food (12-2.30, 6-9) ~ Restaurant ~ (01852) 200233 ~ Children welcome ~ Local live music 1st Fri of month during summer ~ Open 10.30-11(11.30 Sat) ~ Bedrooms: /£118B

BADACHRO NG7773 Map 11

Badachro Inn

2½ miles S of Gairloch village turn off A832 on to B8056, then after another 3¼ miles turn right in Badachro to the quay and inn

The superb waterside setting is enough in itself to take you out of your way, but there's a lot more here to reward you for the detour. The black and white painted cottagey inn has a long unpretentious bar with a relaxing local atmosphere, and the buzz of conversation you'd expect – fishing and boats; gentle eavesdropping suggests that some of the yachtsmen have been calling in here annually for decades. There are some interesting photographs and collages on the walls, and they may put out daily papers. There's a quieter dining area on the left, with a couple of big tables by the huge log fire. Good enjoyable bar food includes home-made soup (£2.35), filled baked potatoes (from £3), home-made pâté (£3.25), sandwiches (from £3.40), locally smoked salmon or herring fillets in four marinades (£4.95), ploughman's (£5.75), haggis, neeps and tatties (£5.95), home-made local salmon and haddock fishcakes with lemon mayonnaise (£6.95), locally caught seafood in a pastry case (£7.15), wild highland venison casserole (£7.25), chicken wrapped in bacon with a wholegrain mustard sauce (£7.45), fresh highland salmon (£8.25), and sirloin steak with a red wine and pepper sauce (£10.95). Well kept changing ales such as Courage Directors, and Isle of Skye Red Cuillin and Black Cuillin on handpump, three dozen whiskies, and a short changing wine list; piped music and dominoes. Casper the pub spaniel is friendly, and other dogs are welcome. There are sturdy tables on a terrace outside the bar which virtually overhangs the water, with more on the attractively planted lochside lawn, and they have homely bedrooms (with a good breakfast). The bay is very sheltered, virtually landlocked by Eilean Horrisdale just opposite. This is a tiny village, and the quiet road comes to a dead end a few miles further on at the lovely Redpoint beach. *(Recommended by Michael Buchanan, Alistair L Taylor, David Wallington)*

Free house ~ Licensee Martin Pearson ~ Real ale ~ Bar food (12-3, 6-9) ~ (01445) 741255 ~ Well behaved children welcome ~ Spontaneous traditional folk music ~ Open 12-12(11.30 Sat); 12.30-11.30 Sun; closed Sun evening at 5 in winter

BRIG O' TURK NN5306 Map 11

Byre 🍽

A821 Callander—Trossachs, just outside village

Set in a lovely secluded spot on the edge of a network of forest and lochside tracks in the Queen Elizabeth Forest Park, this carefully converted pub (its name means cowshed) is ideally situated for walking, cycling, and fishing. Inside, the beamed bar is cosy and spotless, with paintings and old photographs of the area, some decorative plates, comfortable brass-studded black dining chairs, an open fire, and rugs on the stone and composition floor. Good, enjoyable, interesting bar food includes french onion soup with thyme, garlic and parmesan shavings (£2.95; cullen skink £3.25), coarse game terrine on warm brioche and orange chutney (£3.25), steamed Shetland mussels with parsley, shallots, garlic and white wine (£4.25), toulouse sausages on spring onion mash and red wine jus (£7.95), chicken marinated with spices and fried with peppers, tomatoes and oregano on tagliatelle (£8.50), cod fillet with a mint and chilli crust on couscous (£8.95), game pie or slow roasted pork hock on pinto beans, grilled chorizo and plum tomato sauce (£9.50), and puddings such as pear and ginger strudel or pecan pie (from £2.95); friendly, helpful service. The more elaborate menu in the no smoking restaurant is popular in the evenings – it's worth booking then. Well kept Heather Fraoch Heather Ale on handpump, and several malt whiskies; traditional Scottish piped music. There are tables under parasols outside. *(Recommended by Guy Vowles, Susan and John Douglas, D P Brown)*

Free house ~ Licensees Jean-Francois and Anne Meder ~ Real ale ~ Bar food (12-2, 6-9) ~ Restaurant ~ (01877) 376292 ~ Children in eating area of bar and restaurant ~ Open 12-3, 6-11(12 Fri and Sat); 12-11 Sun; closed Mon

BROUGHTY FERRY NO4630 Map 11

Fishermans Tavern ◖ £ 🛏

12 Fort St; turning off shore road

Just yards from the seafront, where there are good views of the two long, low Tay bridges, this friendly town pub looks most attractive from the outside, and has extended into the adjacent cottages. There's a welcoming atmosphere and a cheery bustle of customers, kept happy by the inviting range of well kept real ales which can change every day, but typically includes Belhaven 80/-, Boddingtons, Caledonian 80/- and Deuchars IPA, and guests like Cotleigh Tawny and Fullers London Pride on handpump or tall fount air pressure. There's also a good choice of malt whiskies, some local country wines, and a draught wheat beer. The little brown carpeted snug on the right with its nautical tables, light pink soft fabric seating, basket-weave wall panels and beige lamps is the more lively bar, and on the left is a secluded lounge area with an open coal fire. The carpeted back bar (popular with diners) has a Victorian fireplace; dominoes and fruit machine, and an open coal fire. Good value lunchtime bar food includes filled rolls or sandwiches (from £1.30), soup (£1.45), burgers (from £2.95), minute steak on ciabatta bread (£3.50), omelettes (£3.75), spicy stuffed peppers (£4.50), breaded haddock or lambs liver and bacon (£5.25), seafood casserole or steak in ale pie (£5.90), rib-eye steak (£7.50), and puddings (£1.90); children's helpings (£3.75). Disabled lavatories, and baby changing facilities. The family and breakfast rooms are no smoking. The landlord also runs the well preserved Speedwell Bar in Dundee. On summer evenings, you can sit at tables on the front pavement, and they might hold barbecues and real ale festivals in the secluded walled garden. You can come here by sea, mooring your boat on the nearby jetty. *(Recommended by Arthur Williams, Andy and Jill Kassube, Nigel Woolliscroft, Susan and John Douglas, Angus Lyon, Vicky and David Sarti, Pierre and Pat Richterich, Paul Roughley, Julia Fox)*

Free house ~ Licensee Jonathan Stewart ~ Real ale ~ Bar food (12-2.30(3 Sun)) ~ (01382) 775941 ~ Children welcome away from bar till 9 ~ Folk music Thurs night ~ Open 11-12(1am Sat); 12.30-12 Sun ~ Bedrooms: £19.50(£35B)/£39(£58B)

CANONBIE NY3976 Map 9

Riverside Inn ♀ 🛏

Village signposted from A7

Set in good walking country, this little dining inn has a new licensee. Tables are usually laid for dining, and many of the meals written up on the two blackboards are made from local ingredients: home-made spicy tomato soup (£2.50), smoked fish pâté (£3.50), potted brown shrimps (£3.95), cumbrian air-dried ham and melon (£4.25), vegetarian homity pie (£5.50), home-made fishcakes with parsley sauce (£5.95), ham and eggs (£6.25), grilled salmon with a basil, pine nut and balsamic dressing (£6.95), organic goosnargh chicken with lemon and rosemary (£10.95), scottish rib-eye steak (£11.95), and puddings such as marmalade bread and butter pudding or chocolate rum cake (£2.95). Well kept Caledonian 80/- and Yates Bitter on handpump, as well as a dozen or so malt whiskies, and a carefully chosen wine list. The communicating rooms of the bar have a mix of chintzy furnishings and dining chairs, pictures on the walls for sale, and some stuffed wildlife; the dining room and half the bar area are no smoking. In summer – when it can get very busy – there are tables under the trees on the front grass. Over the quiet road, a public playground runs down to the Border Esk (the inn can arrange fishing permits). *(Recommended by Hazel and Michael Duncombe, David Watkinson, Canon David Baxter, GSB, Roger Everett, R T and J C Moggridge, Peter F Marshall)*

Free house ~ Licensee Edward Baxter ~ Real ale ~ Bar food ~ Restaurant ~ (01387) 371512 ~ Well behaved children welcome ~ Open 12-2.30, 6.30-11; closed 25 Dec, 1 Jan ~ Bedrooms: £55B/£70B

Pubs with outstanding views are listed at the back of the book.

CARBOST NG3732 Map 11

Old Inn

This is the Carbost on the B8009, in the W of the central part of the island of Skye

You'll need to keep your eyes peeled to find this straightforward old stone house, as there isn't an obvious sign, but once you've arrived, fine terrace views of Loch Harport and the harsh craggy peaks of the Cuillin Hills more than compensate for any wrong turns along the way. It's usefully placed for walkers and climbers, and whisky buffs will be pleased to hear that the Talisker here comes fresh from the distillery just 100 yards away; there are guided tours (with samples) in summer – except on Saturdays. The three simple areas of the main bare-boards bar are knocked through into one, and furnished with red leatherette settles, benches and seats, amusing cartoons on the part-whitewashed and part-stripped stone walls, and a peat fire; darts, pool, cribbage, dominoes, TV and piped traditional music. A small choice of bar meals might include sandwiches, soup (£2.10), vegetable samosa with curry dip (£3.25), crispy camembert and brie with bramble jelly (£3.50), burgers (from £5.25), vegetable goujons (£5.75), haddock (£5.95), daily specials such as haggis, neeps and tatties or pasta bake (£5.95), and venison in port and red wine sauce (£7.95), and puddings (£2.75). Non-residents can come for the breakfasts if they book the night before, and the bedrooms in a separate annexe have sea views. They also have a bunkhouse and shower block for the loch's increasing number of yachtsmen. Note the reduced opening in winter. (Recommended by Nigel Woolliscroft, Vicky and David Sarti)

Free house ~ Licensee Deirdre Morrison ~ Bar food (12-2.30, 6.30-10) ~ (01478) 640205 ~ Children in eating area of bar till 8 ~ Open 11-12(11.30 Sat); 12.30-11 Sun; 11-2.30, 5-11 in winter; closed Mon-Weds during Jan and Feb ~ Bedrooms: £28S/£53B

CAWDOR NH8450 Map 11

Cawdor Tavern ⊕

Just off B9090 in Cawdor village; follow signs for Post Office and village centre

Those of you who enjoy the odd dram of whisky will be spoilt for choice at this welcoming Highland village pub, with over 100 to pick from – including some rare brands. The rather modern frontage hides some surprisingly elegant fittings inside, including some beautiful oak panelling in the substantial rather clubby lounge, gifted to the tavern by a former Lord Cawdor and salvaged from the nearby castle; more recent panelling is incorporated into an impressive ceiling. The public bar on the right has a brick fireplace housing an old cast-iron stove, as well as elaborate wrought-iron wall lamps, and an imposing pillared serving counter. Enjoyable bar food at lunchtime includes soup (£2.30), sandwiches (from £2.65), warm crab tart (£3.95), thai chicken strips or grilled goats cheese and fennel salad (£4.25), filled baked potatoes (£4.50), ploughman's (£4.75), venison sausage and mash (£5.95), haddock in beer batter with home-made tartare sauce (£6.95), and grilled gammon with an orange and madeira glaze (£7.40), with evening dishes such as crab and salmon with white wine and cream in a choux bun (£4.95), mini seafood platter (£4.85), chicken breast filled with haggis and a Drambuie and mushroom cream sauce (£9.25), fillet of Shetland salmon on wilted spinach with a tomato and garlic cream sauce (£9.45), and roast breast of guinea fowl with black pudding and a mushroom and whisky sauce (£10.25), and daily specials such as crab and prawn risotto with pesto marie rose or pigeon breast on puy lentils with port jus (£3.95), half a pot roast pheasant with onions and shallot reduction (£9.95), and duck breast on home-made rhubarb chutney with claret gravy (£10.75); puddings such as home-made cheesecake, home-made apple pie or chilled lemon posset with orange shortbread (from £3.15). The restaurant is partly no smoking. Well kept Aviemore Stag and Worthingtons, and a guest from Black Isle, Isle of Skye or Orkney on handpump; darts, pool, cribbage, dominoes, Jenga, board games, cards, fruit machine, juke box, TV, and piped music. There are tables on the front terrace, with tubs of flowers, roses, and creepers. (Recommended by Andy and Jill Kassube, John Shields, B, M and P Kendall, Mr and Mrs D Moir, Derek Thomas)

Free house ~ Licensee Norman Sinclair ~ Real ale ~ Bar food (12-2, 5.30-9) ~ Restaurant ~ (01667) 404777 ~ Children welcome away from public bar ~ Open 11-11(12.30 Sat); 12.30-11 Sun; 11-3, 5-11 in winter

CREEBRIDGE NX4165 Map 9
Creebridge House Hotel 🛏

Minnigaff, just E of Newton Stewart

Set in three acres of gardens and woodland, and surrounded by plenty of things to do, this sizeable country house hotel is an increasingly popular place to stay; they can arrange fishing, walking, pony-trekking, and free golf at the local golf course. The welcoming and neatly kept carpeted bar has well kept Criffel, Cuilhill (and an interesting cask lager called Galloway Gold) from the Sulwath brewery, 25 miles away, along with seasonal guests such as Caledonian Deuchars IPA and Fullers London Pride, about 30 malt whiskies, and that great rarity for Scotland, a bar billiards table; good proper coffee. There are plans to refurbish the public rooms. Under the new licensee, enjoyable brasserie-style food includes soup (£2.95), lunchtime sandwiches (from £2.95), prawn and roast red pepper cheesecake (£4.25), game terrine with port and red onion marmalade (£4.75), deep-fried fresh haddock (£6.95), tagliatelle with crisp vegetables in a fresh coriander sauce (£7.95), shank of scotch lamb braised in red wine (£10.25), steaks (from £11.50), breast of duck on puy lentils with a gin and redcurrant sauce (£13.95), and puddings such as chocolate roulade or strawberry and Cointreau cheesecake (£3.95); roast Sunday lunch, and they plan to hold jazz brunches every last Sunday of the month. Comfortably pubby furniture, and unobtrusive piped music. The garden restaurant is no smoking. Tables under cocktail parasols out on the front terrace look across a pleasantly planted lawn, where you can play croquet. *(Recommended by Christine and Neil Townend, Julie Hogg, Alain Weld, Stan and Hazel Allen, Mike and Sue Loseby)*

Free house ~ Licensee Joanne Allison ~ Real ale ~ Bar food (12-2, 6(6.30 Sun)-9) ~ Restaurant ~ (01671) 402121 ~ Children welcome ~ Open 12-2.30, 6-11(12 Sat); 12.30-2.30, 6.30-11(may open all day soon) Sun ~ Bedrooms: £59S/£98S

CRINAN NR7894 Map 11
Crinan Hotel 🍴 🛏

A816 NE from Lochgilphead, then left on to B841, which terminates at the village

The two stylish upstairs bars of this beautifully positioned hotel are the best spots for soaking up the cheering bustle of the entrance basin of the Crinan Canal, with picture windows making the most of the marvellous views of fishing boats and yachts wandering out towards the Hebrides. The simpler wooden-floored public bar (opening onto a side terrace) has a cosy stove and kilims on the seats, and the cocktail bar has a nautical theme with wooden floors, oak and walnut panelling, antique tables and chairs, and sailing pictures and classic yachts framed in walnut on a paper background of rust and green paisley, matching the tartan upholstery. The Gallery bar is done in pale terracotta and creams and has a central bar with stools, Lloyd Loom tables and chairs, and lots of plants. Sophisticated bar food might include home-made soup with freshly baked bread (£3.50), scottish farmhouse cheddar with fig chutney and oatcakes (£4.50), grilled arbroath smokie with tomato butter (£7.50), Loch Etive mussels with garlic and cream or good sausages with chive mash and onion jus (£8.50), fish of the day (£10.50), 10oz Aberdeen Angus rib-eye steak with sauce béarnaise (£12.50), and puddings (£3.50). You can get sandwiches and so forth from their coffee shop. A good wine list, around 30 malt whiskies, and freshly squeezed orange juice. The restaurants are very formal. Breakfasts can be outstanding. Many of the paintings are by the landlord's wife, artist Frances Macdonald. *(Recommended by Nigel Woolliscroft; also in* The Good Hotel Guide*)*

Free house ~ Licensee Nicolas Ryan ~ Bar food (12-2, 6.30-8.30) ~ Restaurant ~ (01546) 830261 ~ Children welcome ~ Open 11-12; closed 25 Dec ~ Bedrooms: £110B/£220B

CROMARTY NH7867 Map 11

Royal 🛏

Marine Terrace

You'll find a genuinely warm welcome at this delightfully old-fashioned hotel which, pretty much in the centre of things, makes an ideal base for exploring this beautifully restored sleepy village at the tip of the Black Isle. Most of the rooms and a long covered porch area look out over the sea, and a couple of picnic-sets outside enjoy the same tranquil view. The comfortable lounge has quite a bright feel, as well as pink painted walls, cushioned wall seats and leatherette armchairs, small curtained alcoves with model ships, and old local photos; piped Scottish music. A room to the right with a fireplace is rather like a cosy sitting room; it leads into an elegant lounge for residents. The basic public bar, popular with locals, has a separate entrance; pool, darts, dominoes, TV, fruit machine, juke box and piped music. Reasonably priced decent bar food includes scotch broth (£2.25), highland pâté (£3.55), local mussels with pâté and tomato sauce (£4.60), ham, chicken and mushroom crêpe or mushroom risotto (£7.30), local trout with prawns (£7.40), tagliatelle with smoked salmon, prawns and herbs or fisherman's pie (£7.95), steaks (from £14.75), daily specials such as haggis balls in Drambuie sauce (£3.95), huge battered cod (£6.75), and pork loin with a tomato and oregano sauce or lamb cutlets with a honey and mint glaze (£7.75), and puddings (£3.25). Belhaven, John Smiths and Tetleys on electric pump, around three dozen malt whiskies, and very friendly, chatty service. Part of the porch (a nice bit to eat in) is no smoking. It's hard to believe Cromarty was once a thriving port; a little museum a short stroll away sparkily illustrates its heritage. You can get boat trips out to see the local bottlenose dolphins, and maybe whales too in summer. More reports please. *(Recommended by Moira and John Cole)*

Free house ~ Licensee J A Shearer ~ Real ale ~ Bar food (12-2(2.30 Sat and Sun), 5.30-9(9.30 Sat and Sun)) ~ Restaurant ~ (01381) 600217 ~ Children welcome ~ Traditional Scottish music weekly in summer ~ Open 11(10 Sat and Sun)-12 ~ Bedrooms: £37.50B/£59.80B

EAST LINTON NT5977 Map 11

Drovers 🍴

5 Bridge St (B1407), just off A1, Haddington—Dunbar

Well run by two sisters, this comfortable old inn stands out for its enjoyable bar food, good choice of well kept real ales and genuinely pubby atmosphere. The main bar feels a bit like a welcoming living room as you enter from the pretty village street, with faded rugs on the wooden floor, a basket of logs in front of the woodburning stove, and comfortable armchairs and nostalgic piped jazz lending a very relaxed feel. There's a goat's head on a pillar in the middle of the room, plenty of hops around the bar counter, fresh flowers and newspapers, and a mix of prints and pictures (most of which are for sale) on the half panelled, half red-painted walls. A similar room leads off, and a door opens out onto a walled lawn with tables and maybe summer barbecues. Changing every week, up to six real ales might include Adnams Broadside, Belhaven Best, Deuchars IPA, Orkney Dark Island, and Shepherd Neame Spitfire; smartly dressed staff provide particularly helpful service. Relying on fresh local ingredients delivered daily (their local meats are excellent), the very good food might include soups such as smoked haddock and potato or creamed carrot and tarragon (from £2.50), home-made chicken liver pâté (£4.50), griddled black pudding and bacon in a creamy pepper sauce (£6), braised sausages in onion gravy and spicy mash (£6.50), steak, mushroom and Guinness pie (£7), thai-style curry of vegetables or salmon fillet on a bed of spinach and mornay sauce (£7.50), roast rib of beef with yorkshire pudding (£8), roast duckling breast in a sweet berry sauce or saddle of rabbit with caramelised carrots and shallots (£13), and puddings such as mango cheesecake with a pomegranate and passion fruit syrup or rich chocolate swiss flan (from £3). Part of the upstairs restaurant is no smoking; dominoes. The gents' has a copy of the day's *Scotsman* newspaper on the wall.

(Recommended by Andy and Jill Kassube, Christine and Malcolm Ingram, Michael Buchanan)

Free house ~ Licensees Michelle and Nicola Findlay ~ Real ale ~ Bar food (12-2, 6.30-10; not Sat evening) ~ Restaurant ~ (01620) 860298 ~ Children welcome ~ Folk and other music Weds evening ~ Open 11.30-2.30, 5-11 Mon; all day till 11 Tues, till 12.30 Weds-Thurs, till 1am Fri-Sat; 12.30-12 Sun; closed 25 Dec, 1 Jan

EDINBURGH NT2574 Map 11
Abbotsford

Rose St; E end, beside South St David Street

The traditional furnishings inside this small single bar pub lend it a pleasingly old-fashioned charm, and indeed among city folk it is something of a long-standing institution. Originally built for Jenners department store, it has a notably pleasant, friendly (and refreshingly uncluttered) atmosphere, with dark wooden half panelled walls, a highly polished Victorian island bar counter, long wooden tables and leatherette benches, and a welcoming log effect gas fire; there are prints on the walls and a rather handsome ornate plaster-moulded high ceiling. Well kept Abbotsford Ale (brewed locally for them), Caledonian 80/-, Crouch Vale Best, Deuchars IPA, and Worthingtons, served in the true Scottish fashion from a set of air pressure tall founts. Good, reasonably priced lunchtime bar food might include sandwiches, soup (£1.50), haggis, neeps and tatties (locals reckon it's amongst the best in town), roast of the day, and vegetable stir fry (all £5.95), and breaded haddock (£6.25). Over 60 malt whiskies, efficient service from dark-uniformed or white shirted staff, and piped music. *(Recommended by Derek and Sylvia Stephenson, Joel Dobris, Paul Roughley, Julia Fox, the Didler, Eric Larkham, Rob Fowell, Darly Graton, Graeme Gulibert)*

Free house ~ Licensee Colin Grant ~ Real ale ~ Bar food (12-3) ~ Restaurant (12-2.15, 5.30-10) ~ (0131) 225 5276 ~ Children must be over 5 in bar ~ Open 11-11; closed Sun

Bow Bar ★ ◧ £

80 West Bow

The cheery hubbub at this traditional pub, handily placed just below the castle, originates solely from the chatty customers and staff, buoyed up by a superb range of drinks and free from the irritations of piped music or noisy games machines. Eight well kept real ales are served from impressive antique tall founts made by Aitkens, Mackie & Carnegie, and typically include Belhaven, Caledonian 80/- and Deuchars IPA, Timothy Taylors Landlord, and various changing guests. The grand carved mahogany gantry has quite an array of malts (over 140) including lots of Macallan variants and cask strength whiskies, as well as a good collection of rums and gins. Basic, but busy and friendly, the spartan rectangular bar has a fine collection of appropriate enamel advertising signs and handsome antique trade mirrors, sturdy leatherette wall seats and heavy narrow tables on its lino floor, with café-style bar seats. Simple, cheap bar snacks such as filled rolls (from £1; toasties from £1.20), and home-made soup or steak and mince pies (£1.20). *(Recommended by Joel Dobris, the Didler, R T and J C Moggridge, Torrens Lyster, Rob Fowell, Eric Larkham)*

Free house ~ Licensee Helen McLoughlin ~ Real ale ~ Bar food (12-3) ~ No credit cards ~ (0131) 226 7667 ~ Open 12-11.30; 12.30-11 Sun

Café Royal

West Register Street

A few doors down from the Guildford Arms (see below), this popular pub was built last century as a flagship for the latest in Victorian gas and plumbing fittings. Consequently, the interesting café rooms have a series of highly detailed Doulton tilework portraits (although sadly they are partly obscured by the fruit machines) of historical innovators Watt, Faraday, Stephenson, Caxton, Benjamin Franklin and Robert Peel (famous here as the introducer of calico printing). The gantry over the big island bar counter is similar to the one that was here originally, the floor and stairway are laid with marble, there are leather-covered seats, and chandeliers hang from the fine ceilings. Well kept Caledonian Deuchars IPA, Courage Directors, McEwans 80/-, and two weekly guest beers on handpump, with about 25 malt whiskies. Bar food is served all day (till 7pm, and with prices unchanged since last year) and includes sandwiches (from £2.25), soup (£2.75), sausages and mash (£4.25), peppered chicken (£5.75) and steak, kidney and barley wine pie (£6.25). Good choice of daily newspapers, TV, trivia game and piped music. There are some fine original fittings in the downstairs gents', and the stained-glass well in the seafood and game restaurant is well worth a look. It can get very busy, and the admirable décor is perhaps best appreciated on quiet afternoons. No children. *(Recommended by Joe Green, Mrs G R Sharman, the Didler, Eric Larkham)*

Scottish Courage ~ Manager Dave Allen ~ Real ale ~ Bar food (11-7) ~ Restaurant ~ (0131) 556 1884 ~ Open 11-11(12 Thurs, 1 Fri, Sat)

Guildford Arms 🍺

West Register Street

With its buoyant atmosphere, excellent range of well kept real ales and magnificent décor, it's not surprising that this Victorian pub is the most popular of our Edinburgh entries. The main bar has lots of mahogany, glorious colourfully painted plasterwork and ceilings, big original advertising mirrors, and heavy swagged velvet curtains at the arched windows. The snug little upstairs gallery restaurant gives a dress-circle view of the main bar (notice the lovely old mirror decorated with two tigers on the way up), and under this gallery a little cavern of arched alcoves leads off the bar; TV, fruit machine, lunchtime piped jazz and classical music. There are often as many as 11 real ales on handpump, most of which are usually Scottish, such as Belhaven 80/-, Caledonian Deuchars IPA and 80/-, Harviestoun Brooker's Bitter and Twisted and Schiehallion, Orkney Dark Island, and changing guests (three of which are always English such as Fullers London Pride, Timothy Taylors Landlord or Yates Bitter); there's also a good choice of malt whiskies. Lunchtime bar food includes soup (£2.20), various types of bread with fillings such as bacon, lettuce and tomato or baked potatoes (from £3.95) chargrilled steak burger (£5.75), breaded haddock or scampi (around £5.75), and daily specials; on Sundays they only do filled rolls. It is very popular, but even at its busiest you shouldn't have to wait to be served. No children. During August they hold a blues and folk festival. *(Recommended by Derek and Sylvia Stephenson, Roger and Jenny Huggins, Richard Lewis, R T and J C Moggridge, Mrs G R Sharman, Eric Larkham, the Didler, Rob Fowell)*

Free house ~ Licensee David Stewart ~ Real ale ~ Bar food (12-2, not Sun) ~ Restaurant ~ (0131) 556 4312 ~ Open 11-(12 Fri and Sat)11; 12.30-11 Sun

Kays Bar 🍺 £

39 Jamaica Street West; off India Street

Although it's usually packed with customers, this cosy and atmospheric little back street pub is bigger than you might think from the outside. It was originally owned by John Kay, a whisky and wine merchant, when wine barrels were hoisted up to the first floor and dispensed through pipes attached to nipples which can still be seen around the light rose. As well as various casks and vats, there are old wine and spirits merchant notices, gas-type lamps, well worn red plush wall banquettes and stools around cast-iron tables, and red pillars supporting a red ceiling. A quiet panelled back room leads off, with a narrow plank-panelled pitched ceiling and a collection of books ranging from dictionaries to 70 year old books for boys on steam trains; lovely warming open coal fire in winter. The interesting range of around eight well kept real ales changes constantly but might include well kept Belhaven 80/-, Boddingtons, Exmoor Gold, Houston Killellan, McEwans 80/-, Orkney Dark Island, Shepherd Neame Spitfire, Timothy Taylors Landlord and Woodfordes Wherry on handpump; up to 70 malts, between eight and 40 years old, and 10 blended whiskies. As well as soup (£1), simple, good value lunchtime bar food includes highly recommended haggis, neeps or mince and tatties, steak pie and filled baked potatoes (£3), lasagne or beefburger and chips (£3.25) and chicken balti (£3.50). Staff are friendly and obliging; TV, dominoes and cribbage. *(Recommended by Eric Larkham, Roger and Jenny Huggins, Peter F Marshall, the Didler, Comus and Sarah Elliott)*

Free house ~ Licensee David Mackenzie ~ Real ale ~ Bar food (12(12.30 Sun)-2.30) ~ (0131) 225 1858 ~ Well behaved children in back room till 6pm ~ Open 12-12(1am Fri and Sat); 12.30-11 Sun

Starbank ♀ ◖ £

67 Laverockbank Road, off Starbank Road; on main road Granton—Leith

There are great views over the Firth of Forth from the windows in the neat and airy bar of this comfortably elegant welcoming pub. It's not just the views that make this pub popular though – they serve around eight well kept real ales from all around Britain on handpump which change continually but might include Bass, Belhaven 80/-, IPA, St Andrews and Sandy Hunters, Broughton Greenmantle, Orkney Dark Island, Timothy Taylors Landlord and Wadworths 6X. There's a good choice of wines too (all 23 are served by the glass), and as many malt whiskies; TV. Served by friendly, helpful staff the good value tasty bar food is all home-made. Nicely presented dishes include soup (£1.50), chicken liver pâté (£2.50), a daily vegetarian dish (£4.25), ploughman's or steak mince and potatoes (£5), roast leg of lamb with mint sauce or supreme of chicken with tarragon cream sauce (£5.50), halibut steak with orange sauce or minute steak with pepper cream sauce (£6.50), and puddings (£2.50). The conservatory restaurant is no smoking; sheltered back terrace. *(Recommended by Ken Richards, Rob Fowell, Ian Phillips, Eric Larkham)*

Free house ~ Licensee Valerie West ~ Real ale ~ Bar food (12-2.30, 6-9; 12.30-9 wknds) ~ Restaurant ~ (0131) 552 4141 ~ Children welcome ~ Jazz 2nd Sun and folk last Sun in month ~ Open 11-11(12 Thurs-Sat); 12.30-11 Sun

ELIE NO4900 Map 11
Ship

Harbour

This welcoming harbourside pub is in a setting that's hard to beat if you like the seaside with tables on a terrace that look directly over Elie's broad sands and along the bay. Tables in the restaurant enjoy the same view – in winter you might spy the pub's rugby team training on the sand while in summer you could find yourself watching their cricket team. The villagey, unspoilt beamed bar has a buoyant nautical feel, with friendly locals and staff, coal fires, and partly panelled walls studded with old prints and maps; there's a simple carpeted back room. The enjoyable bar dishes could include soup (£2), lunchtime sandwiches (from £3.25), haggis, neeps and tatties (£3.75), potted shrimps (£3.90), steak and Guinness pie (£7.50), hazelnut croquettes with mushroom sauce or smoked haddock and broccoli pie (£8.50), sole fillets with parma ham (£9.50), pork fillet with pesto (£11) and steaks (from £13) with puddings (£3.50); children's menu (£3.95). They do a good Sunday lunch, occasional barbecues in summer. Well kept Caledonian Deuchars IPA and half a dozen malt whiskies; darts, dominoes, captain's mistress, cribbage and shut the box. Plain but well equipped bedrooms are next door, in a guesthouse run by the same family. *(Recommended by R M Corlett, Ken Richards, Dr D J and Mrs S C Walker, Susan and John Douglas, M S Catling, Vicky and David Sarti)*

Free house ~ Licensees Richard and Jill Philip ~ Real ale ~ Bar food (Apr-Sept 12-2.30, 6-9.30; Oct-Mar 12-2, 6-9(9.30 Fri and Sat); 12.30-2.30 ~ Restaurant ~ (01333) 330246 ~ Children in family room and restaurant ~ Open 11-12; 11-1 Fri and Sat; 12.30-12 Sun; 11-11 winter; 12.30-11 Sun winter; closed 25 Dec ~ Bedrooms: £25B/£50B

The ◖ symbol shows pubs which keep their beer unusually well or have a particularly good range.

FORT AUGUSTUS NH3709 Map 11

Lock

Formerly a post office, this traditional village pub is well placed at the foot of Loch Ness, set right by the first lock of the flight of five that starts the Caledonian Canal's climb to Loch Oich. Attracting a good mix of regulars and boating people, the unpretentious, comfortable bar has a gently faded décor, with some stripped stone, a newish flagstone floor, big open fire, and unobtrusive piped music; well kept Caledonian 80/-, Deuchars IPA and maybe Orkney Dark Island on handpump, and a fine choice of about 100 malt whiskies (in substantial measures). Generous helpings of reasonably priced food include soup (£2.35), lunchtime toasted sandwiches (£2.95) and baguettes (£5.95), with other dishes such as home-made wild venison pâté (£4), mussels in white wine, garlic and cream (£4.95), lamb casserole (£8.75), venison or seafood stew (£9.50), orkney poached salmon in prawn and dill sauce (£9.75), steaks (from £12.50), and daily specials, including a catch of the day; quite a bit of the space is set aside for people eating. The fish dishes – particularly good in the upstairs restaurant – are very fresh indeed, and no wonder: Mr MacLennen has his own fishmonger's shop nearby. The upstairs restaurant and part of the bar are no smoking (the rest of the pub can get smoky during busy periods). Summer evenings are a good time to visit when you can listen to their live folk music (Mon-Weds) and they now have summer barbecues with various types of burger such as steak, venison or boar. *(Recommended by Ron and Marjorie Bishop, P R and S A White)*

Free house ~ Licensee James MacLennen ~ Real ale ~ Bar food (12-3, 6-(8 in winter)10) ~ Restaurant ~ (01320) 366302 ~ Children welcome ~ Folk music Mon-Weds evenings Jun-Sept, and in winter Sat ~ Open 11-12(11.45 Sat; 11 Sun)

GAIRLOCH NG8077 Map 11

Old Inn ♀ 🍴 🛏

Just off A832/B8021

Nicely placed at the bottom of Flowerdale Glen, this 18th-c inn (partly rebuilt after a fire five or six years ago) is tucked comfortably away from the modern waterside road, but only yards away from the little fishing harbour, and handy for pleasant beaches. Picnic-sets are prettily placed outside by the trees that line the stream as it flows past under the old stone bridge, and on the opposite side are more trees with high crags above. There are pleasant wooded walks up the glen, the ancestral home of Clan MacKenzie, with quite a few things to look out for. Inside, the two smallish rooms of the quiet lounge bar are pleasantly furnished, and nicely decorated with paintings and murals. Changing well kept real ales are a major feature, with anything from three to a dozen on offer, and some preference for dark ales; regulars are Courage Directors, Isle of Skye Red Cuillin and Blind Piper (the hotel's own blend of Isle of Skye ales, rather in the way that Broadside was originally a blend of other Adnams ales, and named after a famed local 17th-c piper), St Andrews, Peterswell and Tetleys, with guests such as Belhaven 60/-, Caledonian Deuchars IPA, Heather and Orkney Dark Island. They have a lot of enjoyable wines by the glass at fair prices, a decent collection of malt whiskies, and do speciality coffees. Fresh locally landed fish is a major food item, with bouillabaisse, seared scallops with lime, garlic and ginger butter, and home-made langoustine ravioli commonly on the board, and mussels, crabs, lobster, skate, haddock and hake often cropping up too. The regular bar menu includes soup (£2.45), cullen skink, falafel and tahine or local calamari with a greek potato and garlic dip (£3.95), fish pie (£6.75), wild venison sausages or fresh vegetarian fettuccine (£6.85), cheese-topped gammon (£6.95) and sirloin steak (£10.50); with puddings including cloutie dumpling and custard (£2.75); children's dishes (£2.99), and sandwiches on request. Both the bistro dining area and the restaurant are no smoking. The landlady (the Pearsons bought the inn a couple of years ago) makes her own chutneys and preserves – and grows many of the herbs used, while they do track down organically grown vegetables. Friendly service; cheerful long public bar, again with two main areas, with darts, dominoes, pool, fruit machine and juke box. *(Recommended by Mike and Penny Sanders, P R and S A White,*

Graham and Elizabeth Hargreaves, Lorna Baxter, John Winstanley, Jenny and Brian Seller)

Free house ~ Licensees Alastair and Ute Pearson ~ Real ale ~ Bar food (12-2, 6-9; 12-10 summer) ~ Restaurant ~ (01445) 712006 ~ Children in eating area of bar and restaurant ~ Scottish music most Fri evenings ~ Open 11-1; 11-12 Sat; 12.30-11 Sun ~ Bedrooms: £33.50B/£66B

GIFFORD NT5368 Map 11
Tweeddale Arms 🏠

High Street

Looking across a peaceful green to the 300-year-old avenue of lime trees leading to the former home of the Marquesses of Tweeddale, this civilised old inn is probably the oldest building in this scenic Borders village. The tasty lunchtime bar food includes dishes such as soup (£1.95), herring fillets in dill and tomato marinade or deep-fried haggis with whisky and onion sauce (£3.95), creamed chicken and asparagus crêpe, baked vegetable crumble or salmon en croûte with white wine sauce (£6.95), pork with plum sauce (£7.25) and sirloin steak (£9.50) with puddings (from £3.25); sandwiches (from £2.50) are available all day (except Sundays). In the evening you may be able to order dishes in the bar from the restaurant. Comfortable and relaxed, the modernised lounge bar has cushioned wall seats, chairs and bar chairs, dried flowers in baskets, Impressionist prints on the apricot coloured walls, and a big curtain that divides off the eating area; dominoes, fruit machine, TV, cribbage, and piped music. Well kept Belhaven Best and guests such as Abbot Ale and Timothy Taylors Landlord are usually a bit cheaper in the public bar than in the lounge; quite a few malt whiskies, including the local Glenkinchie; cheerfully efficient service. If you're staying, the tranquil hotel lounge is especially comfortable, with antique tables and paintings, chinoiserie chairs and chintzy easy chairs, an oriental rug on one wall, a splendid corner sofa and magazines on a table. *(Recommended by Chris Rounthwaite, Brian and Lynn Young, Nigel Woolliscroft, Derek Thomas, Mr and Mrs R M Macnaughton, Dr G E Martin)*

Free house ~ Licensee Wilda Crook ~ Real ale ~ Bar food ~ Restaurant ~ (01620) 810240 ~ Children in restaurant and eating area of bar ~ Open 11-11(12 wknds) ~ Bedrooms: £42B/£65B

GLASGOW NS5865 Map 11
Auctioneers £

6 North Court, St Vincent Place

With their wonderful collection of eye-catching junk these splendidly converted auction rooms are well worth a visit. Inside, the main high-ceilinged, stone-flagged room has snug little areas around the edges made out of the original valuation booths, so it's easy to find a secluded corner. Plenty of antiques are dotted about as if they were for sale, with lot numbers clearly displayed. You'd probably be most tempted to bid for the goods in the smarter red-painted side room, which rather than the old lamps, radios, furnishings and golf clubs elsewhere has framed paintings, statues, and even an old rocking horse, as well as comfortable leather sofas, unusual lamp fittings, a big fireplace, and an elegant old dresser with incongruous china figures. There's quite a bustling feel in the bar (especially in the evenings), which has lots of old sporting photos, programmes and shirts along one of the panelled walls. Well kept Deuchars IPA, Orkney Dark Island and maybe a guest on handpump, and over 25 malt whiskies; friendly, helpful service, big screen TVs (popular for big sporting events), fruit machine, video game, trivia, piped music. Served most of the day, bar food includes soup (£2.35), potato skins filled with haggis (£3.65), fish and chips (£4.50), rump steak or cajun chicken (£5.25) and mixed grill (£5.50). Sir Winston Churchill and William Burrell are just two of the figures who passed through when the place was still serving its original purpose, the latter returning a painting because he couldn't afford it. The Counting House (another impressive conversion) is just around the corner. *(Recommended by Richard Lewis, David Carr)*

Bass ~ Manager Michael Rogerson ~ Real ale ~ Bar food (12-8.45(9.45 Sat)) ~ Restaurant ~ (0141) 229 5851 ~ Children in eating area of bar till 5pm ~ DJ last Fri of month ~ Open 12-11(12 Thurs-Fri); 11-12 Sat; 12.30-11 Sun; closed 25 Dec and 1 Jan

Babbity Bowster 🍴 ♑ £

16-18 Blackfriars Street

This lively but stylish 18th-c town house is welcoming and cosmopolitan, with something of the feel of a continental café bar. The simply decorated light interior has fine tall windows, well lit photographs and big pen-and-wash drawings in modern frames of Glasgow and its people and musicians, dark grey stools and wall seats around dark grey tables on the stripped wooden boards, and an open peat fire. A big ceramic of a kilted dancer and piper in the bar illustrates the 18th-c folk song (Bab at the Bowster) from which the pub takes its name. The bar opens on to a terrace with tables under cocktail parasols, trellised vines and shrubs, and adjacent boules; there may be barbecues out here in summer. Popular, well presented bar food includes several hearty home-made soups in two sizes (from £1.75), toasted sandwiches (from £3.50), haggis, neeps and tatties (£4.50; they also do a vegetarian version), stovies (£4.95), cauliflower moussaka (£5.95), good daily specials such as rabbit and red wine casserole (£6.50), and evening tapas (from £2.50). There are more elaborate meals in the airy upstairs restaurant. Well kept Caledonian Deuchars IPA and Belhaven IPA alongside well chosen guests such as Church End Cuthberts and Durham Magus on air pressure tall fount, a remarkably sound collection of wines, malt whiskies, cask conditioned cider, and good tea and coffee. Enthusiastic service is consistently efficient and friendly, taking its example from the vivacious landlord. They have live Celtic music on Saturday evening; dominoes. The bedrooms aren't huge and could do with being freshened up. *(Recommended by David Edwards, Vicky and David Sarti, Nigel Woolliscroft, David Carr)*

Free house ~ Licensee Fraser Laurie ~ Real ale ~ Bar food (12-11) ~ Restaurant ~ (0141) 552 5055 ~ Well behaved children away from main bar ~ Folk sessions Sat afternoon ~ Open 11(12.30 Sun)-12; closed 25 Dec ~ Bedrooms: £50S/£70B

Counting House ◧ £

24 George Square

Astonishingly roomy and imposing, this relaxed, popular place is a remarkable conversion by Wetherspoons of what was formerly a premier branch of the Royal Bank of Scotland. The lofty, richly decorated coffered ceiling culminates in a great central dome, with well lit nubile caryatids doing a fine supporting job in the corners. There's the sort of decorative glasswork that nowadays seems more appropriate to a landmark pub than to a bank, as well as wall-safes, plenty of prints and local history, and big windows overlooking George Square. Away from the bar are several carpeted areas (some no smoking) with solidly comfortable seating, while a series of smaller rooms, once the managers' offices, lead around the perimeter of the building. Some of these are surprisingly cosy, one is like a well stocked library, and a few are themed with pictures and prints of historical characters such as Walter Scott or Mary, Queen of Scots. The central island servery has a good range of well kept ales on handpump, such as Caledonian 80/- and Deuchars IPA, Courage Directors, Theakstons Best, and a couple of guests such as Timothy Taylors Landlord or Tomintoul Wildcat, with a good choice of bottled beers and malt whiskies, and 12 wines by the glass. The usual Wetherspoons menu includes soup (£2.39), filled rolls (from £2.79), burgers (from £4.99), scampi (£4.99), chicken balti or vegetable tandoori (£5.49), steaks (from £5.99), daily specials, and puddings (from £2.29). Fruit machine. Friendly service though it may take a while to get served. No children. *(Recommended by R T and J C Moggridge, Richard Lewis, Klaus and Elizabeth Leist, David Carr)*

Wetherspoons ~ Manager Stuart Coxshall ~ Real ale ~ Bar food (11-10; 12.30-9.30 Sun) ~ Restaurant ~ (0141) 248 9568 ~ Open 11(12.30 Sun)-12; closed 25 Dec

GLENDEVON NN9904 Map 11

Tormaukin ♀ ⇌

A823

Within an hour's drive of more than 100 golf courses, including St Andrews, this isolated old drovers' inn is very handily positioned for the ardent golfer. Comfortable and spotlessly kept, the softly lit bar has plush seats against stripped stone and partly panelled walls, ceiling joists, log fires, and maybe gentle piped music. Enjoyable bar food includes a few traditional Scottish foods such as black pudding and haggis in filo pastry (£3.95), home-made minced steak and mushroom bridies (£7.95) and steak and haggis (£13.95), as well as other dishes such as soup (£2.40), trout and lime pâté with oatcakes or grilled goats cheese with roasted vegetable salad (£4.25), pork and apple sausages with liver (£7.95), spicy lamb meatballs with couscous or coriander flavoured crêpes filled with stir-fried vegetables (£8.50), chicken with cream cheese and pesto (£9.75) or duck stir fry with yellow bean sauce (£11.50), and puddings such as scotch pancakes with bananas and rum or steamed marmalade pudding (from £3.95); children's menu (from £2.95), good breakfasts. Well kept Harviestoun Bitter and Twisted, Timothy Taylors Landlord and a guest on handpump, a decent wine list, quite a few malt whiskies, and several vintage ports and brandies; attentive service, even when they're busy. Some of the comfortable bedrooms are in a converted stable block, and they have a self-catering chalet for weekly lets; two new bedrooms have their own sun deck. Loch and river fishing can be arranged. A popular stop on one of the most attractive north-south routes through this part of Scotland, it offers plenty of good walks over the nearby Ochils or along the River Devon. *(Recommended by Mr and Mrs R M Macnaughton, W K Wood, R T and J C Moggridge, Derek and Sylvia Stephenson, Susan and John Douglas)*

Free house ~ Licensee Isadora Simpson ~ Real ale ~ Bar food (12-2, 5.30-9.30; 12-9.30 Sun) ~ Restaurant ~ (01259) 781252 ~ Children welcome ~ Fri Jazz and Tues folk Oct-Mar ~ Open 11-11(11.45 Sat); 12-11 Sun; closed four days in Jan ~ Bedrooms: £55S/£85B

GLENELG NG8119 Map 11

Glenelg Inn ⇌

Unmarked road from Shiel Bridge (A87) towards Skye

Getting to this inviting old inn is quite an adventure, with the single-track road climbing dramatically past heather-strewn fields and mountains with spectacular views to the lochs below. Glenelg is the closest place on the mainland to Skye (there's a little car ferry across in summer) and on a sunny day, tables in the beautifully kept garden have lovely views across the water. Instantly welcoming, the unspoilt green-carpeted bar has an overwhelming impression of dark wood, with lots of logs dotted about, and a big fireplace – it feels a bit like a mountain cabin; there are only a very few tables and cushioned wall benches, but crates and fish boxes serve as extra seating. Black and white photos line the walls at the far end around the pool table, and there are various jokey articles and local information elsewhere; pool and fruit machine. Making very good use of fresh local ingredients (though make sure you order on time), a blackboard lists the very short range of enjoyable bar meals such as soup (£2.50), filled rolls or ciabattas (from £4), crisp coated local crab cakes with chilli sauce (£5), fresh local devilled herring with salsa (£7) and spiced duck breast with fruit sauce (£9); in the evening they do an excellent four-course meal in the no smoking dining room (£25). A good choice of malt and cask strength whiskies; enthusiastic service. They may occasionally have fiddlers playing in the bar; if not, the piped music is in keeping with that theme. They can organise local activities, and there are plenty of excellent walks nearby. The bedrooms are excellent (the price includes dinner), and certainly much improved since Dr Johnson wrote 'We did not express much satisfaction' after staying here in 1773. *(Recommended by Alistair L Taylor, Olive and Ray Hebson; also in The Good Hotel Guide)*

Free house ~ Licensee Christopher Main ~ Bar food (not Nov-March) ~ Restaurant ~ (01599) 522273 ~ Children away from main bar ~ Open 12-2.30, 5-11(12.30 Sat); 12-2, 7-11 Sun; closed Sun and lunchtimes Nov-March winter ~ Bedrooms: £72B/£144B

HADDINGTON NT5174 Map 11
Waterside
Waterside; just off A6093 at E end of town

This long two-storey white house is a lovely place for a sunny summer's day, when tables outside let you enjoy the view looking across the water to a church and narrow little bridge. The setting is captured rather well on an unusual glass engraving in the comfortably plush carpeted bar, which also has swagged curtains around little windows, lamps on the window sills beside square wooden tables, a woodburning stove, and quite a mix of decorations on the walls (among the prints and pictures is a CD presented to them by the singer Fish). Across the hall a similar room has bigger tables and long cushioned benches, and there's a more formal stone-walled conservatory. Several tables have reserved signs as most people come here to eat from the good bistro menu, which could include soup (£2.50), chicken and mushroom pancake or deep-fried haggis in whisky sauce (£3.50), mussels (served as requested, £4.50), cajun chicken (£7.25), steak, onion and ale pie (£7.50), salmon salad or various curries (£7.95), lamb cutlets (£8.95), and steaks (from 12.95); if you ask they will make you a sandwich (from £2.95). Adnams Broadside, Caledonian Deuchars IPA and 80/- and Timothy Taylors Landlord on handpump; good range of wines. There's a family connection with the Drovers at East Linton. If you're driving, the gap under the adjacent bridge is very small; it's much nicer to park a short distance away and walk. On Sundays in fine weather you might be lucky enough to see a jazz band or an accordion player and dancing on the side terrace. *(Recommended by R M Corlett, Tom and Ruth Rees, Brian and Lynn Young)*

Free house ~ Licensee Jim Findlay ~ Real ale ~ Bar food (12-2, 5.30-10; 12.30-9 Sun) ~ Restaurant ~ (01620) 825674 ~ Children welcome ~ Open 11.30-2.30, 5-11; 11.30-11 Sat; 12.30-11 Sun; closed 25 Dec and 1 Jan

HOUSTON NS4166 Map 11
Fox & Hounds ◀
Main Street (B790 E of Bridge of Weir)

This cheery village pub is the home of the Houston brewery, so you can expect to find a very well kept pint of Barachon, Formakin, Killellan and St Peters Well alongside Texas (their seasonal beer), or a couple of guests such as Timothy Taylors Landlord on handpump; also half a dozen wines by the glass, and around 100 malt whiskies. The lively downstairs bar has pool and fruit machines and is popular with a younger crowd, and the clean plush hunting-theme lounge has comfortable seats by a fire and polished brass and copper. The wide range of decent bar food might include soup (£2.25), deep fried mushrooms stuffed with red peppers and pesto or haggis (£2.95), home-made aubergine bake or apple, celery and mushroom stroganoff (£6.95), oxtail casserole, prawn and smoked salmon salad or lamb shank with minted mash and rosemary jus (£7.95), calves liver with charred bacon, mash and onion gravy (£9.50), steaks (from £9.50); puddings such as spotted dick (from £2.95). There's a more elaborate menu in the upstairs restaurant; no smoking areas in lounge and restaurant. *(Recommended by Angus Lyon)*

Own brew ~ Licensee Jonathan Wengel ~ Real ale ~ Bar food (12-2.30, 5.30-10; 12-10 wknds) ~ Restaurant ~ (01505) 612448 ~ Children in restaurant and lounge bar till 8pm ~ Quiz Tues and Sun evening ~ Open 11-12(1 Fri and Sat); 12.30-12 Sun

INNERLEITHEN NT3336 Map 9

Traquair Arms 🍺

Traquair Rd (B709, just off A72 Peebles—Galashiels; follow signs for Traquair House)

This pleasantly modernised inn is a hospitable place to visit especially since the good bar food is served almost all day. Using lots of fresh local ingredients, enjoyable meals might include home-made soup (£2.10), filled baked potatoes (from £2.95), king prawn and chilli kebab (£3.95), omelettes (from £4), haggis sausages (£5.95), steak and ale pie (£6.65), Finnan savoury (made with smoked haddock, onions, local cheddar and double cream, £6.75), grilled escolar with coriander butter (£6.95), salmon, tomatoes and limes in filo pastry (£8.95), duck with apricot and brandy sauce (£9.25), and steaks (from £11.95), specials such as boston bean casserole (£5.25) and fresh salmon fishcakes (£5.85); puddings (from £2.10). Locals and visitors alike gather around the warm open fire in the simple little bar where they serve well kept Broughton Greenmantle and (from nearby Traquair House) Traquair Bear plus a guest from Broughton on handpump; several malt whiskies and draught cider; piped music. Even when they're busy service is friendly and efficient. A pleasant and spacious dining room has an open fire and high chairs for children if needed; all the dining areas are no smoking. Comfortable bedrooms. *(Recommended by Fiona Dick, Barclay Price, Chris Rounthwaite, Comus and Sarah Elliott, Stan and Hazel Allen, D P Brown, Alan J Morton)*

Free house ~ Licensee Dianne Johnston ~ Real ale ~ Bar food (12-9) ~ Restaurant ~ (01896) 830229 ~ Children welcome ~ Open 11(12 Sun)-12; closed 25 and 26 Dec, 1-4 Jan ~ Bedrooms: £45S/£70B

INVERARAY NN0908 Map 11

George £

Main Street East

A central part of this little Georgian town stretched along the shores of Loch Fyne in front of Inveraray Castle, this comfortably modernised inn has been run by the same family for more than 130 years. The friendly stone-flagged bar has a charmingly traditional feel with exposed joists, old tiles and bared stone walls, some antique settles, cushioned stone slabs along the walls, nicely grained wooden-topped cast-iron tables, lots of curling club and ships' badges, a cosy log fire, original flagstones. The good value, generous lunchtime bar food includes soup (£1.95), ploughman's (from £3.50), steak and kidney dumplings (£4.75), home-made lasagne (£5.50), fresh battered haddock (£6.25) and Loch Fyne seafood platter (£6.75), with evening dishes such as gammon steak with cumberland sauce (£6.95), rack of lamb (£8.75), Loch Fyne salmon with scallops and prawns (£9.75) or steak (£11.50); daily specials, good local cheeses, and a choice of coffees. The two real ales are rotated from a range of 10, and might typically include Caledonian Deuchars IPA or Houston Barochan on handpump; over 80 malt whiskies. Good, friendly service, darts, pool, dominoes, and juke box; no bar games in summer. The bar can get a little smoky at busy times. Readers have really enjoyed staying here; some of the individually decorated bedrooms have antique furnishings and big bathrooms. It's well placed for the great Argyll woodland gardens – the rhododendrons are at their best in May and early June; good nearby walks – you may spot seals or even a basking shark or whale. *(Recommended by Derek Harvey-Piper, Derek Thomas, Mrs M A Cameron, Derek Stafford, Andy, Julie and Stuart Hawkins, Neil and Anita Christopher)*

Free house ~ Licensee Donald Clark ~ Real ale ~ Bar food (12-9) ~ Restaurant ~ (01499) 302111 ~ Children welcome ~ Open 11(12 Sun)-12.30; closed 25 Dec and 1 Jan ~ Bedrooms: £30B/£65B

Please tell us if any Lucky Dips deserve to be upgraded to a main entry – and why. No stamp needed: The Good Pub Guide, FREEPOST TN1569, Wadhurst, E Sussex TN5 7BR or contact our web site: www.goodguides.com

INVERARNAN NN3118 Map 11

Inverarnan Inn £

A82 N of Loch Lomond

'Interesting', 'atmospheric' and 'full of character' are typical of the comments that we get from readers about this distinctively Scottish 16th-c house. Reminiscent of a fusty baronial hall, it has lots of tartan, stuffed animals and whisky galore, the staff wear kilts to serve, and the long bar feels unchanged for at least the last hundred years (some of the furnishings and fittings look as if they could have been around even longer). Log fires burn in big fireplaces at each end, and there are green tartan cushions and deerskins on the black winged settles, Highland paintings and bagpipes on the walls, and a stuffed golden eagle on the bar counter. Lots of sporting trophies (such as a harpooned gaping shark), horns and so forth hang on the high walls of the central hall, where there's a stuffed badger curled on a table, and a full suit of armour; piped music is, of course, traditional Scottish. A wide range of good malts – 60 in the gantry and 60 more in stock, Fraoch Heather Ale, and farm cider. Bar food includes broth or toasted sandwiches (£1.95), vegetable haggis (£2.30), steak and Guinness pie, mince and tatties or haddock and chips (£5.25) and fillet steak (£10.95). Tables outside on a back terrace, with more in a field alongside – where you might come across a couple of geese; a stream runs behind. *(Recommended by Mike and Lynn Robinson, C J Fletcher, Nigel Woolliscroft, David Edwards, A York)*

Free house ~ Licensees Stephen Muirhead and Mr Love ~ Real ale ~ Bar food (12-8.15) ~ Restaurant ~ (01301) 704234 ~ Children in eating area of bar and restaurant ~ Open 11-11(12 Sat); 12.30-11 Sun; closed 25 Dec ~ Bedrooms: £23/£55B

ISLE OF WHITHORN NX4736 Map 9

Steam Packet £ 🛏

Harbour Row

Absorbing views of the picturesque working harbour (where there's usually quite a bustle of yachts and inshore fishing boats) from the large picture windows of this friendly modernised inn make it an enjoyable place to spend an afternoon. Inside, the homely low-ceilinged bar is split into two: on the right, plush button-back banquettes and boat pictures, and on the left, green leatherette stools around cast-iron-framed tables on big stone tiles, and a woodburning stove in the bare stone wall. Bar food can be served in the lower-beamed dining room, which has excellent colour wildlife photographs, rugs on its wooden floor, and a solid fuel stove, and there's also a small eating area off the lounge bar. Good value meals might range from filled rolls (from £1.55) and soup (£1.95), to deep-fried brie with cranberry sauce (£3.95), haggis (£4.75), chicken and leek pie or vegetable lasagne (£4.95), moules marinières (£5.25), mushroom ravioli with three cheese sauce, chicken curry or haddock stuffed with prawns, cheese and mushrooms (£5.95), chicken with bacon in apricot and brandy sauce (£7.25), hearty seafood platter (£10.95) and steaks (from £11.50), local cheeses, children's menu (from £1.50). Unusually, you can take food away. Well kept Theakstons XB on handpump, with a guest such as Black Sheep Bitter or Caledonian Deuchars IPA and two dozen malt whiskies. Helpful service from pleasant staff; pool and dominoes. Dogs welcome. White tables and chairs in the garden. The back bar and conservatory are no smoking; the main bar can sometimes be smoky. Every 1½ to 4 hours there are boat trips from the harbour; the remains of St Ninian's Kirk are on a headland behind the village. Their two new bedrooms overlook the harbour. *(Recommended by Mike and Lynn Robinson, Stan and Hazel Allen, Francis and Deirdre Gevers-McClure, B, M and P Kendall, Mike and Sue Loseby)*

Free house ~ Licensee John Scoular ~ Real ale ~ Bar food (not 25 Dec) ~ Restaurant ~ (01988) 500334 ~ Children away from bar ~ Open 11(12 Sun)-11(12 Sat); closed Mon-Thurs 2.30-6 in winter ~ Bedrooms: £25B/£50B

We now have a web site: www.goodguides.com

ISLE ORNSAY Map 11
Eilean Iarmain ♀ ⇌

Signposted off A851 Broadford—Armadale

Overlooking the sea in a picturesque part of Skye, this welcoming hotel forms part of Fearann Eilean Iarmain, a traditional estate covering 23,000 acres. With their own oyster beds, their own blend of whisky, Te Bheag, and friendly staff whose first language is predominantly Gaelic, this attractively positioned place exudes a thoroughly Scottish charm. Every day a diver is sent to collect fresh scallops. Changing daily, enjoyable bar food might include lunchtime sandwiches, langoustine spiced consommé (£2), local mussels in white wine and garlic cream (£4), cannelloni with mixed vegetables and herby tomato sauce topped with mozzarella (£7.50), grilled pork chop on apple and garlic mash with calvados sauce or local salmon wrapped in banana leaf with red pimiento olive couscous and beurre blanc (£8.50), pheasant breast with wild mushroom and garlic cream or snapper with roast butter nut squash (£9.50), rib-eye steak (£11.95), and puddings such as strawberry meringue roulade and vanilla and caramel mousse (from £3); children's menu. The bustling bar has a swooping stable-stall-like wooden divider that gives a two-room feel: good tongue-and-groove panelling on the walls and ceiling, leatherette wall seats, brass lamps, a brass-mounted ceiling fan, and a huge mirror over the open fire. There are about 34 local brands of blended and vatted malt whisky (including a splendid vatted malt, Poit Dhubh Green Label, bottled for them but available elsewhere), and an excellent wine list; darts, dominoes, cribbage, and piped music. The pretty, no smoking candlelit dining room has a lovely sea view past the little island of Ornsay itself and the lighthouse on Sionnach built by Robert Louis Stevenson's grandfather (you can walk over the sands at low tide); new, very comfortable and well equipped bedrooms in a converted stable block across the road have the same outlook. The most popular room has a canopied bed from Armadale Castle. *(Recommended by Nigel Woolliscroft, Guy Vowles, Lt Col M Turner, Lorna Baxter, John Winstanley, John Rahim)*

Free house ~ Licensee Sir Iain Noble ~ Bar food ~ Restaurant ~ (01471) 833332 ~ Children in restaurant, eating area of bar and family room – must leave bar by 8 ~ Open 11-1(12.30 Sat, 11.30 Sun) ~ Bedrooms: £90B/£120B

KELSO NT7334 Map 10
Queens Head ♀ £ ⇌

Bridge Street (A699)

There's an individualistic new landlord in this Georgian coaching inn, which is very popular locally for lunch. The roomy and attractive back lounge has a comfortable mix of modern and traditional furnishings, and there's a lively local feel in the small simpler unpretentious streetside front bar. A wide choice of good, generously served home-made food includes over a dozen tapas dishes (£1.40-£3.50), soup (£2.50), baguettes (from £3), filled baked potatoes (from £3.50), chilli (£6.50), crab salad (£7.25), curries or half a chicken with couscous, chick peas and harissa (£8.95) and rib-eye steak (£10.50). Well kept Courage Directors and around 15 wines by the glass; darts, pool, dominoes, fruit machine, TV, and piped music; they can arrange golf, fishing and horse riding. *(Recommended by Brian and Lynn Young, Nigel Woolliscroft, Mr and Mrs R M Macnaughton)*

Free house ~ Licensee Mr Heisler ~ Real ale ~ Bar food (12-2, 6.30-9.30(6-9 winter)) ~ Restaurant ~ (01573) 224636 ~ Children in restaurant ~ Open 12-2, 5-11(1 Fri-Sun); closed 25-26 Dec ~ Bedrooms: £25S/£50S

KENMORE NN7745 Map 11
Kenmore Hotel ⇌

A827 6 miles W of Aberfeldy

Quietly old-fashioned and civilised, this small hotel is beautifully set in a pretty 18th-c village by Loch Tay – and predates the village by a couple of centuries.

Pencilled on the wall above the big log fire in the main front bar, in Burns' own unmistakable handwriting, is his long poem 'Admiring Nature in her wildest grace' – a tribute to the beauty of the area. This is a comfortable room, with a cosily old-fashioned upmarket feel, armchairs upholstered in a heavy blue and green tartan to match the curtains, and blue and white china with lots of more or less antique fishing photographs on the cream walls above the panelled dado. Afternoon tea with shortbread in here is a relaxing treat after a day on the hills (from £2.25). A brand new carpeted light airy dining bar at the back has sliding glass doors opening out onto a terrace overlooking the Tay (the back garden has the same views, and the hotel leases fishing rights from the Kenmore estate) and is furnished in a traditional style, with painted Anaglypta walls, wall lighting and a good mix of upholstered bar stools, captain's chairs and more conventional seating; pool table, winter darts, TV, fruit machine and piped music. The short range of bar snacks includes sandwiches (from £2, baguettes from £2.50), soup (£2.25), hot dogs (£2.50) and peppered mackerel (£3.40), with more elaborate restaurant meals such as roasted Tay salmon with roasted pepper salsa (£8.25), venison loin on red cabbage with redcurrant and Drambuie sauce (£13.75) and duck breast with port, wine and plum sauce topped with cashew nuts (£14.95). *(Recommended by Peter Salmon, James Oliver, Michael Porter, Susan and John Douglas)*

Free house ~ Licensee Mr Hiroz ~ Bar food (12-10(9 in winter)) ~ Restaurant ~ (01887) 830205 ~ Children welcome ~ Mon evening three-course meal and cabaret ~ Open 11-11(12 Sat); 12.30-12 Sun ~ Bedrooms: £45B/£70B

KILBERRY NR7164 Map 11
Kilberry Inn
B8024

New licensees at this whitewashed inn are working hard to maintain the excellent standards established by the previous licensees. The road here is single-track, so a very leisurely drive allows you to make the most of the breathtaking views over rich coastal pastures to the sea and the island of Gigha beyond. The pub is so remotely set that local produce often arrives by taxi. You'll know you've arrived when you spot the old-fashioned red telephone box outside which was inherited from the pub's days as a post office. There's a warmly social buzz in the small relaxed beamed and quarry tiled dining bar, tastefully and simply furnished, with a good log fire. No real ale, but a good range of bottled beers and plenty of malt whiskies. The family room is no smoking. Bar food might include tomato, mozzarella and basil salad, wild mushroom risotto and smoked haddock and prawn chowder (from £2.95), macaroni cheese or courgette, pepper and feta quiche (£5.50), sausage pie (£6.95), fried salmon with lemon butter (£8.95), venison pie (£9.95) and puddings such as walnut tart with crème fraîche or lemon meringue pie (from £2.75). They appreciate booking if you want an evening meal. It's a nice place to stay with neat, cosy bedrooms. *(Recommended by Justin Hulford, G C Buckle, Norman Stansfield, Stuart Turner, Dr G E Martin)*

Free house ~ Licensees Mr and Mrs G Primrose ~ Bar food (12-2, 7-9; 12-6 Sun) ~ Restaurant ~ (01880) 770223 ~ Well behaved children in family room ~ Open 11-11; 12-6 Sun; closed Sun evening, late Oct-late Mar ~ Bedrooms: £30.40S/£60.80S

KILMAHOG NN6108 Map 11
Lade ♀
A84 just NW of Callander, by A821 junction

The main draw to this cosy pub is the wide range of popular home-made bar food. The choice ranges from soup (£1.99), lunchtime sandwiches (from £3.95) and smoked salmon (£5.25) to main meals such as haggis, neeps and tatties or steak pie (£5.85), several vegetarian dishes such as garlic and herb quorn, brie and broccoli pithiviers or vegetable bourguignon (£6.50), specials such as salmon in oatmeal (£7.95), and 10oz Aberdeen Angus sirloin (£13.95); children's menu. Well kept changing ales include Broughton Greenmantle, Isle of Skye Red Cuillin, Orkney Red

MacGregor and Tomintoul Stag on handpump, and a wine list strong on New World ones; piped Scottish music. The main carpeted dining bar has blond wood chairs around pine tables, with beams, some panelling, stripped stone and Highland prints; a no smoking room opens on to the terrace and attractive garden, where they have three ponds stocked with fish; dogs welcome. It's best to check winter Sunday opening hours before visiting. The pub is set in the beautiful richly wooded surroundings of the Pass of Leny, with high hills all around and the Trossachs not far off. *(Recommended by George and Jean Dundas, Mr and Mrs Richard Osborne, Mr and Mrs R M Macnaughton, Dr J D Bassett, Derek and Sylvia Stephenson, David Watkinson, GSB)*

Free house ~ Licensee Paul Roebuck ~ Real ale ~ Bar food (12-2.30, 5.30-8.30) ~ Restaurant ~ (01877) 330152 ~ Children in eating area of bar ~ Saturday ceilidhs ~ Open 12-3, 5.30-11; 12-12 Sat; 12.30-11 Sun; closed 1 Jan

KINGHOLM QUAY NX9773 Map 9
Swan
B726 just S of Dumfries; or signposted off B725

In a quiet spot overlooking the old fishing jetty on the River Nith, just upstream from the head of the estuary, this well looked-after small hotel is popular even mid-week as a friendly dining pub. Served in the well ordered lounge or at busy times in the restaurant, the food includes soup (£2), sandwiches (from £2.75), spinach cannelloni (£5.95), battered haddock (£6), braised beef or chicken in cream and mushroom sauce (£7.95), daily specials such as steak pie (£5.95) or seafood salad (£6.50) and good puddings such as banoffi pie (£2.80). They also do high teas. The neat and comfortable public bar has well kept Theakstons Best on handpump, and good house wines. The staff are very friendly; TV and quiet piped music. There are tables out in a small garden, which has a play area. We haven't yet heard from readers who have stayed in the bedrooms here, but this would be a handy base for the Caerlaverock nature reserve with its vast numbers of geese. *(Recommended by Philip and June Caunt, Michael Buchanan, John and Christine Lowe)*

Free house ~ Licensees Billy Holesky and Tracy Rogan ~ Real ale ~ Bar food (12-2, 5-8.30) ~ (01387) 253756 ~ Children welcome till 8.30 ~ Open 11.30-2.30, 5-11(12 Fri); 11.30-11 Sun; closed 25, 26 Dec, 1 Jan

KIPPEN NS6594 Map 11
Cross Keys 🛏
Main Street; village signposted off A811 W of Stirling

Now under new licensees, this relaxed and comfortable 18th-c inn is popular with locals and its brightly lit exterior makes a welcoming sight on a cold winter night. The straightforward but welcoming lounge has a good log fire, and there's a coal fire in the attractive family dining room. Good generously served food from a daily changing menu, using fresh local produce might include leek and spinach soup (£2), herring fillet marinated in mild mustard sauce (£3), lambs liver and bacon (£5.30), steak and mushroom pie or breaded haddock (£6.50), beef stroganoff or smoked salmon platter (£6.95), grilled sirloin (£10.75), and puddings such as strawberry and mandarin cheesecake or chocolate profiteroles (from £3.25); smaller helpings for children. Well kept Belhaven 80/- and IPA on handpump, and around 30 malt whiskies; dominoes and TV in the separate public bar. The garden has tables and a children's play area. *(Recommended by Chris Saville, Pat and Tony Martin)*

Free house ~ Licensees Mr and Mrs Scott ~ Real ale ~ Bar food (12(12.30 Sun)-2, 5.30-9) ~ Restaurant ~ (01786) 870293 ~ Children in eating area of bar and family room ~ Open 12-12(1 Sat); 12.30-12 Sun; cl 2.30-5.30 in winter; closed Mon in Jan ~ Bedrooms: £25B/£50B

Children – if the details at the end of an entry don't mention them, you should assume that the pub does not allow them inside.

KIPPFORD NX8355 Map 9

Anchor ⇐

Off A710 S of Dalbeattie

Overlooking the big natural harbour and the peaceful hills beyond, this waterfront inn has a particularly lively atmosphere in summer, although even when it gets really busy service remains cheerfully efficient. The traditional back bar has built-in red plush seats, panelled walls hung with nautical prints, and a coal fire. The no smoking lounge bar, more used for eating, has comfortable plush banquettes and stools and lots of prints and plates on the local granite walls; there are a few more tables in a snug; piped music. Generously served decent bar food might include home-made soup (£1.90), sandwiches (from £2), fresh breaded haddock (£5.95), home-made steak or fish pie (£6.50), chicken burritos or lamb noisettes (£8.50), monkfish (£9.50), 20oz T-bone steak (£11.95) and jumbo crevettes in garlic butter (£12); the upstairs function room acts as a dining overflow with table service in summer (must book for a table here). Well kept Boddingtons, Theakstons Best with a guest such as Flowers Original on handpump, cocktails and lots of malt whiskies. The games room has a juke box, TV, football table, fruit machine, video game, and board games. Seats outside. The recently renovated bedrooms have lovely views, and the surrounding countryside is good for walks and birdwatching. *(Recommended by Stan and Hazel Allen, Pat and Tony Hinkins, B, M and P Kendall, Mike and Sue Loseby)*

Free house ~ Licensee Mark Charlloner ~ Real ale ~ Bar food (12-2.30, 6-9.30 (they may finish earlier in winter)) ~ (01556) 620205 ~ Children welcome ~ Open 11(12 Sun)-12; 12-3, 6-11 in winter; closed 25 Dec ~ Bedrooms: £30B/£60B

KIRKTON OF GLENISLA NO2160 Map 11

Glenisla Hotel ⇐

B951 N of Kirriemuir and Alyth

The new licensees at this welcoming 17th-c former coaching inn, which is set in one of the prettiest Angus Glens, are keen to promote local produce, with the beers, wines, and cheeses all coming from nearby suppliers. It's therefore not surprising that the pub has a strong feeling of being at the centre of local life. The well kept Independence and Lia Fail from the small Inveralmond brewery in Perth are served alongside a guest such as Houston Jock Frost, local fruit wines and 60 or so malts. The simple but cosy carpeted pubby bar has beams and ceiling joists, a roaring log fire (sometimes even in summer), wooden tables and chairs, decent prints and a chatty crowd of locals; a garden opens off it. The lounge is comfortable and sunny, and the elegant high-ceilinged dining room has rugs on the wooden floor, pretty curtains, candles and fresh flowers, and crisp cream tablecloths. Very good bar food might include soup (£2.65), Orkney fish platter (£4.45), penne in tomato and basil sauce (£5.75), Loch Fyne kippers (£5.95), haddock and chips or steak pie and chips (£6.25), mixed grill (£6.95) and Aberdeen Angus steak and a glass of beer or wine (£11); the restaurant is no smoking. A refurbished stable block has darts, pool, alley skittles, dominoes and cribbage. The comfortable bedrooms are attractively individual. There are good surrounding walks, and they can arrange fishing in local lochs. *(Recommended by David Carty, Vicky and David Sarti, Paul Roughley, Julia Fox)*

Free house ~ Licensees Ian and Anne Kemp ~ Real ale ~ Bar food (12-2, 6.30-8.30) ~ Restaurant ~ (01575) 582223 ~ Children welcome ~ Open 11-11(12 Sat); 12.30-11 Sun; 5-11 wkdys in winter; closed 25, 26 Dec ~ Bedrooms: £31B/£28B

LINLITHGOW NS9976 Map 11

Four Marys ⬤ £

65 High St; 2 miles from M9 junction 3 (and little further from junction 4) – town signposted

This bustling town pub is popular for its good range of well kept ales and cheery welcoming atmosphere. The 16th-c building takes its name from the four ladies-in-waiting of Mary Queen of Scots, who was born at nearby Linlithgow Palace, and there are masses of mementoes of the ill-fated queen, such as pictures and written records, a piece of bed curtain said to be hers, part of a 16th-c cloth and swansdown vest of the type she's likely to have worn, and a facsimile of her death-mask. The L-shaped bar also has mahogany dining chairs around stripped period and antique tables, a couple of attractive antique corner cupboards, and an elaborate Victorian dresser serving as a bar gantry. The walls are mainly stripped stone, including some remarkable masonry in the inner area; piped music. Alongside Belhaven 70/-, 80/- and St Andrews and Caledonian Deuchars IPA, four constantly changing guests on handpump might include Black Sheep, Jennings Crag Rat, Marstons Pedigree and Timothy Taylors Landlord. During their May and October beer festivals they have 20 real ale pumps and live entertainment; friendly bar staff. Simple bar food includes sandwiches (from £1.95), haggis, neeps and tatties (£4.95) and fresh smoked or fried haddock (£5.25); part of the pub is no smoking. When the building was an apothecary's shop, David Waldie experimented in it with chloroform – its first use as an anaesthetic. Parking can be difficult. *(Recommended by R J Walden, Andy and Jill Kassube, Brian and Lynn Young)*

Belhaven ~ Manager Eve Forrest ~ Real ale ~ Bar food (12-2.30, 5.30-8.30; 12.30-8.30 Sun) ~ Restaurant ~ (01506) 842171 ~ Children in restaurant ~ Open 11-11(11.45 Thurs-Sat); 12.30-11 Sun; closed 1 Jan

LYBSTER ND2436 Map 11
Portland Arms 🛏️

A9 S of Wick

This staunch old granite hotel which was built as a staging post on the early 19th-c Parliamentary Road has been very attractively refurbished since the last edition of the *Guide*. They've created a cosy country kitchen room with an Aga, pine furnishings and farmhouse crockery in what was the cocktail bar, and the bar has been smartened up into a bistro with warm colours and fabrics, solid dark wood furnishings, softly upholstered chairs and a cosy fire. Improved bar food includes crispy haggis and spinach won tons with mint cream sauce or marinated wild mushrooms on cracked wheat salad (£3.90), Caithness crab tart with light chilli oil (£4.50), cannelloni filled with spicy bean, vegetable and tomato ragoût topped with spicy cheese sauce (£8.50), trout fillets on sautéed leeks on an open pastry case with white wine sauce (£9.50), fried duck breast on a (large!) slice of goats cheese gnocchi with game jus (£10.50), fish of the day, and puddings (£3.50); friendly, helpful staff. They keep 40 or more malt whiskies (beers are keg); dominoes, trivia, piped music. This, our most northerly main entry, is a good base for exploring the spectacular cliffs and stacks of the nearby coastline, and they can arrange fishing and so forth. *(Recommended by Alan Wilcock, Christine Davidson, Fiona Dick, Barclay Price, Ron and Sheila Corbett, Moira and John Cole; also in* The Good Hotel Guide*)*

Free house ~ Licensee Mark Stevens ~ Bar food (12-9) ~ Restaurant ~ (01593) 721721 ~ Children welcome ~ Open 12-12(11.45 Sun) ~ Bedrooms: £48B/£68B

MELROSE NT5434 Map 9
Burts Hotel 🍽️ 🛏️

B6374, Market Square

Melrose is perhaps the most villagey of the Border towns, and this comfortably civilised hotel is an ideal place to stay while you discover its charms. Always busy and cheerful, the friendly L-shaped lounge bar has lots of cushioned wall seats and windsor armchairs on its turkey carpet, and Scottish prints on the walls; the Tweed Room and the restaurant are no smoking. Well kept Belhaven 80/-, Caledonian Deuchars IPA and a guest such as Broughton Greenmantle on handpump, over 80 malt whiskies, and a good wine list; dominoes. Food here is consistently good, but it's best to arrive early or book. Promptly served by professional, hard-working staff, the inventive bar menu might include soup (£2.50), fried cod and smoked haddock fishcakes with spiced red pepper cream or carpaccio with parmesan flakes and dressed leaves (£4.25), breaded haddock or vegetable tortilla (£7.25), chicken breast wrapped in bacon sliced over a tomato and pesto fondue or warm pork salad with cherry tomato, mushrooms and grapes with sweet mustard dressing (£8.25) and puddings such as warm treacle tart or dark chocolate and orange marquise with a ragoût of seasonal fruits and minted mascarpone (£4.25); extremely good breakfasts. The owners here have been providing personal, attentive service for more than 30 years now, and have attracted a good few loyal devotees along the way. There's a well tended garden (with tables in summer). An alternative if distant way to view the town's striking abbey ruins is from the top of the tower at Smailholm. *(Recommended by B, M and P Kendall, Joel Dobris, Chris Rounthwaite, Mr and Mrs R M Macnaughton, Julie Hogg, Alain Weld, Mrs J H S Lang, Ted Tomiak, Peter F Marshall, Jack and Heather Coyle, Nigel Woolliscroft, George and Jean Dundas)*

Free house ~ Licensees Graham and Anne Henderson ~ Real ale ~ Bar food (12-2, 6-9.30(6-10 Fri, Sat)) ~ Restaurant ~ (01896) 822285 ~ Children welcome ~ Open 11-2.30, 5-11; 12-2.30, 6-11 Sun; closed 26 Dec ~ Bedrooms: £52B/£92B

MOUNTBENGER NT3125 Map 9
Gordon Arms
Junction A708/B709

Over one hundred and sixty years ago, the 'Ettrick Shepherd' James Hogg recommended that this very inn should keep its licence, which Sir Walter Scott, in his capacity as a justice and who also knew the inn, subsequently granted. Today, it remains a welcome sight amidst splendid empty moorlands, providing cheap accommodation for hill walkers, cyclists and fishermen in its bunkhouse in addition to the hotel bedrooms. Letters from Scott and Hogg are displayed on the walls of the comfortable public bar, along with an interesting set of period photographs of the neighbourhood (one dated 1865), and some well illustrated poems; winter fire. Well kept Broughton Merlins Ale and maybe a guest on handpump and lots of malt whiskies. Bar food includes soup (£2.25), toasted sandwiches (lunchtime only, from £3.50), ploughman's (£4.50), home-made steak pie or chicken breast stuffed with haggis (£6.50), fresh Yarrow trout fried in capers, butter and lemon juice (£6.95) and weekend barbecue; darts. *(Recommended by Dr Travers Grant)*

Free house ~ Licensees Mr and Mrs Krex ~ Real ale ~ Bar food (11-9) ~ Restaurant ~ (01750) 82222 ~ Children welcome ~ Open 11-11(12 Sat) ~ Bedrooms: £26/£42S

OBAN NM8630 Map 11
Oban Inn
Stafford Street, near North Pier

There's a good-natured bustling atmosphere at this late 18th-c harbourside local. The down to earth beamed downstairs bar has small stools, pews and black-winged modern settles on its uneven slate floor, blow-ups of old Oban postcards on the cream walls, and unusual brass-shaded wall lamps. The smarter, partly panelled upstairs bar has button-back banquettes around cast-iron-framed tables, a coffered woodwork ceiling, and little backlit arched false windows with heraldic roundels in aged stained glass; the children's area is no smoking. Well kept McEwans 70/- and 80/-, and a large selection of whiskies. Very hard-working friendly staff serve good value straightforward lunchtime bar food including all day winter breakfast (£2.49), moules marinières (£3.25/£6.50), 8oz steak (£3.99), lasagne or huge haddock in beer batter (£5.25) and beef and ale pie or breaded scampi (£5.50); fruit machine, juke box, and piped music. *(Recommended by Gordon Stevenson, Nigel Woolliscroft, Susan and John Douglas, George Atkinson, Mr and Mrs T B Staples)*

Scottish Courage ~ Licensee Erica Mouat ~ Real ale ~ Bar food (11(12.30 Sun)-10) ~ (01631) 562484 ~ Children welcome till 8 ~ Open 11-12.45; 12.30-12.45 Sun

PITLOCHRY NN9162 Map 11
Killiecrankie Hotel 🍴 🛏

Killiecrankie signposted from A9 N of Pitlochry

The lovely peaceful grounds of this splendidly set and very well run country hotel, with a putting course, croquet lawn, dramatic views of the mountain pass and sometimes roe deer and red squirrels, seem to stretch for miles. Inside, the attractively furnished bar has some panelling, upholstered seating and mahogany tables and chairs, as well as stuffed animals and some rather fine wildlife paintings; in the airy conservatory extension (which overlooks the pretty garden) there are light beech tables and upholstered chairs, with discreetly placed plants and flowers. Served by friendly staff, reliably good bar food might include soup (£2.75), enjoyable tapas (£5.50), spinach and feta goujons or cumberland sausage with apple and walnut coleslaw (£7.50), tagliatelle with roasted vegetables, black olives and parmesan (£7.95), game casserole (£8.25), 10oz rib-eye Aberdeen Angus steak (£12.50, and puddings such as mixed red berry terrine with fruit coulis and cream or syrup sponge pudding (£3.95). The restaurant – rather formal – is no smoking. Decent wines, around two dozen malt whiskies, coffee and a choice of teas. Please note – the bedroom prices below include dinner and breakfast. *(Recommended by Andrew and Catherine Gilham, Norman Stansfield, Karen Eliot, Fiona Dick, Barclay Price; also in* The Good Hotel Guide*)*

Free house ~ Licensees Colin and Carole Anderson ~ Bar food (12.30-2, 6.30-9.15) ~ Restaurant ~ (01796) 473220 ~ Children in restaurant (must be over 5) and eating area of bar ~ Open 11-2.30, 5.30-11; 12-2, 6.30-11 Sun; closed Jan, and Mon and Tues Dec-Mar ~ Bedrooms: £89B/£178B

Moulin 🍺 🛏

Kirkmichael Rd, Moulin; A924 NE of Pitlochry centre

The traditional pubby atmosphere at this imposing white painted 17th-c inn owes much to the well kept real ales on handpump which are brewed in the little stables across the street: Braveheart, Moulin Light, Ale of Atholl and the stronger Old Remedial; group brewery tours by arrangement. Although the building has been much extended over the years, the bar, in the oldest part of the building, still seems an entity in itself. Above the fireplace in the smaller room is an interesting painting of the village before the road was built (Moulin used to be a bustling market town, far busier than Pitlochry), while the bigger carpeted area has a good few tables and cushioned banquettes in little booths divided by stained-glass country scenes, another big fireplace, some exposed stonework, fresh flowers, and local prints and golf clubs around the walls; bar billiards, shove-ha'penny, cribbage, dominoes and fruit machine. A wide choice of enjoyable bar food includes soup (£2.25), lunchtime sandwiches and baked potatoes (from £3.75), ploughman's (£3.95), Isle of Skye mussels (£4.50/£6.50), haggis and neeps (£5.45), stuffed peppers (£6.50), game casserole or grilled salmon (£6.95), and puddings such as chocolate and nut ice-cream cake or honey sponge and custard (£2.50); prompt friendly service. They keep around 40 malt whiskies. Picnic-sets outside are surrounded by tubs of flowers, and look across to the village kirk. They offer good value three-night breaks out of season. Rewarding walks nearby. *(Recommended by Louise English, Darly Graton, Graeme Gulibert, Susan and John Douglas, Paul Roughley, Julia Fox, David Carty, Andy and Jill Kassube, Derek and Sylvia Stephenson, Peter Salmon, Simon Chell, P R and S A White)*

Own brew ~ Licensee Heather Reeves ~ Real ale ~ Bar food (12-9.30) ~ Restaurant (6-9) ~ (01796) 472196 ~ Children in eating area of bar and restaurant ~ Open 12-11(11.45 Sat) ~ Bedrooms: £25B/£50B

If you stay overnight in an inn or hotel, they are allowed to serve you an alcoholic drink at any hour of the day or night.

PLOCKTON NG8033 Map 11
Plockton Hotel ⇌

Village signposted from A87 near Kyle of Lochalsh

Delightfully set in a lovely Scottish National Trust village, this warmly welcoming little hotel forms part of a long, low terrace of stone-built houses. Tables in the front garden look out past the palm trees and colourfully flowering shrub-lined shore, and across the sheltered anchorage to the rugged mountainous surrounds of Loch Carron. The comfortably furnished, bustling lounge bar has window seats looking out to the boats on the water, as well as antiqued dark red leather seating around neat Regency-style tables on a tartan carpet, three model ships set into the woodwork, and partly panelled stone walls. The separate public bar has pool, darts, shove-ha'penny, dominoes, and piped music. Very good, promptly served bar food includes home-made soup (£2.25, with their own bread), lunchtime sandwiches and filled baked potatoes, Talisker whisky pâté (£3.75), a vegetarian dish of the day (£5.95), west coast haddock and chips (£6.25), herring in oatmeal (£6.50), prawns fresh from the bay (starter £6.75, main course £13.50), chicken stuffed with smoked ham and cheese in sun-dried tomato and basil sauce (£9.50), good steak platters (from £9.95), grilled turbot in orange butter (£10.50), and seafood platter (£15.75); children's menu. It's worth booking, as they do get busy. Good breakfasts; the new Courtyard restaurant is no smoking. Caledonian Deuchars IPA on tall fount air pressure, bottled beers from the Isle of Skye brewery, a good collection of malt whiskies, and a short wine list. More than half of the new bedrooms with bathrooms in the adjacent building have sea views. A hotel nearby has recently changed its name to the Plockton Inn, so if this is where you're headed don't get the two confused. *(Recommended by Sally Causer, Simon Chell, Peter F Marshall, David and Heather Stephenson, P R and S A White, Nigel Woolliscroft, Julie Hogg, Alain Weld, Lorna Baxter, John Winstanley)*

Free house ~ Licensee Tom Pearson ~ Real ale ~ Bar food (12-2.15, 6-9.15) ~ Restaurant ~ (01599) 544274 ~ Children in eating area of bar and restaurant ~ Open 11-12(11.45 Sat); 12.30-11 Sun ~ Bedrooms: £35B/£70B

PORTPATRICK NW9954 Map 9
Crown ★ ⇌

North Crescent

Tables in front of this friendly hotel, which is centrally situated in a delightful harbourside village, and only a stone's throw from the water's edge, allow you to make the most of the evening sun and the comings and goings on the water, especially on a Thursday when the little fishing fleet comes in. Inside, the rambling old-fashioned bar has lots of cosy nooks and crannies, and the partly panelled butter-coloured walls are decorated with old mirrors which have landscapes painted in their side panels. Served by obliging staff, good bar food includes sandwiches (from £2.30; toasties from £2.45), soup (£2.65), and extremely fresh seafood such as local prawns, lobster, and monkfish tails and scallops (platter for two people, £23); good breakfasts. Well kept Boddingtons, a carefully chosen wine list, and over 70 malt whiskies; fruit machine and maybe piped music. An airy and very attractively decorated early 20th-c, half no smoking dining room opens through a quiet no smoking conservatory area into a sheltered back garden. *(Recommended by Stan and Hazel Allen, John Knighton, John Robertson, Andy, Julie and Stuart Hawkins, Joy and Peter Heatherley, Mike and Sue Loseby)*

Free house ~ Licensee Mr A Schofield ~ Real ale ~ Bar food (12-10) ~ Restaurant ~ (01776) 810261 ~ Children welcome ~ Folk most Fridays ~ Open 11-11.30; 11-12 Sat; 12-11 Sun; closed 25 Dec ~ Bedrooms: £43B/£72B

You are allowed 20 minutes after 'time, please' to finish your drink – half an hour if you bought it in conjunction with a meal.

SHIELDAIG NG8154 Map 11
Tigh an Eilean Hotel 🛏

Village signposted just off A896 Lochcarron—Gairloch

This welcoming place is in a beautiful position, looking over the forested Shieldaig Island to Loch Torridon and then out to the sea beyond. It's primarily a hotel with a small village bar attached but it's a very comfortable place to stay, with easy chairs, books, a woodburning stove and a well stocked help-yourself bar in the neat and prettily decorated two-room lounge, and an attractively modern dining room specialising in tasty and good value local shellfish, fish and game. The bar is very simple, with blue brocaded button-back banquettes in little bays, and picture windows looking out to sea; winter darts, bar billiards and juke box. The short choice of simple, quickly served bar food might include sandwiches (£1.95), soup (£2.35), crab bisque with home-made bread (£3.75), steak and ale pie (£6.95), fish of the day (£7.25), prawns in garlic butter (£7.95), seafood stew (£9.50). A sheltered front courtyard has four picnic-sets and wall benches. The National Trust Torridon estate and the Beinn Eighe nature reserve aren't too far away. *(Recommended by Lorna Baxter, John Winstanley, Norman Stansfield, Peter F Marshall, Angus and Rosemary Campbell; also in* The Good Hotel Guide*)*

Free house ~ Licensee Cathryn Field ~ Bar food ~ Restaurant ~ (01520) 755251 ~ Children in eating area of bar and restaurant ~ Open 11-11; 12.30-10 Sun; closed 3-5 Nov-end Feb ~ Bedrooms: £49.50B/£110B

SKEABOST NG4148 Map 11
Skeabost House Hotel ★ 🛏

A850 NW of Portree, 1½ miles past junction with A856

There are glorious views over Loch Snizort from this splendidly grand-looking, civilised hotel which is set in 12 acres of secluded woodland and gardens, is said to have some of the best salmon fishing on the island and has a nine hole golf course. The bustling high-ceilinged bar has a pine counter and red brocade seats on its thick red carpet, and a fine panelled billiards room leads off the stately hall. A wholly separate public bar has darts, pool, TV, and even its own car park. Well kept Hebridean Gold and Red Cuillin from the Isle of Skye Brewery, plus a fine choice of over 100 single malt whiskies, including their own and some very rare vintages. Served in the spacious and airy conservatory, bar food includes home-made soup (£2.20), fried haggis balls with spicy tomato sauce (£2.50), stilton and chestnut pâté (£2.60), cottage pie (£4.95), grilled salmon fillet with lemon sauce (£5.50), beef in Guinness with a large yorkshire pudding (£6.50) and scampi (£7.50). All the eating areas are no smoking and it's best to dress fairly smartly in the main dining room. Bedrooms are comfortable and attractively furnished and the breakfasts excellent. *(Recommended by Norman Stansfield, Karen Eliot, Mrs J H S Lang, Vicky and David Sarti, Graham and Elizabeth Hargreaves, Tony Walker)*

Free house ~ Licensee Michael John Heaney ~ Real ale ~ Bar food (12-2, 6.30-9) ~ Restaurant ~ (01470) 532202 ~ Children welcome ~ Open 12-3, 5-12; 12-1 Sat (11 Sun); closed 7 Jan-1 Mar ~ Bedrooms: £52B/£90B

ST MONANCE SO5202 Map 11
Seafood Restaurant & Bar 🍴

16 West End; just off A917

The excellent seafood in the back restaurant of this rather ordinary-looking place is very much the centre of attention here, and though you're still welcome to come just for a drink, it's probably now best to think of this even at lunchtimes as a (good) restaurant. Then, they offer a two-course meal for £14 (three-course, £18), with dishes such as asparagus, celeriac and chilli soup, cod with cajun spices with a thai coconut sauce, scallops with a saffron and sun-dried tomato risotto and a mango, sweet pepper and chilli salsa and roast gressingham duck with red wine and cranberry jus. In the evenings they do food only in the airy restaurant (except in summer when you can generally eat outside on the charming terrace), with its big windows overlooking the harbour and the Firth of Forth; meals then might include three Kilbrandon oysters (£3), grilled turbot fillet with sauteed fennel and bok choi (£14.50), pan-fried lamb with butter beans (£15.50), shi-itake mushroom risotto with balsamic dressing and roast cherry tomatoes (£11.50), puddings such as prune and armagnac pudding with banana ice cream and butterscotch sauce (£5.15) and a fine selection of cheeses from a delicatessen in St Andrews (run by the owner's mother). It is advisable to book tables in the restaurant – even mid-week. The snug front bar is immaculate yet warmly cosy, the well polished light wooden panelling and fittings and lack of windows creating something of a below-decks feel even if there are no dripping wellies and waterproofs present that day. On the mantelpiece above a smart tiled fireplace is a gleaming ship's bell, and there are a few seafaring models and mementoes on illuminated shelves, as well as turn-of-the-century photos of local life. Well kept Belhaven 80/- and a summer guest such as Wadworths 6X on handpump; also a wide range of wines, around 30 malt whiskies (including a malt of the month), freshly squeezed fruit juices, and a range of teas, coffees and infusions. Very friendly service. *(Recommended by Susan and John Douglas, Ken Richards)*

Free house ~ Licensee Tim Butler ~ Real ale ~ Bar food (12-2 7-9) ~ Restaurant ~ (01333) 730327 ~ Children in restaurant ~ Open 12(12.30 Sun)-3, 6-11 Sat; closed Mon

STONEHAVEN NO8493 Map 11
Lairhillock ♀

Netherley; 6 miles N of Stonehaven, 6 miles S of Aberdeen, take the Durris turn-off from the A90

A good place to come for a decent meal, this friendly extended country pub is smart but relaxed, with a traditional atmosphere that remains welcoming, even at its busiest. The cheerful beamed bar has panelled wall benches, a mixture of old seats, dark woodwork, harness and brass lamps on the walls, a good open fire, and countryside views from the bay window; there's an unusual central fire in the spacious separate lounge. A good choice of well kept ales might include Courage Directors, Belhaven 80/-, Marstons Pedigree and Timothy Taylors Landlord and guests such as Heather Ale on handpump, over 50 malt whiskies, and an extensive wine list; cheery efficient staff, a nice pub cat, darts, cribbage and dominoes. Good, freshly prepared bar food might include soup (£2.25), king prawns gambas (£5.75), a changing terrine or pâté (£4.35), filled baguettes (£4.65), lunchtime ploughman's (£5.95), steak and ale pie (£7.95), stir fry of monkfish and crayfish tails (£9.75), chicken stuffed with haggis in light whisky sauce or braised leg of lamb with red wine, rosemary and root vegetables (£8.95), maybe ostrich fillet steaks (£10.95), and puddings such as cheesecake or banana and butterscotch sundae (from £2.95); Sunday buffet lunch (£7.95). A separate thoughtful children's menu is now available, including wild boar sausages and mash (£3.50) and spicy spare ribs (£2.95). The cosy, highly praised restaurant is in an adjacent building. There are panoramic views from the no smoking conservatory. *(Recommended by R T and J C Moggridge, Susan and John Douglas)*

Free house ~ Licensee Roger Thorne ~ Real ale ~ Bar food (6-9.30(wkdys) and 6-10(Fri-Sat)) ~ Restaurant ~ (01569) 730001 ~ Children welcome ~ Open 10.30-2.30, 5-11; 11-12 Sat; 11-11 Sun

SWINTON NT8448 Map 10
Wheatsheaf ⑪ ⟺

A6112 N of Coldstream

Scotland Dining Pub of the Year

Extremely well run, this has excellent food, service to match, and a nice seting in a pretty village surrounded by rolling countryside, just a few miles away from the River Tweed. At lunchtime, the daily changing menu might include sandwiches, soup (£2.80), aubergine and parmesan melanzane (£4.25), sautéed mushrooms and bacon in a filo pastry basket (£4.70), fillet of salmon with tomato salsa (£8.95), corn-fed chicken in a red wine and mushroom sauce (£7.90), local wild boar sausages with red wine and mushroom sauce (£7.90), and deep-fried fillet of haddock in a crispy beer batter (£6.75), with evening dishes such as roast loin of highland venison in a juniper and quince sauce with spiced poached pear (£14.90), chargrilled scotch fillet steak on a Glenmorangie whisky and honey mustard sauce (£15.85), filo pastry gateau with grilled goats cheese, pine nuts and stir-fried vegetables on a cream, mushroom and brandy sauce (£9.45), and scrumptious puddings such as lemon and almond cake with mascarpone ice cream (£4.00). Booking is advisable, particularly from Thursday to Saturday evening. Caledonian Deuchars IPA and a guest such as Broughton Clipper on handpump, a decent range of malt whiskies and brandies, good choice of wines, and cocktails. Service is helpful, unhurried and genuinely welcoming. The carefully thought-out main bar area has an attractive long oak settle and some green-cushioned window seats, as well as wheelback chairs around tables, a stuffed pheasant and partridge over the log fire, and sporting prints and plates on the bottle-green wall covering; a small lower-ceilinged part by the counter has pubbier furnishings, and small agricultural prints on the walls – especially sheep. The front conservatory has a vaulted pine ceiling and walls of local stone, while at the side is a separate locals' bar; cribbage and dominoes. The garden has a play area for children. The dining areas are no smoking. They do very good breakfasts. *(Recommended by Walter and Susan Rinaldi-Butcher, Brian and Lynn Young, Derek and Sylvia Stephenson, Jack and Heather Coyle, Willie Bell, Christine and Malcolm Ingram, Darly Graton, Graeme Gulibert, George and Jean Dundas, Chris Rounthwaite, RJH; also in* The Good Hotel Guide*)*

Free house ~ Licensee Alan Reid ~ Real ale ~ Bar food (12-2, 6-9.30) ~ Restaurant ~ (01890) 860257 ~ Children in eating area of bar and restaurant ~ Open 11-2.30, 6-11; 11-2.30 6-11 Sat; 12.30-2.30, 6.30-10.30 Sun; closed Sun evening in winter; closed Mon ~ Bedrooms: £50S(£50B)/£80S(£80B)

TAYVALLICH NR7386 Map 11
Tayvallich Inn 🍴

B8025, off A816 1 mile S of Kilmartin; or take B841 turn-off from A816 2 miles N of Lochgilphead

Fresh seafood brought in by local fishermen from the bay of Loch Sween just across the lane is the highlight of the menu at this simply furnished café/bar, with lovely views over the yacht anchorage and loch from its terrace. The choice typically includes good haddock and chips (£4.95), fried scallops (£13.50), mussels (£7.90), cajun salmon with black butter (£10.50), specials such as fillet of beef stroganoff (£11) and a variety of white fish, depending on what's been caught; other bar food includes soup (£2.20), chicken liver pâté (£3.85), stir-fried vegetables (£4.95), home-made burgers (from £5.20), chicken curry (£6.25), sirloin steak (£12.95) and puddings (£3.20); children's helpings. All the whiskies are Islay malts; they also do fresh milk shakes. Service is friendly, and people with children are very much at home here. The small bar has local nautical charts on the cream walls, exposed ceiling joists, and pale pine upright chairs, benches and tables on its quarry-tiled floor; darts, dominoes, cards. It leads into a no smoking (during meal times) dining conservatory, from where sliding glass doors open on to the terrace; there's a garden, too. *(Recommended by Mr and Mrs R M Macnaughton, Nigel Woolliscroft, Dr G E Martin)*

Free house ~ Licensee Jilly Wilson ~ Bar food (12-2, 6-8.30) ~ Restaurant (from 7) ~ (01546) 870282 ~ Children welcome ~ Open 11-12(1 Fri); 11-1 Sat; 12.30-12 Sun; 11-2.30, 6-11(winter wkdys) 11-2.30, 5-1(winter Fri-Sat) 12.30-2.30, 5-12 (winter Sun)

We mention bottled beers and spirits only if there is something unusual about them – imported Belgian real ales, say, or dozens of malt whiskies; so do please let us know about them in your reports: www.goodguides.com

THORNHILL NS6699 Map 11
Lion & Unicorn
A873

Parts of this attractive building date back to 1635, and in the restaurant you can see the original massive fireplace, six feet high and five feet wide. It's warm and friendly, with the licensees keeping the atmosphere aglow even when the cosy log fires are out of season. The constantly changing bar menu is a big draw here, and might at lunchtime include soup (£2.30), fried potato skins (£3.25), baked potatoes (from £4), steak pie (£5.75), scampi (£6.20), and Aberdeen Angus steaks on big sizzling platters (from £10.95). Daily specials may include roast lamb with cherry and orange glaze (£7.50) and salmon steak with greenlip mussels and cream sauce (£7.95); you can eat from the restaurant menu in the bar, and they're fairly flexible with what's on the menu. The open-plan front room has a warm fire, beams and stone walls, and comfortable seats on the wooden floors, and they now do a real ale such as Belhaven or Harviestoun. The beamed public bar has stone walls and floors, and piped music, juke box, pool, fruit machine, TV, darts and dominoes. The restaurant is no smoking. Very nice in summer, the garden has a play area, and maybe barbecues in good weather. The reasonably priced bedrooms have now been refurbished to a high standard (too recently for us yet to have reports from readers who've used them). (Recommended by Ian Baillie, Tom and Rosemary Hall, F Smyth, R J Walden, Nick Holding)

Free house ~ Licensees Fiona and Bobby Stevenson ~ Real ale ~ Bar food (all day in summer, 12-3 in winter) ~ Restaurant ~ (01786) 850204 ~ Children welcome ~ Open 11-12(1 Sat); 11-12 Sun

TUSHIELAW NT3018 Map 9
Tushielaw Inn 🛏
Ettrick Valley, B709/B7009 Lockerbie—Selkirk

This friendly inn by Ettrick Water is a good base for walkers or for touring. The unpretentious but comfortable little bar draws a mix of customers, from hang-gliders to hikers, with Broughton Best, decent house wines, a good few malts, an open fire, local prints and photographs, and several antiques; darts, cribbage, dominoes, shove-ha'penny, TV and piped music. Decent bar food includes soup (£2.75), lunchtime filled baguettes (from £4), ploughman's (£5), nut fettuccine (£5.50), deep-fried haddock or home-made steak and stout pie (£6), Yarrow trout with creamy mustard sauce (£7.50), chicken in a lemon and tarragon sauce (£7.50), and Aberdeen Angus steaks (£11.50). The dining room is no smoking. There are tables on an outside terrace. Simple but comfortable bedrooms, and the inn has its own fishing on Clearburn Loch up the B711. (Recommended by John and Margaret Mitchell, Lorna Baxter, John Winstanley, Paul S McPherson, Mr and Mrs T Christian, E D Bailey)

Free house ~ Licensee Gordon Harrison ~ Real ale ~ Bar food ~ Restaurant ~ (01750) 62205 ~ Children welcome ~ Open 12-2.30 Mon and Fri-Sun, 6.30-11; cl Mon-Weds Dec-Mar winter ~ Bedrooms: £30B/£46B

ULLAPOOL NH1294 Map 11
Ferry Boat 🍽 🛏
Shore Street; coming from the S, keep straight ahead when main A835 turns right into Mill Street

The unassuming two-roomed pubby bar has brocade-cushioned seats around plain wooden tables, quarry tiles by the corner serving counter and patterned carpet elsewhere, big windows with nice views, a stained-glass door hanging from the ceiling and a fruit machine; cribbage, dominoes and piped music. Friendly staff often offer you a healthy pre-buy sample of one of the three changing well kept ales such as Black Isle Red Kite, Isle of Skye Red Cuillin and Wadworths 6X on handpump. Filling up with a good mix of locals and tourists, this room is particularly lively on summer evenings, when the only food available is in the very upmarket no smoking restaurant; evening bar food is served in winter and at other quieter times. The more peaceful inner room has a coal fire, a delft shelf of copper measures and willow-pattern plates. Enjoyable bar lunches include soup and sandwiches (£2.20), ploughman's (£4.20), venison pâté (£4.50), haggis, neeps and tatties (£5.25), aubergine charlotte (£6.25), pork and leek pie (£6.50) and puddings (£2.50). People in wheelchairs feel perfectly at ease in the bar here. Dogs welcome. In summer you can sit on the wall across the road and take in the fine views to the tall hills beyond the attractive fishing port, with its bustle of yachts, ferry boats, fishing boats and tour boats for the Summer Isles. *(Recommended by Michael Buchanan, Ian Baillie, Paul Thompson, Anna Blackburn, Darly Graton, Graeme Gulibert, Chris Saville)*

Free house ~ Licensee Richard Smith ~ Real ale ~ Bar food (12(12.30 Sun)-2.30, 7-9.30 (Restaurant in summer only)) ~ Restaurant ~ (01854) 612366 ~ Children in eating area of bar and restaurant ~ Thurs evening folk music ~ Open 11-11; 11-11 Sat; 12.30-11 Sun; closed 25-26 Dec ~ Bedrooms: £25B/£50B

Morefield Motel ⊕

North Road (A835)

This is an unexpected place to find such good fresh fish and seafood; word has got around, but the friendly, unflappable staff take the hungry crowds in their stride. Depending on availability, the generously served meals might include hot-smoked salmon (£6.25), fresh langoustine platter (£6.75), popular battered haddock (£7.25), seafood thermidor (£9.25), a marvellous seafood platter (£18.75), and daily specials such as plump hand-dived scallops in champagne sauce (£9.25) or monkfish tails with parma ham, again in champagne sauce (£11.95). Non-fishy dishes also feature, such as soup (£2.50), fillet steak with haggis and Drambuie sauce (£14.95), and various vegetarian meals such as vegetable champignon in flaky pastry (£7.95). The smarter Mariners restaurant has a slightly more elaborate menu. In winter the diners tend to yield to local people playing darts or pool. Two well kept changing ales such as Isle of Skye Black Cuillin and Teuchter on handpump, decent wines and a wide range of malt whiskies and ports, some nearly 30 years old; friendly tartan-skirted waitresses. The L-shaped lounge is mostly no smoking, and the restaurant is totally; piped music. There are tables on a terrace. The rooms are simple, but breakfasts are enjoyable. *(Recommended by Karen Eliot)*

Free house ~ Licensee David Caulfield ~ Real ale ~ Bar food (12-2, 5.30-9.30) ~ Restaurant ~ (01854) 612161 ~ Children in eating area of bar ~ Open 11(12 Sun)-12; 11-2.30, 5-12 winter ~ Bedrooms: £25B/£50B

WEEM NN8449 Map 11
Ailean Chraggan ♀ ⇨

B846

This small and welcoming family-run hotel is an enjoyable place to stay, with good food, and chatty locals in the bar. Breakfasts are hearty, and dogs can stay too, but must have their own bedding. The changing menu, in either the comfortably carpeted modern lounge or the mainly no smoking dining room, might include soup (£2.45), sandwiches (from £2.60), fresh sardines with coriander butter (£3.95), moules marinières (£4.65), spinach and onion tart (£4.15), baked salmon stuffed with spinach and fennel (£8.75), sea bream with lemon sauce (£10.75), duck breast with honey sauce or venison steak with sweet and sour red cabbage (£10.95), and puddings such as mississippi mud pie with home-made marshmallow ice-cream (£4.25)). There is a separate children's menu (£3.95). Very good wine list, around 100 malt whiskies; winter darts and dominoes. Two outside terraces (one with an awning) enjoy a lovely view to the mountains beyond the Tay, sweeping up to Ben Lawers (the highest in this part of Scotland). *(Recommended by Susan and John Douglas, Chris and Sue Bax)*

Free house ~ Licensee Alastair Gillespie ~ Bar food ~ Restaurant ~ (01887) 820346 ~ Children welcome ~ Open 11-11; closed 25, 26 Dec, 1, 2 Jan ~ Bedrooms: £42.50B/£85B

Lucky Dip

Besides the fully inspected pubs, you might like to try these Lucky Dips recommended to us and described by readers (if you do, please send us reports: www.goodguides.com).

ABERDEENSHIRE
Aboyne [NO5298]

☆ *Boat* [Charleston Rd, off A930]: Remodelled country inn by River Dee, lounge bar with log fire and Scottish décor, pictures and brasses, maybe model train running around the walls (makes itself heard when in steam), spiral stairs to large upstairs area used as overflow for diners; good fresh food from delicious stovies up, three changing real ales such as Bass, Inveralmond and Isle of Skye, games in public bar; bedrooms (*J F M and M West, Sue and Andy Waters, LYM, R E Wolfendale*)

Braemar [NO1491]

Invercauld Arms [A93]: Wide choice of bar lunches from good soup and sandwiches up in interestingly decorated tartan-carpet bar of large hotel, decent wine, spoilt for choice on whiskies; bedrooms (*J F M and M West*)

Crathie [NO2293]

Inver [A93 Balmoral—Braemar]: 18th-c inn by River Dee, sensitively refurbished under new management, pleasant bar, quiet lounge with open fire, good range of reasonably priced home-cooked food from excellent toasties up, friendly attentive service, lots of whiskies; bedrooms (*J F M and M West, Miss J C Fawcett*)

Fraserburgh [NJ9966]

Findlays Uptown [Smiddyhill Rd/Boothby Rd]: Hearty welcome, huge choice of food in conservatory and dining room, superb Aberdeen Angus steaks, fresh local fish; busy wknds, booking advised; bedrooms planned (*Ian and Sandra Thornton*)

Memsie [NJ9663]

Heath-Hill [B9032, SW of Fraserburgh]: Good food in bar, conservatory and restaurant, esp succulent steaks and big mixed grill, welcoming licensees, several dozen malt whiskies; busy wknds, booking advised; new bedrooms (*Ian and Sandra Thornton*)

Mintlaw [NJ9948]

Country Park Inn [Station Rd (A950 W)]: Good value food from hearty soups to main dishes using local produce, largely no smoking dining area, well stocked bar usually with two changing real ales; busy wknds (*Ian and Sandra Thornton*)

Oldmeldrum [NJ8128]

Redgarth [Kirk Brae]: Good-sized comfortable lounge, traditional décor, well kept changing ales such as Caledonian 80/-, Flowers Original, and Timothy Taylors Landlord, good range of malt whiskies, nicely presented food inc good puddings, more intimate restaurant, cheerful landlord and helpful friendly service; gorgeous views to Bennachie, immaculate bedrooms (*Callum and Letitia Smith-Burnett*)

ANGUS
Dundee [NO4030]

Hogshead [Union St]: Good simple bar food inc good range of ciabatta sandwiches, up to six real ales (*Andy and Jill Kassube*)

Jute Café/Bar [Nethergate]: Unusual trendy new pub/restaurant in new arts centre, laid back during the day and lively at night; good upmarket food (not cheap), huge windows, modern furniture (*Sooz Coghlan*)

Trades House [Nethergate]: Sumptuously converted bank, no expense spared, oak panelling, marble columns, lovely stained glass showing various trades, engraved mirrors, leather wall seats, handsome tables on striking marble and mosaic floor; imaginative lunchtime food from sandwiches up (also Sun afternoon), efficient staff; disabled access and facilities, open all day till midnight, full of young people and loud music Fri/Sat night (bouncers then), quiet other times (*Susan and John Douglas*)

St Cyrus [NO7464]

St Cyrus Hotel [A92]: Good range of good inventive food in welcoming bar and large adjacent dining room, modern décor though old hotel, plenty of locals, old-fashioned village; bedrooms (*J F M and M West*)

ARGYLL
Bridge of Orchy [NN2939]

☆ *Bridge of Orchy Hotel* [A82 Tyndrum—Glencoe]: Comfortable bar with nice views, wide choice of good food in not overly large helpings, warm atmosphere, particularly well kept Caledonian 70/-, Deuchars IPA and 80/-, dozens of malt whiskies, good choice of house wines, interesting mountain photographs; comfortable well decorated bedrooms, good value bunkhouse, spectacular spot on West Highland Way (*R T and J C Moggridge, Paul Fairbrother, Helen Morris, Mr and Mrs Maurice Thompson, David Edwards*)

Glencoe [NN1058]

☆ *Clachaig* [old Glencoe rd, behind NTS Visitor Centre]: Spectacular setting, surrounded by soaring mountains, extended inn doubling as mountain rescue post and cheerfully crowded with outdoors people in season, mountain photographs in flagstoned walkers' bar (two woodburners and pool), pine-panelled snug, big modern-feeling dining lounge; hearty snacks all day, wider evening choice, lots of malt whiskies, well kept ales such as Arrols 80/-, Ind Coope Burton and Orkney Dark Island, unusual bottled beers, annual beer festival; children in no smoking restaurant; live music Sat; simple bedrooms, nourishing breakfast, self catering (*Bob and Lisa Cantrell, LYM, David Edwards, Paul Fairbrother, Helen Morris*)

Kilmelford [NM8412]

☆ *Cuilfail* [A816 S of Oban]: Former coaching inn in attractive setting, cheerful stripped-stone pubby bar with light wood furnishings in inner eating area, welcoming family service, good food in bar and restaurant, well kept McEwans and Youngers No 3, fascinating range of malt whiskies, charming garden across road; comfortable bedrooms (*LYM, Nigel Woolliscroft*)

Kilmun [NS1582]
Cot House [Sandbank; foot of Loch Eck]: Cosy lounge decorated with slabs of cedar, good value bar food (esp mussels), well kept 80/- and the pub's own Eck'ythump, good choice of wines and whiskies; four well equipped reasonably priced bedrooms with own bathrooms *(Chris Richards)*
Port Appin [NM9045]
☆ *Pier House*: Beautiful location, recently refurbished small bar with attractive terrace, very good seafood restaurant, good service, Scottish real ale, room with pool table; comfortable bedrooms, good breakfast *(Andy, Julie and Stuart Hawkins, Lorna Baxter, John Winstanley, Dr G E Martin)*
Tarbert [NR8467]
☆ *Tarbert Hotel* [Harbour St]: Lounge with log fire and attractive easy chairs off pleasant little cocktail bar, woodburner and old fishing photographs in small public bar, good bar food inc fresh local seafood and memorably comprehensive Scottish cheeseboard, good restaurant; comfortable bedrooms overlooking quiet harbour *(Meg and Colin Hamilton)*

AYRSHIRE
Coylton [NS4219]
Finlayson Arms [Hillhead]: Proper two-bar pub with decent décor, good value generous food; bedrooms *(Bill and Sheila McLardy)*

BANFFSHIRE
Aberlour [NJ2642]
Mash Tun [Broomfield Sq]: Extensively refurbished friendly former village station building, well kept Belhaven and two guest beers, bottled wheat beers, good range of malt whiskies (handy for Whisky Trail), good varied food; children welcome *(Adrian Cammack)*
Cullen [NJ5167]
Cullen Bay [A98 W]: Good locally produced food inc good value Sun lunch, plenty of malt whiskies, beautiful bay view from conservatory dining area; comfortable bedrooms *(Ian and Sandra Thornton)*
Royal Oak [A98 W of Banff]: Good bar food inc local dishes such as cullen skink and beef olives, real ales such as Belhaven and Orkney Dark Island, low-priced house wines; comfortable bedrooms with own bathrooms, not far from seafront *(Derek and Sylvia Stephenson)*

CLACKMANNANSHIRE
Sauchie [NS8994]
Mansfield Arms [Main St]: Friendly and cheerful family-run local with enjoyable cheap home-made food in beamed and panelled dining room with heavy mahogany tables, simple public bar *(Ian and Nita Cooper)*

DUMFRIESSHIRE
Eskdalemuir [NY2597]
☆ *Hart Manor*: This beautifully set hotel has just been reopened after refurbishment by the friendly Leadbeaters, who won our title of Scottish Dining Pub of the Year for their

previous Kilberry Inn, and though it's not open at lunchtimes it should be well worth visiting for an evening meal, or a stay *(anon)*
Moffat [NT0905]
Balmoral [High St]: Comfortable open-plan bar with lots of tables and raised end area, enjoyable low-priced plentiful food all day inc high tea, well kept Caledonian 80/- and Greenmantle, quick attentive uniformed staff; open all day *(Rob Fowell, Hazel and Michael Duncombe)*
Moniaive [NX7790]
☆ *George* [High St]: 17th-c inn with interesting no-frills old-fashioned flagstoned bar of considerable character; well kept beer, decent wine, friendly staff and locals, log fire; most days except at quietest times of year have reasonably priced lunchtime food; simple bedrooms *(Stan and Hazel Allen, LYM)*

DUNBARTONSHIRE
Balloch [NS3981]
Tullichewan [Fisherwood Rd, by stn]: Attractive big hotel opp boat trip pier, comfortable drawing-room feel in lounge bar (children allowed) with enjoyable food from soup and sandwiches to steak, small dining room, separate big restaurant, keg beers; bedrooms *(Ian Baillie)*

FIFE
Aberdour [NT1985]
Aberdour Hotel [High St (A921)]: Cosy nicely decorated hotel bar with open fire, red plush banquettes, friendly service, good choice of whiskies, real ales such as Caledonian, Courage or Theakstons, good choice of food at pub prices in restaurant; open all day Thurs-Sun; bedrooms *(Andy and Jill Kassube)*
Anstruther [NO5704]
☆ *Craws Nest* [Bankwell Rd]: Well run and handsomely placed hotel, very popular lunchtime with older people for good value bar meals inc outstanding fresh haddock (these available early evening too); light long lounge with 1970s echoes, comfortable banquettes, photographs, paintings for sale, polite smartly dressed staff; keg beer; comfortable bedrooms in modern wing *(Paul and Ursula Randall, Vicky and David Sarti, Christine and Neil Townend)*
☆ *Dreel* [High St W]: Cosy ancient building in attractive spot with garden overlooking Dreel Burn, plenty of timbers, small two-room bar, back pool room, open fire and stripped stone in atmospheric dining room, pleasant conservatory eating area, good generous varied bar food inc fresh fish lunchtime and evening, well kept local and guest beers, welcoming efficient staff, biscuits for dogs; popular with locals, open all day *(Dr D J and Mrs S C Walker, F Sutcliffe, Callum and Letitia Smith-Burnett)*
Ceres [NO4011]
Meldrums [Main St]: Small hotel's cottage parlour bar, pleasant atmosphere, clean and attractive beamed dining lounge with good choice of well prepared and presented

reasonably priced bar lunches, prompt friendly service even when busy, maybe well kept Courage Directors; well appointed bedrooms, peaceful village *(Paul and Ursula Randall)*
Crail [NO6108]
Golf [High St S]: Welcoming service and freshly cooked good value hearty standard food inc high teas in recently airily refurbished dining rooms, small and basic beamed locals' bar, good range of malt whiskies, coal fire; simple comfortable bedrooms, good breakfast *(anon)*
Dunfermline [NT0987]
Somewhere Else [Guildhall St]: Belhaven Best, good value home-made soup and generous sandwiches, local customers; handy for the Abbey *(R T and J C Moggridge)*
Falkland [NO2607]
Maltbarn [Main St, Newton]: Old village pub now concentrating on good food heavily influenced by Scandinavian landlady, inc good value soup and smorgasbord lunch, nice atmosphere, friendly helpful service, no smoking area; some tables outside *(A Kerr)*
☆ *Stag* [Mill Wynd]: Cosy long low white-painted 17th-c house in delightful setting opp charming green, round corner from medieval village square; dimly lit and pubby, with dark wooden pews and stools, exposed stone, copper-topped tables, stone fireplace, antlers and line drawings on wall, and some stained glass above bar; friendly helpful staff, Ind Coope Burton, coffee cocktails, decent food (not Tues or Sun eve), toasted sandwiches and take-away pizzas available most of day, helpful service, dining room with masses of posters; bar billiards, fruit machine, TV, unobtrusive piped music, children welcome *(Susan and John Douglas, BB)*
Guard Bridge [NO4519]
Guard Bridge Hotel [Main St]: Enjoyable straightforward bar food all freshly cooked by landlord (so may be a wait) inc fresh fish and good puddings, small dark bar, friendly service *(Roger Everett)*
Kinghorn [NT2687]
Auld Hoose [Nethergate]: Warm welcome, up to four well kept ales such as Arran Dark and Caledonian Deuchars IPA, sandwiches *(Andy and Jill Kassube)*
Kingsbarns [NO5912]
☆ *Cambo Arms*: Friendly small inn with real fires in armchair lounge and simple front bar, well kept Belhaven 80/-, St Andrews and a guest beer, homely books and pictures, short choice of light bar lunches, good evening menu in tiny restaurant – good home cooking using much local produce and steaks from own beef herd; well equipped bedrooms in former back stables/outbuildings *(Paul and Ursula Randall)*
Kirkcaldy [NT2791]
Harbour Bar [High St]: Emphasis on half a dozen or more well kept changing ales such as Exmoor, Houston, Oakham and York, good range of malt whiskies, panelled lounge with harbour and other local pictures, long basic bar, straightforward fresh food, very friendly landlord *(Roger and Jenny Huggins)*
Lundin Links [NO4002]
Old Manor [Leven Rd]: Elegant hotel with

good fairly priced seafood choice in bistro, plainly but sensibly furnished bar in separate building; comfortable bedrooms with own bathrooms looking over golf links to sea *(Andy and Jill Kassube)*
St Andrews [NO5116]
Drouthy Neebors [South St]: Food all day from nachos and enterprising baguettes to main dishes, also children's; up to six real ales inc Broughton *(Andy and Jill Kassube)*
West Port [South St]: Stylish and minimalist modern bar in handsome Georgian house, European newspapers, board games, bagels and croissants as well as interesting lunchtime sandwiches, good vegetarian choice, fine range of coffees all day, good Pacific rim restaurant up a few steps (with Stannah lift for disabled), friendly efficient staff, live music Sun night, large attractive garden *(Susan and John Douglas)*

INVERNESS-SHIRE
Fort William [NN1174]
Grog & Gruel [High St]: Done out in cosy traditional alehouse style, friendly helpful service, changing well kept ales such as Houston, Orkney Raven and Timothy Taylors Landlord, barrel tables, upstairs restaurant with wide range of good value food all day from baguettes up; piped music, machines; children welcome, live music nights; in pedestrian part *(David Edwards, George Atkinson)*
Inverie [NG7600]
☆ *Old Forge*: Utterly remote waterside pub with fabulous views, comfortable mix of antique furnishings, lots of charts and sailing prints, good warm atmosphere, open fire, good reasonably priced bar food inc fresh local seafood, even two real ales in season, also lots of whiskies and good wine choice; restaurant extension, open all day, late wknds, occasional live music and ceilidhs; the snag's getting there – boat (jetty moorings), Mallaig ferry three days a week, or 15-mile walk through Knoydart from nearest road *(Nigel Woolliscroft)*
Inverness [NH6645]
Blackfriars [Academy St]: Exceptional choice of well kept real ales such as Black Isle and Broughton, good value food from baguettes up, colourful local atmosphere *(Andy and Jill Kassube)*
☆ *Clachnaharry Inn* [A862 NW of city]: Cosily dim beamed bar, simple top lounge, more comfortable bottom lounge with picture windows looking over Beauly Firth, particularly good value freshly cooked bar food, half a dozen well kept ales from Caledonian, Skye and Tomintoul breweries inc Clachnaharry Village, Cuillin Hills and Skye Porter (some tapped from cask); small garden by single-track railway, lovely walks by big flight of Caledonian Canal locks *(Andy and Jill Kassube, David Wallington)*
Harlequin [1-2 View Pl, top of Castle St]: Downstairs bar with enjoyable lunchtime food, good restaurant upstairs; terrace with castle view *(MM)*

Kingussie [NH7501]

☆ *Royal* [High St]: Big former coaching inn brewing half a dozen or so well made and interesting Iris Rose real ales and lager in the former stables; also 200 malt whiskies, standard well priced food inc good generous baguettes, friendly helpful staff, spacious open-plan bar with plush banquettes and stage for evening entertainment, no smoking area; juke box; children welcome, open all day; bedrooms, handy for Highland Folk Museum *(Jenny and Brian Seller, Peter Salmon, BB, Andy and Jill Kassube)*

Scot House [Newtonmore Rd]: Good bar food esp baked potato skins; bedrooms *(Paul S McPherson)*

Laggan [NH6194]

Monadhliath [Laggan Bridge (A86/A9)]: Hotel with public bar, useful lunch stop, McEwans 80/- etc, good coffee, standard pub food, fair prices; bedrooms *(Mr and Mrs Richard Osborne)*

Mallaig [NM6797]

Marine Hotel [Station Rd]: Comfortable hotel lounge bar (up steep stairs) overlooking fishing harbour and beyond to Small Isles and Skye, good lunchtime bar food inc melt-in-mouth local smoked salmon, courteous service, enjoyable evening restaurant, basic public bar downstairs (notable for its stuffed gannet in full flight); keg beers, piped music; bedrooms, in centre of fishing village *(George Atkinson, Nigel Woolliscroft, Olive and Ray Hebson)*

Tigh-a-Chlachain [side street up hill from harbour]: Friendly and comfortable two-room pub, pleasant food and atmosphere, pool; children welcome *(anon)*

West Highland Hotel: Old-fashioned hotel notable for views to Skye and the Small Isles, comfortable lounge bars, food inc good fresh crab sandwiches; bedrooms *(Nigel Woolliscroft)*

Onich [NN0261]

Nether Lochaber Hotel [A82]: Well kept Bass and good food at sensible prices in friendly little hotel's charming side bar (from outside looks like a shed); bedrooms, with good value set dinner *(Michael Buchanan)*

Spean Bridge [NN2491]

☆ *Letterfinlay Lodge* [A82 7 miles N]: Well established hotel, lovely view over Loch Lochy from big picture-window main bar, small smart cocktail bar, wide food choice from sandwiches up, friendly service; keg beers but good malt whiskies, no smoking restaurant, children and dogs welcome, pleasant lochside grounds, own boats for fishing; clean and comfortable bedrooms, good breakfast, dog baskets available; gents' have good showers and hairdryers -- handy for Caledonian Canal sailors *(LYM, Chris and Sue Bax)*

KINCARDINESHIRE
Catterline [NO8778]

☆ *Creel*: Cosy bar with real fire, big lounge with friendly cat and plenty of tables, good generous food esp fresh local crabs and lobsters in bar and small seaview restaurant (booking advised),

well kept Maclays 70/-, welcoming landladies; bedrooms, old fishing village *(Ian and Sandra Thornton)*

KINROSS
Kinnesswood [NO1703]

Lomond [A911 Glenrothes—Milnathort, not far from M90 junctions 7/8]: New owners doing even better fresh food from sandwiches up in bar and restaurant of well appointed and friendly small inn with lovely sunset views over Loch Leven, well kept Belhaven, Jennings and guest beers such as Greene King Abbot, decent wines, log fire; comfortable bedrooms *(Peter F Marshall, Ron and Marjorie Bishop)*

KIRKCUDBRIGHTSHIRE
Auchencairn [NX8249]

☆ *Balcary Bay Hotel* [about 2½ miles off A711]: Beautifully placed hotel with honest reasonably priced well prepared food from soup and open sandwiches up (inc huge child's helpings) in civilised but friendly bar and in small conservatory with idyllic views over Solway Firth, prompt friendly service even when busy; tables on terrace and in gardens in peaceful seaside surroundings; keg beers; comfortable bedrooms, cl Oct-Mar *(R Davies, John Knighton)*

Colvend [NX8555]

Clonyard House: Attractive small hotel nr Solway coast, welcoming bar well used by locals, good choice of inexpensive food in spacious rooms off and conservatory, splendid puddings, half price for children for most dishes, decent wines, whiskies and coffee, friendly staff, separate no smoking restaurant; has enchanted tree; dogs welcome; bedrooms *(Stan and Hazel Allen)*

Dalry [NS2949]

☆ *Clachan* [A713 Castle Douglas—Ayr]: Attractively refurbished yet pleasantly traditional, very friendly and hospitable, two log fires, well kept Belhaven, enjoyable food from good sandwiches and toasties up, interesting fishing and shooting décor; bedrooms with own bathrooms *(Peter and Sue Goold)*

Gatehouse of Fleet [NX5956]

☆ *Murray Arms* [B727 NW of Kirkcudbright]: Pleasantly relaxed inn with wide choice of good honest value for money food all day inc good buffet with seafood, meats, lots of salads, cheeses and puddings, well kept ale such as McEwans and Theakstons XB, lots of malt whiskies, decent reasonably priced wines, interesting layout of mainly old-fashioned comfortable seating areas inc one with soft easy chairs, friendly attentive service, games in quite separate public bar, elegant restaurant; children welcome, big comfortable bedrooms *(B, M and P Kendall, LYM)*

Twynholm [NX6654]

Star [just off A75; Main St]: Attractive lounge bar, wide food choice lunchtime and evening, helpful friendly service, well kept Caledonian 80/-, several wines by the glass, lots of whisky miniatures; opp new David Coulthard Museum *(B, M and P Kendall)*

MIDLOTHIAN
Balerno [NT1666]
Grey Horse [Main St (off A70)]: Small late
18th-c stone-built pub with unspoilt panelled
bar, friendly lounge, Belhaven, Boddingtons
and Caledonian Deuchars, dominoes, cards;
open all day *(the Didler)*
Johnsburn House [Johnsburn Rd]: Lovely old-
fashioned beamed bar in 18th-c former
mansion with masterpiece 1911 ceiling by
Robert Lorimer; four well kept changing ales
such as Caledonian Deuchars and Orkney Dark
Raven, coal fire, panelled dining lounge with
good food inc shellfish, game and vegetarian,
more formal evening dining rooms; children
welcome, open all day wknds, cl Mon *(the
Didler)*
Cramond [NT1876]
☆ *Cramond Inn* [Cramond Glebe Rd (off A90 W
of Edinburgh)]: Softly lit little rooms with good
range of well prepared sensibly priced food inc
interesting snacks, comfortable brown-and-
brass décor, traditional English-style pub
furnishing but Scottish bric-a-brac, two good
coal and log fires, friendly service by
extraordinarily long-serving barman and other
staff, Sam Smiths OB; very popular for business
lunches and with retired couples at lunchtime
(babies welcome too); in picturesque waterside
village *(Hazel and Michael Duncombe, LYM)*
Edinburgh [NT2574]
☆ *Athletic Arms* [Angle Park Terr]: Unpretentious
pub famous for its perfectly kept McEwans 80/-
from island servery's impressive row of tall
founts – up to 15 red-jacketed barmen keep it
flowing on Tynecastle and Murrayfield football
and rugby days; glossy grey partitions, guest
beers, good value all-day snacks, dominoes in
side room with bell-push service, cribbage,
darts, piped music, TV, fruit machines; no
children *(the Didler, LYM, Eric Larkham)*
☆ *Bannermans* [Cowgate]: Warren of simple
crypt-like flagstoned rooms under some of the
tallest buildings in the Old Town, with barrel-
vaulted ceilings, bare stone walls, wood
panelling and pillars at front, medley of
interesting old furnishings; well kept
Caledonian 80/-, Deuchars IPA and guests in
one room, around 30 malts; lively enough
during the day, with fruit machine, piped music
and maybe big screen TV during sporting
events; younger crowd in evenings, with DJs,
discos, live music and karaoke; children
allowed till 6, bar snacks 12-5, open all day till
1am *(LYM, Klaus and Elizabeth Leist, R T and
J C Moggridge, Eric Larkham, Joel Dobris)*
☆ *Bennets* [Leven St]: Elaborate Victorian bar
with wonderfully ornate original glass, mirrors,
arcades, panelling and tiles, well kept
Caledonian Deuchars and other ales from tall
founts (even the rare low-strength Caledonian
60/-), lots of uncommon malt whiskies, bar
snacks and simple lunchtime hot dishes;
children allowed in eating area lunchtime, open
all day, cl Sun lunchtime *(LYM, the Didler)*
Berts Bar [William St]: Well done up in
traditional style, with well kept ales such as
Caledonian Deuchars IPA, McEwans 80/- and

Orkney Northern Lights, good range of tasty
straightforward food, long narrow bar, room
off with rugby shirt collection *(Roger and Jenny
Huggins)*
Black Bull [Grassmarket]: Long narrow T & J
Bernard pub, part boards and part carpeted,
tiers leading up to bar serving well kept
McEwans and Theakstons, raised seating area,
usual food; disabled facilities *(Eric Larkham)*
☆ *Canny Man* [Morningside Rd]: Good bustling
atmosphere, all sorts of interesting bric-a-brac,
ceiling papered with sheet music, good bar food
inc formidable open sandwiches, well kept
Scottish beer, huge choice of whiskies, cheap
children's drinks, very friendly staff *(Marianne
and Peter Stevens, Rick Lippiett)*
Cloisters [Broughton St]: Parsonage turned
friendly alehouse, mixing church pews and
gantry recycled from redundant church with
bare boards and lots of brewery mirrors;
Caledonian Deuchars and 80/-, interesting guest
beers, friendly atmosphere, food inc lunchtime
toasties; lavatories down spiral stairs; open all
day, folk music Fri/Sat *(the Didler, Eric
Larkham)*
Deacon Brodies [Lawnmarket]: Entertainingly
commemorating the notorious highwayman
town councillor who was eventually hanged on
the scaffold he'd designed; ornately high-
ceilinged city bar, long counter, good value
food in comfortable upstairs waitress-service
dining lounge *(Dave Braisted, BB)*
☆ *Dome* [St Georges Sq/George St]: Opulent
Italianate former bank, huge main bar with
magnificent dome, elaborate plasterwork and
stained glass; central servery, pillars, lots of
greenery, mix of wood and cushioned wicker
chairs, Caledonian Deuchars IPA and 80/-,
smart dining area with interesting food; smaller
and quieter art deco Frasers bar (may be cl
some afternoons and evenings early in week)
has atmospheric period feel, striking
woodwork, unusual lights, red curtains, lots of
good period advertisements, piped jazz, daily
papers, same beers – also wines (rather pricy)
and cocktails; complex includes hotel bedrooms
(Doug Christian, BB, Mrs G R Sharman)
Ensign Ewart [Lawnmarket, Royal Mile]: last
pub on right before castle]: Charming old-
world pub handy for castle (so can get very
full), huge painting of Ewart at Waterloo
capturing the French banner (it's on show in
the castle), real ales such as Caledonian
Deuchars and 80/- and Orkney Dark Island,
wide range of whiskies, usual food lunchtime
and some summer evenings, friendly efficient
staff; juke box, fruit machine, traditional music
most nights; no children, open all day *(Eric
Larkham)*
Halfway House [Fleshmarket Cl]: Tiny single-
room pub on steep steps between Market St
and Cockburn St, very friendly and welcoming,
lots of railway memorabilia *(Eric Larkham)*
Kenilworth [Rose St]: Friendly Edwardian pub
with ornate high ceiling, carved woodwork and
tiles, huge etched brewery mirrors and
windows, red leather seating around tiled wall;
central bar with Marstons Pedigree, Orkney

Dark Island and guest beers, hot drinks inc espresso, good generous bar food lunchtime and evening, quick friendly service, back family room; piped music, discreetly placed games machines, TV; space outside in summer, open all day *(the Didler)*

Malt & Hops [The Shore, Leith]: Good choice of beers, interesting things to look at *(Eric Larkham)*

McCowans Brewhouse [Fountainpark, Dundee St]: Part of leisure/entertainment complex on site of former Scottish & Newcastle brewery; brews its own good beers in visible microbrewery (explanatory tours available), the No 3 following the original Youngers recipe without additives, good food, mix of carpet and bare floor, mezzanine with interesting breweriana inc models and interactive displays; piped music, TV; open all day *(Eric Larkham)*

☆ *Milnes* [Rose St/Hanover St]: Well reworked and extended in 1992 as traditional city pub, rambling layout taking in several areas below street level and even in yard; busy old-fashioned bare-boards feel, dark wood furnishings and panelling, cask tables, lots of old photographs and mementoes of poets who used the 'Little Kremlin' room here, wide choice of well kept mostly Scottish Courage beers with unusual guest and bottled ones, open fire, good value lunches inc various pies charged by size; cheerful staff, lively atmosphere, esp evening *(the Didler, BB)*

Rutland [Rutland St]: Large, congenial and comfortable, with good service, good food choice from bar snacks to meals in upper restaurant, wide drinks choice *(E G Parish)*

☆ *Ship on the Shore* [The Shore, Leith (A199)]: Unpretentious waterside bar with nautical paraphernalia and some old shop signs and so forth, well kept Caledonian Deuchars IPA and occasional local guest beers, food from sandwiches to popular Sun breakfast, inc good locally caught fish and seafood in nicely panelled dining room with more dockland memorabilia; piped music, traditional games; tables outside, fine ship model as inn sign *(Ian Phillips, David Atkinson, Dr C C S Wilson, LYM)*

☆ *Standing Order* [George St]: Former bank in three elegant Georgian houses, grandly converted by Wetherspoons, imposing columns, enormous main room with splendidly colourful and elaborate high ceiling, lots of tables, smaller side booths, other rooms inc two no smoking rooms with floor to ceiling bookshelves, comfortable green sofa and chairs, Adam fireplace and portraits; civilised atmosphere, good value food (inc Sun evening), coffee and pastries, real ales inc guest beers such as Archers Village and Tomintoul Black Gold and Lairds from very long counter; extremely popular Sat night; disabled facilities *(R T and J C Moggridge, Simon and Amanda Southwell, G Coates, BB)*

Steading [Hill End, Biggar Rd (A702)]: Popular modern pub, several cottages knocked together at foot of dry ski slope, a dozen well kept changing Scottish and English real ales inc

Timothy Taylors Landlord, friendly staff, reasonably priced usual food 10-10 in cheerful bar, upstairs restaurant and conservatories *(Michael Buchanan, Andy and Jill Kassube, Christine and Neil Townend)*

White Hart [Grassmarket]: Basic and easy-going, with relaxing atmosphere, well kept Bass and Caledonian ales, usual food, pavement tables; one of oldest pubs here *(Eric Larkham)*

Musselburgh [NT3472]

Volunteer Arms [N High St; aka Staggs]: Same family since 1858, unspoilt busy bar, dark panelling, old brewery mirrors, great gantry with ancient casks, Caledonian Deuchars, 60/- and 80/- and guest beers; open all day (not Tues/Weds, cl Sun) *(the Didler)*

MORAYSHIRE

Elgin [NJ2162]

Thunderton House [Thunderton Pl]: Friendly and popular 17th-c town-centre pub, sympathetically refurbished in 19th-c style, good value tasty pub food, Bass and Caledonian Deuchars IPA, quick friendly service, children's room *(Malcolm M Stewart)*

Findhorn [NJ0464]

☆ *Crown & Anchor* [off A96]: Friendly family pub, good value food all day inc imaginative and children's dishes and tender Aberdeen Angus steaks (model train takes orders to kitchen), four changing real ales such as Orkney, huge log fire in lively public bar, separate lounge; children welcome, most bedrooms comfortable, good boating in Findhorn Bay (boats for residents) *(Andy and Jill Kassube, P R and S A White, J V Dadswell, LYM, Mr and Mrs W D Borthwick)*

Kimberley: Unpretentious, with friendly staff, weekly changing guest beers, good generous food esp fresh seafood, jovial company; children welcome *(Robin and Sally Halbert and family)*

Lossiemouth [NJ2270]

Skerry Brae [Stotfield Rd]: Views over golf links to Moray Firth, good usual food; bedrooms *(Andy and Jill Kassube)*

Nairn [NH8856]

Invernairne [Thurlow Rd]: Two well kept changing ales such as Skye Red Cuillin and freshly made food lunchtime and evening from sandwiches to full meals in plush carpeted partly panelled bar, comfortable and friendly, with roaring log fire; provision for wheelchairs, well behaved children welcome, big garden with putting green, well equipped bedrooms, some overlooking sea *(Andy and Jill Kassube)*

PEEBLESSHIRE

Leadburn [NT2355]

Leadburn Inn [A701/A703/A6094, S of Penicuik]: Friendly and attractive country inn, obliging staff, food from potato wedges through haggis to steaks, two real ales such as Caledonian and Criffel; comfortable bedrooms *(Andy and Jill Kassube)*

Peebles [NT2540]

Park Hotel [Innerleithen Rd]: Hotel not pub,

but does good bar meals; bedrooms *(Olive and Ray Hebson)*

PERTHSHIRE
Bridge of Cally [NO1451]
Bridge of Cally Hotel: Lovely wooded riverside position overlooking bridge, tables in peaceful garden stepped down to river, homely bar with sofas, club fender around nice stone fireplace, old photographs, cheap food, friendly service, well kept Maclays Wallace; bedrooms *(Susan and John Douglas)*
Callander [NN6207]
Waverley [Main St]: Clean and friendly with good quick service, good value snacks from nicely presented sandwiches up, well kept Caledonian 80/- and Harviestoun Bitter & Twisted Original, Ptarmigan and Arran Blondie; nearly opp Rob Roy centre *(Derek and Sylvia Stephenson)*
Errol [NO2523]
Old Smiddy [The Cross, High St (B958 E of Perth)]: Attractive heavy-beamed bar with assorted old country furniture, farm and smithy tools inc massive bellows, good home-made food inc fresh local ingredients and interesting recipes, well kept interesting local Ossian ale, lots of country wines, decent coffee, friendly attentive service; pleasant village setting, open all day Sun, cl Mon/Tues lunchtime *(Susan and John Douglas)*
Loch Tummel [NN8460]
☆ *Loch Tummel Inn* [B8019 4 miles E of Tummel Bridge]: Lochside former coaching inn with great views over water to Schiehallion, big woodburner in cosy partly stripped stone bar with antlers and fishing tackle, gingham-covered tables, well kept local Moulin ales, good food inc home-smoked salmon, no music or machines; attractive bedrooms with log fires – even an open fire in one bathroom, fishing free for residents *(LYM, Bob and Caroline Collins, Jules Akel)*
Meikleour [NO1539]
☆ *Meikleour Hotel* [A984 W of Coupar Angus]: Two lounges, one with stripped stone, flagstones and armour, another more chintzy, both with open fires, helpful friendly service, good bar food inc fine range of open sandwiches and lunchtime snacks, well kept Maclays 70/-; fruit machines, back public bar; pretty building, picnic-sets in charming garden with tall pines and distant Highland view; nr famous 250-yr-old beech hedge over 30 m (100 ft) high *(Susan and John Douglas)*
Pitlochry [NN9358]
Old Mill [Mill Lane]: Comfortable dining pub with enjoyable food, four real ales, draught continental beers, good wine choice, lots of malt whiskies *(Graeme Smith, Don Campbell)*

RENFREWSHIRE
Balmaha [NS4290]
Oak Tree: Recently opened inn on Loch Lomond's quiet side, named for the 300-year-old oak cut for its bar counter; wide choice of food inc good soups, vegetarian and haggis, Caledonian Deuchars IPA, pleasant tartan

décor, restaurant; plenty of tables outside, children welcome, bedrooms, bunkhouse *(Ian Baillie, Rona Murdoch)*
Blanefield [NS5579]
Carbeth Inn [A809 Glasgow—Drymen, just S of B821]: Low whitewashed pub with emphasis on enjoyable food in lounge and family room, well kept Belhaven 80/-, unusual pine-panelled bar with high fringe of tartan curtains, woodburner or log fires throughout; lots of tables outside, open all day; bedrooms *(Ian Baillie, LYM)*
Drymen [NS4788]
☆ *Clachan* [The Square]: Lively cottagey pub, licensed since 1734, friendly and welcoming; original fireplace with side salt larder, tables made from former bar tops, former Wee Free pews along one wall; enjoyable simple food in tartan-carpeted lounge, well kept Belhaven Best, 80/- and Stout, lots of old local photographs; piped music; on green of attractive village, handy for Loch Lomond and Trossachs *(Mr and Mrs J McRobert)*
Fintry [NS6287]
Culcreuch Castle [Kippen Rd]: Handsome and interesting hotel with two real ales and good value food in bar, decent wines, good service, grand restaurant; self catering lodges *(Guy Vowles)*
Glasgow [NS5965]
Blackfriars [Bell St]: Lively fusion of bare-boards tavern and cosmopolitan café, well kept ales such as Belhaven 60/-, Caledonian Deuchars IPA, Houston Killellan, Ind Coope Burton and Tetleys, continental draught and bottled beers, farm cider, plenty of wines by the glass and malt whiskies, friendly service, cheap bar lunches, evening snacks and pizzas, lots of events posters, daily papers, candles on tables; TV, piped music, loudish some evenings; Sun night basement comedy club, Sat band nights *(David Carr, Richard Lewis)*
☆ *Cask & Still* [Hope St]: Comfortable and welcoming, with some 200 interesting malt whiskies, bare boards and panelling, big carpets, raised back leather seating area, reasonably priced food all day (menu limited evenings), well kept ales such as Caledonian 80/-, McEwans 80/-, Orkney Dark Island and Theakstons Best, friendly staff; open all day *(Richard Lewis, Dr and Mrs A K Clarke, BB)*
Clockwork Beer Co [1153 Cathcart Rd]: Comfortable brightly decorated two-level café-bar with microbrewery on view brewing interesting Lager, Amber IPA, Red, fruit beers, wheat beers and special ales, also six or more weekly-changing guest beers on tall fount air pressure, very good range of continental beers, farm cider, speciality fruit schnapps, Scottish and other country wines, good conventional wines, masses of malt whiskies, interesting fruit juices; good reasonably priced food all day, half helpings for children, good vegetarian choice, friendly service, daily papers, spiral stairs to gallery with TV, piano, games tables, books, toys and no smoking area; jazz Tues, open all day, disabled facilities *(Richard Lewis)*
Drum & Monkey [St Vincent St]: Former bank,

with island bar and lots of mahogany, great atmosphere esp lunchtime with cheap quickly served filling snacks, friendly helpful staff, real ale on tall founts *(Dr and Mrs A K Clarke)*

Hogshead [Queen St Stn]: Costa coffee-bar downstairs, comfortable real ale tavern upstairs, half a dozen or more well kept beers, bottled Belgians, good food choice, lots of prints, daily papers, friendly efficient staff, no smoking area; open all day *(Richard Lewis)*

☆ *Horseshoe* [Drury St, nr Central Stn]: Classic high-ceilinged pub with enormous island bar, gleaming mahogany and mirrors, snob screens and all sorts of other Victorian features; friendly jovial staff, well kept Bass and Caledonian Golden Promise, lots of malt whiskies; games machines, piped music; amazingly cheap food in plainer upstairs bar, no smoking restaurant (where children allowed); open all day *(Richard Lewis, David Carr, LYM)*

MacLachlans [W Regent St]: Brews its own ales such as IPA, 80/- and Elderberry Wheat Ale, using organic ingredients, also Belhaven and wide choice of bottled beers, generous tasty organic food inc interesting dishes *(David Edwards)*

Old Printworks [North Frederick St]: Hogshead-style pub with usual wide choice of well kept beers inc microbrews, also Belgian bottled beers, country wines; interesting two-level building keeping features of former trade, lots of bare stone, brick and ironwork, good lunchtime menu, friendly staff; open all day, disabled ramp *(Richard Lewis)*

Station Bar [Port Dundas Rd]: Railway and boat prints and photographs, well kept Caledonian Deuchars IPA and two guest microbrews (one Scottish, one from the south), welcoming helpful staff, lunchtime snacks; two TVs, juke box, games machine; open all day *(Richard Lewis)*

Tennants [Byres Rd]: Big lively high-ceilinged local with ornate plasterwork, panelling, paintings, well kept Caledonian Deuchars IPA, 80/- and Golden Promise, Broughton Greenmantle and Old Jock and several interesting changing guest ales, also several dozen good malt whiskies, decent house wine, quick good-humoured service, cheap usual lunchtime food; open all day *(Bruno Garcia)*

Three Judges [Dumbarton Rd, opp Byres Rd]: Around nine quickly changing real ales from small breweries far and wide (they get through several hundred a year, and will let you sample) in well run open-plan pub with small leather-seat side area, friendly landlady and locals (with their dogs), hundreds of pumpclips on the walls; games machine, juke box, paperback exchange, live music nights, open all day *(Richard Lewis, Nick Holding)*

Toby Jug [Waterloo St/Hope St]: Bare boards, panelling, barrels and some alcove seating, more tables in slightly raised back area, cask tables in standing part, lots of toby jugs, old Glasgow pictures, good value straightforward lunchtime food, four well kept changing ales from small Scottish breweries, friendly staff;

open all day *(Richard Lewis)*

Uisge Beatha: Dimly lit bar with old furniture and animal heads, several dozen malt whiskies, well kept ales inc Caledonian Deuchars, good value lunchtime food, kilted waiters; live music Weds *(Bruno Garcia)*

Lochwinnoch [NS3558]

Brown Bull [Main St]: Traditional village inn restored with restraint, stripped stone, beams and pews, welcoming landlord, fine range of whiskies and real ales such as Belhaven IPA, Caledonian Deuchars IPA, and Auld Simon brewed for the pub, friendly local feel; beautiful countryside, nr Castle Semple RSPB reserve *(Angus Lyon)*

Strathblane [NS5679]

Kirkhouse [Glasgow Rd (A81)]: Small bar, big restaurant area with vast range of good generous if not cheap food inc some exotic dishes, decent wine, good service *(Hazel and Michael Duncombe)*

ROSS-SHIRE

Kyle of Lochalsh [NG7627]

Lochalsh Hotel [Ferry Rd]: Enjoyable simple food inc tasty sandwiches at tables or in armchairs of large, friendly and civilised hotel lounge bar, pleasant views of Skye; bedrooms *(Joan and Tony Walker)*

Lochcarron [NG9039]

Rockvilla: Light and comfortable bar in small hotel, loch view, quick friendly service, good choice of food inc sandwiches and some local specialities; bedrooms *(Tony Walker)*

Poolewe [NB8580]

Pool House: Hotel in lovely setting on Loch Ewe, nr Inverewe Gardens, good if not cheap food esp fish in spacious and comfortable dining lounge, McEwans beer, good service, immaculate lavatories; tables out by water, bedrooms *(Michael Buchanan)*

Tore [NH6052]

Kilcoy Arms [A9 just N of Inverness]: Cosy bar with open fire and dining area, large maps of Scotland, good range of malt whiskies, local beer on tap, good home cooking, hospitable licensees; three comfortable bedrooms, own bathrooms *(John and Jill Walker)*

Ullapool [NH1294]

☆ *Ceilidh Place* [West Argyle St]: Arty celtic café/bar with art gallery, bookshop and coffee shop, regular jazz, folk and classical music, informal mix of furnishings, woodburner, side food servery with wide choice from home-made soups to monkfish and steaks, no smoking conservatory restaurant with some emphasis on fish, children in eating areas; tables out on terrace, comfortable bedrooms, open all day *(Lorna Baxter, John Winstanley, Peter F Marshall, LYM)*

ROXBURGHSHIRE

Ancrum [NT6325]

Cross Keys [off A68 Jedburgh—Edinburgh]: Pleasant village green setting, locals' bar and three lounge/dining bars of varying smartness, friendly helpful staff, well kept Caledonian Deuchars IPA and 80/-, enjoyable food with some imaginative dishes and fresh local produce inc good well priced Aberdeen Angus steaks; games room, nice back garden *(Brian and Lynn Young, Philip Bardswell)*

Kelso [NT7334]

☆ *Cobbles* [Belmont Pl]: Small two-room dining pub with wall banquettes, some panelling, warm log and coal fires, wide choice of good value food inc interesting dishes; very courteous quick service, real ales such as Caledonian Deuchars and McEwans 70/- and 80/-, decent wines and malt whiskies; piped music; disabled lavatory *(Brian and Lynn Young, James Nunns)*

Kirk Yetholm [NT8328]

☆ *Border* [The Green]: Welcoming end to 256-mile Pennine Way walk (Pennine Way souvenirs for sale), beams, flagstones, etchings, murals and open fire, pleasant unpretentious atmosphere, friendly management, well kept Belhaven, wide choice of well cooked generous food in main dining room, small rooms off bar or conservatory; picnic-sets on terrace, good bedrooms *(Joel Dobris, David and Heather Stephenson, Brian and Lynn Young, John and Sheila Lister)*

Lilliesleaf [NT5325]

Cross Keys: Small pleasant 200-year-old stone and plaster pub in attractive village, two clean and comfortable rooms with solid beams, real fires and old photographs, friendly landlord, good value menu and specials inc good soup, well kept Greenmantle and McEwans 80/-, fruit machine but no piped music *(Brian and Lynn Young)*

St Boswells [NT5931]

☆ *Buccleuch Arms* [A68 just S of Newtown St Boswells]: Civilised sandstone inn emphasising wide choice of imaginative well prepared bar food (inc Sun), sandwiches all day; Georgian-style no smoking plush bar with light oak panelling, well kept Greenmantle, restaurant, tables in garden behind; children welcome, bedrooms *(GSB, Chris Rounthwaite, LYM, Joel Dobris)*

SELKIRKSHIRE
Ettrickbridge [NT3824]
Cross Keys: Good atmosphere, efficient service, good standard food; bedrooms *(A N Ellis)*

STIRLINGSHIRE
Stirling [NS7993]
Portcullis [Castle Wynd]: Beside castle, overlooking town and surroundings; friendly service, pleasant atmosphere, nice choice of sandwiches, enjoyable hot dishes, well kept ales such as Aviemore and Orkney Dark Island; spacious bar with open fire and good choice of whiskies; good bedrooms *(Andy and Jill Kassube)*

☆ *Whistlebinkies* [St Mary's Wynd]: Former 16th-c castle stables, looking old outside, but plushly modern inside, three comfortable levels, some bargain dishes on mostly standard menu, quite a few mirrors, lots of posters and leaflets for local and student events; friendly helpful staff, a couple of real ales such as Belhaven 80/-

(emphasis on lagers and whiskies), newspapers; piped pop music (even in the lavatories), big TV, weekly quiz night, some live music; tables on informal sloping garden behind, handy for castle and old town *(Michael Butler, BB, Ian and Nita Cooper, Nick Holding)*

WIGTOWNSHIRE
Portpatrick [NX0154]
Harbour House [Main St]: Bright and friendly modern bar, good value food, welcoming staff and locals; dogs welcome (Gem is the pub dog), cheery Weds winter quiz night; good-sized simple bedrooms overlooking harbour *(Andy, Julie and Stuart Hawkins)*

SCOTTISH ISLANDS
ARRAN
Brodick [NS0136]
Brodick Bar [Alma Rd]: Tucked away off seafront and recently redecorated, with wide choice of food, McEwans beers *(Ken Richards, John Knighton)*
Kingsley: Well run and attractive open-plan bar with good home cooking lunchtime and evening inc choice of soups, well kept local Arran ale as well as McEwans 70/- and 80/- and Theakstons, around 40 malt whiskies, wide choice of wines, pleasant bay views; bedrooms *(Ken Richards)*

BARRA
Castlebay [NL6698]
Castlebay Hotel: Great harbour view, usual food, big but cosy and lively bar with pool etc; decent bedrooms *(Nigel Woolliscroft)*

HARRIS
Rodel [NG0483]
Rodel Hotel [A859 at southern tip of South Harris]: Reopened after refurbishment, good bar; bedrooms *(Don Campbell)*

MULL
Tobermory [NM5055]
Western Isles [Strongarbh]: Good sensibly priced food and drink, great view of mountains and wind-tossed boats; bedrooms *(Meg and Colin Hamilton)*

ORKNEY
Stromness [HY2509]
Stromness Hotel [Victoria St]: Upstairs harbourside bar and dining area with great views over Scapa Flow, good interesting food inc plenty of local fish and seafood, good value wines, staff attentive and friendly even when busy; bedrooms *(Anne and Barry Coulton)*

SKYE
Ardvasar [NG6203]
☆ *Ardvasar Hotel* [A851 at S of island, nr Armadale pier]: Comfortably modernised white stone inn with lovely sea and mountain views, enjoyable home-made food (children welcome in eating areas), prompt service, lots of malt whiskies, two bars and games room; TV, piped music; comfortable bedrooms, open all day

(Mr and Mrs A J Newport, John and Elspeth Howell, Vicky and David Sarti, G and J E Nichol, LYM)

Duntulm [NG4173]

Duntulm Castle Hotel: Good bar food, great views of the castle and sea; bedrooms *(Nigel Woolliscroft)*

Portree [NG4843]

Pier Hotel [Quay St]: Down-to-earth boatmen's bar, language to match sometimes, welcoming landlord, interesting murals, occasional live music, pipers during Skye games week; keg beers; simple good value harbour-view bedrooms *(Nigel Woolliscroft)*

Stein [NG2556]

☆ *Stein Inn* [end of B886 N of Dunvegan]: Down-to-earth small 17th-c inn delightfully set above quiet sea inlet, tables out looking over sea to Hebrides (great sunsets), peat fire in flagstoned and stripped-stone public bar, really welcoming licensees and locals, well kept Isle of Skye Cuillin Red, good malt whiskies, good value bar food (in winter only for people staying) inc huge three-cheese ploughman's; recently renovated bedrooms *(Vicky and David Sarti, Nigel Woolliscroft, LYM)*

SOUTH UIST

Eriskay [NF7910]

Am Politician: Modern bar a virtual museum to the sinking of the *Politician* of *Whisky Galore* fame – the boat is still visible at low tide; good local seafood, original bottles of the salvaged whisky on show – they collect around £1,500 when they come up for sale *(Nigel Woolliscroft)*

Pollachar [NF7414]

☆ *Polochar Inn* [S end of B888]: Comfortably modernised and extended 17th-c shoreside inn in great spot (though things bound to change with completion of Eriskay causeway), glorious views to Barra and Eriskay, dolphins, porpoises and seals; big public bar with pubby atmosphere, separate dining room, good bar meals running up to Aberdeen Angus steaks; very helpful friendly staff and locals (all Gaelic speaking); 11 well renovated bedrooms with own bathrooms, good breakfast *(James Nunns, Nigel Woolliscroft, Jack and Heather Coyle)*

ST KILDA

St Kilda [NF0999]

Puff Inn [Village Bay, Hirta]: Britain's most remote pub, in effect a working men's club manned by volunteers among those stationed out here (£1 for a month's membership); cheap bottled and canned beers and good choice of whiskies, memorable bay view from end of deserted village street; open lunchtime, teatime and late into night *(Nigel Woolliscroft)*

If a service charge is mentioned prominently on a menu or accommodation terms, you must pay it if service was satisfactory. If service is really bad you are legally entitled to refuse to pay some or all of the service charge as compensation for not getting the service you might reasonably have expected.

Wales

Four pubs here have been in each year's Guide since it started 20 years ago: the interesting and ancient Olde Bulls Head in Beaumaris, the Dinorben Arms at Bodfari (lovely surroundings, great range of whiskies), the welcoming Pen-y-Gwryd up in the mountains above Llanberis, and (run by Franco and Ann Taruschio throughout that time until their very recent retirement) the restauranty Walnut Tree at Llandewi Skirrid – still very good under its new owners. Joining these old stagers are one or two newcomers, or pubs back in these pages after a break: the relaxed and civilised Old Black Lion in Hay-on-Wye, the canalside Coach & Horses at Llangynidr, the classy Glasfryn in Mold (a warm-hearted dining pub) and the idiosyncratic Tafarn Sinc at Rosebush (a nice surprise). Other pubs on fine form here these days are the waterside Penhelig Arms in Aberdovey (very reasonable prices for such good fresh fish), the cheerful Sailors Return in Beaumaris, the Ty Gwyn in Betws-y-Coed (very enjoyable, but clinging to its place in the Guide by the skin of its teeth, as you have to eat or stay overnight, you can't just have a drink), the bustling Carew Inn opposite the imposing ruins of Carew Castle, the ancient Pendre at Cilgerran (extraordinarily cheap good food), the Bear in Crickhowell (an all-round favourite), the Nantyffin Cider Mill just outside that little town (excellent food, largely using local organic produce), the charming little Rose & Crown at Graianrhyd (bargain food), the Pant-yr-Ochain near Gresford (imaginative food in this stylish dining pub), Kilverts in Hay-on-Wye (friendly and informal, a nice place to stay), the Castle in Llandeilo (bargain food, excellent beer), the Queens Head near Llandudno Junction (consistently good food), the Open Hearth near Pontypool (the best place for real ales in the area), the Sloop at Porthgain (a well placed seaside family all-rounder), the friendly Clytha Arms near Raglan (good food and drink), the bustling Royal Oak in Saundersfoot (good beer, lots of fresh fish in summer), the pretty thatched Bush at St Hilary (nice food in a proper old-fashioned pub), the Armstrong Arms at Stackpole (good value food in a lovely spot), the Star in Talybont-on-Usk (a thorough-going beer lover's pub with bargain food), and the Nags Head in Usk (a Food Award this year). It is the Nags Head in Usk, run by the same friendly family for many years, which is our Wales Dining Pub of the Year. In the Lucky Dip section at the end of the chapter, pubs to watch are, in Clwyd, the Sun at Rhewl; in Dyfed, the Druidstone Hotel at Broad Haven, Neuadd Fawr at Cilycwm, Dyffryn Arms at Cwm Gwaun, White Hart at Llanddarog and Plantagenet House in Tenby; in Mid Glamorgan, the Black Cock near Caerphilly, Prince of Wales at Kenfig and Travellers Rest at Thornhill; in Gwent, the Skirrid at Llanfihangel Crucorney, Greyhound at Llantrisant Fawr, Red Hart at Llanvapley and Cherry Tree at Tintern; in Gwynedd, the Kings Head in Llandudno; and in Powys, the Red Lion at Llanfihangel-nant-Melan and Dragons Head at Llangenny. Drinks prices in the province are lower than the national average; the Nags Head at Abercych, brewing its own beer, was particularly cheap. Besides the two long-standing local breweries Brains (who now also brew the Buckley beers) and Felinfoel, the newer Tomos Watkins and Bullmastiff beers are well worth looking out for.

ABERCYCH SN2441 Map 6
Nags Head
Off B4332 Cenarth—Boncath

This traditional ivy-covered pub is beautifully set next to a river and in the evenings the front is lit by fairy lights. It's very lively here given the size of the village and its tucked away position, and the dimly lit beamed and stone-flagged bar attracts a real mix of ages and accents. There's a comfortable old sofa in front of its big fireplace, clocks showing the time around the world, stripped wooden tables, a piano, photos and postcards of locals, and hundreds of bottles of beer displayed around the brick and stone walls; piped music, TV. A plainer small room leads down to a couple of big dining areas (one of which is no smoking), and there's another little room behind the bar. As well as their own brewed Old Emrys (named after one of the regulars) the landlord stocks around four beers from brewers such as Wye Valley and Abbot. Bar food includes soup (£2.95), crispy whitebait (£3.75), spinach and cottage cheese pancake (£6.25), battered cod, steak and ale pie or chicken and leek suet pudding (£6.50), gammon steak or lamb korma (£6.95), smoked haddock and cod pancake (£7.25) and 10oz sirloin (£10.25) and puddings (£2.95); at busy times staff may find it hard to cope. Across the peaceful road outside are tables under cocktail parasols looking over the water, as well as a number of nicely arranged benches, and a children's play area. There may be barbecues out here in summer. *(Recommended by John and Enid Morris, Stephen, Julie and Hayley Brown, Andrew Hodgkins, David Twitchett, Paul Hopton)*

Own brew ~ Licensee Steven Jamieson ~ Real ale ~ Bar food (12-2, 6-9, not 25 Dec) ~ Restaurant ~ (01239) 841200 ~ Children in eating area of bar and restaurant ~ Open 11.30-3, 6-11; 11.30-11 Sat; 11.30-10.30 Sun

ABERDOVEY SN6296 Map 6
Penhelig Arms 🍴 🍷 🛏
Opposite Penhelig railway station

In summer you can enjoy the high quality, generous bar food at this mainly 18th-c hotel on their terrace by the harbour wall which has lovely views across the Dyfi estuary. Fresh fish, delivered every day by the local fishmonger, is a big draw and there are usually 12 or so fish dishes to choose from in the evening, with a couple less at lunchtime. They serve the same menu in the bar and restaurant and the very reasonably priced menu changes quite frequently but might include pea and mint soup (£2.50), sandwiches (from £2.95), duck slices with chicory and apple in pink peppercorn and balsamic dressing or griddled halloumi cheese with roast peppers (£4.25), grilled lambs liver and bacon or chicken cooked in lemon sauce with cardamon and ginger (£7.95), seared salmon fillets, roast pork wrapped in bacon with mustard and caper sauce, lamb cutlets with rosemary gravy or baked cod with a stilton crust with italian salsa verde (£8.50); puddings such as rhubarb crumble or blackcurrant mousse with cassis (£3.25); good selection of British cheeses (£3.95). Their two-course Sunday lunch is a good deal (£9.95). The excellent, expanding wine list numbers about 250 bins, with over 40 half bottles, and about a dozen by the glass; they also have two dozen malt whiskies, fruit or peppermint teas, and various coffees. The small original beamed bar (which they plan to refurbish) has a cosy feel with winter fires, and three changing real ales such as Abbot Ale, Brains Rev James Original and Tetleys on handpump; dominoes. Service is friendly and attentive. The separate, newly refurbished restaurant is no smoking. Sea views from the comfortable bedrooms; new ones have balconies. *(Recommended by David Heath, Sue and Bob Ward, A Boss, Di and Mike Gillam, Revd D Glover, Dr M Owton, John Sandilands, Mike and Wena Stevenson, Mrs J Street)*

Free house ~ Licensees Robert and Sally Hughes ~ Real ale ~ Bar food ~ Restaurant ~ (01654) 767215 ~ Children in eating area of bar and restaurant ~ Open 11-4, 5.30-11; 12-4, 6-10.30 Sun ~ Bedrooms: £61S/£108B

ABERYSTWYTH SN6777 Map 6
Halfway Inn

Pisgah (not the Pisgah near Cardigan); A4120 towards Devil's Bridge, 5¾ miles E of junction with A487

There's free overnight camping for customers at this enchanting old place. In summer the panoramic views down over the wooded hills and pastures of the Rheidol Valley are lovely and in winter, when it's warmed by a nice log fire, it's full of genuinely old-fashioned and peaceful charm. The atmospheric beamed and flagstoned bar has stripped deal tables and settles and bare stone walls, as well as darts, pool, dominoes, trivia and piped music (popular folk and country), and well kept Badger Dorset Best, alongside Felinfoel Double Dragon, Hancocks HB and maybe a guest on handpump. There might be up to four draught ciders, and a few malt whiskies. Generously served with fresh vegetables, bar food includes soup (£1.75), filled baked potatoes (from £2.25), breaded plaice (£4.95), ploughman's or puff pastry filled with brie, broccoli and onion sauce (£5.50), home-made steak and ale pie or lasagne (£5.95), 8oz sirloin (£9.95), daily specials such as chicken in cider sauce (£5.95) and venison casserole in red wine (£7.50); home-made puddings. There are picnic tables outside, as well as a very simple play area, a nursery, and a baling rail for pony-trekkers. *(Recommended by Howard England, Guy Vowles)*

Free house ~ Licensee David Roberts ~ Real ale ~ Bar food ~ (01970) 880631 ~ Children in eating area of bar and restaurant ~ Open 12-2.30, 6.30-11; 12-2.30, 7-10.30 Sun; closed lunchtimes in Jan and Feb ~ Bedrooms: /£38S

BEAUMARIS SH6076 Map 6
Olde Bulls Head ♀

Castle Street

Visited by Samuel Johnson and Charles Dickens, the quaintly old-fashioned rambling bar of this smart, cosy, partly 15th-c hotel has lots of reminders of its long and interesting past. Amidst the low beams and snug alcoves are a rare 17th-c brass water clock, a bloodthirsty crew of cutlasses, and even the town's oak ducking stool, as well as lots of copper and china jugs, comfortable low-seated settles, leather-cushioned window seats and a good open fire. As well as Bass and Worthington Best and a guest such as Brains St Davids Ale on handpump, they serve nearly a dozen wines by the glass and freshly squeezed orange juice. They don't do food in the bar, but you can eat in the very popular no smoking brasserie behind. The menu might include soup (£2.75), sandwiches (from £3.75), ham hock terrine with corn salad or roasted fresh asparagus with grilled goats cheese (£4.25) ploughman's (£4.95), smoked haddock and prawn gratin in cream and mushroom sauce (£5.75), ricotta ravioli with chorizo, smoked bacon and passata (£5.95), duck confit with hoi sin sauce, vegetables and steamed pancakes (£6.25) and braised lamb steak on potato and spinach hash (£7.20) with puddings such as spotted dick (from £3.15), and daily specials; vegetables are extra. There's also a smart no smoking restaurant. The entrance to the pretty courtyard is closed by the biggest simple hinged door in Britain, and the straightforward but pleasing bedrooms (with lots of nice little extras) are named after characters in Dickens's novels. *(Recommended by Mike and Lynn Robinson, Jean and Douglas Troup, John and Lis Burgess, Sally Anne and Peter Goodale, Steve Whalley, Darly Graton, Graeme Gulibert, David Jeffreys; also in* The Good Hotel Guide*)*

Free house ~ Licensee David Robertson ~ Real ale ~ Restaurant ~ (01248) 810329 ~ Children must be over 7 in restaurant ~ Open 11-11; 12-10.30 Sun; closed 25 Dec evening ~ Bedrooms: £55B/£85B

Sailors Return

Church Street

Although the friendly, helpful staff are still here, this bright and cheerful pub has been taken over by new licensees. More or less open-plan, it's often full of diners of all ages, especially in the evenings (lunchtimes tend to be quieter); you can book the tables in the dining area on the left. Furnishings include comfortable richly coloured banquettes, with an open fire in winter. There's a quaint collection of china teapots, and maps of Cheshire among the old prints and naval memorabilia; the Green room to the left of the bar is no smoking. Bar food includes soup (£2.50), sandwiches (from £2.80, baguettes £3.85), garlic mushrooms (£3.95), vegetable lasagne (£5.95), roast chicken (£6.75), gammon steak with egg and pineapple (£7.45), sirloin steak (£10.25), and daily specials such as steak and ale pie (£6.95), mediterranean chicken (£7.25) and poached salmon (£7.95) with puddings (£2.95); children's meals (£3.25). Well kept Bass and a guest on handpump; unobtrusive piped music. Parking can be difficult. *(Recommended by J S M Sheldon, Albert and Margaret Horton, Sharon Holmes, Tom Cherrett, Jim Abbott, Peter and Anne Hollindale, Michael Buchanan)*

Free house ~ Licensee Mrs E Rigby ~ Real ale ~ Bar food (11.30(12 Sun)-2, 6-9(9.30 Sat), not 25 Dec) ~ Restaurant ~ (01248) 811314 ~ Children in eating area of bar ~ Open 11.30-3, 6-11; 12-3, 6-10.30 Sun ~ Bedrooms: /£55S

BETWS-Y-COED SH7956 Map 6
Ty Gwyn
A5 just S of bridge to village

It's just as well that this well run, cottagey coaching inn serves such good, imaginative food and is well placed for the area's multitude of attractions – the terms of the licence are such that you can't just pop in for a drink, you must eat or stay overnight to be served alcohol. Generous bar food could include tasty home-made tomato and courgette soup (£2.75), sautéed spicy crab cakes or local smoked duck breast (£4.50), mixed chinese vegetable stir fry (£9.95), welsh lamb with roast onion marmalade or springbok medallions with port, peppercorn and ginger jus (£11.95), local pheasant braised with beaujolais and wild mushroom jus or fresh grilled lemon sole with apple thermidor (£12.95) with specials such as kangaroo au poive or jumbo crab thermidor. There's a genuinely welcoming atmosphere in the beamed lounge bar, which has an ancient cooking range worked in well at one end, and rugs and comfortable chintz easy chairs on its oak parquet floor. The interesting clutter of unusual old prints and bric-a-brac reflects the owners' interest in antiques (they used to run an antique shop next door); highchair and toys available. Wadworths 6X and maybe a guest such as Boddingtons on handpump, very good, friendly staff, and maybe two friendly cats; piped music. Part of the restaurant is no smoking. *(Recommended by David Edwards, Mike and Maggie Betton, Mervyn and Susan Underhill, Herbert and Susan Verity, Mr and Mrs S Mason, KC, Christopher and Jo Barton)*

Free house ~ Licensees Tim and Martin Ratcliffe and Nichola Bradbury ~ Real ale ~ Bar food ~ Restaurant ~ (01690) 710383 ~ Children in eating area of bar and restaurant ~ Open 12-2, 6.45-11.30(11 in winter); closed Mon-Weds in Jan ~ Bedrooms: £17(£20S)/£35(£56S)(£74B)

BODFARI SJ0970 Map 6
Dinorben Arms ♀
From A541 in village, follow Tremeirchion 3 signpost

Clinging to the side of a mountain next to a church near Offa's Dyke, in its lovely setting this attractive black and white inn is well worth a visit – they also have an incredible range of over 250 malt whiskies (including the full Macallan range and a good few from the Islay distilleries). Whisky aside, there are plenty of good wines (with several classed growth clarets), vintage ports and cognacs, quite a few unusual coffee liqueurs and well kept Batemans XB, Greene King Old Speckled Hen and Tetleys along with a weekly changing guest on handpump. Three warmly welcoming neat flagstoned rooms which open off the heart of this carefully extended building are full of character. As well as a glassed-over old well there are beams hung with tankards and flagons, high shelves of china, old-fashioned settles and other seats, and three open fires; there's also a light and airy garden room; piped classical music. There are lots of tables outside on the prettily landscaped and planted brick-floored terraces, with attractive sheltered corners and charming views, and there's a grassy play area which – like the car park – is neatly sculpted into the slope of the hills. Bar food includes steak and kidney pie or breaded plaice (£4.85), broccoli and cream bake (£5.25), welsh lamb chops (£7.95) and steaks (from £6.95); daily specials; they do buffets (£8.95-£13.95). *(Recommended by Mark and Diane Grist, KC, Christopher and Jo Barton, Margaret and Andrew Leach, Basil Minson)*

Free house ~ Licensee David Rowlands ~ Real ale ~ Bar food (12-2.30, 6-10, all day Sun) ~ Restaurant ~ (01745) 710309 ~ Children in eating area of bar and restaurant ~ Open 12-3.30, 6-11; 12-11 wknds

BOSHERSTON SR9694 Map 6
St Govans Country Inn £
Village signed from B4319 S of Pembroke

Usefully placed in a lovely area, this comfortably modernised inn is popular with walkers and climbers. Quite close by there's a many-fingered inlet from the sea, now fairly land-locked and full of water-lilies in summer, and the huge sandy Broadhaven beach, while some way down the road terrific cliffs plunge to the 5th-c St Govans Chapel which nestles at their base by the sea. The south wall of the bar is decorated with murals of local beauty spots painted by the landlord's son; lots of good climbing photos. Stone pillars support the black and white timbered ceiling of the spacious bar which has a log fire in a large stone fireplace, plenty of button-back red leatherette wall banquettes and armed chairs around dimpled copper tables; TV, pool, dominoes, fruit machine, juke box and board games. Straightforward bar food includes sandwiches, their speciality cawl (£2.35), ploughman's (£3.95), cumberland sausage (£3.75), gammon steak or fresh local trout (£6.95) and daily specials such as steak and kidney pie or spinach and feta goujons (£4.95), and thai red chicken (£5.95) with puddings such as treacle tart (£1.95); three-course roast on Sunday (£5.95). The dining area is no smoking. Bass, Fullers London Pride, Worthington and a local guest on handpump, also about a dozen malt whiskies. There are picnic-sets on the small front terrace; dogs are welcome in the stable bar. *(Recommended by Ken Richards, Mr and Mrs J E C Tasker, Charles and Pauline Stride, Jenny and Brian Seller)*

Free house ~ Licensee Warren Heaton ~ Real ale ~ Bar food (not 25 Dec) ~ Restaurant ~ (01646) 661643 ~ Children welcome till 9pm ~ Open 12-3.30, 6.30-11; 11-4, 6-11.30 Sat; 12-4, 6.30-11 Sun; 12-3, 7-11 winter ~ Bedrooms: £25S/£44S

CAREW SN0403 Map 6
Carew Inn
A4075, just off A477

This friendly, simple old inn, just opposite the imposing ruins of Carew Castle, is so popular that in summer they put a marquee in the garden to help accommodate the crowds. The atmosphere is cheery and welcoming, the landlady enjoys chatting to customers and the staff are friendly. The little panelled public bar and comfortable lounge are full of character with old-fashioned settles, scrubbed pine furniture, and interesting prints and china hanging from the beams. The no smoking upstairs dining room has an elegant china cabinet, a mirror over the tiled fireplace and sturdy chairs around the well spaced tables. Generous portions of reasonably priced bar food include lunchtime sandwiches (from £2.95) and ploughman's (£3.95) and other dishes such as smoked mackerel pâté and toast (£3.50), deep-fried camembert with mango chutney (£3.95), thai red curry (£6.95), mushroom and chestnut parcel (£7.95) and steaks (from £10.95) and specials such as baked crab ramekin (£3.95), salmon fillet in chive sauce (£7.95), greek lamb with mint and yoghurt and chicken breast stuffed with garlic and cheese (£7.95), and puddings such as home-made fruit crumble or mince tart (£2.75). The menu may be more limited at Sunday lunchtime, when they have a choice of roasts. Changing beers on handpump might include well kept Brains Reverend James and Tomas Watkins OSB and maybe a guest such as Fullers London Pride; sensibly placed darts, dominoes, cribbage, piped music. Dogs in the public bar only. The back garden overlooks the castle and a remarkable 9th-c Celtic cross, has a wheelchair ramp and is safely enclosed, with a wendy house, climbing frame, slide and other toys. Seats in a pretty little flowery front garden look down to the river where a tidal watermill is open for afternoon summer visits. They have live music every Thursday evening and Sundays in the school holidays. *(Recommended by the Didler, Tony and Wendy Hobden, N H E Lewis, John and Christine Lowe, David and Michelle Bailey, Pamela Goodwyn, David Jeffreys)*

Free house ~ Licensee Mandy Hinchliffe ~ Real ale ~ Bar food (12-2.30, 6-9) ~ Restaurant ~ (01646) 651267 ~ Children in eating area of bar and restaurant ~ Entertainment Thurs evening and Sun in school holidays ~ Open 11-11; 12-10.30 Sun; 11.30-2.30, 4.30-11 wkdys winter; closed 25 Dec

CILGERRAN SN1943 Map 6
Pendre 🍴 🍺 £
High Street, off A478 2¼ miles S of Cardigan

The price of the well presented home-made bar food at this very friendly, ancient pub (said to be one of the oldest in west Wales) continues to amaze readers. All main courses are £4 and might include trout with apple and marmalade cream, mushroom stroganoff, pork with spiced cabbage and onions in mild mustard sauce or roasted chicken in honey and pink peppercorn sauce. Starters range from £1.50 for pâté with whisky mango chutney to £2.50 for soup with cheese and toast or poached prawns with sesame toast. Puddings might include bread and butter pudding or apple banana and marmalade crumble (£1.75) as well as unusual home-made ice creams such as chocolate digestive, turkish delight and mince pie and brandy (from £1.75). The original bar area has massive stripped 14th-c medieval stone walls above a panelled dado, with elbow chairs and settles, and some beautifully polished slate flooring. Besides the comfortable lounge bar, there's a restaurant area. Well kept Tomos Watkins OSB and Whoosh on handpump and possibly a guest in summer; prompt welcoming service; shove-ha'penny, cribbage, fruit machine and darts in the public bar. A small terrace has sturdy tables, and there are more and an enclosed play area in the garden. The other end of the town leads down to the River Teifi, with a romantic ruined castle on a crag nearby, where coracle races are held on the Saturday before the August bank holiday. The local wildlife park nearby is well worth a visit, and this is a good area for fishing. *(Recommended by Steve and Liz Tilley, Richard Siebert, Susan Williams, AA, Giles and Liz Ridout, Brian and Carole Polhill, George Atkinson, John Hillmer)*

Free house ~ Licensees Debra and Jeff Warren ~ Real ale ~ Bar food (12-2, 6-8.30; Sun 7-8.30, not lunchtime) ~ Restaurant ~ No credit cards ~ (01239) 614223 ~ Children in eating area of bar and restaurant ~ Open 12.30-3, 6-11; 12-3, 7-11 Sun; if it's quiet 12-2, 6-9.30 winter ~ Bedrooms: £15(£25S)/£30S

CRESSWELL QUAY SN0406 Map 6
Cresselly Arms
Village signposted from A4075

Seats outside this traditional Welsh-speaking, creeper-covered local face the tidal creek of the Cresswell River and, if the tides are right, you can get here by boat – an approach that adds to the uniquely timeless appeal of the place. There's a relaxed and jaunty air in the two simple comfortably unchanging communicating rooms, which have red and black flooring tiles, built-in wall benches, kitchen chairs and plain tables, an open fire in one room, a working Aga in the other, and a high beam and-plank ceiling hung with lots of pictorial china. A third red-carpeted room is more conventionally furnished, with red-cushioned mate's chairs around neat tables. Well kept Worthington BB and a guest are tapped straight from the cask into glass jugs by the landlord, whose presence is a key ingredient of the atmosphere; fruit machine and winter darts. *(Recommended by the Didler, John and Enid Morris, Pete Baker, Mr and Mrs A Craig)*

Free house ~ Licensees Maurice and Janet Cole ~ Real ale ~ No credit cards ~ (01646) 651210 ~ Open 12-3, 5-11; 11-11 Sat; 12-3, 6(7 winter)-10.30 Sun; closed 25 Dec evening

CRICKHOWELL SO2118 Map 6

Bear ★ ⑪ ♀ ◧ ⛨

Brecon Road; A40

It's worth making a detour to visit this perfectly run old coaching inn with readers continuing to praise the excellent food, service and atmosphere here. Beautifully made using plenty of local ingredients, regularly changing bar meals might include soup (£2.95), sandwiches (from £3.25), welsh rarebit with grilled smoked bacon (£4.25), chestnut mushrooms stuffed with garlic butter, coated in herb breadcrumbs (£4.95), mussels in leek, saffron and garlic cream sauce (£5), ploughman's (from £5.75), faggots in onion gravy (£5.95), goats cheese and fried onion pie with baked ratatouille (£7.75), braised lambs hearts in red wine and black pudding sauce (£7.95), baked fresh salmon fillet with basil leaves in filo pastry with pesto cream sauce (£8.50) and delicious puddings such as treacle sponge pudding or plum terrine wrapped in marzipan (£3.50) or home-made ice creams (£2.95); they've a good range of Welsh cheeses. Their Sunday lunch is very popular. There's a calmly civilised atmosphere in the comfortably decorated, heavily beamed lounge, which has lots of little plush-seated bentwood armchairs and handsome cushioned antique settles, and a window seat looking down on the market square. Up by the great roaring log fire, a big sofa and leather easy chairs are spread among the rugs on the oak parquet floor; antiques include a fine oak dresser filled with pewter and brass, a longcase clock and interesting prints. The family bar is partly no smoking. Well kept Bass, Hancocks HB, Greene King Old Speckled Hen and a guest on handpump; malt whiskies, vintage and late-bottled ports, and unusual wines (with about a dozen by the glass) and liqueurs, with some hops tucked in among the bottles. Their apple juice comes from a mountainside orchard a few miles away. Service is swift and friendly even at really busy times. The back bedrooms – particularly in the quieter new block – are the most highly recommended, though there are three more bedrooms in the pretty cottage at the end of the garden. Lovely window boxes, and you can eat in the garden in summer; disabled lavatories. *(Recommended by Dr and Mrs A K Clarke, Richard Siebert, Tony Hobden, Darly Graton, Graeme Gulibert, David and Nina Pugsley, Denys Gueroult, Giles and Liz Ridout, June and Mike Coleman, P Fisk, Keith and Katy Stevens, Tony and Wendy Hobden, Piotr Chodzko-Zajko, Mel and Billie Tinton, H L Dennis, Christopher and Mary Thomas, Franklyn Roberts, Colyn Withers, John and Sheila Lister, David and Susan Grey, Eric Markland, David Jeffreys, Pamela and Merlyn Horswell; also in* The Good Hotel Guide*)*

Free house ~ Licensee Judy Hindmarsh ~ Real ale ~ Bar food (12-2, 6-10) ~ Restaurant ~ (01873) 810408 ~ Children in eating area of bar and must be over 5 in restaurant ~ Open 10.30-3, 6-11; 11.30-3, 7-10.30 Sun ~ Bedrooms: £52B/£68B

Nantyffin Cider Mill ⑪ ♀ ◧

1½ miles NW, by junction A40/A479

Particularly good, imaginative food and an attractive position facing the River Usk make this handsome, very restaurranty, pink-washed inn somewhere that readers keep coming back to. Using wherever possible local and organic meat and vegetables – quite a lot comes from a relative's nearby farm – the carefully thought-out menu changes all the time, with dishes such as home-made soup (£3.50), moroccan lamb in filo pastry with couscous (£5.50), fresh crab cakes with orange coleslaw (£5.75), italian balsamic pot-roast chicken (£10.50), braised lamb shank with rosemary and garlic sauce and herb mash (£10.95) and rib-eye steak with tarragon sauce (£14.95), and daily specials such as leek risotto cake filled with goats cheese and butternut squash or roast pork loin with apple and black pudding (£9.95), turbot (£14.95) and dover sole (£15.95); they now do a really good value weekday two-course lunch (£7.50). Service is first-class and very well organised. The place is smart and civilised in a brasserie style, with a woodburner in a fine broad fireplace, warm grey stonework, cheerful bunches of fresh and dried flowers, and good solid comfortable tables and chairs. The bar at one end of the main open-plan area has Buckley IPA and two guests such as Felinfoel Double Dragon and Tomos Watkins on handpump, as well as thoughtfully chosen New World wines (a few by the glass or half bottle), popular home-made lemonade and pimms in summer, and hot punch and mulled wine in winter. A raftered barn with a big cider press has been converted into quite a striking no smoking restaurant. The river is on the other side of a fairly busy road, but there are charming views from the tables out on the lawn above the pub's neat car park. A ramp makes disabled access easy. *(Recommended by Ivor and Shirley Thomas, Mike and Mary Carter, Darly Graton, Graeme Gulibert, David and Nina Pugsley, Denys Gueroult, R Mathews, Christopher and Mary Thomas, Paul Boot, Catherine and Richard Preston, Joyce and Maurice Cottrell, Rob Holt, N H E Lewis, John and Enid Morris, Mrs S E Griffiths, Steve and Liz Tilley, Bernard Stradling, Richard Siebert, Eric Markland, David Jeffreys, Paul Hopton)*

Free house ~ Licensees Glyn Bridgeman and Sean Gerrard ~ Real ale ~ Bar food (12-2.30, 6.30-10) ~ Restaurant ~ (01873) 810775 ~ Children welcome ~ Open 12-3, 6(7 Sun)-11; closed Mon; closed Sun night winter

EAST ABERTHAW ST0367 Map 6
Blue Anchor ★ ◗
B4265

Readers agree that you cannot help but be impressed by the charming picture-book exterior of this enchanting thatched and creeper-covered stone pub. Parts date back to 1380 and the warren of snug, low-beamed rooms is full of character: nooks and crannies wander through massive stone walls and tiny doorways, and there are open fires everywhere, including one in an inglenook with antique oak seats built into its stripped stonework. Other seats and tables are worked into a series of chatty little alcoves, and the more open front bar still has an ancient lime-ash floor; darts, dominoes, cribbage, fruit machine, and trivia machine. Their new chef hopes to change the menu which, as we went to press, included sandwiches (from £2.50), soup (£2.50), filled baked potatoes (from £3.50), pheasant and chestnut terrine (£3.50), Welsh faggots or home-made chicken and coconut curry (£5.50), home-made steak and kidney pie or grilled hake fillet (£5.75) and rump steak (£7.50); puddings such as apple and blackberry pie (£2.95); it's best to book for their Sunday roast (no bar food then). Well kept Buckley Best, Marstons Pedigree, Theakstons Old Peculier, Wadworths 6X and a couple of changing guests on handpump; friendly service from cheerful staff. Rustic seats shelter peacefully among tubs and troughs of flowers outside, with more stone tables on a newer terrace. From here a path leads to the shingly flats of the estuary. The pub can get very full in the evenings and on summer weekends, and it's a shame the front seats are right beside the car park. *(Recommended by Giles and Liz Ridout, David and Nina Pugsley, Steve Thomas, the Didler, David Carr, Deborah and Ian Carrington, P J Holdsworth, David and Kay Ross, David Jeffreys)*

Free house ~ Licensee Jeremy Coleman ~ Real ale ~ Bar food (12-2, 6-8; not Sat evening, not Sun) ~ Restaurant ~ (01446) 750329 ~ Children in eating area of bar and restaurant ~ Open 11-11; 12-10.30 Sun

GRAIANRHYD SJ2156 Map 6
Rose & Crown £
B5430 E of Ruthin; village signposted off A494 and A5104

Handy if you're in the Clwydian Hills, the bar of this remotely set pub sparkles with carefully chosen eclectic bric-a-brac. One small room has hundreds of decorative teapots hanging from its beams, the other has steins and other decorative mugs; there are 1950s romantic prints, Marilyn Monroe memorabilia, antlers, china dogs, highly ornamental clocks, a fiddling cherub, cottagey curtains and two cheerful coal fires. The informal young landlord and friendly locals help create a warm, inclusive atmosphere. Well kept Flowers IPA, Marstons Pedigree and Wadworths 6X on handpump, tea and coffee; darts, dominoes, pool, fruit machine. There may be a wait for the tasty bar food (cooked by the landlord) which includes soup (£1.90), burgers (from £2.20), brandy and herb pâté (£3.50), mushroom stroganoff (£4.95), breaded scampi, lasagne or steak and kidney pie (£5.25), goulash or lamb rogan josh (£5.50), trout with almonds (£6.95), 10oz sirloin steak (£8.95) and mixed grill (£12.50). Occasional well reproduced piped pop music goes well with the very relaxed chatty atmosphere. Picnic-sets out on a rough terrace by the car park have pretty hill views. Before you come here do check the opening times below. *(Recommended by KC)*

Free house ~ Licensee Tim Ashton ~ Real ale ~ Bar food (12-2, 6-10) ~ (01824) 780727 ~ Children welcome ~ Open 4-11 Mon-Thurs, 12-11 Fri; 1-11 Sat; 1-10.30 Sun

GRESFORD SJ3555 Map 6
Pant-yr-Ochain ♀

Off A483 on N edge of Wrexham: at roundabout take A5156 (A534) towards Nantwich, then first left towards the Flash

Readers are consistently pleased with the imaginative food at this spacious old country house which stands in its own beautiful grounds with a small lake and lovely trees. The popular, daily changing menu might include carrot and orange soup (£3.25), sandwiches (from £3.95), black pudding and bacon fritter with glazed apple and cider sauce (£4.50), ploughman's (£5.95), scotch salmon with red onions, capers and crème fraîche (£6.45), deep-fried goats cheese and roasted red pepper in filo pastry (£7.95), turkey, smoked bacon and mushroom casserole with a savoury herb scone (£8.95), baked cod fillet with sun-dried tomato crust in creamy parsley sauce (£9.95) and braised lamb shoulder with red onion mash (£10.95) with puddings such as warm apple and sultana crêpe or sticky toffee pudding (£3.95). The place has been thoughtfully refurbished to give a gently up-market atmosphere – it almost seems more like a manor house than a typical pub. The light and airy rooms are stylishly decorated, with a wide range of interesting prints and bric-a-brac on the walls and on shelves, and a good mix of individually chosen country furnishings including comfortable seats for relaxing as well as more upright ones for eating. There are good open fires, and the big dining area is set out as a library, with books floor to ceiling. They have a good range of decent wines, strong on up-front New World ones, as well as Boddingtons, Flowers Original, locally brewed tasty Plassey Bitter and Timothy Taylors Landlord and a guest such as Charles Wells Bombardier, and a good collection of malt whiskies. Service is friendly and efficient; one room is no smoking. The toilets and kitchen have been redecorated. *(Recommended by Martin Weinberg, Mr and Mrs A H Young, Paul and Margaret Baker, Paul Boot, MH, BD)*

Brunning & Price ~ Licensees Graham Arathoon and Lynsey Prole ~ Real ale ~ Bar food (12-9.30) ~ Restaurant ~ (01978) 853525 ~ Children in eating area of bar till 6pm ~ Open 12-11; 12-10.30 Sun

HALKYN SJ2172 Map 6
Britannia £

Britannia Pentre Rd, off A55 for Rhosesmor

The licensees of this welcoming old farmhouse hope to add a pair of donkeys to their collection of two tame goats Fleur the Oxford Sandy and Black, several sheep and lambs and various breeds of ducks and chickens. On a clear day the fabulous views from the partly no smoking dining room and the terrace usually stretch as far as Liverpool and the Wirral, and you may be able to pick out Blackpool Tower and Beeston Castle. There's a friendly atmosphere in the snug unspoilt lounge bar which has some very heavy beams, with horsebrasses, harness, jugs, plates and other bric-a-brac; there's also a games room with darts, pool, dominoes, fruit machine, TV, juke box and board games; piped music. Generous bar food includes home-made soup (£1.30), sandwiches served on Rhes-y-Cae bread (from £3.25), black pudding and mustard sauce (£3.05), mushroom and stilton bake (£4.50), cumberland sausage (£4.75), poached salmon fillet or battered chicken fillets (£4.95), beef and beer pie (£5.50), lamb steak marinated in honey or pork escalopes in pepper sauce (£6.05), daily specials; children's meals (from £1.70). Well kept Lees Bitter and Mild and maybe a seasonal brew on handpump; a choice of coffees. You can usually buy fresh eggs here. *(Recommended by KC, A J W Smith, Dave Irving, MLR)*

Lees ~ Tenant Keith R Pollitt ~ Real ale ~ Bar food (12-2, 7-9, not Mon or Tues in winter) ~ Restaurant ~ (01352) 780272 ~ Children welcome away from main bar ~ Open 11-11; 12-10.30 Sun

HAY-ON-WYE SO2342 Map 6

Kilverts 🛏

Bullring

After a successful browse around the many bookshops in this pretty old town, this friendly, informal hotel is a perfect place to spend the afternoon reading. The atmosphere is calm and relaxed with a nice mix of locals and visitors and service is welcoming and efficient. The airy high-beamed bar has an understated civilised feel, with some stripped stone walls, *Vanity Fair* caricatures, a couple of standing timbers, candles on well spaced mixed old and new tables, and a pleasant variety of seating. Bass, Hancocks HB and Greene King IPA on handpump, farm cider, an extensive wine list with about a dozen by the glass, and really good coffees; maybe piped pop radio. Well prepared bar food from a thoughtful menu includes lunchtime filled baguettes or sandwiches (from £2.75), home-made soup (£3), chargrilled vegetables with goats cheese and red chilli salsa (£4.95), ploughman's (from £5.95), spinach and mushroom roulade filled with cream cheese and chives with sweet peppers and basil (£9.95), baked salmon with tarragon butter cream sauce (£10.95) and steak or lamb chops (£10.95) with evening dishes such as baked chicken breast stuffed with sun-dried tomatoes, ricotta and parma ham with shallot and capsicum cream sauce (£11.95) or roast duckling with orange and ginger sauce (£12.50); blackboard specials might be moules marinières (£4.50) or braised rabbit with mustard and apple sauce (£8.95). There are tables out in a small front flagstoned courtyard; they don't mind dogs. *(Recommended by Andrew and Catherine Gilham, Giles and Liz Ridout, Darly Graton, Graeme Gulibert, Franklyn Roberts, Jacquie and Jim Jones, Ian Phillips, Jayne and Peter Capp)*

Free house ~ Licensee Colin Thomson ~ Real ale ~ Bar food ~ Restaurant ~ (01497) 821042 ~ Children in eating area of bar ~ Open 9-11; 10-10.30 Sun; closed 25 Dec ~ Bedrooms: £40S/£70S(£80B)

Old Black Lion 🍴 🛏 🍷

Lion Street

Oliver Cromwell is thought to have stayed in this partly 13th-c inn. The comfortably old-fashioned civilised bar has candles on old pine tables, casting a rosy glow over the black panelling, oak and mahogany bar counter, and two timber and glass screens. They serve well kept Wadworths 6X, Wye Valley Supreme and a remarkably good beer brewed for them by Wye Valley; good value wines, friendly staff. The wide range of enjoyable (if not cheap) generous food could include soup (£3.50), lunchtime sandwiches (£3.75), baguettes from £5.50), ploughman's (£5.95) with other bar food (from £8.75) such as beef and ale pie, moroccan lamb with couscous and fish pie. The menu in the cottagey no smoking restaurant which can be eaten in the bar includes dishes such as warm smoked trout salad (£5.59), goats cheese with tomato in filo pastry (£5.85), banana and pineapple curry served in half a pineapple (£9.95), wild boar steak (£13.50), guinea fowl supreme filled with garlic, or welsh lamb (£14.50) and quite a few fresh fish specials such as trout, monkfish and bass; puddings such as Tia Maria meringue and bread and butter pudding (from £3.95); Sunday roast. Tables out behind in a sheltered terrace. The comfortably creaky bedrooms have been recently refurbished; decent choice of hearty breakfasts. They can arrange trout and salmon fishing rights on the Wye as well as pony trekking and golf. *(Recommended by Nick and Meriel Cox, Giles and Liz Ridout, Peter Meister, Sue Demont, Tim Barrow, John and Enid Morris, David and Nina Pugsley, Keith Allen, Bob and Val Collman, Pam and David Bailey)*

Free house ~ Licensee Vanessa King ~ Real ale ~ Bar food (12-2.30, 6.30-9.30) ~ Restaurant ~ (01497) 820841 ~ Children over 5 away from main bar ~ Open 11-11; 12-10.30 Sun ~ Bedrooms: £40B/£70B

LITTLE HAVEN SM8512 Map 6
Swan £

Point Road; village signposted off B4341 W of Haverfordwest

Right on the coastal path, in one of the prettiest coastal villages in west Wales, this charming little inn has good views across a broad and sandy half-sheltered cove to the sea from seats in its bay window, or from the terrace outside. The affable landlord cooks the enjoyable bar food (only served at lunchtime) which includes sandwiches (from £1.95), home-made soup (£3.95), cawl – traditional welsh lamb and vegetable soup (£3.95 – with cheese on the side £4.25), ploughman's (from £4.75), crab bake (£5.25), sardines grilled with spinach, egg and mozzarella (£5.50), locally smoked salmon or fresh local crab (£6.95), home-made puddings (from £2.75), and one or two daily specials such as lasagne or bobotie (£4.50); no credit cards. You'll have to book if you want to eat in the Victorian-style restaurant. Well kept Buckleys Reverend James, Greene King Abbott and Worthingtons Best on handpump and a good range of wines and whiskies from the heavily panelled bar counter; prompt service. The two communicating rooms have quite a cosily intimate feel, comfortable high-backed settles and windsor chairs, a winter open fire, and old prints on walls that are partly stripped back to the original stonework. No children, dogs or dirty boots. Parking can be a problem in summer when you may have to use the public car park at the other end of the village. *(Recommended by George Atkinson, Mrs J Kendrick, Jim Abbott, John and Christine Lowe, Giles and Liz Ridout, Deborah and Ian Carrington, John and Enid Morris, Jayne and Peter Capp)*

James Williams ~ Tenants Glyn and Beryl Davies ~ Real ale ~ Bar food (lunchtime only) ~ Restaurant ~ No credit cards ~ (01437) 781256 ~ Open 11.30-3, 6-11; 12-3, 7-10.30 Sun; closed evening 25 Dec

LLANBEDR-Y-CENNIN SH7669 Map 6
Olde Bull

Village signposted from B5106

Inside this charming little 16th-c drovers' inn some of the massive low beams in the knocked-through rooms were salvaged from a wrecked Spanish Armada ship. There are also elaborately carved antique settles, a close crowd of cheerfully striped stools, brassware, photographs, Prussian spiked helmets, and good open fires (one in an inglenook); darts, dominoes, cribbage. Large helpings of home-made bar food include soup (£1.95), filled baguettes (from £2.50), pâté (£2.50), smoked mackerel (£3), king prawns in filo pastry with plum sauce (£3.50) ploughman's, steak and kidney pie or mushroom stroganoff, coronation chicken, battered cod or pork chops with apple sauce (£5.95), halibut steak with lobster sauce (£8.50) and 10oz sirloin (£10.95) with puddings (£2.50); children's meals (£2.50). Well kept Lees Bitter and Mild on handpump from wooden barrels, and several malt whiskies; welcoming service. Two no smoking restaurants. The pub is popular with walkers and, perched on the side of a steep hill, it enjoys splendid views over the Vale of Conwy to the mountains beyond, especially from seats in the particularly lovely herb garden, or the big wild area with waterfall and orchard. Lavatories are outside. *(Recommended by Mike and Wena Stevenson, John Fazakerley, Tracey and Stephen Groves)*

Lees ~ Tenants John and Debbie Turnbull ~ Real ale ~ Bar food ~ Restaurant ~ (01492) 660508 ~ Children welcome ~ Quiz Thurs ~ Open 12-11(10.30 Sun)

LLANBERIS SH6655 Map 6
Pen-y-Gwryd ◖ £ ⇦

Nant Gwynant; at junction of A498 and A4086, ie across mountains from Llanberis – OS Sheet 115 map reference 660558

Isolated high in the mountains of Snowdonia, this magnificently set old inn doubles up as a mountain rescue post. It's been a great favourite among mountaineers for generations – the team that first climbed Everest in 1953 used it as a training base, leaving their fading signatures scrawled on the ceiling. It's a really hospitable welcoming place with friendly, obliging staff (they may make you something to eat even when they're not normally serving food). One snug little room in the homely slate-floored log cabin bar has built-in wall benches and sturdy country chairs to let you gaze at the surrounding mountain countryside – like precipitous Moel-siabod beyond the lake opposite. A smaller room has a collection of illustrious boots from famous climbs, and a cosy panelled smoke room more climbing mementoes and equipment. Served only at lunchtime, you order the generous helpings of good value, home-made bar food from a hatch: the limited menu might include sandwiches (£1.75), pea soup (£2), an enormous ploughman's (£3.50), cold meats with home-made bread (£3.50), cold pork, turkey and cranberry pie (£4), diced lamb in red wine and paprika, steak, mushroom and ale pie or fried chicken breast in white wine, onion and mushrooms (£4.50); home-made puddings such as apple pie and crumble (£2). You will need to book early if you want to stay here. Residents have their own charmingly furnished, panelled sitting room and a sauna out among the trees, and in the evening sit down together for the hearty and promptly served dinner; the dining room is no smoking. In addition to well kept Bass, home-made lemonade in summer and mulled wine in winter, they serve sherry from their own solera in Puerto Santa Maria; table tennis, darts, pool, bar billiards, table skittles, and shove-ha'penny. Note the winter opening times. *(Recommended by Michael Buchanan, Mike and Mary Carter; also in* The Good Hotel Guide*)*

Free house ~ Licensee Jane Pullee ~ Real ale ~ Bar food (lunchtime) ~ Restaurant (evening) ~ No credit cards ~ (01286) 870211 ~ Children welcome ~ Open 11-11(10.30 Sun); closed Nov-Dec, Mon-Thurs Jan-Feb ~ Bedrooms: £24(£29B) /£48(£59B)

LLANDEILO SN6222 Map 6
Castle ◼ £

113 Rhosmaen St

At this former home of the Tomos Watkins Brewery, you can be sure of finding the beers well kept, and friendly knowledgeable bar staff are happy to talk about Brewery Bitter, Merlins Stout, OSB, Whoosh and the five seasonal brews. The tiled and partly green-painted back bar is the most atmospheric room, with locals sat round the edge chatting, a big fireplace with stuffed animal heads above it. A more comfortable carpeted bar at the front has smarter furnishings, and there's also a side area with a sofa, bookshelves, old maps and prints, and an elegant red-painted dining room with fresh flowers on the tables. The very reasonably priced, well presented bar food includes sandwiches (from £1.80), filled baguettes (from £2), home-cooked ham (£2.75), ploughman's with Welsh cheeses (£3.75), smoked salmon and prawn platter, spicy chicken curry or lasagne (£4.50), steak and stout pie (£4.95), beef strips with mushrooms and paprika (£7.50) and puddings such as home-made toffee vanilla mousse or raspberry cheesecake (from £2) and a local cheese platter (£3.50). An outside area with tables leads off here. Set up here five years ago by Simon Buckley, Tomos Watkins now supplies some 654 pubs. A noticeboard in the hallway has newspaper cuttings charting the growth of the brewery, and its success in helping promote Welsh real ales. *(Recommended by Joan and Michel Hooper-Immins, the Didler, Mike Pugh, R J Cox, Christopher and Jo Barton, Mr and Mrs J Brown, Nigel Espley, Liane Purnell, Andrew Hodgkins)*

Free House ~ Licensee Mr Buckley ~ Real ale ~ Bar food ~ Restaurant ~ (01558) 823446 ~ Children welcome ~ Folk Fri evening ~ Open 11-11; 12-10.30 Sun

LLANDEWI SKIRRID SO3416 Map 6
Walnut Tree ★ ⑪ ♀

B4521

The Taruschios have at long last retired from this hillside inn which they made nationally famous for first-class Italian food. The good news is that the people who have taken over are still earning warm praise from readers. It is a very restauranty place and meals aren't cheap but they are excellently made, combining southern

European leanings with first-class fresh and often unusual ingredients. Dishes might include warm crab tart with crème fraîche and grilled cucumber (£7.75), crispy belly of pork with fennel, lemon and caper berries (£8.25), potato gnocchi with duck sauce (£13.50), fried cod with artichokes, spunta potatoes, pancetta and black olives (£16), roast free range chicken with borlotti beans (£15.75), roast duck breast with sweet and sour cherries and locally smoked eel (£16.50), with puddings such as baked chocolate tart with orange marmalade and crème fraîche (£5.50) or hot fresh figs with mascarpone, balsamic and honey (£6); best to book to be sure of a table. The tempting choice of wines has particularly good Italian ones and the house wines by the glass are good value. The small newly repainted, white-walled bar has some polished settles and country chairs around new larger tables on its flagstones, and a log-effect gas fire. It opens into an airy and relaxed dining lounge with dark wooden chairs and tables. There are a few white cast-iron tables outside in front. *(Recommended by Franklyn Roberts, Bernard Stradling, John Close, John Kane, Joyce and Maurice Cottrell, Clare and Paul Howes, Richard Siebert)*

Free house ~ Licensees Stephen Terry and Francesco Mattioli ~ Restaurant ~ (01873) 852797 ~ Children welcome ~ Open 12-3, 7-11; 12-3 Sun; closed all day Mon (except bank hol lunchtime) and Sun evening

LLANDRINDOD WELLS SO0561 Map 6
Llanerch 🍺 £

Waterloo Road; from centre, head for station

Set in a quiet leafy spot on the edge of this spa town, with peaceful mountain views over the Ithon Valley, the front play area and orchard give this rambling 16th-c inn the feel of a country pub. A nice place to enjoy a drink in fine weather is the terrace, which leads to the garden where there are boules in summer (they have a Monday night league). Inside, the cheerfully bustling squarish beamed main bar is well liked by locals and has old-fashioned settles snugly divided by partly glazed partitions, and a big stone fireplace that's richly decorated with copper and glass; there are more orthodox button-back banquettes in communicating lounges (one of which is no smoking till 8pm). Bar food includes soup (£2.50), filled baps (from £2.50), filled baked potatoes (£3.25), ploughman's (£3.50), fisherman's pie (£4.75), chicken curry or steak, kidney and mushroom pie (£5.50), pork stroganoff (£6.50), lamb steak baked in garlic, redcurrant and rosemary sauce (£7.95), 8oz sirloin (£8.50), and daily specials such as smoked mackerel (£3.95), lemon sole or chicken in white wine, mushroom and rosemary sauce (£6.95); Sunday roast (£5.50). Well kept Hancocks HB and two regularly changing guests on handpump; piped music. Popular with a pleasant mix of ages including quite a few youngsters, the pub can get busy on Friday and Saturday evenings. A separate pool room has a fruit machine, darts and dominoes. *(Recommended by R T and J C Moggridge, R Mathews, Stuart Turner, Joan and Michel Hooper-Immins)*

Free house ~ Licensee John Leach ~ Real ale ~ Bar food (12-2.15, 6-9) ~ Restaurant ~ (01597) 822086 ~ Children in eating area of bar and restaurant ~ Entertainment the third Thurs of month ~ Open 11.30-3, 6-11; 11.30-11 Sat; 12-10.30 Sun ~ Bedrooms: £37.50S/£59B

LLANDUDNO JUNCTION SH8180 Map 6
Queens Head 🍽 ♀

Glanwydden; heading towards Llandudno on B5115 from Colwyn Bay, turn left into Llanrhos Road at roundabout as you enter the Penrhyn Bay speed limit; Glanwydden is signposted as the first left turn off this

The enjoyable, generous bar food is what draws customers to this modest-looking village pub. Served by polite efficient staff, the weekly changing menu (made with lots of fresh local produce) might include dishes such as soup (£2.95, local fish soup £3.25), open sandwiches (from £4.10), smoked goose breast with peach and apple chutney (£5.25), fresh potted Conwy crab (£4.95), pancakes filled with mushrooms and asparagus with napoli sauce (£7.25), steak and mushroom pie (£7.95), lamb cutlets with plum and port sauce (£9.50), steaks (from £11.75) and seafood platter (£13.50). Tempting puddings include pecan pie and oranges in Cointreau (£3.50). Though there is quite an emphasis on dining, locals do come in for a drink; well kept Ind Coope Burton and Tetleys and maybe a guest on handpump, decent wines including several by the glass, several malts, and good coffee (maybe served with a bowl of whipped cream and home-made fudge or chocolates). The spacious and comfortably modern lounge bar has brown plush wall banquettes and windsor chairs around neat black tables and is partly divided by a white wall of broad arches and wrought-iron screens; there's also a little public bar; the dining area has a no smoking section; unobtrusive piped music. There are some tables out by the car park. No dogs. *(Recommended by KC, Joan E Hilditch, Denis and Dorothy Evans, Maysie Thompson, R C Wiles, Sharon Holmes, Tom Cherrett, Paul Boot, Mike and Wena Stevenson)*

Punch ~ Lease Robert and Sally Cureton ~ Real ale ~ Bar food (12-2.15, 6-9; 12-9 Sun) ~ Restaurant ~ (01492) 546570 ~ Children over 7 welcome in eating area of bar and restaurant ~ Open 11.30-3, 6-11; 11.30-10.30 Sun; closed 25 Dec

LLANFERRES SJ1961 Map 6
Druid 🏠
A494 Mold—Ruthin

The long-standing staff and landlord at this extended 17th-c inn do their best to make sure that their customers feel at home. The generously served, interesting range of changing bar food might include soups (£2.60), very good granary baps filled with mozzarella and mushrooms, chicken fillet and lemon mayonnaise or pepperoni and mozzarella (£3.95), good vegetarian dishes like mixed vegetables in a creamy chilli sauce (£7.95), and main courses such as steak and oyster pie or chicken fillet with creamy chilli sauce (£8.95), halibut supreme or braised shoulder of welsh lamb with mint and tarragon gravy (£10.95) and duck breast with oriental mushroom sauce (£13.50); plentiful, fresh vegetables. Tables outside sheltered in a corner by a low wall with rock-plant pockets make the most of the view looking down over the road to the Alyn Valley and the mountains beyond, as does the broad bay window in the civilised, smallish plush lounge. You can also see the hills from the bigger beamed and characterful back bar, also carpeted (with quarry tiles by the log fire), with its two handsome antique oak settles as well as a pleasant mix of more modern furnishings. The attractive dining area is relatively smoke-free. Well kept Burtonwood Top Hat and Ridleys Rumpus on handpump, two dozen or so malt whiskies and wine list; the recently refurbished games room has darts and pool, along with dominoes, shove-ha'penny, bagatelle, Jenga and other board games; TV and maybe unobtrusive piped music. The bedrooms have been redecorated. *(Recommended by KC, Mark Powell, Mike and Maggie Betton, John Dowse, Michael Doswell, Graham and Lynn Mason, Ian Jones)*

Burtonwood ~ Tenant James Dolan ~ Real ale ~ Bar food (12-2.30, 6-10; 12-10 Sat, Sun and bank holidays) ~ Restaurant ~ (01352) 810225 ~ Children away from main bar ~ Piano sing-along first Sat of month ~ Open 12-3, 5.30-11; 12-11 Sat; 12-10.30 Sun ~ Bedrooms: £30(£32B)/£38.50(£45B)

LLANGEDWYN SJ1924 Map 6
Green
B4396 SW of Oswestry

Only just inside Wales, this country dining pub is in a very picturesque spot just opposite the village green. Spotlessly kept, it is nicely laid out with various snug alcoves, nooks and crannies, a good mix of furnishings including oak settles and attractively patterned fabrics, and a blazing log fire in winter; there's a pleasant evening restaurant upstairs. Good home-made food includes lunchtime sandwiches (from £1.60) and ploughman's (£3.95), soup (£2.25), steak and kidney pie, chicken curry or lasagne (£5.95) and daily specials such as devilled kidneys (£6.45), ham and mushroom pancakes (£6.95) or pork tenderloin with cheese and mushroom sauce (£9.45). Well kept Boddingtons, Charles Wells Bombardier, Tetleys, Woods and a guest such as Abbot Ale on handpump, Somerset farm cider in summer, a good choice of malt whiskies, and a decent wine list; friendly quick service. Darts, dominoes, fruit machine, TV and piped music; the restaurant is no smoking. It's on a well used scenic run from the Midlands to the coast, so it can get busy in summer – and that's when its attractive garden over the road comes into its own, with lots of picnic-sets down towards the river. The pub has some fishing available to customers, a permit for the day is £4. *(Recommended by Nigel Woolliscroft, A J Bowen)*

Free house ~ Licensee Gary Greenham ~ Real ale ~ Bar food (12-2, 6.30-10(9 Sun)) ~ Restaurant ~ (01691) 828234 ~ Children welcome ~ Open 11-3, 6-11; 11-11 Sat; 12-10.30 Sun

LLANGYNIDR SO1519 Map 6
Coach & Horses ⌂

Cwm Crawnon Road (B4558 W of Crickhowell)

Decked with flowers in summer, this welcoming old coaching inn is an ideal base for walking the Monmouth to Brecon Canal. Inside, the spacious open-plan carpeted lounge has small armchairs and comfortable banquettes against the stripped stone walls, and winter walkers appreciate the large open fire. A handy choice of generous bar food includes pasties (from £1.50), sandwiches (from £2.50), filled baguettes (from £3), ploughman's (£3.75), and several chicken curries or perhaps vegetable moussaka (from £7.50). As well as lots of fresh fish on the specials board which could include salmon and asparagus bake (£4.95) or cod and prawn mornay (£9.95), there are other dishes such as roast duckling with orange sauce (£11.95) or grilled lamb chops (£9.95) with puddings such as lemon brûlée (£3.75); no smoking area in restaurant. Well kept Bass, Hancocks and a guest such as Timothy Taylors Landlord on handpump; pool, fruit machine, video game and TV and piped music. There are plenty of tables across the road on a well fenced lawn running down to a lock and moorings. They do good hearty breakfasts. *(Recommended by Peter and Audrey Dowsett, Norman and Sarah Keeping, David and Teresa Frost, Mr and Mrs A Corbett)*

Free house ~ Licensee Derek Latham ~ Real ale ~ Bar food ~ Restaurant ~ (01874) 730245 ~ Children welcome ~ Open 12-11; 11.30-10.30 Sun ~ Bedrooms: £22.50(£28.50B)/£40(£50B)

LLANGYNWYD SS8588 Map 6
Old House £

From A4063 S of Maesteg follow signpost Llan ¼ at Maesteg end of village; pub behind church

You can now sit outside and enjoy the views from the new eating area at this picturesque, thatched pub which stocks an incredible range of more than 350 whiskies. Inside, there's a pleasant atmosphere and, although it's much modernised, the two cosy rooms, which date back to 1147, still have some comfortably traditional features. The two bars are decorated with high-backed black built-in settles, lots of china and well polished brass around the huge fireplace, shelves of bric-a-brac, and decorative jugs hanging from the beams. Well kept Brains, Flowers Original and IPA and a guest such as Shepherd Neame Spitfire on handpump, and a choice of wines by the glass. Served by friendly staff, the very reasonably priced, tasty bar meals include filled rolls (£1.30), soup (£2), baked potatoes (from £2.25), garlic mushrooms (£3.35), fresh grilled sardines (£3.50) ploughman's (£4), salads (from £4.90), all day breakfast, steak and ale pie or chicken or beef curry (£4.95), wild mushroom lasagne (£5.25) and steaks (from £12.25), puddings from the trolley (£2.60) and daily specials including some fish dishes. An attractive conservatory extension leads on to the garden which has a children's play area, and a soft ice-cream machine; piped music. The Welsh inn sign with a painting of the Mari Lwyd refers to the ancient Mari Lwyd tradition which takes place here at Christmas. Half the pub is no smoking. *(Recommended by R Mathews)*

Whitbreads ~ Lease Richard and Paula David ~ Real ale ~ Bar food (11-10) ~ Restaurant ~ (01656) 733310 ~ Children welcome away from main bar ~ Open 11-11; 12-10.30 Sun

LLANNEFYDD SH9871 Map 6
Hawk & Buckle

Village well signposted from surrounding main roads; one of the least taxing routes is from Henllan at junction of B5382 and B5429 NW of Denbigh

Handy if you're in the area, this welcoming little hotel run by new licensees is perched over 200m up in the hills. In clear weather, the well equipped, comfortable modern bedrooms boast views as far as the Lancashire coast and you may even be able to spot Blackpool Tower 40 miles away. There's an eye-catching mosaic mural on the way through into the back bedroom extension. The long knocked-through black-beamed lounge bar has comfy upholstered settles around its walls and facing each other across the open fire, and a neat red carpet in the centre of its tiled floor. The buzzy locals' side bar has pool and unobtrusive piped music. Bar food includes dishes such as toasted sandwiches (£2.95), ploughman's (from £3.95), mushroom and nut fettuccine (£6.95), local lamb chops (£6.95), and fresh local trout or salmon (from £7.95); the dining room is no smoking. Wine list, keg beers. *(Recommended by D J Hulse, Maysie Thompson)*

Free house ~ Licensees Paula and Fred Hunt ~ Bar food ~ Restaurant ~ (01745) 540249 ~ Children in eating area of bar and restaurant ~ Open 12-2.30, 7-11(10.30 Sun); open Weds, Sat and Sun only in winter; closed Mon, Tues and Thurs; 25 and 26 Dec ~ Bedrooms: £40B/£55B

LLANYNYS SJ1063 Map 6
Cerrigllwydion Arms

Village signposted from A525 by Drovers Arms just out of Ruthin, and by garage in Pentre further towards Denbigh

This atmospheric old place has a delightfully rambling maze of little rooms, filled with dark oak beams, a good mix of seats, old stonework, interesting brasses, and a collection of teapots. Their reasonably priced lunchtime snacks are popular and besides soup (£1.95), sandwiches (from £2), baguettes (from £2.25), baked potatoes (from £2.35), they include cumberland sauage with apple sauce (£4.85) and home-made steak and ale pie (£5.25) while other dishes might be deep-fried camembert with cranberry sauce or prawn cocktail (£3.55), salmon fillet in prawn and cream sauce (£7.25), duck in port and brandy sauce (£9.45), slow roasted lamb in mint and redcurrant sauce (£9.75) and a big mixed grill (£10.95); the restaurant is no smoking. It may be worth booking at busy times. As well as well kept Bass and Tetleys on handpump they keep a good choice of malt whiskies, liqueurs and wines; darts and unobtrusive piped music. Across the quiet lane is a neat garden with teak tables among fruit trees looking across the fields to wooded hills. The adjacent 6th-c church has a medieval wall painting of St Christopher which was discovered under layers of whitewash in the 1960s. *(Recommended by Joan E Hilditch, KC)*

Free house ~ Licensee Brian Pearson ~ Real ale ~ Bar food ~ Restaurant ~ (01745) 890247 ~ Children in restaurant ~ Open 12-3, 7-11(10.30 Sun); closed Mon

LLWYNDAFYDD SN3755 Map 6
Crown

Coming S from New Quay on A486, both the first two right turns eventually lead to the village; the side roads N from A487 between junctions with B4321 and A486 also come within signpost distance; OS Sheet 145 map reference 371555

There's a good fun, well maintained play area for children at this attractive white painted 18th-c pub, while adults can enjoy the well landscaped, tree-sheltered garden with its delightfully placed picnic-sets on a terrace above a small pond, among carefully chosen shrubs and flowers. Large helpings of enjoyable, home-made bar food, served by friendly staff, include soup (£2.95), prawn cocktail (£3.65), pizzas (from £5.95), lasagne, aubergine, courgette and mushroom korma or steak and kidney pie (£6.35), steaks (from £9.25) and daily specials prepared from local produce such as wild rabbit, orange and red wine casserole (£6.85), cajun pork steak with coriander and chilli salsa (£7.65) and seared swordfish steak (£7.85); children's meals. They do a roast on Sunday lunchtimes when the choice of other dishes may be limited. The friendly, partly stripped-stone bar has red plush button-back banquettes around its copper-topped tables, and a big woodburning stove; piped music. Very well kept Flowers IPA and Original and guests such as Brains Reverend James Original and Tomos Watkins OSB on handpump, a decent range of wines and malt whiskies; good selection of liqueur coffees. The side lane leads down to a cove with caves by National Trust cliffs, very pretty at sunset. *(Recommended by Stephen, Julie and Hayley Brown, V and M Bracewell, Giles and Liz Ridout, David and Michelle Bailey)*

Free house ~ Licensee Ian Green ~ Real ale ~ Bar food (12-2, 6-9) ~ Restaurant ~ (01545) 560396 ~ Children in family room and eating area of bar ~ Open 12-3, 6-11(10.30 Sun); closed Sun evening Nov-Easter except Christmas holidays

MOLD SJ2465 Map 6
Glasfryn ♀

Raikes Lane, Sychdyn (the old main road N to Northop, now bypassed by and just off the A5119)

Recently attractively converted by the same group which runs the Pant-yr-Ochain at Gresford, this large former farmhouse is now a popular bistro-style dining pub. Judging by the full car park and the heaving bar, it's also the favoured local port of call for people just in search of a chatty drink in congenial surroundings – including refugee luvvies and lawyers from the theatre and court in the Civic Centre just down the road. There's plenty of space and quiet corners in the rooms which open off here, with an informal and attractive mix of country furnishings and interesting decorations, and the bright young staff stay charming, attentive and helpful even when it is busy. A wide choice of inventive and beautifully presented if not exactly hearty food typically includes soup (£3.25), sandwiches (from £3.50), roast pear and stilton tartlet (£3.95), deep-fried black pudding and chorizo sausage fritter with potato salad and mustard dressing (£4.25), ploughman's (£5.95), salmon and smoked haddock fishcakes (£6.75), moussaka (£7.75), braised lamb shoulder in honey and mint sauce or grilled trout fillet (£10.95); puddings such as chocolate tart with white chocolate sauce (£3.95). Well kept real ales such as Timothy Taylors Landlord, Shepherd Neame Spitfire and Plassey Bitter on handpump, and a good range of tempting wines by the glass, served generously; around 100 whiskies. There are sturdy timber tables out on a big terrace with superb views to the Clwydian Hills – idyllic on a warm summer's evening. *(Recommended by Michael Sprackling, Dr Phil Putwain, Paul Boot, KC, Mrs P A King)*

Brunning & Price ~ Manager Duncan Lockhead ~ Bar food (12-9.30(9 Sun)) ~ (01352) 750500 ~ Children welcome away from bar till 6pm ~ Open 11.30-11; 12-10.30 Sun

MONKNASH SS9270 Map 6
Plough & Harrow ◀

Signposted Marcross, Broughton off B4265 St Brides Major—Llantwit Major – turn left at end of Water Street; OS Sheet 170 map reference 920706

The main bar of this basic but very atmospheric, unspoilt country pub seems hardly changed over the last 60 or 70 years. Dating from the early 12th c and originally part of a monastic grange, the stone walls are massively thick. The dark but welcoming main bar (which used to be the scriptures room and mortuary) has a log fire in its huge fireplace with a side bread oven large enough to feed a village, as well as a woodburning stove with polished copper hot water pipes. The heavily black-beamed ceiling has ancient ham hooks, there's an intriguing arched doorway to the back, and on the broad flagstones is a comfortably informal mix of furnishings that includes three fine stripped pine settles. Aside from the straightforward bar food they serve nine well kept real ales, often with some unusual ones; these might include Baths Ales Gem Bitter, Burton Bridge Bitter, Cottage Golden Arrow, Greene King Abbot Ale, Hancocks HB, Shepherd Neame Spitfire and Timothy Taylors Landlord on handpump or tapped from the cask; also real cider and country wines. The room on the left has daily papers, darts, dominoes, and piped music. Although it's very quiet on weekday lunchtimes, the pub can get crowded and lively at weekends when it's popular with families. There are picnic-sets in the small front garden. It's in a peaceful spot not far from the coast near Nash Point and it's an enjoyable walk from the pub down to the sea, where you can pick up a fine stretch of the coastal path. *(Recommended by David Carr, David and Nina Pugsley, Steve Thomas, R Michael Richards)*

Free house ~ Licensee Andrew David Davies ~ Real ale ~ Bar food (12-2, 6-9, not Sat and Sun evening) ~ Restaurant ~ (01656) 890209 ~ Children welcome ~ Entertainment Sun evening ~ Open 12-11(10.30 Sun)

OLD RADNOR SO2559 Map 6
Harp 🛏

Village signposted off A44 Kington—New Radnor in Walton

Fortunately there's plenty of seating outside this perfectly situated old hilltop inn, (either under the big sycamore tree, or on the side grass, where there's a play area) so you can properly soak up the marvellous views over the Marches. It's full of character inside, where sociable locals gather in the old-fashioned brownstone public bar which has high-backed settles, an antique reader's chair and other elderly chairs around a log fire; TV, cribbage, dominoes. The snug slate-floored lounge has a handsome curved antique settle and a fine inglenook log fire, and there are lots of local books and guides for residents; friendly licensees. Well kept Shepherd Neame and possibly a locally brewed beer; French organic wines. Reasonably priced bar food includes filled baguettes (from £3.50), ploughman's (£4.75), pork and herb sausages (£4.75), home-made quiche (£5.50), lasagne or cod and chips (£6.75), with more elaborate dishes in the restaurant. Readers have really enjoyed staying in the pretty bedrooms; generous breakfasts. There's an interesting early organ screen in the 15th-c turreted church next door; good nearby walks. Do check the opening times given below. *(Recommended by J C Davies, Mrs J Finch, DC, Lynn Sharpless, Bob Eardley, Jane and Daniel Raven, Mr and Mrs H H Smith)*

Free house ~ Licensees Erfye Protheroe and Heather Price ~ Real ale ~ Bar food (12-2, 7-9 wknds; 7-9 wkdys, not Mon) ~ Restaurant ~ (01544) 350655 ~ Children welcome ~ Open 6-11; 12-3, 6-11 Sat; 12-3, 6-10.30 Sun; closed 25 Dec ~ Bedrooms: £30/£50(£57B)

PEMBROKE FERRY SM9603 Map 6
Ferry Inn

Nestled below A477 toll bridge, N of Pembroke

This honest, welcoming old sailor's haunt overlooking the Cleddau estuary has quite a nautical feel. The bar has a bustling pubby atmosphere, lots of seafaring pictures and memorabilia, a lovely open fire, and good views over the water; fruit machine, unobtrusive piped music. Using local produce wherever possible, large portions of good bar food include quite a bit of fresh fish. The menu might have dishes such as smoked mackerel or chicken liver pâté (£3.95), vegetable kiev (£5.50), deep-fried scampi (£5.95), lamb kebabs (£6.50), salmon fillet poached in white wine with hollandaise sauce (£7.95) and sirloin steak (£8.95) with daily specials such as plaice (from £6.95), dressed crab or lemon sole (from £7.50) and dover sole (from £8.95). Well kept Bass, Felinfoel Double Dragon and a weekly changing guest such as Morrels Oxford Blue on handpump, and a decent choice of malt whiskies; friendly knowledgeable staff. When the weather's fine, the terrace by the water is a nice place to sit. *(Recommended by M G Hart, Ian Jones, Mike and Sue Loseby, David Jeffreys)*

Free house ~ Licensee Colin Williams ~ Real ale ~ Bar food (12-2, 7-10(9 Sun)) ~ Restaurant ~ (01646) 682947 ~ Children in eating area of bar and restaurant ~ Open 11.30-2.45, 6.30(7 Mon)-11; 12-2.45, 7-10.30 Sun; closed 25 and 26 Dec

You can send us reports through our web site: www.goodguides.com

PONTYPOOL ST2998 Map 6
Open Hearth ◖

The Wern, Griffithstown; Griffithstown signposted off A4051 S – opposite British Steel main
entrance turn up hill, then first right

This friendly, well run local is the best place for real ale in the area with up to 250
different types of beer a year. The eight well kept beers on handpump could include
Archers Golden, Greene King Abbott, RCH Pitchfork and Wye Valley Best as well
as four weekly changing guests such as Burton Bridge Brew and Moors Chandos
Gold; they also have a good choice of wines and lots of malt whiskies. Reliable good
value bar food includes filled rolls (from £1.60), soup (£2.15), filled baked potatoes
(from £2.85), vegetable stir fry (£4.50), various curries (from £5.60), lasagne
(£5.75), steak and ale pie (£5.95), chicken breast braised in white wine, mushrooms
and cream (£7.35), and sirloin steak (£11.20); good, friendly service. The
comfortably modernised smallish lounge bar has a turkey carpet and big stone
fireplace, and a back bar has leatherette seating; cribbage, dominoes, and piped
music. The downstairs no smoking restaurant is something of a local landmark.
Seats outside overlook a shallow overgrown stretch of the Monmouthshire &
Brecon Canal; there's a play area in the garden which has shrubs and picnic-sets, and
boules in summer. *(Recommended by R Mathews, Tony Hobden, R T and J C Moggridge,
Mike Pugh)*

*Free house ~ Licensee Gwyn Phillips ~ Real ale ~ Bar food (11.30-2, 6.30-10) ~
Restaurant ~ (01495) 763752 ~ Children welcome away from main bar ~ Open
11.30-4, 6-11; 11.30-11 Sat; 12-4.30, 7-10.30 Sun*

PORTHGAIN SM8132 Map 6
Sloop

Off A487 St Davids—Fishguard

Run by the same family since 1743, this long, white-painted pub has plenty of tables
on a terrace overlooking the harbour, with heaters for cooler weather. It's popular
with families, there's a relaxed atmosphere, and the staff are helpful and efficient.
The plank ceilinged bar has quite a bit of seafaring memorabilia around the walls,
from lobster pots and fishing nets, through ships' clocks and lanterns, to relics from
wrecks along this stretch of coast. Locals collect around the bar counter which serves
well kept Felinfoel Double Dragon, Wadworths 6X, Worthingtons Best and a
changing guest such as Abbot Ale on handpump. Down a step another room leads
round to a decent sized eating area, with simple wooden chairs and tables, cushioned
wall seats, a help-yourself salad counter, and a freezer with ice creams for children;
one area is no smoking; piped music. Readers really like the generous bar food
which includes soup (£2.95), lunchtime sandwiches (from £2.40, readers recommend
the fresh crab £3.90), tasty moules marinières with good crusty bread (£4.50),
ploughman's (£5.50), steak, kidney and mushroom pie or home-made vegetable
lasagne (£6.50), home-made macaroni and seafood bake (£6.90), steaks (from
£11.45); the changing specials board has good fresh fish dishes (from £8); puddings
such as hot apple and caramel pie (from £2.90). Rather than having a number for
food service, many of the tables are named after a wrecked ship. A well segregated
games room with juke box, fruit machine, darts, pool, dominoes, Scrabble and a TV
is used mainly by children. Good nearby coastal walks. It can get very busy here in
summer. *(Recommended by Norma and Keith Bloomfield, John and Enid Morris, Mike and
Wena Stevenson, Dr Tom Solomon, Sue Demont, Tim Barrow, Geoff and Angela Jaques, Mike
Pugh, David and Michelle Bailey, Jayne and Peter Capp)*

*Free house ~ Licensee Matthew Blakiston ~ Real ale ~ Bar food (12-2.30, 6-9.30) ~
(01348) 831449 ~ Children welcome ~ Open 11-11; 12-4, 5.30-10.30 Sun*

> People don't usually tip bar staff (different in a really smart hotel, say). If you
> want to thank them – for dealing with a really large party say, or special
> friendliness – offer them a drink.

PORTHMADOG SH5639 Map 6

Ship ◖

Lombard Street; left turn off harbour road, off High Street (A487) in centre

Known locally as Y Llong and built in 1824, this relaxed local on a quiet little street near the centre is the oldest pub in town. They serve six well kept real ales on handpump which as well as Greene King IPA and Old Speckled Hen, Ind Coope Burton and Tetleys Dark and Mild could include a guest such as Abbot Ale; over 70 malt whiskies. There's a laid-back feel in the two dimly lit roomy bars which have lots of attractive ship prints, photographs and drawings, quite a bit of brass nautical hardware, and candles in bottles. It's sturdily furnished, with pews, mate's chairs and so forth, and there are good fires in winter; TV, silenced fruit machine, dominoes. A wide choice of reasonably priced, nicely cooked bar food includes soup (£2.25), pâté of the day (£3.25), vegetable roast with couscous and mango and lime sauce or thai red vegetable curry (£7.85), moules marinières, grilled tuna steak, cuban lamb or steak and kidney pudding (£8.95) and gammon hock with white bean sauce (£9.85); look out for their very good value two for one specials; children's meals (from £3.25). There's also an attractive no smoking bistro-style back restaurant. Service is friendly and efficient, and helpful to families. The lounge bar is no smoking. It's not a long walk from the Ffestiniog Railway terminus. They hold a beer festival the first two weeks of March. *(Recommended by Bob and Val Collman, Jim Cowan, Jane Scarrow, Stephen Hughes)*

Punch ~ Lease Robert and Nia Jones ~ Real ale ~ Bar food (12-2, 6.30-9; 12-4 Sun, not Mon and Tues in winter) ~ (01766) 512990 ~ Children in eating area of bar at lunchtimes ~ Open 11-11; 12-4 Sun; closed Sun in winter and during school term time

PRESTEIGNE SO3265 Map 6

Radnorshire Arms ⌸

High Street; B4355 N of centre

It's a shame that we don't have more reports from readers on this rambling, timbered old inn. Although part of a small chain of hotels, it's full of old-fashioned charm and individuality and discreet modern furnishings blend in well with venerable dark oak panelling, latticed windows, and elegantly moulded black oak beams, some decorated with horsebrasses. Some of its tremendous history was uncovered during renovations which revealed secret passages and priest's holes, with one priest's diary showing he was walled up here for two years. They serve well kept Cains and Peter Yates on handpump, several malt whiskies, local wine, morning coffee and afternoon tea. Bar food includes soup (from £3.45), wraps with fillings such as chicken tikka or prawn cocktail (£4.05) and filled baguettes (£4.25), as well as dishes such as hot welsh rarebit with bacon or wild mushroom ragoût with rice (£4.25), chef's roast of the day, tuna steak with roasted pepper or beef wellington with shallots (£9.25), fried duck breast with spicy fruit salsa (£11.95) and puddings such as chocolate and rum truffle torte or bread and butter cheesecake (from £3.50), local cheese platter (£4.15); children's menu (£3.99). Every day except Sunday they also do a good value two-course snack lunch for £5; welcoming attentive service; separate no smoking restaurant. There are some well spaced tables on the sheltered flower-bordered lawn, which used to be a bowling green. *(Recommended by John Whitehead)*

Free house ~ Licensee Philip Smart ~ Real ale ~ Bar food ~ Restaurant ~ (01544) 267406 ~ Children in eating area of bar and restaurant ~ Open 11-3, 6-11; 11-11 Sat; 12-10.30 Sun ~ Bedrooms: £60B/£68.50B

RAGLAN SO3608 Map 6

Clytha Arms Ⓨ ◖ ⌸

Clytha, off Abergavenny road – former A40, now declassified

Very reasonably priced considering the high quality, and made using lots of fresh local ingredients, the delicious bar food at this graciously comfortable, fine old county inn is really enjoyed by readers. Generously served dishes could include soup (from £4.50), bacon, laverbread and cockles, black pudding with apple and potato mash, faggots and peas with beer and onion gravy (£5.95), three cheese ploughman's or wild mushroom ragoût with pasta (£6.50), wild boar sausages with potato pancakes (£6.75), smoked salmon and scrambled egg (£7.20), daily specials such as spaghetti with bacon and cockles (£6.25) and grilled salmon and prawn salad (£7.25). Not content with serving really good bar food they have a well stocked bar too, with well kept Bass, Bulmastiff Gold, Felinfoel Double Dragon and three interesting changing guest beers on handpump, as well as Weston's farm cider, a changing guest cider, and home-made perry, and the extensive wine list has a dozen or so by the glass. There are usually a couple of locals in the carefully refurbished bar which has a good bustling atmosphere, solidly comfortable furnishings and a couple of log fires; darts, shove-ha'penny, boules, table skittles, cribbage, dominoes, draughts and chess. The exceptionally helpful staff and interested licensees make this such a nice place to stay; the two labradors, Beamish and Stowford, are nicely welcoming too. Don't miss the murals in the lavatories. This lovely building stands in its own extensive well cared for grounds which are a mass of colour in spring. *(Recommended by Bruce Bird, David and Nina Pugsley, Mike and Wena Stevenson, Richard Hoare, the Didler, Stephen, Julie and Hayley Brown, Charles and Pauline Stride, I J and N K Buckmaster, Tony Hobden, James Morrell, Geoffrey and Penny Hughes, Mr and Mrs H D Brierly, Mike Pugh, Mike and Sue Loseby, Eric Markland, Graham and Lynn Mason)*

Free house ~ Licensees Andrew and Beverley Canning ~ Real ale ~ Bar food (not Mon lunch or Sun evening) ~ Restaurant ~ (01873) 840206 ~ Children in eating area of bar and restaurant ~ Open 12-3.30, 6-11; 12-11 Sat; 12-4, 7-10.30 Sun; closed Mon lunchtime except bank holidays ~ Bedrooms: £45B/£60B

RED WHARF BAY SH5281 Map 6
Ship ◖

Village signposted off B5025 N of Pentraeth

This 18th-c inn, run by the same friendly family for nearly 30 years, is old-fashioned and interesting inside, with lots of nautical bric-a-brac in big welcoming rooms on each side of the busy stone-built bar counter, both with long cushioned varnished pews built around the walls, glossily varnished cast-iron-framed tables and welcoming fires. Outside, tables on the front terrace are ideally placed to enjoy the view which stretches down along 10 square miles of treacherous tidal cockle-sands and sea, with low wooded hills sloping down to the broad bay. Changing bar food might include sandwiches (from £2.05, baguettes from £3.95), soup (£2.80), welsh goats cheese and couscous salad (£4.80), potted smoked trout (£4.85), grilled local chilli sausages with penne and spicy tomato sauce (£6.75), wild mushroom and fennel risotto (£6.85), fish casserole with tagliatelle and pesto (£6.95) or roast chicken breast with creamy leek sauce (£7.25) and puddings such as brandy snap basket or rum chocolate truffle torte (£3.65); cheerful service. It can get quite crowded here and you'll need to arrive early for a table on weekends. The family room, dining room and cellar room are no smoking. Very well kept Friary Meaux, Ind Coope Burton, Tetley Mild and a guest such as Brains Bitter on handpump; a wider choice of wines than usual for the area (with a decent choice by the glass), and more than 50 malt whiskies. Dominoes, piped music. There are rustic tables and picnic-sets by an ash tree on grass by the side. *(Recommended by Dylan William, Robert Davis, Dave Braisted, Bob and Val Collman, Denis and Dorothy Evans, Mr and Mrs B Hobden, Darly Graton, Graeme Gulibert, Michael Buchanan)*

Free house ~ Licensee Andrew Kenneally ~ Real ale ~ Bar food (12-2.30, 6.30-9.30; Sun 12-9) ~ Restaurant ~ (01248) 852568 ~ Children in eating area of bar, restaurant and family room ~ Open 11-11; 12-10.30 Sun; 11-3, 6.30-11 wkdys winter

---

Cribbage is a card game using a block of wood with holes for matchsticks or special pins to score with; regulars in cribbage pubs are usually happy to teach strangers how to play.

ROSEBUSH SN0729 Map 6
Tafarn Sinc
B4329 Haverfordwest—Cardigan

Surely this can't be a pub – this big corrugated iron shed, painted a dark maroon? But it is, and not at all the locals-only social club sort of place that your initial misgivings suggest, as you stand outside wondering whether you dare go in. Go on! It's not exactly elegant, but really interesting inside, almost a museum of local history, with plank panelling, an informal mix of chairs and pews, woodburners and a piano. This used to be a railway halt, left behind when this loop of the line closed over 60 years ago, and it's been more or less re-created, even down to life-size dummy passengers waiting out on the platform, and the sizeable garden periodically enlivened by the sounds of steam trains chuffing through (actually broadcast from a replica signal box). The atmosphere in the bar is cheerful and friendly, with welcoming staff, well kept Bass, John Smiths, Worthingtons and a beer named Cwrw for the pub, and good value well cooked straightforward food; there's a no smoking dining room. Unfortunately the licensee refused to answer any of our questions so we cannot give any details for this intriguing place. *(Recommended by Jim Abbott, the Didler, Rev Michael Vockins, David and Michelle Bailey, Eileen Wilkinson, Richard Siebert, John and Enid Morris, David Twitchett)*

(01437) 532214

SAUNDERSFOOT SN1304 Map 6
Royal Oak ♀ ◖
Wogan Terrace (B4316)

The eight or so fresh fish dishes that they serve at this bustling pub, well placed in the centre of the village above the harbour, increases to over a dozen in the summer. There might be john dory (from £6.95), plaice (from £7.95), haddock or grilled hake with chilli sauce (£9.95), lemon sole (£10.95), halibut with lobster and prawn sauce or monkfish (£11.95) and grilled bass (£13.95); prices are variable depending on the catch. A good choice of other bar food includes lunchtime sandwiches (from £2.95) and hot filled baguettes or baked potatoes (from £3.95), ploughman's (£4.95), red thai vegetable curry or beer battered cod (£6.95), steak and bacon pie (£7.25), braised lamb shank with thyme and parsnip mash (£8.95), wild mushroom and brandy strudel (£10.95) or steaks (from £11.50); puddings such as syrup sponge pudding or chocolate biscuit brandy bar (from £3.15). Although the staff will try their best to squeeze you in, it may be worth booking in season. It's efficiently run, staff are pleasant and attentive even in the middle of the holiday season, and in the small public bar (which has a TV and dominoes) the locals are chatty. There's a buoyant atmosphere in the dining area and carpeted no smoking lounge bar, which has captain's chairs and wall banquettes. Well kept Ansells Bitter, Marstons Pedigree and Worthingtons and a couple of guests such as Greene King Abbot and Old Speckled Hen on handpump, 25 malts, and an interesting choice of wines with a dozen by the glass; piped music in the lounge bar. In summer the outside tables get snapped up quickly; they have overhead heaters for cooler weather. *(Recommended by John Burgess, Robin and Janice Dewhurst, Lesley Bass, the Didler, John Hillmer)*

Free house ~ Licensees R J, T L and T S Suter and D J Kirkpatrick ~ Real ale ~ Bar food (12-10) ~ Restaurant ~ (01834) 812546 ~ Children in eating area of bar and restaurant ~ Open 11-11; 12-10.30 Sun

SHIRENEWTON ST4894 Map 6
Carpenters Arms ◖
B4235 Chepstow—Usk

There's plenty to see in this pleasant country inn and it's worth wandering around the hive of small interconnecting rooms before you settle. Collections range from chamber-pots and a blacksmith's bellows hanging from the planked ceiling of one lower room, which has an attractive Victorian tiled fireplace, to chromolithographs of antique Royal occasions under another room's pitched ceiling (more chamber-pots here). Furnishings run the gamut too, from one very high-backed ancient settle to pews, kitchen chairs, a nice elm table, several sewing-machine trestle tables and so forth. Readers enjoy the reasonably priced bar food which includes sandwiches (from £1.40), filled baked potatoes (from £2.50), ham and eggs, pheasant casserole or liver and bacon (£5.25), steak and mushroom pie (£5.95), chicken in leek and stilton sauce (£6.75) and fresh salmon (£6.95). The atmosphere is pleasantly pubby – it's popular with locals enjoying some of their seven well kept real ales which include Brakspears, Flowers IPA, Fullers London Pride, Marstons Pedigree, Theakstons Old Peculier, Wadworths 6X and a guest such as Abbot Ale on handpump, as well as a good selection of around 50 malt whiskies; cheerful service, shove-ha'penny, cribbage, dominoes, table skittles, bar billiards, backgammon and piped pop music. Originally a smithy, the pub has an eye-catching array of hanging baskets outside; handy for Chepstow. *(Recommended by Mike and Mary Carter, Dr and Mrs R E S Tanner, David and Nina Pugsley, M G Hart, C H and B J Owen, R T and J C Moggridge)*

Free house ~ Licensee James Bennett ~ Real ale ~ Bar food (not Sun evening) ~ No credit cards ~ (01291) 641231 ~ Children in family room ~ Open 11-2.30, 6-11; 12-2.30, 7-10.30 Sun

ST HILARY ST0173 Map 6
Bush

Village signposted from A48 E of Cowbridge

The comfortable and snugly cosy low-beamed lounge bar of this old-fashioned 16th-c thatched pub has a very friendly atmosphere, and a pleasant mix of locals and visitors. With stripped old stone walls, and windsor chairs around copper-topped tables on the carpet, the public bar has old settles and pews on aged flagstones; darts, TV, cribbage, dominoes and subdued piped music, and a warming wood fire. Readers praise the good value, enjoyable bar food which includes sandwiches (from £1.95), soup (£2.75), laverbread and bacon (£3.25), welsh rarebit (£3.75), spinach and cheese crêpe (£3.95), ploughman's (£3.95), trout fillet grilled with bacon (£4.50), liver with onion gravy (£4.95), chicken curry and rice or steak and ale pie (£5.50), mixed grill (£7.95), and specials such as seafood crêpe or tagliatelle provençale (£5.95); smaller helpings for children. The locally popular restaurant is no smoking, as is the lounge bar at meal times. Well kept Bass, Hancocks HB, and Worthingtons on handpump or tapped from the cask, with a range of malt whiskies and a farm cider; efficient service. There are tables and chairs in front, and more in the back garden. *(Recommended by Steve Thomas, Derek Stafford, David and Nina Pugsley, R T and J C Moggridge, Alan Sinclair, M G Hart, M Joyner, David Jeffreys)*

Punch ~ Lease Sylvia Murphy ~ Real ale ~ Bar food (12-2, 7-9; 12.15-2.45, 6.30-8.30 Sun) ~ Restaurant ~ (01446) 772745 ~ Children welcome ~ Open 11.30-11; 12-10.30 Sun

STACKPOLE SR9896 Map 6
Armstrong Arms

Village signposted off B4319 S of Pembroke

This rather Swiss-looking pub does good, hearty bar food, perfect after a walk along the sandy beaches, through the woodland or along the craggy cliffs of the Stackpole estate. Reasonably priced dishes, served by cheerful black-and-white uniformed waitresses, might include soup (£3.25), tasty steak baguette (£5.50), mushroom stroganoff, chicken and vegetable lasagne, moules marinières or pint of prawns (£5.95), steak and ale pie (£7.75), lemon sole grilled with prawn and lemon butter (£8.95). One spacious area has pine tables and chairs, with winter darts and pool, but the major part of the pub, L-shaped on four different levels, is given over to diners, with neat light oak furnishings, and ash beams and low ceilings to match; piped music. At busy times you may find it hard to get a table in some parts of the pub if you're not eating. Well kept Buckley Best, Reverend James and a guest and several malt whiskies. There are tables out in the attractive gardens, with colourful flowerbeds and mature trees around the car park. Dogs welcome in bar and garden. *(Recommended by R J Herd, Ian Jones, Rita Scarratt, Lesley Bass, Mike and Sue Loseby, David Jeffreys, Paul Hopton)*

Free house ~ Licensees Margaret and Valerie Westmore ~ Real ale ~ Bar food (not Sun lunchtime) ~ Restaurant ~ (01646) 672324 ~ Children welcome till 8.30pm ~ Open 11-3, 6-11; 12-3, 6-10.30 Sun; 7-11 winter; closed Sun evening and Mon Jan-Feb

TALYBONT-ON-USK SO1122 Map 6

Star ✦ £

B4558

They serve between six and twelve continually changing well kept real ales at this old-fashioned canalside inn from brewers such as Batemans, Bullmastif, Felinfoel, Shepherd Neame, Wadsworths and Wye Valley; farm cider on handpump. Unashamedly stronger on character than on creature comforts, there's a bustling local atmosphere in the several plainly furnished pubby rooms which radiate from the central servery, including a brightly lit games area with pool, fruit machine, TV and juke box; cheering winter fires, one in a splendid stone fireplace. Reasonably priced, straightforward bar food includes sandwiches (£2), soup (£2.50), ploughman's (£4), with a few home-made dishes such as broccoli, cheese and potato pie, chicken curry or hungarian pork goulash (£5.50), chicken breast in leek and stilton sauce or gammon steak (£7.50) as well as faggots, peas and chips or salmon fishcakes (£4.50) and sirloin steak (£8.50). You can sit outside at picnic-sets in the sizeable tree-ringed garden. This simple but beautifully set village, with both the Usk and the Monmouth & Brecon Canal running through – you can walk along the tow path – is surrounded by the Brecon Beacons national park. *(Recommended by the Didler, Colin Parker, Franklyn Roberts, Jean and Richard Phillips, Gill and Rob McCubbins, J P Humphery, Tony Hobden)*

Free house ~ Licensee Joan Coakham ~ Real ale ~ Bar food ~ (01874) 676635 ~ Children welcome ~ Rock and Blues Weds evening ~ Open 11-3, 6.30-11; 11-11 Sat; 12-3, 6.30-10.30 Sun ~ Bedrooms: /£45S

TALYLLYN SH7209 Map 6

Tynycornel ⇌

B4405, off A487 S of Dolgellau

Peacefully nestling below high mountains, the attractively planted side courtyard of this comfortably civilised hotel is a lovely place for afternoon tea. Inside, though it's not at all pubby, it's relaxed and friendly, with deep armchairs and enveloping sofas around the low tables, a central log fire, and big picture windows looking out over the water as well as big bird prints, local watercolours, and a good range of malt whiskies (the serving bar, with keg beer, is tucked away behind). Efficient uniformed staff serve the nicely cooked bar food which includes sandwiches (from £2.30), deep-fried Welsh cheese (£3.95), ploughman's (£5.95), battered cod (£6.25), ham and eggs (£6.75), herring salad (£6.95) and daily specials such as curry (£6.75), fresh crab (£6.95) and beef in red wine and Guinness in a yorkshire pudding (£8.50); no smoking restaurant and conservatory. Guests have the use of a sauna and fishing facilities, and can hire boats on the lake. Cadair Idris opposite has splendid walks and behind is Graig Goch. *(Recommended by W H and E Thomas)*

Free house ~ Licensee Thomas Rowlands ~ Bar food ~ Restaurant ~ (01654) 782282 ~ Children welcome ~ Open 11-11; 12-10.30 Sun ~ Bedrooms: £48.50B/£97B

Please keep sending us reports. We rely on readers for news of new discoveries, and particularly for news of changes – however slight – at the fully described pubs. No stamp needed: The Good Pub Guide, FREEPOST TN1569, Wadhurst, E Sussex TN5 7BR or send your report through our web site: www.goodguides.com

TY'N-Y-GROES SH7672 Map 6

Groes 🍽 🍷 🛏

B5106 N of village

This well run old dining pub has magnificent views over scenic reaches of the Conwy River and the distant mountains, while the seats outside are a good place to sit and appreciate the pretty back garden with its flower-filled hayricks. First licensed in 1573, it claims to be the first licensed house in Wales. The homely series of rambling, low-beamed and thick-walled rooms are beautifully decorated with antique settles and an old sofa, old clocks, portraits, hats and tins hanging from the walls, and fresh flowers. A fine antique fireback is built into one wall, perhaps originally from the formidable fireplace which houses a collection of stone cats as well as winter log fires. A good range of bar food made with lots of local produce might include soup (£2.95), sandwiches (from £3), Welsh cheese board (£5.75), soup and a sandwich (£5.95), lasagne (£7.25), fishcakes (£7.50), steak and kidney pot with thyme dumplings (£7.75), crispy roast duck (£10.95) and steaks (from £12) with daily specials such as vegetable and mushroom pasta bake (£7.25), dijon chicken (£8.25), Welsh lamb steak (£9.25), salmon fillet with hollandaise sauce (£8.50) and seafood platter (£14); lots of delicious puddings such as lemon and ginger sponge and hot bara brith and butter pudding (£3.75); tempting home-made ice creams with unusual flavours such as honey and lemon or fragrant rose. Well kept Ind Coope Burton and Tetleys, a good few malt whiskies, kir, and a fruity pimms in summer; cribbage, dominoes and light classical piped music at lunchtimes (nostalgic light music at other times). It can get busy but the friendly, efficient staff cope very well. It's a lovely place to stay with good views from the spotlessly kept bedrooms (some with terraces or balconies). There's an airy verdant no smoking conservatory, seats on the flower decked roadside. (*Recommended by John and Christine Lowe, Keith and Margaret Kettell, A J Bowen, Joan E Hilditch, Mrs M A Cameron, Brian and Janet Ainscough, H Bramwell, Paul Boot, Mike and Mary Carter, Pat and Tony Hinkins, Mr and Mrs McKay, Michael Buchanan*)

Free house ~ Licensee Dawn Humphreys ~ Real ale ~ Bar food (12-2.15, 6.30-9) ~ Restaurant ~ (01492) 650545 ~ Children under 10 in family room till 7.30pm, over 10 in restaurant ~ Open 12-3, 6.30(6 Sat and Sun)-11 ~ Bedrooms: £64B/£81B

USK SO3801 Map 6

Nags Head 🍽

The Square

Wales Dining Pub of the Year

Run by the warmly welcoming Key family for 35 years, this relaxed old coaching inn serves tasty, unusual bar food with lots of seasonal game. Daily specials might include pheasant in port and duck in Cointreau (£10.50), stuffed partridge, a brace of quail with appropriate eggs, superb venison steaks with sauté potatoes, or guinea fowl in wine (£12), and other dishes such as home-made rabbit pie (£6.80), local salmon or wild boar in apricot and brandy sauce (£12), while the bar menu includes such things as snails and frogs legs (£4.80) alongside familiar staples like soup (£3), battered cod (£5.80), steak pie (£5.80) and vegetable pancake (£6.50). You can book tables, some of which may be candlelit at night; piped classical music. The traditional main bar is full of character, with a huge number of well polished tables and chairs packed under its beams, some with farming tools, lanterns or horsebrasses and harness attached, as well as leatherette wall benches, and various sets of sporting prints and local pictures, amongst which are the original deeds to the pub. Well kept Brains SA, Buckley Best and Reverend James on handpump, served by courteous, friendly staff – it's the sort of place where they greet you as you come in, and say goodbye when you leave. Hidden away in a corner at the front is an intimate little corner with some African masks, while on the other side of the room a passageway leads to the pub's own busy coffee bar, open between Easter and autumn. Built in the old entrance to the courtyard, it sells snacks, teas, cakes and ice cream. Tables from here spill out on to the pavement in front. A simpler room behind the bar has prints for sale, and maybe locals drinking. In summer, the centre of Usk is full of hanging baskets and flowers, many of them looked after by the landlord; the church is well worth a look. *(Recommended by Robert Mansfield, Mike Pugh, Sue and Ken Le Prevost, Jenny and Chris Wilson, David and Nina Pugsley, Michael and Caroline Cordell, Charles and Pauline Stride, Christopher and Mary Thomas, Andrew Williams, Eryl and Keith Dykes, Peter and Audrey Dowsett, Andrew and Catherine Gilham, Eric Markland, Graham and Lynn Mason, Ian Phillips)*

Free house ~ Licensees the Key family ~ Real ale ~ Bar food (12-2, 6-9.30) ~ Restaurant ~ (01291) 672820 ~ Children welcome ~ Open 11-3, 5.30-11; 12-3, 6-10.30 Sun

Lucky Dip

Besides the fully inspected pubs, you might like to try these Lucky Dips recommended to us and described by readers (if you do, please send us reports: www.goodguides.com).

ANGLESEY

Menai Bridge [SH5572]
☆ *Liverpool Arms* [St Georges Pier]: Good cheap fresh food from generous sandwiches up (fish pies and fishcakes particularly well liked) in cheerful relaxed four-roomed local, well kept Greenalls and a guest beer, decent wines, prompt welcoming service even when busy, low beams, interesting mostly maritime photographs and prints, panelled dining room, conservatory catching evening sun, no music; one or two tables on terrace *(Jeff Davies, Glenys and John Roberts)*

CLWYD

Betws-yn-Rhos [SH9174]
☆ *Wheatsheaf*: Well furnished old-fashioned two-bar 17th-c inn with friendly service, well kept beers, wide choice of reasonably priced food inc bargain suppers for two, good log fires; good value bedrooms, lovely village *(C M Miles, J B Towers, BB)*
Broughton [SJ3263]
Spinning Wheel [Old Warren; old main rd towards Buckley]: Early 19th-c black and white building, copper and brass decorations, emphasis on wide choice of good freshly made well served food in big eating area, friendly efficient staff, good choice of beers and malt whiskies; piped music *(MH, BD, Graham and Lynn Mason, Nigel Pittman)*
Brynford [SJ1875]
Llyn y Mawn [B5121 SW of Holywell]: Charming comfortable country pub based on 15th-c coaching inn with sympathetic extension (inc evening restaurant), friendly staff and locals, new chef doing good generous food with fresh veg, well kept ales inc Brains Buckley and three changing guests, summer farm cider; quiz night, good music night 1st Sun of month *(Jamie MacKay, Mr and Mrs L Simpson)*
Burton Green [SJ3558]
Golden Groves [Llyndir Lane, off B5445 W of Rossett]: Relaxed timbered pub in lovely setting, partly knocked-through rooms dating from 13th c, open fires, comfortable settees and settles, plates, horsebrasses, figures carved in the beams; friendly staff, Marstons Best and Pedigree, good range of well priced wines, good value food, restaurant, children welcome, piped

music; large attractive streamside garden with play area, open all day summer wknds *(LYM, Mr and Mrs G Owens)*
Coedway [SJ3415]
☆ *Old Hand & Diamond* [B4393 W of Shrewsbury]: Attractive recently refurbished pub popular for good food inc succulent local lamb and game in small back bar, dining area and restaurant, well kept Bass, Worthington BB and guest beers such as Woods Shropshire Lad, log fire, smaller back bar, friendly service, no music; attractive beamed bedrooms with pristine bathrooms, tables outside, lots of climbing roses and hanging baskets *(Albert and Margaret Horton, Mrs Caroline Gath)*
Cross Lanes [SJ3746]
Kiln: Good choice of enjoyable food inc interesting dishes with fresh veg, decent wines, filter coffee *(Rita and Keith Pollard)*
Gwaenysgor [SJ0881]
☆ *Eagle & Child*: Welcoming and spotless early 19th-c pub, shining brasses and plates, generous freshly cooked good value food, Bass, good service, exemplary lavatories; attractive floodlit gardens, in hilltop village with fine views *(C M Miles, J B Towers)*
Gwernymynydd [SJ2161]
Owain Glyndwr [Glyndwr Rd, off A494 at Rainbow Garage W of Mold]: Hard-working new licensees, very friendly and helpful, well kept ales inc Wadworths 6X, enjoyable food inc Sun lunch, upstairs restaurant with lovely views; bedrooms, cl Mon-Sat lunchtimes *(Basil Minson)*
Hanmer [SJ4639]
☆ *Hanmer Arms*: Relaxed and pleasantly uncrowded country inn with good range of reasonably priced straightforward food inc popular Sun lunch (advisable to book), friendly staff, well kept bar, Tetleys-related ales, big family dining room upstairs, no music; neat and attractive garden, with church nearby making a pleasant backdrop; comfortable good value bedrooms in former courtyard stable block, pretty village *(MH, BD, Anthony Barnes)*
Higher Kinnerton [SJ3361]
Royal Oak [Kinnerton Lane, off A55/A5104 SW of Chester; also signed off A483]: Ancient picturesque coaching inn with good choice of interesting food in dining area, decent wines,

helpful staff, friendly atmosphere, lots of small rooms, log fires, settles, low oak beams hung with jugs, teapots, copper kettles and chamber-pots, interesting collection of soda syphons; tables in small garden, barbecues and play area *(D J Knight)*

Lixwm [SJ1671]
Crown: Well kept early 17th-c village inn, good choice of wine and of real ale inc changing guest beers, good value food cooked to order every evening and wknd lunchtimes, pleasant licensees, nice atmosphere; children allowed in dining room, open all day Sun, cl wkdy lunchtimes; colourful front flower tubs and baskets; bedrooms *(C M Miles, J B Towers)*

Llandegla [SJ1952]
Plough [Ruthin Rd]: Cosy and well run locally popular dining pub, well kept Robinsons, good value generous home-made food inc good range of fresh fish, large dining room; piped music; nr Offa's Dyke Path *(Nigel Pittman)*

Llanelian-yn-Rhos [SH8676]
☆ *White Lion* [signed off A5830 (shown as B5383 on some maps) and B5381, S of Colwyn Bay]: Family-run 16th-c inn, traditional flagstoned snug bar with antique settles and big fire, dining area on left with jugs hanging from beams, teapots above window, further comfortable more spacious dining area up broad steps, wide choice of good reasonably priced bar food from sandwiches and big tureen of home-made soup up, good service, well kept Marstons Bitter, Pedigree and a seasonal beer, good range of wines, lots of malt whiskies, grotto filled with lion models; dominoes, cribbage, piped music; children in eating areas, rustic tables outside, good walking nearby, comfortable bedrooms *(Mr and Mrs David B Meehan, C M Miles, J B Towers, Michael and Jenny Back, Betty Laker, LYM)*

Llangollen [SJ2142]
Corn Mill [Dee Lane]: Striking converted watermill, interesting combination of original features with new construction, attractive and comfortable interior, enterprising and enjoyable food, good range of real ales, good wines; young staff, TV; lovely spot, tables out on terrace above River Dee *(P and M Rudlin, Mrs P A King)*

Lloc [SJ1476]
Rock [St Asaph Rd (A5151)]: Bright décor, enjoyable food *(C M Miles, J B Towers)*

Mold [SJ2464]
Bryn Awel [A541 Denbigh rd nr Bailey Hill]: Consistently good value dining pub, good choice of satisfying food, huge helpings, attentive service, cheerful bustling atmosphere, attractive décor, good no smoking area; piped music can be intrusive *(KC)*

Northop [SJ2468]
☆ *Soughton Hall*: Country pub in attractive and extensively renovated stable block, bare boards and massive beams, well kept real ales inc one brewed by Plassey for the pub, impressive choice of wines, freshly made food in bar and upstairs bistro, helpful and friendly staff; beautiful park and drive to parent country house hotel with bedrooms *(MLR)*

Rhewl [SJ1744]
☆ *Sun* [off A5 or A542 NW of Llangollen]: Unpretentious little cottage in lovely peaceful spot, good walking country just off Horseshoe Pass, relaxing views from terrace and small pretty garden; simple good value generous food from sandwiches to good Sun lunch, well kept Worthington BB and a guest such as Plassey Cwrw Tudno, chatty landlord, old-fashioned hatch service to back room, dark little lounge; outside lavatories, Portakabin games room – children allowed here and in eating area; open all day wknds *(KC, Joan and Michel Hooper-Immins, LYM, MLR)*

Ruthin [SJ1258]
Olde Anchor [Dog Lane]: Black and white timbered former coaching inn, lots of flower baskets, welcoming licensees, open fire, well kept Bass and Worthingtons, reasonably priced bar food, popular restaurant using local produce well; bedrooms good value, attractive country town *(Janet and Peter Race)*

St Asaph [SJ0374]
Red Lion [Gemig St]: Good home cooking, well kept ales such as Marstons, Tetleys and Theakstons, welcoming landlord *(Christopher and Jo Barton)*

Wrexham [SJ3450]
Albion [Pen y Bryn]: Slightly Victorian feel in traditional plainly comfortable main bar, particularly well kept Lees, friendly staff, back games bar; cheap bedrooms *(Pete Baker)*

DYFED

Broad Haven [SM8614]
☆ *Druidstone Hotel* [N of village on coast rd, bear left for about 1½ miles then follow sign left to Druidstone Haven – inn a sharp left turn after another ½ mile; OS Sheet 157 map ref 862168, marked as Druidston Villa]: Very unusual and a special favourite for many; only its club licence rules it out of the main entries – you can't go for just a drink and have to book to eat there (the food is inventively individual home cooking, with fresh ingredients and a leaning towards the organic; restaurant cl Sun evening); a lived-in informal country house alone in a grand spot above the sea, with terrific views, spacious homely bedrooms, erratic plumbing, folksy cellar bar, well kept Worthington BB tapped from the cask, good wines, country wines and other drinks, ceilidhs and folk jamborees, chummy dogs (dogs welcomed), all sorts of sporting activities from boules to sand-yachting; cl Nov and Jan; bedrooms *(Andrew Humble, Charles and Pauline Stride, Norma and Keith Bloomfield, LYM, John and Enid Morris)*

Burton [SM9805]
Jolly Sailor: Great views of River Cleddau and toll bridge, riverside garden tables, Worthington real ale, quite a range of food *(Jenny and Brian Seller)*

Caio [SN6739]
☆ *Brunant Arms* [off A482 Llanwrda—Lampeter]: Unspoilt pretty village local covered with flowers; welcoming and chatty, with well kept Boddingtons and Tomos Watkins, good

layout inc pews, good value generous food inc prime welsh black steak (best to book for small eating area), good service, interesting egg cup collection; pool table and juke box, quiz nights; bedrooms good value, good walks *(Guy Vowles, Michael and Carol Wills)*

Capel Bangor [SN6580]

☆ *Tynllidiart Arms* [A44]: Quaint roadside cottage with woodburner in big stripped-stone bare-boards bar, has its own tiny brewery (in what used to be the gents') with four well kept ales inc a Stout, good friendly landlord, nice atmosphere, limited good well presented food, also large upstairs dining room; well behaved children and dogs allowed *(Gwyneth and Salvo Spadaro-Dutturi)*

Carmarthen [SN4120]

Mansel Arms [Mansel St]: Local and guest real ales, good reasonably priced food; handy for market *(E W and S M Wills)*

Cilycwm [SN7540]

☆ *Neuadd Fawr*: Welcoming Welsh-speaking village local, new licensees gaining good reputation for their home-made food; simple old-world furnishings, cheerful atmosphere, maybe lively impromptu sing-song Sun night; good spot by churchyard above River Gwenlas, among lanes to Llyn Brianne *(Kate Morgan, BB)*

Cwm Gwaun [SN0035]

☆ *Dyffryn Arms* [Cwm Gwaun and Pontfaen signed off B4313 E of Fishguard]: Classic unspoilt country tavern, very basic and idiosyncratic, run by same family since 1840 – charming landlady Bessie has been here over 40 years herself; 1920s front parlour with plain deal furniture inc rocking chair and draughts-boards inlaid into tables, coal fire, well kept Bass and Ind Coope Burton served by jug through a hatch, good sandwiches if you'e lucky, time-warp prices, Great War prints and posters, very relaxed atmosphere, darts; pretty countryside, open more or less all day (but may close if no customers) *(David and Michelle Bailey, the Didler, LYM)*

Cwmbach [SN4802]

Farriers Arms [B4308 Llanelli—Trimsaran]: Plush split-level lounge/dining area with wood and dark wallpaper, decent food, well kept ales such as Everards, Greene King, Marstons and Tomos Watkins, high wooden settles in small stripped stone bar with TV, big informal garden with covered barbecue area, bridge over trout stream to play area and tables well spread in woodland glade *(Michael and Alison Sandy)*

Cwmdu [SN6330]

☆ *Cwmdu Inn* [5 miles N of Llandeilo, a mile W of B4302 (Talley rd)]: In row of cottages, shop and post office, like the pub owned by National Trust; tiny old-fashioned bar, dining room little bigger with log fire in vast inglenook, basic furnishings on great flagstones, good low-priced generous food, limited beers; attractive setting by bridge *(Neville and Anne Morley)*

Fishguard [SM9537]

☆ *Fishguard Arms* [Main St, Lower Town]: Tiny timeless front bar with Worthington BB and a couple of guest beers served by jug at unusually

high counter, open fire, rugby photographs; cheap snacks, very friendly staff, traditional games and impromptu music in back room with big window overlooking river *(E W and S M Wills, LYM, the Didler)*

☆ *Ship* [Newport Rd, Lower Town]: Cheery landlord, lots of atmosphere and seafaring locals in dim-lit red-painted local nr old harbour, well kept Bass tapped from the cask, homely food (not wknds), coal fire, lots of boat pictures, model ships; children welcome, toys provided *(the Didler, LYM)*

Goginan [SN6981]

Druid: Well kept Brains in friendly roadside pub *(Gwyneth and Salvo Spadaro-Dutturi)*

Haverfordwest [SM9515]

☆ *Georges* [Market St]: Massive choice of generous home-made food using good meat, fresh veg and good vegetarian range, in attractive Celtic-theme bar with character stable-like furnishings, informal relaxed atmosphere, quick friendly service even when busy, well kept Marstons Pedigree, a seasonal Wye Valley Dorothy Goodbodys and a guest beer, good wine list (esp New World), more sophisticated evening restaurant; lovely walled garden, no dogs, Celtic arts shop in front *(Betsy and Peter Little, Andrew Humble)*

Lamphey [SN0100]

Dial: Big light and airy bar and adjacent family dining room with show of decorative plates, good varied home-made food inc some enterprising specials, Bass, Hancocks HB and Worthington, good value house wine, friendly attentive staff, games room with pool; maybe 60s piped music; small front terrace, bedrooms *(Jim Abbott, Dr Roger Turner)*

Letterston [SM9429]

Harp [A40 Haverfordwest rd]: Dining pub with dark wood and careful décor in smart lounge bars and restaurant, good well presented food inc lots of fresh fish, real ales such as Ansells, Greene King Old Speckled Hen and Tetleys, friendly efficient service even on busy nights, simple pleasant public bar with pool table; open all day *(David and Michelle Bailey)*

Llanarthne [SN5320]

☆ *Golden Grove Arms* [B4300 (good fast alternative to A40)]: Wide choice of good food in bar and restaurant inc some sophisticated dishes, and friendly helpful service, in nicely laid out child-friendly inn with roomy lounge, open fire, well kept Brains Buckley Best and Rev James, good wine list, huge play area; Tues folk night; bedrooms *(LYM, Nigel Espley, Liane Purnell)*

Llanddarog [SN5016]

☆ *White Hart* [just off A48; aka Yr Hydd Gwyn]: Bustling thatched stone-built dining pub brewing its own Coles Cwrw Blasus and other imaginative ales inc a surprisingly successful beetroot beer, heavy beams hung with bric-a-brac, 17th-c carved settles, two stone fireplaces (one with motorised spit), L-shaped dining area hung with Welsh tapestries and farm tools, friendly landlady, landlord cooks wide range of above-average generous food running up to good fish and

sizzling venison, sandwiches too; piped
nostalgic music (even in the garden) *(Mike
Pugh, Michael and Alison Sandy, Mr and
Mrs J E C Tasker)*

Llandeilo [SN6222]
White Horse [Rhosmaen St]: Busy local with
well kept changing real ales *(the Didler)*

Llandovery [SN7634]
Red Lion [Market Sq]: One basic but
welcoming room with no bar, well kept Brains
Buckley and guest beers tapped from the cask,
friendly and individual landlord; cl Sun, may
close early evening if no customers *(the Didler,
BB)*

Llangadog [SN7028]
Castle Hotel [A4069 SW of Llandovery;
Queens Sq]: Easy-going pub full of curios and
stuffed animals and birds, friendly licensees,
well kept Welsh beer, food inc some interesting
dishes and local wild trout; good value
bedrooms, big breakfast *(Rita Scarratt)*

Mathry [SM8732]
☆ *Farmers Arms* [Brynamlwg, off A487
Fishguard—St David's]: Carefully renovated by
newish local licensees, cosy and homely bar,
wide choice of reasonably priced hearty food
inc good crab sandwiches, local fish and lamb,
well kept real ales, attentive staff, children
welcome in large dining conservatory; tables in
small walled garden safe for children, open all
day in summer, interesting woodworker's opp
*(Trevor Owen, Sue Demont, Tim Barrow,
Deborah and Ian Carrington)*

Myddfai [SN7730]
☆ *Plough*: Relaxing old pub in prettily set Brecon
Beacons village, friendly staff and locals, big log
fire in cosy, quirkily shaped and beautifully
kept beamed bar, home-made food here and in
restaurant, changing real ales such as Brains
Revd James, attentive service, amiable dog,
games room; bedrooms cheap, clean and simple
(O Johansen)

Narberth [SN1114]
☆ *Angel* [High St]: Interesting changing real ales,
good food choice inc lots of local fish, Welsh
lamb, help-yourself salad bar, children's dishes
and good value Sun lunch, pleasant relaxed
surroundings with almost a hotel feel in lounge
bar, quick friendly and helpful service; pub
pianist, fairly handy for Oakwood theme park
and other attractions *(Howard James)*

Nevern [SN0840]
☆ *Trewern Arms*: Extended inn in delightful
setting nr notable church and medieval bridge
over River Nyfer, dark stripped-stone slate-
floored bar, rafters hung with rural bric-a-brac,
high-backed settles, plush banquettes, usually
several Whitbreads-related ales, efficient helpful
staff, food ordered from bright modern kitchen,
restaurant; games room; tables in pretty garden,
comfortable bedrooms, big breakfast *(LYM,
Mike and Wena Stevenson, Dick and
Madeleine Brown)*

Pelcomb Bridge [SM9317]
Rising Sun [A487 NW of Haverfordwest]:
Attractive and welcoming, generous freshly
made food particularly good for the area, real
ale; two bedrooms *(Mrs N W Neill)*

Pembroke [SM9801]
Freshwater Inn [Freshwater East]: Village pub
with lovely bay views from lounge, simple bar
food inc fresh fish, Felinfoel Double Dragon,
Two Cannon Extra and a guest beer such as
Theakstons Old Peculier, dining room, pool in
public bar; well behaved children welcome,
tables outside, busy summer evenings *(Jim
Abbott)*

Rhos [SN3735]
Lamb [A484 Carmarthen—Cardigan]: Two
large rooms with sofas and dining tables, well
kept Banks's Bitter and Mild, efficient friendly
service, appetising food, large restaurant; good
value bedrooms *(Stephen, Julie and Hayley
Brown)*

Solva [SM8024]
Cambrian [Lower Solva; off A487
Haverfordwest—St Davids]: Attractive and
neatly kept dining pub much enjoyed by older
people (perhaps a bit stiff for others); clean and
warm, food inc authentic pasta, fresh fish and
popular Sun lunch, decent Italian wines,
Tetleys-related ales, efficient service, log fires;
piped music, no dogs or children *(Mr and Mrs
A Craig, E G Parish, Mr and Mrs R Woodman,
John Hillmer)*
Harbour House [Main St]: Popular and nicely
worn in, in good harbourside setting with
splendid views, warm friendly atmosphere,
good range of beers and of reasonably priced
freshly made food from quickly served
sandwiches up, attentive staff, children's area
with pool table; public bar can be smoky; tables
on terrace, bedrooms *(George Atkinson, Ian
and Deborah Carrington, Betsy and Peter
Little)*

St David's [SM7525]
Farmers Arms [Goat St]: Cheerful and busy
low-ceilinged pub by cathedral gate, cosy
separate areas, wide choice of good value
straightforward food from sandwiches to
steaks, well kept Flowers and Wadworths 6X,
chatty landlord; cathedral view from tables in
tidy back garden *(Deborah and Ian Carrington)*
Old Cross [Cross Sq]: Hospitable hotel, reliable
food inc good ploughman's with local cheese,
sensible prices, attentive service, good position –
get there before the tourist coaches arrive; dogs
allowed, nicely shaded tables on small lawns of
lovely front garden, bedrooms *(George
Atkinson)*

St Florence [SM0801]
Old Parsonage Farm: Lively family pub with
plenty of games machines etc in back bar, TV
and so forth, food from well filled toasties up;
tables in garden, bedrooms *(M G Hart)*

Tenby [SN1300]
☆ *Plantagenet House* [Quay Hill]: Unusual well
renovated and civilised medieval building on
two levels, with marvellous old chimney, three
floors with stripped stonework, tile and board
floors, candles on tables, piped music, cane
furniture, interesting low-priced food inc fine
soups, good baguettes, fresh local crab and fish,
Welsh cheeses; friendly service, Flowers
Original and Wadworths 6X (licence allows
alcohol service only with food, hence no main

entry), upstairs restaurant; fine Victorian lavatories; open all day in season, but cl lunchtime out of season (George Atkinson, Pamela Goodwyn)

Tregaron [SN6759]
Talbot [The Square]: Friendly and thoughtful service in character bar, good range of food from snacks to full meals, well kept Greene King and other real ales; interesting town (Gordon Neighbour, Guy Vowles)

GWENT

Abergavenny [SO3014]
Hen & Chickens [Flannel St]: Small well used traditional local, Bass and Brains, basic wholesome cheap lunchtime food (not Sun), friendly staff, popular darts, cards and dominoes (Pete Baker, the Didler)
Lamb & Flag [Llanwenarth; A40, 2 miles NW]: Wide range of generous good value food inc lots of puddings in roomy and comfortable modern plush lounge bar or two dining rooms, well kept Brains Bitter and SA, good service, picture-window hill views; children welcome, high chairs; open all day in summer, tables outside with play area; comfortable bedrooms (Joan and Michel Hooper-Immins)

Bassaleg [ST2787]
Tredegar Arms [handy for M4 junction 28; A468 towards Caerphilly]: Whitbreads Wayside Inn with wide range of well cooked food inc interesting dishes, good range of reliably well kept real ales, enthusiastic landlord, pleasant eating area, family and outdoor areas (no dogs allowed in garden) (Nigel Clifton, Alan Sinclair)

Bettws Newydd [SO3606]
☆ Black Bear [off B4598 N of Usk]: Busy cottage-style pub in tranquil village, good if not cheap food in bar and big formal eating area, enterprising game and seafood dishes, cheaper separate snack menu; tiled floor, big wooden tables, piano, lots of brasses, and well kept changing ales such as Bath PA and SPA; picnic-sets by road, more in sloping side garden (the Didler, BB, Colin McKerrow)

Caerleon [ST3693]
Wheatsheaf [Llanhennock, N]: Unspoilt ancient-seeming pub with country views, cosy and friendly bar and snug, good collection of small plates and mugs, good value food (not wknd evenings or Sun lunchtime), real ales such as Bass; children welcome, tables in garden with ducks, cat and play hut (Richard C Morgan)

Chepstow [ST5394]
Castle View [Bridge St]: Opp the castle and its car park, hotel bar with white-painted walls and some exposed stonework, plush chairs and stools, standard bar food inc good sandwich range, well kept Wye Valley Hereford PA from small bar counter, daily papers; tables in attractive garden, bedrooms (BB, Ian Phillips)

Fleur-de-lis [ST1695]
Coal Hole [Gellihaf; A4049 towards Pontllanfraith]: Friendly stripped stone pub bustling at lunchtime, wide food choice running up to steaks, Bass and Hancocks HB (Ian Phillips)

Grosmont [SO4024]
☆ Angel: Welcoming little ivy-covered 17th-c village local on attractive steep single street within sight of castle, seats out by ancient market cross beside surprisingly modern little town hall; friendly local atmosphere, several changing well kept ales from Tomos Watkins and (brewed for the pub) Wye Valley, Bulmer's cider, good value food (not Thurs pm) inc speciality sausages, cheery service, big Welsh flag; TV, separate room with pool and darts, a couple of tables and boules pitch behind (C H and B J Owen, R T and J C Moggridge, BB, David and Elizabeth Briggs)
Cupids Hill Inn [B4347 N]: One for lovers of unspoilt pubs, basic cottage bar on very steep hill in pretty countryside, old settles by fire, low white ceiling, one keg beer, cider, table skittles, dominoes, cribbage; in same family for nearly a century (BB, the Didler)

Llanfihangel Crucorney [SO3321]
☆ Skirrid [signed off A465]: One of Britain's oldest pubs, dating partly from 1110; ancient studded door to high-ceilinged main bar, stone, flagstones and panelling, dark feel accentuated by furniture inc pews (some padded), huge log fire; full range of Ushers beers, helpful staff, good generous bar food from big sandwiches up, fresh veg, reasonable prices, new dining room; open all day summer, children welcome, tables on terrace and small sloping back lawn, well equipped bedrooms (Keith Allen, Eryl and Keith Dykes, Giles and Liz Ridout, Richard and Ann Higgs, LYM, Charles and Hylda McDonald)

Llangattock Lingoed [SO3620]
☆ Hunters Moon: Attractive and child-friendly pub in glorious country nr Offa's Dyke, newly refurbished beamed and flagstoned bars dating from 13th c and keeping old features; has had good home-made food inc home-made relishes and chutney for ploughman's, perfect veg, well kept changing ales such as Bath IPA and Gem and Fullers London Pride, and good house wines, but change of landlord summer 2001 – too late for any news of new regime; tables out on deck, bedrooms (BB, Christopher and Jo Barton, John and Audrey Coupe)

Llangybi [ST3797]
White Hart: Delightful 12th-c monastery building, part of Jane Seymour's dowry; well done usual food, good range of well kept real ales, friendly locals (C H and B J Owen)

Llanthony [SO2928]
Abbey Hotel [Llanthony Priory; off A465, back rd Llanvihangel-Crucorney—Hay]: Enchanting peaceful setting in border hills, lawns among Norman abbey's graceful ruins; basic dim-lit vaulted flagstoned crypt bar, well kept Brains and maybe a guest beer, farm cider in summer, simple lunchtime bar food, no children; occasional live music, open all day Sat (and Sun in summer – much its best time of year); cl Mon-Thurs, Sun evenings in winter; evening restaurant, bedrooms in restored parts of abbey walls, great walks all around (LYM, the Didler)

Llantrisant Fawr [ST3997]
☆ Greyhound [off A449 nr Usk]: Prettily set

17th-c country inn very popular for wide choice of consistently good home cooking at sensible prices; spacious attractive open-plan rooms, hill views, friendly helpful staff, well kept Flowers Original, Greene King Abbot, Marstons Pedigree and Wadworths 6X, log fires; lovely hanging baskets, gardens attractive even in winter, good bedrooms in small attached motel *(Charles and Pauline Stride, Gwyn Berry)*

Llanvapley [SO3714]

☆ *Red Hart* [B4233 Abergavenny—Monmouth]: Friendly country local, neat and clean, with good log fire, well kept Bass, Hancocks HB and guest beers such as Cottage Golden Arrow, good food, chatty landlord, stripped stone walls with copper and china plates, sizeable plush dining room, separate pool room; picnic-sets on sloping back lawn and terrace, dogs allowed, nice spot by cricket pitch in interesting village with Saxon church, cl Mon *(Gwyneth and Salvo Spadaro-Dutturi, BB)*

Mamhilad [SO3004]

Horseshoe: Pleasant roomy bar with well kept Bass and Hancocks HB, lots of malt whiskies, friendly and very helpful licensees, usual food inc generous sandwiches; lovely views, particularly from tables by car park over road; play area *(Tony Hobden)*

Star: Friendly, comfortable and straightforward, coal fire in one bar, woodburner in another, Bass and Hancocks HB with a guest such as Sharps, good bar food; 200 yards from canal *(Tony Hobden)*

Monkswood [SO3402]

☆ *Beaufort Arms*: Refreshingly unspoilt, with well kept ales such as Bass and Marstons Pedigree, decent wines, warmly welcoming atmosphere, interesting food inc fresh fish and game (must book Fri/Sat evenings); Fri quiz night, well behaved children allowed, tables in garden, cricket pitch behind *(Gwyneth and Salvo Spadaro-Dutturi)*

Monmouth [SO5009]

Gockett [Lydart; B4293 2 miles towards Trelleck]: Extended child-friendly country food pub with light and airy raftered room on left, sliding doors to pleasant garden, no smoking dining room with low beams, some stripped stone, coaching prints and log fire, well kept Bass and a guest such as Hook Norton; bedrooms with own bathrooms, good breakfast *(BB, Keith Allen, LM)*

Newbridge on Usk [ST3894]

New Bridge: Fine spot by bridge with view over Usk valley, good reasonably priced food, friendly professional staff, restaurant *(Neville and Julia Lear)*

Pandy [SO3322]

Lancaster Arms [A465]: Welcoming local, useful reasonably priced food stop for walkers, well kept real ales *(Nick and Meriel Cox)*

Rhyd-y-Meirch [SO2907]

☆ *Goose & Cuckoo* [up cul-de-sac off A4042 S of Abergavenny]: Genuinely friendly licensees in tiny unspoilt country pub in beautiful alpine setting, simple but interesting good value food inc home-made ice cream, well kept real ales inc Brains SA, good coffee, lots of whiskies; dogs

on leads allowed, handy for hill walks *(Eddy and Anna Street, Guy Vowles)*

Talycoed [SO4115]

☆ *Halfway House* [B4233 Monmouth—Abergavenny; though its postal address is Llantilio Crossenny, the inn is actually in Talycoed, a mile or two E]: Pretty wisteria-covered 17th-c pub in attractive countryside, softly lit snug bare-boards bar with brasses around nice old stone fireplace, wall settles, antique high-backed settles in back area, nice collection of cigarette pub cards, cosy plush little no smoking dining room with sporting and other prints, black kettles around hearth, well kept Bass and Felinfoel Bitter and Double Dragon, darts, quiet piped radio, outside gents', picnic-sets on front terrace and in neatly kept garden; cl lunchtime Mon-Fri winter *(Sarah Smith, Caroline Cofman, BB)*

The Narth [SO5206]

Trekkers [off B4293 Trelleck—Monmouth]: Log cabin high in valley, unusual and welcoming, esp for children; lots of wood with central fire, helpful licensee, good value generous food (maybe not in winter) inc vegetarian and fun ice creams, well kept Felinfoel Double Dragon, Freeminers and a guest beer, good small wine list, skittle alley family room, facilities for the disabled; dogs, long back garden, open all day Sun *(LM, Guy Vowles)*

Tintern [SO5301]

☆ *Cherry Tree* [Devauden Rd, off A466 about ¾ mile W of main village]: Quaint and friendly country pub under newish young landlord but still unspoilt, steps up to plain front room, huge helpings of generous simple food, well kept Hancocks HB tapped from the cask, farm cider, milk shakes, cards and dominoes, bar billiards in second room; children welcome, charming garden, quiet spot by tiny stream *(Pete Baker, the Didler, Phil and Sally Gorton, Piotr Chodzko-Zajko)*

☆ *Moon & Sixpence* [A466 Chepstow—Monmouth]: Flower-decked small pub, attractively furnished and largely smoke-free, with lots of beams and steps, one room with sofas and easy chairs, natural spring feeding indoor goldfish pool, good value food, well kept Bass and other ales such as Brains SA and Revd James, Greene King Abbot and Hook Norton, friendly service; pleasantly soft piped music; tiny windows, but nice view from verandah over abbey and River Wye, good walks *(Neil and Anita Christopher, Emma Kingdon)*

Trelleck [SO5005]

☆ *Village Green* [B4293 S of Monmouth]: Unflashy old building with cosy and pretty little front bar, welcoming licensees, good freshly made food using local produce from sandwiches up, wonderful puddings, well kept Bass and Worthington, good wines, quick service, prints, lots of dried flowers, comfortable beamed restaurant/bistro; bedrooms in well converted former stables *(Lesley Goodden)*

Trelleck Grange [SO5001]

☆ *Fountain* [minor rd Tintern—Llanishen, SE of

village]: Unassuming inn tucked away on back country road, dark-beamed bar, roomy and comfortable dining room, wide range of good value food inc good fresh sandwiches, fish and popular Sun lunch, cheerful patient staff, well kept Boddingtons and Wadworths 6X, decent malt whiskies and wines; maybe nostalgic piped pop music, darts; children allowed away from bar, small sheltered garden with summer kids' bar; bedrooms *(S H Godsell, BB, John and Kathleen Potter)*

Usk [SO3801]

☆ *Castle Inn* [Twyn Sq]: Relaxed and jaunty front bar with sofas, locals reading newspapers, interesting carved chair and comfortable window seats, big mirrors, lots of dried hops, generous well served food all day, well kept changing ales such as Bass, Fullers London Pride and Timothy Taylors Landlord, freshly squeezed orange juice, a couple of cosy little alcoves off dark dining room; piped music may be loud; tables in garden behind *(BB, R T and J C Moggridge, Ian Phillips, Peter and Audrey Dowsett)*

Greyhound [Chepstow Rd, edge of town]: Neat, tidy and very welcoming, well kept changing ales such as Hardington, Smiles and Wye Valley, huge blackboard choice of generous reasonably priced tasty food (less choice Sun); a place women feel comfortable in *(Peter and Audrey Dowsett)*

☆ *Royal Hotel* [New Market St]: Popular and unchanging country-town inn with traditional fixtures and fittings, collection of old crockery and pictures, old-fashioned fireplaces, comfortable wooden chairs and tables, filling food inc wider evening choice (not Sun) and popular Sun lunch (booking also advised Sat), well kept Bass, Hancocks, HB and Felinfoel Double Dragon from deep cellar, friendly service; piped music; well behaved children welcome, has been cl Mon lunchtime *(LYM, Chris Flynn, Wendy Jones, Anthony Barnes)*

GWYNEDD

Beddgelert [SH5948]

☆ *Tanronen* [A498 N of Porthmadog]: Comfortably and attractively refurbished hotel bar, good choice of good value bar food, attentive staff, well kept Robinsons, restaurant; walkers welcome; good bedrooms overlooking river across road, or fields and mountains behind *(Dave Braisted, BB)*

Betws-y-Coed [SH7956]

Pont y Pair: Good food such as red snapper on fettuccine, Tetleys, decent wine *(Adrian and Felicity Smith, KC)*

Capel Curig [SH7258]

☆ *Bryn Tyrch* [A5 W of village]: Comfortable country inn popular with walkers and climbers, Snowdon Horseshoe views from big picture windows, relaxed understated furnishings inc homely sofas, coal fire, magazines and outdoor equipment catalogues, pool table in plain hikers' bar, generous wholesome food with strong vegetarian/vegan emphasis, lots of coffee blends and Twinings teas, well kept Castle Eden, Flowers IPA and Wadworths 6X; tables

outside, steep little streamside garden over road, children welcome, bedrooms, open all day *(Tracey and Stephen Groves, Jenny and Brian Seller, Mr and Mrs McKay, LYM)*

Cobdens: Very informal and welcoming, reasonably priced food inc home-made bread, well kept local Cambrian and Scottish Courage beers, pleasant staff, bare rock in back bar; lovely river scene across road, good walks all around; bedrooms, well behaved dogs allowed *(Derek Stafford, Paul Thompson, Anna Blackburn)*

Capel Garmon [SH8255]

☆ *White Horse* [signed from A470 and A5 at Betwys-y-coed, towards Llanrwst]: Dark-beamed inn dating from 16th c, comfortable and homely, with log fires, well kept Bass and Worthington BB, wide choice of good value food, good amiable service even when very busy, prettily refurbished cottage restaurant, games in public bar; bedrooms small and simple but comfortable (quietest in new part), fine countryside with magnificent views *(Mr and Mrs S Mason)*

Conwy [SH7878]

Bridge [Rose Hill St]: Well run hotel with Marstons and guests beers, good choice of reasonably priced food inc plenty of vegetarian and even vegan dishes, particularly friendly helpful licensees; bedrooms *(John Andrew)*

Llandudno [SH7882]

Fat Cat [Mostyn St]: One of a small chain of café-bars, bare boards, pictures and books, good value food all day (bookable tables in back eating area), changing guest beers, Hoegaarden on draught; lively young bustle at night *(Mike and Wendy Proctor)*

☆ *Kings Head* [Old Rd, behind tram stn]: Rambling pretty pub, much extended around 16th-c flagstoned core, spaciously open-plan, bright and clean, with comfortable traditional furnishings, interesting old local tramway photographs, red wallpaper, dark pine, wide range of generous food (busy at night, so get there early), well kept ales such as Jennings Cumberland, eclectic choice of wines in friendly-sized glasses, quick friendly service, huge log fire, smart back dining room up a few steps; children welcome, open all day in summer, seats on front terrace overlooking quaint Victorian cable tramway's station (water for dogs here) *(Kevin Blake, Peter F Marshall, Mike and Wendy Proctor, LYM, H Bramwell)*

Llandwrog [SH4456]

☆ *Harp* [½ mile W of A499 S of Caernarfon]: Welcoming lounge bar with irregular shape giving cosy corners, well kept ales such as Black Sheep and Mutleys Revenge, good value usual food inc Sun roast, helpful landlord and friendly bilingual parrot, daily papers and magazines, cheerful separate dining room; picnic-sets among fruit trees, well equipped cottagey bedrooms overlooking quiet village's imposing church, good breakfast *(Mike and Wena Stevenson, Michael Buchanan, BB)*

Maentwrog [SH6741]

Grapes [A496; village signed from A470]: Rambling old inn crowded with families in summer, hearty bar food, four changing beers, over 30 malt whiskies, stripped pine pews, settles, pillars and carvings, good log fires, interesting juke box in public bar, intriguing collection of brass blowlamps, no smoking lower dining room, conservatory; bedrooms, disabled lavatories, open all day, views of trains on Ffestiniog Railway beyond pleasant back terrace and walled garden *(Mike and Wena Stevenson, Ray and Jacki Davenport, Tracey and Stephen Groves, LYM)*

Penmaenpool [SH6918]

☆ *George III* [just off A493, nr Dolgellau]: Lovely views over Mawddach estuary from attractive inn with extended no smoking bottom public bar with beams, flagstones and stripped stone (children allowed here) and civilised partly panelled upstairs bar opening into cosy inglenook lounge; decent food in bar and restaurant, well kept ales such as John Smiths, good choice of wines by the glass; open all day, sheltered terrace, good walks, good bedrooms inc some in interesting conversion of former station on disused line *(Mike and Wena Stevenson, Tracey and Stephen Groves, LYM, Aidan Wallis, Mike and Mary Carter)*

Porthmadog [SH5639]

Station Bar [Harbour Stn]: Particularly well kept beer, tables on platform terrace *(Tracey and Stephen Groves)*

Tremadog [SH5640]

☆ *Golden Fleece* [off A487 just N of Porthmadog; Market Sq]: Neat stone-built inn on attractive square, friendly attentive staff, well kept Bass and Marstons Pedigree, decent wines, cosy partly partitioned rambling beamed lounge with open fire, nice little snug (reserved seats for regulars Fri/Sat night), enjoyable separate back bistro (children allowed here and in small family room), good value generous bar food inc fish, quick friendly service, games room, intriguing cellar bar, tables in sheltered inner courtyard; bedrooms and flats *(LYM, W B and E Cantillon)*

MID GLAMORGAN

Caerphilly [ST1484]

☆ *Black Cock* [Watford; Tongwynlais exit from M4 junction 32, then right just after church]: New landlord doing enjoyable low-priced food from huge baguettes up, well kept Bass and Hancocks HB, friendly staff, neat blue-plush bar with open fire in pretty tiled fireplace, interesting brass-tabled public bar, large brightly lit back dining extension; children welcome, sizeable terraced garden among trees with barbecue and good play area for under-9s, up in the hills, just below Caerphilly Common *(BB, David and Nina Pugsley, Piotr Chodzko-Zajko)*

Pontygwindy Inn [Pontygwindy Rd]: Extended pub popular for good value food, massive helpings, smiling efficient staff, well kept Brains SA, Hancocks HB and Greene King Old Speckled Hen, three-level restaurant with hayloft feel *(Joan and Michel Hooper-Immins)*

Kenfig [SS8383]

☆ *Prince of Wales* [2¼ miles from M4 junction

37; A4229 towards Porthcawl, then right when dual carriageway narrows on bend, signed Maudlam and Kenfig]: Interesting ancient pub among sand dunes, nicely upgraded without harming character, friendly new landlord, wife does good reasonably priced food inc fish specials, well kept Bass, Worthington and weekly guest ales tapped from the cask, good choice of malt whiskies, traditional games, upstairs dining room for summer and busy wknds; handy for nature reserve and walks, children welcome *(John and Joan Nash, the Didler, David Carr, LYM)*

Llwydcoed [SN9704]

Red Cow [Merthyr Rd (B4276 N of Aberdare)]: Friendly neatly kept traditional pub, cosy and comfortable, large bar and restaurant, with well kept Brains SA and Hancocks HB, low-priced generous food inc Fri-Sun carvery, helpful landlord, no juke box or machines; large garden *(John and Joan Nash)*

Machen [ST2288]

White Hart [White Hart Lane, off A468 towards Bedwas]: Now brewing its own interesting beers, with guest beers too from small servery down panelled corridor; unusual welcoming bar and lounge full of salvaged ship memorabilia, recently restored ceiling painting, log fire, generous wholesome bar meals (Sun lunches only, but at bargain price); annual beer festival, garden with play area, bedrooms *(Emma Kingdon, G Coates, Mike Pugh)*

Rudry [ST1986]

☆ *Maenllwyd*: Comfortably furnished olde-worlde lounge in low-beamed Tudor pub with log fires, very wide choice of good reasonably priced food, well kept ales inc Theakstons, good choice of wines, friendly staff, spacious restaurant; can be very busy Fri/Sat; provision for children, good walks *(David and Nina Pugsley, Rob Holt, LYM)*

St Brides Major [SS8974]

Farmers Arms [Wick Rd]: Friendly food pub opp lovely reed-fringed pond with swans and ducks, a walk from the sea; wide choice of good reasonably priced food inc interesting dishes, helpful staff, real ales such as Courage Best and Ushers Best and Founders; can get crowded, esp Sun lunchtimes; beautiful hanging baskets and floral milk churns *(Miss Elaine Pugh, Ian Phillips)*

Thornhill [ST1484]

☆ *Travellers Rest* [A469 towards Caerphilly]: Attractive old thatched stone-built hilltop pub, carefully extended as Vintage Inn dining pub with wide choice of generous good value usual food all day, Bass, Hancocks HB and maybe a guest beer, good sensibly priced wine choice, good service, daily papers and magazines; huge fireplace and nooks and crannies in atmospheric low-beamed bar on right, other bars more modernised, with great views over Cardiff; piped music, very busy wknd, no bookings; open all day, tables out on grass, good walks *(David and Nina Pugsley, Ian Phillips)*

Treoes [SS9478]

Star [off A48 Cardiff—Bridgend]: Busy bar,

homely and friendly welcome, hard-working enthusiastic chef/landlord doing good reasonably priced food inc Sun lunches, stripped stone dining room, well kept Brains Arms Park, wide range of wines, helpful service; lovely quiet village (beyond large industrial estate) *(David and Nina Pugsley, H L Dennis)*

POWYS
Brecon [SO0428]

☆ *Camden Arms* [Watton]: Smartly refurbished free house, some good furniture inc sofa and dresser with books off main bar, good range of beers, named house wines, impressive blackboard food choice, very efficient service; games room, three sleepy dogs *(Jean and Richard Phillips, Peter and Audrey Dowsett)*
George [George St]: Spacious town centre pub with attractive dining conservatory, simple bar, well kept Greene King Abbot, Tetleys and Tomos Watkins OSB, wide blackboard choice of reasonably priced food all day inc ploughman's with local cheeses and generous salads, simple bar, attentive service; very busy Sat night, tables outside *(Peter and Audrey Dowsett, Tony Hobden)*
Carno [SN9697]
Aleppo Merchant [A470 Newtown—Machynlleth]: Plushly modernised stripped stone bar, small lounge with open fire, no smoking area, games in public bar, decent reasonably priced food from sandwiches to steaks, Boddingtons, occasional guest beer, restaurant (well behaved children allowed here), tables in garden; piped music; bedrooms *(LYM, John Kane, Mike and Wena Stevenson)*
Crickhowell [SO2118]

☆ *White Hart* [Brecon Rd (A40 W)]: Homely bar with stripped stone, beams and flagstones, well kept Brains Bitter, Buckley Best and Revd James, usual food from lunchtime sandwiches up in eating area (with TV) off one end, or sizeable no smoking restaurant; pub games, may be piped classical music, quiz night Mon; children in eating areas, open all day Sat, some tables outside *(Roger and Jenny Huggins, Tony Hobden, LYM, Gareth and Joan Griffith, Peter and Audrey Dowsett)*
Derwenlas [SN7299]

☆ *Black Lion* [A487 just S of Machynlleth]: Cosy and peaceful 16th-c country pub, welcoming new licensees, heavy black beams, thick walls and black timbering, attractive pictures and lion models, tartan carpet over big slate flagstones, great log fire, popular straightforward food inc vegetarian and good steak and kidney pie, well kept Tetleys, decent wines; piped music; garden up behind with play area and steps up into woods; bedrooms *(Christopher Tull, BB)*
Glasbury [SO1739]

☆ *Harp* [B4350 towards Hay, just N of A438]: Snug welcoming log-fire lounge with eating areas, good value straightforward food inc children's (children very welcome), well kept ales inc Brains, pool in airy games bar, picture windows over garden sloping to River Wye; tables on terrace, good value simple bedrooms,

good breakfast *(Pam and David Bailey, Peter Meister, LYM)*
Maesllwch Arms [B4350, just off A438]: Large building with two bars and roomy dining room, wide choice of very generous reasonably priced food, well kept Bass, Hancocks HB and Robinsons, good friendly service; bedrooms *(C H and B J Owen, LYM, Tim and Catherine Jones)*
Hay-on-Wye [SO2342]

☆ *Blue Boar* [Castle St/Oxford Rd]: Good choice of generous straightforward home cooking (not Sun evening) in light and airy long dining room with food counter, lots of pictures for sale, bright tablecloths and cheery décor, big sash windows, good coffees and teas, also breakfasts; separate dim-lit panelled bar with pews and country chairs, friendly helpful landlord, log fire, splendid ciders inc organic, well kept ales such as Brains SA and Hancocks HB, decent wines; children welcome, maybe quiet piped classical music *(BB, Sue Demont, Tim Barrow, Bruce Bird)*
Three Tuns [Broad St]: Basic unfussy pub with fireside settle and a few old tables and chairs in tiny dark quarry-tiled bar in one of Hay's oldest buildings, charming veteran landlady (whose parents ran the pub before her) knowledgeable about local history, ciders from barrels on the counter, maybe Wye Valley real ale from a polypin, Edwardian bar fittings, lots of bric-a-brac, daily papers, interesting old stove, some fresh flowers; no food *(Pete Baker, the Didler, Darly Graton, Graeme Gulibert)*
Howey [SO0559]
Drovers Arms [off A483 S of Llandrindod Wells]: Welcoming and homely, with good blackboard range of enjoyable food largely using local produce; good value comfortable bedrooms *(Iain and Jean Coupe)*
Hundred House [SO1154]
Hundred House Inn: Attractive, clean and interesting pub full of curios, consistently well kept Bass and Hancocks HB with interesting guest beers, good wine list, decent food, welcoming staff, small dining room, big garden with play area; children welcome *(J P Shucksmith)*
Llanafan Fawr [SN9655]
Red Lion [B4358 SW of Llandrindod Wells]: Old whitewashed pub, front bar, tables in two rooms off and extra dining area, cheerful friendly landlord, good freshly prepared generous food; adjoining holiday cottage, tables by roadside, very small village *(Maurice and Della Andrew)*
Llanfihangel-nant-Melan [SO1858]

☆ *Red Lion* [A44 10 miles W of Kington]: Warm and friendly stripped-stone 16th-c roadside pub with good freshly made food in roomy main dining area beyond standing timbers on right, smaller room with small pews around tables, well kept changing ales such as Hook Norton, decent wines, sensible prices, good service, some tables in front sun porch, back bar with pool; comfortable simple chalet bedrooms, handy for Radnor Forest walks, nr impressive waterfall, cl Tues-Thurs lunchtime, Tues evening *(BB, Lawrence Bacon, Jean Scott, Richard Siebert, Carol Evans)*

Llanfrynach [SO0725]

☆ *White Swan* [signed from B4558, just off A40 E of Brecon bypass]: Rambling dining pub with good food, rambling bar with flagstones and partly stripped walls, softly lit alcoves, roaring log fire, Greene King Old Speckled Hen and Wadworths 6X, no smoking area in restaurant; children welcome, charming terrace overlooking peaceful paddocks, cl Mon/Tues and maybe in Jan *(LYM, Darly Graton, Graeme Gulibert)*

Llangattock [SO2117]

Horseshoe [off B4558]: Popular lunchtimes for good value food such as a thoroughgoing welsh rarebit, well kept Bass and Hancocks HB *(Tony Hobden)*

☆ *Vine Tree* [signed from Crickhowell; Legar Rd]: Well run small and simple pub with emphasis on good interesting generous food in bar and restaurant inc local meat and veg, fresh fish from Cornwall; pleasant service, well kept Fullers London Pride and Wadworths 6X, good coffee, coal-effect gas fire; children welcome, tables out under cocktail parasols with lovely view of medieval Usk bridge *(Jean and Richard Phillips, Tony Hobden, LYM, Dr Oscar Puls)*

Llangenny [SO2417]

☆ *Dragons Head*: Prettily set in scenic vale, charming licensees, peaceful two-room bar with low beams, big woodburner, pews, housekeeper's chairs and a high-backed settle among other seats, two attractive restaurant areas, wide choice of home-made usual food from sandwiches up, good choice of well kept reasonably priced real ales inc Brains Buckley Revd James; picnic-sets in garden and over road by stream, open wknd summer afternoons if busy enough *(Mr and Mrs N Todd and family, LYM, Pat and Roger Fereday, N Parnaby, Stefan Simms, Keith Allen)*

Llangorse [SO1327]

Castle Inn: Smallish friendly stone local with cosy and comfortable flagstoned main bar, side room set out more for eating; wide choice of good food to suit hungry walkers, well kept Brains SA and Dark, Buckleys and Tomos Watkins ales *(Geoff Pidoux)*

☆ *Red Lion*: Comfortable lounge and big neatly kept bar, efficient friendly service, good straightforward food at sensible prices, well kept Brains, farm cider; attractive spot by stream through village, bedrooms *(Geoff Pidoux, BB)*

Llanwenarth [SO2714]

☆ *Llanwenarth Arms* [A40 Abergavenny—Crickhowell]: Popular and beautifully placed riverside inn dating from 16th c but much modernised since, good food in light and airy modern restaurant, some dark wood in well stocked bar, very good service, daily papers, children welcome (high chairs available); 18 comfortable bedrooms overlooking Wye, splendid views from conservatory and terrace down to water and across hills *(Chris Flynn, Wendy Jones, BB)*

Llanwrtyd Wells [SN8746]

☆ *Neuadd Arms* [The Square]: Comfortably well worn in lounge with big log fire and local pictures, separate tiled public bar with craft tools and splendid row of old service bells, well kept reasonably priced ales such as Badger, Felinfoel Double Dragon and Fullers London Pride, lots of unusual bottled beers, warmly welcoming helpful staff, laid-back atmosphere, popular food inc vegetarian and theme nights; beer festivals, various other events; bedrooms pleasant and well equipped; tables out on front terrace, engaging very small town – good walking area, mountain bike hire *(George Atkinson, Dr and Mrs P Johnston, BB)*

Llowes [SO1941]

☆ *Radnor Arms* [A438 Brecon—Hereford]: Well run and attractive country inn with very wide choice of good food served in local pottery from good filled rolls and inventive soups to fine restaurant-style dishes, with dozens of puddings; ancient cottagey bar with beams and stripped stone, very welcoming, with well kept Felinfoel and log fire, two small dining rooms, tables in imaginatively planted garden looking out over fields towards the Wye; cl Sun pm, Mon (exc bank hols) *(C H and B J Owen)*

Llyswen [SO1337]

Bridge End: Friendly genuine village pub with enjoyable simple inexpensive food, good service, Hancocks HB, decent house wine, good coffee, coal fire; lovely flower tubs and window boxes; nr high Wye bridge with pleasant views *(Keith Allen, Ian Phillips)*

Griffin [A470, village centre]: Charmingly peaceful country inn under new management, good local atmosphere and fine log fire in friendly bar, Brains real ales, children in eating areas; comfortable bedrooms, tables outside *(David and Nina Pugsley, Jayne and Peter Capp, LYM)*

Montgomery [SO2296]

Bricklayers Arms [Chirbury Rd (B4386)]: Good interesting carefully prepared food using fresh produce mainly from local smallholdings, real ales such as Boddingtons and Worthington, cheerful smallish bar with pine tables in dining area, linen-set restaurant; dates from 15th c, picnic-sets out in front *(Lisa Harrop)*

Crown [Castle St]: Simple friendly local with just a couple of tables in lounge, good value popular food inc bargain Sun roast, really obliging service, Worthington *(D W Stokes)*

☆ *Dragon* [Market Sq]: Well run 17th-c tall timbered hotel with attractive prints and china in lively beamed bar, attentive service, well kept Woods Special and guest beer, good coffee, sensibly priced food from sandwiches to steaks inc vegetarian and children's, board games, unobtrusive piped music, restaurant; jazz most Weds, open all day; comfortable well equipped bedrooms, very quiet town below ruined Norman castle – pleasant place to stay *(Lesley Goodden, LYM)*

Pencelli [SO0925]

Royal Oak [B4558 SE of Brecon]: Two small simple bars, welcoming service, well kept Boddingtons and Flowers and farm cider, good home-made food Thurs-Sat pm and wknd lunchtimes inc half-price children's helpings, log fires, polished flagstones, simple dining room; charming terrace backing on to canal and fields, lovely canal walks and handy for Taff Trail *(Tony Hobden)*

Pontdolgoch [SO0193]

Talk House [A470 NW of Caersws]: Tastefully refurbished, with friendly efficient service, plenty of locals, good choice of eclectic Welsh and modern British cooking by landlady's husband, good choice of beers and particularly of wines, restaurant overlooking large pleasant garden; new bedrooms *(Marie and David Turner, Barbara and Martin Rowbottom)*

Rhayader [SN9767]

Lion Royal [West St]: Old-fashioned coaching inn with long-serving landlady, leather club chairs, small sofa and carved settle in lounge with big inglenook, unusual carved oak dresser and hunting prints, corridor with serving hatch, small simple bar with lion-etched windows, Woodhampton Jack Snipe, friendly weimaraner, no piped music; bedrooms, stabling for trekking ponies *(BB)*

Triangle [Cwmdauddwr; B4518 by bridge over Wye, SW of centre]: Small mainly 16th-c pub with good snacks and meals lunchtime and early evening, friendly non-local licensees, separate dining area with view over park to Wye; three tables outside *(Keith Allen)*

Three Cocks [SO1737]

Old Barn [A438 Talgarth—Hay-on-Wye]: Long spacious converted barn with central bar, good choice of low-priced food from sandwiches up, four well kept real ales, very friendly staff; two pool tables, SkyTV; seats outside with good play area and barbecue, open all day at least in summer (can be very busy Sun, cl Mon lunchtime); parent inn across rd has reasonably priced clean and tidy bedrooms with good breakfast *(C H and B J Owen, LYM)*

SOUTH GLAMORGAN

Cardiff [ST1776]

Cayo Arms [Cathedral Rd]: One of the few pubs tied to Tomos Watkins, five of their ales kept well, two areas separated by ironwork, comfortable seats inc fine old wooden armchairs, lots of prints, lunchtime food, friendly staff, daily papers; tables out in front, open all day *(Richard Lewis)*

Cottage [St Mary St, nr Howells]: Proper down-to-earth pub with well kept Brains SA, Bitter and Dark Mild and good value generous home-cooked lunches, long bar with narrow frontage and back eating area, lots of polished wood and glass, good cheerful service, relaxed friendly atmosphere (even Fri/Sat when it's crowded; quiet other evenings), decent choice of wines; open all day *(Sue Demont, Tim Barrow, Steve Thomas, Andrew and Catherine Gilham, Mike and Wendy Proctor)*

Halfway [Cathedral Rd]: Comfortably refurbished popular local with good helpings of low-priced bar food, well kept Brains Bitter, SA and Buckleys Dark, reasonably priced wine, coal-effect gas fires, rugby memorabilia; skittle alley *(Sue Demont, Tim Barrow, Ian Phillips)*

Pantmawr Inn [Tyla Teg, off Pantmawr Rd, Rhibwina; handy for M4 junction 32]: Small comfortable local in attractive former period farmhouse, friendly new landlady, well kept Bass and Hancocks HB, bottled Worthington White Shield, good value food; shame about the SkyTV; sizeable secure garden, in 1960s housing estate *(Simon P Bobeldijk, Mr and Mrs M Dalby)*

Prince of Wales [St Mary St/Wood St, nr station]: Very large stylish Wetherspoons cinema/theatre conversion, largely smoke-free, subdued dark brown and cream décor, historical photographs, good choice of very pocket-friendly beers inc Brains SA, usual food; disabled facilities *(Colin and Peggy Wilshire, Richard Lewis, Joyce and Maurice Cottrell, Alan Sinclair)*

Vulcan [Adam St]: Largely untouched Victorian local with good value lunches (not Sun) in sedate lounge with some original features inc ornate fireplace, well kept Brains Bitter and Dark Mild, maritime pictures in lively sawdust-floor public bar with darts, dominoes, cards and juke box; cl Sun pm, cl 7.30 other nights exc Fri *(Pete Baker)*

Cowbridge [SS9974]

☆ *Bear* [High St, with car park behind off North St; signed off A48]: Neatly kept old coaching inn with Brains Bitter and SA, Hancocks HB, Worthington BB and a guest beer, decent house wines, friendly young staff, three bars with flagstones, bare boards or carpet, some stripped stone and panelling, big open fires, busy lunchtime for usual bar food from sandwiches up; children welcome; barrel-vaulted cellar restaurant, bedrooms quiet and comfortable, CCTV in car park *(Steve Thomas, LYM)*

Craig Penllyn [SS9777]

Barley Mow: Pleasant surroundings, good value standard food, no smoking dining room, friendly informal service, no loud music *(A Jones)*

Lisvane [ST1883]

Ty Mawr Arms [follow Mill Rd into Graig Rd, then keep on]: Large neatly kept country pub with fairly wide food choice, well kept changing real ales, friendly service, several comfortable rooms, one with big open fire; great views over Cardiff from attractive garden *(LYM, Alison and Mike Stevens)*

Llancadle [ST0368]

☆ *Green Dragon* [village signed off B4265 Barry—Llantwit just E of St Athan]: Cheerful traditional bar on left with hunting and other country prints, copper, china and harness, well kept Bass, Hancocks HB and an interesting guest beer, friendly uniformed staff, maybe piped pop music; good value generous usual food inc huge mixed grill, comfortably relaxed dining lounge on right with nice pictures; picnic-sets on covered back terrace *(BB, LYM, A Jones)*

Michaelston-y-Fedw [ST2484]

Cefn Mably Arms [a mile off A48 at Castleton]: Brightly furnished local with very friendly service, well kept Bass and Hancocks HB, enjoyable freshly made food inc fish in bar and

restaurant, tables in garden – country setting
(*R Michael Richards*)

WEST GLAMORGAN
Bishopston [SS5789]
☆ *Joiners Arms* [Bishopston Rd, just off B4436
SW of Swansea]: Thriving local brewing their
own good Bishopswood beers, also well kept
guests such as Charles Wells Bombardier,
Marstons Pedigree and John Smiths; clean and
welcoming, with quarry-tiled floor, traditional
furnishings, local paintings and massive solid
fuel stove, good cheap simple food lunchtime
and early evening inc curries, sizzler dishes and
OAP lunches Sat; children welcome, open all
day Thurs-Sat – the rugby club's local on Sat
nights; parking can be difficult (*LYM, Michael
and Alison Sandy*)
Black Pill [SS6190]
Woodman [A4067 Swansea—Mumbles]:
Popular chain pub with several sensibly
furnished raised areas, airy restaurant and
conservatory, good value bar food inc bargain
meals and carvery (need to book Sun lunch),
well kept Wadworths 6X, pleasant service
(*Tom Evans*)
Craig-y-Nos [SN8416]
Gwyn Arms [A4067 Swansea—Brecon]: Idyllic
riverside setting, bigger than it looks from
outside, with two floors, big well spaced tables
for good range of generous food inc fresh fish,
Whitbreads and some local ales, friendly
efficient staff; handy for country park and Dan-
yr-Ogof caves, children welcome, open all day
(*David and Michelle Bailey*)
Llangennith [SS4291]
Kings Head: Old two-bar village pub with good
choice of notable food esp fresh local fish such
as bass and flounder, friendly Australian staff,
good range of well kept beer, good wine
selection; children allowed (not intrusively),
large terrace not far from beach (*Michael
Jefferson, Dave Irving*)
Llanmadoc [SS4393]
Britannia [the Gower, nr Whiteford Burrows –
NT]: Almost as far as the roads go on the
Gower peninsula, busy summer pub with tables
in front, and plenty more behind in neatly kept
big back garden with flowers, aviary, lots of
play equipment, maybe ducks, donkeys and a
goat — and great estuary views; popular

standard food with some nice vegetarian dishes,
Brains beers, gleaming copper stove in beamed
and tiled bar with old tables, a settle, a few
farm tools and pool table, steps up to smarter
lounge with lots of blowlamps and such,
restaurant beyond (accordionist Sat night);
children welcome, open all day Fri/Sat (*BB,
Michael and Alison Sandy*)
Newton [SS6088]
Newton Inn [New Well Lane]: Under new
management and recently refurbished; good
range of local real ales and decent wine, good
reasonably priced lunchtime bar food
(*R B Mowbray*)
Oxwich [SS4986]
Oxwich Bay Hotel: Large and attractive bar
with beautiful bay and beach views, current
chef doing above-average food all day here and
on tables in well kept garden, efficient friendly
helpful staff; good for families, bedrooms
(*A S and P E Marriott*)
Pontardulais [SN6003]
Fountain [Bolgoed Rd; handy for M4 junction
47, via A4240/A48]: Good dining pub with
good value food in bar and rustic-theme raftered
restaurant inc lots of fish, interesting veg, home-
made puddings, well kept ales such as Batemans
XXXB and Greene King Old Speckled Hen;
comfortable bedrooms with big breakfast (*Steve
Chambers, R T and J C Moggridge*)
Pontneddfechan [SN9007]
Angel: Welcoming 16th-c inn, comfortably
opened up and popular with locals, light and
airy, with well kept ales such as Boddingtons
and Wadworths 6X, plenty of dining tables,
separate flagstoned hikers' bar; lots of flowers
in front, tables on terrace; bedrooms, good
walks inc the waterfalls (*T R and B C Jenkins*)
Reynoldston [SS4789]
☆ *King Arthur* [Higher Green, off A4118]:
Bustling local atmosphere in well placed hotel
with country-house bric-a-brac and log fire in
timbered main bar, back family summer dining
area (games room with pool in winter), food
from lunchtime baguettes to popular Sun lunch,
attentive friendly staff, well kept Bass, Felinfoel
Double Dragon, Worthington Best and maybe
a guest beer, no smoking restaurant; piped
music; children in eating areas, tables outside
with play area, open all day, bedrooms (*David
and Nina Pugsley, LYM*)

Post Office address codings confusingly give the impression that some pubs are in
Gwent or Powys, Wales when they're really in Gloucestershire or Shropshire
(which is where we list them).

Channel Islands

Almost all our recommended pubs are on Jersey. It's just the Fleur du Jardin which flies the flag for Guernsey's pubs – and flies it very proudly, as the Fleur is doing very well this year, with good interesting food, comfortable bedrooms and a pretty garden that does its name justice. It gains our accolade of Channel Islands Dining Pub of the Year. On Jersey, the ancient Les Fontaines in St John is great for a touch of old-fashioned local atmosphere. The candlelit Admiral in St Helier is an impressive pub, with lots of interesting memorabilia, and the Tipsy Toad Town House there is a nice lively all-rounder. The very friendly Rozel Bay Hotel at Rozel has a good fish choice. The Old Portelet Inn up above the St Brelade beaches is good for families, and good value. And La Pulente handsomely placed on St Ouens Bay beach has enjoyable food. In the Lucky Dip section at the end of the chapter, we'd particularly pick out the Original Wine Bar in St Helier. Drinks prices here are well below mainland levels, typically saving about 30 to 35p on a pint of beer. The main pub owner, Jersey Brewery (which also owns Guernsey Brewery, and distributes real ales brewed by its Tipsy Toad brewpub), has just done a deal with Bass which should help to widen beer choice on the islands, though the choice of mainland beers is already quite respectable.

GREVE DE LECQ Map 1
Moulin de Lecq

Popular with visitors and locals alike, this black-shuttered old mill has a massive restored waterwheel still turning outside, with its formidable gears meshing in their stone housing behind the bar. Nicely presented, generous bar food might include soup (£1.95), deep-fried camembert with a raspberry dip (£2.95), ploughman's (£4.75), chicken stir fry (£5.50), vegetable lasagne (£5.75), garlic king prawns (£8.95), and steaks (from £8.95). The bar has plush-cushioned black wooden seats against the white-painted walls and a good log fire in winter; piped music, cribbage, dominoes. Well kept Guernsey Sunbeam Bitter, Bass and two guests from breweries such as Brains and Mauldons on handpump. There are picnic-sets under cocktail parasols on the terrace and there's a good children's adventure playground. The road past here leads down to pleasant walks on one of the only north-coast beaches. The Germans commandeered the mill during the Occupation of Jersey (they used it to generate power for their searchlight batteries in this part of the island). *(Recommended by M G Hart, Ian Phillips, Phil and Heidi Cook, S Palmer)*

Free house ~ Licensee Shaun Lynch ~ Real ale ~ Bar food (12-2, 6-9) ~ Restaurant ~ (01534) 482818 ~ Children welcome ~ Wknd entertainment in summer ~ Open 11-11

KING'S MILLS Map 1
Fleur du Jardin ⊕ ♀ 🛏

King's Mills Road

Channel Islands Dining Pub of the Year

Not only is this old-fashioned inn set in one of the prettiest spots on the island, but the two acres of gardens surrounding it are lovely with picnic-sets among colourful borders, shrubs, bright hanging baskets and flower barrels. The attractive, cosy rooms have low-beamed ceilings and thick granite walls, and a good log fire burns in the public bar (popular with locals), and there are individual country furnishings in the lounge bar on the hotel side. As well as sandwiches (from £2.25) and soup (from £2.50), good, interesting bar food could include cajun spiced chicken pieces with sweet chilli (£4.25), steak, kidney and mushroom pie cooked in Guinness (£5.75), red thai vegetable curry (£5.95), butterfly chicken breast cooked in garlic butter (£6.75), their popular whole Guernsey chancre crab salad (£8.25) and steaks (from £10.95) with specials such as fricassee of baby leeks, mushrooms and shallots in cream sauce with sun-dried tomatoes (£7.45), roast pheasant with onion marmalade (£9.95) and sautéed scallops with whisky and dill sauce (£11.95); puddings such as warm ginger sponge and ice cream (from £3.75). Well kept Guernsey Sunbeam and a seasonal guest like Summer Ale or Winter Warmer on handpump, and a decent wine list with around 17 wines by the glass (most by small or large glass); friendly efficient service; unobtrusive piped music. Handily, they have a large car park; there is a swimming pool for residents. *(Recommended by Julian Dalman, Sue and Bob Ward, Ian Phillips)*

Free house ~ Licensee Keith Read ~ Real ale ~ Bar food (12-2, 6-9.30) ~ Restaurant ~ (01481) 257996 ~ Children welcome ~ Open 11-3, 5-11.45; 12-3, 6-11 Sun; closed evenings 25 and 26 Dec ~ Bedrooms: /£39B

ROZEL Map 1
Rozel Bay Hotel

Run by a very friendly landlord this pub, set on the edge of a sleepy little fishing village just out of sight of the sea, has attractive steeply terraced hillside gardens where they hold summer barbecues. The bar counter and tables in the cosy small dark-beamed back bar are stripped to their original light wood finish, and there is an open fire, old prints and local pictures on the cream walls, and dark plush wall seats and stools. Leading off is a carpeted area with flowers on big solid square tables; darts, pool, cribbage and dominoes in the games room; piped music and TV. The bar and restaurant menus are the same and sensibly priced dishes include home-made soup (£2.95, fish soup £5.95), sandwiches (from £3.25), mussels with smoked salmon and cream (£4.25), grilled goats cheese (£4.95), sausage and mash or steak and kidney pie (£6.95), steaks (from £9.95) and a choice of around eight fresh fish dishes such as red mullet, bass or scallops (£9.95) and half lobster (£12.50); specials such as grilled Jersey plaice with lemon butter or spiced lentil cakes with sweet chilli relish (£6.95) and chicken wrapped in bacon with tomato fondue (£7.95); home-made puddings such as date and sponge pudding and crème brûlée (£2.50). Bass, Courage Directors and a guest like Wadworths 6X kept under light blanket pressure. *(Recommended by Ian Phillips, S Palmer)*

Randalls ~ Lease Ian King ~ Real ale ~ Bar food ~ Restaurant (not Sun evening) ~ (01534) 863438 ~ Children welcome ~ Open 10-11; closed evening 25 Dec

ST AUBIN Map 1
Old Court House Inn 🏠

There are wonderful views past St Aubin's fort right across the bay to St Helier from this charming 15th-c inn. The building has an interesting past – the front part used to be the home of a wealthy merchant, whose cellars stored privateers' plunder alongside more legitimate cargo, while the upstairs restaurant still shows signs of its time as a courtroom. Overlooking the tranquil harbour, the conservatory now houses the Westward Bar – elegantly constructed from the actual gig of a schooner. The main basement bar has cushioned wooden seats built against its stripped granite walls, low black beams, joists in a white ceiling, a turkey carpet and an open fire. A dimly lantern-lit inner room has an illuminated rather brackish-looking deep well, and beyond that is a spacious cellar room, open in summer. Enjoyable bar food includes soup (£2.75), baguettes (from £3.95), vegetable lasagne (£4.95), grilled goats cheese with roasted red pepper dressing or scampi (£5.50), moules marinières (£5.75), cumberland sausage and mash (£6.75) or Jersey plaice (£10.50); two-course lunch (£12.95). In the evening you can eat anything from their à la carte menu in the pub. Well kept Marstons Pedigree and a guest such as Courage Directors on handpump; TV and piped music. It can be difficult to park near the hotel. *(Recommended by Ian Phillips)*

Free house ~ Licensee Jonty Sharp ~ Real ale ~ Bar food (12.30-2.30, 7.30-9.30) ~ Restaurant ~ (01534) 746433 ~ Well behaved children welcome away from main bar ~ Open 11-11.30 ~ Bedrooms: £50B/£100B

ST BRELADE Map 1
Old Portelet Inn
Portelet Bay

There's a sheltered cove right below this marvellously positioned 17th-c ex-farmhouse, reached by a long flight of steps with views across Portelet (Jersey's most southerly bay) on the way down. Welcoming to families, as well as an outdoor play area there's also a supervised indoor one (entrance 50p). The picnic-sets on the partly covered flower-bower terrace by a wishing well are a good place to relax and there are more seats in the sizeable landscaped garden with lots of scented stocks and other flowers. Inside, the low ceilinged, beamed downstairs bar has a stone bar counter on bare oak boards and quarry tiles, a huge open fire, gas lamps, old pictures, etched glass panels from France and a nice mixture of old wooden chairs. It opens into the big timber-ceilinged no smoking family dining area, with standing timbers and plenty of highchairs. Generous helpings of bar food served by the friendly and efficient, neatly dressed staff include sandwiches (from £1.70; open ones from £2.70), home-made soup (£1.80), filled baked potatoes (from £3.90), chilli nachos (£3.99), ploughman's (£4.55), steak and mushroom pie (£5.80), tortelloni ricotta or seafood egg noodles (£5.99), cajun king prawns (£7.20) and sirloin steak (£7.99) with puddings such as chocolate fudge cake (from £2.25). Children's meals (£2.25) and baby food; large range of liqueur coffees and hot chocolates. Well kept Boddingtons, Courage Directors, and a guest such as Flowers or Wadworths 6X on handpump, kept under light blanket pressure, and reasonably priced house wine; plenty of board games in the wooden-floored loft bar; fruit machine, TV, cribbage, dominoes, and piped music. Disabled and baby changing facilities. *(Recommended by M G Hart, Ian Phillips, Phil and Heidi Cook)*

Randalls ~ Manager Tina Lister ~ Real ale ~ Bar food (12-2, 6-9, not 31 Dec evening) ~ (01534) 741899 ~ Children welcome ~ Live music two nights a week in summer ~ Open 10.30-11; 11-11 Sun

Old Smugglers
Ouaisne Bay; OS map reference 595476

In a scenic position on the road down to the beach, this welcoming, laid-back pub was originally old fishermen's cottages. Until after World War II it also had a stint as a small residential hotel. Inside, the bar is made up of thick walls, black beams, open fires, and cosy black built-in settles. Well kept Bass and two guests such as Ringwood Best and Greene King Old Speckled Hen on handpump; sensibly placed darts as well as cribbage and dominoes. Enjoyable bar food includes home-made soup (£2), ploughman's (£4), hot brie sweet and sour coulis (£4.25), filled baked potatoes and burgers (from £4.50), steak, Guinness and mushroom pie (£5.25), crispy duck breast with orange and brandy sauce or chicken breast filled with banana with coconut crumble in mild curry sauce (£6.95), steaks (from £7.95) and king prawns and hot garlic butter (£8.25) with specials such as cantonese chicken (£7.25) and half lobster salad (£9.75). A room in the restaurant is no smoking. Some attractive public gardens are near by. *(Recommended by Ian Phillips, S Palmer)*

Free house ~ Licensee Nigel Godfrey ~ Real ale ~ Bar food (12-2, 6-9; not Sun evening Oct-Mar) ~ Restaurant ~ (01534) 741510 ~ Children welcome ~ Open 11-11.30

You can send us reports through our web site: www.goodguides.com

ST HELIER Map 1
Admiral £

St James Street

One reader writes that this impressive, candlelit pub is the shiniest place he has ever seen. Inside, there's lots of dark wood panelling, attractive solid country furniture, and heavy beams – some of which are inscribed with famous quotations – as well as plenty of interesting memorabilia and curios including old telephones, a clocking-in machine, copper milk churn, enamel advertising signs (many more in the small back courtyard which also has lots of old pub signs) and an old penny 'What the Butler Saw' machine; daily papers to read. Reasonably priced bar food includes home-made soup (£2.20), filled baked potatoes (from £3.25), half a spit-roast chicken or home-made steak in ale pie (£4.95), daily fresh fish and vegetarian dishes, sirloin steak (£6.95), and puddings (£2.50); three-course Sunday lunch (£8.95). Well kept Boddingtons and a monthly guest on handpump; dominoes, cribbage, TV, and piped music. Outside, the flagged terrace (with plastic tables) is quite a suntrap in summer. *(Recommended by Ian Phillips)*

Randalls ~ Manager Joanna Lopes ~ Real ale ~ Bar food (12-2, 6-8; not Fri evening or Sat and Sun) ~ Restaurant ~ (01534) 730095 ~ Children welcome ~ Open 11-11; closed 25 Dec

Tipsy Toad Town House £

New Street

Bar food prices have not changed at this attractive two-floored 1930s pub in more than two years. Straightforward dishes include soup (£1.80), lunchtime baguettes (hot or cold from £1.85), filled baked potatoes (from £2.50), spaghetti bolognese (£3.75), chicken curry (£4.25), pork fillet (£4.75) and deep-fried cod or nachos with spicy beef and melted cheese (£4.95) and chicken or beef fajitas for two (£12). Their à la carte menu has lots of fresh fish and daily specials on the blackboard; children's meals. The traditional downstairs bar has old photographs, solid furnishings, some attractive panelling and stained glass, and heavy brass doors between its two main parts to allow in more light. Upstairs has at least as much space again and is carefully planned with a lot of attention to detail; baby changing facilities and high chairs. There's a no smoking area in the restaurant. Tipsy Toad Ale and Jimmys Bitter, and sound house wines; fruit machine, large TV and piped music. It can get busy in the evenings. *(Recommended by Sarah Smith, Ian Phillips)*

Jersey ~ Manager Martin Kelly ~ Real ale ~ Bar food (12-2.15, 6.30-9.15; not Mon evening or Sun) ~ Restaurant ~ (01534) 615000 ~ Children welcome ~ Open 11-11

ST JOHN Map 1
Les Fontaines

Le Grand Mourier, Route du Nord

Particularly enjoyed by locals – listen out for the true Jersey patois – the best part of this former farmhouse is the distinctive public bar, and particularly the unusual inglenook by the large 14th-c stone fireplace. To get there look out for the worn, unmarked door at the side of the building, or as you go down the main entry lobby towards the bigger main bar go through the tiny narrow door on your right. There are very heavy beams in the low dark ochre ceiling, stripped irregular red granite walls, old-fashioned red leatherette cushioned settles and solid black tables on the quarry-tiled floor, and for decoration antique prints and staffordshire china figurines and dogs; also old smoking chains and oven by the granite columns of the fireplace. The main bar is clean and carpeted, with plenty of wheelback chairs around neat dark tables, and a spiral staircase leading up to a wooden gallery under the high pine-raftered plank ceiling. A bonus for families is Pirate Pete's, a supervised play area for children (entry 50p for half an hour), though children are also welcome in the other rooms of the bar. Straightforward bar food includes soup (£1.80), sandwiches (from 2.20), ploughman's (from £4.80), cumberland sausage (£5.50), battered cod (£5.85), steaks (from £8) and specials such as steak and kidney pudding (£5.80), chicken piri piri (£6), baked lamb shank with mash (£7) and lobster or crab salad (from £9). One large area is no smoking; piped music. Courage Directors, and Wadworths 6X on handpump, kept under light blanket pressure. Seats on a terrace outside, although noisy lorries from the nearby quarry can mar the atmosphere; close to some good coastal walks. *(Recommended by Ian Phillips, Philip and June Caunt)*

Randalls ~ Manager Hazel O'Gorman ~ Real ale ~ Bar food (12-2.15, 6-9, not 25 Dec) ~ Restaurant ~ (01534) 86270 ~ Children in eating area of bar and restaurant ~ Open 11-11, only 2 hrs 25 Dec

ST OUENS Bay Map 1

La Pulente

Start of Five Mile Road; OS map reference 562488

After a stroll along Jersey's longest beach opposite, this welcoming, civilised pub is a good place to stop for a meal – especially at sunset when the views are terrific. Run by a friendly licensee, the public bar has a surfing theme with photographs and prints on the walls, while upstairs, the carpeted eating area with ragged walls and scrubbed wood tables leads off onto a balcony, where you can sit overlooking the bay; there are also views of the sea from the lounge and conservatory. As well as sandwiches and baked potatoes (from £3.50), enjoyable bar food could include chicken and leek terrine (£4.50), ploughman's (from £5), well liked beer-battered cod with mushy peas (£6.75), roasted chicken breast, asparagus and leek tart with chive mash (£8), home-made bass, salmon and cod pie or lamb navarin with cabbage mash (£8.25) or sirloin steak with thyme pepper sauce (£9.95) with specials such as roasted chicken with king prawns (from £8) and lobster and crab (from £9.50); children's meals (£3). Well kept Bass and a guest on handpump. *(Recommended by Phil and Heidi Cook, Ian Phillips)*

Randalls ~ Manager David Bell ~ Real ale ~ Bar food (12-2.30, 6-8.30) ~ (01534) 744487 ~ Children welcome until 9pm ~ Live music Fri evenings ~ Open 11-11

Lucky Dip

Besides the fully inspected pubs, you might like to try these Lucky Dips recommended to us and described by readers (if you do, please send us reports: www.goodguides.com).

GUERNSEY
Castel
☆ *Hougue du Pommier* [off Rte de Carteret, just inland from Cobo Bay and Grandes Rocques]: Civilised hotel's roomy partly no smoking beamed bar, sporting prints, trophies and guns, snug area by log fire in big stone fireplace, conservatory with cane furniture, food in bar and restaurant; popular with elderly folk but children welcome, apple trees shading tables on neat lawn, more by swimming pool in sheltered walled garden, and under trees in flower-filled courtyard, pitch-and-putt golf, attractive bedrooms, no dogs; cl Sun evening *(Sue and Bob Ward, Ian Phillips, LYM)*
Vazon Bay Hotel [Vazon Coast Rd]: Wide choice of good food, Randalls and Sam Smiths beers, clear view of sea wall; bedrooms *(Gordon Neighbour)*

JERSEY
Gorey
Village Pub [Gorey Common]: Recently comfortably refurbished, cheerful and welcoming, with basic bar food *(S Palmer)*
St Aubin
Tenby Bars [Le Boulevard, towards St Helier]: Overlooking harbour, with food (till 8) running up to bass and steaks, real ales such as Courage Directors, Theakstons Best and Wadworths 6X, picnic-sets out on smallish terrace; parking can be difficult *(Ian Phillips)*
St Helier
☆ *Original Wine Bar* [Bath St]: Informal and welcoming, with casual décor and comfortable sofas and armchairs, good choice of interesting lunchtime food (not Sun), real ales such as Brains, Jersey Brewery, Tipsy Toad, Breda Dutch lager, good wines, coffees and teas, friendly efficient service, relaxing cheerful atmosphere, no smoking area *(BB)*

Overseas Lucky Dip

We're always interested to hear of good bars and pubs overseas – preferably really good examples of bars that visitors would find memorable, rather than transplanted 'British Pubs'. A star marks places we would be confident would deserve a main entry. Note that the strong £ currently makes the best bars in foreign capitals (often very pricy) a good deal more accessible than previously.

ARGENTINA
Buenos Aires
Posadas Bar [Posadas 1402, Recoleta]: Café-bar with usual draught beers, sandwiches etc, mezzanine seating, tables out under trees on pavement *(Ian Phillips)*
La Angostura
Cerveceria del Bosque [Cerro Belvedere/Avenida los Arrayanes]: Small bar in touristy building of varnished tree-trunks, local El Bolson microbrew, other bottled beers and snacks; tables outside, town on W end of Lago Nahuel Huapi *(Ian Phillips)*

AUSTRALIA
Hervey Bay
Blazing Saddles [140 Freshwater St, Torquay; Queensland]: Outback-theme bar and grill, lots of pioneer artefacts from windpump and mining tools to an armoured Ned Kelly, big room with pine walls, hardwood furniture, good choice of reasonably priced food inc children's, usual drinks, piped music, TV *(CMW, JJW)*
Mudgee
Lawson Park Hotel [Church St; NSW]: Restaurant behind usual small smoky bar, good DIY barbecue inc huge cheap steaks *(C and R Bromage)*
Taylors Arm
Pub With No Beer [signed off Pacific Highway at Macksville; NSW]: Rambling old verandahed pub immortalised in song by Slim Dusty and Gordon Parsons, full of bric-a-brac, huge club badge collection, central fire, good helpings of good food wknds and hols, games machines, piped country music (maybe live wknds); barbecues, playground, bedrooms *(CMW, JJW)*

BELGIUM
Bruges
☆ *Brugs Beertje* [Kemelstraat, off Steenstr nr cathedral]: Small friendly bar known as the Beer Academy, serving over 300 of the country's beers, most of them strong ones, in each beer's distinctive glass; table menus, helpful English-speaking staff, good basic bar food; open from 4, can get a bit smoky later *(Mike and Wendy Proctor, Bob and Lisa Cantrell, Mrs M Thomas)*

Craenenburg [Markt]: Large bar with own little turret, quiet and refined, Leffe, Hoegaarden and Jupiter, coffee and cakes, daily papers, leather walls, stained-glass window medallions – and beyond, the bustling passing scene *(Mike and Wendy Proctor, Ian Phillips)*
Dyver [Dyver]: Opulent Flemish décor, canal view, bistro by day with 70 different beers; smarter restaurant atmosphere evenings *(Dr and Mrs A K Clarke)*
Erasmus [Wollestraat 35]: Welcoming modernish hotel, mix of old and new décor inc intricate seasonal decorations, good choice of helpfully described beers, enjoyable food *(Mike and Wendy Proctor)*
☆ *Garre* [1 de Garre, off Breidelstraat]: Attractive and welcoming 16th-c timbered building, stripped brickwork, upper gallery, elegant but very relaxed, well over 100 mainly local beers inc five Trappists and its own draught beer – each well served in its own glass with cheese nibbles; knowledgeable helpful staff, unobtrusive piped classical music, light snacks; children welcome *(Dr and Mrs A K Clarke)*
Brussels
Au Bon Vieux Temps [rue Marché aux Herbes 12]: Dark woodwork, beautiful stained glass, old tables, wide range of beers *(Sue Demont, Tim Barrow)*
De Toone [6 Impasse Schuddeveld, off 21 Petite Rue des Bouchers]: Really a puppet theatre at least at night, down dark passage; good bar area with huge log fire, puppets for sale (some huge) hanging from ceiling, stage room with retractable seating, no smoking area; shortish choice of good interesting beers, some food *(Sue Demont, Tim Barrow)*
Imaige Nostre-Dame [Impasse des Cadeaux, rue du Marché aux Herbes]: Dark, relaxed, intriguing, tucked down alleyway nr Grand Place; wide range of beers, open till midnight *(Sue Demont, Tim Barrow)*
Kartchma [Pl du Grand Sablon]: Small two-level bar, trendier than many, yet preserving its impressive art nouveau façade; usual wide range of beers, seats outside *(Sue Demont, Tim Barrow)*
☆ *Mort Subite* [R Montagne aux Herbes Potagères; off Grand Place via Galeries St

Hubert]: Under same family since 1928, long fin de siècle room divided by two rows of pillars into nave with two rows of small polished tables and side aisles with single row, huge mirrors on all sides, leather seats, brisk uniformed waiters and waitresses scurrying from busy serving counter on right; lots of beers inc their own Gueuze, Faro, Kriek, Pèche, Cassis and Framboise brewed nearby, good straightforward food inc big omelettes and local specialities such as brawn and rice tart, no piped music *(Sue Demont, Tim Barrow, Joan and Michel Hooper-Immins)*

CANADA
Banff
Num-Ti-Jah Lodge [Banff National Park, Alberta; W of Highway 93 S of Bow Summit]: Simple oasis in this culinary wilderness, good food and Canadian wine in pleasant room with vernacular décor, polite, friendly and efficient staff *(Dennis Jenkin)*
Granville Island
Bridges [Vancouver]: Great spot by wonderful food markets and craft shops, tables out overlooking harbour; good beers, friendly service, generous food *(Tim and Ann Newell)*
Jasper
Jasper Park Lodge [Alberta]: Good bar snacks and local wine in hotel's bar lounge, friendly prompt service; bedrooms *(Dennis Jenkin)*
Kootenay
Kootenay Park Lodge [Kootenay National Park, Alberta; Highway 93, off Route 1 or 1A Banff—Lake Louise]: Small simple hotel with good food and Canadian wine in attractive main room with hunting trophies etc, polite friendly service; bedrooms, superb scenery on the way *(Dennis Jenkin)*
Ucluelet
Canadian Princess [Vancouver Island, BC]: Ship serving as pub, restaurant and hotel, welcoming staff, good snacks and decent wine *(Dennis Jenkin)*
Vancouver
Steamworks [375 Water St]: Lovely spot overlooking harbour, good pubby feel, own beers (interesting to see the vats and smell the hops), very friendly efficient service, good food from burgers to oysters Rockefeller and steaks *(John Evans)*
Victoria
Empress [Vancouver Island, BC]: Appropriately decorated Bengal Lounge in luxurious hotel does good informal meals, huge helpings, very friendly efficient staff; also a fine stylish if expensive restaurant, good bedrooms *(Dennis Jenkin)*
Spinnakers [Catherine St; BC]: Busy brewpub with great views of Inner Harbour and Olympic Mountains, esp from partly enclosed upper terrace; lots of wood, long upstairs bar, choice of own-brewed ales (using equipment from England), lagers, seasonal barley wines and local berry fruit beers, wicked cocktails, food in bar and restaurant, also deli, gift shop and Internet access; bedrooms *(Martin and Karen Wake)*

CANARY ISLANDS
Brema Baia
Pulpo [Playa de los Cancajos; Palma]: Delicious fresh fish, local wine and lagers in beach bar/restaurant on quiet unspoilt bay with black sand and rocks *(J F M and M West)*
Fuerteventura
Beer Garden [Centro Comercial]: Garden bar, British-owned but not making a fuss about it, British and Spanish beers, wide food choice from meat pies to deep-fried squid *(Colin Gooch)*

CZECH REPUBLIC
Prague
Branicky Sklipek [Vodickova 26, Nove Mesto]: Busy dining bar with Branik Pale and Dark; open all day *(the Didler)*
Bubenicku [Myslikova]: Small many-roomed local, Gambrinus beers, food all day *(the Didler)*
Budvarka [Wuchterlova 22, nr Vitezni Namesti]: Busy two-room pub supplied handily by three nearby breweries, food inc local carp; open all day *(the Didler)*
Cerneho Vola [Loretanske Namesti 1]: Up steps above castle, friendly and jolly, beams, leaded lights, long dark benches or small stand-up entrance bar, good Kozel Pale and Dark 12 black beer, and Velkopopovicky Korel lager, local snacks; can get very busy (though rarely too touristy), cl 9 *(Hallgeir Dale, the Didler)*
Cerny Pivovar [Karlovo 15, Nove Mesto]: Stand-up self-service café with local beers, superb prices; restaurant part open from mid-morning *(the Didler)*
Europa Café [Vaclavske Namesti, by Europa Hotel off Wenceslas Sq]: Good value food and Radegast beers from waiters and waitresses in time-warp café, small admission charge when nicely dated trio playing; open 7am-midnight *(the Didler)*
☆ *Fleku* [Kremencova 11, Nove Mesto]: Brewing its own strong flavoursome black Flekovsky Dark 13 since 1843 (some say 1499); waiters will try to sell you a schnapps with it – say Ne firmly; huge, with benches and big refectory tables in two big dark-beamed rooms – tourists on right with 10-piece oompah band, more local on left (music here too), also courtyard after courtyard; good basic food – sausages, pork, goulash with dumplings; open early morning to late night, very popular with tourists wknds *(the Didler)*
Havrana [Halkova 6]: Pleasant bar open 24 hours (night surcharge), with Kozel beers *(the Didler)*
Houdku [Borivojovo 693, Zizkow]: Typical of this working suburb's many basic honest bars, crowded and noisy early evening, Eggenberg Pale and Dark – never an empty glass; open all day till 9 *(the Didler)*
Jama [V Jame 7, Stare Mesto]: Busy studenty local, Elvis Presley posters, Western piped music, Samson Pale 12 ; open till late, occasional jazz *(the Didler)*
Kocovra [Nerudova 2, Mala Strana]: Long narrow three-room pub behind big black door,

quiet and relaxing; Budvar 12 and Pilsner Urquell 12 , good basic Czech food *(the Didler)*

Krale Jiriho [Liliova 10, Stare Mesto]: 13th-c stone-arched cellar bar with Hendrix and Clapton pictures, maybe loud piped music; Platen Pale and Dark; can get crowded; open 2pm-midnight *(the Didler)*

☆ *Medvidku* [Na Perstyne 5, Stare Mesto]: Superb busy old bar in red light district, namesake bears etched in stone over entry, lots of copper in left bar, bigger right room more for eating (good food, lots of Czech specialities); excellent Budvar Budweiser *(the Didler, Hallgeir Dale)*

Milosrdnych [Milosrdnych 11, Stare Mesto]: Busy three-room local nr St Agnes Convent (now an art gallery), good beers inc Pilsner Urquell, Gambrinus and maybe Primus Pale 10; open all day *(the Didler)*

Na Kampe [Na Kampe 15]: Ancient tiled-floor bar in nice spot below Charles Bridge, very popular and friendly; scrubbed furniture, Gambrinus Dark and Pale and Pilsner Urquell 12, good food from snacks such as skvarky (pork cracklings) to restaurant dishes; open all day *(the Didler)*

Nadrazni Pivnice [Pikovicka 2, Branik]: Very basic early-hours station bar with very cheap beer from nearby Branik Brewery, breakfast dumplings, live music Weds afternoon *(the Didler)*

Novomestsky Pivovar [Vodickova 20, Nove Mesto]: Fine brewpub opened 1994 in unlikely spot off shopping arcade, small long dark bar with copper vessels producing unfiltered Novomestsky Pale, restaurant down steps; open all day *(the Didler)*

Opera House Bar [nr Revolution St/Wenceslas Sq]: Down steps and corridor to back, interesting tiled room, art deco, Pilsner Urquart Light and Dark, good food choice; also classic upper room, mainly for food *(the Didler)*

Pinkasu [Jungmannovo Namesti, Nove Mesto]: Historic beer hall with white-coated waiters serving armfuls of luscious beers – esp Pilsner Urquell, others constantly changing; low prices, good food, also small back bar and upstairs drinking room; open all day *(the Didler)*

Radegast Pivnice [Templova, Stare Mesto]: Low narrow beer hall, cheap Radegast Pale 10 and 12 , excellent value food all day, service quick even when very busy; open all day *(the Didler)*

Snedeneho [1st left over Charles Bridge]: Tiny bar, quiet and friendly, with Budvar Pale and Purkmistr Dark and Pale, lots of old photographs, old record player in window; downstairs restaurant *(the Didler)*

Staropramenu [Nadrazni 102, Smichov]: Tap for nearby Staropramen Brewery, has even their rare Dark; small no-nonsense stand-up bar, or waiter-service dining room with excellent very cheap meat and dumpling dishes; open all day, cl till 3 wknds *(the Didler)*

Svateho Tomase [Letenska 12]: Fascinating arched cellars of ancient Augustine monastic building, very popular with tourists; great beer range inc Budvar, Ferdinand, Krusovice and Radegast, superb menu; not cheap; maybe concerts in adjoining gardens, open all day *(the Didler)*

Vahy [Nadrazni 88, Smichov]: Nice location, good food, Gambrinus Pale; open all day from 6am *(the Didler)*

☆ *Zlateho Tygra* [Husova 17, Stare Mesto]: 13th-c cellars with superb Pilsner Urquell 12 and eponymous Golden Tiger served by white-coated waiters; sometimes a queue of locals even before 3pm opening, and no standing allowed, but worth the wait (don't be put off by Reserved signs as the seats aren't usually being used till later – and they do make tourists feel welcome) *(the Didler, Hallgeir Dale)*

FRANCE

Calais

Alexandra [1/3 Digue Gaston Berthe]: Smart small corner bar overlooking harbour and shipping, Kanterbrau on tap, bottled beers, coffee and snacks *(Ian Phillips)*

Cognac

Coq d'Or [Pl François 1er]: Imposing fin de siècle bar/brasserie with vast mosaic golden cockerel over entrance, usual French and Belgian draught beers, lots of bottled ones, good wines, daily papers; fish and shellfish specialities *(Ian Phillips)*

La Rochelle

Au Bureau [Quai Dupérré]: Modelled on Edwardian pub, in excellent spot overlooking inner harbour; good food esp moules, friendly staff, lots of bottled beers as well as continental draughts *(Ian Phillips)*

Les Echelles

Auberge du Morgue [RN6]: Landlord knowledgeable about wines of Savoie, good food, log fire; simple bedrooms, handy for local gorges and caves, and fishing *(Mrs Jane Kingsbury)*

Lille

Trois Brasseurs [rue de Tournai, opp Gare de Flandres]: Brews its own beers and also keeps many other local ones; good usual snacks and friendly service *(Mr and Mrs A G Leece, Ian Phillips)*

Paris

Bowler [rue d'Artois]: Friendly Adnams pub just a couple of streets off Champs Elysées, their Best and Broadside on handpump, mix of locals and ex-pats but few tourists *(Simon Chell)*

Ribeauville

Bar St Ulrich [Pl de la République]: Six interesting draught beers, a hundred bottled inc fruit beers and rarities, dozens of whiskies, all described really carefully – most impressive; all-wood interior, tables outside overlooking the fountain in the square *(Tom McLean)*

GERMANY

Heidelberg

Vetter Brauhaus [centre]: Good traditional dishes served in cast-iron frying pans, good beers brewed on the premises *(PACW)*

Hersching

Sea Hof: Typical Bavarian restaurant nr the lake, good atmosphere, well cooked nicely served food inc local asparagus speciality in season *(Joyce and Maurice Cottrell)*

Munich

Ratskeller [Marien Platz]: Thoroughly Bavarian, with interesting food running to tempura veg (German menu has wider choice than English); beautiful courtyard, tables under parasols *(Joyce and Maurice Cottrell)*

Schwetzingen

Schwetzinger Brauhaus [Schlossplatz, opp castle]: Sizeable newish brewpub, big copper brewing vessels part of bar décor, good traditional food all day, good blond, dark and seasonal beers, tables outside; no credit cards *(PACW)*

GREECE

Ouranoupolis

Athos Taverna [by Avra Hotel, just outside centre]: Decent house white wine as well as reliable Boutari bottled wines, good fish and lamb, very friendly staff, some sea views *(Ian Phillips)*

IRELAND

Baltimore

Algiers [Co Cork]: Friendly pub in small fishing village (touristy in summer), nautical memorabilia, bare boards, metal-topped tables, good food inc local whiting, good Murphys and Guinness, also Bulmer's farm cider *(Jonathan Smith)*

Bushes Bar: Antique harbourside bar with maritime theme, popular for good seafood from crab sandwiches up *(Nigel Woolliscroft)*

Belfast

☆ *Crown* [Gt Victoria St, opp Europa Hotel]: Well preserved bustling 19th-c gin palace with pillared entrance, opulent tiles outside and in, elaborately coloured windows, almost church-like ceiling, handsome mirrors, individual snug booths with little doors and bells for waiter service, gas lighting, mosaic floor – wonderful atmosphere, very wide range of customers (maybe inc performers in full fig from Opera House opp); good lunchtime meals inc oysters, Hilden real ale, open all day; National Trust *(Mark and Diane Grist)*

Rotterdam [Pilot St]: Unchanging authentic Belfast pub surrounded by docks redevelopment, nightly live music and lively chat, competent friendly staff *(Mark and Diane Grist)*

Cape Clear Island

Ciaran Danny Mikes: Bar food, restaurant; entertainment; bedrooms *(Nigel Woolliscroft)*

Club Chlérre: Very lively, enjoyable food, formal and impromptu music sessions *(Nigel Woolliscroft)*

Night Jar: Good bar food, friendly atmosphere, musicians always welcome *(Nigel Woolliscroft)*

Cashel

Pat Fox's [Main St; Co Tipperary]: Great welcoming bar with hurling memorabilia, beautifully served stouts, lunchtime soup and sandwiches, also morning coffee, afternoon tea; centre of picturesque town *(Andy and Jill Kassube)*

Cloghroe

Blairs [Co Cork]: Well known for good food from interesting sandwiches to restaurant dishes; handy for Blarney Castle *(Andy and Jill Kassube)*

Clonakilty

De Barra [Pearse St; Co Cork]: Unspoilt, with thriving atmosphere, local photographs and memorabilia, bare boards, popular food, good Guinness, lots of whiskeys, nightly folk music *(Jonathan Smith)*

Cobh

Donnachies [Middleton St; Co Cork]: Panelling, bare boards and log fire in huge cast-iron fireplace, warm welcome for all, tip-top stouts, live music most Sats, frequent impromptu sing-songs and music sessions *(Mairead Burke)*

Dingle

Dick Macs [opp church; Co Kerry]: Great atmosphere in former old-fashioned haberdasher's shop, cha ming exterior and delightful inside, good stouts, many whiskeys, friendly staff; mainly standing room around central area with singing, whistle-playing, story-telling etc *(Jonathan Smith)*

Lord Bakers [Main St; Co Kerry]: Beautifully presented full-tasting food esp seafood and local lamb in plush comfortable bar and restaurant, welcoming landlord, no smoking areas *(Jonathan Smith)*

Dublin

Auld Dubliner [Anglesea St, Temple Bar]: Crowded typical Irish pub, friendly staff, enjoyable food from sandwiches up, very laid-back atmosphere, good music *(Sally Anne and Peter Goodale)*

Bruxelles [Harry St, off Grafton St]: Cosy, popular and friendly upstairs Victorian bar with dark panelling, mirrors, picture wall tiles and outstanding Guinness, quick service even on very busy lunchtimes, food inc home-made burgers and sausages; downstairs much more modern, Celtic symbols, grey/black/red décor, seats in alcoves and around central pillars, dim lighting; rock music can be very loud *(Chris Raisin, P A Legon, Jim Abbott)*

Clontarf Castle [Castle Ave]: Pub bar, medieval-style carvery bar, good pub food, open fire, lively bustle, friendly staff, restaurant; comfortable bedrooms *(Sally Anne and Peter Goodale)*

Doheny & Nesbitt [Lower Baggot St, by the Shelburne just below St Stephens Green]: Friendly traditional pub, originally a grocer's, close to Irish Parliament; Victorian bar fittings, two rooms with marble-topped tables, wooden screens, old whiskey mirrors etc; mainly drink (inc good Guinness) and conversation, but has good value Irish stew; live music, can get very busy but worth the wait *(Chris Raisin, Andy and Jill Kassube)*

Guinness Storehouse [St James Gate Brewery]: Not a pub but trendy new exhibition on firm's history, brewing and advertising campaigns (taking over from former Hopstore), gift shop; worth a visit for the great views from 7th-floor tasting bar – Guinness at its best

(Chris Raisin, Sharon Holmes, Tom Cherrett)
McDaids [Harry St, off Grafton St]: Ornate late 19th-c building, traditional furnishings and character, lively atmosphere, well looked after Guinness, Irish music most nights – can get busy; was haunt of Brendan Behan and Patrick Kavanagh *(Chris Raisin, Andy and Jill Kassube)*

☆ O'Donoghues [Merrion Row, off St Stephens Green]: Small old-fashioned Victorian bar with dark panelling, mirrors, posters and snob screens, musical instruments and other bric-a-brac on ceiling, bank-note collection behind long side counter; great atmosphere, good friendly service even when busy, popular with musicians – maybe an impromptu riot of Celtic tunes played on anything from spoons to banjo or pipes; fine Guinness, gets packed but long-armed owner ensures quick friendly service; plainer back bar has live music too; open all day *(Chris Raisin, Arby)*

O'Neills [Suffolk St]: Large early Victorian pub, lots of dark panelling and cubby-holes on different levels off big bar, good lunchtime carvery (go around 2 to avoid the crush; it's on all day Sun), good value doorstep sandwiches and home-made soup, good Guinness *(Chris Raisin, Sharon Holmes, Tom Cherrett)*

Oliver St John Gogarty [Anglesea St, Temple Bar]: Large bustling bare-boards bars, bric-a-brac inc bicycle above counter, good Guinness, generous, good if not cheap food in fairly small cosy upper-floor restaurant (former bank, interesting preserved features) and at lunchtime in main bar, very friendly efficient service; live music upstairs *(Stephen, Julie and Hayley Brown, Sharon Holmes, Tom Cherrett, Chris Raisin, Jim Abbott)*

Palace [Fleet St, Temple Bar]: Splendidly unspoilt Victorian bar standing out from the ersatz 'craic' elsewhere in Temple Bar, with snob screens, rooms through etched-glass doors, tiny snug, plainer back room; good Guinness *(Chris Raisin, Arby)*

Porter House [Parliament St, nr Wellington Quay]: Vibrant three-storey modern pub, lots of pine and brass for café-bar feel, brewing half a dozen good beers inc Porter, Stout, Lager and usually a cask-conditioned real ale, dozens of foreign bottled beers; high tables and equally high seats, good food from ciabatta sandwiches to steaks, upstairs restaurant; live music, can be standing room only wknds *(Andy and Jill Kassube, Steve Whalley, Chris Raisin, C J Fletcher)*

Smythe [Matahide]: Good American-style chargrills, quick and friendly helpful service, good pubby bare-boards atmosphere; live music Mon *(Sally Anne and Peter Goodale)*

Stags Head [Dame Court, off Dame St]: Imposing frontage for elegant upmarket pub with lofty main bar, supposedly Dublin's oldest, lots of carved mahogany, etched mirrors, stained glass, whiskey vats, huge stag's head over huge marble bar, cosy leather-seat back snug with dark panelling and glass ceiling, downstairs music bar; good Guinness, plain food inc sandwiches; can get very busy indeed, signposted by a pretty mosaic in Dame St *(Jim Abbott, Chris Raisin)*

Dun Laoghaire
Purty Kitchen: Well run, with good food and beers; handy for ferry *(Alan Clark)*

Duncannon
Strand Tavern [Co Wexford]: Welcoming recently refurbished seafood restaurant and bar on beach road, good well priced food, good Guinness, pool, TV *(Gwyneth and Salvo Spadaro-Dutturi)*

Kinsale
Jim Edwards [Co Cork]: Good food from oysters and grilled crab claws to steaks, nice puddings; charming fishing village *(Andy and Jill Kassube)*

Naas
Thomas Fletchers [Main St; Co Kildare]: Traditional old-fashioned bar partitioned into three simple areas, one with two carved mahogany alcoves, big whiskey vats set into wall behind bar, good Guinness; good mature barmen *(Jim Abbott)*

New Ross
Mannions [Mount Elliot (N25); Co Wexford]: 19th-c country pub with bare boards and open fires, enjoyable food inc good choice of sandwiches *(Andy and Jill Kassube)*

Roundstone
Shamrock [Co Galway]: Pine seating on stripped pine floors in real Irish bar with warm welcome, high ceilings, log fire; good value food, well served Guinness; children and small well behaved dogs welcome *(Gwyneth and Salvo Spadaro-Dutturi)*

Sherkin Island
Jolly Roger: Oldest pub here, overlooking harbour, bar food all year, good summer music *(Nigel Woolliscroft)*

Murphys: Newly renovated, great harbour views, good bar food, cycle hire, open all day *(Nigel Woolliscroft)*

Thomastown
Long Man of Kilfane [Dublin Rd (N9); Co Kilkenny]: Busy roadside pub with popular home cooking inc lots of fresh veg; live music wknds *(Andy and Jill Kassube)*

Tramore
Seahorse [Co Waterford]: Comfortable little pub, thriving atmosphere, wide choice of enjoyable food, quick friendly service, good Beamish, Guinness and Murphys, lots of whiskeys, tea and coffee all day, upstairs dining overspill; TV, piped music; children welcome *(Jonathan Smith)*

Waterford
Egans [Barronstrand St]: Good food (till 8) and very good service in city-centre bar *(Andy and Jill Kassube)*

T & H Doolan: Dark old pub said to include fragment of 1,000-year-old city wall, leaded windows, flagstones, friendly welcome, fine Guinness, rare whiskeys, speciality coffees and mixed drinks, food too; Irish music Thurs *(Gwyneth and Salvo Spadaro-Dutturi)*

ISLE OF MAN
Glenmaye [SC2480]
Waterfall [Shore Rd, just off A27 3 miles S of Peel – OS Sheet 95 map ref 236798]: Above the

beautiful Glenmaye, convenient for walkers on the coastal path, and named for the waterfall nearby; very popular, warm and welcoming, with good service, good value food served piping hot inc sizzlers and very popular Sun lunch (get there early), well kept Cains, Tetleys and sometimes local Okells ale *(Prof Chris Bucke, James Nunns, B, M and P Kendall)*

Port Erin [SC2069]
Cherry Orchard [Bridson St]: Red plush Morello Bar with decent food inc very generous veg, Okells and Guinness; self-catering apartments *(B, M and P Kendall)*

MAJORCA
Escoria
Escorca [Carretera 710 Soller—Pollenca nr Km 25 sign]: Farm tools in unspoilt rustic bar, tender and succulent country food in beamed restaurant built into cliff, very local wine; lovely mountain views from terrace, cl Thurs *(Susan and John Douglas)*

NETHERLANDS
Amsterdam
Café Belgique [Gravenstraat]: Tiny friendly traditional bar, up to 80 Belgian beers inc over 40 Trappists, snacks inc Trappist and Dutch cheese and biscuits; very popular with British visitors *(Sue Demont, Tim Barrow, Karen Sadler, Guy Platt, Michael Doswell)*
Café de Pilsgen [Gravenstraat]: Huge range of draught and bottled beers in endearingly traditional 'brown café' with attractive balcony *(Stephen, Julie and Hayley Brown)*
☆ *Café Hoppe* [Spuistraat 18-20]: Probably Amsterdam's most famous 'brown café', its huge old-fashioned bar busy from early morning till late at night, with lots of atmosphere, staggering range of gins and whiskies as well as fine beers from delft handpumps, good food; one part traditional, with sand on floor, heavy leather portière and standing only, the other with tables and chairs; in good weather most customers are out on pavement *(Stephen, Julie and Hayley Brown)*
Café Karpershoek [Martelaarsgracht 2]: Authentic old-fashioned 'brown café' dating from 1629, even sand on the floors; very welcoming, usual range of lagers and genevers, good sausages *(Nigel Woolliscroft)*
Elfoe Gebod [Zeedijk]: Classy panelled bareboards 'brown café' with good range of local beers *(Dr and Mrs A K Clarke)*
Gollem [Raamsteeg 4]: Dark, friendly and slightly raffish, blackboards around walls listing vast beer range *(Sue Demont, Tim Barrow)*
Het Molenpad [653 Prinsengracht]: Appealing old-fashioned café/bar on one of the most attractive canals, good cheap imaginative sandwiches and other reasonably priced food, well kept Dutch and Belgian beers inc Leffe Blond; busy evening *(Michael Doswell)*
The Hague
Café Oudemol [Oude Molenstraat]: Tiny café-bar with great atmosphere, masses of interesting Belgian and Dutch beers, good wines, hospitable owners, enjoyable tapas; good piped jazz *(Nigel Woolliscroft)*

NEW ZEALAND
Christchurch
☆ *Oxford on the Avon* [opp Victoria Park]: Busy bar and cafeteria, huge range of excellent value straightforward food from breakfast on inc lovely carvery lamb, good range of nicely served local beers, decent wine by the glass, friendly helpful service, quite a pub-like atmosphere; tables out by the river with evening gas heaters *(Joyce and Maurice Cottrell)*
Coromandel Town
Pepper Pot: Warm atmosphere, esp with the log fire; good fish and seafood such as oysters and smoked salmon *(Joyce and Maurice Cottrell)*
Greytown
Green Man [South Wairarapa]: Recently refurbished turn-of-the-century inn nr centre of oldest NZ inland settlement, fine range of beers on tap as well as bottled (and plans for an attached microbrewery), also good wine choice, interesting well prepared reasonably priced bar food; bedrooms, tables outside *(James Scott, Jane Kaytar)*
Kaikaro
Craypot Café: The place for crayfish, also other good food; relaxed local atmosphere *(Joyce and Maurice Cottrell)*

PORTUGAL
Lisbon
Cervejaria da Trindade [Rua Nova da Trindade 20]: Beautifully tiled early 19th-c beerhouse brewing its own full-flavoured light and dark beers, traditional food inc crab and steaks in two main eating rooms *(Simon and Amanda Southwell)*
Portugalia Espelho d'Agua [waterfront, nr discoveries monument]: Modern beerhouse with big windows overlooking River Tagus, lots of glasses decorating ceiling, its own light and dark beers, speciality steaks *(Simon and Amanda Southwell)*

SOUTH AFRICA
Franshoek
Quartier Français [High St]: Nice bar in pleasant mid-sized hotel, fantastic food, great wine list, wonderful service, stylish décor, log fires throughout, seats outside; bedrooms *(Andy Sinden, Louise Harrington)*
Hout Bay
Dunes [beach rd, off Beach car park just before Chapmans Peak Hotel]: Informal bar and restaurant with great atmosphere, fabulous views from upstairs verandah, good beer and wine choice, creative food; busy chip-loving parrot, seats out overlooking play area *(Andy Sinden, Louise Harrington)*
Johannesburg
Bellinis [just off Oxford Rd, Illovo]: Popular bar and restaurant with great service and food esp steak and rocket salad with fries; seats outside *(Andy Sinden, Louise Harrington)*
Knysna
Belvedere Manor [off road to George, about

2 miles out]: Hotel among upmarket homes in wildlife sanctuary (no dogs allowed), good choice of beers and wines in small bar, charming owners and staff, good food, large swimming pool and terrace overlooking landscaped grounds and lagoon, abundant bird life; cottage accommodation; boat trips to Featherbed nature reserve (*Andy Sinden, Louise Harrington*)

Langebaan

Pearlys [by beach car park]: Informal friendly bar on beach of shallow lagoon, warm for swimming, great food choice from pizzas to steaks and fish, lots of beers inc Guinness and maybe English beers, friendly waiters; seats out on partly screened deck; on edge of West Coast National Park, renowned for flowers (July-Sept) and birds (*Andy Sinden, Louise Harrington*)

Noordhoek

Red Herring [off Chapmans Peak Drive from Hout Bay: follow Noordhoek sign off, then first right, then Red Herring is signed to the left after 500 yards; if Chapmans Peak Drive is closed, go via Silver Mine]: Upstairs bar with verandah and fine views of the incredible white sand beach, wide food choice inc very good pizzas, good range of lagers and wines, seats downstairs outside and in; sports TV, three welcoming dogs (*Andy Sinden, Louise Harrington*)

SPAIN
Barcelona

Café Zurich [overlooking Catalunia Sq]: Good roomy bar, cheap local beer (*Stephen, Julie and Hayley Brown*)

Elisabets Bar [Elizabets]: Good tapas, very cheap (*Stephen, Julie and Hayley Brown*)

Txapela [Passeig de Gracia]: Huge range of good tapas (*Stephen, Julie and Hayley Brown*)

SWEDEN
Lund

John Bull [Banforget, across from Grand Hotel]: Well done traditional British pub with turkey carpet, brass rail and footrests etc, even an advertisement for an eisteddfod in Wales; good choice of British beers in bottle and keg, also Guinness etc (*Derek Stafford*)

TENERIFE
Adeje

Otelo [Barranco del Infierno]: Magnificent views from verandah and restaurant, good food and drinks, low prices; handy for gorge walks (*J F M and M West*)

THAILAND
Phuket

Salsa [Thaweewong Rd (Patong Beach Rd), Patong]: Comfortable air-conditioned oasis of calm in this Blackpool of Phuket, reasonably priced drinks inc local Singha lager (*Jenny and Brian Seller*)

USA
Anchorage

Glacier Brewhouse [737 West 5th Ave, corner 5th and H; Alaska]: Noisy, lively and fun, brewing several good beers inc British-style ones, Stout, a fruit beer, and one or more real ales, also enjoyable food inc good fresh fish, with plenty of wines by the glass (*John Evans*)

Denver

Buckhorn Exchange [1000 Osage St; Colorado]: Classic Old West saloon opened in 1871, lots of appropriate artefacts and game trophies, plenty of spirits and beer; besides alligator, buffalo, elk and rattlesnake, the menu even has Rocky Mountain oysters – don't even ask what they are (*David M Johnson*)

Pints [221 West 13th Ave]: Nearly 200 malt whiskies, and brew their own British-style real ales, good food, darts, UK pool tables, British juke box – anything from bagpipes to the Stones (*David M Johnson*)

Disney

Big River Grill & Brewing Works [Boardwalk, 2101 N Epcot Resort Blvd; Florida]: Good food from superb burgers through big salads to tuna steaks, up to five beers brewed here, marvellous outdoor eating area (*Andy and Jill Kassube*)

Greenville

Brandywine Brewing Co [Rte 52; Delaware]: Good food from sandwiches to traditional regional dishes, children's menu, high-ceilinged open restaurant with private booths; several good beers from their own microbrewery (tours available) (*PACW*)

Modesto

St Stans [821 L St]: American food, their own German-style beer on tap, bar with high stools and tables, also small booths, charming atmosphere, separate restaurant; good live music Weds-Sat (*Roger and Jenny Huggins*)

New York

Commonwealth Brewing Co [10 Rockefeller Plaza]: Large, very clean and comfortable upmarket brew-restaurant, massive visible microbrewery producing excellent beers such as Gotham City Gold; excellent food too (generally have to book at lunchtime) (*PACW*)

Heartland Brewery [1285 6th Avenue/51st St]: Very friendly, cosy and comfortable, brewing its own India PA, Red Rooster, Harvest wheat beer and Oatmeal Stout; good food from seafood to strip steak (*Andy and Jill Kassube*)

Times Square Brewery [160 W 42nd St]: Bustling circular bar with visible microbrewery producing four good beers inc Times Square PA, Bock, Pilsner and Highlands 60/-; good reasonably priced bar food (*Andy and Jill Kassube*)

Philadelphia

City Tavern [138 South 2nd St; Pennsylvania]: Reconstruction of late 18th-c tavern, decent traditional food of that era served by period-dress staff, some interesting beers (inc one using a George Washington recipe) (*PACW*)

Dock Street Brewery [Dock St]: Good beers from visible brewing vessels, good food range, darts and pool (*PACW*)

San Francisco

Steelhead Brewing Co [353 Jefferson]: A stroll from Pier 39 on Fishermans Wharf (two hours' free parking for customers), with view behind glass of microbrewery producing changing range of six beers from stout to wheat beer, inc some cask-conditioned versions on handpump such as excellent dry-hopped Bombay Bomber (tasting set of six small glasses available); also other draught and bottled beers; well spaced tables in big room, happy relaxing atmosphere mingling sea air with hops; another branch at Burlingame Station *(Roger and Jenny Huggins)*

Seattle

Hales Brewery [Leary Way; Washington]: Good real ales brewed by Gales-trained owner, not over-hopped or too strong (a common fault in the region), inc IPA, HSB, Moss Bay Extra, Celebration Porter, and seasonal brews such as Wee Heavy and Irish (a Dark Mild); good food *(Martin Corey)*

Murphys [45th and Meridian]: Long-standing pillar of NW microbrew movement, two real ales, also keg microbrews, ciders, Guinness and Murphys, good fresh fish and chips, sandwiches and burgers, darts, live music *(Martin Corey)*

Sedona

Cowboy Club [Arizona]: Bare boards and plank walls, well padded green leather seats, stools at long bar with buffalo horns and hats behind it, good buffalo burgers and chilli, two Oak Creek beers brewed at the pub; beautiful spot surrounded by red rock *(Roger and Jenny Huggins)*

Tacoma

Swiss Tavern [19th and Jefferson; Washington]: Fine choice of well kept regional microbrews, keg imports such as Boddingtons and Guinness, good local wines, very good sandwiches and pasta, darts and pool; no spirits, live music several nights a week *(Martin Corey)*

West Chester

Iron Hill [W Gay St; Pennsylvania]: Good generous competitively priced fresh food inc imaginative dishes, good beers brewed here inc interesting experimental brews, some live entertainment; other branches opening on Pennsylvania/Delaware border *(PACW)*

Wilmington

John Harvards Brew House [Rte 202, opp Doubletree Inn; Delaware]: Convenient for local hotels, with good food and a good range of beers *(anon)*

Special Interest Lists

Pubs with Good Gardens
The pubs listed here have bigger or more beautiful gardens, grounds or terraces than are usual for their areas. Note that in a town or city this might be very much more modest than the sort of garden that would deserve a listing in the countryside.

Bedfordshire
Milton Bryan, Red Lion
Ridgmont, Rose & Crown
Riseley, Fox & Hounds

Berkshire
Aldworth, Bell
Ashmore Green, Sun in the Wood
Crazies Hill, Horns
Frilsham, Pot Kiln
Hamstead Marshall, White Hart
Holyport, Belgian Arms
Marsh Benham, Red House
Waltham St Lawrence, Bell
West Ilsley, Harrow
Winterbourne, Winterbourne Arms

Buckinghamshire
Bolter End, Peacock
Ford, Dinton Hermit
Hambleden, Stag & Huntsman
Skirmett, Frog
Waddesdon, Five Arrows
Weston Underwood, Cowpers Oak

Cambridgeshire
Elton, Black Horse
Fowlmere, Chequers
Heydon, King William IV
Madingley, Three Horseshoes
Swavesey, Trinity Foot
Wansford, Haycock

Cheshire
Aldford, Grosvenor Arms
Bell o' th' Hill, Blue Bell
Bunbury, Dysart Arms
Lower Peover, Bells of Peover
Macclesfield, Sutton Hall Hotel
Weston, White Lion
Whiteley Green, Windmill

Cornwall
Helford, Shipwrights Arms
Philleigh, Roseland
St Agnes, Turks Head
St Kew, St Kew Inn
St Mawgan, Falcon
Tresco, New Inn

Cumbria
Barbon, Barbon Inn
Bassenthwaite Lake, Pheasant
Bouth, White Hart

Derbyshire
Birch Vale, Waltzing Weasel
Buxton, Bull i' th' Thorn
Hathersage, Plough
Melbourne, John Thompson
Woolley Moor, White Horse

Devon
Avonwick, Avon
Berrynarbor, Olde Globe
Broadhembury, Drewe Arms
Clyst Hydon, Five Bells
Cornworthy, Hunters Lodge
Dartington, Cott
Exeter, Imperial
Exminster, Turf Hotel
Haytor Vale, Rock
Lower Ashton, Manor Inn
Lydford, Castle Inn
Newton Abbot, Two Mile Oak
Sidford, Blue Ball
South Zeal, Oxenham Arms

Dorset
Christchurch, Fishermans Haunt
Corfe Castle, Fox
Plush, Brace of Pheasants
Shave Cross, Shave Cross Inn
Sturminster Newton, Swan
Tarrant Monkton, Langton Arms
West Bexington, Manor Hotel

Essex
Castle Hedingham, Bell
Chappel, Swan
Coggeshall, Compasses
Feering, Sun
Great Yeldham, White Hart
Hastingwood, Rainbow & Dove
Mill Green, Viper
Nounsley, Sportsmans Arms
Paglesham, Plough & Sail
Stock, Hoop
Wendens Ambo, Bell

Gloucestershire
Blaisdon, Red Hart
Brockhampton, Craven Arms
Ewen, Wild Duck
Great Rissington, Lamb
Gretton, Royal Oak
Kilkenny, Kilkeney Inn
Kingscote, Hunters Hall
Nailsworth, Egypt Mill
North Nibley, New Inn
Old Sodbury, Dog
Tewkesbury, Olde Black Bear
Withington, Mill Inn

Hampshire
Alresford, Globe
Bramdean, Fox
Itchen Abbas, Trout
North Gorley, Royal Oak
Ovington, Bush
Owslebury, Ship
Petersfield, White Horse
Steep, Harrow
Tichborne, Tichborne Arms
Whitsbury, Cartwheel
Woodgreen, Horse & Groom

Herefordshire
Aymestrey, Riverside Inn
Much Marcle, Slip Tavern
Sellack, Lough Pool
Ullingswick, Three Crowns
Woolhope, Butchers Arms

Hertfordshire
Ayot St Lawrence, Brocket Arms
Little Hadham, Nags Head
Perry Green, Hoops
Potters Crouch, Holly Bush
Sarratt, Boot
St Albans, Rose & Crown

Isle of Wight
Chale, Clarendon (Wight Mouse)
Shorwell, Crown

Kent
Biddenden, Three Chimneys
Bough Beech, Wheatsheaf
Boyden Gate, Gate Inn
Chiddingstone, Castle
Dargate, Dove
Fordcombe, Chafford Arms
Groombridge, Crown
Ickham, Duke William
Newnham, George
Penshurst, Bottle House
Ringlestone, Ringlestone
Selling, Rose & Crown
Toys Hill, Fox & Hounds
Ulcombe, Pepper Box

Lancashire
Darwen, Old Rosins
Newton, Parkers Arms
Whitewell, Inn at Whitewell

Leicestershire
Barrowden, Exeter Arms
Braunston, Old Plough
Exton, Fox & Hounds
Medbourne, Nevill Arms
Old Dalby, Crown

Lincolnshire
Coningsby, Lea Gate Inn
Lincoln, Victoria
Newton, Red Lion
Stamford, George of
  Stamford

Norfolk
Brancaster Staithe, Jolly
  Sailors
Letheringsett, Kings Head
Reedham, Ferry Inn
Ringstead, Gin Trap
Snettisham, Rose & Crown
Stow Bardolph, Hare Arms
Titchwell, Manor Hotel
Woodbastwick, Fur &
  Feather

Northamptonshire
East Haddon, Red Lion
Farthingstone, Kings Arms

Northumbria
Anick, Rat
Belford, Blue Bell
Blanchland, Lord Crewe
  Arms
Diptonmill, Dipton Mill Inn
Dunstan, Cottage
Greta Bridge, Morritt Arms
Thropton, Three Wheat
  Heads

Nottinghamshire
Caunton, Caunton Beck
Colston Bassett, Martins
  Arms
Kimberley, Nelson &
  Railway
Nottingham, Via Fossa
Upton, French Horn
Walkeringham, Three Horse
  Shoes

Oxfordshire
Binfield Heath, Bottle &
  Glass
Broadwell, Five Bells
Burford, Lamb
Chalgrove, Red Lion
Chinnor, Sir Charles Napier
Clifton, Duke of
  Cumberlands Head
Finstock, Plough
Fyfield, White Hart
Highmoor, Rising Sun
Hook Norton, Gate Hangs
  High, Pear Tree

Maidensgrove, Five
  Horseshoes
South Stoke, Perch & Pike
Stanton St John, Star
Swalcliffe, Stags Head
Tadpole Bridge, Trout
Watlington, Chequers
Woodstock, Feathers

Shropshire
Bishop's Castle, Castle Hotel,
  Three Tuns
Cressage, Cholmondeley
  Riverside
Heathton, Old Gate
Hopton Wafers, Crown
Norton, Hundred House

Somerset
Axbridge, Lamb
Combe Hay, Wheatsheaf
Compton Martin, Ring o'
  Bells
Freshford, Inn at Freshford
Monksilver, Notley Arms
Rowberrow, Swan
Shepton Montague,
  Montague Inn
South Stoke, Pack Horse

Staffordshire
Onecote, Jervis Arms
Salt, Holly Bush

Suffolk
Bildeston, Crown
Brome, Cornwallis
Dennington, Queens Head
Hundon, Plough
Lavenham, Angel, Swan
Laxfield, Kings Head
Rede, Plough
Walberswick, Bell
Westleton, Crown

Surrey
Charleshill, Donkey
Compton, Withies
Hascombe, White Horse
Mickleham, King William IV
Pirbright, Royal Oak
Worplesdon, Jolly Farmer

Sussex
Alfriston, George
Amberley, Black Horse
Ashurst, Fountain
Berwick, Cricketers Arms
Blackboys, Blackboys Inn
Byworth, Black Horse
Danehill, Coach & Horses
Elsted, Three Horseshoes
Firle, Ram
Fletching, Griffin
Fulking, Shepherd & Dog
Hammerpot, Woodmans
  Arms
Heathfield, Star
Henley, Duke of Cumberland
  Arms
Houghton, George & Dragon

Milton Street, Sussex Ox
Oving, Gribble Inn
Rushlake Green, Horse &
  Groom
Scaynes Hill, Sloop
Seaford, Golden Galleon
Singleton, Fox & Hounds
Wineham, Royal Oak

Warwickshire
Edge Hill, Castle
Ilmington, Howard Arms

Wiltshire
Alvediston, Crown
Berwick St James, Boot
Bradford-on-Avon, Cross
  Guns
Brinkworth, Three Crowns
Chicksgrove, Compasses
Ebbesbourne Wake,
  Horseshoe
Lacock, George, Rising Sun
Little Cheverell, Owl
Netherhampton, Victoria &
  Albert
Norton, Vine Tree
Salisbury, New Inn
Seend, Barge
Woodborough, Seven Stars

Worcestershire
Bretforton, Fleece
Welland, Anchor

Yorkshire
East Witton, Blue Lion
Egton Bridge, Horse Shoe
Heath, Kings Arms
Penistone, Cubley Hall
Scawton, Hare
Sutton upon Derwent, St
  Vincent Arms

London
East London, Prospect of
  Whitby
North London, Spaniards
  Inn
South London, Crown &
  Greyhound, Founders
  Arms, Ship
West London, Colton Arms,
  Dove, White Swan,
  Windsor Castle

Scotland
Ardfern, Galley of Lorne
Arduaine, Loch Melfort
  Hotel
Badachro, Badachro Inn
Creebridge, Creebridge
  House Hotel
Edinburgh, Starbank
Gifford, Tweeddale Arms
Glenelg, Glenelg Inn
Haddington, Waterside
Kilmahog, Lade
Pitlochry, Killiecrankie
  Hotel

Skeabost, Skeabost House
  Hotel
Thornhill, Lion & Unicorn

Wales
Aberystwyth, Halfway Inn
Bodfari, Dinorben Arms
Crickhowell, Bear, Nantyffin
  Cider Mill
Llandrindod Wells, Llanerch
Llangedwyn, Green
Llangynidr, Coach & Horses
Llwyndafydd, Crown
Mold, Glasfryn
Old Radnor, Harp
Presteigne, Radnorshire Arms
Rosebush, Tafarn Sinc
St Hilary, Bush
Stackpole, Armstrong Arms
Ty'n-y-groes, Groes

Channel Islands
King's Mills, Fleur du Jardin
Rozel, Rozel Bay Hotel

Waterside Pubs
*The pubs listed here are right
beside the sea, a sizeable
river, canal, lake or loch that
contributes significantly to
their attraction.*

Bedfordshire
Linslade, Globe
Odell, Bell

Berkshire
Great Shefford, Swan

Cambridgeshire
Cambridge, Anchor
Sutton Gault, Anchor
Wansford, Haycock

Cheshire
Chester, Old Harkers Arms
Wrenbury, Dusty Miller

Cornwall
Bodinnick, Old Ferry
Cremyll, Edgcumbe Arms
Helford, Shipwrights Arms
Mousehole, Ship
Mylor Bridge, Pandora
Polkerris, Rashleigh
Port Isaac, Port Gaverne Inn
Porthallow, Five Pilchards
Porthleven, Ship
St Agnes, Turks Head
St Ives, Sloop
Tresco, New Inn

Cumbria
Ulverston, Bay Horse

Derbyshire
Hathersage, Plough
Shardlow, Old Crown

Devon
Avonwick, Avon
Dartmouth, Royal Castle
  Hotel

Exeter, Double Locks
Exminster, Turf Hotel
Noss Mayo, Ship
Topsham, Passage House
Torcross, Start Bay
Tuckenhay, Maltsters Arms

Dorset
Chideock, Anchor
Lyme Regis, Pilot Boat

Essex
Burnham-on-Crouch, White
  Harte
Chappel, Swan

Gloucestershire
Ashleworth Quay, Boat
Tewkesbury, Olde Black Bear
Withington, Mill Inn

Hampshire
Alresford, Globe
Bursledon, Jolly Sailor
Langstone, Royal Oak
Ovington, Bush
Wherwell, Mayfly

Herefordshire
Aymestrey, Riverside Inn

Isle of Wight
Bembridge, Crab & Lobster
Cowes, Folly
Seaview, Seaview Hotel
Ventnor, Spyglass

Kent
Deal, Kings Head
Faversham, Albion
Oare, Shipwrights Arms

Lancashire
Garstang, Th'Owd Tithebarn
Little Eccleston, Cartford
Liverpool, Baltic Fleet
Manchester, Dukes 92
Whitewell, Inn at Whitewell

Lincolnshire
Brandy Wharf, Cider Centre

Norfolk
Reedham, Ferry Inn

Northamptonshire
Oundle, Mill

Nottinghamshire
Nottingham, Via Fossa

Oxfordshire
Oxford, Isis Tavern
Tadpole Bridge, Trout

Shropshire
Cressage, Cholmondeley
  Riverside
Ludlow, Unicorn
Shrewsbury, Armoury
Whitchurch, Willey Moor
  Lock

Somerset
Churchill, Crown

Staffordshire
Onecote, Jervis Arms

Suffolk
Chelmondiston, Butt &
  Oyster

Warwickshire
Lapworth, Navigation

Wiltshire
Bradford-on-Avon, Cross
  Guns
Seend, Barge

Worcestershire
Wyre Piddle, Anchor

Yorkshire
Hull, Minerva
Newton on Ouse, Dawnay
  Arms
Whitby, Duke of York

London
East London, Grapes,
  Prospect of Whitby
North London, Waterside
South London, Anchor, Bulls
  Head, Cutty Sark,
  Founders Arms, Horniman,
  Ship
West London, Bulls Head,
  Dove, White Swan

Scotland
Ardfern, Galley of Lorne
Arduaine, Loch Melfort
  Hotel
Badachro, Badachro Inn
Carbost, Old Inn
Crinan, Crinan Hotel
Edinburgh, Starbank
Elie, Ship
Fort Augustus, Lock
Glenelg, Glenelg Inn
Haddington, Waterside
Isle of Whithorn, Steam
  Packet
Isle Ornsay, Eilean Iarmain
Kenmore, Kenmore Hotel
Kingholm Quay, Swan
Kippford, Anchor
Plockton, Plockton Hotel
Portpatrick, Crown
Shieldaig, Tigh an Eilean
  Hotel
Skeabost, Skeabost House
  Hotel
St Monance, Seafood
  Restaurant & Bar
Tayvallich, Tayvallich Inn
Ullapool, Ferry Boat

Wales
Aberdovey, Penhelig Arms
Cresswell Quay, Cresselly
  Arms
Little Haven, Swan
Llangedwyn, Green
Llangynidr, Coach & Horses
Pembroke Ferry, Ferry Inn

Pontypool, Open Hearth
Red Wharf Bay, Ship
Talyllyn, Tynycornel

Channel Islands
St Aubin, Old Court House
Inn
St Ouens Bay, La Pulente

Pubs in Attractive Surroundings
These pubs are in unusually attractive or interesting places – lovely countryside, charming villages, occasionally notable town surroundings. Waterside pubs are listed again here only if their other surroundings are special, too.

Bedfordshire
Linslade, Globe

Berkshire
Aldworth, Bell
Frilsham, Pot Kiln
Waltham St Lawrence, Bell

Buckinghamshire
Frieth, Prince Albert
Hambleden, Stag &
Huntsman
Little Hampden, Rising Sun
Skirmett, Frog
Turville, Bull & Butcher
Weston Underwood,
Cowpers Oak

Cambridgeshire
Castor, Fitzwilliam Arms
Elton, Black Horse

Cheshire
Barthomley, White Lion
Bunbury, Dysart Arms
Langley, Leathers Smithy
Lower Peover, Bells of Peover
Whiteley Green, Windmill
Willington, Boot

Cornwall
Chapel Amble, Maltsters
Arms
Helston, Halzephron
Lamorna, Lamorna Wink
Porthallow, Five Pilchards
Ruan Lanihorne, Kings Head
St Agnes, Turks Head
St Breward, Old Inn
St Dominick, Who'd Have
Thought It
St Kew, St Kew Inn
St Mawgan, Falcon
Tresco, New Inn
Trevaunance Cove,
Driftwood Spars

Cumbria
Askham, Punch Bowl
Bassenthwaite Lake, Pheasant
Boot, Burnmoor

Bouth, White Hart
Broughton Mills, Blacksmiths
Arms
Buttermere, Bridge Hotel
Caldbeck, Oddfellows Arms
Chapel Stile, Wainwrights
Coniston, Black Bull, Sun
Crosthwaite, Punch Bowl
Dent, Sun
Elterwater, Britannia
Garrigill, George & Dragon
Grasmere, Travellers Rest
Hawkshead, Drunken Duck,
Kings Arms
Hesket Newmarket, Old
Crown
Ings, Watermill
Langdale, Old Dungeon
Ghyll
Little Langdale, Three Shires
Loweswater, Kirkstile Inn
Melmerby, Shepherds
Seathwaite, Newfield Inn
Troutbeck, Queens Head
Ulverston, Bay Horse
Wasdale Head, Wasdale
Head Inn

Derbyshire
Brassington, Olde Gate
Froggatt Edge, Chequers
Hardwick Hall, Hardwick
Inn
Hathersage, Plough
Kirk Ireton, Barley Mow
Ladybower Reservoir,
Yorkshire Bridge
Little Hucklow, Old Bulls
Head
Litton, Red Lion
Monsal Head, Monsal Head
Hotel
Over Haddon, Lathkil
Woolley Moor, White Horse

Devon
Beer, Dolphin
Blackawton, Normandy
Arms
Branscombe, Fountain Head
Buckland Monachorum,
Drake Manor
Chagford, Ring o' Bells
Exminster, Turf Hotel
Haytor Vale, Rock
Holbeton, Mildmay Colours
Horndon, Elephants Nest
Iddesleigh, Duke of York
Kingston, Dolphin
Knowstone, Masons Arms
Lower Ashton, Manor Inn
Lustleigh, Cleave
Lydford, Castle Inn
Peter Tavy, Peter Tavy Inn
Postbridge, Warren House
Rattery, Church House
Slapton, Tower
Stokenham, Tradesmans
Arms

Two Bridges, Two Bridges
Hotel
Widecombe, Rugglestone
Wonson, Northmore Arms

Dorset
Askerswell, Spyway
Corfe Castle, Fox
Corscombe, Fox
East Chaldon, Sailors
Return
Plush, Brace of Pheasants
Worth Matravers, Square &
Compass

Essex
Fuller Street, Square &
Compasses
Little Dunmow, Flitch of
Bacon
Mill Green, Viper
Paglesham, Plough & Sail

Gloucestershire
Ashleworth Quay, Boat
Bisley, Bear
Bledington, Kings Head
Brockhampton, Craven Arms
Chedworth, Seven Tuns
Chipping Campden, Eight
Bells
Cold Aston, Plough
Coln St Aldwyns, New Inn
Great Rissington, Lamb
Guiting Power, Hollow
Bottom
Miserden, Carpenters Arms
North Nibley, New Inn
Sapperton, Bell
St Briavels, George
Winchcombe, Old Corner
Cupboard

Hampshire
Alresford, Globe
Crawley, Fox & Hounds
East Tytherley, Star
Fritham, Royal Oak
Hawkley, Hawkley Inn
Micheldever, Half Moon &
Spread Eagle
North Gorley, Royal Oak
Ovington, Bush
Petersfield, White Horse
Tichborne, Tichborne Arms
Woodgreen, Horse &
Groom

Herefordshire
Aymestrey, Riverside Inn
Craswall, Bulls Head
Dorstone, Pandy
Much Marcle, Slip Tavern
Ruckhall, Ancient Camp
Sellack, Lough Pool
Titley, Stagg
Walterstone, Carpenters
Arms
Weobley, Salutation
Woolhope, Butchers Arms

Hertfordshire
Aldbury, Greyhound
Sarratt, Cock

Isle of Wight
Chale, Clarendon (Wight Mouse)

Kent
Brookland, Woolpack
Chiddingstone, Castle
Groombridge, Crown
Newnham, George
Selling, Rose & Crown
Toys Hill, Fox & Hounds
Tunbridge Wells, Mount Edgcumbe Hotel

Lancashire
Blackstone Edge, White House
Conder Green, Stork
Downham, Assheton Arms
Entwistle, Strawbury Duck
Fence, Forest
Little Eccleston, Cartford
Newton, Parkers Arms
Uppermill, Church Inn
Whitewell, Inn at Whitewell

Leicestershire
Barrowden, Exeter Arms
Exton, Fox & Hounds
Glooston, Old Barn
Hallaton, Bewicke Arms
Upper Hambleton, Finches Arms

Lincolnshire
Aswarby, Tally Ho

Norfolk
Blakeney, White Horse
Blickling, Buckinghamshire Arms
Brancaster Staithe, Jolly Sailors
Burnham Market, Hoste Arms
Heydon, Earle Arms
Horsey, Nelson Head
Thornham, Lifeboat
Woodbastwick, Fur & Feather

Northamptonshire
Chapel Brampton, Brampton Halt
Harringworth, White Swan

Northumbria
Allenheads, Allenheads Inn
Blanchland, Lord Crewe Arms
Craster, Jolly Fisherman
Diptonmill, Dipton Mill Inn
Great Whittington, Queens Head
Haltwhistle, Milecastle Inn, Wallace Arms
Langley on Tyne, Carts Bog Inn

Matfen, Black Bull
Romaldkirk, Rose & Crown
Stannersburn, Pheasant

Nottinghamshire
Laxton, Dovecote

Oxfordshire
Burford, Mermaid
Chalgrove, Red Lion
Checkendon, Black Horse
Chinnor, Sir Charles Napier
Great Tew, Falkland Arms
Maidensgrove, Five Horseshoes
Oxford, Isis Tavern, Kings Arms, Turf Tavern
Shenington, Bell
Swalcliffe, Stags Head

Shropshire
Bridges, Horseshoe
Cardington, Royal Oak
Wenlock Edge, Wenlock Edge Inn

Somerset
Appley, Globe
Axbridge, Lamb
Batcombe, Three Horseshoes
Blagdon, New Inn
Combe Hay, Wheatsheaf
Cranmore, Strode Arms
Exford, White Horse
Luxborough, Royal Oak
Stogumber, White Horse
Triscombe, Blue Ball
Wells, City Arms
Winsford, Royal Oak

Staffordshire
Alstonefield, George

Suffolk
Dennington, Queens Head
Dunwich, Ship
Lavenham, Angel
Levington, Ship
Snape, Plough & Sail
Walberswick, Bell

Surrey
Abinger Common, Abinger Hatch
Blackbrook, Plough
Cobham, Cricketers
Dunsfold, Sun
Mickleham, King William IV
Reigate Heath, Skimmington Castle

Sussex
Alfriston, George
Amberley, Black Horse
Billingshurst, Blue Ship
Burpham, George & Dragon
Burwash, Bell
East Dean, Tiger
Fletching, Griffin
Fulking, Shepherd & Dog
Heathfield, Star

Henley, Duke of Cumberland Arms
Lurgashall, Noahs Ark
Milton Street, Sussex Ox
Rye, Mermaid
Seaford, Golden Galleon
Wineham, Royal Oak

Warwickshire
Edge Hill, Castle
Himley, Crooked House
Warmington, Plough

Wiltshire
Alvediston, Crown
Axford, Red Lion
Bradford-on-Avon, Cross Guns
Ebbesbourne Wake, Horseshoe
Lacock, Rising Sun
Wootton Rivers, Royal Oak
Wylye, Bell

Worcestershire
Broadway, Crown & Trumpet
Kidderminster, King & Castle
Pensax, Bell

Yorkshire
Appletreewick, Craven Arms
Beck Hole, Birch Hall
Blakey Ridge, Lion
Bradfield, Strines Inn
Buckden, Buck
Burnsall, Red Lion
Byland Abbey, Abbey Inn
Cray, White Lion
East Witton, Blue Lion
Heath, Kings Arms
Hubberholme, George
Langthwaite, Charles Bathurst
Lastingham, Blacksmiths Arms
Levisham, Horseshoe
Litton, Queens Arms
Lund, Wellington
Masham, Kings Head
Middleham, Black Swan
Muker, Farmers Arms
Osmotherley, Golden Lion
Ramsgill, Yorke Arms
Ripley, Boars Head
Robin Hood's Bay, Laurel
Shelley, Three Acres
Starbotton, Fox & Hounds
Terrington, Bay Horse
Thornton Watlass, Buck
Wath in Nidderdale, Sportsmans Arms
Widdop, Pack Horse

London
Central London, Olde Mitre
North London, Spaniards Inn
South London, Crown & Greyhound, Horniman, Windmill

Scotland
Applecross, Applecross Inn
Arduaine, Loch Melfort
  Hotel
Brig o' Turk, Byre
Crinan, Crinan Hotel
Haddington, Waterside
Kenmore, Kenmore Hotel
Kilberry, Kilberry Inn
Kilmahog, Lade
Kingholm Quay, Swan
Mountbenger, Gordon Arms
Pitlochry, Killiecrankie Hotel
Tushielaw, Tushielaw Inn

Wales
Aberystwyth, Halfway Inn
Bosherston, St Govans
  Country Inn
Carew, Carew Inn
Crickhowell, Nantyffin Cider
  Mill
Llanbedr-y-Cennin, Olde Bull
Llanberis, Pen-y-Gwryd
Llangedwyn, Green
Old Radnor, Harp
Red Wharf Bay, Ship
Talyllyn, Tynycornel

Channel Islands
St Brelade, Old Portelet Inn,
  Old Smugglers
St John, Les Fontaines

Pubs with Good Views
*These pubs are listed for their
particularly good views,
either from inside or from a
garden or terrace. Waterside
pubs are listed again here
only if their view is
exceptional in its own right –
not just a straightforward sea
view, for example.*

Berkshire
Chieveley, Blue Boar

Cheshire
Higher Burwardsley,
  Pheasant
Langley, Hanging Gate,
  Leathers Smithy
Overton, Ring o' Bells
Willington, Boot

Cornwall
Cremyll, Edgcumbe Arms
Ruan Lanihorne, Kings Head
St Agnes, Turks Head
St Dominick, Who'd Have
  Thought It

Cumbria
Cartmel Fell, Masons Arms
Hawkshead, Drunken Duck
Langdale, Old Dungeon
  Ghyll
Loweswater, Kirkstile Inn
Troutbeck, Queens Head
Ulverston, Bay Horse

Wasdale Head, Wasdale
  Head Inn

Derbyshire
Foolow, Barrel
Monsal Head, Monsal Head
  Hotel
Over Haddon, Lathkil

Devon
Postbridge, Warren House

Dorset
West Bexington, Manor
  Hotel
Worth Matravers, Square &
  Compass

Gloucestershire
Cranham, Black Horse
Gretton, Royal Oak
Kilkenny, Kilkeney Inn
Sheepscombe, Butchers Arms

Hampshire
Beauworth, Milbury's
Owslebury, Ship

Herefordshire
Ruckhall, Ancient Camp

Isle of Wight
Bembridge, Crab & Lobster
Carisbrooke, Blacksmiths
  Arms
Ventnor, Spyglass

Kent
Penshurst, Spotted Dog
Tunbridge Wells, Beacon
Ulcombe, Pepper Box

Lancashire
Blackstone Edge, White
  House
Darwen, Old Rosins
Entwistle, Strawbury Duck
Newton, Parkers Arms
Uppermill, Church Inn

Leicestershire
Loughborough, Swan in the
  Rushes
Saddington, Queens Head

Norfolk
Blickling, Buckinghamshire
  Arms

Northumbria
Anick, Rat
Haltwhistle, Wallace Arms
Seahouses, Olde Ship
Thropton, Three Wheat
  Heads

Oxfordshire
Cuddesdon, Bat & Ball

Shropshire
Cressage, Cholmondeley
  Riverside

Somerset
Blagdon, New Inn

Shepton Montague,
  Montague Inn

Suffolk
Erwarton, Queens Head
Hundon, Plough
Levington, Ship

Sussex
Amberley, Sportsmans
Byworth, Black Horse
Elsted, Three Horseshoes
Fletching, Griffin
Henley, Duke of Cumberland
  Arms
Houghton, George &
  Dragon
Icklesham, Queens Head
Milton Street, Sussex Ox

Wiltshire
Axford, Red Lion
Box, Quarrymans Arms
Lacock, Rising Sun

Worcestershire
Pensax, Bell
Wyre Piddle, Anchor

Yorkshire
Appletreewick, Craven Arms
Blakey Ridge, Lion
Bradfield, Strines Inn
Kirkham, Stone Trough
Langthwaite, Charles
  Bathurst
Litton, Queens Arms
Shelley, Three Acres
Whitby, Duke of York

London
South London, Anchor,
  Founders Arms

Scotland
Applecross, Applecross Inn
Badachro, Badachro Inn
Crinan, Crinan Hotel
Cromarty, Royal
Edinburgh, Starbank
Glenelg, Glenelg Inn
Isle Ornsay, Eilean Iarmain
Kilberry, Kilberry Inn
Pitlochry, Killiecrankie
  Hotel
Shieldaig, Tigh an Eilean
  Hotel
Tushielaw, Tushielaw Inn
Ullapool, Ferry Boat
Weem, Ailean Chraggan

Wales
Aberdovey, Penhelig Arms
Aberystwyth, Halfway Inn
Bodfari, Dinorben Arms
Halkyn, Britannia
Llanbedr-y-Cennin, Olde Bull
Llanberis, Pen-y-Gwryd
Llanferres, Druid
Llangynwyd, Old House
Llannefydd, Hawk & Buckle
Mold, Glasfryn

Old Radnor, Harp
Talyllyn, Tynycornel
Ty'n-y-groes, Groes

Channel Islands
St Aubin, Old Court House
Inn

Pubs in Interesting Buildings
*Pubs and inns are listed here
for the particular interest of
their building – something
really out of the ordinary to
look at, or occasionally a
building that has an
outstandingly interesting
historical background.*

Berkshire
Cookham, Bel & the Dragon

Buckinghamshire
Forty Green, Royal Standard
of England

Derbyshire
Buxton, Bull i' th' Thorn

Devon
Dartmouth, Cherub
Harberton, Church House
Rattery, Church House
Sourton, Highwayman
South Zeal, Oxenham Arms

Hampshire
Beauworth, Milbury's

Lancashire
Garstang, Th'Owd
Tithebarn
Liverpool, Philharmonic
Dining Rooms

Lincolnshire
Stamford, George of
Stamford

Northumbria
Blanchland, Lord Crewe
Arms

Nottinghamshire
Nottingham, Olde Trip to
Jerusalem, Via Fossa

Oxfordshire
Banbury, Reindeer
Fyfield, White Hart

Somerset
Norton St Philip, George

Suffolk
Lavenham, Swan

Sussex
Rye, Mermaid

Warwickshire
Himley, Crooked House

Wiltshire
Salisbury, Haunch of Venison

Worcestershire
Bretforton, Fleece

Yorkshire
Hull, Olde White Harte

London
Central London, Black Friar,
Cittie of Yorke
South London, George

Scotland
Edinburgh, Café Royal,
Guildford Arms

**Pubs that Brew their
Own Beer**
*The pubs listed here brew
their own beer on the
premises; many others not
listed have beers brewed for
them specially, sometimes an
individual recipe (but by a
separate brewer). We
mention these in the text.*

Berkshire
Frilsham, Pot Kiln

Cambridgeshire
Peterborough, Brewery Tap

Cornwall
Helston, Blue Anchor
Trevaunance Cove,
Driftwood Spars

Cumbria
Cartmel Fell, Masons Arms
Cockermouth, Bitter End
Coniston, Black Bull
Dent, Sun
Hawkshead, Drunken Duck
Hesket Newmarket, Old
Crown
Tirril, Queens Head

Derbyshire
Derby, Brunswick
Melbourne, John Thompson

Devon
Branscombe, Fountain Head
Hatherleigh, Tally Ho
Newton St Cyres, Beer
Engine

Hampshire
Cheriton, Flower Pots
Southsea, Wine Vaults

Herefordshire
Aymestrey, Riverside Inn

Kent
West Peckham, Swan

Lancashire
Manchester, Lass o' Gowrie,
Marble Arch
Uppermill, Church Inn

Leicestershire
Barrowden, Exeter Arms
East Langton, Bell

Oakham, Grainstore
Somerby, Old Brewery

Lincolnshire
South Witham, Blue Cow

Northumbria
Diptonmill, Dipton Mill Inn

Nottinghamshire
Nottingham, Fellows Morton
& Clayton

Shropshire
Bishop's Castle, Six Bells,
Three Tuns
Wistanstow, Plough

Staffordshire
Burton upon Trent, Burton
Bridge Inn
Eccleshall, George

Suffolk
Earl Soham, Victoria

Sussex
Oving, Gribble Inn
Pett, Two Sawyers
Seaford, Golden Galleon

Warwickshire
Sedgley, Beacon
Shustoke, Griffin

Yorkshire
Cropton, New Inn
Ledsham, Chequers
Linthwaite, Sair
Sheffield, Fat Cat

Scotland
Houston, Fox & Hounds
Pitlochry, Moulin

Wales
Abercych, Nags Head

**Open All Day (at least in
summer)**
*We list here all the pubs that
have told us they plan to stay
open all day, even if it's only
Saturday. We've included the
few pubs which close just for
half an hour to an hour, and
the many more, chiefly in
holiday areas, which open all
day only in summer. The
individual entries for the pubs
themselves show the actual
details.*

Bedfordshire
Biggleswade, Brown Bear
Linslade, Globe
Stanbridge, Five Bells

Berkshire
Boxford, Bell
Cookham, Bel & the Dragon
Hare Hatch, Queen Victoria
Inkpen, Swan
Peasemore, Fox & Hounds

Reading, Sweeney & Todd
Sonning, Bull
Swallowfield, George &
Dragon
West Ilsley, Harrow
Woodside, Rose & Crown

Buckinghamshire
Easington, Mole & Chicken
Skirmett, Frog
Wooburn Common,
Chequers

Cambridgeshire
Cambridge, Anchor, Eagle
Peterborough, Brewery Tap,
Charters
Wansford, Haycock

Cheshire
Aldford, Grosvenor Arms
Astbury, Egerton Arms
Barthomley, White Lion
Bunbury, Dysart Arms
Chester, Old Harkers Arms
Cotebrook, Fox & Barrel
Daresbury, Ring o' Bells
Higher Burwardsley,
Pheasant
Langley, Leathers Smithy
Lower Peover, Bells of Peover
Macclesfield, Sutton Hall
Hotel
Nantwich, Crown
Peover Heath, Dog
Plumley, Smoker
Tarporley, Rising Sun
Whitegate, Plough
Whiteley Green, Windmill
Willington, Boot

Cornwall
Bodinnick, Old Ferry
Cremyll, Edgcumbe Arms
Edmonton, Quarryman
Helston, Blue Anchor
Lamorna, Lamorna Wink
Lostwithiel, Royal Oak
Mitchell, Plume of Feathers
Mithian, Miners Arms
Mousehole, Ship
Mylor Bridge, Pandora
Polperro, Old Mill House
Port Isaac, Golden Lion, Port
Gaverne Inn
Porthleven, Ship
St Agnes, Turks Head
St Ives, Sloop
St Kew, St Kew Inn
St Mawes, Victory
Tresco, New Inn
Truro, Old Ale House

Cumbria
Ambleside, Golden Rule
Askham, Punch Bowl
Broughton Mills, Blacksmiths
Arms
Buttermere, Bridge Hotel
Caldbeck, Oddfellows Arms

Cartmel Fell, Masons Arms
Chapel Stile, Wainwrights
Coniston, Black Bull
Coniston, Sun
Crook, Sun
Crosthwaite, Punch Bowl
Dent, Sun
Elterwater, Britannia
Garrigill, George & Dragon
Grasmere, Travellers Rest
Hawkshead, Kings Arms
Heversham, Blue Bell
Keswick, Dog & Gun
Kirkby Lonsdale, Snooty Fox
Langdale, Old Dungeon
Ghyll
Little Langdale, Three Shires
Loweswater, Kirkstile Inn
Penrith, Agricultural
Seathwaite, Newfield Inn
Sedbergh, Dalesman
Threlkeld, Salutation
Tirril, Queens Head
Troutbeck, Queens Head
Ulverston, Bay Horse,
Farmers Arms
Wasdale Head, Wasdale
Head Inn

Derbyshire
Ashbourne, Smiths Tavern
Beeley, Devonshire Arms
Buxton, Bull i' th' Thorn, Old
Sun
Buxworth, Navigation
Castleton, Castle Hotel
Derby, Alexandra
Derby, Brunswick, Olde
Dolphin
Eyam, Miners Arms
Fenny Bentley, Coach &
Horses
Foolow, Barrel
Froggatt Edge, Chequers
Hardwick Hall, Hardwick
Inn
Hathersage, Plough
Hope, Cheshire Cheese
Ladybower Reservoir,
Yorkshire Bridge
Litton, Red Lion
Monsal Head, Monsal Head
Hotel
Over Haddon, Lathkil
Shardlow, Old Crown
Wardlow, Three Stags Heads
Whittington Moor, Derby
Tup
Woolley Moor, White Horse

Devon
Branscombe, Masons Arms
Cockwood, Anchor
Dartington, Cott
Dartmouth, Cherub, Royal
Castle Hotel
Exeter, Double Locks,
Imperial, White Hart
Exminster, Turf Hotel

Haytor Vale, Rock
Horns Cross, Hoops
Iddesleigh, Duke of York
Lustleigh, Cleave
Lydford, Castle Inn
Newton Abbot, Two Mile
Oak
Newton St Cyres, Beer
Engine
Noss Mayo, Ship
Postbridge, Warren House
Sidford, Blue Ball
Stoke Gabriel, Church House
Topsham, Passage House
Torcross, Start Bay
Tuckenhay, Maltsters Arms
Two Bridges, Two Bridges
Hotel
Ugborough, Anchor
Wonson, Northmore Arms
Woodland, Rising Sun

Dorset
Ansty, Fox
Askerswell, Spyway
Bridport, George
Burton Bradstock, Anchor
Chideock, Anchor
Christchurch, Fishermans
Haunt
Corfe Castle, Greyhound
East Chaldon, Sailors Return
Furzehill, Stocks
Lyme Regis, Pilot Boat
Sturminster Newton, Swan
Tarrant Monkton, Langton
Arms
West Bexington, Manor
Hotel
Worth Matravers, Square &
Compass

Essex
Burnham-on-Crouch, White
Harte
Chappel, Swan
Moreton, White Hart
Stock, Hoop
Stow Maries, Prince of Wales
Wendens Ambo, Bell

Gloucestershire
Awre, Red Hart
Barnsley, Village Pub
Bisley, Bear
Brimpsfield, Golden Heart
Broad Campden, Bakers
Arms
Chedworth, Seven Tuns
Chipping Campden, Eight
Bells
Coln St Aldwyns, New Inn
Ewen, Wild Duck
Ford, Plough
Guiting Power, Hollow
Bottom
Kingscote, Hunters Hall
Littleton-upon-Severn, White
Hart

North Nibley, New Inn
Old Sodbury, Dog
Oldbury-on-Severn, Anchor
Sheepscombe, Butchers Arms
Tetbury, Gumstool
Winchcombe, Old Corner
  Cupboard
Withington, Mill Inn
Woodchester, Royal Oak

Hampshire
Bentworth, Sun
Boldre, Red Lion
Bursledon, Jolly Sailor
Droxford, White Horse
Fritham, Royal Oak
Itchen Abbas, Trout
Langstone, Royal Oak
North Gorley, Royal Oak
Owslebury, Ship
Petersfield, White Horse
Rotherwick, Coach & Horses
Southsea, Wine Vaults
Wherwell, Mayfly
Winchester, Wykeham Arms

Herefordshire
Aymestrey, Riverside Inn
Craswall, Bulls Head
Dorstone, Pandy
Ledbury, Feathers
Lugwardine, Crown &
  Anchor
Walterstone, Carpenters
  Arms
Weobley, Salutation

Hertfordshire
Aldbury, Greyhound, Valiant
  Trooper
Ashwell, Three Tuns
Ayot St Lawrence, Brocket
  Arms
Bricket Wood, Moor Mill
Hertford, White Horse
Knebworth, Lytton Arms
Perry Green, Hoops
Sarratt, Cock
Watton-at-Stone, George &
  Dragon

Isle of Wight
Arreton, White Lion
Bembridge, Crab & Lobster
Carisbrooke, Blacksmiths
  Arms
Chale, Clarendon (Wight
  Mouse)
Cowes, Folly
Rookley, Chequers
Shalfleet, New Inn
Ventnor, Spyglass

Kent
Bough Beech, Wheatsheaf
Chiddingstone, Castle
Deal, Kings Head
Fordcombe, Chafford Arms
Groombridge, Crown
Hawkhurst, Queens

Iden Green, Woodcock
Ightham, George & Dragon
Ightham Common, Harrow
Langton Green, Hare
Oare, Shipwrights Arms
Penshurst, Bottle House,
  Spotted Dog
Ringlestone, Ringlestone
Smarden, Chequers
Tunbridge Wells, Beacon,
  Mount Edgcumbe Hotel,
  Sankeys

Lancashire
Bispham Green, Eagle &
  Child
Blackstone Edge, White
  House
Chipping, Dog & Partridge
Conder Green, Stork
Croston, Black Horse
Darwen, Old Rosins
Entwistle, Strawbury Duck
Fence, Forest
Garstang, Th'Owd Tithebarn
Goosnargh, Horns
Little Eccleston, Cartford
Liverpool, Baltic Fleet,
  Philharmonic Dining
  Rooms
Longridge, Derby Arms
Lytham, Taps
Manchester, Britons
  Protection, Dukes 92, Lass
  o' Gowrie, Marble Arch,
  Royal Oak
Newton, Parkers Arms
Raby, Wheatsheaf
Ribchester, White Bull
Stalybridge, Station Buffet
Uppermill, Church Inn
Yealand Conyers, New Inn

Leicestershire
Belmesthorpe, Blue Bell
Braunston, Old Plough
Clipsham, Olive Branch
Empingham, White Horse
Hallaton, Bewicke Arms
Loughborough, Swan in the
  Rushes
Newton Burgoland, Belper
  Arms
Oakham, Grainstore
Somerby, Old Brewery
Stretton, Ram Jam Inn
Upper Hambleton, Finches
  Arms
Wing, Kings Arms

Lincolnshire
Grantham, Beehive
Lincoln, Victoria, Wig &
  Mitre
South Witham, Blue Cow
Stamford, Daniel Lambert,
  George of Stamford

Norfolk
Bawburgh, Kings Head

Blakeney, Kings Arms
Brancaster Staithe, Jolly
  Sailors, White Horse
Burnham Market, Hoste
  Arms
Larling, Angel
Letheringsett, Kings Head
Mundford, Crown
Norwich, Adam & Eve, Fat
  Cat
Reedham, Ferry Inn, Railway
  Tavern, Old Brewery
  House
Snettisham, Rose & Crown
Swanton Morley, Darbys
Thornham, Lifeboat
Tivetshall St Mary, Old Ram
Upper Sheringham, Red Lion
Winterton-on-Sea,
  Fishermans Return

Northamptonshire
Chacombe, George &
  Dragon
Chapel Brampton, Brampton
  Halt
Oundle, Mill, Ship

Northumbria
Allendale, Kings Head
Blanchland, Lord Crewe
  Arms
Carterway Heads, Manor
  House Inn
Craster, Jolly Fisherman
Greta Bridge, Morritt Arms
Haltwhistle, Wallace Arms
Matfen, Black Bull
New York, Shiremoor
  Farm
Newcastle upon Tyne,
  Crown Posada
Seahouses, Olde Ship
Shincliffe, Seven Stars
Thropton, Three Wheat
  Heads

Nottinghamshire
Beeston, Victoria
Caunton, Caunton Beck
Elkesley, Robin Hood
Kimberley, Nelson &
  Railway
Nottingham, Fellows Morton
  & Clayton, Lincolnshire
  Poacher, Olde Trip to
  Jerusalem, Vat & Fiddle,
  Via Fossa
Upton, French Horn

Oxfordshire
Banbury, Reindeer
Burford, Mermaid
Chipping Norton, Chequers
Cuddesdon, Bat & Ball
Cuxham, Half Moon
Exlade Street, Highwayman
Finstock, Plough
Great Tew, Falkland Arms
Hook Norton, Pear Tree

Maidensgrove, Five
  Horseshoes
Oxford, Isis Tavern, Kings
  Arms, Turf Tavern
Shipton-under-Wychwood,
  Lamb
South Stoke, Perch & Pike
Stanton St John, Talk House
Thame, Swan
Wootton, Kings Head

Shropshire
Bishop's Castle, Three Tuns
Bridges, Horseshoe
Bromfield, Cookhouse
Ironbridge, Malthouse
Norton, Hundred House
Shrewsbury, Armoury
Wentnor, Crown

Somerset
Bath, Old Green Tree
Churchill, Crown
Clapton-in-Gordano, Black
  Horse
Exford, White Horse
Huish Episcopi, Rose &
  Crown
Norton St Philip, George
Rudge, Full Moon
South Stoke, Pack Horse
Sparkford, Sparkford Inn
Stanton Wick, Carpenters
  Arms
Wells, City Arms

Staffordshire
Alstonefield, George
Eccleshall, George
Onecote, Jervis Arms
Salt, Holly Bush

Suffolk
Brome, Cornwallis
Butley, Oyster
Chelmondiston, Butt &
  Oyster
Cotton, Trowel & Hammer
Lavenham, Angel
Laxfield, Kings Head
Snape, Plough & Sail
Walberswick, Bell

Surrey
Abinger Common, Abinger
  Hatch
Betchworth, Dolphin, Red
  Lion
Elstead, Woolpack
Hascombe, White Horse
Laleham, Anglers Retreat
Leigh, Plough
Pirbright, Royal Oak
Reigate Heath, Skimmington
  Castle

Sussex
Alfriston, George
Amberley, Black Horse,
  Bridge
Barnham, Murrell Arms

Berwick, Cricketers Arms
Burwash, Bell
Chiddingly, Six Bells
East Dean, Tiger
Fairwarp, Foresters Arms
Firle, Ram
Fletching, Griffin
Fulking, Shepherd & Dog
Hartfield, Anchor
Horsham, Black Jug
Houghton, George & Dragon
Icklesham, Queens Head
Kingston Near Lewes, Juggs
Lewes, Snowdrop
Oving, Gribble Inn
Pett, Two Sawyers
Punnetts Town, Three Cups
Rye, Mermaid
Scaynes Hill, Sloop
Seaford, Golden Galleon
West Ashling, Richmond
  Arms
Wilmington, Giants Rest

Warwickshire
Aston Cantlow, Kings Head
Berkswell, Bear
Birmingham, Fiddle & Bone,
  Tap & Spile
Brierley Hill, Vine
Coventry, Old Windmill
Dunchurch, Dun Cow
Edge Hill, Castle
Hatton, Falcon
Himley, Crooked House
Lapworth, Navigation
Stratford-upon-Avon,
  Garrick

Wiltshire
Box, Quarrymans Arms
Bradford-on-Avon, Cross
  Guns
Devizes, Bear
Fonthill Gifford, Beckford
  Arms
Hindon, Grosvenor Arms,
  Lamb
Lacock, George, Red Lion,
  Rising Sun
Malmesbury, Smoking Dog
Netherhampton, Victoria &
  Albert
Norton, Vine Tree
Salisbury, Haunch of
  Venison, New Inn, Old Ale
  House
Seend, Barge
Semley, Benett Arms
Sherston, Rattlebone

Worcestershire
Bewdley, Little Pack Horse
Bretforton, Fleece
Broadway, Crown &
  Trumpet
Forhill, Peacock
Kempsey, Walter de
  Cantelupe

Kidderminster, King & Castle
Ombersley, Crown & Sandys
  Arms, Kings Arms
Pensax, Bell

Yorkshire
Asenby, Crab & Lobster
Aysgarth, George &
  Dragon
Beck Hole, Birch Hall
Beverley, White Horse
Blakey Ridge, Lion
Boroughbridge, Black Bull
Bradfield, Strines Inn
Buckden, Buck
Burnsall, Red Lion
Coxwold, Fauconberg Arms
Cray, White Lion
Crayke, Durham Ox
Cropton, New Inn
East Witton, Blue Lion
Egton Bridge, Horse Shoe
Ferrensby, General Tarleton
Harome, Star
Heath, Kings Arms
Heckmondwike, Old Hall
Hubberholme, George
Hull, Minerva, Olde White
  Harte
Kettlesing, Queens Head
Kirkbymoorside, George &
  Dragon
Langthwaite, Charles
  Bathurst
Ledsham, Chequers
Leeds, Whitelocks
Linthwaite, Sair
Linton, Windmill
Masham, Kings Head
Muker, Farmers Arms
Osmotherley, Golden Lion
Penistone, Cubley Hall
Pickering, White Swan
Pickhill, Nags Head
Pool, White Hart
Ripley, Boars Head
Ripponden, Old Bridge
Robin Hood's Bay, Laurel
Settle, Golden Lion
Sheffield, New Barrack
Thorganby, Jefferson Arms
Thornton Watlass, Buck
Wass, Wombwell Arms
Whitby, Duke of York
Widdop, Pack Horse
York, Tap & Spile

London
Central London, Albert,
  Archery Tavern, Argyll
  Arms, Bishops Finger,
  Black Friar, Cittie of Yorke,
  Cross Keys, Dog & Duck,
  Eagle, Grapes, Grenadier,
  Guinea, Jerusalem Tavern,
  Lamb, Lamb & Flag, Lord
  Moon of the Mall, Moon
  Under Water, Museum
  Tavern, Nags Head,

O'Hanlons, Old Bank of England, Olde Cheshire Cheese, Olde Mitre, Red Lion, Seven Stars, Star, Westminster Arms

East London, Prospect of Whitby

North London, Chapel, Compton Arms, Flask, Holly Bush, Olde White Bear, Spaniards Inn, Waterside

South London, Alma, Anchor, Bulls Head, Crown & Greyhound, Cutty Sark, Fire Station, Founders Arms, George, Horniman, Market Porter, Ship, White Cross, Windmill

West London, both Anglesea Arms, Atlas, Bulls Head, Churchill Arms, Dove, Havelock Tavern, White Horse, White Swan, Windsor Castle

Scotland

Aberdeen, Prince of Wales
Applecross, Applecross Inn
Ardfern, Galley of Lorne
Arduaine, Loch Melfort Hotel
Badachro, Badachro Inn
Brig o' Turk, Byre
Broughty Ferry, Fishermans Tavern
Carbost, Old Inn
Cawdor, Cawdor Tavern
Crinan, Crinan Hotel
Cromarty, Royal
Edinburgh, Abbotsford, Bow Bar, Café Royal, Guildford Arms, Kays Bar, Starbank
Elie, Ship
Fort Augustus, Lock
Gairloch, Old Inn
Gifford, Tweeddale Arms
Glasgow, Auctioneers, Babbity Bowster, Counting House
Glendevon, Tormaukin
Haddington, Waterside
Houston, Fox & Hounds
Innerleithen, Traquair Arms
Inveraray, George
Inverarnan, Inverarnan Inn
Isle of Whithorn, Steam Packet
Isle Ornsay, Eilean Iarmain
Kelso, Queens Head
Kenmore, Kenmore Hotel
Kilberry, Kilberry Inn
Kilmahog, Lade
Kingholm Quay, Swan
Kippen, Cross Keys
Kippford, Anchor
Kirkton of Glenisla, Glenisla Hotel

Linlithgow, Four Marys
Lybster, Portland Arms
Mountbenger, Gordon Arms
Oban, Oban Inn
Pitlochry, Moulin
Plockton, Plockton Hotel
Portpatrick, Crown
Shieldaig, Tigh an Eilean Hotel
St Monance, Seafood Restaurant & Bar
Stonehaven, Lairhillock
Tayvallich, Tayvallich Inn
Thornhill, Lion & Unicorn
Ullapool, Ceilidh Place Ferry Boat, Morefield Motel
Weem, Ailean Chraggan

Wales

Abercych, Nags Head
Beaumaris, Olde Bulls Head
Bodfari, Dinorben Arms
Carew, Carew Inn
Cresswell Quay, Cresselly Arms
East Aberthaw, Blue Anchor
Graianrhyd, Rose & Crown
Gresford, Pant-yr-Ochain
Halkyn, Britannia
Hay-on-Wye, Kilverts, Old Black Lion
Llanberis, Pen-y-Gwryd
Llandeilo, Castle
Llandrindod Wells, Llanerch
Llandudno Junction, Queens Head
Llanferres, Druid
Llangedwyn, Green
Llangynidr, Coach & Horses
Llangynwyd, Old House
Mold, Glasfryn
Monknash, Plough & Harrow
Pontypool, Open Hearth
Porthgain, Sloop
Porthmadog, Ship
Presteigne, Radnorshire Arms
Raglan, Clytha Arms
Red Wharf Bay, Ship
Saundersfoot, Royal Oak
St Hilary, Bush
Talybont-on-Usk, Star
Talyllyn, Tynycornel

Channel Islands

Greve de Lecq, Moulin de Lecq
King's Mills, Fleur du Jardin
Rozel, Rozel Bay Hotel
St Aubin, Old Court House Inn
St Brelade, Old Portelet Inn
St Brelade, Old Smugglers
St Helier, Admiral, Tipsy Toad Town House
St John, Les Fontaines
St Ouens Bay, La Pulente

Pubs with No Smoking Areas

We have listed all the pubs which have told us they do set aside at least some part of the pub as a no smoking area. Look at the individual entries for the pubs themselves to see just what they do: provision is much more generous in some pubs than in others.

Bedfordshire

Biddenham, Three Tuns
Broom, Cock
Houghton Conquest, Knife & Cleaver
Keysoe, Chequers
Linslade, Globe
Milton Bryan, Red Lion
Ridgmont, Rose & Crown
Turvey, Three Fyshes

Berkshire

Ashmore Green, Sun in the Wood
Boxford, Bell
Cookham, Bel & the Dragon
Crazies Hill, Horns
Frilsham, Pot Kiln
Hamstead Marshall, White Hart
Hare Hatch, Queen Victoria
Inkpen, Swan
Marsh Benham, Red House
Peasemore, Fox & Hounds
Sonning, Bull
Stanford Dingley, Bull, Old Boot
Swallowfield, George & Dragon
Waltham St Lawrence, Bell
West Ilsley, Harrow
Yattendon, Royal Oak

Buckinghamshire

Bolter End, Peacock
Ford, Dinton Hermit
Forty Green, Royal Standard of England
Great Hampden, Hampden Arms
Haddenham, Green Dragon
Little Hampden, Rising Sun
Long Crendon, Angel
Preston Bissett, White Hart
Prestwood, Polecat
Skirmett, Frog
Turville, Bull & Butcher
Waddesdon, Five Arrows
Weston Underwood, Cowpers Oak
Wooburn Common, Chequers

Cambridgeshire

Barnack, Millstone
Bythorn, White Hart

Cambridge, Anchor,
  Cambridge Blue, Eagle,
  Live & Let Live
Castor, Fitzwilliam Arms
Elsworth, George & Dragon
Fowlmere, Chequers
Gorefield, Woodmans
  Cottage
Heydon, King William IV
Hinxton, Red Lion
Huntingdon, Old Bridge
  Hotel
Keyston, Pheasant
Madingley, Three Horseshoes
Newton, Queens Head
Peterborough, Brewery Tap
Spaldwick, George
Stilton, Bell
Swavesey, Trinity Foot
Thriplow, Green Man
Wansford, Haycock

Cheshire
Aldford, Grosvenor Arms
Aston, Bhurtpore
Bell o' th' Hill, Blue Bell
Bunbury, Dysart Arms
Cotebrook, Fox & Barrel
Daresbury, Ring o' Bells
Higher Burwardsley,
  Pheasant
Langley, Hanging Gate
Lower Peover, Bells of Peover
Over Peover, Olde Park Gate
Overton, Ring o' Bells
Peover Heath, Dog
Plumley, Smoker
Weston, White Lion
Whiteley Green, Windmill
Willington, Boot
Wincle, Ship
Wrenbury, Dusty Miller

Cornwall
Bodinnick, Old Ferry
Chapel Amble, Maltsters Arms
Constantine, Trengilly
  Wartha
Cremyll, Edgcumbe Arms
Edmonton, Quarryman
Egloshayle, Earl of St Vincent
Helston, Halzephron
Ludgvan, White Hart
Mitchell, Plume of Feathers
Mithian, Miners Arms
Mylor Bridge, Pandora
Philleigh, Roseland
Polperro, Old Mill House
Port Isaac, Golden Lion, Port
  Gaverne Inn
Ruan Lanihorne, Kings Head
St Agnes, Turks Head
St Breward, Old Inn
St Mawes, Victory, Falcon
Treburley, Springer Spaniel

Cumbria
Ambleside, Golden Rule
Appleby, Royal Oak

Armathwaite, Dukes Head
Barbon, Barbon Inn
Bassenthwaite Lake, Pheasant
Beetham, Wheatsheaf
Bouth, White Hart
Broughton Mills, Blacksmiths
  Arms
Buttermere, Bridge Hotel
Caldbeck, Oddfellows Arms
Casterton, Pheasant
Chapel Stile, Wainwrights
Cockermouth, Bitter End
Coniston, Black Bull, Sun
Crook, Sun
Crosthwaite, Punch Bowl
Dent, Sun
Elterwater, Britannia
Garrigill, George & Dragon
Grasmere, Travellers Rest
Hawkshead, Drunken Duck,
  Kings Arms
Hesket Newmarket, Old
  Crown
Heversham, Blue Bell
Ings, Watermill
Keswick, George
Kirkby Lonsdale, Snooty Fox
Langdale, Old Dungeon
  Ghyll
Little Langdale, Three Shires
Loweswater, Kirkstile Inn
Melmerby, Shepherds
Penrith, Agricultural
Seathwaite, Newfield Inn
Sedbergh, Dalesman
Stainton, Kings Arms
Tirril, Queens Head
Troutbeck, Queens Head
Ulverston, Bay Horse
Wasdale Head, Wasdale
  Head Inn
Winton, Bay Horse
Yanwath, Gate Inn

Derbyshire
Ashbourne, Smiths Tavern
Barlow, Trout
Beeley, Devonshire Arms
Birch Vale, Waltzing Weasel
Birchover, Druid
Brassington, Olde Gate
Buxton, Bull i' th' Thorn
Castleton, Castle Hotel
Derby, Alexandra,
  Brunswick, Olde Dolphin
Eyam, Miners Arms
Fenny Bentley, Coach &
  Horses
Froggatt Edge, Chequers
Hardwick Hall, Hardwick
  Inn
Hassop, Eyre Arms
Hathersage, Plough
Hognaston, Red Lion
Hope, Cheshire Cheese
Kirk Ireton, Barley Mow
Ladybower Reservoir,
  Yorkshire Bridge

Melbourne, John Thompson
Milltown, Miners Arms
Monsal Head, Monsal Head
  Hotel
Over Haddon, Lathkil
Whittington Moor, Derby
  Tup

Devon
Ashprington, Durant Arms
Axmouth, Harbour Inn
Berrynarbor, Olde Globe
Blackawton, Normandy
  Arms
Branscombe, Fountain Head,
  Masons Arms
Broadhembury, Drewe Arms
Buckland Brewer, Coach &
  Horses
Buckland Monachorum,
  Drake Manor
Chagford, Ring o' Bells
Cheriton Bishop, Old Thatch
  Inn
Chittlehamholt, Exeter Inn
Clyst Hydon, Five Bells
Cockwood, Anchor
Coleford, New Inn
Cornworthy, Hunters Lodge
Dalwood, Tuckers Arms
Dartington, Cott
Dartmouth, Cherub, Royal
  Castle Hotel
Doddiscombsleigh, Nobody
  Inn
Dolton, Union
Drewsteignton, Drewe Arms
East Prawle, Freebooter
Exeter, Imperial, White Hart
Exminster, Turf Hotel
Harberton, Church House
Haytor Vale, Rock
Horns Cross, Hoops
Kingsteignton, Old Rydon
Kingston, Dolphin
Lustleigh, Cleave
Lydford, Castle Inn
Marldon, Church House
Newton St Cyres, Beer
  Engine
Noss Mayo, Ship
Peter Tavy, Peter Tavy Inn
Sheepwash, Half Moon
Sidford, Blue Ball
Slapton, Tower
Sourton, Highwayman
South Zeal, Oxenham Arms
Staverton, Sea Trout
Stockland, Kings Arms
Stokeinteignhead, Church
  House
Stokenham, Tradesmans Arms
Tipton St John, Golden Lion
Topsham, Passage House
Torcross, Start Bay
Totnes, Kingsbridge Inn
Two Bridges, Two Bridges
  Hotel

Umberleigh, Rising Sun
Widecombe, Rugglestone
Winkleigh, Kings Arms
Woodland, Rising Sun

Dorset
Ansty, Fox
Askerswell, Spyway
Burton Bradstock, Anchor
Cerne Abbas, New Inn
Chideock, Anchor
Christchurch, Fishermans
  Haunt
Church Knowle, New Inn
Corfe Castle, Greyhound
Corscombe, Fox
Cranborne, Fleur-de-Lys
East Chaldon, Sailors Return
East Knighton, Countryman
East Morden, Cock & Bottle
Evershot, Acorn
Furzehill, Stocks
Lyme Regis, Pilot Boat
Marnhull, Blackmore Vale
Plush, Brace of Pheasants
Puncknowle, Crown
Shave Cross, Shave Cross Inn
Stratton, Saxon Arms
Tarrant Monkton, Langton
  Arms
Uploders, Crown
Upwey, Old Ship
West Bexington, Manor
  Hotel

Essex
Arkesden, Axe & Compasses
Birchanger, Three Willows
Burnham-on-Crouch, White
  Harte
Castle Hedingham, Bell
Chappel, Swan
Clavering, Cricketers
Coggeshall, Compasses
Fingringhoe, Whalebone
Gosfield, Green Man
Great Yeldham, White Hart
Horndon-on-the-Hill, Bell
Little Dunmow, Flitch of
  Bacon
Moreton, White Hart
Wendens Ambo, Bell
Youngs End, Green Dragon

Gloucestershire
Ashleworth, Queens Arms
Awre, Red Hart
Barnsley, Village Pub
Bisley, Bear
Blaisdon, Red Hart
Bledington, Kings Head
Bourton-on-the-Hill, Horse
  & Groom
Box, Halfway Inn
Brimpsfield, Golden Heart
Chedworth, Seven Tuns
Chipping Campden, Eight
  Bells
Coln St Aldwyns, New Inn

Cranham, Black Horse
Duntisbourne Abbots, Five
  Mile House
Dursley, Old Spot
Great Rissington, Lamb
Gretton, Royal Oak
Kilkenny, Kilkeney Inn
Kingscote, Hunters Hall
Littleton-upon-Severn, White
  Hart
Meysey Hampton, Masons
  Arms
Miserden, Carpenters Arms
Nailsworth, Egypt Mill
Naunton, Black Horse
North Cerney, Bathurst Arms
Oakridge Lynch, Butchers
  Arms
Old Sodbury, Dog
Oldbury-on-Severn, Anchor
Sheepscombe, Butchers Arms
St Briavels, George
Tetbury, Gumstool
Tewkesbury, Olde Black Bear
Todenham, Farriers Arms
Winchcombe, Old Corner
  Cupboard
Withington, Mill Inn

Hampshire
Alresford, Globe
Arford, Crown
Beauworth, Milbury's
Boldre, Red Lion
Bramdean, Fox
Buriton, Five Bells
Bursledon, Jolly Sailor
Cadnam, White Hart
Crawley, Fox & Hounds
Droxford, White Horse
East Tytherley, Star
Eversley, Golden Pot
Hawkley, Hawkley Inn
Itchen Abbas, Trout
Langstone, Royal Oak
Longstock, Peat Spade
Mapledurwell, Gamekeepers
Micheldever, Half Moon
  & Spread Eagle
North Gorley, Royal Oak
Ovington, Bush
Petersfield, Trooper
Petersfield, White Horse
Pilley, Fleur de Lys
Rotherwick, Coach &
  Horses
Southsea, Wine Vaults
Sparsholt, Plough
Winchester, Wykeham Arms

Herefordshire
Aymestrey, Riverside Inn
Brimfield, Roebuck
Craswall, Bulls Head
Dorstone, Pandy
Ledbury, Feathers
Lugwardine, Crown &
  Anchor
Much Marcle, Slip Tavern

Pembridge, New Inn
Sellack, Lough Pool
St Owen's Cross, New Inn
Titley, Stagg
Ullingswick, Three Crowns
Upton Bishop, Moody Cow
Wellington, Wellington
Weobley, Salutation,
  Butchers Arms, Crown

Hertfordshire
Aldbury, Greyhound, Valiant
  Trooper
Ashwell, Three Tuns
Ayot St Lawrence, Brocket
  Arms
Bricket Wood, Moor Mill
Hertford, White Horse
Knebworth, Lytton Arms
Little Hadham, Nags Head
Perry Green, Hoops
Reed, Cabinet
Sarratt, Boot, Cock
St Albans, Rose & Crown
Watton-at-Stone, George &
  Dragon

Isle of Wight
Arreton, White Lion
Bembridge, Crab & Lobster
Bonchurch, Bonchurch Inn
Carisbrooke, Blacksmiths
  Arms
Chale, Clarendon (Wight
  Mouse)
Cowes, Folly
Rookley, Chequers
Seaview, Seaview Hotel
Shalfleet, New Inn
Shorwell, Crown
Ventnor, Spyglass

Kent
Boyden Gate, Gate Inn
Chiddingstone, Castle
Deal, Kings Head
Groombridge, Crown
Ickham, Duke William
Ightham, George & Dragon
Newnham, George
Oare, Shipwrights Arms
Penshurst, Bottle House,
  Spotted Dog
Sandgate, Clarendon
Smarden, Chequers
Ulcombe, Pepper Box

Lancashire
Bispham Green, Eagle &
  Child
Blackstone Edge, White
  House
Chipping, Dog & Partridge
Conder Green, Stork
Croston, Black Horse
Downham, Assheton Arms
Entwistle, Strawbury Duck
Fence, Forest
Little Eccleston, Cartford
Liverpool, Baltic Fleet

Longridge, Derby Arms
Manchester, Lass o' Gowrie
Mellor, Oddfellows Arms
Newton, Parkers Arms
Raby, Wheatsheaf
Ribchester, White Bull
Uppermill, Church Inn
Yealand Conyers, New Inn

Leicestershire
Barrowden, Exeter Arms
Belmesthorpe, Blue Bell
Braunston, Old Plough
Clipsham, Olive Branch
East Langton, Bell
Exton, Fox & Hounds
Glooston, Old Barn
Gumley, Bell
Hallaton, Bewicke Arms
Hose, Rose & Crown
Loughborough, Swan in the
 Rushes
Lyddington, Old White Hart
Market Overton, Black Bull
Newton Burgoland, Belper
 Arms
Old Dalby, Crown
Saddington, Queens Head
Sibson, Cock
Somerby, Old Brewery,
 Stilton Cheese
Stretton, Ram Jam Inn
Thorpe Langton, Bakers
 Arms
Upper Hambleton, Finches
 Arms
Wing, Kings Arms

Lincolnshire
Allington, Welby Arms
Brandy Wharf, Cider Centre
Castle Bytham, Castle Inn
Coningsby, Lea Gate Inn
Corby Glen, Woodhouse Inn
Dyke, Wishing Well
Gedney Dyke, Chequers
Grimsthorpe, Black Horse
Lincoln, Wig & Mitre
Newton, Red Lion
South Witham, Blue Cow
Stamford, Daniel Lambert

Norfolk
Bawburgh, Kings Head
Blakeney, Kings Arms, White
 Horse
Brancaster Staithe, Jolly
 Sailors, White Horse
Burnham Market, Hoste
 Arms
Burnham Thorpe, Lord
 Nelson
Cawston, Ratcatchers
Erpingham, Saracens Head
Horsey, Nelson Head
Itteringham, Walpole Arms
Larling, Angel
Letheringsett, Kings Head
Mundford, Crown

Norwich, Adam & Eve
Reedham, Ferry Inn, Railway
 Tavern, Old Brewery
 House
Ringstead, Gin Trap
Snettisham, Rose & Crown
Stiffkey, Red Lion
Stow Bardolph, Hare Arms
Swanton Morley, Darbys
Titchwell, Manor Hotel
Tivetshall St Mary, Old
 Ram
Upper Sheringham, Red Lion
Warham, Three Horseshoes
Winterton-on-Sea,
 Fishermans Return
Woodbastwick, Fur &
 Feather

Northamptonshire
Badby, Windmill
Chacombe, George &
 Dragon
Clipston, Bulls Head
East Haddon, Red Lion
Great Oxendon, George
Harringworth, White Swan
Oundle, Mill, Ship
Sulgrave, Star
Woodnewton, White Swan

Northumbria
Allenheads, Allenheads Inn
Aycliffe, County
Belford, Blue Bell
Carterway Heads, Manor
 House Inn
Chatton, Percy Arms
Craster, Jolly Fisherman
Dunstan, Cottage
Great Whittington, Queens
 Head
Greta Bridge, Morritt Arms
Haltwhistle, Wallace Arms
Hedley on the Hill, Feathers
Matfen, Black Bull
New York, Shiremoor Farm
Newton-on-the-Moor, Cook
 & Barker Arms
Rennington, Masons Arms
Romaldkirk, Rose & Crown
Seahouses, Olde Ship
Shincliffe, Seven Stars
Stannersburn, Pheasant
Thropton, Three Wheat
 Heads

Nottinghamshire
Beeston, Victoria
Caunton, Caunton Beck
Colston Bassett, Martins
 Arms
Kimberley, Nelson &
 Railway
Laxton, Dovecote
Nottingham, Fellows Morton
 & Clayton, Lincolnshire
 Poacher, Olde Trip to
 Jerusalem

Oxfordshire
Banbury, Reindeer
Barnard Gate, Boot
Binfield Heath, Bottle &
 Glass
Blewbury, Blewbury Inn
Broadwell, Five Bells
Buckland, Lamb
Burcot, Chequers
Burford, Lamb, Mermaid
Caulcott, Horse & Groom
Chalgrove, Red Lion
Chinnor, Sir Charles
 Napier
Chipping Norton, Chequers
Clifton, Duke of
 Cumberlands Head
Cuddesdon, Bat & Ball
Cuxham, Half Moon
Exlade Street, Highwayman
Fifield, Merrymouth
Fyfield, White Hart
Great Tew, Falkland Arms
Highmoor, Rising Sun
Lewknor, Olde Leathern
 Bottel
Maidensgrove, Five
 Horseshoes
Murcott, Nut Tree
Oxford, Isis Tavern, Kings
 Arms, Turf Tavern
Ramsden, Royal Oak
Shipton-under-Wychwood,
 Lamb, Shaven Crown
South Stoke, Perch & Pike
Stanton St John, Star
Tadpole Bridge, Trout
Wigginton, White Swan
Woodstock, Feathers
Wootton, Kings Head

Shropshire
Bishop's Castle, Castle Hotel,
 Six Bells, Three Tuns
Bromfield, Cookhouse
Cardington, Royal Oak
Heathton, Old Gate
Hopton Wafers, Crown
Ironbridge, Malthouse
Longville, Longville Arms
Ludlow, Unicorn
Much Wenlock, George &
 Dragon
Norton, Hundred House
Wenlock Edge, Wenlock
 Edge Inn
Wentnor, Crown

Somerset
Appley, Globe
Axbridge, Lamb
Batcombe, Three Horseshoes
Bath, Old Green Tree
Blagdon, New Inn
Bradley Green, Malt Shovel
Castle Cary, George
Combe Hay, Wheatsheaf
Compton Martin, Ring o'
 Bells

Cranmore, Strode Arms
Doulting, Waggon & Horses
Dowlish Wake, New Inn
East Lyng, Rose & Crown
East Woodlands, Horse & Groom
Exford, White Horse
Freshford, Inn at Freshford
Hallatrow, Old Station
Huish Episcopi, Rose & Crown
Kingsdon, Kingsdon Inn
Langley Marsh, Three Horseshoes
Monksilver, Notley Arms
North Curry, Bird in Hand
Norton St Philip, George
Rudge, Full Moon
Shepton Montague, Montague Inn
Stanton Wick, Carpenters Arms
Stoke St Gregory, Rose & Crown
Wells, City Arms

Staffordshire
Alstonefield, George
Burton upon Trent, Burton Bridge Inn
Butterton, Black Lion
Cheadle, Queens at Freehay
Onecote, Jervis Arms
Wetton, Olde Royal Oak

Suffolk
Bramfield, Queens Head
Brome, Cornwallis
Butley, Oyster
Chelmondiston, Butt & Oyster
Dunwich, Ship
Erwarton, Queens Head
Framsden, Dobermann
Hundon, Plough
Lavenham, Angel, Swan
Levington, Ship
Lidgate, Star
Rattlesden, Brewers Arms
Snape, Crown, Golden Key, Plough & Sail
Southwold, Crown
Stoke-by-Nayland, Angel
Swilland, Moon & Mushroom
Thorington Street, Rose
Tostock, Gardeners Arms
Walberswick, Bell
Westleton, Crown
Wingfield, De La Pole Arms

Surrey
Abinger Common, Abinger Hatch
Betchworth, Red Lion
Blackbrook, Plough
Charleshill, Donkey
Cobham, Cricketers
Elstead, Woolpack

Laleham, Anglers Retreat
Pirbright, Royal Oak
Worplesdon, Jolly Farmer

Sussex
Alciston, Rose Cottage
Amberley, Black Horse, Bridge, Sportsmans
Billingshurst, Blue Ship
Blackboys, Blackboys Inn
Burwash, Bell
Byworth, Black Horse
Chidham, Old House At Home
Cowbeech, Merrie Harriers
East Chiltington, Jolly Sportsman
Elsted, Three Horseshoes
Firle, Ram
Horsham, Black Jug
Houghton, George & Dragon
Icklesham, Queens Head
Lewes, Snowdrop
Lodsworth, Halfway Bridge Inn
Lurgashall, Noahs Ark
Milton Street, Sussex Ox
Nuthurst, Black Horse
Oving, Gribble Inn
Pett, Two Sawyers
Punnetts Town, Three Cups
Rye, Mermaid
Seaford, Golden Galleon
Singleton, Fox & Hounds
Tillington, Horse Guards
Trotton, Keepers Arms
Wilmington, Giants Rest

Warwickshire
Alderminster, Bell
Aston Cantlow, Kings Head
Berkswell, Bear
Coventry, Old Windmill
Dunchurch, Dun Cow
Edge Hill, Castle
Great Wolford, Fox & Hounds
Hatton, Falcon
Himley, Crooked House
Ilmington, Howard Arms
Little Compton, Red Lion
Long Compton, Red Lion
Sambourne, Green Dragon
Stratford-upon-Avon, Garrick
Welford-on-Avon, Bell

Wiltshire
Alvediston, Crown
Axford, Red Lion
Beckhampton, Waggon & Horses
Berwick St John, Talbot
Brinkworth, Three Crowns
Corton, Dove
Devizes, Bear
Ebbesbourne Wake, Horseshoe
Ford, White Hart

Great Hinton, Linnet
Hindon, Grosvenor Arms
Kilmington, Red Lion
Lacock, George, Red Lion
Limpley Stoke, Hop Pole
Lower Chute, Hatchet
Netherhampton, Victoria & Albert
Norton, Vine Tree
Poulshot, Raven
Rowde, George & Dragon
Salisbury, Haunch of Venison, New Inn
Seend, Barge
Sherston, Rattlebone
Whitley, Pear Tree
Wootton Rivers, Royal Oak
Wylye, Bell

Worcestershire
Birtsmorton, Farmers Arms
Bransford, Bear & Ragged Staff
Bredon, Fox & Hounds
Bretforton, Fleece
Crowle, Old Chequers
Flyford Flavell, Boot
Forhill, Peacock
Kempsey, Walter de Cantelupe
Ombersley, Crown & Sandys Arms, Kings Arms
Pensax, Bell
Welland, Anchor
Wyre Piddle, Anchor

Yorkshire
Appletreewick, Craven Arms
Beverley, White Horse
Boroughbridge, Black Bull
Bradfield, Strines Inn
Buckden, Buck
Burnsall, Red Lion
Byland Abbey, Abbey Inn
Carlton, Foresters Arms
Carthorpe, Fox & Hounds
Coxwold, Fauconberg Arms
Crayke, Durham Ox
Cropton, New Inn
Dacre Banks, Royal Oak
Egton Bridge, Horse Shoe
Fadmoor, Plough
Ferrensby, General Tarleton
Goose Eye, Turkey
Harome, Star
Heckmondwike, Old Hall
Hetton, Angel
Hull, Minerva
Kirkbymoorside, George & Dragon
Kirkham, Stone Trough
Langthwaite, Charles Bathurst
Lastingham, Blacksmiths Arms
Levisham, Horseshoe
Leyburn, Sandpiper
Linthwaite, Sair
Linton, Windmill

Litton, Queens Arms
Lund, Wellington
Masham, Kings Head
Newton on Ouse, Dawnay Arms
Nunnington, Royal Oak
Osmotherley, Golden Lion
Penistone, Cubley Hall
Pickering, White Swan
Pickhill, Nags Head
Pool, White Hart
Ramsgill, Yorke Arms
Ripponden, Old Bridge
Sawley, Sawley Arms
Scawton, Hare
Settle, Golden Lion
Sheffield, Fat Cat, New Barrack
Sinnington, Fox & Hounds
Sutton upon Derwent, St Vincent Arms
Terrington, Bay Horse
Thorganby, Jefferson Arms
Thornton Watlass, Buck
Wass, Wombwell Arms
Wath in Nidderdale, Sportsmans Arms
Whitby, Duke of York

London
Central London, Argyll Arms, Lamb, Lord Moon of the Mall, Moon Under Water, Old Bank of England, Westminster Arms
East London, Prospect of Whitby
North London, Waterside
South London, Anchor, Crown & Greyhound, Founders Arms
West London, Bulls Head, White Horse, Windsor Castle

Scotland
Aberdeen, Prince of Wales
Applecross, Applecross Inn
Arduaine, Loch Melfort Hotel
Brig o' Turk, Byre
Broughty Ferry, Fishermans Tavern
Canonbie, Riverside Inn
Cawdor, Cawdor Tavern
Creebridge, Creebridge House Hotel
Crinan, Crinan Hotel
Cromarty, Royal
East Linton, Drovers
Edinburgh, Abbotsford, Starbank
Fort Augustus, Lock
Gairloch, Old Inn
Glasgow, Auctioneers, Counting House
Glenelg, Glenelg Inn
Haddington, Waterside

Houston, Fox & Hounds
Innerleithen, Traquair Arms
Isle of Whithorn, Steam Packet
Kenmore, Kenmore Hotel
Kilberry, Kilberry Inn
Kilmahog, Lade
Kingholm Quay, Swan
Kippford, Anchor
Kirkton of Glenisla, Glenisla Hotel
Linlithgow, Four Marys
Lybster, Portland Arms
Melrose, Burts Hotel
Oban, Oban Inn
Pitlochry, Killiecrankie Hotel
Plockton, Plockton Hotel
Shieldaig, Tigh an Eilean Hotel
Skeabost, Skeabost House Hotel
St Monance, Seafood Restaurant & Bar
Swinton, Wheatsheaf
Tayvallich, Tayvallich Inn
Thornhill, Lion & Unicorn
Tushielaw, Tushielaw Inn
Ullapool, Ceilidh Place, Ferry Boat, Morefield Motel
Weem, Ailean Chraggan

Wales
Abercych, Nags Head
Aberdovey, Penhelig Arms
Aberystwyth, Halfway Inn
Beaumaris, Olde Bulls Head, Sailors Return
Betws-y-Coed, Ty Gwyn
Bodfari, Dinorben Arms
Bosherston, St Govans Country Inn
Carew, Carew Inn
Cilgerran, Pendre
Cresswell Quay, Cresselly Arms
Crickhowell, Bear
Crickhowell, Nantyffin Cider Mill
Gresford, Pant-yr-Ochain
Hay-on-Wye, Kilverts, Old Black Lion
Llanbedr-y-Cennin, Olde Bull
Llanberis, Pen-y-Gwryd
Llandeilo, Castle
Llandrindod Wells, Llanerch
Llandudno Junction, Queens Head
Llangynwyd, Old House
Llannefydd, Hawk & Buckle
Llanynys, Cerrigllwydion Arms
Llwyndafydd, Crown
Llyswen, Griffin
Pontypool, Open Hearth
Porthgain, Sloop
Porthmadog, Ship
Presteigne, Radnorshire Arms
Raglan, Clytha Arms

Red Wharf Bay, Ship
Saundersfoot, Royal Oak
St Hilary, Bush
Stackpole, Armstrong Arms
Talyllyn, Tynycornel
Ty'n-y-groes, Groes

Channel Islands
St Brelade, Old Portelet Inn, Old Smugglers
St Helier, Admiral, Tipsy Toad Town House
St Ouens Bay, La Pulente

Pubs close to Motorway Junctions
The number at the start of each line is the number of the junction. Detailed directions are given in the main entry for each pub. In this section, to help you find the pubs quickly before you're past the junction, we give the name of the chapter where you'll find the text.

M1
6: Bricket Wood, Moor Mill (Hertfordshire) 2 miles
13: Ridgmont, Rose & Crown (Bedfordshire) 2 miles
18: Crick, Red Lion (Northamptonshire) 1 mile
24: Kegworth, Cap & Stocking (Leicestershire) 1 mile; Shardlow, Old Crown (Derbyshire) 2.25 miles
26: Kimberley, Nelson & Railway (Nottinghamshire) 3 miles
29: Hardwick Hall, Hardwick Inn (Derbyshire) 4 miles

M3
5: Rotherwick, Coach & Horses (Hampshire) 4 miles
6: Mapledurwell, Gamekeepers (Hampshire) 3.5 miles
9: Itchen Abbas, Trout (Hampshire) 4 miles

M4
9: Holyport, Belgian Arms (Berkshire) 1.5 miles; Bray, Crown (Berkshire) 1.75 miles
12: Stanford Dingley, Bull (Berkshire) 4 miles
13: Winterbourne, Winterbourne Arms (Berkshire) 3.5 miles; Chieveley, Blue Boar (Berkshire) 3.5 miles
14: Great Shefford, Swan (Berkshire) 2 miles;

Lambourn, Hare &
Hounds (Berkshire)
3.5 miles
17: Norton, Vine Tree
(Wiltshire) 4 miles
18: Old Sodbury, Dog
(Gloucestershire) 2 miles

M5
6: Crowle, Old Chequers
(Worcestershire) 2 miles
7: Kempsey, Walter de
Cantelupe (Worcestershire)
3.75 miles
9: Bredon, Fox & Hounds
(Worcestershire) 4.5 miles
16: Almondsbury, Bowl
(Gloucestershire) 1.25 miles
19: Clapton-in-Gordano,
Black Horse (Somerset)
4 miles
28: Broadhembury, Drewe
Arms (Devon) 5 miles
30: Topsham, Passage House
(Devon) 2 miles; Topsham,
Bridge (Devon) 2.25 miles;
Woodbury Salterton,
Diggers Rest (Devon)
3.5 miles; Exeter, White
Hart (Devon) 4 miles

M6
16: Barthomley, White Lion
(Cheshire) 1 mile; Weston,
White Lion (Cheshire)
3.5 miles
19: Plumley, Smoker
(Cheshire) 2.5 miles
33: Conder Green, Stork
(Lancashire) 3 miles
35: Yealand Conyers, New
Inn (Lancashire) 3 miles
40: Penrith, Agricultural
(Cumbria) 0.75 mile;

Yanwath, Gate Inn
(Cumbria) 2.25 miles;
Stainton, Kings Arms
(Cumbria) 3 miles; Tirril,
Queens Head (Cumbria)
3.5 miles; Askham, Punch
Bowl (Cumbria) 4.5 miles

M9
3: Linlithgow, Four Marys
(Scotland) 2 miles

M11
7: Hastingwood, Rainbow
& Dove (Essex) 0.25 mile
8: Birchanger, Three Willows
(Essex) 0.8 mile
10: Hinxton, Red Lion
(Cambridgeshire) 2 miles;
Thriplow, Green Man
(Cambridgeshire) 3 miles
11: Little Shelford,
Navigator (Cambridgeshire)
2.5 miles

M25
8: Reigate Heath,
Skimmington Castle
(Surrey) 3 miles;
Betchworth, Dolphin
(Surrey) 4 miles
10: Cobham, Cricketers
(Surrey) 3.75 miles
13: Laleham, Anglers Retreat
(Surrey) 5 miles
18: Chenies, Red Lion
(Buckinghamshire) 2 miles

M27
1: Cadnam, White Hart
(Hampshire) 0.5 mile;
Fritham, Royal Oak
(Hampshire) 4 miles
8: Bursledon, Jolly Sailor
(Hampshire) 2 miles

M40
2: Forty Green, Royal
Standard of England
(Buckinghamshire) 3.5
miles; Bolter End, Peacock
(Buckinghamshire)
4 miles
6: Lewknor, Olde Leathern
Bottel (Oxfordshire)
0.5 mile; Watlington,
Chequers (Oxfordshire)
3 miles; Cuxham, Half
Moon (Oxfordshire)
4 miles
11: Chacombe, George &
Dragon
(Northamptonshire)
2.5 miles
15: Hatton, Falcon
(Warwickshire) 4.6 miles

M42
2: Forhill, Peacock
(Worcestershire) 2 miles

M45
1: Dunchurch, Dun Cow
(Warwickshire) 1.3 miles

M48
1: Littleton-upon-Severn,
White Hart
(Gloucestershire) 3.5 miles

M50
3: Upton Bishop, Moody
Cow (Herefordshire)
2 miles

M56
11: Daresbury, Ring o' Bells
(Cheshire) 1.5 miles
12: Overton, Ring o' Bells
(Cheshire) 2 miles

Report Forms

Report forms

Please report to us: you can use the tear-out forms on the following pages, the card in the middle of the book, or just plain paper – whichever's easiest for you, or you can report to our website, www.goodguides.com. We need to know what you think of the pubs in this edition. We need to know about other pubs worthy of inclusion. We need to know about ones that should not be included.

The atmosphere and character of the pub are the most important features – why it would, or would not, appeal to strangers, so please try to describe what is special about it. In particular, we can't consider including a pub in the Lucky Dip section unless we know something about what it looks like inside, so that we can describe it to other readers. And obviously with existing entries, we need to know about any changes in the décor and furnishings, too. But the bar food and the drink are also important – please tell us about them.

If the food is really quite outstanding, tick the FOOD AWARD box on the form, and tell us about the special quality that makes it stand out – the more detail, the better. And if you have stayed there, tell us about the standard of accommodation – whether it was comfortable, pleasant, good value for money. Again, if the pub or inn is worth special attention as a place to stay, tick the PLACE-TO-STAY AWARD box.

If you're in a position to gauge a pub's suitability or otherwise for disabled people, do please tell us about that.

Please try to gauge whether a pub should be a main entry, or is best as a Lucky Dip (and tick the relevant box). In general, main entries need qualities that would make it worth other readers' while to travel some distance to them; Lucky Dips are the pubs that are worth knowing about if you are nearby. But if a pub is an entirely new recommendation, the Lucky Dip may be the best place for it to start its career in the *Guide* – to encourage other readers to report on it.

The more detail you can put into your description of a Lucky Dip pub that's only scantily described in the current edition (or not in at all), the better. A description of its character and even furnishings is a tremendous boon.

It helps enormously if you can give the full address for any new pub – one not yet a main entry, or without a full address in the Lucky Dip sections. In a town, we need the street name; in the country, if it's hard to find, we need directions. Even better for us is the post code. If we can't find out a pub's post code, we no longer include it in the *Guide* – and the Post Office directories we use will not yet have caught up with new pubs, or ones which have changed their names. With any pub, it always helps to let us know about prices of food (and bedrooms, if there are any), and about any lunchtimes or evenings when food is not served. We'd also like to have your views on drinks quality – beer, wine, cider and so forth, even coffee and tea; and do let us know if it has bedrooms.

If you know that a Lucky Dip pub is open all day (or even late into the afternoon), please tell us – preferably saying which days.

When you go to a pub, don't tell them you're a reporter for the *Good Pub Guide*; we do make clear that all inspections are anonymous, and if you declare yourself as a reporter you risk getting special treatment – for better or for worse!

Sometimes pubs are dropped from the main entries simply because very few readers have written to us about them – and of course there's a risk that people may not write if they find the pub exactly as described in the entry. You can use the forms at the front of the batch of report forms just to list pubs you've been to, found as described, and can recommend.

When you write to The Good Pub Guide, FREEPOST TN1569, WADHURST, East Sussex TN5 7BR, you don't need a stamp in the UK. We'll gladly send you more forms (free) if you wish.

Though we try to answer letters, there are just the four of us – and with other work to do, besides producing this *Guide*. So please understand if there's a delay. And from June till September, when we are fully extended getting the next edition to the printers, we put all letters and reports aside, not answering them until the rush is over (and after our post-press-day late summer holiday). The end of May is the cut-off date for reports for the next edition (we can still cope with reports to our web site during the following weeks). However, the earlier we get them, the more consideration we're able to give them.

We'll assume we can print your name or initials as a recommender unless you tell us otherwise.

I have been to the following pubs in *The Good Pub Guide 2002* in the last few months, found them as described, and confirm that they deserve continued inclusion:

PLEASE GIVE YOUR NAME AND ADDRESS ON THE BACK OF THIS FORM

Pubs visited continued...

Your own name and address *(block capitals please)*

Please return to
The Good Pub Guide,
FREEPOST TN1569,
WADHURST,
East Sussex
TN5 7BR

I have been to the following pubs in *The Good Pub Guide 2002* in the last few months, found them as described, and confirm that they deserve continued inclusion:

Continued overleaf

PLEASE GIVE YOUR NAME AND ADDRESS ON THE BACK OF THIS FORM

Pubs visited continued...

Your own name and address *(block capitals please)*

Please return to
The Good Pub Guide,
FREEPOST TN1569,
WADHURST,
East Sussex
TN5 7BR

REPORT ON *(pub's name)*

Pub's address

☐ **YES Main Entry**   ☐ **YES** *Lucky Dip*   ☐ **NO don't include**
Please tick one of these boxes to show your verdict, and give reasons and descriptive comments, prices etc

☐ Deserves Food award   ☐ Deserves Place-to-stay award   2002:1

PLEASE GIVE YOUR NAME AND ADDRESS ON THE BACK OF THIS FORM

✂ -

REPORT ON *(pub's name)*

Pub's address

☐ **YES Main Entry**   ☐ **YES** *Lucky Dip*   ☐ **NO don't include**
Please tick one of these boxes to show your verdict, and give reasons and descriptive comments, prices etc

☐ Deserves Food award   ☐ Deserves Place-to-stay award   2002:2

PLEASE GIVE YOUR NAME AND ADDRESS ON THE BACK OF THIS FORM

Your own name and address *(block capitals please)*

DO NOT USE THIS SIDE OF THE PAGE FOR WRITING ABOUT PUBS

✂ ....

Your own name and address *(block capitals please)*

DO NOT USE THIS SIDE OF THE PAGE FOR WRITING ABOUT PUBS

IF YOU PREFER, YOU CAN SEND US REPORTS THROUGH OUR WEB SITE:
www.goodguides.com

REPORT ON *(pub's name)*

Pub's address

☐ **YES Main Entry**   ☐ **YES** *Lucky Dip*   ☐ **NO don't include**
Please tick one of these boxes to show your verdict, and give reasons and descriptive comments, prices etc

☐ Deserves Food award   ☐ Deserves Place-to-stay award   2002:3

PLEASE GIVE YOUR NAME AND ADDRESS ON THE BACK OF THIS FORM

✂

REPORT ON *(pub's name)*

Pub's address

☐ **YES Main Entry**   ☐ **YES** *Lucky Dip*   ☐ **NO don't include**
Please tick one of these boxes to show your verdict, and give reasons and descriptive comments, prices etc

☐ Deserves Food award   ☐ Deserves Place-to-stay award   2002:4

PLEASE GIVE YOUR NAME AND ADDRESS ON THE BACK OF THIS FORM

Your own name and address *(block capitals please)*

Pub: ?

YES MAIN ENTRY   ☐   YES Lucky Dip   ☐   NO don't include
Please tick one of these boxes to show your verdict, and give reasons and description, prices etc

DO NOT USE THIS SIDE OF THE PAGE FOR WRITING ABOUT PUBS

✂ ....

Your own name and address *(block capitals please)*

Pub: ?

☐ YES MAIN ENTRY   ☐   YES Lucky Dip   ☐   NO don't include
Please tick one of these boxes to show your verdict, and give reasons and description, comments, prices etc

DO NOT USE THIS SIDE OF THE PAGE FOR WRITING ABOUT PUBS

IF YOU PREFER, YOU CAN SEND US REPORTS THROUGH OUR WEB SITE:
www.goodguides.com

REPORT ON *(pub's name)*

Pub's address

☐ **YES MAIN ENTRY**   ☐ **YES** *Lucky Dip*   ☐ **NO don't include**
Please tick one of these boxes to show your verdict, and give reasons and descriptive comments, prices etc

☐ Deserves FOOD award   ☐ Deserves PLACE-TO-STAY award   2002:5

PLEASE GIVE YOUR NAME AND ADDRESS ON THE BACK OF THIS FORM

REPORT ON *(pub's name)*

Pub's address

☐ **YES MAIN ENTRY**   ☐ **YES** *Lucky Dip*   ☐ **NO don't include**
Please tick one of these boxes to show your verdict, and give reasons and descriptive comments, prices etc

☐ Deserves FOOD award   ☐ Deserves PLACE-TO-STAY award   2002:6

PLEASE GIVE YOUR NAME AND ADDRESS ON THE BACK OF THIS FORM

Your own name and address *(block capitals please)*

DO NOT USE THIS SIDE OF THE PAGE FOR WRITING ABOUT PUBS

✂ ....

Your own name and address *(block capitals please)*

DO NOT USE THIS SIDE OF THE PAGE FOR WRITING ABOUT PUBS

IF YOU PREFER, YOU CAN SEND US REPORTS THROUGH OUR WEB SITE:
www.goodguides.com

REPORT ON *(pub's name)*

Pub's address

☐ **YES Main Entry**   ☐ **YES** *Lucky Dip*   ☐ **NO don't include**
Please tick one of these boxes to show your verdict, and give reasons and descriptive comments, prices etc

☐ Deserves Food award   ☐ Deserves Place-to-stay award   2002:7

PLEASE GIVE YOUR NAME AND ADDRESS ON THE BACK OF THIS FORM

✂ -

REPORT ON *(pub's name)*

Pub's address

☐ **YES Main Entry**   ☐ **YES** *Lucky Dip*   ☐ **NO don't include**
Please tick one of these boxes to show your verdict, and give reasons and descriptive comments, prices etc

☐ Deserves Food award   ☐ Deserves Place-to-stay award   2002:8

PLEASE GIVE YOUR NAME AND ADDRESS ON THE BACK OF THIS FORM

Your own name and address *(block capitals please)*

DO NOT USE THIS SIDE OF THE PAGE FOR WRITING ABOUT PUBS

✂ ....

Your own name and address *(block capitals please)*

DO NOT USE THIS SIDE OF THE PAGE FOR WRITING ABOUT PUBS

IF YOU PREFER, YOU CAN SEND US REPORTS THROUGH OUR WEB SITE:
www.goodguides.com

REPORT ON *(pub's name)*

Pub's address

☐ **YES MAIN ENTRY**   ☐ **YES** *Lucky Dip*   ☐ **NO don't include**
Please tick one of these boxes to show your verdict, and give reasons and descriptive comments, prices etc

☐ Deserves FOOD award   ☐ Deserves PLACE-TO-STAY award   2002:9

PLEASE GIVE YOUR NAME AND ADDRESS ON THE BACK OF THIS FORM

✂ ⌿ ⌿ ⌿ ⌿ ⌿ ⌿ ⌿ ⌿ ⌿ ⌿ ⌿ ⌿ ⌿ ⌿ ⌿

REPORT ON *(pub's name)*

Pub's address

☐ **YES MAIN ENTRY**   ☐ **YES** *Lucky Dip*   ☐ **NO don't include**
Please tick one of these boxes to show your verdict, and give reasons and descriptive comments, prices etc

☐ Deserves FOOD award   ☐ Deserves PLACE-TO-STAY award   2002:10

PLEASE GIVE YOUR NAME AND ADDRESS ON THE BACK OF THIS FORM

Your own name and address *(block capitals please)*

DO NOT USE THIS SIDE OF THE PAGE FOR WRITING ABOUT PUBS

%

Your own name and address *(block capitals please)*

DO NOT USE THIS SIDE OF THE PAGE FOR WRITING ABOUT PUBS

IF YOU PREFER, YOU CAN SEND US REPORTS THROUGH OUR WEB SITE:
www.goodguides.com

REPORT ON *(pub's name)*

Pub's address

☐ **YES Main Entry** ☐ **YES** *Lucky Dip* ☐ **NO don't include**
*Please tick one of these boxes to show your verdict, and give reasons and
descriptive comments, prices etc*

☐ Deserves FOOD award ☐ Deserves PLACE-TO-STAY award 2002:11

PLEASE GIVE YOUR NAME AND ADDRESS ON THE BACK OF THIS FORM

REPORT ON *(pub's name)*

Pub's address

☐ **YES Main Entry** ☐ **YES** *Lucky Dip* ☐ **NO don't include**
*Please tick one of these boxes to show your verdict, and give reasons and
descriptive comments, prices etc*

☐ Deserves FOOD award ☐ Deserves PLACE-TO-STAY award 2002:12

PLEASE GIVE YOUR NAME AND ADDRESS ON THE BACK OF THIS FORM

Your own name and address *(block capitals please)*

DO NOT USE THIS SIDE OF THE PAGE FOR WRITING ABOUT PUBS

✂ ....

Your own name and address *(block capitals please)*

DO NOT USE THIS SIDE OF THE PAGE FOR WRITING ABOUT PUBS

IF YOU PREFER, YOU CAN SEND US REPORTS THROUGH OUR WEB SITE:
www.goodguides.com

REPORT ON *(pub's name)*

Pub's address

☐ **YES MAIN ENTRY** ☐ **YES** *Lucky Dip* ☐ **NO don't include**
Please tick one of these boxes to show your verdict, and give reasons and descriptive comments, prices etc

☐ Deserves FOOD award ☐ Deserves PLACE-TO-STAY award 2002:13

PLEASE GIVE YOUR NAME AND ADDRESS ON THE BACK OF THIS FORM

--✂

REPORT ON *(pub's name)*

Pub's address

☐ **YES MAIN ENTRY** ☐ **YES** *Lucky Dip* ☐ **NO don't include**
Please tick one of these boxes to show your verdict, and give reasons and descriptive comments, prices etc

☐ Deserves FOOD award ☐ Deserves PLACE-TO-STAY award 2002:14

PLEASE GIVE YOUR NAME AND ADDRESS ON THE BACK OF THIS FORM

Your own name and address *(block capitals please)*

DO NOT USE THIS SIDE OF THE PAGE FOR WRITING ABOUT PUBS

✂ ....

Your own name and address *(block capitals please)*

DO NOT USE THIS SIDE OF THE PAGE FOR WRITING ABOUT PUBS

IF YOU PREFER, YOU CAN SEND US REPORTS THROUGH OUR WEB SITE:
www.goodguides.com

REPORT ON _(pub's name)_

Pub's address

☐ **YES MAIN ENTRY**   ☐ **YES** _Lucky Dip_   ☐ **NO don't include**
Please tick one of these boxes to show your verdict, and give reasons and descriptive comments, prices etc

☐ Deserves FOOD award   ☐ Deserves PLACE-TO-STAY award   2002:15

PLEASE GIVE YOUR NAME AND ADDRESS ON THE BACK OF THIS FORM

REPORT ON _(pub's name)_

Pub's address

☐ **YES MAIN ENTRY**   ☐ **YES** _Lucky Dip_   ☐ **NO don't include**
Please tick one of these boxes to show your verdict, and give reasons and descriptive comments, prices etc

☐ Deserves FOOD award   ☐ Deserves PLACE-TO-STAY award   2002:16

PLEASE GIVE YOUR NAME AND ADDRESS ON THE BACK OF THIS FORM

Your own name and address *(block capitals please)*

DO NOT USE THIS SIDE OF THE PAGE FOR WRITING ABOUT PUBS

✂ ....

Your own name and address *(block capitals please)*

DO NOT USE THIS SIDE OF THE PAGE FOR WRITING ABOUT PUBS

IF YOU PREFER, YOU CAN SEND US REPORTS THROUGH OUR WEB SITE:
www.goodguides.com

Maps

Contents

The South-West and Channel Islands   Map 1

Southern England   Map 2

The South-East   Map 3

Central and Western England   Map 4

Central England and East Anglia   Map 5

Wales   Map 6

The North-West   Map 7

Eastern England   Map 8

The North-West and Scotland   Map 9

The North-East and Scotland   Map 10

Scotland   Map 11

Greater London   Map 12

Central London   Map 13

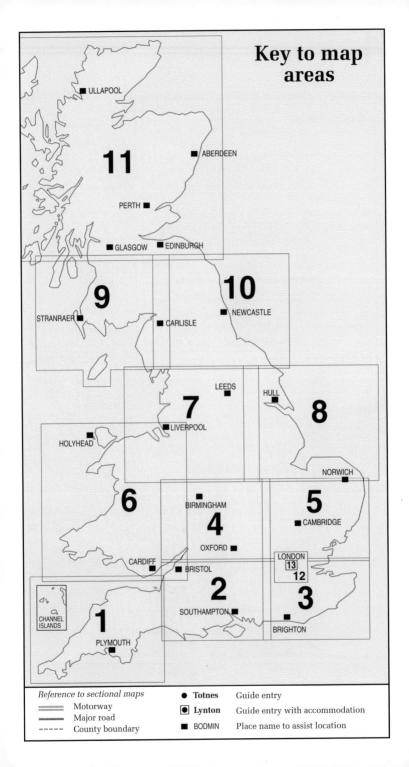

Key to map areas

Reference to sectional maps

~~~~~~~~ Motorway
————— Major road
– – – – County boundary

● **Totnes** Guide entry
◉ **Lynton** Guide entry with accommodation
■ BODMIN Place name to assist location

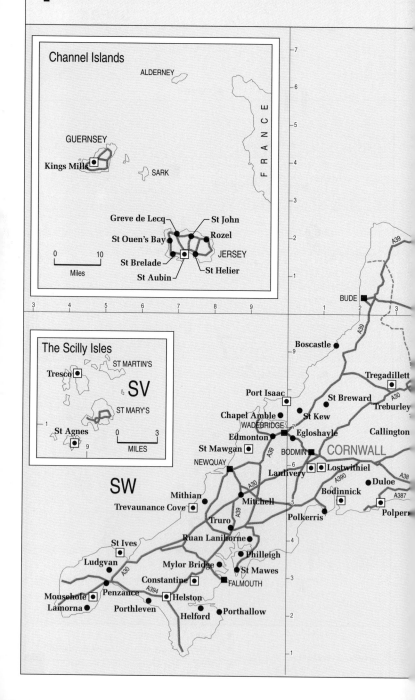

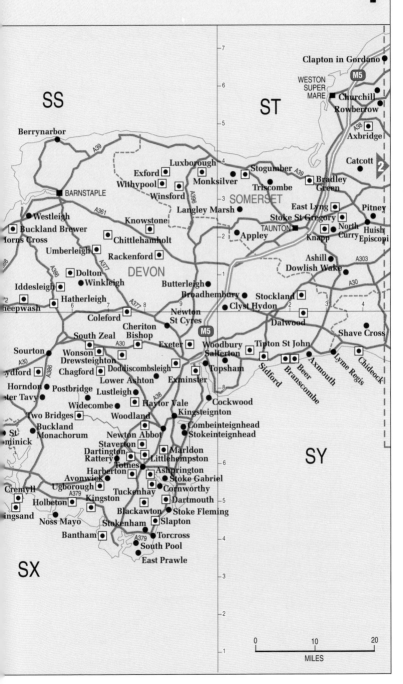

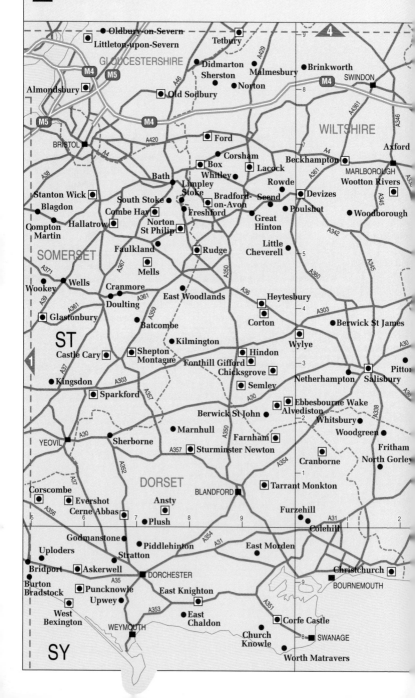

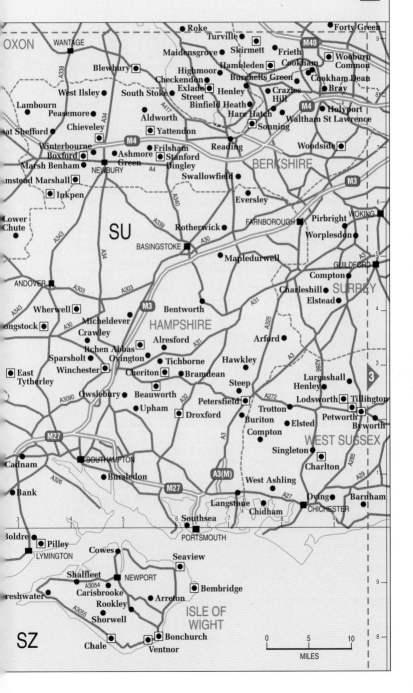

2

OXON WANTAGE

Roke
Turville
Forty Green

Maidensgrove Skirmett Frieth M40
Highmoor Hambleden Cookham Wooburn Common
Blewbury
Checkendon Burchetts Green Cookham Dean
South Stoke Exlade Street Henley Crazies Hill Bray
West Ilsley
Binfield Heath M4
Lambourn Aldworth Hare Hatch Holyport
Peasemore Waltham St Lawrence
Chieveley Yattendon Sonning
at Shefford Frilsham Reading Woodside
Winterbourne Ashmore Stanford BERKSHIRE
Boxford Green Dingley
Marsh Benham NEWBURY Swallowfield M3
mstead Marshall A4
Inkpen Eversley
A340
Lower Chute SU Rotherwick FARNBOROUGH Pirbright WOKING
A339 Worplesdon
Mapledurwell A30
BASINGSTOKE GUILDFORD
A34 Compton
ANDOVER A303 Charleshill SURREY
A303 Elstead
A343 Wherwell M3 Bentworth
ongstock Micheldever HAMPSHIRE Arford
Crawley Alresford
Itchen Abbas A31 Hawkley
Sparsholt Ovington Tichborne Lurgashall
East Tytherley Winchester Cheriton Bramdean Henley
Steep Lodsworth Tillington
Owslebury Beauworth Petersfield Trotton Petworth
Upham Droxford Buriton Elsted Byworth
Compton
M27 WEST SUSSEX
SOUTHAMPTON Singleton
Cadnam Bursledon A3(M) Charlton
Bank M27 West Ashling
Langstone Oving Barnham
Southsea Chidham CHICHESTER A29
PORTSMOUTH

Boldre Pilley Cowes
LYMINGTON Seaview
Shalfleet NEWPORT
Carisbrooke Bembridge
reshwater Rookley Arreton
A3055 Shorwell ISLE OF WIGHT
SZ Chale Bonchurch
Ventnor

0   5   10
MILES

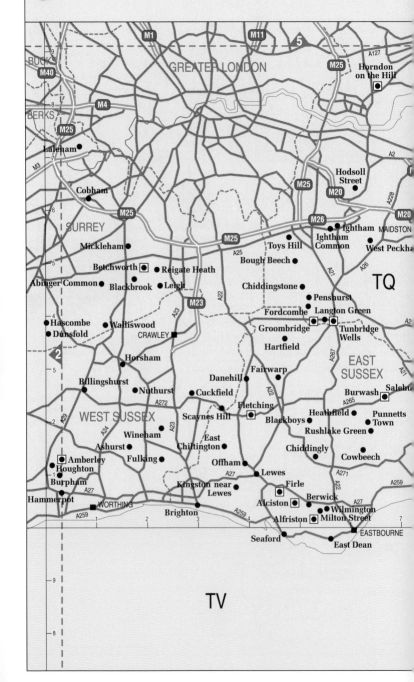

3

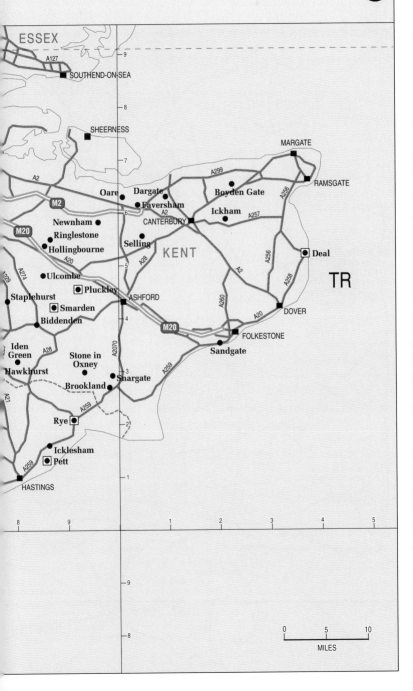

3

ESSEX

A127

■ SOUTHEND-ON-SEA

■ SHEERNESS

MARGATE ■

A299

■ RAMSGATE

A2

M2

Oare ● Dargate ●   Boyden Gate ●

● Faversham

A2

Newnham ●   CANTERBURY ■   Ickham ●   A257

M20

Ringlestone ●

A256

Hollingbourne ●   Selling ●   KENT   A256   ◉ Deal

A20   A28   A258

A274   A2   TR

Ulcombe ●

A229

Staplehurst ●   ◉ Pluckley

Smarden ◉   ASHFORD ■   A260

Biddenden ●

M20

Iden   A28

Green ●   Stone in   A2070   DOVER ■

Hawkhurst ●   Oxney ●   FOLKESTONE ■

A21   Brookland ●   Snargate ●   Sandgate ●

A259

Rye ◉

A259

● Icklesham

A259   ◉ Pett

■ HASTINGS

0   5   10
MILES

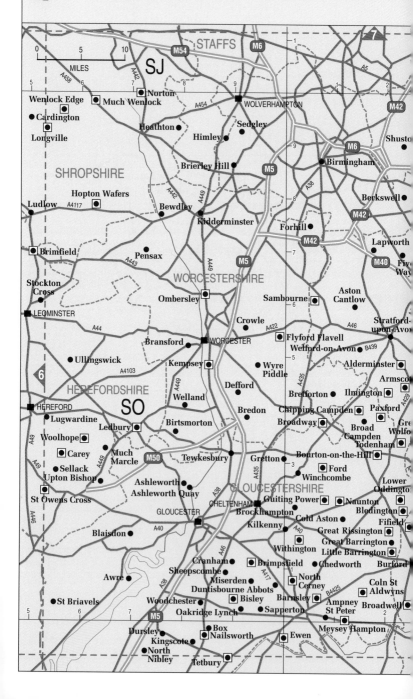

4

STAFFS

M54 M6

0   5   10
MILES

SJ

A458   6   A42   7   8   9

M42

Wenlock Edge • • Much Wenlock • Norton
• Cardington   A454   WOLVERHAMPTON
                    Heathton •   Sedgley •   M6   Shusto •
Longville
            Himley •   Birmingham •
SHROPSHIRE   Brierley Hill •   M5   Berkswell •
                                                                M42
        Hopton Wafers •   Bewdley •   Forhill •   Lapworth •
Ludlow • A4117   M42
                    Kidderminster •   7   M40   Fi
• Brimfield   A443   Pensax •   A449   M5   Way
                                                                        Aston
Stockton   WORCESTERSHIRE   Cantlow
Cross   Ombersley •   Sambourne •   6   Stratford-
• LEOMINSTER   A44   Crowle •   A422   A46   upon-Avo
            Bransford •   WORCESTER •   Flyford Flavell •   Welford-on-Avon   B439
• Ullingswick   Kempsey •   Wyre   5   Alderminster •
HEREFORDSHIRE   A4103   Piddle •   Armsco
                                    Defford •   Bretforton •   Ilmington •   A429
• HEREFORD   SO   Welland •   Chipping Campden •   Paxford •
• Lugwardine   Birtsmorton •   Bredon •   Gre
Woolhope •   Ledbury •   Broadway •   Broad   Wolfo
    • Carey   Much   Campden
Sellack •   Marcle   M50   Tewkesbury •   Gretton •   Bourton-on-the-Hill •
Upton Bishop •   Ford   Lower
St Owens Cross •   Ashleworth •   A435   3   Winchcombe •   Oddingto
                    Ashleworth Quay   GLOUCESTERSHIRE   Naunton •
        CHELTENHAM •   Guiting Power •   Bledington •
Blaisdon •   GLOUCESTER •   Brockhampton •   Cold Aston •   Fifield •
        A40   Kilkenny •   A40   Great Rissington •
                    Withington •   Great Barrington •
Awre •   Cranham •   Brimpsfield •   Little Barrington •
        Sheepscombe •   Miserden •   Chedworth •   Burford •
St Briavels •   Duntisbourne Abbots •   North   Coln St
            Woodchester •   Bisley •   Cerney •   Aldwyns •
        Oakridge Lynch •   Barnsley •   Ampney   Broadwell •
                    Sapperton •   St Peter
Dursley •   Box   Meysey Hampton •
    Kingscote •   Nailsworth •   Ewen •
North
Nibley   Tetbury •

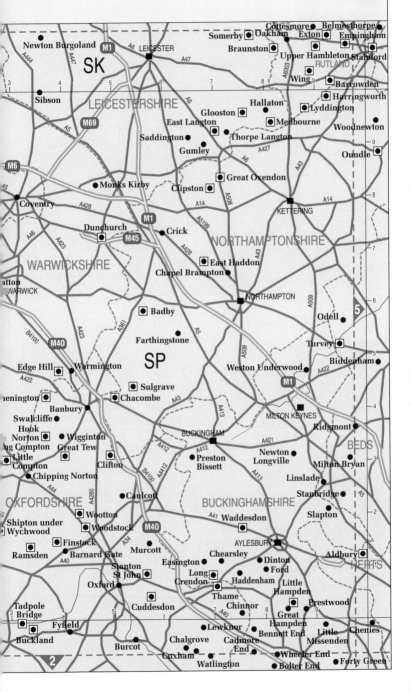

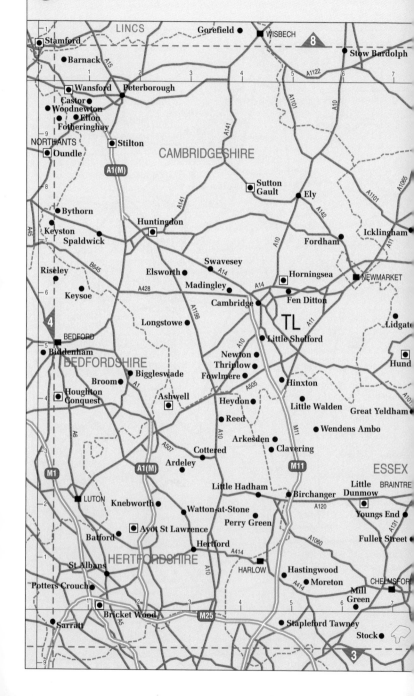

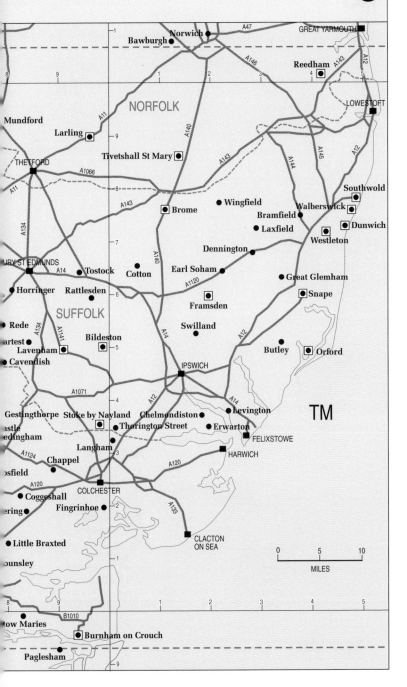

5

Norwich
Bawburgh
GREAT YARMOUTH
Reedham
LOWESTOFT
NORFOLK
Mundford
Larling
A11
THETFORD
A1066
Tivetshall St Mary
Southwold
Walberswick
Wingfield
Brome
A143
Bramfield
Dunwich
Laxfield
Westleton
Dennington
A140
Earl Soham
Great Glemham
BURY ST EDMUNDS
A14
Tostock
Cotton
A1120
Snape
Horringer
Rattlesden
Framsden
SUFFOLK
Swilland
Rede
Bildeston
A14
Butley
Orford
artest
Lavenham
Cavendish
IPSWICH
A1071
A12
Gestingthorpe
Stoke by Nayland
Chelmondiston
Levington
A14
TM
astle
edingham
Thorington Street
Erwarton
FELIXSTOWE
Langham
HARWICH
A1124
Chappel
A120
osfield
A120
Coggeshall
A133
ering
Fingrinhoe
Little Braxted
CLACTON
ON SEA
ounsley
0   5   10
MILES
ow Maries
B1010
Burnham on Crouch
Paglesham

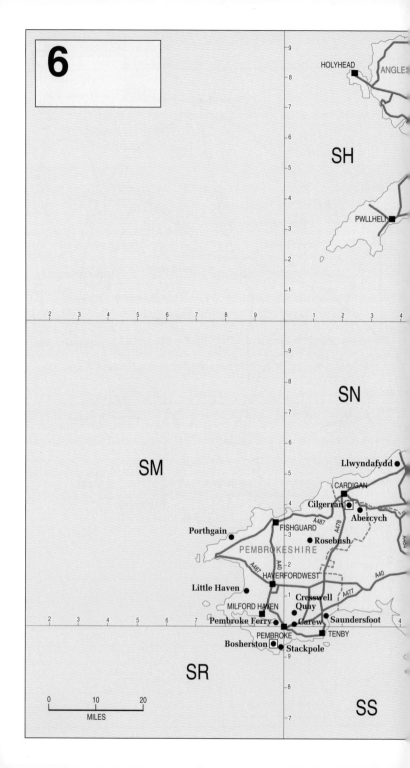

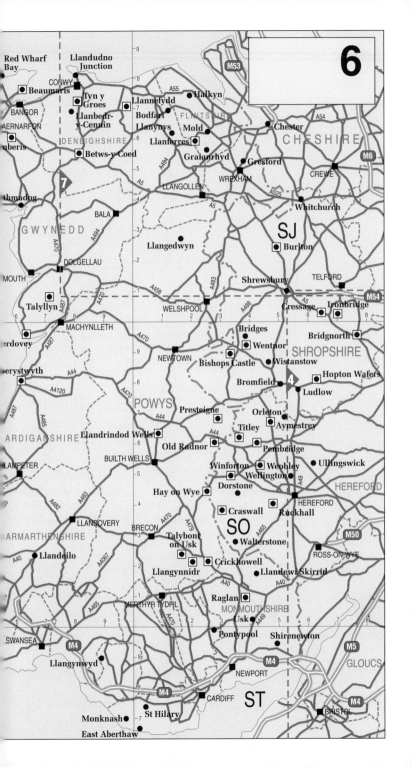

7

9

8

Casterton

Beetham

Ulverston
Kirkby Lonsdal

Dalton-in-Furness
Nealand Conyers

7

BARROW-IN-FURNESS

M6

A65

Settle

6

SD

5

Conder Green

LANCASHIRE

0   10   20
MILES

Garstang
A6
Whitewell
Newtor

4

Chipping
Downham

Little Eccleston
Goosnargh
Longridge
Fer

BLACKPOOL
Wharles
Ribchester

M55

3

PRESTON
M65

Lytham

Croston
Darwen
Entwh

2

SOUTHPORT
A59
Mawdesley
Belmont

Bispham Green
GREATE

MANCHES

1

M58
A6
M61

8   9   1   2   3

M6
A580
M

MERSEYSIDE

M62

9

Liverpool

Daresbury

Llandudno
Junction
M53
CHESHIRE

8

CONWY
Raby

Overton
Plumley
Lowe
Peove

Tyn y Groes
A55
Bodfari
Halkyn
M56
Over Peover
Pe

Llanbedr-
y-Cennin
Llannefydd
Whitegate
Hi

7

Llanferres
FLINTSHIRE
Chester
Willington
Cotebrook

DENBIGHSHIRE
A525
Tarporley
Bunbury
Barthor

Betws-y-Coed
A494
Llanynys
Aldford
Handley
Nantwich
We

6

Graianrhyd
Higher Burwardsley
A49

Gresford

A5
WREXHAM
Bickley Moss
Wrenbury

5

BALA
LLANGOLLEN
SJ
Bell o' th' Hill
Aston
M

A5

4

Whitchurch
A41
A53

GWYNEDD

3

6

A483
A528
A49
A41

POWYS

2

Burlton
A494
A495
A5
SHROPSHIRE

Shrewsbury

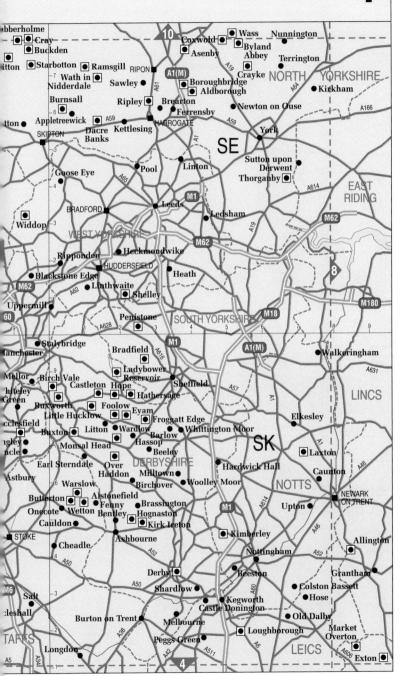

bberholme
Cray
Buckden
litton
Starbotton
Wath in
Nidderdale
Burnsall
Appletreewick
tton
SKIPTON
Ramsgill
RIPON
A1(M)
Sawley
Ripley
Brearton
Ferrensby
HARROGATE
Dacre
Banks
Kettlesing
Coxwold
Asenby
Wass
Nunnington
Byland
Abbey
Terrington
Crayke
NORTH YORKSHIRE
Kirkham
Boroughbridge
Aldborough
Newton on Ouse
York
SE
Goose Eye
Pool
Linton
Sutton upon
Derwent
Thorganby
EAST
RIDING
BRADFORD
Leeds
Ledsham
Widdop
WEST YORKSHIRE
M1
M62
M62
Ripponden
Heckmondwike
Blackstone Edge
HUDDERSFIELD
Linthwaite
Heath
Uppermill
Shelley
60
Penistone
SOUTH YORKSHIRE
M18
M180
Stalybridge
Bradfield
M1
A1(M)
Walkeringham
anchester
Mellor
Birch Vale
Castleton
Ladybower
Reservoir
Sheffield
LINCS
hiteley
Green
Hope
Hathersage
Foolow
Eyam
Buxworth
Little Hucklow
Buxton
Litton
Wardlow
Barlow
Froggatt Edge
Whittington Moor
Elkesley
Hassop
Monsal Head
Beeley
Laxton
SK
Earl Sterndale
Over
Haddon
DERBYSHIRE
Milltown
Hardwick Hall
Caunton
Astbury
Warslow
Birchover
Woolley Moor
NOTTS
NEWARK
ON TRENT
Butterton
Alstonefield
Brassington
M1
Upton
Onecote
Fenny
Bentley
Hognaston
Cauldon
Kirk Ireton
Allington
STOKE
Cheadle
Ashbourne
Kimberley
Nottingham
Salt
leshall
Longdon
Derby
Shardlow
Burton on Trent
Melbourne
Peggs Green
Kegworth
Castle Donington
Old Dalby
Loughborough
Beeston
Grantham
Colston Bassett
Hose
Market
Overton
LEICS
Exton

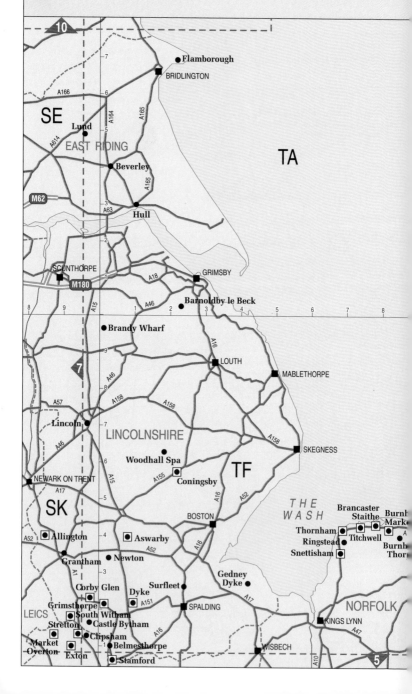

10

● **Flamborough**
■ BRIDLINGTON

A166

SE

A614

A164

A165

● Lund
5

EAST RIDING

6

7

● **Beverley**

A165

TA

M62

3
A63

● **Hull**

2

SCUNTHORPE ●
M180

A18

■ GRIMSBY

A15

A46

1

● **Barnoldby le Beck**

8   9   2   3   4   5   6   7   8

● **Brandy Wharf**

9

A46

A16

7

■ **LOUTH**

8

■ MABLETHORPE

A57

A158

A158

● **Lincoln**

A46

7

LINCOLNSHIRE

A158

6

● **Woodhall Spa**

A155

◻ **Coningsby**

■ SKEGNESS

TF

■ NEWARK ON TRENT

A17

5

A15

A16

A52

SK

■ BOSTON

T H E
W A S H

Brancaster
Staithe

Burnh
Mark

● **Allington**

4

◻ **Aswarby**

A52

A16

Thornham ◻ ◻◻◻ ● Burnh
Ringstead ◻   Titchwell   A
Snettisham ◻

● Newton

● Grantham

A1

Corby Glen ◻
Surfleet ●
Gedney
Dyke ●

Dyke ◻

LEICS

Grimsthorpe ◻
South Witham ◻
Stretton ● Castle Bytham ●
Market ● Clipsham ●
Overton ◻ Belmesthorpe ●
Exton ◻ Stamford

A151

A16

■ SPALDING

A17

NORFOLK

■ KINGS LYNN

A47

1

■ WISBECH

A10

5

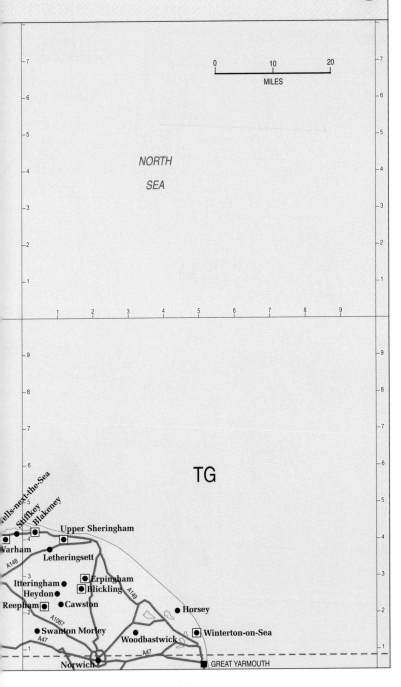

8

0   10   20
MILES

NORTH

SEA

TG

Wells-next-the-Sea
Stiffkey
Blakeney
Upper Sheringham
Warham
Letheringsett
A148
Erpingham
Itteringham
Blickling
Heydon
A149
Reepham
Cawston
A1067
Horsey
Swanton Morley
Winterton-on-Sea
A47
Woodbastwick
Norwich
A47
GREAT YARMOUTH

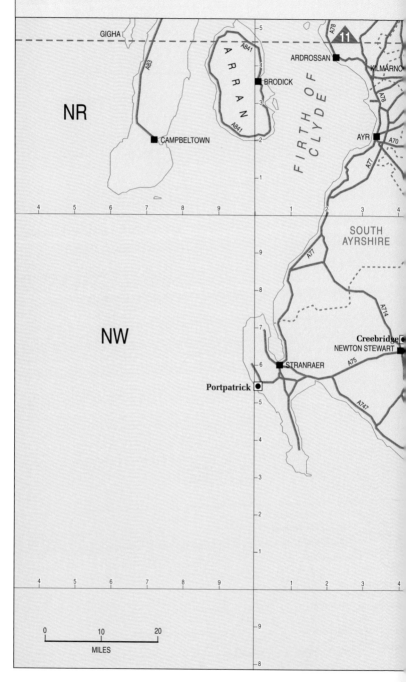

GIGHA

A841

ARRAN

A83

BRODICK

NR

CAMPBELTOWN

A941

FIRTH OF CLYDE

11

ARDROSSAN

KILMARNO

A78

A78

AYR

A70

A77

SOUTH AYRSHIRE

A77

A714

Creebridge

NEWTON STEWART

A75

STRANRAER

Portpatrick

A747

NW

0   10   20
MILES

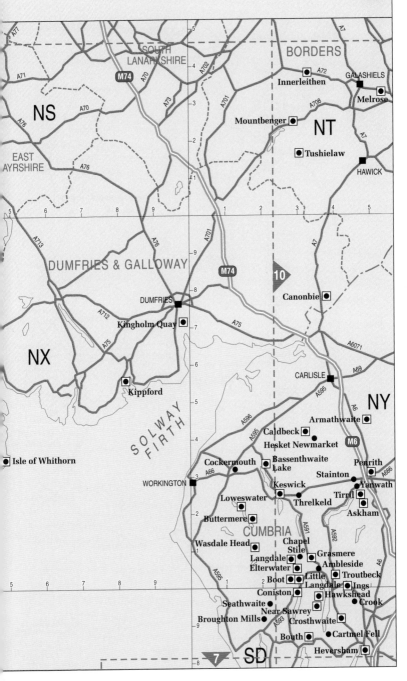

A77

SOUTH
LANARKSHIRE

BORDERS

M74

A70

A71

A70

A72 Innerleithen

GALASHIELS

A76

A73

A701

A702

A706

Melrose

NS

EAST
AYRSHIRE

A76

Mountbenger

NT

A7

A76

Tushielaw

HAWICK

5   6   7   8   9   1   2   3   4   5

A713

A76

A701

A7

DUMFRIES & GALLOWAY

M74

10

9

A76

A712

DUMFRIES

Canonbie

8

A75

A6071

Kingholm Quay   7

NX

Kippford

CARLISLE

A69

A596

6

A595

NY

A6

5

A596

Armathwaite

Isle of Whithorn

SOLWAY
FIRTH

Caldbeck

M6

Penrith

Hesket Newmarket

A66

Cockermouth

Bassenthwaite
Lake

Stainton

A595

Yanwath

3

WORKINGTON

Keswick

Tirril

A696

A595

Loweswater

Threlkeld

Askham

2

Buttermere

CUMBRIA

A591

A6

Wasdale Head

Chapel
Stile

Grasmere

Langdale

Ambleside

Elterwater

Little

Troutbeck

Boot

Langdale

Ings

1

Coniston

Hawkshead

Crook

A595

Seathwaite

Near Sawrey

Crosthwaite

9

Broughton Mills

A593

Cartmel Fell

Bouth

Heversham

8   SD

5   6   7   8   9

7

10

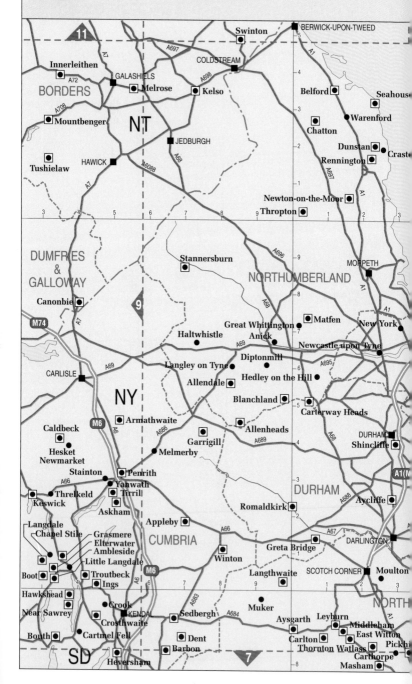

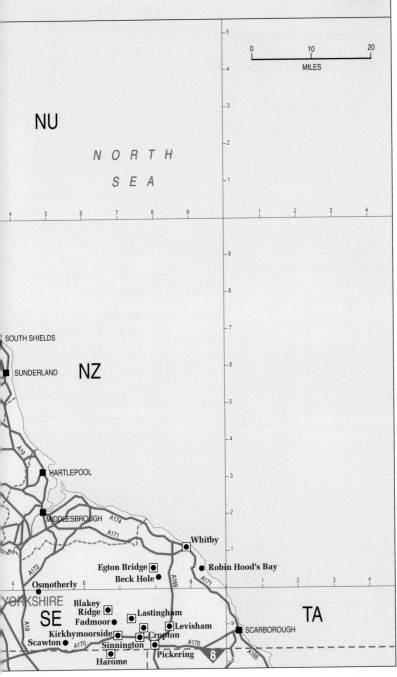

NU

N O R T H

S E A

NZ

SOUTH SHIELDS

■ SUNDERLAND

■ HARTLEPOOL

■ MIDDLESBROUGH A174

A171

● Whitby

● Robin Hood's Bay

Egton Bridge ◉
Beck Hole ●

Osmotherly ●

YORKSHIRE

SE

Blakey
Ridge ◉
Fadmoor ●

◉ Lastingham

◉ Levisham

Kirkbymoorside ◉
Scawton ● A170
Sinnington ◉
Cropton ◉

● Harome

Pickering ◼ 8

TA

■ SCARBOROUGH

A170   A165

0   10   20
MILES

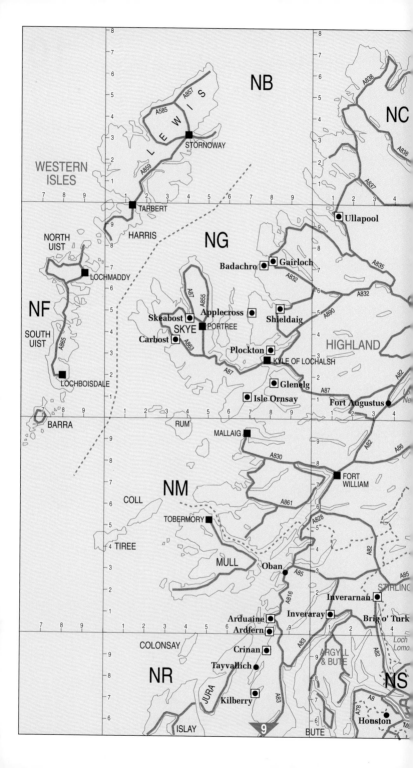

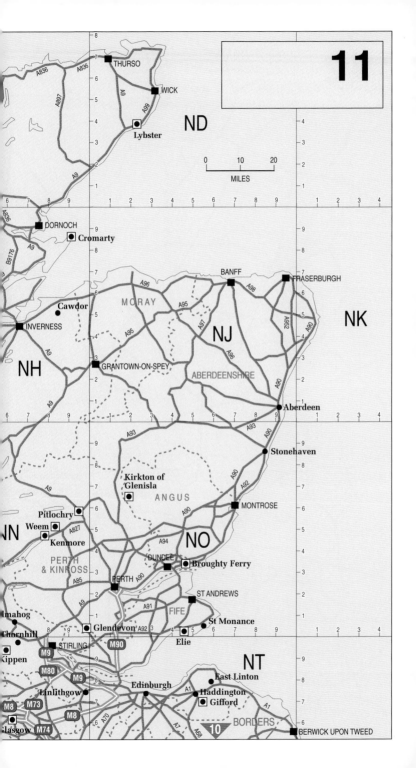

11

THURSO
WICK
Lybster
ND

DORNOCH
Cromarty

BANFF
FRASERBURGH
MORAY
Cawdor
INVERNESS
NJ
NK
GRANTOWN-ON-SPEY
ABERDEENSHIRE
Aberdeen
NH

Stonehaven
Kirkton of
Glenisla
ANGUS
MONTROSE
Pitlochry
Weem
Kenmore
NO
DUNDEE
Broughty Ferry
PERTH
& KINROSS
PERTH
ST ANDREWS
imahog
FIFE
St Monance
Chornhill
Glendevon
Elie
ippen
STIRLING
M90
NT
M80
M9
East Linton
Linlithgow
Edinburgh
Haddington
Gifford
M8
M73
M8
A70
BORDERS
lasgow
M74
10
BERWICK UPON TWEED

0   10   20
MILES

A836 A836
A887
A9
A99
A9
A836
B9176
A9
A96
A96
A95
A97
A95
A9
A98
A952
A90
A96
A90
A93
A90
A93
A90
A92
A90
A94
A90
A85
A9
A91
A92
A827
A9
M90
A70
A7
A68
A1
A1

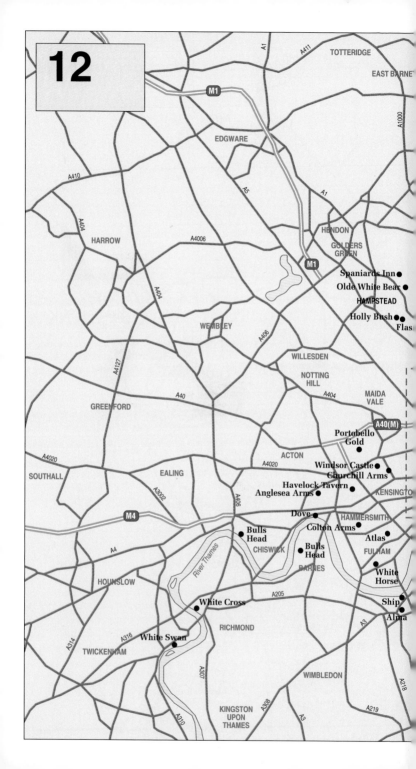

12

TOTTERIDGE
EAST BARNET

EDGWARE

HENDON
GOLDERS
GREEN

HARROW

Spaniards Inn ●
Olde White Bear ●
HAMPSTEAD

WEMBLEY

Holly Bush ●●
Flas

WILLESDEN

NOTTING
HILL

MAIDA
VALE

GREENFORD

ACTON

Portobello
Gold
●

Windsor Castle ●
Churchill Arms ●
Havelock Tavern ●
Anglesea Arms ●

SOUTHALL

EALING

KENSINGTON

Dove ●

HAMMERSMITH

Colton Arms ●

Bulls
Head ●

CHISWICK

Bulls
Head ●

Atlas ●

FULHAM

BARNES

White
Horse ●

HOUNSLOW

White Cross ●

A205

Ship ●
Alma ●

RICHMOND

White Swan ●

TWICKENHAM

WIMBLEDON

KINGSTON
UPON
THAMES

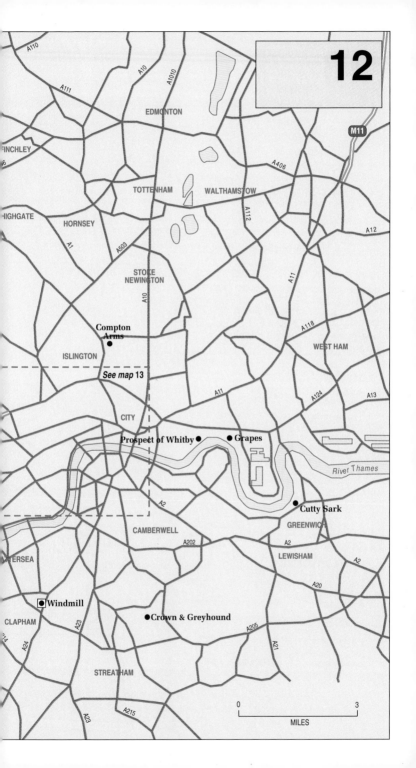

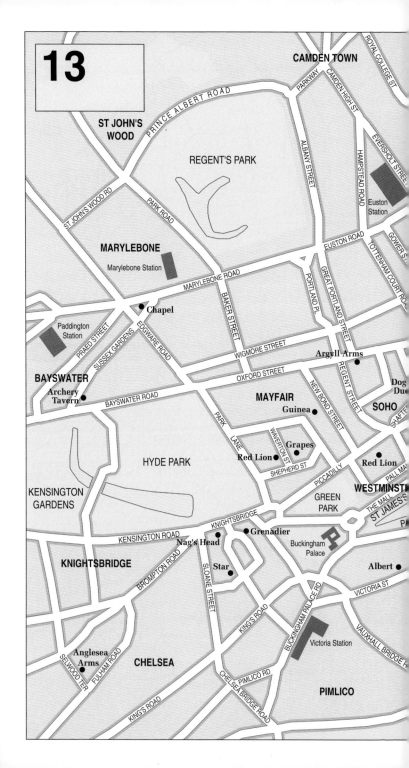

CAMDEN TOWN

ROYAL COLLEGE ST

PARKWAY

CAMDEN HIGH ST

EVERSHOLT STREET

PRINCE ALBERT ROAD

ST JOHN'S
WOOD

ALBANY STREET

HAMPSTEAD ROAD

REGENT'S PARK

GOWER ST

Euston
Station

ST JOHN'S WOOD RD

PARK ROAD

EUSTON ROAD

TOTTENHAM COURT ROAD

MARYLEBONE

PORTLAND PL

GREAT PORTLAND STREET

Marylebone Station

MARYLEBONE ROAD

BAKER STREET

PRAED STREET

EDGWARE ROAD

Chapel

Paddington
Station

SUSSEX GARDENS

WIGMORE STREET

Argyll Arms

REGENT STREET

BAYSWATER

OXFORD STREET

NEW BOND STREET

**Dog
Duc**

SOHO

**Archery
Tavern**

BAYSWATER ROAD

MAYFAIR

Guinea

SHAFTE

PARK LANE

WAVERTON ST

Grapes

Red Lion

SHEPHERD ST

Red Lion

HYDE PARK

PICCADILLY

PALL MA

WESTMINST

KENSINGTON
GARDENS

GREEN
PARK

THE MALL

ST JAMES'S

P

KNIGHTSBRIDGE

Grenadier

KENSINGTON ROAD

Nag's Head

Buckingham
Palace

BROMPTON ROAD

Star

Albert

KNIGHTSBRIDGE

SLOANE STREET

VICTORIA ST

BUCKINGHAM PALACE RD

KING'S ROAD

VAUXHALL BRIDGE R

Victoria Station

**Anglesea
Arms**

SELWOOD TER

FULHAM ROAD

CHELSEA

CHELSEA BRIDGE ROAD

PIMLICO RD

PIMLICO

KING'S ROAD

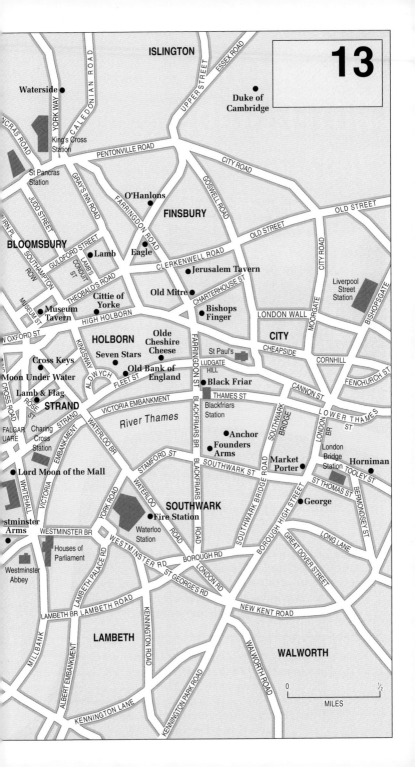

13

ISLINGTON

Waterside

Duke of Cambridge

YORK WAY

CALEDONIAN ROAD

ESSEX ROAD

UPPER STREET

King's Cross Station

PENTONVILLE ROAD

CITY ROAD

NCRAS ROAD

St Pancras Station

GRAY'S INN ROAD

O'Hanlons

FARRINGDON ROAD

FINSBURY

GOSWELL ROAD

OLD STREET

OLD STREET

CITY ROAD

JUDD STREET

BLOOMSBURY

GUILDFORD STREET

SOUTHAMPTON ROW

THEOBALD'S ROAD

Lamb

Eagle

CONDUIT ST

LAMB'S

Cittie of Yorke

CLERKENWELL ROAD

Jerusalem Tavern

Old Mitre

CHARTERHOUSE ST

Bishops Finger

LONDON WALL

Liverpool Street Station

BISHOPSGATE

MUSEUM STREET

Museum Tavern

HIGH HOLBORN

N OXFORD ST

HOLBORN

Seven Stars

Olde Cheshire Cheese

FARRINGDON ST

St Paul's

CITY

MOORGATE

CHEAPSIDE

CORNHILL

FENCHURCH ST

Cross Keys

KINGSWAY

ALDWYCH

Old Bank of England

LUDGATE HILL

CANNON ST

LOWER THAMES ST

Moon Under Water

CROSS ROAD

Lamb & Flag

ROSE ST

FLEET ST

Black Friar

THAMES ST

Blackfriars Station

SOUTHWARK BRIDGE

LONDON BR

STRAND

VICTORIA EMBANKMENT

River Thames

BLACKFRIARS BR

FALGAR UARE

Charing Cross Station

STRAND

WATERLOO BR

Anchor

Founders Arms

London Bridge Station

Horniman

Lord Moon of the Mall

EMBANKMENT

VICTORIA

YORK ROAD

WATERLOO ROAD

STAMFORD ST

BLACKFRIARS ROAD

SOUTHWARK ST

Market Porter

ST THOMAS ST

TOOLEY ST

BERMONDSEY ST

WHITEHALL

stminster Arms

WESTMINSTER BR

SOUTHWARK

Fire Station

SOUTHWARK BRIDGE ROAD

George

BOROUGH HIGH STREET

GREAT DOVER STREET

Houses of Parliament

Westminster Abbey

WESTMINSTER RD

Waterloo Station

LAMBETH PALACE RD

LAMBETH BR

LAMBETH ROAD

BOROUGH RD

LONDON RD

ST GEORGE'S RD

LONG LANE

NEW KENT ROAD

MILLBANK

ALBERT EMBANKMENT

LAMBETH ROAD

KENNINGTON ROAD

LAMBETH

WALWORTH

KENNINGTON PARK ROAD

WALWORTH ROAD

KENNINGTON LANE

0   ½

MILES

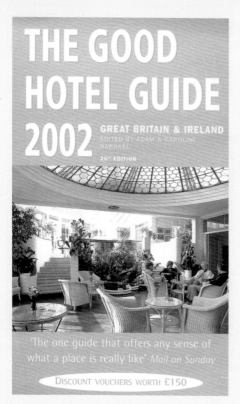